Encyclopedia of the Great Plains

Encyclopedia of

A PROJECT OF THE CENTER FOR GREAT PLAINS STUDIES   University of Nebraska—Lincoln

the Great Plains

DAVID J. WISHART, EDITOR

University of Nebraska Press   LINCOLN & LONDON

The *Encyclopedia of the Great Plains* was produced from 1995 to 2003 with financial support from the National Endowment for the Humanities in the form of two major grants as well as the funds for the cumulative index. Generous support was also provided by the Nebraska Humanities Council; the government of Canada, through the Canadian Embassy in Washington DC; the University of Nebraska Foundation, which raised matching funds from its own endowment, and from Cliff's Foundation, D. B. and Paula Varner, and Frank Hilsabeck; and the Vice Chancellor for Research, the Arts and Sciences Deans Office, the Humanities Center, and the Center for Great Plains Studies, all at the University of Nebraska–Lincoln.

Library of Congress
Cataloging-in-Publication Data
Encyclopedia of the Great Plains /
David J. Wishart, editor.
    p. cm.
Includes index.
ISBN 0-8032-4787-7 (hardcover : alk. paper)
1. Great Plains—Encyclopedias. I. Wishart, David
J., 1946–
F591.E4856 2004
978'.003—dc22   2003021037

Contents

Project Staff

EDITOR
David J. Wishart. University of Nebraska–Lincoln

REGIONAL EDITORS
Pamela H. Brink.
    Associated Authors and Editors, Inc. Lubbock, Texas (Southern Plains)
Nancy Tystad Koupal.
    South Dakota Historical Society. Pierre, South Dakota (Northern Plains)
Theodore D. Regehr.
    University of Calgary and University of Saskatchewan (Prairie Provinces)

ASSOCIATE EDITORS
J. Clark Archer. University of Nebraska–Lincoln
Frances W. Kaye. University of Nebraska–Lincoln
Martha H. Kennedy. Library of Congress
John R. Wunder. University of Nebraska–Lincoln

PROJECT MANAGERS
Scarlett Presley (1995–1999)
Sonja Rossum (1999–2002)

RESEARCH ASSISTANTS
Beth Ritter (1995–1999)
Akim D. Reinhardt (1996–1997)
Pekka Hämäläinen (1996–1998)
Sonja Rossum (1997–1999)
April L. Whitten (1997–1998)
Robert Watrel (1998)
Mark R. Ellis (1999–2001)
Charles Vollan (2000–2002)

ADMINISTRATIVE ASSISTANT
Gretchen Walker

Acknowledgments

The *Encyclopedia of the Great Plains* was conceived in 1989 by John R. Wunder, director of the Center for Great Plains Studies at the University of Nebraska–Lincoln. The Center for Great Plains Studies, under the direction of James Stubbendieck since 1997, has served as the home of the project, which continues the center's mission to foster knowledge of the Great Plains region.

As editor, I am indebted to the scholars who worked with me on this project and made it such a rewarding experience. The regional editors, Pamela Brink, Nancy Tystad Koupal, and Theodore Regehr, championed their causes and provided insiders' knowledge and understanding of their sections of the Plains. They were deeply involved in the conceptualization of the project and contributed entries as well. The associate editors, all from the University of Nebraska–Lincoln, assisted in many ways: they wrote entries and, in addition, J. Clark Archer served as cartographic consultant, Martha Kennedy (now at the Library of Congress) selected much of the artwork, Frances Kaye wrote the essay on Literary Traditions and was an additional consultant for the Canadian part of the region, and John Wunder coauthored the grant applications to the National Endowment for the Humanities. The two project managers were indispensable to the project. Scarlett Presley set up the database that allowed each entry to be tracked at each stage of the editing process. With research assistant Beth Ritter, she got the encyclopedia off the ground by establishing our system of successive contacts with authors and setting a steady course when we really weren't sure of what we were doing. Then Sonja Rossum, who had started as a research assistant (and would later do much of the cartography), took over as project manager. Sonja became, as we all acknowledged, the "brains behind the operation." We all feel fortunate to have worked with her. Gretchen Walker, secretary at the Center for Great Plains Studies, served as administrative assistant during the many years of production, calmly handling the recurring financial crises. The research assistants did the detail work in the library, identified entries, advised me on content and editing, and in most cases, wrote entries themselves. I hope the other assistants will forgive me for singling out Pekka Hämäläinen, Mark Ellis, and Charles Vollan, not only for their longevity on the job, but for their deep knowledge of the Great Plains, which is a credit to the historian's craft. My good fortune continued in the closing stages of the project when three fine editors, Lona Dearmont, Mary Hill, and Joeth Zucco refined the finished product. I am especially grateful to Joeth Zucco, who coordinated the editing of the 5,112 manuscript pages with patience and skill.

Finally, I want to thank all the authors, many of whom are fellows or associate fellows of the Center for Great Plains Studies. They did their work for no real reward other than to be participants in a project that they thought worthwhile. I hope that when they see the *Encyclopedia of the Great Plains* they will consider that their time was well spent.

David J. Wishart, Editor
University of Nebraska–Lincoln

Using the Encyclopedia

The *Encyclopedia of the Great Plains* is organized thematically and alphabetically. There are twenty-seven chapters, ranging in alphabetical order from African Americans to Water. Each chapter is introduced by a major essay, a synthesis of the topic, and contains individual entries of varying length, which are arranged alphabetically. Altogether there are 1,316 entries contributed by almost 1,000 scholars.

This thematic organization has both advantages and disadvantages. The primary advantage is that it gives the encyclopedia an interpretive function which is lacking in purely alphabetical works: the very division into such chapters as Agriculture, Native Americans, Gender, and Images and Icons is a partial analysis of the character of the Great Plains region. The main disadvantage was the difficulty of deciding where to place entries that could very well fit in a number of chapters and, associated with this, how to make sure that readers can readily find the information that they need. The entry on Drought, for example, in the Water chapter, could also logically fit in the Agriculture, Images and Icons, or Physical Environment chapters. Consequently, we have made a concerted effort to guide the reader to the entries.

The easiest way to locate an entry is to go to the general index, where every entry is alphabetically listed in bold lettering. The general index also includes a listing of every person, event, and place that is featured in the encyclopedia but is not the subject of specific entries. These appear in normal lettering. For quick reference, a list of entries is placed at the beginning of each chapter, following the title page. Finally, throughout the encyclopedia, at locations where readers might seek an entry that has been placed elsewhere, there is a cross-reference to the actual placement. So, for example, a reader seeking Charlie Parker in the African Americans chapter, would find:

PARKER, CHARLIE
See MUSIC: Parker, Charlie

Note, in this context, that we have placed most entries on African Americans, Asian Americans, Hispanic Americans, and Native Americans in their particular chapters rather than scattering them throughout the encyclopedia in chapters such as Politics and Government, Music, and Art. In doing this, we wanted to emphasize the contributions of these peoples—contributions that have often been overlooked—to the shaping of the Great Plains. Yet in some cases—Charlie Parker in Music, for example, Jim Thorpe in Sports and Recreation, or Malcolm X in Protest and Dissent—we judged that their con-tributions were of such great national significance that they needed to be placed in the relevant topical chapter.

In the biographical entries we have chosen to use popular forms of names in the title and to provide the full formal name in the text. It seemed more likely that someone would look for "Carson, Johnny" rather than "Carson, John William" or for "Calamity Jane" rather than "Canary, Martha." In almost all the biographical entries we have provided the precise dates and places of birth and (if relevant) death. In these, and all other entries in the encyclopedia, information is believed to have been accurate as of August 1, 2003.

The author's name and affiliation, or place of residence, are given at the end of each essay and entry. Also at the end of all the essays and many of the entries are cross-references to related entries in other chapters. A short bibliography, intended to direct the reader to additional information on the topic, is also provided for the essays and most entries.

Our objective in producing this encyclopedia is to give definition to a region that has traditionally been poorly defined. To achieve this goal, we have strived to be as inclusive as possible: inclusive in topics, from the physical environment to the humanities; inclusive geographically, from Texas to Alberta and from the Rocky Mountains to the Missouri River; inclusive temporally, from Paleo-Indians to the 2000 census; and inclusive ethnically, racially, and by gender. We have thrown a wide net, and it is our hope that we have captured most of what is vital, and interesting, about the Great Plains.

The Great Plains Region

"The Great Plains . . . feel at times like an almost forgotten region—and yet there are wonders in it."—Larry McMurtry

When we applied to the National Endowment for the Humanities for a grant to fund the *Encyclopedia of the Great Plains*, reviewers wanted to know just where the region is located and what makes it special. This confirms Larry McMurtry's thinking, expressed in the above quote, that the Great Plains is a forgotten region, but it was also a reasonable request, prior to dispensing money, and we set about meeting the requirement.

Any region is both a real place and an intellectual concept. In that sense, a region is the equivalent of the historian's period: a region is the division of space into recognizable units, just as a period is the division of time into recognizable segments. Both are classification schemes, generalizations that aid in the understanding of complex reality. The challenge is to identify the characteristics of the human and physical environments that constitute a region and to establish boundaries for that distinctive portion of the earth's surface. Even the South—perhaps the most readily recognizable North American region—lacks definitive boundaries. In the groundbreaking *Encyclopedia of Southern Culture*, for example, the editors make no attempt to delimit their region except to say that the South is wherever southern culture is found. In our case, such a creative evasion would not have satisfied the reviewers, so we set about tracing the evolution of the concept of the Great Plains region, identifying the physical, historical, and cultural characteristics that together define its regional character, and specifying boundaries which, if not hard and fast, are logical.

In this introductory essay, written nine years later, I keep the framework of that original grant proposal, but I can now add substance by drawing from the vast storehouse of information and analysis created by the almost 1,000 scholars who participated in the making of the *Encyclopedia of the Great Plains*.

The region now recognized as the Great Plains has been characterized in many ways, not all of them laudatory. Part of the region was branded the Great American Desert following the explorations of Zebulon Pike (1806) and Stephen Long (1820), though this aspersion was never widely accepted by the American public. Labeling the Great Plains the "buffalo commons," a failed agricultural experiment in a land that should be put back in grass, continues the tradition of maligning the region, in the sense that it negates the people who call it home.

The actual term, "Great Plains," has been used to describe the grasslands of North America since at least the mid-nineteenth century, but it only gained widespread acceptance in the 1930s. In 1931, geographer Nevin Fenneman began his book, *Physiography of Western United States*, with a lengthy discussion of the "Great Plains Province," a physical region of great diversity, yet sufficiently distinctive from surrounding areas to merit separate identification. Also in 1931, historian Walter Prescott Webb propelled the Great Plains into the public imagination with his contention that the grasslands to the west of the ninety-eighth meridian—which he characterized as a treeless and largely unwatered land—demanded fundamental changes in "ways of life and of living" before they could be settled by European Americans. In that same decade of the 1930s the Great Plains became known as a problem region, the home of the Dust Bowl. The region received more attention than it wanted in Pare Lorentz's documentary *The Plow that Broke the Plains*, made for the Farm Security Administration in 1936, and in *The Future of the Great Plains*, a report submitted to President Roosevelt in December of that same year. Through such publicity, the Great Plains became inscribed on the map of American regions, on a par with the Midwest, New England, and the South, and it has persisted. It is there in the geography textbooks, in the scholarly literature on American regionalism, in more popular works like Ian Frazier's *Great Plains*, and on the landscape throughout this vast area on billboards, motel signs, and business marquees.

What are the criteria for identifying the Great Plains as a region? One starting point is climate, specifically climatic variability. Rainfall varies from more than thirty inches a year in eastern Kansas to less than fifteen inches a year in the lee of the Rocky Mountains. Droughts of thirty-five or more consecutive days can be expected annually, with frequency increasing from east to west, and drought periods of sixty to seventy days are experienced about every ten years. Extended periods of drought, such as in the 1890s, 1930s, and 1950s, take on the dimensions of severe natural disasters, causing agricultural failure and depopulation. Native Americans, as well as European American settlers, were confounded by such periodic drought, as in the dry, warm period between 1439 and 1468 when Upper Republican peoples were forced to abandon their agricultural villages in the Central Great Plains. Similarly, the dry years of the early 1890s caused the failure of many settlers on the western Plains, settlers who had only just arrived in the good years of the 1880s and had no reserves when the drought hit. As climatologist Charles Warren Thornthwaite explained in 1941, in the wake of the Dust Bowl, it was this uncertainty that made staying on the Great Plains difficult: "In a desert you know what to expect of the climate and plan accordingly. The same is true for the humid regions. Men [and women] have been badly fooled by the semiarid regions because they are sometimes humid, sometimes desert, and sometimes a cross between the two." Add to this the other climatic hazards of high winds, tornadoes, extreme temperatures, blizzards, and destructive hail, and the tenuousness of settlement in this transitional region becomes understandable.

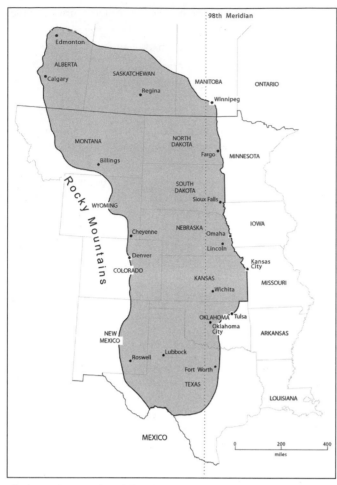

The Great Plains region as defined by the Encyclopedia of the Great Plains

The transitional character of the physical environment of the Great Plains posed another problem for its inhabitants. Thin ribbons of woodlands trace rivers like the Missouri, Platte, and Saskatchewan out into the grasslands of the Great Plains, and the Canadian Prairies are girdled on the north by the Parkland Belt, a mixed prairie and woodland zone that grades into the coniferous forests of the northlands. However, compared to neighboring regions to the east and west, the Plains have few trees. This caused difficulties for Native Americans like the Pawnees and Omahas, who had to move their villages every few years as the local already sparse timber was depleted. It also caused difficulties for early European American settlers who had to improvise by building houses of sod, hay, and clay, and use buffalo dung for fuel. The problem persisted until the railroads were firmly in place, allowing the big lumber companies of St. Paul and Winnipeg to extend their market areas to the west.

A third environmental challenge of the Great Plains was, and is, sheer distance. West of the Missouri in the United States and of the Great Lakes in Canada, the waterways were navigable only for the trappers' and Indians' bullboats and canoes. There were no convenient westward-flowing rivers like the Ohio or Tennessee to channel settlers into the heart of the Great Plains. The Missouri River was navigable for shallow-draft steamboats to the mouth of the Yellowstone after 1832,

but there were frequent groundings and sinkings, and only the earliest American emigrants to the Great Plains (into eastern Kansas and Nebraska in the late 1850s and early 1860s and into southeastern Dakota Territory for a brief time in the 1860s) came by water. Indians partly overcame distance by adopting the horse in the seventeenth and eighteenth centuries. Americans had to wait for the coming of the railroads in the 1860s before they could break free from the Missouri River. Distance remained a serious problem until the 1920s, when automobiles came into common use, revolutionizing mobility and allowing a new flexibility in settlement decisions. But even today the friction of distance and the "social costs" of space (e.g., providing education, electricity, and now broadband Internet access to widely dispersed residents) are compelling features of Plains existence. Isolation is still a reality of life, especially in the wide interstices between the main lines of transportation and settlement.

Of course to many Plains residents the wide-open spaces, even the isolation from neighbors and towns, are regional characteristics to be celebrated, not endured. There may be no doctor within fifty miles and no longer an available bus system, but there is a close connection to the land and a deep sense of place that is often absent in more urbanized areas. Plains residents who have returned to the region after living elsewhere often speak of how much they had missed such simple pleasures as being waved to (generally a single finger barely lifted from the steering wheel) on the country roads.

The vast distances, the flowing grasslands, the sparse population, the enveloping horizons, and the dominating sky (the Plains landscape is really largely skyscape) convey a sense of expansiveness, even emptiness, which is another defining characteristic of the Great Plains region. It's hard to capture a Plains scene in a photograph, for example, because, as Jonathan Raban puts it, there is "more space than place." Norman Henderson, like Raban, an astute contemporary explorer of the Plains, writes that it is difficult to capture the essence of the region in words on paper because "the grasslands are a feeling more than a view."

Novelists such as Willa Cather and O. E. Rölvaag dwelled upon the impact of the overwhelming expansiveness on settlers. In *Giants in the Earth*, Rölvaag's epic novel of pioneer settlement in southeastern Dakota Territory in the 1870s, the woman of the household, Beret, is driven to distraction by the "nameless, blue-green solitude, flat, endless, still, with nothing to hide behind." This was a common reaction of the European American settlers who came out of humid, forested environments; they called it "loneliness," a reaction to too much space and one's own meager presence in it. It is still a common reaction to the sweeping horizons of the Great Plains. Other peoples, however, including the Kiowas, who migrated from the headwaters of the Yellowstone to southwestern Oklahoma, embraced the openness of the grasslands with a sense of emancipation, preferring plains to claustrophobic mountains and woodlands.

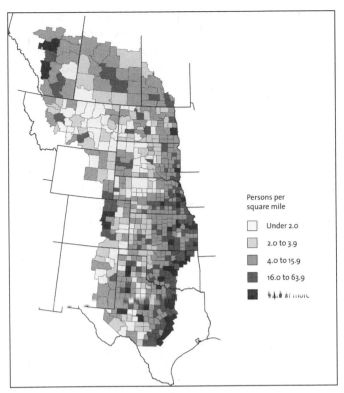

Population density in the Great Plains, by county and census division, in the United States (2000 census) and Canada (1991 census)

Modern geographers have also identified the absence of features as an integral part of the regional character of the Great Plains. To John Hudson, the essence of South Dakota is "captured by pictures of nothing—absolutely nothing, except maybe a telephone pole sticking up over the grain-fields and perhaps a lone elevator on the horizon." Yet on a smaller scale, between the observer and the horizon, there is a wealth of detail. The Great Plains may well lack trees, but there is a rich and diverse array of grasses, forbs, and animal life. An acre of tallgrass prairie, for example, is home to approximately 100 species of grasses and forbs, and every square yard of that prairie teems with insect life, including millions of tiny springtails (*Collembola*) in the rich dark soil.

Despite the demanding environment, the Great Plains has long been a magnet for settlers. Paleo-Indians were attracted to the grasslands at least 12,000 years ago to hunt such mammals as mastodons, mammoths, and bison. In the eighteenth century, the massive bison herds that thundered over the grasslands, and the horse, which allowed more bison to be taken and their meat and hides transported, drew Native Americans like the Lakotas (Sioux) into the region. After the Civil War, when the bison herds were decimated, the void was filled by cattle driven up from Texas and shipped in from elsewhere. The fertile promise of the soil made it worthwhile for farmers to take their chances with drought and loneliness: Per Hansa, Beret's driven husband in *Giants in the Earth*, saw not the desolation of an austere plain, but soil so black and rich that he squeezed it in his hands and watched it fall through his fingers like gold. And indeed, the Great Plains is the granary of North America.

From the earliest Native peoples to contemporary populations, Plains residents have taken up the environmental challenges and, in doing so, have created over time a region with its own identity, its own particular ways of life. No region, of course, is entirely distinct from surrounding regions, especially in contemporary North America where powerful leveling forces of mass media and corporate marketing are at work. Nevertheless, there are specific characteristics of human occupancy that permit the recognition of a particular Great Plains geography.

No other North American region was so fundamentally shaped by railroads. With the exception of the Selkirk settlement in the Red River Valley of the North after 1811, the Texas Hill country in the 1840s, eastern Nebraska and Kansas in the late 1850s and early 1860s, and the Black Hills in the 1870s, European Americans and European Canadians followed the railroads into the Great Plains. The implications of this, as far as regional development was concerned, are many. The railroads accentuated the east-west orientation of Plains settlement, producing a series of economic hinterlands that were, and are, linked to cities mainly to the east of the region (e.g., Winnipeg, Minneapolis–St. Paul, Chicago). They were not only transportation lines carrying grain out and manufactured products in but also active agents of colonization. They recruited widely for settlers—German Russians were particularly favored, because they had prior knowledge of how to farm the grasslands—to fill their large government land grants. They were the main determinant of the location, morphology, and landscapes of Plains towns, many of which have a characteristic T-shape, with the main street bisecting the tracks. They also named the towns, towns like Ismay, Montana, which was an amalgamation of Isabel and May, the names of the daughters of Albert J. Earling, president of the Milwaukee Road. The railroads were responsible for building too many towns, many of which have long since disappeared, or survive only as a single operating business, the grain elevator (which was also the business that got the towns started). Probably no other region of North America has so many ghost towns; there are an estimated 6,000 in Kansas alone. Finally, the railroads meant that Plains settlement, once started, was rapid. On the Canadian Prairies, for example (and the same could be said for other early-twentieth-century Plains frontiers in the Texas Panhandle and eastern Montana), communities, to use Paul Sharp's words, "sprang up almost full-grown." They went into old age quickly too, as rural populations thinned with agricultural mechanization, leaving main street stores closed, their windows covered with paper.

Because the Canadian and American settlement of the Great Plains was late, following the railroad, the region reflects the diverse ethnicity of immigrants who came to North America in the last decades of the nineteenth century and the first few decades of the twentieth century. Local ethnic distinctiveness remains an important part of Plains regionalism, enriching the dominant stamp of native-born American and Canadian pioneers who followed generally latitudinal routes of migration into the area. Fully 71 percent of North Dakotans were foreign-born, or the children of foreign-born, in 1910, mainly Norwegians, Germans, and German Russians. German Russians also came to Nebraska; Swedes to South Dakota and Kansas; and Doukhobors, Ukrainians, and Hutterites to the Prairie Provinces, to name only a few groups and a few places. Add to these African Americans, who first came in substantial numbers to the plains of Kansas as Exodusters in the 1870s; the south to north migration of Latinos, which gathered force in the late nineteenth century and continues today; and Chinese and Japanese settlers who originally entered the Plains from the west. All these groups brought their particular values and material culture to the Great Plains, with lasting effects on the landscape, patterns of religion, foodways, and language. Although diverse ethnicity is an integral ingredient of the character of many North American regions, especially in the large cities, no other extensive region in North America has the complex ethnic mosaic that distinguishes the Great Plains, especially the Northern Great Plains and Prairie Provinces.

Nor does any other North American region, with the notable exception of the Southwest, retain the stamp of the Indigenous Americans as emphatically as the Great Plains. Native peoples have continuously inhabited the Plains for at least 12,000 years. In the late eighteenth and early nineteenth centuries, only decades before the advent of European American settlement, Indians from the eastern United States were still migrating to the Great Plains, first of their own free will (the Lakotas and Crows, for example) and then, in the 1820s and 1830s, under the force and duress of the removal policy, which made refugees of peoples like the Cherokees. In the Plains, these immigrants competed for space and resources with Indigenous peoples such as the Pawnees and Osages. When Native Americans, encircled by European American settlers, were forced to give up their ancestral lands in the second half of the nineteenth century, they remained on the Great Plains, either on reservations that were remnants of their former territories, or amassed in Indian Territory (later Oklahoma). In the Prairie Provinces, First Nations ceded their lands to the government in a series of treaties between 1871 and 1877, before the main rush of immigration. Like their American counterparts, they retained reserves on the Plains and continue to be a major component of Plains identity. This is a component that will only increase in importance, because Native peoples are increasing faster than Plains population as a whole, and they are a young population, with growth built in to their demographic structure.

The list of defining characteristics could go on. The region has been, and continues to be, mainly a producer of raw materials for others to refine. Furs were the first such product, then cattle, corn, wheat, oil, gas, and coal. There is significant manufacturing on the Great Plains, mainly agriculturally based and mostly small scale, but the percentage of total employment in manufacturing is well below the national averages of Canada and the United States. The Great Plains can also be defined by its demographic structure: no other region of North America has a higher percentage of aged population. In many Plains communities, the young have departed, drawn to opportunities outside the region, leaving farms without the next generation and schools closed for want of students. This was not always the case, of course. The Great Plains was settled by young families, but the aged structure of Plains population now makes the region more dependent on government transfer payments (Medicare and social security, for example) than any other in North America. The Great Plains has also been a significant source of protest, as in North Dakota in 1916 when the Nonpartisan League gained control of the legislature and temporarily wrested control of credit and elevators from Minneapolis corporate power. Three years later, while the Nonpartisan League was still in power in North Dakota, to the north of the forty-ninth parallel one of the largest general strikes in North American history was staged in Winnipeg, shutting down factories, newspapers, telephones, and transportation. Protest in the Great Plains has come from all shades of the political spectrum: from socialist and communist activists like Oscar Ameringer and Ella "Mother" Bloor, to right-wing constitutionalists like the Freemen of Montana, to ethnic insurgents like Métis leader Louis Riel, and legal challenges like the landmark case, *Brown v. The Board of Education of Topeka*. Protest, of course, is not particular to the Great Plains, but there is a tradition in the region, and it is yet another defining trait.

No region, of course, is a discrete entity, and the authoritative lines on a map belie the reality of transitions and gradations on the ground. In fact when fifty different delimitations of the Great Plains were mapped by Sonja Rossum and Stephen Lavin, the nebulous nature of regional boundaries became very clear. Yet we felt it was important to define the boundaries of the purpose of this study—to specify the portion of North America that we recognize as the Great Plains.

The western boundary, following the Rocky Mountain front from Alberta to New Mexico, is the least ambiguous limit of the Great Plains. Indeed, there are few regional boundaries anywhere that are as decisive as the discontinuity between plains and mountains in Colorado and Alberta. But even the western boundary is blurred in places: in the Wyoming Basin, for example, where the Great Plains rise to more than 7,000 feet and merge less perceptibly with the Rocky Mountains, or in Montana, where extensions of the Rocky Mountains, such as the Little Rockies, interpenetrate with the Plains. Still, differences in elevation, vegetation, and human occupancy (specifically, the widely discontinuous settlement patterns in the Rocky Mountains) demarcate the Great Plains from the regions to the west.

The northern boundary in Canada is also quite distinct, tracing the line between the Parkland Belt of mixed woodland and grassland and the boreal forest of the north. The Parkland Belt of Alberta, Saskatchewan, and Manitoba, since the time

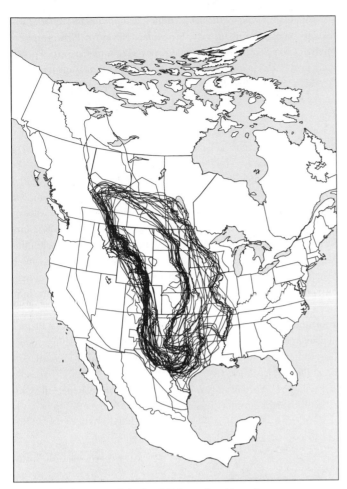

Fifty published versions of the Great Plains regional boundary

when Assiniboines and Crees followed bison herds, has been functionally integrated with the Prairies. This integration persisted through the fur-trade period and into the subsequent era of agricultural settlement. Canadian scholars are in accord on this matter.

Scholars also agree that there are more similarities than differences in land and life on either side of the forty-ninth parallel, marking the international boundary between the United States and Canada. Indians and fur traders crossed the border with impunity in the first half of the nineteenth century, and even after 1880, when the railroads connected the Canadian Prairies and the northern American Plains to their respective eastern control points (mainly Winnipeg and Minneapolis), parallel developments and common experiences were the norm. Land laws and settlement systems were similar. Both sections experienced agrarian protest movements and the drought and depression of the 1930s. Each had its open-range cattle era, and the Canadian grasslands were largely stocked from Montana. Similarly, there was a large influx of Americans into the Canadian Prairies in the two decades preceding World War I. No doubt, the North American Free Trade Agreement (NAFTA) will result in even more interaction between these two national components of the same geographic region.

A strong case can also be made for a distinctive southern boundary of the Great Plains. Physiographically the Great Plains is pinched out at the Rio Grande by the convergence of the Coastal Plain and the Mexican Highland section of the Basin and Range Province. Climatically the lands to the south of the Rio Grande are true desert. The southeastern edge of the Great Plains is marked by the prominent Balcones Escarpment, which was, historically, also a cultural divide marking the western extent of the cotton belt and the South.

This leaves the eastern boundary of the Great Plains, which is not a sharply defined line but an almost imperceptible transition zone from the more humid South and Midwest. The difficulty in identifying the eastern entry onto the Plains was described by Robert Pirsig as he rode his motorcycle west from Minnesota into North Dakota. "There is no one place or sharp line where the Central Plains [i.e., the Midwest] end and the Great Plains begin," observed Pirsig. "It's a gradual change like this that catches you unawares, as if you were sailing out from a choppy coastal harbor, noticed that the waves had taken on a deep swell, and turned back to see that you were out of sight of land." The key landscape evidence for Pirsig was that there were fewer trees on the Great Plains and those that were there had been introduced. The "greenness" encountered farther east had also paled, the streets of the towns were wider, the buildings more run-down. Pirsig concluded that there was less concern with "tidily conserving space" on the wide-open Great Plains.

To compensate for this geographical nebulousness, Plains scholars have sought to define the eastern margin by an arbitrary line, generally the 98th meridian, less frequently the 100th meridian. Perhaps a better definition of the eastern boundary would use a combination of physical, historical, and geopolitical factors. Our boundary follows the eastern border of the states of North Dakota, South Dakota, Nebraska, and Kansas, including these entire units in the region. These states were organized and settled later than the adjoining states to the east, and their institutions and iconographies give them a coherence that should not be divided. The rationale for the eastern boundary in Manitoba is based on physical and economic geography: Eastern Manitoba is part of the Laurentian Shield and its orientation is to Northern Ontario, not the Prairie Provinces. Eastern Oklahoma and eastern Texas are also excluded from the Plains because of overwhelming evidence that historically, environmentally, and culturally their orientation is to the South.

For some purposes in the encyclopedia, these boundaries will be transgressed to deal with particular features of adjacent areas that have significance to the development of the Great Plains, or to include entries that are simply too tempting to be left out! Kansas City, Missouri, for example, a major control point for the development of the Central Plains, is included in the Cities and Towns chapter, and Kansas City Jazz and film director Robert Altman, both products of the Missouri side of the river, are also subjects of entries. Moreover, because no region exists in a geographic vacuum, national and even international trends that have affected life on the Great Plains are often taken into account.

Yet our main concern is with the people, places, and events associated with the territory enclosed by the boundaries on the map. And what a rich tapestry of life that is. Five presidents of the United States and three prime ministers of Canada have come from the Great Plains. Great athletes like Jim Thorpe, Jim Ryun, and Gordie Howe rose from Plains communities. Celebrated writers such as Langston Hughes, Ralph Ellison, Wallace Stegner, Louise Erdrich, and Tillie Olsen were shaped by their years on the Plains. Movie stars, from Buster Keaton and Louise Brooks to Marlon Brando and Tommy Lee Jones, and musicians like Buddy Holly, Charlie Parker, Peggy Lee, and Neil Young spent their formative years in the Great Plains. Events of lasting historical importance, such as the Wounded Knee Massacre, the North-West Rebellion, and the Tulsa Race Riot took place in the Great Plains. And Plains women, including Emily Murphy, Kate Barnard, and Annie Diggs, pioneered the struggle for women's rights in North America.

What Ian Frazier says of the Plains—that "[t]hey're so big you can never know all there is to be known about them" is true. But with the *Encyclopedia of the Great Plains*, the product of the knowledge of so many scholars, we can at least give the reader the opportunity to know much more than was known before about this fascinating North American region.

David J. Wishart, Editor
University of Nebraska–Lincoln

Dawson, C. A. *Group Settlement: Ethnic Communities in Western Canada*. Toronto: Macmillan, 1936. Fenneman, Nevin M. *Physiography of Western United States*. New York: McGraw-Hill Book Co., 1931. Frazier, Ian. *Great Plains*. New York: Farrar, Strauss and Giroux, 1989. Friesen, Gerald. *The Canadian Prairies: A History*. Lincoln: University of Nebraska Press, 1984. Henderson, Norman. *Rediscovering the Great Plains: Journeys by Dog, Canoe, and Horse*. Baltimore MD: Johns Hopkins University Press, 2001. Luebke, Frederick C. "Regionalism and the Great Plains." *Western Historical Quarterly* 15 (1984): 19–38. McMurtry, Larry. Review of *On the Rez*, by Ian Frazier. *The New York Review of Books*, February 10, 2000, 26–28. Pirsig, Robert M. *Zen and the Art of Motorcycle Maintenance*. Toronto: Bantam Books, 1974. Raban, Jonathan. *Bad Land: An American Romance*. New York: Vintage Books, 1996. Rölvaag, O. E. *Giants in the Earth*. New York: Harper and Row, 1955. Rossum, Sonja, and Stephen Lavin. "Where Are the Great Plains? A Cartographic Analysis." *Professional Geographer* 52 (2000): 543–52. Sharp, Paul F. "The Northern Great Plains: A Study in Canadian American Regionalism." *Mississippi Historical Review* 39 (1952): 51–76. Thompson, John Herd. *Forging the Prairie West*. Toronto: Oxford University Press, 1998. Thornthwaite, C. Warren. "Climate and Settlement in the Great Plains." In *Climate and Man: Yearbook of Agriculture, 1941*. Washington DC: Government Printing Office, 1941: 177–87. Webb, Walter Prescott. *The Great Plains*. New York: Grosset and Dunlap, 1931. Wilson, Charles R., and William Ferris. *Encyclopedia of Southern Culture*. Chapel Hill: University of North Carolina Press, 1989.

Encyclopedia of the Great Plains

African Americans

Benjamin Pap Singleton and S. A. McClure, emigrants leaving Nashville, Tennessee, April 15, 1876

AFRICAN AMERICANS

There has long been an important African American presence in the Great Plains. African Americans were there in the early years of exploration, through the conflicts over slavery in Kansas, on the cattle drives, and in the celebrated black frontier regiments. As "Exodusters" they were part of the pioneer settlement of the region, and in the twentieth century they moved to new urban frontiers in Plains cities. As elsewhere in the country, African Americans have been victimized on the Plains, most drastically in the Tulsa Race Riot of 1921. But the Great Plains has also seen some of their greatest triumphs, such as the victory in *Brown v. The Board of Education of Topeka*, which set in process the desegregation of schools. African Americans' triumphs have also been expressed in the people—Malcolm X, Gordon Parks, and Charlie Parker, to mention only a few—who have risen from the Great Plains to make their mark on history.

Beginnings

African Americans were not a major presence in the Great Plains until after the end of Reconstruction in 1877, but that does not mean they played an insignificant role in shaping the early history of the region. As early as the 1530s Esteban (*Estevanico*), an African slave, was a member of the ill-fated expedition of Cabeza de Vaca across the Texas plains. From 1804 to 1806, York, William Clark's slave, was part of the celebrated Lewis and Clark expedition from St. Louis to the Pacific and back. The fur trapper Jim Beckwourth, son of a Virginia plantation owner and a slave woman, first crossed the Great Plains in 1824 heading for the beaver streams of the Rocky Mountains. Beckwourth spent the remaining forty-two years of his life in the Great Plains and elsewhere in the West, living as a trapper, adopted Crow Indian, and guide. Edward Rose was also an African American fur trapper. Rose first went up the Missouri River in 1807, and he remained a key figure in the fur trade until his death at the hands of Arikaras in 1832.

"Aunt" Clara Brown was another African American pioneer. Brown was born a slave in Virginia around 1800 and lived as a slave in Kentucky until she bought her freedom in 1857. Two years later she joined a wagon train of gold prospectors and headed to Denver, where she opened a laundry and established a Sunday school. She was also instrumental in bringing other African Americans to Denver and establishing one of the first black communities on the Plains.

Bleeding Kansas

Still, there were few African Americans, slave or free, in the Great Plains at the onset of the Civil War. Nebraska, for example, reported eighty-two African Americans in 1860, mainly free, and an 1856 count in Kansas listed 400 African American slaves. Despite these relatively small numbers, slavery was the crucial conflict in the initial development of these territories. The 1854 Kansas-Nebraska Act was intended to be a compromise between southern and northern interests, leaving the population of each territory to vote to permit, or prohibit, slavery. But by allowing the extension of slavery to be decided by a few thousand voters at the eastern edge of the Great Plains, Congress upset the balance between North and South and precipitated the Civil War.

The conflict centered on Kansas. Many of the early residents were from the Midwest. They were antislavery Free Soilers, but they were often also antiblack; they wanted neither enslaved nor free African Americans in their prospective state. They were mobilized by the results of the 1854 territorial election that sent a proslavery representative to Congress and elected a proslavery governor, largely because advocates of slavery had poured across the border from Missouri to vote. In retaliation, two antislavery factions united to form the Topeka Movement (or Free State Party), in effect creating two competing governments in Kansas. The Topeka Movement uneasily contained genuine abolitionists as well as those who sought a general exclusion of all African Americans from Kansas. The abolitionists triumphed in 1861 when, after the secession of the South, Kansas was admitted into the Union as a free state.

The antislavery debate was not limited to politics but raged among ordinary citizens across the land. Free Soilers, centered in Lawrence, raided slave auctions, while rampaging Missourians attacked that city on May 21, 1856, burning the Free State governor's house to the ground. John Brown was the most widely known figure to emerge from "Bleeding Kansas." Brown was an abolitionist who believed in the liberation of slaves at all costs, and his violent raids on slavers in Kansas and elsewhere brought him to national prominence as a hero in the North and a pariah in the South.

The Civil War raged mainly to the east of the Great Plains, although a brutal, desultory guerrilla war between proslavery raiders from Missouri and Free State militia from Kansas reprised the terror of the 1850s in that border zone. Meanwhile, many African Americans from Kansas fought for their freedom in the East, a freedom attained through the enactment of the Emancipation Proclamation on January 1, 1863.

Cowboys, Soldiers, and Settlers

The end of the Civil War marked the beginning of a growing African American population in the Great Plains, as emancipated slaves moved out of the South. Black cowboys worked the trail drives north from Texas, African American army regiments were assigned to the Plains, and in the late 1870s African American settlers—known as Exodusters—homesteaded in the region.

It is estimated that in the decades following the Civil War about 9,000 African Americans rode the cattle trails north from Texas to the railheads in Kansas and Nebraska and to the military posts and Indian reservations on the Northern Great Plains. This accounts for about one-quarter of all the trail hands during the open-range era. Some worked in all-black outfits, but nearly all outfits had at least one African American. They were employed mainly as wranglers (the toughest job on the trail) but also as cowhands and cooks. Rarely, except in outfits that were all African American, were they foremen or bosses. There is no evidence, however, that they faced wage discrimination. In fact, African Americans probably faced less discrimination on the trail drive, where they ate and slept alongside European Americans and Hispanic Americans, than in any other context in the nation at that time. Once in town, however, segregation in separate hotels, restaurants, and brothels was the norm.

In 1866 Congress authorized the creation of six African American regiments to patrol the Great Plains. The most renowned was the Tenth Cavalry Regiment, formed at Fort Leavenworth, Kansas, and given authority over Kansas, Oklahoma, New Mexico, and Arizona. Called "buffalo soldiers" by Plains Indians because of the color and texture of their hair, the African American soldiers accepted the name as a badge of respect and adopted the buffalo as the main character of their coat of arms. The all-black Ninth Cavalry and Twenty-fourth and Twenty-fifth Infantry Regiments also served throughout the Plains, engaging in campaigns against Native Americans, building military posts, erecting telegraph lines, and corralling horse thieves. These regiments earned respect for future generations of African Americans in the military. The four regiments had the lowest desertion rates in the Army of the West, and from their ranks eventually came eighteen congressional Medal of Honor winners. Nevertheless, at the places where they were garrisoned—Fort Hays, Kansas, for example—they were frequently embroiled in violent clashes with local settlers, clashes prompted by the settlers' racism and by a more general animosity between soldiers and civilians.

The first substantial growth of the African American population in the Great Plains occurred after 1877 when the Democrats returned to power in the South and, with the acquiescence of Republican president Rutherford B. Hayes, set about reversing the gains that Southern blacks had made during Reconstruction. Repressive laws curtailed African American political, civil, and economic rights and reduced many blacks to landlessness as they labored as sharecroppers, often on the same plantations where they or their parents had been slaves. Here, indeed, was a pool for migration.

Benjamin "Pap" Singleton, from Tennessee, realized that emigration was the solution to the problem of landlessness and that the Great Plains beckoned. In 1879 Singleton and his Edgefield Real Estate and Homestead Association began recruiting African Americans to move to the Singleton Colony in Dunlap, Kansas. By 1880, through the efforts of Singleton and other individuals, 9,500 Exodusters had moved to Kansas, mainly from Texas, Mississippi, and Louisiana.

Nicodemus, perhaps the best known of

the African American towns in Kansas, was founded on the semiarid plains of western Kansas in 1877. The first settlers were from Kentucky. By 1880 the African American population of the town had swelled to 452, and it boasted three general stores, a post office, three churches, and three hotels. Nicodemus actually worked well as an interracial settlement, with businesses and associations being run by both European Americans and African Americans. After an early boom, however, the town's fate was sealed in 1888 when it failed to land a rail connection, and many of its residents moved elsewhere. Nicodemus remains a small town, but it continues to function as a focal point for African Americans in western Kansas.

Oklahoma Territory was another attractive destination for the Exodusters in the late nineteenth century. The opening of the unassigned portion of Oklahoma Territory to homesteaders on April 22, 1889, created a land rush in which African Americans fully participated. At least thirty predominantly African American towns were established from 1889 to 1916 in what would become the state of Oklahoma in 1907. One of these was Langston in western Oklahoma. Langston was established in 1890 by Edward P. McCabe, who had previously been one of the founders of Nicodemus. By 1892 Langston had become the site of the Colored Agricultural and Normal School, and soon the town had the highest literacy rate in the territory. Like Nicodemus, Langston's growth stalled when the railroads chose to go elsewhere, but it is still the site of Langston University, Oklahoma's only predominantly African American university.

Smaller numbers of African American settlers moved to Nebraska and points north. These areas were simply too far from the source of migration in the South. North Dakota, for example, had only 113 black settlers in 1880 and 617 by 1910.

Farther north, the Exoduster wave of immigration reached the Prairie Provinces of Canada in 1908. These settlers were again fleeing persecution, this time from the racist government that came to power with statehood in Oklahoma in 1907. In the years before statehood, African Americans in Oklahoma Territory had been relatively few—about 8 percent of the population—but many were successful farmers, businessmen, and community leaders. Their very success bred opposition in the European American community. Against a backdrop of increasing violence, including lynchings, the Democratic Party gained power in 1907 by campaigning against racial equality. Subsequently, Oklahoma segregated railroads and other facilities and restricted suffrage. Within a period of three years, approximately 1,300 African Americans migrated from Oklahoma to Canada, settling primarily around Edmonton. They were mainly skilled farmers who settled in rural areas, but by 1911 there were also 72 African Americans in Calgary and 208 in Edmonton. However, their reception in Canada was no better than it had been in Oklahoma. In fact, the Canadian government actively opposed the immigration and even sent agents to Oklahoma to stop it. These efforts essentially halted African American immigration to the Prairie Provinces in 1911.

Urban Migration and Racial Violence

At the beginning of the twentieth century, almost 90 percent of African Americans lived in the South, a distribution extending from Virginia to East Texas and largely reflecting the geography of plantation crops, especially cotton. They lived mainly in rural areas. By 1970 only 50 percent of African Americans remained in the South. In one of the great migrations in U.S. history, African Americans left the rural South for the cities of the Northeast, Midwest, and, after 1945, the West. They were pulled by job opportunities, direct recruitment, and the promise of a better future. They were pushed by disenfranchisement and persecution in the South, as well as by the mechanization of agriculture. The Great Plains, with its predominantly agricultural economy, was generally marginal to this migration, but Plains cities in particular saw significant increases in black population over the course of the twentieth century.

World War I, with its increased industrial production and labor demands, was the initial stimulus for the movement of African Americans out of the South. Viewed at the state level, the Great Plains was not greatly affected. No Plains state kept up with the national average of black population increase from 1910 to 1920. At the city level, however, the population composition of the Great Plains was changing. Fort Worth, Oklahoma City, Tulsa, Kansas City, Denver, and Omaha all saw rapid increases in their African American populations. From these populations, increasingly concentrated in segregated neighborhoods, came vibrant cultural achievements and long-lasting community institutions, but they were also targets for discrimination and racial violence, particularly when the job market contracted.

This was the situation in Omaha in September 1919. Omaha's African American population had doubled during the previous decade, climbing to more than 10,000. Many were recent migrants from the South, attracted by jobs on the Union Pacific Railroad or in the Union Stock Yards and, initially at least, by the absence of Jim Crow laws that had plagued them in their previous home. But increased visibility brought discrimination. In 1916, for example, the Union Pacific replaced its black janitors with Japanese, and separate rental listings for African Americans restricted their housing choices to the downtown, in the thriving and violent red-light district. Crimes by African Americans soared, and the *Omaha Bee* seemed to take a delight in publicizing them.

In this atmosphere of racial tension, an atmosphere further heated by returning servicemen who could not find jobs, an African American named Will Brown was jailed at the Douglas County courthouse, allegedly for raping a white woman. On September 26 and 27, 1919, the *Omaha Daily Bee* ran incendiary headlines accusing Brown of the crime. On September 28 a mob of more than 4,000 men and women pulled Brown from the courthouse, hung him from a lamppost, riddled his body with bullets, then burned him on a bonfire while posing for the cameras. This was one of eighteen lynchings of African Americans in Nebraska from 1889 to 1919.

One of the reasons African Americans had left the South was to flee "southern justice," but in Omaha in 1919—and in Tulsa in 1921—they encountered treatment that was no better. It is worth noting that on May 19, 1923, Malcolm Little was born in Omaha. Little's family moved on within the year, to Milwaukee, then to Lansing, Michigan, but it was Omaha that was the birthplace of the great black nationalist Malcolm X.

Achievements in the Arts

Fortunately, racial violence was not the only outcome of African American migration to the Great Plains. The concentration of African Americans in Plains cities encouraged the formation of institutions that would contribute significantly to the future drive for civil rights. The Lincoln (Nebraska) Urban League, for example, provided social services to the city's African American population from 1932 to 1954 and fought for equal opportunity in employment and integration in housing. And it was the Great Plains, specifically Kansas City, that produced the most influential strains of that purely American art form, jazz.

Kansas City jazz was influenced by southern blues, ragtime, and the small band ensembles of New Orleans. Its immediate predecessor was the territory bands that flourished in the Great Plains during the 1920s. Many Kansas City jazz musicians of the 1930s, including Bill "Count" Basie, learned their art in territory bands. Basie's band, including Lester Young on tenor saxophone and Walter Page on bass, remains an influence on contemporary big bands. Kansas City jazz had its fluorescence in the 1940s, with Charlie Parker as its greatest native son.

The Great Plains was also home for fourteen years to the African American novelist and filmmaker Oscar Micheaux. Micheaux homesteaded in Gregory County, South Dakota, in 1904, and his first novel, *The Conquest: The Story of a Negro Pioneer* (1913), was virtually an autobiography of this experience. After writing two other novels, Micheaux moved into filmmaking. He wrote, directed, and produced more than forty-four films. He continued making low-budget films until 1948, often returning to the Great Plains setting. Micheaux's work was largely unappreciated in his lifetime (he died in 1951), but he has since been honored for being a pioneer in African American cinema.

The painter and muralist Aaron Douglas and the Pulitzer Prize–winning poet Gwendolyn Brooks are also major figures in the heritage of the arts on the Plains. Both were born in Topeka, Kansas; Douglas in 1899 and Brooks in 1950. Gordon Parks, the acclaimed photographer, filmmaker, composer, and writer, is also a native of Kansas. Born in Fort Scott in 1912, the largely self-educated Parks was a photographer for *Life* magazine for two decades and was the first African American to direct Hollywood movies. The writers Langston Hughes and Ralph Ellison were also products of the Great Plains.

Civil Rights

During the decades of the 1920s through the 1950s, the Plains African American population as a whole continued to grow but at a rate lower than the national average. In Texas, African Americans followed cotton out onto the High Plains. Throughout the Central and Southern Great Plains, major cities experienced a significant increase in the total number, and percentage, of African American residents. By 1960 Denver's African American population had risen to 35,261, or just over 7 percent of the city's total population. More than 95 percent of Colorado's African American population lived in that city. Other Plains cities with major African American concentrations in 1960 included Fort Worth, with 56,922 African Americans, or 16 percent of the total population; Oklahoma City with 42,282, or 13 percent of the population; and Kansas City, Missouri, with 84,191, or almost 18 percent of the city's population. In general, the number and percentage of African Americans in each Plains state declined with distance from the South. North Dakota had only 777 African Americans in 1960, barely one-tenth of a percent of the total population.

As elsewhere in the nation, African Americans in Great Plains cities were relegated to overcrowded ghettos and segregated in underequipped schools. While such institutional racism did not lead to riots, such as those seen in Chicago and Detroit, growing African American dissatisfaction was expressed in significant ways in the Great Plains. The Plains was the setting for one of the most celebrated cases in the history of American jurisprudence and for two of the earliest sit-ins that sparked the civil rights movement. The United States Supreme Court's May 17, 1954, decision in *Brown v. The Board of Education of Topeka* set forth the legal justification for the end of Jim Crow segregation. The case was actually a fusion of separate cases from South Carolina, Virginia, Delaware, and Washington DC as well as Kansas. The Kansas case was on appeal from federal district court on behalf of twelve African American parents and their nineteen children who were denied access to white schools in Topeka. Thurgood Marshall successfully argued that separate school facilities were a detriment to African American children and were therefore unequal, contradicting the guarantees of the Fourteenth Amendment. Chief Justice Earl Warren guided the decision. Even after this decision, however, school desegregation was a battle fought state by state, but the case inspired the eventual dismantling of segregated practices in American restaurants, buses, and parks.

Although overshadowed by the 1960 sit-in

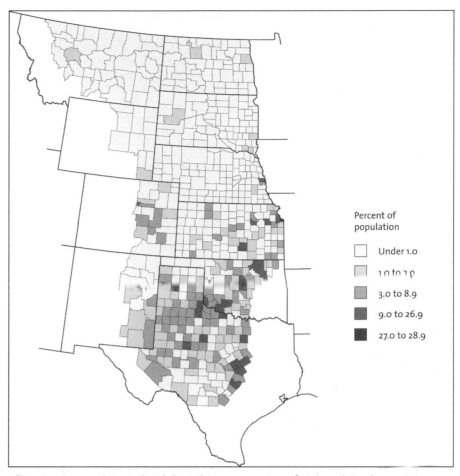

African American population in the U.S. Great Plains as a percentage of total population, by county, in 2000

Percent of population

- Under 1.0
- 1.0 to 2.9
- 3.0 to 8.9
- 9.0 to 26.9
- 27.0 to 28.9

by African American youths at a Greensboro, North Carolina, segregated lunch counter, two earlier sit-ins in Oklahoma City and Wichita were important actions in the movement for African American social justice. Wichita was a booming city in 1958, with a developing aircraft industry that created jobs and attracted workers, including African Americans. But Wichita was also a segregated city where African Americans were not welcome in white elementary schools, restaurants, and other public places. In the spring of 1958 the Wichita Youth Council of the NAACP decided to integrate downtown lunch counters, beginning with the Dockum Drug Store. The nonviolent sit-in began on July 12 and continued until August 7, when the manager of the Dockum Drug Store capitulated and opened service to everyone regardless of race. Just two weeks later, the Oklahoma City Youth Council successfully staged a lunch-counter sit-in at the Katz Drug Store. There can be little doubt that these actions in the Great Plains, news of which diffused widely through the NAACP youth network, inspired later sit-ins in St. Louis, Chicago, and Greensboro.

The *Brown* decision and the Wichita and Oklahoma City sit-ins are landmarks in the civil rights movement in the Great Plains, but in the decades since, in every community that has a substantial African American population, leaders have striven to achieve social justice, economic gains, and political representa-

tion. Their efforts have met with success. In 1991, for example, Wellington Webb, a staunch civil rights advocate, was elected mayor of Denver. Yet despite the gains, African Americans remain one of the poorest segments of the Plains population. In 1990, for example, in Kansas and Nebraska, almost one-third of African Americans lived below the poverty level.

Population Geography

The population of African Americans in Great Plains states continued to increase during the latter half of the twentieth century. In 2000 the African American population of Texas stood at 2.4 million, an increase of 102 percent since 1960. Corresponding totals and percentage increases for other Plains states in 2000 are Oklahoma with 261,000, a 70 percent increase; Kansas with 154,000, a 68 percent increase; Nebraska with 69,000, a 136 percent increase; South Dakota with 4,700, a 322 percent increase; and North Dakota with 3,900, a 402 percent increase. Only in Texas did African Americans make up more than 10 percent of the total population in 2000, and in that case most were located to the east of the Great Plains.

An analysis of the map drawn from 2000 census data reveals that the African American population in the U.S. Great Plains, as a percentage of county population, declines with distance from the South, the original source region. In the Great Plains proper, counties where African Americans account for more than 10 percent of the total population are either large cities, such as Kansas City, Kansas, and Omaha, or are near military bases, such as Fort Sill in southwestern Oklahoma. The African American concentration in north-central Oklahoma includes large city populations in Tulsa and Oklahoma City but is also an inheritance from nineteenth-century slave and free-black settlement in Indian Territory. In recent years, smaller cities such as Lincoln and Topeka have also seen sizable increases in their African American populations. The Northern Great Plains remains an area of few African Americans. In the Prairie Provinces of Canada, African Americans, including immigrants from the Caribbean, are only a fraction of a percent of the total population. More than 80 percent of them live in the large cities, especially Calgary and Edmonton.

Viewed at the national scale, the Great Plains, along with the intermontane West, have the lowest populations of African Americans. Nevertheless, African Americans, from fur trappers to contemporary musicians and politicians, have played an important role in shaping the culture of the Great Plains, and this contribution will certainly continue to be made in the future.

See also LAW: *Brown v. The Board of Education of Topeka*; Jim Crow Laws / LITERARY TRADITIONS: Ellison, Ralph / MUSIC: Parker, Charlie / PROTEST AND DISSENT: Malcolm X.

Malcolm Yeung
Evelyn Hu-DeHart
University of Colorado at Boulder

Athearn, Robert G. *In Search of Canaan: Black Migration to Kansas, 1879–1880.* Lawrence: Regents Press of Kansas, 1978. Bogle, Lori. "On Our Way to the Promised Land: Black Migration from Arkansas to Oklahoma, 1889–1893." *The Chronicles of Oklahoma* 72 (1994): 160–77. Buecker, Thomas R. "Prelude to Brownsville: The Twenty-fifth Infantry at Fort Niobrara, Nebraska, 1902–1906." *Great Plains Quarterly* 16 (1996): 95–106. Hamilton, Kenneth Marvin. *Black Towns and Profit: Promotion and Development in the Trans-Appalachian West.* Urbana: University of Illinois Press, 1991. Katz, William Loren. *The Black West.* Seattle: Open Hand, 1987. Kluger, Richard. *Simple Justice: The History of Brown vs. Board of Education and Black America's Struggle for Equality.* New York: Alfred A. Knopf, 1976. Leckie, William H. *The Buffalo Soldiers: A Narrative of the Negro Cavalry in the West.* Norman: University of Oklahoma Press, 1967. Mellinger, Philip. "Discrimination and Statehood in Oklahoma." *The Chronicles of Oklahoma* 49 (1971): 340–78. Menard, Orville D. "Tom Dennison, the *Omaha Bee*, and the 1919 Omaha Race Riot." *Nebraska History* 68 (1987): 152–63. Mihelich, Dennis N. "The Formation of the Lincoln Urban League." *Nebraska History* 68 (1987): 63–73. O'Brien, Claire. "'With One Mighty Pull': Interracial Town Boosting in Nicodemus, Kansas." *Great Plains Quarterly* 16 (1996): 117–29. Painter, Nell Irvin. *Exodusters: Black Migration to Kansas after Reconstruction.* New York: Alfred A. Knopf, 1976. Parker, Keith D. "African Americans and the Great Plains: An Introduction." *Great Plains Quarterly* 16 (1996): 83–84. Rice, Marc. "'Frompin' in the Great Plains: Listening and Dancing to the Jazz Orchestras of Alphonso Trent, 1925–44." *Great Plains Quarterly* 16 (1996): 107–15. Walters, Ronald. "The Great Plains Sit-In Movement, 1958–1960." *Great Plains Quarterly* 16 (1996): 85–94. Winks, Robin W. *The Blacks in Canada: A History.* Montreal: McGill-Queen's University Press, 1997.

AFRICAN AMERICAN COWBOYS

Both scholars and popular writers have studied African Americans in the cattle industry of the Great Plains, but a review of such works reveals that the image outweighs the reality. This is not to say that African Americans historically did not have an important role in the cowboy culture of the Great Plains. In fact many, if not most, of the Texas and Indian Territory outfits that participated on the long overland drives to the Kansas railheads employed African Americans whose skills (working cattle, caring for horses, working as blacksmiths or cooks) were essential to the operation. But what is perhaps most striking is that while our popular historical image of the cowboy is of a nameless, unassuming, white southerner, most of the handful of black cowboys who are known have received much individual notoriety.

When African American cowboys entered the Great Plains after the Civil War to work on the long overland drives that linked Texas to the Kansas railheads, they were merely continuing a centuries-old pattern rooted in the American South, Mexico, the Caribbean, southern Iberia, and perhaps even West Africa. In fact, Terry Jordan, a geographer who has thoroughly studied the diffusion and material culture of cattle ranching, notes that African slaves were the *vaqueros* for the herds in southwestern Spain by the sixteenth century. This African labor-based Iberian model was transferred first to the Caribbean, and from there to Mexico and the North American Atlantic coast, where it eventually combined with Germanic- and Celtic-derived cattle-herding traditions. Spanish outposts in Florida and Louisiana sporadically reinforced the Iberian system, but by the early eighteenth century the South Carolina Back Country, swarming with wild cattle that were periodically rounded up by slaves, emerged as the principal core area for what would become the most common pre-cotton land use in the piney woods of the Gulf Coastal Plain. As Jordan explains, this Caribbean-derived lowland South cattle frontier led west to Louisiana, where it merged with Spanish and French traditions, all the while using African labor.

Abolition and a surplus of unemployed southern whites apparently changed the cowboy stereotype to the white version just prior to the long overland drives in the Great Plains and the establishment of ranches across the West. With plenty of whites competing for work, the African American cowhand became more of an anomaly in the Great Plains by the mid-1870s. But anomalies are often remembered, and plenty of African American cowboys entered regional folklore. Folk memory and white writers have preserved many infamous black gunfighters and murderers, such as Ben Hodges of Dodge City and Cherokee Bill, who terrorized Indian Territory. Ample nicknames persist, like One Horse Charley and Bronco Sam; others received the appellation "Nigger" so-and-so, which was tacked onto the first names of Newt Clendenen, Bob Leavitt, and many others.

The most famous African American cowboys were those who gained notoriety in show business Westerns, usually for their roping and riding abilities. Nat Love (aka Deadwood Dick), perhaps the most photographed black cowboy of the Great Plains, became famous as a trick roper in the Black Hills. Henry Clay, a trick roper who performed with Will Rogers, was another. Clay worked for the Miller Brothers' 101 Ranch in north-central Oklahoma in the 1890s and early 1900s. The 101, which is credited with institutionalizing professional rodeo (as well as the competitive "fancy dance" of Indian powwows), employed

Adjusting saddle stirrups at a Colored Rodeo Association of Denver event, September 1948

George Hooker, a trick rider, as well as probably the most famous black cowboy, Bill Pickett. Pickett was a native of East Texas who resided for much of his life in Indian Territory. He joined the 101 in the 1890s and became the star of its touring Wild West show. Pickett traveled with the 101 to Chicago, New York, and London and is widely credited with inventing the rodeo sport of "bulldogging," called steer wrestling today. Pickett called it bulldogging because, after jumping from his horse, grabbing the steer's horns, and twisting its neck, he followed the habit of an East Texas cow dog and sunk his teeth into the steer's nose to bring the animal down.

Although the dust of illiteracy, legend, and racism surely obscures a clear view of the real lives and contributions of African American cowhands of the Great Plains, we can safely assume that most were not as simple as the bloodthirsty, comical, or flamboyant stereotypes that folklore and white popular history suggest. We should respect their known presence, celebrate a few, and recognize that we will probably never know much of the reality.

See also FILM: Miller Brothers / SPORTS AND RECREATION: Rodeo / TRANSPORTATION: Cattle Trails.

Brad A. Bays
Oklahoma State University

Durham, Philip, and Everett L. Jones. *The Negro Cowboys.* New York: Dodd, Mead and Company, 1965. Hanes, Bailey C. *Bill Pickett, Bulldogger.* Norman: University of Oklahoma Press, 1977. Jordan, Terry G. *North American Cattle Ranching Frontiers. Origins, Diffusion, and Differentiation.* Albuquerque: University of New Mexico Press, 1993.

AFRICAN AMERICAN NEWSPAPERS

The first African American newspaper was founded in 1827 when *Freedom's Journal* began publication in New York. Twenty-seven years later, the first African American newspaper appeared in the Great Plains when the *Herald of Freedom* began on October 21, 1854, at Wakarusa, Kansas Territory. Unfortunately, editor G. W. Brown's venture had to overcome bad weather, supply shortages, and other strings of bad luck before he could publish his second issue. A scarcity of readers then added to his misfortunes.

In fact, sufficient readers did not begin to arrive until 1877, heeding the call from Benjamin "Pap" Singleton, a former slave from Nashville, Tennessee, to come to Kansas. With continuing westward migration came the fighting spirit typical of the black press. It was displayed at Topeka in 1894 when the *Kansas Blackman* began publication. Editor W. B. Driver said that his paper was published solely in the interest of "negroes," and he used his newspaper's name to encourage black financial support.

Another African American newspaper, the *State Ledger,* under the editorship of Fred Jeltz, had been trying for two years to convince black Kansans to reject racial boundaries and instead embrace the idea that *all* citizens are Americans. The *Kansas Blackman's* name and editorial policy contradicted those ideas, Jeltz argued, and thus should be eliminated from black society. Jeltz's attacks against that newspaper, the editor, and his philosophy became so relentless that the *Kansas Blackman* folded within four months.

The fighting spirit was nowhere stronger in the Great Plains than in Oklahoma, where in 1914 Roscoe Dunjee began the *Black Dispatch.* When questioned about his newspaper's name, Dunjee said it was used to dignify a slur. Along with the name, however, was an editorial philosophy of a newspaper for all the people, equal rights for all, and opposition to the practice of favoring one race at the expense of another. Dunjee's goal was to right any wrongs he confronted, editorially attacking anyone, whether governor, commissioner, army, or navy, whose policies, he felt, infringed on civil rights. Dunjee was not hesitant to seek the truth and place the results before the public.

When it came to finding the truth or writing editorials, Dunjee was known internationally. Even readers who might rejoice to see the *Dispatch* run out of business admitted that you may not like what Dunjee had written, but you read every word, despite his disregard for brevity. Others agreed that what he wrote was sometimes so embarrassingly accurate that the glare of the misdeed was most distressful when seen in print.

The black press did not spread throughout the Great Plains. It followed the path of the migration to Kansas, northwestern Texas, central Oklahoma, and eastern Nebraska. Black editors were few, but they were feisty and they hoisted the fighting flag wherever they migrated.

Before the civil rights movement of the 1950s and 1960s, the traditional white press did not cover much news about African Americans, but many white editors and publishers eventually began to lure the best black reporters and editors to the large dailies. African American readers then shifted to the white press as its primary source for news.

Once the black press no longer needed to function as a fighting press, it assumed a responsibility for reporting community news. More than 300 African American newspapers began publication after the civil rights movement. Of that number, nearly 200 still exist within thirty-six states and the District of Columbia, three of them functioning as dailies. Florida, with eighteen, has the largest number, followed by Illinois with twelve. Within the Great Plains, only two states still have African American newspapers—Oklahoma with four and Kansas with one.

Charles A. Simmons
University of Central Oklahoma

Pride, Armistead S. "A Register and History of Negro Newspapers in the United States: 1827–1950." Ph.D. diss., Northwestern University, 1950.

AFRICAN AMERICAN PIONEERS

Black men and women appeared much earlier in this continent's history than is generally acknowledged. An African-born slave, Esteban (*Estevanico*), accompanied the Spanish explorer Cabeza de Vaca across the southern Texas plains. African Americans were also part of Coronado's expedition through the Central Great Plains in 1540–42. At the advent of Americans in the Great Plains, York, a black servant to William Clark, was a member of the Lewis and Clark expedition through the Plains to the Pacific and back. And Isaiah Dorman, a guide and explorer who worked among and against Native Americans for twenty years, ended his life as the only African American casualty at the Battle of the Little Bighorn in Montana in 1876.

The first significant migration of African Americans into the Great Plains began in 1857, when fugitives from the slave state of Missouri crossed into eastern Kansas Territory where free-state forces were dominant. By 1865 nearly 9 percent of the population of the new state of Kansas was African American, the highest proportion ever reached in Kansas. Most lived in the developing urban areas of eastern Kansas, including Leavenworth, Wyandotte County, and North and South Lawrence. A few pushed as far west as the Neosho Valley.

A large infusion of blacks into the Great Plains occurred after the Civil War with the establishment of the all-black Ninth and Tenth Cavalry Regiments and the Twenty-fourth and Twenty-fifth Infantry Regiments, with the Ninth and Tenth—the "buffalo soldiers"— being particularly influential. These regiments, which served throughout the Plains, absorbed thousands of men who would have otherwise returned to their homes in a time of few jobs and economic depression.

At the same time, western territories were looking for new residents as they sought statehood, and "Exodusters"—black men and women who moved mainly to Kansas and Oklahoma—added their numbers to the growing populations of all colors. For example, Benjamin "Pap" Singleton, a former slave, recruited 200 to 300 black settlers to his Cherokee County Colony in southeastern Kansas in the 1870s. About 6,000 Exodusters moved to Kansas in 1879, when "Kansas fever" was at its peak. Every county in central Kansas had African American settlers by 1885, though regionally they were only a small proportion of the total population.

African American settlers also moved to Nebraska during the early 1880s, settling in Custer, Dawson, and Hamilton Counties. A black community was established near Overton, Dawson County, by a group of ex-slaves who had escaped into Canada and returned to the United States after the Civil War. This community thrived for several decades until the passage of the Kinkaid Act in 1904 enticed many to take out 640-acre homesteads in Nebraska's Sandhills. By 1917 nearly 100 families had settled primarily in Cherry County along a stretch of the North Loup River.

Thousands of black and Hispanic cowboys worked in the Great Plains during the late 1800s and early 1900s. Employed because they had "horse sense," gained from working on farms in the South and on antebellum ranches in the Southwest, these men were snapped up by ranching operations that were growing rapidly to meet the demands of large populations who desired inexpensive meat. Mexican "vaqueros" were the main models for the American cowboy, but African American men who were eager and experienced cattle workers and African American former cavalry and infantry soldiers also rode the range. By the late 1870s, when the open-range cattle industry was at its peak, as many as 9,000 of an estimated 35,000 cowboys were African American.

The development of railroads and towns in the Great Plains after 1870 offered employment to African American cowhands, miners, nannies, small business owners, oxen drovers, freighters, cooks, railyard workers, section crews, and entertainers. Professional employment as dentists, doctors, nurses, ministers, merchants, and teachers gave African Americans positions of authority and influence. Clara Brown established herself as a prominent business entrepreneur and philanthropist in Denver in the late 1860s, and Dr. M. O. Ricketts became the first African American graduate of the University of Nebraska's College of Medicine in 1884 and later a state legislator.

Outside large cities, many black pioneers settled in towns near military forts or railroads. Though their numbers were relatively few, some African American families established ranches. Daniel Webster "80-John" Wallace was the scion of a cattle family in West Texas. Alonzo Stepp and James Edwards started cattle operations in Wyoming that grew to a substantial size in the first half of the twentieth century.

The railroads in particular offered employment opportunities to black men and—to a lesser degree—women. Though the "front end" jobs of engineer, fireman, and administrator were taken by European Americans, the "rear end" occupations of cook, porter, and conductor were left for men and women of color. Later, many of these workers would establish ancillary businesses such as laundries, food preparation, and maid services.

Lawmen such as Bass Reeves, Zeke Millar, and Bob Fortune were feared emissaries of the law in northern Texas and Oklahoma, working for the "Hanging Judge," Isaac Parker. Some black men also veered to the other side of the law, becoming bandits, bank robbers, and outlaws of all stripes. At least one of the "Black Barts" of the Dakotas was an African American.

Nat Love, or "Deadwood Dick," if his autobiography can be believed, personified the African American experience in the Great Plains. An ex-slave, he rubbed shoulders with outlaws and lawmen in Dodge City in 1869, rode the Chisholm Trail as a cowpuncher, became a rodeo champion in Deadwood City in the 1870s, and ended up as a Pullman porter.

Pioneering was difficult for anyone, regardless of skin color, yet these black trailblazers were in evidence from southern Texas to Edmonton and from Denver to Kansas City.

They were, in essence, everywhere that other pioneers chose to work and prosper. Sometimes they succeeded, and sometimes they failed, but it was the true legacy of the frontier experience that hard times were visited evenly on all who came West.

Jack Ravage
University of Wyoming

Durham, Philip, and Everett L. Jones. *The Negro Cowboys.* New York: Dodd, Mead, 1965. Ravage, John W. *Black Pioneers: Images of the Black Experience on the North American Frontier.* Salt Lake City: University of Utah Press, 1997. Shortridge, James R. *Peopling the Plains: Who Settled Where in Frontier Kansas.* Lawrence: University Press of Kansas, 1995.

AFRICAN CANADIANS

Between 1905 and 1912 some 1,500 African Americans migrated to the Plains region of Canada. They came from Oklahoma, although a few families were from Kansas and Texas. They settled in small, rural communities in the Canadian provinces of Saskatchewan and Alberta.

The first black farmers began arriving in 1905. They appear to have been lured north by reports of good agricultural land being available. During the late nineteenth and early twentieth centuries, the federal government of Canada launched an extensive campaign in the U.S. Midwest and Great Plains to attract experienced farmers. Advertisements flooded regional newspapers, pamphlets were widely distributed, and Canadian exhibits were regular features at state and local agricultural fairs. The Canadian advertising did not mention race as a factor in determining who would be allowed to settle in the northern dominion.

The trickle of black farmers into western Canada increased substantially when Oklahoma became a state in 1907. The Oklahoma Democratic Party campaigned for delegates to the Constitutional Convention, and later the first state legislature, on a "Jim Crow" segregation platform. Their racist appeals were effective and, once elected, the Democrats moved quickly to implement a range of racial segregation measures. Black Oklahomans reacted to these developments by organizing, petitioning, boycotting, protesting, and launching court challenges. Their tactics were no more successful in the new state than they had been elsewhere in the South. This led some of them to leave Oklahoma, and one of their destinations was the much-promoted lands available in western Canada.

The movement north was renewed in 1910 when Oklahoma Democrats moved to disenfranchise African Americans. Black Americans had traditionally voted for Lincoln's party, the Republicans. Their votes, when combined with a sizable white Republican minority in Oklahoma, always presented a challenge to the Democrats' political hold on the state. Three years after they segregated African Americans in public services, the Democrats eliminated the black voter from the state's political scene.

White western Canadians shared many of their American neighbors' racial attitudes,

though they rarely expressed them as violently. They reacted overwhelmingly against the black migration and successfully petitioned their federal government to stop African Americans from coming north. At first the Canadian federal authorities tried to discourage blacks by not sending information to prospective African American settlers and by delaying their entry at the border. These methods were only partially effective, and eventually the Immigration Branch of the Canadian Department of the Interior sent two agents to Oklahoma to try to stop black settlers from leaving for Canada. One of these agents was particularly effective, probably because he was himself black, and by late 1911 the African American migration from Oklahoma was ending. Still concerned about possible migration, the Canadian federal cabinet approved an order barring blacks from entering Canada. When the work of the agents in Oklahoma proved to be successful, the order was quietly repealed.

African Americans who managed to get through Canada's immigration barriers appear to have avoided heavily settled areas on the Canadian Plains, possibly in an effort to minimize contact with whites. The areas where they chose to settle were remote, even by the standards of the settlement era. Black farmers headed to the alternating bush and meadowlands that form the northern boundary of the Canadian Great Plains. The principal settlement in Saskatchewan was along the North Saskatchewan River, north of the town of Maidstone. In Alberta, African Americans fanned out from Edmonton, forming an arc of settlements at Breton, Lobstick Lake, Wildwood, and Amber Valley.

African American families in western Canada went to work immediately, transforming the bush and meadowlands into productive farms. It was hard work, and they had to learn new ways of farming. Black pioneers had farmed cotton and tobacco in Oklahoma but now had to make a transition to raising grain and livestock.

Their hard work eventually paid dividends, and within a decade of initial settlement most black farmers were well established. Within those years they also began to create the institutions that gave substance to their Canadian communities. One particularly important social institution was the school, because a large number of children had come north and were soon joined by brothers and sisters born in Canada. African Americans soon learned that they were not completely isolated from white society, and that racially mixed schools were as delicate an issue for whites living north of the forty-ninth parallel as for those south of it. Black children were barred from one Alberta school, while another African American community in Alberta organized its own separate school. In Saskatchewan black children were segregated in their own school for several years.

As with so many rural areas across the Great Plains, African American communities began losing their young people to the economic lure of the cities. Yet racial prejudice was also common in the cities of the Canadian Plains during the early twentieth century, and the new African Canadians found that they were limited to jobs in construction, cartage and hauling, and meatpacking. African Canadians also found that railroading was one of the few industries open to them, and blacks from western Canada (like their counterparts in the United States) found steady employment as porters, although the more lucrative and prestigious position of conductor was closed to them for decades. These African Canadian railroad families gradually relocated across the country, and today the descendants of western Canada's black pioneers are found in railroad centers such as Vancouver, Calgary, Winnipeg, Toronto, and Montreal.

While they faced persistent racial prejudice, black pioneers and their offspring quickly identified with their new country. Perhaps there was no better indicator of that allegiance than the readiness with which young African Canadians volunteered for the Canadian armed forces during World Wars I and II. Black Canadians served their country with distinction during both conflicts.

African Americans who migrated to Saskatchewan and Alberta were seeking a refuge from the racism they had experienced in the United States. They headed north to a region that must have seemed both different and tragically familiar. They learned new ways of farming and how to deal with a different government. Unfortunately, they also encountered another variety of the racism they had fled. Their African Canadian descendants have taken up the struggle for equality and respect, and are calling upon a historical legacy to help them in that struggle.

R. Bruce Shepard
University of Saskatchewan

Painter, Nell Irvin. *Exodusters: Black Migration to Kansas after Reconstruction.* New York: Alfred A. Knopf, 1976. Shepard, R. Bruce. *Deemed Unsuitable.* Toronto: Umbrella Press, 1997. Winks, Robin. *The Blacks in Canada: A History.* New Haven CT: Yale University Press, 1971.

ALL-BLACK TOWNS

African Americans left the South for the "promised land" of the West in ever-increasing numbers after the Civil War. Economic hardship, racial violence, and intolerance prompted this vast migration from states such as Mississippi, Louisiana, Tennessee, Texas, and Arkansas. With leadership from Pap Singleton and Henry Adams, the "Exodusters" settled mainly in Kansas in 1879–80, though the movement had began a few years earlier and lasted into the next decade. The opportunity to own land attracted many of these people to the Great Plains. Reports directed back to the South claimed that landownership was a simple and cheap prospect.

By 1881 African American emigrants had established twelve agricultural colonies in Kansas: Nicodemus, Hodgeman, Morton City, Dunlap, Kansas City–area Colony, Parsons, Wabaunsee, Summit Township, Topeka-area

Town council, Boley, Oklahoma, ca. 1907–10

Colony, Burlington, Little Coney, and the Daniel Votaw Colony. Another settlement, the Singleton Colony, seems to have never really been a viable community. Many of the other colonies lasted only a few years. The town of Nicodemus, on the other hand, founded a few years before the large exodus, prospered into the twentieth century. African Americans also established colonies in Nebraska, including the town of Dewitty. They migrated to western New Mexico, too, creating settlements such as Blackdom and Dora. Oliver Toussaint Jackson established the settlement of Dearfield, Colorado, in 1910, one of the last African American Plains agricultural communities. Many African Americans dispersed elsewhere throughout the Plains; most worked the land like their white counterparts.

During a fifty-five-year period following the end of the Civil War, African Americans built more than fifty identifiable communities in Oklahoma. Some sprouted and quickly vanished; others still survive. Achieving freedom after the Civil War, former slaves of the Cherokees, Creeks, Seminoles, Chickasaws, and Choctaws also formed towns in Indian Territory. When the U.S. government allotted land to individual Native Americans, most Indian "freedmen" chose land next to other African Americans. Their farming communities sheltered self-governed economic and social institutions, including businesses, schools, and churches. Enterprising businessmen set up every imaginable kind of business, including publishing concerns whose newspapers advertised in the South for settlers.

More African Americans settled in Oklahoma Territory with the land run of 1889, which offered "free land" to non-Indians. E. P. McCabe, former state auditor of Kansas, helped found the all-black town of Langston. By means of the *Langston City Herald*, which his traveling agents circulated around the

South, he and other leaders hoped to bring in large numbers of African Americans whose growing political power would secure their prosperity and safety. McCabe never accomplished his goal of creating an African American state. Nevertheless, dozens of black communities sprouted and flourished in the rich topsoil of the new territory and, after 1907, the new state.

In Oklahoma and Kansas, African Americans lived relatively free from the prejudices and brutality common in racially mixed communities of the Midwest and the South. Cohesive all-black settlements offered residents the security of depending on neighbors for financial assistance and the economic opportunity provided by access to open markets for their crops.

Marshalltown, North Fork Colored, Canadian Town, and Arkansas Colored existed as early as the 1860s in Indian Territory. Other Indian Territory towns that no longer exist include Sanders, Mabelle, Wiley, Homer, Huttonville, Lee, and Rentie. Among the Oklahoma Territory towns that no longer exist are Lincoln, Cimarron City, Bailey, Zion, Emanuel, Udora, and Douglas in old Oklahoma Territory. Surviving towns include Boley, Brooksville, Clearview, Grayson, Langston, Lima, Redbird, Rentiesville, Summit, Taft, Tatums, Tullahassee, and Vernon. Boley, the largest and most renowned of these was twice inspected by African American educator Booker T. Washington, who lauded the town in *Outlook Magazine* in 1908.

Immediately after statehood in 1907 the Oklahoma legislature passed Jim Crow laws, and many African Americans became disenchanted with the new state. A large contingent relocated to western Canada, forming colonies such as Amber Valley, Alberta, and Maidstone, Saskatchewan. Another exodus of African Americans from the United States occurred with the "Back to Africa" movements of the late nineteenth and early twentieth centuries. A large group of Oklahomans joined the ill-fated Chief Sam expedition to Africa. Other Plains African Americans migrated to colonies in Mexico.

The collapse of the American farm economy in the 1920s and the advent of the Great Depression in 1929 spelled the end for most all-black communities. The all-black towns were, for the most part, small agricultural centers that gave nearby African American farmers a market for their cotton and other crops. The Depression devastated these towns, and residents moved west or migrated to metropolises where jobs might be found. Black towns dwindled to only a few residents.

As population dwindled, so too did the tax base. In the 1930s many railroads failed, isolating small towns from regional and national markets. This spelled the end of many of the black towns. During the Depression, whites denied credit to African Americans, creating an almost impossible situation for black farmers and businessmen. Even Boley, one of the most successful towns, declared bankruptcy in 1939. Today, only a few all-black towns survive, but their legacy of economic and political freedom is well remembered.

Larry O'Dell
Oklahoma Historical Society

Crockett, Norman. *The Black Towns*. Lawrence: Regents Press of Kansas, 1979. Hamilton, Kenneth Marvin. *Black Towns and Profit: Promotion and Development in the Trans-Appalachian West, 1877–1915*. Urbana: University of Illinois Press, 1991. Taylor, Quintard. *In Search of the Racial Frontier: African Americans in the American West, 1528–1990*. New York: W. W. Norton, 1998.

BASEBALL, INTERRACIAL

Interracial baseball was prevalent in the Great Plains at the same time that other social interaction between African Americans and whites was virtually nonexistent. While Jim Crow segregation prevented African Americans from fully enjoying their constitutional liberties, black baseball players routinely experienced equality on the baseball fields of the Great Plains. It was common for all-black teams such as the San Angelo Sheepherders or Kansas City Colts to play against all-white teams such as the Duncan (Oklahoma) Cementers or the Arkansas City (Kansas) Dubbs.

Beginning around 1920, and increasingly thereafter, residents of the Great Plains could watch baseball contests between local all-black teams as well as barnstorming (touring) black teams that challenged local white teams. The all-black Wichita Monrovians, who played in the professional Colored Western League (founded in 1922) along with all-black teams from Oklahoma City, Omaha, Coffeyville, Topeka, Independence, and Kansas City (Kansas), often played white teams throughout the Plains because additional games provided players the opportunity to earn extra money. Barnstorming tours were also common and included many professional black teams, including the Cuban All Stars and the Kansas City Monarchs—the top team in the Negro

National League in the 1920s and 1930s. Despite the segregation that isolated white and black Americans in everyday life, the baseball diamond proved to be a place where diverse people could compete on an equal basis.

The extent of racial toleration on the baseball field is evident from the game that took place in 1925 between the all-black Wichita Monrovians and the all-white Wichita Ku Klux Klan Number 6 team. The game was played without violence, and the Monrovians prevailed ten to eight. Another sign of racial toleration on the baseball fields of the Great Plains was the existence of an entire racially integrated league in North Dakota in the early 1930s. The league included many players from the Negro National League, including Hall of Famer Satchel Paige, who played for the integrated Bismarcks and was paid $400 a month and given a car by the team owner.

The expansion of integrated regional baseball continued in 1934 when the organizers of the *Denver Post*'s semiprofessional baseball tournament invited the Kansas City Monarchs to be the first all-black team in the tournament's nineteen-year history. The Monarchs finished second and set the stage for future black teams to participate in Plains baseball tournaments. In 1935 the magnitude of racial toleration in baseball in the Plains was displayed in Wichita at the first National Semi-Pro Baseball Tournament. Four different racial groups competed among the thirty-two teams in the tournament. The Memphis Red Sox, San Angelo Sheepherders, Denver Stars, Texas Centennials, and Monroe Monarchs were all-black teams. The Nipponese Stars from California were Japanese and the Stanolind Indians from Oklahoma were Native American. The most diverse team was the tournament champion, the Bismarcks, who featured five white players and six black players, including Satchel Paige, who pitched in the decisive championship game.

Despite the presence of interracial baseball, the Great Plains was not a haven of racial tolerance in the Jim Crow era. Racial toleration in baseball in the Great Plains existed because African Americans represented only a tiny fragment of the total population and were consequently not considered a threat to the existing social order. Interracial and integrated baseball flourished there because the presence of black and white players together did not challenge the racist segregation that existed outside the lines of the ballfield.

See also SPORTS AND RECREATION: Baseball.

Jason Pendleton
Lawrence, Kansas

Bruce, Janet. *The Kansas City Monarchs*. Lawrence: University Press of Kansas, 1985. Pendleton, Jason. "A Jim Crow Strikes Out: Interracial Baseball in Wichita, Kansas 1920–1935." *Kansas History* 20 (1997): 86–101. Rogosin, Donn. *Invisible Men: Life in Baseball's Negro Leagues*. New York: Atheneum, 1983.

BECKWOURTH, JAMES (1798–1866)

Born a slave to his mulatto mother, Miss Kill, and plantation owner Sir Jennings Beckwith on April 26, 1798, in Fredericksburg, Virginia,

James Pierson Beckwourth became a famous African American mountain man. In 1810 the Beckwiths moved to St. Louis, where Beckwourth received his freedom. He joined Gen. William H. Ashley's fur-trapping expedition to the Rocky Mountains in 1824, working as a horse buyer, blacksmith, and trapper. Beckwourth fought against the Blackfeet in 1827–28, before being adopted into Crow chief Big Bowl's band. He married several Crow women while working as a trader for Kenneth McKenzie and the American Fur Company in the 1830s.

Beckwourth served under the command of Gen. Zachary Taylor in the Second Seminole War in Florida in 1836–37, worked as a trader for Andrew Sublette and Louis Vasquez along the Santa Fe Trail at Bent's Fort and Taos, and married a Spanish woman. In 1842 he built a trading post on the Arkansas River and founded the settlement of Pueblo, Colorado. He raided horses from Mexican ranchos, participated in the California insurrection in 1845–46, joined the gold rush in 1848, and opened a trail, later known as Beckwourth Pass, through the Sierras.

His 1854 account of his life earned him a reputation as a liar because he exaggerated his role in many events. He later supplied miners in the Pikes Peak gold rush and guided the army in the Sand Creek Massacre. After serving as scout at Fort Laramie, Beckwourth returned to live among the Crows, where he died in 1866.

Jay H. Buckley
Brigham Young University

Beckwourth, James P. *The Life and Adventures of James P. Beckwourth, Mountaineer, Scout, and Pioneer, and Chief of the Crow Nation of Indians, as Told to Thomas D. Bonner*, edited by Delmont R. Oswald. Lincoln: University of Nebraska Press, 1972. Oswald, Delmont R. "James P. Beckwourth." In *The Mountain Men and the Fur Trade of the Far West*, edited by Le Roy R. Hafen, vol. 6: 37–60. Glendale CA: Arthur H. Clark, 1968.

BLACK REGIMENTS

In recent years, military and African American historians have discovered a common interest in the black regiments that served in the American West. The term "buffalo soldier," a phrase originally employed by the Plains Indians to denote a black cavalryman, colloquially has come to describe all African Americans who served in the frontier army during the late nineteenth century. Impressed with the record of black troops in the Civil War, Congress in 1866 created six new regular army regiments, two cavalry and four infantry, that consisted entirely of African American men. After an 1869 consolidation, four black regiments, the Twenty-fourth and Twenty-fifth Infantries and the Ninth and Tenth Cavalries, comprised nearly 10 percent of the western army. Serving in racially segregated regiments, always under the command of white officers, black soldiers laid telegraph lines, protected railroad crews, escorted military prisoners, and performed numerous other tasks that made settlement of the Plains possible.

Buffalo Soldiers of the 25th Infantry, some wearing buffalo robes, Fort Keogh, Montana, 1890

Immediately following their arrival, black soldiers experienced trouble with white civilians. At Fort Hays, Kansas, for example, an ongoing feud with local townspeople culminated in the lynching of three black infantrymen in January 1869. Discrimination and violence plagued their service at places like Forts Larned and Leavenworth in Kansas and Fort Concho in Texas. Empowered by their roles as U.S. soldiers, African American servicemen often defied western communities' racial mores by patronizing saloons, brothels, and other "white" establishments, resulting in armed conflict. The military's relationship with civilian settlements generally had never been peaceful, and the presence of armed blacks only intensified the friction. As a result, commanders took special pains to station black companies in areas remote from white populations. The Twenty-fourth Infantry, for example, spent more than a decade stationed in West Texas and on the Mexican border, fighting Indian raiders and recalcitrant outlaw gangs. Indian Territory became another assignment for black regiments. There, troops enforced government policy on reservations and prevented encroachment from white ranchers and farmers. Despite concentrations in these areas, however, companies of buffalo soldiers were stationed throughout the Plains until the late 1880s. As agents of federal expansion, African American recruits, many of whom had only recently left slavery, were often responsible for dispossessing Native Americans and relocating them to reservations. Evident contradictions in this situation did not seem to deter them from performing official duties.

Black troops did display considerable loyalty toward each other. Their desertion rates consistently were far below those of white troops, and their high reenlistments allowed them to benefit from the presence of many seasoned veterans in their regiments. For all the danger, prejudice, and sheer boredom that characterized their service, black soldiers developed strong bonds based on uniform and

race, which made the frontier army one of the more attractive options available to African American males in the late nineteenth century.

James N. Leiker
University of Kansas

Billington, Monroe Lee. *New Mexico's Buffalo Soldiers, 1866–1900.* Niwot: University Press of Colorado, 1991.
Leckie, William H. *The Buffalo Soldiers: A Narrative of the Negro Cavalry in the West.* Norman: University of Oklahoma Press, 1967.

BROOKS, GWENDOLYN (1917–2000)

Gwendolyn Brooks was born in Topeka, Kansas, on June 7, 1917, to native-born Kansans Keziah Corine Wims and David Anderson Brooks. Her mother was born in Topeka, Kansas, attended Topeka High School and Emporia Normal, and later became the fifth-grade teacher of Monroe School in Topeka. Her father was born in Atchison, Kansas, but his family moved to Oklahoma when he was nine, and he remained there until he completed high school. He then attended Fisk University in Nashville, Tennessee, where he planned to pursue a medical career, but he left the university at the end of his first year. David and Keziah met during the summer of 1914 and married in July 1916. Gwendolyn, one of their two children, was born June 7, 1917, in Topeka, Kansas. The family relocated to Chicago when Gwendolyn was five weeks of age, and she lived there for the remainder of her life, developing a fierce identity as a Chicagoan.

Gwendolyn's parents recognized her early talents in creative expression and nurtured her desire to write. Her mother regularly relieved her of household chores and taught her the art of oral recitation during Gwendolyn's preschool years. Likewise, her father, who revered books and education, provided her with a writing desk and bookcases to house her growing collection of literary works. Brooks began rhyming around the age of seven and compiling poetry notebooks by eleven. Brooks's first poem, "Eventide," was published in *American Childhood* magazine in 1930. By 1934 Brooks had become a regular contributor to the *Chicago Defender* newspaper and, in a two-year period, published more than seventy-five poems in the weekly poetry column "Lights and Shadows."

Brooks attended public schools in Chicago and graduated from Forrestville Elementary School, Englewood High School (1934), and Wilson Junior College (1936). In 1938, when they were both twenty-one years old, Gwendolyn Brooks married Henry Lowington Blakely II, and together they had two children, Henry III and Nora. Their first home was a kitchenette apartment, located at 43rd and South Park on Chicago's South Side. In 1941 Brooks had her first formal poetry lessons when Inez Stark Cunningham, a Chicago socialite and editor of *Poetry: A Magazine of Verse*, volunteered to teach a poetry class at Chicago's South Side Community Art Center. Out of this affiliation, Brooks broadened her poetic traditions and techniques and, in 1943, won the Midwestern Writers Conference Poetry Award.

During her life, Gwendolyn Brooks published more than twenty books, including poetry, prose, fiction, and autobiography. Her first poetry collection was *A Street in Bronzeville* (1945); her second one, *Annie Allen* (1949), won her the Pulitzer Prize in May 1950. She was the first black writer to win the prize. She published one novel, *Maud Martha* (1953), a children's poetry collection, *Bronzeville Boys and Girls* (1956), and a third volume of poetry, *The Bean Eaters* (1960). Brooks remains highly acclaimed for her adroitness in merging character vignettes developed from the society that surrounded her and intertwining those stories with the complex structures of European poetic forms like the sonnet, folk and literary ballads, terza rima, and rhyme royal. Additionally, she honed the rhythmic flow of form using rhetorical strategies like anaphora, alliteration, and polyptoton. In much of her poetry after *In the Mecca* (1968), Brooks was not as form-conscious, often employing free verse to tell a succinct story but still manipulating story and structure with the flourish of repetition, as in anadiplosis and epistrophe, in place of her former strict metrical lines.

Brooks was highly acclaimed for her poetry and was the poet laureate of Illinois from 1968 to 2000. She held the post of distinguished professor of English at Chicago State University from 1989 to 2000. In 1985 she became the 29th Consultant in Poetry to the Library of Congress. She was a member of the American Academy and Institute of Arts and Letters; the recipient of the National Endowment for the Arts Lifetime Achievement Award in 1989; the only American to receive the Society for Literature Award, University of Greece, 1990; the National Endowment for the Humanities' Jefferson Lecturer, 1994; and a National Book Awards Medalist for Distinguished Contribution to American Letters, 1994. In 1995 she received the National Medal of Arts at the White House; in 1998 she was inducted into the International Literary Hall of Fame for Writers of African Descent; and in 1999 she was inducted as the sixty-fifth poet into the Academy of American Poets. She died in her Chicago home on December 3, 2000.

B. J. Bolden
Chicago State University

Bolden, B. J. *Urban Rage in Bronzeville: Social Commentary in the Poetry of Gwendolyn Brooks, 1945–1960.* Chicago: Third World Press, 1999. Melhem, D. H. *Gwendolyn Brooks: Poetry and the Heroic Voice.* Lexington: University Press of Kentucky, 1987.

BROWN, "AUNT" CLARA (1803–1885)

"Aunt" Clara Brown, between 1875 and 1880

"Aunt" Clara Brown was born in Tennessee in 1803 to slave parents, who were sold to separate owners when she was only three. She went with her mother to the home of Ambrose Smith, a farmer in Logan County, Kentucky. Smith, a kindly man and a devout Methodist, took Clara and her mother to his church services.

Clara was eighteen and a tall, strong woman with warm brown eyes when the Smiths bought an eighteen-year-old carpenter slave, Richard. When he and Clara fell in love, they were encouraged to marry and produce children to work the Smiths' farm. They were separated when Clara was sold to George Brown. Following southern custom, she, like other mature female slaves, was called "Aunt" and given the last name of her new owner. The Browns liked Clara's intelligence and spunk and helped her buy her freedom. She moved to St. Louis, where Missouri law protected free blacks. She later went with the Browns when they emigrated to Kansas. There she joined a wagon train headed to Colorado, earning her way as a cook. She arrived at Denver in June of 1859.

Denver's first-recorded black woman, Aunt

Clara opened a shop as a laundress, worked hard, and scraped together $5,000 to go back to Logan County, Kentucky, to look for her husband, children, and friends. She returned to Colorado with one daughter and other relatives and friends newly freed from bondage.

Aunt Clara moved to Central City and resumed her laundering work, toiling long hours and denying herself any luxuries. With the money she saved she funded the construction of St. James Methodist Church, which thrives to this day. She died in her sleep on October 23, 1885. At her burial at Denver's Riverside Cemetery, Colorado governor James B. Grant, Denver mayor John L. Routt, and other dignitaries praised Aunt Clara as "the kind old friend whose heart always responded to the cry of distress, and who, rising from the humble position of slave to the angelic type of noble woman, won our sympathy and commanded our respect."

Thomas J. Noel
University of Colorado at Denver

Bruyn, Kathleen. *"Aunt" Clara Brown: Story of a Black Pioneer.* Boulder: Pruett Publishing Co., 1970.

BROWN V. THE BOARD OF EDUCATION OF TOPEKA

See LAW: *Brown v. The Board of Education of Topeka*

CHRISTIAN, CHARLIE (1916–1942)

Charles Henry Christian was born to musical parents in Bonham, Texas, on July 29, 1916. His father, Clarence James, played trumpet, and his mother, Willie Mae, played piano. They are known to have played professionally in silent-movie theaters. Charlie had two elder brothers—Edward (born 1906), who was a fine pianist, and Clarence (born 1911), who occasionally played string bass and violin.

In 1918 Clarence, Charlie's father, became blind following an unknown illness. As a direct result the family moved from Bonham to live in Oklahoma City. Charlie started first grade in 1923 at Douglass School but apparently didn't attend school too often, preferring to earn money on the streets playing his ukulele.

He spent the Depression years playing in a variety of bands and at diverse locations. In 1930 Charlie played at Honey Murphey's Club with members of his brother Edward's band, together with members of McKinney's Cotton Pickers Orchestra, which included Don Redman. By 1932 Charlie had left school and become a full-time musician, playing wherever he could to earn a living but mostly with his brother Edward's band, which varied between four and thirteen pieces. T-Bone Walker tells of coming to Oklahoma City in 1933 with the Lawson Brooks Band and playing with Charlie on the streets as a duo. They had a bass and guitar and would play, sing, and dance together. When T-Bone had to leave town suddenly, Charlie took his place in the band. By 1935 Charlie was a regular member of the Rhymaires Orchestra, which was featured at

the Ritz Ballroom, broadcasting weekly over local radio. In 1936 Charlie played at the Texas Centennial celebrations, from which he returned with the Alphonso Trent Band. During the winter of 1936–37 Charlie played with the Trent band in Casper, Wyoming, and at a lengthy engagement in Deadwood, South Dakota. From the summer of 1937 on, Charlie was featured on electric guitar with the Anna Mae Winburn Orchestra. The band, based in Omaha, Nebraska, traveled extensively, going as far afield as Illinois and Minnesota in 1938. Charlie also played a residency with the Alphonso Trent Sextet in Bismarck, North Dakota, in the summer of 1938.

Charlie's big break came in July 1939 when, following a recommendation by Mary Lou Williams, John Hammond of Columbia Records, on his way to oversee a Benny Goodman recording session in Los Angeles, stopped in Oklahoma City to audition Charlie and his sextet. A short time later Charlie received a telegram from Hammond telling him to come to Los Angeles to play with Benny Goodman. Fortunately for the world of jazz, Charlie became a featured member of the Goodman Sextet, recording regularly and being heard weekly on radio broadcasts transmitted throughout the United States. After the reopening of Minton's Playhouse in October 1940, Charlie was co-opted into the house band and played almost every evening, following his work with Goodman, with such bebop luminaries as Dizzy Gillespie, Thelonious Monk, and Kenny Clarke.

In July 1941 Charlie was hospitalized with a recurrence of tuberculosis. He died in Seaview Sanitarium on Staten Island on March 2, 1942. With his tragic early death, jazz lost one of its great innovators, the man who brought the electric guitar into the forefront of popular music.

Peter Broadbent
Barry, Vale of Glamorgan, United Kingdom

Broadbent, Peter. *Charlie Christian.* Blaydon UK: Ashley Mark, 2002.

CIVIL RIGHTS

African Americans in the Great Plains were subjected to some of the same racial discrimination they faced in the South. They have often been denied equal opportunities, experienced violence, and been victimized by racial profiling. The Great Plains has also been the setting for important legal cases and protest movements of the civil rights movement.

Racial unrest and violence against African Americans were widespread in the United States during the early twentieth century. From individual lynchings to mob violence against entire communities, whites lashed out against African Americans. Between 1917 and 1923 the United States experienced a series of deadly race riots. From Tulsa, Oklahoma, to Omaha, Nebraska, and many communities in between, African Americans were attacked, beaten, and killed by mobs. Tulsa was the site of one of the deadliest race riots in American history. On May 31 and June 1, 1921, white

African American men and women demonstrate in Denver, Colorado, for complete integration in schools, May 16, 1968.

mobs attacked Tulsa's black community, destroying thirty-five city blocks and killing indiscriminately. Official counts list only thirty-nine deaths, but historians' and witnesses' accounts push the potential number of deaths up to 300. During the 1990s steps were taken to rectify the wrongs perpetrated against Tulsa's African American population. Seventy-five years after the fact, and six decades after his death, J. B. Stradford, a black Tulsa businessman, was cleared of charges connected to the riot. Descendants of Stradford traveled from around the country to witness a ceremony in October 1996 in which authorities absolved him of charges that he had incited the riot. The Race Riot Commission was established in 1997 to investigate the riot and pay restitution to survivors. In 2001 a report was submitted to the Oklahoma legislature recommending the direct payment of reparations to the survivors.

An important step in the battle for civil rights was the 1954 Supreme Court decision in *Brown v. The Board of Education of Topeka*. This case was one of five segregation lawsuits selected by the NAACP in 1950 to challenge the "separate but equal" rule in the federal courts. On May 17, 1954, Chief Justice Earl Warren read the Court's decision, which was that "separate but equal" did not belong in public education. Although this landmark legal triumph did not instantly end school segregation, it destroyed the constitutional foundation upon which legalized segregation rested and made future gains possible.

In the late 1950s, however, many Great Plains communities still denied African Americans access to the same schools, churches, restaurants, and other public accommodations used by whites. Within this setting, young African Americans in Wichita, Kansas, and Oklahoma City, Oklahoma, launched what may have been the first sit-ins of the civil

rights movement. Beginning on July 12, 1958, several Wichita youths, under the direction of the local NAACP Youth Council, began a sit-in at the Dockum Drug Store in order to end the city's segregation policy. The Wichita sit-in ended on August 7 when the store announced that all customers would be served without regard to race. Spurred on by the victory in Wichita, eight Oklahoma City youths entered the Katz Drug Store on August 19 and requested service. After just two days the store desegregated its lunch counter. Great Plains sit-ins undoubtedly influenced the larger sit-in movement that swept through the South in 1960.

During the 1960s black student unions emerged on college campuses to challenge racial inequalities in the educational system. The black student union at the University of Kansas, for example, demanded, among other things, the establishment of a black studies department, institutional commitment to the recruitment and retention of black students, the hiring of African American faculty and administrators, and the formation of an all-black pompon squad in protest of the university's all-white squad. In response, the University of Kansas opened the Office of Minority Affairs in 1969 and one year later created the Department of African and African American Studies. Black student unions also appeared on high school campuses. The activism of Lawrence (Kansas) High School's black student union led to the introduction of black history courses and a black American heritage week, black representation on cheerleading squads, and the formation of the Lawrence Branch of Concerned Black Parents, Inc.

More recently, the National Conference on Race and Ethnicity in American Higher Education (NCORE) has worked on civil rights issues in higher education. Founded in 1988 by the University of Oklahoma College of Continuing Education, NCORE assists institutions of higher education by creating inclusive educational environments, programs, and curricula, improving campus racial and ethnic relations and expanding opportunities for educational access and success by culturally diverse and traditionally underrepresented populations. NCORE attracts more than 1,500 students, scholars, administrators, policymakers, and civil rights leaders each year.

By the 1990s many people opposed affirmative action policies. In 1996 the United States Supreme Court let stand a state court ruling in *Hopwood v. University of Texas* that led to the end of affirmative action in Texas public colleges and universities. The number of African Americans at the University of Texas law school dropped sharply. The Supreme Court's ruling also had a national impact. It triggered California's Proposition 209 in 1997, outlawing the use of gender and race in hiring, contracting, and university admissions.

A more recent civil rights issue is the racial profiling of African Americans. An example of this in the Great Plains occurred in August 1998 when Rossano V. Gerald and his young son Gregory crossed the Oklahoma border

into a nightmare. A career soldier and a highly decorated veteran, Gerald, a black man of Panamanian descent, was stopped twice in thirty minutes by the highway patrol. During the second stop, which lasted two-and-a-half hours, troopers terrorized Gerald's twelve-year-old son with a police dog. Troopers placed both father and son in a closed car with the air conditioning off and fans blowing hot air, warning that the dog would attack if they attempted to escape. Halfway through the episode, perhaps realizing the extent of their lawlessness, the troopers turned off the patrol car's video evidence camera.

Another example of racial profiling took place at Oak Park Mall in Overland Park, Kansas. The mall security officer in Dillard's department store harassed two black women and accused them of shoplifting. It turned out that the two women were innocent and the security guard was profiling African Americans under the instructions given to him by Dillard's management. The two women filed a discrimination lawsuit and were awarded $1 million by the jury in December 1997.

The battle for civil rights in the Great Plains has had its own particular history, but it is not fundamentally different from the national trend. The perception that only the South was racist is a myth of the American past. In fact, the struggle for civil rights is an American journey, involving all American regions.

See also LAW: *Brown v. The Board of Education of Topeka*.

Jacob U. Gordon
University of Kansas

Harrison, Maureen, and Steve Gilbert, eds. *Civil Rights Decisions of the United States Supreme Court: The 20th Century.* San Diego: Excellent Books, 1994. Orum, Anthony M. *Black Students in Protest: A Study of the Origins of the Black Student Movement.* Washington DC: American Sociological Association, 1972. Walters, Ronald. "The Great Plains Sit-in Movement, 1958–60." *Great Plains Quarterly* 16 (1996): 85–94.

COLEMAN, ORNETTE (b. 1930)

Avant-garde saxophonist-composer Ornette Coleman, born in Fort Worth, Texas, on March 19, 1930, came to the attention of the jazz world in a 1959 groundbreaking engagement at the Five Spot Club in New York City. Although reflecting the southwest rhythm-and-blues tradition of his native Texas, Coleman's radical improvisational approach allowed him to shift his music's flow and density at will by dispensing with fixed harmonic patterns and structural forms. This approach was later formulated in his "harmolodic theory." Coleman's tumultuous improvisations, despite their irregular shapes and jagged lines, often possessed a haunting lyrical beauty as well as emotional directness.

The saxophonist's unorthodox approach, emphasizing collective rather than solo improvisation, divided the jazz world. Detractors, including jazz giants Miles Davis and Charles Mingus, described his music as cacophony and called him a *poseur*. Boosters, including Leonard Bernstein and Gunther Schuller, hailed him as a genius. His influential 1959–60 group (with trumpeter Don Cherry, bassist Charlie Haden, and drummer Billy Higgins) was documented in two landmark 1959 albums, *The Shape of Jazz to Come* and *Change of the Century*. The aptly titled *Free Jazz* (1960), a thirty-seven-minute collective improvisation for double jazz quartet, was equally influential. In addition to alto saxophone, his primary instrument, Coleman has performed on violin and trumpet. Among his best-known compositions are "Lonely Woman," "Ramblin," and "Blues Connotation."

Although his influence has ebbed, especially with the revival after 1980 of older jazz styles, Coleman has successfully employed his "harmolodic" approach in the electric-funk group, Prime Time. Still, Coleman's reputation rests on his status as a key innovator of 1960s' "free jazz" with its freewheeling ensemble improvisations, open-ended plastic forms, and "dissonant" tonal clashes. Among Coleman's many honors is a MacArthur Foundation Fellowship.

Chuck Berg
University of Kansas

Litweiler, John. *Ornette Coleman: A Harmolodic Life*. New York: William Morrow, 1993.

DOUGLAS, AARON (1899–1979)

Aaron Douglas was the leading visual artist of the Harlem Renaissance. Born on May 26, 1899, Douglas attended high school in his hometown of Topeka, Kansas, and received his art training at the University of Nebraska, graduating with a bachelor of fine arts degree in 1922. Douglas had arrived at Nebraska without his high school records, ten days into the term. Still, he was warmly welcomed, and he considered his years at Nebraska one of the more positive times in his life. Douglas worked as an art teacher at Lincoln High School from 1923 to 1925, then moved to Harlem.

Within weeks of his arrival in Harlem, Douglas was recruited by the NAACP's W. E. B. Du Bois, editor of *The Crisis*, and Charles S. Johnson, director of the Urban League and editor of *Opportunity*, to contribute illustrations to their journals. Douglas quickly became one of the leading artists in the New Negro movement, or Harlem Renaissance. Within this largely literary movement, Douglas was specifically hired to create a visual message for a public that had grown dramatically as black migration to the North increased during World War I. *The Crisis* had a national readership, and any illustration Douglas made would be seen in libraries, schools, and homes across the country. Douglas tried to reach this new black middle-class public—a public that was difficult to define and locate—by creating a new, positive, African-influenced black image for his audience.

He wanted to change the way blacks were depicted in art, and to bring the language of African art first to Harlem and then to the whole country. Douglas's growth and experimentation can be traced in his magazine illustrations, which were some of his most forceful and interesting works. Through them he evolved his artistic language, a distinctive language immersed in African art. His illustrations, blending art deco, cubism, and West African sculpture, are clean and bold, often showing a few simple figures or illustrating a basic idea. In his first year in Harlem he won three prizes for his work.

Douglas's Harlem years were filled with commissions for illustrating books and painting murals, most notably his 1934 *Aspects of Negro Life*, which was commissioned for the Public Works Administration for the Countee Cullen Branch of the New York Public Library. Douglas left Harlem in 1937, and in 1939 became the founding member of the Art Department at Fisk University. He chaired that department for almost three decades. Douglas died in Nashville on February 2, 1979.

Amy Kirschke
Vanderbilt University

Kirschke, Amy H. *Aaron Douglas: Art, Race and the Harlem Renaissance*. Oxford: University Press of Mississippi, 1995.

ELLISON, RALPH

See LITERARY TRADITIONS: Ellison, Ralph

EXODUSTERS

Tens of thousands of African Americans moved into the Great Plains to begin new lives during the last three decades of the nineteenth century. These Plains settlers have often been referred to as Exodusters. Beginning in the 1870s and continuing into the 1890s, the Exodusters settled in all Great Plains states and territories, even as far north as Canada, but Kansas and what would become Oklahoma Territory were the main destinations.

Several factors—both push and pull—help explain this sudden and massive migration. Shortly after the end of the Civil War, western territories and states searched for ways to entice prospective settlers. Increased populations would bring statehood for territories and profits for land speculators and railroads, who owned a great deal of land and property. Territorial and state governments and the U.S. Congress passed a variety of land acts and other provisions to attract people to the region. The 1862 Homestead Act, for example, opened up opportunities for African Americans just as for other Americans. Local governments, private individuals, and companies also disseminated elaborate brochures, and newspaper and periodical advertisements solicited black individuals and families to relocate to the Plains. The often-unscrupulous western developers targeted African Americans because of a belief that they would be easy to attract with offers of free or low-cost land. Seldom did boosters and speculators admit that farming conditions, climate, and access to water were not what these immigrants were used to.

Although territorial and federal governments offered inducements to African Americans, a more immediate cause of black migration was the dire conditions of the post-Reconstruction South. The end of Reconstruction in 1877 led to increased racial violence, disfranchisement, loss of civil rights, and lack of economic opportunity for southern blacks. These hardships, combined with rumors of free transportation, free land, and even monetary gifts, led to a massive migration of African Americans to the Great Plains during the late 1870s. Men such as Henry Adams of Louisiana and Benjamin "Pap" Singleton of Tennessee organized and led large numbers of southern blacks to Kansas. Singleton made several trips to Kansas during the early 1870s and helped found several black colonies.

The migrations of 1879—in which 6,000 African Americans settled in Kansas—took on a religious tone. African American migrants saw themselves as taking part in a biblical exodus, with Kansas as the promised land. In 1879, often referred to as the Exodus Year, more than 20,000 black men, women, and children passed through St. Louis to Kansas and points west. Many never reached Kansas, settling instead in urban areas such as Kansas City, Missouri. More than 6,000, however, settled in rural Kansas towns, including all-black towns such as Nicodemus. This Plains town, platted in Graham County, Kansas, in 1877, is the best-known black town in the Great Plains. By 1879 it had a population of more than 600, making it the largest community in Kansas north of the Kansas Pacific Railroad. While Nicodemus was a major destination, it was only one of many all-black towns established in the Central Plains in the last decades of the nineteenth century. Other black towns included Langston, Oklahoma, founded in 1890; Boley, Oklahoma, founded in 1904; and Dewitty, Nebraska, also founded in 1904.

The Exodusters often had dreams of re-creating the lush farmlands of their native states only to find that the unpredictable climate of the Great Plains thwarted their ambitions. By the late 1800s many had returned to their home states, but some, as in Nicodemus, learned to adapt to the new environment, use fertilizers, build water-diversion channels, and survive the harsh winters. The pioneers of African American settlement in the Great Plains—the Exodusters—anticipated the much larger black migrations from the South after 1910, migrations that were increasingly directed at large Plains cities.

Jack Ravage
University of Wyoming

Athearn, G. Robert. *In Search of Canaan: Black Migration to Kansas, 1879–1880*. Lawrence: Regents Press of Kansas, 1978. Painter, Nell Irvin. *Exodusters: Black Migration to Kansas after Reconstruction*. New York: Alfred A. Knopf, 1976.

FIELDS, MARY (ca. 1832–1914)

Mary Fields was one of the most colorful characters in the history of the Great Plains. Various descriptions of her claim that she was six feet tall, weighed over 200 pounds, smoked homemade cigars, and carried a pair of six-shooters and a ten-gauge shotgun. She never married or had children. She gained widespread fame, and the nickname "Stage Coach Mary," for deftly maneuvering U.S. mail stagecoaches and freight wagons over daunting mountain trails.

Born into slavery around 1832 in Tennessee, Mary Fields gave meaning to her freedom at the earliest opportunity by migrating to Toledo, Ohio, where she worked for the Ursuline Convent. In 1884 Mother Amadeus of the Ursuline Convent founded the St. Peter's Catholic Mission School in Montana. Three years later Mary Fields joined her there. For the next ten years she provided protection for the nuns and the school and drove a supply wagon hauling essential freight and other goods. Mary chopped wood, did rudimentary carpentry, and whatever else was necessary to ensure the smooth functioning of the nuns' enterprise.

Mary Fields's temper was as legendary as her ability to get hard jobs done. Indeed, one altercation almost proved her undoing. Bishop Filbus N. E. Berwanger fired Mary from her position with the nuns following a shootout with a cowpuncher that left her unharmed and the cowpuncher slightly wounded and greatly embarrassed. Mary never allowed social conventions or expectations of feminine behavior to circumscribe her. Rather, she carved a space for herself that allowed her the freedom to exploit both her penchant for hard work and her desire to help others.

She settled in a town in Cascade County, Montana, where she was the only black resident. With some money from the nuns, she opened a café and became an avid supporter of the local baseball team. The restaurant failed because Mary fed too many who could not pay, and besides, her cooking was unremarkable. Mary took the closing of her restaurant in stride, and for a brief time she subsisted by doing laundry. She never made enough to be considered rich, but she was reasonably content. Her zest for life enthralled the local community. When her laundry burned down the townsfolk pitched in and helped her rebuild it. The owner of the Cascade Hotel and the local saloons all allowed Mary Fields ready access to their facilities, privileges denied to women in general.

In 1895 Mary secured a job delivering mail for the U.S. postal services, and she continued to do so into her seventies. Citizens marveled at her fierce determination to deliver, on schedule, letters and parcels without concern for weather, the ruggedness of the mountain trails, or the remoteness of the homes and outposts that relied on dependable means of communication in order to process land claims. Without doubt, her work facilitated central Montana's development. Mary Fields died in 1914 of liver failure. Neighbors buried her in the Hillside Cemetery in Cascade. A simple wooden cross marks her grave.

Darlene Clark Hine
Michigan State University

Hine, Darlene Clark, and Kathleen Thompson. *A Shining Thread of Hope: A History of Black Women in America.* New York: Broadway Books, 1998. Miller, Robert. *The Story of Stagecoach Mary Fields.* Englewood Cliffs NJ: Silver Burdett Press, 1995.

GREAT PLAINS BLACK MUSEUM

The Great Plains Black Museum at 2213 Lake Street in Omaha, Nebraska, has one of the largest repositories of historical materials and resources on the African American experience in the United States. The museum opened in the historic Webster Telephone Exchange building in February 1976 with more than 10,000 rare books, artifacts, magazines, documents, letters, pictures, and other memorabilia from Mrs. Bertha Calloway's private collection. The museum was also supported by a $101,000 grant from the board of the American Bicentennial Administration. Other financial support has come from private contributions, voluntary donations, and state agency grants.

From its inception, the central mission of the museum has been the preservation and enhancement of knowledge about the history and culture of African Americans in the Great Plains. Today, the museum has more than 100,000 items, displayed in several galleries, depicting the diversity of the African American experience in the region. The exhibits are grouped into several divisions, each displayed in a separate room. The military room, for example, houses pictures, clothing, correspondence, wills, medals, discharge papers, and other documents. Other divisions are devoted to African and African American arts and artifacts, African American women of the Great Plains, rare books, church and religion, and music and entertainment. There are also exhibits on African American homesteaders and a section commemorating African American political leaders in the region.

See also EDUCATION: Museums.
Daniel Boamah-Wiafe
University of Nebraska at Omaha

Calloway, Bertha W., and Alonzo N. Smith. *Visions of Freedom on the Great Plains: An Illustrated History of African Americans in Nebraska.* Virginia Beach VA: Donning Company Publishers, 1998.

HARRIS, WYNONIE (1913–1969)

Blues singer Wynonie Harris was a leading figure in black music during the 1940s and early 1950s, and he developed a style that had a considerable influence on early rock and roll. A handsome man with striking blue-gray eyes and a flashing smile, and with a voice powerful enough to project over driving horn-led bands, Harris was renowned as a charismatic performer on stage and as a hard-drinking hell-raiser and ladies' man off stage. He became best known for his humorous, often risqué songs such as "Good Rockin' Tonight," "All She Wants to Do Is Rock," "Grandma Plays the Numbers," and "Bloodshot Eyes."

Harris was born in Omaha, Nebraska, on August 24, 1913, the illegitimate offspring of an African American mother and a Native American father. He worked as a dancer for several

Wynonie Harris on stage with the Lucky Millinder band, June 1944

years before becoming a singer. Influenced and inspired by Jimmy Rushing and Big Joe Turner, both big-voiced blues singers from Kansas City, Harris learned his craft in the clubs on Omaha's Near North Side, in particular Jim Bell's Harlem Club. By the early 1940s he was calling himself "Mr. Blues" and was a regular attraction at the Club Alabam on Los Angeles's Central Avenue. His big break came in 1944 when he was invited to join Lucky Millinder's big band as the featured male singer. With Millinder he recorded "Who Threw the Whiskey in the Well," which became a number-one hit on the black music charts. Thereafter, Harris worked as a single, playing residencies at the country's leading black nightclubs and touring frequently. His greatest commercial success came after he signed with King Records in 1947 and recorded "Good Rockin' Tonight." From then until 1952 a string of hit records made him one of the biggest-selling artists among African American record buyers.

Harris's brand of good-time blues was a direct precursor of 1950s rock and roll. Elvis Presley, who recorded his own version of "Good Rockin' Tonight" in 1954, is reputed to have adopted some of his stage movements after seeing Harris perform. Wynonie Harris himself, however, was too old, too raunchy, and too rooted in black musical traditions to appeal to rock and roll's white teenage audience. Harris never gave up the music business completely, but from the mid-1950s onward he worked mostly outside music. He died of throat cancer in Los Angeles on June 14, 1969.

Tony Collins
London, England

Collins, Tony. *Rock Mr. Blues: The Life and Music of Wynonie Harris.* Milford NH: Big Nickel Publications, 1995.

HUGHES, LANGSTON (1902–1967)

Langston Hughes

Born in Joplin, Missouri, on February 1, 1902, Langston Hughes was raised primarily in Lawrence, Kansas, by his part-Indian maternal grandmother, who instilled in him a love of stories and of his people, and who often covered him at night with the bullet-torn cape of her first husband, who died in John Brown's raid at Harper's Ferry. A world traveler, Hughes was a key figure in the Harlem Renaissance of the 1920s—and one of the few to continue to actively publish and lecture after that movement ended—and is considered a major modern American writer.

Versatile and prolific, Hughes forged and maintained an international reputation for nearly half a century. A poet, novelist, playwright, essayist, short-story writer, autobiographer, columnist, editor, translator, and author of children's books, Hughes published more than fifty volumes of prose and poetry during his lifetime, beginning at age nineteen with the often-anthologized poem "The Negro Speaks of Rivers" (1921).

Distinguished by his innovative adaptations of jazz and blues musical forms in his poetry—and by his love for the common black folk who are its subject—Hughes is also well known for his fictional creation Jesse B. Semple, or Simple. Through this endearing "everyman" figure, Hughes explored seriously, yet with characteristic humor, some of the most important questions of his day.

Although sometimes criticized for his art, which in his early years was denounced by some critics for its portrayal of "unsophisticated" lower-class black urban life, and later for his politics, which are considered by many to be naive, Hughes encouraged a number of younger African American writers, including Alice Walker, and continues to hold a prominent place in American literature. He died in New York City on May 22, 1967.

Connie R. Schomburg
Midland Lutheran College

Rampersad, Arnold, ed. *The Collected Poems of Langston Hughes.* New York: Alfred A. Knopf, 1994. Rampersad, Arnold. *The Life of Langston Hughes.* 2 vols. New York: Oxford University Press, 1986, 1988.

JIM CROW LAWS

See LAW: Jim Crow Laws

JOHNSON, NOBLE (1881–1957)

Noble M. Johnson, the first major African American movie actor, was born in Colorado Springs on April 18, 1881. His father was a successful racehorse owner and trainer. Johnson attended public schools in Colorado Springs (Lon Chaney Sr. was a classmate) until the age of fifteen, when he struck out across the country, following the racing circuit, training horses, and working as a cowboy. Back in Colorado Springs in 1909, he filled in for an injured actor, playing an Indian, in a Lubin Film Manufacturing Company Western, and his career path was set.

Johnson made several films for Lubin before joining with several other African Americans (including his brother George) to organize the Lincoln Motion Picture Company in 1916. Noble was the company's original president and acted in its first three films. But he was also getting roles in Universal Studios's serials and was pressured by that studio to resign from Lincoln in 1918. From that point on, Noble Johnson was a Hollywood actor.

Light-skinned and athletic, Johnson was cast in a great variety of often-major roles. He appeared in *Four Horsemen of the Apocalypse* (1921), *The Navigator* (1924), *Ben Hur* (1925), *King Kong* (1933), and *She Wore a Yellow Ribbon* (1949). In a business characterized by racial discrimination, Johnson played Native Americans, Latinos, Asians, and other "exotics" but was never billed as African American or identified with African American roles. He died in 1957, and his memory has faded, despite the success and longevity of his career.

David J. Wishart
University of Nebraska–Lincoln

Leab, Daniel J. *From Sambo to Superspade: The Black Experience in Motion Pictures.* Boston: Houghton Mifflin Company, 1975. Sampson, Henry T. *Blacks in Black and White: A Source Book on Black Films.* Metuchen NJ: Scarecrow Press, 1977.

KING CURTIS (1934–1971)

Saxophonist King Curtis was born Curtis Ousley in Fort Worth, Texas, on February 7, 1934. He spent his formative years surrounded by Texas blues and swing, mainstream jazz, and gospel music. After high school he followed in the footsteps of Illinois Jacquet, the Houston-born innovator of the saxophone style known as "honking," to join vibraphonist Lionel Hampton's jazz band in California. He finally settled in New York in 1952.

In New York, King Curtis shaped his stylistic influences into a fusion of jazz and the popular "honking and shouting" of the rhythm-and-blues (R&B) tenor saxophone. He recorded a small number of mainstream jazz albums and

in 1958 led his own jazz group. In the 1960s he was a prominent innovator of "soul jazz," which combined his early Texas influences of gospel, blues, and jazz. His first major solo success came with "Soul Twist," which reached the top of the R&B billboard charts in 1962; five years later he had another hit with "Memphis Soul Stew." Unlike his R&B contemporaries, he developed a sound on the saxophone that could be as subtle as it was raucous.

King Curtis also garnered recognition as an R&B and soul studio-musician, becoming Atlantic Records' house tenor-saxophonist and bandleader for Aretha Franklin. His career came to an abrupt end in 1971 when he was murdered in front of his Manhattan home.

Christopher Steinke
Harvard University

Gillett, Charlie. *The Sound of the City.* London: Souvenir Press, 1983. Shaw, Arnold. *Honkers and Shouters: The Golden Years of Rhythm and Blues.* New York: Macmillan Publishing Company, 1978.

LITTLE, CLEAVON (1939–1992)

Cleavon Little

Cleavon Jake Little, stage, screen, and television actor, was born in Chickasha, Oklahoma, on June 1, 1939. His father was a native Mississippian and his mother was a Texan. Both parents were of African and Native American ancestry. Cleavon attended grade school in Chickasha, but the family moved to the Linda Vista section of San Diego, California, in 1953. There, Cleavon went to Kearny High School from 1954 to 1957 and was active in several school drama productions. From 1957 to 1960 he took classes at San Diego City College and from 1962 to 1965 he attended San Diego State University, where he earned a bachelor of arts degree in speech therapy with a minor in dramatic arts. His first job was as a speech therapist at a developmental disabilities center, but he dreamed of becoming a professional actor.

His opportunity came when he entered

a nationwide competitive talent search for promising actors sponsored by ABC Television. Cleavon was one of sixteen selected out of 25,000 applicants to receive a full scholarship to the Academy of Dramatic Arts in New York City. While still at the academy he displayed his talents in Shakespeare's *A Midsummer Night's Dream* and *Othello*. He received the academy's highest honors, the Charles Jehlinger Award, when he graduated in 1967. Off Broadway he appeared in *Americana Off Broadway* (1966), *MacBird* (1967), and *Scuba Duba* (1967). Cleavon went on to act on Broadway in *Jimmy Shine* with Dustin Hoffman (1968), *Someone's Comin' Hungry* (1969), and *Ofay Watcher* (1969). In 1970 he won a Tony Award for best actor in a musical (for *Purlie*). Cleavon considered his best works to be *I'm Not Rappaport* (1985) and his one-man show *All God's Dangers* (1989). His 1991 appearance as a guest star in Judd Hirsch's TV series "Dear John" won him an Emmy.

Altogether, Cleavon Little appeared in seventeen movies from 1970 to 1991, but he is remembered most for his hilarious role as mild-mannered Sheriff Bart in *Blazing Saddles* (1974). This quintessential actor of theater, film, and television died of cancer in Sherman Oaks, California, on October 22, 1992. The American Academy of Dramatic Arts set up an endowed scholarship in his name in 1994.

Melvin R. Sylvester
Long Island University
C. W. Post Campus

Cleavon Little, Archival Student File, American Academy of Dramatic Arts, New York City.

LOVE, NAT (1854–1921)

Nat Love (Deadwood Dick), between 1870 and 1890

Also known by his nickname Deadwood Dick, Nat Love was born a slave in 1854 in Davidson County, Tennessee. At the age of fifteen he ventured to the Great Plains where, like many ex-slaves, he found work in the cattle industry. For twenty years he worked on cattle ranches in the Texas Panhandle and Arizona. Love participated in the great cattle drives of the 1870s, driving herds to Dodge City, Kansas, and to mining camps in Montana and the Black Hills. While in Deadwood, Dakota Territory, in July 1876, he reportedly earned the nickname Deadwood Dick after winning a riding, roping, and shooting competition. Love retired from the cattle industry in 1890 and went to work as a porter for the Denver and Rio Grande Railroad. His last job was as a bank guard in Los Angeles.

Love is best known for his autobiography, *The Life and Adventures of Nat Love, Better Known in the Cattle Country as Deadwood Dick* (1907). Unfortunately, the book is highly exaggerated, and it is difficult to separate truth from fiction. Inspired by the Western dime novels of the period, Love describes himself as the best cowboy, best shooter, and hardest drinker on the western frontier. The real life of Nat Love, therefore, is difficult to trace. Nonetheless, the book is high adventure and includes colorful western personalities such as Billy the Kid, Jesse James, and Buffalo Bill Cody. Love reportedly married a woman named Alice in 1889 and had one child. He died in 1921 in Los Angeles, California.

Mark R. Ellis
University of Nebraska at Kearney

Katz, William Loren. *The Black West.* New York: Doubleday, 1971. Love, Nat. *The Life and Adventures of Nat Love, Better Known in the Cattle Country as Deadwood Dick.* New York: Arno Press, 1968.

MALCOLM X

See PROTEST AND DISSENT: Malcolm X

McDANIEL, HATTIE (1895–1952)

In the post–Civil War period, Kansas became the new promised land for recently freed slaves. This was John Brown country, and African Americans believed they would be treated more fairly here than in the South. They traveled by railroads, rivers, and on foot. The Missouri, Kansas, and Texas Railroad ran through Emporia, with easy transfers to the Atchison, Topeka, and Santa Fe Railroad for points west, including Wichita and Fort Collins. Two of the black settlers who came to Wichita, Kansas, were Mr. and Mrs. Henry McDaniel. Henry, originally from Virginia, and Susan (nee Holbrook), from Tennessee, ultimately had a family of thirteen children, most of whom died at birth or shortly thereafter. Their youngest, Hattie, was born on June 10, 1895. The family moved to other places in the Great Plains: first to Fort Collins, Colorado, and then to Denver, the city Hattie McDaniel always considered to be her hometown.

Hattie became an internationally known movie star. She began her professional career in a band; she was the first African American woman to sing on the radio. She started appearing in movies in the early 1930s. Her

Hattie McDaniel, 1939

greatest film achievement was her role as Mammy in *Gone with the Wind* (1939), for which she won an Academy Award for best supporting actor. This was the first time an African American had won an Oscar. Altogether, she played in about 100 films, with only half of them attributed. After *Gone with the Wind*, Hattie was much in demand, and she made at least one movie a year during the 1940s (except 1945), including *In This Our Life* (1942) and *Since You Went Away* (1944).

In 1947 she began starring in *Beulah*, which became the most popular radio program in the United States. She was scheduled for a television version of *Beulah* but fell ill with breast cancer. Hattie McDaniel died on October 26, 1952, and was buried in Rosedale Cemetery in Los Angeles.

Carlton Jackson
Western Kentucky University

Jackson, Carlton. *Hattie: The Life of Hattie McDaniel.* Lanham MD: Madison Books, 1990.

McSHANN, JAY (b. 1916)

Emerging in the 1930s from the blues-drenched soil of eastern Oklahoma, Jay McShann quickly established himself as a dominant Kansas City pianist, rivaled only by Mary Lou Williams and Count Basie. His "band that swung the blues" formed in 1939 and included some of the finest musicians of the area. It was this band's recordings, in 1941, that gave Charlie Parker his first national exposure. McShann continues to be active at the beginning of the new millennium, his diverse styles constituting a lexicon of twentieth-century jazz and blues pianism.

Jay McShann was born in Muskogee, Oklahoma, on January 12, 1916. Muskogee, a town of 30,000, was also the home of guitarist Barney Kessel, bassist Aaron Bell, and tenor saxophonist Don Byas, all important jazz men. It was with Byas that McShann began his professional career in 1931; by 1937 he was fronting his own bands in the Kansas City area. By then, McShann had become a versatile pianist, combining his blues background of barrelhouse and boogie-woogie (influenced by Pete Johnson) with a percussive, jazz comping style characterized by dense, chordal textures. Though most associate McShann with small groups, particularly those with bassist Gene Ramey and drummer Gus Johnson, his most famous band, formed in 1939, was a large ensemble that boasted such outstanding sidemen as trumpeters Orville "Piggy" Minor and Buddy Anderson, trombonist Bob Mabane, and saxophonist Charlie Parker, as well as blues shouter Walter Brown. Later recordings for Decca in Wichita, Kansas, and Dallas, Texas, yielded such classic numbers as "Swingmatism," "Confessin' the Blues," and "Hootie Blues," several of which contained the proto-bop solos of nineteen-year-old Charlie "Yardbird" Parker.

Bolstered by the success of the Decca recordings, especially "Confessin'," which sold over 5 million copies, McShann moved to New York in 1942 to open at the Savoy opposite Lucky Millinder's orchestra. McShann's powerful blues-style-based jazz was still relatively unknown outside the Midwest, but the band garnered rave reviews from the critics. McShann returned to the recording studio in 1942, adding "Sepian Stomp" and "Jumpin' the Blues" to jazz posterity. After this session, the band began to break up, and McShann was drafted in 1944.

Returning to music after the war, McShann preferred playing with small groups, working as leader and accompanist with such artists as blues shouters Big Joe Turner and Jimmy Witherspoon and swing violinist Claude "Fiddler" Williams. In 1959 McShann returned to Kansas City, which is still his home. Much of his playing, including at many major European jazz festivals, was with Williams and drummer Paul Gunther. McShann also began to develop his singing, fashioning a raspy blues timbre reminiscent of Turner and Walter Brown. In 1978 he was featured with the Lincoln (Nebraska) Symphony Orchestra in Robert Beadell's work *Variations for Jazz Trio, Flugelhorn and Strings*. Also that year, accompanied by Paul Gunther and Randy Snyder on bass, McShann was profiled in *Hootie's Blues*, a film by Bart Becker and Michael Farrell. McShann is also a major participant in the documentary *The Last of the Blue Devils* (1979). In honor of his contribution to music in Kansas City, by proclamation of the governor, March 3, 1979, was designated "Jay McShann Day."

See also CITIES AND TOWNS: Kansas City, Kansas and Missouri / MUSIC: Kansas City Jazz.

Randall Snyder
University of Nebraska–Lincoln

MICHEAUX, OSCAR (1884–1951)

Oscar Micheaux was born on January 2, 1884, in Metropolis, Illinois. The details of his early life are obscure, but he may have worked in Chicago as a stockyard hand and Pullman porter. Inspired by Booker T. Washington's philosophy of economic empowerment through landownership and black business development, Micheaux took out a homestead in 1904 on part of the Rosebud Reservation in South Dakota. After establishing a successful farm, despite the attempts of his white neighbors to sell him inferior farming equipment and animals, the death of his wife during childbirth, and the hostile physical environment, Micheaux turned to writing novels that reflected his experiences: *The Conquest: The Story of a Negro Pioneer* (1913); *The Forged Note: A Romance of the Darker Races* (1915); *The Homesteader* (1917); and *The Wind from Nowhere* (1941). He considered these novels as another business venture; he controlled their production from start to finish by submitting to the press printworthy originals of his manuscripts, paying in cash for their publication, and distributing them door-to-door to African Americans throughout the Midwest and South. His novels appealed to African Americans because they presented a critique of black urban life and offered a solution: they should abandon the cities and look to the Great Plains as a place where they could build an alternative to American urban society.

Micheaux's attempts to popularize his novels led him to filmmaking. In 1918, having established the Western Book and Supply Company in Sioux City, Iowa, to produce and distribute his novels, he was contacted by George P. Johnson, general booking manager of the black-owned and operated Lincoln Film Company of Los Angeles, California. Johnson, who also operated an office in Omaha, Nebraska, had read *The Homesteader* and raised the possibility of producing a film version. In May 1918 Micheaux traveled to Omaha to sign a contract with Johnson to film *The Homesteader*. But Micheaux's desire to supervise the actual filming of the production, combined with his lack of experience in directing, caused the contract to fall through.

So Micheaux formed his own film company, the Micheaux Film and Book Company, with offices in Sioux City and Chicago. As he had done previously with the Western Book and Supply Company, Micheaux sold stock in the newly formed film and book company to white farmers around Sioux City. He finally raised enough money from selling shares to produce *The Homesteader* as an eight-reel film in 1918. In all, Micheaux would produce more than forty-four all-black-cast films nationally, some of which were distributed in Europe. His films were widely distributed because of his refusal to propagandize them. He felt that black people did not want racial propaganda like that evident in many of the films produced by Hollywood and some of the white independents. Instead, they wanted a good story—films that reflected the social, economic, and political conditions under which African Americans existed in America.

Taken to task for casting light-skinned African Americans in leading roles, for imitating the manners and speech of white society, and for using his people as "plastic" models, Micheaux did not attempt to shield himself from criticism. Writing in the *Philadelphia Afro-American* on January 24, 1925, Micheaux commented, "I do not wish anyone to construe this as a request for the suppression of criticism. Honest, intelligent criticism is an aid to the progress of an effort. The producer who has confidence in his ideals, politics [sic] constructive criticism. But he also asks fairness, and fairness in criticism demands a familiarity with the aims of the producer, and a knowledge of the circumstances under which his efforts were materialized." Nonetheless, many of his critics categorized his films as second-rate "underground" films.

These criticisms ignore the fact that Micheaux produced films under difficult circumstances. He always lacked the funds necessary to achieve high technical standards, to produce special effects, and to stage massive action scenes. He usually did all the work in his productions except for perfunctory tasks. He wrote scenarios, supervised filming, and handled the bookkeeping. His pictures took an average of ten days to shoot and usually cost between $10,000 and $20,000. Once the production of a film was under way, Micheaux would often make a contract with a theater to supply him with money in return for the theater receiving first screening rights. He would take several of the actors with him on the train to visit prospective patrons. The actors would perform a couple of scenes from the script for the theater manager while Micheaux emphasized the importance and marketability of the script.

In 1920 Micheaux's brother, Swan, joined him as manager of the Micheaux Film and Book Company. In 1921 the corporation had a cash dividend of 25 percent and established an office in New York City. The distribution and financial office remained in Chicago under supervision of Swan Micheaux and Charles Benson. Micheaux was enterprising enough to secure a number of firms to distribute his films: Tiffany Tolliver and W. R. Crowell distributed his films in the East from a branch office in Roanoke, Virginia, while A. Odanes, owner of the Verdun Theater in Beaumont, Texas, distributed the films in the Southwest.

Between 1918 and 1931 Micheaux produced twenty-seven films, most of which were silent. His first all-sound feature was *The Exile* (1931), which was made from his novel *The Homesteader*. Between 1931 and 1940 he produced and directed sixteen all-sound features. In 1948 he wrote the screenplay for and directed *The Betrayal* for Astor Pictures Corporation. The screenplay was adopted from Micheaux's novel *The Wind from Nowhere*; it was his last known film activity. This film opened in a white movie theater in downtown New York to poor reviews. Lack of financial resources forced Micheaux to file a voluntary petition of bankruptcy in 1948.

When Micheaux died in Charlotte, North Carolina, on March 25, 1951, his film corporation was virtually bankrupt. Nevertheless, Oscar Micheaux's entrepreneurial activities won him the distinction as the first independent African American film director and producer. His legacy is kept alive through the Micheaux Film Society of Oakland, California.

Chester J. Fontenot Jr.
Mercer University

Bogle, Donald. *Toms, Coons, Mulattos, Mammies and Bucks.* New York: Viking Press, 1973. Cripps, Thomas. *Slow Fade to Black.* New York: Oxford University Press, 1977. Fontenot, Chester J. Jr., "Oscar Micheaux: Black Novelist and Filmmaker." In *Vision and Refuge: Ethnic Writers on the Great Plains*, edited by Frederick Luebke. Lincoln: University of Nebraska Press, 1980: 109–25.

OMAHA RACE RIOT

During the frenzy of a riot in Omaha, Nebraska, on September 28, 1919, Will Brown, an African American, was lynched near the Douglas County courthouse. He was accused of raping Agnes Loebeck, a white woman. Identified by Loebeck and Milton Hoffman, the young man with her on the night of the alleged attack, Brown had been taken to the police station and then transferred to the courthouse jail. On Sunday morning, the twenty-eighth, a crowd of mostly young men gathered at a school on the south side and was led downtown by Hoffman, adding followers as it progressed.

Earlier in the afternoon the situation seemed nonthreatening, but it turned ugly as time passed and more people appeared on the scene. From 300 at the school, the crowd increased late in the day to an estimated 4,000 at the courthouse. Demanding that Brown be handed over to them, the demonstrators turned on the police and set the courthouse on fire. When firefighters appeared, their hoses were cut into pieces by rioters who had broken into nearby hardware stores and stolen axes as well as firearms. Mayor Edward P. Smith was at the scene and came out of the courthouse at about 10:30 P.M. to try to restore order. He became a target of the mob and was nearly lynched himself before being rescued.

The mob then turned its attention back to Brown, who along with other prisoners had been taken to the roof of the courthouse as the fire spread. Finally the rioters achieved their goal and Brown was taken and reportedly handed over the heads of the rioters down the stairs. By the time the ground floor was reached, he had likely been beaten to death. Hoisted into the air on a lynch rope, his swaying body was then riddled with bullets. Not yet satisfied, the crowd pulled his corpse to a nearby intersection where he was burned, and what remained of Will Brown was then towed about downtown Omaha. The victim's death certificate gave his age as "about 40," marital status unknown, birthplace left blank, and the principal cause of death bullet wounds and strangulation.

During the night federal troops restored order, and in the morning, armed with machine guns, they guarded downtown streets. Several arrests were made in the following days for complicity in the riot, but a grand jury's deliberations resulted in only a few indictments of little consequence.

Omaha was not the only city where rioting blighted the summer and fall of 1919. Chicago and Washington DC, among others, had outbreaks of racial violence and deaths. But in Omaha racial tensions may have been orchestrated for political purposes. A reform movement's candidates had been elected in 1918, defeating the political machine headed by Thomas "Old Man" Dennison that had dominated city hall for two decades. Direct accusations by church leaders and an assessment by Gen. Leonard Wood assigned responsibility for the lynching to political ambition. They asserted that to discredit the reformers, Dennison and his newspaper ally, the *Omaha Bee*, exaggerated crime and racial tensions to create the atmosphere that exploded on September 28, 1919. Two years later voters restored the Dennison slate to office. Will Brown appears to have been the victim of political machinations as well as racial prejudice.

See also CITIES AND TOWNS: Omaha, Nebraska.

Orville D. Menard
University of Nebraska at Omaha

Menard, Orville D. *Political Bossism in Mid-America: Tom Dennison's Omaha.* Lanham MD: University Press of America, 1989. Menard, Orville D. "Tom Dennison, the Omaha Bee, and the 1919 Omaha Race Riot." *Nebraska History* 68 (1987): 152–65.

PARKER, CHARLIE

See MUSIC: Parker, Charlie

PARKS, GORDON (b. 1912)

Gordon Parks overcame barriers of race and poverty to become a noted photographer, writer, filmmaker, composer, and painter. He was born on November 30, 1912, and grew up the youngest of fifteen children in a poor farm family in Fort Scott, Kansas. During his midteens his mother's death led him to leave Kansas to live with relatives in St. Paul, Minnesota. He stayed there briefly before entering a nomadic phase during which he traveled through much of the United States and later the world. Parks played piano in brothels, learned to play the trumpet, and began composing music while trying to finish high school. A stint singing and composing for a band took him to New York City. When the band's demise left him stranded and penniless, he joined the Civilian Conservation Corps in 1933. He later worked as a waiter on the North Coast Limited, a luxury train that ran from Chicago to Seattle.

In 1938, within a year of buying his first camera at a pawnshop, Parks had his first photographic exhibit in an Eastman Kodak store in Minneapolis. He quickly developed his photographic skills through incessant work, including shooting events at Chicago's South Side Community Art Center, fashion spreads for department stores, portraits of wealthy families, and photo essays about poverty on Chicago's South Side. His work documenting poverty earned Parks a Julius Rosenwald fellowship, which he used to train with Roy Emerson Stryker at the Farm Security Administration (FSA) in Washington DC. After Parks left the FSA he moved to Harlem and freelanced for *Glamour* and *Vogue*. He joined *Life* in 1948 and contributed to the magazine for more than twenty years. Parks launched his publishing career in 1947 with *Flash Photography*, an instruction manual. He later wrote a novel, *The Learning Tree* (1963), about growing

Gordon Parks, in the director's chair

up as an African American in rural Kansas, various books of poetry and photographs, and two memoirs, *A Choice of Weapons* (1966) and *Voices in the Mirror: An Autobiography* (1990).

Parks began consulting in the film industry during the 1950s and became the first black director of a major motion picture when he brought *The Learning Tree* to the screen in 1969 for Warner Brothers–Seven Arts. He continued directing with *Shaft* (1971), *Shaft's Big Score* (1972), *Super Cops* (1974), *Leadbelly* (1976), and *The Odyssey of Solomon Northrup* (1983), among others. In addition to directing, Parks wrote the screenplay and musical score for *The Learning Tree* and wrote the score for *Shaft's Big Score*. He also composed a piano concerto and the music and libretto for *Martin*, a five-act ballet tribute to Martin Luther King Jr. In recent years Parks has moved to abstract color photography, using paint and computer technology to alter his photos.

Todd M. Kerstetter
Texas Christian University

Parks, Gordon. *A Choice of Weapons*. New York: Harper and Row, 1966. Parks, Gordon. *Half Past Autumn: A Retrospective*. Boston: Bullfinch Press, 1997. Parks, Gordon. *Voices in the Mirror: An Autobiography*. New York: Doubleday, 1990.

PICKETT, BILL (1870–1932)

Credited with inventing bulldogging (steer wrestling), Willie M. "Bill" Pickett performed with Wild West shows and rodeos for several decades. In recognition of his athletic prowess and crowd-pleasing abilities, in 1971 he became the first African American cowboy inducted into the National Rodeo Cowboy Hall of Fame in Oklahoma City.

One of thirteen children, Pickett was born in Travis County, Texas, thirty miles northwest of Austin. His ancestry was African American, Caucasian, and Cherokee. Growing up in rural Texas ranch country, Will, as he was known in his youth, learned to read brands and toss a rope. By his own account, one day he watched a small dog bite a cow's lip and successfully control the large animal. Pickett decided that he could do likewise and first demonstrated his lip-biting technique to a group of cowboys in 1881.

Pickett worked on various central Texas ranches during the late 1880s and 1890s. He married Maggie Turner in 1890 and together they raised nine children. In partnership with his brothers, he started the Pickett Brothers Bronco Busters and Rough Riders Association in Taylor, Texas, advertising that "We ride and break all wild horses with much care. Catching and taming wild cattle a specialty."

During the early 1900s Pickett demonstrated his toothy bulldogging technique at county fairs and other gatherings throughout the Great Plains. In 1904 he performed at Cheyenne Frontier Days. The following year Pickett joined the famous Miller Brothers' 101 Ranch Wild West Show. Over the next several years he performed with Tom Mix, Guy Weadick, Milt Hinkle, and other Wild West show stars. Later Pickett estimated that he bulldogged some 5,000 steers during his long career.

While working with the 101 outfit, Pickett became known as Bill rather than Will. Strong, athletic, compact (five feet seven inches, 145 pounds), and mustachioed, he dressed like a Spanish bullfighter. The 101 program listed him as "the Dusky Demon who throws steers with his teeth." In late 1908 he brashly agreed to take on a Mexican fighting bull. The bull gored both Pickett and his prized mount Spradley, one of several times that Pickett was injured.

In the 1920s Pickett mostly retired from competitive bulldogging but continued to give exhibitions. He starred in a few Western movies that showcased his rodeo feats. Pickett returned to work for Zack Miller and continued to break horses. His wife's death in March 1929 devastated Pickett, but he continued to work on the Miller ranch. He died at the 101 Ranch on April 2, 1932, after being kicked in the head by a horse. Miller's eulogy aptly summarized Pickett's achievements as the "greatest sweat and dirt cowhand that ever lived—bar none."

See also FILM: Miller Brothers / IMAGES AND ICONS: Wild West Shows.

Richard W. Slatta
North Carolina State University

Hanes, Bailey C. *Bill Pickett: Bulldogger*. Norman: University of Oklahoma Press, 1977, 1989. Johnson, Cecil. *Guts: Legendary Black Rodeo Cowboy Bill Pickett*. Fort Worth: Summit Group, 1994. Russell, Don. *The Wild West: A History of the Wild West Shows*. Fort Worth: Amon Carter Museum, 1970.

SANDERS, BARRY (b. 1968)

Barry Sanders, who was born in Wichita, Kansas, on July 16, 1968, is considered one of the

Barry Sanders, 1988

greatest running backs to ever play football. Following a noteworthy high school career, Sanders was not widely recruited by the major colleges because of his relatively diminutive stature (five feet eight inches). However, Oklahoma State University took a chance on the small but determined Sanders. After two years as one of the best kick-return specialists in college football, in 1988 Sanders had the most prolific season running the football in college football history. That year Sanders ran for 2,628 yards, a National Collegiate Athletic Association record, and scored thirty-nine touchdowns, winning the Heisman Trophy as the nation's best player. Sanders was taken as the third choice in the 1989 National Football League (NFL) draft by the Detroit Lions, for whom he played ten seasons. During his NFL career Sanders rushed for 15,269 yards and was the NFL Rookie of the Year in 1989 and the Player of the Year in 1997.

Sanders's legacy as a running back is as one of the most elusive runners in the game, and his misdirection-runs at both the college and professional levels continue to be seen on "highlight reels" when great running backs are discussed. Following the 1998 season Barry Sanders surprised the football world by retiring from the NFL needing less than 1,500 yards to become the most prolific runner in NFL history. Sanders continues to reside in the Detroit area, although he remains active in the Wichita area through his generous support of his home church.

G. Allen Finchum
Oklahoma State University

Oklahoma State 2001 Football Media Guide. Stillwater: Oklahoma State University Athletic Department, 2001.

SAYERS, GALE (b. 1943)

Though he played just four full seasons in the National Football League (NFL), Gale Eugene Sayers, born May 30, 1943, in Wichita, Kansas, ran his way to historical prominence with the Chicago Bears from 1965 to 1971. Sayers's talents were first realized in Omaha, Nebraska, where he was a standout in football and track at Central High School. After receiving a scholarship to play football at the University of Kansas, he earned All-American status as a halfback in 1963 and 1964. As a Jayhawk he amassed 2,675 rushing and receiving yards, averaged 6.5 yards per carry, and was named first-team All–Big Eight three years straight. In his sophomore campaign, Sayers gained 1,125 yards on 158 carries to lead the nation with a 7.1-yard average.

Sayers's success carried over into the NFL, as he lived up to high expectations of him as the Bears' first pick and the fourth overall pick of the 1965 draft. With a combination of balance, speed, and instinct, the six-foot 200-pound Sayers established himself as the premier running back of his time. While playing in just sixty-eight games, equivalent to fewer than five seasons today, Number 40 compiled 9,435 all-purpose yards, recorded fifty-six career touchdowns, and broke four NFL records and tied two more. He still shares a record with

Dub Jones and Ernie Nevers for scoring six touchdowns in one game. He ran for four, caught one, and returned a punt for another record against the San Francisco Forty-niners on December 12, 1965. That same year he led the NFL with twenty-two touchdowns, a rookie record. Sayers not only stood out as a halfback, but his elusiveness on the field also led to dominance as a punt- and kickoff-return specialist. He holds the record for highest average yardage per kickoff return in a career, at 30.6 yards, and is tied with Ollie Matson for returning six kickoffs for touchdowns. He led the NFL with a 31.2-yard average in 1966, and his career best, a remarkable 37.7 yards, came a year later.

Sayers won two rushing titles in 1966 and 1969 (1,231 and 1,032 yards, respectively), rushed for 100 yards or more in twenty games, averaged five yards per carry, and was named Rookie of the Year. In five professional bowl-game appearances, he was named Most Valuable Player three times. Two severe knee injuries cut his career short, and he was forced to retire in 1971. At thirty-four years old, he became the youngest inductee into the NFL Hall of Fame in 1977. Since his retirement from football, Sayers has become a successful businessman as head of Crest Computer Supplies, a Skokie, Illinois–based company.

See also SPORTS AND RECREATION: Football, American.

Nathan E. Odgaard
Kansas City Kansan

Sayers, Gale, with Al Silverman. *I Am Third*. New York: Viking Press, 1970.

SCOTT FAMILY

The Scott family of Topeka, Kansas, has earned a special place in the legal culture of the Great Plains. Three generations of attorneys have come from their ranks, and among their achievements is their successful effort to secure the educational equality of all American children.

Elisha Scott Sr. (1890–1963) was born in Memphis, Tennessee, the youngest of thirteen children. Eventually, the Scott family made their way to Topeka, settling on Lane Street in West Topeka. His mother was employed as a domestic worker and his father sold coal by the bushel and herded cattle. Elisha Scott's life was shaped not only by his hard-working parents but also through the efforts of a local, well-respected minister, the Rev. Charles Sheldon. Reverend Sheldon replaced Scott's worn clothing and made sure he had a few dollars in his pocket, but his crucial act of generosity came when he paid Scott's tuition at the Kansas Technical Institute, an all–African American vocational school. In 1916 Scott graduated from Washburn College with a degree in law. He was the only African American in his graduating class and only the third African American to graduate from Washburn Law School.

Scott went on to become one of Topeka's most prominent attorneys. His courtroom flair gained him national exposure. It was not uncommon for his mail to be addressed simply as "Colored Lawyer, Topeka." Scott was known for taking cases that seemed impossible to win. He used every legal maneuver available to secure an acquittal. His financial breakthrough came in the mid-1920s when he successfully represented a group of African American and Native American clients from Oklahoma and Texas who had been driven off their land. As it turned out, the land was rich in oil.

Scott and his wife, Esther, had three sons, John, Charles Sr., and Elisha Jr., who would grow up to join their father in the family law firm. John J. Scott (1919–1984) received his formal education at Topeka High School and the University of Kansas. After graduation, John followed in his father's footsteps and in 1942 entered the law school at Washburn University. He completed only two years before he was called for active duty in World War II. In 1946 Scott returned to Washburn University to complete his law degree. He graduated on June 8, 1947, and joined the family law firm. Charles Scott Sr. (1921–1989) also attended Topeka Public Schools and graduated from Topeka High School. In 1940 he began pursuing a career in law by enrolling at Washburn, only to be interrupted by World War II. During the war he was assigned to the all-black Second Calvary Division and served in southern France. Charles Scott and his father enjoyed an especially close relationship, especially during wartime. In 1946, after the war, Charles Scott reenrolled in Washburn University and acquired his law degree in 1948. From there he joined the family firm.

During his initial years in private practice, Charles Scott Sr. and his father were successful in securing the racial integration of elementary schools in South Park, Johnson County, Kansas. Later, Charles and John represented plaintiffs in several cases that sought to allow blacks access to swimming pools, theaters, and restaurants in Topeka. In 1951 Charles and John Scott were among the attorneys who represented the NAACP in filing their landmark case, *Brown v. The Board of Education of Topeka*. Although the case was unsuccessful in district court, it was won on appeal in a unanimous decision by the U.S. Supreme Court on May 17, 1954, and the principle of racially diverse learning environments was established.

Only in their early thirties, Charles and John had gained national attention as a result of the *Brown* case. They probably could have practiced law anywhere. Charles chose to stay in Topeka to pursue civil and human rights issues, while John relocated to Washington DC, where he took a position in the Department of the Interior as assistant solicitor.

Charles Scott Jr. (b. 1948) also followed in the footsteps of his father. In 1979 Charles, an attorney in private practice in Kansas City, Kansas, together with two local Topeka attorneys and representatives of the American Civil Liberties Union (ACLU), petitioned the federal court to reopen the original *Brown* case. Their purpose was to determine if Topeka Public Schools had ever in fact complied with the Supreme Court's ruling of 1954. The petition

to reopen was in direct response to a school-district policy allowing enrollment based on parental choice rather than neighborhood boundaries. As a result, Topeka schools were once again placed under legal scrutiny. In 1992 they were ordered by the federal court to develop a plan to remedy all vestiges of school segregation. The solution included constructing three magnet schools, one of which is named for the Scott attorneys.

See also LAW: *Brown v. The Board of Education of Topeka*.

Cheryl Brown Henderson
Brown Foundation for Educational Equity,
Excellence and Research

SINGLETON, PAP (1809–1892)

Benjamin "Pap" Singleton planted black separatist colonies in Kansas and distinguished himself as a spokesperson for the "Exodusters." Born into slavery in Davidson County near Nashville, Tennessee, Singleton escaped in 1846 to Detroit, Michigan, where he helped fugitives find refuge in Canada. After the Civil War he returned to Nashville, but the growing pervasiveness of segregation, black codes, and lynching violence soon convinced him that African Americans could not trust elected officials to safeguard citizenship rights in the South. In 1874 he banded with eight associates and organized the Edgefield Real Estate and Homestead Association to encourage a cooperative migration to the Kansas plains.

The group held an emigration convention in 1875, but poverty and conflicting reports about the suitability of the Great Plains for settlement prevented them from making an immediate move. In late 1876, however, Singleton agreed to bring settlers to railroad land in Cherokee County in southeastern Kansas, and in early 1877 African American colonists began arriving to build the Singleton Colony north of Baxter Springs. High land prices ensured the colony's rapid demise, so in 1878 Singleton redirected his attention toward the unsold Kansas Reservation trust lands in Morris and Lyon Counties and planted a second Singleton Colony around the village of Dunlap. While the second colony survived and became home to the Presbyterian Church's Freedmen's Academy of Dunlap, Kansas, the 1879 arrival of the Exodusters diverted Singleton away from western colonization and pushed him toward the goal of national race unity.

Singleton became a self-appointed spokesperson for the Exodusters and in 1880 declared during testimony before the U.S. Senate that he was the father of the entire migration. In 1881 he capitalized on his newly won fame by organizing the Colored United Links (CUL) in Topeka, Kansas, which he hoped would grow to unite African Americans across the United States in the cooperative development of black-owned industrial enterprises and educational facilities. The CUL never expanded far beyond its Plains headquarters and soon fell into decline. Singleton devoted his remaining years to organizing or speaking out on behalf of separatist and colonization movements like Kansas City's United Transatlantic Society. In 1889 Singleton raised his voice for the final time when he advised African Americans to migrate to the Southern Plains and help turn part of the Oklahoma Territory into an all-black state. He reportedly died in St. Louis in 1892.

Gary R. Entz
McPherson College

Entz, Gary R. "Image and Reality on the Kansas Prairie: 'Pap' Singleton's Cherokee County Colony." *Kansas History* 19 (1996): 124–39. Hickey, Joseph V. "'Pap' Singleton's Dunlap Colony: Relief Agencies and the Failure of a Black Settlement in Eastern Kansas." *Great Plains Quarterly* 11 (1991): 23–36. Painter, Nell Irvin. *Exodusters: Black Migration to Kansas after Reconstruction*. Lawrence: University Press of Kansas, 1986.

THOMPSON, ERA BELL (1905–1986)

The distinguished journalist, editor, and author Era Bell Thompson was born in Des Moines, Iowa, on August 10, 1905. Her family moved to Driscoll, North Dakota, in 1917, and her "love affair" with the state began. She attended the University of North Dakota for two years and received her bachelor of arts degree from Morningside College in Sioux City, Iowa, in 1933. She later pursued graduate study at the Medill School of Journalism at Northwestern University. Following the publication of her early autobiography *American Daughter* (1946), which she wrote while holding a Newberry Library Fellowship, John H. Johnson hired her in 1947 as associate editor of *Ebony*. She served as the co–managing editor of this magazine from 1951 to 1964, at which point she became the international editor of Johnson Publishing Company, a position she maintained until her death. In 1954 her book *Africa, Land of My Father* appeared, and in 1963 she co-edited *White on Black*.

Thompson received honorary doctorate degrees from Morningside College (1965) and the University of North Dakota (1969). Her numerous awards include the Bread Loaf Writers Conference Fellowship (1949), National Press Club Citation (1961), Iota Phi Lambda Outstanding Woman of the Year (1965), the Society of Midland Authors' Patron Saints Award (1968 for *American Daughter*), and Theodore Roosevelt Roughrider Award, North Dakota's highest honor (1976). The Black Cultural Center at the University of North Dakota was renamed for her in 1979. Thompson died on December 30, 1986, and was buried in her family's plot in Driscoll, North Dakota.

Çigdem Üsekes
University of North Dakota

Anderson, Kathie R. "Era Bell Thompson: A North Dakota Daughter." *North Dakota History* (1982): 11–18. Riley, Glenda. "American Daughters: Black Women in the West." *Montana: The Magazine of Western History* 38 (1988): 14–27.

TULSA RACE RIOT

On the night of May 31, 1921, in one of the worst episodes in Oklahoma and Ameri-

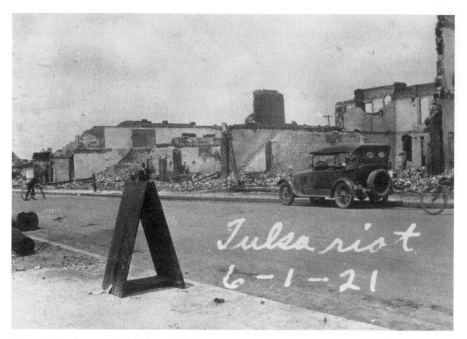

Burned ruins after race riot in Tulsa, Oklahoma, June 1, 1921

can history, Tulsa exploded in violence that scarred the city forever. Although many details of the riot are shrouded in controversy, what is known is that about thirty-five blocks in the African American district were destroyed and at least thirty-nine people—and probably considerably more—lost their lives. The white mob torched the influential black business district known as "Deep Greenwood," and all African Americans who did not flee or get killed were arrested. It took the arrival of the National Guard and martial law to bring order to the violence-torn city.

The Jim Crow climate in Oklahoma and in much of the nation at the time set the tone for Tulsa's riot. Oklahoma had its share of lynchings and racial violence prior to 1921 and after, and the Ku Klux Klan was just gaining a foothold in the young state. Tulsa's African Americans, many of them returning World War I veterans, had a new sense of pride (as well as training), and numerous organizations, including Cyril Brigg's national group, the African Blood Brotherhood, preached self-reliance and the need for community defense. The black press in Oklahoma, and especially A. J. Smitherman's *Tulsa Star*, also advocated protecting family and community. Smitherman had witnessed other racial conflicts prior to Tulsa's catastrophe. In one case in Okmulgee, Oklahoma, he saw a white mob back down from a group of armed blacks who were protecting their houses. This lesson, and also the failure of Oklahoma City authorities to stop a lynching of an African American less than a year before, and the lynching of a white person who was pulled out of the Tulsa jail in 1920, increased the determination of Tulsa's black leaders not to let an African American lynching occur in their city.

On May 30, 1921, Dick Rowland, an African American shoe-shiner, went to the Drexel Building to use the restroom. The closest "colored" restroom was located on the top floor of

the building. Speculation after the riot suggested that Rowland tripped as he entered the elevator and grabbed the arm of the elevator operator, Sarah Page, who then screamed. Whether this is actually what happened is not fully known. It has also been suggested they had an ongoing relationship. The next morning Tulsa police arrested Rowland for attempted rape. The *Tulsa Tribune* printed an article titled, "Nab Negro for Attacking Girl in Elevator," and may have included an even more incendiary article in the editorial section, but all known *Tribune* copies are missing this entry. These news stories aroused both sections of the town.

A large group of whites surrounded the courthouse and jail on the night of May 31. Armed African Americans twice went to the courthouse offering to help protect Rowland. Their second appearance sparked mayhem as a shot scattered the crowd. Skirmishes between blacks and whites occurred from the courthouse back to the African American neighborhoods. Whites broke into stores to get arms and ammunition, and many were sworn in as special deputies. Sporadic fighting lasted through the night. In the middle of the night Tulsa officials sent a telegram to Oklahoma City requesting help from the National Guard.

At dawn the next morning, June 1, a whistle reportedly blew signaling the white invasion of North Tulsa. One controversy surrounding the riot has been the extent to which machine guns and airplanes were used during the battle for Greenwood. Both were present, and there is evidence that explosives were dropped from planes, though the planes seemed to have been used mainly for reconnaissance. The outnumbered African Americans tried to defend their homes, but the invaders descended, burning and looting. Among the African Americans killed was A. C. Jackson, a nationally renowned black surgeon. Others fled north out of the city, but many were arrested and detained at the convention center and later at a ballpark and the fairgrounds. The National Guard arrived at 9:15 that morning, and Gen. Charles Barrett declared martial law at 11:29. By this time the riot had nearly run its course.

African Americans in Tulsa faced an uphill struggle after the riot. The city government enacted a fire-ordinance restriction to stop the rebuilding process. African American lawyers fought and won the fire-ordinance battle, but many North Tulsans were homeless through the winter and lived in tents and makeshift homes. Greenwood did rebuild and, some contend, became more prosperous than before 1921, but no insurance claims were ever paid to the holders nor did the city pay restitution. Urban renewal later leveled North Tulsa a second time.

In 1997 the Oklahoma legislature established a Race Riot Commission to study the violence of the 1921 race war. In 2001 the commission submitted an official report of its findings to the legislature and recommended reparations be paid to the survivors of Oklahoma's—and one of the nation's—worst civil disturbances.

See also CITIES AND TOWNS: Tulsa, Oklahoma.

Larry O'Dell
Oklahoma Historical Society

Ellsworth, Scott. *Death in a Promised Land: The Tulsa Race Riot of 1921*. Baton Rouge: Louisiana State University Press, 1982. Franklin, John Hope, and Scott Ellsworth, eds. *The Tulsa Race Riot: A Scientific, Historical, and Legal Analysis*. Tulsa: A Report Submitted to the Tulsa Race Riot Commission, 2000. Parrish, Mary E. Jones. *Race Riot 1921, Events of the Tulsa Disaster*. Tulsa: Out on a Limb Publishing, 1998.

WARE, JOHN (1845–1905)

By 1885, only three years after migrating to the foothills southwest of Calgary, Alberta, former slave and experienced cowboy John Ware had earned a reputation as the "best rough-rider in the North-West." Despite being nicknamed "Nigger John," contemporary accounts suggest that over time the color of his skin had less influence on how people perceived him than did his renowned strength, riding skills, and gentlemanly demeanor.

Born in South Carolina in 1845, John Ware was freed from slavery at the end of the Civil War. By the late 1870s he had gained valuable experience in Texas as a cowhand and herdsman. In 1882, at the end of a long and arduous cattle drive from Montana to southwestern Alberta, Ware decided to stay in the area when he learned that employment opportunities with the large cattle companies were plentiful for experienced cowboys. By 1890 Ware was able to purchase his own ranch in the foothills, and in 1900 he moved with his wife and children to his second and last ranch, situated along the Red Deer River, east of Brooks, Alberta. John Ware died as a result of a riding accident on September 11, 1905.

John Ware's personality and reputation as a successful horseman and rancher accorded him much respect and admiration during his twenty-three years in the region. After his death a creek, a coulee, a mountain, and eventually a folk song were given his name.

Dawn Nickel
University of Alberta

Winks, Robin W. *The Blacks in Canada*. Montreal: McGill-Queen's University Press, 1997.

WATTS, J. C. (b. 1957)

Born in a poor part of a poor town on November 18, 1957, Julius Caesar Watts made football his ticket out of Eufaula, Oklahoma. The first stop was Norman and the University of Oklahoma, where he led Sooner teams to Orange Bowl championships in 1979 and 1980. Six years in the Canadian Football League followed before he returned to Norman and became a Baptist youth minister. Previously a Democrat, Watts switched to the GOP in 1989 and won election to Oklahoma's corporation commission in 1990. In 1994 he announced his candidacy for the Fourth District's open congressional seat and won handily. J. C. Watts and Connecticut's newly elected Gary Franks thereby became the first black Republicans in the U.S. House of Representatives since 1935. Franks lost in 1996, leaving Watts the lone African American Republican in Congress.

Nationally, his star rose quickly. After a powerful address at the 1996 Republican National Convention, Watts joined Bob Dole's campaign and was the party's choice to answer President Bill Clinton's 1997 State of the Union address. Secure at home, he spent much of the 1998 campaign season speaking on behalf of Republican candidates everywhere. All of this prepared him to be a prime beneficiary of the subsequent shake-up in the Republican leadership. On November 18, 1998, Watts unseated Ohio's John Boehner by a count of 121 to 93 to become chairman of the House Republican Conference. It was his forty-first birthday. Not yet in a third term, in 2000 J. C. Watts had become the fourth-ranking leader of the House majority party. In January 2003 Watts retired from Congress and accepted positions on the board of directors of Dillard's and as national chairman of GOPAC, a national education organization for Republican state and local candidates.

Danney Goble
University of Oklahoma

WEBB, WELLINGTON AND WILMA (b. 1941; b. 1943)

Wellington and Wilma Webb are Denverites who began their public careers as community activists in the 1960s. Wellington's service began with his election from District 8 on the city's northeast side to the Colorado House of Representatives in 1972. Wilma's began with her appointment to the House from the same district in 1980, to which she was subsequently elected following King Trimble's resignation to run for the Denver city council. Since then they have held local, state, and federal government positions and have been active in the Democratic Party. Indeed, Wilma has held positions in the party up to and including party secretary.

From 1977 to 1981 Wellington served as the regional director of the U.S. Department of Health, Education, and Welfare, and from 1981 to 1987 as the director of the Colorado Department of Regulatory Agencies. In 1987 he was elected auditor of the city of Denver, remaining in that post until 1991 when he was elected mayor, an office for which he had first campaigned in 1983. He was the first African American mayor of Denver. He was reelected twice and concluded his third and final term in July 2003. Wilma was reelected fives times as the state representative for District 8, resigning after her husband's election as mayor. Perhaps her most significant achievement was Colorado's recognition and celebration in 1984 of a state holiday on Martin Luther King Jr.'s birthday, after a ten-year struggle that she spearheaded.

William M. King
University of Colorado at Boulder

Denver Magazine 16 (April 1986): 28–33. *Denver Post Magazine*, March 28, 1993: 11–13. *Rocky Mountain News Sunday Magazine*, October 20, 1991: 12M–14M.

WEST, CORNEL (b. 1953)

Theologian, public intellectual, and formerly professor of Afro-American Studies and religion at Harvard University, Cornel West is also highly regarded as a philosopher. In July 2002 West returned to Princeton University, where he received his doctorate, as Class of 1943 University Professor of Religion. Part of a group of influential contemporary African American scholars, Cornel West strives to close those gaps he perceives in the work of the older generation of African American intellectuals and political activists. This accounts for the eclecticism of his work and for his mix of academic scholarship with activist immersion in the matters of everyday life or, as he calls it, the human condition.

The grandson of a Baptist minister, West was born in Tulsa, Oklahoma, on June 2, 1953, and brought up under the religious influence of the Baptist Church. His religious upbringing opened his eyes early to the theme of justice in an unjust world. The marginalization of Native Americans and African Americans to the racially and economically defined periphery of Oklahoma provided him with the existentialist notions of tragedy in the American social-political landscape.

By the time West arrived at Harvard in 1970, he was already an emboldened and eloquent young man who felt no restraint in expressing his opposition to injustice and criticizing the ideas of preceding leaders of the black movement. West has been particularly critical of W. E. B. Du Bois, who had argued that the way for African Americans to break out of oppression and marginalization was to embrace the values of white America. At Harvard, West majored in religion while also studying philosophy. Graduating in 1973, he pursued a doctoral degree in philosophy at Princeton where he came under the influence of Richard Rorty and the new trajectory of pragmatism. Two of West's works, *Post-Analytic Philosophy* (1985) and *The American Evasion of Philosophy* (1989), reflect Rorty's belief that the dominant American academic practice operates, at best, with cynicism about the social conditions of the nation and evades the real problems at the heart of American society. In the latter work, West explores the history of American pragmatism stretching from Ralph Waldo Emerson to Richard Rorty as a response to the social problematic of American society. He returns to these themes frequently in his later writings, notably in *Keeping Faith: Philosophy and Race in America* (1993).

But West's wide popularity comes mainly from his speeches and writings for a general audience, themselves the result of his mission, like his mentor Rorty's, to see philosophy break free from the privileged confines of the academy. Philosophy, in his view, must engage the social tragedies of suffering and despair faced everyday by those who are alienated from society and dispossessed of their fundamental material, social, and spiritual rights.

The greatest influence on West, as he himself admits, is Anton Pavlovich Chekhov. Like Chekhov, the Russian physician and writer, West steps outside his exclusive professional engagements in order to embrace the plight of everyday folks by using the privileges of his own public image and visibility. West's concern is first and foremost with the shifting yet unending bondage of African Americans—from the hot sun of the plantations in a quasi-feudal system to the proletariat conditions of an industrialized America. It is this condition that, in his view, brings forth the idea of community and the necessity of oppositional intellectual groupings within the academy.

D. A. Masolo
University of Louisville

Gordon, Lewis R. *Existentia Africana: Understanding Africana Existential Thought*. New York: Routledge, 2000.

WHITE PRIMARY

See LAW: White Primary

YORK

(ca. 1770s–ca. 1815/1832)

Born into slavery in the 1770s, York achieved fame as the sole African American member of the Lewis and Clark expedition. Virginia plantation owner John Clark selected young York as his son William's body servant, a position of status and privilege, around 1784 when the Clark family moved to the Falls of the Ohio River (Louisville) where they established the Mulberry Hill plantation. William Clark inherited the Clark estate, including York, in 1799. Meanwhile, York married a slave on a nearby plantation.

From 1804 to 1806 York joined his master as a member of the Lewis and Clark expedition. Presumably, York was the first African American to travel through the Northern Plains. He enjoyed the same freedoms as the other men, which enabled him to make considerable contributions to the success of the expedition. York carried a rifle for hunting and protection, went on reconnaissance missions, and cast his vote on selecting a winter campsite near the Pacific Ocean.

When the expedition returned, York did not want to go back to the confines of slavery, nor did he want to be separated from his family in Kentucky by moving with Clark to St. Louis. Clark considered selling York, but decided to discipline him through beating, confinement, hiring him out, and lending him to his family in Kentucky. Sometime after 1815, Clark either had a change of heart or simply relented to York's demands for freedom. Clark manumitted York, providing him with six horses and a wagon to operate a freighting service between Nashville, Tennessee, and Richmond, Kentucky. York struggled to survive, a free man in the slaveholding South, before presumably dying of cholera in Tennessee sometime between 1815 and 1832. The Lewis and Clark Bicentennial Commission plans to confer enlisted man status posthumously on York.

See also EUROPEAN AMERICANS: Lewis and Clark.

Jay H. Buckley
Brigham Young University

Betts, Robert B. *In Search of York: The Slave Who Went to the Pacific with Lewis and Clark*. Boulder: Colorado Associated University Press, 1985.

Agriculture

Grain elevators, southwestern Alberta, 1955

AGRICULTURE

The Great Plains is an agricultural factory of immense proportions. Between the yellow canola fields of Canada's Parkland Belt and the sheep and goat country of Texas's Edwards Plateau, more than 2,000 miles to the south, lie a succession of agricultural regions that collectively produce dozens of food and fiber products. The most important Great Plains crop is wheat. Although the United States and Canada together produce slightly less wheat than China (the world's leading wheat grower), the two North American countries account for more than half of the world's wheat exports. Barley, canola, corn, cotton, sorghum, and soybeans grown in the Great Plains also reach markets around the world.

Agriculture has long been the life force of the Great Plains economy. Although manufacturing employs more people than agriculture in some parts of the Great Plains today, many urban industries rely on the region's farms and ranches for the raw materials they process. One has to look back several thousand years, to a time when plains inhabitants were mainly nomadic hunters, to find an era when agriculture did not figure prominently in the region's pattern of human occupation. Some Native North American groups depended on agriculture as much as the European Americans who displaced them.

Native American Agriculture

Cultivation of domesticated plants was a relatively late innovation in the Great Plains compared to the southeastern and southwestern regions of North America. By A.D. 850, semisedentary horticultural villages dotted the banks of the Missouri River and its tributaries as far north as the Knife River in present-day North Dakota on the Northern Plains. These settlements were a result of migration and diffusion from the Mississippian cultural complex to the east. However, agriculture in the Great Plains has always been a risky business threatened by drought, grasshoppers, and early frosts. For that reason early farmers did not depend entirely on the produce of their gardens; rather, they hunted bison and other game and supplemented their diets with meat and diverse wild plants.

Villages were located on the bluffs and terraces overlooking the gardens, which were carved into the fertile floodplains below. Maize was the most important food crop produced, but gardens also included a wide variety of beans and squash. Some of the earliest domesticates on the Plains were amaranth, chenopods, and sunflowers. Tobacco, central to ritual life in many tribes, was a highly valued crop and trade item as well. The annual cycle of village life revolved around the planting, hoeing, harvesting, and processing of their crops. The architecture, implements, and other technologies associated with this early agricultural lifestyle in the Great Plains were remarkably uniform: semisubterranean earth lodge villages, bison scapula hoes, and ceramic pots used to cook corn and beans.

One of the secrets of the longevity of this lifestyle among Native groups was the sophisticated risk-management strategies employed by the farmers, who were mostly women. Archaeological and ethnographic records reveal careful development of a wide variety of maize, beans, and squash, specifically selected to produce under different conditions. The Mandans, for example, planted at least thirteen varieties of corn at the time of contact with European Americans. In addition, their gardens were widely dispersed geographically and were intercropped. For example, beans were planted among the corn because beans returned essential nitrogen to soils depleted by corn production.

The first harvest of the season was the green corn harvest, which typically began in mid-August. The green corn was roasted or boiled, shelled using clam shells, and spread out to dry in the sun. Corn was used sparingly when other foods were available. The dried corn was usually boiled with beans, squash, or dried meat. Occasionally, it was processed with mortar and pestle to make cornmeal. Particularly good ears were chosen carefully and saved as seed corn for the following year's gardens.

The major harvest of the season was the ripe corn harvest in late September and October. The corn was husked, and fifty or more brightly colored ears were braided together and hung on drying scaffolds in the villages. After the corn was dried, it was stored either in parfleches or in the numerous bell-shaped cache pits located under the floors of the earth lodges. The cache pits could hold twenty to thirty bushels of corn, beans, sunflower seeds, dried pumpkins, or squash. Yields varied from year to year and from region to region, but most fields produced an average of twenty bushels per acre. A good harvest encouraged mutually beneficial trading with the bison-hunting nomads of the Plains.

Early Commercial Agriculture

Some crops perform better in one environment than in another. This obvious fact was learned early in the European American settlement of the Great Plains, and it has been relearned in various ways since. Not only is the Plains region too dry on average for the production of a number of crops, but it also receives a highly variable amount of moisture from year to year. Thus, even crops that do not demand significant amounts of moisture may wither in certain years when moisture is insufficient. Corn became the staple crop of European Americans who learned how to cultivate it from the Native peoples along the Atlantic seaboard. As migrants moved westward into the Great Plains after 1854, they brought with them familiar "American" practices such as raising livestock, which also required that they produce a corn crop for feed.

Corn and wheat became the most important crops of the Plains, just as they had been in the more humid eastern states. The importance of hogs in the Middle West was paralleled by beef cattle in the Great Plains, and cattle typically were fattened for market on corn just like hogs. Wheat was not grown for consumption by farm animals, but rather as a cash crop that would bring the farmer a sure return at the market. Farming practices introduced to the Great Plains by settlers coming from the East thus involved no radical changes in established patterns.

When new lands that had never been cultivated were put into crops by homesteading farmers, it was necessary to "break" the land with a large plow that was capable of turning over the thick prairie sod. Breaking the land was demanding work that required many teams of draft animals. Broken land often was planted with sod corn, which tolerated weeds. After a few years of cultivation, however, the land surface was easily worked with smaller farm implements, and a variety of food crops including wheat, flax, and corn could be planted.

Several traditions of wheat culture were brought to the Great Plains. Early settlers from Minnesota, Ontario, Wisconsin, and places farther east brought spring wheat to the Northern Great Plains and the Canadian Prairies, where it was (and still is) the most common variety grown. It is planted in the spring as soon as fields are dry enough to work and harvested in the fall before the weather turns cold. In Canada, Marquis wheat, a hard northern spring variety, became the preferred crop.

In the Central Great Plains the original bread-grain crop was soft winter wheat, which was brought to Kansas by migrants from Pennsylvania, Ohio, and Missouri. Winter wheat is sown in the fall, allowed to overwinter in the ground, and then resumes its growth the following spring. It is typically harvested in the early or midsummer months.

A third type of wheat, Turkey Red wheat, was brought to central Kansas in the early 1870s by German Mennonites who had recently immigrated from southern Russia. This was a hard winter wheat that produced a superior bread grain, like the hard spring wheats of the north. Turkey Red wheat eventually became the favored variety in the Central and Southern Great Plains.

The first cattle to graze the pastures of the Great Plains were the mixed breeds that were brought to the Americas by the Spanish. These mixed-blood (or *criollo*) cattle were a unique breed from the West Indies that had evolved as the result of crossbreeding. Of the *criollo* cattle, the best-known were the semiwild Texas longhorns. Beginning in the 1860s longhorns were rounded up in Texas for trail drives north to railheads in cities such as Abilene and Dodge City, Kansas, and then shipped east.

Although the longhorn's story forms a colorful chapter in the history of the Great Plains, they were not economically important after the 1880s. Cattle and sheep breeds introduced from England and Scotland were the foundation stock of most herds from the middle of the nineteenth century onward. Sheep grazing was especially well suited to the shortgrass prairies of Wyoming, Montana, and Alberta. Cattle breeds, such as the Aberdeen Angus and Hereford ("whiteface"), were brought to the Great Plains by cattlemen who in the early years of settlement sought to establish large herds on millions of grazing acres. The ranching style they introduced was implemented over much of the western shortgrass Plains, especially in the Dakotas, Wyoming, and Alberta.

Many of the early sheep ranchers and cattle barons were from Scotland and Ireland where pastures were far better suited to grazing animals than to raising crops. Thus the Scots and Irish continued a long-established tradition by focusing on livestock rather than crop production on the Plains. It was settlers from England, Germany, and the agricultural lands of central and eastern Europe who brought a knowledge of crop farming with them, and it was they who introduced most of the varieties of wheat to the Great Plains. They continued the tradition of agriculture they had practiced in Europe.

Droughts

Livestock grazing is less affected by drought than is crop farming, but it was farming that inspired the large number of settlers to come to the Great Plains during the second half of the nineteenth century. The region's agricultural history has frequently involved attempts to cope with droughts. Unpredictable dry years can lead to a series of crop failures and, eventually, the failure of settlement itself.

Early farmers on the Plains had poor weather records to guide them in choosing the best crops to plant. They selected the crops with which they had success elsewhere, but their previous farming experience was not always a reliable guide. For example, in the 1870s and 1880s farmers in Kansas debated whether to plant winter wheat or corn as their primary crop. Wheat was harvested early in the season, before summer droughts did their worst damage. Corn was subject to summer drought but was less affected by spring freezes because it was planted later, after the ground was warm. As a result, the best wheat crops frequently came during years when corn suffered. Droughts in the 1890s heralded a period of decline in the number of acres devoted to corn production in the Great Plains; the trend was not reversed until irrigation became more common in the 1960s.

The most drought-resistant crops often have been the ones that have triumphed in the Great Plains. Sorghum (or milo) was introduced on the Plains because it produces grain under the same drought conditions that cause corn to wither. Sorghum became a major source of cattle feed in the Southern Great Plains after seed companies introduced it in an improved, hybrid form in Texas and Oklahoma in the 1950s. Most varieties of wheat and barley are fairly drought tolerant; consequently these crops are grown in the drier, western plains. Corn, soybeans, cotton, and sugar beets demand a great deal of moisture. These crops are always irrigated when grown in the drier, western parts of the region but are grown frequently on the eastern Plains, where irrigation is not a necessity.

The causes of prolonged drought are not well understood. Wet and dry years often come in series that span several seasons. Persistent droughts occurred during the 1890s and 1930s and in response both of those decades witnessed an abrupt outward-migration of people from the Plains. The most serious problems developed in southwestern Kansas, eastern Colorado, and the Oklahoma and Texas Panhandles, an area that became known as the Dust Bowl in the 1930s because the combination of drought, overcultivation, and excessive grazing had removed so much of the plant cover that soil surfaces became completely open to wind erosion.

Attempts to make rain by cloud seeding were once seen as a means to combat drought, but today the more common approach is to use irrigation where possible. If water resources are lacking, however, drought still represents a major hazard to Great Plains agriculture.

Agricultural Technology

Although the agriculture undertaken by European American settlers involved little more than the simple transfer of familiar practices and cultures from one environment to another, the special needs of farming in the Plains soon became evident. New strategies evolved to cope with the environment from the 1860s onward.

Some innovations included new types of farm implements. The self-scouring steel plow was an invention demanded by the prairie because the thick, black sod was too difficult to turn with the smaller, cast-iron plows farmers were accustomed to using. Steel plows were invented in the Middle West just prior to the European American settlement of the Great Plains. The invention of barbed wire in the 1870s also took place outside the Great Plains, but it similarly had an impact on the Plains

region because it made it possible to fence millions of acres quickly and cheaply in areas where timber or hedges for fencing were unavailable.

Other innovations involved new systems for managing water resources. Windmills made it possible to pump water at remote locations, and thereby to control the grazing patterns of large herds of cattle. The introduction of steam threshing engines in the 1890s required that a supply of fuel be available, but in the Great Plains the firewood commonly found in other regions was lacking. Coal was also often unavailable. The solution was to build straw-burning steam engines that consumed the wheat straw, the principal by-product of threshing.

Still more specific innovations in crop farming were made in the late nineteenth and early twentieth centuries. Known under the general heading of dry farming, these methods involved a scientific approach to conserving soil moisture in areas where, by then, it was known that precipitation was often inadequate. Included under the practices of dry farming is the custom of "alternate fallow"—leaving strips of land unused between cultivated strips, or alternating fields and fallow from year to year so that two years of moisture are available for a single year's crop demand. Cultivating to control moisture-robbing weeds also proved beneficial. Deep plowing, subsurface compaction, and a variety of other methods were similarly introduced to combat the negative effects of inadequate moisture.

Dry farming is, in some respects, a passive technology in terms of environmental adaptation. Irrigation, however, is a much more direct approach to overcoming environmental limits. Irrigation was not widespread in the Great Plains before the middle of the twentieth century. What little irrigation there

The importance of Great Plains agriculture

was had to be located on gently sloping river floodplains where water, diverted from a river channel upstream, could flow across fields and eventually drain back into the main channel farther downstream. In the United States, the federal government's policies related to land and reclamation encouraged the construction of dams and diversion projects on smaller streams; in Canada, the Canadian Pacific Railway promoted large river diversions for irrigation in the early twentieth century. But prior to the 1960s irrigation was limited by the availability of streamside locations—the only place irrigation was feasible so long as dams, canals, and lateral channels were the only means for distributing water.

New technology provided an economical means for expanding irrigation after 1960. Deep wells were drilled and powerful electric pumps brought groundwater up to the surface. The wells fed surface sprinkler systems that moved across fields automatically. With sprinkler irrigation, it became possible to raise almost any feed grain. Once irrigation was in place, corn, the most valuable grain on which to fatten livestock, began to replace the more drought-resistant grain sorghums, although sorghum itself quickly became an irrigated crop as well.

As a result of these developments it became possible for Great Plains farmers to fatten larger numbers of cattle with locally produced feed grains. The typical pattern of shipping young cattle from the Plains to midwestern feedlots went into decline as more and more cattle were born, raised, fed, and slaughtered within the Great Plains itself. The result was a westward pull on the beef packing industry. About half of the major beef packing companies in the United States relocated to the Great Plains during the 1970s and 1980s.

In the 1930s farmers began to implement a variety of techniques to control soil erosion. Contour plowing was an early technique that prevented gullying on steeper slopes. Even seemingly small innovations helped, such as the now-common practice of leaving crop residues on fields after harvest to combat blowing soil conditions. Windbreaks, whether planted as rows of trees in shelterbelts or as strips of perennial grasses along narrow paths within fields, also curtail wind erosion. In the Great Plains today farmers no longer plow their fields annually. Rather, they disturb the soil as little as possible from year to year by working it with smaller cultivating implements and controlling weeds with chemicals.

Contemporary Agricultural Problems

The public's concern with environmental issues in recent years has led many to question the nature of some common farm practices in the Great Plains. Nitrification of groundwater supplies is one such example. Nitrification results from the continued application of nitrogen fertilizers that are used to increase yields of crops such as corn. With increased amounts of fertilizers, pesticides, and herbicides in the environment, some groundwater supplies have become contaminated, especially in areas

where irrigation is in heavy use, such as the Platte River Valley of Nebraska.

Animal manure was once spread over croplands to increase soil fertility on the farms where livestock were penned for feeding. Large, modern Great Plains feedlots produce far more animal wastes than local fields can use, and this has created a serious problem in waste disposal. Water pollution problems have multiplied as a result of large feedlots and the heavy use of chemical fertilizers.

Agricultural scientists have urged a return to crop rotation practices, whereby a fixed sequence of crops is grown on the same field over a series of years. Some crops, such as alfalfa, are planted to replenish soil fertility; others such as corn, are planted for feed; and still others, such as rye, are planted as a means to "rest" the land between years of more nutrient-demanding crops. But crop rotation is uncommon on irrigated fields in the Central Great Plains, most of which are used to produce corn every year. It is also uncommon in dryland wheat farming in the Prairie Provinces of Canada.

Irrigated land is expensive, so a higher return per acre is generally expected. The introduction of less intensive means of production is often resisted in areas that rely on irrigation. If too much irrigation water is diverted from streams, or if groundwater levels are lowered to the point that subsurface streams cannot feed ponds, streams, and rivers, then surface wetlands will dry up and wildlife numbers will decline.

One of the most difficult problems of Great Plains agriculture has actually been its very success. Since the 1930s national policies have been enacted to regulate overabundant crops that would depress the market and drive the price down to a level below farmers' costs of production. Both the Canadian and the U.S. governments have experimented with ways to increase grain exports overseas as one means of coping with oversupplies at home. Other government programs, such as the Soil Bank, enacted in the United States in 1957, have focused more on the conservation of land resources. Under the Soil Bank, and the Conservation Reserve Program that succeeded it, marginal land, such as that most susceptible to erosion, has been taken out of production by paying farmers not to cultivate it.

Agricultural Regions of the Great Plains

Great Plains agriculture varies throughout the region according to the nature of the physical environment, the demand for farm products, and the crop and livestock preferences of local ranchers and farmers. There are eleven major agricultural regions within the Great Plains. From north to south they are the (I) Parkland Belt, (II) Canadian Prairies, (III) Northern Spring Wheat Region, (IV) Unglaciated Missouri Plateau, (V) Sandhills, (VI) Eastern Feed Grains and Livestock Region, (VII) Winter Wheat Region, (VIII) Irrigated High Plains, (IX) Upland Cotton Region, (X) Irrigated Valleys, and (XI) Rangelands. Within these eleven regions are numerous subregions that have special defining characteristics as well.

The Parkland Belt (I) is the northern limit of prairie vegetation and, except for the outlier of the Peace River wheat country, is the northern limit of successful agriculture in North America. The term "parkland" suggests the open nature of the landscape, which consists of expanses of tall grass dotted with groves of aspen and spruce trees. Soils of the Parkland Belt are known as Luvisols in the Canadian system of soil nomenclature. Luvisols are fertile soils associated with broadleaf forests. Although the Parkland's growing season is quite short, the region normally receives more precipitation than does the Canadian Prairie region which forms the Parkland's southern limit. Many portions of the Parkland were settled ahead of the adjacent Canadian Prairie for this reason, although the earliest settlements were made along the line of the Canadian Pacific Railway. European settlers (of whom the Ukrainians are the best known) and the Métis people from Manitoba established agriculture in the Parkland zone at the end of the nineteenth and beginning of the twentieth centuries.

Canola, not wheat, is the crop favored to advance the agricultural frontier northward in Canada because it produces well in a short season of long summer days. The oilseed produces valuable forage and its seedpod yields a highly unsaturated cooking oil. Canola, as well as sunflower oil, is gaining great popularity around the world, and Canada exports large quantities of both to the United States, Europe, and Asia.

The Canadian Prairies agricultural region (II) consists of the large, triangular-shaped zone of grain production bounded roughly by Calgary, Edmonton, Saskatoon, Winnipeg, and the boundary with the United States (the forty-ninth parallel). Hard, red spring wheat is the most important crop here, followed by barley, canola, oats, and a variety of other small grains. Canadian Prairie wheat was traditionally hauled by rail through Winnipeg (the region's major wheat marketing and trading center) to the Lake Superior port of Thunder Bay (formerly, Port Arthur and Fort William), loaded aboard ship, and sent to Liverpool or to other European markets. Today much of the wheat from the Prairie Provinces moves westward to ocean ports in British Columbia for shipment to Asia. Despite being the world's largest wheat producer, China consumes more than it can grow and greatly depends on wheat from Canada to make up the difference.

Chernozemic soils—deep, dark-colored, and high in nutrients—are an important basis for the wheat crop of the Prairie Provinces. About one-half of Canada's total agricultural land in the Prairie Provinces consists of chernozemic soils. It is the same type of soil that is found in the principal wheat-raising areas of the Ukraine, an area that is climatically similar to the southern portions of the Prairie Provinces.

The Canadian Prairie region was less wooded than the Parkland to the north, and the Canadian Pacific Railway, linking the coasts after

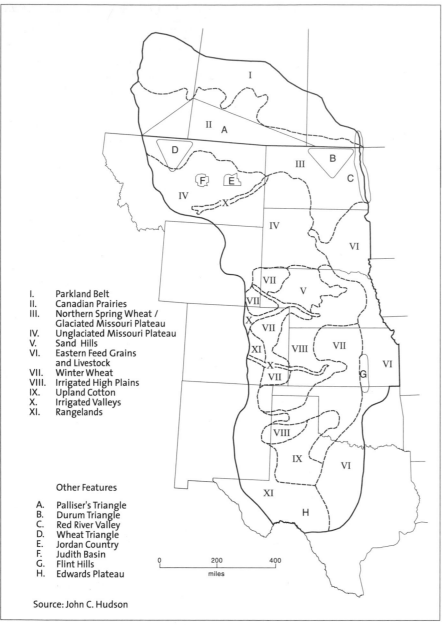

I. Parkland Belt
II. Canadian Prairies
III. Northern Spring Wheat /
    Glaciated Missouri Plateau
IV. Unglaciated Missouri Plateau
V. Sand Hills
VI. Eastern Feed Grains
    and Livestock
VII. Winter Wheat
VIII. Irrigated High Plains
IX. Upland Cotton
X. Irrigated Valleys
XI. Rangelands

Other Features

A. Palliser's Triangle
B. Durum Triangle
C. Red River Valley
D. Wheat Triangle
E. Jordan Country
F. Judith Basin
G. Flint Hills
H. Edwards Plateau

Source: John C. Hudson

Agricultural regions of the Great Plains

its completion in 1885, channeled settlement away from the Prairie and into the Parkland Belt. The Prairie region had received unfavorable comment in an early survey conducted by John Palliser and Henry Hind between 1857 and 1860. Much of the prairie was described by Palliser as "sterile with scanty pasturage." The innermost portion of the Prairie region, which thereby became known as Palliser's Triangle, received little European settlement until the first two decades of the twentieth century. The European immigrants immediately began producing wheat, and by 1930, Palliser's Triangle was a significant wheat-growing region. Today Canada's Prairie Provinces export quantities of wheat not only to Europe and Asia, but also to the United States. The North American Free Trade Agreement (NAFTA) has made it possible for the lowest cost producers to capture markets on either side of the forty-ninth parallel.

The Northern Spring Wheat region (III) of the United States is physically similar to the Canadian Prairies. Spring wheat is the major crop of North Dakota and much of Montana. Barley, durum, flax, sunflowers, oats, and other small grains are also produced.

U.S. breweries depend on the barley grown in Montana and North Dakota just as U.S. pasta manufacturers rely on the durum grown in North Dakota's Durum Triangle in the central and northeastern part of the state. The Red River Valley of the North, along the Minnesota–North Dakota border, also produces wheat, but it is best known for its crops of sugar beets and potatoes that grow on the almost perfectly flat surface that once formed the bed of glacial Lake Agassiz. Fargo, Grand Forks, Minot, and Great Falls are the major cities of the region; however Minneapolis has long functioned as the control point of the Northern Spring Wheat farming system. In

the nineteenth century super-sized farm units known as "bonanza farms" were established in the Red River Valley of the North, where wheat monoculture was practiced on a large scale.

The glaciated portion of the Missouri Plateau, with its fertile soils and smooth topography, is part of the Northern Spring Wheat region. The broad platform of sedimentary rock formation stretches hundreds of miles east of the Rocky Mountains across the steppes (grasslands) of Montana, Wyoming, and the Dakotas. It is an eastward-sloping surface of low relief that is covered, especially in its northern sections, with a mantle of glacial materials from which the deep, black, grain-producing soils were formed. In the U.S. system of soil nomenclature these soils are known as Borolls (a type of Mollisol), the equivalent of the chernozemic soils of Canada and the Ukraine. Borolls provide an adequate supply of nutrients for a variety of small grains throughout the growing season.

Montana's Wheat Triangle, an area of particularly productive grain crops bounded by the cities of Shelby, Havre, and Great Falls, lies at the edge of the glaciated Missouri Plateau and the Northern Spring Wheat region. It was one of the last portions of the Great Plains to be settled, chiefly between 1910 and 1920. Like the grain exports of the Canadian Prairies to the north, most of Montana's wheat and barley exports are directed toward Asia.

The Unglaciated Missouri Plateau (IV), in contrast, is primarily a region of livestock grazing. It has only limited areas suitable for crop farming, and within these areas dry farming is standard. The unglaciated plateau's soils are of several types, but nearly all of them are inferior to those that have developed on the glaciated Missouri Plateau. The unglaciated area's slopes are also steeper and more easily eroded. North and South Dakota's badlands are part of the Unglaciated Missouri Plateau. Here, along the White River in South Dakota and the Little Missouri River in North Dakota, steep, easily eroded slopes preclude agriculture, except in the broader valleys and on the grass-covered tablelands where grazing is possible.

The present course of the Missouri River roughly marks the eastern limit of glaciated topography. In South Dakota the portion of the state west of the glacial border is known as West River country and in North Dakota it is referred to as the Missouri Slope. In both states there is a markedly lower population density on the unglaciated portions of the Missouri Plateau, corresponding to a ranching rather than farming economy. Much of the Unglaciated Missouri Plateau was part of the Great Sioux Reservation until it was broken into six separate reservations in 1888. The relinquished Native American lands were opened to European American settlement. Early homesteaders tried to raise crops on the inferior West River and Missouri Slope soils, but most of the area proved to be submarginal for grain production.

A similar history of agricultural failure

is found in the Jordan Country (Garfield County) of Montana, a largely unpopulated stretch of rough rangeland that lies on the divide between the Missouri and Yellowstone Rivers north of Miles City. Attempts to raise wheat in the Jordan Country, as in the West River of South Dakota, were unsuccessful, and the lands reverted to cattle and sheep range by the 1950s. This was one of America's last agricultural frontiers, one that had only a brief "season of hope" before hard environmental realities were understood.

Some parts of the Unglaciated Missouri Plateau have better soils and are suitable for dry-farmed grain crops. One of these districts is the Judith Basin, a highland wheat- and barley-growing region between Billings and Great Falls that was settled during the decade centered on World War I.

The Sandhills (V) is a 20-million-acre region of grass-covered sand dunes in north-central Nebraska that is devoted almost entirely to livestock grazing. Agricultural settlers came to the Sandhills during the so-called Kinkaid Era after 1904 when enlarged homesteads (640 acres) were granted in the sandy hill country. But wherever the land was broken for planting, wind erosion soon deflated the ground surface and new sand dunes began to accumulate along fence lines. Cattle ranching, which had traditionally been the major land use, was quickly reestablished.

Today, the Sandhills region has some of the largest cattle ranches in the United States. Typical ranches are tens of thousands of acres in size. The only crop of significance is hay, baled from meadows—where it grows wild—that surround the region's many east-flowing streams or surface lakes, formed where the water table intersects the surface. Sandhills cattle ranching has the look of the open range, even though most of the land is fenced and privately owned. A mark of the sparse population in this area is that signposts are to ranches more often than to towns.

The Eastern Feed Grains and Livestock region (VI) covers much of the eastern margins of the Central Great Plains. It consists of several important subregions, but throughout it has a mixed farming system that emphasizes both crop and livestock production.

From eastern South Dakota, across eastern Nebraska, and south across Kansas to Oklahoma and Texas, a version of Corn Belt agriculture dominates the landscape. Beef cattle feeding, hog raising, and corn, soybean, and sorghum production are the backbone of the farm economy. While irrigation is found in a few areas within this region, the climate is not dry enough to require irrigation in most years. For that reason, paradoxically, agriculture here remains vulnerable to drought, but its mixed nature means that farmers have the means to ride out some bad years because their operations are comparatively diversified.

In Kansas this region is bordered on the west by the Flint Hills where crop agriculture is largely confined to valley bottoms while livestock grazing occupies the uplands. Upland soils are relatively thin and unsuited for cultivation. For many years young cattle from the dry, western ranges of the Great Plains have been shipped to the Flint Hills for pasturing on grass before being grain-fed for market. Flint Hills pastures are burned regularly to increase the nutritive value of grasses for livestock.

The Winter Wheat region (VII), concentrated in central Kansas but extending from southern Nebraska to the Texas Panhandle, is the nation's breadbasket. In some years nearly three-quarters of the wheat produced here is in excess of domestic demand. For this reason, much of the crop is exported, principally through the Gulf Coast ports to Europe, Africa, South America, but also to Asia.

German Mennonites from southern Russia introduced (probably unknowingly rather than deliberately) most of the strains of hard winter wheat to this area in the late 1870s. Kansas, which had previously been known as a corn state, soon became a major wheat producer. Winter wheat production is concentrated between Wichita and Dodge City, Kansas, near Enid, Oklahoma, and north of Amarillo, Texas, but large wheat fields are ubiquitous from central Kansas to eastern Colorado.

As a crop, wheat is not as profitable as feed grains like corn or sorghum. For this reason, and because it requires less water to produce, it is rarely economical to irrigate wheat. So where irrigation water is unavailable in the Central Great Plains, wheat farming remains the best option. In most respects soils of the spring and winter wheat region are quite similar and are associated with grassland vegetation. Ustolls, a warm and dry variation of the fertile Mollisol, are the typical soils of the winter wheat region.

Because large acreages mean a sparse rural population, many wheat farmers in the High Plains prefer to live in town rather than on their farms. "Suitcase farmers" or "sidewalk farmers," as such absentee operators are known, live on their farms only a few weeks each season when work needs to be done. Suitcase farming is especially characteristic of the drier, high-drought-risk winter wheat areas of eastern Colorado and western Kansas.

Also a producer of feed grains and livestock, the Irrigated High Plains (VIII) is the newest agricultural region of the Great Plains. It is here that irrigated grain crops are raised to supply local beef feedlots. Sprinkler irrigation fed by deep-well pumps offers the means to produce feed grains in a climate that, by itself, could not sustain crops like corn more than one year in five on average. Central to southwestern Nebraska, western Kansas, eastern Colorado, and the panhandles of Oklahoma and Texas—all areas that had been marginal even for wheat in some years—experienced an intensification of agriculture with the introduction of sprinkler irrigation in the 1960s. Much of the nation's beef industry is now concentrated in this region.

The Upland Cotton Region of the Southern Plains (IX) consists of several separate areas of cotton culture in Texas and Oklahoma. Short-staple upland cotton, the variety used for making coarser cotton goods such as denim, is grown both under irrigation and with dry-farming techniques. Migrants from the southeastern cotton districts of the United States brought cotton farming to Texas and Oklahoma early in the twentieth century.

The Texas High Plains has a long enough growing season for cotton, but its precipitation is insufficient to produce a crop in many years. Especially after the Dust Bowl years, and as pump irrigation was introduced, both cotton and grain sorghum became irrigated crops in this region. Plowed ground is especially prone to soil erosion here, and soil conservation measures, such as surface corrugation to reduce wind speed at the ground, are a common sight. Despite these problems, the Texas Panhandle remains the single largest concentration of cotton acreage in the United States. Farmers began diversifying in the 1970s with the development of viticulture.

Irrigated Valleys (X) comprise a discontinuous but distinctive agricultural region within the Great Plains. Unlike the Irrigated High Plains, where pump irrigation feeds sprinklers supplying water to feedgrain crops, the traditional irrigated valleys of the Great Plains still rely on ditch irrigation and produce a variety of food and feed crops. Sugar beets are grown in these older, valley-based irrigation districts. While technically a food crop (from which ordinary table sugar is refined), sugar beet tops and waste also provide livestock feed. Sugar beets are produced in nearly all of the irrigation districts of the Great Plains and are grown unirrigated in the Red River Valley of North Dakota and Minnesota.

Crosscutting the Unglaciated Missouri Plateau in Montana is the Yellowstone River Valley, which, in its downstream portions, is a corridor of irrigated agriculture dominated by sugar beets and alfalfa. The Yellowstone River has remained undammed, but smaller dams constructed across numerous Yellowstone tributaries channel water to streamside fields. Irrigation provides its greatest benefit to hot regions where water evaporates quickly, however, and thus the Yellowstone irrigation district has few counterparts located this far north in latitude.

The most productive of the Great Plains irrigated corridors is the Platte River Valley of Nebraska, Wyoming, and Colorado. Downstream from the city of North Platte, where the South Platte and North Platte Rivers join, ditch irrigation is practiced within a region where pump irrigation is also available. Nebraska's irrigated Platte River Valley is one of the most productive feedgrain regions of North America. Corn and sorghum crops grown here are sold to local feedlots or are exported from ports on the Pacific Coast.

The North Platte River Valley extends irrigated agriculture into eastern Wyoming. The most intensive irrigation district of the North Platte River Valley is the Scottsbluff Lowland near Scottsbluff and Gering, Nebraska, where sugar beets and feedgrains are the principal crops. Irrigation in the South Platte

River Valley is now functionally part of a much larger scheme. Completed in the 1950s the Colorado–Big Thompson project captures water from the upper tributaries of the Colorado River, sends it through a tunnel in the Front Range of the Rocky Mountains, and distributes it to farms in the Colorado Piedmont. The South Platte River thus became the principal drainage outlet for the irrigated Colorado Piedmont.

The irrigated Piedmont is Colorado's most important agricultural region. Irrigated crops grown near Greeley and Fort Morgan, Colorado, include onions, pinto beans, sugar beets, corn, and alfalfa. Feedgrains and sugar beets grown in the Piedmont are the basis for its cattle feeding industry. Feedlots near Greeley are often cited as the world's largest.

Smaller in area, but also productive, is the Arkansas River Valley irrigation district that stretches downstream from Colorado into western Kansas. Grain sorghum, sugar beets, onions, and cantaloupe are the principal crops of this region. Water diverted from the Arkansas River is the principal source of irrigation, although underground wells supply additional water as well.

Rangelands (XI) are found throughout the Great Plains, primarily wherever rough, steep, stony, or broken land predominates. Areas with low mountains or rugged terrain include the Cypress Hills in Alberta and Saskatchewan and most of the Unglaciated Missouri Plateau. Other areas, such as the Great Divide Basin of Wyoming, are poorly drained and experience high evaporation rates producing saline residues in soils and making the ground surface unsuited for raising crops even with irrigation. Cattle and sheep grazing are the only forms of agricultural activity associated with these areas. Much of the land remains in the public domain.

South of Colorado Springs, the Piedmont lowland disappears at the eastern margin of the Front Range and is replaced by rangelands of comparatively high elevation. Across New Mexico and into Texas, the western limit of the Great Plains consists of dry, broken land suitable only for grazing. Upstream tributaries of the Canadian, Cimarron, Red, and Pecos Rivers are, in places, incised hundreds of feet into the High Plains rock formations.

South of the Pecos River in Texas is a large limestone plateau, underlain by springs and caverns, which is unsuitable for crop farming but excellent for grazing. This is the Edwards Plateau (sometimes designated as the Edwards and Stockton Plateau). Soils are thin and the vegetation cover has a subtropical, savanna-like appearance. The largest concentration of sheep and goats in the United States is found here. The Edwards Plateau is also the world's leading center for the breeding of Angora goats.

Despite the nearly ubiquitous importance of grain crops in the Great Plains, variations in the physical environment and the timing and nature of human settlement activities have created an ever-changing mosaic of agricultural land use that today stretches from Alberta to Texas. Some crops, such as corn, are of native origin although they are grown today on a vastly increased scale of production. Others, such as sorghum and soybeans, have exotic origins. Sorghums are native to Africa, while soybeans originated in China. Great Plains livestock herds are based on cattle and sheep breeding efforts that trace back to England, Scotland, and Ireland. And Great Plains farm families have ethnic roots that extend to many parts of Europe.

In this region were brought together, by various groups of people at various times, the successful ingredients of food and fiber production that now provide a basis for the United States' and Canada's great agricultural abundance. The two countries' favorable balance of trade in foodstuffs helps earn foreign exchange that makes it possible to import other goods from around the world. As a world supplier, the Great Plains ships agricultural products in all directions—south to the Gulf of Mexico, west to the Pacific Ocean ports, east via the Great Lakes to the Atlantic, and even north through Hudson Bay. The region's strategic importance will likely continue well into the future. Agriculture, the Great Plains' most important industry, will continue to provide the basis for its economic growth.

See also IMAGES AND ICONS: West River Country / INDUSTRY: Feedlots; International Trade; Meatpacking / PHYSICAL ENVIRONMENT: Palliser's Triangle; Sandhills; Soils / WATER: Irrigation.

John C. Hudson
Northwestern University

Drache, Hiram. *The Day of the Bonanza: A History of Bonanza Farming in the Red River Valley of the North.* Fargo: North Dakota Institute for Regional Studies, 1964. Foth, Henry D., and John W. Schafer. *Soil Geography and Land Use.* New York: John Wiley, 1980. Green, Donald E. *Land of the Underground Rain: Irrigation on the Texas High Plains, 1910–1970.* Austin: University of Texas Press, 1973. Hargreaves, Mary W. *Dry Farming in the Northern Great Plains, 1900–1925.* Cambridge: Harvard University Press, 1957. Hewes, Leslie. *The Suitcase Farming Frontier: A Study in the Historical Geography of the Central Great Plains.* Lincoln: University of Nebraska Press, 1973. Hudson, John C. *Making the Corn Belt: A Geographical History of Middle-Western Agriculture.* Bloomington: Indiana University Press, 1994. Jordan, Terry G. *North American Cattle Ranching Frontiers: Origins, Diffusion, and Differentiation.* Albuquerque: University of New Mexico Press, 1993. Kraenzel, Carl F. *The Great Plains in Transition.* Norman: University of Oklahoma Press, 1957. Mackintosh, W. A. *Prairie Settlement: The Geographical Setting.* Toronto: Macmillan, 1934. Malin, James C. *Winter Wheat in the Golden Belt of Kansas.* Lawrence: University Press of Kansas, 1944. Nelson, Paula M. *The Prairie Winnows Out Its Own: The West River Country of South Dakota in the Years of Depression and Dust.* Iowa City: University of Iowa Press, 1995. Shannon, Fred A. *The Farmer's Last Frontier: Agriculture, 1860–1897.* New York: Harper, 1968. Sherow, James Earl. *Watering the Valley: Development along the High Plains Arkansas River, 1870–1950.* Lawrence: University Press of Kansas, 1999. Webb, Walter P. *The Great Plains.* New York: Ginn & Co., 1931. Worster, Donald E. *Dust Bowl: The Southern Plains in the 1930s.* New York: Oxford University Press, 1979.

AGRIBUSINESS

See INDUSTRY: Agribusiness

AGRICULTURAL ADJUSTMENT ADMINISTRATION

A decade-long agricultural depression sparked by plunging crop and livestock prices inspired President Franklin D. Roosevelt and New Deal reformers in 1933 to implement the Agricultural Adjustment Administration, the first federal program to limit agricultural production. The dramatic expansion of exports during World War I—beef exports increased more than 100 percent, wheat exports more than doubled, and oats exports soared more than 2,400 percent—led to record prices and the cultivation of millions of acres of previously unused land. With peace and the recovery of European agriculture, demand and prices dropped quickly: corn fell from $1.20 per bushel in 1917 to 26 cents in 1921, while wheat, hogs, and cattle fell to prewar averages. At the same time, the earning power of the nation's farmers declined, land prices plummeted, and thousands of Great Plains banks failed.

The generally booming national economy made it easy to ignore the farmers' plight, but when the stock market crash of 1929 sparked the Great Depression, the Democratic administration elected in 1932 turned its attention to agriculture, passing the Agricultural Adjustment Act (AAA) during the frantic "100 Days." The bill drew on earlier attempts to help farmers achieve parity, a complex formula in which the prices farmers earned for their products would fluctuate depending on the prices of goods they bought, with the years 1909–14 considered "normal." Previous attempts, such as the McNary-Haugen Bill, had proven politically untenable, but the mounting crisis in agriculture forced Roosevelt to take the dramatic step of involving, for the first time, the federal government directly in the economic decisions made by farmers. The AAA initially paid farmers to reduce production of seven major commodities—including corn, cotton, and wheat—and later added eight more, including cattle. Administered by county extension agents and farmers committees, the program was paid for by a tax on processors of agricultural products.

Farmers welcomed the government checks that helped them survive the drought and grasshoppers plaguing the Great Plains in the 1930s; in some areas, 80 to 90 percent of the population relied on federal relief. Of particular value to Plains farmers were the massive livestock-buying programs of the mid-1930s. Responding to the unprecedented drought and dust storms of 1934 and 1935, the government purchased seven million cattle, sending them to greener pastures or slaughtering and distributing them to needy families through other federal agencies. Despite the popularity of these government payouts, rising food prices, payments that tended to favor landlords over tenants, and the failure of the AAA to raise prices to anything actually approaching parity limited the overall success of the program.

The Supreme Court ruled the AAA unconstitutional in *United States v. Butler* (1936), but Congress quickly replaced it with the Soil Conservation and Domestic Allotment Act and with a second Agricultural Adjustment Act in 1938. The AAA and its successors continued to focus primarily on commercial producers, sustained the policies of acreage limitation and price supports in the form of government loans, and helped convert marginal croplands to grass and forage for livestock. This massive government involvement in the economic lives of Great Plains farmers is the most prominent legacy of the AAA.

See also POLITICS AND GOVERNMENT: New Deal.

James Marten
Marquette University

Danbom, David B. *Born in the Country: A History of Rural America*. Baltimore MD: Johns Hopkins University Press, 1995. Lowitt, Richard. *The New Deal and the West*. Bloomington: Indiana University Press, 1984. Perkins, Van L. *Crisis in Agriculture: The Agricultural Adjustment Administration and the New Deal, 1933*. Berkeley: University of California Press, 1969.

AGRICULTURAL COMMODITY MARKETS

See INDUSTRY: Agricultural Commodity Markets

AGRICULTURAL EXTENSION SERVICE

Created to help farmers rationalize and modernize their operations, the Agricultural Extension Service (AES) is a cooperative venture between federal, state, and local governments; land grant colleges and universities; and agricultural experiment stations. Growing out of late-nineteenth-century farmers institutes, efforts by reformers like Dr. Seaman Knapp, and concerns raised by the Country Life Commission of 1908, the extension service received federal funding with the 1914 Smith-Lever Act. Individual states, counties, and farmers organizations such as the Farm Bureau also provided funding over the years.

State extension offices and county agents conducted research and provided expertise on farm management; Plains-worthy strains of grasses and small grains; animal husbandry; marketing and bookkeeping; and controlling pests like gophers, grasshoppers, and Russian thistle. Agents also supervised clubs for boys and girls and developed home extension programs for farm wives. The larger mission of the AES included not only aiding rural Americans in improving their agricultural operations but also developing local leadership and improving the quality of rural life through better health and community activities.

The extension service expanded quickly during World War I, when the Food Production Act of 1917 provided funds for extension agents in each county in the United States. But the long agricultural depression that followed challenged the assumptions and even the survival of the AES in many Great Plains states. By the early 1930s, many counties had closed their extension offices. In South Dakota, for instance, only sixteen counties—about a quarter—had AES agents by late 1932, while nationally the number of agricultural agents and home extension agents declined by one-third and one-half, respectively.

Even as the Depression and the drought of the 1930s created an unprecedented crisis for Great Plains farmers, it reinvigorated the extension service, which implemented the Agricultural Adjustment Administration in 1933. Agents' heroic coordination of life- and farm-saving federal programs tempered most farmers' traditional mistrust of federal bureaucracies, including the extension service. In addition, state legislatures placed the AES on a much more stable financial footing. Over the next several decades, state and county agents once again mobilized farmers for a world war; helped farmers adapt to technological and chemical innovations and make the transition in livestock production from the open range to the farm; extended its mission to urban gardeners; and became involved in environmental issues, as in Montana, where the AES helped reclaim land marred by open pit coal mining.

Nearly a century after the extension service appeared, it remains a largely local bureau dedicated to education rather than policymaking, with two-thirds of its nearly 17,000 employees working at the county level. The top programming priorities remain agriculture and home economics, with 4-H/Youth programs a close third, and community development fourth. Although federal funding has been reduced in recent years, the AES is still cooperatively sponsored by federal, state, and county governments. The traditional focus on education—through small group demonstrations, one-on-one contacts, publications, and other mass media outlets—continues to shape extension activities.

James Marten
Marquette University

Brunner, Edmund, and E. Hsin Pao Yang. *Rural America and the Extension Service: A History and Critique of the Cooperative Agricultural and Home Economics Extension Service*. New York: Columbia University, 1949. Kappel, Tana, ed. *From Sod-Busting to Satellites: 100 Years of Agricultural Research and Extension in Montana*. Bozeman: Montana State University, 1993. Scott, Roy V. *The Reluctant Farmer: The Rise of Agricultural Extension to 1914*. Urbana: University of Illinois Press, 1970.

AGRICULTURAL METEOROLOGY

Agricultural meteorology is the behavior of the atmosphere in relation to crops and soils. In the Great Plains, agriculture is dependent on the atmosphere in many ways. The atmosphere, in turn, links the Great Plains to other parts of the globe. This linkage is forged by air masses entering and leaving the region. These air masses provide plants with a dynamic and renewable source of carbon dioxide and water and modify other contributing factors, such as light and leaf temperature.

With no geographic barriers to the movement of Arctic air from the north or Gulf air from the south, Great Plains weather is characterized by alternate intrusions of warm and cold air, and the region therefore experiences high variability in temperature, cloudiness, humidity, and precipitation during all seasons. Temperatures are harsh during winter, particularly in the Northern Plains, where perennial plants retreat into dormancy and farmers grow annual crops, like spring wheat. Summer provides desirable temperatures for plant growth and development.

The energy required to successfully grow wheat, corn, soybeans, hay, and other crops mainly comes from abundant sunshine. Of course, without the atmosphere to absorb energy and emit a portion of it back to the earth (the greenhouse effect) the surface temperatures would be too low to support life. The atmosphere also exchanges energy through contact with the underlying surface of the ground as air masses pass through the region. This amount of energy is governed by the speed, humidity, and temperature of the air and the temperature and humidity of the underlying surface. Changes in the Plains landscape from natural grasslands to managed croplands, pastures, and windbreaks altered the disposition of atmospheric energy in the local climate. Irrigation also changes the local climate: in a dry field much of the energy goes into heating the overlying air, whereas in an irrigated field much of the available energy goes into evaporation and transpiration.

Growing season precipitation accounts for a large fraction of the annual precipitation. Soil moisture is frequently depleted during the growing season but replenished during winter and early spring, thereby providing a buffer to plants against dry weather that may occur early in the growing season. Evaporation from soils and transpiration from plants draw on stored soil moisture and increase with greater plant biomass, higher temperatures, solar radiation, and wind speed. Evaporation and transpiration decrease with increases in atmospheric humidity. Drought occurs when soil moisture falls below the amount required to meet the crops' need for water.

The main influence of the atmosphere on agriculture is the control exerted by the water and energy on crop production. The atmosphere, however, has other impacts on agriculture. For example, in wet periods the frequent formation of dew on plant leaves (leaf wetness) will increase crop damage due to plant diseases. Drought conditions favor other pests, like spider mites in corn.

Agricultural meteorologists monitor weather in order to quantify both the potential resources and possible damages associated with the dynamic atmosphere. Proper use of this information in decision making can both reduce risk and increase profit associated with agriculture, thus contributing to the goal of sustainable agricultural production in the Great Plains.

See also PHYSICAL ENVIRONMENT: Climate.
Kenneth G. Hubbard
University of Nebraska–Lincoln

Rosenberg, N. J., B. L. Blad, and S. B. Verma. *Microclimate: The Biological Environment*. New York: John Wiley and Sons, 1983.

AGRICULTURAL PRICE SUPPORTS

Since the 1930s the United States and Canada have operated agricultural price-support programs. The intent has been multifaceted, but primarily the purpose has been to manage agricultural output levels in order to increase the price per unit and thereby raise the net income of farmers.

In the United States, the Agricultural Adjustment Administration was formed in 1933, after commodity prices fell by more than 50 percent from 1929 to 1932. Farmers were experiencing negative net farm income year after year, trying desperately, and often unsuccessfully, to avoid bank foreclosure. Farmers continued producing even though there were no markets for what was already in hand.

This desperate situation of chronic overproduction by U.S. producers led to the Agricultural Adjustment Act of 1933, which established government supply management for, initially, seven major farm commodities: wheat, corn, cotton, rice, tobacco, milk, and hogs. The arguments for establishing these programs and continuing them since have largely centered upon the farmer's poor bargaining power in the marketplace, the belief that agriculture has a constant propensity to overproduce, and the need for price stability.

Commodity programs in the United States have not been without critics, who have argued that artificially high prices have weakened the competitiveness of the United States in the world market. They have also argued that the programs have contributed to the trend toward fewer and larger farms since payment flows have tended to be directly proportional to production volume. Thus, critics believe the programs have led to impractical and unsustainable solutions.

While the intent was similar, Canadian efforts to support prices have taken a much different strategy. Canada historically has not restricted the production of individual grains and has not idled cropland. Instead it has relied on the Canadian Wheat Board (CWB) to set the marketing and export policy for its major agricultural grains. Using this single-seller agency and heavily regulated producer quotas, it has accomplished a price support system for Canadian producers in its three Prairie Provinces.

A second means by which Canada has influenced the income of agriculture producers has been through heavily subsidized rail transportation services for grain movement. In essence, the rates are in relation to the distance from the Prairie Provinces to the key ports, thus equalizing the terms for producers across the entire grain-producing region. In so doing, Canadian crop production took on a geographic configuration far different from what it would have been without graduated transportation subsidies.

Farm commodity programs have had a major impact in the Great Plains, wherever wheat, corn, and other feed grains are dominant crops. Program participation by Plains farmers has been relatively high, which has led to a major income transfer into the economies of rural counties. In fact, in many years U.S. farm price-support programs have constituted from one-third to one-half of net farm income in many Plains states. These payments reached record highs in 2000, when direct government payments represented $28 billion—61 percent—of the U.S. total net farm income of $46 billion. And in several of the Plains states, the government payment component was 75 percent or more of the total state net farm income. Canadian programs have had similar impacts on producer income levels in the Prairie Provinces. Moreover, the layers of regulatory and compliance detail attached to program participation in the United States and Canada have significantly shaped cropping patterns and land-use practices. Conservation management practices have been instituted over time using the economic incentive of farm program participation.

Over the course of the last two U.S. farm programs of 1996 and 2002, substantial changes in strategy have taken place. In contrast to earlier efforts to manage supply levels and therefore increase commodity prices, the intent has now shifted to allow more farmer freedom of production levels and to rely on a market clearing system driven heavily by global forces of international trade. The result has been more volatile and generally lower commodity price levels for those crops covered by the programs. In turn, direct and price deficiency payments are now being made to farmer producers relative to their production volume to maintain income levels. The level of these payments has been substantial in recent years, and dependency upon them among producers is very high. In fact, crop producers across the U.S. Great Plains could be said to be on "economic life support" via these programs as market prices of major commodities have fallen below unit cost of production.

Because the current 2002 U.S. farm program is scheduled to continue for at least the next five years, the economic safety net legislation is in place for the near-term future. However, given the larger economic and political uncertainties facing this nation, there is no guarantee that future funding will be at the initial levels proposed. If budget constraints force cutbacks, this safety net could begin to unravel.

For the Plains economy, which remains heavily tied to production agriculture, the implications of this change could be profound. If U.S. federal farm transfer payments drop significantly in the face of low commodity prices, farm income variability from year to year and from one producer to the next will magnify. Canadian producers may well face similar challenges from these economic forces. Those producers with expertise in risk management and astute marketing will be able to survive economically and perhaps even thrive, while others without these skills and resources will likely exit production agriculture at accelerating rates. There will also be some others who will focus more on agricultural products (i.e., organic products marketed direct from the farm) than agricultural commodities and find economically viable niches, but their numbers are likely to be modest in the context of the entire agricultural sector. In sum, entire farming communities and regions within the Plains may be economic winners or losers depending upon the adjustments they are willing and able to make as the history of agricultural farm programs transitions and the structure of the agricultural sector evolves.

Bruce Johnson
University of Nebraska–Lincoln

Cramer, Gail L., and Eric J. Wailes. *Grain Marketing*. Boulder CO: Westview Press, 1993. Paarlberg, Don. *Farm and Food Policy: Issues of the 1980s*. Lincoln: University of Nebraska Press, 1980.

ALFALFA

Alfalfa (*Medicago* sp.), a valuable forage crop, is grown widely throughout the Great Plains under both irrigated and dryland conditions. Alfalfa is a perennial with a deep-penetrating taproot, which gives it considerable resistance to drought. The plant needs a deep, well-drained soil with a pH level that is near neutral or slightly above for maximum production. When planting alfalfa into soils that have not grown the crop for many years, the seeds are commonly inoculated with an effective strain of *Rhizobium* bacteria for nodulation and thus nitrogen fixation.

Alfalfa is often characterized into northern, southern, or intermediate types based on their degree of winter hardiness. The less winter-hardy types produce higher yields because they recover and grow more rapidly after cutting, but they will not survive the cold winters of the Northern Plains. In the Southern Great Plains, where there is a long growing season, five to seven cuttings may be taken per year, whereas in the north there may be only two or three cuttings. In the Northern Plains, where winter killing could be a problem, the last cutting occurs about four weeks before the first killing frost in order for the plants to manufacture and store sufficient carbohydrates and to develop cold resistance. With the availability of new disease-resistant cultivars, better adapted to wider climatic conditions, and with high levels of soil fertility, greater flexibility in fall cutting schedules is possible.

Alfalfa is grown primarily for hay, but it is also widely used for pasture. Additional uses include ensilage, green chop, dehydrated meal, green manure, and seed production. Alfalfa hay—if harvested to preserve its nutritive value—is a highly nutritious and palatable feed for livestock. To maintain the high nutritive value of the stems and leaves and produce high yields, fields are harvested when about one-tenth of the stems have open flowers. Alfalfa is a superior pasture legume for numerous classes of livestock because of its high quality, high yield, and wide adaptation. It is an economical source of protein and provides a greater degree of flexibility in use than most forage plants. Grazing-type alfalfa cultivars have been developed more recently. Compared to cultivars grown for hay, these cultivars have broader and deep-set crowns,

Alfalfa harvest, Huntley Irrigation Project, Montana, 1914

more branched rooting, and do not release all regrowth buds at the same time. One disadvantage of alfalfa for pasture is that it can cause bloat in cattle and sheep; however, bloat can be minimized by certain practices, such as growing alfalfa in combination with grasses.

Alfalfa is susceptible to various diseases and insects. Resistance to many of these pests has been incorporated into the new cultivars. Most other insects and some diseases of economic importance can be controlled through the careful use of pesticides and harvest management.

Martin A. Massengale
University of Nebraska–Lincoln

Graber, L. F. "A Century of Alfalfa Culture in America." *Agronomy Journal* 42 (1950): 525–33. Hanson, A. A., ed. *Alfalfa and Alfalfa Improvement.* Madison WI: American Society of Agronomy, 1988.

AMERICAN AGRICULTURAL MOVEMENT

See PROTEST AND DISSENT: American Agricultural Movement

ANTI-CORPORATE FARMING LAWS

See LAW: Anti-Corporate Farming Laws

BARBED WIRE

Barbed wire signaled the end of the Old West and the beginning of modern ranching. Its advent during the 1870s and 1880s sounded the death knell for the trail drive and the open range and allowed the expansion of farming. Cattlemen at first resented barbed wire, but after a decade of wrangling over access to water and grasslands and waging fence-cutting wars, they acknowledged its benefits and adopted the newfangled fencing.

No single person invented barbed wire, but in 1874 Joseph F. Glidden of DeKalb, Illinois, was the first to receive a patent for his innovation, a double strand of twisted wire interspersed with shorter lengths wrapped around it to form barbs. A few run-ins with the barbs convinced even stubborn critters to avoid the fence. Glidden dubbed his design "the Win-

ner," a name that proved prophetic. He joined forces with a local merchant, Isaac L. Ellwood, to manufacture the Winner; soon they counted among their customers 150 railroad companies, who used the fence to protect their tracks from herds running free. Eventually more than a thousand barbed-wire designs flooded the market, many with colorful names such as Split Diamond, Necktie, Buckthorn, Arrow Plate, and Spur-Rowel.

In one persuasive incident in downtown San Antonio in 1878, barbed-wire salesman John W. "Bet-a-Million" Gates successfully corralled a herd of rambunctious longhorns inside a fence of Glidden's wire, which, he bragged, was "light as air, stronger than whisky, and cheap as dirt." Ranchers all across the Great Plains had to acknowledge that Gates's claims were true. They also appreciated barbed wire's availability in a region short on wood for fences, its resilience in extreme weather, and its ease of installation. Most importantly, it permitted the selective breeding of stock. The legendary plainsman Charles Goodnight, for example, was able to maintain a pure strain of imported English Herefords and to develop the "cattalo," a buffalo-shorthorn cross.

Not all of the consequences of barbed wire were good. Large outfits could better afford both the fencing and the labor to erect it; smaller-scale ranchers were enraged to find themselves cut off, overnight, from once-public water holes, pastures, and trails. In Texas angry cowboys struck back at cattle barons with nighttime wire-snipping raids. By 1883 the attacks had escalated into violence, forcing the Texas Rangers to patrol dozens of hot spots and prompting the state legislature to declare fence cutting a felony (a law that still stands today). And during severe blizzards throughout the Plains, drift fences—intended to prevent herds from drifting off the ranch—instead proved fatal to livestock, which headed south by instinct, only to pile up at the wire and freeze by the thousands.

Today barbed wire is a fixture of the Great Plains. Cowboys have long counted among their regular duties the erection, inspection,

and repair of fence line. The open range has long been closed, but barbed wire's story is preserved in two archives, the Kansas Barbed Wire Museum in LaCrosse and the Devil's Rope Museum in McLean, Texas.

Anne Dingus
Austin, Texas

McCallum, Henry D., and Frances T. McCallum. *The Wire That Fenced the West.* Norman: University of Oklahoma Press, 1965. Slatta, Richard W. *The Cowboy Encyclopedia.* New York: W. W. Norton & Company, 1994.

BARLEY

Fields of barley are an increasingly common sight in the Northern Great Plains. The major barley-growing provinces and states include Alberta, Saskatchewan, Manitoba, North Dakota, and Montana. In Alberta, for example, in 1997 5.6 million acres were seeded to barley, a crop acreage exceeded only by wheat. North Dakota, with 2 million acres under barley in 1998, produces almost one-third of the national output.

Barley is most famous for its use as malt in the brewing and spirits industries. But due to high-glucan and dietary fiber fractions in some types of barley, there is a growing interest in barley in the food industry. Barley is also widely used as a feedgrain and for silage (conserved green matter). Beef cattle fed on barley have similar rates of weight gain as those fed on corn, and dairy cows fed barley silage have similar gains as those fed alfalfa silage.

There are two main types of barley, six-rowed and two-rowed. Six-rowed barley has three kernels at each node of the head, and with two sides to every head, appears to have six kernels in a row around the head. Two-rowed barley has one kernel at each node, appearing to have only two kernels in a row. Barley comes in both hulled and hulless forms. Hulless barley is similar to wheat in that the hull is removed, exposing the kernel, during threshing. Hulless barley is associated with reduced manure production, an important consideration for intensive livestock production where disposal of manure is costly and difficult. From the beer in your glass to the meat on your plate, barley has an important role to play in its production.

Patricia Juskiw
Alberta Agriculture,
Food and Rural Development
Field Crop Development Centre

BONANZA FARMING

In 1864 the U.S. Congress provided an extensive land grant to aid in financing the Northern Pacific Railway Company (NP). When the NP encountered financial difficulty in the Panic of 1873, it sought to shed its indebtedness by exchanging land for its bonds and preferred stock. It encouraged large-scale agriculture in the Red River Valley of the North. There, the almost totally flat, treeless, fertile, stoneless prairie was ideal for establishing showcase farms called bonanzas. After 1875 these bonanzas became the subject of national farm periodicals and were visited by business and political leaders of the United States and Europe. A total of ninety-one farms, ranging from 3,000 to 100,000 acres, qualified as bonanzas. Nearly all of them were located within forty miles of the Red River.

The bonanzas relied on professional farm managers. To achieve maximum efficiency, they specialized in the continuous cropping of wheat, which was well suited to the area. By concentrating on one crop, a limited number of implements were needed—plows, harrows, seeders, binders, and threshing machines. The bonanzas were worked by migrant laborers, ranging from as few as 15 to as many as 1,000 per farm. They lacked experience in operating machinery, so they were divided into teams of five to twenty men under a supervisor who was referred to as the binder boss or plow boss, depending on the job.

For ease of management, the farms were broken down into divisions of 5,000 acres or less. A work unit consisted of one worker with a plow, a seeder, and a binder with at least five horses. Each worker generally was expected to handle 250 acres of crops. Extra workers and horses were employed for seeding and harvesting. Bunkhouses and dining halls were erected, for management knew that good food and facilities were sound economic practices that helped to retain the workforce. Young women did the domestic work and, like the men, often were newly arrived immigrants.

After harvest the migrant laborers moved to other areas, often to the forests of Michigan, Minnesota, and Wisconsin to spend the winter working in logging camps. The logging companies often rented the horses for use in the forest. In the off-season only a few laborers remained on the bonanzas to repair machinery, ship grain, care for horses, and keep records.

Virtually all the bonanza farms were located on the odd-numbered sections of the railroad grant lands. The government reserved the even-numbered sections for homesteaders. Homesteaders did not like the bonanza farmers because they did not do business locally and did not take part in the local schools or social institutions.

Changing world conditions and a surplus of wheat, which caused a decline in prices, made the bonanzas less profitable. New tax laws discriminated against them. Migrant seasonal labor became less plentiful and more costly. All of the above made it difficult for the business-operated bonanzas to compete with homesteaders. By 1920 the bonanza era had ended. Some bonanzas were subdivided and sold on contract-for-deed agreements or were rented to smaller scale farmers. Only a few of the bonanza holdings remain intact today, operating much differently than the originals.

Hiram M. Drache
Concordia College

Drache, Hiram M. *The Day of the Bonanza: A History of Bonanza Farming in the Red River Valley of the North.* Fargo: North Dakota Institute for Regional Studies, 1964.

Branding a calf, Fort Berthold Indian Agency, North Dakota, 1948

BRANDING

Livestock branding was introduced to the Americas in 1520 by the Spanish explorer Hernando Cortez. Branding, like ranching practices in general, spread to south Texas and the Great Plains from Mexico and the southeastern United States. At that time the southern method, which used British-derived designs of block letters and Arabic numbers, prevailed. Spanish designs became so rare in the Great Plains that the term "Mexican brand" was the only description needed to locate stray animals.

In the open-range system on the Plains, brands were burned into the cattle, usually at the spring roundup. A small September roundup was the time to brand the mavericks, cattle that had been missed in the spring. Brands were registered at the county seats in the districts where the cattle were pastured.

A number of different methods, from paint to acid branding, have been tried in applying a brand to live animals. The hot-iron brand and the freeze brand are the methods most commonly used today. The hot-iron method uses an iron heated by fire or electricity to burn the hide, leaving a permanent scar. Freeze branding creates a brand by depigmentation, whereby the pigment-producing cell in the hide of an animal is destroyed by the application of intense cold, leaving the hair to grow out white. Generally, the hot-iron branding method is the preferred form of identification on cattle. The freeze branding method is used more often to brand horses.

A livestock brand is considered a nonreplaceable form of permanent identification of ownership and a deterrent to theft. A hot iron brand is highly visible and difficult to alter; a freeze brand is also highly visible but is more easily altered. In the early days of branding livestock, a running iron, a straight piece of heated metal, was commonly used to legiti-

mately brand livestock. However, it was also used to alter an original brand on stolen or strayed animals. The running iron was used to draw the brand on the animal, unlike the present-day preshaped branding iron, which merely stamps the brand on the animal.

State livestock agencies, livestock associations, and Canadian provinces are now responsible for recording brands in the respective state or province. Only one brand of a particular design, configuration, and location is allowed in each state or province, except in Texas, where brands are recorded county by county. A brand may be composed of capital letters, numbers, characters, and/or pictures in many different combinations and locations. The location on the animal where a brand may legally be applied is generally limited to the shoulder, rib, and hip. A properly recorded brand is considered personal property and is subject to sale, assignment, transfer, devise, and descent as personal property. Brands are a road map of an animal's history and tell a story of its owners. They are considered an animal's only return address home. Brands are usually read from left to right, top to bottom. The livestock brand "B-V" would be read and defined as a "B bar V straight away."

It is important to properly register a livestock brand and keep it in good standing, as state and province laws require brands to be renewed on a regular basis. Presently, New Mexico is the only state in the Plains that has a mandatory cattle-branding law, requiring each cattle owner to brand all cattle in his or her possession with their properly recorded livestock brand. Livestock branding continues to be vital in determining ownership, returning strays or stolen livestock to their rightful owners, and serving as a deterrent to theft.

Steven F. Stanec
Nebraska Brand Committee

Jordan, Terry G. *North American Cattle-Ranching Frontiers*. Albuquerque: University of New Mexico Press, 1993. Yost, Nellie Snyder. *The Call of the Range*. Denver: Sage Books, 1966.

BUFFALO RANCHING

Most people are aware of the near extermination of the Plains buffalo (*Bison bison*) in the 1870s from a high point population of perhaps 40 million in the mid-1800s. Not so widely known is the story of the restoration of the Plains buffalo and the expanding buffalo ranching scene today.

From an estimated 1,500 animals around 1900, buffalo numbers have expanded to a current U.S. population of approximately 300,000, with roughly 40 percent located in the Great Plains region. The 1996 Canadian Census of Agriculture reported an additional 45,235 bison were being raised on 745 farms across Canada. Alberta, with 334 farms and 22,782 bison, is by far the leader in production. Canadian numbers include both the Plains bison and the indigenous Woods bison subspecies.

In the United States, government herds, both state and federal, have remained relatively constant in number over the past thirty years. The percentage of buffalo owned and managed by private individuals has grown dramatically and now represents approximately 90 percent of the total population. This change in the percentage of buffalo that are privately owned has been accompanied by a shift toward treating the animal as domestic livestock by many producers.

The National Buffalo Association was founded in 1966. Its primary goal was to promote the marketing of buffalo meat and by-products. In 1974 the American Bison Association was founded and took a more aggressive approach to the raising and marketing of the animal. In 1995 the two organizations combined to form the National Bison Association (NBA). The NBA represents more than 2,000 producers, ranging from many who raise just a few animals (fifty or less) to several large ranches each raising thousands of animals. The large, and many moderate-size, ranches typically finish animals in feedlots and market the meat on a large scale to restaurants and the public. One cooperative in New Rockford, North Dakota, processes about 10,000 animals per year.

Producers in the NBA have been increasing research into the formulation of feeds and selection of breeding stock to improve the meat-producing ability of the buffalo. They do not support the use of hormones and other such feed additives. The NBA sponsors a Gold Trophy show and sale annually in Denver in connection with the National Western Livestock Show.

Numerous state and regional associations have sprung up across the country and the Great Plains to assist in regional production and marketing. Another philosophy gaining renewed interest since the 1990s places emphasis on a more natural approach to the management, raising, and finishing of buffalo.

The Great Plains Buffalo Association was formed in 1996 to network grass-fed, grass-finished-oriented producers.

In 1992, another influential organization entered onto the buffalo industry scene. That year Native American tribes formed the Inter-Tribal Bison Cooperative (ITBC). Now numbering about fifty tribes nationwide, with more than half of them in the Great Plains region, the ITBC's goal is to restore buffalo to reservation lands. The cooperative also takes a more spiritual approach to the management of buffalo. Respect for the animal and the environment is central to the tribes' care of the buffalo. With substantial land resources, the ITBC is becoming an increasingly important player in the marketing of buffalo products.

T. R. Hughes
Crawford, Nebraska

CAMPBELL, HARDY WEBSTER
(1850–1937)

Hardy Webster Campbell was the Great Plains's greatest exponent of dry farming, which he termed "scientific soil culture." According to historian Walter P. Webb, Campbell was to tillage what William Jennings Bryan was to politics—its apostle.

Born in Montgomery Center, Vermont, on July 21, 1850, Campbell homesteaded in the James River valley, Dakota Territory, in 1879 and began observations that led to his codification of the Campbell System of farming without irrigation in semiarid regions. The principles of his system were deep plowing in the fall, subsurface packing with a packer he designed, light seeding, thorough cultivation before and after seeding, and summer fallowing, with thorough tillage (which he called "summer culture") during the fallow period. Campbell believed his system would make family farming feasible on the Plains.

Campbell publicized his methods through journals, books and pamphlets, associations, demonstrations, and lecturing. His best-known books were the four editions of his *Soil Culture Manual* (first published in 1902). Journals he started include *The Western Soil Culture* and *Campbell's Scientific Farmer*. Campbell founded the Western Agricultural Improvement Society in 1895. More important was the Dry Farming Congress, founded in Denver in 1907. It originated as his personal promotional vehicle, but it grew beyond his control, with agricultural scientists getting involved and questioning his methods. He carried on most of his demonstration farming and technical lecturing for western railroads, including the Northern Pacific, Burlington, Soo Line, Elkhorn, Union Pacific, Santa Fe, and Southern Pacific. He also lectured for the Alberta Department of Agriculture in 1906–7.

Campbell lived his later years in obscurity in California and died there in 1937. His death certificate identified him only as a fireman for the Southern Pacific.

Thomas D. Isern
North Dakota State University

Campbell's subsurface packer

Hargreaves, Mary Wilma M. *Dry Farming in the Northern Great Plains, 1900–1925*. Cambridge: Harvard University Press, 1957. Hargreaves, Mary W. M. "Hardy Webster Campbell (1850–1937)." *Agricultural History* 32 (1958): 62–65.

CANOLA

Canola is the product of several species of the *Brassica* genus (primarily *B. campestris* and *B. napus*). The name is derived from *CAN*adian *O*il *L*ow *A*cid. First commercially cultivated in Canada in the 1970s, canola is rapeseed which has had erucic acid and glucosinolates removed through breeding and selection. Production in the Great Plains is concentrated in the Prairie Provinces. In 1997 Saskatchewan led in both acreage (5.6 million acres) and production (2.7 million tons), closely followed by Alberta (4 million acres and 2 million tons), and more distantly by Manitoba (2.3 million acres and 1.4 million tons). By comparison, relatively small amounts of canola are grown in adjacent areas of North Dakota and Montana, but virtually none is grown farther south in the Great Plains.

Canola plants can be either fall-sown or spring-sown. When seeded in the fall, canola grows until cold weather makes it go dormant. It begins to grow again early in the spring. Fall-sown canola is more productive if it can survive the winter. Breeding work is being done to increase winter survival. The plants bloom in early May with small yellow flowers. The small, dark, shiny seed is similar to the mustard seed.

Canola is raised for the production of oil and protein. The oil is marketed as a "heart healthy" cooking oil because of its favorable fatty acid profile. The meal that remains after extracting the oil is high in protein and is used as an animal feed supplement.

See also INDUSTRY: Oilseeds.

Lenis A. Nelson
University of Nebraska–Lincoln

CATTLE GUARDS

See FOLKWAYS: Cattle Guards

CATTLE RANCHING

Perhaps no other activity has so well defined the character of the Great Plains in literature, movies, and the national psyche as cattle ranch-

Cattle ranching

ing. Ranching, as it developed on the Plains, was well adapted to the physical environment. Cattle were able to consume the nutrient-rich grasses, just as the bison had. Even today, grass is the most important natural resource for ranchers, and little tillage agriculture takes place in order to sustain the herds.

Cattle ranching in the Great Plains of the United States and Canada differs from the raising of beef cattle on small farms farther east. In the Great Plains it is the primary activity, not an adjunct to farming, and it is conducted on horseback (and, more recently, out of a pickup truck). Nearly 50 percent of beef cattle in the United States are raised in the Great Plains, and 33 percent of Great Plains ranches have 1,000 or more cattle. Sixty percent of Canada's beef cattle are raised in the Prairie Provinces, but the average number of cattle per ranch is slightly less than in the United States.

Although modified by Californian and midwestern involvement, Great Plains cattle ranching was formed primarily by Texan influences. The impetus for cattle ranching in the Great Plains began just south of the Edwards Plateau in Texas. In a diamond-shaped area reaching south of San Antonio to Mexico, free-roaming cattle of Spanish bloodlines existed in large numbers by the early 1800s. Texans returning home after the Civil War rounded up as many of these cattle as they could in an attempt to make money. Some started ranches in Texas. Others drove their newfound herds north to the railhead at Sedalia, Missouri. As the railroad and farmers pushed westward, cattle were trailed to terminals at Abilene, Newton, Ellsworth, and Dodge City, Kansas. From the railhead, cattle were shipped east, where they brought as much as $4.75 per hundredweight in 1884.

Prices varied considerably depending on the quality of cattle shipped and where they were shipped, but the profit margin was high enough during the cattle-trailing period from 1866–90 that more than 5 million head were moved out of Texas to eastern markets and to ranges farther north in the Great Plains. For all of its glory, however, cattle trailing was not cattle ranching but merely a prelude to large, permanently established cattle ranches that developed late in the trailing period.

Ranches were established throughout the Great Plains from Texas to the Prairie Provinces. Ranching in Canada developed coincident with that in the United States and was not simply an extension of the cattle business north of the border. A major difference between the two countries was that a government program in Canada allowed up to 100,000 acres to be leased to ranchers, while early ranchers and other, sometimes foreign, interests ran large numbers of cattle on huge tracts of grassland in both countries. The Texas-based XIT Ranch controlled 3 million acres in Texas and another 2 million acres in Montana. The Hash Knife Ranch near Belle Fourche, South Dakota, ran 96,000 cattle.

In the United States, Texas served initially as a mild-weather breeding ground from which cattle were sold to ranchers farther north. The open range of the Northern Great Plains was the fattening ground. Roundups were performed in the spring to brand and count the cattle and in the fall to cut out the beef cattle to be sold at market. The roundups completed in the late 1800s were the same in principle, and much the same in practice, as contemporary roundups. Indeed, striking similarities exist between the calendar of ranch activities in 1890 and that of today. Then, as now, the cycle was closely tied to the seasons and the

grass that provided the main source of food for the cattle. The feeding of hay and grain supplements on contemporary ranches has only slightly altered the basic cycle.

The annual sequence of events varies in timing and technique from Texas to Canada but is similar in purpose and structure throughout the region. During the coldest months of the year, cattle remain on those areas of the range that offer some protection from the elements. This can include rolling topography close to the ranch that provides a natural barrier to wind and snow. This is also the time when supplemental feeding is most important, especially if heavy snow cover makes it difficult for cattle to graze. Cattle from backgrounding operations, where cattle are kept over winter, are marketed during the first three months of the year.

Calving season can begin as early as the last week in January and continue until June. This is frequently a time of round-the-clock work for ranchers when they ride close to the herd to watch for any cow that may have difficulty calving. If the cows are located at some distance from the base ranch, cowboys may be hired to help watch the herd on a daily basis and then return to their homes at night. When old enough, the calves are branded, vaccinated, and eartagged, and bull calves are castrated prior to trailing them to summer pasture around the middle of June when grasses are reaching their peak. In early summer, the job of putting up hay for the winter begins in earnest, and, depending on the precipitation and the type of grass or legume, this work may continue well into the fall.

In the fall, cattle are rounded up from the summer pasture and given necessary vaccinations, while calves are weaned. In operations that do not background calves, steer calves weighing 600–800 pounds are shipped to market in early to mid-October. By November, the cattle are moved to winter pasture in protected areas or areas of the ranch that were not grazed during the summer and fall during the normal rotation of pastures. Winterfeeding begins and continues through February if conditions demand it.

Of the different types of agricultural operations in the Plains, ranching has changed the least in the last century. While, in essence, it remains a straightforward method of producing food, the adjustments and techniques needed to maintain an efficient and environmentally sustainable outfit are more complex than before. Ranchers must contend with drought, cattle diseases, predators, and government intervention, just as in the past. Modern ranchers must also be concerned with changing technologies and the vagaries of market demand for red meat. Still, most operators consider cattle ranching a lifestyle as well as a business. With proper management, ranching is a productive and attractive activity in semiarid environments like the Great Plains.

See also IMAGES AND ICONS: Cowboy Culture.

Kenneth C. Dagel
Missouri Western State College

Jordan, Terry. *North American Cattle Ranching Frontiers.* Albuquerque: University of New Mexico Press, 1992.

Schlebecker, John T. *Cattle Raising on the Plains 1900–1961.* Lincoln: University of Nebraska Press, 1963.

CENTER FOR RURAL AFFAIRS

The Center for Rural Affairs, established in 1973 in Walthill, Nebraska, was created through the vision of two VISTA volunteers, Don Ralston and Marty Strange. The center established its reputation early as an agricultural advocate with a conscience and a strong, independent voice on agricultural matters throughout the Great Plains and beyond.

The center immediately confronted several agricultural issues with serious economic, social, and environmental overtones. Taking issue with irrigation in the fragile Nebraska Sandhills, large-scale hog confinements, and the decline of independent banking in rural Nebraska, it earned a reputation for sound research and honest, practical, and fair solutions. Subsequently, research expanded into global warming, rural economic development policy, unfair livestock markets, and federal farm policy. Most recently the center has examined the structure of agriculture and new marketing opportunities for family farmers.

Advocacy is equally important to the center's history and character. Major policy thrusts include tax reform and school finance in Nebraska as well as conservation and fairness in federal farm policy. The center has worked alone and with others to invigorate and broaden the meaning of sustainable agriculture and to hasten its acceptance in the agricultural community.

Engaging people to find their own solutions has been another major thrust of its work. When the energy crisis of the 1970s created an opportunity for small farms to demonstrate appropriate technology, the center created the nation's first on-farm research program with the Small Farm Energy Project. The Rural Enterprise Assistance Project (REAP) builds on the entrepreneurial assets of rural people and helps communities to support them. And the Land Link program connects retiring farmers with beginning farmers, placing farmland in the next generation's hands. The center sponsors a total of eight such projects to help build rural communities and family farms. Truly one of a kind, the Center for Rural Affairs is a leader in advocating social and environmental justice in rural America.

Marie Powell
Center for Rural Affairs

CONSERVATION RESERVE PROGRAM

The Conservation Reserve Program (CRP) was one provision of the 1985 Food Security Act designed to protect erosion-prone cropland in the United States. The program includes highly erodible land or land with excessive erosion. The Great Plains, which contains more than 23 million acres of erosion-prone land and is sometimes called the "CRP Belt," played a major role in this program.

Corn Produced for Grain in the United States, 1997

State	Harvested acres thousand acres	Total production thousand bushels
Nebraska	8,725	1,151,700
South Dakota	3,400	333,200
Kansas	2,700	386,100
Colorado	1,030	150,380
Texas	907	167,814
North Dakota	605	59,895
Oklahoma	129	20,606
New Mexico	85	14,875
Wyoming	57	7,695
Montana	14	1,890
Great Plains total	17,651	2,294,155
U.S. total production	73,720	9,365,574

The CRP provided farmers the opportunity to receive land rental payments for developing a ten-year contract with the U.S. Department of Agriculture (USDA) to take highly erodible land out of production by planting a permanent cover of grass, legumes, or trees. The CRP program learned from some of the mistakes of the Soil Bank program of the late 1950s and early 1960s. For example, only 25 percent of land in any county could be placed in the program in order to eliminate drastic repercussions on the local agricultural industry.

More than 20 million acres in the Great Plains were placed under protective CRP cover at some time during the 1990s. The average rental rate was around $43 per acre. Texas, North Dakota, Montana, Colorado, and Kansas retired the most acres into CRP. Although modified, with increased emphasis on environmental issues and water quality, CRP continues to operate, with many contracts extending beyond 2010. Critics have considered CRP to be an expensive program, with minor effects on reducing production and stabilizing farm income, but it has been very successful in reducing soil erosion, improving wildlife habitat, and increasing the quality of soil, water, and air in the Great Plains.

Edward J. Deibert
North Dakota State University

CORN

Corn is the only major cereal crop whose origin can be claimed by the Western Hemisphere. Centuries before Europeans "discovered" the Americas, corn played a major role in the Mayan, Aztec, and Incan civilizations in Central and South America. The earliest archaeological evidence of corn was found in Mexico's Valley of Tehuacan and was dated at about 5000 B.C.

Those who appreciate the importance of this grassy species to American agriculture sometimes refer to corn as the King of American Crops. Native Americans more commonly used the term *maize*, "that which sustains life." The Swedish botanist Karl Linnaeus gave corn its botanical name, *Zea mays* L. The Greek word *zeo* also means "to live." After seeing maize for the first time, European settlers called it "Indian corn" in an attempt to compare the crop to the small grains grown in Europe that they called corn. Following corn's "discovery," the crop quickly spread to Europe, Africa, and Asia. Today, most of the world still refers to the crop as maize, but the United States simply calls it corn.

Corn has been grown in various areas of the Great Plains for many centuries. At the beginning of the nineteenth century, for example, Pawnee Indian women had ten pure varieties of corn. In today's modern agriculture, corn continues to play an important role throughout the ten states that comprise the American Great Plains. Approximately 24 percent of the total U.S. corn acreage and production occurs in the Great Plains, with more than 80 percent of that accounted for by Kansas, Nebraska, and South Dakota. Nebraska, itself, has nearly nine million acres under corn each year and an annual total production of more than one billion bushels of the golden grain. Corn production in the Canadian Great Plains is more limited because corn is not well adapted to the cooler and shorter growing seasons there. In 1997 Manitoba produced about 60,000 acres of corn for grain, with a total production of about six million bushels. Corn production in Alberta and Saskatchewan is even less extensive. Corn production is also limited in the dry western Plains states of New Mexico, Wyoming, and Montana.

Corn produced in the Great Plains, like that of the rest of the U.S. Corn Belt, is used in many ways. The majority of the crop is used as a feed grain for livestock and poultry production. About 20 percent of the grain is exported to other countries around the world. The remainder of the corn produced in the Great Plains is processed into various food and industrial products such as ethanol fuel, high fructose syrup, food grade and industrial starches, and human foodstuffs.

Many of the factors that influence the production of corn vary dramatically throughout the Great Plains. Because of the extensive north-south orientation of the Great Plains, one of the most variable factors is the length and warmth of the available growing season. Corn planting can begin in March in the warmer areas of the Southern Great Plains, while significant corn planting efforts do not typically begin in the Northern Great Plains until early May because of cooler temperatures. Harvesting of corn for grain typically begins as early as late August in Texas and as late as October in North Dakota. At first glance, the early harvest times in Texas seem odd in that much of the available growing season is not used. However, planting date and hybrid selection are managed by corn producers to avoid the occurrence of the critical corn pollination stage during the hottest, most stressful times of midsummer. Consequently, corn pollination in Texas occurs in mid- to late June rather than the relatively hotter late July to early August period.

The second major effect of differing growing season lengths is on the adaptability of corn hybrid maturities. Producers in the Southern Great Plains can grow corn hybrids with a much longer maturity cycle than those in the Northern Great Plains. Compared to hybrids that require less time to mature, the long season hybrids typically have greater yield potential, are taller and leafier plants, and have greater tolerance to disease and insect stress.

Seasonal rainfall varies more from east to west than from north to south across the Great Plains, with the majority of the Great Plains area rainfall patterns generally unable to supply the twenty to twenty-five inches of water required to produce a corn crop. Consequently, irrigation is a very important crop management technology and tool for corn production throughout the Great Plains. More than 50 percent of the harvested acreage and 65 percent of the total grain production in the Great Plains is produced under irrigation. In fact, only the Dakotas do not produce a major share of their corn under irrigation. The impact of irrigation on corn grain yields is dramatic for the whole region (157 versus 75 bushels per acre, irrigated versus dryland), but especially so for Colorado, Texas, and New Mexico, where dryland corn grain yields average less than 30 percent that of irrigated corn.

See also WATER: Irrigation.

R. L. Nielsen
Purdue University

Hardeman, Nicholas P. *Shucks, Shocks, and Hominy Blocks*. Baton Rouge: Louisiana State University Press, 1981. Sprague, G. F., and J. W. Dudley, eds. *Corn and Corn Improvement*. Madison WI: American Society of Agronomy, Monograph 18: 1988.

CORPORATE FARMING

Corporate farming has always played a significant role in Great Plains agriculture. This is explained in part by the scale of the production of agriculture that exists in the Plains region of the United States and Canada. Agricultural production units in the Plains are typically much larger in acres and in dollar volume of production than their counterparts in other parts of North America. In order to be economically viable, both cropland and livestock production units often extend over thousands of acres and generate annual sales values of a million dollars or more. Because of sheer size, these units are frequently multi-

family that are efficiently transferred from one generation to the next. Therefore, there are economic as well as tax reasons to operate within a corporate form of organization rather than as a single proprietorship. In short, corporate agriculture often makes sense in the Plains.

Family-farm corporations are a frequent and socially accepted component of Plains agriculture in both the United States and Canada. However, the two countries part company in their historical attitudes toward nonfamily corporate agriculture. While Canada has essentially taken a laissez-faire attitude toward nonfamily corporate agriculture, in large areas of the United States there remains a pervasive opposition to this form. Moreover, the opposition essentially exists in the Plains states.

Of the nine states in the United States that restrict corporate farming either by state statute or constitutional mandate, eight lie within the Plains region. In fact, the very roots of anticorporate farm sentiment were historically centered in North Dakota and eventually spread as far south as Oklahoma. When insurance companies began foreclosing on small farmers in the depression years of the 1930s and taking title to thousands of acres of land, it was seen as a threat to the deep-seated values and livelihood of working-class farm people. Similarly, when the first signs of a more industrialized agriculture began appearing in the 1960s, public reaction was strong. Many of the states that did not have corporate farming restrictions on the books instituted state statutes at that time. In Nebraska, citizens even voted corporate farming restrictions into the state constitution when the legislature failed to enact statutory restrictions.

Today, as the more advanced stages of an industrialized type of production agriculture are manifest in the form of mega-sized and vertically integrated livestock production units, Plains people are again reacting with a populist response. Nonfamily corporate agriculture is seen as a threat to the values and beliefs of a Plains culture that remains tied to the land. These are people whose ancestors migrated here a century ago and tenaciously settled the region, making it the productive agricultural area it is today. It was built in the context of family-farm agriculture and close-knit rural communities, which wove a social fabric of mutual support and care. There was a sense of place and connectedness that could be comprehended and lived within. Now, partly as a result of large-scale industrialized production agriculture, with its lower labor requirements, Plains people see their social fabric unraveling: young people migrate to urban centers, main street businesses close for want of customers, and schools and hospitals struggle to keep their doors open.

Yet, for a variety of economic reasons, corporate farming lends itself well to Plains agriculture. Large capital investment and intricate vertical integration with input suppliers as well as with processors and end consumers seem to be the emerging agricultural structure of the twenty-first century. Finding mar-

ket niches with new or value-added products is part of this new world of production agriculture. In this context, a corporate form of organization may facilitate the infusion of outside capital, the improvement of resource management, and the merging of nonfamily partnerships into new and profitable business ventures—in short, it may be more an antidote than a poison for a rapidly changing Plains agricultural economy. Nonfamily corporate agriculture may actually enhance rather than harm the sustainability of rural economies.

In sum, the fate of the Great Plains in the twenty-first century may well rest on what happens to the structure of its production agriculture. The key question is: Can corporate farming strengthen the rural economy without depopulating and compromising the viability of the communities?

See also INDUSTRY: Agribusiness.

Bruce Johnson
University of Nebraska–Lincoln

Johnson, Bruce B. "Corporate Restrictions in U.S. Production Agriculture: Economic Implications." *Journal of American Society of Farm Managers and Rural Appraisers* (1995): 21–26.

COTTON

Cotton, *Gossypium hirsutum* L., was introduced to the High Plains of Texas near Lubbock in 1901. That year, Will Florence, who had migrated from Stonewall County, Texas, planted ten acres and harvested two bales. By 1928, 1.6 million acres of cotton were being grown in the eighteen counties surrounding Lubbock. Cotton has since become a major commodity on the High Plains of Texas, Oklahoma, and New Mexico, with minor acreage in Kansas. Approximately five million acres are planted each year in the Southern Great Plains. Because of drought, hail, or other production hazards, only about 80 percent of planted acres are harvested each year. Lint yields range from 125 pounds per acre, when grown without supplemental irrigation, to 1,000 pounds per acre when grown with irrigation. About 40 percent of the cotton grown on the Southern Great Plains is irrigated. Production hazards include abiotic factors such as drought, hail, excess rainfall, heat, cold, and blowing sand. Biotic production hazards include weed competition; insects such as aphids (*Aphid gossypii* Glover), bollworm (*Helicoverpa zea* Boddie), and boll weevil (*Anthonomus grandis* Boheman); seedling diseases; verticillium wilt (*Verticillium dahliae*); and rootknot nematode (*Meloidogyne incognita*).

Cotton evolved in Mexico and was introduced to the continental United States by Native Americans in present-day New Mexico, hundreds of years before Europeans arrived on the continent. The Spanish grew cotton in Florida in 1556, and cotton culture was reported in Virginia in 1621, North Carolina in 1664, Louisiana in 1697, Mississippi in 1722, Alabama in 1728, Georgia in 1734, and southeast Texas in 1821. The establishment of cotton

Cotton field, West Texas

culture on the Plains had much to do with invasion of the Mexican boll weevil into Texas in 1892. During the ensuing three decades, entrepreneurial cotton producers moved to the Southern Great Plains and the Southwest in efforts to find a region where the boll weevil could not survive. This strategy worked well for West Texas and Oklahoma until the 1990s, when the boll weevil became established on the High Plains of Texas. The producer-driven boll weevil eradication program promises to rid the United States of this devastating pest.

Cotton is planted when the soil temperature at planting depth reaches 65°F at 10 A.M. for three consecutive days, combined with a favorable, long-range forecast. Thus, the majority of cotton on the Southern Great Plains is planted in May and early June. Given favorable temperatures, moisture, and nutrients, the cotton plant will produce its first fruit form, or flower bud—also called a square—about thirty-five days after planting, its first open flower about sixty days after planting, and its first open boll about 100 days after planting. Cotton is a botanically indeterminate plant that continues to grow vegetatively while growing reproductively. With a normal weather pattern, cotton production on the Southern Great Plains requires about 140 days from planting to maturity.

The mature cotton plant is treated with a chemical defoliant to remove the leaves, a source of trash that would lower the quality and value of the harvested product. Southern Great Plains producers then may apply a desiccant to dry the plants, thus making them more brittle in preparation for harvest. While most U.S. cotton is harvested by a spindle picker that theoretically removes only seedcotton, most of the Southern Great Plains crop is harvested with a stripper machine that removes seedcotton, burs (structures that encase the seedcotton), unopened bolls, and sometimes other plant structures such as branches or bark. This type of harvester is required because Southern Great Plains producers plant cultivars that have "storm-proof" bolls. Such cultivars have open bolls (e.g., mature bolls ready for harvest) where the seedcotton does not fluff and the dry boll structure remains relatively closed at maturity, thus preventing the seedcotton from shattering during high winds and other inclement weather.

Seedcotton, containing both lint and seeds, is taken from the farm to a gin where the seeds and lint are separated. Gin-run seeds are composed of three products: linters, hulls, and kernels. Linters are short fibers that did not elongate into spinnable fibers and the stubble of longer fibers removed in the ginning process. Linters are used in a number of products, including plastics, solid rocket propellants, rayon, paints, and photographic film. Linters are removed as a by-product of the crushing process to produce cottonseed oil. This oil is used as cooking oil and in a number of processed products such as mayonnaise and salad dressing. The remaining hulls are used as filler in feed, mulch, and poultry litter. The meal and cake remaining after oil extraction is used in fertilizer and feed. In 2000 most of the cottonseeds produced in the Southern Great Plains were used as direct feed for cattle. Cottonseeds, regardless of marketing channel, make up about 10 percent of the farm value of the crop.

The primary product of cotton production is its spinnable fibers, or lint. These fibers comprise about 33 percent of the weight of seedcotton. Lint is packaged at the gin into 480-pound bales and transported to mills that combine bales from around the world having similar and desired quality parameters for the mill's yarn product. The raw cotton is spun into 100 percent cotton yarn or combined with man-made fibers or other natural fibers to produce blended yarns. These yarns are then woven into a number of products, from diapers to designer wear.

The cotton industry in the United States yielded more than $40 billion in revenue in 1997. This industry involved over 38,000 businesses (of which 35,000 were farms) that employed more than 443,000 people. In Texas, Oklahoma, and New Mexico, 14,185 businesses (including 13,422 farms) employing 71,909 individuals were involved in cotton production and processing in 1997, generating $4.5 billion in revenue.

See also INDUSTRY: Cotton Industry.

C. Wayne Smith
Texas A&M University
John R. Gannaway
Texas A&M Agricultural Research and Extension Center

Haldenby, R. "A Century of Cotton Production in the High Plains of Texas." *Tulia (Texas) Herald*, December 1, 1999. Smith, C. Wayne, and J. Tom Cothren, eds. *Cotton.* New York: John Wiley & Sons, 1999.

CUSTOM COMBINING

Custom combining, the harvesting of grain crops by itinerant combine crews, not only plays an important role in production on the Plains but also is the basis for a distinctive style of life rooted in the family business.

Prior to the advent of the combined harvester, or combine, small grains on the Plains were harvested with binders or headers and then threshed with stationary separators powered by steam or gas traction engines. Labor was a mix of migrant, local, and family sources. Farmers owned the harvest machinery; custom operators owned the threshing machinery. Combines were first used in the winter wheat areas of the Central Plains in the 1920s and, with windrowers as complements, were adopted in the spring wheat areas of the Northern Plains and Prairie Provinces some twenty years later. Farmers generally owned their own combines, and the flow of migrant labor diminished.

The shortage of labor and machinery during World War II, coupled with the wartime resurgence of wheat production, precipitated custom combining, as harvesters took to the roads on itineraries stretching from Texas to Saskatchewan. Perhaps 500 machines were in itinerant operation in 1942, and in 1947 researchers documented more than 8,000 in Kansas. The most dramatic episode of the war era was the Massey-Harris Self-propelled Harvest Brigade of 1944, when Massey-Harris of Toronto received a special allocation of steel to put 500 additional custom combines into the field.

The 1947 film *Wild Harvest*, starring Alan Ladd, Robert Preston, and Dorothy Lamour, depicted custom harvesters as a wild bunch, and indeed, the early years were marked by men traveling without families. The business persisted, however, and underwent a transformation into a stable, family-oriented enterprise. Custom combining survived for two reasons, the first being that it was a sound, economical adaptation of practice in regional agriculture. It freed farmers of the necessity of capital investment in combines and allowed maximum use of these valuable machines. The second reason was that, like farming, custom combining became a family tradition, with outfits and routes passed down through the generations.

Custom combiners operate along defined routes harvesting mainly for the same farmers year after year. They charge for their work by the acre, with additional charges for high yields and bushel charges for hauling. Families and crews are housed in trailer homes. An important change in operations took place beginning in the 1960s with the advent of irrigated feed grains, corn, and milo on the Southern Plains. This encouraged most custom operators to curtail the northern ends of their itineraries and take on lucrative fall harvesting on the Southern and Central Plains.

A major study of custom combining in 1971 found 3,431 outfits transporting 7,551 combines, but numbers have decreased slowly since then. In particular, the international aspect of the business has diminished. Combine crews were allowed to cross the boundary between the United States and Canada under an executive agreement of 1942 and annual renewals thereof, but fewer than seventy do so today. An organization of American operators called U.S. Custom Harvesters, formed in 1983, has opposed Canadian crews operating in the United States. The Association of Canadian Custom Harvesters, formed the same year, has defended the Canadians' right to work there.

The greatest number of custom combiners comes from the Southern and Central Plains—over the years some 30 percent from Kansas, 30 percent from Oklahoma, and 10 percent from Texas. Prominent among them are Mennonite operators from central Kansas, who entered custom harvesting as a strategy for extending their agricultural way of life.

Thomas D. Isern
North Dakota State University

Isern, Thomas D. *Custom Harvesting on the Great Plains: A History.* Norman: University of Oklahoma Press, 1981. Lagrone, William F., and Earle E. Gavett. *Interstate Custom Combining in the Great Plains in 1971.* Washington DC: Economic Research Service, U.S. Department of Agriculture, 1975.

DRAFT ANIMALS

Draft animals were the most important piece of farm capital and motive power for transportation in the Great Plains in the premechanization period. These work animals—principally horses, oxen, and mules—were used initially to pull wagons to the Plains and then to pull plows and other farm equipment once the settlers arrived.

Many factors came into play when deciding which type of draft animal to use for the westward trek. Oxen were used most often because they were relatively inexpensive to purchase and could be easily sold or used for food at the final destination, thus serving as a "store of value" for the family's wealth. This final attribute was important because an enormous amount of a family's total wealth, in many cases up to 50 percent, was tied up in the value of the draft animals. If on the trek west a horse broke its leg, an extremely large proportion of a family's wealth would be lost. However, if an

ox broke its leg much of the value could be salvaged in the form of meat, either for personal consumption or through sale.

Once at the final destination oxen were then used to plow the prairie sod. This task was one where the ox had a distinct advantage over both the horse and the mule because of its greater strength and torque power. However, after the sod had been turned settlers usually sold or consumed their oxen. From that point on they relied on either horses or mules for their motive power. Both of these animals were better suited to the daily farming chores of the Great Plains, but because horses were less costly than mules they were overwhelmingly preferred on Plains family farms. The more expensive and more resilient mule tended to be used on farms where there were large numbers of hired hands who had less incentive to care for the owner's work stock.

Oxen were used predominately in the early years of Plains settlement, comprising about one-third of all draft animals in 1860. Their numbers declined rapidly thereafter, and they accounted for only about 3 percent of Plains draft animals by 1890. Horses took their place, increasing from 59 percent of all draft animals in 1860 to 89 percent in 1890. The number of mules remained consistently small, varying from 7 to 10 percent between 1860 and 1890. In the early years of the twentieth century, the internal combustion engine signaled the end of the draft animal era on the Plains, though horses are still used extensively in modern-day ranching.

Kyle D. Kauffman
Wellesley College

Kauffman, Kyle D. "Why Was the Mule Used in Southern Agriculture? Empirical Evidence of Principal-Agent Solutions." *Explorations in Economic History* 30 (1993): 336–51. Kauffman, Kyle D., and Jonathan J. Liebowitz. "Draft Animals on the United States Frontier." *Overland Journal* 15 (1997): 13–26.

DRYLAND FARMING

Dryland farming is practiced in the semiarid American Great Plains and Canadian Prairies whereby the soil is cultivated in ways that conserve precious moisture. For generations European Americans coming to the Great Plains of North America labored to squeeze the most out of a land often short on rainfall.

In the late nineteenth century various factors combined to make the Plains a more attractive agricultural base. The "closing of the American frontier in 1890" (according to the Bureau of the Census), rising land prices, and subsequent fears of a food shortage led to a drive to settle new lands. The populist unrest of the 1890s convinced some that lower farming costs on cheaper lands could support a prosperous class of pioneers. In the United States, before World War I, railroads, banks, grain elevators, and businesses used modern advertising methods to attract farmers to new lands in the Plains. In the Canadian Prairies the government actively encouraged settlers to semiarid lands as well. Higher grain prices, and increased land costs in more humid areas, propelled thousands of early-

twentieth-century pioneers into the Great Plains to attempt dryland farming.

Dryland farming theories varied, but at the heart of the publicity were claims that farmers could cultivate the land to capture and conserve the scarce moisture in the Plains soil. It was billed as a "climate-free" system of agriculture. Dryland farmers used deep plowing in the fall to enable grain roots to use the moisture, harrowing after rains to allegedly conserve moisture under the top soil, packing the subsoil to prevent infiltration, and leaving fields fallow in the summer. Drought-resistant grains, such as Turkey Red wheat and sorghums, were promoted. Without conclusive proof, supporters publicized dryland-farming methods as scientifically feasible. Proponents such as Hardy Webster Campbell of South Dakota and the Dry Farming Congress assured settlers that the western Plains and Prairies could be broken and profitably farmed using this system. In 1909 and 1910 Congress passed the Enlarged Homestead Acts, giving each settler 320 acres of free land on which to build a dry-farming empire. Marginal areas in North Dakota, eastern Montana, and the western Southern Plains exploded with settlers, cattle, and acreage brought into cultivation.

Dry-farming methods offered a mixed performance after World War I. During the early 1920s some farm experts believed that, despite the harsh climate and irregular rains, farmers could use drought-resistant wheat strains, relatively cheap operating costs (enabled by new machines), and large-scale acreages to make profits. However, after World War I the hazards of pushing conventional farming into the semiarid zones of the Plains became increasingly apparent. Periodic drought and low grain prices bankrupted thousands of dryland farmers. Up to three-quarters of those who homesteaded in some areas of the Northern Plains before World War I left their claims by the early 1920s. The ensuing drought and depression of the 1930s were also disastrous as thousands more farm families, lured by the promise of cheap lands and quick profits in the 1910s and 1920s, were forced off the land. Many of these farms were simply deserted. In Garfield County, for example, in the rangeland and dry farming country of eastern Montana, the population dropped from 5,368 in 1920 to 4,252 in 1930 and 2,641 in 1940, and it has been going down ever since.

Today, much of the land opened for dryland farming before World War I has reverted back to grazing or has been added to the national grassland system. However, adaptive farm families on large acreages using modern machinery and methods can still reap large crops of wheat, even in years affected by drought. Those who have the savings, capital, and are supported by government agricultural programs can manage some profits and stability. Despite the marginal environment and fluctuating grain prices, dryland farming still supports Plains farm families, but their numbers are dwindling.

Michael J. Grant
Lincoln, Nebraska

Hargreaves, Mary W. M. *Dry Farming in the Northern Great Plains, 1900–1925.* Cambridge: Harvard University Press, 1957. Hargreaves, Mary W. M. *Dry Farming in the Northern Great Plains: Years of Readjustment, 1920–1990.* Lawrence: University Press of Kansas, 1993. Jones, David C. *Empire of Dust: Settling and Abandoning the Prairie Dry Belt.* Edmonton: University of Alberta Press, 1987.

DUST BOWL

See PHYSICAL ENVIRONMENT: Dust Bowl

EXOTIC ANIMALS

Exotic animals, animals living outside their native areas, are increasing in number in the Great Plains. These additions to hunting, ranching, and farming operations, plus rare species in private preservation efforts, are mainly hoofed animals of wildlife species with antlers or horns. A few novel domestics, like llamas, join the mix. In the early 1990s, ostriches, emus, and rheas were also promoted, but markets for these large, flightless birds are more limited than for hoofed exotics.

Exotics are raised variously for meat, feathers, hides, eggs, and, in the case of the emu, for oil that is used in cosmetics. Within the Great Plains, exotics activity varies with environment and politics. Texas, with huge, private ranches and varied environments, stresses all types and has the most animals (15,735, representing fifty-six varieties, in Great Plains counties). Species on the Texas Plains include aoudad (*Ammotragus lervia*) from North Africa, axis deer (*Axis axis*) from India and Sri Lanka, blackbuck antelope (*Antilope cervicapra*) from India, fallow deer (*Dama dama*) from Europe and Asia Minor, red deer (*Cervus elaphus*) from Europe, and various forms of ibex and wild goat (*Capra* spp.) from Asia and Africa. In New Mexico, free-ranging aoudad predominate. There, the state dominates exotics activity, and public hunting is the objective. Northward, the main species are winter-hardy deer, such as fallow and red deer. These are mainly found in the drier western zones of the Northern Plains and in Canada where agricultural alternatives are fewer. Canadian exotics farming is an addition to more prevalent experiments with farming, herding, or culling native wildlife.

Increasing numbers of wildlife ranches, deer farms, and escaped exotics have prompted restrictions to prevent disease and interbreeding with native fauna. Wildlife departments often disapprove of exotics because of these negative possibilities or the added competition for space or forage. Thus, it is agricultural rather than wildlife interests that are promoting growth of exotic activity in the Great Plains.

Elizabeth Cary Mungall
Texas Woman's University

Mungall, Elizabeth Cary, and William J. Sheffield. *Exotics on the Range: The Texas Example.* College Station: Texas A&M University Press, 1994. Traweek, Max S. *Statewide Census of Exotic Big Game Animals.* Austin: Texas Parks and Wildlife Department, 1995.

Hog exhibit, Shawnee County, Kansas, 1918

FAIRS

As carnivals ready rides to serve eager customers, youths finish grooming livestock for judging, and community groups tidy fundraising booths, excitement builds as communities anticipate the opening day of their annual fair. The constancy of fair activity from early settlement through today attests to their importance as economic, social, and cultural events, as well as their ability to adapt to the changing needs of Plains residents.

Early agricultural fairs were significant events in fledgling Great Plains communities. As settlement spread, town boosters competed to attract as many new immigrants to an area as possible. Started and funded mainly by merchants and stockbreeders, fairs became impressive showcases for the production capabilities of an area's fertile soil. Piles of lush apples—the bigger the better—visually guaranteed a region's potential and proclaimed that success was only a matter of hard work. Every local, state, and regional promoter tried to make their fair exhibits the most enticing, since boosters knew the economic benefits of promoting a fair "open to the world."

Though organized mainly by merchants, early agricultural societies needed farmers to enter their crops and animals for display and judging, and farmers attended fairs to socialize and see the bounty of new consumer products. Horse racing, carnivals, and sideshows provided something for everyone and increased gate receipts. When confronted with bad weather or cycles of drought and depression, which kept attendance down, fairs struggled to maintain financial stability.

Among unusual fairs on the Plains were the Indian International Fairs in Muskogee, Indian Territory (now Oklahoma), which began in 1874, and the Trans-Mississippi and International Exposition in Omaha, Nebraska, in 1898, which included an Indian Congress. The congress took on a Wild West show atmosphere with sham battles staged to increase gate receipts.

Fairs changed significantly between 1900 and 1950. During the two world wars, agricultural production was critical in both the United States and Canada, and Great Plains communities celebrated agricultural successes at their fairs. Instead of the promotional events of earlier days, fairs became more educational, highlighting agricultural production, education, and pride of place. To aid fairs financially, many states legislated tax support, and in Canada, provincial governments and towns provided assistance grants.

Since World War II fairs have met the changing needs of Great Plains residents. As the number of farmers declined and the size of farms increased, fair organizations adjusted. Agriculture is still featured, with shining new implements on display and awards for crops and animals, but fairs now serve mixed purposes for more diverse communities. Contemporary fairs often celebrate a cultural heritage tied to the pioneer image of the Great Plains featuring cowpokes, rodeos, and saddle club events. Famous country-western stars attract fairgoers from large urban areas and rural settings alike.

Despite changes in organization, emphasis, and funding, Great Plains fairs have endured. From the Texas State Fair to the Calgary Exhibition and Stampede, fairs remain community celebrations where agricultural products of the region are displayed, and where friends and neighbors socialize, gossip about town events, see the sights, encounter new experiences, and refresh some awareness of who they are and where they live.

Cathy Ambler
Kansas State Historical Society

Ambler, Cathy. "The Look of the Fair: Kansas County Fairscapes, 1854–1994." Ph.D. diss., University of Kansas, 1996. MacEwan, Grant. *Agriculture on Parade: The Story of Fairs and Exhibitions of Western Canada.* Toronto: Thomas Nelson and Sons, 1950. Neely, Wayne C. *The Agricultural Fair.* New York: Columbia University Press, 1935.

FAMILY FARM

Americans have long cherished the family farm as the place where the patriotic virtues of rugged individualism, hard work, and self-sufficiency are practiced best. This institution was identified as early as the eighteenth century by Thomas Jefferson and J. Hector St. John de Crevecoeur and later by Frederick Jackson Turner who made the family farm the centerpiece of his "frontier thesis"; by novelists Hamlin Garland, Willa Cather, and Wallace Stegner; by modern activists like Wendell Berry and Wes Jackson; and by agricultural philosopher Paul B. Thompson. Overall, the family farm has persisted for more than a hundred years on the Plains as a decentralized cottage industry in an increasingly industrialized world. In Canada, for example, more than 99 percent of farm businesses are family operations.

Traditionally on the family farm, household members owned the land, and everyone, including women and children, worked the farm. Its sweat equity and cash flow depended upon its own resources. The family farm stood for cherished rural values of conservation, frugality, responsibility, honesty, dignity in work, belief in community, concern for future generations, neighborliness, and self-reliance. It was institutionalized by the Land Ordinance of 1785, which privatized the public domain, and by the classic 160-acre quarter section provided by the Homestead Act of 1862. The expansion of family farms across the United States was not significantly modified until the end of public land sales in 1935. Similarly, in the Prairie Provinces, the Dominion Lands Act of 1872 promoted settlement and family farms with virtually free provisions of 160-acre homesteads.

On the semiarid Great Plains, family farmers faced great challenges because of the climate extremes and repeated droughts. During the Dust Bowl of the 1930s, almost half of U.S. Plains farms were abandoned. Family farmers who remained became clients of government aid, which is a necessary ingredient of survival even today. Compared to 1950, half the number of Great Plains farmers worked the same amount of land in 1980, and the number will likely be halved again by the end of the first decade of the twenty-first century. During the twentieth century, large-scale, centralized, industrial agriculture gradually replaced family farms to produce most of the nation's food and fiber. This put the family farm at risk. While 94 percent of U.S. farms were still small family farms in 1998—those with less than $250,000 gross receipts annually and with a net cash income of less than $23,000—they received only 41 percent of all farm receipts.

Family farming might survive into the future through niche agriculture, based on low capital investment, intensive labor and management, and high value crop and livestock production. Such specialty farming includes direct marketing of organic foods, new-generation cooperatives and enlargement of local farmers' markets, subscription farming, and farm-to-chef direct marketing, all outside the industrialized food stream. Family farming, which still works the majority of the nation's farm acreage, can also promote sustainable agriculture and reap significant environmental benefits by on-site management of soil, water, and wildlife. Family farming continues to be a major source of images, metaphors, myths, and realities about the intimate bond between humanity and the wider natural world.

See also EUROPEAN AMERICANS: Land Laws and Settlement / LAW: Anti-Corporate Farming Laws.

John Opie
New Jersey Institute of Technology

Comstock, Gary, ed. *Is There a Moral Obligation to Save the Family Farm?* Ames: Iowa State University Press, 1988. Opie, John. *The Law of the Land: Two Hundred Years of American Farmland Policy.* Lincoln: University of Nebraska Press, 1987. Strange, Marty. *Family Farming: A New Economic Vision.* Lincoln: University of Nebraska Press, 1988.

FARM CONSOLIDATION

Although the Great Plains region of North America was largely settled by 1900, farm numbers continued to grow during the first third of the twentieth century, peaking at nearly 1.7 million in 1935. Average farm size was 355 acres in the U.S. Great Plains, and 221 acres (in 1941) in the Canadian Prairie Provinces. During the ensuing six decades, farms grew larger and fewer in number. By 1992 only 646,000 farms remained; there were 502,000 farms in the ten U.S. Plains states, averaging 1,020 acres, and 144,000 Prairie Province farms averaging 952 acres in 1991. This process of farm consolidation was the product of a number of economic and environmental forces that affected all of North America. The effect on Great Plains farms varied considerably from place to place, both in timing and intensity.

Farm expansion was primarily a product of scale economies, mostly related to the impact of mechanization and technological change in agriculture and in the national economy. Increasingly during the twentieth century, farmers had to compete with the booming manufacturing sector for workers. Laborsaving technologies, particularly tractors, were adopted mostly because farmers were unable to secure a sufficient labor supply at an affordable cost. However, machinery was most cost-effective when fully used. A new tractor or hay baler could be more easily paid for if the farmer had more land on which to use it. Thus, machinery purchased to solve a labor supply problem put upward pressure on farm size, as farmers sought to maximize their return on investment.

Farm consolidation was mostly a product of the expansion of some family-owned operations and the demise of others. In the last thirty years of the twentieth century some high-profile corporate farming operations were established in the Great Plains. Most were associated with cattle feedlots, confinement hog production, or center-pivot irrigation. However, the role of nonfarm corporations in agriculture is considerably less important in the Great Plains than elsewhere in North America: corporate farming in the Plains is mostly conducted by family corporations.

The pressure to expand was exacerbated by drought and depression during the 1930s. As crop yields and prices fell and as some marginal cropland was abandoned, farmers in the most drought-stricken areas either had to expand their operations to maintain adequate income or drop out of farming. In the western and southern Great Plains states, farm numbers plummeted between 1935 and 1959. New Mexico lost more than 60 percent of its farms in that twenty-four-year period; Oklahoma and Texas lost 55 percent; Colorado and Wyoming lost more than 45 percent. Farm consolidation was not confined to these states. Farmers dependent on livestock production were especially hard hit. In some counties in the Nebraska Sandhills and in southwestern Kansas average farm size had more than doubled by 1950, and farm numbers had decreased accordingly.

In Oklahoma and Texas, the Depression put almost unbearable pressure on tenant farmers. Farm numbers in these two states dropped by 23 percent between 1935 and 1945, but the number of tenant farmers was cut almost in half. Whereas 58 percent of all farms were operated by tenants in 1935, only 38 percent were tenant-operated in 1945. A few of those tenants became owners, but most were squeezed out of agriculture altogether.

Farmers in the more humid eastern reaches of the Plains were less affected by expansionary pressures because they were able to counter the "cost-price squeeze" by intensifying their operations. In humid, crop-producing areas the adoption of tractors during the 1930s and 1940s freed up land that had been used to feed horses. Increased use of fertilizer and improved seed varieties raised total production without adding more acres to the farm. These options, largely unavailable to livestock producers who dominated the drier sections of the Plains, resulted in only modest changes in farm numbers and size in the eastern third of the Dakotas and Nebraska, and northeastern Kansas. Average farm size increased less than 20 percent in many eastern counties before 1950.

Subsequently, however, and especially after 1959, this area experienced rapid farm expansion, and consolidation shifted dramatically from the livestock counties of the south and west toward the cash-crop and mixed agriculture region of the Central and Northern Plains. Corn Belt farmers had already adopted most of the yield-enhancing technologies and had converted pastureland to crops. Farm expansion was the only means remaining to increase farm output and income.

Farms reliant on corn production were particularly affected. Between 1959 and 1978 nearly all counties in this formerly stable area saw farm size increase by 40 to 80 percent. A typical example is Hall County, a corn-producing county in east-central Nebraska. Between 1930 and 1950, average farm size grew by only 12 percent, from 199 acres to 222 acres; but between 1959 and 1978, farm size jumped 46 percent, from 262 acres to 382 acres. The 1,628 farms in the county in 1930 had been cut nearly in half to 860 by 1978.

Meanwhile, with the recovery from the 1950s drought, ranchers had some opportunities to intensify use of marginal lands, and technological change did not produce the same pressures to expand operations as was the case in the Corn Belt counties. After 1959, farm expansion was quite modest in western and southern Plains counties, and in some areas, farm size actually decreased and farm numbers increased.

After the mid-1970s farm numbers changed relatively little in the Great Plains. Prior to 1974, farm numbers dropped by 10 percent or more in nearly every five-year period. As of 1992, there were only 9 percent fewer farms in the U.S. Plains states than there had been in 1974. Certain external factors may have reduced expansionary pressures in the last third of the twentieth century. Center-pivot irrigation technology provided some farmers with intensification opportunities, which reduced the need to acquire more land. Rural industrialization and other nonfarm employment opportunities resulted in a dramatic increase in the number of farm women holding jobs off the farm. The number of farm men employed in nonfarm enterprises much or all of the year grew substantially in this period. Nonfarm wages provided many families with additional income even without farm expansion and allowed some smaller farms to stay in business.

This is not to say that farm consolidation is a thing of the past. Low commodity prices, larger machinery, and limited opportunities to expand revenues without more land all put pressure on farms to expand. In a region where most land is already in farms, expansion of one farm necessarily comes at the expense of others. Larger farms translate into fewer farms. Whether the forces that provide alternatives to consolidation will continue to stabilize farm size and numbers is difficult to predict. Technological changes in food production and the market prices of agricultural products will certainly affect whether smaller farms will survive or sell out to their expanding neighbors.

Bradley H. Baltensperger
Michigan Technological University

Baltensperger, Bradley H. "Farm Consolidation on the Northern and Central Great Plains." *Great Plains Quarterly* 7 (1987): 256–65. Baltensperger, Bradley H. "Larger and Fewer Farms: Patterns and Causes of Farm Enlargement on the Central Great Plains, 1930–1978." *Journal of Historical Geography* 19 (1993): 299–313. Shover, John L. *First Majority, Last Minority: The Transforming of Rural Life in America.* DeKalb: Northern Illinois University Press, 1976.

FARMERS ALLIANCE

See PROTEST AND DISSENT: Farmers Alliance

FARMERS HOLIDAY ASSOCIATION

See PROTEST AND DISSENT: Farmers Holiday Association

FARM IMPLEMENTS

See INDUSTRY: Farm Implements

FARM INHERITANCE PRACTICES

See FOLKWAYS: Farm Inheritance Practices

FARM SECURITY ADMINISTRATION

The Farm Security Administration (FSA) was created through the Bankhead-Jones Farm Tenant Act in September of 1937, in order to deal with the chronic poverty of American independent farmers and migrant farm laborers. This act created the FSA out of the Resettlement Administration, which President Franklin Roosevelt had launched via an executive order in the spring of 1935.

The FSA's activities fell into two chief categories: rationalization of farming in order to increase its efficiency and decrease cyclical agricultural booms and busts and elevation of public awareness of the problems confronting farmers, especially in the Dust Bowl–ravaged Southern Plains. In order to achieve the former goal, the FSA sponsored fragmentary land-use reform, provided loans which Farmers Unions used to build cooperatives, and offered rehabilitation and settlement camps for a limited number of migrant farmworkers. FSA-sponsored photography documented the struggles of farmers and migrant farm workers, and included the work of Dorothea Lange, Walker Evans, Ben Shahn, Roy Striker, and Marion Post Wolcott. The FSA also sponsored Pare Lorentz's influential documentary, *The Plow That Broke the Plains* (1936). In the Great Plains, the FSA helped launch irrigation projects, most notably on the Platte River in Nebraska and the Colorado River in Texas. It also offered soil conservation assistance and loans at 3 percent to farmers, while sponsoring continued research into the causes and outcomes of the ecological crisis of the Dust Bowl in the region.

The Farmers Home Administration Act of 1946, signed into law by President Harry S. Truman, abolished the FSA and created the Farmers Home Administration (FHA) in its place.

See also ART: Dust Bowl Photographers / FILM: The Plow That Broke the Plains.

Catherine J. Lavender
The College of Staten Island of
the City University of New York

Baldwin, Sidney. *Poverty and Politics: The Rise and Decline of the Farm Security Administration.* Chapel Hill: University of North Carolina Press, 1968. Lowitt, Richard. *The New Deal and the West.* Bloomington: Indiana University Press, 1984. Worster, Donald. *Dust Bowl: The Southern Plains in the 1930s.* New York: Oxford University Press, 1979.

FEEDLOTS

See INDUSTRY: Feedlots

FERTILE BELT

See IMAGES AND ICONS: Fertile Belt

FERTILIZED ACREAGE

Fertilizer use plays an essential role in maintaining the agricultural productivity of the Great Plains. Eliminating fertilizer in just one year would reduce corn yields by 40 percent and wheat yields by 10 percent. Fertilizer use in the region has increased dramatically in recent decades. From 1975 to 1995, nitrogen fertilizer (the most commonly used fertilizer on the Plains) use increased by more than 250 percent, phosphorus fertilizer use by about 50 percent, and potassium fertilizer use by more than 1,200 percent. The Canadian Prairie Provinces use about one-third of the total fertilizer applied in the Great Plains region. The most common forms of fertilizer used in the region are urea and anhydrous ammonia as nitrogen forms, monoammonium phosphate as phosphorus fertilizer, and muriate of potash as potassium fertilizer. Manure is also used as a fertilizer and soil amendment on cropland located near livestock production facilities.

Fertilizer utilization practices change from north to south in the Great Plains. Farmers tend to apply more fertilizer prior to planting and to apply more fertilizer through irrigation systems in the southern part of the region. In the Northern Great Plains, more fertilizer is applied at planting or after planting, and applying the fertilizer in a concentrated band is more common (as opposed to a broadcast application). In addition, the use of phosphorus fertilizer declines in the Southern Plains, where it is more common for farmers to apply nitrogen fertilizer at rates that are below those recommended by agricultural laboratories and crop consultants. Geographically, areas where more than 90 percent of harvested cropland is fertilized include the Red River Valley of the North and adjacent eastern North Dakota and many counties in a belt stretching from central Nebraska through central Oklahoma.

The type of crops grown has a significant impact on fertilizer use in the Great Plains. Farmers tend to apply higher rates of nitrogen fertilizer and use phosphorus and potassium more often in corn production than in winter wheat production. There is good reason for this: corn removes considerably higher levels of these nutrients from the soil than does wheat. Soil testing is recommended as a basis on which to make fertilizer decisions. Great Plains farmers tend to use soil testing more in cornfields (49 percent) than in winter wheat fields (18 percent). Since corn requires a higher investment and has higher potential for economic return, this makes good economic sense.

Irrigation also has a significant impact on fertilizer use. Irrigated crops produce higher yields and remove more nutrients from the soil than dryland crops. Therefore, farmers tend to apply phosphorus fertilizer more often and apply greater amounts of nitrogen and potassium fertilizer to irrigated crops. Irrigated corn is soil-tested more commonly (84 percent) than dryland corn (29 percent). In general, more profitable crops are usually managed more intensely and fertilized more heavily.

Jessica G. Davis
Colorado State University

FLAX

Flax (*Linum usitatissimum*), a native of Asia, is the source plant for the production of linen, linseed oil, edible flax, and coarse and fine paper products. Among these products, the most important has been linseed oil, long used in the manufacture of paint, varnish, and lacquers. Flax is also used to produce linoleum, oilcloth, and printer's ink, although its importance has waned with the advent of more synthetic materials and increased use of soy-based inks.

Flax has traditionally been planted as a fiber crop, where the plants are tall (up to four feet), and as an oilseed crop (linseed oil, edible flax). Fiber flax was raised in the United States from 1658, when it was first introduced in the colonies, until about 1956. All flax fiber used for paper production is now imported from Canada.

The flax production area in North America has shifted north since 1945. The 146,000 acres of flax harvested in the United States in 1997 is a drastic drop from the 6.2 million acres harvested in nineteen states in 1943. The United States currently ranks sixth in world flax production, while neighboring Canada ranks first. Flax is ideally suited to the cool spring temperatures and moderate summer temperatures found in the Northern Great Plains of the United States and the Prairie Provinces of Canada. In 1997, 1,946,000 bushels of flax were harvested in North Dakota, South Dakota, and Minnesota, while 35,928,571 bushels were harvested in Manitoba, Saskatchewan, and Alberta.

See also INDUSTRY: Oilseeds.

Kenneth C. Dagel
Missouri Western State College

Mitchell, E. J. *Flax Facts*. Minneapolis: Japs-Olson Press, 1944.

GARDINER, JIMMY (1883–1962)

James Garfield (Jimmy) Gardiner was born on November 30, 1883, in Hibbert Township, Ontario. On August 14, 1901, he moved west to his uncle's home at Clearwater, Manitoba, where he worked as a hired man and finished high school. Three years later he moved west again, to that part of the Northwest Territories that would become Saskatchewan in 1905.

Following twelve years as representative and minister in the Saskatchewan legislature, Gardiner became premier in 1926. His first premiership, lasting until 1929, occurred during a period of prosperity in the wheat-based provincial economy, while his second, from 1934–35, featured a devastated Saskatchewan agricultural economy. His move from provincial to federal politics in 1935 launched a record-setting twenty-two-year career as Minister of Agriculture. Gardiner first focused on creatively using the Prairie Farm Rehabilitation Act—with which his name became synonymous—to provide financial, water resource, and land-use planning assistance to Prairie farmers. Later, he pushed the Agriculture Ministry to the front of the national policy process, developed close advisory relationships with Canada's major farmers' organizations, and became the leading voice for agriculture in national politics.

Gardiner is also remembered for his use of patronage in the Liberal Party machine provincially and federally, his political abilities within the federal cabinet, and his oratory in parliament. As a cautious reformer within Canada's dominant political party, he strenuously opposed the social democratic Cooperative Commonwealth Federation's attempts to become the major voice of the common people in rural Saskatchewan. Personal ambition and a desire to win westerners and "the people" back to the Liberal banner following the CCF victory in Saskatchewan in 1944 led him to stand, unsuccessfully, for the federal Liberal leadership in 1948. Following electoral defeat in 1958, Jimmy Gardiner returned to his Saskatchewan farm at Lemberg until his death on January 2, 1962.

See also POLITICS AND GOVERNMENT: Cooperative Commonwealth Federation.

David Laycock
Simon Fraser University

Smith, David, and Norman Ward. *Jimmy Gardiner: Relentless Liberal*. Toronto: University of Toronto Press, 1990.

GOATS

It is safe to say that goat production has never been a major enterprise in the United States or Canada. Goats can be generally classified based largely on their function, including fiber types (Angora and Cashmere), dairy types (Alpine breeds plus Nubian), those kept primarily for meat production (Spanish or brush goats, and more recently the Boer), and those kept as laboratory animals or pets (Dwarf or Pygmy).

In the United States the goat population reached its high point around 1965, when Angoras numbered approximately six million. The termination of an incentive program, coupled with a declining demand for Mohair, has decimated the industry in recent years, with numbers in 1998 at less than one million. There has, however, been an increase in the number of goats kept for meat production. This increase has been fueled by a need to replace the Angora for use in grazing management and the identification of a growing ethnic market for goat meat. Recent immigrants from goat-consuming regions (such as the Middle East) to the Prairie Provinces, for example, have stimulated the goat meat industry there. About one-third of Canada's goat population is now in the Prairie Provinces. In the United States it is expected that the major concentration of goats on the Plains will continue to be in the Edwards Plateau and adjacent regions of Texas, where they are an important component of the grazing system and make a significant contribution to ranching income.

The goat, along with certain game species, represents the best ecological fit in the semiarid regions of the Great Plains, and the potential for their exploitation in this region is great. However, this potential is not likely to be realized unless some serious problems can be solved. These include fencing, predation, and grazing policy on federal lands. Finally, if these regions were used to their potential to produce meat or fiber from goats, the supplies would far exceed present known market outlets or demands.

The use of goats in the larger Great Plains region will likely be restricted to smaller private landholdings or to strategic uses for vegetative management. There is a great potential for use of the goat (and to a lesser extent sheep) for reducing fire hazards in forest areas by removing a part of the fuel base, reducing vegetative competition in reforestation efforts (especially conifer forests), and controlling certain noxious plant species, such as leafy spurge (*Euphorbia esula* L.).

Maurice Shelton
Texas Agricultural Experiment Station
San Angelo, Texas

Shelton, Maurice. "Goat Production." In *Encyclopedia of Agricultural Science*, edited by Charles J. Arntzen. San Diego: Academic Press, 1994. Walker, John W., S. L. Kronberg, S. L. Al-Rowaily, and N. E. West. "Comparison of Sheep and Goat Preferences for Leafy Spurge." *Journal of Range Management* 47 (1994): 429–34.

GRAIN GROWERS ASSOCIATIONS

See PROTEST AND DISSENT: Grain Growers Associations

GRAIN PROCESSING

See INDUSTRY: Grain Processing

HAY

Approximately 65 million tons of perennial legume and grass hay crops are produced annually on about 30 million acres of the Great Plains in the United States and Canada. Within the United States, this includes 24 million tons of alfalfa hay produced on 9 million acres and 26 million tons of grass hay produced on the remaining 14 million acres. Variations in length of growing season, soil fertility, available water, and plant species produce wide variations in the yield of hay crops in the Great Plains. Depending on the year, an additional 15 to 20 million tons of hay baled from crop aftermath and annual grass crops could be added to the total. Sixty-five million tons of stacked hay would extend 27,357 miles (10 percent more than the distance around the equator), if packaged as large rectangular bales (1,800 pounds) and loaded on standard forty-eight-foot semitrailers at the rate of twenty-four bales per trailer!

Alfalfa hay production ranges from five harvests (10 tons per acre) on intensively managed, irrigated stands in the Southern Great Plains to only one harvest (1.5 tons per acre) from dryland stands in the higher elevations and latitudes of the north. An improved, cool season perennial grass such as Timothy may yield as much as 5 tons per acre from one harvest with intensive fertilization and irrigation in the northern latitudes. Average yield of native grass hay in the Central Great Plains, harvested once per season, is less than a ton per acre, but yield could be double or greater with above-average precipitation. In the Southern Plains, intensively managed stands of an improved, warm season perennial grass (i.e. Bermuda grass) may yield 5 to 7 tons per acre in one growing season. Because of its bulk and relative ubiquitous occurrence, most hay is consumed locally, except when adverse conditions, such as drought, necessitate shipments from surplus to deficit areas.

Alan Gray
University of Wyoming

More, Kenneth, and Michael Collins, eds. *Forages.* Ames: Iowa State University Press, 1995.

HIND, CORA

See GENDER: Hind, Cora

IRRIGATION

See WATER: Irrigation

THE LAND INSTITUTE

The Land Institute is a nonprofit organization that was established in 1976 on 370 acres near Salina, Kansas. It operates four programs devoted to sustainable agriculture and human communities.

The research program in Natural Systems Agriculture (NSA) has been exploring a new agricultural model that mimics the native prairie ecosystem in order to develop a biodiverse, perennial grain agriculture that preserves soil, requires minimal or no fossil fuel inputs, yields adequately, and does not rely on harmful synthetic chemicals for fertility or pest management. A formal advisory board of sixty-four researchers in the fields of agronomy, ecology, and other sciences assists in setting the program's research agenda. NSA fellowships are offered to graduate students to foster relevant research done either at the fellow's home institution or at the Land Institute.

Since 1992 the Sunshine Farm Research Program has been investigating the possibilities of farming without fossil fuels, synthetic fertilizers, or pesticides by using renewable energy technologies and innovative management practices to raise crops and livestock typical of Great Plains agriculture. The goal of this ten-year project is to examine the energetics of food production and its ecological costs.

The Intern Program, begun in 1983, annually provides stipends for eight graduate-level students who spend ten months as research assistants in NSA and the Sunshine Farm. The program focuses on the broader issues of sustainable society and agriculture as well.

The Rural Community Studies Program, situated in the small town of Matfield Green in the Kansas Flint Hills, has been examining community viability along ecological lines rather than conventional economic ones. The program aims to maximize possibilities for cultural innovation in rural agricultural communities. Recent efforts include a small conference center, an education program for teachers and school administrators, and research into "ecological community accounting" that will measure the flow of energy and materials into and out of the community.

Marty Bender
The Land Institute

Jackson, Wes. *Becoming Native to this Place.* Lexington: University Press of Kentucky, 1994. Soule, Judith D., and Jon K. Piper. *Farming in Nature's Image.* Washington DC: Island Press, 1992.

MILLET

Millet is a generic term meaning "small seed." Three types of millet are grown in North America: proso millet (*Panicum mileacium*), foxtail millet (*Setaria italica*), and pearl millet (*Pennisetum americana*). Proso millet is a short season plant that does well in low rainfall areas (fifteen to twenty inches annual precipitation). The seed is shiny white or red and is a large component of birdseed. It is also used for livestock and poultry feed. Proso millet is grown primarily in eastern Colorado, western Nebraska, and North and South Dakota.

Foxtail millet is grown in many parts of the world for forage and grain. In the United States, the forage is usually dried for hay and the seed is used in finch food because it is smaller than proso seed. Foxtail millet is grown in the Central and Northern Great Plains.

Pearl millet is grown and used for human consumption in Africa and for both forage and grain in the United States. Pearl millet forage is very productive in the southeastern United States. There has recently been interest in the use of the seed of pearl millet as a livestock feed because of newer hybrids that are highly productive. The greatest use of pearl millet for grain is in Nebraska and Kansas.

Because millet is grown by dryland farming there is considerable variation from year to year in production and yield per acre. For example, in 2002, 450,222 acres were planted to proso millet in Colorado, Nebraska, South Dakota, and North Dakota, but because of prevailing drought conditions only 220,000 acres were harvested. This yield was only 12 bushels per acre, compared to the 33 bushels per acre yield of 2001.

Lenis A. Nelson
University of Nebraska–Lincoln

NATIONAL FARMERS UNION

See PROTEST AND DISSENT: National Farmers Union

NATIVE AMERICAN AGRICULTURE

Prior to white contact, Native American agriculture in the Great Plains differed little from farming practices east of the Mississippi River. On the Northern Plains the Mandans and Hidatsas cultivated corn, beans, and squash for their essential food needs. Women, who were expert geneticists, cleared the land and planted, cultivated, and harvested the crops, then stored the surplus in jug-shaped pits. They and other village-based Plains Indians, such as the Pawnees, used floodplain terraces for cropland. The tough prairie sod prevented cultivation of the uplands. Family fields were small, generally less than four acres. Nomadic Plains tribes, such as the Crows and Lakotas (Sioux), traded buffalo meat and hides to the farming peoples for vegetables.

During the nineteenth century the acquisition of Native American lands by the federal government, and its distribution to settlers, led to the creation of reservations where missionaries and government agents attempted to teach Native Americans European American agricultural traditions. A similar policy was instituted in Canada on reserves created in the 1870s and 1880s. Agents often violated Indian culture by providing instruction to men, who viewed agriculture as women's work. Agency farmers also promoted wheat over traditional crops and insisted on row cultivation rather than the intercultivation methods that had traditionally been used.

Often reserves and reservations were located in areas where land could not support agriculture beyond the subsistence level. Both governments also failed to provide adequate equipment, seeds, and training to enable the transition to the new system. On the Canadian reserves, for example, farmers who were supposed to instruct Native Canadians were generally from Ontario and knew nothing of the conditions in the Prairie Provinces.

By the 1880s, in the United States, pressure by settlers for reservation lands became acute and Congress responded with the General Allotment Act (also known as the Dawes Act) in 1887, which provided for the allotment of land to individual tribal members. Under this legislation, each head of household received a plot of land, generally 160 acres, leaving the remainder of the reservations to be sold as surplus lands. Individuals who took allotments would receive title to their land after a trust period of twenty-five years. The Canadian reserves were also allotted. The U.S. and Canadian governments proposed to teach Native peoples to become self-sufficient farmers on their allotments, but they failed to back the policy with the necessary resources. In 1906 Congress passed the Burke Act, which enabled the secretary of the interior to declare an allotted farmer competent to manage his or her own affairs before the end of the trust period. Landowners who were declared competent received title to their lands and often sold it, a process that further hindered the successful development of Native American agriculture.

During the 1930s the federal government attempted to aid Plains Indian farmers by providing cattle to help build tribal herds, and several tribes organized livestock associations to improve breeding and marketing practices. By the end of World War II, however, high crop and livestock prices accelerated white demands to lease or purchase Indian lands because, it was claimed, they were not being cultivated or grazed to capacity. After 1945 only the white farmers who could command the necessary capital and credit, and who had access to new forms of science and technology and large acreages, could earn a profit from commercial agriculture. Native Americans in the Great Plains remained subsistence farmers, if they practiced agriculture at all. In 1970, for example, only 9 percent of Native Americans on the North Dakota reservations of Fort Berthold, Fort Totten, Turtle Mountain, and Standing Rock were farmers or farm managers.

At the beginning of the twenty-first century, on many reserves and reservations in the Great Plains, Native American agriculture has nearly ceased. There are important exceptions, of course, such as Montana Reserve in Alberta, which has a successful ranch and feed operation. But many tribes have leased their reservation lands to white farmers and ranchers, and millions of acres of allotted lands have been sold and passed from Indian control. The problems of government-imposed inheritance laws, which divided land holdings into tracts too small for profitable cultivation, and inadequate capital, credit, and education, as well as insufficient machinery, seeds, fertilizer, irrigation, and managerial experience, remain unresolved. As a result, most Native Americans in the Great Plains live in rural areas but are not farmers.

See also LAW: Dawes Act.

R. Douglas Hurt
Iowa State University

Baillargeon, Morgan. "Native Cowboys on the Canadian Plains." *Agricultural History* 69 (1995), 547–62. Hurt, R. Douglas. *Indian Agriculture in America: Prehistory to the Present*. Lawrence: University Press of Kansas, 1987.

PRAIRIE FARM REHABILITATION ADMINISTRATION

The Prairie Farm Rehabilitation Administration (PFRA) is a branch of the Canadian government's Department of Agriculture and Agri-Food. It was established in 1935 to secure the rehabilitation of the drought and soil-drifting areas in the provinces of Manitoba, Saskatchewan, and Alberta and to develop and promote within these areas systems of farm practice, tree culture, water supply, land utilization, and land settlement that would afford better economic security to the agricultural population.

Over the years, PFRA's mandate evolved along with the agricultural sector. It now works in all agricultural regions of the three Prairie Provinces and the Peace River region of British Columbia, offering its services through its headquarters in Regina, Saskatchewan, and through a network of twenty-two district and five regional offices, a shelterbelt center, eighty-seven community pastures, and two irrigation crop diversification centers.

PFRA's services for resource care (soil and water) and rural development include technical expertise on land and water resource management, land-use planning, crop diversification, irrigation development, environmental analysis, shelterbelt and wildlife habitat plantings, and water quality analysis. It offers technical and financial assistance to develop water supplies (dugouts, wells, dams, and water pipelines) and improve or protect the quality of surface and groundwater resources. It delivers water from Canada-owned and -operated reservoirs to irrigation projects and numerous communities in southwestern Saskatchewan. It provides tree and shrub seedlings for farmyard, field, and wildlife habitat plantings. And it oversees the management and operation of eighty-seven community pastures as well as the management of federal-provincial agreements, programs, and projects related to soil and water resource care and rural growth.

See also WATER: Bow River Irrigation Project.

Bill King
Prairie Farm Rehabilitation Administration
Regina, Saskatchewan

Gray, James H. *Men against the Desert*. Saskatoon, Saskatchewan: Western Producer Prairie Books, 1967.

RANCHES

The day of the cattlemen, of trail drives and open range, lasted only about two decades, from 1866 to about 1887, in the Great Plains. The cattlemen then adjusted to the new era of fence laws, barbed wire, and quarantine laws by gaining control of vast areas of rangeland in the Texas Panhandle, the Nebraska Sandhills, eastern Wyoming, and other parts of the Plains, which, because of aridity and isolation, were not attractive to homesteaders. By manipulating land laws such as the Timber Culture Act (1873) and the Forest Lieu Act (1897), they were able to own the land along the water courses and lakes and, therefore, have undisturbed use of the intervening range. On the U.S. Plains, at least, ranchers sometimes used violence to maintain their operations; more often, however, they relied on the abilities of their ranch managers to adapt to the changing times, and some of the early enterprises continue to prosper.

In the Texas Panhandle, the XIT ("ten counties in Texas")Ranch, run by a Chicago business coalition, eventually extended over more than three million acres and had a herd of more than 150,000 head, watched over by more than a hundred ranch hands. The huge spread was gradually sold to ranchers and farmers over the course of the first half of the twentieth century. The King Ranch in southeast Texas, founded by Richard King and Mifflin Kennedy, who later divided their holdings, covered one million acres in 1852. King's widow, Henrietta, operated the ranch after 1885. Other large Texas ranches, founded in the decades after the Civil War, include the JA, the Pitchfork, and the 6666. The JA was founded by Charles Goodnight in 1877, with financial backing from Irishman John G. Adair (hence the name and brand). The JA encompassed 1.3 million acres in Palo Duro Canyon and grazed 100,000 cattle in the early 1880s. It remains a working ranch today. So too do the Pitchfork and 6666 Ranches, which are both headquartered near Guthrie, Texas, and known for their quality cattle and American quarter horses.

George Washington Miller and his sons' 101 Ranch in northeastern Oklahoma, with 110,000 acres, rodeos, and Wild West shows, is another famous Plains ranch. The 101 remained intact until surviving son Zach was obliged to sell at a bankruptcy auction in 1931. In northwestern Kansas, C. P. Dewey and his son Chauncey controlled 700,000 acres, about half of which they owned and the remainder they leased from private owners or the federal government. Other notable Central Plains ranches include the Colorado spread operated by John Iliff until his death in 1878 and the 150,000-acre Spade Ranch in the Nebraska Sandhills. Iliff's methods reveal how ranchers in the United States controlled large amounts of territory in the nineteenth century. Iliff owned 105 scattered parcels of land, totaling only 15,588 acres, but by strategically locating his parcels along rivers and streams he was able to control a ranching territory of about 6,000 square miles, extending from Greeley to the eastern border of Colorado.

The Swan Land and Cattle Company, headquartered at Chugwater, Wyoming, which operated for more than seventy years and at its peak held as many as 110,000 head of cattle, serves as an example of the strong-arm techniques sometimes used by ranchers to control large amounts of land. In 1894 Alexander Swan hired noted gunman Tom Horn to kill rustlers and homesteaders, both of whom threatened Swan's large operation. Other cattlemen used equal or even greater violence, the best-known example being the infamous Johnson County War (1892) in north-central Wyoming, when vigilantes, hired by large-scale ranchers who were members of the Wyoming Stock Growers Association, "invaded" Johnson County, searching out, and in two cases killing, small operators who were suspected of rustling. The Swan Land and Cattle Company has since been divided into smaller ranches, and its original buildings are in disrepair.

The Matador Land and Cattle Company, founded by five Americans in northwest Texas along the Pease River in 1879, was taken over in 1882 by Scottish investors. Scottish ownership continued until the 1950s (with Murdo Mackenzie particularly influential), as the company acquired grazing lands throughout the Northern Great Plains and into Saskatchewan. The huge estate was divided into smaller holdings and sold after the 1950s.

In the Prairie Provinces, adapted land laws and low population densities made ranching a more regulated enterprise than it was south of the forty-ninth parallel. Under the Land Act of 1881 ranchers could make twenty-one-year leases of up to 100,000 acres at one cent per acre, provided that the rancher kept one cow for every twenty acres of land. Alberta's Bar U Ranch, operated by George Lane, one of Canada's Big Four ranchers, served as the center of an empire that consisted not only of short-grass ranches, but also farms, meatpacking factories, and flour mills. It was renowned for breeding cattle and Percheron horses. The Bar U Ranch, under new ownership, remains an active ranch more than 120 years after its founding.

Today Great Plains ranchers drive the rough terrain of their spreads in air-conditioned four-wheel drive pickups or sport-utility vehicles. At holding pens and feeder yards eighteen-wheelers take on cattle then speed down interstates en route to distant markets or slaughterhouses. Ranchers watch price fluctuations and futures markets on television monitors linked to satellites. They express concern about new cattle afflictions, such as the dreaded mad cow disease. Membership in cattle associations and beef producer organizations is a necessity. Yet most carry the spirit and tradition of nineteenth-century ranches in their hearts, and ranching remains as much a way of life as a business.

Paul D. Travis
Texas Woman's University

Dary, David. *Cowboy Culture: A Saga of Five Centuries.* New York: Alfred A. Knopf, 1981. Jordan, Terry G. *Trails to Texas: Southern Roots of Western Cattle Ranching.* Lincoln: University of Nebraska Press, 1981. Starrs, Paul F. *Let the Cowboy Ride: Cattle Ranching in the American West.* Baltimore MD: Johns Hopkins University Press, 1998.

RANGE MANAGEMENT

Management of rangelands is based on ecological principles that ensure sustained health and productivity of range ecosystems. Rangeland is a noncultivated land type on which the native vegetation includes grasses, sedges, broadleaf herbaceous plants, and shrubs. It is the dominant land type in the Great Plains, comprising about 50 percent of the total land area. Livestock grazing has been the primary rangeland use in the Great Plains since the beginning of European American settlement, and range management has always been closely linked to the livestock industry. The livestock industry started in the Southern Plains in the 1700s and in the early 1870s moved into the Northern and Central Plains. By the mid-1990s, Great Plains rangeland supported about 40 to 50 percent of the beef cattle of the United States and about 75 percent of Canada's. With proper range management for livestock production, the integrity of rangelands and the potential for other uses are not compromised. Great Plains rangelands are important for wildlife habitat, watershed protection, recreation, and preservation of genetic diversity. Management targeted toward

such uses or values is critical on public lands, and ecotourism, wildlife viewing, and fee hunting are important sources of income for private landowners in many states.

Most rangelands in the Great Plains are grasslands, although other range types, such as savannas, shrub lands, woodlands, and wetlands, are important regionally or locally. Great Plains grasslands include tallgrass prairie, mixed prairie, shortgrass prairie, and fescue prairie. Distribution of grassland types is largely related to gradients in annual precipitation from east to west (ten to forty inches) and, to a lesser extent, temperature gradients from north to south (68°F to 85°F in July). The tallgrass prairie once covered the eastern quarter of the Great Plains and was dominated by warm-season grasses, including big bluestem (*Andropogon gerardii*), little bluestem (*Schizachyrium scoparium*), and indiangrass (*Sorghastrum nutans*). Today most of the tallgrass prairie is cultivated for row-crop production, except for the Flint Hills of Kansas, where the shallow soils have restricted cultivation. The mixed prairie occupies the central third of the Great Plains and is dominated by cool-season grasses in the north and warm-season grasses in the south. The mixed prairie is the most important range type for livestock production in the United States, although small grains are also grown on much of the area. The shortgrass prairie extends west from the mixed prairie to the Rocky Mountains and is recognized by its low stature and the dominance of two shortgrasses, buffalograss (*Buchloe dactyloides*) and blue grama (*Bouteloua gracilis*). Plant and animal production is limited by water availability. The fescue prairie is on the northern boundary of the mixed prairie in Canada and is extensively cultivated for crop production.

Condition of rangelands is evaluated based on measures of ecosystem health and production (e.g., soil surface conditions and species composition). Range condition generally was low in the Great Plains by the early twentieth century because livestock mismanagement, cultivation and abandonment, and drought resulted in low plant cover, wind and water erosion, and proliferation of invasive and low quality plants. Aggressive management efforts by the private and public sectors have improved range condition significantly over the past sixty years. Only 6 percent of the rangeland in the Northern Great Plains is classified in poor condition, although 25 percent in the Southern Great Plains is in the poor category.

Tools used to maintain or improve range condition include proper grazing management, prescribed burning, herbicide application, and reseeding. Proper stocking rate for the various range sites is the key to successful management of grazed rangelands. Development of grazing systems involving rotation of livestock through two or more pastures also plays an important role in maintaining or improving range condition. Rotational grazing provides forage plants with critical rest periods that allow for recovery after grazing. Fire, a natural component of most range eco-

systems, is commonly used under prescribed conditions to control invasive plant species, such as junipers (*Juniperus* spp.) and introduced bromegrasses (*Bromus* spp.). Herbicides are an important alternative for control of many broadleaf herbaceous plants and such woody plants as honey mesquite (*Prosopis glandulosa*) in the Southern Great Plains. Although expensive, reseeding native species may be an alternative for extremely depleted sites; however, risk of failure increases under drier conditions. Overall, range ecosystems such as the Nebraska Sandhills demonstrate that when management practices are properly applied, range ecosystems can be used for production purposes while sustaining ecological integrity.

See also PHYSICAL ENVIRONMENT: Grasses.

Walter H. Schacht
University of Nebraska–Lincoln

Holechek, Jerry L., Rex D. Pieper, and Carlton H. Herbel. *Range Management: Principles and Practices.* Upper Saddle River NJ: Prentice Hall, 1998. Samson, Fred B., and Fritz L. Knopf, eds. *Prairie Conservation.* Washington DC: Island Press, 1996. Vallentine, John F. *Range Development and Improvements.* San Diego: Academic Press, Inc., 1989.

RYE

Rye (*Secale cereale* L.) is one of the small grains grown in the Great Plains. It is a winter annual, planted in the fall, and is the hardiest of the small grains. Rye does well in cool climates (optimum temperature 55°F to 65°F) and tolerates most adverse weather. It is often grown on light, sandy soil, when weed problems are present or when the soil is low in fertility. The major disease problem is ergot, a fungus that replaces kernels with a hard, black growth. Rye grain is similar to wheat in size and composition but is lower in protein. Bread made from only rye is a small, dark, compact loaf, so in North America it is generally blended with wheat to produce a loaf that is more acceptable to the consumer.

Due to its hardiness, winter rye is commonly grown in the northern parts of the Great Plains. Rye was never the dominant crop, and acreage of rye has declined over the course of the twentieth century. In Saskatchewan, for example, the leading rye-producing province in Canada, acreage fell from 1.2 million in 1921 to 225,000 in 1993. In Saskatchewan, North Dakota, and South Dakota (generally the leading rye producer in the United States), the crop is grown for its grain.

In general, acreage and production decreases southward down the Great Plains. In 1992, South Dakota had 55,000 acres under rye, Nebraska 17,384 acres, and Kansas 6,993. In Oklahoma and Texas, rye is planted for two purposes. First, it provides ground cover during the winter and reduces erosion and loss of nutrients by leaching. Second, rye provides considerable winter grazing for cattle. Very little of this rye is harvested for grain.

Dale Reeves
South Dakota State University

SASKATCHEWAN WHEAT POOL

Created in 1924, the Saskatchewan Wheat Pool has for decades been Canada's largest agricultural enterprise. The company is democratically controlled by Saskatchewan farmers. The history of the Saskatchewan Wheat Pool can be divided into four phases. First was the founding era of 1924–31, when the cooperative bought and marketed to overseas customers a large proportion of the Prairie wheat crop. The Depression and the 1940s were a period of readjustment, during which the company largely surrendered its original role as a marketer of grain to the Canadian Wheat Board, an organization whose history is intertwined with that of the pool. The war was followed by a long period of dominance and growth as a grain handler, marketer of livestock and specialty crops, and general-interest farm organization. A new phase in the company's history began in 1996 when most of its stock was converted to publicly traded shares.

Activist farmers who were upset with existing grain companies and cooperatives organized the pool in 1923–24. Most farm organizations at the time favored a government-run wheat board to market their crops, but they turned to cooperative action when governments were unresponsive. A faction invited Aaron Sapiro, a California-based lawyer and advocate of pooling, to visit the Prairies in 1923. Sapiro's speeches and ideas proved to be the catalyst for the organization of three wheat pools in Alberta, Manitoba, and Saskatchewan. The 1923 pooling drive in Saskatchewan failed, perhaps due to lukewarm support from provincial leaders and to the formidable contracts that required farmers to pledge all their wheat for a five-year period to the pool and which were void unless 50 percent of acreage was signed up. The second drive in 1924 was a mass effort of community mobilization: 45,725 farmers pledged their 6,433,779 acres of wheat, meeting the target and bringing the pool into existence. From 1924 to 1931, the pool worked with its sister organizations in Alberta and Manitoba through the Central Selling Agency to market a majority of the Prairie wheat crop, wherever possible directly to overseas customers, and to build or purchase networks of storage elevators.

The stock market crash of 1929 caught the pools overextended, as grain prices fell below the level already advanced to farmers; the pools made matters worse by buying more grain in an attempt to influence prices. In 1931 the Canadian government intervened to provide financial guarantees for the pools and took over the sale of their inventories. Government involvement eventually culminated in the creation of the modern Canadian Wheat Board—ironically, what farmers had wanted in the first place. The pool, meanwhile, was converted from a world grain trader to a heavily indebted Saskatchewan elevator company. The pool's response not only preserved the cooperative, but it cemented its place as the province's most important agricultural institution. While repaying its debts, the pool became a crucial agent of adult education. Pool field staff gave talks, showed films, and helped set up consumer cooperatives and credit unions in small towns across Saskatchewan.

From the 1940s to the 1980s, the pool extended its elevator network (handling up to two-thirds of the annual grain crop), branched out into new or expanded lines of business such as livestock marketing and farm supply, and consolidated its position as the spokesperson for Saskatchewan farmers. The pool's model system of member education and delegate democracy was studied by cooperatives around the world; pool annual meetings were a kind of farmers parliament where important issues of provincial, federal, and international policy were debated. Since the pool was both Saskatchewan's largest business corporation and a farm interest group with 60,000 members, it developed considerable influence in provincial politics. Its weekly newspaper, the *Western Producer*, remains the most important farm paper in Canada.

The cooperative could not, however, escape the dominant agricultural trends. Low farm incomes created pressure to operate on low margins; rural depopulation left the pool with fewer and aging members. Pool managers and leaders became concerned in the late 1980s with the cooperative's debt burden, resulting from an aging membership entitled upon retirement to share payouts. At the same time, they saw a need for investment and expansion to meet the challenges of transnational competitors and new agricultural markets. As a result, the cooperative, with the approval of farmer delegates, transformed its ownership structure in 1996. Voting shares—class A shares—were retained only by farmer-members, but virtually the entire capitalization of the company was converted into nonvoting class B shares that were tradable on the Toronto Stock Exchange. The pool remained farmer-controlled, but its owners were now a noncongruent body of investors. Along with the share conversion, the pool undertook an ambitious program to consolidate its handling facilities in a smaller number of larger and more modern elevators, to invest in value-added processing subsidiaries and joint ventures, and to expand outside Saskatchewan and outside Canada.

See also MEDIA: *Western Producer.*

Brett Fairbairn
University of Saskatchewan

Fairbairn, Garry. *From Prairie Roots: The Remarkable Story of Saskatchewan Wheat Pool.* Saskatoon: Western Producer Prairie Books, 1984. Fowke, V. C. *The National Policy and the Wheat Economy.* Toronto: University of Toronto Press, 1957. MacPherson, Ian. "Missionaries of Rural Development: The Fieldmen of the Saskatchewan Wheat Pool, 1925–1965." *Agricultural History* 60 (1986): 73–96.

SHEEP

More than 20 percent of the sheep in the United States are located in Great Plains states, mainly in the drier western reaches. Six of the top ten states in sheep production are in the Plains: Texas (1), Wyoming (2), Montana (5), South Dakota (6), Colorado (7), and New Mexico (8). Colorado is also ranked first in commercial sheep slaughter.

Sheep production in the Great Plains states is extremely diverse. It varies from large extensive range sheep operations in West Texas, western South Dakota, eastern Montana, Wyoming, and New Mexico to more intensively managed flocks in the farming areas of North and South Dakota, Nebraska, Kansas, and Oklahoma. As a general rule, the productivity of pasture or forage crops dictates the maximum levels of productivity that a sheep producer can achieve and thus the type of operation best suited to the area. Production goals for sheep units in the Plains vary from commercial sheep operations to purebred or registered seed stock operations to operations catering to 4-H and FFA market sheep projects.

In areas of low rainfall, such as West Texas, limited feed resources restrict production potential. Since in these areas expected outputs are low, production systems are extensive and resource inputs are minimized. Sheep numbers are large in order to offset the low level of outputs per animal unit. Although in these operations lamb production still accounts for the majority of the income (usually 70 to 80 percent), wool provides a more significant contribution to the total income of the enterprise than in the systems to the east.

In the farming areas of the Great Plains states, forage production capability of the land is not limited and thus sheep production systems involve intensely managed operations with much greater levels of output: production goals may approach up to 200 pounds of lamb per ewe per year. This usually involves a smaller total number of ewes per operation than on the western Plains. In many instances, these operations involve a greater reliance on harvested feed. And they tend not to be complete economic units but are used to support other farm income. The sheep will often use land, labor, and feed resources which otherwise may go unused on many farming and ranching operations.

Because of the proximity of the major slaughter plants in the United States (particularly in eastern Colorado and western Iowa) and the vast feed resources, lamb feeding is an important industry in the Great Plains states and provinces. Feeding centers are located in Colorado, Wyoming, South Dakota, and Alberta. In addition, there is an active farmer-feeding industry in the farming areas of the Great Plains states. In some instances, it is beneficial for farmers to use a livestock fattening enterprise as a method to market their grain.

Rodney W. Kott
Montana State University

SHELTERBELTS

See PHYSICAL ENVIRONMENT: Shelterbelts

SOIL BANK

The Soil Bank Program was conceived in the early 1950s when grain storage facilities full of crop surpluses dotted rural America. Surpluses lowered prices and reduced farm income, and a program was needed to stabilize the market. In 1956, Congress passed the Soil Bank Act to reduce surpluses by lowering acres of the major crops, thus keeping production in line with demand, and to encourage conservation of soil, water, and forest resources. Spring and winter wheat, corn, grain sorghum, and cotton were the majors crops targeted for reduction in the Great Plains.

One part of the program, acreage reserve, was a temporary measure to reduce surpluses by making cash payments for crops taken out of production. These yearly set-aside acres were left idle and could not be cropped, hayed, or pastured. The program also included a voluntary conservation effort, often referred to as the Soil Bank, which was a long-term process aimed at diverting crop production land to conservation uses.

Under the Soil Bank Program, the Agricultural Stabilization and Conservation Service (ASC) entered into three- to ten-year contracts with landowners to set aside planted acres. The farmers received in return an annual payment based on the quality of the land (average payment was around $12 per acre). They agreed to maintain the land in an approved conservation practice (predominantly grass in the Great Plains) and not harvest a crop, cut timber or hay, or graze the area. Nearly 29 million acres were placed in the Soil Bank program, the majority of which were located in the Great Plains. Texas and North Dakota had the highest participation in the program, putting aside as much as 10 percent of their total cropland. More than 300,000 contracts with an annual payment exceeding $300 million occurred in some years.

The Soil Bank provided a guaranteed, risk-free farm income with little work. Because the amount of acres that could be contracted was not limited, the program had negative social and economic effects on many parts of the Plains. Decreased agricultural production resulted in reduced crop handling services and processing activities. Landowners in the Soil Bank Program often moved outside the area, taking along spendable income, or sometimes competed for off-farm employment. Local resentment developed against Soil Bank farmers who retired all their land and received payment for doing nothing. The positive impacts included crop surplus reduction, conservation of soil and water, and development of wildlife habitat.

Edward J. Deibert
North Dakota State University

SORGHUM

Sorghum (*Sorghum bicolor* [L.] Moench) is a major food, feed, and fiber crop of northeast African origin. It is considered the world's fifth most important cereal. In the United States sorghum grain is primarily a feed crop, while in Africa, Asia, and parts of Latin America its primary use is as a food. The United States accounts for about 9 percent of the

Production of hybrid grain sorghum on the Texas High Plains

world's sorghum acreage and 25 percent of grain produced. Kansas, Nebraska, and Texas yield about 80 percent of the sorghum produced in the United States.

Modern grain sorghum is a product of human ingenuity. Cultivated sorghum has morphologically distinct, genetically diverse races that can be intercrossed. The species is a self-pollinating perennial that is grown in temperate areas as an annual, but it is handled as a cross-pollinating crop for hybrid production. Sorghum is especially useful in areas too hot and too dry for crops such as corn. It is classified into four groups: grain sorghum, which includes old types such as kafir, milo, and feterita, as well as dwarf combine-type hybrids grown primarily for grain; forage sorghum, which are types grown primarily for forage, silage, or molasses; grass sorghum, types grown for hay and pasture; and broom corn, which possess long, stiff panicle branches that are used to make brooms.

Identification of cytoplasmic-genetic male sterility in the 1950s led to development of grain, forage, and grass hybrids. Grain sorghum hybrids are of a plant height suitable for combine harvest. The grain may be processed in several ways depending on use as a feed (cattle, poultry, or swine) or food. Forage type hybrids often contain high stalk sugar and are used as silage. Grass or grazing hybrids are fine leaved, thin stemmed, and used primarily for grazing, green-chop, hay, or green manure. Grain yield of sorghum has more than tripled since hybrids became commercially available in 1956. The dramatic increase in grain yield may be attributed to improved plant genetics—causing significant improvements in adaptation, maturity, stalk quality, insect resistance, disease resistance, grain quality, and drought tolerance—and improved management, including herbicides, fertilizer, irrigation, and soil and water conservation practices. Sorghum may be rotated with other crops—for example, a sorghum-fallow-wheat

rotation or cotton-sorghum rotation depending on the location. More sorghum is grown dryland than irrigated. Sorghum produces excellent irrigated yields, although irrigated acreage has declined as producers shift production to higher value crops.

Sorghum acreage declined from 18.3 million acres in 1983 to 9.4 million acres in 1998. Declines have been particularly marked in Kansas. Primary factors are the 1985 Farm Bill, which placed sorghum at a comparative disadvantage relative to corn, and improvements in corn drought tolerance that enabled corn to move into marginal production regions traditionally planted in sorghum. However, no other crop has the versatility of sorghum for diverse production systems, range of planting dates, and maturity. Producers turn to sorghum when other crops fail due to drought or other factors and sorghum will remain key to Great Plains crop production in the twenty-first century.

Gary C. Peterson
Texas A&M University Agricultural Research and Extension Center, Lubbock

Bennett, William F., Billy B. Tucker, and A. Bruce Maunder. *Modern Grain Sorghum Production.* Ames: Iowa State University Press, 1990. Doggett, H. *Sorghum.* New York: Longman Scientific and Technical, 1988.

SOYBEANS

Soybean (*Glycine max*), native to China, is a relatively new crop to the Great Plains, where there was no appreciable production prior to 1950. Since 1950, the production area has increased rapidly to more than 12 million acres in the U.S. Great Plains in 1998, which is about 18 percent of the national production area. The production is largely in the eastern Great Plains, due to the higher annual precipitation and the greater likelihood of rainfall during the critical pod elongation stage, which occurs in early August. Little soybean production occurs in the western Great Plains and the Canadian Prairie Provinces because of the short growing season (in the north), low annual precipitation, and low probability of rainfall during early August. Major production problems are water and high-temperature stress during the growing season. Only a few insect and pest problems cause sporadic yield losses. The most common pest problems are *Phytophthora* root and stem rot, bean leaf beetle, and soybean cyst nematode.

Since soybean is grown most widely in the eastern Great Plains, it does not overlap greatly with the region's large wheat acreage. Soybean is most commonly grown as a rotational dryland crop with corn, grain sorghum, and winter wheat, and is the third most important grain crop in the region, following wheat and corn. Soybean is produced as a cash crop, with the production being shipped by rail or truck to crushing plants. The major food end products are cooking oil, margarine, shortening, and emulsifiers. Soybean is also widely used as a high protein livestock feed supplement. Nonfood end uses include plastics and coatings, lubricants, diesel fuel substitute, carrier for pesticides, dust suppressant in grain handling, and printing ink.

The soybean production area within the Great Plains is concentrated in Nebraska and South Dakota, with 60 percent of the total, while production in Oklahoma and Texas is quite small. The highest yields—45 bushels per acre in 1998—are in Nebraska, largely because approximately one-third of the soybean production area is irrigated. Yields of approximately 25 bushels per acre are common in North Dakota, Oklahoma, and Texas. Soybean yields in the Great Plains average approximately 10 percent less than in the Corn Belt states, where higher, more uniformly distributed annual precipitation occurs.

See also INDUSTRY: Oilseeds.

Stephen C. Mason
University of Nebraska–Lincoln

Wilcox, J. R., ed. *Soybeans: Improvement, Production, and Uses*. Madison WI: American Society of Agronomy, 1987.

SUGAR BEET PROCESSING

See INDUSTRY: Sugar Beet Processing

SUGAR BEETS

Sugar beet (*Beta vulgaris*) is one of the world's two sources of sucrose. Sugar beets are grown in almost all temperate areas of the world and are produced in North America from southern Canada to Mexico at elevations ranging from sea level to near 7,000 feet. In the United States, sugar beets are produced in fourteen states on more than 1.46 million acres, yielding annual output of more than 3.8 million tons of sucrose. Farm gate value (the value of the product when it leaves the farm and before value-added processing, wholesaling, and retailing) to producers is more than $1.1 billion. Sugar beets are grown under dryland conditions in Michigan, Ohio, Minnesota, and eastern North Dakota, and under irrigation in western North Dakota, Montana,

Sugar beets, Huntley Irrigation Project, Montana, 1906

Wyoming, New Mexico, Colorado, Nebraska, Idaho, Oregon, Washington, and California.

Sugar beet production in the Great Plains region accounts for more than 64 percent of the United States total. The crop has been an important part of the farm economy in eastern Colorado and western Nebraska since 1890. Commercial production in the Red River Valley of the North began in 1925. The Minnesota–North Dakota production area that includes the Red River Valley of the North now has nearly 46 percent (667,000 acres) of U.S. acreage; other Great Plains states contribute another 17 percent of the nation's production. Production areas involving western Nebraska and adjacent Colorado and Wyoming annually plant approximately 150,000 acres, and the production areas in the Yellowstone, Missouri, and Bighorn valleys of Montana, Wyoming, and western North Dakota plant approximately 120,000 acres. In 1998 the only sugar beet factory in Texas was closed due to chronically high disease losses. Sugar beet production in Canada is centered in Taber, Alberta, and has recently been targeted for expansion by the minister of agriculture.

The sugar beet is a biennial, cross-pollinated plant whose growth is favored by medium- to light-textured soils with a 6.0–7.5 pH and warm bright days and cool nights. Sugar beets require significant nitrogen—150 to 200 pounds per acre—for maximum production. Nitrogen levels must be carefully monitored since excess nitrogen at harvest will reduce both sugar content and quality. Sugar content in roots can be as high as 22 percent, but commercial production generally ranges from 12 to 20 percent. Two major innovations were critical to the modern culture of this crop: the discovery of cytoplasmic male sterility in the 1940s by Dr. W. F. Owens allowed the production of high yielding hybrids, and the discovery of monogerm seed in 1948 by Drs. V. F.

and Helen Savitsky eliminated the need for hand thinning. Since the late 1960s all sugar beet crops in the United States are planted with monogerm, hybrid seed. Harvesting has been done entirely by machines since the early 1950s.

All sugar beets are grown under contract with sugar companies or grower cooperatives. Typically, a minimum of 25,000 to 30,000 contracted acres are needed to support a sugar processing plant. In the Great Plains region seeding generally starts in March and is finished in early May. After harvest, beets are stored in piles until they are processed during a 60- to 200-day processing period. Sugar beets are almost always grown in rotations of two to three or more years. Shorter rotations lead to depressed yields because of fungal and virus diseases, the sugar beet cyst nematode (*Heterodera schacctii*), insects, and weeds. Historically the most important diseases are Cercospora leaf spot, curly top virus, rhizomania (beet necrotic yellow vein virus), powdery mildew, Rhizoctonia crown and root rot, and Aphanomyces black root. Insect pests include sugar beet root maggot, sugar beet root aphid, armyworms, cutworms, aphids, and leafhoppers. Weed management is critical to high yields of this important Plains crop.

See also HISPANIC AMERICANS: *Betabeleros* / INDUSTRY: Sugar Beet Processing.

Barry Jacobsen
Montana State University

Cooke, D. A., and R. K. Scott, eds. *The Sugar Beet Crop*. London: Chapman and Hall, 1993. Whitney, E. D., and J. E. Duffus, eds. *Compendium of Beet Diseases and Insects*. St. Paul: APS Press, 1986.

SUITCASE FARMING

Suitcase farming was, and to a limited degree still is, carried on by farmers living more than one county away from the land they farm. The

Breaking sod in Greeley County, Kansas, May 1925

term was used as early as 1930 by the county agent for Greeley County, in western Kansas, although its characteristics were not defined. The pattern, or basic ecology, of early suitcase farming can be generalized in this way: Cheap level grazing land in a zone of recurring drought, a moderate distance west of established wheat country that was already largely mechanized, was invaded by farmers with tractors and other farm machinery in a speculative westward advance. The plow-up was so substantial that a suitcase-farming frontier can be recognized that included most of west-central and southwestern Kansas and small areas in Colorado.

After an interruption by the drought and depression of the 1930s, and the restrictions of World War II, including gasoline rationing and scarcity of machinery and parts, a second advance of similar character carried wheat farming still farther west, mainly into east-central Colorado. Kiowa County was affected most. Farmers from northwestern Oklahoma, the Texas Panhandle, and urban bases in front of the Rockies, in some cases former residents, were involved, along with Kansans.

The decline in suitcase farming, due to unprofitable operation, preference for local operators, and locally to irrigation, already apparent in the 1960s, has continued, so that now suitcase farming is mainly a fleeting memory in the history of settlement and agriculture in the Central Great Plains. In aiding great plow-ups, suitcase farming doubtless contributed to Dust Bowl conditions in the 1930s and in the mid-1950s, but probably its most lasting effect was to extend the production of hard winter wheat westward several hundred miles.

Leslie Hewes
University of Nebraska–Lincoln

Hewes, Leslie. *The Suitcase Farming Frontier: A Study in the Historical Geography of the Central Great Plains.* Lincoln: University of Nebraska Press, 1973.

SUNFLOWERS

Native Americans domesticated the sunflower, a native of the Great Plains. They used the seed for food, extracted oil from them for paints, and used bloom petals for dye. The wild form, *Helianthus annuus* L., is still common throughout the Great Plains in cultivated fields, pastures, gardens, roadsides, and other disturbed sites. The plants provide cover, and the seeds furnish energy and protein for a wide range of wildlife species, but they are considered weeds because they compete with cultivated crops.

Cultivated sunflowers are grown as either an ornamental plant in the landscape or as an agronomic crop used for its edible seed or extractable oil. Ornamental sunflowers have been developed to produce blooms of magenta, white, and orange and to reach heights of one to fifteen feet. They are commonly used in the back of garden beds for height, color, and texture, or as screens and alongside fences. Kansas, the Sunflower State, has adopted it as its state flower.

Agronomic sunflower production is divided into two market classes, oil and confectionery. Most of the acreage in the Great Plains is planted with the oil type. The oil is used primarily in cooking and baking. Confectionery types are grown for the edible roasted seed. Acreage in confectionary sunflowers is contracted with processing companies and is subject to strict guidelines. Confectionery seeds not meeting the guidelines go into birdseed markets. Recently, a third market class has developed based on specialty cooking oil markets.

Sunflowers in the Great Plains are grown under both irrigation and dryland-farming methods but mainly under dryland farming. Yields under irrigation are typically double those of dryland. Although sunflowers are cultivated in significant amounts in western Kansas and Nebraska, eastern Colorado, and parts of the Texas Panhandle, U.S. production is dominated by South Dakota and, especially, North Dakota. In Canada, fully 90 percent of national production comes from central Manitoba.

Sunflowers work well in rotation with winter wheat, as a wheat-fallow-sunflower rotation. In this system two crops are harvested in a three-year period. They are sown in May and harvested in late September or October. Sunflowers should be planted into a firm seedbed when soil temperatures are above 50°F. They grow best on medium-textured soils, such as loams. Planting is done with a row crop planter equipped with special plates or with a grain drill. Seeding rates are 14,000 to 21,000 plants per acre under dryland conditions and 20,000 to 25,000 plants per acre under irrigation. Sunflowers are harvested with the use of a combine with special extensions (sunflower pans) in front of the cutter bar.

The sunflower, being native to the region, is vulnerable to a wide array of insects and diseases that can cause serious economic yield reductions. Common insect pests are the sunflower seed weevil, sunflower moth, grasshoppers, and the sunflower head clipper weevil. Common diseases are stalk and head rot, rust, Phoma black stem, and downy mildew.

See also INDUSTRY: Oilseeds.

James Schild
University of Nebraska–Lincoln

Schild, Jim, Dave Baltensperger, Drew Lyon, Gary Hein, and Eric Kerr. "Sunflower Production in Nebraska." G91–1026, University of Nebraska, 1991. McMullen, Marcia P. "Sunflower Production and Pest Management." *Extension Bulletin 25.* North Dakota State University, 1985.

SUSTAINABLE AGRICULTURE

To maintain human economic activity and quality of life in the Great Plains, it is essential to develop a strategy that efficiently uses and conserves natural resources over the long term. Agriculture provides the opportunity to use the water, soil, and other renewable resources of the Plains, but strategies and systems for crop, forage, and livestock production need to be designed for maximum sustainability. This means an agriculture that does not overly exploit or deplete these resources, an agriculture that is productive, economically sound, environmentally benign, and socially viable. One of the most successful models that meets these criteria, including maintaining rural communities, is a sustainable agriculture based on renewable resources, private farm ownership, and family farming units.

What defines the Plains climate for agriculture is a rate of evapotranspiration (water loss from soil and plants) that exceeds the rate of rainfall for an important part of the crop-growing season. There are many ways to compensate for this adverse climate, all involving capturing and storing moisture in the soil so that it will be available when crops are growing. They include reduced or zero tillage during land preparation, choosing crops that have low water needs, planting lower crop populations that will use less water, and managing weeds in a way that limits their water use. Application of chemical herbicides, coupled with minimum or zero tillage, can drastically reduce water loss from the soil surface, but there is the potential hazard of chemical contact by human applicators or nontarget members of the ecosystem. Woody perennial windbreaks can reduce transpiration from crops and increase production. A combination of these water-saving and harvesting methods makes maximum possible use of accumulated water storage from snow and rain.

Irrigation was long used in the Great Plains by Native Americans and later by European American immigrants who settled near rivers. There is now a large irrigated acreage in Nebraska, western Kansas, the Texas Panhandle, and southern Alberta. Although some acres depend on surface water supplies that are renewed each year, a large portion of irrigation in the Central and Southern Plains comes from the Ogallala Aquifer. During the past two decades this source of groundwater has been seriously depleted, especially in the Southern Plains. Farmers there have shifted from irrigated corn to less demanding crops such as grain sorghum and cotton. The Ogallala Aquifer is recharged through the Sandhills of Nebraska and from playa lakes on the Southern Plains, and thus can recuperate if irrigation is curtailed. Deeper aquifers below the Ogallala are composed of fossil water that, once depleted, is lost. Although irrigated production of cereals such as corn, grain sorghum, and wheat has been profitable over the past five decades, it is unlikely that production will continue, because Plains farmers have to compete with farmers farther east in the United States and in other countries with better rainfall conditions and much lower production costs. It is likely that scarce irrigation will be used only on specialty, higher-value crops in the future, hence the importance of sustainable agriculture.

Sustainable agriculture generally includes such production practices as crop rotation, integrated pest management, soil fertility that depends to the greatest extent possible on legumes and grasses in the sequence, and a minimum program of tillage that helps prevent soil erosion. Many proponents maintain that raising livestock as an integral component of the system is essential to long-term soil fertility and sustainability. Livestock provide a ready outlet for green forages and hay and speed the cycling of nutrients by consuming these forages and leaving manure in the fields. They also can graze crop residues in place, making use of such forages and cycling nutrients through manure. Composting animal manures and urban organic wastes is another method of returning important nutrients to the land and building soil organic matter. Although much of the nitrogen and some other elements are lost during the composting process, the nutrients are present in a more stable condition that makes them less susceptible to loss from the system after incorporation into the soil.

To be sustainable, an agricultural system must be economically viable in both the short term and the long term. Thus it is essential to design systems that enhance the resources on which productivity is based rather than pursuing a simplified system that exploits nonrenewable resources such as fossil fuels and sacrifices long-term sustainability for short-term gain. Federal price-support programs for specific crops distort the long-term biological and ecological realities, since farmers feel forced to seek monoculture strategies that maximize short-term gains. Likewise, short-term rental or lease agreements for land provide little incentive for the operator to conserve soil and focus on the future value of this resource. For these reasons, an agriculture based on family farm ownership and entrepreneurship seems the most likely to provide stability in food production and conservation of resources.

Social viability of rural communities is the final dimension of sustainable agriculture. When farms in the Great Plains were consolidated over the past century, the result was fewer people on the land as well as fewer in rural communities to provide support services and social infrastructure. Many small towns in the Plains have disappeared. In part this is a natural consequence of mechanization of agriculture, with fewer hands needed to till and harvest. It is also a result of improved transportation, since commodities can now be marketed over a wide area rather than depending on a local elevator or other buyer. On the business side, it is clear that the larger the farm the less the reliance on local services—pesticides, fertilizers, and equipment now may be purchased from a several state area rather than from the local dealer. The impact of large farms is loss of local business and consequently the loss of other rural infrastructure: churches, schools, medical facilities, entertainment, in short the loss of community. Such a system is clearly not sustainable from the family standpoint, and an agriculture that depends on distant ownership and minimum-wage jobs does not promote conservation of natural or human resources. Building systems that add value to products locally, that generate both food and income for local residents, and that cycle dollars around in the community, rather than extracting them from the land and people, can lead to a more sustainable agriculture and food system for the Great Plains.

See also CITIES AND TOWNS: Small Towns / WATER: Irrigation; Ogallala Aquifer.

Charles A. Francis
University of Nebraska–Lincoln

Edwards, Clive A., Rattan Lal, Patrick Madden, Robert H. Miller, and Gar House, eds. *Sustainable Agricultural Systems.* Ankeney IA: Soil and Water Conservation Society, 1990. Francis, Charles A., Cornelia B. Flora, and Larry D. King. *Sustainable Agriculture in Temperate Zones.* New York: John Wiley & Sons, 1990. Hegyes, Gabriel, and Charles Francis. *Future Horizons: Recent Literature in Sustainable Agriculture.* Lincoln: Center for Sustainable Agricultural Systems, University of Nebraska–Lincoln, 1997.

SWAN, ALEXANDER (1831–1905)

Alexander Hamilton Swan was born in 1831 in Greene County, Pennsylvania. He moved to Cheyenne, Wyoming, in 1873 and soon after, with other family members, established one of the largest cattle companies in the West, the Swan Brothers Cattle Company. Alexander, who managed the business, started with 3,000 head of cattle in 1873 on Chugwater Creek in southeastern Wyoming, where he established the Two Bar Ranch. By 1882 Swan's herd numbered 33,000 head. The next year he formed the Swan Land and Cattle Company and sold the corporation to Scottish investors for $2,550,825. As manager of the corporation, Swan organized four other cattle companies, including the Wyoming Hereford Ranch just east of Cheyenne. Swan was the first rancher to introduce purebred Herefords from England to the United States. Under Swan's management, the Swan Land and Cattle Company holdings expanded to more than one million acres and reportedly carried 110,000 head of cattle. Swan's influence stretched east as well where he was involved in the building of the massive Union Stockyards in Omaha, Nebraska.

Swan was also active in politics. As a Republican he was elected in 1877 to the council in the fifth Wyoming legislative assembly, but he was defeated in 1880 when he ran as a delegate to Congress. His ranching success came to an abrupt end through a combination of overstocking, overgrazing, and the disastrous winter storms of 1886–87, which killed an estimated 300,000 to 400,000 head of cattle in Wyoming. Swan filed for bankruptcy. His detractors accused him of inflating the head count of his herds and poor managerial practices. Swan was sued by his own corporation and replaced by John Clay, a harsh critic of Swan and his business operations. Swan left Cheyenne and died in obscurity in Ogden, Utah, in 1905.

Mark Elliott
Laramie County Community College

Burroughs, John R. *Guardian of the Grasslands.* Cheyenne: Pioneer Printing Stationery Co., 1971. Clay, John. *My Life on the Range.* Norman: University of Oklahoma Press, 1962. Woods, Lawrence M. *Wyoming Biographies.* Worland WY: High Plains Publishing Co., 1991.

SWATHER

See INDUSTRY: Swather

SWINE

Great Plains states account for approximately 16 percent of U.S. swine production, with Nebraska, Oklahoma, and Kansas in the top ten producing states. Nebraska leads other Plains states, but Oklahoma has seen the fastest increase in production in recent years. In Canada, the Prairie Provinces contribute almost 40 percent to national swine production.

Massive restructuring and technological changes are taking place in the swine industry in both countries. Production has moved indoors to large confinement units with improved management, breeding, and nutrition practices that have allowed more efficient production. This restructuring has resulted in much larger hog operations but on fewer farms in the Great Plains.

In the United States, there has been a tremendous increase in corporate hog farms, or private farms raising hogs on contract for swine companies. These changes have been particularly marked in Texas, Oklahoma, Kansas, and Colorado. In Oklahoma, swine companies own approximately 90 percent of the hog population. By contrast, in Nebraska most of the swine production is still dominated by individual farmers, though this is now changing.

Traditionally, hog production on the Plains was based in diversified family farms, which often used home-raised grain, primarily corn or sorghum grain, for feed. These operations were usually "farrow-to-finish." The sows were bred and farrowed and the pigs fed to market weight, currently 240 to 280 pounds. Today many of the new swine facilities have three sites. At one site, sows, usually 600 or more, are bred and farrowed. The pigs are weaned at two to three weeks of age and moved to another site called a nursery, where they live in environmentally controlled housing and are fed specially prepared starter diets until they are nine to ten weeks of age and weigh approximately 50 pounds. The third site consists of buildings where the pigs are fed out to market weight. The three-site production facilities break up the disease cycle and allow more specialized management and more efficient use of labor.

The future of the swine industry looks promising in the Great Plains, but it will continue to consolidate on fewer farms with more intensive management systems. Corporate or contract hog production will probably increase, although the largest independent hog operations will still be able to compete. Future expansion will be slowed down or prevented in some areas by opposition from localities and environmental groups. Stricter local and federal environmental regulations are also being implemented.

William G. Luce
Oklahoma State University

Canadian Pork Council. *Statistics Canada*, Ottawa, 1997. U.S. Department of Agriculture. *Hog and Pig Report.* Washington DC, 1997.

TAYLOR GRAZING ACT

Public agency management of the federal grazing lands began with the passage of the Taylor Grazing Act on June 28, 1934, as dust from the worst storms in the nation's history settled on Washington DC. Enacted after decades of rangeland deterioration, conflicts between cattle ranchers and migratory sheepherders, jurisdictional disputes, and states' rights debates, the act and its amendments ended free access to the range. The purposes of the act were to stop injury to the public lands; provide for their orderly use, improve-

ment, and development; and stabilize the livestock industry dependent on the public range. The new law effectively closed the rangelands to homesteading in the Dakotas and western states.

The act as amended in 1936 established grazing districts on the vacant, unappropriated and unreserved lands of the public domain: fifty-nine districts encompassing 168 million acres of federal land and 97 million acres otherwise owned. The act, as amended in 1939, established grazing advisory boards, primarily composed of livestock owners. Board duties included the allocation of permits and the determination of boundaries, seasons of use, and the carrying capacity of the range. This gave rise to the Federal Range Code and the criticism by some commentators that the advisory boards constituted a private government.

A new permit system granted grazing privileges by preference to ranchers who had actually used a grazing district's land during a priority period before 1934. Owners of land or water rights who could support livestock on base ranches during seasons when herds were not on the grazing districts were favored; those without property were not. Technically, the grazing permit is a revocable license under the law, not creating any right, title, interest, or estate in or to land, but it is considered by many to be a unique form of ownership, constituting a property right of the utmost importance.

The act created the Grazing Service, but inadequate funding prevented effective observation and evaluation of range use. Permitted animal unit months were set at preexisting 1934 stock levels. Efforts to reduce stock levels inevitably failed. The Grazing Service and General Land Office were consolidated in 1946 to form the Bureau of Land Management, which continues today to administer grazing lands not in the national forests.

The basis for grazing fees has always been controversial. Initially fees were set to cover only administrative costs. Western senators have opposed increasing the fees, despite obvious shortages of administrative resources, arguing that costs are higher on lower quality lands and fees comparable to those charged by the Forest Service would be unfair. Other legislators and groups interested in conservation and recreation have called for increased fees as a condition for larger appropriations. The 1970 Public Land Law Review Commission and a 1986 study by the General Accounting Office recommended raising the fee to fair market value. Efforts in the Department of the Interior to increase fees, however, were abandoned after the 1994 election.

Subchapter IV of the Federal Lands Policy and Management Act of 1976 and the Public Rangelands Improvement Act of 1978 have superceded the Taylor Grazing Act. Measuring carrying capacity, determining a viable basis for grazing fees, incorporating public participation into land management decisions, and balancing competing demands

for access all continue to challenge rangeland policymakers.

See also POLITICS AND GOVERNMENT: New Deal.

Laurence A. Clement Jr.
Kansas State University

Clawson, Marion, and Burnell Held. *The Federal Lands: Their Use and Management.* Lincoln: University of Nebraska Press, 1957. Coggins, George Cameron, and Robert L. Glicksman. *Public Natural Resources Law.* St. Paul: West Group, 1998. Foss, Phillip O. *Politics and Grass: The Administration of Grazing on the Public Domain.* Seattle: University of Washington Press, 1960.

TEXAS FEVER

Texas, or Spanish (as it later came to be called), fever was first detected in Pennsylvania in 1796, following the delivery of cattle from South Carolina. On the Plains, this infectious bovine disease, particularly prevalent in Texas, was influential in the development of the cattle trails and cow towns of the Great Plains.

The longhorn cattle from the Southern Plains that carried the disease were immune to its fatal effects, but the domestic cattle of the Midwest were not. The problems caused during the 1850s by the smaller droves of cattle passing through Missouri on their way to eastern markets were multiplied greatly when tens of thousands of Texas longhorns were trailed to Sedalia in 1866. The hostility of the Missouri legislature and local farmers resulted in the closing off of Missouri as a shipping point and the opening of the Kansas cow towns, led by Abilene in 1867.

Dispute over the cause of the disease between Texas drovers, whose cattle showed no symptoms, and local stockmen, many of whose cattle died, led to the establishment of quarantine lines that prohibited the importation of Texas cattle unless they had been wintered over in the north. In 1885 the entire state of Kansas was closed to Texas cattle, interrupting the trail drives and contributing to the demise of the cattle trailing business. The cause of the fever—a tick that was host to a microscopic organism that attacked the bovine spleen—was not discovered until 1889. Dipping vats and insecticides eventually replaced quarantine lines as the most effective method of controlling the spread of the disease, although the Kansas City stockyards maintained separate areas for southern and northern cattle well into the twentieth century.

One of the last major outbreaks of Texas fever on the Plains occurred in 1919 when a shipment of faultily dipped Texas cattle arrived in Wabaunsee County, Kansas, for summer grazing in the Flint Hills.

See also TRANSPORTATION: Cattle Trails.

James Hoy
Emporia State University

UNITED FARMERS OF CANADA, SASKATCHEWAN SECTION

See PROTEST AND DISSENT: United Farmers of Canada, Saskatchewan Section

VITICULTURE

Viticulture flourished in the Great Plains during the last half of the nineteenth century, especially in Kansas, Nebraska, and Texas, due to the wine-growing traditions introduced by European immigrants and the promotional efforts of Thomas V. Munson of Texas, one of the nation's leading viticultural authorities. However, the industry was destroyed by "Dry" interests and Prohibition and did not revive until the 1970s, when the United States became involved in a wine-growing boom that spread to most states.

A short growing season in the Northern Plains of the United States and the Prairie Provinces of Canada limits viticulture to cold-tolerant American table grapes or hybrid wine grapes, which are of little commercial significance. Viticulture is most prominent in the Southern Plains, where the industry focuses almost solely on *vinifera*, or European, wine grapes for premium wine production. Texas leads in wine grape growing in the Great Plains. High Plains farmers in Texas have long been interested in finding alternative crops to cotton or grain sorghum that require less water from the dwindling Ogallala Aquifer, and many have planted five to ten acres of wine grapes as a water-conserving, high-value, supplemental crop. The arid/semiarid climate of West Texas is conducive to growing *vinifera* grapes, a fact already proven by turn-of-the-century experiments. The region has impressive natural advantages (warm days, cool nights, low humidity, high elevation, fewer harmful insects and diseases) over more humid or higher-latitude regions. The only significant climatic problems are the erratic weather and occasional damage from late spring frosts. Texas usually ranks about fifth in the United States in wine grape acreage and produces more than a million gallons of wine a year. Over 80 percent of its more than 3,000 vineyard acres are located on the Southern Plains and in the Pecos Valley. All of Texas's five designated American Viticultural Areas and about half of its twenty-seven wineries are located in West Texas or the Hill Country, either within or on the fringes of the Plains.

Viticultural acreage on the Southern Great Plains continues to expand, and Texas's wine-growing industry alone employs more than 2,200 people and has an estimated total economic value of over $100 million per year. Legal impediments in some Plains states are doubtless more important than adverse physical factors in inhibiting the spread of viticulture in the region.

Otis W. Templer
Texas Tech University

Peters, Gary L. *American Winescapes: The Cultural Landscapes of America's Wine Country.* Boulder co: Westview Press, 1997. Templer, Otis W. "The Southern High Plains: Focal Point of the Texas Wine Growing Industry." In *Viticulture in Geographic Perspective: Proceedings of the 1991 Miami AAG Symposium,* edited by Harm J. de Blij. Miami: Miami Geographical Society, 1992, 97–110.

WHEAT

What is commonly recognized as a kernel of wheat is the caryopsis or fruit of a plant of the genus *Triticum* from the grass family (Gramineae). Biologically the purpose of the caryopsis is to reproduce the plant. Humans recognized the food value of wheat, which today is one of the most important cultivated crops in the world. Commercially in the United States, wheat is classified based on seed coat color (red or white), kernel texture (hard or soft), and growth habit (winter or spring). In the Great Plains three market classes of wheat are typically grown: hard red winter wheat, hard red spring wheat, and durum wheat. Hard red winter and hard red spring wheats (species *Triticum aestivum* L.) are called common or hexaploid wheats and have forty-two chromosomes; durum wheat (*Triticum durum* Desf.) is a tetraploid wheat having twenty-eight chromosomes. Hard white wheat, with winter and spring habit cultivars, is another market class of wheat that is increasing in commercial popularity in the Plains.

Cultivation of wheat in the Central Great Plains began in earnest when Russian Mennonite immigrants brought the hard red winter wheat variety (Turkey Red) to Kansas around 1874, although wheat was grown in Kansas prior to this. Turkey Red proved to be well suited to the environment of south-central Kansas and diffused from there. Agricultural records from 1900 show that Turkey Red (or its sibling Crimea) was also grown in Nebraska and Oklahoma Territory. Today Colorado, Kansas, Oklahoma, Nebraska, and Texas primarily grow hard red winter wheat. Texas and Oklahoma, and to a lesser extent Kansas, also use wheat stands for grazing cattle. Montana and South Dakota grow both hard red winter and hard red spring wheats (as well as some durum wheat) with records of such cultivation dating from 1841 in Montana and the 1890s in South Dakota. North Dakota produces hard red spring and durum wheat; records indicate production of Fife and Bluestem hard red spring types as early as 1879. Production of wheat in the Canadian Prairie Provinces started after the Dominion Lands Act of 1872 and the westward expansion of the Canadian Pacific Railway brought in settlers. Hard red spring and durum wheats are primarily grown because of the short growing season in the region. The Prairie Provinces now produce hard red spring wheats, spring white wheats, durum wheats, and some red winter wheats.

Conditions under which wheat is grown are extremely diverse throughout the Plains. Wide ranges exist in rainfall amounts, altitude, daytime and nighttime temperatures, soil conditions, and farming practices. Also, the types and severity of diseases and insects that attack wheat are many and varied. Winter wheat is planted in fall and harvested in late spring to early summer; it requires a cold period in order to produce grain in the spring (vernalization) but must possess tolerance to adverse winter conditions (winter hardiness). Wheat is usually harvested when the moisture content is about 10 to 16 percent. Winter wheat harvest typically begins in May in Texas and is usually handled by custom harvest crews with combines who move north as the grain ripens. Spring wheat and durum wheat are planted in April or May then harvested in late summer. In the Canadian Prairie Provinces, seeding occurs during May and June. Harvest can begin as early as August and usually runs well into September. Swathing, where wheat is cut at physiological maturity then threshed after drying in the sun, is a common harvesting practice on smaller farms in North Dakota and Canada; however, combining of wheat is increasing there.

Grain yield is influenced by both genetic and environmental factors. Average yield ranges from twenty to forty bushels per acre across the Plains, though in 1997 yields as high

Wheat harvest near Chilocco, Oklahoma, July 1984

as eighty bushels per acre were reported. Major increases in grain yield occurred when farmers shifted from tall to semidwarf varieties, which produce less straw and more kernels per plant. The short stature plants are also sturdier thus more resistant to lodging (falling over). This transition began in the late 1960s in the Northern Great Plains and was completed in the Southern Great Plains by the early 1980s. Once wheat is harvested, it is stored on the farm or taken directly to an elevator for storage or sale. On-farm storage is more prevalent in the Northern Plains. In 1997, approximately 79 million seeded acres produced nearly 65 million metric tons of wheat in the Great Plains.

While much of the wheat is consumed domestically, both the United States and Canada are major exporters. Domestic uses include animal feed, starch and gluten production, industrial applications, seed wheat, and most importantly, milling into bakery flours. Hard winter and hard spring wheats are noted for having high protein content and are typically used for making pan and hearth breads, hard rolls, bagels, buns, other yeast leavened products, and all-purpose flour. Durum wheat is used almost exclusively for making pasta products such as spaghetti and macaroni. In an average year, about 40 percent of the wheat grown in the Great Plains is exported. International customers purchase U.S. and Canadian wheat for such products as pan and hearth breads, French breads, steamed breads, chapatis, flat breads, Asian style noodles, pasta products, and indigenous traditional foods.

See also INDUSTRY: Grain Processing; Swather.

Patrick J. McCluskey
Kansas State University

Bartholomew, David M. et al. *Marketing Kansas Wheat.* Kansas State Board of Agriculture, 1959. Pomeranz, Y. *Wheat: Chemistry and Technology.* St. Paul: American Association of Cereal Chemists, 1988.

WILDLIFE AND AGRICULTURE

Habitat destruction, degradation, and fragmentation, brought about primarily from agricultural development, have greatly changed the landscape of the Great Plains and, concomitantly, the wildlife that reside there. More than 325 million acres in the Great Plains are farmed. Only 1 percent of the original tallgrass prairie remains. The oak savanna, small in area in the Great Plains, is also greatly reduced. Both ecosystems were largely converted to farms. The mixed grass prairie has been impacted to a lesser extent, although it also has been substantially reduced. The shortgrass prairie is relatively intact, although portions have been degraded through overgrazing and fire suppression. Mixed grass and shortgrass prairies that were grazed were less severely altered by agriculture. Wetlands were drained, converted to agriculture, or lost due

to lowering the water table caused by irrigation. Habitat fragmentation may result in the demise of area-sensitive species (those needing a minimum size habitat). Further, isolation of habitats makes it easy for small populations to become extinct and difficult for colonizers to repopulate an area.

Prior to European American settlement the Great Plains was teeming with wildlife: large ungulates such as bison, pronghorns, deer, elk, and bighorn sheep; predators, such as wolves, grizzly bears, and black bears; prairie dogs in the billions; and numerous turkeys and prairie chickens. Millions of acres of wetlands provided breeding habitat for waterfowl and resting and feeding areas for other migratory birds. All that changed with settlement by European Americans. The large ungulates were decimated through wanton shooting, unregulated harvest, and as a military strategy to deprive Native Americans of a source of food. Although this was not the direct effect of agriculture, the decline of those animals was seen as necessary so that cattle could flourish and the prairie could be converted to farmland. Predators perceived as a threat to livestock or animals that competed for forage with livestock were eliminated; or at least, efforts were made to eliminate those animals.

Relatively few species are endemic, or unique, to the Great Plains. Endemic birds that are declining include mountain plover, Sprague's pipit, Cassin's sparrow, and lark bunting. Endemic mammals that are declining include white-tailed jackrabbit, Franklin's ground squirrel, black-tailed prairie dog, and swift fox. Two birds native to the Great Plains—McCown's longspur and the ferruginous hawk—experienced an increase in population over the past twenty-five years. Both species are characteristic of shortgrass prairies and thrive in moderate to heavily grazed systems.

The Great Plains now consists of extensive areas of cultivated crops. The net result of this habitat uniformity has been a loss of richness in the number of species. At a distance croplands may appear like grasslands, but their management results in barren areas after harvest. Existing small areas that cannot be farmed because of thinness of soil or terrain, as well as areas that have been planted with trees, create "edge," which is ideal habitat for some species. Examples of species that have responded positively to farm habitats include ring-necked pheasants (an exotic), northern bobwhite, blue jay, house sparrow (another exotic), raccoon, opossum, red fox, and coyote.

In turn, wildlife has a significant impact on agriculture. In the United States, annual losses of agriculture to wildlife are about $500 million, with over half of that attributed to damages to field crops. Economic benefits from wildlife are also substantial. For example, estimated annual benefits associated with white-tailed deer in the United States are nearly $20

billion. However, those benefits are diffuse and shared by various businesses and communities, whereas damages impact the agriculturalist directly.

See also PHYSICAL ENVIRONMENT: Endangered Species.

Ronald M. Case
University of Nebraska–Lincoln

Licht, Daniel S. *Ecology and Economics of the Great Plains.* Lincoln: University of Nebraska Press, 1997. Noss, Reed F., and Allen Y. Cooperrider. *Saving Nature's Legacy: Protecting and Restoring Biodiversity.* Washington DC: Island Press, 1994. Samson, Fred B., and Fritz L. Knopf, eds. *Prairie Conservation: Preserving North America's Most Endangered Ecosystem.* Washington DC: Island Press, 1996.

WOMEN IN AGRICULTURE

See GENDER: Women in Agriculture

XIT RANCH

The XIT Ranch encompassed more than three million acres across ten counties on the Llano Estacado in western Texas. Considered the largest cattle ranch in the world, the XIT also leased land in the Dakotas and in Montana. The XIT stretched for more than 200 miles in the Texas Panhandle and had 575 miles of outside fence. The first 22,000 cattle arrived from Fort Concho in 1885 and the number maintained on the XIT eventually grew to 150,000. The ranch, which employed as many as 100 cowboys, was organized into seven divisions with a headquarters at Channing. The brand XIT was the idea of Ab Blocker, a trail driver who persuaded management that any good brand should be easy to make with a simple iron, but also be difficult to brand over by rustlers.

The land the XIT was established on was sold by the state of Texas to the Chicago-based Capitol Syndicate Company in 1882. This became the Capitol Freehold Land and Investment Company, Ltd., in 1885, which included investors from the United States and Britain. The Syndicate Company received title to the land in exchange for constructing a new capitol building in Austin. The Capitol building, completed in 1888, ultimately cost $3,224,593.45, which meant the Syndicate Company paid $1.07 per acre for the land that would become the XIT. Because of the high price of land and the declining prices of cattle, the XIT was dismantled in the early twentieth century. The last XIT cattle, 13,560 head, were sold in November 1912, and the vast ranch was sold in large parcels to other ranchers and in small acreages to farmers from 1901 to the 1950s.

Kenneth C. Dagel
Missouri Western State College

Haley, J. Evetts. *The XIT Ranch of Texas and the Early Days of the Llano Estacado.* Norman: University of Oklahoma Press, 1953. Nordyke, Lewis. *Cattle Empire: The Fabulous Story of the 3,000,000 acre XIT.* New York: William Morrow and Company, 1949.

Architecture

Old Germantown bank, Garland, Nebraska

ARCHITECTURE

In what sense can we speak about an architecture *of* the Great Plains? Such a narrative would necessarily derive from essential characteristics of the whole place—flora and fauna, climate and weather, geology, topography, and horizon—and would address building with compelling reference to this ground. Alternatively, we might speak of architecture *on* the Plains, using spatial location as our primary criterion. Either approach might work, but this essay will follow the former, first because the region is defined, in good part, by properties of the natural place, and second because architecture, at root, creates cultural places *within* natural place.

Acknowledging natural place as the ground for architecture changes the perspective on our view of building. Congruence between these "two" places can be discerned by thinking of both in terms of form and structure or, metaphorically, as mind and body. Though it is not possible to conclude an entirely homogeneous interpretation of building from the diverse constructions on the Plains, this approach forces us at least to think about architecture and place in other than human-centered terms. This perspective reveals an incongruence between the two aspects of place that was present from the very beginning of European American entry to the Plains. This story is at variance with those we have heard before.

Ancient Place

Original peoples evolved within an architecture of place. Because the Plains region includes many places and peoples, a diverse realization of architecture occurred. This resulted in part from materials variability, in part from prevailing climatic conditions, and in part from evolving cultural preferences.

A defining characteristic of all prehistoric architecture in the region was the use of construction materials taken directly from the place. Grasses played important roles, particularly in the tallgrass areas, where they were utilized for thatching, matting, and underlay and as wattling for clay-daubed walls. The most spectacular use was the historic Wichita lodge of the Southern Plains, though pole-and-grass huts may also have found early use in widely scattered Central Plains locations.

Similarly, grassland soils played a role in most of the more substantial constructions. Partially excavated interiors were characteristic of many permanent lodges. Some early square and rectangular houses utilized wall systems of closely spaced posts that were wattled and daubed with clay. Clays were also used in the southwestern Plains to plaster floors, make wall bricks, and raise puddled walls. Highly consolidated soils or sedimentary rocks were utilized principally along the High Plains of the western part of the region. Caves formed by the erosional undercutting of streams were home to early big-game hunters along the northwestern Plains from 5,000 to 10,000 years ago. Later cave sites have been located all across the western margins of the

region. Stone masonry dwellings were built in the rugged canyon lands and escarpments of the southwestern Plains. The use of soils culminated in the earth lodge.

Plains fauna also provided raw materials for construction. Bison skins were used from historic times back into the more distant past, perhaps as many as 5,000 years ago on the plains of southern Alberta. The historic tipi is the evolved descendant of a long line of skin lodges.

The extensive repertoire of walling material contrasted with a limitation in roof structure. A scarcity of forested areas limited the location, size, and duration of permanent settlements. Temporary campsites and smaller lodges built of poles with mat, grass, bark, or skin coverings could utilize woods such as willow in more widely scattered locations. But substantial lodges needed large trees for posts, beams, and rafters; permanent villages were therefore built near major wooded streams and rivers.

The formal aspects of this early architecture are more difficult to determine than its structure. Evidence gleaned from archaeological investigation is difficult to interpret, especially in projecting three-dimensional forms from two-dimensional remains. Nevertheless, two distinct patterns, one of circular forms and the other of rectilinear forms, can be broadly discerned.

The oldest remains are found along the western High Plains, where ubiquitous rock circles mark the base of what were circular lodges. Rocks were used to secure the covering of the lodge to the ground or perhaps to stabilize the poles of the structure. Ancestral in design to the historic era tipi, these structures are oldest and most numerous on the Alberta Plains and become more widely scattered and presumably later to the south. The more recent circles mark larger lodges than earlier ones—the adoption of the horse by nomadic peoples increased the size of lodge that could be transported.

In aggregate, the rock circles also reveal the size and configuration of villages, which evidently varied from just a few to hundreds of lodges and from random configurations to villages composed of linear and segmental arrangements. Occupation of some villages was also associated with other great rock formations, most notably, the giant circular works that today are called medicine wheels. These sacred sites apparently served advanced astronomical functions. One of the most spectacular is atop Medicine Mountain in the Bighorn range of present-day Wyoming.

Among the oldest of the rectangular-pattern houses were those constructed at the beginning of the second millennium of the current era along the middle Missouri River of contemporary North and South Dakota. These semisubterranean houses had floors one or more meters below the surface, with entrance through the southerly end of the house via a long, covered ramp. A slightly raised platform usually occupied the entrance end and sometimes extended along the sides. The hearth was

along the long axis. Structurally, these houses appear to have been gable-roofed buildings, supported by ridgepoles and side walls built of closely spaced posts.

Entirely different rectangular houses have been unearthed in the southwestern Plains. Dating from nearly the same time, one built in the upper Washita River drainage contained a central hearth and two central posts. This plan is similar to lower Arkansas valley Caddoan houses of the mid–thirteenth through mid–fourteenth centuries. Closely spaced posts around the perimeter indicate wall lines and narrow, protruding entrance passages. The roof was likely hipped and thatched, while walls appear to have been closed with wattling.

More ubiquitous was a square, four-post lodge that appeared throughout the Central and Southern Plains from the tenth through the fifteenth centuries and that came to be adopted along the middle Missouri River somewhat later. Built with considerable variation in size and detail, this house type appears to be an enlarged version of the two-post rectangular house, constructed with a hipped or pyramidal roof. The nearly square plan typically had rounded corners with walls of closely spaced posts that undoubtedly were wattled and daubed. On the western portions of the Central Plains they were built on or near the surface, while to the east they were semisubterranean.

Initially, square houses were not oriented to any particular direction, but over time the four posts came to be set at the semicardinal points. As the structure was reoriented, the entrance vestibule was typically built facing east. The commodious interiors utilized a variety of features, such as benches and screens, to divide the space into different compartments. Square-lodge villages were typically located on the first or second terraces of rivers and streams, while the village pattern, regardless of size, tended to organically follow the terrain of the terrace. Fortifications were rare except in the middle Missouri region of the Northern Plains, and there they protected only a portion of the extended village.

Perhaps the most distinctive adaptation of the four-post square house occurred along the southwest margins of the Plains in the upper Canadian drainage of what is now the Panhandle of Texas. Particularly interesting are villages in the Antelope Creek basin, where the house was oriented to the cardinal directions and had a very low, east-facing entrance passage. The house floor incorporated raised benches with storage bins. Another raised platform, either protruding into the house or occupying a projecting extension of the west wall, was often found opposite the door. Hearths were centrally located.

Construction technology further distinguishes these houses. Walls were built of puddled clay or clay bricks alternating with horizontal stone slabs. Occasionally, vertical posts were used to stabilize the clay walls. Most interesting was the use of various forms of rock foundations and footings: single or double

Sioux tipis, Fort Buford, Dakota Territory, May 1881

rows of vertical stone slabs set into the ground, the latter with rubble fill, comprised the most unusual system.

Village patterns were also distinct. In several, lodges were built contiguously into large communal blocks that seem to have been a function of choice and not of site limitation. Room configuration was complex. Circular rooms served as antechambers to one square house in each block, possibly indicating some kind of communal function.

Other multichamber complexes were built farther to the northwest along the upper reaches of the Canadian and Arkansas drainages and to the east along Ladder Creek, a tributary of the Smoky Hill River (in contemporary New Mexico, Colorado, and Kansas, respectively). The latter, a pueblo-like construction, dates to after the Pueblo Revolt of 1620. Known as El Cuartelejo, it was associated with the Plains Apache.

Even as the house-pattern preference of the Plains villages coalesced around the four-post square lodge, a shift toward a circular plan had already begun. Four-post circular lodges, presumably walled with wattle and daub like their square counterparts, were occasionally found as minority forms within some square-house villages. Examples from about A.D. 1000 to 1400 appeared along the Salt Creek drainage of the Smoky Hill River in what is now western Kansas and along Muddy Creek in the South Loup River system of present-day Nebraska. Other early circular lodges existed to the south of the High Plains rock-circle clusters in the rugged Apishapa Canyon of the upper Arkansas River in present-day southeastern Colorado. Dating from the latter half of the thirteenth century, these were single- and multichamber dwellings constructed of upright stone slabs. They varied in size from postless and single-post to four-post structures; the latter seems to anticipate four-post circular earth lodges.

The circular earth lodge itself apparently appeared after 1450 and was common until the European American invasion. This house type was adopted by virtually all the semisedentary communities from the Central Plains northward. It was like earlier square lodges in the utilization of the four interior posts, the central hearth, the extending entrance vestibule, and the system of roof rafters. Aside from its plan, major distinctions from its predecessors occur in the perimeter structural system and the earthen covering. In structure, vertical wall members were replaced with a post-and-beam system, and roof rafters rested on the beam rather than on a wall plate. Wall members were leaners that rested against the perimeter beam. The space beneath these leaners, to the outside of the posts, was used for a variety of purposes, including sleeping platforms, storage, and altars.

Other lodge types of the protohistoric period adopted the circular form as well. Hunting camp lodges along the middle Missouri of

the Northern Plains were built with four center posts whose beams supported leaners that peaked like a tipi and marked a circle on the ground. Central Plains Apaches built seasonal lodges that made the circular motif more explicit. There the imprint of the leaners was mirrored in the internal structure, where typically five and sometimes six interior posts were set in a circle around the hearth. The entrance was less an appendage than a protuberance of the curvilinear form.

On the Southern Plains another circular lodge emerged that became a Plains house type of importance equal to the earth lodge. Known primarily from historic Wichita structures, the thatched or grass lodge utilized wall-roof poles set firmly into the ground, bent across an internal post-and-beam system, and tied together at the peak. Light horizontal stringers were tied to these "rafters" to strengthen the frame and provide support for bundled grass thatch. Another set of stringers was applied over the thatch to help secure it to the frame. Older grass lodges in the Red River valley along the Texas-Oklahoma border apparently were built upon a four-post plan. The evolved Wichita house, however, utilized a circular, multipost system that retained some of the significance of the old four-post lodge in the designation of principal posts for the four directions.

A similar evolution occurred with the earth lodge into the historic period, at least among some tribes. Protohistoric Pawnee villages in the lower Loup River valley of present-day Nebraska were composed of four-post circular lodges, while historic Pawnee lodges utilized from six to eight or twelve interior posts set in a circle. This was also the case with historic Omaha lodges. Thus, while four-post circular lodges continued to be built on the Northern Plains, in the Central and Southern Plains four-post structures gave way to multipost circular structural systems that reflected the circle described by the external walls.

While the full meaning of this evolution cannot be known, some significant patterns

Pawnee earth lodge, ca. 1871

can be discerned. Three principal architectural forms share the multipost—or multipole—circular configuration. All three utilized exterior surfaces that were, in essence, angular projections that began the vaulting over of the dwelling from the plane of the earth. Neither wall nor roof in the Western sense, these surfaces formed a continuous vaulting of the dwelling that projected upward from a circle inscribed on the earth. The whole material body of the Plains was also reflected in these forms: soil, the geological and biological basis for the life of the place, was reflected in the earth lodge; grass, the principal flora of the Great Plains, was reflected in the thatched lodge; and bison, the principal faunal life of this place, was reflected in the skin lodge.

In a real sense, the mind of original Plains peoples converged with the body of the place and evolved a climactic Great Plains architecture. The shapes and cycles of things were echoed in the evolved architecture. The vast expanses of the Plains are defined by the circular horizon, and from the horizon vaults the still more vast sky. Within this expanse the rhythmic cycles of the cosmos—of the earth, moon, sun, and stars—are plainly evident. Here the great circle of the terrestrial world, the horizon, marked the boundary of place. Native peoples reflected the shape of the place in forms that mirrored the place. Cycles and the place were celebrated in material form—from lodges to medicine wheels and from great camp circles to contemporary dance arbors.

Disembodiment

Further evolution of Native architecture was eclipsed by the rapid conquest of the Plains by European Americans, who defined the place from a distance. Disembodied, abstract concepts—following the Cartesian lead—took power and control over the ancient evolved body of the place, and anthropocentric priorities began to rift the place to pieces, first in mind, then in body.

The Great Plains was objectified on desks in Washington and Ottawa, fueled by concepts of property and reports from scientific and military expeditions. New territories were defined by imaginary lines such as those drawn in abstract space using the global grid. This grid became part of the "architectural" transformation of the Plains; its extension via government surveys imposed a uniform Cartesian net over the whole of the "flat" and "empty" land. Ultimately, the cultural expression of these lines effected the complete transformation of place, with property lines determining the limits of thought.

Three institutions—the fur trade, the military, and the railroad—cleared the way for European American resettlement and the final phases of disembodiment. Though the early architectural presence of these institutions gave an appearance of being in place due to their use of local materials, their architectures quickly evolved into modern facilities of extraction in keeping with their institutional intent. Their mature architectural forms reflected the power their enterprises had over the body of the place.

Fur traders, here to strip the Plains of its fur- and skin-bearing animals, were the first to make permanent constructions. Early Missouri River posts were typically built of horizontal logs cut from the forested valley. Fontenelle's post at Bellevue (1822), in present-day Nebraska, consisted of individual buildings set around a loose, partially fenced courtyard. Its otherwise benign appearance was belied by the size of its warehouses. Later constructions such as those at Fort Union at the mouth of the Yellowstone (established in 1828) were formally designed, fully stockaded compounds. The head trader's house there is an early example of the elite colonial designs that quickly made their way onto the Plains.

Other fortified compounds were built, beginning in the 1830s, as new centers of extraction were established on the western High Plains. Wood was not abundant there, so clay technologies adopted from Hispanic sources were utilized. From Bent's Fort on the Arkansas northward to Fort John on the North Platte, the spread of southwestern construction techniques was made possible by an abundance of clays and a liberal use of Latino labor. Built as variations on the Spanish presidio, the adobe forts embodied corporate power with controlled, hierarchical plans that only looked premodern because of their old structural systems.

The second wave of corporate technology was associated with U.S. military campaigns. Pursuit of the nomadic western tribes for the security needs of traveling European Americans led to the initial establishment of numerous temporary posts. Selective adoption of premodern techniques facilitated construction where the preferred materials were rare or nonexistent: adobe masonry and panel-wall log construction are just two examples. Seldom were these valued for permanent installations. Lumber was imported as soon as possible, and by the turn of the twentieth century brick veneers were used extensively to lend an aura of permanence and substance to the most important posts.

Unlike the compounds of the fur traders, military architecture on the Plains was rarely fortified; industrial weapons technologies obviated this need. Drawn from Anglo-American architectural traditions, forts were orderly collections of individual buildings, hierarchically arranged and properly attired. Commanding officers' quarters were patterned after the hierarchical central-passage houses of eastern merchants. Though often scaled back to one and a half stories in height, their symmetrical facades and front galleries symbolically reinforced the government's role of establishing control over the region.

The technology that made the army's wholesale importation of construction materials practical, the railroad, also made the extensive European American resettlement of the region possible and did so in a fashion that significantly increased the pace of transformation. Railroads also controlled the location and character of the resettlement. Extensions into "unsettled" country allowed them to establish stops, to plat and own towns, and to control the towns' development. Rail towns were laid out following a small repertoire of plans, all focusing on the depot as the central place. Control of these geometric plats allowed railroads to shape the character of towns by deciding which lots were sold for what purposes and in what order. Business districts were created in immediate proximity to the depot, while churches and residential lots were pushed to the periphery.

The depot was the most intentionally symbolic structure. Plains railroads adopted standard plans that allowed for a variety of selections depending upon the position of the community within the economic structure of the corporation. Noteworthy among Plains designs was the residential depot, which provided housing for agents in locales that were not yet developed. The most common of these had living space on the second floor above passenger waiting rooms and agent offices.

Standard plans gave way to custom designs in communities that established themselves as significant economic entities. Elite designs created symbolic images for both the community and the corporation. This became problematic after World War II, when passenger service declined or ceased altogether. Corporations often quickly removed passenger stations, so that today the sight of a depot is rare and rarer still in its original location. Given the depots' prominent siting, their removal has often left significant gaps in the urban landscape.

An even greater impact of rail technology was in the movement of people and goods. This contribution to the disembodiment of original place facilitated the commodification of agriculture, with its widespread replacement of native flora and fauna. In addition to stockyards and trackside corrals, the most permanent and symbolic of the structures of disembodiment was the grain elevator. The early stacked-lumber elevators have largely disappeared except, perhaps, in more remote regions of the Northern Plains and Prairie Provinces. Victims of truck transport and corporate consolidation, the wooden structures were replaced with larger facilities built of reinforced concrete. The most substantial of these are in gateway cities along the fringes of the region. As the largest and most monumental constructions in the region, they symbolize the region's modern role as grain supplier to the world.

Another architectural result of this activity was the emergence of sod-wall construction. Utilized over vast areas of the central and northern farming Plains, it flourished with increasing European American settlement in the 1870s and followed wherever the prairies were broken. Its success as a building technology relied upon the manufacture of the steel plows needed to cut the tough prairie-grass roots; its demise rested upon Anglocentric notions of "proper" dwelling construction, the proliferation of industrial building technologies, and the destruction of the native prairies.

Replacement

The rest of the architectural story is dominated by the importation of building materials and abstract architectural ideas. The materials needed to accommodate Anglo-American ways of building did not exist in quantity in the Plains, so the new architectural body turned its back on the region. The story is one of replacement.

The existing place didn't feel like a potential home to European Americans, who had mostly been a people of the forest, first in Europe and then in America. On the Plains everything was strange and seemingly empty; as one early traveler put it, a single tree would have been enough to relieve the pain of loneliness and desolation. That tree would also have provided the preferred building material of the newcomer, and so wood, in the form of imported lumber, became critical to the replacement.

Though some wood was processed locally in river towns, regional riparian stands of timber, following the decimation wreaked by overland travelers, the army, the railroads, and the telegraph, were insufficient to meet anything but rudimentary local needs. Exogenous lumber was first supplied by steamboat, and some precut houses were imported during the first years of settlement. But it was the completion of the transcontinental railroads that started the massive importation of lumber into the Plains. The resettlement was built from the body of the upper midwestern and southern forests, and the trackside lumberyard became another symbol of European American resettlement.

Prior to the official opening of the Plains, the evolution of American wooden building had begun to standardize around light frame construction with nail joinery. Locally, however, framing initially followed diverse patterns. Heavy braced frames continued to be built for a time by easterners and some Germans, but increasingly these were superseded by modern light wooden frames. Idiosyncratic hybrid framing was not uncommon, but eventually the technology settled on more or less standard balloon and western platform frames.

The thought behind the replacement was as out of place as the lumber, and this was reflected in the forms the replacement took as well. In the more heavily settled sections of the region the superimposed spatial grid influenced the character of the new landscape from the beginning. Roads, fields, fences, lanes, farms, schools, churches, and towns all became subsets of the grid. Terrain and waterways no longer ordered culture or formed place; section roads and property lines did. In the farming countryside checkerboard fields planted in straight monocultural rows drilled the modern mechanistic order into the land itself. The place became changed at ever deeper levels.

Architectural form followed from the same mind that overlaid the landscape with the abstract grid. Though this modern, abstract mind held sway over the Plains, some communities initially embraced a wider variety of attitudes. Architecturally, before the final triumph of national modernism a more diverse presence established heterogeneous places throughout the region.

Diversity

For a time the Great Plains was inhabited by an international community—a historically contingent, multicultural presence of quite different and sometimes opposing belief systems. Their initial constructions represented a wide array of responses to the challenge of making place. Foreign immigrants often built in old ways that were familiar and comfortable. The transference of old forms was restricted by the extent a material was available to build in the traditional way. If it was not, or if one were instead attempting to conform to emerging national standards, then the old form was either abandoned for a new one built of lumber or it was modified to accommodate the new material.

When we think in regional architectural terms, we naturally look to the materials that form the body of the place, and here, due to notoriety, the sod wall comes first to mind. Its utilization across a broad expanse of the farming Plains, irrespective of culture, made the sod-wall dwelling a true regional vernacular of the replacement. The nature of the material's association with disembodiment, however, precluded its utility beyond the first or second generation of houses. Constructions of baled biomass (hay and straw), perhaps the only regional architectural invention, might have provided a sustainable counterpart to sod, though it appeared too late and in areas too sparsely settled to have had an immediate impact. Its recent resurgence is another matter.

Less popular than sod but still widespread were various clay-wall technologies. Unfired clay found use in brick masonry, puddled-clay, and rammed-earth constructions; its many iterations were known by diverse terms, depending upon the culture that utilized the technique. The clay technologies were primarily culture-bound, and while they were preadapted to the Plains environment, their adoption by others appears to have been only idiosyncratic. Black Sea Germans, Czechs, Poles, Ukrainians, and Hispanics were among the dominant builders in clay.

Diversity was also a theme in the utilization of other native materials. Variation in the type, quantity, and quality of stone led vernacular and elite masons to a remarkable variety of construction in surprisingly widespread locales, virtually everywhere sufficient veins of good-quality rock were found near the surface. Where quantity and quality supported commercial quarrying, elite buildings were constructed. High-quality architectural work can be found everywhere stone was used, but probably nowhere in such concentrations as in the Sioux Quartzite areas of southeastern South Dakota or the Flint Hills of eastern Kansas, where sophisticated dressed ashlar work was common.

Perhaps most surprising for the "treeless" Plains was the extent of log construction during the early settlement period. Diversity arose from the multicultural background of builders and the mixed flora of the region. Most of the log-timbering methods known to have been brought to America, as well as those that evolved on the continent, were utilized on the Plains.

Two factors influenced the use of native material: the first in which the "pioneer" was forced as a matter of necessity and a second in which settlers chose native material as a matter of preference. The former was spatio-temporally restricted to the ever-shifting line of resettlement. Few surviving constructions were built from strict necessity, and most of what remains derived from cultural preference. These were built predominantly by Germans, German Russians, Poles, Czechs, Finns, Hispanics, and Ukrainians.

Cultural diversity was also reflected in architectural form, especially among rural folk and the more conservative immigrants and during the first, second, and sometimes third generations of dwelling construction. Usually the diversity was the result of the direct transplantation of Old World forms.

Though dwelling types were all within a familiar western mold, the constructions of foreign-born settlers were often noticeably distinct from those of the native-born. Many early dwellings were built along ancient plans that accommodated preferred ways of living. Most of these modest dwellings were characterized by the presence of principal rooms—called halls in the English American tradition—and open plans that allowed direct entry into these rooms, preserving old, intimate relationships between the house and the land. The most prominent of the traditional builders were the Germans, German Russians (both Black Sea and Volga), Czechs, Poles, Ukrainians, and Danes. Their old plans were modified, with rare exception, by the adoption of American cast-iron stoves for heating and cooking. The abandonment of old-style hearths, stoves, and ovens did change the interior character of dwellings and often necessitated modifications to traditional foodways. Some built larger, more modern Old World dwellings, while others such as the Volga Germans and Danes chose from American house types that closely resembled familiar European forms.

Though some Anglo-Americans initially built traditional houses (usually a hall-and-chamber house), most erected modernized plans that abandoned halls in favor of kitchens and parlors. Other principal features of this modernization, whatever the kind of house, included the use of multiple thresholds and the accommodation of bedrooms and dining rooms—all reflective of the increasing dwelling size and room specialization characteristic of modern society's movement toward privacy, individuality, and separation from the land. Most of the early modern houses were variations on popular Georgian planning and formal symmetry. Later settlers adopted house types derived from rapidly changing national architectural fashion. The specific sequences of both the foreign- and native-born developments varied depending upon where and when initial settlement took place.

National Modernity

In the main, however, the architectural story of the Great Plains after European American immigration was about an architecture that just happened to be built on the Plains. In the broad sweep it was not substantially different from that developed anywhere else in the United States. There is no reason to retell that story here using local examples. It is, however, important to at least acknowledge the surge of national modernity as it played out on the Plains.

Easterners wasted little time in setting forth the national parameters within which this new place was to be defined; lumber was first, and the architectural pattern book was second. Mass-produced pattern books made the transference of formal architectural ideas out of place possible. Designs no longer needed to respond to locale; rather, they became abstractions that could be built on any "site," anywhere. Pattern books by eastern and British architects had already been a means for expressing and disseminating elite architectural ideas before initial resettlement began. Stylish houses could be and were built soon after the various territories were opened.

By the turn of the twentieth century, books by architects such as Chicagoan William Radford were produced for more popular consumption. Mail-order catalogs were likewise published by retailers like Sears and Montgomery Ward, offering not only designs but also precut materials ready for shipment. Soon local builders and lumberyards produced catalogs depicting their own repertoire of house designs. These were increasingly built in tracts of similar or identical dwellings.

National and "progressive" trends in farm building design were also perpetuated through the state and national agricultural journals that proliferated from the late nineteenth century. Following trends established earlier in architectural publications, they offered advice on lifestyle as well as technical information on buildings. Land-grant universities published technical leaflets with designs for essential farm and ranch building needs. The impact of these was substantial, and from around 1900 onward the agricultural landscape became architecturally more homogenized.

As the demand for architectural and engineering services increased, especially in the cities, more architects from the East migrated west. Some were trained under the apprenticeship system, while others, both native- and foreign-born, had also received academic training. Custom buildings of increasing structural competence and design sophistication were soon raised on the Plains, beginning in the boom years of the 1880s. By the next century academic training was virtually the norm. Education was provided by leading schools in the East, technical universities in Europe, and the Ecole des Beaux-arts in Paris. Some Beaux-arts-trained architects such as Thomas Kimball of Omaha were native sons who returned home after completing their schooling to contribute to the development of the region.

Local apprenticeship systems produced an extensive lineage of architectural practice that became the foundation for the licensed practitioners of the twentieth century. By midcentury several state land-grant and provincial universities had established architecture schools. Some local architectural firms have become national and even international concerns, made possible by the ideological trends of modernity and a globalizing economy.

Great Plains architectural output from the beginning of the replacement replicated abstract, national, and modern trends. Essential influences emanated from eastern cities, then from Chicago, then from the Pacific Coast, and finally from avant-garde Europe. Plains architects creatively adapted national and international design ideology to local problems, especially in the cities and for elite clients. Most moved freely from style to style (a legacy, first promoted by pattern books, of reductionism applied to architecture that divorced the design of a facade from the function and structure of the building) and have done so in every era to the present. Architects were often imported from cities like Chicago, Minneapolis, Kansas City, St. Louis, and New York for the most prestigious commissions.

While society's attitudes toward the modern were national, there was no tendency toward a national style following European American entry to the region. The national classical revivals of the first half of the nineteenth century were on the wane when resettlement commenced, and what followed was a rapid succession of stylistic gyrations. The first to proliferate on the Plains was the Queen Anne; it was a style with national extent, but it lacked national meaning. On the Plains the ethno-English associations of the style were vague; its popularity was more related to a booming economy, ideas of modern "progress," and incipient suburbanization—all concepts that had national overtones of their own. Otherwise, architectural style changed like the prairie winds with the fickle tastes of consumer capitalism.

Excellent products of these multifarious national and international trends dot the landscape, interspersed with delightful local and popular versions. But anything that might be suggestive of a distinct architectural character in the region was more the result of historical contingency. Boom periods—via the sheer quantity of construction—established an initial character to rural and urban landscapes that was distinct from older areas, east or west. These remain present in most locales that peaked economically before the current era. Communities that experienced continued growth typically replaced the replacements and now are tending to resemble the "anywhere" landscapes so emblematic of our time. In this kind of setting, individual monuments serve as symbols of place.

Differentiation

Two forms of architectural differentiation appeared during the first part of the twentieth century. The first sought explicit ethnocultural meanings. Designs generated by some foreign immigrants as they emerged from the background of settlement and forged a greater cultural presence on the land created distinctive local environments. Their architectural differentiation was more pronounced in a host environment dominated by revivals intended in part—via adoption of very selective European and American sources—to create the solidification of cultural hegemony. The second was intended to be a resistance to modernity, an attempt to reground architecture in nature and place through a revival of vernacular design, craft tradition, and, if not indigenous materials, at least the use of natural materials.

Ethnic architectural emergence by some groups appears less culture bound than the result of individual or community tastes and idiosyncrasies; these groups tended to assimilate quickly, with a concomitant architectural melding into the host landscape. Among them, however, Swedes did participate in an Academic form (a self-consciously learned and sophisticated approach to the revisioning of earlier styles) of what has been dubbed "National Romanticism" via the Augustana Synod architect Olof Z. Cervin of Rock Island, Illinois. His picturesque churches drew inspiration from national revivals then current in the Nordic countries. The most explicit of his work was the yellow brick, stepped-gable campus of the Bethphage Mission in Kearney County, Nebraska. Danes also drew inspiration from the revivals in their homeland, though in a more provincial mode. This was evident in picturesque designs for folk schools such as at Nysted in Nebraska, but a more ubiquitous if less obvious ethnic presence was provided especially by Grundtvigian Danish churches, gymnasia, and other community buildings whose interiors were richly walled and ceiled in wood. This harking back to a distant forested past—and recalling wooden seafaring vessels—represents a distinct architectural expression on the Plains.

Also provincial but more a part of an Old World cultural continuum than a revival was the adoption of simplified baroque designs for the community buildings of freethinking Czechs. This "rustic" baroque was part of a nearly three-century extension of the European style. The latest Plains example was the 1921 Kollár Hall near Dubois, Nebraska. The later Orthodox churches of Ukrainian settlers in the Prairie Provinces were also continuations of traditions that had been perpetuated earlier in pioneer church buildings. The free expressions of Alberta architect Father Philip Ruh stand out, such as his Ukrainian Catholic Church of the Immaculate Conception of 1930 at Cooks Creek, Manitoba. In it Ruh retained the multipart articulated massing of traditional churches topped with domes (though not onion domes) but departed from tradition in his Germanic decorative embellishment.

More Academic in origin and related to the immigration of trained architects was the appearance of two German American national styles. Designs based upon the German Gothic were unobtrusive in the American context. Major examples of this *Spitzbogenstil*, or pointed-arch style, were built in German settlements throughout the region: Sioux Falls architect Joseph Schwarz's Holy Family Catholic Church (1903–6) in Mitchell, South Dakota, and J. P. Guth's St. Johns German Evangelical Lutheran Church of 1902 near Lyons, Nebraska, are representative of two common variations. The second, the *Rundbogenstil*, or round-arch style, was more than an ecclesiastical style. Breweries and other commercial and public buildings in German-dominated places were often constructed in this popular style. Frederick W. Paroth's St. Elizabeth Catholic Church at Auraria, Colorado (1898), Anton Dohman's St. Mary's Abbey Church at Richardton, North Dakota (1905–9), and Omaha's Anheuser Busch Beer Depot (1887) are exemplary of a very large repertoire of such designs.

The impetus toward national styles throughout Europe in the nineteenth century grew from emerging nation-state identity, an issue many immigrants brought with them. But the impulse applied equally to the dominant culture in the United States. By the turn of the twentieth century, a Georgian Colonial Revival coalesced that had national overtones among the native-born. Domestically, the style, reinforced in part by xenophobia, segued into various English Period house styles around World War I, then expanded to include period house choices from the western Europe of the old immigration.

Multiplicity was the rule for the nondomestic architecture of the first half of the twentieth century as well, but it was really a focus on taste and massive scale associated with the Academic trend in architecture that characterized American national romanticism of this period. Styles were chosen based upon often-vague notions of association—sometimes institutional, sometimes personal. Thus it could happen that an Academic skyscraper adorned in the Gothic Revival—a sort of "cathedral of commerce"—could appear a few blocks from a new Gothic Revival church, with no apparent contradiction in meaning. Whatever the associations, they may never have been known to the community at large. Such was probably the case with the appearance of the Romanesque Revival for many Catholic churches of this period. Derived from the Italian mode, the style flowed from Vatican influences within the religious hierarchy. To outsiders, taste and substance were probably the primary indicative aspects of Academic national romanticism. Though lacking in substance, this taste was promoted through a series of national expositions, including the Trans-Mississippi and International Exposition of 1898 in Omaha.

Another impulse of the trend toward associational design was a return to American regional culture. The lack of a prior European American presence on the Plains, however, was problematic. There was no regional style here to revive. One solution to this deficit was the use of imagination. Coronado's trek into the Southern Plains provided sufficient impetus for Omahans Thomas Rogers Kimball and Archbishop Richard Scannell to conjure the Spanish Colonial Revival as a style appropriate to the Central Plains. Kimball's St. Cecilia's Cathedral in Omaha of 1905–59 initiated an identity with the American Southwest before Goodhue's national popularization of the style at the 1915 Panama-California Exposition in San Diego. Spanish influences were more prominent on the Southern Plains, where the baroque also found expression in a variety of eclectic designs such as the city hall and auditorium of 1927 in Wichita Falls, Texas, by Lang & Witchell in association with Voelcker & Dixon.

The restrained mission style was more popular, again particularly on the Southern Plains, where it was adopted by the Southern Pacific and Santa Fe Railroads as part of their corporate identities. The Santa Fe station at Great Bend, Kansas, is perhaps exemplary. Kansas City architect Louis Curtiss's more inventive reprisals of southwestern forms such as his 1907 depot and hotel at Syracuse, Kansas, and the 1909–11 Lubbock, Texas, depot are probably high points of this kind of regional identity. As remote as these associations seem today, they do appear more grounded, at least in the South, than the more imaginary associations drawn directly from the Mediterranean such as the 1918 Broadmoor Hotel in Colorado Springs.

The various forms of romanticism held sway side by side with the California Craftsman styles that were popularized in the Plains in the Bungalow movement of the 1910s and 1920s. Craftsman houses were unlike the period revivals in that they lacked cultural roots in the American scene. They were similar to them, however, in a favoring of craftsmanship and vernacular design as well as a philosophical intent to reground buildings in nature. The import of both movements from the East and West Coasts, however, merely continued the trend of building out of place. Neither style's attempts to build with indigenous materials were very successful. With rare exceptions, these buildings were little more than philosophical statements lacking connection to the Plains.

During this period indigenous materials were used almost exclusively in recreational architecture such as the river rock constructions at the Medicine Park Resort in southwestern Oklahoma, the earthen shelters of Emiel Christensen's private retreat, PaWiTo, along the Platte River in Nebraska, and the occasional public works project. Exceptions, however rare, can always be noted. A short-lived river rock vernacular developed on the Plains near Medicine Park, Oklahoma, and here and there distinctive porches appeared on bungalows throughout the region; those built with glacial erratics are probably the most spectacular.

One Chicago influence was related to the Craftsman style in a general way. It was felt in the Plains to an extent in Prairie-style adaptations that borrowed superficial motifs for application to otherwise derivative Colonial and catalog forms. The style probably had the closest theoretical affinity to what might have been a Plains architecture but was fully realized by only a smattering of buildings. This, in spite of the fact that the Plains boasted examples of both Frank Lloyd Wright's earlier and later Prairie houses: the Sutton house of 1905 in McCook, Nebraska, and the Allen house of 1915 in Wichita, Kansas. Fundamental Prairie-style forms—such as low, horizontal, hip-roofed houses—reappeared after World War II with the popularization of suburban ranch-style houses. But these were principally unrelated to the earlier movement and had their genesis on the Pacific Coast.

Beyond these halting movements, an impetus toward regional differentiation simply never materialized, other than through individual efforts. The ephemeral Corn Palace at Mitchell, South Dakota, and the Texas Spring Palace at Fort Worth are two unconventional examples. Both were built to celebrate a kind of cyclical architectural stylishness with their annually changing facades of modern products derived from the body of the Plains; at Mitchell, however, the motifs are applied to a building designed following Moorish sources. More permanent regional motifs appear in places with varying degrees of appropriateness and success. The cowboys and Indians at the Frontier Hotel in Cheyenne (1936) and the architectural inscriptions utilized on the Natrona County Courthouse in Casper, Wyoming, are examples. The cowboy and Indian had appeared earlier as incised sculpture on the frontispiece of the Panhandle-Plains Historical Society Museum of 1932 at Canyon, Texas. Architect E. F. Rittenberry also incorporated the sculpted head of a longhorn steer and a gridwork of local cattle brands surrounding the entrance.

Perhaps no effort surpassed that of architect Bertram Goodhue for the Nebraska State Capitol. It was not regional in style but was an effort to generate monumental form that was responsive to the Plains landscape. Though much about its design and embellishment was anticipated by the local elite, it came to Goodhue alone to conceive of the broad horizontal base and landmark tower in terms that were modern and more explicitly symbolic of place. Goodhue's genius needed an equal in local visionary Hartley Burr Alexander to develop the thematic elaboration of the building. His plan for the murals, mosaics, exterior sculpture, and inscriptions was broadly historical, occasionally transcendental, and firmly rooted in the ethnocentric milieu. Themes associated with place were prominent.

However one might criticize the Canyon and Lincoln buildings today (or even the one at Mitchell), they provide occasions for looking back at place, at least toward cultural place. All three are expressions of regional identity that are still locally revered. But the thinking behind their expression was as fleet-

Nebraska State Capitol

ing as a late summer thunderstorm. Modern thinking never really looked back at place again. (I. M. Pei's National Center for Atmospheric Research at Boulder may be an exception of a different sort.)

Hypermodernity

Both the Canyon and Lincoln buildings were reflective of an emerging modern style. In spite of its initial theoretical concern with "space," even European modernism in the Plains ultimately continued to promote a progressive and reductive architectural style. This cause has been taken up with even more seriousness by so-called postmodern (really hypermodern) developments, in which now, quite literally, decorated facades and the seeking of new forms have again become principal architectural problems.

Other aspects of modernism's focused reductionism have different consequences. We can look to a further loss of the sense of body in place that might have been anticipated by one of the region's most noted modernists, Norman, Oklahoma's Bruce Goff. The philosophical and psychological split of mind from body that has informed this essay and that rift site from place could be exaggerated by Goff's free expressions, which seem to have been made possible only by the prior abstract detachment of site from place. He further pursued architecture as a container split apart from the outside, a container in which the appearance of nature, if it were allowed at all, would be thoroughly domesticated and constrained from the inside.

This latter aspect of Goff's production raises issues concerning a hypermodern extension of the replacement. Of what we can say is left of spontaneous Great Plains place (topography and atmosphere), neither seems destined to survive our assault. Suburbanization's sprawl-

ing consumption of land increasingly results in the massive replacement of terrain and topsoil. Topography is forced into the flat linear conditions of abstract space and the engineer's drawing board and then is sometimes mechanically reintroduced to add "character" to the new, designed landscape.

Concerning atmosphere, the replacement further affects human embodiment in place. The main vehicle for this effort is air conditioning, a technology that, no matter how desirable under acute health-related conditions, conflicts with atmospheric place beyond the effects of consumption and pollution. Hypermodern promotion of air conditioning, designed within a very narrow and absolute "comfort zone," serves to further human disembodiment through a more anesthetized disengagement from place than ever before.

See also IMAGES AND ICONS: Corn Palace / INDUSTRY: Fur Trade, Lumberyards / NATIVE AMERICANS: Paleo-Indians, Pawnees, Sacred Geography, Wichitas / WAR: Frontier Forts.

David Murphy
Nebraska State Historical Society

Boddy, Trevor, ed. "Special Issue on Prairie Architecture." *Prairie Forum* 5, no. 2 (1980). Erpestad, David, and David Wood. *Building South Dakota: A Historical Survey of the State's Architecture to 1945*. Pierre: South Dakota State Historical Society Press, 1997. Henderson, Arn, Frank Parman, and Dortha Henderson. *Architecture in Oklahoma: Landmark and Vernacular*. Norman OK: Point Rivers Press, 1978. Henry, Jay C. *Architecture in Texas, 1895–1945*. Austin: University of Texas Press, 1993. "Historic Places: The National Register for Nebraska." *Nebraska History* 70, no. 1 (1989). Nabokov, Peter, and Robert Easton. *Native American Architecture*. New York: Oxford University Press, 1989: 122–73. Noel, Thomas J. *The Buildings of Colorado*. New York: Oxford University Press, 1997. Sachs, David H., and George Ehrlich. *Guide to Kansas Architecture*. Lawrence: University Press of Kansas, 1996. Starr, Eileen F. *Architecture in the Cowboy State, 1849–1940: A Guide*. Glendo WY: High Plains Press, 1992. Upton, Dell,

ed. *America's Architectural Roots: Ethnic Groups That Built America*. Building Watchers Series. Washington DC: Preservation Press, 1986: 100–165.

ARBORETUMS

The term *arboretum*, a place where woody (tree, shrub, and vine) plants are grown for scientific study and/or educational purposes, is often used interchangeably with *botanical garden*. A botanical garden may also include herbaceous (nonwoody) plants and may have an arboretum collection as part of its program.

In the Great Plains, arboretums and botanical gardens are vital components in the residents' quality of life; they have long taken their cultivated plantings seriously. Arbor Day, an annual tree-planting day now observed throughout the United States and in several other countries for the purpose of foresting, reforesting, or beautifying was first advocated by Julius Sterling Morton of Nebraska. In 1872 Nebraska was the first state to recognize Arbor Day.

Arboretums and botanical gardens in the Great Plains serve varied purposes: for ornamental demonstration plantings suited to particular climatic conditions; for plant hardiness and variety improvement research; for environmental, conservation, and plant science studies; and for recreation and aesthetics. They can be as urban as the Denver Botanical Garden, as rural as the Dyck Arboretum of the Plains in Hesston, Kansas, as nonnative as the Nikka Yuko Garden in Lethbridge, Alberta.

Education is an important mission of all arboretums and botanical gardens. The Morden Arboretum in Manitoba, occupying about 60 acres of a 640-acre federal government research farm started in 1915, evaluates and develops hardy landscape plants and in turn works closely with industry to disseminate information. The Cheyenne Botanic Gardens in Wyoming, started in 1976 and operated by the city park system, serves the community as a source of horticultural demonstration and education in its 6,800-square-foot passive solar greenhouse and outdoor gardens.

Nebraska and Oklahoma have distinctive network systems of arboretum sites across their states. The Nebraska Statewide Arboretum, started in 1978, has forty-eight diverse affiliated sites, including the University of Nebraska Botanical Garden and Arboretum on two Lincoln campuses, featuring hardy and experimental plantings to enhance the teaching, research, and public service mission of the institution. The Nebraska Statewide Arboretum is also involved in rare plant conservation as an affiliate of the national Center for Plant Conservation. The Oklahoma Botanical Garden and Arboretum, started in 1991 by Oklahoma State University at Stillwater, has thirteen affiliate sites, including the Myriad Botanical Gardens and Crystal Bridge in downtown Oklahoma City.

Plant collections exist in nearly all areas of the Great Plains. University campus sites include McCrory Gardens/South Dakota Arboretum at South Dakota State University in Brookings, Patterson Garden at the University of Saskatchewan in Saskatoon, and Devonian Botanic Garden at the University of Alberta in Edmonton. Independent organizations operate the historic International Peace Garden on the border between North Dakota and Manitoba, and Botanica, the Wichita Gardens in Kansas. Province, city, and university interests operate the 2,300-acre Wascana Centre in Regina, Saskatchewan. The Fort Worth, Texas, Botanical Garden, started in 1933 and operated by the city park system, is the oldest of its kind in the Southern Great Plains. Plant evaluation trials are conducted at the North Dakota State University Research Arboretum.

The trend in landscape design today is one of developing a regional style. In the Great Plains, this approach includes using more native plants in a less formal design.

See also ASIAN AMERICANS: Nikka Yuko Garden / IMAGES AND ICONS: International Peace Garden.

Twyla Hansen
Nebraska Wesleyan University

BALED BIOMASS BUILDINGS

The idea of using bales of hay as building blocks emerged in the North Platte River valley after the appearance of mechanical baling equipment in the latter half of the nineteenth century. Although there were relatively few baled hay buildings, the technique was nonetheless a significant architectural innovation of the Great Plains.

Processed from the material body of the place (usually from either prairie flora or agricultural waste), the technology came to be centered in the Sandhills of Nebraska. Other structures were built on the nearby High Plains of Nebraska, Wyoming, and South Dakota. The historic period of importance dates from about 1900 to 1940, but a contemporary resurgence—principally using oat, wheat, and rye straw—has already surpassed the original in numerical and spatial significance.

Bales were used structurally as giant building blocks, stacked in the running bond common to masonry construction, with the constituent materials positioned either vertically or horizontally in the block. Bales were set in either mud or concrete mortar or were simply stacked one upon another. Wooden or metal rods often pinned the bales together and secured window and door frames to the walls. Plates were likewise fastened to the tops of walls. Roofs were most often of the hipped type, which allowed for even compression along all walls and obviated the need to raise the wall high into a gable end. After a short period of settling or sometimes an extended period of occupancy, the exterior of the bales was fitted with chicken wire and then plastered with clay, lime, or cement stucco. Interior walls were typically lime plastered.

Buildings constructed from bales were economical structures with outstanding thermal qualities. Sturdy far beyond expectation, properly built and maintained structures have an indefinite life span. One century-old dwelling still stands west of Alliance, Nebraska. Evidence exists that the material in old baled buildings does not readily deteriorate, and cattle will still eat hay from old bales. While most constructions were intended as dwellings, others were used as schools, a service garage, a two-story restaurant, and a church.

The postmodern resurgence of the technology emanated from research by folklorist Roger L. Welsch, principally from articles that appeared in the 1973 alternative publication, *Shelter*. Most contemporary buildings use bales either as infill for post-and-beam structures or veneering for light wooden frames, but structural bale walls, now dubbed the "Nebraska style," also enjoy renewed popularity. The renaissance is centered in the American Southwest but is significantly international in scope. The diffusion back into the Plains began in the 1990s.

See also FOLKWAYS: Welsch, Roger.

David Murphy
Nebraska State Historical Society

Myhrman, Matts, and Judy Knox. "A Brief History of Hay and Straw as Building Materials." *Last Straw* 1 (1993): 1, 4–5, 18–19; 2 (1993): 16–17, 19, 23; 6 (1994): 17–18. Steen, Athena Swentzell, Bill Steen, and David Bainbridge. *The Straw Bale House*. White River Junction VT: Chelsea Green Publishing Company, 1994. Welsch, Roger L. "Sandhill Baled-Hay Construction." *Keystone Folklore Quarterly* 15 (1970): 16–34.

BARNS

The barn is the defining architectural feature and the central focus of the Great Plains farm. Most Great Plains barns were multipurpose buildings designed for hay storage and shelter for draft horses and cows. Variations include dairy (milking) barns, sheep barns, and barns designed primarily for grain storage.

Barn design is influenced by the origins and traditions of the barn owner and builder, the type of agriculture for which the barn is used, and the building materials that are available locally. The first settlers in the Great Plains brought with them barn-building traditions from Europe and eastern North America, but the scarcity of timber in the Great Plains inhibited the building of the large, multistory, multipurpose, timber-frame barns that were common farther east. Post-and-beam barns constructed of heavy timbers with mortise-and-tenon joints are rare in the Great Plains.

Barn building in the Great Plains did not really take off until the coming of the railroads, which increased the availability of dimension lumber and wire nails. These changes in transportation and building technology, combined with the invention of the hay fork and hay track for loading hay in the barn, resulted in a revolution in barn design. The old, heavy, timber-frame construction was abandoned in favor of the lighter, more versatile balloon framing using dimension lumber.

The typical late-nineteenth- to early-twentieth-century barn of the Great Plains is a rectangular two-story structure, consisting of a low-ceilinged main floor topped by a huge haymow. The main floor is divided into stalls for draft horses or mules and a few dairy cows as well as bins for grain. The development of the double-sloped gambrel roof, which is most frequently associated with barns today, allowed as much as 50 percent more hay storage than the single-sloped gable roof and eliminated crossbeams, allowing for efficient use of a hay track to load hay. The desire for ever larger clearspan space in the haymow eventually led to the development of arched roofs constructed of rounded trusses, which became popular in the first few decades of the twentieth century.

Another common barn design in the Great Plains is the midwestern three-bay barn, also called the feeder barn or hay barn. This light timber-frame barn is divided into three sections, or bays, under a long, sloping gable roof. The center section is used for floor-to-ceiling hay storage. The two side bays hold stalls for animals and sometimes bins for grain storage. This style of barn was popular

Dairy barn, Kranzburg, South Dakota

with farmers whose main need was for a dry storage area for hay rather than for livestock shelter.

Land-grant universities had a widespread influence on early-twentieth-century barn design in the Great Plains. Agricultural engineers developed innovative building designs for all types of farming purposes. They designed special barns for housing dairy cows, hogs, and horses and for storing hay, grain, and machinery and distributed the plans to farmers nationwide through the cooperative extension service. With the availability of ready-made plans and even mail-order barns, barn design became more standardized throughout the country, although regional variations and ethnic building traditions continued well into the twentieth century. The stone barns in the Flint Hills of Kansas and the log barns of the Laramie Plains of Wyoming are two examples of Plains regional variations based on available building materials and local building traditions.

An example of the influence of the land-grant universities is the Wisconsin dairy barn. Although dairy farming is not extensive in the Great Plains, this standard dairy barn still appears as a feature of the Great Plains landscape. Built to specifications provided by the University of Wisconsin–Madison, the dairy barn is distinguished by its rectangular shape (generally, 36 feet wide and up to 100 feet long), north-south orientation, and rows of small windows along the basement walls. The low stable area, designed for milking cows, was topped by a large gambrel roof, which provided ample storage space for hay. As silos gained popularity in the late nineteenth century, they were attached to the end or the side of the dairy barn.

Round and polygonal barns were also designed by agricultural engineers at land-grant universities and promoted as efficient for milking cows and feeding cattle. Although these unusual barns are not common, all Plains states have a few examples. Most are now considered local landmarks, and many have been actively preserved.

Most barns were built by farmers themselves, sometimes with the help of professional barn builders. Some builders developed distinctive styles that can still be recognized in certain localities. While most barns have little ornamentation, elements of architectural styles such as Italianate scroll work, Gothic pointed gables, and even western false fronts were sometimes incorporated into barn design. Some barns also display evidence of regional craftsmanship in brick, stone, and woodwork. Cupolas, used for ventilation, provided the farmer or barn builder with an opportunity to add a special flourish to the barn to distinguish it from those around it.

By the 1950s construction of the multistory barn had virtually ceased and was replaced by the single-story pole barn. Unlike the traditional American barns, which housed several activities under one roof, modern pole barns are specifically designed for a single purpose. They feature huge, open interior spaces, allowing easy access for large machinery. In spite of the predominance of metal-clad pole buildings on farms across North America, the traditional gambrel-roofed barn persists as the symbol of American agriculture, appearing in everything from advertising of farm products to logos of agricultural organizations and corporations.

The decline in the number of farms and in farm acreage in the Great Plains has resulted in the loss of many traditional barns. Even on working farms, these barns face an uncertain future. Barns designed specifically for the storage of loose hay or the hand milking of cows outgrew their original usefulness decades ago. When the tractor replaced the draft horse for plowing and other farm chores, stalls for horses were no longer needed. Farmers found haymows inefficient and sometimes structurally inadequate for storing baled hay. As agriculture became more specialized, many farmers sold their livestock altogether, and barns that had once been the center of the farm operation stood empty.

In spite of the widespread loss, there are still many traditional barns in use across the Great Plains. Some have remained in constant use and have been adapted to fit the changes in agricultural practice and technology. For instance, on many dairy farms, wooden stalls gave way to stanchions and later free stalls, and mechanical milking and waste removal systems were added and improved over the years. In some cases a new milking parlor was built, and the old barn is now used for housing dry heifers and raising calves. In the Northern Plains, where many farmers have sold all their livestock and produce only crops, traditional barns have been converted to store large quantities of hay or grain or to shelter farm equipment. These changes usually involve enlarging doorways and sometimes raising or removing the haymow floor to open up the interior space.

The sheer size of barns and their simple, functional design have made them treasured architectural landmarks as well as utilitarian structures. While many barns have been lost to development or neglect, a significant number of farmers across the country have maintained their older barns and adapted them for modern farming uses.

Mary M. Humstone
National Trust for Historic Preservation

Gyrisco, Geoffrey M., ed. *The Farm Landscape: A Bibliography of the Architecture and Archaeology of Farmsteads and Settlements in Wisconsin and in the Areas of Origin of Its Settlers in the United States and Europe.* Madison: State Historical Society of Wisconsin, 1997. Halsted, Byron David. *Barn Plans and Outbuildings.* New York: Orange Judd Company, 1918. Noble, Allen G., and Hubert G. H. Wilheim, eds. *Barns of the Midwest.* Athens: Ohio University Press, 1995.

BLACK SEA GERMAN ARCHITECTURE

Black Sea German immigrants who moved from southern Russia to the Northern Great Plains in the late nineteenth and early twentieth centuries carried a blend of German and Russian culture that distinguishes them from neighboring ethnic groups. One component of this culture is a basic vernacular architecture that was executed in a variety of ways by individual builders.

These buildings are not the ephemeral sod structures commonly associated with Great Plains settlement; rather, skillful builders used a range of materials from clay and rammed earth to stone and balloon-frame construction. Fundamental to all the buildings except frame is a basic clay mixture that serves as a load-bearing material in walls, as a mortar, and as filler between floor joists. Puddled clay is a freehand method of construction that utilizes no wooden forms to erect load-bearing walls. Instead, clay is piled directly on the foundation up to a height of about thirteen to eighteen inches. Stones are often combined with the clay in regular courses near the exterior surface of walls to serve as filler. *Batsa* is the term used to describe sun-dried bricks made of puddled clay. They are shaped by pressing the clay into wooden molds to form bricks ranging in length from ten to eighteen inches. Rammed-earth walls are formed by piling puddled clay between vertical wooden forms and compressing the clay with a hand-held ramming device. Masonry construction employs puddled clay as mortar in load-bearing walls of either coursed rubble or field-stone. Traditional balloon-frame construction is also used, in some cases with batsa bricks placed between the studs of the exterior wall to serve as insulation.

Black Sea German houses represent an unusual synthesis of German, Russian Ukrainian, and other western European architectural features. Their domestic architecture developed through an integration of specific morphological prototypes expressed in the form, scale, function, and materials of each building. A typical house is distinguished by its one-story height with a loft and an attached vestibule (*vorhausl*) on the long side leading into the kitchen. The rather narrow, rectangular shape is covered with a gable roof. A smaller two- or three-room dwelling is known as a *semelanka*, while larger house-barn combinations, which provide living quarters for people and animals under a single roof, are called *kolonistenhaus*.

Rooms are subdivided by partitions made of wood, puddled clay, and batsa, creating houses two or three bays wide and one or two rooms deep. A central kitchen is typically flanked to the left by a parlor or living room (*stube*) and sometimes by a storage or sleeping room on the right. Some dwellings have a black kitchen (*schwarze kuche*), a small, centrally located, six-foot-square room that functions as a separate space for preparing and cooking food. Abutting the black kitchen and heating the parlor and rear bedroom (*kammer*) is a large clay oven (*bachofen*), which is distinctively Black Sea German. The spatial arrangement of the black kitchen and bachofen is not uncommon in many regions of western Europe; the form was subsequently transplanted through the Black Sea region to several settlement areas in the Northern Plains.

See also EUROPEAN AMERICANS: German Russians.

Michael H. Koop
Minnesota Historical Society

Koop, Michael H. "An Analysis of German-Russian Houses in South Dakota Based on Their Origin, Form and Materials." Master's thesis, University of Wisconsin–Madison, 1989. Schnurr, J. *Heimatbuch der Deutschen aus Russland*. Stuttgart: Landsmannschaft der Deutschen aus Russland, 1967–68. Sherman, William C. "Prairie Architecture of the Russian-German Settlers." In *Russian-German Settlements in the United States*, edited by Richard Sallet. Fargo: North Dakota Institute for Regional Studies, 1974: 185–95.

BRICK MASONRY

Brick masonry—more precisely, construction utilizing modular fired-clay products—is one of many building technologies found in the Great Plains. Bricks are the product of a complex manufacturing process that converts naturally occurring raw clay into an inert, vitrified building material by baking it to very high temperatures (kiln firing). The quality of the finished product (in terms of hardness, uniformity, and color) varies widely, based on the raw clay "body," the method and conditions under which the bricks are fired, and the chemical or mineral impurities present in the clay. Colors typically tend toward either a buff tan color or a reddish color range. Masonry is regarded as a highly desirable building material in the Great Plains, as elsewhere, because of its durability and fire resistance as well as the expression of permanence it conveys.

Reasons for the prevalence of brick masonry in the Great Plains include the time frame of settlement, environmental requirements, and the imported skills and traditions of ethnic groups that settled on the Plains. In many locations the earliest buildings were constructed of other available materials, but after settlements became better established the second generation of buildings often included brick masonry in combination with more costly ornamental stone masonry. Masonry is a relatively massive material with good thermal performance where temperature varies widely from day to night. Brick is inherently fire resistant, a characteristic important in both tightly grouped buildings in urban commercial districts and isolated buildings in the countryside. Many communities adopted building codes mandating masonry construction in downtown locations after disastrous fires like the Great Fargo Fire of 1893 in North Dakota.

The type of clay used to make bricks is present in many Great Plains locations. Immigrants to the Plains (particularly those from northern Europe) were familiar with methods necessary to make bricks and often selected town sites where clay was available and where there were suitable fuels for firing kilns. German Americans in particular had a fondness for brick masonry in buildings. Early brick making sometimes entailed firing piles of hand-molded bricks in the open, referred to as a scove kiln or a clamp. This method was soon supplanted by beehive-shaped kilns, which were fired intermittently, and eventually by industrialized tunnel kilns, which were fired continuously. By 1900 there were more than twenty brick manufacturers in North Dakota alone. Now there are fewer than a dozen manufacturers on the entire Northern Plains.

Brick-making technology led to the design and construction of many types of masonry buildings, including civic and commercial buildings, schools, churches, and a variety of agricultural structures (structural clay-tile silos, grain storage buildings, and rural creameries). Use of brick to construct houses in the Great Plains has been relatively uncommon, but in certain localities significant concentrations of brick residences do occur in both towns and rural areas. Notable examples include areas of German American settlement in river valleys where brickyards are situated, continuing a pattern found farther east in the Minnesota River valley and along the Missouri River near Hermann, Missouri. Similar patterns of brick production, distribution, and usage occur from the Prairie Provinces to the Southern Plains, with the extent of brick masonry diminishing as one moves farther westward onto the Plains. Buildings that appear to be of primarily brick masonry construction were often actually constructed using a mixture of available materials, commonly including wood-floor framing. Brick buildings were generally limited to about four stories in height, which made them relatively well suited to the scale of buildings in most Great Plains cities and towns.

Brick masonry buildings range from the vernacular to high-style buildings designed by professionally trained architects like Frank Lloyd Wright. Historically, ornamentation tended to be accomplished less by molding unique, individual pieces of brick than by the patterns in which the bricks were assembled. Detailed features of brick masonry buildings thus reflect the skill of the masons who erected them and the aesthetic judgment of the architects who designed them.

Steve C. Martens
North Dakota State University

Foster, Joseph Arnold, ed. *Accounts of Brick Making in America Published between 1850 and 1900*. Claremont CA: Privately published, 1971. McKee, Harley. *Introduction to Early American Masonry*. Washington DC: National Trust for Historic Preservation, 1973. Noble, Allen G. *Wood, Brick, and Stone*. Amherst: University of Massachusetts Press, 1984.

CEMETERIES

Rural cemeteries in the Great Plains are familiar, ritual landscapes that serve a fundamental human need for remembrance, commemoration, and spiritual healing. Historically, people have sought out places of natural beauty as burial sites and attempted to cultivate natural beauty according to a sense of ritual order they regarded as appropriate. Cultural notions about death and the commemoration of departed loved ones make cemeteries rich places in which to look for expressions of cultural meaning. The mosaic of burial traditions in

Haskell County, Kansas, 1941

the Great Plains is as varied as other cultural indicators. Observers of the Great Plains landscape can discern a range of cemetery types, including cemeteries associated with country churches, designed or otherwise planned secular cemeteries in many towns and cities, and cemeteries with distinctively ethnic characteristics. A more recent phenomenon in Great Plains cemeteries, as elsewhere, is the lawn cemetery or memorial garden with minimally visible, flat stone markers.

The most widespread and familiar cemetery tradition on the Plains is cemeteries alongside country churches connected with a particular religious denomination and a specific congregation. These cemeteries have often outlasted the churches themselves after their congregations have dwindled. Country church cemeteries display an orderliness according to rules that vary with religious sect. Many Catholic cemeteries, for example, exhibit perimeter rows of trees and occasional walking paths that connect stations of the cross. Some church cemeteries historically encouraged burial plots grouped according to family, while others simply allocated each grave site in chronological sequence based on the order in which members of the community died. Most cemeteries adjacent to country churches were laid out according to a simple, classical sense of order, generally symmetrically and in straight rows, often alongside a straight access driveway.

A romantic, Victorian vision of death permeated many social groups at the time communities were being established in the Great Plains. In the mid-1800s landscape architects in large eastern cities designed cemeteries according to a newly conceived cemetery-planning tradition called the "Rural Romantic" cemetery movement. These picturesque, naturalistic cemeteries were widely copied and adapted in parklike cemeteries constructed in the Great Plains around the turn of the twentieth century, particularly in towns but also in some country cemeteries. In addition to less formal arrangement, Rural Romantic cemeteries often display tranquil water elements, weeping trees and groupings of plants with varied textures, and overtly reflective markers with symbolic meanings. In general, plant materials in Great Plains cemeteries include more diverse and prized cultivars than one might expect to find in the surrounding landscape. Cemeteries change significantly over the seasons as graves are marked with holiday decorations.

Ideas about cemeteries and burial practices are persistent over time, and there is good indication that ethnic populations on the Plains adhered to conservative funerary customs imported directly from native homelands. Ethnicity and religious affiliation clearly influenced the layout of rural cemeteries. Czech American cemeteries on the Plains (including cemeteries designed by secular associations and those consecrated by more traditional Catholic congregations) were laid out in a highly formalized order, with a gridded configuration and a formal allée, or double row of trees, flanking the driveway. Moravian cemeteries were customarily divided into choirs, grouped by age, gender, and marital status. German Americans, Black Sea German Americans, and Ukrainian Americans consecrated some of the most austere, strikingly powerful, and isolated cemeteries, reflecting previous settlement experiences and the harsh circumstances of life in the Great Plains. Handcrafted wrought-iron crosses are a conspicuous feature marking graves in these cemeteries. On the Southern Plains, Hispanic cemeteries, or *camposantos*, reflect traditions of burial in which individual graves are differentiated with low fences (termed *cerquitas*) and niches for sacred reliquary objects. The scraped or swept grave, often attributed to African influences, is a distinctive tradition in cemeteries on the Southern Plains. Other common characteristics of African American burial grounds are the use of homemade grave markers, mounded earth over graves, and "found object" grave decorations such as bottles and light bulbs. Distinctive ethnic traditions can be observed in cemeteries established by many other groups.

In addition to location and overall layout, cemeteries are made distinctive by the features and details constructed within them. Typically, grave markers in most Great Plains cemeteries are made of stone, although there are many examples of wooden, concrete, and wrought-iron markers. Iconographic symbolism often coincides with one of the three traditions described above. In classical church cemeteries, upright stones with family names can be expected. Many Rural Romantic cemeteries include benches for reflection, obelisks, and markers either in the shape of broken tree trunks or topped with urns covered by a draped cloth. Messages inscribed on grave markers range from cowboy epitaphs to academic poetry, memorial photographs, and beautifully composed foreign-language remembrances. Other constructed features include perimeter fences, setting the cemetery apart from its surroundings, and distinctive ornamental gates that often bear the name of the cemetery or congregation. Many local and state historical societies have genealogy interest groups that specialize in informative cemetery grave marker research and inventories.

See also FOLKWAYS: Grave Markers.

Steve C. Martens
North Dakota State University
Nancy Volkman
Texas A&M University

Jackson, Kenneth. *Silent Cities: Evolution of the American Cemetery*. New York: Princeton Architectural Press, 1989. Sloane, David C. *The Last Great Necessity: Cemeteries in American History*. Baltimore MD: Johns Hopkins University Press, 1991. Zelinsky, Wilbur. "Unearthly Delights: Cemetery Names and the Map of the Changing American Afterworld." In *Geographies of the Mind: Essays in Historical Geosophy*, edited by David Lowenthal and Martyn J. Bowden. New York: Oxford University Press, 1976: 171–96.

CLAY CONSTRUCTION

Soils with clay content suitable for building purposes are found throughout the Great Plains. The most prolific use of these was in the industrial manufacture of fired brick, which flourished in countless brickyards around the region from the early years of European American settlement through the first decades of the twentieth century. The earthen construction described here, however, refers to materials used in traditional, preindustrial technologies.

Four techniques predominated. Most common was sun-dried brick, in which clay was first worked into molds, later removed and allowed to dry in the sun, then laid up to form walls. A second was the puddled-clay wall, which was built up from large lifts of clay that were shaped after the clay had set. Rammed-earth construction used puddled clay that was packed or stamped between a formwork. Numerous variations on these techniques are known, including the use of clay lumps and the incorporation of field stones into rammed walls. A fourth technology, wattle and daub, utilized a wooden framework—often of woven materials—in and over which puddled clays were packed to form a reinforced massive wall. Clays were also commonly used as plasters for walls, roofing membranes, finishes, and masonry mortars.

The manner of processing the clay was similar in all cases. Varying quantities of clayey soil and water were mixed together by hand, animal power, or some mechanical device, fusing the soil particles and producing a dense composition ideal for building purposes. Other materials such as straw, grass, manure, and sand were often added to the mix to improve performance. The most common processing method was to mix the materials in a pit near the building site.

Earthen building in the Great Plains occurred in multiple waves. The oldest involved wattle-and-daub walls constructed by Indigenous peoples in the Central and Southern Plains. The most pronounced of these were evident in square and early circular lodges built between 500 and 1,000 years ago.

Initial European American expansion into the western and southwestern Plains was built upon the adoption of Hispanic adobe brick technology by fur traders. Their construction facilitated by imported Latino labor, these architectural forms often imitated the fortified Spanish presidio. The earliest examples were built by trader John Gantt and his competitor, the Bent, St. Vrain & Company. Gantt's Fort Cass was built in 1834, while Bent's Fort followed closely; both were located along the upper Arkansas River. Bent's Fort was state of the art for the fortified trading post. It was a large presidio built by laborers from Taos; its form and construction influenced a number of later trading posts. By 1838 four more adobe forts had been built along the upper South Platte. Along the upper North Platte River, Forts Platte and John, both adobe-walled trading posts, were completed by 1841.

Adobe construction spread farther with the adoption of the technique by the United States Army. Recommendations concerning the utility of adobe bricks in the West did not appear until 1848, coincidental with but unrelated to the adobes' first military use on the Plains in what became Nebraska. There their use was recommended by an old trader with experience in adobe construction, Andrew W. Sublette, then a captain under the command of Lt. Daniel P. Woodbury at the new Fort Kearny. Their first adobe construction was a large storehouse, completed in November 1848. In 1849 Woodbury purchased the American Fur Company's adobe Fort John and renamed it Fort Laramie. By 1852 a number of new adobe buildings had been constructed at the post. Other forts were eventually constructed, in whole or in part, of adobe all over the region.

The final waves of earthen construction appeared quite independent of the earlier ones. Foremost among the European builders were Black Sea Germans. During their three-generation stay on the steppes of Russia they learned the local building methods, including the manufacture of *kohlsteine*, or sun-dried bricks (called *batsa* in South Dakota), puddled clay, and rammed-earth techniques. Earthen construction was introduced wherever Black Sea Germans settled, from Kansas to North Dakota. Mennonites in Marion County, Kansas, used both clay brick and rammed earth, while puddled clay, clay lumps, and rock-filled rammed earth were also used in the North and South Dakota settlements.

Other major introductions were made by Czechs and Poles. The five-room Polish house constructed in 1882 by Mary Zwfka Roschynialski in Sherman County, Nebraska, was built of puddled clay. The Czech structures were located in South Dakota and Nebraska and were of sun-dried brick, rammed earth, and puddled clay (*hlinêný*). Other immigrants also used clay technologies, including Germans and Danes. In North Dakota Ukrainians introduced post-and-earth construction, a form similar to wattle and daub. This technology included wattle—or lathe—between earth-fast posts, with packed clay between the lathes in a kind of rammed-earth fashion, before finishing with clay plaster both inside and out.

The last introduction of earthen building

emanated again from the Hispanic Southwest, with the early-twentieth century immigration of Latinos from Mexico, New Mexico, and Texas to the west-central High Plains of Nebraska and Colorado. Their first adobe dwellings were of the familiar flat-roofed variety, with projecting vigas, while later houses were built with the gabled roofs common to the host culture. Large hoppers rather than pits were used to mix the clay.

Though clays were widely available and eminently suitable for construction, both structurally and as thermal mass, on the Plains, little or no influence was ever exerted on the architecture of the region outside of the source introductions. While much Anglo-American literature claimed to have "discovered" and initially promoted clays for building purposes prior to the opening of the Plains, some authors changed course and criticized mud bricks as worthless for construction before settlement had commenced, deterring earthen materials' potential evolution into a regional vernacular architecture.

David Murphy
Nebraska State Historical Society

Koop, Michael H., and Stephen Ludwig. *German-Russian Folk Architecture in Southeastern South Dakota.* Vermillion: South Dakota State Historical Preservation Center, 1984. Murphy, David. "Building in Clay on the Central Plains." In *Perspectives in Vernacular Architecture*, edited by Thomas Carter and Bernard L. Herman. Columbia: University of Missouri Press for the Vernacular Architecture Forum, 1989: 3: 74–85. Valdez, Anthony Arnold. "Hispanic Vernacular Architecture and Settlement Pattern of the Culebra River Villages of Southern Colorado (1850–1950)." Master's thesis, University of New Mexico, Albuquerque, 1992.

COLD WAR ARCHITECTURE

The proliferation of tract housing, the popularization of fallout shelters, and the construction of missile bases were all a result of shifts in the American and Canadian outlook during the cold war. The rise of suburbs and the construction of large military facilities during and after World War II changed greatly the architectural fabric of the Great Plains. The mass-produced housing of Levittown, New York, was the model for the construction of subsequent suburbs, including those in the Great Plains. William Levitt, the builder, used methods that had been developed by the military during World War II for the rapid construction of installations. Levitt popularized off-site prefabrication and task specialization in the construction of postwar housing that was intended to supply the needs of returning servicemen.

Ranch-style houses are typical of the 1950s developments outside the larger cities of the Great Plains. Most of these homes are one story, with a low pitched roof and a wide eave overhang. They also lack the formalized spaces of earlier eras. This absence of dining rooms, hallways, and elaborated entryways made these houses less expensive to build. Picture and ribbon windows are often present. An attached or built-in garage is also typical, a physical manifestation of the importance of cars in suburban living.

With the deterioration of relations between the Soviet Union and the United States in the late 1950s and early 1960s came the threat of nuclear war and the need for fallout shelters. In a 1959 publication the Office of Civil and Defense Mobilization provided plans and installation instructions for four different types of fallout shelters: a basement shelter constructed with concrete blocks, an aboveground double-wall shelter constructed with concrete blocks, a prefabricated metal shelter, and an underground concrete shelter. Advertisements for houses constructed in the 1950s and 1960s suggested that shelters could be included in new home construction at a nominal cost.

Public and private shelters usually relied on barrier shielding. This shielding, usually thicknesses of concrete or earth, was intended to provide protection by absorbing part of the radiation generated by a nuclear explosion. Due to their additional mass, multistory buildings were believed to provide the most protection. Based on this idea, shelters were established in the lower levels of schools and office buildings.

Active bases and missile sites of the Strategic Air Command are still present throughout the Great Plains. Many of the buildings are unassuming in appearance, with one- or two-story structures belying the presence of a multilevel complex below the surface. The initiation of the intercontinental ballistic missile (ICBM) program represented both a physical and a psychological shift in land use in the Great Plains. F. E. Warren Air Force Base outside of Cheyenne, Wyoming, was selected as the first ICBM complex in 1957. ICBM complexes were also constructed at the Mead Ordnance Depot and at Offutt Air Force Base in Nebraska. Early complexes, housing Atlas squadrons, included a launch operations building, three launch and service buildings, a power plant and pump house, storage magazines, and a tower, all enclosed within a security fence. The buildings are monolithic and industrial in appearance. The launch operations and launch and service buildings were constructed of concrete. The silos are of semihardened concrete, capable of withstanding overpressures of twenty-five pounds per square inch. Auxiliary buildings, such as those found at the entry to the facility, were generally wood frame clad with corrugated metal. While the first facilities emphasized centralized placement, later facilities utilized plans that separated launch control centers and missile silos over large areas.

Other ICBM programs included Shark, Thor, Jupiter, Titan, Minuteman, and Peacekeeper. The Minuteman B missile was installed from 1958 to 1962 in 200 silos scattered across 8,000 square miles. Minuteman B was replaced by the Minuteman III in 1973. Minuteman III and Peacekeeper are active programs. Some abandoned Atlas and Titan facilities have been remodeled into homes in several states, including Kansas.

See also IMAGES AND ICONS Missile Silos / WAR: Cold War.

Dori M. Penny
Larson-Tibesar Associates

Martin, Thomas L., Jr., and Donald C. Latham. *Strategy for Survival.* Tucson: University of Arizona Press, 1963. May, Elaine Tyler. *Homeward Bound: American Families in the Cold War Era.* New York: Basic Books, 1988. Office of Civil and Defense Mobilization. *The Family Fallout Shelter.* Washington DC: Government Printing Office, 1959.

COMMERCIAL ARCHITECTURE

Buildings designed specifically for commercial and related business functions appeared early and figured prominently in the settlement of the Great Plains. Stores, banks, office blocks, restaurants and bars, and hotels were all well-defined types by the mid–nineteenth century, when the region was opened to European American settlement. While many new settlers took up agriculture and lived dispersed on the land, others came to pursue trades and professions and were actively engaged in town building. In many parts of the Great Plains the competition among nascent communities was intense. Many boosters harbored visions of their towns becoming metropolises in the span of a generation, just as had occurred to midwestern centers such as Chicago and St. Louis.

Virtually from the inception of settlement, a principal business street began to emerge in Great Plains towns. This first-generation growth was impermanent in both intent and appearance. Buildings were generally of wood-frame construction and were utilitarian in character, with little or no embellishment. They were also modest in size, occupying only a portion of their lots and seldom exceeding one or two stories. Like the businesses they held, these buildings were initial ventures; it was presumed they would be replaced later by more substantial quarters.

The overplatting of towns in the Great Plains led to many instances where communities fell far short of original expectations. At the same time, hundreds of places did advance to the second generation of growth, which entailed permanent commercial buildings erected approximately two to four decades after initial settlement. The new buildings were generally of substantial masonry wall construction. They consumed the full width and much of the depth of their lots and boasted ornamental fronts, often with cast- or stamped-iron details. The majority of these buildings were two stories tall; some, especially those housing hotels, theaters, and fraternal organizations, were three or four stories. Only in the largest cities such as Omaha were greater heights reached before the turn of the twentieth century.

Second-generation buildings were tightly clustered for purposes of convenience but also out of a collective desire to make the community appear impressive. As in towns farther east, these commercial centers rose as symbols of attainment and potential for their communities. Individual design and group arrangement emulated established urban models; only the character of overall development—the wide main street, the low density of surrounding residential areas, the expansiveness of open space beyond—distinguished Plains towns from older cities to the east. Aspirations of metropolitan stature began to dissipate by the early twentieth century, as the industry needed to sustain large concentrations of people failed to materialize.

The region supported few true cities; in numerous cases town centers did not expand significantly during the decades that followed. Instead, commercial development was a process of small, incremental changes to the existing fabric, many of them in response to functional demands. The growth of retailing, for example, led to the construction of new department stores and, by the 1920s, the remodeling of others to accommodate emerging national chains such as Montgomery Ward and J. C. Penney. With the rapid rise of electrification and telephone networks, utility companies often erected fancy new quarters. In the late nineteenth century many towns of 2,000 people or more had at least one theater, often called an opera house. Many opera houses were later supplanted by movie theaters, with exotic fronts and interior spaces. The hotel was often the largest, best-appointed building in town. Between 1900 and 1950 and especially during the 1920s, with the proliferation of automobile travel, imposing multistory hotels were erected with elaborate public rooms. The automobile also led to the creation of new building types, including sales and service facilities, filling stations, and tourist courts.

Until the 1960s most downtowns retained the business functions that served their communities and the rural areas beyond. But even by the 1920s small-scale business dispersal was evident in the larger towns. Many of these facilities were modest, purveying routine goods in residential neighborhoods. Clusters of more than two or three commercial buildings were rare except in cities or in districts catering to large numbers of college students. While most filling and service stations were concentrated in the center, growing numbers were dispersed, primarily along main routes through the community. These arteries also attracted tourist courts, which generally were sited near the periphery.

Substantial changes occurred to the appearance, configuration, and siting of commercial buildings during the second half of the twentieth century. Designs sporting the abstract vocabularies of modernism, rare in the region before World War II, had become ubiquitous for buildings of all types by the 1950s. Many commercial establishments already standing were given new veneers, often covering the entire facade. Spiraling demand for space to accommodate motorists led to the demolition of existing buildings for parking lots. Banks erected conspicuous new quarters on the edge of downtown in what had been residential blocks. Business development away from the center grew. By the 1960s shopping centers had emerged to challenge the downtown's hegemony, and the continued development of such places has led to the decay or a much narrower focus of commercial functions in the core. Commercial centers in

many small towns have been rendered redundant by improved highway access to regional facilities in larger communities. As pronounced as such shifts have been, they embody national characteristics no less than did the commercial center of the nineteenth century.

See also CITIES AND TOWNS: Main Street; Small Towns.

Richard Longstreth
George Washington University

Hudson, John C. *Plains Country Towns.* Minneapolis: University of Minnesota Press, 1985. Larson, Paul Clifford, ed. *The Spirit of H. H. Richardson on the Midland Prairies: Regional Transformations of an Architectural Style.* Ames: Iowa State University Press, 1988. Longstreth, Richard. *The Buildings of Main Street: A Guide to American Commercial Architecture.* Washington DC: Preservation Press, 1987.

CORN PALACE

See IMAGES AND ICONS: Corn Palace

COUNTRY CLUB PLAZA

Announced in 1922 and begun according to a substantially revised plan the following year, Kansas City, Missouri's Country Club Plaza was the most ambitious and the most influential comprehensively planned retail complex realized in the United States before the mid–twentieth century. Through this work, real estate developer J. C. Nichols became the nation's foremost exponent of a revolutionary new approach to the creation of business centers, an approach that has had a profound impact on the American landscape since World War II.

While not the first example of its kind, the plaza far exceeded any precursors in the scope and detail of its program. The complex was conceived to encompass more than 200 retail outlets and approximately the same number of professional offices and other services for the consumer public. Planned in conjunction with Nichols's vast Country Club District, the plaza was intended eventually to serve a population of tens of thousands from that precinct and other parts of the metropolitan area as well.

Nichols's plans broke with convention in several important ways. First, the plaza was planned as a physically unified entity: buildings and all other components of the landscape were designed to present a harmonious ensemble that would be visually distinct and engaging. Second, the complex was planned to have a unified tenant structure: businesses were carefully selected not only for the quality of the goods and/or services they purveyed but also in terms of how each contributed to the greater whole. Third, this ensemble would operate in a coherent manner under the auspices of a single management office and a business association to coordinate hours, special events, and advertising, among other features. Fourth, rather than having a defined center, with a hierarchy of land values based on proximity to it, all property in the Plaza would be of more or less equal importance in order to foster market return. Fifth, the com-

plex was oriented to motorists rather than to public transportation routes. Streets were unusually numerous and wide to facilitate movement and parking. Buildings could be no more than two stories high to preclude vehicular congestion as well as to equitably distribute land value. In 1928 two parking lots were added in prime locations, to be followed by several others designed to facilitate access. Finally, all these objectives were possible because every aspect of the scheme was undertaken by the J. C. Nichols Company, which retained ownership of the property and control of the operation.

The plaza was designed to be built incrementally as demand in the Country Club District and other outlying areas increased. Construction was brought to a halt by the Great Depression, then resumed in the late 1930s. Numerous additions were made following World War II and fewer in recent years. Through the years the plan has been fluid and dynamic, adjusting to ongoing change.

Nichols intended the plaza to complement rather than compete with the downtown shopping district. Early tenants mostly retailed high-end specialty and convenience goods. By the late 1930s a few chain stores had been included. During the postwar years branches of several major downtown stores and a large Sears unit were added, rendering the complex a more significant regional destination.

Nichols was instrumental in advancing the term *shopping center* for his unusual venture. Within a few years of its commencement, the plaza began to be emulated by other developers, and it soon acquired legendary status. Although the layout and exuberant Spanish baroque–inspired imagery were no longer considered relevant in the postwar era, the success of the plaza's underlying concept had a decisive impact on the proliferation of shopping centers nationwide.

See also CITIES AND TOWNS: Kansas City, Kansas and Missouri.

Richard Longstreth
George Washington University

Longstreth, Richard. "The Diffusion of the Community Shopping Center Concept during the Interwar Decades." *Journal of the Society of Architectural Historians* 56 (1997): 268–93. Longstreth, Richard. "J. C. Nichols, the Country Club Plaza, and Notions of Modernity." *Harvard Architecture Review* 5 (1986): 120–35. Worley, William S. *J. C. Nichols and the Shaping of Kansas City.* Columbia: University of Missouri Press, 1990.

CZECH ARCHITECTURE

Ethnic Czechs from the historic provinces of Bohemia and Moravia brought diverse architectural traditions to the Great Plains. They were part of a general emigration that began after the Peasant Uprising of 1848 and surged after emigration became legal in 1867. Czechs on the Plains clustered in large settlements in southeastern and south-central South Dakota, north-central and northwestern Kansas, and all over Nebraska. Later settlements were established in central and north-central Oklahoma. The diversity of their architectural tradition resulted from many factors but primarily from the dominance of the emigration by small farmers and cottagers with their varied provincial cultures.

An ancient preference for log construction was transferred to the Plains by skilled Czech carpenters. Log dwellings (*roubený dům*) were characterized by wall beams planked on the inside and outside faces, then set with full dovetail notches and chink spaces between the beams. Interior log partitions were dovetailed through the exterior walls, and many structures utilized mortised vertical timbers for door and window jambs. Several incorporated the old common rafter roof with tie beams, while most adopted the simple American rafter roof secured to the wall plates. Outbuildings were often built in the same fashion, though for these other variants also occurred, such as saddle, V, and full dovetail corner timbering on unplanked beams.

Some Moravians built earthen walls for their dwellings (*hliněný dům*). The most common technique utilized unfired clay brick, but puddled clay and rammed earth were not uncommon. As Czechs adopted light frame construction, brick, puddled-clay, and lime mortars were used as nogging between the studs for stability and thermal mass. Other masonry construction was utilized by Czechs from both provinces. Skilled masons commonly employed rubble, coursed rubble, and occasionally ashlar work for limestone walls. High Plains Czechs in Kansas built with sod.

Though considerable provincial variation in house type existed in the way of room size, configuration, and nomenclature, the distinctive Czech tradition is evident as variations on the quintessential Czech house (*Středočeský dům*), a type common in the heart of Bohemia. Its tripartite arrangement (*trojdílný dům*) was comprised of a main room or hall (*světnice*), a narrow central entrance chamber and fire room (*síň*), and a small storage chamber (*komora*). In old times the síň was subdivided to provide for a kitchen (*černá kuchyně*) at the back, but on the Plains that practice was abandoned with the adoption of American cast-iron stoves. The Pechan house in Yankton County, South Dakota, is the only tripartite dwelling known to have subdivided a kitchen in this manner.

Numerous first-generation houses were built as single-room dwellings comprised exclusively of the světnice; these often became the basis for an expanded house. Two-room variations (*dvojdílný dům*) were the most popular, with both an old type (composed of síň and světnice) and a new American type (světnice and komora) being built in large numbers. The latter type simply eliminated the technologically redundant síň and moved the single threshold to the big room. This dwelling was similar to another ancient type that included doors into both rooms. Derived from the house with attached stall, on the Plains the smaller space of this double-door type took the role of principal room.

In most Czech lands, houses were oriented with their narrow gable ends facing the public street. Typically symmetrical, this gabled facade (*štít*) continued to be built as the "front" wall in North America. If decoration was present at all, it was focused on this gable. On the Plains, where farms were dispersed rather than tightly clustered into rural villages, the front gable was often reoriented to the rear, where it faced the farmyard. Thresholds were in the side of the house, also oriented toward the farmyard or toward a small courtyard if in an urban setting.

The old practice of attaching farm buildings to the house and creating single-unit courtyard farmsteads was abandoned on the Plains, where land seemed limitless. Following American practices, farm buildings were built as detached structures, though often these were initially modeled along traditional lines; separate stables, cowsheds, and hay barns were built instead of the single multifunctional American barn. The first "barn" in Valley County, Nebraska, was a traditional three-stall stable with walls raised half a story in height to accommodate a diminutive hayloft. Other remnant examples of the old practices exist, such as the Veselý house with its attached cowshed in Knox County, Nebraska, and the long Merkwan "barn" in Bon Homme County, South Dakota, with its linearly attached storeroom, cowshed, and stables.

Early modernized houses retained traditional characteristics while becoming modestly enlarged. Most common was the one-and-one-half-story cross-wing house (*uhlový dům*), which provided bedrooms in the loft and a kitchen, parlor, and chamber (storage room, often with a bed) on the first floor. Typically, this house was still built with a single threshold, now into the kitchen, the new principal room of the modern dwelling. By the early twentieth century other houses were copied from American models, though interiors often continued to accommodate traditional living practices by emphasizing kitchens and dining rooms as principal spaces. These houses also continued to be built with facades facing the farmyard.

Also distinctive was the public landscape created by the ideologically diverse Czechs, who included freethinkers, Catholics, and Protestants. Old animosities among these groups produced separate cemeteries, which served symbolic, ceremonial, and even nationalistic functions. A fourth kind, a community cemetery with a more inclusive intent (*Česko-Slovanský hřbitov*), initiated efforts at ethnic cohesiveness. Many of the cemeteries, particularly the national cemeteries of the freethinkers (*Česko-Národní hřbitov*), were distinctly designed and landscaped, while others also exhibited homeland features such as curbed and planted graves, cast- and wrought-iron crosses, and Hussite iconography. Elaborately crafted iron entrance gates were typical.

While church architecture was primarily denominationally derived, freethinking and Sokol (gymnastic society) halls often followed popular Czech styles. The most distinctive of these were latter-day American versions of the provincial baroque style (*venkovské barok*) that had become popular in the Czech agricultural villages after enclosure. The overt nationalistic associations of these designs on the Plains were in direct contrast to the Renaissance Revival of the elite national movement in Bohemia, where the baroque carried negative associations with the Counter Reformation. Many variations on the baroque were built, from the simple lunette fronts of halls such as Sladkovský at Pishelville (1882), to the modeled facade and doubly curved dormer of the 1903 Bílá Hora hall at Verdigre, both in Nebraska.

Built following the multifunctional model of the vernacular opera house (albeit in a distinctly noncommercial mode), the public halls of Sokols and Czech fraternal organizations served a variety of community needs, including dances, speeches, funerals, gymnastics, and banquets. Most contained full stage facilities for the popular Czech national theatrical performances. These interiors focused on a proscenium arch with its locally painted curtains, which usually portrayed Czech landscapes and symbolic scenes. Few new halls have been built since the 1880–1920 period, but most of those extant are still in use.

See also EUROPEAN AMERICANS: Czechs.

David Murphy
Nebraska State Historical Society

Frolec, Václav, and Josef Vaeka. *Encyclopedie lidová architektura*. Praha: SNTL—Nakladatelství technické literatury, and ALFA—Vydavateľstvo technickej a ekonomickej literatúry, 1983. Murphy, David. "Dramatic Expressions: Czech Theatre Curtains in Nebraska." *Nebraska History* 74 (1993): 168–82. Murphy, David. "*Jejich Antonie*: Czechs, the Land, Cather, and the Pavelka Farmstead." *Great Plains Quarterly* 14 (1994): 85–106.

DANISH ARCHITECTURE

Danish architecture in the Great Plains reads as a minority report. The number of Danes coming to the region was always small in comparison to other immigrant groups, and the fact that they tended to settle individually rather than in concentrated ethnic communities makes them relatively invisible on the landscape. Several Danish cultural strongholds do exist near and on the Plains: the area around Tyler in western Minnesota is one; another is found in the vicinity of Elkhorn and Kimballton in western Iowa; and another lies in the area around Dannebrog, Dannevirke, and Nysted in Howard County, Nebraska. Wherever they ended up, however, the Danes, like many other immigrants, constructed buildings that mirrored in their diversity the turbulent conditions under which they were conceived.

Danish emigration occurred largely in the years between 1870 and 1920 and was directly linked to the social upheavals caused by industrialization. As production shifted from farm to factory, people in the Danish countryside found themselves on the move, seeking employment first in their country's urban centers and then, after finding jobs there insufficient to match the demand, overseas. It was a time of great change: not only were people physically removed from familiar surroundings, but traditional practices of all kinds were being replaced by newer and more modern ways associated with the urban bourgeoisie. Architecturally, change came in the form of new popular designs flooding in from all sides that challenged the older folk forms associated with the increasingly discredited rural past. The Danes who came to the Great Plains left behind a building tradition very much in flux, and to make things more confusing, they were greeted in their new homes by even more architectural choices. It is not surprising that Danish architecture in the Great Plains and everywhere else the Danes went defies easy description.

Like most Plains settlers, Danish families were forced on arrival to live in dugouts or sod houses that lacked, due to their size and circumstance, a clear national or ethnic affiliation. As the occupation became more firmly established, however, architectural expectations increased, and a great number of permanent buildings, including farmhouses and outbuildings, stores, town houses, churches, and schools, were erected. These buildings display remarkable variety in design and execution, but they generally adhere to a strong progressive ethic lodged within the immigrant community. There are instances where older Danish folk traditions were followed, particularly in the use of half-timber, wattle-and-daub, and unfired clay brick construction. But such practices were extremely rare and found only in the first generation. Most Danish immigrants appear to have chosen, like their European neighbors, the new balloon-frame structural system or, more infrequently because of its high cost, fired brick. The same willingness to experiment with new ideas is found in the designs for the buildings as well.

Danish houses fall into three general categories: houses with origins in Danish nineteenth-century popular culture; houses that are American in origin but nevertheless strongly reminiscent of turn-of-the-century Danish designs; and, finally, houses that have no connection to Denmark whatsoever. This last group is by far the largest, suggesting that most Danish immigrants simply adopted whatever American house forms were popular at the time they arrived. In the 1870s a range of classically inspired rectilinear houses like the hall-parlor type prevailed; in the 1880s and 1890s Victorian cottages were the answer; and after 1900 it was foursquares and bungalows. Although Danish decorative elements and furnishings were often retained on the inside, the exterior treatments betray a strong interest within the immigrant population in affiliating with the dominant culture.

When houses do have Danish references, they are almost always to modern rather than traditional sources. For example, a number of immigrants from Denmark during the 1870s and 1880s built distinctive houses that are three rooms wide and one or two rooms deep and have symmetrically tripartite neoclassical facades. These buildings differ significantly from typically two-room-wide American forms but are not traditionally Danish

either. Rather, they refer to a house form that was introduced into Denmark only during the second quarter of the nineteenth century and championed as a symbol of economic achievement by members of the emerging merchant and farmer classes. Transplanted to the Great Plains, the houses granted their occupants both economic status and national ethnic identity. The same connection is found, albeit more indirectly, in the second category of Danish houses. In the Elkhorn/Kimballton area, for example, Danish immigrants mostly built American-style houses. One of these houses, a one-and-a-half-story bungalow with a front wall dormer, appears strikingly similar to the house with a gable roof and front dormer that was gaining popularity in turn-of-the-century Danish suburbs. In Denmark the house usually faced away from the street, with the main entrance opening onto a protected courtyard while in the Great Plains region, according to American convention, the house and front door directly addressed the street.

Other kinds of buildings demonstrate a similar spirit of progress. Danish stores were aligned along the main street and follow the American one- or two-part commercial block variety. Danish churches are similarly non descript; except for a few Lutheran churches that have Flemish-inspired, stepped-gable parapets and crenellated towers, the predominant design for religious buildings in Danish immigrant communities was the ubiquitous gabled rectangle with engaged front tower form. Although usually clothed in standard American architectural garb, Danish folk schools, part of a sweeping attempt at reforming the educational system, are another feature of the Danish architectural landscape that should be recognized.

One other aspect of the Danish architectural experience involves the self-conscious revival of ethnic identity during the second half of the twentieth century. By the 1950s most Danish families had become so thoroughly assimilated into American life that little or no connection remained with their ancestral homeland. Since most actual sources of ethnic identity had been abandoned, new ones had to be created, and this the descendants of immigrants did by self-consciously highlighting elements of the traditional national culture like costume and food at family and community celebrations. The residents of Elkhorn, Iowa, have gone a step further in dressing up their main street stores in pseudo-Danish half-timbering, moving a Danish windmill to the town park, and commissioning for the town a replica of the famous Little Mermaid statue.

See also EUROPEAN AMERICANS: Danes.

Thomas L. Carter
University of Utah

Betsinger, Signe. "Danes in Iowa and Minnesota." In *To Build in a New Land: Ethnic Landscapes in North America*, edited by Allen G. Noble. Baltimore MD: Johns Hopkins University Press, 1992: 211–25. Carter, Thomas. "Danes." In *America's Architectural Roots: Ethnic Groups That Built America*, edited by Dell Upton. Washington DC: Preservation Press, 1986: 115–23. Faber, Tobias. *Danish Architecture*. Copenhagen: Danske Selskab, 1978.

DAVIS AND WILSON

Architect Ellery Lothrop Davis (1887–1956) executed a broad spectrum of projects, ranging from residences to educational buildings to military facilities, in Lincoln, throughout Nebraska, and around the Plains region from 1909 until his death in 1956. Davis was born in Florida, son of mathematics professor Ellery Williams Davis. Professor Davis relocated to Lincoln to join the University of Nebraska staff in 1893 and was later dean of the College of Arts and Sciences. Ellery graduated from the University of Nebraska in 1906 and from the School of Architecture at Columbia University in 1909. He returned to Lincoln and commenced his architectural career, working briefly as a draftsman for George Berlinghof, then joining him in partnership. The German-born and -schooled Berlinghof had settled in Nebraska in the early 1880s and enjoyed considerable success throughout the region, especially in public commissions such as libraries and county courthouses, before moving to Lincoln in 1905.

The seven-year partnership of the young American and the middle-aged German was highly productive, resulting in major, lasting structures such as the University of Nebraska College of Law, Lincoln High School, Miller and Paine Department Store, and Security Mutual Building (now called CenterStone), all in Lincoln. Their public buildings continued the skillful neoclassicism of Berlinghof's earlier work, while their retail and office structures reflected the tall commercial buildings of Chicago.

Berlinghof and Davis ended their partnership in 1917, and both men's practices apparently were curtailed during World War I. In 1919 Davis hired navy veteran and University of Nebraska graduate Walter F. Wilson (1893–1970) as a draftsman. By 1921 Davis and Wilson's collaboration had blossomed into a durable partnership. From the beginning, public schools were a mainstay of the Davis and Wilson practice for communities throughout Nebraska. In Lincoln the partnership built numerous elementary and junior high schools and the district's next three high schools in 1939, 1955, and 1966. Nebraska colleges and universities also became major clients, led by the University of Nebraska, where the firm's many projects included Memorial Stadium, Morrill Hall, the Coliseum, the Student Union, and Love Memorial Library. Their broad practice also produced excellent churches, such as Lincoln's Gothic Revival Westminster Presbyterian and Byzantine-flavored Temple B'nai Jeshurun (both 1924); handsome Period Revival houses in Lincoln and elsewhere; and large and small commercial buildings. The Stuart Building in downtown Lincoln (1927–29) is a twelve-story, mixed-use structure combining a large movie theater, shops, and offices (now apartments), crowned by a clubhouse, and featuring Lincoln's only gargoyles.

Ellery L. Davis went into early retirement for health reasons in 1931, five years before his son Ellery Hall Davis entered the firm after also graduating from Columbia. Wilson sustained the firm through the Great Depression but prepared to close in 1942 due to the wartime cessation of private construction. However, military projects supplanted private commissions, and Ellery L. rejoined Wilson in 1942 to develop Buckley Army Air Field near Denver. The enlarged firm also worked as engineers or architects for several Nebraska military installations.

After the war the firm's practice again broadened to governmental, educational, hospital, industrial, and commercial buildings throughout Nebraska. A Colonial Revival chapel for Hastings College in 1948 was a stylistic exception, as the firm's work became predominantly International Style. Ellery L. Davis died in 1956, and Walter Wilson retired in 1965. In 1968 the firm was renamed Davis/Fenton/Stange/Darling to reflect ownership by Ellery H. Davis, William M. Fenton, James H. Stange, and Howard Darling. In 1994 the name was simplified to Davis Design, which in 2003 remained the dean of Lincoln architectural firms.

Edward F. Zimmer
Lincoln/Lancaster County Planning
Department

DEPRESSION ARCHITECTURE

New Deal agencies during the administration of President Franklin D. Roosevelt reshaped the public landscape of the Great Plains. From 1933 to 1942 the Federal Emergency Relief Administration (FERA), the Public Works Administration (PWA), the Civilian Conservation Corps (CCC), and the Works Progress (later Work Projects) Administration (WPA) placed a federal facade on the region's public architecture.

Architectural historians identify two primary substyles associated with New Deal architecture: Government Rustic, which is associated with many parks projects of the CCC and the National Park Service during these decades, and PWA or WPA Modern, with the designation depending on the sponsoring agency.

Government Rustic grew out of park designs based on the natural resources and landscape of the mountain West and the Adirondacks of New York. At first glance, the exposed log beams and rough stonework characteristic of the style have little association with the rolling prairies of the Great Plains, but once the National Park Service in 1938 published its architectural guides, *Park and Recreation Structures* and *Park Structures and Facilities*, Government Rustic became codified as the only proper park architecture. Government Rustic style reflected a close relationship to nature not only in the materials used in the buildings but also in how the structures seemingly rose from the ground themselves, linking the style to the design ideas and assumptions of master Prairie school architect Frank Lloyd Wright. The stone and log interpretive pavilion at the Double Ditch Village State Historic Site near Bismarck, North Dakota, is similar in its material and construction to many other Government Rustic structures found in the region's state and federal parks.

The design inspiration for PWA Modern style came from several sources, including the Art Deco and Art Moderne movements of the late 1920s and early 1930s and the patriotic iconography of New Deal agencies such as the National Recovery Administration. By mixing concrete, steel, local building materials, patriotic imagery, classical motifs, and the forms and details of modern architecture, PWA Modern blended the old and new so that buildings were visually modern yet also evoked the past. The Municipal Coliseum in Fort Worth, constructed as part of the Texas Centennial celebration, mixes historical images, local building materials, and Art Deco design in classic PWA Modern fashion.

County courthouses located throughout the Plains document the popularity of PWA or WPA Modern style. In Casper, Wyoming, the Natrona County Courthouse, designed by Karl Krusmark and Leon Goodrich, imaginatively ties together the past and present by using frontier images and quotations on the building's modern-styled facade. The Sheridan County Courthouse in Plentywood, Montana, is much more restrained in its modern styling, reflecting both the isolated location of the county seat and the county's limited financial means. The New Deal–sponsored courthouses symbolized more than the federal presence; they also reminded depressed residents of the national government's commitment to the region and the residents' ever-deepening dependence on the largesse and policies of the federal government. In this way the courthouses symbolically confronted the much-prized independence of westerners because their commanding presence within the local townscape ironically spoke more of dependence than independence.

There was more to the New Deal landscape of the Plains than new public parks and courthouses. Post offices, city halls, and community halls were constructed in many smaller towns; most of these buildings still serve their original purpose. Schools were priority projects for many state FERA agencies; in North Dakota, for example, FERA built 8 schools and renovated 1,604 others. The PWA and WPA built hundreds of other schools, often in popular revival styles. The PWA-sponsored Holmes School in Lincoln, Nebraska, was in a restrained Colonial Revival style, while the PWA school in Fort Scott, Kansas, was a full statement of Colonial Revival design, complete with finials, cupola, and Palladian windows. The WPA school in Kadoka, South Dakota, reflects a Pueblo Revival design quite out of place in its Black Hills setting. The popularity of the revival styles also was evident in the many new classrooms, libraries, stadiums, and auditoriums constructed on college and university campuses. Besides the new education buildings, the addition of libraries and community buildings such as the Art Deco–styled Sonotorium (an outdoor theater) in Kearney, Nebraska, and the new Art Museum in Wichita, Kansas, enriched town life.

New Deal agencies also transformed much of the infrastructure of Plains agriculture, industry, transportation, and urban services. In Montana's lower Yellowstone River valley, CCC work crews improved and expanded existing irrigation projects of the U.S. Reclamation Service. Modern bridges, new highways, airports, sidewalks, and sewage treatment plants improved urban living. Dam and powerhouse construction on rivers such as the Colorado, Missouri, and North Platte improved urban water supplies, provided more water for irrigation, and created new sources for electricity. At some projects, modernity and tradition existed side by side. The dam and town site at Fort Peck, Montana, contained a Swiss chalet–like theater, which is strangely out of place on the flat, treeless prairie of eastern Montana and stands in sharp contrast to the modern concrete and steel spillway of the dam.

Efforts at historic preservation and land conservation, often in association with park development, were widespread. At the Chateau de Mores, a historic house museum in Medora, North Dakota, WPA-funded employees, working together with state historical society officials, cataloged artifacts, furnished the house, and developed its first interpretive tours. Land reclamation efforts led by the CCC created most of the region's initial wildlife reserves and migratory refuges, expanded existing shelterbelts while creating many new ones, and planted trees in reforestation and town beautification schemes.

The impact of New Deal agencies in the Great Plains landscape was immense and long-lasting. The most architecturally imposing public buildings in many of the region's towns date to that era, while the reordered landscapes represented by dam reservoirs, new parks, and urban infrastructure shape everyday perceptions and experiences.

See also POLITICS AND GOVERNMENT: New Deal.

Carroll Van West
Middle Tennessee State University

Cutler, Phoebe. *The Public Landscape of the New Deal.* New Haven CT: Yale University Press, 1985. Short, C. W., and R. Stanley-Brown. *Public Buildings: Architecture under the Public Works Administration, 1933 to 1939.* Washington DC: Government Printing Office, 1939. West, Carroll Van. " 'The Best Kind of Building': The New Deal Landscape of the Northern Plains, 1933–1942." *Great Plains Quarterly* 14 (1994): 129–41.

DOW, WALLACE (1844–1911)

Born in Croydon, New Hampshire, on September 22, 1844, Wallace Leroy Dow learned building skills by working in his father's Newport, New Hampshire, contracting business. In 1873 Dow formed his own contracting company there and was involved in the construction of several public buildings. He also studied under his uncle Edward Dow, who operated a successful architecture firm.

Wallace Dow moved to Pierre, Dakota Territory, in October 1880. He relocated to Yankton in the winter of 1880–81 and maintained an architectural and contracting office there until 1883. Dow's first major job was supervising the construction of John M. Allen's design for the original Main Building (now the Conservatory of Music) at Yankton College. Beginning in 1882 Dow served as architect for the territorial penitentiary at Sioux Falls. During his time in Yankton, Dow also designed the first structure at the Territorial Hospital for the Insane.

In 1883 Dow moved his offices to Sioux Falls and dominated the architectural field in South Dakota during the 1880s and 1890s. He was well connected to the Republican territorial and state governments, so there is hardly a state institution dating from the late nineteenth century that does not have at least one Dow building.

Dow was a versatile designer, at home with all the popular styles of his time. He utilized local quartzite and jasper in many of his most striking commissions. Quartzite was particularly suited to the masonry Romanesque style popularized by H. H. Richardson in the 1870s and 1880s. One of Dow's most important commissions, the Minnehaha County Courthouse in Sioux Falls (1889–92), is a tribute to Richardsonian design rendered in massive rough-finished quartzite blocks. Dow was also an early advocate of concrete. His design for the South Dakota Pavilion at the 1893 Columbian Exposition was composed entirely in precast concrete panels attached to a wooden frame.

Dow retired in 1905, but he remained active. He had patented a device for making concrete blocks in 1904, and he spent his later years promoting concrete building technology as the owner of the Prefection Block Machine Company. He died in Sioux Falls on July 5, 1911.

Michael Bedeau
Idaho State Historic Preservation Office

DUBOIS, WILLIAM (1879–1953)

William Robert Dubois was the most prolific designer of public, commercial, and residential buildings in Wyoming during the first half of the twentieth century. His architectural legacy is still evident throughout the Cowboy State. Dubois also designed buildings in Nebraska, Colorado, and South Dakota.

Born in Chicago on November 15, 1879, Dubois received his formal training there and subsequently worked for an architectural firm in Albuquerque, New Mexico. He came to the Great Plains in 1901 as the supervising architect responsible for the construction of the Carnegie Library in Cheyenne. Dubois decided to remain in Cheyenne and establish an architectural practice.

Although his clientele varied, he is best known for his public buildings—federal, state, county, and city. The architect's most memorable Wyoming state government buildings include the Supreme Court Building (1935–36), the east and west wings of the state capitol (1915–17), and several structures on the University of Wyoming campus in Laramie, including Hoyt Hall (1921), the Student Union, and women's and men's residence halls (1927).

The state also selected Dubois to design numerous institutional structures: the City-County (1918) and Federal Office (1932) Buildings in Cheyenne and the Albany County Courthouse (1931–32) still function as governmental structures.

Dubois's compositions reflect a keen awareness of architectural trends. He was a proficient designer who utilized architectural styles from Romanesque Revival (Wyoming State Penitentiary Guard Quarters/Powerplant) to neoclassical (City-County Building, Cheyenne) to Restrained Classicism (Albany County Courthouse) to Moderne (Laramie Municipal Building). Generally, his public buildings are characterized by formalism and symmetry and are rectilinear in form. While his earliest designs illustrate a commitment to neoclassicism, they also reflect familiarity with popular commercial design. Although the exterior of Cheyenne's Plains Hotel is a straightforward symmetrical terra cotta–clad structure embellished by a heavy neoclassical cornice typical for 1910, the hotel's interior decor once revealed a remarkable interweaving of western and Native American motifs. Dubois's work also reveals a love of details and a skill in embellishing his designs, as exemplified by the Supreme Court Building's Art Deco–embossed metal ornaments. Clearly, Dubois chose designs that suited his clientele. They were popular, affordable, and well built. Over the years Dubois designed more than 100 residences, twenty-seven schools, four Carnegie Libraries, and six churches. He also designed numerous fraternal, commercial, hotel, and apartment buildings.

In addition to his flourishing architectural practice, Dubois served in the Wyoming legislature for ten years. In 1903 he was elected to the Wyoming House of Representatives and served three sequential terms; six years later he was elected to the Wyoming Senate in 1909 for two terms. His leadership skills extended to the Cheyenne Chamber of Commerce and other civic organizations. As an accomplished organist, Dubois demonstrated his talents in churches and fraternal organizations and assisted religious institutions in purchasing organs. William Dubois died on May 31, 1953.

Eileen F. Starr
National Park Service

William R. Dubois Architectural Collection, Wyoming State Archives, Cheyenne. Starr, Eileen. *Architecture in the Cowboy State, 1849–1940: A Guide.* Glendo WY: High Plains Press, 1992.

EARTH LODGES

The earth lodge was the dominant dwelling of Central and Northern Great Plains village Indians. Earth lodges were circular, dome-shaped dwellings with heavy timber superstructures mantled by thick layers of earth. The type emerged in the 1500s and persisted into the reservation era. Tribes most frequently associated with earth-lodge architecture include the Mandans, Hidatsas, Arikaras, Pawnees, Otoes, Kansas, Omahas, and Poncas, although several other groups also adopted the style.

The origins of the earth lodge are not entirely clear, although it was certainly a Northern Plains innovation. Between A.D. 1000 and 1400, horticultural villagers in the Central Plains built square houses. During the same time, Northern Plains villagers constructed rectangular structures. Although these types of houses are frequently called earth lodges, they were not; rather, they were vertical walled with thin coverings of wattle and daub or thatch. A few oval to circular structures appeared in northern Nebraska and central South Dakota in the 1400s, but their floor plans do not reflect the fully developed earth-lodge style. The earliest true earth lodges were built in central North Dakota and northern South Dakota Missouri River villages in the early 1500s by the ancestors of the Mandans and Arikaras. The earth lodges were thicker and more insulated than the earlier square or rectangular dwellings and were a response to the cooling temperatures of the Neoboreal ("Little Ice Age") climatic regime.

The Mandans, Hidatsas, and Arikaras all constructed earth lodges in the sixteenth century. This architectural style rapidly diffused from the upper Missouri as additional sedentary tribes migrated onto the Plains from the south and east and adopted the form. To the south the Pawnees were firmly established in central Nebraska by 1600 and living in earth-lodge villages. Archaeological and ethnohistorical evidence establishes that the Otoes, Omahas, and Poncas were living in earth-lodge villages on the eastern margins of the Central Plains by 1700. The Cheyennes briefly adopted earth-lodge architecture in the mid–eighteenth century during their occupancy of eastern North Dakota. Some circular floor-plan structures encountered by archaeologists working at seventeenth- and eighteenth-century villages of Central Plains tribes such as the Wichitas and Kansas are most likely not earth lodges but grass- or thatch-covered houses. Mississippian sites in the southeastern United States occasionally yield earth lodge–type ceremonial structures. The most fully documented are at Ocmulgee National Monument, Georgia. The relationship, if any, between these and the Plains dwellings is unclear.

Earth-lodge construction began with the excavation of a shallow circular area typically less than one foot in depth with a diameter varying between twenty and sixty feet. Heavy vertical timbers served as central roof supports. The Northern Plains earth lodges almost always had four center posts. The Pawnees, Omahas, Otoes, and other Central Plains tribes used four, six, eight, ten, and even twelve center posts. Center posts were forked at the top and connected by horizontal beams. A secondary row of posts was set around the perimeter of the floor pit several feet inside the wall. These were shorter than the center posts but also connected at the top by a series of horizontal cross-stringers. A series of closely spaced sloping posts spanned the area from the top of the stringers to the ground outside the house pit. Rafters extended in spokelike fashion from the top of the wall stringers to the horizontal beams connecting the center posts. The rafters did not extend across the full radius of the house in order to allow room for construction of a fireplace smoke hole. Thatching and then layers of thick sod and grass covered the sturdy superstructure. A sloping or vertical-walled short entry passage extended from one side of the lodge, typically the south or east.

Interior features included a central fire basin, one or more deep food storage chambers, and altars. Storage chambers were bell shaped, narrow at the lodge floor and expanding to three to five feet at their bases, and were five to eight feet deep. Such pits were later used for trash disposal. The Hidatsas called the space between the outer vertical posts and the exterior leaners an *atuti*. This area was used for placement of beds and storage of firewood, tools, weapons, and other personal items. Beds were either on the ground or on elevated platforms. Sleeping quarters were generally on the ledge between the outside of the house pit and the edge of the leaners. The central portion of the earth lodge was used for food preparation and social activities. The back wall opposite the entry passage often featured an altar or sacred area. One or more extended families occupied the earth lodge, which could house up to sixty people. Villages consisted of at least a dozen earth lodges and in many cases of more than a hundred. It was not uncommon for villages to be home to several thousand people. Earth lodges were often closely spaced, and during times of conflict an earth or timber fortification wall surrounded the community.

The earth lodge formed the central focus of many aspects of Plains horticultural village life. For some tribes, at least, the structures held important symbolic religious, astronomical, and social significance. In Pawnee cosmology the earth lodge was symbolically considered the heavens. Mandan and Hidatsa lodges also had sacred symbolism attached to them, and special earth lodges were reserved for ceremonial activities such as the Mandan Okipa (a four-day ceremony of renewal).

John R. Bozell
Nebraska State Historical Society

Ahler, Stanley A., Thomas D. Thiessen, and Michael K. Trimble. *People of the Willows: The Prehistory and Early History of the Hidatsa Indians*. Grand Forks: University of North Dakota Press, 1991. Nabokov, Peter, and Robert Easton. *Native American Architecture*. New York: Oxford University Press, 1989. Wilson, Gilbert L. *The Hidatsa Earthlodge*. Anthropological Papers of the American Museum of Natural History 33 (1934).

FARMSTEADS

Farmsteads, varying in form and function, are one of the most important components of the Great Plains landscape. The open, relatively treeless land and extreme climate of the Great Plains greatly affected the design of farmsteads built by the first generation of European American homesteaders. Since most homesteaders had little money, they used readily available materials such as stone, mud, and sod to construct a shelter to live in while they proved their claim. Homesteaders typically built small, rectangular (ten by twelve feet was a common size), single-story, one-room shacks or dugouts in a hillside. Livestock shelters were often lean-tos attached to the house or simple structures located a short distance away from the shack or dugout.

Many ethnic groups used architectural styles and building materials common to their homelands in their new farms. For example, Ukrainians in east-central Alberta built clay-plastered log homes with a three-bay plan of two rooms on either side of a main hallway. These features and details such as a large clay oven (*pich*) and a low sloping berm (*pryzba*) built along the base of outer walls to shed water were taken directly from farmhouses in the Galicia and Bukovyna districts of the Ukraine, the previous home of these settlers. Danish immigrants in southeastern South Dakota made bricks from Missouri River bottomland clay to build structures similar to the ones they had left behind in Denmark. Their farmhouses had distinctive arched window-top trim, and they built T-shaped barns with space for horses, cows, and grain or hay storage.

Once settlers proved claims and decided to stay and farm, they needed to expand and improve shelters for their means of production, products, and families. This second stage of farmstead construction coincided with the scientific farming movement from the late 1880s to the early 1920s. Institutions dedicated to agriculture such as government agencies, colleges, regional fairs, and farm journals and newspapers formed during this period promoted enhanced technology, beautification, efficiency, safety, and hygiene in all areas of farm operation. Circulars from agencies such as the United States Department of Agriculture and assorted state university agricultural experiment stations covered topics such as farmyard layouts and building details that could improve livestock health by increasing ventilation and sunlight in a barn.

The second-generation farmstead complex of this era usually consisted of a farmhouse, a large main barn, and smaller outbuildings like machine sheds and shelters for specific groups of livestock such as chicken coops and swine barns. Sometimes the original claim shack was incorporated into the new farmhouse or reused as an outbuilding. Ethnic building techniques and details largely disappeared as farmers covered over dirt and log walls with clapboard siding. Balloon frames of dimension lumber replaced sod, earth, stone, and log walls in new construction. Many of these farmhouses were unadorned, vernacular structures featuring rectangular or L-shaped plans, one- or two-story wood-frame construction, gable or hip roofs, and wood siding. Farmers with more money often built their own interpretations of popular late-nineteenth- and early-twentieth-century styles such as the Victorian/Queen Anne, foursquare, and bungalow or else purchased a house kit from retailers such as Sears, Roebuck and Company in the United States or Eatons of Canada. The front facade and formal entrance usually faced the road, while the everyday entrance was on a side facade and often led into the kitchen. Growing farm families sometimes built a house for the next or the previous generation near the original farmhouse.

Barns and outbuildings became taller and wider and were located farther from the house. Improved truss and rafter systems enabled farmers to build barns that were wind resistant and had tall, clearspan second stories for hay storage. These gambrel- and Gothic arch–roofed barns were just one of many new building types that were a product of this era. Round barns with central interior silos and circular stall arrangements also were promoted as an ideal solution for efficient livestock feeding. The farmyard, essentially nonexistent in most original homesteading complexes, became an important feature of the farm landscape during this time. Many were U-shaped or rectangular, with buildings facing toward the center. The farmhouse, located some distance away from the outbuildings, often had a lawn and gardens facing the road. Some farmyards had a grove of trees to one side for wind protection.

This expansion, improvement, and homogenization of the Great Plains farm continued until the bottom dropped out of the farm economy in the early 1920s and the subsequent Great Depression and extreme weather conditions of the early 1930s forced many families to abandon their farms. Increased mechanization meant that it took fewer people to operate a farm. All these factors contributed to a large decline in the rural population during the 1930s.

Farms surviving into the 1940s were much larger in area and more automated than their predecessors. Expensive new machinery that had to be operated over large tracts of land to be cost-effective required shelters larger than traditional machine sheds. The pole building, a single-story metal structure with a very shallow pitched gable roof supported by poles, was introduced after World War II for machinery and crop storage and for housing livestock. These buildings are still popular.

The trend toward larger farms and a smaller rural population continues today. Many operators live in town and either rent land or work for large corporations with massive landholdings. However, many Plains family farms do survive, and some retain architectural evidence of their earlier years.

See also AGRICULTURE: Family Farm; Suitcase Farming.

Stephanie Ahrendt
Newport News, Virginia

Jacon, Steph, and Allyson Brooks. *Homesteading and Agricultural Development Context*. Vermillion: South Dakota State Historical Preservation Center, 1994. Martynowych, Orest T. *The Ukrainian Bloc Settlement in East Central Alberta, 1890–1930: A History*. Historic Sites Service Occasional Paper no. 10. Edmonton: Alberta Community Development, Historic Sites Service, 1985.

FINNISH ARCHITECTURE

In common with the architecture of other ethnic groups that settled in the Great Plains, Finnish architecture included a mixture of old and new: traditional Finnish uses and techniques were often combined with American building practices and needs. Distinctive Finnish log construction techniques were only manifested in areas with suitable timber resources, which were quite rare on the Plains.

The earliest Finnish settlers were no different from their fellow pioneer settlers who chose to settle in the Great Plains: many lived in "soddies" and dugouts until they could construct more substantial residences. The majority of structures were of frame construction that followed American building practices, and a few were of stone. In areas of abundant timber, Finns built in the traditional Nordic manner—with closely fitted, horizontally stacked logs held together by wooden pins and elegant corner-notching systems—as they did throughout Finland and the Great Lakes region of North America. Significantly, no farm or ranch site was a direct transplant of Finnish architecture to North American soil; instead, contemporary building methods and prefabricated materials and features were commonly combined with Nordic construction techniques. For a period of time, there appears to have been some attempt to lay out the buildings on farms and ranches in open courtyard arrangements, a feature common in some areas of Finnish migration.

One building traditional and unique to Finns was the sauna; it flourished in a variety of materials, including frame, earth, metal, concrete block, railroad tie, and traditional log. Early Finnish immigrants are known to have heated their saunas with buffalo and cow chips. In towns, the sauna was built as a communal commercial building and revealed the greatest variety in form and materials. Many surviving family saunas are frame and followed the traditional two-room layout for bathing and changing purposes. A few adaptations included attached chicken coops to keep valuable poultry warm in the harsh Plains winters. Evidence also survives of a few older smoke (*savu*) or chimneyless saunas.

Surveys conducted to date reveal that the most important concentrations of traditional log structures were built in the Black Hills of South Dakota and the Little Belt Creek valley of Montana, the latter area termed Korpivaara (wilderness hill) by local Finns. These regions provided pine, spruce, and cedar logs for building construction. Less information is available about Finnish architecture in the Prairie Provinces, but Saskatchewan's New Finland community is known for the number of poplar or aspen log buildings constructed by early immigrants.

The Buskala ranch, located in the Black Hills, is an excellent example of Finnish log architecture. Henry and Anna Buskala and their two sons moved to the site in 1901 after residing in several mining towns. The ranch structures, most built prior to 1910, were organized around two yards. The domestic yard included a two-story house, the original sauna, a privy, and a root cellar, while the larger animal yard consisted of a cow and hay barn, a calf barn/stable, and the corral. Hay bins and a field hay barn (*lato*) were situated half a mile from the house, whereas the other buildings show a mixture of American and Finnish features; the lato not only was a very rare architectural feature in the Great Plains, but it was a direct transplant from Finland. By 1918 the Buskalas had added a blacksmith shop, a granary, and a new sauna to the building ensemble. The rather large number of individual structures, most of relatively modest size, also reflected agricultural practices in Finland.

Finnish settlement in Montana's Korpivaara community followed a similar pattern: after working in mining towns, some Finns developed homesteads along the three-mile-long valley. Korpivaara includes evidence of six ranches displaying sophisticated Nordic building methods; many structures reveal frequent use of the toothed-corner notch, a type seldom found elsewhere in America. During the early period of homesteading (1895–1915), Finns typically constructed three or four small log buildings and cleared six to thirty-five acres of land for cultivation. During the subsequent development phase (1915–30), the cultivated acreage increased, a large dwelling unit replaced the initial residence, and as many as ten log buildings were added.

Farther north, the buildings in New Finland, Saskatchewan, were constructed of poplar logs cut from the Qu'Appelle River valley. Because poplar proved difficult to shape and work, chinking made of clay and straw was used between the logs. The earliest buildings included sod roofs covering a layer of birch bark, while the houses often were distinguished by their whitewashed exteriors and interior walls. Locally available ocher was mixed with kerosene or turpentine to make red barn paint. Although many of New Finland's log buildings have disappeared, several farms and ranches—some of which now embrace three or more sections of land—still display at least one extant structure.

Churches and ethnic halls were common features of many ethnic settlements on the Plains. Finns constructed a variety of these buildings, many in frame. Temperance and workers halls and cooperative stores, mills, creameries, and grain elevators were common features in the Finnish settlement landscape. Finns, along with their Nordic neighbors on the Plains, were somewhat more prone than other groups to develop cooperative businesses, including threshing companies, which have left no material remains. In rural South Dakota Finnish Apostolic Lutheran churches developed a new religious architecture, most likely in response to the ecclesiastical independence afforded them in America. Simple and austere, the remaining early Apostolic church at Savo Township, South Dakota, reflects the simplicity and antiliturgical beliefs of its members.

Finnish settlement in the Great Plains is distinguished by its simultaneous maintenance of tradition and adaptation to American and Canadian architectural practices. In most areas Finns replicated the pattern of other immigrant groups: they put up buildings identified as American or Canadian, but beneath them lies an ethnic pattern of communal settlement, economic interdependence, religious and political affiliation, and family association. In rural areas with abundant timber, however, Finns constructed buildings that reflected their Nordic background, a practice that continued well into the 1920s. Today, the only Finnish architectural tradition to survive is the ever-adaptable sauna, which has moved from a singularly ethnic tradition to a common international fixture of wealthy homes, hotels, and spas.

See also EUROPEAN AMERICANS: Finns.

Arnold R. Alanen
University of Wisconsin–Madison
Carolyn Torma
American Planning Association

Sanford, Dena Lynn. "Finnish Homesteads in Montana's Little Belt Creek Valley: Korpivaara's Vernacular Building Tradition." Master's Thesis, University of Oregon, 1991. Sutyla, Charles M. *The Finnish Sauna in Manitoba.* Ottawa: Canadian Centre for Folk Culture Studies, National Museums of Canada, 1977. Torma, Carolyn. "The Architecture of Finnish Settlement in South Dakota." In *Finns in North America*, edited by Michael G. Karni, Olavi Koivukangas, and Edward W. Laine. Turku, Finland: Institute for Migration, 1988: 99–119.

FORT ARCHITECTURE

In the nineteenth century, army posts throughout the Great Plains region varied widely in appearance, reflecting the lack of a centralized design authority. Post commanders exercised great latitude in construction decisions, often relying on poorly trained lieutenants who designed buildings and oversaw their construction. Low levels of funding forced these officers to rely on available materials and expertise, resulting in a diverse array of architecture within forts as well as among them. Nonetheless, two aspects of fort design were consistent: the general layout and the expression of the military hierarchy in the architecture of the quarters.

Contrary to the usual image of a fort, stockades were rare, especially in the Great Plains, where wood was hard to obtain. Examples of perimeter vertical-log stockades include Fort Phil Kearny in present-day Wyoming and Fort Rice, North Dakota, as well as Canadian North-West Mounted Police forts of the 1870s such as Fort Macleod, Alberta, and Fort Walsh, Saskatchewan. Without a stockade, a fort could be entered at any point; access was not controlled. All forts had a parade ground, an open space in the center where troops could assemble. The primary buildings—officers' quarters, barracks, headquarters building, guardhouse—faced this parade ground, with secondary structures, including stables, workshops, laundresses' quarters, and hospital, behind it.

The only published army regulation concerning the architecture of a fort allocated the

Fort Sill, Indian Territory, 1871

number of rooms by rank, limiting lieutenants, for instance, to one room plus a kitchen. As a result, the highest-ranking officer at a post had the largest house. Officers' quarters were domestic in appearance, with front porches, gable roofs, and picket-fenced yards. Often, lower-ranking officers occupied double quarters with separate entrances. Barracks were long, one- or two-story structures, with their broad fronts facing the parade ground. One open room served as the dormitory for an entire company; mess halls and kitchens were in separate structures, in wings off the rear, or on the first floor of two-story buildings. Designs for these buildings originated at the post, and the quartermaster general could approve or reject them.

The individuality of the forts was particularly evident in the building materials employed. The army authorized permanent forts to be built of stone or brick. Temporary forts—which was the designation of most forts in the Great Plains, despite their decades-long utilization—could employ stone only if it were cheaper than alternatives. Troops built wood-framed buildings with board-and-batten or clapboarded walls, as at North Platte Station, Nebraska, on the Union Pacific Railroad line. Cruder, quicker wood buildings included "picket" or "stockade" buildings constructed of small-diameter vertical logs, as at Fort Richardson, Texas. Panel construction—horizontal logs let into vertical posts, which fashioned short timber into long buildings—proved to be the most expedient form of log construction, as seen at Fort Robinson, Nebraska.

Because of the scarcity of wood throughout much of the region, army officers sought alternative materials. Adobe—earth formed into bricks and dried in the sun—found extensive use at forts ranging from Fort Davis, Texas, to Fort Laramie, Wyoming, and Fort Shaw, Montana. The army also experimented

with concrete construction. Officers at Sidney Barracks, Nebraska, in 1872 used a "lime-grout" mixture of lime, sand, aggregate, and no cement. Soon after, officers at Fort Laramie, Wyoming, and Fort Hartsuff, Nebraska, constructed most of their new buildings of concrete.

In 1882 Commanding General William T. Sherman outlined his plans for concentrating his troops in the West into fewer, larger posts. By 1891 111 western forts had been reduced to 62. The quartermaster general's office took an active role in rebuilding the posts, producing standardized plans by the mid-1890s. These new brick buildings—barracks as well as officers' quarters—were spacious and imposing. The standardized plans employed a Spanish Colonial appearance for forts in the southwestern Plains, including Fort Sill, Oklahoma, and an English Colonial Revival style for the rest, including Fort D. A. Russell in Wyoming. Buildings at different posts now resembled each other closely; for example, designs for buildings at Fort D. A. Russell served as models for other forts across the country, including the officers' quarters at Fort George Wright, Washington, and the commanding officer's quarters at Fort Totten, North Dakota. Use of standardized designs issued from Washington DC continued through the twentieth century, resulting in an increasingly uniform military architecture nationwide.

See also WAR: Frontier Forts.

Alison K. Hoagland
Michigan Technological University

Anderson, Thomas M. "Army Posts, Barracks and Quarters." *Journal of the Military Service Institution of the United States* 2 (1882): 421–47. Risch, Erna. *Quartermaster Support of the Army, 1775–1939.* Washington DC: Center for Military History, U.S. Army, 1962. Robinson, Willard B. *American Forts: Architectural Form and Function.* Urbana: University of Illinois Press, 1977.

FOUCART, JOSEPH (1848–1917)

The remarkable visual character of the urban streetscape of Guthrie, Oklahoma, was dominated by the influence of the European architect Joseph Foucart, who was born in Arlon, Belgium, on November 14, 1848. Founded on April 22, 1889, by a land run, Guthrie was a designated town site within a parcel opened for homesteading in the center of Indian Territory. By nightfall the dusty prairie had been transformed into a bustling town of more than 10,000 people. The pace of development in Guthrie was staggering: frame buildings were under construction the next day; the first masonry building was completed within a month; in June an electric streetcar system was franchised; and by the end of summer both the electric power plant and the waterworks were operating. Foucart practiced architecture in this bustling environment from 1889 to 1907. The original town site is now designated a National Historic District.

Foucart's buildings in the commercial district of Guthrie reflect the writings of the French architectural theorist Eugène Viollet-le-Duc, with an emphasis on structural determinism and Gothic styling. The buildings have load-bearing masonry walls that are penetrated with arched openings, with the lintels often accented by contrasting stone to signify their structural importance. Pilasters and engaged piers are expressed as vertical supports, and in some cases cast-iron columns are used in a completely undisguised manner. Foucart's designs reveal a predilection toward the Gothic. They are often asymmetrical, yet the most telling Gothic element—the pointed arch window—is missing completely. In its place are rounded arches and keyhole-shaped arches that evoke a Muslim feeling. The domes on the turrets and oriels on some of his buildings suggest a Russian influence. There is also a suggestion of influence by the American Romanesque Revival architect H. H. Richardson, with the rough-cut stone walls and arched windows that combine stone lintels with voussoirs of contrasting color.

One of Foucart's most prominent early buildings is the Grey Brothers Block. The lower part of the facade is pierced by several large arched openings with rough-cut lintels. The rhythm of the second floor then changes to a series of closely spaced double-hung windows, each crowned with a panel of patterned and corbeled brick. At the cornice is an elaborate sheet-metal band composed of a small-scale decorative motif and accented by large pinnacles that extend both above and below the band. The effect is one of a progression of elements defined by different visual scales and textures, ranging from large, rough elements at the bottom to small, smooth elements at the top.

Another important early building is the De-Ford Building. Foucart created an asymmetrical composition of tall, narrow-arched windows and crowned it with a profusion of sheet-metal ornament. The ornament, like the pattern of the windows, is also asymmetrical, with a pyramidal form poised over the stair leading to the second floor as if to provide a visual landmark signifying entry. In the side facade of the building Foucart abruptly changed the pattern, and the arched windows at the second story are much wider, with several smaller keyhole windows lighting the lower floor.

The State Capital Publishing Company was one of his most important commissions. Built in 1902, it is remarkable for the simplicity and subtlety of the wall surfaces, fenestration, and details. The primary facades are unusually flat and restrained. Because of the facade's austerity, the open, three-dimensional tower is a powerful sculptural counterpoint that draws immediate attention to the corner of the building.

During the last decade of the nineteenth century and the first decade of the twentieth, Foucart became the premier architect of Oklahoma Territory. He received important commissions outside of Guthrie, including the library for Oklahoma A & M College at Stillwater. Foucart moved to Sapulpa, Oklahoma, shortly after statehood (1907). Although he continued to practice, his buildings in Sapulpa do not have the vigor of his earlier work.

See also IMAGES AND ICONS: Boomers.

Arn Henderson
University of Oklahoma

Henderson, Arn. "Joseph Foucart, Territorial Architect." In *Of the Earth: Oklahoma Architectural History*, edited by Howard L. and Mary Ellen Meredith. Oklahoma City: Oklahoma Historical Society, 1980. Henderson, Arn, with Frank Parman and Dortha Henderson. *Architecture in Oklahoma: Landmark and Vernacular*. Norman OK: Point Riders Press, 1978.

GERMAN ARCHITECTURE

During the nineteenth century, particularly after the Civil War, Germans in large numbers streamed into the Great Plains from the eastern United States, Canada, and Germany and created a distinctive German American architecture throughout the region. Although modified significantly by dominating environmental, cultural, social, technological, and political influences and reduced in quantity and distribution through use and obsolescence, remnants of this architecture still exist in thousands of churches, barns, houses, and commercial buildings from Canada to Texas.

Whether in city or country, German immigrants settled the Great Plains in Catholic and Protestant enclaves, and, through the powerful nexus of religion, language, and architecture, their churches functioned as cultural centers of German American life. The most widely distributed German church architecture in the Great Plains is *Rundbogenstil*, a Romanesque Revival architecture that the Bavarian architect Friederich von Gärtner (1792–1847) used in the Ludwigskirche, the Bavarian Court and State Library, and the Ludwig Maximilian University in Munich. Roman in origin, the Rundbogenstil church featured the basilica plan with prominent half-circle or segmented arches that form doors, windows, and cornices on plain building surfaces of brick or stone.

By the second half of the nineteenth century, Rundbogenstil architecture in religious and commercial buildings had spread throughout Germany and widely throughout the Great Plains. St. Bonaventure Catholic Church in Raeville, Nebraska, constructed of brick by the Omaha architect Jacob M. Nachtigall in 1917, is a Rundbogenstil church with arcades of arched openings on its towers and west entry and along its aisled nave, transepts, and apse. There is a series of corbeled arches on its cornice. The twin, cross-gabled, polygonal spires of this Nebraska church are characteristic of many churches in Germany and the Great Plains. A typical smaller variant is the Evangelische Lutherische Dreieinigkeits Kirche, a stone Rundbogenstil church with a single tower built in the shape of a cross in Grand Island, Nebraska, by German-born masons William and Jacob Scheffel from 1894 to 1896. These masons carved elaborate, half-round arches over doors and windows that open into an aisled church with a nave, transept, chancel, and U-shaped balcony. Stained-glass windows with German inscriptions also frequently characterize Rundbogenstil churches on the Plains. For example, St. Anthony of Padua Catholic Church in Wichita, Kansas, built in 1905 and called the "German Church," displays magnificent stained-glass religious scenes that were designed in Germany, shipped in pieces, and reassembled in grand windows under round-arched openings of brick.

Unfortunately, many Plains Rundbogenstil churches, built to symbolize a vibrant German American culture and to last an eternity, are being closed for lack of priests. Many other distinctive examples of late-nineteenth- and early-twentieth-century German Rundbogenstil architecture survive in brick and stone industrial and commercial buildings in a variety of urban settings.

Germans who settled in rural areas expressed their ethnic heritage in a rich vernacular architecture consisting of barns and other farm buildings such as springhouses, granaries, and cribs. The German bank barn originated in southern Germany and Switzerland and was built extensively by Germans who migrated west from the Middle Atlantic cultural hearth into the northern half of the Great Plains. This gabled barn is rectangular in form, and one of its long sides is built into a bank or earthen ramp that leads to the main floor of the structure, consisting of a central threshing bay, a hay-storage bay, and a grain-storage bay. Openings placed strategically in the storage bays allow feed to be dropped into the lower story, which is usually divided into numerous sections of various sizes to feed and shelter different kinds of animals, especially cattle, milk cows, and horses. The foundations of these barns are often thick limestone walls that enclose the lower story while supporting the main floor. The expansive two-story space of the main floor is usually formed by a massive structure of hand-hewn or -sawn wooden posts and beams; diagonally placed corner, wall, and roof braces; and girts, purlins, and rafters that have been mortised, tenoned, and

pegged together in a manner common for centuries in Germany and Central Europe. The exterior skin of these large barns is usually vertical board nailed to structural members, and roofs are board with wooden shingles or metal sheathing. Sometimes the German bank barn has a forebay that extends the main upper floor in a cantilever over the first-floor wall on the downside of the hill and gives outside shelter to animals below.

Another German barn type is the double crib barn, which originated in German-speaking areas of the Alps, was transported almost without change by German speakers into the Middle Atlantic and Upland South of North America, and was diffused from there throughout the South and into the Southern Great Plains, especially Texas. This barn has two square cribs separated by an open driveway that runs transversely to the gable roof. The doors to the cribs most often face the interior driveway. The cribs are usually composed of logs connected at the corners with round or V notches, and the spaces between the logs typically are not chinked.

Although more Germans immigrated to the North American Plains than any other ethnic group, the heritage of German house types and domestic construction details is relatively thin and often misunderstood. The most widely built rural house type in Germany was the *Wohnstallhaus*, or barn house, which sheltered humans and animals under one roof. Although there are rare examples of this house type from the Canadian Prairie Provinces and the Northern Plains, most Germans followed English precedent in their new country by separating their houses from their barns and adopting house types of the dominant American culture such as the symmetrically composed, central hall, I house, or hall and parlor house. Even then, however, German Americans often expressed their own cultural preferences, including their off-center doors, main entries into kitchens, central chimneys with stoves, half-timbered walls, V-notched or dovetailed corners in log structures with hewn stone chinking between the logs, casement windows, and exterior plastering.

One descendant of the Wohnstallhaus that frequently goes unrecognized and is confused with similar house types among other ethnic groups is the German American two-door house. This type was common in rural Germany from the seventeenth to the twentieth century and can be found in significant numbers nearly everywhere Germans settled, from the eastern seaboard to the Plains. This rectangular, gable-roof, balloon-frame house is usually covered with clapboard, although the oldest examples are sometimes half-timbered structures filled with nogging. The house varies from one and a half to two stories and has two entries on the front long side, a front porch, and a kitchen ell or shed addition in the back with a porch. One entry led to a formal parlor (seldom used except for special family events), and the other entry led to a much-used informal parlor or living room. The living room had a stair to the second floor and interior doors that opened to the formal parlor and to the kitchen in the back.

See also EUROPEAN AMERICANS: Germans.

Dennis Domer
University of Kansas

Domer, Dennis. "Genesis Theories of the German-American Two-Door House." *Material Culture* 26 (1994): 1–35. Leiding, Gerlinde. "Germans in Texas." In *To Build in a New Land: Ethnic Landscapes in North America*, ed. Allen G. Noble. Baltimore MD: Johns Hopkins University Press, 1992: 362–78. Pierson, William H., Jr. "Richard Upjohn and the American *Rundbogenstil*." *Winterthur Portfolio* 21 (1986): 223–42.

GOFF, BRUCE (1904–1982)

Bruce Goff is regarded as a major visionary architect. His imaginative designs are an extension of precepts of organic architecture developed by Louis Sullivan and Frank Lloyd Wright. Born in Alton, Kansas, on June 8, 1904, Gott was raised mainly in Tulsa, Oklahoma. He began his career in architecture at age twelve with a part-time drafting job. He established himself as an imaginative designer and was responsible for several notable buildings in Tulsa during the 1920s. His Boston Avenue Methodist Church (1926–28) is regarded as one of the most significant twentieth-century churches.

Goff practiced and taught in Chicago during the 1930s and served in a construction battalion in Alaska with the U.S. Navy during World War II. He practiced briefly in San Francisco before returning to Oklahoma in 1946 as a professor of architecture at the University of Oklahoma. Later that year he was appointed chairman of the school, a position he held until 1955. Beginning in the 1940s Goff's architectural expression became increasingly diverse. Central to his philosophy was the uniqueness of both clients and building sites as primary determinants of design. Yet despite the visual diversity of his buildings, there are common characteristics that establish a sense of continuity and inform us of his ideals.

The most prominent characteristic of his residential work is a reliance on several alternative modes of geometry to organize floor plans. Goff would frequently develop a plan derived from a primary geometric form, such as a circle, triangle, or hexagon, with the interior volume defining a vertical axis. Other characteristics include an open plan with visual extensions into adjacent spaces and a concern for spatial modulation. The concept of interior furnishings as an integral and built-in part of the architecture is another characteristic. Natural light in Goff's buildings is often introduced by skylights or clerestories, and views from the interior to the exterior, especially on the front facade, are often restricted. Many of his houses have exaggerated eaves with a thin edge that evokes a feeling of lightness. Facades are highly articulated, and materials are rich in pattern, texture, and color. Water, in the form of interior or exterior pools, is another element of many designs, for Goff had a particular fascination with reflectivity.

The Bavinger House, completed in 1955 on a rural site in Norman, Oklahoma, is regarded as one of Goff's premier designs. The plan of the house is a logarithmic spiral built of rubble sandstone inset with blue-green cullets. The spiral wall appears to emerge from the earth and wrap around a central mast more than fifty feet in the air. The roof of the house is a warped plane suspended from the central mast. Interior "rooms" are defined as a series of platforms suspended within the spiraling space. Each of these platforms is accessible by stairs that wrap around an interior wall of the spiral as it converges on the central mast. The lowest platform, located at the wide part of the spiral, is a conversation area raised slightly above the floor. Above are platforms that function as sleeping areas and an uppermost platform that is a glass-enclosed studio. Each of these platforms also contains a copper-covered storage cylinder. Collectively, this ensemble of elements—platform and cylinder—establish a dominant rhythm that, like the enclosing spiraling space, ascends upward. Contrasting with these repetitive geometric elements, the floor below is a collage of field-stone, irregular planter beds, and pools of water with goldfish.

Goff left the university in 1955 and relocated his practice in Bartlesville, Oklahoma. He later established his office in Kansas City for several years before moving to Tyler, Texas, where he continued to work until his death on August 4, 1982. During the last quarter-century of his career he continued to develop much impressive work, including the Japanese Pavilion of the Los Angeles County Art Museum.

Arn Henderson
University of Oklahoma

DeLong, David G. *Bruce Goff: Toward Absolute Architecture*. New York: Architectural History Foundation and MIT Press, 1988. Saliga, Pauline, and Mary Woolever, eds. *The Architecture of Bruce Goff, 1904–1982: Design for the Continuous Present*. Chicago: Art Institute of Chicago and Prestel-Verlag, 1995. Welch, Philip B. *Goff on Goff: Lectures and Conversations*. Norman: University of Oklahoma Press, 1996.

GRAIN ELEVATORS

The grain elevator is a facility that stores dry, small cereal grains; it handles grain in bulk rather than in bags or sacks, and it stores, moves, and processes grain vertically. Vertical handling and storage are desirable because grain flows by gravity in tall, narrow bins, and thus less power and labor are needed. Grain elevators emerged in the second half of the nineteenth century in North America when agriculture shifted from a subsistence-based to a cash-market economy as wheat farmers of the Great Plains states and provinces began mass, long-distance distribution of their produce.

All grain elevators consist of several components. The workhouse contains the lower floors, while the headhouse (cupola) consists of two to five upper stories. The workhouse name is derived from the fact that much of the receiving and unloading operations take place on the work floor of the first story, where the elevating (lifting) process begins. The headhouse is so named because the head drive of the vertical conveyor system is located there. The workhouse and the headhouse are collectively referred to as the mainhouse.

The workhouse is the heart of the grain elevator. It contains a "boot" into which farmers dump their crop and a vertical belt-and-bucket conveyor that lifts the grain from the boot to the headhouse, from which it is spouted to a series of walled bins for bulk storage. At the bottom of the bins are openings out of which the grain empties into chutes connected to waiting transportation such as trucks and railroad cars.

Grain elevators can be classified according to arrangement of elevating machinery and storage bins, construction materials, and function. There are two classes of arrangement: self-contained, where the elevating machinery, distributor, spouting system, and storage bins are located in the mainhouse; and the annex, where elevating machinery, distributor, and spouting system are in the mainhouse, while storage is in bins connected to the mainhouse by external spouts and conveyor systems. In the latter system, grain is moved from the mainhouse to the annex bins by an overhead horizontal conveyor belt with a tripping device that directs it into the designated bin. Grain is moved from the annex bins to the mainhouse on a horizontal conveyor belt below the bins.

The first stage in grain elevator architecture was the vernacular iron-clad wood type. Constructed by local farmers and carpenters without a standardized plan or blueprint, the structures emphasized function over form. There are two subtypes based on framing. The studded type consists of balloon construction, also used in residential and commercial building. The cribbed type has walls of two-inch-thick planks, ranging from four to ten inches wide depending upon the height of the elevator. These are laid flat, spiked through one another, and overlapped at the corners. Cladding of one-by-six-inch lapped boards is used for both subtypes. Distinctive features of the iron-clad wood elevator include tie-rods extending through internal bins that are anchored to horizontal braces on the exterior walls and the galvanized iron or tin cladding applied to the exterior walls. Cladding was used for weatherproofing as well as to protect the wood from sparks discharged from coal-powered locomotives passing nearby.

The design and scale of the iron-clad wood elevator include a rectangular-shaped workhouse, forty to sixty feet high and surmounted by a two- or three-story rectangular full or partial headhouse approximately fifteen to twenty feet high. Gable roofs are common for both workhouse and headhouse. Internal features include up to as many as twenty cribbed bins of various capacities for storing and blending the grain, the boot pit (the central dump that receives the grain), the wood elevator leg (the shaft that houses the belt-and-bucket conveyor system), the distributor wheel that directs movement of grain to vari-

CO-OP concrete elevator, built in 1935

ous bins, and the wood spouting system that channels grain to bins or load-out chutes. Depending upon the size of the structure, total storage capacity ranges from 10,000 to 50,000 bushels.

From the beginning of commercial agriculture in the Great Plains, the iron-clad wood elevator was the primary hub for the grain storage and shipping industry. Railroads often provided land (right-of-way) for its construction as well as grain cars suited for transporting locally produced grain to distant markets.

Because of the skyrocketing insurance rates for wood elevators, elevator owners and builders experimented with other materials, such as steel and clay tile. Concrete, however, became the material of choice by 1900 because it eliminated the twin dangers of weevils and fire and thus reduced insurance costs. Cylindrical-shaped concrete structures were an engineering innovation when introduced to the grain industry. The slip-form technology used in their construction produces a tank in one solid and continuous piece of concrete without joints and patches. The technique consists of a concentric double-ring form into which concrete is poured. As the concrete in the lower part of the ring sets, the forms are jacked upward, and more concrete is added. This process is continued until the desired height is reached. The walls, six to eight inches thick, are reinforced with vertical and horizontal steel rods (I beams).

Grain elevators can be classified into four types based on function. The first and most numerous is the country, or local, elevator sited along railroad tracks in the small towns of the Great Plains. Because of the large quantities of grain produced in the surrounding countryside, farmers need local storage facilities to handle surplus production before shipping it to domestic or international markets. Country elevators allow local producers to hold their grain for a better price, protect it against waste and spoilage, accommodate

large quantities of grain during a peak harvest season, and charge lower storage rates than terminal elevators.

The terminal elevator receives grain via rail or truck from the country elevators. These towering bins, up to 150 feet high and arranged in long, parallel lines, have the capacity to hold several million bushels of grain. After receipt of the grain from country elevators, terminal operators sell huge shipments to flour manufacturers or store the grain for later sale to domestic and foreign buyers.

A third type is the processing elevator. Rather than grain storage, its goal is to process the grain within or near the facility into a finished product and series of by-products for either human or livestock consumption. Processing elevators consist of two subtypes, the flour mill and the feed mill. The flour mill elevator classifies and blends wheat for milling and is designed to transfer wheat to a nearby flour mill, where the milling process is completed. The storage tank arrangement of a flour mill elevator is comprised of a variety of bin sizes to hold different grades of wheat used for producing different types of flour. The turning-over process is important in a flour mill elevator in order to retain well-conditioned wheat during prolonged periods of storage. Therefore, flour mill elevators require a complex network of vertical and horizontal conveyors to withdraw wheat from any bin and send it to another. Flour mill elevators also feature specialized equipment concerned with testing and cleaning raw grain such as laboratories, dampers, washers, and driers.

The feed mill elevator normally handles, in addition to wheat, a variety of grains, including corn, oats, and soybeans. Because of this, the feed mill elevator's internal storage must be arranged to provide bins of varying sizes to accommodate different types of grain. Feed mill elevators require different types of space, chutes, and auxiliary buildings such as load-out chutes and docks for both sacked

and bulk feed, packing rooms, and warehouses for sacked-feed storage. Moreover, formula-feed mixing plants are connected to the elevator if this process is not completed within. Finally, feed mill elevators also contain specialized equipment, including corn shellers, cob crushers, roller mills, aspirators, sacking spouts, and batch mixers, which blend mineral supplements and other grains according to customer formulas.

There are two noticeable differences between grain elevators in the Canadian Prairie Provinces and those elsewhere in the Great Plains. First, wood elevators remain more numerous in the Canadian provinces, although this is expected to change as they are replaced by the concrete version. Second, the exterior of Canadian wood elevators is usually painted. Colors vary according to company ownership; however, red, silver, white, and brown are the most common.

Whether wood, tile, or concrete, the grain elevator continues to dominate the visual landscape of the Great Plains, where it has played a significant role in the economic life of small towns for more than 100 years.

George O. Carney
Oklahoma State University

Carney, George O. "Grain Elevators in the United States and Canada: Functional or Symbolic?" *Material Culture* 27 (1995): 1–24. Clark, Charles S., ed. *Grain Elevators of North America.* Chicago: Grain and Feed Journals Consolidated, 1942. Riley, Robert B. "Grain Elevators: Symbols of Time, Place, and Honest Building." *American Institute of Architects Journal* 66 (1977): 50–55.

GREENE, HERB (b. 1929)

Herb Greene is an architect, painter, and author who developed a highly original interpretation of organic design. Born in Oneonta, New York, on September 13, 1929, Greene studied with the architect Bruce Goff at the University of Oklahoma and practiced architecture in Texas, Oklahoma, and Kentucky. He returned to the University of Oklahoma to teach in 1957 and was later a professor of architecture at the University of Kentucky until 1982. Two Oklahoma houses built in the late 1950s—the Joyce House in Snyder and the Greene House in rural Norman—reflect the synthesis of aesthetic and philosophic ideals of his mature work.

The Joyce House, built on a bluff strewn with large granite boulders and with distant views of flat grasslands, represents a synthesis of both site characteristics and the clients' desire to include their collection of antique furniture in the design. The unrestricted views of the surrounding landscape dictated walls of wood and glass placed upon a pedestal of granite to accommodate the unusual collection of furniture. Moreover, the design strategy suggested a high degree of contrast with multidirectional meanings. The anchoring pedestal of granite contrasts with the floating roof above. The upper walls of wood, modulated to accommodate stained-glass windows, are terminated with a winglike mansard protecting the glass walls on the lower floor. The scaly and articulated form of the asymmetrical exterior, with its animalistic, hornlike roof drain, is further contrasted with the smooth, white, crystalline wall forms of the symmetrical interior. At the very center of the octagonal plan is a fountain and pool of water, placid and in contrast to the arid landscape beyond.

The Greene House, built as a family home, is a more complex design than the Joyce House. The two-story, wood-frame house atop a prairie knoll extended Greene's interest in creating an architecture composed of diverse and ambiguous metaphors. The inclusion of diverse elements is, theoretically, an attempt to express meaning through an organic process of cognition. Central to this concept, which Greene derived from Alfred North Whitehead, is the notion that any object is not a static entity but has multiple aspects that are apparent by various cues that can be measured against our own emotional and intellectual experiences.

In the Greene House, forms that are both barnlike and creaturelike are organized into a synthesis of images. The elliptical shape is a form that presents the least surface to Oklahoma storms approaching from the southwest. The color and texture of the house echo the farm buildings of the region. The animal metaphor is also an apparent attempt to make reference to both the living and the passage of time. The weathered boards and shingles on the exterior sustain the metaphors of both creature and barn and relate to the forms of ravines and windblown grass of the landscape. The design reflects deliberate suggestions of opposites. Even the sheet-metal canopy, with its insectlike legs, suggests contradictions. As the canopy climbs upward to hover over the roof, it is transformed into a machined element like a rocket about to launch.

Both the Joyce House and the Greene House are complex and mysterious images. Philosophically, the images suggest associations with regional history, ecology, the passage of time, and pathos. Certainly, they are profound statements of the traditional elements of architecture (form, space, texture, and color), but the arrangement and juxtaposition of images encourage contemplation. Greene constructed an ensemble of startling metaphors and thereby invites speculation into meaning by drawing upon the past experiences of the beholder.

Arn Henderson
University of Oklahoma

Farmer, John. *Green Shift: Toward a Green Sensibility in Architecture.* Oxford: Butterworth-Heinemann, 1996.
Greene, Herb. *Mind and Image: An Essay on Art and Architecture.* Lexington: University Press of Kentucky, 1976.
Greene, Herb, and Nanine Hilliard Greene. *Building to Last: Architecture as Ongoing Art.* New York: Hastings House, 1981.

HERMINGHAUS, ERNST (1890–1965)

Born December 31, 1890, and raised in Lincoln, Nebraska, Ernst H. Herminghaus became in 1915 the first practicing landscape architect residing in Nebraska. His design career spanned fifty years and included landscape projects for the Nebraska State Capitol, Lincoln's Pioneers Park, and numerous private gardens.

Herminghaus graduated in horticulture from the University of Nebraska in 1913 and from the landscape architecture program at the Harvard Graduate School of Design in 1915. An enthusiastic plant expert, Herminghaus taught landscape design and history in the University of Nebraska's architecture program during the early 1930s. During both world wars, Herminghaus worked on designs for military bases at Hastings, Nebraska, and Hanford, Washington, and in Alaska and England.

Because he learned design under Frederick Law Olmsted and Henry Vincent Hubbard at Harvard, Herminghaus's designs for Pioneers Park and private residences read like a Beaux-arts pattern book for landscapes. Herminghaus used Pioneers Park's rolling topography to highlight a series of sequential views within and beyond the park. Distant views focused on the Nebraska State Capitol tower, and internal views terminated at large sculptures. The park's first 160 areas are exclusively devoted to a series of carefully linked, informally planted spaces. Tight spatial control in this rural park was created by dense plantings of conifers. Expression of his rich plant vocabulary resulted in a varied palette of deciduous trees and shrubs. Pioneers Park has been placed on the National Register of Historic Places.

Herminghaus's 1933 plan for the Nebraska State Capitol grounds reveals that he understood the visual needs of the building and landscape better than the architects. Elements of the plan include a broad lawn with carefully placed deciduous trees and a foundation planting of large evergreens. The lack of ornamental shrubs keeps the viewer focused upon the building's rich architectural detail. However, in the capitol's interior courtyards the full ornamental expression of Herminghaus's horticultural knowledge is seen in formal plantings of bright seasonal flowers and diverse shrub borders. Herminghaus's Nebraska State Capitol landscape plan was the state's largest planting project up to that time.

Herminghaus was more than a mere technician. He was also a teacher, and he inspired humanistic goals in his design work. After his death on September 20, 1965, in Newton, Connecticut, Ernst Herminghaus's ashes were scattered in Pioneers Park.

Richard K. Sutton
University of Nebraska–Lincoln

Sutton, Richard K. "Ernst Herminghaus, Landscape Architect." *Nebraska History* 66 (1985): 372–91.

HISPANIC ARCHITECTURE

Mexican pioneers first introduced their adobe building tradition to the Plains in the 1830s. Later, in the mid-1890s California Mission Revival style initiated the self-conscious use of Hispanic imagery for commercial, civic, and residential purposes. Mexican and Mexican American workers recruited to the region by agricultural interests and the railways after

Administration Building, Texas Tech University, William Ward Watkin, architect

1900 were first provided with rudimentary housing but in time developed their own distinctive *colonias* and barrios. These manifestations of Hispanic architecture have been strongest on the southern and western reaches of the Great Plains but have echoed north at least into the Dakotas. However, the relation of the houses built and lived in by Mexican Americans—the primary Hispanic residents of the Great Plains—to self-conscious Hispanic Revival–style buildings has often been tenuous.

Workmen hired from New Mexico in the early 1830s constructed Bent's Fort in southeastern Colorado of adobe, following the Spanish Mexican presidio plan of an enclosed quadrangle with rooms one deep on each side and two towers at opposite corners. Bent's Fort was the model for six fur-trading forts built over the next ten years along the South and North Platte Rivers in northeastern Colorado and southeastern Wyoming. The U.S. Army adopted adobe as the most cost-effective material for its installations on the Central and Southern Plains from the late 1840s into the 1870s. However, only at Fort Mitchell, in western Nebraska, did the army also adopt the quadrangle plan.

Between the mid-1830s and 1900, mestizos from north-central New Mexico pushed into southeastern Colorado and the panhandles of Texas and Oklahoma, while Tejano settlers moved up the Rio Grande and the Pecos River onto the Southern Plains in Texas. Both groups carried the Spanish Mexican vernacular building tradition of massive load-bearing walls. These were primarily built of adobe, although they could also be made of unfinished stone, vertical posts, or hewn horizontal logs, all finished with earthen plaster. Log or milled beams topped by branches or milled decking and a layer of earth formed the typical flat roofs. Most houses were two to four rooms, each with an exterior door and arranged in single file or L-shaped plans. After 1865 carpenter Greek Revival detailing and gabled and hipped roofs of wood or corrugated metal were added to this owner-built vocabulary.

While most early Plains towns took their architectural inspiration from Europe and the East, Spanish Mexican borderlands history made the romantic evocation of Hispanic styles plausible, especially on the Southern Great Plains. The Texas and Colorado state buildings at the 1893 Chicago World's Fair evoked this Spanish heritage, and around 1897 the Santa Fe Railway adopted the California Mission style for its depots and track-side Harvey House hotels as part of its campaign to attract tourists from the Midwest.

Most popular from 1900 to 1925, the Mission style employed buff brick or light stuccoed walls, red tile roofs, arched porches, curved and stepping parapets fronting gable ends, and occasional towers patterned on Spanish missions. While the Mission-style basics of stucco and red tile continued after 1920, mixtilinear parapets became less common, and a richer vocabulary of cast stone and glazed terra-cotta ornament based on the baroque churches of Mexico and Spain provided the predominant accents for Spanish Colonial Revival buildings. This Mission–Spanish Colonial genre was adopted primarily for train depots, hotels, tourist courts, movie theaters, sanitariums, veterans hospitals, Catholic churches, suburban homes, and both public and mission church schools, especially those for Mexican or Indian students. Texas Tech University in Lubbock adopted Spanish Colonial Revival for its campus in the 1920s.

The related Pueblo Revival style, developed primarily in New Mexico in the second decade of the twentieth century, incorporated elements of the flat-roofed, multistory Pueblo villages and the carved corbel brackets and adobe of early Spanish missions. The style was used for public buildings, hotels, and Indian schools in the Great Plains. An occasional aficionado of Santa Fe and Taos might also build a Pueblo-style suburban home. Although the projecting log *vigas* of the Pueblo style and the simple curved and stepping Mission parapets occasionally echoed the Mexican American owner-built vernacular, those commissioning and designing the great majority of Hispanic Revival buildings were non-Hispanics.

Even as the Mission style gained popularity about 1900, workers recruited from Mexico and the Southwest were provided rudimentary housing: tents and boxcar houses next to rail yards and scrap-lumber shacks for migrant farm laborers. In the 1920s, as laborers in the sugar beet fields of Colorado, Wyoming, Nebraska, and the Dakotas sought year-round residence, the Great Western Sugar Company responded by developing a series of workers colonies. Apparently built by the workers themselves in the off-season, the housing employed the flat-roofed adobe vernacular tradition.

In medium-size and large communities, once workers secured permanent employment they quickly moved out of company housing and into working-class districts. Their barrio communities took names like Guadalupe, Little Mexico, Argentine, Santa Fe, El Hueso, and Chihuahua Hill. Workers often rented existing two-room cottages, shotgun houses, and modest bungalows. The desire for home ownership, however, led many extended families to pool their resources and purchase a house. Some families built cottages to the rear from lumber, used railroad ties, rails, and corrugated sheet metal that might house newly arrived relatives or be rented to produce extra income. Some families created enclosed compounds with packed dirt patios to the rear and defined their front yards with low chain-link and wrought-iron fences or concrete block walls. Barrios are often distinguished by shrines to the Virgin of Guadalupe, Chicano murals, and vibrant red, turquoise, and pastel colors.

Today, many descendants of Mexican American pioneers and of the first Mexican immigrants to the Great Plains have entered integrated, middle-class suburbs, where the generic Mission style of Taco Bell and scattered Mediterranean-style houses hint at the region's Hispanic heritage. In the barrios and on the fringes of small agricultural communities, the current generation of Mexican and Central American immigrants who help support the restaurants, construction trades, and food-processing and meat-packing plants still face chronic problems of substandard and overcrowded housing.

Chris Wilson
University of New Mexico

Murphy, David. "Building in Clay on the Central Plains." In *Perspectives in Vernacular Architecture III*, edited by Thomas Carter and Bernard L. Herman. Columbia: University of Missouri Press, 1989: 74–85. Pratt, Boyd C. "Homesteading the High Plains of New Mexico: An Architectural Perspective." *Panhandle-Plains Historical Review* 63 (1990): 1–33. Wilson, Chris. "When a Room Is the Hall: The Houses of West Las Vegas, New Mexico." In *Images of an American Land: Vernacular Architecture in the Western United States*, edited by Thomas Carter. Albuquerque: University of New Mexico Press, 1997: 113–28.

KIMBALL, THOMAS ROGERS
(1862–1934)

For more than a century the buildings of Thomas Rogers Kimball have graced the landscape of Nebraska and surrounding states. His architecture has a refined character that reflects his highly developed training. Kimball was born in Linwood, Ohio, into an influential railroad family in 1862. In his early teens the family moved to Omaha, where he completed his high school education. His formal education in architecture began at the University of Nebraska (1878–80). He continued his studies at the Cowles School of Art in Boston (1883–84), at the Massachusetts Institute of Technology (1885–87), and finally with the artist Henri Harpignies in Paris (1887). Through this training Kimball learned to visualize structures in three dimensions, and he was able to design in many architectural styles.

Over the course of forty-four years Kimball's buildings changed the skyline of Omaha. Major structures include the Omaha Public Library (1892), the Burlington Station (1896), the Omaha Country Club (1900), St. Cecilia's Cathedral (1905–59), Philomena's Church and School (1908), the Fontenelle Hotel (1913), and the Omaha World-Herald Building (1915). Outside of Omaha, Kimball designed many important government and commercial structures, including the Lincoln, Nebraska, Telephone Building (1894), the Dome Lake Club, Sheridan, Wyoming (1895), the Hall County Courthouse, Grand Island, Nebraska (1901), the Battle Mount Sanitarium, Hot Springs, South Dakota (1902), and the Second Church of Christ Scientist, Minneapolis, Minnesota (1928).

Kimball achieved a national prominence. In 1896 he and his Boston partner, C. Howard Walker, were selected as the architects in chief of the 1898 Trans-Mississippi and International Exposition held in Omaha. In 1901 he was selected a fellow of the American Institute of Architects, and in 1909 he was appointed by President Theodore Roosevelt to the Commission of Fine Arts. Walker and Kimball were reunited in 1903 as members of the 1904 St. Louis Louisiana Purchase Exposition Architectural Board, and they designed the Electricity Building for the exposition. Kimball served as president of the American Institute of Architects from 1918 to 1920.

One of Kimball's major contributions to architecture was made behind the scenes in 1919, when he was asked to write the design program for the Nebraska State Capitol Commission. In this capacity he gave the architects full freedom and flexibility, ultimately resulting in Bertram Grosvenor Goodhue's magnificent structure.

David L. Batie
East Carolina University

Haynes, James B. *History of the Trans-Mississippi and International Exposition of 1898.* Omaha: Committee on History, 1910. Thomas Rogers Kimball Collection, Nebraska State Historical Society, Lincoln.

LANDSCAPE ARCHITECTURE

Landscape architecture is the art and science of planning, design, and management of both human-made and natural outdoor environments. It has strong ties to horticulture, recreation, architecture, civil engineering, urban planning, natural resources, social sciences, humanities, and the arts. Licensure in the profession is required in all Great Plains states and provinces except Colorado, North Dakota, Saskatchewan, and Alberta. Landscape architecture focuses on the development of landscapes, though significant emphasis in the profession also occurs in the preservation and management of recreational and historical resources. These factors tend to associate landscape architecture in the Great Plains with larger cities and with notable national, state, provincial, and local parks.

Landscape architecture developed in three overlapping phases in the Great Plains. The first period, from about 1860 to 1920, coincided with initial European American settlement and involved landscape architects from outside the region. During the second phase, from about 1920 to 1970, Plains landscape architects were often associated with multidisciplinary architecture and engineering firms. More recently, a third phase has been characterized by work done by landscape architects trained in programs in the Great Plains.

Early projects in the Great Plains were designed by consultants from eastern cities. In the late nineteenth century, for example, the extensive parks and boulevard system in Omaha was planned by H. W. S. Cleveland from his Chicago office. During this early period, landscape architects were also often involved with the beautification of parks developed by railroad companies, planning graveyards in the "rural cemetery" style, and designing gardens for wealthy patrons. Later, during the Great Depression, the Work Projects Administration hired landscape architects to plan state and municipal parks in the Great Plains. Mount Rushmore National Memorial and Wind Cave National Park in South Dakota, for example, are enhanced with good site design by landscape architects. The International Peace Garden, straddling the forty-ninth parallel between Canada and the United States, is a particularly special achievement, featuring gardens of hardy plants in a severe climate. It was designed by Henry Moore.

Landscape architects have been integral in improving waterfront areas in Plains cities. Combining resource conservation and public recreation goals, landscape architects designed the Red River Corridor and Winnipeg River Walk in Manitoba, the Westcan Center in Regina, Saskatoon, river walks in Calgary and Edmonton, Alberta, the River Front in Wichita, Kansas, and the South Platte River Restoration in Denver, Colorado.

The work of Ernst Herminghaus, who designed the Nebraska State Capitol grounds and Pioneers Park in Lincoln, Nebraska, Gerald Kessler, engineer and landscape architect with the Kansas City, Missouri, Parks Commission who planned that city's parks and boulevard system, and the firm of Hare and Hare, which coordinated with architect J. C. Nichols to create the plaza in Kansas City, Missouri, all deserve special mention. Hare and Hare was the first significant Great Plains landscape architecture firm, and its projects can be found throughout the region, including plans for Kansas City parks, the University of Nebraska campus, the Villa Philbrook in Tulsa, and the Civic Center, capitol sites, and park system in Oklahoma City.

The first Great Plains university program in landscape architecture was founded in 1924 at what is now Kansas State University in Manhattan. This remained the only Plains program until the University of Manitoba in Winnipeg initiated one in 1969. Subsequently, Texas Tech in Lubbock (1970), the University of Colorado–Denver (1981), Colorado State University in Fort Collins (1982), Oklahoma State University in Stillwater (1983), North Dakota State University in Fargo (1991), and the University of Oklahoma in Norman (1995) have developed accredited programs. Landscape architecture in the Great Plains is now homegrown.

See also IMAGES AND ICONS: International Peace Garden.

Richard K. Sutton
University of Nebraska–Lincoln

Lee, Janice, David Boutros, Charlotte R. White, and Dean Wolfenbarger, eds. *A Legacy of Design: An Historical Survey of the Kansas City, Missouri, Parks and Boulevard System, 1893–1940.* Kansas City MO: Kansas City Center for Design Research, 1995. Tishler, William, ed. *Midwestern Landscape Architecture.* Urbana: University of Illinois Press, 2000.

LAYTON, SOLOMON (1864–1943)

Solomon Andrew Layton was a prolific architect of early statehood Oklahoma. Twenty-two of his buildings are listed on the National Register of Historic Places, a record unmatched among the state's architects. Born in Red Oak, Iowa, on July 22, 1864, he died in Oklahoma City on February 6, 1943.

Layton began practice in Denver in 1887 and moved to El Reno in central Oklahoma in 1902. Three years later he moved to Oklahoma City, where he headed an architectural firm until his death. Alone and with different partners, he designed more than 100 public, educational, and commercial buildings (a majority of which remain) and many private residences. Layton powerfully influenced the buildings of early statehood Oklahoma. His works are recognized for their endurance and for setting a standard of stability and rich design that continues to enhance the built environment.

Among Layton's accomplishments are the Oklahoma State Capitol, the governor's mansion, more than one-fifth of the state's seventy-seven county courthouses, and at least forty-five Oklahoma City public schools, including the city's first six junior high schools and first five high schools. In addition, Layton designed several corporate headquarters, office buildings, department stores, mental hospitals, a museum, correctional facilities, and public and private higher education projects. Fourteen downtown Oklahoma City highrises built from 1909 to 1929 were designed by the Layton firm. Layton took advantage of new oil wealth to grace his projects with marble, limestone, sculpted terra-cotta, and often opulent interiors.

On the University of Oklahoma main campus at Norman, Layton fashioned original sections of the library, the administration building, and the football stadium, all still in use. The Layton firm designed the original College of Medicine and Children's Hospital at the University of Oklahoma Health Sciences Center in Oklahoma City. Both were still used in the early twentieth-first century. The Oklahoma State Capitol (designed with S. Wemyss Smith and built from 1914 to 1917) is a neoclassical structure with four-story-tall Corinthian columns on all sides. The interior was altered to gain space in the 1930s to the 1950s but has since undergone a historical restoration. Oklahoma City Central High, Oklahoma's first four-year high school, built in 1908–9, illustrates the adaptability of Layton's works. Abandoned as a sprawling inner-city school in the 1970s, it was remodeled as Southwestern Bell Telephone headquarters. The 1936 Oklahoma County Courthouse in downtown Oklahoma City is a monument of Depression-era Art Deco. The Skirvin Hotel (1911) is famous for its oilman founder, William Balser Skirvin, and his daughter, Perle Mesta, Washington DC social leader and minister to Luxembourg from 1949 to 1953. The Skirvin sheltered royalty, U.S. presidents, and early cattle and oil barons. The 1910 Baum

Daily Oklahoman Building, Oklahoma City, Oklahoma

Building, one of Oklahoma City's first high-rises, was patterned after the doge's palace in Venice. Along with Layton's elaborately ornamented Patterson Building and Halliburton Department Store, the Baum Building fell victim to urban renewal.

The neoclassical Shrine Auditorium (1925–26), later remodeled as the Journal Record Office Building, Central High (Southwestern Bell), and the original Oklahoma Publishing Company headquarters are three Layton works on the National Register to survive the April 19, 1995, terrorist bombing of the A. P. Murrah Federal Building in downtown Oklahoma City. The Shrine Auditorium and the publishing building suffered extensive damage; Central High sustained less damage. Yet all three remained structurally sound in the late 1990s. Central High and the publishing buildings have since been restored, and the Shrine Auditorium is being incorporated into the bombing memorial as an interpretive museum, with full restoration scheduled.

See also PROTEST AND DISSENT: Oklahoma City Bombing.

Mary Jo Nelson
Edmond, Oklahoma

Nelson, Mary Jo. "Solomon Layton: Architect." In *Of the Earth: Oklahoma Architectural History*, edited by Howard L. and Mary Ellen Meredith. Oklahoma City: Oklahoma Historical Society, 1980: 87–104. Williams, Robert L. "Solomon Andrew Layton." *Chronicles of Oklahoma* 22 (1944): 122–24.

LITERARY ARCHITECTURE

The term *literary architecture* can be defined in a number of ways. Three definitions can serve as points of reference on a continuum. The first definition focuses on architecture—structural design—in Great Plains literature. The structures that people live in are frequently a concern, especially in stories of the first European settlers. The dugouts and sod houses originate out of necessity, not preference. The settlers' wives especially resist living in the ground itself. Their reluctance springs not only from the inconveniences associated with setting up housekeeping in dark, leaking, bug-infested structures but, more important, from their cultural antipathy to living like burrowing animals and thereby becoming beastlike, uncivilized. O. E. Rölvaag's novel *Giants in the Earth* (1927) is a classic example of this aspect of literary architecture. As Per Hansa pursues his grandiose dreams of a prairie kingdom, his wife, Beret, equates their sod house on the open prairie with cultural isolation and psychological erasure.

A second definition refers to works in which the design and building of a house form a central theme. In some instances, the conflict centers on the woman's dream of the amenities realized in a clean, fashionable frame house, while the man focuses on the acquisition of land and the equipment necessary to realize financial security. Ironically, once the family's homestead is established and the fine house is built, the structure often becomes a symbol not of fulfillment but of entrapment or pride, as in Frederick Manfred's novel *This Is the Year* (1947). The grand house begins to crumble as soon as it is completed, a reminder of European Americans' misplaced confidence in their ability to control natural forces in the Great Plains. In other novels, the house becomes a trap or a garrison that not only protects the characters from the threatening landscape but also isolates them from social contact with the developing community, as in Martha Ostenso's *Wild Geese* (1925). In some instances, the fortresslike structure provides a site for predation and greed, as in Mari Sandoz's novel *Slogum House* (1937). This theme of enclosure is reworked by authors such as Wright Morris in *The Home Place* (1948) and *The World in the Attic* (1949) and by Larry Woiwode in *Beyond the Bedroom Wall* (1975).

A third definition focuses on the literary structure of Great Plains works themselves. Most Great Plains writers are aware of the complex relationship between the geography of place and the social structures that people create around themselves and in their communities. Although there are many variations, the conflicts—and characters' reactions to them—fall into some familiar patterns. The most common conflict juxtaposes a character who focuses on the land's promise of abundance or wealth against another's insistence on the primacy of societal values: home, family, community. Because Great Plains literary works are about a place that seems spare, the style of Great Plains fiction is also deceptively plain, but, like the intricate roots of prairie grasses, this plain style is often the result of the deliberate planning of a literary work's structure. Willa Cather codified this definition of literary architecture in her essay "The Novel Démeublé" (1922). In the "unfurnished" novel, Cather declared, the artist's aim is not to re-create a realistic world but to select material and present it by a "suggestion rather than by enumeration." A work of art should enable the reader to "feel what is on the page" without having it specifically named. In Great Plains literature, the focus on the elemental struggle to survive and the parallel need for personal fulfillment within a community has created a body of carefully designed works. Cather's own novels are perhaps the best illustration of this third definition of literary architecture. Her deceptively simple stories reveal, upon examination, layers of "felt" but unarticulated realities. Other authors, most notably Wright Morris, have recast this unfurnished style in the postmodern age, relying on the reader's knowledge of the region's apparently simple surface and its underlying complexities as well as the Great Plains literary tradition to provide the framework for an appreciation of the region's literary architecture.

See also EUROPEAN AMERICANS: *Giants in the Earth*.

Diane Dufva Quantic
Wichita State University

Lutwack, Leonard. *The Role of Place in Literature*. Syracuse NY: Syracuse University Press, 1984. Quantic, Diane Dufva. *The Nature of the Place: A Study of Great Plains Fiction*. Lincoln: University of Nebraska Press, 1995. Thacker, Robert. *The Great Prairie Fact and Literary Imagination*. Albuquerque: University of New Mexico Press, 1989.

NATIVE AMERICAN CONTEMPORARY ARCHITECTURE

Before the 1960s and after the demise of traditional architecture, little attention was paid to cultural relevance when designing housing and other structures on Indian reservations. Assimilative pressures, financial exigencies, and supposed efficiency led to reservation housing that was built to resemble housing for other groups, however different the cultural contexts. The standardized buildings also ignored differences in natural environments. Reservation cultural centers and urban social service centers, if built at all, were usually vernacular structures with little indication of the culture in question.

In the late 1960s and early 1970s Native Americans and Canadian First Peoples began to consider ways in which their cultural expressions could help them overcome difficulties in their private and community lives. Language revival, religious renewal, and other recalled traditions were brought into service. Economic development grants made it possible to use the marketing of heritage to generate employment on reservations in need of jobs. Greater public awareness of past social injustices and a new emphasis on group identity rather than the "melting pot" ideology created a favorable background for efforts to make architecture, as the setting for life, more relevant to the traditions of Native American users. Not all Native American groups are creating specifically Native American modern architecture, but many are, and in increasing numbers.

Cultural relevance can be suggested quickly by adding ornament to a standard building, for example. It can be achieved more substantially by reproducing or paraphrasing building types such as earth lodges and brush shelters that predated the arrival of European American settlers. Architects may use traditional building materials and may align their structures with the movements of the stars and other natural forces. Douglas Cardinal, a Canadian Métis, designs curvilinear forms for both Indigenous and immigrant clients that remind observers of the massive contours of bison or eroded rocks. Some clients and architects prefer to use symbolic forms, incorporating numerological patterns or the shapes of animals or medicine wheels, hoping that the values inherent in the symbols can be transferred to the users. Still others incorporate traditional patterns of use into the building plans, adding ceremonial rooms, central gathering areas, and meditation chambers to schools and hospitals. They may take into account customary desires to observe events in groups, standing, instead of in fixed rows of seats. They may also accommodate Native peoples' reticence when meeting strangers or the need for storage of crafts and hunted food. Some buildings have been designed by communal processes rather than by standard European American professional practices.

Oglala Lakota College, Piya Wiconi Building, Pine Ridge Reservation, South Dakota. Hodne-Stageberg, architects

Some tribes restrict culturally appropriate efforts to buildings erected for the direct benefit of all tribal members, including schools, clinics, tribal office buildings, cultural and religious structures, and urban social and service centers, while excluding casinos. Other tribes include windows, trees, and other plantings in casinos, suggesting links between Native Americans and nature and implying that a casino, the "new buffalo," benefits the tribe and is therefore respectable.

In the past decade the United States Department of Housing and Urban Development has become more sensitive to the need for inexpensive housing that also supports customary patterns of Native American life. Multigenerational families and issues of courtesy and privacy are now taken into account. The department has sponsored or encouraged construction with natural materials and with centralized and other unconventional plans inspired by preference polls of prospective residents. Not all tribes take advantage of the department's initiatives, and the available funds cannot meet the urgent need for low-income reservation housing units and the repair of existing ones.

Museum buildings and tourist facilities are especially likely to embody aspects of Native American culture or tradition, because one major aim is to celebrate the distinctiveness of the historic cultures in question. Construction of tribal museums has been stimulated recently by the Native American Graves Protection and Repatriation Act of 1990, which provides for the return of artifacts and human remains to descendants of their original owners. There is no standard museum plan, so the sponsors can build innovative forms or reproduce older ones.

Ceremonial buildings, by contrast, must adhere to certain physical patterns lest the ritual action be hindered. Other religious buildings too, such as the Native American Church at Wounded Knee, South Dakota, are usually traditional in form, though not always in materials. Glass walls or steel beams, for instance, may be used to enlarge such buildings, to economize, or to improve safety.

One design problem is that many Plains people traditionally lived in portable and temporary structures that cannot easily be evoked by fixed buildings made of permanent materials. For this reason, Denby Deegan (Arikara-Sioux) and Dennis Sun Rhodes (Arapaho) have substituted symbolic forms such as the medicine wheel at Deegan's Four Winds School at the Fort Totten Reservation in North Dakota or Sun Rhodes's prairie-side facade (under Thomas Hodne's supervision) for the Piya Wiconi Building at Oglala Lakota College on the Pine Ridge Reservation in South Dakota. Peter Kommers used the morning star to generate a design for the Northern Cheyenne Heritage Center in Lame Deer, Montana. A design by Mark Hoistad for the Omaha interpretive center in Macy, Nebraska, includes totems evoking clan warriors and references to the cosmos reflected in a camp circle as well as a conical container for the sacred pole.

Problems connected to culturally appropriate design include locating sensitive architects (there are still few Native Americans in the profession), securing funds, making decisions by consensus, and devising forms that reflect the cultures. Not all tribal members understand the symbolism in proposed designs, but most will respond favorably to buildings that honor age-old customs and revere traditional patterns of life.

See also CITIES AND TOWNS: Reservation Towns.

Carol Herselle Krinsky
New York University

American Indian Council of Architects and Engineers. *Our Home: A Design Guide for Indian Housing*. Washington DC: National Endowment for the Arts–Design Arts Program, 1994. Krinsky, Carol Herselle. *Contemporary Native American Architecture: Cultural Regeneration and Creativity*. New York: Oxford University Press, 1996. Landecker, Heidi. "Designing for American Indians." *Architecture* 82 (1993): 93–101.

NATIVE AMERICAN TRADITIONAL ARCHITECTURE

Native Americans were living two distinct life styles in the Great Plains at the time of first contact with European Americans. Tribes along the eastern edges of the Plains were practicing a semisedentary lifestyle, relying on agriculture for part of their subsistence. Tribes farther west were leading a more mobile lifestyle based on hunting and gathering. These two adaptations are reflected in distinctive patterns of architecture.

The agriculturists developed more permanent structures. These included earth lodges in the Central Plains and farther north along the Missouri River. The prototype earth lodge was probably first developed as an adaptation to a more northerly climate by northward-moving ancestral Pawnee and Arikara groups around A.D. 1200. This architectural style then spread to neighboring groups, including the Mandans, Hidatsas, Omahas, Poncas, Otoes, and Kansas by the eighteenth century.

The Pawnee/Arikara earth lodge was constructed by first digging a circular pit thirty to fifty feet in diameter and eighteen inches deep. The central framework consisted of four to eight large center posts, which held up the rafters of the domed roof. An outer circular row of posts held the lower end of the rafters. The rafters were covered with willow branches, a layer of grass, and a thick layer of earth. The earth covering and subsurface floor made the structure easy to heat in the winter and allowed it to stay cool in the summer. The circular roof had a central opening at the peak to allow smoke to exit. An entranceway extended to the east for several feet. The earth lodge was home to from thirty to fifty people, depending on the size of the structure. Larger structures were also used for religious ceremonies.

Pawnee earth-lodge symbolism was highly developed. The dome of the roof was the sky, and the circular wall of the earth lodge was the horizon. The house was divided symbolically into four quadrants, each with a center post represented by a symbolic color, wood, animal, and weather pattern. The house was divided into the male east half and the female west half. The west half of the lodge was symbolized by the Evening Star and contained the sacred altar with a bison skull and the sacred bundle with its ears of Mother Corn hanging above. The east half was symbolized by the Morning Star, the god of light, fire, and war. Each morning when the Morning Star rose in the eastern sky it shot beams of light through the entranceway across the lodge to light the fire, symbolizing the first union of the Morning Star with the Evening Star in an act of cosmic procreation. The earth lodge also acted as an astronomical observatory for the village priests. Observations of star positions were made through the central smoke hole, and each of the eighteen to twenty outer wall posts and the four center posts was associated with a star.

On the Southern Plains, the Wichitas, Hasinais, and Caddos built conical-shaped grass lodges with double-curve profiles and wooden frames. Two kinds of grasses were used in constructing these dwellings: the external roof was thatched with coarse Prairie grasses, while the interior walls were sealed over with softer grasses from riverbanks. The walls rested on dozens of poles that were bent and bound together at the top. This structure in turn leaned against an interior ring of posts and beams. The frame, which could be sixty feet in diameter, was tightened with horizontal sapling stringers. The grass lodge could be transformed into a cool summer dwelling by exposing the lower ribs. Traditionally, the grass lodges had no smoke holes; instead, the smoke seeped through the grass roofs.

The tipi was used from the Prairie Provinces to the Southern Plains. The tipi is an inverted cone, steeper on the windward side, with an off-center smoke hole at the top. Overall, the floor plan is subcircular. Two types of tipi architecture are recognized: a four-pole framework was more common on the Northern Plains among groups like the Sarcees, Blackfoot, and Crows, and a three-pole variety was more common on the Southern and Central Plains among the Kiowas, Apaches, Arapahos, Lakotas, and Cheyennes. The agricultural groups on the eastern Plains also used the three-pole variety when hunting bison.

Covering for the conical-pole framework was originally made of tanned bison hides sewn together. Before the advent of the horse, when dogs pulled the travois made of tipi poles and loaded with the tipi cover and other belongings, six to ten bison hides were used in the average tipi. Later, horses allowed larger tipis to be moved. Canvas began to replace bison hides for covering the tipi in the late nineteenth century. Some tipi covers were painted to represent events of importance in the owner's life, including a defining vision. In most societies the tipis were owned by the men but were constructed, assembled, and disassembled by the women. Tipi poles were generally lodgepole pine on the Central and Northern Plains, with red cedar more common on the Southern Plains.

The Plains Indians utilized several types of temporary or specialized structures, the most famous of which was the Sun Dance lodge. The centerpiece of the Sun Dance lodge was a forked cottonwood trunk, which directed the dancers' focus toward the sky and the deity. From the center pole, sapling rafters radiated to a circular fence forty to fifty feet in diameter. The side fence and sometimes the rafters were covered with leafy branches. The interior design was dominated by a low, circular barrier of brushes that separated the dancers from the altar, fire pit, drummers, and singers in the middle. Like the earth lodges, grass lodges, and tipi, the Sun Dance lodge opened to the east, toward the rising sun.

See also RELIGION: Sun Dance.

Steven R. Holen
University of Nebraska State Museum

Nabokov, Peter, and Robert Easton. *Native American Architecture*. New York: Oxford University Press, 1989. Weltfish, Gene. *The Lost Universe*. Lincoln: University of Nebraska Press, 1997.

NEBRASKA STATE CAPITOL

The present Nebraska State Capitol was authorized by the legislature in 1918 as a memorial replacement of the crumbling second capitol. The Nebraska State Capitol Commission adopted Omaha architect Thomas Rogers Kimball's novel procedure for the choosing of an architect. They pitted three Nebraska architects against seven invited outsiders in a double-blind competition: anonymous submissions to an unidentified panel of judges. Each architect submitted with his drawing a 500-word essay describing the use of a sculptor, a muralist, and a landscapist in the realization of the building on its site. Bertram Grosvenor Goodhue's tall shaft in the center of a three-story square base won the judges' immediate acceptance as symbolizing the upward aspirations of a people dwelling on the level Plains. Construction began in 1922, and the building was dedicated in 1934, each year's building progress precisely accommodated to the annual legislative appropriation. Goodhue died in 1924, leaving his office and the commission to supervise the building's completion.

The building integrates a variety of monumental architectural styles. The shaft recalls the Pharos lighthouse at Alexandria, the north front has the form of the Great Temple of Amon at Karnak, the balustrades and capitals are elements of classical temples, and the vaulting and rotundas are modeled on Byzantine and Gothic structures. The stone was quarried in Italy and Indiana, and the woods and metals were specifically chosen for their uses. Fixtures and decorations incorporate Plains-specific motifs such as maize and the buffalo head as well as more traditional elements such as the fasces.

Goodhue had for twenty-five years integrated the sculpture of Lee Lawrie into his buildings. In 1921 he added young mosaic muralist Hildreth Meiere to his artistic collaboration. In 1923 he added University of Nebraska philosophy professor Hartley Burr Alexander as "thematic consultant." Initially hired to write inscriptions, his pointed criticisms of the Lawrie flying buffalo led to an invitation to rewrite the artistic program. He then worked intensively by mail with Meiere and Lawrie from their first drawings to the final placement of their works in the building.

From a distance, the first feature of this integrated and collaborative artistic program seen above the gold-leafed dome is *The Sower*, a huge figure by Lawrie (inspired by French sculptor Aimé Millet) whose seeds, visually and symbolically, bring the Plains to life. The cornice relief panels that circle the building depict the history of western law. Near the north steps are four balustrade reliefs in the Mayan style that represent the buffalo and maize as sacred gifts to Native cultures. The entrance to the building is surmounted by a relief that depicts against a gold background the arrival of pioneer settlers to the Plains. The floors of the Great Hall and Rotunda are paved in black-and-white mosaics that render cosmic and geologic evolution in a dramatic form, including precise copies of drawings by

E. H. Barbour of the Nebraska State Museum of fossils discovered in the Plains. In the East Chamber the ceiling mosaics are in the style of Sioux painting and beadwork and depict a hunt, hoeing, a war party, and a council fire.

Alexander's inscriptions, while recalling classical and traditional sources, express his conception of the state as a collective body rediscovering its common goals in the building of its "House of State." The thematic program, left unfinished in 1934, was completed in 1996 with the dedication of eight murals by Omaha artist Stephen Roberts in the Memorial Chamber.

Robert Haller
University of Nebraska–Lincoln

Luebke, Frederick, ed. *A Harmony of the Arts: The Nebraska State Capitol*. Lincoln: University of Nebraska Press, 1990. Whitaker, Charles Harris, ed. *Bertram Grosvenor Goodhue, Architect and Master of Many Arts*. New York: Press of the American Institute of Architects, 1925.

PUBLIC BUILDINGS

Public buildings such as schools, libraries, city halls, and courthouses are the physical embodiment of pride, stability, and cultural enlightenment. They functionally acknowledge and aesthetically symbolize the foundations of civil life in a community.

The need for universal public education was well established by the time immigrants began to settle the Great Plains. At that time a basic knowledge of reading, writing, and elementary arithmetic was considered a sufficient minimum. Facilities to accommodate these requirements were generally very modest, often temporary structures built by the fledgling communities utilizing indigenous materials such as logs, sod, and even baled hay. Few of these early buildings survive.

During the frontier period many school buildings were barely suitable for educational functions, due primarily to a lack of design and building expertise. Consequently, educational reformers focused attention upon rectifying common deficiencies in illumination, heating, sanitation, and furnishings by developing design guidelines and creating standardized plans. At the same time, state and provincial governments began to assert their influence upon the design of school buildings.

One of the earliest and most basic purpose-built designs for education was the one-room schoolhouse. A small rectangular structure with a gable roof, it became a ubiquitous feature of the rural Plains landscape. Based upon a common plan, the vast majority were of wood-frame construction, although some were constructed of brick or stone where available. Likewise, many medium-size schools were based upon standardized plans. Characteristically rectangular in configuration, many of these buildings were organized around a central hall flanked by several rooms and accommodating stairs to a basement and upper floor. Exterior composition was typically symmetrical, with emphasis upon vertical proportions, the latter frequently accentuated by a central tower. Popular Victorian styles considered appropriate for schools at this time included Italianate, Second Empire, and Romanesque. By the turn of the century the formal classical styles were widely favored for their more pretentious symbolism and distinctive monumental character.

During the early decades of the twentieth century, preparation of the citizenry for an increasingly complex society transformed the mission and magnitude of education. More sophisticated school subtypes evolved to satisfy new educational requirements, ranging from the nursery school to the junior high school and vocational high school. Special-use rooms were required for instruction in science, fine and performing arts, physical education, home economics, and vocational training. The compact but rather confining rectangular plan of earlier years gave way to increasingly flexible T-shaped and courtyard plans. The elevations of these more complex configurations accommodated a variety of stylistic variations, including the Late Gothic Revival, which was popularly associated with educational buildings ranging from grade schools to collegiate institutions.

The architectural character of schools in the Great Plains continued to evolve after World War II, paralleling changes in educational philosophy, technology, and design. Elementary and high schools were typically sited on tracts of land large enough to accommodate generous playgrounds and outdoor athletic facilities. Their designs were characterized by open-space planning, spreading classroom wings, and clearly articulated special-use facilities. Designs in the 1950s and 1960s were distinctly modern, emphasizing efficiency and displaying a functional, almost industrial image. Glass curtain walls, simple brick facades, and flat roofs were characterizing features that were used extensively.

School design in recent decades features a return to subtle historical references in material usage and decorative details, a utilization of the latest advances in building technology, plans based on the concept of learning communities, and an increasingly sensitive response to environmental issues. On the other hand, shifting rural and suburban populations and obsolescent educational facilities have resulted in the closing of many older school buildings and their conversion to offices and housing.

An interest in establishing libraries also accompanied immigrants to the Great Plains. Small collections of books were housed wherever unused space was available such as the rear of a store or the corner of a church basement. These modest collections were frequently the property of local citizens such as women's groups whose goal was to improve the cultural climate of the community. The greatest momentum for founding public libraries in the region occurred between the 1890s and World War I.

After the turn of the century the Carnegie Foundation provided funding and stimulated the construction of many libraries in the Great Plains region of Canada and the United States. In 1911 the foundation published a set of design standards for these libraries. The favored scheme was a rectangular, one story building set on a raised basement and entered from a small vestibule. The Carnegie Endowment program placed almost no restrictions on exterior design, but the overwhelming majority exhibited the influence of classicism, which gained widespread popularity following the World's Columbian Exposition of 1893.

Prior to World War II, library design was characterized by a bias for monumentality, modest attention paid to function, and meager consideration given to future expansion. After 1950 the use of fixed book stacks and walls gave way to a more spatially open, functionally flexible, and user-friendly design. In recent decades the information explosion, new technology, provision for the handicapped, and population growth have forced additional changes upon libraries. In larger cities the main downtown library may be retained, but new satellite branches are being constructed in the suburbs. The exterior appearance of these new buildings varies considerably, partially due to changing attitudes regarding the symbolism considered appropriate for a contemporary public building. Monumentality, once very much in favor for civic architecture, has given way to an imagery that is less formal and imposing. Common interior features include innovations in illumination, environmental control, and flexibility in the functional use of space.

Governmental buildings made their appearance early in the settlement of the Great Plains. In Canada the municipal building, or town hall, was the primary symbol of government after the provincial capitol. Sparsely populated rural communities and townships constructed small, unimposing structures that accommodated only the most basic functions of local government, but by the end of the nineteenth century the largest Plains towns were erecting monumental city halls following European precedents. In addition to providing for governmental activities such as a council chamber, offices, and courtroom, many city halls also housed a public auditorium for cultural events and a variety of additional civic amenities.

In the United States the county courthouse emerged as the most important symbol of government, second only to the state capitol. It was commonly believed that a building displaying a dignified and monumental character was appropriate for the transaction of county business, security of public records, and administration of justice. The courthouse commanded a place of honor in the town plan and typically occupied a full city block. One of the most distinctive spatial arrangements features the courthouse in the midst of the business district surrounded on four sides by commercial buildings. Status within the anonymous grid was also achieved by siting the building on a hill or at the end of a prominent street or vista.

The function of the courthouse changed little during the nineteenth and first half of the twentieth centuries, during which time the spatial arrangement tended to follow a distinctive pattern. Offices for the daily business of elected officials were usually located within a rectangular plan, the more significant activities being located on a raised first floor and the remainder placed in the basement. The second floor accommodated the most important public space, the courtroom, and related functions.

Nineteenth-century governmental buildings revealed evidence of the prevailing Victorian styles, including the Italianate and Second Empire. The Gothic style was quite popular in Canada but seldom utilized in the United States due to its religious connotations and the desire to separate church and state. During the 1880s the round arch, or Romanesque, style was widely favored for its solid, dignified appearance. The overwhelming majority of governmental buildings built between the turn of the century and the 1930s exhibit the influence of classicism.

Since World War II many city halls and county courthouses have been remodeled or replaced. The design of new governmental buildings tends to be significantly affected by functional and economic factors. In contrast to the pride and optimism expressed in much traditional civic architecture, the scale and imagery of many contemporary governmental buildings resemble the sobriety and efficiency characteristic of today's utilitarian office blocks.

See also EDUCATION: One-Room Schoolhouses.

Keith Sawyers
University of Nebraska–Lincoln

Kalman, Harold D. *A History of Canadian Architecture.* Toronto: Oxford University Press, 1996. Maddex, Diane, ed. *Built in the U.S.A.: American Buildings from Airports to Zoos.* Washington DC: Preservation Press, 1985.

RAILROAD DEPOTS

During the era when railroads were the main method of transportation in the Great Plains, the railroad depot was both the economic and social gateway to the community it served. The railroad station, whether a roughly hewn shack or an ornate masonry structure, was the place where people could assemble to board a train for faraway places or welcome arriving travelers. It provided a central delivery point where a community's life-sustaining goods could be shipped or delivered by rail. And in the period from approximately 1865 to 1920 it served as a place where people could come to hear the news of the day, socialize with others, or simply be entertained by the daily arrival and departure of the trains.

When railroad builders first pushed their lines west across the Plains, they realized the importance of establishing railroad stations approximately every ten miles. The concept of having closely spaced stations made sense at a time when farmers used horse-drawn wagons to deliver their goods for shipment by rail. These stations also served as communication points for dispatching trains, fueling facilities for steam locomotives, and potential town sites that could provide future revenue for the carrier.

For isolated communities established on the Plains prior to the arrival of a railroad, obtaining a railroad station once the tracks did arrive in the area was vital to their continued existence. Quite frequently, local citizens and railroad officials disputed the exact location of the town's depot. Most often, the railroad won out. And if the depot was located at some distance from the original town site, residents would usually relocate to the depot site.

In their initial rush to lay tracks, railroad companies often hastily used portable shacks or old boxcar bodies as the first depot for a new community. If the community grew into an established town, the initial roughshod structure was replaced with a frame depot of a standard design adopted by the particular rail carrier. These designs allowed depots of nearly identical appearance to be cheaply and efficiently constructed at hundreds of towns along the lines of a rail system. Minor changes in design were made to conform to the needs of a particular station site; for example, station buildings in more isolated areas had living quarters for the station agent.

Most depots constructed for small towns otherwise followed the combination station plan devised by railroad architects. This combination design essentially provided all railroad services for the public under one roof. A ticket and work office for the agent was most often situated in the center, flanked by a passenger waiting room and a freight room for express shipments. As business grew at some stations, a separate building for freight business was established.

Major railroad companies of the Great Plains such as the Atchison, Topeka and Santa Fe in the United States and the Canadian Pacific in Canada came to be closely identified with their standard design depots (much as fast food restaurants are today). However, as towns grew, local promoters often pressed railroad officials to replace their community's old wood depot with a larger and more ornate building of brick or stone. The railroad station was the first impression that travelers received of a town, and citizens obviously wanted their station to reflect a prosperous image. Railroad officials would sometimes comply, especially if the community was a vital center for railroad operations such as a county seat or college town.

The rise of competing forms of transportation in the early to mid–twentieth century eventually all but eliminated the railroad depot as a Great Plains landmark. Passenger trains and branch lines were abandoned as first the automotive age and then the Great Depression cut into railroad profits. Fewer freight trains were needed as steam locomotives were replaced by diesel engines that could pull longer trains. New communication technologies eliminated the need for an agent to be employed at each town. All these factors prompted the major railroad companies serv-

ing the Great Plains region to close almost all their remaining railroad stations by the late 1970s.

Currently, a limited number of Plains depots remain open to the public in communities that have government-subsidized passenger train service. But the majority of extant station buildings have been acquired by private citizens or public municipalities and converted to other uses. A number of these structures now serve as museums devoted to a time when adventure began or ended on a railroad station platform.

See also TRANSPORTATION: Railroads, United States; Railways, Canada.

James J. Reisdorff
David City, Nebraska

Grant, H. Roger. *Kansas Depots*. Topeka: Kansas State Historical Society, 1990. Grant, H. Roger, and Charles W. Bohi. *The Country Railroad Station in America*. Boulder CO: Pruett Publishing Company, 1978. Potter, Janet Greenstein. *Great American Railroad Stations*. New York: John Wiley and Sons, 1996.

RANCH ARCHITECTURE

Great Plains ranches can best be viewed as a built environment consisting of hay fields, pastures, ditches, corrals, fences, dugouts, wells, roads, and a variety of buildings. The ranch landscape is, in turn, an integral part of a broader ranch culture that includes occupational skills such as branding and fencing, traditional crafts such as saddle making and cooking, folk art forms such as barn dances and yard art, esoteric folk speech, and many other elements.

Plains ranch culture has its origins in Mexican haciendas, which were well established in southern Texas by the 1700s. Haciendas were large land grants with complexes of buildings that were essentially villages, including a large house and many outbuildings, cisterns, wells, ditches, fences, and corrals. Often the haciendas also included a church.

American ranchers in Texas continued to organize their ranches this way, since the hacienda was well adapted to the Great Plains environment and to ranching. As ranches spread north onto the Central and Northern Plains in the late nineteenth century, migrants from the East, South, Midwest, and Europe brought traditional forms and technologies that influenced the architecture.

Typically, the earliest ranchers relied on readily available construction materials such as wood, stone, mud, and sod. Ranchers also built with scrap material: unused buildings were torn down for their materials or moved to a neighboring ranch, a tradition that persists today. With the arrival of railroads in the 1860s, the choice of construction materials and of plans for ranch buildings expanded dramatically. Mass-produced products such as windows, doors, molding, and construction materials changed the character of ranch architecture. Land-grant universities produced numerous publications through their experiment stations and extension offices, as did agricultural journals. By the twentieth century, information on scientific farming

and ranching practices from both academic and popular sources offered designs for barns, poultry houses, corrals, and other buildings. The Midwest Plan Service, a consortium of universities that shared agricultural information, including building plans, began in the 1920s. It continues to offer plans of pole barns and many other structures today.

The architecture and arrangement of ranches are, above all, utilitarian. Buildings tend to be clustered parallel and perpendicular to each other, in a linear or rectilinear plan. Most open toward the entrance of the cluster; some open toward its center. Barns and stables, with their attached systems of corrals and outbuildings, are most often located in front of the living area, so that a visitor passes them on the way to the house. The living area, including house and bunkhouse, is set farther back and often surrounded by trees and gardens. Ranch buildings tend to be near streams or rivers or at least a well, and irrigated hay fields are adjacent to the buildings. Unirrigated pasturelands are farther out, with line cabins (distant shelters for ranch hands) if the ranch is big enough to need them.

Within ranch complexes, the number and type of buildings vary according to the function of the ranch (sheep, horse, cattle, cow-calf, or yearling), the size of the ranch, the date of construction, the ethnic origin of the builder, and the location. Generally, the number of buildings has decreased from the nineteenth century on, as rural electrification and the availability of consumer goods have reduced the necessity for specialized structures such as icehouses, root cellars, and blacksmith shops.

Like other ranch buildings, houses were functional. Often, a homesteader's cabin was a single room or dugout made from available materials such as sod, dimension lumber, or railroad ties. Before widespread industrialization, traditional forms passed down through generations dictated the overall plan of ranch houses. They were not always simple, however; in southeastern Wyoming, for example, wealthy British remittance men built elaborate, stylish mansions. At successful ranches, fashionable houses were constructed from designs found in pattern books, with manufactured decorations. Only occasionally were architects retained to design individual houses or barns.

Barns, stables, loafing sheds (which afford protection for animals), and the networks of fences and corrals to which they are connected are the working heart of most ranches. The appearance and design of a barn depend upon the barn's function and construction materials, the ethnicity of the builder, and the latest trends in the scientific agricultural community. Most ranch barns are used to keep horses and store hay, tack, and other equipment, including tractors. Common barn types include three-bay barns and transverse-crib barns, which range in length from three cribs to as many as twenty. As with houses, earlier barns tended to follow folk modes, while later barns were often built with manufactured components and influenced by academic and government publications. Technological changes over time such as the addition of silos or mechanized hay carriers and forks affected the design. Large barns may also serve as social centers, where ranch families gather for dances.

Ranches may have many other outbuildings, including sheds of various kinds, open-faced stables, dugouts used for storage, chicken coops, springhouses, storehouses, and garages. Ranches also have a variety of fences and corrals, loading docks, gates, ditches for irrigation of hay fields, hay stackers, windmills, water tanks, and cisterns. Some structures such as dance halls, corrals for spring brandings and auctions, rodeo grounds, and dipping vats reflect the communal activities that take place at ranches.

Like any business, ranching has changed with the times. Many modern ranches have prefabricated trailers, modular houses, or Quonset huts. Older buildings may be abandoned, moved, put to other uses, or torn down to save on property taxes. Although most ranches still have horses, motorized vehicles have reduced their numbers and made large horse barns unnecessary. Many traditions persist, however, including overall organization. Computers and other new technology, changes in public land policies, the increased importance of agribusiness, and other factors will continue to change the face of Plains ranching.

See also AGRICULTURE: Cattle Ranching; Ranches.

Timothy H. Evans
Western Kentucky University
Eileen F. Starr
National Park Service

Graham, Joe S. *Hecho en Tejas: Texas-Mexican Folk Art and Crafts*. Denton: University of North Texas Press, 1991. Noble, Allen G. *Wood, Brick and Stone: The North American Settlement Landscape*. Amherst: University of Massachusetts Press, 1984. Starrs, Paul F. *Let the Cowboy Ride: Cattle Ranching in the American West*. Baltimore MD: Johns Hopkins University Press, 1998.

RELIGIOUS ARCHITECTURE

The practice of religion in the Great Plains has been diverse, and the historical evidence of worship displays a rich variety of physical expression. Among the Native inhabitants of the Great Plains, religion was intertwined with nature. Prominent landscape features such as mountains and buttes were venerated as sites possessing spiritual significance. An efficient form of mobile architecture was devised by the Omahas, who created a special tent for housing their Sacred Pole. Permanent structures for the practice of religious ceremonies were also erected by Plains Indians such as the willow sweat lodge of the Lakotas. Indian settlements attracted Christian missions as European immigrants pushed into the Great Plains. For the most part, the rude structures associated with these religious activities were short-lived. Notable exceptions were the Spanish Colonial missions, which continue to grace the southern fringes of the Great Plains in Texas and New Mexico.

The influx of immigrants into the Great Plains of Canada and the United States during the nineteenth century resulted in the creation of numerous local church organizations, and buildings to accommodate worship soon followed. The character of many of these early churches, regardless of denomination, was similar—a rectangular, one-room wooden building capped with a gable roof. A slightly more elaborate version included a central bell tower, the lower portion of which served as an entrance vestibule. Modesty of means and the use of pattern books contributed to a significant degree of homogeneity in the general appearance of the building type during this period. The style preferred for these structures was Gothic Revival, an imagery associated with European Christianity, but most attempts to acknowledge this precedent were pale imitations of the style as practiced in the older metropolitan areas of North America. Scarce resources limited use of the Gothic design vocabulary; for example, the pointed arch above door and window openings might appear only on the front elevation. The interiors of these early churches were generally lacking in spatial development and ornamentation. Furthermore, the functional anonymity of the room and the mobility of the sparse furnishings allowed some fledgling frontier communities to temporarily utilize the building for the secular activities associated with a municipal hall, courtroom, or school until resources allowed for the construction of these special-use facilities.

By the end of the nineteenth century many former frontier communities had grown in both population and financial resources. Consequently, attention was directed toward the design and construction of more sophisticated houses of worship. Congregations erected churches that reflected both their wealth and the history of their beliefs. Guided by the romantic influences of the era, the more conformist denominations such as Roman Catholic, Lutheran, Episcopalian, and Canadian Anglican favored the Gothic Revival, Romanesque Revival, and occasionally the neoclassical Revival styles that were associated with the rituals and rich historical traditions of the European Christian church. Methodists, Presbyterians, Baptists, Congregationalists, and some of the newer denominations frequently took liberties with their interpretations of the traditional Gothic, Romanesque, and Classical styles as well as employing more original nineteenth-century styles such as the High Victorian, Gothic, and Queen Anne. In the process they generated diverse and less historically accurate versions of the precedents, the latter modified to express more contemporary values.

Noteworthy deviations from the popular revival styles of the period were to be found in the interpretations of the Byzantine style employed in Jewish synagogues and the churches built by both Eastern Catholic and Orthodox congregations. Predominantly located in the Northern Great Plains and Prairie Provinces, Eastern Catholic and Orthodox churches in particular were characterized by impressively crafted wood construction, complex massing, and picturesque domes crowning the roofs above the nave and chancel.

More specific distinctions in the architecture of the various denominations resulted from their differing beliefs and rituals of worship. These differences were especially evident in the design of church interiors, the two basic concerns being a recognition of those emotive factors that influenced the worshipers' feelings such as illumination, color, and proportions, especially height, and liturgical factors related to the actions, symbols, and furnishings that defined and facilitated the process of worship.

Prior to the 1960s the plan and spatial configuration of conformist churches placed emphasis upon a celebration of the sacraments in an environment designed to enhance the sense of mystery accompanying rituals and the hierarchical separation between the clergy and laity. Two traditional configurations were most commonly employed. The basilican plan consisted of a rectangular nave, which accommodated seating for the congregation, and a chancel, which was separated from the nave by an arched opening and raised floor. Approached by steps, the chancel was reserved for the clergy and contained the high altar against the rear wall. In the cruciform plan the longer portion contained the nave, the short projection at the top of the cross contained the chancel, and the projections to the left and right, the transepts, held secondary altars.

The spatial complexity and opulence of these interiors could be enhanced by the addition of side aisles, a tall nave illuminated by clerestory windows, stained glass, liberal use of three-dimensional detailing, elegant furnishings, and decorative ceiling and wall surfaces. A characterizing feature of Episcopal and Canadian Anglican churches was the extended length of the chancel. This space accommodated a choir, the seating of which was split into two segments facing one another across an aisle that terminated at the altar. The interiors of Eastern Catholic and Orthodox churches were distinguished by domes that spatially defined the nave and chancel. Typically, the chancel was separated from the nave by an elaborately decorated icon screen that obscured the congregation's view of the altar.

The layout and spatial design of nonconformist churches such as Methodist, Baptist, Presbyterian, and Congregationalist placed emphasis upon the spoken word. This led to the abandonment of traditional elongated plans in favor of a square auditorium configuration that greatly enhanced acoustics and sight lines. Other features borrowed from auditorium design included a gently sloping floor and a fan-shaped seating arrangement that focused attention upon a raised platform containing the pulpit and choir. All these features were ideally suited to a room created for preaching.

During the last half of the nineteenth century a design scheme called the Akron plan was widely used by many Protestant congregations. It typically consisted of the auditorium arrangement of seating and platform plus a large adjacent room separated from the main meeting hall by a moveable partition. This multipurpose room served several functions. When the dividing partition was opened the room could accommodate overflow seating for the auditorium. When closed the partition defined a space used for Sunday school classes. The appearance of a church utilizing the Akron plan was distinctive and usually asymmetrical. The main entrance to the auditorium was typically through a tall corner tower. This arrangement was particularly appropriate for a corner lot and invited direct access from both streets. A secondary entrance was marked by a shorter tower positioned between the auditorium and the Sunday school.

In the years following World War II the superiority of historical precedents influencing both style and hierarchical organization in the design of conformist churches was questioned. Modernization of Roman Catholic churches was accelerated following the Vatican Council II in the early 1960s. The latter resulted in a massive program of remodeling existing churches and rethinking the design of new churches. Interior design changes included reducing the dominance of the high altar in favor of a more communal altar or table situated at the front of the chancel or in the midst of the seating area. Further diminishing of the hierarchical separation of clergy and laity was reinforced by utilization of the auditorium seating plan. This has produced a blurring of the historical distinctions between conformist and nonconformist church interior layout and exterior massing.

Recent trends in the design of religious architecture in the Great Plains reveal a movement away from the conservatism of the past and toward a search for spatial and liturgical compositions compatible with the evolving views of contemporary religious worship. Meanwhile, significant shifts in population linked to social and economic changes resulted in the abandonment of many older churches throughout the Great Plains during the last half of the twentieth century. Finding new uses for these redundant but culturally significant buildings presents a challenge to the communities in which they are located.

See also RELIGION: Distribution of Religions.

Keith Sawyers
University of Nebraska–Lincoln

Kalman, Harold D. *A History of Canadian Architecture.* Toronto: Oxford University Press, 1996. Maddex, Diane, ed. *Built in the U.S.A.: American Buildings from Airports to Zoos.* Washington DC: Preservation Press, 1985.

ROADSIDE ARCHITECTURE

Roadside architecture refers to businesses and building types that evolved in response to the automobile. The most significant occurrence of these buildings, therefore, has been within highway corridors. The Great Plains was crossed by numerous historic highways,

Waltz Service Station, Lincoln, Nebraska, February 1937

including overland trails and railroads. Automotive highways represent twentieth-century additions to these established routes; these in turn were superseded by interstate highways after 1950. Most of the historic highways were east-west federal transcontinental routes such as U.S. 20, U.S. 30, and U.S. 40. Early north-south transcontinental routes such as U.S. 75 and U.S. 81 are less well known. Other early-twentieth-century automotive highways such as the Yellowstone Trail and Route 66 were regional routes primarily associated with tourist traffic.

Highways changed rapidly through time, as did corresponding roadside architecture; early routes and related businesses were often bypassed. However, many types and periods of roadside architecture existed simultaneously, so buildings continued to evolve stylistically. The necessity of providing basic services such as repairs, gas, food, and lodging resulted in the emergence of distinctive building types as the automobile gained predominance after about 1920. Other, more novel businesses with specific architectural forms developed in response to the automobile, including tourist or roadside attractions, drive-in restaurants, and drive-in movie theaters.

Roadside architecture—whether gas station, combination restaurant/gas station, or motel—often adopted regional references based on local vernacular traditions as interpreted for commercial or corporate enterprises. The automobile traveler crossing the Great Plains, for example, could find a sod house or covered wagon tourist stand or a tipi village motel. Such businesses, however, designed to attract passing traffic, were not constrained by historic or geographic accuracy. Many highways through the Great Plains also featured Dutch windmill gas stations and Spanish mission-style motel courts.

Throughout the largely rural expanse of the

Great Plains roadside accommodations were initially limited. Early travelers relied on established businesses for food and other supplies, carried camping gear, or stayed at existing hotels in cities and towns along the route. But communities quickly responded to the increasing numbers of automobile travelers and provided free campgrounds in public parks or designated areas. Campgrounds led to commercial enterprises such as cabin camps that provided auto camping areas and included simple frame one-room cabins. A store with gas pumps and a separate shower/restroom building were often part of the complex.

Cabin camps and available hotels developed into a building type—the motel—that was specifically designed to accommodate automobile travelers. Although many motels featured individual units, they were often arranged into U- or L-shaped courts connected by enclosed garage spaces. Later (although all forms existed concurrently), the motel evolved into a single-story connected building with an attached or separate office constructed of a uniform material such as brick. Integral garage spaces were no longer part of the building; instead, automobiles were parked outside individual units. Freestanding neon signs adjacent to the highway became typical features. A more ephemeral feature of many motels was landscaping, typically a centrally located flower garden or decorative shrubs and trees around individual units.

During the emergent years of the automobile, gas stations and service stations evolved from existing buildings. Livery stables, typically simple frame commercial buildings, added automotive services. Separate buildings soon emerged. In the 1920s throughout the Great Plains these structures were similar to surrounding commercial buildings—frame, brick, or concrete block—identified by advertising signs or, more significantly, by one- or two-bay service entrances on the main facade. Early freestanding gas stations were usually small buildings with canopies, gas pumps, and a small interior office area. Service bays were attached to the main building, generally one square or rectangular bay distinguished by garage doors. As gasoline companies took over along major highways, building designs and logos became standardized. Small picturesque gas stations became outmoded and were replaced by larger porcelain-enamel rectangular or square buildings with office, food, restrooms, and service bays contained within one building.

Drive-in restaurants and drive-in movie theaters developed exclusively in response to the automobile. Although both of these forms enjoyed a period of popularity in the Great Plains as elsewhere, the novelty soon faded, leaving many such businesses abandoned. Drive-in restaurants were characterized by a freestanding building that initially provided curbside service. The novelty of these businesses was in placing an order from and being served in the car. The limitations imposed by the Great Plains climate, however, resulted in either an expansion of indoor seating or a truncated commercial season. Similar to gas stations, roadside restaurant design soon became standardized.

Drive-in theaters originated in the 1930s and reached their peak of popularity and expansion during the 1950s. Because of the amount of land they required, drive-ins were located at the edges of towns, typically on major highway commercial corridors. The enormous screen faced inward to the parking stalls, which fanned outward to the edges of the complex. The inward-facing screen, often oriented along the major thoroughfare, served as a large sign advertising the theater name. Others with the screen located inside the complex utilized freestanding signs that were visible to traffic from either direction. Again, because of the climatic rigors of the Great Plains, drive-ins were seasonal businesses. Unlike drive-in restaurants, the vast amount of land required for drive-in theaters often resulted in developmental pressure, particularly along highway commercial strips. This pressure, combined with the faddish nature of their existence, often led to their complete obliteration in less than a generation. By 2000 no more than a handful remained open in the Great Plains.

Examples of roadside architecture, from early motels with connected garage stalls, to small cottage-style gas stations, to abandoned drive-in movie theaters, still stand on the landscape of the Great Plains. An architectural phenomenon intrinsically linked with the automobile and associated highway systems, roadside architecture has characteristically changed rapidly, and it continues to evolve.

See also FOLKWAYS: Roadside Attractions / TRANSPORTATION: Automobiles.

Carol Ahlgren
National Park Service

Belasco, Warren J. *Americans on the Road: From Autocamp to Motel, 1910–1945*. Cambridge MA: MIT Press, 1979. Jakle, John A. *The Tourist: Travel in Twentieth Century North America*. Lincoln: University of Nebraska Press, 1985. Liebs, Chester A. *Main Street to Miracle Mile; American Roadside Architecture*. Baltimore MD: Johns Hopkins University Press, 1995.

SCHWARZ, JOSEPH (1858–1927)

Born in New York City on February 22, 1858, Joseph Schwarz moved with his family to La Crosse, Wisconsin, in 1861. He trained in the family firm as a cabinetmaker and later worked for a contracting company. Schwarz moved to Dakota Territory in the early 1880s. By 1887 he was a practicing architect in Sioux Falls.

A devout Catholic, Schwarz was long associated with the Diocese of Sioux Falls. Between 1895 and 1924 he designed at least twenty Catholic churches in South Dakota and Nebraska as well as schools and parish houses. Schwarz preferred the Gothic style for his churches, a design aesthetic that met with approval from the mostly German and Czech parishioners. His most notable church buildings include St. Mary's in Salem, South Dakota (1896); St. Wenceslaus' in Tabor, South Dakota (1898–99); Saints Peter and Paul in Bow Valley, Nebraska (1903); and Holy Family in Mitchell, South Dakota (1903–6).

Two of Schwarz's sons, both trained architects, joined the firm after 1900, and their designs began to shift toward classical motifs. Also at this time the firm began to receive significant public commissions. Several of the most noteworthy are the Carnegie Library in Sioux Falls, South Dakota (1903); Sioux Falls High School (1906); the Lyon County Courthouse in Rock Rapids, Iowa (1915); and the administration building at South Dakota State University in Brookings, South Dakota (1912–18). Joseph Schwarz died in Sioux Falls on December 26, 1927.

Michael Bedeau
Idaho State Historic Preservation Office

SOD-WALL CONSTRUCTION

Probably no building technology is as synonymous with the Great Plains as the sod wall. This construction material was mined from the surface strata of Plains soils, complete with the roots and rhizomes of prairie grasses and forbs. The structural strength of the material was derived from the root mass, whose interlocking structure composed significantly more than half of the soil strata.

The area of shortgrass and mixed-grass Great Plains prairies constitutes the principal region of sod-wall construction. While a few examples are known to have been built from true prairie sods in eastern Nebraska, Iowa, and southwestern Minnesota, these are generally exceptional. (Whether this is for historical or environmental reasons has not been determined.) Some true prairie grasses such as big bluestem (*Andropogon gerardi*) were popular for sod-wall construction in mixed prairie environments where these grasses extended westward along valleys.

The diverse expanse of the Great Plains affords many different habitats for grassland vegetation. Grass communities preferred for sod-wall construction were sod-forming varieties rather than bunchgrasses. Any level or nearly level site with a contiguous stand of a dominant, sod-forming grass provided suitable material, but preferred stands were often found in moist valleys, lowlands, or larger sinks known as buffalo wallows. Under locally advantageous conditions, bunchgrasses such as the adaptive little bluestem (*Andropogon scoparious*) might even be present in a sod-forming habitat.

Buffalo grass (*Buchloe dactyloides*) was one of the most important grasses of the High Plains of Nebraska, Kansas, and Colorado, where it was often found in pure stands. Its sod is extraordinarily dense, with a structure of fine but very tough and wiry roots spreading widely in all directions. Together with the roots of adjacent plants, buffalo grass forms a dense, multidirectional mat with considerable tensile strength. This root system allowed for the cutting of bricks of great dimensional stability.

Little systematic investigation has been made into the biological composition of sods in actual walls. Existing data come from reminiscences. While many of these suggest that pure stands of certain grasses were used, most of them likely describe the predominant grass in a mixed community. In the Central Plains grasses most commonly used included bluestems, buffalo, prairie cordgrass (*Spartina pectinata*), and wheat, Indian, and wire grasses.

The antecedents for sod construction on the Plains are still shrouded in mystery. Several studies have speculated on origins, but none has been able to prove its theory. It is unlikely that sod construction originated from immigrant introduction or "pioneer ingenuity" or that it was copied from the membranes of Native American earth lodges. Early observations of the material do not offer reliable evidence or provide clues. Sod walls were often referred to as "dobes" by early observers, and after the proliferation of sod-wall construction, many clay-walled buildings came to be called "soddies."

The earliest reliable account of the use of sods for building comes from Fort Kearny on the Platte River in present-day central Nebraska. There, in 1848 Lt. Daniel P. Woodbury started his troops preparing adobe bricks but later shifted their effort to the cutting of sods in order to speed construction. The technology appears to have diffused from there up and down the Platte River valley and then to near and distant places around the Great Plains. The diffusion, however, was concentrated in the Central Great Plains.

Reminiscences and photographs of sod buildings appeared in the latter part of the nineteenth century, and these, together with numerous extant structures, allow description of a technology that evolved into the twentieth century. Early photographs of older structures suggest that the sod was cut with spades, the sod blocks approximating the size of adobe bricks. Often these blocks depict very crude construction. Eventually, blacksmiths and others designed customized plows not to break the sod but to carefully turn it in order to later cut it into building blocks. These ultimately led to the development of the "grasshopper" plow, which produced large blocks of uniform cut that greatly enhanced the quality of construction. By the 1880s this plow appears to have completely supplanted all older cutting technologies. The great diffusion of sod-wall construction followed the development of this specialized plow, which was manufactured in and distributed widely throughout the Central Plains.

Sod was used to construct a wide variety of house types as well as numerous other buildings, although multiple-story buildings were rare. Plowed bricks—"prairie marble"—were laid in masonry fashion grass side down, the first layer typically on undisturbed soil that had been cleared and leveled. Walls were commonly built two bricks wide with staggered joints and bond courses. Each course was leveled with soil. The use of lumber as a leveling device near midwall became a prominent part of the evolved technology. Roof structures, almost exclusively hipped, used dimensional lumber and wood shingles. Walls constructed for permanent abodes were hard plastered inside and sheathed with a variety of materials outside to prevent erosion. Finished with wood floors and plaster ceilings, interiors were like any other American house of the period except for their greater thermal comfort.

Americans unfamiliar with earthen construction initially experienced great difficulty building good-quality structures. Considerable experimentation was required to perfect the technique, which often seems to have been accomplished by specialized local builders. In other cases, individuals built two or more structures before achieving a size and quality that allowed occupation of the same building for more than a few years.

Like other American uses of native materials, sod was considered a temporary and undesirable method of construction. Most soddies were occupied for only a short period before they were replaced with industrial light-frame constructions. Some others, however, were occupied for decades by owners who overcame the stigma of living in "dirt" houses and who valued the thermal and economic advantages of the sod house. The evolved technology was thoroughly American and became, though fleetingly, a significant regional vernacular.

David Murphy
Nebraska State Historical Society

Alberts, Frances Jacobs, ed. *Sod House Memories*. Hastings NE: Sod House Society, 1972. Weaver, J. E., and F. W. Albertson. *Grasslands of the Great Plains: Their Nature and Use*. Lincoln NE: Johnsen Publishing Company, 1956. Welsch, Roger L. *Sod Walls: The Story of the Nebraska Sod House*. Broken Bow NE: Purcells, 1968.

STATE AND PROVINCIAL CAPITOLS

Capitols in the Great Plains region include eight in the United States and three in Canada. They range in date of design from 1866 to 1932, spanning the Gilded Age, the neoclassicism of the American Renaissance, and international modernism. All three of the Canadian capitols are unicameral, as is the Nebraska State Capitol, the only example in the United States. The others are bicameral.

Soon after becoming a state, the Kansas legislature formed a Capitol Commission in 1866 and elected Col. J. G. Haskell to the post of state architect. He provided a design to be built in parts (it took nearly fifty years to complete) in Topeka based largely on the plan of the United States Capitol. It included two wings, one each for House and Senate, and a central block topped by a dome on a columned drum. The same model was used in 1886 for Elijah E. Myers's Colorado Capitol in Denver; for David W. Gibbs's plan for the capitol in Cheyenne, Wyoming, completed in 1890; for Charles E. Bell and J. H. Kent's design used in 1898 in Helena, Montana; and for Charles E. Bell's plan for the South Dakota Capitol in Pierre in 1907. The model was followed in Oklahoma City in a 1914 design by Solomon Layton and S. Wemyss Smith, although that capitol lacked the planned dome until 2002. The neoclassical vocabulary and central dome of these plans were also used in the three Canadian provincial legislative buildings: by Edward and William S. Maxwell in 1907 in Regina, Saskatchewan; by A. M. Jeffers and John Chalmers in Edmonton, Alberta, in 1908; and by Frank W. Simon in Winnipeg, Manitoba, in 1912.

The two capitols to break with this tradition are those designed by Bertram Grosvenor Goodhue in Lincoln, Nebraska, in 1922 and by John Holabird and John W. Root Jr. in Bismarck, North Dakota, in 1932. Each uses an office-tower block above a base block rather than a dome. Each breaks with neoclassicism, the former in a style that combines ancient, Byzantine, classical, and Gothic elements and the latter in a strongly modernist idiom, the International Style.

A key problem for all the architects of capitols was how to represent the unique identity of the state or province. The most common method was to use local materials—stone for both interiors and exteriors and sometimes wood for interiors. Despite a legislature's preference for the fashionable architectural styles of the era and a respect for precedents in British, American, and French political traditions, architects did not want to repeat their predecessors, especially their own earlier designs. Thus, Bell in South Dakota and Myers in Michigan in 1871, Texas in 1882, and finally Colorado in 1886 developed, varied, and refined earlier efforts.

Another key means of state identity was ornamentation. Sculptures (e.g., oil wells, wheat, bison), adorn these architectural frames. Murals are the most popular means of presenting the stories of the pioneers. A key element in most capitols is a figure atop the dome. Golden men and women are most common, especially those representing classical deities; in some cases, Native peoples are also depicted, usually in postures of nobility.

All plans provide a variety of ways for visiting citizens to be impressed by the grandeur of their political entity while allowing politicians and bureaucrats to work largely unseen by the public.

Great Plains capitols are unique in three respects. First, because the three Canadian Prairie buildings were designed within five years of each other, they are different from other earlier or later provincial capitols. Second, the materials and ornamentation reflect each capitol's regional identity. Finally, originality is greatly evident in the Great Plains capitols, especially in Oklahoma City, Bismarck, and Lincoln. State legislatures preferred to choose local architects. Despite the fact that the most renowned architects of their day were not chosen, some of the most exuberant and innovative capitols in North America were erected.

William Paul Thompson
University of Manitoba

Hitchcock, Henry Russell, and William Steele. *Temples of Democracy*. New York: Harcourt Brace Jovanovich, 1976. Kalman, Harold. *A History of Canadian Architecture*. Toronto: Oxford University Press, 1994.

STONE MASONRY

During the early years of settlement, from the Provinces of Canada to the Edwards Plateau in Texas, the lack of timber forced settlers to construct their buildings and fences from other local materials. Though sod houses and dugouts served in some places, stone, when available, was the material of choice.

In central Kansas a Cretaceous limestone (Fencepost limestone) lies near the surface on the divides and is exposed in stream valleys. It forms a layer of uniform thickness of about nine inches and, when freshly quarried, is soft enough to be sawed, carved, notched, drilled, or otherwise worked with simple hand tools. The stone's standard thickness and coloration and its almost universal use impart to the entire region an element of uniformity and a unique folk character that have survived to the present. Many houses and barns, churches and stores, outbuildings and bridges, fences and curbstones display the same characteristics of color, texture, and dimension.

Quarrying required nothing beyond simple hand tools and strong backs. First the overburden was removed and the level face of the stratum exposed. The drilling buck, a homemade rig with sawhorse legs at one end and a hand-pedaled drill at the other, was used to bore holes into the stratum. Next, wedges, called plugs, were driven into the drill holes to cleave the rock from its stratum. Once cloven, the stone blocks were finished with dressing hammers and frequently textured with a variety of chisels into a number of simple designs. Smooth-textured finishes were ordinarily applied to stones to be used in chimneys, window and door lintels, and building corners. Often the stone for these applications was simply scraped smooth and offered an interesting contrast to the rough-hewn quality of the natural face used for the remainder of the building. Occasionally, the face was pitted with a punch, imparting a primitive decorative feature. Stones were laid one tier upon another mortar; powdered shale was used for chinking the joints.

The stone houses of central Kansas fall into several basic design classes. These include the simple cabin, the two-story L or T plan, and the one- or two-story square design with either mansard or pyramidal roof. Many variations appear within these generalized classes, but character, individuality, and ethnic affinity were achieved by the treatment of the appurtenances rather than by any overt distinction of the basic design. Stone houses were common to most ethnic groups.

With the completion of local rail service lines, lumber became competitive with stone, and in the late 1920s the use of stone was generally discontinued. When it was replaced, the old stone house was often left standing to be put to a variety of uses. It was, after all, nearly as difficult to remove as it had been to build.

L. Carl Brandhorst
Western Oregon State College

Brandhorst, L. Carl. "Settlement and Landscape Change on a Subhumid Grassland: Lincoln County, Kansas." Ph.D. diss., University of Nebraska, 1974. Muilenburg, Grace, and Ada Swinford. *Land of the Postrock*. Lawrence: University Press of Kansas, 1975.

SWEDISH ARCHITECTURE

Swedish immigrants moved particularly to the Northern Great Plains, especially North and South Dakota, although a good number of communities also took root in the Prairie Provinces and the Central Plains states of Kansas and Nebraska. For example, the Swedish settlement of Lindsborg in central Kansas formed in the late 1850s and the 1860s. Now about two thirds of Lindsborg's more than 3,000 inhabitants claim Swedish ancestry. The western reaches of the Plains and the states of Texas and Oklahoma attracted relatively few Swedes.

For Swedes, as for other settlers, a dugout or sod house often served as their first dwelling. Sod blocks, used like bricks, were a cheap building material, and a house could be constructed by the settler within a week. In time, the dugout or sod house might be replaced by a log cabin and relegated to shelter for animals. Whether sod house or log cabin, the Swedish single-room cottage was the model, with one big room (*stuga*) serving as an all-purpose room, with a corner fireplace, small entrance hall, and perhaps a small storage room behind.

Replacing the sod house or log building with a frame house was an important step in the development of the pioneer homestead. Numerous architectural plan books published in the latter part of the 1800s presented a "picturesque" American architecture with elements of Swiss and English rural building techniques as well as the Gothic style. The next step toward the industrialized building process was prefabricated houses, available from mail-order companies in the early 1900s. The standard patterns for frame buildings and houses

built of bricks and stones resulted in a definitive break with the old building traditions.

Churches built by early Swedish immigrants generally were copies of the vernacular church styles of the homeland. One of the most outstanding examples is the Bethany Lutheran Church in Lindsborg. It bears a strong resemblance to the cathedral of Karlstad in Värmland, Sweden, where the majority of the people in Lindsborg have their ancestry. The church was built in 1874 of brown sandstone, but in 1904 it was plastered with stucco and painted white. Also in Lindsborg the McPherson County Old Mill Museum includes the Swedish Pavilion. Designed by the Swedish architect Ferdinand Boberg (1860–1946) and built in Sweden, the pavilion is a reproduction of a Swedish manor house. The building contains a large main room and two wings. It was shipped in pieces to the 1904 Louisiana Purchase Exhibition in St. Louis. Later, it was moved to Lindsborg in sections and rebuilt at Bethany College, where it was used as an infirmary and for classrooms. In 1969 the Swedish Pavilion was moved to its present location and renovated. The pavilion represents a Swedish building tradition that is rare among Plains pioneer buildings and serves to remind Swedish Americans of the traditions of their home country.

See also EUROPEAN AMERICANS: Swedes.

Lena Palmqvist
Nordiska Museet

Lindquist, Emory. *Smoky Valley People: A History of Lindsborg, Kansas*. Lindsborg: Bethany College, 1953. Palmqvist, Lena. *Swedes, America's Architectural Roots*. Washington DC: National Trust for Historic Preservation, 1986. Winquist, Alan H. *Swedish American Landmarks*. Minneapolis: Swedish Council of America, 1994.

TANKHOUSES

Tankhouses are outbuildings constructed to provide water storage for domestic consumption and to insure dependable water pressure. The basic design is simple and straightforward—a large water tank (2,000 to 3,000 gallons) sits on an elevated platform some twenty to forty feet in height. Usually both the tank and the tower structure are enclosed. The area inside the tower is used for a workshop or storage or occasionally as a dwelling area. Wood is used most frequently in the construction of a tankhouse, although in some areas stone, brick, masonry block, or a combination of these materials is employed. Square, straight tower construction is most common in the Great Plains, but tapered towers are found occasionally, and in Nebraska circular towers occur in some counties.

In the Great Plains the construction of tankhouses dates from the 1880s and 1890s, although it occurred earlier in eastern Corn Belt states and in California. Notable, although modest, concentrations of tankhouses are in western Kansas and eastern Colorado, in Nebraska, and in central Texas. Initially, windmills provided the power needed to pump well water into the tanks, and both freestanding and attached windmills were constructed. Later, the availability of internal combustion

engines and electric power from rural electrification projects provided alternative power sources, and windmills fell increasingly into disuse. The development of the hydropneumatic pump ended tankhouse construction by allowing water to be pumped directly from wells into homes under pressure. Some tankhouses are still used for their original purpose, but most have either fallen into disuse, been razed, or been converted to other uses.

Robert B. Kent
University of Akron

Boucher, Aaron S., and Robert B. Kent. "Tankhouses in Nebraska: Distribution, Construction Styles, and Use." *Material Culture* 24 (1992): 43–58. Kent, Robert B. "Tankhouses on the High Plains of Western Kansas and Eastern Colorado." *Material Culture* 24 (1992): 33–41.

TIPIS

Tipis are the conical skin- or canvas-covered dwellings used by the Plains Indians as permanent or seasonal dwellings. The Sioux word *tipi* literally translates as "used to live in." In the nineteenth century each tipi accommodated, on average, eight to ten adults and children. Minimally, tipis consist of a number of long, thin poles placed vertically to form a conical framework, a hide or canvas cover, and tent pegs, rocks, or sod used to hold the cover to the ground.

The framework of tipis consists of peeled poles trimmed of all knots and branches and thinned at the base. Tipis normally utilize fifteen to twenty-five poles, two to adjust the smoke flaps and the rest for the frame. The poles are tied together at the peak of the cone, but poles extend several feet beyond the point where they cross. Size is limited by available pole size. An eighteen- to twenty-foot-diameter tipi uses sixteen to eighteen poles, each twenty-two to twenty-five feet long. Some tribes, particularly the Crows, preferred longer poles that extended higher above the cover. The poles were usually two to three inches in diameter where they crossed and three to six inches at their butts.

In many parts of the Northern Plains, lodgepole pine was the preferred tree for poles because it tends to grow tall and straight and requires less thinning at the base. Where lodgepole was not available, other conifers such as yellow pine, tamarack, and cedar were used, but these were normally heavier or required more trimming.

The tipi cover was made by piecing together hides or lengths of canvas. Buffalo hides were used until the second half of the nineteenth century, when they were gradually replaced by canvas. The hides were thinned, tanned, and cut to the desired shapes. The entire cover is a semicircle with a smoke flap on each side of the center point. The radius of the semicircle is close to the basal diameter of the finished tipi. A traditional tipi with a diameter of fifteen to sixteen feet required thirteen to sixteen buffalo hides. A modern tipi with a diameter of eighteen feet requires sixty-eight square yards of canvas.

Some tipi covers were painted. The painting was done before the tipi was erected. Designs included geometric shapes, sacred animals important to the designer, legends, and battle scenes. Women usually made, erected, dismantled, and maintained tipis, but men painted the designs, and the overall design was exclusive to the painter. The Kiowas of the Southern Plains and the Blackfeet of the Northern Plains were particularly renowned for their painted tipis.

Plains Indians set up tipis by first lashing three or four poles to form the frame. Most Siouan-speaking groups used a three-pole frame, whereas western Plains tribes such as the Crows and Blackfeet favored the four-pole frame. The remaining poles are placed on the frame, and the cover is stretched over the poles. The cover is laced together in the front of the tipi from the ground to the smoke flaps, leaving an opening for the doorway. The final step is to secure the bottom of the cover to the ground. Today, tipis are tied down with tent pegs. In the past, stones or sod blocks often secured the base of the cover. When the tipi was removed, the rocks were rolled off the cover and left as circular alignments, now called tipi rings. These provide the main archaeological evidence of early tipi use.

Tipis are not perfectly circular. The poles on the back are usually slightly closer to the center, creating a steeper surface. This produces a slightly tilted cone, with the steeper back side facing windward and a more gradual slope on the leeward side with the doorway. This arrangement improves stability in strong winds. The difference between the long and short axis is less than 10 percent, and the floor plan is slightly egg shaped.

Tipis are, surprisingly perhaps, quite heavy. The poles for an average tipi weigh around 400 pounds, and a hide cover adds another 100 to 150 pounds. When Plains Indians acquired the horse, they could travel ten to fifteen miles a day using the poles as a travois and putting portions of the cover on each travois. Before the horse, however, dogs were the only pack animals, and it was a strenuous job for a family to move 500 to 600 pounds of tipi poles and cover, plus another 100 pounds or more of bison robes, stored food, and personal possessions five or six miles a day.

Tipis have probably been used since the Middle Archaic period, about 4,000 years ago. Most archaeological evidence dates to the period 2,500 to 500 years ago. Tipi use increased steadily over time and was probably one of the major factors that enabled more intensive and specialized use of the open Plains. Virtually all tribes in the Great Plains from Texas to southern Canada used tipis. Eastern Plains groups who lived in earth-lodge villages used them seasonally when hunting; western Plains hunting and gathering groups used them as year-round dwellings.

Tipis were ideal, adaptable dwellings for the seminomadic Plains Indians. They could be taken down or erected in a few hours and moved to anywhere the group chose to set up camp. They could be adapted to accommodate the number of occupants. In inclement weather they could be modified to include liners and insulation, and, with an internal fire, they offered protection from strong winds and frigid temperatures.

Today, tipis are important symbols of ethnic and tribal identity. They symbolize adherence to traditional ways, evoking lifestyles that persisted for centuries but that have since been effaced. Nevertheless, tipi designs, the knowledge of how to erect tipis, and the right to paint them remain a prized part of the rich Plains Indian heritage.

Ken Deaver
Sherri Deaver
Billings, Montana

Ewers, J. C. *The Blackfeet: Raiders on the Northwestern Plains*. Norman: University of Oklahoma Press, 1958. Frison, G. C. *Prehistoric Hunters of the High Plains*. New York: Academic Press, 1978. Laubin, Reginald, and Gladys Laubin. *The Indian Tipi: Its History, Construction, and Use*. Norman: University of Oklahoma Press, 1977.

TOURIST ARCHITECTURE

Tourists of the Great Plains have both created and encountered a distinctive built environment. In one sense of the term, the first tourist architecture in the region embraced the natural landmarks that travelers named during their overland journeys, places like Chimney Rock in Nebraska and Register Cliff in Wyoming, where travelers carved their names, addresses, and destinations. Later, as railroads crisscrossed the Plains, company officials realized that travelers looked for a West that conformed to preconceived images and ideas. Rustic-style resort hotels and cabins were built in vacation destinations, while railroad depots often reflected a Spanish Colonial or Pueblo Revival style in their design. For example, the Northern Pacific Railway depot in Bismarck, North Dakota, is a striking Spanish Colonial gateway to the city, even if that style has no compelling historical associations with the state.

Yet it was automobile travel that would create the most distinctive aspects of tourist architecture in the Great Plains. The first transcontinental highway, the Lincoln Highway (later designated U.S. 30), passed through the heart of the region. Later came famous roads such as Route 66 and U.S. 40. In their wake came service stations that initially were flashy, eye-catching buildings designed to grab the attention of speeding motorists. The soaring column of the Tower Station, built in 1936 along Route 66 in Shamrock, Texas, was an instant landmark. During the 1930s and 1940s, however, these individualistic designs gave way to the standardized plans of the major petroleum companies. Revival designs, especially reflecting Colonial and Tudor styles, created an image of homelike comfort and convenience. After World War II, standardized designs, like those from Texaco and Standard Oil, used streamlined building forms, striping, and glossy enamel wall surfaces to turn service stations into virtual three-dimensional corporate billboards. By the 1950s a corporate stamp marked the roadside landscape, replacing the unpredictable yet visually exciting designs of earlier auto travel.

The pattern of evolving design conformity documented in service stations is also found in the designs of motels and restaurants, two additional key buildings of the modern roadscape. Motels proliferated across the regional landscape in the late 1940s and 1950s. Some of these early designs, like the Alamo Court motels in Texas, reflected both historical places and revival styles like Spanish Colonial. But by the 1960s major hotel-motel chains dominated the market, and their similar standardized designs varied little, no matter the location. By the end of the twentieth century, even the brightly colored signs once associated with motels, like those of the early Holiday Inns, were gone, replaced by the large, plastic, fluorescent-lit signs that now clutter interstate exits.

The history of restaurant design along the region's roadsides is a similar story of evolving architectural conformity. Distinctive roadside places like Ole's Big Game Tavern in Paxton, Nebraska, still serve travelers on older federal highways, but these restaurants are few and far between compared to the innumerable McDonalds and Burger Kings lining the main streets and interstates of the Great Plains.

See also INDUSTRY: Tourism / TRANSPORTATION: Lincoln Highway; Route 66.

Carroll Van West
Middle Tennessee State University

Hokanson, Drake. *The Lincoln Highway: Main Street across America*. Iowa City: University of Iowa Press, 1988. Jakle, John A., and Keith A. Sculle. *The Gas Station in America*. Baltimore MD: Johns Hopkins University Press, 1994. Jennings, Jan, ed. *Roadside America: The Automobile in Design and Culture*. Ames: Iowa State University Press, 1990.

TRADING POSTS

During most of the fur trade era in the Great Plains, trading post architecture typically followed a ground plan ultimately derived from military fortifications, thus the common use of the word "fort" in trading post names. The strong, defensive nature of trading posts was a by-product of the very nature of the trade. For the (typically) European American builders, the fortified post provided asylum from a rough and dangerous world far from the comforts of home. The fortified architecture also afforded protection for valuable trade goods and provided sanctuary from sometimes hostile Native American trading partners. Native American traders coming to the post may have perceived conflicting messages of promise and threat in the strong defensive character of the fort. The structures were a source of seemingly endless material goods, but the goods could only be acquired from heavily armed and sometimes incomprehensible traders.

Trading posts typically incorporated a structural assemblage encompassed by a square or rectangular palisade. This enclosure was generally constructed of vertical timbers set in a trench and about twelve to eighteen feet in height. Two square bastions or blockhouses were often built on opposing corners of the palisade. More rarely, these had a circular floor plan. The bastions generally had a pitched roof and loopholes from which small cannon and shoulder arms could be fired. To impede hostile intruders from climbing over the top, palisade pickets were occasionally sharpened or surmounted with chevaux-de-frise (crossed, pointed sticks). A gallery (or building roofs in smaller posts) was usually built about four to five feet below the top of the pickets to allow sentries to patrol and fire from the palisade perimeter.

Inside the palisade, buildings were raised around a commons area or open courtyard outfitted with cannon and flagpole. In smaller forts, buildings were constructed directly against the palisade's interior walls. Larger posts usually had structures set out from the palisade with the space between the palisade and structures frequently used for storage or as stables. A house, or "mansion," for the bourgeois or fort superintendent, generally the most imposing structure in the complex, was usually placed opposite the main entrance to the post and would have been the first structure seen by those entering. It often displayed painted wooden siding. Aside from serving as a home for the superintendent, clerks, and guests, the mansion would house the post's business office and dining hall. A separate kitchen was placed behind or near this building. The remaining three sides of the courtyard incorporated ranges of lesser structures. These were usually constructed more crudely without siding and left unpainted. Earth or sod was most commonly the roofing material of choice for these buildings. Structures in the ranges served the trading company as icehouse, powder magazine, employee residences, fur storage, trade and dry goods storage, blacksmith shop, and trade store.

With rare exceptions, trading posts were constructed according to vernacular building traditions common to the region in which they were raised. Aside from typical notched-log structures, vernacular French Métis construction methods were commonly employed in the Canadian Plains. *Poteaux en terre* (posts in earth) structures utilized a wall or building frame of vertical whole or split timbers placed into trenches in the ground. A more challenging construction method was *poteaux sur sole* (posts on sill), which placed vertical posts on wood or stone sills to prevent wood rot and thus provide greater structural endurance. Spaces between vertical framing were packed with mud and grass (*bouzillées*) or stone and plaster mortar (*pierrottées*).

Another common construction method seen on the Canadian Plains was Red River frame, or *pièce sur pièce* (timber on timber). Like poteaux sur sole, this French Métis construction method used vertical logs raised on a wooden sill. In this instance, however, the vertical members were grooved. Spaces between vertical members were filled with horizontal logs whose tongues or tenons were inserted into the vertical grooves to make a wall. Interior walls were commonly plastered and whitewashed.

Occasionally, adobe was used in the construction of trading posts on the Northern Plains (e.g., Fort William, North Dakota). This building material was more commonly used on the Southern and Central Plains, reflecting the greater Hispanic influence in these regions. Examples of adobe trading posts include Fort John (later Laramie) in Wyoming, Fort John in Nebraska, and Bent's Fort in Colorado. Adobe provided an excellent substitute for wood in the relatively dry climate of the High Plains, an area with few trees. Aside from its excellent insulating qualities, adobe construction allowed more free-form structures. Bent's Fort, for example, had circular bastions and generally displayed an abundance of curved structural elements. As such, it had a less forbidding look to it than Fort Union in North Dakota, for example.

Trading posts in the Great Plains were generally of three types, their structural complexity reflecting their position in the fur trade business hierarchy. At the pinnacle of the hierarchy was the major post. These fortified complexes (such as Fort Union, North Dakota, and Fort Garry, Manitoba) functioned as the regional headquarters of a company or trading outfit. They supplied and directed the trade of a number of subsidiary trading posts and wintering posts. Like posts subsidiary to them, however, major posts also served as a center for trade over an extensive area with one or more Native American bands. Major posts were usually quite large, imposing in appearance, and designed to last for a relatively long period of time.

Subsidiary posts such as Fort McKenzie, Montana, and Fort Qu'Appelle, Saskatchewan, were under the administration of a major post. Subsidiary posts were located in the general wintering area of an individual tribal group or band and operated year-round. Although usually smaller in size than the major posts, they were fortified similarly. In keeping with their secondary status, subsidiary posts were constructed more simply and usually built to last for a much shorter duration.

Wintering houses were the smallest and most temporary of trading posts. Administratively situated under one of the other two kinds of posts, they tended to be unfortified and often consisted of little more than a rude log cabin or even a skin lodge. Wintering houses generally formed the "front line" of the fur and bison robe trade, and as such they were usually placed in or near the village of a nomadic group. Since the nomads rarely wintered in exactly the same place from year to year, these establishments typically served the trade for a single trading season. Small-scale independent trading companies tended to resort to this type of post as a necessity, their financial resources being too meager to allow construction of larger palisaded posts.

Fortified trading posts in the Central and Southern Plains were largely replaced by small entrepreneurial operations during the 1840s. The large trading posts of the previous era were similarly reduced in scale to small log or adobe structures. On the Northern and Cana-

dian Plains, however, large enterprises continued to operate fortified trading posts for several decades past the demise of their southern cousins. By 1870, however, even that region's elaborate trading posts were being replaced by small posts comprised of simple, unfortified log structures similar to those that had been built on the Southern Plains in previous decades.

See also INDUSTRY: Fur Trade.

William J. Hunt Jr.
National Park Service

Burley, David V., Gayle Horsfall, and John Brandon. *Structural Considerations of Métis Ethnicity: An Archaeological, Architectural, and Historical Study.* Vermillion: University of South Dakota Press, 1992. Chittenden, Hiram M. *The American Fur Trade of the Far West.* Lincoln: University of Nebraska Press, 1986. Moore, Jackson W., Jr. *Bent's Old Fort: An Archeological Study.* Denver: State Historical Society of Colorado, 1968.

UKRAINIAN ARCHITECTURE

Ukrainian immigrants, mostly peasants from eastern Galicia and northern Bukovyna in western Ukraine, settled large areas of the Canadian Plains from 1892 to 1914. Almost all came to North America to seek free 160-acre homesteads in the "bush country" of the aspen Parkland Belt in Canada's Prairie Provinces, but some were also induced to settle in the Belfield area of southwestern North Dakota by American land agents. In Canada they established a series of large, ethnically homogeneous bloc settlements that stretched northwest from southeast Manitoba, through central Saskatchewan, into east-central Alberta. The Dominion Lands Act of 1872, which governed the disbursement of homesteads in Canada, required that all applicants reside upon their homestead for at least three years before full title was granted. This made it impossible for settlers to replicate the villages they had known in Europe. Nevertheless, chain migration created loose groupings of settlers from the same villages or regions, which encouraged perpetuation of Old Country cultural traits in the newly settled territories.

The first shelter built by a Ukrainian pioneer was often a simple sod-roofed dugout, called a *zemlyanka* or *burdei*, patterned on the temporary shelters used by shepherds in the Carpathian Mountains of western Ukraine. These dwellings provided shelter for the first year or two until a more substantial house could be built. The first true houses showed considerable variation in style according to the builder's region of origin but followed a general pattern: a south-facing, two- or three-roomed, single-story log house plastered and lime washed on the exterior with a low, overhanging, hip or hipped-gable roof and a central chimney. This type of house predominated in Ukrainian rural districts until the late 1930s. Abandoned examples may still be seen, and some modernized versions are still in use.

The aspen parkland provided an array of building materials similar to those of the western Ukraine. Aspen, poplar, birch, tamarack, and spruce were all used in place of the hardwoods of Europe. Slough grass was commonly used as an acceptable substitute for rye straw in thatching. Other materials remained unchanged: clay, fieldstones, chopped straw, lime, and horse or cow dung.

Log construction was the norm in the homeland and in North America, although where Ukrainians settled in timber-scarce areas wattle-and-daub construction was sometimes employed. Three methods of log building were used: horizontally laid logs, post and fill, and vertical logs. The diameter of available timber determined the method used. In areas with mature stands of spruce, logs were squared and corners dovetailed. Generally, poplar logs were merely scaled and corners saddle notched. Where mature timber was more scarce, post and fill was used: load-bearing vertical logs were mortised, and short, small-diameter, or misshapen logs were slotted in as fill. In a few areas where fire had destroyed all good building timber, walls were made of small-diameter logs placed vertically on a wood sill.

Generally, both interior and exterior walls were plastered with a mix of clay, chopped straw, and horse or cow dung. The plaster was anchored to the wall either by pegs driven into the logs or by a lattice of willow fixed into place before the application of the mud plaster. All plaster was invariably coated with a white lime wash.

High, steeply pitched, thatched, hipped, or hipped-gable roofs were most common in the pioneer era. Wood shingles were introduced in the 1920s. Roofs were then lowered and changed to the gable form, but the pronounced eave projection on all sides was maintained. Settlers from Bukovyna commonly extended the eave up to three feet at the front, supporting it with ornate eave brackets and four vertical posts to create an open porch.

House dimensions varied but generally were about twenty-six to thirty feet by twelve to seventeen feet, with the ratio of the side to the front about 1:1.8. Space was divided into the west *mala khata* (little house) and the east *velykha khata* (big house). The front entrance opened into the *mala khata*. In early buildings, this room, which was the center of daily activities, housed the large clay stove (*pich*) with a wide sleeping shelf. These stoves were quickly replaced by lighter and smaller cast-iron store-bought stoves. The *velykha khata* was reserved for formal occasions. Icons were placed along its east wall. A central hallway was a common feature.

Construction of ancillary farm buildings followed that of the house, though they were more likely left without plaster or paint. Usually, such buildings were arranged in the form of a square, with the house forming one side.

Acculturation showed in second-generation buildings, when two-story frame houses were built that still retained the traditional floor plan. In some small service centers, commercial false fronts were grafted onto the gable ends of traditional log buildings. Decor and use of space within the house were the two elements most resistant to acculturation; the preference for blue and green as decorative trim colors survived structural and stylistic changes, as did the use of the east-facing wall for placement of religious icons and, later, family photographs.

Churches built by Ukrainian immigrants during the pioneer era were invariably copies of the vernacular church styles of the homeland. Built by settlers from sometimes inexact recollection, they imbued the new landscape with a strong Slavic element. On occasion, the ancient styles of the Carpathian mountain churches were built, but the Russian Byzantine style, which was then replacing the older forms in the homeland, was more common. Pioneer churches were distinguished by their separate bell towers, log construction, and adherence to homeland regional styles. Ornate pear-shaped *banyas* (Byzantine domes) were sometimes added to early buildings but were more usually an integral feature of second-generation churches built on a tripartite plan. Architect-designed churches using balloon-frame, brick, or concrete construction did not generally appear until the 1930s.

See also EUROPEAN AMERICANS: Ukrainians.

John C. Lehr
University of Winnipeg

Darlington, James W. "The Ukrainian Impress on the Canadian West." In *Canada's Ukrainians: Negotiating an Identity*, edited by Lubomyr Luciuk and Stella Hryniuk. Toronto: University of Toronto Press, 1991: 53–80. Lehr, John C. "Ukrainians in Western Canada." In *To Build in a New Land*, edited by Allen G. Noble. Baltimore MD: Johns Hopkins University Press, 1992: 309–30. Rotoff, Basil, Roman Yereniuk, and Stella Hryniuk. *Monuments to Faith: Ukrainian Churches in Manitoba*. Winnipeg: University of Manitoba Press, 1990.

VOLGA GERMAN ARCHITECTURE

Volga German folk buildings represent an unusual synthesis of central European and Russian building forms and construction methods. Not unlike the Black Sea German settlers in the Great Plains, the Volga River immigrants relied upon homeland prototypes in the development of a distinctive architectural heritage.

The first permanent houses built by Volga Germans in Russia, called *semelanka*, were built according to an official plan devised by the Colonists Welfare Office. The characteristic semelanka was a two- and often three-room dwelling of one story with a gable roof and central chimney. The gable end faced the street, and the entrance to the house was along the side facing the courtyard. The semelanka was later replaced with the more spacious *kolonistenhaus*, a long, narrow house that combined both living quarters and barns under a single roof. The kolonistenhaus was characteristically tripartite in plan but two rooms deep and with space for six or more rooms.

Volga Germans throughout the Plains region and especially in Kansas and Nebraska built both the one- and one-and-one-half-story rectangular four-room with central chimney house they had known in Russia. The Volga preference for the hipped roof is also evident in their houses, although the gable-roofed variant is common as well. Although Volga Germans in the Great Plains used construction materials similar to those used by Black Sea Germans such as *batsa* (sun-dried bricks made from puddled clay), Volga builders in Colorado, Kansas, and Nebraska also used limestone when available. Both log and stone had been common building materials in Russia.

In addition to expressing their traditional preferences through house form and use of materials, Volga Germans also demonstrated their cultural identity in urban areas by establishing compact villages with gridlike street patterns. In the South Bottoms neighborhood of Lincoln, Nebraska, existing lots were subdivided, resulting in an extremely compact settlement of narrow parcels. The long, narrow lots facilitated the construction of traditional houses oriented with their gables facing the street. When settlers in Marion County, Kansas, laid out the town of Gnadenau, the land was divided into twenty narrow parcels, each containing sixteen acres. Four sections surrounding the village were also divided among the twenty village settlers. A single east-west road bisected the village, and all houses were constructed on the north side of the road. Despite having a church, several stores, and two schools, the village was disbanded a few years later. Although the Kansas village failed, it nevertheless represents efforts by Volga Germans to maintain a strong sense of community and, more important, to resist change and slow assimilation into mainstream American society.

See also EUROPEAN AMERICANS: German Russians.

Michael H. Koop
Minnesota Historical Society

Petersen, Albert J. "The German-Russian House in Kansas: A Study in Persistence of Form." *Pioneer America* 8 (1976): 19–27.

WAREHOUSE DISTRICTS

In the last half of the nineteenth century, as settlement moved westward, an intriguing building type called the warehouse, or jobbers, district developed in "gateway cities" in the Great Plains. These districts marked the establishment of an urban presence in the Great Plains. Where they remain today, they are among the strongest and richest of central business neighborhoods.

At their peak in the 1860s, there were over sixty such districts in the Great Plains and Midwest. This number had declined to twenty by 1930, and today only a handful remain with their original integrity intact. Plains cities notable for the development of these districts include, from north to south, Winnipeg, Manitoba; Sioux City, Iowa; Omaha and Lincoln, Nebraska; and St. Joseph and Kansas City, Missouri.

"Jobbers' Canyon," looking south along Ninth Street from Farnam Street, Omaha, Nebraska

A number of factors in the transport of goods and services came together to create the need for and configuration of these districts. Where there was a break in a method of transport (e.g., from cart to water or water to horse), a settlement usually occurred. When there was a break in the ownership of the goods transported, a commercial area developed. Thus in the Great Plains a number of gateway cities developed where these changes in transport and ownership occurred.

Farming and settlement development in the Great Plains created a large demand for goods. Originally, these were stockpiled in East Coast warehouses and shipped via wagon and river to various western settlements and outposts. With the development of the railroad and the telegraph in the 1850s and 1860s, it was possible to do the "jobbing" of goods from the Midwest rather than from East Coast locations. Merchants communicated their orders by wire. The goods could then be shipped efficiently by rail to gateway points, where they were stored for sale and then transshipped to smaller wholesalers and retailers scattered throughout the region. This situation created a demand for large storage buildings and was the economic force that produced a warehouse district. This commercial engine roared from the 1850s to the crash of 1893, then revived around 1900 and continued through the 1920s. Then, because of trucking and transportation changes, the need for large jobbing areas and their distinctive buildings slowly disappeared.

The architectural style of the warehouse buildings varied from austere brick boxes that were relatively unadorned to rich examples of Renaissance Revival and Richardsonian Romanesque. A typical district, like Omaha's, was a mix of building styles. The architectural strength of these areas lay not so much in the individual buildings as in the collective character of the districts they formed. In general, they were laid out on a grid pattern, filling whole blocks from curb to curb and ranging up to eight or nine stories high. This height, combined with their street-level activity around office areas, loading docks, and traffic, created a strong urban character. In many cases, these buildings provided the most identifiable "city element" of their communities as well as the richest architecture.

The need for large floor areas and the strict functional requirements dictated some unique structural solutions. Also, encouraged in part by the tremendous amount of rebuilding required after the Chicago fire of 1871, many innovative engineering and construction solutions developed that spread throughout the Midwest and Great Plains. The Chicago architectural firms of Burnham and Root and Adler and Sullivan were early leaders in these engineering and architectural advancements.

The structure of a typical warehouse included exterior brick bearing walls with heavy timber columns and joists with wood flooring. Heavy timber, with large cross sections of wood, proved to be more fire resistant than cast iron, which would warp and sag at temperatures at which wood was still noncombustible. Toward the end of the warehouse era a new structural system developed in reinforced concrete. Pioneered by Deere and Company of Moline, Illinois, and their in-house architect, Oscar Eckerman, this system consisted of brick bearing walls with reinforced columns and flat concrete slabs. The flat-slab technology eliminated the height requirement of beams and joists and developed the most efficient floor areas for high-volume storage. This system was also virtually fireproof, and, concurrently, many innovative fire safety details were developed, such as fireproof exit stairs and stand pipes for water distribution.

The functional requirements that produced the warehouse districts declined from the 1920s on. The districts slowly fell into disuse until the early 1970s, when they were rediscovered for a variety of retail, commercial, and housing activities. Today, warehouse districts are enjoying a rebirth, and where they remain they still represent some of the best architecture and urban character of Great Plains cities.

See also CITIES AND TOWNS: River Towns.
George A. Haecker
Bahr Vermeer and Haecker Architects

Eaton, Leonard K. *Gateway Cities and Other Essays*. Ames: Iowa State University Press, 1989.

WATER TOWERS

See WATER: Water Towers

WINDMILLS

See IMAGES AND ICONS: Windmills

WOODEN FRAMES

Wooden-frame structures are among the oldest made by human beings for physical shelter, storage of goods, and protection of livestock. Immigrants from the forested regions of western and northern Europe brought traditions of building with wood to North America in successive waves of immigration from the seventeenth through the twentieth centuries. Pioneer settlement of the Great Plains by Americans, Canadians, and European immigrants occurred from the 1850s to the 1920s, just as new American industries directly facilitated the construction of wooden buildings.

After about 1870, steam-powered sawmills in the upper Midwest were mass-producing building materials for wooden-frame structures, supplanting low-production lumber mills powered by local streams and rivers. Beginning in the 1830s eastern manufacturers produced iron nails, and by the 1890s wire steel nails were available. Transport of these construction materials on navigable waterways, mainly the Missouri, supplied major distribution centers in the region. Then, after 1860, railroad lines diffused building materials to new communities throughout the Great Plains. Every fledgling railroad town on the Plains had its lumberyard.

European American settlers often followed traditional methods of building learned in eastern Canada and the United States or in Europe. Timber-frame structures were typically composed of eight-by-eight-inch corner posts, three-by-five-inch studs, and four-by-four-inch rafters. Builders used hand tools to prepare each unit of the frame according to proportionate size and scale, finished the units with appropriate mortise-and-tenon cuts, and joined sections of the frame with these joints. Timber-frame structures required at least one year for the thick members of the frame to cure, weeks for skilled carpenters to cut joints, and a crew of five to six workers to set sections of the frame in place. Plains settlers used this framing technique for houses, inns, commercial buildings, and larger outbuildings on farms, especially barns.

Braced-frame structures were used for buildings of two or more stories such as stores, warehouses, and imposing dwellings. A braced-frame structure consisted of moderate-size milled-lumber members of six-by-six-inch posts, two-by-six-inch studs, and two-by-four-inch rafters. Posts and studs were usually mortised into a heavy sill and plate and, like other sections of the frame, nailed in place. To reinforce the structure, carpenters installed a diagonal brace at the top and bottom of the frame at each corner of the external wall. This method of framing satisfied conservative builders' preferences for a strong timber frame while taking advantage of some of the efficiencies of building with milled lumber and nails.

Balloon-frame construction developed when dimension lumber became available throughout the region during the 1860s. A balloon-frame structure is composed of lightweight four-by-four-inch corner posts, two-by-four-inch studs, and two-by-four-inch rafters nailed together at every joint, creating a basketlike network of components that reinforce and strengthen each other in an integrated series of structural relations. Balloon-frame buildings are identified by an uninterrupted rise of the two-by-four-inch vertical studs nailed to the sill at the foundation and to the plate at the top. Studs are doubled at the corners and at door and window openings to reinforce these sections of the frame. The interval between each stud is sixteen inches on center in order to receive forty-eight-inch-long lath used as support for the interior plaster walls and ceilings. Door and window openings are usually thirty-two inches wide to preserve the sixteen-inch spacing of the studs. Carpenters nail floor joists measuring two by eight inches or two by ten inches to the studs along the exterior side walls. First-story joists are positioned on the sill; second-story joists are supported by a horizontal ledger or ribbon that is nailed to the vertical studs. In order to stiffen these parts, builders nail diagonal bridging between each joist. A subfloor layer of rough boards of one by eight inches, surfaced with one-by-six-inch clear pine boards or narrow strips of hardwood, serves as the flooring. Builders enclose the exterior of the frame with a layer of one-by-eight-inch to one-by-ten-inch boards and cover that sheathing with shiplap siding. Rafters measuring two by six inches or two by four inches, nailed to the plate at twenty-four-inch intervals, are covered with roof boards and surfaced with shingles made of wood or asphalt.

Wall and roof surfaces of balloon-frame structures enclose a rectangular space covered by a saddle roof or a square space spanned by a pyramidal roof. Elevations of balloon-frame houses vary from one to two and a half stories. Scale ranges from simple one- or two-room structures to elaborate asymmetrical extensions of enclosed spaces. This type of wooden frame best suits the needs for economical houses and the skills of local carpenters and builders. Balloon-frame commercial structures that fit narrow business lots can rise from one to three stories and are shaped as extended rectangles spanned by a saddle roof. This sloping roofline is usually concealed by a false-front street facade that rises to the full height of the structure and is crowned with a horizontal cornice the full width of the facade to give the impression of a building constructed according to traditional classical design.

See also INDUSTRY: Lumberyards.

Fred W. Peterson
University of Minnesota, Morris

Peterson, Fred W. *Homes in the Heartland: Balloon Frame Farmhouses of the Upper Midwest, 1850–1920*. Lawrence: University Press of Kansas, 1992. Rempel, John I. *Building with Wood and Other Aspects of Nineteenth-Century Building in Central Canada*. Toronto: University of Toronto Press, 1980. Upton, Dell. "Traditional Timber Framing." In *Material Culture of the Wooden Age*, edited by Brooke Hindle. Tarrytown NY: Sleepy Hollow Press, 1981: 33–96.

WRIGHT, FRANK LLOYD (1867–1959)

The work of America's most renowned architect, Frank Lloyd Wright, spanned a period from the late nineteenth century through World War I, the Great Depression, and World War II and did not end until his death in 1959. Although Wright's primary focus was on domestic buildings, his contributions to public architecture were also significant. His work was based on the principles of "organic architecture," which he defined as "profoundly interrelated, one thing to another, consistent as a whole." Wright was born in Richland Center, Wisconsin, on June 6, 1867. He learned architecture through apprenticeship in Madison, Wisconsin, and, after 1887, in Chicago, especially at the firm of Adler and Sullivan.

Wright's work first gained significant attention in the early years of the twentieth century with his development of the Prairie style in Chicago, Illinois. Prairie style is characterized by sweeping horizontal lines, broad eaves, and low-pitched hip roofs. Wright continued to develop the Prairie style until he reached its zenith with the Robie House (1909) in Chicago. The next two decades of Wright's work revealed a stylistic shift into more regional themes until the 1930s, when he started work on his Usonian houses. Wright saw a need for inexpensive housing for the average American, and his Usonian work was a response to that need. Still based on the principles of organic architecture, the Usonian house is characterized by a modular system of design and construction, inexpensive materials, and manufactured components.

Wright's work in the Great Plains closely reflects the evolution of his work as a whole. Only about half of the nineteen projects he designed for the Great Plains were actually carried through to construction. Of these, the Sutton House (1905) in McCook, Nebraska, was the first. The Sutton House is a fine example of the evolving Prairie style and anchors Wright's work in the Great Plains. The Sutton House was followed by the Allen House (1915) in Wichita, Kansas. Built for Henry J. Allen and his family, its mature masonry work and other details make it a significant example in Wright's development of the Prairie style. The Richard Lloyd Jones House (1929) in Tulsa, Oklahoma, was a significant departure for Wright in his domestic architecture. Built for Wright's cousin, the house was based on the themes Wright had used earlier in his California houses. Although the design was altered during construction, the Community Church (1940) in Kansas City, Missouri, is attributed to Wright. Two houses built in Kansas City, the Sondern House (1939) and the Adler House (1948), are good examples of Wright's more evolved Usonian ideas.

Wright's most significant work in the Great Plains, the Price Tower (1954) of Bartlesville, Oklahoma, is a striking example of his mature thinking and an embodiment of his ideals. Standing nineteen stories above the rolling hills of northeastern Oklahoma, it makes a dramatic counterpoint to Wright's earlier domestic work. The design for the tower was actually first conceived for St. Mark's in the Bouwerie project (1929) in New York. That project was never realized, and Wright resurrected the concept for the Price Tower twenty-five years later.

The Juvenile Cultural Center (1957) in Wichita, Kansas, is another of Wright's nonresidential works. The Kinney House (1957) in Amarillo, Texas, the final example of Wright's work in the Great Plains, embodies his mature ideas concerning the Usonian house and was completed just two years before his death in Phoenix on April 9, 1959.

Randy G. Stramel
Architectural Alliance, Ltd.

Futagawa, Yukio, and Bruce Brooks Pfeiffer. *Frank Lloyd Wright*. Tokyo: A.D.A. Edita, 1984–85. Storrer, William Allin. *The Architecture of Frank Lloyd Wright: A Complete Catalog*. Cambridge MA: MIT Press, 1978. Twombly, Robert C. *Frank Lloyd Wright: An Interpretive Biography*. New York: Harper and Row Publishers, 1973.

Art

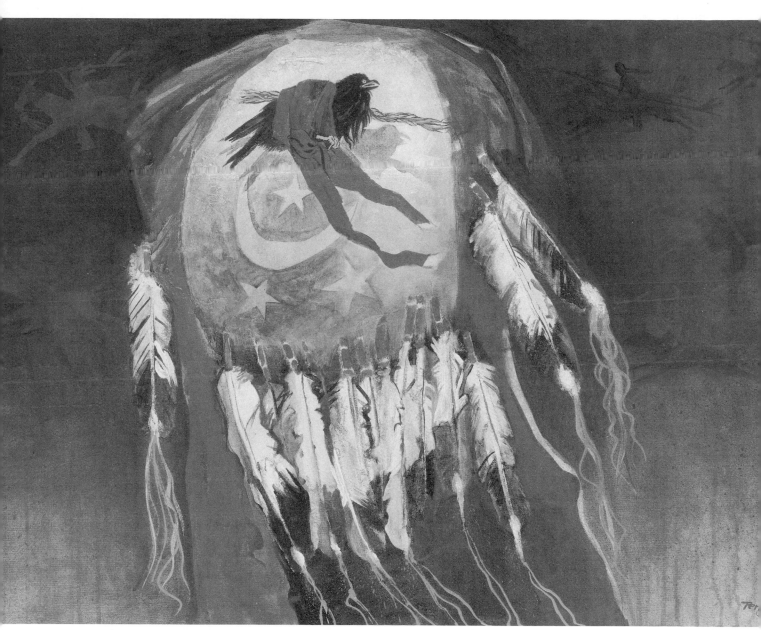

Robert Lee Penn. Nightshield, *1990. Acrylic on canvas.*

Art 105

ART

The Great Plains has presented artists with challenges unlike those of most other regions. Lacking most of the visual elements that traditionally comprise landscape compositions, the terrain can seem utterly devoid of artistic subject matter, empty and uninspiring to those who attempt to portray it. Over time, however, artists have adapted to the Plains' unique qualities in a wide array of interesting ways that offer insights into both the development of the area and its peoples and the special character of the place. And even though the region's sheer extent and distance from major urban centers have tended to relegate it to the "margins" of the art world, artists in the Plains have established a strong visual heritage through other subjects and activities in addition to depictions of their region's landscape. The Great Plains is not often acknowledged for its aesthetic achievements, but it has a rich artistic history that deserves to be better known.

Cultural Contrasts

In visual art Native American and European American traditions differ to such a degree that their imagery is usually considered separately; they are often studied as two distinct specialties within the history of art. These cultures, with very different notions of vision, representation, and relationships to the land, have responded to the world in accordance with their own conceptions of space and humanity's place within it. As a result, each group's art remained distinctive until the mid-twentieth century, when cross-cultural influences began to have an impact. The differences between Native American and European American art, which range from the most basic qualities to the most profound aesthetic issues, compromise comparisons and even parallel discussions of the two to the point of diminishing the integrity of both. This is nowhere more apparent than in the art of the Great Plains, where contrasts of media, styles, subject matter, and perceptions of the land between the two groups have been as polarized as their different value systems and traditional ways of life.

Native Plains art differs from European American imagery stylistically, functionally, and conceptually. Pictorially representing ideas and visual surroundings symbolically rather than literally or "naturalistically," Native Plains artists did not attempt to directly transcribe the appearance of the natural world according to European techniques of perspective. Also, rather than being separated from everyday life within a hierarchical value system that creates artificial divisions between "high art" and lesser manifestations, art within Native traditions is an integral part of societal activities, both everyday and ceremonial.

Plains imagery that precedes European American contact is today extremely rare; it was usually constructed of organic materials that were not long lasting, and it was not considered "art" in the same sense that Europeans conceive the term. Until almost this century it has not been considered unique or valuable apart from its ritualistic or functional purpose and was therefore not usually preserved and revered as collectible. Some European and American visitors to the Plains region in the mid–nineteenth century did collect artifacts of various sorts from the Native peoples, and while those activities were not comprehensive and systematic and were often for anthropological or scientific purposes rather than aesthetic ones, their efforts, and those since, have preserved a variety of objects that give a glimpse into traditional Native Plains imagery. Prehistoric rock carvings and paintings (petroglyphs and pictographs) also survive at several sites throughout the Plains, although very little is known of their origins or intended meanings. Efforts to understand the significance of art in Native American life have been hampered by this scarcity of early examples as well as by the extreme differences between European and Native American concepts of art. Although the impulse behind creating imagery in Native cultures was undeniably inspired by aesthetic considerations as well as by symbolic and ritualistic ones (all of which offer important insights into their artistic and cultural significance), the later exhibition of these objects as museum collections of "art" tends to remove them from their original contexts and can misleadingly present them within a foreign value system, one that considers art primarily something to be *looked at* rather than integrated into the daily activities of its creators, as was originally intended. At the same time, however, the art establishment and its marketplace have provided Native American artists an important outlet for the expression and preservation of their traditions, a means by which their cultures can be understood and appreciated by a wider public. They have also provided some economic support, which in turn encourages additional creative activities within tribal communities.

Native American and European American art forms do share at least one important characteristic that is integral to understanding the significance of their creation in the Plains region. Both cultures created and used imagery, although not exclusively in either case, to document life experiences. Because the land was fundamental to these experiences in both cultures, this basic relationship can serve as a touchstone for discussions of their art.

Plains Indian Art

Plains Indians were, of course, not a single group but rather many different peoples who inhabited an extremely large territory. While they shared certain aspects of lifestyle, their visual imagery, its specific symbolism, meaning, and function, differed according to tribe and even according to individual artists in the same tribe. Comprehensive accountings of their histories and the myriad of specific objects would require separate studies for each group, but because they all had their origin in the same region some generalities can be made.

Plains bison hunters moved frequently; therefore, other than the petroglyphs and pictographs inscribed on rocky outcroppings, their art was necessarily portable. Ranging from large painted tipis to small personal amulets, decorated clothing, shields, and even horses and their own bodies, their media and the uses to which they were put were extremely varied, a diversity demonstrating the richness of the people's creative responses to their environments and experiences.

A large percentage of Native Plains imagery was and continues to be symbolic of sacred events, rituals, and natural forces, which could include everything from celestial bodies and weather to the indigenous animals of the region. Often stylized into schematic diagrams, the representation of these objects on personal and communal belongings could, it was believed, transfer the power of these forces into forms that would protect the user from harm, bring health and prosperity, or appease the spirits and encourage them to provide for the people of the tribe. Some symbols and their subjects or referents were ubiquitous and relatively unchanging; others were highly specialized and designed for specific events or for particular uses. Common among Plains cultures are animal symbols and representations, especially those of the bison, which was a staple of their lives. Other animals were also revered for their special traits. Birds, for example, with their ability to fly, were considered especially powerful since they could transcend the earth, and among these the eagle, with its majestic size and fierceness, was held in highest regard. These and other animals were not only represented in Plains art in pictures and sculptured effigies; their hides and feathers were used as functional and ritual objects as well. In this way the elements of the natural world were both depicted in and part of Native American art, a duality that was both symbolic and practical in the people's creative expression of life and their understanding of it.

Unlike the European tradition, in which the making of art is mainly reserved for a gifted few, most if not all members of Plains tribes incorporated art into their daily tasks and became artists in various ways. Women adorned clothing, baskets, and other personal and household objects with symbolic and decorative imagery made from quills, beads, hides, and other elements that were often dyed with natural colors, and men were responsible for a wide variety of artistic creations, from objects for ritualistic purposes and the painting of their own bodies for ceremonies, hunts, and battles to the inscription of tipis and hides with diagrams and narratives of important events in their lives and those of their tribes. Objects for particularly important purposes would be made by shamans, who were endowed with special gifts of wisdom or healing abilities, but even children were sometimes invited to sculpt small clay animal figures, which would be used in ceremonials. All were taught to understand the relationship between the natural world and the artistic interpretation of it.

Although nothing was ever entirely removed from its spiritual dimension in Native life, actual events were also recorded in pictorial imagery through a more purely narrative format. Calendar hides painted by elders, for example, documented years of history, and although these were not designed according to a standardized hieroglyphic system, they could be read almost as written chapters of tribal life over the course of time. Important ceremonies, battles, hunts, tragedies, storms, and other notable events were the main subjects of these paintings, which augmented the oral tradition of passing stories and communal history from one generation to the next. Individual warriors might also record especially notable encounters, gatherings, and conflicts in paintings, creating a visual document of personally significant occurrences that were used not simply as memory "books" but for important ceremonials. When Native Americans were incarcerated toward the end of the nineteenth century, this tradition served as the basis for smaller ledger drawings that depicted battles between various Plains tribes and the U.S. Army. Named for the paper upon which they were drawn, which was taken from ledgers at the prisons or reservation schools, these drawings form an important record of Native Americans' reactions to the violent disruption of their traditional ways of life.

While the natural world was always the most important subject for Native American art, representations of landscape in the European sense did not exist until late in the nineteenth century and after prolonged contact between the two cultures. The Native concept of nature was not human centered, and thus the tradition of portraying a landscape from a fixed, individual point of view, looking across a scene toward the horizon, was foreign and inconceivable. In place of this "magisterial gaze," a socially constructed concept that has contributed much to the development of Europe and the United States and from which the artistic technique of linear perspective evolved, Native Americans held the idea of the sacred wheel, a cosmic view in which all of nature is integrated and humans are merely one part of a living entity, no more powerful or significant than other things in the world. Because of this philosophy, in traditional Native American representations of nature horizon lines are rarely if ever found; more often, symbols and representations of humans and animals appear to float without a sense of specific location, as if the entire universe is their home. Within the epic expanse of the Great Plains, where the horizon seems to merge with the sky in all directions, this conjoining of land with the cosmos must have seemed an especially appropriate and true representation of the place, even if it does not coincide with the more familiar modern conception of the Plains as an expansive terrain represented by a line running horizontally across a picture.

Since their relegation to reservations, Plains Indians have had to accommodate extraordinary disruptions of their way of life, assimilate

Oscar Howe. Calling on Wakan Tanka, 1967. Casein on paper.

vastly different worldviews and patterns of behavior, and endure the loss of both physical and psychological links to the past. While this has altered their art profoundly (including its increasing commercialization), Native American artists have continued to draw upon their traditional cultures for inspiration even as they have incorporated a new array of materials, subjects, and visual vocabularies into their work. First encouraged in mission schools to learn drawing and later trained in art schools, they have become increasingly familiar with modern artistic concepts and methods. But they continue as well to utilize imagery that links them with their historic traditions and spiritual values. Their work today is a blending of cultures, both visual and social, but, no less than the art of their forebears, it is a unique expression of their identity as artists of the Great Plains.

European Encounters

Although Europeans encountered the Great Plains as early as the 1540s, the first non-Native artists (if early cartographers are not counted) did not arrive until the 1830s. Intent on documenting the appearance of the landscape and its inhabitants for distant audiences rather than incorporating it into an Indigenous society, they worked within a set of values, aspirations, and media entirely different from that of their Native American contemporaries. Their reactions to the terrain were conditioned both by their previous experiences and by their aesthetic preconceptions, and thus they were ill-prepared for the Great Plains landscape. Nothing, except perhaps the boundless ocean, to which the land was often likened, was familiar about the endless treeless vistas that stretched from horizon to horizon, and since their artistic training had taken place in regions that were more visually varied, many early artists in the Plains despaired

at the grassland's lack of subject matter for pictures. The Great Plains, labeled the "Great American Desert" in 1820 by Stephen Long's government-sponsored expedition, seemed to many an aesthetic desert that offered little to artists.

The standard reference for nineteenth-century European American artists who traveled West was the European landscape tradition and its accompanying art theory. These theories and practices had been conceived, of course, for European terrain, which has nothing in common with the Great Plains. This pictorial tradition was premised on the notion of *prospect*, a concept with multiple meanings, both physical and philosophical. At its most basic, referring to a point of view (usually elevated) from which a landscape is viewed, the term implies a human-centered universe, a fixed point of reference that endows the individual with essential power to envision, imagine, and even create the scene that lies ahead. Derived from this fundamental concept are additional connotations that include, among other things, the idea of futurity or potential as well as specific artistic interpretations: "prospect pictures" standardized the representation of terrain into balanced compositions framed with trees and rocks and guided by meandering paths or streams, a gradual movement toward a horizon that was pleasantly glowing with the promise of opportunity. As "prospects," these views offered to audiences a carefully conceived version of visual ownership, a psychological claiming of the land's future and their role within it.

All these issues and traditions directly affected the ability of artists to creatively respond to the Great Plains landscape. Simply stated, the grasslands of central North America seemed to have no prospects. They had no elevated vantage points from which to survey a scene, no variegated vistas that would charmingly direct the gaze through space, and, just as important, they seemed to have no obvious economic potential for a people more accustomed to forestlands linked by navigable waterways. Artists were at a loss both because they had so little with which to fill their canvases and because they knew that viewers expected landscape paintings to imply the promise of the American continent. The Great Plains seemed empty and desolate, hardly the sort of landscape that would fulfill the desires of an eager nation looking west for its future.

This perception of vacancy was, of course, misguided. A region of tremendous variety of many sorts—culturally in its human diversity, zoologically in its animal populations, climatologically with its extremes of weather and dramatic storms, and botanically with its infinitude of grasses—the Plains offer both great expanse and extraordinary subtlety, a combination that is exceptionally difficult to appreciate without long and thoughtful exposure. And to artists intent on finding compositional subject matters that would intrigue their eastern audiences before they themselves returned home, the special aesthetics of the place more often than not went undiscovered and undocumented. Almost none of the sizable number of paintings of the grasslands produced in the nineteenth century depict the expansive landscape without including something to break the monotony of the expanse.

Only in recent years, with the advent of modernist abstraction, which suits the terrain's minimal offerings, coupled with the increasing appreciation of the region's ecosystem and its relative solitude, have painters and viewers begun to appreciate the Great Plains for their own special characteristics. Until then most artists felt compelled to fill the region's emptiness or, alternately, transform it into an idealized vision of their own making.

Expeditions and Excursions

The first European American artists to travel through the Great Plains did so in the company of expeditions, either government or private, and this trend continued until well after the Civil War. Federally sponsored artists were charged in their commission with portraying the scenery and its inhabitants for official reports to be used in policy decisions that would determine the future development of the region. But artists who traveled privately did so for a number of purposes. Most famous of these, both for his expansive route and for his dedication to his subject matter, was Pennsylvanian George Catlin (1796–1872), who journeyed throughout the Plains in 1832 and 1834 on a personal mission to visit and visually document as many of the Native American peoples as possible before, as he foresaw, their way of life was destroyed. To the north, Paul Kane (1810–71) followed Catlin's example by creating an "Indian Gallery" of portraits and landscapes from the Prairie Provinces. In 1833–34 Karl Bodmer (1809–93), a Swiss artist, made his only visit to America in the company of Prince Maximilian of Wied-Neuwied, an

ethnographer studying Native cultures who needed paintings to illustrate the book he would write upon his return. Bodmer's beautiful watercolors, mostly Indian portraits and river views, established a standard for all artists who would follow. In 1837 Alfred Jacob Miller (1810–74) accompanied Scottish nobleman Sir William Drummond Stewart across the Central Plains to the Rocky Mountains. Stewart wanted souvenirs to decorate his castle back home, and Miller's work is correspondingly romantic, both stylistically and thematically.

Other than Catlin, who had relatively little artistic training and was thus less hampered by aesthetic theory and precedents, none of these artists, even Bodmer and Miller, who produced a large number of evocative paintings of the region, portrayed the landscape in its pristine form without something in the composition to provide it with visual interest. This would be the norm for more than 100 years, as artists struggled to enliven their views and to endow the seemingly empty Plains with prospects, even if they were of the artists' own making.

Animals, Indians, and the travelers themselves formed important early subjects. Bison were especially exotic and appealing, and one of the most frequent subjects was the bison hunt, with Indian horsemen engaged in the chase. Prairie fires were another popular theme, often filled with running animals chased by flames and smoke, an eerie and dramatic sight that never failed to evoke awe in those who witnessed those events. Increasingly, scenes of frontier life, usually highly contrived, dominated the images and appealed especially to eastern audiences, as the paintings were exhibited widely and reproduced in readily available publications and prints by lithographic firms such as Currier and Ives. Guidebooks also became immensely popular, as much for their illustrations as for their text, and, especially after the completion of the transcontinental railroad in 1869, these helped shape the expectations of thousands of immigrants who moved into the Plains after the Civil War. Artists often worked on commission for these publishers, and, in the days before copyright enforcement, their work was also frequently shared among publishers or redrawn by other artists in a variety of formats for reprinting.

The Settlement Period

A major change in the portrayal of the Great Plains occurred with the arrival of the settlers, who dramatically altered the landscape and its prospects. With the advent of overland routes such as the Oregon Trail in the 1840s and then with railroads in the 1860s, coupled with the 1862 Homestead Act, which made landownership available to a wide populace, the influx of Europeans and Americans into the region that had first been a trickle became a virtual flood. The prospects of the Great Plains began to improve, and their image evolved from the "Great American Desert" into the "Breadbasket of America." For the Native peoples it

was a harrowing period of loss and despair as their homelands were even more conclusively encroached upon, their livelihoods destroyed, and their ways of life irrevocably altered.

For artists, however, these events meant new subjects and new audiences. Photographers like Solomon Butcher (1856–1927) in Nebraska in the 1880s recognized an opportunity in the new settlers, and his work appealed to people's fascination with his still-new medium that could in a matter of minutes capture both a likeness and their pride in home ownership. He and other entrepreneurs traveled throughout the Plains photographing the homesteaders and their farms. Occasionally, they established studios in the burgeoning towns in the region. Their work has become a valuable historical record of the early American settlement period. In their photographs we see the range of pioneer living conditions in the Plains, from the sod houses of the new arrivals to the frame dwellings of those more established. We also witness the diversity of the people, from newly freed slaves who claimed their own land to European immigrants only recently off the boat. Meanwhile, William Henry Jackson's (1843–1942) photographs of Plains Indians depict the twilight of a way of life that was being effaced. In all these views the sense of place is almost palpable, with the settlements perched tenuously on the expansive Plains, but the insights into the individuals are equally compelling, whether it is hope on the faces of the new landowners or despair on the faces of those dispossessed.

Painters were also inspired by the settlers and gratified by their ability to transform the terrain into scenes not unlike those of more traditional landscape art; at last the artistic prospects of the land and its economic potential were improving. Scenes of verdant fields, locomotives, and farmers at work helped convey these developments to eastern audiences and satisfied the local inhabitants that their efforts were indeed contributing to the progress of the country. The land was taking shape—literally—as what had previously been seamless prairie was conformed to section lines and plowed fields, creating the first blocks of what now appears from the sky to be an earthly quilt.

Although turn-of-the-century viewers did not have the benefit of airplanes, of course, aerial portraits of the landscape were available to Plains audiences through artistic renderings. Throughout the settlement period bird's-eye town views drawn from maps, with careful perspective manipulations to enhance the appearance of each building, were extremely popular and were used as promotional objects by ambitious city planners, civic organizations, and entrepreneurs. A clever adaptation of the eighteenth-century English prospect pictures, which were essentially estate portraits for wealthy landowners, these town views, with their clear delineations of streets, homes, businesses, and surrounding territory, offered a unique sense of ownership to the inhabitants, a feeling of civic pride as they witnessed the expanse of their towns. The surrounding land beyond the last homes not only suggested the local terrain but also implied a stake in the future potential of the community's growth. This innovative form of depicting the Plains persists to this day in an updated version; contemporary farms are routinely photographed from the air, and landowners regard the framed prints as prized possessions.

Cowboy Art and the Great Plains

Even more than the landscape and its cultivation, the most enduring visual image of the Great Plains remains the western ideal of cowboys, Indians, and cavalry. Although precedents had been established for these themes in the 1840s and 1850s, mostly by eastern artists, the "golden age" of western art that codified these indelible symbols actually occurred during a relatively brief period, from the late 1880s through the turn of the century, *after* the Plains had been essentially fenced and domesticated and its Indigenous populations reduced and relegated to ever-shrinking reservations. Inspired by the rapidly disappearing ways of life, as the cattle drives were replaced by railroad shipping, the cavalry campaigns disappeared, and the tribes were subdued, artists such as Frederic Remington (1861–1909) and Charles M. Russell (1864–1926), among others, dedicated their art to heroic masculine action in the Plains, struggles between humans and animals, and the conflict of cultures. The compelling power of this subject matter, enhanced by their dramatic representations of it, established a standard to which all subsequent art of the region would be compared. Russell had been a working cowboy and lived in Montana, but Remington and many of his colleagues such as Charles Schreyvogel (1861–1912) were easterners, and their work, produced in New Jersey and New York studios, ignored the rapid industrialization that much of the terrain they were portraying was actually experiencing. While they were careful to be accurate with details such as clothing and movement, the histrionic compositions of these artists were largely invented and thus portrayed a mythic region that relied as much on romance and nostalgia for its appeal as on fact. Their legacy, however, has been so profound that most Western movies have ascribed to their model, sometimes quite directly, and these representations have determined the identity of the West and the Great Plains for a large viewing audience. Today their emulators are numerous, most notably in the organization known as the Cowboy Artists of America, whose members continue to propagate the ideal of the cowboy and the heroic battles of the Plains tribes through representational imagery.

By the end of the nineteenth century, artists in the Great Plains knew that a new era was upon them. As the focus of the region changed from establishing communities to sustaining them, it became clear that the region would once again be redefined in a new, more modern image. The emphasis, by neces-

Charles M. Russell. Smoking Up, 1904. Bronze.

sity, would have to be on connections with the nation and the world as a whole—for trade, for culture, and for identity itself. While this promised to bring even greater bounty to the region as it positioned itself as the country's agricultural heartland, the transition also posed risks, as dependence upon distant regions became ever more important. This was no less true for artists in the Great Plains as they worked to strengthen their own connections with the larger art world and position their work within it.

Art Culture in the Great Plains

As one of the last major areas of the United States to be settled, the Great Plains was correspondingly slow in developing the trappings of cultivated society, including artistic organizations such as museums, galleries, and societies to support and encourage the development of artists and their work. As soon as statehood was granted, however, which occurred at different times in different parts of the Great Plains, efforts were initiated to establish institutions that would substantially contribute to the region's cultural future. Art museums took time, but private collections were assembled in some places such as Omaha and Winnipeg relatively early, and these as well as public collections supported by civic groups and wealthy philanthropists evolved into today's museums.

Colleges and universities, many of which were founded through federal land grants at the time of statehood, however, offered art departments very early and were an important catalyst for the production of paintings and sculptures as well as for the training of local artists. Their dominance as centers of art activities in the Plains has remained, even as museums, galleries, and specialized art schools have become more common throughout the region.

Women were especially prominent in these developments and, surprisingly perhaps, formed the majority of the art faculties of state universities in the Plains in the early years.

The University of Nebraska, for example, had a strong art program as early as the 1880s, and it was dominated by women, both in the professoriat and the student ranks. This was true as well throughout the Plains, although as the schools developed and grew, men would increasingly take the women's places on the faculty by the 1920s. Far from being amateurs, many of the early female artists in the Plains came from or went on to study at prestigious schools such as the Chicago Art Institute, the New York Art Students League, and in Paris, especially at the Académie Julian, which admitted women beginning in the 1860s. Their high level of expertise established a strong foundation for the growth of art within their home region. Characteristically, the careers of these women have been overshadowed by those of their male colleagues, but recent studies have begun to recognize their achievements and abilities.

Women contributed to the growth of art in the Plains in other ways as well. They organized art societies, art clubs, and exhibitions of art from national collections as well as from local artists and frequently were the guiding forces behind the establishment of the region's major museums. For example, a well-known painter in Oklahoma, Nan Jane Sheets (1889–1976), served as cosupervisor and then supervisor of Oklahoma's Works Progress Administration (WPA) art program during the Great Depression. She also established an art gallery in Oklahoma City with federal funding in 1935. Even after losing funding with the termination of the program in 1942, she managed to keep it open as the Oklahoma City Art Center, the forerunner of the Oklahoma City Art Museum.

While women worked in similar capacities nationwide, their prominence in the Plains states seems to have been especially significant. They may have had a longer and consequently greater impact in the Great Plains because the cultural institutions there were slower to mature than on the coasts, providing the women with more time before men recognized the importance of their activities and moved into positions of authority, but much research remains to determine this. Lack of male competition may have also been a factor in women's abilities to become cultural entrepreneurs and successful artists, perhaps because of a gender bias against artistic culture in these frontier states that would have relegated it primarily to the women's sphere. Nevertheless, the status of art within the Great Plains today—its prominent art academies and university programs and museums that rank among the country's finest—is certainly due to a large degree to the farsighted early women artists and philanthropists who made the region their home.

Canadian Art of the Plains

Canadian art of the Plains has a history similar to its counterpart in the United Sates, albeit, of course, with its own unique circumstances and character. First portrayed relatively sporadically by a few intrepid individuals such as

Peter Rindisbacher (1806–34), who settled briefly near the Red River in Manitoba, or artists who accompanied exploring expeditions such as W. G. R. Hind (1833–89), the landscape became a major component of a few artists' work such as that of Paul Kane, who, after meeting George Catlin in London in 1843, followed the elder artist's example and made extensive travels through the Canadian Prairies, creating both a visual and a written record. Despite these efforts, however, the northern grasslands did not receive significant attention until the Canadian Pacific Railway began providing a means of easy access to the Plains in the 1870s and 1880s. To promote the line the company provided artists with free passes to travel its route, and this benefit, coupled with the patronage of a burgeoning popular press, a government eager to promote settlement in the western provinces, and a growing nationalism in the wake of the 1867 confederation that declared Canada a unified commonwealth of the United Kingdom, encouraged Canadian artists to look to their own landscape for pictorial inspiration. A number of them, including Sydney P. Hall (1842–1922), Frederick Verner (1836–1928), Edward Roper (1857–91), and Augustus Kenderdine (1870–1947), are known for their portrayals of northern grasslands. A particular standout is Toronto artist Charles W. Jefferys (1869–1951), who not only devoted a number of his important canvases to the Plains in the 1910s but also wrote compellingly of the terrain's innate challenges and its significance to a national art, inspiring many younger artists to explore the region's visual potential.

By the early part of the twentieth century, especially through the work of the Group of Seven, members of which first exhibited together in 1920, Canadian painting became noted for its landscape imagery. With a few exceptions, such as some of the canvases of A. Y. Jackson (1882–1976), these artists focused their work on the rocky, northern Canadian Shield region rather than on the Plains. However, other painters increasingly realized the visual power of the Prairie Provinces; an increasing number of artists embraced modernism's minimalist aesthetic and followed the lead of Robert Hurley (1894–1980), who devoted thousands of images to the flat land of Saskatchewan after the 1930s.

The Dust Bowl
Apart from the nineteenth century and its dramatic scenes of cowboys, Indians, and bison, no other period has left as enduring a characterization of the Great Plains as the Great Depression, when years of drought and poor land management turned the western grasslands into the Dust Bowl. Farmers throughout the Plains were forced off their land by the thousands, and workers of all sorts faced unemployment. Along with this widespread suffering, however, art actually flourished, drawing new attention to the central states and developing cultural institutions within them. Regional subjects were accorded new appreciation: gripping depictions of the

John Steuart Curry. Spring Shower; Western Kansas Landscape, 1931. Oil on canvas.

difficult conditions throughout the Middle West and South in paintings and photographs captivated American audiences, and federal relief programs brought new attention to the region's communities through special programs and investments that, among other things, fostered the production of art and encouraged related activities. Just as important, many of the works produced in the Great Plains or by artists from the area during this period have become the archetypal images of the period and a testament to the region's enduring significance to the nation.

The artistic style known as regionalism was not limited to the central states, and indeed it had urban and coastal practitioners who portrayed their own locales, but much attention in both the art community and the country as a whole became focused on the Midwest and the Plains through the art of Kansan John Steuart Curry (1897–1946), Missourian Thomas Hart Benton (1889–1975), and Iowan Grant Wood (1882–1942). Their work, which usually depicted down-home themes and idealized landscapes in an accessible, representational style, seemed wholly American in style and sentiment and indicative of the core of national life, even if it did not usually portray the difficulties of the time. Although only a few artists held the spotlight, regionalism was widespread, and many artists throughout the Plains states adopted it during the 1930s and 1940s. It suited the temper of the time well with its dedication to local subjects and its ability to simultaneously meld the ideal and the real in ways that seemed to many to be more relevant than modernist abstraction. While the emphases of artists varied, from idyllic, pastoral scenes of bounty to harsher realities, some of the most effective works concerned the effects of the Dust Bowl. As much as any other subject since the days of the bison, the widespread devastation peculiar to the Great Plains offered artists in the region a new subject matter that could define their

sense of place and convey to others the power of the landscape within which they lived.

Many of these images were produced independently, without federal assistance, but the WPA began an aggressive campaign in 1933 for reemployment and revitalization throughout the United States. Programs for artists were included among these efforts. Most famous was the Treasury Department's mural project, which decorated post offices and other official buildings throughout the country, but other opportunities were equally exciting, offering painters, sculptors, photographers, graphic designers, and other artists the means for income and the promise of commissions they would never have received otherwise. The programs also brought an unprecedented viability to regional art, including that of the Plains. Federal funding, for example, sponsored traveling exhibitions and established galleries where none had previously existed, introducing original art to a wide spectrum of the populace. Art education programs offered jobs for artists and encouraged creative activities among many, both children and adults, who had never attempted them before. Some of these programs, such as the Oklahoma City Art Center (now the Oklahoma City Art Museum), were maintained after the federal subsidies were discontinued and have become the principal art institutions in their communities.

In what became one of the most familiar programs of the New Deal art initiatives, the Farm Security Administration (FSA) enlisted corps of photographers to travel throughout the hardest hit agricultural areas to document local conditions. From their work emerged some of the most memorable images of the Plains. Dorothea Lange's (1895–1965) *Tractored Out* (1938) and Arthur Rothstein's (1915–1985) gripping image of a farmer and his son running to their house, half buried beneath a sea of dust (1936), for example, are just two of the most famous of the thousands of images produced by this program. These evocative depictions of the Great Plains are today still widely recognized and not only stand as testimony to the most desolate period in the region's history but also attest to the enduring ability of the art of the region to symbolize the state of the country.

Contemporary Art in the Great Plains

Although diversity of artistic subject matter has existed since artists began living in the Great Plains, as life there has become more cosmopolitan, art there has correspondingly grown and developed. With increased ease of travel, the publication of excellent art books and catalogs, the prevalence of television and increasingly the Internet, the growth of art schools and university programs, and the development of active museums, artists and the public today have easy access to art of other regions and countries, and the Great Plains has become no less central to the development of visual culture in the United States and Canada than any other area.

The notion of regionalism in art, which was never an insular concept, is more than ever a matter of choice. As the world becomes more culturally connected and increasingly homogenized, however, the appeal of local identity, artistic and otherwise, becomes more powerful. Increasingly, a number of artists, museums, and galleries in the Great Plains are recognizing this potential and focusing their attention on art of their own region. Institutions such as the Museum of Nebraska Art in Kearney, the National Cowboy Hall of Fame in Oklahoma City, the Center for Great Plains Studies at the University of Nebraska, and others are demonstrating the vitality and richness of the local landscape and its inhabitants and history through art and scholarship.

Artists too, now freed from the constrictions of European theory and the prejudices it carried against planar terrain, are recognizing the visual power of the Great Plains in new ways. With the advent of minimalist abstraction and the more recent return to figurative representation, the art world can finally accept the openness of the landscape and recognize the sublimity it has always offered.

In the final decades of the twentieth century a host of artists, working in a range of media from traditional painting and photography to installations, rediscovered the region and provided new insights into its visual, environmental, and cultural complexity. Their work sometimes celebrates its visual breadth in spectacular dimensions and panoramic scope, as in the work of Nebraska painter Keith Jacobshagen (b. 1941) and the 360-degree photographs of Gus Foster (b. 1940), in which the epic sweep of the horizon and the dominance of the sky overwhelm human scale. In other instances the land's ecological richness is the subject, as artists such as Terry Evans (b. 1944) explore the fragile relationship of the densely integrated foliage and its substructure to the health of the land and its inhabitants.

There is also a new appreciation of the epic poetry of fire as it rages through the grasses or

Keith Jacobshagen. Havelock Elevator, Evening of Ash Wednesday, *1993. Oil on canvas.*

the peacefulness of different times of day, but just as significant in contemporary Plains art is the human presence, which increasingly dominates the landscape in so many ways. Photographers Robert Adams (b. 1937) and Frank Gohlke (b. 1942) and painter Harold Gregor (b. 1929), for example, draw our attention to the often unsettling relationship between people and nature in the Plains through images of suburban sprawl, abandoned towns, and endless views of pristine farm fields where prairie grasses once grew. In their work, as in most recent art of the region, the real and the ideal, the Plains and the spectacular, are conjoined in ways that are often unsettling, provoking a reconsideration of the land and its vulnerability and our ability to inhabit it in sustainable ways.

Finally, environmental art is also emerging as a new art form in the Plains, which now, as every air traveler recognizes, appears as a giant patchwork quilt. Some farmers, ranchers, and "earth artists" such as Stan Herd (b. 1950) are emulating this effect in giant multiacre portraits and plowed pictures. The pictorial prospects of the region have multiplied beyond anything early artists could have imagined. As those who live in the Great Plains have always known, the region of waving grasses and endless horizons is hardly a vacant plain. It is a vibrant place of many visions.

See also EDUCATION: Museums; National Cowboy Hall of Fame and Western Heritage Center / IMAGES AND ICONS: Emptiness; Flatness; Remington, Frederic / NATIVE AMERICANS: Astronomy / PHYSICAL ENVIRONMENT: Dust Bowl / POLITICS AND GOVERNMENT: New Deal.

Joni L. Kinsey
University of Iowa

Kinsey, Joni L. "Cultivating the Grasslands: Women Painters in the Great Plains." In *Independent Spirits: Women Painters of the American West, 1890–1945*, edited by Patricia Trenton. Berkeley: University of California Press and the Autry Museum of Western Heritage, 1995: 242–73, 289–92. Kinsey, Joni L. "Not So Plain: Art of the American Prairies." *Great Plains Quarterly* 15 (1995): 185–200. Kinsey, Joni L. *Plains Pictures: Images of the American Prairie.* Washington DC: Smithsonian Institution Press, 1996. Kinsey, Joni L., Rebecca Roberts, and Robert Sayre. "Prairie Prospects: The Aesthetics of Plainness." *Prospects: An Annual of American Studies* 21 (1996): 261–97. Lamar, Howard. "Seeing More Than Earth and Sky: The Rise of a Great Plains Aesthetic." *Great Plains Quarterly* 9 (1989): 69–77. Maurer, Evan M., ed. *Visions of the People: A Pictorial History of Plains Indian Life.* Minneapolis: Minneap-

olis Institute of Arts, 1993. Nottage, James. *Prairie Visions: Art of the American West.* Topeka: Kansas State Historical Society, 1984. Rees, Ronald. *Land of Earth and Sky: Landscape Painting of Western Canada.* Saskatoon, Saskatchewan: Western Producer Prairie Books, 1984. Stein, Roger. "Packaging the Great Plains: The Role of the Visual Arts." *Great Plains Quarterly* 5 (1985): 5–23. Thacker, Robert. *The Great Prairie Fact and Literary Imagination.* Albuquerque: University of New Mexico Press, 1986.

ADAMS, ROBERT (b. 1937)

For more than thirty years Robert Adams has made photographs that describe the beauty of the land as well as the inexorable impact of human activity upon it. His earlier photographs, as seen in the monographs *Denver: A Photographic Survey of the Metropolitan Area* (1977) and *From the Missouri West* (1980), have been described as bleak and forlorn. They address the manifestations of unchecked growth: tract housing, strip malls, storage buildings, construction sites, and scarred land. Later work, as found in *Perfect Times, Perfect Places* (1988) and *Listening to the River* (1994), is perhaps more celebratory of the space and vistas of the High Plains, with attention given to the unifying element that graces all his work: the enduring beauty and revelatory quality of light.

Born in Orange, New Jersey, on May 8, 1937, Robert Adams moved with his family to Colorado in 1952. He lived in the Denver area until leaving for college in California, where he eventually earned a doctorate in English. Adams returned to Colorado in 1962 to accept a teaching position at Colorado College in Colorado Springs. Dismayed by the increasing destruction of familiar territory, he began photographing as a way to express both outrage and hope. He was sufficiently encouraged by the support of John Szarkowski at the Museum of Modern Art and increasing acceptance of his work to leave the teaching profession and devote his energies to his photographic endeavors. His work has been widely exhibited and was included in *New Topographics: Photographs of a Man-Altered Landscape*, a major exhibition held at the George Eastman House in 1975. With twenty-two publications of writing and imagery, Robert Adams continues to be a major influence in contemporary photography as well as on our thinking toward the land we occupy.

Gary Huibregtse
Colorado State University

Adams, Robert. *To Make It Home: Photographs of the American West*. New York: Aperture, 1989. Adams, Robert. *What We Bought: The New World*. Hanover, Germany: Spectrum-Internationaler Pries für Fotografie der Stiftung Niedersachsen, 1995. Green, Jonathan. *American Photography*. New York: Harry N. Abrams, 1995.

ALLEN, TERRY (b. 1943)

Terry Allen, whose genres include musical and visual arts, theater, film scripts, radio, and various collaborations, may be a Renaissance man in the sense of being a revivalist. His works have roamed topics as diverse as a hitchhiking Jesus, political terrorists, West Texas hookers, wrecks of art trucks, and a twelve-year body of work, *Youth in Asia*, on the Vietnam War.

Shortly after his birth on May 7, 1943, in Wichita, Kansas, Terry Allen's family moved to Lubbock, Texas. In the 1950s the Allen family's dance hall featured blues, country, and early rock 'n' roll and played a major role in shaping the teenage Allen as well as in desegregating Lubbock culture. Leaving Lubbock for Los Angeles, Allen earned a B.F.A. at Chouinard Art Institute in 1966. He continued creating visual arts while teaching at Chouinard and, through the 1970s, at California State University in Fresno. Allen now lives in Santa Fe, New Mexico.

His recording career took off with the 1975 LP *Juarez*, which included in its packaging six original lithographs. Allen has also produced albums, collaborating with Jo Harvey Allen, David Byrne, Joe Ely, Jimmie Dale Gilmore, Butch Hancock, Wayne Hancock, and others. His most recent album (1999) is titled *Salivation*.

Throughout his career Allen has blended the visual and audio, forming works of irony and humor. He utilizes many mediums, from printmaking and painting to installation and public sculptural commissions. *Corporate Head*, for example, completed in 1991 for Citicorp Center in Los Angeles, realistically shows an attaché case carrying a bronze businessman whose head is imbedded in a stone pier on the ground floor. The George Bush Intercontinental Airport in Houston houses Allen's 3,600-square-foot sculpture installation *Countree Music*, which includes a music collaboration with Joe Ely and David Byrne. On the floor, continents surround Houston as the center of the world. A bronze-cast thirty-foot oak tree rises from the center, and from each continent an indigenous instrument plays as people walk over.

Since 1966 Allen's art has been included in more than 50 one-person exhibitions and 150 group shows, including the São Paulo Biennial, and the Whitney Biennial. His awards include a Residency Fellowship from the Wexner Center for the Arts in 1992, a Guggenheim Fellowship in 1986, a Bessie Award in 1986, and National Endowment for the Arts Fellowships in 1970, 1978, and 1985.

Mo Neal
University of Nebraska–Lincoln

ART MUSEUMS

The appearance and growth of museums of art in the Great Plains have taken place mainly in recent decades. Although nearly 100 museums devoted to the collection and display of art in one form or another can be counted in the region at present, it should be recognized that they are frequently of an embryonic nature—historic houses, collections of popular or Native American art, exhibition facilities without permanent collections, and gallery adjuncts to teaching institutions. The collections themselves have ranged from work produced by local artists, to collections of American art as a whole, to the more restricted range of the art of the American West, to the art of Native Americans. Collections of modern and contemporary art have been the last to appear, evidence as they are of the transcending of the historically regional characteristic of the Great Plains.

Outstanding among the institutions located from Edmonton, Saskatchewan, to Marfa, Texas, are the collections of Native American art at the Buffalo Bill Historical Center in Cody, Wyoming, the Denver Art Museum in Denver, Colorado, and the Philbrook Museum of Art and the Gilcrease Museum in Tulsa, Oklahoma. Important collections of the art of the American West, especially in its pioneer phase, are located at the Glenbow Museum in Calgary, Alberta (which also specializes in the art of Canada's First Peoples), the Joslyn Art Museum in Omaha, Nebraska, and the Woolaroc Museum in Bartlesville, Oklahoma. Collections of the work of individual artists, important to the history of the region, are those devoted to Harvey Dunn at the South Dakota Memorial Art Center in Brookings, South Dakota; Oscar Howe at the University Art Galleries in Vermillion, South Dakota; Sven Birger Sandzén at the Birger Sandzén Memorial Gallery in Lindsborg, Kansas; and Charles M. Russell at the C. M. Russell Museum in Great Falls, Montana, and the Center for Great Plains Studies Art Collection in Lincoln, Nebraska. A museum devoted exclusively to the art of a single state is a recent development of the Museum of Nebraska Art in Kearney.

Some of the museums of the Great Plains region have developed holdings of national importance. Among them are the collections of American art of the twentieth century at the Sheldon Memorial Art Gallery in Lincoln, Nebraska, at the Wichita Art Museum in Wichita, Kansas, and at the Amon Carter Museum in Fort Worth, Texas. The Winnipeg Art Gallery, the nation's first civic art gallery, houses the world's largest collection of contemporary Inuit art. The arts of Europe, Asia, Africa, and Latin America are represented by works of world-class quality in the collections of the Nelson-Atkins Museum in Kansas City and the Kimbell Art Museum in Fort Worth.

Norman A. Geske
Lincoln, Nebraska

AUDUBON, JOHN JAMES

See PHYSICAL ENVIRONMENT: Audubon, John James

BODMER, KARL (1809–1893)

Karl Bodmer, painter of perhaps the finest of all Plains Indian portraits, was born on February 11, 1809, in Zurich, Switzerland, where he received artistic training from his uncle, landscape painter and engraver Johann Jakob Meyer.

In 1832 naturalist and explorer Prince Maximilian of Wied-Neuwied contracted Bodmer's services for an expedition to North America. Their journey lasted from July 1832 to July 1834, but the most important phase began in April 1833, when they set out on a voyage up the Missouri River by steamship and, later, keelboat. During stops at trading posts and encampments, Bodmer composed watercolor portraits of Omaha, Dakota, Assiniboine, Atsina, Mandan, Hidatsa, and Blackfeet chiefs and warriors but occasionally women and children as well. He also painted village scenes, ceremonies, and a wide variety of landscapes. In August 1833 Maximilian and Bodmer reached Fort McKenzie, near present-day Great Falls, Montana, but, faced with menacing warfare among the Blackfeet, they turned back a month later. Spending the harsh winter of 1833–34 in Fort Clark near present-day Bismarck, North Dakota, the two central Europeans established a warm rapport with the Mandans and Hidatsas. Artistically and scientifically, their stay at Fort Clark was the most fruitful part of their journey. The masterful—and ethnographically accurate—watercolor, *Interior of a Mandan Earth Lodge*, for example, was sketched over a period of several months during their time at Fort Clark.

After their return to Europe, Bodmer worked for a decade preparing a deluxe edition of Prince Maximilian's *Travels in the Interior of North America*, first published in German in 1839 but promptly translated into French and English and illustrated with eighty-one hand-colored aquatints based on Bodmer's watercolors. Maximilian's narrative has long been one of the most important sources for western history and ethnography, while Bodmer's aquatints provided some of the most striking and well-known images of Plains Indians. The work, however, sold poorly, and Bodmer later rued his involvement as an irretrievable loss for his career.

In the 1850s Bodmer settled outside Paris, affiliating himself with the Barbizon school of landscape painters. Over the next decades he achieved a creditable reputation as a painter of forest scenes, and his engravings regularly appeared in French illustrated magazines. Now and then Bodmer may have nostalgically recalled his American adventures, but for him the United States was only an episode in a career focused on wholly different interests. Bodmer spent his last years in dire poverty, estranged from his family, and he died in relative obscurity in Paris on October 30, 1893.

After Maximilian's death, the prince's diaries and notebooks and Bodmer's nearly 400 original watercolors and sketches vanished into the Wied family archives and were only rediscovered after World War II. In 1962 the Northern Natural Gas Company of Omaha, Nebraska, purchased this collection, which its successor, the Enron Corporation, donated to the Joslyn Art Museum in 1986, where it had been on permanent loan.

Karl Bodmer was a consummate landscape artist who captured often-haunting images of Missouri River scenery and the vast prairies. However, it is the Indian portraits for which he is most remembered. Despite his lack of previous training in portraiture, Bodmer captured the physiognomies, ornamentation, and attire of Native Americans with exceptional detail and accuracy, and in his works his subjects display the vitality one associates with the finest portraiture. Less well known than his flamboyant contemporary, George Catlin, Bodmer nevertheless was a far superior artist.

See also EUROPEAN AMERICANS: Prince Maximilian of Wied-Neuwied.

William J. Orr
Foreign Service of the United States

Bodmer, Karl. *Karl Bodmer's America*. Lincoln: University of Nebraska Press, 1984. Thomas, Davis, and Karin Ronnefeldt. *People of the First Man: Life among the Plains Indians in Their Final Days of Glory*. New York: E. P. Dutton, 1976.

BUGBEE, H. D. (1900–1963)

At the suggestion of his cousin, cattleman T. S. Bugbee, Harold Dow Bugbee came to Clarendon in the Texas Panhandle from Lexington, Massachusetts (where he was born on August 15, 1900), with his parents in 1914. He studied at Texas A&M College in 1917 and the Cumming School of Art in Des Moines, Iowa, in 1920. Each fall, until the late 1930s, Bugbee traveled to Taos to paint with his fellow artists "Buck" Dunton, Frank Hoffman, Leon Gaspard, and Ralph Meyers, often packing into the mountains to paint with either Meyers or Dunton. Advised by Panhandle-Plains cattlemen Frank Collinson and Charles Goodnight and inspired by the example of his idol, Charles M. Russell, Bugbee portrayed historic and then-contemporary Southern Plains life, including cowboys, Native Americans, and flora and fauna of the region.

By the mid-1920s galleries in Denver, Chicago, Kansas City, and New York handled Bugbee's work. In 1933, with the Great Depression and decreasing picture sales, Bugbee turned to magazine illustration, a practice he maintained for some eighteen years. He did pen-and-ink illustrations for *Ranch Romances*, *Western Stories*, *Country Gentleman*, and *Field and Stream*, among others. Additionally, Bugbee also illustrated a number of significant books on western history, including J. Evetts Haley's *Charles Goodnight: Cowman and Plainsman* (1936), Willie N. Lewis's *Between Sun and Sod* (1938), and S. Omar Barker's *Songs of the Saddlemen* (1954). He also continued to make easel paintings.

Under Roosevelt's New Deal, Bugbee painted the first of five murals for the Panhandle-Plains Historical Museum's Pioneer Hall in 1934. He later painted additional murals for the Amarillo Army Air Field and a set of murals on Native American life for the Panhandle-Plains Historical Museum. He exhibited at the Tri-State Fair at Amarillo, the Fort Worth Frontier Centennial Exposition in 1936, the Greater Texas and Pan-American Exposition at Dallas in 1937, and in the annual West Texas art exhibitions in Fort Worth. He also had numerous solo exhibitions in Texas and exhibited in Taos. In 1951 Bugbee became the first curator of art at Panhandle-Plains, a position he held until his death at Clarendon on March 27, 1963. More than 230 Bugbee works are part of the museum's collection.

Michael R. Grauer
Panhandle-Plains Historical Museum

McClure, C. Boone. "Harold Dow Bugbee: A Biographical Sketch." *Panhandle-Plains Historical Review* 30 (1957): 55–67.

BUTCHER, SOLOMON (1856–1927)

Solomon D. Butcher's photographs made the sod house an American icon. No other photographer captured settlement in the Great Plains with such insight into the experience of homesteading.

Butcher was born on January 24, 1856, in Burton, Virginia. His father moved the family to Illinois four years later, and it was there that Butcher spent his childhood and first learned the science of photography. Butcher spent one term at the Henry Military School in Henry, Illinois, but soon gave that up to work as a traveling salesman.

In 1880 Butcher's father again moved on, this time to Nebraska. Solomon gave up his job as a salesman and went along. It took them approximately six weeks to reach the northeastern corner of Custer County, where Butcher's father, Butcher himself, and his brother George, who also made the trip, filed homestead claims. It took Butcher only two weeks to realize he was not made for homesteading, and he returned his claim to the government. There followed a brief attempt at the study of medicine in Minnesota, marriage, and his return to the Sandhills of Nebraska.

By the fall of 1882 Butcher was teaching school and trying to amass enough money to purchase land and photographic equipment. Shortly thereafter he opened what became the first photographic gallery in Custer County, Nebraska. Over the next few years, Butcher moved his family from town to town, never quite escaping from financial ruin. But in 1886, possibly driven by depression over yet another financial crisis, Butcher struck on an idea: he would produce a photographic history of Custer County, Nebraska. For almost three decades, he traveled across the Nebraska Sandhills photographing homesteaders in their environment. He did more than take portraits of people; he placed them within the context that defined their existence. Butcher understood the commitment it took

to homestead, and he also realized that this experience was short-lived and would never happen again.

The sheer volume of images produced by Butcher offers an unparalleled look at the life of homesteaders. Butcher's care to include the landscape, the sod house, and the saplings so carefully tended speaks to his desire to record the space, not just the face, of homesteading. He recorded the impact of homesteading, not just the act. Butcher practiced environmental portraiture at its finest. In some photographs the people are such a small part of the image that they are barely detectable. In others they take center stage but are surrounded by the material trappings of homesteading: stoves, birdcages, tables, chairs, photographs of absent family members.

Butcher created a detailed and comprehensive view of homesteading, but his images also offer insight into the craft of photography in the late nineteenth century and open the door to countless stories about the settlers themselves. Through his images we are transported to the mud and sweat that was the settlement of the Great Plains. Solomon Butcher died in Greeley, Colorado, on May 26, 1927.

See also ARCHITECTURE: Sod-Wall Construction / PHYSICAL ENVIRONMENT: Sandhills.

Jill Marie Koelling
Nebraska State Historical Society

Butcher, Solomon D. *Pioneer History of Custer County, Nebraska and Short Sketches of Early Days in Nebraska*. Broken Bow NE: Solomon D. Butcher and Ephraim Swain Finch, 1901. Carter, John E. *Solomon D. Butcher: Photographing the American Dream*. Lincoln: University of Nebraska Press, 1985.

BYWATERS, JERRY (1906–1989)

As an artist, art critic, museum director, and art educator, Williamson Gerald Bywaters, known as Jerry Bywaters, reshaped art in Texas. The son of Porter Asburn and Hattie Williamson Bywaters, he was born in Paris, Texas, on May 21, 1906. After graduating from Southern Methodist University (SMU) in 1926, he traveled in Europe, Mexico, and New England and studied at the New York Art Students League. Upon his return to Dallas, Bywaters became a spokesman for a group of young artists, including Alexandre Hogue, Otis M. Dozier, and Everett Spruce, who found inspiration in the Texas landscape.

Bywaters produced a significant body of landscape, still life, and portrait paintings, lithographic prints, and public murals. Most of his works were produced between 1937 and 1942. His paintings include *Self-Portrait* (1935), *Sharecropper* (1937), and *On the Ranch* (1941), now at the Dallas Museum of Art; *Where the Mountain Meets the Plains* at SMU; and *Oil Field Girls* (1940) at the Jack S. Blanton Museum of Art, the University of Texas. A regionalist, Bywaters's work is characterized stylistically by a cohesive concern for local subjects portrayed with strong compositions, clear light, and earthy colors.

Bywaters successfully competed in federally sponsored New Deal mural competitions: he completed six projects in Texas, including a series of panels in collaboration with Alexandre Hogue at the Old City Hall in Dallas; a series of panels at the Paris Public Library; one mural each in the post offices of Trinity, Quanah, and Farmersville; and three murals in the Parcel Post Building in Houston. As art critic for the *Dallas Morning News*, Bywaters wrote hundreds of articles in the 1930s. He served from 1943 to 1964 as director of the Dallas Museum of Fine Arts while teaching at SMU. As director, Bywaters recognized the educational possibilities of the art museum and produced several excellent exhibitions. In the mid-1950s he faced accusations that the museum was exhibiting works by Communists; undaunted, Bywaters and his colleagues upheld the standard of freedom of expression. At SMU he served as chairman of the Division of Fine Arts and director of the Pollack Galleries at the Owens Fine Arts Center.

Bywaters wrote and produced catalogs for exhibitions, published an art magazine, and edited art books. His work with the *Southwest Review* included writing articles on the development of regional art as well as serving as art editor and illustrating articles. After retirement from SMU, he served as regional director of the Texas Project of the Archives of American Art, Smithsonian Institution, and continued to curate exhibitions. In 1981 Bywaters presented SMU a gift of his papers to form the Jerry Bywaters Collection on Art of the Southwest. In 1972 he was elected a life member of the Dallas Art Association; in 1978 he received the Distinguished Alumni Award from SMU; in 1980 the Texas Arts Alliance recognized him for distinguished service to the arts in the state; and in 1987 SMU acknowledged his distinctive career with an honorary doctorate. Until his death on March 7, 1989, Bywaters lived in Dallas with his wife of fifty-eight years, Mary McLarry Bywaters.

Francine Carraro
Texas State University–San Marcos

Carraro, Francine. *Jerry Bywaters: A Life in Art.* Austin: University of Texas Press, 1994.

CALGARY GROUP

The Calgary Group was an informal, loosely structured group of artists with modernist concerns working in Calgary in the late 1940s. They responded to what they saw in Alberta as a lack of understanding concerning new developments in art. Key members included Marion Nicoll, Maxwell Bates, and Jock Macdonald.

In 1947 Macdonald, before leaving Calgary to head the Ontario College of Art, heralded the group in an article that appeared in the periodical *Canadian Art*. Stating that Alberta's altitude, climate, and geographical variations—ranging from mountains and foothills to prairie—represented the most desirable environment in which to foster artistic creativity, Macdonald asserted that the province was indeed beginning to produce its own distinctive art. The Calgary Group, he added, was characterized not by a single style or outlook

but by its interest in contemporary expression. Also in 1947, members of the group exhibited works at the Vancouver Art Gallery. The exhibition later traveled to Saskatoon. This show led the curator, G. H. Tyler, to praise the new directions being taken by these Albertan artists, whom he identified as having departed from the artistic dominance within the province of artists such as Walter Phillips, H. G. Glyde, and A. C. Leighton. The following year, an exhibition review in the *Saskatoon Star-Phoenix* identified the Calgary Group's traveling art exhibition, which was en route to the central provinces at that time, as being the first western art show to travel to the older provinces. Again the work was praised and its experimental nature commented upon.

In addition to the artists mentioned above, others who exhibited with the Calgary Group included H. B. Hill, Wesley Irwin, Luke and Vivian Lindoe, Janet Mitchell, Cliff Robinson, Roy Stevenson, and Dorothy Willis. The group does not seem to have lasted more than a few years and, as Macdonald stated, never had a defined program holding its artists together. It may be seen, then, as a group of artists held together loosely and for a short period of time during the postwar period by a desire to showcase the newer tendencies found within Albertan art, a desire that was seen as timely by many.

Joan Greer
University of Alberta

J. S. "The Calgary Group at the Art Centre." *Saskatoon Star-Phoenix*, September 11, 1948: 1, 6. Macdonald, James W. G. "Heralding a New Group." *Canadian Art* 5 (1947): 35–36. Snow, Kathleen M. *Maxwell Bates: Biography of an Artist.* Calgary: University of Calgary Press, 1995.

CAMERON, EVELYN (1868–1928)

An English aristocrat who settled in Montana in 1889, Evelyn Cameron spent more than three decades documenting the settlement of the Great Plains with arresting photographs and diaries. Cameron was born Evelyn Jephson Flower on August 26, 1868, near London. She married Scotsman Ewen Cameron, and they honeymooned in 1889 in the United States, hunting in the Great Plains. The Camerons were smitten by the badlands and undulating prairies of southeastern Montana. They decided to stay and raise polo ponies for export to Great Britain, eventually settling on a spread near Terry, a rough-and-tumble town that Evelyn described in her diary as "rather lively of late, cowboys shooting here, there & everywhere."

Making a living was tough in the hardscrabble hills. The Camerons' polo-pony enterprise failed, and they lost the rest of their money during the Panic of 1893. To make ends meet, Evelyn sold vegetables and took in boarders. She did all the domestic chores as well as jobs considered "man's work": branding cattle, breaking horses, chopping wood, and cleaning stables. Ewen had persistent health problems and was of little help. He spent most his time observing and writing about wildlife.

Despite the hardships, Evelyn loved ranch

life. Photography, which she learned from one of her boarders, became a passion. Soon she was focusing her camera, a plate Kodet, on the sweeping Plains and its inhabitants, including wildlife. She had no telephoto lens, so she had to sneak up on many of the wild animals she photographed. Ewen used her photographs to illustrate his articles. Evelyn's great achievement, however, was to capture the immensity of Montana's space in a small photographic print. She would use a line of cattle or a string of horses on the horizon to measure the vastness, or she would let a small scene in the foreground, like a corral, contrast with the openness beyond. Evelyn also recorded the hardness of pioneer life on this twentieth-century frontier, the settlers' small plain shacks dwarfed by the surrounding landscape.

As the Camerons' financial situation worsened, they relied increasingly on income from Evelyn's photography. She charged a quarter apiece for pictures or three dollars for a dozen. Using a new Graflex camera with a nine-inch Goerz lens, which she bought in 1905 for the princely sum of $225.50, Evelyn worked on commission for the Chicago, Milwaukee, St. Paul and Pacific Railroad, making the harsh land of eastern Montana look seductive to homesteaders.

The Camerons moved to several different ranches in search of more bountiful land. They started their fourth and last ranch in 1907 within sight of the Yellowstone River. Ewen's condition grew worse, despite Evelyn's patient care, and he died of cancer in 1915. Evelyn continued on alone, "as busy as a one-armed man with hives," as she put it. Her fortitude, resourcefulness, and independence were widely admired. An Englishwoman who met Evelyn described her as the "most respected, most talked of" woman in Montana. Evelyn became a U.S. citizen in 1918. Ten years later, on the day after Christmas, she died of heart failure.

Evelyn might have faded into the mists of history had not Donna Lucey, a New York editor who visited Montana in 1978 in search of photographs for a book on pioneer women, discovered a huge stash of Cameron's negatives and diaries in the basement of a neighbor of the photographer. Evelyn's photographs, negatives, diaries, and other personal effects were donated to the Montana Historical Society in Helena. The Prairie County Museum in Terry, Montana, also has a gallery of Evelyn's photographs.

Gayle Shirley
Montana Secretary of State's Office

Lucey, Donna. *Photographing Montana, 1894–1928: The Life and Work of Evelyn Cameron.* New York: Alfred A. Knopf, Inc., 1990. Raban, Jonathan. *Bad Land: An American Romance.* New York: Vintage Books, 1996. Shirley, Gayle. "Evelyn Cameron, Frontier Photographer." In *More Than Petticoats: Remarkable Montana Women.* Helena MT: Falcon Publishing, 1995: 74–83.

CARHENGE

See IMAGES AND ICONS: Carhenge

CATLIN, GEORGE (1796–1872)

George Catlin, artist and visionary, achieved fame for his gallery of Indian portraits and scenes based on his travels in the American West from 1832 to 1836. Born in Wilkes-Barre, Pennsylvania, on July 26, 1796, Catlin trained as a lawyer before moving to Philadelphia in 1821, determined to make his mark as an artist. He specialized in miniature portraits, exhibited regularly, and, despite some evident technical limitations, became a member of the Pennsylvania Academy of the Fine Arts in 1824. Bored with portraiture, he was already nurturing the idea of becoming a historical painter when he moved to New York in 1827 and the next year married Clara Gregory. He found his direction as an artist, he recalled, after encountering a visiting delegation of Indians and concluding on the spot that painting the Indians in their western wilderness would be his life's work.

Confident his efforts would command public support, Catlin moved to St. Louis in the spring of 1830 and two years later fully launched his career as an Indian painter when he boarded a steamboat for the 1,800-mile journey up the Missouri River to Fort Union, in the heart of Indian country. His five-month excursion yielded 170 paintings, with Crows, Blackfeet, and Mandans prominently featured. Subsequently, Catlin toured the Southern Plains (1834) and traveled up the Mississippi (1835–36), painting as he went. He described his experiences in letters to the newspapers, collected in 1841 as *Letters and Notes on the Manners, Customs, and Condition of the North American Indians*, and between trips exhibited his growing collection as Catlin's Indian Gallery. Besides more than 300 portraits of men and women from some fifty tribes, he displayed 200 paintings of western Indians engaged in their daily activities.

Catlin rightfully insisted that he was the first European American artist to offer the world a representative picture of Indian life based on personal observation. He characterized the West as "a vast country of green fields, where the *men* are all *red*"—an apt description of his landscapes and group scenes. They were rendered in shorthand fashion, though he had a knack for the distinctive features of costume and terrain. Catlin's real gift was portraiture. His style was idiosyncratic, and he struggled, often unsuccessfully, to master anatomy. But he captured individual likenesses, and his artistic deficiencies never compromised his obvious admiration for the subjects before him.

Catlin formed his Indian Gallery without government patronage but turned to Congress in May 1838, confident it would reward his enterprise by purchasing his collection. Repeatedly frustrated in this hope, he commenced a lecture career that eventually transformed him into a full-time showman rather than the disinterested advocate for Indian rights he always fancied himself to be. Certain he would find a more receptive audience in Europe, he moved his family to England in November 1839, then to Paris in 1845. Despite flattering attention from crowned heads and commoners, a book recounting his experiences abroad (*Notes of Eight Years' Travels and Residence in Europe, with His North American Indian Collection*, 1848), private commissions, and numerous get-rich-quick schemes, Catlin slid into financial ruin. In 1852 his creditors seized his Indian Gallery. Bereft of his life's work, Catlin entered a period of relative obscurity and some remarkable accomplishments. He painted a second Indian gallery of nearly 300 oil "cartoons" recapitulating his original collection and another 300 showing Indians of the Northwest Coast and South America encountered on three trips he made in the 1850s. He also published several books, including two directed at younger readers (*Life amongst the Indians*, 1861, and *Last Rambles amongst the Indians of the Rocky Mountains and the Andes*, 1867), and an important ethnographic study amplifying observations made among the Mandan Indians in 1832 (*O-Kee-Pa*, 1867). In 1871, after an absence of more than three decades, Catlin returned to the United States and exhibited his Cartoon Collection in New York and Washington DC. He died in Jersey City on December 23, 1872.

Today, visitors to the National Museum of American Art and the National Gallery of Art can sample both Catlin collections in the capital city of a nation that never extended him patronage but now treasures his enduring contribution to the American heritage.

Brian W. Dippie
University of Victoria

Dippie, Brian W. *Catlin and His Contemporaries: The Politics of Patronage*. Lincoln: University of Nebraska Press, 1990. Reddin, Paul. *Wild West Shows*. Urbana: University of Illinois Press, 1999. Truettner, William H. *The Natural Man Observed: A Study of Catlin's Indian Gallery*. Washington DC: Published for the Amon Carter Museum of Western Art, Fort Worth, and the National Collection of Fine Arts, Smithsonian Institution, by the Smithsonian Institution Press, 1979.

CURRY, JOHN STEUART (1897–1946)

John Steuart Curry and his admirers stressed his connections with his birthplace, a farm near Dunavant, Jefferson County, Kansas, where he was born on November 14, 1847, just as it was his paintings of rural Kansas that brought him national fame. However, in a typical pattern, his career as a regionalist painter began only when he left Kansas.

After classes from 1916 to 1918 at the Chicago Art Institute, Curry moved to New York in 1919 and studied with magazine illustrator Harvey Dunn. His apprenticeship led to a successful seven-year career illustrating short stories for periodicals like the *Saturday Evening Post*, during which time he moved to Westport, Connecticut, home to a bohemian artists colony. There writers like Van Wyck Brooks introduced him to the regionalist aim of creating a distinctive and authentic American culture based on artists who were an organic part of a community and who represented their own experience in it. The artist who was responsive to and shaped by the customs and traditions of a particular place would naturally produce an American art that was inseparable from ordinary people's experience within the same community.

After a stint in 1926–27 studying the figure in Vasily Shukayev's studio in Paris, Curry returned and painted his first regionalist subject, *Baptism in Kansas* (1928). It and pictures like *Tornado over Kansas* (1929) instantly succeeded with influential eastern critics and patrons who admired Kansan traditions and communities for their differences from the uniformity and commercialism of modern mass culture. Gertrude Whitney posed with *Baptism* at the opening of the Whitney Museum of American Art in 1931; by 1934 Curry was on the cover of *Time*, anointed with Grant Wood of Iowa and Thomas Hart Benton of Missouri as the midwestern leaders of a new American art movement, distinct from French modernism and abstraction.

Under the New Deal, the Departments of Justice and the Interior in Washington DC hired Curry from 1936 to 1938 to paint mural cycles on themes like the Oklahoma land rush and the freeing of the slaves. But Curry's dealers and friends sought to bolster his regionalist credentials by bringing him back to the Midwest, and in 1936 Curry accepted the position of artist in residence at the University of Wisconsin's College of Agriculture, where he fulfilled the requirement to develop regional art as a force for improving rural culture. Curry's *Ajax* (1936–37), which shows a monumental Hereford bull rising in massive proportions above a flat landscape, in many ways fulfilled the goal of regional art: communities that raised scientifically bred herds of cattle would have their ideal of beauty celebrated on their walls.

Curry also sought validation from his home state of Kansas but with less success, as his choice of subjects was seen there as closer to negative provincial stereotyping. In 1937 he was commissioned to paint murals for the Kansas State Capitol in Topeka, but his depiction of Kansas history—including abolitionist John Brown and soil erosion—met with such hostility that the murals were never completed. Curry stayed at the University of Wisconsin until his death on August 29, 1946, and his success encouraged the incorporation of an arts curriculum at other land-grant universities.

Wendy J. Katz
University of Nebraska–Lincoln

Junker, Patricia, ed. *John Steuart Curry*. New York: Hudson Hills Press, 1998. Kendall, M. Sue. *Rethinking Regionalism: John Steuart Curry and the Kansas Mural Controversy*. Washington DC: Smithsonian Institution Press, 1986. Schmeckebier, Laurence. *John Steuart Curry's Pageant of America*. New York: American Artists Group, 1943.

DOUGLAS, AARON

See AFRICAN AMERICANS: Douglas, Aaron

DUNBIER, AUGUSTUS (1888–1977)

Augustus W. Dunbier, one of Nebraska's most prominent artists in the early and mid–twentieth century, was a prolific oil painter who maintained studios in Omaha from 1916 until his death on September 11, 1977. He was known for his colorful landscapes, still lifes, portraits, and figures in an impressionistic style.

Dunbier was born on a farm in Polk County, Nebraska, on January 1, 1888. At age sixteen he moved with his parents to Germany, where from 1907 to 1914 he was enrolled at the Royal Academy in Düsseldorf. He later studied at the Chicago Art Institute. Dunbier returned to Nebraska just before World War I and opened his Omaha studio. In 1932 he married Lou Eckstrom from Newman Grove, Nebraska, and they had one son, Roger.

In Omaha Dunbier earned a living from the sale of his paintings, many of them portraits of prominent persons, and by teaching at the YMCA and later from his home studio at 914 North 49th Avenue. He also conducted workshops all over Nebraska except in Lincoln, where he appears to have been unwelcome because of what was regarded as his old-fashioned painting style and his vocal disdain of the university's growing modernist art collection.

The majority of Dunbier's landscapes, numbering several thousand, were painted in his home state, where the artist loved the hills and trees, lakes and rivers, farm scenes, and cityscapes. He completed most of these landscapes outdoors, taking no more than several hours for each work. In the evenings he frequently would carve a frame for the painting made that day, and he often commented that it took him longer to carve and gild a frame than to paint a painting. Paintings by Augustus Dunbier are in the Joslyn Art Museum in Omaha, Nebraska, the Sheldon Memorial Art Gallery in Lincoln, and the Museum of Nebraska Art in Kearney, where a Dunbier retrospective exhibition was held in 1994.

Lonnie Pierson Dunbier
Scottsdale, Arizona

Hooley, Renee. *Western Art Digest* 14 (1987): 66–71. Robinson, Natalie U. *Southwest Art* 18 (1989): 60–64.

DUNN, HARVEY (1884–1952)

Harvey Thomas Dunn gained a high reputation during his lifetime as a magazine illustrator, war artist, and art teacher, but his long-term significance became apparent only after his death, as appreciation grew for the prairie scenes he had painted during the last three decades of his career. Donated to South Dakota State College in 1950, two years before his death, these evocative oil paintings might earlier have gained him recognition along with Thomas Hart Benton, Grant Wood, and John Steuart Curry as a leading regionalist artist had the art world been more aware of them.

Harvey Dunn was born on March 8, 1884, on a rural homestead near Manchester in eastern Dakota Territory, the son of William Thomas Dunn and Bersha Dow Dunn, who had moved there from Wisconsin. Uninterested in farming and fascinated with drawing, he obtained his first art training in the preparatory department at South Dakota Agricultural College in Brookings before going on

for further instruction at the Chicago Art Institute and from the famous illustrator Howard Pyle in Wilmington, Delaware.

After opening his own studio near that of his former teacher, Dunn became immediately successful as a magazine illustrator for *Scribner's*, *Harper's*, the *Saturday Evening Post*, and other publications. He was in great demand from advertising agencies as well. The drawings and paintings he executed as one of eight official artists assigned to the American Expeditionary Force in France during World War I are among our most important documents of that conflict.

After the war, magazine illustrating held less appeal for Dunn, and he devoted increasing amounts of time to teaching (his students included Dean Cornwell and John Steuart Curry) and painting prairie scenes of the area in which he had grown up. Dunn died of cancer at his Tenafly, New Jersey, home on October 29, 1952. In later years Dunn's paintings were frequently used in books and articles as illustrations depicting life on the Plains around the turn of the century.

John E. Miller
South Dakota State University

Howell, Edgar M. "Harvey Dunn: The Searching Artist Who Came Home to His First Horizon." *Montana* 16 (1966): 41–56. Karolevitz, Robert F. *Where Your Heart Is: The Story of Harvey Dunn, Artist*. Aberdeen SD: North Plains Press, 1970.

DUST BOWL PHOTOGRAPHERS

On the Southern and Central Great Plains, the Great Depression of the 1930s was compounded by the Dust Bowl, a combination that put great stress on the people of the region as well as the federal government, which sought to alleviate their suffering. Working under Roy Stryker, primarily under the Farm Security Administration (FSA), a small group of talented photographers, including Walker Evans, Dorothea Lange, Marion Post Wolcott, John Vachon, Russell Lee, and Arthur Rothstein, documented the human, natural, and economic devastation of the region in photographs printed in federal publications as well as in a wide variety of newspapers and magazines. Stryker explicitly directed his photographers to document the tragedy and also show the need for and effectiveness of expensive, agriculturally oriented government relief programs.

The most important Dust Bowl photographer, both in terms of technical ability and time spent in the region, was Arthur Rothstein. Rothstein joined the project in 1935, immediately following his graduation from Columbia University. He traveled the Plains from 1936 to 1940. Rothstein's early role and technical abilities gave him considerable influence on the artistic direction of the federal program. He was deeply influenced by the 1936 documentary *The Plow That Broke the Plains* and adopted its visual perspective and persuasive intent. His works were gritty, taking advantage of the ability of black-and-white film to capture the contrast between light and

dark. His realistic style, seemingly documentary, was chosen to enhance the believability of his work.

Under Stryker and Rothstein, government photographers stressed images of poverty and destruction from 1935 to 1937. Russell Lee worked in Texas and Oklahoma, although he concentrated on the Northern Great Plains. His 1939 series, *Part of Mays Avenue Camp, Oklahoma City, Oklahoma*, reveals that even late in the Depression poverty continued to plague the region.

The work of government photographers was sometimes controversial, which is hardly surprising, given the persuasive intent of the assignment. Arthur Rothstein's work proved to be the most controversial. Rothstein was involved in a political controversy during the 1936 presidential election when the conservative *Fargo Forum* criticized him (and, by extension, the Roosevelt administration) for his repeated use of a cow skull to dramatize the bleakness of the Plains. The story spread. Many newspapers later retracted the story, following Stryker's justification of the skull's artistic use, but the reputation of the government photographers suffered. Rothstein's most famous image, *Farmer and Sons Walking in the Face of a Dust Storm, Cimarron County, Oklahoma* (1936), showing a farmer and his two young sons leaning into the wind as dust swallows their outbuildings, has also proven controversial. Other images taken on the same day but with clear skies and an apparent absence of dust belie Rothstein's claim that he took the photograph without staging.

While most of the Dust Bowl photographers worked for the federal government, others worked for private publications. Dorothea Lange worked sporadically for the federal government, but only a small portion of her work covers the region. Among these, produced independently of federal efforts, was *An American Exodus* (1939), which includes bleak scenes of life in the Southern Plains that explain why people would travel great distances to California to live in camps and work in such miserable conditions. Margaret Bourke-White, also considered to be a major Dust Bowl photographer, worked for *Fortune*, which commissioned her to photograph the Deep South. Her most famous photographs, included in *You Have Seen Their Faces* (1937), were taken in the American South but have often been perceived as being set in the Dust Bowl.

Just as the Dust Bowl passed, so too did the need to justify government programs or document rural suffering in the region. After 1937 emphasis shifted to the more positive effects of government relief efforts, with fewer scenes of economic and environmental distress.

See also AGRICULTURE: Farm Security Administration / FILM: *The Plow That Broke the Plains* / PHYSICAL ENVIRONMENT: Dust Bowl.

Charles Vollan
University of Nebraska–Lincoln

Curtis, James. *Mind's Eye, Mind's Truth:* FSA *Photography Reconsidered*. Philadelphia: Temple University Press, 1989. Fleischhauer, Carl, and Beverly W. Brannon, eds. *Documenting America, 1935–1943*. Berkeley: University of California Press, 1988.

EMMA LAKE ARTISTS' WORKSHOPS

Artist workshops have been held at Emma Lake, Saskatchewan, since 1935. Augustus F. (Gus) Kenderdine, an artist trained at the Académie Julian in Paris and an instructor in the fledgling Department of Art at the University of Saskatchewan in Saskatoon, established a summer art camp on an eleven-acre boreal forest peninsula on the shores of Emma Lake. He convinced Dr. Walter Murray, first president of the University of Saskatchewan, that the art camp could perform a vital role in the offerings of the department, and in 1936 the Murray Point Art School at Emma Lake was officially incorporated as a summer school program. Participants were teachers and artists who came from all over the province to learn how to teach art in Saskatchewan schools.

After Kenderdine's death in 1947, a new generation of Saskatchewan artists came of age or moved into the province, including Kenneth Lochhead, Arthur McKay, Ronald Bloore, Ted Godwin, and Douglas Morton—popularly referred to as the Regina Five. In 1955 Kenneth Lochhead, director of the Regina College School of Art, proposed a two-week workshop at Emma Lake to follow the Murray Point Art School classes. The workshop concept, based on modernist art, was established to keep Prairie artists in touch with art centers such as New York and Toronto. The internationally renowned Emma Lake Artists' Workshops became an established annual event and continued virtually unchanged until the last workshop was held in 1995.

Since the mid-1960s the site has also been a provincial research area under the auspices of the University of Saskatchewan Department of Biology for biologists and other researchers. It is the most northerly field station in Saskatchewan and one of the few sites in Canada that specifically examines the boreal forest. It was declared as a game preserve in 1962. In 1989 the site was officially designated as Emma Lake Kenderdine Campus in recognition of Gus Kenderdine. Currently, the site thrives as a summer campus for artists workshops for both university and community programs.

Kate Hobin
University of Saskatchewan

Kate Hobin Papers, Emma Lake Kenderdine Campus Files, Community Arts Program, Extension Division, University of Saskatchewan, Saskatoon. O'Brian, John, ed. *The Flat Side of the Landscape—The Emma Lake Artists' Workshops*. Saskatoon, Saskatchewan: Mendel Art Gallery, 1989.

EVANS, TERRY (b. 1944)

Terry H. Evans has been photographing the landscape and people of the Plains for much of her adult life. She lived in Salina, Kansas, for twenty-six years before moving to Chicago, where she currently resides. Best known for her photographs of the prairie in both its pristine and its altered states, she continues to develop, expanding the geographic and aesthetic parameters of her art.

Evans was born on August 30, 1944, in Kansas City, Missouri. From the age of four she loved to draw and paint, and she was encouraged in these interests by her parents, Norman and Dale Holt, who had a photography studio in Kansas City for many years. Evans completed a bachelor of fine arts degree in drawing and painting at the University of Kansas, Lawrence, but not until her last semester in college did she begin to take photographs. At that time she had the rare opportunity to photograph presidential candidate Robert F. Kennedy during his 1968 visit to the campus. From this experience Evans perceived the extraordinary access that photography gives viewers to special situations. She never had a formal course in photography and cites her father as her main teacher. The work of Charles Harbutt and James Enyeart was also influential.

In her first decade as a photographer, Evans concentrated on exploring the life conditions of poor people, farm people, her own family, and the inhabitants of her hometown in Kansas. In the years since, her work has been shaped mainly by the landscape of the Plains, an environment characterized by unexpected beauty and shaped by often overwhelming natural forces and human activity. In building her understanding of this complex environment, Evans has employed varied approaches that range from close-ups of diverse prairie plant and animal life, including root systems of grasses, to vistas framed at ground level, to stunning aerial views.

Within Evans's aerial photographs, which capture current conditions of the Plains landscape, the viewer can also catch sight of historic alterations of the land. These include paths worn by animal movements, indentations made by long-abandoned dwellings, patterns wrought by agriculture and military shooting ranges, and many more irregular forms and lines made by forces of nature. The conjunctions of such telling details in her aerial views highlight relationships between the past and present and between nature and humans, sometimes resulting in striking abstract designs. Believing that a single image can never suffice to represent her subject, Evans makes images of forms and visual rhythms that stretch to the edges of and sometimes beyond the frame in both her aerial and other scenes. For example, *Chase County, South of Matfield Green, Kansas, 1993*, presents a panoramic view of a prairie landscape in three images that are not strictly continuous yet appear harmoniously connected: late afternoon sunlight burnishes stands of Indian grass in the foreground; across all three panels autumnal light throws the land behind the grasses into a deep horizontal shadow; the same light also illuminates the gentle golden rise of land in the far distance; contrasting bands of shadow and light unify the three panels and reinforce the horizontal character of the grassland, which is bereft of human presence and nearly reduced to essentials that verge on the abstract. Evans takes care, however, to include details such as the slightly

mounded landforms in the background of the frame on the far right, details tied inextricably to the land's subtle beauty.

Evans's photography has been exhibited widely. Recently, the Smithsonian's Museum of Natural History organized *In Place of Prairie*, a nationally touring solo exhibition of her work. Her books are *Prairie: Images of Land and Sky* (1986), *Disarming the Prairie* (1998), and *The Inhabited Prairie* (1998). Her works are held in, among others, the National Museum of American Art, Washington DC; the Museum of Modern Art, New York; the Baltimore Museum of Art; the Chicago Art Institute; the San Francisco Museum of Art; the Sheldon Memorial Art Gallery, University of Nebraska–Lincoln; and the Spencer Museum of Art, University of Kansas at Lawrence. She received a John Simon Guggenheim Memorial Fellowship in 1996. Recently, Evans has been making a photographic study of Matfield Green and is completing an aerial survey of the prairie from Canada to Texas. Evans distinguishes herself as a photographer by the sheer volume of outstanding images she has made that collectively embrace a photographic vision of Plains landscape that is extraordinarily and appropriately broad.

Martha H. Kennedy
Library of Congress

Brown, Turner, and Elaine Partnow, eds. *Macmillan Biographical Encyclopedia of Photographic Artists and Innovators*. New York: Macmillan Publishing Company, 1983. Kinsey, Joni L. *Plain Pictures: Images of the American Prairie*. Washington DC: Published for the University of Iowa Museum of Art by the Smithsonian Institution Press, 1996.

FARNY, HENRY (1847–1916)

Henry François Farny was one of the first artists to make a career painting Great Plains Indians. Born at Ribeauvillé, Alsace, on July 15, 1847, Farny emigrated with his family to the United States in 1854. He traveled to Fort Yates in Dakota Territory in 1881 and came into contact with the Sioux, whom he sketched. From that point the focus of his work became the western landscape and Indians. His paintings are rarely topographical but often recall the upper Missouri and Platte River valleys, the Wichita Mountains in Oklahoma, and the Rockies. The paintings are almost always populated with nostalgically situated Plains Indians painted in exquisite and accurately rendered—albeit occasionally out of context—detail. It should not be forgotten that Farny was trained in a European tradition that valued imagination and creativity; his work strove to create an effect of a past age rather than historical documentation.

Although he traveled frequently, Farny worked exclusively out of the studio and was at his best when painting either the Sioux or the Apaches in what he considered their traditional territories. He exhibited widely in the United States, France, and Germany. His painting *Danger* (1888) won a bronze medal at the 1889 Exposition Universelle in Paris. He is perhaps best known for the pathos of *The Song of the Talking Wire* (1904), which portrays an uncomprehending Sioux with his ear to a telegraph pole. Farny died in Cincinnati on December 23, 1916.

John Wilson
Cincinnati, Ohio

Carter, Denny. *Henry Farny*. New York: Watson-Guptill Publications, 1978.

FITZGERALD, LIONEL LEMOINE (1890–1956)

Lionel LeMoine FitzGerald was a member of Canada's Group of Seven, joining in 1932. In 1933 he became a founder of the Canadian Group of Painters. FitzGerald was born in Winnipeg on March 17, 1890. After study in Winnipeg and Pittsburgh and at the Art Students League in New York in 1921 with Boardman Robinson and Kenneth Hayes Miller, FitzGerald joined the Winnipeg School of Art in 1924 and became its principal in 1929. He held that position until 1947.

FitzGerald's art is distinguished by its precise, often pointillistic, technique, poetic intensity, quiet tone, and subtle color. He explored the light and feeling of space on the Prairies, often using the area around his home in St. James, Manitoba, near Winnipeg. Located there for most of his career (though stimulated by visits in the 1940s to British Columbia, where he met Lawren Harris, a fellow member of the Group of Seven), he sought the "inner life of things."

In the 1950s FitzGerald turned to abstraction to express himself, but most critics agree that he was a typical Prairie artist. Lawren Harris believed that the brittle clarity of the atmosphere of the Prairies was reflected in FitzGerald's landscapes. In the catalog for the FitzGerald memorial exhibition, Ferdinand Eckhardt, director of the Winnipeg Art Gallery, wrote in 1958 that FitzGerald's work was typical of the Prairie Provinces "not only in subject matter but also in its simplicity, intensity, and friendly atmosphere." However, Alan Jarvis, director of the National Gallery of Canada, in the same catalog described FitzGerald's art as classical in a modern sense: "It was highly personal, sensitive and fastidious." He also stressed its universal significance. FitzGerald also painted nudes and still lifes. Among his well-known works is *Doc Snyder's House* (1931), now at the National Gallery of Canada, Ottawa. FitzGerald died in Winnipeg on August 5, 1956.

Joan Murray
Robert McLaughlin Gallery

L. L. FitzGerald 1890–1956: A Memorial Exhibition. Exhibition Catalog. Ottawa: National Gallery of Canada, 1958.

FOLK ART

See FOLKWAYS: Folk Art

FOLK DANCE

See FOLKWAYS: Folk Dance

GILCREASE, THOMAS (1890–1962)

Thomas Gilcrease was known as a collector of Americana at a time when few others were interested in the art, documents, and artifacts of the Western Hemisphere. Eventually, his collection expanded to include nearly 10,000 works of art, a library of 100,000 items, and more than 250,000 artifacts. In 1949 he opened a public museum on his estate in Tulsa, Oklahoma, to showcase his collection.

Gilcrease was born in Robilene, Louisiana, on February 8, 1890. His early life in the Creek Nation of Indian Territory was marked by little formal education and much hard work. While still in his teens, his life changed dramatically when the allotted land he had received as a result of his Creek tribal membership became part of a major oil field in Oklahoma. Gilcrease proved to be a skillful businessman, expanding his original holdings and founding the Gilcrease Oil Company in 1922. During the 1920s and 1930s extensive travel in Europe and visits to European museums inspired him to initiate his own collection. Pride in his Native American heritage and interest in the history of the American West provided a focus for his collecting activities.

By the late 1930s Gilcrease was spending most of his time developing the collection. In the early 1950s, faced with increasing debts relating to acquisitions for his museum, Gilcrease offered to sell the entire collection in order to keep it intact. In 1954 Tulsans supported a bond issue for the payment of Gilcrease's debts and the acquisition of the collection. Gilcrease allocated oil revenues to the city of Tulsa until the income equaled the amount of the bond, a goal that was achieved in the early 1980s. Thomas Gilcrease died on May 6, 1962, in Tulsa.

See also EDUCATION: Museums.

Sarah Erwin
Gilcrease Museum

GILDER, ROBERT (1856–1940)

Robert Fletcher Gilder once identified himself as a journeyman printer by trade, despite the fact that he had a successful career as a professional journalist in Omaha, Nebraska, and achieved lasting recognition as an artist and archaeologist. He painted many Nebraska and western landscapes that were admired, exhibited, and collected during his lifetime. Gilder's paintings capture many aspects of the beauty and subtle variety of the Plains landscape and contribute notably to the region's artistic legacy.

Born October 6, 1856, the son of a minister, in Flushing, Long Island, New York, Gilder attended public schools in Newark and New Jersey and the Gunnery School in Washington, Connecticut. He studied painting under August Will, a Jersey City painter of urban scenes who directed a school in New York City. After arriving in Omaha in 1887, Gilder worked at the *Omaha World Herald*, first as a typesetter, then as a reporter and editor for the newspaper during a career of nearly twenty-five years before he retired in 1919.

The extent of Gilder's formal artistic training with Will remains unknown; he may have been largely self-taught. Friend and fellow Nebraska artist Augustus Dunbier (1888–1977) believed Gilder may have been influenced by Omaha artist J. Laurie Wallace. He often worked outdoors and drew inspiration primarily from the Missouri River basin, especially the Fontenelle Forest area. He also made many paintings of the desert landscape of Arizona as well as scenes in California and Connecticut. His technique can be described as impressionist in that he concentrated on the atmosphere or feel of particular places, sought to capture their natural appearances during brief periods of time, and used bright pigments in broken, broad brushwork. In an untitled winter landscape of 1914 he sensitively rendered the season's cold pale light, which casts faint shadows of trees on a riverbank. In *Shadow of the Bridge* (n.d.), a view of Omaha seen from across the Missouri River, the blue shadows of the bridge cut bold diagonals across the canvas to the blue horizontal of the river, above which the city skyline rises. Known especially for his winter landscapes, which were avidly collected by Omahans, Gilder also painted autumn and spring scenes. An example such as *Passing Storm* (c. 1916), with its heavy lavender gray clouds lifting to disclose clear sky, reveals his skillful use of color, brush strokes, and composition to depict rapidly shifting atmospheric conditions. Broad and broken brushwork, strong but not overstated color, and tight composition characterize many of his best paintings.

Gilder exhibited regularly at Whitmore's Art Gallery in Omaha and had his work shown in Arizona, California, St. Paul, Minnesota, and New York City. Modest, energetic, and consistent in the quality of his work even late in his life, he produced thirty-four paintings the summer before he died in Omaha on March 7, 1940. Nebraska's major art museums, private collections, and several public schools hold examples of his work, in addition to Amherst College and the St. Paul Institute.

See also MEDIA: *Omaha World-Herald*.

Martha H. Kennedy
Library of Congress

Gerdts, William H. *The Plains States and the West: Art across America: Regional Painting in America*. New York: Abbeville Press, 1990. Geske, Norman A. *Art and Artists in Nebraska*. Lincoln: Sheldon Memorial Art Gallery in association with the Center for Great Plains Studies, 1983.

GILPIN, LAURA (1891–1979)

Photographer Laura Gilpin was born on April 22, 1891, in Austin Bluffs, Colorado, just north of Colorado Springs. She was given a Brownie camera for her twelfth birthday, and by the time she was seventeen she was experimenting with Autochromes, an early form of color photography. In 1916 she moved to New York and, using money from her own Colorado poultry business, enrolled in the Clarence H. White School of Photography. There she acquired her skills, but it was in the Southwest and the southwestern Great Plains that she found her subject.

Gilpin returned to her native Colorado Springs, established a professional photographic business, and began photographing the prairies of eastern Colorado. She would remain a landscape photographer for sixty years, becoming the first American woman to devote herself to that art. As her interest in the cultural dimensions of the landscape grew, Gilpin expanded her work to embrace prehistoric sites, contemporary Native American settlements, and the communities of people living and working along the Rio Grande. She addressed these topics in her four major books (*The Pueblos: A Camera Chronicle*, 1941; *Temples in Yucatan: A Camera Chronicle of Chichén Itzá*, 1948; *The Rio Grande: River of Destiny*, 1949; and *The Enduring Navaho*, 1968), each of which explores the interactions between people and their physical environment and focuses on the ways in which the landscape shapes cultural patterns even as people reshape their physical surroundings. Gilpin moved to Santa Fe, New Mexico, in 1945. In her later years, an emerging market for fine art photography brought renewed attention to her life's work. Gilpin died on November 30, 1979, in Santa Fe. She bequeathed her photographic estate to the Amon Carter Museum, Fort Worth, Texas.

Martha A. Sandweiss
Amherst College

Laura Gilpin Photographs and Papers, Amon Carter Museum, Fort Worth. Sandweiss, Martha A. *Laura Gilpin: An Enduring Grace*. Fort Worth: Amon Carter Museum, 1986.

GOHLKE, FRANK (b. 1942)

Born in Wichita Falls, Texas, on April 3, 1942, artist-photographer Frank Gohlke took up the medium in the mid-1960s while a graduate student in English literature at Yale University. Encouraged and influenced by photographers Walker Evans and Paul Caponigro, he initially worked under the sway of New England's thick woods and rolling hills. Yet Gohlke found his true artistic voice after moving to Minneapolis in 1971. Drawn to a bundle of grain elevators near his new home, he began what became a six-year photographic meditation that explored how these great behemoths have come to define the landscape, acting as focal points for regional communities.

Gohlke gained national acclaim in 1975 as one of the nine photographers featured in the influential exhibition *New Topographics: Photographs of the Man-Altered Landscape*. The artists in this show were heralded for bucking the fine art landscape tradition by drawing attention to the often-prosaic beauty of the built environment. The following year Gohlke contributed to the Seagram Corporation's renowned Courthouse Project, photographing courthouses in North Texas. In 1984 he took part in the "Contemporary Texas" photographic project. He also has completed extensive photographic series on the aftermath of the 1980 Mount St. Helens eruption in Washington and the Sudbury River in Massachusetts.

A potent sense of place marks the core of Gohlke's art. Reflecting his Plains roots, his work is infused with quiet, an appreciation for space and balance, and a recognition of the fragility of humanity's relationship with nature. Time also is important. For every photograph capturing a moment like a flash of lightning or a signpost acutely bent by tornado winds, he offers elegiac visions of ordinary structures, objects, and places. At times his work comes infused with a wry humor. In this personal nexus he seeks to clarify how we come to define what we call home.

John B. Rohrbach
Amon Carter Museum

Gohlke, Frank. *Landscapes from the Middle of the World, Photographs 1972–1987*. San Francisco: Friends of Photography, 1988. Gohlke, Frank. *Measure of Emptiness: Grain Elevators in the American Landscape*. Baltimore MD: Johns Hopkins University Press, 1992.

GREENER, CHARLES THEODORE (1870–1935)

Charles Theodore Greener's oil paintings of the area surrounding his Redfield, South Dakota, home made him a leading regional artist during the early twentieth century. His realistic prairie landscapes, painted in soft brush strokes, capture the beauty of the region's wide-open spaces, depict panoramic sunsets and sunrises, and render ordinary scenes that include geese, coyotes, hunting dogs, and other inhabitants of the Plains.

Greener was born on March 16, 1870, in a log house in Grant County, Wisconsin, the second oldest of seven children of Christian and Albina Greener. The family moved to Hand County, Dakota Territory, in 1883 and eight years later settled in Faulkton, which Greener made his home for the rest of his life. Largely self-taught as an artist, he received formal training at the University of North Dakota and at schools in Cincinnati, Minneapolis, and Galesburg, Illinois. His work was displayed at the World's Columbian Exposition in Chicago in 1893. In 1906 Faulk County commissioned him to paint the murals for its new courthouse. He was one of two artists representing South Dakota in 1915 at the St. Paul Institute's first survey of northwestern painting, and he gained national recognition in 1932 by being selected for an exhibit entitled *The American Scene* in Indianapolis.

Greener supplemented his small income from commissions and sales of his paintings through a variety of business ventures, including a photo shop and a combined novelty and grocery store. In 1900 he married W. Florence Jones; they had one child, Dorothy. He engaged actively in community affairs, serving as a deacon in the Congregational church, singing in the church choir, and joining the Masonic Lodge. He was a member of the city council at the time of his death on July 4, 1935.

John E. Miller
South Dakota State University

Lewis, Dale. "Early South Dakota Artist Is Regaining Popularity." *Dakota West* 12 (1986): 20–22.

HENRI, ROBERT (1865–1929)

Robert Henri was a renowned American painter and teacher in the late nineteenth century and first quarter of the twentieth century. He was born Robert Henry Cozad in Cincinnati, Ohio, on June 24, 1865. His father, John J. Cozad, a riverboat gambler and land speculator, settled and developed present-day Cozad, Nebraska. Robert spent his early years on the family ranch and attended school in Cozad. The family hastily left the Plains in 1882 when Robert's father killed one of his workers in self-defense.

Robert Henri—the name he adopted because of fear of repercussions from the Cozad incident—enrolled in the Pennsylvania Academy of the Fine Arts in 1886 and studied under Thomas P. Anshutz. In 1888 he made the first of a number of visits to Europe when he studied with Adolphe William Bouguereau at the Académie Julian in Paris. He found the teaching in Paris to be stifling, but he was inspired by the masterpieces in the Louvre and, subsequently, by the works of Diego Velázquez and Frans Hals.

Henri taught in Philadelphia, New York, and Paris. He encouraged his students to seek the freedom of individual expression and to break from the European academies' and the National Academy of Design's conformity to tradition. Young artists who were influenced by his teaching include William Glackens, George Luks, Everett Shinn, and John Sloan, later members of the Eight, or Ashcan school. Stuart Davis, George Bellows, and Edward Hopper were also inspired by his teaching.

Although Henri's reputation was based mainly on his teaching, he painted many fine landscapes, cityscapes, and portraits, including hundreds of portraits of Irish children. He painted with energetic brushwork, using a dark palette with sharp contrasts of light and shade, as seen in *Girl in Wedding Gown* (1910). Henri continued to receive honors for his work right up until his death on July 12, 1929, in New York.

Gary Zaruba
University of Nebraska at Kearney

Henri, Robert. *The Art Spirit*. New York: Harper and Row, 1984. Homer, William Innes. *Robert Henri and His Circle*. Ithaca NY: Cornell University Press, 1969. *Robert Henri*. Exhibition Catalog. Lincoln: Nebraska Art Association, 1971.

HERD, STAN (b. 1950)

Since the late 1970s Stan Herd has created monumental portraits and other images by plowing, planting, and mowing on tracts of farmland in the Great Plains.

Born in 1950 in Protection, Kansas, and raised in an area that was formerly Kiowa hunting grounds, Herd has frequently chosen his subjects and perfected his methods to reflect his admiration for Native American spiritual attitudes toward the land as well as his concern for contemporary environmental issues. As a youth Herd was struck by images of the colossal pre-Columbian drawings on the desert floor of the Andes Mountains and later by his aerial view from a small plane of a farmer turning over the rich Kansas earth. Herd's first project, completed in 1979, was a portrait of the Kiowa chief Satanta, whose heroic exploits had made him a symbol among the Kiowa of resistance to European American encroachment. Herd began by gridding off a pencil sketch from a photograph of Satanta and transferring this scheme to the land by means of numbered flags. The artist then followed these guides on tractor, pulling a brace of disc rotors behind him to etch the final image into the soil. Herd soon discovered the challenge posed to his image by the vagaries of weather and unpredicted wild plant growth and in the course of ensuing projects would learn ways to gain more control over the ecology of his earth art. This included abandoning for the most part his "subtractive" plowing method in favor of images produced through the strategic plantings of crops, as, for example, his *Sunflower Field* of 1985 (?).

Herd's special concern for the struggles of Native peoples to maintain their culture is exemplified in *Little Girl in the Wind* (1990), a portrait of a Kansan Kickapoo woman and the first of a planned Nation's Portrait series addressing the hardships of Indigenous women in their lands of origin. In a similar vein, *Medicine Wheel* (1992) was a cooperative venture with faculty members Dan Wildcat and Leslie Evans of Haskell Indian Nations University. Conceived as a Native American response to the quincentennial celebrations of Columbus's arrival in the New World, the wheel was dedicated with a Flame Spirit Run during which Native American leaders carried flames from the circle's center outward in the four compass directions. As intended, *Medicine Wheel* has since become a place of prayer and meditation for all peoples of the surrounding community.

One issue Herd has continually wrestled

Stan Herd. Sunflower Field, *near Eudora, Kansas, 1986.*

with is the relationship between art and the business world. In 1988 he created *Cola Wars* for the Ottawa, Kansas, Arts Council. First etching the outline of two crushed Coke and Pepsi cans in a field, Herd then gathered close to 1,000 volunteers wearing all red or blue clothing to temporarily fill in the images of the cans. The anticommercial intention of this living earth sculpture was to emphasize how advertising produces a throw-away consumer culture, resulting in a landscape blighted with trash. Nevertheless, in subsequent years Herd has come to accept the occasional necessity for corporate patronage, carefully screening for companies he deems socially responsible and that offer artistically challenging projects. In considering his first such venture, *Absolut Vodka* (1990), Herd was impressed with the activism in Iroquois Native American issues evinced by the CEO of Absolut's American distributing company.

Herd's recent projects include the whimsical *Ancient Fish Maze*, an image after the 80-million-year-old fossils of *Xiphactinus* found in Kansas. Cut from a dormant alfalfa field outside Lawrence, the contours of the prehistoric fish are filled in with a complex maze design. A portrait of Amelia Earhart, commissioned by the aviator's hometown of Atchison, Kansas, to celebrate the 100th anniversary of her birth, is taking shape from native stone and perennial grasses and will be the artist's first truly permanent land work. As with many of Herd's projects, numerous assisting volunteers make the Earhart portrait a community-wide effort.

See also GENDER: Earhart, Amelia.

Michael C. Dooley
University of Iowa

Herd, Stanley J. *Crop Art and Other Earthworks.* New York: Harry N. Abrams, 1994. Kinsey, Joni L. *Plain Pictures: Images of the American Prairie.* Washington DC: Published for the University of Iowa Museum of Art by the Smithsonian Institution Press, 1996.

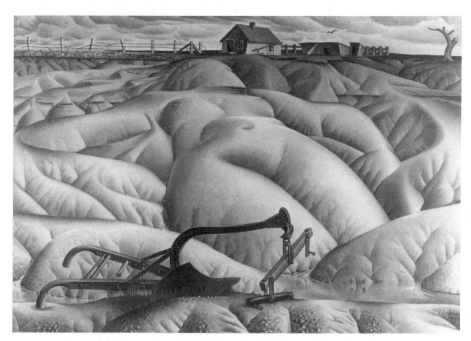

Alexandre Hogue. American 1898–1994. Erosion No. 2. Mother Earth Laid Bare, *1936. Oil on canvas.*

HOGUE, ALEXANDRE (1898–1994)

American artist Alexandre Hogue is known primarily for his paintings of the Dust Bowl of the 1930s. Hogue was one of the few painters of the period to acknowledge the conditions of the Southern Plains during the Great Depression, and his works are considered both accurate and provocative. His concern with the environment and with humans' relations with it endures as a major theme in his work.

Born in Memphis, Missouri, on February 22, 1898, Hogue grew up in Denton and Dallas. He worked briefly (1921–25) in New York as a graphic designer and then returned to Texas, where he established himself as an artist, teacher, and writer. His explorations of the landscape along with his interest in Native cultures and their attitudes toward nature formed an artistic credo that emphasized not only the beauty of the land but also the effects upon it of human activities.

In his travels through the region he witnessed the development of the Dust Bowl, and in 1932 he began his series on the ecological disaster unfolding before him. *Dust Bowl* (1933, Smithsonian Museum of American Art), *Drouth Stricken Area* (1934, Dallas Museum of Fine Art), and *Drouth Survivors* (1936, destroyed in 1948, formerly in the Musée National d'Art Modern, Paris) all show a landscape described by Hogue as a "lush grassland" transformed into a desertlike place scarcely able to sustain life of any kind. Tractors and dead cattle half-buried in sand dunes, an abandoned farm with its broken windmill and dust-filled water trough, and the eerie light of a dust-choked, sandy, and barren ranch—all these images created an apocalyptic iconography that Hogue used to convey the reality of the situation on the Plains as well as his condemnation of the farming and ranching practices that had created it. Unlike the photographers of the Farm Security Administration, who also documented Depression

Era conditions, Hogue expressed little sympathy for the families forced off the land by the Dust Bowl (in fact, they do not appear in his work) but instead made it clear that he held humans accountable for their deliberate misuse of the land.

Perhaps the grimmest and most accusatory painting is *Mother Earth Laid Bare* (1938, Philbrook Museum of Art Museum, Tulsa), in which overproduction of the land and disregard for the forces of nature are clearly presented as acts of desecration. In contrast to other painters of the period such as Grant Wood and Thomas Hart Benton, who generally treated their region as a place of hope, good values, and productivity, Hogue presents a sobering view of a land exhausted and ruined by the failure to acknowledge and respect nature. Later works from the 1950s on were less condemnatory but continued to express the artist's reverence for nature, even at times in an abstract style. His series of drawings, pastels, and paintings on the Big Bend landscape (c. 1960–c. 1990) especially demonstrate the persistence of this theme.

In addition to his career as an artist, Hogue was an important teacher in the region, notably as head of the art department at the University of Tulsa (1945–68). During the 1930s he was a leader in one of the most active regional groups, known as the Dallas Nine, and was also a founder (1938) of the Lone Star Printmakers. Hogue died in Tulsa on July 22, 1994.

See also PHYSICAL ENVIRONMENT: Dust Bowl.

Lea Rosson DeLong
Des Moines, Iowa

DeLong, Lea Rosson. *Nature's Forms/Nature's Forces: The Art of Alexandre Hogue*. Norman: University of Oklahoma Press; Tulsa: Philbrook Museum of Art, 1984. Hogue, Alexandre. "Progressive Texas." *Art Digest* 10 (1936): 17–18. Stewart, Rick. *Lone Star Regionalism: The Dallas Nine and Their Circle*. Dallas: Dallas Museum of Art, 1985.

HOUSER, ALLAN (1914–1994)

One of the most influential Native American artists of the twentieth century, Houser was of Chiricahua heritage; his grandfather was warchief Mangus Coloradas, and his granduncle was Geronimo. Houser was born in Apache, Oklahoma, on June 30, 1914, and grew up near Fort Sill. His early life was filled with stories of Chiricahua resistance. In the 1930s he attended the Indian School in Santa Fe, working with Dorothy Dunn in the Studio. The flat, two-dimensional painting style developed there was too restrictive for Houser, although he executed various Studio-style murals, including some in the Department of the Interior Building in Washington DC. He studied muralism with Olaf Nordmark, who suggested that he turn to sculpture. Beginning in wood, Houser quickly explored other materials, including bronze, marble, and steel. He taught at the Inter-Mountain Boarding School in Utah between 1951 and 1961 and in Santa Fe at the new Institute of American Indian Arts from 1962 to 1975. The institute was founded on principles that Houser held to be deeply important: that Native American artists should be encouraged to explore their cultural heritage as well as to create art in keeping with their own individual goals and self-expression. At sixty-one, he officially stopped teaching to devote his energies to his own art, but he never stopped helping students.

Numerous awards filled his life, including a Guggenheim Fellowship (1948) and the French Palmes d'Académiques (1954) for his exemplary work as both artist and teacher. He was inducted into the Oklahoma Hall of Fame and, in 1992, was the first Native American to receive the National Medal of Arts. His unceasing experimentation and creativity were expressed in subject matter that ranged from representations of Native figures of the past to contemporary abstractions without recognizable imagery. Houser died on August 22, 1994, in Santa Fe.

Joyce M. Szabo
University of New Mexico

Allan Houser (Ha-o-zous): A Life in Art. Exhibition Catalog. Santa Fe: Museum of New Mexico, 1991. Perlman, Barbara H. *Allan Houser (Ha-o-zous)*. Boston: David R. Godine, 1987. *The Studio of Allan Houser*. Exhibition Catalog. Santa Fe: Wheelwright Museum of the American Indian, 1996.

HOWE, OSCAR (1915–1983)

Internationally acclaimed Yanktonai Nakota painter Oscar Howe was a major force in the evolution of the Native American fine arts movement. In the 1950s and 1960s Howe led his generation in the transition from the highly prescribed Studio style to greater personal expression and active engagement with mainstream modern art.

Oscar Howe was born on May 13, 1915, at Joe Creek on the Crow Creek Reservation in South Dakota. His Indian name, Mazuha Hokshina, translates as Trader Boy, which proved particularly appropriate given his lifelong commitment to bridging Native American and European American cultures. Howe came from a distinguished Yanktonai family that included hereditary chiefs and noted orators. At age seven Howe was sent to the Pierre Indian School, which was administered by the Bureau of Indian Affairs on a military model that actively promoted assimilation. Serious health problems interrupted Howe's education, but he subsequently graduated from the school in 1933. Howe enrolled in the Santa Fe Indian School in New Mexico in 1935, two years after Dorothy Dunn had established an innovative art program known as the Studio. Here he was one of a select group of young artists to receive the training and encouragement necessary to pursue careers in art. Howe graduated in 1938 as salutatorian of his class.

Returning to South Dakota, Howe taught art at the Pierre Indian School until 1940, when he joined the WPA South Dakota Artist Project, illustrating several books and painting murals in Mitchell and Mobridge. In 1942 he was drafted into the U.S. Army and served for three and a half years with combat forces in Europe. Honorably discharged in 1945, Howe returned to his art and in 1947 won the grand prize at the second annual National Indian

Oscar Howe in his studio at the University of South Dakota, ca. 1968

Painting Competition at the Philbrook Museum of Art in Tulsa, Oklahoma. With the prize of $350, he married Adelheid Hample, whom he had met in Germany; their only child, Inge Dawn, was born in 1949. Howe attended Dakota Wesleyan University in Mitchell on the GI Bill, receiving a bachelor of arts degree in 1952. During this period, the artist began designing the murals for Mitchell's "world-famous" Corn Palace, a commission he executed annually until 1971. Howe once again returned to Pierre, South Dakota, between 1953 and 1957 and taught high school art. He entered the master of fine arts program at the University of Oklahoma, graduating in 1954. In 1957 Howe accepted a position as professor and artist in residence at the University of South Dakota in Vermillion, beginning a distinguished twenty-five-year tenure at that institution.

These were the artist's most productive years, marked by over sixty solo exhibitions, fifteen grand or first-place prizes, and numerous awards. By this time, Howe had rejected the last vestiges of the Studio style for strong colors, pulsating space, dynamic movement, and a high degree of abstraction. *Sioux Seed Player* (1974), a casein painting on paper, is an excellent example of Howe's mature style. Masterfully executed, the painting is intensely pristine and compositionally complex, but its most compelling feature is its dynamism. Utilizing highly colorful flat shapes, Howe created a fluid, ambivalent, and virtually pulsating spatial illusion that is unique in Native American art.

A signature event in Howe's life, often cited as helping to change the direction of Native American art, occurred in 1958. That year the artist challenged the jurors at the Philbrook's annual National Indian Painting Competition after they assessed one of his more abstract submissions as not Indian enough to qualify for an award. In a justifiably famous letter, Howe advanced the cause of personal expression, with the result that a new experimental category was added to future competitions—a decision that was a powerful incentive to younger artists.

During his life Howe was honored with the Dorothy Field Award from the Denver Art Museum (1952); the Mary Benjamin Award from the Museum of New Mexico, Santa Fe (1960); the Waite Phillips Trophy for Outstanding Contributions to American Indian Art from the Philbrook Museum of Art, Tulsa (1966); the South Dakota Governor's Award for Creative Achievement (1973); and the Golden Bear Award from the University of Oklahoma (1978).

Oscar Howe retired from the faculty of the University of South Dakota in 1980 and was recognized with a major retrospective exhibition that toured nationally between 1981 and 1983. After a prolonged illness, he died on October 7, 1983. Throughout his life, Oscar Howe demonstrated a strong connection with the land of his forebears and passionately advanced the creation of a Northern Plains style of Native American fine arts. Today his aesthetic leadership is widely acknowledged, and his work is celebrated for its revolutionary impact and its assertion of the creative vitality of Native American art in contemporary culture. Howe's achievements are memorialized with major collections of his work in South Dakota at the Oscar Howe Art Center in Mitchell, the South Dakota Memorial Art Center in Brookings, and the Oscar Howe Gallery and Archives at the University Art Galleries in Vermillion, South Dakota.

See also IMAGES AND ICONS: Corn Palace.
John A. Day
University of South Dakota

Dockstader, Frederick J., ed. *Oscar Howe: A Retrospective Exhibition.* Tulsa: Thomas Gilcrease Museum Association, 1982. Howe, Oscar. *Oscar Howe, Artist of the Sioux.* Vermillion SD: Oscar Howe, 1974. White, Mark Andrew. "Oscar Howe." *American Indian Art Magazine* 23 (1997): 36–43.

HOWLING WOLF (1849–1927)

Active in the Southern Plains wars, then incarcerated at Fort Marion in St. Augustine, Florida, between 1875 and 1878, Howling Wolf was a Southern Cheyenne warrior and noted artist who was born in 1849. He and his father, Eagle Head, were undoubtedly at the Sand Creek Massacre in 1864, and Howling Wolf subsequently engaged in various battles, successfully counting coup or completing his first culturally recognized brave action on a war party led by the Bowstring warrior Lame Bull in May 1867. Howling Wolf became a secondary Bowstring leader before being selected, together with seventy-one other Southern Plains warriors and chiefs, for exile to Fort Marion, Florida.

Arguably the single most important Plains artist who worked on paper during the late nineteenth century, Howling Wolf is the only artist known to have created drawings during the prereservation era, on the reservation, and at Fort Marion. Using available paper, often lined accountants' ledgers, Plains men drew images of their battles and horse raids in much the same manner they did on hide robes. Howling Wolf's drawings from the first half of the 1870s not only reflect Plains systems

of representation, with emphasis on the identity of protagonists and important actions, but also demonstrate experimental creativity and great skill. At Fort Marion he, like many of the younger prisoners, made drawings for various reasons, including to sell to tourists. His Florida drawings are generally nostalgic views of home or records of the men's new experiences rather than battle images. The few drawings he made following his release in mid-1878 demonstrate additional changes in subject and style that may be attributed to the vastly different life of the reservation and to many of the unique experiences he had in the East. Howling Wolf died in Oklahoma on July 5, 1927.

See also WAR: Sand Creek Massacre.
Joyce M. Szabo
University of New Mexico

Petersen, Karen Daniels. *Howling Wolf: A Cheyenne Warrior's Graphic Interpretation of His People.* Palo Alto CA: American West Publishing Company, 1968. Szabo, Joyce M. *Howling Wolf and the History of Ledger Art.* Albuquerque: University of New Mexico Press, 1994.

JACKSON, WILLIAM HENRY (1843–1942)

William Henry Jackson's career as a photographer and painter spanned more than seventy years, during which he recorded the vast beauty of the western landscape, Native American life, and the expansion of European Americans into the Great Plains and the West. According to the family Bible, Jackson was born in Keeseville, New York, on April 14, 1843. He inherited his rootlessness from his father, who moved the family six times before William Henry was ten. After serving in the Civil War with the Twelfth Vermont Volunteers, he went to the Great Plains in 1866 and worked as a teamster hauling freight out of Nebraska City. Jackson made many sketches of his early travels in the Great Plains that would later serve as references for his paintings. With his brother he bought a photography studio in Omaha in 1867 and spent the next few years photographing local residents, the Indigenous peoples, the construction of the Union Pacific Railroad, and the settlement of the Great Plains. His photographs of the Pawnee villages and people around 1870, during their final years in Nebraska, are especially evocative.

In 1870 he joined the Hayden Geological Survey as its official photographer and worked for the next eight years documenting the West and Southwest. His photographs of the Yellowstone area influenced Congress's decision to designate the nation's first national park in 1872, and his widely distributed photographs gave Americans a visual knowledge of the Great Plains and West. The quality of his work, considering the equipment and glass plate developing process of Jackson's time, is noteworthy.

From 1879 to the mid-1920s, Jackson devoted his career to commercial photography: he opened a photography studio in Denver, made a photographic survey of railroads around the world, contributed frequently to

William Henry Jackson, 1924

Harper's Weekly, served as photographer for the World's Columbian Exposition in Chicago, and made photographic prints and postcards for the Detroit Publishing Company.

After his retirement in 1924, Jackson painted numerous watercolors and oil paintings, some of which were based on his experiences in the Great Plains and West. The oil painting *Pawnee Indian Village* (1930) is representative. Many others were scenes from the Oregon Trail, which preceded his own time on the Plains. He was mainly self-taught as a painter, although his photography experience gave him compositional skills, and he had become a close associate of the artist Thomas Moran while working on the Hayden survey. Jackson's watercolor paintings have a singular appearance. They are typically small and packed full of subject matter, and they have a pale pastel appearance created by adding white to the transparent medium. He continued painting and writing until his death in New York City on June 30, 1942.

Gary Zaruba
University of Nebraska at Kearney

Hales, Peter B. *William Henry Jackson and the Transformation of the American Landscape.* Philadelphia: Temple University Press, 1988. Jackson, William Henry. *Time Exposure: The Autobiography of William Henry Jackson.* New York: Putnam's Sons, 1940.

JACOBSHAGEN, KEITH (b. 1941)

A notable development in the artistic climate of the Great Plains in the decades following World War II has been the appearance of a whole generation of painters of the prairie landscape: Robert Sudlow, Anne Burkholder, James Butler, Hal Holoun, Ben Darling, Ernest Ochsner, and Keith Jacobshagen. Among them Keith Jacobshagen has attained recognition on the national scene with paintings of exceptional quality. His is not the landscape of the regionalist thirties, dominated by a dry realism and ravaged by climate and social neglect. Instead there is deeply personal, even intimate perception at work. The landscape is rich with the textures of weather, season, and growth. His viewpoint is one of patient absorption, an immersion in the specifics of time and place and, in particular, the hours of the early evening.

Jacobshagen was born on September 8, 1941, in Wichita, Kansas. A graduate of the Kansas City Art Institute (1965) and the University of Kansas at Lawrence (1968), he came to the faculty of the University of Nebraska–Lincoln in 1968 still working in the academic version of current abstract expressionism. Soon thereafter he centered his personal concern on the rural landscape around him, and his work took on the qualities that have identified him among his contemporaries as a master of the minutiae of the subject—of cloud, smoke, the haze of distance. In some of his works he has specified in marginal notations the date, the time of day, the very sounds and smells of being in that place. Most particularly, he has matched the implied complications of the presence of people on the land to the natural drama of the sky.

Norman A. Geske
Lincoln, Nebraska

Geske, Norman A. *Art and Artists in Nebraska.* Lincoln: Sheldon Memorial Art Gallery in Association with the Center for Great Plains Studies, University of Nebraska–Lincoln, 1983.

JEFFERYS, CHARLES W. (1869–1951)

Born in Rochester, England, on August 25, 1869, Charles William Jefferys immigrated with his family to Philadelphia in 1875. He moved to Canada in 1878 and settled in Toronto three years later. He took evening classes at the Ontario School of Art and Design (now known as the Ontario College of Art and Design), had a five-year apprenticeship with the Toronto Lithographic Company, and received art lessons from accomplished Canadian painter George A. Reid. Under the instruction of C. M. Manly of the newly formed Toronto Art Students League, which he joined in 1888, Jefferys gained fundamentals and sound practices that were the foundation of his work throughout his life. He became Canada's earliest and most influential historical illustrator and muralist.

When Jefferys first journeyed to the Prairie Provinces, the vastness and simple beauty of the landscape shattered his stifling commitment to detail, a commitment engendered by his career as a reportage illustrator and spare time spent capturing the rugged yet intricate details of the Ontario landscape. Jefferys's first Prairie visit marked the beginning of a prolific and creative episode in his artistic life.

During the early 1900s Jefferys journeyed across Canada as an official illustrator for numerous Canadian magazines, playing a key role in recording the development of the West. When he first arrived in the southern regions of Saskatchewan and Alberta Jefferys was awestruck by the wide-open spaces and expansive skies. The subtle but complex palette of prairie colors offered artistic opportunities that rivaled other rocky outcroppings of the Canadian Shield.

His first Prairie painting, *Afternoon in the Wheat Fields* (1906), was completed during a visit to Portage-La-Prairie in northwestern Winnipeg, Manitoba. This work inspired his first large oil painting, entitled *Wheat Stacks on the Prairie* (1907), and both are examples of his exploration of this newly discovered and rich palette. Also from this period and in this vein are *Western Sunlight (Last Mountain Lake)* and *A Storm on the Prairie (Allegro Maestoso)*, both from 1911. The latter two oils mark the artist's maturation in this subject matter.

A pioneer in Canadian landscape painting, Jefferys inspired the Group of Seven and their followers through his support of native Canadian subject matter. He died in Toronto on October 8, 1951.

Suzanne Hepburn
Trianon Gallery

Brown, Craig. *The Illustrated History of Canada.* Toronto: Key Porter Books, 1997. Reid, Dennis. *A Concise History of Canadian Painting.* Toronto: Oxford University Press, 1973. Stacey, Robert H. *C. W. Jefferys.* Ottawa: National Gallery/National Museums of Canada, 1985.

JIMENEZ, LUIS

See HISPANIC AMERICANS: Jimenez, Luis

JONES, JOE (1909–1963)

Although not well known today, Joe Jones rose to national prominence as an artist during the Great Depression in the United States. Born in St. Louis on April 7, 1909, this grandson of a stonemason and son of a house painter used his humble beginnings and political beliefs to fashion a persona as a working-class hero that befitted the times. In the early 1930s the twenty-year-old was working alongside his father painting houses when he began to draw attention in local art circles for his works on canvas, produced without the benefit of formal training. But his middle-class backers began to retreat as the young artist became as notorious for his controversial political activities as he was for his paintings. Jones's flight to New York to escape local prosecution on a charge of spreading Communist propaganda proved to be a wise career move.

His first one-man show in the spring of 1935 at the American Contemporary Art Gallery received rave reviews. His social protest paintings such as *We Demand*, which depicts a workers' demonstration, and *American Justice*, which features a lynching, garnered the most attention. However, his next exhibition, *Paintings of Wheatfields*, at the Walker Gallery in January 1936, showed him moving in a less controversial direction. These tranquil scenes of farmers at work in their fields brought the self-proclaimed "professor of wheat" five prestigious federal contracts for murals in post offices in the Midwest and the Great Plains, commissioned by the Treasury Section of the Fine Arts, a New Deal program that sought to bring art to the public while employing struggling artists.

While he was in the Plains Jones painted the oil on canvas works *Turning a Corner* (1939) in Anthony, Kansas, and *Men and Wheat* (1940) in Seneca, Kansas. Deftly balancing the restraints of the administration's guidelines, the local postmaster's needs, and the awkward constraints of the site, Jones produced typical regionalist rural scenes, depicting man, machine, and landscape working together in harmony. But beyond the mythic ideal of

Joe Jones. American Farm, *1936. Oil and tempera on canvas. 30 x 40 inches (76.2 x 101.6 cm).*

a bountiful nature, Jones's compositions frankly reveal humanity's mark upon the environment—the lush fields are being thoroughly stripped by the anonymous workers, their figures merging with the dominating forms of modern machinery. The artist expressed his desire to portray both the importance of wheat to Kansas and the image of people at work in the murals. But as social realism fell out of fashion in the 1940s, Jones abandoned the working hero, focusing instead on the portrayal of the landscape for corporate clients such as *Fortune* magazine and Standard Oil. He died of a heart attack in New Jersey on April 9, 1963.

See also POLITICS AND GOVERNMENT: New Deal.

Louisa Iarocci
Boston University

Marling, Karal Ann. "Joe Jones: Regionalist, Communist, Capitalist." *Journal of the Decorative and Propaganda Arts 1875–1945* 4 (1987): 46–58. Marling, Karal Ann. *Wall-to-Wall America: A Cultural History of Post-Office Murals in the Great Depression.* Minneapolis: University of Minnesota Press, 1982.

KANE, PAUL (1810–1871)

Paul Kane is regarded as one of the founding fathers of Canadian art. Born at Mallow, Ireland, on September 3, 1810, he immigrated to Upper Canada with his family around 1819. He started his artistic career in the 1820s as a decorative furniture painter and later advertised as a coach, sign, and house painter. By the second half of the 1830s he was making his living as an itinerant portrait painter in a number of American cities, including Detroit, Michigan, and Mobile, Alabama. Kane traveled in Europe from 1841 through 1843 studying great art, a tour that was the fulfillment of a long-cherished dream. Following a brief return to portrait work in the United States, Kane arrived back in Canada in 1845 with a mission that would remain his passion for the remainder of his life.

Between 1845 and 1848 Kane undertook two westward journeys from Toronto to sketch the western landscape and the manners and customs of the First Peoples. He returned to Toronto with more than 500 landscape and cultural heritage sketches and within one month opened an exhibition of 240 sketches. This display was Kane's first solo exhibition and one of the first public one-person exhibitions to be held in Canada. He received high praise in newspaper reviews, and the exhibition increased public appreciation for Canadian painting.

Field sketches, however, were only the first step toward the fulfillment of Kane's vision. That vision was realized through the patronage of the Honorable George William Allan, barrister, senator, mayor of Toronto, and president of the Western Canada Savings and Loan Company who gave Kane the resources he needed to produce a cycle of 100 paintings to serve as his record of mid-nineteenth-century landscapes and Indigenous life.

Kane's second journey, from 1846 to 1848, took him as far west as the Pacific Ocean. He spent thirteen months on the Plains sketching the Métis, Sioux, Crees, Assiniboines, and Blackfoot. More than 160 sketches executed in

Paul Kane. Cree Indians Travelling. *Plains Cree. North Saskatchewan River, 1848–1856. Oil, (912.1.49).*

pencil, watercolor, and oil on paper represent invaluable documents of mid-nineteenth-century Plains Indian culture and landscape. The sketches also inspired the oil paintings that he later executed in his Toronto studio, but these, rendered in the contemporary European romantic style, are considerably less important as historical records.

In June 1846 Kane arrived at the Red River Settlement on the Red and the Assiniboine Rivers. Kane's sketch of the settlement represents a view from the bank of the Red River and depicts a number of significant landmarks, such as the St. Boniface Cathedral and Upper Fort Garry. The oil painting (1848–56) represents a similar scene, although the viewer has been securely placed back from the river. The cattle shed and log raft in the foreground and the distant buildings of settlement and commerce in the middle ground embody "progress" and a tamed landscape.

The oil painting *Indian Summer on the Saskatchewan* (1848–56) exemplifies Kane's desire to represent the scenery of the Plains. The oil image is inspired by nature, and details are taken from field sketches; however, the balanced placement of the trees and valley banks, the easy slope into the distance, and the pervasive yellow glow endow the painting with a melancholy, retrospective cast characteristic of romantic artistic conventions.

Kane's tendency to depict the romantic is likewise shown in the oil painting *Cree Indians Travelling* (1848–56). The 1846 sketch of the same title is the basis for the oil painting, although in the painting Kane made a number of changes to the overall composition. The vegetation and human activity in the foreground as well as the middle-ground break of color between the landscape and the sky are conventions in the picturesque style and illustrate Kane's subjective vision and his rendering of the imaginative truth.

In his oil paintings, although they are informed by his sketches, Kane harmonized with expressions of current artistic conventions. In his field sketches, on the other hand,

Paul Kane. Cree Indians Travelling. *Plains Cree. North Saskatchewan River, September 1846. Pencil on paper, September 1846 (946.15.102).*

Kane left a record rich with depictions of Plains landscape and cultural history. The artist died in Toronto on February 20, 1871.

Kenneth R. Lister
Royal Ontario Museum

Harper, J. Russell. *Paul Kane's Frontier*. Fort Worth: Amon Carter Museum of Western Art, 1971. Kane, Paul. *Wanderings of an Artist among the Indians of North America*. Mineola NY: Dover, 1996. MacLaren, I. S. "Journal of Paul Kane's Western Travels." *American Art Journal* 21 (1989): 23–62.

KIOWA SIX

The Kiowa Six, sometimes erroneously called the Kiowa Five, had a profound impact on the development of Native American easel painting. The five most commonly known artists in the group are Jack Hokeah (1900–1969), Monroe Tsatoke (1904–37), Spencer Asah (1906–54), James Auchiah (1906–74), and Stephen Mopope (1900–1974). The sixth member was a woman, Lois Smoky (1907–81).

Painting was an important and honored aspect of traditional Kiowa culture. Men painted calendars, chronological records of important events that affected the group as a whole, and records of an individual's heroic deeds. Women usually confined their artistic expression to beading. These early Kiowa artists all spoke Kiowa and were actively involved in traditional Kiowa culture, despite the forced acculturation of the period.

In order to "civilize" and Christianize the Kiowas and turn them into American capitalists, the Kiowa reservation in western Oklahoma was allotted in 1900. Each tribal member received 160 acres. The remaining 480,000 acres of "excess" land were sold to white settlers in 1906. European American education became mandatory. The six Kiowa artists attended St. Patrick's Mission School near Anadarko, Oklahoma. There they were given English names and taught English and how to do manual service jobs. Upon leaving school these artists returned to their community.

At this time Susie Peters was the Indian Service field matron at Anadarko. She is still remembered there for her concern for and support of many Kiowas. By 1920 she had organized a group of Kiowa artists that included the Kiowa Six. She did not give them lessons in art but encouraged them in their work. She also provided them with paints and drawing paper, which, for the most part, they had not had access to previously. During this period these six artists developed what is commonly referred to as the Kiowa style. Like traditional Kiowa painting, the figures in these paintings were drawn on a plain background. Within the lines color was used as a flat filler. This opaque paint was more solid than traditional vegetable dyes or pencil and ink. Partly because of this technique, Kiowa-style paintings, commonly of individual dancers or ceremonies, emphasize design.

Susie Peters also attempted to market the works of the Kiowa artists in both Oklahoma and New Mexico, and she brought them to the attention of Oscar Jacobson, director of the art department at the University of Oklahoma. In 1927 Jacobson arranged for Stephen Mopope, Monroe Tsatoke, Spencer Asah, and Jack Hokeah to use facilities and supplies at the University of Oklahoma under the guidance of Edith Mahier. Jacobson, however, insisted that they be given no formal instruction. Later, these four artists were joined by Lois Smoky and James Auchiah.

Jacobson, in contrast to Susie Peters, had the contacts to successfully market the artists and their works. Six months after the arrival of the first group of Kiowa artists at the University of Oklahoma, a traveling sales exhibition was organized. Within a year the artists' works had been sold, and an even larger exhibition was mounted. A mere eighteen months after he came to know the artists Jacobson arranged for thirty-five watercolors to be exhibited at the International Congress in Prague, Czechoslovakia, and for a folio of their work to be published in France.

Starting with an exhibition in New York in 1931, the decade of the 1930s was a period of further recognition by European Americans of the beauty of early Kiowa easel painting. The artists were also commissioned under the Public Works of Art Project (PWAP) to paint a number of murals, a medium ideally suited to the Kiowa style with its flat color areas. Other murals were commissioned for the State Historical Building in Oklahoma City and the Department of the Interior Building in Washington DC. The five Kiowa men were involved in these mural projects. Lois Smoky was not. After marrying and having children, she turned her artistic talent to the traditional Kiowa woman's art of beadwork.

The Kiowa Six were among the first Native American painters to be recognized by the European American community. Their work was the model for what is commonly referred to as the traditional flat style, which was refined and developed by Dorothy Dunn at the Indian School in Santa Fe, New Mexico.

See also GENDER: Field Matrons / NATIVE AMERICANS: Kiowas.

Lydia L. Wyckoff
Philbrook Museum of Art

Wyckoff, Lydia L., ed. *Visions and Voices: Native American Painting*. Albuquerque: University of New Mexico Press, 1996.

MILLER, ALFRED JACOB (1810–1874)

Alfred Jacob Miller, born in Baltimore on January 2, 1810, to George Washington Miller and Harriet Jacob, was one of the earliest trained artists to cross the Great Plains. Following study in Paris and Rome in 1833, the young Miller returned to Baltimore and established a studio. After his parents died, Miller left Baltimore and moved to New Orleans in the spring of 1837.

That is where he met Capt. William Drummond Stewart, the second son of Scottish nobility, veteran of the Napoleonic Wars, sportsman, and a seasoned traveler who had attended the annual rendezvous of fur trappers and traders in the Rocky Mountains on several occasions. Stewart planned to attend the 1837 rendezvous and, thinking that it might be his last, employed young Miller to document the trip.

Miller arrived in St. Louis in April 1837. There he visited with Gov. William Clark, the prominent explorer and superintendent of Indian Affairs, and spent time in Clark's museum in preparation for the trip. Stewart and Miller left Westport in May, along with forty-five men and twenty carts loaded with trade goods to exchange for pelts at the rendezvous. They followed the Kansas and Little Blue Rivers to the Platte River, with Miller documenting every segment of the trip. They took the North Fork of the Platte past Chimney Rock, Scotts Bluff, and Fort Laramie, all of which Miller rendered in colorful watercolor. He also depicted Independence Rock, Devils Gate, Split Rock on the Sweetwater River, and the Continental Divide, arriving, finally, at Horse Creek in the Wind River Mountains, where trappers and Indians had gathered for the 1837 rendezvous.

Miller remained at the rendezvous for about three weeks. Following another couple of weeks hunting in the mountains with Stewart, Miller returned to New Orleans to begin working on the paintings that Stewart had commissioned. Stewart, meanwhile, had learned that his older brother John had died, that he had inherited the family estates and titles, and that he must soon return to Murthly Castle, the family estate just outside of Perth, Scotland.

Miller had made dozens of sketches. From them he first prepared a small album of eighty-seven wash and watercolor sketches for Stewart and then set to work on several large oil paintings that Stewart intended as decoration for Murthly. Stewart loaned eighteen of Miller's oils to the Apollo Gallery in New York for exhibition from May to July 1839 before shipping them to Scotland. Miller accepted Stewart's invitation to come to Murthly to continue his painting and remained there for approximately a year, painting both western and religious scenes. He returned to Baltimore in the spring of 1842 and spent the remainder of his life there.

The 1837 trip was the only western journey that Miller made, but he kept his field sketches and continued to fulfill commissions from them throughout his life. The most notable commission was that of William T. Walters, who ordered 200 watercolors from 1858 to 1860. Miller also sold several paintings to Charles Wilkins Weber that were chromolithographed for his books, *The Hunter-Naturalist: Romance of Sporting; or, Wild Scenes and Wild Hunters* and *The Hunter-Naturalist: Wild Scenes and Song-Birds*.

Miller saw the West through the lens of the romantic artist, depicting the many Indians at the rendezvous as noble savages and the Plains and mountains as a garden. There are large collections of his work at the Joslyn Art Museum in Omaha, the Walters Art Gallery in Baltimore, and the Gilcrease Museum in Tulsa. He died in Baltimore on June 26, 1874.

Ron C. Tyler
University of Texas at Austin

Troccoli, Joan Carpenter. *Alfred Jacob Miller: Watercolors of the American West.* Tulsa: Gilcrease Museum, 1990. Tyler, Ron. *Alfred Jacob Miller: Artist as Explorer.* Santa Fe NM: Gerald Peters Gallery, 1999. Tyler, Ron, ed. *Alfred Jacob Miller: Artist on the Oregon Trail.* Fort Worth: Amon Carter Museum, 1982.

NATIVE AMERICAN TRADITIONAL ART

Before Europeans introduced glass beads, metal cones, ribbons, and cloth, Plains Indians decorated themselves, their clothes, and their household belongings with paint, stone, bone and shell beads, animal teeth, and other natural materials. They also carved and painted human and animal figures and various symbolic designs on boulders and rock walls. In the Central and Northern Plains, some groups used stones to create outline figures of medicine wheels, humans, and animals. Shells with faces carved in them and sculptures of buffalo demonstrate that carving, although a minor art form, was done before the introduction of metal tools.

The great diversity in rock-art styles suggests that there were many different tribes or groups inhabiting the Plains. Each region has its own distinct style, and scholars have named and described the works from each area. In the northwestern Plains, works believed to date from between 1000 and 1700 have a recognizable Plains Indian style that connects well to later art forms. Called "Ceremonial" by scholars, the early designs consist of simple outline figures of humans and animals. Some humans are depicted with rectangular bodies, V-shaped necklines, and round heads. Others have large round bodies with arms and legs. The decorations on the bodies suggest that they represent shields, and the designs are referred to as shield-bearing warriors. Animals are shown with elongated, rounded bodies with stick legs and well-defined horns or antlers. Symbolic ribs often appear inside the animal bodies.

Later rock art continued the stick-figure techniques but presents them in much more action oriented scenes. This style has been called "Biographical." Hunting and battle scenes seem to tell stories of actual events. Scenes dating from postcontact times show rectangular-bodied, round-headed warriors brandishing guns and riding horses. Similar scenes appear on the earliest known buffalo robes and men's shirts. A robe collected by Meriwether Lewis and William Clark on their trip up the Missouri River in 1804 shows the same kind of round-headed, rectangular-bodied stick figures as the rock art.

The earliest art, whether rock art or items collected by visitors to the tribes, contains the basic elements of Plains Indian art and shows that the attitudes and aesthetics were very different from European art. Unlike European art, which included large paintings, sculptures, and buildings designed to be regarded as art, Plains Indian art was an integral part of everyday life. Dresses, robes, moccasins, tipis, and rawhide containers were functional whether they were decorated or not, but the decorations enhanced the object and brought pleasure to the people who saw and used them. Both men and women took pride in being well dressed and living among beautiful things.

The designs that were used on clothing and household objects often had spiritual or sacred aspects that connected the creator or the user to tribal beliefs about the world. Plains Indian cosmologies were highly complex, and very simple abstract designs may have had multiple meanings. One common Northern Plains design was a circle composed of elongated triangles painted to look like feathers. The feathered circle represented both the sun and the eagle-feather headdress worn by a successful warrior.

Colors were associated with directions, and directions were associated with sacred beings, whose behavior influenced humans. Using the right color could bring blessings from the spiritual beings. Many different Plains tribes believed that the thunderbird, often shown as a winged, hourglass-shaped figure, caused thunder by shaking its wings. If the bird appeared to a man in a vision or dream, the man could depict the being on a shield, and this would protect him and increase his chances of success in hunting and warfare.

Native American art also differed from European art in its lack of concern with realism. Today, many people still think that an artist should be able to make a tree look just like a tree, but Plains Indians did not think that way. Because the designs often represented mystical or cosmological elements, realism was not a concern. Depicting a thunderbird as an hourglass had the same meaning as showing a bird with widespread wings. Nor was realism necessary to meet the needs of biographical art. A stick figure wearing a distinctive headdress or carrying a unique shield was immediately recognizable. Since realism was not a goal, European ideas of perspective and spatial ordering were not a part of Native American art. When a man painted his war exploits on his robe, he placed the scenes anywhere he thought they looked best, paying little attention to the shape of the robe or how the activities would be seen by others. Because Plains Indian art was so different from what people trained in the European tradition were used to, they considered the Indigenous art childlike or primitive and paid little attention to its meaning.

Another characteristic of Plains Indian art was the fairly strict division between art made and used by men and art made and used by women. Although men and women sometimes cooperated, women usually painted or quilled very balanced, controlled geometric designs on dresses, moccasins, robes, bags, and containers. Men were responsible for the human and animal figures that appeared in the biographical or cosmological art, but women's art had sacred meanings too. Designs placed on women's clothes symbolized prayers for a long life and healthy children. Quillwork was considered a sacred art that a woman had to have the right to do, or disaster would result. Cheyenne and Lakota women gained the right to do quillwork by becoming members of societies in which the art was taught. A woman who excelled in quillwork or other women's arts was publicly honored in the same way as a successful warrior.

The advent of glass beads and other new materials brought changes to the arts, but these were not as immediate or as far-reaching as one might think. Traditional ideas about art were maintained. Women skilled in sewing porcupine quills found that glass beads were not much different and continued to use the old designs. In the Southern Plains, where the porcupine was not found and quillwork had not been developed, the tribes made sparing use of beads and continued to color their clothes with yellow or green paint. In the Central and Northern Plains, however, tribes like the Lakotas and Assiniboines covered large portions of their garments with beaded designs reminiscent of quillwork. In painting, Indian men adopted the European idea of shading to make forms more realistic but did not use perspective or focal points in their work. In the middle to late nineteenth century men began to use paint, colored pencils, and crayons on paper to record scenes of tribal life. Called ledger paintings because many were done on the lined pages taken from account books, these works continued the traditions of earlier times and formed a link to modern Plains Indian painting.

See also GENDER: Native American Gender Roles.

Mary Jane Schneider
University of North Dakota

Berlo, Janet, ed. *Plains Indian Drawings, 1865–1935: Pages from a Visual History.* New York: Harry N. Abrams, 1996. Berlo, Janet, and Ruth B. Phillips. *Native North American Art.* New York: Oxford University Press, 1998. Keyser, James. "A Lexicon for Historic Plains Indian Rock Art: Increasing Interpretive Potential." *Plains Anthropologist* 32 (1987): 43–71.

O'KEEFFE, GEORGIA (1887–1986)

Born in Sun Prairie, Wisconsin, in 1887, Georgia O'Keeffe was the second child of Francis O'Keeffe and Ida Totto O'Keeffe. Perched on the prairie, Sun Prairie was a typical nineteenth-century farming community. O'Keeffe lived on her family dairy farm until she was twelve, when she went away to school, first to Chatham Academy in Virginia and then to the Chicago Art Institute in 1905 and the New York Art Students League in 1907. The O'Keeffe family fortunes declined, and in 1915 she was forced to leave school in New York and take a teaching job in Columbia, South Carolina. While she was there, O'Keeffe revised her work, using simple abstract forms and a limited palate. Her goal was to express emotion or emotional states using abstraction.

O'Keeffe's first experience of the Great Plains came in 1912, when she took a position as an art educator in the Amarillo public schools. After less than a year she left after battling with the state education commission over textbooks. But her love for the land had been established. In 1916 O'Keeffe moved to Canyon, Texas, and became the head of (and the only faculty member in) the art department at West Texas State Normal School. She disliked the small town, but she was inspired by the wide horizons and the overarching sky. The openness of the space changed her work, and she began to paint the infinite variations of light coming onto the Plains, especially at sunrise and sunset. The clouds of dust that arose from the herds of cattle being herded through town gave her new sources of abstract shapes.

The imagery of these paintings in Texas ranged between realistic and abstract forms with allusions to the land. She produced them on whatever paper was available as she wandered the land, inspired by the power and beauty of the Plains. North Texas, she would write in 1919, was the only place she really felt at home.

O'Keeffe's mature style was fully developed when she moved back to New York in the summer of 1918. In 1924 she married Alfred Stieglitz, the influential photographer and owner of Gallery 291. Critics at the time discussed O'Keeffe's work in terms of feminine forms, but many of the allusions were to landforms. Other critics pointed to evidence of Orientalism and Art Nouveau, the dominant art movements of her youth, and to the influence of her most important teacher, Arthur Wesley Dow, whose dictum, that all things must be done beautifully, stayed with her all her life. All these influences are important, but landscape, especially the Plains landscape, was vital to her art.

After 1929 O'Keeffe began spending her summers in New Mexico, eventually (in 1949) buying property in the village of Abiquiu, near Santa Fe. Her love of the land is evident in the New Mexico paintings, in which, once again, landforms are dominant. After her death on March 6, 1986, O'Keeffe's estate formed the basis of the Georgia O'Keeffe Foundation. In 1997 the Georgia O'Keeffe Museum, dedicated solely to O'Keeffe's legacy, opened in Santa Fe. She is one of a few women artists in the world to be so honored.

See also PHYSICAL ENVIRONMENT: Caprock Canyonlands.

Ellen Bradbury
Santa Fe, New Mexico

Giboire, C. *Lovingly, Georgia: The Complete Correspondence of Georgia O'Keeffe and Anita Pollitzer.* New York: Simon and Schuster, 1990. O'Keeffe, Georgia. *Canyon Suite.* New York: George Braziller, 1995.

PEALE, TITIAN RAMSAY (1799–1885)

Titian Ramsay Peale, naturalist, scientific illustrator, and explorer, meticulously depicted the birds, insects, and plants of the Central Plains with high-quality sketches and paintings during the 1820s and 1830s.

Peale was born on November 2, 1799, in Philadelphia, the son of Charles Willson Peale, an artist who founded the Philadelphia (or Peale's) Museum. From an early age he demonstrated an unusual ability as a naturalist and artist. Peale's first exploration came on an 1817 trip to eastern Florida and the Sea Islands of Carolina. Then, in 1819, he was appointed as the assistant naturalist for Maj. Stephen H. Long's scientific expedition. Ordered to explore the Central Plains and the major streams that crossed it, the scientists began their journey aboard the steamboat *Western Engineer.* They halted for the winter of 1819–20 near present-day Fort Calhoun, Nebraska. The next summer Long led the group overland along the Platte River to the Front Range of the Rockies. For three months they observed, mapped, sketched, and gathered plant and animal specimens, returning along the Arkansas and Canadian Rivers. Because of the scarcity of water and trees on the Plains they traversed, the explorers labeled the region the Great American Desert.

Peale's ensuing reputation as a scientific illustrator resulted from the 122 paintings and drawings he made while on the expedition. His work included colored plates of birds drawn for Alexander Wilson's *American Ornithology* (1824–33) and of insects for Thomas Say's multivolume *American Entomology* (1824–28). For the next several decades he remained one of the top scientific illustrators of the flora and fauna of the Central Plains while serving as the curator of Peale's Museum and also designing coins for the U.S. Mint. He joined Charles Wilkes's 1838–42 scientific expedition to the Pacific, but conflicts with Wilkes prevented a definitive publication of his drawings from the voyage. Peale then worked for the U.S. Patent Office until his retirement in 1873. He died on March 13, 1885, in Philadelphia.

See also WAR: Long, Stephen.

Roger L. Nichols
University of Arizona

Poesch, Jessie. *Titian Ramsay Peale, 1799–1885 and His Journals of the Wilkes Expedition.* Philadelphia: American Philosophical Society, 1961. Porter, Charlotte M. *The Eagle's Nest: Natural History and American Ideas, 1812–1842.* Tuscaloosa: University of Alabama Press, 1986.

PENN, ROBERT LEE (1946–1999)

From the late 1960s until his death on February 7, 1999, Robert Lee Penn was one of the most outstanding Northern Plains Indian artists of his generation.

Penn was born in Omaha, Nebraska, on May 3, 1946, to an Omaha father and Brulé Lakota mother. He grew up on the Winnebago Indian Reservation in Nebraska and the Rosebud Reservation in South Dakota, a background that would define his cultural roots and his art. During his years as a student at the University of South Dakota (1967–72), Penn began his formal art studies with the renowned Yanktonai Nakota artist Oscar Howe. After graduation, Penn continued his creative efforts while working as an illustrator, designer, and teacher. Over a period of twenty-five years he exhibited his work regularly in numerous one-man exhibitions and many others.

Penn mastered the technical means of drawing, watercolor, and painting and used them to express his very personal experience of being a traditional Indian in contemporary America. He considered that, as a Native American in contemporary society, his role was that of both artist and interpreter, using his art to convey cultural themes. His work is characterized by sure drawing combined with a strong sense of color and dynamic design, which he used to eloquently express the vital juncture between Plains Indian worlds, past and present.

Evan M. Maurer
Minneapolis Institute of Arts

Maurer, Evan M. *Visions of the People: A Pictorial History of Plains Indian Life.* Minneapolis: Minneapolis Institute of Arts, 1992.

RANNEY, WILLIAM (1813–1857)

William Tylee Ranney, born in Middletown, Connecticut, on May 9, 1813, achieved a substantial reputation as a genre artist specializing in hunting and western scenes prior to his death in Hoboken, New Jersey, on November 18, 1857, at the age of forty-four.

Since he was born and died in the East, Ranney's affinity for western subjects requires explanation. The war for Texas independence lured him west in 1836, when he was an art student in Brooklyn, and he spent a formative year in the Southwest that left no impression on his work as a portraitist and painter of history and genre scenes until 1846, when the annexation of Texas and the Mexican War created a demand for western subjects. Unlike George Catlin, Ranney was not a painter of Indians. He concentrated on white pioneers and, a contemporary thought, "caught the spirit of border adventures."

Ranney's style was highly refined if rather static, and he was adept at the precise detail dear to genre painting with its focus on everyday life. His western scenes depicted parties of pioneer men and women on the move and picturesque frontier types sometimes fighting Indians, more often gossiping in and meandering through a spacious land tinted in sunset colors. Though his only personal experience was in Texas, Ranney generalized the settings in his western paintings. Texas became the "broad prairie" in *The Retreat* (1850), which showed three trappers fleeing from pursuing Indians across an open country devoid of shelter, and in *Advice on the Prairie* (1853), which showed a party of emigrants listening raptly to a veteran plainsman tell them of what lay ahead. Ranney, in short, worked his own variations on the West as a theater for perilous adventure and as a prospective paradise for those who dreamed of a land of milk and honey.

Brian W. Dippie
University of Victoria

Dippie, Brian W. *West-fever.* Los Angeles: Autry Museum of Western Heritage in Association with the University of Washington Press, 1998. Grubar, Francis S. *William Ranney: Painter of the Early West.* New York: Clarkson N. Potter, 1962.

REAUGH, FRANK (1860–1945)

Called the "dean of Texas painters," Frank Reaugh was born near Jacksonville, Illinois, on December 29, 1860. In 1876 he and his family settled on a farm near Terrell, Texas. His mother taught him natural history, and his father taught him to work with his hands. Later, Frank made his own picture frames and patented several inventions.

Reaugh honed his skills by copying reproductions from popular magazines, and he taught himself cattle and sheep anatomy. He also sketched longhorn cattle that were brought up from South Texas to fatten on the prairies nearby. As early as 1883 Reaugh began sketching—often from the saddle—cattle drives and roundups near Wichita Falls. He later enlarged and refined his sketches in his studio, creating paintings such as *The One-O Roundup* (1894). Reaugh's formal studies began at the St. Louis School of Fine Arts in 1884–85 and continued at the Académie Julian in Paris in 1888–89. While in Europe he copied paintings in the Louvre and studied paintings in Belgium and Holland. Reaugh exhibited widely, including at the World's Columbian Exposition, the National Academy of Design, the Pennsylvania Academy of the Fine Arts, the Chicago Art Institute, and the Louisiana Purchase Exposition. He also joined the Society of Western Artists, exhibiting with them all over the United States.

Reaugh continued his annual sketching trips to the Texas Plains until he was almost eighty. He had been taking students, including Alexandre Hogue and Florence McClung, on trips there since 1910. Reaugh died in Dallas on May 6, 1945, and is buried in the Terrell cemetery. The Panhandle-Plains Historical Museum at Canyon, Texas, is the repository for Reaugh's works and papers.

Michael R. Grauer
Panhandle-Plains Historical Museum

Grauer, Michael R. "Frank Reaugh: The Dean of Texas Artists." *Persimmon Hill* (1994): 50–55. Haley, J. Evetts. *F. Reaugh: Man and Artist.* El Paso TX: Herzog, 1960.

REGINA FIVE

The Regina Five were a loose group of abstract painters based in Regina, Saskatchewan, although only three were natives of the Prairies. The members were Ronald Bloore (b. 1925), Ted Godwin (b. 1933), Kenneth Lochhead (b. 1926), Arthur McKay (b. 1926), and Douglas Morton (b. 1926). They took their name from a 1961 exhibition organized by the National Gallery of Canada, *Five Painters from Regina*. All were associated with the art school at the University of Saskatchewan, Regina Campus, or with its annual artists' workshops at Emma Lake, Saskatchewan. Lochhead, the head of the school, and McKay, an instructor, were instrumental in recruiting important American artists and art critics to lead the summer workshops. Abstract artist Barnett Newman and critic and abstract proponent Clement Greenberg particularly influenced the Regina Five.

The five did not think of themselves as a group and indeed had markedly different styles, although they had certain similarities such as the use of flat, muted color. For the space of roughly three years, from 1961 to 1964,

they were considered very avant-garde. Art critics marveled at the fact that they came from the isolated Prairies. Then, in 1964, two of the group left Regina, and Lochhead and McKay had works in Clement Greenberg's badly received Los Angeles show. From that point the group lost its influence, and its members went on to pursue separate careers. At Expo 67 only two of their works were shown—in the section for historic Canadian art.

Donna Bowman
University of Regina

Chabun, Will. "'The Regina Five': Art, Politics and History." *Regina Leader Post*, February 8, 1997: A7. *Five Painters from Regina.* Exhibition Catalog. Ottawa: National Gallery of Canada, 1961. Leclerc, Denise. *The Crisis of Abstraction in Canada: The 1950s.* Ottawa: National Gallery of Canada, 1992.

REMINGTON, FREDERIC

See IMAGES AND ICONS: Remington, Frederic.

RINDISBACHER, PETER (1806–1834)

Peter Rindisbacher was born on April 12, 1806, in Berne, Switzerland. In the summer of his twelfth year he toured the Bernese Alps and studied art with Swiss miniature painter Jacob S. Weibel. Fifteen-year-old Peter began painting the Canadian West when his family arrived at Lord Selkirk's colony on the Red River, near present-day Winnipeg, Manitoba, in 1821, more than a decade before American artist George Catlin reached the upper Missouri River country.

The trading post at the Red River settlement bartered with Assiniboine, Ojibwa, and Sioux peoples, all of whom are portrayed in Rindisbacher's detailed sketches and vivid watercolors. He was a skilled draftsman, and his paintings are well composed. His artwork provides an accurate record of the dress and daily life of the Native peoples such as a Sioux bow hunter on snowshoes pursuing a buffalo or a Chippewa family traveling by canoe. Rindisbacher was the first European American artist to capture life inside a tipi, in his *Scene in an Indian Tent* (ca. 1824). His best-known work, *The Murder of David Tully and Family by the Sissatoons, a Sioux Tribe* (ca. 1823–30), chronicles the dramatic deaths of former members of the settlement in 1823.

After barely surviving at the Red River colony and following the destructive flood of 1826, the Rindisbacher family made their way to Wisconsin, living there for three years before moving to St. Louis in 1829. During the next four years, a number of lithographs and engravings of Rindisbacher's work appeared in the *American Turf Register and Sporting Magazine*, published in Baltimore. He died August 15, 1834, at the age of twenty-eight of unknown causes.

See also EUROPEAN AMERICANS: Douglas, Thomas (Earl of Selkirk).

Ken Rogers
Bismarck Tribune

Josephy, Alvin M., Jr. *The Artist Was a Young Man: The Life Story of Peter Rindisbacher.* Fort Worth: Amon Carter Mu-

seum, 1970. Nute, Grace Lee. "Peter Rindisbacher, Artist." *Minnesota History* 14 (1933): 283–87. Vazulik, Johannes W. "Peter Rindisbacher's Red River Watercolors at the West Point Museum." *North Dakota History* 64 (1997): 20–29.

ROCK ART

Rock art in the Great Plains consists of both petroglyphs (markings that have been pecked, scratched, incised, or abraded on natural rock surfaces) and pictographs (painting on nonportable rock surfaces). Petroforms (sometimes called geomorphs, in which large stones or boulders have been used to outline anthropomorphic, zoomorphic, or geometric forms) are found primarily in the northeastern U.S. Plains and southern Saskatchewan. Petroglyphs and/or pictographs have been recorded in all states of the Great Plains. Rock art was noted in the journals of European American explorers, but it was not until the 1930s that petroglyphs and pictographs were thoroughly documented and interpreted for professional publication.

The placement of petroglyphs and pictographs is highly variable in the Great Plains. In the Northern Plains rock art is found in and around major geologic uplifts, especially where rock surfaces are exposed on canyon walls and in rock shelters. On the open Plains rock art is found on sandstone or limestone where streams have cut the underlying bedrock and on boulders on talus slopes and hogbacks. Petroglyphs on isolated boulders also occur along the Missouri River in the Dakotas, in southern Alberta and Saskatchewan, and in central Texas and southern Oklahoma. Rock art in the Central Plains is rarer; however, protohistoric and early historic Native Americans used rock shelters intensively in the Dakota sandstone of the Smoky Hills region of north-central Kansas, where they depicted representational images. Native Americans also made petroglyphs on sandstone bluffs in central Oklahoma. In the Northern Plains some rock art is believed to be associated with bison jumps and kill sites. It is generally acknowledged, however, that in prehistoric social environments the role of rock art as a means of communication varied with its social context. The places where it was produced are usually understood to have had special meanings and functioned, along with myths and stories, to maintain social cohesion.

Despite difficulties in the accurate dating of rock art, it is known that some of the oldest rock art in the Plains is found in the Black Hills of western South Dakota, eastern Wyoming, and the Wyoming Basin. These areas have rock art thought to predate 10,000 B.P. and also contain sites ranging through the Archaic period (7500–2000 B.P.). The art is primarily on exposed vertical cliffs and at the base of canyon walls. Zoomorphic figures, usually wapiti (elk) or mountain sheep, are the predominant representations. Some depictions of hunting are found, such as game nets or corrals and the spearing of animals by humans. Some of the most heavily varnished petroglyphs depict apparent hoof prints, vulvas, and grooves. Pictographs depicting orange to light red finger

Rock art, southeastern Colorado, Fort Carson Military Reservation.

lines and handprints in central Montana are believed to be more than 3,000 years old.

Archaic hunters and gatherers in southern Texas, where the Pecos River, Devils River, and Rio Grande meet, created rock art—considered to be some of the most impressive prehistoric art in the world—in dry rock shelters. Dramatic polychrome pictographs of detailed life-size human-feline composites and anthropomorphic figures with feathers, wings, claws, horns, and weapons are documented. The oldest rock art, the Pecos River style, is nearly 4,000 years old. Farther north along the Pecos River at Lewis Canyon are more than 250 pictograph sites and more than 900 petroglyphs. The petroglyphs, many on flat rock surfaces, consist of abstract geometrical designs and representational figures of human hands as well as deer, bison, and bird feet. Depictions of atlatls, a weapon of the Archaic, suggest, in association with other cultural remains, production of the petroglyphs between 9,000 and 1,000 years ago. In some of the older glyphs human figures appear to brandish some kind of lance or other weapon. Rock shelters in the Wichita Mountains of Oklahoma contain near life-size anthropomorphic figures and geometric petroglyphs painted with red and yellow ochre.

Pictograph images of animals and anthropomorphs on a massive schist formation at Long Lake along the Manigotagan River in southern Manitoba are thought to have been produced during the middle to late Archaic. In the Milk River valley of southern Alberta a complex of 93 sites and 280 separate rock art panels constitutes one of the largest concentrations of rock art in the Northern Plains. This area, the Writing-on-Stone Provincial Park, includes petroglyphs ranging from up to 1000 years old through the postcontact period (A.D. 1725–1850). Boulder alignments, many considered solstice-aligned configurations, are found in southern Saskatchewan. Some of the alignments were probably constructed 2,000 years ago; others, based on astronomical calculations, may have been constructed in the eighteenth and nineteenth centuries.

Rock art in southeastern Colorado, including many zoomorphic or anthropomorphic representations, has been intensively studied, especially in the rock shelters of the Purgatoire River area. Some rock art in this area is associated with rock structural remains that suggest Native American vision quest activities. Ages of these images range from the middle Archaic (c. 3500 B.P.) to the late Ceramic stage (c. 250 B.P.). A cluster of dry caves and rock shelters in the canyon country of Black Mesa in the Oklahoma Panhandle contain petroglyphs and pictographs of bison and anthropomorphs, associated with perishable artifacts such as sandals, basketry, and skin bags, that range in age from the late Archaic through the Woodland (A.D. 200–1000). The Black Hills of South Dakota include many examples of prehistoric rock art. Stylistic analyses suggest that a chronological sequence of rock art, ranging from the late Paleo-Indian to the early historic period, is reflected in at least seven distinct styles of petroglyph and pictograph imaging. Pecked petroglyphs are also documented, especially in Whoop-Up Canyon in the Black Hills.

The diversity of prehistoric rock art in the Great Plains is indicative of the region's varied modes of social organization and economic systems. Advances in the technology of direct dating will help in assigning rock art to its cultural affiliations, but an understanding of why the markings were made in the places they occur will challenge researchers for years to come and, indeed, may never be known.

See also NATIVE AMERICANS: Paleo-Indians
Ralph J. Hartley
Midwest Archeological Center

Francis, Julie E., and Lawrence L. Loendorf. *Ancient Visions: Petroglyphs and Pictographs of the Wind River and Bighorn Country, Wyoming and Montana.* Salt Lake City: University of Utah Press, 2002. Kirland, Forrest, and W. W. Newcomb Jr. *The Rock Art of Texas Indians.* Austin: University of Texas Press, 1967. Sundstrom, Linea. *Rock Art of the Southern Black Hills.* New York: Garland, 1990.

RUSSELL, ANDREW J. (1829–1902)

Born on March 20, 1829, in Walpole, New Hampshire, Andrew Joseph Russell apprenticed with a local artisan in Nunda, New York, and began his professional career painting portraits and landscapes for influential men in railroading and politics. He recruited for the Union army, was elected company captain, and served in the defenses of Washington in 1862. Brig. Gen. Herman Haupt appointed him government photographer on March 1, 1863, and he served in Virginia as acting quartermaster to the United States Military Rail Road Construction Corps until September 9, 1865.

To encourage settlement and investment in the West, Union Pacific vice president Thomas C. Durant commissioned Russell to document the transcontinental railroad. During 1868 the photographer lived in the construction camps and periodically sent his negatives east for printing as stereographs. He returned to New York in December and published *The Great West Illustrated* in the spring. On his second trip west he photographed Omaha and the growing Nebraska towns of Fremont, Columbus, Grand Island, and North Platte on his way to the joining of the rails at Promontory, Utah, on May 10, 1869. Thousands of newspaper readers viewed his images and read his description of the ceremony in *Frank Leslie's Illustrated*. The center spread—*East Meets West at Laying of Last Rail*—became historic immediately. During the summer Russell camped in the Wasatch and Uinta Mountains and then took the train to California; in December he returned to Omaha. Russell established the Decoration and Designing Company in New York City after his publishing partnership failed in 1870. He worked as a photojournalist for Frank Leslie and died in Brooklyn of congestive heart failure on September 20, 1902.

Susan E. Williams
Oakland, California

Combs, Barry B. *Westward to Promontory.* New York: Crown Publishers, 1986. Naef, Weston, and James N. Wood. *Era of Exploration: The Rise of Landscape Photography in the American West, 1860–1885.* New York: Metropolitan Museum of Art, and Buffalo: Albright-Knox Art Gallery, 1975. Williams, Susan E. "The Truth Be Told: The Union Pacific Railroad Photographs of Andrew J. Russell." *View Camera* (January–February 1996): 36–43.

RUSSELL, CHARLES M. (1864–1926)

Charles Marion Russell, born in St. Louis, Missouri, on March 19, 1864, is today known worldwide as Montana's "cowboy artist." The third of six children, he grew up in comfortable circumstances, but he was a misfit—a dreamer who struggled with school and at an early age set his heart on going west. In 1880 his parents yielded to his desire and, just before his sixteenth birthday, granted him permission to accompany a sheepman they knew to Montana Territory. After a stint with a professional meat hunter, Kid Russell (as he came to be known) in 1882 hired on as night herder on a trail drive from Billings to the Judith

Basin. Cattle driving and cowboying fit Russell's romantic temperament, and for the next eleven years (apart from the summer of 1888, which he loafed away sketching Indians in Alberta), he "sung to the horses and cattle," earning a reputation as an amusing raconteur with an exceptional gift for portraying the life around him.

Russell's small watercolor *Waiting for a Chinook*, which shows a starving cow surrounded by hungry wolves, summed up the devastating winter of 1886–87 on the Northern Plains and brought him his first real recognition as an artist. In 1893, persuaded that the open range cattle industry was finished, Russell took up his art full time and in 1896 married Nancy "Mame" Cooper, an unsophisticated eighteen-year-old with a head for business and drive and ambition enough for both of them. She assumed management of his career, encouraging him in 1904 to make the first in a series of professional trips to New York City, where he met professional illustrators, editors, and publishers who shared his enthusiasm for western subjects. After a one-man exhibition at the Folsom Galleries in New York in 1911, Russell branched out, exhibiting at the inaugural Calgary Stampede in 1912—his first international exposure—and, significantly, at London's Doré Galleries in 1914.

By then Russell was an established artist. Though he did little illustration, his paintings became familiar to the world through postcards, calendars, and color reproductions. Especially adept at modeling, Russell had his first bronze cast in 1904, contributing to the opinion after Frederic Remington's death in 1909 that he was America's most accomplished western artist. Russell's repertoire was set early. He added other subjects to it (mountain men, hunting dramas in the high country, wildlife studies, North-West Mounted Police in action, some shooting scrapes), but the body of his work consisted of cowboy scenes, equally divided between roping and riding pictures, and Indian scenes, including buffalo hunts but mostly showing parties of warriors moving across open space or perched on bluffs, surveying the land below that once was theirs. Indeed, the commemorative, nostalgic tone of these pieces defined the entire body of Russell's work and his commanding theme: "the West that has passed."

Escalating prices followed Russell's rise to prominence. By 1920, when the Russells began spending their springs in California, a major oil painting commanded $10,000. Other celebrities were drawn into his orbit (Hollywood movie stars, popular writers, and every western artist of his day), and the rich and influential became his patrons. But Charlie Russell was a homebody at heart. He was always most comfortable visiting with friends in Great Falls, where he and Mame had lived since 1897, shooting the breeze outside a saloon or cigar store with cronies from his rangeland days, and passing his summers at Bull Head Lodge, his cabin built in 1905 at the foot of Lake McDonald in what became Glacier National Park. He liked his simple,

homespun routine, telling the yarns that were published in two "joke books," *Rawhide Rawlins Stories* (1921) and *More Rawhides* (1925), and collected in *Trails Plowed Under*, a Western classic that appeared in 1927, the year after Russell died (on October 24) and was buried in Great Falls.

Charles M. Russell remains one of the most beloved of westerners, admired as much for his sense of humor, his basic decency, and his fierce loyalty to a time and a place as for the artwork enshrined in museums across America. His modest home and log cabin studio in Great Falls bespeak a humble man who made great things out of the ordinary clay of human experience, closely observed and lovingly recorded.

Brian W. Dippie
University of Victoria

Dippie, Brian W., ed. *Charles M. Russell, Word Painter: Letters 1881–1926*. Fort Worth: Amon Carter Museum in Association with Harry N. Abrams, 1993. Dippie, Brian W., ed. *Charlie Russell Roundup: Essays on America's Favorite Cowboy Artist*. Helena: Montana Historical Society Press, 1999. Taliaferro, John. *Charles M. Russell: The Life and Legend of America's Cowboy Artist*. Boston: Little, Brown and Company, 1996.

SANDZÉN, SVEN BIRGER (1871–1954)

Sven Birger Sandzén was one of the premier landscape painters of the Great Plains during the first half of the twentieth century. Born in Blidsberg, Sweden, on February 5, 1871, Sandzén left in 1894 for the small town of Lindsborg, Kansas, founded twenty-five years earlier by Swedish Lutherans. There he intended to teach at Bethany College and pursue his art in the American West. As a student of drawing and painting in Stockholm and Paris, Sandzén valued the European tradition, but he was also eager to experience the liberating influence of the open prairies. Over the next sixty years he produced an estimated 2,800 oil paintings, 400 watercolors, 330 prints, and 5,600 sketches.

Best known are the landscapes, whose thick,

vigorously applied paint in vivid colors reveal Sandzén's passionate response to nature. He was thrilled by the clear atmosphere and "glorious scenery" he found in Kansas, particularly the Smoky Hill River valley, where he lived, and farther west in Graham County. Sandzén was deeply impressed by rolling hills and ravines, and he cherished other commonplace features of the region such as cottonwood trees, sandstone boulders, and pioneer homes. He was also a consummate professional with a strong sense of civic responsibility. He taught art at Bethany College for over half a century, wrote articles for newspapers and magazines, and helped establish numerous organizations such as the Kansas Federation of Art and the Prairie Print Makers. Sandzén's legacy in Lindsborg lives on through the art department at Bethany College, his recently restored house and studio, and the Birger Sandzén Memorial Gallery, opened in 1957. Sandzén died in Lindsborg on June 22, 1954.

Bruce R. Kahler
Bethany College

Diffily, John. "Birger Sandzén 1871–1954: Through the Corridor of Nature." *Southwest Art* 13 (1983): 42–51. Lindquist, Emory. *Birger Sandzén: An Illustrated Biography*. Lawrence: University Press of Kansas, 1993. Birger Sandzén Papers, Birger Sandzén Memorial Gallery Archives, Lindsborg KS.

STANLEY, JOHN MIX (1814–1872)

John Mix Stanley was one of a number of painters who came west in the first half of the eighteenth century to paint what they believed were the last days of the Native Americans. Born in Canandaigua, New York, on January 14, 1814, Stanley progressed from painting signs to painting portraits and landscapes. He was enamored with George Catlin's works and followed his example, retracing some of the same ground and even painting portraits of the same people.

Stanley traveled throughout Indian Territory from 1842 to 1845. In 1846 he accompanied

John Mix Stanley. Herd of Bison Near Lake Jesse, *ca. 1853. Color lithograph.*

American soldiers during the Mexican War, arriving in Santa Fe just weeks after Stephen Watts Kearny's Army of the West. Kearny hired him as a topographical draftsman, and Stanley fought in battle under Kearny in San Diego. Probably the most traveled of western artists, Stanley soon made his way to Oregon, where he narrowly avoided being killed in the Whitman massacre. He spent one year in Hawaii before returning to New York in 1850. There he began the first of several unsuccessful attempts to sell Congress his "Indian Gallery," approximately 150 paintings done in Indian Territory and the Southwest. Unable to sell his paintings to the government, he accepted an offer by the Smithsonian Institution to house his works. In 1853 he joined the northern railroad survey headed by Isaac Stevens, producing sixty images that were printed in the official reports of the expedition, several of which are of Great Plains scenes.

His western travel behind him, Stanley moved to Washington DC, where he further labored to sell his paintings to Congress. Stanley never again traveled among the Native Americans, but he continued to paint them, based on memory and imagination. Like Catlin, Stanley believed that the Native Americans were incompatible with American civilization and would fade away, a process he believed inevitable and ultimately just.

Exhibiting great realism, in part because he was one of the first artists to base his work on photographs, which he began using in the late 1840s, Stanley's works show greater skill than those of Catlin. *The Trial of Red Jacket* (1868) is his best-known work. Stanley's "Indian Gallery" was lost in the great Smithsonian Institution fire of January 1865, and a second fire that year at the New York City museum of P. T. Barnum, followed by an 1872 fire in his own studio, destroyed most of his remaining works. Stanley died of heart failure in Detroit, Michigan, on April 10, 1872, still hoping for compensation for his destroyed work. His remaining works are housed in the Smithsonian Institution; the Gilcrease Museum in Tulsa, Oklahoma; the Detroit Institute of Arts; the Stark Museum of Art in Orange, Texas; and the Buffalo Historical Society.

Charles Vollan
University of Nebraska–Lincoln

Dippie, Brian W. *Catlin and His Contemporaries: The Politics of Patronage.* Lincoln: University of Nebraska Press, 1990. Taft, Robert. *Artists and Illustrators of the Old West, 1850–1900.* New York: Bonanza Books, 1953.

TALLCHIEF, MARIA (b. 1925)

Born in Fairfax, Oklahoma, on January 24, 1925, Elizabeth Marie Tall Chief became the first American classical dancer to earn international acclaim as a prima ballerina. Her parents, Alexander Joseph Tall Chief and Ruth Parker, had acquired their wealth from Osage oil money, and from her early years Elizabeth Marie was schooled in music and dance. In 1930 Ruth moved the family to Hollywood, California, specifically to advance the music and dance careers of Elizabeth Marie and her younger sister Marjorie. Elizabeth Marie's talents as a pianist and dancer blossomed, and by her senior year at Beverly Hills High School she had chosen ballet for her career.

Elizabeth Marie joined the Ballet Russe de Monte Carlo in 1942 and gained soloist status in 1943, the same year she changed her name to Maria Tallchief. Following her 1946 marriage to George Balanchine, the Russian-born choreographer acclaimed as the father of American ballet, Tallchief became the first American featured as a guest artist with the Paris Opera Ballet. She joined Balanchine's Ballet Society in 1947 and contributed to the company's development into the New York City Ballet the following year. Tallchief was featured in twenty-two major works created by Balanchine and is recognized as the prototype for what is known today as the "Balanchine ballerina." During her career with the New York City Ballet, which ended in 1965, she appeared as guest artist with companies such as the American Ballet Theatre during its 1958 Russian tour and the Royal Danish Ballet. In addition to honors bestowed on her by the Osage Nation, the state of Oklahoma, and the dance world, Tallchief was named Indian of the Year in 1963. She received the Capezio Award in 1965, a Kennedy Center Honors in 1996, and a National Arts Award in 1999.

Lili Cockerille Livingston
Tulsa, Oklahoma

Livingston, Lili Cockerille. *American Indian Ballerinas.* Norman: University of Oklahoma Press, 1997. Reynolds, Nancy. *Repertory in Review: 40 Years of the New York City Ballet.* New York: Dial Press, 1977.

THOMPSON, BRADBURY (1911–1995)

Bradbury Thompson, the eminent American graphic designer, was born in Topeka, Kansas, on March 25, 1911. In 1934 he graduated from Washburn College, where he served as the graphic designer and editor of the college publication. His major was in economics, but his editorial design work presaged his brilliant career in visual communications design. He also developed his visual discipline during these years by working as a draftsman for roads and bridges.

From 1938 to 1962 Thompson designed *Westvaco Inspirations for Printers*, the innovative arts journal of the West Virginia Pulp and Paper Company (Westvaco). It was at this time that he developed his unique style of visual graphic design, which included the experimental use of four-color printing, typography, and photo reproduction. Westvaco provided him with unlimited paper stocks and advanced printing processes; however, the company's budget for illustration was nonexistent. Thompson creatively solved this problem by adapting engravings, photographs, and artwork from advertising agencies, museums, and magazines.

After World War II Thompson worked as a freelance designer in New York. He was art director of *Mademoiselle* magazine and design director of *Art News* from 1945 to 1972. He also designed the format of various publications, including the *Smithsonian Magazine*. Another accomplishment was his design of more than ninety U.S. postal stamps.

In 1979, drawing from the experience he had accumulated at Westvaco and in the magazine trade, Thompson completed the design of the Washburn College Bible in 1979. He used the flush-left, ragged-right style of modern typesetting, and the lines of text are broken into individual phrases according to speech cadences, making reading easier while also providing a clearer meaning. His significant contribution to this project was to follow historical typographic traditions while also advancing typographic standards and incorporating them into modern visual themes. Thompson died on November 1, 1995.

Ron Bartels
University of Nebraska–Lincoln

Carter, Rob. *American Typography Today.* New York: Van Nostrand Reinhold Company, 1989. Meggs, Philip B. *A History of Graphic Design.* New York: Van Nostrand Reinhold Company, 1983. Thompson, Bradbury. *Bradbury Thompson: The Art of Graphic Design.* New Haven CT: Yale University Press, 1988.

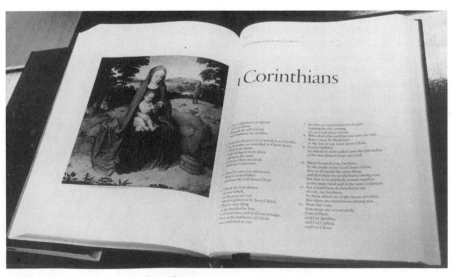
Washburn Bible designed by Bradbury Thompson, 1979

WEIDMAN, CHARLES (1901–1975)

Born in Lincoln, Nebraska, on July 22, 1901, Charles Weidman was a leading figure in the development of American modern dance. Weidman's father was a civil engineer who also served as Lincoln's fire chief, and his mother was a former roller-skating champion. Influenced, perhaps, by his father's engineering background, the young Weidman showed a strong interest in architecture. But his passion turned to dance in 1916 after seeing a performance by the Denishawn Company, the pioneering American modern dance troupe founded by Ruth St. Denis and Ted Shawn. Dance was a field in which Weidman felt he could use his love of architecture, his sense of humor, and his newly discovered dance talents together in the design and creation of dances.

In 1920, after studying dance locally with Eleanor Frampton, Weidman left Lincoln for Los Angeles to study at the Denishawn School. Recognizing Weidman's extraordinary talent as a mimic, Ted Shawn choreographed solos for him, putting to use his expressive face and gestures and his sense of humor. In the Denishawn Company, Weidman worked with other young American dance artists who were beginning to explore their own kinds of movement and choreography, including Martha Graham and Doris Humphrey. In 1927 Weidman and Humphrey left the Denishawn Company to form their own school in New York. A year later they presented their first concert. The Humphrey-Weidman Dance Company reflected the differences in the two directors' choreographic styles, with Weidman's comic and mimetic talent complementing Humphrey's serious dramatic works. The dual directorship of a company was unique in dance and continued for two decades.

Audiences enjoyed Weidman's wit and humor in works such as *The Happy Hypocrite* (1931), in which he used pantomime gestures to convey the story, then exaggerated the gestures into dance movements. His work also had a serious side, shown throughout his career in dances commenting on human behavior and social morality. In 1936 he presented a trio of dances titled *Atavisms*. Two of the works were humorous: *Bargain Counter*, in which rapacious shoppers stampeded a beleaguered salesclerk, and *Stock Exchange*, a satire of the cutthroat business and personalities of high finance. The third work, however, *Lynchtown*, inspired by an actual incident in Nebraska, depicted the infectious hatred that turns individuals into a violent mob. Many of Weidman's other works also show the influences of his Nebraska childhood and his attachment to his family. Autobiographical dances such as *On My Mother's Side* (1940) and *And Daddy Was a Fireman* (1943) combined poignant and tender reminiscences in dance with touching moments of humor. His past also was the inspiration for one of his most popular works, *Flickers* (1941), a piece poking fun at the Hollywood silent films of his childhood.

The Charles Weidman Dance Company was formed in 1945 as Weidman continued to work on his own after a serious illness forced Doris Humphrey to stop performing. His humor, wit, and satire in dance were widely recognized in the theatrical arena, bringing jobs choreographing for opera, Broadway musicals, and dance revues. Weidman's openness to experimentation and his movement inventiveness made his choreography and teaching important influences on the next generation of dancers and dance teachers. He taught at Bennington College, the summer gathering place for the early creators of American modern dance in the mid-1930s, as well as at other universities and colleges.

One of Weidman's innovations was the development of a movement form he called "kinetic pantomime." He began by discarding the convention of using pantomime gestures solely to tell a story or for dramatic effect. Instead, he based the technique on gestures that evolved out of movement itself and relied on movement to connect one gesture to another, a concept that helped pave the way for later developments in the field of performance art. Weidman also pioneered mixed-media theater when he joined with Mikhail Santaro in the late 1950s. They later formed the Expression of Two Arts Theater, experimenting with performance works that attempted to make connections between graphic art and dance.

Throughout his career, Weidman returned periodically to his native Lincoln, teaching and giving workshops in performance and choreography. Continuing to work as a choreographer, performer, and teacher, he maintained an active interest in new explorations in dance until his death in New York City on July 15, 1975. The Charles Weidman Dance Foundation in New York is dedicated to the preservation of his work and his contributions to dance.

Lisa A. Fusillo
University of Nebraska–Lincoln

Cohen, Selma Jean. *Doris Humphrey, an Artist First.* Princeton NJ: Princeton Book Company, 1995. Lloyd, Margaret. *The Borzoi Book of Modern Dance.* New York: Alfred A. Knopf, Inc., 1949; reprint, New York: Dance Horizons, 1970.

WHITTREDGE, WORTHINGTON (1820–1910)

Worthington Whittredge, the American landscape artist, was born on May 22, 1820, on a farm near Springfield, Ohio. He began his career in Cincinnati, then spent a decade in Düsseldorf and Rome before settling in 1861 in New York City, where he became a leading member of the Hudson River school.

Spurred on perhaps by Albert Bierstadt, whom he had befriended in Europe, Whittredge joined Gen. John Pope on an inspection tour of the Central Plains in 1866 that left Fort Leavenworth, Kansas, in early June for Fort Kearney, Nebraska Territory, then followed the Oregon Trail and South Platte River to Fort Collins and Denver, Colorado Territory. These areas provided him with most of his western subjects. From there the expedition went to Santa Fe, Albuquerque, and Fort Union, New Mexico, before returning to Fort Riley, Kansas, via the Old Santa Fe and Cimarron Trails. He returned for shorter visits in 1870 in order to sketch some trees near Fort Collins for his major work *Crossing the Ford* (1868–70) and again the following year to the Denver area.

Unlike Bierstadt, Whittredge was impressed not by the lofty height of the Rockies but by the breadth of the Plains, and the mountains provide no more than a backdrop in most of his paintings. The western pictures before 1870 are filled with romantic imagery inspired by the poems of William Cullen Bryant, who decisively influenced Whittredge's Hudson River pictures, while the later ones retain the freshness of his oil sketches, from which they are often nearly indistinguishable. The artist relied on his experiences in Europe to describe the Plains, but his paintings are mainly distinctive for an uncommon directness and lyricism that reflect his personality. He paid particular attention to conditions of light and atmosphere. Native Americans, however, served mainly to set the scene, and he had little interest in recording their ways of life, which he nevertheless depicted accurately. Whittredge built up a sizable stock of subjects showing the Plains and foothills of the Rockies, but in his large canvases he concentrated mainly on variants of several favorite compositions: *On the Plains* (1872), *Crossing the Platte River* (1872–74), and *On the Cache La Oudre River* (1876).

Despite his success in treating western landscapes, Whittredge stopped painting them after 1876, when his art underwent a major change under the impact of French Barbizon painting, especially the light-filled style of Charles Daubigny. Along with the other Hudson River painters, Whittredge was soon eclipsed by the American Barbizon school, but he remained a respected member of the New York art community until his retirement in 1900. He died on February 25, 1910, in Summit, New Jersey, where he had lived since 1880.

Anthony F. Janson
University of North Carolina–Wilmington

Janson, Anthony F. *Worthington Whittredge.* Cambridge: Cambridge University Press, 1990.

WIMAR, CARL (1828–1862)

Charles "Carl" Wimar was born on February 19, 1828, in Siegburg, near modern-day Bonn, Germany. He came to St. Louis in 1843, studying there under Leon de Pomarede. His early paintings of Native Americans were based on images from popular literature rather than firsthand knowledge. He earned his first public notice after returning to Germany to study at the Kunstakademie in Düsseldorf. Returning to the United States in 1856, he decided to gain a more authentic knowledge of the country and of Native Americans. Like John Mix Stanley, Wimar relied on his own photographs as the basis of his paintings. From 1858 to 1860 Wimar traveled with parties of the American Fur Trading Company up the Mississippi, Missouri, and Yellowstone Rivers. He also accompanied shipments of annuities to tribes along the Missouri River. He used these experiences as the basis for a more realistic approach to tribal subjects.

As he came in contact with Native Americans his subject matter grew less romantic, shifting from themes of tribal war, buffalo hunting, and conflict with European Americans to the changing western landscape and the decline of tribal peoples and cultures in the face of European American expansion. In these years Wimar also painted several detailed panoramas of the Missouri River and the tribes living along its banks, the last large-scale works completed before European American colonization permanently altered tribal life there. Although known for his accurate portrayal of costumes and gestures, Wimar remained a romantic in his choice of themes. His most famous works include *Indian Approaching Fort Benton* (1859) and the important *Attack on an Emigrant Train* (1856), considered to be a prototype of the wagon train attack painting.

Wimar was commissioned by the city of St. Louis to paint murals for the city courthouse with western themes, all of which have since been destroyed. He died of tuberculosis in St. Louis, Missouri, on November 28, 1862.

Charles Vollan
University of Nebraska–Lincoln

Stewart, Rick, Joseph D. Ketner II, and Angela L. Miller. *Carl Wimar: Chronicler of the Missouri River Frontier*. New York: Harry N. Abrams, 1991.

WOLCOTT, MARION POST (1910–1990)

Marion Post Wolcott is best known for the social documentary photographs she made for the Farm Security Administration (FSA) during the later part of the Depression, including work in the Great Plains. She was born Marion Post in 1910 in Montclair, New Jersey. Her older sister Helen was considered the more artistic and was encouraged toward a career in the arts, becoming well known for her portraits of Native Americans done for the Department of the Interior in the 1930s and 1940s. Marion was sent to a series of

Marion Post Wolcott. Freight train and grain elevators in Carter, Montana, August 1931.

boarding schools and eventually attended the New School for Social Research and New York University, intending to teach. On a visit to Vienna in 1933 she was introduced to photography and was strongly attracted to its immediacy and power.

After she returned to the United States Marion held a series of jobs until she was hired by the FSA to photograph farm problems and general rural life in America. She worked for the agency from July 1938 until November 1941, traveling thousands of miles through the South, New England, and the West. On June 6, 1941, she married Lee Wolcott, an administrator for the Department of Agriculture, and, at his insistence, her credits were changed on all her photographs to retroactively reflect her married name.

In the fall of 1941 she set out on her last major photographic expedition for the FSA, covering Colorado, Nebraska, Montana, Idaho,

and, briefly, California. Although she was unfamiliar with the region, her Plains work is some of her best, emphasizing the openness of the land and the relative insignificance of the human impact upon it. She succeeded in capturing the sense of space and distance by using roads, telephone poles, long trains, and grain elevators as compositional devices.

Wolcott retired from professional photography in 1941, raised a family of four children, was recognized late in life as a significant contributor to American photography, and died in 1990.

See also AGRICULTURE: Farm Security Administration.

F. Jack Hurley
University of Memphis

Hurley, F. Jack. *Marion Post Wolcott: A Photographic Journey*. Albuquerque: University of New Mexico Press, 1989.
Stein, Sally. *Marion Post Wolcott: FSA Photographs*. Carmel CA: Friends of Photography, 1983.

Asian Americans

City commissioners and local Chinese delegation, Calgary, Alberta, October 13, 1901

ASIAN AMERICANS

In 1870 the first "Chinaman" set foot on the streets of Denver, Colorado. A local paper described him as "a short, fat, round-faced, almond-eyed beauty," and added that he "appeared quite happy to get among civilized people." Despite this kind of ridicule, the Chinese of Denver soon became an essential element in the city's urban economy. They provided domestic services to a primarily male population for an affordable price, services that had not been available before the Chinese arrival. From that time on, the Asian presence in Denver and in many other parts of the Great Plains has been a permanent fixture.

But if one were to open a Denver history book, or any history book about the Great Plains for that matter, one would be hard-pressed to find more than one or two pages written on Asians. This marginalization from the pages of history is a clear injustice to a people who have been fundamental to the development of the region. From the late-nineteenth-century Chinese, who did the vast majority of the region's laundry, to the present-day Southeast Asians who have revitalized city neighborhoods and provided a workforce for the region's meatpacking industry, Asians have made and continue to make vital contributions to the prosperity and growth of the Great Plains.

Chinese Pioneers

The Chinese were the first Asian immigrant group to reach the region. Settling originally in the California goldfields, they began moving eastward in the 1860s following railroad construction and mining opportunities. From California they moved to Nevada, Montana, Wyoming, and then Colorado. Although the first Chinese came to the Western Plains to work on the railroads and in the mines, the vast majority who followed these pioneers came to fill the empty economic niche in laundry work and other domestic services, a necessity in the rough-and-tumble, predominantly male frontier towns. By 1880, for example, Denver had a thriving Chinese community of 238, of whom more than 80 percent worked as laundrymen. In other towns such as Deadwood, South Dakota, Chinese opened restaurants, general provision stores, and opium dens. The Plains' Chinese population gradually began to move farther east, providing similar urban services along the way. By 1890 there were 224 Chinese in Nebraska, and by 1920, 261 had settled in Oklahoma.

Chinese also migrated to the Prairie Provinces of Canada. The majority settled in large cities such as Edmonton and Calgary, Alberta, while others settled in smaller urban communities such as Lethbridge and Medicine Hat, Alberta. Many were brought in by American contractors (especially the Minnesota firm of Langdon and Shepard) to lay the tracks of the Canadian Pacific Railway in the years 1881 to 1883. Many of the laborers were recruited directly from the United States, and some returned to the United States after the contract ended. After 1883 the Canadian Pacific Railway recruited directly from Canton and Hong Kong, as well as from Vancouver. By 1900 Calgary had become home to approximately eighty Chinese who worked as laborers, cooks, and domestic servants.

Despite being invaluable to the Great Plains urban economy, the Chinese were still subject to discrimination. White workers blamed Chinese for the slow economy and resented Chinese competition, particularly in the mining industry. Politicians stoked this volatile issue in order to gain the labor vote. As a result, towns often practiced discriminatory taxation and passed economic sanctions against the Chinese.

There were times when these discriminatory measures did not satisfy a town's populace and violence ensued. On Sunday, October 31, 1880, for example, a group of several hundred white males incited an anti-Chinese riot that resulted in the death of one laundryman and the destruction of Denver's Hop Alley. The immediate cause was a bar fight between two Chinese and two whites, but the underlying cause was the anti-Chinese agitation of the local Democratic Party and labor organizations. A similar incident occurred in Calgary. On August 2, 1892, a mob of more than 300 destroyed Chinese laundries after learning that four Chinese who had been quarantined for smallpox had been released. In both cases, authorities were exceedingly slow to react.

The best-known and bloodiest action against the Chinese in, or near, the Great Plains occurred in September of 1885 in Rock Springs, Wyoming. A few months earlier, the Union Pacific Coal Division had brought in about 300 Chinese to work in the local mines, an action that infuriated local white workers. On September 2, two white miners found that the seam to which they had been assigned was already being tapped by two Chinese miners. The enraged miners proceeded to rally other white miners, and by early afternoon a mob of 150 moved on Rock Springs' Chinatown, slaughtering residents at every opportunity. At day's end, twenty-six Chinese were dead and fifteen others were wounded. Government troops eventually restored order and helped company officials to reinstate Chinese in the mines. To this day, the Rock Springs massacre stands as one of the most brutal manifestations of American opposition to the Chinese presence.

The Chinese were not always passive in the face of such oppression. They used the legal system as a means of resistance and sometimes even won their cases. In 1882, for example, local authorities accused Yee Shun of murdering a fellow Chinese in Las Vegas, New Mexico. Although the court eventually found Yee Shun guilty, the defense team achieved a legal victory of immense proportions for all Chinese in America. They were able to overturn a prior ruling prohibiting Chinese from testifying in court.

Another legal victory for the Chinese occurred in Regina, Saskatchewan, in 1907. On the morning of August 8, nine patrons of the Capital Restaurant became ill after eating porridge. Local authorities soon discovered that Charlie Mack, the Chinese cook of a competing restaurant, had poisoned the porridge. Mack disappeared before he could be arrested, causing the local authorities to detain the entire male Chinese population of Regina in an effort to extract information concerning his whereabouts. The Chinese, encouraged by their lawyers, prosecuted the local officials. They won their case, received a small indemnity, and had the satisfaction of seeing Regina's police chief removed from office.

By 1890 the Chinese population in the Great Plains had peaked. Every state, territory, and province in the region had Chinese residents. Soon afterward, however, this population began to decline, especially in Colorado, Wyoming, and Montana, the states where the largest settlements had been concentrated. The decline followed a national trend that had begun with the 1882 Chinese Exclusion Act and continued in the early twentieth century with the passage of the 1902 Chinese Exclusion Act, a congressional bill that made permanent the 1882 act. Because most Chinese in the United States, including the Great Plains, were male, and because immigration had been banned, there was little natural population growth. Under the circumstances, community roots never had a chance to take hold, and they withered quickly after 1902. Similarly, Canada imposed restrictions on Chinese immigration in 1903 and 1923. The legislation virtually halted Chinese immigration until 1947, when it was repealed.

Japanese: From Farms to Internment

With the decline in the Chinese population, industrialists and growers needed a new source of cheap labor. They turned to newly arrived Japanese immigrants. Between 1880 and 1900, yearly Japanese immigration to the United States increased from 148 to 24,326. Although most Japanese settled in Hawaii and California, a good number moved to the Great Plains. Like the Chinese before them, the Japanese followed rail, mining, and agricultural work to Montana, Wyoming, and Colorado. By 1910 Japanese migrants also began moving to Nebraska and Kansas to pursue sugar beet work and to coastal Texas to cultivate rice.

One immigrant, Naokichi Hokazano, was particularly instrumental in bringing Japanese to the Plains. Arriving in Denver in 1898, Hokazano promptly contracted seventy Japanese to harvest 1,200 acres of sugar beets that he owned. Hokazano has been criticized by Asian American historians for exploiting the labor of his countrymen by paying them substandard wages. Nevertheless, he was responsible, at least in part, for the increase in Japanese migration from the West Coast to the Great Plains. By 1909, of the 3,500 Japanese in Colorado, almost 2,000 were connected to the sugar beet industry.

Within twenty years, through skill, enterprise, and hard work, several of these immigrants became successful landowners and farmers, a pattern of upward mobility first seen in California. The Japanese in this economic sector were so successful that many competing white farmers gave up, leaving the industry open to further Japanese control. These pioneers of Colorado agriculture irrigated, and thus made arable, much of the land in the northeast corner of the state. Today, they are honored in the state capitol building, where Naokichi Hokazano is memorialized in a stained-glass window.

Japanese also started urban businesses and organized civic institutions. By 1916 they owned sixty-seven stores in Denver and had founded the Japanese Methodist Church and the Denver Buddhist Church. In Scottsbluff, hub of Nebraska's sugar beet industry, Japanese settlers started the Japanese-language newspaper *Neshyu Jibo* (*Nebraska News*) and founded the Japanese Association of Nebraska. In Texas, Japanese dominated the nursery industry.

Like the Chinese before them, Japanese also settled in the Prairie Provinces of Canada, moving into southern Alberta shortly after the turn of the century. They migrated mainly from British Columbia and the United States. As in the United States, they worked in the mines, on railways, and in agriculture and were quite often recruited by labor supply companies. In 1907 the Canadian Nippon Supply Company recruited a large group of Japanese to work in the mines near Lethbridge, Alberta. The following year, Nippon Supply sent 300 more workers to the Lethbridge mines. Unfair treatment by their employers and by fellow countrymen working for labor supply companies prompted Japanese laborers to organize labor unions soon after their arrival in the Prairie Provinces. It was not until the 1920s, however, that Japanese workers were accepted as equals, with equal pay, to white workers.

As in the American Great Plains, Japanese in the Prairie Provinces made their greatest contribution in agriculture. In 1907 the Canadian Pacific Railway recruited 370 Japanese workers through the Nippon Supply Company to build irrigation ditches. The Raymond Knight Sugar Company recruited 100 Japanese workers in 1908 and another 105 in 1909. The workers remained wage laborers for only a few years, however, as they soon began to lease and, on occasion, buy their own tracts of land. These successful Japanese pioneers eventually established permanent communities with their own newspapers, churches and temples, and social organizations.

Their success in farming prompted a more virulent racism. In the early 1920s, following the example of California, the states of Montana, Wyoming, Nebraska, and Texas passed legislation barring Japanese from owning or leasing land. Colorado was the only Plains state with a significant Japanese population that did not pass an alien land law. This was one reason why more Japanese moved to Colorado than elsewhere in the Great Plains, and why Japanese Coloradans were so successful in agriculture.

The worst act of discrimination perpetrated against Japanese Americans—an act

that did not bring an official apology from the United States until August 10, 1988—came during World War II. On February 19, 1942, President Franklin Delano Roosevelt signed Executive Order 9066 allowing for the internment of all Japanese within a designated militarized zone. While this zone was located primarily on the West Coast, "suspected" Japanese community leaders throughout the nation were also interned, including those in the Plains.

Rev. Hiram Hisanori Kano of Nebraska, for instance, was arrested on the day of the Pearl Harbor attack. He was held in a Santa Fe, New Mexico, internment camp until 1944. Kano and other community leaders were imprisoned merely on suspicion of disloyalty. Elsewhere in the Great Plains anti-Japanese hysteria led to house searches by the FBI, often carried out in a demeaning and destructive manner.

The Plains was the site of one of the largest internment camps in the United States, Granada, Colorado (also called Amache). Heart Mountain, Wyoming, another large camp, was just to the west of the Plains. Several smaller camps were also located in the region. At one such camp in Lordsburg, New Mexico, in the early morning of July 27, 1942, an army guard shot and killed Hirota Isamura and Toshira Kobata as they were being delivered for internment. The guard insisted that Isamura and Kobata were trying to escape, although several eyewitness accounts maintained otherwise. The guard went unpunished.

Meanwhile, as fellow Japanese Americans were being imprisoned, young *nisei* (second-generation Japanese Americans) served in the American military with distinction. One of them, Ben Kuroki of Hershey, Nebraska, came home with a distinguished war record only to find himself ostracized for being Japanese. This discrimination led Kuroki to campaign against the injustices of internment.

The long-overdue apology for internment came only after a hard-fought redress effort by Japanese Americans. Bill Hosokawa, a resident of Denver and himself a veteran of internment, was particularly instrumental in gaining this apology. Hosokawa was interned at Heart Mountain in Wyoming, where he published the camp newspaper. After his release Hosokawa became active in the Japanese American Citizens League (JACL), the organization primarily responsible for redress. Hosokawa also became the *Denver Post*'s first foreign correspondent, and he covered the Korean War in this capacity. Later in his career he became the *Post*'s Sunday magazine editor and then the assistant managing editor. His career as a journalist made him JACL's selection to write a history of second-generation Japanese Americans called *Nisei: The Quiet Americans* (1969).

Hosokawa and the JACL are at the center of a five-decade-old controversy that has divided the Japanese American community. During the months preceding internment, the JACL took the stance that cooperation with the government's internment plans was a necessary

evil that Japanese Americans would have to endure in order to demonstrate their loyalty. This stance has not been popular with the more militant members of the Japanese American population who argue that it was in essence a sellout. This controversy continues to this day and has been fervently taken up by third-generation Japanese Americans, the *sansei*.

Japanese Canadians were also persecuted during World War II, and again the Great Plains, securely in the heart of the country, was the setting for their forced relocation. In 1942, 20,881 Japanese, 75 percent of them Canadian citizens, were taken from their homes and moved to detention camps in the interior of British Columbia and to sugar beet farms in Manitoba and Alberta. Many of the relocated Japanese Canadians worked for individual farmers, but others were gathered into huge "prisoner of war" camps at Lethbridge and Medicine Hat. The Canadian government sold off their assets—farms, homes, fishing boats—and used the proceeds to finance the internment. At the end of the war, Japanese Canadians were given the choice of either returning to a devastated Japan or moving permanently to the Prairie Provinces or eastern Canada. Most chose the latter option.

The discrimination did not end with the war. In 1946 the Canadian government tried to deport 10,000 Japanese Canadians, and only an international outcry prevented this infamy. Japanese Canadians did not regain their status as Canadian citizens until 1949.

Late Twentieth-Century Developments

In 1965 the U.S. Congress passed an Immigration Reform Act. By removing racially based quotas, promoting family reunification as a priority, and encouraging the immigration of professionals, the act opened the way for a great increase in Asian immigration to the United States, including the Great Plains. As a result the Plains has experienced a recent influx of Filipinos, Koreans, Chinese, and South Asians (Indians and Pakistanis). Each of these ethnic groups has thriving communities in major Plains cities. In 2000 the Denver metropolitan area, for instance, had an Asian population of approximately 63,000, Dallas–Fort Worth had an Asian population of close to 195,480, and Oklahoma City had an Asian population of almost 18,000. Chinese and Koreans have played a significant role in reviving small businesses in urban areas. Filipinos have mainly entered the professional ranks. And Indians, in addition to being both shopkeepers and professionals, have built an occupational specialty in the small-motel industry. Chinese and Indians, in particular, are well represented in higher education and the high-technology industry.

Similar circumstances have resulted in a significant increase in Asian numbers in the Canadian Prairie Provinces. As of 1991 Alberta was home to 71,635 Chinese, 16,310 Filipinos, and 54,750 South Asians; Manitoba was home to 11,145, 22,045, and 24,465, respectively; and Saskatchewan was home to 7,550, 1,635, and

11,285, respectively. In recent years a large number of Chinese left Hong Kong in anticipation of the July 1997 takeover by the People's Republic of China. Canadian immigration policy encouraged the immigration of wealthy Hong Kong investors by granting automatic residency to any person investing $1 million in the Canadian economy. Most Asians have settled in urban areas, particularly Edmonton, Calgary, and Lethbridge. The presence of the Nikka Yuko Garden in Lethbridge, one of the most authentic Japanese gardens in North America, is visual evidence of the importance of the Japanese presence in the Prairie Provinces.

Also in the recent years, the Great Plains has attracted large numbers of refugees from Southeast Asia. Subsequent family reunification has swelled their numbers. Having been forced to flee their homelands due to war, several million have made new homes in the United States and Canada. They migrated in two waves, one in 1975 and the other starting in 1979 and continuing to the present. The first wave consisted primarily of the highly educated or professionals fleeing from Vietnam and, in smaller numbers, from Cambodia. By contrast, the 1979 wave consisted mostly of farmers and rural dwellers from Vietnam, Cambodia, and Laos. While U.S. relief agencies intended to relocate these refugees to all parts of the nation, the majority have gathered in only a few states—California, Texas, Washington, Oregon, and Minnesota. Thus, although the Plains' Southeast Asian population is relatively small, it is growing and certainly an invaluable contributor to the region's social and economic fabric.

In at least four Plains cities—Denver, Oklahoma City, Tulsa, and Wichita—Southeast Asians have formed communities with populations of more than 1,000. These communities have started to form civic organizations that address the multiplicity of adjustment problems faced by refugees. The Oklahoma Vietnamese, for instance, formed the Vietnamese American Association (VAA) in 1978. To date the VAA has offered English classes and job training, placement, and upgrading services. The VAA has been so successful that the federal government has used it as a model for its national program.

In Denver, Southeast Asians have also formed community organizations. Led by a first-wave refugee, Khan Penn, the Cambodian community formed the Colorado Cambodian Community (CCC) in 1976. The CCC emphasizes the preservation and observation of cultural traditions and revolves to a large extent around the Buddhist temple. These sorts of community activities also serve to ease the adjustment of Cambodian refugees although not in as concrete a manner as the VAA in Oklahoma City.

Southeast Asians have noticeably affected the demographic makeup of some Plains regions. For example, more than 100 Laotians settled in the small town of Tecumseh, Nebraska, between 1982 and 1992. In the late 1990s they accounted for about 6 percent of

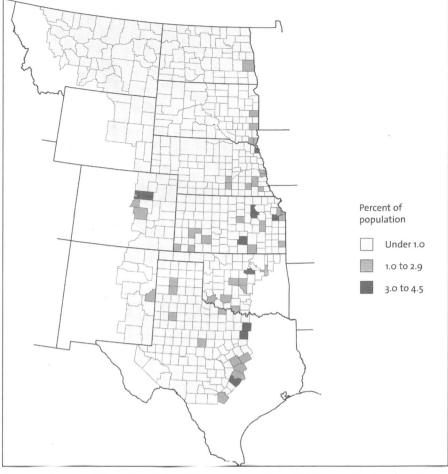

Asian American population in the U.S. Great Plains as a percentage of total population, by county, in 2000

the town's population and more than 17 percent of its schoolchildren. Refugees often move to small towns like Tecumseh in order to escape the more economically competitive environments of large cities. In many instances they are also recruited by local industries, such as Tecumseh's Campbell Soup canning factory. Garden City, Kansas, has seen similar changes as more than 1,000 Vietnamese migrated into the city, mainly to work in local meatpacking companies.

Southeast Asian numbers in the Plains are growing at a rapid rate. In Colorado, for instance, 7,210 Vietnamese, 1,320 Cambodians, 1,202 Hmong, and 1,996 Laotians were noted in the 1990 census. More than 97 percent of these groups lived in urban areas, particularly in Denver. Similar situations can be found in Nebraska although on a smaller scale. More than 2,600 Southeast Asians lived in the state in 1990, of whom 1,800 were Vietnamese. The Vietnamese numbers grew to 6,364 by 2000. In Colorado, according to the 2000 census, Vietnamese were the second-largest Asian ethnic group after Koreans. In Kansas the Vietnamese population of 11,623 (2000) made it the single largest Asian ethnic group. In 2000 the total Southeast Asian population in Kansas numbered more than 15,000. A similar demographic situation existed in Oklahoma. There, the Vietnamese numbered 12,566 in 2000, with the total Southeast Asian population amounting to more than 15,000.

The significant numbers of Southeast Asians have not only revitalized the meatpacking industry and other labor-intensive industries in the Plains but have also reenergized key segments of urban economies. In Denver, for instance, the entrepreneurial drive of Vietnamese refugees invigorated a slumping Chinatown economy. They opened new restaurants and groceries, an immigrant entrepreneurial staple, and they own and operate beauty parlors, nightclubs, coffee shops, and jewelry stores, to name only a few enterprises. Southeast Asians have also contributed significantly to the success of Denver's high-tech industry. A large number, if not a majority, of assembly-line workers in this industry are Southeast Asian.

Asian Americans have clearly played a significant if not always acknowledged role in the history of the American and Canadian Great Plains. This role dates back to the time of Chinese railroad construction workers and miners and Japanese agricultural laborers. Today, although Asian Americans constitute no more than 5 percent of the population of any Great Plains county, Asian Americans are essential to the regional economy. Southeast Asians are contributing to the growth of communities that otherwise might be declining, and in urban areas such as Denver, Colorado, and Lethbridge, Alberta, Asian Americans are contributing to the rejuvenation of the urban economy. Asian Americans have been, and will continue to be, integral actors in the history of the Great Plains.

See also AGRICULTURE: Sugar Beets / CITIES AND TOWNS: Calgary, Alberta; Denver, Colorado / WAR: World War II

Malcolm Yeung
Evelyn Hu-DeHart
University of Colorado at Boulder

Barth, Gunther. *Bitter Strength: A History of the Chinese in the United States, 1850–1870*. Cambridge: Harvard University Press, 1964. Culley, John J. "Trouble at the Lordsburg Internment Camp." *New Mexico Historical Review* 60 (1985): 225–48. Daniels, Roger. *Concentration Camps, North America: Japanese in the United States and Canada during World War II*. Malabar FL: R. E. Krieger Publishing Co., 1989. Fairbairn, Kenneth J., and Hafiza Khatun. "Residential Segregation and the Intra-Urban Migration of South Asians in Edmonton." *Canadian Ethnic Studies* 21 (1989): 45–64. Ichioka, Yuji. *The Issei: The World of the First Generation Japanese, 1885–1924*. New York: Free Press, 1988. Iwaasa, David. "Canadian Japanese in Southern Alberta: 1905 through 1945." In *Two Monographs on Japanese Canadians*, edited by Roger Daniels. New York: Arno Press, 1978. Kano, Hiram Hisanori. *A History of the Japanese in Nebraska*, edited by Jean and Sheryll Patterson-Black. Scottsbluff NE: Scottsbluff Public Library, 1984. Muzney, Charles C. *The Vietnamese in Oklahoma City: A Study in Ethnic Change*. New York: AMS Press, Inc., 1989. Ralph, Martin G. *Boy from Nebraska: The Story of Ben Kuroki*. New York: Harper and Brothers Publishers, 1946. Sontag, Deborah. "New Immigrants Test Nation's Heartland." *New York Times*, October 18, 1993. Storti, Craig. *Incident at Bitter Creek: The Story of the Rock Springs Chinese Massacre*. Ames: Iowa State University Press, 1991. Takaki, Ronald T. *Strangers from a Different Shore: A History of Asian Americans*. Boston: Little, Brown, 1989. Wortman, Roy. "Denver's Anti-Chinese Riot, 1880." *Colorado Magazine* 42 (1965): 275–91. Wunder, John R. "Law and the Chinese in Frontier Montana." *Montana: The Magazine of Western History* 30 (1980): 18–31.

AMACHE INTERNMENT CAMP

On February 19, 1942, President Franklin D. Roosevelt issued Executive Order 9066 authorizing the removal of more than 110,000 Americans of Japanese ancestry from their homes on the West Coast of the United States. Under the auspices of the War Relocation Authority (WRA), the federal government eventually imprisoned these Japanese Americans, two-thirds of whom were native-born citizens, in ten internment camps—Manzanar and Tule Lake in California, Jerome and Rohwer in Arkansas, Colorado River (Poston) and Gila River in Arizona, Central Utah (Topaz) in Utah, Heart Mountain in Wyoming, Minidoka in Idaho, and Amache (Granada) in Colorado.

Camp Amache, located in southeastern Colorado, had been under construction for only two months when the first 212 prisoners arrived from California on August 27, 1942. Although only a portion of the camp was habitable, the Western Defense Command refused to alter its schedule of removals. By the end of September nearly 5,000 people were in camp, and within six months the population of Amache exceeded 7,500. Camp Amache virtually overnight had become the tenth-largest city in the state. But it was a peculiar city. Hastily built, enclosed by barbed wire, and still unfinished when the bulk of the evacuees arrived, it had only the most rudimentary fa-

Granada Relocation Center, Amache, Colorado, June 1943

cilities. Even with the internees themselves assisting the WRA in various construction projects during these early months, mess halls were inadequate, bathhouses were without water, toilets were unsightly and unsanitary, and drinking water had to be trucked in from the nearby town of Granada.

In spite of the treatment they were accorded, or perhaps because of it, the men and women of Amache proceeded quickly to set up a system of democratic self-government. The camp charter, which had been drafted by early November 1942, was prefaced with a preamble that began with the words "We the People of Granada Relocation Center" and continued self-consciously to echo phrases contained in the preamble to the Constitution of the United States. As specified in the charter, a popularly elected community council, consisting of one representative from each of the twenty-nine blocks into which Amache's 348 barracks were organized, formed the core of camp government. It was responsible for establishing local ordinances, appointing an eight-member judicial commission to preside over all cases except felonies, and naming a fifteen-member arbitration commission to settle civil disputes.

Within a year after the charter had received the approval of the WRA, life in Amache assumed a semblance of normality: a police force of sixty men and a fire department of twenty-four to thirty men, assisted by a corps of voluntary firemen, were fully operational; the camp post office handled 2,500 letters and 400 packages daily; the *Granada Pioneer* spread the news to approximately 3,000 readers on a biweekly basis; a 150-bed hospital, staffed by five internee doctors and twenty-five nurses or nurse's aides, in conjunction with an outpatient clinic, treated 800 patients a week; a dental clinic with seven internee dentists dealt with 125 emergency cases daily; the local public library accumulated a collec-

tion of more than 4,500 books; and the education system enrolled 1,900 students in various grade levels ranging from preschool to senior high school. Because a workforce of nearly 3,500 internees formed the backbone of all of these enterprises, WRA officials, with apparently little sense of the irony of the situation, were quick to announce that the program of "rehabilitating" the evacuees was progressing smoothly and that therefore the majority of those interned would soon be qualified to enter the "mainstream of normal American life."

What perhaps impressed WRA authorities most were the successes of the camp farm and cooperative. The farm, which was the largest employer at Amache, encompassed some 10,000 acres, two-thirds of which were under irrigation at any given time. Contrary to the predictions of many local growers, the Amache farmers raised bumper crops of alfalfa, corn, and sorghum which, when coupled with harvests of head-lettuce, celery, spinach, onions, and lima beans, enabled them to export railroad carloads of produce to points outside Colorado. In 1943 alone, the total value of crops grown at Amache was $190,000. The cooperative begun in January 1943, the Amache Consumers' Enterprises, Inc., was similarly successful. With a membership in excess of 2,300 internees, the co-op brought into camp everyday items and services available to Americans on the outside. In its first year of operation, the co-op grossed more than $362,000 and became one of the largest organizations in the state.

But life at Amache in 1943 was not entirely reassuring to WRA officials. In February the WRA and the War Department jointly began to register all adults in the ten internment camps in the United States. As part of the registration procedure, internees were required to complete a questionnaire whose primary purpose was to measure "loyalty." Question 27 asked the internees whether they were willing to serve in the armed forces, and question 28 asked them whether they were willing to forswear any form of allegiance to the emperor of Japan. Based on the answers respondents gave to these two loaded questions, WRA officials segregated "loyals" from "disloyals." At Amache, the result was the removal of a small group of "disloyals" to Tule Lake, California, and the arrival of the first group of "loyals" from Tule Lake in September 1943. Eventually, more than 1,000 Tule Lake internees were relocated to Amache. James G. Lindley, the director of Camp Amache, was not pleased with the exchange. Loyalty aside, the "Tuleans," Lindley said, were troublemakers who resented internment and were unwilling to forget the "wrongs" they had suffered.

To Lindley's dismay, the Tule Lake contingent soon dominated the community council and voiced challenges not only to his policies but also to those of the federal government. Most notably, some of the former Tule Lake internees questioned the federal government's policy of drafting *nisei* men into military service while holding them and their families prisoners. Despite such protest, 494 men from Amache served in the military of a nation that classified them as "undesirable aliens." Thirty-eight of them earned combat decorations for exemplary conduct under fire; thirty-one were killed in action.

The courage and sacrifices of these men and the other Japanese American soldiers of the 442nd Regimental Combat Team and 100th Infantry Battalion accelerated the pace of the federal government's program to close the nation's internment camps. However, in late 1944 there were still more than 6,100 internees at Amache. In January 1945 the government lifted its ban on resettlement on the West Coast, and in March the WRA announced that it was no longer necessary for internees to secure prior approval of their relocation plans. By this time, those remaining at Amache were apprehensive about leaving camp, fearful of what awaited them on the outside. The *Denver Post* had only recently referred to them as "Japanese enemies," local farmers now complained about them possessing the best farmland in the state, the Colorado House of Representatives passed a bill (defeated in the Senate) banning ethnic Japanese from owning land in the state, and local merchants in nearby towns still posted "No Japs Allowed" signs in their windows. Not until October 15, 1945, two months after the end of the war in the Pacific, did the last internees leave Amache. "What does America mean to you?" Marion Konishi, valedictorian of Amache High School, asked her classmates in 1943. It is a question that should resonate with us all.

See also WAR: World War II.

Mel M. Yazawa
University of New Mexico

Thompson, William Takamatsu. "Amache: A Working Bibliography on One Japanese American Concentration Camp." *Amerasia Journal* 19 (1993): 153–59. War Relocation Authority. Granada Relocation Center. *Amache, Colorado.* Granada, 1943.

People of Asian Ethnic Origin
Living in Canadian Metropolitan Centers, 1991

	Calgary	Edmonton	Regina	Saskatoon	Winnipeg
Chinese	32,515	32,960	2,490	3,155	10,445
Japanese	1,880	1,090	100	175	980
East Indians	14,945	15,120	1,050	835	6,130
Filipino	7,805	7,055	555	765	21,720
Total Asian	77,145	78,690	6,440	6,530	48,815

ASIAN CANADIANS

People of Asian origin comprise a small but notable and increasingly important segment of the population in the three Canadian Prairie Provinces. Before 1951 the Canadian government sought to restrict Asian immigrants. The first Chinese and Japanese immigrants to Canada were almost all laborers building the railways or working in the mines. Many returned home after the transcontinental railways were built, but others stayed. The majority tried to establish themselves in British Columbia or Ontario. Some, however, remained in the cities, towns, and villages on the prairies. Most Chinese and Japanese in the Prairie Provinces before World War II established or worked in laundries, restaurants, market gardens, and confectioneries. They faced systemic and persistent discrimination and kept to themselves as much as possible, living mainly in segregated areas of the larger urban centers or in their places of business in the smaller rural towns and villages. World War II marked a decisive turning point for Japanese Canadians. In 1941 the Canadian government decided to remove all those of Japanese origin from a so-called security zone in western British Columbia. These people were first placed in internment camps in the British Columbia interior and in other camps established during the 1930s for single, unemployed men. Labor shortages, particularly in the labor-intensive sugar beet industry on irrigated land in southern Alberta, resulted in a relocation of many Japanese internees to assist in farmwork. Several Japanese Canadian authors, most notably historians Ken Adachi and Ann Gover Sunahara and novelist Joy Kogowa, have documented that sad chapter in the history of their people. A few Japanese farmers began cultivating sugar beets in southern Alberta even before the war, and others found opportunities to enter that branch of farming as a result of their wartime experience as farm laborers.

The reluctance of the federal government to allow the Japanese to return to their prewar homes in British Columbia persuaded many to remain in Alberta, where they established a good reputation and achieved moderate success as farmers. Others entered the professions. A strong Japanese community remained, particularly in the Lethbridge area. After the war the Japanese Canadians expressed their appreciation for the opportunities afforded them in southern Alberta by creating and opening to the public a beautiful Japanese garden and park in the city of Lethbridge.

The postwar economic boom, chronic labor and capital shortages, and changing attitudes resulted in dramatic changes in Canadian immigration policy after 1951. Specifically, immigration restrictions against immigrants from Asian countries were eased. The majority of these new immigrants established themselves in Vancouver, Toronto, and Montreal, but some also found their way to cities on the Prairies. There the new Chinese and Japanese immigrants revitalized, not always without conflict, old, established ethnic communities while East Indian and Vietnamese immigrants created new ones.

The more recent immigrants have found integration into Canadian society easier than did their predecessors, but in all the Prairie cities, and in many of the towns and villages, distinctive Asian restaurants as well as cultural, social, and religious organizations enhance the richness and diversity of prairie society.

Ted D. Regehr
University of Saskatchewan
and University of Calgary

Adachi, Ken. *The Enemy That Never Was: A History of the Japanese Canadians.* Toronto: McClelland and Stewart, 1976. Buchignani, Norman, and Doreen M. Indra. *Continuous Journey: A Social History of South Asians in Canada.* Toronto: McClelland and Stewart, 1985. Li, Peter. *The Chinese in Canada.* Toronto: Oxford University Press, 1988.

ASIAN EXCLUSION LEGISLATION

The treatment of Asian immigrants in the nineteenth century by federal, state, and local governments, as well as by the public at large, represents a bitter underside to U.S. and Canadian history. In response to the demand for cheap labor, Chinese first immigrated to the United States in significant numbers during the middle of the nineteenth century. They were instrumental in completing the transcontinental railroad and contributed greatly to the mining industry in the West.

It is well known that after the Civil War, greater legal freedoms for African Americans came with the abolition of slavery and the implementation of the Reconstruction amendments to the U.S. Constitution. Far less known, however, is the Chinese misfortune that mounted during this same period. In California, the home of many Chinese immigrants, partisan political concerns, along with labor unionism, figured prominently in the often-violent anti-Chinese movement. The American West as a whole experienced over 150 anti-Chinese riots during the 1870s and 1880s. The most destructive Great Plains riot broke out in Denver on October 31, 1881, leaving one Chinese person dead and causing over $50,000 in damage. Calgary experienced a similar riot in 1892.

In the first comprehensive federal immigration law, Congress in 1882 barred virtually all Chinese immigration to the United States and also excluded criminals, prostitutes, "lunatics," "idiots," and the poor. The courts upheld this and future Chinese exclusion laws. In the famous Chinese Exclusion Case (1889), the U.S. Supreme Court concurred with Congress that the presence of "foreigners of a different race" who "will not assimilate with us" was "dangerous to the peace and security" of the United States. Canada also sought to restrict Chinese immigration. Beginning in 1885 Chinese immigrants were forced to pay an entry fee, or "head tax," to enter the country. Because the head tax did not completely eliminate Chinese immigration, the fee was raised in 1903 to $500; the following year the number of Chinese immigrants fell from more than 4,700 to 8. Canada barred all Chinese immigration on July 1, 1923, a day Canadian Chinese refer to as "Humiliation Day." Discriminatory Canadian legislation directed at the Chinese was not repealed until 1947.

As a result of restrictive immigration legislation, the Chinese population in the Great Plains declined after 1890, while Japanese migration to the region increased, especially to Colorado and Nebraska in the United States and to Alberta in Canada. Both nations, however, soon extended the exclusion laws to effectively bar immigration from Japan and persons of Asian ancestry from *any* nation. For example, the Gentleman's Agreement between the United States and Japan in 1907–8 severely restricted immigration from Japan. A similar agreement between Canada and Japan limited the number of Japanese male immigrants to 400 annually; in 1928 Japanese immigration was further reduced to 150 per year. The U.S. Immigration Act of 1917 expanded Chinese exclusion to prohibit immigration from the "Asiatic barred zone," including the vast majority of Asia. A 1924 law, best known for creating the discriminatory national origins quota system, excluded from admission noncitizens "ineligible to citizenship," which directly affected Asian immigrants who could not naturalize and become citizens.

Other provisions of the immigration and nationality laws reinforced the anti-Asian sentiment reflected in the exclusion laws. For example, the U.S. Supreme Court interpreted the law allowing "white" immigrants and persons of African ancestry (after the Civil War) to naturalize as barring Asian immigrants from naturalizing. In *Ozawa v. United States* (1922), for example, the Court held that a Japanese immigrant, as a nonwhite, could not naturalize and thus could not become a citizen. Consequently, before repeal of the whiteness requirement for naturalization in 1952, Asian immigrants could not vote or enjoy other rights associated with U.S. citizenship. In Canada the Chinese did not gain suffrage until 1947. The children of Asian immigrants

born in the United States or Canada, however, became citizens at birth.

Several states, particularly in the West with its growing Japanese population in agriculture, enacted "alien land laws" in the early twentieth century that barred the ownership of certain real property by immigrants "ineligible to citizenship." Racial animus combined with economic factors fueled passage of the laws. Influenced by California's alien land laws of 1913 and 1920, Texas, Nebraska, New Mexico, and Kansas enacted similar laws during the 1920s; only Colorado and the Dakotas did not. Alien land laws did not disappear until the 1950s in most western states.

Over the course of the twentieth century, the U.S. Congress slowly relaxed the Asian exclusion laws. During World War II, pressures to end the prohibition on Chinese immigration to the United States grew as it became increasingly embarrassing for the government to prohibit immigration from China, a valued ally in the war effort. In response to foreign policy concerns, Congress in 1943 allowed China a minimum quota of 105 immigrant visas per year.

Despite this meager liberalization of the law, the Immigration and Nationality Act of 1952 carried forward the bulk of the national origins quota system that drastically limited immigration from Asia as well as from southern and eastern European. Not until 1965, as the civil rights movement forever transformed the nation, did Congress repeal the last vestiges of the Asian exclusion laws. Restrictions on Chinese immigration to Canada were completely removed by 1967. Since the 1960s immigration to the United States and Canada from Asia has increased dramatically, as has the overall Asian American population of the two countries.

Kevin R. Johnson
University of California, Davis

Hing, Bill Ong. *Making and Remaking Asian America through Immigration Policy 1650–1990*. Stanford CA: Stanford University Press, 1993. Salyer, Lucy E. *Laws Harsh as Tigers: Chinese Immigrants and the Shaping of Modern Immigration Law*. Chapel Hill: University of North Carolina Press, 1995. Takaki, Ronald. *Strangers from a Different Shore: A History of Asian Americans*. New York: Little, Brown and Co., rev. ed. 1998.

BUDDHISM

See RELIGION: Buddhism

CALGARY CHINATOWN

The first small concentration of Chinese in Calgary developed on the eastern edge of downtown at the end of the nineteenth century. Riots broke out in 1892 when some of the Chinese were discovered to have smallpox, and the Chinese population had to be protected by the police. In 1901 another area of concentration, again mostly a handful of residences, laundries, and restaurants, developed on the southwestern edge of downtown, on the other side of the railway tracks, when a local minister helped the Chinese obtain rental property. In 1910 soaring property values

in the city led to the sale of the properties rented by the Chinese. But this time local Chinese businessmen were able to buy land, and they reestablished themselves on the northern fringe of downtown near the Bow River, on Centre Street between 2nd and 3rd Avenues, an area little valued because it was prone to flooding.

This area of concentration did grow slightly to include neighboring blocks as the population of Chinese in Calgary grew from 485 in 1911 to 1,054 in 1931. But additional growth was limited, because of the national prohibition on Chinese immigration, and because of the tendency for the Chinese to establish small businesses in suburban areas, which allowed little chance for community roots to grow. But by 1961 immigration regulations were relaxed and the census identified 2,232 Chinese in the city of a quarter of a million inhabitants. Chinatown contained approximately two-fifths of this total and had eleven different social associations, a school, two Chinese Christian churches, and thirty businesses, a majority of which were restaurants or other food businesses.

During the 1960s a series of transportation and slum clearance programs threatened to destroy Chinatown. But vigorous lobbying by the Sien Lok Society, founded in 1968 by a group of Chinese businessmen and professionals, suggested that business and residential redevelopment should be initiated by Calgary's Chinese population and should reflect the area's heritage. These ideas were formalized by the city's 1976 Design Brief for the area. The streets were given Chinese names, and street furniture and new buildings adopted Chinese motifs, styles, and preferred colors, such as red and gold. The climax of the redevelopment was the creation of a cultural center that was a replica of the Temple of Heaven in Beijing, built by craftsmen imported from China. Opened in September 1992, the building contains a Chinese library, recreation hall, meeting rooms, Saturday language school, and restaurant and gift shop, and is actively used by the city's Chinese community.

Chinatown is no longer home to the majority of Calgary's Chinese population, whose numbers had grown to more than 50,000 by 1996. Most live in suburbs, especially Edgemont, Huntington Hills, and Marlborough. Chinatown now has 1,400 residents—less than 3 percent of the city total—housed mainly in three high-rise apartments. Ninety percent of these are of Chinese ethnic origin and more than half are senior citizens. However, Chinatown has seen a remarkable increase in commercial activity. It has expanded along Centre Street to 4th Avenue and neighboring streets to form a six-block commercial area, with interior malls and a wide variety of and a large number of businesses. Nevertheless, the historic concentration on restaurants and retail food outlets is still present, accounting for a quarter and a fifth of the businesses, respectively.

Planning surveys have shown that almost three-quarters of the shoppers in Calgary's

Chinatown are from outside the area, but two-thirds of the total are of Chinese ethnic origin, which shows that the area acts as a commercial core for the dispersed Chinese population, as well as for the city as a whole. However, new concentrations of Chinese businesses have recently developed: one is across the Bow River along Centre Street north to 16th Avenue and the others are in suburban locations, especially in Pacific Plaza and International Avenue in the eastern part of Calgary. Yet Chinatown is still the largest concentration of Chinese businesses in the city, and the presence of professional activities and social organizations provides it with a high degree of institutional completeness. Chinatown is no longer a historic ghetto. It acts as a refuge for the Chinese elderly, contains an invented symbolic core for Calgary's dispersed community, and is a distinctive, yet specialized ethnic business area.

Wayne K. D. Davies
University of Calgary

CHINESE

During the summer of 1875, Sin Goon, a Chinese immigrant, arrived in the Great Plains in search of a prosperous town where he could open a laundry. While traveling through Nebraska he visited the nascent railroad town of North Platte. Impressed with the town's possibilities as a growing commercial center on the transcontinental line, Goon opened what was probably the first Chinese-owned business in western Nebraska.

Sin Goon was one of the relatively few Chinese who chose to settle in the Great Plains during the nineteenth century. In 1870, for example, no Chinese lived in either Nebraska or Kansas. By 1890 census takers enumerated only 214 in Nebraska and 93 in Kansas. The Canadian Plains attracted even fewer Chinese during this period. Only 80 Chinese lived in Calgary in 1900. Chinese immigrants, who began arriving in the United States around 1850, tended to settle in the far western states, primarily California. They came to the United States as sojourners, with the intention of making a fortune and then returning home. Thus, the first Chinese immigrants worked in the mining regions of the American West. Only the western fringe of the Great Plains offered Chinese immigrants opportunities in mining: Colorado, the Black Hills, Montana, and Wyoming. Denver quickly gathered the largest concentration of Chinese in the Plains; in 1890 almost 1,000 Chinese lived in "Hop Alley," the city's Chinatown.

While mining was the original economic attraction for Chinese immigrants, they also played an important role in nineteenth-century railroad construction, particularly on the Canadian Plains. Between 1881 and 1883 Chinese contract laborers helped build the Canadian Pacific Railway across the Prairies. Most Chinese returned home or migrated to the United States after the railroad was completed, but many settled permanently in Prairie cities such as Edmonton, Calgary, and Medicine Hat.

Service industries provided yet another economic opportunity for Chinese immigrants. Chinatowns in Denver; Butte, Montana; Deadwood, South Dakota; and Calgary supported a wide variety of Chinese-owned laundries, restaurants, gambling houses, and mercantile businesses. During the 1870s and 1880s enterprising Chinese entrepreneurs like Sin Goon left the Chinese enclaves of the mining West and opened service businesses in Plains towns such as North Platte, Nebraska, and Wichita, Kansas. Because Great Plains communities could support only a limited number of service-oriented businesses, Chinese businessmen were scattered across the Plains, often living alone and distant from fellow countrymen. In 1890, for example, Nebraska's railroad towns generally had one or two Chinese laundries and perhaps a Chinese restaurant: two Chinese lived in Sidney, two in North Platte, one in Lexington, two in Kearney, and three in Grand Island.

While the Chinese may have found economic opportunity in Great Plains communities they still could not escape from the racism, discrimination, and violence that plagued the Pacific and Rocky Mountain West. By the 1870s economic depression and racism produced a virulent anti-Chinese movement in California, which then spread to other regions of the American West. Towns such as Los Angeles, Tacoma, and Seattle witnessed anti-Chinese riots; in 1871 Los Angeles mobs killed twenty-two Chinese. The Great Plains was not immune to such intolerance. In 1880 rioters destroyed Denver's Chinatown, killing one Chinese launderer, while in 1885 at Rock Springs, Wyoming, a mob killed twenty-six Chinese miners. Although less violent than their American counterparts, Canadians also repressed their Chinese population. On August 2, 1892, for example, a Calgary mob destroyed the city's Chinese businesses. Sin Goon also experienced intolerance and violence in North Platte. Just weeks after his arrival Goon was warned to leave town by the non-Chinese launderers. When Goon refused, his competitors hired thugs to break the windows of his laundry. Goon hastily left North Platte, but instead of abandoning the Plains he moved down the Union Pacific line and opened another laundry in Grand Island.

After 1890 the Chinese population in the Plains began to decline, largely the result of the Chinese Exclusion Act of 1882, which nearly halted all Chinese immigration to the United States. As a "bachelor society" with few women, the Chinese population in the United States could not sustain itself by natural increase. Between 1890 and 1900 the Chinese population in the United States fell from 105,828 to 74,013. During these same years Nebraska's Chinese population fell from 214 to 190 while Colorado's dropped from 1,398 to 960.

Chinese immigration to the United States did not resume until after 1947, when prohibitive immigration restrictions were lifted. Further immigration reform in both the United

States and Canada during the 1960s sparked a new wave of immigration from China, primarily professionals and businessmen. As Sin Goon had done in the 1870s, Chinese returned to the Plains in search of economic opportunities. In the early twenty-first century, Plains towns such as Denver, Fort Worth, and Oklahoma City in the United States and Calgary, Edmonton, and Lethbridge in Canada have thriving Chinese communities, composed of women and children as well as men, and of scientists and doctors as well as launderers and restaurateurs.

Mark R. Ellis
University of Nebraska at Kearney

Courtwright, Julie. "A Slave to Yellow Peril: The 1886 Chinese Ouster Attempt in Wichita, Kansas." *Great Plains Quarterly* 22 (2002): 23–33. Li, Peter. *The Chinese in Canada*. Toronto: Oxford University Press, 1988. Wortman, Roy. "Denver's Anti-Chinese Riot, 1880." *Colorado Magazine* 42 (1965): 275–91.

DEADWOOD CHINATOWN

Joining another western gold rush, Chinese began to arrive in the Black Hills, Dakota Territory, from Montana, Colorado, and Wyoming in the mid-1870s. Their population soon increased to nearly 300. Most of them resided in the Deadwood-Lead area. Although some of the Chinese engaged in placer mining, an overwhelming majority of these Asian immigrants found their calling in service businesses. Encountering relatively mild racial prejudice, the Chinese immigrants were able to open their businesses anywhere in the region. Chinese-owned washhouses and restaurants dotted the city of Deadwood.

Nevertheless, the voluntary congregation of Chinese in residences resulted in a distinctive ethnic quarter. Located along Main Street and at the northern end of Deadwood, the so-called Chinatown was actually a multiethnic community that sheltered Chinese, African Americans, and European Americans. Contemporary Black Hills residents often called that section "Badland" because it was where all the "bad" groups stayed, such as prostitutes, gamblers, outlaws, African Americans, and Chinese. The legendary and notorious Calamity Jane once lived in a shack in Chinatown. Curious European Americans and Native Americans occasionally visited the place and patronized the Asian business establishments seeking cultural exchange or vice. Since Dakota Territory placed no restrictions on foreign ownership of property, the Chinese owned most of the houses and stores in Chinatown. From the late 1870s to the 1910s, Deadwood Chinatown functioned as the social and cultural center for the Chinese immigrants in the entire Black Hills region.

Over the years Deadwood's Chinatown, like many other frontier communities, survived flood, fire, and violence. By the 1910s most of the Chinese had left the Black Hills due to the decline of the mining industry and the local economy. As a result of the dwindling population, Deadwood's Chinatown gradually faded away. Today, frontier Deadwood Chinatown has become part of the local legend.

See also IMAGES AND ICONS: Deadwood, South Dakota / GENDER: Calamity Jane.

Liping Zhu
Eastern Washington University

Anderson, Grant K. "Deadwood's Chinatown." *South Dakota History* 5 (1975): 266–85. Liestman, Daniel D. "The Chinese in the Black Hills, 1876–1932." *Journal of the West* 27 (1988): 74–83.

DENVER BUDDHIST TEMPLE

The Denver Buddhist Temple was established by a branch of the Jodo Shinshu, one of Buddhism's largest sects in Japan, founded by Shinran Shonin in the thirteenth century. Economic conditions in Japan in the nineteenth century drove many Japanese immigrants to North America seeking employment in farming, mining, and railroad construction. Records indicate the first Japanese settlers in Colorado arrived before 1886; a Japanese cultural society was founded in Denver about 1904.

Shin Buddhism followed the settlers to Colorado, and on March 13, 1916, Rev. Tessho Ono, a graduate of Kyoto Imperial University, inaugurated a church attended by 250 Japanese immigrants. The Denver Buddhist Church served also as community center for many lonely Japanese. Eventually, membership spanned the region, including Colorado, Nebraska, Wyoming, New Mexico, Montana, and Texas. The early ministers of the Denver Buddhist Church traveled widely, visiting parishioners, comforting the sick, and performing memorial services for the dead. From the beginning, the church organized cultural events that supported traditional values while Japanese assimilated into American culture. Youth groups such as the Young Buddhist Association (eventually the YMBA and YWBA) and Sunday schools sponsored oratorical contests, ballroom dancing, beauty pageants, and a night school. Eventually, a Sunday school curriculum was supplied by the Buddhist Churches of America, headquartered in California, guiding immigrant parents in the religious education of their children. By 1934, under the leadership of Rev. Yoshitaka Tamai, there were fourteen branch temples within a 600-mile radius of Denver, and 300 families were listed as members.

World War II and its anti-Japanese sentiment were difficult for the Colorado Japanese community. Travel was restricted and finances were threatened, but most avoided the internment imposed on their West Coast compatriots. In 1944 a church delegation sought an additional English-speaking minister and brought to Colorado Rev. Noboru Tsunoda, a second-generation Japanese who had been interned in a camp. After the war, as many as 20,000 Japanese moved into the state to work on farms. Church membership soared. At the same time, European Americans took an interest in Buddhism and in Japanese culture, and myriad groups from Christian churches, civic organizations, and schools visited the church, resulting in an increase in non-Japanese membership.

Determined to realize its dream of building, the community raised $150,000 to purchase land in downtown Denver. In 1949 they dedicated their new church and created a regional organization called the Tri-State Buddhist Church. Over the next fifteen years the Denver church added offices, Sunday school rooms, a residence for ministers, an auditorium, and a high-rise apartment building, Tamai Towers, for subsidized housing. Eventually, commercial establishments rented space, creating Sakura Square, a Japanese cultural presence in downtown Denver.

In a pattern consistent with national Shin Buddhist trends, membership in the Denver church has declined since the 1950s. In 1977 the Denver Buddhist Church became the Denver Buddhist Temple. In 2001 the Denver temple had an official membership of 454 and had informal affiliated communities in Wyoming, Nebraska, New Mexico, Texas, and Oklahoma; two Denver ministers serve nine affiliated temples with a total of 214 members and visit distant communities annually.

Judith Simmer-Brown
Naropa University

Bloom, Alfred. "Shin Buddhism in America: A Social Perspective." In *The Faces of American Buddhism*, edited by Charles S. Prebish and Kenneth K. Tanaka. Berkeley: University of California Press, 1998: 31–48. Watada, Matajiro, ed. *A History of Fifty Years of the Tri-State Buddhist Church, 1916–1966*. Denver: Tri-State Buddhist Church, 1968.

DENVER CHINATOWN

Chinese laborers working on various railroads that traversed the Great Plains made Denver's Chinatown their favorite haunt. In February 1870 the Colorado Territorial Legislature passed a resolution encouraging Chinese to immigrate to the area as a means of meeting its chronic shortage of laborers, especially in the agricultural sector. With the decline of gold mining on the West Coast and the completion of the transcontinental railroad, many Chinese went to Colorado seeking better economic opportunities.

By the fall of 1870 there was a small settlement of forty-two Chinese men and women formed along Wazee (a term that probably meant "Chinese") Street in Denver. This constituted the center of Denver's small Chinese community. (Denver's Chinatown was also known as "Hop Alley," a derogatory term that referred to the presence of opium dens that were entered from the alleyways.) During the 1870s Denver, along with its Chinese community, experienced an economic boom and an increase in population when gold was discovered in the Rocky Mountains. On the eve of the anti-Chinese riot (October 31, 1880), there were 238 Chinese in Denver (approximately 39 percent of all the Chinese in Colorado). In 1890 the Denver Chinese community reached its apex with 980 residents.

As was the case with Chinatowns throughout the country, Denver's Chinese community was a "bachelor society," consisting of predominantly young men. Because of the small

number of women, the Chinese community was unable to have a traditional family life and to reproduce itself. Racism prevented the Chinese from entering most occupations and forced 80 percent of them to work washing laundry by hand. The rest found other occupations, mainly within the Chinese community. As a result of the Chinese Exclusion Act of 1882 and the introduction of steam laundries, the Chinese community began to decline. By 1940 there were only 110 Chinese left, and they were forced to disperse when the city razed the few buildings remaining in Denver Chinatown as part of its urban renewal program.

See also CITIES AND TOWNS: Denver, Colorado.

William Wei
University of Colorado at Boulder

Ourada, Patricia K. "The Chinese in Colorado." *Colorado Magazine* 29 (1952): 273–84. Wei, William. "The Anti-Chinese Movement in Colorado: Interethnic Competition and Conflict on the Eve of Exclusion." *Chinese America: History and Perspectives* 9 (1995): 179–97.

DENVER'S ANTI-CHINESE RIOT

On the afternoon of October 31, 1880, a mob descended on Denver's Chinatown. Within hours the mob destroyed businesses, residences, and killed one Chinese resident. Denver's riot was one of 153 anti-Chinese riots that swept through the American West during the 1870s and 1880s. Because so few Chinese settled in the Great Plains during the nineteenth century, however, the Denver riot was one of two major anti-Chinese incidents to strike the region (the other was in Calgary in 1892).

The Chinese had experienced discrimination and violence since 1849 when they first arrived in California. They were driven out of California mines by the "foreign miner's tax" and also experienced outright violence (a Los Angeles mob killed twenty-eight Chinese in 1871). By the late 1870s the anti-Chinese movement had entered national politics. Fearful that cheap Chinese labor would threaten the white working class, Denis Kearney, an Irish immigrant and founder of the Workingman's Party, led a campaign to ban Chinese immigration. During the presidential election of 1880 Chinese immigration became an important issue when Winfield Hancock, the Democratic candidate, supported a ban on Chinese immigration.

Colorado was not immune to anti-Chinese agitation. In 1874 white miners drove 160 Chinese out of Nederland, and in 1879 the people of Leadville were proud to announce that they had no Chinese living in their community. By 1880 the anti-Chinese movement had reached Denver, a city with 238 Chinese residents. During the presidential election of 1880, Denver's *Rocky Mountain News*, a staunchly Democratic paper, launched an anti-Chinese campaign, igniting Denver's working class. In its October 23 issue, for example, the newspaper called the Chinese the "Pest of the Pacific" and pointed out that if they invaded Colorado in greater numbers, white men would starve and women would be forced into prostitution.

Other editorials attacked the opium dens located along Hop Alley in Chinatown. On October 28 the *Rocky Mountain News* reported that there was open talk in Denver of running the Chinese out. The night before the riot, supporters of the Democratic Party marched through the streets, many carrying anti-Chinese banners.

Denver was ready to explode. The spark that ignited the riot came on the afternoon of October 31 when several intoxicated white men entered a saloon and began harassing two Chinese. The Chinese patrons retreated out the back door but were pursued and assaulted. Soon after, a crowd composed mostly of Irish laborers gathered near the scene of the crime. By two o'clock the crowd had turned into a mob of 3,000, and Denver's police force, which was understaffed and without a police chief, was unable to control the masses. The mayor called on the fire department to help with crowd management and then tried to persuade the mob to disperse. When the crowd shouted down the mayor, he ordered the fire department to disperse them with water hoses. Enraged by the soaking, the crowd hurled bricks and rocks at the firemen and then turned their rage on Chinatown. They sacked businesses, burned homes, and attacked innocent victims. By early evening rioters had burned every laundry in Chinatown. When the mob found Sing Lee, a laundryman, they pounced on him, kicking him as he lay on the ground. The helpless laundryman was dragged down the street with a rope around his neck and eventually was beaten to death.

A few Denverites stood up to the mob and protected their Chinese friends. Several citizens hid Chinese friends in their homes. Jim Moon, a gambler of ill repute, held off a mob bent on burning out a Chinese laundry. With a revolver leveled at the crowd and using forceful language, Moon single-handedly dispersed the crowd. In another act of bravery, Liz Preston, the madam of a brothel, and ten of her employees protected several terrified Chinese. Armed with shotguns, champagne bottles, and high-heeled shoes, the women forced the crowd to retreat. Preston's brothel served as a safe haven for Denver's Chinese during the riot; at least thirty-four Chinese waited out the riot inside her parlor.

In the heat of the riot the mayor appointed Dave Cook, a Denver fireman, as acting police chief, and he quickly appointed 125 special policemen to help reestablish order. Police officers rounded up the Chinese and lodged them in the county jail for their own protection. With law enforcers finally on the streets, the crowd slowly disappeared into the night. By eleven o'clock Cook reported that Denver's streets were quiet.

Authorities kept the Chinese locked in the county jail for several days. On November 4 they were released, only to find their businesses, homes, and temples destroyed. Estimates of the total damage exceeded $53,000. The Chinese consul in San Francisco requested reparation payments from the federal government and the city of Denver. His re-

quests were denied. To add further insult to the Chinese victims, Denver's rioters escaped punishment. Those who had been jailed during the riot were released for lack of evidence, and Sing Lee's murderers were acquitted in February 1881. Despite the violence and destruction of their property, many Chinese remained in Denver. They rebuilt their businesses and homes along Hop Alley, and by 1890 more than 980 Chinese lived in Denver. Chinatown remained a part of the Denver landscape until 1940 when it was razed in the name of urban renewal.

See also CITIES AND TOWNS: Denver, Colorado.

Mark R. Ellis
University of Nebraska at Kearney

Wortman, Roy T. "Denver's Anti-Chinese Riot, 1880," *Colorado Magazine* 42 (1965): 275–91. Wunder, John R. "Anti-Chinese Violence in the American West, 1850–1910." In *Law for the Elephant, Law for the Beaver: Essays in the Legal History of the North American West*, edited by John McClaren. Pasadena CA: Ninth Judicial Circuit Historical Society, 1992: 212–36.

FEMALE EMPLOYMENT ACT

In February of 1912 the Saskatchewan legislature enacted the Female Employment Act, which made it illegal for "any Japanese, Chinaman or other Oriental person" to employ or offer lodging to any "white woman or girl." The legislation resulted from, in a general sense, the adoption in Saskatchewan of pronounced anti-Chinese ideas, current especially on the West Coast, and from an almost pathological fear of miscegenation. However, the trigger was a seemingly innocuous incident in Moose Jaw involving a Chinese restaurant owner who rapped with a broom handle the ankle of a white woman (and former employee) who was blocking a doorway in his establishment. This incident, for which the restaurateur was convicted of indecent assault, occurred less than a week before the introduction and passage of the act.

The owners of two restaurants in Moose Jaw, with the financial help of other Chinese businessmen and the active support of their white female employees, unsuccessfully challenged the act before the courts, claiming that it infringed on federal powers. The act's scope was reduced in 1913 when an amendment confined the prohibition to Chinese, and again at the end of World War I when another amendment allowed the owners of restaurants and laundries to employ white females if they obtained a yearly license from the municipal council.

It was a demeaning experience to apply for such a license, and by no means guaranteed to be successful. The effect of the act was to discourage such businesses, commonly run by Chinese, from employing white females and to contribute to the marginalization of the Chinese in Saskatchewan. Of course the act also limited employment opportunities for "white women and girls," and it was this that ultimately led to the act's repeal in 1969.

Ken Leyton-Brown
University of Regina

Leyton-Brown, Ken. "Discriminatory Legislation in Early Saskatchewan and the Development of Small Business." In *Proceedings of the Seventh Annual Conference of the International Council for Small Business–Canada*. Regina: ICSB-Canada, 1991: 252–71.

HOSOKAWA, WILLIAM (b. 1915)

William Hosokawa, January 1943

William K. Hosokawa was not born in the Great Plains—he was born on January 30, 1915, in Seattle, Washington—but he moved to the region as a young man and spent more than forty years as an award-winning journalist for the *Denver Post* and historian for the Japanese American Citizens League (JACL).

Hosokawa's parents were first-generation Japanese immigrants (*issei*). As a youngster Hosokawa spoke Japanese and did not learn English until he attended public school. From an early age he had an interest in writing. He served as the sports editor for his high school newspaper and later at the University of Washington wrote for the student newspaper and for Seattle's *Japanese American Courier*. After graduating in 1937 with a bachelor's degree in liberal arts and a minor in journalism, the young journalist married Alice Tokuko Miyake and moved to Asia where he worked as managing editor for the *Singapore Herald* (1939–40) and then as a writer for the *Shanghai Times* (1940–41). With tensions increasing between the United States and Japan in 1941, however, Hosokawa returned to Seattle just weeks before Pearl Harbor.

Like most West Coast *nisei* (second-generation Japanese Americans) Hosokawa and his family were forced from their Seattle home by the federal government and sent to internment camps. While being held at the Heart Mountain Relocation Camp in Wyoming, Hosokawa continued writing by editing the camp newspaper. Hosokawa was released in 1943 and took a job in Iowa as a copy editor for the *Des Moines Register*. In 1946 he moved his family to the Great Plains, where he began a long career with the *Denver Post*. Throughout his newspaper career there he held a variety of positions: war correspondent in Korea (1950) and Vietnam (1964), associate editor (1963–77), editorial page editor (1977–83), and columnist (1983–92). Hosokawa also taught journalism at the University of Northern Colorado, University of Colorado, and University of Wyoming.

Hosokawa has written several important books on the Japanese American experience. His most important works include *Nisei: The Quiet Americans* (1969) and JACL *in Quest of Justice* (1982), both of which chronicle the history of the Japanese American Citizens League and its quest for redress for internment during World War II. He also coauthored *They Call Me Moses Masaoka* (1987) with Mike Masaoka, the leader of the JACL. Hosokawa has won awards from the Colorado Society of Professional Journalists (1976) and the Denver Press Club (1985), and in 1990 he received an honorary doctorate from the University of Denver. Hosokawa is retired and lives in Denver.

See also MEDIA: *Denver Post.*

Mark R. Ellis
University of Nebraska at Kearney

JAPANESE

The first generation of Japanese immigrants, known as *issei,* originally came to the Great Plains as sojourning contract laborers for railroad or mining companies in the late 1890s and early 1900s; few other occupations were open to them. After completing their contracts, many worked for farmers and meatpackers, and eventually some became owners of small businesses and farms. By 1910 Montana, Wyoming, and Colorado each had a Japanese population of between 1,500 and 2,500. The other Great Plains states each had fewer than 1,000 Japanese. In Canada, most of the early Japanese immigration was to British Columbia. In the early 1900s the Canadian Pacific Railway recruited many Japanese immigrant workers, especially Okinawans. Just before World War II there were more than 550 Japanese in Alberta and 40 in Manitoba.

The Oriental Trading Company brought Japanese railroad gangs to Montana for the Great Northern Railroad in 1898 and provided as many as 6,000 workers to eight other railroad companies in Montana, Idaho, and North Dakota. Other Japanese workers built railroads in Colorado, Nebraska, and South Dakota. *Issei* were brought to the Great Plains by labor contractors called *keiyaku-nin,* who recruited and transported the laborers to work sites and negotiated labor conditions with employers. Contractors also served as foremen, supervisors, and translators, and they kept a portion of the workers' wages for their services: a contractor for the Northern Pacific Railroad, for example, charged each worker ten cents out of their $1.10 daily wage. Most *issei* were bachelors who lived in boxcars in despicable conditions, often developing illnesses from overwork and malnutrition.

Issei first engaged in agriculture as contract laborers. While European Americans could obtain land through the Homestead Act or outright purchase, the majority of Japanese Americans remained tenants because of the alien land laws of several states. These prohibited the acquisition of land for "aliens

ineligible for citizenship"—a racist constitutional interpretation that until 1952 limited citizenship to "free white person[s]" and "persons of African nativity or descent." In the Great Plains, Japanese Americans mainly grew sugar beets but gradually diversified by adding potatoes and beans as they acquired larger acreages. In the early 1900s the Great Western Sugar Company in Billings, Montana, and Scottsbluff, Nebraska, specifically encouraged Japanese production of sugar beets. In Colorado, Naoichi Hokazono advanced the sugar beet venture by cultivating 2,000 acres near Greeley using Japanese contract laborers. *Issei* farmers also made Rocky Ford, Colorado, famous for quality cantaloupes. Altogether, between 1907 and 1909, *issei* farmers in Colorado increased their total farming acreage by 131 percent.

Miners were the other major pioneering group of *issei* to first reach the Great Plains. In 1909 there were 300 Japanese miners in Colorado from a total of 3,555 Japanese Americans in the state. In Wyoming, Japanese miners, who worked in at least seven mines, joined the white labor union. *Issei* also entered the meatpacking industry in the Great Plains when labor contractor Kinji Okajima brought in 120 strikebreakers to an Omaha packinghouse and another 100 strikebreakers during Kansas City's 1904 Armour meat packinghouse strike.

Denver became home to the largest Japanese American community in the Great Plains. Although Denver's Japanese town survives in greatly reduced form, its cultural and religious institutions once served much of the Great Plains. Denver's Tri-State Buddhist Church, established in 1916, grew to serve a 600-mile radius, extending into Nebraska and Wyoming, with fourteen branch churches in 1934. Tamai Towers, a senior citizens' home, stands in Denver's Sakura Square to honor Rev. Yoshitaka Tamai, who dedicated his life to ministering to his dispersed Great Plains congregation. Farther east, Japanese communities developed in Nebraska in the cities of Omaha, Lincoln, North Platte, Scottsbluff, and Mitchell. Rev. Hiram Hisanori Kano, a minister of the Episcopal Church in Nebraska and leader of the Japanese agricultural community, received an early graduate degree in agriculture from the University of Nebraska. A farmer himself, he later established the Japanese colony of Dutton Ranch in Hebron, Nebraska. Kano and members of the Nebraska Japanese Improvement Association achieved a minor victory when the state's land law was widened to include aliens, not just those eligible for citizenship, and leases were extended from two to five years.

During World War II approximately 120,000 Japanese Americans on the West Coast were forced to leave their homes and were sent to temporary detention centers operated by the army and then to one of ten concentration (a term now preferred to internment) camps operated by the War Relocation Authority. Two of these camps were located in or near the Great Plains—Heart Mountain near Hunt, Wyoming, and Amache near Granada, Colo-

rado. The Japanese Americans and Japanese Canadians living in the Great Plains were not forcibly relocated, apart from several *issei* leaders, including Reverend Kano. The governors of the Great Plains states, with the exception of Colorado's Ralph Carr, may have had some responsibility for the system of concentration camps because they opposed settlements of unguarded Japanese among the general population in their states. The Justice Department's Immigration and Naturalization Service (INS) also operated several smaller camps for *issei,* which detained such "security risks" as community leaders, Japanese-language teachers, and newspaper editors. Several INS camps were located in the Great Plains, including those at Bismarck, North Dakota, and Crystal City, Texas.

Japanese Americans were able to leave the concentration camps once they secured college admission, army service, or army clearance. This led to increased Japanese American student enrollment at some Great Plains colleges, particularly in Colorado and Nebraska. Japanese Americans were also furloughed temporarily from the camps to work on sugar beet farms in the surrounding areas. The Canadian government, as a part of its own forced relocation, also sent some 3,600 Japanese Canadians to work in harsh conditions on sugar beet farms in Alberta and Manitoba. Many *nisei* (second-generation Japanese Americans) from the Great Plains also served in the much-decorated 442nd Regimental Combat Team. The sacrifices of soldiers of the 442nd and the exploits of Nebraska war hero Ben Kuroki are credited as part of the reason for the amelioration of anti-Japanese racism.

Although the majority of the removed Japanese Americans returned to the West Coast, third- and fourth-generation Japanese Americans are now part of the fabric of life in the Great Plains, serving as city council leaders, editors, professors, and farmers. According to the 2000 census, 17,120 Japanese citizens and Japanese Americans live in Texas, 11,571 in Colorado, 2,505 in Oklahoma, 1,935 in Kansas, 1,582 in Nebraska, 1,964 in New Mexico, and 1,906 in other Great Plains states. Canada's 1996 census reveals that 8,280 Japanese and Japanese Canadians reside in Alberta, 1,670 in Manitoba, and 415 in Saskatchewan.

See also WAR: World War II.

Noriko Asato
University of Nebraska–Lincoln

Daniels, Roger. *Asian America: Chinese and Japanese in the United States since 1850.* Seattle: University of Washington Press, 1988. Iwata, Masakasu. *Planted in Good Soil: A History of the Issei in United States Agriculture.* New York: Peter Lang, 1992. Takaki, Ronald. *Strangers from a Different Shore.* New York: Penguin Books, 1989.

KANO, FATHER HIRAM HISANORI
(1889–1986)

Hiram Hisanori Kano was born into a Japanese noble family on January 30, 1889. His warlord father was the governor of the province of Kagoshima and a member of the Japanese parliament. As the second son in the family, young Kano was not required to follow his father's career. Instead, he chose to study agriculture at the Imperial University in Tokyo, where he graduated with a bachelor of science degree in 1916. Kano eventually found his way to the Great Plains after William Jennings Bryan, a family friend, convinced his father that he could receive a better agricultural education in the United States. With a handwritten note from Bryan in his pocket, Kano journeyed to Lincoln, Nebraska, where in 1918 he earned a master's degree in agricultural economics at the University of Nebraska.

In 1919 Kano married Ai "Ivy" Nagai in Seattle; the couple had two children. He put his agricultural education to good use when he bought a 300-acre farm near Litchfield, Nebraska. Kano became active in the Japanese Americanization Society, teaching English and working as an intermediary or translator for immigrants. In 1921 Kano and Rev. George Allen Beecher, the Episcopal bishop for western Nebraska, successfully defeated a bill introduced in the Nebraska legislature that would have barred Japanese residents from owning property and serving as legal guardians of their children. During the 1920s Kano became active in the Episcopal Church, working with Japanese living in the Platte River valley. He was ordained a deacon in 1928 and became a priest in 1936.

Kano's life took a dramatic turn on December 7, 1941, when the Japanese attacked Pearl Harbor. After conducting services in North Platte, Nebraska, that Sunday morning, he was arrested by local police and interrogated by federal agents. Because of his family ties to the Japanese government and his position as a leader of Japanese immigrants in the Great Plains, federal authorities deemed Kano a threat to national security and sent him to an internment camp. While being held away from his family, Kano taught English classes to fellow internees. In 1944 he was released and allowed to move his family to Nashota, Wisconsin, where he entered a seminary, earning another master's degree in 1946. Returning to Nebraska, Kano worked as an Episcopal missionary among Nebraska's Japanese residents until his retirement in 1957. After leaving the priesthood, Kano moved to Fort Collins, Colorado, where he and his wife bought a small farm. Kano died on October 24, 1988.

Mark R. Ellis
University of Nebraska at Kearney

Kano, Hiram Hisanori. *A History of the Japanese in Nebraska*. Lincoln: Nebraska Committee for the Humanities, 1984.

KOGAWA, JOY NOZOMI (b. 1935)

The Japanese Canadian writer and activist Joy Kogawa is best known for her novel *Obasan* (1981), which was based on her own experiences as a captive in a Canadian internment camp during World War II. The book won *Books in Canada* First Novel Award and Canadian Authors Association Book of the Year Award.

Kogawa was born in Vancouver on June 6, 1935, a second-generation Japanese Canadian (*nisei*). During World War II she and her family, together with more than 20,000 other Japanese Canadians, were shipped to detention camps in the interior of the country. Kogawa was sent first to Slocan, British Columbia, then to Coaldale, Alberta. In *Obasan*, the adult Naomi, as an activist seeking justice for the victims of internment, reconstructs what had happened to her as a child as she scrutinizes the records that document this dark period of Canadian history.

Kogawa studied education at the Universities of Alberta (1954) and Saskatchewan (1968) and taught elementary school in Coaldale for a year. Her first book of poetry, *The Splintered Moon*, was published in 1967. She subsequently published three other collections of poetry. She has written three other novels since *Obasan*, two of which also feature Naomi. Like her main character, Kogawa has campaigned tirelessly for the rights of Japanese Canadians, so much so that in a 1988 interview she expressed concern that her writing would be overwhelmed by her political commitment. Her most recent novel, *The Rain Ascends* (1995), moved away from the previous autobiographical character of her fiction to tackle an equally charged subject matter: the abuse of children by clergymen.

David J. Wishart
University of Nebraska–Lincoln

Williamson, Janice. *Sounding Differences: Conversations with Seventeen Canadian Women Writers*. Toronto: University of Toronto Press, 1993: 148–59.

NATIONAL JAPANESE AMERICAN STUDENT RELOCATION COUNCIL

The National Japanese American Student Relocation Council was the primary civic organization that helped 4,000 *nisei* (second-generation Japanese Americans) leave concentration camps and enter some 600 colleges and universities in states outside the Pacific Coast exclusion zones (California and western Washington, Oregon, and Arizona) during World War II.

In 1942 the U.S. government uprooted over 120,000 Japanese Americans from their West Coast homes "for their security" and sent them first to army-administered assembly centers and then to more permanent concentration camps (euphemistically called relocation camps or internment camps) operated by the War Relocation Authority (WRA). *Nisei*, who were American citizens by birth, outnumbered the first generation (*issei*) by more than 30,000; their median age was seventeen. More than 2,500 *nisei* had been attending college in Pacific Coast states at the beginning of the war. Although college admission and work release were the only initial ways to leave the camps, many colleges refused to accept any *nisei*. The Relocation Council, a collective of several regional organizations, began operations on May 29, 1942, with Robbins W. Barstow, president of Hartford Seminary, as the first national director. The group was supported by the YMCA, the YWCA, church groups (especially Quakers), government agencies, educators, and the Japanese American Citizens League. The three major functions of the Council were to coordinate with the FBI and the WRA to obtain clearance for the *nisei* and for the colleges that accepted them, to raise funds for scholarships, and to work with Japanese Americans in the camps to increase morale and encourage the pursuit of higher education.

Between July 1942 and July 1946 more than fifty institutions of higher learning in Great Plains states accepted a total of 991 students: 505 in Colorado, 197 in Nebraska, 83 in Wyoming, 73 in Texas, 42 in Kansas, 30 in Montana, 29 in South Dakota, 22 in Oklahoma, and 10 in North Dakota. The University of Nebraska was one of the first universities to respond to the *nisei*'s plight, admitting 80 students by 1943. The university had originally decided on a cap of 10 students but gradually increased this to 120. Five of the major participating institutions—University of Colorado, University of Denver, Denver Art Institute, Colorado State College of Education, and Colorado State College of Agriculture and Mechanical Arts—were located in Colorado, reflecting Gov. Ralph Carr's hospitable attitude toward Japanese Americans.

Not all the *nisei* students were admitted with the help of the council; some applied independently, inspiring other *nisei* to pursue higher education. Recently, however, Gary Okihiro has argued that, although the work of the Student Relocation Council was antiracist, by working closely with the WRA it assisted the government's policy of relocating Japanese Americans and therefore accepted the racist implication that the Japanese Americans themselves were to blame for the reaction against them.

Noriko Asato
University of Nebraska–Lincoln

James, Thomas. "Life Begins with Freedom: The College Nisei, 1942–1945." *History of Education Quarterly* 25 (1985): 155–74. O'Brien, Robert W. *The College Nisei*. Palo Alto CA: Pacific Books, 1949. Okihiro, Gary Y. *Storied Lives: Japanese American Students and World War II*. Seattle: University of Washington Press, 1999.

NIKKA YUKO GARDEN

Japanese Gardens exist in all parts of the world, and the Great Plains states and provinces host some of the finest examples. Though there are important gardens in Sioux Falls, South Dakota, and in Devon near Edmonton, as well as other Plains cities, the preeminent example is the Nikka Yuko Garden (*Ni* for *Nihon* [Japan], *Ka* for Canada, *Yuko* for widespread friendship) in Lethbridge, Alberta.

Japanese gardens occur in several different formations. Meditation gardens are for quiet contemplation, rather than for walking, and consist of flat, dry-raked gravel with beautiful "island" stones irregularly placed in the sand or gravel area. Certain elements pertain to the basic cosmic forces seen in all gardens—namely the air, earth, fire, and water as universal components. Some of these elements occur as garden furniture or in the form of other features such as lanterns (fire), ponds (water), stones (earth), and of course the omnipresent air. Nothing in nature is absolute; hence dry gardens contain some water—usually in a *tsukubai* (basin) in one part of the garden. In the case of the Nikko Yuko, water additionally is suggested by the *shakkei* (borrowed landscape) view of a nearby lake.

Strolling gardens can also feature *roji*, which include hills, streams, ponds, waterfalls, and pathways. The latter give access to all these beautiful aspects of nature as expressed within the traditions of the Japanese garden.

Another form of the garden is the *cha-niwa* (tea master's garden). It is always small, never pretentious, reserved in its nature, and minimal in its number of plants. Some *cha-niwa* are single-plant gardens reduced to the barest essentials. Plants in this type of garden are indicative of the immediate area and never rare or exotic. The tea ceremony forms the ultimate aesthetic occasion in Japanese art and it takes place in a *cha shitso* (tea house) in a tea master's garden, usually within a larger Japanese garden. Its simplicity causes this form of garden to be the one most easily understood of all the various forms of the Japanese garden.

The Nikka Yuko Garden in Lethbridge contains most of the above-mentioned characteristics in an area slightly larger than three-and-one-half acres. The garden was established in November 1964 and was two years in construction. Dr. Tadashi Kubo of Osaka, Japan, who earlier had built a Japanese garden in San Diego, California, was instrumental in the Lethbridge project. He was assisted by Masami Sugimoto and Dr. Bob Hironaka of Lethbridge during the two-year construction phase. Mountains of earth were moved, distant stones were donated and brought to the site, and a water-circulation system was developed. A garden was born.

Plants were donated. A pebble-picking picnic produced bushels of stones from the Oldman River for the *ariso* beaches of the garden's pond. The necessary wooden structures were built in Japan and shipped to Canada. Prince and Princess Takamatsu of Japan officially opened the garden on July 14, 1967, Canada's centennial year. The dream of a fine Japanese garden in the Plains had come true—a place of peace and quiet, of *wabi* (beauty in simplicity)—in the vastness of the Alberta prairie.

Lennox Tierney
University of Utah

POISON PORRIDGE CASE

In August of 1907 some patrons of a Regina restaurant fell ill while eating breakfast and were diagnosed as suffering from arsenic poisoning. Three later died. Suspicion immediately fell on Charlie Mack, the Chinese owner of an older, neighboring restaurant. His business was known to have suffered because of competition from the newer establishment, and he had access to the oatmeal that had been found to contain arsenic.

The police, however, were unable to locate him, and public dissatisfaction with their lack of results finally prompted the police to take extraordinary measures. In a midnight raid they rounded up the entire male Chinese population of Regina and took them to city hall, apparently believing that they were conspiring to hide Charlie Mack. The operation was not a success, though; Charlie Mack was never apprehended. Moreover, fourteen of those taken into custody sued the police officers involved in the raid, the mayor of Regina, and the attorney general of Saskatchewan, alleging that they had been falsely arrested and unlawfully confined. The authorities at first refused to take the suit seriously, but the complainants persisted (though the attorney general was later dropped from the case) and they eventually won their case. They collected substantial damages, and the affair cost the chief of police his job. The most important result, though, was to deter police from taking such indiscriminate action against the Chinese community in the future, and to demonstrate that the courts of Saskatchewan were able, and in this case willing, to protect the rights of all of Saskatchewan's citizens.

Ken Leyton-Brown
University of Regina

Leyton-Brown, Ken. "The 'Poison Porridge' Case: Chinese and the Administration of Justice in Early Saskatchewan." *Great Plains Quarterly* 12 (1992): 99–106.

SOU, CHIN LIN (1837–1894)

One would have trouble explaining "westward expansion" to Chin Lin Sou. Chin was a Cantonese immigrant in his twenties when he came to San Francisco in the early 1860s fleeing the bloody civil war that started with the T'ai P'ing Rebellion of 1850. By 1864 the Central Pacific Railroad's Charles Crocker employed hundreds of overseas Chinese workers. "Crocker's Pets," as they were called, blasted grades and cuts through Donner Pass in the Sierras and on across Utah's Great Basin. From that memorable time in his life, Chin's "frontier" pushed east rather than west.

Following the driving of the "golden spike" at Promontory Point, Utah Territory, on May 10, 1869, Chin Lin Sou found himself in the employ of Gen. Grenville Dodge's Union Pacific Railroad, working to bring its tracks up to government standards. This opportunity brought him across the Rocky Mountains to the Great Plains of Nebraska. In 1870 a group of Denver businessmen, including H. A. W. Loveland, financed the construction of the Denver Pacific Railroad, a north–south line connecting Denver and Colorado to the transcontinental trunk line at Cheyenne, Wyoming. Chin served as a foreman of the Chinese labor crew that brought the project in under budget.

Chin Lin Sou stayed in Colorado, locating in Central City, where he made modest profits in mining investments. Sometime in the late 1870s he was financially able to bring his family from China. They settled in Denver where, by 1880, he operated several businesses. He likely witnessed the terrible "Hop Alley" riots on October 31, 1880, when irate white residents burned and pillaged the Chinese neighborhood of downtown Denver along 18th and Lawrence Streets. Chin died in 1894 a pillar of Denver's Chinese community. He was buried in the city's Riverside Cemetery. Today a stained-glass window portrait in the Colorado state capitol commemorates Chin Lin Sou as Colorado's leading Asian pioneer leader.

See also CITIES AND TOWNS: Denver, Colorado.

John H. Monnett
Metropolitan State College of Denver

Melrose Francis. "Rocky Mountain Memories." *Rocky Mountain News*, May 20, 1984. Monnett, John H., and Michael McCarthy. *Colorado Profiles: Men and Women Who Shaped the Centennial State.* Niwot: University Press of Colorado, 1996.

TERRITORY OF NEW MEXICO V. YEE SHUN

Territory of New Mexico v. Yee Shun (1884) is a landmark case that established the right of Chinese Americans to participate in the American constitutional system. For the first time, an American court of last resort guaranteed non-Christian Chinese and other Asian Americans the right to testify in courts of law.

On the evening of February 24, 1882, a young Chinese man, Yee Shun, exited a train in Las Vegas, New Mexico Territory, and walked to a nearby laundry. He had been on his way to a job at a Las Vegas hotel but had decided instead to travel on to Albuquerque. He stopped in Las Vegas because he wanted to make sure that his mail could be forwarded, and so he sought to find his local contact. There were four Chinese men gathered at the laundry. The owner indicated that he could escort Yee Shun to meet his friend, but before he could do so, another Chinese man, Jim Lee, came into the room from the back and two shots rang out. Jim Lee was shot dead, the owner was wounded, and the others, including Yee Shun, escaped. Yee Shun was apprehended and charged with second-degree murder.

At the trial, crucial testimony came from Jo Chinaman, one of the men who had been present inside the laundry. He testified that he had seen Yee Shun pull out a gun and shoot Jim Lee. Before his damning testimony, Jo Chinaman had been asked if he was a Christian and whether he understood the oath to tell the truth. He replied that he was not a Christian and that he did not understand the oath, but that he would tell the truth. The judge deemed this sufficient to allow the testimony, and a jury of twelve Mexican Americans found Yee Shun guilty of murder. Yee Shun's attorney appealed the verdict to the New Mexico Territory Supreme Court on the basis that Chinese witnesses who were not Christians could not take the oath, and therefore their testimony could not be allowed. It should also be noted that Jo Chinaman had been at the laundry to force the owner to sell, and when the police arrived he said he knew nothing about the murder.

The territorial Supreme Court heard the

case and decided that Chinese could in fact testify in New Mexico's courts as long as the court inquired as to the custom the witness would invoke in his culture when testifying and confirmed that the witness believed an oath to be binding on his conscience. After *Yee Shun* more states and territories soon began to allow Chinese to testify in their courts. Prior to the decision, only Nebraska, Colorado, and Texas in the Great Plains protected the Chinese right to testify, and they did so through their state constitutions. The only other western states guaranteeing Chinese testimony were Nevada and Oregon. Only Kansas continued to question whether Chinese Americans might testify at all. In 1909 Nebraska used the *Yee Shun* decision to guarantee the right of Japanese Americans to testify in American courts, the first such decision made by a state or federal court.

For Yee Shun, this important breakthrough in Asian American civil rights was of no avail. He was sentenced to life in prison and transported to Leavenworth, Kansas (New Mexico did not have a secure prison and contracted with the state of Kansas to hold its prisoners). Yee Shun then lost his appeal, and sometime after being informed of this decision, in the early morning hours of September 11, 1884, he committed suicide by hanging himself in his cell with a rope fashioned from his bed linens.

John R. Wunder
University of Nebraska–Lincoln

Wunder, John R. "Chinese in Trouble: Criminal Law and Race on the Trans-Mississippi West Frontier." *Western Historical Quarterly* 17 (1986): 25–41. Wunder, John R. "*Territory of New Mexico v. Yee Shun* (1882): A Turning Point in Chinese Legal Relationships in the Trans-Mississippi West." *New Mexico Historical Review* 65 (1990): 305–18.

VIETNAMESE

Significant numbers of Vietnamese first appeared in the American and Canadian Great Plains following the fall of the U.S.-backed Saigon government in 1975 and the resettlement of the first wave of Southeast Asian refugees in America. Many of these early refugees were educated military officers or professionals who had worked closely with Americans in Vietnam. In Kansas, Catholic sponsors helped the first newcomers obtain jobs and eventually establish businesses, while Catholic refugees provided clergy for the priesthood and sent their children to Catholic schools. Other denominations or interfaith councils have also provided continuing help and support to newcomers, as well as educating an often-unfriendly public about the reasons for refugee presence in Plains communities.

Government policy in both Canada and the United States at first emphasized dispersal of the refugees to encourage assimilation and avoid overburdening individual communities. The availability of sponsors and employment determined locations for refugee resettlement. After initial placement, however, many refugees made their own decisions about where to live and work, and most preferred to live in such areas as eastern Canada and California,

Vietnamese fan dancers, Garden City, Kansas, ca. 1990

which quickly developed sizable Vietnamese communities. With the exception of Texas, which has consistently hosted the second-largest Vietnamese population in the United States since 1980, American Great Plains populations of Vietnamese are generally low today (less than 1 percent of state populations), though they may be higher in some localities and especially urban settings.

The situation is rather different in the Canadian Prairie Provinces. According to the 1991 census, of the 94,255 Vietnamese living in Canada, 20,210 lived in the Prairie Provinces, and 15,135 in Alberta alone. Almost all live in the larger urban centers and many operate restaurants or other small businesses. One significant difference between the American and Canadian situations is that there was already a core of approximately 1,500 young and well-educated Vietnamese in Canada in 1975. They had come as students to study at French Canadian universities, and they early established a strong cultural and religious presence. Subsequently, the Vietnamese integrated relatively easily into Canadian economic, social, and cultural life.

Settling near relatives or friends was nearly always a consideration for newcomers, as were employment opportunities. Refugees to the American Great Plains sought manufacturing or other jobs in Kansas City, Wichita, and Denver, while meatpacking plants in smaller communities presented opportunities for others. Limited in their work options by the language barrier, as well as by problems of transferring skills and verifying credentials, refugees arriving during the 1970s and 1980s struggled to support themselves. Meatpacking, though unpleasant and dangerous, allowed newcomers to accumulate the capital to buy a house, start a business, or extend their education and training; meatpackers deliberately recruited refugees as a source of cheap, docile labor. One of the earliest groups of Vietnamese to arrive in Kansas was sponsored by a

meatpacking plant near Wichita. Others soon followed, and the expansion of meatpacking in southwest Kansas in the 1980s brought several thousand Vietnamese to the small towns of Liberal, Dodge City, and Garden City. In addition to the smaller meatpacking towns, urban areas throughout the Great Plains, such as Lincoln, Nebraska, quickly developed Vietnamese populations.

The first-wave pioneers who arrived in 1975 were followed in the 1980s by a prolonged and socially diverse flow of Vietnamese and other Southeast Asian refugees, the so-called boat people who fled from communist Vietnam on fishing boats and other barely seaworthy craft. Vietnamese refugees included Catholics and Buddhists, highly educated professionals, and relatively less educated farmers and fisher folk from rural areas. The refugees faced severe challenges, ranging from near-universal feelings of grief and survivor guilt due to their loss of or separation from close family members to the frustrations of making a living in an unfamiliar and sometimes hostile environment. In spite of these difficulties, most Vietnamese have survived—and some have prospered— due to extremely hard work and the mutual support of family and friends.

By the end of the 1980s Vietnamese were moving out of the meatpacking towns of southwest Kansas to other states and locations: some to California to rejoin relatives and friends, others to Texas or Louisiana to take up shrimping or seafood processing. Some who left later returned, either to Wichita, home to a large Vietnamese population, or to one of the meatpacking towns to earn more capital. Parents discouraged by their own attempts to move beyond low-wage, entry-level jobs saw the education of their children as a primary goal.

At the beginning of the twenty-first century the flow of Vietnamese with the legal status of refugee has almost ended, though for many years former refugees, now citizens, have been able to sponsor family members as immigrants to both Canada and the United States. Urban Vietnamese populations are growing from both natural increase and immigration. The most fortunate early arrivals have established successful businesses, educated children through college, and are in some cases ready to retire. In Alberta, Vietnamese are now represented in the provincial legislature. A whole generation of Vietnamese American children has grown up in the Great Plains, as evidenced by the Vietnamese student associations at most universities in this region.

Janet E. Benson
Kansas State University

Benson, Janet E. "Garden City, Kansas: Vietnamese Refugees, Mexican Immigrants, and the Changing Character of a Community." In *Manifest Destinies: Americanizing Immigrants and Internationalizing Americans*, edited by David W. Haines and Carol A. Mortland. Westport CT: Praeger Publishers, 2001: 39–54. Dorais, Louis-Jacques. *The Cambodians, Laotians and Vietnamese in Canada*. Ottawa: Canadian Historical Association, 2000. Stull, Donald D., Janet Benson, Michael J. Broadway, Arthur L. Campa, Ken C. Erickson, and Mark A. Gray. *Changing Relations: Newcomers and Established Residents in Garden City, Kansas*. Report no. 172. Lawrence: University of Kansas Institute for Public Policy and Business Research, 1990.

WONG, FEE LEE (WING TSUE)

(ca. 1846–1921)

Between 1848 and 1900 some 200,000 Cantonese were brought to the United States by labor contractors. Put to work at menial jobs in mining camps and on railroad construction crews, they moved eastward from California in the wake of new gold strikes. Some of them, including Fee Lee Wong, found their way to the Black Hills of Dakota Territory during the 1875–76 gold rush.

Hundreds of gold-hungry prospectors hastily erected rough cabins and tents along Whitewood and Deadwood Creeks in narrow Deadwood Gulch. By the late 1800s the north end of the mining camp's main street was a noisy, bustling Chinese village where Fee Lee Wong, better known as Wing Tsue, established his thriving business. His shop at 566 Main Street stocked a wide selection of Chinese foods and herbs, novelties, silk, tea, porcelain,

Wong family

and other luxury import gifts. Wing Tsue's name was listed in the 1880 census along with 212 other Chinese, most of them young men in their twenties and thirties. Actual numbers were probably much higher.

Although most of Deadwood's Chinese returned home or moved on to larger cities as the gold rush waned, Wing Tsue remained for forty years, becoming a prominent and respected businessman. When he brought his wife, Hal Shek Wong, from China, he announced she would be pleased to receive wives of his white business friends in their home on New Year's Day. In her book *Old Deadwood Days*, Estelline Bennett described the luxuriously appointed Wong home and said Mrs. Wing Tsue herself was "the loveliest bit of exquisite china I ever saw."

The Wong children, two sons and four daughters, attended Deadwood's public schools and Sunday schools. Records of Mount Moriah Cemetery show the burial of an eleven-month-old child of Wing Tsue on January 30, 1895, and the removal of the body

in 1904. Another daughter, born in 1900, died in 1902.

According to a family biography compiled by his grandson, Wing Tsue took his family back to China in 1902, then had difficulty re-entering the United States two years later. Intervention by a U.S. congressman allowed him to return to Deadwood. The First National Bank of Deadwood bought the Wing Tsue building for $1,055 in 1915 when the Chinese merchant defaulted on the loan. The family left Deadwood for the final time in 1919, after Wing Tsue suffered a stroke at a meeting of the Society of Black Hills Pioneers. He died in Canton, China, in 1921 at the age of seventy-five.

See also IMAGES AND ICONS: Deadwood, South Dakota.

Rena Webb
Rapid City, South Dakota

Bennett, Estelline. *Old Deadwood Days*. New York: J. H. Sears, 1928. Fielder, Mildred. *The Chinese in the Black Hills*. Deadwood SD: Centennial Distributors, 1982.

Cities and Towns

Main Street, Topeka, Kansas, ca. 1870

CITIES AND TOWNS

Cities were crucial to the European colonization of the Great Plains, yet when measured against the power of the protean natural environment, cities would play little direct role in defining the perceived human character of the region. Therein lies the paradox of urbanism in this vast territory of America, and its explanation is profoundly geographical. The primacy of cities for the region's actual development rests on two themes: the fundamental importance of urban markets in the American East and overseas in stimulating the huge demand for agricultural and mineral products that the Great Plains could satisfy, and the urban-based management of the very colonization system employed to settle people on the Plains. Furthermore, railroads, those avid servants of cities, brought settlers to the region and simultaneously provided them with an instant network of new urban sites to coordinate the supply of economic and social services the region required. On the other hand, the geographical logic of those supply lines placed the largest cities at the very rim of the region, if not wholly outside it, and so the Great Plains has evolved virtually as the hole in the urban "doughnut" of America. Consequently, the urban culture of the Great Plains is overwhelmingly a small-town culture in which attitudes and outlook are much closer to those of the rural vastnesses of their immediate trade areas than to the tempo and timbre of the big-city urban web that surrounds them on practically all sides. Only on the Canadian Prairies—unlike the American Great Plains, surrounded on all sides by terrain ill suited for the building of cities—is the hole-in-the-doughnut simile less appropriate.

Great Plains Towns in a Continental Context

Towns and cities in the American and Canadian Great Plains are among the youngest urban foundations on the continent. Few cities can trace their urban existence further back than 1860, and many towns in the region were founded as recently as the early decades of the twentieth century. Amarillo and Lubbock, Texas, Wichita, Kansas, and Regina and Saskatoon, Saskatchewan, the only sizable cities centrally on the Plains, were founded in 1887, 1890, 1873, 1882, and 1883, respectively. Associated with the youth of the region's urban places is the low level of urbanization overall. In the four states that are wholly contained within the region (North and South Dakota, Nebraska, and Kansas), only 49.5 percent of the population at the end of the twentieth century lived in metropolitan areas, as opposed to 79.8 percent nationally, and only five urban areas in these four states exceeded 100,000 residents. It requires no further statistics to establish that the Great Plains is a region in which large cities are only marginally important, but those geographically peripheral cities loom large socially and economically within the actual urban pattern of the region.

The other overarching characteristic of Great Plains urbanism is the enduring asymmetry of its spatial structure and national connections. The Plains was settled from the East, and its towns and cities have historically looked east for markets, sources of supply, and general inspiration. The immediate ties of commerce and urban culture on the Plains are to the large metropolises of the Middle West and, more distantly, the northeastern seaboard. Minneapolis, to take the most pronounced case, has long enjoyed an extraordinary westward reach in its economic dominance of the Northern Plains, making not only all of North and South Dakota tributary to its businesses and banking services but also the entire state of Montana. Not only Billings,

at the western edge of the Plains, but Butte and Missoula in the mountains have stronger business ties to Minneapolis than to Seattle, only a third of the distance away. Similarly, within the Plains states, urban trade areas have long been hugely skewed to the west: in South Dakota, Mitchell newspapers in the 1920s were read as far west as Philip, which is three times closer to Rapid City than to Mitchell. In the Canadian Prairies, because of the triangular shape of the region, such skewedness tends to be to the northwest or north of the key urban centers.

The long distances between towns and the low population densities within so much of

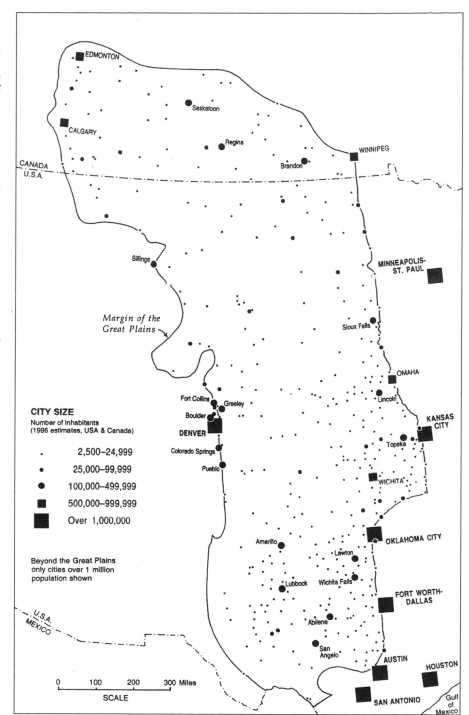

Cities of the Great Plains

the region dictate that its towns and cities fulfill only a restricted range of economic and social functions, and customers seeking advanced services such as high-tech medical attention, wider consumer choice, and major sporting events often need to travel to the large cities on the region's margins to obtain them. Since the development of hub-and-spoke service in the deregulated airline industry, residents south of the forty-ninth parallel have had to endure decidedly poor and remote air service. For the same reasons, manufacturing is an insignificant component of most towns and cities of the region, except for oil and gas processing in the Canadian provincial centers of Calgary and Edmonton. Industrial activity, if it is based on exports at all, is generally extremely small-scale or devoted to repair rather than fabrication. As such, urban life tends to be replicative rather than innovative and best developed in the gateway cities on its margin. These, then, are some of the abiding features of urban life in the Great Plains seen within a wider context.

Periods of Urban Life

Notwithstanding the comparative recency of towns and cities as historical artifacts in the Great Plains, their appearance on the physical landscape and in the social fabric of the region should be seen as the product of a fairly complex phasing in time and space. It is reasonable to recognize four broad phases in that emergence: town life in places established during the river and droving regime (1850s–1870s); town life during the phase of railroad colonization (1870s–1910s); urban life during the period of early-twentieth-century modernity (1910s–1950s); and, latterly, the era of urban polarization and retreat (1950s–present). Plainly, such historical distinctions are but a convenience for general understanding. The key processes attached to each phase can be found in adjacent phases, particularly when one considers geography: developments had a way of spreading from east to west over time, though very unevenly, and the retreat of urban life appears to be progressing, with similar unevenness, from west to east. It is revealing nonetheless to consider these four phases as distinct periods of social experience in the Great Plains, because each has left its own characteristic marks on the landscape and echoes within the composite outlook of the region's population.

Urban origins in the Great Plains predate the railroad. This may seem obvious, but it deserves emphasis because the greatest flows of population into the region occurred during the railroad period and thus shaped the "majority" experience that became handed down as lore through the generations. Before the 1850s, urbanism in the Great Plains was represented largely by the wealth the fur trade bestowed on St. Louis, Winnipeg, and Edmonton. As the tide of European American settlement pushed up the Missouri River and territories were organized across the Plains proper, river towns appeared on the west bank of the Missouri in Kansas and Nebraska during the 1850s. Thus, a narrow zone on the eastern margins of the Plains urbanized under a steamboat regime (essentially, a potamic or water-based colonization system), supplying both military forts planted deep on the frontier as well as the overland freighting trade, cattle droving, and the first tentative farm settlements. Towns were laid out with grandiose plats from Wyandott to Leavenworth, Atchison, Bellevue, Nebraska City, Omaha, and Florence. The river-port system was extended upriver into Dakota Territory, with Yankton and Vermillion founded around 1858, as well as along the lower reaches of the Kansas River.

These river towns owed their morphology and social character largely to their eastern predecessors on the Mississippi and Ohio Rivers, but they represented also the western limit of this type of urban function as transshipment points between waterways and wagon trails. The utility of great rivers as localizing arteries of commerce and population dispersion, so fundamental to America as far west as Missouri, fell foul of the shallow river conditions and uncertain water levels of the Great Plains. Settlement would have stalled had the railroads not caught up with potamic colonization on the middle Missouri River during the late 1860s. Nevertheless, the river towns of the Plains add depth to the urban record of the region and echo an early affiliation with water routes that would soon be lost.

Railroads could cross dry terrain with virtual impunity, and they spearheaded an unprecedented wave of urban and rural settlement across the Great Plains from the 1870s well into the twentieth century. This is the great era of town construction from scratch. This second and dramatic phase of Plains urbanization witnessed a standardization and corporatization of town founding, inasmuch as railroad companies developed something of a science in planting towns at suitable distances along their lines in hopes of generating maximum traffic and perfected the art of controlling the supply of key urban equipment such as grain elevators, stockyards, coal and lumberyards, banks, and hotels, many financed and owned by businessmen in midwestern centers such as Minneapolis and Chicago. In the Canadian Prairies the pattern was slightly different, owing to the direct role of the national government in developing the railroads. However, there was no lack of uniformity in the planning and look of Prairie towns north of the forty-ninth parallel.

During this period, regional differences in the density and location of urbanization across the Great Plains became quite evident. At first, the drive to complete several transcontinental railroad trunk lines produced lonely linear corridors of towns at several latitudes across the Plains. Then, as the continental wheat belt bifurcated into two zones and surged northwestward into the Dakotas and Canadian Prairies and southwestward into Kansas, dense networks of rails and shipping towns arose in their midst. But try as they might, settlers could not establish a firm foothold in certain areas, and the West River country of North and South Dakota and the Sandhills of Nebraska would stand out as inimical to town development. Farther west, north, and south, the rangelands that stretch from Montana to Texas and the southern portion of the Canadian Prairies, which the Palliser expedition described as an extension of the Great American Desert, also proved hostile to more than minimal railroad service, and, consequently, they saw infrequent town foundations.

However, all this became framed by the heady growth of the gateway cities, those "hinge" nodes that sort the traffic between the Great Plains and their neighboring regions. The trunk railroad pattern ensured that eventually towns like Calgary and Edmonton, Billings, Cheyenne, and Denver would prosper along the western border, while Winnipeg, Fargo, Omaha, Kansas City, Wichita, Oklahoma City, and Fort Worth would rise on the eastern margin.

During the opening two decades of the twentieth century railroads overpenetrated the productive portions of the Great Plains, a miscalculation that the first droughts of the period would dramatize. This is the last time new towns would be added to the region's network. The period lasting roughly from 1910 to 1950 can be distinguished and lent some coherence by its mixed signals of progress and retardation. While the limits were being tested, both by the last pioneering generation on the farms and by the overconfident and often overextended railroads, the era also witnessed the seepage of modernity into the entire region. Automobiles, electricity, radio, the movies, modern hospitals, and college education spread their influence across the Plains, simultaneously bringing hope of a better life from the outside as well as reinforcing how relatively backward many areas on the Plains were by comparison with more settled areas.

In the same period that agricultural science was assisting in diffusing better farming methods applicable to the dry Plains and strong demand and bumper crops produced occasional good economic times, other forces were conspiring to sort out the town system of the Great Plains in an ominous way. The mail-order business, for one, undercut the commerce of local store merchants. The "viability" of farm trade centers across the region became the worrisome watchword of the new rural sociologists, and the first patterns of differential growth between small towns and larger centers became clear. The diffusion of the automobile decreased physical isolation but simultaneously increased the geographical consolidation of retailing and other services in fewer, larger places.

After the Second World War, patterns of small-town decline across the Great Plains intensified, and they have continued unabated to the present. Broad changes in the continental organization of farming, wholesaling, and retailing have produced in this region, as elsewhere, fewer and larger farms, mechanized production requiring less labor, and a steady migration of farm and small-town people to the cities within and beyond the region. Family cars and trucks only permit the heavier concentration of services in a sparser network of towns spaced at ever greater driving distances away.

This fourth period of urban life in the Great Plains has produced, then, an intractable implosion of the region's urban pattern. Generations of investment in town buildings, streets, plantings, special facilities (most forlornly, the schools) lie bleaching under the open prairie skies in numberless towns too small to hold their populations. By the end of the twentieth century, very few towns under 15,000 inhabitants showed any ability to grow, and only cities at the geographical margins or with specific and solid functions such as in government, education, or health seem able to keep pace with national norms. The result is a scramble among the region's cities to chase growth for its own sake, competing within the national urban system for business investments at the risk of their tax base, while midsize cities soak up the small-town migrants discouraged by job losses and limited economic and social horizons in the small towns of their birth. The region is urbanizing at an unprecedented rate (given the ratio of city dwellers to rural residents) while losing the vast majority of its once-urban places. No other region in North America is undergoing quite this transformation. Since midcentury the Plains has been experiencing the "hollowest" era of its urban history, but it may also be qualitatively the best.

The Origins of Individual Urban Places
It is a commonplace to characterize urban life in the Great Plains almost exclusively on the basis of its small towns and to speak of the huge sameness among them as if they differed no more from each other than one generic strip mall from the next. The first tendency likely derives from the fringe position of most of the region's bona fide large cities. Denver is, after all, no more the metropolis of the High Plains portion of eastern Colorado than it is the capital of mountainous western Colorado. Kansas City also serves two regions of different economy and culture. The region's large cities seem more simply members of the national urban system, more preoccupied with global positioning than with representing the interests of their nearby Plains hinterlands, so the "Plains country town" does sterling duty as the "default" urban symbol for the region. But even if this is so, the standard image is misleadingly simplistic. Not all Plains cities and towns were platted by railroad tycoons, milked for their income, and cast to the winds when no longer useful.

A few Plains urban locations can trace their essential locations to early trading posts in the fur trade and forts guarding western trails, and to this day their proximity to water and to suitable crossing points for wheeled traffic explains more fully their specific siting than any subsequent feature. Winnipeg, Manitoba; Edmonton, Alberta; Pierre, South Dakota; Fort Benton, Montana; and Leavenworth, Kansas,

serve as ready examples. To these can be added a number of river towns sited as suitable places for emigrant provisioning and agricultural trade such as Atchison, Lawrence, and Topeka, Kansas. This type is distinguished by huge urban plats designed for speculative land sales and boosterism, and it prefigured those of the railroad era. But even before the railroad arrived, spreading agricultural settlement stimulated the creation of "inland towns" (i.e., located away from navigable rivers), vast numbers of which failed to survive, but a goodly number that did, such as Bottineau and Cando, North Dakota, invariably did so by attracting a railroad.

The railroads greatly augmented the frequency and density of speculative railroad towns on the Plains. Some independent townsite promoters thought it was sufficient to announce the mere existence of town plats on their land, but this rarely sufficed to attract settlers and generally dissuaded railroads. Promotion was most successful when undertaken by the railroads themselves, for they controlled both local land sales and connection with the wider world. The key to understanding the relation of speculative towns to the railroad is the alignment of railroad tracks within the plats; by definition, a railroad town is one wholly oriented to the axis of the rails, with its linear "railroad reserve." All other plan patterns denote some more complicated history of town and railroad.

Two other types of town origin loom large in the Great Plains. Towns founded as county seats declare this fact through the designation of a public square reserved for the county courthouse. Many actual county-seat towns lack such features because they were founded without such ambition, and numerous country towns contain such squares even though political history was not to bless them with

the hoped-for prize. Presence and absence of such prominent elements in the built form of Plains towns echo the history of such aspirations and the geographical pattern of their outcome. In most cases, the primacy of commerce relegated the courthouse square to a peripheral position within the town plan.

Last among the key types of town origins are mining and oil towns. Here the striking features are the often-chaotic patterns produced by boom conditions, especially when aided by restricted sites, such as in the Black Hills of South Dakota. Awkward topography and rapid, unplanned growth have given places like Deadwood and Lead quite singular curving and terraced townscapes. Often, mining settlements were strictly company towns, though such origins did not always guarantee regular plans and coherent development.

Despite the diversity of urban origins, however, their initial distinctions have often barely endured, if at all. Subsequent development has had a way of generalizing if not standardizing the layout and built form as well as the social composition and community dynamics of many Plains towns. This has produced a high degree of geographical homogeneity among them, regardless of function or size, and has encouraged the emergence of a strong urban stereotype of the small town on the Plains.

Urban Roles and Town-Country Relations
This stereotype of the Plains small town transcends population size, although a town's size clearly betrays the accumulation of functions that it performs within the region's urban network. The largest cities on the Plains are the entrepôt towns, "gateway" cities that not only act as bulking and processing centers for crops and livestock raised on the Plains for onward shipment to distant markets in the

Union Pacific Railroad depot (built 1886), looking west, Cheyenne, Wyoming

County courthouse and surrounding business district, Weatherford, Texas

East but also handle through traffic. One cannot stand on the street bridges that pass over the railroad yards in Cheyenne, Wyoming, and Fargo, North Dakota, and fail to appreciate that the Great Plains is a vast transit region, a geographical obstacle to freight passing across the continent from end to end. Such traffic is almost irrelevant to the region, except that its maintenance provides some local jobs. But these gateway cities are more than entrepôts: they are also hubs for people and goods originating and terminating somewhere not too far away on the Plains; most strikingly, now they are portals for air travel.

The purpose of towns and cities on the Plains has always been primarily to organize the export of crops, livestock, and minerals from the region. This necessitates a mostly dispersed rural population to produce the materials and supply centers to provide the essentials of life to that dispersed population. Hence, "shipping" is the key function of all such places, regardless of scale. Location on the transportation arteries of this system has always been the essence of their success, first and last via the railroad system, from the first boisterous frontier cow towns to the prosaic farm or ranch towns of today.

The smallest shipping points represent towns—one can hardly call them that—with a couple of grain elevators, a repair garage perhaps, and a hundred or so residents. Farther up the size scale are towns that can still boast a grocery store, gas station, maybe a bank, and some other businesses and support a population of several hundred. Beyond this, there is one standard function that boosts such towns into another league: a few hundred towns have county-seat status. Serving as centers of county government provides work for a small host of professionals, including engineers, lawyers, accountants, politicians, and office workers whose combined income supports a

thousand residents or more and a correspondingly wider range of stores and other social services. Often, county towns contain courthouses with eye-catching classical or modern architecture: the higher the Plains (i.e., the more westerly the location), the lower the pretension. With just these three lower rungs of the Great Plains urban hierarchy, we have accounted for the vast majority of urban places in the whole region.

Between the small service centers and the gateway cities, the hierarchy supports a few medium-size cities that derive their importance from special functions. These are the state capitals, college towns, and mineral towns that dot the region with a casual regularity. Only five capitals of the ten states with territory in the Great Plains are situated well within the Plains proper. Colleges, particularly public institutions, share with other state facilities such as prisons and medical centers the historical function of ensuring the permanent decentralization of state expenditures. Only the mineral towns, whether mining gold or pumping oil, obey geology and cluster where the deposits have been found, in the Black Hills of South Dakota or the gas and oil fields of the Permian Basin. The size and facilities of all these places with special functions create a different local culture, sometimes more cosmopolitan, sometimes even more tenuous than that of farm and ranch urbanism. Midland, Texas, for example, headquarters of Permian Basin oil power, was obliged to promote itself as a retirement town and convention center due to the decline of oil prices after 1986 and the subsequent contraction of the industry. The future of Lead, South Dakota, is even more precarious, following the announcement in 2000 that its renowned Homestake Gold Mine was phasing out operations.

What is strikingly absent from the Plains, however, is large-scale urban manufacturing.

Early city boosters may have hoped for the expansion of the national manufacturing belt into the region, but its remoteness from the majority of the nation's urban demand guaranteed that it would never really develop heavy industry. Pueblo, Colorado, has had a steel industry since the 1880s, but this is an exception (and even there employment has fallen from more than 9,000 in the 1950s to fewer than 700 in 2000). Manufacturing logic has always placed most final-stage processing and fabrication close to the markets rather than the raw materials. While meatpacking decentralized westward onto the Plains during the twentieth century, attracting especially Latino workers, it does not pack the economic punch of car plants or steelmaking.

People Attracted to Great Plains Towns

Plains towns, like their surrounding rural areas, acquired their early populations from three distinct sources: Indigenous peoples, native-born migrants from the East and Midwest moving farther west, and foreign-born immigrants arriving especially from northern and eastern Europe. Long-established ethnic groups have contributed significant populations to local towns in areas where they have been well represented, such as Native Americans in eastern Montana, North and South Dakota, and Oklahoma, Hispanics in northeastern New Mexico, West Texas, and southeastern Colorado, and African Americans in eastern Oklahoma. American migrants from states to the east have maintained broad though somewhat mixed zones of latitudinal movement, so that settlers of eastern and central Canada, New England, and upper Midwest heritage were more likely to settle on the Northern Plains, those of "North Midland" origin on the Central Plains, and those from the South on the Southern Plains. Into this mixture, Europeans came in large numbers, filling up the open frontier especially in the Prairie Provinces and the Dakotas but also localities farther south, often in response to vigorous promotional efforts.

The "latitudinal" transfer of population to the Canadian Prairies a century ago from Ontario and points east was even more pronounced than south of the border precisely because of the linear structure of Canada's human geography. This was especially so for the English-speaking Canadian and British migrants, who, because of advantages of language and petty capital, could often form a wide and deep small business class that populated the towns of all sizes across the region. Nevertheless, this western border was nonideological and porous, and many settlers of British, Canadian, American, and continental European stock drifted easily back and forth between American Plains and Canadian Prairies.

Over time, there have been subtle shifts in the social composition of Plains towns. Early on, Canadian and American migrants often made up the bulk of the small merchant class because they brought trading experience and some capital to the frontier towns. Slowly, as young country people moved to town, the business class broadened its ethnic complexion, while retired farmers from strongly ethnic country communities added further to the social diversity of the towns. Suggestive is the proportion of businessmen of Norwegian to Anglo stock in three North Dakota counties with strong Norwegian representation, judged by the ethnicity of advertisers in county atlases in the early twentieth century. The Grand Forks County atlas of 1909 contains the names of ninety Anglo businessmen to fifty-three of Norwegian stock, and the McHenry County atlas of 1910 shows forty-seven of Anglo background and thirty of Norwegian stock. By 1929, however, the Bottineau County atlas was listing only thirty-eight Anglo businessmen to seventy-six of Norwegian extraction. Crude though these comparisons are, they lend some credence to the notion that Plains towns gradually extended participation to the would-be entrepreneurs of their hinterlands. Such opportunities often provided staging points for family members to migrate farther up the regional and national urban ladder.

Three Plains Urban Archetypes

The comparative diversity of urban roles performed by towns on the Plains might suggest any number of "typical" towns for the region. The dominating image of the "plains country town," on the other hand, works hard against that. What follows is an attempt to recognize at least a trinity of typical Plains towns, the better to capture some of the diversity already noted while concentrating on characteristics readily apparent to anyone with an attentive eye. Although they are selective, these types—the gateway city, the plains country town, and the ethnic town—exist clearly in the landscape.

THE GATEWAY CITY

It is virtually impossible to approach the Great Plains from either east or west by train today (using what is left of the fabled passenger rail network of bygone days) without passing through one of the region's gateway cities. Even using superhighways, one enters the region by skirting the edges of one or another of these great entrepôts. They have preserved, indeed enhanced, their historic regional roles while adding new ones pertinent to the information age. What do these gateway cities look like, how are they laid out, and what are their distinctive features?

However much the central skyline of the gateway city center resembles that of all other self-respecting American downtowns, with its tall office buildings and hotels, its ring of parking lots, and the awkward architectural remains of a once-thriving shopping district, what typifies the gateway city is the scale and land-use dominance of freight-handling facilities and warehouse districts. Most gateway centers have modernized their transportation zones, placing them recurrently on or near the urban fringe to gain the space for the vast operations needed. These outlying districts are impressive enough, but the long history of transfer functions can be found even closer to

hand, in the near-central railroad depots and brick warehouse districts that still lurk near the old downtown, now often transformed into funky entertainment districts for tourists and locals alike. Many such districts have lost numerous structures, victims of bulldozer redevelopment before old brick became fashionable. But the remaining warehouse quarters of cities such as Omaha, Denver, Fort Worth, Fargo, Cheyenne, and Billings, to name a few, stand as testimony to the specialized role these places have long played in the national system of cities.

The wholesale warehouse districts have always been tied to the railroads, and even today, with the importance of truck shipments and intermodal transport, that link survives intact. Winnipeg boasts a great array of railroad yards and transfer facilities, far more extensive than in most other cities of its population size.

Gateway cities that collect the produce of the corn and wheat belts also sport impressive stands of grain elevators, not just the two or three silos of the country shipping point but huge regiments of cylindrical concrete towers, taller than any office block in town, that march across and blot out the horizon, as in Atchison, Kansas, and Enid, Oklahoma. Gateway towns opposite ranching areas used to boast massive stockyards, such as at Fort Worth and Omaha, but they are now victims of a westward decentralization of slaughtering. Even here, however, the cultural heritage of such facilities lives on in the urban folk life of such places, sustained by the nostalgia of country and western music or perhaps a famed steakhouse.

Not only the physical equipment of railroad and truck transshipment distinguishes these cities but also their historical occupational profiles and still distinctive business and political cultures, with hotels catering to visitors to the cities' wheat exchanges and stockmen's clubs, where deals still get made. In a world of corporate globalism, more of the action is tak-

ing place elsewhere, but the original purposes of these gateway cities have yet to be wholly eclipsed. Many have begun to market their special character for tourists, even at the risk of bowdlerization. But theatrics apart, what remains undisputable about the Plains gateway city is its long involvement in transport, transfer, and storage and its geographical function as the eye of the needle through which all the produce of the Plains is threaded on its way to distant processing and divided profit. The Plains gateway cities are large enough each to have a peculiar morphology, but, at base, the essential features are common to all of their class.

THE PLAINS COUNTRY TOWN

The scale of the Plains country town is personal. It is, in its archetypal form, small enough to be walked through from end to end in a few minutes. It is also virtually predictable in its contents and layout. Whether a "parallel" town, a "T-town" (referring to the axes of railroad reserve and commercial core), or a fusion of the two patterns, the Plains country town is like some outsize combination of a child's erector set, wooden play blocks, and model train layout. Invariably stamped on the prairie as if with a cookie cutter by a railroad department or a speculative land company and named after the railroad's owner or other such chance association, the town pays almost total obeisance to the railroad tracks.

The genre can be encapsulated in its essentials by the case of Bradshaw, Nebraska, in 1889. Founded in 1879 by the Burlington and Missouri River Railroad Company, the town site had a population of 150 residents the very next year. Created to serve the farmers of western York County, about fifty-five miles west of Lincoln, Bradshaw in 1889 offered three grain elevators along the tracks, together with the train depot and a small stockyard. Railway Street ran like a cordon along the railroad reserve, from which sprang Lincoln Street, the business thoroughfare—all one and a half

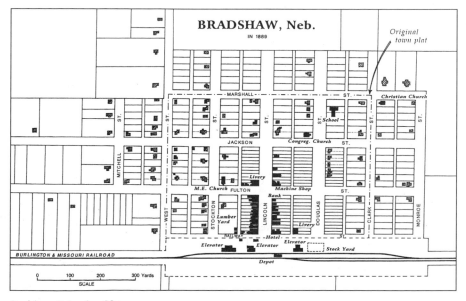

Bradshaw, Nebraska, 1889

blocks of it. There was a lumberyard, a hotel, a bank, two liveries, thirty business buildings, three churches, a school, and eighty-nine residences. Strikingly, while the business district was compact, reflecting the importance for merchants of proximity to the railroad and other businesses, the town's residential space was loose. After only ten years of life and with 112 empty building lots still available in the "Original Town," landowners felt it essential to plat four "additions," more than doubling the lotted area of the town. Forty-one residences lolled over this additional territory, their owners quite unable to contemplate settling on the still vacant land of the Original Town.

Such was the planning and early development history of Bradshaw. Vary the orientation by which the tracks pass through the locality, shift the street alignments accordingly so that they meet at some angle, but no matter what adjustments are made, this is the physical blueprint for tens of thousands of "towns" planted upon the soil of the Great Plains. As speculations, their future was subject to the fortunes of remote markets, railroad politics, and sometimes chicanery, and thousands failed almost before they had started. Importantly, though, here was a model plan, infinitely expandable should the town succeed, simple, orderly, but allowing for the disorder of individual choice, and a perfect mechanism for transferring the risks of urban growth to the shoulders of optimistic settlers while relieving them of a sizable chunk of their initial capital. Town boosting had long become a high art in American life by the time the Plains were settled, and its exquisite delineation on the ground can be found right here. Bradshaw in 1889, even in its elegant simplicity, was a cipher for all the utilitarian philosophy of urbanism that played itself out like a hapless tide across the Great Plains.

THE ETHNIC TOWN

The ethnic town or, more often, village is the third recurrent urban archetype of the Great Plains. Consistent with the small scale of most "urban" places on the Plains, many small urban centers have emerged and even survived as de facto ethnic towns, representative of the high concentration of ethnic settlement in the surrounding countryside, sometimes even remaining virtually exclusive to one group. The larger cities have developed their varied neighborhoods of immigrant complexion, from Calgary to Kansas City, but these seem little different from those of big cities all over the nation. It is precisely on the Plains proper, where the relative recency of concentrated ethnic settlement has preserved a sharper ethnic imprint on the landscape than in most older sections of the two countries, that one can find still viable, if not always vibrant, ethnic towns. Their comparative isolation favored slower national integration, and some groups have resisted assimilation through various habits and attitudes, hence the survival to this day of numerous small but stubbornly distinctive and self-conscious ethnic enclaves throughout the Great Plains.

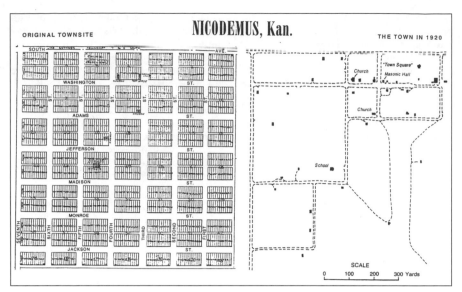

Nicodemus, Kansas

The Canadian Prairies and the Northern Plains of the United States stand out in this respect, given their availability for settlement during the last great tides of agrarian immigration from central, eastern, and northern Europe around the turn of the twentieth century. From the Ukrainian, German, Scandinavian, and French Canadian tracts around Edmonton to the Doukhobor districts north of Saskatoon and the French Canadian and Mennonite settlements in the southern and western hinterlands of Winnipeg, small urban centers with names like Wostok, St. Alphonse, and Halbstadt dot the western Canadian landscape. In their churches and ethnic business names, if not always in other features, they display their ethnic affiliation, indeed, their urban purpose. Farther south, the pattern is repeated from North Dakota to central Kansas and even in Oklahoma and Texas. Few travelers can fail to observe the Native American characteristics of towns serving Indian populations in Oklahoma such as Okmulgee, where the old Creek Council House graces the courthouse square, or Tahlequah, where street signs are bilingual. Likewise, the cultural character of the Volga German communities of Ellis County, Kansas, finds expression in the unexpected and strikingly tall Catholic church steeples of Pfeifer, Liebenthal, St. Catharine, and, most dramatically, the "Cathedral of the Plains" at Victoria (Herzog).

Nicodemus, Kansas, stands as a celebrated all-black town settled by "Exodusters" in 1877. Founded as a speculative town site to attract blacks from the South, it was paired as a business enterprise with Hill City, a town twelve miles to the west in Graham County intended for white settlers. Twelve years later, the Union Pacific Railroad bypassed Nicodemus and connected Hill City, which consequently became the county seat. Thereafter, Nicodemus stagnated, losing most of its businesses to nearby Bogue and to Hill City. Notable are Nicodemus's long but narrow town lots, which measure 25 by 160 feet. The modal urban lot width in the Great Plains is closer to 50 feet.

While Hill City also has 25-foot-wide lots, the early town plan there included city blocks reserved for a school and a courthouse, amenities lacking in the Nicodemus plan, the purest expression of monetized land. While Nicodemus never filled up the plat, it hung on as a social center for the surrounding African American farming community and in 1976 was designated a national historic landmark for its significance in interpreting the nation's cultural heritage. To this day, Emancipation Day is celebrated on the informal "town square."

City Building and Urban Culture

The progress of American urbanism in the Great Plains is measured for the most part in the diffusion of amenities, technical accomplishments, and stylistic fashions over time from the largest trendsetting metropolises of the nation—New York, Chicago, St. Louis, and their ilk—to the gateway cities and medium-size centers of the region. It is hardly to be expected that great new urban innovations would emanate from the modest cities of the Plains. Nevertheless, Plains urbanism was developed in the late nineteenth century by the most routinized and relentless booster program up to that period. Because the Great Plains was so vast and seemingly so underdeveloped, boosting was particularly required in order to steer capital into the region and attract settlers.

In some ways, Plains urban centers were designed and built with "cutting-edge" concepts on a tabula rasa. Even today, commercial districts and residential sections reflect the new norms of building technology, design, and furnishings current during the period from the 1890s through the 1920s. Since the first wooden merchant structures lasted at least a few years, most of the more substantial buildings that replaced them came in the twentieth century. Where high-rise business structures were built, they sported the new wide, Chicago-style windows that let in light rather than the narrow, New York–influenced vertical windows long popular in the East. Residences featured the latest in standard manufactured design, and Plains towns must account for a disproportionate national share of the mail-order homes shipped by Sears, Roebuck and Company and its competitors.

Occasionally, Plains cities claimed national attention for some avant-garde creation, which is best illustrated in the case of two state capitols. By 1918 Nebraska's capitol was deemed insufficient, and, following a national competition won by Bertram Grosvenor Goodhue, in 1922 construction began on the present mini-dome-capped skyscraper edifice, with Art Deco decoration produced by local artists. North Dakota followed in 1931, when fire destroyed the existing traditional capitol, opting for a spartan, slablike office high-rise building designed by a consortium of local and Chicago architects. Such choices reflect the ethos of modernity that was permeating the Plains in the early twentieth century and a certain rejection of unnecessary frills in favor of functionalism. By and large, however, such banner projects found few echoes in the private sector, and on the residential front, most urban neighborhoods, of whatever social class, have tended to exude a comfortable, traditional normality of external appearance while displaying internal modernity in proportion to economic capacity. Much of this stems from the relative homogeneity of income in Plains towns, where the extremes of urban wealth generated by high industrialism have generally been absent or muted. Only the banker's house, the doctor's house, and the funeral home stand out as conspicuous ornaments in many a Plains country town. And only rarely does a public building seek to astound, as the Corn Palace in Mitchell, South Dakota, in a folksy way surely does.

In public infrastructure, Plains cities have performed close to the national average for their size. A late start in city building for most towns meant that the thresholds of population needed to capitalize services such as electric power plants, street railways, telephones, and modern hospitals kept these places from being precocious centers of innovation. But in terms of their own development, many such services came sooner in the experience of residents than they had in older cities. Street railways are a good indicator: while Plains cities were not innovators in this realm, they adopted the technology with eagerness. Street railways came early in the individual history of Plains towns because their fast initial growth promised the patronage needed to sustain the railways. Installations were so numerous in towns below 5,000 population, however, that many failed and caused the towns to wait a number of years before reinstallation was successful. In other respects, urban centers on the Plains generally attempted to participate in urbanistic novelties in proportion to their size and enterprise. Most cities of any size, for example, display some of the boulevards and curving drives so fashionable in the trendsetting metropolises of the East and Far West, even if on a modest or token scale.

Generalizations

Risking dispute through inevitable selectivity, several generalizations about urbanism in the Great Plains might be proposed here. First, the past is still young in Plains towns and cities, and it is not very important while economic growth is apparent. The past becomes more important when growth subsides and economic stress increases, because it offers a validation of prior accomplishments and a means to recapitalize the built environment through historic preservation and tourist edification. Some of the striking public sculpture to be found in some Plains towns featuring heroic ox teams plowing the prairies (in Fargo, North Dakota) or cowboys herding steers (Billings, Montana, and Dodge City, Kansas) now seeks to develop this urban theme.

Second, in county seats on the Plains, government functions are generally secondary to commercial ones, so it is very rare, in contrast to such places in older sections of the nation, to find the courthouse square the central focus of the town; rather, it is the railroad and its shipping facilities that define the town and attract the business district, leaving the civil government precinct well off to the side in the town plat.

Third, the size and variety of urban equipment in the Great Plains is inversely proportional to altitude. Generally, the farther west towns are located, the more limited are the size, number, and architectural pretension of their business buildings and government installations. In western North Dakota, for example, some county courthouses are almost indistinguishable from neighboring real estate agencies and grocery stores. In the western Canadian north–south corridor from Edmonton to Lethbridge, however, many quite pretentious public buildings stand in contrast to this rule.

Fourth, the formal urban threshold is set comparatively low in the Great Plains, and for historical reasons. Incorporation laws in several Plains states, for example, permit places to be regarded as "cities" at population levels far below the national norm. Kansas provides the most extreme case, allowing settlements of as small as 300 inhabitants to incorporate as cities. Elsewhere in the modern world, such places would be considered mere hamlets or villages. Indeed, even in Kansas they are usually that, despite their legal status.

Fifth, many rim cities and state and provincial capitals are prominent in service functions such as health facilities, insurance companies, and educational campuses, drawing from sometimes-enormous tributary areas. Billings, Montana, offers hospital facilities that would scarcely be found in cities of comparable size in, say, Illinois, because distances on the Plains are so large and such cities few and far between. Conversely, and sixth, trans-shipment and wholesale activities are more significant than manufacturing. This imbalance suggests the extent to which Plains urban centers are more dependent on the outside world than those in denser settled regions, a characteristic once shared with the traditional South but no longer.

Seventh, all cities and towns actually on the Plains are close to the countryside, in a mental sense, through their intimate economic ties and the remoteness of sophisticated urban distractions. A broadly engendered "small-town *mentalité*" exists even in the larger centers, reinforced by migration patterns from the rural areas and knowledge of their rural constituencies' demands for cultural inspiration.

Lastly, Great Plains urbanism is a kind of derivative and dependent urbanism. There is comparatively little that was, or is, original, self-sustaining, or generative about urban life in the Great Plains. In terms of the two nation-states across which the Great Plains extend, their urban landscapes reflect classically those of internal colonization. Nevertheless, they represent an extraordinary production of urban life across a vast land.

See also AFRICAN AMERICANS: Exodusters / ARCHITECTURE: Grain Elevators; Nebraska State Capitol; Public Buildings; Warehouse Districts / EUROPEAN AMERICANS: Settlement Patterns, Canada; Settlement Patterns, United States / IMAGES AND ICONS: Corn Palace; Deadwood, South Dakota / PHYSICAL ENVIRONMENT: Palliser's Triangle / TRANSPORTATION: Railroads, United States; Railways, Canada.

Michael P. Conzen
University of Chicago

Artibise, Alan F., ed. *Town and City: Aspects of Western Canadian Urban Development*. Regina: University of Regina, Canadian Plains Research Center, 1981. Bennett, John W., and Seena B. Kohl. *Settling the Canadian-American West, 1890–1915: Pioneer Adaptation and Community Building: An Anthropological History*. Lincoln: University of Nebraska Press, 1995. Hamilton, Kenneth Marvin. *Black Towns and Profit: Promotion and Development in the Trans-Appalachian West, 1877–1915*. Urbana: University of Illinois Press, 1991. Haywood, C. Robert. *Victorian West: Class and Culture in Kansas Cattle Towns*. Lawrence: University Press of Kansas, 1991. Hudson, John C. *Plains Country Towns*. Minneapolis: University of Minnesota Press, 1985. Melnyk, Bryan P. *Calgary Builds: The Emergence of an Urban Landscape, 1905–1914*. Calgary: Alberta Culture, Canadian Plains Research Centre, 1985. Mothershead, Harmon. "River Town Rivalry for the Overland Trade." *Overland Journal* 7 (1989): 14–23. Nelson, Paula M. *After the West Was Won: Homesteaders and Townbuilders in Western South Dakota, 1900–1917*. Iowa City: University of Iowa Press, 1986. Reps, John W. *Cities of the American West: A History of Frontier Urban Planning*. Princeton NJ: Princeton University Press, 1979. Schellenberg, James A. *Conflict between Communities: American County Seat Wars*. New York: Paragon House, 1987. Stock, Catherine McNicol. *Main Street in Crisis: The Great Depression and the Old Middle Class on the Northern Plains*. Chapel Hill: University of North Carolina Press, 1992. Tauxe, Caroline S. *Farms, Mines, and Main Streets: Uneven Development in a Dakota County*. Philadelphia: Temple University Press, 1993. Toms, Donald D. *The Flavor of Lead: An Ethnic History*. Lead SD: Lead Historic Preservation Commission, 1992. West, Carroll Van. *Capitalism on the Frontier: Billings and the Yellowstone Valley in the Nineteenth Century*. Lincoln: University of Nebraska Press, 1993. Wetherell, Donald G., and Irene R. A. Kmet. *Town Life: Main Street and the Evolution of Small Town Alberta*. Edmonton: University of Alberta Press, 1995.

ABILENE, TEXAS

Abilene, Texas, a town of 117,111 in 1999, is located 150 miles west of Fort Worth at the junction of Interstate 20 and U.S. Highways 277 and 83. It was one of many towns that came into existence as the Texas and Pacific Railway made its way west to California. What made Abilene different from and more successful than other railroad towns was the aggressiveness of the people who lived there. From the beginning, they promoted Abilene as the "Future Great City of West Texas." Local ranchers and businessmen C. W. Merchant, John Merchant, John N. Simpson, and John T. Berry persuaded H. C. Withers, town-site locator for the railroad, to select a site in northeastern Taylor County for the new town, ignoring the already established community and county seat, Buffalo Gap. A tent city of 300 was already established when the first town lots were auctioned on March 15, 1881. Some 200 people spent $51,000 to become a part of the new city. Before long, Abilene had two newspapers, an imported sheriff (John J. Clinton from Dodge City, Kansas), public schools, and churches. In 1883 Abilene won the election to become the new county seat.

Religion has always been an important part of the community. In 1891 the first of three church-related universities, Simmons College (later Hardin-Simmons University), was established. Abilene Christian University originally opened in 1906 as Childers Classical Institute and was followed in 1923 by McMurry University. Subsequently, they were joined by branches of Cisco College and Texas State Technical College. The abundance of Christian universities has led some to say that Abilene is the buckle on the Bible Belt of the South. There is no doubt that the universities have had their impact on the city; they are a major economic asset and help make Abilene an education center.

In the late nineteenth century, as the Texas Plains were being settled, Abilene boosters unashamedly promoted their city, running promotional trains from Fort Worth to give people the opportunity to settle in this "Eden of the West." This boosterism made Abilene the center of what is called today the "Big Country." By the early twentieth century, Abilene had developed an ample water supply, public utilities, streetcars, and a fairly dependable economy based on farming and ranching, including sheep. The Abilene Epileptic Asylum, known today as the Abilene State School, was built in 1899 and, along with the West Texas Rehabilitation Center and two major hospitals, made Abilene a major medical center for the region. Abilene also quickly developed into a center for wholesale and retail trade, transportation, media, and cultural events as well as the headquarters for independent oil operators after the oil boom of the 1920s, which had more than doubled the population to 23,175 by 1930.

However, it was World War II that put Abilene on the map. The arrival of Camp Barkeley and Tye Army Air Field in 1940 brought 1.5 million soldiers as well as millions of dollars into the city. The closing of Barkeley at the end of World War II spurred civic leaders to diversify Abilene's economic base, but they never lost sight of what a military installation had done for the economy. In 1952 their lobbying efforts proved successful when Congress approved the construction of Dyess Air Force Base in Abilene. The air force base, along with the Nike and Atlas missile installations in the early sixties, put Abilene into another economic boom that only temporarily subsided in the late sixties before resuming once again during the oil crisis of the 1970s. The oil industry stimulated a rapid growth in manufacturing, banking, and construction. Oil, however, has always been a fickle economic base, and declining prices in the 1980s once again set Abilene scrambling to shore up its economic livelihood.

In the 1990s Abilene turned the declining downtown area into a historic district, anchored by the Grace Cultural Center and Museums of Abilene complex and promoted by an art walk. Old railroad buildings have been transformed into a restaurant, candy factory, and tourist information and Chamber of Commerce center. Minor-league baseball and hockey teams have complemented the strong Abilene Philharmonic Orchestra, opera association, ballet company, and theater groups as entertainment attractions. The LaJet Classic, held at the Fairway Oaks Golf and Racquet Club since 1981, was on the PGA tour for about ten years. The Abilene Convention Center brings all types of organizations to the downtown area, while the Taylor County Coliseum has become the center for horse shows and rodeos. The ruins of Fort Phantom Hill north of Abilene and Buffalo Gap Historic Village just south of the city add to the cultural attractions.

B. W. Aston
Hardin-Simmons University

Downs, Fane, ed. *The Future Great City of West Texas, Abilene, 1881–1981.* Abilene TX: Richardson, 1981. Duff, Katharyn, and Betty Kay Seibt. *Catclaw Country: An Informal History of Abilene in West Texas.* Burnet TX: Eakin, 1980. Lack, Paul, Paul Jungmeyer, Robert Sledge, and Fane Downs. *The History of Abilene.* Abilene TX: McMurry, 1981.

ALL-BLACK TOWNS

See AFRICAN AMERICANS: All-Black Towns

AMARILLO, TEXAS

Located in the center of the Texas Panhandle, Amarillo, with a population of almost 175,000 in 2000, straddles the Potter and Randall county line and serves as the seat of government for Potter County. The population is 77 percent white, 15 percent Latino, 6 percent African American, and a small percentage of other groups. It is a marketing point for cattle, wheat, corn, sorghum, natural gas, oil, and helium. Amarillo is a crossroads and has served that function throughout its history.

When the Fort Worth and Denver Railway, after a delay during the depression of the 1870s, resumed its northwestward march into the Texas Panhandle, James T. Berry, a real estate promoter, led a group of merchants from Colorado City to establish a new town site along the railroad route. In 1887 they laid out a grid of streets near Amarillo Lake, also known as Wild Horse Lake. At first called Oneida, the town's name was soon changed to Amarillo, which means "yellow" in Spanish. Supposedly, Spanish shepherds or traders had previously named the area for an abundance of yellow flowers or perhaps for the yellow soil of the creek banks. Local cowboys, having been promised a town lot by Berry, cast the decisive votes for Amarillo as the new county seat on August 30, 1887. This political designation, along with the railroad and the supply of water, gave Amarillo the necessities of life.

The railroad arrived in 1887, bringing merchants, cattle buyers, and settlers. By 1890 Amarillo was one of the world's busiest cattle-shipping points. The town site lay on low ground, however, and after soaking rains in the spring of 1889 the town was moved to a higher location established by rancher Henry B. Sanborn and barbed wire–fencing magnate Joseph F. Glidden. The railroad opened a second depot, and voters transferred the county seat in 1893. Citizens incorporated the town in 1899 and established a council-manager form of city government in 1913, a system used to the present day.

Amarillo continued to grow. Three more rail lines had arrived by 1903. In the first decade of the twentieth century Amarillo acquired a hospital, an independent school district, an electric service, a trolley system, a public library, and a rowdy bowery. Although the population reached 9,957 in 1910, it was still a raw town, as Mary H. Turner of Chicago observed in 1902. Men spoke only about the cattle business; there were no sidewalks and no trees; rattlesnakes sunned themselves on the small golf course; and a black bull wandering the streets opened home fence gates in order to eat the planted flowers.

Oil explorers found natural gas near Amarillo in 1918 and petroleum in 1921. The nearby Cliffside gas field, with its high natural helium content, began producing in 1927 and resulted in the construction of a federal government helium plant four miles west of town. The government produced the inert gas until 1970, when an excess of helium in the nation made production unnecessary. Amarillo still bills itself as the "Helium Capital of the World." After the dust storms and poverty of the Great Depression, World War II brought economic relief in 1942 with the opening of the Amarillo Army Air Force Field for training pilots and the nearby Pantex Ordnance Plant for producing bombs. The airfield closed in 1946, reopened in 1951, and then closed again in 1968. The federal government converted the Pantex plant in 1951 to the production and deconstruction of chemical and nuclear explosives. Fears about radioactive poisoning and reports of unsafe environmental conditions have resulted in occasional protests and have left a shadow of concern that remains to the present time. Still, the Pantex plant was Amarillo's largest employer, and there has been relatively little pressure on Pantex to prioritize environmental protection.

After a decline in population of 8 percent following the closing of the airfield, Amarillo's population had rebounded to 149,230 by 1980. In 1971 the city took over a part of the airfield for an airport, which is now served by six passenger airlines, and Interstates 40 and 27 now traverse the city, dividing it into quarters. Natural gas, petroleum, cattle, agriculture, and transportation remain Amarillo's main economic supports.

David G. McComb
Colorado State University

Henderson, H. Allen. "Amarillo, Texas." In *The New Handbook of Texas*, edited by Ron Tyler. Austin: Texas State Historical Association, 1996: 1: 140–42. Key, Della Tyler. *In the Cattle Country: History of Potter County*. Amarillo: Tyler-Berkley, 1961. Price, B. Byron, and Frederick W. Rathjen. *The Golden Spread*. Northridge CA: Windsor Publications, 1986.

BILLINGS, MONTANA

Billings, located in south-central Montana, is the state's largest city, with a population of 89,847 in 2000. Billings is the seat of Yellowstone County (2000 population, 129,351). To the north of the city stands the Rimrocks, a sandstone formation that rises approximately 300 feet above the Yellowstone valley; to the south lies the Yellowstone River. With abundant game and the Yellowstone River, the site of present-day Billings was a center for hunting and trading well before homesteaders established a permanent settlement there in 1877. The original town of Coulson was served by steamship but was overshadowed when a town site was chosen along the newly developed Northern Pacific Railroad in 1881. The city was named for Frederick Billings, president of the Northern Pacific Railroad. Early historical figures include Calamity Jane and Wild Bill Hickok.

As the largest city within a 500-mile radius, Billings is a major regional service center for the Northern Plains and Rocky Mountains. Economic activities include medical and retail services, oil refining, agricultural processing, telecommunications, and tourism. Educational institutions include Montana State University–Billings and Rocky Mountain College. Billings is also the location of regional offices of federal and state agencies.

Billings and Yellowstone County have experienced substantial growth in recent years, predominantly on limited available river valley farmland. In general, environmental issues, including land use, water resources, and wildlife management, are controversial. City and county governments are challenged by the prospects of planning and growth management in a state with little historic success in those endeavors. In addition to low-density suburban development on the city's edge, downtown Billings experienced significant redevelopment in the 1990s after a two-decade decline in retail and business activities. The city center is now home to numerous art galleries, museums, and restaurants.

Annual events include the North American

Livestock Exposition and the Montana Fair, the largest annual agricultural fair in the state. Billings is home to several museums. The Western Heritage Center, a regional history museum, is located in the original Parmly Billings Library building, a structure that was designed by the Frederick Billings family to replicate the library at the University of Vermont. The Peter Yegen Jr. County Museum, which focuses on frontier history, is located at the top of the Rimrock cliffs, immediately adjacent to Billings Logan International Airport. The recently renovated and expanded Yellowstone Art Museum is located in the former county jail and is one of the largest contemporary art museums in the western United States.

Attractions within an hour's drive of Billings include the Pryor and the Beartooth Mountains, the Little Bighorn Battlefield National Monument, the Bighorn National Recreation Area, Pictograph Cave State Park, and Chief Plenty Coups State Park. Thirty miles east of Billings stands Pompeys Pillar National Monument, where William Clark chiseled his first initial, last name, and the date, July 25, 1806, in the sandstone formation. This is the only remaining physical evidence of the Lewis and Clark Expedition. The site is owned by the Bureau of Land Management and has been recommended for status as a national monument.

See also MEDIA: *Billings Gazette.*

Mark Guizlo
Montana State University–Billings

Small, Lawrence. *A Century of Politics on the Yellowstone*. Billings MT: Rocky Mountain College, 1983. West, Carol Van. *Capitalism on the Frontier: Billings and the Yellowstone Valley in the Nineteenth Century*. Lincoln: University of Nebraska Press, 1993. Winks, Robin. *Frederick Billings: A Life*. New York: Oxford University Press, 1991.

BISMARCK, NORTH DAKOTA

The capital of North Dakota and seat of Burleigh County, Bismarck is located in the south-central part of the state on the eastern bank of the Missouri River. Its sister city, Mandan, is situated on the opposite western shore in Morton County. Though originally a rich agricultural center and regional river and railroad transportation hub, during the last quarter of the twentieth century Bismarck evolved into a diversified regional medical, governmental, industrial, and technological center.

Bismarck was founded in 1873, the child of both Missouri River steamboat transportation and late-nineteenth-century Great Plains railroad expansion. Originally called The Crossing, the town was a strategically located port for steamboats, which carried upriver immigrants, and military supplies. In 1872 Camp Greeley (later Camp Hancock) was built by the military as a warehouse and supply depot for troops that were protecting the Northern Pacific Railroad survey crews. Indeed, the town was at one time named Edwinton after the railroad's first chief engineer, Edwin Johnson. However, the financially distressed railroad's need to attract German bond investors induced the railroad's board of directors in 1873 to rename the city Bismarck in honor

of Germany's "Iron Chancellor," Otto von Bismarck-Schönhausen.

Bismarck was named the capital of Dakota Territory in 1883, and when Congress passed the 1889 Omnibus Bill, dividing the territory into North and South Dakota, the city became the capital of the new state. The city was officially incorporated in 1875, adopted the commission governing structure in 1913, and began operating under a home rule charter in 1986.

Bismarck grew from a Dakota river town of 1,200 in 1874 to a metropolitan center with a population of 55,532 in 2000. Much of the recent growth has centered around the city's development into a regional health center, with two major hospitals, allied and independent clinics, health-care services, and nursing and elder-care facilities. The next largest employers are federal, state, county, and city governments. Bismarck also functions as a wholesale and retail center, serving a trade area of a 100-mile radius with more than 170,000 customers. The city's growing technology and energy industries are other major employers.

Bismarck has also become a regional education center, with a comprehensive two-year college, Bismarck State College, the Benedictine-founded University of Mary, and an intertribal United Tribes Technical College. In addition to these institutions, there are two colleges of nursing, a school of respiratory care and radiological technology, a university graduate center, and the Bismarck campus of the University of North Dakota School of Medicine.

Long the center of state politics, Bismarck is home to the state's Heritage Center, the law library, the penitentiary, and the Bank of North Dakota. The bank, chartered in 1919 to promote the state's agriculture, commerce, and industry, is the nation's only state-owned bank. Bismarck's most recent national accomplishment was being named an all-American city in 1997.

Bismarck offers a wealth of cultural organizations and activities for its citizens, including an arts and galleries association, art schools, summer musical productions, amateur theater, a symphony orchestra, dance studios, men's and women's choruses, and a national tribal powwow. The city owns and manages 2,525 acres of park facilities, including forty-eight parks, thirty miles of recreational trails, and one of the nation's fifty Millennium Legacy Trails.

Bismarck's historical connections with the Custer legacy center on its proximity to his command post at Fort Abraham Lincoln and its status as the port for the famous steamboat, the *Far West*, whose epic journey to transport the wounded from the Little Bighorn battlefield in 1876, a distance of 900 miles in fifty-four hours, stands unrivaled in Missouri River steamboating history.

See also MEDIA: *Bismarck Tribune.*

J. Michael McCormack
Bismarck State College

Bird, George F., and Edwin J. Taylor Jr. *History of the City of Bismarck: The First 100 Years, 1872–1972*. Bismarck ND: Bis-

marck Centennial Association, 1972. Bismarck-Mandan
North Dakota Community Profile. Bismarck: Bismarck-
Mandan Area Chamber of Commerce, 2000. Robinson,
Elwyn B. *History of North Dakota.* Lincoln: University of
Nebraska Press, 1966.

BRANDON, MANITOBA

Brandon, the "Wheat City," is located on the Assiniboine River in southwestern Manitoba. It is the second largest urban place in Manitoba. Although Manitoba was founded in 1870, the current site of Brandon as well as most of its hinterland were not included in the province until expansion took place in 1881. This territorial growth was closely related to the building across the Prairies of the Canadian Pacific Railway. Incorporated in 1882, Brandon was founded in May 1881 as a divisional point by the railway's Gen. Thomas Rosser.

Brandon grew rapidly, reaching a population of 15,000 by World War I. Following the initial boom, growth was slow but steady, the population total reaching 20,000 only in the late 1940s and just under 40,000 by 1996. However, recent developments have led to a projected population of 45,000—and even 50,000 by some boosters—in the next few years.

Brandon has principally acted as a service center for its agricultural hinterland. It has never had any of the advantages for manufacturing that are noted by location theorists. Many of the industries such as flour milling that were built during the early growth period were closely related to the agricultural base. This trend has continued to the present. Simplot Chemicals and Ayerst Organics have boosted the industrial sector in Brandon, and the opening of a huge pork-processing plant by Maple Leaf led to the recent boosting of Brandon's population projections.

Politically, Brandon can be characterized as a rather conservative city within a more conservative area of the province. However, in the recent past the city has acted more like Winnipeg and other Manitoba urban areas in its electoral behavior. In 1969 the New Democratic Party won the provincial riding of Brandon East and added the other city riding of Brandon West. Although later this seat reverted to the Progressive Conservative Party, the New Democratic Party won both Brandon East and Brandon West when it swept back into provincial power in 1999.

The future of Brandon seems more secure than that of many of the surrounding smaller settlements, as it is likely to continue to grow in population as well as to continue to dominate its trade area of approximately 200,000 people, which it serves as a service and education center. In this context, Brandon University, Assiniboine Community College, a federal experimental farm, and an Agricultural Extension Center are valuable assets, along with various other branches of the provincial government. Brandon is trying to improve its image as a pleasant place to live and as a place in which to retire. It is also trying to attract tourists by developing a parks and recreation area along the Assiniboine River.

Calgary, Alberta

As the face of agriculture changes regionally, it is possible that "Wheat City" will become a misnomer and that "Pork City" might become more appropriate. For the most part, however, the face that Brandon presents to the world is likely to change more in detail than in grand sweep.

John C. Everitt
Brandon University

Welsted, John, John Everitt, and Christoph Stadel, eds. *Brandon: Geographical Perspectives on the Wheat City.* Regina: University of Regina, Canadian Plains Research Center, 1988. Welsted, John, John Everitt, and Christoph Stadel, eds. *The Geography of Manitoba: Its Land and Its People.* Winnipeg: University of Manitoba Press, 1997.

CALGARY, ALBERTA

The administrative city of Calgary had a population of 876,519 in April 2001, with another 70,000 in the surrounding metropolitan area. Calgary has been one of the fastest growing centers in Canada, increasing from 139,000 in 1951 to 403,000 in 1971, 592,000 in 1981, and 711,000 in 1991. In the 1996–2001 period the city grew by more than 109,000 people, two-thirds of whom were in-migrants. It is now Canada's sixth largest metropolitan area and second largest in area, covering 278.5 square miles.

The city owes its origin to the fort established by the North-West Mounted Police in 1875 at the confluence of the Bow and Elbow Rivers near the junction of the Prairie grasslands and the forested Foothills belt fringing the Rocky Mountains. Calgary occupies an area of mainly flat postglacial lake deposits at a height of 3,400 feet downtown, with relief provided by the scarps of the incised river valleys and glacial overflow channels and the eastern outliers of the Foothills belt. The city has a cold and dry continental interior climate—the typical Calgary day has an open blue sky, and the mean precipitation level is only fourteen inches. Locally, the altitude, which reduces summer temperatures and the number of frost-free days, and warm chinook winds, which moderate the cold winter climate, also exert their influence.

The transcontinental Canadian Pacific Railway reached Calgary in 1883, creating a small service center that was incorporated as a town in 1884. Despite its designation as a city in 1896, the center only contained 4,000 people by 1901, since most of the surrounding area was still sparsely populated and dominated by large cattle ranches to the west. The influx of pioneering farming families led to Calgary's first major boom as a regional service center based on agricultural processing and railway marshaling industries. A central business area emerged, with buildings built of distinctive local sandstones. By 1911 the population had reached almost 44,000 and a decade later was over 63,000, making Calgary the eighth largest city in Canada.

The discovery in 1914 of the Turner Valley gas and oil field, thirty miles to the southwest, led to Calgary's rise as the administrative center of the industry. Major oil and gas discoveries in other parts of Alberta after World War II fueled a boom in the industry, but the head offices remained in Calgary despite the expanded national and international roles of the oil companies. The result is that Calgary has always had a significant role as a corporate headquarters center. The city is home to 103 of the top 800 companies in Canada, as ranked by revenue, compared to greater Toronto with 234, greater Montreal with 104, and Vancouver with 51. Most of these head offices and their ancillary companies in law, finance, geology, surveying, and transportation remain downtown, along with government offices and other service industries. Hence Calgary's city center—a distinctive modern high-rise complex with 32 million square feet of office space and more than 106,000 workers—has remained the city's primary center of employment.

Calgary's government structure consists of an elected mayor and fourteen councilors elected on a ward basis. Calgary's concentrated high-rise downtown contrasts dramatically with the low-density sprawl of the rest of the city, which explains why the city has the highest per capita car ownership and gas consumption in Canada. Yet strong planning controls by its unicity government structure have meant that suburban residential development has been based on detailed community plans for more than forty years. A distinctive feature of Calgary's suburban development has been the creation of residential areas anchored by a recreational complex, nine built around artificial lakes and six around golf courses. The city also has more than 130 residential community associations, most of which have their own community halls. Although these associations occupy a relatively small role in most people's lives, they are routinely consulted on planning developments, and they play an active role in recreational and social provision. When added to the participation of the Calgarians in other associations, the city has produced one of the highest levels of citizen volunteerism in cities in the Western world.

In view of the corporate basis of the city, it is not surprising to find that its employment structure is dominated by services: in 1996 only 9.4 percent of employed people were in manufacturing, 6.7 percent in construction, and 12.0 percent in transportation and communication. Most of the industrial activity is located in a distinctive sector extending southeast from the inner city. The oil industry has attracted one of the highest concentrations of computer power on the continent, which has stimulated a rapidly growing electronic- and technology-based sector, with more than 30,000 jobs. Another important amenity is the University of Calgary, which had a student enrollment of 24,000 and an external research budget close to $100 million in 2000. The 1990s also saw the city develop as a transportation and depot hub for western Canada, although it no longer has a regular passenger rail service. Its airport, with more than seven million passengers per year, is the fourth largest in Canada.

Calgary has traditionally been peopled by immigrants of British and Irish descent, who accounted for 83.6 percent of the population by 1921. There was also a strong American presence, since 21 percent of Alberta's residents at the time were born in the United States and had joined the pioneering rush to the Canadian Prairies. Americans were also attracted to the oil industry, both in an administrative capacity and in exploration and production. After World War II the ethnic balance changed as new immigrants from western and northern Europe moved to the city. By 1971 only 56 percent of the residents had a British Isles ethnic background, another 21 percent were of German, Scandinavian, and Dutch origin, while 3.9 percent and 2.4 percent were of Ukrainian and Italian origin, respectively. Since the 1980s the immigration streams have altered again. The 1996 federal census revealed that 20.8 percent of the city's population was born outside Canada, and a third of this number come from a variety of Asian countries. The largest Asian group, numbering approximately 50,000 in 1996, are the Chinese. Most are scattered throughout the city, although there is still a significant concentration in a redeveloped Chinatown on the edge of downtown that contains a large number of restaurants, businesses, high-rises, and a re-creation of Beijing's Temple of Heaven as a cultural center.

The proximity of the city to the Rocky Mountains and its national parks means that Calgary has become a gateway for recreational visits to the area. In addition, the Winter Olympics of 1988 gave the city world exposure and left a significant heritage in world-class winter sports facilities in the city and vicinity. The presence of a ranching industry in the foothills to the west provides a link to the past, but the ranching economy of the city has long since disappeared. However, the annual Calgary Stampede is still a major presence that keeps the heritage alive. During Stampede week the majority of people in the city, whatever their ethnic heritage and occupation, take pride in dressing up in cowboy costumes, giving the city a distinctive if invented tradition and character. This image has been enhanced by the recent development of Spruce Meadows, just outside the city boundary to the south, which now hosts some of the world's premier horse jumping events.

The annual re-creation of Calgary's cowboy past may provide an easily recognizable image but should not be allowed to conceal the city's true character of a modern, affluent, corporate metropolis. It has virtually no slum areas, a 68 percent home ownership figure, one of the highest rates of postsecondary educated people in Canada, and a median annual income of $50,000 per census family in 1996. Calgary is also characterized by large amounts of recreational space, especially along the major rivers and in a series of parks, of which Nose Hill is the largest. Calgary's recent growth has made it a demographically young city, and only 8.7 percent of the population is over sixty-five years of age. The result is a dynamic and increasingly cosmopolitan center, a city with high levels of amenity but one still intimately linked to the oil and gas industry, despite recent trends in economic diversification.

See also ASIAN AMERICANS: Calgary Chinatown / SPORTS AND RECREATION: Calgary Winter Olympics.

Wayne K. D. Davies
University of Calgary

Bradley, Andrew. *Calgary: A Photographic Essay*. Canmore, Alberta: Altitude Publishing Canada Ltd., 2002. Lloyd, Tanya. *Calgary*. Vancouver, British Columbia: Whitecap Books, 2000. Tivy, Patrick. *Portrait of Calgary*. Canmore, Alberta: Altitude Publishing Canada Ltd., 1995.

CALGARY CHINATOWN

See ASIAN AMERICANS: Calgary Chinatown

CASPER, WYOMING

Casper sits at several crossroads, literally and figuratively. From its origins as a trading and army post at a ford on the North Platte River, it has grown into a modern city of about 50,000 people. Located at an elevation of about one mile above sea level, Casper stretches out along the river and is growing toward the base of 8,000-foot Casper Mountain to the south of the city.

Casper is at a geological crossroads, sitting on the Casper Arch, which separates the Powder River Basin from the Wind River Basin. This is a low saddle in the Rocky Mountains that continues to provide a natural topographic funnel for travelers heading west. Long before European Americans settled the area, Native Americans traveled through the region on their way from the Great Plains to the mountains and basins of the Middle Rocky Mountains. The attraction then as now was the ease of travel provided by the broad basins and the abundant local resources, especially water. The first permanent occupation was a bridge and trading post built by Louis Guinart in 1859 to provide support and a river crossing for travelers on the Oregon, California, Mormon, Pioneer, and Pony Express Trails and access to the nearby Bridger and Bozeman Trails. Casper is still a crossroads, the point of connection for Interstate 25, U.S. 20 and U.S. 26, and Wyoming 220.

Casper is also at a crossroads economically, struggling with the transition from the boom-and-bust cycles of the petroleum and minerals (coal, uranium, trona, bentonite, and clay) industries to a rapidly developing service and manufacturing economy. The city is a regional service center for central Wyoming. The Wyoming Medical Center provides sophisticated medical care for the region. Casper College, a comprehensive community college, and the University of Wyoming Upper Division Center combine their resources to provide an ever-expanding number of educational opportunities. Medical, legal, banking, and recreational services, along with retail sales and light manufacturing, are slowly replacing petroleum and minerals as the economic base. In 1999 the service sector accounted for almost 30 percent of total employment, having increased its share by almost one third over the decade, while mining employment (including oil and gas) stood at barely 7 percent of the total and had declined by almost 10 percent during the 1990s. Oil, gas, and minerals continue to be an important part of the economic picture, but it is apparent from the lack of impact on Casper of the current coal bed methane boom that Casper can no longer be considered a petroleum and minerals boomtown.

The culture of Casper is very much like the culture of many western towns, with one foot firmly planted in the Old West and one stepping toward the New West. Wingtips and cowboy boots mingle together at local watering holes, tapping in rhythm to both country western and rock. Nothing illustrates Casper's position at the cultural and economic crossroads better than the following juxtaposition. Casper is now the host city for the College National Finals Rodeo, which each year in June fills the town with cowboys and cowgirls from around the nation. Contrast that Old West picture with the high technology, New West scene created by a crowd of locals who recently gathered on a sage-covered dune just north of town to witness the test firing of Wickman Aerospace's latest rocket engine for NASA.

Jerry E. Nelson
Casper College

Casper Zonata Club. *Casper Chronicles*. Casper WY: Casper Zonata Club, 1964. Mead, Jean. *Casper Country: Wyoming's Heartland*. Boulder CO: Pruett Publishing Company, 1987.

CATTLE TOWNS

Often referred to (less respectfully) as "cow towns," cattle towns were small frontier settlements whose entrepreneurial existence depended heavily on the trade in free-range cattle. A typical cattle town lay at the junction of railroad and livestock trail. It provided facilities for the reception of herds driven up from the south, their sale, and their transportation to urban meatpackers, to midwestern cattle feeders, or to the ranchers of the Central and Northern Plains. While their principal commodity was cattle, horses destined for ranch use provided an important secondary commerce. Although Ogallala, Nebraska, was also a noted cattle town, the most famous were those of post–Civil War Kansas, each served by a trail from Texas.

The first was Abilene, organized as a market for Texas stock in 1867. It flourished until farmers overran its outlying ranges, ending its access to the trail. Ellsworth and Wichita then assumed roles as major cattle towns. From 1872 through 1875 these two—urged on by rival railroads—competed for the trade. Ultimately, rural settlement closed them both. Dodge City became a cattle town in 1876. A severe drought, temporarily retarding the advance of the agricultural frontier, extended its life as a Texas cattle market until 1885. Caldwell flourished from 1880 through 1885. Kansas finally closed its borders to direct importation of Texas cattle, ending the careers of both Dodge and Caldwell.

Local politics at the cattle towns tended to center on conflict between critics and defenders of the cattle trade. Critics consisted of two groups. Farmers feared trampled crops and the fatal effects of "Texas fever" on domestic livestock. Many townspeople opposed the saloons, professional gambling, and prostitution apparently required by cattlemen and off-duty cowboys. Businessmen invariably closed ranks against outlying farmers but tended to factionalize on moral reform. Three political positions emerged. Traditionalists fond of a lingering frontier ambience resisted all change. Moderate reformers, mainly leading business and professional men, favored ameliorative measures: multiple police officers to enforce tough gun control laws, thus ensuring that good order accompanied commercial sin; monthly tax assessments on saloonkeepers, gamblers, and prostitutes to help finance close police supervision (police salaries typically constituted a town's largest budget item); and, as far as possible, the segregation of brothels and dance houses from the main business district. Finally, there were the radical reformers, chiefly evangelicals who grew increasingly active after Kansas adopted liquor prohibition in 1880. With the saloons of Dodge and Caldwell now egregiously illegal, local opponents of all social immorality ral-

lied under the antiliquor banner. Although women reportedly comprised the hard core of antiliquor crusaders, a male element eventually resorted to violence to achieve reform. In 1885 arsonists destroyed much of Dodge City's business district in an apparent attempt to rid it of saloons and brothels; simultaneously, a group lynched a Caldwell bootlegger as a warning to other violators of the liquor law.

But the legendary street homicide associated with the cattle towns has been very much overdrawn by novelists, screenwriters, and journalists. Between 1870 and 1885, including justifiable killings by the police, only forty-five adults died violently at the five major Kansas cattle towns, an average of 1.5 fatalities per cowboy season. Recent efforts by scholars to exaggerate this low body count through the use of criminologists' "per 100,000 population" ratio have proved statistically fallacious. Nobody died in a Hollywood-style duel. Fewer than a third of the victims returned fire; a number were not even armed. Four deaths were accidental shootings. Famous "bad men" (the term *gunfighter* had not yet been innovated) accounted for few deaths. John Wesley Hardin killed a man snoring too loudly in an adjoining hotel room; Wyatt Earp (or another policemen) killed a carousing cowboy; Bat Masterson dispatched the murderer of his brother; Wild Bill Hickok killed two men, one—a security guard—by mistake. In large part, the low cattle town body count resulted from businessmen's fear of violence, which not only could escalate into property damage but could also deter the in-migration of substantial citizens and capital investment. But potential violence always presented something of a quandary for cattle town elites. Business leaders felt it necessary to suppress the disorder to which drunken and high-spirited visitors were prone but to do so without causing Texas drovers to take their business elsewhere. Only the end of cattle trading in each town resolved this dilemma.

See also IMAGES AND ICONS: Dodge City, Kansas / TRANSPORTATION: Cattle Trails.

Robert R. Dykstra
Worcester, Massachusetts

Dykstra, Robert R. *The Cattle Towns*. New York: Alfred A. Knopf, Inc., 1968. Dykstra, Robert R. "Overdosing on Dodge City." *Western Historical Quarterly* 27 (1996): 505–14. Dykstra, Robert R. "To Live and Die in Dodge City: Body Counts, Law and Order, and the Case of *Kansas v. Gill*." In *Lethal Imagination: Violence and Brutality in American History*, edited by Michael A. Bellesiles. New York: New York University Press, 1999: 210–26.

CHEYENNE, WYOMING

Cheyenne, the capital city of Wyoming, is located in Laramie County on the semiarid High Plains at an elevation of 6,100 feet. In 2000 the city's population was 53,000. The Union Pacific Railroad gave birth to Cheyenne during the summer of 1867 when its chief engineer, Maj. Gen. Grenville M. Dodge, selected and surveyed the site as a supply depot. The city was named for the Cheyenne Indians, who ranged in the area and had engaged in hostilities with Dodge. The name Cheyenne is probably a Lakota term meaning "people of different speech" or "red talkers." The town literally sprang into existence, engulfed by numerous barkeeps, gamblers, merchants, and prostitutes who inhabited the "Hell on Wheels" communities that traveled with the construction gangs of the railroad. By November 13, 1867, when the first train arrived, Cheyenne's population had grown rapidly to 4,000. At first, the city was part of the Dakota Territory, but in 1869 Cheyenne was selected as the territorial capital of the newly established Wyoming Territory. A few miles northwest of the city the army built Fort D. A. Russell and Camp Carlin, a major quartermaster supply depot.

In 1875, with the discovery of gold in the Black Hills, Cheyenne became an outfitting center for miners and stage passengers on their journey to the mines. The railroad was also essential in the development of the prosperous Wyoming livestock industry, and Cheyenne became the center of the territory's cattle boom. Wealthy ranchers built luxurious homes in a neighborhood dubbed Millionaires' Row and mingled at the elegant Cheyenne Club. Because of its rapid birth and ability to recover from periodic economic slumps, Cheyenne was called the "Magic City of the Plains." As the city matured during the territorial period (1869–90), it also developed a reputation as a social and cultural center. The city was notable for its opera house, the Atlas Theater, the Cheyenne Club, the Inter-Ocean

A stereograph of Cheyenne, Wyoming, 1869

Hotel, numerous retail businesses, and more than forty lavish mansions. The success and wealth of the city attracted western legends such as Wild Bill Hickok, Calamity Jane, Buffalo Bill Cody, Tom Horn, and Wyatt Earp, who rode shotgun on the Cheyenne–Black Hills stage.

Historically, government has been an important economic base of Cheyenne, especially after the creation of the state of Wyoming in 1890. Among the city's prominent politicians and judges have been Joseph M. Carey, U.S. attorney for the territory of Wyoming, justice of the Wyoming Supreme Court, territorial delegate to Congress, U.S. senator, and Wyoming governor; Willis Van Devanter, who held the positions of chief of the territorial court and federal court justice and was appointed to the U.S. Supreme Court in 1910; and Francis E. Warren, a rival to Joseph Carey who was perhaps Cheyenne's most distinguished citizen. He served as territorial governor, first governor of the state of Wyoming, and U.S. senator for thirty-seven years.

Transportation has always been an important economic and cultural stimulus for Cheyenne. For years Cheyenne was a repair terminal and passenger depot for the Union Pacific. As the railroad's impact on the community subsided, Cheyenne benefited from its location along the Lincoln Highway, the nation's first coast-to-coast automobile thoroughfare, and today the city has the advantage of being at the junction of Interstates 80 and 25. Its economic base still includes agriculture, cattle, sheep, and the railroad, but its major economic benefits derive from the presence of federal and state governments and Warren Air Force Base. Cheyenne's most important tourist attraction is the Frontier Days rodeo, popularly known as the "Daddy of 'Em All." Regarded as one of the largest and oldest continuous rodeos in the country, Frontier Days held its first Wild West celebration on September 23, 1897.

See also POLITICS AND GOVERNMENT: Warren, Francis / SPORTS AND RECREATION: Rodeo / TRANSPORTATION: Dodge, Grenville

Mark Elliott
Jim Johns
Laramie County Community College

Adams, Judith. *Cheyenne: City of Blue Sky*. Northridge CA: Windsor Publications, 1988. Carley, Maurice, William Dubois, and Katherine Halverson. *Cheyenne: The Magic City of the Plains*. Cheyenne WY: Cheyenne Centennial Committee, 1967. Field, Sharon Lass, ed. *History of Cheyenne, Wyoming*. Dallas: Curtis Media Corporation, 1989.

COLLEGE TOWNS

More than a dozen Great Plains cities and towns owe their development and contemporary character to the presence of colleges or universities. College towns like Lawrence, Kansas, Brookings, South Dakota, and Chadron, Nebraska, while distinct from one another because of the different nature of the schools located in them, are nonetheless similar in many ways to hundreds of other cities nationwide that are dominated by institutions of higher education. With their youthful and

Aggieville (Manhattan) is a blur of activity after a 1984 Kansas State victory in football over the University of Kansas.

comparatively diverse populations, highly educated workforces, relative absence of heavy industry, and presence of cultural opportunities unusual for cities of their size, these towns stand apart from the rest of the region.

As elsewhere in the United States, many colleges on the Plains were founded outside the largest cities, so they came to have a controlling influence over the places where they were located. Colleges were placed in smaller towns not because, as is often assumed, college founders had an antiurban attitude but because small towns actively pursued colleges as a way to assure their economic survival. Rarely did the municipality that won designation as seat of a college have any special locational advantages. More often than not, it was successful because it offered the largest amount of money and the biggest plot of land or was politically adept. Backroom deals and unethical behavior were common. Town leaders in Lawrence, for example, bribed legislators deciding where to locate the University of Kansas for $4 a vote.

Most college towns remained relatively small places, with the college often serving as but one part of a diversified economy, until after World War II, when a college degree increasingly came to be viewed as a prerequisite for success. Enrollments boomed through the mid-1970s, and college towns grew rapidly as a result. As higher education institutions fueled local economic development, town leaders began to resist less desirable types of industry, and college towns became more one-dimensional in the process. To some degree, they resemble company towns, with the college as the number one employer, biggest property owner and landlord, and most powerful political force. In many, the majority of the population has some connection to the college. In Vermillion, South Dakota, a town of fewer than 10,000 residents that is home to the University of South Dakota, students and staff number more than 8,000.

The most fundamental difference between college towns and the rest of the Great Plains is demographic. In a region that is growing older, college towns are ever young. Nearly half the residents of Manhattan, Kansas, home of Kansas State University, are eighteen to twenty-four years old. While many towns on the Plains are losing people, college towns are growing. The population of Brookings, home of South Dakota State University, grew 14 percent between 1990 and 2000. In a region that has long battled brain drain, college towns again are an exception. In Laramie, Wyoming, home of the University of Wyoming, 40 percent of adults have a college degree. College towns are also comparatively cosmopolitan. Students at Oklahoma State University come from fifty states and 116 countries. Residents of Stillwater, where Oklahoma State University is located, are three times more likely than Oklahomans in general to have been born outside the United States.

The nature of higher education institutions and the people associated with them give college towns distinctive personalities. Most are regional cultural centers, with the college campus serving as the focus of such activity. With their concert halls, theaters, museums, sports stadiums, parklike landscapes, and busy calendars of events, campuses serve not only as environments for learning but also as public spaces. At the University of Oklahoma in Norman, for example, the Catlett Music Center hosts concerts several nights a week. Two campus art museums feature regular exhibits. The university recently opened a thirty-eight-million-dollar museum of natural history. Millions of people visit Norman every year to attend football games, an annual medieval fair, and other campus events.

The university influence is also significant off campus. Nearby shopping areas strongly reflect the ever-changing tastes of young people and the nonmainstream orientation of many academics. In some college towns, such as Manhattan and Norman, commercial districts have developed next to campus that are separate from the city's downtown. Certain types of businesses tend to be unusually plentiful in college town business areas: bookstores, coffeehouses, T-shirt stores, bike shops, ethnic restaurants, health food stores, and, most conspicuously, bars. There are eighteen bars in a six-block area of Manhattan's Aggieville district.

The social differences that exist in college towns have also led to the emergence of distinctive residential landscapes. The large number of students is marked by the high-rise dorms of campus, the faux classicism of "fraternity row" (for example, University Avenue in Grand Forks, North Dakota), and the disheveled rental houses of the "student ghetto" (for example, Lawrence's Oread neighborhood). Most college towns also have at least one campus-adjacent neighborhood that is home to concentrations of faculty and administrators. Characterized by tree-lined streets and stately homes, these neighborhoods were often marketed directly to professors; in Norman, one such subdivision was platted as Faculty Heights.

College towns are also relatively unconventional places. The sexual revolution first played out in college towns as diverse as Lawrence, which had an active gay rights organization as early as 1970, and Chadron, home of tiny Chadron State College, where a local theater drew national attention in 1969 when it began showing X-rated movies to a largely student audience. Lawrence was a center of the 1960s counterculture and, since that time, has maintained its reputation for liberalism, once electing a state representative known as "Marijuana Mike," successfully fighting development of a suburban shopping mall, and voting disproportionately for left-leaning presidential candidates like Ralph Nader. It has nurtured poets, artists, musicians, and eccentrics. Suggestive of the different character college towns possess in a largely conservative region, a 1980s Lawrence rock band penned a song paying tribute to the distinctive nature of the Kansas college town. It was entitled "Berlin on the Plains."

See also EDUCATION: Land-Grant Universities.

Blake Gumprecht
University of South Carolina

COLORADO SPRINGS, COLORADO

Colorado Springs, although dominated by and identified with Pikes Peak, is located on the western edge of the Great Plains. The city was founded in 1871 by a consortium of investors led by William Jackson Palmer, a Civil War hero and railroad builder. Since then Colorado Springs has grown from a small tourist town to a metropolitan area of over half a million people.

Prior to the 1850s the area was traversed by Native Americans, fur trappers, and Spanish military expeditions. Zebulon Pike led the first U.S. government exploration to this re-

Colorado Springs, Colorado, between 1880 and 1910

gion in 1806. Later explorers included Stephen Long in 1820 and Kit Carson and John Charles Frémont in the 1840s. Anglo-American ranchers and a few merchants settled in the area after the discovery of gold to the north in 1859.

Colorado Springs was the crown jewel of Palmer's north–south railroad, the Denver and Rio Grande. He oversaw the development of the initial 2,000-acre plat and championed Colorado Springs as a well-planned community. The town's treeless prairie environment was modified through an active tree-planting program that transformed the appearance of its wide thoroughfares. An extensive irrigation works was constructed, and large tracts of land were donated for city parks and Colorado College. As the city grew steadily in its first two decades, Palmer invested in opulent hotels and sanitariums.

In the early 1890s gold was discovered at Cripple Creek to the west of Pikes Peak. Colorado Springs was transformed, as it provided transportation, milling services, and coal for the gold mines. During a thirty-year mining boom the city, home to fifty millionaires by 1900, became an internationally known health resort, playground, and elite enclave. Philanthropic millionaires such as Spencer Penrose and Winfield Scott Stratton established institutions that are still important today. Penrose, for example, was instrumental in forming the Cheyenne Mountain Zoo and the Fine Arts Center, and Stratton founded the Myron Stratton Home for orphaned children. New elite neighborhoods such as the upscale suburb of Broadmoor, which included a lavish casino and recreation complex, were developed. Tourism continued to be an important part of the economy. The health benefits of the climate were extolled for victims of tuberculosis, leading to the development of several

tuberculosis sanitariums. During the Great Depression the so-called lungers were an essential part of the city's economic base.

World War II signaled another change in the city's economy with the establishment of Camp Carson, later Fort Carson, as an army training center, bringing almost 30,000 soldiers into the area. The military fueled much of the economic and population growth for the remainder of the twentieth century. Two U.S. Air Force bases, the North American Air Defense Command, and the United States Air Force Academy became the engine of the regional economy and infused millions of dollars into the local economy annually. The growth and development of the community thus became linked to national policy and government largesse. In addition, high-tech firms associated with the military/industrial complex were attracted to the city by billions of Defense Department contract dollars. The rapid population growth of the city has led to the development of low-density suburbs, spreading eastward on the Plains. Consequently, infrastructure problems, especially transportation issues, and associated air pollution problems are important issues today.

See also EDUCATION: United States Air Force Academy.

Steven Jennings
Robert P. Larkin
University of Colorado at Colorado Springs

Huber, Thomas P. *Colorado: The Place of Nature, the Nature of Place.* Niwot: University Press of Colorado, 1993. Sprague, Marshall. *Newport in the Rockies: The Life and Good Times of Colorado Springs.* Athens: Ohio University Press/Swallow Press, 1987. Wyckoff, William. *Creating Colorado: The Making of a Western American Landscape 1860–1940.* New Haven CT: Yale University Press, 1999.

COUNTY SEATS

Approximately 500 counties exist in the Great Plains, and each of them has a county seat, that is, a city or town designated as the county's center for local government.

The county-centered Virginia system had a stronger influence upon the organization of local governments during U.S. westward expansion than the town-centered system begun in colonial New England. Although townships do exist in states as far west as Nebraska and the Dakotas, they are clearly less important than the county unit. The prevailing form of county government in the Great Plains included locally elected commissioners and a number of elected county executive officers operating from the courthouse of the county seat. State or territorial legislation also generally recognized the importance of popular sovereignty in selecting which town became the county seat.

With few exceptions, the county seat was (or became, after it was selected as the county capital) the town with the largest population. In a few cases, when the largest town lacked a central location, the county seat went to a smaller town nearer the county center. Examples of leading cities failing to become county seats include Coffeyville and Pittsburg in Kansas and Crete and Norfolk in Nebraska.

The likelihood for future growth of a town chosen by a county-seat election often led such elections to be highly disputed. In some cases (such as in Pratt, Stevens, and Wichita Counties in Kansas), battles between rival towns resulted in deaths. More commonly, a raiding party from a town seeking to become the new county seat (often following a disputed election) forcibly seized the county records from a rival town. This was the case in at least twenty different counties in Nebraska and the Dakotas.

The rapid settlement of the Great Plains led to the organization of many counties within a few years. For example, all of the counties in northwest Texas were organized in the same year, 1876, and in 1873 no fewer than 45 counties (of the 120 now existing in North and South Dakota) were organized in Dakota Territory. Rapid settlement and county organization were leading factors in the most violent county-seat controversies, often pitting very young towns (and sometimes only projected locations for towns) against each other. Most of the "county-seat wars" (as the more bitter controversies have been called) occurred in the Great Plains during the last quarter of the nineteenth century.

Few county seats were changed during the twentieth century, though this has happened in several cases when strong population growth of one town supported its claim to county-seat honors. This occurred in Logan and Morton Counties in western Kansas as late as the 1960s, when new county seats were located at Oakley and Elkhart, respectively. With very few exceptions, however, the counties and county seats that had been established by the early twentieth century have remained unchanged.

See also POLITICS AND GOVERNMENT: Civil Divisions of Government.

James A. Schellenberg
Indiana State University

Kane, Joseph Nathan. *The American Counties*. New York: Scarecrow Press, 1983. Schellenberg, James A. *Conflict between Communities*. New York: Paragon House, 1987.

DEADWOOD CHINATOWN

See ASIAN AMERICANS: Deadwood Chinatown

DEADWOOD, SOUTH DAKOTA

See IMAGES AND ICONS: Deadwood, South Dakota

DENVER, COLORADO

Denver, the capital of Colorado, was established by a party of prospectors on November 22, 1858, after gold was discovered at the confluence of Cherry Creek and the South Platte River. The town founders named the dusty crossroads after James W. Denver, governor of Kansas Territory, of which eastern Colorado was then a part. Other gold discoveries sparked a mass migration of some 100,000 people in 1859–60, leading the federal government to establish Colorado Territory in 1861.

The "Mile High City's" aggressive leadership, spearheaded by William N. Byers, founding editor of the *Rocky Mountain News*, and Territorial Governor John Evans, insisted on the removal of the original inhabitants, Cheyennes and Arapahos, from the area. Denverites then built a network of railroads that made their town the banking, minting, supply, and processing center for Colorado and neighboring states. Between 1870, when the first railroads arrived, and 1890, Denver's population grew from 4,759 to 106,713. In a single generation it became the second most populous city in the West, second only to San Francisco. Although initially founded as the main supply town for Rocky Mountain mining camps, Denver also emerged as a hub for High Plains agriculture, with breweries, bakeries, and meatpacking and other food-processing plants as well as farm and ranch equipment, barbed-wire, and windmill manufacturing.

Economic depression during the 1890s and repeal of the Sherman Silver Purchase Act in 1893 abruptly ended Denver's first boom. Growth began again after 1900 but at a slower rate. Stockyards, brickyards, canneries, flour mills, and leather and rubber production powered the city. Of the many Denver-area breweries, only Coors has survived, and it is now the nation's third largest producer.

Regional or national headquarters of many oil and gas firms fueled much of Denver's post–World War II growth and resulted in an eruption of forty- and fifty-story high-rises downtown in the 1970s. Denver's economic base has also come to include skiing and tourism, electronics, computers, aviation, and the nation's largest telecommunications center. As the regional center of a vast mountain and Plains hinterland, Denver boasts more federal employees than any city except Washington DC. Since the 1940s, the large federal center, augmented by state and local government jobs, has stabilized the city's boom-and-bust cycle, but an overreliance on a nonrenewable resource returned to haunt the city during the 1980s oil bust. When the price of crude oil dropped from $39 to $9 a barrel, Denver sank into a depression, losing population and experiencing the highest office vacancy rate in the nation. Prosperity has since returned.

Visually, Denver is notable for its predominance of single-family housing and its brick buildings. Good brick clay underlies much of the area, while local construction lumber is soft, scarce, and inferior. Even in the poorest residential neighborhoods, single-family detached housing prevails, reflecting the western interest in "elbow room" as well as the spacious, relatively flat High Plains site, where

Denver, Colorado

sprawling growth in all directions except west is unimpeded by geographic obstacles.

Denver always has been obsessed with transportation systems. Fear of being bypassed began early when railroads and later airlines originally avoided Denver because of the 14,000-foot-high Rocky Mountain barrier just west of town. To secure Denver's place on national transportation maps, the city opened a new five-billion-dollar airport in 1995. The fifty-five-square-mile Denver International Airport is the nation's largest in terms of area and capacity for growth, prompting boosters to call it the world's largest. Denver is a sprawling city in a state of long distances and mountainous obstacles. To tackle those distances and tough terrain, Coloradoans have become dependent on cars. Denver has one of the highest per capita motor vehicle ownership rates in the country, with almost one licensed vehicle for every man, woman, and child. In the 1990s Denver built an outer ring of freeways, which immediately became congested. Even after the Regional Transportation District began building a light-rail system, highway congestion has remained the number one complaint of many Denverites.

By 2000 the metro area had reached a population of 2.1 million, three-fourths of whom live in the suburban counties of Adams, Arapahoe, Boulder, Denver, Douglas, and Jefferson. Roughly 20 percent of the core city population have a Spanish surname, 13 percent are African American, 2 percent Asian, and 1 percent Native American. Denver has elected Latino (Federico Peña, 1983–91) and African American (Wellington Webb, 1991–2003) mayors in recent years and has enjoyed relatively smooth race relations. Notable institutions in the city include the Denver Museum of Natural History, the Denver Public Library, the Colorado History Museum, the Denver Art Museum, and the Denver Center for the Performing Arts as well as the U.S. Mint and major-league baseball, basketball, football, hockey, and soccer teams.

The "Rocky Mountain Metropolis" boomed during the 1990s as the eastern suburb of Aurora became Colorado's third largest city and the western suburb of Lakewood became the fourth largest. Even the core city and county of Denver gained population in the 1990s for the first time since the 1970s, climbing to 555,000 in the 2000 census. Thanks to landmark districts preserving venerable business and residential areas as well as the 1990s opening in the core South Platte River valley of Coors Baseball Field, Elitch Gardens Amusement Park, Ocean Journey Aquarium, the Pepsi Athletic Center, and many new housing projects, downtown Denver is booming along with its suburban fringe at the dawn of the twenty-first century.

See also AFRICAN AMERICANS: Webb, Wellington and Wilma / ASIAN AMERICANS: Denver Chinatown / HISPANIC AMERICANS: Peña, Federico / MEDIA: *Denver Post*.

Thomas J. Noel
University of Colorado at Denver

Leonard, Stephen J., and Thomas J. Noel. *Denver: Mining Camp to Metropolis*. Niwot: University Press of Colorado, 1990.

DENVER CHINATOWN

See ASIAN AMERICANS: Denver Chinatown

DODGE CITY, KANSAS

See IMAGES AND ICONS: Dodge City, Kansas

EDMONTON, ALBERTA

Edmonton is the capital of the province of Alberta and the dominant urban center for the central and northern regions of the province and for much of Canada's Far North. In 1996 the population of the city proper stood at 616,306 and of the greater metropolitan area at 862,597.

The city is situated on the North Saskatchewan River in the Parkland Belt region of the Canadian Prairies. This strategic location made it an attractive site for fur trading, and in 1795 the Hudson's Bay Company built the first Fort Edmonton downstream from the present city. The last post to bear that name was built in 1830, by which time Edmonton had emerged as one of the company's most important inland depots. Following the transfer of company territory to Canada in 1870, speculators and merchants promoted Edmonton as a future agricultural center, but the first trans-Canada railway crossed the Prairies 200 miles to the south, where the rival city of Calgary emerged. A branch line from Calgary in 1891 failed to cross the river into Edmonton, giving rise to the south-side upstart of Strathcona. Few agricultural settlers reached the district, with the result that Edmonton-Strathcona had a population of only 4,000 by 1901.

The following decade brought explosive growth. Two new transcontinental railways reached Edmonton, and settlers swarmed into the surrounding hinterland. Led by Frank Oliver, an Edmonton newspaperman, politician, and booster, the city outmaneuvered Calgary to become the capital of the new province of Alberta in 1905 and the site for the University of Alberta in 1909. The construction of a high-level railway bridge across the river facilitated the amalgamation of Edmonton and Strathcona in 1912. By 1916 the population of the city had reached 54,000, but by then rapid growth had already ended. Most of the surrounding hinterland had been settled, and a speculative real estate bubble burst in 1913. Recession gripped the agricultural economy after the World War I. Although growth and prosperity resumed in the mid-1920s, the Great Depression soon brought the return of hard times.

World War II stimulated new growth when American money and manpower poured into the city to launch three major wartime projects: the Alaska Highway, which would provide an alternate supply route to that state safe from Japanese attack; the Canol Pipeline, which carried petroleum from northern Canada to Alaska; and the North-West Staging Route, a series of northern airports constructed to shuttle aircraft to the Soviet Union under lend-lease. These projects gave the

city the expertise and economic base to become a major oil service center following the Leduc strike of 1947. While Calgary remained the financial and corporate headquarters for the petroleum industry, Edmonton became more important for oil field supply, refining, petrochemical manufacturing, and pipeline construction.

Geographically, the city has sprawled in typical North American fashion, with major arterial roads leading to suburbs clustered around shopping centers. The most impressive of these, West Edmonton Mall, was completed in stages and in 1985 became the largest shopping center in the world. The regional planning commission established by the province in 1950 also encouraged the development of satellite communities beyond the city. These included the industrial complex at Fort Saskatchewan, the airport center of Leduc, and major residential communities like Sherwood Park and St. Albert.

While the city attracted many newcomers from outside the region, much of its postwar growth also came from rural depopulation in Alberta. Arrivals from the many ethnic settlements in the rural hinterland ended the overwhelming dominance of the city by people of British origins. Symbolic of this change was the populist mayor of Ukrainian descent, William Hawrelak, who was elected for various terms from the 1950s to the 1970s in spite of corruption scandals. Since then, the city has also attracted immigrants from the Far East and India.

Although the collapse of oil prices in the early 1980s jolted the city economically, it recovered quickly and began to diversify. Today there are many more industries and information-based services unrelated to agriculture or petroleum. In addition to its economic, political, and educational importance, the city is also a major cultural and recreational center. Attractions include a symphony, opera, theater, art galleries, space science center, and provincial museum. Festivals devoted to culture and recreation are held almost continuously throughout the summer months, including Klondike Days and the Fringe Theater. The city also boasts superb facilities for amateur and professional sports, and citizens take great pride in the championship dynasties established by the Edmonton Grads in basketball, the Edmonton Eskimos in football, and the Edmonton Oilers in hockey. With its steep banks, the river valley remains the dominant element in the city landscape, and it features vast wilderness parks and golf courses connected by a network of recreational trails.

See also INDUSTRY: Petroleum, Canada / MEDIA: *Edmonton Journal* / SPORTS AND RECREATION: Edmonton Grads.

Paul Voisey
University of Alberta

Hesketh, Bob, and Frances Swyripa, eds. *Edmonton: The Life of a City*. Edmonton: NeWest Press, 1995. MacGregor, James G. *Edmonton: A History*. Edmonton: Hurtig, 1975. Smith, P. J., ed. *Edmonton: The Emerging Metropolitan Pattern*. Victoria: University of Victoria, 1978.

FARGO, NORTH DAKOTA

Fargo, located in east-central North Dakota on the banks of the Red River, is the largest city in North Dakota, with a population of 90,599 in 2000, an increase of 22 percent over 1990. Adjacent cities include Moorhead, Minnesota (population 32,177), and West Fargo, North Dakota (estimated population 14,940). The population of the Fargo-Moorhead metropolitan statistical area (Cass County, North Dakota, and Clay County, Minnesota) is 174,367.

Fargo sits on clay-loam soil from ancient Lake Agassiz, which resulted from melting glaciers 12,000 years ago. The soil's fertility and depth drew settlers to the region's bonanza farms of the late 1800s. Fargo served as a railroad distribution point for new settlers and as a grain-shipping terminal. The city, platted in 1871 and incorporated in 1874, was named after William G. Fargo, a Northern Pacific Railroad director and founder of the Wells-Fargo Express Company. In 1885 Fargo had a population of 7,394, and by 1920 it was the largest city in North Dakota, with 21,961 people.

Fargo is the seat for Cass County and is host for several state and federal government facilities such as the new federal courthouse, named after U.S. senator Quentin Burdick. It is served by the Burlington Northern and Santa Fe Railway, Amtrak, and the Hector International Airport and is at the intersection of Interstates 29 and 94. Fargo hosts 4,056 business establishments. The adjacent cities of Moorhead, with 1,101 businesses, and West Fargo, with 550 businesses, bring the area total to 5,707 establishments. Although agriculture is a dominant industry, other industries also are vital to the area's economy. For example, Fargo is a regional health-care center, with three medical facilities: Dakota Heartland Health System, MeritCare Medical Center, and the Veterans Affairs Medical Center. Other major employers include North Dakota State University, Blue Cross Blue Shield of North Dakota, American Crystal Sugar Company, Great Plains Software, First Bank System, and Case Corporation.

About 30 percent of the city's employment is in the service industry, followed by wholesale and retail trade with 29 percent (the West Acres Shopping Mall is a regional draw). The remaining employment is in government, manufacturing, mining, construction, finance, insurance, real estate, transportation, utilities, and communications. Fargo and Moorhead together have a labor force of 103,120 employees, with 99,950 in nonagricultural employment.

The area is home to several colleges, universities, and vocational schools. North Dakota State University is the state's land-grant university, with a student enrollment of over 9,600. Minnesota State University–Moorhead has an enrollment of 6,700 students. Concordia College, a Lutheran liberal arts college, has nearly 3,000 students. Northwest Technical College–Moorhead provides training for 1,400 students. The area's primary and secondary public school system serves nearly 22,700 students. In addition, there are nine

Aftermath of a fire in Fargo, North Dakota, June 7, 1893

private and parochial school facilities that serve more than 2,000 students.

Churches and religious institutions play an important role in the community. There are about 125 congregations in the Fargo-Moorhead area, with about 32 percent of the members in Catholic churches, 49 percent in Lutheran churches, and the remaining 19 percent in churches of other denominations. Additionally, there are two Jewish synagogues and meeting places for those of other faith traditions.

Fire destroyed almost the entire city on June 7, 1893, and floods have plagued Fargo, including one in 1897 and another in 1997. These events resulted in rebuilding booms that shaped the city's architecture. A tour of the city's homes and buildings reveals Classical Revival architecture from the postfire construction, Richardsonian Romanesque in many of the downtown buildings constructed after the turn of the century, and Art Moderne in buildings from the mid-1920s to 1940. Popular vernacular styles and period revivals can be seen throughout residential neighborhoods.

The FargoDome is the largest indoor multipurpose facility in the Northern Plains and hosts athletic events, concerts, trade shows, and conventions. Bonanzaville, U.S.A., adjacent to the Red River Valley Fairgrounds, is a reconstructed pioneer town with turn-of-the-century houses and stores. The Heritage-Hjemkomst Interpretive Center in Moorhead, with a replica Viking ship and Norwegian stave church, highlights the area's Scandinavian heritage. Other facilities include the Plains Art Museum and Red River Zoo.

Fargo is home to the Fargo-Moorhead Symphony, which presents symphonic and chamber orchestral works, and the Fargo-Moorhead Community Theatre, which offers plays and theatrical training. Sports teams include the Beez (minor-league basketball), the Ice Sharks (hockey), the RedHawks (minor-league baseball), and the Fargo Freeze (indoor football). The community's artistic and sports atmosphere has produced celebrities like singer Bobby Vee and baseball player Roger Maris.

Several magazines and organizations have ranked Fargo-Moorhead in lists of the most kid-friendly, best small place to live, safest, best place to raise a family, best for working mothers, and best place to start a career.

See also MUSIC: Vee, Bobby / WATER: Floods.

Gary A. Goreham
North Dakota State University

Crossings: A Photographic Document of Fargo, North Dakota. Fargo: Institute for Regional Studies, North Dakota State University, 1995. Roberts, Norene A. *Fargo's Heritage.* Fargo ND: Fargo Heritage Society, 1983.

FORT WORTH, TEXAS

On June 6, 1849, Maj. Ripley A. Arnold positioned forty-two men of Company F of the U.S. Second Dragoons on the Clear Fork of the Trinity River, his mission that of guarding East Texas settlers against Indian incursions. Within two months he relocated his men to a more advantageous spot, a high bluff overlooking the river, and designated this site as Camp Worth in honor of Brig. Gen. William Jenkins Worth, who had distinguished himself in the recent Mexican War. Three months later, on November 14, 1849, the War Department officially named this area Fort Worth, thereby establishing a permanent outpost on the north-central Texas frontier.

During the 1850s Fort Worth struggled to survive. Even though the army evacuated the area for a string of forts farther west in 1853, residents John Peter Smith opened a school, Julian Field a flour mill, and Henry Daggett and Archibald Leonard department stores. In 1856 these early settlers also persuaded the

Butterfield Overland Mail and the Southern Pacific Stage Line to use the town as a western terminus on the California route, and they waged a bitter but successful fight in 1860 to have Fort Worth replace the nearby town of Birdville as the county seat.

Then came the Civil War and the aftermath of Reconstruction (1861–74)—and even greater struggle. With young men joining the Confederate army, with money a scarcity on the Texas frontier, and with food and supply shortages increasingly apparent, the citizenry barely survived. By 1866 the population had dropped to a low of 175. As a result, Fort Worth soon assumed the title of "Panther City," suggesting that its environs were so placid and its ambience so dull that citizens had discovered a panther sleeping on the streets.

After 1873 this image changed. Because of the efforts of merchants Jacob Samuels, William Jesse Boaz, and William Henry Davis, banker Khleber M. Van Zandt, and newspaperman Buckley B. Paddock, Fort Worth was incorporated, and, with a mayor-council form of government, the city began to grow. In 1876 the Texas and Pacific Railway designated Fort Worth as its eastern terminus, in part because cowboys rested there before continuing to drive cattle northward along the Chisholm Trail to railheads in Kansas and Missouri. As a consequence, meatpacking became the principal local business, culminating with the establishment of Swift and Armour meatpacking plants in 1902. This, together with other economic enterprises that prospered because of the city's eight railroads, stimulated growth, so that by 1900, with a population of 26,668, Fort Worth was the fifth largest city in the state. Residents proudly proclaimed Fort Worth as the "Queen City of the Prairies."

Fort Worth continued to expand and prosper in the first half of the twentieth century. It became a military and defense center, benefiting from military contracts and associated personnel. During World War I the U.S. Army established Camp Bowie in the western part of the city, where 100,000 soldiers received instruction and training; the U.S. Air Force also converted three airfields into aviation-training establishments. In 1942, after the outbreak of World War II, Consolidated Vultee Aircraft Corporation (later bought out by General Dynamics and still later by Lockheed-Martin) became the largest aircraft manufacturer in the area; and in 1948 a bomber military operation became Carswell Air Force Base, home to the Strategic Air Command's B-36 bombers.

Other ingredients also guaranteed continued growth. With the discovery of oil in West, Central, and East Texas prior to and after World War I, oil-refining corporations such as Sinclair, Texaco, and Humble (later Exxon) selected Fort Worth as a home base and made it a center for oil exchanges and field equipment. Equally important was the leadership of Amon G. Carter, who directed the economic and political fortunes of the city. Besides building the *Fort Worth Star-Telegram* (its logo is "Fort Worth, Where the West Begins"), he directed the construction of Casa Mañana (theater-in-the-round) and of the Texas Frontier Centennial in 1936 to rival the state fair in nearby Dallas. As a result of his forceful guidance, the city received much-needed federal funds during the Depression. Carter was largely responsible for a number of Public Works Administration and Work Projects Administration projects, most of which still exist: Will Rogers Memorial Center (an auditorium), the Botanical Gardens, the John Peter Smith Hospital, a public library, forty-eight public schools and playgrounds, low-cost housing, a high school gymnasium, and the largest high school football stadium in the state (Farrington Field). Carter also promoted the Southwestern Exposition and Livestock Show (initiated in 1896), which has continued to grow in popularity.

After the death of Amon Carter in 1955, James Claude "Jim" Wright assumed the political mantle for Fort Worth. In 1954 he was elected to the Twelfth Congressional District, encompassing Fort Worth and surrounding cities. In 1977 he became Democratic majority leader and in 1987 Speaker of the House of Representatives. As a result, Fort Worth received favorable congressional attention. Through his initiatives in the 1960s, federal funds helped rejuvenate and preserve the historic north side, where unemployment had risen to more than 20 percent after the Swift and Armour meatpacking plants closed in 1962. During the 1960s and 1970s Wright also effectively championed Fort Worth as a military center by maintaining and expanding Carswell Air Force Base and by securing lucrative Pentagon contracts for companies such as General Dynamics and Bell Helicopter. Through his leadership, Fort Worth obtained federal and state funds for significant flood-control projects, for the construction of U.S. highways (I-20, I-30, and I-35) that crisscrossed the city, and for the Federal Center in the downtown area, which in turn attracted other government agencies. In 1974 Wright, together with local and state officials, dedicated the Dallas–Fort Worth International Airport, the fourth largest air terminal in the world.

As a result of such leadership, continuing with businessmen such as Perry Bass and his four sons, Fort Worth has continued to expand significantly. From 1950 to 2000 the population increased from 277,047 to 534,694, making Fort Worth the fourth largest city in the state.

See also INDUSTRY: Petroleum, United States / MEDIA: *Fort Worth Star-Telegram.*

Ben Procter
Texas Christian University

Knight, Oliver. *Fort Worth: Outpost on the Trinity.* Norman: University of Oklahoma Press, 1953. Pate, J'Nell. *Livestock Legacy: The Fort Worth Stockyards, 1887–1987.* College Station: Texas A&M University Press, 1988. Sanders, Leonard. *How Fort Worth Became the Texas-most City.* Fort Worth: Amon Carter Museum, 1973.

GHOST TOWNS

Ghost towns—towns that are extinct or so diminished in population and function as to be virtually extinct—are the most common category of towns in the Great Plains. Daniel C. Fitzgerald, author of *Faded Dreams*, estimates that there are 6,000 such places in Kansas alone. Towns withered on the land and disappeared from the maps even in the very first years of Plains settlement as speculative ventures failed or highly mobile populations moved on to better opportunities, generally to the west. (For example, Omadi in northeastern Nebraska, founded in 1856, emptied out to the Colorado gold mines in 1859.) Ghost towns are still being created as the rural population that once sustained them thins, leaving schools and stores closed, young people gone, and perhaps only an elevator or a church as a reminder of a more vibrant past.

In the Rocky Mountains the archetypical ghost town was the product of a collapsed mining boom, and there are examples of such towns in the Great Plains also. Hundreds of Black Hills mining towns lasted only as long as the gold, often only months. In Crawford County in southeastern Kansas, dozens of clapboard company towns sprang up during the coal boom of the early twentieth century, went into protracted decline in the 1930s, and disappeared when the mine shafts were sealed. Just to the south, in Cherokee County, a similar cycle in lead and zinc mining left towns like Treece (which once sustained a population of 749) abandoned. Farther south again, oil towns (like Three Sands in Noble County, Oklahoma, founded in 1921) started quickly, roared briefly, then, as the oil and gas became too expensive to tap, went into a long decline.

In the Great Plains, however, the characteristic ghost town is the diminished rural service center. After farm mechanization reduced the need for labor on the land and automobiles increased the distance that farmers could travel to the elevator and implement store, there were simply too many of these towns, which had been founded during the horse-and-buggy era when farmers needed local access to goods and services. The first towns to drop out of the network were the "inland towns," those places that never secured a railroad and that were, therefore, at a great competitive disadvantage. As John C. Hudson shows in his detailed study of town building and competition in northern North Dakota in the late nineteenth and early twentieth centuries, farmers would generally make a longer trip to a railroad town to buy cheaper goods rather than shop locally at the more expensive inland town store. Consequently, the inland towns went under. Many successful railroad towns of the late nineteenth century such as Blaine in Pottawatomie County, Kansas, also fell victim to transportation changes. After the 1930s, as railroad companies consolidated their lines, Blaine was left stranded inland. Its grass-covered Main Street is now deserted and lined with crumbling buildings that once housed hotels, livery stables, retail outlets, and a bank. Only the St. Columbkille Catholic Church remains (albeit with drastically reduced services) to recall the better times.

The number of towns in the Great Plains continues to decrease as the rural population shrinks. In North Dakota all but six of the fifty-three counties lost population during the 1990s. Nelson County, for example, in the northeastern part of the state, suffered a 17 percent population decline during those years. There, the neat Norwegian town of Whitman is not yet a ghost town, but it is heading in that direction: its four bars, two general stores, and grain elevator are closed; deaths far exceed births; the Lutheran church still offers services but only to twelve members.

Towns like Whitman are still greatly valued by their residents not just for nostalgic reasons but as good places to raise a family. But in those parts of the Plains too far from prosperous cities to serve as dormitory suburbs, from the major highways to reap the benefits from gas stations, restaurants, and motels, and from the "oases" where abundant surface or groundwater provides the irrigated agriculture that sustains feedlots, implement dealers, and grain processing, many of the settlements seem destined to dwindle, eventually to join the ranks of ghost towns.

David J. Wishart
University of Nebraska–Lincoln

Fitzgerald, Daniel C. *Faded Dreams: More Ghost Towns of Kansas*. Lawrence: University Press of Kansas, 1994. Hudson, John C. *Plains Country Towns*. Minneapolis: University of Minnesota Press, 1985. Kilborn, Peter T. "Boom in Economy Skips Towns on the Plains." *New York Times*, July 2, 2000: 1, 13.

GRAND FORKS, NORTH DAKOTA

Located at the confluence of the Red River of the North and the Red Lake River on the North Dakota–Minnesota boundary, Grand Forks is one of the most flood-prone communities of North Dakota. Although a difficult site, the city's general situation has been favorable since the 1860s for development as the major commercial center for northeastern North Dakota and northwestern Minnesota.

Trade and transportation have always been important to Grand Forks. European fur traders visited the area in 1734, but continuous European American settlement only began with the creation of a steamboat-refueling station in the mid-1860s. The first town-site plat was recorded in 1875, and the city was incorporated in 1881. The St. Paul, Minneapolis, and Manitoba Railway came in from the east in 1880; the Northern Pacific Railroad entered from the south in 1882. Regional wholesaling functions became significant in the early 1890s as the region's settlement increased by immigration, notably of Norwegians. Between 1890 and 1910 Grand Forks tripled in population to reach 12,478 people.

Population growth and economic prosperity increased and fluctuated from the 1920s through the 1950s with the region's wheat, potato, and sugar beet–based economy. In 1956 Grand Forks Air Force Base opened, sparking a boom in population and retailing during the 1960s and 1970s. Concurrently, enrollment growth was substantial at the University of North Dakota, and medical services also expanded, making Grand Forks a regional health-care center. Population had reached 43,765 by 1980 and 49,425 by 1990.

The 1990s were a time of economic turbulence. Drops in retail and holiday spending by Canadians, formerly a major component of the local economy, had adverse effects, as did the personnel reduction from post–cold war mission changes at the air force base. Compounding economic uncertainty were the farm crisis of the late 1990s and the population decline of the Devils Lake Basin, a major part of the city's trade hinterland. Then came the flood of 1997, the community's most devastating natural catastrophe to date. Damage to the metropolitan area of Grand Forks (which includes East Grand Forks, Minnesota) amounted to almost $3.8 billion.

Although seriously damaged by the flood, the city has bounced back remarkably in terms of the built environment, thanks to massive amounts of federal and private aid. A long-range flood protection program is under way that consists of expansion of dikes and abandonment of the most flood-prone areas. Rebuilding of the central business district has been extensive, as has the increase in residential areas within the southern and western parts of the city. Currently, the city of Grand Forks covers 17.38 square miles and is expected to continue to grow in area, but it is struggling to resume its population growth.

See also WATER: Floods.

Douglas C. Munski
University of North Dakota

Grand Forks Centennial Committee. *They Came to Stay: Grand Forks, North Dakota Centennial 1874–1974*. Grand Forks, 1974. LeFever, Julie, John Bluemle, and Ryan Waldkrich. *Flooding in the Grand Forks–East Grand Forks, North Dakota and Minnesota Area*. Bismarck: North Dakota Geological Survey, 1999. Orvik, Jan, and Dick Larson. *The Return of Lake Agassiz: The University of North Dakota and the Flood of 1997*. Grand Forks: University of North Dakota Press, 1998.

GREAT FALLS, MONTANA

Great Falls, Montana, is situated at the upper end of a series of cataracts that begin at Black Eagle Falls and extend a dozen miles downstream to the largest drop in the Missouri River (given the name Big Falls by Meriwether Lewis), the site of present-day Ryan Dam. Nez Percé and Flathead Indians regularly defied the Blackfoot and entered the Plains from west of the mountains in search of bison, which were abundant in the vicinity of the site of the present city. Another attraction was the shallows situated just upstream from present-day downtown Great Falls, in those days the only practical place to cross the Missouri for forty miles in either direction.

In the heart of Blackfoot country and off the track for road freighters, who gave a wide berth to the deep cuts and coulees formed by the Missouri's feeder streams, the site of the future city remained virtually devoid of permanent occupation by Native Americans and settlers alike until Paris Gibson, a wool merchant and pioneer sheep rancher, founded the town in 1884. He had read the Lewis and Clark journals and came to see the falls for himself. Impressed with their beauty and their industrial potential, he convinced his friend, railroad magnate James Hill, to invest in the town site and urged him to extend his railroad through the new city on its way to the Pacific. Hill made the investment, but to Gibson's chagrin Hill subsequently chose a more northerly route for his transcontinental railroad (the Great Northern) so that the main line bypassed the town. Nonetheless, Gibson proceeded to supervise the symmetrical platting of streets and avenues, laid out on north–south and east–west axes with fourteen lots to the block, each lot precisely 50 by 150 feet. Gibson saw to the inclusion of parks and insisted on planting trees in abundance along the town's streets and avenues. Great Falls was a planned town—a businessman's town, different in style and character from mining camps and cattle towns that had sprung up of their own volition. This difference was noted by another of Gibson's friends, the famed cowboy artist Charlie Russell, who lauded Gibson for his work in founding the city.

Great Falls served from the first as a trade center for area farmers and ranchers, and Gibson and his partners saw to the building of dams to harness waterpower within a decade of the city's founding. Silver smelting emerged early on, and despite the repeal of the Sherman Silver Purchase Act in 1893 and other subsequent setbacks in the crusade to put silver at the center of the country's monetary system, the smelting industry survived and expanded, with copper becoming the predominant product during an era of industrial expansion. The 506-foot "Big Stack" dominated the city's skyline from the time of its completion in 1908. The smelter closed in 1980, and demolition of the landmark stack two years later marked the end of an era during which the smelter had been the single greatest source of industrial jobs for generations of Great Falls residents.

With the loss of the smelter and the effects of repeated drought years during the 1980s, Great Falls faced difficult times. However, other foundations of the local economy remained in place. One such was Malmstrom Air Force Base, established during World War II as the East Base to serve as a ferrying point for lend-lease aircraft headed for the Russian front via Alaska and Siberia. During the cold war era it continued as a missile base. From the first the military's presence had a significant social as well as economic impact. It brought to Great Falls significant numbers of people from many parts of the country, resulting in an increased population and a more diverse social and cultural milieu.

Other institutions also continued to bolster the local economy. National chains added to the number of large retail discount stores in Great Falls during the 1980s and 1990s, serving customers drawn from throughout the northern and central parts of Montana. Major medical and educational facilities have remained in place, and the state university system has steadily increased its presence in the city. During the late 1990s two new interpretive centers were built, one dedicated to the Lewis and Clark Expedition and the other to the Native American *pishkun*, or bison kill site, located not far from town. These joined the C. M. Russell Museum to attract increasing numbers of tourists to the city.

A number of factors combined to stem the initial steep declines following the closing of the smelter and the years of drought and agricultural depression. Great Falls entered the new millennium in a modest growth mode, with its most recent population at 56,690, drawing the city virtually even with where it stood in 1980 before the smelter closed.

See also TRANSPORTATION: Hill, James.

William J. Furdell
University of Great Falls

Frohlicher, S. V. *Stone Age to Space Age in 100 Years: Cascade County History and Gazetteer.* Great Falls MT: Cascade County Historical Society, 1981. Furdell, William J. "The Great Falls Home Front during World War II." *Montana: The Magazine of Western History* 48 (1998): 63–73. Furdell, William J., and Elizabeth L. Furdell. *Great Falls: A Pictorial History.* Virginia Beach VA: Donning Company Publishers, 1984.

"HELL ON WHEELS" TOWNS

When the Union Pacific Railroad crossed the Plains, large numbers of workers, hangers-on, and purveyors of vice congregated in temporary boom communities known as "Hell on Wheels." With few towns in existence along the Union Pacific line, there was little for the men to do, so professional gamblers, saloon keepers, and prostitutes filled the void in entertainment, building a reputation that lasts to the present. By no means, though, did all activity revolve around vice. In longer-lived towns, literary clubs, religious gatherings, theatrical offerings, and other activities were common. Two communities coexisted in the Hell on Wheels towns: the raucous railroad builders and their followers and the business-oriented class who hoped to remain and build permanent communities.

The men building the Union Pacific Railroad were often Irish immigrants, and many were Civil War veterans of both Confederate and Union sympathies. They were young and often single, a combination that encouraged violence and the available vices. Besides the inevitable prostitutes, other female residents were teachers, actresses, laundresses, cooks, and hotel operators, but women were still few in number.

The first "Hell on Wheels" town began near Fort Kearny, Nebraska Territory, in August 1866, when the Union Pacific line met Dobeytown, a settlement that existed to provide for the soldiers' more earthy needs. Fort Kearny (later just Kearney) and North Platte, Nebraska; Julesburg, Colorado; Cheyenne, Laramie, Green River City, and Benton, Wyoming; and Bear River City and Corrine, Utah, were among the primary towns.

Tent city, 16th Street, Cheyenne, Wyoming, 1867

A Hell on Wheels town was founded when the line of the railroad became apparent. At that point, merchants, aided by information provided by railroad officials, and the more enterprising residents of the last town moved to establish a community they hoped would be permanent but was usually temporary. Within a few weeks, residents of the last town would follow, leaving behind a small number of people who hoped to found a permanent city—North Platte declined in this manner from a population of a few thousand to less than 200. Sometimes departing residents left only trash and mud chimneys behind. The new community sprang to life as merchants of everything from the mundane to the scandalous quickly set up shop to receive the workers they knew would soon arrive. Town populations could rise from zero to thousands within a few days.

Few permanent structures were built in the towns. Most were tents with possibly a wooden front wall to give the appearance of solidity. Others were prefabricated and crude, designed to be taken apart and put together rapidly. Only in towns like Cheyenne, which had been earmarked as a repair center, did lasting buildings rise.

The towns provided virtually every service a construction worker might want, from dentistry and legal advice to gambling and prostitution. Saloons existed in large numbers. A tent more than 100 feet long, known as the "Big Tent," provided one notable place to drink and gamble as it followed the line. Dance houses provided relatively wholesome contact with women, while houses of prostitution also thrived. Vice was lucrative and found a ready market.

Merchants along the line made large fortunes, providing goods not only to residents of the towns but also to military posts and the established city of Denver. Large capital-intensive firms, such as dry goods and banking concerns, followed the line from bases in Denver, Chicago, and Omaha. Freighting companies worked to connect the cities on the line with Denver and with towns ahead of the track. Some towns, including Cheyenne, featured multiple newspapers, but most had only the "Press on Wheels," otherwise known as the *Frontier Index*, which followed the line from Fort Kearny to Bear River City.

While the towns violated the sexual and moral codes of the era despite the existence of law enforcement officers, quasi-legal and legal courts, and several vigilance committees, there was far less violence and open disregard for convention than has been supposed. Newspaper accounts show that while fights and killings did occur, they did not do so on a daily basis, despite repeated references in the historiography to phrases like "a man for breakfast."

The traditional view that the towns lasted only one or two months is only correct for the later towns, built when the speed of construction was greatest. Several towns endured, including Kearney and Julesburg, both of which had already existed in some form, and Cheyenne and Laramie, which were chosen by the Union Pacific for repair facilities or terminals of branch lines. Others, including Bear River City, disappeared, leaving behind little more than a lingering reputation.

The Union Pacific's Hell on Wheels towns seem to have been a unique phenomenon. They did not exist on the Central Pacific Railroad, which was built to meet the Union Pacific from Sacramento, California, to Promontory Point, Utah. The largely Chinese workforce of the Central Pacific was less violent, drunken, and ill behaved than that of the Union Pacific, and the builders of the Central Pacific appear to have exerted far greater control over their line. The contemporaneous Union Pacific–Eastern Division (later the Kansas Pacific) likewise was not known for producing wild construction towns. There were previously existing towns, however, such as Wallace and Hugo, Kansas, that provided similar services.

For the builders of the Union Pacific these towns were necessary—supplies and workers needed to be organized in convenient locations. The theft of Union Pacific property, attempts to squat on company land, and the atmosphere of violence and disorder, however, made the towns an example no other line would follow.

Charles Vollan
University of Nebraska–Lincoln

KANSAS CITY, KANSAS AND MISSOURI

Kansas City owes its fortunes to its geography, since it is located precisely where the Missouri River stops flowing to the south and begins to stretch out eastward. In 1833 this fortunate situation was enhanced when J. C. McCoy found a rock ledge that could serve as a natural boat landing. McCoy connected the landing by trail to his new settlement at Westport, creating one of the best jumping-off points for western land routes. The present-day Kansas City, Missouri, city center was incorporated in 1850. At around the same time settlement was beginning along the river bottoms in Wyandotte County just across the border in the state of Kansas. So from the 1850s on there were two Kansas Cities, divided by the Missouri-Kansas state line, and both grew from a consolidation of villages rather than from a single unit.

The construction of the Hannibal Bridge across the Missouri River in 1869 (the first railroad bridge to span the river) allowed Kansas City to develop quickly as a grain- and meat-processing center. The meatpacking industry began on the Kansas side of the river, as did the Santa Fe Railroad shops and yards, and this area became the home of several important ethnic populations, notably, Slavic, Hispanic, and African American. The African American population was increased by the arrival of the "Exodusters" from the South in the 1870s. African Americans established newspapers, churches, and a university in Kansas City, Kansas, during the late nineteenth century, but it was their twentieth-century contributions in both Kansas Cities that have been the most long lasting. From 1908 to 1955 Kansas City, Missouri, was home to the Kansas City Monarchs, one of the best teams in the Negro baseball league. Beginning in the 1920s Kansas City developed its own style of jazz, which was so popular that at one time there were more than fifty jazz clubs, located mainly between Twelfth and Eighteenth Streets on the Missouri side of the river. Kansas City barbeque is another mainly African American contribution.

Kansas City, Missouri, had also established itself as the "Gateway to the Southwest," with important rail connections and the industries that profited from them. Between 1880 and 1890 the population doubled, and in the next two decades ambitious plans for a network of boulevards and parks were established and eventually implemented. Suburbanization began in the 1920s with the creation of large residential districts mainly to the south of the downtown area. J. C. Nichols was the most successful real estate developer of this period. He created the Country Club Plaza, the first shopping center in the nation. The plaza has several notable features: it was designed in the 1920s with free parking lots placed around its periphery, and it was originally the home of a number of branch stores from the downtown area, serving as a model for retail suburbanization across the United States.

Prosperity ended with the Depression, but while the population stagnated, Kansas City, Missouri, benefited from a number of federal building initiatives, including a new post office (1933), a municipal auditorium (1935), and a new federal courts building (1933). It also profited from planned expansion. Unlike many older cities such as St. Louis that are hemmed in by surrounding counties, Kansas City, Missouri, was able to expand in an extraordinary fashion during the second half of the twentieth century, increasing in size from 60 square miles in 1940 to 130 square miles in 1960 and 316 square miles in 2001. The population of Kansas City, Missouri, stood at 435,000 in 2000.

During the Depression, Kansas City, Kansas, benefited mainly from a large levee development project. During World War II many firms produced munitions, engines, and the landing craft for the Normandy invasion, and after the war the city's industrial base began to diversify even more. Kansas City's industries now include Hallmark Cards, H & R Block, Kansas City Southern Industries, Ford Motor Company, and General Motors. The famous Kansas City stockyards are now virtually closed.

Kansas City, Kansas, has a population of 143,000, leaving Wichita as the largest city in Kansas. But if the explosive suburban growth seen in Johnson County, Kansas, in the 1980s and 1990s was added to the population of Kansas City, Kansas, it would be Kansas's largest city. Johnson County and Wyandotte County display the sharpest divide in social geography in Kansas. Wyandotte County's population is long established and mainly blue collar, with a large minority component. By contrast, Johnson County's population consists mainly of affluent, recently arrived, middle-class white residents.

Following the nationwide trend of the 1980s and 1990s, the urban school systems in both Kansas Cities now have a majority of African American and Hispanic students. But the two cities present other distinct contrasts. Kansas City, Missouri, known as the "City of Fountains," is currently undergoing urban revitalization in many of its downtown neighborhoods, notably at Westport and near the Plaza. In the late 1990s Union Station was remodeled into a science museum with funds supplied by both city and county taxpayers. Kansas City, Kansas, has not been able to attract as many new residents or new businesses as its neighbor, but it maintains its distinct social heritage and several of its historic ethnic neighborhoods, notably, Strawberry Hill. The entire metropolitan area now contains fifteen counties, thirty-five communities in two states, and nearly two million people.

See also AFRICAN AMERICANS: Baseball, Interracial / ARCHITECTURE: Country Club Plaza / INDUSTRY: Hallmark Cards, Inc. / MUSIC: Kansas City Jazz.

Karen J. De Bres
Kansas State University

De Bres, K. "Kansas City Urban Sites: Historical and Modern." *Papers and Proceedings of the Applied Geography Conference* 19 (1996): 299–305. Shortridge, J. "New Introduction." In *The WPA Guide to 1930s Kansas*, Lawrence: University Press of Kansas, 1984.

LAWTON, OKLAHOMA

Situated in southwestern Oklahoma between the ninety-eighth and ninety-ninth meridians, roughly nine miles from a small cavalry post, Lawton resulted from acts of Congress in 1900 and 1901 that eliminated the Kiowa, Comanche, and Apache Reservation by allotting every family 160 acres and opening the surplus land to non-Indian settlement under the provisions of the homestead and town-site laws. By March 1901 federal officials had completed the task of Indian allotment, and on July 4, 1901, President William McKinley declared the area ready for settlement.

To avoid the confusion and chaos that had previously accompanied the establishment of counties and county seats in Oklahoma Territory, the secretary of the interior was empowered to divide the former reservation into counties and to specify the names and locations of the county seats. The Interior Department was also vested with the responsibility for platting each county seat. In accordance with Congress's provisions, the sale of commercial and residential lots in Lawton was to be done by public auction under the direction of the Department of the Interior. The bidding for town lots began on August 6, 1901. The rapid, orderly sale of town lots spurred the formation of a local government. On September 28, 1901, Lawton became an incorporated city with a mayor-council system of government. In 1911 Lawtonians switched to the commission plan of government, but in the 1920s city government reverted to the mayor-council form. Finally in 1972, Lawton voters adopted the current structure of city manager, mayor, and city council.

Lawton's initial boomers never imagined that the nearby fort would have a decided impact on the future of the new town. They envisioned that Lawton would become mainly a commercial hub for the surrounding agriculture hinterland. However, the designation of Fort Sill as a field artillery center changed the outlook of the community. From 1909 onward, the city's population and economy have been closely tied to the level of activity of Fort Sill, and although some economic diversification has occurred, Fort Sill remained the biggest employer in the community in 1998. From 1940 to 1970 the city more than quadrupled its size, swelling from 18,055 to 74,470. Much of this growth stemmed from the expansion of Fort Sill. Subsequent reduction in military spending has halted Lawton's population explosion. After 1970 the city's population increased more slowly, reaching 81,110 in 1998.

Lawton did experience some economic change during this same period as it developed new industries. The construction of a Goodyear tire factory during the 1970s helped to wean the city from its dependence on Fort Sill; currently, Goodyear represents the second largest employer in Lawton. The city also functions as a regional health-care and higher education center and continues to act as a retail hub for surrounding counties in southwestern Oklahoma. In addition, the adjacent Wichita Mountain Wildlife Refuge draws thousands of tourists to the city each year.

See also WAR: Military Bases.

Suzanne Jones Crawford
Cameron University

Crawford, Suzanne Jones. "L. M. Gensman: A Study of an Early Twentieth Century Western Attorney." Ph.D. diss., University of Oklahoma, 1980. Stevens, M. David. *Lawton–Ft. Sill: A Pictorial History*. Virginia Beach VA: Donning Company Publishers, 1990.

LINCOLN, NEBRASKA

In 1859 a group of settlers gathered in southeastern Nebraska Territory on the banks of Salt Creek and founded the hamlet of Lancaster. They had aspirations that Lancaster would grow into a manufacturing center based on local salt deposits, aspirations that came to nothing. But by 1866 the hamlet was named the county seat, and a year later, when Nebraska attained statehood, the site was formally selected as the capital and renamed in honor of President Abraham Lincoln. The settlement was incorporated in 1869.

The city grew rapidly, attracting one railroad by 1870 and seven by 1900. In addition to its governmental function, Lincoln became home to meatpacking, agricultural-processing, and printing industries and the first of many insurance companies by the 1880s. Diversity was recognized early on by the Nebraska legislature's donation of a site for the African American congregation of the Quinn Chapel African Methodist Episcopal Church, in 1873. The city's population grew rapidly to 55,000 in 1890, then declined during the depression of the 1890s. Recovery was slow at first, but Lincoln's population then increased during every decade of the twentieth century, reflecting the diversified economic base, which furnished jobs, and the attractive living environment. By 2000 the city's population had reached 209,192, having grown at an annual rate of 1.6 percent over the previous three decades.

As the seat of state, city, and county governments, Lincoln remains a major administrative city. It has a mayor-council form of local government and the option of home rule under the Nebraska constitution, which authorizes the city to operate under its own charter. The University of Nebraska, established in 1869, Nebraska Wesleyan University, and Union College give the city its identity as a university town. A mix of manufacturing, transportation, trade, commerce, insurance, health, and other service industries characterize the contemporary diversified economy of the city.

The premier work of architecture in the city is the Nebraska State Capitol, designed by architect Bertram Grosvenor Goodhue. The First Plymouth Congregational Church, the old university library (Architectural Hall), and the William Jennings Bryan House are also noteworthy and among several buildings listed on the National Register of Historic Places. Distinguished architects Phillip Johnson and I. M. Pei designed the Sheldon Memorial Art Gallery and Sculpture Garden and the National Bank of Commerce, respectively. Another local point of interest, Pioneers Park, designed by landscape architect Ernst H. Herminghaus (who also laid out the state capitol grounds), lies at the fringe of the city.

Prominent historical residents of Lincoln include John J. Pershing, commander of American forces in Europe during World War I; William Jennings Bryan, orator, U.S. congressman, and three-time Democratic Party presidential candidate; Charles Dawes, vice president under Calvin Coolidge in 1924; Willa Cather, Nebraskan author and 1895 graduate of the University of Nebraska–Lincoln; George Beadle, Nobel Prize–winning biologist; and Roscoe Pound, legal scholar, dean of the University of Nebraska Law College, and dean of Harvard Law School.

See also ARCHITECTURE: Herminghouse, Ernst; Nebraska State Capitol / LITERARY TRADITIONS: Cather, Willa / POLITICS AND GOVERNMENT: Bryan, William Jennings / WAR: Pershing, John J.

N. Brito Mutunayagam
Abigail Posie Davis
University of Nebraska–Lincoln

Clerk of the Legislature, ed. *Nebraska Blue Book 1998–1999*. Lincoln NE: Unicameral Information Office, 1999. Copple, Neal. *Tower on the Plains: Lincoln's Centennial History, 1859–1959*. Lincoln NE: Lincoln Centennial Commission Publishers, 1959. McKee, James L. *Lincoln, the Prairie Capital: An Illustrated History*. Woodland Hills CA: Windsor Publications, 1984.

LUBBOCK, TEXAS

Lubbock, Texas, a city of 193,000 inhabitants in the heart of the Llano Estacado of West Texas, traces its roots to a country store that George Singer established in 1882 along the upper Brazos River. The tiny store attracted area cowboys and a few overland travelers but little else.

Eight years later, however, and a few miles away, two groups of promoters established separate towns, Lubbock and Monterey. A compromise was needed, for everyone understood that both communities, fewer than three miles apart but divided by a shallow canyon of the Brazos, could not survive. In December 1890, having reached an accommodation, the promoters, led by W. E. Rayner, Frank Wheelock, and Rollie Burns, agreed to a third site, and a new town, also called Lubbock, appeared south of the canyon where they thought a railroad might pass through the area.

They chose well. Situated on the High Plains some 3,200 feet above sea level, the new town attracted businessmen, farmers, and ranchers. Early in 1891 more than 100 people lived in the town, and in the spring it won election as the political seat of Lubbock County. Before winter Lubbock contained several stores, churches, a newspaper, and a school.

Drought and depression slowed Lubbock's growth, however, and its population in 1900 was fewer than 300 inhabitants. The Santa Fe Railroad arrived, finally, in 1909, and Lubbock immediately entered a boom period. As crop farming increased, farmer-settlers replaced ranchers in the area, and additional railroads reduced the city's isolation. In response, Lubbock's population more than doubled between 1910 and 1920, and the city soon became known as the "Hub City of the Plains."

In the 1920s Lubbock enjoyed a second boom. Texas Technological College, which became Texas Tech University in 1969, was the major cause. Established in 1923, the college grew remarkably in students, faculty, and facilities, continuing its expansion through the 1930s and afterward. Owing in part to the university, Lubbock today enjoys a large symphony orchestra, two ballet companies, several theater groups, and many libraries and museums.

In 1940 the city's population reached 32,000, including about 1,600 Latinos and 1,000 African Americans. During World War II Lubbock expanded again as the city became an important military center. The region's mild weather and sunny skies made it ideal for Reese Air Force Base, an air training station. Before it closed in 1997, the air base, with its personnel and large civilian workforce, greatly enhanced the city's economy and contributed to its cultural and social evolution.

After World War II Lubbock developed into a major agribusiness center. In the 1950s the city produced pumps, tubular goods, sprinklers, farm equipment, fertilizers, and pesticides. With its large processing plants, it became a national marketing center for cotton. Continued population expansion in the 1960s encouraged the founding of a second college, Lubbock Christian University. In 1970 the city's population stood at 150,000 people, with more than 31,000 Latinos and nearly 11,000 African Americans.

A tornado in 1970 leveled a residential area just north of downtown Lubbock, killing twenty-six people and injuring many others. The tornado destroyed 1,046 homes, damaged 8,000 others, and left 1,800 people homeless. It also damaged some 600 businesses. Lubbock citizens rebuilt the area with a large civic-center complex and memorial. The rebuilding process plus the construction in the 1970s of Texas Tech University's Health Sciences Center, a large teaching hospital, and the expansion of the city's other hospitals made the city a major medical center. By the 1980s Lubbock was home to 292 industrial concerns, and it served a wholesale and retail area covering much of West Texas and eastern New Mexico. It became the world's leading center of cottonseed production.

Lubbock's cultural roots reach back to agrarian southern traditions. Its citizens are conservative in politics and informal in dress and lifestyle, but Lubbock's society is entirely modern. Its largest minority groups, Latinos and African Americans, influence the political and cultural life of the city, and their social and economic successes have helped to move Lubbock into the modern era and into a dominant position on the southern High Plains.

See also INDUSTRY: Cotton Industry.

Paul H. Carlson
Texas Tech University

Abbe, Don, Paul H. Carlson, and David J. Murrah. *Lubbock and the South Plains: An Illustrated History*. Tarzana CA: Preferred Marketing, 1995. Graves, Lawrence, ed. *A History of Lubbock*. Lubbock: West Texas Museum Association, 1959. Graves, Lawrence, ed. *Lubbock from Town to City*. Lubbock: West Texas Museum Association, 1986.

Main Street, Florence, Kansas

MAIN STREET

Main Street is the heart and soul of all Great Plains towns and cities, the starting point from which all towns in this region began. The combination of community development, economic growth, and the love-hate relationship with the automobile makes the Great Plains Main Street distinctive from other Main Streets in North America.

Main Street is a planned development that integrates traffic, commercial markets, and public open space. The most common characteristic of Great Plains Main Streets is that they are part of a grid system of streets. Main Street is the spine within a series of streets arranged in a perpendicular pattern. The benefits of a grid pattern of streets allows for an efficient flow of traffic and maximizes building access from the street. Main Streets also share the following types of land uses: commercial space for trade and banking; government space for governance and justice; public open space for celebrations and festivals; and churches for religious, educational, and town meetings. All of these land uses were tightly confined to a few blocks for several reasons. First, communities just getting started had limited resources. Consequently, Main Streets initially developed within a couple of blocks in order to handle the most immediate community needs. Second, most Great Plains Main Streets were developed at a time when commerce was primarily regional in focus and did not require a large amount of space or infrastructure to support area businesses. Finally, since Main Streets were not built in an era of modern telecommunication capabilities, most community life was handled directly through face-to-face interactions, which were more easily accommodated by a densely organized Main Street where everything was in easy walking distance.

In addition to meeting local community needs, Main Streets were also developed to generate economic resources. The economic attractiveness of the Main Street design is two-fold. First, organizing a community around Main Street provided local buildings with easy customer access from the street. Buildings that are easily accessible from the Main Street thoroughfare generate more revenue and have a higher real estate market value than buildings that are located on less traveled arterial routes. Second, the grid pattern of streets made it easier for towns to accommodate new growth. All a town needed to do to grow was to expand its infrastructure of roads and utilities by adding another block along Main Street. The ease of Main Street expansion made real estate speculation less risky because block sizes were standardized and new developments were anchored by the established activity already on Main Street. In some cities, like Topeka, Kansas, Main Street grew solely by real estate development. Plains railroad towns are another example of towns developing on a Main Street schema for real estate speculation.

Much of the current demise of Main Streets came about through the combination of mass ownership of automobiles and a changing economy that dictated a new logic in the development and organization of town space. Beginning in the 1920s, automobiles became more prevalent due to their increasing affordability and dependability. Motorists' demands for decreasing traffic congestion and improving vehicle access to buildings resulted in reconfiguring Main Streets to accommodate the car. Main Streets were retrofitted for this rising mobility through widening the street, adding traffic signals, and providing more on-street and off-street parking. By the end of World War II, the attractiveness of high-density Main Streets had come to an end. The advent of mass automobile ownership required buildings to be more accessible to cars than to pedestrians. The requirement of parking spaces forced buildings away from the street and set them, almost as a backdrop, behind the parking lot. Also, streets had to be widened even more, and the stoplights had to be calibrated to allow for a tolerable flow of vehicular movement along Main Street and to prevent unacceptable levels of traffic.

In some Great Plains communities, Main Streets became economically obsolete because of their existing dense configuration of buildings arranged along a narrow high-traffic corridor. In such places, Main Streets never grew beyond their original buildings. The impacts of telecommunications and the economic postwar boom in the 1950s and 1960s also created demand for more decentralized Main Street space. Commerce from the 1950s to the early 1970s was no longer dependent on face-to-face transactions. Decisions could be made and business deals closed with the interested parties being physically in two different parts of the world. In addition, regional economic systems were becoming more national and international, requiring larger facilities that could not be accommodated in the old Main Street system of spaces. It was becoming less cost-effective for businesses to be located in Main Street buildings with high rents, limited space (especially for storage), and inconvenient parking.

For other communities, the commercial decline of their downtown Main Streets was the result of an overly successful planned and managed Main Street. In these cases, the grid pattern of streets with Main Street as the lynchpin was so successful that it drew people and economic development out of the Main Street core to the suburban fringe. Main Street grew beyond the downtown to become the arterial spine of suburbanized sections of the city, accommodating higher traffic densities and lower building densities such as the suburban shopping mall. Lincoln, Nebraska, is one example of a popular Main Street that expanded out to the suburban fringe, carrying development away from the original downtown section.

A revival of the original pedestrian-based Main Street system has been gaining momentum since the 1970s. This revival was fueled by international trends such as rising gasoline costs, renewed appreciation for historically significant buildings, antisuburbanization sentiment, and, more recently, computer and telecommunication innovations that make businesses less tied to suburban commercial spaces. The rekindling of the Main Street spirit has also been supported by the cooperative efforts of individual entrepreneurs, local civic groups, and national organizations like the National Trust for Historic Preservation. After years of neglect and countless facade modifications, old Main Street buildings are now being restored and maintained according to their original design. Perkins, Oklahoma, is one example of a town working to restore historically significant buildings on its Main Street. The town's restoration efforts are nicely illustrated in the 1993 refurbishing of the Baker's Store Building, built in 1890 on the corner of Main and Thomas. Through such community revitalization, Great Plains residents are once again making Main Street the heart and soul of their community.

See also ARCHITECTURE: Commercial Architecture.

John Gaber
Auburn University

Liebs, Chester. *Main Street to Miracle Mile: American Roadside Architecture.* Boston: Little, Brown, 1985. Reps, John. *The Forgotten Frontier: Urban Planning in the American West before 1890.* Columbia: University of Missouri Press, 1981.

MIDLAND, TEXAS

Midland, located at an altitude of 2,779 feet on the southern edge of the Great Plains, is doubly distinguished as a modern and wealthy oil capital and as one of the most isolated urban areas in the United States. The major metropolitan centers of Dallas–Fort Worth, Austin, San Antonio, El Paso, and Albuquerque are all over 300 miles away. Midland shares its isolation, its airport, its oil and gas economy, and a standard metropolitan area designation with its nearby sister city, Odessa. Much of the world links the two cities with a common name, Midland-Odessa. The surrounding oil-producing region of West Texas is known as the Permian Basin in recognition of the subterranean oil-bearing geological strata deposited by ancient seas during the Permian Era.

Although Midland was founded in 1885 as a ranching and agricultural depot on the Texas and Pacific Railroad, where its midway location between Fort Worth and El Paso inspired its name, the city's growth and development since the 1920s have depended disproportionately on oil and natural gas. After major oil field discoveries throughout the Permian Basin during the 1920s, the city quickly developed into the regional headquarters for one of the most important oil-producing regions of the United States. Odessa, in contrast, developed into much more of a blue-collar city, becoming home to thousands of workers in the oil fields and related activities. Despite cycles of boom and bust in the "awl bidness," Midland has steadily grown to a population of approximately 97,000, combined into an Odessa-Midland population of approximately 225,000.

One prominent family name in Midland now belongs to the history of the nation. President George H. W. Bush arrived in the Permian Basin with his young family in the early 1950s, living briefly in Odessa and then in Midland for most of the decade. With some investment money in hand, Bush learned the oil business during one of its periods of rapid development. He was part of a stream of new arrivals from out of state who brought a high level of education and managerial expertise to the area. George and Barbara Bush's son George W. Bush grew up and attended several grades of public school in Midland. He was destined to become governor of Texas and the first presidential son since John Quincy Adams to follow his father to the White House. Some years after the family moved their oil interests to Houston, George W. returned to the city he still considers his hometown to start his own career in the oil business. Midland is also the hometown of President George W. Bush's wife, Laura.

Drivers approaching the city on Interstate 20 might well marvel at the tall business towers rising in a dense cluster from the arid West Texas plains. Those taking time to visit would probably be equally surprised to discover a well-planned city with many amenities usually associated with a much larger population. Inside the commercial and residential areas, most signs of the West Texas desert quickly disappear. Elegant and comfortable residential areas display ample evidence of the city's oil wealth along wide and well-landscaped streets. Residents often praise the sheer convenience of everyday life in Midland, where traffic jams are almost nonexistent and modern retail shopping and dining facilities developed rapidly during the 1990s.

The 2000 census reported a Midland population that was about 75.5 percent white, 29 percent Hispanic, and 8 percent African American. School enrollment figures since then, however, indicate a rapidly changing demography. The Hispanic population, in particular, is increasing rapidly, a change that is already reflected in local civic and school board elections.

In compensation for Midland's distance from the rest of the world, much attention has been paid to surface and air transportation. In addition to Interstate 20, the city is encircled and connected to Odessa by a system of modern expressways that stimulated the remarkable commercial and retail boom of the 1990s. A glance at the map of North America reveals the inspiration for another transportation project that is under way for the Midland area. The city lies almost exactly at the midpoint of the most direct potential corridor between Dallas–Fort Worth and the large northern Mexican industrial city of Chihuahua. In the spirit of the North American Free Trade Agreement, a coordinated plan called La Entrada al Pacífico is already under way in both Texas and Mexico to build modern highway links between Midland and Chihuahua.

Midland has long been a regional air transportation center. During World War II the site of the present airport was a major military pilot-training facility. Today Midland International Airport serves a vast area of West Texas, including much of the trans-Pecos region. It is the closest full-service airport to Big Bend National Park, about a four-hour drive away. In 1991 the airport became home to the American Airpower Heritage Museum. With special emphasis on the preservation of World War II aircraft, the museum holds the largest private collection of these planes in the United States. Many of the aircraft are maintained in flying condition and are the focus of the annual October Airshow.

Given Midland's location in the desertlike chaparral of West Texas, with an average annual rainfall of only twelve to fourteen inches, visitors are often surprised at the amount of irrigated agriculture that is visible to the north and east of the city. The crops, which typically are cotton, alfalfa, and pecans, depend on water from the Ogallala Aquifer, which extends hundreds of miles north into the Great Plains and reaches its southern extent a few miles south of the city. Until recently, Midland was heavily dependent on wells for its municipal water supply. By the 1990s, however, pure water began reaching the city via a 150-mile pipeline from Lake Ivey in Central Texas.

Midland's premier educational facility is Midland College, a comprehensive two-year community college on a spacious, parklike campus on the northern edge of the city. A branch campus of the state university, the University of Texas of the Permian Basin, offers a variety of baccalaureate and graduate-degree programs at its campus in Odessa. Midland's high schools, along with those of Odessa, have become nationally famous for the intensity of their annual football jousts. H. G. Bissinger's 1990 book, *Friday Night Lights*, has brilliantly documented this rivalry and the culture that has developed around it.

Despite its prominence, football is not the only diversion available to Midlanders. Low humidity and mild winters make other outdoor activities such as tennis and golf attractive year-round. When the flat and virtually treeless plains occasionally become too monotonous, many Midlanders have discovered that relief is only a short drive away, at least in Texas miles. The alpine resorts of Cloudcroft and Ruidoso, New Mexico, are close enough for a Midland colony of vacation homes, while Guadalupe National Park and the cool, green Davis Mountains are barely three hours away. The Nature Conservancy of Texas has recently established the Davis Mountains Preserve in the heart of this range, providing Midlanders and other West Texans an opportunity for increased awareness of the ecology and diversity of their region.

See also IMAGES AND ICONS: Friday Night Football / INDUSTRY: Petroleum, United States / POLITICS AND GOVERNMENT: Bush, George H. W.; Bush, George W.

Jerry Franks
Midland College

Bissinger, H. G. *Friday Night Lights: A Town, a Team, and a Dream.* New York: HarperCollins, 1990. Olien, Roger M., and Diana Davids Olien. *Oil Booms: Social Change in Five Texas Towns.* Lincoln: University of Nebraska Press, 1982.

ODESSA, TEXAS

Odessa is a city of 95,700 inhabitants, located centrally in the Permian Basin of West Texas. It sits nearly equidistant from both El Paso and Fort Worth and serves as the county seat for Ector County. The city, which shares its name with Odessa, Ukraine, started as 640 acres in Survey 27 in 1876. Jay Gould's Texas and Pacific Railroad Company, which reached the survey in 1881, provided the impetus for further settlement. In 1886, when the population was only sixty, the Texas and Pacific transferred the acreage to John Hoge of Ohio, who then formed the Odessa Land and Townsite Company. Advertising in 1888 about the new town of Odessa on the Staked Plain of West Texas ensured eastern readers of cheap homes, provisions for religious and educational facilities, and the intentional absence of saloons. By 1890 there were 224 inhabitants; thirty-five years later, there were still only 750 residents of Odessa.

Population growth accelerated with the 1926 discovery of oil in Ector County and subsequent discoveries in nearby counties. The industry that emerged had its origins in the Permian Sea, which covered the area before dinosaurs made their appearance on the earth. As the waters eventually receded, the decaying plant and animal life became over time the future oil reserves. It was not until after the worst of the Depression that the burgeoning petroleum industry came into its real strength. Odessa's proximity to the oil fields and railroad made it the choice location to service and supply the wells, and Odessa and Midland together are jointly referred to as the Petroplex. Additionally, Odessans have experimented since initial settlement with livestock ventures. Early attempts at sheep raising failed due to barbed wire, which closed off the range. Cattle ranching strengthened over time and remains a vibrant business today. Football was introduced to the town in 1923 to encourage young men to stay in school. Today, Odessa is nationally known for its highly competitive football program: Permian High captured the Texas state high school title six times from 1964 to 1991, and Odessa High was champion in 1946.

In 1927 the town became a city when it incorporated, receiving its charter and electing its first mayor. But its development and growth still came in spurts, largely dependent on the oil economy and available accommodation. Such booms and busts continue to influence the area. It was during one such boom in 1948 that President George H. W. Bush and his family lived and worked in Odessa. They spent one year in the city before moving to Midland.

Modern Odessa, while still dependent on oil and cattle, continues to evolve. The Permian Basin International Oil Show, first begun in 1940, continues to be held biennially, but Odessa is also working to diversify its economy by attracting other businesses and industries. And although the city's first college was burned to the ground in 1892, possibly in response to the saloon debate, today there are two thriving institutions of higher learning: Odessa College and the University of Texas of the Permian Basin. Possibly, the area's oldest point of interest is the meteor crater created some 20,000 years ago but only declared a national landmark in 1965: the Odessa Crater measures 550 feet in diameter and is purported to be the second largest in the country.

See also IMAGES AND ICONS: Friday Night Football / INDUSTRY: Petroleum, United States.

Linda D. Brown
Odessa College

Justice, Glenn. *Odessa: An Illustrated History.* Chatsworth CA: Windsor Publications, 1991. Sheppard, John Ben. *Odessa 100: An Informal History.* Odessa TX: Exchange Club, 1981. *Texas: The New Town of Odessa.* Odessa TX: Odessa Land and Townsite Company, 1888.

OIL BOOMTOWNS

Beginning in the 1890s, oil fever spread expectations of new growth and money across the Great Plains from the eastern parts of Kansas and Texas. Oil seeps and folds and faults in the layered limestone beds of the Flint Hills looked promising to both oil scouts and geology professors at the University of Kansas. Prairie Oil Company, correctly suspected to be allied with the Standard Oil Company of John D. Rockefeller, brought twenty experienced drillers from older fields in Pennsylvania to Neodosha, Kansas. In 1893 they completed the first commercial well in the giant midcontinent collection of fields that would eventually arc southward through Oklahoma to Abilene, Texas. A lively oil industry also developed in the Prairie Provinces.

The Plains were open to high hopes, exploration for oil, and speculative investments. Oil was found in Central Texas, just to the east of the Plains, at Corsicana in 1894. Discovery wells were subsequently drilled in Indian Territory and Texas. As new fields were found, schemes to solicit investment money for oil development became particularly active in Fort Worth, Texas. Later, Calgary, Alberta, developed a similar collection of brokers selling leases and shares in new oil companies, some of which were paper creations aimed at gullible purchasers.

In the United States, the production of oil from states west of the Mississippi River exceeded that of the eastern states by 1904. At that time, interest focused on the Osage Hills in Indian Territory near the Kansas border. A major discovery in the Turner Valley of Alberta, just to the south of Calgary, in 1914 started a rush to develop the large new oil reservoir. In both the Prairie Provinces and Kansas, large amounts of natural gas were also found. Towns and cities began to enjoy heat and lighting from natural gas as pipelines fanned out across the Plains. With new discoveries, especially in North Texas and the Permian Basin of West Texas, a chain of booming oil towns appeared from the far southern reaches of the Great Plains to its northern margins.

Black-and-white photographs taken in the oil boomtowns show landscape images of raw wood, angular steel, and legions of grimy, exhausted men staring blankly into the camera. Heavily laden wagons threaded for miles along rutted roadways hauling pipe and supplies. Other pictures of intensely worked early fields show scars, scrapes, roads, trenches, and blast holes in the land similar to some of the battlefields of World War I. The boomtowns filled with men who worked, slept, ate and imbibed, celebrated, waited for mail, prayed with oil field preachers, and occasionally fought each other. Women and children found it difficult to fit into these places of bad housing, incessant noise, invasive lights, dangerous machinery, fires, toxic flammable gases, explosions, unsanitary conditions, and high prices, but surprising numbers of them endured the hardships of oil field life as they migrated with their husbands or fathers from one new field to the next. However, the harshness of such a life was reflected in high divorce rates, especially in the early development periods of isolated fields like the Permian Basin.

Tents were often the only accommodation for workers and families, even through cold, windy Plains winters. Heating the tents was hazardous. Unpainted wood weathered quickly on the storefronts of boomtown Main Streets. Two-room shotgun shacks or moveable boxcar houses sufficed as housing in some of the boomtowns and across the producing fields. Wells were drilled alongside existing houses in towns such as Burkburnett, Texas, which was deluged by oil boomers in 1917. Most boomtowns had the same look and feel: temporary, muddy, dusty, noisy, and forlorn. The towns were often mired in mud, some of which came from the slush pits that collected wastes from the wells. Electric lights hanging high on the oil rigs gave the nighttime illusion of a carnival spread across the Plains.

In the 1920s the large oil companies began building camps for workers and families in an attempt to improve living conditions in the new fields. Life in these camps was preferred over the tents or boomtown housing, even though most camps only provided a few rows of houses painted white with green or orange roofs. Outdoor toilets were the rule, but even these were unavailable in many camps and towns, leaving people to their own devices, usually vacant lots or empty fields. Contagious diseases, including tuberculosis and diphtheria, spread rapidly in such conditions.

Many people came to the boomtowns to make money in service occupations, most of which were as legitimate as running retail stores, hotels, and restaurants and teaching school. Some came to practice lucrative illegal activities such as bootlegging liquor, gambling, and prostitution. "Jake joints" sold Jamaican Ginger, an illegal alcoholic product well known for paralyzing the legs of those who drank too much of it.

The Turner Valley of Alberta had its own collection of oil boomtowns such as Longview (dubbed Little New York) and Royalties (Little Chicago), with seedy suburbs such as Banana Flats and Whiskey Row. The valley quickly filled with development. One area of the valley, with its numerous gas flares, became known as Hell's Half Acre. The same name described a few blocks of saloons in Fort Worth, Texas.

For the Great Plains, oil and gas development meant frontiers in a new guise. Some towns appeared and became small cities; others quickly disappeared. The fields needed a few larger places to serve as regional oil field support centers for equipment and services. Examples include Odessa, Texas, and Wichita, Kansas. Others, like Fort Worth, Texas, Oklahoma City, Oklahoma, and Calgary, Alberta, became even larger oil and gas logistical centers, with central supply houses, technical services, and homes for families as workers were able to drive farther to work in the fields on improved highways. At the eastern margins of the Great Plains, two major management and finance centers—Dallas, Texas, and Tulsa, Oklahoma—became the hometowns of wealthy oil investors who founded their own corporations—Harry Sinclair, J. Paul Getty, and H. L. Hunt, among others. The population shifts prompted by oil development jolted Great Plains farm and ranch people, as did the grimy landscapes filled with manic activity and so completely defined by their function that their form and appearance became a kind of ingrained tattoo.

Boomtowns such as Borger, Texas, and Kiefer, Oklahoma, earned reputations for violence, but most injuries and deaths were caused by dangerous jobs around large, moving equipment or explosions in the oil fields rather than from fighting in the streets or saloons. A distinction can be made between some Texas and Oklahoma towns, with their whiskey celebrations in saloons and dance halls, and more staid Kansas towns, with their clear ideas of propriety and personal conduct. Everywhere, life in the fields discovered after World War II was milder than in the early boomtowns.

The early Plains boomtowns, mainly those in Texas and Oklahoma, became a popular setting for fictional stories. A singular theme, the corrupting influence of oil money, was emphasized repeatedly in novels and movies, with iconography and imagery drawn from the stereotypical early boomtowns. This simplified representation became the standard view of all oil towns across the Great Plains. The 1941 Hollywood movie *Boom Town*, set in Burkburnett, Texas, is typical. The central figure drills his first well with stolen money, rejects his oil field partner and his wife, and enjoys the sweet life with lots of booze and a new romantic liaison. After losing his fortune, he sheds the evil of oil money with the help of his old friend and long-suffering wife, then returns to the true values once again to drill another well.

See also FILM: Oil Field Films / INDUSTRY: Petroleum, Canada; Petroleum, United States.

Gary L. Thompson
Norman, Oklahoma

Landrum, Jeff. *A Photographic Essay of the Burkburnett Oil Boom*. Wichita Falls TX: Humphrey Printing Company, 1982. Olien, Roger M., and Diana Davids Olien. *Oil*

Booms: Social Change in Five Texas Towns. Lincoln: University of Nebraska Press, 1982. Rister, Carl. *Oil: Titan of the Southwest*. Norman: University of Oklahoma Press, 1949.

OKLAHOMA CITY, OKLAHOMA

Oklahoma City, like San Francisco and Denver, was an instant city. On the morning of April 22, 1889, the future site of the town was an unbroken level prairie lying in a loop of the North Canadian River; by that evening between 6,000 and 10,000 people populated the site. Unlike the people who settled San Francisco and Denver, however, the settlers of Oklahoma City were not lured by the promise of precious metals. Rather, it was the lure of land and the promise of future prosperity that made Oklahoma City a boomtown. The land had belonged to the Creeks and the Seminoles, but in 1889 the United States acquired title to the "Unassigned District," and on April 22 of that year the land was opened for homestead settlement in the first of a series of "runs."

Oklahoma City would become the largest urban center and the most important trade headquarters in central Oklahoma. After 1895, Oklahoma City was served by four railroads, which enabled local wholesale merchants to extend their trade areas. Easy transportation also facilitated the growth of flour and cottonseed oil mills. In May 1909 representatives of the Chicago packing firm of Nelson, Moriss and Company met with a large number of Oklahoma City businessmen to consider the possibility of constructing a packing plant. The businessmen offered a cash bonus of $300,000 and property concessions, and the company built the plant. A second packing plant soon followed. By 1910 these two plants and the attendant holding yards employed more than 4,000 people. In 1910 Oklahoma City became the permanent state capital, which also provided employment for many city residents. The village had quickly grown into a city of 64,000, and much of the impetus for growth had come from dynamic early leaders such as Charles Colcord, Henry Overholser, Hugh M. Johnson, Anton H. Classen, and E. K. Gaylord.

Stimulated by World War I, Oklahoma City boomed, and by 1920 the population had increased to 91,295. The metropolitan area contained 400 manufacturing plants, a similar number of jobbing houses, and 1,100 retail establishments. After World War I the economy became increasingly diversified: the city continued to serve as a processing center for agricultural products, but there were also new iron and steel plants and factories producing furniture, clothing, and electrical equipment. Various large utility companies and brokerage houses established their headquarters in the downtown area, and, most significantly, in the late 1920s a gusher oil field was discovered and developed on the east side of the city. This discovery led to an oil boom that would make Oklahoma City a leading center of the nation's petroleum industry.

The Great Depression had a chilling impact on Oklahoma's two primary economic activities, agriculture and oil. The crisis was so deep that the chamber of commerce advised residents not to invite their relatives or friends to move to the city unless they had a job, and in 1931 the community budget allocated $338,092 of its $450,565 for relief activities. However, although the Depression slowed economic growth in Oklahoma City, it did not stop it: more than 367 new businesses were established in 1931 alone.

But again it was war—World War II—that stimulated growth. Led by business and civic leaders R. A. Singletary, Stanley Draper, Samuel W. Hays, Frank Buttram, Harvey P. Everest, and Dan Hogan, Oklahoma City secured Tinker Air Force Base. By the 1970s Tinker was the city's and the state's largest single employer, with some 22,500 civilian workers and about 3,000 air force personnel and an annual payroll of almost $300 million. Along with further economic development in iron and steel and the electronics industry, Oklahoma City also expanded physically in the 1960s. The city annexed a large number of surrounding areas, increasing in size from about 310 square miles in 1960 to about 635 square miles in 1970. Its population continued to grow, reaching 403,484 in 1980.

Unlike many cities in the 1960s, Oklahoma City was not rocked by violent social upheavals. Clara Luper, sponsor of the NAACP Youth Organization, led a generally peaceful sit-in movement that integrated most restaurants and other public facilities in the late 1950s. Integration of Oklahoma City schools by busing in the 1960s, however, did create turmoil and protest.

In the 1970s and early 1980s Oklahoma City reaped the economic and social benefits of a growing oil industry and the construction of a General Motors plant. Unfortunately, the collapse of Penn Square Bank and problems in

Oklahoma City, Oklahoma Territory, 1889

the oil industry slowed city growth for much of the 1980s. On April 19, 1995, Oklahoma City gained prominence that it did not want when the Alfred P. Murrah Federal Building was bombed and destroyed, killing 168 people. In 2000 the population of Oklahoma City proper was 450,000, with more than one million people living in the entire metropolitan statistical area.

See also ARCHITECTURE: Layton, Solomon / INDUSTRY: Petroleum, United States / PROTEST AND DISSENT: Oklahoma City Bombing.

John Thompson
Oklahoma Christian University

Meredith, Howard L., and George H. Shirk. "Oklahoma City: Growth and Reconstruction, 1889–1939." *Chronicles of Oklahoma* 55 (1977): 293–300. Scott, Angels C. *The Story of Oklahoma City.* Oklahoma City: Times Journal Publishing Company, 1939. Stewart, Ray P. *Born Grown: An Oklahoma City History.* Oklahoma City: Fidelity Bank, 1974.

Omaha, Nebraska, 1900

OMAHA, NEBRASKA

Omaha was founded in 1854, but its roots date from 1846, when the westbound Mormons entered the area. From 1846 to 1848 Winter Quarters, in modern northern Omaha, was the Mormon departure point for the Salt Lake valley. Because Winter Quarters was on Omaha Indian land, the Mormons were eventually obliged to make their nearby settlement of Kanesville, Iowa, their jumping-off point. In 1853 Kanesville was renamed Council Bluffs, and, although the Mormon preeminence in the community passed, the town remained a gateway to the Platte River valley, the easiest overland route west.

The Kansas-Nebraska Act of 1854 unleashed the energies of town-site promoters who saw great futures for communities on the western bank of the Missouri River. Omaha, Nebraska Territory, was the product of such promoters in Council Bluffs. A short distance south of Omaha was Bellevue, a trading post, Indian agency, and mission dating from the early 1820s. This settlement's established position made it a logical site for the territorial capital, but Governor Francis Burt's death soon after his arrival in Bellevue aided Omaha's ambitions. Acting Governor Thomas B. Cuming Jr. championed Omaha, where he convened the first territorial legislature in 1855. Despite opposition from residents south of the Platte, Omaha remained Nebraska's capital until statehood in 1867.

The capital was crucial to Omaha's early development; moreover, proximity to the Platte valley made the town an outfitting point for westbound travelers and a center of stagecoach operations and wagon freighting. The Rocky Mountain mining boom in 1859 created close ties between Omaha and Denver. Down the Missouri, Nebraska City became the territory's principal wagon-freighting center and Omaha's key rival. However, in 1863 President Lincoln designated Iowa's border adjoining Omaha as the eastern terminus of the Union Pacific Railroad. The construction of that line between 1865 and 1869 assured Omaha's leadership in Nebraska and its regional importance.

Railroads now tied Council Bluffs to Chicago, and the completion of the Union Pacific bridge between Omaha and Council Bluffs in 1872 secured the future of both communities as rail centers. The construction of other trans-Missouri lines soon expanded Omaha's trade sector beyond the service area of the Union Pacific and augmented Omaha's ties to the Plains and the West. These links enabled Omaha to become a smelting center and were the prelude to the building of the Union Stockyards in 1884 and South Omaha's rapid evolution as a packing center.

The 1880s brought the greatest population increase in Nebraska's history, and Omaha more than tripled in size. Hard times in the 1890s halted this boom, yet the "Magic City" of South Omaha, driven by meatpacking, grew more than threefold. Indeed, the problems of the nineties encouraged Omaha to create the Knights of Ak-Sar-Ben (reverse spelling of Nebraska), a civic group that fostered closer relations with the city's trade area. From its founding in 1893, the Commercial Club (now the Greater Omaha Chamber of Commerce) promoted business ties between Omaha and other towns in Nebraska and adjoining states and took an active interest in the region's agriculture. Extolling western development, in 1898 Omaha hosted the Trans-Mississippi and International Exposition, which drew some 2.6 million people.

In 1900 Omaha, with a population of 102,555, ranked behind San Francisco, Kansas City, and Denver as the fourth largest trans-Missouri city, just ahead of Los Angeles. Despite its recent origin, South Omaha had a population of 26,001. The establishment of the Omaha Grain Exchange in 1903 and growing wholesale enterprises further emphasized the city's ties to the Central Plains. Omaha absorbed South Omaha in 1915, and with its established economic base, the city grew gradually.

In 1910 some 53.7 percent of Omaha's residents and about 64.2 percent of South Omaha's residents were foreign-born white or had at least one parent born outside the United States. Persons of German, Scandinavian, Czech, Irish, Polish, and Italian background were numerous. The African American population increased significantly between 1910 and 1920. South Omaha's anti-Greek riot in 1909 and the lynching of African American men in 1891 and 1919 in Omaha were the worst manifestations of ethnic prejudice. As the civil rights movement grew during the mid–twentieth century, African Americans sought an end to employment and housing discrimination. There were serious episodes of racial confrontation in 1966, 1968, and 1969. As the twentieth century closed, the key development in Omaha's ethnic profile was a growing Hispanic population.

Preparation for World War II brought the Glenn L. Martin Bomber Plant to Fort Crook, adjoining Bellevue. At its peak, the plant employed 14,572 workers, and its closing at war's end briefly threatened the local economy. However, the cold war and the establishment of Strategic Air Command headquarters at Offutt Air Force Base on the plant's site kept the Bellevue-Omaha area crucial to American defense. This major military presence outlasted the cold war, and Bellevue's growth became part of the general development of metropolitan Omaha. From a 1940 population of 1,184, Bellevue grew steadily and has become Nebraska's third largest city.

By 1955 Omaha was the world's leading livestock market and meat-processing center, but between 1967 and 1976 labor costs, outdated plants, and environmental problems resulted in a drastic decline in the local packing industry. Marketing changes contributed to the end of the Omaha Grain Exchange in 1985 and the departure of the stockyards in 1999. Yet diversity continued to mark Omaha's economic development as service enterprises flourished. Information technology became a major feature of the city's livelihood, although at times Omaha's location has been a challenge to its growth as a corporate headquarters. In 2000 the metropolitan area had a population of 629,294.

See also AFRICAN AMERICANS: Omaha Race Riot / MEDIA: *Omaha World-Herald* / WAR: Strategic Air Command.

Harl A. Dalstrom
University of Nebraska at Omaha

Larsen, Lawrence H., and Barbara J. Cottrell. *The Gate City: A History of Omaha*. Lincoln: University of Nebraska Press, 1997.

PIERRE, SOUTH DAKOTA

Pierre (pronounced "pier") is located in central South Dakota on the eastern bank of the Missouri River. Its sister city, Fort Pierre, is across the river on the western bank. Incorporated in 1883, Pierre is both the state capital of South Dakota (since 1889) and the seat of Hughes County. The boundary dividing mountain and central time zones follows the Missouri River, placing Pierre and Fort Pierre in different time zones.

The area around Pierre was originally a major fortified center of the Arikara Indians. In 1804 Lewis and Clark held council with three Teton Sioux chiefs at the mouth of the Teton (Bad) River near the future site of Pierre. In 1832 the American Fur Company established Fort Pierre at the site. The fort was a major trading post for the middle Missouri River region until 1855, when it was sold to the U.S. Army. During the Black Hills gold rush (1876–85) Pierre was a transportation and freighting outpost for miners and supplies. The city boomed with the arrival of the railroad in 1880, becoming an important commercial center for the local farm and ranch economy. Pierre has continued to grow in population, increasing from 3,235 in 1890 to 13,876 in 2000.

Today Pierre's economy centers on state and county government, agriculture (primarily grains and beef cattle), tourism, and recreation (fishing and hunting). State government is the city's most important economic activity. Products manufactured in Pierre include electrical and irrigation equipment. Printing is also a major economic activity.

Located six miles north-northwest of Pierre is the Oahe Dam, the eighth largest dam in the world by volume. The dam is a major flood-control and power production unit on the Missouri River; the power plant has a total peaking capacity of 826,000 kilowatts. Behind the 245-foot-high dam is Lake Oahe. Its waters stretch 231 miles upstream and cover 374,000 acres of land.

The city is served by the Pierre Regional Airport, the Dakota, Minnesota, and Eastern Railroad, and U.S. Highways 14 and 83. Pierre is home to the Indian Learning Center, a boarding school for Native Americans in grades one through eight. The region is also served by Capital University Center, which provides access to programs from three state universities. Major tourism and recreation attractions in Pierre and the surrounding area include the Cultural Heritage Center, the South Dakota Discovery Center and Aquarium, the state capitol, the Fighting Stallions Memorial, the Verendrye Museum (in Fort Pierre), the Oahe Dam and Visitors Center, the Farm Island State Recreation Area, and the Fort Pierre National Grassland.

Edward Patrick Hogan
South Dakota State University

Hogan, Edward Patrick, and Erin Hogan Fouberg. *The Geography of South Dakota*. Sioux Falls SD: Center for Western Studies, 1998. Schell, Herbert S. *The History of South Dakota*. Lincoln: University of Nebraska Press, 1968.

PUEBLO, COLORADO

Pueblo, at an elevation of 4,695 feet, is located in southern Colorado, 40 miles south of Colorado Springs and 110 miles south of Denver. Over the years, Pueblo has experienced a slow but steady growth to a population of 102,319 in 2000. Latinos comprise approximately 50 percent of the city's population. The remainder is extremely diverse, and diversity has been a common theme since the city's inception. While the city has been aggressive in pursuing economic development in recent years, most locals do not want to see a dramatic population increase. Part of Pueblo's attractiveness is its manageable size combined with its urban amenities.

Pueblo has a rich history. Its location at the junction of Fountain Creek and the Arkansas River has made it suitable for settlements. As early as the sixteenth century Spaniards were in the area. The French established a trading post around 1740. In the late fall of 1806, after the United States acquired the region through the Louisiana Purchase, Zebulon Pike set up a defensive position in what is now Pueblo before beginning his unsuccessful attempt to climb the mountain that bears his name, Pikes Peak. In the 1840s fur traders built Fort Pueblo, and, later in the decade, the explorer John C. Frémont visited the area. In a sad incident in 1854 Ute Indians massacred a group of settlers at Fort Pueblo. The name Pueblo would continue with the establishment of the city in the 1860s. As is often the case, the city planning was an imprecise process. It was not until the twentieth century that three distinct settlements became one town. In the twentieth century Pueblo's greatest disaster was the flood of 1921, during which there was a catastrophic loss of life and property.

Following the gold rush of the late 1850s Pueblo became a natural site for ranching, farming, and sheepherding. The arrival of the railroad in 1876 created a varied economy. Gen. William Jackson Palmer, a prominent southern Colorado entrepreneur and the founder of Colorado Springs, played a prominent role in constructing a steelworks. Completed in 1882, the steelworks and its laborers have had an integral role in the economic and social life of the city. At times, more than half of Pueblo's population worked in the steel mill. More recently, Pueblo's economy has become more diversified. Some of the largest employers are in the medical, educational, industrial, governmental, and telemarketing fields. Pueblo is also home to the U.S. Army Chemical Depot, the Federal Consumer Information Office, and the University of Southern Colorado. In politics, Pueblo has developed into a Democratic enclave in a generally Republican state. The city is usually a campaign stop for national Democratic figures.

Notable personalities include Thomas M. Bowen, a hard-drinking lawyer who received the Medal of Honor during the Civil War and eventually became a judge and U.S. senator. Ed "Dutch" Clark was an all-American football player who set rushing records that stood for over thirty years with the Detroit Lions. Points of interest in the Pueblo area include Lake Pueblo State Park, San Isabel National Forest, and the City Park complex (which includes the Pueblo Zoo). Pueblo is also home to the Colorado State Fair.

Frederick C. Matusiak
University of Southern Colorado

Dodds, Joanne West. *They All Came to Pueblo: A Social History*. Virginia Beach VA: Donning Company Publishers, 1994. Stone, Wilber Fisk, ed. *History of Colorado*. Chicago: S. J. Clarke Publishing Company, 1918. Whittaker, Milo Lee. *Pathbreakers and Pioneers of the Pueblo Region*. Pueblo: Franklin Press, 1917.

RAPID CITY, SOUTH DAKOTA

Rapid City is located in southwestern South Dakota on the eastern edge of the Black Hills. Incorporated in 1882, the city is the county seat of Pennington County. During the Black Hills gold rush Rapid City flourished as a commercial center. In 1886 Rapid City became the first city in the region serviced by a railroad, guaranteeing its survival. The darkest day in the history of the city came on June 9, 1972, when heavy rains caused flash floods that killed over 200 people. In 2000 Rapid City's population was 59,607.

By 1880 the Black Hills gold rush had waned, and cattle ranching became the primary economic activity; its importance to the local economy has continued into the twenty-first century. Rapid City also serves the surrounding area as a trade and transportation center for ranching, agriculture, lumbering, and mining. The Bureau of Reclamation's Rapid Valley irrigation project has enhanced agricultural productivity. Major minerals mined or quarried in the area include gold, silver, uranium, mica, limestone, sand and gravel, and gemstones. Manufacturing activities in this rapidly growing city include flour milling, dairy and meat products, wood millwork, wooden furniture, gun stocks, small arms ammunition, gold and silver jewelry, uniform manufacturing, circuit boards, construction materials, steel fabrication, packaging, concrete, and limestone products. Banking and finance are also major economic activities.

The invention of the automobile and President Calvin Coolidge's popularization of the Black Hills brought tourists to the region. Rapid City is the gateway to numerous Black Hills attractions, including Mount Rushmore National Memorial, Wind Cave National Park, Devils Tower National Monument, Badlands National Park, and Jewel Cave National Monument. Other local tourist attractions include the Black Hills National Forest, Custer State Park, Crazy Horse Monument, the Sturgis

Motorcycle Rally, and the town of Deadwood. Rapid City is also home to The Journey, a major museum complex that houses the South Dakota Museum of Geology, the Sioux Indian Museum, the Archaeological Research Center, the Minnilusa Pioneer Museum, and the Duhamel Collection.

Rapid City is served by the Rapid City Regional Airport, the Dakota, Minnesota, and Eastern Railroad, U.S. Highways 14 and 16, and Interstate 90. Ellsworth Air Force Base, located northeast of the city, is a major air command installation and a significant source of employment. Educational institutions include the South Dakota School of Mines and Technology, the National American University, and the Western Dakota Technical Institute.

See also: PHYSICAL ENVIRONMENT: Black Hills / SPORTS AND RECREATION: National Parks; Sturgis Motorcycle Rally.

Edward Patrick Hogan
South Dakota State University

Hogan, Edward Patrick, and Erin Hogan Fouberg. *The Geography of South Dakota*. Sioux Falls SD: Center for Western Studies, 1998. Schell, Herbert S. *The History of South Dakota*. Lincoln: University of Nebraska Press, 1968.

REGINA, SASKATCHEWAN

Regina, the capital of Saskatchewan, is a prime example of a community overcoming the disadvantages of geography through both good fortune and great effort. The site possessed few natural advantages, situated as it was on a poorly drained treeless plain, with a shallow creek littered with the bones of buffalo slaughtered by Métis and Indians its only source of water. Yet the decision of the Canadian Pacific Railway to abandon its originally surveyed route along the North Saskatchewan River in favor of one straight west from Winnipeg would set into motion a chain of events leading to the selection of this most unlikely location as the capital of Canada's Northwest Territories. Battleford, the original capital of the territories, was deemed by the Dominion government and the railway to be too far from the main line. They wanted the capital to be at a central position in order to have adequate communications with the East. Edgar Dewdney, the lieutenant governor of the territories, lobbied for the location of this new capital on a tract of land owned by him and a number of associates, but eventually the railway chose a location for a station and town site two miles to the east. Dewdney was mollified to some extent when the government decided to build the North-West Mounted Police barracks and the lieutenant governor's residence on his property. The railway surveyed the site, laying out some 13,000 lots during the fall and winter of 1882–83, and the new capital was named after Queen Victoria.

Regina's fortunes were closely tied to agricultural development, but settlement lagged for almost twenty years because of poor crops, a limited local market, lack of local capital, and continuing settlement of the American West. After 1900 better harvests and increasing prices for wheat, cheaper transportation rates, and a massive immigration to the Canadian West solidified its status as a key urban center in the region. In 1902 the Canadian Pacific Railway granted Regina local distributing freight rates and special rates on farm machinery, which reduced the cost of shipping to the city, making it more competitive with Winnipeg, the regional metropolis. The city was also designated a customs port of entry that year, which prompted a number of agricultural machinery businesses, including Massey Harris and International Harvester, to establish distributing operations. Regina's security as a government center was ensured when it was made the capital of the new Province of Saskatchewan in 1905. New lines built by the Canadian Northern and the Grand Trunk Railways to different regional centers expanded the city's hinterland. As a result of these developments, the population of Regina had increased from 2,249 in 1901 to more than 30,000 a decade later.

Yet like its neighbors, Regina would struggle in its attempts to attract industry because of its distance from major markets, the prohibitive costs of power, and the stiff competition offered by other cities in the limited provincial market. As a result, Regina's development was locked into the boom-and-bust nature of the wheat monoculture. The city did benefit from its position as political capital, a factor that played a major role in the location decisions of the Saskatchewan Wheat Pool and various banks and credit unions. Yet the decline of wheat prices, triggered by global depression, combined with drought and grasshopper and rust infestations devastated the city during the 1930s. The Depression witnessed the emergence of a loose alliance of farm and labor movements in the province, and in 1933 the Cooperative Commonwealth Federation was formed and held its first national convention in Regina, drafting the socialist political charter that became known as the Regina Manifesto.

The fortunes of the city have continued to be tied to agriculture, although less so than before because of the development of industries linked to potash and oil discoveries throughout the province and a growing internal market. While potash and mineral development have combined with the high-tech sector to propel Saskatoon to a position of primacy, Regina has benefited more directly from the province's oil boom. Petroleum from Alberta's oil fields transported to eastern Canada via the Interprovincial Pipeline was first refined in Regina in 1950. Oil from western Saskatchewan was first refined in Regina in 1954, but because of its high sulphur content much of the light and medium crude found in the province is shipped elsewhere. The more viscous and heavy oil found in western Canada is now refined in the upgrading facility built in Regina in the 1980s. The oil boom's most important legacy was the Interprovincial Steel and Pipe Construction Company, built in Regina in the late 1950s, the largest single manufacturing enterprise in Saskatchewan and the only steel mill in western Canada.

With a present population of just over 195,000, the city has continued to benefit from its status as provincial capital, securing the crown corporations and administrative expansion associated with the growth of the welfare state. The most visible manifestation of its association with government is the development of the 2,300-acre park centered around Wascana Lake, an artificial creation made possible by the damming of Wascana Creek, whose grounds provide a setting for the Legislative Building and government offices, the University of Regina, the Saskatchewan Centre of the Arts, museums, galleries, and a science center. Administered jointly by the city, the province, and the university since 1962, the park provides a wide range of recreational activities and has won prizes for its design all over the world.

In addition to its political function, Regina has continued in its role as a regional service and distribution location and in this context has become the western Canadian call center for large companies such as Sears Canada and Royal Bank. It has recently become the headquarters for Crown Life Insurance Company and AgrEvo Incorporated, one of the world's largest chemical crop protection companies. In addition, the university's new research park has begun to attract some high-tech companies linked to the computer and petroleum industries. Yet like other Prairie cities, Regina still relies heavily on resource-based industries and thus is affected greatly by changing world markets.

See also INDUSTRY: Petroleum, Canada / MEDIA: *Leader-Post* (Regina) / POLITICS AND GOVERNMENT: Cooperative Commonwealth Federation.

Randy William Widdis
University of Regina

Brennan, J. William. *Regina: An Illustrated History*. Toronto: James Lorimer and Company, 1989. Drake, Earl. *Regina: The Queen City*. Toronto: McClelland and Stewart Ltd., 1955. Riddell, W. A. *Regina: From Pile o' Bones to Queen City of the Plains*. Burlington: Windsor Publications Ltd., 1981.

RESERVATION TOWNS

The U.S. federal government, railroads, traders, tribal governments, individual Indian proprietors, and missionaries all took part in the planning of towns on Native American reservations in the Great Plains. Prior to allotment, reservation towns were often located on rivers for trading purposes, near missions, or near Bureau of Indian Affairs agencies. As railroads extended through reservations and lands were opened to non-Indians through "surplus" lands acts, new towns were incorporated along railroads and in central places on reservations. Some reservation towns grew haphazardly until incorporation; when gridiron plans were superimposed on the landscape. Others were planned prior to settlement, again commonly laying streets in the four cardinal directions. Regardless of their planning, reservation towns serve as bases for both Indian and non-Indian communities throughout the Great Plains today.

The functions of reservation towns vary from being the seat of tribal governments to being central places for rural Indian and non-Indian populations and bases for economic development. Some towns are largely populated by Indians and house the tribal governments and Bureau of Indian Affairs agencies. For example, Agency Village, Lake Traverse Reservation, South Dakota, was the site of the old Bureau of Indian Affairs agency. After a surplus lands act opened the reservation in 1892, the Bureau of Indian Affairs moved the agency to Sisseton, South Dakota, six miles north of the old agency. Nonetheless, the tribe continued to hold its annual *wacipi* at the old agency site. In the 1960s the tribal government moved its headquarters back to the old agency and named the town Agency Village. This move enabled the tribe to create its own place on the reservation separate from the town of Sisseton, which was populated largely by non-Indians by the 1960s. Today, Agency Village houses one of the tribe's gaming operations, the tribal community college, the wacipi arena, a tribal elementary and secondary school, the offices of the tribal government, and many low-income housing units.

Other reservation towns, especially on the western Great Plains, are populated by both Indians and non-Indians and provide goods and services to vast rural areas. Eagle Butte, South Dakota, houses the tribal government and Bureau of Indian Affairs agency for the Cheyenne River Sioux Tribe. The town provides goods and services to people within the 2.8 million–acre reservation. The landscape of the town reflects the presence of the tribal government, with building after building on the main street displaying the seal of the tribal government. The tribal government owns the telephone authority, the cable company, a hotel, a grocery store, and a small strip mall that service both Indian and non-Indian populations within the reservation.

Reservation towns that are close to major Plains population centers are likely to house casinos today. The economy of Flandreau, South Dakota, a town of 2,400 residents, mostly non-Indians, has become increasingly tribally driven and dependent upon gaming. At the southwestern corner of the town is the Flandreau Santee Sioux's small reservation and large casino. The Royal River Casino has expanded in recent years and now employs some 300 people. The proximity of Flandreau to Sioux Falls, South Dakota, has enabled the casino to achieve some level of success. Through this success, the tribe has funneled money back into the Flandreau community, thus changing this place through economic development and grants.

Like most Plains small towns, those on reservations have a Main Street, often perpendicular to railroad tracks. The tribal government and Bureau of Indian Affairs offices are located on or near the main street, as are other major tribal services. Low-income housing provided by the tribal housing authority,

Housing and Urban Development, or Habitat for Humanity is located in developments on the outskirts of the typical reservation town.

See also NATIVE AMERICANS: Reservations.

Erin Hogan Fouberg
Mary Washington College

Bays, Brad A. *Townsite Settlement and Dispossession in the Cherokee Nation, 1866–1907*. New York: Garland Press, 1998. McCormick, Kathleen. "In the Clutch of the Casinos." *Planning* 63 (1997): 4–6. Reps, John W. *Cities of the American West: A History of Frontier Urban Planning*. Princeton NJ: Princeton University Press, 1979.

RIVER TOWNS

As European American settlement moved onto the edges of the Great Plains in the 1840s and 1850s, American entrepreneurs from St. Louis transformed the fur-trading network of forts and outposts along the upper Missouri River into a system of river towns that served both as outfitting centers at the termini of the major overland trails that crossed the Plains and trading centers that connected settlers to the national market. In the 1830s, while regular St. Louis boats ran only out to the terminus of the Santa Fe Trail at Westport, Missouri, other St. Louis boats traded as far north as Forts Lisa, Pierre, Mandan, and Union. Increased traffic along the overland routes to the west in the 1840s and the opening of Kansas and Nebraska Territories in 1854 triggered the development of the river towns of Kansas City, Missouri; Kansas City, Atchison, and Leavenworth, Kansas Territory; and Brownville, Nebraska City, and Omaha, Nebraska Territory. After Dakota Territory was opened in 1861, Yankton, Chamberlain, and Pierre and later Mandan (Bismarck) and Williston (near Fort Union) all emerged as river towns in the 1860s. The navigability of the Yellowstone River in Montana reinvigorated Fort Benton and led to the establishment of Miles City, Coulson City (and later nearby Billings), and Bozeman as river towns in the late 1860s and 1870s.

The history of each river town varied with the timing of the arrival of the steamboat and the arrival of the railroad there or at towns farther north. With the arrival of steamboats, Kansas City, Atchison, Leavenworth, Nebraska City, and Omaha and later Yankton and Bismarck each became a terminus and outfitting center for a major overland route to the West. In each case, the discovery of gold, whether in Colorado in 1858, Montana in the 1860s, or the Black Hills in the 1870s, deepened the town's outfitting function. In the 1850s St. Joseph, Missouri, and Atchison and Leavenworth, Kansas, became the headquarters for major freight and mail companies providing shipping services to the West. Both Omaha, the territorial capital located at the terminus of the Platte River route, and its rival, Nebraska City, after 1858 the outpost of a freighting company from Leavenworth at the terminus of the northern route to the Rockies, enjoyed a decade of prosperity as river towns. Farther north, freight companies at Sioux City, Iowa, and Yankton and Bismarck, Dakota Territory,

vied with each other for the Montana and Black Hills gold trade in the 1860s and 1870s. As settlement increased around each place, the town became a depot for shipments between St. Louis merchants and farmers and landlocked towns in the hinterlands.

At each river town, however, the heyday of the steamboat trade was short-lived. The arrival of the railroad at Kansas City in 1854, St. Joseph in 1858, Council Bluffs in 1867, and Omaha and Sioux City in 1868 intersected and truncated the St. Louis–controlled urban system extending up the river. As St. Louisans were cut out of their river trade, the new railroad terminus replaced St. Louis as the steamboating entrepôt to the north until it too had its trade cut off by a railroad arriving at some town upriver. For example, when the railroad reached Sioux City, Iowa, in 1868 it became the upriver steamboat entrepôt until the railroads reached Yankton and Bismarck in 1873. They in turn enjoyed their heydays as entrepôts only until the railroad reached Pierre and Chamberlain and later Fort Benton in the 1880s. On the river below, steamboating declined into local or secondary freight service, thus ending its significance in each river town's economy.

The history of most of these river town outposts followed a similar scenario, varying only in the timing of their development as river towns and the arrival of the railroads. A river town was a particular kind of urban trading center along one of the great interior rivers of North America or their tributaries to and from which steamboats transported goods, services, and passengers. The river and the steamboat were the lifeblood of the classic river town. Its economy was defined by the seasonal rise and fall of the river. During the brief spring navigation season on the Missouri, steamboats delivered and picked up tons of produce at the wharf or adjacent warehouses or factories. The river was the Main Street and the levee was the front door of the typical river town. Near the wharf stood mills and factories to process the products of the hinterland. In larger towns, hotels, saloons, and taverns adjacent to the levee became the focal point of a vibrant river-town culture. Nearby, lower-income workers and transients and, especially in towns from Kansas City to Omaha, African American residents usually crowded into cramped living quarters. Farther back from the river, merchants and professionals, the social elite, lived in elaborate row buildings and houses, often built in a steamboat architectural style, interspersed with churches.

This spatial differentiation was often reflected by a hierarchical society. In most river towns a small booster elite ruled as a political and social oligarchy over a diverse local population. Though some river towns developed a reputation for tolerating deviant social behavior, the social elite usually ruled indirectly through a working-class boss who controlled the local political machine and the police to protect and support the city's wide-open vice business. By the later nineteenth century, some river towns such as Kansas City and Omaha developed into railroad and manufacturing gateway cities and entrepôts of the Great Plains. Most stagnated and settled for slower growth as secondary or local railroad and manufacturing centers. Riverfronts once crowded by steamboats and then railroads evolved in the early twentieth century into warehouse and industrial districts that cut the river off from the city. Periodic floods and shifting economic conditions caused many manufacturers to relocate and railroads to shut their lines, gradually leaving most river fronts underused or vacant. Only since the 1980s have some former river towns and cities tried to reclaim riverside lands as industrial or corporate parks, public parks, or sites for gambling casinos (and their adjacent parking lots), but in both Omaha and Kansas City the riverfront remains an underused industrial district and railroad right-of-way, inaccessible to most residents, who have long since turned their backs on the river to live and work farther and farther out in the suburban and fringe city hinterland.

See also ARCHITECTURE: Warehouse Districts.

Timothy R. Mahoney
University of Nebraska–Lincoln

Larsen, Lawrence H. *The Urban West at the End of the Frontier.* Lawrence: Regents Press of Kansas, 1978. Lass, William E. *A History of Steamboating on the Upper Missouri River.* Lincoln: University of Nebraska Press, 1962.

ROSWELL, NEW MEXICO

Roswell, the largest New Mexico city in the Great Plains, is situated in the Pecos Valley. It grew out of the Indian wars and the cattle kingdom of the 1860s. The army established Fort Stanton in the Mescalero Apache country in 1855 and the Bosque Redondo Reservation in 1863 at Fort Sumner for Mescaleros and Navajos. Texas cattlemen then drove their longhorns into the territory to feed the soldiers and Indians, with Charles Goodnight and Oliver Loving blazing their famous trail in 1866, followed by John Chisum the next year. In 1870 Van Smith built a hotel/saloon and a store near the confluence of the Pecos River and the Rio Hondo to serve the drovers passing through on the cattle trails. He secured a post office for Roswell in 1873 and named it for his father. Smith did not advance the town, but Joseph Lea arrived in 1877 and began to develop the area. Later generations would call him the "Father of Roswell."

There were few settlers in the area by 1890, but events that stimulated growth began that year. Well drillers discovered artesian water in 1890, and farmers started producing excellent alfalfa and apples. Residents organized Chaves County, incorporated Roswell (population 343 in 1890), and founded New Mexico Military Institute, all in 1891. James Hagerman built the Pecos Valley Railway to Roswell from the south in 1894, then extended it northeastward to Amarillo in 1899. With the local farming and outside connections, Roswell's population reached 2,049 in 1900, and the town

government was reorganized as a city in 1903. Roswell continued to grow rapidly, reaching 6,172 in 1910 and 13,482 by 1940.

Roswell Army Airfield (RAAF) was opened in 1942, and the Roswell prisoner of war camp billeted 4,800 Germans during World War II. In 1947 RAAF personnel recovered the remains of what true believers call an unidentified flying object. The "flying saucer" allegedly crashed near Roswell, and the aliens on board were killed—the so-called Roswell Incident. RAAF became Walker Air Force Base (WAFB) in 1948. Federal authorities installed missile silos around WAFB in the early 1960s but soon dismantled them. The closing of WAFB in June 1967 was a tremendous economic blow to Roswell, as the declining population figures for 1960 and 1970—39,593 and 33,908—attest. Undeterred, Roswell turned the former base into the Roswell Industrial Air Center, with the city airport, a bus factory, a college, and many other installations. Retirees attracted by the salubrious climate have also been an important factor in the city's recovery.

Roswell's economy is still dependent upon agriculture. Chaves County is a leading producer of beef, sheep, wool, alfalfa, and cotton. After 1960 area farmers added the production of pecans, chilies, and especially dairy products. More than forty dairies, most of them established after 1980, operate in the Roswell area. One of their markets is the world's largest mozzarella factory near the city.

An annual celebration of the Roswell Incident has made the city a tourist destination and stimulated the building of a new convention center and many new motels in the 1990s. The population stood at 45,293 in 2000.

See also IMAGES AND ICONS: Roswell Aliens.
Elvis E. Fleming
Historical Society for Southeast New Mexico

Fleming, Elvis E., and Minor S. Huffman, eds. *Roundup on the Pecos.* Roswell NM: Chaves County Historical Society, 1978. Fleming, Elvis E., and Ernestine Chesser Williams. *Treasures of History.* Roswell NM: Historical Society for Southeast New Mexico, 1991, 1995. Shinkle, James D. *Fifty Years of Roswell History, 1867–1917.* Roswell NM: Hall-Poorbaugh Press, 1964.

RURAL-URBAN POPULATION CHANGE

In this synthesis of historical demographic trends in rural and urban areas of the Great Plains, an updated version of the regional definition used by the Economic Research Service of the Department of Agriculture is used. In all, 484 counties in eleven states are included, all of them within the boundaries delineating the Great Plains region. Comparisons are offered for those portions of the Great Plains in Canada.

In the United States, counties are subdivided into metropolitan and nonmetropolitan based on the 1993 Office of Management and Budget definition. Metropolitan areas contain a core county with a city of at least 50,000 and any adjacent counties that are socially and economically integrated with the urban county. To avoid problems of compatibility over time, any county classified as metro-

politan in 1993 is here considered metropolitan throughout the entire study period, even though it might have been nonmetropolitan under an earlier definition. Of the 484 Great Plains counties, 444 are classified as nonmetropolitan and 40 as metropolitan. The terms *metropolitan* and *urban* are used interchangeably here, as are the terms *nonmetropolitan* and *rural*. Such usage is consistent with the extensive research literature examining recent population redistribution trends but differs from the Census Bureau definition of urban, which includes individuals residing in places of 2,500 or more.

In 1870 approximately 127,000 people lived in the Great Plains of the United States. The population grew rapidly over the next six decades. By 1930 more than 6.8 million people resided in the region. Migration fueled much of this population gain as the great agricultural potential of the region attracted millions of settlers. Natural increase also contributed to the rapid population gains, as high rural fertility produced a significant excess of births over deaths.

In 1870 nearly 80 percent of the Plains residents lived in rural areas; in 1930 almost 74 percent of the Plains population still lived in rural areas, which had gained more than 4.9 million residents during the period. Places that were urban or would soon become urban grew by 1.8 million during the same period. However, after 1930 the growth patterns in urban and rural areas diverged: the rural population peaked in 1930, whereas the urban population continued to grow.

Between 1930 and 1940 the American Great Plains suffered a population loss of 208,000. More than 75 percent of the counties in the region lost population during the decade. Most of the loss resulted from net out-migration. The Great Depression and severe drought forced many rural families to abandon farms, stores, and other enterprises. In such a difficult situation, parents chose to have fewer children, resulting in a lower rate of natural increase. Population declines were most severe in rural areas, which lost 363,000 residents; fewer than 20 percent of the nonmetropolitan counties gained population. For example, in the Texas Panhandle, twenty-three of thirty-two counties lost population; the nine that gained were oil- and gas-producing counties. By contrast, the urban counties of the region added 154,000 people.

Growth resumed again during the 1940s, when the region as a whole gained 558,000 residents. Natural increase fueled almost all of this growth. Migrants continued to leave the rural areas, attracted by the recovering industrial sector of the nation's cities. The growth that did occur was selective geographically: only 35 percent of the counties actually gained population, and nearly all of that growth was in urban areas. Overall, urban counties gained 631,000 residents, more than enough to offset the 72,000-person loss in rural areas. Only about 31 percent of the rural counties grew during the decade, compared to 78 percent of the urban counties.

Population growth accelerated during the 1950s. However, the substantial gain of 1.1 million was concentrated in only 35 percent of Plains counties. All of this growth resulted from the substantial natural increase associated with the baby boom, because the region actually experienced a net migration loss of 322,000. Though the region as a whole gained population, rural areas saw a slight population decline during the 1950s caused by a staggering migration loss of 753,000. This loss represents 16 percent of the population residing in rural areas at the beginning of the decade. The exodus of young adults was particularly severe: rural areas lost more than 229,000 twenty- to twenty-nine-year-olds between 1950 and 1960, or 44 percent of the age group. Because this age group produces most of the children, the out-migration had significant demographic implications and represented a substantial loss of human capital.

Between 1960 and 1970 the population of the Great Plains grew by only 385,000, the smallest decennial gain on record, apart from the 1930s. Natural increase was sufficient to offset net out-migration (611,000) in the area as a whole, but overall only 23 percent of the counties experienced population gain. While the rural population declined by 231,000 in the 1960s, the urban population grew by 668,000. The rural losses resulted from a net outflow of 708,000, which was only partially offset by natural increase. By contrast, urban areas gained 97,000 by migration and 571,000 by natural increase. By the end of the 1960s the population residing in metropolitan areas of the Great Plains exceeded that in rural areas for the first time in history.

At the national level, the 1970s witnessed a remarkable nonmetropolitan demographic turnaround characterized by widespread in-migration and substantial population increase. The Great Plains participated in this reversal of trends to a certain extent. Rural population grew for the first time in four decades. However, the rural gain of 241,000 was almost entirely due to natural increase. Out-migration continued from rural areas, albeit at a dramatically reduced rate. In contrast, urban areas had a net migration gain of 473,000 and a natural increase gain of 486,000. This substantial urban growth, coupled with modest rural growth, produced an overall population gain of nearly 1.2 million in the 1970s.

The turnaround did not last long. The region only grew by 379,000 during the 1980s, and only 21 percent of the counties increased their populations, the fewest in history. Out-migration again became common in the 1980s, with a net loss of 562,000. The population grew modestly because births exceeded deaths and offset out-migration. Both rural and urban areas of the Great Plains suffered migration losses during the 1980s. However, the magnitude of the rural losses was much greater. Rural areas experienced a net migration loss of 519,000 people compared to an urban loss of only 42,000.

During the 1990s nonmetropolitan America experienced a rural rebound. Some evidence of this rebound is reflected in the demographic patterns of the Great Plains, which as a whole experienced net in-migration, primarily in the metropolitan areas. Rural areas continued to experience net out-migration, though at a rate considerably below that of the 1980s, and many rural areas close to urban centers gained population because of their appeal as residential and employment centers. Still, Plains rural population grew by only 42,000 between 1990 and 1998. Long years of out-migration of young people from rural areas had left few adults to produce children. Metropolitan areas of the Great Plains, on the other hand, enjoyed both significant net in-migration and substantial natural increase in the 1990s. From 1990 to 1996, for example, net migration gain in the Denver region was 175,000, making it one of the fastest growing metropolitan areas in the United States.

Generally similar demographic trends have occurred in the Prairie Provinces. Initial settlement was largely rural but later than on most of the Great Plains. About two-thirds of all homestead entries on the Canadian Prairies from 1870 to 1930 were registered in the fifteen years before World War I. Rural population has diminished since the 1930s, but the declines have not been uniform. Rural areas close to Canadian urban centers and those with scenic or economic advantages were less likely to lose population. Metropolitan areas on the Canadian Great Plains gained population, as did their U.S. counterparts. For example, Calgary, Alberta, known as the "Energy Capital of Canada," has been one of the fastest growing cities in Canada since the 1940s. In 1941 Calgary's census metropolitan area (CMA) population was 93,000; by 1981 this figure had risen to 625,966. In 1996 Calgary's CMA population was 821,628, making Calgary the sixth largest CMA in Canada. Canada also enjoyed a similar rural turnaround during the 1970s. However, again as in the case of the United States, the impact of the turnaround was considerably less pronounced on the Plains than it was elsewhere in Canada.

In sum, the patterns of population change in the Great Plains over the past 130 years have been complex. From 1870 to 1930 the population of the U.S. Great Plains grew significantly, with most of the growth occurring in areas that remain rural to this day. As late as 1930, 75 percent of the Plains population was rural; thereafter, the rural population generally diminished, while the urban population grew dramatically. In 1998 nearly 61 percent of the 11.1 million people of the U.S. Plains lived in metropolitan areas. Only 4.4 million remained in rural areas, down from a peak of 5 million in 1930. Since 1950 the rural Great Plains of the United States have suffered a net migration loss of 2.1 million people, many of them young adults. This loss of so many potential parents has now drained much of the demographic resilience from the rural Plains. As a result, more than 200 of the 444 rural counties in the Great Plains had more deaths than births between 1990 and 1998. The proportion of Great Plains counties with such natural decrease is greater than in any region of the country at any time in history.

Kenneth M. Johnson
Loyola University Chicago

Albrecht, Don E. "The Renewal of Population Loss in the Non-Metropolitan Great Plains." *Rural Sociology* 58 (1993): 233–46. Carlyle, William J. "Rural Population Change on the Canadian Prairies." *Great Plains Research* 4 (1994): 65–87. Johnson, K. M. "When Deaths Exceed Births: Natural Decrease in the United States." *International Regional Science Review* 15 (1993): 179–98.

SAN ANGELO, TEXAS

The city of San Angelo is located at the confluence of the North and South Concho Rivers near where the 100th meridian and the thirty-first line of latitude intersect. This part of Texas was once the homeland of the Jumano Indians. The region around this modern-day city became a center of European activity in the 1620s, when Spanish missionaries began ministering to local Indian groups. The permanent settlement of San Angelo may be dated to 1867, when the U.S. government established Fort Concho as part of a series of forts intended to protect westering settlers. In 1870 a San Antonio entrepreneur named Bart DeWitt purchased land along the Concho River (and opposite Fort Concho) with intentions of founding a town, but the village struggled in its early years. Initially, it survived by meeting the numerous needs of military personnel and their families.

One reason why San Angelo struggled during its early years was that most local commercial establishments were located at the nearby village of Ben Ficklin, the center of a stage line extending into California. But a devastating flood in 1882 destroyed that tough little way station, and six years later the Santa Fe Railroad connected San Angelo to the outside world and ensured its growth. The city by the Conchos flourished.

While Fort Concho had provided much of the economic stimulus for San Angelo during its early days, that ended when the federal government closed the installation in 1889. (In the 1980s and 1990s city officials restored the fort. It is now a main point of interest for tourists.) By the late nineteenth century, San Angelo had become a major center for sheep and cattle ranching. In the early 1900s farmers in surrounding areas began growing cotton, and that enterprise also proved profitable. Wildcatters struck oil in areas close to the city in the early 1920s, and the oil industry stimulated economic growth: banks, department stores, construction, and real estate activity boomed. The San Angelo economy early became diversified, and diversification has been sustained with the later addition of more than 120 manufacturing plants, modern medical facilities, and a military presence in the form of Goodfellow Air Force Base.

Among the notable figures who have played a hand in shaping the city's destiny is Margaret A. Shannon, a philanthropist whose large fortune funded the establishment of the Shannon Medical Center in 1932; it remains among the most important medical facilities in West

San Angelo, Texas, ca. 1886

Texas. After World War II, Houston Harte arrived in the city to become the editor of the *San Angelo Standard-Times*. He became involved in historic preservation, founded his own profitable private businesses, and participated in numerous civic causes. During a period of almost three decades in the late twentieth century, Dr. Lloyd D. Vincent transformed the local junior college into Angelo State University, which had an enrollment of 6,300 in 2000.

San Angelo's population growth has reflected its economic development. Between 1920 and 1930, as the oil boom struck, the city's population more than doubled to 25,309. The establishment of Goodfellow Air Force Base in 1950 resulted in another growth spurt, with the population climbing to 52,093 by 1950. The diverse economy and San Angelo's attractiveness as a retirement center have kept the population curve rising—to 73,240 in 1980, 84,474 in 1990, and 88,439 in 2000.

Elvis E. Fleming
Historical Society for Southeast New Mexico

Clemens, Gus. *The Concho Country*. San Antonio: Mulberry Books, 1980.

SASKATOON, SASKATCHEWAN

Saskatoon, the largest city in the province of Saskatchewan, with a population of 220,000, has experienced both stunning growth and marked stagnation during its relatively short history. The community was founded in 1882 by John Lake, who came to the Canadian Northwest to examine the land granted by the Dominion government to the Toronto-based Temperance Colonization Society and to choose a site for the administrative center of the colony. Lake and his compatriots selected a spot along the South Saskatchewan River, where the banks on both sides were low enough to provide a crossing. Legend has it that the original location on the east side was named Saskatoon after the berries growing on the bushes beside the river.

After the influx of the first Temperance Colony settlers in 1883, the community grew very slowly. The leaders of the colony realized that their isolation hindered development,

and they lobbied hard for a rail connection. Their efforts paid off in 1887 when the government granted the Qu'Appelle, Long Lake and Saskatchewan Railway and Steamboat Company a land subsidy of 6,400 acres per mile to build a rail line from the main Canadian Pacific Railway line to Prince Albert, across the river at Saskatoon. The railway decided to locate its station on the lower western bank where there was easier access to water for the steam locomotives. In response, the society surveyed a new town site with the station at its center, and the original settlement was allowed to languish.

The coming of the first railway line did not spur significant development, but it did make Saskatoon a shipping center, increasing the importance of the Battleford Trail, and it made possible the export of three commodities: buffalo bones, cattle, and grain. Yet with a population of only 113 in 1901, Saskatoon was stagnating. At this point a number of factors ensuring an incredible burst of growth came into play.

Among the most important was the 1902 purchase of over one million acres of land between Regina and Saskatoon from the railway and the Dominion government by the Saskatchewan Valley Land Company, a colonization company organized by midwestern capitalists. It was the settlement of land by American immigrants, among other groups, that would provide the hinterland so necessary to the community's growth. The local economy also received a boost with the arrival by rail of the Barr colonists, drawn from industrial cities of England, in 1903. Over 1,500 colonists disembarked from the train and were outfitted by local merchants before making their way west to the Lloydminster area.

The major impetus for growth came from 1908 to 1914, when the Grand Trunk Pacific and the Canadian Pacific Railways constructed new lines to Saskatoon, making the city the self-proclaimed "Hub of the Prairies." With the coming of the railways, the wholesale-retail function expanded, and Saskatoon became the major distribution center for central Saskatchewan. Much of the capital financing new businesses came from Britain, France, and Holland as well as from eastern Canada. In 1906 Saskatoon became a city when it joined with Nutana, the original settlement on the eastern

bank, and Riverdale, the village created by Barr colonists who had remained in the area. The crowning glory for the city was being awarded the provincial university in 1909, an achievement that would generate employment and provide a cultural focus for its inhabitants. Its population grew to more than 12,000 by 1911 and more than doubled during the next ten years.

All of this development took place within a context of the integration of the Canadian West into the national and world economic systems. Saskatoon was well located on a good site and far enough away from Winnipeg and Edmonton to capture its own significant hinterland. But like other Prairie communities, its fortunes would rise and fall with that of the wheat economy. During the periodic global recessions of the 1920s and the Depression the following decade, growth declined. Efforts to diversify the economy by industrializing were relatively unsuccessful because of a lack of water power produced from a river whose flow was too slow in the winter, Saskatoon's isolation from large markets, and the lack of investment occurring during times of economic recession. Saskatoon did manage to attract some industry, however, including Quaker Oats, Robin Hood Flour, and the Massey Harris and Rumely farming implement companies.

It was only after World War II that Saskatoon would enlarge its industrial base, an expansion founded initially on the mining industry. By the end of the 1940s five potash mines were operating in Saskatoon's vicinity, making the city the "Potash Capital of the World." The local economy diversified as a result of increasing exploitation of oil and minerals in the western and northern parts of the province, respectively. By the 1960s manufacturing had become increasingly important as chemical, textile, fiber optics, steel fabrication, and a host of other food-processing, engineering, and machinery industries established themselves. Since the 1990s there has been a significant development of high technology, with biotechnology, computer software, microelectronics, aerospace, pharmaceutical, and animal health firms locating in the university's research park. Major businesses, including Northern Telecom, Develcon Electronics, and Advanced Data Systems, have located in the city. All this has resulted in Saskatoon increasing its population more than 300 percent between 1951 and the present. Yet even as the city diversifies and expands its economic base, it and other communities in the province still rely overwhelmingly on a resource sector that has proven to be increasingly fragile in a fast-changing world.

See also INDUSTRY: Biotechnology; Potash; Potash Corporation of Saskatchewan / MEDIA: *Star-Phoenix* (Saskatoon).

Randy William Widdis
University of Regina

Delaney, William, John Duerkrop, and William Sarjeant. *Saskatoon: A Century in Pictures*. Saskatoon: Western Producer Prairie Books, 1982. Kerr, Don, and Stan Hansen. *Saskatoon: The First Half Century*. Edmonton: NeWest Press, 1982. Peel, Bruce, and Eric Knowles. *The Saskatoon Story, 1882–1952*. Saskatoon: General Printing and Bookbinding Company, 1952.

Sioux Falls, South Dakota

SIOUX FALLS, SOUTH DAKOTA

Strategically located in southeastern South Dakota at the junction of Interstates 29 and 90, the city of Sioux Falls is positioned for the future to take advantage of the expanding trading opportunities with Canada via I-29 and the coast-to-coast trade between Boston and Seattle by way of I-90. The city takes its name from a series of falls on the Big Sioux River located north of the present downtown area.

It is believed that Native Americans inhabited the falls area for at least 1,500 years before the arrival of European explorers. The first verified visit of non-Indians to the specific site was not by European explorers but by members of the U.S. Army led by Capt. Joseph Allen on September 12, 1844. Several years later, in 1856 and 1857, land speculators from Iowa and the territory of Minnesota arrived at the falls to lay out town sites. This early attempt at settlement proved premature because the Sioux Uprising of 1862 forced the abandonment of the area. Only with the building of Fort Dakota in 1865 did the settlers feel safe to return.

The reestablishment of Sioux Falls did not lead to a dramatic increase in population, but it did result in the town becoming the county seat of the newly created Minnehaha County in 1868. Not until the first railroad arrived in Sioux Falls in June 1878 did the town's population begin to grow dramatically; by 1890 there were 10,177 inhabitants in the city. At the same time Sioux Falls earned the distinction of being the largest city in South Dakota, a title the city has since held; in 2000 the city's population was 124,000.

The city's economy has always been intertwined with the agricultural economy of the region. In 1909 this relationship was made manifest when John Morrell and Company established a large meatpacking plant in Sioux Falls, and in 1917 the Sioux Falls Stockyards were created. With the reputation of having

built Sioux Falls, the Morrell Company provided good-paying jobs and served as the major employer of the community for most of the twentieth century.

Beginning in the 1980s, the dominance of the Morrell Company in the Sioux Falls economy began to fade as the city started a conscientious effort to diversify and expand its economy. In 1981 the New York City–based Citibank Corporation moved its credit card–processing center to Sioux Falls because of the city's favorable business climate and the passage of special banking legislation by the state legislature. Following the example of Citibank, other financial institutions soon followed. The 1980s also witnessed the expansion of the local hospitals, Sioux Valley and Avera McKennan, transforming Sioux Falls into a regional medical center. At the end of the decade, Hutchinson Technology, a computer technology company, arrived in Sioux Falls.

The city gained national recognition for its economy and quality of life when *Money* magazine in 1992 declared Sioux Falls to be the number one community in the United States.

See also MEDIA: *Argus Leader* (Sioux Falls).

Kermit L. Staggers
University of Sioux Falls

Fanebust, Wayne. *Where the Big Sioux River Bends: A Newspaper Chronicle*. Sioux Falls SD: Minnehaha County Historical Society, 1985. Olson, Gary D., and Erik D. Olson. *Sioux Falls, South Dakota: A Pictorial History*. Virginia City VA: Donning Company Publishers, 1985. Smith, Charles A. *A Comprehensive History of Minnehaha County, South Dakota*. Mitchell SD: Educator Supply Company, 1949.

SMALL TOWNS

Small towns in the Great Plains generally developed as a result of a connection to a transportation network that linked the town and the surrounding area to the more densely settled regions to the east. The basic economic role of most small towns was and still is to serve as nodes of collection for agricultural

goods produced in the region for transport outside the region and as supply centers for area residents. Resource extraction is the economic basis for several communities, but this is a far less common role. Northwestern North Dakota, for example, has a network of towns dedicated to coal mining, and southern Saskatchewan has multiple communities engaged in mining potash, but resource-oriented towns are vastly outnumbered by agricultural towns.

The early small towns (Nebraska City in Nebraska Territory and Yankton in Dakota Territory, for example) developed along the Missouri River, but it was the railroads that were responsible for the creation of the greatest number of small towns on the Plains. Railroad officials or their agents spaced communities at specific intervals along lines in an effort to maximize economic efficiency. The distance a farmer could transport grain to an elevator determined the space between each elevator and thus between each accompanying town. This town pattern, introduced in the latter decades of the nineteenth century, is still evident today: grain elevators remain the dominant town feature looming on the horizon at regular intervals as one travels through the region.

Standardized morphology characterizes railroad communities. Towns bisected by tracks, Main Streets perpendicular to the tracks in a T-town pattern, and Main Streets crossing the tracks are all characteristic forms on the Plains. The ascendancy of towns along rail corridors occurred largely at the expense of small towns dependent on river transportation, especially those unable to attract the new mode of transportation. Today, however, the importance of the railroad for each community is vastly diminished from the days when the railroad was often the sole connection to the larger world.

The transportation revolution in the twentieth century altered the economic foundation of Great Plains communities. The rise of the automobile and the construction of a road network have been the greatest factors affecting the fate of these small communities. The automobile allowed rural consumers as well as residents of small trade centers to bypass local merchants in favor of cheaper and larger selections in higher-order regional centers or even metropolitan areas. In South Dakota and Nebraska, where license plates designate the county in which a car is registered, rural consumers can be easily identified in the parking lots of malls in Rapid City, Sioux Falls, Lincoln, and Omaha. With the railroad tracks grassed over or torn up altogether and with residents shopping—and attending school—in larger towns, many small towns (particularly those under 500 population) have gone into protracted decline. Their Main Streets have a gap-toothed appearance, with a significant number of buildings abandoned or in a state of disrepair.

The case of Purcell, Oklahoma, thirty miles south of Oklahoma City, serves as an example of how outside forces buffet small places.

Tribune, Kansas

Founded by the Santa Fe Railroad in 1887, the town became a major node of the railroad in southern Oklahoma. Purcell weathered the Great Depression better than many small communities on the Southern Plains, but most of the employment related to the railroad was consolidated in Oklahoma City after the end of World War II. A line, still used, passes through town. Its main function now is the transportation of agricultural goods to the national market. No longer tied to the fortunes of the railroad, the community was forced to adjust to a new role in order to survive. Today the local chamber of commerce touts Purcell's proximity to Interstate 35 and the Oklahoma City metropolitan area as assets. While Amtrak has a stop in Purcell, most of the functions related to the railroad are long gone, and tourism is now the main source of revenue. The town's Main Street reflects this tourist orientation. Businesses designed to capture the tourist dollar such as antique shops are interspersed among businesses catering to the local residents such as lawyers and insurance offices.

A second challenge for small towns is the impact of agricultural restructuring. As farms and ranches in the region become larger in size and fewer in number, the total number of spenders and consumers in the small towns decreases. The slow decline in the number of jobs in the area affects the communities in a manner similar to towns dependent on a declining mining sector, although the slide is much more gradual. The decreasing number of dollars spent in town from the hinterland drastically impairs the economic health of the community.

A variety of efforts may be made to add jobs to a town and arrest its decline. While many small or medium-size meat-processing facilities have operated in Plains towns for decades, several experienced dramatic change after meat-processing companies constructed large facilities in their communities. As older, higher-wage facilities in the eastern Midwest

closed, new plants opened in cities such as Lexington, Nebraska, Garden City, Kansas, and Guymon, Oklahoma. The influx of people to these communities in the years immediately following the construction of the plants greatly altered their ethnic character. For example, Lexington had a population of 6,601 in 1990. Ten years later, the population had increased to 10,011, of whom 5,121 were Hispanic. Changes in the composition of school population, religion (especially increased Roman Catholicism), cuisine, the visible landscape, and many other aspects of life have enriched places like Lexington, but the rapidity of change has also brought stress to long-established residents for whom continuity was long the norm.

Small towns that diversify economically tend to be more secure. For instance, the presence of a state or private college provides insulation from shifts in the agricultural economy. Communities also seek economic diversity by competing with each other for new correctional facilities. Prisons virtually guarantee a constant payroll for the community, with wages that are usually higher than those paid by existing local jobs. Sterling, in northeast Colorado, is one such place that succeeded in attracting a prison and is now tied to the criminal justice economy of the state.

Today several of the towns with the brightest prospects are those that lie along a major transportation corridor such as one of the interstates crossing the Plains. For these towns, the market comes to them in the form of motel and restaurant customers or truck repairs and gasoline sales. Towns adjacent to a metropolitan area have also prospered. A significant segment of workers residing in such towns departs to the nearby city for daily employment. Dell Rapids, South Dakota, for example, is twenty miles north of Sioux Falls by interstate or U.S. highway. Many of its 3,000 residents commute to Sioux Falls, helping to buoy the economy and maintain the population base of the town. The economic base of Dell Rapids

has shifted from its traditional agricultural and quarrying roles to that of a commuter exurb.

From their inception to the present day, small towns in the Great Plains have been economically bound to the metropolitan areas of Canada and the United States. Whether they served (or still serve) as bases of resource extraction or as points of collection for agricultural goods, a main purpose was and is to move raw materials out of the region to the more densely settled areas of each country. Processing and refining activities were generally located on the margins of the Plains or outside the region. The new meat-processing plants represent an overall shift of placing value-added industry on the Plains, at least for one economic function. However, the processing centers require large markets to consume their products; thus the linkages to higher-order places remain fundamentally unchanged. In a similar fashion, the new prisons are linked to metropolitan areas in the sense that a significant portion of the incarcerated population originates from the cities. Therefore, much of the recent economic development of prospering small towns on the Plains is still dependent on their ties to larger places.

Matthew R. Engel
University of Nebraska–Lincoln

Hudson, John C. *Plains Country Towns.* Minneapolis: University of Minnesota Press, 1986. Hurt, Douglas A. "Railroad Influence on a Small Town Main Street: A View of Purcell, Oklahoma." *North American Geographer* 1 (1999): 64–79. Stull, Donald D., Michael J. Broadway, and David Craig Griffith, eds. *Any Way You Cut It: Meat Processing and Small-Town America.* Lawrence: University Press of Kansas, 1995.

T-TOWNS

T-towns were founded in the Great Plains in the second half of the nineteenth century as market centers for farmers. They developed in the shape of a T, with the railroad constituting the top bar and Main Street and the commercial area the perpendicular.

As Americans pushed westward in the nineteenth century the shape and format of their settlements changed along with their needs and the environment. In the Old Northwest and the South the pattern of town development usually took the form of a square. If the town was the county seat, the courthouse stood in the center; if not, the municipal hall or some other civic institution was located there. Commercial buildings surrounded the square, and residential areas developed on a grid pattern following the survey lines laid out in the Basic Land Ordinance of 1785. Some courthouse-square towns are found in the Great Plains in areas such as southeastern Nebraska, where some settlement preceded the railroads, but most Plains settlements accompanied or followed the rail lines and took the T-town shape.

As the rail lines extended westward, opening the Plains to grain farming and ranching, there was a need for market centers. Developers followed the team-haul principle for determining the location of these centers: a team could haul a wagonload of wheat five miles round-trip in one day; a ten-mile distance required an overnight stay. Thus elevators and, subsequently, towns sprang up across the Great Plains along the railroad right-of-ways approximately every ten miles. On the Rock Island line in Kansas, for example, from its division point in Herington eastward, Latimer, White City, Dwight, and AltaVista lie approximately ten miles from each other. In White City, also on the Kansas-Texas (Katy) division of the Missouri Pacific Railroad, the rails with the elevator near the depot provided the link with the outside world. Its primary street, McKenzie, ran westward from the depot, and commercial buildings sprang up on both sides of this main thoroughfare. When the Rock Island built northeast to southwest on the western edge of the town some fifteen years after the Katy, it confirmed the future of McKenzie as the "downtown" artery, with a depot at each end. In other towns with only one railroad in the early period, the end of the commercial zone was often marked by a public building, perhaps the county courthouse, as in the case of Council Grove, Kansas, and Bismarck, North Dakota.

The T-towns were outlets for the farmers' grain and service centers for their needs. Farmers hauled their wheat to market during the cold winter months and returned with a load of lumber and groceries. The lumberyard was second only to the grain elevator as a dominant feature of these towns, because almost all of the lumber had to be imported by rail to construct Plains town and country buildings. The local bank that financed both rural and urban needs often was the sole brick or stone structure in town, a sign of its security and stability. Most of the wooden commercial buildings, including the requisite hotel for drummers and transients and the mercantile stores, were standardized so that as needs changed over the years different kinds of merchants could utilize them. A smithy might be converted into a creamery, a lodge hall, an automobile garage, and finally a movie theater.

With the advent of the internal combustion engine, the technological revolution in agriculture, and the closing of many rail lines, many T-towns lost their economic foundation. Farmers were able to travel to the county seat or other larger centers for machinery parts, and while they were there they did their shopping in the supermarket and, eventually, the regional Wal-Mart. The team-haul principle had given rise to many Plains towns during the nineteenth century, but by the mid-twentieth century many of these towns had become obsolete, and they dwindled along with their commercial outlets. A few of them survived by aggressively seeking light industry or by fostering tourism through a museum and antique shops. Some, like Lincoln, Nebraska, thrived as government and university centers. Most that had blanketed the Plains, though, went the way of the horse and buggy and became relics of Great Plains settlement,

standing as a mute reminder to the old-timers of dreams gone awry.

R. Alton Lee
University of South Dakota

Hudson, John C. *Plains Country Towns*. Minneapolis: University of Minnesota Press, 1985. Lee, R. Alton. *T-Town on the Plains*. Manhattan KS: Sunflower University Press, 1999.

TOPEKA, KANSAS

Overland transportation was key to the origins and development of Topeka. When Kansas Territory opened for settlement in 1854, the banks of the Kansas River attracted permanent residents some sixty miles above its mouth. There a military road connecting Fort Leavenworth and the Santa Fe Trail crossed the Oregon Trail. But more than geography explained the city's development. The nine men who jointly founded Topeka on December 5, 1854, shared a desire to profit from town-lot speculation and a bias against slavery spreading to the Central Great Plains. As a result, Topeka came to represent the free-state side in the violence that made "Bleeding Kansas" the prologue to the Civil War.

After territorial fights over slavery were resolved in Topeka's favor, civic leaders made the city a political center, both as a county seat and the new capital, when Kansas gained statehood early in 1861. They also worked to make their frontier village a commercial center by tapping into the national expansion of railroads. The first Union Pacific train reached Topeka on New Year's Day, 1866. Subsequently, Cyrus K. Holliday, an original town founder, organized the Atchison, Topeka, and Santa Fe Railroad in 1868 and began laying tracks to the southwest, ultimately extending the city's connections to the Pacific.

Jobs created by processing regional agricultural products such as meatpacking and flour milling as well as building and repairing rail rolling stock stimulated population growth. Two additional railroads, the Rock Island and the Missouri Pacific, arrived in the 1880s. With the influx of German immigrants from Russia and Freedmen fleeing worsening conditions in the South, Topeka became an economically dynamic and ethnically diverse center.

International recognition for the city came in 1897 when Charles M. Sheldon published *In His Steps*, an influential Christian social novel. In the early twentieth century, Samuel J. Crumbine pioneered public health reform. That tradition would be enriched when Dr. C. F. Menninger and his two sons opened the Menninger Clinic in 1920 and the Menninger Sanitarium in 1925 and made Topeka a world-famous center for the study of psychiatry.

Natural disasters—floods in 1903 and 1951 and a tornado in 1966—rearranged land-use patterns, while mobilization for World War II brought new industries to the city's periphery. Postwar annexations and suburban housing developments pushed city limits outward. With the beginnings of the interstate highway system, I-70 cut a swath through the middle of Topeka in the 1960s, prompting urban re-

newal activities that displaced business from the downtown to the suburbs.

Local efforts to challenge racial segregation again brought national attention when in 1954 the case of *Brown v. The Board of Education of Topeka* initiated school integration throughout the nation. State government's expansion in the 1960s assured that Topeka's population would remain stable at about 120,000 for the balance of the century. By the century's end, the Kansas state capital had become a western edge city for the Kansas City bistate metropolitan area.

See also EDUCATION: Menninger, Karl / LAW: *Brown v. The Board of Education of Topeka* / RELIGION: Sheldon, Charles / TRANSPORTATION: Holliday, Cyrus K.

William O. Wagnon Jr.
Washburn University

Bird, Roy D. *Topeka: An Illustrated History of the Kansas Capital*. Topeka KS: Baranski Publishing Company, 1985. Bird, Roy D., and Douglass W. Wallace. *Witness of the Times: A History of Shawnee County*. Topeka KS: H. M. Ives and Sons, 1976. Giles, F. W. *Thirty Years in Topeka, 1854–1884: A Historical Sketch*. Topeka KS: Geo. W. Crane and Company, 1886.

TULSA, OKLAHOMA

Tulsa, located on the Arkansas River where it bends to flow south, is Oklahoma's second largest municipality and the principal urban center for the state's northeastern region. In 2000 the population of Tulsa proper was almost 400,000 and of the greater metropolitan area 803,000.

The Lochapokas, a band of Creek Indians who endured their own "trail of tears" to Indian Territory in 1836, first settled the area and named their settlement Tallasi. Unable to pronounce Creek properly, whites called the settlement Tulsi or Tulsa. The community remained isolated and experienced little growth until after the Civil War, when Reconstruction agreements and land allotments forced upon the Creeks by the federal government opened the area to white settlement. In 1882 the Frisco Railroad made Tulsa a terminus, and the town became the hub for the region's cattle industry.

It was a series of oil discoveries in northeastern Oklahoma between 1901 and 1907 (the largest being the Cushing field) that really transformed Tulsa by bringing a flood of laborers, speculators, and financiers. The city's population surged from 7,298 in 1907 to 72,000 in 1920. As the epicenter for the midcontinent field, Tulsa was labeled the "Oil Capital of the World." Companies like John D. Rockefeller's Prairie and Gas Company, the Texas Company (now Texaco), and Gulf Oil operated out of Tulsa. Pipelines reached out, carrying crude to Port Arthur, Texas, Whiting, Indiana, and Baton Rouge, Louisiana. By 1927 Tulsa was headquarters of 1,500 oil-based companies. Those who profited most from oil built extravagant homes. One such subdivision, Maple Ridge, became a national historic site.

Besides the prosperity and progress of the 1920s, Tulsans created and experienced one of the nation's worst acts of terror against African Americans. On June 1, 1921, deputized and armed white mobs invaded and shot, robbed, and burned their way through Greenwood, the city's northern African American section. Planes dropped turpentine bombs, and machine gunners shot fleeing residents. Thirty-five city blocks were razed. At least thirty-nine and probably many more black Tulsans were murdered. Not a single individual was brought to justice. A state investigation in 2000 recommended reparations to survivors and their descendants. Racism persisted as Tulsa became a hotbed of Ku Klux Klan activity during the 1920s.

The collapse of the petroleum industry in 1930 accentuated the Great Depression's effect on the city. But, as with many western cities, World War II defense industries rescued Tulsa, stimulated and diversified its economy, and transformed its demography. Tulsa became a leading manufacturer of military aircraft and home to companies like Douglas Aircraft. Tulsa was also a training center for British, Canadian, and American pilots at the Spartan Aircraft Company and School. Cold war defense spending and a prospering aeronautical industry confirmed the city's renewed prosperity, making Tulsa the regional center of aviation production (with companies like North American and McDonnell-Douglass) and commercial services (American Airlines). Prosperity also led to Tulsa being labeled "America's Most Beautiful City" in 1957.

During the 1960s and 1970s Tulsa, like other American cities, became the victim of suburban sprawl, with new suburbs clustered around new commercial centers. The suburbanization resulted largely from white flight to the south and east. The result created many Tulsas: North Tulsa was predominantly African American, West Tulsa stayed working class, East Tulsa grew with the expanding middle class, and South Tulsa remained predominantly upper class. The federal government also made Tulsa one of ten urban centers selected for the program to relocate Native Americans during the 1950s and 1960s; Tulsa now has the highest per capita Native American population of any metropolis. Tulsa continues to attract immigrants from a variety of ethnicities. Recent grassroots and municipal-level efforts have begun to unite the various Tulsas.

Today, numerous industries and information-based services unrelated to oil, agriculture, or aviation are located in Tulsa. In addition to its economic, political, and educational prominence, Tulsa is also a major cultural center. It is home to two world-class art museums, the Philbrook Museum of Art and the Thomas Gilcrease Museum, which boasts one of the world's largest and most prestigious collections of western and Native American art and artifacts. Tulsa is the smallest American metropolis to support professional full-time ballet and opera companies as well as a symphony orchestra. Professional hockey, baseball, and soccer teams make Tulsa their home. In the 1970s the "Tulsa sound" of J. J. Cale and Leon Russell greatly influenced rock music, and the musical scene remains important today. Music and cultural festivals include Oktoberfest, Reggaefest, the Juneteenth Blues and Jazz Festival, the Greenwood Jazz Festival, and the Tulsa University Powwow. Because of the high quality and diversity of life there, Tulsa has been labeled an all-American city.

See also AFRICAN AMERICANS: Tulsa Race Riot / ART: Gilcrease, Thomas / INDUSTRY: Petroleum, United States.

S. Matthew DeSpain
University of Oklahoma

Debo, Angie. *Tulsa: From Creek Town to Oil Capital.* Norman: University of Oklahoma Press, 1943. Ellsworth, Scott. *Death in a Promised Land: The Tulsa Race Riot of 1921.* Baton Rouge: Louisiana State University Press, 1982. Goble, Danney. *Tulsa!: Biography of the American City.* Tulsa OK: Council Oak Books, 1997.

URBAN COMMUNITIES

See NATIVE AMERICANS: Urban Communities

URBAN INDIAN RESERVES

Reserve towns are not as prevalent on the Canadian Prairies as reservation towns are on the U.S. Plains. However, the recent development of urban Indian reserves is unique. In 2000 there were fourteen urban reserves in Saskatchewan, one each in Manitoba and Alberta, with more in the planning stage. The number of urban reserves in the Canadian Prairies will continue to increase.

Following the treaty process (1871–77), many reserve surveys allowed for the development of village sites. Churches and the Hudson's Bay Company, for example, often secured lots on reserves, and over time small villages grew around them. Non-Indian town sites on alienated reserve lands were established as a result of the land rush accompanying the building of the Canadian Pacific Railway. Many Indian reserves within the railway belt were subject to expropriation for railway right-of-ways or to accommodate growing municipalities. The town of Hobbema (population 9,000), for example, is situated on lands once reserved for the Samson First Nation in the Bear Hills (Maskwacîsihk), Alberta. The reserve was surveyed in 1881 but a few years later fell within the reach of the proposed Edmonton-Calgary line. Reserve lands were expropriated or surrendered to accommodate the line and siding (train station landings and town sites).

Often urban pressures resulted in the loss of entire reserves. Papascase First Nation was surveyed in 1884 well beyond the city limits of Edmonton, but the railway line and the urban explosion soon targeted it for future development. Within a few years most of the band members enfranchised (withdrew from treaty), and their reserve was surrendered. The Mill Woods area, south of 51st Avenue and north of the Tourist Information Centre, sits on the surrendered Papascase reserve. Often First Nations surrendered reserves after relentless pressures from government officials and local settlers; sometimes the legalities of the appropriations were questionable.

In Saskatchewan, very few reserves were established near settler villages and towns largely because federal Indian policies for the Prairies were developed to facilitate clearing the fertile region for railway and settlement and to suppress First Nations' resistance to treaties and their demands for the creation of a large Cree-Assiniboine territory in the southern Prairies. The Plains Cree movement was crushed in 1885, and the disbanded dissenters were removed to small, isolated reserves north of the railway belt.

More recently, urbanization and economic diversification trends have precipitated First Nations' investments in urban properties. Currently, there are two types of urban First Nations landholdings: those subject to municipal jurisdiction like other private holdings, and those that have been converted to Indian reserve status, now referred to as urban reserves.

The process by which lands are converted to reserve status is defined by two instruments: section 9.3.2 of the 1987 Additions to Reserves Policy of the Department of Indian Affairs and Northern Development, and article 9 of the 1992 Saskatchewan Treaty Land Entitlement Framework Agreement, a comprehensive land claims agreement between Saskatchewan First Nations, the federal government, and the province of Saskatchewan. Both instruments were precipitated by First Nations' specific and Treaty Land Entitlement claims. Once transformed into Indian reserves, urban reserves are subject to the Indian Act and have the same legal status as rural Indian reserves: they are held in trust by the federal government, fall under First Nations jurisdiction, and are exempt from municipal and provincial taxation and most laws.

While formal agreements between First Nations and municipalities are not required, they are encouraged and are becoming the norm. Comprehensive agreements between First Nations and municipalities address a range of substantive issues: the application and enforcement of provincial and municipal laws and their compatibility with First Nations bylaws; compensation for lost tax revenue; First Nation taxation jurisdiction over Indian and non-Indian residents; service delivery (for example, sewage, water, garbage disposal) to urban reserves; and dispute-resolution mechanisms.

In January 1997 the Centre for Municipal-Aboriginal Relations (CMAR) was created by the Federation of Canadian Municipalities and the Indian Taxation Advisory Board. CMAR serves as a clearinghouse and resource center and undertakes applied research in the area of municipal-Aboriginal relations.

See also NATIVE AMERICANS: Reserves.

Winona Wheeler
Saskatchewan Indian Federated College

Barron, F. Laurie, and Joseph Garcia, eds. *Urban Indian Reserves: Forging New Relationships in Saskatchewan.* Saskatoon: Purich Publishing, 1999. Tobias, John L. "The Subjugation of the Plains Cree, 1879–1885." *Canadian Historical Review* 64 (1983): 519–48.

WICHITA, KANSAS

From a trading and hunting outpost of 600 people when it emerged as an incorporated town from the former Osage reservation in 1870, Wichita prospered through changes, reinvented itself often, and served, by the turn of the twenty-first century, a metropolitan area of 500,000 people. It was by turns, and among other things, the premier cattle town of Kansas (1870s), the fastest growing city in the United States (1880s), the broomcorn-jobbing capital of the nation (1910s), the "Air Capital of the World" (1920s), a major defense manufacturing center (1940s), an entrepreneurial incubator for fast food franchises and other businesses (1950s and 1960s), and a regional center for medical care and research (1970s and 1980s).

Like many Plains cities, Wichita's strength has been in the energy and vision of its people. Joseph McCoy organized the cattle trade there. Marshall Murdock of the *Wichita Eagle* attracted attention by calling his hometown the "New Memphis of the American Nile" and the "Peerless Princess of the Plains." Mary E. Lease formed her Populist rhetorical style in local debates. Carrie Nation made national headlines by discovering that Wichita was not respecting the Kansas prohibition ordinance. William Coleman's Wichita gasoline lantern plant made his name a household word. A. A. Hyde invented Mentholatum, the "little nurse for little ills," in Wichita. Matty Laird, Walter Beech, Lloyd Stearman, Clyde Cessna, and William Lear were only some of those who made aviation history there. Wichita was an early leader in government innovation through establishing a city commission (1909) and a city manager system (1917). Even earlier (1887), the town had extended the municipal franchise to women. Paul Wellman was a popular western historian. Louise Brooks of Wichita became a major movie star. Frank and Dan Carney founded Pizza Hut in a small brick building in Wichita in 1958. Sam Ramey took his Wichita State education on to international opera stardom. Runner Jim Ryun broke the four-minute mile in high school and must surely be ranked as the nation's all-time greatest miler. Nancy Kassebaum pioneered among women in the Senate.

Wichita seemed to learn from its reverses. In the 1890s it lost one-third of its population and one-half of its valuation yet attracted aviation and other industries in the early twentieth century to grow again. During the Great Depression, although its population stabilized at 100,000, local people preserved the aircraft business, and, with that industry as a base, World War II contracting led to a doubling of the population within a decade.

In the late twentieth century Wichita became more diverse—in population, in business, and in social and cultural focus—than it had been traditionally. During World War II its lack of Asian residents had been an argument for making it a defense center, and the black population was never over 5 percent until the 1960s. That changed, and in 2000 Asians and African Americans constituted, respec-

tively, 4 percent and 11.4 percent of the city's population. Wichita has three times in recent decades been recognized as an All-American City in national competition, reflecting its cultural resources, clean environment, and continuing entrepreneurial spirit.

See also INDUSTRY: Coleman, William; Pizza Hut / PROTEST AND DISSENT: Lease, Mary Elizabeth; Nation, Carry / WAR: World War II / SPORTS AND RECREATION: Ryun, Jim.

Craig Miner
Wichita State University

Bentley, O. H. *History of Wichita and Sedgwick County.* Chicago: C. F. Cooper and Company, 1910. Miner, Craig. *Wichita: The Magic City.* Wichita KS: Wichita–Sedgwick County Historical Museum, 1988.

WICHITA FALLS, TEXAS

According to tradition, the land where the city of Wichita Falls is presently located, in southeastern Wichita County, Texas, was acquired in a poker game by one John A. Scott of Mississippi in 1837. In fact, Scott acquired the tract by purchasing Texas land certificates, which he packed away and promptly forgot. Years later the certificates were rediscovered by Scott's heirs, who commissioned M. W. Seeley to map out a town site in the tract on the Wichita River. As platted by Seely in July 1876, the town site included the location of a small waterfall on the Wichita River that was later washed away, several named streets, and a town square. In a fanciful drawing that accompanied the plat, Seeley also included an imaginary lake, a steamboat on the river, and warehouses laden with cotton and other goods. The town never became a steamboat shipping center, although railroads were later very important to its development.

The first permanent settlers were the Barwise family of Dallas. They first came to the town site on an exploring trip in 1878 and returned to stay the following year. The first public school opened in the fall of 1880, and the first church, First Methodist, was formally organized in 1881. By that time, according to various reports, there were between eight and thirteen families living within the town site.

In 1881 and 1882 the residents of Wichita Falls induced the Fort Worth and Denver Railroad, then building tracks west out of Fort Worth, to run its line through the town by offering substantial property concessions along the right-of-way. The arrival of the first train on September 27, 1882, triggered a boom in the sale of town lots. Also in 1882 the first manufacturing concern, a shingle and sorghum mill, was established along with the first lumberyard. J. A. Kemp, later to become one of the most prominent of the town's promoters, arrived in 1883 and soon established a general merchandise store. Wichita Falls became the county seat of Wichita County in November 1883.

The city of Wichita Falls was officially incorporated on July 29, 1889. Soon the economy was stimulated by the arrival of more railroads, making the town a transportation and supply center for northwest Texas and

southern Oklahoma. By 1890 the population was 1,987, and as the town continued to grow its leaders recognized the need for a reliable water supply. The Lake Wichita project was completed in 1891. It remained the primary source of water for drinking and irrigation as well as a major recreation site until the 1920s. Lake Kemp was added during the twenties, followed by Lake Kickapoo in 1947 and Lake Diversion in 1960. Currently, the primary water supply comes from Lake Arrowhead, constructed in 1966.

By 1907 the population of Wichita Falls was 5,055, and the economy was firmly based upon railroads. The infrastructure was also growing: in 1909 Wichita Falls boasted 30 miles of sidewalk, 5 miles of sewers, and more than 100 businesses. A streetcar system also appeared with an extension to Lake Wichita, which made the lake a recreation center. Soon a hotel, domed pavilion, racetrack, boardwalk, and vacation cottages sprang up. The lake remained the center of leisure activity for the city until well after World War I, even though the hotel was destroyed by fire in 1915.

Wichita Fall's first newspaper was the *Wichita Falls Mirror*, printed by Steve Reynolds in the early 1880s. Dr. H. A. Lewis started the *Wichita Falls Herald*, which was later owned by F. F. Dougherty and Ed Howard. The *Times*, founded in 1887 by Sam Bell Thomas, was purchased by Howard in 1897. He organized the Times Publishing Company in 1904 and began printing the *Daily Times* and the *Record News*. Those two papers continued to appear separately until 1987, when they were combined into one morning paper.

The opening of the Electra oil field in 1911 triggered a shift in the economic base. By 1913 the North Texas fields were producing 46 percent of all the oil in Texas, and refineries began to appear in Wichita Falls in 1915. Then came the discovery of the Burkburnett fields in 1918. By 1920 there were nine refineries and forty-seven factories within the city. The oil boom also produced a building boom. More than a dozen major building projects were inaugurated in the downtown area during the early twenties. In addition, the city added a municipal auditorium in 1927 and an airport in 1928. It also adopted the city manager form of government.

The population of Wichita Falls in 1930, on the eve of the Great Depression, was 43,607. The Depression slowed growth but did not stop it, thanks in part to a major oil discovery at nearby Kamay in 1938. In 1940 the population was 55,200. Bank deposits exceeded $36 million, and there were 92 miles of paved streets, 77 manufacturing establishments, 127 wholesale outlets, and 741 retail stores. In 1941 the economy was bolstered by the opening of Sheppard Field, an army air corps training facility. By May 1945, when the base reached its peak strength, 46,650 army personnel were stationed there. The base was deactivated on August 31, 1946, but reopened as Sheppard Air Force Base in August 1948. It continues to function as a major training center for air force technicians and a flight training center for NATO.

Wichita Falls reached its peak population of 110,100 in 1955, then went into gradual decline. By 1960 the population had dropped to 101,724, and while oil production in the area still ranked eighth in the state, it would soon be eclipsed by other areas. Also, by 1962 oil-refining activity had practically ceased. Recognizing that change was in the air, the city's leaders formed Industrial Development, Inc., which sought to diversify the economy by attracting other types of industries. In 1970 Industrial Development, Inc., merged with the chamber of commerce under the name Board of Commerce and Industry. This organization was successful in attracting fifteen new industries during the 1970s, including Pittsburgh Plate Glass, Certain Teed, Washex, Howmet Turbine, AC Spark Plug, and Ciba-Geigy. These successes produced great optimism that the new trend would continue, but instead it had petered out by the early eighties. Meanwhile, because of the construction of a large shopping mall in the southwestern part of the city, the downtown collapsed as a viable shopping area.

Wichita Falls was devastated on April 10, 1979, by one of the largest tornados on record. Sweeping through the southern part of the city, the storm destroyed 20 percent of all dwellings in town, destroyed numerous business establishments, killed 46 people, and injured 3,200 more. Within three years, most of the damage had been repaired. Also, the boom in oil prices during the early eighties caused a brief flurry of activity in business. But in the mideighties, when oil prices slumped again, the economy stagnated.

In the 1990s Wichita Falls showed signs of recovery. New businesses entered the economy, there was a building boom, and the population soared over 100,000 for the first time in twenty years, reaching 104,192 in 2000.

See also INDUSTRY: Petroleum, United States.

Kenneth E. Henrickson Jr.
Midwestern State University

Auty, Michael. *Wichita Falls: A Century of Photographs.* Wichita Falls TX: Midwestern State University Press, 1982. Kelly, Louise. *Wichita County Beginnings.* Burnet TX: Eakin Press, 1982.

WINNIPEG, MANITOBA

Winnipeg is located at the extreme northeastern edge of the Great Plains, on the bed of ancient glacial Lake Agassiz, at the interface of the Laurentian Shield and Prairies, and at the confluence of two great rivers of the Plains, the Red and Assiniboine. The city centers Canada's eighth largest metropolitan area in a province that centers the country. It is the capital of Manitoba, the so-called Keystone Province, and it is possibly the province more than the city itself that has in the past been more strongly connected with the Great Plains, reinforced by the prominent featuring of the bison as the provincial animal symbol.

Winnipeg itself has always had aspirations well beyond Manitoba and well beyond provincial status. Its early boosters envisaged a commercial metropolis on the Chicago model, serving the Canadian Prairies and the Northern Great Plains. Winnipeg was named during the 1860s for one of the two large lakes to its north. Even though the naming of Winnipeg is thought by some to have been a joke (the name comes from the Cree word for muddy or murky water—the low-lying settlement was prone to flooding and was often coated with gumbo), the name stuck and indeed became a point of pride, especially when the fledgling province, at the city's incorporation in 1873, tried to rename it Assiniboia. The latter actually became the appellation for the young city's first region, extending across most of the southern half of what is now the Prairie Provinces. From its beginning Winnipeg treated this macroregion as its incipient hinterland, casting itself as the independent commanding metropolis.

In 1870 a tiny unincorporated Winnipeg, with a population of no more than a few hundred, became the provincial seat of government simply by virtue of hosting Fort Garry, an early fur-trading hub. Its aggressive business elite ensured that no rival of any consequence would emerge, and to this day Winnipeg enjoys exceptional primacy in the provincial urban system. However, Winnipeg's early ascendancy is mainly associated with the emergence of the Canadian Prairies as the "Breadbasket of the British Empire." The colonial overseers described Winnipeg as the "buckle of the wheat belt" and the "bull's-eye of the Dominion."

Winnipegers themselves cast their city in even grander roles as the "Heart of the Continent" and the "Gateway to the West." The years from 1875 to 1915 were indeed heady times: the city enjoyed rapid growth, especially after the arrival of the railway in 1881. Winnipeg's population increased rapidly, reaching 42,340 by 1901. It was then touted, quite plausibly, as the "Chicago of the North"; but it was not to be, and at times it has seemed more likely that Winnipeg would become the "Detroit of the North." Some blame the 1919 Winnipeg General Strike; others point to a particularly long and deep depression following the opening of the Panama Canal. Competition from more westerly cities was certainly a factor.

Winnipeg's star can now be seen to have been in relative decline for most of the twentieth century. Other, more western centers have steadily eroded Winnipeg's initial expansive Prairies hinterland; Calgary, in particular, has eclipsed Winnipeg as the dominant Prairie commercial metropolis, but Regina, Saskatoon, and Edmonton have also played their competing parts. The city has steadily slipped in rank, from third largest in Canada (after Montreal and Toronto) in 1911, to fourth in 1941, to eighth in 1996 (with a population of 618,477). Nevertheless, Winnipeg does possess a remarkably diversified economy, with considerable economic activity—a condition of dynamic stability that puts its now slow growth in a more tolerable perspective.

Many influential Winnipeggers have difficulty facing their distinctly reduced circumstances and in taking a more inclusive provincial perspective. Their provincial brethren often diagnose them as having a pronounced case of "perimeteritis," an inability to see beyond the perimeter highway that surrounds and roughly delimits the city. But this condition is actually still as much one of overlooking the rest of Manitoba as it is the inward looking of self-preoccupation. And, intriguingly, it seems to be leading to an outlook that is much more inclusive of a Great Plains perspective.

Winnipeg boosters now tend to embrace not so much a national but a continental (the Americas) frame of reference, with a more north–south than east–west orientation. For example, the city has hosted the Pan-Am Games twice (1967 and 1999) and is now reconnecting with the Great Plains by its enthusiastic participation in the development of the midcontinent corridor concept, which links Manitoba with Mexico. This concept and Winnipeg's aspiration to become a meeting place on a continental scale have been given expressive form since 1990 in the pride-filled redevelopment of The Forks at the junction of the Red and Assiniboine Rivers. Given over to the railway for much of the city's history, the site is again a humanized place of quality, eliciting considerable affection from current residents as it connects to the city's presettlement Aboriginal roots, a heritage that plays a large part in the future now unfolding.

See also MEDIA: *Winnipeg Free Press* / PROTEST AND DISSENT: Winnipeg General Strike.

Ian Wight
University of Manitoba

Artibise, Alan F. J. *Winnipeg: A Social History of Urban Growth, 1874–1914.* Montreal: McGill-Queen's University Press, 1975. Dafoe, Christopher. *Winnipeg: Heart of the Continent.* Winnipeg: Great Plains Publications, 1998. Morton, W. L. *Manitoba: A History.* Toronto: University of Toronto Press, 1957.

Education

Rural school near Osnabrock, North Dakota, between 1900 and 1909

Education 193

EDUCATION

Education has always been part of human life in the Great Plains, a means of passing on necessary skills, values, and history. While today we tend to think of education in formal terms that include institutions and administrative structures, Native peoples had well-established means of transferring knowledge between generations long before Europeans arrived. For pioneers, education in the form of schooling was fundamental to the "civilization" they carried with them. Schools were among the first institutions established, and as society matured, so did the levels of education. Within a decade of initial settlement and often much earlier, states and provinces in the Great Plains had institutions of higher education. Throughout the region today, an energetic system of education exists. Virtually all children attend elementary schools, most graduate from high school, and many have attained at least some postsecondary schooling.

This level of education has not been easily secured. The story of education in the Great Plains has been one of reform and resistance over the past two centuries.

The earliest European and American educators in the Plains were missionaries who were motivated to bring Christianity to Native peoples through education. Later reformers determined that schooling would not only be the best way to separate Indians from their traditional cultures, thereby assimilating them, but it would also instruct African Americans and immigrants about their place in society. Reformers also sought ways to improve education: they legislated compulsory education and longer school terms and pushed for vocational training, adult education, and, in rural areas, agricultural education and eventually school consolidation. In an attempt to improve the quality of education, reformers also promoted formal teacher training. Many reforms met resistance from the outset as parents challenged the implementation of schooling as well as attempts to alter it. Sometimes, they simply refused to participate; at other times, they used the courts to contest school practices.

Schooling Indians

The first attempts at formalizing education in the Great Plains involved the long tradition of ministry to Native peoples. Much of the story of "educating the Indians" centered on replacing long-standing customs with indoctrination. Missionaries accompanied the fur trade in Canada's earliest years, and the tie there between religion and Indian education was strong until the 1970s. Similarly, in the United States missionaries were present at the earliest stages of exploration and settlement. When the United States forcibly removed Native Americans from the eastern woodlands to the Southern and Central Great Plains, missionaries followed them. By the 1830s missionaries were present in many parts of the region. In both countries the federal government relied on various religious organizations to help administer Indian policy, particularly education.

Indian parents waiting for children who will be going home for summer vacation, Birtle Residential School, Manitoba, 1904

Strategies for Indian education have followed a common pattern throughout the Great Plains: initial contact with Native peoples and attempts to bring them to Christianity and European-derived values; day schools on reservations; boarding schools that took children from their families, first on the reservation and then off; integrating Indian children into public schools; and, most recently, admitting tribal influence back into education.

By the mid–nineteenth century, provisions for education had become commonplace in treaties negotiated between Indians and whites. Tribal peoples sought skills to help them deal with a rapidly changing world, and, for different motives, politicians, missionaries, and humanitarians believed education would ease that transition. At first, missionaries established day schools near villages where children could attend and still reside at home. Day schools were strongly preferred by parents, so much so that when negotiations were under way in a series of treaties between Canadian and First Nations leaders in the years following Confederation, local education was a consistent demand. Such schools were also cheap to administer, and missionaries and government officials hoped that the children would take their newfound ideas back to their families and thus accelerate assimilation for everyone. These hopes were not fulfilled; far from assimilating their parents, children often held tenaciously to traditional values. Neither bureaucrats nor missionaries ever understood that Indian parents wanted whatever advantages education might bring but steadfastly rejected the underlying principles of assimilation that went hand in hand with schools.

By the 1870s boarding schools had become a cornerstone of Indian education in both Canada and the United States. At first, educators built boarding schools near the reserves or reservations. When close proximity to tribal and family influences proved too strong, perpetuating old ways, missionaries and government officials decided that total separation was necessary. The thinking was that only by

disconnecting children physically as well as culturally from their families would they learn the educational and economic skills necessary for assimilation into society. Although the tactics they used proved execrable, educators' primary concern was how to prepare Indian children for the world they would face as adults, a world that could not rely on the buffalo hunt.

The first and probably best known off-reservation boarding school in the United States was Carlisle Indian Industrial School, located in rural Pennsylvania, far from the homes of Great Plains children who were sent there. Carlisle opened in 1879, and over the next two decades an additional twenty-five off-reservation boarding schools, all located in the West, were established. Almost a third were in the Great Plains: Chilocco, Indian Territory (1884); Genoa, Nebraska (1884); Lawrence, Kansas (1884); and Pierre (1891), Flandreau (1893), Chamberlain (1898), and Rapid City (1898), South Dakota. In 1883 the Canadian Parliament approved funding for three off-reservation schools dedicated to industrial education, all in what was then the Northwest Territory: Battleford and Lebret, Saskatchewan, and Dunbow, Alberta. Other industrial schools were subsequently established at Elkhorn, Manitoba (1888), and at Red Deer (1893) and Regina (1895), Saskatchewan. These schools initially provided agricultural skills to boys; later, girls also attended and were taught mainly domestic skills.

The children found much to dislike about attending boarding schools. Often their hair (their specific identity) was cut, and they were obliged to wear uniforms. They were also forced to abandon their Native languages. They were lonely and found life at the residential schools harsh. Not only was the labor physically hard, but it was also designed to train them in tasks and gender roles that paralleled white society and contradicted their own. Punishments for even minor infractions were severe. Scores of children ran away, and many died, particularly from contagious diseases, which spread rapidly in the crowded conditions.

Indian parents were ambivalent about boarding schools. Over time, many had come to believe that their children needed to learn nontraditional skills to survive in their changing world. Tribal leaders sometimes actively sought schooling with great hopes that it would help preserve tribal autonomy. At the same time, they detested teaching methods that relied on punishment and coercion, and they missed their children during the long absences. Many resisted sending their children to school even though their refusal led to punishments such as having their annuities withheld.

By the late 1890s, however, there was growing concern about residential schools. Humanitarians and policy makers, both outside and inside the government in Canada and in the United States, voiced opinions that policies aimed at educating Native peoples were dismal failures, particularly at boarding schools. Although it would take several years before they were closed, the period between 1900 and 1920 marked a shift in policy away from off-reservation schools.

The first four decades of the twentieth century were turbulent times for Indian education. Growing criticism since the turn of the century, combined with constant financial woes, brought a major reorganization of Indian schooling in Canada in 1910. Industrial education lost its privileged status and after that date received no extra funding. In the United States more and more Indian children attended public schools, for which school districts received per capita payments. Criticism also led to the closing of the Carlisle Indian Industrial School in 1918. Continuing financial problems during World War I, the 1920s, and the Great Depression resulted in greatly reduced funding for Indian education. Nevertheless, the proportion of Indian children in school increased during this period. Taken together, Canadian day and boarding schools were, by 1910, providing education to about half (54.4 percent) of the 20,000 school-age Indian children, although in the northern districts attendance was erratic because many Natives there continued to follow a hunting-and-gathering lifestyle. In the United States in 1913 about 75 percent of the 65,000 school-age Indian children attended. By 1927 Canadian enrollment proportions equaled those of the United States. Nonetheless, the goal of that education, assimilation, was not achieved.

A number of reports, both private and government-sponsored, concluded that even after several years at school, few Native Americans had achieved the necessary skills to succeed in the larger society. At the same time, throughout the Great Plains, additional criticisms were leveled at federal policies regarding education. One criticism pointed to the unhealthy conditions at the schools, which resulted in much illness and death. Dr. P. H. Bryce, a medical examiner for Canadian Indian Affairs, concluded a study in 1904 of the devastating health conditions in residential schools. None of his recommendations were implemented.

A second and new criticism was directed at the central objective of the education programs: destruction of Indian culture. In the United States this criticism culminated in the report entitled *The Problem of Indian Administration* (known as the Meriam Report after its chief investigator, Dr. Lewis Meriam), published in 1928, which provided, among other topics, a detailed description of life for Native American children in boarding schools. The Meriam Report also influenced the appointment of John Collier as commissioner of Indian Affairs in 1933, a post he held for the next dozen years. Under his direction, federal Indian policy radically changed, particularly in education. He instituted instruction in Native American languages and required teachers to develop curricula about Indian culture. He also closed boarding schools in favor of day schools.

Between World War II and the emergence of Native American and First Nations activism in the 1960s, both countries tried to find ways to reshape policy regarding education. In the United States a new policy, aptly named "termination," sought to end federal responsibility and jurisdiction over many tribal nations. Families were encouraged to leave reservations and relocate in cities, where, theoretically, they would become part of mainstream society. The results were disastrous. Unwelcome in urban schools, Native Americans came to be the most poorly educated people in the United States by the 1950s.

In Canada too First Nations children academically lagged behind their contemporaries in public schools. The Canadian government, in cooperation with provincial education authorities, radically changed its policy. Indian students would attend provincial elementary and high schools. Mainstreaming the students would take them away from the poorly staffed, inadequately equipped, heavily church-oriented day schools and thereby speed up assimilation. In many ways, the attempt to mainstream these children was quite similar to the rejected boarding schools. They faced long bus rides or, once again, living away from their families. This shift in policy proved no more successful than had previous plans in terms of academic achievement or assimilation. Indian students enrolled in large numbers, but few completed high school, and even fewer matriculated.

The social activism of the 1960s led Indians in both Canada and the United States to demand control of their own education programs. In specific legislation passed in the United States in the 1960s and 1970s, especially the Bilingual Education Act of 1968, the Indian Self-Determination and Education Assistance Act of 1975, and the Education Amendments Act of 1972, Indian parents gained control over the money spent for schools and for the first time in many generations could help determine the education of their children. At the same time, education in Canada became more Indian centered. The Department of Indian Affairs and Northern Development adopted a policy on education that shifted much responsibility to local communities and demanded new curricula, instruction in Native languages, and a focus on Native culture.

The same activism that led First Nations peoples to demand control over elementary and secondary education made them seek access to and representation in higher education, both in Canada and the United States. Programs in "Native studies" or "Native American studies" were developed in colleges throughout the Great Plains in the 1970s. Not content with representation in the curriculum, Native Americans also successfully demanded that programs be developed *for* them as well as *about* them. At the University of Regina, for example, the Indian Cultural College receives federal funding. In the United States, federal legislation such as Title III of the Elementary and Secondary Education Act of 1965, the Indian Education Act of 1972, and the Indian Self-Determination and Education Assistance Act of 1975 support institutions for Native students. Thus by the 1980s education for Indian children throughout the Great Plains was more clearly grounded in tribal society than at any time since 1850.

The Development of Public Schools

With European, American, and Canadian settlement of the Great Plains came school systems that replicated seasoned educational models in the East. In copying existing modes of education, Great Plains settlers maintained a link to the places they had left. They also shared the belief that schools would moderate the instability associated with migration to the frontier. Schooling was to provide children with an understanding of reading, writing, and arithmetic as well as a patriotic sense of their country's history. Students were also expected to grasp the virtues of the work ethic and Christian values as a route to success. While settlers in both countries borrowed heavily from existing school practice, there were also differences. In the United States central issues included the philosophy of education and who had access to schooling; in Canada a major concern was the role religion and language played in public education.

By the 1860s, when pioneers began to settle the Great Plains, the United States had established a school system that drew funding from property taxes to provide free education to all children through eight grades. That model would eventually extend through high school. Even access to higher education was relatively inexpensive in the Great Plains. In the belief that an educated public was necessary to uphold democracy, public lands were set aside to support education. Pioneers were quick to set up schools, and western legislatures just as quickly established the framework to guide and fund the schools. In most U.S. territories, public schooling of some sort was available within the first year of settlement. The territory of Nebraska, for example, was opened to settlement in 1854, and the territorial legislature approved a school system the following year. Many school systems, however, existed only on paper because land sales and tax funds often could not support a school. In such cases, private schools, both religious and secular, or subscription schools (schools organized by individual communities) often met the needs of students.

Over the long term, as territories became more densely populated, formal public education spread. Then, with statehood, legislatures once again mimicked eastern structures, establishing departments of public instruction and creating hierarchies to direct education. At the top was the state superintendent of public instruction, followed by county superintendents who were responsible for administering several local schools, which in turn had boards of education. Even with formal structures in place, public education frequently was sketchy, especially for rural children, who seldom had a school close by. Even in 1918 many rural schools on the Northern Great Plains had no wells or indoor plumbing. Such schools were generally one-room shacks, sometimes with a basement that served as poor accommodation for a lonely teacher.

Manitoba had established schools in 1819 along the Red River settlement, and the Church of England and the Hudson's Bay Company established the first school in Saskatchewan in 1840. However, the commitment to public education was not initially as deeply entrenched in the Prairie Provinces as in the United States. Until the 1840s, when Egerton Ryerson, superintendent of education for Canada West, initiated a reform of education in the new province of Ontario, schooling in the Canadian colony copied the British model, which provided schooling based primarily on social class. Ryerson borrowed ideas from European and American educators to design a centralized system of education that used property taxes to provide free schooling. His innovations were not enthusiastically received, but he steadfastly worked to bring various schools under control. Beginning in 1841 with the Common School Act, Ryerson tried to initiate a uniform school system based on the sale of public lands with local or municipal councils serving as boards of education. Subsequent school acts in 1846 and 1850 were aimed at school administration and how to fund education so that all children could attend. Ryerson's structure was embodied in the British North America Act in 1867 and was in place as the territories in the West were first settled and later sought admission to the Dominion.

Language and religion also distinguish the schools set up in Canada from those in the United States. In the Canadian West both Catholics (mainly French speaking) and Protestants (mainly English speaking) have had an active voice in staffing classrooms and determining curriculum; in the United States, by contrast, such decisions had long rested in civil hands. Recognizing the importance of private religious schools that were already in place, the Manitoba Act ensured that minority rights were retained. The implementation of this system was left to the new legislatures, and it took different forms in each of the Prairie

Provinces. In 1871 the Manitoba legislature created a provincial board of education to direct schools and oversee funding. At the local level, various denominations managed their respective schools, and appointed officials oversaw the public schools. This dual school system also existed in the Northwest Territory, which in 1905 was split into Saskatchewan and Alberta. These two provinces also inherited already-functioning school systems and, like Manitoba, created centralized departments of education, with a minister at the top and locally elected boards of trustees in the various communities that were responsible for operating the schools. Over time, however, language became a more important issue than religion as new immigrants from central Europe added to the population mix. In Saskatchewan a provincewide dual system persisted, with each system receiving tax support, while Alberta adopted a system based on central administration that permits local options for separate schools.

Educators' strong beliefs in the power of schooling to transform cultural norms and to bring about social change is evident in a series of reforms in the late nineteenth and early twentieth centuries. None of these reforms was initiated in the Great Plains; rather, educators there were influenced by the larger forces for change in that period.

Forming a national identity and inculcating in future citizens the responsibilities that accompany that citizenship have long formed a cornerstone of educational reform. Such beliefs underlay the origins of public schools in the United States, and patriotic themes had been central in the curriculum there since the 1840s. Concerns about patriotism and about national identity were heightened by the massive immigration from eastern and southern Europe after 1900. Canadians also utilized schools to encourage nationalism, but until after World War I, that nation was part of the British Empire. Only in the 1920s did educators develop a curriculum that focused more closely on Canadian history, replacing stories of English patriotism with Canadian examples.

In addition to designing a curriculum that encouraged nationalism, school reformers were determined that students would be in school and for longer periods of time. School superintendents at all levels throughout the Great Plains successfully pushed for laws that required attendance and lengthened the school year. By 1920 all states and provinces in the Great Plains had compulsory education laws, but even then, in many cases, that law required attendance for only three months each year. In towns, where the population was larger and children had fewer work responsibilities, school terms were much longer, often eight or nine months.

Concerned about the quality of education in rural areas, where attendance was erratic and staffing a constant concern, reformers began to push for consolidation based on the argument that the districts could not afford to maintain distant schools with compara-

ble curriculum. Annual reports written by state superintendents of public instruction throughout the Great Plains sung the praises of school consolidation. Such praise fell on the deaf ears of parents and their elected legislators, who ignored or rejected this reform well into the twentieth century. World War II, however, hastened the consolidation of rural schools and the standardization of the length of the school term for all students—roughly nine months long.

High school education also came quickly to the towns and cities of the Great Plains, encouraged by the influx of new settlers in the early twentieth century and by changes in the role of the high school in education. In the mid–nineteenth century high schools were viewed as a course of study only for those students who were college bound, but over time they came to be seen as the logical completion of public schooling instead of simply a prep school for college. As a result, the curriculum changed radically. Rather than courses solely in the liberal arts and sciences, high schools began to offer classes in vocational and business education. Students could graduate ready to enter the workforce. Some historians have argued that this development was closely tied to the needs of industry and that immigrant children in particular were tracked away from college and into vocational, technical, or commercial education. Whether these charges are valid for the Great Plains is difficult to discern.

What is clear is that students and their parents valued a high school education. Since the 1940s the demand for high schools to provide rural students the same multipurpose education that their contemporaries in towns and cities receive has led to regional high schools that enroll students from several rural districts. By the end of World War II most young people in the Great Plains received at least some secondary education. This, of course, often involved long-distance transportation to schools, frequently as far as fifty miles each way every day in sparsely populated areas such as the Nebraska Sandhills or eastern Montana. Many rural children boarded in towns in order to complete the program. This was still the case in 1981 in Jordan, the county seat of Garfield County, eastern Montana, where a dormitory was attached to the only high school serving this vast space.

Teacher preparation was a central aim of the first high schools, especially in the stages of rapid immigration in the late nineteenth and early twentieth centuries. School administrators throughout the region lamented the shortage of trained teachers. High schools seemed to provide an obvious solution. There, as they completed their own public schooling, young people, primarily young women, could also pick up pedagogical skills to enter elementary classrooms. Hundreds of young women in the Great Plains taught during a summer term in a rural school and worked on their own diplomas during the regular term. Many high schools also provided specific courses in teacher training, particularly in Canada, where normal schools as separate institutions were less common than in the United States.

In addition to teacher training, many high schools provided instruction in other vocations. Schools that emphasized business or commercial education prepared graduates for various aspects of office work; others focused on technical skills to train students for industrial work. In 1910, for example, Winnipeg had a composite high school that offered commercial and technical programs in addition to academic courses. The Technical Education Act of 1919 gave federal money to provinces that provided such training.

As important as teacher training, agricultural education was also offered in high schools throughout the region. The Agricultural Instruction Act of 1913 provided federal funding to Canadian provinces to encourage high schools that taught agricultural science and farm mechanics. In 1917 the United States followed suit with the Smith-Hughes Act.

Colleges and Universities
Just as Plains settlers were quick to establish public schools, they also wanted institutions of higher education. Most states provided for state universities in their constitutions; some even planned such institutions during the territorial period. Dreams about higher education were fostered by federal support. Recognizing the importance of higher education, the federal government set aside two townships (sections 16 and 36) as an endowment for a university when a state was admitted to the Union. As with public education, the state could use whatever funds the land generated to support higher education. In some states, like Wyoming, the land set aside was rich in minerals and has provided substantial funds to the state university. Most other states were not so fortunate. The Morrill Act of 1862 provided additional lands (30,000 acres for each representative and senator for each state) to support higher education, specifically in agriculture and mechanical arts. The timing of this legislation was fortuitous for the Great Plains, and states such as Kansas, Colorado, Texas, and Oklahoma developed strong "A&M" programs. In the Dakotas, Montana, and Wyoming, these two provisions were supplemented by the Land Act of 1881, which held back land from sale during the territorial days so that states would have access to it after statehood. As a result, all Great Plains states were able to develop public systems of higher education.

Like elementary education, funding for higher education was seldom sufficient, and for many years these universities existed only on paper. Nevertheless, as population increased and parents and students came to demand higher education, the necessary public structures were put in place. In addition to these public institutions, dozens of privately endowed colleges and universities dot the American Great Plains. North Dakota, for example, has ten accredited institutions of higher education: one is private, three are church supported, and the remainder are state schools. Of

the twenty-three accredited schools in Kansas, two thirds (sixteen) are religious.

One group that benefited from early planning for higher education in the United States was women. Because the legislation establishing land-grant institutions did not prohibit women's matriculation, when these schools did open, women took advantage of the opportunity and enrolled in large numbers. In the first years more women than men attended. While these legal provisions were not unique to the Great Plains, women there were among the first to profit from the broadened access to education.

Ideological differences about who should obtain a college education also influenced higher education in Canada, where matriculation has been more difficult. Nevertheless, all three Prairie Provinces established universities shortly after admission to the Dominion and have received federal funding. Moreover, agricultural education at the university level, while primarily a responsibility of the province rather than the federal government, has been a central component of postsecondary schooling. Agricultural education in Manitoba, for example, is centered at the Manitoba Agricultural College, established in 1906 and since 1924 a part of the University of Manitoba. In Saskatchewan and Alberta agricultural studies have been part of the provincial universities from the beginning. Like American land-grant universities, the University of Saskatchewan was located where land was readily available for farming, animal science, and experimental agriculture and today retains its reputation as an "ag school." As part of the Agricultural Schools Act, Alberta also opened agricultural schools at Vermilion and Olds in 1913.

Proportionally fewer students attended the Prairie Province universities than those on the American Plains until the 1950s, when increasing urbanization, industrialization, and expanded communication demanded a more highly trained workforce. These economic demands, combined with a shift in consciousness that more students should have the opportunity for higher education, resulted in the creation of more colleges and universities in the Prairie Provinces.

Vocational Education
Despite the courses historically offered to high school students to prepare them for the workforce, many were unable to find jobs. Some students dropped out before completing the high school program, but others who did earn their diplomas found that a gap existed between the training they received and the skills required on the job. To meet the needs of both workers and employers, vocational and technical training has been available since the late nineteenth century in Canada and the United States. Initially, this training was a responsibility of the provinces or states. As early as 1911 Saskatchewan passed legislation authorizing a course in manual training. About a decade later, the federal government also became involved. The Technical Education Act (1919)

provided shared funding for provinces that established technical schools.

Responsive to the need for an adequately trained workforce, federal governments in Canada and the United States have continued to provide funds to build schools that are strictly vocational, especially during World War II and the postwar years. Canada's Vocational Training Co-ordination Act of 1942 provided a strong impetus to the provinces to establish facilities for postsecondary vocational training. The act offered federal funds to help such programs, and the Prairie Provinces quickly took advantage of it and set up vocational schools in several communities, especially to meet the needs of returning veterans. In 1948, for example, the Manitoba Technical Institute opened at Winnipeg. Other federally funded schools were established in Brandon and The Pas. Continued enrollment, coupled with demands for a broader curriculum, had by the late 1960s modified the original mission of these schools from strictly vocational training to include some liberal arts courses. Saskatchewan also took advantage of the Vocational Training Co-ordination Act and set up vocational training at Moose Jaw, Prince Albert, Saskatoon, and Regina. Following Manitoba's pattern, the school at Prince Albert added liberal arts courses and evolved into a community college.

Agricultural Extension and Education
In keeping with the spirit of agricultural education, reformers sought the means to transfer academic research to the men and women on farms. Funded by both federal and state or provincial governments, these programs provide a variety of services, including personal contacts as well as demonstrations and lectures. Specialists were trained to address issues of importance to rural families, including diverse topics such as pesticides and hybrid corn as well as sanitary measures for food preservation and better-laying chickens. The Hatch Act of 1887 funded agricultural experiment stations that would demonstrate new techniques and crops in the United States. Since then, government support for agricultural education has generally increased. A formal division of the Department of Agriculture, the Cooperative Extension System, was created in 1914 (the Smith-Lever Act). The same legislation transferred federal money to the states to organize agricultural clubs for girls and boys, which, in the 1920s, became known as 4-H Clubs. Agricultural clubs for Canadian youth started at the same time and in the early 1930s organized nationally as the Canadian Council on Boys' and Girls' Clubs.

Teacher Training and Professionalism
Reformers have always looked to teachers as the main purveyors of educational norms, and for more than a century they have been concerned about how to provide an adequately prepared teaching force. State and provincial legislatures began to demand that teachers receive some sort of formal instruction and pass tests aimed at ensuring a qualified teach-

ing force. In the United States teachers were trained in departments of education at state universities. More important in staffing classrooms, however, were the normal schools established throughout the Great Plains in the last decades of the nineteenth century. Massive immigration from border states and provinces and from Europe mandated more teachers, especially for the elementary grades. The first was Kansas State Normal School, which initially enrolled students in 1865, followed by Nebraska State Normal School at Peru in 1867. Other states in the region did not establish schools for another twenty years. One of these, Colorado State Normal School at Greeley, which opened in 1891, became known for its innovative methods and stood out in the first quarter of the twentieth century as one of the leading teachers colleges in the nation. In western Canada, teacher training was often offered as part of the high school curriculum, but there too separate schools prepared teachers to meet increasing standards. Saskatchewan created normal schools when it became a province in 1905.

At the same time that school reformers tried to improve the teaching force, teachers formed professional organizations to further their own interests. They too were interested in curricular change and compulsory education. The Alberta Teachers' Association was particularly active in politics in the 1920s and 1930s. A number of the association's members were elected to positions of power, and they were able to change both the structure of and curriculum in public schools. Perhaps more important, they were able to make clear that the association represented the teachers. Teachers associations were never as politically strong in the United States, but, like their counterparts in Canada, they fought for tenure, retirement, hospitalization, and fair pay.

Resistance

Not everyone agreed with the developments in education. There have been resistance and challenge from the earliest days, and they continue to the present. A central issue is minority school rights.

The first resistance came from Native peoples who rightly saw the imposed education systems as direct attacks on their ways of life. Immigrants also resisted the forces of assimilation. While settlers willingly migrated into the Great Plains, many insisted on retaining their own cultures, especially their language and religion. Because of the religious pluralism in the United States, religion was rarely the crucial issue for immigrants. Moreover, until recently it has always been clear that English would be the sole language. The main exception is Spanish, which in the Texas, New Mexico, and Colorado Plains is in widespread use. Attempts to preserve bilingualism, which emerged in the 1960s and 1970s, have been hampered by contemporary nativism, which calls for "English only."

In contrast, issues of religion and language in the Prairie Provinces have been contested since settlement. The best-known conflict is the "Manitoba schools question." Reflecting the ethnic mix of the population as well as tradition, the federal legislation that separated Manitoba from the other western territories protected the educational rights of Protestants and Roman Catholics when schools were first established but did not make provisions about language. Respective boards of education administered each set of schools and received tax support, but in 1889 the more populous Anglo-Protestant residents determined to abolish tax support of Roman Catholic and French-language schools. French Catholics naturally objected that their constitutional rights were being abridged. After years of litigation, a compromise in 1897 resolved that Catholic teachers would be hired if there were sufficient students to teach. Moreover, if ten or more students in a school spoke another language, instruction might be in that language. Because of the massive immigration to Manitoba between 1890 and 1910, this compromise led to linguistic disarray. By then instruction was being held not only in English and French but also in German, Ukrainian, Polish, Icelandic, and Scandinavian languages. Several factors encouraged the provincial government in 1916 to repeal the bilingual section of the school law.

Minority school rights in the United States have been most successfully won through the courts. Access to equal education has been a central issue for African Americans since Reconstruction. Jim Crow legislation by 1900 had firmly established the concept of "separate but equal" education in Great Plains states and elsewhere. In Oklahoma segregated schools were written into the first state constitution in 1907. Since the 1930s civil rights organizations, particularly the National Association for the Advancement of Colored People (NAACP), have filed lawsuits under the equal protection clause of the Fourteenth Amendment. Many of these cases had their origins in the Great Plains. The first focused on access to postgraduate programs where none existed or where those that did could not offer equal facilities like libraries. In *Sweatt v. Painter* (1950), the Supreme Court ruled that African Americans must be admitted to the University of Texas law school; in *McLaurin v. Oklahoma State Regents* (1950) the Court determined that African Americans must be admitted to graduate school. The most far-reaching of the NAACP cases was *Brown v. The Board of Education of Topeka* (1954), which overturned the separate but equal concept and concluded that race could not be used to determine which schools students would attend. Equal access has not translated into equal education, however, especially in regard to funding. In many Plains states where a proportion of the financing for public education rests on property taxes, great disparities exist between rich and poor districts.

Contemporary concerns about minority rights focus on the curriculum, both in content (especially evolution versus creation) and pedagogy (whole language versus phonics and spelling skills). Neither issue is new. Concerns about content reach back decades, as do arguments about how students should learn. What is new is the increasing number of families who homeschool their children.

Conclusion

To a large extent, the school systems that emerged in the Great Plains mirrored those in eastern Canada and the United States. But to conclude that education in the Great Plains simply replicated earlier models ignores the unique and sometimes controversial issues that shaped education there. One contentious issue involved schooling for the Aboriginal population. The large Indigenous population, there either by long custom or by removal, could not be ignored. The Great Plains provided a crucible for working through conflicting ideologies about the role and scope of education for Native Americans and First Peoples. Today, after many failures, that education rests once more in the hands of the various tribes.

Other issues that have played out in the Great Plains focus on the rights of minorities to education. In Canada that issue has centered on language and religion; in the United States, on the access of African Americans first to graduate training and later to public schools. Finally, the access of American women to higher education at state-supported institutions, which took place first in the Great Plains, distinguishes the region. Many recent pressures have also been important in shaping education: more ardent demands by minorities for civil rights and, especially on the American Plains, the increasing role of the courts in education. Today education and schools continue to confront the same issues of two centuries ago: what is the purpose of education, and who controls it?

See also AGRICULTURE: Agricultural Extension Service / GENDER: Hooker, Evelyn / HISPANIC AMERICANS: *Escuela Tlatelolco* / LAW: *Brown v. The Board of Education of Topeka*; *Meyer v. Nebraska*; North Dakota Anti-Garb Law / NATIVE AMERICANS: Assimilation Policy.

Kathleen Underwood
University of Texas at Arlington

Adams, David Wallace. *Education for Extinction: American Indians and the Boarding School Experience, 1875–1928.* Lawrence: University Press of Kansas, 1995. Axelrod, Paul. *The Promise of Schooling: Education in Canada, 1800–1914.* Toronto: University of Toronto Press, 1997. Barman, Jean, Yvonne Herbert, and Don McCaskill, eds. *Before Canada: Toward an Ethnohistory of Indian Education.* Vancouver: University of British Columbia Press, 1986. Bruno-Jofre, Rosa del C. *Issues in the History of Education in Manitoba: From the Construction of the Common Schools to the Politics of Voices.* Lewiston NY: Mellon, 1993. Burchart, Ronald E. "Education and Culture in the Trans-Mississippi West: An Interpretation." *Journal of American Culture* 3 (1980): 351–73. Campbell, John Martin. *The Prairie Schoolhouse.* Albuquerque: University of New Mexico Press, 1996. Friesen, Gerald. *The Canadian Prairies: A History.* Toronto: University of Toronto Press, 1984. Gaskell, Jane S., and Arlene Tigar McLaren, eds. *Women and Education: A Canadian Perspective.* Calgary: Detselig Enterprises, 1987. Gulliford, Andrew. *America's Country Schools.* Washington DC: Preservation Press, 1984. Jones, David C., Nancy M. Sheeban, and Robert M. Stamp, eds. *Shaping the Schools of the Canadian West.* Calgary: Detselig Enterprises, 1979. Miller, J. R. *Shingwauk's Vision: A History of Native Residential Schools*. Toronto: University of Toronto Press, 1996. Sheehan, Nancy M., J. David Wilson, and David C. Jones, eds. *Schools in the West: Essays in Canadian Educational History*. Calgary: Detselig Enterprises, 1986. Titley, E. Brian, and Peter J. Miller, eds. *Education in Canada: An Interpretation*. Calgary: Detselig Enterprises, 1982. West, Elliott. *Growing up with the Country: Childhood on the Far Western Frontier*. Albuquerque: University of New Mexico Press, 1989.

ABBOTT, EDITH (1876–1957)

Edith Abbott was among the most important Americans who were involved in the establishment of social work as a profession—a profession akin to those of law, medicine, and theology, requiring not merely the "good intentions" of its practitioners but a scrupulous intellectual education and a rigorous practical training. As the first woman to become the dean of a major American university graduate school (University of Chicago, School of Social Service Administration), Abbott prepared several generations of social servants to assume what she called "the grave responsibility of interfering with the lives of human beings."

Abbott was born in Grand Island, Nebraska, on September 26, 1876. She grew up in a family of social activists that included her younger sister (and lifelong professional colleague), Grace Abbott, the great American champion of children's rights. Edith and Grace Abbott were the daughters of Elizabeth Griffen, an early leader of the Nebraska suffrage movement, and of O. A. Abbott, a pioneer lawyer who was the first lieutenant governor of Nebraska. Describing the sisters' unusual upbringing amid family guests such as Susan B. Anthony and Lucy Stone, Edith Abbott later said, "We were brought up to stand by our guns, popular or not—and if unpopular, so much the better!"

In 1906 Edith Abbott, having earned a doctorate in economics at the University of Chicago, was awarded a trip to England, where she lived in a settlement house and came into contact with the famed socialists Beatrice and Sidney Webb of the Fabian Society. Abbott's successful studies in London led to a teaching post at Wellesley College in Massachusetts and, soon thereafter, the opportunity to return to Chicago to become a resident of Jane Addams's Hull House.

Edith Abbott's first book, the influential *Women in Industry*, was published in 1910. It was at about this same time that she joined the faculty of the Chicago School of Civics and Philanthropy. She was a key figure in the 1920 effort to move this institution of social work training to the University of Chicago, where it was renamed the School of Social Service Administration (SSA). Abbott thereafter led the SSA to become one of the first programs of social work—perhaps the very first—at a great American university. She became dean of the school in 1924.

For many years, through the Great Depression, Edith Abbott worked closely with her sister, Grace (then the highest-ranking woman in the federal government), to combat a wide array of social ills. It was through their joint efforts that many early forms of social welfare, some of which have been credited with leading to the New Deal programs that helped end the Great Depression, were begun. The Abbott sisters formed a complementary team, with each providing an invaluable and unique service. As Edith Abbott put it, "I could assemble the facts and write a report, but Grace had the gift of applying the proper legislative remedy."

Edith Abbott continued to publish important books on immigration, the tenements of Chicago, American pioneers in social welfare, and the philosophy of social welfare education. She was the cofounder in 1927 of the publication *Social Service Review* and was also its longtime editor; she was named president of the American Association of Schools of Social Work from 1925 to 1927; she was appointed to the Wickersham Commission (the National Committee on Law Enforcement and Observance) in the late 1920s; and she was the president of the National Conference of Social Work in 1937.

In 1942 Abbott retired from her position as dean of the SSA. She served as dean emeritus and continued teaching until 1952, when she returned to her hometown, where she died on July 29, 1957.

At the time of Edith Abbott's death, Wayne McMillen of *Social Service Review* wrote, "History will include her name among the handful of leaders who have made enduring contributions to the field of education. Social work has now taken its place as an established profession. She more than any other one person gave direction to the education required for that profession. Posterity will not forget achievements such as these."

See also POLITICS AND GOVERNMENT: Abbott, Grace.

John Sorensen
New York, New York

Papers of Grace and Edith Abbott, Regenstein Library, University of Chicago. Costin, Lela. *Two Sisters for Social Justice: A Biography of Grace and Edith Abbott*. Urbana: University of Illinois Press, 1983. Sorensen, John. "My Sister and Comrade: A Radio Portrait of Grace Abbott." Nebraska Public Radio, Lincoln, 1997.

ADULT EDUCATION

Adult education in the Great Plains has a long and rich history. Unlike many other geographical regions of the United States, where learners and providers of adult education programs enjoy close proximity, the large landmass and relatively sparse population of the Great Plains have resulted in the development of many distinctive educational delivery systems.

Historically, the critical challenge for adult education providers in the Great Plains has been to develop a system of sound educational options and strategies that allow access to their resource base and at the same time overcome the fundamental barrier to participation that is posed by the substantial distances that exist between their location and potential adult students. The work of the Cooperative Extension Service with regard to community and leadership development, 4-H, the agricultural experiment station initiatives, and correspondence study, an early form of self-paced learning, are among the most notable examples of these efforts.

Presently, distance-based learning activities that are delivered via two-way interactive video or Web-based coursework to the increasingly large number of adults in the region who have access to the Internet are among the most significant ways in which adult education degrees as well as personal and professional development offerings are being provided to residents of the Great Plains. In addition, on-site, off-campus college and university courses and other types of mediated self-directed instructional activities associated with the outreach mission of the region's many land-grant universities as well as the applied research and development endeavors of the Cooperative Extension Service, which provides educational and research services to agriculturally related interests of the Great Plains, continue to be among the key means by which new knowledge is disseminated throughout the region.

See also AGRICULTURE: Agricultural Extension Service.

W. Franklin Spikes
Kansas State University

Knowles, M. S. *The Adult Education Movement in the U.S.* Melbourne FL: Krieger, 1983. Merriam, S. B., and P. M. Cunningham, eds. *Handbook of Adult and Continuing Education*. San Francisco: Jossey-Bass, 1989.

ART MUSEUMS

See ART: Art Museums

BEADLE, WILLIAM H. H. (1838–1915)

William Henry Harrison Beadle was born on the frontier in Parke County, Indiana, on January 1, 1838. His father wanted him to farm, but he had dreams of an education. He studied civil engineering at the University of Michigan, graduating in 1861. He then enlisted in the Union army and by the end of the war had risen to the rank of brigadier general. Beadle followed this experience with a law degree from the University of Michigan in 1867 and practiced briefly.

Beadle combined his skills to draft the school lands provision at the South Dakota Convention of 1885. The impetus for this provision came from his appointment by President Grant in 1869 as surveyor general of the Dakota Territory, where he met with settlers face to face and saw state-appropriated lands being taken by entrepreneurs. General Beadle was convinced that school lands were a trust for future generations and should be sold at their appraised value and never for less than $10 an acre. State legislators thought this to be an exaggerated figure, but history soon proved Beadle to be right. Shortly thereafter, the Dakota land boom started, and with settlers immigrating at a rate of several thousand per year, there was increased demand for teachers, schools, and school lands. Beadle ensured that sections 16 and 36 in every township in the state were set aside as an endowment for public school purposes. His efforts have long since been vindicated, with the current amount realized from the sale of these lands standing at $125 million. Leasing or loaning these lands in the future could further produce some $7.5 million per annum.

Beadle ended his career as president of the Madison State Normal School (now Dakota State University) from 1889 to 1906 and as a professor of history until his retirement in 1912. He died on November 15, 1915, in San Francisco.

Devon Jensen
University of South Dakota

South Dakota Beadle Club. *Permanent School Fund in South Dakota and the Beadle Club.* Aberdeen SD: North Plains Press, 1976.

BLANTON, ANNIE WEBB (1870–1945)

Annie Webb Blanton was a recognized international leader in education, a teacher, a suffragist, and the first woman in Texas elected to a statewide office. The twin daughter of early Texas pioneers Thomas Lindsay and Eugenia Webb Blanton, she was born in Houston on August 20, 1870. She had six siblings: her twin, Fannie, who died at age twelve, two other sisters, and three brothers. After early education in Houston and at La Grange (Texas) High School, she began teaching in a small school in Pine Springs, Fayette County, where her special interest in rural education began. In 1888, with both parents deceased, she moved to Austin and taught in elementary schools and later in Austin High School to support herself while studying at the University of Texas. She graduated in 1899 with a bachelor of literature degree.

Blanton taught English in Denton at North Texas State Normal (now the University of North Texas) from 1901 to 1918. While there she was active in the Texas State Teachers Association and was elected its first woman president in 1916. She also served as vice president of the National Education Association for three terms, 1917, 1919, and 1921. A strong advocate of equal rights for women, she entered Texas politics in 1918 and was elected state superintendent for public instruction in the first election in which Texas women had the right to vote. Her accomplishments included adoption of a system of free textbooks, revision of teacher certification laws, efforts to improve rural education, increased salaries for teachers, increase in length of the school term, and passage of the Better Schools Amendment to remove state constitutional limitations on tax rates for local school districts.

After serving two terms, Blanton ran unsuccessfully for the U.S. Congress in 1922 and then returned to the University of Texas at Austin for a master's degree in 1923. Here she began teaching as adjunct professor of school administration. In 1926 she took a leave of absence to attend Cornell University for a doctorate in rural education and rural sociology, which she received in 1927. She returned to Austin and in 1933 became professor of rural education, the third woman to receive the rank of full professor at the University of Texas.

In 1929, at her residence in the Faculty Women's Club near the campus, she founded the Delta Kappa Gamma Society, an honor society for women teachers that in 2001 had an international membership of 143,951. She was author of several books, including textbooks. Texas public schools in Austin, Dallas, and Odessa and a residence hall at the University of Texas bear her name. She died in Austin on October 2, 1945, and was buried in Oakwood Cemetery.

Margaret C. Berry
Austin, Texas

Cottrell, Debbie Mauldin. *Pioneer Woman Educator: The Progressive Spirit of Annie Webb Blanton.* College Station: Texas A&M University Press 1993. Holden, Eunah Temple. *Our Heritage in the Delta Kappa Gamma Society.* Austin TX: Delta Kappa Gamma Society, 1970.

BOYS TOWN

Founded in Omaha, Nebraska, in 1917, as a residence for young homeless males, Boys Town today is a youth care network with multiple services and locations. It originated with the work of Father Edward Flanagan, an Irish-born Catholic priest who aided unemployed men in Omaha. Flanagan soon turned his attention to the young boys who arrived at his Workingmen's Hotel, many of whom were referred there by local social agencies and legal authorities. Flanagan was determined to provide the home he was certain these boys deserved and required, and his operation quickly outgrew two consecutive houses in Omaha. In 1921 he acquired Overlook Farm on the western outskirts of the city, where Boys Town grew and stands today as an incorporated village.

Father Flanagan's often-quoted motto, "There are no bad boys," was evident in the development and operation of Boys Town. The nonsectarian home was open to boys of all races and religions. There were no fences surrounding the grounds, the premise being that only those who wanted to be there should be. There was no physical punishment for misdeeds; rather, education and guidance were the hallmarks of the institution. There was also hard work, as each resident had regular chores in addition to studies, participation in athletic events, and attendance at religious services. Experience in citizenship was provided through election of a mayor, council, and commissioners among the residents.

Father Flanagan sought funds and recognition for Boys Town through several public enterprises. A traveling show with the boys, billed as the "World's Greatest Juvenile Entertainers," toured the Great Plains. Flanagan himself hosted a nationally syndicated radio program. The Boys Town choir was organized in the 1930s, performed around the nation, and made several recordings. The Boys Town football team also became a respected athletic

power. Great attention came to Boys Town in 1938 with the film *Boys Town*, starring Spencer Tracy and Mickey Rooney. Tracy won an Academy Award as best actor for his portrayal of Father Flanagan. His Oscar is displayed today in the Boys Town Hall of History.

Since Flanagan's death in 1948, Boys Town has continued his basic philosophy. In 1979 it expanded its services to include girls. And in 2000 seven out of ten residents voted to change the name to Girls and Boys Town. Today approximately 500 young people are in residence at any given time, receiving schooling and services until they can return to their families. The original dormitories have been replaced with seventy-six homestyle residences, each with six to ten youths living with a married couple. The campus (now a National Historic Landmark) covers approximately 900 acres, including a working farm, Catholic and Protestant chapels, Father Flanagan's home, middle, high, and vocational schools, a post office, and meeting facilities. Also headquartered in Omaha are child care and training programs and the Boys Town National Research Hospital, which specializes in children with communication disorders.

Boys Town's services and programs extend far beyond its Great Plains origins, with facilities in thirteen states and Washington DC as well as a national hotline serving all of North America. Boys Town administrators estimate that in one year they provide direct or indirect care to approximately 1.1 million children. This influence helps make Boys Town one of Nebraska's leading tourist attractions, where visitors are greeted with one of the famous statues of one boy carrying a smaller one on his back with the caption, "He ain't heavy, Father . . . he's m' brother."

Susan K. Wunder
University of Nebraska–Lincoln

Hickey, Donald R. *Nebraska Moments: Glimpses of Nebraska's Past.* Lincoln: University of Nebraska Press, 1992: 197–205. Oursler, Fulton, and Will Oursler. *Father Flanagan of Boys Town.* Garden City NY: Doubleday, 1949.

BROWN V. THE BOARD OF EDUCATION OF TOPEKA

See LAW: *Brown v. The Board of Education of Topeka*

CANADIAN PLAINS RESEARCH CENTER

The Canadian Plains Research Center (CPRC) is the longest serving research institute at the University of Regina, Saskatchewan, with a broad mandate to develop an understanding and appreciation of the Canadian Plains region. The center also cooperates with U.S. scholars on issues relevant to the broader North American Great Plains.

CPRC works to develop a community of students of the region, including staff from Prairie universities, governments, and other institutions and members of an interested public; to provide services to Prairie institutions and researchers; to study and help solve problems of the region, its people, and its resources; and to initiate, undertake, encourage, and support research and scholarly work on all aspects of Prairie life.

The center delivers four specific programs. The Canadian Plains Studies Program is a graduate program that facilitates the interdisciplinary studies of students pursuing their masters and doctorates on topics relevant to the Canadian Plains. More than thirty-five students have been supported through the program. The Research Fellow Program, established in 1983, has provided support to more than forty scholars conducting research relevant to the Canadian Plains. The Publication Division is a university press, established in 1973, that publishes eight to ten scholarly books per year, with a total of more than 130 titles. The press also publishes *Prairie Forum*, a multidisciplinary journal on topics of relevance to the Canadian Plains region. Finally, the Geographic Information Systems Division is a group of research and technical staff and facilities that support education and research in the spatial distribution of resources, both physical and cultural.

As part of its original and continuing education and community outreach mandate, the CPRC also organizes, facilitates, and partners with other organizations in delivering numerous conferences, symposia, workshops, lectures, meetings, and seminars. The CPRC also presents the Woodrow Lloyd Occasional Seminar Series, in which leading scholars present topics relevant to the Canadian Plains, and administers a trust fund dedicated to advancing communication and education about conservation issues in Saskatchewan.

David A. Gauthier
University of Regina

CENTER FOR GREAT PLAINS STUDIES AT EMPORIA STATE UNIVERSITY

The Center for Great Plains Studies, officially sanctioned at Emporia State University by the Kansas board of regents in 1977, was conceived by history professor Patrick O'Brien some three years earlier. The center, established with the assistance of a grant from the National Endowment for the Humanities, has a three-part mandate: to offer academic programs, to promote public service activities, and to foster and support research on all aspects of the people, culture, and land of the Great Plains, from Texas to Canada. The ultimate goal of this mandate is to increase awareness, understanding, and appreciation of the Great Plains.

From the beginning, pedagogy has been a major function of the center. Courses on Great Plains topics from a variety of disciplines in the arts, humanities, and sciences were developed and continue to be offered, both on campus and on location. Particular emphasis has been on literature and folklore, history and the social sciences, geology, and the biological sciences. The most innovative course offering was the Great Plains Semester, during which students devoted an entire semester to study of the history, anthropology,

and literature of the Great Plains, combining classroom instruction with field trips to six Plains states. Offering seminars and summer courses on Plains topics for elementary and secondary teachers is an ongoing activity of the center. The center publishes and distributes *Tales out of School*, which contains pedagogical topics and suggestions for public school teachers.

In the area of public service the Center for Great Plains Studies has hosted presentations by scholars from around the nation and as far away as Australia. It also cooperates with local arts agencies in sponsoring exhibits and performances by Plains artists. "Plains Talk," a series of public service announcements, is made available to radio stations in the Great Plains, and the center has produced national award–winning programs for local-access cable television. The center also supports a Friends of the Plains organization, comprised of both academics and community members.

In addition to *Tales out of School* and the *Great Plains Newsletter*, the Center for Great Plains Studies publishes a multidisciplinary scholarly journal, *Heritage of the Great Plains*, whose contents range from ethnobotany, to original historical source materials, to literary criticism, to comparative studies of grasslands in other parts of the world.

James Hoy
Emporia State University

CENTER FOR GREAT PLAINS STUDIES AT THE UNIVERSITY OF NEBRASKA–LINCOLN

The Center for Great Plains Studies at the University of Nebraska–Lincoln is the oldest and largest interdisciplinary regional research and teaching center in the United States. It was founded by Paul A. Olson and chartered in 1976 by the board of regents of the University of Nebraska. Two grants from the National Endowment for the Humanities and many donations received through the University of Nebraska Foundation financed the center's beginnings. Continued support is provided by the Friends of the Center for Great Plains Studies. The purpose of the center is to foster the study of people and the environment in the Great Plains. The center's activities embrace the three-part mission of education, research, and service of a comprehensive land-grant university. The center is administered in the College of Arts and Sciences.

The center's Great Plains Art Collection includes significant paintings, sculptures, and photographs of the region and the American West and a library of western Americana. Several exhibits each year feature portions of the twelve-million-dollar permanent collection as well as works from other institutions and individuals. The exhibits are displayed in the center's Christlieb Gallery, located in Hewit Place, which was constructed in 2000.

The center has 180 fellows elected from the four campuses of the University of Nebraska. Fellows conduct research, teach, and provide service directly relating to the Great Plains.

A twelve-member board of governors elected from the fellows provides advice to the center's director. Academics at other institutions may be elected as associate fellows.

Undergraduate students may major or minor in Great Plains studies, and masters and doctoral candidates may specialize in Great Plains studies. The monthly Paul A. Olson Seminars in Great Plains Studies present topics of interest to students, faculty, and members of the community. The annual symposium addresses regional topics and attracts a regional, national, and international audience. Research and creative activity includes publication of the refereed journals *Great Plains Quarterly*, devoted to regional essays in the humanities, and *Great Plains Research*, which examines the natural and social sciences. *Plains Song Review* publishes essays, poems, and short stories by students and regional authors. The thirteen-volume *Journals of the Lewis and Clark Expedition*, edited by Gary Moulton, was completed in 2001. This *Encyclopedia of the Great Plains* is also a project of the Center for Great Plains Studies.

James Stubbendieck
University of Nebraska–Lincoln

CHAUTAUQUA

Beginning in the late nineteenth century, first communities and then touring companies presented a combination of public humanities and entertainment programs that were labeled Chautauquas. The term originates from the educational seminars held first in 1874 at a site near Chautauqua Lake in southwestern New York State.

The Chautauquas that appeared in the Great Plains borrowed the name but drew greater inspiration from the public lyceums that had spread from New England through much of urban America before the Civil War. Chautauqua organizers hoped to bring education and intellectual stimulation to their communities. Scholars, actors, speakers, and exhibits dominated the typical program. The Chautauquans presented plays, reenacted historic speeches, and offered lectures on topics of general interest. They shared the stage with politicians as well, who used Chautauquas to reach a wider public.

The first Chautauquas were held during the summer months in the Great Plains after 1880 and came about through the work of local community leaders. Often, many of the first community organizers had become familiar with the Chautauqua Literary and Scientific Circle (CLSC). The CLSC, which began in 1878 and had more than 2.5 million members by 1900, was a study program designed to bring educational opportunities and enlightenment to individuals who lacked the chance to gain an education through traditional avenues. At first the community-based Chautauquas copied the New York Chautauqua Institute. A combination of professionals and locals provided the talent. Community leaders organized financial support. Larger communities that could afford to hire more recognized per-

Chautauqua tent, Kearney, Nebraska, ca. 1890

formers and presenters such as Carry Nation and William Jennings Bryan attracted large crowds.

Attempts were made by different Chautauqua groups across wider regions to coordinate their organization, fund-raiding, and scheduling of program content. Disagreements between local promoters undermined these efforts. Private companies that offered packaged programs appeared after 1900. These companies coordinated the performers and the themes and then booked their Chautauquas in strings of communities. The standard Redpath Chautauqua, developed by the Redpath Lyceum Bureau in 1904, was one of the first to tour parts of the Great Plains. By 1919 community organizations typically relied on one or more circuit Chautauqua companies to provide programming.

The circuit Chautauquas provided a wider variety of presentations. However, competition from motion pictures and radio reduced popular support for Chautauquas. Improved transportation, in particular, the spread of automobiles, made it easier for consumers to seek out entertainment rather than wait for it to appear as part of a touring program. While a collection of communities maintained their Chautauquas into the 1930s, the Great Depression undermined what financial and popular support remained.

A modern revival of the Chautauqua form, with scholars representing historical characters, began in North Dakota in 1974. In this incarnation, Chautauquas serve as a public humanities program. A consortium of humanities councils sponsors a touring Chautauqua in the Great Plains each summer. The content and the characters presented, organized around a central theme, change each year.

Daniel Lewis
California State Polytechnic–Pomona

Case, Victoria, and Robert Ormand Case. *We Called It Culture: The Story of Chautauqua.* Garden City NY: Doubleday and Co., 1948. Harrison, Harry P., as told to Karl Detzer. *Culture under Canvas: The Story of Tent Chautauqua.* New York: Hastings House Publishers, 1958. Tapia, John E. *Circuit Chautauqua: From Rural Education to Popular Entertainment in Early Twentieth Century America.* Jefferson NC: McFarland and Co., 1997.

CLIFFS NOTES

Cliff Hillegass was born in 1917 in the Great Plains of Nebraska in the town of Rising City. He graduated from Rising City High School, entered Midland College in Fremont, Nebraska, and, after graduation, began graduate work as an assistant in geology at the University of Nebraska in Lincoln.

After a stint in the Army Air Corps in the 1940s Hillegass began work at Long's Book Store, which soon was renamed Nebraska Book Company, a firm that is among the nation's largest handlers of used books. He rose rapidly through the ranks and became a buyer of used textbooks throughout a large portion of the United States. Because of the company's widespread wholesale network, his enthusiasm, and his grasp of the value of books, Hillegass became friends with bookstore managers from coast to coast. These close business friendships became the lynchpins that would later help him launch Cliffs Notes.

In the late 1950s, while Hillegass was visiting Jack Cole, a Canadian book dealer, Cole suggested that Hillegass publish a line of literary study guides similar to Cole's Notes. Cliff liked the idea, returned to Nebraska, borrowed money, and arranged with Boomers Printers to publish 4,000 copies each of sixteen of Cole's top-selling Shakespeare titles. Many book dealers were dubious about the venture, but, because of their longtime friendship with Hillegass, they agreed to stock Cliffs Notes, which were boxed and shipped from Hillegass's basement in Lincoln, Nebraska.

Cliffs Notes were an immediate success—so much so that the business moved from the basement to a large warehouse in downtown Lincoln. The series continued to prosper, doubling in sales every year, and numerous employees were added to the firm, including professional editors, a consulting editor, and many university professors as writers. Along the way, competing firms began selling literary study guides (in the early 1970s, for example, there were thirteen competitors), but Cliffs Notes outsold them all and survived to become the generic term for all study guides.

Today, Cliffs Notes are sold all over the world, and many of the titles have been translated into other languages. In the United States they are often used as a teaching tool in high schools and are recommended or required reading for many university graduate courses. Cliffs Notes remained a Lincoln, Nebraska, firm until it was acquired by IDG Books Worldwide, Inc., in 1998 and operations were moved to Indianapolis, Indiana. Cliff Hillegass died in Lincoln, Nebraska, on May 5, 2001.

James L. Roberts
University of Nebraska–Lincoln

COLLEGE TOWNS

See CITIES AND TOWNS: College Towns

DISTANCE EDUCATION

Distance education is characterized by a physical separation between learner and teacher or learner and institution. The Great Plains proved to be an ideal setting for the development of distance education programs owing to its large area and small population.

The earliest form of distance education in the Great Plains was that of faculty members from land-grant institutions traveling around their states by horse or rail to offer instruction to residents. In the 1890s correspondence education programs, first pioneered by a private institution, the University of Chicago, began developing at major state universities in the Midwest. By World War I correspondence was the dominant form of distance education in the Great Plains.

Practitioners of distance education took advantage of new technologies as they emerged: radio in the 1920s, television in the 1950s, satellite delivery in the 1980s, and computer-based instruction in the 1990s. As each delivery technology emerged, it was incorporated into the overall strategy of distance education. Rather than succeeding generations of technology replacing prior technologies, new technologies added to the delivery arsenal available to practitioners.

Although the first distance education efforts were aimed at the postsecondary marketplace, lifelong learning was always an important concern. Noncredit courses covering everything from the arts, to horticulture, to various trades and skills were offered, regardless of the decade or the technology. In the 1990s one of the greatest areas of growth, in terms of both programs and users, was in the elementary and secondary education arena.

James E. Sherwood
University of Nebraska–Lincoln

EASTMAN, CHARLES (1858–1939)

Dr. Charles Alexander Eastman (Ohiyesa) devoted his entire life to helping Native Americans. He believed that Indians could retain their beliefs, but they also needed to selectively adopt non-Indian ways in order to function in the dominant culture. This was the message he often presented in his lecturers and his eleven books and numerous articles. Elaine Goodale Eastman, his non-Indian wife, assisted him in his publications.

Eastman was born near Redwood Falls, Minnesota, on February 19, 1858, and raised in the traditional manner of a Santee Sioux hunter and warrior. His life drastically changed at age fifteen, when his recently Christianized father convinced Eastman to join him at Flandreau, Dakota Territory, and enroll in Flandreau Mission School. For the next seventeen years Eastman attended a number of schools, including Santee Normal Training School and Dartmouth College, ultimately receiving his medical degree from Boston University School of Medicine in 1890.

His first of several government appointments was as Indian physician at Pine Ridge Agency, South Dakota (1890–93), where he witnessed the massacre at Wounded Knee. Other government positions were outing agent at Carlisle Indian Industrial School, Pennsylvania (1899), Indian physician at Crow Creek Agency, South Dakota (1900–1903), head of the project to revise the Sioux allotment rolls (1903–9), and Indian inspector (1923–25). At times, he clashed with his white superiors regarding policies. His nongovernment work included a brief medical practice in St. Paul, Minnesota (1893), serving as Indian secretary of the International Committee of the YMCA (1894–98), and representing Santee Sioux claims in Washington DC. For several years, the Eastman family ran a summer camp near Munsonville, New Hampshire.

As an active Indian reformer, Eastman helped found and later served as president of the Society of American Indians. He condemned reservation conditions, supported Indian citizenship, and called for the abolition of the Bureau of Indian Affairs. In his final years, Eastman continued to present lectures and worked with the YMCA and Boy Scouts of America and on several research projects. In 1933 he was awarded the first Indian Council Fire Medal for his lifelong work in addressing Indian and white relations. Eastman died in Detroit, Michigan, on January 8, 1939.

See also GENDER: *Eastman, Elaine Goodale.*

Raymond Wilson
Fort Hays State University

Eastman, Charles Alexander (Ohiyesa). *Indian Boyhood.* New York: Dover Publications, 1971. Wilson, Raymond. *Ohiyesa: Charles Eastman, Santee Sioux.* Urbana: University of Illinois Press, 1983.

ESCUELA TLATELOLCO

See HISPANIC AMERICANS: *Escuela Tlatelolco*

FRONTIER COLLEGE

Conceived in protest more than a century ago, Frontier College is Canada's oldest national adult literacy organization. At the dawn of the twentieth century the factories, mines, farms, and railways that were shaping Canada's future required an army of workers. Immigrants poured into the country, many often poor, uneducated, and illiterate. Alfred Fitzpatrick, a former Presbyterian minister from Pictou, Nova Scotia, decided to take literacy and the advantages of education to the workers. He recruited university students for his Canadian Reading Camp Association (later named Frontier College in 1919) and sent them to isolated locations to labor with the workers during the day and to teach them at night. They became known as laborer-teachers. Male laborer-teachers worked on steel gangs and section crews for the Canadian National Railway, while women laborer-teachers worked alongside Prairie women during the grain harvests. Whatever work they did, they brought with them literacy and, in some cases, social reform.

After World War I Frontier College was authorized by the Canadian government to grant university degrees, making it Canada's only "national university." By the 1930s the degree-granting concept had been terminated, and laborer-teachers worked in Relief Camps for the unemployed and later, during World War II, on the Alaska Highway. By the 1950s and 1960s, as sophisticated machinery reduced the need for manual labor, Frontier College turned to community development and projects with Canada's First Nations. In 1977 Frontier College was recognized by the United Nations with the UNESCO prize for education and literacy. Beat the Street, a literacy program of street people working with street people, was begun in Regina and Winnipeg in the 1980s.

Since 1987 Canadian university students calling themselves Frontier College associates have been working in Alberta, Saskatchewan, and Manitoba to address issues of literacy and poverty. The Student Centred Individualized Learning Programme (SCIL), developed by Frontier College, has allowed learners across the country to set up and monitor their own programs. Frontier College continues to respond to the challenge that founder Alfred Fitzpatrick made to all Canadians: to take education to those who do not have it, whoever and wherever they may be.

James H. Morrison
Saint Mary's University

Frontier College Papers, National Archives of Canada, Ottawa. Krotz, Larry, comp., with Erica Martin and Philip Fernandez. *Frontier College Letters: 100 Years of Teaching, Learning and Nation Building.* Toronto: Frontier College Press, 1999. Morrison, James H. *Camps and Classrooms: A Pictorial History of Frontier College.* Toronto: Frontier College Press, 1989.

INDIAN BOARDING SCHOOLS, UNITED STATES

Indian boarding schools, a primary focus of federal Indian policy beginning in the late 1870s, were designed as instruments for the assimilation of Native Americans into American society and were established on and off reservations throughout the United States, especially in the Great Plains. Boarding schools first appeared on reservations in 1877, but, beginning in 1879, policy makers seeking higher potential for assimilation channeled their efforts into building them off the reservations. By 1900 officials had reversed their decision, disturbed by the high costs associated with these schools, and, until 1923, they renewed support for on-reservation boarding and day schools. In 1923 pressure from Indian rights activists led the government to decrease its role in Indian education and, with the passage of the Indian Reorganization Act in 1934, to withdraw even further.

From the early nineteenth century, philanthropists and political leaders promoted assimilation through education as the most humane approach to the "Indian problem." Education was initially left to missionaries and philanthropists, who, with the support of church denominations and the government's "civilization" fund, established schools along with missions among Plains Indians during the 1830s. Mission schools remained an important component of Indian education—and assimilation—policy throughout the century, though they declined in importance after 1873, when direct federal financial support was removed. The federal government did, however, continue to contract with religious denominations to support mission schools, but their era was over.

The federal government moved to fill the gap. In 1870 Congress initiated an annual appropriation of $100,000 for Indian education. By 1893 the annual appropriation had risen to $2.3 million. The bulk of the money went to establishing day schools on or near Indian villages and later on reservations. By 1870 48 day schools were in operation, and the number had risen to 147 by 1900; the majority were on reservations in the Great Plains.

But reformers were not entirely satisfied with day schools. The reservation environment, to which the child returned daily, undermined the process of assimilation. By the end of the 1870s policy makers were promoting reservation boarding schools as a solution to the shortcomings of the day schools; they viewed these schools—and the resultant separation of Indian children from their families—as a superior context for changing children's attitudes, values, and habits. Like the day schools, which still received support, the majority of reservation boarding schools were built in the Great Plains.

As the idea of reservation boarding schools took hold, so too did the idea of federally operated schools off reservations. These schools followed the model of Richard Henry Pratt's Carlisle Indian Industrial School, founded in Pennsylvania in 1879, with an initial enrollment recruited from the Plains. The children received instruction in academic subjects (English, arithmetic, and geography) and also worked on manual labor projects. Boys labored in the fields, in construction, and in the blacksmith's shop; girls were taught to cook, clean, and sew. The objectives were to instill a work ethic, individualism, and other tenets of American civilization and to suppress all that was Indian.

Federal off-reservation boarding schools first appeared in the Great Plains in 1884 with the opening of Chilocco in Indian Territory near the Kansas border, Genoa in Nebraska, and Haskell in Lawrence, Kansas. Plans were soon under way to expand further. Pratt had urged officials to build off-reservation schools only in completely white communities, as far away from reservation influence as possible, but policy makers were concerned about the cost of transporting Indian children long distances. To save money they decided to build schools closer to the reservations, and in 1882 congressional authorization to use vacated military buildings reinforced this decision.

By the end of the 1880s seven federal off-reservation boarding schools were in operation nationally, enrolling more than 1,800 Indian children. In the 1890s eighteen more were built, including those at Pierre, Flandreau, Chamberlain, and Rapid City, South Dakota. By the end of the century there were also forty-three reservation boarding schools on the Plains and sixty-seven day schools. The on-reservation boarding schools were mainly located in North and South Dakota and Indian Territory; South Dakota, with its eight reservations and large Indian population, had the bulk of the day schools.

Enthusiasm for federal off-reservation boarding schools quickly faded after the turn of the twentieth century. In 1901 Commissioner of Indian Affairs William Jones expressed alarm that $45 million spent on 20,000 Indian children had produced little evidence of assimilation. His 1904 annual report emphasized the necessity of utilizing existing reservation boarding and day schools more effectively. Arguing that these schools were no less effective than the off-reservation schools for assimilation, Jones proposed a hierarchy of existing schools that would provide the greatest opportunity for assimilating the best students with the greatest potential for surviving in the white world.

The building phase was over. Thereafter, Indian education policy deemphasized off-reservation schools. Policy makers argued that Indians were incapable of (more accurately, resistant to) the rapid assimilation envisioned by Pratt and noted that most Indians educated in the system of schools returned to the reservation. With this shift in emphasis, the number of boarding schools began to decline, and by 1920 seven of the federal off-reservation schools, including the flagship Carlisle as well as Chamberlain, had closed.

By the 1920s the long-lasting and unsuccessful assimilation policy was in decline. John Collier's American Indian Defense Association, founded in 1923, worked for the next decade to change the focus of federal Indian policy from destruction of Native cultures to respect for individual Indian self-identity. Collier became commissioner of Indian Affairs in 1933. In 1934 the passage of the Wheeler-Howard Indian Reorganization Act established a "New Deal" for Native Americans, providing for tribal landownership, self-government, control of Indian education, and the closing of many of the remaining federal off-reservation boarding schools. The Great Plains education map is now dotted with reservation community day schools, Bureau of Indian Affairs postsecondary schools (for example, Haskell Indian Junior College), and tribally controlled community colleges such as Sinte Gleska on Rosebud Reservation in South Dakota, the first Indian-run college to offer bachelor's degrees. The off-reservation boarding schools at Flandreau and Pierre, however, continue to operate.

See also NATIVE AMERICANS: Assimilation Policy.

Ronald C. Naugle
Nebraska Wesleyan University

Adams, David Wallace. *Education for Extinction: American Indians and the Boarding School Experience, 1875–1928.* Lawrence: University Press of Kansas, 1995. Hoxie, Frederick E. *A Final Promise: The Campaign to Assimilate the Indians, 1880–1920.* Lincoln: University of Nebraska Press, 1984. U.S. Department of the Interior. *Annual Report of the Commissioner of Indian Affairs to the Secretary of the Interior.* Washington DC: Government Printing Office, 1877–1932.

INDIAN RESIDENTIAL SCHOOLS, CANADA

The modern phase of Canada's residential schools system for First Nations children emerged in the 1880s in the Prairie Provinces, and several of the institutions would continue to exist in that region after the government of Canada decided to phase out the institutions in 1969. Missionaries and colonial governments had experimented with boarding schools for Native children as early as the French colonial regime of the seventeenth century, and other custodial institutions were initiated by Protestant missionary organizations in eighteenth-century colonial New Brunswick and early-nineteenth-century Upper Canada (Ontario). However, the modern era of residential schooling in Canada began in the Prairies in 1883 as a direct consequence of the treaties that Canada had negotiated with the First Nations between 1871 and 1877. The system began slowly in the Prairies in 1883, spread to British Columbia in the 1890s, and expanded to the far North and the northerly regions of Ontario and Quebec in the twentieth century. At the height of the residential school system in the 1920s, more than half of the eighty institutions were located in the three Prairie Provinces.

Indian residential schools were joint operations of the federal government and the major Christian churches. The government authorized the creation of schools, provided partial funding for their operation, specified curricula and standards of care, and, in general, oversaw their operation as a system. The day-to-day running of the institutions was in the hands of the churches, with approximately 60 percent of the schools operated by the Roman Catholic Church (mainly through the Oblates of Mary Immaculate and female religious orders), about 30 percent by the Anglican Church, and the remainder by the Methodists and Presbyterians. (The Methodists and most Presbyterians united with the Congregationalists in 1925 to form the United Church of Canada.) Church missionary bodies concentrated on selecting personnel, particularly principals, subject to the approval of the government. A constant source of tension between missionaries and the government was the level of state funding, which was never adequate to cover most of the costs of the schools. The various churches also tended to regard one another with denominational hostility, resulting in a competition for recruits to populate their schools.

The strong emphasis placed by the missionaries on sectarian attitudes toward denominational rivals and the aggressive proselytization of the students under their care constituted but one of the many grievances that both residential school students and their families had with the system. Inadequate government funding, especially from the 1890s to the latter part of the 1950s (the government began to improve financing after 1956), led to overwork of the students and inadequate care in diet, accommodation, clothing, and amenities such as recreational equipment. The root of the funding problem was government reluctance to spend much on the First Nations, principally because Canadian society placed little value on Native peoples, and the fact that the per capita funding mechanism that was used induced missionaries to place a greater emphasis on keeping student places in the schools filled than on providing adequate care.

Since, like American schools, Canadian residential schools operated until the 1950s on the half-day system, the administrators had ample occasion to overwork the students. The half-day system theoretically taught both usable job skills and rudimentary academic learning by having students in the classroom half the day and engaged in work in fields, barns, kitchens, and workrooms the other half. In reality, the half-day system proved a means of extracting student labor to keep the underfunded schools running. Besides excessive work and ethnocentrically focused religion, the schools stimulated opposition by providing inadequate care at the best of times and serious physical, emotional, and sexual abuse at the worst. These ills, in conjunction with the obvious fact that the schools were not succeeding as pedagogical, evangelical, or vocational-training operations, provoked strong and organized First Nations opposition by the 1940s. After much hesitation, largely caused by vigorous Roman Catholic opposition to closure, the government decided in 1969 to phase out the schools. Some schools persisted into the 1980s, and a few continued to operate under First Nations control until the 1990s.

In the twenty-first century Canada's resi-

Father and children attending Qu'Appelle (Saskatchewan) Industrial School, ca. 1900

dential schools are a festering legal and political problem for Canadians. By the end of 2000 more than 6,200 individual lawsuits involving some 7,200 individuals had been filed against the government and, in some cases, the missionaries; they allege abuse, both physical and sexual, and cultural loss. The number of suits continues to increase weekly. One law firm in the Prairie Provinces is handling over half the suits.

See also NATIVE AMERICANS: Assimilation Policy.

J. R. Miller
University of Saskatchewan

Miller, J. R. *Shingwauk's Vision: A History of Native Residential Schools.* Toronto: University of Toronto Press, 1996. Milloy, J. S. *A National Crime: The Canadian Government and the Residential School System, 1879 to 1986.* Winnipeg: University of Manitoba Press, 1999. Titley, E. Brian. "Industrial Schools in Western Canada." In *Schools in the West: Essays on Canadian Educational History,* edited by Nancy M. Sheehan, J. Donald Wilson, and David C. Jones. Calgary: Detselig Enterprises, 1986; 133–54.

LAND-GRANT UNIVERSITIES

The Morrill Act, signed into law by Abraham Lincoln on July 2, 1862, set aside public lands for the establishment of land-grant universities. The act came from a movement favoring practical scientific and industrial education for American working classes. Led by Congressman Justin Morrill of Vermont, the land-grant idea emerged as a reaction against the classical curriculum that dominated traditional institutions. Sparked by advancements in science prior to 1850, reformers sought a system that could build upon the resourcefulness of industrial classes. Morrill, himself the son of a blacksmith, believed in better educational opportunities for the children of artisans, farmers, and laborers. He believed that a true democracy meant educating everyone, not just those who sought careers in law, politics, and the ministry. Morrill was also influenced by a crisis of declining agricultural productivity on American farms. He learned about the advances in scientific agriculture in Europe and believed that similar practices could be applied in the United States, especially as it expanded westward into new agricultural areas. The Morrill Act was passed the same year as the Homestead Act, thus further encouraging agricultural development in the Great Plains.

President James Buchanan had vetoed Morrill's first land-grant bill in 1857 on the grounds that higher education should be left to the states. Morrill was also hindered by southerners' skepticism of the expansion of federal powers and the bill's perceived favoritism toward northern states and territories. After the Civil War began, Morrill introduced the bill again in 1861 to a more receptive, northern Congress. Morrill set aside for every state the sale of 30,000 acres for each representative and senator to endow and support land-grant universities. The act allowed for teaching a classical curriculum, but the emphasis was on agriculture, mechanical arts (engineering), and military tactics. Ironically, western states that later benefited from the Morrill Act were some of its loudest detractors in the beginning. Westerners feared that all of the public lands would be taken from their states. Kansas senator James Lane offered an amendment that limited the land claimed in any one state to one million acres. With that amendment, the bill was passed.

During the Civil War, only two states, Iowa in 1862 and Kansas in 1863, passed land-grant resolutions. Not until after 1865 could most states refocus their attention on higher education. Kansas was the first Plains state to take on the conditions of the Morrill Act, with the Kansas State Agricultural College (Manhattan), founded in 1863. Nebraska was next, with the University of Nebraska (Lincoln), founded in 1869. Other Plains states and territories followed, with Texas A&M University (College Station) in 1876; Colorado State University (Fort Collins) in 1879; South Dakota State University (Brookings) in 1881; the University of Wyoming (Laramie) in 1887; North Dakota State University (Fargo) in 1890; and Oklahoma State University (Stillwater) in 1890. Since the land-grant universities were founded to be the agriculture and mechanical schools, some states established separate state universities with an emphasis on liberal arts. Kansas, Oklahoma, and South Dakota, for example, each established two universities, one land-grant and one state university. Nebraska and Wyoming combined both the land-grant purpose and liberal arts into one consolidated university.

The land-grant curriculum focused on practical, scientific education. Besides mechanical arts, the curriculum could include agriculture, pharmacology, and, for women, domestic economy. Military training was also required of male students, and many of those soldiers and officers later served in the Spanish-American War and both world wars. In the Great Plains, institutions focused on agricultural studies, which included efficient crop production, animal science, dairying, and plant biology. In the twentieth century, agriculture science expanded to include genetics, hybridization, fertilizer production, and veterinary medicine. Women were included in the land-grant mission through domestic or home economics programs, because efficient farms also needed educated farm wives.

Land-grant universities were progressive not only in their approach to practical education but also because they admitted women and people of color; all students received free tuition and subsidized rail travel. These institutions struggled financially and academically before 1900, and some critics claimed that young people never returned to farm work after attending college, thus defeating the very purpose of the land-grant mission. Even if that was the case, land-grant institutions continued to reach out to rural, agricultural populations. In 1887 Congress passed the Hatch Act to stimulate research in agriculture science through the creation of experiment stations at which students and professors could apply new knowledge toward efficient farm production. Students even lived and worked on model farms that allowed them to use their classroom education in a working and productive farm setting. The Hatch Act expanded the role of land-grant universities through research contributions to agricultural science that continue to this day.

In 1890 the second Morrill Act was passed, providing additional land-grant endowments. States that made distinctions of race in admissions could not receive the funds, so the act allowed for the creation of separate land-grant universities for blacks. The founding of many all-black colleges after 1890 included two in the Great Plains: Prairie View A&M University in Texas and Langston University in Oklahoma. All other Plains land-grant institutions continued to admit black students. It was not until 1994 that Congress passed the Equity in Educational Land-Grant Status Act, which created land-grant colleges for Native American populations. Plains states benefited most from this, with a majority of Indian land-grant colleges located in South Dakota (four), North Dakota (five), Montana (seven), Nebraska (one), and Kansas (one).

The desire to extend land-grant education to a broader population led to the creation of the Cooperative Extension Service as part of the Smith-Lever Act of 1914. Because practical education was still unavailable to many, cooperative extension sought to disseminate information to a wider population, especially in agriculture, home economics, and rural energy. Extension programs especially benefited Plains states, with their large geographic areas and scattered rural populations. Today, extension programs continue to take education to distant farm areas.

In the twentieth century, land-grant universities expanded their missions beyond the agricultural scope of the nineteenth century. Not strictly agriculture and mechanics schools anymore, land-grant universities also developed arts, humanities, and social science programs. Graduate programs were established

in most departments on land-grant campuses. Further, land-grant universities endeavored to carry on in their purpose of providing public, democratic, and practical education to a larger population. Broad admissions standards, low tuition costs, cooperative extension programs, and agricultural experiment stations are some of the methods used by land-grant institutions to make education widely available to many in the Great Plains.

Andrea G. Radke
Brigham Young University

Cross, Coy F. *Justin Smith Morrill: Father of the Land-Grant Colleges.* East Lansing: Michigan State University Press, 1999. National Association of State Universities and Land-Grant Colleges. *The Land-Grant Tradition.* Washington DC: Government Printing Office, 1995. Nevins, Allan. *The Origins of the Land-Grant Colleges and State Universities.* Washington DC: Civil War Centennial Commission, 1962.

LIBBY, ORIN (1864–1952)

Orin Grant Libby was born on June 9, 1864, on a farm near Hammond, Wisconsin. After receiving his diploma from River Falls State Normal School in 1886, he taught in Wisconsin high schools until 1890. Entering the University of Wisconsin as a junior, he was awarded a bachelor of letters degree in 1892. He remained in Madison and was among the first graduate students of the historian Frederick Jackson Turner. Libby's doctoral dissertation, entitled "The Geographical Distribution of the Vote of the Thirteen States on the Federal Constitution 1787–8," may be the most important single contribution ever made to the interpretation of the movement for the federal Constitution.

After receiving his doctorate in 1895, Libby remained at Wisconsin for seven years as an instructor, teaching history and pursuing his interests in birds and bird migration. In 1902 he accepted the position of professor and chair of history at the University of North Dakota in Grand Forks, a position he held until he retired in 1945 at the age of eighty-one.

Realizing on his arrival that the young state's history was still in the making, Libby turned to researching the history of North Dakota, thereby earning the title the "Father of North Dakota History." He reorganized the State Historical Society, served as its secretary for more than forty years, and, until his retirement, edited the society's journals, the *Collections* and the *North Dakota Historical Quarterly.* He created the State Museum, the State Historical Library, and the State Park System. In 1907 Libby helped organize the Mississippi Valley Historical Association, and in 1903 he organized the North Dakota Audubon Society.

Libby spent thirty-five years researching the visit in 1738 of Pierre Gaultier de Varennes, sieur de La Vérendrye, and his sons to the Missouri River in what is now North Dakota. A recognized authority on North Dakota's Native Americans, Libby cleared the Arikara scouts who had served under Lt. Col. George Armstrong Custer at the Battle of the Little Bighorn of the charge that they had acted cowardly and had been responsible for the de-

feat of Maj. Marcus Reno's men. In 1912 Libby interviewed the nine surviving scouts and published his findings in *The Arikara Narrative of the Campaign against the Hostile Dakotas, June, 1876.* Recently reissued to favorable reviews, Libby's account cannot be disregarded in any serious study of the Battle of the Little Bighorn.

Throughout his life, Libby recorded the memories of the state's early inhabitants, their relatives, and their descendants; excavated for artifacts and remains of historic sites; photographed log cabins, sod houses, and dugouts; collected letters, photographs, diaries, Indian legends, newspapers, and documents; and encouraged the writing of lodge, church, community, and county histories. Little of North Dakota's history escaped his interest and efforts.

Orin Grant Libby died on March 29, 1952, at the age of eighty-seven. He was survived by wife, Eva Cory Libby, daughter, Margaret, son, Charles, and four grandchildren. He was buried in Memorial Park Cemetery in Grand Forks.

See also WAR: Little Bighorn, Battle of the.
Gordon L. Iseminger
University of North Dakota

Libby, Orin Grant. "The Geographical Distribution of the Vote of the Thirteen States on the Federal Constitution 1787–8." *Bulletin of the University of Wisconsin* (1894): 1–116. Libby, Orin G., ed. *The Arikara Narrative of Custer's Campaign and the Battle of the Little Bighorn.* Norman: University of Oklahoma Press, 1998.

LIBRARIES

Little is known of the earliest libraries in the Great Plains, but they probably resembled antebellum collections elsewhere in book-scarce frontier communities. Nascent frontier communities established private libraries such as those in the village of Omaha, Nebraska, where in 1856 residents wanted to boost settlement and provide competition for saloons. These libraries laid the foundations for public libraries once legislation allowed for municipal support of publicly held, free-circulating libraries.

By the time settlers migrated to the Great Plains, the library movement in North America was already maturing from its British and Colonial New England origins as parochial, mercantile, and social into a profession led by public and college librarians. Events such as the establishment of the American Library Association (ALA) in 1876 and Melvil Dewey's founding of the first modern library school at Columbia University eight years later signified this homogenization of "library economy," which Dewey summarized as providing "the best reading for the largest number at the least expense."

Development of libraries varied in each community, often depending on the energy of social reformers possessed by the "library spirit." Many libraries owe their origins to women's clubs, which raised funds for reading rooms by memberships, lectures, and bake sales before turning their library over to the city. Such gifts were often prompted by the desire for matching grants offered by Andrew Carnegie and other philanthropists to construct local temples of knowledge.

Statehood was another factor in the growth of libraries, as legislatures allowed communities to raise mill levies for their support. This legislation varied in each jurisdiction. In Oklahoma, for example, school districts were originally charged with library operation in 1889. It wasn't until 1901 that the territorial legislature allowed cities with a population over 2,500 to charge a mill levy to support publicly held libraries. The small size of many Great Plains communities likely retarded library development, because numerous communities could only afford small collections that opened for just a few hours and were staffed by "born" librarians rather than trained ones.

The establishment of the Laramie County Library in Cheyenne, Wyoming, in 1886 pioneered the first county library system, which since has become the model for modern library service in North America. In Saskatchewan the province not only allowed municipalities to tax for library support in 1905 but also offered an additional grant; however, library development was slow until the province's Commonwealth Cooperative Federation government created the Regional Library in 1950. Readers in the Southern Great Plains were further disadvantaged by Jim Crow laws, which segregated libraries and left many African Americans without access. For example, racial conflict, masquerading as an anti-Communist crusade, led to the downfall of Bartlesville, Oklahoma, librarian Ruth Brown in 1950. After thirty years of service, Brown was fired for ostensibly circulating subversive materials, but the real reason was her affiliation with the Congress of Racial Equality.

State library commissions were also strong promoters of public libraries. For example, North Dakota's Public Library Commission, established in 1907, operated traveling libraries (cases with sixty books or fewer on loan to communities for up to six months) and advised communities on library development. These traveling libraries contributed to the hunger for reading in rural parts of the state. A year later the commission established the Legislative Reference Bureau, which was based on Wisconsin's progressive example. However, in 1919 the commission became involved in a political fight between the Nonpartisan League and opponents over "socialistic" books in traveling libraries. As a result of the weakened Library Commission and the end of Carnegie grants to libraries, little progress was made in providing service to rural parts of North Dakota until counties received permission to operate libraries in 1945. Sparse populations and an aversion to taxes, though, meant that few such initiatives passed until the 1955 Library Services Act, which supported rural library development as part of federal initiatives during the cold war to improve education and literacy. Throughout the Great Plains, federal aid through the WPA and other agencies created during the Great Depression provided extension librarians to many rural communities that previously were without service.

Among the first libraries in the Plains were state and territorial ones that grew on the exchange of government documents. The dates of establishment for these early libraries are Texas (1846), New Mexico (1850), Kansas (1855), Nebraska (1856), Colorado (1863), South Dakota (1865), Montana (1865), Manitoba (1870), Wyoming (1871), Oklahoma (1893), Alberta (1906), North Dakota (1907), and Saskatchewan (1953). Other special libraries in the Great Plains also developed, including law libraries, medical libraries, and corporate information centers. The history of the Great Plains is preserved in many state and provincial historical society libraries and archives as well as in the Dwight D. Eisenhower Library and Museum (Abilene, Kansas), the Johnson Presidential Library (College Park, Texas), and the Bush Presidential Library (Austin, Texas), which are operated by the National Archives and Records Administration. These libraries, together with local and academic libraries, are repositories for books, periodicals, and archival papers that encompass the print culture of the Great Plains.

The largest collections in the Plains are those of the research universities of the states and provinces. In good years these libraries grew along with their fledgling institutions of higher learning. Indeed, their growth was instrumental in the growth of all Plains libraries, because their librarians taught in the pioneering programs of library schools, pioneered library legislation on the state level, and encouraged the state library associations that fostered professional librarianship. Research libraries at state schools, inspired by the vision of the Morrill Act of 1862, not only provide material for students and faculty but also offer service to citizens through reference assistance and book circulation via interlibrary loan. Special collections and archives at research libraries contribute to the preservation of the cultural life of the Great Plains. The extensive papers and correspondence of writer Mari Sandoz, for example, are at the University of Nebraska–Lincoln. The Harry Ransom Humanities Research Center at the University of Texas at Austin is one of the world's richest collections of archives and manuscripts, including those of New Mexico author Alice Corbin Henderson, and papers of writers D. H. Lawrence, Tennessee Williams, Isaac Bashevis Singer, and publisher Alfred A. Knopf. Some of the more important special collections at Canadian university libraries include the papers of the Thistledown and Turnstone regional literary presses and the diaries of Icelandic immigrant Símon Símonarson at the University of Manitoba, members of the Regina Five art movement at the University of Regina, and author W. O. Mitchell at the University of Calgary.

Professional education for librarianship has been available in the Great Plains since Gertrude Shawan established a ten-week sequence at Kansas State Normal School (later Emporia State University) in 1902. It was typical of the apprentice classes run by larger public and academic libraries from which early library workers were recruited. Unlike many schools that were closed as education became more professional, the School of Library and Information Management at Emporia State University survived and now offers professional master's and doctoral degrees. Library science was also taught at the University of Denver between 1932 and 1985 and again after 1995. The predecessor to the School of Library and Information Studies at the University of Oklahoma was established in 1929, and the University of Alberta established a graduate program in 1968. Texas is unique in that it has three professional schools, two at the University of North Texas in Denton and one at the University of Texas at Austin. Many other colleges, especially normal schools, once offered teacher-librarian courses to prepare school librarians, but these were not graduate programs accredited by the ALA.

Although recent library literature focuses on technological developments, historical reflection suggests that libraries' traditional functions of providing access to information and recreation perhaps have not changed greatly. However, libraries and archives are increasingly faced with questions of how to preserve both digital and paper records of life in the Great Plains as well as offer access to the wider world.

Andrew B. Wertheimer
University of Wisconsin–Madison

Passset, Joanne E. *Cultural Crusaders: Women Librarians in the American West, 1900–1917*. Albuquerque: University of New Mexico Press, 1994. Robbins, Louise S. *The Dismissal of Miss Ruth Brown: Civil Rights, Censorship and the American Library*. Norman: University of Oklahoma Press, 2000.

LORENTINO, DOROTHY SUNRISE
(b. 1912)

Dorothy Sunrise Lorentino opened the door for public school education for Native Americans and educated a nation. The extraordinary contributions to education of this Lawton, Oklahoma, native began with a battle. At the age of six she was denied access to the Cache Public Schools because of her heritage as a Comanche Indian. She and her parents made a twenty-mile train ride to Lawton, Oklahoma, where her father sued the school district for refusing to admit Native American children to public schools. Lorentino's father won the lawsuit in 1918. Prior to this ruling, all Native American children were required by law to attend only Bureau of Indian Affairs schools.

Lorentino later graduated from the Indian boarding school at Chilocco and earned a bachelor's degree from Northeastern Oklahoma A&M in Talequah in 1938 and a master's degree from the University of Oregon in 1947. Before retiring in 1972, Lorentino taught special education for thirty-four years on reservations in Arizona and New Mexico and later in the public schools of Salem and Tillamook,

Oregon. Following her retirement, she continued teaching by substituting at public schools, and she taught the Comanche tribal language and songs to members of her tribe.

Lorentino earned many awards throughout her career as a teacher. In 1997 she became the first Oklahoman and Native American to be inducted into the National Teachers Hall of Fame. Other honors include the National Indian Education Association's Elder of the Year, the Delta Kappa Gamma Society Lifetime Award, and Outstanding Woman of Comanche County. In 1996 Cache High School initiated the Dorothy Sunrise Lorentino Award to be presented annually to the Native American graduating senior who best exemplifies the qualities for which Lorentino stands.

Cora Z. Hedstrom
National Teachers Hall of Fame

McLAURIN V. OKLAHOMA STATE REGENTS

Working with the National Association for the Advancement of Colored People (NAACP), black Oklahomans in the 1940s increasingly tested laws and state policies that upheld segregation, including segregated education. While Oklahoma had a relatively small African American population (about 8 percent at the time of statehood in 1907), a majority of early white Oklahomans had southern roots and thoroughly embraced the concept of white supremacy.

The first legislature, meeting in 1907, had established separate schools for African Americans and heavy fines for administrators, teachers, and students who broke the law. In the state's higher education system the all-black Langston A&M College, created during the territorial era, offered African Americans many programs leading to a bachelor's degree, but Langston had no graduate programs. Instead, the state provided out-of-state educational grants for African American students who wished to go to graduate school. Approximately 2,000 black Oklahomans received such grants between 1907 and 1946. However, such a system was not acceptable to many of the state's African American students, one of whom was George McLaurin, an instructor at Langston who wished to pursue a graduate degree within the state.

McLaurin became a pioneer in the national civil rights movement when he, along with five other African Americans, applied for admission to the all-white University of Oklahoma's graduate program in January 1948. Denied admission, McLaurin applied again in September. Still denied, he sought a remedy in federal court, which ordered the university to admit McLaurin. The ruling, however, did not specifically void the state's segregation laws.

University president George Lynn Cross, who did not personally oppose integration, worked with regents to admit McLaurin while also obeying the state's segregation laws. However, the implemented plan was dehumanizing. The university made arrangements for McLaurin to take his courses in room 104 in the Carnegie Building. Workers constructed an alcove (the NAACP's lawyer, Thurgood Marshall, who, with Robert L. Carter and Amos T. Hall, argued the case before the Supreme Court, called it a "broom closet"), with wooden railings that separated McLaurin from the rest of the class. He had a separate entrance and exit to and from the hall. McLaurin also found that the university had given him a separate-but-equal men's room, a separate table in the student union, a separate table in the campus cafeteria, and a separate library study table with his name on it. These arrangements satisfied neither McLaurin nor the NAACP, whose legal appeal argued that such on-campus segregation hampered McLaurin's ability to study, to take part in class discussions, and to interact further with other students. On June 5, 1950, the U.S. Supreme Court agreed and ordered the university to end the on-campus segregation of McLaurin.

With this victory, *McLaurin v. Oklahoma* joined a train of precedents, including *Missouri ex. rel. Gaines v. Canada* (1938), *Sweatt v. Painter* (a 1950 Texas case), and *Sipuel v. Board of Regents University of Oklahoma* (1945), which integrated the University of Oklahoma Law School and led to the Supreme Court's historic *Brown v. The Board of Education of Topeka* decision of 1954 and the eventual integration of schools nationwide.

James M. Smallwood
Oklahoma State University

Fisher, Ada Lois Sipuel. *Matter of Black and White: The Autobiography of Ada Lois Sipuel Fisher.* Norman: University of Oklahoma Press, 1996. Franklin, Jimmie Lewis. *Journey toward Hope: A History of Blacks in Oklahoma.* Norman: University of Oklahoma Press, 1982. Smallwood, James. *Blacks in Oklahoma.* Stillwater: Oklahoma State University Press, 1981.

MENNINGER, KARL (1893–1990)

One of the most distinguished and influential American psychiatrists of the twentieth century and cofounder with his father of the Menninger Clinic (later Foundation), Karl Augustus Menninger was born July 22, 1893, in Topeka, Kansas. After graduating from the University of Wisconsin, Menninger attended Harvard University, receiving his medical degree in 1917. Menninger's father, Dr. C. F. Menninger, had already established his practice in Topeka, and, influenced by the family arrangement of the Mayo Clinic, he had planned on his son joining him in practice. This Karl Menninger did, but not as his father had foreseen. While at Harvard, Menninger's chief influence was Elmer Ernest Southard, a professor of neuropathology. Southard turned Menninger's interest toward mental health, and after his return to Topeka Menninger steered the direction of the joint practice toward psychiatry.

In 1920 father and son founded the Menninger Clinic, thus initiating the younger Menninger's long and productive career in Kansas. Five years later, the clinic was complemented by the Menninger Sanitarium in Topeka, and in 1926 the Menningers started the Southard School for children with psychological problems. In 1941 the clinic and sanitarium, by then among the most prestigious in America, were reorganized into the not-for-profit Menninger Foundation. In 1942 Menninger and his brother William, who had also joined his father in the enterprise, established the Topeka Institute for Psychoanalysis. After World War II, during which Menninger had been sent to Europe to assess the need for psychiatric care of military personnel, Karl Menninger became manager of the nation's largest Veterans Administration hospital, Winter Hospital, in Topeka, where students at the newly founded Menninger School of Psychiatry trained.

Menninger's approach to psychiatry during these years became increasingly Freudian. He underwent analysis in 1930 with Chicago psychoanalyst Franz Alexander and again in the early 1940s in New York with Ruth Mack Brunswick. He not only applied these psychoanalytic concepts in his clinical practice but also reflected them in his prolific writing. In 1930 he published *The Human Mind*, which became a best-seller and a Book-of-the-Month Club selection, the first work by a serious psychiatrist to achieve such popularity. In it, he developed a style that would mark much of his work: the ability to translate abstract concepts into vivid, concrete cases. His second book, *Man against Himself* (1938), a study of suicide, describes the power of the death instinct when it is directed inward: the externally aggressive will to kill combined with the internal desire to be killed and to die. In addition to the psychiatric books that Menninger continued to publish throughout his life, he also popularized psychiatry in a column about child rearing that he wrote from 1929 to 1942 in *Household* magazine and in a short-lived advice column in the *Ladies' Home Journal* (1930–32). In a speech honoring Menninger at the Smithsonian Institution, Erik Erikson said that he "translates Freud into American literature. He is not a popularizer, but an enlightener."

Menninger was a crusader not only for Freud and for enlightenment about mental illness but for social issues as well. Early in his career his causes were directly related to psychiatry. He was chair of the first commission to investigate the role psychiatrists play in legal proceedings, and in 1946 he chaired an investigatory panel studying conditions in Kansas mental hospitals. Later in life he turned his attention to matters such as capital punishment (in 1968 he published *The Crime of Punishment*), child neglect (in 1966 he founded The Villages, Inc., a Topeka group home for homeless children), and the mistreatment of Native Americans. In 1978, at the age of eighty-five, he was appointed co–project director of a federal program to develop programs and housing for five southwestern Native tribes.

Menninger was married twice. In 1916 he married Grace Gaines, with whom he had three children: Julia, Robert, and Martha. They divorced in 1941. Later that year he married Jeanetta Lyle, who was to become his collaborator on many projects, including cowriting his third book, *Love against Hate*, in 1942. They adopted a daughter, Rosemary, in 1948.

In 1981 President Jimmy Carter honored Karl Menninger with the Medal of Freedom for his long career and invaluable contributions to American life. Menninger is the only psychiatrist ever to be so recognized. Menninger died of abdominal cancer in a Topeka hospital in July 1990, just four days short of his ninety-seventh birthday.

Howard J. Faulkner
Washburn University

Faulkner, Howard J., and Virginia D. Pruitt, eds. *The Selected Correspondence of Karl A. Menninger*. Columbia: University of Missouri Press, 1995. Friedman, Lawrence. *Menninger: The Family and the Clinic*. Lawrence: University Press of Kansas, 1992. Hall, Bernard. *A Psychiatrist's World*. New York: Viking Press, 1959.

MORRILL ACT

The Morrill Act was passed by Congress and signed into law by President Abraham Lincoln on July 2, 1862. It authorized the establishment of land-grant colleges in every state of the Union and specified that each state be granted 30,000 acres of public land for each member of Congress and Senate for "the endowment, support, and maintenance of at least one college in each state where the leading object shall be, without excluding other scientific or classical studies, to teach such branches of learning as are related to agriculture and the mechanic arts, as the legislatures of the states may respectively prescribe, in order to promote the liberal and practical education of the industrial classes in the several pursuits and professions of life." A slightly different version had been vetoed by President James Buchanan in 1859, the opposition asserting that the proposed land grants would be an invasion of the domestic rights of the states.

Scrip—certificates of possession—were issued on federal lands in new states when no public lands in established states were available. How the land or scrip was to be disposed of was left to state discretion, but the grants did not turn out to be the bonanza that the founders had hoped for. The pressure for immediate funds glutted the market with huge blocks of scrip. The concurrent railroad grants and the inauguration of homesteading in 1862 depressed land prices, and the unsettled financial state of the nation in the 1860s and 1870s further lowered land values. State officials often seemed to have little appreciation of the possibilities of the act and used the grants to secure ready money by quick sale. Established states—Pennsylvania, Massachusetts, and Ohio in particular—were inefficient in disposing of the land, but nine other states received more than the established minimum of $1.25 per acre. Western states generally managed their land above the minimum price. In Nebraska, for example, no school land was disposed of for less than $7.00 an acre.

In time, every state and three U.S. territories established new colleges or combined the land-grant college with existing institutions. Twenty separate colleges of agriculture and mechanic arts were founded, eight in the Great Plains. They were Colorado Agricultural and Mechanical College, Fort Collins (1870); Kansas State Agricultural College, Manhattan (1863); Montana State College, Bozeman (1893); New Mexico College of Agriculture and Mechanic Arts, Las Cruces (1889); North Dakota Agricultural College, Fargo (1890); Oklahoma Agricultural and Mechanical College, Stillwater (1891); South Dakota State College of Agriculture and Mechanic Arts, Brookings (1881); and Agricultural and Mechanical College of Texas, College Station (1871). Two states in the Great Plains used the federal grants to found state universities. They were the University of Nebraska (Lincoln) in 1869 and the University of Wyoming (Laramie) in 1887.

The importance of the land-grant college to American society is hard to exaggerate. The curriculum of American higher education was broadened to include not just the orthodox classics and mathematics but also mechanical, agricultural, and other subjects of assumed immediate utility. The student body was widened to include not just the Christian gentlemen whom Christian colleges traditionally prepared for public service but all persons who through ability and ambition might contribute in a variety of ways to the public welfare. Through the influence of the land-grant colleges and state universities, high schools were established, and their standards were set across the nation. The colleges stimulated a spirit of regional pride centered on these local schools. Women as well as men were invited to attend by the introduction of courses in home economics, and coeducation became standard. Both federally and locally, society was committed to the support of universities, whereas earlier universities and colleges had relied heavily though not exclusively on religious affiliations. Education was secularized. Research became a requisite part of higher education through the model of scientific investigations. With the Hatch Act of 1887, which established experiment stations at land-grant colleges, the federal government assumed some financial responsibility for both general and specialized research. The various states became similarly committed to the support of both basic and applied research. The Jeffersonian ideal of an aristocracy of talent was given a practical means of achievement. The land-grant college was, and still is, a major agency for upward mobility in a democratic world and a lasting and fundamental part of Great Plains education.

Robert E. Knoll
University of Nebraska–Lincoln

Eddy, Edward Danforth, Jr. *Colleges for Our Land and Time: The Land-Grant Idea in American Education*. New York: Harper and Brothers, 1957. Nevins, Allan. *The State Universities and Democracy*. Urbana: University of Illinois Press, 1962. Ross, Earl D. *Democracy's Colleges: The Land-Grant Movement in the Formative States*. New York: Arno Press, 1969.

MUSEUMS

There are more than 1,000 museums in the Great Plains, and they tell many stories—how the region was formed, the history of its Indigenous inhabitants, the process of exploration and settlement by immigrants.

The center of the continent is marked by the Geographical Center Historical Museum (Rugby, North Dakota), in the heart of the Great Plains. Some museums document the big changes in the region. The Royal Tyrrell Museum of Paleontology (Drumheller, Alberta) presents a vivid picture of evolution in the Great Plains, from bacteria to dinosaurs. The changes wrought by western agricultural practices are depicted in the Cattle Raisers Museum (Fort Worth, Texas), the Canadian National Historic Windmill Centre (Etzikom, Alberta), and the National Agricultural Center and Hall of Fame (Bonner Springs, Kansas). The Gem of the West Museum (Coaldale, Alberta) tells the interrelated story of irrigation and European settlement. Museums devoted to the settlers include trail sites, sod houses, historic buildings, pioneer villages, and shrines to cowboys and farmers. The Great Plains is dotted with historic forts and military museums, including the Fort Casper Museum (Casper, Wyoming), the Fort Concho National Historic Landmark (San Angelo, Texas), and the Little Bighorn Battlefield National Monument (Crow Agency, Montana). In Oberlin, Kansas, the Last Indian Raid Museum commemorates the last battle between settlers and Native Americans in the state (in 1878); the French Legation Museum (Austin, Texas) recalls Texas as a French colony. Cowboy museums include the National Cowboy Hall of Fame and Western Heritage Center (Oklahoma City, Oklahoma), the Boot Hill Museum (Dodge City, Kansas), and the Pro Rodeo Hall of Fame and Museum of the American Cowboy (Colorado Springs, Colorado).

Museums devoted to the ethnic heritage of Great Plains inhabitants include El Museo Latino and the Great Plains Black Museum (Omaha, Nebraska), the National Hall of Fame for Famous American Indians (Anadarko, Oklahoma), and the Seminole Nation Museum (Wewoka, Oklahoma). The Trembowla Cross of Freedom, Inc., Museum (Dauphin, Manitoba) celebrates the first Ukrainian settlement in North America. The Calgary Chinese Cultural Centre and the Beth Tzedec Heritage Collection (a Jewish museum) are in Calgary, Alberta.

Other museums interpret modern agents of change. Chevyland U.S.A. (Elm Creek, Nebraska) features a working collection of all Chevrolet models. The petroleum industry is the subject of the Norman #1 Museum in Neodesha, Kansas (site of the first commercial oil well west of the Mississippi) and the Iraan Museum (in Alley Oop Fantasy Land Park, Iraan, Texas). The rise of suburbia is detailed in the Johnson County Museum (Shawnee, Kansas). The museum's collection includes a fully furnished all-electric house from the 1950s, with reenactors portraying family members.

Great Plains museums also record the changes in particular places that have shaped local history. There are hundreds of small mu-

Royal Tyrrell Musuem, Drumheller, Alberta, July 1989

seums and historic sites such as the Grant County Museum (Elgin, North Dakota) and the Rocky Ford Historical Museum (Rocky Ford, Colorado), often run entirely by volunteer labor. These institutions preserve local heritage. In all, about 77 percent of Great Plains museums are history museums, historic sites, and general museums devoted to one place or region. Some are comprehensive institutions with large-scale exhibitions, collections, archives, and conservation facilities such as the Kansas Museum of History (Topeka, Kansas), the Nebraska State Museum (Lincoln, Nebraska), and the Panhandle-Plains Historical Museum (Canyon, Texas). Most history museums are smaller, such as the Middle Border Museum of American Indian and Pioneer Life (Mitchell, South Dakota) and the Otoe County Museum of Memories (Syracuse, Nebraska). The Tsa Mo Ga Memorial Museum (Plains, Texas) receives only about thirty visitors a year.

Several Great Plains museums are known worldwide as research institutions. Among these are the Natural History Museum and Biodiversity Research Center at the University of Kansas (Lawrence, Kansas), the Joslyn Art Museum (Omaha, Nebraska), and the Kimbell Art Museum (Fort Worth, Texas). About 8 percent of Great Plains museums are art museums. Another 3 percent focus on natural history, 2 percent are devoted exclusively to Native Americans, and 4 percent are zoos or botanical gardens. Specialized museums (7 percent) include the World Figure Skating Museum and Hall of Fame (Colorado Springs, Colorado) and Big Well, a museum about the world's largest hand-dug well (Greensburg, Kansas). The Parade of Presidents Wax Museum is in Keystone, South Dakota.

Although most museums are federal, state, or local nonprofit institutions, some are private tax-exempt corporations. These may be large—the Harold Warp Pioneer Village Foundation (Minden, Nebraska) numbers among its collections at least 350 cars, 50,000

historical items, and a Norman Rockwell collection. Most are smaller and more modest in scope such as the Galloping Road Compound and Poker Alley at Harbor Ranch (Dripping Springs, Texas).

The Great Plains has museums devoted to famous people. Two museums honor former president Dwight Eisenhower, the Eisenhower Birthplace State Historical Park (Denison, Texas) and the Dwight D. Eisenhower Library and Museum (Abilene, Kansas). Others include the Dalton Defenders Museum (Coffeyville, Kansas), the Buddy Holly Center (Lubbock, Texas), the Billy the Kid Museum (Fort Sumner, New Mexico), and the Jim Thorpe Home (Yale, Oklahoma). The Emmett Kelly Historical Museum is in Sedan, Kansas; the Will Rogers Memorial is in Claremore, Oklahoma; the Martin and Osa Johnson Safari Museum, Inc., is in Chanute, Kansas; and the O. Henry House and Museum is in Austin, Texas.

The spirit of Willa Cather thrives in museums. Her childhood home (the Willa Cather State Historic Site) and other locations in Red Cloud, Nebraska, invoke her writings. The stories of her immigrant characters are told in diverse places such as the Museum of the American Historical Society of Germans from Russia (Lincoln, Nebraska) and the Wilber Museum (Wilber, Nebraska).

Some Great Plains museums feature decidedly singular pursuits. These include the Enchanted World Doll Museum (Mitchell, South Dakota) and the National Museum of Woodcarving (Custer, South Dakota). Turner's Curling Museum (Weyburn, Saskatchewan) has a collection of 3,800 curling pins. The National Museum of Roller Skating (Lincoln, Nebraska) exhibits skates from 1819 to the present.

A few museums are monuments to American eccentricity, including the Garden of Eden, a house built from limestone logs surrounded by an allegorical sculpture garden (Lucas, Kansas). The Robert L. More Bird Egg

Collection (Vernon, Texas) houses 10,000 bird eggs. The Great Plains is the birthplace of Kool-Aid, which is depicted in an exhibit in the Hastings Museum (Hastings, Nebraska). This is a big museum in a small community, with three floors of exhibits and an IMAX theater. The museum's founder is buried in the basement.

Among the most specialized Great Plains museums are the Museum of Independent Telephony and the Greyhound Hall of Fame (both in Abilene, Kansas) as well as the Boys Town Hall of History (Boys Town, Nebraska). There is America's Shrine to Music Museum (Vermillion, South Dakota), the William A. Quayle Bible Collection at Baker University (Baldwin, Kansas), and the Strategic Air Command Museum (Ashland, Nebraska). The Soukup and Thomas International Balloon and Airship Museum is in Mitchell, South Dakota; the Appaloosa Horse Club Senior Citizens Museum and Archives can be found in Claresholm, Alberta.

What all of these museums have in common is their commitment to study, preserve, and exhibit real things, be they hubcaps, projectile points, fossil sea urchins, or rubber horseshoes. A museum gives its audience a sense of place and purpose. Museums interpret the past to inform the future.

See also FOLKWAYS: Roadside Attractions.

John E. Simmons
University of Kansas

The Official Museum Directory. 31st ed. Washington DC: American Association of Museums, 2001.

NATIONAL COWBOY HALL OF FAME AND WESTERN HERITAGE CENTER

There's no better place to learn about the history and art of the West than the National Cowboy Hall of Fame and Western Heritage Center, a sprawling, 80,000 square-foot museum located atop Persimmon Hill overlooking old Route 66 in Oklahoma City, Oklahoma. The center attracts about 350,000 visitors each year.

The center, founded in 1955, was the dream of the president of Lee Jeans, Chester A. Reynolds. A Kansas City, Missouri, entrepreneur, he had long been concerned about preserving the country's western heritage. When the museum officially opened in 1965, actor John Wayne was parade marshal. He served on the center's board of directors for more than a decade, and his numerous collections are among the museum's treasures. Dedicated to the memory of those who settled the West, the museum quickly began to acquire, catalog, and exhibit art, artifacts, and archival material that pay homage to America's favorite icon, the American cowboy.

Separating myth from reality has always been one of the center's major missions. The reality is found in three major halls of fame, all within the institution. The Hall of Great Westerners honors those who have made significant contributions to the development of the West. The Hall of Great Western Performers honors those who have contributed to the Western genre on stage, screen, and television. Its inductees are honored each year during the Academy Awards–style Western Heritage Awards ceremony. The Rodeo Hall of Fame honorees, chosen by the Rodeo Historical Society, are honored each October. The American Rodeo Gallery displays memorabilia of these rodeo greats.

Reality and myths mingle in the museum's western art collection, including works by such famous artists as Charles M. Russell, Frederic Remington, Albert Bierstadt, and William R. Leigh. The work of contemporary artists is found in the center's Prix de West Collection, honoring the annual Prix de West Award winner during the Prix de West Invitational Exhibition. Held each June, the exhibition features the work of more than ninety of the country's most prominent western artists.

Among recent additions to the museum's showcase of western art and artifacts is the Arthur and Shifra Silberman Native American Art Gallery, which presents a narrative from ledger art to contemporary Indian work. The American Cowboy Gallery traces cowboy culture from its vaquero roots to today's cowboy. The Western Entertainment Gallery highlights the films of early Western movie stars. Prosperity Junction, an authentic turn-of-the-century western town, shows how communities developed in the Old West. The Children's Cowboy Corral provides an interactive experience about western legends.

A constantly changing exhibition schedule explores aspects of the West from fashion, cowboy gear, and photography to notables such as Hopalong Cassidy and Frederic Remington. Special events round out the museum's program, including the annual Chuckwagon Gathering and Children's Festival, a biannual Cowboy Poetry Festival, a Visions of the West Gala honoring patrons, and Michael Martin Murphey's Cowboy Christmas Ball.

What often impresses visitors most is the sense of monumentality that the museum now expresses in its massive *Canyon Princess, Welcome Sundown,* and *End of the Trail* sculptures that are among the first works of art greeting guests. What often lingers with them is the memory of viewing the five monumental western landscape triptychs painted by Wilson Hurley. These massive paintings, housed in the Sam Noble Special Events Center, serve as true "windows to the West" for museum visitors.

See also IMAGES AND ICONS: Cowboy Culture / SPORTS AND RECREATION: Rodeo.

> *M. J. Van Deventer*
> *National Cowboy and Western Heritage Museum*

Van Deventer, M. J., ed. *Visions of the West: A Tribute to Leadership.* Oklahoma City: National Cowboy Hall of Fame, 1997.

NATIONAL RANCHING HERITAGE CENTER

Stories of the pioneers who notched a home out of the western wilderness are preserved at the National Ranching Heritage Center in Lubbock, Texas. This museum interprets western heritage through the preservation of more than thirty-five early ranch structures from some of the country's most historic ranches. Lifestyles, music, art, and craftsmanship are demonstrated through special programs, exhibits, and annual events that promote education and interest in ranching history and perpetuate time-honored ranching customs.

The National Ranching Heritage Center displays the evolution of ranch architecture from the late 1700s through the early 1900s. Each building (a bunkhouse, barns, dugouts, windmills, rustic homes, a one-room schoolhouse, a blacksmith shop, a steam engine, a depot, a Spanish fortress blockhouse, the Queen Anne–style home of a wealthy rancher, and more) is authentically restored and furnished and reflects the geography of its original location and the local materials available for its construction.

Some 90,000 people from throughout the nation and abroad visit the National Ranching Heritage Center each year to tour the fourteen-acre Proctor Park historical site and view permanent displays and temporary exhibits. Some 8,000 students from Texas and New Mexico enhance their classroom study each year with memorable history education experiences gained through their visits. More than 200 volunteers help to ensure that guests enjoy their time at the Heritage Center.

The concept of a complex to preserve the history of ranching was approved by the Texas Tech University board of regents in the mid-1960s. They saw the National Ranching Heritage Center as a way of preserving significant evidence of the history of ranching and development of the West. The new facility opened during formal ceremonies from July 2 to 4, 1976, attended by dignitaries from throughout the world and highlighted by the arrival of the Bicentennial Longhorn Trail Drive.

On June 1, 1998, Texas Tech separated the National Ranching Heritage Center from the university's museum to provide greater visibility and identity for the facility. Special events and programs were developed, including a Ranch Dance series, new children's membership organization and activities, and Grand-Day, on which visiting children are accompanied by a grandparent or older relative. Recognition programs include the Boss of the Plains Award, presented to an individual who has contributed greatly to the success of the museum, and the Golden Spur Award, which is annually presented to one of the nation's outstanding ranchers.

See also AGRICULTURE: Ranches / ARCHITECTURE: Ranch Architecture.

> *Marsha Gustafson*
> *National Ranching Heritage Center*

NORTH DAKOTA INSTITUTE FOR REGIONAL STUDIES

Located in Fargo, the North Dakota Institute for Regional Studies was founded at North Dakota State University (NDSU) in 1950 to stimulate and coordinate scholarship, research, and publications that foster understanding of regional life in the Northern Plains and Prairies and related regions of the world. In keeping with the land-grant university tradition, both knowledge and application are encouraged by institute programs.

Collections, publications, outreach, and the Center for Social Research are the major activities supported by the institute. Institute research collections and archives related to the Plains experience are housed in the NDSU Library under the curation of library staff. The publications program, which includes monographs, occasional papers, and hardcover and paperback books related to Plains life, is housed in the College of Arts, Humanities and Social Sciences. Outreach activities include radio and television production, public programs, and oral history. The Center for Social Research conducts ethnographic and survey research in the rural and urban Plains. The institute codirectors are the director of the NDSU Library and the dean of the College of Arts, Humanities and Social Sciences. The institute houses a small publications endowment and the Gunlogson Fund for Plains research.

The North Dakota Institute for Regional Studies is the oldest Plains studies center in the United States and houses the only university-based press in North Dakota. Recent publications include *Aristocrat of the West* by Larry Wowoide (2000), *Unwanted Bread: The Challenge of Farming and Ranching* by Sheldon Green and James Coomber (2000), and *Dakota Circle: Excursions on the True Plains* by Tom Isern (2000).

> *Thomas J. Riley*
> *North Dakota State University*

ONE-ROOM SCHOOLHOUSES

One-room schoolhouses once were a common feature in the Great Plains. One teacher, typically a young, single woman, taught farm children in grades one through eight in a small building on the prairie. Often the teacher had only an eighth-grade education herself. Still, rural children got a basic education good enough to produce a literacy rate that was higher than that in many other parts of the nation.

Support for rural public schools originated with the federal Land Ordinance of 1785, which began the land surveys that laid out townships and sections across the growing nation. Every township was to consist of thirty-six sections containing 640 acres each. Section 16 and later, in 1848, section 36 were set aside to support schools. By the early 1900s one-room schoolhouses dotted the countryside throughout the Great Plains and the Midwest to such an extent that the heartland contained nearly half of the more than 200,000 one-room schools nationwide. These schools were not only the center of learning for the community but also the center of the community as a whole. Community meetings, worship services, weddings, family celebrations, and

Glenwood School near Hoople, North Dakota, 1899

funerals were held at the school, often the only public building in the area.

The first schools were built of readily available material. On the Plains, that may have been sod or, in more wooded areas, logs. Some schools were little more than dugouts. Eventually, wood frame and even brick became the common mode of construction. As they were often poorly insulated, one-room schools were hard to heat, and inefficient wood- or coal-burning stoves were common fixtures. Teachers had to open the school, start the fire, and handle all the custodial duties. Restrooms were outhouses. Water came in by pail from a neighboring farm until a well was dug. Still, students learned the basics: reading, writing, and spelling were the common subjects. Math, history, geography, and handwriting usually filled out the curriculum. Students committed the lessons to memory, then recited them from the front of the room. By the end of the eighth grade students had heard the same lessons many times over.

The decline of rural schools began with President Theodore Roosevelt's appointment of the National Commission on Country Life in 1908. The commission set about to improve the quality of life—and education—in rural America. With the advent of better roads and automated transportation, school consolidation led to the first wave of elimination of one-room schools, often after a bitter debate that pitted farmers against their cousins in town.

One-room schools struggled through the Great Depression. In the aftermath of World War II many one-room schools were eliminated as mobility became more common, mechanization increased farm size and reduced farm numbers, and the migration of population from rural to urban areas accelerated. In the state of Kansas, for example, half of

the state's one-room schools were closed between 1945 and 1950.

The rapid elimination of country schools continued over the next decade. By 1958 some Great Plains states had all but eliminated them entirely, while other states still operated hundreds but not thousands as they once had. By the mid-1980s fewer than 1,000 one-room schools could be found throughout the nation, and more than half of these were located in three Great Plains states: Montana, Nebraska, and South Dakota.

Today, many of the few existing one-room schools are threatened with extinction. Those that remain, however, have moved past the basics to include computer literacy as well as the three R's.

Milan Wall
Heartland Center for Leadership Development

Fuller, Wayne E. *One-Room Schools of the Middle West.* Lawrence: University Press of Kansas, 1994. Gulliford, Andrew. *America's Country Schools.* Washington DC: Preservation Press, 1984. U.S. Department of Education. *Rural Education: A Changing Landscape.* Washington DC: Government Printing Office, 1989.

POUND, LOUISE (1872–1958)

Louise Pound was a scholar, teacher, and athlete who established the scholarly study of American speech and folklore. Pound signed her letters with the symbol for the British pound sterling with a likely sense of self-approbation. She was a pragmatic woman who chose to remain at the University of Nebraska in the city of her birth (June 30, 1872) for half a century despite an international reputation.

At a time when ambitious women were not welcome in the academy, Pound was aware that a strong social and familial base in a relatively new western city like Lincoln would give

her a grounding as firm as the three-story house in which she continued to live with her sister, Olivia. They had inherited the house from their father, Stephen Bosworth Pound, a lawyer, district court judge, and state senator, and their mother, Laura Biddlecomb Pound. The sisters, together with their brother, Roscoe (who became a leading legal theorist), had been educated at home by their mother, whose special interests were German language and literature as well as botany, to which she contributed by finding previously unidentified prairie flowers in the company of her children. After two years at the university's preparatory Latin school, Pound enrolled as a freshman at the university, from which she received a bachelor's degree with a diploma in music (piano) in 1892, having been class orator and poet. Pound earned her master's degree from the University of Nebraska in 1895.

Reinforcing her sense of self-worth was Pound's astonishing ability at a variety of sports, including figure skating. As an undergraduate Pound became women's state tennis champion and university champion in men's singles and doubles, for which she earned a man's varsity letter. Pound also earned a string of bars for "century runs" (cycling 100 miles in twelve hours) and was variously coach, captain, and member of a women's basketball team that she strongly encouraged to play to win. (She later took issue with Mabel Lee over women's physical activity for fitness rather than for competition.) For more than twenty-five years Pound was a ranking women's golfer, and in 1955 she became the first woman elected to the Nebraska Sports Hall of Fame.

Pound's academic capabilities as well as her impatience to get things done were signaled by her decision to get her doctorate from a German university. She went to Heidelberg, where she acquired the degree in two semesters rather than the usual seven. A considerable portion of Pound's academic work may be described as taxonomic in methodology (a familiar mode for her time), but she was also alert to and influenced by what was happening in adjacent fields such as botany as it was being redefined by Charles Bessey. Despite a heavy teaching load at the University of Nebraska, Pound published an impressive amount of scholarly work distinguished by common sense, as can be seen in her amusing piece on "Lovers' Leaps" in the posthumously published *Nebraska Folklore* (1959). H. L. Mencken acknowledged his debt to her in *The American Language: An Inquiry into the Development of English in the United States* (1962) when he wrote that her "early work put the study of current American English on its legs." That Pound was an advocate of women's education is demonstrated by her willingness to speak to women's groups throughout the state, and she probably influenced many mothers to send their daughters to the university. As a gadfly she strove to improve the position of women at the University of Nebraska. In 1955, at eighty-two, she was also elected the first woman president of the Modern Language Association, which may have assuaged her disappointment at never having been chair of the English department, although outsiders often assumed she was. Pound died in Lincoln on June 28, 1958.

See also LAW: Pound, Roscoe.

Evelyn Haller
Doane College

Haller, Evelyn. "Louise Pound's Work in Nebraska Folklore." *Nebraska Humanist* 7 (1984): 44–47. Louise Pound Papers, Nebraska State Historical Society, Lincoln.

ROE CLOUD, HENRY (1884–1950)

Born on the Winnebago Reservation in northeastern Nebraska on December 28, 1884, to parents who still lived mainly by hunting and trapping, Henry Roe Cloud went on to become, in Commissioner of Indian Affairs John Collier's words, the "most important living Indian."

Henry Roe Cloud was originally called *Wohnaxilayhungah*, or Chief of the Place of Fear. He was given the name Henry Cloud by a reservation school administrator. Later, while an undergraduate at Yale, he was adopted by Dr. and Mrs. Walter C. Roe, and he joined their name to his own. Cloud graduated from Yale in 1910, the first Native American to do so, and he added to his credentials a bachelor of divinity degree from Auburn Theological Seminary in 1913 and a master's in anthropology from Yale the following year.

Though educated in American institutions and convinced that Native Americans should strive to succeed within American society, Roe Cloud was also a Native American activist. As an undergraduate at Yale, he campaigned successfully for the return of Geronimo's Apaches from Fort Sill, Oklahoma, to the Mescalero Reservation in New Mexico. Also while an undergraduate, he was instrumental in the founding of the Society of American Indians, which advocated higher education for Native Americans. Roe Cloud's persistent hope was that Native Americans could become self-sufficient through education. In 1915 Roe Cloud founded and became president of the Roe Indian Institute in Wichita, Kansas, the first college preparatory school for Native Americans in the United States. The school operated until 1935, though in 1931 Roe Cloud arranged for its takeover by the board of the national missions of the Presbyterian Church as his obligations and ambitions at the national level of federal Indian affairs multiplied. One of those ambitions, to become commissioner of Indian Affairs, was never realized, but he played a key role in the preparation of the Meriam Report (1928), which starkly revealed the failings of the federal Indian policy. As a Progressive and New Dealer, he supported Collier's reforms in the 1930s, including the Indian Reorganization Act of 1934.

In 1933 Collier appointed Roe Cloud head of Haskell Institute (Kansas), the largest of the Bureau of Indian Affairs's off-reservation high schools. Cloud's two years at the school were difficult as he fought to integrate Native American traditions into the curriculum and

to broaden the existing focus on vocational education. He was appointed supervisor of Indian education in 1936 and superintendent of the Umatilla Reservation in Oregon in 1939, but again he was disappointed when he failed to secure a position on the Indian Claims Commission, and in these later years he felt that he was shunted aside by the bureau. Henry Roe Cloud died in Siletz, Oregon, on February 9, 1950.

David J. Wishart
University of Nebraska–Lincoln

Crum, Steven. "Henry Roe Cloud, a Winnebago Reformer: His Quest for American Indian Higher Education." *Kansas History* 11 (1988): 171–84.

SCHOOL CONSOLIDATION AND REORGANIZATION

School districts proliferated during the settling of the Great Plains. As the region became sprinkled with small communities and rural settlements, school districts were formed. Geographic distance, the platting of agricultural land in large sections, and a widely dispersed population all combined to make the rural school the only viable way to deliver education to the children of an expanding agricultural population. The increase in school districts was also accelerated by state policies. Later, as the region's population declined, the number of schools followed suit. In the period of decline, population decreases and waves of consolidation efforts have worked to reduce the number of school districts.

Up to the time of the Dust Bowl and the Great Depression, the region sustained large numbers of school districts. In the peak year of 1924 there were 56,121 school districts in Great Plains states, with Kansas alone having 9,326. The Canadian Prairie Provinces showed a similar pattern: by the 1930s Saskatchewan reported 4,000 school districts and Manitoba 1,700. Significant population declines followed the droughts and economic crisis that struck the Great Plains in the thirties. By the end of the 1960s the states and provinces of the Great Plains had closed many of their school districts. In the U.S. portion of the region, by 1968 only 4,822 school districts remained.

The school districts that sprang up in the Great Plains were filled with thousands of one-teacher country schools. By 1931, of the 143,391 one-teacher schools in existence in the United States, more than 41,000 were located in the rural parts of the Great Plains, with Kansas leading the numbers with 6,983 and Nebraska close behind with 6,136. State policies encouraged the formation of school districts. In Kansas a county superintendent could create school districts as long as there were fifteen persons of school age in the new district. In South Dakota residents could petition a county board for a new school as long as there were seven children living within three miles of the proposed school. In Colorado a majority of local voters could create a district. State educational policy was compatible with the economic development policies of the settlement era, policies that sought to populate the Great Plains region.

In the 1920s and 1930s states began exercising their constitutional authority to organize school districts differently. In some states the boundaries of the town or community became coterminous with the boundaries of the school district. Some states created county boards with the authority to consolidate schools in their jurisdictions. Outside the Plains, the state of Washington set up a commission to oversee consolidation plans in the 1940s. In the Great Plains region, Colorado, North Dakota, and Kansas followed suit. Beliefs about what constituted an adequate educational program drove these efforts. Small schools simply could not provide the range of curricula that educational experts had determined should be offered.

Beginning in the early thirties, as dirt roads gave way to paved streets and automobiles facilitated travel to district commercial centers, school districts began to disappear on the prairie and in very small communities. This disappearance was hastened by successive waves of consolidation efforts. The first reorganization period was characterized by a national initiative to reduce the number of rural country schools. Small elementary districts, with their classic one-room schoolhouses, were combined with larger K-12 districts. By 1970 only 1,572 one-teacher schools remained in the Great Plains states, and Kansas, the leader in such schools in 1931, had none. A second wave of consolidation efforts began in the 1960s with what was called the Great Plains School District Organization Project. Funded by federal dollars under Title V of the Elementary and Secondary Education Act of 1965, this project set out to provide both an educational argument and an economic case for consolidating school districts into larger administrative units. This consolidation effort met with stiff resistance and generated heated debate, and the Great Plains District Organization Project did not immediately lead to large numbers of school district closures. But school districts have since declined in number as pressure to consolidate has continued unabated from state agencies and educational experts. In the 1980s and 1990s the successful reorganization of school districts was carried out by state legislatures as almost all of the states and Canadian provinces forced the realignment of school district boundaries.

Throughout this period there has been resistance. Representatives of rural communities and small towns have argued that a school district is an essential part of their economic and cultural well-being. Supporters of consolidation efforts typically argue that economies of scale as well as adequate educational programming demand consolidation into larger administrative units. No definitive research has established that one particular organizational scheme of education works better than another. The forces that now buffet rural schools are mainly economic. Dependent more and more upon state sources of funding, since a sparse population no longer supports a property tax base to provide for rural education, rural schools have an uncertain future in the Great Plains.

Miles T. Bryant
University of Nebraska–Lincoln

Dawson, Howard. "Trends in School District Reorganization." *Phi Delta Kappan* 32 (1951): 302–7. Phillips, Charles. "District Reorganization in Canada." *Phi Delta Kappan* 32 (1951): 308–12. Purdy, Ralph. *The Great Plains School District Reorganization Project*. Lincoln: Nebraska Department of Education, 1968.

SCHOOLS OF MUSIC

See MUSIC: Schools of Music

STATE AND PROVINCIAL HISTORICAL SOCIETIES

"Here open to all is the history of this people." This phrase, carved in stone at the entrance to the Nebraska State Historical Society library/archives building in Lincoln, emphasizes a key characteristic of state and provincial historical organizations in the Great Plains region of the United States and Canada. In contrast to their counterpart institutions in other parts of the country, and especially in the East and South, state and provincial historical organizations in the Middle West and Great Plains developed as publicly supported institutions or government agencies open to all rather than private, members-only organizations.

Beginning in 1854, only eight years after it was first organized, the State Historical Society of Wisconsin became the first statewide historical organization to receive a regular state appropriation. The Minnesota Historical Society, established in 1849, eventually followed the Wisconsin model, as did most state historical organizations in the Great Plains region, including Montana, founded in 1865, Kansas (1875), Nebraska (1878), Oklahoma (1893), South Dakota (1901), and North Dakota (1905). In other Plains states organizational structures may have differed, but the established tradition of public support and open public access remained.

Nearly all of these organizations began as research libraries that published books and journals and held scholarly meetings that sometimes lasted several days. As time passed, they grew and developed into large, multifaceted agencies with statutory authority to operate museums and historic sites, conduct extensive archaeological investigations, hold the state's public record archive, and offer a wide variety of public educational programs for people of all ages. During the second half of the twentieth century these organizations often were designated as the agency responsible for administering the federal historic preservation programs within that state. As a result, many of the state historical societies in the Middle West and Great Plains regions rank among the largest historical organizations in the United States. Annual budgets measured in millions of dollars and staffs of well over 100 employees are typical.

In Canada the provincial museums perform many of the same functions as state historical societies in the United States, but there is usually more emphasis on the development of large-scale museums and publication and archaeological programs. Public archives, historic sites, and historic preservation programs are the responsibility of other units of the provincial or federal Canadian government. The tradition of open public access and strong public financial support, however, is as consistent in Canada as it is in the Great Plains region of the United States.

These state and provincial historical organizations have been preeminent in serving the interests of their entire state or province through the extensive programs and services they provide for every segment of the population, including academic scholars, genealogists, local historians, and students. Of special interest are the journals published by these institutions. *Montana: The Magazine of Western History*, *Kansas History: A Journal of the Central Plains*, *Nebraska History*, *Chronicles of Oklahoma*, *South Dakota History*, and *North Dakota History: A Journal of the Northern Plains* are among the more popular historical publications available. The historical societies truly are full-service institutions open to all, usually at little or no cost because of the public financial support they receive.

The physical location of many state or provincial historical society buildings adjacent or in close proximity to the state or provincial capitol symbolically reflects the importance of its heritage to that state or province. In several instances, such as in Nebraska, these historical organizations are also near the state's primary institution of higher education. Throughout the Great Plains region of the United States and Canada these state and provincial historical societies are large, complex, multifaceted institutions that rank among the leading historical organizations of both nations.

Lawrence Sommer
Nebraska State Historical Society

Alexander, Edward P. "The Rise of American History Museums." In *Leadership for the Future*, edited by Bryant F. Tolles Jr. Nashville: American Association for State and Local History, 1991: 5–19.

TRIBAL COLLEGES

Thirty-eight tribal colleges across the United States and Canada enroll 30,000 students from more than 200 Native American and First Nations tribes. Tribal colleges are unsurpassed in their ability to provide the knowledge and skills Indian students need to become successfully employed, and their job placement rates are high. In addition, 42 percent of graduates from these colleges continue their education in other postsecondary institutions. Indian students who transfer from tribal colleges are four times more likely to complete four-year degree programs than those who enter mainstream institutions as freshmen.

Twenty-five tribal colleges are located in the Great Plains: seven in Montana, five in North Dakota, four in South Dakota, three in Alberta, two in Nebraska, two in New Mexico, one in Kansas, and one in Saskatchewan.

Maskwacîs Cultural College in Alberta was the first tribally controlled college in Canada. In July 1988 the Legislative Assembly of Alberta passed the Maskwacîs Cultural College Act, which established the college as a private postsecondary institution with authority to grant certification to students at the certificate and diploma levels. Since then, Maskwacîs Cultural College has grown to offer nine one- and two-year program certificates and eight bachelor's degrees. Founded in 1884 as an Indian boarding school, Haskell Indian Nations University in Lawrence, Kansas, became the first federally chartered Indian college in the United States in 1970. Two tribally controlled colleges in the Great Plains were founded in 1971: Oglala Lakota College in Kyle, South Dakota, and Sinte Gleska University in Rosebud, South Dakota. Most recently, Little Priest Tribal College was chartered in Winnebago, Nebraska, in 1996.

In the United States tribal colleges are situated on land that is considered to be federal trust territory. This means that individual states are not required to provide any funding, making most tribal colleges dependent upon the federal government's treaty obligation and trust responsibility to provide education for Native American tribes. With unemployment on Native American reservations ranging from 30 to 70 percent, the greatest challenge faced by administrators, faculty, staff, and students at tribal colleges is funding. This is reflected in the White House Executive Order on Tribal Colleges and Universities (1998), which lists increasing core funding for operations as the first priority for the thirty federal departments and agencies involved in tribal college education.

The mission statements of the twenty-five tribal colleges in the Great Plains stress three fundamental concepts. First, all of the colleges focus on the importance of students understanding their sense of self-identity. For example, Dull Knife Memorial College in Lame Deer, Montana, states that the college operates "in the belief that all individuals should be treated with dignity and respect." A second common concept emphasized by tribal colleges is the preservation and perpetuation of their Native cultures. Blackfeet Community College in Browning, Montana, for example, which serves students from both Montana and Canada, states that, "most importantly, it is the mission of Blackfeet Community College to serve as a living memorial to the Blackfeet Tribe, in preserving the traditions and culture of a proud and progressive people." Finally, tribal colleges stress the importance of students being able to understand the differences between Native culture and Western society. For example, Cankdeska Cikana Community College in Crow Agency, Montana (formerly Little Hoop Community College), states that "the mission of Cankdeska Cikana Community College is to provide comprehensive post-secondary education which addresses both traditional and contemporary aspects of learning. The College focuses on educating our students to live successfully by assisting each in reaching a goal that is desirable and attainable for their needs in this multi-cultural world." These examples, or philosophies, may well explain why tribal colleges are so successful in educating Native peoples.

Charles A. Braithwaite
University of Nebraska–Lincoln

American Indian Higher Education Consortium and the Institute for Higher Education Policy. *Tribal Colleges: An Introduction*. Washington DC: Tribal College Research and Database Initiative, 1999.

UNITED STATES AIR FORCE ACADEMY

In 1949, two years after the establishment of an independent air force, Secretary of Defense James Forrestal appointed a board of educators to review the education of core armed forces officers. The board, headed by Dwight Eisenhower and Robert Stearns, both university presidents, advised creating a separate institution to meet the needs of the new air service. Overtaken by events in Korea, the recommendation languished until 1954, when Congress authorized Secretary of the Air Force Harold Talbott to select the United States Air Force Academy (USAFA) site. After exhaustive consideration of 580 possible locations in 45 states, three—Colorado Springs, Colorado; Alton, Illinois; and Lake Geneva, Wisconsin—were submitted to Secretary Talbott for final site selection. Colorado's enthusiastic support influenced the outcome. In July 1955 the first cadets entered temporary quarters at Lowry Air Force Base in Denver while permanent facilities were being constructed.

The Cadet Wing moved to the USAFA grounds in August 1958. The following spring 206 cadets graduated and were commissioned. As cold war tensions increased following the Cuban missile crisis, authorized wing strength nearly doubled to 4,417 cadets. The first female cadets graduated with the class of 1980.

The USAFA campus is nestled among 18,000 acres fronting the Rocky Mountain's Rampart Range. Its most endearing landmark is the Cadet Chapel, architect Walter Netsch Jr.'s innovative design of glass, aluminum, and steel. The chapel's seventeen spires dominate the cadet quadrangle and inspire the institution's "Commitment to Excellence." That commitment, despite occasional scandal, has resulted in more than thirty Rhodes scholars and critical leadership for the youngest military service.

William E. Fischer Jr.
Ottawa, Canada

Cannon, M. Hamlin, and Henry S. Fellerman. *Quest for an Air Force Academy*. Colorado Springs: USAFA, 1974.
Fagan, George V. *The Air Force Academy: An Illustrated History*. Boulder CO: Johnson Books, 1988.

WOMEN IN HIGHER EDUCATION

Women felt the importance of higher education almost as soon as the first settlers arrived in the Great Plains. Plains immigrants brought with them democratic ideals rooted in the need for public education. By the late 1840s and 1850s only a few scattered communities in the eastern Plains had established primary schools. After the Civil War, increased Plains settlement prompted more school building. Public education was not yet compulsory in the United States, but communities took the initiative of organizing schools. Local districts often hired teachers from among the young, unmarried daughters of homesteaders, especially in the wake of the post–Civil War shortage of male teachers. Since new teachers were often young and uneducated themselves, the need for institutionalized teacher training arose early.

The first opportunities for women in higher education emerged as part of this need for teacher training. In rural areas, teachers had little or no access to institutional education, so for Plains women, "normal" training and

teacher institutes provided an early opportunity for higher education. Normal schools and teacher-training institutes, founded in the United States since the early nineteenth century, went west with the settlers. However, it was not until the late 1860s that Plains states and territories established normal schools such as Nebraska State Normal School in Peru (1867). By the 1870s counties throughout the Plains were holding teacher institutes during the summer months for educating schoolteachers. Little better than high schools, these institutes offered a form of higher education to rural women. Also called county institutes, by the 1890s they became union normals and/ or junior normal schools after many counties were brought under one, consolidated summer training session. It was mainly women who attended these institutes because the teaching profession became increasingly feminized in the late nineteenth century.

Around 1910 many Plains states consolidated normal training under state jurisdiction with the establishment of state teachers colleges. States then assumed more control over these colleges by incorporating them within the state university systems by the 1930s. After World War II education standards began to require a bachelor's degree for teacher certification. Today, many women college students obtain teaching certificates through bachelor programs in primary and secondary education at state and land-grant universities, where they dominate the programs.

University education for women had important beginnings in the Great Plains. The Morrill Act of 1862 set aside lands for each state or territory to establish a university for the education of the agricultural and industrial populations. Although coeducation was not required by the Morrill Act, by 1890 every state included the admission of women in its land-grant charter. The first Plains land-grant institution to admit women was Kansas State Agricultural College (Manhattan), founded in 1863. Others followed: the University of Nebraska (Lincoln) in 1869; Texas A&M University (College Station) in 1876; Colorado State University (Fort Collins) in 1879; South Dakota State University (Brookings) in 1881; the University of Wyoming (Laramie) in 1886; North Dakota State University (Fargo) in 1890; and Oklahoma State University (Stillwater) in 1890. By 1890 coeducation was a recognized norm in Great Plains higher education.

Since coeducation was not yet overwhelmingly accepted in America, the admission of women students was an important experiment for Plains women. Women's education fit easily into the land-grant mission because agricultural populations included farmers' wives and daughters as well as those single women who farmed for themselves. Domestic economy training, later known as home economics, provided for the making of scientific farm wives. Land-grant universities in the Plains were some of the first in the world to offer professional domestic economy training to female students. Kansas Agricultural College in Manhattan, later Kansas State Univer-

Cadets in front of the USAFA Cadet Chapel, Colorado Springs, Colorado

sity, offered a domestic economy department in 1871, the first of its kind at a public institution in America. Other land-grant institutions were sometimes slow to establish a domestic economy department, instead offering women students the traditional, classical-based curriculum of Latin, Greek, history, and literature. By the 1890s, however, most domestic economy departments were firmly in place.

Domestic economy programs began with the basic courses of cooking and sewing. As departments expanded, courses included nutrition, sanitation, hygiene, air circulation, plumbing, dairying, poultry, dressmaking, millinery, child care, nursing, and horticulture or house gardening. What made land-grant universities unique is that men and women students together studied basic science courses like chemistry and biology. In the upper-class years, students divided into separate coursework based upon gender: mechanical arts (engineering) and agriculture for men and domestic economy for women. While domestic economy courses built upon the scientific foundation women had received with their male colleagues, the practical application of that science was directed toward women's roles as housewives. For instance, chemistry was applied toward the study of nutrition for healthy meal preparation. Although most land-grant women used their training for domestic purposes, a few women built upon their undergraduate backgrounds in chemistry and biology to pursue graduate degrees in those sciences.

While higher education for women in the Plains centered mostly around domestic economy, many women chose to pursue the traditional classical curriculum. Since the land-grant universities were founded for scientific training, some states established separate state universities with an emphasis on liberal arts. For example, the University of Kansas, the University of Oklahoma, the University of South Dakota, and the University of North Dakota were all founded as liberal arts alternatives to their states' land-grant universities. At these state universities, women could study history and literature and receive teacher training. Other states like Nebraska and Wyo-

ming combined both the land-grant purpose and liberal arts into one consolidated university where women could choose between domestic arts and liberal arts. Women like Willa Cather at the University of Nebraska chose the literary option instead of the domestic arts program. Other important women who made names for themselves at universities in the Plains included Grace Hebard as a historian at the University of Wyoming and Rachel Lloyd as a botanist at the University of Nebraska.

In the Canadian Plains, women entered higher education in various private colleges and seminaries for women prior to 1900. Provinces founded public coeducational universities after 1900 with the establishment of the University of Manitoba (Winnipeg) in 1900, the University of Alberta (Edmonton) in 1908, and the University of Saskatchewan (Saskatoon), which opened with fifty-eight men and twelve women students in 1909. These Canadian universities had programs similar to the American state universities for studying liberal arts, and most had established domestic economy programs for women by the 1920s.

Native American and African American women also found opportunities for higher education in the Plains. Since most of the land-grant institutions were open to anyone regardless of race, a few nonwhite women attended. Most Native women entered all-female seminaries and academies, like the Chickasaw Female Indian Academy in Oklahoma. These academies provided language, domestic economy, and teacher training for Native women. A few Native American women with means went east for higher education, like Susan and Marguerite LaFlesche of the Omaha nation, who attended the Hampton Normal and Agricultural Institute in Virginia. Black women who could not find adequate training in the Plains also enrolled in eastern universities. By the late 1890s, in order to accommodate the need for African American women teachers at segregated Plains schools, Texas and Oklahoma founded black-only normal schools. The second Morrill Act of 1890 created land-grant universities for African Americans, including Prairie View A&M University in Texas and the

Colored Agricultural and Normal University in Oklahoma, today known as Langston University, where women could obtain domestic economy and liberal arts education.

The history of women's experiences in Great Plains higher education is an especially important one to the overall history of women's education in America. Many Plains institutions, both land-grant and state universities, were some of the first public institutions in America and in the world to be coeducational. Further, women's entrance into scientific studies like chemistry and biology was pioneered in the Plains, especially in land-grant education. Enrollment for women students in the nineteenth century hovered at around 25 to 30 percent of all university students, and that percentage gradually increased through the twentieth century. Today, female enrollment at Plains universities is just under 50 percent, with a higher representation for women in specific areas of study such as home economics, family sciences, history, English, music, and art. Women are still underrepresented in fields such as agriculture, veterinary science, engineering, math, and biological sciences as well as in chemistry. Plains universities are now seeking to increase female enrollment in graduate programs, law schools, and medical and dental programs. In 2001 at the University of Nebraska, for example, women constitute 53 percent of all graduate students and 43 percent of the students in law and architecture but only 32 percent of the dental and medical students. With recruiting programs, scholarship opportunities, teacher training, distance education, and collegiate preparation in high schools, Plains women continue to expand their presence in Great Plains higher education.

Andrea G. Radke
Brigham Young University

Cordier, Mary Hurlbut. *Schoolwomen of the Prairies and Plains: Personal Narratives from Iowa, Kansas, and Nebraska.* Albuquerque: University of New Mexico Press, 1992. Myres, Sandra L. *Westering Women and the Frontier Experience 1899–1915.* Albuquerque: University of New Mexico Press, 1982. Vaughn-Robertson, Courtney Ann. "Sometimes Independent but Never Equal—Women Teachers, 1900–1950: The Oklahoma Example." *Pacific Historical Review* 53 (1984): 39–58.

European Americans

Youngsters line up for a parade, Lindsborg Celebrations, Lindsborg, Kansas, 1961

EUROPEAN AMERICANS

European immigrants and their descendants created an archipelago of ethnic communities in the Great Plains largely between 1860 and 1930, although agricultural settlement began as early as 1811 in the Earl of Selkirk's colony in the Red River Valley of the North and the 1830s in the German Hill Country of southern Texas. Even earlier, European explorers and fur traders had penetrated most parts of the Great Plains. Within the flood of settlement spreading out onto the Plains after 1860 were distinctive streams of immigrants that fed ethnic communities that would survive as cultural islands for decades to come. These European immigrants, like the migrants from the eastern and central United States and Canada, encountered an unforgiving physical environment that demanded changes in their cultures, distinctive ways of life, and farming practices. Over time, depending on the volume and longevity of the migration streams and on the stability of the communities, American-born generations preserved some of their parents' cultures while adopting North American ways and creating new patterns of their own. They contributed to the successful development of new systems of agriculture on the western grasslands, actively participated in the political life of Canada and the United States, and met the challenges posed by World War I, which became the first major test of loyalty to their new homeland. In doing so, they redefined the meaning of what was required to be American or Canadian.

Creating an Archipelago of Communities

Migrations created these distinctive cultural communities, and a number of other factors determined whether these communities waxed or waned. The volume of immigration to a given destination was important in forming a significant spatial cluster, and spatial clustering was another key factor. If the area had previously been largely unsettled, then immigrants might be able to realize their goal of a homogeneous community. Furthermore, if new settlers shared a common set of values and goals, and if they had a strong leader, then the likelihood of the ethnic community's success also increased. Conversely, if the migration stream was heterogeneous and heading for diverse destinations, with little interest in clustering, then it was less likely that a successful ethnic community would emerge. Proximity to a major urban center from which metropolitan cultural values emanated might weaken the cultural distinctiveness of an ethnic community. If the rate of geographic mobility was high, as it usually was in North America, then a community's longevity could be shortened and its cohesiveness weakened. However, a continuing stream of new immigrants into the community would counteract the outflow of settlers, and in those cases a transfusion model might be used to explain the continuing vitality of the community.

Streams of European immigration fed the newly formed communities in the Great Plains. A general distinction is drawn between

Immigrant woman and children in front of Winnipeg Station, Manitoba, ca. 1909

the waves of transatlantic migration before the economic depression of 1893–96 and those between 1896 and 1914. The earlier waves carried large numbers of Germans and Scandinavians, mostly to the Great Plains of the United States; the later waves carried immigrants from central and eastern Europe, mostly to the Canadian Prairies. Before 1893 the grasslands in the United States were the strongest magnet for transatlantic migrants, but by 1890 opportunities had diminished there, so that after the depression of the 1890s the Canadian Prairies represented new opportunities not only for Ukrainians, Poles, Russians, and Hungarians from Europe but also for settlers coming northward from the American Plains. Indeed, the years between 1896 and 1914 saw considerable longitudinal relocation within the grasslands as farmers sought new possibilities in the "Last Best West." New restrictive immigration policies in both the United States and Canada in the years after World War I curtailed further European immigration to the Great Plains.

Ethnic communities in the Plains were created in part by immigrants coming directly from Europe and in part by settlers from older, well-established communities in the central Midwest and eastern Prairies. Some immigrants began farming in established communities in Illinois, Wisconsin, Iowa, Minnesota, or Manitoba, where they worked as farmhands and earned enough cash to purchase a farm of their own farther west. In many cases individual families or several families traveled in hopscotch fashion across the Midwest before they arrived on the western fringe of settlement. The successful creation of new settlements, however, was not the result of haphazard migration. Communities were most often the result of careful planning under the auspices of a church leader, a group of businessmen, or with the assistance of a rail-

road company. Frequently, the stated goal was a homogeneous community that would provide economic security (and implicitly, emotional and spiritual support) for the families arriving on the frontier. The concept of the homogeneous ethnic community was supported by railroad companies, which saw its advantages for promoting land sales, but it was an idea that was not always welcomed by government.

The U.S. government tended to promote the individual landowner, and it did not assist in the creation of homogeneous ethnic settlements in the Great Plains, whereas the Canadian government adopted a policy of assisting such settlements, at least in the early years, by making block land grants to immigrants. The arrival in the Plains of large numbers of Mennonites in the early 1870s from southern Russia highlighted the differences between the approaches of the two countries. President Ulysses S. Grant refused to assist in creating the homogeneous settlements that the Mennonites desired. Such communities could be formed by Mennonites homesteading government lands and by purchasing intervening railroad lands, but they would have to do it without government support. The Canadian government, however, set aside two large blocks of land in southern Manitoba exclusively for Mennonite settlement. Within twenty years, however, the Canadian government had changed its mind and thereafter discouraged large block settlements, although it made a brief exception in the case of Doukhobor communities after 1900.

Railroads played an important role in the creation of ethnic-group communities in the Plains. Not only did they advertise widely in western and then eastern Europe, but they also worked energetically with leaders in both Europe and U.S. midwestern communities

Settlers from the United States crossing the Canadian prairie

to organize group migrations to the western grasslands. Thus, Swedes in Chicago and Galesburg, Illinois, worked with the Union Pacific in the late 1860s to found Lindsborg, the initial magnet for the development of a broad swath of Swedish communities in central Kansas. Canadian railways and land companies joined forces to sell lands to German Catholics migrating from Minnesota in the first decade of the twentieth century to create the large St. Peter's colony in central Saskatchewan and St. Joseph's colony along the Saskatchewan-Alberta border. The railways also influenced the location of ethnic communities: after 1870 railways replaced rivers as the major routeways along which settlers traveled to the agricultural frontier, and railways created towns along the tracks to serve as markets and supply points for the surrounding agricultural hinterland.

Ethnic communities in the Great Plains often began with the creation of daughter colonies, the offspring of communities in the eastern and central Midwest and Manitoba. Frequently, church leaders organized the initial settlement and negotiated with the railroads for favorable terms of transportation and land purchase. Through an intricate network of contacts extending to Europe, pastors also attracted new immigrants to emerging settlements. Thus, the populations of young communities were often comprised of newly arrived Europeans as well as those who had lived for several decades in North America. In the case of the Canadian Prairies there were fewer daughter colonies, and less east–west migration, than in the United States. Nevertheless, in both countries, the new communities often included families with some previous farming experience in North America.

Environmental Adaptation
Few European immigrants, regardless of time spent in North America, had adequate experience to prepare them for the Plains environment. Conditions were markedly different from the central Midwest and vastly different from their homelands in northern and west-

ern Europe. Only those who came from eastern and southern Europe, especially from the Russian steppes, had encountered environments with similar challenges to farming. The grasshopper plagues that swept the Plains states in 1874 and 1876 were only one of the many natural hazards to induce fear, anxiety, and discouragement. Prairie fires, violent thunderstorms, occasional tornadoes, sudden blizzards, and hailstorms were among the most disturbing of nature's trials to test the pioneers' mettle. Perhaps most unsettling of all was the persistent and subtle problem of drought. Changes in the amount of moisture available for crop growth due to differential rates of evapotranspiration stymied not only the immigrant but also American farmers in the Plains. In the Canadian Prairies these problems were compounded by the short growing season and the danger of spring and fall frosts.

The physical landscape created its own psychological stresses. The very flatness of the Western Plains created a sense of anomie even in the most closely knit ethnic communities. A great dome of sky stretched to the seemingly endless horizon, accentuating the smallness of the human scale and the vulnerability of human endeavors. The human landscape further unsettled those who were used to the compact, tightly defined geography of the densely populated European lowlands. As the grasslands were domesticated, field boundaries and roads accentuated a new rectilinear geometry in the landscape that heightened the sense of alienation and intensified the differences from the European homeland. There was no way that the Old Country patterns of social life and economic activity could be replicated in the Great Plains.

Economic forces also bore down heavily on settlers. The pioneer phase of settlement was shorter in the Plains than it had been in the central Midwest: the influence of market pressures on farming were brought to bear more rapidly than farther east as railroads increasingly penetrated the American Plains in the two decades following the Civil War. In the Canadian Prairies, both settlement and the railroads mainly came later, after the 1896 depression, and European farmers, many with only limited experience of the pressures of commercial agriculture, had to adjust rapidly to the demands of the North American marketplace. European ways of doing things, including European patterns of farming, could not survive for long in the face of an austere natural environment, changing mortgage rates, and fluctuations in the market price of farm produce. New systems of cropping and livestock farming necessarily had to be adopted in the Plains.

On first arrival, some European settlers tried to generate cash with a specialty crop or activity that would help them get on their feet until the farm became fully operational. Swedes grew broomcorn, for example, while Mennonite communities produced watermelons and silkworms in the earliest days. Other specialty crops included sunflowers, tobacco, and sugar beets. Ukrainians in Canada gathered ginseng root as a means of earning cash in the first years. Soon, however, immigrant communities adopted one or both of the great cash crops grown in the central Midwest and carried out onto the Plains—wheat and corn. Over time the viability of these two major cash crops would be tested by drought, and farmers adopted new crops resistant to moisture shortages (such as alfalfa and sorghum) or more suited to the short growing season on the Canadian Prairies (such as fast-maturing wheat and the hardy grains). Immigrants, especially those coming from southeastern Europe, where environmental conditions most closely approximated conditions in the Plains,

Galician woman delivering milk, Manitoba, ca. 1890–1910

often led the way in developing dryland farming techniques and other innovative strategies. Much has been made of the German Russian Mennonites' role in introducing hard winter wheat in central Kansas, which led to the growth of the winter wheat belt in Kansas and Oklahoma, but of more lasting importance was their ability to figure out new patterns of cropping and livestock farming and new dryland farming techniques, the best approaches to agriculture for more than fifty years from North Dakota to Oklahoma. American farmers, as well as other European immigrants, soon learned from the German Russians' success. European immigrants learned to become flexible, giving up the labor-intensive methods they brought with them and adopting the extensive-farming approaches that were better suited to the Plains. Similarly, on the Canadian Prairies new strains of fast-maturing wheat were the key to success in commercial agriculture among immigrant communities in the years before and after World War I.

Transfer from one physical environment to another produced radical changes in the immigrants' cultures. The majority of Europeans encountered not only a different physical environment but also a different economic system from those they had known in the Old Country. Fairly rapidly the immigrants dropped the distinctive crops and European patterns of farming and adopted North American cash crops, then took out mortgages to expand and mechanize their farm operations and to provide for a new generation of farmers. In short, they quickly embraced the North American world of commercial agriculture and profit maximization, and in doing so they accepted the culture of North American consumerism, thereby modifying their traditional values according to their new circumstances.

Cultural Transformation

The issue of cultural transformation is one of the most complex problems faced by scholars in studying how Europeans became North Americans. The outward manifestations of cultural transfer from the European homeland have been readily identified and have survived for decades in the landscape of the Plains. Germans in the Texas Hill Country built half-timbered and stone houses and lines of rock fences, Mennonites attempted to duplicate village patterns of settlement in reconstructing their communities in Manitoba and Kansas in the 1870s, Scandinavian communities had their distinctive smokehouses, and immigrants from Russia built summer bake ovens outside the farmhouse to cope with summer heat. But deep-seated changes in the cultures of the immigrants—in their mores and most closely held values—are not so easily identified, measured, and tracked in the adaptation to the new milieu.

These mores and values were reflected in the religious beliefs of the community, with the church playing a defining role, frequently circumscribing the behavior of its members. In German Catholic and Lutheran communities the churches defined moral behavior in ways that clearly reflected their European antecedents. German churches were perhaps less restrictive and their members more permissive than in other churches. The Swedish Lutheran Church has been described as straitlaced and puritanical in the early years: dancing, drinking, and card-playing were forbidden, a clear example of the transfer of mores directly from Sweden. The most extreme examples of this transfer can be found among Anabaptist groups such as the Mennonites. Church music, dancing, and smoking were outlawed, although the use of alcohol was permitted. Over time these patterns changed as the church relaxed its strictures: German gospel hymns were allowed by the late 1890s and social constraints on youthful Mennonite behavior were also loosened. Some Mennonites swung toward temperance and against the repeal of Prohibition in the 1920s as part of a drift toward Americanization. In general, however, churches acted as a disciplinary and conservative force in preserving the core values of communities well into the twentieth century.

Immigrants were mostly drawn from the conservative peasant class in Europe, and that conservative outlook persisted for generations in North America. Historian Oscar Handlin even suggested that immigrants became more conservative than their relatives who remained in Europe. That conservatism was reflected not only in religious practices but also in social and economic behavior. The foreign-born were more fiscally conservative, less keen to borrow than their American-born neighbors. Such traits, stemming from their peasant backgrounds, stood them in good stead in their struggle to establish themselves in the Plains. Norwegians, who had no experience making a living in grasslands, survived because of habits of industry, frugality, and perseverance, as well as community cohesiveness. Swedes were also described as patient, honest, and persistent, as well as hardheaded, stubborn, contentious, and tightfisted! Germans were recognized as tidy, careful, and efficient, with a strong interest in maintaining family continuity on the farm. The degree of community cooperation varied from community to community but was strongest among the Mennonites. All of these traits reflected the European peasant traditions from which Plains settlers were drawn.

The transition from European peasant to North American commercial farmer wrought fundamental changes in the immigrants' values. As their financial condition improved and farmers increasingly developed an expendable income, their pastors and priests railed against the inroads of consumerism and the loss of traditional spiritual values. As pioneer farmers expanded their operations and took out mortgages, they were increasingly drawn into the world of cash crops and profit maximization. The rise of economic individualism within immigrant communities meant a weakening of community cooperation and communal responsibility, although the sense of community did not disappear entirely. Families slowly adopted new goals in this world of capitalist agriculture, among them a concern for continuity on the family farm. The old peasant desire for land, for a farm they could call their own, survived the transition to commercial agriculture.

To be sure, elements of their old cultures survived in the transfer from life in Europe to life in the Great Plains, but survival was a selective process. Crops that were environmentally suitable and for which there was a market demand continued to be grown. Patterns of life that could be incorporated within a dispersed homestead settlement pattern also persisted. But the distinctive practices of religious worship and the constraints on individual behavior slowly changed with time as moral values and moral responsibility adapted to the North American social and economic milieu. Gradually, the values and behavior of a small bourgeois class living in small Plains towns became the norm for the upwardly mobile in rural communities, especially as the second generation came of age. These adjustments marked the first stages in the assimilation of the immigrants.

Assimilation

The term assimilation refers to the process whereby immigrants entered the mainstream and became indistinguishable from other members of American or Canadian society. In the United States, Frederick Jackson Turner proposed that the western frontier acted as a crucible in which immigrants shed their European heritage and intermarried to create a new nation of Americans. His "frontier thesis," however, was more a statement of ideals than an observation of reality: he seemed to ignore the presence of large, clustered ethnic settlements on the grasslands where assimilation, insofar as it existed at all, proceeded at glacial speed. But where the migration streams to frontier communities were heavily mixed and where the Europeans demonstrated a weak interest in clustered settlement, assimilation could be fairly rapid. Certainly, the adoption of the English language was necessary in small, dispersed communities because it gave the European immigrant access to a wider world of commerce, politics, and North American culture.

Biological assimilation presents a more complex picture than does linguistic assimilation. Religion represented a major barrier to intermarriage, particularly between Protestant and Catholic immigrants and to a much lesser degree within various branches of the Protestant faith. Although the rate of exogamy (marriage across national lines) was moderately high within groups of Catholic immigrants, relatively few Catholics married their predominantly Protestant American neighbors. But even among Protestant immigrants, relatively few married Americans—those from the British Isles led the way, followed by the various Scandinavian groups; few Slavic immigrants engaged Americans in marriage. On the other hand, biological assimilation was fairly rapid in small communities where the choices were limited: immigrants were obliged to find marriage partners among their American or other European neighbors. For many immigrant groups, however, exogamy was generally discouraged; it was even considered a sin among the Dutch of Montana. After World War I the rate of biological assimilation slowly began to increase, but not until well after World War II did exogamy rates in most European ethnic groups rise above 50 percent.

By contrast, European immigrants quickly adopted American material culture. The use of distinctive architectural styles and materials in home building soon gave way to the construction of American houses. Exceptions to this general rule can be found among Mennonite and Ukrainian settlers, especially on the Canadian Prairies. In the American Plains the Mennonites discarded their Russian-style houses with thatched roofs, in addition to the farm tools and implements they had brought over, within twenty years of their arrival. The rectangular survey system in both Canada and the United States was a powerful influence in molding the European immigrant to North American ways of economic individualism and shaping both the structure and operations of the farm.

The rate of assimilation among immigrant groups varied according to the community's size, location, and whether it was rural or urban. Generally, the pressures as well as the attractions to join the mainstream were greater in towns than in rural areas. Much also depended on the degree to which each group was perceived to be acceptable by mainstream society. British immigrants were ranked first. Scandinavians were also valued and assimilated readily, and arguments have been advanced that Swedes assimilated more rapidly than Norwegians and vice versa. Danes were thought to be more clannish, and Germans seemed to remain aloof longer than others. The Irish had encountered rejection in the cities of the Atlantic seaboard, but in the Plains resistance to them was much modified. French Canadian communities in Kansas and North Dakota were small, and they too assimilated fairly quickly. Strongly sectarian groups such as the Mennonites, Amish, Doukhobors, and Hutterites consciously resisted assimilation in varying degrees, and in many cases still do.

The Canadian Prairies presented a different milieu from that of the American Plains. The Prairies were opened for agricultural settlement just after Canadian Confederation in 1867, which recognized that the Dominion had two founding nations, France and Britain. A balance was supposed to be maintained between the two cultures in this keystone region within Canadian confederation, but it never was. The French established a small toehold in Manitoba in the 1870s and 1880s, but it was English Canadian farmers, particularly from Ontario, who shaped the social life and the economy of the Prairies, far out of proportion to their numbers. Citizens of the Dominion thought of themselves as British rather than Canadian in the final decades of the nine-

Doukhobor village of Vosnesenya, Thunder Hill Colony, Manitoba

teenth century and well into the twentieth century (a distinctive Canadian identity did not appear until after World War I and even then developed slowly). Certainly after 1890, when the railway network was being built, the British norm was in the ascendancy in the Prairie region. British immigrants, of course, were seen as the most desirable. But the large German Catholic colonies in Saskatchewan were peopled by settlers who had come from Minnesota expressly to resist assimilation, and they stood apart. New immigrant groups who arrived after 1896, such as Ukrainians and Doukhobors, were subjected to vilification in the local press. They clearly were not wanted by the local "host society." Indeed, on the Canadian Prairies one could make the case for ethnogenesis rather than assimilation among many European groups.

Ethnogenesis

Ethnogenesis is the process whereby immigrants transformed themselves, became members of an ethnic group, and developed a distinctively new culture and identity. The new culture was not a replica of their Old World culture because social, economic, and especially physical environmental conditions in North America were so different from what they left behind. Immigrants often tried to retain their European language because it fostered cohesion within the community, defining their culture and identity. They clung to their churches, even though churches were subject to splits and schisms on the frontier. They married within their own group and discouraged exogamy. They easily yielded to change only in matters of material culture as they adapted to the new conditions and opportunities. They clustered in fairly homogeneous settlements because they could maintain essential services such as churches and schools and eventually institutions of mutual assistance. The larger these homogeneous settlements the easier it was for the ethnic community to develop "institutional completeness."

The ability of ethnic groups to create homogeneous settlements with a substantial "critical mass" was very important for ethnogenesis. Germans and Scandinavians, for example, streaming into the Upper Midwest and then into the Plains, homesteaded quarter-sections and later purchased the intervening railroad lands for themselves and their children, thereby creating solid ethnic settlements. As noted above, Mennonite leaders failed to persuade American federal officials to help them create exclusively Mennonite settlements. In Canada they succeeded, and the government set aside blocks of townships for Mennonite settlement in the 1870s. But by the turn of the century Canadian officials had rejected the notion of block settlements, and so newly arrived German Catholics from Minnesota settled in Saskatchewan without government block grants; instead, they followed the usual American pattern of combining homesteads with railroad lands to create homogeneous communities. Large homogeneous clusters provided advantages such as ease of communication, mutual assistance, and a population large enough to facilitate endogamy.

Survival of the language is often taken as a marker of the strength of ethnogenesis within a community. Men adopted English fairly rapidly, while women, bound to the domestic domain, retained the mother tongue and passed it on to the children. Churches also acted as a bulwark against the assimilative forces of the public school; pastors were determined to keep the traditional language alive by using it in church services and teaching it in Sunday schools, summer schools, and in after-school classes. The various branches of the Lutheran Church in German and Scandinavian communities were particularly active in preserving their mother tongues, whereas the Roman Catholic Church often, though not always, encouraged the adoption of English as a means of achieving unity among their nationally diverse adherents. The major challenge to linguistic survival came in 1917 as the United States entered World War I and a new form of nativism appeared as an anti-German campaign. Nevertheless, in many communities sermons continued to be delivered in the old language until the 1930s.

An ethnic community fostered cooperation during the pioneer period and facilitated the development of social and other services in later years as the community matured. The first concern of settlers may have been to create churches and schools, but soon other institutions appeared that brought stability and enhanced the security of the community. Colleges for training teachers were soon established, ensuring a continuing ethnic presence in local schools. Local banks organized by successful immigrants made credit available to fellow farmers, while general stores and hotels proudly announced the ethnic origin of the owner in the hope of attracting customers. In time hospitals, orphanages, and old folks' homes were built to cater to community needs. Musical groups and athletic clubs provided social opportunities for young people in the community. Consequently, some ethnic communities developed an institutional completeness that reduced needy immigrants' dependence on external services, thereby reinforcing their distinctive identity and keeping them within the ethnic fold.

Churches played a central role in the formation of a clustered ethnic community, not only because they provided religious services and could control the local public school system, but also because they exercised powerful social controls and exerted pressures to conform within the community. Perhaps the most extreme examples were (and to a degree, still are) found in Mennonite, Hutterite, and Doukhobor communities, but the pattern was also observed among others. The exercise of such power brought with it hazards, for it could lead to schism and disunity. In fact, religious fracturing was occasionally evident on the frontier and may be understood as yet another facet of ethnogenesis, as immigrants adjusted to their new circumstances and subconsciously began to work out a new identity for themselves. Most important, however, the churches fostered a sense of cohesion and preserved a sense of cultural identity, in addition to maintaining moral standards of behavior within ethnic communities in the Great Plains —just as they had done in the parent communities of the eastern Midwest.

Leadership was also tremendously important in the creation and survival of ethnic communities. Churches, though an important source, were not the sole source of leadership candidates within these communities. Teachers, newspaper editors, and occasionally politicians emerged as leaders. But lay leaders rarely challenged the religious leadership. Indeed, the two categories were not mutually exclusive—some of the early political leaders among the Swedes in Kansas were Lutheran pastors. Newspaper editors created a unique form of leadership, publishing foreign-language papers that linked local communities to a network of ethnic communities across the Plains and even eastward throughout the Midwest. These networks were often sustained by familial ties, especially where daughter colonies had been created. They kept local readers informed of events far beyond the local community and in doing so connected it to a wide network of communities of their own kind, whether German, Swedish, Norwegian, Danish, or Irish, scattered across North America. The conscious realization that other communities survived elsewhere in the West and Midwest was an important factor in ethnogenesis and in the emergence of ethnic block voting in regional and national elections.

Political Participation

Newly arrived immigrants usually had little concern for politics beyond local concerns such as operating schools, but as their communities matured they were increasingly drawn into national political issues. The arcane debates over monetary issues, for example, were initially beyond their comprehension, but local social and cultural issues engaged their avid attention. Several sectarian ethnic groups (Hutterites, Doukhobors and some Mennonites at first) did not participate in the political arena: they refused to vote, hold public office, or engage in public litigation. Within two decades, however, as Mennonite isolationism broke down and as they realized the necessity of protecting their school system, they were drawn into politics. The issues that became lightning rods for ethnic political participation were prohibition, women's suffrage, and state regulation of parochial schools, although when the financial crisis of the late 1880s and the depression of the 1890s threatened foreclosure of their mortgages, many ethnics abandoned their traditional party affiliations and supported the Populist wildfire sweeping the Plains states.

The Republican Party attracted many foreign born in the years before and during the Civil War because of the immigrants' revulsion to slavery. The Germans in Texas rejected not only slavery but also secession from the Union and conscription in the Confederate army. As the northern Plains states were settled in the decades after the Civil War the majority of new immigrants continued to embrace the Republican Party. Protestant immigrants joined the Republican Party, while Catholic immigrants tended to become Democrats. There were exceptions, however. Some German Methodists joined the Democratic Party whereas French Canadians were mostly Republican. In Canada, British immigrants tended to be solidly Conservative. Later immigrants found the Liberal Party more welcoming.

The decade of the 1890s was a fractious one in the United States as the economic bubble burst and depression set in. Many ethnics were shaken loose from their traditional political affiliations when mortgage rates escalated and farm loans were foreclosed. Although many in ethnic communities were wary of the new radicalism (some thought it a front for a new form of nativism), which ran counter to the fundamental conservatism of the immigrant property owner, populism did indeed make inroads. The rockbed republicanism of Swedes and French Canadians in Kansas, for example, fractured as they flocked to the Populist cause.

Even Kansas-German farmers abandoned their loyalty to the Republican Party, although they drew the line with "Yellin'" Mary Lease on the grounds that a woman's place was in the home. Populists even found support among ethnic communities in the cities of the Western Plains.

Prohibition was another issue that shook ethnic communities loose from their traditional allegiances. Here the clash was between cultures—North American puritanism versus European immigrant culture. Most foreign-born thought the idea of prohibition was ridiculous. But the situation was complex, and a division occurred largely along religious lines: Methodists, Evangelicals, and Baptists were in favor whereas Catholics, German Lutherans, and Mennonites opposed prohibition. German Catholics, Bohemian Catholics, German Lutherans, and Volga Germans were opposed while German Methodists and Swedish and Norwegian Lutherans supported prohibition. When Kansas went dry in 1889 many Germans defected to the Democratic Party. In Nebraska they played a crucial role in defeating prohibition in 1890. The general German opposition to prohibition was sustained through the first two decades of the twentieth century, even when the United States officially adopted the policy.

The other major cultural clash occurred over women's right to vote. On this issue Germans of all denominations were fairly well united against suffrage. Their stance was shared by Mennonites and many Scandinavians. Increasingly, though, Germans stood out among the ethnic communities as opponents on the battle lines that marked the clash between immigrant and American culture. In part, this was because Germans unified to make their voice effective in American politics.

In 1901 the German-American Alliance was founded as a cultural and political organization determined to preserve German culture, especially the German language, and to create a unified voice in the political arena for the protection of those issues Germans held dear. Branches were established in various Great Plains states and were effective in preserving the German parochial school system, both Catholic and Lutheran, and in opposing prohibition and women's suffrage. When World War I broke out in Europe, they were passionate in their support for the fatherland and opposed war loans and the shipment of arms to the French and British. They declared their loyalty to the United States but also insisted on American neutrality in Europe's war. All that changed when the United States entered the war in April 1917. World War I was to become a major watershed not only for Germans but also for other European ethnic groups in the Great Plains.

In the United States both major parties attracted immigrant support, but on the Canadian Prairies the two major parties were deeply divided on the question of immigration. The Conservatives encouraged immigration from Britain during the 1870s and 1880s when the Prairies were being opened for settlement. When the Liberals took power in 1896, a young lawyer from the Prairies, Clifford Sifton, became minister in charge of immigration and encouraged opening the doors to peasant farmers from eastern and central Europe, especially from the Ukraine. The level of vitriol in public discourse between the Liberal *Winnipeg Free Press* and the Conservative *Winnipeg Telegram* underscored policy differences between the two major parties and within the host society forming on the Prairies. These divisions did not lessen after 1914, and the two issues of prohibition and suffrage were intimately interwoven in Canadian Prairie politics during the war years.

Support for suffrage and attacks on alcoholism and prostitution were part of a reform program launched by Anglo-Canadian women on the Prairies with the support of farmer organizations in the years before World War I. The large number of immigrants, newly arrived in western Canada, were not yet ready to join the movement, especially when suffrage was introduced in 1916. Older immigrant groups such as the Scandinavians would be included but not the rough-hewn newcomers. Although young Ukrainian women began to engage in public discussions as early as 1912, they were encouraged to emulate their Anglo-Canadian models but not to expect the same rights. Furthermore, alcoholism had been a major scourge in some Ukrainian communities in Manitoba—and local legend has it that the anti-Prohibition industry that funneled supplies across the United States border in the 1920s and 1930s originated here. Clearly, in the Anglo-Canadian view, the morals of these new immigrants would have to be much improved before full British rights could be extended to them, long after the war had ended.

World War I Watershed

The outbreak of war in Europe in 1914 had an immediate effect on Canadian immigrants, particularly those of German origin. A strong anti-German sentiment swept across the country, including the Prairies, as German-language schools were ordered to use English and German-language newspapers were closed. It was not just German-speaking Canadians who felt the force of anti-German sentiment. Those from any part of the Austro-Hungarian Empire were suspect. Ukrainians, in particular those with ambitions to establish a Ukrainian republic and those who were socialists, were rounded up and put in detention camps. However, the rights of pacifist groups such as the Mennonites, Amish, and Hutterites to refuse military service were upheld.

South of the forty-ninth parallel a policy of neutrality prevailed until April 1917, when the United States entered the war. Meanwhile, those of German ancestry, including the Mennonites, were far from cowed. The threat of an attack on the fatherland united Germans in the United States as never before. They insisted that the United States should remain neutral and avoid foreign entanglements. The German American press attacked the Ameri-

can media and President Woodrow Wilson for their apparent tilt toward Britain. German American communities also raised funds for the German Red Cross. In the election of 1916 Germans voted Republican, although Mennonites voted Democratic in the belief that President Wilson would keep the United States out of the European war.

The Germans and German-speaking peoples in the Plains were not alone in lining up on the German side during the initial years of the war. Scandinavians generally supported the German cause, especially Swedes, although Danes were bitterly divided on the issue. The Irish in Butte, Montana, also supported the German side, in large measure because of their fierce anti-British sentiment.

When the United States entered the war, loyalty to Germany was incompatible with loyalty to the United States. A new American organization, the National Security League and its offshoot the American Defense League, raised a voice that spread virulent superpatriotism and intensified anti-German hysteria. The superpatriots attacked the use of the German language in schools as unpatriotic. The use of German in churches also came under attack. German was forbidden in the pulpit in Montana and a Lutheran pastor in Texas was whipped when he continued to preach in German. Church congregations varied in their response to these pressures, but of all the churches the German Lutherans were most resilient.

Pacifist groups such as the Mennonites were doubly vulnerable, not only because of their use of German in church and school but also because of their pacifist principles. While some Mennonite youths from liberal congregations were willing to perform military service, there were many who strenuously adhered to traditional nonviolent principles. Occasionally violence erupted. The refusal of conscientious objectors to accept military service resulted in their vilification, and their patriotism was called into question. In North Dakota the Hutterites, who resolutely refused military service, were in an impossible position, and many of their young men were beaten and imprisoned for their pacifist principles. Many moved north into the Canadian Prairies. In Kansas some Mennonites who balked at buying war bonds were threatened by local mobs, and a few were tarred and feathered.

Although the United States entered the war later than Canada, the reaction to "enemy aliens" in the Plains was more virulent than on the Prairies. To be sure, the Canadian government created a register of enemy aliens that required surrender of firearms, monthly reporting of their whereabouts, and suppression of foreign-language journals. But Canada admitted Hutterite refugees from the Dakotas despite the opposition of Canadian veterans' organizations, and Canadian Mennonites fared better than their American cousins during the war. As the war continued, however, Canada also turned up the heat on enemy aliens in 1917 and 1918. Most discrimi-

natory of all was the Canadian Wartime Elections Act of 1917, which deprived naturalized citizens of enemy origin of the right to vote. In April 1918 all exemptions to military service were canceled except those for Mennonites and Doukhobors. Some zealous local boards even tried to draft them. Heavy restrictions were placed on all foreign-language presses in September 1918, by which time German newspapers in western Canada had ceased publication. Pressure on German language and culture continued to build on both sides of the border as the war continued.

After the war ended, discriminatory attitudes toward foreign languages continued, and many ethnic communities accelerated their adoption of English. Non-English languages, including French, were suppressed in Prairie public schools, and "Canadianization" became the order of the day. English Canadian nativism briefly reared its ugly head on the Prairies and targeted French Canadians because of the conscription crisis in Quebec during the war. In the United States foreign-language instruction declined precipitously after the war and many parochial schools adopted English. Although the German-language press rebounded to an extent after the war, the number of German-language church periodicals and trade journals dwindled during the 1920s to about one-quarter of their prewar numbers. German churches in the United States (Catholic and Lutheran) fell into the hands of leaders committed to Americanization during the 1920s, so that foreign-language use in church services and on tombstones gradually declined. During this decade the English-language press and radio made significant inroads into ethnic homes.

In politics, ethnic communities retained a distinctive perspective. They could not forget the discrimination they had experienced during the war, and the politics of revenge was practiced, for example, when the German areas of Nebraska returned huge Republican majorities after the war. In 1920 especially, Germans were not so much pro-Harding as anti-Wilson. But the deepest crisis faced by German communities was one of regional leadership. The Burgersbund replaced the old German-American Alliance in the Midwest, but the new leadership was weak. Consequently, the Germans and Mennonites supported presidential candidate Robert La Follette and his League for Progressive Political Action in 1924 and were ineffective in both major parties. They continued to oppose prohibition and women's suffrage.

Efforts to organize and unify the ethnic voice in regional and national elections failed in the 1930s as assimilation swamped ethnic identities. The failure of leadership among Germans permitted the success of Nazi sympathizers within those communities in the 1930s when Germans in general were anti-Roosevelt. The onset of World War II, however, found ethnic communities solidly within the national camp, and there was no repeat of the internal conflicts and hostilities that had marked entry into World War I. So much assimilation had taken place during the 1920s and 1930s, and so much suffering had been endured during the Great Depression, that ethnic communities blurred the boundaries that separated their identities from that of the mainstream host society.

With the possible exception of Ukrainian communities on the Prairies, where distinctive religious practices and language retention remained strong, immigrant communities in the Plains and Prairies saw a decline in ethnic solidarity. The use of Swedish and other foreign languages in Sunday church services, for example, declined in the early 1930s, and support for summer-school language instruction withered during the Depression. Second- and third-generation farmers of foreign origin in the Plains and Prairies were faced with acute problems of farm survival, during which feelings of community solidarity were strengthened, especially among sectarian ethnic groups. But in those difficult years many had come to think of themselves increasingly as Americans or Canadians.

Europeans in Urban Centers in the Plains

The vast majority of European immigrants to the Plains and Prairies lived in rural communities: they had been drawn to North America because of the opportunities in farming. Usually, small service centers emerged in which American-born merchants and professionals provided services. But if the town served a large, ethnically homogeneous community, then European immigrants would set up a general store, provide legal, banking, and other services, publish newspapers, and become community leaders. Thus, the ethnic group developed institutional completeness within these small towns. These good burghers also "set a tone"—maintained standards of behavior that became the norm for their rural cousins. Examples of such towns might include the Swedes in Lindsborg, Kansas; Germans in Humboldt, Saskatchewan; Mennonites in Steinbach, Manitoba; and the Norwegians in Northwood, North Dakota. European immigrants in the hundreds of small service centers scattered across the Plains played a key role in setting social standards and in sustaining networks of contact throughout rural communities.

A few immigrants were drawn to employment opportunities in small mining communities in the Plains. Deposits of coal and lead were exploited in southeastern Kansas in the 1870s and Oklahoma in the 1880s. Italians, who seldom went into farming, were attracted to Krebs, Oklahoma, as early as 1875 and dominated later mining communities in the state such as McAlester and Coalgate. The Irish overwhelmed the mining community of Butte, Montana, to an extraordinary degree: they owned the mines, supplied the labor, and controlled the unions and local politics until the turn of the century when Finns and Italians began to compete with them in the labor market. But in general the Irish were not drawn to mining. Italians and Poles, on the other hand,

were enticed by mining companies from Oklahoma to the Crowsnest district in Alberta, particularly after 1896 when immigration from eastern and southern Europe burgeoned.

The largest urban ethnic communities were found in the major transportation centers that served as gateways to the Plains—Kansas City, Omaha, and Winnipeg. Each ethnic group developed a niche in the labor market, working in the warehouse district, in meatpacking plants, or in small manufacturing enterprises such as brewing or brickmaking. Newcomers tended to cluster in the early years of settlement in these growing cities, but large ethnic ghettos rarely persisted as they did in eastern cities. An exception was Winnipeg, where distinctive Slavic and Jewish settlements emerged in the "North End." The ethnic and class divisions in Winnipeg were especially marked as Germans and Scandinavians blended into the Anglo-Canadian majority, who also formed the city's elite. During the famous General Strike of 1919, however, Jewish and other east European immigrants joined forces to challenge the power elite in a rare display of labor solidarity, despite attempts to denigrate the strike as anti-British and antidemocratic.

Conclusion

The strategies and concepts that scholars have used to study the adaptation of European immigrants to North American society have changed over the decades. In midcentury, scholars such as Oscar Handlin focused on the social transformation of European peasants and proletariat as they created new homes in North America. In the last thirty years of the twentieth century scholarly focus shifted to the enduring cultures of these European immigrants. New emphases will no doubt emerge in the decades to come as the processes of modernization are brought into the discussion. One of the most interesting new concepts to be introduced to ethnic studies is that of the localization of culture. The concept offers the possibility of fresh insights into how Europeans transformed both themselves and North Americans.

Localization of culture refers to the ability of immigrants to embed their values deeply in a locality, not only at the level of the family or small group but also at the broader community or county level. If an ethnic group is sufficiently numerous it may take control of the local institutions of governance, education, and politics and infuse them with a distinctive character, thereby creating a "charter culture." The charter culture is reflected in the modes of social control and conformity, the public morality, the priorities in resource allocations, and the patterns of checks and balances in daily life that distinguish one locality from another. Thus, a myriad of local cultures is created, which in turn affects the development and course of mainstream culture and which ultimately may explain the evolution of its regional variants.

One of the most distinctive and as yet unexplained patterns within the Great Plains is the regional variation in sociopolitical perspec-

tives that, for want of better terms, we may label conservative and liberal. In Kansas and Nebraska one thinks of the Bible Belt and the political support of fiery radio broadcaster Father Coughlin and Republican presidential candidate Alf Landon in the 1930s. It contrasted sharply with the so-called Red Belt of the Dakotas and Minnesota, which found expression in the political views of Henry Wallace and, later, Eugene McCarthy and George McGovern. On the Canadian side of the border there was a Bible Belt in Alberta associated with the Social Credit Party of Bill Aberhart and Ernest Manning, which contrasted sharply with the "social gospel" of Tommy Douglas and the Cooperative Commonwealth Federation in Saskatchewan. The links between these political philosophies and various branches of Christianity are easy to establish. The links to ethnic communities, and particularly to their deeply held values, are not yet clearly established. But the concept of localization of culture offers much potential for exploring those links and for clarifying the contribution that ethnic communities have made to regional and mainstream culture and politics.

Localization of culture is but one of several perspectives used in studying the making of new Americans and new Canadians in the Great Plains. The adjustment of immigrants to their environment, their assimilation or ethnogenesis, and their influence on the political, social, and cultural life of this broad region all represent other perspectives. But there can be no doubt that European immigrants made a distinctive contribution to Plains life, both in rural and urban communities. The constant ebb and flow of population, as farmers and urban workers and their families left for new frontiers farther west, or for other opportunities in nascent towns and cities, resulted in the creation of a network of family ties, ecclesiastical connections, and institutional links that strengthened and deepened the culture and identity of each community. The evidence remains to this day, for example, in western Kansas where, due to rural population decline, German Russians travel twenty or thirty miles to come together and maintain churches and social institutions and so sustain their culture. It may sometimes seem as if European cultures are fading from the bright patchwork of ethnic communities of a century ago, but the reality may also be that all along they have been forming mainstream culture as their own.

See also IMAGES AND ICONS: Last Best West / LAW: *Meyer v. Nebraska* / MEDIA: Immigrant Newspapers / POLITICS AND GOVERNMENT: Democratic Party; Liberal Party; Populists; Republican Party / RELIGION: Doukhobors; Hutterites; Mennonites / TRANSPORTATION: Railroad Land Grants.

Aidan McQuillan
University of Toronto

Conzen, Kathleen N. "Mainstreams and Side Channels: The Localization of American Cultures." *Journal of American Ethnic History* 11 (1991): 5–20. Conzen, Michael P. "Ethnicity on the Land." In *The Making of the American*

Landscape, edited by Michael P. Conzen. London: Unwin Hyman, 1990: 221–48. Dawson, Carl A. *Group Settlement: Ethnic Communities in Western Canada*. Toronto: MacMillan Publishing Company, 1936. Emmons, David M. *The Butte Irish: Class and Ethnicity in an American Mining Town, 1875–1925*. Urbana: University of Illinois Press, 1989. Handlin, Oscar. *The Uprooted: The Epic Story of the Great Migrations that Made the American People*. New York: Grosset and Dunlap, 1951. Hudson, John C. "Migration to an American Frontier." *Annals of the Association of American Geographers* 66 (1976): 242–65. Lehr, John C., and D. W. Moodie. "The Polemics of Pioneer Settlement: Ukrainian Immigration and the Winnipeg Press." *Canadian Ethnic Studies* 12 (1980): 88–101. Loewen, Royden K. *Family, Church and Market: A Mennonite Community in the New and Old Worlds, 1850–1930*. Urbana: University of Illinois Press, 1993. Luebke, Frederick. *Germans in the New World: Essays in the History of Immigration*. Urbana: University of Illinois Press, 1990. McQuillan, D. Aidan. *Prevailing over Time: Ethnic Adjustment of the Kansas Prairies, 1875–1923*. Lincoln: University of Nebraska Press, 1990. Nugent, Walter T. K. *The Tolerant Populists: Kansas Populism and Nativism*. Chicago: University of Chicago Press, 1963. Schlichtmann, Hansgeorg. "Ethnic Themes in Geographical Research on Western Canada." *Canadian Ethnic Studies* 9 (1977) 9–41. Shortridge, James R. "The Heart of the Prairie: Culture Areas in the Central and Northern Great Plains." *Great Plains Quarterly* 8 (1988): 206–21. Turner, Frederick Jackson. "The Significance of the Frontier in American History." *Annual Report*. American Historical Association (1893): 199–227.

ANGLO-CANADIANS

The influence of immigration and ethnicity on the American and Canadian portions of the Great Plains has been profound and diverse. Although European migration to this region has received considerable attention, little is known about the experiences of Canadian migrants, both those crossing the international border and those moving westward within their country of birth. This is explained primarily by the scarcity of data on internal migrants, although their experience can be reconstructed through manuscript censuses, homestead records, and local histories. The neglect of the Canadian immigrant experience in the United States is explained in part by the assumption that Canadians, Anglo-Canadians specifically, experienced rapid assimilation because they shared the same language and many other attributes with the host society. Yet Anglo-Canadian immigrants invite examination because they played an important role in the settlement of the American Great Plains, particularly in the northern half where they comprised a significant percentage of the foreign population during the period of initial settlement.

North–south intermingling within this region occurred well before European permanent settlement, as the American and British fur-trading systems converged along the upper Missouri River at the villages of the Mandans and Hidatsas in what is now west-central North Dakota. Prior to 1800 several fur-trading posts run by Hudson's Bay and North West Companies had established operations in the northern Red River Valley. Anglo-Ontarians, many of whom had been living in Manitoba, made their way south to the Pembina District of Minnesota Territory early in

the nineteenth century, but their numbers were small. Pembina, located adjacent to the international border, became the center of a vast trade territory whose main commerce was in furs taken from the Northern Plains and western Canada. Beginning in 1843 oxcarts operated by Hudson's Bay Company traveled from Fort Garry and Pembina to St. Paul carrying furs east and finished products west. An important player in this trade was Norman Kittson, originally from Quebec, who later moved to St. Paul where he and three other prominent Canadian-born businessmen—Donald Smith, James J. Hill, and George Stephen—developed steamboat and railroad transportation links that would open up the Northern Plains for settlement. These developments stirred American capitalists to look beyond the border and extend their empires into western Canada, but the trade monopoly of Fort Benton in Montana and the grand schemes of St. Paul businessmen were ended with the building of the Canadian Pacific Railway.

It has been estimated that from 1861 to 1931 the net migration of Canadians to the United States totaled over two million, with the greatest flow occurring in the 1880s. Emigration from Canada during the latter part of the nineteenth century was framed by three concurrent processes: the decomposition of rural society, a sluggish pace of industrial development in the midst of a global recession, and the expansion of urban-industrial opportunities in nearby border states. While most Anglo-Canadians located in towns and cities in states such as Michigan, New York, and Massachusetts, considerable numbers traveled farther afield to the Great Plains. Many Canadians intent on taking up land in Manitoba following the passage of Canada's Homestead Act (1872) were attracted by intervening opportunities in Dakota Territory and changed their travel plans accordingly. The well-publicized Dakota land boom of 1879–86 proved especially tantalizing to Canadians. By 1879 Canadians, many of Scottish descent, settling along the northern part of the Red River were so numerous that more Canadian than American money circulated there.

An important factor in the settlement of Canadian and other immigrant groups in the Dakota Territory (and also in Kansas) in the late 1860s and 1870s was the development of a

railroad system that provided a critical link between farmers and markets. Between 1870 and 1890 more than 120,000 Canadian-born chose the American Plains over Canada, with present-day North Dakota being the most important destination within the region. As a consequence, more is known about the anglophone Canadian experience there than in any other in the American Plains states. Most Canadians migrating directly to North Dakota came from three major source regions in Ontario: the Huron Tract, Glengarry County, and Bruce and Grey Counties, all areas experiencing significant population pressure. Many others from Ontario and other parts of eastern Canada lived in states such as Michigan and Illinois before settling in North Dakota. Those who came to homestead settled primarily along the Red River and the northern border, a pattern that still dominated in 1910. Transplantation of Ontario communities, as evidenced in the adoption of Canadian place-names, was made possible by processes of chain and cluster migration.

Anglo-Canadians in North Dakota as elsewhere displayed little attachment to group symbols or institutions. The host society associated them with their British roots, as did many of the Canadians themselves. It was generally easier for Canadians to adapt to an Anglo-American way of life where Yankee traditions shaped the banks, businesses, schools, and politics. In fact, a significant number of Anglo-Canadians, again primarily from Ontario, came to North Dakota to take advantage of the business opportunities accompanying the opening of a new frontier. Anglo-Canadians in Grand Forks, for example, mirrored the American occupational profile more than any other immigrant group. Yet residential clustering in farm communities and in the small towns of the region ensured that members of this group interacted at both social and economic levels. As elsewhere in the United States, kinship and kith connections played an important role in both location decisions and adaptation experiences among Anglo-Canadians. In addition, a high degree of endogamy existed among this group in North Dakota, although less so than for the Scandinavians and Germans.

For many Anglo-Canadians, North Dakota would only be a temporary stage in their life-long migration. Many eventually left the Red

Canadian-Born by State
Great Plains, 1850–1930 Census Years

State	1800	1850	1870	1880	1890	1900	1910	1920	1930
North Dakota		1,458	906	10,678	23,045	28,166	21,507	15,743	12,509
South Dakota					9,493	7,044	6,010	4,462	3,414
Nebraska		438	2,635	8,622	12,105	9,049	7,335	5,780	4,410
Kansas		986	5,324	12,536	11,874	8,538	7,188	5,352	4,068
Oklahoma					420	1,807	2,871	2,489	2,146
Texas	137	458	597	2,472	2,866	2,949	3,534	4,200	4,563
New Mexico			125	227	681	764	1,023	738	618
Colorado			607	4,749	9,142	9,797	9,581	7,642	5,845
Wyoming			329	475	1,314	1,248	1,431	1,440	1,144
Montana			1,172	2,088	9,040	13,826	13,842	14,700	11,193

River Valley because of increasing land prices and mortgage rates and a series of poor crops. Some of this group tried their luck in the western part of the state, especially after 1904–5, when both the Soo and Great Northern Railroads built lines into the area. But the state's efforts to settle its western half met with strong competition from Canada. Given the poor quality of the generally drier land in western North Dakota and the lure of cheap homestead land north of the border, many ex-Canadians, as well as others from the state and elsewhere throughout the region, crossed the boundary into Saskatchewan and Alberta. The migration focus at the turn of the century was on the Last Best West, and eastern Canadians intent on farming shifted their attention toward the Canadian Prairies.

Little is known about Canadians in other states, but it is likely that many of the same experiences were repeated throughout the Great Plains. Today, the Anglo-Canadian presence is less visible throughout the region, as U.S. regulations have restricted the number of immigrants, and those who do emigrate from Canada generally choose to locate in urban regions with a more diverse economic base. Yet since the Canada–U.S. Free Trade Agreement and the North American Free Trade Agreement went into effect in 1989 and 1994, respectively, the flow of goods between the two countries has increased even as the movement of people has slowed considerably. Canada is the top export market for most of the states in the Plains, and much of their agricultural, energy, and transportation needs are in turn supplied by Canada. Thus, the tradition of close links between people living on both sides of the boundary within this international region continues today, even though the nature of this relationship has changed.

See also IMAGES AND ICONS: Last Best West / INDUSTRY: NAFTA.

Randy William Widdis
University of Regina

Hudson, John C. "Migration to an American Frontier." *Annals of the Association of American Geographers* 66 (1976): 242–65. Widdis, Randy W. *With Scarcely a Ripple: Anglo-Canadian Migration into the United States and Western Canada, 1880–1920.* Montreal: McGill-Queen's University Press, 1998. Wilkins, Robert W., and Wynona Huchette Wilkins. *North Dakota: A Bicentennial History.* New York: W. W. Norton, 1977.

CANADIAN MOSAIC

See IMAGES AND ICONS: Canadian Mosaic

CEDARVALE COMMUNIST COMMUNITY

One of the most unusual foreign settlements in the Great Plains in the nineteenth century was a utopian socialist commune established by Russian exiles on former Osage Indian lands near Cedarvale in southern Kansas. Its inspiration goes back to members of the Russian intelligentsia, led by Alexander Herzen and Michael Bakunin, and their reception of the ideas of French socialists such as Fourier and German romantic philosophers during the 1830s and 1840s. This generation of thinkers was followed by one of activists, inspired especially by Nicholas Chernyshevsky and Peter Lavrov (the "sons" of Ivan Turgenev's *Fathers and Sons*), who sought implementation of basic reforms and socialist ideals based on the example of Russian peasant collectives. But this was not easy to accomplish in an autocratic empire, even during the relatively liberal reign of Alexander II (1855–81). Some, therefore, went in search of greater freedom for experimentation abroad.

One of these was a former army officer and surveyor of Baltic German background, Vladimir Geins. Due to American sympathy toward Russia during the Crimean War and Russian support of the Union during the Civil War, literature about the United States was abundant. Geins and his wife set out for the "land of *social* opportunity" in 1868, first settling in Jersey City, then joining an established commune in Missouri as Wilhelm and Maria Frei, which was soon Americanized to William and Mary Frey. Owing to disputes among the group and the opening up of Osage land, the Freys, with a few other American and Russian followers, moved to Kansas in 1871 to found the "Progressive Communist Community" at Cedarvale.

Though small—fifteen members at the most—and relatively remote, it became well known for its mixture of Russian atheistic populists and American Christian socialists, its adherence to "modern" ideas such as vegetarianism and, for a few, nudism, and its promotional and educational efforts. In 1875 Frey began publishing *The Progressive Communist,* a monthly newsletter that circulated to other communities such as Oneida and Brook Farm. The Kansas commune was also distinguished by some of its members, such as Ukrainian writer Gregory Machtet, Nicholas Chaikovsky, who played a leading role in the Russian Revolution in 1917, and Vladimir Dobroliubov, the brother of Chernyshevsky's associate.

In 1879 disagreements and financial pressures came to a head, and the community dissolved. The Freys lived for a short time at the New Odessa colony in Oregon, then spent their remaining years in London, from where William carried on a widely publicized correspondence with Leo Tolstoy. Machtet and Chaikovsky returned to Russia to write of their experiences and suffer long periods of forced exile in Siberia.

Norman E. Saul
University of Kansas

Frey, William. Papers. Manuscript Division, New York Public Library, New York. Saul, Norman E. *Concord and Conflict: The United States and Russia, 1867–1914.* Lawrence: University Press of Kansas, 1996. Yarmolinsky, Avrahm. *A Russian's American Dream: A Memoir on William Frey.* Lawrence: University Press of Kansas, 1965.

CORONADO (ca. 1510–1554)

Francisco Vásquez de Coronado explored the American Southwest and the Great Plains from 1540 to 1542. As a younger son born into a family of the lesser nobility in Salamanca, Spain, Coronado was given a limited portion of the family estate by the laws of primogeniture and entail. Seeking to improve his fortune, this poor gentleman joined the retinue of Antonio de Mendoza, New Spain's first viceroy. Shortly after his arrival in Mexico City in 1535, Coronado married Doña Beatriz, one of five daughters of Alonso de Estrada, treasurer and governor of the colony in the 1520s and reputed to be the illegitimate son of Ferdinand II of Aragon (1479–1516). Coronado's marriage elevated his social status and allowed him to enjoy half the tribute of the Indians of the town and province of Tlapa, granted to the couple by his wealthy mother-in-law. Favored by the viceroy, Coronado became a member of the municipal council of Mexico City before being appointed governor of the northwestern province of Nueva Galicia in 1538.

From the time of Columbus's discovery, the impulse for exploration was grounded in mistaken medieval geographical theory and legendary tales of rich kingdoms. The search led by Coronado for the gold of the Seven Cities of Cíbola and Quivira had its origins in European legend, a tall tale told by an Indian in Mexico, and the disastrous expedition led by Pánfilo de Narváez to Florida in 1528. When four survivors of the Narváez expedition arrived on the northern frontier of Nueva Galicia, their tale of adventure and subsequent report to Viceroy Mendoza set the stage for the Coronado expedition.

The desire of the Franciscan order to peacefully convert the Indians of the north and the dream of finding "another Mexico" by the conquistadors led to at least two reconnoitering expeditions by Franciscan friars. The alleged discovery of Cíbola by Fray Marcos de Niza, who described the humble Zuñi village of Hawikuh as a city of fine appearance larger than Mexico City, persuaded the viceroy to send Coronado north with an army of 300 Spaniards and some 800 Indians on February 4, 1540. Fray Marcos acted as chief guide but returned to Mexico after Cíbola was reached and proved to be a crowded little village lacking wealth.

After choosing winter quarters on the Rio Grande, the Spaniards met an Indian slave at Pecos who told them of large settlements to the east rich in gold and silver. In the spring of 1541 this Indian, called the Turk, led the expedition on a fruitless quest into the Great Plains. Coronado reached Golden Quivira in the vicinity of Great Bend, Kansas, only to find a Wichita Indian village of grass lodges. After wintering in New Mexico, Coronado, disillusioned, in ill health, and 50,000 ducats poorer, led the disappointed army back to New Spain. After being replaced as governor of Nueva Galicia in 1544, Coronado returned to Mexico City, where he acted as councilman until his death.

Coronado's quest for golden kingdoms was a failure, but his journey through the present states of Arizona and New Mexico, the Texas Panhandle, and the Great Plains of Oklahoma and Kansas gave the European world geographical knowledge of these hitherto unknown regions. Moreover, reports of the expedition described the way of life of the sedentary and hunting tribes the Spaniards encountered and the flora and fauna seen in that country. Further, the fantasy of Quivira persisted and would be joined to utopian dreams of spiritual conquest between 1542 and 1580. The final result would be the colonization of New Mexico and the mission system, the chief institution responsible for the extension of Hispanic culture onto Spain's northern frontier.

See also IMAGES AND ICONS: Quivira.

Ralph H. Vigil
University of Nebraska–Lincoln

Bolton, Herbert E. *Coronado: Knight of Pueblos and Plains.* Albuquerque: University of New Mexico Press, 1949. Hammond, George P., ed. *Narratives of the Coronado Expedition, 1540–1542.* Albuquerque: University of New Mexico Press, 1940. Hodge, Fredrick W., ed. *Spanish Explorers in the Southern United States, 1528–1543.* New York: Barnes and Noble, Inc., 1953.

CZECHS

Czechs were among the largest groups of continental European immigrants to settle on the American Great Plains from 1865 through 1914. Of the more than 620,000 Americans who reported Czech to be their mother tongue in the 1920 census, 22.8 percent, or 141,782, lived in the six Great Plains states from Texas through North Dakota. Ten years earlier, 125,140 citizens in the same states constituted 23.6 percent of all Czech Americans nationwide. Of the latter group, 72.8 percent resided in Nebraska and Texas and the remaining 27.2 percent in Oklahoma, Kansas, and the Dakotas. An additional 5,308 Czech Americans in 1910 lived in the states of New Mexico, Colorado, Wyoming, and Montana. Of these residents, a majority had settled on the High Plains. Within the above ten states, at least 90 percent of all Czech Americans resided east of the 100th meridian and primarily in eastern and southeastern Nebraska, east-central Texas, central Oklahoma, north-central Kansas, southeastern South Dakota, and eastern North Dakota. Almost all of these citizens lived on farms or in small towns. In this enormous ten-state area, the only city with a large Czech American population was Omaha, which ranked fourth nationally in this regard after Chicago, Cleveland, and New York City. From the 1870s to the 1950s Omaha was second only to Chicago as an American Czech-language publishing center and home to the *Hospodář,* the largest Czech-language agricultural periodical in the world.

By contrast, few Czechs migrated to the Canadian Plains, or to Canada as a whole, before U.S. immigration quotas in 1921 and 1924 made Canada a more attractive destination. The 1921 census put the national Czech population at only 8,840. Yet Czechs were present in the Canadian Plains as early as the 1880s: Kolin in Saskatchewan was probably the first settlement. By the early twentieth century Winnipeg had a significant Czech population. Most of these early settlers were farmers, miners, and artisans. Among the Czechs who migrated to the Prairie Provinces in the 1920s were sugar beet farmers who settled around Lethbridge, Alberta.

Like many European immigrants of the period 1865 through 1914, most Czechs departed from regions characterized by "agricultural overpopulation." The typical Czech immigrant couple left a farm of ten to fifty acres in size that was not large enough to support a family. Other landless Czech immigrants seldom had capital and usually sought employment in large industrial cities, notably Chicago, where one in four Czech Americans resided by 1920. In the trans-Missouri West, Bohemian Czechs predominated in Nebraska, South Dakota, Kansas, and Oklahoma, whereas Moravian Czechs were more numerous in Texas and North Dakota.

Czech immigrants were divided not only by social class, occupation, and regional origin but also by religious differences. At least half of all Czech immigrants up to 1914 were "freethinkers" (*svobodomyslné Češi*) who chose not to affiliate with any organized religion and who established fraternal and benevolent associations to advance many of the same goals as those promoted by churches: fellowship, community solidarity, and civic service. Outstanding among these associations were the Sokol, dating from 1862 in Bohemia and 1864 in the United States, and the various benevolent associations, including the ČSPS (*Česko-slovanský podporuicí spolek* or Czecho-Slavic Benevolent Society) and its trans-Mississippi offshoots and rivals, the ZČBJ (*Západní česká bratrská jednota* or Western Bohemian Fraternal Association), founded in Omaha in 1897, and the SPJST (*Slovanská podporuicí jednota státu Texasu* or Slavonic Benevolent Order of the State of Texas), founded in 1898 and affectionately referred to as the "Special People Jesus Sent to Texas." The founding of the ZČBJ by trans-Mississippi members of the ČSPS reflected their desire to admit women to membership on the same terms as men and to obtain lower insurance premiums for western lodge members, who tended to be younger and have longer life expectancies than eastern industrial workers.

Nearly half of all Czech immigrants were practicing Catholics, who established Czech-speaking parishes in almost all urban and rural areas with sizable Czech populations. Protestants numbered no more than 5 percent of the Czech American population and organized independent congregations only in Texas. In the other Great Plains states, fledgling Czech Protestant congregations developed with the support of mainline Protestant denominations, notably the Presbyterians. After several decades of acculturation, tens of thousands of Czech freethinkers and their descendants joined liberal Protestant denominations or returned to their ancestral Catholic faith. Czech-speaking Jews usually affiliated with local synagogues and other Jewish organizations, and some, like the Rosewater and Brandeis families in Omaha, rose to positions of political and commercial leadership.

Similar social, occupational, and religious divisions were evident among the tens of thousands of Czech immigrants who came to the United States immediately after World War I and before the immigration quotas. The most recent waves of Czech immigrants—in 1938–39, 1948, and 1968—fled Nazi or Communist oppression and included a larger percentage of professional and managerial people. These waves flowed heavily into the largest American and Canadian metropolitan areas.

Three times—after 1914, 1939, and 1948—Czech Americans, regardless of occupation or religious outlook, made common cause with a majority of Slovak Americans. Their first joint effort supported the Czechoslovak National Council abroad during World War I in its successful effort to establish an independent Czechoslovak republic. In early September 1914 Czech Americans in Omaha conducted the first public subscription of funds to support Czech interests against the Austro-Hungarian government. The Czech National Bazaar of Freedom (*Český národní bazar svobody*) in Omaha in September 1918 was the largest of many American fundraisers for the Czechoslovak independence movement led by T. G. Masaryk.

After Nazi Germany's occupation of Bohemia and Moravia on March 15, 1939, Americans of Czech and Slovak ancestry, including Roman Hruska from Nebraska, met at the University of Chicago to help former Czechoslovak president Edvard Beneš organize a Czechoslovak government in exile and work for the restoration of Czechoslovak independence. Similarly, during the cold war, many Czech American and Slovak American organizations welcomed immigrants who had fled from Czechoslovakia after the Czechoslovak communist coup of February 1948. These organizations also helped expose Czechoslovak communism's ongoing corruption, mendacity, and disregard for human rights. The restoration of democracy and a market economy to the Czech Republic and Slovakia after November 1989 facilitated an intensification of personal and institutional contacts between Americans of Czech ancestry and the citizens of the Czech Republic.

See also ARCHITECTURE: Czech Architecture.

Bruce M. Garver
University of Nebraska at Omaha

Garver, Bruce. "Czech-American Freethinkers on the Great Plains, 1871–1914." In *Ethnicity in the Great Plains,* edited by Frederick Luebke. Lincoln: University of Nebraska Press, 1980: 147–69. Gellner, John, and John Smerek. *The Czechs and Slovaks in Canada.* Toronto: University of Toronto Press, 1968. Jerabek, Esther. *Czechs and Slovaks in North America: A Bibliography.* New York: Czechoslovak Society of Arts and Sciences in America and Czechoslovak National Council of America, 1976.

DANES

Place-names with a Danish ring, such as Dannevirke, Nebraska, and Viborg, South Dakota, testify to the founding of Danish settlements during the chief migration of Danes to the Great Plains of the United States from 1860 to 1895. Most of these settlers were dispossessed farmers taking advantage of the 1862 Homestead Act, which made possible their dream of landownership. The establishment of railroads provided additional incentive for emigration, as large tracts of land owned by the railroad companies were made available and transportation was provided. Unlike their Nordic neighbors, the Danish settlers tended to scatter widely, with no more than 11 percent of the total settling in one state. In Kansas, for example, a number of settlements were the result of Danes fleeing Prussian rule of their home province of North Schleswig in the wake of Denmark's 1864 war with Prussia. During the first decade of settlement survival was difficult. Cultivation methods learned at home were useless on prairie land, where wheat and corn were the main crops. In Danevang, Texas, the southernmost Danish settlement in the Plains, the techniques for growing cotton had to be learned. One aspect of their traditional farming system of cooperatives did transfer, however, and the impact of Danish dairy cooperatives can still be seen today.

Settlements in North Dakota and the Canadian provinces of Alberta and Saskatchewan represent the second migration of the Danes, many of whom were forced to leave the midwestern states as a result of rising land prices. Favorable Canadian homestead legislation added to the pull of the north. In addition, the United States' enactment of restrictive immigrant quotas in 1924 diverted a significant number of prospective emigrants to Canada. Settlements in such cities as Omaha and Calgary reflected the increasing occupational diversity of the immigrants, from commerce to the professions, which contributed to wider settler dispersion.

Nevertheless, by the early twentieth century immigrants in both rural and urban areas had established their own churches and folk schools, many clergy-inspired, as well as fraternal societies, including the Danish Brotherhood, social clubs, and newspapers. The *Danish Pioneer*, the largest Danish newspaper, was founded in Omaha in 1872 and is still being published. An 1894 split within the Danish Lutheran church in North America led to the formation of two organizations serving the Danes. One branch was headquartered at Blair, Nebraska. Its seminary, Trinity College, also at Blair, evolved into a liberal arts college, Dana College, which today houses an impressive archival collection related to Danish immigration to North America. The Dana Folk School in Calgary is also associated with the Blair synod. The other branch, shaped by the thought of N. F. S. Grundtvig, an influential Danish pastor and educator, saw as a major part of its mission the preservation of Danish language and heritage via the founding of colonies. Settlements such as Danevang, Texas, and Dagmar, Montana, and folk schools like Dalum Folk School in Dalum, Alberta, were the direct results of its support. Almost all the folk schools were forced to close in the 1930s due to the Depression and poor enrollment.

Today's chain of Danish brotherhood and sisterhood lodges and social clubs, located in Canada and throughout the United States,

serve to maintain and promote Danish heritage and culture. So does the Federation of Danish Associations in Canada. The Danes of the Great Plains have made major contributions to American and Canadian life and culture. Two Danes of exceptional talents were Niels Hansen, a distinguished pioneering horticulturist associated with South Dakota State College, and Gutzon Borghlum, the sculptor known for his monumental carvings on Mount Rushmore in North Dakota.

See also ARCHITECTURE: Danish Architecture / IMAGES AND ICONS: Mount Rushmore National Memorial.

Marianne Stølen
University of Washington

Bender, H., and B. Flemming Larsen, eds. *Danish Emigration to Canada*. Aalborg, Denmark: Danes Worldwide Archives, 1991. Hvidt, Kristian. *Flight to America: The Social Background of 300,000 Danish Emigrants*. New York: Academic Press, 1975. Nielsen, George R. *The Danish Americans*. Boston: Twayne Publishers, 1981.

DOUGLAS, THOMAS (EARL OF SELKIRK)
(1771–1820)

Thomas Douglas, Fifth Earl of Selkirk, organized the first European settlement colony in the Northern Great Plains. He was born at St. Mary's Isle, Scotland, on June 20, 1771, the youngest son in a large family. In 1806 he was elected to the House of Lords, but his main interest lay in settlement schemes. In *Observations on the Present State of the Highlands of Scotland* (1805) Selkirk proposed government-sponsored emigration as a solution to poverty and potential rebellion incited by "progressive" land use. Unable to secure official support, he pursued private projects in Upper Canada. Selkirk intended to help Highlanders who had been displaced by large-scale sheep farming to preserve their language, cultural identity, and allegiance to the crown by relocating them within the British Empire. In 1811 Selkirk acquired Assiniboia from the Hudson's Bay Company, a land grant for peasants dispossessed of their homes during the Highland clearances. Selkirk's grant encompassed 116,000 square miles of present-day Manitoba, Ontario, Saskatchewan, North Dakota, and Minnesota—an area five times the size of Scotland.

Inspired by Sir Alexander McKenzie's glowing description in *Voyages from Montreal* (1801), Selkirk focused his efforts on the rich agricultural potential of the Red River Valley, which fell within the chartered land of the Hudson's Bay Company. Selkirk gained influence in the company through marriage and major stock purchase. With the company experiencing financial difficulties, caused in part by their rivalry with the North West Company, Selkirk successfully argued in favor of an agricultural settlement. The Red River Valley offered abundant natural resources, was an ideal staging ground for fur-rich western regions, and settlement would interfere with the North West Company's trade. Recruited in the Highlands, settlers first arrived at the confluence of the Red and Assiniboine Rivers

(present-day Winnipeg) via Hudson's Bay in 1812. Despite extreme hardship in an isolated, harsh environment, and Selkirk's failure to obtain military protection, the population of the Red River Settlement grew to several hundred by 1816. With aid from local Saulteaux and Métis, settlers wintered at the buffalo feeding grounds near the confluence of the Red and Pembina Rivers, where they constructed Fort Daer, the first European settlement in present-day North Dakota.

In 1815 Selkirk arrived in North America to attend to court proceedings in the escalating dispute over jurisdiction between the Hudson's Bay and North West Companies. Before these issues could be resolved legally, the trade feud became violent. In the Seven Oaks Massacre on June 19, 1816, Métis (debatably armed and encouraged by Nor'westers) burned houses and crops, killing twenty-one settlers and dispersing the colony. Selkirk spent the summer of 1817 at Red River Settlement negotiating a treaty with the Indians and trying to secure the colonists' title to the land, before returning to Montreal. That year colonists returned, greatly encouraged by Selkirk's visit to the Red River.

Having taken direct charge in the offensive against the North West Company, Selkirk overstepped his authority and became deeply entangled in an exchange of charges and countercharges that would absorb his intellectual and financial resources for the brief remainder of his life. Weakened by consumption, he returned to England in 1818. He traveled to France seeking better health but died there in 1820. The following year the trading companies merged. Although the colony continued to face environmental hardships, it slowly grew. In the late 1830s Selkirk's Settlement began to thrive when an overland route tied the settlement to the growing outpost of St. Paul on the Mississippi River.

See also WAR: Seven Oaks Massacre.

Anne Kelsch
University of North Dakota

Bumsted, J. M., ed. *The Collected Writings of Lord Selkirk*. 2 vols. Winnipeg: Manitoba Record Society, 1984. Gray, John M. *Lord Selkirk of Red River*. East Lansing: Michigan State University Press, 1964. Selkirk Papers. Provincial Archives of Manitoba, Winnipeg.

FIDLER, PETER (1769–1822)

Peter Fidler's service to the Hudson's Bay Company spanned the three most important periods of the fur trade. He was the last of the company's winterers; later he faced the cutthroat opposition of the North West Company in its richest fur region; and in the last years of his life he helped to organize and sustain the Red River colony.

In 1788 nineteen-year-old Fidler left his native Derbyshire, signed on as a laborer with the Hudson's Bay Company, and traveled that summer to York Factory. A year later he accompanied William Tomison up the Saskatchewan River and spent the winter as "writer" at South Branch House, the position filled by David Thompson three years before. Philip

Turnor, the company's surveyor since 1778, taught Fidler and Thompson the elements of navigation and cartography at Cumberland House during the winter of 1789–90. These months of intensive instruction were to be Turnor's most important contribution to the scientific knowledge of the continental interior. From that moment to the end of their active lives, his two students would keep detailed journals, map the vast extent of the British fur trade, and survey for new communities at the edges of its settled occupation.

The following year Fidler paddled with Turnor as far as the North West Company post of Ile à la Crosse, where they stayed as guests of the rival company and then pushed on to survey access to Great Slave Lake. In 1791–92 Fidler wintered with a band of Chipewyans, learning their language and sharing their way of life. The following winter he spent almost five months with the Peigans as they moved along the front ranges of the Rocky Mountains. The Hudson's Bay Company practice of sending young employees alone or in pairs to live with Native bands dated from Anthony Henday's inland journey from York Factory in 1754–55. By Fidler's time, trading posts extended European organization to the Athabaska region and the upper Saskatchewan watershed. These inland posts, rather than York Factory, were Fidler's points of departure, and his time with each band was much shorter than for previous generations of winterers, from Henday to Tomison. After 1793 the practice was discontinued.

Fidler spent the next nine years, from 1793 to 1802, at posts west of Lake Winnipeg and along the Saskatchewan River. Slowly he gathered information from his own surveys and from Native cartographers, which he compiled in a large map of the Plains. Fidler's own map, sent to the company's London Committee and then forwarded to Aaron Arrowsmith, has not survived; Arrowsmith probably discarded it when he copied its line of the Rockies south to Chief Mountain, and its delineation of the upper Missouri watershed, onto the 1802 version of his *Map Exhibiting all the New Discoveries of the Interior Parts of North America*. Three years later Lewis and Clark consulted Arrowsmith's map on their way up the Missouri; they were dismayed that the map did not seem to show the river and the mountains accurately. Since they knew the source of Arrowsmith's information, the captains instantly doubted Fidler's "varacity." But the tracing of the Missouri watershed was conjectural, as clearly shown by Arrowsmith's dotted lines. And the Rockies that Fidler had in constant view from November 1792 to March 1793 do form a band of parallel ranges quite unlike the uplands and outcrops of the mountains to the south. Fidler's navigational skills as he made a running survey of the front ranges were in no way inferior to those of the Corps of Discovery.

Fidler spent four winters, from 1802 to 1806, at Lake Athabaska, sandwiched between posts of the North West Company and Alexander Mackenzie's XY Company. Although his win-

terer's knowledge of the Chipewyans' language and customs was an advantage, Fidler suffered brutal harassment from the other companies and traded few furs. The next few years spent at Cumberland House and Ile à la Crosse were more peaceful for him, although rivalry intensified and the resources of each company were strained by the need to manage trade across the continental divide as well as the difficult access to Athabasca.

The Hudson's Bay Company responded to the competition by cautiously following established routes and by attempting to diversify its trade (lumber, foodstuffs, and mining, as well as furs). Lord Selkirk's scheme of a colony at Red River seemed to fit well with this new policy: it could provide pemmican for brigades traveling long distances and it could be a center of farming and some manufacturing as well as administration of "northern" trade (the Athabaska and Saskatchewan districts). In 1812, after a year in England, Fidler led settlers from York Factory to Red River. The following year he began to survey lots, and from 1814 to 1816 he worked hard to keep the settlement going despite Métis hostility and opposition from the North West Company. In the summer of 1817 a treaty was signed extinguishing Aboriginal rights to the colony's surveyed territory in return for a yearly rent to be paid to the bands of Cree and Ojibwa who had formerly lived there. Fidler made a copy of the treaty and continued to survey lots in the colony. The settlers now numbered more than 200, and the colony's existence was no longer threatened.

Fidler spent the remaining years of his life at posts west of the colony. He was offered retirement with no diminution of his salary of £100 but preferred to continue as a clerk. He met George Simpson, just arrived from London as governor of Rupert's Land, and lived to see the collapse of the North West Company in 1821. Just before his death at Fort Dauphin, on December 17, 1822, Fidler formally married the mother of his fourteen children, of whom eleven survived him. His complicated will was broken in 1827 and his carefully amassed fortune of £1,900 was distributed among these survivors. The numerous descendants of Peter Fidler now form one of the leading Métis families of western Canada.

See also INDUSTRY: Hudson's Bay Company.

Barbara Belyea
University of Calgary

Belyea, Barbara. "Mapping the Marias." *Great Plains Quarterly* 17 (1997): 165–84. J. G. MacGregor. *Peter Fidler, Canada's Forgotten Surveyor, 1769–1822*. Calgary: Fifth House, 1998.

FINNS

Overall, the Great Plains served as home for small numbers of Finns in the United States, although their communities played a relatively greater role in Canada's total Finnish settlement picture. About 300,000 Finns immigrated to the United States between 1864 and 1914, with massive emigration beginning in the 1890s. The Finnish population of the

American Great Plains peaked at some 3,000 individuals in 1910, or only slightly more than 2 percent of the nation's total population of 130,000 foreign-born Finns. A small trickle of Finns began to make their way to Canada during the nineteenth century, but the majority of these 118,000 émigrés arrived between 1900 and 1930 and during the 1950s. In 1921 over 16 percent (2,100 individuals) of Canada's total foreign-born population of 12,155 Finns resided in the Great Plains; by 1931 the number of Plains Finns had grown slightly to 2,400, but this figure represented only 8 percent of Canada's foreign-born Finnish population of 30,355 people.

The first Great Plains Finnish settlement emerged in 1878 at Poinsett (now Lake Norden) in Hamlin County, South Dakota; most of Poinsett's early Finnish population arrived from the copper-mining towns of northern Michigan. Four years later a Finnish land agent who worked for the Chicago, Milwaukee, and St. Paul Railroad recruited a number of Finns to Frederick in Brown County, South Dakota. Soon thereafter, Finnish settlements also appeared in western South Dakota: at Lead and nearby mining towns in Lawrence County; at Snoma and Newell in Butte County; and at Buffalo and Cave Hills in Hardin County. By the mid-1880s Finns were also moving to Dickey County, North Dakota, located just north of Frederick, South Dakota. Other Finns subsequently settled in the North Dakota counties of Logan, Emmons, Towner, Rolette, Burleigh, and Mountrail. The Rolla–Rock Lake community in Rolette and Towner Counties, initially settled in 1896, soon evolved into North Dakota's largest Finnish colony. Other Finns moved to Montana's Cascade and Fergus Counties, while a small number settled in scattered areas of Wyoming and Colorado.

Canadian Finns established their initial Great Plains enclave in 1887 at New Finland (Uusi Suomi), located along the Qu'Appelle River in southeastern Saskatchewan. After 1889 New Finland's population expanded when agents of the Canadian Pacific Railway who wished to attract Finns from Minnesota and the Dakotas selected it as a colonization site. Western Saskatchewan began to be homesteaded in 1905 by Finns who settled in and around the communities of Elbow, Rock Point, and Outlook on the *Coteau*. Additional Finnish settlements established at Dunblane and Dinsmore after 1909 included several Finns who had been politically radicalized by their experiences on Minnesota's Mesabi Range. A much smaller concentration of Saskatchewan Finns was also found in Turtle Lake just northwest of North Battleford. In Alberta a group of visiting delegates from Finland chose the Red Deer district in 1899 as a potential Finnish settlement node; three years later the first immigrants began to move to the Sylvan Lake–Eckville area located just west of Red Deer. Immigrants also moved to other scattered places in Alberta, including Radway, Stettler, Foremost, and the Three Hills–Trochu area. For many years Winnipeg was the only large

Great Plains city with a noticeable Finnish population.

Virtually all Finnish Great Plains communities included one or more immigrant churches, the vast majority Apostolic Lutheran, Suomi Synod Lutheran, or National Lutheran congregations. Finnish temperance and socialist halls served as gathering places for social and political events, provided libraries for avid readers, and accommodated discussion and drama groups, bands, and athletic and gymnastic teams. Cooperative retail stores and grain elevators provided immigrants with a modicum of economic security. One institution, the Knights of Kaleva, which eventually spread to Finnish communities throughout North America, was organized in the Western Great Plains town of Belt, Montana, in 1898. A sister society, the Ladies of Kaleva, was also formed in Belt six years later. Intended to improve the image of Finns in America, the Knights and Ladies of Kaleva employed rituals derived from the *Kalevala*, the national folk epic of Finland.

The majority of Finnish settlers who immigrated to the American Great Plains arrived before they had exposure to the radical movements that dominated Finland and the Great Lakes region during the early twentieth century. In Canada, however, most Great Plains communities were settled by immigrants who arrived from Finland after 1900; several of these enclaves—especially those on the Coteau—were much more likely to include institutions that expressed the views of a radicalized population. Overall, it is obvious that despite their relatively small numbers, the Finns of the Great Plains reflected the general Finnish settlement picture of North America.

See also ARCHITECTURE: Finnish Architecture.

Arnold R. Alanen
University of Wisconsin–Madison

Anderson, Alan B., with Brenda Niskala. "Finnish Settlement in Saskatchewan: Their Development and Perpetuation." In *Finnish Diaspora I: Canada, South America, Africa, Australia and Sweden*, edited by Michael G. Karni. Toronto: Multicultural History Society of Ontario, 1981: 155–82. Roinila, Mika. "A Century of Change: The Rolla/Rock Lake Finnish Settlement of North Dakota." *Finnish Americana* 11 (1995–96): 32–40. Warwaruk, Larry. *Red Finns on the Coteau*. Saskatoon, Saskatchewan: Core Communications, Inc., 1984.

FRENCH CANADIANS

Of the role of French Canadians in the Great Plains two things are certain. Their impact was significant but their legacy is tenuous. Despite some toponymical traces, historical memory of them is disappearing.

The French Canadians were among the first Europeans to contact the First Nations of the Plains, initiating commercial activity and contributing to early understanding of the geography of the region. In the seventeenth century, French Canadian men, seeking adventure, wealth, and freedom from the restraints of colonial society in the valley of the St. Lawrence, headed west, reaching the Great Plains by the early eighteenth century.

In times of French and British predominance, the availability of this choice irritated European administrators and visitors, who resented the French Canadians' clear spirit of independence.

The territorial interest and trading activity of France in North America changed significantly at the end of the War of Spanish Succession. By the Treaty of Utrecht (1713), the French withdrew from Newfoundland and most of Acadia and acknowledged English control of the Hudson's Bay watershed. Threatened by the strategic losses in the Gulf of St. Lawrence, and hemmed in by the Thirteen Colonies and the English on Hudson's Bay, French explorers and traders diverted their activity to the Western Plains.

The travels and trade of the La Vérendryes exemplify this new orientation. Born in Trois Rivières in 1695, Pierre Gaultier de Varennes, the Sieur de la Vérendrye soldiered in France, then returned to Canada. In 1726 he engaged in the fur trade north of Lake Superior. In the 1730s and 1740s he and his sons traveled farther west, reaching the lower Saskatchewan River and Missouri River, in present-day North Dakota. In 1742 his sons Louis-Joseph and François crossed the Plains, probably reaching present-day Wyoming and certainly returning by way of present-day South Dakota.

As French coureurs de bois, then voyageurs after the British conquest of Canada, French Canadians were the proletariat in the fur trade economy. They worked as canoemen, transporting European goods west and pelts east, and labored as guides, interpreters, porters, traders, negotiators, and intermediaries between the Native peoples and Europeans. The expeditions of Peter Pond, Alexander Mackenzie, Lewis and Clark, and John Charles Frémont, among others, depended upon French Canadians' muscle power, as well as their invaluable practical understanding of the climate and environments of the region and the languages and cultures of the Plains peoples.

One notable French Canadian impact was the creation of the Métis, a unique syncretic and Indigenous Plains people who were the offspring of French traders and Native women. The Métis, who combined Christian and Native spirituality and spoke a mix of Ojibwa, Cree, and French languages, lived, traveled, and traded mostly in the Canadian Plains. They were displaced by the disappearance of the buffalo and the development of the agricultural frontier in the late nineteenth century. Resisting such change, their greatest leader, Louis Riel, praised as a visionary or excoriated as a traitor, might better be seen as the personification of this cultural synthesis. Riel was executed at Regina on November 16, 1885, only days after the driving of the last spike of Canada's first transcontinental railroad. The contribution of Riel and his people remains a source of deep controversy.

French Canadians never perceived the Great Plains primarily as a place of settlement and always preferred regions closer to home. Quebec did experience important internal

and external migration of population between 1850 and 1930, and some French Canadians moved west to the Prairie Provinces. Most, however, chose the comfort of contiguity, either in Montreal or regions such as the Laurentians, the Saguenay River, and the Gaspé Peninsula. Beyond Quebec thousands went to the industrializing towns of New England or the lumbering regions of Ontario.

Some directed movement to the Prairie Provinces was sponsored by the Roman Catholic Church and individual clergymen, partly to attract French Canadians away from the lure of a multireligious and unilingual United States. While even today scattered French Canadian agricultural settlements exist in the provinces of Manitoba, Saskatchewan, and Alberta, their rate of assimilation to the prevailing English-speaking culture is the highest of any of the French-speaking minorities in Canada.

Assimilation of French speakers in Canada outside Quebec is a serious concern, and it is especially critical in the west. The *Francomanitobain*, *Fransaskois*, and *Franco-albertain* minorities continue to make heroic efforts to preserve their French language and culture. While the absolute number of French speakers in Canada, not including Quebec, is increasing slightly, their proportion to the even faster growing English-speaking majority is in decline. In the mid–twentieth century, they comprised 7.25 percent of the total population, while by 1996 they were only 4.5 percent. With smaller numbers and a more dispersed population in the Canadian West, the pressure of assimilation there is even greater. One measure is the percentage of those who attend French-speaking schools. Despite the constitutional reaffirmation of their right to education in French and the creation of education divisions and construction of more schools since the 1980s, as of 1996 in the Prairies only about 16 percent of those who had the right to do so actually attended such schools. In Manitoba, where their population is more concentrated, about 4,500 students, or slightly less than 30 percent of the school-age French-speaking minority, are taught in their own language. Farther west, these percentages decline dramatically to 12 percent in Saskatchewan and less than 8 percent in Alberta.

Historical literature on the French Canadians in the Great Plains is uneven. Despite some admirable academic studies of specific aspects, mostly focusing on Canada, to date a comprehensive synthesis of their experience in the Great Plains region does not exist. Material written in French in the late nineteenth and early twentieth centuries was mostly mythological, stressing heroic explorers and saintly churchmen. Now frequently written by local enthusiasts, contemporary material in that language is often anecdotal and genealogical in approach, as well as antiquarian and nostalgic in value. Substantial historical writing of the Plains in English, both in the United States and Canada, often refers only slightly to French Canadians. Lack of familiarity with the language of that minority hampers western historians' access to the French-speaking part of the history of the Plains. Given the danger of the assimilation of the French Canadians in the Great Plains and the present condition of current scholarship, one may well wonder if such a history will ever be written.

See also NATIVE AMERICANS: Métis.

Stephen Kenny
University of Regina

GERMAN RUSSIANS

German Russians are a unique group of Germans who lived in Russia after the 1760s and began their immigration onto the Great Plains in the 1870s. In 1762 Catherine the Great of Russia launched an aggressive campaign to entice skilled farmers into the Volga region to turn the area into a productive agricultural region and to create a human buffer zone against the persistent threat of Asian marauders. She offered transportation money and various privileges: freedom of religion, no military service, protection of culture and language, and the option to leave if they became unhappy with their situation. Approximately 23,184 settlers took advantage of the offer. The greatest number came from areas heavily damaged by years of war—Hess, the Rhineland, and the Palatinate. Between 1764 and 1768, 104 mother colonies along the Volga River were settled. Between 1804 and 1824 more Germans, mostly from the Danzig region of West Prussia, accepted the same privileges from Czar Alexander I and began farming colonies along the north littoral of the Black Sea.

In the late 1860s, as the trend toward nationalism swept across Europe, Alexander II began to rescind German Russian privileges; by 1871 the only privilege left was their opportunity to leave. The first wave of emigration out of Russia corresponded with the grace period before conscription into the Russian army began. Between 1873 and 1914 approximately 115,000 German Russians immigrated to the United States and about 150,000 to western Canada.

German Russians settled in the Great Plains as they had in Russia, according to their Evangelical, Catholic, or Mennonite faith. In towns where German Russians from more than one village congregated they tended to cluster together, reproducing their home villages in Russia, and for the first few generations there was little intermarriage between groups. The tradition of large families also continued—eight children or more was not uncommon.

Railroad companies were instrumental in moving the German Russians onto the Plains with offers of cheap land. The land tenure system in Russia, however, often determined the ability to farm in the Plains. Those from the Volga region lived under the *muir* system, where land was held in common by the colony and distributed according to family size. Without money from land sales in Russia to purchase railroad land, and with homesteading mostly taken, Volga Germans often found work in Plains railroad towns as day laborers

German Russians hoeing beets somewhere in western Nebraska, early 1910s.

or as migrant farm workers. Over time, some families were able to save enough money to purchase farms.

Terms of immigration to Russia during the era of Alexander I did allow Black Sea German Russians to buy and sell land. Although not wealthy, these German Russians often purchased farmland or started businesses in town when they arrived in the Plains. Those who worked the land found the Plains environmentally similar to their Russian homeland, and the crops and agricultural practices they had developed to cope with those semiarid conditions worked well on their new Plains farms.

According to 1910 U.S. census data (here aggregated by country), of the approximately 101,808 German Russians who lived in the states that are wholly or partly in the Great Plains region, nearly 85 percent lived in the Plains proper. The largest concentration of German Russians was in North Dakota (31,910), followed by Kansas (15,311), South Dakota (13,189), and Nebraska (13,020). Of the states in which the Great Plains is only partly included, 5,138 German Russians lived in the Colorado Plains from a state total of 13,616; 78 percent of Oklahoma's German Russians (4,159) found land in the Plains after Oklahoma Territory opened up to white settlement; and 60 percent of Montana's German Russian population (1,309), 76 percent of Wyoming's (578), and 46 percent of New Mexico's (106) lived in the Plains portions of those states.

Accurate statistical data on German Russians immigrating to Canada are more difficult to determine. It is estimated, however, that by 1910 approximately 44 percent of all German settlers in western Canada were Germans from Russia. Movement into Canada began in 1874 when Mennonite settlers, denied their request for closed, block settlements in the United States, chose to settle the Prairies of southern Manitoba. Although disapproving of block settlements, the Canadian government was anxious to populate the new province and granted the Mennonites their request. This set the precedent for the creation

of a mosaic of sizable ethnic islands in the Canadian Prairies. While some mixed-group settlements were established, most of the German Russian groups settled in block communities that were based on religion—Catholic, Evangelical, or Mennonite—and area of origin in Russia—Black Sea or Volga region.

The success of the Mennonite farmers attracted the attention of prospective immigrants from Russia as well as second- and third-generation German Russians from the United States. By 1962 Saskatchewan had 132 German Russian settlements, Manitoba had 27 settlements (and also the largest number of mixed settlements within a province), and Alberta had 14 German Russian settlements.

Overall, Black Sea Germans found it easier than Volga Germans to assimilate into Plains communities. Because of their location in Russia close to the trade centers of the Black Sea, they were more familiar with modern capitalist trends. The Volga Germans, by contrast, had lived isolated in the interior for almost 100 years. Their lack of familiarity with capitalist society inhibited assimilation. Their reluctance to learn English, as well as their premodern work habits—pulling children out of school to work and women working alongside men in the beet fields—were significant factors in the discrimination against them.

Until 1914, as immigrants worked frantically to bring other family members out of Russia, the flow of new Germans from Russia onto the Plains helped to replenish their Old World culture. World War I effectively ended immigration and encouraged assimilation; however, strong German Russian communities still exist.

See also ARCHITECTURE: Black Sea German Architecture; Volga German Architecture.

Renee M. Laegreid
University of Nebraska–Lincoln

Bassler, Gerhard. *The German Canadian Mosaic Today and Yesterday: Identity, Roots, and Heritage.* Ottawa: German-Canadian Congress, 1991. Hale, Douglas. *The Germans from Russia in Oklahoma.* Norman: University of Oklahoma Press, 1980. Koch, Fred C. *The Volga Germans in Russia and the Americas from 1763 to the Present.* University Park: Pennsylvania State University Press, 1977.

GERMANS

Immigrants from the German-speaking areas of Europe (the various German states were united politically only after 1871) comprise one of the most significant elements of the population of both the United States and Canada. Germans began to arrive in North America as early as the late seventeenth century, but the overwhelming majority came between 1840 and 1890, "pushed" out of mainly northwestern Germany because of the disruption of traditional ways of life by the advent of factory modes of production, and "pulled" to North America (especially the American Midwest and the Great Plains during this period) by both real and perceived opportunities for economic betterment, due in large part to the prospects presented by landownership.

Immigrants from the German lands accounted for at least six million of those who entered the United States between 1830 and World War II, or about one in five. During most of this period Germans outnumbered any other single immigrant ethnic group, and their share of the total foreign-born in the country was never less than one-quarter. The influence of such a large immigration on the ancestral makeup of the United States is clearly reflected in late-twentieth-century census data. In 1980, for example, just over 26 percent of those sampled in the long form reported German ancestry, the largest of any single ancestral group. The number of Germans who immigrated to Canada is much smaller, and they mainly arrived between 1870 and 1935, with an interruption during World War I when Germans were barred from entry into the country. Returns from the 1996 census reveal that about 10 percent of the Canadian population claims German ethnic origin, but the numbers are much higher in the Prairie Provinces of Saskatchewan, Alberta, and Manitoba (29, 23, and 19 percent, respectively). In these provinces most "German" immigrants, however, were in fact German Russians who emigrated primarily from southern areas of the Ukraine.

One of the distinguishing characteristics of the German population in North America (especially in comparison to other immigrant groups) has been its relative degree of cultural diversity, reflected especially in the number of Christian denominations to which Germans belonged. In part this reflects patterns that had developed over centuries in Germany, whose population came to include nearly every variety of Christianity—from Catholics, Lutherans, and Reformed groups to more radical Anabaptist pietistic movements such as Amish, Mennonites, Schwenkfelders, and the Moravian church. It is not surprising, then, that nearly all of these denominations were represented among the German immigrant population in North America. The occupational profile of German immigrants was diverse, but like those of other western and northern European immigrants, it was dominated by farmers. This is largely because the process of immigration tended to be highly selective,

Burlington and Missouri Railroad lands advertisement in German

drawing from specific socioeconomic strata. Those Germans who immigrated to North America during the nineteenth century, as revealed in recent detailed studies of German transatlantic migrations, mainly were small-time farmers, landless sharecroppers, and servants (maids and farmhands), all of whom had been negatively affected by the social and economic disruptions that accompanied industrialization. While many came over in small family groups, a good number were young, single men and women traveling alone. A common theme underlying German immigration to North America was chain migration, the process by which generations of immigrants moved between two locales over a period of decades, creating transatlantic kinship and place-specific linkages, which often resulted in the transplantation of whole communities overseas.

German immigrants participated in the settlement and expansion of the agricultural frontier in the American Great Plains from the second half of the nineteenth century on, but their numerical presence in this frontier was not nearly as large as in the midwestern one that had come before it. Their presence in the region during the early phases of frontier expansion immediately after the Civil War was limited largely to the prairies of eastern Dakota Territory, Nebraska, and Kansas, as well as parts of central Texas. With the exception of Volga Germans (who came from a physical environment similar to the Plains), the semiarid steppe grasslands in the western Great Plains were much less attractive to most German immigrant farmers, whether migrating from the Midwest or Germany.

At the regional level, Germans, like other population groups, were attracted to the lure of free or cheap land in the Plains, largely as a result of the Homestead Act of 1862. At the local level, however, settlement patterns reflected the influence of such processes as chain migration and boosterism on the part of railroad agents and land speculators. These processes tended to direct migrants and immigrants to specific locales and resulted in literally hundreds of German ethnic "islands," particularly in the eastern Great Plains. Once a community nucleus had been established by the first generation of frontier settlers (often centered around an ethnic church), subsequent generations of migrants and immigrants, attracted to a place inhabited by those speaking a similar language or dialect, practicing a specific faith, or even hailing from the same region or village in Germany, filled in surrounding areas until an ethnic community—perhaps several townships or even a county in size—had been established. By 1910 German-born immigrants comprised an average of about 9 percent of the total population in the Great Plains states, with North Dakota registering the highest number (18 percent) and Oklahoma and Texas the fewest (5 percent).

The settlement of German immigrants in the Hill Country of central Texas differed significantly from that in the Midwest and elsewhere in the Great Plains proper. There, immigrants were participants in a short-lived but nevertheless highly influential planned settlement venture founded in 1842 in Hessen-Nassau by members of the nobility as a private joint-stock company. Among the goals of this so-called *Adelsverein* (union of nobles) were the alleviation of poverty and overpopulation among German peasants on the nobles' lands and the creation of new markets for goods by transplanting Germans to south Texas. The company obtained from the Republic of Mexico a two-million-acre grant situated in the Southern Plains of West Texas, and between 1844 and 1846 shipped about 10,000 Germans from many areas of central and northern Germany to Galveston through the port of Bremerhaven. Unfortunately, the company went bankrupt in 1846 before most had even arrived in the proposed area of settlement. Many became stranded along the way and settled in present-day Mason, Gillespie, Kendall, and Comal Counties at the edge of the Southern Plains, where most became successful farmers. Despite this setback, individuals and families continued to migrate to the German Hill Country on their own throughout the 1850s and 1860s. By 1857 it was estimated that 35,000 to 40,000 German-born immigrants lived in Texas; in 1850 they comprised between 60 and 80 percent of the total population in the four counties mentioned above.

In Canada, the Canadian Homestead Law of 1872 (which offered 160 acres of land for only $10) succeeded in attracting thousands of German immigrant farmers to the Prairie Provinces of Alberta, Saskatchewan, and Manitoba. Overwhelmingly, these Germanic immigrants were German Mennonites from eastern Europe and southern Russia. In 1874 alone, 7,000 German Mennonites established several villages near Winnipeg along the Red River. But starting in the late 1880s thousands of ethnic Germans who belonged to traditional religions such as Lutheranism and Catholicism began to immigrate to the Prairies from parts of eastern and central Europe and Russia, where they had been colonists in the early and middle decades of the nineteenth century. A smaller number came directly from Germany or migrated from Ontario or the United States. By 1911, 14 percent of Saskatchewan's population was German-born. Interrupted by World War I, immigration from Germany resumed after the war, and between 1919 and 1935 more than 90,000 German-speaking persons arrived in Canada. Fifty percent again came from eastern Europe and Russia, half came directly from Germany, and seven of every ten were farmers. German settlement processes in the Canadian Prairie Provinces tended to mirror those in the American Great Plains, with chain migration working to direct immigrants to specific small ethnic communities populated by those with similar religious and linguistic backgrounds, as well as similar geographic origins in Europe.

See also ARCHITECTURE: German Architecture.

Timothy G. Anderson
Ohio University

Conzen, Kathleen Neils. "Germans." In *Harvard Encyclopedia of American Ethnic Groups*, edited by Stephan Thernstrom. Cambridge: Harvard University Press, 1980: 405–25. Jordan, Terry G. *German Seed in Texas Soil: Immigrant Farmers in Nineteenth-Century Texas*. Austin: University of Texas Press, 1966. McLaughlin, K. M. *The Germans in Canada*. Ottawa: Canadian Historical Association, 1985.

GIANTS IN THE EARTH

Written by a Norwegian-born professor of Norwegian at St. Olaf College in Minnesota, Ole Edvart Rölvaag's novel *Giants in the Earth* (1927) tells of the hardships and triumphs of a group of Norwegian immigrants to the southeastern Dakota Territory in the 1870s. These men and women, who had formerly been fishermen in northern Norway, have to adjust to the vast expanse of the sea of grass in which they find themselves as well as to isolation, loneliness, a harsh climate, and a host culture that regards their national characteristics as a nuisance at best and threatening at worst.

The characters respond to their new circumstances in various ways. Per Hansa, the male protagonist, exemplifies both the daring of a skilled fisherman and the thirst for material advancement of a would-be Yankee. Severely criticized by the author, Per Hansa finally loses his life, in large measure as a result of his hubris. His friend Hans Olsa, in contrast, has neither Per Hansa's intelligence nor his daring, but he steadfastly works his land until struck down by illness. The women characters in the book are neither as daring nor as well suited to Plains life as the menfolk. Per Hansa's wife, Beret, the novel's most memorable character, suffers from a severe depression, which Rölvaag suggests has multiple causes: some of her choices while in Norway, her husband's decision to move the family to America, and the loneliness of the Plains. Although the Norwegian immigrants of *Giants in the Earth* are ultimately successful in their quest for a new and materially better life, the emotional and spiritual price of their success is very high indeed.

See also LITERARY TRADITIONS: Rölvaag, O. E.

Jan Ivar Sjåvik
University of Washington

Haugen, Einar. *Ole Edvart Rölvaag*. Boston: Twayne Publishers, 1983. Paulson, Kristoffer F. "Ole Rölvaag's *Giants in the Earth*: The Structure, the Myth, the Tragedy." *Norwegian-American Studies* 34 (1995): 201–15. Simonson, Harold P. *Prairies Within: The Tragic Trilogy of Ole Rölvaag*. Seattle: University of Washington Press, 1987.

HENDAY, ANTHONY (1725–?)

Anthony Henday, the younger son of a farm family on the Isle of Wight, is said to have been outlawed for smuggling (a common occupation on the island) before he signed with the Hudson's Bay Company in 1750. For several years he worked as a common laborer at York Factory, then volunteered to travel inland from the bay with a Native band from the Saskatchewan River. James Isham, the chief factor, based his plan of sending company employees to winter inland on the journeys of Henry Kelsey and William Stewart; he saw this practice of wintering as a response to the British government's demand for exploration as well as to French commercial rivalry west of Lake Winnipeg. After his first trip inland, Henday worked as a netmaker and then returned to the Saskatchewan River in 1759–60. For the next two years, serving at York Factory and its satellite Severn House, Henday was occasionally given greater responsibility. When the company refused the salary he demanded, Henday claimed his back pay and left the service. Nothing more is known of him.

Henday is remembered for his first trip inland. He left York Factory on June 26, 1754, equipped with a small consignment of trade goods, a supply of paper, and a "boat compass" by which he was to determine his route. When he set out Henday knew nothing of canoe travel, nor could he speak the language of his companions. Even so, he managed the arduous tracking and portaging necessary to reach the Saskatchewan River, where the canoes were abandoned and they met the rest of the band. Henday joined a "family," or tenting group, including a woman referred to as his "bedfellow." Henday's journal describes his acculturation to this Plains band, his growing skill at hunting, his pleasure at feasts. At the same time, he fretted that his companions refused to hunt more animals than were needed for their own use.

Isham considered the purpose of Henday's trip inland to have been fulfilled when the young man met with leaders of the "Archithinues," Natives who did not trade at the Hudson Bay forts and whose language was unfamiliar. In one version of his journal, Henday persuaded them to make the long journey east; in another version the Archithinue chiefs answered him that they could not paddle, or eat fish, or leave the buffalo. After a winter spent "pitch[ing] too & fro to Get furrs and provisions," Henday's band assembled on a riverbank, built canoes, and paddled down to Hudson Bay. They arrived at York Factory on June 23, 1755.

Presumably Henday brought with him a journal of his year inland and a map of the region he had visited. Neither document has survived. Four copies of the journal are extant, three of them copied by Andrew Graham, the clerk at York Factory, and a fourth made for Graham by an unknown copyist. The earliest copy, sent to the London Committee of Hudson's Bay Company a few weeks after Henday's return, reports that he had success in urging the Archithinues to trade and in preventing his companions from exchanging their best furs at French posts along the Saskatchewan River. The other three copies are found in Andrew Graham's compilation of his memoirs and other documents, written and rewritten over a period of thirty years and called "Observations on Hudson's Bay." In Graham's "Observations," Henday cannot persuade the Archithinues to trade, nor can he prevent the band he has wintered with from trading at the French posts. Other problems presented by the four extant texts are discrepancies in the courses and distances that chart Henday's route, and in the designation of landmarks he noted along the way.

Henday's journal was published in 1907 as an article in *Transactions of the Royal Society of Canada*. The text was the last of Graham's copies in the "Observations"—a text that the editor never saw, copying as he did a late-nineteenth-century copy of Graham's copy of Henday's holograph. Gradually the other surviving texts came to light: by 1931 three were known to exist, and in 1968 a fourth was found in the company archives. Nevertheless, historians and anthropologists continued to rely on the *Transactions* text and to draw inferences from its all-too-vague statements. By 1969 the accepted story was as follows: Henday traveled with some Crees from the Saskatchewan watershed up to The Pas, Manitoba, then across to the Battle River to his meeting with Blackfoot leaders south of Red Deer, Alberta. After viewing the Rocky Mountains from a nearby hill, Henday's Crees drifted north to the Beaver Hills east of Edmonton, Alberta, and built canoes on a bank of the North Saskatchewan River. When the ice broke up, they returned to York Factory after passing two French forts on the Saskatchewan River.

However, if all four texts are considered and wishful inferences are rigorously excluded, no consistent account of Henday's movements or activities is possible. The four extant texts are rife with differences and contradictions that no honest, scholarly treatment can rationalize or reconcile. Exactly where Henday went, whom he met, and what trading success he had must remain at best uncertain and on most points unknown. His journal is an enduring puzzle, a lesson in the textual limits of historical research.

See also INDUSTRY: Hudson's Bay Company.

Barbara Belyea
University of Calgary

Barbara Belyea, ed. *A Year Inland: The Journal of a Hudson's Bay Company Winterer.* Waterloo, Ontario: Wilfrid Laurier University Press, 2000.

HUNGARIANS

Hungarians, people from east-central Europe who speak a Finno-Ugric language unrelated to any of the Germanic, Slavic, and Romance languages, immigrated to North America in several waves after the mid-nineteenth century.

First came the "Forty-eighters" following the failure of the Hungarian Revolution of 1848–49. They were about 4,000 strong and mostly represented Hungary's gentry class. Although enthusiastically received, by virtue of their social background most of them were unable to fit into America's rugged society of self-made men. Consequently, following the Austro-Hungarian Compromise of 1867, which made them partners in the Austro-Hungarian Empire, many repatriated to Hungary. While in the United States, they generally stayed on the East Coast. The only exceptions were those few who settled in Chicago, St. Louis, Davenport (Iowa), and on an ephemeral farm community in southeastern Iowa called New Buda.

The Forty-eighters were followed by the 650,000 to 700,000 immigrants who arrived between 1880 and 1914 for economic reasons. Although they came as temporary guest workers, three-fourths of them stayed. Barely literate peasants, they went to work in the coal mines, steel mills, and industrial plants of New York, New Jersey, Pennsylvania, Ohio, Illinois, and Indiana. Their intention was to accumulate enough capital to repatriate and to make themselves into prosperous farmers or well-to-do artisans. For this reason few settled in the country's agricultural regions, including the Great Plains, where the accumulation of capital was much more difficult. The only exceptions were those peasants who after 1885 migrated from the United States to Canada and settled in the region between Winnipeg and Calgary, where they tried to establish themselves as prosperous tobacco farmers. The earliest of these Hungarian settlements in Manitoba (Hunsvalley) and Saskatchewan (Esterházy, Kaposvár, Otthon, Békevár) were established at the initiative of Paul Oscar Esterházy (1831–1912).

The quota laws of 1921 and 1924 and the Great Depression drastically lowered the number of Hungarian immigrants to the United States to a total of just under 40,000 during the 1920s and 1930s. At the same time, immigration to Canada increased. Whereas before World War I only 8,000 Hungarians had entered Canada, during the interwar years their numbers more than quadrupled to 33,000. With the exception of a few hundred highly skilled scientists and scholars who fled Hungary in the late 1930s because of the spread of Nazism, interwar Hungarian immigrants, although more mixed socially, still came for economic reasons.

Following World War II, two major waves of political immigrants entered the United States and Canada: the "displaced persons," or DPS, between 1948 and 1953, and the "Fifty-sixers," or "Freedom Fighters," between 1956 and 1960. These two immigrant waves brought about 65,000 émigrés to the United States and nearly 50,000 to Canada. The DPS represented Hungary's elites while the Fifty-sixers were mainly technocrats who left in response to the defeat of the anti-Soviet and anti-Communist uprising that began on October 23, 1956.

According to the U.S. census of 1990 and the Canadian census of 1991, the Hungarian population of the ten states (Kansas, Nebraska, South Dakota, North Dakota, Texas, New Mexico, Oklahoma, Colorado, Wyoming, Montana) and the three provinces (Saskatchewan, Manitoba, Alberta) in the Great Plains was 138,710, but only two-fifths of these were exclusively of Hungarian extraction. About 76 percent of them lived in two states (Texas and Colorado) and two provinces (Alberta and Saskatchewan). The remaining 24 percent resided in the remaining eight states and one province, where the Hungarian population ranged between 1,398 (South Dakota) and 8,070 (Manitoba).

By virtue of the fact that three-fourths of these Hungarians live in two states and two provinces that are only partly in the Great Plains, the actual number of Hungarians living in the region is probably considerably less than 138,710. For this reason there is little organized Hungarian activity in the Great Plains except in the urban centers on the region's peripheries—Denver and Dallas in the United States and Calgary, Edmonton, Regina, and Winnipeg in Canada. Of these centers of Hungarian life, Calgary, home to about a dozen Hungarian cultural associations, is probably the most important.

Steven Béla Várdy
Duquesne University

Puskás, Julianna. *Ties That Bind, Ties That Divide: 100 Years of Hungarian Experience in the United States,* translated by Zora Ludwig. New York: Holmes and Meier Publishers, Inc., 2000. Tezla, Albert. *The Hazardous Quest: Hungarian Immigrants in the United States, 1895–1920.* Budapest: Corvina Press, 1993. Várdy, Steven Béla. *The Hungarian-Americans.* Boston: Twayne Publishers, 1985.

ICELANDERS

About one-quarter of Iceland's small population, already shrunken by famine, disease, and volcanic disaster, immigrated to the middle of the North American continent in the last three decades of the nineteenth century. Since they left a treeless place where the only real crop was native grass, the landscape of the Great Plains seemed less strange and forbidding to them than to the many immigrants who had left more temperate wooded places on the European continent. Icelanders expected harsh and lengthy winters in the New World, and of course the Great Plains fulfilled those expectations. The torrid summers surprised but did not delight them. In Iceland the temperature seldom rose above 60°F.

In the Old Country, these immigrants had been mountain sheep farmers and, on the coast, fishermen, egg gatherers, and seabird catchers. In good years they ate salt fish, smoked mutton, and hard tack. Though they did harvest the native grasses, they had never planted a crop, tasted pork, or seen a gathering of more than three or four cows at a time (and those usually old milkers).

The earliest immigrants located in Spanish Fork, Utah, and Washington Island in Lake Michigan, but the great bulk of the 16,000 immigrants moved to the Great Plains. In the United States they settled on farms in Lyon and Lincoln Counties in western Minnesota, the terminus of the railroad in 1875. A few years later they colonized the northeastern counties of North Dakota (then Dakota Territory), settling mostly around Mountain and Cavalier on the old shore of Lake Agassiz at the western edge of the Red River Valley.

The bulk of the Canadian immigration, beginning in 1873, went north of Winnipeg to the interlake country, where the Canadian government had established New Iceland. The harsh climate and infertility of the district soon promoted a migration to better land in the North Dakota settlements, to Glenboro and Brandon in Manitoba, to Wynyard in central Saskatchewan, and finally, in 1888, to Markerville, Alberta, eighty miles north of Calgary. Some Icelanders continued west to the Pacific, establishing settlements between Seattle, Washington, and Vancouver, British Columbia, but most seemed more comfortable with long views, grass, and wind. Winnipeg, to this day, boasts the largest concentration of Icelanders in any city outside Reykjavik.

By the beginning of the twentieth century, the immigration was substantially complete. A half dozen towns and districts in the Great Plains had assumed an Icelandic identity, and the countryside there was populated by families with names like Gislason, Gottskalkson, and Thorbjornsson. The Icelanders were unusual among immigrants in their literacy and their devotion to books and learning. Hardly an immigrant chest, no matter how poor the owner, was without the Icelandic sagas and a handful of favorite Icelandic poets. As the generations passed, the Icelanders sent their children off to university—an unattainable dream in the Old Country—where they became mostly lawyers, judges, teachers, and journalists, sometimes of great distinction. The Icelanders preferred such vocations to business or farming. Vilhjalmur Stefansson, born in 1878 in New Iceland, left North Dakota to become one of the most famous Arctic explorers of the twentieth century, but even he is best remembered for the quality of his prose.

This small immigrant community's great legacy to the Plains is to have produced three of the best Icelandic poets of the twentieth century. They all lacked formal schooling but were well-read men of the laboring class, one a hired man, the other two farmers. K. N. Julius (1860–1936) of Mountain, North Dakota, was the first light-verse satirist in modern Icelandic: many of his humorous poems describe immigrants' struggles with English. Guttormur Guttormsson (1878–1966) of Riverton, Manitoba, was a panegyrist in Old Icelandic poetic forms of Canadian nature. And Stephan G. Stephansson (1859–1927) of Markerville, Alberta, considered by Icelanders to be one of the giants of their literature, was a great innovator in language and a profound philosophical thinker. All three wrote in their beloved Icelandic but greeted their neighbors in accented English. In the subsequent generations, Icelandic, like all immigrant languages, steadily evaporated in the New World. The descendants of these great poets must now read them in translation. Still, their works stand on as monuments to the Icelandic heritage in the Great Plains.

Bill Holm
Minneota, Minnesota

Arnason, David, and Vincent Arnason, eds. *The New Icelanders*. Winnipeg: Turnstone Press, 1994. Palmer, Howard. "Escape from the Great Plains: The Icelanders in North Dakota and Alberta." *Great Plains Quarterly* 3 (1983): 219–33. Walters, Thorstina. *Modern Sagas: The Story of the Icelanders in North America*. Fargo: North Dakota Institute for Regional Studies, 1953.

IMMIGRANT NEWSPAPERS

See MEDIA: Immigrant Newspapers

IMMIGRATION BOARDS

The peopling of the Great Plains in the United States was significantly fueled by the promotional activities of state and territorial immigration boards. Following the Civil War many U.S. citizens looked for a fresh start in the sparsely populated Plains. Overpopulation and a lack of land on which to build a livelihood also influenced many Europeans to emigrate and create a new life for themselves in the opened tracts of the Great Plains. The Homestead Act of 1862 provided another major impetus by giving any U.S. citizen, or alien who intended to become a citizen, 160 acres of land.

Developed settlements encouraged law and order, provided entrepreneurial opportunities in agriculture and industry, and offered better methods of reliable transportation for the new transplants. The railroads promoted settlement by providing land along their tracks and by mounting vigorous advertising campaigns. Attracting immigrants to the Plains was economically important for land companies, as well as for the already settled residents of the territories and many newly organized states. In the early 1870s, for example, the community of Yankton paid local merchants who were in New York on business to meet incoming steamships and make a pitch to immigrants—particularly German Russians, who knew how to farm the prairie—to settle in southeastern Dakota Territory. Many state or territorial governments established boards or

bureaus of immigration to foster the settlement of the Plains.

The immigration boards advertised primarily in the United States and Europe through newspapers and pamphlets and by setting up exhibits at World Fairs and various conferences. Colorado's immigration board was typical of these government agencies. In 1872 the Territory of Colorado established the Board of Immigration to promote Colorado as an attractive and desirable locality for those seeking homes, to supply immigrants with full and authoritative information, and to aid and facilitate their journey to the territory. Similarly, the Dakota Territory's legislature set up an Immigration Bureau in January of 1871, headed by a commissioner who published promotional pamphlets and spent time in New York competing with agents from Kansas and Nebraska for potential Plains settlers. The size of the bureau was increased to five in 1875, including a German who was responsible for immigrants disembarking from steamboats in New York and from trains in Chicago, and a Norwegian who was assigned to attract Scandinavians. The bureau operated until 1877, by which time immigration had its own momentum, prompted by settlers' letters back to the Old Country.

For most people, moving to the Great Plains was difficult, not least because of the environmental challenges. Information about the climate and living conditions was particularly helpful for many prospective settlers. Immigration handbooks and publications provided necessary facts, but they sometimes exaggerated the qualities of the environment and the settlements in order to attract more people. These handbooks became an important genre of literature throughout the latter part of the nineteenth and early part of the twentieth centuries. Although the immigration boards were not above overrating their advertised regions, most agencies published credible and honest information so that the newcomers would be successful in their pursuits. A failed settlement, after all, could not significantly contribute to the growth and development of the region.

Erin McDanal
Colorado State Archives

Board of Immigration. Collection. Colorado State Archives, Denver. Greenleaf, Barbara Kaye. *America Fever: The Story of American Immigration*. New York: Four Winds Press, 1970. Schell, Herbert S. *History of South Dakota*. Lincoln: University of Nebraska Press, 1961.

IRISH

Between 1800 and 1920 Ireland was the most emigration-prone of all European countries. Political and religious repression under British rule, rapid population growth, periodic famines, and the absence of domestic industrialization prompted approximately eight million Irish women and men to seek a better life abroad. Before the Great Famine of the 1840s, Canada was a favored destination of this exodus, while the majority of postfamine emigrants were attracted to the United States.

When the Great Plains of both countries was opened up after about 1860, it was not surprising that the Irish, with their long tradition of migration in search of economic opportunities, were conspicuous agents in the westward spread of white settlement. Like many other newcomers, the Irish sought to mitigate the dislocation of transatlantic mobility by transplanting core elements of their traditional culture to their new environment. Consequently, the settler societies that emerged in the Great Plains north and south of the forty-ninth parallel owed much to the traditions, institutions, and ideological orientations of the Irish.

The agricultural potential of the Canadian Prairies was first noted by Capt. John Palliser in 1857, and over the next decades fellow Irishmen Millington Synge, John Macoun, and Clifford Sifton worked to promote the settlement of the region. When the initial pioneer phase was completed in 1911 the Irish were a significant element within the emerging provincial mosaics. Almost 160,000 people, comprising 13.1 percent of the population of Manitoba, 12.2 percent of Saskatchewan, and 10.9 percent of Alberta, were of Irish ethnicity. Approximately 10 percent of these were Irish-born, but the majority—more than 65 percent—were the descendants of earlier Irish emigrants to eastern Canada, with Ontario being the largest source. The remainder came from the United States. Although spread across a range of occupational categories, the Irish who migrated to the Canadian Prairies were motivated primarily by the desire to own land. In 1911 more than two-thirds lived in rural areas and were either homesteaders or farm laborers working to accumulate the resources necessary to begin homesteading.

As with the larger Canadian Irish population, Protestants outnumbered Catholics by a margin of two to one among the western Irish, and typical also was their respective attachment to two peculiarly Irish institutions—the Orange Order and the English-speaking Roman Catholic Church. Both of these had evolved over centuries in the homeland as expressions of Irish Protestant and Catholic cultures, and they subsequently became vehicles for the intergenerational transmission of these two Irish identities throughout the diaspora. Because of their early arrival on the Prairies, these institutions became forums for integrating the Irish with other nationalities, promoting social cohesion in ethnically diverse frontier societies. Although frequently at loggerheads with each other on sectarian grounds, the Protestant and Catholic Irish were nevertheless in agreement on the desirability of cultural conformity and the primacy of the English language in the creation of a new western Canadian identity.

The experiences of the Irish who settled in the American Great Plains were even more varied than those of their counterparts north of the border. As early as the 1820s Irish lumbermen were following the timber trade west through Illinois, Michigan, and Wisconsin, and by the 1860s significant numbers of Irish families were homesteading in Nebraska,

Kansas, and Texas. Railroad construction, on the Kansas Pacific for example, brought more Irish to the Plains, and others came with the military. Eventually, Irish founded such Plains towns as Garryowen, South Dakota, O'Neill, Nebraska, and Chapman, Kansas, and there was a major Irish immigrant presence in such cities as Denver and Omaha. In Omaha, for example, in 1880, Irish occupied 44 percent of the city's blocks, with a concentration around the Union Pacific rail yards.

The vast majority of the Irish who settled in the American Plains were Roman Catholics who came directly from Ireland, and the Church remained central to their communal lives. The fate of the homeland was also an abiding concern. Thus, radical Irish nationalist organizations found strong support among Irish Americans in the Plains, and these served to promote both Irish particularism and working-class militancy. Because of their numbers and organizational cohesion, the Irish became a dominant force in local politics at the turn of the century, and this brokerage position allowed them to act as Americanizers of other European ethnic groups that subsequently migrated west.

An analysis of Irish settlement in the Great Plains suggests that the popular stereotype of eastern urbanization and ghettoization represents only one dimension of the North American Irish diaspora. Although anti-Irish prejudice lingered as a structural barrier, especially in the United States, the Irish nevertheless possessed certain advantages. Early arrival, white skin, Christian adherence, proficiency in the English language, familiarity with the democratic process, and the ability to exploit a wide range of economic opportunities all presaged success. Thus, the Irish must be viewed as central agents in the massive continental transformation represented by the creation of white, Christian, commercial settler societies in the Canadian and American Great Plains during the second half of the nineteenth century.

Michael Cottrell
University of Saskatchewan

Cottrell, Michael. "The Irish in Saskatchewan, 1850–1930: A Study of Intergenerational Ethnicity." *Prairie Forum* 24 (1999): 185–209. Fitzgerald, Margaret, and Joseph A. King. *The Uncounted Irish in Canada and the United States.* Toronto: P. D. Meaney Publishers, 1990.

ITALIANS

Italian immigrants entered the Great Plains first as missionaries such as Fra Marco da Nizza (1495–1558) and Eusebio Francisco Kino (1645–1711), and later as adventurers such as Count Leonetto Cipriani (1816–1888) and Italian American Charles Siringo (1855–1928). Since Italy was not a unified country until the Risorgimento (1860–70), early sojourners were either in the service of Spain or France or were individual agents. In the mid-1800s the combination of economic and political conditions encouraged some Italians, like the six officers and enlisted men in Gen. George Armstrong Custer's Seventh Cavalry Regi-

Italian-owned Val Verde Winery, Del Rio, Texas

ment, to find adventure on the Plains. After 1869 the transcontinental rail line brought Italian journalists and tourists to the Great Plains; their letters and published travel memoirs provided information about the people, geography, and potential jobs to countrymen back home.

Italian emigration began in earnest in the late 1880s, when political and economic upheaval coincided with natural disasters. A rapid rise in Italy's population increased pressure on the land, which in many areas had been farmed to the point of exhaustion; years of poor rainfall contributed to famines and poverty; and in 1887 a devastating outbreak of malaria left 21,000 dead. Leaving one's village in search of work in other parts of Europe was a tradition in Italy. Between 1886 and 1890, however, there was a significant increase in emigration from Italy, and by 1890 immigration to America surpassed movement to other parts of Europe. Until 1886 Italian immigrants were predominantly from the Piedmont, Venetia, and Lombard areas in northern Italy. By the 1890s, however, 90 percent of those leaving were from the south, or *mezzogiorno*, especially Abruzzi, Calabria, Campania, and Sicily. From 1891 to 1910, the years of heaviest Italian emigration, 880,908 immigrants came to the United States. Although exact numbers are difficult to determine, approximately 24,000, or about 3 percent of the total, moved to the Great Plains. During this same period approximately 62,633 Italians, roughly 4 percent of the total immigrant population, moved to Canada, with 6,650, or about 10 percent of them, finding their way onto the Plains.

Perhaps as many as 70 percent of Italian immigrants were *contadini*, peasants who in Italy had lived in town and farmed a few acres in the surrounding countryside. With few exceptions, Italian immigrants on the Plains came to work in railroad and mining camps or as urban laborers. Railroad and mining companies recruited heavily to bring Italian

workers to the Plains, offering cheap transportation and higher wages than in Italy. In a few instances *padroni* such as Antonio Cordascoi, the Montreal labor broker for the Canadian Pacific Railway, directed immigrants to jobs on the Canadian Plains, but most Italians found work through word of mouth.

In the states of the Great Plains, according to 1910 census data (here aggregated by country), Colorado had the largest total population of Italians (14,375), with approximately 6,885 living in the Plains. In Texas 1,554 of the total number of Italians (7,190) lived on the Plains, and in Montana 2,568 out of all Italians (6,592) made the Plains their home. In Nebraska 66 percent of the state's 3,799 Italian immigrants lived in the city of Omaha and another 14 percent in Lincoln, with the remainder scattered throughout the state. Seventy-five percent of the 3,517 Italian immigrants in Kansas lived in that state's southeastern coal-mining district. In Oklahoma, 72 percent of the state's total Italian immigrants (2,564) lived in the Great Plains. In Wyoming 1,086 of the statewide total (1,962) were in the Plains, and in New Mexico 1,237 out of a total of 1,958 Italians were in the Plains. In South Dakota the 1,158 Italians lived mainly on land along the rail lines, and in North Dakota 1,262 Italian immigrants were recorded in 1910, although by 1920 only about 400 remained in the state.

Prior to 1880, Canadian immigration policy restricted southern European settlement; it was not until 1881, when construction of the Canadian Pacific Railway increased demand for unskilled labor, that Italians began to emigrate in large numbers, increasing from an average of 360 per year to more than 1,000 per year, with a peak of 27,704 in 1913. The immigration pattern was similar to that in the United States; the majority of Italians who ventured into the Canadian Plains found jobs with the railroad or in the coalfields. One notable difference was that Canadian Italians would often move on, to Toronto, Montreal,

Vancouver, or the United States, to avoid harsh winters and to find work. It was not until the Canadian mines began to close in the 1940s that the numbers of Italians in Plains urban areas, particularly Edmonton and Winnipeg, began to accumulate in appreciable numbers. Between 1945 and 1960, in both Canada and Italy, immigration policies encouraged a new wave of immigration to Canada, consisting mainly of skilled laborers. Although as many as two-thirds of these new immigrants stayed in the larger eastern cities, urban centers on the Plains such as Calgary, Edmonton, and Winnipeg experienced substantial population growth. For example, Winnipeg's Italian population increased from 1,743 in 1951 to 4,216 in 1961.

All across the Great Plains, Italians worked together to help newly arrived immigrants find jobs and places to live. Small boarding houses provided familiar food, language, and a comforting family atmosphere. Churches and schools were quickly established, as were mutual aid societies, such as the Dante Alighieri Society and the Christopher Columbus Society. The societies also served as sites for labor union meetings in mining regions. "Little Italy" neighborhoods developed in urban areas such as Omaha, Edmonton, and Sheridan, Wyoming. Italian-English newspapers were published in Omaha and Edmonton. Many Italians who decided to remain in the Plains gradually worked up from their initial menial jobs to own shops, farms, or businesses and became active in local politics. As many as 50 percent of all Italian immigrants, however, returned to Italy once they had saved money to buy land or improve their ancestral farm.

In both Canada and the United States, immigration legislation in the 1920s and early 1930s, combined with Benito Mussolini's efforts to reduce emigration, dramatically reduced the flow of Italian immigrants, although the movement was never eliminated entirely. By the late twentieth century, Italian immigrants were no longer *contadini* looking for manual work or skilled workers arriving with families, but were university students and professionals searching for educational and career opportunities difficult to find in Italy.

See also FOLKWAYS: Siringo, Charles.

Renee M. Laegreid
University of Nebraska–Lincoln

Carbone, Stanislao. *Italians in Winnipeg: An Illustrated History*. Winnipeg: University of Manitoba Press, 1998. Kathka, David. "The Italian Experience in Wyoming." In *Peopling the High Plains: Wyoming's European Heritage*, edited by Gordon Olaf Hendrickson. Cheyenne: Wyoming State Archives and Historical Department, 1977: 67–94. Rolle, Andrew. *Westward the Immigrants: Italian Adventurers and Colonists in an Expanding America*. Niwot: University Press of Colorado, 1999.

JEWS

Anti-Semitism and lack of economic opportunities caused about 1.25 million Jews to leave Europe for North America between 1880 and 1914. Jewish immigration to the Great Plains during these years was either kin-based or

Purim parade, Denver, Colorado, March 23, 1973

promoted by agencies such as the Hebrew Immigrant Aid Society and the Industrial Removal Office. Additional influxes followed World War II, with smaller numbers arriving from the Soviet Union after 1975 and from Russia after 1989. Jewish settlement in the Great Plains, with notable exceptions, has been urban. Routes of access for most Jewish immigrants were east to west across both Canada and the United States, and for smaller numbers, north from the port of Galveston, Texas.

Early Jews on the Plains were peddlers serving Native Americans and homesteaders. Most Jews subsequently settled in small towns, where they established retail dry goods stores, clothing and grocery stores, wholesale houses, and, along the rail lines, scrap metal operations. They gradually gravitated to larger cities with better Jewish communal infrastructures. The minimum critical mass necessary to maintain substantial Jewish communal organizations appears to be about 1,000 Jews. Second and third generations gravitated toward law, teaching, and medicine, and later into the corporate world.

Plains cities with significant Jewish populations include Winnipeg, Manitoba; Calgary, Alberta; Regina, Saskatchewan; Billings, Montana; Omaha and Lincoln, Nebraska; Wichita, Kansas; Oklahoma City, Oklahoma; and Amarillo and Fort Worth, Texas. Still, the Jewish presence in the Great Plains has never been more than 2 percent of the general population, and it is much less than this in rural areas. Ninety-six percent of Manitoba's Jews, for example, live in Winnipeg.

As settlement increased, Jewish organizations proliferated in Plains cities. These included welfare organizations, houses of worship, free loan societies, and, in the larger cities, Jewish community centers. Local organizations had regional, national, and international connections. The Anti-Defamation

League, Workmen's Circle, and the World Zionist Organization, women's groups like Hadassah, National Council of Jewish Women, and synagogue sisterhoods, and men's groups like B'nai B'rith linked Plains Jews through education, activism, and philanthropy to New York, Palestine, and Israel. Reform Temples were linked to Cincinnati; Conservative, Orthodox, Reconstructionist, and Lubavitch were linked to New York. To ameliorate isolation Jewish youth and adults were encouraged through these organizations to meet coreligionists in Kansas City, Chicago, and New York. Jews in smaller towns maintained contacts with rabbis, synagogues, and family and friends in the closest urban area.

Although rural Jewish populations were never large, as part of the "back-to-the-land movement" of the 1880s, Jews took up farming on homesteads with start-up loans from agencies such as Cincinnati's Hebrew Union Agricultural Society, Chicago's Jewish Agriculturalists' Aid Society of America, and the Jewish Agricultural and Industrial Aid Society. In Canada the government offered incentives, including exemption from military service, to attract Jewish homesteaders. New Jerusalem, founded in 1882 in Saskatchewan, was one of the earliest Plains Jewish settlements. In North Dakota the first settlements were around Painted Woods and Devils Lake. After 1900 Burleigh County in central North Dakota became the focus of Jewish settlements. By 1910, the peak year, North Dakota had 250 Jewish homesteads with 1,200 individuals. Other Plains settlements were at Touro, Leeser, Beersheba, Lasker, Gilead, Montefiore, and Hebron in Kansas, and at Cotopaxi, Colorado. However, no more than 10 percent of the Jewish families stayed on the farms for ten years; at the most 2 percent passed ownership to a second generation. Lack of money and experience was a problem, and many sold their homesteads when they received titles after the five-year residency and used the money to set up businesses in Plains towns, or else they left the region altogether. Often only a Jewish cemetery survives as a reminder of the Jewish homesteading movement. More enduring and successful were individual entrepreneurs like southern Wyoming sheep farmer Isadore Bolten and the Wolf family who ranched in Albion, Nebraska, for more than seventy-five years.

In the cities, Jews participated widely in politics and intellectual life. Jewish politics in Winnipeg had a radical cast. In American politics Jews served as mayors, members of the House of Representative and Senate, and justices on state supreme courts. Tillie Olsen, one of the most significant Jewish writers, lived in Omaha, Nebraska, in the 1920s. In the latter part of the twentieth century, centers for Jewish studies were established in several Plains universities, deriving much of their financial support from prominent Jewish philanthropists.

See also LITERARY TRADITIONS: Olsen, Tillie / RELIGION: Judaism.

Oliver B. Pollak
University of Nebraska at Omaha

Libo, Kenneth, and Irving Howe. *We Lived There Too: In Their Own Words and Pictures—Pioneer Jews and the Westward Movement of America, 1630–1930.* New York: St. Martin's Press, 1984. Rikoon, S. Sanford. "The Jewish Agriculturalists' Aid Society of America: Philanthropy, Ethnicity, and Agriculture in the Heartland." *Agricultural History* 72 (1998): 1–32. Schulte, Janet E. "Proving Up and Moving Up: Jewish Homesteading Activity in North Dakota, 1900–1920." *Great Plains Quarterly* 10 (1990): 228–44.

KELSEY, HENRY (ca. 1667–1724)

Famous as the first Englishman to have seen the buffalo, in 1684 the London-born Kelsey was apprenticed to the Hudson's Bay Company and sailed to York Factory, its fur trade post on the west coast of Hudson Bay. The Hudson's Bay Company's strategy was to build posts at the mouths of rivers flowing into the bay and there await the Indians who came down the rivers from the interior. To encourage such a trade, the company required employees who were skilled in Indian languages and willing to travel inland. As these proved hard to find, company directors were happy to learn that "the boy Henry Kelsey [was] a very active lad delighting much in Indians' company, being never better pleased than when he is traveling amongst them."

On June 12, 1690, Kelsey set forth from York Factory with a group of Indians who had come to the post to trade. Without their help, and that of the other Indian men and women with whom Kelsey traveled, his great journey would not have been possible. George Geyer of the Hudson's Bay Company reported that Kelsey "cheerfully undertook" the expedition. Kelsey himself recorded that it was "with a heavy heart" that he headed off to the "Inland Country of Good Report [which] hath been by Indians but by English yet not seen." On July 10 he reached a place he named Deering's Point, now generally believed to have been near The Pas, Manitoba, on a bend of the Sas-

C. W. Jefferys. Kelsey Sees the Buffalo, *August 1691.* 1928 calender illustration

katchewan River. He spent the winter of 1690–91 in the neighborhood and returned there in the spring, where he received orders and a fresh supply of trade goods from Geyer. Equipped with such items as guns, Brazilian tobacco, and a brass kettle, he began the second stage of his journey to "discover and bring to a Commerce the Naywatame poets." (Linguistic evidence has identified these people as Siouan-speaking, perhaps the Hidatsas.)

It is not likely that Kelsey's route will ever be definitely established. There is a well-argued case that he traveled south of what is now the town of Hudson Bay, Saskatchewan, as far as the Yorkton area and ventured into both the Beaver and Touchwood Hills. What is beyond doubt is that he was the first European to see the Northern Plains and to witness a buffalo hunt, conducted on foot by people among whom the horse had yet to be introduced. Kelsey did reach the Naywatame, although he was unable to persuade them to suit the interests of the Hudson's Bay Company by concentrating less on making war and more on hunting beaver. Nonetheless, he returned to York Factory in the summer of 1692 "with a good Fleet of Indians," much to Geyer's pleasure.

Kelsey remained in the employ of the Hudson's Bay Company until 1722 as a trader, mariner, and administrator. He served not only at York Factory but also on James Bay and the east coast of Hudson Bay. In 1718 he was named governor of all Hudson's Bay Company posts on the bay. He was recalled to England in 1722 and died in London in 1724.

During his years with the Hudson's Bay Company Kelsey made several trips back to England, two of them when he had the misfortune to be taken by the French when they captured and then recaptured York Factory. In 1698 he married Elizabeth Dix of East Greenwich. The couple had two daughters and a son.

In 1926 a Major A. F. Dobbs of Carrickfergus presented to the Public Record Office of Northern Ireland a collection of papers, among them a manuscript volume titled "Henry Kelsey his Book," now usually known as "The Kelsey Papers." This is thought to have

come into the possession of the family in the time of Arthur Dobbs, a vigorous critic of the Hudson's Bay Company in the mid-1700s. The volume includes Kelsey's journals of his 1690–92 expedition and his 1689 journey to the Barren Lands, as well as his account of some of the customs and religious practices of the Plains Indians. Kelsey also wrote a Cree vocabulary, published by the Hudson's Bay Company and long thought to have been lost, until it was identified in the 1970s among the holdings of the British Library.

It is for what he saw that Kelsey is remembered. We think of him as a man privileged to have seen the Northern Plains and their peoples as they once were. Yet we should also acknowledge that he traveled not primarily as a recorder and observer but as a trader, devoted to the interests of England and the Hudson's Bay Company. He came to the Plains to change what he saw even as he was seeing it.

See also INDUSTRY: Hudson's Bay Company.

Anne Morton
Hudson's Bay Company Archives

Davies, K. G. "Henry Kelsey." *Dictionary of Canadian Biography* 2 (1969): 307–15. Epp, Henry, ed. *Three Hundred Prairie Years: Henry Kelsey's "Inland Country of Good Report."* Regina: Canadian Plains Research Center, 1993. Warkentin, John. *The Kelsey Papers.* Regina: Canadian Plains Research Center, 1994.

LAND LAWS AND SETTLEMENT

In both Canada and the United States, the federal governments acted as huge real-estate dealers transferring the public domain to settlers who would, ostensibly through their labor, enrich both themselves and their respective nations. The problem with these land-transfer systems, at least as far as the Great Plains was concerned, was that the basic 160-acre settlement unit was devised for a humid environment, not for a subhumid environment where agriculture was a more extensive—and more precarious—enterprise. There was also the problem of speculation, which held land out of actual settlement; many of the land laws were easily manipulated for such a purpose and some seemed to be actually designed for it.

The United States' system had its origins in the Land Ordinance of 1785 which, after subsequent modifications, established an orderly procedure for the alienation of public lands: acquire the lands through cessions from Native Americans; survey them into townships of thirty-six one-square-mile sections, each containing quarter sections of 160 acres; reserve sections 16 and 36 for future sales to support schools (such lands are still being sold off for this purpose); and sell the remaining land to settlers through public auction or through regional public land offices. The exception to this general land alienation system in the Great Plains was Texas, which kept title to its own public lands when it entered the Union. There, the land was sold as a source of revenue and disposed of in land grants for various social purposes. Texas did, however, adopt the same survey system.

Before the Homestead Act of 1862, the main

type of sale was through preemption, which was codified in the Preemption Act of 1841. By the terms of the act, an adult could settle on the public domain and secure title to 160 acres by improving the land and paying $1.25 an acre within twelve months. Preemption and the much-abused military bounty land warrants, which were designed to provide soldiers with homes but were transferable and could therefore be amassed in bulk by speculators, were the principal methods of acquiring land in areas of eastern Nebraska and Kansas settled before 1862.

That year, the Homestead Act inaugurated the era of virtually free land for the settler, providing 160 acres for a minimal registration fee and the promise to live on the land and improve it for five years, at which time a patent was issued. After six months settlers who wanted to secure title could purchase the land at $1.25 an acre (perhaps to sell at a profit later). Settlers soon had other options for securing Plains land. Following the 1862 Morrill Act, which allocated public lands to the states for the purpose of supporting agricultural colleges, settlers could purchase scrip, which then could be used to buy land at $1.25 an acre. Again, speculators acquired large amounts of the scrip and bought considerable acreages in the Plains, which they held until land values rose and then sold for a profit. Settlers also had the option of adding to their holdings by locating in railroad land grants, which were given to railroad companies to subsidize construction. By the acts of 1862 and 1864, for example, the Union Pacific Railroad was granted all the odd-numbered sections in every township in a twenty-mile zone on either side of the tracks. Clearly, land near the railroads, the connection to markets and supplies, was in great demand; free homestead sections in the land grants were taken first, giving the characteristic checkerboard settlement pattern, until filled in by the later purchase of railroad sections.

In the Canadian Plains, the Dominion Lands Act of 1872, which followed the Canadian government's acquisition of Rupert's Land from the Hudson's Bay Company, was modeled on the American land survey and free homestead system. The same 640-acre section and thirty-six-section township survey was adopted, and so the rectangular grid came to dominate the entire Great Plains, with profound and inestimable effects on ways of living ever since. A similar free homestead system was inaugurated, but with a "proving-up" time of only three years. Also, as in the United States, two sections (11 and 29) were designated school lands in each township, and following its 1881 charter the Canadian Pacific Railway was given the odd-numbered sections in a land grant extending twenty-four miles on either side of the tracks across the Prairies. "Indemnity selection" allowed the Canadian Pacific to go outside the forty-eight-mile strip if there was not sufficient good land within it. Significant differences from the United States' system were evident in the provision of 160 acres of lands, or

$160 in scrip, for Métis, who had preceded the survey, and the reservation of lands—section 8 and three-quarters of section 26 in each township, amounting to more than seven million acres in Manitoba, Saskatchewan, and Alberta—for the Hudson's Bay Company as compensation for the relinquishment of Rupert's Land. The Canadian government, determined to attract immigrants to the Prairies, also made block settlement grants to ethnic groups such as Russian Mennonites and Icelanders, a practice that was not endorsed in the U.S. Great Plains.

Even before John Wesley Powell, in his 1878 *Report on the Lands of the Arid Region of the United States*, drew attention to the unsuitability of the standard land system for the country west of the 100th meridian, new land laws were being specifically adapted to the Great Plains. In 1873 Congress passed the Timber Culture Act, which was designed to promote the planting of trees in the Great Plains and also, theoretically, to increase rainfall by accelerating transpiration rates. The act stipulated the planting and cultivation of forty acres of trees (later reduced to ten acres) over a period of ten years (later reduced to eight), after which the settler would receive a patent for 160 acres. Most timber claims were filed in the Central and Northern Great Plains. (After 1873, therefore, the Plains settler could legally acquire 480 acres of public domain through the Homestead, Preemption, and Timber Culture Acts for only $200.) However, the fact that only a small proportion of timber entries were carried through to patent indicates the difficulty of fulfilling the provisions of the act in a subhumid environment, but it indicates even more the convenience of the law for the small-scale speculator: settlers could use 160 acres rent-free and tax-free for ten years with no intention of acquiring a patent. At the Cheyenne Land Office in Wyoming Territory, for example, 290,278 timber filings had been made by 1888 but only 65,265 were ever patented. The flawed legislation was repealed in 1891.

Other acts enlarged the size of the holdings that settlers could obtain cheaply or without cost. The Desert Land Act of 1877, which applied to the territories of New Mexico, Wyoming, Montana, and Dakota (and more generally throughout the West), allowed settlers to file on 640 acres for a payment of twenty-five cents an acre. Title could be obtained in three years for an additional payment of $1 an acre and proof of irrigated cultivation. Only one-fourth of the entries in the Great Plains resulted in titles. In 1904 the Kinkaid Act offered settlers in the Nebraska Sandhills 640 acres on homestead terms, and in 1909 the Enlarged Homestead Act increased the free acreage more widely to 320 acres. Under the stimulus of the 1909 act, the plains of eastern Montana in particular filled up with farmers hoping to make a future by dry-farming wheat on their 320 acres. More homestead entries were made there in 1910 alone than in all of the preceding three decades. Montana and the High Plains states of Wyoming, Colorado, and New Mexico were also the main targets of

the Stock Raising Homestead Act of 1916, by which settlers could acquire 640 acres of non-irrigable land for the purposes of stock raising and the cultivation of forage crops. But often the settlers had no experience in farming, and almost always they were undercapitalized. In Montana the drought of 1918 put an end to the dreams of many, and many others who "stuck" through that crisis failed in the 1920s and 1930s.

In the Prairie Provinces also, attempts were made to ensure that settlers could acquire a 320-acre holding rather than the clearly inadequate 160 acres. Successful settlers were allowed, through "preemption rights," to file on an adjacent quarter if it was not occupied. Settled farmers, having accumulated some capital, were also encouraged to buy Canadian Pacific Railway lands, and many did, especially after 1908 when the remaining odd-numbered sections were put on the market at reasonable prices. Still, by 1910 in much of the Prairie Provinces and elsewhere in the Plains, even 320 acres was a small holding and hardly adequate for efficient production.

The rate of failure in both the Canadian and U.S. Great Plains points to the overextension of farming that the liberal land laws had encouraged. The gap between the number of land entries and the number of patents issued was glaring: in the Dominion Lands, for example, only 40 percent of homestead entries culminated in a title, and an unknown portion of those that did quickly passed into the hands of speculators. The end of the Dominion policy came in 1930, with the completion of transfer of remaining lands and resources to the provincial governments. In the United States the Taylor Grazing Act of 1934 withdrew from homesteading virtually all the remaining desirable land, though the 1862, 1909, and 1916 acts, which had drawn so many settlers to the Plains, were not repealed.

See also EDUCATION: Morrill Act / TRANSPORTATION: Railroad Land Grants.

David J. Wishart
University of Nebraska–Lincoln

Gates, Paul W. "Homesteading in the High Plains." *Agricultural History* 51 (1977): 109–33. Martin, Chester. *"Dominion Lands" Policy.* Toronto: McClelland and Stewart Ltd., 1973. McIntosh, C. Baron. "Use and Abuse of the Timber Culture Act." *Annals of the Association of American Geographers* 65 (1975): 347–62.

LEWIS AND CLARK

Meriwether Lewis (1774–1809) and William Clark (1770–1838) were the first Americans to investigate the Great Plains. Both men were born in Virginia (Lewis near Charlottesville on August 17, 1774, and Clark in Caroline County on August 1, 1770) and served in the army together briefly in the mid-1790s. Clark resigned his commission and returned home in 1796, while Lewis continued in military service and in 1801 became President Thomas Jefferson's private secretary. In 1803 Jefferson placed Lewis as leader of the Corps of Discovery, and Lewis offered Clark an invitation to greatness as co-commander. In the nearly two and a half years on the expedition, the two men shared command responsibilities and a friendship that has become legendary.

The men's conclusions about the region were more optimistic than some later explorers and tended to support a garden concept of the region. As the men entered the Plains environment in the summer of 1804, they had a chance to test this idea. Beyond the Platte River, terms like "high and dry" were more frequent than the usual "beautiful and well-watered," but their impressions did not change greatly. Indeed, it was the profusion of wildlife that caught their attention rather than the endless grassland and semiarid climate. Fascinated by the varied animal life, the captains wrote scientific descriptions of a host of Plains animals. Moreover, they told of vast numbers of bison. And it was the captains' reports of abundant beaver that sent fur trappers into the interior. From the party's Fort Mandan, in present-day North Dakota, Lewis penned this overall impression: "This immense river so far as we have yet ascended, waters one of the fairest portions of the globe, nor do I believe that there is in the universe a similar extent of country, equally fertile." This positive evaluation of the Plains resulted from a river-bottom perspective—a fact that prejudiced Lewis's opinion.

As the explorers turned west in the spring of 1805, the terrain became more arid, treeless, and rugged. Nonetheless, along the riverbanks Lewis still sighted groves of trees, and in the underbrush he saw thick stands of berry-laden bushes. New animals, like bighorn sheep, were seen farther west, and the famed grizzly bear appeared. The men discounted stories about its ferocity, but after several bouts with bears, Lewis concluded, "I must confess that I do not like the gentlemen and had reather fight two Indians than one bear." As the party moved into a harsher terrain, Lewis's evaluations of the land became increasingly bleak, until he finally called the region a "desert barren country." The negative appraisals were restricted, however, to the far northwestern edge of the Great Plains.

Lewis and Clark's meetings with Plains Indians focused on two principal goals. One was diplomatic—to apprise the tribes of United States' sovereignty under the Louisiana Purchase and to explain the purposes of their mission. They also wanted to establish intertribal peace. It is doubtful that many Plains Indians understood the purpose of exploration, nor did they grasp the idea of diplomacy outside of trade. Lewis and Clark envisioned trade in the long run; the Indians desired an immediate exchange of goods. Lewis and Clark wanted to expand the United States' commercial influence, while Plains Indians wanted the best goods at the lowest price from the most dependable supplier. Nor were the Indians ready to talk of peace with their traditional enemies without some assurance of security. Lewis and Clark could not give that.

The commanders' other function was ethnographic—to gather information about tribes in order to increase knowledge. In this regard, Lewis and Clark interviewed Indians and resident traders, reported on observations, participated in Indian activities, and collected cultural objects. The captains did their best work in recounting objective matters and describing external cultural aspects. They were not as good at relating ritualistic behavior or subjective matter, and they misunderstood or misinterpreted some activities. They also missed some important ceremonies due to timing. Nevertheless, they rose above the prejudices of their time and left a valuable ethnographic legacy.

After the expedition Lewis became governor of Louisiana Territory but did not fare well. Mounting difficulties in St. Louis and disputes with federal officials sent him to Washington in 1809. Along the way, plagued by multiple problems, he took his life on the Natchez Trace in Tennessee on October 11. Clark, on the other hand, lived a prosperous and productive life as a politician and public servant, most notably as superintendent of Indian affairs in St. Louis, where he died on September 1, 1838.

See also IMAGES AND ICONS: The Garden.

Gary Moulton
University of Nebraska–Lincoln

Ambrose, Stephen E. *Undaunted Courage: Thomas Jefferson and the Opening of the American West.* New York: Simon and Schuster, 1996. Moulton, Gary, ed. *The Journals of the Lewis and Clark Expedition.* Lincoln: University of Nebraska Press, 1983–1999.

MALLET BROTHERS

Pierre and Paul Mallet were French Canadians who led the first successful European expedition across the Great Plains to Santa Fe. Born in Montreal to Pierre Mallet and Madelaine Tuvée DuFresne, the brothers were frontiersmen who moved to Illinois in about 1734. In 1739 they led a group of seven other men up the Missouri River in search of Santa Fe. Confused about the geography of the Great Plains, they traveled all the way to present-day South Dakota before friendly Arikaras and Skidi Pawnees put them on the right road. They returned downriver to an Omaha village in what is now northeastern Nebraska, where they purchased horses for their overland trip. Using existing trails, and with the help of a Native American guide for part of the journey, they traveled first to the Pawnee villages in central Nebraska, then south through Kansas and western Oklahoma to Santa Fe.

In spite of the fact that they lost most of their trade goods while crossing the Kansas River, the Mallets and their companions were welcomed in Santa Fe, where they spent the winter. In 1740 they returned to Louisiana rather than Illinois, carrying letters from the lieutenant governor of New Mexico and from a priest, both of whom encouraged trade between the French and Spanish colonies. Jean-Baptiste LeMoyne de Bienville, the governor of French Louisiana, prepared a summary of the Mallet journal, which is fortunate because the journal was later lost, and so the summary is the primary source of information about the route taken by the Mallets.

French colonial officials were very interested in trade with the Spanish and in the remote possibility of conquering the Spanish silver mines that lay somewhere south of Santa Fe. Within three months of the arrival of the Mallets in New Orleans, a new expedition led by Fabry de la Bruyère set out up the Arkansas and Canadian Rivers. Bruyère's expedition did not get past eastern Oklahoma, however, and the Mallet brothers appear to have fought continually with him over how best to proceed. Eventually, Fabry turned back while the Mallets pressed on, only to lose their trade goods this time in the Canadian River, whereupon they too turned back. French attempts to penetrate to New Mexico then languished for a decade. In 1750, however, the new governor of Louisiana, the Marquis de Vaudreuil, sent Pierre Mallet west for a third time. On the way Comanches robbed him of his trade goods and most of his official documents. On his arrival in Santa Fe, he was arrested as an illegal intruder and sent to jail in Mexico City, where he disappears from the documentary record. Paul Mallet remained behind in Louisiana, where the last documentary record of his life has him living with a wife and three daughters at the Arkansas Post.

Although none of the three expeditions led by the Mallet brothers was economically successful, their endeavors are recorded in several place-names, including the Canadian River and the Bayou Mallet and Bois Mallet, both in Louisiana.

Donald J. Blakeslee
Wichita State University

Blakeslee, Donald J. *Along Ancient Trails: The Mallet Expedition of 1739.* Niwot: University Press of Colorado, 1995. Folmer, Henri. "The Mallet Expedition of 1739 through Nebraska, Kansas, and Colorado to Santa Fe." *Colorado Magazine* 16 (1939): 163–73.

MAXIMILIAN, PRINCE OF WIED-NEUWIED (1782–1867)

Prince Maximilian Alexander Philipp of Wied-Neuwied was a German explorer and naturalist who traveled through the United States in 1832–34. He became well known for his studies of the Northern Plains Indians, especially the Mandans and Hidatsas.

Prince Maximilian was born the eighth of eleven children on September 23, 1782, in the city of Neuwied, Germany. His parents were Friedrich Carl Count of Wied-Neuwied (1741–1809) and Louise Wilhelmine Countess of Sayn-Wittgenstein-Berleburg (1747–1823). The most influential people in Maximilian's career were Johann Friedrich Blumenbach, the Enlightenment's leading theorist on comparative anthropology, and naturalist Alexander von Humboldt, who became his mentor and friend after they met in Paris in 1814.

Whenever Prince Maximilian was free of military service in the Prussian army, he diligently pursued his scientific studies. He learned his skills as a naturalist mainly on his own, but he also enrolled at the University of Göttingen in 1811–12 to study under Blumenbach. In 1815, encouraged by Humboldt, Maximilian led his first major expedition to Brazil, where he studied the flora and fauna of the Mata Atlantica and Indigenous peoples such as the Botocudo, Purí, and Pataxo. Upon returning to Germany in 1817, Maximilian devoted himself to the analysis of his Brazilian experience, which culminated in the two-volume *Journey to Brazil in the Years 1815–17* (1820–21).

In the late 1820s Maximilian began preparations for a second major expedition. Originally he played with the idea of exploring Labrador or the Kirgisian Steppe in Russia, but by 1830 he had decided to travel to North America. One stated purpose of this journey was to continue his investigation of the flora and fauna of the Americas, but he also intended to study the Indigenous cultures of North America and compare them with those of southeastern Brazil. In May of 1832 Maximilian, accompanied by the Swiss painter Karl Bodmer, left Europe for the United States, where they arrived in early July. After a tour of eastern cities they traveled west. Because of a serious illness resembling cholera, Maximilian was forced to stay the winter of 1832–33 in New Harmony, Indiana, where he enjoyed the company of fellow naturalists Thomas Say and Charles Alexandre Lesueur.

In the spring of 1833 Maximilian finally arrived in St. Louis, where he made arrangements to travel up the Missouri with boats belonging to the American Fur Company. After short stops at Forts Pierre, Clark, and Union, Maximilian arrived at Fort McKenzie, the westernmost point of his expedition, in August of 1833. Originally Maximilian wanted to extend his studies farther upriver into the Rocky Mountains, but the hostility of the three Blackfeet tribes forced him to reconsider this plan. After about five weeks of fieldwork around Fort McKenzie, Maximilian returned to Fort Clark to stay for the winter of 1833–34. There he devoted his time to a thorough study of the Mandans and Hidatsas and to a less complete analysis of the nearby Arikaras.

In his travel accounts Maximilian routinely described the physical appearance of the Indigenous peoples he encountered, then concentrated on recording their customs, languages, and cultures, including one of the most important ceremonies of the Mandans, the *Okipa*. Maximilian's visit to the upper Missouri came at a time when the fur trade was altering the social, political, and cultural characteristics of the Northern Plains tribes, and he recorded many of these changes, even though he was not always aware of their significance. His travel writings also reinforced the Romantic interest in the "noble savage," an invented image that had fascinated intellectuals throughout Europe since the late Renaissance.

In April of 1834 the Prince journeyed back to the East Coast, then on to Europe in July. As soon as he returned to Neuwied, Maximilian began the synthesis of his expedition, which culminated in the publication of the two-volume *Travels in the Interior of North America* (1839–41). In the years following, and until a few years before his death on February 3, 1867

in Neuwied, he continued to publish articles on his North American experience. Maximilian's legacy survives in the nomenclature of Plains plants and animals (for example, the sunflower *Helianthus maximilianii* and the Cretaceous saurian *Mosasaurus maximiliani*).

See also ART: Bodmer, Karl / INDUSTRY: American Fur Company / RELIGION: Okipa.

Michael G. Noll
Valdosta State University

Roth, Hermann Josef, ed. *Maximilian Prinz zu Wied: Jäger, Reisender, Naturforscher, Fauna und Flora in Rheinland-Pfalz*, Beiheft 17. Landau: Gesellschaft für Naturschutz und Ornithologie Rheinland-Pfalz e.V., 1995. Schach, Paul. "Maximilian, Prince of Wied (1782–1867): Reconsidered." *Great Plains Quarterly* 14 (1994): 5–20.

MORES, MARQUIS DE (1858–1896)

The Marquis de Mores was a part-time resident of the Badlands of western Dakota Territory for only three years, 1883–86, but the French nobleman left his mark on the region's history. The village he founded and named after his wife, Medora, is a thriving tourist site where the tall, brick chimney of his meatpacking plant still stands as a lonely symbol of his ambitious business enterprises.

Born in Paris on June 14, 1858, Antoine-Amedee-Marie-Vincent-Amat Manca de Vallombrosa was well educated and fluent in English, German, and Italian. He fell in love with a young American woman, Medora von Hoffman, the daughter of a wealthy New York banker, and they were married on February 15, 1882, in Cannes, France. Working in his father-in-law's Wall Street bank, de Mores looked for investment opportunities, and in April 1883 he chose a site near the Little Missouri River in the Dakota Badlands as the place to make his entrepreneurial dreams a reality. He formed a corporation known as the Northern Pacific Refrigerated Car Company and began buying cattle and building abattoirs, a meatpacking plant, and a railway spur to provide growing eastern markets with fresh meat shipped directly from the range in refrigerated railcars. In addition, the Marquis built a large home (today known as the Chateau de Mores State Historic Site), a hotel, a Roman Catholic church, blocks of businesses, and a brick home for his in-laws. Many of the structures still stand.

The Marquis and his family typically spent part of the year, from the late spring to the early fall, in Medora, where despite the challenges of his cattle and ranching operations, the Marquis found time, money, and energy to invest in sheep and horses, ship salmon in from the Columbia River, and begin a stage and freight line between Medora and Deadwood in present-day South Dakota. Though the Marquis had the financial backing of his father-in-law, his many business ventures failed: opposition from other meat dealers in Chicago and New York limited his beef distribution efforts, and the stage line lost its bid for the mail contract, which left it unprofitable. Though the Marquis participated in stockmen's associations and entertained guests such as fellow rancher Theodore Roosevelt, he

could not escape controversy. Charged with the 1883 murder of a Badlands cowboy, Riley Luffsey, the Marquis was tried and acquitted three times. The de Mores family left Medora in the fall of 1886, but the Marquis continued to attract attention. When he moved from the United States to France, his anti-Semitic positions and views on social reform brought him disapproval and arrest. In June 1896 he was killed in North Africa and was buried in Cannes, France.

Janet Daley
State Historical Society of North Dakota

Arnold O. Goplen. *The Career of the Marquis de Mores in the Badlands of North Dakota*. Bismarck: State Historical Society of North Dakota, 1994. Virginia Heidenreich-Barber, ed. *Aristocracy on the Western Frontier: The Legacy of the Marquis de Mores*. Bismarck: State Historical Society of North Dakota, 1994. D. Jerome Tweton. "The Marquis de Mores and His Dakota Venture: A Study in Failure." *Journal of the West* 6 (1967): 521–34.

NORWEGIANS

Though the total number of Norwegians in both the United States and Canada is small, Norway is second only to Ireland in the percentage of its population who emigrated from Europe. Norwegian immigration to North America in the modern era began in 1825. Before the Civil War, Norwegian settlement centered in Wisconsin, with large settlements also forming in neighboring Iowa and Minnesota, although some Norwegians settled as far south as Texas. After the Civil War, Norwegians followed the railroads westward onto the Northern Great Plains. Some came directly from Norway; others had been born in places such as Houston and Fillmore Counties in southeastern Minnesota, or Mitchell and Worth Counties in northern Iowa, and had moved on to the next available land.

Of all the states, North Dakota was, and remains, the most Norwegian in proportion to its total population. Traill County, in the middle of the Red River Valley, between the cities of Fargo and Grand Forks, was 74 percent Norwegian in 1880. By 1900 Norwegians comprised almost one-fourth of the state's population. Norwegians settled almost the entirety of the Goose and Sheyenne River valleys in the eastern half of the state and spread out along the Souris River in the western part of the state. They were successful farmers, quickly adjusting to Plains agriculture. In the early years the men supplemented their incomes by working as carpenters, teamsters, and railroad laborers, and single women took jobs in towns, often as maids or cooks. The large Norwegian presence in northwestern North Dakota led to the claim (a Plains tall tale) that one could walk from the Garrison Dam to the state's northwest corner without leaving land owned by ethnic Norwegians.

North of the forty-ninth parallel, Saskatchewan was the most Norwegian province by the turn of the twentieth century. When the Canadian Pacific Railway reached Calgary, entrepreneurs sought to create a fortune by providing lumber for settlers on the treeless prairie. They recruited workers from the midwestern lumber city of Eau Claire, Wisconsin, creating a Norwegian colony in Calgary in the 1880s. Most of those born in Norway came to Canada by way of the United States; on the other hand, many Norwegians who came to the United States first landed in Quebec, because of its proximity to Norway, before going to the Midwest and the Great Plains. Of the 88,558 people of Norwegian origin living in Canada in 1931, almost 82 percent lived in the provinces of Alberta, Saskatchewan, and Manitoba.

For most Norwegians religion played a central role in community and private life. The Norwegian state church was Lutheran, and in the Great Plains most Norwegians remained Lutheran. But this apparent source of cultural unity was also one of division, as Norwegians founded fourteen different Lutheran synods, or denominations, all claiming to be Lutheran. Many of these competing synods later merged into larger organizations that are now part of the multiethnic Evangelical Lutheran Church in America. The different synods were maintained by an assertive and vigorous clergy who promoted an active cultural awareness.

In addition to the church, two other organizations maintained and fostered Norwegian culture in the Great Plains. The *bygdelag* movement was a distinctive Norwegian organization formed by immigrant families and their descendants from a specific Norwegian valley, fjord area, or community district. They tended to be a rural phenomenon and to have a religious orientation. A strong attachment to the local Norwegian community from which they came was the major motivation behind the creation of the *bygdelag*. In contrast, the Sons of Norway tended to be an urban organization, a fraternal and secular society offering life insurance to its members. Clergy often attacked the Sons of Norway as a secret society similar to the Masonic order.

The Norwegians' ethnic identity is a curious combination of pride and humility. Though a church or Sons of Norway lodge may still serve a traditional meal of *lutefisk* and *lefse*, most Norwegians are culturally assimilated. The creation and continued existence of the *bygdelag* and the Sons of Norway are indicative of cultural pride. On the other hand, Norwegian humor tends to poke fun at fellow countrymen, usually named Ole, Lars, or Lena.

John M. Pederson
Mayville State University

Loken, Gulbrand. *From Fjord to Frontier: A History of Norwegians in Canada.* Toronto: McClelland and Stewart Ltd., 1980. Lovoll, Odd. *The Promise of America: A History of the Norwegian-American People.* Minneapolis: University of Minnesota Press, 1984. Thorson, Playford V. "Scandinavians." In *Plains Folk: North Dakota's Ethnic History,* edited by William Sherman and Playford V. Thorson. Fargo: North Dakota Institute for Regional Studies, 1988: 188–257.

POLES

Poles first began to settle in the Great Plains in the 1870s, and today their Polish American children and grandchildren are found throughout the region, both in identifiable ethnic communities and as individuals. Although the first permanent Polish community in America was established at Panna Maria on the Texas Gulf Coast in 1854, significant Polish immigration to the United States did not begin until the 1870s and continued until the passage of laws in 1922 and 1924 reducing immigration from eastern and southern Europe. Polish immigration resumed after World War II with the arrival of war refugees and veterans of the Polish army. The liberalization of immigration laws in 1965 restarted a small trickle of immigration, which grew with political upheaval in Poland in the 1980s and continued with renewed economic immigration in the 1990s.

Prior to significant Polish settlement in the Great Plains, the region was visited by only a few Poles. One was Karol (Charles) Radzimiński, a political refugee from the failed 1830–31 November Uprising against Russian rule in Poland, who joined the U.S. Army and served along with several dozen fellow Polish refugees in the Mexican War. After the war, Radzimiński helped explore and map parts of Texas and Oklahoma and assisted in the demarcation of the new U.S.-Mexican boundary. Like many Europeans, Polish visitors to America were strongly attracted to the West. Among the most famous of these visitors was the Nobel Prize–winning author Henryk Sienkiewicz, who traveled parts of the Great Plains in the mid 1870s and met with Lakota Indians.

Major Polish settlements in the Great Plains began in the 1870s in central Nebraska and eastern North Dakota. The central Nebraska colonies were formed in Howard, Greeley, Valley, and Sherman Counties as a planned colonization effort of the Polish Roman Catholic Union of America, a Chicago-based fraternal association, and the Burlington and Missouri River Railroad Company. Beginning in 1877 the colonies were advertised in the Polish-language papers as similar to the black-earth regions of Ukraine. Leaders of the organization envisioned the Nebraska colonies as a potential Polish oasis where immigrants could be delivered from the perils of the industrial cities. Lack of resources, and Polish immigrants' preference for wage-labor jobs in the factories and mines of the East and Midwest, frustrated these plans, but the Nebraska colonies nevertheless attracted significant settlement in more than a dozen small Catholic parishes.

Although sporadic colonization efforts among Polish immigrants continued into the 1920s, other major settlements, such as the communities in the Red River Valley of the North, were formed by the more gradual process of chain migration. Beginning first on the North Dakota side and later on the Minnesota side, Polish immigrants established about ten parishes, the largest being St. Stanislaus in Warsaw, North Dakota, founded in 1883. Small Polish farming communities were also founded in Kansas, Oklahoma, eastern Montana, and South Dakota. On the Canadian Prairies, Poles settled in Manitoba (where some 40,000 Polish Canadians were reported to reside by the 1950s), Saskatchewan, and Alberta and were often found among the more numerous Ukrainian Canadians.

Although most Polish communities in the Great Plains were agrarian, industrial communities formed as well, especially around extractive industries. Poles mined coal in Oklahoma, Colorado, and Alberta and smelted zinc in Oklahoma. In many cases, Polish miners came from Pennsylvania. The largest urban communities were created around meatpacking industries, especially in Kansas City and Omaha. By the 1930s the Polish community near the Omaha stockyards was estimated at about 10,000, grouped around three main Roman Catholic parishes, and was the largest Polish community in the Great Plains.

In the first and second generations of settlement, these scattered Polish communities in the United States were tied to the much larger Polish centers of Chicago, Milwaukee, and the Twin Cities through family bonds or via Polish-language newspapers such as *Wiarus* (*The Faithful One*), *Rolnik* (*The Farmer*), *Gazeta Polska Narodowa* (*Polish National Gazette*), *Zgoda* (*Harmony*), or *Naród Polski* (*The Polish Nation*). Omaha had the critical mass to support its own newspaper, *Gwiazda Zachodu* (*The Western Star*), which was published weekly from 1904 to 1945. In Canada the *Gazeta Katolicka* (*Catholic Gazette*) was published in Winnipeg after 1908. Winnipeg's Polish community, reinforced by World War II–era refugees, is home to the newspaper *Czas* (*The Times*).

After World War II, aside from a number of refugee priests who came to serve in Great Plains dioceses, there was little immigration to these Polish communities, although some postwar and Solidarity-era immigrants did settle in Dallas, Denver, Omaha, Calgary, and Winnipeg. The children and grandchildren of the earlier immigrants learned English, but in most of the small communities Polish continued to be used in the home and in church at least into the 1950s. The distinct Polish American culture created by the immigrants remains viable in some of the larger concentrations of settlement, as attested to by active Polish fraternal societies in North Dakota and the opening of a Polish cultural center in Ashton, Nebraska, in 2000.

See also: MEDIA: Immigrant Newspapers.

John Radzilowski
University of Minnesota

Bernard, Richard M. *The Poles in Oklahoma.* Norman: University of Oklahoma Press, 1980. Niklewicz, F. *Polacy w Stanach Zjednoczonych.* Green Bay WI: n.p., 1937. Radzilowski, John. "A New Poland in the Old Northwest: Polish Farming Colonies on the Northern Great Plains." *Polish American Studies* 59 (2002): 79–96.

SCOTS

Frontiersmen of Scottish origin were attracted to the Great Plains long before the region was permanently settled by European Americans. Americans and Canadians of Scottish descent were among the first to venture into the area,

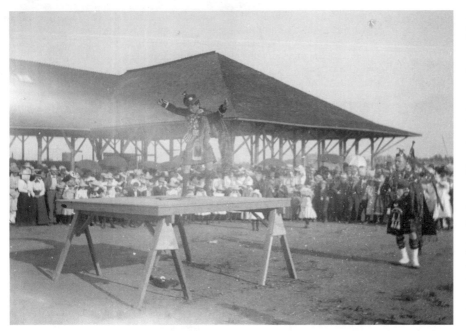

A woman dancing the Highland fling in Scottish costume, Denver, Colorado, between 1904 and 1910

and if those of Ulster Scots heritage such as Kit Carson and Davy Crocket are included, the numbers become still more impressive.

The Hudson's Bay Company and its rivals for the fur trade recruited much of their staff either directly from Scotland—particularly from the Orkney Islands—or from the largely Highland Scots population of Glengarry County in eastern Ontario. But the Hudson's Bay Company did not remunerate its workers very well, and a considerable number of dissatisfied former company employees transferred to the American Fur Company, including Kenneth McKenzie, the "King of the Missouri," who presided over the fur trade on the Northern Great Plains in the 1830s from his base at Fort Union. The Hudson's Bay Company continued to actively seek employees in Scotland until well after World War II, long after its economic interests had shifted from the fur trade to land development and department store investments. Highlanders were also a major component of the Earl of Selkirk's Red River Settlement, founded in 1812.

Other Scots who made their mark in the Great Plains were political refugees such as Allan Pinkerton, the founder of the well-known detective agency, who emigrated to North America as a result of his involvement in radical politics in Glasgow in 1842. Scottish investors financed much of the cattle boom of the 1880s in the Great Plains. The Matador Land and Cattle Company, founded by two Americans and later sold to a consortium of Dundee businessmen, was one of the most significant and long-lasting ranching corporations. Under the management of Murdo Mackenzie, a native of Tain, in Rosshire, Matador extended its operations from Texas to New Mexico, Oklahoma, Nebraska, South Dakota, Montana, and Saskatchewan. The Scottish-owned Matador landholdings in Texas were not bro-

ken up until 1951. Other Scots of note in the livestock industry included the Eighth Earl of Airlie, who chaired the Prairie Land and Cattle Company and the Dundee Land Investment Company, and John Sutherland Sinclair, a North Dakota rancher who had emigrated in 1875 at the age of seventeen. It has been estimated that in the late 1870s and 1880s three-quarters of all foreign investment in ranching in America came from Scotland. Scots also invested in mortgage companies, mining, and railroads, many of which were also financed in Scotland.

Scotland provided more than its share of migrants in the late nineteenth and twentieth centuries. While an increasing proportion of these migrants came from urban communities in lowland Scotland and gravitated to major cities in the United States and Canada, many also headed to the Great Plains seeking land. The Montana writer Ivan Doig, in his novel *Dancing at the Rascal Fair* (1987), describes the emigration of an apprentice wheelwright and a wheelworks clerk from the Scottish county of Forfar to "Scotch Heaven" in northwestern Montana. Doig's Angus MacCaskill and Rob Barclay must have been typical of many Scots artisans who saw a bright future in the ownership of land, which was virtually impossible in Scotland, where the tenanted farms were rarely offered for sale. Artisans and skilled farmworkers, who were numerous in Scotland during the nineteenth century, often found emigration to the Great Plains a much more attractive proposition than the alternatives open to them at home. They applied the skills learned in their homeland to stock farming and crop production, and although new methods of dryland farming had to be learned, the industrious producer could hope to make a success as a landowner in the Great Plains. One of these emigrants, the South Dakota rancher Scotty

Philip (a native of Auchness, near Lossiemouth), was instrumental in saving the Plains bison from extinction.

See also AGRICULTURE: Ranches / INDUSTRY: McKenzie, Kenneth.

Ronald M. Sunter
University of Guelph

Donaldson, Gordon. *The Scots Overseas*. London: Robert Hale, 1966. Jackson, W. Turrentine. *The Enterprising Scot: Investors in the American West after 1873*. Edinburgh: Edinburgh University Press, 1968. Pearce, W. M. *The Matador Land and Cattle Company*. Norman: University of Oklahoma Press, 1964.

SETTLEMENT PATTERNS, CANADA

The two-year-old Dominion of Canada purchased that part of the Great Plains that extended north of the forty-ninth parallel from the Hudson's Bay Company in 1869. Peopling this region with farm families, connecting it to Central Canada with a railroad, and exploiting the region's resources were the goals of the "National Policy," Canada's western development strategy. Migrants from Europe, the United States, and from Maritime and Central Canada reshaped this expanse into the Prairie Provinces: Manitoba (1870), Saskatchewan (1905), and Alberta (1905).

Ironically, given Canada's determination to differentiate the Canadian West from the American West, Canadian settlement and development policy copied basic U.S. models. The Dominion Lands Act of 1872, like the U.S. Homestead Act, gave would-be farmers 160 acres if they "proved up": planted crops, built a shack, and survived on the homestead for three years. As in the United States, the routes the railways chose shaped the broad patterns of settlement in the Canadian Plains. Also as in the United States, Canada subsidized privately owned railways. The Canadian Pacific Railway, completed in 1885, received generous gifts of public land and public money. By 1915 the Canadian Pacific had been joined by two new transcontinentals, the Grand Trunk Pacific and the Canadian Northern Railway, supported by government guarantees of their corporate bonds. Soon bankrupt, the new railways were nationalized between 1917 and 1923 as Canadian National Railways.

Until the late 1890s European settlement of Canada's Prairie West proceeded slowly. Most settlers who moved west came from the eastern provinces, a majority of them from Ontario. For complex reasons, one of which was English Canadian hostility, only small numbers of French Canadians migrated west. The region had only 31,000 farms in 1891, and the total non–First Nations population had grown only to 251,000, compared to the combined population of Montana and North Dakota of 334,000 in 1890. Most embarrassing was that the U.S. census showed that a tenth of these North Dakotans and Montanans had migrated south from Canada.

Slower population growth made the Canadian government more generous toward block settlement by ethnic groups than was its U.S. counterpart. Two communities of Mennonites were attracted to Manitoba in 1874 with promises of freedom from military service, subsidized ocean passage, and grants of twenty-five townships on the east and west sides of the Red River. The U.S. government refused to allow village settlement on homestead lands, but the Canadian government agreed to a "hamlet clause": Mennonite families could live in a village away from the land they farmed and earn title without fulfilling the usual residence requirements.

Like the Mennonites, other minorities were pushed to the Canadian Prairie West by conditions in their homelands and pulled by the liberality of the Canadian government. In 1877 Icelanders settled a block grant on the west shore of Lake Winnipeg. Mormons moved north from Utah to evade a U.S. antipolygamy law; their capital and experience enabled them to buy and irrigate railway lands in southern Alberta, and Canada took no action against polygamy. Attracted by assurances that they could preserve their cultural distinctiveness, Jewish homesteaders abandoned North Dakota to create six agricultural colonies in Manitoba and Saskatchewan, and 1,700 Hutterites left South Dakota for Manitoba and Alberta.

After 1900 a surging export-oriented wheat economy initiated massive migration to what Canadian immigration pamphlets called the "Last Best West." Regional population leaped to almost two million in 1921, and from 5 percent to 22 percent of Canada's total population. Prairie prosperity persuaded emigrants from the eastern provinces to migrate west within Canada rather than to depart for the United States. But four out of ten in the region in 1921 came from outside Canada: from the British Isles, every country in Europe (Canadians did not think of Britain as part of Europe), or the United States. Canadian immigration policy was unrestrictive, with one massive exception: immigration laws kept low the numbers of people of color—Chinese, Japanese, and South Asian.

The newcomers came as individuals or in families, but no longer did they come as whole villages. Canada's magnanimity toward other ethnic groups was motivated by desperation; when the Canadian West became more attractive to migrants, policies became less generous and less flexible. The 7,400 Russian Doukhobors who settled in north-central Saskatchewan in 1899 were denied the privilege of proving up their lands collectively and had their homestead entries universally canceled in 1907. Informal block settlement continued; however, Department of the Interior officials encouraged Ukrainian migrants from the Austro-Hungarian Empire to choose homesteads in the parkland belt, which fringed the prairies to the north, close to countrymen with whom they shared a language. Their established Ukrainian neighbors would help impoverished newcomers through their first winter without any cost to the government, and their segregation averted friction with English-speaking Canadians.

Ukrainian homesteaders also became seasonal workers for the railways and resource industries. Although Canada officially sought farmers from Europe, after 1906 more European immigrants were actually unskilled workers destined for the same sort of work than they were homesteaders or farm workers. Half or more of those who came were not "immigrants" at all, but sojourners who sought work in North America intending to return to Europe. A durable ethnic pecking order evolved in the region: English-speaking Canadians, Britons, and Americans nearest the top, Swedes, Norwegians, and Protestant Germans (until World War I) next, and the laborers and peasant homesteaders from eastern Europe at the bottom.

This ethnically diverse population set the Prairie Provinces apart from the rest of Canada, and to a lesser extent from adjacent states of the United States. English-speaking westerners wanted to force European immigrants to speak English and to conform to British Canadian values, but the sheer numbers of immigrants limited their capacity to do so. The ethnic segregation of both the countryside and the cities of the Prairie Provinces also worked against the assimilation of European immigrants. There were striking differences in the rural and urban populations of particular ethnic groups. More than half of British Isles immigrants lived in cities and towns, but two-thirds of those from the United States were farmers and three-quarters of Ukrainians lived in the countryside.

In the rural Prairie Provinces, ethnic background, time of settlement, available capital, and differing local environments created different agricultural patterns. A handful were large-scale farmers like American immigrant Charles S. Noble, who cultivated 30,000 acres of southern Alberta in 1917, when the average farm was less than 300 acres. Much more numerous were the near-peasant families like the Ukrainian settlers of southeastern Manitoba or northeastern Alberta, who hewed homesteads from the aspen parkland belt, where they found the wood and water that they needed for almost self-sufficient agriculture. Between these extremes were the families in the parkland belt and the river valleys who attempted diversified farming on mixed farms like the ones that they had grown up on in Ontario or the United States. Finally, in the dry plains closest to the Canada-U.S. boundary were the grain growers. For most farm families the goal was economic independence in order to sustain and reproduce the family. Settlers did not set out alone into the unknown, but traveled west with family and friends. The rural society that migrants fashioned in the Canadian Prairie West before 1920 retained elements of traditional rural societies alongside elements of modern industrial society. Settlers within the region shared the settlement experience, cooperated with their neighbors to harvest and to thresh, and took part in the same community activities.

A recession in 1912–13 interrupted immigration to the Prairie Provinces. World War I, which for Canada began in August 1914, stimulated the economy but made migration across the Atlantic impossible and discouraged American immigration. War also made the relationship between immigrant minorities and the English-speaking majority more difficult. English-speaking westerners saw the war as a patriotic duty to the British Empire and a struggle for democratic principles, but their conduct was most undemocratic. Manitoba in 1916 and Saskatchewan in 1918 abolished the educational rights of linguistic minorities and made public schools unilingual; French was treated as a "foreign" language and was eliminated along with German and Ukrainian. English-speaking westerners also enthusiastically supported the wartime internment of Ukrainian immigrants, who posed absolutely no threat, and welcomed the disenfranchisement of naturalized "enemy aliens" in the federal election of 1917.

Over nativist opposition, the flow of immigrants resumed in the mid-1920s. The sources of the flow shifted. Many fewer migrants came from Britain and very few from the United States, and a majority came from central and eastern Europe. Shut out of the United States by the quota system introduced in 1924, Poles, Ukrainians, Mennonites, Czechs, German Russians, and Hungarians chose the Canadian West. The federal government allowed the Canadian Pacific and the Canadian National Railway to recruit immigrants in Europe to do pick-and-shovel work in the resource industries, to work the grain harvest, and to start small farms on quarter-sections in the parkland belt, purchased on time from the railway companies.

Ethnic diversity made the Prairie West polyglot, but it could not make it pluralistic. In Saskatchewan the Ku Klux Klan flourished briefly by connecting nativism and anti-Catholicism. English-speaking westerners attempted to force the newcomers into the mold of Anglo-conformity. But immigrant ethnic identities persisted, not as static transplantations from the Old Country but as identities relocated to and reconstructed within western Canada. Ethnic minorities acculturated to English as necessary but spoke their mother tongue at home: the census reported that in Saskatchewan 70 percent of Germans and more than 90 percent of Ukrainians continued to do so in 1941. They married endogamously in ethnic churches, belonged to ethnic fraternal societies, and maintained distinctive residential and occupational patterns. The minority ethnic identities measured by these demographic characteristics persisted in the Canadian Prairie West longer than they did in Plains states for several structural reasons, including primarily rural residence in Canada, formal and informal block settlement, and the longer continuation of wide-open immigration. Eventually, immigrant communities negotiated their own relationship with Canada and with the dominant British Canadian culture. In the Prairie West, immigrant communities themselves invented the Canadian "multicultural mosaic" three decades before governments discovered and sanctioned it.

Without New Deal programs to entice or

compel small-scale farm families off the land, the economic crisis of the 1930s did not produce an exodus from the Prairie Provinces as it did in the Great Plains states. Some farm families in the Dust Bowl areas stuck it out through drought and depression; others made new farms in the northern reaches of the parkland belt or in Alberta's Peace River country. Not until World War II, which began for Canada in 1939, did military service and jobs in wartime industries initiate the migration of hundreds of thousands of young women and men out of the countryside, and often out of the region. This rural depopulation has continued; in 1996 the three Prairie Provinces had only 132,000 farms as compared to 301,000 in 1936, when the total number of farms reached its peak.

The proportion of immigrants to Canada who chose the Prairie West as their destination fell from more than one in two before 1930 to about one in seven after 1950. The total population of the Prairie West fell from 21 percent of Canada's population in 1941 to 16 percent in 1971, where it has remained. The largest numbers of immigrants who chose the Prairie Provinces in recent decades have come from South, Southeast, or East Asia; 7 percent of Alberta's population traced its origins to these parts of the world in 1996. The collapse of the former Soviet Union and of Yugoslavia also brought small migrations to the Prairie Provinces from longer-established ethnic groups. Whatever their origins, recent immigrants settled overwhelmingly in the large cities—Calgary, Edmonton, or Winnipeg.

Changes in immigration patterns, migration from country to city, and internal migration within the region have profoundly transformed the three Prairie Provinces. Manitoba and especially Saskatchewan experience continued out-migration to Alberta, to the cities of Edmonton and Calgary in particular. The 2001 census showed that Alberta has more than half of the regional population of more than five million. It also showed that, although the Prairie Provinces contain 80 percent of Canada's agricultural land, the number of farm families continues to diminish as a once rural region becomes ever more urban.

See also ASIAN AMERICANS: Asian Canadians / IMAGES AND ICONS: Canadian Mosaic; Last Best West / TRANSPORTATION: Railways, Canada.

John Herd Thompson
Duke University

The Canada Yearbook. Ottawa: Statistics Canada, 1867–2000. Kerr, Donald, and Deryck W. Holdsworth. *Historical Atlas of Canada*. Vol. 3, *Addressing the Twentieth Century 1891–1961*. Toronto: University of Toronto Press, 1990. Lehr, John C., and Yossi Katz. "Crown, Corporation and Church: The Role of Institutions in the Stability of Pioneer Settlements in the Canadian West, 1870–1914." *Journal of Historical Geography* 21 (1995): 413–29.

SETTLEMENT PATTERNS, UNITED STATES

The dominant settlement patterns of the Great Plains of the United States reflect both an initial 1800s pioneer landscape and subsequent changes: the evolution of the region's landscape is a continuing process.

The pioneer settlement process divided the grasslands of North America into a vast checkerboard where squares were separated by section lines, which became roads, field divisions, county lines, and even state lines. The artificially imposed matrix of the U.S. Public Land Survey System, originating with the Ordinance of 1785, obliterated the natural landscapes known to the Native Americans. Six-mile-square townships were divided into thirty-six one-mile-square sections of 640 acres. European-style *strassendorf* villages or earlier New England–style village commons were virtually unknown, since the Homestead Law of 1862 required that homesteaders live on the land they claimed.

The homesteaders flowed into the Great Plains from a wide variety of origins. Native-born Americans moved in generally latitudinal directions from former homes in the eastern United States into the Plains. The children of former pioneers from New York, born in southern Wisconsin in the 1840s and 1850s, were the first American settlers in Dakota Territory in the 1870s and 1880s. To their south, a mixture of settlers from New York, New England, and Pennsylvania pioneered in a belt from Ohio to Iowa, then sent their children on to settle western Nebraska, southern Dakota Territory, and northern Kansas. "Midlanders" from Ohio, Indiana, and Illinois constituted a major flow into Kansas, but that state's southern part in particular was filled from the Upper South, from Missouri, Kentucky, southern Indiana, and southern Illinois. Farther south, in the late-settled American frontiers of Oklahoma and the Texas High Plains, the latitudinal migration was again evident, with settlers coming from Tennessee and the Deep South. African Americans also settled in considerable numbers in Kansas and Oklahoma after the Civil War. Several African American homesteader communities survive.

The population geography was diversified by settlers from Europe. Chain migration, in which early settlers wrote back to the home folks in Scandinavia, Germany, Russia, and the Austro-Hungarian Empire to encourage their migration, led to many ethnic colonies throughout the Plains, many of which survive in some form to the present. In general, the percentage of European-born settlers and their children decreased from north to south. Notable among these groups were the German Russians, who brought hard red winter wheat seed to central Kansas and laid the foundation for the winter wheat belt. Scandinavians overflowed to the Dakotas and Montana from Minnesota and produced a Viking veneer over the Northern Plains. In Kansas and Nebraska, high school teams are still known by such names as the Swedes or Cossacks depending on the origins of the original homesteaders. In Oklahoma, the land rush produced an ethnic pattern that reflected Native American, Confederate refugee, and European origins. On the Texas Plains the pattern was initially dominated by people of southern U.S. and Mexican origin: in the Texas Panhandle in 1880, for example, about

two-thirds of the population had origins in the eastern United States, mainly from the South, while one-fifth of the population was Mexican, mainly from New Mexico. The Latino component of the Plains population continued to grow rapidly during the twentieth century, with a core area in the New Mexico and Texas Plains but also forming a major presence in eastern Colorado, southeastern Kansas, the meatpacking towns of Nebraska, and elsewhere throughout much of the region. This Latino immigration, and a growing Asian population, continue the tradition of a region enriched by waves of migration.

In most areas, homesteaders in the nineteenth century located on dispersed farms of a quarter-section (160 acres). There were occasional interspersed rural schools, churches, and post offices. Initial building construction often utilized native sod, since lumber was not available. Barbed wire fences were used to divide fields because rails were not available either. Sod homes were often replaced by relatively expensive lumber construction as soon as railroads and improved finances made it possible.

The initial village pattern consisted of service centers at critical stream fords and at the intersections of wagon and horse trails. As railroad expansion spread a vast web of iron rails across the Plains, new sites emerged, since steam locomotives required water every eight to ten miles. These watering spots became the nuclei from which permanent villages, towns, or cities emerged. Here sprouted railroad depots, water towers, grain elevators, stockyards, stores, schools, and churches—facilities to enable the dispersed homestead farmers to obtain their supplies, market their products, and provide for their basic living needs. Early communities vied with each other for the right to be the county seat, and occasionally heated battles occurred. Such a role was perceived as essential if a place was to become dominant in the future urban hierarchy.

As the twentieth century progressed, depression and dust bowl conditions modified the settlement pattern, initiating significant changes that continue to the present. Rural free mail delivery led to the discontinuance of many of the open-country post offices. Farm consolidation led to the abandonment of many section-line roads, and operations that were originally farms became ranches. Removal of much of the rural population led to the consolidation of rural schools and churches. The advent of larger railroad steam engines, and then of diesel engines, decreased the need for water-tower villages—only the grain elevator survives in many diminished places. Additionally, improved highways and the use of trucks doomed many of the branch railroads and the villages they served.

The present settlement pattern of the Great Plains reflects this consolidation process and some unique situations. As the farm population consolidated, the need for service centers declined and a few strategically located centers (often county seats) emerged as the dominant centers. This pattern reflects to some extent the division of the Plains into irrigated and nonirrigated areas, with denser settlement patterns in the irrigated oases of the river valleys and High Plains Aquifer.

The original Plains peoples, the Native Americans, remain an important and rapidly growing component of the region's population, especially on the Northern Plains and in Oklahoma. On the reservations, residential villages of Native Americans are interspersed with farms, often occupied by European Americans, which were homesteaded as "surplus" lands or purchased as allotments in the decades following the Dawes Act of 1887. On some reservations, for example the Devils Lake Sioux Reservation in North Dakota, more than three-quarters of the land is owned by non-Natives.

There are some places where the postconsolidation pattern offers some semblance of a European-style settlement pattern. In the German Russian Hutterite colonies of the Dakotas and Montana, large blocks of land were purchased and central residential areas for communal living were constructed. Vagaries of the Great Plains climate and the quest for profit led some large-scale operators to develop "suitcase" and "sidewalk" farming operations. In suitcase farming, the operator has widely spread grain operations necessitating overnight trips for farming. In sidewalk farming, more localized dispersion makes living in a town feasible but still permits scattered fields, so that at least some will escape localized drought and hail hazards. Both types of operations have led to the semblance of a compact farming-village settlement pattern.

The settlement patterns of the Great Plains reflect the sum total of the effects of these ongoing processes. Native Americans, who only 150 years ago were the region's sole inhabitants, have been relegated to relatively small areas. Throughout the region a pattern of large-scale farms is interspersed with abundant artifacts of a much denser network of farmsteads, railroads, and villages. At regular intervals surviving towns continue to offer supplies, markets, and life services to an increasingly diverse population.

See also AGRICULTURE: Suitcase Farming / CITIES AND TOWNS: Small Towns / TRANSPORTATION: Railroads, United States.

John L. Dietz
University of Northern Colorado

Hudson, John C. "Who Was 'Forest Man'? Sources of Migration to the Plains." *Great Plains Quarterly* 6 (1986): 69–83. Kraenzel, Carl F. *The Great Plains in Transition.* Norman: University of Oklahoma Press, 1955. Shortridge, James R. *Peopling the Plains: Who Settled Where in Frontier Kansas.* Lawrence: University Press of Kansas, 1995.

SIMPSON, GEORGE (1787–1860)

Sir George Simpson, in his role as governor of the Hudson's Bay Company territories in North America from 1826 to 1860, had a major impact on the development of the Canadian Prairies. He visited the region frequently, inspecting posts, meeting with the chief factors who supervised each district, organizing the government of the Red River Settlement in Assiniboia (which the Hudson's Bay Company had originally granted to the Earl of Selkirk in 1812, then reacquired in 1836), or simply passing through rapidly, as he did on his journey to the Columbia River in 1824–25.

Simpson was suited for a life spent in remote places (although after 1833, following his marriage to his cousin Frances Ramsey Simpson, he was based at Lachine, near Montreal), having been born in distant Rosshire, Scotland, in 1787. As a young man he clerked for a London firm that did business in the West Indies. He must have impressed, because in 1820 the Hudson's Bay Company sent him to Canada as a possible replacement for Governor William Williams, who seemed likely to be arrested in the conflict with the North West Company. After the two companies amalgamated in 1821, Simpson was appointed governor of the Northern Department. Five years later he was put in charge of the entire North American operations.

Governor Simpson was an autocratic administrator who prioritized economy and efficiency. Immediately following the 1821 merger he inaugurated a series of reforms akin to modern-day corporate restructuring. He radically reduced the number of employees, closed unproductive posts, and overhauled the transportation system. He cut back on gift-giving and the provision of credit to the Native trappers and curtailed the use of alcohol as a trade inducement, ostensibly for the Native people's own good but also to economize. And, with considerable insight, he worked to put the fur trade on a sustained-yield basis: Native trappers were encouraged to rotate their trapping grounds, to refrain from taking cub beaver, and to trap different animals in alternating seasons to allow populations to recover. Recognizing that it would be difficult to force the Native peoples to adopt such alien conservation practices, Simpson also periodically opened and closed trading posts to draw the Native people to different trapping grounds, thus achieving the same goals. In the region between the South Saskatchewan and Missouri Rivers, however, where competition with American traders was intense, he suspended conservation measures and set out to create a "fur desert" that would keep Americans out. Simpson's management systems worked: from 1825 to 1860 Hudson's Bay Company stockholders never earned dividends of less than 10 percent a year.

Simpson was knighted in 1841 for his service to the Hudson's Bay Company and his contributions to exploration. He died of apoplexy in Lachine on September 7, 1860, leaving behind a considerable fortune, as well as five legitimate and, from his "country marriages," five illegitimate children.

See also INDUSTRY: Hudson's Bay Company.

David J. Wishart
University of Nebraska–Lincoln

Ray, Arthur J. *Indians in the Fur Trade: Their Role as Trappers, Hunters, and Middlemen in the Lands Southwest of Hudson Bay, 1660–1870.* Toronto: University of Toronto Press, 1974.

SPANIARDS

From the Andean highlands and central Mexico to the northern reaches of the upper Rio Grande, Spanish citizens worked to meet the crown's unquenchable thirst for mineral wealth, new lands, and Catholic converts. However, while Spain's efforts proved successful elsewhere, they were met with sound defeat in the Great Plains. The story of Spaniards in the Great Plains, therefore, is mainly one of Spanish explorers.

The first Spaniards to reach the Great Plains (the specific geography of their route is unknown) were Álvar Núñez Cabeza de Vaca, Andrés Dorantes, and Castillo Maldonado, along with Estevan, an African Arab. They were the only survivors of the disastrous Panfilo de Narváez expedition. Their eventful journey—from about 1529 to 1536—back to what is now Mexico took them across the Southern Plains of Texas. Cabeza de Vaca and his men arrived in Mexico City claiming to have seen such marvels as herds of buffalo and cities of gold. The reports quickly led the Spanish crown to commission an expedition to secure the purported riches.

In the same manner as other Spanish conquistadors before him, Francisco Vásquez de Coronado set out north from Mexico in 1540 with hopes of attaining great wealth and fame. His initial goal was to find the fabled Seven Cities of Cíbola. He found instead Pueblo villages lacking in any great wealth. Disillusioned at not finding the seven golden cities, he was easily persuaded (by the stories of an Indian slave) to continue his search in a more easterly direction. In 1541 Coronado and thirty of his men struck out across the Llano Estacado looking for Quivira, another illusionary place of wealth. Quivira turned out to be only the grass lodges of the Wichitas, near Great Bend, Kansas. Disappointed again, he retreated to New Mexico. His report to the crown indicated that while the country was of great agricultural potential and similar to Spain, it held no place for Spaniards; simply put, there was no gold.

It was almost two centuries after Coronado before Spaniards again pushed deep into the Great Plains. In 1720 Don Pedro de Villasur was sent to investigate French activities in the Central Plains. His expedition took him as far north and east as the Platte River in central Nebraska, where his party was attacked and defeated by Otoes and Pawnees. This disaster marked the end of the Spanish presence in the Central Plains, except for fur traders, most notably the Missouri Fur Company under Manuel Lisa, who pushed up the Missouri River from St. Louis in the late years of the eighteenth century and early years of the nineteenth century. Spain primarily focused its attention on maintaining sovereignty over the Southern Plains of New Mexico, Colorado, Oklahoma, and Texas.

While Spaniards persevered as explorers, they failed miserably as Great Plains settlers. Permanent Spanish settlement on the Plains did not begin until 1757. In a deceptive ploy aimed at forming an alliance against their archenemy the Comanches, the Lipua Apaches petitioned the Spanish government to establish a mission on the banks of the San Saba River near present-day Menard, Texas. The settlement was a failure, however, because few Apaches converted to Catholicism, and on March 16, 1758, the Comanches attacked the village, killing all but four residents and burning the mission buildings to the ground. For approximately ten years the Spanish government tried to resurrect the mission community, but to no avail. The settlement was finally abandoned in 1770, thus ending Spain's attempt at founding a mission settlement in the territory of the Plains Indians. In 1786 the Spanish entered into a treaty with the Comanches, which ushered in a period of accommodation and trade, rather than settlement, on the Southwestern Plains.

By 1821, the year in which political control of the Southern Plains was transferred to the newly formed Mexican government and the Santa Fe Trail opened, the region was still unsettled by Spaniards. Hispanos (Spanish Americans) had spread their sheep operations east into the Great Plains from the upper Rio Grande, occupying a territory that would, by 1900, extend out into the Texas and Oklahoma Panhandles, but that was the extent of the Spanish influence.

Despite the best efforts of the Spanish crown, permanent Spanish settlements in the Great Plains failed for at least four reasons. First, there was little to attract Spanish citizens to the Great Plains. Expeditions became tedious marches through a vast, seemingly empty land, where nothing of value was found to warrant the price of settlement. Second, the Spanish system of employing Indian labor could not be applied to the mobile people of the Plains. The Plains Indians were too nomadic and too independent to be restricted to settlements. Third, the Plains Indians quickly and violently opposed Spanish infiltration. After the Apaches acquired the horse in 1684 and the Comanches in about 1714, they no longer tolerated the Spaniards invading their land. Finally, despite the fact that they alone among European colonizers were accustomed to arid climates, Spaniards regarded the physical environment as too inhospitable. The barren Llano Estacado of west Texas, for example, was perceived as nothing more than a transition zone, a land to be politically controlled but not necessarily settled. Spain preferred to use the Great Plains as a buffer zone protecting its northern colonies from French and, later, American interference.

Today, the Spanish legacy in the Great Plains has all but faded. Hispanos still live, as minorities, in Plains towns such as Roswell, New Mexico, and Pueblo, Colorado, but their numbers have been surpassed by the inmigration of Latinos since World War II.

See also HISPANIC AMERICANS: Hispano Homeland; San Sabá Mission and Presidio.

Jeffrey S. Smith
Kansas State University

Vigil, Ralph H., Frances W. Kaye, and John R. Wunder. *Spain and the Plains: Myths and Realities of Spanish Exploration and Settlement on the Great Plains*. Niwot: University Press of Colorado, 1994. Webb, Walter Prescott. *The Great Plains*. New York: Grosset and Dunlap, 1931. Weber, David J. *The Spanish Frontier in North America*. New Haven CT: Yale University Press, 1992.

SWEDES

Swedes settled the U.S. Great Plains and Canadian Prairies as a part of their mass migration to North America from the 1860s on, many coming via settlements in Illinois, then the cradle of Swedish America. They followed the river valleys and railways, many enticed by propaganda from the states, railroads, and steamship companies, or by the individual efforts of ethnic colonizers and churchmen. Old established settlements in the eastern Plains and Prairies gave birth to new colonies farther to the west; in addition, many immigrants settled directly from Sweden.

The Swedish-born population peaked in the period 1890 to 1910, with most subsequent migration flowing from farming communities to urban areas such as Winnipeg, Fargo, Omaha, and Kansas City. In 1930 the Swedish-born population was most apparent in Nebraska (12 percent of the foreign-born), Kansas (10.5 percent), South Dakota (10 percent), North Dakota (8 percent), and Texas (4.1 percent). At that time, the Swedes outnumbered all other Scandinavian groups in Nebraska, Kansas, Texas, and Oklahoma. Swedes operated mixed grain, livestock, and wheat farms, worked as contractors and builders, and quickly became upwardly mobile in the professions, especially the second generation. Swedes established many ethnic institutions such as hospitals, schools, clubs, and newspapers. Of those who had a religious affiliation, most were Augustana Lutheran, Mission Covenant, Methodist, or Baptist. At present, Texas leads the Plains states in the absolute number of persons of Swedish heritage, though most Swedes in Texas are outside the Plains, followed by Nebraska and Kansas. Nebraska, North Dakota, and South Dakota have the highest percentage of Swedes compared to other ethnic groups. Traditional ethnic festivals such as *Midsommar* and Santa Lucia are celebrated at various places throughout the region.

Sven Magnus Swenson, leader of a contingent from Nässjö, Sweden, established a colony of Swedes on the fertile, waxy prairies of eastern Texas in the 1860s. Blanketing Travis and Williamson Counties, the Swenson settlement today is the largest contiguous Swedish settlement in Texas. Wheat farming, cattle breeding, and cotton production were the early pursuits. The old settlements of East Texas generated offshoots elsewhere, and today people of Swedish heritage are found in most Texas counties. Their urban presence is greatest in Austin, Houston, and Galveston. Swedish Lutherans founded Trinity College at Round Rock, and Swedish Methodists founded Texas Wesleyan College at Austin. Swedes in Oklahoma have been relatively few in number, with the overwhelming share of them in Oklahoma City and Tulsa.

Swedish settlers in Kansas mainly followed the Kansas, Big Blue, and Republican River valleys west. Today, persons of Swedish ancestry are in nearly all Kansas counties, with the greatest concentrations in McPherson, Saline, Wyandotte, Shawnee, Osage, Republic, and Riley Counties. Mariadahl, the oldest Swedish enclave, was established in the Big Blue Valley in the 1850s. The First Swedish Colonization Company, founded in Chicago in 1868, was instrumental in establishing the Lindsborg Colony (Saline and McPherson Counties), today the largest rural concentration of Swedes in Kansas. The largest urban concentrations are in Kansas City, Topeka, and Salina, all important transit cities in the early phases of Swedish migration. From eastern Kansas and Lindsborg the Swedes dispersed westward, establishing Swedesburg and Walsby on the Republican River, as well as a spattering of settlements elsewhere identified by names like Stockholm. Bethany College, founded in 1881 in Lindsborg, is one of the Swedes' most notable and enduring contributions.

Swedish Americans are found throughout Nebraska, but the heaviest concentrations are in the eastern urban centers of Omaha and Lincoln. In 1930 more than 10 percent of the population of Omaha was Swedish-born. Large rural settlements coalesced at Wahoo, Malmo, and Swedeburg in Saunders County, just west of Omaha; Oakland in Burt County; Polk, Swedehome, and Stromsburg in Polk County; and Axtell and Holdrege in Kearney and Phelps Counties, respectively. The Swedes founded Lutheran College at Wahoo, Immanuel Deaconess Institute in Omaha, Bethphage Mission for tuberculosis patients at Axtell, a children's home at Holdrege, and hospital facilities sponsored by the Swedish Covenant Church and Augustana Synod.

Swedish migration into the Dakotas was primarily individual, not group, so extensive colonies like those in Kansas and Nebraska were never formed. Swedes followed the Northern Pacific and Great Northern Railroads and settled in farm and small-town settings among the more numerous Norwegians. Harwood, dating from 1870–71, is the oldest Swedish settlement in North Dakota. Swedes have a notable presence in Fargo, Grand Forks, Minot, Bismarck, and Williston, as well as in smaller places like Finley, Prosper, Sheyenne, and Kenmore. In South Dakota the Swedes are most numerous in Sioux Falls and elsewhere in Minnehaha County. Swedes also settled in considerable numbers in the Dalsburg and Komstad districts in Clay County near Vermillion; Alcester and Big Springs in adjacent Union County; and in other eastern districts.

Most Swedes migrated to the Canadian Prairies via the northern United States. They followed the tracks of the Canadian Pacific and Canadian National Railways, mostly westward from Winnipeg, and took up residence alongside other Nordic migrants, especially the Norwegians. They avoided the dry prairies, settling the parklands of mixed grass–woodlands, and established themselves as lumbermen and agriculturists in mostly mixed farm and wheat operations. The Swedish element gravitated toward the professions in Prairie towns and cities. In 1930, 40 percent of the Swedes in Manitoba lived in Winnipeg and its suburbs, most of them employed as industrial, craft, and railroad workers. Logan Avenue emerged as the hub of the Swedish enclave in Winnipeg. Sizable rural enclaves emerged at Lac du Bonnet and Teulon–Norris Lake near Winnipeg; Eriksdale, Lillesve, and Erickson-Scandinavia north of Winnipeg; and Stockholm and Percival in Saskatchewan. In 1930 Swedes constituted 0.8 percent of the foreign-born population of the Canadian Prairies. Their largest absolute numbers were in Saskatchewan and Alberta. In recent years Swedish Canadians, like other Canadians, have been drawn to the oil industries in the Calgary and Edmonton regions.

See also ARCHITECTURE: Swedish Architecture.

Ann M. Legreid
Central Missouri State University

Benson, Adolph B., and Naboth Hedin. *Americans from Sweden*. New York: J. B. Lippincott, 1950. Kastrup, Allen. *The Swedish Heritage in America*. St. Paul MN: North Central Publishing Company, 1975. Nelson, Helge. *The Swedes and Swedish Settlements in North America*. New York: Bonnier, 1943.

THOMPSON, DAVID (1770–1857)

David Thompson was schooled for a career in the Royal Navy; at the end of the Seven Years War, when the navy was downsized, he was apprenticed instead to the Hudson's Bay Company. His first years in the fur trade were spent at the bay and along the North and South Saskatchewan Rivers. At the inland posts he was caught up in the rivalry between the Hudson's Bay Company and Canadian traders who had recently joined together as partners in the North West Company. In 1778–88 the young man went "a full month's march at about fifteen miles a day . . . over a fine country" west–southwest of the river posts in order to trade with "Peeagans" camped along the front ranges. Thompson's rudimentary knowledge of Cree allowed him to converse with Sark-a-map-pee, an old man who had personal experience of the Plains tribes' shifting alliances and the smallpox epidemic of 1781. Five years later Peter Fidler, a fellow Hudson's Bay Company apprentice, also wintered with "Peeagans" and served at the Saskatchewan River posts.

A broken leg forced Thompson to winter at Cumberland House, which he wrote, "by the mercy of God turned out to be the best thing that ever happened to me." He and Fidler studied surveying with Philip Turnor, sent from England to verify claims of Peter Pond's map of Northwest America. Both apprentices became accomplished surveyors and cartographers. But after ten years of routine inland trade Thompson grew impatient to explore and chart beyond the Hudson's Bay Company's trading frontier. In 1797 he left his winter post in the "Rat Country" west of Hudson Bay and joined the North West Company.

In order to regulate their southwest trade, the partners from Canada commissioned Thompson to ascertain the positions of the Missouri and Mississippi headwaters relative to Lake Superior and Lake of the Woods. As of 1792 the forty-ninth parallel had been proposed as the western boundary between British and American territories. This line would replace the earlier treaty of 1783 that agreed on a border along the supposed northerly source of the Mississippi near Lake of the Woods.

Thompson's route for this survey lay south to the Assiniboine River and south again to Turtle Mountain and the Souris River. He and his nine men walked overland in December storms, finding little shelter or wood and few animals to hunt. The only advantage to traveling so late in the season was a lowered risk of running into "Sieux," who would have opposed their trade with the "Mandanes." On December 30, 1797, Thompson arrived at the first of five villages of "Mandanes" and "Willow" or "Fall Indians" located near the junction of the Missouri and Knife Rivers. He stayed for two weeks, long enough to map the region, compile a vocabulary, and inquire how the hundreds of domed houses were built. Thompson wrote that his time was "spent in noticing their Manners and conversing about their Policy, Wars, Country, Traditions, &c &c." Watchful for the interests of the North West Company, he concluded that "no hopes could be entertained of their ever coming to our Settlements to Trade—indeed they seem to have but little that is valuable to us." Nothing in this remark indicates awareness of the importance of the villages in a long-distance network of Native trade. In 1803 Samuel King would use Thompson's survey of this region as well as Fidler's information on the upper Missouri to draw a map for Lewis and Clark. The American explorers wintered at the "Mandane" villages in 1804–5.

Soon after his return to the Assiniboine River in the spring of 1798, Thompson set out again to discover the source of the Mississippi, which he identified as "Turtle Lake in Latitude 47.39.15 N Longitude 95.12.45 W." As Thompson explained, the supposition of a more northerly source was due to "the Fur Traders . . . counting every pipe a League of three miles at the end of which they claimed a right to rest and smoke a pipe. By my survey I found these pipes to be the average length of only two miles, and they also threw out of account the windings of the River." This location, while not exact, at least placed the Mississippi well south of Lake of the Woods and was crucial in promoting the forty-ninth parallel as the international boundary across the Plains.

Unlike these two trips of 1797–98, Thompson's later explorations west of the continental divide were once more subordinated to his role as trader. From 1807 to 1812 Thompson worked to establish a new fur-trade department between two Rocky Mountain passes and the mouth of the Columbia River. He also surveyed this region, later incorporating his regional charts into three huge manuscript maps of the continent from Hudson Bay and

the Great Lakes to the Pacific Ocean. The historical construction of a "race to the sea," which places Thompson a poor third behind the Corps of Discovery and the Astorians, misreads Thompson's fur-trade role and his most important contribution to western exploration: his patient, meticulous mapping of the Columbia River from source to sea.

Thompson retired from the fur trade in 1812 but continued survey work for the international border along the Great Lakes and in Lower Canada. His hope of a comfortable settled life vanished with poor investments; he was still camping with survey crews when he was well past sixty years of age. In 1845 he began a commentary on his years in the fur trade, based on the journals he had kept during that period. The fluent, poetic style of this text has made it a favorite among exploration accounts since its publication in 1916. Some of his journals have also been edited: these terse, detailed, professional records are of great interest to regional and fur-trade historians.

See also POLITICS AND GOVERNMENT: Forty-ninth Parallel.

Barbara Belyea
University of Calgary

Thompson, David. *Columbia Journals*, edited by Barbara Belyea. Montreal: McGill-Queen's University Press, 1994. Thompson, David. *Narrative*, edited by Richard Glover. Toronto: Champlain Society, 1962. Wood, W. Raymond, and Thomas D. Thiessen. *Early Fur Trade on the Northern Plains: Canadian Traders among the Mandan Indians, 1738–1818*. Norman: University of Oklahoma Press, 1985.

UKRAINIANS

Ukrainians from the provinces of Galicia and Bukovyna, two rural backwaters of the Austro-Hungarian Empire, settled large areas of the Canadian Prairies and some small areas of the Northern Great Plains. They were pushed to migrate by poor economic conditions. Most land in western Ukraine was owned by the aristocracy; peasant farms were mostly fragmented, small, and inefficient. Even for those with land, the system of inheritance promised to reduce the size of their offsprings' holdings. For most peasants the economic outlook was dismal.

In 1880s Germans from Galicia had emigrated to Alberta. News of their progress reached Ivan Pylypiv in Nebyliv, Kalush County. Contemplating emigration, Pylypiv and another Nebyliv peasant, Vasyl Elyniak, traveled to Canada in 1891 to visit the Alberta German colony at Josephburg. They returned to bring out others to settle at Star, near Josephburg, in 1892. By 1895 chain migration had brought in some thirty-eight families, all from Nebyliv and the neighboring district.

In 1895 Dr. Josef Oleskiv, a professor of agriculture at Lviv who was concerned about the growing emigration of Ukrainians to Brazil, published a pamphlet, *Pro vilni zemli* (*About free lands*), advising against emigration to Brazil and suggesting Canada as an alternative. After a visit to Canada he gave it his endorsement in *O emigratsii* (*On emigration*), a pamphlet widely circulated in western Ukraine.

Oleskiv hoped to secure exclusive rights to manage Ukrainian emigration to Canada so as to prevent the emigration of unprepared or undesirable settlers. The Canadians balked at this, but they nevertheless cooperated with him. The emigrants he recruited were regarded as the best-prepared and best-led Ukrainian settlers to enter Canada.

Oleskiv's work triggered a surge of emigration to Canada in the late 1890s, over which he soon lost control. Lured by visions of free land, and often with unrealistic expectations of rapid economic progress, thousands of Ukrainians from Galicia and Bukovyna emigrated to Canada. Before 1905, families seeking land predominated; thereafter, single men, many of whom sought work in western mines and cities before taking land, formed the majority. A small proportion, a few hundred at the most, were lured to North Dakota by American agents in Winnipeg. By the time the outbreak of war in Europe halted emigration in 1914, some 170,000 Ukrainians had arrived in Canada.

Ukrainians settled in a series of large blocks that arced across the northern fringe of the aspen-parkland belt from southeastern Manitoba through Saskatchewan into central Alberta. This distinctive pattern of settlement resulted from the interplay of an array of forces: the environmental preferences of the immigrants; their economic circumstances upon arrival; the immigrants' desire to settle alongside their friends, relatives, and countrymen; the presence of German-speaking settlers from Ukraine (with whom they could communicate); the availability of off-farm work; and the concern of the Canadian government to prevent the growth of massive blocks of foreign settlers. Unchecked chain migration worried Canadian officials because it created massive blocks of Ukrainian settlements. Only with great difficulty were newcomers induced to pioneer in new areas to create new settlement nuclei, thereby fragmenting Ukrainian settlement and facilitating assimilation.

Ukrainian settlers resisted placement on the open prairie since the vast majority were from the wooded foothill regions on the eastern flank of the Carpathians and so had no experience of steppeland agriculture, nor did they have sufficient capital to contemplate immediate entry into commercial agriculture. Instead they chose to occupy wooded lands that were often marginal in terms of their long-term agricultural potential but offered a wide resource base for those bent on self-sufficiency and mixed farming. Wood was seen as a vital resource for building, fencing, and use as fuel. Long-term economic progress was sacrificed to secure immediate survival. Most Ukrainian settlers were dependent on off-farm work to generate capital for farm development, and for decades they "worked out" on threshing crews, railroad construction gangs, and in regional resource industries.

Ukrainian settlements were also shaped internally by chain migration. Immigrants from Galicia, mostly Ukrainian Catholics, settled separately from those from Bukovyna, who were mostly Ukrainian Orthodox. Further groupings by district, village of origin, and extended family were also common.

The interwar years brought a second, smaller wave of immigration from Ukraine to western Canada. Some homesteaded on the agricultural margins but most gravitated to the cities, where they joined established Ukrainian communities. Farm consolidation and opportunities in urban centers saw Ukrainian rural communities decline, while the proportion of Ukrainians in the parkland cities of Winnipeg, Saskatoon, and Edmonton increased dramatically. The postwar years saw a third wave of Ukrainian immigration into Canada, of which a small proportion gravitated to Prairie cities. The Ukrainian community still reflects its origins in its internal divisions on the basis of religious affiliation, political orientation, and, to some extent, time of immigration.

See also ARCHITECTURE: Ukrainian Architecture.

John C. Lehr
University of Winnipeg

Kaye, Vladimir J. *Early Ukrainian Settlements in Canada, 1895–1900.* Toronto: University of Toronto Press, 1964. Lehr, John C. "Peopling the Prairies with Ukrainians." In *Canada's Ukrainians, Negotiating an Identity*, edited by Lubomyr Luciuk and Stella Hryniuk. Toronto: University of Toronto Press, 1991: 30–52. Martynovytch, Orest. *Ukrainians in Canada: The Formative Period 1891–1924.* Edmonton: Canadian Institute of Ukrainian Studies Press, University of Alberta, 1991.

VÉRENDRYE FAMILY

Pierre Gaultier de Varennes, the Sieur de la Vérendrye, was born in Trois Rivières, Canada, on November 16, 1685. He served briefly in the army, married in Quebec in 1712, and fathered four sons and a daughter. The rest of his life was devoted to the western fur trade and exploration. In 1727 he was appointed commandant of the Posts of the North, which then consisted of three forts on the west side of Lake Superior. From that beginning, he established a string of small forts that extended deep into the Plains north and west of Lake Superior in what is now southern Ontario and Manitoba. These forts established the claim of New France to this western country and challenged the English fur traders based at Hudson Bay. He and his sons went on to be the first Europeans to explore what is now southern Manitoba and western North and South Dakota.

La Vérendrye and his sons established Fort St. Pierre in 1727, Fort St. Charles in 1732, Fort Maurepas in 1734, Fort Dauphin about 1741, and finally, Fort La Reine on October 3, 1738. Fort La Reine was on the Assiniboine River directly south of Lake Manitoba. On October 18, 1738, La Vérendrye, two of his sons, and a party of about fifty men moved southwest from Fort La Reine. Accompanied by Assiniboine Indians who joined them on the march, they reached the Mandan villages near the junction of the Heart and Missouri Rivers on December 3. After a brief trading session, he left two men there to learn the Mandan language and, seriously ill, departed on the 13th.

In 1742 his two younger sons, François and Louis-Joseph, returned to the Mandan villages, and on July 23 they struck out to the southwest, eventually approaching some high, wooded mountains. Most historians believe these mountains were the Black Hills of South Dakota, although they may have been the Big Horn Mountains of northern Wyoming. Because of the generalized nature of their narrative it is impossible to be certain either of their destination or the identity of most of the Indian tribes they met during their travels. Whatever their route, it is certain that they returned to the Mandans by way of the mouth of the Bad River, near what is now Pierre, South Dakota, for the discovery there in 1913 of a lead plate left by their party provides the only indisputable point of reference for their eleven-month expedition from the Mandan villages.

The brothers had hoped to discover the "Western Sea," and their long search was a disappointment both for their father and his superiors. La Vérendrye was recalled and replaced as commandant in 1744. Much of his exploration had been done at his own expense, and he was deeply in debt. When his successor left the post two years later, La Vérendrye resumed his former position, but his explorations were over. Before his death on December 6, 1749, La Vérendrye was awarded the coveted Cross of St. Louis. He had opened the Canadian West for the French but they ignored his explorations, and it was left to the British to occupy the Prairie Provinces of Canada. His trials, expenditures, and sacrifices for New France had been in vain.

W. Raymond Wood
University of Missouri–Columbia

Burpee, Lawrence J. *Journals and Letters of Pierre Gaultier de Varennes de la Vérendrye and His Sons.* Publications of the Champlain Society, vol. 16. Toronto: Ballantyne Press, 1927. Smith, G. Hubert. *Explorations of the La Vérendryes in the Northern Plains. 1738–1743*, edited by W. Raymond Wood. Lincoln: University of Nebraska Press, 1980.

VIAL, PEDRO (ca. 1746–1814)

Born in Lyons, France, around 1746, Pedro (Pierre) Vial was one of the earliest European explorers and trailblazers on the Southern Plains. From 1787 to 1809 he served as a guide, interpreter, negotiator, and pathfinder in the Spanish Borderlands. Little is known of Vial's early life, but by the early 1770s he was probably trapping on the Missouri River. During the 1770s he lived periodically with various Southern Plains Indians, plying his trade as a gunsmith. Vial's relationship with Plains Indian tribes would help him during his many journeys across the Plains in later years.

Vial made his first trip across the Plains in 1786–87, when Texas governor Domingo Cebello commissioned him to find a route between the Spanish provincial capitals of San Antonio, Texas, and Santa Fe, New Mexico. Vial left San Antonio on October 4, 1786, with a single companion and a packhorse. The pair headed north and then followed the Red and

Canadian Rivers across the Plains, reaching Santa Fe on May 26, 1787. Although the trail he established was not a direct route and would be rerouted the following year, Vial was the first European to travel overland between the two settlements.

Using Santa Fe as a home base after 1787, Vial traversed the Plains on numerous occasions in the service of Spain. In 1788, for example, he blazed a trail from Santa Fe to Natchitoches (Louisiana). Concerned with American activity in the trans-Mississippi region, New Mexico governor Fernando de la Concha assigned Vial in 1792 to find a route from Santa Fe to St. Louis. He and two companions left Santa Fe on May 21, crossing the Plains via the Canadian, Arkansas, and Kansas Rivers; much of this route comprised the later Santa Fe Trail. On his return trip, Vial went up the Missouri River to the mouth of the Little Nemaha River (present-day Nebraska) where he established relations with the Pawnee Indians. Between 1795 and 1806 he visited Pawnee territory at least four times: in 1795 the Spanish government sent him to negotiate a peace treaty between the Pawnees and Comanches, and in 1805 he went back to find out about the Lewis and Clark expedition. Vial apparently retired from government service in 1809 and settled permanently in Santa Fe. He did not marry and had no children. Pedro Vial died there in October 1814.

Mark R. Ellis
University of Nebraska at Kearney

Bannon, John Francis. *The Spanish Borderlands Frontier: 1513–1821.* Albuquerque: University of New Mexico Press, 1974. Loomis, Noel B., and Abraham P. Nasatir. *Pedro Vial and the Roads to Santa Fe.* Norman: University of Oklahoma Press, 1967.

VILLASUR, PEDRO DE

(ca. late seventeenth century–1720)

Don Pedro de Villasur, a Spanish government official and military officer, led a disastrous expedition north into modern Nebraska in 1720. Born a Castilian nobleman in the late seventeenth century, he died on August 13, 1720, in a battle against Pawnee and Otoe Indians. In the early eighteenth century he reached the Americas, where he became a sublieutenant at El Paso, then later a war captain and alcalde at Santa Barbara, Nueva Vizcaya. By 1719 he had risen to be lieutenant governor of New Mexico. To find out what their French rivals planned to the north, Governor Antonio Valverde de Cosio sent Villasur, an inexperienced officer, on a reconnaissance mission.

The expedition, consisting of forty-two veteran soldiers, three settlers, sixty Pueblo Natives, chaplain Juan Minguez, chief scout Jose Naranjo, and interpreter Jean L'Archeveque, set out on June 16, 1720, from the Santa Fe presidio. They crossed the Sangre de Cristo Mountains, then moved north to modern Pueblo, Colorado. From there they pushed across the Plains of eastern Colorado to the South Platte River, which they followed to the Platte and down into what is now eastern Nebraska. There, Villasur sent a captive Pawnee to parley at a nearby village.

Negotiations with the Pawnees collapsed after two days. The other officers convinced Villasur that the situation had reached a crisis, and they retreated fifty miles upstream to the Loup River near modern-day Columbus, Nebraska. That night the sentries heard noises in the dark, but Villasur responded only by sending Pueblos to look around. In the early morning of August 13, 1720, while the groggy Spanish rounded up their horses, a united band of Pawnees and Otoes attacked. Most of the Pueblos escaped, while the disoriented Spaniards milled around on foot and fell victim to the attackers' musket fire. Thirteen soldiers and one settler managed to escape, but they left behind forty-five dead, including eleven Pueblos and thirty-two Spaniards, Villasur among them. All the survivors were wounded, but the attackers themselves had suffered so heavily that they could not give chase.

Subsequently, many Spaniards seriously questioned Valverde's decision to allow an inexperienced lieutenant such as Villasur to lead such an important mission, blaming this officer's mistakes in leadership for the massacre. Valverde was found guilty of negligence by a court of inquiry but had only to pay a small fine. Despite its tragic end, Villasur's expedition remains important because it was the most northerly penetration by the Spanish into North America and the only Spanish incursion into Nebraska.

Steven Jackman
University of Nebraska–Lincoln

Hotz, Gottfried. *The Segesser Hide Paintings: Masterpieces Depicting Spanish Colonial New Mexico.* Santa Fe: Museum of New Mexico Press, 1991. Jones, Oakah L. *Pueblo Warriors and Spanish Conquest.* Norman: University of Oklahoma Press, 1966. Thomas, Alfred B. *After Coronado: Spanish Exploration Northeast of New Mexico, 1696–1727.* Norman: University of Oklahoma Press, 1935.

WELSH

The Welsh are one of the least numerous of the ethnic groups that settled in the Great Plains. The peak of immigration of the Welsh to America was at the beginning of the twentieth century, but the ten American states of the Great Plains showed only 7,259 people born in Wales at this time, with another 542 in the Canadian Prairies, but as the latter area was settled the Canadian numbers grew to 3,597 in 1911 and 5,980 in 1921. However, all these figures are probably underestimates since the Welsh were often grouped with the English or British ethnic categories. In recent censuses the numbers of Welsh recording a single ancestry are among the lowest of all ethnic groups, due to high levels of intermarriage with other peoples and cultural absorption.

Although the numerical contribution is small, the Welsh have made important contributions to the development of the region. Several of the earliest European pioneers in the exploration and mapping of the northern reaches of the Great Plains, including David Thompson and John Thomas Evans, came from Wales. But it was the development of agricultural settlement in the region that at-

tracted significant numbers of Welsh people. The largest and most persistent of the agricultural concentrations are in Emporia, Kansas, beginning in 1856–58, and Edmunds County, South Dakota, beginning in 1883, with several other smaller clusters, such as Arvonia, Kansas, and Richardson County, Nebraska, forming in the 1860s and 1870s. Small concentrations of Welsh miners were also attracted to Coal and Pittsburg Counties in Oklahoma after 1880 and Cambria County in Wyoming after 1867.

In Canada also, two rural settlement areas associated with the Welsh stand out. The Wood River area east of Ponoka in Alberta developed in 1900–1905 and attained a peak of around 200 people in 1910. Although some of the settlers had been born in Wales, many were American-born (mainly in Kansas and Nebraska), so the Wood River settlement was largely a Welsh American initiative. Of the two original Welsh chapels, Zion still survives, although regular services ended in 1995. Another Welsh area, of approximately the same size, was established near Bangor, Saskatchewan, in 1902–3, but again these were largely first- and second-generation Welsh, this time from Patagonia, Argentina. The concentration of names of Welsh origin still survives in the area, and services are still held in two of the original four churches, Llewellyn Bethel United and St. David's Anglican, although the use of Welsh died out in the 1930s.

The fact that these two primary rural settlements in the Canadian Prairies were settled by Welsh from outside Wales indicates the pull of other areas upon potential Welsh immigrants to the Great Plains. However, the negative comments about working conditions in western Canada from a group of young Welshmen who worked on the construction of the Crowsnest Pass railway line west of Lethbridge in 1897–98 might have also discouraged potential Welsh immigrants. Their complaints received wide publicity in Britain and led immigrant agents to try to cover up the bad news. Nevertheless, small numbers of Welsh continued to immigrate to the coal-mining areas and also to the bigger cities, many of which had Welsh churches by the 1920s.

Vestiges of the Welsh cultural heritage still survive in many areas, such as the celebration of St. David's Day on March 1 in Emporia, Kansas, and the annual Gymanfa Ganu, a chapel-based singing festival in Ponoka, Alberta, in August. In mining areas the Welsh often played an important part in political and workforce activity, for many of the Welsh had known the value of union activity in their homeland. But many of the Welsh were also known for their piety, so in most settlement areas and the bigger cities Nonconformist chapels were built and became the focus of Welsh cultural life.

Unfortunately, the small size of most of the Welsh rural settlements, their distances apart, and the inability to reinforce cultural heritage through continued emigration from the homeland led to the decline in cultural separateness. In addition, the loss of the Welsh language in many of the industrial areas of Wales and the decline of the Nonconformist religion provided a further blow to the distinctiveness of Welsh immigrants. In industrial areas, the limited economic life of most mines exacerbated the problem of cultural survival, for people were forced to move on once the mine was exhausted. In most large cities in the region the same decline in cultural identity can also be seen, and the Welsh churches that were the focus of communities closed in the decades before and after World War II. However active Welsh societies can still be found in most large cities, while the Welsh passion for rugby led many immigrants to promote the game, especially in Canada. But it is new immigrants from Wales in the cities, often in teaching or skilled worker positions, who have helped keep the Welsh heritage alive, while many Welsh societies have been reinvigorated or even re-created in the last two decades because of a greater interest in cultural heritage.

Wayne K. D. Davies
University of Calgary

Davies, Wayne K. D. "The Welsh in Canada: A Geographical Overview." In *The Welsh in Canada*, edited by M. Chamberlain. Swansea UK: Canadian Studies in Wales Group, 2002: 1–48. Williams, J. G. *Songs of Praise: Welsh Rooted Churches beyond Britain*. Clinton NY: Gwenfrewi Santes Press, 1996.

Film

Red River

Film 255

FILM

The Great Plains has inspired a long and rich tradition of cinema and have produced a remarkably deep pool of actors and filmmakers. Westerns derive much of their force from the vastness of the Plains landscape, a suitably grand setting for the conflict between good and evil. The pioneer film is based on the immigrants' struggle with this harsh yet fertile environment, and the Plains has also been a classic setting for the small-town movie, claustrophobic even in those wide-open spaces. Significant documentaries and realistic dramas have conveyed the exploitation of the region's inhabitants by external forces as well as their efforts to resist those forces. And a galaxy of stars has risen from Plains cities, towns, and farms, from Lon Chaney (born in Colorado Springs in 1883), Roscoe "Fatty" Arbuckle (Smith Center, Kansas, 1887), and Buster Keaton (Piqua, Kansas, 1895) to Dennis Hopper (Dodge City, Kansas, 1936), Demi Moore (Roswell, New Mexico, 1963), and Brad Pitt (Shawnee, Oklahoma, 1963).

While it is the American rather than the Canadian Plains that has produced the stars (Rod Cameron of Calgary notwithstanding), it is mainly the Prairies that have developed a genuine Plains aesthetic in film. Indeed, the very first Great Plains films depicting life on the Prairies were made in 1897 by Manitoba farmer James Freer. Films set in the American Plains have been overwhelmed by Hollywood pretensions. Even a revisionist Western like *Dances with Wolves* (1990) is a distortion, albeit a spectacular one, of the history of the region and of the Native Americans, to whom the director, Kevin Costner, tries to pay homage. Filmmaking in the Prairie Provinces has also been influenced by Hollywood distribution monopolies, but because of the support of the National Film Board of Canada (established in 1939) and of the provincial governments, the opportunity has been there for the production of Prairie feature films and documentaries that are made in the region. Consequently, it is that part of the Great Plains that is most likely to see its history and culture on the big screen without translation by Hollywood.

Actors and Filmmakers

Perhaps if any region is thoroughly investigated the result will be the same, but it does seem that an inordinate number of actors and directors have come from the Great Plains. Stars were born the length and breadth of the region, from Edmonton, Alberta (Michael J. Fox, 1961) to San Saba, Texas (Tommy Lee Jones, 1946), and from Denver, Colorado (Douglas Fairbanks Sr., 1883) to Kansas City, Missouri (Jean Harlow, 1911). Investigate any subregion of the Plains, and the depth of film talent becomes evident. Omaha, Nebraska, for example, was home to two-time Oscar winner Marlon Brando (1924), to the debonair and light-footed Fred Astaire (1899), to the sensitive and tragic Montgomery Clift (1920), and to that durable tough guy, Nick Nolte (1941).

Piqua, Kansas, birthplace of Buster Keaton

In rural Nebraska were born Henry Fonda (Grand Island, 1905), who played perhaps his finest role as Tom Joad, the displaced Plains farmer in *The Grapes of Wrath* (John Ford, 1940); *The Fugitive*, David Janssen (Naponee, 1930); *Our Man Flint*, James Coburn (Laurel, 1928); leading man Robert Taylor (Filley, 1911); Tony- and Academy Award–winning actress Sandy Dennis (Hastings, 1937); B-movie stars Hoot Gibson (Takamah, 1892) and Coleen Gray (Staplehurst, 1922); torch-song diva Ruth Etting (David City, 1896); master comedian and stuntman Harold Lloyd (Burchard, 1888); and movie mogul Darryl Zanuck (Wahoo, 1902).

Many of these Plains people did not stay long in the region, but surely the Plains stayed in them. Buster Keaton, for example, spent his early years in the tiny railroad town of Piqua in southeastern Kansas serenaded by piercing whistles, screeching brakes, and clanging bells. Even though the Keatons—small-time performers in ten-cent shows—moved to New York in 1899, when Buster was four, these memories stayed with him all his life, and many of his films, including perhaps his greatest, *The General* (1926), feature trains. In his autobiography, *My Wonderful World of Slapstick* (1967), Keaton recounts how Pickway (Piqua) was virtually blown away by a tornado soon after he was born. Like the trains, Plains winds stayed with him: how else to account for the daredevil scene in *Steamboat Bill* (1927), when Keaton is tumbled through River Junction by a howling wind, until finally he is enveloped by the falling facade of a two-story building, a small window passing around him and, literally (for this was not a camera trick), saving his life.

Other filmmakers from the Great Plains have dealt more explicitly with their Plains

upbringing. Gordon Parks, the youngest in a family of sixteen children, was born in 1912 and grew up in the segregated small town of Fort Scott, Kansas. It was a racist town, and the family's clapboard house was crowded, but in his autobiographical novel, *The Learning Tree* (1963), and in the lyrically beautiful film of the same name that he produced and directed in 1969 as Hollywood's first African American director, the memories of his Plains upbringing are also affectionate. The place was a learning tree, his mother had told him, and trees bear both good and bad fruit.

Parks gratefully left Fort Scott for Minnesota in 1927, probably passing through Kansas City, where Robert Altman was then two years old. Altman grew up in comfortable, middle-class circumstances and learned his trade directing industrial films and television series and commercials in Kansas City in the early 1950s. Perhaps it was because of the central location of that city, at the crossroads between North and South, East and West, that Altman would go on to become the preeminent director of films that explore and dissect American dreams, mythologies, and hypocrisies. His first film and one of his later feature films were set in Kansas City. His teenage hoodlum film, *The Delinquents* (1956), was shot in his hometown, and he left for Hollywood as soon as it was finished. In 1996 Altman made *Kansas City*, evoking the city of his youth with its gangsters, crooked politicians, and, most of all, its vibrant jazz scene. Using local musicians, Altman reprised the jazz sessions he had caught as a teenager in the Kansas City clubs, making us all wish we had been there. Another two of his more than thirty feature films—*Buffalo Bill and the Indians* (1976) and *Come Back to the Five and Dime, Jimmy Dean, Jimmy Dean* (1982)—also have Plains settings.

A filmmaker doesn't have to be from the Plains, of course, to make a Plains movie. Two of the most significant Plains films of recent years, the documentary *Incident at Oglala* and the feature film *Thunderheart*, both released in 1992 and both set on Pine Ridge Reservation in South Dakota, were made by Michael Apted, an Englishman.

Great Plains Films

Innumerable mainstream Hollywood films have been set in the Great Plains. The grand finales of *North by Northwest* (Alfred Hitchcock, 1959) and *Close Encounters of the Third Kind* (Steven Spielberg, 1977) are played out in spectacular Plains settings (Mount Rushmore, South Dakota, and Devil's Tower, Wyoming, respectively), although these are not otherwise Plains films. On the other hand, many Plains films such as *Oklahoma!* (Fred Zinneman, 1955) and *Oklahoma Crude* (Stanley Kramer, 1973) were actually filmed elsewhere (the former in Arizona and the latter in Stockton, California).

The Western is the genre most clearly associated with the Plains. Many Westerns are actually "placeless," taking place in what Richard Slotkin calls "mythic space." Precise locations are often ambiguous, because the West in such films is too big for any one place. The "place-lessness" is accentuated by the fact that many Westerns were filmed on stage sets. Yet many Westerns, while retaining their mythic qualities, are clearly set in the Great Plains and depict events in Plains history, albeit refracted through a lens. These include cattle-drive films such as Howard Hawks's *Red River* (1948), which is based on the opening of the Chisholm Trail in the 1860s. In the film, a tough older man, Thomas Dunson (John Wayne), and a sensitive young man, Matthew Garth (Montgomery Clift, in his first movie role), are pitted against each other over whether to drive the herd to the old destination at Sedalia, Missouri, or to the new railheads in Kansas. The competition heads toward a showdown, but the gunfight never materializes, because the honorable Dunson cannot kill his "spiritual" son. Many other cattle-drive films similarly combine personal drama and historical epic, but none as effectively as *Red River*. *The Virginian* (Victor Fleming, 1929; Stuart Gilmore, 1946) is also a Western with a Plains setting (Medicine Bow, Wyoming) and again the classic Western theme: the rugged, innocent, and honorable cowboy confronted with a moral dilemma.

Homesteader films, another aspect of the Western genre, are often set in the Plains. One of the earliest, *The Homesteader* (1917), was by an African American, Oscar Micheaux, who had actually homesteaded in South Dakota in the first years of the twentieth century. Based on his own novel of the same name (1917), Micheaux tells the story of an African American settler who makes good and is involved in an interracial love affair. Written, produced, and directed by Micheaux and filmed in Gregory County, South Dakota, this was the first feature film made entirely by African Americans.

The homesteader tradition has continued into recent decades—battling the Plains environment is an enduring theme in literature (e.g., O. E. Rölvaag's *Giants in the Earth*, 1927) and film. The classic film of Prairie Provinces settlement, *Drylanders* (Donald Haldone, 1963), is a saga of homesteading in southern Saskatchewan from the late nineteenth century to the 1930s. The first film produced by the National Film Board of Canada, *Drylanders* stayed close to historical reality, from the initial sod house to the dust storms of the 1930s. The poignant film *Heartland* (Richard Pearce, 1979) slowly and gracefully traces the tribulations of a housekeeper and her daughter who move to frontier Wyoming to work for a dour rancher (played by Rip Torn) and end up finding affection. Terrence Malick's haunting *Days of Heaven* (1978), the story of a steelworker and his lover who flee Chicago after a fight (murder?) to work as itinerant laborers in the wheat fields of the Texas Panhandle in the years just before World War I, is also a homesteader film. After all, this area was, along with eastern Montana, a twentieth-century Plains frontier. The film, shot in Alberta, captures the unpredictability of the

Plains environment in a sequence of close-ups that show a wheat seed germinating deep in the fertile soil and then, months later, a wheat kernel being devoured by a grasshopper, one of millions that have descended to strip the fields to the ground.

There are, of course, numerous films about the conflicts between European Americans and Native Americans in the Great Plains. These movies, like the writing of history itself, tell as much about the times in which they were made as they do about the times they portray. During the course of fifty years in movies, Plains Native Americans have gone from "savage" to "noble survivor," while at the same time Gen. George Armstrong Custer has gone from conquering hero to arrogant fool. Significant Plains films in this transition include *Soldier Blue* (Ralph Nelson, 1970), which graphically depicts the atrocities of the 1864 Sand Creek Massacre, and Arthur Penn's audacious *Little Big Man* (also 1970), which takes the 120-year-old Jack Crabb through virtually every event of the Plains Indian wars. However, these films are as much about Vietnam and My Lai as they are about Native Americans. *Dances with Wolves*, for all its romanticizing and revising of Plains Indian life (Pawnees were hardly the aggressors in their conflicts with Lakotas), goes farther than most other Westerns by giving Native American actors prominent roles and by employing Lakota in the dialogue, with English subtitles. In many respects, Costner's film can be seen as a successor to Elliot Silverstein's *A Man Called Horse* (1970), which also uses Native American actors and language as the setting for a European American's heroics and distorts history in the process.

The end of the West, leaving its people dislocated, is another classic theme in Plains Westerns, and Texas is a favorite setting. The best example, perhaps, is *Hud* (Martin Ritt, 1963), which was adapted from Larry McMurtry's novel *Horseman, Pass By* (1961). *Hud* features the conflict between an honorable old man (played by Melvyn Douglas), who has an abiding pride in the Texas ranch he has built over the years, and his cynical son (Paul Newman), who values nothing. The passing of the West here is associated with the loss of principles and the severing of the attachment to the land. *Giant*, which won an Academy Award for director George Stevens in 1956, covers some of this same territory, both actually and figuratively. Set and filmed in West Texas, *Giant* follows Bick (Rock Hudson) and Leslie Benedict (Elizabeth Taylor) through the transition from big ranching money to big oil money that took place from the 1920s to the 1940s. A central figure, Jeff Rink (played rather movingly by James Dean in his last acting role), represents the loss of humanity that comes with wealth. Another theme is the caste system, in which Mexicans are relegated to a servile role and to segregated, poverty-stricken living conditions. Yet on this issue the film ends on an optimistic note, as Bick finally rejects the racism he has grown old with. The prejudices, conflicts, and accommodations between European Ameri-

cans and Latinos (and in this case African Americans too) are also featured in John Sayles's *Lone Star* (1996), a penetrating analysis and gripping account of contemporary life in fictional Rio County, located at the southern extremity of the Great Plains, where the Edwards Plateau meets the Rio Grande.

The end of the West is a central theme in *The Last Picture Show* (Peter Bogdanovich, 1971), also the best of another Plains genre, the small-town movie. Adapted from another McMurtry novel, this film, suitably shot in black and white, is a painful and moving look at a small Texas town in decline. It tells the coming-of-age stories of two young men whose energy and hopes are in stark contrast to the lives of boredom and deceit led by the town's adults. The only saving grace is Sam the Lion (played by Ben Johnson, who had himself grown up in the small Plains town of Foraker, Oklahoma), who runs the movie house and provides a link to the town's more vibrant past. But the movie house closes (the last film shown is *Red River*), and Sam dies, leaving only a dusty cocoon of a place.

Even as historic Westerns have declined in popularity in recent decades, the end-of-the-West movie remains an effective theme, a poignant evocation of the loss of a purportedly simpler and more noble way of life before the forces of modernism. The best recent example is Stephen Frears's *The Hi-Lo Country* (1999), a story of friendship between two cowboys, Big Boy (Woody Harrelson) and Pete (Billy Crudup), set on the Plains of eastern New Mexico in the years immediately following World War II, when the cattleman and the cattle drive were giving way to the corporation and the truck.

The Plains is also a favorite setting for road movies, providing the spaces that must be crossed to escape circumstances or to find redemption. *Badlands* (Terrence Malik, 1973), loosely based on the Charles Starkweather murder spree, *Thelma and Louise* (Ridley Scott, 1991), which feminizes this generally male genre, and the humorous and uplifting *Pow-Wow Highway* (Jonathan Wacks, 1988), the story of the spiritual quest of a young Northern Cheyenne man from his impoverished Montana reservation to New Mexico via the sacred Bear Butte, all involve flights by automobile across the Plains.

Some of the most important Plains films deal with the exploitation of the region by outside forces and the political responses of the people. The opening scene of *The Grapes of Wrath*, where Tom Joad walks across the flat Plains landscape, evokes a sense of exposure and vulnerability and prepares the viewer for the exodus of the Joads from Oklahoma to California. Four years before Ford's classic, Pare Lorentz's documentary, *The Plow that Broke the Plains*, had blamed the machine for the Dust Bowl and the ruin of families like the Joads. This powerful piece of propaganda (made for the Resettlement Administration) depicted an army of huge tractors moving across the land, tearing through the virgin sod and exposing the soil to the winds. Lorentz backed off, however, from blaming the economic forces behind those machines.

There is no backing off in John Hanson and Rob Nilsson's *Northern Lights* (1979). The directors use footage of North Dakota farm families shot by Nilsson's grandfather between 1915 and 1921 as background for the story of the rise of the populist Nonpartisan League. The film conveys better than any other the feel of the Northern Plains landscape and the lives of farm families at the mercy of eastern industrialists. A similar subject, the life of a prairie farmer, is covered in *Paper Wheat* (Albert Kish, 1979), which is set in Saskatchewan and was another production of the National Film Board of Canada.

There are also Plains films that stand alone, outside of any genre. *The Wizard of Oz* (Victor Fleming, 1939) is such a film, unless, of course, it too is a road movie, from black-and-white Kansas to Technicolor Oz and then back to "no place like home." The film is based on the book *The Wonderful Wizard of Oz* (1900) by L. Frank Baum, who spent three years in South Dakota during the drought and economic depression of the late 1880s and early 1890s. Just as the book is often seen as a critique of the politics of the 1890s, the movie can also be perceived as an allegorical commentary on the 1930s political scene. Opening in the sepia-toned Dust Bowl of Kansas, it takes the viewer to a blooming land transformed by Franklin Roosevelt's New Deal.

Images of the Great Plains in Film

Popular images of places are probably shaped more by movies than by any other medium, and often those images have little to do with historical or geographical reality. "Hollywood's Canada," for example, is made up of wild and impenetrable forests populated by scarlet-clad Mounties. The Prairies, apparently too tame and unexciting for Hollywood, were rarely used as a film setting. Two useful studies of Hollywood's Oklahoma (one by Jack Spears, the other by Thomas Bohn and Joseph Millichap) provide an opportunity to focus on one Plains state and its celluloid image.

Most of the (at least) fifty-five feature films that deal with Oklahoma concentrate on historical themes of settlement. The land rush of 1889 and the oil boom of the early twentieth century are favorite motifs. The other major event in Oklahoma's history, the relocation of Native Americans to then Indian Territory, is not such a popular theme. This is not surprising, because the traditional objective has been to glorify the "winning of the West," using Oklahoma as the setting, not to expose the brutality and dire consequences of Native American relocation. Most of the movies are less about the actual place than about the American ideology of taming the frontier. The best movie in this tradition is *Cimarron* (Wesley Ruggles, 1931), which won three Academy Awards in 1931, including best picture. This sprawling epic takes a pioneer Oklahoma family from the land rush through the emergence of the state to the oil fields and burgeoning cities of the 1920s, along the way editorializing on prejudice against Jews and Native Americans and corruption in state government. Despite such qualifications, the message is one of successive frontiers offering opportunity to enterprising Americans.

There is, however, an ambivalence in the movie image of Oklahoma. Oklahoma is the verdant land—"a colorful picture postcard," to use Spears's words—of the musical *Oklahoma!*, but it is also the derelict oil fields of *Tulsa* (Stuart Heisler, 1949), the ruined soil and lives of *The Grapes of Wrath*, and the small-town confinement of *The Dark at the Top of the Stairs* (1960), which was based on the play by Kansan William Inge and directed by fellow Kansan Delbert Mann. This ambivalent image—garden and desert—can be extended to cover the entire Plains region. Its roots go back as far as Zebulon Pike, who in 1806 compared the Southern Plains to the Sahara, and Lewis and Clark, who saw extraordinary fecundity during their passage along the eastern edge of the Central Plains in 1804.

Filmmaking in the Great Plains

Just like the Plains automobile companies that turned out small numbers of distinctive cars until the 1920s, when Detroit took over and they went under, so small filmmaking companies produced movies in various parts of the Plains until they succumbed to the Hollywood studio system.

One of the earliest Plains film companies was founded by "Buffalo Bill" Cody in Denver in 1913, with financial backing from the *Denver Post*. The Colonel William F. Cody (Buffalo Bill) Historical Pictures Company's sole achievement, if that is the correct word, was *The Indian Wars* (1914), which purported to give an accurate representation of four key battles: Summit Springs (1869), Warbonnet Creek (1876), the Mission (1890), and Wounded Knee (1890). The film was shot at the sites of the battles and featured, in addition to Cody, Lt. Gen. Nelson Appleton Miles, troops from the Twelfth U.S. Cavalry, and more than a thousand Lakotas. *The Indian Wars* was screened in Washington DC, Denver, and Omaha, Alliance, and Chadron, Nebraska, in 1914 before being mired in controversy and withdrawn from circulation. The government may have thought that the military was presented as too much the aggressor at Wounded Knee, Native Americans resented their portrayal as "savages," and the public simply did not think much of the entire production.

A year later, the Black Hills Feature Film Company had its brief moment of glory in the northwestern Nebraska town of Chadron in 1915 with the production of the silent Western *In the Days of '75 and '76*. The company was organized by the townspeople, in particular, the chief of police, James O. Hartzell, whose wife wrote the script and whose daughter played the lead role of Calamity Jane. A more experienced company, Harman Brothers Film Manufacturers of Omaha, was brought in for technical advice. Shot in the nearby Nebraska Pine Ridge country and the Black Hills of South Dakota and using only local talent, the seven-reel film was completed in a month. It premiered to an enthusiastic audience, anxious to catch glimpses of themselves and their acquaintances, at Chadron's Rex Theater on September 24, 1915, and subsequently played at nearby frontier towns in Nebraska, Wyoming, and South Dakota. It was a typical Western genre film of the times, with saintly heroes, vile villains, gambling, shootouts, and friendly and hostile Indians. Within a year the film had dropped out of sight, and so had the Black Hills Feature Film Company.

Similar companies flourished briefly throughout the Plains in the first two decades of the twentieth century. Oklahoma seems to have had more than its share, perhaps because the frontier was living history in this newest state, and former outlaws could parlay their established fame into acting. William M. Tilghman, for example, a famous frontier marshal, moved effortlessly into directing silent Westerns for the Oklahoma Natural Mutoscene Company in 1908. The first, *The Wolf Hunt*, shot in the Wichita Mountains, was screened by President Theodore Roosevelt in the East Room of the White House in 1909. The film featured former outlaw Al Jennings, by then a lawyer in Lawton. Jennings, a poor actor, went on to a Hollywood career. Tilghman's second film, *The Bank Robbery* (1908), starred Jennings as his outlaw self as well as Comanche chief Quanah Parker and many citizens of Cache, where it was shot. Clearly, occupational mobility was a feature of frontier life, and the distinction between movies and real life was blurred.

The Lincoln Motion Picture Company was the most important of the early film companies to be associated with the Plains. A young Omaha, Nebraska, mailman, George P. Johnson, and his film actor brother, Noble (both Plains born, in Colorado Springs), formed the company in 1915 in an effort to free African American filmmakers from dependence on European American financiers and to combat the racist stereotypes propagated by D. W. Griffith's *The Birth of a Nation* (1915). Noble ran the studio in Los Angeles while George promoted and distributed their films from Omaha. In its movies and by its example, the Lincoln Motion Picture Company proclaimed that African Americans had every right to participate fully in American life. But the Johnsons constantly had to struggle to obtain financing, and by 1920 they were competing not only against the European American movie establishment but also against other African American companies, including that of Oscar Micheaux. There was simply not enough ticket-buying money in the African American community to support such enterprises, and in 1922 the Lincoln Motion Picture Company folded.

In the Prairie Provinces, Calgary emerged as a center of film production between 1919 and 1923 due to the entrepreneurship of Earnest G. Shipman ("Ten Percent Ernie"), who located there after obtaining the film rights to James Oliver Curwood's stories. Shipman produced five profitable films and a sixth that was a financial disaster. He left the business, and Prairie filmmaking declined.

In subsequent years, despite the suffocating dominance of Hollywood, films have continued to be made locally in the Great Plains. Often they are associated with film schools and public television stations. An annual Great Plains Film Festival is now held at the University of Nebraska–Lincoln to showcase Plains filmmakers and films. Texas has a thriving film industry, but its hub is Austin, outside the Plains proper. North of the forty-ninth parallel, film cooperatives and corporations in Winnipeg, Regina, Saskatoon, and Calgary are taking advantage of federal and provincial funding to create television dramas and documentaries (and occasionally low-budget feature films) on Prairie Province topics and in Prairie Province settings.

Meanwhile, the Plains continue to produce movie stars and filmmakers, and directors continue to be attracted to the region for its epic landscapes, dramatic (and unfurling) history, and mythic resonances.

See also AFRICAN AMERICANS: Micheaux, Oscar; Parks, Gordon / CITIES AND TOWNS: Small Towns / LITERARY TRADITIONS: Baum, L. Frank; Inge, William; McMurtry, Larry; The Western / PHYSICAL ENVIRONMENT: Dust Bowl / PROTEST AND DISSENT: Nonpartisan League.

David J. Wishart
University of Nebraska–Lincoln

Berton, Pierre. *Hollywood's Canada: The Americanization of Our National Image*. Toronto: McClelland and Stewart Limited, 1975. Bohn, Thomas W., and Joseph Millichap. "Film Images of Oklahoma." *Film and History* 10 (1980): 83–89. Cripps, Thomas. *Slow Fade to Black: The Negro in American Film, 1900–1942*. London: Oxford University Press, 1977. Eisloeffel, Paul J., and Andrea I. Paul. "Hollywood on the Plains: Nebraska's Contribution to Early American Cinema." *Journal of the West* 33 (1994): 13–19. Etulain, Richard W. "Recent Interpretations of the Western Film: A Bibliographical Essay." *Journal of the West* 22 (1983): 72–82. Hilger, Michael. *From Savage to Nobleman: Images of Native Americans in Film*. Lanham MD: Scarecrow Press, 1995. Horne, C. S. "Interpreting Prairie Cinema." *Prairie Forum* 22 (1997): 135–51. Katz, Ephraim. *The Film Encyclopedia*. 2nd ed. New York: Harper Collins, 1994. Keaton, Buster, with Charles Samuels. *My Wonderful World of Slapstick*. London: George Allen and Unwin, 1967. McGilligan, Patrick. *Robert Altman: Jumping off the Cliff*. New York: St. Martin's Press, 1989. Parks, Gordon. *Voices in the Mirror: An Autobiography*. New York: Doubleday, 1990. Paul, Andrea. "Buffalo Bill and Wounded Knee: The Movie." *Nebraska History* 71 (1990): 183–90. Slotkin, Richard. "John Ford's *Stagecoach* and the Mythic Space of the Western Movie." In *The Big Empty: Essays on Western Landscapes and Narrative*, edited by Leonard Engel. Albuquerque: University of New Mexico Press, 1994: 261–83. Spears, Jack. "Hollywood's Oklahoma." *Chronicles of Oklahoma* 67 (1989–90): 340–81.

ALTMAN, ROBERT (b. 1925)

One of the prime architects of a renaissance in American independent filmmaking in the 1970s, Robert Altman has chronicled in his own idiosyncratic way the vagaries and varieties of the American experience. He was born in Kansas City, Missouri, on February 20, 1925. He recalls that his formative youthful experiences—particularly his frequenting of the jazz districts around 18th and Vine and the movie theaters near his Brookside neighborhood home—provided him with what he calls his "chips," his "attitudes" toward life and art.

After serving as a B-24 pilot during World War II, Altman returned to Kansas City, where he began making industrial films for the Calvin Company. He made two locally financed features, *The Delinquents* (1956) and *The James Dean Story* (1957), then departed to Los Angeles, where he began directing for the television series *Alfred Hitchcock Presents*, *The Rifleman*, and *Combat!* His breakthrough film was *M*A*S*H* in 1970, which he quickly followed up with several "antigenre" films, *McCabe and Mrs. Miller* (1971), *The Long Goodbye* (1973), *Thieves Like Us* (1974), and *Nashville* (1975). He won the Palme d'Or Award at the Cannes Film Festival for *M*A*S*H* and the New York Critics' Film Circle Award for best director for *Nashville*.

Altman returned to his hometown in 1996 to make *Kansas City*, a portrait of the town's milieu of jazz, corrupt politics, and rampant gangsterism in the mid-1930s—a summation of his thematic preoccupation with loose ends and failed hopes, served up with his trademark eccentric, semi-improvisational style (which he compares to the solo riffs of the jam sessions he heard as a youth in the Kansas City clubs). *Kansas City* may be his most autobiographical film, drawn as much from his own memories as from the historical record. With his characteristic relish for paradox, Altman admits the film is hardly factual but insists it is "truthful."

John C. Tibbetts
University of Kansas

Jacobs, Diane. *Hollywood Renaissance*. New York: A. S. Barnes and Company, 1977. McGilligan, Patrick. *Robert Altman: Jumping off the Cliff*. New York: St. Martin's Press, 1989. Tibbetts, John C. "Robert Altman: After Thirty-Five Years Still the 'Action Painter' of American Cinema." *Literature/Film Quarterly* 20 (1992): 36–42.

ARBUCKLE, FATTY (1887–1933)

Actor, director, screenwriter, and Hollywood outcast, Roscoe Conklin Arbuckle was born in a sod house on his parents' farm near Smith Center, Kansas, on March 24, 1887. His father never liked farming, and a decade later he uprooted the family and moved to California.

Neither Roscoe's parents nor his siblings were heavy, but Roscoe quickly grew into his nickname (a nickname he hated), surpassing 200 pounds by the time he was twelve. Nevertheless, "Fatty" was agile, and by the time he was fifteen he was performing in vaudeville up and down the West Coast as acrobat, singer, and magician. His break came in 1908, when he was hired as an extra by the Selig Polyscope Company, and he began a slow transition from vaudeville to motion pictures, appearing in numerous one-reel comedies. In 1913 he joined Mack Sennett's Keystone Studios and was soon a star, acting alongside, among others, Charlie Chaplin. After 1916 he wrote, directed, and acted in innumerable films, launching the career of his fellow Kansan, Buster Keaton, in one of them (*The Butcher Boy*, 1917). Arbuckle's popularity soared; so did his salary, to $7,500 a week by 1920.

His fall was meteoric. On September 4, 1921, at an alcohol-soaked party at a San Francisco hotel, the aspiring actress Virginia Rappe went into convulsions after allegedly being raped by Arbuckle. Five days later she died, and Arbuckle was charged with murder. He was eventually acquitted, but his career was ruined. In the following years he directed films under a pseudonym and seemed to be on the verge of making an acting comeback when, in the early morning of June 29, 1933, in New York City, he fell victim to a heart attack.

David J. Wishart
University of Nebraska–Lincoln

Young, Robert, Jr. *Roscoe "Fatty" Arbuckle: A Bio-Bibliography*. Westport CT: Greenwood Press, 1994.

ASTAIRE, FRED (1899–1987)

No one knows what possessed Fred Astaire to put on a pair of ballet slippers in an Omaha dance studio at the age of four and begin his long journey to stardom. It happened at the turn of the century at Chambers Dancing Academy, where Astaire's sister, Adele, took dance lessons. Astaire often accompanied his mother or father to the studio to pick her up. The young lad, not surprisingly, had no interest in dancing. In his autobiography, *Steps in Time*, Astaire wrote: "Dancing was merely something my sister did, something that all little girls did. I let it go at that and the hell with it." Unbeknownst to Astaire at that time, dancing would consume his life and help him create an entertainment legacy that includes more than forty Hollywood films.

The son of an Austrian beer salesman, Astaire was born Frederick Austerlitz in a humble bungalow not far from downtown Omaha on May 10, 1899. The house still stands at 2336 S. 10th Street, but without any marker of its historical significance. The family moved to the north side of Omaha near the old Storz Brewery when Astaire was about a year old. The dilapidated brewery still stands, but the two homes where the Austerlitzes lived, 1429 N. 19th Street and later 1426 N. 19th Street, are gone. Astaire recalled very little of his early years in Omaha, except the sound of rumbling locomotives in the nearby railroad yards and taking Sunday afternoon buggy rides with his father to a local cigar store.

When he was four years old, Astaire and his sister boarded a train with their mother and headed for New York and professional dance training. Their father stayed behind and sent money to help the family. It was in New York that the two children began their dancing careers. According to legend, their first job was in a Keyport, New Jersey, theater, where they danced on a large wedding cake as bride and groom. Astaire wore what would eventually become his trademark tails, white tie, and top hat. They got $50 for their efforts.

Astaire spent his early youth traveling the Orpheum circuit as a vaudeville act with his sister. They played in Omaha and possibly

Lincoln, which also had an Orpheum Theater. "We played every rat trap and chicken coop in the Middle West," Astaire recalled in his autobiography. He and his sister danced on Broadway but split up their act in 1932, when Adele married a British nobleman. Like most stars, Astaire made his way to Hollywood.

After a screen test, one talent scout infamously wrote: "Can't act. Can't sing. Balding. Can dance a little." For a scrawny guy who was never much of a looker, Astaire danced with the crème de la crème of silver screen stars: Audrey Hepburn, Cyd Charisse, Judy Garland, and Eleanor Powell, to name only a few. Most notably, he partnered Ginger Rogers in ten films, beginning with *Flying Down to Rio* in 1933. His film career spanned fifty years (1931–81), and for all of them he was a star. He won almost every movie award, including an honorary Academy Award in 1949. He legitimized dance in movies, his repertoire spanning tap, ballet, and jazz. He choreographed all his own work, and he made it look effortless. A national chain of dance studios now carries the Astaire name.

The Adele and Fred Astaire Ballroom, which takes up most of the top floor of the historic Storz Mansion at 3708 Farnam Street, stands as the only memorial to his Omaha beginnings. Despite his accomplishments and his status as one of the greatest figures in entertainment history, Astaire remained a modest man. "I don't understand what people see in me," he wrote. "I don't look like a movie star and I don't act like a movie star. I'm just an old So and So from Omaha." Fred Astaire died in Beverly Hills, California, on June 22, 1987.

Al J. Laukaitis
Lincoln Journal Star

Astaire, Fred. *Steps in Time*. New York: Harper, 1959.
Basinger, Jeanine. "Astaire, Fred." In *International Dictionary of Films and Filmmakers*, edited by Nicholas Thomas. Detroit: St. James Press, 1992: 3:34–36.

AUTRY, GENE (1907–1998)

Gene Autry's career spanned some sixty years in the entertainment industry, encompassing radio, recordings, motion pictures, television, rodeo, and live performances. He also became a broadcast executive and major league baseball team owner. He is the only entertainer to have five stars on Hollywood's Walk of Fame. In his ability to transcend media and in the sheer scope of his output, Autry is unsurpassed as a popular image maker of the American West.

Born in Tioga, Texas, on September 29, 1907, Orvon Gene Autry spent most of his boyhood north of the Red River in Ravia, Oklahoma. He bought his first guitar for $8 at the age of twelve and began to sing in local drugstores and nightspots. By the late 1920s he was working as a telegrapher for the Frisco railroad and moving from town to town in Oklahoma. While he was singing and playing in the Chelsea office one night, he was discovered by the great cowboy humorist, Will Rogers. Rogers advised the young Autry to try radio, and the rest is history.

Gene Autry and Champion, ca. 1947

Autry began his radio career in 1928 with station KVOO in Tulsa as "Oklahoma's Yodeling Cowboy" and made his first recordings a year later. His first hit came in 1931 with *That Silver-Haired Daddy of Mine*, the first record ever certified gold for having sold more than a million copies. Autry made his film debut as a dude ranch cowboy singer in the 1934 Ken Maynard film *In Old Santa Fe*. In 1935 he made his first starring appearance in the science fiction Western serial *The Phantom Empire*. Autry's hugely successful movie formula combined Hollywood elements with his Plains upbringing: a mixture of flashy image and down-home sense. Other important ingredients were his singing; his trusty horse, Champion; and his faithful comic sidekick, Smiley Burnette (played by Pat Buttram). The combination proved irresistible to Depression-ridden audiences. By 1937 Autry was "America's Favorite Cowboy," voted the number one Western star by the theater exhibitors of America. He remained in first or second place among cowboy stars in terms of box office draw until he retired from motion pictures in 1953.

The successful Hollywood singing cowboy did not forget his roots. Many of his films, with titles such as *Red River Valley* (1936), *Yodelin' Kid from Pine Ridge* (1937), *Blue Montana Skies* (1939), and *Sunset in Wyoming* (1941), were set on the Plains. The effect of his upbringing on his creative output can also be seen in the frequent references to the Southern Plains in Autry's songs. He surrounded himself with Oklahomans: Bev Barnett, his publicity director; the Marvin brothers (Frankie and Johnny) and Jimmy Long, collaborators on many of his songs; and Jimmy Wakely and Johnny Bond, who played with Autry for years, all hailed from the Sooner State. His first wife, Ina Mae Spivey, Long's niece, whom Autry married in 1932 and who played a large part in his success until her death in 1980, came from Duncan.

In 1941 Autry purchased a 1,360-acre spread in the foothills of the Arbuckle Mountains, just west of Berwyn, Oklahoma, as the headquarters and winter home for his traveling rodeo. He named it the Flying A Ranch and Rodeo. Soon after, Berwyn changed its name to Gene Autry. The small Oklahoma town maintains a museum devoted to the man it honors. Autry also toured the Plains states extensively with his rodeo in the 1940s and 1950s, usually appearing in small towns before packed audiences.

In total, Autry appeared in 93 feature films and made 635 recordings, more than 300 of which he wrote or cowrote. His best-known movies were based on his hit records, including *South of the Border* (1939), *Back in the Saddle* (1941), and *Strawberry Roan* (1948). His recordings have sold more than 60 million copies and brought him more than a dozen gold records. Autry's beloved Christmas and children's records, *Here Comes Santa Claus* (1947) and *Peter Cottontail* (1950), went platinum (for more than two million copies sold), while *Rudolph the Red-Nosed Reindeer* (1949) remains the second best selling single of all time (behind only Bing Crosby's *White Christmas*), with sales totaling more than 30 million.

In addition to his movie and recording success, Autry's *Melody Ranch* was heard weekly over the CBS Radio Network between 1940 and 1956. During World War II Autry enlisted for service on the air during a broadcast of the show. Sgt. Gene Autry served his country as a flight officer with the Air Transport Command. From 1943 until 1945 he flew large cargo planes in the China-Burma-India theater. When the war ended, Autry was assigned to Special Services and toured with a USO troupe in the South Pacific before resuming his movie career in 1946.

Realizing that the days of the B-Western were numbered, in 1950 Autry became one of the first major film stars to move into television. For the next five years he produced and starred in ninety-one episodes of *The Gene Autry Show* as well as producing such popular television series as *Annie Oakley*, *The Range Rider*, *Buffalo Bill Jr.*, and *The Adventures of Champion*. In the late 1980s Autry and his former movie sidekick, Pat Buttram, hosted ninety-three episodes of the *Melody Ranch Theatre* show, spotlighting the telecasting of his old Republic and Columbia movies.

In 1961 Autry's great love of baseball prompted him to purchase the American League's California Angels (renamed the Anaheim Angels in 1996). He held the title of vice president of the American League until his death. Among the many hundreds of honors this son of the Plains received were induction into the Country Music Hall of Fame, the Nashville Songwriters' Hall of Fame, the National Cowboy Hall of Fame, and the National Association of Broadcasters Hall of Fame. He also was honored by his songwriting peers with a lifetime achievement award from the American Society of Composers, Authors and Publishers.

A long-cherished dream came true with the opening in Los Angeles in November 1988 of the Gene Autry Western Heritage Museum (renamed the Autry Museum of Western Heritage in 1995). Autry stated: "It has always been my intention to build a museum which would exhibit and interpret the heritage of the West, and show how it has influenced America and the world." The Autry Museum is now acclaimed as one of the foremost museums of the American West, with important collections of art, artifacts, and documents, drawing millions of visitors from around the world. Jackie Autry, whom he married in 1981, serves as chairman of its board of directors.

Autry's extraordinary life ended at his home in Los Angeles on October 2, 1998 after a long illness. He was ninety-one years old.

Kevin Mulroy
University of Southern California

Gene Autry Collection, Autry Museum of Western Heritage, Los Angeles. Autry, Gene, with Mickey Herskowitz. *Back in the Saddle Again*. Garden City NY: Doubleday, 1978. Rothel, David. *The Gene Autry Book*. Madison NC: Empire Publishing Company, 1988.

BEERY, WALLACE (1885–1949)

Wallace Beery, the burly actor who made his name in films playing a lovable slob, was born in Kansas City, Missouri, on April 1, 1885. He started in show business in 1901 as an elephant trainer, rising to become elephant manager at Ringling Bros. by 1904. Beery played in road-show musicals and Kansas City theater until 1913, when he began acting in Essanay film comedies. His career in the movies began in drag, playing Sweedie, a Swedish maid.

In 1920s silent films Beery mixed rugged parts such as that of the menacing Magua in *The Last of the Mohicans* (1920) with comedies before developing what became his characteristic role—the scoundrel with a heart of gold—in *Beggars of Life* (1928). The advent of sound opened up new horizons for his acting, and he made his best films and became a major star in the 1930s. He was nominated for an Oscar for his convict role in *The Big House* (1930), and he shared (with Frederic March) a best actor award for his performance with child actor Jackie Cooper in *The Champ* (1931). The role for which he is probably best remembered, however, is pirate Long John Silver in *Treasure Island* (1934).

Beery continued making at least one film a year during the 1940s. His last (and 252nd) film was *Big Jack*, which was released in 1949, the year he died (on April 15) in Beverly Hills, California. Beery was married to actress Gloria Swanson from 1916 to 1918, and his brother (Noah Sr.) and nephew (Noah Jr.) were also actors.

David J. Wishart
University of Nebraska–Lincoln

Gallagher, John A. "Beery, Wallace." In *International Dictionary of Films and Filmmakers*, edited by Nicholas Thomas. Detroit: St. James Press, 1992: 3: 87–90.

BRANDO, MARLON (b. 1924)

Marlon Brando was born on April 3, 1924, in Omaha, Nebraska, to Dorothy Pennebaker Brando and Marlon Brando Sr. The Brandos had two other children, Jocelyn and Frances. Marlon's bully of a father was a salesman; his eccentric mother was an actress with the local community theater. Both had drinking problems. Descended from Irish immigrants, the family had been living in Nebraska for generations. Brando spent the first six years of his life in Omaha in a large wood-shingled house on a quiet street lined with elm trees. His earliest memories recall the sweet fragrance of fresh-cut hay and lilies of the valley and the grating sound of boots on frozen snow on a frigid Plains winter day. In 1930 his father took a job in Evanston, Illinois, and the family left Nebraska behind.

In 1943, when he was nineteen years old, Brando moved to New York City and began studying acting at the Dramatic Workshop of the New School for Social Research. His teacher, Stella Adler, had studied with Konstantin Stanislavsky, the director, acting theorist, and founder of the Moscow Art Theatre. In 1944, when he was twenty years old, Brando had his Broadway debut as Nels in the Richard Rodgers production of *I Remember Mama*. The play ran for two years. This was followed by performances in 1946 in Maxwell Anderson's *Truckline Cafe*, George Bernard Shaw's *Candida*, and Ben Hecht's *A Flag Is Born*. In 1947 Brando was chosen for the role of Stanley Kowalski in Tennessee Williams's *A Streetcar Named Desire*, directed by Elia Kazan. The Broadway premiere was a tremendous success. Marlon Brando became a star celebrated by audiences and critics alike.

In 1950 Marlon Brando began his career as a film actor. He brought his acting style and his training from Elia Kazan and the Actors Studio to the screen. In his film debut in Stanley Kramer's *The Men*, he played an embittered paraplegic. He prepared for the role by spending a month in a hospital ward for the rehabilitation of paraplegics. Brando was subsequently nominated for a best actor Academy Award for four successive years: for his performances as Stanley Kowalski in *A Streetcar Named Desire* (1951), Emiliano Zapata in *Viva Zapata!* (1952), and Marc Anthony in *Julius Caesar* (1953). He won the award for his portrayal of Terry Malloy, under the direction of Elia Kazan, in *On the Waterfront* (1954).

In 1971 Brando won his second Oscar for his powerful performance as Don Corleone, the patriarch of the Corleone crime family in *The Godfather*. In 1972 he was nominated for another best actor Oscar for his role in Bernardo Bertolucci's controversial *Last Tango in Paris*. In 1989 Brando gained another Oscar nomination for best supporting actor in *A Dry White Season*. He has continued to make films.

Through all of life's vicissitudes Marlon Brando has remained the quintessential film actor. He revolutionized the concepts of film acting yet repeatedly dismissed acting as a waste of precious time and life. Deeply and actively committed to humanitarian causes, he has vigorously used his heroic status to publicly advance civil rights, from joining Dr. Martin Luther King's march on Washington to his refusal to accept his Oscar for *The Godfather* as a way of protesting the treatment of Native Americans.

Carol Penney
University of New Haven

Brando, Marlon, with Robert Lindsey. *Brando: Songs My Mother Taught Me*. Toronto: Random House, 1994. Tanitch, Robert. *Brando*. London: Studio Vista, 1994. Vineberg, Steve. *Method Actors*. New York: Schirmer, 1991.

BROOKS, LOUISE (1906–1985)

Louise Brooks, ca. 1928.

Actress, dancer, and writer on film, Louise Brooks is perhaps best known for her role as Lulu in the silent film *Pandora's Box* (1929). She was born Mary Louise Brooks on November 14, 1906, in Cherryvale, Kansas, to Leonard and Myra Brooks, a lawyer and touring speaker, respectively. Her first stage role was at age four; she later performed as a dancer at local clubs and fairs in southeastern Kansas. At age fifteen Brooks joined the Denishawn Dance Company, the leading modern dance troupe in America. After two years with Denishawn, Brooks left the company and landed parts as a chorus girl in George White's Scandals and as a specialty dancer in the Ziegfeld Follies. She had the distinction of being the first person to dance the Charleston in London.

Brooks's performance in the Follies led to a tryout in the movies. Her early films include *The American Venus* (1926), *It's the Old Army Game* (1926), *The Show-off* (1926), and *Love 'Em and Leave 'Em* (1926), all of which were social comedies typical of the era. Subsequent dramatic roles include *A Girl in Every Port* (1928), *Beggars of Life* (1928), and *The Canary Murder Case* (1929). Brooks appeared as Lulu, a femme fatale, in G. W. Pabst's German production of *Pandora's Box* in 1929, one of the great films of the silent era. She also starred in Pabst's *Diary of a Lost Girl* (1929) and in the French production *Prix de beauté* (1930).

Brooks's career had declined by the mid-1930s. After a brief sojourn in Wichita, the once-celebrated actress settled in New York City, where she lived for more than a decade in obscurity. She later moved to Rochester, New York, and began writing; her first article appeared in 1956. Over the next three decades, Brooks contributed numerous essays to various film journals. Her highly acclaimed 1982 book, *Lulu in Hollywood*, includes essays about her life and the careers of other movie stars. Brooks's legendary beauty and distinctive bob hairstyle have been celebrated in numerous films, plays, novels, poems, comic strips, artwork, and songs. She died of a heart attack in Rochester on August 8, 1985.

Thomas Gladysz
Louise Brooks Society

Brooks, Louise. *Lulu in Hollywood*. New York: Knopf, 1982. Jaccard, Roland. *Louise Brooks: Portrait of an Anti-Star*. New York: Zoetrope, 1986. Paris, Barry. *Louise Brooks*. New York: Knopf, 1989.

BUTLER, HUGO (1914–1968)

Hugo Butler wrote motion picture stories and scripts for three decades. Born in Calgary, Alberta, on May 4, 1914, he soon abandoned the Canadian Prairies. His British parents divorced after World War I, and his father, Frank Butler, who worked for the Canadian Pacific Railway, relocated to Hollywood and a career as an actor and writer, while young Hugo moved with his mother to Victoria, British Columbia.

After studying journalism at the University of Washington, Butler left without a degree for a junior writer's job at MGM. Credited with eleven movies there, he specialized in adapting children's classics. He soon joined the fledgling Screen Writers Guild, while his father opted for the rival, industry-endorsed Screen Playwrights Inc. Hugo Butler's cowritten story, *Edison, the Man* (1940), earned an Academy Award nomination. Four years later, as a guild vice president, he presented the writers Oscars, one to his father. His postwar credits include scripts directed by Jean Renoir and Joseph Losey, among them Losey's *The Prowler* (1950), which Butler cowrote with Dalton Trumbo, though he received sole credit, fronting for the blacklisted Trumbo.

Butler and his wife, Jean Rouverol Butler, were active Communist party members, and they were identified to the House Committee on Un-American Activities in 1947. They fled a 1951 HUAC subpoena with their children, choosing exile in Mexico over Butler's native Canada, because Butler disliked Canada's cold climate. Butler continued to write pseudonymously for Luis Buñuel and Robert Aldrich, contributed to scripts without credit, and codirected two documentaries as Hugo Mozo (Hugo the Houseboy). In Italy in the 1960s he wrote again for Aldrich and the also-exiled Losey. Returning to Hollywood in 1964 and about to rise from the blacklist with Aldrich's *The Legend of Lylah Clare* (1968), cowritten with his wife, Butler died in Los Angeles on January 7, 1968, of a coronary occlusion after

several years' struggle with arteriosclerotic brain disease.

In 1997 his rightful credits were restored to five films cowritten during the blacklist. Butler's films include *The Adventures of Huckleberry Finn* (1938), *A Christmas Carol* (1938), *Lassie Come Home* (1942), *The Southerner* (1945), *The Big Night* (1951), *The Adventures of Robinson Crusoe* (1953), *World for Ransom* (1954), *Torero!* (1956), *Los pequeños gigantes/How Tall Is a Giant?* (1958), *La joven/The Young One* (1960), *Eva* (1962), and *Sodom and Gomorrah* (1963).

Blaine Allan
Queen's University

Conrad, Randall. "No Blacks or Whites: The Making of Luis Buñuel's *The Young One*." *Cineaste* 20 (1994): 28–34. McGilligan, Patrick, and Paul Buhle. *Tender Comrades: A Backstory of the Hollywood Blacklist*. New York: St. Martin's, 1997. Rouverol, Jean. *Refugees from Hollywood: A Journal of the Blacklist Years*. Albuquerque: University of New Mexico Press, 2000.

CHANEY, LON (1883–1930)

Lon Chaney

Famous star of silent motion pictures, Lon (Leonidas) Chaney was dubbed "The Man of a Thousand Faces" for his elaborate makeups. He was born to deaf-mute parents in Colorado Springs on April 1, 1883. His acting career began in 1902 with comic operas for the Colorado Springs Opera House. After touring with several musical comedy troupes, he joined Fischer's Follies of Los Angeles in 1912. Chaney began to do bit parts for the Universal Film Manufacturing Company in 1912, and he used novel makeups in films as early as *The Sea Urchin* (1913), in which he played a hunchback. His breakthrough role was as a con man pretending to be crippled in *The Miracle Man* (1919).

In 1923 Chaney starred in *The Hunchback of Notre Dame*, and his incredible makeup and performance as Quasimodo vaulted him to

fame. He achieved superstardom in *The Phantom of the Opera* (1925), arguably the most famous of all silent films. The remainder of his career included many macabre roles at MGM, often teamed with director Tod Browning, including *The Unholy Three* (1925), *The Unknown* (1925), *London after Midnight* (1927), and *West of Zanzibar* (1928). Some of his best performances, however, came in his non-makeup roles: as a tough drill sergeant in *Tell It to the Marines* (1927) and as a detective in *While the City Sleeps* (1928). Chaney appeared in only one sound film, a remake of *The Unholy Three* (1930), before dying of lung cancer on August 26, 1930. He appeared in approximately 160 films. His only child, Creighton, appeared in numerous horror films, billed as Lon Chaney Jr.

Jon C. Mirsalis
Emerald Hills, California

Blake, Michael F. *Lon Chaney: The Man behind the Thousand Faces*. New York: Vestal Press, 1990.

CIMARRON

Released in 1931, *Cimarron* was directed by Wesley Ruggles, with a script by Howard Estabrook and Edna Ferber, based on her novel. The film won Academy Awards for best picture, art direction, and adapted screenplay.

One of the earliest epic films of the sound era, *Cimarron* (Spanish for "wild and unruly" and the name of a river in Oklahoma and Kansas) traces the history of the state of Oklahoma through its first forty years, beginning with the great land rush of April 22, 1889, when two million acres were opened to settlement. Although cheated out of his claim, Yancy Cravat (Richard Dix), a lawyer and newspaperman, moves his wife, Sabra (Irene Dunne), and child from her family's home in Wichita to the instant boomtown of Osage, Oklahoma. Well liked by nearly everyone, Cravat metes out two-gun justice to the town bully during a church meeting in the town's gambling tent and later kills an old friend who has become an outlaw. Lured by the spirit of adventure, Cravat abandons his family and lights out for the Cherokee Strip when it opens in 1893. Besides raising their two children, Sabra publishes Yancy's newspaper, leaving his name on the masthead. He returns after serving in the Spanish-American War and runs unsuccessfully for governor when the territory becomes a state in 1907. Once again he takes off for new adventures, leaving the paper in his wife's hands. By 1929 Oklahoma is in an oil boom, Osage is a modern city, the newspaper is a success, and Sabra, never giving up hope for her husband's return, has been elected to Congress. While touring the oil fields with other dignitaries she discovers her mortally injured husband, now an anonymous drifter hired as a roughneck. In the final shot, a statue unveiled in the city park honoring Oklahoma pioneers bears an unmistakable resemblance to Yancy Cravat.

Cimarron is the saga of the last frontier and the building of an empire. As seen in consecutive shots of its main street, Osage transforms in stages from tents and hastily thrown up shacks to a bustling modern city with automobiles, streetcars, and skyscrapers. The film also includes the theme, common in many Westerns, of the passing of the West from wide-open spaces to settled farms and towns. Yancy civilizes Osage with his six-gun, and he consistently stands for tolerance and progressive policies toward Native Americans. Ironically, it is practical Sabra, much less tolerant and more conventional in her attitudes about race and society, who is eventually elected to Congress, while her husband dies in obscurity.

Today the film looks slow, stilted, and talky, and Dix's performance, filled with histrionics, seems almost a self-parody. In addition, humor based on racial and physical stereotypes may make modern audiences wince. The opening scene of the 1889 land rush, however, is one of the most exciting action sequences in cinema. Unfortunately, nothing else in the film has so much energy.

See also IMAGES AND ICONS: Boomers.

William M. Wehrbein
Nebraska Wesleyan University

Fenin, George N., and William K. Everson. *The Western: From Silents to the Seventies.* New York: Grossman, 1973.
Wright, Will. *Six Guns and Society: A Structural Study of the Western.* Berkeley: University of California Press, 1975.

CLIFT, MONTGOMERY (1920–1966)

A major film star from the late 1940s through the early 1960s in such widely admired movies as *Red River* (1948), *A Place in the Sun* (1951), and *From Here to Eternity* (1953), Montgomery Clift set the standard for the new breed of Hollywood stars who emerged in the post–World War II era. Clift's casual attire, preference for life in New York instead of California, and belief that an actor owes nothing to the public except a good performance quickly became de rigueur attitudes for American actors wishing to be taken seriously.

Clift was born Edward Montgomery Clift in Omaha, Nebraska, on October 17, 1920. His family had no roots in the Great Plains. Clift's father, William, a Tennessean by birth, served for several years as vice president of the Omaha Trust Company. A 1921 Omaha city directory lists the Clift family residence at 3527 Harney Street. Clift's mother, Ethel, a Philadelphian, disliked Omaha, and when Clift was a small child the family relocated to Chicago. In the early 1930s they settled permanently in New York City, where Clift's father set up a lucrative investment counseling firm.

In 1934 Clift made his professional acting debut in a summer stock production of *Fly Away Home*, a new comedy by Dorothy Bennett and Irving White. When *Fly Away Home* moved to Broadway in January 1935, Clift remained in the cast and was launched on a career as a Broadway juvenile. Broadway productions he appeared in include *Jubilee* (1935), a Cole Porter musical, and *There Shall Be No Night* (1940), a Pulitzer Prize–winning drama by Robert E. Sherwood. A chronic case of amoebic dysentery exempted Clift from military service in World War II. Throughout the war years Clift continued with his Broadway career in Thornton Wilder's *The Skin of Our Teeth* (1942), Lillian Hellman's *The Searching Wind* (1944), and Elsa Shelly's *Foxhole in the Parlor* (1945). Clift's final Broadway appearance came in the drama *You Touched Me!* by Tennessee Williams and Donald Windham in the fall of 1945.

In 1946, after having spurned earlier offers from Hollywood due to his reluctance to sign a long-term contract with a movie studio, Clift accepted director Howard Hawks's offer of a principal role in the independently produced film *Red River*, a psychologically centered Western about a young man (Clift) and an older man (John Wayne) in conflict over leadership of a cattle drive. While *Red River* was entangled in legal and financial difficulties that delayed its release, Clift went to Europe to star in *The Search*, a low-budget semidocumentary about an American soldier working with displaced children in war-ravaged Germany. Released in the spring of 1948 to laudatory reviews, *The Search* introduced Clift to the moviegoing public and earned him a best actor Academy Award nomination. Finally released in September 1948, *Red River* was a critical and box office smash that firmly established Clift as an important new star. Publicity material presented Clift as the son of a Wall Street stockbroker and rarely mentioned his early years in Omaha. Clift considered himself a New Yorker, and in interviews he never suggested that his Nebraska birth had any effect on his life or acting style.

In 1953 Clift earned another Academy Award nomination for his portrayal of a sensitive young soldier in *From Here to Eternity*. After this Clift's career faltered because of his extreme choosiness in regard to scripts and his increasing problems with alcohol and prescription drugs. Injuries suffered in a 1956 auto accident blunted his finely turned facial features, and he began appearing in character parts that incorporated his now-battered appearance. Clift's later films include *Suddenly Last Summer* (1959), *The Misfits* (1960), *Judgement at Nuremberg* (1961), and *Freud* (1962). Clift died of a coronary occlusion at his home in New York City. His final film, *The Defector*, a low-budget spy thriller, was released posthumously in the fall of 1966.

Mary C. Kalfatovic
Arlington, Virginia

Bosworth, Patricia. *Montgomery Clift: A Biography.* New York: Harcourt Brace Jovanovich, 1978. Montgomery Clift Papers, New York Public Library for the Performing Arts, New York City. Kalfatovic, Mary C. *Montgomery Clift: A Bio-Bibliography.* Westport CT: Greenwood Press, 1994.

CODY, IRON EYES (1907–1999)

Iron Eyes Cody was best known as the "Crying Indian" in the Keep America Beautiful advertising campaign of the 1970s, but his Hollywood credits span eight decades of film and television history. His place and date of birth are disputed, as is his ancestry, but he claimed that he was born in Oklahoma in 1907 to Cree and Cherokee ancestors. Whatever the case, he spent most of his life in Hollywood or on location. He is credited in forty-seven movies and performed uncredited in at least that many more. He not only acted in but also worked as a consultant for films such as *The Oregon Trail* (1959) and *The Unconquered* (1947). He counted among his friends film legends Gary Cooper, Tim McCoy, Cecil B. De Mille, John Ford, and many others.

One of Cody's first films was *The Covered Wagon* (1923). When the film premiered at Grauman's Chinese Theater, Cody was one of fifty Native Americans from the film who provided a prologue filled with Native American dancing and music. Cody danced and told stories in sign language, which Tim McCoy "translated." From that point on, Iron Eyes Cody was one of the most visible Native Americans in the entertainment industry.

About his involvement in the stereotypical depictions of Native Americans, Cody said, "When I first started in the film business, I had no power and was there to do what I was told: to make *exciting* Western entertainment. And in the days of the big studios, you either did what you were told or you didn't work. So we made movies, we 'gave them what they wanted,' as movies always did and continue to do." Cody died on January 4, 1999, in Los Angeles, California.

Jacquelyn Kilpatrick
Governors State University

Cody, Iron Eyes. *Indian Talk: Hand Signals of the American Indians.* Healdsburg CA: Naturegraph Publishers, 1970.
Cody, Iron Eyes, and Collin Perry. *Iron Eyes: My Life as a Hollywood Indian.* New York: Everest House, 1982.

COOPER, GARY (1901–1961)

Gary Cooper, the son of English immigrants, was born Frank James Cooper in Helena, Montana, on May 7, 1901. His lawyer father, Charles Cooper, in addition to owning a ranch outside of Helena, served for a time as a member of the Montana State Supreme Court. Young Frank loved the western life; hunting, fishing, riding, and the natural grace we associate with his screen persona doubtless relate to his being so at home in the outdoors.

After high school, Cooper, who aspired to become a political cartoonist, bounced from college to college until he found himself in Los Angeles, where his lanky frame (he was nearly six feet three inches tall), stunning good looks, and horse-riding ability helped him to win numerous roles in a series of B-Westerns. His break as an actor came in 1926, when Cooper, whose agent had changed his screen name to Gary, was cast as one of the leads in Henry King's silent film *The Winning of Barbara Worth*. But 1929 was his watershed year, with his performance in Victor Fleming's adaptation of Owen Wister's classic Western novel *The Virginian*. This film marks the advent of the distinctive Cooper hero, an identity from which he rarely deviated during his thirty-six-year career.

The Gary Cooper hero is characterized by a seemingly simple and naive, almost awkwardly shy and soft-spoken persona, equally appealing to both men and women, whose authentic nature emerges only when his sense of honor and his personal courage are challenged by a significant moral crisis. In *The Virginian* the eponymous hero, now a ranch foreman, is forced to preside over the hanging of his cattle rustler best friend, Steve (Richard Arlen). In slow close-up director Fleming focuses on the agonized face of the Virginian as Steve is hanged and captures brilliantly the grief, suffering, and profound solitude of the conscience-stricken Cooper hero, for whom the virtuous life always exacts a heavy cost.

Although only a third of Gary Cooper's films were Westerns, he is best identified as a Western star, perhaps because in all his films he is so closely associated with certain qualities of the West that have been derived from our indigenous historical, literary, and folkloric traditions. Indeed, the Cooper hero may have been the most unaffectedly natural, the most enduringly appealing and admirable, of the great masculine American character types.

In 1937, for example, Cooper made one of his most popular Westerns, *The Plainsman*, a Cecil B. De Mille adventure epic based very loosely on the lives of Wild Bill Hickok (Cooper), Calamity Jane (wonderfully played by Jean Arthur), and Buffalo Bill (James Ellison). Despite the film's historical inaccuracies and genial superficiality, Cooper, in his heroic portrayal of Indian fighter Bill Hickok, manages to endow it with considerable gravity and good sense. The viewer is ultimately startled by Hickok's death at the hands of Jack McCall in Deadwood, South Dakota, only because he seems so completely in control of his own life. And yet a fatal aura of fragile, wounded humanity surrounds him even in this generally winsome film, if only because Hickok's relationship with Calamity Jane is marred by a previous betrayal, and, like the Virginian, he has lost another friend, Buffalo Bill, this time to marriage.

The Cooper hero emerges more profoundly in a far superior film, *The Westerner* (1940), directed by William Wyler. There Cooper's representative Western type (it is interesting that, more than any other Western actor, he could play types, like a "Virginian," a "Plainsman," a "westerner," or, much later, a "Man of the West") subdues a deranged father-figure, the fanatical Judge Roy Bean (Walter Brennan), in such a way that we feel both the justice of Bean's downfall and the terrible loss for the westerner that that just downfall entails.

Gary Cooper gave his greatest performance as Will Kane, the ravaged hero of the cold war classic *High Noon* (1952), for which he won his second Academy Award (the first was for *Sergeant York* [1940]). Betrayed and driven to the brink of despair by his fellow citizens in the ugly, dusty Plains town of Hadleyville, Will Kane walks its lonely streets in his solitary struggle against the evil Frank Miller gang. Ultimately, he is forced to confront Miller by himself, and he does so with Odyssean cleverness and intelligence. Finally, at film's end, his enemies vanquished, in one of the most bitterly cynical moments in any Western, Kane

contemptuously hurls his marshal's tin star into the dust of Hadleyville as he and his wife, Amy (Grace Kelly), the only person who has finally come to his aid, leave the town and ride out onto the prairie.

Bertolt Brecht once remarked that Gary Cooper was the world's greatest actor because he was never guilty of acting. Cooper's natural affability and goodness of spirit, mixed with a complex moral seriousness, all helped to define his iconic "Americanness" as he strove in film after film to embody our national character at its ideal best. He set a standard no American star has ever matched. "Just make me the hero," Cooper once remarked to a director before he had even seen a script. The director did make him the hero, and so, of course, did we the audience throughout his exemplary career. Gary Cooper died on May 13, 1961, in Beverly Hills, California.

John L. Simons
Colorado College

McDonald, Archie P. *Shooting Stars: Heroes and Heroines of Western Film.* Bloomington: Indiana University Press, 1987. Swindell, Larry. *The Last Hero: A Biography of Gary Cooper.* Garden City NY: Doubleday and Company, 1980. Warshow, Robert. *The Immediate Experience.* Garden City NY: Doubleday and Company, 1962.

CUSTER FILMS

Hollywood has never felt particularly compelled to film its representations of Bvt. Maj. Gen. George Armstrong Custer's last battle at the Little Big Horn anywhere near where the actual epic 1876 battle occurred. But it is surprising to note that in at least some instances a few celluloid Custers and Sitting Bulls actually performed their cinematic battles before the cameras at various locales somewhere in between the Rocky Mountains and the muddy waters of the Missouri River.

On film George Armstrong Custer almost always has wielded an anachronistic saber, worn the wrong uniform, flown the wrong flags, and fired inaccurate pistols. But sometimes, in spite of a lack of historical accuracy, Custer's Last Stand on film has created a unique audience-pleasing celluloid world of its own making. Most film professionals take the viewpoint that historical films are more about the perception of history, not about documentary duplication of the event. And these very same directors, producers, writers, and actors have been more than willing to knowingly bend, alter, and even fabricate Custer filmland fiction to further a pet political viewpoint, give a vicarious thrill, or make a fast box office buck. Trying to convey a real sense of the Plains Indians Wars of the 1870s to an impressionable public has seldom been their concern.

The very first Custer film, William Selig's *Custer's Last Stand* (1909), utilized footage of a reenactment shot near the real Montana battle site intercut with scenes done in Selig's Chicago studio. But it didn't take long for early producers to discover the balmy climate of Southern California. The very next Custer

film, Thomas Ince's 1912 production of *Custer's Last Fight*, was lensed amidst the rolling hills of Santa Monica. Ince had convinced the 101 Wild West Show troupe to winter in California so he could make use of their performers and rolling stock in a series of frontier-themed films.

Of the sixty-seven motion pictures and thirty-some television representations of Custer, at least a handful were actually filmed in southeastern Montana or nearby South Dakota, the real-life haunts of the Seventh Cavalry and their Sioux and Cheyenne adversaries. *In the Days of '75 and '76* (1915) was filmed in South Dakota utilizing a local National Guard unit to portray Custer's Seventh Cavalry. Victor Mature's thespian representation of *Chief Crazy Horse* in Universal's 1957 film of the same name shot its brief Little Big Horn sequence right in the middle of the Black Hills.

Central Oregon was an adequate visual substitute for the Little Big Horn valley in *The Flaming Frontier* (1926) and Walt Disney's *Tonka* (1958). *The Scarlet West* in 1925 and *The Last Frontier* in 1926 opted for the picturesque mesas of southwestern Colorado and southeastern Utah. *Bob Hampton of Placer* (1920) did an unusual combination of filming on the Blackfeet Reservation near Glacier National Park, Montana, and Fort Huachuca in southern Arizona, where the all-black enlisted men of the famed Tenth Cavalry stood in for the Seventh Cavalry in vast panoramic shots filmed from high atop a hovering signal balloon.

Cecil B. De Mille's 1936 epic, *The Plainsman*, staged most of the film's large-scale battle scenes with a second unit near the Tongue River in Montana, only to see most of that footage then used as back projection for principal scenes filmed at sound stages on the Paramount lot in Los Angeles. When Paramount revisited the Custer battle with *Warpath* in 1951, the same Tongue River area was used again along with a partial reconstruction of Fort Abraham Lincoln built at the Montana State Fairgrounds in Billings.

The most famous celluloid Custer motion picture, Errol Flynn's starring vehicle *They Died with Their Boots On* (1941), was shot exclusively on the Warner Bros. Studio Ranch in Agoura, California, a scant twenty miles from Warner's main lot in the Los Angeles suburb of Burbank. No film has had more influence on the public's perception of Custer than this epic, until the release of *Little Big Man* in 1970. If Errol Flynn's Custer is rambunctious and overzealous, he is also loyal and courageous, all traits that, whatever else his faults, the real Custer exhibited time and again. If the film is incredibly inaccurate history, the tone of Flynn's characterization still rings quite true of the real man.

Since 1970 filmmakers have tried to get as close to filming on the real battlefield as possible. *Little Big Man* (1970), ABC's miniseries of Evan Connell's best-selling book, *Son of the Morning Star* (1991), and TNT's cable television movie *Crazy Horse* (1995) were all shot in the Billings and Hardin areas, just a stone's throw away from the hallowed marble markers on the real Custer Hill. But in 1997, when Robert Redford wanted to feature the current Little Big Horn National Battlefield in his contemporary western *The Horse Whisperer*, he had his art director build a modern-day representation near Livingston, Montana, 140 miles west of the actual location.

Perhaps therein lies the magic of Hollywood's enduring fascination with Custer. Whether Custer is a hero or a villain, a major character or a minor supporting player, his buckskin jacket and long hair are immediately recognizable. For some these objects represent the white man's sins; for others they are the visual representation of heroic legend and myth. Custer's appeal on a medium like film is obvious; he is the most adaptable of visual symbols that represent the American West. Villain, hero, fool, misunderstood warrior, whatever the times have called for, filmmakers have molded George Custer into the figure that best suited their needs. There is no reason to think that will change in the future.

See also IMAGES AND ICONS: Custer, George Armstrong.

Dan Gagliasso
National Cowboy Hall of Fame

Dippie, Brian W. *Custer's Last Stand: Anatomy of an American Myth*. Missoula: University of Montana Press, 1976. Gagliasso, Daniel L. *The Celluloid Custer*. Lincoln: University of Nebraska Press, 2000. Hutton, Paul Andrew. "Correct in Every Detail." *Montana, the Magazine of the Western History* 41 (1991): 28–54.

DANCES WITH WOLVES

Kevin Costner's Academy Award–winning *Dances with Wolves* (1990) is likely the most powerful cinematic reminder of the grandeur of the prairie that once spanned the heart of the North American continent. Although best known for its revisionist treatment of Indians (Lakota Sioux) in the last years of and just after the Civil War, *Dances with Wolves* offers many scenes that help convey the color, breadth, and vastness of the Great Plains. *Dances* was shot on location for five months in South Dakota, and the centerpiece of the film is an extended buffalo hunt during which Costner's character, Lt. John J. Dunbar, kills a wounded buffalo that threatens a young Sioux and is then informally initiated into the tribe. For the hunt, Costner took his actors and crew to a 62,000-acre ranch northwest of Pierre, South Dakota. Holding 3,500 head of bison, the ranch offers visiting hunters the chance to shoot bison at $1,500 a head.

Exploiting wide-screen cinematography and an epic format more common to the 1950s and 1960s, *Dances* is a finely crafted film. The acting is outstanding in a genre not known for patient explorations of character; the cinematography of a reimagined Great Plains, cavalry blues, Sioux buckskin and face paint, and horses, wolf, and buffalo blend a wide-screen lushness with the austerity of a nature documentary; the editing is expert; and the gliding camera complements the restrained performances of all the actors. Many scenes and moments use little or no dialogue, encouraging attention to imagery, sound effects, and a now-alien aural environment. Early in the film, Dunbar silently brushes his hand across the waist-high grasses of the prairie. Later in the film, we see Kicking Bird (Grahame Greene) repeat the gesture. The parallelism provides a powerful evocation of the sublime force of the great prairie on people of the period. While classic Westerns had most often been set in valleys over which the Rockies towered or amidst the other-worldly landscapes of Monument Valley, *Dances with Wolves* carefully and quietly evoked the grandeur of a more subtle geography, where muted earth tones and the big sky dominate.

In November 1993 ABC broadcast a longer version of *Dances* that incorporated footage left out of the original American theatrical release. Much of the material, nearly an hour long, expanded on themes established in the first film. More environmental destruction is seen. A white hunting camp on sacred Sioux grounds is strewn with animal carcasses and empty whisky bottles. The prior inhabitants of Fort Sedgewick are shown, isolated on the Plains and surrounded by Indians, the remainder of the command reduced to savage living in cliff-side dugouts—a dark contrast to Dunbar's successful transition to nature and Indian ways. A recent treatment of the "vanishing American" narrative, *Dances* ends, unsurprisingly, far above the Plains, with Dunbar and his bride, Stands with Fists, ascending a remote, snow-covered mountain, their tribe hunted by the army, the prairie no longer a refuge from accelerating encroachment.

Robert Baird
University of Illinois

Bird, Elizabeth S. *Dressing in Feathers: The Construction of the Indian in American Popular Culture*. Boulder CO: Westview Press, 1996. Blake, Michael. *Dances with Wolves*. New York: Ballantine, 1988. Rollins, Peter C., and John E. O'Connor, eds. *Hollywood's Indian: The Portrayal of the Native American in Film*. Lexington: University Press of Kentucky, 1998.

DAYS OF HEAVEN

Days of Heaven, written and directed by Terrence Malick and released in 1978, is perhaps the most pictorially beautiful depiction of the Great Plains ever created on film. Set in the Texas Panhandle at the onset of World War I but actually filmed in the wheat fields of Alberta, the film reflects Malick's sensitivity to a landscape he knows well, having worked on the wheat harvest as a teenager, following it from his native Texas north to Canada.

Like his first film, *Badlands* (1973), which was based on the Charles Starkweather/Caril Fugate murder spree across Nebraska in the late 1950s, *Days of Heaven* employs voice-over narration, emphasizes the setting, and centers on poor and uneducated characters. But *Days of Heaven* is more generalized and distanced, almost mythic. This quality is effected by a number of elements: the plot, based on the tragic love triangle of Bill, Abby, and "the Farmer," unfolds episodically but with implacable inevitability; there is a preponderance of long shots; dialogue is held to a minimum; water, fire, and a plague of locusts are important to the visual presentation; the characters are often backlit (with the sun behind them, they are virtually silhouetted) and thus depersonalized; and much of the shooting was done at the "magic hour" right after sunset, producing a clear and lonely light.

Nestor Almendros, the film's internationally renowned cinematographer, explained that *Days of Heaven* was shot in Alberta because it was a Hutterite area, largely untouched by modern influences. The Hutterites' wheat was longer than conventional wheat varieties, their silos were red, and collectors among them were in possession of steam tractors and cutters. This landscape evoked the Plains of the early twentieth century.

Perhaps because of this pastoralism, some critics have thought that the film lacks any political view of the impoverished farmworkers, but this judgment is debatable. The film's

Days of Heaven

title sequence is a montage of black-and-white still photographs of turn-of-the-century urban poor people taken by Lewis Hine, among other noted photographers, followed by the opening sequence of a Chicago steel mill that shows Bill (Richard Gere) in an argument with the foreman that leads to his flight by freight train to the wheat fields. In the fields we see harvesters' pay docked by the farm foreman for a "short line" a little while before the Farmer's accountant tells him that he's becoming the richest man in the county. The voice-over of Bill's sister Linda (Linda Manz) includes lines such as "the rich got it figured out" and "some got more than they need, others less." This is not to suggest that *Days of Heaven* is primarily a progressive political film; rather, the issue of class is an aspect of the whole.

If *Days of Heaven* has a problem it is with the whole. Its elliptical plot—the love story of Bill, Abby (Brooke Adams), and the Farmer (Sam Shepard)—does not sustain the tenor of the film because the characters lack depth of development. What is compelling is the cycle of Plains seasons—the harvest, winter snow, the emergence of spring shoots—with its eloquently rendered evocation of the natural order.

June Perry Levine
University of Nebraska–Lincoln

Denby, David. "Museum Piece." *New York* (September 25, 1978): 138–40. Fox, Terry Curtis. "The Last Rays of Light." *Film Comment* (1978): 27–28. Riley, Brooks. "Nestor Almendros Interviewed." *Film Comment* (1978): 28–31.

DENNIS, SANDY (1937–1992)

The actress Sandy Dennis, whose nervous and fragile screen persona had very little to do with the real person, was born in Hastings, Nebraska, on April 17, 1937. Her father was a postal clerk. At the age of fourteen, after watching Kim Stanley and Joanne Woodward in the television production *A Lady of Property*, she realized that her calling was acting. Her talent quickly became evident. She played leading roles in high school plays and in the Lincoln Community Theater; at the age of nineteen she left Nebraska for New York City and a distinguished career in acting.

Within three months Dennis had won her first professional role as a thirteen-year-old in Henrik Ibsen's *The Lady from the Sea*. She studied with Lee Strasberg at the Actors Studio and secured major roles in Broadway plays in the early 1960s. By 1964 she had collected two Tonys and a New York Drama Critics Poll Award.

Dennis's movie breakthrough came in 1967, when she played Honey, the whimpering wife of the young faculty member in *Who's Afraid of Virginia Woolf*. She won an Academy Award for best supporting actress for her performance. Other critically acclaimed performances in comedies and dramas on stage and screen followed, but her popularity declined in the 1970s and 1980s, partly because she refused to glamorize her appearance. Her final film role was in 1991 in Sean Penn's *The Indian*

Runner, fittingly set in Dennis's home state of Nebraska.

Dennis was briefly married to her longtime companion, jazz musician Gerry Mulligan, from 1975 to 1976. However, a self-described "solitary person," she seemed to be more comfortable in the company of cats and dogs than of people. Sandy Dennis lived the final years of her life with her mother in Westport, Connecticut, where she died of ovarian cancer on March 2, 1992.

David J. Wishart
University of Nebraska–Lincoln

DISNEY, WALT (1901–1966)

After creating Mickey Mouse in 1928, Walt Disney proceeded in his cartoons, movies, television shows, and theme parks to establish an entertainment empire, dedicated to re-creating American popular culture in Disney's own image. Walt was essentially a product of his midwestern upbringing. Born in Chicago on December 5, 1901, the fourth son of Elias and Flora Disney, he grew up in two Missouri towns, rural Marceline and urban Kansas City, where he acquired the background experience and moral outlook—Protestant values, indomitable self-reliance, a sturdy work ethic, and a distrust of outsiders—that would pervade all of his work.

Disney began as a cartoonist and animator from 1921 to 1923 for Kansas City Film Ad and for his own company, Laugh-O-Gram, producing animated advertisements for local theaters and a series of fairy tales for national distribution. Before he left Kansas City for good in 1923, he had gathered around him a circle of friends and associates who would, either as colleagues or eventual competitors, follow him to Los Angeles and collectively change the face of American animation: Ub Iwerks (thereafter Disney's chief technical supervisor), theater organist Carl Stalling (who would later join the Warner Bros. cartoon unit as its principal composer), Fritz Freleng (later a cartoon producer for Warner Bros. and for his own Depatie-Freleng company), and Hugh Harmon and Rudolph Ising (later the heads of Harmon-Ising animation, which originated the *Bosco* cartoons and the *Merrie Melodies* series for Warner Bros.).

In important respects, Walt never really left Kansas City and the Midwest behind. By all accounts, his early years working on his father's farm near Marceline, Missouri, were filled with pain and hardship, dominated by his abusive father. Yet he transformed and idealized this miserable experience into a fantasy of life in a picturesque, turn-of-the-century small town—with its town square, bandstand, and quaint shop fronts—that appears in virtually all the Mickey Mouse cartoons (beginning with *Steamboat Willie* in 1928) and in dozens of live-action feature films and television shows, including *So Dear to My Heart* (1946), *Pollyanna* (1960), *Mary Poppins* (1964), and the *Mickey Mouse Club* series in the 1950s. Significantly, it was Marceline's Main Street that Disney reconstituted into the "Main

Street" of the theme parks in Anaheim, Orlando, Paris, and Tokyo, the only area through which every visitor must pass. This obsession with order and detestation of dirt points up the midwesterner's ambivalent attitude toward the soil, the fertile ground from which both food springs and encroaching weeds must be cleared away, and it is most graphically demonstrated in the substantial amount of screen time (fully one-third of the total film) devoted to Snow White's instructions to the Seven Dwarfs about how best to clean up their cottage. Walt insisted with equal fervor on tidying and cultivating his own media image as a plainspoken interpreter of cultural artifacts like classical music and great works of literature, diluting and packaging them in forms accessible to the great American mass audience. Although he died on December 16, 1966, this process, dubbed the "Disneyfication" of America, continues. He embodies the energy that once settled the New World, plowed it under, paved it over, and pushed its frontiers ever westward and that now busily reconfigures it into myth and memory.

John C. Tibbetts
University of Kansas

Schickel, Richard. *The Disney Version*. New York: Simon and Schuster, 1968. Shortridge, James R. *The Middle West: Its Meaning in American Culture*. Lawrence: University Press of Kansas, 1989. Smoodin, Eric, ed. *Disney Discourse: Producing the Magic Kingdom*. New York: Frederick Ungar, 1978.

DRYLANDERS

Drylanders (1963) was the first feature film made by the National Film Board of Canada. Directed by Don Haldane, it chronicles thirty years in the lives of a family who homestead, farm, live, and suffer under the power of nature in the Great Plains. The film was made on location in the Swift Current area in southwestern Saskatchewan in 1961, premiered there in 1963 to an enthusiastic audience, and went on general release in 1964. Originally planned as a television program for the Canadian Broadcasting Corporation, which showed little interest in it, it became a ninety-five-minute black-and-white feature, which was reduced to seventy minutes for general release and is now available in four parts for teaching English as a second language.

The story is organized in two major sequences, 1907–9 and 1928–38. It begins in the spring of 1907 after the terrible winter of 1906–7, when Dan (James Douglas) and Liza Greer (Frances Hyland) and their two small sons arrive at their quarter section, which is a survey post, the major feature on that treeless land. There is a sod house building bee, a dance, a blizzard, and the first crop—and the hail that destroys it. That sense of hope and disaster is a prelude to the more devastating second sequence: the bumper crop of 1928 is followed by the great drought, during which the younger son (Don Francks) leaves for the city, the older son (William Fruet) stays (though there is only dust), neighbors leave, the father dies without hope, and the rains come, leaving Liza to say at the end of the film, "We're starting over again."

Between these two sequences a long montage, sometimes using license plates to chart the passage of time, disposes of World War I, in which the eldest son fights, his marriage, and the many years of good times on the farm. The montage, however, is out of sync with what goes before and comes after—the sequences that evoke an emotional response to the joys and tribulations of the Greer family. Are those invisible twenty years part of the twenty-five minutes Haldane was forced to cut? There is a successful second montage of the younger son walking the city; the closed warehouses, shut gates, soup kitchens, owners shaking their heads, letters home, riding the rail, and so on succeed, in the method of Eisenstein, to create a powerful metaphor for the unemployed single man in the city.

Drylanders is a film about farmers and nature, not about farmers and markets. There are haunting images of the Greers against the beautiful and harsh environment: the oxen and cart against a prairie sunset, the father disappearing over a snowbank in a blizzard, the dust swallowing house and barns, the lone farmer standing tall in the field. There are, however, no banks, no cost-price squeeze, no grain exchange, and no farmer protests. We know the drought eats money as well as hope, but there's no boom-bust to accompany it.

The film is really about the human heart and farming the Great Plains, not about the balance sheet. A central theme is hope and its obverse, despair, which is the trajectory the father suffers. It is his optimism and hope that bring the family west and help him survive the growing skepticism of his wife and early setbacks. When he loses all hope during the Depression and dies in 1938 after years of despair, that's a terrible pattern of defeat offset only by his wife's growing resolve to stay in the place she hated and now calls home no matter what. When the minister tells her not to lose hope, she replies, "Trouble with hope is it has to be fed," and of Dan's death she says, "The prairie had betrayed him." In *Drylanders* no one wins easily.

In style *Drylanders* is a film that declares itself a film, in its voice-overs, balancing of light and shade, elaborate camera angles, long montage sequences, and obvious symbolism and poetry. There is a great deal of pleasure to be gained from its style, from the photography of Reginald Morris, the music of Eldon Rathburn (who scored more than a hundred films at the National Film Board from 1944 to 1976), the literate script of Charles Cohen, and the acting, especially that of Frances Hyland (whose "educated" pronunciation seems right for a woman of 1907), though all the performances are good.

The film must finally be judged on its ability to move us, to make us feel the hope and despair of the homesteader and farmer in the Great Plains, in this case, the prairie of Saskatchewan. That opening night audience in Swift Current felt that emotion.

Don Kerr
University of Saskatchewan

Evans, Gary. *In the National Interest: A Chronicle of the National Film Board of Canada from 1949 to 1989.* Toronto: University of Toronto Press, 1991. Morris, Peter. *The Film Companies.* Toronto: Irwin, 1984.

FAIRBANKS, DOUGLAS, SR. (1883–1939)

A major force in the motion picture industry in the 1910s and 1920s, Douglas Fairbanks is best remembered for his swashbuckling costume pictures. He was born Douglas Elton Ulman on May 23, 1883, in Denver, Colorado, the last of three children to Ella and H. Charles Ulman. After his father deserted the family, he was raised by his mother, who reassumed the surname of her first husband, Fairbanks. The family relocated to New York City in 1900, and young Doug began appearing in a succession of light comedies on Broadway. By 1914 he had established himself as a leading performer in satiric comedies like *The Show Shop* and *The New Henrietta*.

Lured to Hollywood in 1915, his buoyant optimism and physical agility transferred easily to the motion picture screen. In just his first year at Triangle–Fine Arts, the spectacular success of open-air adventures like *The Lamb* (1915) and *The Good Bad Man* (1916) and farcical comedies like *His Picture in the Papers* and *American Aristocracy* (1916) encouraged him to form his own production company, the Douglas Fairbanks Film Corporation. Two years later he joined Mary Pickford (soon to become his second wife), Charles Chaplin, and D. W. Griffith at United Artists, through which he released his legendary swashbuckling costume pictures, including *The Mark of Zorro* (1920), *The Three Musketeers* (1921), *Robin Hood* (1922), *The Thief of Bagdad* (1924), and *The Black Pirate* (1926). After the box office failure of his first talkie, *The Taming of the Shrew* (1929), costarring Mary Pickford, his career trajectory faltered, and he retired from the screen after making *The Private Life of Don Juan* (1934) in England. Restless to the end, he divorced Pickford in 1936, married again a year later, and, after years of traveling and a series of half-hearted business ventures, died in his sleep of a heart attack in the early morning hours of December 12, 1939.

Fairbanks remains the very embodiment of energy and optimism. In action and philosophy his was the poetry of pose, the strut of sentiment. He was an equal opportunity enthusiast who played no favorites in the democracy of delights. He pulled high-fives with the world and claimed its privileges. An influential businessman as well as a film celebrity, he helped found the Academy of Motion Picture Arts and Sciences (serving as its first president), promoted the importation and distribution in America of international art house films like Eisenstein's *Potemkin* (1925), and encouraged technical innovations in the film industry like the Technicolor process (which he employed in *The Black Pirate*).

His upbringing in Colorado and stage training in New York City lent his work a peculiar blend of western vigor and eastern attitude. Particularly in the cycle of Westerns he made from 1915 to 1919, East meets West and civilization collides with nature in imaginative and entertaining ways. In pictures like *The Lamb* and *The Mollycoddle* (1920), he's an effete aristocrat tested by the rigors of cowboy life. In *The Good Bad Man* and *The Half Breed* (1916) he's a bandit and an Indian, respectively, seeking the legitimacy of society. And in *Wild and Woolly* (1917) and *Knickerbocker Buckaroo* (1919) he erases altogether the boundaries that separate the cowboy from the clubman. Shot on locations in prairie Kansas, the desert Southwest, and the Grand Canyon, these films provide spectacular scenic arenas for his boundless energies and flamboyant acrobatics. In a typical moment from *The Mollycoddle*, he stands poised on the rim of the Grand Canyon, suddenly raises his hands, and shouts, "Hurrah for God!" It's a defining moment.

John C. Tibbetts
University of Kansas

Schickel, Richard. *His Picture in the Papers.* New York: Charterhouse, 1973. Tibbetts, John C. "The Choreography of Hope: The Films of Douglas Fairbanks, Sr." *Film Comment* 32 (1996): 50–55. Tibbetts, John C., and James M. Welsh. *His Majesty the American: The Films of Douglas Fairbanks, Sr.* Cranbury NJ: A. S. Barnes, 1977.

FILM COMPANIES

The contribution of the Great Plains to the heritage of cinema is not limited to the native-born individuals such as Buster Keaton and Marlon Brando who made names for themselves in Hollywood. Not only was the Plains used for "location" filming in mainstream theatrical releases, newsreels, and documentaries, but the region was also home to many motion picture producers, both companies and individuals.

Motion picture technology was born in the 1890s in North America primarily through the work of Thomas Edison and his employees. The key was the invention of flexible photographic film, created by the Eastman Kodak Company for use in still cameras. Innovations abounded in the early years, but soon after the turn of the twentieth century the 35-mm film format was well established as a standard in America (by 1910, motion picture film was Kodak's best-selling product).

At the same time, motion pictures became an increasingly popular form of entertainment, and entrepreneurs were more than willing to exploit the trend. Public houses (particularly opera houses) were converted to accommodate movie projection, and new theaters were built. Pioneering Colorado filmmaker Harry Buckwalter described the situation in 1907: "The picture show business has developed into a most astonishing industry throughout the country. Everywhere it is flourishing. . . . It is the poor man's grand opera."

In 1915 the *Omaha World-Herald*, believing that the movies' influence on the public was significant, launched a weekly review page. By 1917 there were nearly 600 movie theaters throughout Nebraska, almost double the number of just a few years before. Motion picture projectors could be found in schools, churches, corporate offices, even in the state penitentiary and the State Hospital for the Insane. This scenario was played out in the rest of the Great Plains as well as throughout the United States.

All this activity was meant to accommodate the flood of films being produced both nationally and locally. In those early years, the large commercial film studios were located in New York, New Jersey, Chicago, and Los Angeles, all quite distant from the Great Plains. But the lure of the Plains was compelling for the fledgling motion picture industry, especially as a setting for that quintessential North American film genre, the Western. Studios like Selig Polyscope, American Biograph, Lubin, Universal, and Famous Players–Lasky all came to the Plains to take advantage of the broad landscape and the genuine pioneering qualities of the locals. Besides bringing Plains scenery to broad audiences, this cinematic activity served to encourage local filmmaking efforts. Photographers, film distributors, and investors set up independent businesses for the production of local motion picture projects, particularly during the 1910s and 1920s. This phenomenon was certainly not specific to the Great Plains; homegrown moviemaking was widespread throughout North America starting shortly after the turn of the century, fueled by the rapidly changing technology of motion picture production and by the great economic promise of the burgeoning motion picture industry. But the Great Plains more than kept abreast of this trend. Notable examples from the region were the Black Hills Feature Film Company (Nebraska), the 101 Bison Studio (Oklahoma), the Rocky Mountain Production Company (Wyoming), and the Jamieson Film Company (Texas), as well as independent filmmakers Harry Buckwalter (Colorado) and James Freer (Manitoba, Canada). Though many intended to capitalize on the Western theme (as did their larger and more famous counterparts), their productions ultimately ran the gamut of film genres, from fictional features, travelogues, and historical reenactments to industrial training, educational, and promotional films. In many cases, the people behind these ventures dreamed of widespread theatrical distribution, but most often their products enjoyed only a limited run within a relatively local geographic area.

In addition to these established production companies, the Great Plains was also home to independent itinerant movie producers who traveled throughout the region and filmed events, promotions, or short fictional pieces for a price. Such films were made in countless venues. They most often resulted in footage of a county fair or other local celebration or pageant (known as actuality footage), but some involved attempts at acting by local residents playing out roles from a prepackaged script (these latter productions are called local talent films).

Capturing the Great Plains on celluloid was limited to professionals only until 1923, when the 16-mm home movie film format was introduced (followed by the 8-mm format in 1932). This put the power of motion picture production in the hands of hobbyists and resulted in unique and voluminous film records of Plains life and culture. After World War II, the amateur 16-mm format gained professional status, leading to a flurry of motion picture production for use in educational, corporate, and recreational settings and in the new film delivery medium of television (the first local TV station within the Great Plains regional borders was WBAP-TV in Fort Worth, Texas; it went on the air on September 29, 1948). During this time, the production of promotional films, public service films, and educational films abounded, as did the capture of daily local events for television news broadcasts. This trend continues today, although celluloid film has been replaced with magnetic videotape.

See also AFRICAN AMERICANS: Johnson, Noble M.; Micheaux, Oscar; Parks, Gordon.

Paul J. Eisloeffel
Nebraska State Historical Society

Horne, G. S. "Interpreting Prairie Cinema." *Prairie Forum* 22 (1997): 135–51. Jones, William. "Harry Buckwalter: Pioneer Colorado Filmmaker." *Film History* 4 (1990): 89–100.

FONDA, HENRY (1906–1982)

Henry Jaynes Fonda, one of America's most beloved screen actors, won the admiration of film fans around the world with an unassuming acting style that was engagingly forthright and sincere. From his Hollywood debut in *The Farmer Takes a Wife* (1935) to his Oscar-winning performance in *On Golden Pond* (1981), Fonda projected a clear-eyed integrity that compelled him to seek the truth and stand up for the little guy.

Born in Grand Island, Nebraska, on May 16, 1906, Fonda moved with his family to Omaha when he was six months old. Intent on a career in journalism, he enrolled at the University of Minnesota. He dropped out after two years and returned to Omaha and a job as an office boy. In 1925 a friend of the family—the mother of then one-year-old Marlon Brando—asked him to act in an amateur production at the Omaha Community Playhouse. Entranced by the theater, Fonda quit his office job to work with the company for three years.

In 1928 Fonda headed to New York to seek his fortune as a professional actor. After several minor Broadway roles, he achieved stardom in *The Farmer Takes a Wife*, his first film role. As a young Hollywood leading man, Fonda at first played opposite established female stars such as Bette Davis in *Jezebel* (1938). The defining moment for Fonda's career came in director John Ford's *The Young Mr. Lincoln* (1939), a role that allowed the actor's aura of midwestern honesty and thoughtful compassion to shine. Other now classic films capitalizing on Fonda's quiet heroism include *The Grapes of Wrath* (1940), *The Ox-Bow Incident* (1943), *My Darling Clementine* (1946), *Twelve Angry Men* (1957), and *Fail Safe* (1964).

Although his international celebrity was a result of his status as a Hollywood star, Fonda's true love was theater, and in 1948 he returned to Broadway for three long-running hit plays, *Mr. Roberts* (1948), *Point of No Return* (1951), and *The Caine Mutiny Court-Martial* (1954). Fonda might never have appeared in movies again had it not been for John Ford, who insisted that he reprise his role of *Mr. Roberts* for the 1955 film adaptation. Thereafter, Fonda shuttled back and forth between New York and Los Angeles. Among his last triumphs were the one-man Broadway show *Clarence Darrow* (1974) and his cutting-against-the-grain villain in film director Sergio Leone's epic *Once Upon a Time in the West* (1969).

In 1981, when he was sick and dying, Fonda agreed to film the adaptation of *On Golden Pond*, which costarred and was produced by his daughter Jane. Teamed with Katharine Hepburn in what proved to be his final role, Fonda was hailed by the critics, the public, and the Academy of Motion Picture Arts and Sciences, which awarded him a best actor Oscar. Fonda also is the father of actor-producer Peter Fonda. Henry Fonda, who was granted a Life Achievement Award by the American Film Institute in 1978, died in Los Angeles on August 12, 1982.

Chuck Berg
University of Kansas

Fonda, Henry. *My Life: As Told to Howard Teichman*. New York: New American Library, 1981. Sweeny, Kevin. *Henry Fonda: A Bio-Bibliography*. New York: Greenwood Press, 1992. Thomas, Tony. *The Films of Henry Fonda*. Secaucus NJ: Citadel Press, 1983.

GALE, DOROTHY

See IMAGES AND ICONS: Gale, Dorothy

GIANT

Edna Ferber's best-selling novel *Giant* (1952) provides the basis for this 1956 film set in Texas and directed by George Stevens. Stevens, who won an Academy Award for best director for *Giant*, was especially lauded for his ability to juxtapose the vast Texas landscape with the narrow-mindedness of the people who lived there. The film's star-studded cast includes Elizabeth Taylor, Rock Hudson, and James Dean. *Giant* was Dean's last film before his fatal car accident, which occurred two weeks after shooting the final scene.

Ferber based the opulent lifestyle portrayed by Bick and Leslie Benedict (Hudson and Taylor) on wealthy Texas ranch owners and oil developers like Bob Kleberg and Glenn McCarthy, who received significant media attention in the 1940s and 1950s, including representation on the cover of *Time* magazine. *Giant* contrasts a materialistic life of lavish dinners, fine clothes, and automobiles with the exploitation of Mexican Americans, whose labor was a significant commodity in the Texas economy. Mexican Americans were still being referred to as "wetbacks" in the U.S. government documents and academic reports that Ferber used as sources in the late 1940s. In addition to the politics of materialism, the film addresses racial and class prejudices directly when the Benedicts' son (played by Dennis Hopper) marries a Mexican woman. The novel and film caused

James Dean in Giant

considerable controversy. Articles in newspapers and magazines, including the *Dallas Morning News* and the *Houston Press*, protested what they considered a stereotypical and exaggerated representation of the Texas culture.

Virginia M. Wright-Peterson
University of Nebraska–Lincoln

Ferber, Edna. *A Kind of Magic.* New York: Doubleday, 1963. Edna Ferber Papers, Wisconsin State Historical Society Archives, Madison. Richie, Donald. *George Stevens: An American Romantic.* New York: Museum of Modern Art, 1970.

THE GRAPES OF WRATH

While John Ford was filming *The Grapes of Wrath* in 1940, St. Louis citizens were dumping the controversial "communist" novel into the Mississippi. Darryl F. Zanuck, head of Twentieth Century Fox, acquired the rights to John Steinbeck's novel, appointed the most respected screenwriter of the time, Nunnally Johnson, to write the script, and then negotiated for what seemed to be the obvious director, John Ford. Henry Fonda coveted the role of Tom Joad so much that he bargained away his career to get the role. But with the Hays Commission criticizing any overt political statement and the novel's controversy, Zanuck was worried about his prize property. Ford took his production inside a sound stage so that no one could interfere. Gregg Toland, whose stylized black-and-white photography would contribute greatly not only to Ford's *The Long Voyage Home* (1940) but also to Orson Welles's *Citizen Kane* (1941), was Ford's cinematographer. Toland's work became part of Ford's translation of Steinbeck's naturalism and pessimism to the screen.

In John Ford's films, one or two protagonists try to maintain their sometimes perverse individuality while helping some nuclear, professional, social, or makeshift family. Often the family or society may incorporate the individual into its mythology and thus guarantee cultural continuity. In John Steinbeck's novel, set in eastern Oklahoma during the Great Depression, family and individuality are crushed by the times. Ford's film doesn't cheat Steinbeck. It recognizes the times and Steinbeck's points (and even his tone), but it maintains Ford's romanticism (a romanticism that would dim with later films).

In the film, Ford and Toland's compositions confine or squeeze the protagonist, Tom Joad, played by Henry Fonda at his iconic best. Ford and Fonda, both cognizant of the dark side of the American male hero, present Tom Joad, a returning convict, in danger of turning sociopathic if not even psychopathic. When Ma Joad (Jane Darwell) first sees him upon his return from prison, she asks, "Did they [the prison, the system] hurt you and make you mean, mad?" From the way that Fonda conducts himself, from Ford's composition, we see that Tom could turn mean or mad. But his madness is the key to his salvation and his transcendence.

Casey, the preacher (John Carradine), becomes a stand-in for John the Baptist and anoints Tom Joad as the visionary. When Casey is killed, Tom, not yet fully aware of his new status, not fully past his psychopathic urges, kills a deputy. Later, fully aware of Casey's vision in his "I'll be there speech" to Ma, Tom becomes Emersonian: "Fella ain't got a soul, just a piece of the big soul. The big soul that belongs to everybody. I'll be all around in the dark." He walks into the dark and disappears, into the compositions that squeezed him. He may die, but he has learned something of a new consciousness, or maybe he has learned to forget his own consciousness in order to become a part of the flow of all life. His sacrifice makes society better. The only false note is the ending, Ma's "We're the People" speech that tries to turn the film into patriotic propaganda. Ford claims Zanuck attached the last scene; Johnson claimed that it was in his original script; Zanuck denied attaching it. In other words, no one claims it, for it smears this epic poem.

Ford's *Grapes of Wrath* is not so much a portrayal of a particular American time and place as a dark, brooding, but ultimately optimistic and poetic vision of America. It shows the way one medium can adopt or adapt from another to produce not a hybrid, not a completely different animal, but a meditation and variation on the tone and theme of the original.

See also IMAGES AND ICONS: Okies / PHYSICAL ENVIRONMENT: Dust Bowl / TRANSPORTATION: Route 66.

Jim Sanderson
Lamar University

Gallagher, Tag. *John Ford: The Man and His Films.* Berkeley: University of California Press, 1986. Place, J. A. *The Non-Western Films of John Ford.* Secaucus NJ: Citadel Press, 1979. Sanderson, Jim. "American Romanticism in John Ford's *The Grapes of Wrath*: Horizontalness, Darkness, Christ, and F.D.R." *Literature/Film Quarterly* 17 (1989): 231–44.

GRAY, COLEEN (b. 1922)

Coleen Gray was born Doris Jensen on October 23, 1922, in Staplehurst, a small town in eastern Nebraska. She attended Hamline University in St. Paul, Minnesota, where she became interested in dramatics. After a series of appearances in little theaters, she landed her first, uncredited role in the Hollywood musical *State Fair* (1945). The following year she had a bit part in yet another musical comedy, *Three Little Girls in Blue* (1946), also uncredited. In 1947, however, she appeared as the honest, faithful wife of criminals in two famous films noir, *Kiss of Death* and *Nightmare Alley*, in which she established herself as a competent actress capable of playing leading roles. Perhaps her most complex role was that of the abusive nurse, Ann Sebastian, in the disturbing noir *The Sleeping City* (1950), about corruption in a large city hospital. She also appeared in many Westerns and action films, among them Howard Hawks's *Red River* (1948), in which she played Fen, the lovely woman whom Thomas Dunson (John Wayne) leaves behind, in effect condemning her to death.

In all, Gray appeared in about thirty-eight motion pictures, making very few after 1960, the year she was cast in the Universal horror film *The Leech Woman*, a mediocre picture in which she was quite good. She continued to appear on television, playing guest roles in various series, but these appearances also diminished, and after 1972 she retired from acting altogether. She made a brief return with a role in *Cry from the Mountain* (1986), made by the Reverend Billy Graham.

Samuel J. Umland
University of Nebraska at Kearney

Katz, Ephraim. *The Film Encyclopedia*. New York: Thomas Y. Crowell, 1979. Silver, Alain, and Elizabeth Ward, eds. *Film Noir: An Encyclopedic Reference to the American Style*. Woodstock NY: Overlook Press, 1979.

HARLOW, JEAN (1911–1937)

Jean Harlow, the platinum blond embodiment of sexual glamour in Hollywood's Golden Age, was born Harlean Carpenter in Kansas City, Missouri, on March 3, 1911. An only child doted upon by her dentist father and domineering mother, Harlean lived in a lavish Kansas City home and summered at her grandparents' twenty-five-room Bonner Springs, Kansas, retreat. Her parents' divorce in 1922 left Harlean alone with her mother, so at sixteen she eloped with wealthy Charles McGrew II and moved to Beverly Hills, California. Her mother followed, broke up the marriage, and persuaded Harlean to find work in films. Assuming her mother's maiden name, stunning Jean Harlow achieved instant stardom in *Hell's Angels* (1930), an aerial drama financed and directed by Howard Hughes.

Two years later, Hughes sold Harlow's contract to Metro-Goldwyn-Mayer, where her knack for comedy surfaced in *Red-Headed Woman* and *Red Dust* (both 1932). Meanwhile, her two-month marriage to MGM executive Paul Bern ended with his suicide in their home. Braving rumors of impotence, bigamy, and foul play, Harlow not only survived the scandal but emerged more popular than ever, becoming one of MGM's most important and beloved stars in hits like *Dinner at Eight* (1933), *Bombshell* (1933), *China Seas* (1935), and *Wife vs. Secretary* (1936). Contrary to her provocative screen persona, Harlow was known to friends and coworkers as "the baby"; at the height of her stardom, she still lived with her mother.

Harlow's private life was chaotic and unhappy. A third marriage to MGM cameraman Harold Rosson in 1933 lasted eight months, while a three-year relationship with actor William Powell was marred by his refusal to marry. Already an alcoholic, at twenty-six Harlow succumbed to kidney failure, the result of an undiagnosed poststreptococcal infection. Her agonizing death on June 7, 1937, was widely attributed to her Christian Scientist mother's refusal to seek medical aid; in truth, doctors were present, and Harlow died in a hospital, but at the time no treatment existed to save her.

Underrated in her own lifetime, Jean Harlow is now considered a unique and irreplaceable talent; once notorious, her bleached hair has become a fashion staple.

David Steen
New York, New York

Steen, David. *Bombshell: The Life and Death of Jean Harlow*. New York: Doubleday, 1993.

HOLLYWOOD INDIANS

In more than a century of film history, the "Hollywood Indian" has rarely reflected the actual Native Americans of the Great Plains.

During the years of silent film production, Native Americans were often played by members of the Sioux Nation. "Extras" were brought in by busload for the films, and producer and director Thomas Ince had a Sioux settlement of "Ince Indians" on the California coast. Even during those years, however, Native American roles of importance were generally played by non-Native actors, and the dress and customs of Native American peoples were depicted in whatever costumes suited the director or set designer's taste and rarely reflected the individual tribes. However, the Hollywood Indian from the 1920s through the 1980s was more likely to resemble a Plains Indian than any other, largely because the American audience quickly grew accustomed to the exotic look of Plains headdresses and breastplates. In 1914, Alanson Skinner, assistant curator of the Department of Anthropology at the American Museum of Natural History, wrote the *New York Times* to complain about these inaccuracies in film costuming, describing the movies as "grotesque farces" in which Delawares were dressed as Sioux and eastern Indians were shown dwelling in skin tipis of the type used only in the trans-Mississippi West.

In 1940 a Cherokee actor named Victor Daniels (aka Chief Thunder Cloud) led a group of actors in applying to the Bureau of Indian Affairs for recognition as the "De Mille Indians," a new tribe composed only of Native Americans who worked in the film industry. While humorous, the application was also an attempt to show the artificiality of the stereotypes found in the film images. The Western imagination is largely visual, and American audiences have over the course of film history generally accepted as reality the Hollywood Indian, whether Noble Savage or Bloodthirsty Savage.

The Native American has often been used as the metaphorical foe in Westerns. For instance, when the Colonel William F. Cody (Buffalo Bill) Historical Pictures Company made *The Indian Wars* in 1914, the secretary of state sent troops and equipment for the filming, Gen. Nelson Miles agreed to appear in the film, and the War Department put the Pine Ridge Sioux (Lakota) at Cody's disposal. Such overwhelming support was due, presumably, to the fact that the film was to be used for War Department records and to enlist recruits to fight in World War I. Later, films such as *Northwest Passage* (1939) would be similarly used to engender a patriotic response in World War II, with the Hollywood Indian standing in for the German soldiers once more.

During the 1950s the images were more likely to be those of the Noble Savage, as Hollywood, experiencing the effects of McCarthyism, used the Native American to represent the oppressed Other. *Broken Arrow* (1950) and *Cheyenne Autumn* (1964) showed the Native American as gallant and dignified in the face of oppression by the dominant culture. *Little Big Man* (1970) and *Soldier Blue* (1970) used Native Americans as metaphors for the Vietnamese, with the message that innocent and noble people were being killed in an unjust war.

Perhaps the most obvious Hollywood Indian appeared in Elliot Silverstein's 1970 film *A Man Called Horse*, which was intended and well publicized as a "sympathetic and accurate portrayal" of the Plains Indians, particularly the Lakota Sioux. However, according to Ward Churchill, a Native American scholar, the film depicted Indians whose language was Lakota, whose hairstyles ranged from Assiniboine to Nez Perce to Comanche, whose tipis were Crow, and whose Sun Dance ceremony was Mandan. Other important distortions include sending an old woman out into a blizzard to die because her only means of support, her son, was killed in a raid. This is in direct opposition to the reverence with which the Sioux peoples hold the elderly.

The Hollywood Indian of the 1980s and 1990s is more likely to be an actual Native American than in previous decades, and a few films have been made that depict Native Americans less stereotypically, although many still include stereotypes old and new (the Natural Ecologist is among the new ones). Although most films that include Native Americans still take place in the past with tribes that are vanishing or have vanished (as the scroll at the end of Kevin Costner's 1990 *Dances with Wolves* indicates), the images of Native America are occasionally more human than stereotypical. Also, more films are being made by Native American filmmakers, so perhaps it is the Hollywood Indian tribe that will soon vanish.

Jacquelyn Kilpatrick
Governors State University

Bataille, Gretchen, and Charles L. P. Silet, eds. *The Pretend Indians: Images of Native Americans in the Movies*. Ames: Iowa University Press, 1980. Churchill, Ward, and Annette Jaimes. *Fantasies of the Master Race: Literature, Cinema and the Colonization of American Indians*. Monroe ME: Common Courage Press, 1992. Kilpatrick, Jacquelyn. *Celluloid Indians: Native Americans in Film*. Lincoln: University of Nebraska Press, 1999.

HOPPER, DENNIS (b. 1936)

Dennis Hopper's childhood (he was born on May 17, 1936, in Dodge City, Kansas) hardly foreshadowed the alienated, counterculture hero he would come to be known as in films of the 1960s and 1970s. In his early teens a family relocation to California made possible his pursuit of a film career. After high school graduation Hopper was awarded a scholarship to San Diego's Old Globe Theatre, where he appeared in a number of Shakespearean roles.

In the 1950s Warner Bros. cast him in a series of supporting roles with James Dean (*Rebel without a Cause* [1955]; *Giant* [1956]). Dean's acting style greatly influenced Hopper, who would later move to New York in order to study method acting at the Actors Studio. He also began a new career as a photographer, a move specifically calculated to teach him the art of filmmaking and a choice that would bring him artistic recognition.

In 1969 Hopper directed and costarred in the acclaimed *Easy Rider*, filmed from a script he had coauthored with Peter Fonda. *Easy Rider* won the prize for best film by a new director at the Cannes Film Festival. Impressed by the low-budget, high-grossing film, Hollywood gave Hopper another chance to direct. The opportunity was squandered on *The Last Movie* (1971), an unsuccessful film that cost Hopper his studio credibility. He continued to work in films, including *Apocalypse Now* (1979), but by 1984 Hopper's history of substance abuse climaxed with his commitment to a psychiatric hospital.

Two years later he began another comeback. In 1986 Hopper won an Academy Award nomination for his role in *Hoosiers* and a best supporting actor award from the National Society of Film Critics for his malevolent role in *Blue Velvet*. A year later he directed *Colors*, his first feature film in sixteen years. Hopper continues to work regularly as a creative artist, most notably, as a character actor.

Karen L. Durst
University of Nebraska–Lincoln

Katz, Ephraim. *The Film Encyclopedia.* New York: Harper Collins, 1994. Rodriguez, Elena. *Dennis Hopper: A Method to His Madness.* New York: St. Martin's Press, 1988.

HUD

The motion picture *Hud* (1963), released by Paramount, directed by Martin Ritt, and starring Paul Newman, Melvyn Douglas, Patricia Neal, and Brandon de Wilde, was based on an early novel by Larry McMurtry, *Horseman, Pass By* (1961). *Hud* was filmed in and around Claude, a small town a few miles east of Amarillo in the Texas Panhandle, and its extraordinary power can be explained by the fact that it is a morality play cast in the form of a family drama about Texas cattlemen.

At the center of the drama is Lon (de Wilde), a parentless teenager who has been raised by his grandfather, Homer Bannon (Douglas), and his uncle, Hud Bannon (Newman), two male role models whose values and ethics are in collision. Alma (Neal), the housekeeper, a woman of quiet beauty and dignity, serves as a surrogate mother for Lon. The dramatic tension resides in the decision Lon will make regarding his role model and hence the set of ethical values and principles represented, on the one hand, by his grandfather Homer and on the other by Hud. The decision to cast Brandon de Wilde, the little boy who so idolized Shane in *Shane* (1953), as Lon underscores the dramatic tension, as *Hud* is largely about the passing of heroes of mythic proportions and the epigones who follow them. Indeed, *Hud* resonates with this particular theme of the Western film, specifically, the passing of a generation that saw itself and the land as inseparable, represented by the laconic Homer and his cattle, and the arrival of a belated, pragmatic generation, represented by the epigone Hud in his misguided desire to drill oil wells.

The film garnered Academy Awards for Patricia Neal, Melvyn Douglas, and cinematographer James Wong Howe. Paul Newman and director Martin Ritt were also nominated for awards, as were the writers of the screenplay,

Irving Ravetch and Harriet Frank Jr. The film was nominated for best art direction and set decoration as well.

See also LITERARY TRADITIONS: McMurtry, Larry.

Samuel J. Umland
University of Nebraska at Kearney

Wiley, Mason, and Damien Bona. *Inside Oscar: The Unofficial History of the Academy Awards,* edited by Gail MacColl. New York: Ballantine Books, 1988.

INCIDENT AT OGLALA

Incident at Oglala is a 1992 documentary detailing the June 26, 1975, slayings of FBI special agents Jack Coler and Ronald Williams in the Jumping Bull compound near Oglala, South Dakota, and the subsequent conviction of Leonard Peltier for the crime. Although James Eagle, Dino Butler, Bob Robideau, and Peltier were charged with the shootings, Peltier was the only one convicted. Directed by Michael Apted and produced and narrated by Robert Redford, the film provides substantial background on the period of high tension on the Pine Ridge Reservation immediately following Wounded Knee II. The film clearly suggests the unscrupulous lengths to which the FBI and government prosecutors went in order to get a conviction. Peltier, who had fled to Canada, was extradited based on sworn affidavits that government prosecutors later admitted to be coerced fabrications.

Besides giving a feel for the conditions on Pine Ridge and an account of the incident, the film includes interviews and statements with key players and witnesses, including Peltier, American Indian Movement members Dennis Banks and Russell Means, William Kunstler, who served as attorney for Butler and appellant attorney for Peltier, and Myrtle Poor Bear, who claims she was coerced into changing her affidavit in order to extradite Peltier. Two assistant U.S. attorneys and one U.S. attorney speak for the government, but no FBI agents speak due to Bureau policy.

The Peltier case is ongoing. Peltier has become a celebrated example of someone considered by many to be a political prisoner. The incidents surrounding the story were also loosely used in Apted's theatrical film *Thunderheart* (1992).

See also PROTEST AND DISSENT: American Indian Movement.

Larry J. Zimmerman
University of Iowa

Messerschmidt, Jim. *The Trial of Leonard Peltier.* Boston: South End Press, 1983.

IN COLD BLOOD

See LAW: *In Cold Blood*

JOHNSON, MARTIN AND OSA

(1884–1937 and 1894–1953)

Photographers, explorers, naturalists, authors, and entrepreneurs, Martin and Osa Johnson captured and presented tens of thousands of images in their twenty-one films,

eighteen books, hundreds of magazine articles, and many vaudeville presentations across America. How these natives of southeastern Kansas—Martin was born in Rockford, Illinois, on October 9, 1884, but grew up in Independence, and Osa Leighty was born on March 19, 1894, in nearby Chanute—came to become celebrated world travelers is a fascinating story.

The Kansas Plains might seem an unlikely stimulus for risk taking, but in 1906 twenty-two-year-old Martin left Independence to travel the South Seas with Jack London. Upon his return to Independence he presented a travelogue of his adventures that attracted the admiration of the equally adventurous sixteen-year-old Osa. They eloped in 1910 and began twenty-seven years of adventure and exploration, documenting their trips to the New Hebrides in the South Seas, Borneo, and Kenya in theatrical feature films like *Among the Cannibal Isles of the South Pacific* (1918), *Simba* (1928), and *Congorilla* (1932). The Johnsons' efforts on behalf of animal preservation, night photography, aerial photography, and camera safaris have influenced later generations of naturalists and photographers. It says a lot about the Johnsons that upon arriving in Africa they planted Kansas sunflowers on the mountain slopes. After Martin's death in a plane crash near Salt Lake City on January 12, 1937, Osa wrote the autobiographical *I Married Adventure* in 1940. She died in New York City on January 7, 1953. The Martin and Osa Johnson Safari Museum in Chanute, Kansas, houses the Johnsons' maps, Native artifacts, personal memorabilia, and dozens of films, which can be viewed in a thirty-seat theater.

John C. Tibbetts
University of Kansas

Froehlich, Conrad. "Martin and Osa Johnson: Adventuring Filmmakers." *Classic Images* 229 (1994): 26, 28, 56. Imperato, Pascal and Eleanor. *They Married Adventure: The Wandering Lives of Martin and Osa Johnson.* New Brunswick NJ: Rutgers University Press, 1992. Johnson, Osa. *I Married Adventure.* 1940. Reprint, New York: Kodansha America, 1997.

JOHNSON, NOBLE M.

See AFRICAN AMERICANS: Johnson, Noble M.

JONES, TOMMY LEE (b. 1946)

Tommy Lee Jones, who was born to working-class parents in the small central Texas town of San Saba on September 15, 1946, has the looks (his face appears to have been chiseled by a dusty Plains wind) and real experience of cattle country that surely would have made him a hero of Westerns had not that genre faded before he became a star (his role in the television movie *Lonesome Dove* [1988] proves this point). Instead, he has become a popular, accomplished, not-quite-leading man in a diverse array of films, including his complex portrayal of murderer Gary Gilmore in *The Executioner's Song* (1982), his inventive character study of Clay Shaw in *JFK* (1992), and his tongue-in-cheek performances in Hollywood action movies like *Men in Black* (1997).

There is no doubt that Jones is a fine actor who through small gestures can make his characters real, and he was honored as such with a best supporting actor Academy Award for his role as Gerard in *The Fugitive* (1994). Yet part of his appeal is that he doesn't seem to take himself seriously. A cum laude graduate in English from Harvard (where he also played football and roomed with Al Gore), he nevertheless still locates "home" as "somewhere between Texas and Mexico"; he likes to play polo, but he also raises cattle on a ranch near San Saba; and he credits his Texas upbringing with giving him the work ethic that carried him through thirty-three feature films by 1998.

David J. Wishart
University of Nebraska–Lincoln

Matthews, Peter. "12 Distinct Species of Maniacal Laughter." *Sight and Sound* 7 (1997): 7–9. Smith, Gavin. "Somebody's gonna give you money, you do your best to make 'em a good hand." *Film Comment* 30 (1994): 30–36.

KEATON, BUSTER (1895–1966)

One of the greatest creators of American silent film comedy, Keaton was born Joseph Frank Keaton in Piqua, Kansas, on October 4, 1895. His father, Joe Keaton, migrated from Indiana to Oklahoma during the land boom of 1889 but soon abandoned homesteading to perform eccentric dances for Frank Cutler's Medicine Show. There Joe met Cutler's daughter Myra, who also performed in the show. In 1894 Joe married Myra and launched his own medicine show in partnership with Harry Houdini, who allegedly suggested the younger Keaton's nickname, Buster.

According to legend, one day while his parents were performing in Kansas shortly before Buster's third birthday, Buster suffered three alarming accidents. First he caught his hand in a clothes wringer, mangling the tip of his right index finger, which had to be amputated. Later the same day, he hit himself near the right eye with a rock while trying to knock a peach out of a tree. Still later, he was sucked out of a window by a tornado, carried three blocks, and deposited on the ground unhurt. Concluding that Buster might be safer onstage, Joe devised the vaudeville act known as *The Three Keatons*, which consisted primarily of an escalating combat between Buster, an unruly child, and Joe, his exasperated Irish father. As "the Human Mop," Buster entertained audiences by tumbling and being flung impassively around the stage, developing acrobatic skills he later used to perform spectacular film stunts.

Largely due to Buster's audience appeal, *The Three Keatons* thrived until Joe's alcoholism made working with him intolerable. When the act broke up in 1917, Roscoe Arbuckle recruited Buster to appear in a series of short comedies for Arbuckle's Comique Film Corporation. To Buster's surprise, the mechanics of filmmaking fascinated him, and he quickly mastered the new medium.

Keaton's greatest achievements are the thirty-two film comedies (nineteen shorts and thirteen features) he made, mostly for his own company, between 1920 and 1929. These films showcase Keaton's trademark character: an unsmiling, hauntingly earnest young man who becomes embroiled in a wide array of bizarre situations, many of them involving machines. Keaton's films are characterized by wry humor, a touch of surrealism, and a vigorous exploration of the possibilities and limitations of film as a medium. Of his feature films, *Our Hospitality* (1923), *Sherlock, Jr.* (1924), *The Navigator* (1924), *The General* (1926), and *The Cameraman* (1928) are especially notable.

In 1928 Keaton made the critical mistake of signing a contract with MGM. As a result, he quickly lost control of his films, whose quality seriously declined, while at the same time his marital and drinking problems increased. Fired by MGM in 1933, the tenacious Keaton nevertheless continued to work, less prominently, as an actor, gag writer, producer, and director. Eventually, he remarried happily and lived to see his films revived in the 1950s and 1960s. This rediscovery of his work brought him renewed, even unprecedented recognition, including a special Oscar in 1960. Buster Keaton died of lung cancer in Woodland Hills, California, on February 1, 1966. A small museum in Piqua recalls Keaton's Plains origins.

Constance Brown Kuriyama
Texas Tech University

Dardis, Tom. *Keaton: The Man Who Wouldn't Lie Down.* New York: Charles Scribner's Sons, 1979. Keaton, Buster, with Charles Samuels. *My Wonderful World of Slapstick.* New York: DaCapo, 1982. Rapf, Joanna E., and Gary L. Green. *Buster Keaton: A Bio-Bibliography.* Westport CT: Greenwood Press, 1995.

THE LAST PICTURE SHOW

In the opening scene of *The Last Picture Show* (1971), directed by Peter Bogdanovich, it appears as if gunshots are echoing through the empty dirt streets of Anarene, Texas. But it is only the backfiring of Sonny Crawford's (Timothy Bottoms) truck, and the viewer is forewarned that though this may look like a frontier town, right down to the tumbleweeds, it no longer has the energy to give rise to a gunfight. The stores are boarded up, the highway sign to Routes 25 and 79 points to the way out, and the Royal, the town's theater, is showing its final movie, Howard Hawks's *Red River*.

The year is 1951, and Sonny and his best friend, Duane (Jeff Bridges), have just lost their last football game, and, like other teenagers in Anarene, they have no idea what to do with their lives. The adults offer no model: there is Ruth Popper (Cloris Leachman), the aging and lonely wife of the boorish coach who finds respite from despair in the arms of Sonny; there is Lois Farrow (Ellen Burstyn), rich and bored and worried that her daughter—the self-centered and manipulative Jacy (Cybill Shepherd)—is following in her footsteps; there are nameless old men who aimlessly gather at the pool hall, its air heavy with dust and tedium; and everywhere there are open secrets and unmentioned infidelities. Only the dignified Sam the Lion (Ben Johnson), a former cowboy and now the theater owner, is a reminder of a more vibrant past. But Sam dies, the movie house closes, Duane heads off to Korea, and Sonny is left with no prospects in this atrophied place.

Director Peter Bogdanovich audaciously (by 1970 nearly all feature films were in color) shot the film in black and white on location in Archer City, which, like the fictional Anarene, lies just to the southwest of Wichita Falls. Bogdanovich and Larry McMurtry wrote the Academy Award–winning screenplay, which was adapted from McMurtry's 1966 novel of the same name. (The screenplay is a less bitter though no less desolate view of McMurtry's hometown of Archer City.) The music of Hank Williams, Hank Snow, and Bob Wills and the Texas Playboys, among others, confirms the time and place. With its unhappy marriages and failed lives, the movie could easily have degenerated into a soap opera, but Bogdanovich's skilled, unobtrusive direction and the superb cast of actors—both Ben Johnson and Cloris Leachman won Oscars and Ellen Burstyn won a New York Film Critics Award for their supporting roles—ensure the authenticity of this sad, elegiac portrayal of the dying days of a Great Plains town.

See also CITIES AND TOWNS: Small towns / LITERARY TRADITIONS: McMurtry, Larry.

David J. Wishart
University of Nebraska–Lincoln

Dawson, Jan. "Review of *The Last Picture Show.*" *Sight and Sound* 47 (1972): 107–8. Lorenz, Janet E. "*The Last Picture Show.*" In *International Dictionary of Films and Filmmakers,* edited by Nicholas Thomas. Chicago: St. James Press, 1990: 1: 497–99.

LITTLE, CLEAVON

See AFRICAN AMERICANS: Little, Cleavon

LITTLE BIG MAN

Little Big Man, released in 1970 and directed by Arthur Penn, is based on a novel of the same title (1964) by Thomas Berger. Berger and Calder Willingham wrote the screenplay. The film, shot on location in Montana and Canada, is a revisionist history of the mythic Old West, reflecting the social turmoil of the late 1960s.

The central character, Jack Crabb (Dustin Hoffman), is nearly 120 years old and in a home, where he relates his life story to a young writer. After his parents are killed by Native Americans on the way west, Jack and his sister are taken into a Cheyenne village. His sister escapes, but Jack is raised Cheyenne, in particular by Old Lodge Skins (Dan George).

The story is braided with characters who move in and out of the narrative as Jack ages. Later "rescued" from captivity, Crabb is caught between the worlds of the Cheyennes and European Americans. He moves through life as a gunfighter, a failed store clerk, a muleskinner, a drunkard, and a military scout, but he always moves back to the Cheyennes in order to center his life. The story is told with hyperbole, as a tall tale would be, but with deft humor and irony.

The entire film is a classic retelling of every Western ever written or made. The segments in the European American world are often the most humorous. Jack's religious education is overseen by a missionary and his lusty wife, who later reappears as a saloon prostitute. He assists a snake oil salesman and is tarred and feathered. His tutelage as a gunfighter is overseen by his "manly" sister, Caroline, and Wild Bill Hickok. His stint as an inept businessman includes his marriage to an ill-tempered immigrant woman, who henpecks him. As a drunkard, he ends up becoming a muleskinner and scout for George Armstrong Custer.

Jack's movement in and out of the Native American world is also humorous, but the Cheyennes are presented as victims. Jack is present at the Sand Creek Massacre, after which he takes a Cheyenne wife, only to see her, her sisters, and his child killed by the Seventh Cavalry on the Washita River. He lives to fight in the Battle of Greasy Grass (Little Big Horn), where a childhood rival rescues him from being killed.

The portrayals of the Old West and Native Americans are exaggerated in every way. The film marks the beginning, however, of showing Native Americans as close to nature, spiritual, and victims of the white man. *Little Big Man* was among the first films that made an effort to be ethnographically accurate in its Native American segments. It may also be the first portrayal of Custer as vainglorious and, by the time of the Washita River massacre and Little Big Horn, a raving lunatic. *Little Big Man* reflects the growing resistance to the Vietnam conflict but also incorporates other themes of the day, including more open sexuality, an exposure of religious hypocrisy, and an awareness of environmental issues.

See also LITERARY TRADITIONS: The Western.

Larry J. Zimmerman
University of Iowa

Kasdan, Margo, and Susan Tavernetti. "Native Americans in a Revisionist Western: *Little Big Man*." In *Hollywood's Indians: The Portrayal of the Native American in Film*, edited by Peter C. Rollins and John E. O'Connor. Lexington: University Press of Kentucky, 1998: 121–36.

LLOYD, HAROLD (1893–1971)

Harold Lloyd has been called the third genius of silent film comedy. The films of Charles Chaplin and Buster Keaton may be better known to modern audiences, but Lloyd's films are equally as innovative and entertaining as those of his famous contemporaries. While Chaplin was the master of pathos, and Keaton deftly battled the machinery of the modern age, Lloyd's Great Plains sensibility allowed him to mine the humor found in day-to-day experiences. His Everyman character paid tribute to the resiliency of the American spirit and the wisdom of everyday people.

Harold Clayton Lloyd was born on April 20, 1893, in Burchard, Nebraska. His father, James "Foxy" Lloyd, was frequently unemployed, requiring the Lloyds to move con-

stantly. Harold acquired his mother Elizabeth's love for dramatics, and when he was twelve years old he performed with a traveling stock company directed by John Lane Connor. In 1910 the Lloyds divorced. Harold and his father moved to San Diego, where Harold once again studied drama with Connor, his mentor. Lloyd's film debut came in 1912, when he landed a small part as a Yaqui Indian in the Edison Company's production of *The Old Monk's Tale*. In 1913 Harold moved to Los Angeles, where he performed in several Keystone comedies. He was also hired as an extra at Universal, becoming friends with another aspiring filmmaker, Hal Roach.

When Roach opened his own studio in 1914, he hired Lloyd to play a character named Willie Work in a series of comedy shorts. Willie Work was quickly replaced by Lonesome Luke, a Chaplinesque character who wore tight-fitting clothes and sported a two-piece mustache. In 1916 and 1917 Lloyd and Roach produced more than a hundred of the Luke action comedies, but Lloyd was never completely satisfied with the character. In 1917 he devised a new character who wore normal-fitting clothes and the black horn-rimmed glasses that soon became Lloyd's comic trademark. A series of short comedies starring Lloyd's new character, often referred to simply as Harold, or "the Boy," soon made the comic star the highest paid actor in Hollywood. In 1921 Roach and Lloyd produced their first feature film, *A Sailor-Made Man*, and Lloyd began outdrawing both Chaplin and Keaton at the box office.

In 1923 Lloyd married Mildred Davis, his leading lady in several films, including the masterpiece *Safety Last*, filmed that same year. Also in 1923 Lloyd and Roach parted company on friendly terms following their final collaboration, *Why Worry?* Lloyd began producing his own films for Pathé and later for Paramount. One of Lloyd's biggest commercial hits, *The Freshman*, was released in 1925. In 1929 Lloyd made the transition into sound films with *Welcome Danger*, but his style of gentle, optimistic comedy was poorly received by Depression audiences. Lloyd made his final film, *Mad Wednesday*, in 1947.

In 1952 Lloyd received a special Academy Award inscribed to a "master comedian and good citizen." In 1962 Lloyd produced a compilation of his work entitled *Harold Lloyd's World of Comedy*, which he presented at the Cannes Film Festival to a rave response. During the 1960s Lloyd traveled to colleges and film festivals, introducing his work to new audiences. Harold Lloyd died of cancer on March 8, 1971. He left over 200 films, more than Chaplin and Keaton combined, documenting his extraordinary contributions to American film comedy.

Keith Semmel
Cumberland College

Brownlow, Kevin, and David Gill, producers. *Harold Lloyd: The Third Genius*. Thames Television Production, 1989. Katz, Ephraim, ed. *The Film Encyclopedia*. New York: Harper Collins, 1994: 833–34.

LOY, MYRNA (1905–1993)

Myrna Loy, Hollywood's top female box office attraction in the mid-1930s, was born on August 2, 1905, on a sheep and wheat ranch near Raidersburg, Montana, where the Rocky Mountains meet the Great Plains. She grew up in nearby Helena in comfortable circumstances, just up the street from another future Hollywood star, Gary Cooper. Her father was a member of the Montana legislature, and early on Myrna developed her own strong political conscience. When her father died in the 1918 flu epidemic, her mother moved the family to Los Angeles, settling in Culver City, near Hollywood.

Long interested in theater and dance, Myrna started doing screen tests when she was eighteen. She landed bit roles in *The Ten Commandments* (1923) and *Ben Hur* (1925) before being typecast as a mysterious vamp in numerous films over the next ten years. Her casting opposite William Powell in *Manhattan Melodrama* in 1934 shattered this stereotype, and in subsequent films, thirteen of them with Powell, she reinvented herself as a witty and beautiful heroine, the model of the "perfect wife." The public loved the image, and in 1936 she was crowned "Queen of the Movies" in a poll, alongside the anointed "King," Clark Gable.

During World War II Loy put her film career on hold and channeled her energies into the Red Cross. She continued her political activism after the war as U.S. representative to UNESCO and as campaigner for John F. Kennedy and Eugene McCarthy in their runs for the presidency. She continued to find time for movies, most notably, *The Best Years of Our Lives* (1946).

Loy was never nominated for an Oscar, but at the 1991 ceremony she was presented with an honorary Academy Award. That same year the Myrna Loy Center opened in Helena with a mission to bring the arts to the citizens of Montana. Myrna Loy died in New York on December 14, 1993.

David J. Wishart
University of Nebraska–Lincoln

Kotsilibas-Davis, James, and Myrna Loy. *Myrna Loy: Being and Becoming*. New York: Alfred A. Knopf, 1987. Thompson, Frank. "Loy, Myrna." In *International Dictionary of Films and Filmmakers*, edited by Nicholas Thomas. Chicago: St. James Press, 1990: 3: 203–6.

MANN, DELBERT (b. 1920)

Delbert Mann, Oscar-winning motion picture and television director, was born in Lawrence, Kansas, on January 30, 1920. He moved to Nashville, Tennessee, as a young boy and graduated from Vanderbilt University in 1941. After serving as a bomber pilot during World War II he earned a master of fine arts degree from Yale's Department of Drama. In 1949 he was invited by Fred Coe, a producer at NBC Television and an old friend, to go to New York and direct live television drama. Among the many productions he directed were *The Petrified Forest* (1955), with Humphrey Bogart and Lauren Bacall, and *Marty* (1953), with Rod

Steiger and Nancy Marchand. *Marty* was so successful as a television drama that Mann was invited to Hollywood to direct the feature film with Ernest Borgnine and Betsy Blair. The film won Academy Awards in 1955 for best picture, best director, and best actor (for Borgnine). Mann directed many other Hollywood films, including *The Dark at the Top of the Stairs* (1960), *The Outsider* (1961), and *That Touch of Mink* (1962).

From the late 1960s through 1994 he directed several television films, including *David Copperfield*, *Jane Eyre*, *The Man without a Country*, *All Quiet on the Western Front*, *All the Way Home*, and, in 1994 at the age of seventy-four, *Lily in Winter*. Typical of the art that was live television drama, the hallmarks of Mann's style lie in character development and realistic drama with an interest in rendering the lives of normal everyday people. The papers of Delbert Mann, from 1947 to 1994, are preserved in the Special Collections Library of Vanderbilt University, Nashville, Tennessee. They consist primarily of the materials generated by Mann's television and motion picture productions, including production papers, scripts and script reports, photographs, videotapes, and scrapbooks.

Catherine L. Preston
University of Kansas

Harwell, Sarah, ed. *The Papers of Delbert Mann: A Manuscripts Catalog.* Nashville: Vanderbilt University, Jean and Alexander Heard Library, 1993. Mann, Delbert. *Looking Back . . . at Live Television and Other Matters.* Los Angeles: Directors Guild of America, 1998.

MCDANIEL, HATTIE

See AFRICAN AMERICANS: McDaniel, Hattie

MCGUIRE, DOROTHY (1918–2001)

Dorothy McGuire was born June 14, 1918, in Omaha, Nebraska, where she grew up. Her acting debut at age thirteen was on the stage of the Omaha Community Playhouse, where she appeared opposite Henry Fonda in *A Kiss for Cinderella*. Like Fonda, also a native Nebraskan, Dorothy McGuire had a warm, engaging personality, an honest, homespun sincerity that was to characterize the roles she played during her highly successful career.

She went to New York, first to work in radio and then on Broadway, getting her start as the understudy to Martha Scott in Thornton Wilder's *Our Town* in 1938. She then toured with John Barrymore in *My Dear Children* and in 1940 was the understudy to Julie Haydon in *The Time of Your Life*. She was chosen by playwright Rose Franken to star in the Broadway comedy *Claudia* (1941) and in 1943 played the role, opposite Robert Young, in David O. Selznick's successful film version. She and Young appeared in the sequel, *Claudia and David*, in 1946, by which time she had also appeared in Elia Kazan's *A Tree Grows in Brooklyn* (1945) and *The Spiral Staircase* (1946), a thriller in which she played a mute servant. She was nominated for but did not win an Academy Award for best actress for her performance in

Gentleman's Agreement (1947), a film about anti-Semitism. In 1947 she also founded the La Jolla Playhouse with Gregory Peck and Mel Ferrer.

She continued to appear in prestigious films —the romantic comedy *Three Coins in the Fountain* (1954) and a drama about Quaker pacifism, *Friendly Persuasion* (1956)—while her versatility as an actress continued to garner praise. Her appeal lay in the way she gave unglamorous, common, hardworking women a beauty and integrity that came from inside, from the spirit. She starred in two classic films by Walt Disney for precisely these reasons: *Old Yeller* (1957) and *Swiss Family Robinson* (1960) were both about the value of family and the difficulties of adolescence. Perhaps because her personal life remained intensely private, her screen persona dominated; she eventually played the Virgin Mary in George Stevens's *The Greatest Story Ever Told* (1965), after which she made fewer and fewer feature film appearances.

In 1976, after an absence of many years, she starred in a revival of Tennessee Williams's *The Night of the Iguana* on Broadway and also began acting in made-for-television features. All her appearances thereafter were in television, the medium in which she continued to work until the late 1980s, when she was in her seventies. Her talent and professionalism placed her in the upper echelon of the best Hollywood film actresses of the century. She died from heart failure in Santa Monica, California, on September 13, 2001.

Samuel J. Umland
University of Nebraska at Kearney

Chaneles, Sol, and Albert Wolsky, eds. *The Movie Makers.* Secaucus NJ: Derbibooks, 1974.

MICHEAUX, OSCAR

See AFRICAN AMERICANS: Micheaux, Oscar

MILLER BROTHERS

The Miller brothers, owners of the 101 Ranch near Ponca City, Oklahoma, created a world-renowned Wild West show. Col. George Washington Miller founded the 101 Ranch in 1893, and upon his death the ranch passed into the hands of his three sons, Zack, Joe, and George. While Zack focused on the ranch's oil development and George on the ranch's finances, Joe developed the *101 Real Wild West Show* and began touring in 1906. The production featured acts by Lucile Mulhall, Buffalo Bill, Geronimo, and Bill Picket. The show helped launch the careers of Tom Mix and Buck Jones.

A number of early Hollywood Westerns were shot on location at the ranch and featured many of the ranch cowboys as stars. Among these was the 1908 production *A Round-Up in Oklahoma*, directed by Oklahoma federal marshal William Tilghman, himself a participant in numerous real adventures. In 1924 Paramount used the ranch to film *North of 36* (1924), based on the Emerson Hough novel of the same name. Other films shot in their entirety or in part on the 101 Ranch were *Trail*

Dust (1924), a tale of the pioneers of the 1870s, and the ten-part series, *Wild West* (1925), a story about a circus and medicine show traveling through Oklahoma in the 1890s and starring dozens of 101 Ranch performers.

The Miller brothers established their own motion picture department in 1911 under the direction of J. B. Kent, a pioneer Oklahoma filmmaker. Their company produced films such as *Setting up the Strip*, *On with the Show*, and *The Cherokee Strip*. Some of the movies were shot on the 101 Ranch, but many others were filmed on sound lots in Los Angeles, in part because the weather was better there. In addition to their own work, the Miller brothers' ranch and show casts starred in several other Westerns, including *War on the Plains* (1912).

In 1924 the Miller brothers purchased the Walter L. Main Circus and combined the two shows. With exotic animals like buffalo, tigers, bears, and alligators, the show became a sensation in the 1920s, and the 101 Ranch hosted famous guests like John D. Rockefeller, Gen. John J. Pershing, and Presidents Theodore Roosevelt and Warren Harding. With the deaths of his brothers, Zack assumed control of the production in the late 1920s, but the Great Depression hit the show and the ranch hard. In 1931 a series of lawsuits were filed against Miller, one patron asking for $80,000 in damages because of personal injury sustained during a show. Poor attendance, debt, more lawsuits, and high traveling expenses forced Miller to sell the show in 1932, and, after a failed attempt by Al Capone to buy the 101 Ranch, the federal government purchased the land in 1937. Zack Miller moved to Texas, where he died in 1952.

See also IMAGES AND ICONS: Wild West Shows.

Stefanie Decker
Oklahoma State University

Collings, Ellsworth, and Alma Miller England. *The 101 Ranch.* Norman: University of Oklahoma Press, 1971. Spears, Jack. "Hollywood's Oklahoma!" *Chronicles of Oklahoma* 67 (1989–90): 340–81. Wallis, Michael. *The Real Wild West: The 101 Ranch and the Creation of the American West.* New York: St. Martin's Press, 1999.

MOORE, DEMI (b. 1962)

Like her contemporary in movie stardom, Brad Pitt, Demi Moore was born in the Great Plains but quickly moved on. She was born Demi Guymes on November 11, 1962, in Roswell, New Mexico. She had a tough upbringing: her mother and father married and divorced twice before separating permanently when Demi was fifteen. By her estimation, she had lived in more than thirty different towns by the time she was twelve. Geographic stability came only in 1975, when she settled in West Hollywood with her mother. At the age of sixteen she began a career as a model, and by the time she was twenty she was acting in movies and the television soap opera *General Hospital*.

Her rise to celebrity status came with her all-too-true-to-life role as a cocaine addict in *St. Elmo's Fire* (1985). Moore quickly overcame her own addiction and with great ambition and energy went on to become one of Hollywood's most bankable stars in the 1990s. Leading roles in *Ghost* (1990), *A Few Good Men* (1992), and *Indecent Proposal* (1993) proved that Moore could indeed act. Posing nude for a *Vanity Fair* cover in 1991 while seven months pregnant only added to her stardom. Her star has, perhaps, temporarily dimmed in recent years because of a series of unfortunate choices of film roles (not least, *Striptease* in 1996).

An intelligent woman with strong ideas of her own (she has been labeled "difficult" because of this), Moore was initially married to rock musician Freddy Moore and was later in a long relationship with Emilio Estevez. In 1987 she married actor Bruce Willis, with whom she has three children. They divorced in 1998.

David J. Wishart
University of Nebraska–Lincoln

MOVIE HOUSES

The first regular cinema opened in Pittsburgh, Pennsylvania, in 1905. Movie houses began appearing in the Great Plains shortly thereafter; for example, the newly incorporated town of Lubbock, Texas, boasted its first movie house, the Orpheum, in 1909. By World War I movie houses were common fixtures in communities across the Plains.

As in the rest of the nation, movie houses provided entertainment for Plains folk, that is, when proprietors could get films. Early newspaper ads promised nightly shows during the week and matinees on Saturday, tempered with the caveat "when available." Nevertheless, even irregular movie schedules provided substantially more entertainment than other sources. Radio would not be widespread on the Plains for another two decades, television for another four. Though many small communities had an opera house, which mostly hosted musicals and drama and variety shows, regular performances were difficult to support, and traveling companies—tent shows and circuses—came to town no more than once or twice a year.

Besides, the movies provided a different kind of entertainment, and that difference was important to the isolated peoples of the Plains. First, the occasion of seeing a movie was a social event in and of itself, a time and place to visit with widely scattered neighbors and friends. But while the movie house was a great place to socialize, Plains folk also found there satisfaction for their staunch independence, that collective character trait that more than any other marks this peculiar American tribe. In the anonymous darkness of the theater, separated by armrests, with all eyes turned toward the images flickering on the screen, moviegoers could escape to a bigger world, a world of their own choosing. Unlike the traveling shows and local stage offerings, which catered to narrow regional tastes and attitudes, motion pictures were crafted for a wide audience. There were new and novel sights and new and novel ideas. In the movie house, the warm smell

Blair Theatre, Belleville, Kansas

of buttered popcorn and the soft mechanical purr of the projector meant magic. If it was hard to keep 'em down on the farm after they'd seen Paree, it was harder still when Paris, and London and Rome and New York, could be seen almost anytime without leaving the county, and for little more than a dime.

But because motion pictures came along at roughly the same time that settlements were still appearing on parts of the Plains, movie houses also had a practical side. Early on, they provided much-needed facilities for public use, with local governments, churches, schools, and civic clubs all relying upon them for meeting space. Soon they became important to the local economy, bringing people to town, then giving them something to do when they got there. Before long, a nice, modern movie house became a necessity to chambers of commerce and other community boosters. Rounding out the practical side of things, movie newsreels were an important source for national and international news until television made them obsolete.

Movie houses retained their central place in Great Plains communities, both large and small, through the Dust Bowl, the Great Depression, and two world wars. In the cities, they remain today in roughly the same numbers. In Lubbock, for instance, the number of inhabitants per movie screen—a notso-scientific but commonsense yardstick—has stayed consistently between 3,000 and 4,000 over the past ninety years.

That said, movie houses themselves have all but disappeared. The newsreels are gone. And if the movies themselves still serve Plains peoples, that service is offered in the sterility of the modern multiscreen cinema or the isolation of the television set. In the cities, small neighborhood theaters have been replaced by large multiscreen facilities. Outside the cities, movie theaters of any kind are rare. Too many people have moved away, and those who remain rent videotapes and purchase satellite receivers.

Yet the movie house isn't quite dead. In Lubbock there's the Cactus; in Claude, Texas, the Gem, which was featured in the movie *Hud*; in Dalhart, Texas, it's the La Rita; and in McCook, Nebraska, the Fox. In communities across the Plains, large and small, old theaters are being renovated and put back to use, though not for the showing of motion pictures. Instead, they're providing venues for plays and concerts and other live performances, and, once again, bragging rights for their towns. Even the Royal Theater, the subject of Larry McMurtry's *The Last Picture Show*, is being rebuilt as an arts center for the town of Archer City, Texas. Perhaps there's some magic still.

Andy Wilkinson
Lubbock, Texas

Graves, Lawrence L., ed. *A History of Lubbock*. Lubbock: West Texas Museum Association, 1962. Grun, Bernard. *The Timetables of History*. New York: Simon and Schuster, 1982. Young, Norma Gene Butterbaugh. *Black Sunday*. Boise City OK: Privately published, 1998.

NOLTE, NICK (b. 1942)

Born in Omaha, Nebraska, on February 8, 1941, Nick Nolte was a star athlete in high school who won a football scholarship to Arizona State University. Over the next several years he drifted in and out of numerous college programs before abandoning plans for a professional football career.

While studying at the Pasadena Playhouse, Nolte came to the attention of a drama coach who encouraged him to study at Stella Adler's Academy. Believing that the coasts were overpopulated with talented actors, Nolte sought opportunities to develop his acting skills with various regional theater companies. He worked for more than a decade with companies in Denver, Chicago, and Minneapolis. After a few minor television roles in the early 1970s, Nolte landed the pivotal role of his career (*Rich Man, Poor Man*, ABC [1976]), which garnered him an Emmy nomination.

Hollywood noticed his phenomenal audience appeal, and Nolte began regular film work. Although much in demand as a romantic lead (*The Deep*, 1977; *Prince of Tides*, 1991), Nick Nolte has almost always shunned purely commercial fare in favor of roles that examine the darker, more troubling elements of the human spirit. As a result, he is more often seen as a complex and often threatening antagonist (*Q & A*, 1990) than a romantic leading man. Even his more romantic turns (as in *Afterglow*, 1997) examine a tortured psyche with enormous depth and realism.

One of the most physically intense and emotionally eloquent contemporary American actors, Nolte continues to produce critically acclaimed performances (*Affliction*, 1998; *The Thin Red Line*, 1999).

Karen L. Durst
University of Nebraska–Lincoln

Katz, Ephraim. *The Film Encyclopedia*. 3rd ed. New York; HarperPerennial, 1998. Macnab, Geoffrey. "Saint Nick." *Sight and Sound* 8 (1998): 6–8.

NORTHERN LIGHTS

Northern Lights (1978), an independently produced film, tells the story of North Dakota farmers who rebel against the economic tyranny of the railroads, grain dealers, and bankers by working for the election of Nonpartisan League candidates in 1916.

A mixture of historical fact and imaginative fiction, the film shows why one individual becomes involved in a radical, grassroots political movement. It begins with shots of Henry Martinson, a lifelong socialist who was in his nineties at the time the film was made. Martinson reminisces about the old days when "we had the powers that be on the run" and then discovers a diary that belonged to the fictional Ray Sorenson. The action flashes back to 1915, when Ray, his brother John, and their father are farming near Crosby, North Dakota. Visiting Nonpartisan League members advocate political changes that will give farmers more control over the grain-marketing process and thus ease their economic troubles. At first Ray is skeptical, but after his father dies and his fiancée's parents lose their farm, he is motivated by these personal losses not only to join the league but also to become an organizer, recruiting new members and campaigning for league candidates. League candidates win the primary election of 1916, but John and Ray receive a letter notifying them the bank is foreclosing on their farm. Martinson concludes the film by reporting the league's victory in the general election of 1916 and hoping that such victories might happen again in the future.

Another major theme of the film is the desire to have a personal life and the sacrifice of that life required by those who commit themselves to a cause. At the beginning of the film, Ray proposes to Inga Olsness. However, as Ray becomes increasingly involved in league activities, they seldom see each other, and their relationship deteriorates. Inga tells a friend that she no longer loves Ray as she once did, and she fears that Ray will always be away from home because the struggle will continue indefinitely. Ray and Inga might eventually get together or they might drift apart, but the disillusioned Inga feels they will never be able to live the better life for which Ray is struggling.

The film was written, directed, produced, and edited by John Hanson and Rob Nilsson through Cine Manifest, a San Francisco–based film collective that was formed to produce socially conscious narrative films. Both Hanson and Nilsson have family connections in North Dakota. A few actors, including Robert Behling, Susan Lynch, and Joe Spano, are professionals, but nonprofessional North Dakotans play the other roles. Most of the film was shot in Crosby and at Bonanzaville, a pioneer village in West Fargo, North Dakota. The North Dakota Humanities Council contributed greatly to the production of the film, which was made with an extremely low budget—a little over $300,000. The film premiered in Crosby in July 1978 and was shown throughout North Dakota and the Midwest before being entered in the Cannes Film Festival, where it won the Camera d'Or (Golden Camera) Award for best first feature film in 1979.

Although *Northern Lights* depicts an actual political movement, viewers will learn little about the Nonpartisan League from it. Martinson, an ardent socialist, is not a good representative of the league's politics, which were much more moderate. None of the league's three main leaders—A. C. Townley, Lynn Frazier, and William Lemke—appears in the film (Lemke is not even mentioned), and it does little more than hint at why the league was in power for only six years. The film has been criticized for showing women only in subservient, passive roles rather than as partners and leaders in the movement. Hanson and Nilsson, however, state that their intent was to create a social documentary that depicts the personal aspects of a political movement rather than a historical documentary.

The style of the film is unusual. The dialogue is extremely sparse, and sometimes the characters speak Norwegian. The film's photography captures both intimate family scenes and the open spaces of the prairie, and the scene that shows people threshing during a blizzard is particularly effective. Photographed by Judy Irola with 16-mm black-and-white film, which created a high-contrast image with rich tones and frequent silhouettes, the film was later blown up to 35 mm for theatrical release, which added to its grainy appearance. Irola also used a relatively old-fashioned camera style: the camera seldom moves, and most action takes place inside the frame. These techniques help create a sense that the film takes place at a much earlier time, and its visual world, which includes hard work, struggles against the forces of nature, and tough economic times, evokes the theme so often repeated in the history of the Great Plains—that of farm families being forced off their farms.

See also PROTEST AND DISSENT: Martinson, Henry; Nonpartisan League.

Eunice Pedersen Johnston
North Dakota State University

Anderegg, Michael. "History, Image, and Meaning in 'Northern Lights.'" *North Dakota History* 57 (1990): 14–23. Dempsy, Michael. "'Northern Lights': An Interview with John Hanson and Rob Nilsson." *Film Quarterly* 32 (1979): 2–10. Jenkinson, Clay. *A Humanities Guide to "Northern Lights."* Bismarck: North Dakota Humanities Council, 1981.

OIL FIELD FILMS

Movies about the discovery and production of oil are usually a subgenre of the Western and often take place in Oklahoma or Texas. From *Boom Town* (1940), with Spencer Tracy and Clark Gable, to *Stars Fell on Henrietta* (1995), with Robert Duvall and Aidan Quinn, the tale of the adventuring wildcatter is always a popular theme. *Giant* (1956) is the best known. Oil production films can start in the Great Plains and go anywhere in the world: *Hellfighters* (1968), *Local Hero* (1983), and the Imax production of *Fires of Kuwait* are examples. Oil field scenes and plot devices also appear in other films such as *Cimarron* (1931), *Hud* (1963), and *The Last Picture Show* (1971).

Since U.S. oil fields and movies are both about a hundred years old, they have coexisted and interacted. Speculators in oil and film know that the odds of bringing in a gusher or a blockbuster are about the same. A great monetary risk is involved; however, in the oil fields as well as the movie studios, the love of the game is supreme. The continuing players love the process and the romance of the search for big-time success.

From silent films to talkies and from black and white to color, oil has been a popular mid-American subject. It is part of the lore of the Plains pioneers. The movies often depict the cattle ranchers versus the sheepmen, farmers, trainmen, and finally oilmen. In many stories of later times (*Hud*, *Stars Fell on Henrietta*, and *Oklahoma Crude*, released in 1973), the rancher must find oil on his property in order to survive because the land has been fenced and the railroads have taken over from the cattle drives. Some of the land has dried up and been farmed out, and the Plains ecosystems have deteriorated. Oil will be the salvation of the entrepreneur and his family.

Women wildcatters sometimes take over as oil prospectors. In *Tulsa* (1949) Susan Hayward goes for oil to avenge the death of her cattle rancher father, and in *Waltz across Texas* (1982) Anne Archer is a modern-day geologist looking for oil and finding romance. In *Lucy Gallant* (1955) Jane Wyman plays the title role of a woman who finds success in selling expensive dresses to the women of an oil town. One line of gowns is even in the colors of oil. Charlton Heston is the love-interest rancher who becomes an oilman.

Since these films are Westerns, the men and women in the oil business are tough and aggressive, coming from strong pioneer stock. Because wealth is at stake, they are clever and conniving. They work hard and play hard at very high emotional levels of romance and adventure. Their fortunes may wax and wane with many highs and lows; however, they survive with great determination and effort. Oil is the black gold, which has a great attraction, and whether they are searching, drilling, hauling, selling, or putting out fires, it is always exciting on the motion picture screen.

Donald E. Staples
University of North Texas

Graham, Don. *Cowboys and Cadillacs.* Austin: Texas Monthly Press, 1983.

OKLAHOMA!

Oklahoma! (directed by Fred Zinneman) was one of the most popular films of the 1950s. The musical, written by Richard Rodgers and Oscar Hammerstein, was based on Lynn Riggs's Broadway play, *Green Grow the Lilacs.* The musical was adapted into a movie in 1955.

The story takes place in Indian Territory (later Oklahoma) during the early 1900s and concerns the rivalry between a cowboy, Curly, and a ranch hand, Jud Frye, for the love of an Oklahoma farm girl, Laurie Williams. While the 1943 Broadway musical was a success for Rodgers and Hammerstein, the film version, starring Shirley Jones (Laurie), Gordon MacRae (Curly), and Rod Steiger (Jud Frye), made *Oklahoma!* an overnight sensation. The film version also included performances by Gloria Grahame, Eddie Albert, and Charlotte Greenwood. Revolutionary for its time, the musical incorporated plot, music, and dance, with choreography by Agnes De Mille. The score of *Oklahoma!* also proved highly popular, including songs such as "Oh, What a Beautiful Mornin'," "The Surrey with the Fringe on Top," "I Can't Say No," and "People Will Say We're in Love." The title song, "Oklahoma," became the official state song. Although the musical presented an idealized story of life on the Plains frontier, the film version was actually shot in Arizona. The film won Academy Awards for best score, best editing, and best sound as well as nominations for best film and cinematography. In 1955 the New York Film Critics Circle named *Oklahoma!* the year's best film.

See also LITERARY TRADITIONS: Riggs, Rollie Lynn.

Stefanie Decker
Oklahoma State University

Bronner, Edwin. *The Encyclopedia of the American Theater, 1900–1975.* New York: A. S. Barnes, 1980. Lynch, Richard Chigley. *Musicals!: A Directory of Musical Properties Available for Production.* Chicago: American Library Association, 1984.

PARKS, GORDON

See AFRICAN AMERICANS: Parks, Gordon

THE PLOW THAT BROKE THE PLAINS

In May 1936, as the people of the Great Plains battled against the combined effects of over-

The Plow That Broke the Plains

production, drought, and depression, the federal government released *The Plow That Broke the Plains.* The film was part of a massive campaign by the federal government to convince farmers and ranchers that the search for windfall profits in the West had resulted in misplaced settlement, misuse of the land, and ultimately the great dust storms that ravaged the Great Plains in the 1930s.

In 1935 Rexford Tugwell, the head of the Resettlement Administration, recruited Pare Lorentz to produce a film that would explain the causes of the Dust Bowl. The film also made a strong case for resettling destitute farmers, for retiring marginal farmland from production, and for restoring grasslands in the West. The twenty-eight-minute film, which cost $19,260 to produce, included a highly emotional musical score by Virgil Thomson and was narrated by Thomas Chalmers. Although the movie industry complained about competition from a government-produced film, *The Plow That Broke the Plains* was shown in independent theaters, school auditoriums, and other public meeting places throughout the country. It was seen by 10 million people in 1937 alone and would become one of the most widely viewed films in American history. The film is still shown to audiences throughout the country to explain the economic and ecological disasters that struck the Plains during the 1930s. The film was, however, instantly controversial. It has since become part of an enduring historical debate about the past and the future development of the Great Plains.

The heart of the controversy about the film, then and now, was the interpretation by Lorentz and other New Deal farm experts that much of the Great Plains was unsuited for agriculture. While soft music plays in the background and scenes of acres of lush, billowy grassland appear on the screen, the film's narrator explains how beautiful the unspoiled Plains had been before the period of European American settlement. Then, as the music grows louder with increasingly harsh tones, the film shows the movement of cattlemen

onto the Plains, the coming of railroads and land speculators, and finally waves of homesteaders and farmers with horses and gang plows breaking up Great Plains grasslands. The film then moves to the World War I era, when farmers enjoyed high prices and seemingly unlimited prosperity. As the music reaches a feverish pitch, the film shows giant plows, often lined up side by side in rows, plowing under millions of additional acres of grassland. Then, after the screen goes momentarily black, the film shifts to the 1930s. The music becomes dirgelike; the Plains are now pictured as a desolate wasteland. A steer's skull, bleached white by the sun, is shown wedged in the dirt. Poor farmers, their homes nearly covered by mounds of dust, are shown running to ramshackle houses to escape the relentless dust storms that sweep across the Plains.

While many contemporaries blamed farmers and ranchers for exploiting, without regard for the environment, the resources of the West to their own advantage, Lorentz focused the blame for the ecological disaster on mechanized agriculture rather than unthinking greed. Still, the message of the film was clear: the great plow-up was a terrible mistake. At the end of the film, as thousands of refugees flee the Plains, the narrator concludes that 40 million acres of land have been totally ruined and another 200 million acres badly damaged. The film ends with a troubling question: "What is America going to do about it?"

While the film was generally hailed as a cinematic triumph, many contemporaries questioned Lorentz's understanding of the history of the Great Plains. First, critics pointed out that Lorentz had deemphasized the impact of the drought and had exaggerated the importance of agricultural expansion to explain the origins of the Dust Bowl. Second, critics contended that Lorentz had created a false impression that the entire Great Plains area was a Dust Bowl. In their view Lorentz had overlooked the diversity and vitality of the Great Plains economy and had undervalued the quality of farm life, even in the Dust Bowl areas, to make the case that substantial areas of the Great Plains should be turned back to grassland. Finally, although Lorentz had generally pictured farmers as victims of modern technology, his critics insisted that he had presented a negative and unfair image of Great Plains farmers, who were, they argued, conscientious stewards of the land. The film's critics insisted that the Plains was suitable for agriculture in spite of the dust storms and that prosperity would return to the farm economy with the return of rain.

It can be argued that the most important impact of the film was that it focused discussion on the future of the Great Plains and underscored the need for a comprehensive soil conservation program. The film, however, obviously did not settle the question about whether land in the Great Plains region, and particularly in the western Plains, should be used for agriculture. The same questions that were debated in the 1930s are still debated today, particularly during periods of drought and low farm prices.

See also MUSIC: Thomson, Virgil / PHYSICAL ENVIRONMENT: Dust Bowl.

Michael W. Schuyler
University of Nebraska at Kearney

Hurt, R. Douglas. *The Dust Bowl: An Agricultural and Social History.* Chicago: Nelson Hall, 1981. Snyder, Ralph. *Pare Lorentz and the Documentary Film.* Norman: University of Oklahoma Press, 1968. Worster, Donald. *Dust Bowl: The Southern Plains in the 1930s.* New York: Oxford University Press, 1979.

PRAIRIE FILMS

The basis of a regional culture is a common history and geography. The history of the Prairies, a history of colonial expansion and exploitation, has provided the basis for many a yarn and many an artistic work. In terms of geography, the look of the land and its unyielding climate have inspired many to write and paint and to make films. It may not be possible to identify a specific type of film called a "Prairie film," but over the years there have been attempts to capture and transmit Prairie culture in cinematic form. A completely satisfying cinematic reflection of the Prairie experience has yet to be created.

With cinema, as with publishing and some forms of visual art, the demands of the marketplace must also be taken into consideration. Certainly, the Prairie region has been its own marketplace. Some films have recuperated their costs within the region. However, production gatekeepers expect financial success, which often means raising money by distribution beyond the Prairies.

When Hollywood became a world center for film production, producers realized that Prairie history and geography could be exploited in one of the most successful film genres: the Western. By the time Edwin S. Porter made *The Great Train Robbery* in 1903, readers of pulp novels had already developed a taste for stories of cowboy heroes and villains, so it made sense to bring these characters to the movie screen. Westerns could also employ the appealing choreography of horse and stagecoach chases, gunfights, and powwows.

Westerns have been successful in the marketplace, but the genre is extremely restrictive in terms of plot conventions. We must look to independent filmmakers to provide us with films that explore the finer aspects of the Prairie experience. Independent filmmakers also have to make money. Production costs for even a short documentary film can be thousands of dollars per minute. Government and private foundations provide some funds for independent production, but they tend to place some creative demands on the filmmaking process. When funding institutions reside outside the Prairies, filmmakers face a battle to tell regional stories that are true to their cultural roots.

Some of the best cinema reflections of the Prairie experience can be found embedded in films whose purpose is not necessarily art but some form of communication or commerce. Educational films, industrial or promotional films, television "movies of the week," and in some cases commercial feature films have contained scenes or elements that could be said to reflect the Prairie experience.

One of the first Prairie films was also one of the first films made in Canada. James Freer, a Manitoba farmer, made a film of farm life in 1898. The film was sponsored by the Canadian Pacific Railway to promote, in England, the sale of land on the Prairies. No prints remain of this first Prairie film, though it has been much talked about, but one can speculate: being a promotional piece, it is unlikely that it contained images of blizzards or other elements illustrating the harder aspects of life on the Prairies during this period.

A long drought in regional production occurred between 1925 and 1950. A few educational films and documentaries appeared, but cinematic storytelling was, for the most part, left to Hollywood. The results have been disappointing in their slavish use of Hollywood conventions and stereotypes.

When television came to the Prairies in the mid-1950s, TV stations produced some documentaries as part of their mandate to reflect the region for their viewers, usually in the form of hard news reportage or promotion of local events and institutions. The National Film Board of Canada offered other opportunities for the representation of Prairie themes and stories. Notable NFB films of the 1950s include *Corral* (1954), about an Alberta cowboy rounding up and breaking wild horses, and *Paul Tomkowicz: Street Railway Switchman* (1954), based on the elderly Tomkowicz's account of working on the Winnipeg street railway line on a cold winter day.

Drylanders (1964), one of the first feature film productions of the NFB, tells the story of a family of settlers who arrive from eastern Canada in the late 1800s to claim a piece of land. The film includes images of the family making their way west with an oxen cart, building a sod hut in which to live during their first winter, welcoming their first bumper crop of wheat, then watching as the land blows away during the "dirty thirties."

The 1970s was a period of expansion of the Canadian motion picture industry. Money was available in the form of loans and tax incentives through the Canadian Film Development Corporation (CFDC), later Telefilm Canada. Some government- and foundation-funded feature films have been successful at telling a Prairie story while managing to make money for their producers. These include *Who Has Seen the Wind* (1977), based on W. O. Mitchell's coming-of-age novel; *The Hounds of Notre Dame* (1981), based on the early years of Père Athol Murray at Notre Dame College in Wilcox, Saskatchewan; and *Why Shoot the Teacher* (1978), based on the Max Braithwaite novel of the same name.

In the 1980s and 1990s film development corporations were formed in Manitoba, Alberta, and Saskatchewan to supplement federal government funding from Telefilm Canada with provincial government funds. The budgets of SaskFilm and other Canadian film agencies help to finance the one-to-four-million-dollar movies of the week destined for the pay television market. These films employ some regional actors and craftspeople and use regional locations. Unfortunately, the locations are seldom identified within these films and instead appear as generic U.S. cities. The stories for these movies are chosen for their wide commercial appeal rather than their regional flair.

Regional filmmakers are unable to gain significant funding for their projects because regional films are not deemed financially viable. Telefilm Canada and provincial film development agencies seldom fund a project unless a large percentage of its budget has been secured from a major broadcaster or distributor. A regional story by a regional writer is less likely to gain the cooperation of a mainstream coproducer or broadcaster.

Clearly, it is up to Prairie filmmakers themselves to depict the Prairie experience in a form that avoids stereotypes but manages to entertain a wide audience well enough to attract adequate funding and distribution both within and outside the region.

Gerald S. Horne
Burnaby, British Columbia

Clandfield, David. *Canadian Film.* Toronto: Oxford University Press, 1987. Horne, G. S. "Interpreting Prairie Cinema." *Prairie Forum* 22 (1997): 135–51. Magder, Ted. *Canada's Hollywood: The Canadian State and Feature Films.* Toronto: University of Toronto Press, 1993.

RED RIVER

This famous motion picture was directed by Howard Hawks, with a script by Charles Schnee and Bordon Chase (from his *Saturday Evening Post* serial) and music by Dimitri Tiomkin. Released in 1948, *Red River* featured John Wayne, Montgomery Clift, Walter Brennan, and Joanne Dru plus a number of actors who appeared in Westerns from the silent film era through the television era. The film was shot at Rain Valley Ranch at Elgin (near Tucson), Arizona.

Lying at the intersection of history and myth, *Red River* is the story of the first cattle drive along the Chisholm Trail from Texas to Abilene, Kansas, and, according to Hawks, the story of Texas's famed King Ranch. Beginning with one cow, which belongs to the orphaned youngster Matt Garth (Clift), and his own bull, Tom Dunson (Wayne) builds a herd of 10,000 cattle on the Red River D ranch north of the Rio Grande. But by the end of the Civil War there is no market for beef in impoverished Texas. In desperation Dunson decides to drive his entire herd north to Sedalia, Missouri, in spite of the dangers of weather, rustlers, Indians, and stampedes. As living and working conditions for his cowboys deteriorate, Dunson becomes more and more tyrannical. In spite of reports of bandits in Missouri and the possibility of an alternative market in Abilene, he continues to drive his men ruthlessly toward the original destination. When Dunson threatens to hang two recaptured deserters Matt seizes control of the drive. Incensed, the wounded Dunson vows to catch up and kill him. Later, the drive encounters a wagon train of gamblers and women headed to Nevada, and cardsharper Tess Millay (Dru) falls in love with Matt. When the drive reaches Abilene they find the railroad and buyers waiting for them, and Matt sells the herd for a good price. Dunson arrives the next day. However, instead of the gunfight that all had expected, neither man will shoot the other. A fistfight ensues that Tess halts by firing a pistol. Tess points out that their actions indicate that Dunson and Matt must actually love each other, and in recognition of the successful completion of the cattle drive, Dunson volunteers to add Matt's "M" to the Red River D brand.

While lacking the iconographic images of John Ford's Westerns, *Red River* has a number of memorable sequences, including the beginning of the cattle drive (a 180-degree pan followed by nineteen insert shots of yahooing cowboys), the crossing of the Red River, the stampede, Wayne reading over the grave of a dead cowboy, cattle herds choking the streets of Abilene, and the climactic fistfight. As in many of Hawks's films, *Red River* includes themes of male camaraderie and professionalism, and the primary relationship is not the one that includes the actress. The conflict between Tom Dunson and Matt Garth is not only generational but reflects the tension between Dunson's virtue of grim individual determination and Matt's "softer" virtues that build community.

William M. Wehrbein
Nebraska Wesleyan University

Bogdanovich, Peter. *Who the Devil Made It*. New York: Alfred A. Knopf, 1997. Mast, Gerald. *Howard Hawks, Storyteller*. New York: Oxford University Press, 1982. McBride, Joseph. *Hawks on Hawks*. Berkeley: University of California Press, 1982.

ROGERS, WILL (1879–1935)

Will Rogers was more than a movie star; he was one of the greatest American show business personalities of the first third of the twentieth century. Born William Penn Adair Rogers at Oolagah in Indian Territory, now Oklahoma, on November 4, 1879, he entered show business in a turn-of-the-century Wild West show, already helping construct the myths of the values and spirit of the Old West of his childhood. Audiences loved him, and so producers brought him to New York City. By 1912 he was bringing the humor of the Great Plains to Broadway; through the late 1910s and early 1920s he reigned as the top attraction of the Ziegfeld Follies. This led to authorship of some 4,000 newspaper columns; a series of influential articles for the *Saturday Evening Post*; popular phonograph records; six books, including *The Cowboy Philosopher on the Peace Conference* (1919) and *Letters of a Self-Made Diplomat to His President* (1926); an NBC radio show; and ultimately to world fame as a Hollywood movie star.

Rogers did not instantly rise to motion picture stardom. Famed producer Samuel Goldwyn signed him to play in silent films, and between 1918 and 1922 he essayed cowboy roles, but his career went nowhere. He needed his verbal wit and humor; silent film titles never captured his presence. While he spent most of his adult life outside the Great Plains, surely his homespun humor was based on a persona of straightforward, unpretentious traits developed from his childhood. For the remainder of the silent film era, Will Rogers returned to the vaudeville stage—except for completing a handful of silent short subjects for Hollywood's Hal Roach Studios.

The coming of talkies enabled Rogers to shine. During the bleak years of the Great Depression he came to represent the common person, the casual humorist and raconteur, the man who clung to the folkways of a mythical nineteenth-century America that seemed so long ago.

From 1930 on Will Rogers was Fox Films' most important movie star. John Ford, the great American film director, best understood Rogers's image and persona and fully exploited them in a series of hometown tales that were as popular as any set of films made during the Great Depression: *Doctor Bull* (1933), *Judge Priest* (1934), and Rogers's best film, *Steamboat 'round the Bend* (1935). Sadly, Rogers's best was his last, and he was at the height of his motion picture popularity when he died in an airplane crash at Point Barrow, Alaska, on August 15, 1935. His final two films, *In Old Kentucky* and *Steamboat 'round the Bend*, were released after the actor's death by the major studio he helped create, Twentieth Century Fox.

Douglas Gomery
University of Maryland

Rogers, Will. *The Autobiography of Will Rogers*. Boston: Houghton Mifflin, 1949. Rollins, Peter C. *Will Rogers: A Bio-Bibliography*. Westport CT: Greenwood Press, 1984. Yagoda, Ben. *Will Rogers: A Biography*. New York: Alfred A. Knopf, 1993.

SAUNDERS, RUSSELL (1919–2001)

Born on a farm near Winnipeg, Manitoba, on May 21, 1919, Russell M. Saunders repeatedly risked his life as perhaps the greatest movie stuntman of Hollywood's halcyon days. As a child he was fascinated by the acrobats in traveling circuses, and he worked on his acrobatic skills until he had achieved Canadian championships in diving and gymnastics. After being rejected by the Canadian Air Force because he was color-blind, he moved to California. There he quickly found his way to Muscle Beach in Santa Monica, where acrobats and body builders performed and paraded. Even in his later years he spent much of his time on the beach, giving free gymnastics lessons to children.

But it was in the movie business that Saunders made his name. He appeared in more than a hundred movies, doubling for stars such as Alan Ladd, Robert Cummings, and Gene Kelly. He was particularly revered by his peers for his ability to capture the exact mannerisms of the stars as he performed the dangerous feats they were unable to do. In *The Three Musketeers* (1948), for example, he jumped from a rooftop, caught hold of a flag, and, as it ripped, swung on the shreds through an open window. In another film as Richard Widmark's double he leaped off a fifty-foot cliff, breaking his arm on a rock in the water. Saunders was also in the climactic fight scene in *Shane* (1953), unknown to audiences, who saw only Alan Ladd and his antagonists in the blur of action. Russell Saunders died in a West Los Angeles nursing home on May 29, 2001.

David J. Wishart
University of Nebraska–Lincoln

SOLDIER BLUE

Soldier Blue (1970), directed by Ralph Nelson, is loosely based on *Arrow in the Sun* (1969), a novel by Theodore Victor Olsen (1932–93), a Wisconsin-born freelance writer of nearly four dozen Western sagas, including the bestsellers *The Stalking Moon* (1965) and *Red Is the River* (1983). As in the film, the novel centers on the fictitious characters of Private Honus Gant, a former schoolteacher from Ohio turned army trooper, and Cresta Marybelle Lee, a young woman from Boston who, while en route to marry an army lieutenant posted on the frontier some years earlier, is captured by a band of Cheyennes and becomes the second wife of the band's leader, Spotted Wolf. After escaping from the Cheyennes, Lee accompanies an army paymaster's detail that includes Private Gant to Fort Reunion, where her fiancé is stationed. When the paymaster's detail is ambushed and wiped out by Spotted Wolf's band, Gant and Lee, the sole survivors, are forced to try to make it to Fort Reunion on their own. They never do, as their fates become linked to Colonel Iverson's brutal attack on Spotted Wolf's village, which brings the film to a brutal, horrifying, and surreal climax.

Soldier Blue is badly flawed by a glaring anachronism, among other inaccuracies. Action portrayed in the novel supposedly takes place roughly in 1877, more than twelve years after Spotted Wolf had witnessed his entire family being murdered at Sand Creek by Col.

John M. Chivington's Colorado Volunteers. Indeed, as we are told in the novel, Spotted Wolf had been instrumental in George Crook's humiliating defeat at Rosebud Creek, Montana, in 1876, and he had been at Little Big Horn too in that same year. Near the beginning of the film we learn that Private Gant's own father had been killed at the Little Big Horn the previous year, yet by the end of the film it is, inexplicably, November 29, 1864, when we relive the gory and ultraviolent (though poorly re-created) Sand Creek Massacre. Colonel Iverson becomes Lieutenant Calley, and *Soldier Blue* becomes an uneasy parallel to My Lai during which U.S. soldiers wantonly rape, murder, and mutilate hundreds of Native American men, women, and children.

See also WAR: Sand Creek Massacre.

R. B. Rosenburg
Clayton College and State University

SPLENDOR IN THE GRASS

Based on an original screenplay by Kansas playwright William Inge, *Splendor in the Grass* (1961) reflects Inge's concerns with the problems and frustrations of small-town life in the Midwest. Determined to shake off his frustrations over his first failure on Broadway, *A Loss of Roses* (1959), Inge went to Hollywood to prepare *Splendor* for Elia Kazan, who had directed Inge's *Dark at the Top of the Stairs* for the stage two years before. Characteristically, the setting is a small Kansas town in the late 1920s (obviously Inge's hometown of Independence, Kansas) where two ill-fated young lovers, Bud Stamper and Deanie Loomis, struggle against the sexual inhibitions and materialistic priorities of their parents. As a result of their enforced separation, Bud goes to Yale and marries someone else, and Deanie goes insane and is confined to a mental hospital after a suicide attempt. At the end, both are forced to accept what has happened and find consolation in poet William Wordsworth's words, "We will grieve not, rather find / Strength in what remains behind."

Although Kazan was anxious to capture the look of Kansas, most of the film was shot on Long Island and Staten Island and in Poughkeepsie and the Filmways Studio in New York City. The role of Deanie was played by a young Natalie Wood, already an established actress. Bud's oppressive oil-rich father was played by Pat Hingle. Warren Beatty, a newcomer from the cast of the failed *A Loss of Roses*, appeared as Bud, and Inge appeared in a cameo role as the Reverend Whiteman. Ironically, the film's theme of the dangers of prudery and hypocrisy led to the excision by the Production Code censors of several scenes thought to be too sexually explicit. Despite some critical cavils (Dwight Macdonald scornfully suggested the film was essentially "an Andy Hardy story with glands"), the film opened to sensational box office returns and earned Inge an Academy Award for his screenplay.

See also LITERARY TRADITIONS: Inge, William.

John C. Tibbetts
University of Kansas

Ciment, Michel. *Kazan on Kazan.* New York: Viking Press, 1974. Inge, William. "A Level Land." In *What Kansas Means to Me,* edited by Thomas Fox Averill. Lawrence: University Press of Kansas, 1991: 153–59. Voss, Ralph. *A Life of William Inge.* Lawrence: University Press of Kansas, 1989.

ROBERT TAYLOR (1911–1969)

Robert Taylor

A film and television star from 1934 to 1969, Robert Taylor achieved renown as one of the most handsome leading men in Hollywood and distinction as one of the most professional actors of his time. Born Spangler Arlington Brugh on August 5, 1911, in Filley, Nebraska, he attended public school in nearby Beatrice, where his father was an osteopath and his mother was an intelligent but ailing housewife. Nicknamed Arly as a youth, he rode a pony, took private cello lessons in Lincoln, participated in drama and music activities, learned to dance, won a state oratorical contest, and made the honor roll. In 1929 he attended Doane College and continued his drama and music interests. For two summers he also performed as part of a musical trio on KMMJ radio in Clay Center, Nebraska. Brugh then followed his cello teacher to Pomona College in Claremont, California, where he graduated in 1933, and was discovered by a Metro-Goldwyn-Mayer talent scout.

During his career, the versatile Taylor appeared in more than eighty motion picture and television films and earned acclaim for his romantic, swashbuckling adventure and Western roles. The first American actor to appear in a film made in England and the first major Hollywood contract star to appear on television, he also set the Hollywood record for longest contract with one studio (twenty-four years with MGM). As a matinee idol in the 1930s, he ranked as the decade's eighth top box office attraction. He was the narrator of Acad-

emy Award–winning feature-length documentaries in 1944 and 1948 and the recipient of a Golden Globe Award in 1954. Taylor also starred in his own weekly television series, *The Detectives,* from 1959 to 1962 and was host and occasional star of *Death Valley Days* from 1966 to 1968.

Offscreen he flew an airplane, served in the United States Navy from 1943 to 1946, disliked Communists, liked steak, and wrote letters. An avid outdoorsman, he rented a cabin near Buffalo, Wyoming, fished on the Rogue River in Oregon, and hunted in Nebraska, South Dakota, and Manitoba. In 1954 he received the first Outdoorsman of the Year Award presented by the Winchester Repeating Arms Company. A gentleman with the many ladies he dated during his Nebraska and Hollywood years, he had no major scandals, though he had brief, discreet involvements with Lana Turner and Ava Gardner during his first marriage, from 1939 to 1951, to Barbara Stanwyck. In 1954 he was remarried at Jackson Lake, Wyoming, to German-born actress Ursula Schmidt Thiess, a *Life* cover girl who bore his son Terence and daughter Tessa. Robert Taylor died of lung cancer on June 8, 1969, in Santa Monica, California. His close friend Ronald Reagan delivered the eulogy.

Taylor was posthumously inducted in 1970 into the National Cowboy Hall of Fame in Oklahoma City, and reviews of the 1,000 best movies in *Magill's American Film Guide* (1983) included seven films in which he starred: *Magnificent Obsession* (1935), *Camille* (1937), *Three Comrades* (1938), *Waterloo Bridge* (1940), *Johnny Eager* (1962), *Quo Vadis* (1951), and *Ivanhoe* (1952). In 1988 Lorimar Telepictures renamed the Metro-Goldwyn-Mayer Administration Building after Taylor. In 1994 the Nebraska State Highway Commission designated the twelve-mile portion of U.S. Highway 136 between Filley and Beatrice as the Robert Taylor Memorial Highway, and the Gage County Historical Society established a permanent exhibit on Taylor.

E. A. Kral
Wilber, Nebraska

Kral, E. A. "Robert Taylor of Beatrice: The Nebraska Roots of a Hollywood Star." *Nebraska History* 75 (1994): 280–91. Quirk, Lawrence J. *The Films of Robert Taylor.* Secaucus NJ: Carol Publishing, 1975. Wayne, Jane Ellen. *The Life of Robert Taylor.* London: Robson Books, 1987.

TELEVISION SHOWS

See MEDIA: Television Shows

WESTERNS

Plains Westerns typically center on two key elements, historical and geographical, each of which assumes importance by virtue of the specific character of the Plains experience.

One of the representative traits of Western films involving or located within the Great Plains is their pronounced obsession with actual historical events and historical characters. This may be so because in the Western film dialectic between East and West, the Plains

FILM : 279

form a sort of Middle Landscape, mixing history and myth, between the more historically mapped East and more exotically romanticized and mythologized West. Real historical events and persons occur much more often in Plains Westerns, which helps to explain why John Ford's silent film epic of the building of the transcontinental railroad, *The Iron Horse* (1924), is filled with so many historical events and characters, many more than any other of his more "western" Westerns. The history, of course, has often been radically altered for narrative, dramatic, and ideological reasons. While it is unusual to find the Civil War, Abraham Lincoln, westward expansion, Wild Bill Hickok, Buffalo Bill, Calamity Jane, the Plains Indian Wars, and Gen. George Armstrong Custer (though most of them appeared together in *The Iron Horse*) all cobbled together as they are in Cecil B. De Mille's wildly improbable, spectacularly inaccurate, action-filled *The Plainsman* (1936), nevertheless, many other Plains films are also based, if ever so loosely, on actual historical events and characters primarily because the Plains Western mixes myth and history more readily than does the Far West Western.

Key Plains historical events include the great pioneer migration after the Civil War (*The Covered Wagon*, 1923; *How the West Was Won*, 1962); the blazing of the great cattle trails (*Red River*, 1946; *Abilene Town*, 1951); the brief career of the Pony Express, an especially popular topic for very early Westerns made by *Great Train Robbery* (1903) director Edwin S. Porter and stars Bronco Billy Anderson and Tom Mix; the founding of cattle towns (*Dodge City*, 1939; *Wichita*, 1955; and many others); the advent of railroads (*Iron Horse*, 1924; *Dodge City* and *Union Pacific*, both 1939) and the telegraph (*Western Union*, 1941); numerous wars with the Plains Indians, the greatest of which and the most prescient and sympathetic to Native Americans is Kevin Costner's *Dances with Wolves* (1990); the Missouri-Kansas border wars (*Dark Command*, 1940; *The Outlaw Josey Wales*, 1976); and historical figures such as Kit Carson, William Clark Quantrill, John Brown, Jesse and Frank James, the Dalton Gang, Wyatt Earp, Bat Masterson, Sitting Bull, Crazy Horse, and many more, all of whom appear in numerous films. Propelled by the mythic and historical provenance of Manifest Destiny and the more literal promise of vast new lands for exploration and settlement, the Great Plains hovered in a special zone of the imagination between myth and history, fact and fantasy, with each feeding the other in rich, energizing, though at times blatantly jingoistic and racist ways.

As is virtually the case with all Westerns, landscape figures prominently in nearly every film, from the very early settler epic, *The Covered Wagon*, through the more racially, culturally, and ecologically sophisticated *Dances with Wolves* and the more gender-conscious *Westward the Women* (1951), *The Ballad of Little Jo* (1993), and *Unforgiven* (1991). Almost no Westerns have been actually shot on location in the Central Plains, though more recently

Montana, Wyoming, and the Canadian Prairies have been used as locations for filming Westerns. Nevertheless, numerous films are able to convey through cinematography and editing a feeling for the oceanic vastness of the Plains, the winds, the droughts, the sudden storms, the vast buffalo herds, and the Native Americans so that a sense of the Plains' dwarfing presence offers a kind of historical and political, moral and spiritual landscape out of which the narratives of the Plains experience emerge. *How the West Was Won* (1962) is a hodgepodge of many Westerns, but its sense of visual space, enhanced by the Cinerama process (note especially Henry Hathaway's section on "The Prairie"), still makes it worth looking at if not listening to. The same is true, although the stories are much more interesting, in the depiction of the Southern and Northern Plains, respectively, in Terrence Malick's sumptuously photographed *Days of Heaven* (1978) and in Michael Cimino's saga of the Wyoming Johnson County War, *Heaven's Gate* (1980).

From the approving heavenly choirs that herald a wagon train's sinuously curved journey across the vast Central Plains at the beginning of Howard Hawks's epic *Red River* (1946) to the journey of a soul broken by war, violence, and personal tragedy in Clint Eastwood's masterly *The Outlaw Josey Wales*, the best directors merge landscape, story, and character in a unified whole. The story of Josey Wales, which begins in catastrophe, ends in a vision of cosmic and comic harmony in nature and in society, closer in kind to a Shakespearean romance than to a traditional Western. Throughout this remarkable pilgrim's progress the landscape continues to underscore the imperatives of both plot and character.

Since all Westerns are about versions and visions of history, no Western can be understood, then, outside of its doubled historical focus on both the remembered and interpreted past and the self-interpreting present. Thus the more "triumphalist" 1930s and 1940s studio Westerns of Cecil B. De Mille (*The Plainsman*, *Union Pacific*) and Raoul Walsh (*The Big Trail*, 1931; *They Died with Their Boots On*, 1941), Howard Hawks (*Red River*), and Michael Curtiz (*Santa Fe Trail*, 1940; *Dodge City*) are placed in sharp relief with films more critical, more conflicted and paradoxically puzzling, of the settling of the West such as Fred Zinnemann's *High Noon* (1952), John Ford's *The Searchers* (1956), filmed in Ford's mythical signature landscape, Monument Valley, but really a story of the arduous post–Civil War settling of Texas, and Arthur Penn's *Little Big Man* (1970).

No film presents a more stark contrast with the lush, lyrical beauty of the epic, mythically charged story of the embodiment of Manifest Destiny, epitomized by *Red River*, than the radically revisionist *High Noon,* a parched and sparse view of the almost unrepresented Plains. The most deliberately *plain* of the Plains Westerns, *High Noon* presents a landscape not seen in many other films, a vision of the end of an era, closer in spirit to a contem-

porary film about the death of the Old West, Peter Bogdanovich's *The Last Picture Show* (1971), than to the more optimistic tradition of the American Western. *High Noon* offers a troubling account of the Plains West in the aftermath of its vitalizing frontier settlement. Topographically, the film's central irony turns on the etiolated city streets of "civilized" (all too civilized) Hadleyville, themselves metamorphosing into a terrifying spatial void, as threatening as the Plains themselves. The town that Marshal Will Kane (Gary Cooper) has tamed and to which he has brought law and order now questions his leadership and turns its back on him in this misanthropic Western. We have come a long way from John Wayne's mythical larger-than-life Tom Dunson in *Red River*, a man who revels in the wild, vitalizing spaces he inhabits, who sees only more and more land in which to "grow good beef for hungry Americans." Will Kane looks outside of Hadleyville—and inside—and sees nothing but nothingness. His Plains America no longer affords a Turneresque vision of the creative fusion of wilderness and society at the edge of the frontier, for in this film each cancels out the other.

The great majority of Plains Westerns, of course, celebrate an expanding, optimistic America, a land of perpetual plenty. But if the Western mirrors American history, and it does, then the Plains Western proffers the same pleasures and discontents we contemplate as we simultaneously look backward and forward at the history of our country through the already passed, always present, prism of the Western film.

John L. Simons
Colorado College

Buscombe, Edward, ed. *The* BFI *Companion to the Western*. New York: DaCapo, 1988. Slotkin, Richard. *Gunfighter Nation: The Myth of the Frontier in 20th Century America*. New York: Atheneum, 1992. Smith, Henry Nash. *Virgin Land: The American West as Symbol and Myth*. Cambridge: Harvard University Press, 1950.

THE WIZARD OF OZ

Rated sixth on the American Film Institute's list of the country's 100 greatest movies, *The Wizard of Oz* has become a defining feature of American culture. From its sepia-toned opening shots of Kansas to its Technicolor fantasy world of Oz, the 1939 Metro-Goldwyn-Mayer production permeates the American imagination with lines such as "Toto, I've a feeling we're not in Kansas anymore" and songs such as "We're Off to See the Wizard." The Cowardly Lion (Bert Lahr), the Scarecrow (Ray Bolger), the Tin Man (Jack Haley), and Dorothy Gale (Judy Garland) sang and danced their way into America's collective imagination in a script adapted from L. Frank Baum's book, with lyrics by E. Y. "Yip" Harburg and a score by Harold Arlen. In the process, Kansas and the Great Plains came to epitomize the drab and ordinary, the foil against which Oz and other parts of America, especially urban areas, seem fantastic and magical.

The Wizard of Oz opened in August 1939, a phenomenal year in movie history—*Gone* with the Wind, Wuthering Heights, Stagecoach, and Mr. Smith Goes to Washington also premiered that year. Nonetheless, The Wizard of Oz, directed by Victor Fleming, captured Academy Awards for best original score and best song ("Over the Rainbow"). Judy Garland also received a juvenile Oscar for her performance as Dorothy. Because the film played to large audiences of children, who did not pay full rates, the production did not make money until it was leased to television in 1956. Running each year on CBS or NBC, the show became standard family viewing fare.

Like the book before it, the film tells a uniquely American fairy tale, and in the new medium Americans related to it in greater numbers. At the same time, its audience broadened throughout the world, largely because, as author Salman Rushdie notes, the film actually improved on a good book, creating a work of art. An important aspect of this film transformation is the much larger role assigned to Kansas and its people. In Baum's book, only six pages in chapter 1 and under twenty lines in the final chapter are devoted to the sun-seared Great Plains. Only Auntie Em, Uncle Henry, Dorothy, and Toto appear. In contrast, the movie introduces three farmhands (played by Lahr, Bolger, and Haley), an itinerant salesman (Frank Morgan), and Miss Gulch (Margaret Hamilton). These characters mirror the most important characters in the Land of Oz. Introducing evil in the person of Miss Gulch and her counterpart, the Wicked Witch of the West, the film takes on an immediacy and drama not possible in the book. The Kansas sequence, shot in black and white and placed in a brown bath to mute the tones, emphasizes the stark difference between the reality of Kansas and the colorful fairyland of Oz.

Whether in Baum's book or the MGM movie, the sharp contrast between Kansas and Oz has always been a defining feature, suggesting that Oz is something more than it seems—a metaphor for America. In 1900, when the book was first published, America's economy was depressed, and Baum's Oz can be interpreted as a parody of America under the influence of the Populist party, which had arisen at the turn of the century to champion farmers and laborers against corporate America. In 1939 the country was in the depths of the Great Depression, and some viewers suggest that MGM's Oz might be a commentary on President Franklin D. Roosevelt's administration. In a 1981 interview in the Washington Post, songwriter Yip Harburg, who had considerable creative freedom on the film, claimed that the Emerald City represented the New Deal. Regardless of specific interpretations, however, both book and movie have lent themselves to political allusion, being recast in each new era. In the 1970s political pundits likened President Richard Nixon to the bogus Wizard of Oz caught behind the curtain in the movie, while illustrator Barry Moser modeled his wood engravings for a 1986 edition of the book on members of the Ronald Reagan White House. First Lady Nancy Reagan was identifiable as the Wicked Witch of the West.

No matter what the political interpretation, the 1939 film evokes a joyful, still innocent, can-do world in which each person already holds the solution to his or her own problems. In setting this up, however, The Wizard of Oz also creates a no-can-do Kansas, a dull drabness in the heart of America, making it one of the most controversial film portrayals of the Great Plains.

See also LITERARY TRADITIONS: Baum, L. Frank / POLITICS: Populists (People's Party).

Nancy Tystad Koupal
South Dakota State Historical Society

Harmetz, Aljean. The Making of "The Wizard of Oz." New York: Alfred A. Knopf, 1977. MacDonnell, Francis. "'The Emerald City Was the New Deal': E. Y. Harburg and The Wonderful Wizard of Oz." Journal of American Culture 13 (1990): 71–76. Rushdie, Salman. The Wizard of Oz. BFI Film Classics. London: BFI Publishing, 1992.

WYATT EARP FILMS

Wyatt Earp, itinerant lawman, gambler, and saloon keeper, was born in 1848 and died in 1929. He served as marshal in several towns in Kansas, but his legendary status rests on an incident in Tombstone, Arizona, that lasted no more than half a minute.

Besides having his own television series, the character Wyatt Earp appears in about twenty motion pictures. In some, nothing more than the character name is used, while in others, Earp is only a minor figure. But four well-known films purport to tell the history of Wyatt Earp. Although the events in these films are inconsistent, all of them emphasize the close relationship between the Earp brothers (Wyatt, Morgan, Virgil, and James), the unlikely friendship between Wyatt and the notorious alcoholic and tubercular gambler John "Doc" Holliday, the stormy relationship between Holliday and his female companion, and Wyatt's own romance with a strange and beautiful woman who arrives on a stagecoach.

My Darling Clementine (1946) is the most economical of the four, beginning when the Earp brothers reach Tombstone and ending immediately after the famous gunfight. Furthermore, the shootout involves only two Earps and Holliday versus four Clantons. From its opening shot of Monument Valley this film is unmistakably a John Ford Western, with its emphasis not on action but on the transition from wilderness and disorder to civilized society. Henry Fonda's Earp has a dry sense of humor and is even a bit playful. While the gunfight that destroys the power of the Clanton family is certainly the climax, the turning point in the film is the dance held at the construction site of a church, emphasized by the long tracking shots of Earp and Clementine (Cathy Downs) walking arm in arm to the camp meeting while the hymn "Shall We Gather at the River" can be heard in the background. At the end of the film the surviving Earps head to California, while Clementine chooses to remain in Tombstone to organize its first school.

Frankie Lane sings a Dimitri Tiomkin ballad over the credits of John Sturges's Gunfight at the OK Corral (1957) that comments on the action throughout the film. The first half recounts the story of Earp's developing friendship with Holliday in Fort Griffin, Texas, and Dodge City. Burt Lancaster is a stolid if somewhat prissy Wyatt Earp who disapproves of the near sadomasochistic relationship between Holliday (Kirk Douglas) and his long-suffering companion, Kate (Jo Van Fleet). Their emotionally charged relationship is a stark contrast to the rather dull and unconvincing romance between Earp and a woman gambler (Rhonda Fleming) he initially disdains. Accompanied by Holliday, Wyatt leaves her to join his brothers in Tombstone, where town marshal Virgil is threatened by a gang of cattle rustlers. After young Jimmy Earp (Martin Milner) is ambushed, the three surviving Earps are joined by Holliday in that final showdown with six members of the Clanton and McLaury gang.

After a montage of historical footage, clips from The Great Train Robbery (1903), and scenes of the cast shot in grainy black and white, Tombstone (1993), directed by George P. Cosmatos, opens as Wyatt and his wife join his two brothers and their wives in Arizona to seek their fortunes. Although they are financially successful, the lawlessness of Tombstone leads Virgil and Morgan to take up the badge again, over Wyatt's objections. Conflict with the outlaw gang known as the Cowboys culminates in an especially quick and ugly gunfight, with three Earp brothers joined by Holliday blasting away at five Clantons and McLaurys at point-blank range. Surviving members of the Cowboys ambush Virgil and kill Morgan, convincing the Earp family to leave Tombstone. But before heading to California, Wyatt secures an appointment as U.S. marshal and heads a posse of loyal followers in an orgy of revenge killings. While Kurt Russell's Earp possesses a cruel streak, he has a rather tender relationship with the deteriorating Holliday (played by Val Kilmer in a flamboyant performance).

Released only nine months after Tombstone, Lawrence Kasdan's Wyatt Earp (1994) takes time telling its story. The film flashes back to the cornfields of Iowa, where Earp's father (Gene Hackman) instills in his many children the primacy of family over all other human relationships. After adventures in California and Wyoming Territory, young Wyatt settles in Lamar, Missouri, to raise a family and read law. When his wife dies of typhoid, a despondent Earp (Kevin Costner) falls into alcoholism and crime until his father arranges for his release from jail. Jumping bail, Wyatt heads west to become a lawman in Wichita and Dodge City, where he is fired for excessive brutality. The story of the Earp family in Arizona parallels rather closely the Tombstone version, but this Wyatt is even colder and more aloof, his life driven primarily by fate rather than choice.

After years of traveling the real Wyatt Earp settled in Southern California and in his later years often hung out with former cowboys who had become extras and wranglers for Hollywood Westerns. When he died both William S. Hart and Tom Mix were pallbearers at his funeral.

See also CITIES AND TOWNS: Cattle Towns / IMAGES AND ICONS: Earp, Wyatt; Holliday, Doc.

William M. Wehrbein
Nebraska Wesleyan University

Faragher, John Mack. "The Tale of Wyatt Earp." In *Past Imperfect: History According to the Movies*, edited by Ted Mico, John Miller-Monzon, and David Rubel. New York: Henry Holt and Company, 1995: 154–61. Parks, Rita. *The Western Hero in Film and Television: Mass Media Mythology*. Ann Arbor MI: UMI Research Press, 1982.

ZANUCK, DARRYL F. (1902–1979)

Darryl Francis Zanuck was born on September 5, 1902, in Wahoo, Nebraska. His father, Frank Zanuck, and his mother, Louise Torpin Zanuck, were an unhappy couple. After the death of an older brother in an accident Darryl became an only child, and when his parents divorced he lived with his mother, dividing the year between Glendale, California, and Oakdale, Nebraska, the home of his maternal grandparents. Though this cannot be verified, Zanuck claimed to have first thought of working in film at the age of seven or eight, when he was hired as a movie extra. Restless and energetic, the diminutive young man lied about his age and at fifteen enlisted in the army. Private Zanuck saw action on the French and Belgian fronts during World War I, and this wartime experience left a strong imprint on his life, later recalled in a number of films, most notably, *The Longest Day* (1962).

After his discharge he worked in a series of unsatisfying jobs. With only an eighth-grade education, he nevertheless persisted as a writer. He finally succeeded in placing some of his short silent scenarios at Universal and the FBO Company (a forerunner of RKO). Often generously borrowing from other film or stage sources, the young writer, barely nineteen, wrote quickly, drawing his inspiration from tabloids and pulp fiction. Hired in 1924 by growth-oriented Warner Bros., his big break came when his wildly successful scenarios made Rin Tin Tin the studio's biggest draw.

Soon an almost atavistic energy and an intuitive grasp of all aspects of filmmaking, absorbed at the studio, caused Zanuck to outgrow his screenwriting limitations (he was notoriously weak with dialogue), and with a string of hits credited to his three screen names, he rose quickly to become Warner's head of production before he was thirty. As production chief he practically invented the genres of the gangster film, the biopic, and the backstage musical. He used his love of tabloid and pulp to turn the American cinema (which was reaching for a new direction with the advent of sound) away from the British-derived gentility of rival producers Irving Thalberg and David Selznick and toward a distinctive but contradictory American world of urban crime and small-town nostalgia. Before he left the studio in a dispute with its difficult owners he had signed a number of memorable stars (James Cagney, Edward G. Robinson, and Barbara Stanwyck among them) and produced a number of legendary films such as *The Jazz Singer* (1927), *The Public Enemy* (1931), and *Forty-Second Street* (1933).

In 1933 Zanuck joined forces with mogul Joseph Schenck to found Twentieth Century Pictures. Two years and more than a dozen hit films later, Zanuck merged his company with Fox Films to form Twentieth Century Fox. From 1935 to 1956, under the title vice president in charge of production, he ruled the studio uninterrupted (except for military service in World War II) and virtually unquestioned. He supervised every detail of every film, creating careers for Tyrone Power, Sonja Henie, Marilyn Monroe, and Betty Grable, and he took several established figures (notably, Shirley Temple and Alice Faye) to new heights of popularity. His studio program was divided between controversial prestige films like *The Grapes of Wrath* (1940) and *The Snake Pit* (1948) and escapist musicals and films of small-town nostalgia. Although Zanuck almost never returned to Nebraska, the imprint of small-town Plains life was always a strong presence in his vision of the cinema. During the studio era, more than a quarter of his studio's films were set in small towns at the turn of the century, giving moviegoers a highly nostalgic, almost regressive vision of a United States that was becoming increasingly urban and populated by non-WASP immigrants.

Leaving Fox in 1956, Zanuck became an independent producer, operating largely out of Paris. But after five failed productions, it appeared as if Zanuck, the recipient of a record three Thalberg Awards and three Oscars for best picture (*How Green Was My Valley*, 1941; *Gentleman's Agreement*, 1947; and *All about Eve*, 1950), had lost his touch. He surprised everyone and made a stunning comeback with his blockbuster version of the D day operation *The Longest Day*. In 1962, with his old studio nearly destroyed by poor management and the costly fiasco of *Cleopatra* (1963), Zanuck ousted the head of the corporation, Spyros Skouras. While he operated from the New York office, he placed his twenty-eight-year-old son, Richard, in charge of the studio. With hits like *The Sound of Music* (1965) and *The Planet of the Apes* (1967) series, it appeared as if Zanuck could go on forever. But a changed set of power relations in the motion picture business and a string of costly box office bombs made in an attempt to imitate *The Sound of Music* resulted in Zanuck's summary dismissal in 1971.

Impaired by Alzheimer's disease, Zanuck was taken back by his estranged wife, Virginia, whom he had left in 1956, and he died quietly out of the limelight on December 22, 1979. At his funeral Orson Welles recalled him as the most gifted Hollywood producer of all, one whose greatest assets were his personal loyalty and his strength in story construction. Few people were able to see past his outlandish mogul behavior (oversized cigars, swinging a polo mallet, an endless string of malapropisms) to observe that Zanuck was one of the industry's most creative and courageous giants. Even though he left the world of the Plains at a young age, of all the old-time producers his voice was the most genuinely American from the inside, a perspective that suffuses almost every film he made. He brought to the American cinema a populist's sense of fair play, a no-nonsense patriotism, a love of simple stories, and a dose of social criticism.

George F. Custen
City University of New York, College of Staten
Island, and Graduate Center of the City
University

Custen, George F. *Twentieth Century's Fox: Darryl F. Zanuck and the Culture of Hollywood*. New York: Basic Books, 1997.

Folkways

The John Curry Homestead, near West Union, Nebraska, 1886

FOLKWAYS

Folkways, the unofficial traditions of a people that are passed on informally from person to person or from one generation to another, are an integral part of the cultural heritage of every group of human beings. Yet no matter how carefully they are passed on, many folkways tend to assume variant forms with each successive performance or retelling. Even members of the same family who know a favorite story will relate the narrative in slightly different ways. Folkways mirror the forces of tradition, but they also reflect the ever-changing nature of culture and the predilections of each new generation of storytellers.

The diverse number of Great Plains folkways matches the diversity and vastness of the region itself. To be sure, many folkways have gone unstudied or unrecorded. Some undoubtedly have vanished without a trace. Others exhibit incredible resilience and have persisted for centuries and even millennia.

Among the earliest known inhabitants of the Great Plains were hunters and gatherers who lived at least 11,500 years ago. These early folk, who pursued mammoths and prehistoric bison, tipped their spears with exquisitely fashioned stone points. Other than their stone-age technology, relatively little is known about the ancient people archeologists refer to as Clovis. Yet there are intriguing hints of Clovis folkways, including the use of stone tool caches, incised bone rods, and red ochre. At the Anzick site near Wilsall, Montana, a whole cache of Clovis projectile points and other artifacts came to light that were colored with red ochre. The Anzick discovery helps us appreciate not only the possible existence of ancient Great Plains folkways but also their time-depth, which extends back many thousands of years.

Definitional Considerations

In 1906 American sociologist William Graham Sumner published *Folkways*, a volume that focused attention on a society's common usages, manners, customs, mores, and morals. To his credit, Sumner deemed such modes of expression as worthy of study. But Sumner did not fully comprehend the complexity of the beliefs and customs that he tried to analyze. He was hindered by both his apparent lack of familiarity with non-American folkways and other prevailing schools of thought that also focused on "folk" phenomena. Nonetheless, Sumner's *Folkways* proved influential, especially in the disciplines of history, psychology, and sociology. The influence extended into many nonacademic areas and even business ventures. In 1949, for example, Folkways Records was established and the company produced numerous recordings that became known all over the world. The term "folkways" soon was heard in many parts of the Great Plains as well. Today, Plains dwellers who never heard of William Graham Sumner or Folkways Records sometimes characterize their traditions as "folkways."

A much older term, and one that is most often used today, is "folklore." This term can be traced back to 1846 in England, and it gained a foothold in North America with the founding of the American Folklore Society in 1888. The parameters of folklore study have been debated and discussed for decades by folklorists. In *The Study of American Folklore* (1986), folklorist Jan Harold Brunvand provides an inclusive but straightforward definition: "Folklore comprises the unrecorded traditions of a people; it includes both the form and content of these traditions and their style or technique of communication from person to person." Brunvand divides the subject matter of folklore into three main categories: oral folklore (e.g., folk narratives, folk speech, proverbs, riddles, traditional rhymes and poetry, folk songs, folk music); customary folklore (e.g., folk beliefs, folk customs and festivals, folk dances and dramas, gestures, folk games); and material folk traditions (e.g., folk architecture, crafts, arts, costumes, and food). Brunvand is well aware that many folk phenomena overlap (as in the case of a folk festival that incorporates folk songs and traditional foods), and thus his divisions serve more as a useful guide rather than a rigid system of classification.

Still another term that is frequently used by contemporary folklorists is "folklife." The word has its counterpart in the Swedish *folkliv*, which dates from 1847. Unlike the terms "folkways" and "folklore," the European-inspired "folklife" emphasizes traditional life within a particular society. In 1976, with the establishment of the American Folklife Center at the U.S. Library of Congress, a new definition of folklife emerged that stressed "traditional expressive culture" as found in a variety of groups: familial, ethnic, occupational, religious, and regional.

Ethnic and Occupational Folklife

Popular misconceptions about the Great Plains abound. One still hears comments that the region is unusually monotonous, in terms of both landscape ("There's not a hill in sight!") and culture ("They all look like northern Europeans!"). Such criticism is in the same vein as much earlier impressions of the region that characterized the Great Plains as the "Great American Desert," where nearly everything (wood, water, people) was found to be sorely lacking.

To the Plains Indians the region was and remains a powerful place for dreams and visions. When European explorers arrived in the Plains, they encountered many Native peoples who were either village-based horticulturalists or nomads who pursued bison and other animals on foot. By the late 1800s, well after the advent of the horse and other, often imposed, changes, the lifestyles of Plains Indian groups had changed dramatically. Despite forced confinement on reservations, and concerted efforts by Americans to destroy their belief systems, Plains Indian peoples and folkways have survived. Beadworking, quillworking, and the making of star quilts are just a few examples of the varied traditional Plains Indians arts and crafts that have passed down from generation to generation. Many oral traditions, like trickster tales and stories of legendary and supernatural beings, are still told by tribal and clan elders, often in the Native language, or sometimes in English with a sprinkling of Native terms to accommodate listeners who have not learned their native tongue.

Spanish-speaking groups in the Great Plains also have preserved many of their folk traditions, most notably in the Southern Plains. Mexican American folklife is enriched by use of the Spanish language, numerous folk beliefs, festive events, and folk religious practices that exist alongside Roman Catholicism, mainstream medicine, and other formal institutions.

On the Northern Plains, where French-speaking fur traders were among the first Europeans to encounter Native peoples, a distinct racial and social group emerged known as the Métis. Ojibwa and Cree traditions mingled with those of the French and with other European folkways as well, most notably Irish, Scottish, and English. The "Michif" language resulted, as did a fondness for fiddling and dancing (in mocassined feet) to the "Red River Jig" and other folk tunes. Today, Métis identity remains strong, and families still converge on "Li Zhour di Lawn" (New Year's Day) and other festive occasions to play music, share stories, and feast on traditional Métis foods like "bullets" (meatballs) and "bangs" (pieces of fry bread).

Numerous ethnic groups have settled in the Great Plains and added to the diversity and richness of prairie folklife. Following the Homestead Act of 1862 in the United States and the Homestead Act of 1873 in Canada, and promotional campaigns by the railroads and other companies, thousands of families took up residence in the Great Plains. Some of these families were Anglo-Americans and Anglo-Canadians who simply migrated west, but many newcomers were immigrants who came from distant lands. One of the largest ethnic groups to settle in the Great Plains were the Germans. Their surnames and accents may have sounded similar to outsiders, but the Germans were unusually heterogeneous in terms of religious and regional traditions. German-speaking Catholics, Lutherans, Baptists, Mennonites, and Hutterites from German and eastern European states, for example, formed separate communities and seldom intermingled.

In the mid 1870s the first Germans from Russia entered the Great Plains. Experienced with growing wheat and living on the treeless steppes of Russia, these settlers soon put down roots in many areas of the Plains. The Black Sea Germans settled primarily in the Dakotas while the Volga Germans established communities in Kansas and other Central Plains states. Russian Mennonites also came to the Great Plains and settled in great numbers in the prairie lands of Manitoba and Saskatchewan. Hutterites (Hutterite Brethren) started out in what is now South Dakota, but many migrated to Canada due to anti-German persecution (mainly because of their refusal

A Métis group performs the Red River Jig.

to serve in the military) and wartime hysteria in 1918. Today, the Hutterites are the most conservative of all the Germans from Russia. They still live in colonies, use German as their primary language, and their lives are steeped in the folk traditions of their Anabaptist forebears.

The Great Plains also attracted large numbers of English, Irish, Scottish, and Welsh settlers who were influential in the development of many towns and small businesses. The Norwegians, Swedes, Finns, and Icelanders were most numerous in the Dakotas and other areas of the Northern Plains, while groups like the Czechs and Poles settled mainly in Nebraska and elsewhere in the Central Plains.

African Americans were in many parts of the Plains as early as the 1860s but a real impetus for settlement occurred in the late 1870s. Thousands of former slaves known as "Exodusters" headed west and established African American communities like Nicodemus, Kansas, and Dearfield, Colorado. As with so many other ethnic groups, those who came later often took up residence in the more densely populated areas of the Great Plains.

Many British and French settlers put down roots in the Canadian Prairie Provinces, but Ukrainian, Hungarian, Romanian, and many other immigrants also established viable communities. When agricultural lands were no longer available for settlement, immigrants continued to stream into Canadian towns and cities. Prairie urban centers such as Calgary, Regina, and Winnipeg all include diverse ethnic communities where folk traditions are integral parts of everyday life. A walk through Winnipeg's historic North End, for example, will take you past the Ukrainian Catholic Saints Vladimir and Olga Cathedral, past the Wawel Meat Market with its displays of buckwheat sausage, and past Gunn's counters of bagels and knishes.

Asian Americans settled in various parts of the Great Plains and have operated farms and businesses for generations. Early Japanese immigrants, for example, worked as manual laborers in the sugar beet fields of eastern Colorado, western Nebraska, and southern Alberta until they accumulated enough money to acquire farms of their own. More recently, Vietnamese, Cambodian, and East Indian immigrants have moved into Great Plains communities, where they keep alive such folkways as silk embroidery, traditional storytelling, and Kathak (Indian) folk dance.

Many ethnic groups of the Great Plains often found it difficult to maintain their folk traditions due to the small number of families involved. In the late 1800s, for example, Russian and Romanian Jews established agrarian colonies in Kansas, Nebraska, North Dakota, and Saskatchewan. Most of these agricultural experiments proved unsuccessful, but the recollections of such endeavors are still kept alive in the folklore of countless families. Linda Mack Schloff, in her book *And Prairie Dogs Weren't Kosher* (1996), reveals a wealth of oral history material and photographs relating to Jewish farmers in the Great Plains.

Just as the Plains attracted many ethnic and religious groups, it also provided a home for individuals of varying occupations. Fur traders, scouts, soldiers, blacksmiths, ranchers, sheepherders, rainmakers, railroad workers, stoop laborers, Canadian Mounties, oil field roughnecks, and a host of other occupational groups all have left their mark on the Great Plains. In the 1800s and early 1900s the most common occupation was that of farmer. But in a region as diverse and vast as the Great Plains, the occupation of farming greatly varied. A person engaged in farming in the Great Plains might be a dryland farmer, an irrigation farmer, a truck farmer, or a part-time farmer or rancher. Farming usually involved

families who, during harvest and at other times of the year, pitched in to keep things running smoothly. Farming was a way of life, not merely an activity. And this type of labor-intensive occupation gave rise to an incredible number of folk traditions. The traditions were most often seasonal in nature and ranged from planting rituals and barn cleanings in the spring, to ditch burnings and hog butcherings in the fall.

Surely no occupational group in the Great Plains has received as much attention as cowboys. This is to be expected when one remembers how important ranching is in the Great Plains. Cowboys have been an integral part of Plains life going back to the great cattle drives of the 1860s and 1870s. Since that time, the image of the cowboy has been romanticized in countless books, television shows, and motion pictures. Seldom is there an opportunity for cowboys to be seen for who they really are—hardworking men and women involved in a folk tradition that brings them into daily contact with cattle and horses. Much of what they know was taught to them by other cowboys—grandparents, parents, friends, or coworkers. Cowboy folklife manifests itself in countless ways, ranging from well-worn cowboy boots and leather chaps to community rodeos and "cowboy lingo."

Although there are many well-known cowboy songs, the popular image of the "singing cowboy" does not fit every Great Plains buckaroo. Like members of other groups, there are those cowboys who sing, others who simply sit and listen, and still others who would prefer to do something like drive cattle rather than serenade them. Recently, there has been great public interest in cowboy poetry, which has ties to the balladlike pieces recited by trail hands a century ago and more. In the 1980s folklorists turned their attention to contemporary cowboy poetry, and there has been a virtual outpouring of published and recited work relating to cowboy folklife. Anthologies of cowboy poetry also have appeared, including Teresa Jordan's *Graining the Mare: The Poetry of Ranch Women* (1994).

Oral Folklore

One of the richest sources of published material relating to Great Plains folkways is oral folklore. This does not mean that there has always been more oral folklore in the Plains than customary folklore or other folk traditions. Instead, it may reflect the interests of early collectors of folklore who emphasized oral forms of traditional expression (e.g., legends, myths, tall tales). In their zeal to collect certain stories, many other traditions went completely unnoticed. This is unfortunate, as the folklore of a group is best understood and appreciated within its cultural context, and this requires the serious investigator to pay close attention to the totality of traditional life.

In terms of oral folklore, one of the best indicators of group identity is folk speech. Native Americans, African Americans, Hispanic Americans, Asian Americans, and European Americans all contributed to linguistic diversity in the Great Plains. Yet over time the Plains experience gave rise to a distinct form of folk speech that revealed an emerging regional identity, no matter what the ethnic or racial background of the speaker. Winfred Blevins, in his *Dictionary of the American West* (1993), includes many examples of Great Plains folk speech: "prairie lawyer" (a coyote); "prairie strawberries" (a humorous name for beans, an old standby); "prairie wool" (another name for buffalo grass); and "prairie cocktail" (a salted and peppered raw egg in liquor or vinegar).

Published collections of Great Plains proverbs and folk expressions are unfortunately rare. Nonetheless, examples of these types of oral folklore can be found in various regional compilations like S. J. Sackett and William E. Koch's *Kansas Folklore* (1961) and Louise Pound's *Nebraska Folklore* (1987). In an essay on Nebraska snake lore, Louise Pound includes a number of folk expressions dealing with snakes, varying from "As crooked as a snake" to "Madder than snakes in haying." Great Plains riddles also are a much-neglected genre, but examples of riddles told and enjoyed by prairie dwellers can be found in *Kansas Folklore* and in more comprehensive collections such as John Greenway's *Folklore of the Great West* (1969). Greenway includes a number of traditional riddles that reflect the realities of rural life: "What walks in the water with its head down?" (Answer: "The nails in a horse's shoe when he walks through the water") and "What goes 'round the house with a harrow after her?" (Answer: "A hen with her chickens—all engaged in scratching up the ground").

Unlike proverbs and riddles, folk narratives have received considerable attention, for the Great Plains is a region of great stories and great storytellers. Among the earliest collections of Great Plains folk narratives are those compiled by anthropologists and other researchers who did fieldwork for the Bureau of American Ethnology. Numerous narratives were recorded in the native languages of Plains Indian storytellers, and these texts comprise a valuable folkloristic and linguistic resource even today. Early writers like George Bird Grinnell, who were intimately familiar with Plains Indian folkways, added richly to narrative collections. Grinnell's early books, including *Pawnee Hero Stories and Folk-Tales* (1889) and *Blackfoot Lodge Tales* (1892), are still in print and widely read.

Plains Indian folk narratives continue to be a focus of interest, both on the part of scholars and the general public. In recent years, collections have appeared that include contemporary narratives told by Native storytellers. An example of one such collection is Keith Cunningham's *American Indians' Kitchen Table Stories* (1992). Native writers also have published a growing number of works that include folk narratives. In many cases, Native American writers provide the all-important cultural context for understanding the role of narratives in contemporary Plains Indian life. A recent example is Delphine Red Shirt's *Bead*

on an Anthill: A Lakota Childhood* (1998), in which she describes the influential way that Plains Indian stories about "Double Woman" and "Iktomi" (Spider) inspired and strengthened her.

For the many ethnic and occupational groups who make the Great Plains their home, folk narratives serve as a rich source of local knowledge that strengthens group identity. But the Great Plains also has folk narratives that transcend ethnic and occupational boundaries. Legends are clearly a case in point. These folk narratives are localized and are related in a conversational style as "true stories." They range from narratives about haunted farmhouses and prairie UFOs to much more mundane subjects, such as cattle theft and runaway tractors. One legend heard all over the Great Plains concerns a rancher who traps a troublesome coyote. He suspects the coyote is a predator and so he ties a stick of dynamite to the coyote's leg, lights the fuse, and quickly releases the animal from the trap. The coyote, confused and frightened, runs under the rancher's new pickup truck. Legend expert Jan Harold Brunvand, in his book *The Choking Doberman* (1984), refers to this folk narrative as "The Coyote's Revenge" and notes its similarity to Native American stories in which the coyote is a perennial trickster.

Another genre of folk narrative that is common to the Great Plains is the tall tale. While not confined to the American and Canadian Plains, the tall tale is completely at home in the land of big skies, baseball-size hailstones, and sizzling summer temperatures. But unlike the legend that elicits gasps and a sense of dread, the tall tale prompts chuckles and belly laughter. The telling of tall tales enables Plains dwellers to poke fun at the larger-than-life forces that face them almost daily. When asked if they are getting enough rain, sunblackened Great Plains farmers might reply: "No, not much at all. Even the carp and crawdads are down to their last canteen." Folklorist Roger Welsch relates this favorite Great Plains tall tale: "Three farmers all died at the same time. All of them wanted to be cremated. One was from Texas, one from Kansas, and the third from Nebraska. The guy from Texas was ashes in two hours—ditto for the Kansan. But they left the guy from Nebraska in for two days, and when they opened the door he jumped out and said, 'My God, two weeks more like this and there won't be any corn crop this year.'" A number of tall-tale publications dealing with the Great Plains and the American West have appeared. Roger Welsch's *Shingling the Fog and Other Plains Lies* (1972) and Robert E. Gard's Canadian classic *Johnny Chinook* (1945) are among the most amusing and comprehensive.

Prairie dwellers have sung songs for centuries and danced to the sound of many musical traditions. Although Native American folk music in the Plains is extremely diverse, intertribal powwow celebrations have done much to bring Native peoples of different backgrounds together. At such gatherings, Indians from the Canadian Prairies and those from

the Southern Plains come into contact and realize there are many similarities they share in common. Numerous powwows take place throughout the Great Plains each year. One of the largest is the Crow Fair at Crow Agency, Montana, which attracts thousands of participants and spectators.

The folk musical traditions of the Great Plains often reveal evidence of cultural borrowing and sharing. In the sugar beet region of the Central Plains states (western Nebraska, northeastern Colorado, and southeastern Wyoming), a distinct type of polka music known as "the Dutch Hop" is still popular. The fast-paced music represents a Volga German folk tradition that exhibits many Russian and other eastern European influences. One of the central Dutch Hop symbols is the *hackbrett* (hammered dulcimer), a handcrafted instrument with eighty wires that the player strikes with two wooden "hammers." The Dutch Hop is perhaps most pronounced in northern Colorado, where, despite an influx of population and unparalleled urban growth, the folk tradition continues to hold its own.

In Spanish-speaking areas of the Central and Southern Plains, many folk musical traditions are in evidence. One of these traditions reflects interesting cultural borrowings. The Mexican American music known as *conjunto* is characterized by a reliance on the button accordion. Those who dance to the lively music of conjunto cannot fail to recognize its similarity to German-style polkas and schottisches that are interspersed with the other numbers. Although conjunto is perhaps most popular in Texas, its influence in the Great Plains extends at least as far north as the prairie lands bordering the Red River in North Dakota, Minnesota, and Canada.

While the musical tastes of Great Plains residents are rich and varied, there are folk songs that have come to be strongly identified with the region. A classic example is the song "Home on the Range," which has its roots in the heart of Kansas. Oceanlike images of a huge, waving sea of grass sometimes appear in the folk songs of the Great Plains. "Bury Me Not on the Lone Prairie," for example, is based on the old English folk song "Ocean Burial."

Many folk songs of the Great Plains have undergone modification to make them more suited to specific locales. Inspired by the tune "Beulah Land," Plains folksingers simply change the opening line (depending on where they reside) and sing something like:

Nebraska Land, Nebraska Land,
As on thy desert soil I stand
And look away across the plains,
I wonder why it never rains. . . .

In the Plains of Saskatchewan, a similar folk song is sung and lyrics are added that give it a distinctive local flavor. Michael Taft, in his *Discovering Saskatchewan Folklore* (1983), includes this verse:

Saskatchewan, the land of snow,
Where winds are always on the blow,
Where people sit with frozen toes.
And why we stay here no one knows. . . .

Customary Folklore

Folk beliefs ("superstitions"), folk customs, weather lore, folk medicine, folk games, seasonal traditions, and life-cycle customs are a few of the many phenomena folklorists refer to as "customary folklore." While these often involve elements of oral lore and even material folk culture, customary folklore typically manifests itself in traditional belief or behavior.

One of the largest collections of Great Plains customary folklore is William E. Koch's *Folklore from Kansas* (1980). This unusually detailed compilation, which includes more than 5,000 individual folklore texts, focuses on folk customs, beliefs, and superstitions. Koch's material covers a wide range of topics: illnesses, making wishes, dreams, luck, plants and planting, hunting and fishing, and even a section detailing beliefs and customs relating to domestic animals and wildlife. Some of the latter traditions reflect an intimate familiarity with cattle country and the Plains environment (e.g., "If you grease a fence after a cow gets cut on it, the cow won't get an infection"; "During a storm, horses always stand with their tails to the wind, and cattle stand with their heads to the wind"; and "Grasshoppers come only in dry years").

Koch also presents many examples of weather lore, and this is indeed a rich source for Great Plains folklore. Plains residents read a variety of "signs" in natural phenomena of all kinds: phases of the moon, the color of the Great Plains sky, the shape of thunderheads and other approaching clouds, even the sudden appearance of bubbles on a stream or pond (which are believed to portend an approaching rainstorm). Louise Pound, in *Nebraska Folklore*, includes a fascinating section on rain lore and rainmaking. From time to time, Great Plains residents believed that rain could be coaxed from the sky by plowing acres of prairie, planting trees, shooting explosives into the sky, and even by setting fire to the prairie itself. Pound does not overlook perhaps one of the most common folk beliefs relating to rainmaking: "Wash and polish your car and you may be sure rain will follow."

Folk medicine also is an important and integral part of customary folklore. Home remedies, herbal recipes, and traditional faith-healing techniques are examples of folk medicine found in the Great Plains. It is not uncommon to find Plains residents who treat certain ailments at home while seeking treatment for other ailments from either folk healers or licensed medical practitioners. Evidently, a range of factors comes into play when deciding how to treat an ailment and whom to seek for appropriate treatment. David E. Jones, for example, worked with a Comanche medicine woman in western Oklahoma. The resulting study, *Sanapia* (1972), provides a fascinating glimpse into the world of a Plains Indian healer who combines elements of Christianity and peyotism alongside traditional Comanche beliefs relating to guardian spirits and vision quests.

In the southern portions of the Great Plains, one still finds much evidence of the Mexican American folk-healing tradition known as *curanderismo*. Unlike the medical care provided by hospitals and licensed practitioners, the Spanish-speaking world of curanderismo is more accessible and personal. Formal appointments and office paperwork are unnecessary and "payments for services" are never demanded. Patrons who are comfortable with the mix of natural remedies and spirituality that the *curanderos* (healers) provide typically leave a donation.

Far to the north, in the Dakotas, a folk-healing tradition very similar to curanderismo is found among the Germans from Russia. *Brauche* is a type of folk healing that makes use of prayers, religious verses, herbs, massage, the "laying on of hands," and other faith-healing techniques. Much like Mexican American curanderos, German Russian "brauchers" accept donations but never demand payment.

Games and traditional forms of recreation in the Great Plains are subjects not overlooked by scholars. Jim Hoy and Tom Isern, in their volume *Plains Folk* (1987), devote attention to many prairie traditions, including folk games and other favorite pastimes. Among them are "Dare Base" (also called "Prisoner's Base"), recess games (like throwing a ball over the schoolhouse and referring to it as "Annie Over" or a similar term), "Fox and Geese," and six-man football.

Seasonal customs and celebrations are common throughout the Great Plains and often are linked with specific ethnic and religious groups. In Lindsborg, Kansas, for example, Swedish Americans celebrate the feast day of Santa Lucia (on the second Saturday of December) with ethnic food, Old Country fiddling, roving carolers, the crowning of Santa Lucia, as well as a number of other activities. Folklorist Larry Danielson offers a richly detailed description and analysis of the celebration in his essay, "St. Lucia in Lindsborg, Kansas" (1991). In Texas especially, but also in Oklahoma, African Americans celebrate "Juneteenth" on June 19, commemorating the Emancipation Proclamation that was read in Galveston on that day in 1865. Public speeches, picnics, parades, ball games, displays of African American arts, and musical entertainment are all part of the celebration.

Life-cycle customs also are found wherever there are families and traditional communities in the Great Plains. An incredibly diverse number of folk traditions surround the various stages of the human life cycle: conception, birth, infancy, childhood, adolescence, adulthood, old age, and death. Sometimes, certain life-cycle events provide an occasion for family members and friends to come together and celebrate, as in the case of christenings, bar mitzvahs, Mexican American *quinceañera* (fifteenth birthday) festivities, weddings, and funerals. Not uncommon in the Great Plains is the tradition of mock weddings, a form of folk drama linked to life-cycle celebrations such as anniversaries and weddings. The mock wedding is characterized by individuals who dress up in old wedding attire and reverse gender roles. Thus, a man may don a bridal gown and tattered veil while a woman will wear a man's oversized suit and even paste on a funny-looking mustache or sideburns. A folk parody of the marriage ceremony takes place, often with some rather colorful and even risqué components.

Michael Taft has documented the mock wedding tradition in his lively and richly illustrated study "Folk Drama on the Great Plains: The Mock Wedding in Canada and the United States" (1989). Taft discovered that while the mock wedding tradition can be found in other parts of North America, this particular folkway has found fertile ground in the Great Plains. One explanation Taft offers for this rather unusual regional phenomenon is that the mock wedding provides a way for Plains women to "express their ambivalent and conflicting roles as farm wives." By means of a humorous and even outrageous parody, the traditional roles of men and women in agricultural communities are turned upside down, played with, and thus reexamined.

Material Folk Traditions

Unlike oral and customary folklore, material folk traditions manifest themselves in tangible ways that can be touched, measured, and even photographed. Yet folklorists do not concern themselves only with the tangible results—or artifacts—for there is always a much larger body of tradition that surrounds a Plains Indian flute, a Doukhobor spinning wheel, or an African American family quilt. Material folk culture takes many forms and includes such wide-ranging traditions as foodways, folk architecture, folk crafts, and folk art.

Traditional foodways of the Great Plains vary tremendously and reflect a rich mosaic of ethnic and occupational tastes. Roger Welsch, in *A Treasury of Nebraska Pioneer Folklore* (1984), includes examples of many regional and ethnic dishes, including "corn coffee," buckwheat cakes, Indian meal mush, wild rabbit, green corn pudding, currant jam, and rhubarb tarts. Traditional foodways serve not only to provide bodily nourishment but also to evoke and maintain a strong sense of group identity. Thus, while certain foods like Bohemian pressed blood sausage, Mexican menudo (tripe soup), or the cowboy dish "prairie oysters" (fried calf testicles) might repulse outsiders, these same culinary creations serve to reinforce feelings of group uniqueness on the part of those who willingly—and happily—indulge themselves.

In terms of Great Plains folk architecture, one of the most enduring symbols of the region is the sod house of the homesteader. This dwelling, as befits its name, was constructed from strips of prairie sod. The thick earthen walls ensured that the occupants would be comfortable during sweltering summers and brutally cold winters. The sod house has its counterpart in the earth lodge of early Plains Indian settled peoples, including the Pawnees, Arikaras, Mandans, and Hidatsas. Adobe-style houses can be found in the Southern Plains, and they remain an integral part of Mexican American folk architecture. In the Northern

"House-barn" structure in a small Mennonite community in southern Manitoba

Plains, the Black Sea Germans and the Ukrainians built homes of sun-dried clay brick that served them especially well during the long cold winters. These homes usually were low earthen structures that blended in well with their grassland surroundings.

In Manitoba and Saskatchewan, Mennonites from South Russia often built long wooden "house barns." This unique type of prairie dwelling consists of a house, barn, and stable—all connected under one roof. In some cases, a "summer kitchen" is built between the main dwelling and the barn, thus connecting the structures in a slightly modified fashion. This type of folk architecture was particularly well suited to the rigors of a northern climate, for the settlers could tend to their horses and other livestock during fierce winter storms without leaving the safety of the connected buildings. Today, a number of these "house barn" dwellings still can be seen in the Canadian Prairies.

Individuals knowledgeable in folk crafts can be found in every Great Plains community. At one time, of course, folk crafts enabled many families to be as self-sufficient as possible. Agricultural tools, cooking utensils, branding irons, wagon wheels, and various other items were made by hand or were crafted by local blacksmiths and wheelwrights. When the desired items were made by folk artisans or other specialists, barter often was possible.

Great Plains ranchers and farmers came up with ingenious devices for making life easier and more satisfying. One such innovation is the cattle guard, which simultaneously serves as both a gate and a fence. While people and vehicles can pass over the horizontal metal bars of the cattle guard fairly quickly, cattle refrain from crossing. Jim Hoy, in his book *The Cattle Guard* (1982), convincingly demonstrates that cattle guards first appeared in the Great Plains about 1905. Like so many folk crafts and folk innovations, the name of the original craftsman who made the first Great Plains cattle guard is unknown.

Just as the makers of various folk crafts often remain anonymous, the same holds true for many types of folk art. There is a thin dividing line between folk craft and folk art, but many scholars argue that in the realm of folk craft, the utilitarian function outweighs aesthetic considerations. A quilt might be considered an example of folk craft if the item is used for purely utilitarian purposes. Yet a quilt that is displayed only on special occasions and is the object of much admiration may be considered folk art. As is so often the case with folklore, the cultural and situational contexts are vitally important in determining the true nature of a folk tradition.

Folk art in the Great Plains takes many forms. Plains Indian artistic traditions, for example, manifest themselves in items like drums, porcupine quillwork, carved pipes, parfleches, and in numerous other ways. Quite often all or most of the raw materials come from natural materials within the Great Plains. Groups who later moved into the Plains, especially European Americans, often had to adapt their artistic traditions to the new surroundings.

Throughout the Great Plains, from the Mexican border to the Prairies of Alberta, Manitoba, and Saskatchewan, numerous examples can be found of a distinctive form of folk art: wrought-iron grave crosses. Usually made by blacksmiths or other metal specialists, these crosses range in size from small children's markers to elaborately crafted iron crosses that stand several feet in height. Although iron grave crosses can be found in many parts of the world, they seem particularly striking when viewed against the open, uncluttered horizon of the Great Plains.

In the Southern Plains, iron crosses are most common in Mexican American cemeteries. In Kansas, they are numerous in the many Volga German settlements around Hays. In the Dakotas and Prairie Provinces, the so-called iron spirits are associated with the Germans from Russia, Ukrainians, Métis, and other ethnic groups. As might be expected, handcrafted iron crosses include an array of ethnic-based and religious symbols, but some crosses also include decorative features strongly reminiscent of the Great Plains: symbols of the sun, sparkling stars, abundant open space, and waving wheat. Most wrought-iron crosses are unsigned and include few words other than the names and dates of the deceased. Yet, like other works of art, the "iron spirits" of the Great Plains compel travelers to stop, take a closer look, and ponder the great mysteries.

Conclusion

Great Plains folkways are so diverse that it is difficult to summarize the region's traditions

Wrought-iron cross on the plains of southwestern North Dakota

A forty-five-foot-high tower of oil cans near Casselton, North Dakota, dating from the Depression era

in a comprehensive fashion. Yet one theme does run through many of the songs and stories of Great Plains people, no matter what the ethnic or occupational background of the folksingers and storytellers. In a land of big skies and seemingly endless horizons, there is a tendency to celebrate and even exaggerate the immensity of the region itself, as well as the numerous challenges it poses to all who call the prairie their home.

Rather than ignore the harsh side of Great Plains life, prairie dwellers tend to confront and even "play up" such hardships as blizzards, droughts, severe heat, extreme cold, hailstorms, and other realities. This tendency manifests itself in a number of distinctive folkways, including the telling of tall tales and the singing of humorous folk parodies about life in the Great Plains.

This emphasis on hyperbole in Great Plains folklore also manifests itself in the large number of "roadside colossi" that can be found throughout the region. As Karal Ann Marling's book *The Colossus of Roads* (1984) illustrates, roadside sculptures are not unique to the Great Plains, but they do assume humorous and rather spectacular forms there. From the Texas Hill Country to the Canadian Rockies, various types of folk monuments can be found along Great Plains highways.

All of this perhaps is to be expected when one considers a Great Plains state like South Dakota, which includes such visual wonders as Mount Rushmore, the Crazy Horse Monument (near Custer), the Corn Palace (Mitchell), and Dinosaur Park (Rapid City). Other Great Plains states are not to be outdone. Near

Alliance, Nebraska, numerous old automobiles and other vehicles form "Carhenge," a gigantic circle of iron and steel that is hauntingly reminiscent of the ancient Stonehenge in England. In Fort Stockton, "Paisano Pete," a statue of a twenty-foot-long roadrunner, welcomes travelers to West Texas.

In Wyoming, a huge likeness of the mythical jackalope (a jackrabbit with antlers) can be viewed in downtown Douglas. Near Rothsay, Minnesota, "the world's largest prairie chicken" stands guard at the eastern edge of the Great Plains. In Jamestown, North Dakota, "the world's largest buffalo" dwarfs a herd of live buffalo that graze nearby. East of New Town, North Dakota, an eye-catching statue of the tall, lanky cowboy Earl Bunyan—the legendary Great Plains brother of the lumberjack Paul Bunyan—waves a branding iron and braces himself against the strong northern winds with a walking cane.

Folk monuments also dot the Canadian Plains, ranging from the twenty-two-foot-high western painted turtle in Boissevain, Manitoba, to the gigantic replica of a Ukrainian *pysanka* (decorated Easter egg) in Vegreville, Alberta. One of the most unusual Canadian folk monuments is the "World's Largest Bunnock" that rises more than thirty feet above the rolling prairies near Macklin, Saskatchewan. The curious onlooker soon learns that a "bunnock" is one of fifty-two horse anklebones that are used in a centuries-old folk game transplanted from the Russian steppes to western Canada. To create the World's Largest Bunnock, the image of an actual horse anklebone was enlarged nearly 100 times and then formed into shape out of metal pipe, chicken wire, and fiberglass. The bunnock monument is illuminated at night and is visible for miles around. As one might expect, Macklin is also the site of the "World Championship Bunnock Tournament," which has been held yearly since 1993.

The presence of so many roadside colossi and folk monuments in the Great Plains should come as little surprise. Plains dwellers know their region is often referred to as "tall tale country." Instead of fighting such a label, many storytellers chuckle and quickly share some favorite "windies" of their own.

Great Plains folkways are as diverse and as dynamic as the region itself. The traditions mirror the experiences of many different groups who have grown accustomed to the great vistas and the even greater uncertainties that surround Plains dwellers on an almost daily basis. Through it all, Plains folk have developed a fierce and begrudging appreciation for their home. The numerous tall tales and humorous folk songs and roadside monuments reflect something else: the ability of Great Plains folk to laugh at adversity and, on occasion, to laugh most heartily at themselves.

See also ARCHITECTURE: Roadside Architecture; Sod-Wall Construction / EUROPEAN AMERICANS: German Russians; Jews / IMAGES AND ICONS: Cowboy Culture / LITERARY TRADITIONS: Cowboy Poetry; Oral Traditions / MUSIC: Hispanic Music; Polka Music / NATIVE AMERICANS: Métis / SPORTS AND RECREATION: Crow Fair / WATER: Rainmaking.

Timothy J. Kloberdanz
North Dakota State University

Blevins, Winfred. *Dictionary of the American West*. New York: Facts on File, 1993. Brunvand, Jan Harold. *The Study of American Folklore: An Introduction*. New York: W. W. Norton Co., 1986. Cunningham, Keith. *American Indians' Kitchen Table Stories: Contemporary Conversations with Cherokee, Sioux, Hopi, Osage, Navajo, Zuni, and Members of Other Nations*. Little Rock AR: August House Publishers, 1992. Danielson, Larry. "St. Lucia in Lindsborg, Kansas." In *Creative Ethnicity: Symbols and Strategies of Contemporary Ethnic Life*, edited by Stephen Stern and John Allan Cicala. Logan: Utah State University Press, 1991: 187–203. Gard, Robert E. *Johnny Chinook: Tall Tales and True from the Canadian West*. London: Longmans, Green and Company, 1945. Greenway, John. *Folklore of the Great West*. Palo Alto CA: American West Publishing Company, 1969. Hoy, James F. *The Cattle Guard: Its History and Lore*. Lawrence: University Press of Kansas, 1982. Hoy, James F., and Isern, Tom. *Plains Folk: A Commonplace of the Great Plains*. Norman: University of Oklahoma Press, 1987. Jones, David E. *Sanapia: Comanche Medicine Woman*. New York: Holt, Rinehart and Winston, 1972. Jordan, Teresa, ed. *Graining the Mare: The Poetry of Ranch Women*. Salt Lake City: Peregrine Smith, 1994. Kloberdanz, Timothy J. "The Daughters of Shiphrah: Folk Healers and Midwives of the Great Plains." *Great Plains Quarterly* 9 (1989): 3–12. Marling, Karal Ann. *The Colossus of Roads: Myth and Symbol along the American Highway*. Minneapolis: University of Minnesota Press, 1984. Pound, Louise. *Nebraska Folklore*. Lincoln: University of Nebraska Press, 1987. Red Shirt, Delphine. *Bead on an Anthill: A Lakota Childhood*. Lincoln: University of Nebraska Press, 1998. Sackett, S. J., and William E. Koch, eds. *Kansas Folklore*. Lincoln: University of Nebraska Press, 1961. Schloff, Linda Mack. *"And Prairie Dogs Weren't Kosher": Jewish Women in the Upper Midwest Since 1855*. St. Paul: Minnesota Historical Society Press, 1996. Sumner, William Graham. *Folkways: A Study of the Sociological Importance of Usages, Manners, Customs, Mores, and Morals*. New York: Arno Press, 1979. Taft, Michael. *Discovering Saskatchewan Folklore: Three Case Studies*. Edmonton, Alberta: NeWest Press, 1983. Taft, Michael. "Folk Drama on the Great Plains: The Mock Wedding in Canada and the United States." *North Dakota History* 56 (1989): 17–23. Welsch, Roger L. *Shingling the Fog and Other Plains Lies: Tall Tales of the Great Plains*. Chicago: Swallow Press, 1972. Welsch, Roger L. *A Treasury of Nebraska Pioneer Folklore*. Lincoln: University of Nebraska Press, 1966, 1984.

ADAMS, RAMON (1889–1976)

Musician, businessman, bibliophile, and lexicographer, Ramon Frederick Adams authored twenty-four books about the West. Born to Cooke M. and Charlie Adams in Moscow, Texas, on October 3, 1889, he attended Sherman Private School in 1903 and Austin College in 1905. Adams dropped out in 1909 but returned and graduated in 1912. He edited *Reveille*, a student publication, in 1907. Adams studied violin under Carl Venth at Kidd-Key College in Sherman and later taught at the University of Arkansas until 1914. Further study in Chicago before moving to North Texas led him to chair the violin department at Wichita Falls School of Music. Later he became well known for accompanying silent films in theaters in Wichita Falls, Fort Worth, and Dallas. A wrist broken while he was trying to crank a Model T Ford forced his retirement from music. With his wife, Allie, whom he had married while in Arkansas, Adams then opened a highly successful candy business in Dallas, first retail and later wholesale. They sold the business in 1955, after which Adams, who had privately published his first book, *Poems of the Canadian West*, in 1919 and sold his first story to *Western Story Magazine* in 1923, devoted himself to book collecting and writing.

Adams's focus on cowboy life took him, with support from various foundations, across the Great Plains from Texas to Montana interviewing and collecting. His books include *Six Guns and Saddle Leather* (1954), an extensive bibliography; *Charles M. Russell, the Cowboy Artist: A Biography* (1948), written with Homer E. Britzman; and *A Fitting Death for Billy the Kid* (1960). Also important are the dictionary *Western Words* (1944); *Come An' Get It* (1952), which features western cooking; and *The Cowboy and His Humor* (1968), which details the entertainments of the old-time cowboy. *Burrs under the Saddle* (1964) points out historically inaccurate passages in Western writing, a passion that drove Adams to extensive reading and research.

Adams won the Dallas Public Library Award in 1965 and received an honorary doctor of letters degree from Austin College in 1968. He died on April 29, 1976, in Dallas and was buried there in Resthaven Memorial Park.

Lawrence Clayton
Hardin-Simmons University

Klinefelter, Karen. "Folklorist Enjoys Third Career." *Dallas Morning News*, October 26, 1969: 38A. Phillips, Edward Hake. "Adams, Ramon Frederick." In *The New Handbook of Texas*, edited by Ron Tyler. Vol. 1: 25. Austin: Texas State Historical Association, 1996.

ANIMAL LORE

Animal lore is the accumulated fact, tradition, and belief about the fauna of a region. Larger animals have a stronger grip on the human imagination. Thus, the buffalo has long been emblematic of the Great Plains. However, farmers and ranchers who know the region best have a rich store of knowledge of smaller animals, including badgers, beavers, bobcats, foxes, lynxes, minks, muskrats, opossums, prairie dogs, rabbits, raccoons, skunks, squirrels, and weasels.

The folkloristic sources of the ideas, images, and stories about wild animals of the Great Plains are many, but four types can be distinguished: oral narratives, popular culture, performances, and elite culture. These categories provide a frame of reference for understanding this body of animal lore.

First are the oral narratives, a key source of ideas about wild animals of the Great Plains. This genre includes the true "stories" people pass on to explain to one another the meaning of a wild animal. It is also the category that has been treated to the most folklore scholarship. Myths are representative of this genre, and there are many Native American myths involving such animals as the deer, coyote, elk, or bear. Myths often explain the origins of geographic features in the remote past. An example is Devils Tower in eastern Wyoming, a large stump-shaped cluster of rock columns, overlooking the Belle Fourche River and rising 1,280 feet above the rolling grasslands. Noted for its magnificence and beauty, this formation has long been a landmark to explorers and travelers heading west from the Black Hills. In Kiowa mythology the striations on the tower were formed when seven young girls, playing far from camp, were chased onto the rock by bears. The rock rose into the heavens where the girls became stars, and the bears, trying to follow, left their claw marks on the surface.

Such legends are also set in the less-remote past. For example, there is a nineteenth-century story about the "white mustang of the prairies," whose coat and tail and mane were pure white. He symbolized freedom and untamed nature in an era before there were barbed-wire fences. Many people claimed to see him, especially on moonlit nights. The white mustang was able to avoid all predators and was never seen for very long at a time. Cowboys tried to capture him, but they eventually realized it was a waste of time because of the white mustang's courage, speed, and intelligence, which always kept him out of the of ropes and bullets.

Popular culture is the second source of ideas about wild animals of the Great Plains. Included in this category are postcards, souvenirs, cartoons, comics, television commercials, print advertising, theatrical films, and mass-circulation magazines. Popular culture provides a repertoire of stories and images to a wide audience. Popular material from commercial culture can be found in abundance, from the Warner Bros. cartoon character Wile E. Coyote to the postcards from Nebraska featuring the "jackalope," a legendary creature combining a jackrabbit with an antelope.

The third source of ideas, images, and stories are the performances that involve somehow an interpretation of a wild animal. Oldest in this category are the Native American performance rituals and dances that involve the armadillo, the coyote, the bear, and the rattlesnake. European American settlers favored participatory dramalike events that began with Buffalo Bill's Wild West show and continue in present-day tourist attractions, rodeos, festivals, museum and zoo programs, hunting expeditions, cooking events, and the like. Significantly, Col. William F. Cody (Buffalo Bill) was always pictured riding a white stallion, recalling that persistent theme in Plains animal lore.

The fourth source of our notions about animals is elite culture, the body of fine literature and fine arts that is the usual subject matter of humanistic study. Fine painting, poetry, novels, and short stories of the Great Plains often feature animals such as Texas longhorn cattle, descended from the wild cattle brought to America by the Spanish, as central symbols in the imaginative landscape of their fictive works. But even here folk ideas are often still present, just recast in more elegant language. In American elite art we can trace the iconography of Great Plains wildlife from the earliest European renditions through the likes of Thomas Hart Benton and Charles Marion Russell up to the present.

See also LITERARY TRADITIONS: Oral Traditions.

Angus Kress Gillespie
Rutgers University

Gillespie, Angus Kress, and Jay Mechling. *American Wildlife in Symbol and Story*. Knoxville: University of Tennessee Press, 1987. Lawrence, Elizabeth Atwood. "The White Mustang of the Prairies." *Great Plains Quarterly* 1 (1981): 81–94. Wilson, David Scofield. *In the Presence of Nature*. Amherst: University of Massachusetts Press, 1978.

BLIZZARD STORIES

The ferocity of blizzards in the Great Plains has entered into the region's folklore through countless stories of tragedy and of survival. The word "blizzard" originated in the Northern Plains during the mid–nineteenth century, perhaps derived from the German *blitzartig*, meaning lightninglike, which accurately portrays the power and swiftness of Great Plains blizzards.

The first documented Plains blizzard in which large numbers of people lost their lives was the January 1872 Buffalo Hunters' Storm, which swept up so quickly that unprepared buffalo hunters, many just arrived from the East, were found dead from the Platte River of Nebraska to the Texas Panhandle. The Easter Storm of April 1873 saw the deaths of not only ranchers and thousands of cattle in the open country of the Central Plains but also a boy in Central City, Nebraska, who died trying to reach a print shop one block away. In the Great Blizzard of 1886, 100 people and 100,000 cattle died in western Kansas during a series of storms that struck less than a week apart. In southwestern Kansas, a man froze to death in a light linen overcoat with a flyer in his pocket advertising Kansas as the Italy of America. A young woman in Clark County, Kansas, became separated from her family on a half-mile journey and died within an arm's length of the door of her brother's house, her hands tangled in her hair.

Arguably the most tragic blizzard of the Plains was the School Children's Storm of January 1888, which struck following an exceptionally warm period. The blizzard hit the Central Plains when schools were letting out, and some teachers, new to the Plains, discounted stories of death during blizzards as simply tall tales and let their children walk home. Other teachers released their students early, hoping they would arrive home before its full fury. However, temperatures quickly plummeted to nearly 40° below zero, and sixty-mile-per-hour winds with snow as fine as sifted flour reduced visibility to practically zero on the open prairie. In Pierce County, Nebraska, a teacher with three students became hopelessly lost walking 200 yards to her boarding place, and they spent the night huddled in a haystack. The children died and the teacher lost both feet to amputation. In Bon Homme County, Dakota Territory, the wind scattered a teacher and her nine students.

They all died and were not found until the snow had melted months later. An old-timer of the community advised watching for circling buzzards to locate the bodies. More than 200 people perished from Saskatchewan to Texas, most of them children of the Central Plains and their parents who went out searching for them.

Although these blizzards brought tragedy to many Plains settlers, stories of survival also fill the pages of Great Plains history. A man in Clay County, Nebraska, survived the Easter Storm of April 1873 by housing his eight-person family, one hog, one dog, all his chickens, and four head of cattle in the same room. In Hastings, Nebraska, during the same blizzard, people needing supplies followed a rope tied between a store and the city well. During the Great Blizzard of 1886, a wandering range steer in Lane County, Kansas, burst through the wall of a sod house and was skinned on the spot, providing steaks to a family running low on food. In the same county, a woman checking on the family cow 100 yards from the house became disoriented, so she tied her shawl to the cow and let it lead her home, where both comfortably waited out the rest of the storm.

The School Children's Storm of 1888 also has heroic stories of survival. In Jerauld County, Dakota Territory, a group of schoolchildren and their teacher held hands to travel the 100 yards to a farmhouse. Missing the house by six feet, they fell into a small ravine but clambered back out to reach a straw pile, where they all survived the night. In Hanson County, Dakota Territory, two men spliced together several coils of clothesline and tied one end to the local mercantile establishment to walk to the schoolhouse, three blocks away, and guide the children back to safety. Although many children died in the storm, others lived, thanks to the efforts of their teachers who sheltered the children safe in the schoolhouse, staying awake all night to keep the stove warm, burning books and furniture when the woodpile ran out. After the wind ripped away part of a sod schoolhouse roof in Valley County, Nebraska, the teenage teacher tied her sixteen students together and safely led them to the house where she boarded, nearly a mile away, prompting the writing of a song Nebraska children still sing in elementary school.

See also PHYSICAL ENVIRONMENT: Blizzards.

Eric F. Grelson
Barksdale Air Force Base

Dick, Everett N. *The Sod-House Frontier, 1854–1898.* Lincoln: University of Nebraska Press, 1979. Miner, Craig. *West of Wichita: Settling the High Plains of Kansas, 1865–1890.* Lawrence: University Press of Kansas, 1986. Sandoz, Mari. *Love Song to the Plains.* New York: Harper Brothers, 1961.

CATTLE GUARDS

A cattle guard is a device of folk technology (although many today are commercially manufactured) that allows automotive traffic to move freely while hindering the passage of livestock. Its essential components are a pit,

Cattle guard

usually constructed of concrete and a foot or more deep, placed across a roadway at the point where it intersects with a fence; a grid of metal bars, pipe or of railroad rails, fastened in parallel fashion across the pit and spaced about three to five inches apart; and a wing on either side that angles up from the edge of the grid to the fence. Hoofed livestock, instinctively wary about insecure footing, are generally deterred by this barrier. Some ranchers have created effective cattle guards by placing fresh cowhides, sheets of tin, or an arrangement of old tires in a gateway.

The cattle guard had its origin in the Great Plains, being independently developed in a number of locations from Texas to North Dakota in the decade beginning around 1905 in response to the introduction of a growing number of automobiles in fenced range country. The immediate progenitor of the automotive cattle guard is the railroad cattle guard, an American innovation dating back at least to 1836. The ultimate progenitor of the cattle guard is the flat stone stile of Cornwall, England, where grids of granite bars placed over pits in public footpaths have been in existence for more than 2,000 years.

Today, cattle guards are found in all fifty states and on every continent. The term "cattle guard" is generally used in the Southern Plains, while from Nebraska north the terms "auto gate" or "car gate" are common. In the Prairie Provinces, a cattle guard usually refers to the railroad variety, while those on highways are called "Texas gates."

James F. Hoy
Emporia State University

Hoy, James F. *The Cattle Guard: Its History and Lore.* Lawrence: University Press of Kansas, 1982.

CHINOOK STORIES

A dry, westerly wind, the adiabatically warmed chinook blows down the eastern face of the Rocky Mountains onto the adjacent foothills and plains. While capable of blowing any season of the year, the chinook's presence is most salient during the winter, when its relative warmth provides a stark contrast to frigid continental-polar air masses. Its ability to melt and sublimate away thick coverings of snow in a matter of days or even hours has led to the common but apocryphal story that chinook is an "Indian" word for "snow eater." In fact, the Great Plains chinook owes its name to the Pacific Northwest fur trade, where a vaguely similar westerly breeze flowed up the lower Columbia River from the vicinity of the Chinook Indian villages; British Canadian and American settlers transplanted the chinook name first to the interior Columbia Plain and then, by the 1880s, to the northwestern Great Plains.

The dramatic changes in winter weather the chinook can bring have made it the inspiration of regional folklore and imagery. Frances Fraser, for example, recounts a Blackfoot story of a boy who gained status among his band by freeing the wind from the custody of the bear in the mountains: "[E]ver since then, the snow can be deep, and the cold bitter, but, in a short while, the Chinook will come blowing over the mountains, and everyone is happy again." The first white settlers likewise celebrated the chinook, making its snow-removing capabilities the stuff of regional environmental legend. Among the frontier yarns that were spun was the story of the man who hitched his team of horses to a post one snowy evening only to awake the next morning to find his horses dangling from the church steeple. Another often-told story describes a horse-drawn sleigh racing a chinook home: as the horses struggled through chest-deep snow, the front runners of the sleigh sloshed through mud while the back runners kicked up dust. Another variant of this story has the man driving the sleigh in front suffering frostbite while his children in back catch sunstroke. More than just a source of amusement, Plains ranchers touted the chinook's snow-removing capabilities as an ally that made available nutritious winter grasses to tender-snouted cattle, thus reducing—or eliminating, as some mistakenly believed—the need for cut hay and winter shelter. The brutal winter of 1886–87 tragically demonstrated that such wishful thinking was naive. As the region's open-range herds were decimated by blizzard conditions, ranchers cast a yearning eye toward the western mountains, sentiments which the *Yellowstone Journal and Live Stock Reporter* captured in a short ad: "WANTED—A rip-roaring, snow-eating, polar-paralyzing chinook. . . . Must have it!" Later, the winter of 1885–87 would be eulogized by Montana cowboy artist Charles M. Russell in a simple sketch of a rib-exposed steer called "Waiting for a Chinook."

While its effects are not entirely benign, with property-damaging gusts that can desiccate and erode farmers' soils, the chinook continued to be celebrated throughout the twentieth century as a welcome winter relief. Such celebration of the mild chinook has been particularly pronounced in southern Alberta, which local boosters, only partially tongue-in-cheek, describe as Canada's "Banana Belt," and which the regional tourism industry officially markets as "Chinook Country." The chinook also is a well-recognized presence among the communities along Colorado's Front Range, even serving for a few years (1969–72) as the name for a Denver-based underground weekly newspaper; as explained in the inaugural issue, *Chinook* was chosen because it is a "warm wind that comes from the mountains. It sometimes brings great upheaval, but more often it brings gentle warmth and good vibrations."

See also PHYSICAL ENVIRONMENT: Chinooks.

Peter S. Morris
Santa Monica College

Burrows, Alvin T. "The Chinook Winds." *Journal of Geography* 2 (1903): 124–36. Fraser, Frances. *The Bear Who Stole the Chinook: Tales from the Blackfoot.* Vancouver: Douglas and McIntyre, 1990. Morris, Peter S. "Regional Ideas and the Montana-Alberta Borderlands." *Geographical Review* 89 (1999): 469–90.

COWBOY CRAFTS

"Cowboy crafts" refers to a group of traditional crafts associated with cowboys and ranchers. Historically, the tools of the cowboy—saddles, bridles, bits, quirts, chaps, boots, hats, branding irons, and other objects—were handmade by cowboys, saddlemakers, or specialized craftsmen working out of saddle shops. Many still are, although mass-produced goods now dominate the lower price ranges.

Most cowboy crafts have roots in the *vaquero* traditions that emerged in Mexico in the sixteenth century as adaptations of Spanish and Moorish horse culture. As American imperialism brought northern Mexico into the United States in the 1840s, much of the occupational lore of vaqueros was adopted by American ranchers. This included techniques for handling horses, cattle and sheep, the construction and layout of ranches, and occupa-

Saddlemaker John King of King's Saddlery, Sheridan, Wyoming

tional folk speech, as well as cowboy crafts. As the ranching industry spread north from Texas and the Southwest during the nineteenth century, all of these traditions spread with it. Most of them continue in altered and localized forms to the present day.

Although many of the simpler crafts (and repairs) are carried out by cowboys in their spare time, the center of cowboy crafts has always been the saddle shop. Large saddle shops existed in Mexico by the sixteenth century, employing many saddle- and harness makers, leather carvers, apprentices, and specialists in related crafts such as silver engraving. All saddles and other products produced in a shop bore its stamp, no matter who actually did the work. This atelier system still exists in large saddle shops throughout Mexico, the United States, and Canada. In addition, cowboys and others sell crafts to the shop or work on consignment.

The western stock saddle is the predominant saddle type in the Great Plains and throughout the West. Much larger and heavier than the English saddle, it is a specialized piece of occupational equipment, meant for extended periods of heavy riding and for cattle herding and roping. Its origins can be traced to the Mexican vaquero saddle of the 1700s. It has large skirts, a deep seat, and a horn for roping. It is a complicated and time-consuming object to put together, consisting of sixty or more parts and requiring dozens of specialized tools.

By the mid- to late nineteenth century, the western stock saddle had developed regional variations throughout the American West, most notably in Texas, California, and the Great Basin. Texas saddles were larger and heavier than other western saddles: skirts were

large, heavy, square, and lined with sheepskin, and riggings (the assemblage of hardware, straps, and cinches that holds the saddle on the back of the horse) were doubled, having both front and rear cinches. With the settlement of the Northern Plains, a distinct variant developed that resembled Texas saddles but with a lower and sturdier horn, a higher seat, and a projecting rim on the cantle known as a Cheyenne roll. In the twentieth century, regional variations in saddle form became less important, while many specialized forms of rodeo and show saddles developed.

The decoration of leather has always been integral to the saddlemaker's craft. This includes the carving and stamping of leather, as well as the use of engraved silver and other minor aspects such as lacing and quilting. Great Plains saddles have generally relied less on silver and more on leather carving than saddles from farther west. Leatherwork patterns vary from basketwork and other geometric designs to intricately carved flowers, wildlife, or scenes of rodeos and ranch life. Fancy carved saddles for use by wealthy ranchers or in parades go back to the seventeenth century, but in the twentieth century became more abundant, commissioned for Hollywood stars or as rodeo trophies. Since the 1950s, Sheridan, Wyoming, and other centers of the craft have specialized in highly decorated "art" saddles and produce a variety of intricately carved leather items, such as briefcases and photo albums. At the same time, many saddlemakers continue to produce less-expensive custom saddles for working cowboys.

After saddles, bits and spurs are the most prestigious cowboy craft. Like saddles, they are generally made by specialists. Also like saddles, their roots lie in eighteenth-century Mexico, and variations developed as they diffused in the nineteenth century into the American West. In general, bits and spurs in the Great Plains were simpler and less decorated than those farther west. Modern bit and spur makers, like saddlemakers, compete with factory goods but continue to thrive, producing highly polished and elaborately engraved silver-plated art objects, as well as undecorated bits and spurs for everyday use.

Although some other cowboy crafts are made by specialists—for example, hats and boots—many others are made by cowboys in their spare time or are produced as a sideline by full-time crafters. These include bridles, belts, billfolds, and other smaller leather items, often carved; soft leather items such as chaps and leather vests; twisted ropes; ropes, horse tack, and decorative items made from twisted rawhide; and items made from dyed horsehair that has been braided, twisted, or hitched into ropes, bridles, hatbands, and jewelry.

One of the most notable developments in late-twentieth-century cowboy crafts was the emergence of art and collectors' markets. Saddles, spurs, and other items from prestigious older saddle shops such as Myres of Texas, Collins of Nebraska, and Meanea of Wyoming command huge prices and are proudly displayed in museums and private collections; the same is true of well-known contemporary shops such as King's Saddlery of Wyoming. Along with "western" paintings, beaded moccasins and silver mounted rifles, they are part of a regional art market, a "taste culture" that characterizes many museums, galleries, and private art collections of the Great Plains and, more generally, the West.

See also IMAGES AND ICONS: Cowboy Culture.

Timothy H. Evans
Western Kentucky University

Dary, David. *Cowboy Culture: A Saga of Five Centuries.* New York: Alfred A. Knopf, Inc. 1981. Evans, Timothy H. *King of the Western Saddle: The Sheridan Saddle and the Art of Don King.* Jackson: University Press of Mississippi, 1998. Rice, Lee M., and Glenn R. Vernam. *They Saddled the West.* Centreville MD: Cornell Maritime Press, 1975.

COWBOY POETRY

See LITERARY TRADITIONS: Cowboy Poetry

DOBIE, J. FRANK (1888–1964)

James Frank Dobie, the beloved best-known popularizer of Texas and ranchland folklore, was born on September 26, 1888, on a small ranch in Live Oak County, Texas. He grew up working as a cowboy on his father's ranch and became a voracious reader. Educated both at home and in a one-room schoolhouse, he lived among Hispanic workers and so became bilingual. As Dobie matured he absorbed the lore, language, and legends of the land and people he loved, developing a strong, liberal philosophy.

Dobie earned a bachelor of arts degree at Southwestern University in Georgetown, Texas, and a master of arts degree at Columbia University in New York City. In 1914, as an English teacher at the University of Texas, Austin, he became involved with the Texas Folklore Society, before enlisting in the army in 1917. He returned to the University of Texas in 1921, and later (1923–25) served as head of the English Department at Oklahoma A&M in Stillwater.

When Dobie and his wife, Bertha, returned to Austin after his time in the service, he resumed teaching English and his well-known class "Life and Literature of the Southwest." He served as editor and secretary of the Texas Folklore Society from 1922 to 1942. Without a doctorate, he was still promoted to full professor in 1933, but his honest, outspoken traits kept him in conflict with his colleagues and administration. He left the university in 1947.

Academic folklorists criticized Dobie for rewriting and editing his sources, and he seldom gave credit to his informants. Nevertheless, Dobie's books (he wrote more than twenty in all, including *Coronado's Children*, which won a Literary Guild award in 1931), were the efforts of a natural-born storyteller, a man who shared with love and reverence the traditions of his heritage, including those of Hispanics and African Americans. A true ranchland Texan, he shared the values of the southwestern Plains. Dobie was awarded the Medal of Freedom, the nation's highest civil honor, on September 14, 1964. Four days later he died in Austin, Texas.

Guy Logsdon
Tulsa, Oklahoma

Abernethy, Francis Edward, ed. *Texas Folklore Society.* Denton: University of North Texas Press, 1992–2000. Bode, William. *A Portrait of Pancho: The Life of a Great Texan.* Austin: Pemberton, 1965. Tinkle, Lon. *An American Original: The Life of J. Frank Dobie.* Boston: Little, Brown and Co. 1978.

FARM INHERITANCE PRACTICES

The transfer of family resources from one Great Plains generation to the next is often difficult and stressful. The farm is perhaps the most difficult of all family resources to pass down because it represents both an economic enterprise and a way of life. The inheritance practices, therefore, go beyond law and cross over into folkways, where the decisions are made in the family, albeit within the wider context of formal legalities.

Typically, two generations are involved in the transfer. The "senior generation"—the family members transferring the farm—may still be principal owners and managers, or they may have already begun to transfer control to someone else. The "junior generation" are the children of the senior generation and the spouses of the children.

When planning the transfer of the family farm, family members often identify specific goals they want to accomplish. For some family members—often those whose farm has been in the family for many generations—ensuring that the family farm remains intact and in the family is an important goal. The maintenance of the family farm as a viable financial entity is often a second goal: the family wants the transfer accomplished in a way that ensures that the junior generation is not burdened by financial costs which prevent the successful operation of the family farm. A third goal is to use the revenues from the family farm to provide an income adequate to support the retirement of the senior generation.

To attain these goals, family members use various principles. First, families sometimes insist on the principle of equality of treatment of the junior generation. Here, families want to ensure that each member of the junior generation receives an equal share of the family farm resources. Goals incompatible with this principle may be sacrificed to ensure equality and fair treatment for each child. If necessary, the farm will be sold and the resulting financial assets evenly divided so that all offspring are treated equitably. Second, some farm families embrace the principle that the "right" to inherit a share of the family farm must be earned. This principle implies that only those who have shown a commitment to the family farm through hard work on the farm have any claim. Providing choice for the junior generation is a third principle that sometimes guides the transfer. Families adopting this principle want to ensure that members of the junior generation have the opportunity to choose their own futures, whether running the family farm or embarking on a nonagricultural career. Fourth, an exchange relationship might be established between the senior and junior generation. One child—typically the eldest son—receives the farming operation but must agree to take care of the parents as long as they live. Siblings of that child might receive a symbolic, but very small, portion of the farm. Finally, families vary in who is permitted to participate in the inheritance decision-making process. Some families insist that only members of the senior generation should be involved. Other families want all immediate family members—the senior generation and the junior generation—to be actively involved. Spouses of the children are explicitly excluded. Some families embrace an inclusive principle. They want all family members—the senior generation, the children of the senior generation, and the spouses of those children—to be involved in the process.

Combining goals can often be unattainable. For example, the use of the farm as a retirement package can preclude the transfer of a financially viable farm to the junior generation. To obtain the financial resources to fund the senior generation's retirement, the junior generation may be required to rent or even buy the farm, thus incurring costs that reduce its financial viability. However, some combinations are compatible. The preservation of the family farm and the maintenance of the family farm as a financially viable economic enterprise are not mutually exclusive. In fact, they are mutually reinforcing.

Prioritizing some goals prevents the adoption of certain principles. For example, passing on a financially viable farm while maintaining the principle of equitable treatment among the members of the junior generation is not always possible. Securing a financially viable operation sometimes requires some members of the junior generation to receive less than other members of the family. However, the selection of certain transfer principles can facilitate the accomplishment of specific goals. The principle specifying that one child will inherit the farm and be required to support the parents is consistent with all three goals: the farm is preserved when the entire farming operation is transferred intact; the farming operation is not financially burdened by the necessity of having to rent, or even buy, the operation from the senior generation; and the farming operation can be considered a retirement package since some farm income must be used to support the parents in their retirement.

Ron G. Stover
Mary Kay Helling
South Dakota State University

Stover, Ron G., and Mary Kay Helling. "Goals and Principles of the Intergenerational Transfer of the Family Farm." *Free Inquiry in Creative Sociology* 25 (1998): 201–12. Stover, Ron G., and Mary Kay Helling. "Transferring the Family Farm." *Extension Extra* 14040 (1996): 1–3.

FARMING LORE

The folklore of farming in the Great Plains is a blend of lore from as far away as Germany and from as close as the Omaha nation along the Missouri River of Nebraska. Farming folklore here is defined as the tales, beliefs, sayings, proverbs, jokes, and songs that are expressed in words and have been learned informally. The lore of the Great Plains is a legacy of migrants from Europe moving across North America and of Native American residents who were already farming, hunting, and passing on their beliefs through oral history.

Farming lore addresses the trip to the place where new immigrants could find land of their own. It is about the myths that developed around women's madness in the Plains, and it is about the growing of food and the dreams that the pioneers had of the future. The lore of farming is mingled with that of ranching in the Great Plains. Following the Civil War, large cattle ranches were established, and then farmers began arriving. These tales and songs often placed the role of cowboys in myth as they worked the Plains from Texas to Alberta. Often the cowboy tales are placed in juxtaposition with those of the farmers who worked the land, providing a more glamorous antithesis to the life of the pioneers.

Settlers' songs depicted a living that was hard and often almost unbearable, as the words to "The Little Old Shanty" reveal:

I am looking rather seedy now while
    holding down my claim,
And the victuals are not always of the
    best. . . .
The hinges are of leather and the windows
    have no glass,
While the board roof lets the howling
    blizzards in.

Against this lament of hardship, the optimism of the settlers is also recorded and passed down, as the song continues:

Yet I rather like the novelty of living in this
    way,
Though my bill of fare is always rather
    tame;
But I'm happy as a clam on the land of
    Uncle Sam.

Other songs such as "Starving to Death on a Government Claim," "But the Mortgage Worked the Hardest," and "Hard Times" depict times of severe hardship.

The hardships of the 1870s and 1880s stimulated the development of the Farmers Alliance. The Alliance organized to regulate railroads, to loosen the hold of merchants on the price of supplies and the marketing system, and to encourage cooperative stores. Songs such as "Marching for Freedom," "Dear Prairie Home," "The Hayseed," "The Pauper's Cowhides," and "The Patches on My Pants" illustrate the unrest felt among the Plains farmers as they were left out of the economic gains of the cities.

Often the lore of farming and ranching was depicted in tales. These were set around the everyday activities of life on a farm. Humor was a common feature of the tales, as in "A Threshing Hoax," in which the protagonist sabotages a competing threshing crew by placing soap in the boiler so the threshing machine would not work. This slowed down the competing crew for a day without causing real damage to the equipment. Tales of grasshoppers and other disasters were also passed on, as in tales of straw being driven through trees by a tornado. These tales used humor to ease the burden of living in the Plains.

Children's games were also illustrative of farming in the Plains. Titles such as "The Farmer in the Dell," brought from England, and love games such as "Round and Round the Valley" showed how mate selection was envisioned and highlighted the joy of being a farmer who produces crops of oats, beans, and barley.

Farming folklore illustrates not only active farming, mate selection, and dreams and desires, but also the prophetic, featuring omens, portents, and signs that farmers and ranchers in the Great Plains used to guide their activities. Prophetic sayings feature weather, marriage and courtship, death and bad luck signs, and cures. Many focused on the unpredictable Plains climate, especially the uncertain rainfall. Sayings such as "If it rains on Easter Sunday, it will rain on seven Sundays after" and "If the rooster crows when he goes to bed, he will get up with a wet head" illustrate the necessary concern with rain. Mate selection was also imbedded in sayings, and the fear of being an unmarried female is the focus on such sayings as "If a girl sits on a chair while someone sweeps under it, she will be an old maid." These prophecies can still be heard, as Great Plains farmers pass on their beliefs about weather and other issues that are beyond their control.

Myths are also part of farming folklore. One particular myth is that of women going insane because of the wind, the cold, the animals, and the loneliness of the vast expanses. Writers of Plains history have often indicated that while life in the Plains was difficult for the men, it was almost unbearable for the women. Although the myth of insane women settlers has been shown to be magnified, the impact of the wind and the austere environment was, and is, wearing and tiring. In notes left in courthouses, or in hospitals throughout the Plains, women cried out for social intercourse that was often many miles away.

The original Plains farm folklore was not European American. The Omahas have tales of agriculture, as illustrated in "Corn Comes to the Omaha." In this tale the Omaha hunters' need for food is lamented, and a young man who goes hunting finds a small bush; the bush flowers and finally grows to mature maize. At the end of the first year the maize is shared with the tribe. Each family receives four kernels of the maize. The following year messages were sent to other tribes. It is through this sharing that corn is believed to have come to the Indigenous peoples of the Plains.

Farm folklore of the Great Plains focuses on the difficulties of first getting to the new homeland, then on settling the land, raising children, and fighting for a political voice in the urbanizing society. The lore depicted in the late 1800s and early 1900s is humorous, humbling, and angry. Yet, while the lore may question the wisdom of remaining in this vast grassland, it also points to the excitement of the challenge and to possibilities for a better future.

Although the early settlers have passed away, and their children and grandchildren have often moved from the Plains, the lore that expressed and supported the beliefs, values, and ways of life of farmers and ranchers is still heard in coffee shops, around sale barns, and at other public gatherings, as Plains folk celebrate the lives they have chosen.

See also IMAGES AND ICONS: Mad Pioneer Women.

John C. Allen
University of Nebraska–Lincoln

Cannell, Margaret. *Signs, Omens and Portents in Nebraska Folklore.* Lincoln: University of Nebraska Studies in Language, Literature, and Criticism, 1933. Welsch, Roger L. *A Treasury of Nebraska Pioneer Folklore.* Lincoln: University of Nebraska Press, 1966, 1984.

FOLK ART

Folk art of the Great Plains is as broad and seemingly limitless as the landscape itself. However, the lines of distinction between what is, and what is not, folk art often blurs, just like the line between the sky and the land in a Great Plains horizon. Yet folklorists generally agree that folk art is a complicated whole comprised of a number of integrated parts, with some more prominent than others.

First, a shared sense of identity among the individuals who comprise a distinctive group is key. The ties that bind the individual to the

Ukrainian Easter eggs made by Angie Chruszch of Belfield, North Dakota

group and are the foundation for tradition include a shared language, culture, ethnicity, history, occupation, community, region, and religion or spirituality. Folk art is rooted in a tradition. The art often serves as a way to reaffirm the individual's group identity, as well as to communicate to others who they are, what they believe, and where they came from.

Second, the process and form of folk art is influenced heavily by a community sense of artistic value that changes and adapts from place to place and through time. That is not to say there is no room for the artist's individual creative expression. There is freedom, but within the boundaries of the community's artistic standards, based on its shared sense of tradition. This applies not only to the form of the art but also to the process by which that art is created. For example, within a community of Ukrainian Easter egg artists, the proper process for the creation of a decorated egg begins with a prayer to the Virgin Mary to guide the hands of the artist.

Third, folk art generally passes from one generation to another informally by way of example, observation, and word of mouth. It is usually learned outside of formal educational settings and institutions. For example, a German Russian blacksmith who makes decorative wrought-iron grave crosses may enlist one of his young sons to help him in the shop. The son soon learns the proper process and form for making cemetery crosses simply by observing and working alongside his father.

Finally, folk art is often part of a larger cultural context. It plays an active role in the lives of the community. Ukrainian Easter eggs are not made just for art's sake. They are taken to the church on Easter Sunday to be blessed by the priest. Some Ukrainian traditionalists will then take one of those eggs and bury it in the corner of one of their fields, thus ensuring a bountiful harvest. Similarly, a Native American ceremonial bag decorated with porcupine quills is not just a piece of art to be admired; it also may be used to hold a sacred pipe that is the focal point of various ceremonies.

Much of the folk art of the Great Plains stems from tribal or ethnic identity. Plains Native American and First Nation groups excel in a wide range of folk arts, from star quilts used in giveaways, naming ceremonies, and even funerals, to basketry, beadwork, and porcupine quillwork used to adorn everything from moccasins to horse masks and cigarette lighters.

The Spanish and Mexican influence, which took root in the Great Plains in the sixteenth and seventeenth centuries, is still found through folk arts, such as intricate needlework and the carving and painting of revered Santos, or images of Catholic saints, by Hispanic folk artists. The French influence, which spread through the fur trade into the Prairie Provinces in the eighteenth century, can still be seen in the jigs, reels, and fiddle music of the Métis people, who are descendants of French, Irish, and Scottish fur traders and Native Americans. The farmers and cowboys who followed in the nineteenth century established enduring occupational folk arts, such as wheat weaving, cowboy poetry, and decorative spur- and saddlemaking.

Subsequent immigration of many eastern and northern European peoples in the late nineteenth century brought to the Plains such folk arts as colorful Polish paper cutting, Norwegian needlework, Czech Easter eggs decorated with designs cut from wheat straw, Greek woodcarving, lively polka music, and much more. Added to this is the relatively recent influx of new immigrants: Cambodians who brought their tradition of story-cloths, Vietnamese who brought the Dragon Dance, Armenians from Azerbaijan who brought copper bas-relief work, and Sudanese and Congolese who brought *adungu* music.

Just as ethnic, tribal, or occupational identity is often at the core of folk art, so too is a sense of religion or spirituality. It is also important to remember that both identity and spirituality are shaped in subtle ways by the natural environment. Thus, the environment has an influence in the shaping of folk arts, especially through time. The natural environment of the Great Plains is one of vastness and distant horizons, with a sun that always looms large. The environment is strong and stark, yet delicate and colorful. People at first glance may see the sameness of an immense sky, but the brilliance of a Plains sunset ends the day. People notice oceans of grass or wheat, but all the while there are tiny, colorful crocus flowers waiting for the watchful eye. The Great Plains is given to periods of boom and bust, to cycles of life and death, flood and drought, to the seasons that are keenly felt, and to renewal. People incorporate what they see and experience around them. The natural environment of the Great Plains gives folk art in this region a distinctive feel. This can be illustrated through examples of motifs from nature found in the folk art of two ethnic and occupational (farming) groups.

The Ukrainian Easter egg tradition is a pre-Christian art form that was tied to spring fertility rituals, in recognition of the cycles of birth, death, and rebirth in nature. Animals, flowers, birds, and insects are some of the nature-theme motifs used in this delicate and colorful tradition, whereby images are applied to an egg through a batik method of dyeing. With the advent of Christianity, that spiritual notion of life after death was readily applied to the crucifixion of Christ. As Ukrainians moved to the Great Plains, they brought with them the Easter egg tradition. Some of the nature-theme motifs used in the Old Country continued in the new. Others were discarded and replaced by motifs more indicative of the artists' new home. Two motifs that have continued, and seem to have grown in popularity in the Plains, reflecting their centrality in the landscape, are those of wheat, a symbol of fertility, and the sun, a symbol of God and rebirth.

The strong, stark German Russian wrought-iron cemetery crosses also often contain motifs from nature. These beautiful crosses are eerily representative of the landscape. Some crosses are made with a half-circle arcing from one end of the horizontal bar to the other like a setting or rising sun on a flat and expansive horizon. Waving upward from the sun are iron strands of wheat. These crosses immortalize silently, yet poetically, the memory of the deceased with symbols representing shared religious beliefs of life after death: a prominent cycle observed in the natural environment that surrounds these Plains folk.

Troyd Geist
North Dakota Council on the Arts

Dorson, Richard M., ed. *Handbook of American Folklore.* Bloomington: Indiana University Press, 1983. Geist, Troyd A. *From the Wellspring: Faith, Soil, Tradition.* Bismarck: North Dakota Council on the Arts, 1997. Sherman, William C., and Playford V. Thorson, eds. *North Dakota's Ethnic History.* Fargo: The North Dakota Institute for Regional Studies and North Dakota Humanities Council, 1986.

FOLK BELIEF

People often use "folk belief" to refer to superstitions, old wives' tales, and unorthodox religious and medical practices. This view of folk belief reinforces a perception of already marginalized people as more exotic and backward than previously imagined. Folk beliefs are better seen as providing insights into how people live their lives and what they think of as important. Understood in this way, folk beliefs and practices provide valuable clues into how people construct their worlds and bring meaning to their experiences.

The folk beliefs of the Great Plains reflect the many groups contained within its vast boundaries. Indigenous peoples, European pioneer settlers, and more recent arrivals such as the Hmong (Laotians) all contribute to the rich cultural heritage of folklife in the Plains. Along with traditional beliefs and practices, each group creates new forms of folk belief through exposure to unfamiliar terrain, conditions, and other groups. Folk beliefs thus reflect a dynamic process of tradition making, with plenty of room for individual variations and stylistic differences along with cross-cultural sharing within the region.

Folk belief takes on a regional flavor through the response of people to their immediate natural world. For instance, weather signs and omens form a vital part of folk belief within the Plains. Examples include "Rain follows the plow," "Heavy fur on animals means a severe winter," and "A tornado never hits the junction of two rivers." Sometimes weather signs are put in the form of rhymes: "Sunset red and morning gray sends the traveler on his way / Sunset gray and morning red keeps the traveler to his bed."

The world encountered by early settlers in the Great Plains was filled with wondrous and formidable creatures, many of which figure prominently in folk belief. One of the more unpleasant aspects of Plains life was the abundance of snakes. Snakes slithered by the hundreds in massive dens, crawled easily through the sod walls of Plains homes, and startled unwary humans and horses alike. A few examples of snake lore include stories about fabled "hoop snakes" and "joint snakes" and beliefs such as "Black snakes will suck cows."

Because of its deadly bite, rattlesnakes hold a special place in Plains snake lore. Kill a garter snake, and you'll get rain. But kill a rattler and get a BIG rain. Watch out for its mate, however, because "everyone knows a rattler's mate will come lookin' for it." A rattler's fangs naturally have special powers: "Be careful about killing a rattler with a lariat. Its fangs might get caught in the rope and bite you when you coil it." If this happens, be sure to apply plenty of "fresh, warm cow dung" to cure it. Ironically, rattlers also serve a medicinal function among Plains folk. To cure a headache, just place a rattlesnake's rattle in your hatband.

Of course, if that doesn't cure your headache, you might try a red bandana, wearing earrings, or finding a person born in October to rub your temples. Folk remedies and charms for good health are abundant throughout the Plains. "Unlucky enough to get a sty? Rub a wedding ring on your eye." Or say this helpful charm: "Sty, sty, come off my eye, and go to the next passerby." Of course, if that passerby gives you a black eye, a silver knife is sure to draw the soreness out! Transference also works well with warts. Should you get warts from playing with a toad, simply sell them to another person or rub them with a penny and give the penny away.

Many folk beliefs and practices deal with luck. Find a "four-leaf clover" or a "red ear of corn" for good. Spill salt and throw some over your left shoulder to avoid bad. Bad luck at cards? "Get up and walk around your chair three times or sit on a handkerchief." Animals bring luck—crickets and rabbit's feet for good and crows bad. Some animals bring both kinds of luck: "If a black cat crosses your path, it's bad," but "If a black cat comes to stay at your house, it's good." Just don't kill it, whatever you do—that's bad. Death, the ultimate bad luck, comes by many signs: birds flying into the house, dogs howling at night, rain in an open grave, and pictures falling from the wall.

Folk beliefs and practices reveal the challenges faced daily by Plains folk. They underscore such things as the importance of good weather for survival, provide ways of dealing with the unexpected, and help cope with the often-precarious conditions of life in the Great Plains.

Nikki Bado-Fralick
Iowa State University

Hoy, Jim. "Rattlesnakes." In *Plains Folk: A Commonplace of the Great Plains*, edited by Jim Hoy and Tom Isern. Norman: University of Oklahoma Press, 1987: 3–4. Sackett, S. J., and William E. Koch, eds. *Kansas Folklore.* Lincoln: University of Nebraska Press, 1961. Welsch, Roger L. *A Treasury of Nebraska Pioneer Folklore.* Lincoln: University of Nebraska Press, 1966, 1984.

FOLK DANCE

Folk dance in the Great Plains has its roots in many traditions and reflects the history and culture of its peoples. Native American dances, with their origins in ritual, ceremonies, and initiation, were passed on from one generation to another. European folk dances evolved in the same way, although they came to serve a social rather than ritual function. In some Plains communities, a specific ethnic identity has continued unbroken to the present. In Lindsborg, Kansas, for example, descendants of Swedish settlers still maintain their tradition of Swedish music, dance, and festivals. Modern technology and communication bring an ever-widening mix of dance from other lands, which reflects the universality of folk dance and the diversity of the American and Canadian nations. However, some uniquely North American forms of folk dance developed in the Great Plains.

The settlers who entered the Great Plains in the nineteenth century brought the dance forms that they knew: the quadrille and the popular couple dances of the time. Farther east, the quadrille, a dance performed by four couples in a square formation, had become increasingly complex. A specific quadrille, the Standard Lancers, for instance, consisted of five different sections; thus, people felt the need of formal instruction under a dancing master to learn and memorize the sequence of figures. A second source of what evolved into square dancing in the Plains was the big circle dances of the Appalachian region. In these dances, alternate couples moved out to the couple on their right, performed a few figures with them, and then moved on to the next couple. A third feature of the square dance was the caller. Since dancing masters and dancing schools were not available to the pioneers, dancers relied on one person to call out the figures. These figures were performed in a four-couple square rather than a big circle, but they still had the visiting-couple format, in which one couple went out and danced various figures with each of the other couples in succession. Interspersed with the square dances were couple dances consisting of simple patterns danced to the rhythms that had become popular in nineteenth-century Europe: the waltz, polka, schottische, and a version of the mazurka called the Varsouvienne.

In the Southern Great Plains these same square dances and couple dances were featured, but there was also a strand of folk dance coming up from Mexico. Both Spanish colonial dances and dances of Mexican influence were popular, many of them done to waltz or polka music. The "fandango," or Spanish ball, was a popular assembly where dancing and socializing took place. However, the opposition of the churches to dancing was particularly strong in Texas, Oklahoma, and Kansas, resulting in the flourishing of "play parties" instead of dances. Another factor in this region was the great distances that separated people, as well as the scarcity of both musicians and women. On the great cattle ranches of West Texas, people would come from fifty miles around if a fiddler were found and a dance scheduled. The furniture would be taken out of the largest room in the house, and the dancing would continue until dawn. Given the gender ratio, men would either wait their turn to dance or put on an apron or tie a scarf around their arm and dance the woman's part. With regional variations, these same square dances and couple dances took hold throughout the Great Plains, including the Canadian Prairie Provinces. In addition to private homes, granges and military posts provided settings for dances and social gatherings.

In the twentieth century these dance forms continued in pockets throughout the Great Plains, but a new approach to folk dancing developed. Researchers, teachers, and recreation leaders revived the dances of the previous century and made them popular once again, but this time as a recreational activity. Researchers also collected ethnic dances in Europe and brought them again to the United States. Over time, square dancing evolved into a highly organized activity with a long sequence of lessons required before dancers could join clubs.

A folk dance that is currently popular in the Plains states is the contra dance, a "longways" dance in which couples face each other in long lines. Contra dancing, which originated in England and was popular in colonial America, employs figures used in square dancing but keeps them to a limited number. It endured in New England and has now become popular across the country. A major feature of contra dancing is the use of live, rather than recorded, music. In the Canadian provinces, club square dancing and international folk are the predominant folk dance activities. All the current folk dance forms—contra, square, and international folk—are sustained by local associations as well as regional and national organizations, some of which produce annual festivals to further promote their activity.

Enid Cocke
Manhattan, Kansas
Susan Sanders
Lawrence, Kansas

Casey, Betty. *Dance across Texas.* Austin: University of Texas Press, 1985. Harris, Jane A., Anne M. Pittman, Marlys S. Waller, and Cathy L. Dark. *Dance a While.* Boston: Allyn and Bacon, 2000. Shaw, Lloyd. *Cowboy Dances.* Caldwell ID: Caxton Printers, 1939.

FOLK MUSIC

Folk music can be defined as music that is perpetuated orally rather than by the use of traditional notation, and whose subject matter reflects the social community within which it exists. The concept of marginalization also enters into the definition of this art form, indicating that some form of isolation from the mainstream—by class, sex, age, race, language, space, time, or religion—has historically influenced the creation of much so-called folk music. Within a climate of relative seclusion, people necessarily create a common musical currency. By this definition, the Great Plains has afforded much opportunity for distinct regional types of music, owing to its vast size and geographical diversity, and indeed the folk music tradition of this region is as varied as the people who populate its prairie landscape. A discussion of the art form is probably best attempted within the context of some of the various influential ethnic groups that originally settled the region: the British settlers throughout the Plains, the Scottish and French influence on the Métis culture in Central Canada, the Hispanic explorers in Texas to the south, and the Ukrainian and Russian tradition in the Prairie Provinces and Northern Plains states.

The British, the most prevalent ethnic group in the Great Plains as a whole, brought with them to North America a long legacy of narrative song. In 1882 the historian and musicologist Francis James Child published a collection called *English and Scottish Popular Ballads* that was revered throughout pioneer America as the primary source of traditional music. Eventually known simply as "Child's ballads," these songs were typically narrative in nature and concerned largely with love affairs and their oft-tragic ends. Other forms of vocal music, including part-songs known as broadside ballads, supplemented this collection. Circulated on large sheets of paper called broadsides, these songs chronicled historical events and described folk heroes such as Jesse James. Dance traditions from the British Isles were also revived, translating into "play-party" songs and square dances, normally accompanied by the guitar, banjo, mandolin, violin, and mouth organ—the main instruments of the American folk experience.

Scottish and Irish fur traders contributed to the Aboriginal musical community in early Canada, deepening its preexisting tradition of balladic storytelling and combining with the vocal and instrumental music of the French voyageurs to create a unique hybrid of music and song that chronicled the history of the Red River Valley of the North region. These traders introduced European fiddles and fiddle music to the Plains in the early 1800s and, when combined with the more organic song tradition of the Native peoples, produced a unique hybrid musical style incorporating elements of both cultures. The fiddle music of the Métis (who emerged from intermarriage between French, Irish, and Scottish traders and Native women) utilized Celtic or French melodies reinterpreted through a distinctive Native musical perspective—characterized by irregular phrase lengths and/or overlapping phrases, reiterated or embellished cadences, variable formal structures, and rhythmic freedom—resulting in the development of a new musical form, specific to the region.

The Hispanic folk music tradition in the Great Plains originated more than 400 years ago when Spanish conquistadors, moving northward from Mexico, explored the southwestern part of the region. The prevalent song forms in the Mexican region, the *corrido* and the *decima*, became popular in southern Texas during the nineteenth century. The corrido typically related a story or event of local or national interest—a natural disaster, the exploits of a hero or villain—and usually adhered to a conventional form, consisting of six sections. The formal opening of the corrido, in which the balladeer called upon the audience to hear his tale, was followed by a section that introduced the song's protagonist and established its setting. The arguments of the hero were then stated, followed by the main plot of the tale. The corrido concluded with the farewells of both the song's protagonist and the balladeer himself. A history of liturgical drama also exists in the Southwest and Southern Plains, dating back to the mystery and miracle plays of medieval Spain. Religious folk plays called *autos*, based upon both Old and New Testament texts and consisting of spoken dialogues alternated with sung portions, are still performed regularly in many communities.

Also prevalent in the Prairie Provinces and Northern Plains states is the heritage of the Russian Doukhobor and of the Ukrainian settlers. Doukhobor music (the word meaning "spirit wrestler" to denote the sects' struggles against the Russian Orthodox Church) is largely choral in nature, passed down without the aid of notation, and encompassing a variety of musical styles from monody to counterpoint. The Ukrainian community also values choral singing in two and three parts, as well as instrumental music played on the *cembale*, *bandura*, and *kobza*.

The influx of diverse cultures to the Great Plains of North America has been, and continues to be, the greatest influence upon its folk music. The ethnic groups discussed here may be easily supplemented by countless other nationalities, producing a truly varied and colorful musical mosaic.

See also EUROPEAN AMERICANS: Ukrainians / MUSIC: Hispanic Music / NATIVE AMERICANS: Métis / RELIGION: Doukhobors.

Donna Lowe
Brandon Folk Music and Arts Festival

Nettl, Bruno. *Folk Music in the United States*. Detroit: Wayne State University Press, 1976. Peacock, Kenneth. *A Survey of Ethnic Folkmusic across Western Canada*. Anthropology Papers, no. 5. Ottawa: National Museums of Canada, 1963. Tawa, Nicholas. *A Sound of Strangers: Musical Culture, Acculturation, and the Post–Civil War Ethnic American*. Metuchen NJ: Scarecrow Press, 1982.

FOLK SONGS

Folk songs are words and music transmitted orally from one generation to another within particular groups; usually there are musical and textual variants of the songs. However, in the twentieth century, recorded sound and the printed word made it possible for folk songs to be learned outside the traditional group experiences, and they also reduced the number of variants that accompanied the oral transmission process. Folk songs can be ballads—songs that tell a story; folk songs can be lyrical—songs that communicate an emotion without necessarily telling a story; and folk songs can be functional—lullabies, songs for dancing, play-party songs, work songs, and songs that enhance other human activities. For many decades it was a common belief that folk songs were perpetuated and sung only by the illiterate and that only art and popular songs had cultural merit. That uninformed criticism has been slow in disappearing.

The groups in which traditional songs evolve are families, communities, churches, occupations, ethnic, regional, and many others. Great Plains folk songs, therefore, are diverse, including a wide variety of Native American songs that were inspired by musical sounds in nature. Other traditional songs, mostly of western European origin, came with the expansion of the western frontier. They include those from Spanish traditions that initially dominated the Southern Plains, but which by the twenty-first century had moved into the central and northern portions of the region. Mexican *corridos* (ballads) and other Hispanic songs are now heard throughout the Great Plains along with Anglo-American and African American spirituals, Czech polkas, Germanic or Scandinavian songs and schottisches, a wide variety of fiddling tunes and styles, blues, Southeast Asian music, *klezmer* (Jewish) music, and the music of numerous other ethnic and immigrant groups. However, the most widely known or recognized folk songs are those that have their origins in English, Scottish, and Irish song.

Folk songs also can be associated with singing styles, influenced by the openness of the Great Plains—no tight throat sounds emerged here—in contrast to the vocals from the mountain regions of the South. Even ethnic groups modified singing styles to the expanses of the Plains by adopting open vocals.

By the 1960s folk songs had acquired a broader definition and included songs that had not gone through the long oral transmission process but were written and/or sung by individuals who referred to themselves as folksingers. A musician with a guitar or at least a banjo singing a ballad was a "folksinger"; often social protest songs were defined as folk songs, even though their life expectancy was sometimes no longer than the duration of the topic being protested. Long before this popular interpretation evolved, however, two specific folk-song groups had emerged from specific Great Plains experiences: cowboy and western songs and songs about the dust storms.

The cattle industry is one of the oldest European American commercial ventures in the Plains, dating back to early Spanish explorations when cattle and horses were brought to the North American continent. The romanticized American cowboy who emerged after the Civil War capitalized on the traditions of the Hispanic industry, using their tools, techniques, and vocabulary. However, cowboy songs came from southern traditions and were based on the old English, Scottish, and Irish songs sung throughout the South. In recent decades, historians and pop culturalists have shown African American influences on traditional cowboy songs, but the western European song style had greater influence on African American song during the late nineteenth century than did African American song style on cowboy songs.

The cowboy idiom did not mature until the early 1870s, at which time songs with a cowboy theme appeared. Cowboys had been singing the popular parlor and folk songs of the day, as well as hymns; in short, a cowboy song was anything a cowboy wanted to sing. The most popular was "The Old Chisholm Trail," an English lyrical song that dates to as early as 1640 and was modified by the cowboy idiom. Most of the songs that came from the post–Civil War trail-drive days were either tragedy or humor, the two faces of drama; there were very few lyrical songs, and most of those were written by unknown poets. However, Montana poet D. J. O'Malley wrote a few poems in the 1880s and 1890s, such as "When the Work's All Done This Fall," that were set to music by unknown musicians. In the early 1900s South Dakota poet Charles Badger Clark Jr. wrote "Border Affair," which was later adapted to a folk song, and New Mexico cowboy N. Howard "Jack" Thorp wrote "Little Joe, the Wrangler" in 1898, which also was adapted to a folk song. Some cowboy folk songs were bawdy, and most working cowboys did not (and do not) have outstanding singing voices. Some of their singing would start a stampede, not settle down the cattle.

The cowboy became the folk hero of the nation, and a romanticized singing cowboy enhanced the image. In the mid-1930s Hollywood developed the singing-cowboy movie genre for Gene Autry, who started his career as the "Oklahoma Yodeling Cowboy." Soon other singing cowboys were featured in the movie houses. Some of the songs they sang, along with those on records, entered the oral transmission process and are considered by some singers to be folk songs; indeed, a few of the songs, such as "Cool Water," "Tumbling Tumbleweeds," or "Riding Down the Canyon," have become traditional songs of the cowboy and the Plains. The cowboy singing and songwriting traditions have been continued into the twenty-first century by numerous performers such as the popular horseman-singer-songwriter Ian Tyson of Alberta.

Cowboys love to dance; each cow town had dance halls, and they were not always associated with saloons. In the 1920s Bob Wills, a fiddle-playing son of a cotton farmer in West Texas, started playing ranch-house dances. His desire to play dances eventually developed a dance genre known as western swing.

While the music has elements of jazz and blues, it actually evolved from the specific merger of cowboy and farmer folk song and instrumentation.

In the early 1930s, when drought struck the Great Plains and continued through the decade, the Southern High Plains was designated the "Dust Bowl." Woody Guthrie was born and reared in Okemah, Oklahoma, but moved to Pampa, Texas, in 1929. There he experienced the Dust Bowl storms that devastated farms, ranches, and towns from Canada to Mexico; his songs "So Long, It's Been Good to Know You," "Talking Dust Bowl," "Do, Re, Mi," "Dust Can't Kill Me," and many more chronicle the era, as does his autobiographical novel, *Bound for Glory* (1943). Guthrie and his Great Plains songs were instrumental in creating the folk-song revival that swept the nation in the 1950s and 1960s. In such ways, the folk songs of the Great Plains are cultural contributions to the world of music, and they will be sung and played as long as there is music in the soul of mankind.

See also FILM: Autry, Gene / MUSIC: Cowboy Music; Guthrie, Woody; Wills, Bob.

Guy Logsdon
Tulsa, Oklahoma

Guthrie, Woody. *Bound for Glory*. New York: E. P. Dutton and Co., 1943. Logsdon, Guy. *"The Whorehouse Bells Were Ringing" and Other Songs Cowboys Sing*. Urbana: University of Illinois Press, 1989. Lomax, Alan. *The Folk Songs of North America*. Garden City NY: Doubleday and Co., 1960.

FOLK SPEECH

Folk speech refers to the dialect, or style of speaking, unique to people living within a geographic area. The folk speech of an area may be differentiated from other regions by variation in grammatical, phonetic (pronunciation), and lexical (word usage) features. Along with other forms of traditional culture, such as music, dance, and folklore, folk speech plays a role in the conservation and perpetuation of Great Plains culture.

In his book *The Great Plains* (1931), Walter Prescott Webb noted that sign language was an essential early form of communication in the Great Plains. Using hand and arm gestures, sign language made intertribal communication possible among Plains Indians. Subsequently, the westward movement of European Americans during the nineteenth century established the basic geographical patterns of speech within the Great Plains that persist to this day. Because of the area's relatively recent settlement (by non-Indians), migration patterns played a more immediate role in influencing contemporary patterns of speech within the Great Plains than in many other parts of North America.

Characterizing the folk speech of the Great Plains presents a significant challenge because the region is a meeting place of several migration streams. Another difficulty is determining what set of words, pronunciations, and grammatical forms are specific to the region. Beginning in the 1940s several regional atlas projects were implemented by dialect geographers and linguists in an attempt to form a baseline of language patterns in the United States. In part because of these efforts, most linguists now recognize North Central, Midland, Southern, and Western dialect areas converging in the Great Plains.

The North Central area extends from the western boundary of North Dakota southward to Sioux Falls, South Dakota. Examples of terms common to the Northern Plains include "soddy" for a house constructed of tough prairie sod and "sodbuster" for the one who breaks the sod. The need for trees in some Northern Plains areas during their settlement years brought legislation to encourage tree planting on "tree claims," a term that persists in the eastern Dakotas to describe woodlots. Another example can be seen in the use of "borrow pit" or "bar pit" as a road-building term that describes a place where earthen material has been removed.

The Midland area, extending westward from Philadelphia and represented in the Great Plains in a zone from Lincoln, Nebraska, southwest toward Amarillo, Texas, is widely considered to be the most important dialect region. This area forms a transition zone between the north dialect stream and the region dominated by southern speech forms. Because it is a transition zone in terms of language features, the Midland region is difficult to distinguish and may be the most unmarked in terms of a unique dialect.

Extending into southern Oklahoma and most of Texas south of Amarillo, the Southern dialect region is the speech region most easily identified by the American public. The vocabulary of this area includes the word "blinky" as an adjective to describe milk that has begun to sour. Another colorful term, "gully washer," refers to an exceptional amount of rainfall, and in Texas a compliment might be paid to someone who was said to be as "handy as hip pockets on a hog." The Spanish language has also had a profound impact on folk speech in this part of the Plains, as represented in terms such as "arroyo," meaning a dry gulch or deep gully cut by an intermittent stream.

The Northern, Midland, and Southern dialect areas merge with Western dialect forms in the western reaches of the Plains. Western dialect terms that mingle within the Great Plains include "corral," "bull snake," and "jerky." Slang terms are also an important part of folk speech, as represented by "Wyoming wind gauge," used for a logging chain on a fence post. Native American and First Nation languages have also influenced Plains folk speech: in the Prairie Provinces, for example, the verb "ponask" has been borrowed from the Cree language to describe the practice of splitting a piece of meat, putting it on a stick, and roasting it over an open fire.

Distinctive folk speech of the Great Plains can also be found within enclaves or ethnic islands. These include places settled by European immigrants who have retained distinctive, yet not necessarily foreign-sounding, elements in their speech. Language retention is important, for example, to many ethnic Ukrainians whose ancestors migrated to Manitoba beginning in the 1890s. In some cases the Ukrainian language has blended with English, as represented in words such as *drúgshtor* (drugstore).

In many cases, unique forms of folk speech in a particular area may have grown out of isolation from mainstream society. During the early years of settlement, particular forms of grammar, word usage, and pronunciations were also born out of necessity or emerged from the imagination of settlers. For example, a tree common to the Plains, the "bois d'arc" (*Maclura pomifera*), was named by the French for the Indian use of *bois* for the wood used to construct the bow (arc). Americanization replaced bois d'arc with "bowdark" and added the term "horse apples" for the bowdark's fruit.

Thomas A. Wikle
Brad A. Bays
Oklahoma State University

Allen, Harold, B. *The Linguistic Atlas of the Upper Midwest.* Minneapolis: University of Minnesota Press, 1976. Bailey, Guy, Tom Wikle, and Lori Sand. "The Focus of Linguistic Innovation in Texas." *English Worldwide* 12 (1991): 195–214. Cassidy, Federic G., ed. *Dictionary of American Regional English.* Cambridge MA: Belknap Press, 1985.

FOLK TOYS

Centuries before the influx of European American settlers, Native Americans of the Great Plains developed hundreds of ingenious and highly differentiated toys to instruct and entertain both the young and not-so-young. Among the most widespread and creative examples were six-foot-long knotted loops, usually of deer hide or rawhide, which were used to produce string figures, variations of the modern "cat's cradle." Play could be solitary, or it might join two persons of different generations passing the intricate loops back and forth (thus, the practice was called "web weaving"). Tribes shared many designs and each produced a variant of the nearly universal cat's cradle. Many Great Plains Native American string figures illustrated tribal histories and folklore, as well as religious narratives.

Other Native American toys both entertained and developed eye-hand coordination. Many were comprised of an eight- to twelve-inch pin of wood, bone, or antler connected by a length of cord to a series of up to nineteen small rings, or to a piece of leather punched with various-sized holes. As the pin is swung upward at arm's length, the rings or leather form a large arc, and when reaching the apex, begin to fall downward. At that instant, the player attempts to thrust the pin through all the rings or through a designated hole in the leather. The considerable deftness and skill required helped train children for spearfishing and hunting.

A related toy combines a hoop with darts. In each variant, whether from the Ojibwas of North Dakota, Lakotas of South Dakota, or Gros Ventres of Montana, a hoop, with a diameter from two-and-three-quarters up to twenty-five inches, fashioned from a thin branch, bone, or supple corn husk, surrounds a central weaving of yarn, string, beads, or rawhide. The weaving divides the hoop's enclosed area into sectors, with a small hole remaining in the center. The target hoop may be set on the ground, suspended from a tree branch, or rolled along the ground. Two players throw sharpened and sometimes elaborately decorated darts, or shoot arrows at the hoop, seeking to hit an exact spot or find the hoop's center. A variation has players throwing short spears instead of darts while running after a rolling hoop.

One of the continent's most ancient toys is the buzzer, a disk-shaped piece of wood, bone, or pottery pierced with two holes, through which a deerskin thong or piece of doubled-over sinew, about two feet long, is passed. The object is placed at the center of the doubled thong and spun rapidly by the winding and unwinding of the thong, with the rhythmic pressure of the hands and arms moving inward and pulling outward on the thong in the manner of playing an accordion. The thong, stretched tight between the hands, supports the buzzer, which functions as a flywheel. The Gros Ventres and the Lakotas used a knee bone or knucklebone as a buzzer; other tribes used painted and patterned wooden disks that would change color (for example, red and yellow becoming orange) and apparent shape as the buzzer spun. The term "buzzer" derives from the sound made while the bone, wood, or pottery piece is rotated clockwise and then counterclockwise at high speed.

Plains Indians also fashioned many designs of spinning tops of wood, bone, and horn; the Crees of Alberta as well as the Crows of Montana and the Lakotas crafted tops of solid horn, which children kept spinning with rawhide whips.

Balls for numerous kinds of play were crafted from hardwood, buckskin filled with rag or animal hair, and even pebbles covered with yarn. In Montana, the Northern Cheyennes and Crows, and in North Dakota the Mandans, developed a soft ball of buckskin, antelope hair, or dyed porcupine quills wrapped with cord, which they kicked gently in the air and caught on the top of the foot. A girl's toy, it was nearly identical to the modern "hacky sack."

Many Plains Indian children fashioned human and animal forms (especially horses and buffaloes) of red-brown sun-dried mud; Lakota children made clay animal forms and mixed vertebra from buffalo, deer, or antelope and their imagination to create "bone ponies." Children would gather the bleached bones into herds or use them in single combat or races. These folk toys were sometimes copied by white settlers' families in the nineteenth century.

Native American dolls were nearly universal, with great variations in design, color, and sophistication. Construction materials ranged from the simplest combinations of fabric tied to a forked stick to finely finished figures with beaded deerskin dresses, sometimes attached to miniature cradleboards. Today, replicas of these latter dolls are sold widely at reservation gift shops.

Great Plains settlers brought with them a small number of notable folk designs from Europe and the eastern United States, including the "limberjack," an Irish and Scandinavian dancing figure used to accentuate Celtic musical rhythms; carved, brilliantly painted Scandinavian toy animals; and carved dolls. Rag dolls had become common in New England following the Revolutionary War, took up little space, and traveled well. But because of the hardships involved in settling the Plains, children's amenities, including folk toys, were often lost.

Folk toys could be constructed by parents or other adults at a final destination once housing, a water supply, and other necessities were established. Miniature cradles and rocking horses were fashioned using a saw, jack-knife, hammer, and nails. Additional sturdy folk toys, including stilts, swings, and seesaws were made on the spot from scraps of available wood, providing years of delight to Great Plains children.

John R. Nelson Jr.
University of Massachusetts–Amherst

Culin, Robert Stewart. *Games of the North American Indians.* Washington DC: Government Printing Office, 1907. Nelson, John R. Jr. *American Folk Toys.* Newtown CT: Taunton Press, 1998. Toelken, Barre. *The Dynamics of Folklore.* Boston: Houghton Mifflin Company, 1979.

FOODWAYS

"Eat beef!" is a common sign found along roadsides and on pickup trucks throughout the Great Plains. Sponsored by local livestock associations, this slogan reflects the dominant ranching economy in the western half of the Plains. It also holds true for consumption. Beef is by far the preferred meat from the Canadian Prairie Provinces to South Texas. In fact, eating this red meat provides a source of regional identity, especially when a state or province name is inserted, as in Nebraska or Alberta beef. A grilled T-bone steak is the preferred cut and preparation method for home and restaurant consumption, but beef also is the focus of foodways events such as chuck-wagon dinners, barbecue contests, and chili cook-offs.

Male-dominated competitive cooking, perhaps inspired by stories from cattle-drive campsites, is a popular activity in the Great Plains. Barbecue contests involve secret dry rubs, marinades, and tangy, tomato-based sauces. These are applied to a wide assortment of beef cuts, with brisket being a popular choice. Chili cook-offs vary in sophistication, from a circuit where contestants collect points to be eligible for a national competition to simpler community social events, such as heritage days. Known regionally as "bowl o' red," chili is composed of meat, tomatoes, chilies, secret ingredients, and sometimes beans simmered together in a large pot.

On restaurant menus, beef in the form of steaks, roasts, and barbecue is regularly supplemented in the Southern Plains by a specialty known as chicken-fried steak. This is tenderized round steak that has been dipped in a liquid (sometimes buttermilk) and seasoned flour, and then fried in a pan. It inevitably is served with mashed potatoes and gravy. Rocky Mountain oysters (also known as calf fries or prairie oysters) are another regional specialty. These are calf testicles that are sliced and fried. The uninitiated may consider this a taboo food, but insiders call it a delicacy. They are served primarily at special events sponsored by lodges. Bison is an alternative red meat that is gaining in status and popularity because of its nutritional value (low fat and less cholesterol) and clever marketing by the North American Bison Cooperative in New Rockford, North Dakota. Wild game also is popular in home cooking. Antelope and elk are preferred on the western, mountainous edges of the Plains and pheasant is preferred in South Dakota.

People in the Great Plains are noted for their inclination toward "meat and potatoes." This diet reflects the European heritage of its settlers in part, but it also provides the high-calorie replenishment needed for the pursuit of vigorous, outdoor labor still common in the Plains. Traditional ethnic foods, such as dumplings, sausages, kolaches, lefse, and lutefisk are today pretty much reserved for holidays, family gatherings, or public ethnic celebrations such as Høstfest in Minot, North Dakota, Czech Days in Tabor, South Dakota, Svensk Hyllningsfest in Lindsborg, Kansas, or Oktoberfest in Fredericksburg, Texas. A notable exception to this rule is Runza, a franchise restaurant out of Lincoln, Nebraska, that is named after a folded pastry sandwich filled with seasoned beef and cabbage that is found in many ethnic cuisines (called a *bierock* by German Russians). Native American food is presented to the public in restaurant settings or at events such as the American Indian Exposition in Anadarko, Oklahoma. An Indian taco (fry bread topped with seasoned meat, lettuce, and tomatoes) is the most popular offering. Mexican cuisine, or Tex-Mex as some call the Americanized version, is now by far the most popular ethnic food in restaurants in the Plains. Two Plains franchises—Taco John's headquartered in Cheyenne, Wyoming, and Taco Cabana of San Antonio, Texas—are indicators of this trend; another is the presence of local taco stands in almost every Southern Plains small town.

Being in the middle of the nation's breadbasket, with wheat fields to the horizon, the northern portions of the Plains are, understandably, home to important milling and food processing centers. Because a triangle of eastern North Dakota has a climate ideal for growing premium Hard Amber durum wheat, pasta has become a local specialty. A grower-owned manufacturing facility, the Dakota Growers Pasta Company, was established in Carrington in 1993.

Throughout the Plains, home-baked products such as bread, buns, cakes, bars, and pies are important. If grilling beef is the competitive venue for men, then pie making serves the same purpose for women. Winning a blue ribbon at the county fair remains a coveted award, and local cafés prominently advertise home-baked pies on the menu board. The favorite pies utilize local fruits in season, including rhubarb in northern places. Chocolate, coconut cream, lemon meringue, pecan, and sour-cream raisin pies are standard throughout the year.

Farmwives in the Plains traditionally prepared large noon meals for threshing crews during wheat harvest time. A significant folklore exists regarding this activity, and it remains a fact of life today. The extra men from the community who helped harvest the wheat are being replaced today by custom cutting crews who travel the Plains with their combines from south to north during harvest season. These crews still must be fed quickly with filling meals, whether it is in the field, farm kitchen, or restaurant.

Although traditional home cooking has persisted in the Plains to a greater degree than in most other parts of the United States and Canada, it is curious that this sparsely settled area is also the headquarters for many franchise restaurants. White Castle, the first of the burger joints, was established in Wichita, Kansas, and Sonic Drive-Ins in Shawnee, Oklahoma. The major cafeteria chains of Luby's and Furr's first operated in San Antonio and Lubbock, Texas, respectively. Pizza Hut began in Wichita, Kansas, Godfather's Pizza in Omaha, Nebraska, Mazzio's in Tulsa, Oklahoma, Mr. Gatti's in Kerrville, Texas, and Valentino's in Lincoln, Nebraska. No franchise seafood restaurants have originated in the Great Plains, as might be expected. More surprisingly, steak chains do not have headquarters in the Plains either. Here the reason is different—the local steakhouse is the place to be.

See also HISPANIC AMERICANS: Mexican American Cuisine / INDUSTRY: Pizza Hut.

Barbara G. Shortridge
University of Kansas

Fertig, Judith M. *Prairie Home Cooking*. Boston: Harvard Common Press, 1999. Powers, Jo Marie, and Anita Stewart. *Northern Bounty: A Celebration of Canadian Cuisine*. Toronto: Random House of Canada, 1995. Wagner, Candy, and Sandra Marquez. *Cooking Texas Style*. Austin: University of Texas Press, 1993.

FUR TRADE LORE

It is possible to identify two categories of fur trade lore, drawn from the first four decades of the nineteenth century when fur traders were the predominant European American presence in the Great Plains. The first category involves the traders' own understandings—largely communicated by word of mouth—of such matters as the geography of the country and the characteristics of the Native inhabitants; the second relates to stories from the fur trade, tales of traders' lives, especially of heroic exploits, which have been passed down over the years in both oral and written forms.

When the fur trade in the American Great Plains first gathered momentum, following the return of Lewis and Clark from their epic journey with news of abundant beaver and otter at the headwaters of the Missouri, there was only a vague understanding of the geography of the region. This explains why Manual Lisa, who organized his first expedition to the Northern Plains in 1807, believed that he could forge a trading connection to Santa Fe from the headwaters of the Missouri. Lisa was possibly influenced by his partner, George Drouillard, whose map of 1808 showed Santa Fe to be only a few days' ride from the headwaters of the Missouri. Such geographic misconceptions were corrected over time through often-bitter experience on the ground.

The discovery—for to Americans in 1824 it was indeed a discovery—of South Pass by a small band of trappers led by Jedediah Smith provides an example of how lore was translated into geographical knowledge. Americans had probably crossed the Rocky Mountains through South Pass in previous years (John Colter in 1807, for example), but there had been no "effective" discovery of this vital gateway to the West. Smith, in the first of his great explorations, remedied that. His party labored through the Badlands of South Dakota in the fall of 1823, then on past the Black Hills to the Wind River Mountains, where they went into winter camp with the Crows. Using sand piled on a bison robe, the Crows modeled the topography of the Rockies, showing the trappers the convenient route around the south edge of the Wind River Range. In March of 1824 Smith and his men struggled through a blizzard to cross South Pass, leading the way for the hundreds of trappers who would trace the Platte and Sweetwater Rivers through the pass to the rendezvous over the next fifteen years and for the far more numerous emigrants to Oregon, Utah, and California who followed in the 1840s.

Traders' views of the Indigenous peoples of the Plains were also lore, in the sense that their appraisals were based not on any objective reality but on the Native group's utility to the fur trade. The traders came to despise the Arikaras—they labeled them the "Horrid Tribe"—because of their resistance to the fur trade, most dramatically in 1823 when they attacked William Ashley's expedition to the upper Missouri, leaving twelve Americans dead. The Arikaras, of course, were only following their own agenda: to preserve their middleman role in the commerce by preventing Americans from opening up their own trade with the upriver Indians. By contrast, the Crows had a good reputation. Their finished furs were regarded as the best in the Plains, and, according to trader Edwin Denig, they never killed Americans and rarely stole from them.

Stories from the fur trade—our inherited fur trade lore—abound. For example, the extraordinary travels of the young Englishman Henry Kelsey, while in the service of the Hudson's Bay Company, are legendary, partly because of their daring, partly because the exact routes are clouded in mystery, and partly because Kelsey's journals were not known to historians until 1926. The fact that the journals were also partly written in crude verse only adds to the mystery. In 1690 Kelsey was sent inland from Hudson Bay to connect distant Indians to the fur trade. Accompanied by Indian guides, Kelsey probably ascended the Saskatchewan River and explored the Canadian Plains over the following two years. He contracted the Assiniboines and maybe the Gros Ventres, and he was the first European to record descriptions of bison and grizzly bears in the Canadian West. Even if some of the more fabulous events associated with his journey are discounted, such as his reputed killing of two grizzly bears with two shots, the sheer accomplishment of his exploration and his easy ability to fit in with the Indians (he knew some Indian languages well) make Kelsey a figure of mythological, as well as historical, importance.

Fact and fiction merge in fur trade accounts, especially in the dramatic memoirs of trappers like Joe Meek and Robert Newell. One book, *The Lost Trappers*, written by David H. Coyner in 1859, was, in the words of the eminent fur trade historian Hiram Martin Chittenden, a "complete fabrication." The remarkable story of Hugh Glass, however, seems to be true, and no other piece of fur trade lore has been so durable. In 1902, when Chittenden wrote his classic *American Fur Trade of the Far West*, the saga of Hugh Glass was an oral tradition among Plains folk. There had also been three written accounts by that time, including one in the *Missouri Intelligencer* in 1829. Subsequently, Glass's exploits were included in numerous fur trade books, retold as an epic narrative poem in John G. Neihardt's *The Saga of Hugh Glass* (1915) and filtered through Hollywood in the film *Man in the Wilderness* (1971), with Richard Harris playing the lead.

The story is this: following the battle with the Arikaras, Hugh Glass (who had been wounded in the fight) set out for the Yellowstone River with a party of trappers led by Ashley's partner, Andrew Henry. Glass, an expert marksman, was sent ahead to hunt and, out there alone, he was attacked by a grizzly bear and her cubs. Part of his throat was torn out and his arms and legs were badly wounded. When the rest of the party caught up, they killed the bear and waited for Glass to die. But Hugh Glass was unwilling to take that final step, so Henry, anxious to get on with business, persuaded two men (one of them a teenager named Jim Bridger) to stay with him, then left for the trapping grounds. A few days later the two men rejoined Henry, reporting that Glass had died.

They were almost right, but Glass was able to crawl to a place where there was a spring and wild cherries and buffaloberries within reach. As his strength slowly returned, he resolved to find the men who had abandoned him and seek revenge. Living on berries, roots, and carcasses of dead animals, he struggled across more than 100 miles to Fort Kiowa, in present-day South Dakota. There, though still badly hurt, he joined another trapping party bound for the upper Missouri, seeking his former companions. He found them at their new post at the junction of the Big Horn and Yellowstone Rivers in December of 1823. Looking like an apparition, Glass walked into the post and up to Bridger, but taking into account his youth, he forgave him. Glass later found the other man who had left him at Fort Atkinson, where he had joined the army, and he too was forgiven. Hugh Glass's luck finally ran out when he was killed by Arikaras in the winter of 1832–33.

Such stories are the stuff of fur trade history. Probably no other period of the American past has been represented so much by lore and so little by systematic analysis. No doubt the latter is needed, but hopefully not at the expense of the drama that characterized European Americans' initial encounter with the dramatic physical and human environments of the Great Plains and Rocky Mountains.

See also EUROPEAN AMERICANS: Kelsey, Henry / HISPANIC AMERICANS: Lisa, Manuel / INDUSTRY: Fur Trade.

David J. Wishart
University of Nebraska–Lincoln

Chittenden, Hiram Martin. *The American Fur Trade of the Far West*. Lincoln: University of Nebraska Press, 1986. Morgan, Dale Lowell. *Jedediah Smith and the Opening of the West*. Lincoln: University of Nebraska Press, 1953. Saum, Lewis O. *The Fur Trader and the Indian*. Seattle: University of Washington Press, 1965.

GHOST STORIES

Characteristic ghost stories of the Great Plains may now be found in collections from Alberta to Texas. This was not always so. People of the Great Plains have traditionally evinced a wry skepticism toward ghosts. Typical is Lisa Hefner, a collector of ghost stories from Kansas. When asked if she believed in ghosts, she responded that she believed in stories. In Nebraska an Omaha Indian expressed dislike for the word "ghost." He said Native Americans preferred to think of these encounters with the dead as grandparents returning to give advice. He said that many times his dead grandfather had returned to guide him to a better way. Nevertheless, everywhere in the Great Plains ghosts are used to explain unexplained sounds, sights, feelings, or movements.

A willingness to believe in ghosts can be a disadvantage. For example, in a story called "The Phantom Piccolo Player," historian Everett Dick tells how one homesteader, haunted nightly by the same melody and, eventually, by gunshots, abandoned his homestead in Dakota Territory. When he returned years later he found the owner of his former claim whistling the same haunting tune. Soon he learned that his erstwhile haunter had been privy to information about where the railroad was to be built and had made a fortune on that knowledge.

From collecting three volumes of ghost stories, mostly from Nebraska and Iowa, storyteller Duane Hutchinson identified several characteristics of Plains ghosts: they seem unable to think; they do not speak and, if approached, they vanish; most often, they seem to be carrying out some task that they repeat mindlessly, trapped in some habitual action; and in a few cases, they respond to shouts and commands to go away and leave the living alone. Furthermore, the costume the ghost wears appears and vanishes with the apparition, which raises the question: are overalls immortal?

In the course of research that took three and a half years, Debra Munn interviewed 137 people and scoured the records of historical societies for evidence of Wyoming ghosts. The ghost stories of Wyoming share attributes of ghost stories everywhere—mysterious footsteps, machines that malfunction, doors that open and close, and rocking chairs that rock with no one in them—but Wyoming ghost stories are also place-specific. There is Dolly Carson's haunted trailer (a common Wyoming house type) in Cody, where her dead husband and mother carry on the feud that defined their living relationship; there is the restaurant on the outskirts of Cheyenne where weary travelers once sought refuge in a Plains blizzard but could never find again; and there is Fort Laramie, with its layers of history, perhaps Wyoming's most haunted site. Of course, some ghosts are purely imaginary: the door at Fort Laramie that kept unlocking itself was only a case of a lock responding to Wyoming's temperature extremes.

In his collection of "eerie true tales" from his native Oklahoma, David Farris documents numerous sightings of UFOs, overgrown fish, and strange beasts, as well as ghosts. Philanthropist Thomas Gilcrease is said to still (forty years after his death) walk the hallways of the Gilcrease Museum, and a phantom hitchhiker—a young boy—has been picked up on a lonely stretch of Highway 20, just east of Clarence, only to disappear mysteriously. Meanwhile, in Ghost Hollow, near Cushing, the old elm that once was a hanging tree glows luminously when there is a full moon.

The farther south you go in the Plains, the more the ghost stories take on a Mexican flavor. This is evident from some of the titles in Docia Schultz Williams's collections from Texas: "The Ghost of San Pedro Playhouse," "Jose Navarro's Haunted Homestead," and "Shadows of El Tropicana." The stories are filled with historical and cultural details and convey the essence of the Plains environment: old army posts molder into the earth; night breezes carry the fragrance of piñon and mesquite; and for those willing to believe, ghosts drift through the West Texas night.

See also ART: Gilcrease, Thomas.

Duane Hutchinson
Lincoln, Nebraska

Farris, David A. *Mysterious Oklahoma: Eerie True Tales from the Sooner State*. Edmond OK: Little Bruce, 1995. Hutchinson, Duane. *A Storyteller's Ghost Stories*. Lincoln NE: Foundation Books, 1989, 1990, 1992. Munn, Debra D. *Ghosts on the Range: Eerie True Tales of Wyoming*. Boulder CO: Pruett Publishing, 1989.

GRAVE MARKERS

In Wyuka Cemetery in Lincoln, Nebraska, an aircraft pioneer is buried beneath the smashed propeller of his plane. Nearby, in Nebraska City, a prominent insurance salesman rests

Portion of the Davis Memorial in Hiawatha, Kansas

next to a life-sized replica of his rolltop desk, and the founder of Arbor Day, J. Sterling Morton, is remembered by an exquisite twelve-foot limestone tree. A Garden City, Kansas, boy who loved his car is buried under the actual engine, and his name appears on the valve cover. Another Kansan, from Attica, used his tombstone to rail against the evils of the Democratic Party. In the small town of Hiawatha a husband and wife are depicted at every stage of their lives together in an enormous ensemble of statuary that cost a fortune during the Great Depression. A young man from Tulsa, Oklahoma, poses on his motorcycle, and an inscription below the porcelain photograph says simply, "I'd rather be drag racing." A traveling salesman from Lincoln, Kansas, is symbolized by a sculpted suitcase and the misspelled inscription, "Here is where he stoped last."

Grave markers are erected for the departed, but it is the living who are truly served by these monuments. Ritual burial of the dead and the marking of this passage are defining phenomena for virtually all of civilization. The humble tombstone provides a venue for the listing of cultural and spiritual values, and a chance for individuals or groups to record their grief and voice their hope. In many cases they also provide humanity with a welcome excuse for artistic expression. In the Great Plains, skillful and passionate people have left such distinctive monuments in the cemeteries that dot the landscape from Texas to Canada.

Although professional sculpture from Europe was sometimes imported by grieving families, most grave markers in the Great Plains were made by vernacular artisans working with local materials. Those in wagon trains and in fly-by-night mining camps carved markers quickly from wood. Immigrant Spanish stonecutters created decorative Catholic crosses, while their northern European counterparts imitated the illustrated tablets of England. Germans who had lost the sponsorship of Catherine the Great emigrated from Russia and erected iron crosses much like those in the Old Country, but in western Kansas many of these were produced using plumbing pipe and other utilitarian provisions. Epitaphs were brought from the British Isles and gradually infused with an American flavor, providing the visitor with a poetic glimpse of the deceased's character, or at least the sensibilities of those who had loved him. Italian immigrants brought a tradition of statuary with them, contributing angels and portraiture, executed in the round. Poorer enclaves and subcultures with no tradition of sophisticated sculpture would resort to concrete and other mixed media, but all of these efforts would shine with creativity compared to the cookie-cutter granite stones that emerged later in the twentieth century.

As might be expected, small town and rural cemeteries bristled with orthodox religious symbolism and Gothic gingerbread. Stones featured the anchor, a symbol of hope, fingers that pointed to heaven, and the weeping willow tree, which, like the Christian church, flourished in every part of the world. Jewish stones abounded with graven images, including the hands of benediction that identifies the Kohanim, the traditional priests of Israel, the lion of Judah, and the cup of the Levites. Later, urban mausoleums sported Egyptian Revival motifs or Art Deco designs. Generic symbols for death, such as the spilled flowerpot, the broken urn, and the inverted torch, appeared as society moved to a more secular view of life. Firemen, policemen, and fraternal organizations set up umbrella monuments to preside over their casualties. The Woodsmen of the World sold insurance policies to thousands of frontier families and erected grave markers in the form of tree stumps or stacked logs with individual names, resembling God's cord wood for the final blaze of judgment. Rows of lambs pointed out the frightful attrition that faced children on the frontier. Young women died in childbirth and were remembered by low-relief roses carved in limestone.

In the mid–twentieth century, cemeteries began to imitate the tract housing of the suburbs, and identical stones made of granite became almost universal. Soon these vertical markers would be laid flat so that lawn mowers could more easily be used. The cemetery became more a business and less a community institution. Finally, tombstones would be eliminated altogether, replaced by plaques and subterranean receptacles for the temporary use of flowers.

Happily, Americans have risen up against this unnatural anonymity. Images on markers are again attempting to portray the individual person, and porcelain photographs have reappeared. In the Great Plains it is now not unusual to see a farmer's grave marker that features his tractor, or some manifestation of the land itself. Outstanding older monuments are finally being sporadically sheltered and preserved. The grave marker is an important way for us to tell the next generation who we were and to help preserve our collective cultural identity.

See also ARCHITECTURE: Cemeteries.

John Gary Brown
Lawrence, Kansas

Ariés, Phillippe. *The Hour of Our Death.* New York: Alfred A. Knopf, Inc. 1981. Jackson, Kenneth T., and Camillo J. Vergara. *Silent Cities: The Evolution of the American Cemetery.* New York: Princeton Architectural Press, 1989. Marion, John Francis. *Famous and Curious Cemeteries: A Pictorial, Historical, and Anecdotal View of American and European Cemeteries and the Famous and Infamous People Who Are Buried There.* New York: Crown Publishers, Inc., 1977.

GRINNELL, GEORGE BIRD (1849–1938)

George Bird Grinnell was not from the Great Plains—he was born into a wealthy family in Brooklyn, New York, on September 20, 1849—but his studies of Plains Indians, and especially his role in the preservation of their histories, are fundamental to the region's legacy.

A mediocre student, Grinnell nevertheless graduated from Yale in 1870. That same year his interest in the Great Plains was kindled during a paleontology expedition along the route of the Union Pacific Railroad when he met William F. Cody and accompanied the Pawnees on a bison hunt. He was with George Armstrong Custer in the Black Hills in 1874 as a naturalist, and later, as editor of *Forest and Stream,* he shaped the early years of the American conservation movement. It was his publications on Native American customs and oral traditions, however, that particularly distinguished his life.

Starting with *Pawnee Hero Stories and Folk-Tales* (1889), and continuing through *Blackfoot Lodge Tales* (1892), *The Cheyenne Indians: Their History and Ways of Life* (1923), and *By Cheyenne Campfires* (1926), Grinnell collected and preserved the Indians' own histories with a sensitivity that was often lacking in the studies done by his contemporaries. While he shared his contemporaries' social Darwinist views that Native Americans had to give way to "civilization," and while he may not, as Richard Levine has argued, really have understood the implications of the "folktales" he collected, Grinnell let the Pawnees, Blackfeet, and Cheyennes tell their own stories, in their own way. Those stories survive as vivid insights into their views of themselves and of their position in nature.

Although he spent portions of most years in the Great Plains learning and recording (and serving as treaty commissioner for the U.S. government), Grinnell continued to be based in New York City. He died there on April 11, 1938, having suffered a series of heart attacks over the previous decade.

David J. Wishart
University of Nebraska–Lincoln

Levine, Richard. "Indians, Conservation, and George Bird Grinnell." *American Studies* 28 (1987): 41–55. Parsons, Cynthia. *George Bird Grinnell: A Biographical Sketch.* Lanham MD: University Press of America, 1992. Reiger, John F. "Dedication to George Bird Grinnell." *Arizona and the West* 21 (1979): 1–4.

HUMOR

Without question, the most common form of folk and popular humor in the Great Plains, and in North America in general, especially in recent decades, is the joke. The form of the joke changed dramatically through the nineteenth and twentieth centuries, the emphasis falling away from style, narrative, and language, sometimes lengthy and humorous throughout, to an almost total reliance on a "punch line," a surprising last line without which the story has little or no humor. That very characteristic is itself parodied and thereby showcased in the so-called shaggy-dog story, in which the requisite punch line is absent or is an execrable pun, less funny than painful. That is, this distortion of the prevailing joke form clarifies and accentuates its usual form. Indeed, at the turn of the millennium, the predominant form of American joke is little more than a punch line ("Did you hear about the blond who . . . ?") or a "riddling" joke, a curious question with a surprise or punning answer, both provided by the joke teller: "What's Polack surf 'n' turf? Carp and kielbasa. How many psychiatrists does it take to change a light bulb? Only one, but the bulb has to *want* to be changed." Plains peoples participate fully in every dimension of humor fashion, from ethnic slurs like the above (which, however, almost inevitably have evolved from esoteric expressions within the derogated ethnic group to become a flag of internal identity and pride) to political slanders, sexist barbs, and topical commentary.

It is impossible to quantify humor in degree, quality, or quantity, but it is suggested here that the Great Plains is distinctive in the cultivation of at least two forms of the joke: the tall tale and the form that is here called "civil ribaldry." Both forms have their longest and strongest traditions in the rural Plains.

Example of Great Plains humor, Yates Center, Kansas, 2001

The tall tale is of course an ancient art, widely spread throughout the world. Alice Fletcher recorded the form during her early observations of the Omaha tribe, and non-Native invaders carried the form with them on horseback and in wagon trains. The true tall tale is not a tale at all, rarely having a narrative element. Nor, strictly speaking, is it a lie, since its exaggerations are so utterly preposterous that no one of normal intelligence or humor could conceivably mistake a true tall tale for a legitimate report—for example, "It was so cold folks went to church just to hear about hell; . . . so dry I saw two cottonwood trees chasing a dog; . . . too windy to load rocks."

Nor are such complaints to be mistaken as true laments. The faces of persons reciting tall tales like the above actually reveal a kind of perverse pride. Indeed, one could legitimately consider them traditional brags: "Living on the Plains is like being hanged . . . the initial jolt is fairly sudden but after you hang there a while, you kinda get used to it" is a manner of bringing attention to one's own courage and strength even while modestly denigrating the geography in question. "Modestly" because the exaggerations and extensions are largely true, if slightly overdrawn! While the tall tale is not unique to the Plains by any stretch of the imagination (so to speak), the form may well have flourished there as nowhere else. This may be because the dramatic extremes of the Plains have driven the boaster to ever greater—and funnier—extremes to match, yet outdo, the truth.

The tall tale is nurtured primarily in rural contexts but finds wider distribution through press releases from elusive tall-tale "contests." (Innocent souls sometimes try to organize formal tall-tale "contests," which almost inevitably fail because the true tall-tale contest never happens and is itself a fiction.) The traditional tall tale, however, falls far short of the

shock value demanded by modern folk and popular culture humor and is appreciated only as a quaint, even childish form.

Far less well known to the general American public, and more clearly a Plains survival, is a humor type that lacks a formal label but may be called "civil ribaldry." These jokes take the form of extraordinarily subtle, distinctly rural narratives. While there is a punch line, unlike the riddling joke, for example, "civil ribaldry" does contain a clear narrative element. The stories, while slightly off-color, can be, and are, told in mixed company, even with children present, without much danger of being understood by the innocent.

Two examples recently collected in the vicinity of Dannebrog, Nebraska, are as follows:

You'll never believe this, Rog, but yesterday I was on the gravel between here and Grand Island and I spotted Kenny L. out disking his fields on his old John Deere . . . and he was stark naked from the waist down. Not a stitch of clothes on below the belt, not even underwear. So, I stopped at the edge of the field and waited until he came back down the row. I waved him down and asked him, "What's this, naked from the waist down like that, Kenny?" He replied, "Yesterday I worked out here on the tractor all day without a shirt on and came home with a stiff neck. This is the wife's idea . . ." (related by Eric Nielsen).

Only a few weeks ago I entered the Dannebrog tavern and found an old friend sitting morosely at the bar. I asked him what the problem was and this is what he said:

I can't rightly say for sure. You know that black mare I was trying to sell? Well, a guy offered me $500 for her, but he said he needed to have a 15 percent discount for paying cash. Well, that was all right by me, but I'm not too good with ciphering, so I couldn't for the life of me figure out 15 percent of $500. So, I took a quick run over to the schoolteacher's house, knocked at her door, and asked her, "Now, if I was to give you $500 for something but need a 15 percent discount for paying cash, how much would you be taking off?" And she said, quick as you can think, "Everything but my socks and earrings." Rog, I'm still trying to figure that one out (name of narrator withheld).

Roger L. Welsch
Dannebrog, Nebraska

Fletcher, Alice C. *Indian Story and Song from North America*. Lincoln: University of Nebraska Press, 1995. Welsch, Roger. *Shingling the Fog and Other Plains Lies*. Lincoln: University of Nebraska Press, 1980. Welsch, Roger, and Linda K. Welsch. *Catfish at the Pump: Humor and the Frontier*. Lincoln: University of Nebraska Press, 1986.

HUNTING LORE

The hunting lore of the Great Plains can be exemplified by three major figures: William F. "Buffalo Bill" Cody (1846–1917), Theodore Roosevelt (1858–1919), and Natty Bumppo, the main character of the Leatherstocking tales by James Fenimore Cooper (1789–1851).

Of course, the myriad tribes of Native Americans were the first inhabitants and hunters of the "Great American Desert," as it was described in some quarters throughout the nineteenth century. The buffalo was their crucial game, providing food and many other products for survival. No part of the animal was wasted, and the symbiotic relationship between the tribe and the buffalo connoted a spiritual link, reflected in many beliefs and legends.

One such legend, related by Buffalo Bill in his autobiography, centers on a creation myth. According to Cody, one night a group of Pawnees came into camp bringing with them a number of large bones, one of which a doctor with Cody's expedition identified as a human thighbone. The Pawnees maintained that the bones belonged to an ancient race of men who inhabited the country and were three times the size of human beings of the day. Any one of these giants could run down a buffalo and tear off its leg with one hand and then eat it as he walked. However, these giant men did not believe in the Great Spirit; they were not intimidated by the thunder and lightning and laughed at it. This angered the Great Spirit, and he sent a great rainstorm that drove the giants to the hills. But the water rose and covered the mountaintops as well, and the conceited giants were drowned. Once the floodwaters receded, the Great Spirit considered that he had made men too large and powerful, and he would henceforth re-create them smaller and weaker. The Pawnees maintained that this was Indian history handed down to them from time out of mind. This explains why men are not like the giants of old and have to work harder to hunt and to live. Cody adds an interesting note to this episode. He remarked that since their expedition had no wagons with them and the thighbone was very large, it had to be left behind.

Probably the most famous account of Buffalo Bill relates how he earned his name. In a contest with William Comstock, who was chief of scouts at Fort Wallace, Kansas, Cody killed sixty-nine buffalo in an eight-hour day, while Comstock shot only forty-six. Cody maintained that during his service to provide meat for the men building the Kansas Pacific Railroad in 1867, he killed 4,280 buffalo. However, Cody's "accomplishments" as a buffalo hunter remain a subject for debate, for the facts are clouded by myth.

Theodore Roosevelt was another hunter figure whose exploits are legendary. He spent two years in the Dakotas, following the deaths of his mother and his first wife, Alice, on the same day in February of 1884. He became a gentleman cattle rancher and found consolation in the hard work and austere landscape. In 1885 Roosevelt wrote an essay on "The Lordly Buffalo" for his book *Hunting Trips of a Ranchman* (1885). He regretted the excesses of the 1870s when the buffalo herds were reduced to near-extinction, but he saw their demise as necessary for the progress of the nation. He also enthusiastically hunted buffalo in a more controlled manner, which he described in great detail in his essay, and sought to preserve them for hunting as a sport. He founded the Boone and Crockett Club and served as its first president. One goal of the club was to preserve large game in America for hunting.

Natty Bumppo, the hero of James Fenimore Cooper's five Leatherstocking tales, is to a large extent a fictional portrayal of Daniel Boone. In *The Prairie* (1827), Natty was an old man in his eighties who had moved ever westward over the course of his life and would die in the Great Plains. He spent the last stage of life in a forest of grass on the Plains, his hunting years at an end. This was a time of American expansion across the continent. The pioneers were seeking new lives as Natty was ending his. He represented a way of life that had all but disappeared, just as his youth and strength were nearly gone. However, he was freed from the confines of time because his hold on mortal life was tenuous. He came to symbolize a nation that had developed and reached out across a continent of dramatic landscapes, unconstrained by any boundaries. He was the hunter scout who opened the path for the march of pioneers who followed.

Lynda Wolfe Coupe
Pace University

Cody, William F. *The Life of Hon. William F. Cody, Known as Buffalo Bill, the Famous Hunter, Scout, and Guide: An Autobiography*. Lincoln: University of Nebraska Press, 1978. Cooper, James Fenimore. *The Prairie: A Tale*. New York: Rinehart, 1960. Roosevelt, Theodore. *Hunting Trips of a Ranchman: Sketches of Sport on the Northern Cattle Plains and the Wilderness Hunter: An Account of the Big Game of the United States and Its Chase with Horse, Hound, and Rifle. 1885*. New York: Modern Library, 1996.

INSECT LORE

The folklore of the Great Plains touches on many insects, including buffalo gnats and Mormon crickets, but no creature so permeates the culture of this region as the grasshopper—and the Rocky Mountain locust (*Melanoplus spretus*) in particular (a locust is a type of grasshopper capable of forming immense, migratory swarms). During periods of favorable weather, these insects erupted from their "permanent breeding zones" in the fertile river valleys and spread over an area of nearly two million square miles. For half a century, outbreaks of this locust devastated farms in every state and province of the Great Plains, and this species was declared the single greatest impediment to the settlement of the region.

Glacial deposits containing frozen locusts in the Rocky Mountains reveal that outbreaks have occurred for at least 1,000 years, but European settlers first reported seeing swarms in 1818. Major outbreaks developed in 1855–57 and 1864–67, but the folklore of this locust was established with the swarms of 1873–78 (1874 was called the "Grasshopper Year" in Kansas). Laura Ingalls Wilder's description, from *On the Banks of Plum Creek*, is classic: "The cloud was hailing grasshoppers. The cloud *was* grasshoppers. Their bodies hid the sun and made darkness. . . . The rasping whirring of their wings filled the whole air and they hit the ground and the house with the noise of a hailstorm. . . . Laura had to step on grasshoppers and they smashed squirming and slimy under her feet."

In fruitless efforts to fight the swarms that stripped the land of all vegetation, shredded laundry, and infested larders, people used smoky fires, burning trenches, and various contraptions, such as a horse-drawn device to scoop and smash the insects. Governments offered bounties for locust eggs ($5 per bushel), and the eggs were even used as a form of local currency. Kansas attempted to assemble a "grasshopper army," requiring every able-bodied male from age twelve to sixty-five to fight the locusts. Townspeople reported that "heavy freight trains were delayed for hours by their [the locusts'] gathering on the track in large numbers, the wheels crushing their bodies and forming an oily, soapy substance, which caused the wheels to spin around and around, with no power to go forward." Some interpreted the swarms as a punishment sent by Providence. This notion was disputed by a state entomologist who headed a section of his report "Not a Divine Visitation."

The catastrophe became the material of tall tales, like the one about a man who, when plowing his field, hung his work jacket on a post, leaving his watch in the pocket. When he came back to get his jacket, all that was left was the watch—because the grasshoppers had eaten his jacket. Another humorous bit of folklore recounted the man who left his team in the field while he went to his well for a drink of water. When he came back the grasshoppers had eaten up the team and harness and were playing horseshoes with the iron shoes the horses had worn.

When the outbreak of the 1870s abated, the Rocky Mountain locust once again concentrated in the fertile river valleys. At the same time, settlers were converging into these regions, converting them into farmland and effectively destroying the habitat needed by the locust during its recession periods. In doing so, farmers managed to inadvertently drive their most severe competitor to extinction, leaving North America without a locust species. The Rocky Mountain locust lives on only in folklore; the last living specimen was collected in 1902.

See also PHYSICAL ENVIRONMENT: Grasshoppers.

Jeffrey A. Lockwood
University of Wyoming

Lockwood, Jeffrey A., and Larry D. DeBrey. "A Solution for the Sudden and Unexplained Extinction of the Rocky Mountain Locust, *Melanoplus spretus* (Walsh)." *Environmental Entomology* 19 (1990): 1194–1205. Welsh, Roger L. *A Treasury of Nebraska Pioneer Folklore.* Lincoln: University of Nebraska Press, 1966.

LOMAX, JOHN A. (1867–1948)

Although best known as the folk-song collector who found Huddie "Leadbelly" Ledbetter in a Louisiana prison, John A. Lomax's pioneering role in cultural preservation was established more than thirty years earlier with the publication of *Cowboy Songs and Other Frontier Ballads* (1910). Born in Holmes County, Mississippi, on September 23, 1867, he was scarcely two when his family moved to Texas, and he always considered himself a native Texan. The social and cultural heritage of the Lone Star State was to have a pervasive influence on his life's work.

In his youth Lomax attended a small frontier "college" in Granbury, Texas, and later taught school for a time. In 1895, when he was twenty-eight, he entered the University of Texas as a freshman and eventually earned two degrees there (bachelor of arts, 1897; master of arts, 1906). He also attended the University of Chicago (1985, 1903) and, ultimately, Harvard University (master of arts, 1907), where he studied comparative literature and balladry under such luminaries as Barrett Wendell and George Lyman Kittredge. From 1897 to 1903 he served as registrar of the University of Texas, and at intervals beginning in 1903 he taught English at the Agricultural and Mechanical College of Texas (later Texas A&M University).

In 1907, supported by Kittredge and Wendell, Lomax began what proved to be one of the first serious, systematic efforts to collect American folk songs. Traveling through the Central Plains and Southwest, sometimes on horseback, he gathered and recorded such now-famous classics as "Home on the Range," "Git Along Little Dogies," and "The Old Chisholm Trail," published three years later, with 109 others, as *Cowboy Songs and Other Frontier Ballads*.

Lomax returned to the University of Texas in 1910. His association with the university shaped both his personal and professional life for many years, although he left or was forced out of positions there no fewer than three times between 1903 and 1925, when he moved to Dallas to accept a job as vice president of the Republic National Bank. At that point his song-collecting activity, which had dwindled over the years, seemed finished.

When the Depression struck, Lomax was in his sixties, in ill health, and mourning the death of his wife. In 1932 his sons, John Jr. and Alan, persuaded him to resume his folk-song lecture tours and fieldwork. Together they mapped out a six-month lecture-and-collecting tour that took them across the nation, restored both Lomax's health and bank account, and set the pattern for the next ten years of his life. From this work came *American Ballads and Folk Songs* (1934) and *Our Singing Country* (1941), which preserved in print such national treasures as "Casey Jones," "Rye Whiskey," "Amazing Grace," "Cotton-Eyed Joe," "Jack o' Diamonds," and many others.

In 1933 Lomax was named curator of the Archive of American Folksong at the Library of Congress. With support from that institution, he and his son Alan made field recording trips throughout the 1930s, pioneering the use of instantaneous disk recording for that purpose and eventually depositing in the archive recordings of more than 4,000 folk songs. Along the way he found time to conduct notorious verbal duels with his critics and detractors, to promote Leadbelly, and to publish seven more books, including his autobiography.

In early 1948 Lomax traveled to Greenville, Mississippi, near his birthplace, for a celebration in his honor. Before the ceremony could begin, he suffered a massive heart attack and died two days later, on January 26, 1948.

See also MUSIC: Cowboy Music.

Nolan Porterfield
Bowling Green, Kentucky

Lomax Family Papers. Center for American History, University of Texas at Austin. Lomax, John, and Alan Lomax. *Cowboy Songs and Other Frontier Ballads.* New York: Collier Books, 1986. Porterfield, Nolan. *Last Cavalier: The Life and Times of John A. Lomax.* Urbana: University of Illinois Press, 1996.

MOCK WEDDINGS

The mock wedding is a folk drama that flourishes in the small communities of the Great Plains and is as strong a tradition today as it was more than 100 years ago. While the drama may take a number of forms, all mock weddings are theatrical parodies of the marriage ritual, in which members of a community dress as a wedding entourage and stage a mock ceremony. Players have specific roles—such as bride, groom, minister, ring bearer, and bridesmaids—and there is usually a script, either written or oral, in which several of the players have speaking parts.

Especially in earlier times, this drama was performed informally by teenage girls as playful preparation for marriage. Children of both sexes also performed mock weddings—often called Tom Thumb weddings—under adult supervision, either as a school play or as part of a fund-raising benefit. Similarly, all-male groups, such as volunteer fire departments, would stage "womenless weddings" as a way of raising money.

While these forms are popular in various parts of North America, there is one kind of mock wedding tradition that is stronger in the Great Plains than in the rest of the continent. This drama involves both men and women ac-

tors who cross-dress, and it is characterized by ad-libbing, bawdy behavior, and general horseplay. Often the bride is a very large man, while the groom is a particularly petite woman. Outrageous costumes, masks, and props usually add to the parodic nature of the performances.

Although this form of mock wedding is sometimes staged as a fund-raiser, it is usually part of a larger community celebration of a marriage or, more likely, a milestone wedding anniversary. As part of a couple's twenty-fifth anniversary, for example, friends, family, and neighbors will hold a celebration. The honored couple may be regaled with speeches (often of a "roast" variety) and locally composed songs or poems. Gifts, food, drink, music, and dancing are all part of this celebration.

Unannounced, a mock wedding procession enters the hall and takes over "center stage." Amid laughter, jeers, and expressions of dismay, the procession arranges itself in a typical wedding tableau. The minister usually begins with a "dearly beloved" speech, a parody of the liturgy. This is followed by the saying of vows, which often reveals embarrassing characteristics or stories about the honored couple, a ring ceremony involving a jar-sealer ring or other sight gag, and the kissing of the bride, which sometimes devolves into a wrestling match. The ceremony might be augmented with other scenes, such as the entrance of a girlfriend with babe in arms.

Obviously, this drama honors the anniversary couple through good-natured mockery. But it is also a form of commentary on rural and agrarian life, especially through some of the vows, which often concern the less savory aspects of farm work ("Do you promise to clean the slaughterhouse mess, and not love and honor your husband any less?"). As women are generally the organizers of mock weddings, these dramas tend to comment on the many roles that women must fulfill on the family-run farm or ranch. The cross-dressing itself emphasizes the blurring of divisions between men's and women's work on the farm. These commentaries are well understood by actors and audience alike.

Michael Taft
American Folklife Center
Library of Congress

Butala, Sharon. *Luna.* Saskatoon: Fifth House, 1988. Taft, Michael. "Folk Drama on the Great Plains: The Mock Wedding in Canada and the United States." *North Dakota History* 56 (1989): 16–23. Taft, Michael. "Men in Women's Clothes: Theatrical Transvestites on the Canadian Prairie." In *Undisciplined Women: Tradition and Culture in Canada,* edited by Pauline Greenhill and Diane Tye. Montreal: McGill-Queen's University Press, 1997: 131–38.

MYTHICAL ANIMALS

The most pervasive mythical animal of the Great Plains is undoubtedly the jackalope. Mounted jackalopes are most often seen hanging from the walls of cafes, taverns, and filling stations throughout the region, while jackalope postcards are a popular tourist item. Most jackalopes have the body and head of a jackrabbit and the antlers of a deer or elk or the horns of a pronghorn antelope, although the "warrior rabbit" of Nebraska and the Dakotas also has pheasant wings and tail feathers. The New Mexico version is sometimes called an "antelabbit."

A large statue of a jackalope is located in Douglas, Wyoming, which claims to be the home of this fabulous beast, the brainchild of two taxidermist brothers, Ralph and Doug Herrick, who created their first one in the 1930s. The antecedents of the jackalope, however, are much older, going back to the Bavarian *wolpertinger* and the French *dahout*. These beasts combine crow or hawk wings, rabbit ears, deer antlers, boar tusks, duck forefeet, rooster hind feet, a foxtail, and a coxcomb, all on a woodchuck body.

A body of lore has grown up around the jackalope: it can mimic the human voice and in earlier times would often sing along with night herding cowboys; jackalopes mate during flashes of lightning; and jackalope milk is credited with the ability to cure everything from rheumatism to snakebite. An exhibit at the Dyche Museum of Natural History on the campus of the University of Kansas displayed not only mounted jackalope and postcards but also a number of mounted cottontail rabbits afflicted with Shope's papillomas, a viral infection that causes skin growths similar to that which forms the outer sheath of the pronghorn on an antelope. Other fabulous creatures reported in the Great Plains include Bigfoot, sighted near McLaughlin, South Dakota, during the early 1980s, and a water monster, nicknamed "SinkHole Sam," which supposedly arose in the early 1950s from an underground cavern in McPherson County, Kansas, when a small lake there was drained.

Most mythical creatures from the Plains are actual animals that have achieved exaggerated proportions, such as stories of snakes the size of boa constrictors. Obvious hoaxes are the postcard versions of giant grasshoppers or saddled jackrabbits being ridden by cowboys, while stories of giant catfish that reside in the deepest waters of the reservoirs that dot the Plains are told for truth. Also told for truth are reports of animals that were once prevalent before being hunted to regional extinction in parts of the Plains, such as bear or mountain lions or wolves.

Finally, individual animals have sometimes taken on mythic status, such as the elusive white mustang that roamed the Central Plains in the last century, or the "Murder Steer" of the southwestern Plains celebrated in folk song. Apparently based on an actual quarrel and gunfight that resulted from an ownership dispute during a roundup, the steer was branded MURDER and set free, whereupon for decades it roamed the range from Texas to Montana, a grim reminder of the consequences of greed and anger.

James F. Hoy
Emporia State University

Dance, S. Peter. *Animal Fakes and Frauds*. Maidenhead UK: Sampson Low, 1975.

NICKNAMES

Nicknames have long been especially popular among two groups: self-promoters and those who consider themselves beyond the limits of ordinary rules of conduct. The Plains, especially in the nineteenth century, was filled with characters who were self-promoters and had a disdain for established authority. William F. Cody was first on the list of self-promoters. "Buffalo Bill" said it all; a little of the reality of the Plains and a lot of its myth and folklore is distilled in this nickname. Less well known today is his Wild West show rival, Gordon William Lillie, or "Pawnee Bill."

The great majority of nicknames, however, went to outlaws such as John Henry "Doc" Holliday (who was a real "Doc," a dentist from Georgia). The Doolin Gang (the "Oklahombres") alone boasted "Dynamite Dan" Clifton, George "Bitter Creek" Newcomb, Richard "Little Dick" West, George "Red Buck" Waightman, and William "Little Bill" Raidler. Those on the side of the law rarely had public nicknames; the Earp brothers, the most famous lawmen of the Plains, did not. Two who straddled the fence between law and lawlessness, however, William Barclay "Bat" Masterson and James Butler "Wild Bill" Hickock, were best known by their nicknames.

Since early Plains society to a degree was one of rough equality, it is not surprising that women used nicknames for the same purposes as men. Martha Canary was every bit as much a self-promoter as Buffalo Bill, and she found that calling herself "Calamity Jane" (ostensibly because she got mixed up in so much trouble) did the trick. As with the men, most of the nicknames of women in the Plains went to those who, if not exactly criminals, were at least on the fringes of proper society, especially the prostitutes and madams. Ella Watson, who earned her nickname "Cattle Kate" because she took cattle (often stolen) in payment for her services, and "Diamond Lil" Powers, the Denver madam, are two of the better-known.

Much of the nicknaming in the Plains has disappeared, but it reminds us that nicknames are means of creating images and public personae, and their bearers wear them proudly, often flaunting society's norms in the process.

Edward Callary
Northern Illinois University

PECOS BILL

Pecos Bill is a semilegendary cowboy-culture hero of the Southwest. According to tales, Bill was the strongest, meanest cowboy west of the Pecos River, the greatest roper and bronc buster and gunfighter. He rode a panther that weighed as much as three steers and a yearling and used a rattlesnake for a quirt. He invented calf roping and branding and built the first six-shooter. He could ride a cyclone while rolling a cigarette with one hand. He dug the Rio Grande one droughty year so he could get water from the Gulf of Mexico up to the Pecos. He staked out New Mexico for his ranch spread and used Arizona as a calf pasture. He became the mythical cowboy supertype.

Bill was born in the early 1830s of pioneer Texas stock. When another family settled fifty miles downriver, his family moved west because of the crowded conditions. Bill fell out of the wagon when it was crossing the Pecos, and because there were so many kids in the family, his folks did not miss him until it was too late to go back. Bill was raised by coyotes, and for food he ran down deer and jackrabbits. Bill was ten years old when a cowboy rode up on him while he was squeezing two bears to death to get meat for supper. The cowboy finally convinced Bill that he was human by pointing out that he had no tail. So Bill threw in with humans and began the adventures that have earned him literary and folkloric fame.

Pecos Bill first came to literary life in an article by journalist Edward O'Reilly in *The Century Magazine* in October 1923. O'Reilly claims to have heard stories about Pecos Bill in his childhood and from cowboys sitting around the chuck wagon. In 1934 Mody Boatright took O'Reilly's stories and expanded them into three chapters of his *Tall Tales from Texas Cow Camps*. Because the only known means of dissemination of Pecos Bill tales has been in published literature, some scholars question the validity of Pecos Bill as a true folk character. The final authority on Texas legends, J. Frank Dobie of the Texas Folklore Society, asserted that Pecos Bill was unknown before O'Reilly's article. Dobie based his judgment on his own encyclopedic knowledge of southwestern folklore and on the fact that O'Reilly once admitted, in a lawsuit against a writer who plagiarized his article, that he had invented Pecos Bill. Pecos Bill seems to have been more the product of journalism than folklore.

F. E. Abernethy
Stephen F. Austin State University

Boatright, Mody. *Tall Tales from Texas Cow Camps*. Dallas: Southwest Press, 1934. Botkin, B. A. "The Saga of Pecos Bill." In *A Treasury of American Folklore*. New York: Crown Publishers, Inc., 1944: 180–85. O'Reilly, Edward. "The Saga of Pecos Bill." *The Century Magazine* 106 (1923): 827–33.

PERSONAL EXPERIENCE NARRATIVES

Personal experience narratives are those that relate an event from the first-person perspective. In the folk tradition of the Great Plains, such narratives have been preserved and transmitted in a variety of modes—via letters and diaries as well as orally—and often function to document the history of the region in miniature.

The most significant contrast between personal experience narratives and other folk-narrative genres has to do with the sense of "private ownership" often attached to personal experience narratives. While other narrative genres follow fairly stable structural and thematic patterns, personal experience narratives—being rooted in the teller's own experiences and perceptions—tend to be idiosyncratic in their form and content, although such narratives can become more traditional in the sense that their form often stabilizes with repetition. Thus, one of the critical functions of personal experience narratives is the role they play in shaping and conveying the identity, values, and aesthetics of their respective tellers. Personal experience narratives play a crucial role in constructing identity; they are one of the primary means by which individuals "perform" their identity for others, and also one of the vital ways in which people construct their own internal sense of identity.

Taken collectively, then, such stories can form a life history of one person, or—if examined in broader contexts—they can help shape family, local, and regional histories. In particular, personal experience narratives as a genre have been taken up for study by those interested in women's history; since the dominant tellers of many traditional folk-narrative genres have been men, scholars have looked to personal experience narratives as an overlooked genre by which women express themselves.

This trend is especially important in terms of the Great Plains, as evidenced by the many recently recovered and published diaries by women journeying west during the age of expansion, as well as by more contemporary life histories of Great Plains women. As Lillian Schlissel notes, aside from the Civil War, "no other event of the [nineteenth] century . . . evoked so many personal accounts as the overland passage." While formally different from orally transmitted personal experience narratives, such literary accounts nevertheless form a critical part of our understanding of Great Plains history and heritage. These historical personal experience narratives, represented in diaries and letters, document perceptions of the Plains and early multiethnic encounters. In her comparative study of women's diaries of the westward journey, for example, Schlissel excerpts the journal of Rebecca Ketcham, a single woman traveling from Ithaca, New York, to Oregon to become a schoolteacher, who—upon realizing she has been charged more than other travelers in her group and made to work as well—decides that she "shall find more time to write hereafter." Schlissel also relates the story of Clara Brown, a slave who—after purchasing her own freedom and setting up a laundry in the mining camps of Colorado—sponsored wagon trains to help other freed slaves to migrate west after the Civil War. These narratives include evocative descriptions of the Plains during this era that capture the sense of newness and inspiration they could evoke, such as this passage recorded by Lydia Allen Rudd during her crossing in 1852: "Left the Missouri river for our long journey across the wild uncultivated plains. . . . As we left the river bottom and ascended the bluffs the view from them was handsome! In front of us as far as vision could reach extended the green hills covered with fine grass."

Many of the personal narratives recounted in such texts can be found in oral tradition and family histories as well. The multitude of similar narratives suggests that the stories are probably apocryphal; even so, they can be very accurate barometers of historical development and change. One such narrative has become so prevalent that it earned its own title of sorts, "Goldilocks on the Oregon Trail." The story recounts the allegedly historical fact of a Native American chief becoming so enamored of a young woman (who invariably has beautiful blonde or red hair) that he offers the men in the party an entire herd of horses, cattle, or some other treasure in exchange for the "exotic" beauty. While this story is told in many families as "true," it clearly cannot be documented; nevertheless, its popularity and themes tell us much about how both early settlers and their contemporary descendants wish to remember, or imagine, Native American reactions to white encroachment. Captivity narratives—again, whether transmitted verbally or in writing—also document one side of the story of early encounters. As such, these types of narrative, true or not, become a significant part of our understanding of Plains history.

Since the inception of the American Folklore Society in 1888, folklorists have been interested in documenting and preserving the customs and oral traditions of Plains Indians, an interest that has resulted in fieldwork recordings and transcriptions that work to balance out Anglo-American narratives of settlement. One of the great ethical dilemmas in early fieldwork with Native Americans, however, was that fieldworkers' own biases led them either to misunderstand or deliberately misrepresent their informants' narratives. Contemporary folklorists and anthropologists collecting personal experience narratives from individuals of all groups, but particularly from traditionally underrepresented groups, are making a more concerted effort to collaborate with their informants in a reciprocal way that allows the person's words to stand on their own. Anthropologist Sally McBeth's collaborative work with Shoshone elder Essie Burnett Horne, for example, represents an attempt to voice a traditionally underrepresented aspect of Great Plains history in as direct and unmediated a way as possible. Horne's life story, which begins on the Wind River Reservation in Wyoming, traces the development of one woman's pan-Indian and pan-Plains identity through her years as a student at the Haskell Indian School in Lawrence, Kansas, to her becoming a teacher herself at Indian schools in Oklahoma and North Dakota, before retiring to the White Earth (Chippewa) Reservation in Minnesota. All along she offers a counternarrative to the Indian schools' policy of assimilation by showing how, instead, the schools allowed "multitribal alliances" to be forged.

Thus, the personal experience narrative, while seemingly simple and limited in scope, can lend tremendous insight not only into the identity of a single person but into the history of the Great Plains itself.

See also AFRICAN AMERICANS: "Aunt" Clara Brown / GENDER: Captivity Narratives.

Rosemary V. Hathaway
University of Northern Colorado

Horne, Esther Burnett, and Sally McBeth. *Essie's Story: The Life and Legacy of a Shoshone Teacher.* Lincoln: University of Nebraska Press, 1998. Schlissel, Lillian. *Women's Diaries of the Westward Journey.* New York: Schocken Books, 1982. Stahl, Sandra Dolby. *Literary Folkloristics and the Personal Narrative.* Bloomington: Indiana University Press, 1989.

PLAINS INDIAN NARRATIVES

For the Indian peoples of the Plains, narratives, or what are often referred to as oral traditions, convey their most cherished values and contribute to the perpetuation of their worlds. The narratives encompass a variety of categories, two of the most prominent being stories of creation and tales of human heroes. While recognizing the rich variation of narratives that issue from the tribal diversity of the region, it can be generalized that creation stories typically involve powerful mythic beings, often identified by animal names, who transform a dangerous world and prepare it for the coming of the human peoples. In the "earth diver" accounts among the Arapahos, Blackfoot, and Crows, for example, mud is brought forth from the bottom of a primordial sea by a waterbird and, with a small piece of the earth, Coyote, or Old Man, fashions the landscape, creates other animals and plants, helps establish various customs and institutions, and ultimately molds from the earth and gives life to the first human beings. These ancient personages simultaneously embrace the traits and qualities of human, animal, and spiritual beings, and, through their deeds, display tremendous transformative powers.

Paramount among these creation mythic beings is the trickster, known by the Blackfoot as Napi or Old Man, by the Crows as Isaahkawuattee or Old Man Coyote, by the Lakotas as Iktomi or Spider, and by many tribes simply as the Coyote. While acknowledged as a benevolent creator, the trickster can also exhibit a self-serving character. Old Man Coyote might attempt to apply deception and trickery to gain a free meal, the woman of his dreams, or some other object of his desires. Yet Coyote's elaborate schemes to outwit an opponent are just as likely to end in failure, with himself being duped by his own trickery and made to look foolish.

Hero tales express the ideals of courage, brotherhood, generosity, and self-effacing valor. In the "Scar Face" (or "Burnt Face") stories of the Blackfoot or Crows, for example, the protagonist finds himself disfigured, poor, and ostracized, and consequently unable to obtain full adult status and marry. Alone, he sets out on a great journey to face seemingly overwhelming obstacles and challenges. Because of his bravery, generosity, and "heart," Scar Face receives a guardian spirit and its powerful assistance, his physical shortcomings are removed and any antagonists overcome, his family position is restored, he is allowed to marry, and he goes on to live a full and bountiful life. In the Blackfoot story, Scar Face, like other culture heroes, also brings an important ceremonial institution, the Sun Dance, to his people.

Embedded within the oral traditions are essential values and discernible lessons. Key among these values is the understanding that the world and its many inhabitants are spiritually endowed and maintained, that the animal peoples share in a fundamental kinship with the human peoples, and that reciprocity is the means by which one should relate to other kinsmen, whether human or animal. An elk is addressed as a "brother" and will offer its meat to a hunter when properly respected. An eagle can become a "father" as a result of the food and water sacrifices offered during a vision quest, and, from the spiritual medicine bestowed during the vision, the eagle can guide, nurture, and bring health to a person throughout his life. From the narratives one learns the likely consequences of being a self-serving Coyote, and from the hero tales one is encouraged to seek the assistance of a guardian spirit and strive to benefit others.

Because the narratives of the Plains Indian emanate from an oral-based medium, the act of storytelling is an essential component of the story. In the past, a storyteller had to have the right to tell stories, typically having inherited the authority. Both men and women could become accomplished storytellers. For most tribes it was only during the winter season, from the first frost in the fall until the first thunder heard in the spring, that the stories of Coyote should be told. Again, acknowledging variation from storyteller to storyteller, it can be said that among the various styles and techniques exhibited by storytellers were the use of repetition of phrases to signal key actions within the narrative, the singing of associated songs, the dramatic use of intonation and pauses, the accentuation of body movement and hand gesturing, and the requirement that listeners of the story affirm their involvement in the story by periodically saying aloud, *ée* (yes), or motioning in some other fashion. Should the storyteller fail to receive such acknowledgments, the telling would immediately cease for the evening.

The act of storytelling is made particularly potent through the use of Native language. For example, when told in the Crow language, the words of the story are understood as having the power to bring forth and manifest that which is being spoken. This pivotal notion is conveyed in the Crow term *dasshússua*, literally meaning "breaking with the mouth." That which comes though the mouth has the power to affect the world. The understanding of the creative power of language, coupled with the various techniques used by storytellers, encourages listeners to become participants within the story, traveling the same trails alongside the Coyote or Scar Face.

In addition to disseminating the knowledge and wisdom brought forth by the heroic and mythic figures celebrated in the narratives, oral traditions have another essential role. The narratives help re-create and revitalize the worlds of the Plains Indians. In the act of telling of the deeds of Coyote and Scar Face, that which is conveyed in word and gesture is brought to life, viewed, and engaged in by the participants in the oral tradition. A landscape is renewed and a people are reinvigorated. Today, the telling of the oral traditions remains an essential act of tribal affirmation, identity,

and perpetuation, and is a testament to the continued vitality of the Plains Indian life.

See also LITERARY TRADITIONS: Oral Traditions / NATIVE AMERICANS: Crows / RELIGION: Sun Dance.

Rodney Frey
University of Idaho

Dorsey, George. *Traditions of the Arapaho*. 1903. Lincoln: University of Nebraska Press, 1997. Lowie, Robert. *Myths and Traditions of the Crow Indians*. 1918. Lincoln: University of Nebraska Press, 1993. Wissler, Clark, and D. C. Duvall. *Mythology of the Blackfoot Indians*. 1909. Lincoln: University of Nebraska Press, 1995.

PLANT LORE

The uses of native plants of the Great Plains for food, medicine, and utilitarian purposes were many and of profound importance to the Native Americans. Plant lore has declined dramatically since European American settlement, and the majority of foods and virtually all medicines today are imported into the region.

The Great Plains has more than 3,000 plant species. All Native American tribes of the region used numerous plant species, totaling in the hundreds. Most of the knowledge of their uses for food, medicine, and utilitarian purposes was held in oral histories, and many Native American uses continue today on Plains reservations. Anthropologists and ethnobotanists have recorded much information on the topic. Not surprisingly, most plants utilized were prairie plants, although some trees and shrubs also had important uses.

More native prairie plants (over 200) have been documented as being used by Plains Indians for medicine than for any other use. Some, such as yarrow (*Achillea millefolium*) and the purple coneflower (*Echinacea angustifolia*), were widely used for their general medicinal qualities. Others, such as locoweed (*Astragalus*), with its toxic amounts of alkaloids and selenium, were used more successfully to treat both internal and external maladies. Most people knew the many common uses of plants, but there were also highly trained individuals, medicine men and medicine women, who had very specific knowledge about plants and used them in spiritual ceremonies for healing.

In most cases, the belief system was that the spirit healed the individual, and that the plant was a vehicle for this process. The major medicinal plant cures of Plains Indian tribes have plausible scientific explanations for their use and effectiveness. Most of them contain active medicinal constituents. It is extraordinary that many of these uses were discovered. Certainly, much learning occurred through trial and error, but Native Americans also believed that knowledge could be gained through dreams and visions, and plant lore was of course handed down, orally, over generations. In fact, the healing systems of Native Americans are ancient and suggest links to Asia. For example, the Pawnees burned the stems of yarrow and leadplant (*Amorpha canescens*) as short punks placed on rheumatic points to relieve pain, a practice known as "moxabus-

tion," which today is almost completely associated with Asian medicine. Only a very few medicinal plants used by Native Americans were adopted by European American immigrants, primarily because the traditions were vastly different and few European Americans were willing to give credence to Native American learning. One that was adopted was the purple coneflower, which has been imported into Europe and more recently been made available commercially in the United States as an immune system stimulant, used primarily to ward off colds.

Food uses of native plants were vitally important to the Great Plains Indians, and played an essential dietary role. More than 120 native prairie plants were used for food. Many plants were used for seasoning, flavors, tea, or nutritional needs (greens in the spring were used to ward off scurvy). The most important native food plant was the prairie turnip (*Psoralea esculenta*). This starchy, leguminous root was eaten as a staple or added to bison stew. It was also dried and traded or stored. The prairie turnip was so important to the Omahas that they determined the route of their summer buffalo hunt in the High Plains by the locations where the women could find the plant. Since wild food procurement was primarily women's work, little of this knowledge was passed on to European immigrants because interaction between Native American women and women settlers rarely occurred.

Native Americans had many other uses for wild plants, such as cattails and rushes for mats, white sage (*Artemisia ludoviciana*) and eastern redcedar (*Juniperus virginiana*) for ceremonial incense, and trees for lodges and firewood. Of course, Native American women had long cultivated corn, beans, squash, sunflowers, and other crops. With European American settlement, large numbers of new cultivars were introduced for farming and gardening, but the diversity and variety have dramatically decreased over the decades, and farmers now only grow a handful of crops (and indeed only a few genetic varieties of a small number of crops). Only a small number of the native plants originally used by Plains Indians —wild plums (*Prunus americana*), chokecherries (*Prunus virginiana*), wild grapes (*Vitis riparia*), and other—are now used for jams, jellies, and wine by the wider population.

Kelly Kindscher
University of Kansas

Kindscher, Kelly. *Edible Wild Plants of the Prairie: An Ethnobotanical Guide*. Lawrence: University Press of Kansas, 1987. Kindscher, Kelly. *Medicinal Wild Plants of the Prairie: An Ethnobotanical Guide*. Lawrence: University Press of Kansas, 1992. Moerman, Daniel E. *Native American Ethnobotany*. Portland OR: Timber Press, 1998.

PLAY PARTY

The play party, a preplanned traditional dance without instruments, was a recreational activity of teenagers and young adults that was once common across the Great Plains and the entire United States. People attending play parties played singing and action games such as "musical chairs" and many other games involving male-female interactions, emphasizing socialization and interpersonal relationships rather than competition, while they shared refreshments and conversation.

Early folklorists, including Ben Botkin, Vance Randolf, and L. D. Ames, analyzed the play party and concluded that it flourished in Anglo-American culture on the western frontier because of the repressive influence of the puritan ethic, especially its opposition to musical instruments. As early as 1949, folklorists began to challenge this widely accepted description by noting that the lack of instruments at the play party might well have been caused simply by a shortage of instruments. Ben Botkin further maintains that the songs of the play party came to the Great Plains with the cattle drives through Texas and Oklahoma, two states where the parties were very popular. He also made the point that despite the play party's Anglo-American origins, African Americans and Native Americans participated in them as well, particularly in the Southern Great Plains. A 1972 article based on field interviews conducted in the mid-1960s concluded that the play party probably existed across America, persisted after the passage of the frontier, experienced revivals that often included instruments, created a complex poetic, and lived on as a substantial contribution to American children's games and folk music. Since that time, however, it seems that the tradition of the play party has faded.

Keith Cunningham
Northern Arizona University

Ames, L. D. "The Missouri Play Party." *Journal of American Folklore* 24 (1911): 295–318. Cunningham, Keith. "Another Look at the Play Party." *Affword* 2 (1972): 12–23. Randolf, Vance. "The Ozark Play-Party." *Journal of American Folklore* 42 (1929): 201–32.

PROVERBS AND PROVERBIAL SAYINGS

The proverbial language of the Great Plains is as varied as the landscape and culture of this vast area of North America that stretches from Canada to Mexico. With English being the dominant language, traditional proverbs and their wisdom, as well as proverbial sayings with their colorful metaphors, were brought to this continent by British settlers and abound throughout the United States and Canada. In fact, such standard texts as "The early bird catches the worm," "First come, first served," and "Honesty is the best policy," as well as such common proverbial sayings as "A feather in your cap," "Hit the nail on the head," and "On the tip of my tongue" are known and used in oral and written communication in all parts of the world where English is spoken. They belong to the basic stock of proverbial utterances in the English language, and they certainly appear frequently in the verbal communication of people living in the Great Plains.

Naturally, not all proverbial texts can be traced back to British sources. Every region, state, province, or country also develops its own homegrown metaphors, which through repeated use develop into new proverbs and sayings. This is also true for the Great Plains,

of course, but it must be noted that it is usually extremely difficult to ascertain the specific regional origin and distribution of proverbial texts. Fortunately, the American Dialect Society undertook a major proverb collection exercise between 1945 and 1985 that resulted in 250,000 references, which have now been registered and annotated in *A Dictionary of American Proverbs* (1992). This massive collection identifies whether a particular text is known generally throughout the United States and/or Canada, and if it is not, locates the state or province where it was collected and registered. Impressive as this information might be, it is nevertheless of limited value since only English-language texts were collected. Foreign-language proverbs and sayings from the various immigrant groups and Native Americans are lacking, and the same is true for many texts from ethnic groups such as African Americans, Mexican Americans, Volga Germans, and Ukrainians in Canada.

For some states, small special proverb collections have been assembled, notably for Colorado, Kansas, Nebraska, and Texas. As expected, they contain primarily standard English proverbs, but there are at least some truly regional texts among them that reflect the life and mores of the inhabitants of the Plains, with its ranches, prairies, wheat fields, horses, and cattle. A few examples from Colorado are: "Money greases the axle," "Keep your feet in the stirrups," "To not have sense enough to pound sand into a rat hole," "As cold as yesterday's pancakes," "Only fools and tenderfeet predict the weather in Colorado," "As big as a horse and almost as smart," and "Lower than a snake's belly in a wagon track." Among the texts collected in Kansas are: "You can build a house but you have to make a home," "Mud thrown is ground lost," and "A dry well pumps no water." From Nebraska stem such proverbs and sayings as "Where there's room in the heart, there's room in the house," "Don't holler before you're hurt," and "As safe as a cow in the stockyards." And the large state of Texas might have originated such proverbial utterances as "Don't waste your ammunition on a dead duck," "To have about as much use for (something) as a hog has for a sidesaddle," "So lazy that grass grows under your feet," and "Don't kick until you're spurred." Of course, there are also such stereotypical sayings as "Rich as a Texan and as full of hot air," "Cold as a well-digger's lunch in Nebraska," and "Hot as corn in Kansas in August." As can be seen, such regional sayings often contain their dose of humor and ridicule, and they can quickly be changed by substituting one state's name for another. Furthermore, it must be kept in mind that the geographical borders of states or provinces do not hinder proverbs and sayings from spreading beyond them. It is extremely difficult to pinpoint the precise origin of any given saying, and it is better to speak of proverbs that are current in a particular region rather than claiming too quickly that they are indigenous to it.

The situation is just as vexing when one considers the proverbs and sayings that the

various immigrant groups brought to the Great Plains. Books have been assembled of Mexican and Spanish proverbs in current use in Spanish in New Mexico, Texas, and southern Colorado. Among this rich verbal lore are proverbs (in English translation) like "Don't look for three feet on a cat," "Whoever is burnt by milk is even afraid of cottage cheese," and "Faces we see, hearts we don't know." The Germans brought along proverbs like "The morning hour has gold in its mouth," "Old love does not rust," and "You can't make good hay from poor grass," and the Swedish settlers still say "Dust is always dust, however near to heaven it may be blown," "A tall house is empty under the rafters," and "No one thinks of the snow that fell last year." Czech immigrants employ proverbs like "Custom is rust that mocks at every file," "The farmer's footprints make the field fertile," and "Young people and dogs take many useless steps in an hour." Among Chinese railroad laborers were such proverbs as "Even dust, if accumulated enough, will form a mountain," "Through old things we learn new things," and "Ten fingers cannot be all the same size." Jewish traders and merchants brought along such Yiddish proverbs as "Dumplings in a dream are not dumplings but a dream," "Words should be weighed and not counted," and "One cannot live by another's wits." And the Ukrainians in Canada still use proverbs like "The plowman has no time for mischief," "The farmer's hands are muddy and black, but his loaves are sweet and white," and "Another's fur coat does not warm you as your own." While most of these proverbs are cited in their original language, some of them have been translated into English over time and have gained a more general currency. This is especially true for the German proverb *Der Apfel fällt nicht weit vom Stamm* and the proverbial saying *Das Kind mit dem Bade ausschütten*, which have become quite well known throughout North America as "The apple does not fall far from the tree" and "To throw the baby out with the bath water."

There are also, of course, the proverbs of African Americans who moved north from Texas all the way to Canada trying to escape prejudice and looking for jobs. Some of their proverbs go back to slavery, such as "Every bell you hear is not the dinner bell" (there was also the "rising bell" in the morning that called the slaves to work) and "The quicker death, the quicker heaven." Other proverbial wisdom from the black experience is shown in such texts as "Scraping on the bottom of the meal bin is mighty poor music," "A robin's song is not pretty to the worm," and "When bugs give a party they never ask the chickens."

But while there are at least some collections of African American proverbs and proverbial sayings from the Plains (primarily Texas), very little is known about the proverbial language of Native Americans. Anthropologists, folklorists, and linguists have hitherto registered only very few proverbs of Native Americans. It is even argued that their tribal languages are basically void of any proverbial language. This is proven false by at least the few texts that have been collected and annotated. From the Crow Indians of Montana are such texts as "When pine needles turn yellow" (a proverbial phrase characterizing an impossibility), "To be like the one who wanted to catch the porcupine" (referring to a person who persists in a hopeless enterprise), and "To be like the turtle that was thrown into the water" (applied to people feigning dislike for what they really crave). The entire stock of Native American proverbs collected thus far does not even number 300, and much work remains to be done to register this treasure trove of folk wisdom among Native Americans of the Great Plains and elsewhere.

The proverbial language of the Great Plains is thus a "mixed bag," to use a folk metaphor. While many texts can be traced back to Anglo-American traditions, the various immigrant groups, as well as Native Americans and African Americans, have also added much linguistic, cultural, and ethnic diversity to this basic stock of proverbs and proverbial sayings. Field research among the inhabitants of the Great Plains would uncover many more hitherto unrecorded proverbs and proverbial sayings that bear witness to the rich and diverse cultural traditions of the heartland of North America.

Wolfgang Mieder
University of Vermont

Glazer, Mark, ed. *A Dictionary of Mexican American Proverbs.* Westport CT: Greenwood Press, 1987. Mieder, Wolfgang. *American Proverbs: A Study of Texts and Contexts.* Bern Switzerland: Peter Lang, 1989. Mieder, Wolfgang, Stewart A. Kingsbury, and Kelsie B. Harder, eds. *A Dictionary of American Proverbs.* New York: Oxford University Press, 1992.

QUILTING

Patchwork quilts came to the Great Plains with the first European settlers who carried them in wagons and on pack mules. During the westward migration, quilts served not only as utilitarian bedding—both as pallets and covers—but as shelter when draped as overnight, tentlike structures and sometimes as doors and room dividers in the rude homes that were erected hastily in the early months of settlement.

Women traveling across the Great Plains during the mid–nineteenth century on the Oregon Trail left many records of quilts in their diaries, letters, and memoirs. Later in the century, when Kansas, Nebraska, and Oklahoma became destinations rather than mile markers on the journey to Oregon or California, women again recorded details of the quilts they brought with them to their new homes. Among surviving writings, however, there is no mention of actual quilt making during the westward migration. There are some references to mending, sewing, and knitting on the road, but not to quilt making. Most healthy emigrants preferred to walk rather than ride in wagons. Moreover, the bumpy ride inside covered wagons made it virtually impossible to sew the precise seams

Star of Bethlehem quilt, made by Maria L. Gear Mook (1833–1914), Johnson County, Nebraska

required for making quilt blocks. On the other hand, women resumed quilt-making activities quickly after reaching their destinations, some almost as soon as they had a roof over their head. For example, according to family tradition, Clarissa Palmer, a homesteader in northwestern Nebraska, fashioned a silk crazy quilt from scraps her family sent to her during the first year she "sat" her claim.

Quilts and quilt makers in the Great Plains are notable for their conservative character and for their tendency to reliably reflect national trends in quilt making. This is not surprising because, by the time women in the Great Plains began making quilts in large numbers during the last quarter of the nineteenth century, an increasing number of national magazines had begun to standardize quilt-making styles and patterns. Women's magazines such as *Godey's Ladies Book*, *Delineator*, *Ladies' Home Journal*, *Woman's Home Companion*, and *McCall's* featured quilt patterns, articles about quilt making, and nostalgic images of old quilts. By the 1920s, newspapers—most notably the *Kansas City Star* but also the *Omaha World-Herald* and Dallas's *Semi-Weekly Farm News*—presented traditional and original quilt patterns on a regular basis and offered patterns that could be ordered from the paper's home office. The availability of patterns from newspapers had an enormous standardizing influence on quilt patterns during the first half of the twentieth century.

The agricultural fair, an established American tradition by the time Kansas, Nebraska, Oklahoma, and the Dakotas were settled, also helped nationalize and standardize aesthetics. Fairs and expositions were eagerly awaited annual events in all settled areas and provided friendly competition, recognition, and an opportunity to display one's needlework skills. Prizewinning quilts, no doubt, inspired imitation.

Quilt making remained a popular pastime in the United States throughout the nineteenth century. In the early 1900s, while much of the country turned to mass-produced woven blankets, the largely rural population of the Great Plains continued to use handmade quilts for bedding. Consequently, quilt making remained a vital part of everyday life in the Plains until the 1940s. Many present-day quilters from the Dakotas to Texas recall learning to sew by piecing blocks for a patchwork quilt. For generations, girls were taught to sew and to quilt by their mothers and grandmothers and were expected to do their share in making quilts and clothing for the family. Young women made quilts in anticipation of the day when they would have homes of their own. Many quilters born during the early 1900s readily recall growing up with a quilt in progress in a quilting frame in their homes. Often the frames were suspended by ropes from the ceiling and were raised and lowered as necessary.

Because quilting had never gone out of style

and quilts had never gone out of use in the largely agricultural Great Plains, the surge of print media attention given to quilts in the first quarter of the twentieth century only reinforced the unflagging interest in quilt making held by rural quilters of the region.

Most surviving nineteenth-century quilts from the Great Plains are star patterns. Star patterns (single and multiple) remained the most popular design among American quilters of European descent until the 1930s. The names of star patterns sometimes varied from state to state: for example, the Bethlehem Star became the Lone Star in Texas, and a four-pointed star pattern became known as Rocky Road to Kansas.

Northern Plains Indian women favored dazzling, large, single-star patterns for their quilts. Quilting, introduced by the wives of missionaries in the late 1800s, sparked a new cultural practice among Plains Indian women of the Dakotas and Montana. Quilts eventually replaced buffalo robes in the wrapping of the dead. Star quilts were, and are, given in celebration at births and to honor loved ones at graduations. And quilts—mainly star designs—always serve as a focal point in the Native Americans' customary "giveaway."

Other quilt patterns and styles enjoyed periods of popularity in the Plains. For example, log cabin quilts and crazy quilts were fad styles that swept the region and the nation between 1870 and 1900. Plains women more often made their crazy quilts of practical wool or cotton fabrics, instead of the silks favored by eastern women. During the 1920s and 1930s a hexagon-based mosaic pattern called Grandmother's Flower Garden, as well as the Double Wedding Ring, Dresden Plate, and Nine Patch patterns rose in popularity. They remained among the most prevalent patterns for quilters of European descent until the 1960s. A resurgence of interest in quilting began in the 1970s and continues in the twenty-first century with quilters from Texas, Kansas, and Nebraska at the forefront of the revival.

See also GENDER: Quilting Circles.

Patricia C. Crews
University of Nebraska–Lincoln

Brackman, Barbara, Jennie A. Chinn, Gayle R. Davis, Terry Thompson, Sara Reimer Farley, and Nancy Hornback. *Kansas Quilts and Quilters.* Lawrence: University Press of Kansas, 1993. Crews, Patricia Cox, and Ronald Naugle, eds. *Nebraska Quilts and Quilt Makers.* Lincoln: University of Nebraska Press, 1991. Yabsley, Suzanne. *Texas Quilts, Texas Women.* College Station: Texas A&M University Press, 1984.

ROADSIDE ATTRACTIONS

What most people mean by "roadside attraction" is a site that has in some way been "framed" and consciously presented to a public audience for visitation and viewing. It is a "roadside" phenomenon both in the obvious sense that it exists in some proximity to regular routes of public movement and in the sense that it has the particular capacity to draw, at least briefly, a traveler's attention away from the goal of reaching an intended destination. The modern roadside attraction

Garden of Eden, Lucas, Kansas

has precursors in such features as wayside chapels along pilgrimage routes and sales exhibits of regional souvenirs along early railway lines (as in some of the Harvey House hotels on the Santa Fe Railroad), but it is primarily a creature of the modern highway and road system. Although roadside attractions are components of a touristic landscape, they are in most cases not primary destinations for recreational travelers. Characteristically, such attractions evoke spontaneous reactions and relatively brief stops rather than preplanned and extended visits.

There are many locations that might or might not be considered a roadside attraction, depending on the qualities one chooses to emphasize. The Great Plains has one of the most notable such cases in Mount Rushmore National Memorial, located in the Black Hills of western South Dakota. While some might argue that its official status as a premier National Park Service site disqualifies it as a "mere" roadside attraction, a good case could also be made that it is the epitome of this landscape genre. The monumental sculptures are elaborately "framed" for viewing and have no other purpose than to induce wonder and perhaps even awe. At the same time, Mount Rushmore is not the primary destination for at least most long-range travelers, and a couple of hours at the site is probably the limit for the typical visitor.

Mount Rushmore has one other quality that links it to the less-spectacular roadside attractions of the Great Plains and elsewhere. Central to its appeal is its inherent strangeness. The uncanny apparition of the gigantic presidential visages in a "wilderness" context is, depending on one's tastes, sublime, inspiring (even religiously so), bizarre, tacky, kitschy, or even frightening or repulsive. Roadside attractions in general are typified by some form of exceptional strangeness or landscape dissonance, though few to the degree of this na-

tional monument. It is this quality that sets roadside attractions apart from some other features of the landscape that might prompt travelers to pause, such as scenic overlooks, historical markers, or war memorials. As moments of arresting strangeness, roadside attractions may be human constructions, like Mount Rushmore, or natural features, like the nation's first national monument, Devils Tower, in northeastern Wyoming, a strikingly uncanny geological formation.

These two monuments are particularly grand examples of one subset of such attractions—the officially endorsed or civic sites that sometimes become signature emblems of the communities that maintain them. The Corn Palace in downtown Mitchell, South Dakota, is a more modest and so perhaps a better representative of this type. With fantastically orientalist architecture and an exterior covered in annually changing murals made entirely of South Dakota corn, seeds, and grains, the building functions mainly as a civic auditorium, sports arena, and agricultural exposition site.

Along with these more or less official attractions, two other types may be distinguished, the commercial and the folk or vernacular. Commercial roadside attractions are perhaps the most pervasive form of this landscape characteristic and the type most associated with the term in the popular imagination. The notion of the "tourist trap," suggesting hokum, hucksterism, and crass commercial interests, is evoked by many sites of this sort, giving them an air of tawdriness and sly deceit. The nineteenth-century dime museum and the carnival sideshow are precursors to this brand of attraction, and the rhetoric of excess—the biggest, the oldest, the first, and so on—is especially prominent in them. Many Plains towns have built gigantic animal sculptures to attract travelers. Jamestown, North Dakota, has a sixty-ton concrete buffalo, reputed to be "the world's largest." Not to be outdone, New Salem, North Dakota, takes pride in "Salem Sue," the world's largest Holstein cow, and in the same state the town of Dunseith is the home to "W'eel," the world's largest turtle. While many travelers perceive such sites only as roadside clutter and tasteless purveyors of garish come-ons, for others they have an appeal as nostalgically seedy alternatives to the plastic, franchised, strip-mall-studded roadside landscape that has become increasingly pervasive in the Great Plains, as elsewhere in North America.

In some cases, sites of this sort have become so notable and elaborated as to transcend the dubious associations of their origins. Wall Drug—now virtually a town unto itself—is perhaps the most famous instance of this phenomenon in the region. Located, like the Corn Palace and Mount Rushmore, along the Interstate 90 corridor in South Dakota (one of the most fertile routes for roadside attractions in the Plains), Wall Drug is especially famous for its novel advertising strategy of posting mileage signs at remote locations around the country and even abroad.

A third subset of roadside attractions includes those sites that arise in vernacular or folkloric contexts and from primarily personal rather than commercial or civic motivations. In many cases they are the products of individual obsession, hobbyist enthusiasm, or private commemoration, and they frequently reflect a folk art aesthetic of playful bricolage. While many such sites remain fairly obscure and available mainly to local travelers, those that become known to a wider public do so, at least at first, more by word-of-mouth communication than by conscious design and advertising. Often produced from inexpensive, low-tech, or recycled materials and with skills learned on the job or through a hobby, such sites become true roadside attractions to the degree that they achieve sufficient flamboyance and public visibility to set them off dramatically from the surrounding landscape.

One of the best-known and most interesting sites in this category is the "Garden of Eden," located in a residential neighborhood of Lucas, Kansas. Growing to remarkable proportions over the years from 1905 until the death of its creator in 1933, the Garden of Eden was produced by Samuel Dinsmoor as a monumental folk sculpture display devoted to biblical and early-twentieth-century political themes (e.g., antitrust advocacy). With its large figures constructed of concrete and overlaid with a sculptural layer of limestone plaster, the Garden is one of the masterpieces of this surprisingly common genre of display environment. It is an excellent example of a personal vision reaching sufficient proportions and notoriety to become one of the premier roadside attractions of the Great Plains.

It is debatable whether the Great Plains is better supplied than other parts of North America with sites of the sort described here. However, it does seem that such instances of cultural strangeness and landscape dissonance stand out with special vividness against the (relatively speaking) neutral background of Plains roadsides.

See also ARCHITECTURE: Roadside Architecture / IMAGES AND ICONS: Corn Palace; Mount Rushmore National Memorial; Wall Drug.

John Dorst
University of Wyoming

Andrews, J. J. C. *The Well-Built Elephant, and Other Roadside Attractions*. New York: Congdon and Weed, Inc., 1984. Clay, Grady. *Real Places: An Unconventional Guide to America's Generic Landscape*. Chicago: University of Chicago Press, 1994. Marling, Karal Ann. *The Colossus of Roads: Myth and Symbol along the American Highway*. Minneapolis: University of Minnesota Press, 1984.

SEASONAL CELEBRATIONS

Seasonal celebrations and festivals are among humanity's most ancient and enduring traditions. It is often no accident that many of the world's oldest and most important religious holidays coincide with, or are directly related to, the cycles and seasons of the natural world. We have always observed the changing seasons with a mixture of anticipation and dread, knowing that our very survival—a bountiful harvest, plentiful herds, or a successful hunt—depends largely on the whims of Mother Nature. We have always celebrated the seasons with occasions of ritual and festival, both expressing relief and giving thanks for the bounty of the land, brought forth by time and our own hard work.

Similar to the range and variety of its folk beliefs, the seasonal celebrations and festivals of the Great Plains reflect the customs and traditions of the many groups contained within its vast boundaries, taking on a regional flavor through the response of people to their immediate natural world. Like others around the world, the folk of the Great Plains have worked to the rhythms of the land, sometimes confronting unexpectedly harsh and even brutal conditions. Both religious and secular festivals typically mark "seasons of work" having to do with agriculture or the care of animals: hunting, planting, harvesting, breeding stock, moving animals from one pasture to another, shearing sheep, and butchering animals that will not be "wintered over." Agricultural survival in the Great Plains requires not only hard work but delicate timing. Tasks of planting and harvesting seldom can wait but must be timed to the whims of rain and sun.

Hard work, harsh conditions, and delicate timing notwithstanding, the seasons in the Great Plains are also accompanied by equally hard play and merry socializing, especially after the work is done. Special foods, songs, games, and customs attend each seasonal celebration. Food and drink are absolutely necessary elements, along with music and dancing. Historically, Plains folk seemed to enjoy just about any excuse to get together and have fun: parades, races, speeches, contests, dressing up (even cross dressing), role reversals, and general carousing typically accompany seasonal festivals.

Spring in the Plains is a time not only for planting but also for celebrating the end of winter and reveling in the sheer joy of being alive. Although seasonal customs change and sometimes pass away with time, children in parts of the Great Plains still dance and sing around the maypole and make May baskets of spring flowers for their neighbors. Bonfire dancing also once accompanied general spring festivities, especially among Swedes, usually at Easter. Ethnic groups such as the Swedes and the Finns contributed their own unique festivals—such as the celebration of Midsummer's Day—to the cultural mix of the Great Plains.

Seasonal work affords plenty of occasions for festive socializing. Often this is a matter of necessity: it takes more than one hand or one family to finish a harvest on time, and the fruits of that harvest provide the means for socializing. Once-common activities such as cornhusking bees, bean picking, pea shelling, and watermelon feeds provided opportunities for women and children to both work and socialize. The women exchanged news and information and checked out prospective mates for their daughters and sons. Seasonal activities and festivals were, and still are, an important part of community building for Plains folk.

Additionally, seasonal work itself is often intertwined with play in the form of games or contests: Who can pick the most corn or harvest the most wheat? Who's the fastest sheep shearer, the best cowpoke? Who makes the best fruit pie or jam? Who can grow the largest pumpkin? Both rodeos and state and local fairs have evolved as premier events in the Great Plains, designed to demonstrate the level of one's skills and to showcase the bounty of the harvest. Even local churches are lovingly decorated with the fruits of the harvest season. The late summer and fall harvest seasons still provide numerous opportunities for both work and festive play, ending with the final twin harvest celebrations of Halloween, with its puckish and unruly mischief, and Thanksgiving, with its solemn and grateful sharing of harvest bounty.

Although many seasonal celebrations of the Great Plains are similar to those found in other parts of the country, Plains folk nevertheless put their own distinctive stamp on the fun. Independence Day has not been the same in Lewistown, Montana, since two desperados tried to hold up the town in 1884. Each year, the whole town reenacts the dastardly crime, complete with the mock shooting of "Rattlesnake Jake" and his partner, and the unfortunate shooting death of the unlucky citizen who just happened to be in the way.

Christmas celebrations also undergo interesting transformations in the Plains. While Santa Claus normally wears a jolly red suit, he is just as likely to be dressed as a rowdy, rollicking cowboy in the Plains. Good little girls and boys leave cookies and milk for Santa. German children in the Plains make sure to leave three ears of corn, one for each of the Three Wise Men, for Santa's reindeer. Christmas dinner is a lovingly prepared feast, but for Swedes in the Great Plains it is literally a smorgasbord, a custom that dates back at least to the time of the Vikings. Where pines and evergreens are plentiful, expect to find Christmas trees with all the usual trimmings. But in Kansas, where such trees were absent, early Plains settlers creatively wove a "Christmas arch" from which to hang their Christmas stockings and gifts.

Above all, the settlers of the Great Plains were "make do" people when it came to seasonal celebrations and festivals, adapting to the demands of the land and crafting new traditions to honor and celebrate the never-ending transformation and renewal of life in the Plains.

Nikki Bado-Fralick
Iowa State University

Johnson, Dorothy M. "Independence Day, 1884!" *Montana* 8 (1958): 2–7. Sackett, S. J., and William E. Koch, eds. *Kansas Folklore*. Lincoln: University of Nebraska Press, 1961. Welsch, Roger L. *A Treasury of Nebraska Pioneer Folklore*. Lincoln: University of Nebraska Press, 1966.

SHIVAREES

Known also as serenading or belling, a shivaree is a noisy, rowdy, and often bawdy community celebration of a marriage. On the wedding night, friends and neighbors would gather outside the couple's bedroom window banging pots and pans, playing musical instruments, sometimes shooting off guns, and demanding entrance to the newlyweds' home. Once inside, the group might play practical jokes on the couple, such as taking the labels off cans, tying bells to the bedsprings, or bringing livestock into the house. The tradition might also include kidnapping one or both of the newlyweds, tying them to trees, dunking them in horse troughs, riding them around town, abandoning them in the countryside, or otherwise disrupting and delaying the wedding night. Despite this rough treatment, newlyweds were expected to act as gracious hosts by offering the group food, drink, and hospitality—or by paying the revelers to leave.

While the tradition as practiced in the Plains was usually a celebration in which the community showed its approval of the marriage, the European roots of this custom were often far from benign. The original "charivari" was usually a form of rough justice wherein neighbors showed their displeasure over an unequal marriage, an improper remarriage, adultery, or a marriage in which there was spousal abuse. In this older tradition, the newlyweds might be publicly humiliated (such as forced to ride backward on a donkey), beaten, or even killed. As a custom in the Plains during the nineteenth and early twentieth centuries, however, the shivaree became associated with neighborliness, community spirit, and the recognition of marriage as a stabilizing factor in frontier society.

Michael Taft
American Folklife Center
Library of Congress

Dary, David. *Seeking Pleasure in the Old West*. Lawrence: University Press of Kansas, 1995. Johnson, Loretta T. "Charivari/Shivaree: A European Folk Ritual on the American Plains." *Journal of Interdisciplinary History* 20 (1990): 371–87. Kinsella, W. P. "Dangerous Consequences." In *The Secret of the Northern Lights*. Saskatoon: Thistledown Press, 1998: 55–66.

SIRINGO, CHARLES (1855–1928)

Cowboy, Pinkerton detective, and western author, Charles Angelo Siringo was the first authentic cowboy autobiographer. His books helped popularize the romantic image of the American cowboy. Born on February 7, 1855, in Matagorda County, Texas, Siringo was introduced to the life of a cowboy at a young age. By the age of eleven he was working on Texas ranches, and during the 1870s he drove cattle north on the Chisholm Trail to the Kansas cattle towns of Abilene and Dodge City. During the late 1870s he helped establish the LX Ranch, a large cattle-ranching operation in the Texas Panhandle. While in West Texas, Siringo reportedly met Billy the Kid, and later he led a posse in search of the outlaw. In 1884 Siringo left the LX Ranch and moved to Caldwell, Kansas, where he opened a general merchandise store. With more time on his hands, he began writing about his experiences as a cowboy. Published in 1885, *A Texas Cowboy; or, Fifteen Years on the Hurricane Deck of a*

Spanish Pony was the first cowboy autobiography and a best-seller. Historian J. Frank Dobie called it the most widely read book on cowboy life. In 1886 Siringo went to work for the Pinkerton Detective Agency. For the next twenty-two years he lived an adventurous life, chasing criminals across the West, infiltrating outlaw gangs and labor unions, and serving as a bodyguard for high-profile clients such as "Big Bill" Haywood.

Siringo resigned from the Pinkerton Agency in 1907, returned to his ranch near Santa Fe, New Mexico, and began writing books about his career as a western cowboy and detective. *A Cowboy Detective* (1912), his second book, was originally titled "Pinkerton's Cowboy Detective." Siringo dropped the word Pinkerton from the title and throughout the text after the agency blocked its publication through legal action. Angered by the Pinkerton's legal attack, Siringo lashed out at the company in his third book, *Two Evil Isms, Pinkertonism and Anarchism* (1915). The book was highly critical of methods used by the Pinkertons, accusing the agency of buying off policemen and politicians, bribing juries, intimidating witnesses, and murder. Once again the agency went to court to block the sale and publication of the book. Frustrated with such legal wrangling, Siringo briefly retired from writing in 1916 and took an assignment as a New Mexico Ranger.

Two years of chasing cattle rustlers and horse thieves across the Southwest, however, was enough to convince the aging Siringo to return to writing. In 1919 he published *A Lone Star Cowboy*, and the following year his *History of Billy the Kid* appeared. In 1922 failing health and financial problems forced Siringo to leave his Santa Fe ranch and move to California, where his children lived. Siringo eventually landed in Hollywood, where he had several small roles in Western movies and served as a consultant for Western actor William S. Hart. Siringo's final book, *Riata and Spurs*, was published in 1927.

Siringo had a difficult married life. His first wife died in 1889, leaving him with a young daughter to raise. A second marriage in 1893 to Lillie Thomas ended in divorce after three years (the couple had a son). Two other marriages each lasted only a few months. Siringo died on October 28, 1928, in Altadena, California.

See also IMAGES AND ICONS: Cowboy Culture.

Mark R. Ellis
University of Nebraska at Kearney

Peavy, Charles D. *Charles A. Siringo: A Texas Picaro*. Austin: Steck-Vaughn Co., 1967. Pingenot, Ben E. *Siringo: The True Story of Charles A. Siringo*. College Station: Texas A&M University Press, 1989.

TALL TALES

Called yarns, lies, windies, or bullshit, tall tales are stories of exaggeration that act like verbal practical jokes. Most often, tellers begin their stories as if relating a true incident, but part way through the tale they stretch the facts beyond credulity, thereby "catching" their lis-

teners, who then appear to be gullible fools. Sometimes, tall tales are traded by two or more tellers as a contest to see who can tell the most artful whopper. In all cases, however, the tall tale is a clever mixture of truth and fiction.

Many of these stories have ancient roots and have migrated far and wide. Consider the tall tale of weather that is so cold that speech freezes, so that you have to wait until spring thaw to hear winter conversations. It is a well-known story in the Plains, but it can be traced back as far as Plutarch (347 B.C.) and has been told throughout Europe and North America. Wherever storytellers have encountered extremes of nature, landscape, or human behavior, they have responded by exaggerating these extremes further through tall tales.

At the same time that the tall tale is an international form of folklore, it is also a marker of regionalism. The explanation for this seeming paradox is that each locality chooses only that part of the great pool of stories which best comments on regional conditions. Thus, people of the seacoast tell tall tales about heavy fog, great fish, and canny mariners. Mountain folk tell of "side-hill gougers"—small animals whose left legs are shorter than their right legs so that they can stand upright in hilly country. And people of the forest lie about trees so big that two gangs of loggers can chop on opposite sides without being aware of each other's existence.

It is no surprise, therefore, that Plains people comment upon their land through a similar selection from the international storehouse of lies. Tales of extreme cold, like the frozen conversation, are common, but the extreme variability of flatland weather generates its own kind of stories. The warm chinook winds that rush down the Rockies into the Plains during wintertime create scenes such as a team of horses struggling through high snow while the driver's cart bogs down in mud, and meanwhile the dog running behind kicks up dust from the dry road. The gumbo mud of springtime causes problems for pigs: the mud builds up on their tails to such an extent that it stretches the skin on their backs so that they can't close their eyes and they often die from lack of sleep. Other tales comment on summer heat and drought ("the day it rained") and the resulting dust storms when gophers are seen ten feet in the air digging down.

If mountain people have side-hill gougers, then Plains folk have "jackalopes"—jackrabbits with antelope prongs on their heads—or their larger cousins, the "elkhares." Prairie grasshoppers grow so big they're mistaken for cattle or airplanes. Venomous snakes strike at wagon tongues, which swell so much they provide enough kindling to last the winter.

In good times, prairie wheat is so thick that it must be swathed twice before it will fall, and cabbages are large enough to shelter pigs from the sun. In bad times, it's so dry that bullfrogs don't know how to swim because they've never had a chance to learn; parents pour water through a screen so that their children will know what rain looks like.

Just as tall tales comment upon the land

and the climate, they also describe regional occupations, especially outdoor, primary-resource industries. For this reason, the tall tale is often seen as a preserve of men, the traditional workers in such occupations, although on occasion women have been known to lie. Farmers tell of strong pitchers who could unload a rack of hay in two forkfuls. Ranchers recall riding on the backs of jackrabbits to herd far-ranging cattle. Oil drillers speak of derricks so tall that they are hinged to let the moon pass.

Sometimes the tellers of these tales turn into folk heroes in their own right, becoming Münchhausens of their particular region or occupation. For example, the oil driller Gib Morgan (1842–1909) was a prodigious teller of tall tales, and he soon became the protagonist in oil-patch stories. Instead of oil, he drilled for cream or champagne, used snakeskins for a pipeline, and when he heard a distant thunderstorm, single-handedly capped a gusher in mid-blow.

Other heroes were entirely fanciful, sometimes the work of popular writers. Although Paul Bunyan was best known in the forests of the East and Midwest, he was also a tall-tale figure in the Plains. In fact, he logged the Northern Plains so completely that the Dakotas are almost devoid of trees. The tall-tale cowboy Pecos Bill was the invention of writer Edward O'Reilly, who probably based his character on Paul Bunyan. Pecos Bill rode tornadoes and lit cigarettes with lightning bolts. At the age of one month, he killed a panther; his life ended when he laughed himself to death looking at a Bostonian in a cowboy suit.

Just as authors have used the tall-tale tradition to their advantage, so too have commercial artists. For example, the art of the taxidermist may be seen in Plains saloons, where stuffed and mounted jackalopes are on display. More popular, however, are tall-tale postcards. Since the early twentieth century, postcard manufacturers have used trick photography to show giant ears of corn (three to a wagon), fur-bearing trout (from especially cold streams), hunters carrying large grasshoppers on poles, and the jackrabbit-riding cowboys mentioned above.

Whether told during roundup or sent as postcards to eastern relatives, the tall tale is a sardonic commentary on the harshness and changeability of life in the Great Plains. Exaggeration allows flatlanders to temper the disappointment of crops that are not abundant, weather that is less than moderate, and occupations that involve more drudgery than heroism. The humor of tall tales resides in a delicate balance of fact and fiction that reflects both the dreams and realities of Plains life.

Michael Taft
American Folklife Center
Library of Congress

Boatright, Mody C. *Gib Morgan: Minstrel of the Oil Fields.* Publications of the Texas Folklore Society, no. 20. Dallas: Southern Methodist University Press, 1945. Halpert, Herbert. "Tall Tales and Other Yarns from Calgary, Alberta." *California Folklore Quarterly* 4 (1945), 29–49. Reprinted in *Folklore of Canada,* edited by Edith Fowke. Toronto: McClelland and Stewart Ltd., 1976: 171–89. Welsch, Roger L. *Shingling the Fog and Other Plains Lies.* Lincoln: University of Nebraska Press, 1980.

TORNADO STORIES

The first written accounts of tornadoes in the Great Plains were from settlements near and along the Missouri River in Kansas during the mid-1800s. On October 25, 1844, a tornado moved northeast from present-day Mission, Kansas, into Missouri. Many pioneer farms were damaged or destroyed. A horrific nighttime tornado struck the Baker home just outside Stanton, Kansas, on June 8, 1860, killing all the family. The local townspeople were unaware of the event until morning, when they saw pieces of the home scattered across the hillside. Another nighttime tornado struck near Galesburg, Kansas, killing three children and injuring their mother in their home. Tales spread about the "night phantom that appeared to be composed of fire."

A small outbreak of tornadoes struck central Kansas on June 6, 1876. One tornado near Salina was reported to look like an elephant's trunk moving side to side for about a half hour. A man was watching this tornado off to his north from the doorway of his home when another tornado approached from the south, destroying the house and killing him. On August 25, 1877, a tornado destroyed two spans of the Union Pacific Railroad bridge that crossed the Missouri River at Omaha. Wrought-iron bars on the bridge were bent and twisted. Eyewitnesses saw an immense cloud traveling down the river lifting water into the funnel. An injured watchman on the east bank of the river boated, then swam, to Omaha to warn the next train leaving town of the destroyed bridge. One of the first tornadoes reported in South Dakota occurred on April 17, 1878. The tornado passed about eleven miles west of Yankton near Olivet, destroying several homes. A wagon was reported to have been thrown two miles. One of the first tornadoes reported in Texas was on April 15, 1879, near Dallas, injuring twenty-five people. Fifteen homes were destroyed and six were damaged by what was reported to be a "green-rimmed cone-shaped tornado which rose and fell moving like a monster wave."

A large tornado outbreak in Kansas, Missouri, Nebraska, and Iowa occurred on May 29 and 30, 1879. John Park Finley, a young army cadet, was dispatched from Washington to conduct a damage survey. Finley recorded numerous eyewitness accounts, documented the time of tornado occurrences, and even calculated the forward speeds of the tornadoes. He described in graphic detail the "agonies of death" experienced by some of the tornado victims: "All of the parties were covered with mud from head to foot; eyes, mouths, and ears filled, and clothing torn into shreds. The mother and two children were left in the rubbish; the former having her head crushed, and her long hair, which reached below her waist, was partly cut and pulled from her head, twisted into a rope, and found several feet from her body. That portion of her hair left upon her head was twisted into little wisps and mixed with mud." He wrote that "the bodies of the children, after having been washed for days, were still covered with specks of fine dirt and leaves which seemed to be driven into the flesh."

One of the most famous tornado stories came from Mr. Will Keller, a farmer near Greensburg, Kansas, who witnessed the inside of a tornado from his cellar on June 22, 1928. He looked up into what appeared to be a hollow cylinder and saw lightning, "which zigzagged from side-to-side." Many tornado stories have involved accounts of plucked poultry, sulfurous odors, and objects being carried great distances. Another fascinating account recalls the tornado that struck the railway station in Elmont, Kansas, on June 5, 1917. The ticket window was blown into a nearby field, where it was found beneath a heavy scale weight. The glass was not even cracked. On April 27, 1942, a frame house was blown away by a tornado that struck Pryor, Oklahoma, leaving a kerosene lamp, still lighted and burning, beneath a nearby tree. Such tornado stories made for good press, and together they constitute a distinctive folklore.

See also PHYSICAL ENVIRONMENT: Tornadoes.

Tim Marshall
Flower Mound, Texas

Flora, Snowden D. *Tornadoes of the United States.* Norman: University of Oklahoma Press, 1953. Grazulis, Thomas. *Significant Tornadoes.* St. Johnsbury VT: Tornado Project of Environmental Films, 1993.

TRICKSTER

The trickster is the embodiment of lawlessness and paradox. He is a divine buffoon, a hero who breaks taboos, a rebel, a coward, and a creator. Trickster helps establish social rules, and he deliberately flouts them. He is commonly depicted as deceitful and humorous. He is amoral, rather than immoral, and he has a voracious appetite for food and sex. In his traditional and mythic incarnations, he is almost always male. As the supreme boundary-crosser, trickster is always *between* classifications—between what is human and what is animal, between what is cultural and what is natural.

Native American tricksters tend to be associated with animal spirits (such as Coyote, Rabbit, or Raven). Their tales are both sacred myths and simple folk tales. Among the Indigenous peoples of the Great Plains, the trickster's name is Old Man (Crow and Blackfoot), Iktomi (Lakota), and Veeho (Cheyenne). The most common incarnation of the Plains trickster, however, is Coyote.

In his various (and strikingly similar) cultural guises, trickster is the self-indulgent clown who dupes women into having sex with him; he steals food from his industrious neighbors; he cross-dresses and becomes temporarily a woman; he dies and is reborn. As expected, his tomfoolery frequently backfires. He juggles his eyes and loses them in a tree; he accidentally sleeps with his wife; he drowns in his own feces; he uses his enormous penis to attack a chipmunk (who in turns bites his penis off to "human" size). Further, trickster is a cultural hero. In some narratives, he creates the Earth; he creates animals or substantially alters their bodies; he steals tobacco from the gods; and, more recently, he tricks the white man.

Symbolically, the trickster is always located at the periphery of the community (though, importantly, never totally separated from it). From this "outer" vantage point, trickster reveals "inner" communal structures. His very presence determines the limits of social boundaries. Trickster thus serves as a political tool with which to subvert (or endorse) social practices. Indeed, trickster continually offers us the possibility of transcending (or renewing) social codes. As such, trickster is arguably an incarnation of creativity itself. At the very least, trickster allows us to poke fun at the powers that restrain us. He reveals the *structure* of social structures and offers us glimpses of new (and terrifying) world orders. Not surprisingly, many contemporary authors use tricksterlike characters as creative forces that both define and critique dominant cultural practices.

Ultimately, the trickster is disturbing, not because of his difference but because of his lack of difference. As purely a cultural construct, the trickster's body is a cultural body—our body. He is always a part of us, and he exists only to be interpreted. And when we interpret trickster, we interpret ourselves. Even though we often attempt to alienate ourselves from the trickster—by making his body grotesque, indistinguishable—wherever we are, there is trickster, laughing at what we've become.

Anthony Farrington
University of Arkansas at Monticello

Babcock, Barbara. "'A Tolerated Margin of Mess': The Trickster and His Tales Reconsidered." In *Critical Essays on Native American Literature*, edited by Andrew Wiget. Boston: G. K. Hall, 1985: 153–84. Ballinger, Franchot. "Living Sideways: Social Themes and Social Relationships in Native American Trickster Tales." *American Indian Quarterly* 13 (1989): 15–30. Radin, Paul. *The Trickster: a Study in American Indian Mythology*. New York: Philosophical Library, 1956.

WELSCH, ROGER (b. 1936)

Nebraska author and folklorist Roger Lee-Flack Welsch has as many alter egos as Nebraska has weather patterns: storyteller, professor, talk show host, originator and first president of the Liars Hall of Fame, raconteur, columnist, Omaha Tribe member, family man, musician, "that guy in the overalls on CBS *News Sunday Morning*," and antique-tractor-hugging collector. Highly sought after as a speaker, and best known for his humorous portrayals of Great Plains characters in the popular press and media, Welsch also has a more scholarly side. He has published important works on tall tales, sod houses, foodways, round barns, and traditional stories of the Omaha Tribe, among others. He was formally adopted into the Omaha's Wind Clan by tribal elders in 1967.

Born on November 6, 1936, Welsch grew up in Lincoln, Nebraska, a member of the city's substantial community of Germans from Russia (Volga Germans). He attended the University of Nebraska, earning both a bachelor of arts (1958) and a master of arts (1960) in German, and then pursued a growing interest in folklore by completing graduate work at the University of Colorado (1962) and at the Folklore Institute, Indiana University (1963–65.) Welsch taught folklore and English at Dana College in Blair, Nebraska, from 1960 to 1964, at Nebraska Wesleyan University in Lincoln from 1964 to 1973, and at the University of Nebraska–Lincoln (UNL) from 1973 to 1988. He remains a UNL adjunct faculty member. Welsch has published many scholarly and popular writings on Great Plains folklore.

He has also played an important role in promoting Great Plains folk traditions by coordinating Nebraska's featured participation in the Smithsonian Institution's 1975 Festival of American Folklife, serving on grant panels for the National Endowment for the Arts (NEA) Folk Arts Program, and successfully nominating Nebraskan Albert Fahlbusch, a Volga German who makes and plays hammered dulcimers, for an NEA National Heritage Fellowship in 1984.

Welsch first came to national prominence, however, as a result of his successful 1972 campaign for a seat on the Lancaster County (Nebraska) Weed Control Authority board on a "pro-weed ticket," reducing the number of native plants defined as weeds. Charles Kuralt, who was at that time still conducting his "On the Road" series for the CBS *Evening News*, got wind of the folklorist-politician and invited Welsch to appear on his show. That meeting began their long-term friendship and working relationship. Welsch became nationally known as the overalls-wearing Nebraska essayist, affably relating stories—"Postcards from Nebraska"—of rural and small-town life in the Great Plains for Kuralt's show, CBS *News Sunday Morning*.

Now living with his wife, artist Linda Welsch, on their tree farm near the small community of Dannebrog (a "star" of many of the "Postcards from Nebraska"), Welsch continues his writing, television, and speaking career. His ability to prosper by doing what he loves is a good example of the "can-do" adaptive spirit he celebrates in the people of the region.

Gwen K. Meister
Nebraska State Historical Society

Welsch, Roger L. *A Treasury of Nebraska Pioneer Folklore*. Lincoln: University of Nebraska Press, 1966. Welsch, Roger L. *Shingling the Fog and Other Plains Lies*. Lincoln: University of Nebraska Press, 1980.

Gender

Patsy Rodgers Henderson, the first Calgary Stampede Queen, 1946

GENDER

Practically this whole study has been devoted to the men. . . . The Great Plains in the early period was strictly a man's country—more of a man's country than any other portion of the frontier. Men loved the Plains. . . . But what of the women?—Walter Prescott Webb, *The Great Plains* (1931: 505)

"I was tricked!" cries the Nebraska woman. "I read 504 pages of *The Great Plains*, the classic work on my environment, trusting that I was gaining insight into my own experience, only to find on page 505 that practically the whole thing applied specifically to men and not to women. I want my time back!"

While there remain scholars inclined to dismiss the gravity of the woman's protest, increasing numbers have granted its validity. They have made a variety of responses to the neglect of women and the representation of the male experience as normative in canonical writings about the Great Plains. The diverse answers to the complaint have formed a body of scholarship dealing with the problem of the inclusion or exclusion of women in texts about the Plains and with the relationship between women and men.

One response has been that women were indeed included in the processes described in *The Great Plains*. Webb just didn't understand that women were present throughout as homesteaders, as fighters, as men's equals. Some who would make this response ask that the woman substitute inclusive language in Webb's writing and try to understand that "man" in English is used in a generic way to include both men and women. Webb overlooked women and we need only write them in. The broad contours of the text stand; the inclusion of women merely strengthens it and makes it more comprehensive.

Others would find nearly as much fault with this response as with the exclusion of women in Webb's account. Their answer to the woman's complaint would affirm it and underscore the difference between men's and women's lives in the Plains and hence the critical necessity of a thoroughgoing consideration of women. From this corner would come the observation that Plains men and women have been different in terms of legal rights, family roles, economic resources, political power, and cultural expectations. Surely this would produce different experiences for men and women in the Great Plains. What needs to be done, they contend, is to study cultural constructions of maleness and femaleness and the effects they have had on the institutions of the Plains. Did the Great Plains shape a sense of maleness and femaleness distinct from that of other regions? How did diverse racial and ethnic groups in the Plains define maleness and femaleness? From this perspective, the canon must be radically revised so that women are included.

In the past twenty-five years, probing into various dimensions of gender has provided intriguing openings for scholars. The study of gender, of cultural constructions of maleness and femaleness, has mainly grown out of the study of women. This scholarship has also contributed to an understanding of racial and ethnic diversity in the Great Plains, although much remains to be done in theorizing the intersection of gender and race.

Life of a Woman Homesteader

In the spring of 1876, eighteen-year-old Luna Kellie packed up her five-month-old baby, Willie, bade her husband, J. T., a sad farewell, and left St. Louis on a train for central Nebraska, where she would prepare for the family's homesteading and wait for J. T. Luna's father had already been lured to a Nebraska homestead through railroad advertising, and he would help to settle the couple. Since both he and J. T. had been railroad workers, they had the advantage of cheap passage to Grand Island, which was the stopping-off point for their homesteading. Luna spent the summer with her father and siblings. In November, after completing a final season of railroad work, J. T. joined them.

February of 1877 found Luna, J. T., and Willie—young, inexperienced, but at least together—striking out on their own Nebraska homestead a few miles from that of Luna's father. They had less than $400 with which to outfit their 160-acre government grant. After digging a shelter out of the side of a hill, they dipped into their cash reserve to buy boards to complete the house, since they could get no sod at that time of year. They also bought a new stove and a few food staples. To begin farming they purchased fifteen steers, a milk cow, and a plow. J. T. traded his watch for an old wagon. With these basics, they began farm life.

Their first reversal of fortune came when a sudden blizzard struck in the night just as they had begun to savor the Nebraska spring and to think about putting their cattle out on the buffalo grass. Hearing the wind, J. T. bolted up in fear of losing the cattle. He and Luna ran out into the night and rounded up all but one of the cattle and drove them into their tiny house. Again and again they chased the last one, but each time they got him closer to the house he ran in the opposite direction. Finally, cold and exhausted, they let him go and returned to bed, where J. T., Luna, and Willie warmed themselves as the cattle pressed in on them. Although J. T. made repeated trips into the blizzard to get the wild steer, he finally gave it up. The three Kellies spent the next day huddled in bed and ate boiled oatmeal with no milk while the cattle occupied most of the room in the house.

Through the summer of 1877 the Kellies worked themselves nearly to death. They had no money at all. A neighbor saved them from starvation by giving J. T. a sack of flour as early pay for harvest work. Luna had a second baby that year. This baby and the one born the following year died early, undoubtedly because overwork and lack of food had dried Luna's milk. Luna survived these deaths, she survived her terror of the rattlesnakes that lurked in the fields around the house, and she survived her despondency at being unable to send her grandmother a birthday greeting because she did not have three cents to buy a stamp. Luna and J. T. pressed on, they had more babies in the following years, and their crops came in as they established themselves and learned farming skills. By the 1880s their farm was producing abundantly and their family was steadily increasing in number.

However, defeat came when their farming operation failed and they lost their homestead, not through acts of God or their own failings, but because they could not turn a profit on their successful production. And here the railroad was to blame. Why? It seemed to be the price gouging inflicted by the railroad. The railroad made money by bringing settlers to Nebraska, by shipping farming tools and supplies west, and by carrying grain to market. Railroad rates were not standardized, and the companies tended to charge higher rates per mile for short, local runs that served small communities than for long runs. Where competition existed, typically in cities, rates were lower than in rural areas. While the railroads extracted high fares from farmers, they offered free passes to politicians and controlled local and state politics through their patronage. The railroad, it seemed, fattened itself on the Kellies' labor, returning only misery to them. Of the railroad Luna wrote, "[T]he minute you crossed the Missouri River your fate both soul and body was in their hands. . . . [T]hey robbed us of all we produced."

Losing the homestead and moving to another farm to begin again, Luna's rage exploded into political action as she joined the Farmers Alliance. She became secretary of the Nebraska Farmers Alliance, and from her farm home she published an Alliance paper that attacked the railroads and the middlemen that profited from the exploitation of farmers. In a rousing speech delivered to the Nebraska Farmers Alliance in 1894, she declared, "[T]he people now know that they have the constitutional right to take the railroads under right of eminent domain and run them at cost in the interest of *all the people*." Later, her hopes for the Alliance and for the populist movement, like her earlier hope of farming prosperity, died a painful death, a disillusion readers can follow through her experience of trying to hold the principles of the farm movement above the egos of its Nebraska leadership, which was male.

Luna's loss of her two babies, the poverty that constricted her spirit, her sadness at her beloved J. T.'s repeated failures, the vulnerability to exploitation by external forces, and her resilience must be recognized as a piece of the Plains experience. Contrary to Webb, the Plains was a woman's country as well as a man's country. Without women such as Luna Kellie, European Americans could not have claimed the Plains.

Putting Women into the Plains Picture

Publication of the stories of Luna Kellie and other Plains women grew out of the 1970s explosion of studies on women that accompanied the revitalization of the feminist movement. Scholars in many disciplines began to notice that women were absent, or only peripherally present, in standard works by such accepted authorities as Webb. The first work on Plains women was compensatory, much of it having to do with European American women in farming. Two articles by Mary W. M. Hargreaves in *Agricultural History*, "Homesteading and Homemaking on the Plains: A Review" (1973) and "Women in the Agricultural Settlement of the Northern Plains" (1976), set the path for further research. These articles placed women in the history of Plains farming, underscored the significance of women's contribution to European American settlement, and pointed to the particular hardships that Plains life imposed on women.

A further step in this compensatory scholarship was more systematic and focused on the exhuming of texts and records of Plains women. Most of the political, military, and commercial records available from the early European American settlement of the Plains are male-centered. Focusing on women meant bringing forward a different set of sources: diaries, letters, church and club records, wills, deeds, court records, local newspapers, advertisements and personal columns in magazines and journals, and oral histories.

Scholars seeking to put women into accounts of the Plains have found them almost everywhere they have looked. For example, women figured in the fur trade, which writers have typically represented in terms of rugged men and growth of capital. Women of the Native Plains nations did some trapping, and they processed skins for trade. In *Many Tender Ties: Women in Fur-Trade Society, 1670–1870*, Sylvia Van Kirk (1980) describes early European traders' practice of taking Native wives, who stabilized ties with Native nations, served as guides and interpreters, provided moccasins and snowshoes, which eased travel on the Northern Plains, supplied pemmican and other local foods, and helped make canoes. Women, as well as men, shaped the dynamics of the fur trade.

In the United States the Homestead Act of 1862 allowed single women as well as men to homestead. Studies of women homesteaders include *Bachelor Bess: The Homesteading Letters of Elizabeth Corey, 1909–1919* (1990), edited by Philip L. Gerber, *The Land of the Burnt Thigh* by Edith Eudora Kohl (1938), and Elaine Lindgren's article "Ethnic Women Homesteading on the Plains of North Dakota" (1989). In Canada, single or married women were not allowed to homestead (although widows and divorced or unwed mothers could). Still, women's participation was central to most family farming operations. Single Canadian women might purchase and operate farms. In *Wheat and Women* (1914), Georgina Binnie-Clark, an Englishwoman with enough resources to buy a Canadian farm and hire most of the labor, wrote about her adventures and gave advice on the economics of running a farm in the years immediately preceding World War I. In addition to their economic contributions, Plains women were active in political struggles—including populist, suffrage, and temperance movements—in both Canada and the United States.

Binnie-Clark wrote that "they realized that what men had done for themselves in agricultural pursuits on the prairie, women could also do for themselves." Like men, women were daring and adventurous; they worked hard to claim the land; they could own property and engage in commerce; and they were as capable of effective political participation as men. Adding women has filled out the picture of the Plains.

But did men and women inhabit different parts of that picture? Following the lead of historian Joan Kelly, who concluded that the existing periodization of European history was not valid from the perspective of women, Plains researchers asked if the accepted historical movements and markers were what in reality moved and marked women's lives. Do we really know that homesteading or populism had the same appeal for the majority of women as for men? What was it that drove women? Elinore Pruitt Stewart's *Letters of a Woman Homesteader* (1914) reveals the importance she placed on human interaction; she shows little concern for politics or empire building. Yet the early-twentieth-century writings of Albertan Nellie McClung, collected in *Our Nell* (1979), indicate that her personal leanings placed her in the woman-centered political struggles of suffrage, temperance, and women's economic rights. Perhaps the gap between the personal and the political was not as wide for women as for men.

From Women to Gender

Are women persons? In 1927, eleven years after western Canadian women had won full suffrage rights, the Supreme Court of Canada was called upon to decide the issue of women's personhood. The question itself is remarkable; the answer, "no," is astonishing. The issue had arisen through the activism of Nellie McClung and other women in the Prairie Provinces who had refused to stay on their side of the line drawn between the world of men and that of women.

The case began in 1916 when Alice Jamieson of Calgary and Emily Murphy of Edmonton were appointed police magistrates, the first women in the British Empire to receive such appointments. On Murphy's first day in court a defense lawyer challenged her authority on the grounds that by law she was not a person. Although the challenge was dismissed, the point was well taken. Under British common law, women were persons in "matters of pains and penalties" but not in "matters of rights and privileges."

The issue lay dormant for several years, then resurfaced in the 1920s when a group of Alberta women wanted the law set right. Their strategy was to advocate a Senate appointment for Murphy. Since the law stipulated that only a "fit and qualified person" was eligible for such an appointment, the question of whether a woman was a person would have to be settled. Any five citizens could request an interpretation. Murphy, McClung, suffrage leader Louise McKinney, legal scholar Henrietta Muir Edwards, and provincial cabinet minister Irene Parlby joined to request a ruling on whether or not women were persons. Although four out of five Supreme Court justices joined in the opinion that they were not persons, the women were accustomed to opposition and they forged ahead by appealing to the Privy Council in London, which at that time had the authority to override Canadian decisions.

In 1929 the women prevailed in the Privy Council and became persons under British common law and hence under Canadian law. It had been a long road to arrive at what would seem to be square one. From the vantage of the twenty-first century, the question seems patently ridiculous, as it did to the five Alberta women at the time. Many men saw it with different eyes. The women were moving toward gender equality before the law. The question of men's and women's legal equality went beyond the rearrangement of women's affairs and into a redefinition of what it meant to be a man as well. If being a person was not coterminous with being a man, then the legal definition of "man" was also being revised. It was a question of gender delineation, and this mattered to both men and women at a deeply personal level.

Two principles are tied up in the recent scholarship using the term "gender." First is the assumption that definitions of maleness and femaleness are culturally defined rather than biologically given. Without denying that men and women are in some ways different, these studies point to the similarities between men and women, which are considerable, and view the construction of gender as a suppression of natural similarities rather than an elaboration of natural differences. Both men and women cry, but European American constructions of gender suppressed the crying of men and accentuated that of women, thereby creating a cultural difference where no biological difference existed. Canadian women who sought to join men in their identities as persons were asking that the accepted understanding of "person" be recognized as a cultural artifact and therefore subject to reasoned modification. Second, as can be inferred in the Canadian judges' opposition to women being persons, gender has to do with both maleness and femaleness and with the constructions arising out of the relations between maleness and femaleness.

While often such questions emerge in esoteric points that seem far removed from the reality of most people's lives, they are embedded in basic social and economic structures. Farming in European American culture is generally associated with males: Asked to draw a picture of a farmer, most European Americans will automatically draw a man. The potential for being a farmer helps to shape male identity for European Americans, and the correlate dissociation of women with farming shapes female identity. This dual classification gives rise to the particular configuration of the family farm. We appreciate the cultural contingency of this arrangement by observing that, in Native American nations that cultivated corn, women had the major farming roles. Asked to draw a picture of a farmer, a Native American would have drawn a woman. What it meant to be a man or woman in these societies was not the same as what it meant to European Americans, and this difference was further reflected in religion, art, and ethical norms.

Drawing on Henry Nash Smith's *Virgin Land: The American West as Symbol and Myth* (1950), Annette Kolodny has underlined the extent to which the westward movement across North America was gendered. In *The Lay of the Land: Metaphor as Experience and History in American Life and Letters* (1975) and *The Land Before Her: Fantasy and Experience of the American Frontiers, 1630–1860* (1984), Kolodny explores gender in myths and symbols of land. At first, men saw the land as maternal and nurturing; later the dominant metaphor changed from the land as Mother to the land as Mistress, a place to be explored and conquered for its material treasures. For women, the dominant metaphor of the new land was the garden, a social setting to be cultivated and adapted for human needs. Kolodny's analysis resonates through writing about the Plains. Various Plains writers, among them Meridel LeSueur, have used the metaphor of the plowed land as the flesh of a woman and the conquering of this virgin land as a triumph of masculinity.

A study of a Kansas farming county extended the significance of gender beyond symbol and metaphor and into the economic and political shaping of Plains life. In "Structure of Agriculture and Women's Culture in the Great Plains" (1988), Cornelia Butler Flora and Jan L. Flora contrasted farming patterns in three ethnic groups: German, Volga German, and American-born (or Yankees). These ethnic groups formed different complexes of gender relations, which affected fertility, labor, and resource allocation. The willingness of the two foreign-born groups to allow their daughters to take domestic service work, thus augmenting farm income, and the unwillingness of the American-born families to do so greatly affected success rates. The Volga Germans had the most staying power on the land, followed by the Germans, with the American-born a distant third. Thus, the evolving ethnic character of the farming community came to derive more from German and Volga German traits than from those of the Yankee farmers. Such studies of gender reveal complexities in the agricultural economy that were not apparent when only men's production was considered.

Gender and Interregional Differences

Not only did cultural configurations of gender modify the cultural landscape of the Plains, but geographic and economic conditions associated with the Great Plains in turn reconfigured gender. For the last 200 years the Great Plains has seen constant migration and readjustment, and studies of gender reflect this continuing change as well as significant continuities with external traditions. People entered the Great Plains from different directions and with different cultural baggage, including gender. In what ways did the Plains rearrange this baggage and in what ways did the constructions that people brought rearrange the cultures of the Great Plains? Some scholars, including Mary Neth in *Preserving the Family Farm: Women, Community and the Foundations of Agribusiness in the Midwest, 1900–1940* (1995) and Katherine Jellison in *Entitled to Power: Farm Women and Technology, 1913–1963* (1993), minimize the specificity of the Plains experience of gender and emphasize instead the continuities between European American patterns in the Midwest and Great Plains. By contrast, Dorothy Schwieder and Deborah Fink in their article "Plains Women: Rural Life in the 1930s" (1988) and Fink in *Agrarian Women: Wives and Mothers in Rural Nebraska, 1880–1940* (1992) argue that gender patterns were reworked in the Great Plains. Rather than emphasizing the continuity arising from shared cultural roots and common federal policy, Schwieder and Fink point to the sparse population and the greater sacrifices required of Plains women and relate this to a reconfiguration of gender. Glenda Riley's *The Female Frontier: A Comparative View of Women on the Prairie and the Plains* (1988) draws out contrasts but considers that in fundamental ways the tasks facing the women in the Midwest and Great Plains were similar. Further comparative work will deepen the understanding of whether and to what extent the Plains experience altered the gender identities of its people.

If the Plains environment did have an effect on gender relations, what was that effect? Scholars disagree. On one hand is the view that for European American settlers the move into the open spaces removed restricting conventions and social controls and opened the way for more egalitarian relationships between men and women. Writing of British women in *A Flannel Shirt and Liberty: British Emigrant Gentlewomen in the Canadian West, 1880–1914* (1982), Susan Jackel found the birth of a feminist consciousness and a collective identity among British women migrants to the Prairies of Canada. Katherine Harris, in "Sex Roles and Work Patterns among Homesteading Families in Northeastern Colorado, 1873–1920" (1984), also presents a case for greater egalitarianism: with homesteading came a muting of gender-role distinctions, shared decision making between husbands and wives, and the accrual of greater power to women because of their acknowledged economic centrality.

In various articles, including "Every Husband's Right: Sex Roles in Mari Sandoz's *Old Jules*" (1983), Melody Graulich makes a contrary argument: with the loosening of social restraints in the West, women were more vulnerable to men's brutality. *Old Jules* (1935), the story of Sandoz's parents' homesteading and marriage in western Nebraska, may be read as a study in gender relations, and not a happy one. Fink's *Agrarian Women* represents another entry in the case against the salutary effects of the Plains for male-female relations. The controversy is complicated by the methodological difficulties in assessing the intimacy of marriages. No one denies that there were good marriages as well as oppressive ones in the Plains, just as there have been in every social setting. The question remains of the effects of the Plains environment on them, and it is a messy and possibly imprudent question. Notwithstanding the enormous problems, including ethical ones, the subject has been broached and has not been laid to rest.

A Harvest Yet to Reap (1976), a collection of early-twentieth-century writings by Canadian Prairie women, describes shifts in the cultural definitions of women as migrants crossed into the Great Plains. Life in the Great Plains at the time of settlement placed its inhabitants under specific constraints. Drawing on studies of Canadian farming and on Marxist theory, Max Hedley's 1981 article "Relations of Production of the 'Family Farm'" theorizes that, through relations of production, the domination of capital in Canadian farming penetrated and marked internal family relations, including those between husbands and wives. As Hedley points out, the idea of the family farm implied collective ownership; the vocabulary of kinship evoked obligations to the farm operation that in an ideal kinship setting would have been reciprocal. However, the demands of a capitalist economic system dictated the subordination of kinship obligations to the imperatives of the cash economy. What a woman wanted and deserved from a marriage partnership became subordinate to the banker's demands on a farmer. *"Other" Voices: Historical Essays on Saskatchewan Women*, edited by David De Brou and Aileen Moffatt (1995), complicates this analysis by pointing out the ethnic diversity present in Saskatchewan alone, and hence the diversity of gender constructions arising from migration to the Plains.

Plains Towns

The Great Plains south of the forty-ninth parallel is as rural as any region of the United States, and except for the major cities of Calgary, Edmonton, and Winnipeg the Prairie Provinces of Canada are also largely rural. The rural ethos has colored all of the institutions in the region. But cities, with their colleges, universities, museums, libraries, orchestras, and opera houses, have also been integral to Plains culture. Women have done much of the building of these institutions and have found employment and influence through them. These institutions have also been points of articulation with the world beyond the Plains. For some women, such as Willa Cather, they have provided routes of departure. Women in the small towns dotted across the map were instrumental in bringing and maintaining churches, which also served as connections to

European and European American cultures to the east and were transmitters of gender norms as well. June O. Underwood's article "Civilizing Kansas: Women's Organizations, 1880–1920" (1984/85) surveys the ways in which Kansas women worked for the reforms associated with the Progressive Era. These included establishing homes for indigent and helpless persons; lobbying for better conditions in county homes and other institutions; working for a broad range of health concerns, including clean water, better nutrition, and more accessible medical care; promoting municipal improvements such as parks, restrooms, and sidewalks; fighting for prohibition; and working for child labor and truancy laws.

Women's suffrage was a burning issue throughout the United States and Canada in the late nineteenth and early twentieth centuries. The Plains protest movements of the time advocated women's suffrage, although the depth of commitment has been questioned. From one point of view the Great Plains, removed from the entrenched prejudices of the East, represented a fertile field for the establishment of equal voting rights. As a territory in 1869 Wyoming became the first government to grant women equal voting rights, and it became a state in 1890 with this voting legislation intact. In Canada, women voted first in the Prairie Provinces and British Columbia. Whether this can be attributed to frontier democracy, however, has been questioned. Julie Roy Jeffrey, in *Frontier Women: The Trans-Mississippi West, 1840–1880* (1979), wrote that when men of the western territories granted women the vote their motivations involved more conservative expediency than altruistic commitment to democracy. In Wyoming, legislators concerned about the sparse and transient population believed that granting the vote to women would attract attention to the territory and draw women to establish domesticity and stability on the frontier. The fragility of women's rights in Wyoming was evident in 1870 when women lost their right to serve on juries. Women serving on a grand jury had upset male politicians by indicting Laramie saloons for doing business on Sunday; the men shut the women down instead of the saloons. It was 1950 before women regained the right to serve on Wyoming juries. Whatever men's motivations for cultivating the appearance of women's equal rights, the gain with suffrage was real, and it happened first in the Great Plains.

In contrast to the image of the Plains town as a setting for the noble causes for which women worked, there has been no shortage of criticism of the Plains town for its crushing of female spirits. Willa Cather's fiction, including *My Ántonia* (1918) and *A Lost Lady* (1923), may be read as a gender critique of Plains towns, as may the life of Cather herself in her Nebraska years, which is analyzed in *Willa Cather: The Emerging Voice* by Sharon O'Brien (1987). Sinclair Lewis's novel *Main Street* (1920) stands as a classic depiction of suffocating conformity imposed on women by small-town society. Although Gopher Prairie, the setting of *Main Street*, is in Minnesota, Lewis wrote that Gopher Prairie was every small town west of the Mississippi. While the subject matter of these disquieting works is unmistakably gendered, they do not picture men as evil agents and women as victims; often it is women rather than men who appear as the enforcers of the deadly social norms.

Race and Ethnicity

Just as gender study has tended to focus on women, considerations of race in the Plains have tended to be about Native Americans, African Americans, and Hispanic Americans rather than European Americans. Moreover, like the studies of European Americans, the studies of these groups have tended to be about men. Anthropologist Robert Lowie's *Indians of the Great Plains* (1954), for example, has indexed entries for women in a work otherwise given over to men. Similarly, the Pulitzer Prize–winning novel of Kiowa writer N. Scott Momaday, *House Made of Dawn* (1966), is unself-consciously male centered.

Researchers have disrupted the conventions of discourse about race, declaring that race exists as a cultural construct rather than as biological fact. While race remains a political and analytical category, its essential significance is as a particular form of ethnicity. Moreover, scholars have found gender and racial constructions to be intimately related. The proclaimed goal of making the Plains safe for European American women justified the isolation of Plains Indians as well as the restrictions on activities of European American women. Yet, as pointed out by Joan Jensen in her publication of Mary Jemison's captivity account (1981) and Glenda Riley in her book *Women and Indians on the Frontier, 1825–1915* (1984), European American women's actual experiences of contact with Indians seldom matched what they had been led to expect. Riley believed that women were more likely than men to revise their views of Indians based on what happened to them personally after they reached the Plains. On the other hand, Van Kirk's study of the Canadian fur trade indicates that in this setting British women were more prejudiced against persons of the original nations than were British men.

While not specifically addressing the Plains, Joan Jensen has pointed to the significance of women's farming as a base of economic power in nations of the southwestern and northeastern United States. Balancing the image of the male warrior and buffalo hunter that has dominated popular representations of Native Americans, Jensen has brought out the economic importance of women as food producers and processors. Contrary to early European American scholarship, which viewed the considerable labor inputs of Native American women as evidence of their debased social position, anthropologists such as Alice Fletcher, Francis La Flesche, and Gene Weltfish, who studied Plains nations, interpreted women's labor as a sign of their economic and social centrality. *The Hidden Half*, edited by Patricia Albers and Beatrice Medicine (1983), shows Plains Indian women from diverse societies to have been major food providers, controllers of assets, decision makers, and central to the political and spiritual functioning of their societies. Although Plains nations were culturally diverse, women usually did most of the perennial labor—including building lodges and tipis, farming, processing hides, and rearing young children.

Native American women writers have provided intimate studies of the world of Plains men and women from the original nations. Ella Cara Deloria's novel *Waterlily*, written in the 1940s and published in 1988, offers a Lakota woman's understanding of women's life among her people in the 1840s and 1850s. *Waterlily* depicts a past in which women occupied a valued and powerful place, notwithstanding the male dominance of the warrior society. Mary Crow Dog's *Lakota Woman* (1991), which is about recent political struggles, represents another powerful study of gender from the perspective of a Plains woman. The fiction of Louise Erdrich explores twentieth-century adjustments made by Chippewa peoples who had been displaced to the Plains from their homes in the Eastern Woodlands.

In addition to the revisions and scholarship critiquing the conventional wisdom about the lives of Native American women of the Great Plains, recent scholarship has dislodged the authority of early observers who pictured the Plains Indian man as a lazy dandy. As David J. Wishart (1995) finds, these early observers failed to understand that men's work took place away from the village. Men's activities were raiding, hunting, defending, trading, and diplomacy. The skewed demographics observed in the nineteenth century, when in many Plains tribes more than two-thirds of the adults were women, are testimony to the physical risk inherent in men's roles. Further, Wishart believes that European American observers also misinterpreted polygyny. Rather than a debasement of women, it was a practical response to the relative shortage of men.

Modern Plains Indians recount a history in which women commanded a great deal of respect; they attribute degradation of Native American women to the postcontact introduction of alcohol and loss of the traditional economic and spiritual nexus. One of the most unpardonable sins of a modern Lakota is to fail to show respect to a senior Lakota woman, thereby acceding to European American norms rather than Lakota order.

Yet the widespread belief in a kinder, more respectful precontact past may reflect modern cultural politics as well as Indian history. Notwithstanding the tendency to attribute gender violence to European influence, reliable historical accounts reveal that Plains Indian women faced violence and death when they violated sexual or familial norms. For both men and women, secure status in the traditional societies appears to have rested on the degree to which they fulfilled moral expectations associated with their respective genders.

Although African American men and women settled in the Great Plains, many of the details of their lives are unexplored. Glenda Riley, who made a brave attempt to include accounts of African Americans in *The Female Frontier*, came up with little information. The largest concentration of black settlers was in Kansas, but small numbers of African Americans settled in other areas of the Plains as well. Race mattered in the Plains and shaped a distinct Plains experience for these settlers as compared to European Americans; nevertheless, African Americans were faced with problems of survival similar to those confronting European Americans. Perhaps the experience of gender for black persons in the Plains was similar to that of European Americans, although available anecdotes provide insufficient basis for firm conclusions.

Similarly on the list of gender studies that have not yet emerged are the early experiences of Hispanic Americans and Asian Americans in the Plains. With so much intriguing work done on gender in these populations in other locations, it is hard to believe that there is nothing to be uncovered that would reveal what the Plains has meant for them both historically and in the present.

Gender and Masculinity

Gender doesn't mean women. A burgeoning body of scholarship has appeared to address the significance of gender in the understanding of male activities as well. Unfortunately, little of this has been about the Plains, although there have been some beginnings. Kolodny's *Lay of the Land* ferrets out male imagery in the conquest of western lands. Elizabeth Atwood Lawrence's *Rodeo: An Anthropologist Looks at the Wild and the Tame* (1982) opens the subject of the significance of maleness for cowboys, and Garrison Keillor's radio program, "Prairie Home Companion," includes an intriguing sequence of gender satire on the lives of the cowboys, which are forever being complicated by the addition of women and social responsibility. Much remains to be explored. The significance of the maleness of the soldier/warrior in European American and Native American cultures must have reached into other social domains and colored gender relations more generally for both. These studies are sorely needed before we can reach a balanced understanding of the significance of gender in the Plains.

Conclusion

Few questions of gender in the Great Plains have been put to rest. They are being revisited in ongoing investigations, and debates are wide-ranging. As with much other scholarship on gender, the Plains research is multidisciplinary. In 1984 a conference in Las Cruces, New Mexico, entitled "Rural Women in Historical Perspective," provided a forum for academics and activists engaged in work on rural women. It drew heavily from the discipline of history, but the scope was broad enough to include anthropologists, sociologists, literary analysts, economists, extension personnel, rural activists, and farm women. The continu-

ing development and evolution of the conference has provided a network for theorists, many of them isolated, addressing questions of gender in the Great Plains. Now, unlike in Webb's day, anyone who writes accounts of the Great Plains and ignores women can expect to get called on it. Beyond that, there is little consensus.

See also ASIAN AMERICANS: Female Employment Act / EDUCATION: Women in Higher Education / FOLKWAYS: Quilting / LITERARY TRADITIONS: Cather, Willa; Erdrich, Louise; Webb, Walter Prescott / PROTEST AND DISSENT: Temperance Movement.

Deborah Fink
Ames, Iowa

Albers, Patricia, and Beatrice Medicine, eds. *The Hidden Half: Studies of Plains Indian Women*. Washington DC: University Press of America, 1983. Binnie-Clark, Georgina. *Wheat and Women*. Toronto: University of Toronto Press, 1979. Corey, Elizabeth. *Bachelor Bess: The Homesteading Letters of Elizabeth Corey 1909–1919*, edited by Philip L. Gerber. Iowa City: University of Iowa Press, 1990. De Brou, David, and Aileen Moffatt, eds. *"Other" Voices: Historical Essays on Saskatchewan Women*. Regina: University of Regina, Canadian Plains Research Center, 1995. Fink, Deborah. *Agrarian Women: Wives and Mothers in Rural Nebraska, 1880–1940*. Chapel Hill: University of North Carolina Press, 1992. Flora, Cornelia Butler, and Jan L. Flora. "Structure of Agriculture and Women's Culture in the Great Plains." *Great Plains Quarterly* 8 (1988): 195–205. Graulich, Melody. "Every Husband's Right: Sex Roles in Mari Sandoz's *Old Jules*." *Western American Literature* 18 (1983): 3–20. Hallett, Mary, and Marilyn Davis. *Firing the Heather: The Life and Times of Nellie McClung*. Saskatoon: Fifth House, 1993. Hargreaves, Mary W. M. "Homesteading and Homemaking on the Plains: A Review." *Agricultural History* 47 (1973): 156–63. Hargreaves, Mary W. M. "Women in the Agricultural Settlement of the Northern Plains." *Agricultural History* 50 (1976): 179–89. Harris, Katherine. "Sex Roles and Work Patterns among Homesteading Families in Northeastern Colorado, 1873–1920." *Frontiers* 7 (1984): 43–49. Jackel, Susan. *A Flannel Shirt and Liberty: British Emigrant Gentlewomen in the Canadian West, 1880–1914*. Vancouver: University of British Columbia Press, 1982. Jeffrey, Julie Roy. *Frontier Women: The Trans-Mississippi West, 1840–1880*. New York: Hill and Wang, 1979. Jellison, Katherine. *Entitled to Power: Farm Women and Technology, 1913–1963*. Chapel Hill: University of North Carolina Press, 1993. Jensen, Joan M. *With These Hands: Women Working on the Land*. Old Westbury NY: Feminist Press, 1981. Kellie, Luna. *A Prairie Populist: The Memoirs of Luna Kellie*, edited by Jane Taylor Nelsen. Iowa City: University of Iowa Press, 1992. Kohl, Edith Eudora. *The Land of the Burnt Thigh*. St. Paul: Minnesota Historical Society Press, 1986. Kohl, Seena B. *Working Together: Women and Family in Southwestern Saskatchewan*. Toronto: Holt, Rinehart and Winston of Canada, 1976. Kolodny, Annette. *The Land before Her: Fantasy and Experience of the American Frontiers, 1630–1860*. Chapel Hill: University of North Carolina Press, 1984. Kolodny, Annette. *The Lay of the Land: Metaphor as Experience and History in American Life and Letters*. Chapel Hill: University of North Carolina Press, 1975. Lawrence, Elizabeth Atwood. *Rodeo: An Anthropologist Looks at the Wild and the Tame*. Knoxville: University of Tennessee Press, 1982. Lindgren, H. Elaine. "Ethnic Women Homesteading on the Plains of North Dakota." *Great Plains Quarterly* 9 (1989): 157–73. Neth, Mary. *Preserving the Family Farm: Women, Community and the Foundations of Agribusiness in the Midwest, 1900–1940*. Baltimore MD: Johns Hopkins University Press, 1995. O'Brien, Sharon. *Willa Cather: The Emerging Voice*. New York: Oxford University Press, 1987. Rasmussen, Linda, Lorna Rasmussen, Candace Savage, and Anne Wheeler. *A Harvest Yet to Reap: A History of Prairie Women*. Lincoln: University of Nebraska Press, 1976. Riley, Glenda. *The Female Frontier: A Comparative View of Women on the Prairie and the Plains*. Lawrence: University Press of Kansas, 1988. Riley, Glenda. *Women and Indians on the Frontier, 1825–1915*. Albuquerque: University of New Mexico Press, 1984. Riley, Glenda. "Women on the Great Plains: Recent Developments in Research." *Great Plains Quarterly* 5 (1985): 81–92. Savage, Candace. *Our Nell: A Scrapbook Biography of Nellie L. McClung*. Saskatoon: Western Producer Prairie Books, 1979. Schwieder, Dorothy, and Deborah Fink. "Plains Women: Rural Life in the 1930s." *Great Plains Quarterly* 8 (1988): 79–88. Stewart, Elinore Pruitt. *Letters of a Woman Homesteader*. Boston: Houghton Mifflin Company, 1914. Underwood, June O. "Civilizing Kansas: Women's Organizations, 1880–1920." *Kansas History* 7 (1984/85): 291–306. Van Kirk, Sylvia. *Many Tender Ties: Women in Fur-Trade Society, 1670–1870*. Norman: University of Oklahoma Press, 1980. Webb, Walter P. *The Great Plains*. Boston: Ginn and Company, 1931. Wishart, David. "The Roles and Status of Men and Women in Nineteenth-Century Omaha and Pawnee Societies: Postmodernist Uncertainties and Empirical Evidence." *American Indian Quarterly* 24 (1995): 509–18.

ALBERT V. ALBERT

In *Albert v. Albert* (1885) the Supreme Court of Montana held that a single incident of physical abuse by a husband against his wife could be deemed to constitute "extreme cruelty" so as to justify the granting of a divorce. The decision arose out of a petition for divorce filed in the Second District Court of Deer Lodge County by Kate Albert against her husband, Charles. Mrs. Albert claimed that she had been repeatedly beaten and whipped by Charles, and that the abuse she had incurred constituted extreme cruelty within the meaning of the applicable common law standards prescribing sufficient cause for the granting of a divorce. Mr. Albert defended his actions by claiming that he had beaten his wife on only one occasion and that he had been justified in doing so because Kate had publicly accused him of adultery.

In its charge to the jury, the trial court sided with Mr. Albert's view of the legal standards applicable to the situation, instructing the jury that even if they found that Mr. Albert had in fact struck his wife on more than one occasion, those actions did not necessarily establish the charge of extreme cruelty. The court further instructed the jury that if they found from the evidence that Mrs. Albert had "provoked" her husband to strike her, then Mr. Albert could be excused for treating her in a harsher manner than would have otherwise been justified. Based upon those instructions, the jury concluded that Mrs. Albert had not established her claim of extreme cruelty and denied the requested divorce decree.

On appeal by Mrs. Albert, the Montana Supreme Court reversed the trial court's judgment. In a decision that represented a significant departure from prevailing judicial interpretations of traditional gender roles and marital relations, the court held that even a single act of physical violence by a husband against a wife constituted sufficient proof of extreme cruelty to justify a divorce decree. The court further held that mere words uttered by a wife against her husband could never provide an excuse for a husband's violent response.

For the next twenty years the Montana Supreme Court's enunciation of this "single incident" standard for extreme cruelty provided the foundation for additional judicial tinkering with traditional legal interpretations of the marital relationship. Some legal historians, for example, point to the *Albert* decision as illustrative of the leading role played by western and Great Plains legal institutions in the evolution of new patterns of judicial recognition for the emerging "cult of true womanhood" and "companionate marriage ideal" of the Victorian period. In 1906, however, the Montana Supreme Court stepped back from the progressivism embodied in *Albert* and reversed itself on the single incident standard. In *Ryan v. Ryan* the court held that *Albert* had been superseded by legislation which provided that only mistreatment resulting in "grievous bodily injury" to a wife could give rise to an action for divorce. In response to *Ryan*, the Montana legislature amended the relevant statute again so as to provide that even the threat of grievous bodily harm would suffice to state a claim of extreme cruelty. Thus, *Albert v. Albert* remains a leading example of the evolving progressivism of Great Plains legal institutions in the reshaping of gender roles and marital dynamics in the late nineteenth and early twentieth centuries.

Mark R. Scherer
University of Nebraska at Omaha

Albert v. Albert, 5 Mont. 577, 6 P. 23 (1885). Petrik, Paula. *No Step Backward: Women and Family on the Rocky Mountain Mining Frontier, Helena, Montana, 1865–1900*. Helena: Montana Historical Society Press, 1987.

BARNARD, KATE (1875–1930)

Catherine Ann (Kate) Barnard is representative of the women in the Great Plains who made a career of social activism on behalf of the poor and vulnerable, voicing the concerns of the working class, minorities, women, and families in agricultural states experiencing rapid development. Kate was born in Geneva, Nebraska, on May 23, 1875, but grew up in Kirwin, Kansas. Her mother died there in 1877. In the mid-1890s she moved with her father, John P. Barnard, to a claim he had staked in the Oklahoma Land Run of 1889. While her father practiced law in Oklahoma City, Kate lived alone on the homestead, enduring the isolation, wind, and hard work, until the claim was secure. She then moved to Oklahoma City and attended St. Joseph's Academy. She taught in rural schools from 1896 to 1899 and then worked as a stenographer before taking charge, in 1905, of the Provident Association of Oklahoma City, a floundering charity organization. Barnard's highly successful appeals for contributions through the *Daily Oklahoman* newspaper turned her home into a distribution center for food, clothing, money, and job-placement information.

Barnard moved beyond charity to activism when she founded the local chapter of the Women's International Union Label League and represented the workers of the Oklahoma City Trades and Labor Assembly in 1905–7. These efforts made her an attractive advocate to socialist and populist political factions. She developed alliances with women's groups such as the Oklahoma Territory Federation of Women's Clubs, and she traveled to several major cities to interview the leaders of national reform organizations, making valuable contacts and gaining firsthand information about the latest social justice measures. As Oklahoma statehood approached in 1907, Democratic Party leaders recognized Barnard's political potential. She represented the women's lobby at the preliminary Shawnee Convention, urging child labor legislation, compulsory education, prison reform, and the creation of an office of commissioner of charities and corrections to oversee these issues. In the state document, members of the constitutional convention worded the description of the commissioner of charities and corrections to include a woman officeholder so that she might have the position. She was such an effective campaigner that she polled more votes from an all-male electorate than any other candidate, including the governor. She was reelected in 1910.

Barnard used her new office as the vehicle to propose aggressive legislation to implement her reforms and to demand adequate appropriations to establish effective social welfare institutions. Her graphic exposures in 1908 and 1909 of the treatment of Oklahoma prisoners in Kansas jails led to the construction of the first state penitentiary at McAlester and to a national reputation as an authority on prison reform. The publicity surrounding her descriptions of the shortcomings of the Oklahoma government's response to the poor and helpless, as well as her outspoken demands for money and action, soon angered party leaders such as William "Alfalfa Bill" Murray, speaker of the Oklahoma House of Representatives. Barnard's prosecution of corrupt, court-appointed "guardians" who dispossessed Indian orphans of valuable land, money, and oil assets led to her political downfall. In retaliation for her interference, members of the state legislature launched an investigation of her office, cut her appropriations, and recommended that the office be abolished. Barnard left political office in 1914, exhausted and ill. In obscurity she continued to advocate on behalf of society's most vulnerable citizens until she died alone in an Oklahoma City hotel on February 23, 1930.

Linda Reese
University of Oklahoma

Crawford, Suzanne, and Musslewhite, Lynn. "Kate Barnard, Progressivism, and the West." In "An Oklahoma I Had Never Seen Before": Alternative Views of Oklahoma History, edited by Davis D. Joyce. Norman: University of Oklahoma Press, 1994: 62–79. Reese, Linda W. *Women of Oklahoma, 1890–1920*. Norman: University of Oklahoma Press, 1997. Short, Julia A. "Kate Barnard: Liberated Woman." Master's thesis, University of Oklahoma, 1972.

BERDACHE

In the seventeenth and eighteenth centuries, French explorers, traders, and missionaries in the Mississippi Valley occasionally encountered Native Americans who could be classified neither as men nor women. They called such individuals *berdaches*, a French term for younger partners in male homosexual relationships. In fact, Plains Indian berdaches are best described as occupying an alternative or third gender role, in which traits of men and women are combined with those unique to berdache status. Male berdaches did women's work, cross-dressed or combined male and female clothing, and formed relationships with non-berdache men.

Plains Indian women often engaged in hunting and warfare, but a female role equivalent to that of male berdaches, although common west of the Rockies, has been documented in the Plains only among the Cheyennes (the *hetaneman*). Even so, some Plains Indian women became notable warriors and leaders and behaved much like berdaches. In the early nineteenth century, Running Eagle of the Piegans wore male clothing on war parties, while Woman Chief of the Crows had four wives.

Male berdaches were known among the Arapahos (*hoxuxunó*), Arikaras, Assiniboines (*wiⁿktaⁿ*), Blackfoot (*ake:śkassi*), Cheyennes (*he'eman*), Comanches, Plains Crees (*ayekkwe*), Crows (*boté*), Gros Ventres, Hidatsas (*miáti*), Kansas (*miⁿquge*), Kiowas, Mandans (*mihdeke*), Plains Ojibwas (*agokwa*), Omahas (*miⁿquga*), Osages (*mixu'ga*), Otoes (*mixo'ge*), Pawnees, Poncas (*miⁿquga*), Potawatomis (*m'nuktokwae*), Quapaws, Winnebagos (*shiángge*), and the various Siouan-speaking tribes (*winkte*, Lakota; *winkta*, Dakota). The two most common reasons cited for individuals becoming berdaches were childhood preference for work of the other sex and/or certain dreams or visions. The Lakotas credited dreams of Double Woman with influencing men to become *winkte*; others credited the Moon. Such dreams also conveyed valued skills—in particular, proficiency in women's arts, such as quilling, tanning, and beading. Among the Dakotas the saying "fine possessions like a berdache's" was the highest compliment one could pay a household.

Berdaches often had distinct religious roles. A Crow *boté* selected the central pole used in constructing Sun Dance lodges. Cheyenne *he'eman* directed the tribe's most important ceremony, the scalp dance. In Hidatsa villages, *miáti* were an "organized group" of as many as fifteen to twenty-five, treated as a "special class of religious leaders." In several tribes, berdaches were shamans and healers. Other skills attributed to berdaches included the ability to foretell the future and convey luck by bestowing obscene nicknames (Lakota), make love magic (Pawnee), and arrange marriages (Cheyenne). By reputation, many Plains berdaches were sexually active. George Catlin illustrated a Sauk and Fox dance in which a berdache is the central figure surrounded by "her" male lovers. Dakota warriors sometimes visited berdaches before joining war parties in the belief that such encounters augmented their masculine ferocity. Prominent warriors and chiefs, including the Omaha American Horse and the Lakota Crazy Horse, had berdaches among their wives.

Some observers have explained berdache roles as niches for males unable to fulfill rigorous standards of Plains masculinity. But as Dakotas told anthropologist Ruth Landes, a distinction was made between men afraid to join war parties and berdaches, who "had a dream." In fact, Plains berdaches were active in all aspects of warfare, from providing assistance on war parties to leading war ceremonies and entering battles (and some Dakota berdaches hunted, even as they maintained tipis that women envied). When the Hidatsa chief Four Bears encountered a Lakota winkte, and his arrow failed to penetrate his robe, the winkte exclaimed, "You can't kill me for I am holy. I will strike coups on you with my digging stick." In 1866 a winkte predicted the success of Lakota and Cheyenne forces against the Americans at Fort Phil Kearny. In 1876 the Crow boté Finds Them and Kills Them killed a Lakota warrior in the Battle of the Rosebud.

In the reservation period, American missionaries denounced berdaches, government agents forced them to do men's work, and boarding-school teachers punished children for inappropriate gender behavior. As European American attitudes toward homosexuality were adopted in Indian communities, families often intervened to prevent their own members from becoming (or behaving like) berdaches. Nonetheless, traditional berdaches like Finds Them and Kills Them successfully resisted efforts to change their lifestyles. In the 1980s anthropologist Walter Williams found individuals on Plains reservations still performing traditional functions of the berdache role.

In the 1990s the term "two-spirit" was introduced by Native Americans as an alternative to berdache, and traditional third gender roles became the subject of renewed interest among Natives and non-Natives alike. As Michael Red Earth, a gay-identified Dakota, writes, "Once I realized that this respect and acceptance was a legacy of our traditional Native past, I was empowered to present my whole self to the world and reassume the responsibilities of being a two-spirited person."

Will Roscoe
California Institute of Integral Studies

Jacobs, Sue-Ellen, Wesley Thomas, and Sabine Lang, eds. *Two-Spirit People: Native American Gender Identity, Sexuality, and Spirituality*. Urbana: University of Illinois Press, 1997. Roscoe, Will. *Changing Ones: Third and Fourth Genders in Native North America*. New York: St. Martin's Press, 1998. Williams, Walter L. *The Spirit and the Flesh: Sexual Diversity in American Indian Culture*. Boston: Beacon Press, 1986.

BINNIE-CLARK, GEORGINA (1871–1947)

Born at Dorset, England, on April 25, 1871, Georgina Binnie-Clark was a journalist who migrated to Canada in 1905 to become an independent farmer. She "caused quite a sensation" in the Qu'Appelle Valley of southern Saskatchewan when she purchased a quarter-section of land. Single, independent women farmers were rare in Prairie Canada. Under the Dominion Lands Act (1872), single women were not eligible for a quarter-section, or

160 acres, of free land from the Canadian government.

Binnie-Clark was determined to make her farm a successful revenue-producing investment so that she could secure independence. Without the free quarter-section of land, she was under a greater financial burden than her male counterparts. She had access to some funds enabling her to buy necessary supplies, farm equipment, and livestock, and to hire labor. But purchasing land forced her to deplete limited capital and make added interest payments. The harvests were also disappointing, making it increasingly difficult for her to cover mortgage costs or meet growing debt payments.

As a result of her experiences selling grain in the open market, Binnie-Clark became a sharp critic of the privately controlled grain-marketing system. In her view the Prairie farmer was not sufficiently aided by either financial institutions or governments. She advocated government regulation of grain marketing and the establishment of government-run experimental farms to serve as models for Prairie women farmers. After the 1908 harvest, Binnie-Clark traveled to Ottawa to discuss with government officials the "claim of women to her fair share" in the homestead lands of Canada. She helped to spearhead the movement calling for application of the free-land provisions of the Dominion Lands Act to women, which converged with other Prairie women's crusades for equal rights before the law, such as the campaigns for dower rights and the voting franchise. The homestead land provision was not open to single women until the lands of the Canadian Prairie were transferred from the federal government to provincial jurisdiction in 1930.

Binnie-Clark wrote many articles in British and American publications. Their purpose was to outline the difficulties and provide guidance through her experiences to other women contemplating owning and operating a farm on the prairie. She was a keen observer of Saskatchewan rural life. Her autobiographical books contain rich detail about the social life and customs, material culture, local politics, and the rhythm of daily farm life. She died in England on April 22, 1947.

David B. Marshall
University of Calgary

Binnie-Clark, Georgina. *A Summer on the Canadian Prairie*. London: Edward Arnold, 1910. Binnie-Clark, Georgina. *Wheat and Women*. Toronto: Bell and Cockburn, 1914. Jackel, Susan. *A Flannel Shirt and Liberty: British Emigrant Gentlewomen in the Canadian North West, 1880–1914*. Vancouver: University of British Columbia Press, 1982.

CALAMITY JANE (1856–1903)

Martha Canary (Calamity Jane), the famous frontierswoman, was born in 1856 in the vicinity of Princeton, Missouri, the eldest daughter of Robert and Charlotte Canary. In 1864 the Canary family joined the gold rush to Montana. Martha's parents died in the West a few years later, and Martha was reported alone in

Calamity Jane

the 1869 census of Piedmont, Wyoming. She evidently became a prostitute, traveling between the bustling new Union Pacific Railroad towns and Wyoming's military posts. At some point she gained her famous nickname, "Calamity Jane," probably based on her propensity for raising a ruckus or because of her calamitous origins. The first published notice of Martha bearing her famous nickname appeared in 1875, when in the capacity of camp follower she accompanied the "Jenney expedition" from Fort Laramie to the Black Hills of Dakota Territory.

Martha's local notoriety increased in 1876 when, again as camp follower, she accompanied Gen. George Crook's command against the Sioux; for the remainder of her life, Martha claimed to have scouted for Crook. Shortly afterward she joined James Butler "Wild Bill" Hickok's wagon train headed for the Black Hills. Though their acquaintance lasted only a few weeks before Hickok was murdered in Deadwood on August 2, 1876, the names of Calamity Jane and Wild Bill Hickok would be joined in folklore.

Martha gained national prominence in 1877 after Horatio N. Maguire penned a colorful account of her in his promotional booklet *The Black Hills and American Wonderland*. His description was appropriated by dime-novelist Edward Wheeler for his new "Deadwood Dick" series, instantly transforming "Calamity Jane" into a nationally known heroine.

Her life was less glamorous than the dime-novel descriptions allowed. She worked as a dance-hall girl, waitress, and laundress, living with a series of male companions she identified as husbands. Following early experiences, she migrated to newly constructed railroad towns, mining camps, and military posts. She followed the Northern Pacific Railroad as it built westward through Montana in the early 1880s, then migrated to the Wyoming region as railroad extensions were built into interior regions. For several years she was the companion of William Steers, a physically abusive railroad brakeman. They were legally married several months after the birth of their daughter, Jessie, in 1887.

In 1895 Calamity Jane made a celebrated return to Deadwood, selling photographs of herself in frontier costume. Publicity led to a contract to tour eastern cities with Kohl and Middleton's dime museums in 1896. Her somewhat fictionalized autobiography, *Life and Adventures of Calamity Jane, By Herself*, was published during this tour for sale to audiences. Afterward Martha returned to Montana, making a subsistence living from sales of her autobiography and photographs and from performing menial labor. A generous woman, she attended people in illness and shared her meager proceeds; an alcoholic, she never held lasting jobs nor accumulated property or wealth.

Exhibiting increasing signs of serious illness, Martha once again received national publicity in 1901 when author Josephine Brake offered her the opportunity to live with her in New York. Upon her arrival there, Calamity Jane was exhibited with Colonel Frederic T. Cummins's "Indian Congress" at the Pan-American Exposition in Buffalo. Unhappy and feeling used, Martha returned to Montana, where her drunken celebrations made her less and less welcome. In December 1902 she departed for the Black Hills, where she died in Terry, near Deadwood, on August 1, 1903. She was buried in the vicinity of Hickok.

See also IMAGES AND ICONS: Deadwood, South Dakota; Hickok, Wild Bill.

James D. McLaird
Dakota Wesleyan University

Etulain, Richard W. "Calamity Jane: Independent Woman of the Wild West." In *By Grit and Grace: Eleven Women Who Shaped the American West*, edited by Glenda Riley and Richard W. Etulain. Golden CO: Fulcrum Publishing, 1997: 72–92. Jennewein, J. Leonard. *Calamity Jane of the Western Trails*. Huron SD: Dakota Books, 1953. Sollid, Roberta Beed. *Calamity Jane: A Study in Historical Criticism*. Helena: Montana Historical Society, 1995.

CAPTIVITY NARRATIVES

Captivity narratives are the accounts written by men and women reporting on their experiences as abductees of Native Americans. From the seventeenth century to the end of the nineteenth century such accounts accompanied the westward-moving frontier, and their storylines, established in the first known captivity narrative by Mary Rowlandson in 1682, remained essentially the same: conflict between the settlers and Indians, capture by the Indians, ordeal at the hands of the captors, and a return to European American society.

In general, male captives adjusted easier to their new lives with Native American peoples than did female captives, who, with very few exceptions, feared for their virtue and prayed for a return to civilization. Through the centuries in these captivity narratives, stock phrases are perpetuated—for example, bashing brains out and burning people at the stake. Their descriptions of elements of the captors' cultures tend to be generic and confusing, but the message is clear: Native American cultures are considered inferior to European American civilization, and Native Americans are perceived as emotionless, cruel, and traitorous. The captives' detailed descriptions of torture scenes and the suffering of women and children provided justification for armed conflict on the western frontier and the displacement of Native Americans, whose voices were very rarely heard in the captivity documents.

Women and children brought civilization to the frontier, and in the minds of their contemporaries, their removal from their fledgling communities represented a basic threat to civilization. It was acceptable to convert Native Americans to Christianity and make farmers of them, and thereby to make them part of the mainstream. Women captives, however, found it impossible to exert a civilizing influence on their captors, and their captivity narratives revealed their belief that Native Americans had to disappear in order for civilization to come. Documents and testimonials attached to the narratives were meant to encourage the reader to believe in the historical truth of the narratives and to treat the information contained therein as fact.

Captivities during the settlement of the Plains were much more widely distributed than those during colonial times, and Plains captivity narratives exerted significant influence on their readers. Stories like Fanny Kelly's painted a vivid picture of Native Americans who rejoiced in the killing of women and children. Kelly despairs as she recognizes her small daughter's scalp and then witnesses the hopelessness of a fellow captive forced to "marry" her captor and the degeneration of a captive who, from infancy, had grown up among the Native Americans. Kelly also described "barbaric" customs and physical assaults. These highly emotional descriptions and reports of repeated treachery by the Sioux helped to convince settlers on the Northern Plains that military expeditions were necessary, and that any sympathy with the Native Americans was misguided. Glenda Riley, in her analysis of women's voices on the frontier and especially in the Southern Plains, reveals accounts that reflect Kelly's attitude, as well as accounts of women who came to an understanding of Native American people and their increasingly desperate situation.

The closing of the frontier and the end of Indian wars in the Plains in the late nineteenth century did not diminish the popularity of captivity narratives. They continued to follow the standard form of the genre, but some elements—for example, the heroism of the captives and their deeds—became more exaggerated. At the same time, portrayals of Native Americans became more sympathetic. Instead of condemning Native American cultures wholesale, they allow some noble characters to emerge. An interesting change in the basic plot of captivity narratives has occurred in the last thirty years with the emergence of romance. The captive remains with her Native American captor and exerts a "civilizing" influence over him and his tribe—she achieves what the earlier woman captive could not. There is also hope for some Native American cultures in these romances. These new conventions are evident in such recent films as *Dances with Wolves* (1990), which, while ethnographically more accurate, as newer audiences demand, romanticizes traditional Lakota culture and also plays on images of the "noble" and the "savage" Native American (the latter in this case are Pawnees). Captivity narratives remain a formula rather than portrayals of complex and contemporary peoples; they deal with the conflict between Native and European Americans in terms entirely satisfying to the latter audience, while denying complexity and contemporaneity to Native American peoples.

See also: FILM: *Dances with Wolves*.
Birgit Hans
University of North Dakota

Kelly, Fanny. *Narrative of My Captivity among the Sioux Indians*. Chicago: Lakeside Press, 1990 [1871]. Riley, Glenda. *Women and Indians on the Frontier, 1825–1915*. Albuquerque: University of New Mexico Press, 1984. Stedman, Raymond William. *Shadows of the Indian: Stereotypes in American Culture*. Norman: University of Oklahoma Press, 1982.

CLEARY, KATE M. (1863–1905)

Detailing the life of small-town pioneers, Kate M. Cleary wrote novels, stories, sketches, and poems about Nebraska in the late 1800s. Born on August 22, 1863, in Richibucto, New Brunswick, Canada, she moved with her mother and two brothers in 1880 to Chicago, where the whole family wrote to support themselves. In 1884 she married Michael Cleary, and the couple moved to the newly founded village of Hubbell, Nebraska. While in Hubbell, the Clearys had six children, losing two daughters within a year of each other. The family moved back to Chicago in 1898.

After nearly dying from childbirth fever in 1894, Cleary became dependent on the morphine that her doctor had given her to relieve the pain. She battled ill health as well as addiction throughout her life, finally admitting herself to the Elgin Asylum for the Insane for drug treatment. After her treatment she separated from her husband and dedicated herself to writing, insisting on supporting the children's private schooling. She died of heart failure in Chicago on July 16, 1905, at age forty-one, just as she had begun negotiating with publisher Houghton Mifflin on a collection of her short stories. It was never published.

Throughout her lifetime Cleary wrote hundreds of stories, which appeared in such diverse outlets as the *Chicago Tribune*, *Cosmopolitan*, and *McClure's*. The best of them are about early Plains settlers, especially the men and women in rural villages. Many of them are realistic or naturalistic depictions of the hardships of western pioneers. Others, however, are humorous and satirical portrayals, gently mocking social pretensions and the idealized Cult of True Womanhood.

Susanne K. George
University of Nebraska at Kearney

George, Susanne K. *Kate M. Cleary: A Literary Biography with Selected Works.* Lincoln: University of Nebraska Press, 1997.

COLBY, CLARA (1846–1916)

Clara Bewick Colby, Nebraska's most prominent suffragist, was a newspaper editor and lecturer whose personal commitment to equal rights resulted in a national career and an international reputation. Born in England on August 5, 1846, she emigrated to Wisconsin in 1854. She entered the University of Wisconsin in 1865 and studied coursework previously offered only to men. Initially denied the right to graduate, she was subsequently recognized as the 1869 class valedictorian and hired as an instructor by the University of Wisconsin. She later left that position over a dispute concerning gender pay equity. In 1872 she married Leonard Wright Colby and moved to Beatrice, Nebraska. The couple adopted a three-year-old boy, Clarence, from an orphan train in 1885. Leonard later (1891) returned from the Wounded Knee Massacre with a Sioux child named Zintkala Nuni (Lost Bird) and adopted her himself while Clara was away lecturing on suffrage issues. Clara and Leonard Colby were formally divorced in 1906.

Colby strove to bring culture to her Plains hometown by establishing a public library and a community theater. In 1878 she invited suffragists Elizabeth Cady Stanton and Susan B. Anthony to lecture in Beatrice. She then began traveling as a national women's suffrage speaker. Colby was one of Elizabeth Cady Stanton's "girls" or "lieutenants." In 1881 she was one of the organizers of the Women's State Suffrage Association in Nebraska and served as its president from 1885 to 1898. In 1883 she became the editor and publisher of the *Woman's Tribune*, a national suffrage newspaper she created to bring events and perspectives to readers in isolated locations. From 1886 to 1889 the *Woman's Tribune* was the official publication of the National Woman Suffrage Association. In 1888 the newspaper was published in a daily edition of 12,500 during the International Council of Women in Washington DC. This was the first time a daily paper for women had been edited and published by a woman. Considered by Susan B. Anthony to be the best writer of the women's movement, Colby was Anthony's first choice as a biographer. In 1889 Colby received the first press correspondent's pass issued to a woman to cover the Spanish-American War. She was one of the members of the Revising Committee of the controversial *Woman's Bible*, published from 1895 to 1898. In 1904 Colby moved to Oregon to continue suffrage work there. The *Woman's Tribune* ceased publication in 1909, although Colby optimistically intended to continue when funds became available.

In the last years of her life, Colby lectured in Britain and other European locations and served as a delegate to the International Moral Education Congress (London, 1908); International Women Suffrage Alliance (Amsterdam, 1908); International Races Congress (London, 1911); International Woman Suffrage Convention (Budapest, 1913); and the International Peace Conference (The Hague, 1913). Clara Bewick Colby died September 7, 1916, in Palo Alto, California, four years before the passage of the Nineteenth Amendment establishing women's suffrage as law.

Laureen Riedesel
Beatrice Public Library

Brown, Olympia, ed. *Democratic Ideals: A Memorial Sketch of Clara B. Colby.* Washington DC: Federal Suffrage Association, 1917. Colby, Clara Bewick. Papers. State Historical Society of Wisconsin, Madison. Jerry, E. Claire. "Clara Bewick Colby and the *Woman's Tribune*, 1883–1909: The Free Lance Editor as Movement Leader." In *A Voice of Their Own: The Woman Suffrage Press, 1840–1910*, edited by Martha M. Solomon. Tuscaloosa: University of Alabama Press, 1991, 110–28.

DIGGS, ANNIE (1848–1916)

Annie LePorte Diggs played a prominent role as a Kansas-based journalist, orator, and political organizer for women's suffrage, the Farmers Alliance, the Populist (People's) Party, and many other causes. The thread that joined all the causes together was her quest for a more equitable distribution of wealth and power.

Born in London, Ontario, on February 22, 1848, and raised in New Jersey, Annie moved to Kansas in 1873. She soon married, bore three children, and found she needed employment to supplement the family income. She chose newspaper work, which threw her among all classes of people. Although she entered the political arena via temperance and religion, a trip to Boston in 1881 convinced her that the reforms she sought were more economic than moral. The Boston trip also marked the beginning of her pattern of leaving Kansas to research social issues, give speeches, and write articles for local and national publications, and then returning to Kansas to organize for major political campaigns.

From the 1880s to 1912, when Kansas finally ratified the women's suffrage amendment, Annie was a leader in the suffrage struggle. For the Farmers Alliance she wrote and lectured on the themes of money, transportation, and land, and pushed for farmers and workers to form a national third party. Her hard work in the development of the Populist Party culminated in her appointment as Kansas State Librarian (1898–1902), the most important governmental office assigned to a Kansas woman by that date. Even after the Populist Party died, she remained committed to its principle of public ownership of public utilities and its mission of bringing justice to the dealings between owners and workers in the realm of industry. Annie Diggs died in Detroit on September 7, 1916.

Joan Stone
University of Kansas

Clanton, O. Gene. *Kansas Populism.* Lawrence: University Press of Kansas, 1969. Weddle, Connie Andes. "The Platform and the Pen: The Reform Activities of Annie Diggs." Master's thesis, Wichita State University, 1979.

EARHART, AMELIA (1897–1937)

Amelia Earhart was a woman who was ahead of her time. She was a pioneer aviator, a pacifist, and a feminist who, although daubed with grease, was unmistakably a lady. Earhart was born July 24, 1897, in Atchison, Kansas. On both sides, her family had been American since before the Revolution. Her maternal grand-

Amelia Earhart in Denver, Colorado, June 3, 1931

father was a judge who was upright, conventional, and moderately wealthy. Her paternal grandfather was a minister, whose saintliness was matched only by his poverty. The judge's gentle, lovable daughter married the minister's brilliant, irresponsible son and the results were Amelia Earhart and her younger sister, Muriel. The girls initially enjoyed an idyllic childhood, spending the school year with their grandparents in Atchison and the summers with their parents in Kansas City. However, when alcoholism caught up with her father it all came apart, and the family drifted around the Midwest, living in poor circumstances. Amelia graduated from high school in Chicago in 1916.

A stint in a Canadian military hospital during World War I left her a confirmed pacifist and gave her a first glimpse of aviation activity, but she did not became involved herself until a few years later when the family moved to California. Her first flight was in 1920, and in 1921 she gained her license from the National Aeronautics Association. The next year she set the women's altitude record (14,000 feet).

In 1928, while working as a social worker in Boston, Amelia had an opportunity that brought her worldwide recognition. A transatlantic flight had been arranged, and the sponsor wanted a woman aboard who not only could fly but also could represent the United States with grace and honor. Amelia was a natural for the position. One of those who interviewed her was George Palmer Putnam of the publishing firm G. P. Putnam and Sons. The success of the flight brought Amelia headlines. Although she had merely been a passenger, she was officially the first woman to fly across the Atlantic.

Taking advantage of her widespread fame, Putnam (whom Amelia married on February 7, 1931) scheduled Earhart for a full program of lectures. In addition, she wrote articles and books to help support her mother and sister. In her works Amelia stressed two themes: first, she advocated aviation as a means of transportation and promoted the unlimited possibilities for flight in general; and second, as a pioneer for women's rights, she strove for the day when women would have the same educational and career opportunities as men.

Earhart loved the beauty of flight and flew whenever she could. Although she set several speed records for women pilots, and in 1931 held the world altitude record for autogyros at 18,451 feet, her specialty was long-range routes, which she saw as heralds of regular commercial routes. On May 20 and 21, 1932, she made her solo transatlantic flight from Newfoundland to Ireland. Early in 1935 she made the first solo nonstop flight from Honolulu to Oakland; later the same year she established another record from Mexico City to New York City.

In 1935 she became affiliated with Purdue University as an aviation adviser and as a counselor for women students. Purdue provided her with a Lockheed Electra as a flying laboratory. That same year, Amelia decided that she had one more flight in her system.

She wanted to fly around the world as close to the equator as possible. Her first attempt, from east to west, ended in March 1937 when her plane ground-looped as she was taking off from Honolulu for Howland Island in the Pacific. She had to start over again after her aircraft was repaired. For various reasons she changed her route to fly from west to east. On this ill-fated flight, she sent back detailed accounts of each leg. She appeared to be doing well, but on the next to the last leg, from New Guinea to Howland Island, Amelia and her navigator, Fred Noonan, disappeared on July 2, 1937. On July 17 they were declared lost at sea.

There the clear stream of Amelia Earhart's life was lost in a swamp of myth and speculation. Figuring out what happened to her has become a sort of cottage industry, with explanations running from the fairly plausible to the frankly incredible. The search to find her plane and body continues, but no one can yet say with any degree of certainty where and why Amelia crashed. The real tragedy was the loss of Amelia Earhart the person: a vivid, likable, and interesting woman who made an invaluable contribution to aviation and women's rights and in the process made herself one of the best-known and best-liked personalities of her time.

Donald M. Goldstein
University of Pittsburgh

Goldstein, Donald M., and Katherine V. Dillon. *Amelia: Life of the Aviation Legend*. Washington DC: Brassey's, 1998. Long, Elgen M., and Maria K. Long. *Amelia Earhart: The Mystery Solved*. New York: Simon and Schuster, 1999. Rich, Doris. *Amelia Earhart: A Biography*. Washington DC: Smithsonian Institution Press, 1989.

EASTMAN, ELAINE GOODALE
(1863–1953)

Elaine Goodale Eastman wrote extensively about Native Americans, both as a collaborator with her husband, Dakota physician and writer Charles Eastman, and under her own name. Born on October 9, 1863, at Sky Farm in the Berkshires of Massachusetts, Eastman wrote poetry as a child, used her literary talents while a teacher of Sioux at Hampton Institute, and sent letters and articles to eastern publications during four years of teaching and supervising Native schools on the Great Sioux Reservation from 1886 to 1890.

At Pine Ridge at the time of the Wounded Knee Massacre, she met and married Dr. Eastman. Thereupon she sacrificed her own literary ambition to further the career of her husband and the cause of his people. When he had difficulty providing for the family, she encouraged him to write stories of his Native childhood, which she edited and published. Together they produced nine books, most under his name alone. He became famous as a writer and lecturer on Native American life, while she remained anonymous at home in Massachusetts caring for their six children. In all this Elaine Eastman exhibited a "feminist Protestant ethic," whereby all the virtues of the Protestant ethic—industry, thrift, and

enterprise—were applied to the service of others, specifically her husband and Native Americans.

Illness, constant financial problems, and the death of a daughter increased the strains on an already troubled marriage, which ended in 1921. The couple neither divorced nor reconciled. Elaine Eastman continued to write until she was almost ninety, drawing material from her own childhood and marriage, as well as from her experience living with and teaching the Sioux. Although her posthumously published memoirs provide a sympathetic and readable account of Sioux life in the 1880s, none of her seven books achieved the success of those published under her husband's name. Elaine Eastman died on December 22, 1953, at Hadley, Massachusetts.

Ruth Ann Alexander
South Dakota State University

Alexander, Ruth Ann. "Elaine Goodale Eastman and the Failure of the Feminist Protestant Ethic." *Great Plains Quarterly* 8 (1988): 89–101. Eastman, Elaine Goodale. "All the Days of My Life." *South Dakota Historical Review* 2 (1937): 171–84. Eastman, Elaine Goodale. *Sister to the Sioux*, edited by Kay Graber. Lincoln: University of Nebraska Press, 1978.

FIELD MATRONS

Field matrons worked for the U.S. Bureau of Indian Affairs (BIA) between 1890 and 1938 in a campaign designed to introduce Native American women to Victorian, middle-class culture. Like the destruction of the collective land base by allotment, the disruption of families by the removal of children to Indian schools, and the steady diminution of sovereignty by federal encroachments, the domestic education of Native American women became, in the hands of the field matrons, yet another tool to destroy tribalism. Convinced that it was possible to "kill the Indian and save the woman [*sic*]," the BIA looked to the field matrons to promote assimilation in reservation communities across the American West.

By the last decades of the nineteenth century, Canadian and American policymakers and reform advocates active in Indian affairs agreed that wholesale "civilization" was the only way to ensure the survival of those remaining Native populations located in the western provinces and states. Only in the United States, though, did a woman-specific assimilation strategy develop. To teach Indian women "to respect and love and seek the ways of White women," the BIA worked with members of Congress, reformers, and missionary activists to create the field matron program.

Sent into the field in 1890, the field matrons eventually worked in nearly every tribal community in the Great Plains, as well as across the West. Those women first employed by the BIA in the late nineteenth century exemplified the era's "certified civilizers." Caucasian, middle class, and single, they were imbued with Christian missionary spirit. As field matrons they spread among the Indians the American gospel of cleanliness, godliness, corsets, femininity, homebound domesticity, and woman's proper sphere. In the early twentieth century, however, the composition of the group changed. The American women becoming field matrons after 1900 coupled their reformist ambition to "do good" with their personal desire to "do well" financially as BIA employees. From the end of World War I until 1938, women motivated by economic gain rather than rescue dominated the field matron corps.

While the BIA heartily encouraged Native women to become advocates for assimilation in their homes and communities, it only reluctantly included them as full partners in the field matron program. The same ethnocentrism that skewed American and Canadian perspectives on Indian traditionalism resulted in restrictions on the employment of "civilized" tribal women. The BIA rarely accepted Native adoptions of the "American way" as trustworthy because, at base, it was deeply suspicious of the very process of cultural change it hoped to promote. The agency restricted tribal women to the position of assistant field matron and only appointed them between 1895 and 1905. Most of these women served in tribal communities located in the Great Plains.

The decision to phase out the field matron program in the 1930s reflected both the waning significance of Victorian domesticity and the desperate need in reservation communities for medical expertise. Appalling public health conditions plagued Native Americans in both the United States and Canada during the late nineteenth and early twentieth centuries. In the United States, tuberculosis and trachoma ran rampant; infant and child morbidity and mortality robbed tribal communities of their future generations; and destitution revealed itself in malnutrition and hopelessness. Field matrons struggled to adapt their positions by teaching seminars on epidemic diseases and prenatal care instead of homemaking. Their efforts saved lives but also led the BIA to conclude that trained nurses were more valuable than assimilation advocates. After 1938 field nurses replaced field matrons as "civilization" took a backseat to Indian public health education and care in the United States.

See also NATIVE AMERICANS: Assimilation Policy.

Lisa E. Emmerich
California State University, Chico

Bannan, Helen M. "'True Womanhood on the Reservation': Field Matrons in the United States Indian Service." SIROW Working Paper No. 19. Tucson: University of Arizona, 1984. Emmerich, Lisa E. "'Right in the Midst of My Own People': Native American Women and the Field Matron Program." *American Indian Quarterly* 15 (1990): 201–16. Emmerich, Lisa E. "'To Respect and Love and Seek the Ways of White Women': Field Matrons, the Office of Indian Affairs, and Civilization Policy, 1890–1938," Ph.D. diss., University of Maryland, 1987.

GAY AND LESBIAN LIFE

Social isolation is a major force in the lives of gay men and lesbians in the Great Plains, especially in small towns and rural areas. This isolation results from the region's great distances and low population density, the conformist and privacy-guarding aspects of rural and small-town life, and the tendency of many gays and lesbians to leave their hometowns for larger cities within and outside the region. In urban places it is generally easier for them to be themselves and to connect with other gays and lesbians.

Though the intensity of this migration has possibly lessened in recent years, it continues, and it helps to foster the idea among many heterosexuals that homosexuality is an exclusively urban phenomenon, irrelevant to rural or small-town life. Many gays and lesbians who stay in their small communities strengthen this belief by concealing their homosexuality, or by denying and suppressing it in order to follow a traditional life pattern that typically includes marriage and child rearing. Growing up in a homogeneous and conformist community, lacking information and openly gay role models, gay and lesbian youth are likely to perpetuate this pattern.

In recent years, with television and other vehicles of popular culture depicting gays and lesbians living openly, gay and lesbian youth are less likely to remain ignorant of, or confused by, their natures and are less susceptible to making life choices that are rooted in concealment and pretense. Internet access to supportive information and social connections is especially valuable to the most isolated gays and lesbians, perhaps reducing their likelihood of attempting suicide or engaging in substance abuse, unsafe sexual practices, or other self-destructive behaviors.

Great Plains culture celebrates individualism, but only within the tightly delimited boundaries of conventional gender identity. Females are allowed somewhat more latitude to stray from the feminine ideal than are males to deviate from the masculine. Especially when it is combined with fundamentalist interpretations of biblical texts and with the puritanism of Judeo-Christian culture, this gender-role rigidity is a powerful enforcer of the heterosexual norm.

No state or provincial government of the Plains region has been progressive in extending full civil rights to gay men and lesbians. In many places, their consensual sexual activity is criminalized, their access to housing and employment is threatened, and the recognition of marriage or domestic partnership for their committed relationships is denied. It is not uncommon for acts of antigay violence to be viewed with indifference or a sense of being deserved. In a widely publicized case, Matthew Shepard was murdered in Laramie, Wyoming, in 1998. Though he was a native of that state, the twenty-one-year-old had attended high school in Europe and had lived on the East Coast. Returning to Wyoming, he brought with him a manner of self-presentation that proved to be fatally at odds with Plains culture: he would not, or could not, conceal his gayness.

Before contact with Europeans, many Native cultures of the Plains accommodated and even valued gender-atypical males and females. Regarded as a blend of woman and man, these individuals were clearly counterparts of contemporary gays and lesbians, but their differences from typical men and women were understood by their tribes to be more complex than simply "sexual orientation." Seen as having special talents, they performed well-defined and respected functions within their communities: artists, healers, mediators, keepers of cultural traditions. As Native cultures have been eroded or destroyed, so have these intermediate gender identities, though some contemporary Native Americans are embracing and reviving them—preferring to call themselves two-spirit rather than gay or lesbian.

Will Fellows
Milwaukee, Wisconsin

Fellows, Will, ed. *Farm Boys: Lives of Gay Men from the Rural Midwest.* Madison: University of Wisconsin Press, 1996. Jacobs, Sue-Ellen, Wesley Thomas, and Sabine Lang, eds. *Two-Spirit People: Native American Gender Identity, Sexuality, and Spirituality.* Urbana: University of Illinois Press, 1997. Loffreda, Beth. *Losing Matt Shepard: Life and Politics in the Aftermath of Anti-Gay Murder.* New York: Columbia University Press, 2000.

GENDER AND SENSE OF PLACE

Women and men experience the Great Plains in very different ways. The characteristics they find appealing or repellent, the reasons they have for being there, even the terms they use to describe Plains life and landscape are distinctly different, almost as if they were describing different worlds. Women often praise the interpersonal qualities of small-town life in the region, such as the closeness of families, the closer intergenerational ties, and the intimacy and helpfulness of the community. In contrast, men typically laud the Plains as an ideal context for work and play, citing independence, opportunity, and freedom to work their own schedules. Women understand the merits men see in Plains life. They describe the flexibility and freedom men enjoy in their work, and how the "frontier" qualities of the Plains appeal to men, but they usually consider these the exclusive domain of males. In fact, many women regard the Plains as primarily a man's place, and they feel more restricted to traditional female roles in work, home life, and community than they would in other places. Plains society does not readily acknowledge it when women share in traditional men's work. For instance, many women work full-time on the family farm but rarely are recognized as farmers.

Men are much more likely than women to find the Plains physically appealing. They get an expansive feeling from the open landscape and regard the remoteness and emptiness of the Plains as a source of welcome solitude, privacy, and freedom from disturbance. Women, in contrast, frequently deride the emptiness and treelessness, report feeling "vulnerable" or "exposed" in the open, and describe the landscape with foreboding terms such as "barren," "desolate," "edge of the earth," or "vast nothingness." They often experience what men affectionately call "solitude" as social isolation, cultural deprivation, and domestic inconvenience.

Distinctions are even more pronounced between men and women who immigrate from outside the Plains. Immigrant men adapt readily to Plains life and typically embrace an exhilarating sense of widened horizons and expanded possibilities. Immigrant women are much more likely to complain of restrictive gender roles, oppressive social norms, social and emotional isolation, and a lack of professional or recreational opportunities. Even after decades of residence, they can suffer from culture and landscape shock, and they often admit to pining for their original homes and richer landscapes.

These responses are especially intriguing in light of the nearly identical gender distinctions that appear in accounts of early European American settlers, especially regarding the landscape. The forces that drew men to, and repelled women from, the Plains in the nineteenth century apparently still operate today. This could be a culturally imprinted contrast in sensitivity or aesthetics, but its endurance suggests that a gender distinction may exist that is deeper than the cultural milieu. Perhaps, as some research suggests, men have an innate preference for open landscapes, and women for shelter. This question may never be answered, but its emergence in the Great Plains offers insight into the relationship between gender and sense of place.

Cary W. de Wit
University of Alaska Fairbanks

de Wit, Cary W. "Women's Sense of Place on the American High Plains." *Great Plains Quarterly* 21 (2001): 29–44.

GENDERED SPACE

Both gender and space in society are abstract concepts that reflect power relations, the gendered division of labor, and societal concepts of propriety. The boardrooms of banks symbolize and enclose more power than small-town kitchens, for example, and each entails a sense of proper activities to be conducted within them. The former space is still more associated with men; the latter, with women. Because the Great Plains is so closely associated with spatial concepts like distance and "wide-open spaces," gendered space has much to do with how Great Plains residents and outsiders understand this region. Great Plains history and literature provide many examples.

Deborah Fink's study of Nebraska farmwives from 1880 to 1940 shows that they were far more socially isolated and restricted in their mobility than were their husbands. Although both husband and wife could take the team and wagon to town, women initially found few spaces accessible to them beyond the general store, and even fewer spaces where mothers could bring small children. Male farmers, in contrast, would frequent various farm supply stores or chat with male friends in the saloon or livery stable—spaces no "respectable woman" would invade. Such experiences further discouraged rural women from traveling beyond their farms, thus limiting their opportunities for friendships with town dwellers

who might have welcomed farm women's visits. The automobile, telephone, and emergence of women's groups (quilting circles, for example) diminished these barriers, essentially by reconfiguring space: the time-distance equation changed and new female spaces developed. Subsequently many farm women took jobs in town, such as teaching school, to supplement the family's agricultural income, and thus they became less isolated than husbands devoted to full-time farming.

Despite many rural women's involvement in the heavy farmwork and men's involvement with domestic chores, farm space still seems gendered to many people: the fields, pastures, and barn are encoded as male space; the house and garden, as female. Thus, European emigrants who had longstanding traditions of women haying and harvesting in the fields faced prejudices from their native-born Anglo-American or Anglo-Canadian neighbors in the Great Plains, who found the immigrants' "foreign" division of space and labor improper.

These social realities encouraged popular legends about the female Plains settler's maladaptation to its wide-open spaces and her preference for the settled East. Willa Cather in her short story "The Wagner Matinee" poignantly describes a former music teacher stranded on an isolated Nebraska farm. The bleakness of her surroundings contrasts with the rich cultural opportunities of Boston, where she weeps during a concert on one of her rare trips away from home. In Hamlin Garland's *Moccasin Ranch*, homestead wife Blanche lives close enough to town to escape her Dakota claim shanty at every opportunity for trips to the post office or general store. When winter blizzards further isolate her, she nearly goes mad and elopes with the storekeeper.

Recent research, however, demonstrates that nineteenth-century women's dread of isolation was by no means universal. Some single women homesteaders associated their remote situations with financial independence and with freedom from excessive social restrictions placed on eastern women. Female travelers from the eastern United States and Europe taking the transcontinental railroad across the Great Plains also sometimes observed the expansive landscape with enthusiasm and expressions of personal release.

Masculine spatial legends equally abound. Most common is the Old West interpretation of the Plains as empty space to be transformed through settlers' ranching, plowing, fencing, railroading, and similar activities. European American men, accordingly, do not merely occupy space, they build it.

Because the meanings of gendered space vary with specific societies, times, and places, how Great Plains residents exemplify them can rapidly change. Today, with more integrated boardrooms and kitchens, fewer gender-segregated spaces exist than in the past; however, the football field (or in Canada, the ice hockey rink) and male locker rooms, the altars of Catholic churches, and meeting rooms of

businesswomen's associations are contemporary examples.

Jeanne Kay Guelke
University of Waterloo

Cather, Willa. "A Wagner Matinee." In *The Troll Garden*. Lincoln: University of Nebraska Press, 1983: 94–101. Fink, Deborah. *Agrarian Women: Wives and Mothers in Rural Nebraska, 1880–1940*. Chapel Hill: University of North Carolina Press, 1992. Garland, Hamlin. *The Moccasin Ranch: A Story of Dakota*. New York: Harper and Brothers, 1909.

HAYES, KATE SIMPSON (1856–1945)

Kate Simpson Hayes, one of the earliest woman authors and journalists in western Canada, was born in Dalhousie, New Brunswick, in 1856 and died on January 15, 1945, in Victoria, British Columbia. Hayes arrived at Prince Albert in 1879. In the mid-1880s, after her marriage failed, she took her two young children and moved to the small Canadian Prairie town of Regina. There she met Nicholas Flood Davin, and their nine-year intimate relationship resulted in the birth of two children out of wedlock.

Following a brief period as proprietress of her own millinery shop, Hayes worked as librarian for the territorial legislature and wrote for the *Regina Leader* newspaper. Much of her work was written under the pseudonym "Mary Markwell." In 1889 she spent several months in North Dakota, reporting on fairs, harvest conditions, and fashion trends. Hayes also wrote plays and comedic sketches, which were performed in a number of prairie communities. Her first book, *Prairie Pot-Pourri*, a collection of poems, stories, and a children's play, was published in 1895. In 1900 Hayes moved to Winnipeg, where she edited the women's page of the *Manitoba Free Press* (later *Winnipeg Free Press*) until 1906. She then traveled to Britain, where she worked for the Canadian Pacific Railway, promoting the emigration of women to western Canada. Kate Hayes was a charter member of the Canadian Women's Press Club in 1904 and served as club president in 1906–7. Her newspaper columns reveal her conservative social views, including her opposition to women's suffrage. Hayes contributed to the *Manitoba Free Press* until 1909, and during 1910–11 was women's editor of the *Ottawa Free Press*. For the remainder of her life Kate Hayes continued to write, supporting herself with her pen until well into her senior years.

See also MEDIA: *Winnipeg Free Press*.

Constance A. Maguire
Regina, Saskatchewan

Hayes, Catherine Simpson. Papers. R-215. Saskatchewan Archives Board, Regina, Saskatchewan, Canada. Maguire, Constance A. "Kate Simpson Hayes, Agnes Agatha Hammell, and the 'Slur of Illegitimacy.'" *Saskatchewan History* 50 (1998): 7–23. Maguire, Constance A. "'Leaving the Hearth Fire Untended': Women and Public Pursuits in the Journalism of Kate Simpson Hayes." *Prairie Forum* 23 (1998): 67–92.

HIND, CORA (1861–1942)

Ella Cora Hind was a pioneer in breaking gender barriers and a lifelong advocate for wom-

Cora Hind

en's rights. She was appointed by J. W. Dafoe as agricultural editor of the *Manitoba Free Press* (later *Winnipeg Free Press*) in 1901, twenty years after she was first refused work there on gender grounds.

Hind was born in Toronto on September 18, 1861. Orphaned in early childhood, she and her two older brothers grew up on their grandfather's mixed farm near Orillia, Ontario. As her grandfather's favorite, Hind learned about agriculture firsthand. Cora was raised by her Aunt Alice, who moved to Winnipeg with Cora in 1882. They lived together until Alice's death in 1908. During Cora's first three decades in Winnipeg, Alice was truly her partner, bringing in an income as a dressmaker, managing Hind's business in her absence, and doing research for Cora's freelance articles.

Cora trained herself to use the new office innovation, the typewriter, and became a clerk for a firm of influential lawyers. In 1893 she set up her own office, acting as public secretary to, among others, a number of farming organizations. Her big break came in 1898 when she traveled west to report for banking and business interests on the effects of a late crop. Her distinguished career in journalism culminated in a tour around the world (1935–37) to report on farming, published as *Seeing for Myself* (1937). Her accurate estimates of crop yields were legendary on both sides of the U.S.-Canadian border.

Hind was granted an honorary doctorate by the University of Manitoba in 1935. When she died in Winnipeg on October 6, 1942, trading at the Winnipeg Grain Exchange was halted for two minutes in her honor.

See also MEDIA: *Winnipeg Free Press.*
Janice Dickin
University of Calgary

Hacker, Carlotta. *E. Cora Hind.* Don Mills ON: Fitzhenry and Whiteside, 1979. Haig, Kenneth M. *Brave Harvest: The Life Story of E. Cora Hind.* Toronto: Thomas Allen Ltd., 1945. Hind, E. Cora. *Seeing for Myself: Agricultural Conditions around the World.* Toronto: Macmillan Publishing Company, 1937.

HIRED GIRLS

The hired girl was in demand on the farms of the Great Plains. Though sought after, she was often spurned if her work habits, language skills, and personal habits did not meet the standards of her employer. In spite of the need for supplemental labor on nonelectrified farms, the supply of girls available to do domestic work between 1870 and 1940 seldom met the demand, perhaps because the hired girl's pay ran about half that of the hired man.

In the Great Plains, hiring out daughters was a common practice among nearly all immigrant ethnic groups. The money they earned usually returned, at least in part, to their families, perhaps to support the educational goals of younger siblings. The work also served as training in running a household, and for those who obtained work in homes of native-born Americans, an opportunity to learn the English language and American-style housekeeping.

The rural domestic was not confined to the house proper. She was especially valued if she could milk cows and separate the cream, feed chickens and gather eggs, harness horses, and perhaps take a few turns in the field. The lack of definition in the job often drove rural girls to urban homes where the pay was better and the tasks limited to the house.

Child care was usually a part of the hired girl's work, and because it interfered with the other assigned duties it was often a major source of discontent. Yet the domestic filled every aspect of the role the farm woman vacated when seasons of intense work, such as harvest, demanded her labor in the fields. For some hired girls, this exposure was enough to convince them to leave farm life behind. City work often led to marriage and life in an urban setting.

The hired girl often went to work at a very young age. Hired girls as young as seven took on child care and minor household and barnyard tasks. Often these very young girls had lost one or both parents or were born out of wedlock and had no place in their mother's subsequent family. By the age of twelve, most young girls were considered capable of managing housework, barnyard chores, and child care for a couple of weeks while a woman recovered from childbirth. After the age of sixteen, young women who had completed their education, or who sought income to support more education, took positions near home or

farther away, with enough understanding of the demand for their labor to arrange for the most advantageous situation. If pay was withheld, the work too demanding, or the atmosphere too oppressive, they could easily find another position. The advantage of mobility might fade for a widow or divorced woman who had to turn to domestic work to support herself and her children.

The demand for domestics in the rural Great Plains guaranteed that women, even those with little education or some social handicap such as an illegitimate child, could find work at any time. The quality of the experience varied with the domestic's age, family status, and ability to maintain some control over the selling of her labor.

Barbara Handy-Marchello
University of North Dakota

Coburn, Carol K. "Learning to Serve: Education and Change in the Lives of Rural Domestics in the Twentieth Century." *Journal of Social History* 25 (1991): 109–22. Dudden, Faye E. *Serving Women: Household Service in Nineteenth-Century America.* Middletown CT: Wesleyan University Press, 1983.

HOOKER, EVELYN (1907–1996)

Born in North Platte, Nebraska, on September 2, 1907, Evelyn Hooker, a pioneer in the scientific study of male homosexuality, revolutionized the psychological establishment's understanding of homosexuality during the second half of the twentieth century. Her research and activism contributed significantly to the modern gay rights movement.

Evelyn Gentry, the sixth of nine children of poor farming parents, was born in her grandmother's home, close by Col. William F. (Buffalo Bill) Cody's, barely eluding the Sandhills sod house in which her family had recently been dwelling. She spent her youth on small farms in northeastern Colorado until her education-minded mother, who had migrated to Nebraska by prairie schooner, moved the family to Sterling in the Colorado Plains, where Evelyn could attend a large and progressive high school. There her teachers encouraged her to apply to the University of Colorado, which she entered on a tuition scholarship in 1924, eventually majoring in psychology.

After completing her master's degree at Boulder in 1930, she pursued doctoral work at Johns Hopkins University, where she earned her doctorate in psychology in 1932. After several years of teaching at small colleges, a bout with tuberculosis, and study and travel in Germany (where she witnessed Nazi repression firsthand), she applied for a position in psychology at UCLA, becoming a research associate through the extension division in 1939. She taught and conducted her research there until 1970, and then pursued private practice for another decade.

Prompted by a gay former student, Hooker began preliminary research with male homosexuals in the late 1940s. In 1953 she applied to the National Institute of Mental Health (NIMH) for a stipend to undertake a comparative study of adjustment in nonclinical homosexual and heterosexual men, which to her surprise was granted, despite McCarthy-era attacks on homosexuals, ubiquitous sodomy statutes, and orthodox psychiatry's conviction that adult homosexual behavior was a serious mental disorder producing severe maladjustment.

Contradicting firmly entrenched psychiatric dogma, Hooker's findings, which were presented at meetings of the American Psychological Association and published from the mid-1950s onward in a succession of rigorously researched articles, demonstrated that there was no distinct male homosexual personality type, that homosexual men were no more inherently abnormal in psychological makeup than their heterosexual counterparts, and that the results of standard projective tests and attitude scales (Rorschachs, Thematic Apperception Tests, and the like) of well-matched heterosexual and homosexual men were, in terms of social adjustment, indistinguishable to expert clinicians. (Other researchers, replicating Hooker's experiments, have repeatedly turned up identical results.) In 1961 she was encouraged to continue her empirical studies of homosexual men through an NIMH Research Career Award.

Years later Hooker was appointed to head the NIMH Task Force on Homosexuality. Among the recommendations of its 1969 report were increased funding for empirical scientific research into homosexuality, repeal of laws criminalizing homosexual acts between consenting adults, and an end to job discrimination based on sexual orientation. In 1973, largely as a result of Hooker's sustained research, members of the American Psychiatric Association voted to remove homosexuality as a pathological condition from its *Diagnostic and Statistical Manual of Mental Disorders*. Two years later the American Psychological Association took a similar stance, and since then, in the spirit of Hooker's groundbreaking work, has become a leading force in the movement for social equality for gay men, lesbians, bisexuals, and transgendered persons. In 1991 the American Psychological Association honored Hooker's "Distinguished Contribution to Psychology in the Public Interest." The University of Chicago's Evelyn Hooker Center for Gay and Lesbian Mental Health was named in her memory.

Evelyn Hooker died in Santa Monica, California, on November 18, 1996.

George E. Wolf
University of Nebraska–Lincoln

Hooker, Evelyn. "The Adjustment of the Male Overt Homosexual." *Journal of Projective Techniques* 21 (1957): 18–31. Hooker, Evelyn. "An Empirical Study of Some Relations between Sexual Patterns and Gender Identity in Male Homosexuals." In *Sex Research: New Development*, edited by John Money. New York: Holt, Rinehart and Winston, 1965: 24–52. Schmiechen, Richard, director. *Changing Our Minds: The Story of Dr. Evelyn Hooker.* 16 mm and videocassette. New York: Changing Our Minds, Inc., 1992.

MAD PIONEER WOMEN

See IMAGES AND ICONS: Mad Pioneer Women

MAIL-ORDER BRIDES

The term "mail-order bride," as it applies to a marriage arranged via correspondence between American men and women in the Great Plains in the nineteenth century, is largely a misnomer. Twentieth-century folklore has it that a homesteader could peruse the Sears and Roebuck or Montgomery Ward catalogs and order a wife to be delivered to his dusty doorstep just as easily as he could order a rifle, stove, or stomach cure, but the truth is far more interesting. Arranged long-distance marriage existed in the Plains in a range of communities, took a number of forms, and grew out of a variety of social, economic, and cultural phenomena, but never involved the literal sale, purchase, or ownership of women, as the term "mail-order bride" suggests.

Among Plains Indians, sight-unseen marriage was frequently arranged with the help of a middleman and could involve the payment of a "bride price," intended to compensate the woman's family for the impending loss of her labor. But intercultural marriage was rare. In 1854, at a peace conference at Fort Laramie, a prominent Cheyenne chief requested of the U.S. Army the gift of 100 white women as brides, but the army refused. Russian immigrants brought with them the tradition of *koopla*, whereby marriage brokers were paid a fee to pair men with potential spouses from the Old Country. Similarly, Chinese and Japanese obtained "picture brides" from their homelands, women whom they had come to know only through grainy photographs. According to historian Glenda Riley, Asian women entered such relationships because of parental pressure, to escape poverty, or to hide a sullied reputation. It was customary for the men to bear all costs, including the woman's passage and any wedding expenses incurred.

During the peak years of overland migration, hundreds of thousands of white women traveled west, but the majority were already married, and it was thought that "suitable" single women did not go west alone. While many cowboys eschewed marriage for perpetual bachelorhood, homesteaders believed that married men made better farmers.

From the 1830s until the turn of the twentieth century, settlers pined for "that useful and essential article of household furniture—a wife." So severe was the shortage of single white women of marriageable age in Nebraska, recounts Mari Sandoz in *Old Jules* (1935), her classic portrait of Plains homesteading, "a man had to marry anything that got off the train."

By 1865 it was estimated that there were as many as 30,000 single women back east, a number augmented by the Civil War widows. The plentitude of bachelors in the Plains—and hence the chance for greater social and economic freedom away from home—beckoned women. Newspapers from Nebraska to Kansas and Wyoming (a state the *Ladies Home Journal* in 1899 declared a heaven for spinsters and widows) began to serve as forums for matchmaking, running regular "matrimonial columns" of paid advertisements, frequently

with accompanying photographs, for example: "A young lady residing in one of the small towns in Central New York is desirous of opening a correspondence with some young man in the West, with a view to a matrimonial engagement. . . . she is about 24 years of age, possesses a good moral character . . . is tolerably well-educated, and thoroughly versed in the mysteries of housekeeping"; or more commonly, "A Bachelor of 40, good appearance and substantial means, wants a wife. She must be under 30, amiable, and musical." Across the Plains there arose a cottage industry of "heart and hand" catalogs, folded double sheets and broadsides devoted entirely to the matrimonial prospects.

Letters were the only means of courtship between potential mates separated by thousands of miles. According to one bride, the Pony Express "took about four weeks to go from east to west," and letters "often came in bundles." Language was a means of persuasion. Illiterate men could dictate their letters to typists who, for a fee, would doctor their sentiments on Remington Standards. Dishonesty was a risk. Men and women could easily misrepresent their physical attributes, their station, or finances. A homesteader who sent his betrothed a train ticket might find that she had turned it in for cash. A 1911 *Wahpeton Times* article tells of a New York girl for whom, upon arrival in Buford, North Dakota, "the spell was immediately broken" when she saw the face of her intended.

The railroad also played an important role in the western diaspora of single women. In 1882 businessman Fred Harvey sought young rural women "of good character, attractive and intelligent" as waitresses in whistlestop cafés along the Santa Fe rail line. Harvey required that they remain single for a year, live in chaperoned dormitories, and entertain callers in "courting parlors." By the turn of the century, he had married off nearly 5,000 so-called Harvey Girls.

By the early twenty-first century, matchmaking not only in the Plains but across the globe had become technically sophisticated. More than 200 so-called mail-order bride companies are available on the Internet, providing, for a fee, pictures of, or arranged meetings with, women from impoverished third world countries. At the millennium, the U.S. Immigration and Naturalization Service estimated that there were 10,000 such marriages per year, although specific numbers for the Great Plains are not available. The contemporary mail-order bride business, with its roots in benign nineteenth-century customs, has been called the "trafficking" and "enslavement" of women, but no clear evidence exists that the contemporary incarnation is different from its antecedents, except that profits from a single business can exceed $500,000 per year and a greater economic, social, and linguistic divide exists between the men and the women they marry.

Julie Checkoway
University of Georgia

Luchetti, Cathy. *"I Do!": Courtship, Love, and Marriage on the American Frontier: A Glimpse at America's Romantic Past through Photographs, Diaries, and Journals, 1715–1915.* New York: Crown Trade Paperbacks, 1996. Makabe, Tomoko. *Picture Brides: Japanese Women in Canada.* Toronto: University of Toronto Press, 1995. Riley, Glenda. *Building and Breaking Families in the American West.* Albuquerque: University of New Mexico Press, 1996.

MCCLUNG, NELLIE (1873–1951)

Nellie Letitia McClung was an internationally known writer, platform speaker, feminist, and social activist whose passion for social transformation in the service of justice was equaled only by the witty, engaging manner in which she delivered her message. A woman of humble beginnings, she went on to achieve tremendous social and political notoriety, and by the end of her life was one of Canada's best-known personages, lovingly known as "Our Nell."

McClung was born Nellie Mooney to a poor farming family in Grey County, Ontario, on October 20, 1873. Lured by the promise of homesteading, her family relocated to Millford, a small settlement in southwestern Manitoba, when Nellie was seven. She became a country schoolteacher by sixteen and was dreaming of "telling the stories of the common people" as a writer when she met Annie McClung, the wife of the new Methodist minister. Annie combined religious conviction with a passion for women's suffrage and temperance activism in a powerful mix that was both compelling and inspiring to the young woman. First a role model for Nellie, Annie became Nellie's mother-in-law in 1896, when Nellie married her oldest son, Wes. Annie was responsible for Nellie's entry into the short story contest that began her formal writing career, and after the publication of Nellie's first novel, *Sowing Seeds in Danny* (1908), she initiated McClung's speaking career by arranging a public reading of that Canadian best-seller in the service of the temperance cause.

McClung moved to Edmonton, Alberta, in 1914, then relocated to Calgary in 1923. She used her literature as a pulpit to preach a text of social change grounded in what she believed was God's intention for Creation, "the even chance for everyone." As the campaign for women's suffrage gathered momentum, she was increasingly in demand as a platform speaker, traveling throughout Canada, and in 1916 and 1917 throughout the United States as well, at the behest of the National American Woman Suffrage Association. Her oratory skills were superlative. Gifted with a devastating wit, she roundly trounced political enemies like the conservative premier of Manitoba, Sir Rodmond Roblin, in her speeches, culminating in the wildly successful "Woman's Parliament" of 1914. This play of role reversals, where men ask a government of women for men's suffrage, is fictionally rendered in McClung's social gospel novel, *Purple Springs* (1921).

McClung went on to write sixteen books (four novels, two novellas, several collections of short stories and newspaper columns, and a two-volume autobiography), as well as a syndicated newspaper column and innumerable magazine articles. Her status as a cultural figure was a key reason she was appointed the only female member of the Canadian Broadcasting Corporation's first board of governors. She maintained her political profile after women's suffrage was achieved, serving as a Liberal Member of the Legislative Assembly (MLA) in Alberta from 1921 to 1926. She was also one of the "Famous Five" Alberta women who in 1929 petitioned the Privy Council in Great Britain in the "Persons Case" to have women declared full legal "persons" in Canada. A lifelong member of the Women's International League for Peace and Freedom, she represented Canada at the League of Nations and was an outspoken opponent of the internment of the Japanese and an advocate for Jewish immigration to Canada during World War II. Finally, she was a religious activist, lobbying tirelessly for the ordination of women in the United Church of Canada, a goal achieved formally in 1934. While she is criticized by some contemporary scholars for her "naive liberalism" and Christian belief, her passionate conviction that the Prairie West should become a "Land of the Fair Deal," and her work toward achieving it, embodied the optimism and determination that mark Plains and Prairie culture, in her day as today. McClung moved to Victoria, British Columbia in 1935, and died there on September 1, 1951.

Randi R. Warne
Mount St. Vincent University

McClung, Nellie L. *In Times Like These.* Toronto: McLeod and Allen, 1915. Savage, Candace. *Our Nell: A Scrapbook Biography of Nellie L. McClung.* Saskatoon: Western Producer Prairie Books, 1979. Warne, Randi R. *Literature as Pulpit: The Christian Social Activism of Nellie L. McClung.* Waterloo: Wilfred Laurier University Press, 1993.

MOCK WEDDINGS

See FOLKWAYS: Mock Weddings

MURPHY, EMILY FERGUSON (1868–1933)

Emily Murphy was the first woman police magistrate in Canada (and probably in the British Empire), a noted suffragist who led in bringing the "Persons Case," an indefatigable worker for the rights of women, and a popular writer both under her maiden name, Emily Ferguson, and the pen name "Janey Canuck."

Emily Ferguson was born on March 14, 1868, to a prominent Protestant Irish family in Crookston, Ontario, and educated at the Bishop Strachan School in Toronto. In 1887 she married the Reverend Arthur Murphy. They were the parents of four daughters, two of whom died in childhood. When her husband was transferred to Winnipeg, Manitoba, she became the literary editor of a local paper. She published her first book, *Janey Canuck Abroad,* in 1902. In 1907, after three years on a homestead near Swan River, Manitoba, the family moved to Edmonton, Alberta, where Murphy lived for the rest of her life. Her second book, *Janey Canuck in the West* (1910), describes some Swan River experiences and expresses her delight with the freedom of Great Plains spaces and people.

From 1910 to 1916 Murphy was one of the most effective workers for suffrage and women's rights in the province, forcing the passage of the Alberta Dower Act in 1911. In April 1916 Alberta became the second province to enfranchise women, and two months later Murphy was appointed police magistrate. Almost immediately a lawyer questioned her eligibility on the ground that a woman was not a "person" in the legal meaning of the word and hence could not serve as a court officer. The Alberta courts upheld a woman's right to serve in 1917. As a police magistrate, Murphy dealt primarily with women and children as both victims and offenders. The twin problems of prostitution and drug addiction particularly gripped her. She organized her friends and social contacts to provide jobs and other support for women trying to leave the street, and in 1922 she published *The Black Candle,* considered to be the first comprehensive book on drug addiction in North America. Like many social reformers of her day, including her close friend Nellie McClung, she advocated birth control and sterilization for "defective" persons. She also advocated for women's right to work and for adequate health care for everyone.

In 1921 Murphy was nominated for the Senate, the appointive upper house of Canada's parliament, but Prime Minister Arthur Meighen refused to appoint her, citing the familiar argument that as a woman, she was not a person under the meaning of the British North American Act, Canada's enabling legislation. With four other leading Prairie suffragists, Murphy petitioned for an interpretation of the act, and finally, on October 18, 1929, the British Privy Council ruled that all women in the British Empire were "persons." Much to Murphy's disappointment, however, she never did become a senator. Party politics decreed that Cairine Wilson would be the only woman appointed to the Senate before Murphy's sudden death in Edmonton on October 26, 1933.

Frances W. Kaye
University of Nebraska–Lincoln

Cleverdon, Catherine L. *The Woman Suffrage Movement in Canada.* Toronto: University of Toronto Press, 1974. Ferguson (Murphy), Emily. *Janey Canuck in the West.* Toronto: McClelland and Stewart Ltd., 1975. James, Donna. *Emily Murphy.* Don Mills, Ontario: Fitzhenry and Whiteside, 1977.

NATIVE AMERICAN GENDER ROLES

Traditionally, Plains Indian gender roles were well defined, and men's and women's responsibilities were equally crucial to the functioning, even the survival, of their societies. Consequently, both men and women were respected for doing their jobs well, although this is not how early European American observers saw it.

Such observers, coming from societies which held that women—gentlewomen, that is—

should be cloistered and protected, were aghast at the workload that Plains Indian women carried. They witnessed them, from varying societies and at various times of the year, clearing fields, planting, hoeing, and harvesting; digging cache pits and storing food; erecting and dismantling lodges and tipis; collecting wild plants and firewood; cooking, hauling water, and washing dishes; transporting possessions, generally on foot, on bison hunts; making household items, including pottery and clothing; and child rearing. This workload increased during the first half of the nineteenth century as the fur trade raised the demands for dressed skins and robes. Meanwhile, the European American observers, often only transitory travelers, saw Indian men sitting around the village or encampment, smoking, gambling, perhaps mending a weapon or caring for a horse. The men seemed to have all the power; the women seemed to do all the work.

Visitors who lived with Plains Indians for more extended periods of time, including early anthropologists like Alice Fletcher, saw a much more complex division of labor and distribution of authority. There is no doubt that Plains Indian women worked hard, but they were held in high esteem for the elemental role they played in supporting village life. Among the farming Indians of the eastern Plains at least, women provided most of the food in most years; even in the bison-hunting societies of the western Plains they provided significant amounts of food through collection of wild plants and berries, and they processed the meat obtained on the hunt.

While it is true that the women generally played a subordinate role in ceremonial life and lacked formal political power (you will look in vain for a Plains Indian woman's signature on a treaty with the United States), they had types of political power that contemporary American women lacked. In the agricultural societies—the Pawnees and Omahas of Nebraska, for example—they owned the lodge, tipi, and its contents; the fields, seeds, and implements of production; and they had the right to trade their surplus crops. On the bison hunts they often made the decision on where to camp, and in the lodge the senior wife (for sororal polygamy was the norm) was the main decision maker. Women also had the right to divorce, and since they owned the lodge, an unkind husband could find himself homeless, with only his horse and weapons to his name. Women were also held in high esteem for their craft work, they played an important role in healing (especially in problems associated with childbirth), and they took care of religious items, a responsibility of the highest order.

Men's roles were equally misunderstood by early European American travelers. Men were responsible for hunting, defensive and aggressive warfare, manufacturing of weapons, and nearly all societywide political and religious operations. Observers who saw Indian men in their villages saw them "off work," although often they did help the women in the fields or

in the construction of a lodge. Men's work took them away from the village, and it was dangerous. They hunted on increasingly contested bison ranges and journeyed hundreds of miles to enemy encampments to steal horses and to win honors. The reciprocity of the gender roles is made clear by the hard facts of Indian demography: in most, if not all, Plains Indian societies in the mid–nineteenth century there were far more women than men. Women often died at an early age, worn down by a life of hard work and frequent childbearing, but men died in greater numbers and at earlier ages, victims of their dangerous occupations. Only in the late nineteenth century, when wars among the tribes and with the United States were curtailed, did the gender ratios equalize. By that time men and women alike were equally likely to die from diseases caused by poverty, such as tuberculosis.

The gender roles devised over generations by traditional Plains Indian societies persisted for so long because they worked to keep the family and the band or tribe intact. In the last decades of the nineteenth century, the Canadian and U.S. governments launched a concerted attack on the traditional roles of Indian men and women: Indian men were to become farmers or blacksmiths, and Indian women were to become housewives, in keeping with European American concepts of "civilized" divisions of labor. Indian extended families were to be fragmented into nuclear families, each occupying an individual allotment. These imposed changes were resisted, but Indian men's traditional roles were fast disappearing, and as the weight of supporting families fell increasingly on the women, so did relative power. This shift has continued to this day.

On Plains reservations and reserves in the early twenty-first century, women are more likely than men to have completed high school and to hold jobs outside the home. They are often the chief providers for the household, while Indian men frequently take over the child care, cooking, and cleaning. Such changes bring with them benefits, such as increased authority for women and closer father-child relationships for men, but they also bring the stresses of added responsibilities and altered self-images.

David J. Wishart
University of Nebraska–Lincoln

Albers, Patricia, and Beatrice Medicine. *The Hidden Half: Studies of Plains Indian Women*. Washington DC: University Press of America, 1983. Billson, Janet Mancini. "Standing Tradition on Its Head: Role Reversal among Blood Indian Couples." *Great Plains Quarterly* 11 (1991): 3–22.

PEATTIE, ELIA (1862–1935)

Elia Wilkinson Peattie was born in Kalamazoo, Michigan, on January 15, 1862, and later moved to Chicago with her parents. In 1883 she married Robert Peattie, a Chicago newspaperman. Later, she and her husband and children moved to Omaha, where from 1889 to 1896 she was an editorial writer and columnist for the *Omaha World-Herald*. While in Omaha, Peattie participated in politics, es-

pecially with William Jennings Bryan; hobnobbed with Willa Cather and Hamlin Garland, among other authors; helped organize Women's Clubs across the state; and actively supported hospitals for unwed mothers, orphanages, relief for the poor and homeless, and day-care centers for Nebraska women. As one of the first western women to write editorial columns that addressed public issues, her outspoken and often irreverent remarks show a side of the frontier often overlooked. Not all pioneer women lived in sod houses and spent their days gathering buffalo chips for cooking. Many western pioneers, like Peattie, lived in fledgling villages and booming cities, and their influence impacted the course of history, too.

Upon her return to Chicago, Peattie became the literary critic for the *Chicago Tribune*, a member of the exclusive literary club Fortnightly, and one of the leaders of Chicago Women's Clubs. She influenced the taste of a wide-reading public until realists such as Theodore Dreiser, whom she labeled a "literary tomcat," rebelled against the prevailing romantics and Victorian sentimentalists. Peattie died on July 12, 1935, while visiting her grandchildren in Wallingford, Vermont.

Throughout her life, Peattie penned hundreds of stories, novels, children's books, poems, essays, and book reviews. Torn between the ideals of the self-sacrificing "True Woman" of Victorian society and the emerging, independent "New Woman" of the early twentieth century, Peattie's life is representative of the struggles of late-nineteenth-century women authors to balance the demands of the home with their careers as writers.

See also MEDIA: *Omaha World-Herald.*
Susanne K. George
University of Nebraska at Kearney

Falcone, Joan. *The Bonds of Sisterhood in Chicago Women Writers: The Voice of Elia Wilkinson Peattie.* Normal: Illinois State University Press, 1992.

PERSONS CASE

The "Persons Case" was raised by five Alberta women and resulted in the October 18, 1929, decision by the British Privy Council that women were legally "persons," not just in Canada but throughout the whole British Empire.

The case had its roots back in 1916, when Emily Murphy took her seat in Edmonton as the first woman police magistrate in the empire. A lawyer against whose client she had ruled claimed that, as a woman, she was not a "person" in terms of the British North America Act, Canada's enabling legislation, and hence was not eligible to serve as a magistrate. The lawyer did not follow up his objection, but ten years later Justice Murphy began to be considered for appointment as Canada's first woman senator. The British North America Act allowed qualified "persons" to sit in the Senate, but an 1876 British court had ruled that "women are persons in matters of pains and penalties, but are not persons in matters of rights and privileges." Murphy joined forces with four others—Nellie McClung and Louise McKinney, both suffrage leaders and former members of the Alberta Legislative Assembly; Henrietta Muir Edwards, an expert on women's legal status; and provincial cabinet minister Irene Parlby—to ask for an interpretation of the act. When the Supreme Court of Canada ruled that women were not "persons" in the senatorial sense, the five women pursued the case to the British Privy Council, then Canada's court of last resort, which eventually admitted that women were "persons."

A statue commemorating the "Famous Five" was erected in Calgary, Alberta, in 1999.

Frances W. Kaye
University of Nebraska–Lincoln

Prentice, Alison, Paula Bourne, Gail Cuthbert Brandt, Beth Light, Wendy Mitchison, and Naomi Black. *Canadian Women: A History*. Toronto: Harcourt Brace Canada, 1996. Savage, Candace. *Our Nell: A Scrapbook Biography of Nellie L. McClung*. Saskatoon: Western Producer Prairie Books, 1979.

QUILTING CIRCLES

Quilting has long been a means of connecting women in the Great Plains. As material objects, quilts connected European American settlers with their past homes. As process, making quilts gave women an acceptable outlet for their creative powers while fulfilling their household duties. Sharing the labor of quilting, through formal and informal quilting circles, relieved the isolation of women's lives. Especially in the early years of settlement, communal quilting activities were inclusive; as the entire quilt had to be quilted in one day, it would have been counterproductive as well as impolitic to leave any neighbor out. It seems likely that European immigrants assimilated the Anglo-American quilt traditions through such gatherings.

Although most quilts were made for domestic use, women also joined to make quilts for public purposes: helping the needy or honoring community leaders through presentation quilts inscribed with the names of the makers. Women's church societies raised money by quilting: a Ladies Aid in Harvard, Nebraska, for example, earned more than $1,400 in seven years through quilting and socials.

Women living in towns who shared an interest—temperance, suffrage, self-improvement, or quilting—found it easier to form organizations than did rural women. A "young ladies crazy patchwork society" in 1884 in Red Cloud, Nebraska, is an early instance of a specifically quilt-related group. When quiltmaking regained popularity in the 1910s and 1920s, better transportation enabled rural women to come together more often. While women still made quilts as individuals, in the 1920s and 1930s they also turned to friends and neighbors who met in many informal clubs, with names like the Willing Workers, the Helping Hands, or the Friendship Club. The hostess at each meeting would "furnish work" for members, who often made the quilt blocks as well as helped to quilt the finished top.

Despite standardizing influences such as quilts pictured in national women's magazines, patterns published by regional media such as the *Kansas City Star*, and kits and patterns distributed through national companies, distinctive styles evolved in some communities. Emporia, Kansas, became a center for some of the finest appliqué quiltmaking of the twentieth century. Some of the Mennonite communities scattered throughout the Great Plains have become known for a style of whole-cloth quilts; auctions of their quilts benefit relief and mission work. Another unusual style, based on the Lone Star design, has evolved among Native Americans on reservations in the Dakotas.

Quiltmaking declined again during World War II, as transportation and materials again became scarce. Still, church sewing societies in rural areas kept the skills, patterns, and traditions alive until the late 1960s, when interest in the past and in handmade things led to a revival of interest that has lasted since that time. Quilt guilds began to form on the local level in the early 1970s and spread to state and national levels. These guilds develop the individual quilter, add to the body of knowledge of quilting, and continue the philanthropic work of the early quilting circles in the Plains.

See also FOLKWAYS: Quilting.

Kari Ronning
University of Nebraska–Lincoln

Brackman, Barbara, Jennie A. Chinn, Gayle R. Davis, Terry Thompson, Sara Reimer Farley, and Nancy Hornback. *Kansas Quilts and Quilters*. Lawrence: University Press of Kansas, 1993. Crews, Patricia Cox, and Ronald Naugle, eds. *Nebraska Quilts and Quiltmakers*. Lincoln: University of Nebraska Press, 1991. Pulford, Florence. *Morning Star Quilts: A Presentation of the Work and Lives of Northern Plains Indian Women*. Los Altos CA: Leone Publications, 1989.

RODEO QUEENS

Rodeo queens appear at rodeos all across the Great Plains. Rhinestone tiaras adorning their hats, and bedazzling in cowgirl regalia, the queens reign over the rough-and-tumble rodeo events. The idea of a ceremonial rodeo queen might seem oddly out of place among the physically demanding performances of cowboys and cowgirls, yet the role of the queen is inextricably linked with the rise of rodeo as a spectator sport in the Great Plains.

The first rodeo queen is believed to have made her appearance at the 1910 Pendleton Round-Up in Oregon, but it took twenty years for the idea to spread. Cheyenne Frontier Days in Wyoming became the next well-known rodeo to have a queen. It is no accident that the first Miss Frontier Days, Miss Jean Nimmo Doubois, appeared in 1931. Local businessmen, worried that the Depression would keep ticket-buying spectators away from the rodeo, devised a competition: the young woman who sold the most tickets would become queen of the rodeo. The selection of a young woman from within the community, and one who did not compete in rodeo events, but instead used her "royal" position to promote the rodeo to a broad audience, was an innovation that worked well and was widely copied.

During the 1940s hundreds of communities throughout the Great Plains began holding their own rodeos. Although the method of choosing a queen varied widely, their purpose was the same—to help sell tickets. Competition was fierce among the towns to pull in large crowds, thereby making the rodeo an economic success, and rodeo queens worked with the town promoters to attract spectators. The role the queens played within their communities depended on the goals of the community sponsoring the rodeo.

In Cheyenne, a large town actively seeking regional and national attention, the role of queen gradually evolved into a rigorous two-year commitment, with activities planned not only in Cheyenne but throughout the country. In 1946 Miss Patsy Rogers was selected by the Calgary Exhibition and Stampede Board to serve as the first Calgary Stampede Queen. Miss Rogers represented the Stampede locally, regionally by traveling to rodeos in the surrounding area, and internationally as a Ranch Girl in Gene Autry's Madison Square Garden and Boston Gardens rodeos. Nebraska's Big Rodeo, held in Burwell, a small community hoping to attract spectators from across the state, often selected its queens from outside Burwell. Ruby Dearmont, Miss Burwell 1949, was one of the very few queens selected from Burwell itself to represent the rodeo. Most common, however, were small-town rodeos where local queens appeared at numerous civic and social functions in town and traveled as visiting royalty to other nearby rodeos. In fact, traveling to promote the rodeo is something that most past rodeo queens recall as an important and exciting part of their responsibilities, even if the travel was only to the next town.

Another type of queen promotion began in the Plains in 1931, when the Texas Cowboy Reunion in Stamford held the first sponsor contest. In a unique promotional twist, Stamford sent out a call to chambers of commerce throughout the region to provide girls to participate in the sponsor event at the Stamford rodeo. Each town was responsible for holding a competition to select a hometown representative; the winner would then compete at the Stamford rodeo in an event specifically designed for them. The contestants were judged on the appearance of their horse, their costume, and horsemanship. The sponsor contests held by these other towns were a remarkably successful mechanism for publicizing the rodeo, and within a few years of its founding the Texas Cowboy Reunion was one of the largest rodeos in the country.

The original intention of the sponsor contest was to "add a little softness to the all-male rodeo." However, the horsemanship part of the competition became increasingly popular. What started as a subjective evaluation of the young women's ability to ride around three randomly placed barrels evolved into a timed event with a standardized cloverleaf pattern. Later named barrel racing, this event remains popular and highly competitive in rodeo today.

A new dimension was added to the rodeo

queen phenomenon in 1955, when the first Miss Rodeo America pageant was held in Casper, Wyoming. Since its inception, twenty-two of the forty-four Miss Rodeo America queens have been from the Great Plains. The first Miss Rodeo Canada also made her debut in 1955. In order to compete for the title, a young woman must be sponsored by a Canadian pro-rodeo association. The Canadian pro-rodeo circuit is centered in the Plains—the easternmost rodeo is held in Morris, Manitoba—so twenty-six of the thirty-three Miss Rodeo Canada queens have been from the region. The role of the national queens is to travel across their respective countries promoting professional rodeo. In the 1960s it became increasingly common for Miss Rodeo America and Miss Rodeo Canada contestants to also participate as athletes in rodeos, usually competing in barrel racing events.

See also SPORTS AND RECREATION: Rodeo.

Renee M. Laegreid
University of Nebraska–Lincoln

LeCompte, Mary Lou. *Cowgirls of the Rodeo: Pioneer Professional Athletes.* Urbana: University of Illinois Press, 1993. Shelton, Hooper. *Fifty Years of a Living Legend: Texas Cowboy Reunion and Oldtimers Association.* Stamford TX: Shelton Press, 1979. Stoeltje, Beverly. "Gender Representations in Performance: The Cowgirl and the Hostess." *Journal of Folklore Research* 25 (1988): 219–41.

SACAGAWEA (ca. 1780–1812)

The only woman on Lewis and Clark's expedition, Sacagawea was a young Shoshone who had been captured by Hidatsa raiders near the three forks of the Missouri River about 1800. She married trader Toussaint Charbonneau sometime before 1804. A son, Jean Baptiste, called "Pomp" by Clark, was born to them in February of 1805. Together, the family traveled from the Mandan-Hidatsa villages in present-day North Dakota to the Pacific and back.

Sacagawea has been the object of considerable myth and misinformation; her contributions to the expedition have been both exaggerated and minimized. Clark thought more of her contributions than did Lewis, though one must consider here the eighteenth-century tendency to discount contributions of non-white peoples. In a letter to Charbonneau after the expedition, Clark wrote, "Your woman deserved a greater reward for her attention and services on that rout than we had in our power to give her." Lewis's view was more dismissive: "If she has enough to eat and a few trinkets I believe she would be perfectly content anywhere."

In fact, Sacagawea's contributions were real: she provided important geographical data to the party at various times, she helped as translator with certain tribes, she rescued important documents during a canoe mishap in May 1805, and, perhaps most important, she gave a friendlier face to the Corps of Discovery. Clark wrote that she "reconsiles all the Indians, as to our friendly intentions, a woman with a party of men is a token of peace."

Sacagawea died of a "putrid fever" in December 1812 near present-day Mobridge, South Dakota, at about age thirty-two. Jean Baptiste and Sacagawea's daughter, Lizette, lived with Clark at St. Louis for a time.

See also EUROPEAN AMERICANS: Lewis and Clark.

Gerald M. Parsons
University of Nebraska–Lincoln

McMurtry, Larry, "Sacagawea's Nickname." *New York Review of Books* 48 (September 20, 2001): 71–72. Moulton, Gary, ed. *The Journals of the Lewis and Clark Expedition.* 13 vols. Lincoln: University of Nebraska Press, 1983–2001. Ronda, James P. *Lewis and Clark among the Indians.* Lincoln: University of Nebraska Press, 1984.

SALTER, SUSANNA (1860–1961)

Susanna Madora Salter was the first woman to become mayor in the state of Kansas, and she was probably the first woman mayor in the United States. Susanna Madora, or "Dora," was born in Ohio on March 2, 1860, and moved to Kansas with her family when she was twelve. At age sixteen she enrolled at Kansas State Agricultural College (later Kansas State University) in Manhattan; she graduated in 1879. In September of 1880 Dora met and married Lewis Salter, son of former lieutenant governor of Kansas Melville J. Salter. Susanna's husband ran a hardware store in the newly established Quaker town of Argonia in Sumner County, Kansas, where Susanna became politically active in the Woman's Christian Temperance Union, founded in 1883.

When Salter was elected mayor in 1887 she received congratulatory telegrams from all over the world. She never campaigned for the position; in fact, by some accounts her name was placed on the ballot as a joke. Women in Kansas had just received the right to vote in municipal elections, and several men in Argonia were determined to embarrass her by placing her name on the ballot. To the surprise of many (herself included), Susanna, aged twenty-seven, received two-thirds of the vote. She served for only one uneventful year and is said to have ceded most of her decision-making power to the men seated on the council. Even though she was encouraged to run for an additional term, Susanna refused because she wished to spend her time with her eight children.

The Salters took out a claim near Alva, Oklahoma, in 1893, following the opening of the Cherokee Strip. After her husband's death in 1916, Susanna moved her family to Norman, Oklahoma, where she lived until her death on March 16, 1961, at age 101.

Suzanne M. Leland
University of North Carolina at Charlotte

Billington, Monroe. "Susanna Madora Salter—First Woman Mayor." *Kansas Historical Quarterly* 21 (1954): 173–83.

SASKATCHEWAN WOMEN GRAIN GROWERS

Founded in 1913, the Women's Section of the Saskatchewan Grain Growers Association played a major role in the advancement of such causes as women's suffrage, public health and medical care, prohibition, the Canadianization of the immigrant, and the propagation of the cooperative ideal. Although born of the Saskatchewan Grain Growers Association, the Prairies' pioneer agrarian organization, with origins that preceded the creation of Saskatchewan (1905), the Women Grain Growers was not its auxiliary. Viewing themselves as both farm women and farmers, the leaders of the Women Grain Growers—most prominent among them Violet McNaughton, Francis Beynon, and Zoa Haight—claimed, and received, full constitutional status with the parent body as well as the right to form their own locals and meet separately if they so desired. Three of their members were also guaranteed seats on the board of directors of the Saskatchewan Grain Growers Association.

By 1919 there were 6,000 women members in the Women Grain Growers and in the locals of the Saskatchewan Grain Growers Association; that is, approximately one in six of the total membership. The Saskatchewan Women Grain Growers became the model on which women's sections of the United Farmers of Alberta, Manitoba, and Ontario was patterned.

Full participation by women in the affairs of the Saskatchewan Grain Growers Association and the Women's Section preceded by six and eight years, respectively, the first exercise of the right to vote by women in provincial and federal politics. As such, any study of women and politics in Canada must give prominence to these agrarian organizations.

Leaders of the Saskatchewan Women Grain Growers played an influential role in the move of traditional farmers to the political left, as witnessed by the introduction of the Wheat Pool in 1924 and the amalgamation of the Saskatchewan Grain Growers Association and the more radical Farmers Union of Canada in 1926. A separate women's section of the new United Farmers of Canada–Saskatchewan Section disappeared after 1930, when that organization experimented—more faithfully on paper than in practice—with an early form of affirmative action.

See also PROTEST AND DISSENT: Grain Growers Associations.

David E. Smith
University of Saskatchewan

Marchildon, Randolph George. "Improving the Quality of Rural Life in Saskatchewan: Some Activities of the Women's Section of the Saskatchewan Grain Growers, 1913–1920." In *Building Beyond the Homestead: Rural History of the Prairies*, edited by David C. Jones and Ian MacPherson. Calgary: University of Calgary Press, 1985: 89–109. Taylor, Georgina M. " 'Ground for Common Action': Violet McNaughton's Agrarian Feminism and the Origins of the Farm Women's Movement in Canada." Ph.D. diss., Carleton University, 1997.

SHIVAREES

See FOLKWAYS: Shivarees

SLAUGHTER, LINDA (1843–1911)

Linda Warfel Slaughter was a journalist, historian, and women's rights advocate in North Dakota. Born February 1, 1843, in Cadiz, Ohio, and educated at Oberlin College, she settled in

Linda Slaughter, ca. 1880.

Bismarck in 1872. She was appointed superintendent of schools for Burleigh County in 1873. Though women could not vote at that time, she was elected to the position several more times until 1882. In 1876 Slaughter was appointed deputy superintendent of public instruction for Dakota Territory.

Slaughter wrote regularly for the *Bismarck Tribune* and other papers. Her fiction was thinly disguised commentary on social life in the military and the politics of the Indian campaigns. Her essays at first criticized women's public suffrage and temperance activities and advocated "true womanhood" as women's proper role.

By the late 1880s Slaughter was a Washington correspondent for Dakota Territory newspapers. By then embracing the women's rights movement, she served as vice president of the Woman's National Press Association, attended the 1888 meeting of the International Council of Women, served on the national executive committee of the National Woman Suffrage Association, supported Belva Lockwood's presidential campaigns, and became an organizer for the Knights of Labor. In 1892 Slaughter attended the Populist Party convention, becoming the first woman to vote in a national convention for a presidential candidate.

In 1889 Slaughter organized the Ladies' Historical Society of Bismarck and North Dakota. As president, she collected and preserved records of North Dakota's early history. In 1895 she negotiated a merger with the fledgling State Historical Society, assuring women the right to vote and hold office in the new organization.

Slaughter continued to write history until very late in her life. Her last articles, four on Sitting Bull for *Sports Afield* (1903–4) and a lengthy piece for the State Historical Society (1906), are on early settlement, military activity, and Indian resistance. She died in St. Cloud, Minnesota, on July 3, 1911.

See also MEDIA: *Bismarck Tribune.*

Barbara Handy-Marchello
University of North Dakota

Burgum, Jessamine Slaughter. *Zezula, or Pioneer Days of the Smokey Water Country.* Valley City ND: Getchell and Nielsen, 1937. Slaughter, Linda Warfel. *Fortress to Farm or Twenty-three Years on the Frontier*, edited by Hazel Eastman. New York: Exposition Press, 1972.

STEWART, ELINORE PRUITT

(1876–1933)

Born in White Bead Hill in the Chickasaw Nation, Indian Territory, on June 3, 1876, Elinore Pruitt Stewart was no stranger to hardship. At eighteen, with both parents dying within a year of each other, Stewart became responsible for six siblings. A few years later, she married and presumably divorced Harry Rupert. In 1906 she moved with her daughter, Jerrine, and two sisters to Denver, where she told everyone that she was a widow. A life of poverty in Denver encouraged her to try homesteading, so in 1909 she answered Clyde Stewart's advertisement for a housekeeper in the *Denver Post*. Stewart and her daughter arrived in Burntfork, Wyoming, in April 1909. In May she filed on 160 acres adjoining Clyde's homestead, and within eight weeks, married her employer. Stewart spent the rest of her life on the ranch, except for a few years when the family moved to Boulder, Colorado, for the children's education. She died in a Rock Springs hospital on October 8, 1933, at the age of fifty-seven.

Stewart's life is not unique, for many women homesteaded as well as became "mail-order brides." However, her contributions to American history and literature are the letters that she wrote to a former employer in Denver, Mrs. Juliet Coney, which were published serially in the *Atlantic Monthly* and then in book form by Houghton Mifflin Company as *Letters of a Woman Homesteader* (1914) and *Letters on an Elk Hunt* (1915). Stewart describes in detail the joys and hardships of homesteading and raising a family on the frontier. Each letter is often a complete narrative in itself; however, together they combine to create a type of story cycle, with characters and themes recurring. Although largely autobiographical, these works were written for publication, and she was known to have "never let the facts get in the way of a good story."

Susanne K. George
University of Nebraska at Kearney

George, Susanne K. *The Adventures of the Woman Homesteader: The Life and Letters of Elinore Pruitt Stewart.* Lincoln: University of Nebraska Press, 1992.

SUFFRAGE MOVEMENT

The suffrage movement—the campaign to secure women's right to vote in federal (presidential) elections—comprised the "first wave" of feminist activism in North America. Several of the Great Plains states (or former territories) and the Canadian Prairie Provinces were the first in their nations to obtain women's suffrage. This largely white middle-class movement constituted one of the hardest-fought struggles for equality in the region. Along with their demand for the vote, suffragists advanced a number of social and moral issues to the forefront of North American political debate.

Many Canadian provinces and U.S. states had granted partial or limited voting rights to women on school, taxes, and bond issues prior to universal suffrage. Canadian women were federally enfranchised in 1918 (women in or connected to the armed forces obtained voting privileges the previous year). In Canada, women's formal enfranchisement began in the Prairie Provinces, largely under the leadership of Nellie McClung. In January 1916 Manitoba became the first province to guarantee women the right to vote and hold provincial office, followed by Saskatchewan, Alberta, and Ontario later that same year.

In the United States, Wyoming Territory led the way by passing presidential suffrage legislation in 1869 (with full women's suffrage ensured with Wyoming's statehood in 1890). This was fifty-one years before ratification of the Nineteenth Amendment (the women's suffrage amendment to the U.S. Constitution). Neighboring states in the Great Plains followed Wyoming, granting full women's suffrage either by constitutional amendment or by legislative enactment: Colorado (1893), Kansas (1912), Montana (1914), North Dakota and Nebraska (1917), and Texas, South Dakota, and Oklahoma (1918). Thirteen out of the fifteen states that had ratified a full suffrage amendment in their state constitutions prior to the federal constitutional amendment were in the western half of the country.

The patterns of the women's suffrage movement, with its roots in eastern cities but its concrete expression in the Plains, Prairies, and other points west, were the result of a number of demographic, political-economic, and social processes. One way of understanding the success of suffrage in Wyoming, for example, is that suffrage was seen as having the potential to attract women settlers and thereby stabilize family life and, eventually, the frontier economy. (Beyond that, the Wyoming territorial legislative body that passed suffrage consisted of only fourteen people!) But while opportunistic politicians may have used suffrage to promote the Prairies and Plains in this way, there is no evidence that the women's vote actually attracted any settlers.

The suffrage movement began in the United States and Canada in conjunction with a number of other moral reform movements of the 1830s and 1840s, including abolition, temperance, and health reform. As middle-class white women's domain was confined more and more exclusively to the home, activism in reform movements became one of the few accepted "careers" open to them. Women's participation in reform movements in many ways did not challenge the division of society into separate spheres, since many women's involvements drew on an ideology of women's superior moral character and virtue in the fight for better schools, health care, and other public social services. Women's suffrage, like these other involvements, was expected to reform politics and thus "civilize" communities.

In Canada, women's service to society, such as their help in settling the Prairies or their sacrifices for the war effort, was a primary argument for women's suffrage. The Woman's Christian Temperance Union (WCTU) was active in Manitoba, where women's "moral authority" to speak for prohibition lent validity to their arguments for the vote. The situation in Kansas was similar: women's struggle for the vote there was tied to their moral arguments, especially to the very active WCTU and abolitionist movements. In Kansas, however, it was also suffrage's identification with prohibition that provoked much hostility toward it and delayed its passage far longer than expected.

The suffrage movement in the Plains and Prairies was also tied to women's participation in rural agrarian reform movements such as the Grange, the Farmers Alliance, and the Populist Party. Colorado's rural populist roots, for instance, combined with its urban radical labor movement, led to the related movement for women's suffrage. When suffrage passed in Colorado in 1893, a wide coalition of support had been established among white middle-class suffrage leaders, men and women in organized labor (such as the Labor Union Party), and rural supporters of agricultural reform.

On one hand, suffrage was a clear indicator of women's rights; many women perceived it as such, and some American women even died for it. Certainly, early suffragists saw voting rights as having a clear political purpose. They managed to establish a feminist discourse in North America that paved the way for a more nuanced feminism later in the twentieth century that was concerned with human rights more broadly. On the other hand, suffrage was not necessarily granted as a "women's rights" issue but was often a cynical and opportunistic political gesture by elite men. "Women's rights" were not necessarily advanced by suffrage, either. In fact, not all women were granted suffrage (Native American and Mexican American women, for example, were not); women's voting patterns turned out to be similar to men's; and the social improvement suffragists fought for largely failed to materialize.

Karen M. Morin
Bucknell University

Beeton, Beverly. *Women Vote in the West: The Woman Suffrage Movement, 1869–1896*. New York: Garland Publishing, Inc., 1986. Cleverdon, Catherine L. *The Woman Suffrage Movement in Canada*. Toronto: Toronto University Press, 1974. Flexner, Eleanor. *Century of Struggle: The Woman's Rights Movement in the United States*. Cambridge: Harvard University Press, 1975.

UNITED FARM WOMEN OF ALBERTA

The United Farm Women of Alberta (UFWA) was the first provincial organization of farm women in Alberta. First established in 1915 as

UFWA meeting group, Heart Lake, Alberta, 1921

an auxiliary to the United Farmers of Alberta (UFA), the women at the 1916 convention voted to make the UFWA a separate organization with its own constitution and direction.

By 1915 many local women's groups were already in place, with distinct names, purposes, and procedures of their own. The UFWA drew from women's experiences in these local groups and from the procedures already developed for the UFA to create a highly centralized organization; most local initiatives were funneled through and directed by the central office and the provincial executive. A yearly program, outlining the content and structure of monthly meetings, was developed at the provincial level and followed faithfully by locals. An information bulletin on each monthly topic was added in 1920. Three provincial committees were formed in 1916 and provincial conveners named to manage them. They focused on health, education, and young people's work, reflecting the organization's focus on "social welfare" and "betterment of rural life." More committees were added over the years as the group broadened its focus to include the legal status of women and children, cooperative marketing, farm safety, and environmental concerns. Issues such as property rights for farm women, reproductive rights, farm economics and marketing, stress in farm families, child care in rural areas, access to affordable medical care, rural depopulation, and loss of schools and services kept the organization lobbying and in advocacy activities for decades, and maintained its reputation as a respected voice for rural communities.

The United Farm Women of Alberta was responsible for innovations such as a Junior Branch for Young People, Farm Young People's Week at the University of Alberta, the first Egg and Poultry Pool established in Can-

ada (1925), Farm Women's Week at Olds Agricultural College, and the first rural chautauqua held in Alberta (1937). The organization was a major contributor to the election campaigns that resulted in UFA governments in Alberta from 1921 to 1935. The organization's first president, Irene Parlby, was appointed as the first female cabinet minister in Canada after winning a seat in the 1921 election.

In 1949 the UFWA became the Farm Women's Union of Alberta (FWUA). Significant achievements of the FWUA include the launching of a magazine for farmers (1949) and building a leadership and citizenship camp for young people in the foothills of the Rockies. In 1970, due to another organizational amalgamation, this time with the Alberta Federation of Agriculture, Unifarm was created, and the women's organization chose the name "Women of Unifarm." Significant achievements of this period include the Matrimonial Property Act (1979), giving women equality in division of marital property; the publication of the eighth edition of their renowned cookbook, which brought the total number of cookbooks sold to more than 100,000 copies; and the introduction of Farm Safety Week and the Farm Safety Hike, which garnered international recognition for the organization.

Nanci Langford
Athabasca University

Carter, Eva. *Thirty Years of Progress*. Calgary: United Farm Women of Alberta, 1944. Cormack, Barbara Villy. *Perennials and Politics: The Life Story of Hon. Irene Parlby, LL.D.* Sherwood Park, Alberta: n.p., 1969. Langford, Nanci L. *Politics, Pitchforks, and Pickle Jars: 75 Years of Organized Farm Women in Alberta*. Calgary: Detselig Enterprises, 1997.

VICTORIAN WOMEN TRAVELERS

"Victorian women travelers" generally refers to professional European and American travel writers, tourists, wives of colonial administrators, and other (mostly) elite women who wrote narratives about their experiences abroad in the nineteenth century. From a "liberal" feminist perspective in Anglo-European scholarship, travel presented one means toward female liberation for middle- and upper-class Victorian women. Many studies from the 1970s onward have demonstrated the ways in which women's gendered identities were negotiated differently "at home" versus "away," thus showing women's self-development through travel. The more recent "poststructural" turn in studies of Victorian travel writing has focused attention on women's diverse and fragmented identities as they narrated their travel experiences. In this framework, emphasis is placed on women's sense of themselves as women in new locations, but only as they worked through their ties to nation, class, whiteness, and colonial and imperial power structures. Much recent work has examined Victorian women travelers' not-so-innocent participation in European empire building, especially in terms of women travelers' ambivalent relationships with Indigenous peoples in Asia, Africa, and the Americas.

In the North American context, attention has been drawn to Victorian women's narratives of travels throughout the American and Canadian West, portions of which describe the Great Plains. (This was stimulated at least in part by western historians' long-standing interest in women settlers' relationships with the land.) Coinciding with advances in transportation technology, particularly in the steamship and railroad, the American and Canadian West was opened for wide-scale tourism and travel by the middle or upper classes in the later Victorian period (1870s in the United States, a decade later in Canada). Oftentimes, foreign visitors from Europe came to the United States and Canada as part of a world tour, and they, as well as east-coast North Americans, took "grand tours" of the continent when the transcontinental railroad lines were completed. For many travelers, the Great Plains was a place en route to the well-advertised scenic attractions of points farther west, such as Yosemite or Vancouver, rather than a destination in its own right. Thus, while many Victorian women travelers commented on the scenery, people, and economic development of the Great Plains in their travelogues, they did so without ever leaving the trains during the portions of their journeys through the region.

There are many exceptions, though. The Englishwoman Lady Rose Pender, for instance, traveled with her husband to inspect the family's investments in Wyoming ranching, and they participated in a cattle roundup in the Niobrara River valley—camping out and "roughing it" for the first time in her life. Pender thoroughly enjoyed this "wild rough life"—the clear air, the stirring scenery, and her feeling of physical well-being and "utter freedom." Mrs. Cecil Hall's 1884 narrative describes her three-month visit to her emigrant brother's farm in Manitoba. Again, what these and other Victorian travelers wrote about the Great Plains depended to a large extent on their routes and destinations. Women's travels through the Plains often followed the transects of the railroads; thus, for instance, those riding the Union Pacific Railroad wrote about Kansas City, Omaha, and Cheyenne, as well as the farms, settlements, train depots, and open country in between. Since it took up to several days to travel from Chicago to Denver by train, oftentimes the women wrote about the (in)adequacy of the train compartments themselves or described their primarily visual (and often bored) experience of passing landscapes. Many travelers expounded at length on the situation of Native Americans, especially Native women, who they sometimes encountered at train depots. British Victorian women travelers' rhetoric about Native peoples often resembled that of Indian reformers of the period.

Karen M. Morin
Bucknell University

Hall, Mrs. Cecil. *A Lady's Life on a Farm in Manitoba.* London: W. H. Allen, 1884. Hardy, Lady Duffus. *Through Cities and Prairie Lands: Sketches of an American Tour.* Chicago: Belford, Clarke and Co., 1882. Pender, Rose. *A Lady's Experiences in the Wild West in 1883.* Lincoln: University of Nebraska Press, 1978.

WOMEN HOMESTEADERS

Thousands of women took advantage of the Homestead Act (1862) that offered free land in the American Great Plains. Women who were single, widowed, divorced, or deserted were eligible to acquire 160 acres of federal land in their own name. The law discriminated against women who were married. A married woman was not allowed to take land in her own name unless she was considered the head of the household. The majority of homesteading women were young (at least twenty-one), single, and interested in adventure and the possibility of economic gain.

Lucy Goldthorpe told how she got caught up in the excitement of the times. "Even if you hadn't inherited a bit of restlessness and a pioneering spirit . . . it would have been difficult to ward off the excitement of the boom." Pauline Shoemaker remarked, "I've done everything else, I might as well try homesteading." Louise Karlson was looking for a good investment: "When in 1908 I heard about the homestead land one could get . . . I thought, here is my chance." A few women homesteaded land to help a male relative expand his acreage. This was the exception rather than the rule, and even in these cases the women usually received some compensation for their efforts.

Homesteading provided widows with an economic opportunity often denied them elsewhere. Many had children to support. Tyra Schanke, when widowed, was left with three children, ages three, four, and five. Kari Skredsvig brought up her seven children on a homestead near Bowbells, North Dakota. Even the elderly women took part in this venture. Anna Hensel was sixty-seven when she immigrated to the United States from Bessarabia in southern Russia. A year later, in 1903, she declared her intent to become a citizen and applied for a homestead in Hettinger County, North Dakota. Women from almost all ethnic groups took advantage of homesteading opportunities. An extensive but not all-inclusive list would include Anglo-Americans, Norwegians, Swedes, Danes, Finns, Hollanders, Icelanders, Germans, Germans from Russia, Bohemians, Poles, Ukrainians, Lebanese, Irish,

Agnes Lamb on the day she filed on her homestead land near the town of Washburn, North Dakota, ca. 1906

English, Scottish, Italian, African Americans, and Jewish Americans.

Although the initial experiences of homesteaders varied considerably, few women or men struck out on such an undertaking by themselves. Settlers usually came with family or friends, but a few managed alone. Kirsten Knudsen left Norway with two other young women, but she came to Mountrail County, North Dakota, by herself. She knew no one and could not speak English. She carried only a letter of introduction to an attorney from a mutual friend.

The length of time it took to "prove up," or receive title to the land, varied over the years. The Homestead Act of 1862 required a five-year residence, but the definition of residence was ambiguous. Some homesteaders left their land for lengthy periods of time to earn money, visit family, or escape severe weather. Others remained on the land most of the time. Shortly after the initial Homestead Act was passed, amendments provided for other ways of "commuting" the claim. One such option allowed the homesteader to reside on the claim for only fourteen months and then pay $1.25 an acre to receive title.

Women who took homesteads tended to "work out" as well. Many of them pursued careers as teachers, nurses, seamstresses, and domestic workers, but a few followed less traditional paths such as journalism or photography. Many eventually married, but some remained single. Those who achieved economic success used their resources in a variety of ways. Some stayed on their homestead and accumulated additional land. Others sold their holdings and invested elsewhere. In some cases homesteaders rented out the land and used the proceeds for personal or family needs. Ida Popp sold her land in Bowman County, North Dakota, and bought land adjoining her husband's claim. Lucy Gorecki traded her 160 acres for a commercial building in Fordville, North Dakota. Anna Mathilda Berg traded her homestead for a boardinghouse in Warwick, North Dakota.

In many ways, women who homesteaded resemble contemporary women. Their schedules were demanding, requiring flexibility, ingenuity, and endurance. Most would be considered community movers and shakers, as their initiatives were instrumental in building schools, churches, and other community institutions.

The homesteading period of history usually brings to mind stories of blizzards, prairie fires, and other catastrophic events. Yet tragedy is but one dimension of human life. To dwell on that aspect is to distort reality. In spite of their heavy demands, many homesteaders found time to devote to music, art, literature, and even poetry. A sense of humor was important in shaping their outlook on life.

Visitors to the homestead of Kirsten Knudsen likely were amazed to hear musical strains from the scores of operas such as *La Traviata* and *Aida* come floating through the prairie air. When Kirsten arrived on her homestead she brought with her the operas, memorized when she had spent time as a chorus girl in the National Theater in Oslo, Norway. Women as well as men were proficient in violin, piano, organ, and other instruments. Anna Zimmerman told of playing for dances with her brother. They both played accordion, violin, and guitar. Anna often played the harmonica and danced at the same time. Homesteading was more than tears and suffering.

A closer look at the lives of women who homesteaded does not reaffirm the old descriptions that characterized them as secondary "helpmates" or reluctant pioneers. Rather, they, along with men, were main characters in the settlement drama.

See also EUROPEAN AMERICANS: Land Laws and Settlement.

H. Elaine Lindgren
North Dakota State University

Fairbanks, Carol. *Prairie Women: Images in American and Canadian Fiction*. New Haven CT: Yale University Press, 1986. Lindgren, H. Elaine. *Land in Her Own Name*. Norman: University of Oklahoma Press, 1996. Muhn, James. "Women and the Homestead Act: Land Department Administration of a Legal Imbroglio, 1863–1934." *Western Legal History* 7 (1994): 283–307.

WOMEN IN AGRICULTURE

The first women farmers in the Great Plains were Native Americans who grew corn, beans, and other crops. Mandan and Hidatsa women who lived near the Missouri River in the Northern Plains, and Pawnee women along the Platte River, tended gardens and controlled the distribution of the crops. A surplus of corn contributed to the creation of trade centers near agricultural villages in the Plains. Though the wars of the late nineteenth century and reservation life contributed to the loss of this important economic role for Indian women, some continued to farm in the twentieth century.

Non-Native women who farmed the Plains, usually with husbands and children, provided labor or management skills for field crops as well as a small, stable income from barnyard and garden surpluses. Women's work in the wheat fields of the Plains was necessary during the early years of settlement, though most American families and some immigrant cultures considered it a temporary departure from desirable gender arrangements. Women plowed, planted, shocked, and pitched wheat bundles, hoed sugar beets, made hay, and hauled rocks out of the fields. Rarely did women have the opportunity to operate early threshing machinery, but they did operate tractors and trucks as soon as those machines became common in the Plains. Some women preferred fieldwork to housework, but others were glad to have their growing children take over in the fields so that they could return to the house, where they generally asserted authority.

Housework, however, cannot be distinguished from farm work. Farm women housed, fed, and cleaned up after hired helpers. In the days before combines, a farm woman who fed the threshing crew, often with the help of neighboring women working in an informal labor-exchange system, reduced the per bushel costs of threshing. Even farm women who did not work in the fields or feed hired help had to arrange their work around the daily and seasonal demands of the farm.

Farmyard work, routine for women until 1945, consisted of planting and tending vegetable gardens, raising chickens for meat or eggs, milking a few cows, separating the cream, and churning butter. In many farm homes these products served family needs as well as provided a surplus for trade at the nearest store. While the income from these commodities was relatively small, it was a reliable source of cash when the field crops failed (a common event on Plains wheat farms) or when crop prices were low.

Women on Great Plains farms apparently felt a greater need for this income than farm women in other parts of the United States, because they raised more chickens per farm and increased poultry production at a greater rate than the U.S. average between 1910 and 1930. They also were more likely to churn butter in the mid-1920s than were farm women elsewhere in the country, who by then were selling milk or cream to commercial creameries. These activities, vestiges of a frontier economy, continued to be economically useful to Great Plains farm families during the Depression. Farms where women continued to pursue productive activities tended to be more prosperous than others and more likely to enjoy continuity of ownership.

Women in the Great Plains also had more children than women in most other parts of the United States. Only the South had consistently higher birthrates than the Great Plains. Though data were collected only irregularly until the 1930s, where figures are available the birthrate tends to be higher in Plains states than in the nation as a whole and for the national rural population specifically. Cultural traditions of many of the Plains ethnic groups probably accounted for some of the tendency toward large families, but large farms requiring a lot of labor and the availability of inexpensive land were contributing factors. With large families, Plains farm women had more housework and greater need for home gardens and poultry and dairy products, but they also more hands to help with the workload.

Plains farm women did not allow distance and cultural differences to interfere with their social interests and obligations. Women organized Ladies Aid societies in rural communities, often before the organization of the church congregation. Rural Ladies Aids served as the social and political center of rural communities, with whole families attending meetings, especially during winter months, and whole communities attending Ladies Aid–sponsored celebrations. Before automobiles were available, women walked, drove wagons, or used farm equipment and draft stock to get to meetings.

Plains farm women sought to improve their economic situation as well as to foster social relationships through organizations such as the Grange, the Farmers Alliance, Farmers Institutes, and the County Extension Service. Though women rarely took a leading role in these organizations (though since the 1980s, the Extension Service has seen more female leadership), they did provide a platform from which women could challenge the notion that farmers were always men and assert their own ideas about women's roles on farms as wives, producers, and operators.

If widowed, farm women often found themselves operating the farms they had previously shared with their husbands. In 1900 farming ranked sixth in a national list of employment for women. However, in the Northern Plains, farming was the second most important job category for foreign-born women. Most of these women were widows past the age of forty.

After World War I the Extension Service encouraged women to give up farmwork and concentrate on housework and child care. After World War II, many women sought off-farm work. In recent years there is a trend toward women becoming actively involved in farming once again.

Barbara Handy-Marchello
University of North Dakota

Handy-Marchello, Barbara. "The Main Stay: Women's Productive Work on Pioneer Farms." *North Dakota History* 63 (1996): 17–27. Jellison, Katherine. *Entitled to Power: Farm Women and Technology, 1913–1963.* Chapel Hill: University of North Carolina Press, 1993. Wilson, Gilbert, ed. *Buffalo Bird Woman's Garden: Agriculture of the Hidatsa Indians.* St. Paul: Minnesota Historical Society Press, 1987.

WOMEN IN HIGHER EDUCATION

See EDUCATION: Women in Higher Education

WOMEN IN THE FUR TRADE

Women played an integral part in the North American fur trade from its inception. Yet the role of women, especially Native American women, has often been ignored in fur trade history. Contrary to the notion that the fur trade was a male-dominated activity, it actually depended upon the participation and labor of Native women for its very survival and economic success. Native women acted as essential producers in the fur trade of the Canadian and American Plains.

European women have appeared very little in fur trade lore. A few French wives may have ventured west with their trapper husbands, and some Hudson's Bay Company officials brought their wives from Europe. White women Narcissa Whitman and Eliza Spaulding acted as observers of the American fur trade when they accompanied a caravan across the Plains and attended the 1836 rendezvous. Two years later, four other white women, Mary Gray, Mary Richardson Walker, Myra Fairbanks Eells, and Sarah Gilbert White Smith, also attended the rendezvous with their missionary husbands. Their detailed journal descriptions of fur trade activities are an important part of the historical record.

Native women were the primary female participants in the fur trade. Plains Indian women married French Canadian, British, American, and Indian employees of the fur companies. As wives and daughters, Native women acted in such important fur trade roles as producers, translators, traders, and guides. Marriage between white men and Indian women encouraged political, social, and economic alliances within the fur trade systems. Marriage *à la façon du pays*, or "according to the custom of the country," served as a unifying bond between European American and Canadian fur traders and Native tribes, with many traders paying a "bride price" for the daughters of important tribal leaders. For example, in 1814 the St. Louis trader Manuel Lisa married Mitain, daughter of an Omaha chief, and secured an alliance that kept the Omahas tied to the United States during the War of 1812 with Britain and also kept their furs flowing to Lisa's post. In spite of cultural differences and the economic motivations, many mixed marriages were stable, loving, and long-lasting. White traders also married the Métis, or mixed-blood, daughters of white-Indian marriages, as a means of improving their status in the fur trade community. However, with the arrival of more European wives in the mid-1800s, Métis wives and children suffered increased discrimination.

Indian and Métis women were instrumental to fur trade success. Whether at forts or in settled communities, at the rendezvous or on hunts, women were participants in fur operations. They actively promoted and benefited from the trade of woolen blankets, cloth, glass beads, steel knives, awls, needles, and pans. In turn, they contributed to the trade's success through varied support roles and especially through the production of furs. Women were, in fact, the primary producers of the fur trade: they trapped the smaller marten for its fur, and they made the moccasins, snowshoes, canoes, and other equipment necessary for travel on winter hunts. For food they hunted small animals, fished, and made pemmican. Most importantly, Native women prepared, or dressed, the bison robes and the beaver and otter pelts for their ultimate use as hats and clothing. Crow women in particular were renowned for production of fine hides and moccasins. Native women may have traded their dressed skins and furs, too, though it has been argued that their status actually decreased with the fur trade, as market negotiations were taken over by Native American men. Certainly, women's workload went up with fur trade demands: tanning a robe was a three-day job, and Indian women aimed at tanning up to thirty-five over a winter season.

Native women also served as important guides and translators to expeditions, most famously, Sacagawea. The lesser-known Thanadelthur, a Chipewyan woman, guided and interpreted for an early expedition of the Hudson's Bay Company. Without fame or salaries, Native women actively contributed to the success of the North American fur trade.

See also INDUSTRY: Hudson's Bay Company / NATIVE AMERICANS: Métis.

Andrea G. Radke
Brigham Young University

Brown, Jennifer, *Strangers in Blood: Fur Trade Company Families in Indian Country.* Vancouver: University of British Columbia Press, 1980. Faragher, John Mack, "The Custom of the Country: Cross-Cultural Marriage in the Far Western Fur Trade." In *Western Women: Their Land, Their Lives,* edited by Lillian Schlissel, Vicki L. Ruiz, and Janice Monk. Albuquerque: University of New Mexico Press, 1988: 199–225. Van Kirk, Sylvia. *Many Tender Ties: Women in Fur-Trade Society, 1670–1870.* Norman: University of Oklahoma Press, 1980.

WOMEN OF ALL RED NATIONS

See PROTEST AND DISSENT: Women of All Red Nations

WOMEN WARRIORS

Raiding and warfare were an integral part of the men's role among Plains Indian nations, but it was by no means uncommon for women to engage in these activities as well. Their motivations were the same as those of the men: revenge, defense, and a desire for prestige and wealth. Most frequently, a woman would join or even lead a war party in order to take revenge for relatives slain by some enemy. Women would also take up arms to defend their camp against hostile intruders. In other cases, women, by means of visions, received the command to go to war. Capturing horses and other property on a raid also brought great prestige to both men and women.

The term "woman warrior," while commonplace, is misleading. To be a warrior was a lifetime occupation for Plains Indian men, but most women who went to war did not pursue a warrior's life permanently. Many women went to war only once or twice in their lives. Others were married and accompanied their husbands on war or raiding parties, especially while the couple was still young and childless. Some women served as sentries and messengers; others fought in battle alongside the men, counted coup, and took scalps. Eventually, they quit warring and raiding, raised children, and did their share of work within the gendered division of labor. In this they differed from the female two-spirits, or *berdaches*, who took up the culturally defined man's role completely and permanently.

In some cases, however, success as a warrior would pave a woman's way to a quasi-masculine role and status. The war deeds of Woman Chief, who lived among the Crow around 1850, were so daring that the men invited her to join their council meetings, where she ranked as the third leading warrior in a group of 160 lodges. She became an accomplished trader and hunter and eventually married four wives, who processed the hides and did the other standard women's chores around her lodge. Another example is Brown Weasel Woman, a Piegan female warrior. A major battle with an enemy tribe brought her—the only female in her tribe's history to be so honored—a man's name, Running Eagle, that was reserved for famous warriors.

The role of the woman warrior was socially accepted wherever it occurred among the Plains nations. The same holds true for other role alternatives in which women could gain prestige by exhibiting behavior culturally defined as masculine. The prestige system of the Plains cultures was clearly male-dominated, centering on warlike activities and personality traits considered masculine. It is true that Plains Indian women could gain great prestige by excelling in women's occupations such as beadwork and agriculture, by assuming certain roles in ceremonies, and by expressing culturally valued ideals of femininity. Yet the masculine prestige system was the measure for both sexes. Even feminine achievements were sometimes expressed in masculine terms. Within that system, however, women could compete for the prestige associated with war and raiding on equal terms with men and did so if they had the inclination.

Sabine Lang
Hamburg, Germany

Hungry Wolf, Beverly. *The Ways of My Grandmothers*. New York: Quill Books, 1982. Lang, Sabine. *Men as Women, Women as Men: Changing Gender in Native American Cultures*. Austin: University of Texas Press, 1998. Medicine, Beatrice. "'Warrior Women': Sex Role Alternatives for Plains Indian Women." In *The Hidden Half: Studies of Plains Indian Women*, edited by Patricia Albers and Beatrice Medicine. Washington DC: University Press of America, 1983: 267–80.

Hispanic Americans

Mexican workers on a train listen to a lecture in Spanish on hoeing and thinning beets, eastern Colorado, ca. 1920.

When Damasso Armendáriz left his South Texas home in 1994 to work at Millard Processing Services in Omaha, Nebraska, he thought he was going to start a life that would offer more than the one he was leaving. After all, the recruiters from the pork-processing plant had promised him free housing and a managerial position. But as soon as Armendáriz stepped into the jam-packed Ford Clubwagon, the vehicle designated to transport Armendáriz and several others from El Paso, Texas, to Omaha, he knew that he had been mistaken. And when he arrived in Omaha, he found to his dismay that his housing consisted of a rundown apartment with bug-infested, torn-up furniture. The promised managerial position did not materialize, and company officials instead placed him on the processing lines, a job that was not only grueling but dangerous. It was a situation shared by the other 800 Mexicans and Mexican Americans working in the plant.

Although Armendáriz's dismal tale took place only six years from the twenty-first century, his experience coming to *El Norte* was not unique. He is but one of many who have migrated from the south to the Great Plains since the sixteenth century. Spaniards, Mexicans, and Mexican Americans, joined recently by Central Americans, have maintained a noticeable presence in the Great Plains for almost 500 years; they have contributed their labor and ideas to building settlements and the Plains economy, and they have enriched its culture.

The Spanish and the Plains, 1540–1821

The Spanish were the first Europeans to recognize the importance of the Plains. Their presence was initially established through the gradual penetration of the Southern Plains by exploration sponsored by the Spanish state and military, wealthy ranchers and miners, and the Catholic Church. Later, Spanish influence emanated from settlements and colonies around the Southern Plains.

It all started in the sixteenth century when Spain, having secured Mesoamerica, turned its colonization machine to the north. Álvar Núñez Cabeza de Vaca, the second-in-command of the ill-fated Pánfilo de Narváez expedition to western Florida, skirted the Southern Plains in his journey from the Texas coast to Mexico City in 1528–36. He brought back rumors of the mythical Seven Cities of Cíbola. To investigate Cabeza de Vaca's report, Viceroy Antonio de Mendoza sent Father Marcos de Niza to the north in 1539. The Pueblo Indians forced Father Marcos to turn back, but his report of Cíbola, a magnificent Rio Grande pueblo larger than any Mexican city, enticed Viceroy Mendoza to appoint Francisco Vásquez de Coronado to lead a large expedition to occupy the region. When Cíbola proved to be but an ordinary pueblo, Coronado took thirty-six men east to the Southern Plains in 1541. There, according to a Pawnee captive nicknamed El Turco, he would find the fabled province of Quivira. From central Kansas,

beyond the land of "cattle and sky" (as the expedition's chronicle described the flat, bison-rich expanses of the Llano Estacado), Coronado eventually found Quivira—a Wichita Indian village with beautiful grass lodges and well-tended cornfields, but no gold.

Coronado returned to Mexico in disgrace, but the notion of wealth and a better life in the north remained alive in New Spain. When France and England entered the colonization race in the late sixteenth century, Spanish officials began to worry that they might penetrate the North American interior and threaten their lucrative mines in northern Mexico. Settlement was needed in the Rio Grande Valley and beyond, and an official competitive settlement contract was announced. After several aborted attempts, Don Juan de Oñate, a wealthy silver baron, took 500 settlers and more than 1,000 head of stock north in 1598 and established a permanent colony in the Rio Grande Valley. In 1609 a mission was built at Santa Fe, which in 1610 became the capital of the new royal province of New Mexico. By the 1620s a modest but entrenched Spanish colony, with missions, ranches, and land grants, had been established in the Rio Grande Valley. Except for a brief interim during the Pueblo Revolt in 1680–92, the colony persisted. The establishment of New Mexico revolutionized life among the Pueblo Indians, who felt the full burden of repressive Spanish colonial rule, but it also had enormous impact on the adjacent grasslands. Due to the proximity of New Mexico to the Southern Plains—only the narrow and relatively passable Sangre de Cristo Range separated them—their histories would be intimately linked.

Meanwhile, rapid French expansion forced the Spanish to act also in the east. By the late 1680s the French were exploring the lower Mississippi Valley, and a few years later the French unsuccessfully tried to plant a colony on the east coast of Texas. New Spain responded by officially creating the province of Texas in 1691 and sending its first governor, Domingo de Terán, to lead church, civilian, and military colonization efforts. Spain moved into East Texas first, and by the 1710s it had established a string of missions at the southeastern edge of the Southern Plains. In an effort to connect northern Mexico with its far-flung Texas outposts, a presidio, San Antonio de Béjar, was built in 1718, followed shortly by a mission, San Antonio de Valero (later called the Alamo). The French threat had created a strong commitment by Spain to settle Texas and to occupy the southern flank of the Plains. For the next 100 years the Texas colony and the Southern Plains would have a complex, fluctuating relationship, which profoundly affected both.

Although the Spanish endured on the borders of the Southern Plains until the collapse of the Spanish Empire in 1821, they never made serious attempts to colonize the grasslands. The nomadic and seminomadic hunters of the Southern Plains—Apaches, Comanches, Wichitas, and others—were an insurmountable obstacle to the Spanish imperial system, which was based on the exploitation of seden-

tary agricultural Indians and their labor. The futility of absorbing the Plains into the empire became painfully clear in the early eighteenth century, when Spain, in an effort to block France's commercial expansion, tried to establish a military presence in the region. Alarmed by reports of French activities among the Pawnees and Apaches, Governor Antonio Valverde y Cosío commissioned Lieutenant Governor Pedro de Villazur to lead an expedition to the Platte River and to determine whether a presidio in southeastern Colorado would serve to eliminate the French threat. In 1720, traveling with sixty Pueblos and forty-two Spanish troops, Villazur marched to the confluence of the Platte and Loup Rivers in central Nebraska, farther than any Spanish expedition from New Mexico would ever travel in the Great Plains. There, Pawnees and Otoes with French guns destroyed them. Villazur was killed along with twenty-nine soldiers, one-third of New Mexico's troops. Humiliated, the Spanish retreated to their existing Rio Grande settlements.

A similar fate ended Spain's attempt to expand its reach north of Texas in the 1750s. Over the years Lipan Apaches, pressured by southward-expanding Comanches, had repeatedly asked for a mission and, thereby, Spanish protection. In 1757 Spanish officials finally responded to the Lipan requests by sending six missionaries and 100 soldiers and their families to build a mission and a presidio on the San Saba River. The site, about three miles east of the present town of Menard, Texas, was chosen because it was suitable for irrigated farming and was near a rich mineral region. Yet within a year, Mission Santa Cruz de San Sabá and Presidio de San Luis de las Amarillas, the only Spanish mission and presidio ever established in the Plains, lay in ruins, destroyed by Comanches, Wichitas, and Hasinais who wanted to prevent the Spanish-Apache alliance. The attempt to extend the Spanish frontier into the Texas Plains ended in utter failure.

The Villazur and San Sabá disasters fundamentally altered the history of the Great Plains. During the remaining years of the Spanish presence in the Americas, New Mexico and Texas devolved into sleepy outposts rather than serving as springboards for Plains colonization. In the 1770s, when New Spain's northern colonies were organized into a huge semiautonomous administrative unit, the *Provincias Internas*, the rationale for the arrangement in New Mexico and Texas was to improve the colonies' defensive, not expansive, potential. But the absence of colonization did not mean that there was no interaction between the Spanish and the Plains. Throughout the Spanish era, trade goods, animals, and microbes were disseminated into the Plains, radically changing both land and life.

Diseases spread from the colonies to the adjacent grasslands, killing tens of thousands of Indians who had no resistance against European microbes. It is not known when the first epidemics struck, but many scholars believe that the Plains Indian population in 1700 was only a fraction of what it was before contact.

But the colonies also benefited the Plains Indians. The most positive exchange was the reintroduction of horses to the grasslands. The first horses probably came to the Plains in the early seventeenth century, but the diffusion accelerated greatly after the Pueblo Revolt, when Pueblos and Plains Indians engaged in active trade in horses left behind by the Spanish. Within a few generations, the Plains Indians reinvented themselves and became some of the most refined hunting and equestrian cultures in history.

In addition to microbes and animals, people crossed the boundaries between the Spanish colonies and the Plains. In the eighteenth and early nineteenth centuries, Comanches sold thousands of Apache and Pawnee captives to New Mexico. The commerce in humans was also encouraged by the *Recopilación* of 1681, which obliged the Spanish to ransom Native Americans enslaved by other Native Americans. Called *indios genízaros*, these captives lacked social status within either Spanish or Puebloan society. With no land or property, genízaros were put in new settlements constructed as frontier outposts on the western Plains border. There they constituted the front line of defense protecting the Spanish presence in the Southwest.

The movement of diseases, horses, and people in and out of the Plains was abetted by economic interaction. Initially, the Spanish–Plains Indian trade grew out of necessity: the Spanish needed Plains goods—hides, dried meat, and tallow—and the Jumanos, Comanches, and other Native American groups were eager to obtain horses, metal goods, and firearms. Later, as Spanish officials realized that the Plains was beyond their military grasp, they attempted to control the Plains Indians through trade. In an effort to block French and, later, American expansion into the Plains and northern Mexico, the Spanish tried to turn the Southern Plains into a buffer zone by drawing the region's Indians into their commercial orbit.

Spurred by these economic and political motives, Spanish–Plains Indian trade flourished, particularly in New Mexico. As they had done for centuries, Plains nomads came every year to Pueblo trade fairs, which in the eighteenth century were increasingly dominated by Spanish merchants. Texas, the poorer of the two colonies, was slower to develop trade with the Plains tribes. There was some trade at San Antonio de Béjar. But in most cases the Indians focused on raiding the poorly protected missions and ranches for horses, mules, cattle, and goods.

Before the 1780s the trade was also often interrupted in New Mexico by raids launched by Comanches and Apaches who were either looking for horses and corn or trying to force the Spanish into more favorable trade arrangements. A new era in Spanish–Plains Indian relations began in 1785-86, when the Spanish governments in Texas and New Mexico signed treaties with the Comanches. The Spanish promised secure trade, gifts, and access to guns, while the Comanches promised

to stop raiding. In addition, both agreed to wage a joint war against the Apaches, which led to sporadic Comanche-Spanish expeditions against the few Apache bands still living on the Plains margins.

The peaceful relations with the Comanches after the 1780s also enticed Spanish and Puebloan traders from New Mexico to venture onto the open grasslands. Known as *comancheros*, these traders flourished in the Plains until the 1870s, exchanging bread, metal, tobacco, guns, ammunition, and alcohol for bison products, horses, and other Plains exports. Contemporaries of the comancheros were *ciboleros*, bison hunters from New Mexico, who made annual winter hunting expeditions to provide meat for their families and hides for a burgeoning Santa Fe–Chihuahua trade. Roaming the Llano Estacado from semipermanent camps, the ciboleros may have taken as many as 25,000 bison hides back to New Mexico during the peak years of the early nineteenth century.

Spain's role in the geopolitics of the Plains was also changing. In 1763, as a result of the French and Indian War, Spain gained Louisiana, which at that time included all of the Great Plains except for the far northern regions. The new geopolitical arrangement allowed the Spanish to relax their frontier defenses in New Mexico and Texas. On the other hand, the southward push of Canada-based British fur traders in the late eighteenth century forced Spanish officials to take action in the Northern Plains. In an effort to block British expansion, the officials promoted trade and exploration along the upper Missouri River, the commercial and transportation artery of the Northern Plains. Enticed by a large cash prize, French and Spanish merchants in St. Louis formed the Missouri Company and sent three exploring parties up the river between 1794 and 1796, reaching as far as the Mandan villages in present-day North Dakota.

In 1800, however, military losses in European wars forced Spain to return Louisiana to France. Spain was soon shocked to find an aggressive republic, the United States, on her *Provincias Internas* border, following Napoleon's sale of Louisiana to the Americans in 1803. Once again, Spain was restricted to the Southern Plains. For the remainder of their tenure in North America, the Spanish made a concerted effort to keep the Americans out of the Southern Plains, which they continued to use as a buffer zone for Mexico's silver mines. Spanish officials, for example, liberally granted licenses to comancheros, for they thought that the itinerant traders could help to gather intelligence on American actions in the Plains. Legally, because France and the United States had not formalized the southern border of the Louisiana Purchase, neither side had a definite claim to the Southern Plains.

The Spanish–Plains Indian interaction remained active until the collapse of the Spanish Empire. A decade of unrest culminated in the Mexican Revolution in 1821, which ended three centuries of Spanish presence in North America. Still, the Spanish legacy was profound. Missions, presidios, and ranches had fixed the Spanish and their institutions and culture on the Plains margins. An amalgamation of the Indigenous peoples and Spanish gave rise to a dynamic mestizo culture, which became an integral part of life in the Plains. Politically, Mexico inherited Spain's claim to a great portion of the Southern Plains, a demand that was confirmed in the Adams-Onís Treaty in 1819, just two years before the end of Spain's hegemony. According to the treaty, American and Spanish possessions were separated in the east by the Sabine River (which still separates Louisiana and Texas) and in the north by the Red River and, west of the 100th meridian, the Arkansas River. Although these boundaries were largely abstractions that ignored Native Americans' territorial claims, the fact that Spain managed to claim such a large portion of the Southern Plains testifies to its significant historical role in the region.

Mexicans and the Plains, 1821–1846

The period of Mexican rule in New Mexico and Texas was marked by growing political instability, economic difficulties, and dismantling of missions, presidios, and other colonial institutions. New Mexico and Texas were isolated from the political core of central and southern Mexico and suffered from a lack of governmental direction and from deteriorating economic systems. Also a reflection of their isolation from Mexico's core areas, New Mexico and Texas began to be pulled into the American orbit. The growing American influence first contributed to the Texas Revolution in 1836, then culminated in the annexation of Texas and New Mexico by the United States in 1845 and 1848, respectively.

Yet these enormous changes created only ripples in the Plains. Throughout the Mexican period, comancheros continued to make trade journeys among Comanches and Kiowas, keeping in place the economic ties between New Mexico and the Plains. Trade, albeit more limited in scope, also continued on the Texas frontier. However, the acute financial problems of the Republic of Mexico made it impossible for the frontier officials to abide by the provisions of the Indian treaties, which prompted the Comanches and Kiowas to escalate their raiding activities in New Mexico and Texas. In Texas an additional problem was the relentless northward and westward thrust of the settlement frontier, which gained momentum in the 1820s as increasing numbers of Americans and Europeans migrated to the province. By 1833 a great portion of the Plains south of the Arkansas River had already been allocated to immigration agents called *empresarios*, although the lands were still under Comanche and Kiowa control. When settlers pushed to the north, the Comanches and Kiowas retaliated with raids. By 1840 raiding had become so widespread that a virtual state of war existed on the New Mexico and Texas Plains border.

The most crucial development of the Mexican period in the Plains was the expansion of the private land-grant system onto the Llano

Estacado. This rose from the dread of American territorial expansion, which was fueled by growing American economic influence in New Mexico after the opening of the Santa Fe trade in 1821. Determined to eliminate the American threat, Mexican governors in the 1820s and 1830s made huge land grants to the Baubiens, Mirandas, and other leading families of New Mexico. The recipients of the grants agreed to put settlers on their lands, which, the governors hoped, would fasten Mexico's hold on the territory and act as a barrier against American expansion. By the early 1840s the whole western flank of the Southern Plains from the Arkansas River to the Canadian River had already been allocated as private grants. Although Indian occupation kept the assigned lands thinly populated, the grants gave the Mexican elite a strong legal claim to large portions of the Southern Plains on the eve of American takeover.

Mexican Americans and the Plains, 1846–1900

The annexation of Texas pushed the United States and Mexico toward war. Mexico had never recognized Texas independence and viewed the annexation as an act of aggression. The United States did recognize the Republic of Texas in 1837: because so many Americans had migrated to Texas, it was considered a logical extension of a growing empire that would eventually reach to the Pacific. The Plains proper, firmly in the possession of the Indians, played a marginal role in this struggle. However, because Texas claimed a southern and western border all the way to the Rio Grande, and because Mexico insisted on the Nueces River, the Southern Plains was involved, at least on the map, in an international conflict. The Mexican American War of 1846–48, although fought outside the Plains, still had enormous ramifications for the region. The Treaty of Guadalupe Hidalgo, which stipulated the terms of the peace, transferred New Mexico and part of Colorado to the United States, extended the Texas boundary to the Rio Grande, and, in effect, placed the Southern Plains within the United States.

At first the United States focused its efforts on the Rio Grande Valley in New Mexico and in the San Antonio region in Texas. The immediate goal was to absorb those economic and population centers into the national system by introducing American jurisdiction, establishing representative governments, controlling the Catholic Church, and remaking land laws. While major economic, social, and political changes were forced upon the Mexican Americans of New Mexico and Texas, they still retained their distinctive culture. They clung to Catholicism, Spanish and Mexican customs, and the Spanish language, and they celebrated Mexican national holidays and built adobe houses. They also demanded power, better living conditions, and fair treatment. During the latter part of the nineteenth century, most of New Mexico's territorial delegates to Washington DC were Mexican Americans. In Texas, Tejano workers organized several strikes.

Meanwhile, the Plains remained a periphery where Mexican-born ciboleros and comancheros could operate relatively undisturbed by the federal government. In fact, the comanchero trade reached its height as late as the 1860s and 1870s, when the comancheros began to traffic in cattle the Comanches stole from Texas ranches. Texas longhorns found a ready market among wealthy New Mexican merchants, who had begun to produce meat for federal beef contractors. Encouraged by the burgeoning trade, comancheros started to build semipermanent trading centers along the well-traveled trade routes of the Llano Estacado. These trading camps, which often featured dugouts, stone houses, and rudimentary irrigation systems, represented the first substantial Mexican American settlements in the Plains.

The confinement of Native Americans on reservations by the mid-1870s paved the way for an even more permanent Mexican American settlement in the Plains. *Pastores* (shepherds) from New Mexico filled the vacuum left by the removed Comanches, Kiowas, and Plains Apaches. Prompted by a growing market for wool in the United States after the Civil War, the pastores expanded their operations from the Rio Grande and Pecos Valleys onto the Llano Estacado, where abundant shortgrasses provided plentiful forage for their herds. Using the traditional Spanish transhumance system, pastores moved their flocks between summer and winter pastures, making large circuits along old Indian and comanchero trails. A mix of merino and Spanish *chaurro* breeds, New Mexican sheep proved to be well adapted to the Plains environment, and their owners thrived.

As the number of pastores on the Llano Estacado grew, they began to congregate into small communities called *plazas*. By the 1880s dozens of small and large plazas were distributed along the Canadian River valley and its tributaries, the core sheepherding region. Besides their function as herding centers, the plazas were nuclei of Mexican American culture in the Plains. A typical plaza featured a single line of adobe or rock houses surrounded by a New Mexican–type stone wall. An irrigation ditch, or *acequia*, provided water for a fruit orchard and small fields of corn, beans, melons, and peppers. Social life revolved around fiestas, all-night *bailes* (dances), traditional Mexican games such as *la pelota* (a form of field hockey), and regular Catholic services (the Catholicism practiced in the plazas could differ considerably from the Catholicism practiced elsewhere in New Mexico and Texas, where there was much more official church control). A nearby cemetery signaled a long-term commitment to the region.

The pastores flourished in the Plains until the mid-1880s, when they were replaced by the expanding open-range cattle industry. By the 1890s only a few pastores remained on their shrinking pastures; most had been eliminated by Anglo-American ranchers' barbed wire, threats, and restrictive laws. Many retreated to

the urban areas of New Mexico, only to return in large numbers to build railroads across the Texas Panhandle in the late 1880s and 1890s. Some pastores remained on the Llano Estacado and began to work for the same cattle barons who had dispossessed them. By the 1880s about one-fourth of all cowboys working on the Plains cattle trails were Mexican Americans. Through their labor, these Mexican Americans made a significant contribution to an industry that had already been heavily influenced by Spanish and Mexican ranching heritage. From the gear and methods used, to its vocabulary, the Anglo-American cattle industry of the Great Plains was built on a Spanish-Mexican foundation. Anglo cowboys, often working alongside *vaqueros*, rode on Mexican stock saddles, garnished their stirrups with "taps" (*tapaderas*), used the lasso (*lazo*) or lariat (*la reata*), collected the animals in annual roundups (*rodeo* or *corruda*), and relaxed by engaging in rowdy drinking binges (*parrandas*).

While Mexican Americans were making important contributions to the social and economic life of the Southern Plains, their hold on the land was slipping away. The Treaty of Guadalupe Hidalgo had promised to respect the landholdings of Mexican citizens, but decisions made in American courts and legislatures undermined the principle. In 1854 the first American surveyor-general to New Mexico discovered multiple claims and overlapping land grants. Confusion governed New Mexican land policy, triggering more claims and divesting many Mexican Americans of their homes and fields. Furthermore, after the introduction of the Homestead Act in 1862, Mexican Americans also had to compete with Anglo farmers for the land.

In 1891 Congress created the Court of Private Land Claims to hear disputes in New Mexico and Colorado. In a few years, Mexican Americans lost more than 33 million acres. Lawyers were paid for their services in land; some attorneys amassed fortunes by taking huge amounts of land from villages as fees. Dispossessed Mexican Americans sought work in Colorado as miners, in Texas as rail workers, and on the Central Plains as *betabeleros*—beet workers, planters, and harvesters.

Mexican Americans did not accept these changes without resistance. In the late 1880s, largely as a response to the uncertainty and corruption surrounding land titles, a group of Mexican Americans and sympathetic Anglos organized a vigilante group called *Gorras Blancas*, or White Caps. Operating mainly in the New Mexico Plains, the Gorras Blancas resisted fencing of the ranges by railroad companies, cattlemen, and other land claimants and sought to protect Hispano land grants. They tore up railroad tracks and fences, formed a local political party, and were instrumental in obtaining legislative action to preserve the grants.

By the end of the nineteenth century, the culture of the Great Plains—its economy, architecture, social customs, and ethnic fabric—displayed strong traces of Spanish and Mexican heritage. This heritage reflected the long tenure of Spanish and Mexican people in and around the region, a tenure that had begun with the first Spanish expeditions in the sixteenth century. Around 1900 a new period began in the history of Mexican Americans and the Great Plains. Before 1900, Spanish, Mexican, and Mexican American influence had emanated to the Plains from the adjacent regions of New Mexico and Texas. In the twentieth century, however, people from all over Mexico and from Central America began to migrate to the Plains in search of employment and to escape the economic or political conditions in their home countries.

Latinos and the Plains in the Twentieth Century

During the twentieth century two important trends emerged with reference to Mexicans and Mexican Americans and the Great Plains. First, they moved more widely throughout the region. Migration to the Central Plains was particularly significant, and that migratory process was different from past migrations. The displacement and the transitory aspects of the migration of Mexicans and Mexican Americans fueled labor abuses and unrest. Some Plains industries, such as meatpacking, became dependent upon Mexican and Mexican American labor. Second, Mexican Americans had begun to infiltrate the power structures of American society, including political offices. This new development reached the highest levels of local, state, and national government. Throughout these changes, Mexican Americans retained significant aspects of their culture, with their music, art, and culture developing regional and national prominence.

Beginning in the 1880s the Mexican population in the Great Plains began to increase, the direct result of a transportation revolution created by the railroad. Between 1882 and 1912 U.S. rail corporations built four lines from the heart of Mexico into California and New Mexico. Following these lines (and often building them) Mexicans traveled to Texas, Colorado, and Oklahoma to work in booming coal and agricultural industries. It was, however, the social upheaval surrounding the Mexican Revolution, which began in 1910, that pushed large numbers of Mexicans into the United States and the Great Plains. The first major wave of immigration started in 1900. Most of these "first wavers" settled in Kansas; a smaller number made their way to other Central Plains states. In 1900 the U.S. census counted only 182 Mexicans in Oklahoma, Kansas, Nebraska, South Dakota, and North Dakota combined. But by 1910 that number had increased to 11,384. Over the course of the following decade, 23,201 Mexicans migrated into these states, and in the 1920s, 32,240 more followed. Actual numbers were much higher; census authorities have noted that these figures represent a gross undercount of migratory Mexican immigrants. Immigration halted in the 1930s, as the Great Depression eliminated job opportunities and some states started repatriation movements, deporting both Mexicans and Mexican

Americans to Mexico. By 1940 this immigration had lowered the region's Mexican and Mexican American population to 8,452.

Most Mexicans in the Plains lived a migratory life. They were mainly males, and they frequently traveled back across the border, visiting the families they had left behind in Mexico. The nature of their employment, moreover, was very transient, so Mexican migrants frequently moved around within the Plains. They labeled themselves *solos*, characterizing the solitary migrant lives that most of these immigrants led. The lives and work patterns of solos, therefore, were the result of several interrelated factors: the labor market, the demands of employers, the convenience of rail travel, and the desire to see their families.

Two other factors influenced the kind of jobs that were made available to Mexican workers. Racism excluded Mexicans from skilled and semiskilled work; only unskilled industrial and agricultural employment remained open. Moreover, not only were the majority of jobs unskilled and poorly paid, but they were also seasonal. Railroad companies, a major employer of immigrants, usually hired from March through May or October. Sugar beet growers, the other major employer, hired in six-month cycles ending in November or December. The seasonal nature of the solos' employment left them with a period of time during which they could return to Mexico or the Southern Plains and see their families. This travel was facilitated by the extensive rail networks that crisscrossed the Plains and extended well into Mexico. While the initial wave of Mexicans came as solos, later waves of migrants settled down permanently. After 1910 railroad companies came to the conclusion that seasonal workers were less profitable than permanent workers—a seasonal worker could easily protest low wages by leaving his job and finding a new one elsewhere. So rail companies began hiring Mexicans in more permanent positions. To encourage this they began transporting entire Mexican families into the United States and settling them in the company's locale. By 1927 sugar beet companies were copying railroad hiring practices. At the end of the decade, the seeds of permanent Mexican American communities in the Central Plains had been planted, and the *colonias* in the Southern Plains were replenished.

Migration patterns varied with the type of employment. Mexicans employed in the rail industry, *traqueros*, crossed the Mexico-U.S. border at El Paso. There they were recruited to work for railroads from all over the nation. Traqueros heading to the Plains traveled first to Kansas City, where most stayed to work for the Santa Fe Railroad. A smaller number moved on to other areas. Betabeleros, laborers in the sugar beet fields, followed a different migratory route. Sugar companies, in particular the Great Western Sugar Company, recruited thousands of Mexicans directly from Mexico and brought them through New Mexico and the Southern Plains. The numbers escalated as the industry grew, increasing significantly when World War I reduced domestic

labor supplies. In 1915 Great Western recruited only 500 Mexican workers; in 1920 the company hired 13,000 Mexicans, and in 1926, 14,500 Mexicans. As with traqueros, betabeleros first gathered in Kansas City. From there, they moved to the beet fields of northern Colorado, Nebraska, Kansas, Wyoming, Montana, South Dakota, and North Dakota. By 1920 Mexicans became synonymous with beet workers in the Plains, and by 1927 they comprised 90 percent of all beet workers in the region.

Despite the different routes of arrival and their uneven distribution over Plains states, betabeleros in the Plains demonstrated a strong working-class solidarity. These workers succeeded in organizing despite their migratory lifestyles and the racism directed against them by employers who had a free hand in using union-busting tactics. The workers first formed organizations such as the *Comisión Honorífica Mexicana* to protest discrimination. By World War I, with encouragement from the Industrial Workers of the World, the betabeleros organized to gain higher wages. In the early 1920s they formed the Mexican Beet Workers Committee, later *Asociación de Betabeleros*, an organization aimed at improving working conditions and ensuring fair employment practices.

At its peak, the Asociación de Betabeleros united some 10,000 workers from Colorado, Nebraska, Kansas, Wyoming, and Montana. When the American Federation of Labor (AFL) rejected their efforts to affiliate, the Asociación aligned instead with communists and socialists to form the United Front Committee of Agriculture Workers in 1932. Although they commanded a formidable membership of 18,000, they were still not able to strike successfully against the powerful sugar companies of the Great Plains.

In 1935 several local beet-worker organizations joined to form the Colorado Conference of Beet Field and Agricultural Unions. They then affiliated with the Agricultural Workers Union, a branch of the AFL. In 1937 these workers left the AFL to affiliate with the United Cannery, Packing, and Agricultural Workers of America (UCAPAWA), a branch of the newly formed Congress of Industrial Organization. UCAPAWA claimed some 18,000 to 20,000 Mexican American beet workers in the Plains, of whom 60 percent were Mexican-born and 40 percent American-born. But like the other efforts at organization, UCAPAWA failed, in this case because of the inept leadership of European American organizers who knew little about the beet industry or Mexican Americans.

Although the majority of Mexican Americans in the Plains were betabeleros and traqueros, some worked in other industries as well. During World War I, Mexican Americans were employed in the meatpacking industry in Kansas, Oklahoma, and Nebraska. In 1921, 200 to 300 Mexican Americans worked in Kansas City plants, and in 1927 approximately 600 worked in the South Omaha stockyards. They also worked in the cotton fields of southern

Oklahoma and the mines of southeastern Oklahoma and southern Colorado. In the mining town of Lafayette, just outside Denver, for example, Mexican Americans composed 52 percent of the miners between 1921 and 1928.

The economic hardships of the Great Depression intensified racist attitudes toward Mexican immigrants. Nativists, many of whom belonged to trade unions, blamed cheap Mexican labor for stealing jobs from "hardworking Americans," meaning Anglos. The U.S. government responded by implementing a program designed to "repatriate" undocumented workers. While for the most part this program did not extend beyond California, Arizona, and the Plains states of Texas and New Mexico, Immigration and Naturalization Service (INS) officials derived the idea of mass deportation from the practices of a Plains city. As early as 1921, metropolitan Denver's county sheriff had independently ordered his law enforcement department to bus undocumented workers back to the Mexican border.

While one segment of the American public was aligned against Mexican immigration, another segment, growers in the Southern Plains, clamored for more low-paid Mexican workers. Manpower shortages during World War II further increased the need for labor. The federal government responded by entering into an agreement with the Mexican government that created what later came to be known as the Bracero Program. Through this 1942 agreement, the Mexican government facilitated the importation of temporary workers in exchange for the guarantee that Mexican nationals would have full protection under federal laws.

The Bracero Program provided much-needed labor to several Plains states. There is, however, a dearth of information about exactly how many braceros entered the Plains, where they went, and in what industries they worked. Texas was probably the only Plains state to receive large numbers of braceros. They faced great difficulties there. Almost from the outset of this program, the Mexican government banned braceros from entering the state because of racial abuses practiced by Texas growers. A similar situation existed in Wyoming. Consequently, after Wyoming received just 650 braceros in 1942 and 1943, the Mexican government prohibited its nationals from working in the state. Both Texas and Wyoming eventually regained access to braceros, and Texas continued to import large numbers until the end of the program in 1964.

Twenty years after the first repatriation program, the federal government mounted yet another initiative to deport undocumented workers, ironically at a time when the Bracero Program was still going strong. "Operation Wetback" began in 1954 and lasted a little over two years. Of the Plains states, only Texas and New Mexico were targeted. In Texas, the INS deported 81,127 "illegals" and intimidated an estimated 500,000 to 700,000 undocumented workers into leaving. Many deported workers simply turned around at the border and reen-

tered the United States. In September of 1956 the INS officially terminated Operation Wetback, proclaiming that it had cleared the targeted states of all undocumented Mexicans. This program had the devastating effect of allowing increased employer exploitation of their Mexican workers. If a Mexican worker were to complain, the employer would simply call the INS.

This abusive treatment of Mexicans and Mexican Americans did not go unchallenged. In the 1960s the Chicano movement started in California and across the Southwest. One valiant effort was that of César Chavez and his United Farm Workers. One of the preeminent leaders in this labor movement, Dolores Huerta, was born in the Plains (in the now-defunct coal-mining town of Dawson, New Mexico, in 1930), though she moved to California as a child. By the end of the decade, Chicano activism focused on three Plains states: New Mexico, Colorado, and Texas. From these states came three dynamic leaders.

Reies López Tijerina was the first of these leaders to emerge. Born in Falls City, Texas, in 1926, Tijerina had labored as a youth on Texas cotton plantations and in Colorado beet fields. He began his political activities in New Mexico in the early 1960s. Aiming to reclaim land in New Mexico stolen from Hispano landowners shortly after the 1848 Treaty of Guadalupe Hidalgo, Tijerina formed the *Alianza Federal de los Pueblos Libres* (Federal Alliance of Free City States). In 1968 Tijerina organized a political party, *Partido Constitucional del Pueblo* (People's Constitutional Party), which received several thousand votes in that year's gubernatorial election. His best-known accomplishments were the 1966 occupation of the Echo Amphitheater in the Kit Carson National Forest and his 1967 raid on the Rio Arriba County Courthouse in Tierra Amarilla, New Mexico, an action aimed at arresting the district attorney.

In 1969 Tijerina's movement came to an abrupt end when U.S. Forest Rangers arrested him and his wife for destroying U.S. forest signs while attempting to occupy the Coyote Campsite, again in the Kit Carson National Forest. After 775 days of incarceration, Tijerina came out of prison repudiating violence. He found upon his release that his position of leadership in the movement had waned. Another activist from the Plains, Rodolfo "Corky" Gonzalez, had simultaneously been developing another strand of the Chicano movement.

Gonzalez, a native of Denver, parlayed his experiences as a professional boxer into a successful political and business career. In the mid-1960s, however, he changed from mainstream politics to activism in an effort to address issues specific to his community. Gonzalez returned to the Denver barrio to organize the Crusade for Justice, a movement for social justice, and to lead protests such as the 1968 West Side High School walkout, which was prompted by the killing of fifteen-year-old Joseph Archuleta by a police officer. He also published an epic poem, "I Am Joaquín," that

became the most inspirational piece of literature in the Chicano movement.

In 1969 Gonzalez organized the Youth Leadership Conference (YLC) in Denver. At this event, he adopted the term "Chicano," meaning a U.S.-born Mexican, and he introduced Mexican Americans to the vision of Aztlán, the mythical Chicano homeland. From that time on, the term "Chicano" and the search to regain Aztlán became the defining characteristics of a movement for social and economic justice among many Mexican Americans of the Plains. A long-lasting legacy of the Crusade for Justice in Denver is the *Escuela Tlatelolco*, a community-controlled alternative school still in operation three decades after its founding in the late 1960s. In 1972, with a mandate from the YLC, Gonzalez organized a Colorado chapter of La Raza Unida, an independent Chicano political party that had been founded in Texas two years earlier.

La Raza Unida was founded in Texas by José Angel Gutiérrez, another important Chicano leader. In 1967, while still a student at St. Mary's University in San Antonio, Gutiérrez organized the Mexican American Youth Organization (MAYO). In 1970, after failing to obtain MAYO representation in city government, Gutiérrez organized La Raza Unida.

La Raza achieved immediate success in the small community of Crystal City in South Texas, located just off the Plains. Here, within one year, Gutiérrez became president of the Zavala County school board, and twenty-three of the twenty-four positions were filled by Chicanos. In 1971 La Raza members moved to expand the party's influence to a statewide level by contesting seats on the Houston, Fort Worth, Dallas, and San Antonio city councils and school boards. In 1972 Ramsey Muñoz ran on the La Raza ticket as the party's Texas gubernatorial candidate, and he experienced greater success than anyone, including La Raza leaders, had expected. That same year La Raza voted to go national, at which time Gonzalez organized the Colorado chapter.

At the beginning of the twenty-first century Mexican Americans and Mexicans continued to occupy many of the same niches in the Great Plains labor market that they had occupied for almost a century. Increasingly, Central Americans joined them in these jobs. Although it is difficult to assign numbers—many are undocumented workers who moved back and forth across the border—it is evident that the majority worked in agriculture, manufacturing, and construction. Meatpacking drew thousands into the region each year. Nowhere did this industry have a greater impact than in Nebraska.

From 1980 to 1990 the number of Mexicans and Central Americans in Nebraska more than doubled. This increase was largely explained by the opening of meatpacking plants in Grand Island, Lexington, Omaha, and other cities. Large companies such as Iowa Beef Packers were attracted to the area by the promise of tax cuts and other benefits. The meatpacking companies relied on and recruited nonunion immigrant labor, particularly Mexicans and other Latin Americans. In the 1970s they paid most of these workers about $6 an hour, substantially less than the $30,000 a year made by unionized meatpackers, and this trend continued into the 1980s and 1990s. Labor recruiting focused on Texas border towns and was so successful by the mid-1990s that 65 percent of all meatpacking workers in Nebraska were of Mexican origin. In Lexington, Nebraska, for example, the Mexican population increased from 6 percent of the town in 1980 to 23 percent in 1993. But there was no job security, the housing provided usually turned out to be dilapidated, and the work itself was grueling and hazardous.

Terrible working and living conditions led to unionization drives in the late 1980s. Two locals of the United Food and Commercial Workers union were particularly active. In 1989 Local 271 attempted to organize the Millard packing plant in Omaha, only to encounter resistance from plant management. This dispute reached the National Labor Relations Board in 1995. Local 22 also attempted to organize several plants, including an Iowa Beef Packers plant in Fremont and a Monfort plant in Omaha. The Monfort effort resulted in a union contract in 1997. Meatpacking plants often responded to union activity by increasing their cooperation with INS officials searching for undocumented workers. The result was an increase in raids on the Mexican communities in the area, and deportations were frequent.

Exploitation of Mexican and Mexican American meatpacking workers was not limited to Nebraska. In Greeley, Colorado, similar conditions existed. Following the temporary shutdown of a Monfort meatpacking plant there in 1980, the local meatpackers' union disbanded, giving Monfort a free hand in its treatment of the new workers the company hired when it reopened in 1982. Monfort started by filling its factories with Mexican and Central and South American workers. Working conditions were no better than at the meatpacking plants in Nebraska, and Greeley city officials were reluctant to take action against Monfort's exploitation of its workers because the local economy relied heavily on the meatpacking industry.

The Hispanic Impact

At the beginning of the twenty-first century, Mexicans and Mexican Americans maintained a significant presence in the Southern Plains. In a broad belt of counties reaching along the western Great Plains from the Mexican border to southern Colorado, "Persons of Hispanic Origin," the designated census category encompassing Mexican Americans, Mexicans, and other Latin Americans, comprised more than 25 percent of the total population. In Texas, Hispanics comprised one-third of the total state population: a number of counties in the Panhandle saw their Hispanic population grow by more than 10 percent from 1990 to 2000. In Colorado, Hispanics made up 13 percent of the total population. In Denver alone there were more than 397,000 Hispanics

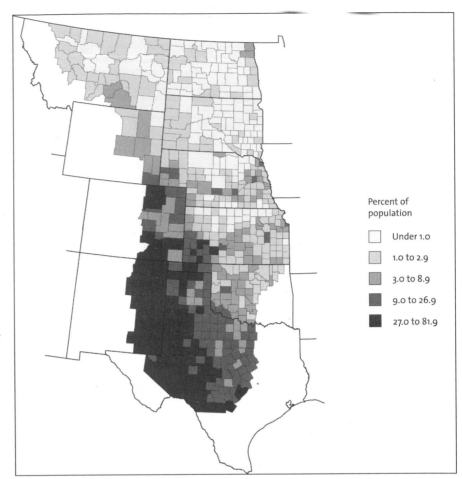

Hispanic population in the U.S. Great Plains as a percentage of total population, by county, in 2000

Percent of population

- Under 1.0
- 1.0 to 2.9
- 3.0 to 8.9
- 9.0 to 26.9
- 27.0 to 81.9

in the 2000 census, comprising almost 19 percent of the city's total population.

These large populations have had an extensive impact on the social, economic, and political makeup of Plains communities. In Denver, for instance, Hispanics have turned their formidable numbers into political representation. Federico Peña, secretary of transportation in President Bill Clinton's first administration and secretary of energy for two years in Clinton's second administration, cut his political teeth in Denver. Originally from Texas, Peña served as Denver's mayor from 1983 until 1990, when he stepped down from that position. As secretary of transportation, Peña turned his position into positive gains for Denver when he helped the city obtain nearly $5 billion in federal funds for a new Denver International Airport.

Other distinguished Mexican American politicians from Colorado include Polly Baca (born in 1943 in Greeley), the first minority woman elected to the Colorado Senate, and Linda Chavez (who was born in Albuquerque in 1947 but grew up in Denver), the highest-ranking woman in the Reagan administration and a leading conservative figure.

In New Mexico, where in 2000 all the Plains counties were more than 25 percent Hispanic, political power for Mexican Americans is deeply rooted. Miguel Antonio Otero (1829–82) served in the territorial legislature, was appointed as territorial district attorney, and was

elected New Mexico's delegate to Congress in 1855. The tradition continued: Mari-Luci Jaramillo (born in 1928 in Las Vegas) was appointed ambassador to Honduras by President Jimmy Carter in 1976, the first Mexican American woman to hold an ambassadorship. Bill Richardson went from New Mexico congressman to serving as ambassador to the United Nations and as secretary of energy in the second Clinton administration. In 2002 he was elected governor of New Mexico.

Numbers and percentages of Hispanics decrease northward up the Plains and eastward away from the linear concentration running from the Rio Grande to Colorado. Persons of Hispanic origin comprise 7 percent of the total Kansas population. Finney County, home to meatpacking plants in Garden City, has Kansas's highest concentration of Hispanics. Voters in Hutchinson, in central Kansas, elected the Great Plains' first Mexican American woman mayor, Frances Garcia, in 1985. In Nebraska, Hispanics constitute 5.5 percent of the total population, but in the Panhandle, the prime sugar-beet-growing region, and in counties with meatpacking activities they are a more significant presence. Moreover, Hispanics are now Nebraska's largest minority population and, with a 338 percent growth from 1990 to 2000, its fastest-growing one. In Oklahoma, Hispanics account for 5 percent of the total population; their numbers are relatively few but the distribution is broad. In only a handful of counties in Oklahoma is the population less than 1 percent Hispanic.

The only other Plains state to have a sizable Hispanic population is Wyoming. Along the sugar beet belt of southern Wyoming, Hispanics comprise between 5 and 25 percent of the population in each county. In the Northern Plains states, there are relatively few Hispanics. Recent (1996) statistics of ethnic origin for the Canadian Prairie Provinces show Alberta with the largest concentration of Hispanics (10,335), but this represents only 0.3 percent of the total population. Manitoba had 2,735 Hispanics in 1996 and Saskatchewan 1,229.

The impact of Mexicans and Mexican Americans on the modernization of the Great Plains has been invaluable. Without their labor there is no doubt that this region would not enjoy the farming and industrial prosperity that it has achieved. One of Colorado's preeminent labor leaders in the postwar era was Mexican-born Tim Flores, who rose from farm laborer in Greeley and brick mason in the Pueblo steel mills to leadership positions in the Colorado Labor Council before his death in 1988.

Their cultural contributions also have enriched the region. The poet Bernice Zamora was born in 1938 in the small town of Aquilar in south-central Colorado and grew up in Pueblo and Denver. The greatest of all women golfers, Nancy Lopez, grew up in Roswell, New Mexico. Tejano music, originating in the Rio Grande Valley at the southern edge of the Plains, and a full range of social and political programming are now widely broadcast on more than forty full-time and scores of part-time Spanish-language radio stations from Texas to Nebraska and Wyoming. And wherever there is a Mexican American population of any significant size, there is a family Mexican restaurant, perhaps the greatest addition to Plains cuisine in the twentieth century. These contributions have not always come easily. Mexican Americans have often been rewarded with racist treatment and second-class citizenship. But like the Chicano activists of the 1960s and 1970s, they will continue to strive for a better life in this region.

The story of the Spanish, Mexicans, and Mexican Americans in the Great Plains is one that features great sacrifice and perseverance. There were dramatic events that shaped migration and settlement, such as the Narváez expedition crashing ashore in Texas, the opening of the Santa Fe Trail, and the establishment of the Bracero Program. There were collisions of empires and economies, such as the Mexican Revolution, the Texas Revolution, the Mexican American War, and the Industrial Revolution. There are cultural continuities, built around faith, song, home, and word. And there are the people—Francisco Vásquez de Coronado and Pedro de Villazur; the traqueros and betabeleros; Federico Peña and Corky Gonzalez; pastores and vaqueros; and, yes, recruited worker Damasso Armendáriz.

See also EUROPEAN AMERICANS: Coronado; Spaniards; Villasur, Pedro de / FOLKWAYS: Cowboy Crafts / IMAGES AND ICONS: Quivira / INDUSTRY: Meatpacking.

Malcolm Yeung
Evelyn Hu-DeHart
University of Colorado at Boulder

Almaráz, Félix D. Jr. "An Uninviting Wilderness: The Plains of West Texas, 1534–1821." *Great Plains Quarterly* 12 (1992): 169–80. Andreas, Carol. *Meatpackers and Beef Barons: Company Towns in a Global Economy.* Niwot CO: University Press of Colorado, 1994. Carranza, Miguel A. "The Hispanic Presence on the Great Plains: An Introduction." *Great Plains Quarterly* 10 (1990): 67–70. Castro, Tony. *Chicano Power: The Emergence of Mexican America.* New York: Saturday Review Press, 1974. Cooper, Marc. "The Heartland's Raw Deal: How Meat Packing Is Creating a New Immigrant Underclass." *The Nation*, February 1997: 11–17. De León, Arnoldo. *Mexican Americans in Texas: A Brief History.* Wheeling IL: Harlan Davidson, Inc., 1999. Garcia, Juan R. *Mexicans in the Midwest, 1900–1932.* Tucson: University of Arizona Press, 1996. González, Nancie L. *The Spanish-Americans of New Mexico: A Heritage of Pride.* Albuquerque: University of New Mexico Press, 1969. Haverlank, Terrence. "The Changing Geography of U.S. Hispanics, 1850–1990." *Journal of Geography* 96 (1997): 134–45. Nostrand, Richard L. *The Hispano Homeland.* Norman: University of Oklahoma Press. 1992. Oppenheimer, Robert. "Acculturation or Assimilation: Mexican Immigration in Kansas, 1900 to World War II." *Western Historical Quarterly* 16 (1995): 429–48. Simmons, Helen, and Cathryn A. Hoyt, eds. *Hispanic Texas: A Historical Guide.* Austin: University of Texas Press, 1992. Smith, Michael. "Beyond the Borderlands: Mexican Labor in the Central Plains, 1900–1930." *Great Plains Quarterly* 1 (1981): 239–51. Weber, David J. *The Spanish Frontier in North America.* New Haven CT: Yale University Press, 1992.

ADAMS-ONÍS TREATY

The Adams-Onís Treaty of February 12, 1819, also known as the "Transcontinental Treaty," which settled border disputes between the United States and the Spanish Empire, proved vital to the nation's security. The catalyst for the negotiations between U.S. Secretary of State John Quincy Adams and the Spanish minister to the United States, Luís de Onís y Gonzalez, was border raids by Seminoles out of Spanish Florida. Once negotiations over Florida commenced, the issue of borders in the Great Plains and Pacific Northwest came to the fore.

Central to Spain's willingness to accept Adams's border demands in the Great Plains was the secretary of state's eventual willingness to give up claims on Spanish Texas. After lengthy negotiations, Adams and Onís established a Louisiana Purchase boundary line that followed the Sabine, Red, and Arkansas Rivers northwest to the forty-second parallel and then straight west to the Pacific. In accepting this line, Spain relinquished all claims to the Pacific Northwest, thereby improving the chances of the United States gaining control of the region.

The most significant element of the treaty was Adams's insistence that the boundary be extended to the Pacific. Adams's skillful negotiations opened the way for the United States to become a transcontinental power. In asserting for the United States a continental presence, Adams secured what he believed to be his most important diplomatic achievement, and one that marked a new era in U.S. history.

Matthew A. Redinger
Montana State University–Billings

Bemis, Samuel Flagg. *John Quincy Adams and the Foundations of American Foreign Policy.* New York: Alfred A. Knopf, Inc., 1949. Brooks, Philip Coolidge. *Diplomacy of the Borderlands: The Adams-Onís Treaty of 1819.* New York: Octagon Books, 1970.

BACA, POLLY (b. 1941)

Polly Baca's career is filled with firsts. She was the first Latino (and the first minority) to be elected to the Colorado Senate and the first Latina to serve in the leadership in any state senate or to be nominated by a major party to run for U.S. Congress (an election she lost).

Baca is a lifelong Coloradan, and most of her public service has been in Colorado. She was born in Weld County on February 13, 1941, and grew up in Greeley and Thornton. In 1962 she received her bachelor of arts degree at Colorado State University. Baca was drawn into politics as part of the first campaign to harness Latino voters, the 1960 "Viva Kennedy" campaign. Her campaign work initiated a series of political jobs, first with unions, then with the Democratic Party and the United Farm Workers. Baca tapped these experiences when she successfully ran for the Colorado House of Representatives in 1974 and the Colorado State Senate in 1978. She left the Colorado legislature to run unsuccessfully for U.S. Congress in 1986. Baca received two appointments in the Clinton administration. In 1993 she was appointed director of the U.S. Office of Consumer Affairs. She left this position in 1994 to return to Colorado as Rocky Mountain regional director for the General Services Administration.

After leaving public service in 1998, she began her own consulting firm and worked as a full-time volunteer with the Center for Contemplative Living, which is dedicated to renewing the contemplative dimension of the Gospels in everyday life. Polly Baca holds honorary degrees from the University of Northern Colorado at Greeley and Wartburg College. In 2000 Baca was inducted into the Colorado Women's Hall of Fame.

Louis DeSipio
University of California, Irvine

BETABELEROS

Throughout the twentieth century Mexican and Mexican American migrant workers were instrumental in the success of the sugar beet industry in the Great Plains. Beginning as early as 1915, corporations such as the Holly Sugar Company and the Great Western Sugar Company increasingly depended upon reliable, experienced, and low-cost labor to cultivate and harvest sugar beets. Recruited from Texas, California, and Mexico, these workers came to be known as *los betabeleros,* the sugar beet workers.

Government-sponsored research and construction of irrigation systems in the 1890s, combined with a sharp rise in the national consumption of sugar at the turn of the century, made the sugar beet industry one of the fastest growing and most successful in the Great Plains. Main growing areas were, and are, eastern Colorado and western Nebraska, the Yellowstone and Bighorn Valleys of Montana and Wyoming, and the Red River Valley of the North. Government and industry cooperated to provide farmers with the much-needed labor in these sparsely populated areas. Two groups of laborers became the working backbone of the industry: German Russians and Mexicans. For example, in 1924 the Great Western Sugar Company brought to Montana's Yellowstone Valley 3,604 Mexicans and 1,231 German Russians to harvest a record 31,000 acres.

While the German Russian immigrants were supported by the sugar beet companies in purchasing their own farms and settling their families permanently, the Spanish-speaking workers were initially hired only as seasonal workers. Before World War I, this strategy kept wages down and eased European American fears of "foreigners" settling permanently in their midst. But by 1922, as the need for field labor increased, the corporations began to recognize that attracting families to "winter over" assured a stable and experienced workforce. In Billings, for example, the Great Western Sugar Company, enlisting the labor of Mexicans, arranged for the construction of up to forty small adobe homes. By 1927 hundreds of these low-cost settlements, known as *colonias*, had been established by the sugar beet companies throughout the Great Plains.

Within the colonias, residents raised animals and planted gardens to supplement their diets, and during the winter those with limited earnings shared resources. But while the colonias provided Latinos with a sense of community and support, they also isolated them from the larger community. Latinos were often banned from public swimming pools, segregated in theaters, and not allowed in certain stores and restaurants. Sugar beet companies worked to allay fears and prejudice directed at the Mexican laborers by citing in their annual reports and publications how essential they were to the success of the industry. Despite the discrimination, the economic hardship, and the backbreaking labor experienced by the *betabeleros*, many returned to work the fields each spring, often renewing previous associations with farmers. Some beet workers even remained with the farmer throughout the year, tending to animals and fences during the winter.

In the Northern Great Plains, the sugar beet season began in mid-April with planting. Workers hoed and thinned from late May to mid-July, weeded through the summer, and harvested and topped the beets in the fall. Stoop labor for planting, weeding, and harvesting, a short-handled hoe for thinning, and a curved knife for topping made for arduous work. For the women, in addition to the work in the fields, the regular household duties of cooking and cleaning made for a "double day." Children, by ages eight or nine, were encouraged to help out and were regularly pulled out of school to help plant and harvest.

The Depression economy of the 1930s created an atmosphere of opposition to the migrant worker. The Great Western Sugar Company elected to hire local workers before those from outside the area, thus discouraging Latino families from remaining. But with the onset of World War II western growers and industries faced serious labor shortages. Congress responded by creating the Bracero Program, which allowed farmers to employ Mexican nationals. From 1943 to 1946 Great Western's Billings district relied on Mexicans to thin and top most of its crop. After 1963, when Congress terminated the Bracero Program, companies continued to rely on Mexican nationals.

In the 1950s, as agriculture was becoming more mechanized, many Latinos began to seek out better-paying, steadier jobs. In Billings, jobs with the railroad or the packing plants offered a positive alternative to working the beet fields. While establishing permanent homes in Billings, Latinos also began working to improve educational opportunities for their children. As early as 1929, associations like the *Comisión Honorífica Mexicana* were formed to organize social and cultural events and assist Latinos in need. In the 1960s *Concilio Mexicano* helped to advocate for jobs and education in the community. In 1971 the Migrant Council was established to provide health, educational, and labor assistance to migrant families.

Despite farm mechanization, increased use of herbicides, and continued restrictions on migrant workers, beet growers still depend on some hand labor. By 1976 the Great Western Sugar Company handed over the job of recruiting and providing migrant workers to the beet growers. Today, migrant workers, mostly Mexican Americans from Texas, still come to the Yellowstone Valley each spring to work the beets. These seasonal workers follow a route that takes them on to other states in the region to pick apples, top and bag onions, and harvest beans before returning to Texas in late fall. The migrant workers of the past, including those who have elected to make a home in this region and those who choose to return each year, continue to make a vital contribution to the economy as well as to enrich the culture of the Great Plains.

See also AGRICULTURE: Sugar Beets / EUROPEAN AMERICANS: German Russians.

Rebecca Berru Davis
Western Heritage Center

Mercier, Laurie. "Creating a New Community in the North: Mexican Americans of the Yellowstone Valley." In *Stories from an Open Country: Essays on the Yellowstone River Valley*, edited by William L. Lang. Billings MT: Western Heritage Press, 1995: 127–47. Valdes, Dennis N. "Settlers, Sojourners, and Proletarians: Social Formation in the Great Plains Sugar Beet Industry, 1890–1940." *Great Plains Quarterly* 10 (1990): 110–23.

BRACERO PROGRAM

Mexican workers, repatriated during the Great Depression, were allowed to enter the United States as temporary contract workers due to the manpower shortage during World War II. The August 4, 1942, bilateral agreement (Public Law 45) between Mexico and the United States (Mexican Farm Labor Program Agreement) assured agricultural employers a steady supply of documented laborers (braceros). In 1943 railroads were allowed to hire Mexican workers as section hands. The first phase of this labor importation ended in 1947. Approximately 253,000 farmhands were recruited in these years, and some 80,000 Mexicans were employed by the rail lines, many of them in the Great Plains. The number that officially entered the United States diminished considerably after the war, but the Korean War and the problems of the ever-increasing numbers of illegal aliens rationalized demands by agricultural employers' associations for legally imported Mexican labor. Formalized by Public Law 78 as a temporary measure in 1951 and periodically renewed, the final phase of this government-sponsored importation program recruited some 4.6 million braceros before it was finally ended in 1964.

Critics of the program called it another federal subsidy to large-scale commercial farm operators. Since the government paid for the recruitment and transportation of contract workers, growers of crops like sugar beets were spared this expense. The agreement provided for a regional prevailing wage and adequate housing, but it was farm employers rather than the government who ultimately set wages and the condition of the labor camps. Mexican workers also acted as "task forces" where domestic laborers threatened to organize for higher wages. Not only did the program adversely affect wages of domestic farmhands, but it may have contributed to an increase of undocumented Mexican workers. On their return to Mexico, legally contracted workers told others of the higher wages available in the United States, which motivated Mexican workers to cross the border illegally. Further, Public Law 78 did not include provisions penalizing employers who hired illegal aliens. In any case, some 3.8 million undocumented Mexican nationals, pejoratively called "wetbacks," were rounded up and returned to Mexico in the 1950s.

Braceros and *mojados* (undocumented workers) not only froze or lowered wages for domestic farmworkers in these years, but undocumented workers were frequently given legal status and entered the program. Texas opted out of the Bracero Program during the war years and instead decided on an open-border policy. When the Mexican government announced it would refuse to send workers to the state, Texas growers recruited Mexican workers by using private contractors. Between 1947 and 1950 some 200,000 undocumented workers, the majority of them in Texas, were legalized by the federal government and admitted into the contract labor program. Mexican Americans in Texas and the Southwest found it hard to compete for jobs, and many left to seek work elsewhere. The need for labor finally persuaded Texas to participate in the Bracero Program in the 1950s.

The Bracero Program benefited large-scale growers of crops rather than small farmers. The braceros themselves formed part of a recent, massive Mexican migration to the United States. Mexican immigration, whether legal or illegal, permanent or temporary, has created low-wage labor pools, legal peonage, social ostracism, and a negative stereotyping of Mexican Americans. Under pressure from organized labor, the National Farmers Union, and concerned religious and social reform groups, Congress finally ended the legal importation of workers under the Bracero Program, which seemed to signal that the formerly open southern border would be harder to cross legally and illegally.

Ralph H. Vigil
University of Nebraska–Lincoln

Craig, Richard B. *The Bracero Program: Interest Groups and Foreign Policy.* Austin: University of Texas Press, 1971. Galarza, Ernesto. *Merchants of Labor: The Mexican Bracero Story.* Santa Barbara CA: McNally and Loftin, 1964.

CENTRAL AMERICANS

Central Americans are one of the fastest-growing Latin American origin groups in the United States. The 1990 U.S. census enumerated 1.3 million persons of Central American origin, of whom slightly more than 1 million were foreign born. Approximately 8 percent of all Central Americans in the United States reside in the ten states of the American Great Plains, the vast majority in Texas.

The isthmus of Central America encompasses the nations of Guatemala, Belize, Honduras, El Salvador, Nicaragua, Costa Rica, and Panama. There are an estimated 36 million people in Central America, most of whom are mestizos, but there also are Indigenous groups, especially in Guatemala, and people of African ancestry in the Caribbean coastal areas. The United Nations projects that this population will increase to 58 million by the year 2025. Poverty is widespread: gross national product per capita in 1997 ranged from a low of $410 in Nicaragua to a high of $3,080 in Panama, compared to $29,080 in the United States. Export agriculture dominates the economies of Central America, with coffee, cotton, bananas, beef, and sugar the leading products. The industrial sector grew during the 1960s and 1970s but remains small. With the exception of Costa Rica and Belize, military governments have been a common feature of the political landscape in the region. Mounting political tensions and public discontent with the ruling regimes in El Salvador, Guatemala, and Nicaragua erupted into civil wars in the late 1970s and early 1980s. The 1990s saw the restoration of peace and the establishment of democratically elected governments in all three countries.

During the worst years of the conflicts the number of immigrants entering the United States from El Salvador, Guatemala, and Nicaragua grew dramatically. Close to two-thirds of the roughly 1 million Central American immigrants included in the 1990 U.S. census arrived between 1980 and 1990. Advocates of U.S. foreign policy in the region argued that immigration from El Salvador and Guatemala was economically motivated, and to support their argument they pointed to well-established patterns of international migration within the region and significant differences in earnings and living standards between the United States and Central America. Critics of U.S. foreign policy viewed Salvadoran and Guatemalan immigrants in the United States as political refugees in search of safe haven. The U.S. government generally denied refugee status to immigrants from the region. In spite of the legal restrictions on immigration to the United States, immigrants from Central America came in large numbers, many without legal documentation.

Central Americans began arriving in the Great Plains in significant numbers during the 1980s as part of a larger stream of foreign-born immigrants attracted to the region by employment opportunities in new or expanding meatpacking plants and other low-wage industries. Intense competition and low profit margins in meatpacking have made the industry very dependent on unskilled immigrant labor. The arrival of Mexican, Central American, and Asian immigrants has transformed many small towns with meatpacking plants, like Lexington, Nebraska, and Garden City, Kansas, into ethnically, linguistically, and culturally diverse communities. The low wages offered by meatpacking plants and the comparatively low skill levels of many Central Americans and other new immigrants have also created greater levels of poverty in these communities.

The relative youth and size of the new immigrant streams have placed strains on the supply of housing, education, medical care, and basic services available in meatpacking communities. School enrollments have soared, creating overcrowding in classrooms, and there is a growing demand for bilingual and English as a Second Language programs. In the area of health care, most of the current demand for services is related to maternal and child health. As the Central American population ages, the demand will eventually shift to health services for adolescents, adults, and the elderly.

Although they represent a small proportion of all Central Americans in the United States, Central American immigrants in the Great Plains, along with other new immigrant groups, will have an increasingly visible impact on the towns and cities they inhabit because of the comparatively small size and previous ethnic homogeneity of these places.

David P. Lindstrom
Brown University

Lamphere, Louise, Alex Stepick, and Guillermo Grenier, eds. *Newcomers in the Workplace: Immigrants and the Restructuring of the U.S. Economy.* Philadelphia: Temple University Press, 1994. Stull, Donald D., Michael J. Broadway, and David Griffith, eds. *Any Way You Cut It: Meat Processing and Small-Town America.* Lawrence: University Press of Kansas, 1995.

CERVANTEZ, PEDRO (1914–1987)

Born at Wilcox, Arizona, on May 19, 1914, artist Pedro Lopez Cervantez took his father's last name—instead of his mother's, as usually dictated by Hispanic tradition—because he had been told of an earlier Cervantes who had been a great man. His mother was a Mexican Indian whose parents ran a pottery at Durango, Mexico, before the Mexican Revolution. Cervantez's father, of Spanish descent, worked for the Santa Fe Railroad at Texico, New Mexico. Pedro Cervantez lived most of his life in Texico and Clovis, New Mexico, and across the Texas border at Farwell. Most of his painting focused on life in the Plains of eastern New Mexico, combining a Regionalist style with a hybrid surrealism.

Cervantez began painting in oils about 1930. He assisted artist Russell Vernon Hunter (1900–1955) on Hunter's mural *The Last Frontier* (1934), a Public Works of Art Project for the DeBaca County Courthouse at Fort Sumner, New Mexico. Allegedly, Cervantez was disappointed in not receiving any credit for his work on the mural. Nevertheless, Hunter continued as his mentor.

Later, Cervantez made easel paintings for the Works Progress Administration's Federal Art Project, exhibiting most of his New Deal productions at the Museum of Fine Arts at Santa Fe. In 1938 Cervantez's work was included in the exhibition "Masters of Popular Painting: Modern Primitives of Europe and America" at the Museum of Modern Art in New York. He was one of the first Hispanic artists in the United States to receive national attention.

Cervantez enlisted in the U.S. Army in 1940 and was stationed in Italy and Germany during World War II. Following the war he worked as a sign painter for the Coca Cola Bottling Company at Clovis for a number of years. He never regained his prewar recognition and never truly returned to easel painting, about which he felt some bitterness. He died at Clovis on July 3, 1987, after many years as a public school custodian. Ironically, some of his New Deal easel paintings hang at Melrose (New Mexico) High School. His paintings were featured in a recent exhibition, "*Sin Nombre*: Hispana and Hispano Artists of the New Deal Era," at the Museum of International Folk Art in Santa Fe.

Michael R. Grauer
Panhandle-Plains Historical Museum

CHAVEZ, LINDA (b. 1947)

Linda Chavez is a prominent conservative intellectual and activist. Her ideas on race and ethnicity in public policy have made an important contribution to the national debate. Chavez is a leading critic of "identity politics" —that is, the idea that racial and ethnic classifications should play an important role in politics, government, and law. Instead, she has advocated assimilation and "color-blind" law.

Linda Chavez was born in Albuquerque, New Mexico, on June 17, 1947. She grew up in Denver, Colorado, and received her bachelor of arts degree from the University of Colorado in 1970. She married Christopher Gersten, who became another important conservative activist, in 1967. Chavez began her political career as a Democrat but became unhappy with the party because she believed it had moved too far to the left. She served in the Reagan administration, first as director of the U.S. Commission on Civil Rights (1983–85) and then as director of public liaison in the White House (1985). She then ran in 1986 for the U.S. Senate in Maryland, winning the Republican nomination in a crowded field but losing in the general election to Barbara Mikulski.

Since then Chavez has mainly devoted her career to writing and speaking on public policy issues. She criticized liberal Hispanic organizations, as well as programs like bilingual education and affirmative action, in her 1991 book *Out of the Barrio: Toward a New Politics of Hispanic Assimilation*. Chavez founded the Center for Equal Opportunity in 1995 and built the organization into a leading conservative think tank. She writes a syndicated weekly column, contributes articles to journals and magazines, and frequently lectures and appears on television and radio.

Roger Clegg
Center for Equal Opportunity

Chavez, Linda. "Our Hispanic Predicament." *Commentary* 106 (1998): 1–4. Chavez, Linda. *Out of the Barrio: Toward a New Politics of Hispanic Assimilation*. New York: Basic Books, 1991.

CIBOLEROS

Hispanic New Mexican hunters and plainsmen, or *ciboleros* (from the New Mexican Spanish *cíbolo*), learned to hunt bison from Native American neighbors in order to provide winter meat for their home villages. Like the Pueblos and Plains Indians, New Mexican Hispanos depended on bison during the late Spanish colonial, Mexican, and territorial eras. The volume and extent of the ciboleros' hunts peaked in the first half of the nineteenth century and declined thereafter as the bison were taken to the brink of extinction.

Ciboleros traditionally hunted bison twice a year. The large-scale autumn hunt took place after crops were harvested. Expeditions from settlements in north-central New Mexico and southern Colorado usually took six weeks to reach the Southern Great Plains, encounter herds, barter with Comanches or Kiowas, hunt, secure and preserve meat, and return before heavy snowfalls. During these autumn hunts, bison were taken for their thick robes as well as for their meat.

The summer hunt took place in June, after spring planting, by which time meat supplies procured the previous autumn were exhausted. Bison meat was of utmost importance for the common people, allowing them to save goat herds for milk and roast kid for special occasions. Only the wealthier classes regularly partook of domestically raised meats.

Each village had an individual hunter who

Cibolero

specialized in running bison on horseback. Specially trained horses were ridden only by the ciboleros and used for only that purpose. The lance and bow and arrow were the main weapons of the hunt; firearms were few and far between in New Mexico until the late nineteenth century. It was a skill and profession that was handed down from father to son, and certain New Mexican families were specialists. Hunters from various villages prepared supplies for the journey and for barter and furnished skinners and camp helpers. The hunters gathered at a predesignated place and chose a *mayordomo*, or foreman, and the expedition proceeded in caravans of oxcarts. Often Hispanos and Pueblos traveled together for mutual safety and cooperation.

The Southern Plains was dominated by the Comanches and Kiowas, who maintained generally good relations with the Pueblos and Hispanos after 1785, when New Mexico governor Juan Bautista de Anza decisively defeated the Comanches, led by Cuerno Verde, and established peace. Barter of New Mexican agricultural products with the Native Americans created goodwill and allowed the ciboleros to enter their traditional hunting lands.

After the bison herds were encountered, each cibolero tied a long rope around his waist in order to remount if thrown during the chase. Commending their souls to God and Santiago (Saint James), they rode into the herds. Selecting choice animals, they lanced the bison or shot arrows, bringing down only as many as their villages needed. This was a dangerous undertaking, and some ciboleros died from being trampled, while others were killed by Indians, especially the Cheyennes, who by 1850 were competing for the diminishing herds. The late Cleofes Vigil of San Cristóbal, New Mexico—poet-troubadour, historian, rancher, and retired railroad worker—often performed ballads about such fatal accidents.

After enough bison were brought down, *agregadores* (helpers) and hunters pitched in, skinning, slicing, and salting meat. After drying, meat was packed in oxcarts for the return.

All the bison parts were used. Aside from the meat, hides were tanned for robes or leather, smoked tongues were traded in Mexico, horns and bones were made into utensils, and the wool was spun into rough cloth or stuffed in mattresses.

The late Cipriano Solano (1870–1967) of Springer, New Mexico, a retired rancher, recalled that near the end of the nineteenth century there were remnant bison herds near Loma Parda, New Mexico, and he described how he had taken a burro to haul the meat back after hunting, and how one cibolero would provide meat for several families for a year. Ciboleros are still remembered in New Mexican folk songs, cultural events, and family oral traditions.

Jerry A. Padilla
Taos, New Mexico

Gregg, Josiah. *Commerce of the Prairies*. Norman: University of Oklahoma Press, 1954. Kenner, Charles L. *A History of New Mexican Plains Indian Relations*. Norman: University of Oklahoma Press, 1969.

COMANCHEROS

The *comancheros* were an ethnically mixed group of New Mexican merchants who in the late eighteenth and nineteenth centuries developed a distinctive form of trade with Comanches, Kiowas, and other Plains Indians. The comanchero trade began after 1786, when the Comanches signed a treaty with Spanish New Mexico and agreed to stop raiding in exchange for trade and gifts. The treaty opened the Southern Plains to New Mexico's traders, who were eager to reactivate the lines of commerce that had been broken during prolonged Spanish-Comanche wars. Trade in the Plains was officially sanctioned in 1789, when Governor Fernando de la Concha allowed the Spanish, Pueblos, and *genízaros* to take their goods out to the grasslands. In their search for mobile hunting bands, these traders sometimes traveled as far north as the Platte River in present-day Nebraska, but their main customers were the numerous Comanche bands of the Llano Estacado. The term *comancheros*, a derivation of their clientele's name, was first mentioned in Spanish documents in 1813 and was popularized in the 1840s by the Santa Fe trader Josiah Gregg.

Each fall, after the harvest, the comancheros loaded their burros and oxcarts (*carretas*) with beads, calico, tobacco, coffee, sugar, kettles, and large butchering knives (*belduques*) and ventured onto the Llano Estacado. A popular trade item was hard-baked corn bread, which was highly desired by Comanches, who needed carbohydrates to balance their bison-based diet. In return, the comancheros received horses, hides, dried meat, tallow, and captives. During the first half-century of the trade, the comancheros remained relatively unorganized. They relied on chance meetings with their clients, and the volume of their business remained low. According to Gregg, they seldom carried more than $20 worth of goods to the Plains. During the Spanish and Mexican periods, the comancheros also suffered from vacillating official policies. At times, the comanchero trade was seen as a means to obtain intelligence on American actions in the Southern Plains, and the officials granted licenses liberally. At other times the officials prohibited the trade, which they correctly thought stimulated Comanche horse raids into Texas and Mexico. The U.S. takeover of New Mexico resulted in stricter licensing policies and other restrictions on the comancheros, whose activities, particularly the ransoming of captives, were abhorred by the Americans.

The comancheros adjusted their commercial strategies to the changing conditions. Beginning in the 1850s they began to buy cattle stolen from Texas ranches by Comanches. The cattle found a ready market among wealthy New Mexican merchants who had begun to supply government beef contractors. Spurred by the new traffic, the comanchero trade was transformed from the unorganized, small-scale operations of the early nineteenth century into a mature commercial institution with fixed marketplaces, an elaborate transportation system, professional traders, and varied merchandise.

The comanchero trade of the 1850s and 1860s revolved around designated rendezvous sites, which featured irrigation ditches, adobe shelters, and other structures, indicating at least semipermanent occupation. The Llano Estacado was dotted with sites such as Tecovas Springs, northwest of present-day Amarillo, Texas; Las Lenguas (or Los Lingos) Creek, the modern-day Pease River; and Yellow House Canyon or Cañón del Rescate (Ransom Canyon), near present-day Lubbock, Texas. Bartering at these rendezvous could take weeks, during which huge amounts of cattle and commodities exchanged hands. Although the trade in subsistence goods persisted, much of the trade was now in firearms, ammunition, whiskey, and other manufactured products. A web of well-established cart roads and smaller pack trails connected the rendezvous to each other and to the Rio Grande Valley. Although the comancheros' practices, by then almost entirely associated with cattle-rustling, were illegal under American law, the attempts to repress them failed, mainly because many army officers had secretly invested in the trade.

The comanchero commerce reached its peak during the Civil War. The relaxation of frontier defenses in Texas allowed Comanche raiders to steal Confederate stock and sell them to comancheros, who in turn sold the animals to Union agents. After the war, the comancheros continued their lucrative operations with Kwahada Comanches, who refused to settle in the reservation that had been assigned to them in 1867. José P. Tafoya and other prominent comancheros amassed large profits, part of which was invested in the sheep industry, ranching, and freighting. But the ethnic, political, and economic niche that had allowed the comancheros to flourish was rapidly vanishing. The bison herds were nearly gone, the Kwahadas were forced into the reservation,

and the U.S. Army intensified its efforts to put an end to the illicit trade. The final blow came in 1874, when the army, guided by imprisoned comancheros, destroyed the last Kwahada strongholds on the Llano Estacado.

See also NATIVE AMERICANS: Comanches / PHYSICAL ENVIRONMENT: Llano Estacado.

Pekka Hämäläinen
Texas A&M University

Haley, L. Evetts. "The Comanchero Trade." *Southwestern Historical Quarterly* 38 (1935): 156–76. Kenner, Charles L. *A History of New Mexican–Plains Indian Relations.* Norman: University of Oklahoma Press, 1969. Levine, Frances. "Economic Perspectives on the Comanchero Trade." In *Farmers, Hunters, and Colonists: Interaction between the Southwest and the Southern Plains*, edited by Katherine A. Spielmann. Tucson: University of Arizona Press, 1991: 155–69.

DE BACA, FABIOLA CABEZA

(1898–1993)

Fabiola Cabeza de Baca was born on the de Baca family land grant on the Llano Estacado in northeastern New Mexico on May 16, 1898. When she was four years old, de Baca's mother died and her paternal grandmother, a traditional Hispana of the *patrón* (elite) class, became her primary caregiver. She grew up speaking Spanish, English, and two Pueblo dialects—Tewa and Tiwa—fluently.

In 1921 de Baca received a degree in pedagogy from New Mexico Normal University and taught in the New Mexico public school system for several years. In 1929 she received a degree in home economics from New Mexico State University in Las Cruces. From 1929 to 1959 she worked as a home demonstration agent for the New Mexico State Extension Service, serving the Hispanic and Pueblo villages of northern New Mexico. There she founded clubs for women and children, taught nutrition, and organized marketing of craft products. In 1939 de Baca married Carlos Gilbert, an insurance agent.

Throughout her career as a practicing home economist, de Baca wrote several books and articles about folkways and culinary traditions among Hispanos. Her 1939 book *Historic Cookery*, based on observations in New Mexico village kitchens, eventually sold more than 100,000 copies. All of her writing furthered her cause of preserving Hispanic traditions and correcting American history, which she felt either neglected New Mexican Hispanos or misrepresented them.

In 1954 she published *We Fed Them Cactus*, her most autobiographical narrative and the book for which she is best known. The title refers to an incident that marked the end of an era for New Mexican Hispanos. Because of social, economic, and natural conditions—drought and the influx of American ranchers and homesteaders in the Plains in the late nineteenth century—her family was forced to feed cactus to their cattle. This tragedy calls attention to the communal bonds of Hispanic tradition and encourages Hispanos to remember a better way of life. Ultimately, *We Fed Them Cactus* imagines an egalitarian society in which all Hispanos, from *empleado* (la-

borer) to *patrón*, live in cultural harmony. Fabiola Cabeza de Baca died in 1993, after spending her final years in a home for the elderly in Albuquerque.

Becky Jo McShane
Salt Lake City, Utah

de Baca (Gilbert), Fabiola Cabeza. *Historic Cookery*. 1939. Reprint, Las Vegas NM: La Galeria de los Artesanos, 1970. de Baca, Fabiola Cabeza. *We Fed Them Cactus*. Albuquerque: University of New Mexico Press, 1954. Poythress, Stephanie. "Fabiola Cabeza de Baca Gilbert." In *Notable Hispanic American Women*, edited by Diane Telgen and Jim Kamp. Detroit: Gale Research, Inc. 1993: 178–79.

EMPRESARIOS

From its independence from Spain until it lost Texas to revolt, Mexico enlisted the aid of *empresarios* to recruit colonists to its sparsely settled province of Texas. The Mexican Colonization Law of August 18, 1824, provided general guidelines for the settlement of remote corners of the new republic and required the individual states to pass their own laws, which the state of Coahuila y Texas did on March 24, 1825. Although the national colonization law gave preference to Mexican citizens, the Colonization Law of Coahuila y Texas invited foreigners to that territory. Individuals could and did migrate to Texas, mostly from the United States, but because of the language barrier and the difficulties in acquiring land through the Mexican bureaucracy, most colonists obtained land in Texas through the offices of the empresarios.

Empresarios were contractors empowered by the government of Coahuila y Texas to recruit specific numbers of families to the territory. Mexican citizens were preferred as empresarios and as colonists, but the majority of the empresarios were from the United States. The empresario received a grant of land on which to settle the colonists he recruited, though he did not, in fact, own this land. It was the empresario's responsibility to survey the land and then issue title to that land. The empresario grants extended northwestward from the Gulf Coast Plain of Texas across the Balcones Escarpment and well into the Great Plains. Most empresarios agreed to recruit 100 families within a six-year span. They also served as immigration agents, determining the moral character of those who wished to enter their colony. The empresarios received no pay or compensation for their endeavors up front. When they had settled at least 100 families within their colonial grant, thus fulfilling their contract, they acquired land of their own. For every 100 families an empresario recruited and settled within Texas, the state gave him five *sitios* (22,140 acres) of pastureland and five *labors* (885 acres) of farmland. An empresario could receive compensation in land for settling up to 800 families, making him a very wealthy man.

The only empresario who received compensation for so many recruited families was Stephen F. Austin. By far the most successful of the empresarios in terms of numbers of colonists settled, Austin put into action the plans of colonization conceived by his father,

Moses Austin. Between 1823, when he recruited 300 families under the old Spanish Imperial Colonization Law and his final colonization contract, Austin settled more than 1,500 families in an area extending from the Texas Hill Country, at the edge of the Plains, to the Gulf of Mexico. No other empresario was able to recruit and settle even one-quarter of this number. Green DeWitt received a contract for 400 families but granted land titles to only 166 families. Some empresarios, such as Dr. John G. Purnell and Benjamin Drake Lovell, were never able to fulfill their contracts. By 1832 the empresarios had signed almost thirty contracts calling for the settlement of more than 10,000 families. But the government of Coahuila y Texas, growing suspicious of increasing Anglo-American influence in Texas, ceased issuing grants after 1832 and finally closed the land offices in November of 1835. The era of the empresarios, the colonizing agents of Texas, came to an end.

John Kelly Robison
Martin Luther University Halle-Wittenberg

Fehrenbach, Theodore R. *Lone Star: A History of Texas and the Texans.* New York: Colliers Books, 1968. Haley, James L. *Texas: An Album of History.* Garden City NY: Doubleday and Co., 1985. Richardson, Rupert Norval, Ernest Wallace, and Adrian Anderson. *Texas: The Lone Star State.* Englewood Cliffs NJ: Prentice-Hall, 1981.

ESCUELA TLATELOLCO

Escuela Tlatelolco was founded during the Chicano civil rights movement of the 1960s by Rodolfo "Corky" Gonzales, Chicano activist and community leader, and it continues to thrive as a private school in Denver, Colorado. Named after the Indian city of Tlatelolco, Mexico and rooted in Aztec history, Escuela Tlatelolco is a community-based school that transforms the pedagogy of oppression into the pedagogy of hope. Its mission is "to liberate the minds of students." Cultural expression and leadership, with emphases on spirituality, moral courage, honorable behavior, and critical thinking, are the values and skills that students are taught, providing them with the means to act upon their world and create social change and justice. Its success has been with those "high risk" students who have failed in traditional public school settings.

Using liberationist Paulo Friere's philosophy, the school's teachers challenge students "to seek out the root causes of oppression." Escuela Tlatelolco's philosophy is based on the understanding that "knowledge without action has no value." It is believed that liberated thinking provides students with avenues to break the social, economic, cultural, and political chains of oppression that keep them in what has been termed "the colonial mentality." Community service is expected, as students engage in changing the social conditions in the community.

Escuela Tlatelolco serves predominantly Chicano and Mexicano youth in prekindergarten through twelfth grade. The newly developed *Circulo Montessori de Tlatelolco*, a comprehensive, community-based pre-Montessori educational center, serves prekindergarten through sixth grade, while the Academia Institute serves middle-school-age youth. The *Segundaria* Program serves high-school-age youth and runs on a year-round schedule. Fully 90 percent of Escuela's students graduate from high school.

Ramon del Castillo
Denver, Colorado

GENÍZAROS

Genízaro was a term used in eighteenth- and nineteenth-century New Mexico for "detribalized Indians," a variety of individuals of mixed Native American, but not Pueblo, parentage who had adopted at least some Hispanic styles of living. They were most common in areas of New Mexico adjacent to the Southern Plains. Genízaros, many of whom were descendants of Native Americans who made their home in the Great Plains, are a little-studied group. They appear to have been a transitional group that appeared and then disappeared as part of the opening, and later closing, of a particular set of frontier relations in New Mexico. Even the origin of the term *genízaro* is controversial.

The more commonly claimed origin is from the term for captive Christians who were forcibly converted to Islam and served as troops in the Turkish army, called *yeni-cheri*, anglicized as janissary. Because of the close phonetic equivalence and because of similar roles played by genízaros in New Mexico, this is assumed to be the genesis of the term. Steven Horvath argues persuasively for a different origin. To the root *geno-*, meaning lineage or race, are added suffixes *-izo* and *-aro*, yielding the Spanish word. It referred to people who were the children of parents from two nations, for example France and Spain, or in New Mexico, Comanches and Pawnees. Writing in 1872, Fray Juan Augustín Morfi explained, "This name is given to the children of the captives of different nations who have married in the province." The term became generic for Native Americans who had been born among nomadic groups, but who lived in New Mexico.

There were two sources of genízaros. First, they might have been taken captive in the many fights with surrounding nomadic groups. Second, they might have been traded (or "rescued") from friendly Indian groups who had taken them captive in their raids on enemies. Typically, they were children or women and were used as servants and laborers. To skirt the legal ban on slavery, they were officially designated as under the protection of a Spanish household, whose head was to train them in Christianity and Spanish culture generally. In practice they were often slaves. They were desirable because of labor shortages, especially in frontier areas. Consequently, their initial commonality was that they had been born Native Americans but lived in Hispanic society and occupied the lowest social strata. Because they often grew up in captivity, they knew little of their natal culture and hence were often described as "detribalized Indians."

Some genízaros eventually earned their freedom and worked as day laborers; a few became landowners or craftsmen. Two avenues to improved status were open to them. They could settle new areas where the Spanish government sought to expand control. Also, men could serve in militia units to fight hostile nomadic Indians. Because of their origins their loyalty was suspect, but they were deemed particularly adept at dealing with or fighting nomadic Indians because of their putative fierceness and because some had at least rudimentary knowledge of one or more languages of nomadic Indians. (This same quality allowed them to participate in locally lucrative but illegal trade with Plains Indians.) Their military role is one basis for the common assumption that *genízaro* was a Spanish term for janissary.

Genízaros who stood out in battles eventually could own land or enter occupations other than day laborer or soldier. Land grants to genízaro settlers typically were along frontiers where fighting was heaviest. Through time others of ambiguous ancestry might join such communities. Thus, genízaro came to refer to anyone of ambiguous ancestry and/or lower status. Eventually, more successful genízaros passed into the general Hispanic population. By the late nineteenth century the term gradually fell into disuse. The term is seldom used today except by historians and genealogists studying New Mexico history.

Determining the number or proportion of genízaros is difficult. First, it was a status individuals sought to hide. Second, it changed through time for individuals and for families. Finally, as both social relations and the terms for various groups evolved, just who should be counted as genízaro changed. Estimates range from less than 10 percent of the settled population to as high as one-third—enough to be an important social component of Hispanic society in colonial New Mexico, especially in its interactions with Native Americans who lived in the Great Plains.

For some individuals genízaro might be a multigenerational transitional status in a passage from Indian to Spaniard. Collectively, they were a buffer group created by the combination of a need for labor and a supply of captives from nomadic Indians. When the flow of captives slowed, and finally ceased, the group was no longer refreshed by new members and gradually disappeared.

Thomas D. Hall
DePauw and Colgate Universities

Gutiérrez, Ramón A. *When Jesus Came, the Corn Mothers Went Away: Marriage, Sexuality, and Power in New Mexico, 1500–1846.* Stanford CA: Stanford University Press, 1991. Horvath, Steven. "The Social and Political Organization of the *Genízaros* of Plaza de Nuestra Señora de los Dolores de Belén, New Mexico, 1740–1812." Ph.D. diss., Brown University, 1979. Magnaghi, Russell M. "Plains Indians in New Mexico, the Genízaro Experience." *Great Plains Quarterly* 10 (1990): 86–95.

GONZALES, CORKY (b. 1928)

Rodolfo "Corky" Gonzales is best known for his contribution to the Chicano movement. Born in Denver, Colorado, on June 18, 1928,

Corky Gonzales (under banner) speaks at war protest in front of the capitol, Denver, Colorado, 1970.

purposely focused on the younger generation of Mexican Americans, finding them receptive to his major themes of Chicano nationalism, self-determination, and cultural and historical pride.

In 1970 Gonzales formed the Colorado La Raza Unida Party, a third-party political organization dedicated to the goals of the Chicano movement. At the party's first national convention in El Paso, Texas, in 1972, Gonzales vied unsuccessfully against Texas La Raza leader José Angel Gutiérrez for the national chairmanship. At issue in the campaign was Gonzales's emphasis on ethnic nationalism against Gutiérrez's political pragmatism.

While becoming a significant public leader of the Chicano movement, Gonzales remained dedicated to his family in Colorado. In 2001 he celebrated more than fifty years of marriage to his wife, Geri Romero de Gonzales, with his eight children, eighteen grandchildren, and many great-grandchildren. Although slowed by a serious automobile accident in 1988 and heart surgery in 1989, Gonzales remains active and is working on his autobiography.

Linda Van Ingen
University of Nebraska at Kearney

Gonzales, Rodolfo "Corky." *Message to Aztlán: Selected Writings of Rodolfo "Corky" Gonzales.* Houston: Arte Público Press, 2001. Marín, Christine. *A Spokesman of the Mexican American Movement: Rodolfo "Corky" Gonzales and the Fight for Chicano Liberation, 1966–1972.* San Francisco: R and E Research Associates, 1977. Vigil, Ernesto V. *The Crusade for Justice: Chicano Militancy and the Government's War on Dissent.* Madison: University of Wisconsin Press, 1999.

GORRAS BLANCAS

This secretive association of hooded night-riders operated in San Miguel, Santa Fe, and Mora Counties, New Mexico, from 1889 to 1891. Comprised of *neomexicanos* (Spanish-speaking New Mexicans), the *Gorras Blancas* took their name from the hooded White Caps of Tuscola, Illinois, who in 1889 made headlines for their destructive raids on the property of local commissioners who were proposing an unpopular drainage canal in their community. Believed to have numbered between 700 and 1,500 members, the Gorras Blancas launched a militant campaign of threats and intimidation against individuals who allegedly had encroached on community land and made that land inaccessible by fencing it off.

In an 1890 publication, the Gorras Blancas declared themselves defenders of "the rights of all people in general, and especially the rights of poor people." They sought favorable adjudication of the contested Las Vegas Land Grant to protect the community's right to use and occupy the land. When legal action failed, however, the Gorras Blancas vowed militant retribution. They cut miles of fence lines, destroyed buildings and farm equipment, and threatened the lives of presumed encroachers and their sympathizers, some of whom were fellow neomexicanos. These actions prompted Governor Lebaron Bradford Prince in 1890 to denounce the Gorras Blancas as a vigilante

Gonzales became one the most dynamic and influential leaders of the Mexican American struggle for self-determination and cultural pride in the 1960s and 1970s.

The son of a migrant father from Chihuahua, Mexico, Gonzales grew up in a Denver barrio amid poverty, discrimination, and hard work. His mother died when he was two years old, leaving Gonzales, the youngest child, in the care of his father and seven siblings. Nicknamed "Corky" at a young age by one of his older brothers, Gonzales spent much of his youth working alongside family members in the sugar beet and potato fields of northern and southern Colorado.

Gonzales attended numerous public schools in the Denver area. In 1944, at age sixteen, he graduated from Denver's Manual High School. Gonzales completed one term at the University of Denver but found the costs of further attendance prohibitive. Nevertheless, he pursued knowledge, learning not only from his experiences and the many people he met but also from reading the likes of Federico García Lorca, Pablo Neruda, John Steinbeck, and Ernest Hemingway. Gonzales's intellectual and creative capacity is evident in his many writings—hundreds of speeches, letters, and editorials, two plays, and many poems. His widely read poem, "I Am Joaquín," first published in 1967, has become one of the major pieces of Chicano literature. Revealing the cultural and spiritual conflicts in the Chicano identity, the poem inspired Chicano pride and activism.

Gonzales developed a strong, charismatic presence early in life. He drew crowds as an amateur boxer and became one of the best fighters of the time. He won the National Amateur Athletic Union Bantamweight Championship in 1947, and until 1955 fought professionally in featherweight divisions, with seventy-five wins, nine losses, and one draw. In 1988 Gonzales was inducted into the Colorado Sports Hall of Fame, the first Latino to be so honored.

Gonzales's first foray into politics centered around the Democratic Party. He campaigned for Quigg Newton for Denver mayor in 1947, and as a district captain in Denver County he organized Latino support for the Democratic Party in the 1950s. In 1960 he led the Colorado "Viva Kennedy" campaign. Gonzales himself ran unsuccessfully for office, including a bid for Denver City Council in 1955, the Colorado House of Representatives in 1964, and mayor of Denver in 1967. In 1965 he was appointed director of Denver's War on Poverty.

Increasingly frustrated by partisan wrangling, Gonzales publicly resigned from the Democratic Party in 1967. He had begun to shift his focus to the Crusade for Justice, which he and other community activists founded in 1966. A grassroots, human-rights cultural center located in Denver, the Crusade for Justice became an important site for Chicano activism. Gonzales represented the organization throughout the nation, as he gave speeches, conducted forums, and otherwise inspired and organized Chicanos to action. Under his leadership, the Crusade for Justice hosted three annual National Chicano Youth Liberation conferences. More than 1,500 Chicano youths attended the first conference in 1969. They produced goals for the Chicano movement and introduced the concept of Aztlán in the document *Espiritual de Aztlán.* Gonzales mob and to take measures securing the safety of local officials. Although at least four dozen of the Gorras Blancas were eventually indicted for their activities, none was convicted.

The Gorras Blancas were reportedly headed by former U.S. Indian agent and Knights of Labor organizer Juan José Herrera (affectionately known as *El Capitán*) and his younger brothers Nicanor and Pablo. It is believed that Juan José may have been inspired by the tactics of the above-mentioned White Caps; however, a surviving family member suggests that Herrera took his inspiration from the hooded Ku Klux Klan.

John Nieto-Phillips
New Mexico State University

Arellano, Anselmo. "The People's Movement: Las Gorras Blancas." In *The Contested Homeland: A Chicano History of New Mexico*, edited by Erlinda Gonzales-Berry and David R. Maciel. Albuquerque: University of New Mexico Press, 2000: 59–82. Larson, Robert W. "The White Caps of New Mexico: A Study of Ethnic Militancy in the Southwest." *Pacific Historical Review* 44 (1975): 171–85. Rosenbaum, Robert J. *Mexicano Resistance in the Southwest: "The Sacred Right of Self-Preservation."* Austin: University of Texas Press, 1981.

GUADALUPE HIDALGO, TREATY OF

Signed on February 2, 1848, the Treaty of Guadalupe Hidalgo officially ended the Mexican American War (1846–48). The treaty required that Mexico cede 947,570 square miles, almost half of its territory, in exchange for peace and $15 million. The United States gained most of what is now the American Southwest and parts of the Great Plains, including New Mexico, Arizona, Utah, Nevada, California, and parts of Wyoming, Colorado, and Oklahoma. The treaty also recognized the annexation of Texas to the United States and set the boundary between the two nations at the Rio Grande.

Key factors leading to the war, as well as the eventual terms of the treaty, included the annexation of Texas by the United States, an almost religious belief in American manifest destiny, and a vulnerable Mexican government. Unfortunately for Mexico, a succession of overthrown presidents had followed its war of independence from Spain, leaving the unstable nation an easy target for American expansionism.

Appointed by President James Polk, Nicholas Trist traveled to Mexico in May 1847 and began diplomatic relations soon after. He and three Mexican peace commissioners eventually signed the treaty at Villa de Guadalupe Hidalgo, but ratification would be an arduous process for both countries. While Mexican officials were outraged about lost territory, Americans were equally disappointed that they would not receive even more of the defeated nation.

Aside from land and money, the treaty dealt with the citizenship and property rights of those living within the transferred territory: Mexican citizens could relocate to Mexico, remain in the territory as Mexican citizens, or become citizens of the United States. The treaty promised these new Americans all rights, including "free enjoyment of liberty and property." The ratification did not, however, include Article 10 of the original document, which had promised to honor Mexican land grants.

Mary E. Adams
University of Oklahoma

del Castillo, Richard Griswold. *The Treaty of Guadalupe Hidalgo: A Legacy of Conflict*. Norman: University of Oklahoma Press, 1990. Gonzales, Manuel G. *Mexicanos: A History of Mexicans in the United States*. Bloomington: Indiana University Press, 1999.

GUTIÉRREZ, JOSÉ ANGEL (b. 1944)

José Angel Gutiérrez, between 1965 and 1980

José Angel Gutiérrez—along with César Chavez, Reies Tijerina, and Corky Gonzales—stands out as an important leader in the Chicano movement of the late 1960s and early 1970s. He was born into a middle-class family on October 25, 1944, in Crystal City, Texas. When he was still in grade school, his father died and young Gutiérrez was forced to work in the fields to help support his family. Despite facing such hardships early in his life, Gutiérrez emerged as a bright student and gifted leader; he served as the student body president of his high school. Gutiérrez earned a bachelor's degree in political science in 1966 from Texas A&I University in Kingsville and a master's degree in the same field two years later from St. Mary's University in San Antonio.

While at St. Mary's Gutiérrez continued his role as a student leader by helping to organize a chapter of the Mexican American Youth Organization. By 1970 Gutiérrez had returned to Crystal City, where he organized the Mexican American population through a new political party, La Raza Unida. With a mobilized Mexican American electorate, Gutiérrez was elected to the city council and later to the school board. From these positions of power, Gutiérrez and other Mexican American leaders enacted changes in the school system, including the introduction of bilingual and bicultural education programs, and improved relations between the Chicano and Anglo communities.

By the mid-1970s Gutiérrez was less involved in politics, but he continued to represent his community. In 1974 he was elected to a judgeship in Zavala County. He also continued his education, earning a doctorate in political science in 1976 from the University of Texas. Gutiérrez served as a judge until 1981 when he resigned to take a teaching position, first at Colegio César Chavez in Mt. Angel, Oregon, and later at Western Oregon State College. By 1986, however, Gutiérrez was back in Texas working on his law degree (which he earned in 1988) at the University of Houston. In 1993 he ran unsuccessfully for Lloyd Bentsen's vacated U.S. Senate seat. Gutiérrez was a professor of political science at the University of Texas at Arlington in 2001.

Mark R. Ellis
University of Nebraska at Kearney

HERRERA, JUAN JOSÉ (ca. 1840s–1902?)

In the late 1880s Juan José Herrera rose to prominence in San Miguel County, New Mexico, as district organizer for the Knights of Labor, or *Los Caballeros del Trabajo*. Known as *El Capitán* by his followers, Herrera's efforts to organize labor and vigilante groups earned him great respect among poor and dispossessed *neomexicanos* (Spanish-speaking New Mexicans), as well as disdain among many Anglo-American settlers, local officials, and landed neomexicanos. From April 1889 and into 1891, he reportedly led the *Gorras Blancas* (White Caps) in an armed campaign against Anglo-Americans and neomexicanos who had presumably encroached on community lands. Although he and several of his followers were arrested for vigilante activities in 1889, none was convicted. Herrera denied association with the Gorras Blancas.

Two years later Herrera was elected probate judge of San Miguel County. His varied background prepared him for popular organizing. A captain in the Union army, Herrera departed from New Mexico in 1866, leaving his wife, Luisa Pinard, and became an Indian agent, traveling among various western states. By the time he finally resettled in New Mexico in 1887, he had learned to speak several Native languages or dialects, as well as French. His command of English, his growing knowledge of the law, and his political instinct served him well in his brief organizing career. According to his descendants, Herrera, who was born sometime in the 1840s, died in relative obscurity in Utah in or about 1902.

John Nieto-Phillips
New Mexico State University

Arellano, Anselmo. "The People's Movement: Las Gorras Blancas." In *The Contested Homeland: A Chicano History of New Mexico*, edited by Erlinda Gonzales-Berry and David R. Maciel. Albuquerque: University of New Mexico Press, 2000: 59–82. Larson, Robert W. "The White Caps of New Mexico: A Study of Ethnic Militancy in the Southwest." *Pacific Historical Review* 44 (1975): 171–85. Rosenbaum, Robert J. *Mexicano Resistance in the Southwest: "The Sacred Right of Self-Preservation."* Austin: University of Texas Press, 1981.

HISPANIC POPULATION GEOGRAPHY

Spanish was the first European language spoken in the Great Plains. In 1540 Francisco Vásquez de Coronado and 1,800 adventurers departed from Tiguex, Nuevo Mexico, in search of the fabled Seven Cities of Cíbola. Coronado then traversed the Texas and Oklahoma Panhandles, the Arkansas River, and much of central Kansas looking for Quivira, another fabled realm of gold. Coronado returned emptyhanded, but the Spanish legacy is evident in Texas place-names such as Llano Estacado, Tierra Blanca, and Palo Duro.

Permanent European settlement of the grasslands began over 300 years later in New Mexico and Colorado. Hispano homesteaders —descendants of Spaniards who settled New Mexico in 1598—migrated from the New Mexican mountains to the High Plains east of Las Vegas, New Mexico, as early as 1823. However, widespread settlement of the Great Plains did not occur until after 1848 when the United States annexed northern Mexico. After 1848 Hispanos established several towns on the New Mexican High Plains, including San Miguel, Sabinoso, and Picacho, and several southern Colorado communities, including Trinidad, Trinchera, and La Plaza de los Leones (Walsenburg). By 1900 approximately 2,000 Hispanos tended sheep and grew vegetables between the Arkansas and Hondo Rivers, an area that was part of the "Hispano homeland."

Hispano migration away from the homeland began after 1900 when European American farmers began irrigating the valleys of the Arkansas and South and North Platte Rivers. European Americans planted sugar beets along the Platte and vegetables along the Arkansas. Increased agricultural production led to labor shortages, and many Hispanos migrated from the homeland to take advantage of the relatively high wages; some migrated as far north as the Red River Valley in North Dakota. Hispano barrios established in the 1920s are still visible around sugar beet factories from Loveland, Colorado, to Scottsbluff, Nebraska.

European American farmers in Texas used water from the Ogallala Aquifer to irrigate thousands of dryland acres on the Llano Estacado and then recruited Tejano laborers from the Rio Grande Valley to work the farms. European Americans also financed railroads to connect Great Plains states, but much of the labor came from Mexico. By 1912 railroad companies were encouraging Mexican families to settle permanently on railroad property near the tracks. By 1930 Mexican railroad workers had established several barrios "on the other side of the tracks" in towns in Oklahoma, Kansas, Texas, and Nebraska. Between 1900 and 1930 what we now call "Latinos"— Hispanos from New Mexico, Tejanos from South Texas, and Mexicans from Mexico—laid track and irrigation pipe and harvested crops from Wyoming to Texas. The Great Depression temporarily halted Latino migration to the Great Plains.

World War II created labor shortages that led in 1942 to Public Law 45 that authorized Mexican workers, braceros, to enter the United States as contract workers. Such contracting continued through the 1940s and was formalized by Public Law 78 in 1951. The Bracero Program recruited Mexican laborers to work in the United States at a guaranteed wage and provided transportation, food, and housing. The Bracero Program institutionalized the Hispanization of certain sectors of the Great Plains economy, especially the Llano Estacado cotton farms. By 1950, 30,000 braceros and Tejanos migrated annually to the Llano Estacado to pick cotton and vegetables. Labor shortages continued after the war because many veterans took advantage of the so-called GI Bill to get an education and leave farmwork.

Although the Bracero Program was abolished in 1964, Great Plains farmers still relied on Mexican labor. In 1965 the U.S. government amended its longstanding immigration quota policy in order to allow an increasing number of Mexican migrants into the country. After 1965 Hispanics began to diversify from agricultural and railroad work and were increasingly employed in factory jobs associated with agribusiness such as beef processing, well-drilling, and pipe-laying. Iowa Beef Processors (IBP) and Monfort (now Con-Agra), among others, needed to replace their diminishing European American workforce and increasingly hired Hispanic laborers in their plants in Omaha, Grand Island, Lexington, and North Platte, Nebraska; Garden City, Kansas; and Greeley, Colorado. IBP, for example, has worked with the Immigration and Naturalization Service (INS) to recruit workers from Mexico and has been discussing the creation of a new bracero-type program.

Diversification of the Latino occupational structure has led to the urbanization of the Hispanic population. Today Latinos live primarily in Great Plains cities—Denver, Greeley, Pueblo, Lubbock, Amarillo, Midland-Odessa, Omaha, and Kansas City. In these cities, Latino-owned businesses have altered the Great Plains urban landscape, with Mexican restaurants, Latino music shops, tortilla factories, Spanish-language theaters and radio stations, and bilingual churches.

Latinos are now an integral part of the labor force in several Great Plains economic sectors, and their cultural imprint is increasingly evident. Mexican restaurants, which not so long ago were considered exotic, are common even in small Plains towns. Around Lubbock, Texas, a "High Plains Mexican food" variant has emerged, and in the South Platte and Arkansas Valleys there is a thriving Hispano cuisine. An essential ingredient of Mexican food—chiles— are now planted extensively along the Arkansas River and handpicked by Mexican immigrants. Chile farms and chile harvest festivals around Pueblo, Colorado, are key components to the revitalization of that city. Politically, Latino participation is most apparent in the Texas High Plains and the Arkansas Valley, where Hispanics now constitute as much as 50 percent of the population. Latino mayors, sheriffs, and business leaders are common in these regions. The economic boom of the 1990s exacerbated Great Plains labor short-

ages, and a willing, mobile population of Mexicans with a history of migration to the Great Plains means that the sounds of Spanish will continue to be heard well into the foreseeable future.

Terrence W. Haverluk
United States Air Force Academy

Haverluk, Terrence W. "The Changing Geography of U.S. Hispanics, 1850–1990." *Journal of Geography* 96 (1997): 134–45. Nostrand, Richard L. "The Century of Hispano Expansion." *New Mexico Historical Review* 62 (1987): 361–86. Smith, Michael M. "Beyond the Borderlands: Mexican Labor and the Central Plains, 1900–1930." *Great Plains Quarterly* 4 (1981): 219–51.

HISPANO HOMELAND

The term "Hispano" is sometimes used as a substitute for "Spanish American," a person who is part of the old and distinctive New Mexico–centered subculture. In colonial times Hispanos settled in the Spanish Borderlands far earlier and became far more numerous than their subcultural counterparts, Tejanos and Californios. When the United States took political control of the Southwest in the nineteenth century, Hispanos escaped the onslaught of Mexican immigrants who engulfed and almost completely absorbed the Tejanos and Californios. Today, subtle cultural differences stemming from earlier colonization and isolation set Hispanos apart from their Mexican-origin brethren. Also, Hispanos are far fewer numerically, with 400,000 Hispanos in greater New Mexico compared to 10 million Mexican-origin people elsewhere in the American Southwest. Significantly, these Hispanos represent America's only surviving Spanish colonial subculture.

The creation of a Hispano homeland is the story of Hispano interaction with four other peoples. In 1598 Spaniards moved in with the Pueblo Indians who occupied the upper Rio Grande basin. The resentful Pueblos staged a successful revolt that sent the Spaniards south in 1680. But the Spanish soldier-settlers soon returned to transform the Pueblo Indian realm into a Hispano "stronghold" during the 1700s. Meanwhile, nomad Indians, the second people, stifled Hispano attempts to expand beyond the Pueblo realm—until about 1790, a turning point in their pacification. After 1790 Hispano sheepmen seeking new grazing lands began to spread east into the Great Plains in a spontaneous village-by-village movement that lasted until 1890. Territorial expansions into the Texas and Oklahoma Panhandles happened quickly in the 1860s and 1870s. Then Anglo-Americans, the third people, moving west with their cattle, blunted—indeed drove back—the Hispano *pastores*. Anglos, who had been arriving in Hispano territory since 1821, continued to come in the twentieth century. Mexicans, the fourth people, also arrived from Mexico and the Southwest. By 1900 the Hispano homeland reached its greatest areal extent as it stretched over parts of five states and was the size of Utah. But the arrival of Anglos and Mexican-origin people especially drove down the Hispano percentage to only onefifth of the region's population.

In the process of colonizing greater New Mexico, Hispanos, acting by themselves, created a special feeling for their milieu, their homeland. The highland environment that they had wrested from the Pueblos required some adjusting to. Their cultural heritage brought from Spain and New Spain made them well prepared to irrigate dryland New Mexico and to build with adobe brick when lacking timber. When lowland pastures dried up in summer, they drove sheep to higher elevations, a Spanish practice called transhumance. But adjusting to bitterly cold winter temperatures required the construction of livestock shelters in addition to corrals, and short growing seasons precluded planting anything but hardy vegetables and deciduous fruit trees. At the same time, Hispanos created a distinctive cultural landscape by building fortified villages for protection from nomadic Indian attack and by laying out long agricultural planting lots so that everyone had access to the irrigation ditch lifeline. Both processes—adjusting to a highland environment and stamping that environment with a unique cultural impress—became central in the Hispanos' bonding with place. Adding to this attachment to place came control of land through land-grant ownership. To this day Hispanos have an uncommonly strong concept of homeland among Americans.

But the homeland that Hispanos so deeply love is by no means uniform. In 1900 three zones representing degrees of Hispano strength clearly existed. The inner half of the homeland constituted a stronghold where Hispanos represented a minimum of 90 percent of the population and where they had political clout but already had lost much economic control. A broken concentric ring beyond the stronghold constituted an "inland," suggesting accurately that Anglos had intruded here to reduce Hispano numbers to between 50 and 90 percent. Anglos in this area shared political control with Hispanos and had pretty much taken over economically. The outer broken ring, called the "outland," represented areas to which economic opportunity had pulled Hispanos from the center. Hispanos had moved "out" to assume jobs as railroad workers, miners, ranch hands, shepherds, and laborers. In the outland, Hispanos owned little land, had virtually no political say and minimal social standing, and constituted a minority population of between 10 and 50 percent.

Since 1900 the three morphological zones have all but disappeared, but their recent existence is useful when explaining the Great Plains segment of the Hispano homeland. Much of the Hispano homeland that now overlaps east into the Great Plains is yesterday's outland. Compared to the long occupation of their highland stronghold, Hispano settlement of the high, flat Plains is relatively recent. They did so either by spreading east in a lightly settled string of villages founded by sheepmen, who were later rolled back by Anglo cattlemen, or by being pulled into the Plains by Anglo economic opportunity. In both cases Hispanos came to represent a mi-nority population that found itself disadvantaged economically, socially, and politically. After World War II the problem was compounded by the arrival of Mexican-origin people in urban centers like Roswell, Clovis, Pueblo, and Denver (which in 1980 were all homeland outliers except Pueblo). Thus, it seems appropriate to characterize the Hispano homeland where it overlaps the Great Plains as an expansion on the periphery of the highland core.

Richard L. Nostrand
University of Oklahoma

Nostrand, Richard L. *The Hispano Homeland.* Norman: University of Oklahoma Press, 1996.

JIMENEZ, LUIS (b. 1940)

Luis Alfonso Jimenez Jr., one of the Americas' most important Hispanic artists, was born on July 14, 1940, in El Paso, Texas. He received a bachelor of science degree in art and architecture from the University of Texas in 1964. The same year, he attended Ciudad Universitaria, Mexico. He has been awarded the prestigious Mid-Career Fellowship Awards at the American Academy in Rome and the National Endowment for the Arts, and the American Institute of Architects Environmental Improvement Award for *Vaquero*, his work of sculpture in Moody Park, Houston, Texas. Numerous other commissions and exhibitions are at institutions such as the National Museum of American Art, Washington DC; New York's Metropolitan Museum of Art; the Art Institute of Chicago; the Modern Art Museum of Fort Worth; the San Antonio Museum of Arts; and the Sheldon Memorial Art Gallery, University of Nebraska–Lincoln.

Jimenez's technique in creating monumental sculptures was learned in the workshop of his father, a sign painter and neon sign maker. He is widely known for his large, public, fiberglass sculptures that are based on a contemporary language and convey a "Tex-Mex" flavor, inviting spirited dialogue not only about their subject matter but also their medium. He incorporates age-old Chicano and Mexican icons that can be thought of in a more popular idiom, and he challenges accepted notions of the definition of art. His vigorous, gestural drawings also are full of a sense of pride in his Latino heritage.

Karen O. Janovy
University of Nebraska–Lincoln

Zamudio-Taylor, Victor. "Chicano Art." In *Latin American Art in the Twentieth Century,* edited by Edward J. Sullivan. London: Phaidon Press, 1996: 318–21.

JUNTA DE INDIGNACIÓN

See PROTEST AND DISSENT: Junta de Indignación

LISA, MANUEL (1772–1820)

In a letter to William Clark, written in 1817, Manuel Lisa offered this self-assessment: "I go a great distance while some are considering whether they will start today or tomorrow. I impose upon myself great privations." Indeed he did. Ambitious and impetuous, Lisa was the first St. Louis trader to respond to Lewis and Clark's revelation of an area "richer in beaver and otter than any country on earth" at the headwaters of the Missouri.

Lisa was born in New Orleans on September 8, 1772, to Christobal de Lisa and Maria Ignacia Rodriquez. He learned his trade on the Mississippi and Ohio Rivers in the 1790s before settling on a Spanish land grant in St. Louis. There he went into direct competition with the resident French trading aristocracy over the commerce with the Osage Indians. But after the return of Lewis and Clark, he turned his sights to the upper Missouri River.

In the spring of 1807 Lisa organized an expedition of about sixty men, which ascended the Missouri and built a trading post, Fort Raymond, at the confluence of the Yellowstone and Bighorn Rivers. From there he dispatched trappers to the Rocky Mountains while plying a successful trade with the Crows. Encouraged by the large quantity of furs they obtained, Lisa returned to St. Louis to mount a larger expedition.

In 1809, 160 men in the employ of Lisa's Missouri Fur Company left St. Louis for the upper Missouri. They established posts along the river for all the Indians who wanted to trade, thus satisfying the Indians' wants and keeping the river open, while at the same time garnering furs. But Lisa's main objective was to trap in the headwaters of the upper Missouri, and there his plans disintegrated. The furs were there, but so were the Blackfeet. When his enterprise was abandoned in the summer of 1810, only thirty packs of beaver had been accumulated, and twenty of his men were dead.

Lisa's trading activities—indeed all the activities of the St. Louis fur trade—were curtailed during the War of 1812. When trade resumed in 1819, Lisa formed a second Missouri Fur Company with the same objectives as the first. But before the enterprise got under way, Lisa contracted a serious illness. The enterprising Spaniard died in St. Louis in the summer of 1820 and was buried in what became Bellefontaine Cemetery. He never realized his ambition to create a fur empire that combined trading along the Missouri River with trapping in the Rocky Mountains, but he left a blueprint that others, like William Ashley, would follow with great success.

See also INDUSTRY: Fur Trade.

David J. Wishart
University of Nebraska–Lincoln

Oglesby, Richard E. *Manuel Lisa and the Opening of the Missouri Fur Trade.* Norman: University of Oklahoma Press, 1963.

LOPEZ, NANCY (b. 1957)

Born on January 6, 1957, in Torrance, California, Nancy Lopez, the daughter of Domingo and Marina Lopez, was a "wunderkind" of golf. When she was very young the family moved to Roswell, New Mexico, where Domingo ran an automobile repair shop. At age eight, Nancy learned the game of golf, carrying her mother's 4-wood and trailing her father as he played the arid municipal course. She developed an unorthodox swing, taking her club back slowly with her arms stretched high over her head, pausing, and then unleashing a powerful downswing.

Lopez won a Peewee League girls' tournament by 110 strokes at age nine (the prize was a Barbie doll), the New Mexico Women's Amateur Tournament at age twelve, and five national and regional junior championships as a teenager. As an amateur, she placed second in the United States Women's Open in 1975 and, while attending the University of Tulsa, captured five collegiate titles. She turned professional in 1977 and in 1978 won nine tournaments, a record-setting five in a row, including the Ladies Professional Golf Association Championship (LPGA). That year she was the leading money-winner, won the Vare Trophy for low scoring average, and was named both Player of the Year and Rookie of the Year.

Ever flashing a telegenic smile, Lopez infused women's golf with an expansive spirit; she became, said one observer, "the whole sport of women's golf." More women took up the game, the media gave increasing coverage to the LPGA tour, and galleries at LPGA events multiplied. Heretofore eclipsed by women's tennis, gymnastics, and running, women's golf was soon equally popular.

Lopez won eight tour events in 1979 but slipped comparatively from 1980 through 1984, claiming two to three titles each year. Contributing factors were a failed marriage to Tim Melton, her pregnancy following her marriage to Ray Knight, a major league baseball player, the flattening of her swing, and stiffer competition on the tour. She returned to preeminence in 1985 when she won five tournaments. She attributed her renewed success in part to Knight, who, understanding the demands facing professional athletes, gave her "peace of mind."

Lopez won thirteen championships from 1986 through 1993 despite cutting her play because of two pregnancies and the demands of domestic life. After 1993 her scoring average remained nearly at old levels, but she did not claim another title until 1997. She has been named Player of the Year four times and was elected to the LPGA Hall of Fame in 1987.

Carl M. Becker
Wright State University

Deford, Frank. "Nancy with the Laughing Face." *Sports Illustrated*, July 10, 1978: 24. Lopez, Nancy, with Peter Schwed. *The Education of a Woman Golfer*. New York: Simon and Schuster, 1979.

MAXWELL LAND GRANT

The Maxwell Land Grant, located on New Mexico's northeastern border with Colorado, possesses one of the most interesting legal histories of any piece of land in the United States. During the latter part of the nineteenth century, the Maxwell Land Grant and Railway Company, a Dutch bond-holding company doing business in the United States, used violent, political, and legal means to extinguish the property rights of hundreds of the grant's residents—Native Americans, former Mexican citizens, and American homesteaders.

Conflicting claims to the land originated in the grant's conveyance in 1841 from the Mexican government to two Mexican citizens, Carlos Beaubien, a prominent Taos merchant, and Guadalupe Miranda, the collector of customs for New Mexico. That conveyance did not specify the exact location of the grant's boundaries or its exact acreage. After the Mexican American War (1846–48), the departure of Miranda, and the death of Beaubien in 1864, Lucien and Luz Maxwell, Beaubien's son-in-law and daughter, took control of the land. Maxwell managed the grant by settling people, raising livestock, planting crops, and engaging in the developing trade with the United States. As sole owners of the land grant, the Maxwells became prominent citizens in the eastern Plains of New Mexico and were famous among Santa Fe Trail traders for their lavish home and lifestyle.

When gold was discovered in 1867 and prospectors swarmed onto their property, the Maxwells became aware of the land's worth and their inability to control its boundaries. Not knowing the extent of their property holdings, they, with the help of Jerome Chalke, who was attempting to broker a lucrative sale, conducted the most accurate survey to date, determining that the grant was 1.7 million acres. In 1869 the Maxwells sold the land to English investors for $1.35 million, or less than $1 per acre. The buyers, well aware of the ill-defined extent of the grant's title, sought to have Congress confirm the grant at 1.7 million acres, thus giving the investors a clear title to the property. Though Congress confirmed the validity of the land title, it did not specify how many acres the grant contained. In 1871, however, Secretary of the Interior Columbus Delano ruled that the grant contained only 97,000 acres, because under the Mexican Colonization Law of 1824 a grant to two individuals had specific acreage limits. Secretary Delano then instructed the Maxwell Land Grant Company to choose 97,000 acres, and he declared the remainder public domain and open to settlement. Faced with this unfavorable legal decision and financial ruin, the company's directors turned to its powerful allies in the Santa Fe Ring (an influential group of politicians and business leaders) to help them preserve their investment. For the next ten years, the Maxwell Land Grant Company waged a political and legal battle to maintain its claim to 1.7 million acres, while at the same time homesteaders were settling across the land grant on what they believed to be public domain.

The legal troubles continued during the 1880s, when the state of Colorado sued the Maxwell Company, arguing that its property claims infringed on the Colorado public domain. The lawsuit, *United States v. Maxwell*, made its way through the court system, eventually landing in the U.S. Supreme Court. In 1887 the Court decided that the boundaries of the land grant were not restricted to a mere 97,000 acres but extended to enclose 1.7 million acres. The effect was that hundreds of settlers, many with final homestead rights, were evicted from their homes. The conflict between the Maxwell Land Grant Company and the settlers came to a violent standoff in the Stonewall Valley War of 1888, in which two men died, many were injured, and the company sustained substantial property damage.

Despite these last violent skirmishes, the Maxwell Company maintained control over the vast estate well into the twentieth century until they sold portions to the Rockefeller-owned Colorado, Fuel, and Iron Company, the Phelps-Dodge Corporation, and other private interests. Today, the largest intact parcels of the land grant are in the Kit Carson National Forest and the adjacent Boy Scouts of America Philmont Scout Ranch.

María E. Montoya
University of Michigan

Maxwell Land Grant Papers, Archive 147, Center for Southwest Research, Zimmerman Library, University of New Mexico. Montoya, María E. *Translating Property: The Maxwell Land Grant and the Conflict Over Land in the American West, 1840–1900*. Berkeley: University of California Press, 2001. Pearson, Jim B. *The Maxwell Land Grant*. Norman: University of Oklahoma Press, 1968.

MEATPACKERS

The employment of Latinos in the meatpacking industry of the Great Plains first took place between 1900 and 1930. Many Mexicans had entered the region to perform sugar beet work for the Great Western Sugar Company. Mexican communities formed near the refineries at sugar-beet-producing centers like Scotts Bluff County, Nebraska, and Weld County, Colorado. By 1927 half of the 58,000 Mexicans employed by the sugar beet industry worked in Wyoming, Colorado, Iowa, and Nebraska. Other Mexican immigrants entered the meatpacking industry after coming to the region through Kansas City, Kansas, to work for the Union Pacific, Burlington Northern, Santa Fe, and other railroads. The Mexican section hands settled in towns along the rail lines like Lawrence, Garden City, and Kansas City, Kansas, and Sidney, Ogallala, Grand Island, and Omaha, Nebraska.

Mexican immigrants obtained work in the slaughterhouses and meatpacking plants of Wilson and Company, Swift and Company, Cudahy, and the Omaha Company in Nebraska, South Dakota, Kansas, and Iowa. They established settlements near the packing plants in Omaha, Kansas City, Sioux City, and Sioux Falls. Many meatpackers and their families became permanent residents of the Great Plains, though large numbers were repatriated to Mexico during the 1920–21 depression and the Great Depression. During and after World War II, Mexican meatpackers in Omaha, Kansas City, and Fort Worth played an important role in the unionizing drives of the Packinghouse Workers Organizing Committee.

The Great Plains meatpacking industry continues to attract Mexicans and other Latinos because of the labor needs of processing

Armour Packing Plant in Kansas City, Kansas

plants that have moved from the big urban centers to the Plains rural areas and small towns like Lexington, Nebraska, and Emporia and Garden City, Kansas. From 1980 to 1990 the beef, pork, and poultry processors in Nebraska, Kansas, and Iowa recruited workers from South Texas and California. The percentage of Latinos throughout the meatpacking industry continues to increase, representing more than 20 percent of the workers in some meat plants, like those in Emporia, to two-thirds in others, like those in Finney County, Kansas. Most workers are young males born in Mexico and in Guatemala. Fewer than half of the Latino immigrant meatpackers have lived in the United States for five years. More than one-third are in the country legally through provisions of the Immigration Reform and Control Act of 1986, while more than one-fourth lack legal residence, resulting in frequent arrests and deportations.

Illness, high injury rates, and stress caused by repetitive work plague meatpackers, who often quit after a few months or are forced off the job by the company. More than two-thirds leave because of poor working conditions. Low wages, limited mobility and advancement, and poor relations with management also account for high turnover rates in this industry. Latino meatpackers are burdened with housing shortages, poor health care and other social services, and racism and discrimination. The passage of "English only" ordinances and other such laws has been prompted by the increasing presence of Latinos in the meatpacking centers of the Great Plains. That presence, however, which is only the latest wave of immigration to a region populated by the descendants of immigrants, is not likely to diminish in the foreseeable future.

See also INDUSTRY: Meatpacking.
Zaragosa Vargas
University of California, Santa Barbara

Gouveia, Lourdes. "Global Strategies and Local Linkages: The Case of the U.S. Meat Packing Industry." In *From Columbus to ConAgra: The Globalization of Agriculture and Food*, edited by Alessandro Bonanno, Lawrence Bush, William Friedland, Lourdes Gouveia, and Enzo Mingione. Lawrence: University Press of Kansas, 1994: 125–48. Lamphere, Louise, Guillermo Grenier, and Alex Stepick, eds. *Newcomers in the Workplace: New Immigrants and the Restructuring of the U.S. Economy*. Philadelphia: Temple University Press, 1994.

MEXICAN AMERICAN CUISINE

Of the familiar ethnic triad of foods in the United States, Mexican American dishes far outdistance those from Italy and China in the Great Plains. This is true both for locally owned restaurants and for fast-food franchises. The cuisine became known because of the region's proximity to the Southwest, and it became popular because it is inexpensive, tastes good, and is filling. The wide diffusion of Mexicans and Mexican Americans throughout the Plains in recent decades has meant that family Mexican restaurants and Mexican grocery stores have come even to small communities, diversifying and enriching the culinary landscape.

What most Plains people are eating is Tex-Mex, a modified version of Mexican food originally adapted to please Anglo palates that preferred less heat and more meat. Some food items, such as tortilla chips, were actually concocted for the U.S. market. The preparation style and ingredient list is different from historic Mexican cooking in that Tex-Mex has more cheese and tomato-based sauces. It differs from Spanish-colonial cooking in its spices, variety of meats, and wheat-based pastries. Tex-Mex has its origins as a lower-class or peasant food, similar in function to Cajun food within southern Louisiana culture. In fact, Tex-Mex food represents such a jumbled mixing of food traditions from several cul-

tures that it is difficult to untangle the regional origins and discuss authenticity. It is truly a hybrid product.

In a restaurant setting, a Tex-Mex meal is invariably initiated by a basket of tortilla chips and fresh tomato salsa, with options for varying degrees of heat. A common meal is a combination plate that might include a beef taco served in a crisp corn tortilla, a chicken enchilada with sauce, a bean burrito wrapped in a flour tortilla, and sides of refried beans and Spanish rice. One end of the plate contains a mound of shredded iceberg lettuce with fresh tomato chunks, and a layer of grated cheese covers everything. Dessert might be sopapillas, while a beverage of choice is often a beer or margarita. Liquid of some kind is essential, as the diner does not always know in advance the heat level of the dish. The ambiance of the restaurant setting is, of course, dependent upon the imagination of the owner, but the decor often includes bright, tropical colors, *ristras* of dried red chiles, painted clay pottery, and ironwork. Mexican music is almost mandatory and is important in conveying the upbeat, festive atmosphere associated with this cuisine.

Three classic Tex-Mex items—tacos, nachos, and chili—have escaped their ethnic origins and become "American." Other foods belonging to this cuisine are more likely to be found in the Mexican American home, although some have begun to be incorporated into restaurant settings as customers demand more variety. Pico de gallo, chicharrón, gorditos, and chalupas are in the process of making it in the commercial world. Others, such as tamales, are often homemade, special-occasion food. Cabrito, offal food, barbacoa, panocha, chorizo, buñuelos, and handmade tortillas all fall mostly in the category of home consumption only. As the Mexican American population becomes more urban, lack of time to prepare labor-intensive dishes and the inability to butcher animals and cook outside in a pit are changing some aspects of the cuisine.

See also FOLKWAYS: Foodways.
Barbara G. Shortridge
University of Kansas

Bentley, Amy. "From Culinary Other to Mainstream American: Meanings and Uses of Southwestern Cuisine." *Southern Folklore* 55 (1998): 238–52. Graham, Joe S. "Mexican-American Traditional Foodways at La Junta De Los Rios." *Journal of Big Bend Studies* 2 (1990): 1–27. Pilcher, Jeffrey M. *¡Que vivan los tamales! Food and the Making of Mexican Identity*. Albuquerque: University of New Mexico Press, 1998.

MISSOURI COMPANY

The Spanish had a tenuous grasp on the upper Louisiana Territory in the waning years of the eighteenth century. The Missouri Company was founded in an effort to exploit its riches. France had ceded Louisiana to Spain in the secret Treaty of Fountainbleau in 1762, although residents of Louisiana did not learn of the transaction until late in 1764, and French control of upper Louisiana was not formally surrendered to Spain until 1770. France regained control in 1800 and sold Louisiana to the United States three years later. During the latter years of the eighteenth century, Spanish officials in St. Louis tried to halt British trade incursions in the area. The Missouri River was the key to Spanish domains west of the Mississippi River, though they were slow to exploit the trade there. Spaniards had not ventured much farther west than the French had before them. But they were competing with British traders from the Mississippi River who were reaching the Omahas and other tribes along the lower Missouri.

On October 15, 1793, François Luis Hector Carondelet, Louisiana's governor-general, and Jacques Clamorgan oversaw the founding of the Company of Discoveries of the Upper Missouri. Although it was later commonly called simply the Missouri Company, it was known under ten variant names. This company of St. Louis merchants was intent on exploiting the fur resources of the upper Missouri River and removing the British threat to Spanish domains. Clamorgan, director of the company, planned to build a series of forts on the Missouri and hoped eventually to extend the company's interests west to the Pacific Ocean.

The new company made its first explorations of the river in the fall of 1794, when Jean Baptiste Truteau ascended as far as present-day central South Dakota. He did not reach the Mandans, but he did build a post on the Missouri, Ponca House, not far from the mouth of the Niobrara. Results were disappointing. In April 1795 the company sent a second and larger expedition upriver under the leadership of a man named Lecuyer. This expedition was a fiasco due to Lecuyer's poor leadership and the hostility of the Poncas.

In July 1795 company officials in St. Louis heard news that threatened to further usurp trade in their domain, news of a direct threat to Spanish control of the upper Missouri River. Two traders from the Mandans had deserted and made their way downriver, where they told the Spanish commandant of upper Louisiana, Zenon Trudeau, about direct trade between Canadian traders and the Mandans, and that the British had built a fort at the villages of the Mandans.

The company concluded preparations for a third expedition, a far larger one, nearly the size of the later Lewis and Clark expedition. The party was under the direction of the Scotsman James Mackay, a former trader in Canada, and John Thomas Evans, a Welshman who had come to the United States seeking the legendary Welsh Indians. Their four vessels and thirty men left St. Louis in August or September 1795. They built a post for the Otoe Indian trade near the mouth of the Platte River, then established Fort Charles not far from present-day Sioux City. In 1796 Evans made his way to the Mandans and expelled the Canadian traders from their trading post, but he decided not to continue on to the West Coast as Mackay had ordered him, and he returned to St. Louis. Mackay had already done so, and the third expedition ended—again, a failure. Any significant Spanish presence on

the Missouri River promptly evaporated, and the Canadians resumed their trade with the Mandans. The expedition's greatest contribution to history was the information it provided for Lewis and Clark seven years later.

The Missouri Company did not long survive these setbacks. Clamorgan was blamed for its losses, but he enlisted the aid of a powerful Canadian trader, Andrew Todd, and expanded operations to the upper Mississippi River. With Todd, he formed a new company —Clamorgan, Loisel and Company—that competed with the Missouri Company, with which he was still associated. When Todd died in 1796 the financially tottering firm was temporarily rejuvenated by St. Louis leaders such as Auguste Chouteau, but under Clamorgan's erratic hand the firm slowly expired and was no longer in operation by the time of the Louisiana Purchase.

See also INDUSTRY: Fur Trade.

W. Raymond Wood
University of Missouri–Columbia

Nasatir, Abraham P. *Before Lewis and Clark: Documents Illustrating the History of the Missouri, 1785–1804.* St. Louis: St. Louis Historical Documents Foundation, 1952. Nasatir, Abraham P. "Jacques Clamorgan." In *The Mountain Men and the Fur Trade of the Far West,* edited by Le Roy R. Hafen, 2: 81–94. Glendale CA: Arthur H. Clark, 1965. Wood, W. Raymond. "Fort Charles, or 'Mr. Mackey's Trading House.'" *Nebraska History* 76 (1995): 2–7.

OTERO, MIGUEL ANTONIO (1829–1882)

Businessman, banker, politician, and railroad promoter, Miguel Antonio Otero was born in Valenica, New Mexico (then a province of the Mexican Republic), on June 21, 1829. Otero was educated in private schools in Missouri, attended St. Louis University, and graduated from Pingree College in Fishkill, New York. He taught briefly at Pingree before returning to Missouri, where he studied law under Governor Trusten Polk. After being admitted to the bar in 1851, Otero returned to New Mexico (by then a U.S. territory) to practice law. He quickly became involved in territorial politics: he served in the territorial legislature, briefly held the position of territorial district attorney, and was elected New Mexico's delegate to Congress in 1855 (he held that position until 1861). While serving in Congress Otero married Mary Josephine Blackwood of Charleston, South Carolina; the Oteros had four children (son Miguel Antonio Jr. was New Mexico Territory's first Hispanic American governor).

Otero focused on a variety of business ventures after leaving Congress. In 1867 he opened a mercantile business in Westport Landing, Missouri, and as the railroad moved west across Kansas he relocated to Leavenworth, Fort Harker, and Hays City. Otero also became active in railroad promotion. He worked for the Atchison, Topeka, and Santa Fe Railroad during the 1870s and he helped organize the New Mexico and Southern Pacific Railroad, which built through New Mexico. At Raton Pass in December 1878, Otero drove the ceremonial spike into the first rail laid in New Mexico. By the late 1870s Otero was living in Las Vegas, New Mexico, and was engaged in

mining, banking, health resorts, and a telephone company. He founded and was the first president of the San Miguel National Bank. Otero died of pneumonia at age fifty-two on May 30, 1882, in Las Vegas.

Mark R. Ellis
University of Nebraska at Kearney

Otero, Miguel Antonio Jr. *Otero: An Autobiographical Trilogy.* New York: Arno Press, 1974. Vigil, Maurilio E. "Miguel Antonio Otero." In *Los Patrones: Profiles of Hispanic Political Leaders in New Mexico History,* edited by Maurilio E. Vigil. Washington DC: University Press of America, 1980: 45–48.

PASTORES

The *pastores* are a little-known Hispanic sheepherding group whose homeland was the grasslands of north-central New Mexico (*Quechero*, or Mescalero Plains). Established there by at least the early nineteenth century, the pastores practiced a transhumance lifestyle with their flocks. The long circuits made in search of pasturage and water for the flocks took males away from their homes for extended periods. For these sheepherders, material possessions were basic and sparse as they traveled hundreds of miles with their sheep. Economically, the pastores were part of either the *partido* system of herd management or a family business that owned and managed the flock. The New Mexico partido system, adapted from that of Spain, was a means of lending capital at interest that allowed a sheepherder to build up his own flock, thereby moving to the family business system.

A burgeoning sheep industry necessitated new, open rangelands that were safe from raids by Native peoples. Despite risks, pastores began their incursion into the upper Canadian River valley of eastern New Mexico by 1849 and the Canadian River valley of the Texas Panhandle in the 1860s. In the middle 1870s, with the removal of the Native peoples and near extermination of the bison herds on which they depended, the vast grasslands of the Texas Panhandle and Southern High Plains became open territory. The value of this area was realized quickly by the pastores as they moved their flocks into the region. Part of a longer circuit bringing the flocks back to New Mexico, family settlements soon lined the Canadian River valley and its tributaries in the Texas Panhandle. By 1880, 340 pastores were in that area. The pastores established small settlements in previously used summer grazing pastures with the intention of remaining in the area on a year-round basis. Known as *plazas*, the largest one (founded by Casimero Romero in 1876) became the town of Tascosa. The Canadian and Red River drainage systems were the primary routes for circuits and settlements.

Pastores sites have been identified in archeological surveys along the middle Pecos River near Santa Rosa, New Mexico, and the Canadian River valley in the Texas Panhandle. Rock corrals were common among a small variety of site types. Rock corrals, used by pastores, have been found in the eastern canyon lands of the Rolling Plains and within the drainages and on the uplands of the Southern High Plains.

The pastores fashioned a distinctive architecture and favored specific topographic and environmental settings. Corrals, built for shelter and protection, were located where abundant pasture and surface water coexisted. The locally available rock used in construction also influenced structure placement. Corrals, built of local materials and without mortar, were of variable size and were square, rectangular, or oval. Rocks were stacked with the larger ones near the bottom and smaller ones on top, and the walls were not faced. The corrals constructed in the various areas were substantial and took time and effort. The majority were single-space enclosures, although partitioned corrals have also been identified. Machine-cut square iron nails (manufactured between 1860 and 1884) have been commonly found within and around the corrals. The settlements made efficient use of available resources within a localized area while providing a safe haven within a controlled pasturage for people and sheep.

Anglo-American cattle ranchers also recognized the value of the vast grasslands, which they used first as open range and then, by 1881, controlled with land titles and barbed-wire fencing. Restrictions on free range, several harsh winters, and a general atmosphere of distrust and dislike between the sheepherders and cattlemen led to a rapid decline of pastores settlements in the region. By 1887 all the plazas were abandoned and most pastores had returned to New Mexico.

During their short tenure on the western Texas Plains, the pastores were always in transition—from seasonal use to permanent settlement to withdrawal from the region. Abandonment was not only quick but also unexpected, brought about by changes over which the pastores had no control. Their influence on the regional culture is neither fully understood nor appreciated. Nevertheless, the pastores' brief presence left its mark on the landscape of the region and influenced early settlement patterns. Plazas became town sites and corrals and camps provided an infrastructure for European American reuse and settlement of the region.

Eileen Johnson
J. Kent Hicks
Museum of Texas Tech University

Archambeau, Ernest R. "Spanish Sheepmen on the Canadian at Old Tascosa." *Panhandle-Plains Historical Review* 19 (1946): 45–72, 96. Hicks, J. Kent, and Eileen Johnson. "Pastores Presence on the Southern High Plains of Texas." *Historical Archaeology* 34 (2000): 46–60. Rathjen, Frederick W. *The Texas Panhandle Frontier*. Austin: University of Texas Press, 1973.

PEÑA, FEDERICO (b. 1947)

Federico Fabian Peña was born and raised in South Texas. By age fifty-two he had logged a distinguished political career as a Colorado state legislative leader, Denver's mayor, and the head of two major federal agencies as a member of President Bill Clinton's cabinet.

Born in 1947 in Laredo, Texas, as one of six children, Federico Peña was raised in an upper-middle-class Hispanic family. His father, a Texas A&M University graduate, was a successful cotton broker. Peña's ancestors had helped in the founding of Laredo, and several held elective posts during the Civil War. His lineage, therefore, was one of both economic and political participation and success.

Peña's early schooling was in English-speaking Catholic schools in Brownsville, Texas, he was a top performer in both academics and athletics. Federico went on to the University of Texas in Austin for his bachelor of science and law degrees (1969 and 1972, respectively). In 1973 he moved to Denver where he worked with the Mexican-American Legal Defense Fund and as a private attorney, focusing primarily on civil rights cases and voting issues.

Federico Peña's elective political career began at age thirty-one in the Colorado House of Representatives. In search of an aggressive leader, the Democrats selected Peña as minority party leader in only his second term. Then, in a surprise move, the promising young lawmaker abandoned legislative life at the end of that term in 1983 to run for mayor of Denver. A virtual unknown, Peña challenged fourteen-year incumbent mayor Bill McNichols and won a close and improbable victory. Peña's campaign slogan was "Imagine a Great City," and it featured a high-energy, street-level approach to politics and an aggressive voter registration drive bolstered by an estimated 4,000 volunteers. The new mayor's first term was rocky; he inherited a municipal budget deficit and a depressed local economy. Peña sought to "open City Hall" and establish a plan for economic recovery, but critics said he was slow to establish his cabinet, and an initial push for a new convention center failed.

In the face of opposition, Peña sought a second term. On the eve of the election he was roughly twenty points down in the polls, but again he won a close election. With an economic strategy in place, and with more experience, Mayor Peña launched a number of extremely successful capital development projects. His reputation solidified, he once again surprised observers by rejecting a run for a third term. Peña had recently married Ellen Hart, a world-class distance runner. They'd begun a family and he wanted more time at home.

But within a year Peña was back in public life, first on President Clinton's transition team, and then for four years as secretary of transportation and two years as secretary of energy. In 1998 Peña returned to Denver with his wife and three young children, entering the business world as senior adviser with Vestar Capital Partners.

Federico Peña's career in politics was marked by major achievements as well as by the criticism that comes with public life. Critics characterized him as indecisive in his first mayoral term, and in his second he was the object of a failed recall movement. But Peña was also the force behind a new Denver airport, convention center, performing arts center, and library, as well as improvements in streets, parks, and neighborhoods. Denver gained a major league baseball team during his tenure. In Washington, Peña successfully reduced government personnel and cost levels and championed the causes of mass transit and technology. He was a relentless champion of civil rights and civil liberties. Peña's expressed philosophy was that personal success flows from hard work and vision, and community success rests upon leadership, inclusion, participation, and investment. The route to Denver's International Airport is along Peña Boulevard.

See also CITIES AND TOWNS: Denver, Colorado.

John A. Straayer
Colorado State University

PLAN OF SAN DIEGO

From 1915 to 1917 the anarchist-inspired Plan of San Diego (named after the small town in South Texas where it was devised) sought to redress the suffering of some ethnic poor in America by creating two new, independent republics from states in the Southwest and the Great Plains where Hispanics, blacks, Native Americans, and Japanese could live free from "capitalist oppression." The plan proposed liberating first, as a Spanish-speaking homeland, the lands Mexico had lost to the United States in 1848, namely Texas, New Mexico, Arizona, Colorado, and California. Then six bordering states, Nevada, Utah, Wyoming, Nebraska, Kansas, and Oklahoma, would be freed and given to blacks and Indians (Japanese could live anywhere). These goals would be achieved by killing all white males over the age of sixteen and would begin with assaults against South Texas.

The plan's ideology derived from the Mexican-origin, Spanish-language anarchist newspaper *Regeneración*, which drew 40 percent of its subscribers from the Great Plains even though it was published in Los Angeles by Ricardo and Enrique Flores Magón. Both men were convicted of violating United States neutrality statutes, in part by inciting the Plan of San Diego. Raiding against the United States from Mexico intensified to the point of contributing to the war crisis between the two countries in the summer of 1916. Early in 1917, when President Woodrow Wilson learned from the intercepted Zimmermann Telegram of a German proposal to return to Mexico lands previously lost to the United States, a proposal similar to that of the Plan of San Diego, it played a role in Wilson's decision to declare war on Germany.

A combination of military and political actions by the United States and Mexico against plan insurgents on both sides of the border defused the movement in 1917. Such success, however, was little appreciated at the time, and the legacy of the Plan of San Diego embittered United States–Mexico relations for seventy years.

James A. Sandos
University of Redlands

Harris, Charles III, and Louis Sadler. "The Plan of San Diego and the Mexican War Crisis of 1916: A Re-Examination." *Hispanic American Historical Review* 57 (1978):

381–408. Sandos, James A. *Rebellion in the Borderlands: Anarchism and the Plan of San Diego, 1904–1923*. Norman: University of Oklahoma Press, 1992.

RANCHING HERITAGE

The origins of ranching in the Great Plains can be traced to those Spanish settlers who first arrived in the Western Hemisphere. Beginning as early as 1500, *vaqueros*, or Spanish cowboys, were engaged in raising cattle for commercial purposes in the Caribbean Islands. During this early period the Spaniards' tradition of open-range herding and horse-mounted drovers was influenced by African ranching techniques. African slaves working as herders introduced the idea of herding the cattle off the range and into pens at the close of each day to keep the animals from straying off the ranch at night. The Africans also contributed several new words to the Spanish lexicon that became commonly associated with the ranching industry. For example, linguists claim that the word "dogie," a term used to describe a motherless calf trailing behind a herd of cattle, originated from the Bombara language of West Africa. Nevertheless, despite such African influences, the Spanish tradition of ranching remained dominant during this early colonial period.

Following in the wake of Hernán Cortés, Spaniards first brought cattle from the Caribbean Islands to the North American mainland when Gregorio Villalobos arrived in 1520 through the port of the Paunco River near present-day Tampico, Mexico. Scholars have substantially documented the early exploits of Spanish conquistadors against the Indigenous people of Mexico, but less known is the Natives' contempt for the Spaniards' cattle that ravaged their agricultural fields, decimating valuable subsistence crops. By 1529 the abundance of livestock in Spanish North America made it necessary to organize the first ranching association, or *mesta*. The mesta required that all ranchers register their brands with the authorities located in Mexico City. The cattle industry quickly became an integral part of the Mexican colonial economy, especially after the mid–sixteenth century, when Spanish silver mines opened in the northern reaches of Mexico. For those Spaniards living in the northern mining camps, beef became a significant part of their diet.

The Spanish tradition of ranching in the American West began when Don Juan de Oñate's men herded more than 1,000 head of cattle across to El Paso del Norte, present-day El Paso, Texas, in April 1598. Later, Spanish missions assembled large herds of cattle in Texas, and by the latter part of the eighteenth century, more than a million head of cattle grazed in the open grasslands between the Nueces and Rio Grande Rivers. It is estimated that in 1770 the mission La Bahia del Espiritu Santo, near Goliad, was running approximately 40,000 cattle between the Guadalupe and San Antonio Rivers.

The famous Texas longhorn breed of cattle evolved from these early Spanish herds. Throughout the 1760s and 1770s vaqueros drove Spanish cattle eastward along trails to markets located in New Orleans. During the American Revolution, Spanish cattle from Texas proved a valuable source of nourishment for Anglo-American settlers living in the frontier regions of present-day Kentucky.

Louisiana was the "middle ground" where Anglos first came into contact with the Hispanic tradition of cattle ranching. Herding cattle was already an established profession of backcountry pioneers in the frontier regions of the southern British colonies in North America. However, the cattle industry in the British colonies differed considerably from the Hispanic tradition of ranching. Anglo ranchers constructed pens that were used to corral their cattle many miles from their established farms. African or mulatto slaves and indentured servants were charged with the care of the animals. Using dogs rather than riding horses to herd the short-horned British cattle, the colonial herders acquired the moniker "cowboys." In their efforts to find fresh grazing land, the Anglo cattlemen, both owner and herder, often found themselves in the vanguard of westward migration.

Shortly after the turn of the nineteenth century, the backcountry drovers crossed the Mississippi River. As eastern ranchers moved farther west, the Anglo tradition of ranching began to merge with the well-established practices of the Spanish vaqueros. The newcomers to the American West learned and adopted the vaquero traditions of horsemanship and roping. Spanish influences on the Anglo cattle culture are clearly evident in the terminology commonly associated with the western cattle industry. Words such as "lariat," "lasso," "rodeo," "bronc," "corral," "sombrero," and "stampede" all have Spanish origins. While scholars credited Anglos with spreading the cattle industry northward to the Great Plains from Texas and Louisiana between 1865 and the 1880s, they also suggest that the American ranchers could not have accomplished this feat without first accepting the Spanish model of ranching. Between 1870 and the late 1880s every American cowboy who went up the Goodnight-Loving Trail to Denver, the Western Trail to Dodge City, and the Chisholm Trail to Abilene used the same techniques the Spanish vaqueros had introduced to North America nearly 300 years before the first railheads emerged on the Central Plains.

The Spaniards made other contributions to the ranching heritage of the Great Plains. In addition to Spanish cattle, the Spaniards brought horses with them to the New World. The Spanish horse, like the longhorn, descended from stock brought into Spain during the eighth and ninth centuries by the invading Moors of North Africa. After the Spanish moved into the Southwest, some of their horses escaped into the wild, multiplied, and formed feral herds that eventually populated the Plains. These wild horses became the American West's famous mustang. The mustang horse became one of the most important components of the Great Plains cattle industry. Both Spanish vaqueros and American cowboys praised the endurance and dependability that the mustangs demonstrated in the rigid daily routines associated with working cattle on the open range.

An aspect of the Hispanic ranching heritage that has received less scholarly attention than the cattle industry is the Spanish sheepherders. Sheepherders used the same basic principles as the cattlemen: they grazed and watered their sheep on the public domain and drove their animals along established trails to reach distant markets.

The Spaniards first introduced sheep into present-day California, Arizona, New Mexico, and Texas as part of the Spanish mission establishments. By 1779 the Hopis were grazing approximately 30,000 sheep, and one mission in California was reported to have 100,000 sheep in its herd. The main center of the Spanish sheep industry, however, was located in New Mexico. Throughout the late nineteenth century the sheep population increased dramatically in the New Mexico Territory. In 1850 there were at least 377,000 sheep raised in the region and by 1880 there were over 2 million sheep grazing the New Mexico countryside. By 1865 herders in New Mexico had moved their sheep north into the eastern ranges of Colorado Territory. During the 1880s Texas became an important center of the sheep industry—more than 8 million sheep grazed the Texas range by the middle of the decade. On a much smaller scale, sheep ranching also developed in Wyoming, Montana, and the Dakotas. In these regions there were no large sheep ranches, but many small commercial enterprises dotted the Northern Plains. Scholars estimate that between 1865 and 1900 approximately 15 million sheep were herded along eastern trails to railheads and feedlots located in Kansas, Nebraska, and Minnesota.

The ranching heritage of the Great Plains thus originated with the first Spanish settlers and continued to develop according to the trends established by the early Spanish vaqueros. The most significant contributions of Hispanic cattlemen involved the introduction of longhorn cattle to the North American Plains and the perfection of the techniques used in moving these rugged animals from one location to the next. The equestrian skills learned from the Hispanic vaqueros proved invaluable to the American cowboys who drove cattle up the trails from Texas through the Plains to railheads in Kansas and Nebraska. The Spanish sheep industry served as the cornerstone of an alternative model of ranching that became economically important to the western regions of the Central Plains. For these reasons, the Hispanic ranching culture was vital in establishing the foundation of a ranching tradition in the Great Plains.

See also AGRICULTURE: Cattle Ranching.

Kenneth W. Howell
Blinn College

Hine, Robert V., and John Mack Faragher. *The American West: A New Interpretive History*. New Haven CT: Yale University Press, 2000. Jordan, Terry G. *North American Cattle-Ranching Frontiers: Origins, Diffusion, and Differentiation.* Albuquerque: University of New Mexico Press, 1993. Webb, Walter P. *The Great Plains.* Boston: Ginn and Company, 1931.

REPATRIATION TO MEXICO

Twice in the twentieth century the United States recruited Mexican workers for seasonal employment on American farms, and twice large numbers of Mexicans were repatriated. The first government-approved recruitment of Mexican workers occurred on May 23, 1917, when the Department of Labor permitted Mexicans to enter the United States to work for farmers for up to one year. Many Mexicans had previously left the United States in the spring of 1917, in part because of rumors that they would be drafted into the army. To replace them, as well as to replace American residents who were drafted, Mexicans were legally admitted.

Mexicans were eager to emigrate. During the Mexican Revolution (1913–20), the seven west-central states of Mexico—Nuevo León, Tamaulipas, Zacatecas, San Luis Potosí, Guanajuato, Jalisco, and Michoacán—were a battleground between the central government in Mexico City and revolutionaries from Mexican border states, and the fighting led most haciendas to reduce their employment. Between May 1917 and June 1920 some 51,000 Mexicans entered the United States legally under these exemptions. Eighty percent were farmworkers, including sugar beet workers in the Great Plains; others worked on the railroads and in mines. Housing and meal arrangements under this program were left to the discretion of employers. As a result, some Mexican workers wound up owing money to farmers at the end of the season. Mexicans continued to migrate north after 1921, so that the number of Mexican-born U.S. residents rose rapidly in the 1920s. However, between 1929 and 1933 an estimated 400,000 Mexicans were returned—voluntarily and forcibly—to Mexico, meaning that more Mexicans were repatriated during these four years than had immigrated in the 1920s.

In 1942 farmers again won permission to recruit Mexican workers, and over the next twenty-two years, some 4.6 million Mexicans were admitted to the United States to do farmwork, under what was called the Bracero Program. At the insistence of Mexico, braceros were not allowed to be employed legally in Texas between 1942 and 1947 because of discrimination there against Mexicans. The Mexican government also prohibited its citizens from working in Wyoming after 1963. Both states eventually regained access to braceros.

There was a major repatriation of Mexicans during the Bracero Program. In June 1954 the Immigration and Naturalization Service launched "Operation Wetback" to ensure that Mexicans employed in the United States had work authorization. "Operation Wetback" began in California, moved to Texas, and then into the Midwest. In coordinated sweeps with state and local law enforcement authorities,

some 1.1 million persons were returned to Mexico in 1954, including at least 20,000 from Chicago, St. Louis, and Kansas City; many Mexicans living in the Midwest left for Mexico before they were apprehended. Apprehended Mexicans were returned to Mexico via Presidio, Texas, because the Mexican city across the border, Ojinaga, had rail connections to the interior of Mexico.

The Bracero Program and "Operation Wetback" are considered mistakes in U.S. immigration policy. The Bracero Program set Mexico-U.S. migration in motion, and "Operation Wetback" allowed the U.S. government to violate the rights of legal immigrants and American citizens in the name of regaining control of its borders.

Philip Martin
University of California–Davis

Galarza, Ernesto. *Merchants of Labor: The Mexican Bracero Story.* Charlotte NC: McNally and Loftin, 1964. Garcia, Juan Ramon. *Operation Wetback: The Mass Deportation of Mexican Undocumented Workers in 1954.* Westport CT: Greenwood Press, 1980. Martin, Philip. *Promises to Keep: Collective Bargaining in California Agriculture.* Ames: Iowa State University Press, 1996.

RICHARDSON, BILL (b. 1947)

Bill Richardson is one of the most prominent Hispanic politicians in the United States, serving in the U.S. House of Representatives for fourteen years as a New Mexico Democrat and, during the Clinton administration, as ambassador to the United Nations (1997–98) and secretary of energy. He was elected governor of New Mexico and took office January 1, 2003.

Richardson was born in Pasadena, California, on November 15, 1947, to an American father and a Mexican mother. He attended a Massachusetts boarding school and then Tufts University, graduating with a bachelor of arts degree in 1970, after which he was drafted as a pitcher by the Kansas City Athletics baseball team (he quit the sport due to an injury). Richardson arrived in Washington DC as a low-level aide in Richard Nixon's State Department, and he later worked on Capitol Hill. His ambition was to run for public office, and in 1978 he moved to New Mexico—a place where he had no roots but where his Hispanic background and Spanish-speaking abilities helped him with voters. In 1980 he challenged Republican congressman Manuel Lujan and ran a strong race in a losing effort. Two years later, reapportionment gave New Mexico an extra House seat, and Richardson was elected to it, representing the northern tier of the state.

As a member of Congress, Richardson won attention for negotiating hostage releases in Iraq, Kashmir, North Korea, and elsewhere. This led to his UN appointment (where he briefly became embroiled in the Monica Lewinsky scandal for holding a job open for her in late 1997). His promotion to energy secretary in 1998 came at a troubled time, right before explosive charges about Chinese espionage at nuclear labs erupted. Although Richardson essentially inherited the problem, he came un-

der sharp attack from Republicans and was frequently criticized for his role in the Wen Ho Lee affair. Soaring gas prices in 2000 also tarnished his reputation. He was talked about as a possible running mate for Al Gore in 2000, but these two controversies forced him from serious contention.

John J. Miller
Washington DC

RIVERA, TOMÁS (1935–1984)

Tomás Rivera is one of the most important writers who emerged from the Chicano movement of the 1960s. A member of a Mexican American migrant farmworker family, he was born in Crystal City, Texas, on December 22, 1935, and grew up in Texas, Iowa, Minnesota, Michigan, Wisconsin, Ohio, and North and South Dakota. His novel, short stories, and poetry portray the experiences of Mexican American families who traverse the Great Plains and Midwest in search of work as farm laborers. Notable about Rivera's work is his commitment to capturing the humanity of workers who must endure inhumane living, working, and traveling conditions. Although some of his narratives and poems are set specifically in Iowa, Minnesota, and Texas, most settings are unidentified, which seems an appropriately general way to represent the common experiences of migrant workers spread throughout the Great Plains, Midwest, and West.

In the novel . . . *y no se lo tragó la tierra* (. . . *And the Earth Did Not Devour Him,* 1971) and the short stories collected in *The Harvest* (1989), Rivera presents Mexican Americans' migratory experiences as haunted by racism and desperate struggles to survive. It is through these portrayals, though, that Rivera manages to present Mexican American migrants as uniquely strong people who refuse to let adversity break their search for better lives.

An important theme in Rivera's work is the devastating effect that migrants' constant mobility has on their sense of home and on their ability to maintain a sense of community among themselves. The poem "The Searchers" (1976) is a powerful meditation on how migrants' meandering precipitates a feeling of alienation from the land they travel over, sleep on, and work on.

Rivera also published several critical essays about Chicano literature, and two years before his death he published "The Great Plains as Refuge in Chicano Literature" (1982). In this essay he elaborates on the conflicting meanings that the Great Plains and Midwest have held for Mexican Americans since the late nineteenth century. He indicates that in the 1880s, Mexican laborers began streaming into the Great Plains and Midwest—which they dubbed simply *El Norte* (the North)—in search of economic opportunity as well as an escape from the particularly cruel treatment they received as laborers on ranches in Texas. In El Norte, Texas Mexicans and Mexican immigrants worked as cowhands, sheep shearers, and railroad hands. Ultimately, Rivera captures the contradictory meanings that the Great Plains and Midwest held for migrant workers when he points out that they were places where Mexicans encountered exploitation, respect, disillusionment, exhausting work, and the prospect of a new life, all at the same time.

Tomás Rivera died in Fontana, California, on May 16, 1984.

Phillip Serrato
Fullerton College

Lattin, Vernon E., Rolando Hinojosa, and Gary D. Keller, eds. *Tomás Rivera, 1935–1984: The Man and His Work.* Tempe AZ: Bilingual Review Press, 1988.

ROMERO, CASIMERO (1833–1912)

Little is known of the early life of Casimero Romero except that he was of Spanish lineage, born in 1833 in New Mexico, and that in his younger years he participated in the comanchero trade and perhaps was a cibolero as well. Evidently he prospered, because by the 1870s Romero, then living in Moro County, was a large-scale sheep rancher. His entrepreneurial eye turned eastward, however, and led him to the Texas Panhandle, where he contributed significantly to the nascent development of the Southern High Plains.

In November 1876 Romero trailed 3,000 head of sheep to the Canadian River valley to take advantage of unoccupied, rich, free grasslands. He built a capacious, sturdy adobe home and, except for a few staples, produced or took from the land everything needed to sustain a good life for his family and workers. Unwittingly, Romero may have inspired the first European Americans to migrate into the Texas Panhandle as residents. Other New Mexican pastores followed Romero and settled along the Canadian River, and the town of Tascosa grew around the Romero plaza.

By the middle 1880s, however, the pastores found themselves unable to compete with cattle ranchers who secured land titles which, backed by barbed wire, enabled them to control access to grass. The pastores had to find other livelihoods. While keeping his Tascosa homestead, Romero turned to a twelve-wagon freighting business connecting the far-flung ranchers and the merchants of Tascosa with their major supply point, Dodge City, Kansas, thereby contributing in a second way to Southern High Plains settlement.

Long-haul freighting declined as railroads crossed the Texas Panhandle and eliminated the need for Romero's service. Romero experimented with an irrigated fruit orchard for a time at Tascosa, but he soon returned to New Mexico. In 1893 he purchased a sheep ranch near present-day Bard and lived there until his death in 1912. He is buried at Endee, New Mexico.

Frederick W. Rathjen
West Texas A&M University

Carlson, Paul H. *Texas Wooleybacks: The Range Sheep and Goat Industry.* College Station: Texas A&M University Press, 1982. Romero, José Ynocencio. "Spanish Sheepmen on the Canadian at Old Tascosa." as told to Ernest R. Archambeau. *Panhandle-Plains Historical Review* 19 (1946): 45–72. Taylor, A. J. "New Mexican Pastores and Priests in the Texas Panhandle, 1876–1915." *Panhandle-Plains Historical Review* 56 (1984): 65–79.

SAN SABÁ MISSION AND PRESIDIO

Franciscan missionaries and Spanish soldiers established Mission Santa Cruz de San Sabá and Presidio de San Luis de las Amarillas on the San Saba River near present-day Menard, Texas, in 1757 to Christianize the eastern (Lipan) Apaches. Though failing to win Apache converts in significant numbers, the attempt brought the Spaniards into conflict with the Comanches and allied "northern tribes." Less than a year after its founding, on March 16, 1758, an estimated 2,000 Indians sacked and burned the log mission. The "protecting" presidio was powerless to intervene. The mission president, Fray Alonso Giraldo de Terreros, Fray José de Santiesteban, and at least six other mission occupants were slain. The mission was never rebuilt.

The presidio commander, Col. Diego Ortiz Parrilla, led a 600-man expedition to punish the attacking Indians in 1759 but was repulsed at the fortified Taovaya (Wichita) village on the Red River. Nineteen Spaniards died and many others were wounded. His failure, added to the mission attack, emphasized the Native American's enhanced warfare capabilities, with Spanish horses and French firearms. Participants in the mission attack included not only Comanches of the Texas High Plains but also members of the Caddoan confederacies of eastern Texas and western Louisiana and the intervening Wichita groups.

Ortiz Parrilla, going to Mexico to report, offered recommendations for dealing with the changes, but he was replaced as the commander. In his stead, Felipe de Rábago y Terán was sent to hold the post and maintain Spanish prestige. The presidio was temporarily abandoned in 1768 and closed for good in 1770. The San Sabá Mission episode signaled Spain's retreat from its northernmost Texas outpost and the reshaping of its entire northern defense system.

See also WAR: San Sabá Mission, Destruction of.

Robert S. Weddle
Bonham, Texas

Weddle, Robert S. *The San Sabá Mission: Spanish Pivot in Texas.* Austin: University of Texas Press, 1964.

SOUTH AMERICANS

Hispanics of South American origin, foreign born or of foreign stock, appear in census figures for the Great Plains from the late nineteenth century on, but their numbers take on significance only in the latter half of the twentieth century.

In general, the South American population in North America has never been substantial. Canadian censuses do not distinguish ethnic categories prior to 1941, and following that date numbers of South Americans are consistently below 1 percent of Canada's total population. From 1890 through 1930 South Americans accounted for an average of only 3.6 percent of the entire Hispanic population of the United States. Census figures range from a low of 4,733 in 1900 to a high of 33,623 in 1930. Of this population during those years, fewer than 1,000 ever settled in the Great Plains. As represented in the 1900 and 1930 census, South Americans on the Plains ranged from 279 to 853 individuals. However, while the numbers are few, the geographic pattern they formed represented a template for the future. Of the ten states and three provinces of the Great Plains, Texas and Colorado consistently accounted for half, or nearly half, of the South American population, with Kansas and Oklahoma trading off as the third most popular destination. The population of New Mexico, while significantly Hispanic, was predominantly Mexican and attracted relatively few South Americans from 1890 to 1930.

The presence of South Americans in the Great Plains increased markedly from 1960 to the present. For the United States as a whole, the number of South Americans increased from 89,000 to more than 1 million persons. For the Great Plains specifically, the relative share of the national total remained nearly constant at 5 to 6 percent, while numbers grew from just over 9,000 to nearly 53,000 persons. The most significant spatial aspect of this population growth is the continuation of the earlier pattern of settlement, but with an even greater concentration in Texas.

As in the earlier census, Texas and Colorado account for the majority of the South Americans in the Plains. From 1960 through 1990 they claimed from 63 percent to just over 85 percent of the Plains total. Again, New Mexico, with only 2 to 4 percent of the Plains total during these decades, is not a significant location for South Americans. A new variant that has emerged in this time frame is the sharp increase in the concentration of South Americans in Texas. In 1960 Texas, Colorado, and Oklahoma combined claimed 75 percent of the South Americans in the Great Plains. By 1990 Texas alone was home to more than 76 percent of the total, and Texas and Colorado together represented over 90 percent of the Plains total.

While actual numbers for some other Plains states increased—in Oklahoma from 1,098 to 2,477; in Nebraska from 307 to 783; in New Mexico from 439 to 1,357; and in South Dakota from 94 to 217—their relative share of Plains South Americans fell as the Texas population surged from 4,374 to 40,521.

What accounts for these geographic patterns is unclear, but statistics on education and occupation suggest some possible answers. Research on Hispanics in the United States by categories indicates that South Americans are much more likely to have a college degree or some education beyond high school than most other Hispanic groups. South Americans are also distinguished by their occupational profile: they are twice as likely to report employment in the managerial, professional, technical, administrative, and sales areas than other Hispanic groups. They are generally not associated with the service area categories of private household occupations or farming, or with other categories of general labor. The demographic data suggest that because Texas and Colorado represent expanding regional hubs of technology, education, and professional occupations, they offer the best prospects for South Americans in the Great Plains.

Roger P. Davis
University of Nebraska at Kearney

Aponte, Robert, and Marcelo E. Siles. "Latinos in the Heartland: The Browning of the Midwest." JSRI Research Report no. 5. East Lansing MI: Julian Samora Research Institute, Michigan State University, 1994. Moreno, Susan E. "U.S. Latinos and Higher Education." IUPLR Briefing Papers, no. 1: 6. Austin TX: Inter-University Program for Latino Research, 1999. Pinal, Jorge del, et al. "We the Americans . . . Hispanics." Washington DC: U.S. Department of Commerce, Economics and Statistics Division, Bureau of the Census, September 1993.

SPANIARDS

See EUROPEAN AMERICANS: Spaniards

SPANISH-COMANCHE TREATIES

In November 1785 several thousand western Comanches congregated at their favorite wintering spot at the Big Timbers of the Arkansas River to discuss important news: after years of tiring mediation, Juan Bautista de Anza, the governor of New Mexico, wanted to negotiate peace with the Kotsoteka, Yamparika, and Jupe Comanches. Although the eastern Comanche bands had already entered into an accord with the Texan Spanish in October, some western bands remained recalcitrant. The opposition centered on Toro Blanco, who was backed by the bands that supported themselves by raiding New Mexican horse ranches. To resolve the deadlock, the peace faction assassinated Toro Blanco and forced his followers to disperse.

In February 1786 Ecueracapa, a Kotsoteka chief representing the peace proponents, arrived in Santa Fe, where he hammered out the treaty stipulations with Governor Anza. The Spanish promised the Comanches free access to New Mexican markets and trade fairs, distribution of presents to friendly chiefs, and regulation of the fairs so that the shrewd New Mexican traders could not cheat their Native clients. In return, the Comanches agreed to stop raiding, to unite behind one principal chief who would negotiate with the Spanish, and to refrain from trading with foreigners, particularly Americans. There also would be a joint Comanche-Spanish war against the Lipan Apaches, whom both parties wanted to expunge from New Mexico's eastern border. The alliance was sealed in an elaborate ceremony at which Anza distributed lavish gifts, including presenting Ecueracapa with a Spanish flag and a saber. The Comanches returned a New Mexican captive and "buried the war."

This Comanche–New Mexican treaty is one of the major turning points in the history of the Southern Plains. It marked a profound change in Spain's Plains Indian policy by ushering in the abandonment of the traditional military approach in favor of a diplomatic-commercial option. This shift pacified the southwestern Plains for over a generation: from 1786 to 1821 accommodation and trade rather than violence defined Comanche–New Mexican relations. On the other hand, the treaty was a disaster to the Lipans, who were soon forced to retreat to the Sangre de Cristo Mountains by the powerful Comanche-Spanish alliance. The counterpart of the 1786 Comanche–New Mexican treaty, the 1785 Comanche-Texan accord, proved less successful. Comanche-Texas trade did increase after 1785, but the province's officials lacked the necessary funds to maintain a consistent Indian policy. As a result, Comanche raids in Texas continued throughout the Spanish era.

See also NATIVE AMERICANS: Comanches.

Pekka Hämäläinen
Texas A&M University

Kavanagh, Thomas W. *The Comanches: A History, 1706–1875.* Lincoln: University of Nebraska Press, 1999.

SPANISH-LANGUAGE PRESS

While not as abundant as in some other areas of the country, Spanish and bilingual newspapers have been published in the Great Plains since at least the late nineteenth century. In the tradition of Native journalism reaching back to the founding of the first press in Santa Fe, New Mexico, in 1834, Casimiro Barela, a settler and Hispanic political leader in southern Colorado, hired exiled journalist José Escobar to publish *El Progreso* in the western Plains town of Trinidad, Colorado, in 1891. After being named Mexican consul for Colorado in 1896, Barela recruited Escobar to edit *Las Dos Repúblicas*, a weekly published in Denver between 1896 and 1898. In addition to consular activities, the paper addressed the potential for trade, industry, commerce, and scientific exchange between Mexico and the United States. Escobar, a poet and writer, added literary criticism and in-depth editorials on the conditions faced by Mexican-origin peoples in the West. Barela moved his press back to Trinidad in 1898, where he continued to publish *El Progreso* until 1901. A second Spanish weekly, *El Anunciador de Trinidad*, was issued in 1904 and was discontinued only in the 1940s.

A sizable population of Mexican immigrant workers and their families emerged in Kansas City, Missouri, between 1900 and 1920. Two brothers, Manuel A. and Juan M. Urbina, began *El Cosmopolita* in 1914 to support *mutualista* (mutual aid) associations working in defense of Kansas City's Mexican residents. In 1915 Jack Danciger, a successful Kansas City entrepreneur with political and business ties to the Mexican community, bought the paper. Danciger and his associates used the paper to promote the sale of goods, merchandise, and beer on both sides of the border. By 1918 *El Cosmopolita* boasted a circulation of 9,000 subscribers, making it one of the largest Spanish-language newspapers in the country. A succession of owners changed *El Cosmopolita*'s editorial stance over the years. The Urbina brothers had supported insurgency in Mexico. When Danciger took over, he moderated this view by supporting Venustiano Carranza's rise to power, a move that was advantageous to Danciger's business interests across the border. In its last year of publication the paper took on a missionary bent when it became the mouthpiece of the *Instituto Cristiano Mexicano*, a Protestant group critical of the role of the Catholic Church in Mexico and among Mexican Americans.

Latino-oriented print media published in Great Plains communities today include *Dos Mundos* (Kansas City, Missouri), *Hola Colorado* and *La Voz* (Denver), *El Nacional* (Oklahoma City), and *Prensa Latina* (Grand Island, Nebraska).

A. Gabriel Meléndez
University of New Mexico

Kanellos, Nicolás. *Hispanic Periodicals in the United States, Origins to 1960.* Houston: Arte Público Press, 2000. Meléndez, A. Gabriel. *So All Is Not Lost: The Poetics of Print in Nuevomexicano Communities, 1834–1958.* Albuquerque: University of New Mexico Press, 1997. Smith, Michael, M. "The Mexican Immigrant Press beyond the Borderlands: The Case of *El Cosmopolita*." *Great Plains Quarterly* 10 (1990): 71–85.

SPANISH WATER LAW

See WATER: Spanish Water Law

TAFOYA, JOSÉ PIEDAD (c. 1830–?)

Sometimes called the "Prince of the Comancheros," José Piedad Tafoya was born in northern New Mexico around 1830. He was in the Great Plains as early as 1859 with his father, who was scouting for a survey party along the Texas–New Mexico border. Although Tafoya owned a large sheep ranch in San Miguel County, New Mexico Territory, by the early 1860s he was heavily involved in the *comanchero* trade on the Texas Llano Estacado—comancheros traded livestock, horses, and manufactured goods with Plains Indians, particularly the Comanches. During the Civil War, when the U.S. military and the Texas Rangers had little control over the Southern Plains, Tafoya operated a trading post in present-day Briscoe County, Texas, where he traded stolen Texas cattle and horses.

Comancheros began losing business during the 1870s Plains Indian Wars. Because of their knowledge of the Southern Plains and familiarity with the Plains Indians, the military enlisted or conscripted many comancheros as guides, interpreters, and scouts. In 1874 Col. Ranald S. Mackenzie allegedly forced Tafoya to serve as a scout in the campaigns against the Comanches. At the end of the Southern Plains Indian Wars, Tafoya and other former comancheros, such as Casimero Romero and Juan Trujillo, herded sheep in the Texas Panhandle. By the early 1880s, however, most had been forced out by large cattlemen, and Tafoya moved his wife and four children back to his ranch in New Mexico. In 1893 the U.S. Court of Claims subpoenaed Tafoya and several ex-comancheros as witnesses for Indian depredation cases. Based upon Tafoya's testimony, Charles Goodnight and other Texas ranchers were awarded $14,176. Tafoya probably spent his remaining years on the family ranch and died in obscurity sometime after 1893.

Mark R. Ellis
University of Nebraska at Kearney

Kenner, Charles Leroy. *A History of New Mexico–Plains Indian Relations.* Norman: University of Oklahoma Press, 1969. Rathjen, Frederick W. *The Texas Panhandle Frontier.* Austin: University of Texas Press, 1973.

TEJANOS

People of Mexican descent who live in Texas, whether native or foreign-born, are generally referred to as "Tejanos" by Spanish speakers. The designation has been used since at least the 1820s. The beginnings of Mexican-origin inhabitants of Texas may be traced to the early eighteenth century, when the Spanish established several permanent settlements in what eventually became the state of Texas. In 1821 Tejanos became citizens of Mexico, in 1836 members of the Republic of Texas, and in 1845, following annexation, citizens of the United States. In the late twentieth century, their numbers approximated five million.

Historically, mainstream society has treated Tejanos as an ethnic/racial group, and much of what is Tejano history consists of resistance (at times violent, but generally peaceful) against such forces as discrimination, racism, labor exploitation, and nativism. But Tejanos have also made a pronounced imprint on the state by helping build its economy, enriching the Texas literary corpus and its musical heritage, contributing to the cultural mosaic that is the Lone Star State, participating in politics (there were more than 2,000 elected Tejano officials in the 1990s), and fighting in every foreign war.

Today, most Tejanos are United States–born. But their adjustment to mainstream society runs the gamut from those who remain culturally "Mexican," to many who feel comfortable being bilingual and bicultural, to those who have become totally Americanized. Mexican Americans considering themselves Tejanos would readily concede their admiration for such aspects of Mexican heritage as the Spanish language, Mexican music, Mexican religious and cultural traditions, fiestas, and Mexican cuisine and folklore. Simultaneously, they embrace most of what is representative of Anglo-American life and culture.

Arnoldo De León
Angelo State University

Benavides, Adán Jr. "Tejano." In *New Handbook of Texas,* 6: 238–39. Austin: Texas State Historical Association, 1996. De León, Arnoldo. *Mexican Americans in Texas: A Brief History.* Wheeling IL: Harlan Davidson, Inc., 1999. Montejano, David. *Anglos and Mexicans in the Making of Texas, 1836–1896.* Austin: University of Texas Press, 1987.

VILLASUR, PEDRO DE

See EUROPEAN AMERICANS: Villasur, Pedro de

ZAMORA, BERNICE (b. 1938)

Chicana poet Bernice Zamora is best known for her collection of poems, *Restless Serpents.* First published in 1976, this collection established Zamora's reputation as an important poet. Zamora was born on January 20, 1938, in the small rural community of Aguilar, Colorado, where her family roots extend back several generations. Her parents, Victor and Marjorie Ortiz, eventually moved the family to Pueblo. The influence of the southern Colorado landscape and its rugged terrain of mountains and volcanoes would become a lasting feature in her work, as would the regional culture.

Zamora received her bachelor of arts degree from Southern Colorado University in 1970, her master of arts degree from Colorado State University in 1972, and her doctorate from Stanford University in 1986. In addition to her career as a poet, Zamora has taught classes in Chicano studies, ethnic studies, and literature at the University of California at Berkeley, University of San Francisco, Santa Clara University, and Stanford University. Zamora has also coedited anthologies of Chicano writing. Her collected poems in *Restless Serpents* were republished with a series of new poems under the title, *Releasing Serpents,* in 1994.

A variety of themes and influences culminate in Zamora's poetry: Chicano cultural traditions, gender discrimination, cultural suppression, labor exploitation, spiritual questions, identity conflict, and love. The regional setting of southern Colorado and, more generally, the American Southwest, figures prominently in her work as she explores such questions. Chicano writers often locate Aztlán, the homeland of the Aztecs, within the region of northern New Mexico and southern Colorado. Zamora integrates Aztec references and images in her writing as she explores themes and questions about cultural heritage and the effects of colonization in the contemporary world of the American Southwest.

Sharla Hutchison
University of Oklahoma

Bruce-Novoa, Juan. *Chicano Poetry: A Response to Chaos.* Austin: University of Texas Press, 1982. Sánchez, Marta Ester. *Contemporary Chicana Poetry: A Critical Approach to an Emerging Literature.* Berkeley: University of California Press, 1985.

Images and Icons

Mount Rushmore National Memorial, 1936

Place imagery is so much a part of everyday life that its importance and function are rarely questioned. Associations between Colorado and mountains, New Orleans and gumbo, and Vermont and quaint small towns seem at once accepted, simplistic, and trivial. Such linkages may indeed be accepted and simplistic, but their function is anything but trivial. Imagery exists, first of all, because almost any physical or cultural landscape is far too complicated to comprehend in its entirety. If we are to talk or think about such places, we are forced to generalize, to create sets of symbols that we believe embody regional essences. When applied to the Great Plains, this geographical "shorthand" includes items such as tornadoes, Frederic Remington paintings, and independent farmers.

Besides providing the generalizations necessary for ordinary conversation, place images also are strong influences on human decision making. It even can be argued that images are more important than facts in this regard. Although nearly everyone today sees the Great Plains as a rural and small-town society, for example, judgments vary on the worth of such ruralism. Some equate it with dullness, others with safety, self-reliance, and friendliness. The ratio between the two evaluations may prompt population redistributions that range between regional abandonment and congestion.

State and local agencies for development and tourism spend millions of dollars annually trying to build, modify, and counteract images for purposes of economic gain. Such efforts are hindered, though, by a scarcity of studies on what the stereotypes of various places actually are and on how the process of image creation works. The survey of Plains symbols offered here is thus more suggestive than authoritative. It draws mostly from thirty years of life in and observation of the region and stresses the views of the immigrant European American and European Canadian populations. Large-scale imagery is discussed first, and then symbols that are more geographically restricted.

Enduring Symbols

In her recent survey of Great Plains literature, Diane Quantic concluded that the most common regional symbols arise from the land itself. This finding is applicable to the entire body of Plains lore. Whether in the reports of early European visitors or in conversation with modern residents, one encounters frequent commentary on the vastness and isolation of this land, on its variable and violent weather, and on its prairie ecosystem. Part of this interest stems from an obvious contrast between the Plains environment and the landscapes of eastern Canada, the eastern United States, and western Europe. The sheer beauty, starkness, and grandeur of this physical world are even more important.

Vastness is perhaps the single most important image. Willa Cather caught the feeling well when she wrote of early Nebraska that it was "not a country at all, but the material of which countries are made." These words carry

From Highway 56, near Gladstone, New Mexico

an expectation for development that has necessarily faded over time, but the grand scale of things remains. "Wide-open spaces" is the term used most frequently to verbalize this mood; the motto "Big Sky Country" that appears on Montana license plates is a close second. Grandness of scale is a concept easy to feel but difficult to crystallize into specific icons. How do you symbolize space? The most realistic depictions, perhaps, are the two largest undissected sections of the region: the High Plains in western Kansas and eastern Colorado and the Llano Estacado (Staked Plains) in western Texas and eastern New Mexico. These can be harsh and lonely places, but Plains people routinely speak of them with pride. For enthusiasts they represent solitude, freedom, and peace, the ultimate experience of open country.

If one moves beyond synecdoche, vastness also is symbolized by particulars of sky and by vertical punctuations to the omnipresence of horizontal space. A view of white cumulus clouds floating across a dome of azure blue is one common idealization, that of a towering steel gray thunderhead another. Spectacular, multiple-hued sunsets resonate still more deeply. They are among the first memorable aspects of the Plains reported by newcomers to the region and one of the sights missed most often by former residents. The use of vertical accents to emphasize a pervasive horizontality is a real-world application of a common practice in art. If the seemingly limitless expanse of the Plains cannot be captured directly by an image, use a counterpoint. The prime examples are grain elevators, windmills, and telephone poles. Elevators and windmills usually are shown standing alone and achieve their power from this starkness. Telephone poles, in contrast, typically are portrayed in groups along a road or railroad track. They convey a sense of space by directing one's eye to the vanishing point on the horizon.

The sky inevitably looms large in the land-

scape of any open environment. It has assumed an even more prominent role in the North American Plains because of its obvious associations with the region's highly variable, seemingly capricious, climate. Weather forecasts are given more air time on radio and television stations in the Plains than elsewhere on the continent, and with good reason. Nowhere else do strongly contrasting air masses have such potential for clashing with one another. Cold, dry polar air encounters no barrier to southward movement here except for, as the saying goes, barbed-wire fences. The same is true for dry tropical air from the American Southwest and for moister air masses from the Gulf of Mexico. Should any one of these three systems dominate for long, the product is drought, flood, or numbing cold. Should unlike masses clash, the results are some of the most vivid icons of Plains life: powerful winds, blizzards, hailstorms, thunderstorms, and, of course, tornadoes.

The role of weather icons has changed over the last century and a half. Winds that whistled through cracks in the house walls reminded many early settlers of the loneliness and harshness of their lives and broke the spirit of some. Hail was sometimes seen as the wrath of God, since it often would destroy promising crops during the peak of their summer growth. These traditional symbolic roles persist but have lessened in the face of a more diverse economy and a more sophisticated technology. Weather icons act today partly as humbling devices for residents, reminders that people do not control their entire destiny. They also are a source of self-esteem. Dakota bumper sticker messages that "−40° keeps out the riffraff" and calm Oklahoma tellings of bizarre tornado stories both imply pride in being able to cope with life in such an unpredictable environment.

Like the sky, the natural ecosystem of the Plains also has produced a set of enduring regional images. Unbroken tracts of bluestem grasses and imposing herds of buffalo and antelope were new experiences for European Americans and European Canadians during the nineteenth century and therefore celebrated. The persistence of these biological features as modern symbols is more complicated. It reflects, in part, the survival of significant areas of the natural grass cover in the Flint Hills of Kansas, in the Sandhills of Nebraska and Saskatchewan, and along the drier western edge of the entire region. The real staying power of these images, though, derives from nativeness, from their harmonious adaptation to the Plains climate. In this way they contrast with and inspire a generation of humans who have begun to see folly in their modern but unrooted lifestyles. Similar, perhaps lesser icons in this vein include cottonwood trees, coyotes, prairie dogs, pheasants, mockingbirds, and meadowlarks.

Early but Transitory Symbols

In contrast with their agreement on the importance of scale and weather to life on the Plains, nineteenth-century European Americans and European Canadians divided sharply along rural-urban lines in their assessments of economic potential. This division hinged on two powerful but opposed symbols: the desert and the garden. The garden idea appeared first when Americans in 1803 touted their newly purchased Louisiana Territory as a land of fertile soil and salubrious climate. This view was quickly overturned, though, by reports from a series of government explorers, each of whom was accustomed to well-watered landscapes. In the most widely circulated of these accounts, Edwin James wrote that the expedition of Major Stephen Long in 1820 had encountered a wasteland that extended 400 miles east of the Rocky Mountains and 500 miles north and south. It was a desolate place, he asserted, whose elevated surface was "barren desert."

Research has shown that belief in James's conception of a "Great American Desert" was strongest in the cities of the American Northeast, especially among people there who opposed westward expansion of the nation. Rural dwellers and those closer to the frontier held the Plains in a much higher regard. This localized optimism became the general American view just after the Civil War. Actual migration to Kansas and Nebraska began on a large scale, and railroad promoters and others eager to attract settlers wrote about the landscape with unbridled enthusiasm. The Plains were now a farmer's paradise, the future garden of the world. Such imagery was as exaggerated as that of the desert had been, of course, but it persisted in the United States until the agricultural depression of the 1920s and through the 1920s in Canada. Displays of cropland bounty prepared for various fairs and expositions served as contemporary icons for this perspective. The best surviving example is the Corn Palace in Mitchell, South Dakota.

Railroads join desert and garden as important but now largely forsaken symbols of the region. As street patterns still attest, steel tracks created most Plains towns. Railroads were the primary promoters of the region, the means by which most settlers arrived, and the economic lifeline that linked local farm products with eastern markets. Like all powerful corporations they aroused mixed feelings on the part of residents, but, in the decades before the age of highways, nothing rivaled their centrality to regional life. The names of the early ones became legendary: Canadian Northern, Canadian Pacific, Great Northern, Kansas Pacific, Northern Pacific, Santa Fe, Texas and Pacific, and Union Pacific.

Early and Persistent Symbols

Perhaps the greatest drought in the recorded history of the Plains began in 1888 and lasted almost continuously until 1900. This disaster, a perversion of the garden imagery, might have prompted a return to desert thinking. Such a course of action was precluded, though, by increasing belief in new, more "scientific" methods of farming. Instead, the combination of drought and technology led to a creative, hybrid symbolization for the agricultural economy. The land still was seen to hold potential riches, but now it would yield them sporadically and only after major inputs of human effort. For Canadians the idea came to be encapsulated by the phrase "next-year country"; Americans usually spoke of a "boom-and-bust" lifestyle.

Three other enduring sets of regional images also stem from early agricultural practices: the cowboy, the yeoman farmer, and a sense of colonialism. The first two of these differ from the symbols discussed previously in that they function on the American (but not the Canadian) national stage nearly as much as they do on the regional one. The Great Plains, in fact, has become a geographical "box" into which residents of the United States have ensconced particular aspects of their perceived national character. So boxed, yeoman wholesomeness, cowboy independence, and similar rural traits can coexist peacefully with contradictory and similarly boxed national images such as the technological power and ethnic diversity associated with eastern cities.

Since the earliest days of the nation, Americans have identified themselves closely with independent farmers who live virtuous lives. The idea was written about with enthusiasm by Thomas Jefferson, encoded into the land laws by the Homestead Act of 1862, and heavily promoted for the Plains as part of the general imagery of the garden. Plains people came to see themselves as the embodiment of yeoman ideals: industrious, honest, humble, and self-reliant citizens who acquired and maintained these values by working for themselves and by being in close contact with the earth. They were living what they understood to be the American dream and were proud of it. Disparities between myth and reality, including high rates of rural tenancy and an overwhelmingly commercial orientation of the farms, were ignored. The imagery was so powerful that residents of small towns and even larger cities adopted it as their own. In this way the symbol became one with the region as a whole. Today it commonly is encapsulated by the phrase "heartland of America" and by a host of rural icons, including red barns, windmills, shocks of wheat, combines, and old pickup trucks.

Plains people allowed themselves to see only one contradiction between yeoman values and reality. Railroads, grain-marketing facilities, and banks held obvious control over their supposedly self-sufficient lives. Residents generalized these forces into an image of a New York or Toronto businessman and delivered high rhetoric on the subject during every national

Abandoned town in western Kansas, a result of the 1890s drought

depression, drought, and glut of grain. The talk, in other words, was nearly continuous. Although weather certainly was not controlled by New Yorkers, and not all grain dealers were unscrupulous, having a scapegoat made Plains people feel better. It still does. Past iconography in this regard has focused on political efforts to limit monopolist power through socialistic reform. The principal symbols in Canada were the Social Credit and the Cooperative Commonwealth Federation Parties. In the United States they were the Populists and the Nonpartisan League. The New Democratic party in Canada and the conspiracy-seeking Posse Comitatus in the United States are more recent manifestations.

Cowboy imagery shares most of its basic values with yeomanry. It adds to these traits a dose of masculinity, of course, including ruggedness of character. This ruggedness supposedly comes from life on the edge of society, where nature is rawer than on a farmer's homestead. It has survived even as the nineteenth-century cowboy has evolved into the twentieth-century rancher. The invention of this virile and largely noble conception of cattle culture has been traced to the pen of Frederic Remington and his popular drawings for *Harper's Monthly Magazine* and *Harper's Weekly* between 1886 and the turn of the century. Its amazing durability as a national symbol is testimony to the values Americans place on vitality and independence. People in the Plains necessarily must share the cowboy icon with residents of the mountain West, but flatlanders feel that they have the controlling interest. Boots, hats, and longhorn steers are associated with Texas more than with any other state, and two Plains cities—Calgary and Cheyenne—host the biggest rodeos on the continent.

More Recent Symbols
The yeoman farmer and the cowboy together served as master symbols for the Great Plains from the beginnings of European American and European Canadian settlement until about 1960. A desire to maintain the self-conception of an independent, hard-working, and honest society was great enough to sustain this imagery through the challenges of major droughts in the 1890s and the 1930s, numerous periods of low prices, and steadily mounting evidence that market forces were far more international than local in scope. Plains residents even clung to the symbols for a while in the face of growing national fascination with gleaming new factories and cities. These old ideals continue as a part of regional identity, but they are faded and must confront a competing set of images.

The countersymbol to the noble yeoman farmer is the hick. On the Plains the transition from the former image to the latter has important roots in the photographs of rural failure made during the years of the Dust Bowl by Dorothea Lange and Arthur Rothstein. Wartime concerns kept this new interpretation of Plains life from capturing the public imagination for a decade or so, but then came the unprecedented rewards of continuing prosperity and modern technology. Urbanized Canada and the United States became synonymous with sprawling suburban houses, leisure time, health insurance, and television. Migration from farm to city increased rapidly, and a contrast between city and hinterland became evident. Rural areas, to urban eyes, now appeared as cultural backwaters; their formerly noble inhabitants looked dull and unsophisticated.

The view that the American Plains no longer was the progressive, vital heartland of the nation grew in the 1960s and 1970s. Outside writers saw the people as conservative and the towns as safe but dull. They labeled the region as a whole "flyover country," implying a culturally barren landscape that must be endured on travels from the modern cities on one coast to those on the other.

Few studies have explored how Plains residents have reacted to the new set of uncomplimentary images. Clearly, though, local people see and understand the implications of out-migration from their counties. They know the mindsets of the vacationers who pass through on their way to somewhere else. Given a choice of places to live in the 1970s, college students from North Dakota said they would opt for Minnesota over their home state. Those from Kansas selected Colorado. Such nonlocal patterns of preference are rare outside the Plains and suggest that regional pride may be weaker here than elsewhere. Some writers even make a case for a collective inferiority complex.

Student polling notwithstanding, it is obvious that pride is far from extinct on the Plains. Recent evidence includes a massive wave of moral outrage that broke across the region in the early 1990s over a seemingly innocent proposal by Frank and Deborah Popper of Rutgers University. These scholars noted the local population declines and suggested a planned approach to its management rather than laissez-faire. Instead of eliciting yawns, however, their vision of a publicly owned "buffalo commons" in the heart of the Plains hit a raw nerve. Local newspapers and speeches have been filled with rebuttals ever since. The Poppers, they say, have badly underestimated Plains grit. As for the phrase "buffalo commons," it has become iconographic: uttered often and always with venom.

Many of the most positive expressions of regional pride in recent decades have been tied to sport. An admiration of physical vigor, once tested by muscular jobs on farm and railroad, underlies this alliance. Professional teams in the region command good followings, but the core of loyalty is more local: high school and university teams in the United States and the junior leagues in Canada. The sport of choice varies across the states and provinces as a reflection of history, climate, and winning tradition. It is football in Nebraska, Oklahoma, and Texas; basketball in Kansas; hockey in the Dakotas and the Prairie Provinces; and rodeo along the western borderland. Nebraskans who wear red university sweatshirts can easily extend the positive feelings associated with Cornhusker football to themselves and to their state; the affection even may carry over to the Plains as a whole.

Evidence exists that Plains residents finally are beginning to see their land more on its own terms and less as a stage for acting out the expectations of others. One sign is a renewed interest taken in regional history. Detailed maps of the Chisholm, Oregon, Santa Fe, and other pioneer trails are in demand. County historical societies thrive, and visitors stream to restorations of nineteenth-century forts, cattle towns, sod houses, and the childhood homes of such place-oriented writers as Willa Cather, Wallace Stegner, and Laura Ingalls Wilder. These activities reflect more than a desire to connect with the past. In a manner similar to that adopted for tornado stories, they also celebrate a people's ability to survive and to prosper in a potentially dangerous environment.

The most direct evidence for a society becoming one with a place may be their acknowledgment and appreciation of an environmental aesthetic. This, too, is becoming more common for Plains people. When strangers are not around, they sometimes will talk about their love for the prairie and its big sky. They do so even though the Plains world lacks mountain ridges, seashores, and the other common cues for beauty. Their emotion is a complex response to the absence of things, to the power of space and solitude. With few material "things" to focus upon, egos begin to melt away. Some call the experience prairie Zen.

The Prairie Provinces
The isolation that is central to any discussion of the Great Plains is doubly applicable to its Canadian section. The Prairie Provinces are squeezed north and south between the border of the United States and the boreal forest; the high Rockies isolate them from Vancouver. More important historically, 1,300 miles of the agriculturally barren Canadian Shield separate Winnipeg from the industrial cities of southern Ontario. People in the Prairie Provinces feel that the national power brokers from Montreal, Toronto, and Ottawa discount their views and goals and see them as second-class citizens. Consequently, their identity has come to be symbolized largely through a series of individuals who have protested against the eastern hegemony.

Louis Riel, after more than a century of mixed evaluation, has emerged as the most important hero of the Prairie Provinces. Two rebellions carry his name, in 1869–70 and in 1885, both aimed at protecting the rights of local people (the Métis) against invaders from the East (Anglo-Canadians). Although government forces technically won both protests, the Métis gained recognition for their preexisting land claims, first in the Red River Valley of the North and then in Saskatchewan. Gabriel Dumont, Riel's military commander during the second rebellion, also has become increasingly admired by modern residents; the site of his defeat at Batoche, Saskatchewan, is visited frequently.

Following the period of major European Canadian settlement from the 1880s to World War I, protests against the eastern establishment began to emanate from all Prairie peoples, not just the Métis. Residents believed that they paid more in taxes to Ottawa than they got back in services. They favored trade reciprocity with the United States but could not prevail over the protectionist national policies of the industrialists in Toronto and Montreal. Such matters came to a symbolic head in 1919 with the Winnipeg General Strike. Demands for old-age pensions and unemployment relief voiced there served as the inspiration, some fifteen years later, for Canada's first socialist party, the Cooperative Commonwealth Federation (CCF).

Depression in the 1930s cemented the budding association between the Prairie Provinces and socialistic politics. An Alberta form, the Social Credit Party, was promoted by radio evangelist William Aberhart. The Saskatchewan equivalent was the CCF. Both won and kept control of their respective provincial governments. Longtime CCF leader T. C. "Tommy" Douglas gained a major national presence as well and sponsored the first public medical insurance plan in North America. CCF influence continues today under the label of the New Democratic Party.

The European Canadian settlement of the Prairie Provinces was promoted even heavier than was the equivalent process in the United States. Physical conditions were rather different, too, with a climate that allowed crop agriculture to exist all the way westward to the Rocky Mountain front (except for southern Alberta). This physical potential for farming gave rise to two enduring descriptive terms: the "Last Best West" and the "fertile belt." Symbolic credit for the successful colonization, however, has been accorded to a particular seed and a particular man. The seed is Red Fife wheat, a variety that matured ten to twenty days faster than did previous wheats and thus ensured reliable yields. The man is Clifford Sifton, a minister of the interior who boldly expanded the recruitment field for Prairie settlers from the United Kingdom alone to the United States, Germany, and eastern Europe. Sifton essentially created the current social and ethnic geography of the region, a rich mosaic that includes the Russian pacifists known as Doukhobors and a huge contingent of Ukrainians. This blend frightened British Canadians at the time, but it since has come to be a proud badge of Prairie regional identity, a Canadian "mosaic." More recent Prairie symbols relate mostly to the achievements of individuals. John Diefenbaker, known for patriotic rhetoric during his tenure as prime minister, is revered today primarily for being the first national leader to have true Prairie roots. Two heroes share the regional hockey glory. Gordie Howe, a former leader in career points for the National Hockey League, was born in Floral, Saskatchewan. Wayne Gretzky, the current career leader in points, achieved his fame with the Edmonton Oilers.

Although outsiders easily lump the Prairie Provinces together, their residents see clear, province-based images. People in Saskatchewan, the most rural of the three units, regularly endure the label of hick. Albertans also are separated out easily. Their grasslands south of Calgary provide a strong cowboy theme. Their oil fields are rich enough to prompt both an increasing devotion to conservative politics and an occasional characterization as "blue-eyed Arabs." The new Reform Party, with an agenda to cut social programs, is based in Calgary.

The Central and Northern Plains States

The imagery associated with the northern half of the American Plains differs only moderately from regionwide generalities. The most distinctive contrasts relate to a relative abundance of broken or hilly terrain. Another set stems from an unusual ethnic mix in the Dakotas. The influence of the rougher landscape is complex but begins with visual distinctiveness. The Flint Hills of Kansas are modest in size but still the most recognized physical division in the state. Nebraska's Sandhills, stretching more than 250 miles east and west, are even more spectacular, and nearly the entire terrain of the Dakotas west and south of the Missouri River varies between moderately dissected and an otherworldly maze of erosion known as the Badlands. True mountain clusters exist as well, several in central Montana and the dramatic Black Hills in western South Dakota.

Almost all these broken lands retain their native covers of grass or forest and are used as pasture for livestock. Stockman images thus are strong, with Wyoming often said to be more dependent on cattle than any other state. Rougher land also has added a growing image of recreation potential to several locations. People drive Nebraska 2 and Kansas 177 to explore the serenity of the Sandhills and the Flint Hills, respectively. They are awestruck by the national parks in both the North Dakota and the South Dakota Badlands, and they can pursue a wide diversity of leisure activities in the Black Hills. Mount Rushmore is a national icon. The regional recreation image also encompasses a series of major reservoirs on the upper Missouri River. Fort Peck Lake has dominated the Montana plains since the early 1940s. Downstream are the "Great Lakes of the Dakotas": Sakakawea, Oahe, Francis Case, and Lewis and Clark.

The symbolic designation of the western Dakotas and eastern Montana as an important part of America's "Indian Country" is still another terrain-related feature. The major Native peoples concentrated there (the Arikaras, Assiniboines, Chippewas, Crows, Gros Ventres, Hidatsas, Mandans, Northern Cheyennes, and especially the Lakotas [or Sioux]) were Plains dwellers at the onset of European American immigration. Their concentration in these rougher lands, though, was mainly a matter of coercion. Icons abound. The Little Bighorn Battlefield National Monument is on the Crow Reservation in Montana, and the grave of Sitting Bull is on the Standing Rock Reservation in North Dakota. The small settlement of Wounded Knee, South Dakota, is symbolic as the site both of a brutal massacre a century ago and of a major protest against federal Indian policy in 1973. Nearby, in the Black Hills, an immense and still unfinished statue of Crazy Horse also serves a dual symbolic role: for a growing racial tolerance in the nation and for an enduring Lakota claim to these mountains as a spiritual center.

Together, the presence of badlands topography, a strong ranching tradition, some 30,000 Native Americans, and mountain scenery in the Black Hills has given South Dakota a positive statewide image that is at least as much western as it is midwestern. This identity contrasts sharply with that of states to its north and south and is one that tourist officials play to regularly and with success. In a recent ranking of "favorite tourist destinations," for example, South Dakota was the only state in the Plains tier to escape the bottom grouping.

North Dakota's image is nearly as distinctive as that of its neighbor to the south but not nearly as marketable. Ethnicity is its focus, in particular, the influx a century ago of some 125,000 Norwegians and 117,000 Russians of German ancestry. Together, these peoples were the core of a foreign stock that constituted an astonishing 71 percent of the state population in 1910. The early Norwegians and German Russians were wary of one another but shared a deep respect for physical work, for farming as a way of life, and for religion. These traits have come to be central to the North Dakota image. The two peoples also were receptive to socialist politics as a means to counter the local influence of eastern capitalists. Their Nonpartisan League, which flourished from 1915 to 1921, has become a major source of state pride. It is honored today through its legacy of government-owned banks and grain elevators.

Nebraska and Kansas lack the ethnic and physical variety of the Dakotas. American settlers in both states came principally from the old Northwest Territory and became known for their close identity with the imagery of garden and yeoman. The special local strength of such belief may derive from timing. This central section of the Plains was occupied earlier than either the Dakotas or West Texas, before droughts and other problems had diminished enthusiasm. Belief also has been augmented by the fact that two of the most powerful writers on Plains agrarianism—Willa Cather and Mari Sandoz—came from Nebraska.

Beyond Cather's fictional characters of Ántonia Cuzak and Alexandra Bergson, the major symbol of pride and identification in the Nebraska Plains is the Sandhills, a magnificent ranching region that occupies most of the north-central portion of the state. The grass there is good, and the people are secure and self-confident. The region typifies pastoralism at its best. Nebraskans also derive satisfaction from their stewardship of the Platte Valley. Whether via the Union Pacific Railroad or Interstate 80, this was and is the most heavily trafficked pathway across the Plains. A list of individual Nebraskans of heroic status would include politicians William Jennings Bryan and George Norris, both champions of public interest legislation, and Tom Osborne, leader of the "Big Red" football dynasty.

The brand of agrarianism found in Kansas long had a puritanical flavor. This self-righteous spirit originated with the territorial victory of free-state forces over slavery ones (symbolized by activist John Brown) and evolved into similar crusades for prohibition (Carry Nation) and other progressive ideas. So long as the nation honored its small-town roots, Kansans felt good about themselves, and they joined their fellow Americans in making Dwight Eisenhower and editor William Allen White into icons of their period. Pride turned into defensiveness, however, when it became clear that most of the nation no longer admired rural virtue. Residents still rankle at every showing of the movie version of *The Wizard of Oz*, easily the most powerful image for the state. In it Kansas is a dull, black-and-white place, far different from the alluring world of Oz. Recent decades have brought more positive thinking back to the state. People tout the corridor of cities along the Kansas River from Manhattan to Kansas City for its blend of sophistication, friendliness, and relatively low cost of living. They show pride in rural roots by transplanting to suburban yards an old standby from the north-central counties: limestone fence posts.

The Southern Plains States

Americans regularly draw a distinction between the Central and Southern Plains at the Kansas-Oklahoma border. The assumption is that Kansans are descendants of a homogeneous immigration from Ohio, Indiana, and Illinois, whereas Oklahomans and Texans represent a mosaic of southerners, Native Americans, and Hispanics. Anyone who believes this and travels through the Panhandle region expecting to encounter a world limited to Baptist and Catholic churches, Native American settlements, and Garth Brooks songs will be disappointed. The local imagery is complicated.

The actual divide in western Oklahoma between settlers of midwestern ancestry and those from the South is near the east-west-running Canadian River. In Texas it is near the Prairie Dog Fork of the Red River even farther south. This pattern was initiated during a series of land rushes that opened most of Oklahoma Territory to European American occupation between 1889 and 1901. Midwesterners, who had lined up on the Kansas border, garnered control of half the acreage before they met the Texans coming north. Life in northwestern Oklahoma and the Texas Panhandle thus differs considerably from that depicted by the images dominant in the rest of their respective states. The limit of midwestern settlement corresponds with wheat as a dominant crop. The same line traditionally marked the southern limit of Republican politics. Amarillo, with its rail connections to Kansas City, and Lubbock, with its major cotton market, nicely symbolize the two orientations.

The older cultural imprint from population origins in the Southern Plains gradually has eroded in the face of more powerful, state-based associations. This is the force that, for outsiders, has repositioned the modern Plains divide at the Kansas-Oklahoma border. Simple examples are the license plates and the stylized tipi designs at roadside rest areas in Oklahoma; both proclaim the state to be Native America. The "Okie" image of Anglo-Oklahoma, drawn originally from the southeastern section of the state, is even more strongly established. This unflattering symbol of rural poverty is far different from that of a Kansas yeoman farmer.

Statewide imagery for Texas, without doubt the most powerful in the nation, emphasizes the perspective of European American settlers and their cattle. By overstating the role of the Plains in state history, this distortion flatters West Texans. Unfortunately, it also misrepresents the true Plains heritage. The contributions of early midwesterners and more recent Hispanics disappear. So do the irrigated cotton fields south of Lubbock and the large herds of sheep and goats kept alongside the cattle on the Edwards Plateau.

The role of cattle culture in the symbolism of the Southern Plains is difficult to overstate. The lawns of the capitol in Austin and Oklahoma City are both graced by statues of cowboys. The mascot of the University of Texas is a longhorn steer, and Oklahoma is home to separate halls of fame for rodeo and cowboys. On an individual level, the most famous Oklahoman remains cowboy humorist-philosopher Will Rogers. And J. Frank Dobie's collected stories of ranch life find a place on nearly every Texas bookshelf.

After cattle, the major images for the region come from the experiences of the Dust Bowl, the oil industry, and football. The Dust Bowl affected all the Great Plains, of course, but because devastation was the worst in the Panhandle area, the stories focus here. These narratives, mostly about hardships and abandonments, effectively ended popular associations between the Southern Plains and yeoman agriculture. The resultant perceptual void well could have been filled by emphasis on the increasingly elaborate irrigation systems of the time, but outsiders, at least, chose to acknowledge only ranching.

Oil and football play related symbolic roles. Their heroes, whether roustabouts, fullbacks, or wildcatters, are males known for physical stamina and courage, not intellectual prowess; they continue the stereotypical mind-set of the cowboy. Regional football attention at the university level focuses on Texas Tech in Lubbock. Oil imagery is concentrated in two locations: the Panhandle field between Amarillo and Kansas and the West Texas field that encompasses Midland and Odessa, Texas, and Hobbs, New Mexico.

Coda

Once established, regional images can take on lives of their own. Most travelers to the Great Plains will have heard about wheat in Saskatchewan or Anglo ranchers in Texas before they actually experience either of these places. With the images firmly in place, these visitors then will look for (if only subconsciously) and almost surely find evidence to support the stereotypes. Just as surely, they may ignore the presence of flax next to the wheat or of a Hispanic irrigation worker beside the rancher. Stereotypes, then, although necessary, can limit our ability to see the Great Plains afresh and for what it really is. We need to know the imagery better so as not to be limited by it.

See also FILM: *The Wizard of Oz* / LITERARY TRADITIONS: Cather, Willa; Sandoz, Mari / PHYSICAL ENVIRONMENT: Dust Bowl; Llano Estacado; Sandhills / POLITICS AND GOVERNMENT: Diefenbaker, John; Eisenhower, Dwight D. / PROTEST AND DISSENT: Nonpartisan League; Riel, Louis.

James R. Shortridge
University of Kansas

Allen, John L. "The Garden-Desert Continuum: Competing Views of the Great Plains in the Nineteenth Century." *Great Plains Quarterly* 5 (1985): 207–20. Avellanet, John R. "Landscape Symbols and Their Role in Establishing Sense of Place: A Case Study of Kansas." Master's thesis, University of Kansas, 1995. Averill, Thomas F. "Oz and Kansas Culture." *Kansas History: A Journal of the Central Plains* 12 (1989): 2–12. Bader, Robert S. *Hayseeds, Moralizers, and Methodists: The Twentieth-Century Image of Kansas.* Lawrence: University Press of Kansas, 1988. Broach, Elise L. "Angels, Architecture, and Erosion: The Dakota Badlands as Cultural Symbol." *North Dakota History* 59 (1992): 2–15. De Wit, Cary W. "Sense of Place on the Kansas High Plains." Master's thesis, University of Kansas, 1992. Emmons, David M. *Garden in the Grasslands: Boomer Literature of the Central Great Plains.* Lincoln: University of Nebraska Press, 1971. Everndell, Neil. "Beauty and Nothingness: Prairie as Failed Resource." *Landscape* 27 (1983): 1–8. Jordan, Terry G. "The Anglo-Texan Homeland." *Journal of Cultural Geography* 13 (1993): 75–86. Logan, Linda. "The Geographical Imagination of Frederic Remington: The Invention of the Cowboy West." *Journal of Historical Geography* 18 (1992): 75–90. Matthews, Anne. *Where the Buffalo Roam: The Storm over the Revolutionary Plan to Restore America's Great Plains.* New York: Grove Weidenfeld, 1992. McLaird, James D. "From Bib Overalls to Cowboy Boots: East River/West River Differences in South Dakota." *South Dakota History* 19 (1989): 455–91. McMurtry, Larry. *In a Narrow Grave: Essays on Texas.* New York: Simon and Schuster, 1968. Quantic, Diane D. *The Nature of the Place: A Study of Great Plains Fiction.* Lincoln: University of Nebraska Press, 1995. Rees, Ronald. *New and Naked Land: Making the Prairies Home.* Saskatoon: Western Producer Prairie Books, 1988. Shortridge, James R. *The Middle West: Its Meaning in American Culture.* Lawrence: University Press of Kansas, 1989. Stein, Howard F., and Robert F. Hill, eds. *The Culture of Oklahoma.* Norman: University of Oklahoma Press, 1993. Wallach, Bret. "Oklahoma: When the Jokes Wear Thin." *Focus* 42 (1992): 32–37. Wilkins, Wynona H. "The Idea of North Dakota." *North Dakota Quarterly* 39 (1971): 5–28.

BILLY THE KID

See LAW: Billy the Kid

BOOMERS

Boomers were settlers who worked for the opening to homesteading of the so-called Unassigned Lands located at the eastern margins of territory taken from the Creeks and Seminoles of Indian Territory after the Civil War.

The early survey of this tract of nearly two million acres in the heart of the future state of Oklahoma led to the plausible assumption that the land was intended for settlement by non-Indians and should be available for homesteading. The claim made in the *Chicago Tribune* in 1879 by Elias C. Boudinot, a prominent Cherokee employed as a railroad attorney, that the land was public domain subject to homesteading apparently led to immediate attempts by would-be homesteaders. Three groups that tried to enter were turned back by U.S. army guards on the northern border during that year. However, David L. Payne, after failing to receive an answer from the U.S. attorney in Kansas as to whether the Unassigned Lands were open to homesteaders, put the matter to a test by leading a group of twenty-one to the vicinity of present-day Oklahoma City. They were removed to Kansas, and Payne was imprisoned for a time. One of the editors of the Boomer newspaper, the *War Chief*, published over a period of years in several places in southern Kansas, was even jailed for rebellion against the United States.

Further efforts at colonization also resulted in eviction to Kansas and arrests. One of the men who joined Payne, W. A. McCurry, took a group claimed to number about 500 deep into the territory before being ejected, and then only after the army unit that discovered the colony had been reinforced. In some cases, women and children were included among the colonists. After Payne's death in 1884, one of his men, William L. Couch, became the main Boomer leader. The last recorded entry of Boomer colonists was in October 1885. By this time, it appeared that homesteading would soon become legal because of political action. An Englishman, Samuel Crocker, aided this effort by extensive lecturing and lobbying. There were probably unreported individual efforts at settlement in addition to the Boomer colonies, but those settlers would have been considered Sooners, and if they had been discovered, they would have been disqualified as homesteaders. When at noon on April 22, 1889, homesteading became legal

by presidential proclamation, the great land "run" was probably much larger because of Boomer efforts.

Payne County bears the name of the Boomer leader, and the words "Boomer" and "Sooner" in the pep yell "Boomer, Sooner, Oklahoma U," long used at the University of Oklahoma, are both proud labels and probably better known than "89er," a name given to those who made the big run.

See also FILM: *Cimarron.*

Leslie Hewes
University of Nebraska–Lincoln

Agnew, Brad. "Voices from the Land Run of 1889." *Chronicles of Oklahoma* 67 (1989): 4–39. Peery, Dan W. "Colonel Crocker and the Boomer Movement." *Chronicles of Oklahoma* 13 (1935): 273–96.

BOOT HILL

In the lore of the Old West, Boot Hill described a cemetery for ruffians with slow trigger fingers who "died with their boots on" or others who succumbed to violent deaths. This distinguished them from decent folk who were put to rest in "hallowed ground" after dying of natural causes. Boot Hill cemeteries can be found throughout the Great Plains and are depicted in gunfighter fiction.

In the modern Great Plains, entrepreneurs have used the Boot Hill concept to lure Old West aficionados to places that depict the mythical West. Tourists can visit Boot Hill graveyards at Dodge City and Hays, Kansas; Ogallala, Nebraska; and Deadwood, South Dakota. Although many places lay claim to the original Boot Hill, debate persists as to which was really the first. Typical tours at such sites include visits to the graves of the most noteworthy local villains, discussions of interesting headstones and other sepulchral monuments, stagecoach rides, and re-created mock gunfights. For example, visitors to the Boot Hill cemetery in Deadwood, South Dakota, can visit the graves of Wild Bill Hickok and Calamity Jane.

The image of Boot Hill has also been used

to peddle a variety of Old West items. Several B-Westerns have used the name in their titles, for example, Ray "Crash" Corrigan's *Boot Hill Bandits* (1942), the 1958 Charles Bronson flick *Showdown at Boot Hill*, and the 1969 spaghetti Western *Boot Hill*. Marketers have also produced Boot Hill western wear, Boot Hill chili sauce, and even Boot Hill motorcycles. Boot Hill remains an enduring icon of the Old West and of the Great Plains.

Michael A. Amundson
Northern Arizona University

BONNIE AND CLYDE

See LAW: Bonnie and Clyde

BREADBASKET OF NORTH AMERICA

For most of its history, the word "breadbasket" was tied to the *consumption* of food, referring since the early 1700s to one's stomach or belly. Not until after World War II did the word's slang usage switch to the *production* side of the food story. Nonetheless, by the end of the twentieth century "breadbasket" was widely used to describe a significant grain-growing region, with the Great Plains offering the prototype example for North America and indeed the world. The Plains "Breadbasket" was one of journalist Joel Garreau's Nine Nations of North America; travel books covering the Plains states commonly tout the unexpected beauty and excitement awaiting the tourist in "America's breadbasket"; and even a fantasy board game called Arduin includes a fictional region called the "Great Grass Plains," which is described as "truly the breadbasket of the country."

While the breadbasket label is relatively recent, the general idea is not. Indeed, the concept of a distant agricultural region providing grain to a food-deficient metropolis is as old as classical Greco-Roman civilization. The mass consumption of pillowy white wheat bread, however, was a modern development of the industrial era. Political-economic changes such as the repeal of Britain's Corn Laws, combined with new technologies such as the railroad, steamship, grain elevator, and combine, effectively opened the once-remote interior grasslands of North America to a global market in gluten-rich hard wheat. Consequently, early pessimism regarding the agricultural potential of the Plains gave way during the mid-1800s to new assessments made by regional boosters such as William Gilpin, the Pacific railroads, and government scientists such as Canada's John Macoun. By the 1870s, optimism about the potential Plains granary provided a powerful counterweight to the Great American Desert idea that had characterized some earlier reports. In fact, the old Desert image became a convenient straw man for the boosters, an excessively pessimistic stereotype against which the region's early agricultural successes shone bright.

Despite frequent calls for greater diversification, wheat was the preferred crop. Relatively cheap and easy to grow and readily

Boomers on Canadian River

transportable to distant markets, wheat offered quick returns and desperately needed cash flow to debt-strapped farmers. Wheat likewise fit the boosters' grand patriotic visions of Plains farmers literally feeding the world, not just with any food but with the staple grain that many Victorians believed provided the key to civilization. Moreover, the very qualities for which the region had long been denigrated, namely, its broad expanses of treeless grassland, were now celebrated as regional virtues, providing the ideal environment for large-scale, mechanized grain production.

By the early twentieth century, the Great Plains granary was widely celebrated across North America. In his 1901 novel *The Pit*, Frank Norris described "waveless tides" of grain springing from the western "wheat belt" and being funneled through Chicago on its way to the "mills and bakeshops of Europe," a "world-force" that was the "Nourisher of the Nations." In 1908 the Canadian government circulated a pamphlet simply titled *Canada: The Granary of the World*, a label echoed at the local scale as cities all across the Plains became the self-proclaimed "Grain Golden City" or the "Garden of the West."

The sharp decline in wheat prices after World War I, followed by the difficult Dust Bowl years of the "dirty thirties," brought an end to the boosters' rhetoric and renewed calls for economic diversification. The number of farms declined as the size of farms increased, and wheat became increasingly supplemented by maize, cotton, and oilseeds. Wheat remains king, however, both on the ground and in the region's psyche. During the 1990s, the winter-wheat belt, centered on Kansas, and the spring-wheat belt, centered on North Dakota and Saskatchewan, combined to produce more than 60 million metric tons per year, most of which was destined for overseas markets. Despite ongoing rural depopulation and the death of the old agrarian dream, the Plains remain a breadbasket, a continental granary feeding the world.

See also AGRICULTURE: Wheat.

Peter S. Morris
Santa Monica College

Morgan, Dan. *Merchants of Grain*. New York: Penguin, 1979. Owram, Doug. *Promise of Eden: The Canadian Expansionist Movement and the Idea of the West, 1856–1900*. Toronto: University of Toronto Press, 1980. Smith, Henry Nash. *Virgin Land: The American West as Symbol and Myth*. Cambridge: Harvard University Press, 1950.

BUFFALO CHIPS

Ruminant manure constituted an important factor in American settlement on the Plains, providing fuel for heat and cooking in the near total absence of wood or coal and serving as a medical specific for injuries and medical complaints ranging from the reattachment of severed members and snake bite to hiccups and sunburn. Travelers on the Plains, European Americans and Native Americans alike, erected cairns of buffalo chips to serve as landmarks. As a fuel, cow and buffalo chips offered the advantage of not throwing sparks into

bedding or clothing, which was especially important in military tents and tipis. One early settler reported, "Don't feel sorry for us cooking with cow chips. They had their advantages—didn't need to use pepper."

Where advantages did not exist, they were invented: a common nineteenth-century mock praise of the Plains celebrated the region as a paradise, "where the wind draws the water and the cows cut the wood." The principal disadvantage of "Plains oak," as it was commonly—and politely—called, was an aversion toward collecting the fuel. The problem is alluded to in the Mormon Trail song "Whoa! Ha! Buck and Jerry Boy." While commenting on an attractive traveler in another wagon, the reporter sings, "Look at her now with a pout on her lips / As daintily with her fingertips / She picks for the fire some buffalo chips." "The Soddy Rally Song" also refers to the problem and its solution with nineteenth-century delicacy: "We Soddies will remember when / No fuel could be found. / Those cows they must have wondered / Why we followed them around." European American women, accustomed to cooking over wood fires in stone and brick fireplaces and taking care that manure was not tracked into their kitchens, were particularly offended to find themselves hauling manure into their homes by the basketload to fuel cooking fires, of all things, in cast-iron stoves. A canon of cow chip desirability for fuel developed: chips from cows grazing on autumn plums and therefore full of hard, hot, and long-burning plum pits were particularly prized and reserved for nighttime and cold weather fires.

Roger L. Welsch
Dannebrog, Nebraska

Dary, David A. *The Buffalo Book*. Chicago: Swallow Press, 1974. Welsch, Roger L. *Sod Walls: The Story of the Nebraska Sod House*. Lincoln: J. & L. Lee Company, 1991. Welsch, Roger L. *A Treasury of Nebraska Pioneer Folklore*. Lincoln: University of Nebraska Press, 1966.

BUFFALO COMMONS

In 1987 Deborah and Frank Popper, New Jersey–based scholars, published an article on the history and environment of the Great Plains. They saw government homestead and railroad settlement policies as having promoted a settlement of the Plains that was far more dense than the resources of the area could support. Droughts of the 1890s and the Dust Bowl years of the 1930s had uprooted a high proportion of Plains residents, and subsequent farm consolidation and mechanization of agriculture led to reduced numbers of farmers and a decline in the small towns that relied on them. The Poppers noted that maintenance of the current population involved depletion of the waters and soils of the Plains and required subsidization of agriculture. They suggested a government-run environmental restoration project that would relocate inhabitants, replant the grasses, restock native animals, and make large sections of the Great Plains a "buffalo commons."

The buffalo commons proposal reinforced

the image of the area between the Missouri River and the Front Range of the Rockies as an "Empty Quarter" marked by lack of population; vast, dry, and treeless distances; and marginal economic enterprises. With the removal of people and the reintroduction of native fauna and flora, the Plains would revert to a primeval prairie, a new Eden attractive to romantic environmentalists.

The Popper proposal has met with intense criticism from many quarters. Principal criticism has focused on deprivatization, an increased governmental role, and failure of the proponents to understand the natural economic adjustments that allow Plains resources to be more efficiently utilized by fewer people. The proposals also ignore the noneconomic factors that hold Plains communities together, including churches, coffee shops, reading groups, and service clubs, as well as the residents' attachment to the region. While the solution of the federalized buffalo commons has been largely rejected, the ideas have been attempted on a small scale. The Houche Ranch in South Dakota and Ted Turner at his Spanish Peaks Ranch near Bozeman, Montana, among others, have attempted to re-create a free buffalo range.

Theodore B. Pedeliski
University of North Dakota

Popper, Deborah E., and Frank J. Popper. "Great Plains: From Dust to Dust." *Planning* 53 (1987): 12–18. Popper, Deborah E., Frank J. Popper, Paul Roebuck, Karen J. Debres, and Bret Wallach. "The Buffalo Commons Debate." *Focus* 43 (1993): 16–27.

CALAMITY JANE

See GENDER: Calamity Jane

CANADIAN MOSAIC

The Canadian Mosaic defines Canadian society as a multicultural collage rather than as a unicultural melting pot. It contrasts Canadian settlement and assimilation policies, particularly in the Great Plains, with those in the United States. Those differences are conveyed in the images of an American ethnic and cultural melting pot and a Canadian Mosaic.

The concept of a Canadian settlement mosaic developed slowly and in part as a reaction against the American frontier thesis advanced by Frederick Jackson Turner in 1891. Turner suggested, among other things, that the free homestead system created mixed communities in which people from many different national, ethnic, racial, and religious backgrounds were transformed into Americans. Canada, on the other hand, allowed block settlements of different religious or ethnic groups. The result was a slower and different process of assimilation.

It was not the intention of the Canadian government to create a polyglot society, but the presence of a large French Canadian population in Quebec, concentrations of people of other ethnic backgrounds elsewhere, and government policies during the last two decades of the nineteenth and the early years of the twentieth centuries to allow prospective settlers on the Prairies to settle in groups, or blocks, resulted in the cultural collage. Maps published by the Department of the Interior early in the twentieth century color-coded each township to show the ethnic or national background of the majority of the people living there. On these maps each township looked like a small tile in a large mosaic.

Government leaders expected immigrants to learn English and to accept British political institutions and values. Public schools were established and, particularly during and immediately after World War I, served as aggressive agents of assimilation. Travel writers, immigration promoters, educators, and social workers in the 1920s and 1930s adopted more selective policies. They gained an appreciation of ethnic foods, dances, songs, folkways, clothing, and special holidays. Increasingly, these came to be seen as distinctive ethnic characteristics worthy of celebration and preservation, provided the immigrants learned enough English to function effectively in Canadian society and became familiar with and accepted British parliamentary institutions of law and governance.

In the 1960s the Canadian federal government, in an effort to placate French Canadian aspirations, initiated measures to make the country more bilingual and bicultural. When federal money was provided to promote the French language and French Canadian culture, other ethnic groups demanded that they too share in this largess. The result was a new Canadian policy of multilingualism and multiculturalism.

The contrasting images of the Canadian Mosaic and the American melting pot identify but probably also exaggerate differences in the acculturation of immigrants into North American societies. A Canadian historian has suggested that assimilative processes are clearly evident on both sides of the border. Like the different ingredients in a stew, the various ethnic groups are being "cooked." The main difference seems to be the degree of nationalist heat applied and the speed with which distinctive cultural characteristics are softened. Certainly, the distinct tiles of an ethnic and cultural mosaic, as drawn in the old Canadian Department of the Interior atlases, no longer accurately portray Canadian Prairie society. The edges are becoming mushy in Canada, while many communities in the United States continue to be shaped and enriched by the diverse cultural traditions and treasures of their immigrant pioneers.

Ted D. Regehr
University of Saskatchewan and
University of Calgary

Gibbon, J. M. *Canadian Mosaic: The Making of a Northern Nation.* Toronto: McClelland and Stewart, 1938. Katz, Yossi, and John C. Lehr. *The Last Best West: Essays on the Historical Geography of the Canadian Prairies.* Jerusalem: Magnes Press, 1999. Royal Commission on Bilingualism and Biculturalism. *The Cultural Contributions of Other Ethnic Groups.* Ottawa: Government of Canada, 1970.

CARHENGE

Carhenge is a remarkable piece of outdoor sculpture in a field just north of Alliance, Nebraska. The piece is composed of thirty-eight cars, dating from the 1950s and 1960s, painted gray, with some upended and partly buried in the ground so that the arrangement of the cars is roughly similar to the arrangement of the stones in Stonehenge, the ancient monument in England.

Jim Reinders and other family members were inspired to create an automotive representation of Stonehenge on Reinders's farm during a family reunion in 1987. The sculpture generated some controversy, with neighbors calling for a junkyard fence to enclose what they perceived as an eyesore on the rural landscape. The conflict was resolved when the city council of Alliance granted a zoning variance, and the site became a popular tourist attraction. It is visited by about 80,000 people annually and is maintained by a nonprofit group, Friends of Carhenge. The ten-acre site is two and a half miles north of Alliance on U.S. Highway 385. The site has parking, shaded picnic tables, and paths for visitors to wander among the cars. Like Stonehenge, Carhenge is home to a number of ceremonies and solstice celebrations.

See also FOLKWAYS: Roadside Attractions.

Mary Ann Vinton
Creighton University

CODY, BUFFALO BILL (1846–1917)

Buffalo hunter, scout, soldier, and western showman, William F. Cody is one of the most widely recognizable figures to emerge from the nineteenth-century Great Plains. More popularly known as "Buffalo Bill," Cody was born on February 26, 1846, in Scott County, Iowa. The Cody family moved to the Great Plains in 1854, settling near Fort Leavenworth, Kansas Territory. When his father, Isaac, died in 1857, Cody left school to help support the family. He held a variety of jobs, including ox-team driver, express messenger (for the transportation firm of Russell, Majors, and Waddell), and Pony Express rider. During the early years of the Civil War he operated with an irregular Kansas-based militia unit, and in 1864 he enlisted as a private in the Seventh Kansas Volunteer Cavalry, seeing action in Missouri, Arkansas, Kansas, and Tennessee. While stationed in St. Louis he met and married Louisa Frederici; the couple had four children.

In the years after the Civil War, Cody ran a hotel, drove a stagecoach, and worked periodically as a scout and guide for the army. In 1867–68 Cody earned the nickname "Buffalo Bill" by supplying buffalo meat to the Kansas Pacific Railroad; he killed roughly 4,280 bison during his eight-month contract. From 1868 to 1872 Cody served as a civilian scout for the Fifth United States Cavalry. He fought in at least nineteen battles against Plains Indians and was awarded the Medal of Honor (though

Col. William F. Cody (Buffalo Bill)

in 1916 a congressional act removed his name and all other civilian winners from the rolls). In 1872 Gen. Philip Sheridan assigned Cody to guide a buffalo hunt for the Grand Duke Alexis of Russia. This highly publicized hunt, along with an 1869 serial story in the *New York Weekly* by dime novelist Ned Buntline (entitled "Buffalo Bill, the King of the Border Men"), made Cody a national hero and helped set the stage for his acting career. Cody made his first stage appearance in 1872, when he appeared in Buntline's *Scouts of the Prairie*. For the next decade Cody scouted for the army, guided hunting parties, and toured as an actor with various shows.

Cody launched his Wild West show on May 17, 1883, in Omaha, Nebraska. Buffalo Bill's Wild West show operated from 1883 to 1913, touring Europe and appearing at diverse American venues, including Madison Square Garden in New York City (1886) and the Chicago World's Fair (1893). In 1899 alone the show traveled more than 11,000 miles and gave 341 performances in 132 cities. Cody's outdoor extravaganza included romanticized reenactments of the Pony Express and the Battle of Summit Springs, horse races, roping demonstrations, gunfights, and target shooting. The cast of characters included Sitting Bull (the Hunkpapa Lakota leader), Annie Oakley ("Little Sure Shot"), and Buck Taylor ("King of the Cowboys"). Although Cody's show was a profitable business operation, he was a poor businessman, and by 1913 his show had failed. Heavily in debt, Cody toured as the "main attraction" for other Wild West shows until 1916.

Cody was both a real frontier hero who participated in the conquest of the American West and a western showman who promoted and perpetuated the "winning of the West" as a romantic venture. Buffalo Bill Cody died in Denver, Colorado, on January 10, 1917.

Mark R. Ellis
University of Nebraska at Kearney

Rosa, Joseph, and Robin May. *Buffalo Bill and His Wild West.* Lawrence: University Press of Kansas, 1989. Russell, Don. *The Lives and Legends of Buffalo Bill.* Norman: University of Oklahoma Press, 1960.

COLONY OF THE EAST

Despite a widespread image as an uninviting desert, the Great Plains was the subject of numerous agricultural "colonization" schemes, beginning in 1811 with Lord Selkirk's colony for displaced Scottish crofters at Assiniboia. Similar projects would continue throughout the nineteenth and early twentieth centuries, particularly after the Plains was claimed as public domain and then granted in sprawling checkerboard blocks to the various Pacific railroad companies. While the primary impetus behind these schemes was to mobilize the most substantial asset possessed by the two federal governments and the railroads—western land—many also promoted the cooperative group settlement of tightly knit ethnoreligious communities.

The predominant Plains-as-colony image, however, stands these forward-looking ideas of national and community development on their head. Rather than a vision of success, the colony metaphor is more often invoked in a story of regional failure. Declining grain prices during the deflationary 1870s and 1880s brought financial ruin to many rural families, just as agricultural settlement was expanding onto the Plains. Rather than abandon the agrarian frontier dream and its hopeful image of a bountiful garden rising amidst the Great American Desert, many on the Plains blamed their region's troubles on the moneyed interests of the East. Eastern banks, railroads, elevator companies, commodities traders, and others formed a "plutocracy" that siphoned off the lion's share of the farmers' hard earned wealth. Even north of the border, where Ontario was long viewed by western boosters as a necessary and welcome metropolitan partner, the East became an amorphous conspiracy whose greed and indifference retarded the growth of Canada's promising Northwest.

This overtly regionalist brand of colonialism peaked during the drought and depression years of the 1930s, after which the Sunbelt rise of the Pacific and Gulf Coasts made stories of an all-powerful eastern conspiracy difficult to support. Rather than truly disappear, though, the Plains-as-colony thesis was transformed. While not dismissing populist concerns with eastern money power, authors during the 1930s and 1940s such as Walter Prescott Webb, Joseph Kinsey Howard, and Bernard DeVoto increasingly looked to nature for the primary factor limiting economic and community development on the Plains. Many of the region's problems certainly could be traced to eastern greed, indifference, and ignorance, they argued, but there was no escaping the Plains' dry climate. Indeed, nature forced Plains residents to accept a devil's bargain of sorts: agricultural settlement in this arid and remote region required the tools provided by eastern industry to produce the crops and transport them to distant markets, which were themselves organized by eastern financial interests.

By century's end, the region's image had returned full circle. Rather than blame greedy eastern or coastal interests, observers such as Donald Worster and Frank and Deborah Popper concluded that the failures of the Plains' rural economies rested on a basic environmental miscalculation and a continent-wide obsession with economic growth at all costs, in which rural residents of the Plains are no less culpable than the metropolitan powers of the coasts. Consequently, federal farming assistance programs and groundwater-mining schemes simply postpone the inevitable retreat of farm communities from the arid Plains. The would-be agricultural colony, in the eyes of many, has become a desert once again.

Peter S. Morris
Santa Monica College

DeVoto, Bernard. "The West: A Plundered Province." *Harper's Monthly Magazine* (August 1934): 355–64. Owram, Doug. *Promise of Eden: The Canadian Expansionist Movement and the Idea of the West, 1856–1900.* Toronto: University of Toronto Press, 1980. Worster, Donald. *An Unsettled Country: Changing Landscapes of the American West.* Albuquerque: University of New Mexico Press, 1994.

CORN PALACE

The Corn Palace is located in Mitchell, South Dakota, in the James River Valley. Mitchell was first platted in 1879. In 1892 the town began a six-day festival at the height of harvest season. One key event during this festival included constructing a simple frame building, the exterior of which was decorated with the principal product of the region—corn. A more permanent structure, replacing a second corn palace, was erected and opened in time for the 1921 festival. Eventually, seating in the building expanded to hold more than 5,000 people. The festival continues today and is typically held during the last week of August and the first week of September.

The structure is built of reinforced concrete. The exterior and interior of the building are covered with corn, sometimes as many as 600,000 ears. In addition, 2,000 to 3,000 bushels of other grains such as flax, rye, wheat, oats, and millet as well as bromegrass, bluegrass, and straw are combined with the corn to depict a different theme each year. The design is usually by local artists and is built upon themes such as "South Dakota Birds," "Salute to Agriculture," and "Youth in Action." Separate shades of corn are used to add depth to the various scenes.

The palace itself has been and still is used for various events besides the annual corn festival. John Philip Sousa's band, Bob Hope, and Lawrence Welk are just a few of the famous acts to have performed there. The Corn Palace is also home to high school and college basketball games—the NBA rookie of the year for the 2000–2001 season, Mike Miller, played his high school games there.

Nicholas J. Aieta
Clarksville, Tennessee

Reese, M. Lisle. *South Dakota: A Guide to the State.* New York: Hastings House, 1952.

COWBOY CULTURE

Today, the culture of America's favorite icon—the cowboy—is known around the world. Other callings that helped shape the West, like lumberjacking, farming, railroading, and hard rock mining, were equally as arduous and often as dangerous, but they pale in comparison to the compelling image of the cowboy. The infatuation with all aspects of cowboy life certainly refutes a statement made by Charles Moreau Harger, who wrote in *Scribner's Magazine* in 1892: "The cow-boy, with his white, wide-trimmed hat, his long leather cattle whip, his lariat, and his clanking spur is a thing of the past." Despite Harger's prediction, cowboy culture continues to have an impact on mainstream culture. Few other western themes have spawned such a rich vocabulary, created such distinctive clothing, or inspired unique genres of literature, poetry, music, and dance.

Cowboys came from many different backgrounds and traditions. Some young cowboys grew up around cattle on western ranches, while others had run away from home or crossed the ocean in search of work and a new life. African American, Native American, Hispanic, and even English and Scottish cowboys worked side by side with native-born white cowboys on Plains ranches and cattle drives. The many faces of the cowboy reflect a more colorful, authentic story of the West than the homogenized image created by novels and movies.

Philip Ashton Rollins, who gave the world its first professional look at cowboy life in his 1922 book, *The Cowboy: An Unconventional History of Civilization on the Old-Time Cattle Range*, recognized the rich Hispanic tradition in cattle ranching by noting that American cowboys "obtained from Mexican sources all the tools of his trade, all technic of his craft, the very words by which he designated his utensils, the very animals with which he dealt." Words such as *cincha* (cinch), *chaparejos* (chaps), *catallerango* (wrangler), *reata* (lariat), *vaquero* (cowboy), and rodeo are Hispanic in origin.

For young cowboys and buckaroos, working cattle was not just a job but also a lifestyle, one that was lived in the freedom of the outdoors and, most of the time, on horseback. Though the seasonal nature of his work might require moving from ranch to ranch, the cowboy could always expect room and board plus his wages. Pay on most ranches ranged from $25 to $40 per month from the 1870s to the turn of the century. The quality of a ranch's bunkhouse and chuck wagon grub often determined how long a cowboy stayed on a particular spread.

Webster's Dictionary does not do justice to a cowboy's interpretation of "culture." For the frontier cowboy, culture meant his horse and saddle, his lariat cracking in the air, and the smell of burning hair and flesh as the red-hot branding iron met the hide of a calf. For a cowboy, culture is sleeping under a blanket of stars, tasting the dust on a long, hot trail drive, smelling thick, steaming coffee on a frosty morning. A cowboy's culture, both historically and in contemporary times, is defined by his tools and its trappings, from custom-made boots and hats to hand-tooled saddles and finely braided *reatas*. The popular appeal of these cowboy accoutrements, in America and abroad, symbolizes the magnetism of the cowboy and his hold on the nation's collective psyche.

By reputation, cowboys never walked if they could ride, so their saddle became their favorite utilitarian possession. Over the course of 150 years, the shape of the western stock saddle adjusted to the needs of the men who worked cattle from horseback. The classic American stock saddle of the 1850s through the 1870s evolved from saddles developed by the *vaqueros* of northern Mexico and California. The saddle had to be a comfortable and secure seat for riders who spent long hours on horseback. The development of a strong pommel, or "horn," and more secure rigging made the western saddle a working platform for roping cattle. Shape and decoration varied according to regional styles or to the amount of equipment to be attached. By 1900 the western stock saddle had evolved into a distinctive and practical piece of equipment that reflected the colorful ranching heritage of each region of the country.

As important to the cowboy as his saddle was his lariat. There were numerous styles and materials—linen, horsehair, women's hair, grass, and leather—but the fancy braided rawhide ropes made by the late Luis Ortega are considered the finest in the world. Ortega also made quirts, hackamores, and hobbles, and his collection of braided rawhide cowboy gear is now preserved at the National Cowboy Hall of Fame in Oklahoma City, Oklahoma.

Even the cowboy's clothing reflected his outdoor lifestyle and regional and cultural background. Freshly creased or crumpled, the cowboy hat is recognized around the world as a symbol of the American West. The Spanish influence was so pervasive in the West that mail-order catalogs as late as 1900 still referred to the hat of the "cow boy" as a *sombrero*.

Regional styles, the environment, and weather often dictated a cowboy's clothing. The type of brush or foliage a cowboy encountered in the course of his work, for example, determined the style of his chaps. By the 1890s commercial products like Stetson hats and Levi Strauss denim "overalls" were marketed specifically for the working cowboy. Eventually, the popularity of rodeo champions and Western movie stars transformed the utilitarian work clothing of cowboys into western fashion. Ten-gallon hats, embroidered shirts, and brightly colored boots are recognized worldwide as distinctly cowboy in origin.

Like hats, chaps, and kerchiefs, boots also had functional origins. Tall, snug-fitting boots with high heels had become the hallmark of Great Plains trail-drive cowboys by the 1870s. Boot makers such as "Big Daddy" Joe Justin set up shop in cow towns, hoping to get a share of the drovers' wages before they headed back to the range. Many of these cobblers drew on a German heritage and made alterations to the classic European riding boot based on suggestions from cowboys. By 1900 the bulky riding boot had transformed into the basic boot pattern recognized today. The twentieth century brought more changes in toe shape, decoration, and materials, elevating the humble boot to the status of folk art and high fashion.

Two elements that have provided flashy elegance in cowboy culture are bits and spurs. Also born of utility and also of Spanish origin, bits and spurs have always been made and used by any culture that relied on the horse for transportation. Still collectors' items, those being made today by master artisans spare nothing to continue the tradition of flamboyant craftsmanship seen in the gleaming embossed silver and hand-tooled leather used to create these original trappings of the cowboy lifestyle.

Some aspects of cowboy life have changed since the nineteenth century. For example, cattle are more often rounded up by cowboys driving pickups than on horseback. But interest in cowboy history and culture is as strong and as diverse as the stories told by old ranch hands while sitting around a campfire singing trail songs or playing checkers or cards in the bunkhouse. Just experience any of the hundreds of cowboy songfests, poetry gatherings, chuck wagon cook-offs, ranch rodeos, collectible shows, and other western happenings, and you will find plenty of living cowboy culture.

See also FOLKWAYS: Cowboy Crafts / HISPANIC AMERICANS: Ranching Heritage / INDUSTRY: Justin, H. J., and Sons.

M. J. Van Deventer
National Cowboy and Western
Heritage Museum

Beard, Casey. *Tools of the Cowboy Trade.* Salt Lake City: Gibbs-Smith Publishers, 1997. Martin, Ned and Jody. *Bit and Spur Makers in the Vaquero Tradition.* Nicasio CA: Hawk Hill Press, 1997. Slatta, Richard W. *The Cowboy Encyclopedia.* Santa Barbara CA: ABC-CLIO, 1994.

CRAZY HORSE MEMORIAL

In the Black Hills, on land taken from the Lakota Sioux, stands a 600-foot mountain. This mountain, blasted away for more than fifty years to expose bare granite, is gradually beginning to represent Crazy Horse, an Oglala Sioux leader and warrior. Korczak Ziolkowski, the self-taught sculptor and artist (born in Boston on September 6, 1908) who started this project has died, but his family is working to keep his dream alive.

Ziolkowski's dream began in the late 1930s, when Henry Standing Bear, an Oglala chief, asked him to create a memorial to Native Americans. Standing Bear wrote, "My fellow chiefs and I would like the white man to know the red man has great heroes too." To honor Standing Bear's wish, Ziolkowski decided to erect a monument—ten times larger than Mount Rushmore—to Crazy Horse, who was born sometime around 1840 and led his people in many fights, resisting white encroachment and refusing to sign treaties. Crazy Horse helped defeat George Armstrong Custer's Seventh Cavalry at the Battle of the Little Bighorn. He was killed at Fort Robinson, Nebraska, in September 1877, reportedly while trying to resist arrest. Crazy Horse remains an important symbol of Native American resistance to European American hegemony.

Ziolkowski dedicated the first blast of the Crazy Horse Memorial in 1948. The monument was just one part of his extensive nonprofit humanitarian project intended to honor Native Americans; Ziolkowski also had intentions to build a museum, university, and medical training center. Only one of his goals ever reached completion, the Indian Museum of North America, which is located below the monument.

The monument can only be what Ziolkowski called a "lineal likeness," since Crazy Horse never allowed anyone to photograph or sketch him. The Crazy Horse Memorial will be the world's largest in-the-round sculpture, measuring 641 feet high and 563 feet long. Four thousand people will be able to stand on his outstretched arm, and below his hand, in three-foot-high letters, a message will read, "My lands are where my dead lie buried."

Although intended to honor Crazy Horse and Native Americans in general, many have questioned the appropriateness of blasting his image out of the sacred Black Hills. According to Virginia Driving Hawk Sneve, Lakotas would rather his image "be cloaked in faceless anonymity to forever symbolize their defeat and the need for inspired leaders once more." However, fifty years after the first blast, Crazy Horse's face was dedicated on June 3, 1998. Some still question whether or not the monument will ever be completed.

See also WAR: Crazy Horse.

Amy Scherer
Reno, Nevada

DeWall, Robb. KORCZAK: *Storyteller in Stone.* Crazy Horse SD: Korczak's Heritage, 1984. Fielder, Margaret. *Sioux Indian Leaders.* Seattle: Superior Publishing Company, 1975. Sneve, Virginia Driving Hawk. *They Led a Nation.* Sioux Falls SD: Brevet Press, 1975.

CUSTER, GEORGE ARMSTRONG
(1839–1876)

George Armstrong Custer, born in New Rumley, Ohio, in 1839, rose to fame as the "boy general" of the Civil War and achieved immortality by perishing with his entire command at the hands of Lakota and Cheyenne Indians on the Little Bighorn River in 1876. He graduated from West Point at the bottom of his class in 1861 but proved himself a fearless fighting soldier in the Civil War. By the age of twenty-three he was a brigadier general of volunteers in the cavalry corps. In a self-designed uniform sparkling with gold, his long blond hair flying out behind him, Custer was the stuff of legend; by the age of twenty-five he was commanding a division. When the war ended he reverted to his regular army rank of captain, and while he would never regain the lofty rank of major general, he was promoted to lieutenant colonel in the newly formed Seventh Cavalry in 1866. After a fruitless campaign against the Southern Plains tribes over the summer of 1867 that culminated in a court-martial and suspension from duty for eleven months, Custer established himself as an Indian fighter on November 27, 1868, with a controversial victory on the Washita River, Indian Territory, during which the Seventh Cavalry destroyed a Cheyenne village, killing 103 men, women, and children.

Following a stint of Reconstruction duty in Kentucky, Custer accompanied his regiment to Dakota Territory in 1873. He led it in the field that summer on the Yellowstone Expedition, designed to clear the way for the construction of the Northern Pacific Railroad through Sioux country, and the following year on an exploratory probe deep into the Black Hills that turned up gold in paying quantities and created intense pressure on lands ceded to the Lakotas by treaty in 1868. The fallout, the Sioux Expedition of 1876, had as its objective the confinement of "hostile" Lakotas on their reservation. Three military columns took the field, the Seventh riding with the Dakota Column under Gen. Alfred Terry. On June 22 Terry sent Custer ahead with 600 men of the Seventh Cavalry and a contingent of scouts. On the morning of June 25, in sight of an enormous Indian camp on the Little Bighorn River, Custer divided his regiment into four battalions and led the five companies under his direct command—211 men—to total annihilation.

Custer's Last Stand became an enduring myth, and Custer himself has represented everything from fearless self-sacrifice (the martyred hero) to reckless incompetence (the egocentric fool). In 1877 Custer's remains were reburied at West Point, where a monument marks his final resting place, though those still fascinated by his fabled Last Stand make their pilgrimage to the Little Bighorn Battlefield National Monument in southeastern Montana.

See also FILM: Custer Films / WAR: Little Bighorn, Battle of the.

Brian W. Dippie
University of Victoria

Dippie, Brian W. *Custer's Last Stand: The Anatomy of an American Myth.* Lincoln: University of Nebraska Press, 1994. Hutton, Paul Andrew, ed. *The Custer Reader.* Lincoln: University of Nebraska Press, 1992. Utley, Robert M. *Cavalier in Buckskin: George Armstrong Custer and the Western Military Frontier.* Norman: University of Oklahoma Press, 1988.

DEADWOOD, SOUTH DAKOTA

A great aura hangs over Deadwood, a small mining town turned gambling town on the western side of South Dakota in the Black Hills. Its two most famous characters, Wild Bill Hickok and Calamity Jane, spent little time in the town but left their legacy there, as both are buried next to each other in the Mount Moriah Cemetery overlooking the main part of Deadwood. Calamity Jane made this request because of her admiration for a

Deadwood City, Dakota Territory, 1876

man she hardly knew. The now-permanent partnership provides one of the main tourist attractions in Deadwood.

The name Deadwood resulted from the stands of timber that were prevalent in the area when the first miners arrived in response to reports of gold from Lieutenant Colonel George Armstrong Custer's party in 1874. A century later, despite being designated a national historic landmark in 1961, the town looked set for extinction.

Deadwood was saved by the statewide referendum of 1988, which legalized gaming. Crucial to the "yes" vote was the stipulation that a portion of the proceeds had to be used for historic preservation. As a result, November 1, 1989, marked the renaissance (or demise, in the eyes of gambling opponents) of Deadwood. Evidence of restoration is apparent everywhere, with brick-paved streets, simulated gas lighting, and mostly stone buildings that follow architectural traditions from the period 1880–1940. Trolley buses are a visual reminder of the vehicles that used to run on rails within the town.

Almost 100 casinos compete for the gambling dollars that keep the legacies of characters like Deadwood Dick, Poker Alice, Potato Creek Johnny, and Preacher Smith alive in this iconic survival of the Old West.

See also ASIAN AMERICANS: Deadwood Chinatown.

Roger P. Miller
Black Hills State University

Bennett, Estelline. *Old Deadwood Days.* New York: J. H. Sears, 1928. McClintock, John S. *Pioneer Days in the Black Hills,* edited by Edward L. Senn. Deadwood SD: J. S. McClintock, 1939. Watson, P. *Deadwood: The Golden Years.* Lincoln: University of Nebraska Press, 1981.

DODGE CITY, KANSAS

Untold millions have formed their views of the Old West from American movies and television series. The global popular culture spawned

by Hollywood now includes an unassailable belief that the region was uniquely murderous, and no locale holds more importance in this popular belief than frontier Dodge City, Kansas.

Today the name of the town that flourished as a Texas cattle market from 1876 to 1885 is widely employed as a cultural metaphor for homicide, anarchy, and depravity. Yet only fifteen adults died violently in Dodge during its cowboy years. In two livestock seasons and probably a third, no adults died violently, and only once did the annual number reach as high as five.

But before becoming a cattle town Dodge had served as a center for the buffalo-hide trade. During its first year its governmental organization was tied up in court. Lacking formal law enforcement, Dodge suffered sixteen to nineteen violent deaths. By mid-1873, however, its county had been organized and a sheriff elected. Not until 1878 is another adult homicide known to have occurred. By then lawmen headquartered there consisted of a deputy U.S. marshal, a sheriff, an undersheriff, as many deputy sheriffs as needed, a city marshal, an assistant marshal, as many policemen as needed, and two town constables. This formidable deployment and the enforcement of gun control largely explain the low body count.

Nevertheless, the anarchy of Dodge's first year lived on in the popular imagination, kept alive by dispatches to eastern newspapers by visitors. Dodge's own lawyer-journalist, Harry Gryden, also exploited its notoriety in such magazines as New York's *Police Gazette.* He proved instrumental in creating the media attention that made Wyatt Earp and Bat Masterson celebrities. During the "Dodge City War" (1883), news stories printed in the Chicago, New York, and other eastern papers reinforced Dodge's national image as the "Sodom of the West."

Gryden died in 1884, but Dodge's business community carried on in his spirit, hosting the first "genuine Spanish bullfight" held on

American soil—a stunt eliciting moral outrage and news coverage from around the nation. It also formed the Dodge City Cowboy Band, professional musicians masquerading as off-duty cowhands who played to enthusiastic audiences in St. Louis, Chicago, and Minneapolis. But with the end of the Texas cattle trade, Dodge's fame declined.

Popular writers occasionally renewed Dodge's name recognition in such mass-circulation journals as *Everybody's Magazine*, the *Saturday Evening Post*, and *Time*. But it was the publication of Stuart N. Lake's bestseller *Wyatt Earp: Frontier Marshal* (1931) that proved decisive in transforming Dodge into a modern tourist destination, a position it has retained to the present. Beginning with the movie *Dodge City* (1939), a number of films collaborated with this effort. More influential was the long-running (1955–75) television series *Gunsmoke*, which gave rise to the metaphoric Dodge among U.S. service personnel in Vietnam: to "get out of Dodge" meant to vacate a dangerous area.

The public perception of Dodge seems unchanged today. Probably of most continuing influence has been "Bloody Dodge City" (1992), an episode of the TV series *The Real West*. The program emphasized violence and ignores the old cattle town's paltry body count. A combination of national media attention and the town's energetic self-promotion ensures that the Dodge of myth and metaphor is here to stay.

Robert R. Dykstra
Worcester, Massachusetts

Christian, Shirley. "Where Wyatt Earp Stood Tall." *New York Times*, January 17, 1999. Dykstra, Robert R. *The Cattle Towns*. New York: Alfred A. Knopf, 1968. Dykstra, Robert R. "Imaginary Dodge City: A Political Statement." *Western Historical Quarterly* 31 (2000): 278–84.

EARP, WYATT (1848–1929)

Peace officer, gambler, stagecoach driver, buffalo hunter, and businessman, Wyatt Earp was a legend in his own time and has since been the subject of countless books, articles, and motion pictures. Portrayed as the prototypical frontier lawman, Earp is one of the most popular, heroic, and enduring images of the American West.

Wyatt Berry Stapp Earp was born on March 19, 1848, in Monmouth, Illinois, to Nicholas and Virginia Earp. A farmer, lawyer, and deputy sheriff, Nicholas Earp raised Wyatt to respect the law. Wyatt grew up in Pella, Iowa, then moved with his family to California in 1864. There he took a job in 1865 with the Banning Stage Line, driving the hazardous sixty miles between San Bernardino and Los Angeles. In 1868, at the age of twenty, Earp operated his own freighting business, delivering supplies for Union Pacific construction crews in Wyoming.

In November 1869 Earp replaced his father, who had moved the family back to Missouri the previous year, as constable of Lamar Township in Barton County. He married

Wyatt Earp

Urilla Sutherland at Lamar in 1870, but his wife died soon thereafter. Widowed at the age of twenty-two, Earp opted for a life of adventure, heading to the Great Plains, where he spent most of the time from 1871 to 1873 hunting buffalo. During the summer of 1873 Earp lived in the Kansas cattle towns, and in April 1875 he briefly served as a peace officer in Wichita. Contrary to the popular image of Earp as a prolific gunfighter, there is no documented case of him being involved in a gunfight before the infamous "showdown" at the OK Corral in Tombstone, Arizona. Over six feet tall, Earp typically subdued drunks and toughs with firm persuasion or a sharp crack to the back of the head with his revolver, a practice known as "buffaloing."

After leaving Wichita in April 1876, Earp's next stop was Dodge City, sometimes called the "Wickedest City in America." The practical duties and challenges facing lawmen in Dodge were similar to those in Wichita: disarming cowboys, keeping the revelry and vice confined to a designated part of town, handling routine street crime, and maintaining peace and order. Earp was praised regularly by the local press for his work on the Dodge City police force from 1876 to 1879.

Earp left Dodge City in the winter of 1879, settling with his brothers James, Virgil, and Morgan in Tombstone, Arizona Territory. There, Earp worked for Wells Fargo, held an interest in the Oriental Saloon, and served as Pima County deputy sheriff. He maintained a close friendship with dentist, gambler, and suspected highwayman John Henry "Doc" Holliday. On October 26, 1881, growing bad blood between the Earps and members of a group of local hard cases and rustlers, the Clanton-led "cowboy faction," erupted in the legendary confrontation outside Tombstone's OK Corral, leaving Billy Clanton and brothers Frank and Tom McLaury dead. Accounts suggest that Earp fired the fatal shot that killed Frank McLaury. Clanton sympathizers later took revenge on the Earps, wounding Virgil and killing Morgan in separate ambushes. In

turn, Wyatt, who was appointed U.S. deputy marshal after the attack on Virgil, is rumored to have killed Frank Stilwell, Morgan's suspected assassin.

If not for the gunfight at the OK Corral, Wyatt Earp might only have been a colorful historical footnote. The transformation of Earp into a folk hero began with the nationwide newspaper coverage of the gunfight and its aftermath and evolved through the writings of Bat Masterson and Earp biographer Stuart N. Lake, whose 1931 *Wyatt Earp: Frontier Marshal* is the source of many of the tall tales embellishing, idealizing, and romanticizing the historical Earp. Earp spent the years after Tombstone pursuing a variety of business ventures and died peacefully in Los Angeles, California, on January 13, 1929.

The historical Earp was a complex individual and certainly no angel. He was tough, pragmatic, and independent, reflecting his environment and times. As a Kansas peace officer, Earp was respected more than feared, making him an effective lawman. After the layers of legend and myth are peeled back, the Wyatt Earp of history remains a strong, compelling symbol of America's frontier heritage.

See also FILM: Wyatt Earp Films.

Derrick S. Ward
Ventura, California

Boyer, Glenn G. *I Married Wyatt Earp: The Recollections of Josephine Sarah Marcus Earp*. Stamford CT: Longmeadow Press, 1994. Lake, Stuart N. *Wyatt Earp: Frontier Marshal*. Boston: Houghton Mifflin Company, 1931.

EMPTINESS

Emptiness defines the Great Plains. The region typically is described by what is *missing*: no trees, no mountains, little water, few people. When travelers dread crossing the Plains, it is the endless space, the passage through "nothing" that they fear. The Plains landscape offers no comfortable niches, no categorical grip, no sense of context, not even convincing evidence of movement. Most North Americans, comfortable in the ornate context of the city, feel uneasy on the Plains. They lose their bearings, their sense of place, and the panoply of stimuli they usually depend upon for a sense of self. Some outsiders simply cannot endure this emptiness. They pay for a plane ticket and avoid the empty drive. In extreme cases, people have given up halfway across, abandoned their cars, and flown home from the nearest airport. Plains residents call the unhinging effect the emptiness can have on outsiders "Plains fever."

Contrary to the typical outsider's perspective, denizens of the Plains are very attached to emptiness. They too describe the advantages of Plains life in terms of absence: no crowds, traffic, city clutter, and obstructions to long views. Many things they cherish are possible only because of these absences—quiet, solitude, lack of encroachment, spectacular skyscapes, and especially "room to breathe." They gain a sense of freedom from the emptiness and relish the ability to drive with little obstruction and without restraint to speed.

Emptiness is the natural order of things to Plains natives, so much so that they complain of feeling "closed in," "claustrophobic," or "suffocated" in more heavily garnished places. The very landscapes that most Americans seek for aesthetic reasons can cause Plains dwellers to recoil. A few days in the mountains, a drive through the overdeveloped East, or a visit to the city can send them running back with relief to the open spaces. In effect, the emptiness makes the Great Plains "somewhere" to its residents as much as "nowhere" to outsiders.

Emptiness affects every facet of Plains life. Much time goes into dealing with empty space; long distances are an everyday reality, and substantial time behind the wheel is essential to social and economic life. The environment cannot be easily divided from daily life and experience, as it can in enclosed places. On the Plains it is not easy to forget that people and their doings are a tiny speck in a vast world. Emptiness thus helps shape the local cosmology and has become an essential part of residents' identity.

Because of their strong identification with emptiness, Plains dwellers take a defensive stance against the typical outsider's view and against urban ideas and culture in general. Urbanites rarely think of flat, empty space as having inherent value and often make policy decisions aimed at filling up that "wasted" space with "useful" things such as landfills, nuclear waste depositories, and wildlife preserves. Plains dwellers are not amused by these proposals and often react passionately to any suggestion that their cherished emptiness is wasted space.

Cary W. de Wit
University of Alaska–Fairbanks

Evernden, Neil. "Beauty and Nothingness: Prairie as Failed Resource." *Landscape* 27 (1983): 1–8. Gohlke, Frank. *Measure of Emptiness: Grain Elevators in the American Landscape.* Baltimore MD: Johns Hopkins University Press, 1992. Norris, Kathleen. *Dakota: A Spiritual Geography.* New York: Ticknor and Fields, 1993.

FERTILE BELT

The term *fertile belt* first appeared in Henry Youle Hind's *Narrative of the Canadian Red River Exploring Expedition of 1857 and of the Assinniboine and Saskatchewan Exploring Expedition of 1858* (1860), the account of his scientific expedition commissioned by the government of the Canadas to explore the possibilities of large-scale agricultural settlement in the Northwest. Hind used the term to refer to a region that he estimated to be 40 million acres in size, of excellent soil and rich pasture that would be ideal for agriculture, stock raising, and settlement, and that stretched in an arc from the American border at the Red River, northwest to the forks of the Saskatchewan River, and then along the North Saskatchewan River to the Rocky Mountains, where, in the foothills, it took a southward turn until it reached the border at 114° west. Hind highlighted and accentuated the fertile belt in his report in two ways: as a yellow band marked "Fertile Belt" on a map drawn by the British cartographer John Arrowsmith to ac-

company the British version of the report and by stating in block letters its importance for agricultural settlement: "IT IS A PHYSICAL REALITY OF THE HIGHEST IMPORTANCE TO THE INTERESTS OF BRITISH NORTH AMERICA THAT THIS CONTINUOUS BELT CAN BE SETTLED AND CULTIVATED FROM A FEW MILES WEST OF THE LAKE OF THE WOODS TO THE PASSES OF THE ROCKY MOUNTAINS, AND ANY LINE OF COMMUNICATION, WHETHER BY WAGON ROAD OR RAILROAD, PASSING THROUGH IT WILL EVENTUALLY ENJOY THE GREAT ADVANTAGE OF BEING FED BY AN AGRICULTURAL POPULATION FROM ONE EXTREMITY TO THE OTHER."

John Palliser, heading a British expedition into the same region that Hind traversed, also in 1857, also recognized the existence of an arc of fertile land and used the term *fertile belt* in his *Report* in 1863. It is possible that Palliser gave Hind the idea of calling the region the fertile belt but was himself cautious in using the term and played down the concept in his *Report*. As a result, his name has become associated with the more sterile land to the south—Palliser's Triangle—believed at the time to be the northern tip of the Great American Desert. Nevertheless, both Hind's and Palliser's reports established the very important generalization of two distinct regions in the Northwest: one containing good agricultural land—the fertile belt—and the other poor agricultural land—Palliser's Triangle. Later promoters of western settlement used such images as the "Rainbow of Rupert's Land," "ordained garden," and "Paradise of Fertility" in reference to Hind's and Palliser's fertile belt.

During the negotiations of the sale of Rupert's Land by the Hudson's Bay Company to the Canadian government in 1869–70, the term *fertile belt* came to be associated with the whole area from the Red River to the Rocky Mountains and from the North Saskatchewan clear down to the American border, including Palliser's Triangle. This was the area referred to in the deed of surrender by which the Hudson's Bay Company retained "one twentieth of the land of the fertile belt" as part of the agreement to sell Rupert's Land to Canada.

Throughout the 1870s, both visions of the fertile belt—as a delineated area north of Palliser's Triangle and as all the land south of the Saskatchewan River—held sway. When exploration and surveying began for a proposed railway through western Canada, reference was frequently made to the fertile belt. Sandford Fleming and George Grant used the term in *From Ocean to Ocean* (1872) to refer only to the Hind-Palliser area, recommending this area as the best route for the proposed railway to follow. The International Boundary Survey of 1872–75 that mapped out the area for homesteading also emphasized the Hind-Palliser concept of a fertile belt. In the words of the survey's chief geologist, C. M. Dawson, the "fertile belt must form the basis of settlement and utilization of the western plains," although Dawson emphasized as well the availability of good agricultural land to the south.

By 1881, however, when the Canadian Pacific Railway Company began construction of its line, Hind's and Palliser's concept of a clearly demarcated fertile belt had given way to one that assumed all the area south of the Arctic to be "fertile," therefore rendering as meaningless the term *fertile belt*. The botanist John Macoun of the Geological Survey of Canada party implied in his *Manitoba and the Great North-West* (1880) that the land previously designated as the arid land of Palliser's Triangle was no less fertile than the fertile belt. He estimated such fertile land as consisting of some 150 million acres—a striking contrast to Hind's original estimate of 40 million acres for his "fertile belt." By 1900 the term had died out, because it implied that the area through which the Canadian Pacific Railway ran was not fertile and therefore unsuitable for agricultural settlement.

See also PHYSICAL ENVIRONMENT: Palliser's Triangle.

R. Douglas Francis
University of Calgary

Hind, Henry Youle. *Narrative of the Canadian Red River Exploring Expedition of 1857 and of the Assinniboine and Saskatchewan Exploring Expedition of 1858.* 1860. Reprint, Edmonton: Hurtig Publishing, 1971. Owram, Doug. *Promise of Eden: The Canadian Expansionist Movement and the Idea of the West, 1856–1900.* Toronto: University of Toronto Press, 1980. Warkentin, John. "Steppe, Desert and Empire." In *Prairie Perspectives 2*, edited by Anthony Rasporich and Henry C. Klassen. Toronto: Holt, Rinehart, and Winston of Canada, 1973: 102–36.

FLATNESS

Only one-twentieth of the Great Plains's surface is flat, yet flatness has long been an important component of the region's image. Why this discordance? The explanation in part is in the region's name.

In 1776 Alexander Henry the Elder delineated cartographically the northern edge of the "Great Plaines," and in 1785 Peter Pond mapped out the northeastern and eastern edge of the "immense Pleins." Both fur traders made it clear that the names applied to a vast region extending westward to the Rocky Mountains and for an unspecified but considerable distance to the south. Whatever the spelling, *plains* became associated with extensive grasslands. That concept may have been received from earlier French traders, as Henry's French spelling suggests. In turn, perhaps the French had been influenced by Native Americans. Crees, for example, used the words "muskuty tuskee" (grassy ground), and, between the North and South Saskatchewan Rivers, Anthony Henday reported in 1754–55 leaving the "Muskuty Plains" that he was conscious of having been on for precisely seventy-eight days.

With the exception of the second quarter of the nineteenth century, when the name "Great American Desert" dominated, "Great Plains" remained the accepted name for the region. Yet, especially for those speaking English as their mother tongue, the term *plains* conveyed and still conveys the interlinked image of flatness, levelness, and openness. It is not strange, therefore, that many expressed surprise on first experiencing Great Plains landscapes. Lodisa Frizzell, an emigrant from Illinois, noted in 1852 that what she saw from the Platte River valley was "not nearly so level as I had supposed," and a London editor, William H. Dixon, observed in 1867 that the "grassy plains" of Kansas were "not level, as many persons think, but rolling uplands."

By the late nineteenth century, eminent scientists felt it necessary to correct the region-wide image. Richard Hinton, special agent in charge of irrigation for the United States Department of Agriculture, cautioned in 1890 that "it must not be imagined that . . . the word Plains imply a vast and perfectly level stretch of country." John Wesley Powell, arguably the best-known field scientist of his generation, observed in 1896 that the region was "in fact a group of elevated plateaus" and that "it would serve to harmonize the nomenclature if the name could be changed from plains to plateaus." But by 1914 the physiographer Nevin Fenneman had reluctantly concluded that "the name Great Plains is so firmly attached to the region by custom that it must be retained."

The false image of flatness is not, however, entirely an accident of nomenclature. There were, and remain, other factors. Pre–Civil War lobbyists for transcontinental railroads promoted the image. In a petition to Congress, George Wilkes argued in 1846 that "a smooth unbroken plain, leading gradually to the culmination of the [South] Pass," afforded a better natural route "for the construction of a railroad than is offered by the same extent of any portion of the globe." Once railroads had been built, however, companies attempted in their publicity to dispel the image of flat, monotonous landscapes. Yet for passengers, the routing of many railroads along the easily engineered divides between valleys reinforced this image. Above the hidden river valleys there were, according to John Lambert in 1854, and for the most part still are "few objects to arrest the eye," and the atmosphere is "so transparent, that it is only the curvature of the earth's surface that limits the view."

This most extensive and recurring of the region's landscape types gave rise to an ocean simile. The waving grass, persistent winds, scudding clouds, all-encompassing sky, long sweeping vistas, pervasive horizon, absence of upstanding features, and general feeling of emptiness created the impression of a land ocean. It was a simile that reinforced the image of flatness, as in the Abbé Emmanuel H. Domenechs's 1860 description of the static landscape of West Texas as "an ocean of dark stunted herbs in which not a single brush or bramble obstructed the view, where nothing marked a beginning or an end, and where all was mute and motionless." While the simile conveyed exaggerated images to people outside the region, the reality sometimes led to the insanity of its residents. Arguably, that condition was a consequence of confinement by an encircling horizon and scenic monot-

ony within it rather than to a geometrically flat world.

G. Malcolm Lewis
University of Sheffield, England

Hammond, Edwin H. *Classes of Land-Surface Form in the Forty-eight States, U.S.A. 1:5,000,000.* Map Supplement no. 4. *Annals of the Association of American Geographers* 54 (1964). Lewis, G. Malcolm. "The Great Plains Region and Its Image of Flatness." *Journal of the West* 6 (1967): 11–26. Lewis, G. Malcolm. "Indian Delimitations of Primary Biogeographic Regions." In *A Cultural Geography of North American Indians*, edited by Thomas E. Ross and Tyrel G. Moore. Boulder CO: Westview Press, 1987: 93–104.

FLYOVER COUNTRY

"Flyover country" is a popular epithet that dismisses the American interior as a region to be passed over or through on the way to someplace else. Thought to be a dominant preconception held by coastal urbanites, the term, or related imagery, is prevalent in contemporary Great Plains writing, where it is used to represent the neglect and ignorance of the region by outsiders. Flyover country captures the views of a coastal elite who see the Great Plains as a vast, boring, featureless expanse of land in between, a place to be passed over as quickly as possible on the way to the mountains or coasts.

Such sentiment has deep roots in American society. A defining characteristic of the Great Plains throughout history has been the mythic role it has played as a transit region from at least the time of the Oregon Trail in the 1840s. A high proportion of transit on the Plains has always moved through rather than to the region, and the Plains have long been considered an obstacle to travel. Flyover country can be interpreted as a jet-age manifestation of this characteristic and belief. While the flyover image may be the creation of outsiders, the term is more commonly used by Plains residents and sympathetic writers to characterize the negative preconceptions of the Plains and to defend regional interests.

David Robertson
University of Oklahoma

Shortridge, James R. "The Expectations of Others: Struggles toward a Sense of Place in the Northern Plains." In *Many Wests*, edited by David M. Wrobel and Michael C. Steiner. Lawrence: University Press of Kansas, 1997: 114–36.

FRIDAY NIGHT FOOTBALL

The old adage that "it's only a game" might apply to checkers or slow-pitch softball but not to Friday night high school football. As immortalized in H. G. Bissinger's *Friday Night Lights*, which follows Permian High School in Odessa, Texas, during the 1988 season, football is not just a game. Instead, football galvanized the community, held it together, and gave it a way to express itself. As exemplified by football, Odessa's values were not pretty. Racism and sexism afflicted the town, which inadequately funded a school system that exempted athletes from even minimal academic achievement, and football was a quasi-religious experience bordering on fanaticism: the 20,000-

seat stadium was a shrine that worshipers packed to capacity, star players were deities; and away games became pilgrimages.

But Texas is an exception, and even within the Lone Star State, West Texas's devotion to football is extreme. Few if any other states are so football crazy. In 1997 163,298 boys played the game there; the next closest was California, with fewer than 93,000, and no other state had more than 50,000. Indeed, during the last several decades interest in football has declined nationwide, falling behind both soccer and basketball in terms of participation among six- to seventeen-year-olds. The Plains states were not immune to the trend. In the mid-1970s as many as 4,000 people attended games at tiny Butner, Oklahoma, but in 1996 the school board abolished football without protest from players or fans. During the 1970s in Lincoln, Nebraska, Seacrest Field filled its 10,000-seat stadium for intense intracity rivalries, but in the mid-1990s no more than 4,000 fans attended such games.

Despite these and other similar examples of fading interest, football remains vibrant across the Plains, where high schools play the game in multiple formations. All Plains states have eleven-man teams, but two also play nine-man (North and South Dakota), five field eight-man squads (Oklahoma, Kansas, Nebraska, Montana, Colorado), and five play six-man football (Texas, Kansas, Nebraska, Montana, Colorado). Canadian schools field twelve-, nine-, and six-man teams.

Each variation comes with different rules, ranging from the size of the field to which players are eligible to catch a pass, as well as a distinct ambience. For instance, in Canadian six-man football the quarterback can directly advance the ball, while in American six-man he must first lateral or hand off before he can get the pigskin back and then advance it. Within the United States, during eleven-man games fans sit throughout the contest and are a considerable distance from the action. But most people watch six-man football standing up, and up close; even though the grandstands are tiny they usually remain half-empty, because fans prefer to mill along the "fences" (often nothing more substantial than a single strand of rope), which are only a few yards from the sidelines. During inclement weather, six-man fans may take refuge in their vehicles, which are parked facing the field and so close to it that they still provide a better view of the game than many people have at large, eleven-man stadiums. When a good play occurs, blaring horns replace cheers as a way of "voicing" approval.

In most Plains towns Friday night lights illuminate a praiseworthy community spirit. Football does indeed bind a community together, especially since the sport involves not only the players but also band members (who usually outnumber the football players), cheerleaders, and spirit squads, with the latter two groups often representing a female elite with a privileged status comparable to that of the players. Families and friends of all the participants mingle in the bleachers, along the sidelines, and at the concession stand, discussing the weather, the crops, business, children, marriages and funerals, their fears, and their dreams.

Yet even in the most admirable circumstances Friday night football hides a dark underside, because players pay a price while undertaking their community-building role. Beneath the glamour lurks untold hours of enervating practice and immense pain, both spiritual and physical. For the losers—young, aggressive, testosterone-laden teenagers who often believe their virility is at stake on the gridiron—defeat can be agonizing, perhaps as hurtful as the broken bones, torn ligaments, and concussions that routinely accompany high school football. Of course, even here the sport reflects Great Plains values, the fervent belief that pain and sacrifice and an intimate knowledge of both success and failure can build character in the best sense of the word, resulting in good citizens.

See also SPORTS AND RECREATION: Football, American; Football, Canadian; Football, Six-Man.

Peter Maslowski
John R. Wunder
University of Nebraska–Lincoln

Bissinger, H. G. *Friday Night Lights: A Town, a Team, and a Dream.* New York: HarperCollins, 1990.

FRONTIER VIOLENCE

When people think of nineteenth-century Great Plains towns such as Dodge City, Kansas, Ogallala, Nebraska, and Deadwood, South Dakota, they often conjure up images of frontier violence. One image that comes to mind is of Marshal Matt Dillon, with six-shooters drawn, facing an unruly cowboy on a dusty street in Dodge City. Someone else might imagine a pair of luckless horse thieves being dispatched by vigilantes in Ogallala. Still another image might be of the cowardly assassination of Wild Bill Hickok by Jack McCall in Deadwood's Saloon #10. Whatever the image, the overall picture is of a Great Plains frontier where violence and disorder ruled the day. No other region of the United States is given this distinction more than the Great Plains.

Why do people perceive the American Great Plains as violent? Nobody pictures the Canadian Plains in the same manner. Instead of gunfighters, highwaymen, and vigilantes, images of the North-West Mounted Police, with their connotations of law and order, define the Canadian Plains. The American Great Plains, however, were never as violent as popular culture assumes. Since the publication of Robert Dykstra's *The Cattle Towns* (1968), scholars have begun, although not without protest, to chip away at the myth of a violent Great Plains. Dodge City, as Dykstra points out, witnessed an average of only 1.5 homicides per year during its ten years as a cattle-trading center; it was hardly a town plagued by lethal violence. Ogallala, Nebraska, the "cowboy capital" of the Cornhusker State and often described as the "Gomorrah of the trail," recorded only six killings during its ten years (1875–84) as an end-of-the-trail cattle town.

The driving force behind the creation of a violent Great Plains has been the media: nineteenth-century newspapers, dime novels, and popular histories and twentieth-century television Westerns and Hollywood. Without the nineteenth-century media and dime novelists, the names of Billy the Kid, Wyatt Earp, Wild Bill Hickok, and Bat Masterson would not be the cultural icons they are today. In 1867 *Harper's New Monthly Magazine* published an article on James Butler Hickok, better known as Wild Bill, and his Great Plains exploits. This widely read article exaggerated Wild Bill's prowess with a gun and the number of men he had killed. He quickly became a frontier hero and a popular subject of dime novelists who pushed the number of Hickok killings higher with each new publication; by the time of his death in 1876 he was credited with more than 100 killings. Thereafter, Hickok became a frontier icon, and the Kansas towns where he lived and worked—Hays, Abilene, and Deadwood—became ingrained in popular culture as places where lethal violence ruled.

Perhaps the most lethal of the Great Plains towns, at least in popular culture, was Dodge City. Founded in 1872 and for more than ten years an end-of-the-trail cattle town, Dodge City became a favorite of eastern journalists. In 1878 the *National Police Gazette* published a story about a Dodge City shooting that introduced Wyatt Earp to the American public. In 1883 news reports about the "Dodge City War" (a nonlethal conflict) were picked up by the Associated Press, sparking nationwide commentary on western lawlessness and confirming in the public mind that Dodge City was in fact the "Sodom of the West." During the twentieth century books such as Stuart N. Lake's *Wyatt Earp: Frontier Marshal* (1931) and popular television Westerns such as *Gunsmoke* kept Dodge City at the forefront of frontier iconography.

To be fair, the Great Plains did experience its share of violence during the first few decades after the Civil War. The federal government fought wars against the Comanches and Kiowas on the Southern Plains and the Lakota Sioux and Cheyenne on the Northern Plains. Wild Bill Hickok, Bat Masterson, and Wyatt Earp patrolled the Kansas cow towns as armed lawmen. Gunmen, lawmen, and innocent bystanders were gunned down on the streets and in the saloons of Dodge City, Ogallala, and Deadwood. And vigilantes hanged and shot victims in every Great Plains state and territory. The problem is that such violent incidents were episodic rather than epidemic and should not be used to define an entire region. The nineteenth-century Plains were probably far less violent than the contemporary South or eastern urban centers such as New York City.

Despite the relatively undramatic historical reality of violence in the Great Plains the public will always believe the myth. Hollywood will continue to make movies about the wild and violent West, popular writers will still produce fictional accounts of gunfighters and lawmen, and untrained historians will continue to define the region through the eyes of Billy the Kid, Wild Bill Hickok, and Wyatt Earp.

Great Plains communities also keep the idea of a violent Great Plains alive and kicking through tourism. While driving across the Great Plains travelers can visit dozens of Boot Hill cemeteries, including those in Ogallala and Dodge City. Abilene, Kansas, offers the Wild Bill Rodeo. In Deadwood, South Dakota, tourists can compete in quick-draw contests at the annual Wild Bill Days or take a tour of Mount Moriah Cemetery, where Hickok is buried next to Calamity Jane. At Dodge City visitors can stay overnight at the Boot Hill Bed and Breakfast while enjoying the annual Dodge City Days. It's hard to blame writers, producers, and Great Plains towns for perpetuating the image of frontier violence. After all, Clint Eastwood will always sell more tickets at the box office as a mysterious gunslinger than as a Plains sodbuster. It's good entertainment, and the public wants their myths and heroes to be left alone.

See also CITIES AND TOWNS: Cattle Towns / LAW: North-West Mounted Police.

Mark R. Ellis
University of Nebraska at Kearney

Dykstra, Robert R. *The Cattle Towns.* New York: Alfred A. Knopf, 1968. Stansbery, Karyn. "The Law at the End of the Trail: Ogallala, 1873–1887." *Nebraska History* 79 (1998): 2–13. Udall, Stewart, Robert R. Dykstra, Michael A. Bellesiles, Paula Mitchell Marks, and Gregory Nobles. "How the West Got Wild: American Media and Frontier Violence." *Western Historical Quarterly* 31 (2000): 277–95.

GALE, DOROTHY

Although *The Wonderful Wizard of Oz* (1900) features Dorothy as the main character, she had no surname until the third Oz book, *Ozma of Oz* (1907). Most readers associate Gale with the cyclone that swept Dorothy to Oz in the first place, but the book in which she is named transports her to Oz via a maelstrom at sea: Dorothy and Uncle Henry are traveling to relatives in Australia so that he can rest from all the hard work he's done on his Kansas farm. But Dorothy Gale and a "gale" of wind make a logical association. Interestingly, when L. Frank Baum was editor of the *Aberdeen (Dakota Territory) Saturday Pioneer*, he published long and frequent accounts of Great Plains weather. In 1879 six Gales of Irving, Kansas, were killed in a nationally famous double tornado. The Kansas state song, "Home on the Range," widely adapted to many locations during the nineteenth century, starts its second verse with "Oh, give me the gale, of the Solomon vale." Perhaps Baum was simply echoing the surname of his mother-in-law, Maude Gage.

However Dorothy came by her last name, she is a famous Great Plains citizen and a true westerner. She is an agent for change: she kills two witches in Oz (one with a house, the other with water, just as many pioneers used those weapons to great effect on the Plains), and she substitutes benevolent rulers in their places. She is loyal to home and once in Oz determinedly sets her mind to returning to it. Nothing sways her resolve. She unites various people and creatures in democratic fashion, she's very practical, she's conscientious and clean (mopping up the "mess" of the melted Wicked Witch of the West), and she acts calmly, without fear, in spite of her age. Finally, she knows life on the Plains, explaining that her desire for a quick return home comes from her assumption that Aunt Em will think she's dead and that the poor woman cannot afford mourning clothes if the crops are no better than they were the year before.

In subsequent books, Baum tired of disasters as vehicles to transport Dorothy to Oz, and he left the Great Plains and Kansas in 1910, in *The Emerald City of Oz*, to take up permanent residence as part of Ozma's court. L. Frank Baum lasted only three years in the Great Plains; Dorothy Gale lasted ten. Together they gave the region one of its admirable citizens, someone with the heart, brains, and courage to thrive in a difficult environment.

See also LITERARY TRADITIONS: Baum, L. Frank.

Thomas Fox Averill
Washburn University

Averill, Thomas Fox. "Oz and Kansas Culture." *Kansas History* 12 (1989): 2–12. Greene, David L., and Dick Martin. *The Oz Scrapbook*. New York: Random House, 1977.

THE GARDEN

For most of the past two centuries, the concept of the Great Plains as a rich and productive garden has been a part of both popular and official iconography of the region. Sometimes sharing space in the minds of North Americans with the counterimage of the Plains as a desert, sometimes standing alone as the prevailing view of the Plains, the view of the garden has been one of the most enduring and compelling images of the western interior of North America between the Mississippi and the Rockies.

Prior to the nineteenth century, views of the land quality of the Plains were sketchy at best, dependent upon brief forays onto the Plains by British, French, and Spanish explorers and available only to those who had access to the records of exploration or their derivative entries in gazetteers, pamphlets, and government documents. These early impressions varied from the pessimistic view of the Plains as a desert contained within British exploratory accounts, through the more-or-less neutral Spanish perspective in which both garden and desert concepts were present, to a French impression that was imbued with notions of interior abundance. These various images were crystallized in the early nineteenth century by Thomas Jefferson, whose politics demanded ample agricultural land for the expansion of the agrarian republic and whose politically risky purchase of Louisiana Territory sought justification in the notion of a land of plenty. It was true that the Plains were treeless, wrote Jefferson, but only because the soil was too rich for the growth of forest trees. President Jefferson's garden was verified for the American public by Lewis and Clark, who described the Missouri River as watering one of the most fertile portions of the globe.

For most of the first two decades of the 1800s, both elite and folk images of the Plains were dominated by the Jeffersonian view. But as military and scientific explorers ventured into the Plains and began to encounter an environment visually and climatically at variance with their eastern woodlands experience, the counterimage of the Plains as desert began to increase its hold over the better-educated and urban segments of society. In maps and books published in the eastern cities of the United States after 1825, the idea of the Great American Desert was advanced. The desert concept was particularly attractive to those who opposed expansion, and for many of the remaining years before the Civil War the images of garden and desert coexisted in American perceptions of the interior. The desert image was favored by the eastern elite, while rural southerners and westerners readily accepted the garden image, which promised a future of agricultural abundance and fueled a steady western expansion.

It was not until after the Civil War that the Plains environment was tested by Americans and the validity of the garden or desert image confirmed by experience. As first the livestock industry and then farmers began to push into the Plains, and as the railroads began to advance across the region from the east, the garden image started to crowd out the desert idea. Part of the swelling garden image was based on the experience of bumper wheat crops in the Central Plains and increasing herds farther west; equally important was railroad and land agent promotional literature that encouraged prospective Plains dwellers to expect the best. And in spite of the droughts and grasshopper invasions of the 1870s and the blizzards of the 1880s, which, respectively, drove out many farmers and forced a spatial restructuring of the livestock industry, the garden image of the Plains persisted until the Dust Bowl of the 1930s. But even glimpses of the gaunt visages of Oklahomans and Kansans leaving the Plains for California did not destroy the garden concept of the Plains. Countering historian Walter Prescott Webb's pessimistic assessment of the Plains as desert, the farmers and government agents of the 1930s almost immediately recognized that the Dust Bowl was the result of human mistreatment of the Plains rather than a limitation in the Plains environment. The next time the rains failed, went both scientific and vernacular opinion, windbreaks planted crosswise of the westerly winds would prevent soil loss.

Well into the latter years of the twentieth century, both official and popular images of the Plains persisted in picturing the Plains as a region of abundance, not scarcity. Recent advocates of the Plains as a "buffalo commons," the decline in Plains rural population, and some diminishing of agricultural expectations notwithstanding, the view of the Plains as garden is still, if not as strong as in Jefferson's day, the enduring image of this region.

John L. Allen
University of Connecticut

Allen, John L. "The Garden-Desert Continuum: Competing Views of the Great Plains in the Nineteenth Century." *Great Plains Quarterly* 5 (1985): 207–20. Bowden, Martyn J. "The Great American Desert and the American Frontier, 1800–1882: Popular Images of the Plains." In *Anonymous Americans*, edited by Tamara K. Haraven. Englewood Cliffs NJ: Prentice-Hall, 1971: 48–79. Smith, Henry Nash. *Virgin Land: The American West in Symbol and Myth*. Cambridge: Harvard University Press, 1950.

GEOGRAPHIC CENTER OF THE UNITED STATES

A point in Smith County, Kansas, north of U.S. 36 on Kansas 281, one mile west of the junction of Kansas 281 and Kansas 191 near Lebanon, is the geographic center of the forty-eight contiguous states. (Once simply called the geographic center of the United States, its title was changed with the statehood of Alaska and Hawaii to specify the forty-eight contiguous states.) This point, halfway between San Francisco and Boston, saw the Pony Express gallop past. Later, the Chicago, Rhode Island, and Pacific Railroad chugged by. About forty-five miles south of the geographic center in southeast Osborne County, five miles east of Kansas 281, is the geodetic center of the North American continent (Luray in Russell County is the closest town). Other places in Kansas also note their "center" status. Kinsley, at the junction of U.S. 56 and U.S. 50, calls itself "Halfway and a Place to Stay," and signage proclaims New York City and San Francisco to each be 1,526 miles away.

Milton Eisenhower thought Kansas was at the heart, geographically and spiritually, of the nation. Kansas remains middle ground, as a mixture of town and country, agriculture and industry, conservative and progressive. William Least Heat-Moon claimed Kansas as archetypal, at the center of what it is, politically and socially, for good and evil, to be American.

Travelers to these centers find themselves in the Great Plains. They become aware of both the centrality of their position and, as the signs proclaim, the distance to places by which many Americans measure their lives. Like many Great Plains symbols, the geographical center is ambiguous: precisely pinpointed, celebrated as representative, but at a great distance, literally and figuratively, from the rest of the United States.

Thomas Fox Averill
Washburn University

Eisenhower, Milton. "The Strength of Kansas." In *What Kansas Means to Me: Twentieth-Century Writers on the Sunflower State*, edited by Thomas Fox Averill. Lawrence: University Press of Kansas, 1991: 105–21. Least Heat Moon, William. "The Great Kansas Passage." In *What Kansas Means to Me: Twentieth-Century Writers on the Sunflower State*, edited by Thomas Fox Averill. Lawrence: University Press of Kansas, 1991: 194–206.

GHOST TOWNS

See CITIES AND TOWNS: Ghost Towns

GRANT, CUTHBERT (1793–1854)

Cuthbert Grant is best known as the captain of the Plains Métis who clashed with the Selkirk settlers at the Seven Oaks Massacre (near present Winnipeg, Manitoba) on June 19, 1816. The Métis victory nearly destroyed the fledgling Red River Colony, which later became the province of Manitoba, and enshrined Grant as the founder of the Métis nation. This sense of Métis nationhood would play a role in the Red River Resistance of 1869–70 and the North-West Rebellion of 1885.

Cuthbert Grant was born in 1793 at Fort de la Rivière Tremblante (Saskatchewan) to Cuthbert Grant Sr., a North West Company (NWC) trader, and a Métis woman of French Cree ancestry. He was sent to Montreal to be educated. In 1810 he joined the NWC, returning to the Northwest in 1812 at a time when the Hudson's Bay Company (HBC) and the NWC were engaged in a fierce competition for fur-trade supremacy in British North America. The NWC tried to use the Métis in their struggles against the HBC by instilling in them the idea that they were a nation with rights to the territory. The NWC also appointed Grant as "Captain-General of all the Half-Breeds" with the intention that he and his Métis kinsmen would destroy the Red River Colony, which was backed by the HBC. The Métis, for their part, needed little encouragement after the colony's governor prohibited the export of pemmican from the district and forbade the hunting of buffalo near the settlement.

The Seven Oaks Massacre began when the colony's governor attempted to stop Grant and his men from carting pemmican out of the country. In this battle Governor Robert Semple and twenty-one of his men were killed but only one of the Métis. This violence, which contributed to the eventual merger of the two fur-trading companies in 1821, vastly increased Grant's prestige among the Métis. For this reason the new HBC tried to use Grant as a means of controlling the Métis and winning them over to the settlement. In 1824 they offered Grant a large land grant at White Horse Plains (part of the Red River Colony) with the hope that he would settle the Métis there and prevent them from trading with the Americans. In 1828 the company also appointed Grant as "Warden of the Plains," paid him a large salary, and allowed him to trade in furs if he would prevent his kinsmen from doing the same.

Grant remained a respected leader and chief of the Métis buffalo hunt until the 1840s, when a younger generation of Métis openly defied his authority to trade furs illegally to the Americans on the upper Missouri. No longer effective, Grant was let go by the HBC, and the rest of his life was fairly uneventful. He died on July 15, 1854, after falling from his horse.

See also NATIVE AMERICANS: Métis / WAR: Seven Oaks Massacre.

Gerhard J. Ens
University of Alberta

Dick, Lyle. "The Seven Oaks Incident and the Construction of a Historical Tradition, 1816 to 1970." *Journal of the Canadian Historical Association/Revue de la Société Historique du Canada*, n.s. 2 (1991): 91–114. MacLeod, Margaret, and W. L. Morton. *Cuthbert Grant of Grantown: Warden of the Plains of Red River*. Toronto: McClelland and Stewart, 1974.

GREAT AMERICAN DESERT

Edwin James, chronicler of Stephen Long's 1820 expedition, formed the image of the Great American Desert (the Plains as a region unfit for American settlement), and geographies published in New England from 1820 to 1835 perpetuated the myth. Elite New Englanders wanted to end westward expansion and its concomitants: new states, senators, and congressmen and thus a diminution of New England's political power. The wish was father to the Federalist myth of the Great American Desert in the New England mind. In the remainder of the East, beyond New England and its extensions, the desert, viewed as lying farther and farther west and increasingly narrow against the Rocky Mountain front from 1845 onward, was only one of a pool of myths about the Great Plains that included the pastoral region and the garden. During the middle third of the century, even among the elite in the South and the interior and especially on the frontier and on the eastern margins of the Great Plains, the desert notion did not exist. The Mormons were the exception: from 1855 to the present, the Great American Desert had become an invented tradition for a majority of their literate public. The Mormon crossing of the Great Plains, relatively easy and uneventful, was transformed by Mormon leaders in the pulpit into a neo-Mosaic traverse of their American Sinai, the Great American Desert east of the Rockies, which, among a number of traditions, proved the Mormons to be God's chosen people, the Latter-day Saints, and their leaders to be inspired by God.

In the Plains region, ignorance of the desert myth changed twenty years into the settlement process as boosters and writers for the railroads and state chambers of commerce published hundreds of pamphlets and books promoting the Plains. The pamphlet writers, many of whom had been educated in the Northeast during the 1840s and 1850s, found it easy to contend that the agricultural frontier now existed 100 miles or so into the Plains of Nebraska and Kansas, which had been labeled the Great American Desert during the writers' youth. The perceived agent of change in the Plains was increased rainfall, caused either by plowing the soil or by tree planting, or a corollary of Manifest Destiny, or a reward from a benevolent God. In the escalation of Plains promotion, the boosters referred to the "conquest" of the Great American Desert and challenged the prospective migrant to go west and further the change. The boosters, local county historians, and Plains newspaper editors of the period from 1870 to 1900 erased the memory of the land actually encountered by the pioneers.

After 1880 Plains pioneers, predominantly midwesterners who had encountered no Great American Desert in their texts in the 1850s and 1860s, conveniently adopted the eastern boosters' textbook desert in their reminiscences recorded for state historical societies and for publishers of county histories. They talked themselves into believing that they had either conquered or disproved the existence of the desert. In effect, they initiated the process of the reinvention of the tradition of the Great American Desert by claiming to have conquered it. The romantic Plains historians from 1885 to 1910 drew on these pioneer recollections without knowing of the self-glorification embedded within them, completed the reinvention of the desert tradition, and propagated it.

In *The Great Plains* (1931), Walter Prescott Webb recapitulated the boosters' rediscovery of the desert in the 1870s; the only difference between Webb's discovery and that of his booster predecessors was that he found in the 1920s references to the Great American Desert in three school geographies from 1840 and 1850. Based upon these, he built a factitious superstructure: the Great American Desert idea did exist in the American mind from 1820 to 1870, was at its most popular in the 1850s, and halted the American frontier. American historians who wrote the school and college textbooks followed Webb's interpretation of the desert myth. The paradox exists, therefore, that during the period from 1820 to 1870, when Webb and his followers claimed that a Great American Desert existed in the American mind, practically nobody, excepting the Mormons after 1855 and a well-educated minority in the Northeast before 1855, believed in the existence of a desert west of the Missouri. The only period during which a belief in either a real or an imaginary Great American Desert in the Great Plains region ever existed consensually in the American mind, and then only among the high-school- and college-educated, was from 1920 to 1970.

See also WAR: Long, Stephen; Pike, Zebulon

Martyn J. Bowden
Clark University

Bowden, Martyn J. "The Great American Desert and the American Frontier, 1800–1882: Popular Images of the Plains." In *Anonymous Americans: Explorations in Nineteenth-Century Social History*, edited by Tamara K. Hareven. Englewood Cliffs NJ: Prentice-Hall, 1971: 48–79. Bowden, Martyn J. "The Great American Desert in the American Mind: The Historiography of a Geographical Notion." In *Geographies of the Mind: Essays in Historical Geosophy in Honor of John Kirtland Wright*, edited by David Lowenthal and Martyn J. Bowden. New York: Oxford University Press, 1976: 119–47. Lewis, G. Malcolm. "Regional Ideas and Reality in the Cis–Rocky Mountain West." *Transactions, Institute of British Geographers* 38 (1966): 135–50.

GUNSLINGERS

Their names still reverberate through the American consciousness—Jack Slade, Wild Bill Hickok, John Wesley Hardin, Bill Longley, Clay Allison, Kid Curry, Ben Thompson, Luke Short, Billy the Kid. These and dozens of other gunslingers like them plied their trade in the Great Plains from Texas and New Mexico in the south to the Dakotas and Montana in the north. They have been romanticized, demonized, and mythologized. Their number of gunfights and killings has been both wildly exaggerated and greatly underestimated. Most deserve their reputations; some don't. They have been written about in the liveliest of narrative and psychoanalyzed in the dullest of prose. They remain figures of legendary proportions, and they continue to capture the American fancy. Why they do so is obvious. The gunslingers put their lives on the line—again and again. Their bravery and coolness under fire, for good or ill, were awe inspiring.

Wild Bill Hickok and Dave Tutt warily eyed each other from opposite sides of a town square. The night before they had argued when Tutt insisted on keeping Hickok's watch as collateral for a gambling debt. Hickok told Tutt not to appear in public wearing the watch if he valued his life. Now Tutt stood across the square, the watch prominently displayed. Suddenly, the two men drew their guns and fired. Hickok's round buried itself in Tutt's heart, and Tutt slumped to the ground dead. Apart from the Civil War and Indian fighting, Dave Tutt was the second of seven men shot to death by Hickok during his days in the West.

Yet Hickok was by no means the leading man killer in the Great Plains. John Wesley Hardin, Bill Longley, and Jim Miller had at least eleven or twelve kills each, and Kid Curry (Harvey Logan) had nine. Some would credit Billy the Kid (Henry McCarty) with six or seven and possibly as many as nine. Several others, including John Selman, Dallas Stoudenmire, and Ben Thompson, had five or six.

These and other gunslingers came from a wide variety of backgrounds and worked in various capacities during their lives on the Plains. Some spent most of their adult lives operating on the side of the law, a few stayed entirely outside the law, and many existed in an extralegal ambiguity resulting from Reconstruction, or feuding ranchers, or political factions criminalizing their opposition. Hickok was born in a small town in Illinois to a father who both farmed and operated a small store, Billy the Kid in New York City to Irish immigrants, Thompson in England to parents who immigrated to the United States, Hardin in Texas to a Methodist minister who rode the circuit, Selman in Arkansas to an English immigrant father, Kid Curry to an Iowa farming couple who died when he was young. Some of the gunslingers had a hardscrabble childhood; others lived a middle-class existence. They nonetheless had much in common. They were brave, had nerves of steel, were expert marksmen, and were fierce when provoked. Some of their gunfights were almost formal affairs of honor, others were drunken saloon brawls, some were part of shootouts involving several participants, and a few, when an enemy's guard was down, were executions.

Another thing most had in common was a violent death. Hickok, Billy the Kid, Hardin, Selman, Kid Curry, Stoudenmire, and Thompson (and most others) were shot to death. Longley and Miller (and a few others) were hanged. Rare was the gunslinger who lived to a ripe old age and died of natural causes. Wyatt Earp did so at eighty, Bat Masterson at sixty-eight.

See also LAW: Billy the Kid; Masterson, Bat.

Roger D. McGrath
Thousand Oaks, California

Miller, Nyle H., and Joseph W. Snell. *Great Gunfighters of the Kansas Cowtowns, 1867–1886*. Lincoln: University of Nebraska Press, 1967. O'Neal, Bill. *Encyclopedia of Western Gunfighters*. Norman: University of Oklahoma Press, 1979. Rosa, Joseph G. *The Gunfighter*. Norman: University of Oklahoma Press, 1969.

HICKOK, WILD BILL (1837–1876)

Wild Bill Hickok

Born in Illinois in 1837 to a farmer and proprietor of a small store, James Butler Hickok grew up to become a gunfighter and lawman of legendary proportions in the West. He served as constable of Monticello, Kansas, in 1858, then worked as a teamster in the Great Plains before serving with the Union army as a wagon master, scout, and spy during the Civil War. Following the war he scouted for Custer's Seventh Cavalry and was a deputy U.S. marshal responsible for capturing army deserters and rustlers of government livestock. In August 1869 he was elected sheriff of Ellis County, Kansas, but that lasted only three months. During 1871 he was town marshal of Abilene. The next several years found him guiding Russian nobles on a buffalo hunt, gambling his way from one cow town to another, and performing in Buffalo Bill's *Scouts of the Prairie* theatrical production. In 1876 he joined the rush to the Black Hills, but he had no luck prospecting and spent most of his time drinking and gambling in Deadwood. While playing cards in the No. 10 Saloon on August 2, 1876, he was shot through the back of the head by Jack McCall. Wild Bill died instantly, still holding his hand of aces and eights.

Hickok was a legendary figure while still alive. He embraced, perpetuated, and added to his own legend and, alternately, was repulsed by it. He was an enigmatic figure who defies simple analysis. One thing is clear. He was a fearsome gunfighter: his accuracy was extraordinary, he shot equally well with either hand, he had great presence of mind in the face of death, and he gave no quarter. He shot to death seven men, not counting those he killed in the Civil War and in Indian fights.

Roger D. McGrath
Thousand Oaks, California

Connelley, William Elsey. *Wild Bill and His Era*. New York: Press of the Pioneers, 1933. Rosa, Joseph G. *They Called Him Wild Bill*. Norman: University of Oklahoma Press, 1964. Rosa, Joseph G. *Wild Bill Hickok*. Lawrence: University Press of Kansas, 1996.

HOLLIDAY, DOC (1852–1887)

John Henry "Doc" Holliday, perhaps the most written about dentist in American history, was one of the most colorful and enigmatic characters on the nineteenth-century frontier. The frail, tubercular Georgian became a popular folk legend after participating in the famous gunfight outside the OK Corral. Holliday's image as a killer and peerless duelist has been embellished through countless newspaper and magazine articles, books, television shows, and motion pictures. While the Doc Holliday of fiction and folklore continues to be an enduring symbol of America's violent frontier past, the historical personality behind the myth remains an elusive, complex figure.

Doc Holliday was born on August 14, 1852, at Griffin, Georgia, the only son of Jane and Henry B. Holliday, a planter, lawyer, and politician. After attending dentistry school, Holliday opened a practice in Atlanta in 1872. Diagnosed with tuberculosis in 1873, he sought a healthier climate farther west. He settled in Dallas, Texas, and became a regular at the local gaming houses. He adapted well to the saloons and gambling halls and eventually became a full-time faro dealer. He left Dallas in 1875 after being involved in a shooting fray. Doc Holliday reportedly spent the years from 1875 to 1879 drifting from one frontier town to another, dealing faro and practicing dentistry in Plains communities such as Denver, Colorado; Las Vegas, New Mexico; Cheyenne, Wyoming; and Dodge City, Kansas. In Dodge he developed a close friendship with city policeman Wyatt Earp, whom he later followed to Tombstone, Arizona.

Holliday has had the reputation of being a superb marksman and one of the most deadly gunfighters of the Old West. Also said to have been handy with a bowie knife, he has been credited with as many as thirty-five killings. For example, he reportedly shot to death a soldier at Jacksonboro, Texas, knifed a gambler in Denver, and killed another man in Las Vegas, New Mexico. These stories have little basis in fact, having been penned years after the alleged acts occurred. Bat Masterson, for example, helped strengthen Holliday's image as a killer in a popular 1907 article. Holliday also helped popularize his own image as a dangerous killer. The frail, chronically ill Holliday was actually a poor shot who carefully nurtured his reputation as a skilled gunman and killer to deter any would-be gambling cheats, thieves, or assorted hard cases. His only documented killing, the shotgun slaying of Tom McLaury, took place during the OK Corral fight.

While Doc Holliday and others might have exaggerated his notorious reputation, he was certainly not all bluff. A product of the southern dueling tradition, Holliday often resorted to violence to settle disputes. For example, when Billy Allen approached him in a Leadville, Colorado, saloon in 1884 to collect a five-dollar bet, the insulted Holliday opened fire, leaving Allen with a nasty flesh wound. Also on October 26, 1881, in the most written about gun battle of the nineteenth-century American West, Holliday stood side by side with the Earp brothers at the OK Corral in a fight that killed three members of the Clanton gang. In the period after the Tombstone gunfight, he was alleged to have helped Wyatt Earp murder Clanton henchmen Frank Stillwell and Florentino Cruz, although he never stood trial for either crime. Doc Holliday died from tuberculosis on November 8, 1887, in Glenwood Springs, Colorado.

See also FILM: Wyatt Earp Films.

Derrick S. Ward
Ventura, California

Jahns, Pat. *The Frontier World of Doc Holliday.* New York: Hastings House, 1957. Myers, John M. *Doc Holliday.* Boston: Little, Brown, 1955.

HOMESTEAD NATIONAL MONUMENT OF AMERICA

Authorized by Congress as a unit of the National Park Service in 1936, Homestead National Monument of America commemorates the development of an agricultural empire based on government disposition of the public domain and the attendant social systems that changed the western United States. The purpose of the monument is to expose visitors to the entire scope and diversity of homesteading throughout the nation, from its nineteenth-century origins to today.

The cry of free land advertised across the nation and abroad motivated American settlers and immigrants to strike out for independent ownership of farms, to free themselves of bondage to authoritarian regimes, and to seek improved economic and social conditions for their children. Through the Homestead Act of 1862, the government granted free land not only to its own citizens but also to those willing to pledge allegiance to a struggling democracy. Approximately three million original entries were filed under the original and amended homestead laws between 1863 and 1960, and 64 percent were successful. The lives of the people forever altered by the effects of the Homestead Act and settlement of the West are commemorated in the preservation of the land, artifacts, and stories at Homestead National Monument of America.

The monument consists of the original 160 acres of land acquired by Daniel Freeman, one of the nation's first homesteaders, on the first day the Homestead Act took effect—January 1, 1863. With the addition of the Freeman School by Congress on September 25, 1970, the purpose of the park was extended to commemorate the educational and social institutions of the early settlers of the Great Plains. The monument is located in Gage County, Nebraska, approximately 50 miles south of Lincoln and 3.5 miles west of Beatrice. Primary road access is via Nebraska 4. The monument, which covers 194.57 acres, is listed in the National Register of Historic Places. Classified structures include the Palmer-Epard Cabin, the Freeman School, locations of former dwellings of the Freeman family, and viable remnants of an Osage orange fencerow.

One hundred acres of restored tallgrass prairie retain their scientific and historic significance. Initiated in 1939, the restoration remains the oldest prairie restoration in the national park system and the second oldest in the nation. Management of the prairie has evolved from early erosion control and stabilization to biological management practices. Two and a half miles of trails circumvent this prairie, which has been designated a Watchable Wildlife area by the state of Nebraska in cooperation with Defenders of Wildlife.

A museum collection of more than 5,000 objects is displayed and stored at the monument's visitors center. It includes artifacts and archival materials that represent the settlement period from 1862 to 1890. Additional collections of artifacts from archaeological investigations in the park are maintained by the Midwest Archeological Center for the National Park Service.

The monument is open daily, except for Thanksgiving Day, Christmas Day, and New Year's Day. Access to all programs is free of charge. Annual celebrations include a storytelling festival in May, demonstrations of farm equipment and Homestead Days in June, ranger-conducted programs during the summer, and a Winter Festival of Prairie Cultures in December. A curriculum-related education program and teacher workshops are offered throughout the year.

See also EUROPEAN AMERICANS: Land Laws and Settlement.

Mark Engler and Beverly Albrecht
Homestead National Monument of America

Gates, Paul W. *History of Public Land Law Development.* Washington DC: Government Printing Office, 1968. Tecklenberg, Robert. *Homestead National Monument of America: An Administrative History, 1962–1981.* Omaha: Midwest Regional Office, 1982.

INTERNATIONAL PEACE GARDEN

The International Peace Garden was created to commemorate more than 150 years of peace between the United States and Canada. Straddling the world's longest unguarded international boundary, it is situated in the scenic Turtle Mountains between North Dakota and Manitoba and halfway between the Atlantic and Pacific Coasts. Just inside the main entrance, beneath the flags of both nations, a marker is inscribed: "To God in his glory, we two nations dedicate this garden and pledge ourselves that as long as man shall live, we will not take up arms against one another."

Inspiration for the garden began with Dr. Henry Moore of Islington, Ontario. On July 14, 1932, his idea became a reality when over 50,000 people gathered to dedicate this monument to peace. Spreading over 2,339 acres, the garden displays a spectacular mosaic of flowers, trees, fountains, and paths. Visitors can stroll through the formal gardens, camp under aspens and oaks, and even get married in the Peace Chapel. The most prominent structure, the Peace Tower, with its four pillars, stands more than 100 feet tall right on the international boundary. More than a horticulturalist's dream, the garden hosts concerts, arts festivals, and renowned youth summer camps in music and athletics. As many as 250,000 people visit the garden each summer and help renew this pledge of friendship between Canada and the United States.

Sonja Rossum
University of Nebraska–Lincoln

"A Garden for Peace." *North Dakota Horizons* 21 (1991): 8–15.

LAST BEST WEST

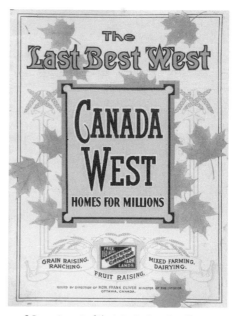

1908 Department of the Interior immigration pamphlet

The "Last Best West" is a slogan popularized by the immigration branch of the Canadian Interior Department in the early twentieth century. The phrase was used in the titles of promotional pamphlets produced by the Canadian government and distributed to potential settlers in Europe and the United States. Designed to dispel negative climatic and cultural preconceptions and extol the virtues of the Canadian Prairie for agricultural settlement, these pamphlets played a significant role in the aggressive immigrant-recruiting campaign staged by Clifford Sifton, minister of the interior from 1896 to 1905. Sifton believed that promoting settlement of the Prairie Provinces was a crucial national enterprise, and the largest infusion of immigrants to the Canadian West occurred during and shortly after Sifton's tenure.

The role of government promotion in influencing the rate of settlement during this period has been debated. It is recognized that a conjuncture of favorable circumstances contributed to western agricultural expansion in the 1890s, including the growing scarcity of free, arable land in the United States, a condition the Canadian government exploited in its advertising campaign. The slogan championed the existence of a pioneering opportunity on the Canadian Prairie at a time when the Plains frontier of the United States was closing. The phrase represents the final chapter in the early promotion and European American settlement of the Great Plains and has become the most notable example of Canadian Prairie boosterism.

See also POLITICS AND GOVERNMENT: Sifton, Clifford.

David Robertson
University of Oklahoma

Berton, Pierre. *The Promised Land: Settling the West, 1896–1914.* Markham, Ontario: Penguin, 1984. Bruce, Jean. *The Last Best West.* Toronto: Fitzhenry and Whiteside, 1976. Friesen, Gerald. *The Canadian Prairies: A History.* Toronto: University of Toronto Press, 1987.

LONGHORN CATTLE

The Texas longhorn (*Bos texanus*) is a breed of cattle that developed largely from feral Andalusian stock in southern Texas. Along with the cowboys who herded and drove them, the longhorns became an American icon. A head-on image of a longhorn, which can have a horn spread of forty inches or more, is emblazoned on countless football helmets, in Texas and elsewhere, and on numerous other products. In Texas alone, twenty-four schools use the longhorn as their mascot. The mere symbol of the longhorn imparts a sense of the adventure, power, strong will, and independence often associated with the frontier spirit.

The longhorn is descended from cattle first found in the Andalusian area of the Iberian peninsula. Living wild in what is now southern Texas for nearly 350 years produced changes in body style and temperament that came to characterize the Texas longhorn breed. The longhorn is famous for its durability on the open range, its resistance to Texas (splenic) fever, and its high reproductive rate. Thousands were rounded up after the Civil War and driven north on the Shawnee (Sedalia), Chisholm, Western, Texas, and Goodnight-Loving Trails and shipped by rail to eastern markets.

The economic benefits derived from more heavily marbled beef and the desire to own more docile animals inspired ranchers to upgrade their cattle with northern European bloodlines, and longhorn numbers declined dramatically after 1888. Through the efforts of several dedicated ranchers since the 1920s, the longhorn has been reestablished in the United States and is maintained by the Texas Longhorn Breeders Association of America. The official Texas longhorn herd is kept at Fort Griffin Historical Park northeast of Abilene.

See also TRANSPORTATION: Cattle Trails.

Kenneth C. Dagel
Missouri Western State College

Dobie, J. Frank. *The Longhorns.* New York: Grosset and Dunlap, 1941. Jordan, Terry G. *North American Cattle-Ranching Frontiers: Origins, Diffusion, and Differentiation.* Albuquerque: University of New Mexico Press, 1993. Rouse, John E. *Cattle of North America.* Norman: University of Oklahoma Press, 1973.

LOVE, NAT

See AFRICAN AMERICANS: Love, Nat

MAD PIONEER WOMEN

Shaped by the spoken and written word, the image of mad pioneer women has been handed down from generation to generation, perpetuating the notion that a large segment of women failed to endure the hardships of the Great Plains settlement experience and were driven insane. Documented accounts include women who suffered depression, took to their beds, committed suicide, killed their children, were locked away in back rooms and attics, and were sent to and died in asylums. Often buried in unmarked graves, their illnesses became dark family secrets, and their individual stories are lost to history.

Although based on fact, the idea that it was primarily women who were driven to madness by the isolation, hardships, and environment of the settlement experience is misleading. Madness was not unique to women, to those isolated in rural environments, to those in the Great Plains, or even to those in America. During the nineteenth century, mental disorders and insanity were not only experienced in the United States and Canada but also appeared to be widespread and were feared to be rapidly increasing in western European countries, including England and France.

The federal census of 1880 suggests that, for undetermined reasons, the number of persons regarded to be insane increased greatly in the United States during the latter part of the nineteenth century. By 1880 most of the insane had been committed to institutions. There were nearly 140 asylums in the United States; 7 were in the Plains states. In Nebraska the 1880 population was 452,402, and 450 of them were recorded as insane. One half of those were women.

As the Great Plains was settled, the building of insane asylums took place as part of the region's development. However, the establishment of insane asylums was not only a response to peculiar frontier needs but also a reflection of the movement to organize special hospitals for the mentally ill across America. Legislative bodies often dealt with widely publicized appropriations for facilities as well as accusations of abuses concerning the mentally ill. Well-meant reforms in the treatment of the insane were undertaken; they generally failed in the face of overcrowding and aging facilities. The life of an occupant was usually one of desolation; as time passed this was accepted as the norm.

Nineteenth-century explanations of pioneer women's mental disorders include the deaths of family members, physical and emotional abuse, substance abuse, poverty, and worry as well as family histories of mental illness. The illnesses of men were often credited to disappointment in love, financial difficulties, and physical illness. Causes of mental illnesses listed by one Plains institution in the settlement years included mania, dementia, general paralysis, melancholia, and intemperance.

Today, cultural change is listed as a major cause of mental disorders. Great Plains pioneer women and men experienced great cultural change in an environment that became a constant reminder of that change. Some were not strong enough to withstand the change and became part of the image of those who were called mad.

Nancy B. Johnson
Central City, Nebraska

Grob, Gerald N. *Mental Illness and American Society, 1875–1940.* Princeton NJ: Princeton University Press, 1983. Johnson, Nancy B. "Crazy Quilt Legacy: Uncovering Myths of Women's Madness on the Plains." Master's thesis, University of Nebraska at Kearney, 1994.

MISSILE SILOS

Across the Great Plains, from northern Colorado into western Nebraska and throughout Wyoming, North Dakota, and Montana, are the missile fields of the United States nuclear program. Each of the three Strategic Missile Wings at Malmstrom Air Force Base, Montana, F. E. Warren Air Force Base, Wyoming, and Minot Air Force Base, North Dakota, has oversight and control over the missile force, which is comprised of Minuteman III and Peacekeeper missiles. Each of these missiles is stored, ready to launch, in its own hardened launch facility, commonly called a missile silo.

Missile silos are scattered across such vast expanses so that potential adversaries would have to target each missile individually. For instance, the missile field of F. E. Warren Air Force Base includes portions of western Nebraska, northern Colorado, and eastern Wyoming, an area of more than 12,000 square miles. A chain-link fence, barbed wire, and an array of motion-detection devices enclose each silo. Armed guards routinely inspect each site and respond immediately to any attempted unauthorized access. Visible from the surface is each silo's 110-ton blast door, which looks like a well-guarded slab of concrete. Stored below is the missile that, in a true launch situation, would emerge after the door was blasted off the silo opening by explosive charges. The missiles are stored underground to provide protection from the elements and from attack. Not much of a silo is visible from above, but the depth of a missile silo that accommodates either a Peacekeeper or Minuteman missile exceeds 100 feet.

See also ARCHITECTURE: Cold War Architecture / WAR: Cold War.

Steve Slate
United States Air Force Academy

MOUNT RUSHMORE NATIONAL MEMORIAL

Mount Rushmore National Memorial, or, as its sculptor, Gutzon Borglum, referred to it, the Shrine of Democracy, was the brainchild of Doane Robinson, South Dakota's poet laureate and superintendent of the State Historical Society. The year was 1923. Robinson's idea was to carve notable western figures on the granite stone spires called the Needles, which rise along one of the highways through the Black Hills. He approached U.S. senator Peter Norbeck with the concept. Robinson believed that South Dakota needed to diversify its economy that at the time was based on mining, which experienced periods of boom and bust, and agriculture, which was suffering. He felt that larger-than-life stone sculptures would draw tourists to the Black Hills. Norbeck had met Gutzon Borglum in 1916 at the Republican National Convention and liked him personally. In the early 1920s Norbeck had been present when Borglum made his pitch to Congress for financial support for Stone Mountain in Georgia, a Confederate memorial. At that time, Borglum was highly respected for the numerous works of art he had already produced. Senator Norbeck felt Borglum was audacious enough and talented enough to take on the challenge of carving huge figures in granite.

Robinson and Norbeck began a letter-writing campaign to convince Borglum to come to South Dakota and take on the project. When Borglum visited South Dakota, he immediately felt that the project should be national in scope and proposed carving larger figures than had ever been carved before and carving them on the side of a mountain. Borglum convinced Norbeck that the sculptures should be of significant presidents. In a letter to the senator, Borglum explained his choices: Washington and Lincoln, "founder" and "savior," respectively; Jefferson, the "first great expansionist"; and Roosevelt, who had "completed commercial control by securing the Panama Canal."

The concept was agreed upon, and a site near the isolated mining town of Keystone was chosen. The formal dedication was held on August 10, 1927, with President Calvin Coolidge in attendance, and carving commenced that year, when Borglum was sixty years old. Work continued until early 1941, when Borglum died. His son, Lincoln, oversaw some finishing work on the mountain, but that work was stopped at the end of October, when the impending war required the conservation of resources.

Borglum had intended to carve more of the presidents' figures and also to carve a vault in the canyon wall behind Mount Rushmore. However, after his death the memorial was not completed according to Borglum's original design. Fortunately, Borglum himself was able to finish the lifelike features of the four presidents.

Each year, more than 2.5 million visitors gaze up at the faces of the Shrine of Democracy. They stand in awe of its magnificence and in appreciation for its remarkable sculptor, Gutzon Borglum, and his truly American image, Mount Rushmore National Memorial.

See also FOLKWAYS: Roadside Attractions / POLITICS AND GOVERNMENT: Norbeck, Peter.

Sheila R. Aaker
Black Hills State University

Shaff, Howard, and Audrey K. Shaff. *Six Wars at a Time*. Darien CT: Permelia Publishing, 1985. Smith, Rex A. *The Carving of Mount Rushmore*. New York: Abbeville Press, 1985.

OKIES

"Okies," as Californians labeled them, were refugee farm families from the Southern Plains who migrated to California in the 1930s to escape the ruin of the Great Depression and the Dust Bowl. The refugees came from several states, including the drought-ravaged corners of Kansas, Colorado, and New Mexico but especially the impoverished parts of Oklahoma (the origin of one fifth of Okies), Texas, Arkansas, and Missouri.

Okies were escaping two distinct although simultaneous and bordering catastrophes, one economic, the other more environmental. Many Okies—families from Arkansas, Missouri, eastern Oklahoma, and East Texas—were not Dust Bowl refugees but instead were tenant-farming casualties of sinking commodity prices and agricultural mechanization during the 1920s. Beef and oil prices plummeted after World War I, and the price of cotton fell from thirty-five cents per pound in 1919 to six cents in 1931. Farmers hung on by expanding production and assuming more debt, prompting widespread foreclosures after 1929. In an effort to raise prices, the Agricultural Adjustment Act of 1933 subsidized landowners to take land out of production, allowing them to mechanize, consolidate holdings, discontinue leases, and evict sharecroppers. This was especially the case in Oklahoma, which had by far the nation's highest rate of farm tenancy.

The Dust Bowl years on the Southern Plains also had economic origins. Mechanization and falling wheat prices in the 1920s combined to fuel the "Great Plow-Up," a decade of aggressive expansion of cultivated acreage during which farmers hoped for a good year that would allow them to recover spiraling debts on new equipment and land. In 1931, however, the rains stopped, and the Great Plains entered a decade-long drought. Suitcase-farming speculators wrote off their investments, but everyone's farms began to blow away in spectacular dust storms in 1932. Families suffered drought, wind, dust, and death from dust pneumonia for half a decade before the horrific dust storms and heat of 1935–36 forced many to abandon their homes and search for a new life in the Golden State. The Dust Bowl exodus reduced the populations of Texas and Oklahoma panhandle counties by as much as one-fourth and killed or stunted numerous towns. The images of the refugees—hungry, gaunt families riding overloaded jalopies over lonely Route 66—remain vivid in the American collective memory.

Predominantly upland southerners, the half-million Okies met new hardships in California, where they were unwelcome aliens, forced to live in squatter camps and to compete for scarce jobs as agricultural migrant laborers. They displaced Mexican workers, but despite the initial fears of landowners that they would demand better working conditions, these conservative, self-reliant, and persevering folk proved even easier to exploit. With many more willing hands than jobs, wage rates dropped. Crowded, filthy squatter camps rose up along the roads and streams of the San Joaquin Valley, leading Californians to attribute the scene to the refugees' own regionally derived ignorance and sloth. Federal relief in the form of labor camps (such as Steinbeck's "Wheat Patch"), dubbed "Little Oklahomas," were hardly effective.

Genuine relief for the Okies arrived in 1940, when federal defense dollars inflated West Coast industries, allowing many to abandon the orchards for shipyards and bomb plants. In fact, while the squatter camps disappeared, the number of people coming to California from the Southern Plains actually increased in the 1940s. These "defense Okies" poured into Los Angeles and Orange County during the war years and continued to take jobs in the state's aeronautical, petroleum, and automotive industries in the 1950s.

The Okie migration brought the dialects, denominations, politics, and attitudes of the Southern Plains to California, where they persist in places like Bakersfield. Although the Okie experience is best described in Steinbeck's works, it also affected popular culture in diverse musical genres, including the ballads of social radical Woody Guthrie, which inspired urban folk and rock music, as well as infusions into country music in the steely, apolitical, bumpkin sound of Buck Owens and the melancholy, oppressed-yet-patriotic ballads of Merle Haggard. Separated by ideology and a generation, both Guthrie and Haggard painted in their lyrics the imagery of a cruel, decadent California and a righteous, nostalgic Oklahoma. That image lasts in the regional meanings of "Okie": a California insult and an endearing nickname in the Southern Great Plains.

See also FILM: *The Grapes of Wrath* / MUSIC: Guthrie, Woody / PHYSICAL ENVIRONMENT: Dust Bowl / TRANSPORTATION: Route 66.

Brad A. Bays
Oklahoma State University

Gregory, James N. *American Exodus: The Dust Bowl Migration and Okie Culture in California*. New York: Oxford University Press, 1989. Shindo, Charles J. *Dust Bowl Migrants in the American Imagination*. Lawrence: University Press of Kansas, 1997. Steinbeck, John. *The Harvest Gypsies: On the Road to the Grapes of Wrath*. Introduction by Charles Wollenberg. Berkeley CA: Heyday Books, 1988.

PASTORAL REGION

The Great Plains was never developed homogeneously, but after the early nineteenth century its image was associated with a sequence of supposed socioeconomic potentials or conditions. During some periods this image was one of limited or even negative potential, as with the Great American Desert in the first half of the nineteenth century and the Nation's Stepchild in the mid–twentieth century. The first of the positive economic concepts was that of the pastoral region, which emerged after the Civil War and climaxed circa 1885, by which date the coequal and approximately contemporary concepts of a pioneer settlement region and a dry-farmed cash grain region were in the ascendancy. Between 1884 and 1887 severe winter conditions or premature chinooks or hot dry summers had affected every part of the pastoral region. Their effects were catastrophic for a type of ranching that during good years had appeared not to require insurance in the form of constructed shelters, supplementary feed, and artificial reservoirs. The climatic disasters, coinciding almost exactly with a national economic depression, quickly weakened the pastoral image.

Especially on the western Great Plains, stock raising had begun slowly with the realization that cattle abandoned or straying from emigrants on trails west not only overwintered but often flourished on the shortgrass divides between valleys. It did not, however, emerge as a dominant economy until the 1870s, when there was an eightfold increase in the number of cattle in the northern and central parts of the region. However, the image was probably stronger than the ranching economy it epitomized. It had been promoted in eastern North America and elsewhere by several books. In *The Central Gold Region: The Grain, Pastoral, and Gold Regions of North America* (1860), William Gilpin devoted a chapter to "Pastoral America." Published on the eve of the Civil War, the book was predictive: "The Great Plains of America" were "not deserts" but formed "the Pastoral Garden of the World," an immense, longitudinally oriented "empire of pastoral agriculture" at the threshold of which the frontier of settlement had just arrived. Once the prediction materialized, James S. Brisbin, in *The Beef Bonanza; or, How to Get Rich on the Plains* (1882), and Walter Baron von Richthofen, in *Cattle-Raising on the Plains of North America* (1885), were particularly important in publicizing it. Von Richthofen, in a brief first paragraph, announced that the "former Great American Desert" had become "the largest and richest grass and pasture region of the world" and that it would "probably soon become the most important beef-producing country of the globe." The image was further strengthened by the associated glamour of the cowboy culture, which was already being promoted in literature. Ironically, further publicity was associated with the demise of ranching in the mid-1880s. Much of the investment and many of the leading participants in ranching were from eastern North America and Europe, and their losses were widely known. Although the ranching economy revived, the powerful icon of a pastoral region was never reestablished.

See also AGRICULTURE: Cattle Ranching.

G. Malcolm Lewis
University of Sheffield, England

Lewis, G. Malcolm. "Regional Ideas and Reality in the Cis–Rocky Mountain West." *Transactions and Papers of the Institute of British Geographers* 18 (1966): 135–50. Lewis, G. Malcolm. "William Gilpin and the Concept of the Great Plains Region." *Annals of the Association of American Geographers* 56 (1966): 33–51.

POTTS, JERRY (ca. 1840–1896)

Jerry Potts was a frontiersman who is generally credited with guiding the North-West Mounted Police to a safe haven when they were completing their trek to the Canadian West in 1874 and with having a long and colorful career as their interpreter and guide.

Potts was born at Fort McKenzie on the Missouri River about 1840, the son of Andrew R. Potts, an American Fur Company clerk, and Namopi'si, or Crooked Back, a Blood Indian. His father was killed shortly after the boy's birth, and young Potts was adopted by Alexander Harvey and later by Andrew Dawson. At the age of twenty-three he killed Antoine Primeau at Fort Galpin and then began to spend more time with his mother's people. During this time he was given the Blackfoot name of Kyiyokosi, or Bear Child.

During the 1860s he took part in several Indian skirmishes, including a major battle between Blackfoot and Crees in which almost 300 of the enemy were killed. Potts took sixteen scalps during the battle. When the North-West Mounted Police marched west in 1874 to bring law and order to the Canadian territory, they became lost and took refuge near the Sweetgrass Hills. Potts was engaged as guide and led them to a site where they built Fort Macleod.

Potts remained with the police until his death at Fort Macleod on July 14, 1896. He was famous for his unerring ability to find his way on the Prairies, even during blizzards, and for his help in maintaining friendly relations between the Mounted Police and Indians of the Blackfoot confederacy.

See also LAW: North-West Mounted Police.

Hugh A. Dempsey
Calgary, Alberta

Dempsey, Hugh A. *Jerry Potts, Plainsman.* Calgary: Glenbow Museum, 1966. Steele, Samuel B. *Forty Years in Canada.* London: Herbert Jenkins, 1915.

PROMOTIONAL LITERATURE

Those with a vested interest in the settlement of the Great Plains, from the railroads to territorial and state governments, faced a daunting challenge. Early explorers and travelers had described the entire region west of the 100th meridian and east of the Rocky Mountains in language that could be charitably described as unflattering. Only one of these descriptions used the phrase "Great American Desert," but few of the accounts spoke favorably of the agricultural potential of the Plains, and some of them were openly despairing of its future as an agricultural region. It may not have been a desert, but it was assuredly desertlike. In sum, the Plains had an image problem that antedated its settlement by decades.

It followed that many of the early promoters of the settlement of the Plains spent as much time trying to break down negative impressions as they did trumpeting the positive features of the region. They employed a variety of tactics. One of them, the most respectable, was to remind interested settlers that the Prairies of Illinois, Iowa, and Minnesota had once been dismissed as infertile because they were relatively treeless. The world knew of the productive capabilities of the Prairies; soon it would know of the equally productive potential of the Plains. At the very least, the absence of timber on the Plains was not disqualifying.

From this good beginning the promotional effort began to veer toward the make-believe if not the openly deceptive. Claims were made that whatever the insufficiency of rainfall on the Plains, the matter would be quickly and easily remedied by the increase in rainfall that would follow settlement. The agent of that increase varied with the promoters. For some, railroad lines and telegraph wires would bring more rain; others maintained that the planting of trees would have the same effect; still others argued that rain would increase as more of the Plains were put under cultivation—in other words, "rainfall follows the plow."

The promoters, particularly the railroads, brought this message to every potential agricultural settler, whether in eastern U.S. cities or in the cities, towns, villages, and farms of Europe. They joined "rainfall follows the plow" with other equally alluring promises. The most important of these was, predictably, the "free" land that came with filing a homestead claim. But there were others: good prices for wheat and corn; cool summers and moderate winters; gentle zephyrs; and perfectly timed precipitation. An advertising blitz was under way, and it was remarkably modern in some of its features. There were no surveys, polls, or focus groups, but the promoters understood what assurances their potential customers for land wanted, and they supplied them. To say that they occasionally stretched the truth would be to understate. Similarly, in the Canadian Prairies the Canadian Pacific Railway tried to erase the image of the area as arid and to attract farm families with the messages of "free homes for all" and abundant "profits of farming."

Economic independence—good crops that brought good prices—was only one of the assurances. Promotional literature thus included frequent references to the "taming" of the West. The image of desertlike sterility was the most stubborn obstacle to overcome, but the image of the West as a place of savage Indians, arrogant and grasping cattle barons, shoot-outs, barroom brawls, and open prostitution had also to be countered. The same pamphlets and books that spoke of wheat yields and prices also included references to schools, churches, the closing of red-light districts and bars, and the removal of "troublesome" racial and ethnic groups: Indians, Mexicans, and Asians.

Much of this aspect of the promotional campaign suggests a gendered approach. It is not that women did not care about free land or wheat prices or that men were not interested in schools and churches, but the promotion emphasis does lend itself to a female interpretation. References to the ethnic and racial "purity" of the new and domesticated West were in the same sections of the promotional literature that contained happy talk of schools, churches, and bridge clubs—the "women's section."

There are two other important points to make in this regard. First, the promoters knew what historians have only recently come to acknowledge: women were equal partners in the decision to migrate. Second, the perceptions of what constituted the women's sphere are revealed: women cared about social amenities. If the agricultural lands as well as the town sites of the Plains were to be promoted and settled, attention would have to be paid to both productivity and domestication, the two parts of the "migration calculus."

Books, gazettes, pamphlets, newspapers, and territorial and state government publications in scores of languages were sent to every corner of the United States and those parts of Europe that seemed promising and where the population was of an "acceptable" standard—Protestant and relatively well-off. In some respects, this was the first organized American advertising campaign, complete with slogans, jingles, and deceptive promises. It cannot be known how many responded or how many of those were able to make a living on the Plains. What can be known is that the Great Plains was the first of America's "frontiers" to be heavily promoted, and the first that needed to be.

See also EUROPEAN AMERICANS: Immigration Boards.

David M. Emmons
University of Montana–Missoula

Bowden, Martyn J. "The Great American Desert in the American Mind: The Historiography of a Geographical Notion." In *Geographies of the Mind: Essays in Historical Geosophy in Honor of John Kirtland Wright*, edited by David Lowenthal and Martyn J. Bowden. New York: Oxford University Press, 1976: 119–47. Emmons, David M. *Garden in the Grasslands: The Boomer Literature of the Central Plains*. Lincoln: University of Nebraska Press, 1969.

QUIVIRA

Rumors of the land of Quivira, one of many fantastic realms of gold sought by Spanish conquistadors, lured the army of Francisco Vázquez de Coronado into the Great Plains in 1541. Soon after the expedition failed to find the mythical Seven Cities of Cibola at Zuni in western New Mexico, the Spaniards received a delegation of Indians from Pecos (Cicuye), who welcomed them to their country. At Pecos the exploring party sent by Coronado met an Indian captive of the Plains whom they called the Turk. After the leaders of Pecos Pueblo persuaded the Turk to lead the Spaniards into the Plains and lose them, he was given to the Spaniards as a guide. On the buffalo plains beyond Pecos, the Turk told the soldiers so many and such great things about his country that they decided to return and report this welcome news to Coronado.

As understood by the Spaniards, in the farther part of the Turk's country there were large settlements and a river two leagues wide with fish as big as horses. The lords of Quivira had large canoes with sails and more than twenty rowers on each side, and their chief lord, a white-haired and bearded man called Tatarrat, worshiped a gold cross and an image of a woman, the ruler of heaven. King Tatarrat napped under a great tree adorned with many gold bells that swayed in the breeze and lulled him to sleep; so rich was the kingdom that everyone had jugs and bowls of gold and ordinary dishes of wrought plate.

After wintering at Tiguex on the Rio Grande, near present-day Albuquerque, the army went in search of Quivira in the spring of 1541. During the journey across the immense plains, Coronado realized that the Turk had deceived him. After sending the army back to Tiguex, he and Fray Juan de Padilla went on with a small company of horsemen and foot soldiers. Using friendly Teyas Indians as guides, Coronado reached Quivira in July and discovered it to be a province of the Wichita Indians in the vicinity of Great Bend, Kansas. These people lived in grass lodges, and their lord wore a copper necklace, but no gold and silver were found. After the Turk was killed for his treachery, Coronado returned to Tiguex, where his soldiers, poorly clothed and covered with lice, fantasized about the vast treasures they might have found had they continued to search for that better land.

Despite Coronado's failure, the chimera of Quivira continued to beckon. In 1593, three years before Juan de Oñate took formal possession of New Mexico, Francisco Leyva de Bonilla led an illegal expedition into the Plains in search of Quivira; he was killed by a companion, and most of his small force were killed by Indians. In 1601 an Aztec survivor of the Bonilla expedition guided Governor Oñate and some seventy men in search of Quivira. The Wichita Indians along the Arkansas River gave them beads before they recrossed the Plains in October. In the 1670s Don Diego de Penalosa, a renegade governor of New Mexico tried by the Inquisition, presented an altered version of the Oñate expedition to the French government; it served, in part, to launch the La Salle expedition and the beginnings of international conflict in the borderlands. As late as 1720 the governor of Coahuila and Texas led 500 mounted troops into East Texas in an attempt to check French defenses beyond the Red River and to discover the rich lands of Gran Quivira.

Quivira and various other illusory golden realms were the products of the mythic imaginary West. Mistaken geographical theory, a thirst for gold, and the utopian dream of friars to convert the Indians made for the invention of America before reality intruded. The search for Quivira, like other fantasies, acted as a motivating force for the discovery, exploration, and eventual settlement of the Western Hemisphere. As America became better known, Quivira and other elusive kingdoms became themes of myth, fable, and fiction.

See also EUROPEAN AMERICANS: Coronado.

Ralph H. Vigil
University of Nebraska–Lincoln

Brandon, William. *Quivira: Europeans in the Region of the Santa Fe Trail, 1540–1820*. Athens: Ohio University Press, 1990. Gandía, Enrique de. *Historia crítica de los mitos de la conquista americana*. Madrid: J. Roldán y Compañía, 1929. Vigil, Ralph H. "Spanish Exploration and the Great Plains in the Age of Discovery: Myth and Reality." *Great Plains Quarterly* 10 (1990): 3–17.

RAINFALL FOLLOWS THE PLOW

The myth that "rainfall follows the plow" began in the late 1800s as new settlers pushed onto the Great Plains. The settlers needed water to transform the prairie into farms. As they crossed the 100th meridian and the twenty-inch rainfall line, settlers persuaded themselves that they were the agents of increased precipitation. Proponents of this theory believed that breaking the prairie sod would allow rainfall to be absorbed into the soil. This moisture would then evaporate into the atmosphere and result in an increase in humidity and rainfall.

Some early explorers and writers had suggested the possibility of altering the Plains by cultivation. Santa Fe trader Josiah Gregg proposed that extensive cultivation of the earth might contribute to the multiplication of showers, and itinerant Englishman Sir Richard Burton pointed to increased rainfall at the Mormon settlements in Utah and attributed the change to cultivation and tree planting.

One of the most widely recognized supporters of the plow theory was Dr. Samuel Aughey Jr., a professor at the University of Nebraska. Professor Aughey wrote numerous articles, addressed the Kansas and Nebraska state boards of agriculture as well as the Nebraska State Legislature, and published a book entitled *Sketches of the Physical Geography and Geology of Nebraska* in 1880. He explained that the soil would absorb the rain like a huge sponge once the sod had been broken. This moisture would then be given slowly back to the atmosphere by evaporation. Each year, as cultivation extended across the Plains, Aughey argued, the moisture and rainfall would also increase until the region was fit for agriculture without irrigation.

Following in Aughey's footsteps was Charles Dana Wilber, who popularized the phrase "rain follows the plow" in his book, *The Great Valleys and Prairies of Nebraska and the Northwest* (1881). Other individuals supporting this theory included H. R. Hilton, a Kansas farmer-agriculturist; Orange Judd, editor and publisher of the *Prairie Farmer* in Chicago; and Professor Frank H. Snow, later chancellor of the University of Kansas.

Railroads, trying to attract settlers to their land grants, also quickly adopted a theory that advocated an increase in rainfall in the Great American Desert, and they used it in their promotional slogans. For example, the Santa Fe Railroad printed a pamphlet showing a Kansas farmer using a steel plow. The pamphlet asks, "Who killed the Great American Desert?" The sturdy yeoman answers, "I did with my team and plow." The railroad also advertised that the rain line was moving steadily westward at the rate of about eighteen miles per annum, keeping just ahead of and propelled by the advancing population. Whenever Professor Aughey spoke, a stenographer employed by the Burlington and Missouri River Railroad was usually close at hand. Copies of his speeches were published and distributed to prospective emigrants in Europe.

The plow theory essentially ended with the severe droughts of the 1890s, although some diehard proponents suggested that this was only because the plowing had not been deep enough.

See also PHYSICAL ENVIRONMENT: Aughey, Samuel, Jr.

M. Jean Ferrill
Northern Michigan University

Emmons, David M. *Garden in the Grasslands*. Lincoln: University of Nebraska Press, 1971. Ferrill, Jean Williams. "The Marginal Lands of Australia and the American West: Some Comparisons in Their Perceptions and Settlement." In *The Process of Rural Transformation*, edited by Ivan Volgyes, Richard E. Lonsdale, and William P. Avery. New York: Pergamon Press, 1980: 68–88.

REMINGTON, FREDERIC (1861–1909)

Although Frederic Remington was the most prolific of all the artists who sought to portray the rapidly changing nature of the peoples and lands west of the Mississippi River in the latter half of the nineteenth century, his talents were not limited to the more than 2,500 paintings, drawings, and illustrations he produced in the last two decades of his life. He also authored a play, eight books, and numerous magazine articles and sculpted twenty-four major bronzes.

Born in Canton, New York, on October 4, 1861, Remington remained throughout his life an easterner, and with the exception of his limited and abortive attempt to raise sheep in Kansas from March 1883 to May 1884, he never lived in the Great Plains. Nevertheless, he became one of the great image makers of the nation's western experience and shaped the manner and vision by which eastern audiences thought about the Great Plains.

After desultory experiences in eastern military schools, Remington enrolled at Yale University in 1878 to study art. Energetic and robust at five feet nine inches and weighing almost 200 pounds, Remington gained more distinction on Walter Camp's 1879 football team than he did for his artistic studies. With the death of his father in 1880, Remington ended his university studies. Upon receiving his inheritance at the age of twenty-one, he invested this $10,000 in a sheep ranch on the fringes of the Flint Hills in Kansas. When this venture failed, he returned to Canton, married Eva Caten, took the balance of his inheritance, and became a partner in a Kansas City saloon. When success again eluded him, and with no discernible future before him as a rancher or saloon keeper, Remington committed himself to becoming an artist.

Within five years, Remington was one of the nation's leading illustrators. His drawings and illustrations appeared regularly in *Harper's Weekly*, *Harper's Monthly*, *Outing*, *Century Magazine*, *Scribner's*, and other major magazines. He also became one of the leading book illustrators of the era, with illustrations in Elizabeth B. Custer's *Tenting on the Plains* (1887), Theodore Roosevelt's *Ranch Life and the Hunting Trail* (1888), Thomas Janvier's *The Aztec Treasure House* (1890), and Henry Wadsworth Longfellow's *Song of Hiawatha* (1890). Seeking to avoid being identified just as an illustrator, he began to work in both oils and watercolors with the hope that he would be recognized as an artist.

In 1889 his dynamic *Dash for the Timber* was exhibited at the National Academy for Design, and the popular and critical reception of this work began to give him the artistic recognition he sought. In this same year his *Lull in the Fight* won a silver medal at the Paris Universal Exposition. Increasingly, his paintings depicted a West that was past. Frequently focusing upon the role of the cavalry in subduing the land and its Native inhabitants, Remington portrayed a West that was wild and antithetical to approaching industrialized civilization. What he admired in the West were mounted warriors, men on horseback. In the emerging tradition of western art, his paintings were both romantic and narrative. They sought to capture a time past and to commemorate it for the present and future. Determined to distance himself from his reputation as an illustrator and always willing to experiment artistically, in 1895 he began to work in bronze. In 1902 his dynamic *Coming through the Rye* demonstrated his growing mastery of this medium.

Remington died on December 26, 1909, near Ridgefield, Connecticut, following complications from an appendectomy.

Phillip Drennon Thomas
Wichita State University

International UFO Museum and Research Center, Roswell, New Mexico

Nemerov, Alexander. *Frederic Remington and Turn-of-the-Century America*. New Haven CT: Yale University Press, 1995. Samuels, Peggy, and Harold Samuels, eds. *The Collected Writings of Frederic Remington*. Garden City NY: Doubleday, 1979. Vorphal, Ben Merchant. *Frederic Remington and the West: With the Eye of the Mind*. Austin: University of Texas Press, 1978.

ROADSIDE ATTRACTIONS

See FOLKWAYS: Roadside Attractions

ROSWELL ALIENS

In early July 1947, an event so spectacular that it sent a shock wave throughout the world occurred in Roswell, New Mexico, and yet another image became associated with the Great Plains. The July 8, 1947, issue of the *Roswell Daily Record* announced: "RAAF Captures Flying Saucer on Ranch in Roswell Region." The article referred to the capture of alien bodies and an alien spacecraft that supposedly crashed just outside of Roswell. The following day the *Roswell Daily Record* reported that the military had emptied the saucer of its occupants. The Roswell Army Airfield first reported capturing a flying saucer and then recanted the story, replacing "flying saucer" with "weather balloon." The U.S. government still maintains that no aliens were found in Roswell.

Walter Haut and Glenn Dennis were active participants in the 1947 event. Walter Haut was the public relations officer assigned to the Roswell Army Airfield. Acting under orders, he reported the initial incident to the *Roswell Daily Record*. Glenn Dennis was the local mortician. Someone from the airfield contacted Dennis and asked him how to preserve a body that had been exposed to the elements and also inquired about the quantity of child-size

State/Province	Nickname	Animal	Bird	Flower	Tree
Colorado	Centennial State	bighorn sheep	lark bunting	columbine	blue spruce
Kansas	Sunflower State	bison	western meadowlark	sunflower	eastern cottonwood
Oklahoma	Sooner State	bison	scissor-tailed flycatcher	mistletoe	redbud
Montana	Treasure State	grizzly bear	western meadowlark	bitterroot	Ponderosa pine
Nebraska	Cornhusker State	white-tailed deer	western meadowlark	goldenrod	eastern cottonwood
New Mexico	Land of Enchantment	black bear	roadrunner	yucca	Piñon
North Dakota	Peace Garden State		western meadowlark	wild prairie rose	American elm
South Dakota	Coyote State	coyote	ring-necked pheasant	pasque flower	Black Hills spruce
Texas	Lone Star State	longhorn and armadillo	mockingbird	bluebonnet	pecan
Wyoming	Equality State	bison	western meadowlark	Indian paintbrush	plains cottonwood
Alberta			great horned owl	wild rose	lodgepole pine
Manitoba			great gray owl	prairie crocus	white spruce
Saskatchewan			sharp-tailed grouse	western red lily	white birch

coffins he had on hand. His curiosity piqued, Dennis traveled out to the airfield to see what was going on. Upon his arrival at the airfield hospital, he discovered chaos. When he began to ask questions, he was physically escorted out of the building. Later that day he met with a friend, a nurse from the hospital, and she told him she had seen aliens. She even drew him a picture on the back of a prescription pad. Her drawing has become the standard image of aliens: short, thin, gray in color, with large heads, no hair or ears, large almond-shaped eyes, holes for a nose, a slit for a mouth, and hands with four elongated fingers and suction cups on the inside tips.

The International UFO Museum and Research Center in Roswell, New Mexico, co-founded by Haut and Dennis, focuses on these events and invites visitors to make up their own minds about what really happened.

Glenda Shafer
International UFO Museum and Research Center

ROUGHNECKS AND ROUSTABOUTS

Roughnecks, skilled members of drilling crews, are employed in the drilling of oil wells. Once the wells are put on-line, roughnecks hurry to find work in the next oil strike. Roustabouts, unskilled laborers, also follow the oil booms; however, they often take work outside of drilling operations and sometimes became more permanent oil-town residents. Many from both groups are young and unmarried men who work hard and spend their money with abandon to relieve the monotony of the work and the often wretched living conditions. Lured by the excitement and adventure of "black gold," they have long migrated from one strike to another throughout the Great Plains, from the Rio Grande of Texas north to the Prairie Provinces of Canada and from the midcontinent region of Oklahoma and Kansas west to the Rocky Mountains. Icons in literature and motion pictures, roughnecks and roustabouts in oil boomtowns such as Whizbang, Borger, Artesia, and El Dorado replaced the earlier cowboys of Abilene and Dodge City,

prospectors from Custer City and Deadwood, and bullwhackers on the Santa Fe Trail and the Platte River Road in the lore of the Great Plains.

A roughneck is expected to handle a number of tasks. He could be a bit dresser in charge of repairing and sharpening drill bits; a brake-out man, who adjusts the heavy tongs used to loosen pipe joints as they are pulled out of the hole; a cathead man in charge of the winch head on the draw-works countershaft of a rotary rig; a chain slinger, back-up man, or C-slinger, who handles the tongs used to hold the lower section of drill pipe while the upper section is unscrewed; a tool dresser or toolie, who assists the driller and keeps the tools in good repair; a floorman or slip puller, who performs general tasks on the floor of a derrick; a lead-tong man, pipe stabber, or pipe racker, who handles the lead tong and stacks pipe. An inex-

The drilling floor of a cable tool-drilling rig

perienced roughneck is known as a farmer. The tool pusher, also called a stud horse, stud duck, or stud terrapin, is in charge of the roughnecks on a drilling crew.

A roustabout, also called a gaffer, assists the drilling foreman with tasks such as feeding fuel to boilers on cable tool rigs or performs general work around producing oil wells and oil company property. A head roustabout is the name given to a district superintendent who oversees several drilling rigs.

See also CITIES AND TOWNS: Oil Boom-towns / INDUSTRY: Petroleum, Canada; Petroleum, United States.

Kenny A. Franks
Oklahoma Heritage Association

Boone, Lalia Phipps. *The Petroleum Dictionary.* Norman: University of Oklahoma Press, 1952. Day, David Talbot. *The Handbook of the Petroleum Industry.* New York: Wiley Publishing Company, 1922. Franks, Kenny A., and Paul F. Lambert. *Voices from the Oil Field.* Norman: University of Oklahoma Press, 1984.

STATE AND PROVINCE SYMBOLS

The Great Plains region has had many symbols thrust upon it, generally from the outside. Often they are pejorative, including Great American Desert, flyover country, and, in its dismissal of the reality of residents in the region, buffalo commons. But the states and provinces that make up the Plains have also chosen their own symbols, from birds and flowers to nicknames and slogans, and, as might be expected, these reflect their environments more accurately than the imposed images. They also present a more positive face to the world.

Quite a few of the symbols, particularly those emblems of identity drawn from the physical environment, are widely represented. For example, the western meadowlark, whose joyous, flutelike song enriches the Plains aural landscape, is the official bird of five Central and Northern Plains states; the honeybee (even though it is a foreign import) is the official insect of four states; the bison, historically the defining symbol of the Plains, is the official animal of three states; and the wild prairie rose of roadsides, pastures, and meadows is the official flower on both sides of the forty-ninth parallel in North Dakota and Alberta. Other environmental symbols—New Mexico's roadrunner, for example—are more geographically specific.

The range of representative symbols is extraordinarily broad, especially in the U.S. section of the Plains. (The approval process in the Prairie Provinces is far more bureaucratic and stringent, resulting in fewer official symbols.) Texas has three state mammals, large (longhorn), small (armadillo), and flying (free-tailed bat); Nebraska has a state soil, the Holdrege series; Texas, North Dakota, and Colorado recognize square dancing as their state dance; New Mexico claims the bizcochito as its state cookie; and Colorado has a state tartan, which, generously, "may be worn by any resident or friend of Colorado, whether or not of Celtic heritage." More ubiquitous icons include state and province flags, seals, mottos, and songs, the last of which have a tendency to nostalgia.

How are these diverse symbols chosen, and why? Economic influence plays a role; hence, milk is North Dakota's official state beverage, in recognition of the importance of the dairy industry. Official flowers and birds are often promoted by women's clubs, and agricultural and conservation societies are often behind the selection of state grasses. Selections are sometimes made more democratically: Nebraska schoolchildren chose the western meadowlark as the state bird, and in 1982 55,000 schoolchildren in 425 Montana schools selected the grizzly bear as the state animal by a two-to-one margin over the elk. Sometimes symbols are chosen by happenstance. In 1956 the North Dakota Motor Vehicle Department put the words "Peace Garden State" on its license plates in recognition of the International Peace Garden, which straddles the international boundary with Manitoba. The name proved so popular that the 1957 legislature made it official. It certainly beats Great American Desert.

David J. Wishart
University of Nebraska–Lincoln

STURGIS MOTORCYCLE RALLY

See SPORTS AND RECREATION: Sturgis Motorcycle Rally

TREE PLANTING AND CLIMATE CHANGE

One method proposed for conquering the arid frontier in the Great Plains was tree planting. Settlers brought with them plant-climate theories whose origins ultimately can be traced to ancient Greece. A belief in trees having a modifying effect on dry lands had become widespread in Europe by the time of Columbus. When European American farmers faced the Great Plains, some optimistically believed that tree planting would turn the Great American Desert into a garden.

Supportive arguments appeared in writings of travelers such as Frederick Olmsted and Ferdinand Hayden as early as the 1850s. It was during the 1870–90 period, however, that the myth of using trees to influence the climate and over a period of years increase the rainfall and improve conditions for agriculture received the most attention. Some influential sponsors of this theory were members of the newly created U.S. Forest Service. The first three chiefs, F. B. Hough, N. H. Egleston, and B. E. Fernow, all authored articles endorsing the benefits of tree planting. Fernow proposed that nature, if left to itself, would forest almost the entire world. Support came from the dean of the Industrial College, Charles E. Bessey, and Agricultural College professor Harvey Culbertson at the University of Nebraska. Bessey told the Nebraska State Board of Agriculture in 1886 that the Plains were dry because they were treeless and advocated tree planting to change this condition. To prove his point, Bessey, with the aid of Fernow, planted the only U.S. man-made national forest (Halsey) in the Sandhills of Nebraska, a forest, it might be added, that has hardly thrived.

State governments recognized the need to encourage tree planting both to attract immigrants and to replace the trees that had been cut by the railroads and military. In 1873 the federal government officially encouraged tree planting with the Timber Culture Act, which required a settler to plant trees on (initially) forty acres of a quarter section in order to secure patent to the land. Introduced by Nebraska senator Phineas W. Hitchcock, the bill carried the argument that growth of timber would not only provide wood but also influence the climate.

New settlers, including Rev. C. S. Harrison, upheld the tree-planting theory. Reverend Harrison founded the town of Arborville, Nebraska, in 1871 and established a tree nursery. He wrote in 1873 that the "desert" would soon be forested to the base of the Rocky Mountains. J. Sterling Morton, Nebraska's secretary of agriculture, continued the crusade of tree planting by launching Arbor Day in 1872. As a result, Nebraska was known as the Tree Planting State long before it became the Cornhusker State. Railroads also supported the benefits of tree planting in order to promote their land sales to prospective settlers.

Tree planting in the Great Plains continued to be supported by many individuals and groups even after the droughts of the 1890s dispelled notions of an improved climate linked to tree planting. Claims, however, became more realistic. It was recognized that trees could have a positive effect on microscale climate, and the beneficial qualities of shelterbelts and windbreaks on the Plains have continued to be emphasized.

See also POLITICS AND GOVERNMENT: Morton, J. Sterling.

M. Jean Ferrill
Northern Michigan University

Bessey, C. "The Grasses and Forage Plants of Nebraska." In *Annual Report of the Nebraska State Board of Agriculture, 1886*. Lincoln: Nebraska State Journal: 208–9. Elliott, R. S. "Climate of Kansas." In *Annual Report of the Board of Regents of the Smithsonian Institution for 1870*. Washington DC: 472–74. Fernow, B. E. "Forest Planting on the Plains." In *Annual Report of the Nebraska State Board of Agriculture, 1890*. Lincoln: Nebraska State Journal: 140.

WALL DRUG

Wall Drug is a world-famous attraction located in Wall, South Dakota. The community of Wall is situated on the east "wall" of the Badlands, just fifty-four miles southeast of Rapid City. Wall Drug began as a country pharmacy serving local farmers and ranchers and the residents of a small, western South Dakota community.

In the early years of the Depression, Theodore Edward Hustead, a recent graduate of pharmacy school, purchased the existing drugstore in Wall using a three-thousand-dollar inheritance from his father. Because local farmers and ranchers were dried out, they had little

Ted Hustead in front of Wall Drug, ca. 1932

money to spend in town. For a number of years, Ted and his wife and partner, Dorothy, noticed a steady stream of autos headed west on Route 16A. The problem was that very few of these autos were taking the time to pull off the two-lane highway. In the summer of 1936, during a particularly hot spell, Dorothy had the inspiration of offering free ice water to travelers. Ted immediately set to work making signs, modeled after the old Burma Shave highway signs. Each phrase of the message was written on a board, and all the boards were then placed along the highway, spaced so that people could read each sign as they drove along. Advertising a free, desirable product to get people into the store proved to be immensely successful. More than sixty years later, with many signs located in far-off places, Wall Drug has grown to a 76,000-square-foot complex that includes two malls. A thirsty traveler can still find free ice water there, along with five-cent coffee.

Sheila R. Aaker
Black Hills State University

Hustead, Ted. "Wall and Water." *Guideposts* (July 1982): 34–37. Jennings, Dana Close. *Free Ice Water! The Story of Wall Drug*. Aberdeen SD: North Plains Press, 1969.

WESTERNS

See FILM: Westerns

WEST RIVER COUNTRY

Travelers heading west in South Dakota on Interstate 90 confront the geographic and cultural distinctiveness of the "west river country" as they cross the Missouri River at Chamberlain. The countryside they have traversed to that point is farm country, albeit increasingly sweeping, open, and treeless. Its talismans are the nineteenth-century white frame houses, the hipped-roof dairy barns, the fenced fields, the familiar crops of corn and soybeans. West of the river the land is starkly higher, drier, rougher, and emptier. Farms and ranches are far fewer, scattered so widely that travelers might scan the horizon in vain for several miles, looking for a telltale grove to mark human habitation. Farm and ranch buildings, when they do appear, are often less substantial than those east of the river. The twentieth-century homesteading frontier that shaped the west river country left its legacy in the small claim shacks that residents cobbled together to create homes and outbuildings once the boom years ended.

The mystique of the west river country lies in its harsh environment and its dramatic history. The Lakota people, nomadic buffalo hunters, skilled horsemen, and feared warriors, claimed the region as their own. When the U.S. government forced them to reservations after Red Cloud's War in 1868, the reservations and west river country became virtually synonymous. The west river country in many minds was the land of "savages." The open range cattle years, though short-lived, brought to the region hard-riding, hard-living ranchers and cowboys who lived without civi-

lization or amenities, wresting their living from cruel nature and glorying in their freedom. The west river country, under their tutelage, became a land associated with physical prowess, self-reliance, and romance.

The final ingredient in the west river mystique came with the homesteading rush after 1900. It brought with it farmers, town builders, speculators, and dreamers—people who came to transform the land they perceived as both a savage and a romantic wilderness. They hoped to create a productive agricultural paradise. They reduced the size of the reservations, fenced the open range, laid railroad tracks, plowed the tough sod, and built market towns across the prairie. But repeated drought and hard times reshaped and reduced their ambitions until mere survival in the face of hardship became their definition of success. The west river country in the farming years became a land of hard work, struggle, and intense pride, virtues still prized there today.

Paula M. Nelson
University of Wisconsin–Platteville

Nelson, Paula M. *After the West Was Won: Homesteaders and Town Builders in Western South Dakota, 1900–1917.* Iowa City: University of Iowa Press, 1986. Nelson, Paula M. *The Prairie Winnows out Its Own: The West River Country of South Dakota in the Years of Depression and Dust.* Iowa City: University of Iowa Press, 1996.

WILD AND SCENIC RIVERS

See WATER: Wild and Scenic Rivers

WILD WEST SHOWS

Wild West shows, including Buffalo Bill's *Wild West*, Pawnee Bill's *Historical Wild West*, Buckskin Bill's *Realistic Wild West*, and the Miller brothers' *101 Wild West Show*, were outdoor spectacles of western pageantry that came out of the Great Plains during the last decades of the nineteenth and first decades of the twentieth centuries. The showmen who created these extravaganzas made Great Plains imagery their stock-in-trade. They paraded figures like the frontier scout, the Plains Indian warrior, and the cowboy hero, touted them as "real" or "authentic," and made them central to popular views about the American West at home and abroad. Their success stemmed from Americans' nostalgia about the passing of the frontier. The shows blended myth and reality in a simplified and patriotic fashion that reinforced popular notions about the nation's Manifest Destiny, identity, and gender roles: they were scripted dramatizations about the "winning of the West."

The character that best symbolized the winning of the West in Wild West shows was the frontier scout. The scout had been a standard hero of dime novels, but he became an even greater heroic icon through the Wild West shows. Showmen like William F. "Buffalo Bill" Cody, Gordon W. "Pawnee Bill" Lillie, Dr. William F. Carver, and similar self-promoters re-created themselves as scouts. They dressed in buckskins, were portrayed as sure and quick with wit and weapons, and assumed a rough-and-tumble facade that idealized west-

ward expansion. They represented the triumph of the forces of good and of civilization, and they were held up to spectators as models of proper American manhood. Conquest of Native Americans was central to such an image, and Cody particularly identified himself this way, even (ironically, given the latter's fate) by associating his image with George Armstrong Custer.

Plains Indians were vital to the success of Wild West shows and were prominent in their advertisements and in the shows. Advertisements for Cody's show enticed crowds to come see the "horde of war-painted Arapahos, Cheyenne, and Sioux Indians," while Lillie employed Osages, Pawnees, and Kiowas in his show. Wild West shows depicted Plains Indian life as the antithesis to "civilized" life. They portrayed Native Americans as savages from a wild land but with a martial spirit that made them worthy adversaries, and so famous warriors became popular figures to include in show casts. Geronimo joined Pawnee Bill's show and was advertised as "The Worst Indian That Ever Lived," and Cody's hiring of Sitting Bull in 1885 led to the Sioux being the most prized Plains Indians in Wild West shows. Always, the role of Native Americans was to attack whites and to be conquered. Many of the great set programs of the Wild West shows—"The Burning of Trapper Tom's Cabin," "The Fight at Wounded Knee," "Capture of the Deadwood Mail Coach," and "The Battle of the Little Big Horn"—featured Plains Indian attacks. These programs demonstrated to viewers that the fight for the West was complete, that force had been necessary, and that victory was certain.

The cowboy hero, perhaps the most recognized icon of the Great Plains, had his beginnings with the Wild West shows. Indeed, before William F. Cody presented William Levi "Buck" Taylor to audiences, there was no popular cowboy hero. Cody and other Wild West showmen made the cowboy a saleable figure. Gradually, cowboys elbowed aside Native Americans and scouts as the major attractions at the shows, especially during the early twentieth century. Cowboys and cowboy skills became central to a myriad of Wild West shows, including the Millers' 101 Ranch show, with its rodeolike performances. It was on the Millers' show that Bill Pickett captivated onlookers with his sanguine art of "bulldogging" and easterner Tom Mix learned the cowboy-entertainer skills that he later transferred to silent Western movies.

The heyday of the Wild West shows ended in 1913, when Cody and Lillie dissolved their merged *Two Bills* show, though Wild West shows continued through the 1930s in combination with rodeos and circuses. Financial problems and the cinema's growing popularity contributed to the shows' demise. Still, before film took over as the vehicle of western imagery, millions of people experienced the "reality" of the Great Plains at various Wild West shows. The Wild West shows moved western life from the realm of history into mythology and popular culture and shaped ideas and images of America's frontier past that persist today.

S. Matthew DeSpain
University of Oklahoma

Moses, L. G. *Wild West Shows and the Image of American Indians, 1883–1933*. Albuquerque: University of New Mexico Press, 1996. Reddin, Paul. *Wild West Shows*. Urbana: University of Illinois Press, 1999. White, Richard. "Frederick Jackson Turner and Buffalo Bill." In *The Frontier in American Culture*, edited by James R. Grossman. Berkeley: University of California Press, 1994: 7–65.

WINDMILLS

Windmills are machines designed to convert the force of the wind into power to be used by humans. In the Great Plains, windmills were used, and continue to be used, primarily to pump water for consumption by people and domestic animals. Windmill installations typically consist of the actual wind machine and a tower (derrick) to support it in the air.

Most windmills used in the Great Plains were of self-governing design. This means that they automatically turned to face changing wind directions and automatically controlled their own speeds of operation to avoid destruction from centrifugal force during high winds. The first commercially successful self-governing windmills in America were invented and patented in 1854 by Daniel Halladay in Connecticut. By 1863 the factory producing Halladay's wind machines had relocated to Illinois, closer to a growing market for windmills in the Great Plains and Midwest.

Windmills started to appear in considerable numbers in the Great Plains during the 1870s, but the heyday for their use spanned the decades from the 1880s to the 1920s. Dozens of companies produced them. In time, tens of thousands of these wind machines came into use, principally for pumping water from drilled wells. A small minority of the early windmills converted the force of the wind into rotary power for operating small farm machines such as feed grinders, corn shellers, and wood saws.

The initial windmills in the Great Plains employed wheels and vanes made from wood, combined with cast iron and steel mechanical components. Manufacturers painted them in bright colors similar to other farm machines. All-metal windmills began appearing in the 1870s, but it was not until the 1890s that

"Currie" windmill pumping water for livestock in Lincoln County, Colorado

they came into widespread use. Production of steel windmills gradually supplanted that of "wooden" mills, although the latter remained available commercially into the 1940s. Starting in the 1920s, some residents of the Great Plains began using specially designed wind machines to produce electricity principally for domestic use.

Over the years windmills became visual icons in the Great Plains. One reason for this phenomenon probably stemmed from their appearance. Windmills on their towers constituted some of the very few vertical elements in the otherwise horizontal Plains environment. Furthermore, many residents of the region associate fond remembrances with windmills and their life-giving water, from cool drinks after long hours of field work to the experience of learning to swim in livestock-watering reservoirs. Many Plains residents to this day express their emotional attachments to windmills as historical and aesthetic survivals connected with earlier times.

Several economic and technological factors contributed to the decline in use of traditional windmills in the Great Plains. The first major competition the wind machines met came from small internal combustion engines, used by some farmers and ranchers for mechanical work, including pumping of water supplies. The decline of agricultural commodity prices in 1921, following World War I, reduced the

ability of people to purchase new windmills, a situation that worsened with general economic depression during the 1930s. The passage of the 1935 Rural Electrification Act enabled many rural people in the Plains to begin securing comparatively inexpensive electricity, which they then often used to operate power pumps, further decreasing demand for windmills.

In the half-century following World War II, windmills remained prominent elements of the built environment in the Great Plains. In most counties in the Plains "windmillers" still continue their business of installing and repairing windmills, which remain available from manufacturers both in the Great Plains and beyond. Because of personal sentiment, many residents in the region have carefully preserved historic windmills as tangible links with their past.

See also INDUSTRY: Wind Energy.

T. Lindsay Baker
Hill College

Baker, T. Lindsay. *A Field Guide to American Windmills*. Norman: University of Oklahoma Press, 1985. Eide, A. Clyde. "Free as the Wind." *Nebraska History* 51 (spring 1970): 25–41. *Windmillers' Gazette* (1982–present).

THE WIZARD OF OZ

See FILM: *The Wizard of Oz*

Industry

Anna Anderson #1, 1905

INDUSTRY

On a lonely stretch of the Trans-Canada Highway, in the heart of what local radio announcers call the "Wheat Belt," a large sign advises motorists that the next turn to the left will take them to the Great Plains Industrial Drive. The sign, on the flat, dusty, and seemingly empty Saskatchewan landscape, looks like a statement of hope rather than of economic developments already realized.

In the popular mind, the Great Plains of North America consists of vast open spaces inhabited by cowboys, wheat farmers, oil-patch wildcatters, and roughnecks. The huge smoke-belching factories and blast furnaces of industrial America and the microchip valleys of modern technology are located elsewhere. The perception is that people living on the Plains produce only raw materials, mainly agricultural, that are shipped in a raw or semiprocessed state to major industrial, manufacturing, and processing centers outside the region.

There is, nonetheless, a great deal of industrial activity in the region if one considers not only the primary and secondary processing and manufacturing, whereby raw materials are converted into finished consumer products, but also the extraction, handling, and marketing of the region's resources and the numerous regional service industries. Developments in the various resource industries are similar in some respects, but there are also important differences, making it necessary to examine them separately.

The Fur Trade

The first major natural resources extracted and exported from large portions of the Canadian Prairies and Northern Great Plains were bison meat and the skins of fur-bearing animals. Furs and later bison robes were exported raw, with only basic processing being done by the Native producers or traders. Final processing and use of the resource occurred mainly outside the Great Plains, while most of the supplies were imported.

The fur and meat trade in the Great Plains began in the 1780s, when the Prairie Provinces became a scene of intense rivalry between the Hudson's Bay and North West Companies. Between 1780 and 1821 both companies established numerous trading posts along the North and South Saskatchewan, Souris, Qu'Appelle, and Red Rivers. These posts furnished sizable amounts of beaver, muskrat, marten, and other skins, but their main function was to procure provisions, primarily pemmican, for trading posts located to the north in the Canadian boreal forests. The traders at these northern posts used the pemmican during their long trips to the primary fur distribution centers on Hudson Bay and in Montreal.

This pattern changed dramatically in the 1820s and 1830s. In 1821 the two rival companies united, making it possible for the reorganized Hudson's Bay Company to establish a monopoly over the fur trade in the Canadian Prairies. The Hudson's Bay Company attempted to take advantage of its monopoly by reducing the number of trading posts and placing the fur production on a more sustained ecological basis. Unfortunately, the attempt came too late. By the 1820s, beaver, the primary hunted animal of the fur trade, had already become virtually extinct in many areas of the Canadian boreal forest and Prairie Provinces. The final blow to the beaver trade came in the 1830s, when European demand for beaver abruptly collapsed due to a change in fashion. To overcome these difficulties, the Hudson's Bay Company shifted its production in the Prairie Provinces from pelts to bison robes, which were in great demand in the rapidly growing industrial centers of eastern North America.

The 1830s also saw an expansion of the American fur trade onto the Northern Plains south of the forty-ninth parallel. American traders had attempted to advance onto the Northern Plains ever since Lewis and Clark had praised the region's rich animal resources, but it was not until after the introduction of steamboat transportation on the Missouri River in the early 1830s that a large-scale U.S. trade in the area became possible. The American fur trade on the Northern Plains was controlled from St. Louis, the artery of the trade was the Missouri, and its main product was bison robes. By the mid-1830s the American Fur Company had established a virtual monopoly over this trade, a position it and its direct successors held until the 1860s. The trade in furs was never a major economic activity on the Southern Plains, where the rivers did not provide reliable year-round navigation and there were fewer animals with rich and thick winter furs.

Ranching

After the demise of the fur trade, a series of developments made possible the emergence of new economic undertakings that exploited other major resources of the region. The new developments making such initiatives possible included the earlier purchase by the United States of the Louisiana Territory from France in 1803, the drawing of the boundary between British and U.S. territory at the forty-ninth parallel in 1818, the acquisition through conquest of northern New Spain by the United States in 1848, the military resolution of the quarrel between the northern and southern states in 1865, the acquisition by Canada of Rupert's Land in 1869, and the military or negotiated subjugation of the Native peoples by 1890. These developments opened the Great Plains to whatever new economic initiatives U.S. and Canadian governments and businessmen thought appropriate.

When they first came into possession of the Plains neither Americans nor Canadians were quite sure what to make of the vast, semiarid lands. Many regarded the Plains, described by Edwin James, chronicler of Stephen Long's 1820 expedition, as the "Great American Desert," as little more than an impediment to national expansion and occupation of the more promising lands on the Pacific slope of the continent. Many early Plains settlers who tried to apply farming methods common in more humid areas failed or paid a very high price for limited success. As a result, the settlement frontier jumped across the Great Plains to the Pacific slope and then worked its way onto the Plains from both east and west. That was followed after the mid-1890s by a massive northward thrust from the United States, augmenting the settlement of the Canadian prairies.

The Plains were very rich in one important resource: there was an abundance of grass, which had sustained enormous buffalo herds for hundreds of years. The destruction of these great herds by the 1880s made possible the raising of domestic cattle on the great open ranges. While there is some disagreement, most historians trace the immediate origins of the Great Plains range cattle industry to the Nueces River valley of southern Texas. That valley is not part of the Great Plains, but, beginning in the 1860s, significant numbers of cattle were driven northward from the Nueces Valley onto the open plains. There the animals mingled with livestock brought in by early settlers and with some of the stock from former Spanish *encomiendas*, or estates. As demand for meat increased with the construction of numerous military posts, the opening up of mining developments in adjacent mountain regions, and the construction of railroads, the size of the herds also increased, and cattlemen extended their operations northward.

Transcontinental railways across the Plains also provided the means to take the cattle to eastern markets, and major cattle drives to rail towns became a much-celebrated aspect of regional life. There was rapid expansion throughout the 1860s and 1870s, and by 1885 some of the ranchers from the Powder River territory of Wyoming began to drive their cattle northward to the summer grazing grounds of the Cypress Hills and the foothills of the Canadian Rockies.

Open range ranching, in spite of the longevity of cowboy myths in Hollywood movies and at regional stampedes and rodeos, remained the primary industry of most of the Great Plains for only two or three decades. And the popular image of the stalwart individualism of the cowboy at one end of the business should not obscure the fact that at the other end ranching was dominated by a few large companies. Closed range ranching, of course, remains an important economic activity in many parts of the region.

Natural and human-made disasters and a growing demand that the cattle ranges be opened to farmers broke up the large operations. Serious overgrazing, combined with a harsh winter in 1885–86, destroyed the herds in Colorado, Kansas, and the Texas Panhandle, with some operators reporting losses of up to 85 percent of their animals. The next winter a similar disaster overtook the ranchers of Wyoming, Montana, and the Dakotas, accounting in part for the driving of cattle from Wyoming into the new ranching frontier of southern Alberta and Saskatchewan. The industry prospered there for a time, but all the remaining large-scale operators in Canada and adjacent U.S. territories faced economic ruin in 1906–7, when an unusually severe winter destroyed their herds.

On some southern ranges sheep replaced the cattle herds, but all grazing operations came under increasing pressure with the arrival of the farmers. Homesteaders and settlers were eager to transform the open cattle ranges into an agricultural garden. In the United States they began to encroach on the grazing lands of the Plains as early as the 1860s, while in Canada the major influx of homesteaders only began in the mid-1890s.

In the contest between ranchers and farmers the operations of the former were relegated to the semiarid High Plains, hilly lands, and other tracts of land not well suited to the cultivation of cereal grains. Later disasters would show that farmers broke vast tracts of marginal land that had to be returned to grazing during the disastrous droughts that periodically afflict the region. During the settlement booms, however, farmers usually had their way, sometimes causing terrible environmental damage that could have been minimized if land best suited for grazing had been left to the ranchers.

Cattle ranching promoted some related business undertakings, most notably meatpacking plants. In the United States the beef-packing industry in the late nineteenth century was dominated by the "Big Five": Swift and Company, Armour and Company, Wilson Packing Company, Morris Packing Company, and Cudahy Packing Company. Kansas City and Fort Worth were the main centers of the industry. In 1903 these companies joined to form the National Packing Company, which controlled the industry until it was dissolved in 1920. Thereafter, the location of packing plants became more diffuse throughout the Great Plains, but these five companies were still in control. Most of the equipment and supplies needed by ranchers and later by the packers and processors were shipped in from outside.

In Canada ranchers supplied meat in the 1880s to railway construction contractors and the federal Department of Indian Affairs. In the late 1890s the Yukon gold rush absorbed much of their produce, but surplus supplies were sent east, either to Toronto or Chicago, until Patrick Burns established meatpacking plants first in Calgary and then in Edmonton and Prince Albert. Burns, however, was more interested in ranching than in meatpacking. Together with fellow ranchers George Lane, A. E. Cross, and Archie McLean, Burns was one of the "Big Four" who created the world-famous Calgary Stampede in 1912. The Burns meatpacking operations were sold in 1928 to the Toronto-based Dominion Securities Corporation. As is the case in the United States, the meatpacking industry in Canada has become more diverse, with strong local companies such as Olympic Meats in Saskatoon and Gainers in Edmonton competing with U.S.-based international companies.

Cattle were significant as a revenue-producing freight for the new railroads. Rail construction and operating crews consumed much of the meat produced by the ranchers, but the railroads, the men who built and financed them, and the construction supplies all came from outside the region. Cattle ranchers, like the fur traders before them and grain farmers later, sold an essentially unprocessed staple commodity in volatile outside markets over which they had little or no control.

On the High Plains, in the interior valleys of the mountain ranges, in the driest regions of the open Plains, and rough country such as the Flint Hills of Kansas, ranching has remained an important industry. Taken together, West Texas, Kansas, and Nebraska remain the largest cattle-producing region in the world, and the industry still exerts a powerful economic and political influence in many parts of the Plains. In most areas it has, nevertheless, yielded its place of economic primacy to cereal agriculture after only two or at most three decades during which the large cattle companies and their individualistic hired cowboys dominated not only the economy but also an entire way of life on the Plains.

Precious Metals

Major mining developments on the Plains and in adjacent territories coincided with the expansion of ranching and provided important markets for the beef raised by the ranchers. The most important discoveries of precious metals in the second half of the nineteenth century, however, occurred in the Rocky Mountains to the west of the Great Plains. There was only one spectacular gold field on the Plains, and that was in the Black Hills of South Dakota, where old Indian legends of important gold deposits were confirmed in 1874. A discovery that year near present-day Custer and others at Deadwood Gulch and Gold Run Gulch in 1876 brought in swarms of prospectors. The Homestake Mine at Lead, South Dakota, employed as many as 500 men in the 1880s and remained until recently one of the most productive gold mines in the United States.

Placer mining was possible for individual prospectors, but the extraction of gold imbedded in rock required expensive crushing, smelting, and refining equipment that only wealthy individuals and large corporations could afford. As a result, gold prospecting, which at midcentury was undertaken by thousands of independent amateurs, became the preserve of large and wealthy corporations. Independents, however, were never entirely driven from the field.

The Great Plains yielded few other precious metals. The great silver discoveries in the mountain states and the contentious "Free Silver" campaigns of Great Plains politicians (which proposed the unlimited coinage of silver in the 1890s) gave that metal a prominence not matched by the actual silver-mining developments in the region. Some rich zinc and pumice deposits were discovered and developed in Kansas, while several Plains states have commercially viable bentonite and other clay product developments. Traces of other precious metals and minerals can be found in a few places, most notably in the Black Hills. The search for precious metals on the Plains resulted in few major discoveries, but it was important because it brought in many would-be miners who took up farming when their dreams of a new bonanza faded. Mining developments in adjacent mountain states also created lucrative markets for the agricultural products of the Plains.

Agriculture

Agriculture became the dominant industry of the American Great Plains and Canadian Prairies during the second half of the nineteenth century and the early decades of the twentieth century. Farming operations had, of course, been carried on in some parts of the Plains for many years. The Indigenous people of the Central Plains, for example, had developed agriculture long before the coming of

The Ellison shaft group, cyanide plants, and the open cut at the Homestake Mine, Lead, South Dakota, between 1940 and 1950

European settlers. Early European American settlers on the Plains often had difficulty making a living from the soil. Coming from more humid and temperate climates, they found it difficult to cope with the drought and heat in the South and with the short frost-free growing season in the North. As a result, subsistence agriculture was all but impossible for non-Native people, while lack of suitable products and the means to bring them to market militated against the development of any form of commercial agriculture, at least until military, mining, and railroad developments provided the needed markets and transportation facilities.

The transcontinental railroads were critically important in the development of Plains agriculture. The Union Pacific Railroad, completed in 1869, was the first to cross the region from east to west. Its construction crews provided lucrative but transitory markets for local farm products. Once built, the railroads provided the necessary means to carry grain grown on the Plains to eastern markets. Thanks to their land grants, the railroads also had a direct interest in bringing in as many new settlers as possible and to see them established so that more traffic could be generated. At least six additional transcontinental railroad lines were built across the Prairies and Plains between 1880 and 1915, while other major railroads provided branch-line facilities and important north–south linkages. The railroads provided the necessary transportation services that made possible the export of wheat from the region and the importation of the needed equipment and supplies that were not produced within the region.

Major grain-handling, milling, and marketing facilities were also needed. Most facilities were established by large corporate interests whose headquarters were located in large urban centers outside the region such as Minneapolis, Milwaukee, and Chicago. Winnipeg was one Plains city that did provide more grain-marketing, wholesaling, and other intermediate economic services. Many of the large grain handling, milling, and marketing companies, whether located within or outside the region, had close financial links with the large and powerful railroad and financial corporations and were consequently often regarded as agents of outside interests.

Successful Plains farming depended on the production and export of wheat. The fortunes of Plains farmers fluctuated with the weather and the price of wheat delivered at Liverpool for distribution throughout the British Isles and northern Europe. Exceptionally strong demand during World War I gave wheat virtually complete dominance of the Plains farming economy. But the wartime bonanza was followed by great market instability in the 1920s, when, twice, the average price of wheat in one year fell to less than half that obtained the previous year. This was followed in the 1930s by the disastrous collapse of world markets when wheat prices fell to a 400-year low and to one-tenth of the record high prices paid in 1919.

These developments demonstrated that what happened beyond the farm gate was often far more important to the success and prosperity of the farm than anything done on the farm. Beyond the farm gate, large impersonal corporations, institutions, and interest groups manipulated market conditions in their own interest, making a mockery of the alleged independence of the individual producers and of the myth that rewards were directly linked to hard work and intelligent management.

The market instability of the 1920s and the disasters of the 1930s convinced many Plains farmers that they had become too dependent on a single export commodity and that they should diversify their economy. In areas where there was sufficient precipitation, most notably in the Red River Valley of the North, sugar beets, oilseeds, vegetables, animal fodder crops, and truck farming supplemented or replaced cereal grains. Irrigation, either through stream diversions, particularly in southern Alberta, or the pumping of groundwater in Kansas, Nebraska, and Texas, made the planting of vast areas of similar crops possible. Elsewhere, poultry, dairy, hog and beef operations, including large feedlot operations in which range cattle were prepared for market, sprang up. In Kansas and Nebraska the decline of wheat as the primary agricultural export commodity led to a revival of corn. Farther south in Texas and New Mexico irrigated cotton, which had gained a hold during World War I, became very important.

A second aspect of regional economic diversification involved the processing of agricultural products grown on the Plains. Instead of sending the produce out in its raw state, efforts were made to do more of the processing in the region. The big slaughterhouses in Chicago and Toronto faced increased competition as new packing plants were built in several of the larger Plains urban centers, often with provincial or state subsidies and tax concessions. Similarly, numerous sugar refineries were built to process locally grown sugar beets. Oilseed-crushing plants and refineries transformed the economies of several communities, and vegetable dehydration plants, particularly those specializing in the manufacture of potato chips, became the economic mainstay of Prairie and Plains towns such as Winkler and Steinbach in Manitoba and Clark in South Dakota. Specialized milling operations facilitated processing of cereal products, while new pelletizing technology created new markets, most notably in Japan, for hay and grass grown on the Plains. Discoveries of huge potash deposits in Saskatchewan and New Mexico provided a new staple export commodity but also facilitated the establishment of chemical fertilizer–manufacturing plants near the mines.

Economic diversification also extended to the establishment of numerous agricultural service industries. Transportation was probably the most important. The railroads provided a wide array of economic services, although their primacy as carriers of goods and

products being shipped into or out of the region declined after World War II, when automotive forms of transportation, supported by massive government highway construction programs, became more important.

Wholesalers and jobbers of all kinds provided other vital economic services for people living on the Plains. These services related to both the assembling and handling of products destined for export and the making of all the arrangements necessary for the importation and distribution of the great variety of supplies needed but not produced by the region's residents. Winnipeg was, for many years, the most important regional wholesale, jobbing, grain-handling, and marketing center in the Prairie Provinces. Later, with the growth of other resource industries, businesses in other Prairie cities such as Calgary and Edmonton provided similar services. In the United States, by contrast, many of these intermediate economic services were provided by businesses in cities such as Denver, Dallas–Fort Worth, Minneapolis, and Chicago, all marginal to or outside of the Great Plains region. In that respect, then, the Canadian Prairie economy became more diversified than the adjoining Plains economy in the United States.

Another important agriculturally related industry is the manufacture and, more importantly, the modification and adaptation of assembly line–produced machines to meet local requirements. A few so-called full-line farm machinery manufacturers located their factories on the Plains, providing an industrial base for places such as Hesston, Kansas, Hastings, Nebraska, and Yorkton, Saskatchewan. Most of the big farm machinery factories remain outside the region. Many mass-produced farm machines, however, require modifications and adaptations to make them suitable for local conditions or specialty crops. As a result, short-line agricultural implement manufacturers have prospered on the Plains, as have small factories manufacturing or adapting other equipment and machinery needed by Plains farmers.

The modification of large assembly line–produced machines has also given a number of Plains industries a profitable niche in the automotive industry, where modifications of trucks and vans for specialized farm, recreational, and other domestic uses are needed. The major factories are located elsewhere, but shops adapting the products of those factories to meet local requirements or to take advantage of reliable and inexpensive regional labor resources have created employment and revenue for many Plains residents.

Agricultural diversification in its various forms has helped to stabilize the Plains economy, but the region remains heavily dependent on the export of agricultural products, and international marketing crises quickly engulf not only the primary producers but also those who serve those producers or process what has been produced. Diversification into nonagricultural products, most notably fossil fuels, has, however, reduced regional economic dependence on agriculture.

Fossil Fuels

The American Great Plains and the Canadian Prairies have exceptionally rich deposits of fossil fuels. The most abundant of these are the coal deposits along the entire eastern slope of the Rockies and in numerous large pockets farther east. Most of the coal found on the Plains, however, is lignite or brown wood coal that has been fossilized to some extent but retains its distinctly wooden texture. It is inferior to anthracite and bituminous coal for heating purposes. The fact that it expands when burning rather than simply burning down evenly increases the risk of explosions when such coal is used to fire steam engines and locomotives. Because of its high sulfur content, lignite coal also produces more pollution than the superior coals. As a result, although substantial income has been derived from the lignite coal mined on the Plains, the availability of superior coals elsewhere has prevented the exploitation of this resource to its full potential. Some of the lignite deposits are sufficiently close to the surface so that strip mining is possible, but there are also deep-seam lignite coal mines on the Plains. Some, most notably those in the Black Hills of South Dakota, produce a much higher quality coal than the strip-mining operations on the Missouri Escarpment. The resource is abundant, but discoveries of huge oil and natural gas deposits, particularly at the northern and southern ends of the Great Plains, have limited the exploitation of the coal resources of the region.

The economies and cultures of Texas, Oklahoma, Alberta, and parts of other Plains states and provinces have been radically altered by the discovery and extraction of these fossil fuels. In the south, the Texas cities of Dallas and Houston, both outside the Great Plains region, have been major beneficiaries of oil developments, but several cities on the Southern Plains, most notably the Texas cities of Midland and Odessa as well as Tulsa and Oklahoma City, owe much of their growth to oil. The boom in Midland and Odessa began in the 1920s with numerous local oil discoveries. Odessa became one of the world's largest inland petrochemical centers during World War II, while Midland became a major administrative center, housing offices of more than 200 oil companies by the 1950s. Although both cities have suffered from fluctuations in the oil industry, they remain important oil centers.

In the north, Calgary and Edmonton, both clearly on the Prairies, became major oil capitals following discovery of the huge Leduc field near Edmonton in 1947. There had, however, been earlier natural gas and oil discoveries near Calgary, which became the site of major head or branch offices, while the major cracking plants and oil-related petrochemical industries (the blue-collar oil businesses) located in Edmonton. Oil has become the single most important source of revenue in Texas and Alberta and has spawned numerous related economic activities. Primary processing is done within the region. Efforts have been made to establish major petrochemical industries in the region, but most are still located elsewhere.

Potash

The discovery of massive deposits of potash, used mainly in the manufacture of fertilizers, has given several regions, most notably Saskatchewan and New Mexico, an important new source of economic activity. Technological difficulties, mainly in the sinking, stabilizing, and waterproofing of shafts through the water-bearing layers of gravel that overlie the potash deposits, created major difficulties in the industry immediately after the discovery of marketable quantities of the mineral. Then the industry was beset for a time in the 1960s and 1970s with serious problems of overcapacity in which the less-efficient New Mexico operators sought to protect domestic American markets from Canadian competition. These problems have, however, been largely resolved as international demand for fertilizer increased and trade barriers were lowered or removed. Most of the product undergoes only primary processing before being exported. There are, however, some attempts to promote further processing of potash and many other staple products of the Plains locally.

Health-Care and Service Industries

The relative isolation of most rural people living on the Plains and their remoteness from many essential services resulted in much unnecessary suffering. Nineteenth-century epidemics that decimated the Native peoples were attributable to diseases against which these peoples could offer little resistance. Later, among the homesteaders, lack of the best available health care made women, children, and the elderly particularly vulnerable, and many an old rural cemetery bears mute witness to these tragedies. It was, therefore, not surprising that Plains and Prairie people became particularly concerned about and demanded improved hospital and medical care.

The desperate conditions during the Great Depression of the 1930s gave a particularly strong impetus to the development of government-supported and -sponsored medical care facilities. The first socialist government elected anywhere in North America, the socialist Cooperative Commonwealth Federation government, which came to office in Saskatchewan in 1944, made improved medical care its most important and controversial priority. It, like other provincial and state governments, supported community-based hospital and health-care organizations and facilities. Then in 1961 the Saskatchewan government introduced a comprehensive government-sponsored medical-care program. Socialized medicine became a very controversial issue in Canada, but before the end of the 1960s the federal government had adopted the main features of the Saskatchewan plan, giving Canada a medical-care system that differed sharply from the one previously in force everywhere in North America and continuing in force in the United States. But even where private medicine remained the norm, governments took measures to assist private and community initiatives and to provide basic health-care services for those most in need.

Health care, including medical research, has become a major industry in all parts of North America. In Canada it is the largest single expenditure in the budgets of both provincial and federal governments, while the privately operated systems in the United States absorb a higher percentage of the gross national product than anywhere else in the world.

Rapidly rising health-care costs associated with new and expensive technological and pharmaceutical developments and changing demographics as young people in large numbers migrate from rural to urban areas, together with growing concern about deficit spending by all levels of government, created a health-care crisis in the 1990s. In the ensuing debates tensions between sparsely settled parts of the country and the larger urban centers and between areas with an aging and declining population and new growth centers have become more intense. The health-care industry will certainly continue to expand, but its development on different sides of the forty-ninth parallel and in lightly settled rural areas compared to larger urban centers may well follow divergent patterns.

Tourism

The Great Plains, with their windswept open spaces, have not benefited as much from the post–World War II development of tourism as have the adjacent mountain states and other regions of more conventional natural beauty. The scenic Black Hills of South Dakota, the rich heritage of Native peoples, the pioneer past, the splendid desert and winter resort country of the southwestern Plains, and the hunting and fishing opportunities of the northern parklands and other fish and game habitats have, however, contributed greatly to a growing Great Plains tourist industry. The great mountain parks and resorts, while outside the Plains region, attract millions of tourists every year, many of whom cross the Plains. And every major city, town, and village along the major freeways in the United States and the Trans-Canada and Yellowhead Highways in Canada offers basic services to tired, hungry, thirsty, or, alas, mechanically disabled tourists. Most of the major tourist routes run in an east–west direction, but Alberta has also become a beneficiary of a strong northward pull as tourists point their horseless carriages and truckers their burdened tractor-trailers toward the glories of that enormous wartime construction project—the Alaska Highway.

Defense Industries

Military activity supported large sectors of the Great Plains economy during the major U.S.–Native American wars. The subjugation of the Native peoples after about 1890 sharply reduced the need for a strong military presence during the mining and agricultural phase of Great Plains development. During and after World War II, however, the strategic location of the region resulted once again in a sharply increased military presence.

American military expenditures in the Pacific Northwest during the war created a major economic boom for Edmonton, the jumping off point for the North, and for major sectors of the Canadian agricultural community, which supplied much of the food required by the incoming American construction workers. The Canadian Prairies also became the primary training ground for the Commonwealth Air Training Program, under which thousands of British, Canadian, Australian, and other prospective military pilots obtained their basic training on the relatively flat terrain. During the cold war numerous electronic surveillance and antiballistic missile sites were built on the American Great Plains. Also in the United States, major defense contractors, often prompted by government incentives to create jobs in economically depressed areas, have established manufacturing, training, and testing facilities in the region. Boeing, for example, has established a major aircraft assembly plant and related facilities in Wichita, Kansas, serving both military and civilian markets.

The end of the cold war and political pressures to reduce government spending have resulted in cutbacks in the defense industry that have had a major impact on those towns and cities such as Lubbock, Texas, and Rapid City, South Dakota, with large military defense industries or nearby major military bases.

New Footloose Industries

Defense industries were only the most notable of many industries that were established wherever they could take advantage of the largest federal, state, provincial, or municipal grants, tax concessions, the provision at public expense of needed economic infrastructure, the availability of cheap or better-qualified workers, and lower costs of living. Modern computer and electronic technology help industries to overcome many of the disadvantages of geographical remoteness. Omaha, Nebraska, for example, is a major telemarketing center.

Efforts to attract major electronic industries, often in close cooperation with local university and research facilities, have given those Plains cities with large university graduate schools, research institutes, or research-oriented military and transportation industries an advantage over other centers lacking these facilities. Thus, for example, Saskatoon, Saskatchewan, has overtaken its rival, Regina, thanks largely to its ability to attract new electronic industries whose research interests are enriched by work done at the well-established University of Saskatchewan and the large "Innovation Place" research park on the sprawling university campus. In Calgary, Alberta, by contrast, the presence of a rapidly increasing number of company head offices has lured key financial, legal, and taxation specialists to the city, which in turn makes the city more attractive to other industries contemplating a move. The premier of Alberta also places much stock in what he calls the "Alberta Advantage." Alberta is the only Canadian province that does not have a provincial sales tax. Neighboring Saskatchewan, where taxes are higher but the cost of living is lower, in part because of the wider array of services offered by the government, promotes those services in efforts to attract "footloose" industries.

The North American Free Trade Agreement has increased competition between Canadian and American states and provinces trying to attract new industries. The United States frequently cites the higher tax burdens in Canada. Canada promotes the public funding of services such as health care, which saves employers from having to provide expensive private health-insurance plans for their employees. Every state and province and most municipalities are eager to attract footloose industries, but the inducements differ widely. Some, for example, stress the better quality of life available because of low pollution levels; others regard the absence of effective environmental legislation as an advantage in the quest for economic diversification and industrialization.

Conclusion

Industrial activity in the Great Plains is mainly concentrated in the extraction, handling, partial processing, and export of a few staple products. Beginning with the fur trade in the North and on through ranching, grain farming, and gas, oil, and other natural resource developments, the region is an economic hinterland that sells its products in outside markets and is dependent on outside suppliers for most manufactured goods and centralized services.

There have been numerous attempts to diversify the regional economy and to establish a broader industrial base, as the numerous sites set aside for such economic development affirm. Those efforts have been most successful in the early processing of locally extracted natural resources and in a variety of businesses that, directly or indirectly, serve the needs of the basic commodity producers. In recent years, more broadly based service industries, most notably tourism and in some places defense, health-care, and electronics establishments, have contributed to regional economic diversification.

The region has a relatively small population. The extractive and primary processing industries, particularly farming, were at one time quite labor-intensive, but mechanization has reduced the number of people needed to sustain the basic regional industries. Regions with small populations tend to be politically weak in countries where political representation and influence are largely based on population. This has fostered periodic populist political protests and revolts against outside influences, particularly against the "big interests," almost all of which have their power bases outside the region. When William Jennings Bryan made his famous "Cross of Gold" speech in the difficult economic years of the 1890s and William Aberhart vehemently denounced the "Fifty Big Shots" during the worst years of the Great Depression, they provided few clear definitions of exactly who those big shots were. It was enough that they and their listeners believed that there were powerful interests that thwarted their region's economic aspirations.

Such sentiments were reinforced by important class differences. The major extractive industries were dependent on the economic services of large corporations, almost all of which had their headquarters outside the region. Local economic activities, however, were dominated by large numbers of small independent operators. Clashes between farmers and transcontinental railroads, between grain handlers, marketers, millers, and brewers, or between the wildcatters and the major oil companies were often a product of divergent interests of regionally based small independent operators and large international capitalist corporations. Small independent operators rarely think of themselves or their economic activities in terms of "class," but in their hostility and suspicion of big business, big government, and big labor they manifest not only regional but also class characteristics.

Industrial development and the attitudes associated with it evolved rather differently in Canada than in the United States. Seymour Lipset, in his book *Continental Divide*, argues that the values and institutions of the two countries are, in some respects, fundamentally different. Both countries, he argues, were products of the American Revolution, but one adopted classical liberal or Whig values and institutions, while the other adhered to classical conservative or Tory traditions. Other writers have challenged such neat dichotomies, but it must be admitted that government involvement in industrial policies, particularly in the promotion and ownership of key economic infrastructures, is more pronounced in Canada than in the United States.

Differences between the regional economies north and south of the forty-ninth parallel may also be due to the major urban centers that were established within the region in Canada but mainly beyond the peripheries of the region in the United States. Both regions depend on large eastern metropolitan centers to meet their major financial, trade, transportation, and manufacturing needs, but on the American Plains the intermediate economic services are provided by cities such as Minneapolis–St. Paul, Chicago, Kansas City, St. Louis, Dallas, Salt Lake City, and Denver, all of which are on the periphery or outside of the Great Plains. In Canada the areas surrounding the Prairies are not suitable for urban development. The Laurentian Shield to the east, boreal forests and tundra to the north, the Rocky Mountains to the west, and the international boundary to the south made it necessary to establish the major intermediate economic urban centers, notably Winnipeg, Edmonton, Calgary, Saskatoon, and Regina, on the Prairies. Consequently, Canadian Prairie cities have become an integral part of the regional economy and identity, while American cities on the periphery of the Plains seem to be more closely integrated into and responsive to national and international economies.

There are thus some differences between

the economies of the two regions. These differences should not, however, obscure the important structural similarities in the regional economies. The most important of those similarities is the reliance on the extraction, partial processing, and export of natural resources and a dependence on outside sources for most manufactured goods. As a result, the motorist who is diverted onto a Great Plains Industrial Drive will find numerous farm and automotive service, machinery, and agricultural processing industries but few of the large factories normally associated with industrialization.

See also AGRICULTURE: Cattle Ranching; Wheat / IMAGES AND ICONS: Colony of the East / POLITICS AND GOVERNMENT: Bryan, William Jennings; Cooperative Commonwealth Federation / PROTEST AND DISSENT: Aberhart, William / TRANSPORTATION: Railroads, United States; Railways, Canada / WAR: British Commonwealth Air Training Plan.

Ted D. Regehr
University of Saskatchewan and
University of Calgary

Eagle, John A. *The Canadian Pacific Railway and the Development of Western Canada, 1896–1914.* Montreal: McGill-Queen's University Press, 1989. Fowke, V. C. *The National Policy and the Wheat Economy.* Toronto: University of Toronto Press, 1957. Lipset, Seymour Martin. *Continental Divide: The Values and Institutions of the United States and Canada.* New York: Routledge, 1990. Nash, Gerald D. *The American West in the Twentieth Century.* Albuquerque: University of New Mexico Press, 1977. Perloff, Harvey, et al. *Regions, Resources, and Economic Growth.* Baltimore MD: Johns Hopkins University Press, 1960. Richards, John, and Larry Pratt. *Prairie Capitalism: Power and Influence in the New West.* Toronto: McClelland and Stewart Ltd., 1972. Robbins, William G. *Colony and Empire: The Capitalist Transformation of the American West.* Lawrence: University Press of Kansas, 1994.

AEROSPACE

As a twentieth-century phenomenon, the Plains aerospace industry evolved from early interest in airline travel as a means to cope with widely separated population centers and the tendency of overland transportation systems to follow traditional east–west routes. As the tempo of air transportation accelerated, pioneering aircraft manufacturers in the Great Plains began to appear, especially during the years following World War I.

A number of builders survived hard years of competition and erratic financing, and major aircraft-manufacturing entities took many years to mature. With its widely scattered population and agrarian focus, the region always presented major problems in acquiring a large force of technically skilled workers, especially in the case of advanced technologies such as aviation. Manufacturers in the area tended to succeed with smaller, less technically advanced aircraft. These "light plane" designs generated growing numbers in the general aviation sector as distinguished from commercial airliners and military aircraft.

The advent of World War II dramatically changed this picture. Many production centers were organized throughout the Great Plains, partly to locate new aircraft plants away from vulnerable sites near coastlines. Thousands of workers relocated near these new plants; many remained in the region. As the cold war era evolved after 1945, national defense requirements kept many of the wartime centers active in the construction of a new generation of military aircraft. Moreover, postwar prosperity provided a rapidly growing market for a variety of new general aviation aircraft and generated a significant backlog of orders for components used in the postwar generation of bigger, faster commercial passenger transports. Also, succeeding generations of aircraft relied increasingly on electronic and computerized equipment. During the mid-1950s, the aerospace industry appeared, indicating growing dimensions of rocketry and space research. Electronics and computer companies proliferated. Smaller, specialized firms like these often succeeded in supplying components and systems management expertise to the aerospace industry, even though the national centers of aerospace production lay elsewhere.

Several of the areas where aviation and aerospace manufacturing occurred were clearly in the Great Plains region. Moreover, a number of metropolitan centers that lay just outside its boundaries began to employ such a large number of aviation workers that their "footprint" clearly affected considerable innumerable employees who actually lived within the Plains.

In Canada, the center of aviation manufacturing remained in the southeastern part of the country. Following World War II, however, military training bases gave momentum to regional fabricators and suppliers. As the oil and gas industries emerged on the Prairies and the population mushroomed, a technical and industrial infrastructure flourished that contributed to the aviation/aerospace industry. These activities emerged in metropolitan areas such as Edmonton and Calgary. Firms in these cities not only built subassemblies for a variety of major eastern Canadian manufacturers but also offered comprehensive electronic technologies for communications and navigational systems.

In the United States, aircraft manufacturing after World War I built on the enthusiasm of wartime aviation and the availability of venture capital. During the 1920s, although a variety of optimistic companies sprang up in several states, manufacturers of general aviation aircraft succeeded most often, especially around Wichita, Kansas. There, the lack of surface transportation and the energy of wildcatters in the oil business created a market for smaller, agile aircraft. Early builders who eventually survived included Beechcraft and Cessna, specializing in general aviation designs intended to carry four to six passengers. During World War II, these companies turned out thousands of primary trainers for military flight schools.

Wartime necessity also stimulated smaller fabricators of aviation hardware throughout the region and brought major manufacturing plants to urban areas such as Omaha and Lincoln, Nebraska, Kansas City, Kansas, and Fort Worth, Texas. Overnight, the latter made Texas one of the largest aircraft production centers in the United States, turning out thousands of trainers, P-51 Mustang fighters, and B-24 Liberator bombers. The area's concentration of suppliers and workers made it a postwar center as well, producing a long line of jet bombers and fighter aircraft such as the Lockheed F-16. Wichita also produced large military aircraft, and new Boeing facilities there continued to build components for B-52 bombers as well as a long line of postwar Boeing transport planes. In Colorado, the Denver-Boulder locale emerged as a postwar center for aerospace research, producing rocket vehicle components and electronic systems for military and civil applications.

In 2000 manufacturers across the region produced light planes, corporate jets, supersonic fighters, space-flight hardware, and a wide range of electronic aerospace products. A number of ventures involved foreign firms, reflecting the era's global economy.

Roger E. Bilstein
University of Houston–Clear Lake

Bilstein, Roger. *The American Aerospace Industry: From Workshop to Global Enterprise.* New York: Twayne/Simon and Schuster, 1996. Launius, Roger D., ed. "The Aerospace Industry in the West." *Journal of the West* 36 (July 1997).

AGRIBUSINESS

The agribusiness industry includes all those activities performed to produce, process, and distribute food and fiber. Harvard's John H. Davis and Ray A. Goldberg first used the term *agribusiness* in 1957, and its scope continues to evolve and now includes the following distinct yet interrelated sectors: inputs, production, processing-manufacturing, and distribution.

The input sectors include those firms that sell feed, seed, equipment, credit, insurance, chemicals, and other inputs to producers. The farmers and ranchers who produce raw commodities comprise the production sector. The processing-manufacturing sector includes those firms that process commodities into basic ingredients and basic ingredients into final consumer products. Finally, the wholesalers, distributors, and retailers who bring finished products to consumers represent the distribution sector.

As agricultural efficiency continues to improve, the number of people engaged directly in production agriculture continues to decline, now accounting for only about 1.5 percent of the U.S. population. However, according to the U.S. Department of Agriculture, as a whole the agribusiness industry is the single largest industry in the U.S. economy, accounting for over 17 percent of employment and over 14 percent of gross national product. Throughout the Great Plains region, agribusiness is an even larger economic engine. For example, 25 percent of the employment in Nebraska is dependent on agribusiness.

Although all four sectors of agribusiness are important in the Great Plains, production and processing-manufacturing form the foundation. In particular, the expansive scope of agribusiness in the Great Plains is driven by the regional importance of agricultural production and the economic necessity of locating a significant share of the input and processing-manufacturing sectors near production. It follows that an appreciation of agribusiness in the Great Plains must begin with an appreciation of agriculture in the Great Plains.

The Great Plains is an important region for the production of many types of livestock, poultry, dairy, and food and feed grains. For example, eastern Nebraska is a major corn- and soybean-producing region, and oats and barley are mainstay crops in North Dakota and the Prairie Provinces of Canada. However, from Texas to the Prairie Provinces, cattle and wheat are the quintessential agricultural commodities of the Great Plains.

Mixed- and shortgrass prairies once dominated the Great Plains, with the tallgrass prairies lying mainly to the east. Climate, most notably rainfall, dictated this delineation. While the original grasslands have largely disappeared, they remain marked by the crops that have replaced them. Corn grows where tallgrass prairies once flourished (and in irrigated outliers farther west), while wheat is the dominant crop of the former mixed- and shortgrass prairies of the Great Plains, with North Dakota, Kansas, and Montana the leading U.S. producers. Similarly in Canada, the Prairie Provinces of Alberta, Saskatchewan, and Manitoba produce twenty times the wheat output of the rest of the nation. The Plains, which once supported North America's great bison herds, are today the epicenter of North American cattle production, led in the United States by Texas, Nebraska, Kansas, and Colorado. In Canada, Alberta is the dominant beef producer, supplying 65 percent of the total market.

While the prominence of the Great Plains in cattle and wheat production is dictated by the characteristics of the land and climate, its relative strength as a food processing-manufacturing region is dictated by economics. Food processors-manufacturers must decide about locating near farm production or near consumer markets. Although the Great Plains is an important region for agricultural production, its sparse population makes it a relatively small consumer market. For example, according to the U.S. Census Bureau, Kansas, Nebraska, Montana, South Dakota, and North Dakota rank thirty-second, thirty-eighth, thirty-ninth, forty-third, and forty-eighth, respectively, in 1998 population estimates. The Prairie Provinces of Canada reflect a similar pattern.

The location of agribusiness processing-manufacturing depends on the costs of transporting farm products to the plant versus finished products to the consumer. If the commodity is bulky and relatively low value compared to the final product, processing-manufacturing will more likely be located near the commodity source. With respect to this economic rule, the two primary commodities of the Great Plains, wheat and cattle, are quite different.

Until the 1950s, flour mills were usually built near growing regions because the rail charge to ship wheat versus flour was about the same. Since then, the rates for shipping flour have risen, relative to the rates for shipping wheat, so more modern milling operations tend to be found near major population centers throughout North America and hence outside the Plains.

Processing of the other major Great Plains commodity, beef cattle, is the dominant agribusiness processing-manufacturing concern in the region, again dictated by economics. It is much less costly to ship processed meat than it is to ship live animals. The beef-processing industry is highly concentrated, with the top four firms accounting for approximately 80 percent of the fed cattle slaughtered in the United States. These four firms—IBP, Cargill's Excel, ConAgra's Monfort, and Farmland—are among the most prominent Great Plains firms in any industry. IBP has major plants in Emporia and Finney County, Kansas, in West Point and Lexington, Nebraska, in Amarillo, Texas, and in Brooks, Alberta. Monfort's main plants are in Greeley, Colorado, Garden City, Kansas, Dumas, Texas, and Grand Island, Nebraska. Excel has plants in Friona and Plainview, Texas, Dodge City, Kansas, Fort Morgan, Colorado, Schuyler, Nebraska, and High River, Alberta, and Farmland's main processing centers are in Liberal and Dodge City, Kansas. Beef represents one of the largest export products from the Great Plains. For example, in 1998 the export value of beef from the United States was $2.3 billion, representing approximately 10 percent of total beef sales, and most of that beef came from the Plains.

Because of their interdependence, the future of agribusiness and of the Great Plains region go hand in hand, and there are significant changes on the horizon. First, like many industries, all sectors of agribusiness are concentrating, resulting in fewer, larger entities. This holds from the farm to the processing plant to the grocery store. Second, as the impact of technology on agribusiness grows, the need for more educated employees also grows. Genetic engineering and precision farming are two prominent examples. Finally, the agribusiness industry must continually adapt to its ultimate customers, who are constantly in flux. Given shifting consumer demographics and dynamic societal influences, change will be the only constant facing the agribusiness industry as it seeks to continue to meet the needs of consumers.

See also AGRICULTURE: Cattle Ranching; Wheat / HISPANIC AMERICANS: Meatpackers.

Tim Burkink
Arizona State University East

Beierlein, James G., Kenneth C. Schneeberger, and Donald D. Osburn. *Agribusiness Management*. Prospect Heights IL: Waveland Press, 1995. Kohls, Richard L., and Joseph N. Uhl. *Marketing of Agricultural Products*. Upper Saddle River NJ: Prentice-Hall, 1998. Madson, John. *Where the Sky Began*. Ames: Iowa State University Press, 1995.

AGRICULTURAL COMMODITY MARKETS

The Great Plains states and provinces are major producers of basic agricultural commodities, including grain, oilseeds, cotton, hay, sugar beets, and livestock. Because the end products into which they are made are critical in meeting basic human needs and because they comprise a relatively small part of total consumer expenditures, the prices of agricultural commodities are highly responsive to changes in supply and demand, with resulting volatility of regional producer incomes. Owing to vagaries of Plains weather, susceptibility of living plants and animals to assorted pests, and highly competitive conditions in the production of most of these commodities, supplies can vary widely from year to year and over longer periods. As foreign markets have become a major outlet for many of the products, demand too has become much more variable. A phase-out of U.S. government supply controls and price supports has brought further price and income variability.

The raw products of agriculture are heavy and bulky relative to their value, and their Plains production locales are far from major centers of national and world demand. Because production is seasonal in the face of ongoing needs, large inventories must be carried from one harvest to the next, and because they are products of biological origin, agricultural commodities are highly perishable. Transportation, storage, and processing are therefore challenging and costly.

In the 1950s and early 1960s, most grain moving off American farms went first to country elevators; from there, usually by rail and in single-car lots, to much larger subterminal or terminal elevators; and, finally, by rail or river barge, to processors. Feed grains often bypassed the system, moving directly from producers to local feeders, and much of the grain was used by producers themselves. Farms have since become larger and more specialized and country elevators fewer and much larger. Long-haul grain shipments now move by rail directly from train-loading country elevators to ports of export or to domestic processing and feed-deficit areas. Short-haul traffic formerly moving by rail now goes mainly by truck. These changes have been prompted by a number of factors: economies of elevator scale; rail innovations such as unit trains, "jumbo" covered hopper cars, automated car-control systems, and suspension of transit billing privileges; abandonment of railroad branch-line trackage; expanded port facilities; larger ocean-going vessels; construction of the U.S. interstate highway system beginning in 1956; opening of the St. Lawrence Seaway in 1957; federal deregulation of both rail and trucking industries in 1980; and growth in foreign demand.

Wheat milling was once done in and near sources of production, much of it in urban centers such as Kansas City and Minneapolis. Trainload shipments in specialized hopper cars have since made it cheaper to ship wheat than milled products, leading mills to relocate to areas of flour demand. Milling has also become more concentrated; the largest four firms had 70 percent of U.S. capacity in 1992. Grain marketing firms have integrated forward into flour milling in both the United

States and Canada, the largest three Canadian firms having 75 percent of that country's capacity at latest count. Canadian millers, unlike those in the United States, are often integrated forward into baking as well. Feed grains were formerly milled in small production-oriented facilities. Today, mills are much larger and fewer in number. Most are located in areas of feed grain production and local livestock feed demand, but some are situated in more distant centers of poultry production in the southeastern United States.

U.S. grain prices were formerly determined largely in cash markets in places such as Minneapolis, Chicago, Kansas City, and Omaha. Now, cash markets are nearly extinct, and price bids at country elevators are based on futures markets in Chicago, Minneapolis, and Winnipeg. Prices for grain moving into ultimate domestic and foreign markets are determined largely by telephoned bids and offers for future deliveries. In Canada, the Canadian Wheat Board has sole marketing authority over barley and wheat, and producer prices for exported grain vary each year only by transportation differentials. The Winnipeg Commodity Exchange has open-market trading of canola, feed barley, feed wheat, and feed oats. The Canada–United States Trade Agreement (CUSTA) and the North American Free Trade Agreement (NAFTA) have reduced government interference in markets on both sides of the border, making the two markets more integrated. Rail shipping rates for agricultural products were traditionally subsidized by the Canadian government under the Crow's Nest Pass Agreement, by which the government funded rail-line construction in return for a ceiling on shipping rates, giving Canadian grain shippers favored access to Pacific Rim markets. The ceilings are now being removed, with resulting diversion of much Canadian wheat across the border to American railroads. Canadian rail system efficiency lags behind that in the United States, and grain moves through country elevators of smaller size and load-out capacities than those south of the forty-ninth parallel.

Innovations in transportation, especially refrigerated railcars, and a gradual westward shift of livestock and feed grains production prompted a westward migration of U.S. livestock markets and slaughter. Chicago, once the nation's largest livestock marketing center, was superseded in the 1950s by Omaha. Peripheral Plains-oriented markets prospered in Sioux City, Kansas City, Fort Worth, and elsewhere. More recently, urban markets and packing houses have given way to slaughter and processing in smaller, rural Plains communities. Direct packer purchases of cattle from producers have supplanted the auction and terminal markets of the past. Packers now disassemble carcasses into "boxed beef" cuts for shipment by refrigerated trucks to retail markets, leaving bone and other waste behind for manufacture into feed and fertilizer. Meatpacking and meat-processing plants and firms have grown sharply in size while shrinking in number; by the 1990s, the four largest packing firms had 82 percent of U.S. beef slaughter and 80 percent of boxed beef production.

See also AGRICULTURE: *Agricultural Price Supports; Wheat.*

Dale G. Anderson
University of Nebraska–Lincoln

Anderson, Dale G. *Transporting Nebraska Grain and Oilseeds: Changing Markets in a Changing World Economy.* Report no. 177. University of Nebraska Department of Agricultural Economics, Lincoln, 1998. Cramer, Gail L., and Eric J. Wailes. *Grain Marketing.* Boulder CO: Westview Press, 1993. Larson, Donald W., Paul W. Gallagher, and Reynold P. Dahl, eds. *Structural Change and Performance of the U.S. Grain Marketing System.* Champaign IL: Prestige Printing, 1998.

AMERICAN FUR COMPANY

Chartered on March 29, 1808, by the New York legislature, the American Fur Company was John Jacob Astor's bid to establish a fur empire that would reach from the Great Lakes to the Pacific Northwest. Astor failed to realize this ambition (his Pacific Fur Company, a worldwide trading scheme pivoted at Fort Astoria at the mouth of the Columbia River, foundered in 1813), but until it suspended payments on September 6, 1842, the American Fur Company dominated the fur trade of the Great Lakes and the Central and Northern Great Plains.

Astor and his right-hand man, Ramsey Crooks, were slow to enter the fur trade of the Great Plains: their policy always was to let others make mistakes first, then move in and take over. Their first tentative move was made in 1821, when the American Fur Company made an arrangement with the St. Louis firm of (Bartholomew) Berthold and (Pierre Jr.) Chouteau to supply their trade goods. Within five years, the American Fur Company had absorbed its competition and established a virtual monopoly over the fur trade from the Platte River to the Canadian boundary and from the Missouri River to the Rocky Mountains. This monopoly would be periodically challenged by pretenders, but the American Fur Company had the resources to outprice and outlast its opponents and the political clout to discredit them.

By 1834 the American Fur Company was operating a network of trading posts that spanned the Central and Northern Great Plains. Three major depots—Fort Union (1829), at the mouth of the Yellowstone; Fort Pierre (1832), near the junction of the Cheyenne and Missouri Rivers; and Fort Laramie (1834), on the North Platte—were the organizational hubs in this system, and numerous regional posts served the trade of specific tribes or bands. No Native Americans who wanted to trade—and by 1834 they all did—were without an outlet. They were the primary producers in a global trading system that began on the Plains with the collection and processing of robes and pelts and ended in the fur marts of London and Leipzig. The Missouri River, with steamboat navigation after 1832, was the artery of the commerce, and St. Louis was its main control point, funneling furs to markets in the eastern United States and Europe and trade goods from Europe and elsewhere to Native American consumers on the Plains. The economic system was regulated by a constant flow of correspondence from the trading posts through St. Louis to Europe and back. The American Fur Company kept an agent, Curtis M. Lampson, in Europe to monitor market conditions and maintained contracts with various European firms for the importation of, for example, beads (Alessandro Bertolla of Venice) and knives and traps (Hiram Culter of Sheffield). This was truly an international enterprise.

In the halcyon years of the early 1830s, the American Fur Company was exporting at least 25,000 bison robes a year from the Great Plains. But even then Astor could see the writing on the wall. Competition, often involving the flagrant use of alcohol as a trade inducement, was escalating, and the price for beaver pelts was falling as silk became the new preferred raw material for top hats. In 1834 Astor, old and ailing, sold the Northern Department of the American Fur Company to Ramsay Crooks and the Western Department to the St. Louis firm of Pratte, Chouteau and Company. Under the direction of Pierre Chouteau Jr., the fur-trade system established by the American Fur Company would continue to operate on the Plains until the 1860s, when it was enveloped by waves of settlers.

David J. Wishart
University of Nebraska–Lincoln

Lavender, David. *The Fist in the Wilderness.* Lincoln: University of Nebraska Press, 1998. Wishart, David. *The Fur Trade of the American West, 1807–1840: A Geographic Synthesis.* Lincoln: University of Nebraska Press, 1992.

AUTOMOTIVE

Never a large industry in the Great Plains, automaking nonetheless flourished until the 1930s. The region's small factories often sold directly to motorists, thereby eliminating transportation costs and agents' markups, and provided services unknown in the East: free driving lessons, lifetime warranties, and sometimes a chance for customers to help build the car they would own.

Nebraska and Kansas each had half a dozen companies that saw serious, sustained production prior to World War II. In Kansas, Topeka's Smith Automobile Company (1902–12) sold 1,200 hand-built autos nationally. The Great Smith's advanced semiautomatic transmission, built-in icebox, and colorful stunts—climbing Pikes Peak in a blizzard, driving six days nonstop on rain-soaked Texas roads—won it many fans.

The lightly populated Dakotas, Montana, New Mexico, Oklahoma, and Wyoming saw little automaking activity. The popular Montana Special, which sold well in Big Sky Country from 1911 to 1916, was actually a Minnesota product. Denver supplied Colorado's best-known autos: the Colburn, famed for racing, and the Fritchle Electric, which Oliver P. Fritchle advertised widely in 1908 during a grueling trek over bad roads from Lincoln, Nebraska, to New York City.

A shift in demand from open to closed cars

and the advent of the moving assembly line forced automakers to invest more heavily in machinery, particularly after World War I. Consolidation marked the 1920s. Except for a few makers of luxury autos (for whom quality, not price, was all-important), smaller factories failed. A few of the region's automakers survived by producing fire engines, truck bodies, street cleaners, and other specialty machines.

Now a few large companies dominate the automobile industry, and manufacturing is concentrated in Ontario, in the case of Canada, and in Michigan and Ohio, in the United States. Great Plains states accounted for just less than 10 percent of U.S. output in 1996. General Motors plants in Oklahoma City, Arlington, Texas (just east of Fort Worth), and Fairfax, Kansas (northeastern Kansas City) and the Ford Motor Assembly Plant in Kansas City, Missouri, are the hubs of the region's production.

See also TRANSPORTATION: Automobiles.

Curt McConnell
Lincoln, Nebraska

Kimes, Beverly Rae, and Henry Austin Clark Jr. *Standard Catalog of American Cars, 1805–1942.* Iola WI: Krause Publications, 1989. McConnell, Curt. *Great Cars of the Great Plains.* Lincoln: University of Nebraska Press, 1995. *Ward's Automotive Yearbook.* Southfield MI: Ward's Communications, 1997.

BANKING

Banking's role in the Great Plains economy has long been important and controversial. Most Great Plains states developed a commercial banking system after enactment of the National Banking Acts of 1863 and 1864. National banks were required to hold relatively large amounts of capital and could not make direct loans to real estate. Nonresidents owned many Great Plains national banks. State banks, which had lower capital requirements and made direct real estate loans, were more numerous in the sparsely settled, agricultural Great Plains and were usually locally owned; successful merchants most commonly started Great Plains banks.

Fearing that nonresidents would gain monopoly control over allocation of bank credit, many states adopted unit-banking policies that prohibited banks from branching. As late as 1980, only New Mexico and South Dakota among Great Plains states allowed branching. Numerous small banks with undiversified loan portfolios dominated Great Plains banking.

The unit-banking system proved to be fragile during economic downturns. After the Panic of 1907, several states experimented with state-run deposit insurance systems as an alternative to branch banking in providing stability to the banking system. Between 1907 and 1917 eight states nationwide adopted deposit insurance systems, including Kansas, Nebraska, North Dakota, Oklahoma, South Dakota, and Texas. Chain banks and multibank holding companies (group banking) also developed as ways to evade restrictions on branch banking.

Citizens Bank, Wharton, Oklahoma Territory, 1894

During the 1920s and 1930s Great Plains banking experienced substantial turmoil. Prices of agricultural products rose during World War I, with a resulting rapid expansion in the number of banks. The postwar collapse of agricultural prices and of land values resulted in numerous bank failures when banks saw the value of their loans dramatically fall. During the 1920s state-run deposit insurance systems may have intensified difficulties by encouraging banks to take too many risks. The banking system further contracted during the early 1930s. In addition to failures of thousands of unit banks, many chain banks and bank holding companies did not survive the Great Depression; however, some continued to play a significant role in Great Plains banking. For example, Minneapolis-based First Bank and Norwest systems both owned many banks in the Dakotas and in Montana.

The banks in the Prairie Provinces of Canada fared much better during the 1920s and 1930s. A merger movement among Canadian banks occurred after 1900. By 1920 Canada had developed a nationwide branch-banking system that was characterized by national diversification and greater stability than in the United States; no Canadian banks failed during the Great Depression.

After World War II, commercial banks continued to provide most non–real estate loans to farmers. Banks gradually increased their farm mortgages, which had substantially dropped during the 1920s and 1930s; however, federal land banks and life insurance companies often provided a larger share of farm mortgages. Banks faced increasing competition from other depository institutions such as savings and loan associations, which emphasized home mortgage loans, and credit unions, which emphasized consumer loans. Commercial banks also became more actively involved in lending to petroleum and natural gas businesses, particularly in Colorado, Oklahoma, Texas, and Wyoming.

Dramatic changes in Great Plains banking occurred after 1980. Relatively high prices for agricultural and energy products caused many

Great Plains banks to expand their lending to these activities during the late 1970s. The recession of the early 1980s combined with falling prices for agricultural and energy products to result in a bust in both sectors. The undiversified loan portfolios of many Great Plains banks resulted in numerous bank failures. This time, many savings and loan associations also failed. Between 1982 and 1994, 2,573 commercial banks and savings and loan associations failed nationwide. Texas alone accounted for more than 30 percent of these failures, while Colorado, Kansas, Nebraska, and Oklahoma combined accounted for more than 14 percent.

Great Plains states responded differently to these challenges. South Dakota changed its usury law and actively sought national credit card operations, particularly Citibank, to relocate and thereby provide jobs. Others reluctantly loosened restrictions on branch banking and passed interstate banking legislation. The 1994 Riegle-Neal Interstate Banking and Branching Efficiency Act effectively removed remaining obstacles to interstate banking.

Since 1980 Great Plains banking has transformed from being predominantly a unit-banking industry to one that includes both statewide branching and interstate banking. Although the total number of banks has declined by more than 30 percent, there has been an increase in the number of bank branches. While an increasing share of bank deposits is under the control of large out-of-state organizations, many smaller community banks continue to flourish because they are able to provide more personalized services, which many customers still prefer, and they remain the best source of information concerning the credit-worthiness of local businesses.

Robert Stanley Herren
North Dakota State University

Doti, Lynne Pierson, and Larry Schweikart. *Banking in the American West: From the Gold Rush to Deregulation.* Norman: University of Oklahoma Press, 1991. Spong, Kenneth, and James Harvey. "The Changing Structure of Banking: A Look at Traditional and New Ways of Delivering Banking Services." *Financial Industry Perspectives* (1998): 1–16.

BIOTECHNOLOGY

Biotechnology, with a particular emphasis on agricultural biotechnology, is a relatively recent but immensely important addition to the industrial base of the Great Plains. The Nature Biotechnology Directory identifies 119 biotechnology companies in the U.S. Great Plains, with 68 in Texas and 30 in Colorado (though not all are located in the Plains portion of these states). Of states that are completely in the Plains region, Kansas has 11 such firms, Nebraska 8, South Dakota 1, and North Dakota none. In the Canadian Prairie Provinces, Saskatchewan is the hub of the industry, and a closer look at agricultural biotechnology there serves to elucidate what is being achieved.

Saskatchewan is the largest producer of food and feed grains among the ten provinces of Canada, and its economy is dominated by agriculture. Saskatoon is a recognized world center for agricultural biotechnology. Sustainable agricultural production is the objective of Saskatoon's agbiotech community as it moves ahead with research and development to improve crops of the Great Plains such as wheat, barley, canola, flax, peas, and beans and to find innovative uses for those crops.

Insect-resistant crops yield 8 to 10 percent more per acre than conventional crops, canola growers gain two bushels per acre with herbicide-tolerant varieties, and a new wheat variety yields 13 percent higher than the best conventional variety. All this can be achieved with reduced mechanical inputs, reduced chemical and fertilizer use, and reduced equipment and labor cost while at the same time promoting environmental stewardship by reducing fuel usage and greenhouse gas emissions and reducing tillage. These agronomic advances represent the first of three waves of agbiotech development, with the second and third waves just beginning.

The second wave of crops being developed in Saskatchewan uses biotechnology to provide improved quality traits, often stacked on top of and incorporating the benefits from the agronomic traits of the first wave such as herbicide tolerance. Seeds with healthier edible oil profiles, high-stearate oilseeds that do not require hydrogenation, improved animal feeding qualities, and special nutritional traits such as high-lysine content are examples.

The third wave of agbiotech products goes beyond food uses of crops into the area of industrial and pharmaceutical products. Within a few years, farmers will be growing ultra-high-value crops that have been engineered to produce biopolymers—plastics from plants, vehicle fuels and lubricants, vaccines for animal and human use, and a whole range of value-added products often collectively referred to as products of molecular farming. Renewable sources of energy and chemical feed stocks from agriculture should become commonplace within the next twenty years.

These second and third wave crops bring with them the decommoditization of crops from the Great Plains as extra value is added to crops that have up until now been sold at generally low world commodity prices. These "designer crops" require segregation during harvest, storage, and transportation in order to preserve their identity and integrity through to the end user, which will in turn change the traditional grain-handling systems of the Great Plains.

Saskatchewan's agricultural biotechnology community is actively involved in all three waves and has grown to a critical mass that now includes some forty biotech companies and institutions that employ approximately 2,000 people. Saskatchewan's agbiotech companies were generating around $150 million in annual sales in the late 1990s. With nearly 40 percent of Canada's agbiotech firms located in Saskatoon, Saskatchewan is the country's top center for agricultural biotechnology. The forty biotechnology enterprises currently (in 2000) operating in Saskatoon are four times the number active in the city in 1994, and new agbiotech companies are being formed at a rate of three or four per year.

More than 100 agbiotech research and development projects are under way at the many research centers in Saskatoon. They include the development of transgenic vaccines for cattle and hogs, the development of probiotic products to enhance gastrointestinal function in animals with the objective of increasing feed utilization, gene mapping in cattle and hogs targeted at increased productivity and improved carcass quality, and improved animal feeds and feed processing. Biotech developments on the crop side include agbiological products such as biofertilizers, biopesticides, and the application of microbial metabolites in both these areas; micropropagation of native trees and grasses for land reclamation; plant growth regulation; genetic engineering for tolerance to crop stress factors such as drought, heat, and cold; herbicide resistance for cereal, vegetable, and pulse crop species; molecular farming to produce therapeutic molecules in oilseeds; development of new crop types such as a new oilseed crop from a member of the mustard family; and the reduction of anti-nutritional compounds in existing crops.

Peter B. McCann
Ag-West Biotech Inc.

BUFFETT, WARREN (b. 1930)

Warren Edward Buffett, businessman and investor, was born August 30, 1930, in Omaha, Nebraska, to Howard Homan Buffett and Leila Stahl Buffett. He is the youngest of three children, with sisters Doris and Roberta. In 1952 he married Susan Thompson. They have three children, Susan, Howard, and Peter. In 2000 Buffett was the second wealthiest individual in the United States.

Buffett attended elementary school in Omaha, then junior high school and high school in Washington DC while his father served as a congressman from Nebraska. During this time, he became interested in business and pursued a variety of money-making ventures, including a newspaper route, a pinball machine business, a Rolls Royce rental business, and used golf ball sales. He also purchased forty acres of farmland for $1,200 in his home state, Nebraska. When he graduated from high school, Buffett had about $6,000 in savings.

In 1947 he enrolled in the Wharton School of Business at the University of Pennsylvania. After two years, he transferred to the University of Nebraska–Lincoln and graduated in 1950 with a degree in business. During his senior year, he read *The Intelligent Investor* by Benjamin Graham, a finance professor at Columbia University in New York. Having tried various investment strategies, Buffett became intrigued and enrolled in the graduate program at Columbia to study under Benjamin Graham. In 1951 he graduated with a master's degree and applied for a job at Graham-Newman, an investment firm. Graham turned him down, so Buffett returned to Omaha to work for his father's brokerage firm. In 1954 Graham offered Buffett a job that he accepted. Two years later, Graham-Newman closed, and Buffett again returned to Omaha. At that time, Buffett started his own investment company, the Buffett Partnership, with $100 of his own money and $105,000 contributed by seven limited partners.

In 1962 Buffett began investing in Berkshire Hathaway, a textile mill located in New Bedford, Massachusetts, gaining control of the firm in 1965. Instead of reinvesting money in textiles, Buffett used capital to invest in other companies. Disappointed with opportunities in the stock market, Buffett ended the partnership in 1969, suggesting to his partners that they either cash out, remain invested with Berkshire Hathaway, or invest in a fund managed by a classmate from Columbia, William Ruane. Buffett retained his shares in Berkshire Hathaway and is currently the chairman and chief executive officer. Berkshire Hathaway, no longer a textile company, is a holding company with investments in Coca-Cola, Gillette, the *Washington Post*, Disney, and other well-known firms. It also owns the Nebraska Furniture Mart, Borsheim's jewelry store, See's Candies, GEICO insurance, Dairy Queen International, and several other businesses.

From 1955 to 1969 the partnership earned an astounding 29.5 percent annual compound rate of return. Since Buffett gained control of Berkshire Hathaway, the average annual gain in net worth is approximately 25 percent compared to the average percentage gain in the S&P 500 of approximately 13 percent. His personal wealth has grown from $9,800 at the time he left Columbia University to about $30 billion in 2000.

Benjamin Graham, Philip Fisher, and Buffett's current partner, Charlie Munger, have influenced Buffett's investment philosophy. Buffett learned from Graham quantitative techniques and the importance of margin of safety, which is the difference between the market value and the intrinsic value of a business. Fisher and Munger stress the importance of business economics and management. Buffett, who uses aspects of both quantitative and qualitative techniques, believes that an investor should understand the business, not worry about stock market volatility, and should buy when the market price is significantly less than the intrinsic value of the business.

Buffett achieves success with hard work, diligence, dedication, honesty, enthusiasm, and humility. These characteristics reflect the spirit and heritage of the Great Plains people. A native Nebraskan, Warren Edward Buffett has earned a place in history as one of the greatest investors of all time.

Thomas Johansen
Fort Hays State University

Hagstrom, Robert G., Jr. *The Warren Buffett Way*. New York: John Wiley and Sons, 1995. Kilpatrick, Andrew. *Of Permanent Value: The Warren Buffett Story*. Birmingham: AKPE, 1998. Lowenstein, Roger. *Buffett: The Making of an American Capitalist*. New York: Doubleday, 1995.

CANADIAN PACIFIC RAILWAY

The Canadian Pacific Railway (CPR) was one of the most important forces in opening up the Canadian Prairies to settlement. What the Hudson's Bay Company did in the late eighteenth and early nineteenth centuries, the CPR did in the late nineteenth and early twentieth centuries.

Following the formation of the Dominion of Canada in 1867, arrangements were made to transfer the Hudson's Bay Company territory, known as Rupert's Land, to Canada. The transfer of this territory, which comprises the present-day Provinces of Manitoba, Saskatchewan, and Alberta, was completed in 1870. In 1871 the colony of British Columbia joined the Dominion under the condition that a railway be built to connect it to the east. After several attempts, including more than five years of construction by the Canadian government, the Canadian Pacific Railway Company was incorporated by act of Parliament on February 17, 1881. At that time the government of Canada gave the new company $25 million and 25 million acres of land in the Plains area between Winnipeg and the Rocky Mountains.

At the start of 1882 the company hired William Cornelius Van Horne as its general manager. Under his leadership, construction proceeded at a record pace, and the first train reached Calgary (now in the province of Alberta but then in the Northwest Territories) in the summer of 1883. On November 7, 1885, the last spike in the main line was driven at Craigellachie in the mountains of British Columbia, and on June 28, 1886, the first through transcontinental train departed Montreal for the Pacific Coast, which it reached six days later.

During the next thirty years the CPR built a network of branch lines that connected many Prairie communities with the main line. Until other transcontinental railways were built, in the first decade and a half of the twentieth century the CPR was the only practical way of reaching the Prairies. Its influence on the pattern of settlement of western Canada from 1885 to 1914 cannot be overestimated.

As the CPR evolved, it began operating ships, both oceangoing and inland, airlines, and road transport as well as a chain of hotels.

By the mid–twentieth century it was advertising itself as the world's greatest travel system and using the slogan "CPR Spans the World." It also began to exploit its oil and mineral resources and involved itself in many other activities besides transportation.

Today the 1881 company still exists as Canadian Pacific Limited and still owns some of the land originally granted. Since the majority of its business is in the West, the company moved its corporate headquarters from Montreal to Calgary in the 1990s. With its large reserves of oil, gas, and coal and its various transportation divisions, including the railway with which it started, Canadian Pacific Limited is still an important component in the ongoing development of western Canada.

See also TRANSPORTATION: Railways, Canada.

Fred F. Angus
Montreal, Quebec

Eagle, John A. *The Canadian Pacific Railroad and the Development of Western Canada, 1896–1914*. Montreal: McGill-Queens University Press, 1989. Innis, Harold A. *History of the Canadian Pacific Railway*. Toronto: University of Toronto Press, 1970.

CENTER PIVOTS

Irrigation equipment in the Great Plains most often refers to center-pivot equipment. A center-pivot irrigation installation consists of a fixed, four-legged pivot structure with a long pipeline to which sprinklers are attached for dispersing water. The pipeline rotates around the central pivot in a straight radial-arm fashion, riding on wheeled tower structures and creating a large irrigated circle pattern on planted crops.

The industry originated in the Great Plains. Frank Zybach, a dryland wheat farmer in Colorado, developed the first system in 1948. The first prototype, made of steel and aluminum, was propelled by piston-driven actuators powered by water pressure from the pivot system water supply. In 1954 Robert Daugherty of Valley Manufacturing acquired the marketing rights to the patent and continued development of the concept over the next ten years, perfecting it into a strong, durable design and establishing an entire industry.

In the thirty years after World War II, more than sixty companies in the United States manufactured center-pivot irrigation systems. Today there are four major suppliers, all located in Nebraska: Valmont (in Valley and McCook, with plants in South Africa, Spain, and the United Arab Emirates), Lindsay (headquarters in Omaha and plants in Lindsay, Nebraska, and France), Reinke (in Deshler), and T-L (in Hastings). These four companies supply 85 percent of the global demand for center pivots and virtually all of the North American market requirement. All four companies go to market through networks of exclusive dealers and distributors. Center pivots are now used in more than 100 countries around the globe.

Major developments in center pivots have included the transition from water power to electric and oil-hydraulic power, the adoption

of durable coatings for the pipes and structure, and the invention of special spans mounted at the end of the pivot arm to cover the corners in square and irregularly shaped fields. Linear move machines are built from the same components but are not fixed to a central pivot. Linear move machines, introduced in the 1970s, proceed in a straight line to cover rectangular fields. Special water application devices for the low-energy precision application of water were introduced in the 1980s. In the 1990s computerized controls were added, along with integration of controls with soil moisture monitoring and weather monitoring capability.

Mechanized pivot irrigation equipment has advantages over other methods of irrigation because of the uniform application of water to large fields, low energy consumption, relatively low cost, and the savings in labor required for irrigation. The average life of a center pivot is more than twenty five years of annual usage, resulting in a very low total lifetime cost of ownership. Its ability to operate over undulating ground gives the additional advantage of not requiring costly land leveling, as is the case with other forms of irrigation. Chemicals can also be applied to the crop through aqueous solution with the irrigation water or by separate spray manifolds mounted on the pipeline structure. Water runoff can be virtually eliminated by the precise application of only the amount of water that can be absorbed by the soil. There is a growing market for mechanized irrigation equipment to dispense wastewater through pivots to irrigate field crops such as alfalfa hay. Large industrial consumers of water such as food processors, paper producers, and municipalities can benefit from the reuse of the water through pivots in such productive ways.

Crops produced under center pivots include fruit tree orchards, commercial turf, high-value vegetables, cotton, and all major commodity grain crops.

See also WATER: Irrigation.

Dennis Schwieger
Valmont Irrigation

CHOUTEAU, PIERRE, JR. (1789–1865)

Pierre Chouteau Jr., familiarly known as "Cadet" (meaning second-born son), was the leading entrepreneur in the Great Plains for much of the first half of the nineteenth century. Son of the St. Louis trader and banker Jean Pierre Chouteau (1758–1849), Pierre was destined to succeed: after all, his family was instrumental in the founding of St. Louis, and, with great enterprise as well as timely switches of political allegiance and strategic marriages, they had amassed a fortune from mining, banking, and the fur trade, a fortune that Pierre would multiply.

He was born in St. Louis on January 19, 1789, and by the time he was fifteen he was engaged in the fur trade with the Osages. In 1810 he left to develop his family's interests in the Dubuque (Iowa) lead mines, but while mining remained an interest for him until the 1850s, his sights were set on the West.

Back in St. Louis in 1812, Chouteau opened a store with the merchant Bartholomew Berthold and began an association with the western fur trade that would last for half a century. The partnership backed Manuel Lisa's trading expedition to the upper Missouri in 1819 and lost heavily. In the maelstrom of competition for the Indian trade that followed, Berthold and Chouteau built trading posts on the Missouri as far north as present-day South Dakota. Gradually, Chouteau eased into an economic relationship with John Jacob Astor's American Fur Company, a relationship that was formalized in 1826 with a merger of interests that left Pierre as head of the company's Western Department.

From that point on, Pierre Chouteau Jr.'s wealth and influence soared. After Astor's retirement from the fur trade in 1834, Chouteau's company (by then Pratte, Chouteau and Company) became the dominant force in the fur trade on the Central and Northern Great Plains, with a network of trading posts stretching from Fort Union (present-day North Dakota) to Fort Laramie (present-day Wyoming). A disastrous overextension of operations into the volatile Rocky Mountain trapping system in 1834 (a rare miscalculation on Chouteau's part) was terminated in 1839. By that time his enterprise was simply P. Chouteau Jr. and Company, and under that name it moved hundreds of thousands of bison robes through St. Louis to the main markets in the eastern United States over the following twenty-five years.

Pierre Chouteau Jr. was a driven man and a ruthless competitor—the epitome of a frontier capitalist. He was also an innovator who, for example, was instrumental in introducing steamboat navigation on the Missouri River in 1832, which revolutionized the scale of the fur trade. He was deeply involved in the negotiation of Indian treaties, in part because of the clauses that mandated the payment of debts to traders. The lucrative and often nefarious business of supplying annuities to Indian reservations was another of his endeavors. Through these and other ventures, he built an estate worth millions of dollars.

In the late 1850s his health began to fail. In 1859 he lost his sight; three years later he lost Emile, his wife of fifty years. Pierre Chouteau Jr. died on September 16, 1865, in St. Louis, a city he had done so much to build.

See also HISPANIC AMERICANS: Lisa, Manuel.

David J. Wishart
University of Nebraska–Lincoln

Lecompte, Janet. "Pierre Chouteau Junior." In *The Mountain Men and the Fur Trade of the Far West*, edited by LeRoy R. Hafen, 9: 91–123. Glendale CA: Arthur H. Clark Company, 1972. Sunder, John E. *The Fur Trade on the Upper Missouri, 1840–1865*. Norman: University of Oklahoma Press, 1965.

CLARK, JIM (b. 1944)

Once a high school dropout in Plainview, Texas, James H. Clark became a university professor, then a business entrepreneur who founded three billion-dollar companies: Silicon Graphics Inc., Netscape Communications Corp., and Healtheon Corp., now Healtheon/Web MD. He is still involved in the latter enterprise, which used the Internet to revolutionize the handling of medical records, In addition, he serves as chairman of MYCFO, an Internet-based money-management firm; Shutterfly .com, a Web site for digital photo hobbyists; and SmartPipes, Inc., a business networking company. He serves on the board of directors of two genetics companies, DNASciences and Kiva Genetics, and is an investor in Shockwave.com, an entertainment site. His customary method of operation is to see an emerging trend, form a company to take advantage of it, then turn its operation over to management professionals.

Jim Clark was born in Plainview, Texas, on March 23, 1944. His mother worked in a doctor's office; his father did odd jobs and had a drinking problem and a violent temper. His parents divorced when he was fourteen, leaving his mother to support the family, which included Jim's brother and sister, on $225 a month. Clark attended Plainview High School but was bored. He was suspended in his junior year for talking back to a teacher. He never returned. Instead, he joined the navy. After completing his four-year hitch, Clark passed his high school equivalency test and entered college. By 1971 he had received a master's degree in physics from the University of New Orleans, and in 1974 he earned a doctorate in computer science at the University of Utah.

By age thirty-six, he was an associate professor of electrical engineering at Stanford University, working in the computer systems laboratory. While in this post, he invented a breakthrough integrated-circuit chip that made possible new developments in three-dimensional graphics. To build upon this invention, he started Silicon Graphics in 1981 and left Stanford. Unfortunately for Clark, the venture capitalist who had helped fund the new company ended up controlling it. Disillusioned and not much richer, Clark next founded Netscape Communications to develop and market an innovative Internet browser created by programmer Marc Andreesen. This time Clark made sure he retained control. When Netscape merged into America Online, he left that association with a personal take of $1.5 billion. This nest egg gave him the operating capital to start his subsequent successful businesses.

Marvin Bryan
Palm Springs, California

Bryan, Marvin. "How to Become a Billionaire: Netscape Founder Jim Clark Tells All." *Profit Magazine* (September 1999): 50–54. Clark, Jim. *Netscape Time*. New York: St. Martin's Press, 1999.

COAL

The Great Plains' coal resources occur in nine major regions, but the bulk of resources and production occurs in the five coal regions of the Northern Great Plains and Prairie Provinces. These five regions, which contain low-rank subbituminous and lignite coals of late Cretaceous to early Tertiary age, are the Great Plains Coal Region of Alberta; the Fort Union Coal Region of western North Dakota, eastern Montana, southern Saskatchewan, and southwestern Manitoba; the North Central Coal Region of north-central Montana; and the Powder River and Big Horn Coal Regions of northern Wyoming and southeastern Montana. Major coal deposits in the Southern and Central Plains include the high-sulfur bituminous coals of eastern Kansas (the Western Interior Coal Region) and north-central Texas (the Southwestern Coal Region), the low-sulfur bituminous coking coal of northeastern New Mexico and southeastern Colorado (the Raton Mesa Coal Region), and the subbituminous coals in the Denver Coal Region of northeastern Colorado and southeastern Wyoming.

Coal has provided a local source of fuel for Great Plains farms, ranches, towns, railroads, and industries from early European American settlement into the modern era. By the end of World War II, production in the Plains had peaked at just a few percent of the more than 600 million tons mined in the United States and Canada. Production bottomed out in the late 1950s and early 1960s, reflecting increasing displacement of coal by oil and gas. Beginning in the late 1960s, however, a growing demand for electrical power, concerns over oil and natural gas supply, and the demand for coals low in sulfur and ash to meet government emissions standards initiated a period of explosive growth in the coal industry. Much of this growth occurred in the Northern Plains and Prairie Provinces in the form of more than twenty new mines, several with adjacent power plants.

Area mining, a type of surface mining used where coal seams are relatively horizontal and the surface terrain is nearly level, accounts for nearly all mining in the Great Plains. Area mining utilizes draglines to remove overburden, and the coal is then removed using power shovels and loaders. As each strip of overburden is removed, it is deposited as a spoil ridge in the area from which coal has already been excavated. Individual dragline cuts may be 100 to 200 feet wide and extend for thousands of feet. Several square miles may be excavated over the life of a mine.

Land productivity and water availability and quality are particularly significant issues in the semiarid range and farmlands of the Northern Great Plains, and mining companies are required to reclaim mined land. To ensure land productivity in mined areas, topsoil and subsoil are removed by scrapers and stockpiled prior to mining. Following mining, the spoil ridges are shaped in a manner reflecting the premining topography, the soil is replaced, and the sites are revegetated. The recontoured spoil density, initially about 25 percent greater than the original material, decreases over time to about 20 percent of the original material. Differential subsidence, with the potential for ponding, salinization, and disrupted cultivation, can be addressed in large part through materials placement and grading practices.

State/ Province	Major coal-producing region	Number of mines	Production millions of tons	Total employment	Reserve base millions of tons	Exports percentage
Kansas	West Interior	3	0.36	67	976	0
Montana	Fort Union North Central Powder River	8	41.00	708	48,815	75
New Mexico	Raton Mesa	1	1.24	40		
North Dakota	Fort Union	6	29.58	657	9,470	0
Wyoming	Powder River Bighorn	20	266.58	2,777	25,971	90
U.S. total		38	388.76	4,249	85,232	
Alberta	Great Plains	6	23.47	2,525	9,367	25
Saskatchewan	Fort Union	4	13.00	513	3,070	0
Canadian total		10	36.47	3,038	12,437	
Total		48	375.23	7,287	97,669	

In the premining landscape, reducing conditions prevail at depths greater than thirty feet, but excavation brings these materials into contact with oxygen. As a result, recharge through spoil banks and newly reclaimed areas produces groundwater characterized by elevated concentrations of dissolved solids, elevated concentrations of sodium and sulfate, and increased alkalinity. In most areas, carbonates and hydroxides provide a high natural buffering capacity that precludes significant acid mine drainage. Surface and groundwater quality improves with time, but the disruption of groundwater flow resulting from the removal of the coal and the aquifers in the overburden cannot be fully remedied within the mined area.

In 1997 Great Plains coal production stood at 375 million tons from forty-eight mines, accounting for nearly 33 percent of the combined U.S.-Canadian output. The 337 million tons produced from the thirty-four mines in Wyoming, North Dakota, and Montana accounted for 78 percent of U.S. low-rank production, 31 percent of total U.S. production, and nearly 90 percent of total Great Plains production. The 36.5 million tons from the ten mines in the Prairie Provinces accounted for 42 percent of total Canadian production and 10 percent of total Great Plains production. New Mexico and Kansas contribute the remaining 1.6 million tons, or 0.4 percent, of Plains production. Mines in Montana and Wyoming are producing at only three-quarters of capacity. Most of the subbituminous coal mined in Wyoming and Montana is shipped out of state for use in coal-fired power plants. In contrast, the lignite of North Dakota and Saskatchewan is mainly utilized by mine-mouth power facilities.

In the Great Plains, 99 percent of coal production is from surface mines. The 85 billion tons in demonstrated surface-minable reserves in the Northern Plains states of the United States, including the 19 billion-ton reserve of the Wyodak seam in the Powder River Coal Region, are sufficient to last for nearly 250 years at current production levels and represent nearly half of the demonstrated surface mine reserves of the United States. Employment at Plains surface mines stood at approximately 7,200 workers in 1997. Productivity levels (tons of coal per miner per hour) for surface mines in 1997 in Wyoming (35.4), Montana (23.6), and North Dakota (17.8) were well above the U.S. surface mine average of 9.5, reflecting economies of scale and relatively low overburden to coal thickness ratios. Coal severance taxes are levied in all states with Plains-based coal production.

The Powder River Coal Region of northeastern Wyoming and southwestern Montana contains North America's thickest and most extensive low-sulfur coal seams, including the seventy-foot-thick Wyodak seam, and the region's 269 million-ton production accounts for 70 percent of Plains production and 23 percent of combined U.S.-Canadian production. Most of the coal is transported out of state, with over half going to just six states in 1997 (Texas, Missouri, Illinois, Oklahoma, Wisconsin, and Iowa). Most Powder River region coal is produced from federal lands.

Great Plains coal resources have also figured in unconventional types of coal-based energy and commodities. Since 1983 lignite from the Beulah-Zap seam in the Fort Union Coal Region has been the feedstock for the large-scale production of substitute natural gas at the Great Plains Coal Gasification Plant near Beulah, North Dakota. The Powder River and Raton Mesa Coal Regions are significant areas of coalbed methane exploration and development. Between 1972 and 1988, a variety of federal and private entities conducted field tests in Wyoming, including tests at two sites in the Powder River Coal Region, designed to evaluate the technical and environmental feasibility of underground coal gasification in low-rank coals. Weathered low-rank coal, known as Leonardite, has been used as an additive in drilling fluids and as a soil amendment. Coal combustion by-products such as fly ash and bottom ash have been used for concrete, engineered fills, aggregate, soil stabilization, and ceramics.

Daniel J. Daly
University of North Dakota

Energy Information Administration. *Coal Industry Annual 1997: U.S. Department of Energy.* Energy Information Administration, December 1998. *Keystone Coal Industry Manual.* Chicago: Intertec Publishing Company, 1998. Wood, G. H., Jr., and W. V. Bour. *Coal Map of North America.* Washington DC: U.S. Geological Survey, 1998.

COLEMAN, WILLIAM (1870–1957)

William Coffin Coleman founded a manufacturing company that became a world leader in the production of camping equipment. Born in Chatham, New York, on May 21, 1870, Coleman grew up in Labette County, Kansas. To earn money as a law student at the University of Kansas in 1900, he began selling a lamp that burned gasoline under high pressure. Sales were disappointing, so he acquired the lamp's patent and redesigned it. Soon he was manufacturing his own version in a small building in Wichita, Kansas.

In 1905 Coleman's arc lanterns lit one of the first night football games ever played—at Wichita's Fairmount College, later Wichita State University. Coleman's lanterns quickly became popular with farmers, campers, and emergency workers. Through the years, he added more products, including heaters and air conditioners. During World War II, American servicemen in Europe and Asia used more than one million of Coleman's ingenious "GI pocket stoves," ranked with the jeep as the one of the most important pieces of noncombat equipment developed during the war.

After William's death in Wichita on November 2, 1957, his son and grandson, Sheldon and Sheldon C. Coleman, managed the Wichita company. By the 1960s their expansion into the camping and recreation products market had made Coleman a household word. In a 1989 hostile takeover, New York investor Ron Perelman acquired the Kansas firm. The Sunbeam Corporation took control in 1998, moving the headquarters from Wichita to Boca Raton, Florida. At that time, Coleman had manufacturing plants in eight states and six foreign countries. The bulk of its employees were in Wichita, making William

Coleman's former company one of Kansas's leading exporters.

Dave Webb
Kansas Heritage Center

Lunday, Sarah. "Shaking up Coleman." *Wichita Eagle*, May 12, 1998: 1A, 4A. Webb, Dave. *399 Kansas Characters*. Dodge City: Kansas Heritage Center, 1994.

CONAGRA FOODS

ConAgra Foods, a diversified foods company headquartered in Omaha, Nebraska, is the second largest food company in North America, operating in 35 countries and employing 85,000 people. Its products span the food chain: ConAgra Foods provides seeds, fertilizer, and chemicals for crops; trades grains, beans, and other agricultural commodities internationally; mills flour, corn, and feed; supplies ingredients to food and beverage processors; and processes beef, pork, lamb, chicken, turkey, seafood, and freshwater fish. ConAgra is the largest supplier in North America to food service operations such as restaurants, cafeterias, and schools. It is also the second largest grocery supplier of frozen, refrigerated, and shelf-stable goods. ConAgra Foods' eighty products include Healthy Choice, Banquet, Swiss Miss, Hunts Tomato, Butterball, Bumble Bee, Wesson Oils, and Country Pride.

ConAgra Foods was incorporated in 1919 as Nebraska Consolidated Mills, the result of a merger of four flour mills across central Nebraska: Ravenna Mill, Hastings Mills, St. Edward Mill, and Glade Milling in Grand Island, where Nebraska Consolidated Foods made its headquarters. A merger with Updike Mills of Omaha in 1922 doubled the company's milling capacity and resulted in moving the headquarters to Omaha. An early success was the development of Duncan Hines Cake Mix in 1951. Nebraska Consolidated Mills's first venture beyond Nebraska was the construction of a flour mill in Decatur, Alabama, in 1941. Its first venture beyond the continental United States was the construction of the Molinos (Mills) de Puerto Rico, which opened in 1959.

In 1971 Nebraska Consolidated Mills was renamed ConAgra, which in 2000 became ConAgra Foods. The company has grown rapidly since 1976, largely through extensive acquisitions, including Peavey, Armour, and Monfort, and now ranks sixtieth overall in revenues on the Fortune 500 list.

William J. Corcoran
University of Nebraska at Omaha

COTTON INDUSTRY

The cotton industry and the Great Plains region are not often viewed as synonymous, but the southern portion of the region constitutes the most concentrated area of cotton production in the world. Cotton production and the industrial base associated with it are concentrated in the southern High Plains of Texas and eastern New Mexico and the Rolling Plains of Texas and Oklahoma. The region consistently produces about 30 to 35 percent of the cotton output of the United States and 5 to 8 percent of the cotton produced in the world. The area of greatest concentration is within 100 miles of Lubbock, Texas, but production extends from the southernmost part of the Plains to as far north as Kansas, although production is extremely sparse north of Plainview, Texas, and Altus, Oklahoma.

Cotton is a multiproduct crop. The primary product is cotton lint, which constitutes about 80 percent of the farm value of cotton production, and the secondary product is cottonseed, which constitutes about 15 percent of the farm value. There are also several by-products. The industry can be characterized as consisting of sectors: production, ginning, warehousing, merchandising, oilseed processing, and textile processing.

The region produces 3.5 to 4.0 million bales of cotton lint each year (each bale weighs 480 pounds), with more than 4.5 million acres planted to cotton and almost 4 million acres harvested each year. The cottonseed production is 1.6 to 1.8 million tons per year. The farm value of cotton production in the region is typically $1.25 to $1.5 billion per year, with a total regional income generated of over $4 billion.

Production occurs under both irrigated and nonirrigated conditions within the region. The crop is typically harvested between mid-October and mid-December using mechanical cotton strippers that remove (strip) all of the material from the cotton stalk, including complete bolls, any remaining leaves, and small stems. Some but not all strippers have field cleaners mounted on them that separate the burrs in the cotton boll from the lint and seed and leave them in the field.

Once harvested, the harvested material (seedcotton) is typically stored in the field in "modules"—eight to twelve bale packed "loaves" of seedcotton of about 20,000 to 25,000 pounds each. These are constructed using module builders. Modules are then picked up with module mover trucks and hauled to a gin for further processing. There are more than 300 of these gin plants within the southern portion of the Great Plains region. They perform the function of separating the lint, seed, and other organic material in the seedcotton. The result is baled lint, which is moved to a warehouse for storage until it is ready to be shipped to a textile plant, and cottonseed, which is sold to a cottonseed oil mill or to a dairy or feedlot for direct consumption by cattle. There are forty-three cotton warehouses within the region and six cottonseed oil–processing plants. The oil mills produce meal for livestock feed, oil for cooking oils, and a range of by-products from linters and seed hulls.

Before cotton leaves the gin, samples are drawn from each bale and sent to a Classing Office operated by the U.S. Department of Agriculture. Each bale is evaluated for fiber color, foreign matter content, length, strength, length uniformity, and micronaire (an indicator of fiber fineness and maturity). The quality information on each bale's sample is placed with the bale, and each bale maintains its individual identity throughout the marketing system until it is consumed by a textile plant. This information plays an important role in determining the most efficient use for the cotton and its market value.

Cotton merchants/shippers, who have more than sixty installations in the region (belonging to a smaller number of firms), perform the functions of buying, selling, and moving cotton lint to the textile user. Their concentration tends to correspond to the location of production. As much as 45 percent of the cotton traded occurs through sophisticated computerized electronic trading systems. Most of the cotton from the region is shipped to the southeastern part of the United States or to foreign buyers. However, there is an expanding textile-processing industry within the southern portion of the region. There are some eleven textile-manufacturing firms within the region, most of them using cotton. Only about 5 percent of the cotton grown in the region is processed into textile products within the region, but this is an increase from about 1 percent fifteen years earlier. Manufacturing and transportation cost advantages in relation to the expanding West Coast and Mexico markets will likely support future growth of textile manufacturing within the region.

See also AGRICULTURE: Cotton.

Don E. Ethridge
Texas Tech University

ETHANOL

Ethyl alcohol (or ethanol, grain alcohol, or C_2H_5OH) is a colorless, sweet-smelling substance. Ethanol production in the form of intoxicating beverages was one of humankind's earliest industrial achievements. Beyond being the key ingredient in alcoholic drinks, ethanol is a solvent and has a growing role as a renewable-source fuel for motor vehicles.

Ethanol can be made synthetically by catalytic reaction of ethylene (from natural gas) with steam. However, most ethanol is made by fermentation of plant material. In fermentation, single-celled yeast organisms consume simple sugars, excreting ethyl alcohol and carbon dioxide. Plants are composed of carbohydrates (compounds containing carbon, hydrogen, and oxygen), and the simple sugars (called monosaccharides) are building blocks for complex carbohydrates like starches, higher sugars, and cellulose. Fruits tend to be rich in sugar, and grains are rich in starch, while straw and wood are dominated by cellulose. Only the monosaccharide sugars are directly fermentable, so natural fermentation requires a sugar-rich fruit (like grapes) for significant alcohol content. To make ethanol from other biomass sources, higher-order plant structures must be broken down to monosaccharides. Specialized enzymes or weak acids are used to break starch and cellulose into monosaccharides before fermentation. After fermentation, the resulting "beer" solution contains a small percentage of ethanol. Solids are filtered out for use as animal feed or fuel, and ethanol is separated from the remaining water by distillation and mole sieve techniques. Ethanol processes are well established for grain feed stocks, and research is improving ethanol yield and energy efficiency. New processes and enzymes are being developed to enable commercial production from cellulosic materials such as grass, straw, and wood.

Fuel ethanol is denatured by blending it with 5 percent gasoline or solvent to render it undrinkable. The denatured product is then blended with petroleum-based gasoline as a high-octane fuel component. American gasoline contains up to 10 percent ethanol, especially in winter months and in areas with serious air pollution. E85 (gasoline with 85 percent ethanol) is used in specially adapted or "flex-fuel" vehicles. The 15 percent hydrocarbon content in E85 is tailored to optimize fuel volatility and inhibit corrosion.

In 2000 American ethanol production was 1.8 billion U.S. gallons with roughly equal amounts used for fuel and for all other purposes. About 7 percent was synthetic, and the rest was the result of fermentation. Of the fermentation ethanol, 90 percent used corn as a feedstock, with the dominant production in Corn Belt states (Illinois, Iowa, Nebraska, and Minnesota). Overall, the Great Plains states supplied 23 percent of American fermentation ethanol. Canadian ethanol production in 2000 was in excess of 160 million U.S. gallons, with 75 percent from Ontario corn and 5 percent from forest products. The remaining 29 percent came from wheat, the dominant grain crop in the Prairie Provinces. Raw grain is bulky and expensive to transport, so most ethanol production plants are located in areas of high grain production or along major transportation routes. In 2000 there were two ethanol production plants in the Prairie Provinces—at Lanigan, Saskatchewan, and Red Deer, Alberta—and nineteen such plants in the American Great Plains, with Nebraska, the leading state, with seven.

Concerns over air pollution, petroleum supply, and greenhouse gas emissions are leading to increased production of biologically based ethanol. Currently, this is raising demand for grain, a major product of fertile lands in the Great Plains region. Future growth of the fuel market and commercialization of cellulose-based ethanol processes are expected to create a demand for cellulosic crops such as switch grass, straw, and poplar wood. These crops grow well on less fertile lands, so their production would provide an alternative industry in Plains areas currently dominated by livestock.

M. David Checkel
University of Alberta

FARM IMPLEMENTS

The production and use of farm implements have always been important in the development of the Great Plains. Current production of farm implements remains an integral part of the regional economy. Dominant sectors include the production of forage and small

Implements store, Greeley, Colorado, ca. 1882

grain harvest equipment, seeding and tillage equipment, irrigation equipment, large tractors, chemical application equipment, and equipment for specialized regional crops such as sugar beets and potatoes. Although the equipment produced reflects regional needs, it is also sold in global markets.

Forage and small grains are important regional crops in the semiarid climate of the Great Plains. Significant manufacturers of harvesters for these crops are located in the Plains. Hay and Forage Industries, formerly Hesston (Hesston, Kansas), produces a major line of hay and forage harvesters. The small round baler, conceived and developed by Nebraskan Ummo Franklin Luebben, was initially produced in Omaha. Manufacturing rights were purchased, and the baler was widely marketed by Allis-Chalmers during the period 1940 to 1960.

New Holland (Grand Island, Nebraska) and Gleaner-AGCO (Independence, Missouri) manufacture combines for grain harvest. MacDon (Winnipeg, Manitoba) makes combine headers. Winds common on the Plains often cause grain stalks to bend over and lodge before harvest. Companies such as Crary (West Fargo, North Dakota) supply attachments to pick up and lift the crop. Massey-Harris developed the self-propelled combine for use in the Great Plains during the late 1930s. It became firmly established during the 1940s, when there was a labor shortage due to World War II, and organized fleets of combines subsequently followed the annual wheat harvest northward.

Seeding and tillage equipment manufacturers have developed a wide variety of drills, air seeders, and planters for both small and coarse grains. Equipment was often originally developed in response to regional climatic needs but is now marketed extensively. Manufacturers include Fleischer (Columbus, Nebraska), Flexi-Coil (Saskatoon, Saskatchewan), Great Plains (Salina, Kansas), Krause (Hutchinson, Kansas), Tye-AGCO (Lockney, Texas), and Wil-Rich (Wahpeton, North Dakota). Some tillage equipment, such as the disk plow and rod weeder (Morris Industries, Yorkton, Saskatchewan), was developed to

conserve moisture and prevent wind erosion. These implements are innovations of Plains manufacturers. For example, Charles Noble (Nobleford, Alberta) developed the Noble blade cultivator during the 1930s in response to Dust Bowl conditions.

Large open fields encouraged steam tractor plowing of the grasslands. Four-wheel-drive tractors with greater than 250 engine horsepower are commonly used on larger farms and ranches. They are produced by Case Corporation, formerly Steiger (Fargo, North Dakota), and New Holland, formerly Versatile (Winnipeg, Manitoba). In response to disreputable marketing of farm tractors early in this century, the Nebraska legislature passed a law in 1919 requiring that all tractors for sale in that state be tested. Although the law was amended in 1986 to permit standardized testing from other facilities, the Nebraska tractor test has been a standard by which most North American tractors are judged.

Chemical application equipment is used for weed control and fertilizer application. Large fields have promoted the development of self-propelled sprayers, such as those manufactured by Melroe (Fargo, North Dakota). Wind-swept Plains topography has influenced the development of drift-control application equipment, such as that produced by Rodgers Engineering (Saskatoon, Saskatchewan).

Equipment for specialized crops grown in parts of the Great Plains is important regionally and is also marketed worldwide. Lockwood Corporation (Gering, Nebraska) manufactures potato production implements, and Woods Equipment (Fargo, North Dakota) markets equipment for sugar beet production.

In addition to larger manufacturers, hundreds of smaller shops throughout the Great Plains build, modify, supply parts for, and repair farm implements. Their presence is evident on the landscape of most Plains towns of any size. Rather particular to this part of North America, a harvest brigade of parts and repair workers follows the annual wheat harvest by custom combine operators from the Texas Panhandle north to the international border.

H. Mark Hanna
Iowa State University

Equipment Manufacturers Institute. *A Presentation of the Equipment Manufacturers Institute on the Occasion of Its 100th Convention, September 25–27, 1993, Fairmont Hotel, Chicago, Illinois.* Chicago: Equipment Manufacturers Institute, 1993. Von Bargen, K., L. L. Bashford, L. I. Leviticus, and W. E. Splinter. "Nebraska Tractor Testing beyond 1985." ASAE Paper no. MCR-86-109. St. Joseph MI: ASAE, 1986.

FEEDLOTS

Grass, corn, and cattle are abundant in the Great Plains. When corn production became efficient, corn was fed to produce rapid and efficient body weight gains in cattle. American consumers developed a taste for "finished beef," which has sufficient marbling to produce the taste and juiciness we have become accustomed to. Cattle feeding based on corn first developed in the Corn Belt, and markets were centered around Chicago. The Corn Belt expanded into the Great Plains due to irrigation, and sorghum was produced in drier areas to substitute for corn in feedlot finishing diets.

In the traditional Corn Belt, cattle were fed in barns and paved feedlots. In the 1950s and 1960s, as the Corn Belt was expanding west, it was established that the drier climate of the Great Plains was appropriate for feeding cattle without the expense of barns and completely paved feedlots. Cattle feeding expanded rapidly in the 1960s, and the majority of U.S. cattle feeding now occurs in the Great Plains, with southwestern Kansas a particularly notable concentration. Similarly, Canadian cattle feeding has also expanded in the Great Plains area.

Today's feedlots range from farmer-feeders to large custom feedlots. Farmer-feeders generally produce most if not all of the corn and forage fed to their cattle and typically own most of the cattle. These feedlots may have capacity for 1,000 to 10,000 cattle at one time. Custom feedlots are generally larger, with numbers up to 100,000 at one time. Cattle are

typically fed for customers who own the cattle. The customer pays for the feed, health supplies, and "yardage"—the cost of facilities, equipment, labor, and so on. The custom feedlot makes a profit by maintaining customer cattle near capacity. The feedlot must operate very efficiently to maintain the customers.

Feedlots vary from simple facilities to sophisticated, computer-operated feedlots with veterinary and nutritionist consultants. Feed is mixed and fed to the cattle two or three times daily with feed trucks. Larger feedlots have feed mills that operate with computers, in some cases unattended by employees. The feed trucks have electronic scales and in many cases onboard computers that are used to record the amount of feed allocated to each pen. These records are then downloaded to the primary computer for accurate recording and billing to customers.

Health of the cattle is monitored daily by a "cowboy crew." These individuals typically ride a horse through each pen of cattle (usually 200 head). Sick animals are removed from the pen and taken to a "hospital" area for treatment and recovery. Innovative feedlots now have mobile hospitals that move to the cattle pens, where the cattle are treated. Most common health problems are respiratory diseases; however, few cattle become sick.

Feedlots typically employ one person for each 1,000 cattle. Primary jobs are feeding and health care, but maintenance and business procedures are also important jobs. Cattle enter feedlots at different ages and weights and spend 100 to 200 days in the feedlot. This diversity is necessary to provide a consistent supply of cattle to consumers. Cattle require forty to sixty bushels of grain while in the feedlot and the equivalent of about one-third ton of hay. It takes about one-half acre of cropland to produce this much feed. Because of the forage used for cows and growing of feedlot cattle,

only two to three pounds of corn are required to produce a pound of finished animal. Typically, feedlots have extensive runoff facilities to ensure that no waste leaves the feedlot uncontrolled to enter surface or groundwater. The waste from the feedlot is returned to the cropland as organic fertilizer. Cattle are typically worth $700 to $900 each at market time. Most feedlots market two and one-half times their one-time capacity. Therefore, a 10,000-head-capacity feedlot would have sales of $20 million per year.

Terry J. Klopfenstein
University of Nebraska–Lincoln

Albin, Robert C., and G. B. Thompson. *Cattle Feeding: A Guide to Management.* Amarillo TX: Trofton Printing, 1996. Ball, Charles E. *Building the Beef Industry.* Denver: National Cattlemen's Foundation, 1998.

FOREIGN INVESTMENT

Foreign investment has long been an economic force in the Great Plains of Canada and the United States. In the 1870s and early 1880s English and particularly Scottish syndicates invested heavily in Plains ranching, only to lose much of their money when the bottom dropped out of the business in 1885–86. At the same time, English investors were buying huge tracts of land from the railroads in Kansas and reselling them to settlers for large profits. North of the forty-ninth parallel, British investors were even more influential. British urban real estate firms controlled much of the early development of Regina, Saskatoon, Winnipeg, and other cities in the Prairie Provinces, and British capital also flowed into the wheat industry and railroad construction.

In the 1990s in the United States as a whole, foreign investment averaged $33.3 billion a year. In Canada, during the same period, annual foreign investment averaged just over $6 billion. In both countries, such investment is concentrated in coastal states or provinces. For example, two-thirds of U.K. investment in Canada (a source that is second only to the United States) goes to Ontario; Alberta, with 8 percent of total U.K. investment, leads other Prairie Provinces. In 1995, in the ten states wholly or partly in the Great Plains of the United States, there were 509,700 jobs in foreign affiliates. These jobs accounted for only 4 percent of total private industry employment in the region, and no state reached the 4.8 percent national average of jobs in foreign affiliates, though Texas was close. Between 1990 and 1995, however, states in the Great Plains saw a 6 percent increase in such employment, outpacing the 4 percent national average. Colorado led the way, with a 28 percent increase, rather evenly divided between foreign investment–generated employment in manufacturing and nonmanufacturing. Oklahoma experienced the greatest decrease in this time period (a 24 percent decline in this type of employment), probably reflecting problems in the volatile energy sector.

There are also significant intraregional variations in sources of foreign investment. The United States is by far the leading source in the

Feedlot east of Dodge City, Kansas

Prairie Provinces. During the 1990s, for example, many of the leading U.S. food-processing firms, including Archer Daniels Midland, Cargill, and ConAgra, Ltd., made significant investments in Alberta. South of the forty-ninth parallel, Canada is the main source of foreign investment in South Dakota, Montana, and Kansas. The United Kingdom is an important source throughout the Plains region, but especially in Wyoming. Japan is important too, but proportionately less so than for the United States as a whole. France and Germany, on the other hand, have a proportionately greater presence on the Plains than they do in the Untied States as a whole.

Foreign investors are drawn to the Great Plains for a variety of economic and political reasons, including a desire to expand their foreign market share, minimize production and transportation costs, take advantage of the availability of skilled labor, and profit from state or province development incentives. The positive effects for the Plains include increased competitiveness in the regional economy, the accumulation of capital and expertise, and, of course, the provision of jobs. Possible negative impacts involve overcapacity, especially in mature industries, and unfair competition due to foreign subsidies and state and province development initiatives.

Roger Riefler
University of Nebraska–Lincoln

Fahim-Nader, Mahnaz, and William J. Zeile. "Foreign Direct Investment in the United States." *Survey of Current Business* 77 (1977): 42–69. Paterson, Donald G. *British Direct Investment in Canada, 1890–1914.* Toronto: University of Toronto Press, 1976. Wilkins, Mira. *The History of Foreign Investment in the United States to 1914.* Cambridge: Harvard University Press, 1984.

FUR TRADE

The historic fur trade in the Great Plains spanned the midcontinent and involved three separate systems: the French and, later, the English fur trade in the Prairie Provinces and on the Northern Plains; the successive French and Spanish, then English and American, fur trades of the Missouri River; and the fur, hide, and skin trade on the Southern Plains. The trade was fueled by businessmen who sought to provide furs and hides necessary for the fashionable clothing and accessories of eastern North America and Europe.

While beaver pelts were generally the most important single item, at least in the Far North, the pelts and hides found in fort warehouses were as diverse as the mammals living on the Plains. They included bison, elk, wolf, fox, rabbit, deer, bear, and, in the Southern Plains, even hedgehog, although many of these pelts were of little value. Goods traded to Native American trappers and hunters were equally varied, depending on wants, style, and time period, but firearms, ammunition, metal containers, glass beads, knives, blankets, and cloth were universally important. Alcohol was also an important trade item in many places. Native Americans were not passive participants in the business, for they had traded extensively among themselves long before the arrival of Europeans and Americans. They were shrewd traders and demanded quality goods.

Beginning in 1727, the Canadian fur trader Pierre Gaultier de Varennes, sieur de La Vérendrye, established a series of posts across what is now south-central Canada, ultimately building Fort La Reine in southern Manitoba. From there he made an expedition to the Mandans on the Missouri River in 1738. A few years later his sons explored as far southwest as the Black Hills of South Dakota. It was not until late in the 1700s, however, that two rival companies, the Hudson's Bay Company and the North West Company, began competing for the trade in the Prairie Provinces. Their goods reached central Canada by canoe from York Factory on Hudson Bay and from Montreal, respectively. Between 1779 and 1821, these companies established more than 100 posts along the North and South Saskatchewan, Qu'Appelle, Souris, and Red Rivers. Although most posts were occupied for only a few years, they linked the region's Native groups—Plains Crees, Assiniboines, Blackfoot, Gros Ventres, and Sarcees—firmly to international fur markets. Beavers were the most lucrative items of the trade. These companies, along with independent traders, also crossed what is now the Canada-U.S. boundary to trade with the Mandans, Hidatsas, and others. The merger of the two companies in 1821 led to domination by the Hudson's Bay Company, which is still in business.

The Missouri River fur trade was rudimentary before 1806, although the lower parts of the river had been explored and exploited by French fur traders in the decades following the discovery of its mouth by Jacques Marquette and Louis Jolliet in 1673. French and, later, Spanish traders penetrated as far north as the Mandans by 1791. English traders also reached the Missouri River tribes, such as the Omahas and Poncas, by ascending the Des Moines River and by traveling overland from Prairie du Chien on the upper Mississippi River. It was only after the return of the Lewis and Clark expedition in 1806, however, that American exploitation of the resources of the Missouri basin began in earnest. In 1807 Manuel Lisa established Fort Raymond at the mouth of the Bighorn River in modern Montana. His enthusiasm for that trade, albeit short-lived, led to the formation by others of the Missouri Fur Company in 1809, one of the first of many successive and overlapping American companies dedicated to the pursuit of furbearers in the Central and Northern Plains. Dugout canoes and keelboats carrying trade goods up the Missouri were replaced after 1832 by steamboats, beginning with the famous steamer *Yellowstone*, which carried goods by the ton in both directions.

The most important of the companies was the American Fur Company founded by John Jacob Astor in 1808. By the early 1830s, a string of the company's posts and those of its competitors lined the Missouri River and its tributaries, the most important of which were Forts Union, Clark, and Pierre. Although many types of furs and skins were produced, bison robes were the dominant product after 1830 on the American Plains. By 1867, with furbearers depleted and the bison all but extinct, even this trade was over. Traders and their kin were replaced by settlers, and their forts were abandoned.

The early trade on the Southern Plains was closely linked to the lower Mississippi River valley. From that center, French and later American traders pushed up the Red and Arkansas Rivers to barter for furs, hides, and deerskins with Caddos, Wichitas, and Comanches. From the late eighteenth century on, *Comancheros*, Pueblo, and Spanish traders from New Mexico journeyed to Comanche camps to trade foodstuffs, tobacco, and manufactured items for bison hides, deerskins, horses, and captives. A new era in the region's trade began in the early 1830s, when Charles and William Bent and Ceran St. Vrain established the prosperous Bent's Old Fort on the upper Arkansas River. The success of Bent's Fort enticed others, and by the early 1840s the fringes of the Plains were dotted with numerous posts operated by merchants from the United States and Texas. The trade collapsed in the early 1850s, when the combined effects of commercial hunting, aridity, exotic bovine diseases, and environmental degradation pushed the massive bison herds into decline.

Although the days when the fur trade was the dominant industry of the Great Plains are long passed, there is still a fur industry in the region, particularly on the Northern Great Plains and in the Prairie Provinces. Trapping is generally a part-time occupation of rural Plains people. Beaver and muskrat are the most important products of a trade that, in the Prairie Provinces, was worth an average of $15 million a year from 1976 to 1986.

See also EUROPEAN AMERICANS: Vérendrye Family / HISPANIC AMERICANS: Missouri Company.

Raymond Wood
University of Missouri–Columbia

Ray, Arthur. *Indians in the Fur Trade: Their Role as Trappers, Hunters, and Middlemen in the Lands Southwest of Hudson Bay, 1660–1870.* Toronto: University of Toronto Press, 1974. Wishart, David J. *The Fur Trade of the American West, 1807–1840.* Lincoln: University of Nebraska Press, 1979. Wood, W. Raymond, and Thomas D. Thiessen. *Early Fur Trade on the Northern Plains.* Norman: University of Oklahoma Press, 1980.

GATEWAY, INC.

Gateway, Inc., a South Dakota company, pioneered direct marketing of computers to individuals for personal applications in their homes. Its headquarters moved from North Sioux City, South Dakota, to San Diego, California, in 1998, but it still maintains its North Sioux City location, as well as a location in Sioux Falls. The company went public in 1993 and is now listed in the New York Stock Exchange as GTW. Formerly known as Gateway 2000, the "2000" was dropped from the name in 1998.

Ted Waitt started Gateway in 1985 in the abandoned farmhouse on his family's cattle ranch with $10,000 capital from his grandmother. Waitt was twenty-three years old. The growth of the company has been remarkable. By 1997 its revenues had reached $6.3 billion. It then ranked seventh among its competitors—behind IBM, Dell, and Compaq but above Apple, NCR, and Silicon Graphics. Gateway has manufacturing facilities in the United States, Ireland, and Malaysia and showrooms, called Gateway Country Stores, in thirty-seven American cities. The number of stores, however, was being greatly reduced in 2003 in an effort to reduce expenses.

Gateway maintains its ties to its Great Plains and cattle ranch roots. The familiar Holstein cow spots on its shipping boxes are known around the world. The spots are prominent in its logo and cover its buildings. In the fall of 2002, Gateway updated its logo with a G (the "power on" symbol on its side) inside a single cow spot.

The company wins numerous industry awards year after year. Its founder, Ted Waitt, is recognized by journalists as one of America's leading executives and strategists.

Harold Christensen
University of Sioux Falls

Dumaine, Bryan. "America's Smart Young Entrepreneurs." Fortune, March 21, 1994: 34–41.

GOODNIGHT, CHARLES (1836–1929)

Charles Goodnight epitomized the plainsman. Born in Macoupin County, Illinois, on March 5, 1836, Goodnight, riding bareback, first came to the Southern Plains of Texas in 1846. During his young adulthood in the Brazos River valley, he worked as a farmhand, freighter, and cowboy. In 1856 Goodnight hired himself out to a local rancher and received every fourth calf as pay. Within a year he had also become a Texas Ranger. Meanwhile, he continued to add to his small herd of cattle, which he moved to Palo Pinto County, Texas.

His eight-year Ranger career, filled with frontier patrols, ended when the twenty-nine-year-old entrepreneur decided to take his 180 head of cattle west to reservation agencies. He became partners with Oliver Loving, a man twenty-five years his senior with experience in driving cattle long distances. The two adventurers planned to trail their combined herd from Fort Belknap, Texas, to Fort Sumner, New Mexico. While preparing for departure, Goodnight invented the chuck wagon by remodeling the back end of an existing wagon into a mess area. In 1866 the two men took 2,000 cattle guided by eighteen cowboys and struck out southwest for the Pecos River, which they would follow north. The 700-mile journey, 96 miles of it without water on the Staked Plains, established the Goodnight-Loving Trail that later extended to Cheyenne, Wyoming.

The two stockmen quickly made a successful second trip but met disaster on their third trip in 1868, when Comanches mortally wounded Loving. Goodnight made three more trips on the trail from 1869 to 1871 while simultaneously operating a corn farm and way station ranch in southeastern Colorado. In 1871 he wed Mary Dyer from Fort Belknap, Texas. Subsequently, they lost their Colorado holdings in the Panic of 1873.

Charles returned to his trail-driving days by blazing the Goodnight Trail from Alamogordo Creek, New Mexico, to Granada, Colorado, in 1875. The following year, he moved his remaining cattle into the Palo Duro Canyon in the Texas Panhandle, where he found a partner in John Adair from Ireland. Their spread, the JA Ranch, eventually covered one million acres and included more than 100,000 cattle. To these cattle, Goodnight added bison from a captive breeding program he had initiated in 1878 at the request of his wife. Goodnight bred bison with cattle, thereby developing the "cattalo." He later abandoned the project, but his knack for cattle breeding resulted in the improvement of his herds with Hereford bulls. In 1880 Goodnight became the inaugural president of the Panhandle Stockman's Association.

Goodnight retired from the JA Ranch in 1888 and within a couple of years purchased a smaller ranch at nearby Goodnight Station. He spent the remainder of his life as a cattle breeder, an active member of the American Bison Society, and a leading citizen. Goodnight died on December 12, 1929, in Phoenix, Arizona. His family buried him next to his wife in Goodnight, Texas. Goodnight was commemorated by the U.S. Postal Service with a stamp and postcard in its 1993 Legends of the West series.

See also AGRICULTURE: Ranches / TRANSPORTATION: Cattle Trails.

Ken Zontek
University of Idaho

Goodnight, Charles, Emanuel Dubbs, and John A. Hart. Pioneer Days in the Southwest from 1850 to 1879. Guthrie OK: State Capital Company, 1909. Haley, J. Evetts. Charles Goodnight: Cowman and Plainsman. Norman: University of Oklahoma Press, 1936. Hamner, Laura. The No-Gun Man of Texas: A Century of Achievement, 1835–1929. Amarillo: Hamner, 1935.

GRAIN PROCESSING

The Great Plains of the United States and Canada form one huge production engine for barley, wheat, and sorghum. Wheat is by far the dominant cereal grain produced, which explains why the Great Plains is commonly referred to as the "Breadbasket of the World." There are three classes of wheat produced in the region. Eastern Alberta, Saskatchewan, southwestern Manitoba, northeastern Montana, North Dakota, northwestern Minnesota, and northern South Dakota are the major production area for hard red spring wheat and durum wheat. Hard red spring wheat is a high-protein wheat used as a blending wheat to upgrade the quality of lower-quality wheats and is also the source of flour for specialty breads such as hard rolls. Durum wheat is the source of semolina, a granular product used in the production of high-quality pasta products. The Plains states from South Dakota to Texas and from Montana to Colorado are the source of hard red winter wheat, a slightly lower protein wheat than hard red spring wheat. The flour from hard red winter wheat is used primarily in the production of pan breads.

In 1998 the United States produced an estimated total of 69.61 million metric tons of wheat. This included hard red winter wheat, hard red spring wheat, soft red winter wheat, soft white wheat, and durum wheat. The Great Plains states of the United States produced 46.14 million metric tons, or 72 percent of that total. Total wheat production in Canada in 1998 was 24.40 million metric tons, with the Prairie Provinces producing 93 percent of that total.

The number of flour mills and total milling capacity in the United States for 1997 were 195 and 1,395,323 hundredweights (cwts), respectively. Much of the milling of the wheats produced in the Great Plains is done either within or relatively close to the grain production states. Plains states had the following number of mills and flour production capacity in 1997: Colorado (4; 22,000 cwts); Kansas (18; 154,640 cwts); Montana (4; 16,880 cwts); Nebraska (5; 26,570 cwts); North Dakota (1; 19,000 cwts); Oklahoma (4; 31,200 cwts); South Dakota (1; 4,000 cwts); and Texas (8; 64,560 cwts). This gives a combined total of 45 flour mills and milling capacity of 338,850 cwts. There is a similar concentration of durum milling in the Plains, with North Dakota (4; 19,555 cwts) the leading state. In all, seven of the twenty-three durum mills in the country are in North Dakota, Montana, and Nebraska. The Prairie Provinces are also an important location for both flour and semolina production. Close to 30 percent of the flour and 40 percent of the semolina milling capacity of Canada are in Alberta, Saskatchewan, and Manitoba.

The three major flour-milling companies in the U.S. Great Plain states are Archer Daniels Midland Milling Company, ConAgra Grain Processing Company, and Cargill Foods Flour Milling. In the Prairie Provinces the leading companies are Archer Daniels Midland Milling Company, CSP Foods, and Robin Hood Multifoods, Inc. The three major durum-milling companies operating in or close to the U.S. portion of the Plains states are Archer Daniels Midland Milling Company, General Mills, and Harvest States. In the Prairie Provinces, durum-milling companies include Ellison Milling Company and Robin Hood Multifoods, Inc.

Wheat milling and flour extraction have come a long way from the days of stone grinding. Today wheat milling is a high-throughput, automated process that extracts flour from the wheat in high volume to meet the needs of the baking industry. An average bushel of wheat weighs sixty pounds, from which the miller hopes to "extract" about forty-five pounds of flour (75 percent) and fifteen pounds of millfeed (25 percent).

When wheat arrives at the mill by truck, ship, barge, or rail, samples are taken to ensure it meets purchase quality specifications for milling and baking or other end use needs.

Results from inspection and quality testing determine how the wheat will be handled and stored. The wheat is blended and stored in large bins on the basis of the desired end product. Grain storage is a critical component of wheat handling to ensure it does not go out of condition prior to milling.

The first step in the milling process is to clean the wheat of extraneous material picked up in the harvesting process. Foreign materials such as metal, sticks, stones, straw, seeds, and other grains are removed in steps by a magnetic separator, vibrating screens, a destoner, a disc separator, and a scourer. Once the wheat is cleaned, water is added to it in precise amounts in a process called tempering. This is done to toughen the bran and mellow the inner portion of the wheat kernel (the endosperm), facilitating separation of the kernel components. Tempered wheat is stored in bins for twelve to twenty-four hours, depending on the class of the wheat. After proper tempering, the wheat passes through an impact scourer (entoleter) that breaks apart and removes unsound kernels and then moves to the grinding bins (large hoppers that feed the wheat to the grinding rolls).

Mill rolls are corrugated and paired, and they counterrotate at different speeds. One pass between the first break rolls begins the separation of the bran, endosperm, and germ. Feeding the tempered wheat to the first break rolls begins a gradual reduction process whereby middlings or coarse particles of endosperm are graded and separated from the bran by sieves and purifiers. Each size is returned to appropriate rollers, and the process is repeated until the desired flour is produced. The flour is then bleached and enriched with three B vitamins (thiamin, niacin, and riboflavin), iron, and folic acid. Family flour for retail sale is packed in 5-, 10-, or 25-pound bags. Bakery flour may be packed in 50- or 100-pound bags or shipped in bulk trucks or railcars.

See also AGRICULTURE: Wheat.

Brendan J. Donnelly
Kansas State University

Grain and Milling Annual. Kansas City MO: Sosland Publishing Company, 1998. *1998 Crop Quality Report.* Washington DC: U.S. Wheat Associates, Inc., 1998.

HALLMARK CARDS, INC.

Joyce C. Hall, born in David City, Nebraska, founded Hallmark Cards, Inc. in 1910. His brother Rollie joined him in 1911, and the two brothers opened up a specialty store in downtown Kansas City, Missouri. The original company was called Hall Brothers, Inc., and the men were jobbers of greeting cards, buying designs created and manufactured elsewhere and then selling them wholesale to drugstores, bookstores, and gift shops.

In 1915 the Hall Brothers changed the scope of their operations after a devastating fire that destroyed the storefront and all of their inventory. The brothers purchased an engraving firm and began creating the first original Hallmark designs. William Hall, who had stayed behind to run a bookstore in the family's hometown of Norfolk, Nebraska, joined Joyce and Rollie in 1921. The company changed its name in 1954 to Hallmark Cards, Inc.

Still privately owned, the company reported consolidated net sales in excess of $3.9 billion in 1998. Hallmark publishes its products in more than thirty languages and distributes them in more than 100 countries. Domestically, the company has approximately 47,000 domestic retail outlets. Hallmark employs almost 21,000 people worldwide, with about 10,000 of them in the Great Plains. The creative staff consists of more than 700 people who produce 30,000 new or redesigned greeting cards and related products annually. In addition to greeting cards, the firm sells holiday ornaments, writing paper, jigsaw puzzles, photo albums, calendars, gift wrap, ribbons, home decor specialty products, party goods, and a variety of other gift items.

Hallmark operates manufacturing plants in Kansas City, Missouri, and Lawrence, Topeka, and Leavenworth, Kansas. Distribution plants are located in Liberty, Missouri, and Enfield, Connecticut. In addition, two of the company's major subsidiaries have operations in the Great Plains. These include Binney & Smith, headquartered in Easton, Pennsylvania, the maker of Crayola, Liquitex, and Silly Putty, and Crown Center, an eighty-five-acre commercial and residential complex adjacent to the Hallmark headquarters in Kansas City. The Crown Center complex attracts more than five million people annually.

David Berkowitz
University of Alabama in Huntsville

Hall, J. C., with Curtiss Anderson. *When You Care Enough.* Kansas City: Hallmark Cards, Inc., 1992. Hallmark Cards, Inc. *Hallmark Press Kit.* Kansas City, Missouri, 1999.

HEADBOLT HEATER

Without a doubt, necessity was the mother of invention in the case of the headbolt heater—necessity and an enterprising man. The necessity was getting a car to start in the frigid North Dakota winter; the man was Andrew Freeman, an electrical engineer who, as general manager of Minnkota Power Cooperative, brought electricity to the rural areas of North Dakota.

The year was 1947, and Freeman, like everyone else in Grand Forks, found that even if he succeeded in getting his car running, it took so much out of the battery that soon the engine was dead. He started experimenting with devices that would heat the engine of his V-8 Ford. At first, using scrap copper tubing as inserts and a ribbon wire heating element from an old flatiron, he devised a method of heating the two hoses that went from the bottom of the radiator to the engine block. On a thirty-degree morning he attached the heating elements to an electrical cord, plugged it in, waited for two hours, and immediately started the engine. Unfortunately, when Freeman tried to install his invention on a neighbor's Plymouth, he found that it did not work; nor was it successful on another neighbor's Chevrolet. So he thought again.

Advertisement for the Headbolt Heater

Freeman concluded that he needed a way to get heat directly to the water in the engine block. He discovered that in most cars the headbolts extended directly into the water. After much experimentation over a period of three years, Freeman developed a system that transmitted electricity via a brass tube through a replaced headbolt into the water. The electric lead extended from the heater through the radiator grill to the outlet.

In 1947, with two colleagues, Freeman formed the Five Star Manufacturing Company of East Grand Forks to manufacture headbolt heaters. The company did not do well at first, not least because there was a manufacturing error in the first 25,000 heaters. But soon the product was refined and the manufacturing process mechanized until the company was turning out 200,000 heaters a year for sale in the United States and Canada. Altogether Freeman estimates that he sold as many as two million headbolt heaters.

Eventually, other types of tank and plug heaters took over, and improvements in engine design diminished their general necessity. Still, engine heaters continued to go by the name "headbolt heaters," which is testimony to the lasting legacy of Andrew Freeman's invention.

Andrew L. Freeman Jr.
Bemidji, Minnesota
David J. Wishart
University of Nebraska–Lincoln

McCutchon, Beverly. *Reflections: Andrew Freeman, 1909–1996.* Grand Forks ND: Minnkota Power Cooperative, Inc., 1996.

HOMESTAKE MINE

Homestake Mining Company began operations in the Black Hills of Dakota Territory (now South Dakota) in 1877 after a group of California miners purchased the Golden Star and Homestake claims for $70,000. These original claims comprised approximately ten acres. By 1999 the Homestake Mine had grown to more than 8,000 acres of patented claims

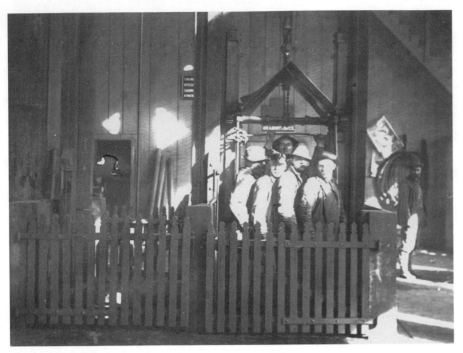
Homestake Mine, ca. 1930

and was the oldest continually operating gold mine in the world.

Located in Lead, South Dakota, Homestake Mine consisted of an "open cut" surface operation as well as an 8,000-foot-deep underground mine. Over the years, the Homestake Mine produced more than 39 million ounces of gold, and there were an additional 4.7 million ounces of proven and probable reserves as of 1997. In 1998 the Homestake Mine experienced major restructuring with the implementation of a new operating plan that was designed to lower production costs in the underground mine from $355 per ounce to $280 per ounce. The company also spent nearly $100 million to reclaim portions of the Whitewood Creek Superfund Site that served as a tailings and municipal waste dump for nearly 100 years.

Homestake Mining Company entered the New York Stock Exchange in 1977. The company had focused solely on gold mining until the 1950s and 1960s, when it delved into uranium, lead, and zinc mining. The company became even more diversified in the early 1980s, when it purchased fossil fuel developments. Homestake also aggressively acquired additional gold mines in Australia and Canada at this time. In early 2001 Homestake ranked as the second largest gold producer in the United States.

The Homestake Mine itself, however, has experienced an interesting turn of events. Despite the new operating plan, falling gold prices and depleted reserves led to cutbacks and ultimately closure of the mine. The Homestake Mining Company removed its last gold ore on December 14, 2001, merged with Barrick Gold of Toronto, ceased mining operations completely on December 31, 2001, then donated the mine for use as an astrophysics laboratory. A small laboratory run by the University of Pennsylvania for nearly twenty years deep in the underground mine served as the nucleus for this newer, larger National Underground Science Laboratory. Work at this new lab would focus on the study of subatomic particles emitted from the sun, called neutrinos, at a depth of 7,400 feet beneath the surface. At this depth, interference from background cosmic radiation is filtered out, allowing only neutrinos to pass through. The laboratory received interim funding in the fall of 2001, and a proposal for the five-year, 281-million-dollar facility was submitted to the National Science Foundation in 2001. The final funding decision is still pending. The National Underground Science Laboratory would hire a number of former Homestake employees and bring in astrophysicists from all over the world, continuing the long and storied legacy of the Homestake Mine. As of April 2003, Barrick Gold had agreed in principle to donate the mine for use as a laboratory, but only if Barrick stockholders were protected from environmental liability for the property.

Steve Anderson
Black Hills State University

HUDSON'S BAY COMPANY

The oldest company in the Prairie Provinces and one of the world's first joint-stock companies, the Hudson's Bay Company has played a major role in Plains history for three centuries, first as a fur-trading company and then as a large retailer, major landowner, and developer.

Charles II of England chartered the company in 1670, granting it exclusive rights to trade in the Hudson Bay drainage basin, a territory that became known as Rupert's Land. The company's monopoly, however, was never safe. Its envoys first visited the Plains in the late seventeenth century to invite Indians to trade at York Factory on Hudson Bay and to monitor competitors from New France. By the 1690s the company had become a major supplier of European goods to the Indigenous peoples of the northern Great Plains. These goods profoundly influenced lifestyles and patterns of trade, warfare, and diplomacy there.

From the 1690s to 1821 the company competed on the Plains with Montreal-based rivals. Like its competitors, it focused primarily on the rich furs of the subarctic, but in response to stiffening competition from Canadian opponents after 1766 the company established permanent posts on the northern margins of the Plains after 1780. This began a period of intense competition, with important implications for the Native peoples of the region. Although traders purchased furs (especially wolf and fox but also some beaver) from the Indians of the Plains, the region was also important as the source of preserved bison meat (especially pemmican) that the Hudson's Bay Company and other companies used to feed their employees in the subarctic. Cree, Assiniboine, and Métis communities supplied most of bison meat, although Blackfoot, Sarcee, Gros Ventre, Mandan, Hidatsa, and Ojibwa groups also traded directly with the company. In 1812 the company established the Red River Colony, the first permanent European American settlement in the northern Great Plains.

When the Hudson's Bay Company and the North West Company merged in 1821, it seemed that the Hudson's Bay Company would finally enjoy its elusive monopoly, but with the border between Rupert's Land and the United States settled at the forty-ninth parallel in 1818, the company faced growing challenges from Métis free traders and American competitors. Before 1818 and even into the 1830s, the company acquired furs trapped well south of the forty-ninth parallel. After 1830, the flow of furs changed. Many Métis employees laid off by the Hudson's Bay Company after the merger settled in the Red River Colony, and the colony became primarily Métis. Increasingly, Red River Métis defied the company by trading furs from Indians and selling them to businesses in the northern United States. Also, the Columbia Fur Company and American Fur Company hired many of the talented traders (such as Kenneth McKenzie) who were released from the Hudson's Bay Company after 1821, and these men helped the American Fur Company establish trading relations with communities such as the Blackfoot and Gros Ventres of the Northern Plains. The Hudson's Bay Company was also hampered by the fact that its supply lines were expensive compared with its Missouri River–based competition, especially when the trade in bulky and heavy buffalo robes became important after the 1830s. Thus, between the 1830s and the 1870s, the competitive position of the Hudson's Bay Company weakened.

In 1870 the company reached an important milestone when it sold Rupert's Land to Canada for £300,000. As part of the agreement, the company retained one-twentieth of the land in the Prairie Provinces, much of which was destined to become prime urban real estate. As a result, the Hudson's Bay Company became a major landowner and important real estate developer. After 1870 the company's trade with incoming settlers grew. Its wholesaling, retailing, and real estate activities quickly dwarfed its diminishing fur-trading operations, and it developed a large chain of department stores across Canada. In the twentieth century, it also expanded its interests into natural resource development, including oil and gas. In 1970 it moved its headquarters from London to Winnipeg, Manitoba. The company's papers, now housed in Winnipeg, are one of the most valuable sources for historians of the Prairie Provinces and Northern Great Plains before 1870.

See also LAW: Pierre-Guillaume Sayer Trial / NATIVE AMERICANS: Métis.

Theodore Binnema
University of Northern British Columbia

MacKay, Douglas. *The Honourable Company*. Toronto: McClelland and Stewart, 1966. Newman, Peter C. *Empire of the Bay: An Illustrated History of the Hudson's Bay Company*. Toronto: Viking Studio Books, 1989. Rich, E. E. *The History of the Hudson's Bay Company 1670–1870*. Toronto: McClelland and Stewart, 1960.

INDUSTRIAL WORKERS OF THE WORLD

See PROTEST AND DISSENT: Industrial Workers of the World

INSURANCE

The Great Plains insurance industry has a spirit and tenacity that reflect the speculative and adventurous nature of the region in which it was born. The Great Plains insurance industry was created by losses from prairie fires, lightning strikes, and windstorms. Other forces such as the uncertainty of crop prices and cattle prices as well as the high costs of farming operations led to the organization of a substantial part of the agricultural community into the Grange and Farmers Alliance movements. From these issues and organizing movements many Great Plains insurance companies were started. Other insurance companies were formed on the principles of cooperation, mutual aid, benevolence, and care for others. Most provided an alternative to the eastern stock insurance companies, which did not understand the Great Plains conditions and whose insurance coverage was unaffordable. Some of the early companies still in business today are Portage Mutual (Manitoba, 1884), Northwest German Farmers Mutual Insurance (South Dakota, 1887), Farmers Alliance Mutual (Kansas, 1888), Kansas Mutual (1895), Wawanesa Mutual (Manitoba, 1896), and the Oklahoma Farmers Union (1907).

In 1998 the Great Plains insurance industry consisted of more than 600 domestic companies writing $35 billion in U.S. property and liability insurance, $133 billion of the U.S. life insurance premiums, and more than $1 trillion in life insurance. There are 87 domestic Prairie Province insurance companies out of more than 200 general Canadian insurance companies. The Canadian companies insure $4 billion worth of Great Plains property and liability (21 percent of the Canadian total) as well as $1 billion in accident and sickness and $3 billion in life insurance.

Losses in the Great Plains are caused by tornados (there were 508 in 1996, or 44 percent of the U.S. total) and strong winds, but the most significant losses result from hail damage. Great Plains property premiums have escalated due to hail losses to real property and autos. As a result of high losses, some companies withdrew from the Great Plains property insurance markets. However, since 1993, most Great Plains insurance companies have become profitable with an acceptable adjusted loss ratio and net investment income. The Great Plains insurance customer continues to receive a high level of service from the insurance industry, and the cost of insurance continues to remain below the U.S. average, with annual auto insurance expenditures of $523 versus the national average of $665. Healthcare costs continue to increase; however, health-care insurance premiums are below the national average. For example, the Great Plains average hospital cost of $749 per patient day in 1999 was well below the U.S. average of $968.

The insurance industry makes a significant contribution to the Great Plains economy: $340 million in life insurance premium taxes and $1.14 billion in property and casualty insurance taxes are paid annually. As employers, Great Plains insurance companies also pay Social Security taxes as well as other taxes, licenses, and fees. The economic multiplier effect results in a substantial economic contribution to the Plains economy. The insurance industry output averages about 2 percent of each state's gross state product.

Changes in U.S. agricultural policy and world agricultural markets have forced Plains farmers to proactively analyze grain markets and manage crop revenue. New crop insurance approaches provide multiperil insurance coverage for crop revenue and market price fluctuations. National and global competition is forcing a revision in underwriting models for personal and commercial lines as Great Plains insurance companies continue to look for better methods to provide affordable and profitable insurance. Technology changes are revising marketing practices as direct marketers such as the USAA Group strive to take advantage of electronic databases and electronic marketing opportunities.

The Great Plains agricultural community, which established the Great Plains insurance industry, continues to decline in employment and in proportion of total value added. It has been replaced by economic clusters of airplane manufacturing, mining, petroleum, and various light global and domestic industries throughout the Great Plains region. In general, the Great Plains continues to be served by domestic insurance companies and independent agents, particularly in the commercial lines, but the trend is to increase personal lines market share by direct writers and national insurance companies. Insurance companies will continue to consolidate, to merge with banks, to demutualize, to market across national boundaries, and to engage in electronic commerce. These trends will challenge the domestic Great Plains insurance market and may ultimately alter the state regulatory management of the industry. The resiliency and tenacity of the Great Plains insurance industry founders will need to be remembered if these challenges are to be successfully met.

James A. Stephens
Emporia State University

The Fact Book 1998: Property/Casualty Insurance Facts. New York: Insurance Information Institute, 1998. *Facts of the General Insurance Industry in Canada*. 24th ed. Toronto: Insurance Bureau of Canada, 1997. *1997 Life Insurance Fact Book*. Washington DC: American Council of Life Insurance, 1997.

INTERNATIONAL TRADE

The international trade of the Great Plains is dominated by Texas, which exports more, by value, of almost every important Plains product than any other state or province in the region. One significant balance in the North is the large amount of Alberta's exports of oil and natural gas. In total, Texas exports almost as much, by value, as all the other Great Plains states and provinces combined.

Texas probably imports more than the other states as well, but there are no estimates of imports by state. This data void is unfortunate, because imports contribute to the standard of living by providing a greater variety of goods at lower costs than we would be able to produce ourselves, and it would be interesting to observe the differences in import patterns across the Plains. These commodity export data also ignore trade in services such as finance, transport, consulting, and tourism. Finally, it should be noted that the data are assembled by state and therefore reflect substantial exports originating outside of the Plains areas of several states. Primary metals and wood products from Alberta and Montana come mainly from their mountain regions, and much of Texas's oil and chemical exports originates in the Gulf Coast region. On a per capita basis, trade appears to be most important to Saskatchewan, Alberta, and Manitoba, in that order. Colorado and Texas are the only Plains states above the U.S. national average of $2,308 worth of exports per person.

Most of the international trade is between the United States and Canada, which are each other's largest international trade partners. The European Union and Japan are the next largest foreign trade partners for both the United States and Canada. These trade patterns have been maintained in the aftermath of the 1989 free-trade agreement between the United States and Canada and after the 1994 implementation of the North American Free Trade Agreement, which included Mexico as well. However, trade with Mexico and the developing countries of Asia and Africa has been growing rapidly, especially in the categories of food and other agricultural products. For example, the largest export market for Kansas hard winter wheat in 2003 was Nigeria.

Commodity Exports of the Great Plains States and Provinces in 1996

State/Province	Total exports U.S. dollars (millions)	Exports per capita U.S. dollars (millions)	Major products
Texas	53,662	2,805	machinery, oil
Colorado	10,749	2,812	machinery
Kansas	5,312	2,065	agriculture
Oklahoma	2,752	834	machinery
Nebraska	2,573	1,557	processed food
New Mexico	935	546	agriculture
North Dakota	632	981	agriculture
South Dakota	422	577	machinery
Montana	358	407	metals
Wyoming	130	270	chemicals, machinery
U.S. total	77,525		
Alberta	22,634	7,950	oil, gas
Saskatchewan	9,197	9,290	grain, oil
Manitoba	4,571	4,031	vehicles, grain
Canadian total	36,402		
Total	113,927		

Despite the significance of international trade for the Great Plains, it pales in significance next to intranational trade. Oil, grain, and livestock products are major exports from the Plains to the East and West Coasts of the United States and Canada, while the Plains imports primarily manufactured products from the more populated areas of the two countries.

The composition of Plains exports partially reflects the resource endowment of this region. Raw and processed agricultural products are major exports from Saskatchewan, North Dakota, Nebraska, Manitoba, and Kansas, metals from Alberta and Montana, and petroleum-related products from Alberta, Saskatchewan, Oklahoma, and Texas. Major metropolitan areas in Colorado, Manitoba, New Mexico, Oklahoma, and Texas, however, have taken advantage of economies of scale and technology to make machinery and equipment their major exports.

Craig R. MacPhee
University of Nebraska–Lincoln

Hayward, David J., and Rodney E. Erickson. "The North American Trade of U.S. States: A Comparative Analysis of Industrial Shipments, 1983–91." *International Regional Science Review* 18 (1995): 1–31. Massachusetts Institute for Social and Economic Research. *National Trade Data Bank, Exports, State of Origin, Series II.* Amherst: University of Massachusetts Press, 1998.

JUSTIN, H. J., AND SONS

More than a century ago, "Big Daddy" Joe Justin never dreamed his boots would become the "Standard of the West." He just knew he did not want to be a cigar maker like his father. Spanish Fort, Texas, south of Red River Crossing on the Chisholm Trail, was a bustling town in 1879 when twenty-year-old H. J. "Joe" Justin arrived from Lafayette, Indiana, with five dollars in his pocket. He began repairing boots. With a thirty-five-dollar grubstake, he soon opened a small shop and made boots for the trail hands. Justin married Annie Allen of Hood County, Texas, in 1886, and the couple's first son, John, was born in Spanish Fort.

When an east–west railroad was built eighteen miles south, Spanish Fort's businessmen moved to the tracks in 1889 and established Nocona. In 1894 Joe and Annie devised a self-measuring kit for ordering boots by mail, and cowboys across the West soon wore Justin boots. The Justin family grew to three boys and four girls. Annie and the children all worked in the boot shop alongside Joe.

The two oldest boys, John and Earl, became partners in 1908 with their father in H. J. Justin and Sons. John and Earl supervised ten to twelve men in the shop, and Joe traveled around the country with boot samples. In 1911 the company did $180,000 in boot business in twenty-six states, Canada, Mexico, and Cuba.

Joe Justin's health began to fail in 1916, and he turned the company over to his sons, John, Earl, and Avis. When Joe Justin died in 1918, his boots were already a legend of the American West. In 1925 Justin's sons moved their growing company to larger quarters in Fort Worth, where better shipping facilities and a ready workforce were available. Their sister, Enid Justin, chose to remain in the old shop and continue production as Nocona Boot Company.

Justin boots continued to grow in popularity, with new styles, stitching, leathers, and lightweight boots—the "Western Gypsy" line—designed especially for women. In 1950 John Justin Jr., Joe's grandson, was named vice president and general manager. He soon took full control of the company. By 1952 company sales topped $1 million for the first time. His innovative ideas on designs, production, and marketing led to H. J. Justin and Sons' continued growth. By 1954 the company was shipping 100,000 pairs of boots a week.

John Justin Sr. worked at the plant until his death in 1959. John Jr. bought the remaining family-owned shares in the company in 1967 and became sole owner. Two years later, Justin became chief executive officer of Justin Industries, Inc., a diversified holding company, with the boot company as one of its four subsidiaries.

Justin Boot Company celebrated its 100th anniversary in 1981, the same year that Justin Industries bought Nocona Boot Company from eighty-year-old Enid Justin. In 1990 Justin Industries added another major competitor to its fold—Tony Lama Boot Company of El Paso, Texas.

John S. Justin Jr. retired as CEO of Justin Industries in 1999. For the first time in 120 years, the reins of management of the boot company passed to the hands of someone other than a member of Joe Justin's family.

Jane Pattie
Aledo, Texas

H. J. Justin and Sons, Archives, Justin Industries, Inc., Fort Worth TX.

KARCHER, JOHN (1894–1978)

John Clarence Karcher, inventor of the reflection seismograph, was born in Dale, Indiana, on April 15, 1894, to Leo and Mary Madlon Karcher and was raised on a farm near Hennessey, Oklahoma. After graduating from Hennessey High School in 1912, he attended the University of Oklahoma, where he received bachelor's degrees in physics and in

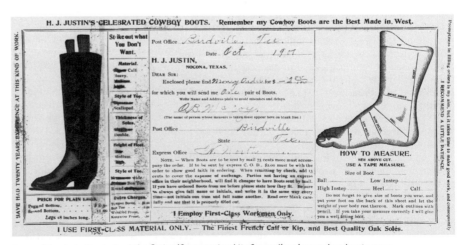

Joe and Annie Justin devised the first self-measuring kits for mail-order cowboy boots, 1907.

electrical engineering in 1916. From Oklahoma he went to the University of Pennsylvania to pursue graduate degrees, completing his doctorate in 1918.

From 1917 onward John Karcher combined his major area of study, physics, with geology, due perhaps to his acquaintance with geologists while at Oklahoma. During World War I, he collaborated with the U.S. navy in trying to develop a method of locating German artillery batteries by tracking the sound and seismic waves that their firing produced. In the process, he was inspired to invent an instrument that could map subsurface geologic structures by measuring blast-induced vertical vibrations in the earth. He subsequently designed, built, and patented the reflection seismograph, or at least an American version of that tool, now an essential aspect of "prospecting" for petroleum reservoirs.

In June 1921 Karcher, several University of Oklahoma professors, and three Oklahoma City oilmen successfully tested the reflection seismograph north of Oklahoma City. In 1925 Karcher combined with Everette L. DeGolyer of Amerada Petroleum Corporation to form Geophysical Research Corporation. For the next few years their crews prospected around Seminole, Oklahoma, and finally identified a structure likely to contain oil. There, in December 1928, Amerada successfully activated the world's first oil well located by reflection seismography.

Karcher's career took off in the late 1920s, when he went into the petroleum production business. His companies, among them Geophysical Service Incorporated (which later was sold and renamed Texas Instruments, Incorporated), Coronado Corporation, Las Tecas Petroleum Company, and Concho Petroleum Company, prospected for oil, drilled the wells, and marketed the product. Karcher received the Anthony F. Lucas Gold Medal, given by the American Institute of Mining, Metallurgical and Petroleum Engineers, for developing the seismograph. John Clarence Karcher died in Dallas, Texas, on July 13, 1978.

Dianna Everett
Oklahoma Historical Society

Green, Cecil H. "John Clarence Karcher, 1894–1978, Father of the Reflection Seismograph." *Geophysics* 178 (1979): 1018–21. Perdue, Richard M. "John Clarence Karcher." In *The New Handbook of Texas*, edited by Ron Tyler et al., 3: 1033. Austin: Texas State Historical Association, 1996.

KOOL-AID

Kool-Aid, the powdered drink mix known to generations of children, was invented by Edwin E. Perkins in Hastings, Nebraska, in 1927. Perkins was born in Lewis, Iowa, in 1889 but spent his youth in the village of Hendley in southwestern Nebraska. While working in his father's general store, Perkins became fascinated with kitchen chemistry experiments, prepackaged foods like Jell-O, and mail-order sales schemes. After World War I, the budding entrepreneur invented a tobacco remedy called Nix-O-Tine, the first of his many patent medicines.

In 1920 Perkins and his new wife, Kathryn "Kitty" Shoemaker, moved to Hastings and expanded the Perkins Products Company, which sold more than 125 household products through direct sales. One of the most popular was Fruit-Smack, a liquid fruit drink concentrate. In 1927 Perkins reconstituted Fruit-Smack into powdered crystals and packaged it in bright paper envelopes. Originally called Kool-Ade, the drink mix was sold in self-service display cartons (another Perkins innovation) in grocery stores and was so successful that the company moved to Chicago in 1931. By the end of the Great Depression, Edwin Perkins owned a suburban mansion and employed hundreds of workers in his factory. In 1953 Perkins retired and sold the company to General Foods, the manufacturer of Jell-O.

Edwin and Kitty Perkins spent their remaining years establishing foundations and making gifts to colleges, hospitals, and other institutions in Nebraska and elsewhere. When he died in 1961, Kool-Aid's inventor, who had lived in a sod house as a child, left an estate worth over $45 million and a product that had become a household name.

Richard C. Witt
Hastings, Nebraska

LUMBERYARDS

Early lumberyards in the Great Plains not only shaped the development of that region but also affected the Great Lakes region and railroad practices. As settlers in the last half of the nineteenth century moved west onto the generally treeless Plains, they sought familiar building materials at lumberyards. During the same period, the pine forests of the Great Lakes region were being rapidly harvested, providing the timber for sale at those yards. Indeed, Great Lakes lumber supplied much of the growing market in the Great Plains, with transportation enabled by a rail network that was expanding west from Chicago and other midwestern cities.

A relationship between railroads and lumber retailers was necessary, since timber usually was sold through "line yards"—multiple facilities owned by various companies and located in towns along a railroad line. But it was an often tenuous association. In general, the preferred site for a lumberyard in a Plains town was on a warehouse lot adjacent to the railroad. Due to their proximity to the tracks, these locations were easy to stock. They also often had good visibility, which helped to generate traffic. However, since those parcels were usually on railroad property, the railroad made the warehouse lot assignments to its best advantage, which often relegated lumber companies to less desirable situations. It was left to Gen. Grenville Dodge, Civil War veteran and engineer in charge of the Union Pacific's late 1860s push across the Plains to Promontory Point, Utah, to argue that lumber and railroad companies should work as partners, because lumber was among those commodities that could attract settlers to a town and thus help generate traffic for a railroad.

Once the site for a yard had been agreed upon (preferably a site without standing water), a stock of lumber was delivered and made available for sale. Until a company was sure that a town's potential for settlement merited investment, initial lumber sales generally occurred without the convenience of an office or lumber shed. If the early sales were satisfactory, a company might construct a small structure, perhaps no bigger than sixteen feet by twenty-four feet and including only a modest office and shed for the finished lumber. If sales did not develop properly, the company could easily load its stock onto a train and move to the next town, losing virtually nothing in the process.

Aside from an office and shed, lumberyards in early Plains towns included a limehouse and lumber piles. Sometimes yard expansion was warranted, and an addition was made to the extant office-and-shed combination. For instance, the sixteen-by-twenty-four-foot structure could be extended to forty feet in length, thus allowing more lumber storage space. The investment a company was willing to make in a yard was commensurate with the perceived potential for lumber sales. Accordingly, larger towns received more substantial yards, which generally included multiple storage sheds, the largest of which could accommodate wagons.

Lumberyards were places at which a significant commodity passed from supplier to consumer. Moreover, they played an important role in the processes that ultimately created the Great Lakes cutover region as well as in the establishment of the early European American built environments in the Great Plains. Despite these extensive effects, the companies that operated the yards had simple objectives: they wanted to get into a town quickly, sell as much lumber with as little investment possible, and then move on to seek fortune elsewhere.

See also TRANSPORTATION: Dodge, Grenville.

John N. Vogel
Heritage Research, Ltd.

Laird, Norton Company Correspondence, Laird, Norton Company Papers, Minnesota Historical Society, St. Paul. Vogel, John N. *Great Lakes Lumber on the Great Plains: The Laird, Norton Lumber Company in South Dakota.* Iowa City: University of Iowa Press, 1992.

McKENZIE, KENNETH (1797–1861)

Kenneth McKenzie was, as fur trade historian Hiram Martin Chittenden put it, "the ablest trader the American Fur Company ever possessed." From his headquarters at Fort Union (which he was instrumental in establishing in 1829) he ruled the fur trade of the upper Missouri in its halcyon days. He pioneered the company's expansion into Blackfeet country with the establishment of Fort McKenzie in 1834; he was, with Pierre Chouteau Jr., the innovator of steamboat navigation on the upper Missouri, which revolutionized the transportation system; and he can even be credited with building what was perhaps the first whiskey still in the Great Plains, an imaginative but illegal and short-lived effort to evade the government's laws against importation of alcohol into Indian Country. McKenzie was like a king at Fort Union: dressed in a fine uniform, he lived in a residence with the rare luxury of glass windows and earned a reputation both as a martinet who brooked no insubordination and as a gracious host who presided over the best table of food and wine in the West.

McKenzie was born in Rosshire, Scotland, on April 15, 1797. He settled in St. Louis in 1822 after serving his apprenticeship in the fur trade with the North West Company. Within a year he was running the Columbia Fur Company, which controlled the trade on the upper Missouri until it was bought out by the American Fur Company in 1827. In the course of the following six years, as head of the Upper Missouri Outfit of the American Fur Company, McKenzie secured the company's virtual monopoly over the fur trade on the Northern Great Plains. By 1834 almost 2,000 packs of bison robes a year were being collected at Fort Union as well as large quantities of beaver, fox, and muskrat skins.

McKenzie retired from the fur trade in 1834, in part because of the furor over his whiskey scheme. In St. Louis he subsequently operated wholesale grocery and liquor businesses and invested in land and railroads. Kenneth McKenzie, "King of the Missouri," died on April 26, 1861. He was survived by his wife, Mary Marshall (whom he married in 1842), and four children in St. Louis as well as by his family from a previous marriage to an Indian woman at Fort Union.

David J. Wishart
University of Nebraska–Lincoln

Chittenden, Hiram Martin. *The American Fur Trade of the Far West.* New York: F. R. Harper, 1903. Mattison, Ray H. "Kenneth McKenzie." In *The Mountain Men and the Fur Trade of the Far West*, edited by LeRoy R. Hafen, 2: 217–24. Glendale CA: Arthur H. Clark Company, 1965.

MEATPACKING

In the last third of the twentieth century the meatpacking industry became a major force in the social and economic transformation of small towns in the Great Plains. From the earliest days of European American settlement, cattle were raised on the Plains' extensive pastureland. The arrival of the railroad allowed cattle to be shipped to stockyards in Chicago, Kansas City, Omaha, Winnipeg, Toronto, and other cities to the east of the Plains. The cattle would then be purchased by packing companies and slaughtered in multistoried facilities located adjacent to the stockyards. A hundred years later, cattle are still raised on the Plains, but they are now fattened in feedlots and sold to nearby packing plants. In 1950 the states that extend north from Texas to North Dakota slaughtered 21 percent of U.S. cattle; by 1997 the corresponding figure was 57 percent. Most of this growth has been concentrated in Texas, Kansas, and Nebraska.

The industry's increasing concentration on the High Plains is attributable to innovations in cattle feeding and meatpacking. In 1950 U.S.-fed cattle production was 4.4 million head; by 1997 the equivalent figure was 13.2 million, with nearly 60 percent of this total being concentrated in Texas, Kansas, and Nebraska. Center-pivot irrigation was introduced to the High Plains in the 1960s, allowing farmers to tap the Ogallala Aquifer and cultivate feed grains. The availability of feed and water attracted the feedlot industry.

The industry's shift to small towns near the Great Plains began in 1961, when Iowa Beef Packers (now known as IBP Inc.) opened its first plant in Denison, Iowa. The company has since grown to become the world's largest red meat producer. The Denison plant, unlike its predecessors, did not use gravity to move the animals through the plant but instead used a "chain" to move individual cattle along a disassembly line. Under this system, workers are stationed along the line and perform the same operation on each animal as it passes by. The fact that workers were required to perform the same task, requiring "less skill" than butchers in the old plants, was used as a rationale by the company to avoid the terms of the industry-wide union master contract and lower its labor costs. By locating the plant close to a source of cattle, the company lowered its transport costs and reduced the shrinkage and bruising associated with shipping cattle long distances.

In 1967 IBP opened a plant in Dakota City, Nebraska, to produce a new product, boxed beef. Instead of shipping carcasses to its customers, IBP removed fat and bone at the plant, thereby retaining valuable waste materials such as entrails (to be used for pet food), and shipped vacuum-packaged portions according to retail specifications. This innovation allowed meat wholesalers and supermarkets to lower their labor costs by eliminating their need for butchers. The combined effect of these cost-cutting innovations was to increase the demand for IBP products, and it responded by building additional large slaughter-capacity plants close to feedlots in the High Plains during the 1970s and 1980s. A plentiful supply of high-quality water is an important requirement for these sites, since between 400 and 600 gallons of water are required per head of cattle slaughtered. This need was met by using the Ogallala Aquifer.

In response to IBP's cost-cutting innovations, some competitors demanded wage concessions or closed plants, while others emulated IBP's High Plains location strategy. Communities generally welcomed the packers with financial incentives such as tax breaks and the construction of supporting infrastructure. These changes were particularly evident in Kansas, which experienced plant closures in Kansas City and Wichita, while new plants were constructed in the southwestern portion of the state in Liberal, Holcomb, Garden City, and Dodge City.

The construction of large slaughter-capacity plants and the adoption of the disassembly line led to increases in both worker productivity and injury rates. The most common injury among line workers is carpal tunnel syndrome, caused by the rapid, repetitive nature of work on the disassembly line. By the 1980s meatpacking had become the most hazardous industry in America. The hazardous working conditions and low pay contribute to high employee turnover. Monthly turnover among line workers in established plants averages between 6 and 8 percent. This means that, in the case of IBP's Holcomb plant, 5,000 workers come and go each year.

Most High Plains towns lack surplus labor to meet the demands of an industry with high employee turnover, so packers recruit workers from beyond the local region. In the early 1980s IBP recruited Southeast Asian refugees; in the 1990s Latinos became the target of recruitment efforts. The influx of new immigrants has transformed small packing towns into multicultural communities and provided a host of challenges to local social service providers in the form of housing shortages, increases in school enrollment and crime, and demand for social assistance and special services.

Canada's beefpacking industry has experienced similar changes. Small, inefficient urban plants have closed, while large slaughter-capacity plants have been constructed in southern Alberta. The packers have been drawn to the province by the availability of fed cattle and water. In 1989 Cargill, the third largest meatpacker in the United States, constructed a plant in High River, thirty miles south of Calgary. Five years later, IBP purchased Lakeside Packers of Brooks, in southeastern Alberta, and immediately announced expansion plans that would result in hiring 2,000 additional workers. High River has avoided many of the social problems associated with U.S. packing plants, as most of its workers live in Calgary and commute to the plant. In Brooks, immigrant families and young adult males from across Canada have moved to the community, straining local services.

See also AGRICULTURE: Cattle Ranching / HISPANIC AMERICANS: Meatpackers / WATER: Ogallala Aquifer.

Michael J. Broadway
Northern Michigan University

Broadway, Michael J. "Following the Leader: IBP and the Restructuring of Canada's Meatpacking Industry." *Culture & Agriculture* 18 (1996): 3–8. Skaggs, Jimmy M. *Prime Cut: Livestock Raising and Meatpacking in the United States, 1607–1983.* College Station: Texas A&M University Press, 1986. Stull, Donald D., Michael J. Broadway, and David Griffith, eds. *Any Way You Cut It: Meat Processing and Small-Town America.* Lawrence: University Press of Kansas, 1995.

MELROE BOBCAT

The Melroe Bobcat, now sold in seventy-five countries through 900 dealerships and celebrated by *Fortune* magazine as one of the 100 best products in the United States, has its origins in Great Plains local enterprise. In 1947 E. G. Melroe, the son of Norwegian immigrants, founded the Melroe Manufacturing Company in the small North Dakota community of Gwinner. Through the 1950s the company thrived on the sales of Melroe's first invention, a windrow pickup device attached to combines that could collect windrows of grain with little loss of kernels. In 1957 Melroe's sons (E. G. Melroe had died in 1955) bought the rights to a homemade three-wheeled loader that had been built by Cyril and Louis Keller of Rothsay, Minnesota. The Kellers became employees of Melroe Manufacturing Company, and the first in a developing line of Melroe Bobcats came off the assembly line.

The Bobcat was initially a three-wheeled light loader that could turn 360 degrees in its own length. By 1963 an additional wheel had added more stability, and the utility of the Bobcat had been proven in industry and construction as well as in agriculture. Refinements in design (for example, a quick-change attachment system was developed in 1973 to make the Bobcat a multijob machine) and diversification of models for different jobs (for example, the Mini-Bob loader was produced in 1971 for work in the most restrictive spaces) have kept the Melroe Bobcat at the forefront of the loader and excavation business.

The Melroe Company, now headquartered in Fargo and with plants in Gwinner and Bismarck, is North Dakota's largest manufacturer, and the Bobcat logo, featuring the head of that tough, agile Plains animal, can be seen on building sites, farms, and industrial operations worldwide.

David J. Wishart
University of Nebraska–Lincoln

MISSOURI COMPANY

See HISPANIC AMERICANS: Missouri Company

NAFTA

The North American Free Trade Agreement (NAFTA), implemented on January 1, 1994, is an agreement to remove most barriers to trade and investment in both goods and services among Canada, the United States, and Mexico. Its purpose is to stimulate economic growth in the three countries and to increase jobs. Full employment in Mexico, for example, will help its economic growth, discourage emigration, and create wealth for Mexican consumers to buy American and Canadian products. Items that now move more freely among the signatory nations include capital, textile products, petrochemicals, automobile components, fertilizers, farm products, and telecommunications. In the case of farm products, for example, some tariffs were removed immediately, and most others are being phased out over a transition period.

In the Great Plains, two trading groups have emerged to take advantage of NAFTA. The Camino Real Economic Alliance (CREA) operates at the western fringe of the Plains, linking forty-five business organizations from Chihuahua, Ciudad Juárez, El Paso, Las Cruces, Albuquerque, and Santa Fe. CREA seeks to strengthen ties between and development of the states of Chihuahua and New Mexico and the region of West Texas. A second group is the Rocky Mountain Trade Corridor (RMTC), which is a membership organization for small businesses throughout the Great Plains. The RMTC convenes seminars on NAFTA and matches its members with business partners in Canada and Mexico.

Outside of these groups, businesses in the Great Plains are trading under NAFTA on their own. On a state-by-state basis, there is a positive trade balance with Canada. The trade balance with Mexico is more mixed. Exports to Mexico in 1994–95 dipped in Kansas, Oklahoma, Nebraska, South Dakota, and Texas but went up in Colorado, North Dakota, Montana, and Wyoming. The freight data for goods shipped to Mexico in 1996 yield a similar picture. At present Texas is positioned to capitalize on the impending boom in Mexico.

What does NAFTA mean to the Great Plains? It means highway construction, bridge maintenance, railway mergers, train coordination, warehousing, and trucking. Congress has set aside $700,000 for highway construction. Interstate 35 will get the lion's share of that money. The Santa Fe Railroad has concluded a merger with Burlington Northern and relocated its corporate headquarters in Texas, a move from which Dallas–Fort Worth will benefit. The Santa Fe must now coordinate its train business with its rival (Union Pacific) to ensure smooth flows of commerce across the Plains. Warehousing facilities are going up in the Great Plains. Big firms have constructed one or two strategically located facilities from which they ship consumer goods. Canadian firms servicing the U.S. market and American firms servicing the Canadian market have erected warehouses in Omaha, Nebraska. Denver, Colorado, Kansas City, Missouri, and Dallas, Texas, have experienced similar growth, a growth that has benefited local economies. Though warehouses attract few workers, the land on which these facilities rest produces property taxes to fund local schools. Trucking is booming on I-29, I-70, and I-35, largely due to NAFTA commerce. But the flow of commerce south to Mexico has been impeded by bottlenecks. In Laredo, Texas, by far the busiest U.S.-Mexican crossing point, cargo lines have tested driver patience. Haulers often have to wait up to ten hours before moving their cargo into Mexico. Trucks have to cross two aging bridges to get to their destinations. The amount of commerce moving into Mexico is also determined by the pace of border inspections.

Beyond the bridge building, the inspectors, and the highway improvements, nagging issues threaten the flow of commerce. American access to Canadian dairy and poultry markets, grain trade between the United States and Canada, and granting access to American beef in Canada head the list.

Ronald C. Griffin
Washburn University

Glick, Leslie A. *Understanding the North American Free Trade Agreement.* Boston: Deventer, 1993. Moss, Ambler H., Jr., ed. *Assessments of the North American Free Trade Agreement.* Coral Gables FL: Transaction, 1993. Riggs, Alvin R., and Tom Velk, eds. *Beyond NAFTA: An Economic, Political, and Sociological Perspective.* Vancouver: Fraser Institute, 1993.

NUCLEAR WASTE SITES

The search for disposal sites for nuclear wastes in the United States has often turned to the Great Plains region; there have been no nuclear waste disposal siting efforts in the Canadian Great Plains. Nuclear waste is generated within the Great Plains by way of activities ranging from nuclear power generation to medical treatment. There are three nuclear power generating plants operating within the Great Plains: Cooper Nuclear Station and Fort Calhoun Station in Nebraska and Wolf Creek Generating Station in Kansas. Each of these serves as a storage location for spent nuclear fuel and low-level radioactive waste (LLRW). The Rocky Flats Nuclear Weapons Plant, located sixteen miles northwest of Denver, manufactured components for nuclear weapons until 1992 but is now scheduled for decommissioning, waste disposal, and environmental cleanup. Many of the universities in the Great Plains dispose of the LLRW generated by their research activities at locations on campus.

There are three main classifications for nuclear waste in the United States: high level, low level, and transuranic. The different waste forms are defined not only by the composition of the material making up the waste but also by the manner by which it is generated (commercial or defense) as well as by whether the federal or state government is responsible for regulating its disposal. High-level and transuranic wastes are defined by the specific composition of the wastes; low-level radioactive waste is defined by what it is not—high-level waste. Each of these wastes is regulated by different laws. Providing disposal capacity for high-level and transuranic wastes is a federal government responsibility; providing disposal capacity for low-level wastes is the responsibility of the state in which the wastes are generated. High-level and transuranic wastes require underground, deep-geologic disposal; disposal of low-level waste is allowed above ground and in shallow-burial trenches.

The first government-sponsored nuclear waste disposal siting effort was in the Great Plains, conducted by the U.S. Atomic Energy Commission. Underground disposal of high-level and transuranic wastes was investigated in the Lyons, Kansas, area in 1970. By 1972 it was determined that the salt mines of the Lyons area did not meet acceptable requirements for the isolation of the waste. Subsequently, an area east of Carlsbad, New Mexico, was identified for consideration in 1974. Dismayed by the slow progress in developing disposal capacity, Congress created the Waste Isolation Pilot Project (WIPP) in 1979, directing that a safe method for the disposal of wastes generated by defense facilities be developed. The WIPP continued to focus on salt formations near Carlsbad. Following eight years of studying the geology and hydrology of the area, construction of the WIPP facility began in 1983; the underground construction was completed in 1989. In May 1998 the Environmental Protection Agency announced that the WIPP met all applicable federal nuclear waste disposal standards. The WIPP began receiving transuranic waste in March 1999.

Prior to 1980, LLRW disposal was primarily a market-driven business. In that year Congress mandated that the states were responsible for providing disposal capacity for LLRW generated within their borders. States were encouraged to band together and form compacts to address this mandate. In 1983 three states of the Great Plains—Nebraska, Kansas, and Oklahoma—joined with Louisiana and Arkansas to form the Central Interstate Low-Level Radioactive Waste Compact. The compact selected U.S. Ecology, Inc., to site, develop, and operate a disposal site for the member states. In December 1987 Nebraska was designated the host state for a disposal site. Approximately one year later, three 320-acre candidate sites in Nebraska were identified for detailed evaluation. These sites were in Boyd, Nemaha, and Nuckolls Counties. Following the designation of the candidate sites, U.S. Ecology discovered and acknowledged a problem with wetlands (over forty-six acres) on the Boyd County site. Nevertheless, in December 1989 the Boyd County site was selected as the preferred site. An application to construct and operate a waste disposal site was filed in July 1990 with the Nebraska Department of Environmental Quality (NDEQ). In January 1993 the NDEQ issued an intent to deny a license because the site did not meet regulatory requirements, the presence of wetlands being the primary reason. Six months later, in an effort to eliminate the wetland problem, U.S. Ecology submitted an amended application for a 110-acre parcel of the original site. Following extensive review and evaluation of that application and after public hearings, the NDEQ in August 1998 again issued an intent to deny the license. By December 1998 a final denial was made because the proposed site lacked sufficient depth to the water table and groundwater discharged to the surface within the site. In 1999 Nebraska formally withdrew from the Central Interstate Low-Level Radioactive Waste Compact, a move that resulted in continued litigation. After twelve years and over $90 million spent, the effort to site, construct, and operate a low-level waste disposal site in Nebraska had not been successful.

There has been organized opposition by citizens living in the areas surrounding all of the proposed nuclear waste disposal sites. Likewise, there has been organized local support for the various siting efforts.

While no nuclear waste disposal sites were operating in the Great Plains at the end of 1998, the WIPP began operations in 1999. Additionally, there are continued efforts to establish low-level waste disposal sites. In 1993 Sequoyah Fuels Corporation of Oklahoma began seeking authorization to dispose of low-level wastes generated during the operation of its uranium conversion plant and its decommissioning at the Gore, Oklahoma, plant site. Waste Control Specialists of Texas, starting in 1995, has been pursuing authorization to include disposal of low-level wastes at a hazardous waste disposal site in Andrews County, Texas.

Diane A. Burton
University of Nebraska–Lincoln

OILSEEDS

The Great Plains is a principal production region for several crops grown for the oil contained in the seed. Changes in U.S. farm legislation and world market conditions may make it possible for oilseeds to become an even more prominent component of the repertoire of crops grown in the Great Plains in the future. Crushing facilities for extracting oil from seeds have been built in the Great Plains, while facilities outside the region convert or incorporate the seed oil into finished products.

Canola (*Brassica campestris* and *B. napus*) is the most widely grown oilseed crop in the Great Plains region of Canada and has increased in popularity among northern U.S. growers. For example, production in North Dakota increased from 18,000 acres in 1991 to more than 400,000 acres in 1997. Canola acreage will expand in the near future, specifically on the Northern Plains and in the Prairie Provinces. Canola oil contains less saturated fat than many other vegetable oils. As a result, consumption of canola oil in the United States has risen dramatically since it was first granted GRAS (generally recognized as safe) status for human food use by the U.S. Food and Drug Administration in 1985. Plant geneticists have altered the fatty acid composition of the seed oil, thus increasing the number of varieties available to growers and oil types available to end users.

Crambe (*Crambe abyssinica*) is grown on around 40,000 acres annually in the Great Plains, all of which are located in North Dakota. Rapeseed (*Brassica campestris* and *B. napus*) is grown on approximately 100,000 acres each year in Canada. The seed oil of both crambe and rapeseed contains erucic acid. This fatty acid is used in the manufacture of slip agents, plasticizers, lubricants, and corrosion inhibitors. Neither rapeseed nor crambe produce seed oil that is suitable for human consumption. Currently, world demand for crambe and rapeseed oil is stable.

Flax (*Linum usitatissimum*) is grown on approximately two million acres in Canada each year. An additional 100,000 to 150,000 acres are produced in the United States, with about 80 percent occurring in North Dakota. Linseed oil (obtained from flax) is used in the manufacture of paints and varnishes. Interest in flax within the health food industry has evolved as the benefits of incorporating flax into the human diet have been identified. The development of flax oil as an edible vegetable oil also has contributed to a renewed interest in flax production.

Mustard (*Brassica juncea* and *B. hirta*) is grown in northern portions of the Great Plains region, primarily in Canada. Production in the United States is mostly limited to North Dakota and Montana, where between 12,000 and 60,000 acres were grown annually between 1991 and 1997. Most mustard is used in the processed meats industry and as a flavoring agent in sauces and condiments. Market demand for mustard presently is stable, with little change anticipated in the near future.

Safflower (*Carthamus tinctorius*) is grown in dry, northern portions of the Great Plains. The area under safflower ranged from 20,000 to 85,000 acres between 1991 and 1997. Most safflower is grown for the vegetable oil market. Worldwide, Japan is the principal importer. Enhanced promotion of traditional safflower oil, which contains a relatively high level of polyunsaturated fatty acids compared to many other vegetable oils, could increase market demand for safflower oil. High-oleic safflower also is being grown.

Sunflower (*Helianthus annuus*) was grown on almost 3.5 million acres of the Great Plains in 1997, primarily in North and South Dakota. Sunflower acreage is expanding, particularly in eastern Colorado and western Kansas. Most of the sunflower is grown for the vegetable oil market. About 20 percent of the sunflower crop is a nonoil type that is eaten as a snack food or sold in the bird food market. Traditional sunflower oil is high in linoleic acid. It is used as a cooking oil, in salad oil, and in the manufacture of margarine. High-oleic sunflower has been developed as a high-value, premium cooking oil. The NuSun sunflower produces an oil with moderate levels of oleic acid and low levels of saturated fats.

See also AGRICULTURE: Canola; Flax; Sunflowers.

Patrick M. Carr
North Dakota State University

Carter, Jack F. "Potential of Flaxseed and Flaxseed Oil in Baked Goods and Other Products in Human Nutrition." *Cereal Foods World* 38 (1993): 753–59. Van Dyne, Donald L., Melvin G. Blase, and Kenneth D. Carlson. *Industrial Feedstocks and Products from High Erucic Acid Oil: Crambe and Industrial Rapeseed.* Columbia: University of Missouri Press, 1990.

PACKARD, DAVID (1912–1996)

David Packard, along with his partner, William Hewlett, established the computer industry giant Hewlett-Packard. Packard was born on September 7, 1912, in Pueblo, Colorado. He attended Stanford University, where he earned varsity letters in football and basketball and graduated in 1934. After several months of graduate work at the University of Colorado, Packard took a job with General Electric in Schenectady, New York, in 1938. That year he married Lucile Salter of San Francisco, whom he had met at Stanford. He returned to Stanford and completed a master's degree in electrical engineering. In 1939 he and fellow graduate student William Hewlett founded Hewlett-Packard with a capital investment of $538. The company's first product was an electrical oscillator, a device for testing audio equipment. Early orders came from the Walt Disney studios.

In 1947 the two inventors incorporated their business, with Packard named as president. Packard served as president until 1964, when he became chairman of the board and chief executive officer. He remained in this position from 1964 until 1969, then took leave to become deputy secretary of defense in the Nixon administration. He served there until 1971. In 1972 he was reelected as chairman of Hewlett-Packard, a position he held until his retirement in 1993. He remained active in the business until his death.

In addition to its products, which include measurement and computational devices used in industry, business, engineering, science, medicine, and education, Hewlett-Packard is known for its innovative management style, known as the "HP way," which is designed to maintain high productivity and employee loyalty. The HP way includes catastrophic medical coverage, flexible work hours, open offices, decentralized decision making, management by objective, employee profit sharing, and discount stock purchases.

Packard was active in business, government, and philanthropy. He was a trustee of Stanford University from 1954 to 1969, a member of the Trilateral Commission from 1973 to 1981, and a member of the White House Science Council and the National Academy of Engineering. He cofounded the American Electronics Association. From 1975 to 1983 he sat on the U.S.-USSR Trade and Economic Council's committee on science and technology, and he was director of the National Fish and Wildlife Foundation from 1985 until 1987. He also served on the President's Council of Advisors on Science and Technology from 1990 until 1992. Through the David and Lucile Packard Foundation, which was established in 1964, he and his wife donated more than $400 million to various charities, community organizations, education, health care, conservation, science, and the arts. In addition to the work of the foundation, Packard personally donated hundreds of millions more, including $300 million to Stanford University. David Packard, a pioneer in the computer industry, died on March 26, 1996, at Stanford University Hospital.

Charles Vollan
University of Nebraska–Lincoln

Packard, David. *The HP Way: How Bill Hewlett and I Built Our Company*, edited by David Kirby and Karen Lewis. New York: HarperBusiness, 1995.

PETRO-CANADA

Petro-Canada is an integrated petroleum corporation based in Calgary, Alberta. It combines "upstream" oil and gas exploration and refining with a "downstream" national chain of service stations. Petro-Canada is the second largest petroleum company in Canada and the largest Canadian-owned operation.

Petro-Canada, founded in 1975 as a petroleum exploration company, was owned by the federal government. During the 1970s and early 1980s, the world was preoccupied with the issues of oil and gas scarcity and cost, and Canada was divided by debates about the effects of foreign ownership as well as by federal-provincial disputes over petroleum taxation and export regulations. As a result, and unlike many "crown corporations" created by federal

and provincial governments in strategic industries in twentieth-century Canada, Petro-Canada was less a conventional state enterprise than an instrument of specific national policy in two key ways. First, Petro-Canada was capitalized by the federal treasury through direct cash transfers rather than by bond issues. The company acquired a number of Canadian subsidiaries of international oil firms, including Atlantic Richfield in 1976, Pacific Petroleum in 1979, Petrofina in 1981, and British Petroleum in 1983. Second, when the government of Canada created a new National Energy Programme (NEP) in 1980, a statist reaction to the energy crisis, the NEP granted Petro-Canada the federal share of oil and gas prospects on all federal crown land, including Arctic and Atlantic offshore prospects as well as a share of Syncrude Canada's northern Alberta bituminous sands synthetic oil.

The federal election of 1984 saw a change of government and national energy policy. The new policies of fiscal restraint, free trade, and privatization reoriented Petro-Canada to a more conventional petroleum company. In 1991 it issued common shares, creating private ownership in about 20 percent of the company. In 1995 a larger issue of shares reduced the federal government stake to below 20 percent. The company acquired other firms, including Gulf Canada's service stations in 1985 and the Amerada Hess holdings in 1995. Petro-Canada is the operator of the large Hibernia oil field, which became the first producing field in the Atlantic offshore in 1997, and is currently developing other offshore fields as well as a new bituminous sands project.

Barry Ferguson
University of Manitoba

Fossum, John E. *Oil, the State, and Federalism: The Rise and Demise of Petro-Canada as a Statist Impulse*. Toronto: University of Toronto Press, 1997. Foster, Peter. *Self-Serve: How Petro-Canada Pumped Canada Dry*. Toronto: Macfarlane, Walter and Ross, 1992. Petro-Canada, Annual Reports, 1976–2000.

PETROLEUM, CANADA

The still-expanding petroleum industry in Alberta has redefined the balance of economic and political power within the Prairie Provinces and the nation. The Western Canada Sedimentary Basin is the chief geologic feature relating to the occurrence of oil and gas. Stretching from Canada's Northwest Territories to South Dakota, it is a large basin within a vast multibasin freeway that extends from the Arctic islands through the Mackenzie Delta and Central Plains in varying widths to the Gulf of Mexico.

The first reported hint of the petroleum wealth hidden beneath the basin's sedimentary strata came from Alexander Mackenzie. He noticed "bituminous fountains" while traveling along the Athabasca River in 1788 and explained that the liquid bitumen, when mixed with spruce gum, produced an excellent caulking compound for canoes. Over the following century many travelers viewed the tar oozing from the rock and sand formation along the riverbank. While some became cap-

tivated by this potential El Dorado in the northern wilderness, until the 1960s the region remained too remote to attract much more than scientific curiosity, especially when there seemed to be promising possibilities in more accessible areas.

The first indication of southern Alberta's petroleum potential came in 1883 and was the unexpected by-product of the Canadian Pacific Railway's search for water along its right-of-way through the dry belt west of Medicine Hat. The company's drilling crew hit a natural gas pocket, and, to their misfortune, the gas ignited and consumed the drilling rig in a great ball of fire. Subsequent discoveries confirmed the location of significant gas fields in the Medicine Hat area, and in 1904 a municipal natural gas company was organized to serve residential and commercial customers. By 1912 both Lethbridge and Calgary were connected by pipeline to southern Alberta's prolific new gas fields. From this humble beginning the industry grew on the strength of continued gas field discoveries and an expanding pipeline network that by the late 1950s spanned the continent.

The recognition that oil could be expected to exist in combination with natural gas prompted a parallel but prolonged search that failed to yield a significant result until the "Dingman discovery" in 1914. Located a short distance southwest of Calgary, the discovery identified what soon became known as the Turner Valley oil field and launched a speculative frenzy that distinguished western Canada's first oil boom. Speculative excess and disappointing results in the field brought the boom to a quick end. Starved for capital, legitimate local petroleum companies made little progress over the following decade.

Further development of the field awaited the arrival of outside capital, which eventually came with Imperial Oil, a subsidiary of Standard Oil of New Jersey. Imperial's interest was stimulated as much by the activities of archrival Shell as by the Dingman discovery. In 1920, to protect its interests in western and northern Canada, Imperial launched an energetic exploration and drilling program along the Mackenzie River in the Northwest Territories, in east-central Alberta, and, under the direction of a new subsidiary company, Royalite Oil Ltd., in the Turner Valley area. Success came first in the North with an important strike at Fort Norman in August 1920, but the location was far too remote, and interest was not rekindled until World War II. Drilling activity in east-central Alberta was unrewarded, but in the Turner Valley, on October 24, 1924, Royalite No. 4 struck oil and ignited Alberta's second oil boom. By year's end thirty-four companies were drilling, and, supported by modest finds, development continued through the 1930s. Although production was very small by Texas or Oklahoma standards, it was sufficient to meet regional demand and to turn Calgary into a minor refining center. Perhaps more important, field development and growing production by 1938 compelled the creation of Alberta's Petroleum and Natural Gas Conservation Board to address various matters of oil field management, especially the contentious issues of market sharing and "waste" gas flaring.

The appointment of the first board chairman, W. F. Knode, formerly of the Texas Railroad Commission, underlines the extent of American influence during the first decades of petroleum production and regulation in western Canada. An important factor shaping the social and regulatory environment, one that distinguishes the Canadian experience, is that, unlike their U.S. cousins, the great majority of Canadian homesteaders held only surface title to their farm and ranch lands. Mineral rights for the most part were retained by the crown, which meant not only a different pattern in the distribution of oil wealth but also that Knode and subsequent Alberta regulators did not have to contend with thousands of ranchers and farmers who held mineral rights and who were inclined to vociferously resist conservation or other measures that would restrict development and production. The regulatory tradition that Knode and his colleagues put in place was perhaps Turner Valley's most important legacy in shaping the pattern of development and production in the big oil fields discovered after World War II.

The turning-point discovery that Albertans had been waiting for since 1914 occurred on February 13, 1947. Located about fifteen miles southwest of Edmonton, Imperial Oil's Leduc No. 1 discovered a prolific new oil field, and the dramatic blowout and fire at Atlantic No. 3 a few months later signaled to the world that the Alberta discovery was in the big league. Turner Valley companies were joined by a host of newcomers from Oklahoma, Texas, and California. The string of big finds that quickly followed launched the province on an oil boom that, with but a few brief interruptions, has continued to the present.

While Alberta's oil and natural gas emerged as a significant contributor to Canada's postwar economic prosperity, the impact at the provincial level was of much greater significance. The provincial economy was transformed. By 1960 the value of exported oil and gas products surpassed the returns earned from agriculture. Alberta's burgeoning oil-fired economy produced the fastest population growth rate of any Canadian province and accelerated the urbanization trend that had begun well before Leduc. The growing petroleum industry shifted the economic center of gravity from the eastern to the western edge of the Prairie region, and Calgary captured Winnipeg's historic role as the region's dominant metropolis.

If oil transformed Alberta's economy, it did not alter the province's political agenda. The politics of wheat and the politics of oil were not dissimilar. Sustained by petroleum revenues and rock-solid electoral support, Alberta's premiers emerged as formidable spokespersons for western and, especially, Alberta's interests. This hypersensitivity is manifest in the battery of provincial legislation put forward with the intent of forestalling federal interference in the

management of the province's oil and gas resources. The bitter confrontation between Alberta and Ottawa over the latter's imposition of the National Energy Policy (1980) ultimately led to a constitutional amendment (section 92A) affirming exclusive provincial control over the exploration, development, and management of nonrenewable natural resources. Alberta's interests, shaped by both the needs of the new economy and historical memory, coalesced to reinforce in post-Leduc Alberta the broad sense of alienation that had developed throughout the preceding decades of agrarian protest.

See also POLITICS AND GOVERNMENT: Alberta.

David H. Breen
University of British Columbia

Breen, David H. *Alberta's Petroleum Industry and the Conservation Board*. Edmonton: University of Alberta Press, 1993. Doern, G. Bruce, and Glen Toner. *The Politics of Energy*. Toronto: Methuen, 1985. Smith, Philip. *The Treasure-Seekers: The Men Who Built Home Oil*. Toronto: Macmillan of Canada, 1978.

PETROLEUM, UNITED STATES

Within a year of completing the first successful crude-oil well in northwestern Pennsylvania in 1859, opportunists from eastern states were drilling for oil in the Great Plains. Using tools and techniques honed in the central Appalachian area, some of these early oil seekers focused their efforts on natural seeps that occurred near the town of Paola in east-central Kansas. Though early wells were unsuccessful, persistence paid off, and in 1893 there was a promising oil discovery near Neodesha, Kansas, that would grow into one of the first commercial oil fields of the Great Plains. Realizing the petroleum potential of the Neodesha area, Standard Oil Company opened a refinery there in 1902 to process the crude oil. This early refinery, though clearly significant to local economic development, was also symbolically important to the region. The refinery

sent a strong signal to prospectors that oil had the potential to become one of the economic foundations of the Southern Great Plains.

Oil and gas fields are volumetrically significant accumulations of hydrocarbon that have pooled naturally in the crust of the earth. The geographic position of these accumulations beneath the U.S. and Canadian Great Plains is due to a coincidence of a number of geologic factors. Among these are a hydrocarbon source rock (usually a shale from which the liquid is initially derived) and a reservoir to house the oil (usually a porous sandstone or limestone layer). Another important factor is a migration pathway for the hydrocarbon to move from the source rock to the subsurface reservoir rock. If one of these factors is absent or incompletely developed, an oil field will not form. Consequently, the present-day distribution of commercial oil and gas fields in the Great Plains is a reflection of where the coincidence of these factors has been most favorable.

Hydrocarbon source rocks are a case in point. The hydrocarbon source rocks present beneath the Great Plains are a reflection of the configurations of at least two ancient inland seaways that extended throughout the Plains and Rocky Mountain regions of North America. Thick intervals of organic-rich mud settled to the bottom of these ancient seaways. Deep burial of this mud within the crust of the earth helped to transform the mud into shales with potent oil- and gas-generating potential. At just the right combinations of temperature and pressure and at different locations throughout the Great Plains, oil was released from these source rocks. Geologic conditions in the Southern Great Plains were especially conducive to the accumulation of hydrocarbons. Consequently, due to differences in geology, discovery dates of commercial quantities of oil differed greatly from state to state.

The earliest commercial oil operation in the Great Plains was the Florence field in Colorado. Though oil was discovered at this site in

Bartlesville, Oklahoma

1862, it was not until the 1880s that both consumer demand and infrastructure were adequate for Florence to become a commercial oil field. Then, following the Neodesha, Kansas, success of 1893, exploratory wells were tapped in surrounding counties in Kansas and Oklahoma. The completion of the Nellie Johnstone No. 1 well in 1897, situated east of the newly founded city of Bartlesville, Indian Territory, marked the first commercial oil well in present-day Oklahoma. Oil production from the Oklahoma Indian Territory officially began in 1901. By the time Oklahoma achieved statehood in 1907, the Southern Great Plains was well on its way to becoming recognized as a major petroleum province.

The Northern Great Plains was not to be outdone. At about the same time that the midcontinent area (North Texas, Oklahoma, and Kansas) was coming into its own, a significant volume of oil was also being produced at Salt Creek field, Wyoming's first major Plains oil field. Natural surface seepages had been noted as early as 1889, and the field became commercially viable in about 1908.

Back in the Southern Great Plains, a North Texas oil boom commenced with discovery of the Electra field in 1911, located to the west of Wichita Falls, Texas. This was followed by numerous other large oil field discoveries between 1911 and 1920 in North Texas, Oklahoma, and Kansas. Many of these oil field discoveries resulted in the rapid development of new town sites or the growth of existing nearby town sites. New oil fields in Texas included Ranger, Breckenridge, Burkburnette, and Northwest Burkburnette. New Oklahoma fields were Cushing, Healdton, Garber, Hewitt, and Burbank. The most impressive new fields in Kansas were Augusta and El Dorado. During this period of rapid oil field discoveries, the Midcontinent was producing 30 percent of the total U.S. crude oil. This total had grown to 56 percent by 1920. In response to these exploration successes, a new pattern of railroad and pipeline transportation systems emerged to support the production, refining, and distribution of crude oil within the Southern Great Plains and to areas located outside of the Great Plains. By 1920, according to the Oklahoma Geological Survey, Oklahoma's crude oil was being processed in about seventy refineries in Oklahoma and surrounding states.

Despite these successes, the consumption of petroleum products after World War I had increased so dramatically that the production and distribution capacity was strained beyond limits. Refiners were unable to obtain adequate supplies of crude oil, and some gasoline stations had to close shop for days at a time. On the heels of this demand for crude oil, Charles N. Gould, former Oklahoma state geologist, discovered one of the world's largest oil and gas districts in the Texas and Oklahoma panhandles—the Panhandle field—in 1920.

The Permian Basin, stretching across West Texas and southeastern New Mexico, was beginning to yield crude oil in this period as well. The first commercial oil well in the Permian Basin, completed in about 1921, was located in Mitchell County, Texas. An oil rush in the Permian Basin began with the completion of the Santa Rita No. 1 well in 1923. This well was located on land granted to the University of Texas in an agreement dating to 1883. The success of the Permian Basin contributed to the growth of the Midland-Odessa area of West Texas, located very near the geographic center of the basin. In 1924 the Permian Basin Artesia field was discovered across the border in New Mexico. Hobbs field was discovered in New Mexico in 1928. Oil production in this portion of New Mexico resulted in population growth for both Artesia and Hobbs, New Mexico.

Following the success of the Florence and Salt Creek fields, other significant oil field discoveries were made in the Northern Great Plains states. However, due to fundamental differences in geologic history, fewer commercially viable fields occur in the Northern than in the Southern Plains. In Montana, the Kevin-Sunburst field, located north of Shelby, was discovered in 1922. The Cutbank field, near Cutbank, Montana, was opened in 1934. In Nebraska, the first successful oil field in the eastern portion of the state was discovered in 1940 at Falls City in Richardson County. In western Nebraska, the first commercially successful well was the Mary Egging No. 1, drilled in Cheyenne County in 1949 by Marathon Oil Company (then known as the Ohio Oil Company). This and adjacent wells were christened the Gurley field. Significant oil production from the Williston Basin of North Dakota began in 1951 with the completion of the Clarence Iverson No. 1 well, located near the towns of Tioga and Minot. In South Dakota, some oil production commenced in 1954 with the discovery of oil in Harding County, located in the northwestern corner of the state.

This regional production, of course, was taking place against a backdrop of the world context of global supply and demand. Following the Panhandle field discovery, coupled with production from other Great Plains fields and other oil-rich regions across America, the United States and the Great Plains entered a period from 1921 to 1940 of petroleum overabundance. Annual production in the United States in 1920 was 443 million barrels and was in balance with demand. By 1923 the volume had expanded to 732 million barrels per year, and the bloated industry headed into a tailspin. Fortunes were lost and dreams crushed during a time that overlapped the Great Depression. From 1945 to 1973 the industry slowly recovered through maintenance of a managed balance between supply and demand. Then from the Arab oil embargo in 1973 to about 1983, the petroleum industry of the Great Plains rode a wave of high oil prices fostered by global fears of oil-supply shortfalls. In 1986, however, oil-rich Saudi Arabia began to increase production in order to gain more control over supply and pricing. This action created an overabundance of oil and placed downward pressure on oil prices. From about 1984 to the present, the petroleum industry has undergone unprecedented global contraction. Emphasis on cost savings has forced the major North American companies to consolidate their operations in Houston, Texas, and Calgary, Alberta. Consequently, the remaining oil and gas wealth of the U.S. Great Plains is mainly the domain of independent investors and the small- to medium-size companies of the region.

The contraction of the industry has been very hard on the economies of the oil field towns that grew up around the industry. For instance, during the oil boom of the seventies, the Permian Basin city of Midland, Texas, was rumored to have more millionaires per capita than any city in the United States. At the beginning of the twenty-first century, however, unemployment there hovered at 9 percent. Economic growth in most of the oil towns in the Southern Great Plains was momentarily stunted by this downturn in the energy industry. Northern Great Plains cities such as Casper and Gillette, Wyoming, and Williston and Dickinson, North Dakota, have also grappled with this economic challenge.

According to U.S. Department of Energy statistics for the year 2000, Texas led both the Great Plains and the nation in daily crude-oil production (1.2 million barrels from the Great Plains, East Texas, and Gulf Coast fields). (One barrel equals forty-two gallons of crude oil.) Oklahoma is ranked fifth in the nation in daily production (191,000 barrels), followed by New Mexico, 184,000 barrels; Wyoming, 166,000 barrels; Kansas, 94,000 barrels; North Dakota, 89,000 barrels; and Colorado, 50,000 barrels. Montana produces 42,000 barrels a day, ranking it thirteenth. Nebraska is ranked twenty-first, with a production rate of 8,000 barrels a day. South Dakota produces 3,000 barrels a day and is ranked twenty-fifth.

Despite years of exploitation, the proved reserves of oil in the Great Plains still tend to be located in the traditional oil-rich areas. In 1999 Texas ranked number one in the nation, with proved reserves of 5,339 million barrels (again, including the Great Plains and other Texas oil provinces). This Texas total is double the reserve estimate for all the remaining areas of the U.S. Great Plains. New Mexico is second in the nation, with proved reserves of 718 million barrels, followed by Oklahoma, with 621 million barrels of reserves. Estimates for other states include Wyoming, 590 million; Montana, 207 million; Colorado, 203 million; Kansas, 175 million; North Dakota, 53 million; and Nebraska, 17 million barrels. South Dakota is estimated to have less than 1 percent of the total U.S. crude-oil reserves. To place these numbers for the U.S. Great Plains into a global context, Saudi Arabia has proved reserves of 262,000 million barrels, or about 25 percent of the estimated proved reserves in the world. Saudi Arabia's oil reserves are fifty times larger than those of Texas.

In the early twenty-first century, the Great Plains oil and gas producers compete on a global stage where market forces and oil-rich countries continue to determine the profitability of the industry. Giant multinational companies and the wealthiest petroleum-producing countries are well poised to take advantage of the latest computer-related technology for the exploration and production of hydrocarbons. These technologies have helped to lower finding costs from $15 per barrel in the 1970s to less than $5 per barrel in 2002. Some of these technologies such as 3D seismic (allowing clearer images of subsurface rocks) and improved drilling methods (directional-drilling capabilities) have helped to lower finding costs in the Great Plains.

In the future, one segment of the industry that may witness continued growth in the Great Plains is the natural gas industry. Natural gas, an environmentally friendly alternative to oil and coal, is growing in importance as an energy source of choice. The rocks of the Great Plains still contain an ample supply of this untapped resource.

Stanley T. Paxton
Oklahoma State University

Mast, R. F., D. H. Root, L. P. Williams, W. R. Beeman, and D. L. Barnett. *Areas of Historical Oil and Gas Exploration and Production in the Conterminous United States* U.S. Geological Survey Geologic Investigations Series, 1-2582, Reston, VA: Department of the Interior, 1998. Owen, E. W. *Trek of the Oil Finders: A History of Exploration for Petroleum.* American Association of Petroleum Geologists, Memoir 6, Tulsa OK, 1975. Yergin, D. *The Prize: The Epic Quest for Oil, Money, and Power.* New York: Simon and Schuster, 1991.

PHILLIPS PETROLEUM

Phillips Petroleum Company is a major diversified energy firm engaged internationally in oil and gas exploration and production. Phillips refines, markets, and transports petroleum, and it also gathers, processes, and markets natural gas, principally in the United States. In addition, the company manufactures and sells chemicals and plastics worldwide.

Two brothers, Frank (1873–1950) and Lee Eldas (1876–1944) Phillips, entered the oil business in 1903. In 1905 they drilled their first gusher when the Anna Anderson No. 1, located in Indian Territory, hit oil on leased land owned by an eight-year-old Delaware Indian girl of that name. The Phillips brothers remained in the oil business until 1915, when they decided to leave petroleum for banking. However, they soon realized that U.S. involvement in World War I would precipitate a steep rise in petroleum demand. They reconsidered their decision to leave the oil business and incorporated Phillips Petroleum Company in Bartlesville, Oklahoma, on June 13, 1917.

After discovery of the huge Panhandle gas field in 1918, Phillips profited from the burgeoning natural gas industry. In particular, Phillips specialized in the extraction of liquids from natural gas. By the mid-1920s, Phillips was the largest producer of natural gas liquids in the United States.

Since the late 1920s, consumers have recognized Phillips for its distinctive Phillips 66 service stations. Phillips originally entered the retail gasoline business to profit from the rapidly increasing demand for automobile fuel. In 1927 Phillips opened its first oil refinery near Borger in the Texas Panhandle, and in the same year the company opened its first service station in Wichita, Kansas.

During the Great Depression, Phillips posted its first loss ($5.7 million), and its stock price fell from $32 to $3 per share. The company persevered. During World War II, Phillips contributed to innovations in synthetic rubber and high-octane aviation gasoline. In the late 1940s Phillips entered the chemical business when it formed Phillips Chemical Company, a wholly owned subsidiary that operated a large facility by the Houston Ship Channel. In the 1950s Phillips began producing a polyolefin plastic trademarked as Marlex. Marlex was the most common plastic used in the manufacture of hula hoops, which became ubiquitous in that decade.

Beginning in the mid-1940s, Phillips explored for petroleum internationally, first in Venezuela, Canada, and Colombia and later in the Middle East. Phillips pioneered the industry in Alaska when it participated in a drilling project at Cook Inlet in 1962 and also at Prudhoe Bay on the North Slope. Phillips's most spectacular discovery was the massive Ekofisk field in the Norwegian sector of the North Sea. Phillips also participated in a project to manufacture and ship liquefied natural gas (LNG) from Alaska to Japan during the late 1960s.

During the 1980s, Phillips Petroleum survived hostile takeover attempts by groups led by T. Boone Pickens Jr. and Carl C. Ichan. Remaining independent was an expensive proposition that tripled Phillips's corporate debt. Phillips's financial condition, exacerbated by turmoil in the oil industry, caused it to either sell off or shut down some of its assets, including fertilizer, carbon black, and synthetic rubber plants. By the 1990s, Phillips had combined restructuring efforts with continued international and domestic business expansion. Phillips celebrated its eightieth anniversary in 1997 and remains the only major U.S. oil company still bearing its founders' name.

Christopher J. Castaneda
California State University, Sacramento

Wallis, Michael. *Oil Man: The Story of Frank Phillips and the Birth of Phillips Petroleum.* New York: Doubleday, 1988. Wertz, William C., ed. *Phillips: The First 66 Years.* Bartlesville OK: Phillips Petroleum Company, 1983.

PIZZA HUT

The international restaurant chain Pizza Hut, Inc., was founded in Wichita, Kansas, by brothers Dan and Frank Carney, students at Wichita State University. With $600 borrowed from their mother, the young men opened a small pizzeria at a busy Wichita intersection on June 15, 1958. They mixed dough in a plastic baby bathtub and gave away pizza slices to attract customers. A family member remarked that their little building looked like a hut, and the name Pizza Hut was born. (This structure has been moved and is preserved on the university campus.)

After just over a year, the Carneys owned five Wichita Pizza Huts. In 1959 they incorporated and opened a franchise in Topeka. Their small chain soon expanded across Kansas and into Oklahoma, Texas, and other states. With the opening of their first Pizza Hut in Canada, they entered the international market in 1968.

By 1971 Pizza Hut had added franchises in Australia and Europe, making it the world's number one pizza restaurant chain in both sales and number of outlets. The next year its stock began trading on the New York Stock Exchange. In 1977 stockholders approved a merger with PepsiCo, Inc., for a reported $300 million.

Both founders left the company (Dan Carney in 1974, Frank in 1980), but PepsiCo retained Pizza Hut's corporate offices in Wichita until 1995, when operations were shifted to Dallas, Texas. Two years later, PepsiCo spun off Pizza Hut and its two other restaurant holdings. As a division of Tricon Global Restaurants, Inc., of Louisville, Kentucky, Pizza Hut, Inc., entered the twenty-first century with more than 10,000 restaurants, 3,000 of them in eighty-six foreign countries.

Dave Webb
Kansas Heritage Center

O'Hara, Eileen. "Pie in the Sky." *Wichitan* (November 1981): 24–26. Webb, Dave. *399 Kansas Characters.* Dodge City: Kansas Heritage Center, 1994.

POST, C. W. (1854–1914)

Charles William Post was a businessman and experimenter who invented and marketed several important breakfast cereals and a coffee substitute. He was born in Springfield, Illinois, on October 26, 1854. He attended school in Illinois, dropping out of Illinois Industrial University after two years. At age seventeen he briefly relocated to Independence, Kansas, where he was a salesman, clerk, and store owner. After his return to Springfield in 1872, he focused on selling and manufacturing agricultural implements as well as inventing his own cultivator, harrow, plow, and haystacker.

Although he was successful, the strain of business life proved too much, and Post suffered a nervous breakdown in 1885. Thereafter, he moved to Fort Worth, where he worked to develop two subdivisions. He suffered a second breakdown in 1891 and moved to Battle Creek, Michigan, home of John Harvey Kellogg's health complex. There he partially adopted Kellogg's beliefs concerning human health. He started his own sanitarium in 1892, also in Battle Creek. In 1894 he invented a coffee substitute called Postum that he insisted had healthful benefits. He soon recognized the potential for a strong market in breakfast cereals and invented Grape-Nuts. He built his own paper mill in 1899 to construct cartons for his cereal. Soon he had a cereal empire. In 1908 he invented the popular Post Toasties. As a result of his activities, Post and Kellogg became lifelong enemies. Post's empire eventually became a part of General Foods.

As a successful businessman, Post served as president of the American Manufacturers Association and the Citizen's Industrial Association, in which, despite the organization's title, he worked to defeat unions and the open shop system. Wealthy enough to pursue his dreams, in 1906 Post returned to Texas, where he hoped to establish a model farming community. In 1907 he bought 225,000 acres in Lynn and Garza Counties, where he established the town of Post City (now Post), Texas. Although he platted out the settlement, planted trees, and built roads and schools, the settlement grew slowly. Post worked to improve the region's prospects, going so far as to conduct long and expensive rainmaking experiments from 1911 to 1914 that failed to produce rain. Post's health began to fail in his later years, and on May 9, 1914, he apparently committed suicide at his home in Santa Barbara, California.

See also WATER: Rainmaking.

Charles Vollan
University of Nebraska–Lincoln

Major, Nettie Letich. *C. W. Post.* Washington DC: Judd and Detweiler, 1963.

POTASH

Potash refers to compounds containing the element potassium such as potassium chloride, potassium sulfate, potassium-magnesium sulfate, potassium nitrate, and mixed sodium-potassium nitrate. The word "potash" comes from an early settler term, "pot-ashes," referring to potassium salts obtained by burning wood in pots. It is called potassium oxide in the ceramics industry.

Potassium is the seventh most abundant element of the earth's crust and is found in all plants and animals and in soils, rocks, minerals, oceans, rivers, and lakes. Potassium is essential for plant and animal growth; consequently, 95 percent of potash production is used as fertilizer or plant food. The remaining 5 percent of potash production is consumed by the chemical industry for a variety of products such as glass, ceramics, soaps and detergents, explosives, dyes, medicines, and alkaline batteries.

Potash is usually mined from underground bedded salt deposits. Shafts are sunk, and the ore is dug out or pumped to the surface through solution mining. Canada leads the world in both production and reserves. The bulk of Canada's potash production (about 9.3 million tons in 1997) and reserves are located in the Great Plains. The potash industry is focused in Saskatchewan, because there the ore deposits are thick and relatively close to the earth's surface; similar but more expensive to mine ore deposits occur in Alberta, Manitoba, North Dakota, and Montana. Currently, about ten mines produce potash in Saskatchewan. Most of the output is exported: about 55 percent to the United States and about 40 percent overseas via Vancouver. The United States is a much smaller potash producer (about 1.6 million tons in 1997), but again, the Great Plains is the leading region. About 80 percent of U.S. production comes from the Carlsbad area of New Mexico.

Grant D. Jackson
Montana State University

The 2000–2005 Outlook for Potash, Soda, and Boratic Minerals in North America and the Caribbean. CD-ROM, Icon Group International, 2001.

POTASH CORPORATION OF SASKATCHEWAN

The Potash Corporation of Saskatchewan, headquartered at Saskatoon and operating six mines in Saskatchewan, one in New Brunswick, and, until its sale in 2000, one in Moab, Utah, is the world's largest fertilizer enterprise. In 1999 the corporation's production of potash stood at 6.4 million metric tons, or 15 percent of the world's output. Potash is a generic term for several types of potassium salts or nutrients essential for modern agricultural fertilizers.

It is estimated that the Potash Corporation of Saskatchewan has 60 percent of the world's excess potash capacity and enough reserves for 1,000 years of production. Potash was first discovered in southern Saskatchewan in 1943, but the first potash mine was not established until 1958, when the Potash Company of America began production of the extensive deposits. Technical difficulties delayed large-scale exploitation until the late 1960s, but by 1971 ten potash mines were in operation in Saskatchewan, a province where there had always been a debate over how best to develop its natural resources.

Allan Blakeney's election as premier of Saskatchewan in 1971 marked the beginning of a long-running feud between the government and the potash producers over an existing prorating plan to control production and price. In 1974 the government instituted a new tax on producers, and in early 1975 it announced plans to create the Potash Corporation of Saskatchewan and nationalize some or all of the province's potash industry. In October 1976 the government purchased its first producing mine, and within two years it controlled 40 percent of the province's capacity.

The defeat of Premier Blakeney and his New Democratic Party in 1982 marked a dramatic political and ideological shift in the province. Premier Grant Devine and the Progressive Conservatives assumed office with a profound faith in the primacy of the market, as did many governments throughout the western democracies at the time. They placed little value on state-run enterprises and proceeded to privatize the Potash Corporation of Saskatchewan through a public share offering. Ironically, it was a New Democratic Party government, led by Roy Romanow, that completed the sale of the Potash Corporation shares that the province had retained after the initial public offering.

See also POLITICS AND GOVERNMENT: New Democratic Party.

Raymond B. Blake
University of Regina

SMALL-TOWN INDUSTRIALIZATION

Towns and villages with populations of fewer than 2,500 people are a common feature of the Great Plains region. Such small towns in the Plains are home to a diverse collection of manufacturing industries producing goods such as animal feeds, toys, antibiotics, potato chips, computers, plywood, leather handbags, and plastic pipe. Manufactured goods primarily are sold in wholesale markets, but a number of small-town firms in the Great Plains sell directly to consumers.

Despite the diversity of products manufactured in small towns in the region, there are some industries that dominate the landscape, based on numbers of establishments. Not surprisingly, a number of these dominant industries are connected to the agricultural base of the region. Of the ten manufacturing industries that account for just over 50 percent of all manufacturing in small towns at the three-digit standard industrial classification (SIC) level, four are agriculturally based: farm machinery production, meat processing, grain products, and miscellaneous food products. The most prevalent industry, however, is not driven by agriculture but by the need for information. The printing and publishing of daily and weekly newspapers account for nearly 13 percent of manufacturing in small towns in the Great Plains region. The production of farm equipment and machinery is the second most common industry in small towns, accounting for approximately 7 percent of all firms.

Small-town manufacturing firms often produce more than one product. For example, since the processes and equipment used for newspaper and commercial printing are very similar, and since small towns may not have enough demand for commercial printing for a stand-alone operation to be successful, many small-town newspapers offer commercial printing services. Farm machinery producers also commonly produce vehicle and engine parts, specialized industrial or commercial machinery, and fabricated metal. Many of these companion products also are related to agricultural facilities and processes. Finally, grain-milling firms may also produce foods such as pasta and crackers in addition to marketing certain pesticides, herbicides, and fertilizers.

The mix of industries does not vary considerably across towns of different sizes. The smallest towns, those with populations below 250, however, have a greater proportion of farm machinery and equipment (often small machine shops) and lumber products firms and a lower proportion of printing and publishing firms when compared to larger towns. There generally is little variation in the type of small-town manufacturing activity taking place across the region. The agricultural base of the region drives much of the activity.

Small-town industries range in size from those employing more than 1,000 workers to home-based businesses employing no paid workers. Nearly 70 percent of all small-town manufacturers employ fewer than ten people. The smallest firms account for nearly three-quarters of manufacturers in towns with fewer than 500 residents and for nearly two-thirds of firms in towns with populations between 2,000 and 2,500.

Employment sizes vary among the most common industries. The vast majority of small-town printing and publishing firms (approximately 90 percent) employ fewer than ten workers. Food-processing firms (including meat processors and grain mills) tend to be larger overall, with about 60 percent employing fewer than ten workers and nearly one-quarter employing from ten to twenty-four employees. Just over half of machinery and equipment producers employ fewer than ten workers, but nearly a quarter employ up to 200. A small number of firms, mainly food processors, actually employ workforces greater in number than the population of the town in which the firms are located. These firms are major employers not only in the towns but also in the areas surrounding them as well.

Relatively few manufacturing industries in small towns are subsidiaries of national or international firms. The largest proportion of this type of subsidiary firm is found in towns with populations from 500 to 1,499. The majority of small-town enterprises, however, are stand-alone profit centers, often sole proprietorships, or subsidiaries of firms located within the same state.

See also: CITIES AND TOWNS: Small Towns.

Lisa Darlington
Matthew A. England
University of Nebraska–Lincoln

Harris Info Source. 1997 Oklahoma Directory of Manufacturers & Processors. Twinsburg OH: Harris Info Source Staff, 1997. Nebraska Department of Economic Development. Nebraska Directory of Manufacturers and Their Products, 1998–1999. Lincoln NE: The Department, 1998. U.S. Office of Management and Budget. Standard Industrial Classification Manual, 1987. Springfield VA: National Technical Information Service, 1987.

SPRINT

Sprint, the global communications company based in Westwood, Kansas, has its rather humble origins in Abilene, Kansas. There, in 1902, Jacob and C. L. Brown chartered the Brown Telephone Company, seeking to target the rural market that tended to be overlooked by the Bell Telephone Company, which dominated the industry. In 1911 the Brown Telephone Company incorporated with three other Kansas independents as the United Telephone Company, making it the second largest such company in the state. The groundwork had been laid for a century of virtually uninterrupted expansion.

By 1925, United Telephone and Electric (UT & E), as it was then called, controlled sixty-eight companies, mainly telephone companies. UT & E rode out the Depression, when millions of impoverished subscribers gave up their phones, and by the 1950s the again-renamed United Utilities was the nation's third largest independent phone company.

United Utilities grew rapidly during the 1960s and 1970s, diversifying its concerns (into telecommunications equipment manufacturing, for example) and modernizing its operations (to dial operation in the 1960s, then into digital systems in the late 1970s). The com-

pany's new name, United Telecom (adopted in 1972), captured its new high-technology image and priorities. In 1986, following the breakup of "Ma Bell," United Telecom and GTE Sprint, the low-cost long-distance telephone company, entered into an equal partnership and immediately took advantage of the nation's new fiber-optic network. In 1991 United Telecom fully acquired Sprint and took the name Sprint Corporation. During the 1990s, Sprint extended its operations globally, entering into agreements with French, German, Canadian, and Mexican communications companies. Sprint has also consolidated its domestic market and now has services in forty-eight states. In all, Sprint, the end product (so far) of the Browns' small Abilene telephone company, serves more than 17 million customers and returns about $17 billion in annual revenues.

David J. Wishart
University of Nebraska–Lincoln

SUGAR BEET PROCESSING

Sugar beets of the *Beta vulgaris* species have a white inner flesh and look more like a large parsnip than a red beet. The sugar beet crop is planted in early spring and harvested in the fall, when it is at maximum sugar content. To grow beets, a farmer signs a contract with a company to plant a certain amount of acreage; usually payment is made by the company on the basis of the sugar content of the beets and also the price of refined sugar sold by the company. Many U.S. sugar companies today are owned by cooperatives made up of beet growers.

Harvesting machines uproot the beets, cut off the tops, and then convey the beets into a truck. The beets are delivered to the factories and receiving stations, where they are dumped either directly into the process or stored in large piles for later use. The sugar factory operates round the clock and must be fed a continuous supply of beets once the "campaign," or processing season, gets under way. Campaign length is usually from 120 to 150 days and even longer in the northern regions.

Upon entering the factory, the beets are washed and sliced into long thin strips called "cossettes." The cossettes then enter the diffuser, where water carries away the sugar in the form of raw juice. The exhausted beet material, called "pulp," goes to the dryer or silo to be sold as livestock feed. After leaving the diffuser, the raw juice is purified with lime and then put through two stages of carbonation in which carbon dioxide gas is added to precipitate the lime and nonsugars. The juice then passes through several filtration steps to remove impurities. This purified juice, called "thin juice," then goes to the evaporators to be concentrated into "thick juice." It is then filtered again to assure purity.

The pure thick juice then enters crystallization, where there are typically three stages: white pan, high raw pan, and low raw pan. The syrups arrive at the vacuum pans, where the liquid is boiled into a thick supersaturated liquid. At just the exact moment in the boiling

stage, the sugar boiler initiates the crystal formation by "seeding" the pan with an extremely fine sugar slurry. The sugar crystals are grown to the proper size, then the mass of sugar crystals is dropped to centrifugal machines to be spun at high speed. The liquid portion, or "mother liquor," is separated from the sugar crystals and saved for further crystallization and sugar removal. The liquid from the final boiling is exhausted of sugar and is called molasses. The molasses is saved for further desugarization and sold as an animal feed by-product.

The final white sugar is centrifuged from the white pan mass and washed. The damp sugar crystals are then sent to the sugar granulator for drying. From the granulator, the sugar goes to packaging, truck, or rail loading or is stored in huge storage silos. It requires approximately forty pounds of sugar beets to produce a five-pound bag of granulated sugar.

In the crop year 2000 more than 32 million tons of beets were harvested in the United States in twelve states. The major sugar beet growing area is the Red River Valley, which straddles the boundary of Minnesota and North Dakota. Nearly half of all the sugar beets grown in the United States come from this area. Among other Plains states, Montana, Colorado, Wyoming, and Nebraska all produce more than one million tons of sugar beets. During the 2000 production year there was a total of ten sugar beet companies in the United States, with a total of twenty-eight operating factories. Of these factories, thirteen are in the Great Plains region. They are located in the states of Colorado, Nebraska, Wyoming, Montana, and North Dakota. The beet sugar companies of the Great Plains include Western Sugar Company, Holly Sugar Corporation, American Crystal Sugar Company, Minn-Dak Farmers Co-op, and Rogers Sugar. There are two sugar beet growing areas in Canada, located in Ontario and Alberta. Canada has one sugar beet factory, located in Taber, Alberta, that annually contributes approximately 10 percent of Canada's total refined sugar production. Despite the above-noted production, the United States and Canada are net importers of sugar.

See also AGRICULTURE: Sugar Beets.

Richard Reisig
Western Sugar Company

SWATHER

A swather, also known as a windrower, is a self-propelled agricultural implement that harvests all types of hay. The introduction of the swather radically altered harvesting techniques in the Great Plains (particularly in South Dakota, North Dakota, northern Nebraska, and southeastern Colorado, where haying is prevalent) and throughout the world. The machine was refined and marketed by an agricultural implement manufacturer in central Kansas whose considerable economic clout resulted directly from the popularity of the swather.

In the nineteenth and early twentieth centuries hay was grown widely on mixed farming operations. It was a profitable crop because it was consumed as feed by horses and mules in cities and rural areas. However, its harvest was time-consuming. A different implement was necessary for each step in the process: mowing the hay, collecting the mowed crop into narrow, elongated piles (windrows) in order to dry it, and—to facilitate drying—"raking" or turning over the windrows. Dry hay is critical to preventing molding once the crop is baled and stored. If the hay is stored when damp, the resulting decomposition can eventually generate enough heat to cause the hay to catch fire.

Hay-harvesting methods were destined to change drastically when Lyle Yost, a Mennonite entrepreneur from Hesston, Kansas, helped form the Hesston Manufacturing Company in 1949. The firm acquired the production rights from a machine-shop owner in Iowa to a device that single-handedly accomplished all the tasks of hay harvesting. Yost's company introduced the "swather" (later renamed the "windrower") in the mid-1950s. In addition to mowing, windrowing, and being self-propelled, the swather has an innovation that enables hay to dry faster and more thoroughly. As the crop is mowed, the stalks are crushed (known as conditioning), allowing the plant's moisture to evaporate more quickly once the hay is stacked in windrows. Ideally, conditioning hay eliminates the need for raking and protects the protein-rich tips and leaves of harvested plants. Today's windrowers are larger and more sophisticated than earlier models, and their central role in haying remains undiminished.

Based largely on the popularity of the swather, Yost's fledgling company eventually employed well over 1,000 people and became an international force in the implement industry. In 1966 the company was renamed Hesston Corporation. In the late 1980s the business underwent major financial restructuring, but it continues to manufacture agricultural implements as Hay and Forage, Inc. Hesston Corporation and its home community, Hesston, became synonymous with hay harvesting. The town of Hesston was transformed from a small farming hamlet into a prosperous suburban-like community by the company's success. Hesston high school sports teams are known as the Swathers, which says much about the influence of Yost, his company, and his hay harvester.

See also AGRICULTURE: Hay.

Steven V. Foulke
Perry, Kansas

Jones, Billy M. *Factory on the Plains: Lyle Yost and the Hesston Corporation*. Wichita KS: Center for Entrepreneurship, Wichita State University, 1987.

TELUS

Telus Corporation is an Alberta–British Columbia telecommunication firm created by the 1999 merger of two province-based companies. It is the second largest telecommunication organization in Canada and one of the largest business operations in Canada headquartered in the West.

Telus's emergence reflects the changing goals of western provincial enterprises and governments and the influence of federal regulations. Until privatized and renamed Telus in 1990, the former Alberta Government Telephones operated from 1908 to 1990 as a provincial crown enterprise regulated and sheltered under a provincial public utilities board. Operating from 1904 to 1999, BC Telephone, renamed BC Telecom in 1992 and a wholly owned subsidiary since 1926 of American utility GTE, was confined to provincial activity under the federal regulation that oversaw private-sector utilities.

In 1988 the Supreme Court of Canada ruled that federal regulation of telecommunication included provincial crown-owned enterprises, and in 1992 the federal regulator, the Canadian Radio-Television and Telecommunication Commission, began allowing interprovincial telecommunication competition. The merger between Edmonton-based Telus and Vancouver-based BC Telecom has enabled Telus to compete nationally with other telecommunication and cable providers for the total market of data, Internet, voice, and wireless communication. Current federal regulation of telecommunication stipulates that rates and ownership structures are controlled but not competition for markets. Telus shares are one-fifth held by Verizon, the successor to GTE and Bell Atlantic. Telus has made major acquisitions in Canada and abroad in order to compete throughout Canada, in the United States, and elsewhere.

Barry Ferguson
University of Manitoba

Babe, Robert. *Telecommunication in Canada: Technology, Industry and Government*. Toronto: University of Toronto Press, 1990. Lens, Jean-Guy. *The Invisible Empire: A History of the Telecommunication Industry in Canada 1846–1956*. Montreal: McGill-Queen's University Press, 2001.

TOURISM

As most travelers in the Great Plains are en route to other places, tourism in the region tends to focus upon transit tourism rather than upon destination tourism. And since the modern "tourist gaze" rarely appreciates the beauty of the Plains landscape, marketable tourist attractions tend to be man-made, emphasizing culture and heritage. The Plains states contain much of the nation's western heritage and numerous Native American sites. All the Plains states now celebrate their Native American heritages, especially the state of Oklahoma. Some tourist sites such as Mount Rushmore National Memorial in South Dakota's Black Hills and the Little Bighorn Battlefield National Monument in Montana are associated with the struggle for ownership and identity between Native Americans and the wider American culture. A more traditional version of the region's settlement history has been and continues to be celebrated and marketed as the principal resource of the Plains tourism industry.

Most of the advertising and state funding for Plains tourism is focused on the frontier and early European American settlement period, which lasted from the 1850s into the beginning of the twentieth century. In Nebraska and Kansas, for example, important pioneer trails such as the Oregon Trail and the Santa Fe Trail are well marked, and former cattle towns are often important tourist destinations. Dodge City, Abilene, and Wichita all contain replicas of the "Front Streets" of the 1870s. Wichita's replica, which includes several original buildings, is the most complete and accurate.

State funding for Plains tourism is often tied to western heritage promotion. In Kansas, for example, when the state legislature first approved $25,000 for tourist promotions in 1953, the funds were specifically set aside to celebrate the state's "western heritage." This policy continues, as exemplified by the 1990s Kansas State Historic Sites Master Plan, which is organized under the title "Kansas; Where the West Begins."

Plains tourism is of particular economic importance to towns and cities located along major transit routes. Billboards advertising the attractions of towns, sometimes hundreds of miles away, attempt to persuade the motorist to stop and spend the night. From south to north the major routes are I-10 and I-20 in Texas, I-35 and I-44 in Oklahoma, I-70 in Kansas, I-80 in Nebraska, and I-90 in South Dakota. Cities that particularly benefit from such motorists include Amarillo, Abilene, Big Spring, and Odessa, Texas; Tulsa and Oklahoma City, Oklahoma; Goodland, Colby, Russell, and Salina, Kansas; North Platte, Kearney, and Grand Island, Nebraska; and Sioux Falls and Mitchell, South Dakota. Williston, Grand Forks, and Minot are also stopover towns in North Dakota. Given the region's propensity for sudden snowstorms in the winter and for tornados and thunderstorms in the summer, many of these cities also benefit from the presence of visitors forced to seek shelter unexpectedly.

Other Plains cities that benefit from tourism are those located on the edge of the region that often host major conferences. These cities include Fort Worth, Kansas City, Denver, and Calgary. In 1998 alone, for example, Calgary hosted 136 conventions, bringing more than 495,000 visitors to the city.

Two other common features of the Great Plains attract local tourists rather than a mix of visitors from within and without the region. Local tourists especially enjoy the reservoirs and lakes constructed by the U.S. Army Corps of Engineers from the 1950s through the 1970s. They are also the major participants in the many small-scale festivals and rodeos as well as the larger state fairs held annually throughout the region.

Great Plains tourism in Texas focuses on the Alamo and the nearby River Walk (Paseo del Rio) in San Antonio. Tourism at the Alamo is centered almost entirely on a traditional American interpretation of the well-known battle and siege. Less contentious is Lyndon B. Johnson National Historic Park, located near Johnson City. The Dallas–Fort

Worth area is home to the Amon G. Carter Museum, an important repository of American western art, as well as Six Flags over Texas, the primary theme park of a major chain. Annual festivals, rodeos, and celebrations take place in a number of cities and towns, with the German towns of New Braunfels (which has built a water park to attract more tourists) and Fredericksburg as examples.

In Oklahoma, many of the tourist attractions feature the state's frontier heritage. Examples include the National Cowboy Hall of Fame and Western Heritage Center in Oklahoma City. Indian City, U.S.A., contains seven restored Indian villages and is but one example of a major policy shift in Oklahoma's tourism, which aims to celebrate rather than downplay the state's extensive Native American heritage. Critics still complain of tourist "commodification" and stereotyping of Native American history. The Chickasaw National Recreation Area, the first national park in the state, contains springs, lakes, and streams. Local festivals include the American Indian Exposition at Anadarko, Will Rogers Days at Claremore, and the Cherokee National Holiday in Tahlequah.

As the boyhood home of a popular American president, Abilene, Kansas, benefits from the Eisenhower library, museum, home, and chapel. Fort Leavenworth and Fort Riley both have museums dedicated to frontier army life. The dinosaur museum in Hayes has been moved from its campus location to a more convenient and larger site next to Interstate 70. Despite some local opposition, a large ranch house and its attendant acres of prairie have been preserved for posterity in Chase County. Kansas festivals include Wah-Shun-Gah Days in Council Grove, Dodge City Days in Dodge City, and Beef Empire Days in Garden City.

Tourism in Nebraska is also often focused on its frontier heritage, with the Harold Warp pioneer village at Minden as one extraordinary example. As in Kansas, nineteenth-century collectors found dinosaur bones in the state. Some of the fossils not shipped back east are on display in Royal. Omaha, the state's largest city, contains, among other tourist attractions, the Henry Doorly Zoo, the Joslyn Art Museum, the Durham Western Heritage Museum, and the renovated Old Market. Nebraska draws tourists to its spectacular annual bird migrations, especially those of the sandhill crane. Annual festivals include the Oregon Trail Days in Gering and Arbor Day in Nebraska City.

Most of South Dakota's tourist attractions, unlike those in other states fully in this region, are natural rather than cultural features. They include the Badlands National Park, Wind Cave National Park, and the Black Hills. The Black Hills is a tourist destination in its own right. Mount Rushmore National Memorial depicts the huge carved granite faces of Presidents Washington, Jefferson, Lincoln, and Theodore Roosevelt. As a partial response to criticism about the use of this site, a monument to Crazy Horse is being created nearby. Festivals in South Dakota include Gold Discovery Days in Custer, the Corn Palace Festival in Mitchell, and the Sturgis Motorcycle Rally.

North Dakota's tourist attractions tend to be located near its major population centers. Theodore Roosevelt National Park is well known for its badlands and diverse animal life. As in most Great Plains states, there are several restored nineteenth-century forts and Native American villages, notably those at Lincoln State Park and at Fargo. Festivals include Roughriders Days in Dickinson, Norsk Hostfest in Minot, and Bonanza Days in Wahpeton.

New Mexico, Colorado, Wyoming, and Montana draw tourists mainly to their western, mountainous portions, but their eastern plains also have much to offer to tourists, particularly if they want to get off the beaten path. Carlsbad Caverns in southeastern New Mexico is both a national park and a world heritage site; its spectacular caves attracted 469,303 visitors in 2000. Nestled in the lee of the Rocky Mountains, Colorado Springs has been a tourist center since the 1870s. North again into eastern Wyoming, the traveler's eye is struck by Devils Tower, the volcanic intrusion that abruptly rises 1,267 feet above the Belle Fourche River. A sacred site to the Kiowas and Comanches, Devils Tower also attracts rock climbers, 4,000 of whom made their way to the top in 1998. In eastern Montana, natural features such as the badlands of Makoshika State Park and historical sites such as the restored Fort Union have much to offer as tourist destinations. One site, Pompey's Pillar, just east of Billings, bears an important latter-day graffiti: William Clark's signature, the only on-site physical evidence of the Lewis and Clark Expedition.

North of the forty-ninth parallel, the same generalization holds true: tourists are attracted to physical settings that, while they may lack the splendor of the mountains, still present drama and beauty, to historical sites, and to the cultural offerings of the cities. The Cypress Hills Interprovincial Park, for example, standing 600 meters above the plains of southwestern Saskatchewan, is an alpine environment of great biotic diversity. Throughout the Prairie Provinces, the rich multicultural heritage finds expression in diverse landscapes and cultural celebrations: at Batoche, in west-central Saskatchewan, for example, Métis culture is reinvigorated each summer with traditional dancing, fiddling, and jigging. The single most important tourist destination in the Prairie Provinces, however, is Calgary, which in 1998 drew more than 4.2 million people who spent more than $629 million Canadian.

Tourism may not be what the Great Plains is known for, yet the attractions are many, and the economic influence is great. Indeed, in Nebraska, for example, tourism ranks only behind agriculture and manufacturing as a source of state income.

See also EDUCATION: National Cowboy Hall of Fame and Western Heritage Center / PHYSICAL ENVIRONMENT: Carlsbad Caverns / SPORTS AND RECREATION: National Parks; Sturgis Motorcycle Rally.

Karen J. De Bres
Kansas State University

De Bres, Karen J. "Cowtowns or Cathedral Precincts? Two Models for Contemporary Urban Tourism." *Area* 26 (1994): 57–67. De Bres, Karen J. "Defining Vernacular Tourism: The View from Kansas." *Annals of Tourism Research* 4 (1996): 945–54. Jakle, John A. *The Tourist: Travel in Twentieth-Century North America*. Lincoln: University of Nebraska Press, 1985.

URANIUM MINING

Several Great Plains states have been home to uranium production since 1945. Beginning in 1947, the Atomic Energy Commission offered government subsidies, including guaranteed prices and discovery bonuses, to stimulate uranium production for America's cold war defense. A uranium rush ensued, and claims were staked throughout the region. Successful mines and processing mills near Edgemont and Pine Ridge, South Dakota, and the Wyoming towns of Shirley Basin, Jeffrey City, and Douglas produced and sold uranium concentrate, or yellowcake, to the federal government. The program was so successful, however, that supply exceeded government demand, and the industry collapsed in the late 1960s.

Following the close of the government program, the energy crisis of the 1970s fueled the expansion of nuclear power plants and created another uranium boom. This time, the mills at Edgemont, Jeffrey City, and Shirley Basin produced yellowcake for commercial power companies. But after environmental fears following the Three Mile Island accident in March 1979 stopped further nuclear generator construction, the industry again collapsed, and most mines and mills were closed by 1985. Since then, the new and comparably inexpensive extraction technique of in situ mining, during which solvents are pumped directly into the underground ore body, allowed to dissolve and leach out the uranium, and then pumped back to the surface, has made Nebraska one of the leading uranium-producing states in the country. Uranium mining is still active in Saskatchewan, but the mines are located to the north of the Plains portion of that province.

Although comparatively little uranium is currently produced in the Great Plains, former uranium mines and mill sites face costly environmental remediation and continuing maintenance and radiation checks.

Michael A. Amundson
Northern Arizona University

Albrethsen, Holger, and Frank E. McGinley. *Summary History of Domestic Uranium Procurement under U.S. Atomic Energy Commission Contracts: Final Report*. Grand Junction CO: U.S. Department of Energy, 1982.

WEATHER INDUSTRY

As the nicknames "Tornado Alley," "Dust Bowl," and "blizzard country" imply, weather has a major impact in the Great Plains. The variety and intensity of Plains weather justify its description as a "climate of extremes." For these reasons, the region is home to a sizable percentage of the country's weather and climate research institutions, government service agencies, and weather information businesses.

Among what is nationally a relatively small sector of specialized business, the "weather industry" in the Plains has a substantial impact, especially in certain local areas. The potential impact of severe weather on such weather-sensitive industries as aviation, highway and rail transportation, insurance businesses, and agriculture creates a high demand for weather data, weather-monitoring equipment, and weather professionals. Private weather enterprises include weather data and hardware vendors, wind energy generation, aviation and agricultural weather forecast services, and even weather modification companies that provide cloud seeding for hail suppression or precipitation enhancement. Television weather coverage in the Plains, with an emphasis on tornado warning dissemination, is extensive and highly detailed, with stations in Oklahoma City, Tulsa, and Wichita devoting more resources to weather coverage than their counterparts in large markets such as Los Angeles, New York, and Chicago.

Significant concentrations of private businesses devoted to weather and climate data analysis and forecasting are found in the Dallas–Fort Worth, Oklahoma City, and Wichita metropolitan areas. Major centers for public weather research include Boulder, Colorado, Lubbock, Texas, Rapid City, South Dakota, and, most notably, Norman, Oklahoma. Numerous agencies of the National Oceanic and Atmospheric Administration (NOAA), a division of the U.S. Department of Commerce, are headquartered in the Plains. The Aviation Weather Center, responsible for worldwide weather forecasting for American civilian airlines, is located in Kansas City, and its military equivalent is in Omaha.

The emergence of Norman as the world's primary center for research, monitoring, and prediction of tornadoes and severe local storms began in 1948 at nearby Tinker Air Force Base, where tornado forecasting was pioneered. The evolution continued in 1964 with the establishment in Norman of the National Severe Storms Laboratory (NSSL), where Doppler weather radar was developed and tested. In 1997, under modernization initiatives of the National Weather Service (NWS), the Storm Prediction Center, responsible for the issuance of severe weather watches and hazardous weather guidance nationwide, relocated to Norman from Kansas City. Additional NOAA agencies, including an NWS office, the NEXRAD (National Weather Service's Next Generation Weather Radar) Radar Operational Support Facility, and numerous federal and state atmospheric research institutes associated with NSSL and the University of Oklahoma, were placed under one cooperative umbrella in 1998 as the Oklahoma Weather Center. The center, with emphasis in the development of numerical forecast models, environmental monitoring systems, tornado research, and severe weather forecasting, directly employs 600 people and injects more than $60 million annually into the economy.

See also PHYSICAL ENVIRONMENT: Tornadoes.

Matthew D. Biddle
University of Oklahoma

England, Gary A. *Weathering the Storm: Tornadoes, Television, and Turmoil*. Norman: University of Oklahoma Press, 1997. Grazulis, Thomas P. *Tornadoes of the United States*. Norman: University of Oklahoma Press, 2000. Penn, David. *Impact of the Oklahoma Weather Center on the Oklahoma Economy*. Norman: Center for Economic and Management Research, University of Oklahoma–Norman, 1998.

WIND ENERGY

The Great Plains has been called the "Saudi Arabia of Wind Energy" because its resources for wind power are so immense, but development of those resources has been slow. Several important long-term factors favor extensive development of the industry in the Plains: wind power is independent of the fluctuations of the world energy market, which many analysts expect to become more extreme; it has a low impact on the environment; and, because wind towers need very small footprints and wind farm wires are underground, it is compatible with grazing, farming, and other Plains land uses. Indeed, for individual farmers and ranchers, wind farm lease royalties can greatly surpass other income.

Through sophisticated engineering of blades and other turbine components, the costs per kilowatt-hour of wind power have been dropping steadily for many years. Only natural gas–burning turbines now produce cheaper power, and high-tech wind turbines are predicted to soon equal their costs—sooner if fossil fuel costs rise, as many expect. In some parts of the Great Plains, wind power is already effectively cheaper than gas when all costs, for example, transportation of fuel, are taken into account. However, Plains state governments, universities, and private utilities have all been slow in recognizing the manifold advantages of wind power for the region. Wind facilities are presently concentrated where state governments have acknowledged the potential of wind power (Texas primarily, but Colorado and Kansas have also offered incentives for "green" power). As of 1999, wind turbine installations also exist in Wyoming, Nebraska, and North Dakota.

According to prospectors who have assessed the Plains winds, North Dakota alone has wind resources that, if harnessed, could provide about a third of the entire country's electricity demand, and the Plains as a whole could provide all the power the country could foreseeably need. However, because of the economics of the electrical industry, wind power is likely to evolve as a largely local institution in the thinly settled Plains. As utilities planners have recently recognized, electrical distribution is more costly than electrical generation. This fact has implications both for generating strategies and for grid planning. For the Plains, it means that wind farm development is likely to be relatively decentralized, a pattern that will minimize grid investment needs. It is also likely to suit the desire of Plains people for local control rather than dependence on distant powerful forces. Because transmission costs and losses favor consumption of power nearer points of generation, state-scale or local generating facilities are probable. They will also have the advantage of increasing local grid reliability in case national power shortages occur. A Danish-owned, thirteen-employee wind machine blade factory has recently been set up in Wisconsin, and other manufacturing and installing companies should follow in the Plains proper. Wind farms provide more numerous jobs per million dollars of investment than any other means of generating power—and without the boom-and-bust pattern of oil and coal. Individual farmers and ranchers with their own turbines will also find themselves able in especially windy spells to sell excess power to the grid through reverse metering.

See also PHYSICAL ENVIRONMENT: Wind.

Ernest Callenbach
Berkeley, California

Righter, Robert W. *Wind Energy in America: A History*. Norman: University of Oklahoma Press, 1996.

Law

Mounted troop of North-West Mounted Police Lancers in front of main gate, Fort Walsh, Saskatchewan, 1878

Law 441

LAW

A legal system is one of the forces that shapes a society and gives it structure. This is true whether one considers very informal legal systems, typical of early tribal communities on the Great Plains, or highly formal systems characteristic of modern urban life. In every case, legal systems have been put in place and designed to preserve established values and ways of behaving and also to achieve desired changes in society—a transformative role too often overlooked. One result of the imbedding of legal systems within societies is that there have been as many systems of law on the Great Plains as there have been communities. This great diversity reflects the richness of the history on the region but has also meant that significantly different legal systems have at times had to coexist. This has not always been easy to achieve, and on occasion it has not even been possible. The result has sometimes been disputes amounting to battles for supremacy between systems and between the communities of which they were a part, though on other occasions mutual modification has provided a more peaceful solution. What has emerged in the modern period is to a great extent a legacy from all that has gone before, a legal system derived predominantly from England's but preserving elements from other European traditions and from Aboriginal systems. It is a system that has been and continues to be shaped by the unique experience and diverse communities of the Great Plains.

Indigenous Law

The legal history of the Great Plains may be said to begin with the first appearance of organized communities in the region thousands of years ago and long before the arrival of Europeans. The very persistence of these communities over time makes it obvious that they possessed systems of law sufficiently flexible and sophisticated to answer the needs of societies ranging from sedentary agricultural groups with comparatively large population centers to scattered bands of nomads who depended primarily on hunting and gathering for their survival. To some extent they all possessed, for example, rules governing interpersonal relations and well-developed ideas about property that regulated access to the resources of the land. Archaeologists have demonstrated that small groups (e.g., individual families) frequently had exclusive or at least first access to the resources in a defined locale. Larger groups (e.g., tribes) likewise occupied defined territories from which they endeavored to exclude others. Unfortunately, little except generalities can reliably be set forth in outlining the finer points of this sort of early legal history and the rules these societies developed to give them structure and cohesion because of the lack of accessible and reliable evidence available to the historian. Unfortunately, this problem is only somewhat abated as we come to consider more recent times and even approach the arrival of Europeans.

In some respects, of course, Native peoples on the Great Plains began to feel the first effects of European influence before—in some cases long before—the actual arrival of the Europeans themselves. The introduction of the horse, new trade goods (notably, firearms), and diseases to which they had little resistance disrupted traditional ways of living and patterns of trade and drastically altered power relationships. The effects of these changes were visible wherever Europeans established themselves, but, like the ripples from a rock thrown in a pond, they spread far and wide, affecting Indigenous people far away from Europeans themselves. Precisely how the societies of the Great Plains adjusted their existing practices to respond to the new realities—or even if they did in every case—is very difficult to determine in the light of existing evidence. There is a body of oral tradition preserved among the various peoples who populated the Great Plains in the years before the arrival of the Europeans, but for very early periods this is a difficult source for historians to use, and it is not always seen as reliable without corroboration.

Nor, it seems, can we say much with confidence about the period when Europeans first had a physical presence, in the form of missionaries, traders, and explorers, on the Great Plains. These harbingers of change produced the first body of written material dealing with the autochthonous population of the Great Plains, but even with this often fascinating body of work in hand the legal historian is too often frustrated. The internal ordering of Indigenous societies was not something in which many of these early writers were interested, and even when it was mentioned, the observers were not always sufficiently sensitive to or even capable of understanding what they saw. With the arrival of larger European populations, though, we are on firmer ground because of the increased abundance of written records and more useful oral accounts.

The latter in particular have proven a valuable source for reconstructing the laws of a number of Plains tribes during the nineteenth century. Both tribes that had a long history on the Plains such as the Blackfoot and those that moved into the region only in the eighteenth century such as the Lakota (Sioux) had to adjust to new realities. The result was approaches to law that share certain broad characteristics such as an emphasis on consensus and restitution. Among the Kiowas of the Southern Plains, for example, there were few conflicts over property, the main exception being horses. Food was shared and stealing was rare. Internal family conflicts were also rare and likely to be settled by reason rather than by law. Criminal actions were deterred by the fear of supernatural reprisal (*taido*). Serious crimes such as murder might result in social ostracism or, if they threatened the integrity of the tribe, in the imposition of the death penalty, a killing "legalized" by the singing of a song, which nullified any supernatural penalty.

There were, however, considerable differences in legal systems (as in most other aspects of life) among Plains Indians. The Kiowas' legal system and, even more so, the Comanches'

were rather informal, certainly when compared to the Cheyennes, to whom Llewellyn and Hoebel attributed a "legal genius." In Cheyenne society, for example, the tribal chiefs had exclusive jurisdiction over punishment of a murderer. Punishment generally meant banishment from the society, though remission was possible after a number of years if the perpetrator was penitent. The Cheyenne legal system, it might be added, had a refined classification system of what constituted murder and what might be excused as a justified killing.

The dynamic and varied Indigenous legal systems held on to much that harked back to traditional times but also demonstrated the ability to respond to new needs. The jurisdiction of the chiefs is a good example of the former, and perhaps the best example of the latter in most tribes, including the Cheyennes, is the increasing power of the warrior societies to make and enforce rules. However, the various tribal systems were eventually to come into conflict with ultimately more domineering legal traditions brought to the region by Europeans.

The Impact of European American Legal Systems

Spain was active in the southern and France and England originally along the eastern and northern parts of the Great Plains. At first directly and later through colonial offshoots in the Americas, these three European powers, with very different legal cultures, began to transform the region. In all cases it was at first the policy of the European and later American powers not to extend their laws to the Indigenous population. In fact, it was recognized, either explicitly or implicitly, that it was neither desirable nor possible to expect the full body of their national law to apply even to those of European extraction. In theory, then, Native peoples would continue to be governed by their own laws, and Europeans and Americans would be subject to "appropriate" European law. In the United States, Indian Country was territory that was outside the organized territories and states. Settlers were forbidden there, and traders could operate only under license. A series of Intercourse Acts, including the 1834 act, which applied to the Great Plains, regulated trade and imposed fines on violations of the rules governing interactions with Native Americans.

This separation of legal domains was often very difficult and sometimes impossible to apply. Which European or American laws were in effect and which were not? Which rules should apply in disputes involving both Indigenous peoples and European Americans? What was to be done with the increasing numbers of people with both European American and Native ancestry? The result of this period of confusion was twofold. In the first place, there is clear evidence that in some cases contact with European Americans and their ways of doing things profoundly modified Indigenous rules and ways of proceeding. For example, alcohol, forbidden through the Intercourse

Acts, continued to flow into the Plains through the fur trade and severely disrupted Native American lives.

But it was the second development that was ultimately to prove more significant. The law of the more powerful party, the European Americans, came to dominate, holding sway in most of the region and over most matters. Indigenous law was, by this steady process, largely marginalized. (Marginalized does not, however, mean exterminated. Indigenous law not only survives but in some jurisdictions—for example, rules concerning access to Native American sacred sites—has been rejuvenated and is even modifying the dominant European-inspired legal system.)

It is difficult to overstate the impact on Indigenous cultures and indeed on the entire ecology of the Great Plains itself that was occasioned by the arrival of large numbers of European Americans coming not simply to explore or trade but also to settle and to make lives for themselves and their children in these new lands. This process began in earnest during the nineteenth century and filled the region roughly from east to west. Friction was often impossible to avoid as the new arrivals sought to take control over the lands and water they needed in order to survive and as a result dispossessed the Native peoples. This process, accomplished by a series of treaties sanctioned by existing European and international law, occasionally led to violence and even wars, especially in the United States but also during two brief episodes in Canada (the Red River Resistance of 1869–70 and the 1885 Riel Rebellion). But these were only the most visible evidences of a kind of low-grade battle that had been in progress for some time as European American and Indigenous ideas about the ownership of property competed.

Traders had earlier confronted the fact that Native peoples often had ideas about private property quite different from their own. This was dealt with in a variety of ways; the Hudson's Bay Company's and American Fur Company's practice of trading literally through a hole in the wall so that their customers had no direct access to the trade goods and could not simply walk off with what they wanted is a good example. This fundamentally different view of property rights remained a source of friction between European Americans and Native peoples as the process of settlement continued and affected everything from land to movables. One particular focus was the horse, which had spread rapidly throughout the Great Plains region after the first Spanish imports had been introduced in the south. Horses became an integral part of the life of many tribes, and possession of horses conferred great status. The result of this was, eventually, a period of near constant raiding—which European Americans, as usual not overly sensitive to Indigenous life and values, termed simply "horse stealing"—during which the aim was to control as many horses as possible. Any and every horse was fair game in this passionate activity, with the frequent result that horses owned by European Americans

were run off by Indians. Unfortunately, what was a serious though in some respects a sporting activity for Native peoples was seen as a very serious crime by European Americans, and only the efforts of the military in the United States and lawmen on both sides of the Canadian-American border prevented more serious problems from developing. They were occasionally thwarted by knowledgeable raiders, who knew they could not be chased across the international boundary, sometimes referred to as the "medicine line."

A second problem, related in the minds of most European Americans but in fact quite distinct, concerned the safety of cattle kept on the open range. Native peoples in the Great Plains depended to some extent on hunting for their subsistence, and in the northern regions, where huge herds of bison wandered the prairies, they were almost entirely dependent on this important source of food and its secondary products. It was difficult to persuade Indian hunters, especially after the destruction of the great bison herds was well advanced, that they should not take the cattle that had replaced them, since hunger and even starvation were often the only alternative to killing cattle.

However, the picture so often presented, at the time and since, of Indians as cattle killers and horse thieves has been greatly overdrawn. They did take both cattle and horses in some numbers, but careful reading of the records of the time makes it clear that European American criminals often found it easy to blame Indians for their own crimes and that many complained of Indian depredations simply because they hoped their respective governments would make good their "losses." In fact, members of the North-West Mounted Police in Canada frequently complained in their annual reports that settlers reported that their animals had been stolen simply so that the police would go out and round up their herds for them in the fall free of charge. In the United States Indian agents often noted that "depredation claims" by settlers seemed to coincide with the arrival of Native American annuity payments.

From the point of view of many in the dominant society, a solution to these and other problems was finally arrived at in both Canada and the United States when the various tribes were confined to lands set aside for them, called reserves in Canada and reservations in the United States. In the United States these areas have preserved an important legal significance, stemming initially from the judgments of Chief Justice John Marshall in the famous Cherokee cases—*Cherokee Nation v. Georgia* (1831) and *Worcester v. Georgia* (1832)—that established the idea of tribes as "domestic dependent nations" possessing limited sovereignty. This sovereignty was further defined by the U.S. Supreme Court in *Ex Parte Crow Dog* (1883), where it was ruled that the United States had no jurisdiction over crimes committed by one Indian against another. Congress subsequently acted to limit this sovereignty, notably, in the Major Crimes Act of

1885, which determined that the United States did have jurisdiction over Indians for seven major crimes, including murder, but it remains an important part of the legal apparatus of the American Plains.

The "checkerboard" nature of landownership patterns on Plains reservations, however (a product of the 1887 Dawes Act, which imposed allotments on the Indians and permitted the sale of "surplus" reservation lands to Americans), makes for extremely complicated jurisdiction in Indian Country. On many Plains reservations, non-Indians own most of the land, the lines between tribal and federal jurisdictions are blurred, and individual states also try to assert their legal and political authority. Landmark cases, including *Montana v. United States* (1981), have revolved around this complex geography and the extent of tribal jurisdiction over nonmembers of the tribe living on or, in that case, fishing and hunting on the reservation. Recent Supreme Court decisions have even led to the "diminishment" of reservations, especially in South Dakota.

In Canada, however, the approach has not been to recognize group rights, and the various tribes and bands have not had any formal power to make and enforce law. This seems to be changing, though, as a result of the current strong movement toward First Nations self-government, a movement at least partly informed by the perception that the American approach has its virtues. This movement was born in the Prairie Provinces, where more than half of Canada's Status Indians reside, but opposition to Native self-government is also greatest in that same region.

The American Legal Frontier

Neither the Spanish nor the French were willing or able to support the large-scale presence in the Great Plains proper that would have led to the institutionalization of their laws there. Texas did later follow some Spanish concepts of family and property laws, including the legalization of adoption and the recognition of woman's rights to property acquired during marriage, and there is a legacy of French civil law, especially in Manitoba. But overwhelmingly, it was English law that was brought to the Plains. The United States, despite its violent separation from England, essentially preserved the English system of laws and extended it to much of the Great Plains. To the north, eventually north of the forty-ninth parallel, the Hudson's Bay Company and later Canada also introduced an English-inspired legal regime.

People of European extraction came to the Great Plains during the nineteenth century in great numbers, and they did so, by and large, to make lives for themselves in this land of endless possibilities. Much has been made of the wild frontier that greeted them, with its violence, its lawlessness, and its "gun-totin'" heroes. Recent scholarship suggests, however, that at least as striking is the underlying "law-mindedness" of its people. Even on the Oregon Trail, cutting through the Central Plains in the 1840s, conduct was regulated by respect for lawful behavior. Constitutions were drawn up to define the rules of traveling, and the sanctity of private property was recognized, even though there was no formal legal machinery governing actions.

Later, during the settlement era, the Great Plains became essentially a ranching and farming frontier inhabited by three related but also distinct groups—cattle ranchers, sheep ranchers, and farmers—and the towns associated with them. It is their often-different needs, and the frequent friction between them, that provides an important backdrop for understanding much of the legal history of the Great Plains during the nineteenth century.

All three systems needed access to land and water. However, the different ways they needed access caused problems that often proved intransigent. The cattle ranchers, who were usually the first on the scene, expected and in fact needed free access to open rangeland and the region's limited water resources. If they had these, their often-huge herds could become the basis of a way of life and also of huge fortunes and great power. However, there were those who threatened all this. Sheep, which cattlemen believed cropped the land so thoroughly that it could not support cattle, and farmers, who plowed the prairie and fenced it in, were perceived as threats to the very survival of cattle ranching, and so the cattle ranchers resisted them (and were in turn resisted by them), resorting to both legal and extralegal means. The legal means included an appeal to appropriate political powers, seeking new laws and better enforcement of existing ones. For one side or the other, this could produce satisfaction or at least livable results. The gradual development of a body of law relating to water rights and water use is the best example of this and a case where the law continues to prove responsive to the ever-changing needs of the region.

The doctrine of riparian rights, whereby the owner of the land bordering a stream had the right to use its water, came west with the earliest settlers. This was, however, a thoroughly inappropriate system in the arid and semiarid lands of the Great Plains and was eventually replaced by what is called the "appropriative system." This system, which was largely put in place by the courts of the western states, protects users of water whether they are located near the source of water or not. The 1882 Colorado Supreme Court case, *Coffin v. Left Hand Ditch Company*, was a key decision in this transition. This approach to water rights and use, modified somewhat in the case of Native American water rights (see the 1908 decision of the Supreme Court in *Winters v. United States*, which reserved water rights for reservations from the time of their establishment), has also been adopted in Canada, though the active and controlling role of the provincial governments there has resulted in its being termed an "allocative system."

The law did not always provide an acceptable solution, however, and the sort of ranching operations that developed during the middle years of the nineteenth century had certain characteristics that meant that problems associated with lawlessness were virtually unavoidable. The best example is rustling, a problem that was met head-on by the ranchers. They could not keep their cattle under constant supervision (that was not compatible with open-range grazing), but they did brand them to establish ownership, and they could see to it that they and the men they hired to help manage their herds carried guns and were prepared to use them. This resort to "self-help" made sense in the absence of reliable policing, as did its elaboration in the form of vigilantism, a kind of cooperative self-help. Such tactics no doubt produced good results at times, but they also posed a danger, since the "might is right" approach could easily lead to excesses and abuses. A group of citizens rounding up rustlers and robbers seemed like a good thing, but without the protections afforded by a fully developed legal system mistakes were unavoidable, and sometimes the innocent suffered, not the guilty. And of course there was a dangerous seduction about the whole process that made armed men operating without the sanction of the law seem an acceptable solution to other perceived problems. The result at times was that weaker groups such as farmers and Chinese could also find themselves the targets of what was sometimes referred to as "rough justice"—something that usually had a lot of the former and very little of the latter.

Another focus of lawlessness during this period was the towns, especially those located at the end of the trails used to bring cattle to the railheads prior to shipping them to market. The end of a long drive brought to these towns a large number of men with money in their pockets and guns at their hips, anxious to blow off steam in the first saloon they'd seen for weeks. The results were predictable (though again, the lawlessness of the cattle towns has been overblown) and, in the eyes of the residents of such towns, highly undesirable. County sheriffs were rare, and townspeople could not rely on the comparatively few federal marshals, so in many cases the solution ultimately adopted was to hire a town marshal. The names of many of these have passed into history—and even into legend. In fact, job mobility between outlaws and marshals was high. Some men, like Wyatt Earp and Bat Masterson, walked both sides of the line. To be successful they had to be willing and able to meet force with force, and since they were usually paid, at least partially, according to the number of arrests made or fines levied, they tended to be extremely aggressive in their work. Their results were often crude, but the work of these men and of the few corporate bodies such as the Texas Rangers was all the more important in light of the virtual absence of proper courts and even the most rudimentary of prison facilities during the early years of settlement.

The Canadian Legal Frontier

During the nineteenth century the lands that were soon to form the Prairie Provinces began to fill with settlers, though much later (mainly after 1880) than was the case in the United States. This timing was important insofar as the legal history of the region is concerned, but it is only one of several factors that explain the significantly different legal culture of the Canadian Plains.

The Hudson's Bay Company, whose charter of 1670 granted the great trading company jurisdiction over a huge area and which extended a poorly defined body of England's laws to North America, was not originally active on the Great Plains. That region was at first completely unknown to Europeans and later was seen as little more than a hinterland of the rich fur-trapping land to the north, but as the trade progressed and as competition with Canadian and later American traders became progressively more fierce, the region was divided up by the company into jurisdictional units. The first rudiments of a justice system were established, notably as a result of English statutes of 1803 (the Canada Jurisdiction Act) and 1821 (An Act for Regulating the Fur Trade) and of the establishment of the Red River Colony by Lord Selkirk in 1811. The forced union of the English Hudson's Bay Company and the Canadian North West Company in 1821—the result of a famous breach of the law, the 1816 Seven Oaks Massacre—ended the worst of the violence that had come to characterize the trade and, more completely though not unambiguously, extended English law and legal institutions to the region. Even so, development of the law was still halting. Something approaching a full-fledged though very poorly functioning justice system did develop at Red River, which had been returned to the control of the Hudson's Bay Company by Lord Selkirk's heirs in 1834. But the Métis population of the colony never really accepted Hudson's Bay Company rule. Their open practice of selling robes and furs to American traders led to the Pierre-Guillaume Sayer trial in 1849. Sayer was found guilty of illegal trading, but, with 300 armed Métis protesting outside the courthouse, he was set free. The Hudson's Bay Company monopoly on trading was broken.

The antipathy of the company toward settlement, its desire to keep all costs to a minimum, and the sense that the days of the great monopoly trading companies were numbered all tended to prevent elaboration of the courts, prison facilities, and other institutions of the Red River Colony, with the result that when the area passed from the company's control to Canada in 1869, the new Dominion found itself inheriting a justice system that existed more in theory than in fact.

In taking up responsibility for these new lands, Canadian authorities had to respond to a number of needs: to avoid the mistakes of American policies, which were seen to have led to a great deal of violence and especially to the Indian Wars; to assert sovereignty against what was perceived to be an expansionist United States; to keep control over a fractious population, some of whom had recently taken up arms in an effort to safeguard their rights under the new political order; to prepare the region for settlement; and to do all this as cheaply as possible. The solution arrived at in 1873 was the creation of the North-West Mounted Police (NWMP), a body designed primarily to act as a police force (but some of whose members served as judges) and to provide prison facilities. The NWMP juggled these various roles effectively and ensured that a comparatively well-developed legal apparatus preceded settlement in most parts of the Canadian Prairies. However, having members perform every role from arresting officer, to witness, prosecutor, and judge, to jailer unavoidably left the NWMP open to accusations of conflict of interest and improper conduct. At times, especially when enforcing unpopular laws such as prohibition, the criticism could be fierce. Nonetheless, when the question of dissolving the NWMP was seriously raised in 1905 (the achievement of provincial status by Saskatchewan and Alberta meant that it was questionable whether a federally controlled police force could continue to operate in the West), a constitutional amendment was introduced to preserve what was, after all, an extremely popular and successful institution. And so the NWMP and the independent courts and prisons that had gradually appeared survived to become the basis of the provincial justice systems of the Canadian Prairies.

Twentieth-Century Developments
In both the American and Canadian sections of the Great Plains the late nineteenth century witnessed dramatic increases in population, the appearance of towns and cities, and the maturing of economies and important social institutions. These developments allowed the transformation of what had been, in a constitutional sense, territorial lands into states, in the case of the United States, and, by the beginning of the twentieth century, into provinces, in the case of Canada. This change was important in the legal sphere since it made the people of the Great Plains responsible to a much greater extent for their own legal institutions, though they were, of course, constrained in all cases by limits inherent in federal statutes. To a large extent, the outlines were already in place, and they were the base on which the future was built. All Great Plains jurisdictions inherited common-law traditions and the broadly similar structures and ways of proceeding those traditions implied. Law was to be made by democratically elected legislators and to a very limited extent by the courts. Courts, both courts of first instance and appeal courts, were to be presided over by judges who were to be impartial and independent and who were not to take a more active role in proceedings than necessary. (There is, however, an important difference between Canada and the United States here, since in Canada judges of all superior courts are appointed by the federal government.) Prisons, both local jails for those serving shorter sentences—generally less than two years—and penitentiaries for those serving longer terms, were there to punish, rehabilitate, and deter,

and they operated along broadly similar lines. Finally, in all states and provinces of the Great Plains, a variety of police forces existed to serve their communities.

These similarities have also extended to include some of the most important uses of law. One of the most long-lived examples of this has been the use of law, albeit not always successful, to protect the perceived collective interests of the inhabitants of the Great Plains. From the Progressives and others in the United States who, beginning in the 1890s, tried to use legal means to control the railways, financial institutions, and other large businesses that seemed to stand against the people's interest to the governments, especially on the Canadian Plains, that pursued some of these same or similar goals during the twentieth century, the Great Plains has produced some of the most significant legal initiatives on the continent (not the least of which is women's suffrage). It should be noted, however, that efforts to use the law to "protect" society have not always been so commendable, and one of the blackest marks on the record of the various Great Plains jurisdictions is the use majorities have made of the full apparatus of the law to deny equality to groups who have at different times been identified as posing a danger. Indigenous peoples had already suffered in this way, but as the nineteenth century came to an end and the twentieth century began other groups—Chinese, Germans, Japanese, and many others besides—were similarly mistreated. For example, all the American Plains states, except Colorado and the Dakotas, introduced "alien land laws" in the early 1920s directed at preventing Japanese Americans from owning land. This is a regrettable record for a region that in other respects—the early achievement of women's suffrage, for example—has been a leader in modern legal development.

Within these broadly similar outlines, however, there was still room for significant variation, which has, in some cases, tended to increase over time, especially when American and Canadian jurisdictions are contrasted. One good example of this is the generally different handling of mineral rights in the two countries. The origin of this difference is that in Canada mineral rights over much of the Great Plains region did not pass to settlers and instead remained vested in the government. This has meant that in Canada the provincial governments (especially since 1930, when the national government finally gave its remaining crown lands to the western provinces) have had a much more direct role to play in the development of extractive industries than is the case in the United States, and it is probably safe to say that there are more differences between Canadian and American law in this area than there are similarities. Moreover, it might be argued that this has contributed to a significantly different perception of the proper role for government in the economy and in society generally and therefore of the proper use of law.

Another instance where there is an apparent difference is in the approach to public pol-

icing. In the United States one encounters forces that serve towns and cities, counties, and states as well as various national bodies—a complex system with many intricacies involving separate and overlapping jurisdictions. In the Prairie Provinces there are only municipal police forces and the Royal Canadian Mounted Police, which is rented by the provinces and numerous smaller municipalities. (Provincial police are allowed under Canada's constitution but were found, after a brief experiment, to be too expensive. Moreover, their primary responsibility, enforcing prohibition, did not ensure their credibility.) However, any differences between Canada and the United States with respect to policing mask broad areas of agreement over questions such as what police ought to do (and not do) and what powers they need. It is probably also accurate to say that citizens of both countries share concerns about the limits that must be placed on police in a free society.

Contemporary Issues
The existence of a generally satisfactory legal system in the various jurisdictions of the Great Plains has not meant the end of the development of law or that no new challenges have arisen. One of the most important has been the question of individual rights and the limits freedom must place on the coercive power of the state. In the United States, individual rights have been guaranteed under the Constitution for more than two centuries, and the nature of these rights has been developed and elaborated by courts for most of that time. Such a process has been much less apparent in Canada, until comparatively recent times. But with the enactment of Canada's Charter of Rights and Freedoms in 1982 as well as provincial human rights legislation, Canadian courts have begun to develop an approach to individual rights that is in some ways reminiscent of the American model. Neither country, though, has been completely successful in identifying and protecting group rights, though things like protection of identified groups in rights legislation and in legal decisions, tribal control of the administration of justice on reservations in the United States, the move toward First Nations self-government in Canada, and the very recent innovation of sentencing circles in western Canada seem to indicate that an approach to law that recognizes that both individual and group rights can be accommodated within modern democratic states.

A second area where both differences and the beginnings of convergence can be detected is in the methods used to choose important officials in the justice system. The strongly democratic character of American selection procedures—either directly through such mechanisms as the election of judges, prosecutors, and high-ranking police officers or more indirectly through public confirmation hearings—has traditionally been rejected by Canadians. Recently, however, a movement, especially strong in western Canada, has begun pushing for a more public appointment process for Canada's judges. But while it seems

Sign behind bar in Birney, Montana, August 1941

likely that Canada's traditionally secretive process will soon undergo some reform, it is extremely unlikely that the final result will be closely modeled on American practices, nor does there seem to be any move to "democratize" other elements of the justice system. Instead, there appears to be more support for increasing the role of supervisory bodies such as police commissions, which have mainly civilian members, and corrective bodies, such as royal commissions, which have, with increasing frequency, been created to look at existing and past problems.

One last trend we might note here is a result of the popular perception of an increase in violent crime, despite statistics that show a steady decrease in such crimes over the last two decades or more. In the United States the response has been a huge increase in the prison population, reflecting higher conviction rates, a more frequent resort to prison time in sentencing, and longer sentences. The prison population in Canada has also increased recently, though to nothing like the degree it has in the United States. The fact that Canada has no death penalty is also a significant difference between the two countries. An important similarity, though, and a very worrying one, is the overrepresentation of minority groups in the region's prisons, be they Latinos, Native Americans, or African Americans in American prisons or Natives in Canadian prisons. This reflects the serious societal problems faced by these groups as well as the unequal treatment they receive from the justice system. Members of such groups are more likely than others to be charged, to be convicted, and to be sentenced to time in prison. They also tend to receive longer sentences. Addressing this problem will be one of the most important challenges of the twenty-first century on the Great Plains as in other parts of the United States and Canada.

See also AGRICULTURE: Branding / ASIAN AMERICANS: Asian-Exclusion Legislation; Poison Porridge Case; *Territory of New Mexico v. Yee Shun* / INDUSTRY: Hudson's Bay Company / NATIVE AMERICANS: Sovereignty / POLITICS AND GOVERNMENT: Forty-ninth Parallel / WATER: Appropriation Doctrine; Riparian Doctrine; Winters Doctrine.

Kenneth Leyton-Brown
University of Regina

Cutter, Charles R. *The Legal Culture of Northern New Spain, 1700–1810.* Albuquerque: University of New Mexico Press, 1995. Knafla, Louis, ed. *Law and Justice in a New Land: Essays in Western Canadian Legal History.* Toronto: Carswell, 1986. Llewellyn, K. N., and E. Adamson Hoebel. *The Cheyenne Way: Conflict and Case Law in Primitive Jurisprudence.* Norman: University of Oklahoma Press, 1941. McLaren, John, et al., eds. *Law for the Elephant, Law for the Beaver: Essays in the Legal History of the North American West.* Regina: Canadian Plains Research Center, 1992. Reid, John Phillip. *Law for the Elephant: Property and Social Behavior on the Overland Trail.* San Marino CA: Huntington Library, 1997. Richardson, June. *Law and Status among the Kiowa Indians.* Monographs of the American Ethnological Society, vol. 1. New York: J. J. Augustin, 1941. Wunder, John, ed. *Law and the Great Plains: Essays on the Legal History of the Heartland.* Westport CT: Greenwood Press, 1996.

ADAMS-ONÍS TREATY

See HISPANIC AMERICANS: Adams-Onís Treaty

ALBERT V. ALBERT

See GENDER: *Albert v. Albert*

ANTI–CORPORATE FARMING LAWS

Corporate farming has long been considered by some to be an economic, environmental, and social threat to family farmers. Advocates of diversified, family-owned and -operated farms point to fifty years of research that indicates that corporate agriculture leads to negative conditions in rural communities, including population decline, lower per capita income, fewer community services, and environmental pollution. During the 1930s, one response to the growth of large corporate farms in the Great Plains was the adoption of laws prohibiting corporations from owning farmland or participating in farming activities. The first such law was adopted in Kansas in 1931, followed shortly thereafter by one enacted in North Dakota in 1932.

In the 1970s other anti–corporate farming laws were adopted in Iowa, Minnesota, Missouri, Oklahoma, South Dakota, and Wisconsin. When Kansas and North Dakota enacted amendments to their anti–corporate farming statutes in 1981, the laws in all eight states became similar in content and form. Beginning in the mid-1970s, several attempts were made in the Nebraska legislature to pass an anti–corporate farming statute, but the efforts failed. As a result, a citizen petition was begun, and in November 1982 Nebraska became the first state to have its anti–corporate farming law placed in the constitution by citizens rather than adopted through statute by a legislature. In 1998 the citizens of South Dakota also amended their constitution through the petition process with an anti–corporate farming law patterned after Nebraska's.

While the anti–corporate farming laws in all nine states contain similar language and a variety of exemptions allowing certain corporations to engage in farming or to own farmland, the laws also differ considerably. For instance, the definition of a family farm corporation, whether the law allows so-called authorized farm corporations, and whether the law prohibits the ownership of livestock as well as farmland are all key issues in interpreting these laws. For instance, in Iowa there are few restrictions on who may qualify as a family farm corporation other than a requirement that 60 percent of the corporation's income must come from farming. But in Nebraska and South Dakota, one of the family members must either reside on the farm or be actively engaged in the day-to-day labor and management of the farm in order to qualify for an exemption.

Debate over the effectiveness and wisdom of anti–corporate farming laws has intensified in recent years as agriculture has become more specialized and concentrated, especially in livestock production. Opponents of anti–corporate farming laws claim the laws limit competition. Proponents of strong anti–corporate farming laws, however, argue that the tax advantages and limited liability available to corporations give them an unfair advantage over individual farmers. Family farm advocates contrast the growth of large, corporately owned operations in states without anti–corporate farming laws with the relative health of family farming in states such as Nebraska that have tough restrictions on corporate farms.

Controversy over anti–corporate farming

laws is expected to persist as the structure of agriculture continues to impact the well-being of rural communities throughout the Great Plains.

See also AGRICULTURE: Corporate Farming.

Nancy L. Thompson
South Sioux City, Nebraska

Pedersen, Donald B., and Keith G. Meyer. *Agricultural Law in a Nutshell*. St. Paul MN: West Publishing, 1995. Stayton, Brian F. "A Legislative Experiment in Rural Culture: The Anti-Corporate Farming Statutes." *UMKC Law Review* 59 (1991): 679–93. Thompson, Nancy L. *Raising Hogs in Nebraska Legally: A Farmer's Guide to Pork Production under Initiative 300*. Walthill NE: Center for Rural Affairs, 1998.

ASIAN-EXCLUSION LEGISLATION

See ASIAN AMERICANS: Asian-Exclusion Legislation

BEAN, JUDGE ROY (c. 1825–1903)

Judge Roy Bean, the legendary "Law West of the Pecos," operated a combination courthouse-saloon on the West Texas frontier near the junction of the Pecos River and the Rio Grande for more than twenty years. Bean was one of the most colorful, individualistic, and controversial personalities on the Great Plains. In terms of his place in American folklore, Bean has been compared to Davy Crockett, Mike Fink, and Paul Bunyan.

Roy Bean was born sometime between 1825 and 1830 in Mason County, Kentucky, to Francis and Anna Bean. At about the age of sixteen, Roy is said to have traveled to New Orleans, where, after alleged complicity in a major French Quarter brawl, he fled the Crescent City to avoid possible legal and extralegal repercussions. Later in his youth Bean reportedly helped run a saloon–trading post with his brother Samuel in Chihuahua, Mexico. There he killed a machete-wielding desperado who attempted to rob the saloon, and Bean once again found himself on the run when the outlaw's friends and relatives vowed revenge. He wound up in southern California sometime in 1850.

The accounts of Roy Bean's exploits in California are deeply imbedded in the state's folklore and early history. They reflect the romanticism of Old California and attempt to portray Bean as a bona fide folk hero, some kind of King Arthur–meets–Mike Fink figure. He is said to have fought a duel on horseback over the affections of the local young ladies of San Diego. After winning the contest and being jailed for dueling, Bean escaped, digging his way out with tools smuggled to him in tamales prepared by sympathetic local girls. Next, Roy Bean and his brother Joshua ran the Headquarters Saloon in San Gabriel, nine miles outside of Los Angeles, until 1852, when Joshua was murdered, allegedly by members of the Joaquín Murrieta gang. After leaving California in the mid-1850s, Bean married, had children, plied numerous trades, and became an embargo runner for the Confederacy on the Texas border during the Civil War.

The legend of Judge Roy Bean developed across the desolate regions of southwestern Texas in 1882, when he was nearly sixty. A shrewd businessman, Bean capitalized on the construction of the Southern Pacific Railroad by establishing a saloon-courthouse at a settlement called Vinegarroon and later at nearby Langtry. Contrary to popular belief, Bean was an authorized justice of the peace with the full power of the law and often a detachment of Texas Rangers to enforce his authority. He was supported by and served the interests of both the government and the wealthy ranch owners who sought increased law and order. Using the 1879 *Revised Statutes of Texas* as his legal guide, Judge Roy Bean performed marriages, held inquests, granted divorces, and tried horse thieves, drunks, and killers for two decades.

The true history of Judge Roy Bean is so intertwined with myth, legend, and folklore that it is difficult to separate fact from fiction. Some of the tales are memorable indeed: Bean fining a corpse $40 for "carrying a concealed weapon"; the large beer-drinking black bear that patrolled his courthouse-saloon and slept at the foot of his bed; his infatuation with the British actress Lily Langtry. (His saloon the Jersey Lily was named for her, but he lied when he wrote her that the town of Langtry, Texas, was named in her honor.) Judge Roy Bean died peacefully in his saloon from "excess of liquor" on March 19, 1903, and was buried at Del Rio, Texas. For better or worse, Judge Roy Bean has become an American folk hero, coming to symbolize the independent, strong, pragmatic, rugged frontier individual, able to stand up against the coarser natural and human elements and prevail.

Derrick S. Ward
Ventura, California

Lloyd, Everett. *Law West of the Pecos: The Story of Judge Roy Bean, the Original Manuscript*. San Antonio: Naylor Company, 1936. McDaniel, Ruel. *Vinegarroon: The Saga of Judge Roy Bean, the Law West of the Pecos*. Kingsport TN: Southern Publishers, 1936. Sonnichsen, C. L. *Roy Bean: Law West of the Pecos*. Lincoln: University of Nebraska Press, 1986.

BILLY THE KID (c. 1856–1881)

Billy the Kid was an outlaw whose legend has come to overshadow any personal or historical significance he may have had. It has not been satisfactorily documented when and where he was born, although it has been established that his actual name was Henry McCarty. In 1880 in Fort Sumner, New Mexico, McCarty (alias Billy Antrim, Henry Antrim, Kid Antrim, Billy Bonney, William H. Bonney, and Billy the Kid) told a federal census taker that he was twenty-five years old, that both of his parents had been born in Missouri, and that he too had been born there. There is no reason to believe he was lying. It can be documented that in 1866 he was living in Marion County, Indiana, with his mother, Catherine McCarty, and his elder brother, Joseph McCarty. Catherine McCarty suffered from tuberculosis, and this may have prompted her to move farther west. In 1873 Billy's mother married William H. Antrim in Santa Fe, New Mexico. Shortly after his mother's death in 1874, he took to wandering and spent two years as a general laborer, cowboy, and teamster in eastern Arizona.

Only four killings can be documented against the Kid. The first occurred in 1877 at Camp Grant, Arizona, when Billy shot and killed Frank "Windy" Cahill after an argument turned violent. The Kid was found guilty of "criminal and unjustifiable" shooting, but he escaped from custody and returned to New Mexico. The Kid's other killings resulted from his involvement in the Lincoln County War, a deadly feud involving local merchant and cattle interests. On one side stood Scottish lawyer Alexander McSween and John H. Tunstall, an Englishman who owned a cattle ranch in Lincoln County. On the other were James Dolan and Lawrence Murphy, merchants in the town of Lincoln. In January 1878 the Kid was working for Tunstall. When Tunstall was murdered by the Murphy-Dolan faction, the Kid and other Tunstall-McSween allies declared themselves "Regulators" and sought revenge.

For the next year bloody retaliatory warfare was waged between the two factions. In early March the Regulators arrested and then killed Dolan associates Frank Baker and Billy Morton, reportedly while the pair were trying to escape. At that point, territorial governor John Axtell declared the Regulators outlaws; after that they were hunted. On April 1, 1878, when Sheriff William Brady and Deputy George Hindman, both Dolan allies, tried to ambush McSween, the Regulators fought back and killed the lawmen. Three days later the Regulators battled "Buckshot" Roberts, a heavily armed bounty hunter, at Blazer's Mill. Roberts and Dick Brewer, a Regulator, were killed in the gunfight. The decisive battle of the Lincoln County War was fought during a five-day shoot-out in Lincoln in July 1878. Sniping went on for four days, with the Regulators trapped inside McSween's house. On the fifth day, after the ineffective U.S. Army arrived, McSween's home was set on fire, and the Kid led a rush out of the burning house. The Kid managed to escape, but McSween and several others were riddled with bullets.

Along with what was left of the Regulators, the Kid was outlawed for good. In December 1880 the newly elected sheriff of Lincoln County, Pat Garrett, and other lawmen captured the Kid at Stinking Springs. There were two federal indictments open against the Kid. The first was for killing Buckshot Roberts, the second was for the death of a clerk on the Mescalero reservation. The prosecution decided that both of these charges would probably result in acquittal, so it was decided to try the Kid for the murder of Sheriff Brady. The Kid was found guilty and sentenced to hang, but he escaped on April 28, 1881, after killing two guards. The Kid was shot to death on the night of July 14, 1881, killed by Pat Garrett during an ambush at old Fort Sumner.

Hundreds of books, motion pictures, radio programs, television programs, and even a ballet have subsequently been inspired by the legend of Billy the Kid. As a legend, the Kid is open to a variety of interpretations, principally as a good man who went bad, as a bad man who remained bad, as a good man who was falsely persecuted. Historians, too, have been guilty of using the Kid's life to prove some thesis or another about his true nature. None of this has anything to do, of course, with the historical Billy the Kid who probably killed only four men, generally in circumstances that might be conceived of as self-defense, and who was unfortunate enough to find himself on the losing side in a mercantile war.

See also WAR: Lincoln County War.

Jon Tuska
Golden West Literary Agency

Fulton, Maurice Garland. *History of the Lincoln County War.* Tucson: University of Arizona Press, 1968. Tuska, Jon. *Billy the Kid: His Life and Legend.* Albuquerque: University of New Mexico Press, 1997.

BONNIE AND CLYDE

Bonnie Parker and Clyde Barrow came of age during the Great Depression and ultimately led authorities on a deadly twenty-seven-and-a-half-month spree of robbery, abduction, and murder between 1932 and 1934. They represented a new breed of bandit: youths, predators really, traversing mostly rural parts of an America not too far removed from the preindustrial Old West but employing the technology of their age such as automatic weapons and automobiles.

Their robberies, though involving banks from time to time, consisted largely of petty thefts, often from grocery stores and filling stations. As thieves they held no notoriety, but as dangerously slippery fugitives, Bonnie and Clyde were something quite apart. Indeed, the inevitability that Clyde Barrow would open fire when cornered and probably succeed in shooting his way out of almost any situation, taking Bonnie with him, was the stuff upon which the legend of Bonnie and Clyde was based. The fact that they were young and by all accounts deeply in love added fuel to the legend. It has also contributed to the ongoing tendency to romanticize their deeds and misdeeds, which is unfortunate. There was nothing romantic about their lives—not for Bonnie and Clyde and certainly not for their victims.

By the time they died in a bloody hail of gunfire on May 23, 1934, Bonnie and Clyde were linked to the deaths of nine lawmen and four or five civilians, depending on the source. Of these, Clyde Barrow probably killed five, perhaps six. The rest were gunned down by accomplices like Joe Palmer, Henry Methvin, and Clyde's brother Buck. Interestingly, Bonnie Parker, despite her image, rarely handled weapons. In fact, there is no hard evidence that she ever shot anyone, except herself once, in the foot, while clowning around with one of Clyde's guns.

Bonnie Parker was born on the Plains on October 1, 1910, in the West Texas town of Rowena. Clyde Barrow was born on March 24, 1909, on the fringe of the Great Plains in Telico,

Bonnie and Clyde on a road between Dallas and Marshall, Texas, shortly after the car pictured was stolen, 1933

Texas, forty miles south of Dallas. There is some debate among family members as to whether he was born in 1909, as is usually cited, or in 1910, as recorded in the family Bible. Nevertheless, by 1922 both families were living in West Dallas, at the time an unincorporated slum of dirt streets and shotgun shacks located just across the Trinity River from downtown Dallas. It was there, at the home of a mutual friend, that Bonnie and Clyde first met. The year was 1930.

Two weeks later, Barrow, already quite involved in crime, was arrested and subsequently sentenced to fourteen years in the Texas penitentiary for burglary and auto theft. In 1932, because of prison overcrowding, he was issued a conditional pardon and released. He quickly rejoined Bonnie and for a time tried to go straight, working at a Dallas glass and mirror company while she waited tables at a cafe near the county courthouse.

Barrow's status as an ex-convict from West Dallas made him the inevitable target of random police roundups and incessant questioning. In March 1932 he was fired from his job because of the bad image he had acquired from being visited so frequently by the police. At that point, Barrow left town and took to crime with a vengeance, swearing he would never be taken alive. Initially, Bonnie accompanied Clyde only sporadically, but by mid-August 1932 she was with him almost constantly, vowing to die with him.

Although many of their more notorious crimes and gun battles took place beyond the Great Plains, Bonnie and Clyde were no strangers to that part of the country, ranging throughout the region from Mexico to Canada. On August 14, 1932, Bonnie and Clyde, along with a friend named Raymond Hamil-

ton, abducted a New Mexico deputy sheriff and drove him all the way to the Texas Hill Country. The lawman had pulled up to the Carlsbad home of Bonnie's aunt to take a closer look at what he correctly identified as a stolen car. Suddenly, he found himself staring down the bore of a shotgun and being loaded into the very car he was trying to investigate. Twelve hours later, the deputy was given a few dollars and released fifteen miles from San Antonio.

On June 10, 1933, Bonnie and Clyde and another cohort named W. D. Jones were involved in a grinding one-car wreck near the Texas Panhandle town of Wellington. Barrow and Jones were thrown free and miraculously escaped injury, but Bonnie was briefly trapped in the car and severely burned. When two lawmen arrived, Clyde and Jones abducted them both and transported them, along with the injured Bonnie, to Erick, Oklahoma, using the officers' own car. Bonnie survived her burns, but subsequently she could neither walk nor stand without some form of support.

Bonnie and Clyde frequently prowled Kansas, which, according to former gang member Ralph Fults, was the best bank-robbing state in the Union because of its numerous straight roads, each intersecting every mile or so with another road, creating a network of escape routes virtually impossible to seal off. Clyde Barrow robbed his first bank in Kansas along with Fults and Hamilton.

In September 1933 Barrow and another pair of accomplices tried to hijack a car from a group of people playing croquet in Meade, Kansas. A woman in the group attacked the outlaws with her mallet, clubbing and capturing one of Barrow's companions. Barrow and the third man managed to escape on foot. On April 29, 1934, Bonnie and Clyde stole a brand new Ford V-8 Deluxe from the driveway of Jesse and Ruth Warren in Topeka, Kansas. The car only had a few hundred miles on the odometer, but when it turned up a little more than three weeks later on a narrow dirt road eight miles south of Gibsland, Louisiana, it had been driven more than 6,000 miles, and Bonnie and Clyde were slumped in the front seat, bloodied and filled with bullet holes. They had finally fulfilled their vows, dying together, violently and in a car, a car stolen on the Great Plains.

John Neal Phillips
Dallas, Texas

Dallas Police Department, File #6048, Clyde Champion Barrow, Texas/Dallas Archives Division, Dallas Public Library. Phillips, John Neal. *Running with Bonnie and Clyde: The Ten Fast Years of Ralph Fults.* Norman: University of Oklahoma Press, 1996.

BREWER, DAVID (1837–1910)

David J. Brewer was born in Smyrna, Asia Minor, on June 20, 1837, the fourth child of Josiah and Amelia Brewer. Josiah was a Congregational missionary; Amelia was from the Field family of Massachusetts, one of the nation's prominent legal families. At the age of fourteen David entered Wesleyan College, then transferred to Yale after two years. He graduated fourth in his class in 1856. His focus was on becoming a lawyer, which led him to his uncle David's office in Albany, where he read law for a year. He then enrolled in Albany Law School and graduated in February 1858.

During law school, David Brewer became sympathetic to the abolitionist cause and opposed to the Kansas-Nebraska Act. The Dred Scott decision added to his frustration. He decided to forgo the security of his uncle's law office and seek his destiny at the focal point of the free-state/slavery conflict—Kansas Territory. He chose the thriving frontier town of Leavenworth as the place to practice law. Brewer's judicial career commenced with his election to probate judge in 1862. After two years in that office, he was elected district judge of Leavenworth and Wyandotte Counties. He took a two-year break from the judiciary in 1868 to be the county prosecutor, then was elected justice of the Kansas Supreme Court in 1870, serving until 1884. Justice Brewer wrote opinions on fraudulent county elections; fraudulent bonds in Comanche County issued before it was populated; bond issues for building railroads; railroad regulation; and the criminal conviction of a cattle rustler captured by Bat Masterson, sheriff at Dodge City. In a child custody case he established the precedent that the welfare of the child was controlling. He also fostered woman's rights by ordering that a woman could hold an elective office even though she could not vote.

David Brewer's work in courts and in the communities of Kansas brought him such favorable attention that in 1884 President Chester A. Arthur appointed him federal circuit court judge for the eighth circuit, comprising the states of Nebraska, Minnesota, Iowa, Missouri, Kansas, Colorado, and Arkansas. He served there until 1889. As circuit judge, Brewer handled a variety of cases. His most controversial decisions were the Wabash Railroad receivership and the injunctions he issued against labor unions. His most high-profile decisions were the Maxwell Land Company cases in New Mexico and Colorado.

When Justice Stanley Matthews of the U.S. Supreme Court died in 1889, President Benjamin Harrison appointed Brewer to the vacancy. He served on the Supreme Court until 1910, writing 533 majority opinions and 57 dissents and concurring in 8 cases. One of his most important decisions was in the Plains case *Kansas v. Colorado* (1904), the beginning of a continuing dispute over Arkansas River water. Here Brewer established some interstate common law in prescribing an equitable apportionment of benefits.

As a noted public speaker in great demand across the country, Justice Brewer was an outspoken advocate for peace. He made exceptions for the Civil War and Spanish-American War on the grounds they were for the noble causes of freeing the slaves and Cubans. He gave unselfishly of his time and dedicated his life to his beliefs. He was complex and sometimes paradoxical, but his faith in the individual was consistent. He thought the true end of government was the protection of the individual, since the majority has the power to take care of itself. He died on March 27, 1910, and was buried in Mount Muncie Cemetery, Leavenworth, Kansas.

Harold S. Herd
Washburn University School of Law

Broadhead, Michael J. *David J. Brewer: The Life of a Supreme Court Justice, 1837–1910.* Carbondale: Southern Illinois University Press, 1994.

BROWNELL, HERBERT, JR. (1904–1996)

Herbert Brownell Jr., attorney general under President Dwight Eisenhower from 1953–57, was born on February 20, 1904, in Peru, Nebraska. Brownell grew up in southeastern Nebraska and earned a bachelor's degree from the University of Nebraska in 1924. He left the Great Plains to attend law school at Yale University. Graduating in 1927, he was admitted to the bar in 1928 and immediately began practicing law in New York City, eventually entering the prestigious law firm of Lord, Day and Lord. Brownell also became involved in New York politics early in his career. At the age of twenty-eight he was elected to the New York assembly, representing Manhattan from 1933 to 1937. From 1938 to 1948 he managed Thomas Dewey's gubernatorial and presidential campaigns, and he briefly served as the chairman of the Republican National Committee (1944–45). During the 1952 presidential campaign, Brownell worked closely with Eisenhower, advising him on convention strategy and the selection of Richard Nixon as vice president. As a reward, President-elect Eisenhower nominated Brownell attorney general.

Brownell's work in the Justice Department revolved around two themes: anti-Communism and civil rights. As a staunch anti-Communist, Brownell resurrected spy cases and accused the Truman administration of being soft on Communism. He also protested a stay of execution for Julius and Ethel Rosenberg, targeted left-wing organizations, attacked labor unions, and proposed to Congress an array of anti-Communist legislation.

At the same time, however, Brownell, more than any other Eisenhower cabinet member, worked to further civil rights. It was Brownell's recommendation, for example, that led to the appointment of Earl Warren to the Supreme Court. Brownell also supported the Supreme Court's decision in *Brown v. The Board of Education of Topeka*. Brownell worked hard to push the Civil Rights Act of 1957 through Congress, which established a Civil Rights Commission and created the Civil Rights Division in the Justice Department. One of his most important accomplishments was advising Eisenhower to intervene and forcefully integrate Central High School in Little Rock, Arkansas.

Brownell resigned as attorney general in October 1957 and returned to private practice in New York City. He and his wife, Doris McCarter, whom he had married on June 16, 1934, in New York City, had four children. Herbert Brownell died on May 1, 1996.

See also POLITICS AND GOVERNMENT: Eisenhower, Dwight D.

Mark R. Ellis
University of Nebraska at Kearney

Brownell, Herbert, Jr., with John P. Burke. *Advising Ike: The Memoirs of Attorney-General Herbert Brownell.* Lawrence: University Press of Kansas, 1993. U.S. Department of Justice. *The Attorney Generals of the United States, 1789–1985.* Washington DC: Government Printing Office, 1985.

BROWN V. THE BOARD OF EDUCATION OF TOPEKA

Long before *Brown v. The Board of Education of Topeka* became part of the national legal landscape, African American parents were initiating court cases to challenge segregated public schools. The first documented school case took place before the Civil War. In 1849, in the case of *Roberts v. The City of Boston*, the Massachusetts courts denied Benjamin Roberts and other African American parents the right to enroll their children in certain Boston public schools. More than thirty years later, African American parents in Kansas took up the cause of gaining equal access to public schools. The free-state heritage, geographical location, and composition of its population positioned Kansas to play a central role in the major questions of educational freedom and equality. In 1868 state law allowed but did not require separate schools. Some schools admitted children without discrimination, and one of the first state superintendents of public instruction, Peter McVicar, vocally opposed segregated schools.

The arrival of the "Exodusters" from the South in the 1870s, however, hardened attitudes toward segregated schools in Kansas. Migration increased the African American population from 627 in 1860 to more than 43,000 by 1880. Because of community sentiment, some schools began to separate children by race. In 1879 the Kansas legislature passed a statute specifically allowing first-class cities (those with populations of 15,000 or more) to operate separate primary schools. This law remained in effect into the 1950s. With the exception of those in Wyandotte County, secondary schools were not segregated in Kansas. For a span of nearly seventy years, from 1881 to 1949, the Kansas Supreme Court became the venue for the constitutional question of public schools and segregation.

During that period the following cases were organized by African American parents across Kansas: *Elijah Tinnon v. The Board of Education of Ottawa* (1881); *Knox v. The Board of Education of Independence* (1891); *Reynolds v. The Board of Education of Topeka* (1903); *Cartwright v. The Board of Education of Coffeyville* (1906); *Rowles v. The Board of Education of Wichita* (1907); *Williams v. The Board of Education of Parsons* (1908); *Woolridge v. The Board of Education of Galena* (1916); *Thurman-Watts v. The Board of Education of Coffeyville* (1924); *Wright v. The Board of Education of Topeka* (1929); *Graham v. The Board of Education of Topeka* (1941); and *Webb v. School District No. 90, South Park, Johnson County* (1949). Individuals or small groups of parents appear to have acted on their own in the earliest cases. In later cases state and national strategies of the National Association for the Advancement of Colored People (NAACP) were clearly at work.

In response to numerous unsuccessful attempts to ensure access to equal opportunities for all children, African American community leaders and organizations stepped up their efforts to change public education. In the fall of 1950 members of the Topeka chapter of the NAACP agreed to challenge again the separate but equal doctrine applied to public education as a result of the 1896 United States Supreme Court ruling in the case of *Plessy v. Ferguson*. Chapter president McKinley Burnett, secretary Lucinda Todd, and attorneys Charles Scott, John Scott, and Charles Bledsoe developed the strategy for this challenge.

The three young attorneys for the Topeka NAACP were graduates of Washburn University and Washburn Law School in Topeka. Lucinda Todd had taught in one of the segregated African American schools but had resigned in keeping with the policy that did not permit married women to teach school. McKinley Burnett was a longtime community activist for the rights of African American people.

From 1948 to 1950 Burnett went before the Topeka School Board to persuade it to end the practice of segregated elementary schools since Kansas law permitted but did not require segregated public schools. The decision to challenge segregation in the courts was a measure of last resort for the NAACP.

The team of Burnett, Todd, Bledsoe, and the Scotts devised a plan that involved enlisting the support of fellow NAACP members and personal friends as plaintiffs in what would be a class action suit filed against the Board of Education of Topeka Public Schools. Lucinda Todd was the first to volunteer on behalf of her seven-year-old daughter. She was eventually joined by a group of twelve parents who agreed to participate on behalf of their children (nineteen children in all). Individuals in the Topeka case moved ahead, unaware that at the same time legal counsel for the NAACP headquarters in New York was representing plaintiffs in school cases from Delaware, Virginia, South Carolina, and Washington DC.

Children of the Topeka plaintiffs had to travel past and away from nearby schools to attend the four schools designated for African Americans. Topeka operated eighteen schools for white children and only four for African American children. In the fall of 1950 the thirteen parents were instructed by the NAACP to locate the white school closest to their home, take their child or children there along with a witness, and attempt enrollment. The parents were denied the right to enroll their children in these schools, a result that provided the attorneys with documentation to file suit. The NAACP case was filed in federal district court in February 1951. At that point, Oliver Brown, the only male among the roster of parents, was designated as lead plaintiff. With that designation, the case became known by his name. In

addition to Brown the plaintiff roster included Darlene Brown (no relation to Oliver), Lena Carper, Sadie Emmanuel, Marguerite Emmerson, Shirla Fleming, Zelma Henderson, Shirley Hodison, Maude Lawton, Alma Lewis, Iona Richardson, Vivian Scales, and Lucinda Todd.

Even though their case met with defeat, the testimony of expert witnesses firmly established that while educators in African American schools held more advanced degrees than their white counterparts, the school buildings for African American and white children in Topeka were substantially unequal. These findings set the stage for a challenge to segregation per se. Under the leadership of Presiding Judge Walter Huxman, who had once served as governor of Kansas, the federal district court ruled in favor of the Topeka Board of Education. Attorneys for the NAACP immediately filed an appeal with the U.S. Supreme Court.

When the Kansas case reached the Supreme Court it was combined with the other NAACP cases from Delaware, South Carolina, Virginia, and Washington DC. The combined cases became known by the Kansas case: *Oliver L. Brown v. The Board of Education of Topeka*. These cases were supported by the NAACP and its executive secretary, Walter White, and were litigated by the daunting legal team of Charles Bledsoe, Harold Boulware, Robert Carter, William T. Coleman, Jack Greenberg, Williams H. Hastie, George E. C. Hayes, Oliver Hill, Charles Hamilton Houston, Thurgood Marshall, James M. Nabrit Jr., Louis Redding, Frank Reeves, Spotswood Robinson, Charles S. Scott, John Scott, U. Simpson Tate, and Franklin Williams.

On May 17, 1954, at 12:52 P.M., the Supreme Court issued a unanimous decision. The Court's verdict was based on arguments presented in the lower courts by social scientists Louisa Holt and Kenneth Clark. As a consequence the Court declared that the separation of children in public schools for no other reason than race was a violation of the Fourteenth Amendment and therefore unconstitutional. In December 1955 the Court directed the country to implement its decision "with all deliberate speed." The Court's edict of 1955 became known as *Brown II*.

To this day, efforts continue in Kansas and across the country to realize the dream of the NAACP. In 1979 a group of attorneys was concerned that a Topeka Public Schools policy allowing open enrollment would lead to resegregation. The attorneys believed that with this type of choice white parents would shift their children to other schools, creating predominantly African American and predominantly white schools, and they petitioned the federal district court to reopen the original *Brown* case to determine if Topeka Public Schools had in fact ever complied with the Court's ruling of 1954. Their case became known as *Brown III*. The attorneys were Richard Jones, Joseph Johnson, and Charles Scott Jr. (son of one of the attorneys in the original *Brown* case) in association with Chris Hansen

from the American Civil Liberties Union in New York. In the late 1980s Topeka Public Schools were found to be in noncompliance. On October 28, 1992, after several appeals, the U.S. Supreme Court denied Topeka Public Schools' petition to once again hear the *Brown* case.

In the absence of another appeal, the Topeka Board of Education was directed by federal district court to develop plans for compliance. In response, three magnet schools were constructed to replace older buildings and expand neighborhood boundaries. These schools are excellent facilities and make every effort to be racially balanced. In recognition of the legacy of the 1954 decision, one of these new schools was named for the Scott family attorneys. Another was named for one of the city's leading African American teachers, the late Mamie Williams.

In 1988, in order to create a living tribute to the attorneys and plaintiffs in the original *Brown* case, the family of the late Oliver L. Brown and other community members in Topeka established the Brown Foundation for Educational Equity, Excellence, and Research. In 1990 the Brown Foundation sought to create a permanent place for the interpretation and commemoration of the landmark Supreme Court decision. On October 26, 1992, after two years of work by the Brown Foundation, President George H. W. Bush signed the *Brown v. The Board of Education* National Historic Site Act to commemorate the landmark Supreme Court Decision.

See also AFRICAN AMERICANS: Civil Rights; Exodusters; Scott Family / CITIES AND TOWNS: Topeka, Kansas.

Cheryl Brown Henderson
Brown Foundation

CATTLE CODES

Cattle laws on the Great Plains trace their origins and their defining elements to similar laws in the eastern United States. The main cattle laws, which are interdependent rules regulating the raising and marketing of livestock, govern fencing, branding, rustling, recording, and strays.

Fencing laws are of two types. The oldest of these, used in northern Europe as early as the fifth century, requires farmers to fence out animals to protect crops. The newer laws, which were adopted in more populated livestock areas beginning in the seventeenth and eighteenth centuries, require livestock owners to fence in their animals. At the time the United States became independent, fencing-in laws had been adopted in England as well as in Spain and its colonies but not in the former English colonies. When American cattlemen came to the Great Plains in the nineteenth century, they brought with them the fencing-out laws of the eastern United States, and they ignored the fencing-in laws that had previously prevailed under Spanish and Mexican rule in Texas and New Mexico.

Although branding was never followed in England, it was a common practice in the English colonies and in the eastern United States after independence. It was similarly used in the Spanish colonies and in Mexico after its independence. However, unlike the practice in Spain and Mexico, livestock owners in the eastern United States were required to use a system of town brands, in addition to their own personal brands, to identify the origin of their animals. Cattle in Salem, Massachusetts, for example, had to be branded with an "S." This same system was adopted on the Great Plains; for instance, the first branding law adopted in Colorado required cattle from Arapaho County to carry an "A" brand.

The parentage of the Great Plains cattle-rustling laws can be traced to the eastern United States because of an anomaly originally peculiar to the rustling law of North Carolina. To convict an individual of altering a cattle brand, North Carolina required a prosecutor to first prove that the original brand was recorded. This same requirement was later adopted in Texas, Colorado, and other parts of the American West. Laws in Texas similarly made illegal the stealing of "neat cattle" and the "altering or defacing" of another's brand. Both of these expressions were copied from statutes in the East.

Early Great Plains recording statutes followed procedures used in the East. As the English had done since medieval times, easterners relied on a toll system for proving ownership of livestock. Anyone moving cattle from one county to another had to register his individual brands in the county he was moving them to. Also, driving cattle without a certified bill of sale (one endorsed by certain town, county, or state officials) was similarly illegal.

Estray statutes, like fencing laws, are of two kinds: those that require finders to advertise found animals and those that require owners to advertise lost animals. In 1747 South Carolina adopted the first estray statute requiring finders to advertise in newspapers of general circulation, a requirement common to all later American estray statutes, including those adopted by Great Plains states. The Spanish colonies and Mexico after its independence used the second kind of estray statute, with one exception. When the Mexican state of Coahuila and Texas adopted a new estray statute in 1835, it required finders to advertise, a procedure familiar to the many American colonists who had recently moved to Texas. When Texas became independent the next year, it kept the "finders must advertise" statute adopted by Coahuila and Texas the year before.

See also AGRICULTURE: Branding.

Ray August
Washington State University

August, Ray. "Cowboys v. Rancheros: The Origins of Western American Livestock Law." *Southwestern Historical Quarterly* 96 (1993): 457–88. Myres, Sandra L. "The Ranching Frontier: Spanish Institutional Backgrounds of the Plains Cattle Industry." In *Essays on the American West*, edited by Harold M. Hollingsworth and Sandra L. Myres. Austin: University of Texas Press for University of Texas at Arlington, 1969: 19–39.

CIVIL RIGHTS

See AFRICAN AMERICANS: Civil Rights

COFFEYVILLE RAID

On October 5, 1892, five dusty horsemen walked their horses through the bustling streets of Coffeyville, Kansas. Dick Broadwell and Bill Powers were professional bandits. The other three men were brothers, Bob, Grat, and Emmett Dalton. All five had bank robbery on their minds.

Bob and Grat had been lawmen briefly, and their elder brother, Frank, had been a well-known U.S. deputy marshal, killed in 1887 in the line of duty while riding for "hanging judge" Isaac Parker. Most of the fifteen Dalton kids turned out well, but for Bob, Grat, and Emmett the lure of easy money was too strong, and it would cost them dearly.

The Dalton boys knew Coffeyville well, for their family had lived nearby ten years before, and so they were surprised to find that Coffeyville's passion for civic improvement had frustrated part of the gang's plans: as part of a design to build gutters and sidewalks, the city fathers had removed the hitching rail to which the outlaws had intended to tether their horses. The gang tied their mounts to a pipe in a narrow alley behind the police judge's house, pulled their Winchesters from their saddle scabbards, and walked down the alley toward Coffeyville's central plaza and the town's two banks.

The gang had enjoyed a brief run of success, with four train robberies in Indian Territory just to the south, but now the law was close behind them. On their last raid, on the Kansas-Texas (Katy) division of the Missouri Pacific Railroad, at Adair, the gang had shot a doctor who did no more than watch them gallop out of town. Now every man's hand was against them, and Bob, the gang's leader, was determined to make one big strike and travel on, far and fast.

They would hit two banks at once, Bob boasted, something not even their famous cousins, the Younger brothers, had ever done, but the raid went bad from the start. In spite of wearing false mustaches and beards, the Daltons were recognized as they walked across the plaza. As Bob and Emmett pushed into the First National Bank and Grat, Powers, and Broadwell entered the Condon Bank, the citizens of Coffeyville armed themselves.

Nobody carried a gun in peaceful Coffeyville, including the town marshal, but two hardware stores had plenty of weapons and handed out guns to anybody who wanted one. There were plenty of takers. Meanwhile, inside the First National, Bob and Emmett forced the staff to hand over more than $20,000. But in the Condon, a young bank teller convinced Grat that the safe—long since unlocked—was on a time lock and could not be opened for ten more minutes. Grat was still staring at the safe when his brothers left the First National and a citizen fired at them.

In the firefight that followed, four townsmen and four bandits died. Young Emmett was the sole survivor of the gang, and he was shot almost to pieces. The local doctor fended off a lynch mob intent on hanging Emmett by telling them that the outlaw would surely die of his wounds. "Are you sure, Doc?" somebody asked. "Hell yes," said the physician. "Did you ever know one of my patients to live?" Somebody laughed, the tension broke, and Emmett survived to spend fifteen years in the Kansas State Penitentiary.

Another brother, Bill, would join gang members who had not participated in the Coffeyville raid. These men carried on the gang's lawless career until all of them, including Bill Dalton, were run down and killed by lawmen.

Robert B. Smith
University of Oklahoma

Barndollar, Lue Diver. *What Really Happened on October 5, 1892.* Coffeyville KS: Coffeyville Historical Society, 1992. Smith, Robert Barr. *Daltons! The Raid on Coffeyville, Kansas.* Norman: University of Oklahoma Press, 1996.

DAWES ACT

Formally titled the General Allotment Act of 1887, the Dawes Act (also commonly referred to as the Dawes Severalty Act) authorized the president of the United States to subdivide tribal reservations into private parcels of land that would then be "allotted" to individual members of each tribe. Designed to detribalize Indians and assimilate them into mainstream white society by transforming them into self-supporting farmers and ranchers, the Dawes Act became one of the most far-reaching and, for Native Americans, disastrous pieces of Indian legislation ever passed by Congress. By the time the allotment process was stopped in 1934, the amount of Indian-held land in the United States had dropped from 138 million acres to 48 million acres, and, of the remaining Indian-owned land, almost half was arid or semiarid desert.

Under the act, heads of families received quarter-section parcels of 160 acres, while other individuals were granted smaller tracts of up to 80 acres. Allotments deemed to be suitable only for grazing were doubled in size. Once the president directed that a particular reservation be broken up pursuant to the act, tribal members were given four years to select their specific allotment. If no such selection was made, the government made the selection for the individual. Each allotted tribal member received a patent, or trust deed, which provided that the United States would hold title to the land in trust for the benefit of the nominal Indian "owner" for a period of twenty-five years. Proponents of the legislation envisioned that during the trust period Indian allottees would adapt to the farming lifestyle and become increasingly self-reliant through the ownership and control of private property. Perhaps most significantly, the act further provided that tribal lands that were unallocated and therefore deemed "surplus" could be offered for sale to non-Indians, with the revenues to be held in trust by the government for the benefit of the tribes.

The Dawes Act affected reservations throughout the Great Plains, except in Indian Territory, which was not subject to allotment until the establishment of the Dawes Commission in 1893 and the passage of the Curtis Act in 1898. For example, the Devils Lake Sioux Reservation in North Dakota was allotted in 1904 over the objections of many of its residents. The allotments amounted to about 136,000 acres, leaving 92,000 surplus acres to be sold to non-Indians. It was through the allotment process that Plains reservations became "checkerboarded" in complex patterns of white-owned private property and Indian trust lands.

Most modern commentators concede that the proponents of the Dawes Act, including its primary legislative sponsor and namesake, Senator Henry L. Dawes of Massachusetts, were motivated by a sincere interest in the well-being and future prosperity of Native Americans. "Reformers" inside and outside the government viewed tribalism and traditional Indian cultural practices as impediments to the long-term survival and "advancement" of Native Americans—obstacles that could only be overcome by breaking up the reservations and forcing Indians to adopt a more "civilized" lifestyle. Other analysts insist that allotment was never intended to be anything more than a disingenuous legal cover for whites who coveted Indian lands. Whatever the appropriate interpretation of the motivations behind the Dawes Act, the allotment era that the act ushered in is today universally viewed as one of the darkest chapters in the annals of federal-Indian relations. Individual landownership was and is contrary to most traditional Native American beliefs and practices. Moreover, many Indians had no desire to become sedentary farmers and were woefully unprepared and ill equipped to succeed in that occupation even if they had wanted to. The value of the parcels of thousands of allottees was quickly dissipated or lost entirely through tax foreclosures, distressed sales, or unfavorable lease arrangements. Millions of surplus acres were sold or leased away by the government as well, and the ultimate effect of the allotment program was to separate Native Americans from millions of acres of their lands without accomplishing any of the "reforms" intended by the act's proponents.

See also NATIVE AMERICANS: Allotment; Assimilation Policy; Reservations.

Mark R. Scherer
University of Nebraska at Omaha

Prucha, Francis Paul. *The Great Father: The United States Government and the American Indians*. Lincoln: University of Nebraska Press, 1986. Washburn, Wilcomb. *The Assault on Indian Tribalism: The General Allotment Law (Dawes Act) of 1887*. Philadelphia: J. B. Lippincott, 1975. Wunder, John R. *Retained by the People: A History of American Indians and the Bill of Rights*. New York: Oxford University Press, 1994.

EX PARTE CROW DOG

In 1883 the U.S. Supreme Court rendered a decision in *Ex Parte Crow Dog* that reaffirmed a basic promise of federal law as it dealt with the Native American nations: that these nations are political sovereigns and have a right to be ruled by their own law in their own land. Within three years the same Court would break that promise, just as the political branches of the government had broken treaties. Nevertheless, *Ex Parte Crow Dog* remains a foundational case for the tradition of legal pluralism that is today manifested in the laws and institutions of Native American sovereigns.

On the afternoon of August 5, 1881, Kangi Sunka (Crow Dog) shot and killed Sinte Gleska (Spotted Tail) on a road in the Rosebud Indian Agency on the Great Sioux Reservation in Dakota Territory. Both men were respected among the Brulé Lakota. At the time of his death Spotted Tail was attempting to maintain a homeland for his people as both a traditional chief and a leader recognized by the Bureau of Indian Affairs (BIA). Crow Dog had ridden with Crazy Horse yet also served several terms as a BIA-appointed chief of Brulé police. The complex forces of culture and politics that pitted these two men as enemies remain a mystery. The facts of their encounter are still disputed: was it assassination or self-defense?

After the death of Spotted Tail the tribal council met and, following Brulé law, sent peacemakers to both families to restore harmony and order. The families agreed to a payment of $600 and gifts of eight horses and one blanket, which were quickly delivered to Spotted Tail's people. Nevertheless, in contravention of prior policy that had honored Native American self-government, Henry Lelar, the acting agent at Rosebud, ordered the arrest of Crow Dog. He was quickly arrested and imprisoned at Fort Niobrara, Nebraska.

Crow Dog's trial in federal court, Dakota Territory, was tainted by strong anti-Indian prejudice. The lead prosecution witness, Agent John Cook, was in Chicago when the killing occurred, but he testified to Crow Dog's political animosity. Crow Dog, ably represented by attorney A. J. Plowman, was allowed to present his claim of self-defense, but Pretty Camp, his wife and an eyewitness, was not allowed to testify. Moreover, there is unsettling evidence of perjury. But all of this factual controversy is beside the point. The claim of federal jurisdiction, the legal power to make and apply law for Indian-to-Indian matters within Indian Country, is the crux of the matter, and the conviction and death sentence given Crow Dog brought the issue to the Supreme Court.

By writ of habeas corpus Crow Dog urged the Supreme Court to deny federal jurisdiction in the matter. At the same time, the BIA and the prosecution, which had orchestrated the arrest and trial as part of a plan conceived as early as 1874 to extend federal law into Indian Country, argued that treaties and statutes provided federal jurisdiction. The federal government made the following argument: section 5339 of the *Revised Statutes* provides for the death penalty for any murder within the jurisdiction of the United States; title 28 extends the general law of the United States to Indian Country, but it has an exception for crimes committed by one Indian against another Indian; that exception was repealed by the treaty of Fort Laramie (1868), which provided that "bad men among the Indians" shall be delivered to the United States; and the act of 1877 (Congress had prohibited further treaty making with Native Americans in 1871) provides that Congress shall "secure to [the Sioux Nations] an orderly government; [and] they shall be subject to the laws of the United States."

The Supreme Court rejected the government's argument, stating that such an understanding would reverse an unbroken policy of respect for Native American sovereignty. First, if "bad men" were not delivered, the treaty called for deductions from annuities due the Lakotas; thus it could not mean "bad men" who acted against other Sioux. Second, the statutory promise of "orderly government" meant a pledge of self-government for the Sioux. Finally, to be "subject to the laws of the United States" meant subject to the power of Congress to make federal Indian law for distribution of sovereignty between Native Americans and the United States, not subject as individuals to the generality of federal law. Crow Dog was granted his release.

Crow Dog returned to the Rosebud Agency. He remained a leader among the Brulé, taking Ghost Dancers into the Badlands in 1890 and refusing an allotment until 1910. The BIA repeatedly sought his removal from the Rosebud Agency. He died there in 1912.

Yet *Ex Parte Crow Dog* was tainted by racism. Its concluding language referred to Native Americans living a "savage life" and having a "savage nature," and it described Native American law as the "red man's revenge." This played into the hands of the Interior Department and the BIA, which had since the late 1870s urged Congress to pass a statute extending federal law to Indian-on-Indian crimes within Indian Country. Two years after *Ex Parte Crow Dog* Congress passed the Major Crimes Act of 1885. The act cut deeply into the promises of self-government and sovereignty by creating federal jurisdiction over seven enumerated crimes when committed by one Indian against another Indian. (Today the statute covers fourteen crimes.)

A year later, in *United States v. Kagama* (1886), the Supreme Court upheld the legality of the act. The Court found a "duty of protection" arising from the "weakness and helplessness" of the Native Americans that granted Congress power despite the lack of any constitutional authority. Civilization was brought to Indian Country in the form of punishment, retribution, violence, and isolation of wrongdoers. The plenary power of Congress over Native American affairs was affirmed, and the people witnessed again the fragile nature of legal promises.

See also NATIVE AMERICANS: Spotted Tail.

John Rockwell Snowden
University of Nebraska–Lincoln

Harring, Sidney L. *Crow Dog's Case*. Cambridge: Cambridge University Press, 1994.

FEMALE EMPLOYMENT ACT

See ASIAN AMERICANS: Female Employment Act

HALL, EMMETT (1898–1995)

Born at St. Colomban, Quebec, on November 9, 1898, Emmett Matthew Hall moved to Saskatoon, Saskatchewan, with his family at age twelve. Later, he studied law at the University of Saskatchewan (he was a classmate of John Diefenbaker), graduating at age twenty-one. While Diefenbaker was prime minister, Hall was elevated to chief justice of Saskatchewan (1961) and to Canada's Supreme Court, where he served from 1962 until his retirement in 1973 at age seventy-five.

This record only partially defines the man, for Emmett Hall served Canada in a wide range of roles. By 1962, with Saskatchewan premier Tommy Douglas, he had developed a comprehensive plan for publicly supported medical care. Diefenbaker then asked him to chair a royal commission on health services, overcome resistance on the part of the medical profession, and design a system of universal health care for all of Canada. Hall's 1964–65 *Report of the Royal Commission on Health Services* was implemented in 1967 under Prime Minister Lester B. Pearson.

While Hall made his mark as the father of medicare, he also reported on primary and secondary school education in Ontario (1968), university organization and structure (1973), railway arbitration (1973), as well as grain handling and transportation (1974). Furthermore, he was a popular and involved chancellor at the University of Guelph (1971–77) and at the University of Saskatchewan (1980–86).

At the time of his death on November 12, 1995, at age ninety-six, Emmett Hall was recognized as an outstanding Canadian. When he retired from the Supreme Court, he was appointed a Companion of the Order of Canada (1974)—the highest honor bestowed by Canada—for his lifetime of service to the law, health services, and education. Hall's incomparable commitment and energy are apparent in the fact that so many of his contributions in health care and education came when he was seventy to eighty-five years old. Modern Canadian society, in large measure, is shaped by the vision of this one man.

See also POLITICS AND GOVERNMENT: Diefenbaker, John.

Linda M. Gerber
University of Guelph

HASKELL, ELLA KNOWLES (1860–1911)

On a December evening in 1889, after Cornelius Hedges and two other Montana lawyers had conducted an unusual bar exam, Hedges wrote in his diary, "Examined Miss Knowles for admission to the Bar and was surprised to find her so well read. She beat all that I have ever examined." Ella Knowles Haskell might have enjoyed that assessment had she ever read it, because the words summarized her life.

Born July 31, 1860, in Northwood Ridge, New Hampshire, Ella Knowles became a woman of many firsts. She would be the first woman to become a lawyer in Montana, the first woman to run for a major political party for state attorney general, and probably the first woman to serve as an assistant state attorney general and represent a state before a state supreme court.

Ella's early years were spent in New Hampshire and Maine, where she embraced education and sought to expand women's rights. At age twenty she entered Bates College as one of its first women students. She graduated in 1884 magna cum laude and started to read law in a New Hampshire law office.

Ella Knowles then developed an illness for which she was advised to move West. In 1888 she arrived in Helena, Montana, and thereafter claimed Montana as her permanent home. After teaching for a year in Helena, she resolved to begin preparing for a legal career by reading law with local attorney Joseph W. Kinsley. In order to practice law, however, Ella had to persuade the Montana territorial legislature to change Montana's law that restricted legal practice to men, and then she needed to pass a bar exam. In February 1889 the legislature revised its laws to allow women to practice law, and that December Ella Knowles easily passed her bar exam.

Knowles opened her own law office in 1891. She prevailed in her first case, suing a black restaurant owner in justice of the peace court on behalf of a Chinese client who had been employed in the restaurant and cheated out of $5 of back wages.

Ella Knowles quickly made a reputation as a progressive and energetic lawyer, and it resulted in her nomination in 1892 by the Populist Party to run for attorney general. Although she came in a close third, losing to Republican incumbent Henri Haskell, she garnered more statewide votes than any other Populist candidate. Prior to the campaign, Haskell had gained authorization to hire an assistant attorney general, and after the campaign he offered the position to Ella Knowles. She accepted and proceeded to represent the state in public lands issues, and she defended the state's anti-Chinese legislation before the Montana Supreme Court. In May 1895 Ella Knowles married Haskell, and as Ella Knowles Haskell she continued to represent the state of Montana until her husband's term expired in 1896.

During these years Ella was active politically. In 1896 she was chosen president of the Montana Women Suffrage Association. That same year she was selected to attend the Populist Party's national convention in Omaha. She went on the stump for William Jennings Bryan in both the 1896 and 1900 presidential campaigns.

In 1897 Ella divorced Henri Haskell and relocated eventually in Butte, where she hung up her shingle once again. Over the next fourteen years she became an expert on mining law, corporate law, and property law. She also accumulated significant wealth from investments in mines and from her corporate work and continued to lecture on woman's rights in Montana, the Great Plains, and the West.

On January 27, 1911, Ella Knowles Haskell died from an infection at her home in Butte at the young age of fifty.

John R. Wunder
University of Nebraska–Lincoln

Larson, T. A. "Montana Women and the Battle for the Ballot." *Montana: The Magazine of Western History* 28 (1973): 24–41. Roeder, Richard B. "Crossing the Gender Line: Ella L. Knowles, Montana's First Woman Lawyer." *Montana: The Magazine of Western History* 32 (1982): 64–75. Wunder, John R. "Law and Chinese in Frontier Montana." *Montana: The Magazine of Western History* 30 (1980): 18–31.

IN COLD BLOOD

In Cold Blood is the compelling and controversial account of the brutal murder of Herb, Bonnie, Nancy, and Kenyon Clutter inside their farmhouse near Holcomb, Kansas, on November 15, 1959, and of their murderers, Richard Eugene Hickock and Perry Edward Smith. Truman Capote's Edgar Award–winning work catapulted him to the peak of his career with its release in 1965. The country was still recovering from the rampage of mass killer Charles Starkweather in Nebraska and Wyoming (he was executed on June 25, 1959) when another horrible slaying traumatized the nation's heartland. The innocence associated with rural America was shattered, and the phrase "it can't happen here" seemingly did not apply anymore.

Shortly after reading about the killing of the Clutter family, Capote, accompanied by his childhood friend, author Harper Lee, traveled to Holcomb on assignment for the *New Yorker* to do his investigative research. He interviewed Dick Hickock and Perry Smith after they were captured in Las Vegas, Nevada, and returned to the Finney County jail. Capote followed their lives for more than five years, from the trial in Garden City and subsequent conviction for first-degree murder, through the numerous appeals, and ultimately to their execution on April 14, 1965, at the state penitentiary in Lansing, not far from where Hickock had grown up in Olathe. Capote watched Hickock die; however, he had grown much too close to Smith, a mixed-blood Western Shoshone from Nevada, to witness his execution, and he ran from the building where the hangings were staged.

The fascination with what transpired that night outside Holcomb in remote southwestern Kansas and the events that followed continues unabated. Within two years after Capote's work was published, a motion picture by the same name was released. The "semidocumentary," directed by Oscar-winner Richard Brooks, received four Academy Award nominations in 1968. More recently, a TV movie aired in 1996, and the A&E Channel featured the Clutter murders and *In Cold Blood* in its *American Justice* series.

In 1997 Doubleday published George Plimpton's book *Truman Capote*. Plimpton, in focusing on Capote through the eyes of those who knew him prior to his death in 1984, explored the author's motives in creating what he claimed was a new genre, the "nonfiction novel." The Modern Library in 1999 ranked *In Cold Blood* 96th among its top 100 nonfiction books.

Guy Louis Rocha
Nevada State Library and Archives

Algeo, Ann M. *The Courtroom as Forum: Homicide Trials by Dreiser, Wright, Capote and Mailer.* New York: P. Lang, 1996. Capote, Truman. *In Cold Blood: A True Account of a Multiple Murder and Its Consequences.* New York: Random House, 1965. Plimpton, George. *Truman Capote: In Which Various Friends, Enemies, Acquaintances, and Detractors Recall His Turbulent Career.* New York: Nan A. Talese/Doubleday, 1997.

INDIAN CLAIMS COMMISSION

In 1946, after decades of periodic debate, the United States established the Indian Claims Commission to give Native Americans their "day in court." The commission operated until 1978. Native American tribes and bands were given five years to register claims with the commission, claims relating to past injustices of federal Indian policy, including lands illegally taken, lands taken for "unconscionably low" compensation, and the government's misuse of Indian monies. Most Native American groups did register claims, and many claims were upheld, but ultimately there was little justice delivered in the process.

The Indian Claims Commission, comprised of three (later four) judges appointed by the president, actually functioned as a court that heard arguments of two adversaries—the Native American claimants and the United States as defendant—and then passed judgment. Awards were monetary only; return of land was expressly excluded. In a typical claim involving land, the Native American claimants had first to prove title to that land, then show that the original compensation paid (generally during the nineteenth century) was significantly below its fair market value at the time of taking. The difference between the fair market value and the original compensation (minus lawyers' fees and other offsets) constituted the award. Once an award was accepted or a case dismissed, then that claim was dead forever. Despite platitudes about "belated justice," the United States primarily intended this to be a wiping clean of the slate of outstanding claims as a prelude to termination—the prevailing policy to eliminate tribes as a separate factor in American society.

Altogether, by the deadline, 176 tribes and bands lodged 370 claims, which were separated into 617 dockets. Plains tribes were well represented. From the Lipan Apaches of southern Texas to the Blackfeet and Gros Ventres of northern Montana and from the Omahas of eastern Nebraska to the Crows of Wyoming, Plains Indians took their grievances to the commission.

In all, eighteen Plains tribes and nations lodged claims. The largest award, $35,060,000 for land primarily in West Texas, went to the Kiowas, Comanches, and Apaches in 1974. Other sizable awards included $15 million (1965) to the Cheyennes and Arapahos for lands in northeastern Colorado and adjacent Wyoming, Nebraska, and Kansas; and $10,242,984 to the Crows (1954) for their traditional homelands in Wyoming and Montana. The smallest award—$2,458—was made to the Poncas of Nebraska in 1965 for an accounting claim. In the most notorious case, involving the Lakotas' (Sioux) 1877 cession of the Black Hills, the Indian Claims Commission's award of $17.5 million (without interest) was appealed and eventually reached the Supreme Court, which ruled in 1980 that, because the taking was unconstitutional, not just inadequate, the Lakotas merited interest on the award from 1877 on. Their award, accumulating to more than $600 million by the late 1990s, sits unclaimed in the U.S. Treasury; the Lakotas want their sacred Black Hills back, not a monetary settlement.

On close analysis, even sizable awards diminished to small payments when they were allocated to individual Native Americans. (Sometimes awards were put into tribal investments, but this was often contentious, because the tribal members who did not reside on reservations would not benefit from reservation development.) The Pawnees of central Nebraska, for example, were awarded $7,316,096 in 1964, largely for lands that had been taken in the nineteenth century for unconscionably low compensation. Of this, the lawyers took $876,897 for fees and expenses, leaving $6,439,199. In March 1964 the tribal council voted to distribute the award (with a small amount of accrued interest) on a per capita basis to the 1,883 enrolled members of the tribe. Each Pawnee received about $3,530—no doubt a boon in (always) hard times, but hardly a redress of past injustices. The Omahas, the Pawnees' traditional neighbors, received even less ($750 for each tribal member) in their 1960 settlement, and each Yankton Sioux accepted $249 in 1960 as a reward for enduring ten years of litigation in their land claims case.

The Indian Claims Commission, therefore, should be viewed more as a continuation of the past than a break from it. As in the nineteenth century, most Plains Indians (and Native Americans elsewhere in the country) felt obliged to accept the United States' definition of what constituted justice. At no stage of the litigation process before the Indian Claims Commission was the value that Plains Indians placed on their lands as homelands taken into account.

David J. Wishart
University of Nebraska–Lincoln

Indian Claims Commission. *Final Report.* 96th Cong., 2nd sess., 1980, H. Doc. 96–383. Lieder, M., and J. Page. *Wild Justice: The People of Geronimo vs. the United States.* New York: Random House, 1997. Sutton, I., ed. *Irredeemable America: The Indians' Estate and Land Claims.* Albuquerque: University of New Mexico Press, 1985.

INDIAN POLICE

Indian police forces first appeared on the Great Plains during the 1830s, when the federal government relocated eastern tribes such as the Cherokees to Indian Territory. Known as the Lighthorse, Cherokee police units performed law enforcement duties similar to their European American counterparts of the period. During the 1860s and 1870s Indian agents throughout the American West began to organize police forces to protect reservations from cattle and horse rustlers, timber thieves, and liquor peddlers. In 1862, for example, the Bureau of Indian Affairs (BIA) agent at the Pawnee Agency in Nebraska created a police force to curb horse thefts. Agents at Red Cloud and Spotted Tail Agencies in northwestern Nebraska created similar forces during the 1870s. These police forces operated autonomously, without federal approval or funding. This changed in 1878, when Congress legitimized Indian police forces by providing funds and operational guidelines. BIA agents quickly organized Native police forces, in part because this increased their influence over reservation affairs and removed the need for military troops. By the end of 1878 police forces operated at twenty-two agencies. Three years later forty-nine of sixty-eight agencies had police forces, and by 1890 the number had risen to fifty-nine.

Indian policemen are often viewed unfavorably by historians. Using examples such as the 1890 killing of Sitting Bull by Standing Rock policemen or the role of BIA police officers at Wounded Knee in 1973, many scholars have portrayed Indian policemen as traitors to their own people. This interpretation fails to acknowledge the origins of police forces. The concept of tribal police forces was not new to Plains Indians. All tribes traditionally had law enforcers. Traditional Lakota law enforcers, known as *akicitas*, enforced tribal laws and customs, policed camp moves, and regulated buffalo hunts. When the first agency police force was organized at Pine Ridge (present-day South Dakota) in 1879, it was the akicitas who filled its ranks, suggesting that the Lakotas may have used this institution to continue their traditional roles.

Indian policemen performed an array of duties. Day-to-day tasks included maintaining law and order in and around the agency, including guarding agency property and storehouses, arresting drunks and gamblers, maintaining the agency jail, and serving as messengers and scouts. Armed and mounted policemen also patrolled reservation boundaries, driving off or arresting stock thieves, liquor peddlers, and timber thieves. More controversial duties sometimes included forcing children to attend agency schools and enforcing bans on polygamy, dancing, and traditional ceremonies. In carrying out their duties Indian policemen were often put in danger. Between 1876 and 1906 at least twenty-four Indian police officers were killed in Indian Territory alone. In the deadliest day for Indian policemen, six members of Standing Rock's Indian police force were killed on December 15, 1890, while attempting to arrest Sitting Bull.

Early Indian police forces were usually poorly equipped. With little federal support, agents were left on their own to arm and clothe

Mounted Dakota Sioux Indian police, Rosebud Agency, South Dakota, 1896

their police officers. Agents at Rosebud and Pine Ridge Agencies, for example, armed their forces with borrowed weapons from nearby Fort Robinson. By the mid-1880s, however, the Department of the Interior was providing standardized uniforms, badges, and weaponry. Dismally low remuneration was another problem. Ranking officers in 1880 earned only $8 a month, while enlisted men received a paltry $5 for a month's labor. Even as late as 1927 many Lakota policemen had to supplement their income by farming. Most forces experienced high turnover rates, because policemen could earn more money as military scouts or laborers.

Each Indian police force looked and operated differently from the others. On Lakota reservations police units operated almost like the military. Pine Ridge's police force regularly drilled under the command of ex–military officers and patrolled reservation boundaries in small mounted squads. Cherokee and Choctaw police officers, however, operated more like a European American constabulary, performing law enforcement tasks as sheriffs and deputies. Police forces also varied in size. Units at Pine Ridge and Rosebud Agencies included the maximum of fifty policemen, while the smaller Cheyenne River Agency had only nine officers on its original force.

The early 1880s were the heyday for Indian police forces on the Great Plains. During these years Indian police forces performed all law enforcement duties on their reservations and operated largely free of federal control. By the mid-1880s, however, federal laws began to encroach on the autonomy of the criminal justice system on reservations. The Major Crimes Act of 1885 gave the federal government jurisdiction in most felonies, limiting the duties of Indian police officers. The Dawes Act further curtailed the authority of Indian police by placing allottees under the jurisdiction of the state in which they resided. By 1900 the large Indian police forces of the 1880s had disappeared. Without federal financial support,

most reservations could employ only one or two police officers by the 1920s; even the largest Lakota reservation employed only seventeen officers. By the 1950s Bureau of Indian Affairs police forces had supplanted most agency forces. In 2000 Bureau of Indian Affairs police forces operated in every Great Plains state except Texas.

Mark R. Ellis
University of Nebraska at Kearney

Ellis, Mark R. "Reservation Akicitas: The Pine Ridge Indian Police, 1879–1885." *South Dakota History* 29 (1999): 185–210. Hagan, William T. *Indian Police and Judges.* Lincoln: University of Nebraska Press, 1980.

JIM CROW LAWS

Elaborate discriminatory laws existed in Great Plains states with large African American populations such as Texas, Oklahoma, and Kansas, while Nebraska, Colorado, Wyoming, and Montana, with smaller minority populations, created limited and often unenforced segregation laws. Because of small African American populations, North and South Dakota created no such laws. Except for Texas and Oklahoma, with their large rural African American populations and Southern views of race relations, Plains states applied segregation laws almost entirely in towns. Other forms of segregation in these states existed as a matter of custom. Hispanic Americans and Native Americans also faced discriminatory laws.

Texas adopted a state constitution in 1876 that required segregated schools for African Americans. Some local school districts also segregated Hispanic students. The legislature in 1876 allowed jury commissions that could eliminate African American jurors. In 1891 the legislature allowed segregated railroad cars. Six years later it outlawed interracial sexual relations. Texas added a constitutional amendment in 1902 requiring a poll tax for voting that fell primarily on working-class African Americans and Hispanics. In 1903 a new election law allowed political parties to exclude minorities from white primaries. Texas strengthened that law in 1923. Several towns segregated public accommodations and transportation. Some West Texas counties excluded African American settlers by customs known as "sundown laws."

The first Oklahoma state constitution in 1907 segregated public schools. The legislature added laws segregating transportation and forbidding intermarriage. Oklahoma later segregated various public accommodations, while some towns segregated residential areas. In 1910 the state adopted a literacy test and a grandfather clause to disfranchise African Americans. Both measures were declared unconstitutional by the U.S. Supreme Court in 1915 in *Guinn and Beal v. United States.*

Segregation laws in Kansas dealt primarily with education. The state constitution of 1859 specified separate African American schools.

Drinking at a "colored" water cooler in a streetcar terminal, Oklahoma City, Oklahoma, July 1939

Soon the Kansas legislature created county school districts in which African Americans could attend white schools if no separate institution existed. In 1874 the state passed a civil rights law that forbade segregated schools. Five years later the legislature revised the school code to allow towns of 15,000 population to establish separate primary schools for African Americans. Secondary schools were segregated only in Wyandotte County. African Americans challenged segregated schools, but the Kansas Supreme Court upheld the segregation statute.

Wyoming passed a law allowing a school segregation law in 1899. In 1913 the state made miscegenation a misdemeanor. Nebraska passed a similar law against miscegenation in 1911. While some de facto segregation existed in the state, no other Jim Crow measures became law in Nebraska.

Montana, with its large Native American population, denied voting rights to persons under federal "guardianship" in 1871 and forbade voter precincts on reservations. In 1889 the state opened voting to all male persons except Native Americans. After the federal Indian Citizenship Act of 1924, Montana divided counties into at-large districts to dilute the impact of Native American voters. In 1937 the state ruled that all deputy voter registrars must be taxpaying residents of their precincts. Since Native Americans were exempt from some local taxes, they could not act as voter registrars, and tribal voter registration was effectively limited.

In the early twentieth century Jim Crow laws on the Plains began to face challenges. Important court cases included those in Texas that outlawed the white primary by the early 1940s. After earlier court cases in Texas eliminated Hispanic school segregation and Texas and Oklahoma cases outlawed segregation at the law school/graduate school level, the U.S. Supreme Court in *Brown v. The Board of Education of Topeka* ruled against legal school segregation on the basis of race in 1954.

See also AFRICAN AMERICANS: Civil Rights.

Alwyn Barr
Douglas Hales
Texas Tech University

Barr, Alwyn. *Black Texans: A History of African Americans in Texas, 1528–1995.* Norman: University of Oklahoma Press, 1996. Svingen, Orlan J. "Jim Crow, Indian Style, 1980s." In *Peoples of Color in the American West*, edited by Sucheng Chan, Douglas Daniels, Mario T. Garcia, and Terry P. Wilson. Lexington KY: D. C. Heath and Company, 1994: 352–63. Taylor, Quintard. *In Search of the Racial Frontier: African Americans in the American West, 1528–1990.* New York: W. W. Norton, 1998.

LAND LAWS AND SETTLEMENT

See EUROPEAN AMERICANS: Land Laws and Settlement

LEAVENWORTH PENITENTIARY

Leavenworth Penitentiary in eastern Kansas was the first of three federal prisons authorized during the 1890s to avoid housing federal prisoners in state prisons known for scandal and mistreatment of inmates. Prisoners have been incarcerated in the Leavenworth area since before Kansas gained statehood in 1861. At that time, a territorial jail there became the first state penitentiary. Congress established the U.S. Army Disciplinary Barracks at Fort Leavenworth in 1874. In 1895 Congress ordered the military prison transferred to the Department of Justice, creating one of the first federal prisons for civilian offenders. (The U.S. government operated a penitentiary in Washington DC from 1831 to 1862 as well as territorial prisons.)

During the next eleven years, inmates marched from the fort to a nearby construction site on the military reservation where they built the Leavenworth Penitentiary according to plans drawn by the St. Louis architecture firm Eames and Young. The lack of skilled labor and the painstaking security measures necessitated by using convict laborers made for slow progress. Inmates began occupying the new facility in 1903, but the population did not transfer entirely from the military prison until 1906. Construction continued, with cell blocks completed by 1919, shoe shops by 1926, a brush and broom factory by 1928, and the offices and rotunda by 1929. The penitentiary became a tourist attraction even as it was being built. The arrival of 200 tourists from Kansas City in a single day in 1910 led the warden to suspend tours temporarily. Planners expected 1,200 cells would accommodate 1,200 prisoners, but crowding led officials to abandon that ideal. As early as 1915 the prison population reached 1,800. By 1925 the population had climbed to 3,262. Continued crowding led to another annexation of the Fort Leavenworth Disciplinary Barracks from 1929 through 1940. At the beginning of the twenty-first century, the penitentiary housed 1,726 inmates.

Todd M. Kerstetter
Texas Christian University

Keve, Paul W. *Prisons and the American Conscience: A History of U.S. Federal Corrections.* Carbondale: Southern Illinois University Press, 1991. McShane, Marilyn D., and Frank P. Williams III, eds. *Encyclopedia of American Prisons.* New York: Garland, 1996. U.S. Department of Justice, Bureau of Prisons. *The Leavenworth Story.* Washington DC: Government Printing Office, n.d.

LOAN ASSOCIATION V. TOPEKA

After the Civil War, capital-scarce states and localities continued the antebellum practice of granting subsidies to encourage business enterprise. Railroads were the principal beneficiaries of such aid. Subsidy arrangements typically took the form of stock subscriptions by local governments, which were paid for by the issuance of negotiable bonds. The bonds were serviced by revenue raised from taxation. State courts generally upheld financial assistance to railroads but insisted that taxes could only be levied for a public purpose. Although not expressly written in federal or state constitutions, this requirement was viewed by judges as an inherent principle of republican government.

As state and local governments lavished aid on businesses, however, courts occasionally groped to fashion some limit on the power of taxation.

Loan Association v. Topeka (1874) marked the Supreme Court's endorsement of the public purpose doctrine as a means of restricting grants of public revenue to private enterprise. As authorized by state law, the city of Topeka donated municipal bonds to an ironworks company to encourage that business to establish shops in the city. The city soon ceased making interest payments. When a bondholder in Ohio sued to collect interest on these bonds, the Supreme Court was called upon to consider the validity of such subsidy arrangements.

Stressing that there were limits on governmental power that "grow out of the essential nature of all free governments," the Supreme Court, in an opinion by Justice Samuel F. Miller, warned: "Of all the powers conferred upon government that of taxation is most liable to abuse." Miller ruled that "there can be no lawful tax which is not laid for a *public purpose*." He then concluded that taxation to aid manufacturing was not for a public purpose and that the municipal bonds were therefore invalid. In reaching this result, Miller was clearly influenced by the perceived excesses of public aid to railroads and seemed determined to draw the line against grants of public revenue to other types of private business. Dissenting alone, Justice Nathan Clifford maintained that courts could only strike down state laws that violated specific constitutional provisions and that it was inappropriate for courts to rely on vague theories of government to curb state legislative taxing authority.

Following *Loan Association* the public purpose doctrine was sometimes invoked to curb use of the tax power to subsidize business enterprise. Moreover, the ruling made clear that the Supreme Court distrusted the judgment of state authorities concerning disbursement of tax revenue and was prepared to render an independent assessment about which projects were for a public purpose. The decision is also significant because the Supreme Court accepted the premise that legitimate government was restrained by certain fundamental if unwritten principles. Thus *Loan Association* paved the way for the Supreme Court to adopt a substantive reading of the due process clauses in the late nineteenth century. Lastly, the case demonstrated that the Court in the late nineteenth century was not following a monolithic course of assisting business enterprise.

James W. Ely Jr.
Vanderbilt University

Fairman, Charles. *History of the Supreme Court of the United States.* Vol. 6, *Reconstruction and Reunion, 1864–88.* New York: Macmillan Publishing Company, 1971. Hovenkamp, Herbert. *Enterprise and American Law, 1836–1937.* Cambridge: Harvard University Press, 1991. Powe, L. A., Jr. "Rehearsal for Substantive Due Process: The Municipal Bond Cases." *Texas Law Review* 53 (1975): 738–56.

LONE WOLF V. HITCHCOCK

Lone Wolf v. Hitchcock (1903) was a U.S. Supreme Court decision that abrogated Native American treaty rights and underscored congressional supremacy (called plenary power) over Indian affairs. Plaintiffs Lone Wolf and several other Indians had sued the defendant, Interior Secretary Ethan Allen Hitchcock, to block allotment of the Kiowa-Comanche-Apache Reservation in southwestern Oklahoma. Kiowa claims, including the condition of article 12 of the Medicine Lodge Treaty (1867) forbidding cession of Indian land unless approved by three-fourths of the tribe's male members, were sidestepped in the Court's opinion. In 1900 Congress had approved a modified 1892 allotment agreement that did not contain sufficient signatures, even with forgeries, and Lone Wolf and his supporters sought judicial relief. Their case had been rejected in federal court in Washington DC and in the District of Columbia Court of Appeals.

The decision was the culmination of a century-long congressional assault on Indian land and treaty rights. The Court held that congressional guardianship over Indian reservation property could not be limited by an Indian treaty and cited its own decree in *Cherokee Nation v. Georgia* (1831) that Congress possessed complete administrative power over Indian tribal property. Referring to the earlier decision in *United States v. Kagama* (1886), the justices upheld congressional supremacy over the nation's "Indian wards," called paternalism, ruling that congressional plenary authority over Indian relations was not subject to judicial oversight or review, since such congressional power was political.

The Court's decision had reverberations far from Lone Wolf's own reservation, which was quickly allotted. The unallotted "surplus" was opened to a tide of non-Indian settlers, who rapidly engulfed tribal lands. Although Indian land division had been under way before the opinion, the judicial pronouncement spurred a frenzy of allotment. Indian land loss increased, not least on reservations on the Northern Great Plains. Indian Office abuses of Indian land, resources, and rights increased in the ensuing years. Indian nations sank deeper into the mire of wardship, subject to virtually unlimited federal authority. The plenary doctrine of *Lone Wolf* dominated federal Indian law and Indian policy for more than half a century. The decree set back the efforts of humanitarian reformers, who advocated modifications in Indian policy. At the same time in the nation's history, the United States acquired its first overseas possessions, following the conclusion of the Spanish-American War. U.S. authorities viewed local island independence in the same light as that of continental Native American tribal independence, as the attitudes visible in the *Lone Wolf* litigation were applied narrowly to the new possessions.

Although officially repudiated in the judicial system since 1980 (*United States v. Sioux Nation of Indians*), the doctrine periodically has been resurrected in defense of denying Indian rights, such as in Indian religious freedom rights and those dealing with sacred sites. The Indian trust funds scandal at the end of the 1990s, involving Bureau of Indian Affairs mismanagement of Indian trust money, was also a long-postponed but direct outgrowth of the *Lone Wolf* decision and its attendant bureaucratic mind-set.

C. Blue Clark
Oklahoma City University

Clark, Blue. *Lone Wolf v. Hitchcock: Treaty Rights and Indian Law at the End of the Nineteenth Century*. Lincoln: University of Nebraska Press, 1994. Wilkins, David E. *American Indian Sovereignty and the U.S. Supreme Court: The Masking of Justice*. Austin: University of Texas Press, 1998. Wyatt, Kathryn C. "The Supreme Court, *Lyng*, and the *Lone Wolf* Principle." *Chicago-Kent Law Review* 65 (1989): 623–55.

LOUGHEED, JAMES (1854–1925)

Sir James Alexander Lougheed was a prominent Calgary lawyer and entrepreneur and, from December 10, 1889, until his death, a member of the Senate of Canada. Of Protestant Irish descent, Lougheed was born in Brampton on September 1, 1854, was raised in Toronto, where he trained as a lawyer, and settled in Fort Calgary in 1883, just as the Canadian Pacific Railway was being constructed there. He married Belle Hardisty, daughter of William Hardisty, a prominent Hudson's Bay Company factor; they eventually had four sons and two daughters.

Lougheed's law practice grew rapidly, particularly as solicitor for the railway, and he invested heavily, and profitably, in Calgary real estate. He constructed numerous rental properties in the downtown area, culminating in the Lougheed Building (1912), an office building with a 1,500-seat theater. Lougheed was leader of the Conservative Party in the Canadian Senate from 1906 until his death, and he was government leader from 1911 to 1921. He served in the federal government under Sir Robert Borden as minister without portfolio (1911–18), minister of soldiers' civil reestablishment (1918–20), and (under Arthur Meighen) as minister of the interior, superintendent general of Indian affairs, and minister of mines (1920–21). Lougheed's diplomatic skills were a great asset in securing the passage of government measures. He always was a vigorous representative of western Canada in Ottawa. Perhaps his greatest work was the resettlement of demobilized soldiers, many of them in western Canada, following World War I. Sir James Lougheed died in Ottawa on November 2, 1925.

David J. Hall
University of Alberta

McKenna, Marian C. "Calgary's First Senator and City Builder: Sir James Alexander Lougheed." In *Citymakers: Calgarians after the Frontier*, edited by Max Foran and Sheilagh S. Jameson. Calgary: Historical Society of Alberta, Chinook Country Chapter, 1987: 93–116. Morton, Desmond, and Glenn Wright. *Winning the Second Battle: Canadian Veterans and the Return to Civilian Life, 1915–1930*. Toronto: University of Toronto Press, 1987.

MACLEOD, JAMES (1836–1894)

Col. James Farquharson Macleod, the second commissioner of the North-West Mounted Police (NWMP), worked tirelessly to establish harmonious relations with the Indian nations of the Canadian Prairie West, only to see his efforts frustrated by a federal Indian policy based on coercion, control, and parsimony.

Born on the Isle of Skye in Scotland on September 25, 1836, Macleod was nine years old when his family moved to a farm north of Toronto in present-day southern Ontario. Although Macleod earned degrees in classics and philosophy and then law, he preferred life in the militia—a passion that was reinforced in 1870, when he was sent west as a member of the Wolseley Expedition to quell the Métis resistance at Red River.

Thanks to his political connections, Macleod secured a commission as superintendent with the fledgling NWMP in May 1873. The following July he was one of 300 Mounties on the so-called Great March from Dufferin, Manitoba, west along the international boundary to southern Alberta. The police had been sent into the western interior to suppress the American whiskey trade on Canadian soil but barely survived the trek across the open, unfamiliar prairie; fortunately, neither the whiskey traders nor the Indians offered any resistance.

Macleod, in command of the force in the absence of the commissioner, lost little time in establishing a police presence in the region; he built posts on the Oldman River (Fort Macleod) in 1874 and in the Cypress Hills (Fort Walsh) and on the Bow River (Fort Calgary) the following summer. He also initiated important contacts with the leading Indians of the area, in particular Chiefs Crowfoot (Blackfoot) and Red Crow (Blood), and secured their support in ending the debilitating whiskey trade. Macleod's attempt to extradite several Americans implicated in the 1873 Cypress Hills massacre, however, ended in failure.

Macleod was appointed NWMP commissioner in July 1876. He was a popular choice because of his Canadian background, and his tenure at the helm of the force was largely preoccupied with First Nations issues. He participated in the signing of the last two major treaties in western Canada: Treaty Six with the Plains Cree at Fort Carlton in August 1876 and Treaty Seven with the Blackfoot Confederacy at Blackfoot Crossing in September 1877. Both Crowfoot and Red Crow attributed their willingness to enter into treaties with the queen's representatives to their friendship with Macleod. The new commissioner also met with Sitting Bull at Fort Walsh in September 1877; he assured the refugee Lakota leader that his people would find sanctuary there but that there would be no government assistance. Finally, as a member of the appointed Northwest Territories council, Macleod sponsored legislation to conserve the dwindling bison herds in order to head off Indian starvation. But the measure came too late, and his visits to Indian agencies throughout the region in 1879—he traveled over 2,000 miles on horseback—confirmed his worst fears.

By 1880 Macleod had become disillusioned with the failure of the Canadian government to honor its treaty obligations. Ottawa, in turn, began to ask questions about his poor management of police funds. Macleod consequently resigned as commissioner that September and devoted his energies to his other major role as stipendiary magistrate. His earlier legal training served him well, for he was appointed to the first territorial supreme court in 1887. But his arduous days on the trail had taken a toll on his health, and Judge Macleod died in Calgary on September 5, 1894.

See also NATIVE AMERICANS: Crowfoot / WAR: Red River Resistance.

Bill Waiser
University of Saskatchewan

Baker, William, ed. *The Mounted Police and Prairie Society.* Regina: Canadian Plains Research Center, 1998. Beahen, William, and Stan Horrall. *Redcoats on the Prairies.* Regina: Centax Books, 1998. Col. J. F. Macleod Papers, Glenbow Archives, Calgary.

MASTERSON, BAT (1853–1921)

The man destined to achieve fame and notoriety as Bat Masterson, frontiersman, lawman, and gunfighter on the frontiers of Kansas and Texas, was born at Henryville, Quebec, Canada, on November 26, 1853. Christened Bartholomew and called Bart or Bat by his family, he chose to use the name William Barclay Masterson throughout his life.

Masterson grew up on farms in New York, Illinois, and Kansas. He left his father's farm in Sedgwick County, Kansas, in 1871 to hunt buffalo and soon gained a reputation as a dead shot and intrepid frontiersman. In June 1874 he was the youngest of twenty-eight buffalo hunters at Adobe Walls, Texas, who withstood an attack and siege by several hundred warriors led by Quanah Parker. Masterson served as a civilian scout in the Red River War of 1874–75. A shooting on January 24, 1876, at Sweetwater (now Mobeetie), Texas, was the basis for his gunfighter reputation. He killed a soldier after the man shot a woman to death and severely wounded Masterson. He served as a city policeman at Dodge City, Kansas, during that town's most uproarious years and was elected sheriff of Ford County before reaching the age of twenty-four. On April 9, 1878, after his brother, Dodge City marshal Ed Masterson, was shot and killed, he avenged that murder by killing one and wounding another of the assailants.

Residing primarily in Colorado after 1880, Masterson returned to Dodge City frequently, most notably as a participant in an 1881 gunfight in the town's plaza in which he shot and wounded a local saloon man and as a member (with Wyatt Earp and other gunmen) of the Dodge City Peace Commission formed in 1883 to protect the interests of gambler Luke Short. In 1902 Masterson left Denver for New York City, where he became a well-known boxing authority and sports columnist. He died on October 25, 1921, in New York and is buried there.

See also IMAGES AND ICONS: Dodge City, Kansas; Gunslingers / WAR: Adobe Walls, Battle of.

Robert K. DeArment
Sylvania, Ohio

DeArment, Robert K. *Bat Masterson: The Man and the Legend.* Norman: University of Oklahoma Press, 1979.

MCLAURIN V. OKLAHOMA STATE REGENTS

See EDUCATION: *McLaurin v. Oklahoma State Regents*

MEYER V. NEBRASKA

In *Meyer v. Nebraska* (1923), the U.S. Supreme Court struck down a Nebraska statute that prohibited the teaching of modern foreign languages in private and parochial elementary schools. The Court held that the statute was unconstitutional because it deprived parents and teachers of liberty and property without due process of law in violation of the Fourteenth Amendment to the U.S. Constitution.

The Nebraska statute was enacted shortly after World War I in response to widespread hostility against Nebraska's large German American community that had arisen as a result of the war. Similar laws were promulgated in many other states. Proponents of these laws argued that they facilitated "Americanization" of children who lived in isolated ethnic communities. German American Lutherans, who challenged the constitutionality of the Nebraska statute and similar laws in companion cases in Ohio and Iowa, contended that their children needed to learn the German language in order to participate in German-language worship at home and in churches. Robert T. Meyer, a teacher in a Lutheran school in Hampton, Nebraska, defied the statute by openly teaching German, as did two other Lutheran parochial schoolteachers in Ohio and Iowa. Meyer argued that it was his religious duty to teach children the religion of their parents in the language of their parents. Since German American Lutheran parochial schools already taught basic curricular subjects in the English language, the Court found that the Nebraska, Ohio, and Iowa statutes did not promote the states' interest in encouraging patriotism and the use of a common language. In a dissent joined by Justice George Sutherland, Justice Oliver Wendell Holmes Jr. argued that the Court ought to have deferred to the legislatures' determination that the statutes were necessary for the protection of the public welfare.

The Nebraska statute and its counterparts in other states were part of a broader nativistic assault on the rights of ethnic Americans that included a widespread movement to destroy parochial education by requiring all children to attend public school. In ruling that parents had a right to control the education of their children unless such education directly threatened the interests of the government, the Court in *Meyer* laid the foundation for its landmark decision in *Pierce v. Society of Sisters*

(1925), which struck down a compulsory public education law in Oregon. In reaffirming *Meyer's* ruling that parents have a constitutional right to control the education of their children, *Pierce* ended the movement for compulsory public education.

The *Meyer* decision was also significant because it was the first case in which the Court invoked the Fourteenth Amendment to protect noneconomic rights against intrusion by the states. Until *Meyer*, the Court generally had struck down only those state statutes that unreasonably interfered with economic activities. In suggesting that the statute unconstitutionally infringed upon both economic rights and noneconomic rights, *Meyer* marked the start of the Court's modern role as a guardian of personal liberties. In sweeping language, the Court held that the Fourteenth Amendment "denotes not merely freedom from bodily restraint but also the right of the individual to contract, to engage in any of the common occupations of life, to acquire useful knowledge, to marry, establish a home and bring up children, to worship God according to the dictates of his own conscience, and generally to enjoy those privileges long recognized at common law as essential to the orderly pursuit of happiness by free men."

Although proponents of parochial education regarded *Meyer* as a victory for religious freedom, the Court in *Meyer* did not rely upon the First Amendment's freedom of religion clause or any other specific provision of the Bill of Rights, which the Court had not yet begun to incorporate into state law. *Meyer's* emphasis on personal liberties, however, presaged the Court's gradual application of the various provisions of the Bill of Rights to the states, beginning later in the 1920s.

While most civil liberties decisions after *Meyer* and *Pierce* have been grounded in specific provisions of the Bill of Rights, *Meyer* remains a precedent for the proposition that there are some constitutional rights that are not found in specific provisions of the Constitution. *Meyer* therefore has served as a cornerstone for the development of the right of privacy. The U.S. Supreme Court relied upon *Meyer* in striking down antiabortion laws in *Roe v. Wade* (1973) and in other decisions concerning various aspects of privacy.

William G. Ross
Samford University

Luebke, Frederick C. "Legal Restrictions on Foreign Languages in the Great Plains States, 1917–1923." In *Languages in Conflict: Linguistic Acculturation on the Great Plains*, edited by Paul Schach. Lincoln: University of Nebraska Press, 1980: 1–19. Ross, William G. *Forging New Freedoms: Nativism, Education, and the Constitution, 1917–1927.* Lincoln: University of Nebraska Press, 1994.

MONTANA V. UNITED STATES

In *Montana v. United States* (1981), the U.S. Supreme Court ruled that the Crow Tribe of Montana did not possess the inherent sovereign power to regulate hunting and fishing by nonmembers of the tribe on lands owned by non-Indians within its reservation boundaries. The decision arose out of a dispute between the Crows and the state of Montana over the question of which entity had jurisdiction to control hunting and fishing within the reservation boundaries and primarily focused on the right to regulate fishing and duck hunting on and around the Big Horn River, which flows through the Crow reservation. The Crows based their claim on their inherent powers of tribal sovereignty and the language of the various treaties that created their reservation and, they argued, gave them ownership of the bed of the Big Horn River. Montana, on the other hand, argued that it took title to the riverbed at the time it became a state and that it had always maintained the authority to regulate hunting and fishing by non-Indians within the reservation.

In an attempt to resolve the conflict, the United States, acting as trustee for the tribe, initiated a lawsuit in 1975 seeking a judicial resolution of both the threshold question of title to the riverbed and the accompanying jurisdictional dispute over hunting and fishing rights. The federal district court ruled in favor of Montana, holding that the state rather than the Crows owned the banks and bed of the Big Horn River. The Ninth Circuit Court of Appeals reversed the district court's decision, holding, with some qualifications, that the treaties establishing the Crow Reservation had vested title to the riverbed in the United States as trustee for the tribe and that the Crows could regulate hunting and fishing within the reservation by nonmembers. In its 1981 decision, the Supreme Court reversed the court of appeals, essentially restoring the district court's judgment in favor of the state of Montana.

Two components of the ruling are key. On the question of title to the riverbed, the Court held that, notwithstanding certain ostensibly contradictory language in the 1851 and 1868 treaties by which the Crow Reservation was formed, title to the riverbed passed to the state of Montana upon its admission into the Union in 1889. With respect to the broader issues of inherent tribal sovereignty, the Court acknowledged that Indian tribes still maintain certain powers of self-government but went on to hold that those powers extend only to the control of "internal relations." Extension of tribal power beyond the realm of internal tribal matters, the Court ruled, would be "inconsistent with the dependent status of the tribes." Finding that control of hunting and fishing by nonmembers on lands no longer owned by the tribe (but still within its reservation) bears "no clear relationship to tribal self-government or internal relations," the Court held that the Crows did not possess the "retained inherent sovereignty" to regulate those activities.

The *Montana* decision and others like it are universally perceived by Native Americans and their supporters as troubling judicial assaults on the remnants of tribal sovereignty, confirming the extremely fragile nature of that sovereignty and reiterating the ultimate power of the federal government to define the precise scope and extent of Indian powers of self-determination.

See also NATIVE AMERICANS: Crows.

Mark R. Scherer
University of Nebraska at Omaha

Bloxham, Steven John. "Tribal Sovereignty: An Analysis of Montana v. United States." *American Indian Law Review* 8 (1980): 175–81. Canby, William C., Jr. *American Indian Law in a Nutshell*. 3rd ed. St. Paul MN: West Group, 1998.

MORRIS, ESTHER (1814–1902)

Esther Morris

When the commissioners of Sweetwater County, Wyoming Territory, approved Esther Morris as a justice of the peace on February 12, 1870, she entered history as the first woman magistrate in the nation.

Morris was born in Spencer, Tioga County, New York, on August 8, 1814. Orphaned at an early age, she learned to support herself and developed a sense of independence. She lived for more than twenty years in Peru, Illinois, where she raised her family. In 1869 she moved west to the rough-and-tumble gold-mining town of South Pass City to join her husband and oldest son, who had moved there the previous year in search of gold. Five months later, women in Wyoming Territory were the first in the nation to be granted suffrage. One of the few advocates of women's rights in the small mining town, Morris was encouraged by local citizens and an influential judge to apply for a vacant justice of the peace position. She was appointed on February 17, 1870.

Justice Morris's first case involved the prosecution of her predecessor, who refused to turn over the court docket to her as a female judge. The case was consequently dismissed without the transfer of the docket, and Morris purchased a new book in which to record her cases. Serving less than nine months, she tried twenty-eight cases, including ten assaults.

Although she chose not to stand for election at the end of her appointed term, Esther Morris earned the respect of the predominantly male, antisuffrage local citizenry. Even though she was erroneously dubbed the "Mother of Woman Suffrage" in turn-of-the-century newspaper and historical reports, she did work diligently for women's rights, and Judge Morris rightfully deserves national attention because of the precedent she set. She died in Laramie on April 2, 1902. Her statue stands in front of the Wyoming State Capitol in Cheyenne.

See also GENDER: Suffrage Movement.

Lois M. Berry
University of Wyoming

Dobler, Lavinia. *Esther Morris: First Woman Justice of the Peace*. Riverton WY: Big Bend Press, 1993. Larson, T. A. *History of Wyoming*. Lincoln: University of Nebraska Press, 1978. Massie, Michael A. "Reform Is Where You Find It: The Roots of Woman Suffrage in Wyoming." *Annals of Wyoming* 62 (1990): 2–21.

NATIVE AMERICAN RIGHTS FUND

The Native American Rights Fund (NARF), based in Boulder, Colorado, is the oldest and largest nonprofit national Indian rights organization in the country. Since its establishment in 1970, NARF has grown from a three-lawyer staff to a firm of forty full-time staff members, with fourteen attorneys. Most of the attorneys and nearly all support staff personnel are Native American. NARF has represented more than 200 Indian tribes located in thirty-one states, including many Native people who are Indigenous to the Great Plains. The hundreds of cases it has handled have involved every major problem and issue in the field of Native American law. The Native American Rights Fund is governed by a thirteen-member board of directors composed entirely of Native people. This board charts the direction of NARF's activities by setting priorities and policies. Board members are chosen on the basis of their involvement in Native affairs, their knowledge of the legal problems facing Native Americans throughout the country, and, most importantly, their dedication to the well-being and survival of Native Americans.

Today, more than fifty-five Indian tribes are an important and integral part of the economic, political, and cultural life of the Great Plains. Most have treaties with the United States that set forth property, political, and legal rights. Each Great Plains state contains Indian reservations that were established by treaties or other federal action and are governed by tribal governments. From legal and political standpoints, each reservation in the United States is a nation within a nation. The power of tribal governments and the jurisdiction over reservation lands among tribal, state, and federal governments are integral aspects of Great Plains governance and are continually being refined by litigation or legislation. At the same time, the protection of and control over the natural resources located on Indian reservations such as water, oil, and natural gas are vitally important to Indian owners. Tribal people are citizens of their respective Indian tribes, the United States, and their respective states, and they aspire to rights of self-determination, tribal sovereignty, cultural rights, and human rights similar to those sought by other Indigenous peoples throughout the world.

NARF attorneys work to tear down barriers to the fulfillment of these rights in Great Plains courtrooms and legislatures. For example, NARF has worked to restore land and federal recognition to the Alabama-Coushatta Tribe, the Kickapoo Tribe, and the Ysleta del Sur Pueblo in Texas and to restore tribal jurisdiction to the Winnebago Tribe in Nebraska. In Oklahoma, NARF has worked to recognize the reservation status of Pawnee lands, to clarify Osage tribal government status, and to confirm Cheyenne and Arapaho tribal oil and gas taxation authority. In the area of human rights, NARF has represented Native American inmates in jails and prisons in North and South Dakota, Nebraska, Kansas, and Oklahoma. It provided legal representation to tribes located in Oklahoma and North Dakota to protect tribal burial grounds from desecration and to repatriate human remains that had been removed from tribal graves and carried away to museums, historical societies, and other institutions. NARF has also represented tribes and students in South Dakota, North Dakota, Oklahoma, and eastern Colorado on education issues relating to public, tribal, and Bureau of Indian Affairs schools. NARF has represented traditional religious practitioners in protecting their freedom of worship at sacred sites in eastern Wyoming, in prisons, and during the worship ceremonies of the Native American Church. These issues illustrate the problems that confront Great Plains Indian tribes in the United States today as Native peoples strive to live according to their traditional ways of life and the aspirations of their forefathers.

See also NATIVE AMERICANS: Reservations.

Ray Ramirez
Walter Echo-Hawk
Native American Rights Fund

NEBRASKA PRESS ASSOCIATION V. STUART

The potential conflict between society's First Amendment right to a free press and a criminal defendant's Sixth Amendment right to a fair trial was addressed by the U.S. Supreme Court in the landmark decision of *Nebraska Press Association v. Stuart*. The grisly case began on the evening of October 18, 1975, when Erwin Simants walked into the home of Henry Kellie, just outside the village of Sutherland, Nebraska, carrying a rifle. Once inside, Simants brutally raped and then murdered Kellie's ten-year-old granddaughter. Later, when other members of the Kellie family arrived home, they found Simants waiting for them. After killing both Henry and his wife, their son, and two other grandchildren, Simants, an unemployed alcoholic, calmly visited both of Sutherland's two bars and then spent the rest of the night outside the Kellie house.

The next morning, Simants was quickly arrested and charged with six counts of first-degree murder. Just as quickly, television and newspaper articles describing the horrific events began to appear. Even before the bodies were removed from the Kellie home, news

agencies from around the country had focused on Sutherland, reporting the multiple homicide. Such widespread media coverage caused concern that public disclosure of highly prejudicial information revealed in Simants's preliminary pretrial hearing would taint potential jurors and prevent a fair trial. As a result, Lincoln County District Judge Hugh Stuart granted the prosecuting attorney's request to gag the press. He strictly prohibited the media from publishing reports of confessions and other details that strongly implicated Simants.

The press complied with Stuart's order but appealed to the Nebraska Supreme Court, claiming the order violated the press's constitutional right to report information disclosed in open court. The media contended that the First Amendment right to a free press necessarily included the right to cover events both in and outside of the courtroom and that this ability was essential to prevent judicial abuse of authority. In contrast, Stuart's counsel argued that Simants could not receive a fair trial without the restrictions. Allowing the press to publish extremely prejudicial information, his defense asserted, would bias potential jurors and preclude their ability to base their decision solely on evidence received in court. Prior exposure to the case through the media, it was argued, would make it impossible to find an impartial jury as guaranteed by the Sixth Amendment.

The Nebraska Supreme Court, after modifying Stuart's order, affirmed it. Eventually, the suit was brought before the U.S. Supreme Court, which reversed the decision, holding that the order did impermissibly restrict free press. The Court acknowledged that prior restraints may be necessary in certain rare circumstances, but the court went on to explain that the presumption against the use of prior restraints can only be overcome by showing that less restrictive alternatives cannot sufficiently protect a defendant's rights. *Nebraska*

Press is often characterized as the most significant First Amendment ruling emanating from Nebraska, and it essentially closed the question of prior restraints in criminal law. As a result, the media enjoy nearly complete discretion over what and when to publish concerning judicial proceedings.

James W. Hewitt
Lincoln, Nebraska

Larson, Milton R. "Free Press v. Fair Trial in Nebraska: A Position Paper." *Nebraska Law Review* 55 (1976): 543–71. Younger, Eric C. "The Sheppard Mandate Today: A Trial Judge's Perspective." *Nebraska Law Review* 56 (1977): 1–22.

NORTH DAKOTA ANTI-GARB LAW

On June 29, 1948, North Dakota voters passed an initiative that prohibited Catholic nuns from wearing their habits while teaching in public schools. Known as the Anti-Garb bill, this law was the culmination of a long battle to drive nuns from public schools. Due to a shortage of qualified teachers and insufficient funding for public education, many states, including North Dakota, had hired nuns to teach in public schools during the first half of the twentieth century. Fearing that the Catholic Church would dominate public education, many communities opposed this practice. North Dakota became the center of opposition on the Great Plains.

While North Dakota schools had employed nuns since 1918, no formal protests appeared in the courts until the 1936 case of *Gerhardt v. Heid*. Filed against three Benedictine sisters who wore their religious garb while employed by the Gladstone school district in Dickinson, North Dakota, this civil case eventually reached the North Dakota Supreme Court. The plaintiffs argued that the primarily Protestant schoolchildren's First Amendment rights to freedom of religion had been violated by constant exposure to their teachers' religious garb. Interestingly, the nuns also invoked the First Amendment, arguing that a ban on

Rev. Mother Carmelita Schaan teaching at Saint Leo's, Minot, North Dakota

wearing habits would be a violation of their right to practice their religion. Because the sisters had not taught religious doctrine or required students to participate in religious activities, the supreme court ruled in favor of the sisters.

The court's ruling did not end protests against the employment of nuns in North Dakota public schools. During the 1940s, for example, the legislature twice failed to pass anti-garb bills. In 1948 an organization known as the Committee for the Separation of Church and State (CSCS), primarily comprised of Protestant ministers, led a campaign to have an anti-garb initiative put to the voters. The real issue was not the clothing worn by the sisters but rather a fear that nuns would impose a sectarian influence on schoolchildren and that the Catholic Church would eventually dominate public education. After collecting more than 100,000 signatures, the CSCS filed a petition with the secretary of state, and the initiative was placed on the ballot for the 1948 election.

In response to the CSCS's initiative drive, a group called the Committee for the Defense of Civil Rights organized to battle the anti-garb bill. Using leaflets, pamphlets, and speeches, both sides waged an intense public campaign, and voters thronged to the polls—10,000 more turned out for the 1948 election than for the previous gubernatorial election. Despite more than 50,000 non-Catholics voting against the initiative, voters passed North Dakota's anti-garb bill.

The anti-garb bill did not immediately drive nuns from public schools. Not until the early 1960s did they disappear from North Dakota's public schools. Those who continued teaching in public schools, however, were forced to alter their teaching attire; some wore green Women's Army Corps (WAC) uniforms. North Dakota's anti-garb bill was an early battle in the debate over religion in public education. Today, the battle has moved to issues such as prayer in public schools and government aid to parochial schools.

Mark R. Ellis
University of Nebraska at Kearney

Grathwohl, Linda. "The North Dakota Anti-Garb Law: Constitutional Conflict and Religious Strife." *Great Plains Quarterly* 13 (1993): 187–202.

NORTH-WEST MOUNTED POLICE

Created by an act of the Canadian Parliament in 1873 as "a Police Force in the North West Territories," the North-West Mounted Police (as it was officially known from 1879 through 1904) was the first version of today's Royal Canadian Mounted Police. The force made its mythic reputation by its actions while policing the Canadian Great Plains from 1874 on as it prepared the West for both the Canadian Pacific Railway (completed in 1885) and the settlers who followed.

The "Great Lone Land" that became the Canadian Prairie Provinces had been held since the late seventeenth century as Rupert's Land by the Hudson's Bay Company. Euro-

pean American fur traders, both passing through and living on the land, worked with Native peoples (mainly Crees) in the trade and together created the Métis as a separate people. Not until 1869, with the transfer of Rupert's Land to the new Dominion government of Canada, was there conflict; the Métis, led by Louis Riel in the Red River Resistance, protested the transfer and instigated a second rebellion in 1885. Prime Minister Sir John A. Macdonald, having expanded his new nation to the Pacific Coast with the promise to British Columbia of an all-Canadian transcontinental railway and very aware of settlement pressures and conflicts between the U.S. Army and Native Americans just south of the "Medicine Line," realized that he needed some agency to govern Canada's vast new territory, prepare for the railway, and defend Canada's sovereignty against American incursion. Upon receiving news of a massacre of Assiniboines in the Cypress Hills during the summer of 1873, Macdonald acted by creating the North-West Mounted Police (NWMP).

Consciously modeled on police forces found elsewhere in the empire, the NWMP was intended to appear British; its constables' characteristic red tunics were chosen to contrast—especially in the minds of Native people—with the blue of the U.S. Army. At the same time, Macdonald carefully styled them as police rather than military so as to keep from alarming the Americans. The 300 new recruits were given a challenging task: police an area of some 300,000 square miles. After organizing in Manitoba over the winter of 1873–74, they set out west in July 1874 on what has come to be known as the "Great March," which, given its numerous difficulties, has usually been seen as epic. Divisions separated in order to set up posts throughout the region, most proximate to the U.S.-Canadian border and with a particular concentration in what is now southern Alberta, the area frequented by American whiskey traders from Fort Benton, Montana.

Once the NWMP was established, the whiskey traders were routed, and peaceful relations with the Natives had been effected, the force set about preparing the way for settlement. Constables were dispatched to smaller and more remote posts and, through a method of regular patrols and central reporting, both got to know their areas and kept their commanders aware of local conditions. Because of personnel limitations coupled with the status each constable had as a de facto justice of the peace (that is, constables who arrested also judged), the NWMP style of policing was in marked contrast to that found south of the border, especially in its initial dealings with Native peoples. "Maintain the Right" is the force's motto, and such was its accomplishment during its first decade.

From its beginning, the NWMP was a cloistered entity whose ongoing existence was not certain, and its first commissioners were concerned with public perception of the force. A newspaper illustrator from the *Canadian Illustrated News* accompanied the Great March west, and from that time on, journalists served

to create and enlarge the myth of the Mounted Police. No single instance made this more evident than Sitting Bull's time in Canada after the Battle of the Little Bighorn in June 1876. Many Native Americans moved north of the border to escape avenging U.S. soldiers. Sitting Bull arrived in 1877. The Lakota leader trusted the Mounted Police, especially Superintendent James Walsh, whom newspapers dubbed "Sitting Bull's Boss." The negotiations between governments—Canada, Great Britain, and the United States—over the "American" Lakotas drew enormous media attention. These episodes, during which the force's actions toward the Native peoples were comparatively and retrospectively positive, are the basis of the Mounted Police's mythic reputation.

By treating people, irrespective of race, fairly, the NWMP reasonably claims a corporate reputation based on the numerous instances of casual and commonplace heroism characterizing its early history generally and its dealings with Native peoples particularly. Such acts in turn suggest a group diligence embodied in the ubiquitous "get their man" cliché. The phrase, coined by an American newspaper and perpetuated by popular writers and Hollywood's twentieth-century infatuation with the North-West Mounted Police, is still used to characterize the force in its present but very different form as a 200,000-strong national force with liaisons in twenty-seven foreign capitals.

See also IMAGES AND ICONS: Frontier Violence.

Robert Thacker
St. Lawrence University

Atkin, Ronald. *Maintain the Right: The Early History of the North West Mounted Police.* New York: John Day, 1973.
Thacker, Robert. "Canada's Mounted: The Evolution of a Legend." *Journal of Popular Culture* 14 (1980): 298–312.
Walden, Keith. *Visions of Order: The Canadian Mounties in Symbol and Myth.* Toronto: Butterworths, 1982.

OVERLAND TRAIL CONSTITUTIONS

Travelers on the Overland Trail to the Pacific, after crossing the Missouri River, entered a territory without enforceable law, courts, or police. Those who journeyed in companies soon discovered the need for government, and, until about 1854, most companies drafted constitutions and sometimes bylaws.

Constitutions were seldom-detailed codes of government. They did not seek to regulate specific behavior but to obtain a reasonable degree of conformity within a social, economic, and legal environment conducive to democracy. Although a few companies had members sign their charters, implying that they thought constitutions were compacts and perhaps even personal contracts, the dominant legal theory was that overland constitutions were organic acts outlining the procedures for identifying and judging unacceptable conduct. Another common operative theory was that companies were organic wholes, peripatetic governments possessing all sovereign authority, a fact demonstrated by those constitutions establishing representative legislatures and authorizing capital punishment. Punishment was seldom inflicted, as offending parties could avoid most physical sanctions (except for the death penalty) by departing from the company. That reality did not undercut but instead reinforced the purpose of constitutions, because they sought social cooperation, not legal discipline. Once a wrongdoer left, harmony was restored. Lack of harmony was the chief cause terminating company governance. When pressures of overland travel destroyed harmony, emigrants knew the constitution no longer functioned.

The legal and social principles shaping constitutional policy on the Overland Trail were based on mediation, not legislation, to obtain harmony within diversity, not unanimity through legislation. These constitutions have a unique importance for American history. There is no more reliable way to measure the constitutional notions of average nineteenth-century citizens than to examine Overland Trail constitutions.

See also TRANSPORTATION: Oregon Trail.

John Phillip Reid
New York University School of Law

Reid, John Phillip. "Governance of the Elephant: Constitutional Theory on the Overland Trail." *Hastings Constitutional Law Quarterly* 5 (1978): 421–43. Reid, John Phillip. *Policing the Elephant: Crime, Punishment, and Social Behavior on the Overland Trail*. San Marino CA: Huntington Library, 1996.

PERSONS CASE

See GENDER: *Persons Case*

PIERRE-GUILLAUME SAYER TRIAL

The trial of Pierre-Guillaume Sayer on May 17, 1849, marked the effective end of the Hudson's Bay Company's trade monopoly in western Canada. Sayer was a Métis who, together with three companions, had traded liquor for furs in defiance of the company's trade monopoly. Most of the Métis were descendants of traders of the North West Company, which had been amalgamated with the Hudson's Bay Company in 1821. The North West Company and its traders had never recognized the legality of the Hudson's Bay Company's monopoly, but after the amalgamation the company was able, for a time, to enforce its monopoly by military means. Most of the Métis chafed under the company's restrictive policies, and their leaders, including Louis Riel Sr. (father of the Métis leader in the 1869–70 and 1885 troubles), appealed to a growing sense of Métis identity and nationalism. They argued that by right of exploration and trade conducted by their fathers and through Native rights derived from their mothers, the Métis should not be subject to the Hudson's Bay Company's restrictive trade policies.

The company's position was weakened in 1848 when the small contingent of British regular troops was withdrawn from Red River. Company officials, who were also the law officers of the colony, nevertheless decided to bring Sayer and his companions to trial. The case was brought before the General Quarterly Court of Assiniboia, but on the day of the trial several hundred well-armed Métis buffalo hunters threatened violence if Sayer and his companions were sent to prison. A jury acceptable to both sides was impaneled and in due course found Sayer guilty but recommended mercy. That recommendation was almost certainly a result of intimidation, since neither the court nor the company had the means to control and subdue the well-armed and angry Métis. Officially, mercy was recommended on the grounds that Sayer believed what he had done was legal.

The Hudson's Bay Company's chief factor at Red River accepted the jury's recommendation. Sayer was allowed to go free, and the charges against his companions were dropped. The Métis, regarding the outcome a a great victory, discharged their guns in delight, shouting "La commerce est libre!" Thereafter, the company undertook no further legal action at Red River to enforce its trade monopoly, relying instead on competitive practices to protect its trade. In practice, the Sayer trial ended the Hudson's Bay Company's trade monopoly. Legally, it only expired twenty years later with the transfer of the territory to the Canadian government.

See also INDUSTRY: Hudson's Bay Company / NATIVE AMERICANS: Métis.

Ted D. Regehr
University of Saskatchewan and
University of Calgary

Morton, W. L. *Manitoba: A History*. Toronto: University of Toronto Press, 1955. Ross, Alexander. *The Red River Settlement*. London: Smith, Elder, 1856.

POISON PORRIDGE CASE

See ASIAN AMERICANS: Poison Porridge Case

POUND, ROSCOE (1870–1964)

Roscoe Pound was a botanist, lawyer, educator, law professor, writer, and legal theorist. A leading American legal scholar of the twentieth century, Pound had a significant impact on American legal culture.

Pound was born in Lincoln, Nebraska, on October 27, 1870. Education was important to the Pound family. Roscoe's mother educated her children at home, infusing in them her love of literature and botany. Pound went on to the University of Nebraska, where he graduated with a degree in botany in 1888. Influenced by his father, Stephen, a prominent Nebraska lawyer and judge, Pound entered Harvard Law School but returned to Nebraska after one year. He continued his study of law—in a law office rather than law school—and in 1890 was admitted to the Nebraska bar. Even while practicing law, however, Pound's interest in botany continued, and in 1897 he earned a doctorate in that subject from the University of Nebraska. Pound taught botany at the university, served as the director of Nebraska's botanical survey, and identified a rare lichen, which was given the scientific name *roscoepoundia*.

Between 1890 and 1906 Pound was active in Nebraska's legal community. In addition to practicing law, he played a key role in the 1900 organization of the Nebraska State Bar Association, drafting the association's constitution and serving as its secretary for six years. In 1901 Pound was appointed a commissioner (temporary appellate judge) to the Nebraska Supreme Court. Finally, in 1903 the University of Nebraska appointed him dean of the law school, a position he held for several years.

Pound drew national attention in 1906 when he addressed the American Bar Association in St. Paul, Minnesota. In this speech Pound outlined his theory of "sociological jurisprudence," arguing that the law was not static but that judges should consider the social and economic consequences of their decisions. Impressed by the young legal scholar, Northwestern University hired him as a law professor. After serving two years there and another at the University of Chicago, Pound took a position at Harvard Law School and went on to become its dean from 1916 to 1936.

Although Pound left the Great Plains in 1907, he continued to have a significant impact on Nebraska's legal community. The University of Nebraska Law School appointed its deans largely based on Pound's recommendations. Pound also periodically returned to the Plains to deliver addresses at the annual meetings of the Nebraska State Bar Association.

Over the course of a multifaceted career, Pound wrote on a wide variety of topics, including botany, criminal law, prison reform, and the organization of courts. The 1959 publication of *Jurisprudence*, a five-volume work, capped a legal career that spanned more than seventy years. Pound died on July 1, 1964, in Cambridge, Massachusetts.

See also: EDUCATION: Pound, Louise.

Mark R. Ellis
University of Nebraska at Kearney

PUBLIC LAW 280

Public Law 280, passed on August 15, 1953, ended federal law enforcement on tribal lands and brought the tribes of five mandatory states—California, Minnesota, Nebraska, Oregon, and Wisconsin—under state civil and criminal jurisdiction. (Alaska was added later.) In theory this termination-era legislation was applied to these states because their state senators had requested the change and because tribal leaders had apparently accepted state control and federal withdrawal. All other states whose constitutions allowed such action were given the option to accept jurisdiction over their reservations. Congressional testimony reveals two primary justifications for the legislation: a feeling that a condition of lawlessness existed on and near reservations and the belief that tribal peoples should be under the same laws and law enforcement as the majority population.

Although the federal government traditionally administered law on Indian reservations, beginning in 1940 it began to give certain states partial or total jurisdiction. Among these states were Kansas and North Dakota (only on the Devils Lake Sioux Reservation). Following passage of PL 280 other Great Plains states attempted to accept some form of jurisdiction over their reservations. North Dakota accepted civil jurisdiction over its tribes, dependent upon tribal consent. Significantly, no tribe there has consented to state control. South Dakota attempted to apply the law multiple times, including unilaterally extending jurisdiction to its reservations, but, between court battles and electoral decisions, it has not been successful in this endeavor.

Both states and tribal peoples immediately noted problems with the law, problems that would lead to virtually continuous disputes both in and outside of courtrooms for the next four decades as well as jurisdictional uncertainty between tribal, city, state, and federal law enforcement agencies. State arguments against the law were almost universally based on the problem of increased cost to local and state governments. Tribal complaints centered on the fact that the law did not require any form of tribal consent.

Nebraska, the lone mandatory Great Plains PL 280 state, experienced such jurisdictional and law enforcement difficulties. Home to the Omahas and Winnebagos, neither Nebraska nor Thurston County (site of the reservations) hired additional law enforcement officers to replace departing federal officers, despite the fact that allotted lands owned by tribal members were taxed. With diminished law enforcement, crime rose on the reservations. In 1957 the state legislature passed a law known as the Indian Bounty Act, supplying state funds for counties with heavy tribal populations and land bases. This act formed the basis of later tribal complaints that county officials unjustly arrested inordinate numbers of Native Americans in order to receive these funds.

Because of widespread discontent on all sides, Congress included a consent clause to PL 280 in the Civil Rights Act of 1968 and also allowed states to retrocede jurisdiction back to the federal government. It did not give tribal peoples in previous PL 280 states power to demand this retrocession, and the prior consent clause did not have any bearing on the states already affected by PL 280. Under this change, the Omahas and later the Winnebagos successfully won retrocession. They have since created tribal courts and police and have completed cross-deputization and concurrent jurisdiction agreements with county, state, and federal authorities.

Charles Vollan
University of Nebraska–Lincoln

Goldberg, Carol. "Public Law 280: The Limits of State Jurisdiction over Indians." *UCLA Law Review* 22 (1975): 535–94. Hansen, Sandra. "Survey of Civil Jurisdiction in Indian Country." *American Indian Law Review* 16 (1990): 319–75.

SILKWOOD V. KERR-MCGEE

See PROTEST AND DISSENT: *Silkwood v. Kerr-McGee*

STARKWEATHER, CHARLES (1938–1959)

Charles Starkweather, Nebraska's most infamous son and one of America's most shocking serial killers, terrorized the Great Plains in the winter of 1957–58 when he embarked on a brutal murder rampage with his fourteen-year-old girlfriend, Caril Ann Fugate. Put to death for his crimes, Starkweather, whose case received unprecedented national media coverage, shocked America out of its 1950s malt-shop innocence and foreshadowed the modern spree killer, whose victims are chosen largely at random to satisfy some deep-rooted hatred of humanity and to settle some secret grudge against society.

Charles was born in Lincoln, Nebraska, on November 24, 1938, the third of seven children of Guy and Helen Starkweather. Guy worked as a carpenter-handyman, Helen as a waitress. By all accounts they were good, decent, loving parents. Starkweather is said to have experienced an ordinary, normal childhood until he began his schooling. From prison, he reflected that his hatred for society was spawned on the kindergarten playground when on his first day of school his fellow classmates mocked his speech impediment and bowlegs, making him feel isolated and different. Starkweather wrote that on that fateful day his heart turned "black with hate and rage," and he vowed revenge.

Starkweather's life between the kindergarten incident and eleven gruesome homicides reflects his antisocial and deeply troubled mind. As a youth he had a hair-trigger temper and was constantly involved in fistfights. A loner and an outcast, Starkweather became obsessed with guns and hunting. He began to idolize and emulate actor James Dean, star of *Rebel Without a Cause*, the 1955 film classic about alienated youth. He adopted Dean's "live fast, die young" credo. He became increasingly disillusioned with his job as a trash collector and in the years before the killings began having terrifying nightmares and vivid, bizarre hallucinations during which he would converse with "Death." Also during this period Starkweather, the shy, withdrawn loner, found a girlfriend in Caril Ann Fugate.

Caril Ann and Charles were soon inseparable. She fit nicely into his paranoid, alienated worldview, willingly adopting and reinforcing his self-imposed exile from mainstream society. Strangely, instead of quelling Starkweather's murderous predilections, his storybook romance with Caril Ann seems to have driven him over the edge, convincing him that the end was near, that he must take action soon. In Starkweather's mind Caril Ann had finally given him "something worth killing for."

Starkweather's murder spree began on December 1, 1957, when he robbed a Lincoln gas station, kidnapped the attendant, Robert Colvert, and shot him to death on a lonely rural road. The murder gave Starkweather a feeling of power; he had operated outside of the law and gotten away with it. Violence erupted once again on January 21, 1958, when Starkweather fought with Velda Bartlett (Caril Ann's mother) over the teenagers' relation-

ship. In a rage, he savagely beat, stabbed, and shot her to death, along with Caril Ann's stepfather and baby sister.

After Starkweather killed Caril Ann's family, the couple kicked off a weeklong frenzy of violence that resulted in another seven homicides. In need of money and supplies, Starkweather killed seventy-two-year-old August Meyer, a longtime family friend, at his rural Lincoln residence. Seventeen-year-old Robert Jensen and sixteen-year-old Carol King were the next victims when, on January 27, Starkweather and Fugate picked up the hitchhiking couple. Starkweather shot Jensen six times in the back of the head and shot and stabbed King repeatedly. Incredibly, Starkweather and Fugate then returned to Lincoln, where they invaded the home of C. Lauer Ward, a wealthy industrialist. Starkweather stabbed and shot to death Lauer, his wife, Clara, and the housekeeper, Lillian Fencl. Loading the Wards' 1956 Packard with food, the couple headed west across the Plains.

By now a major manhunt was in progress. The Nebraska National Guard cruised Lincoln streets in jeeps fitted with machine guns. Parents armed with guns escorted their children to and from school. Aircraft searched for the Wards' black car, while authorities initiated a block-to-block search. Meanwhile, Starkweather and Fugate made it to Wyoming on January 29 and were in search of a car that authorities would not recognize. Merle Collison, a traveling salesman who was sleeping in his car alongside the highway, became the final victim when he refused to surrender his car. Starkweather was captured shortly thereafter by Wyoming authorities and extradited to Nebraska.

Starkweather and Fugate were charged with first-degree murder, convicted, and sentenced, Fugate to life in prison, Charles Starkweather to death. He was executed in Nebraska's electric chair on June 25, 1959. Caril Ann Fugate was paroled on June 20, 1976, after seventeen years of imprisonment. She continues to proclaim her innocence, denying complicity in the killings.

Derrick S. Ward
Ventura, California

Allen, William. *Starkweather: The Story of a Mass Murder*. Boston: Houghton Mifflin, 1976. Newton, Michael. *Waste Land: The Savage Odyssey of Charles Starkweather and Caril Ann Fugate*. New York: Simon and Schuster, 1998. O'Donnell, Jeff. *Starkweather: A Story of Mass Murder on the Great Plains*. Lincoln NE: J. and L. Lee Company, 1993.

TEXAS RANGERS

The Texas Rangers are the oldest state law enforcement agency in the United States. Throughout their storied history they have gone through several transformations and have performed an array of duties. A symbol of the American West and immortalized in film and print, the Texas Rangers have a worldwide reputation and are mentioned in the same breath with elite law enforcement agencies such as the Royal Canadian Mounted Police and Scotland Yard.

Texas Rangers, between 1890 and 1900

The origins of the Texas Rangers date back to 1823, when Stephen F. Austin appointed ten frontiersmen to defend the nascent Texas settlements from Indian attacks. These early ranger companies operated as loosely organized and irregular units until 1835, when a more permanent body was created. When the Texas Revolution broke out in 1836, the rangers served in a limited capacity as scouts, couriers, and escorts. Several rangers died defending the Alamo.

The Texas Rangers played an important role in defending the frontier under the Lone Star flag of the Republic of Texas. Under the leadership of Capt. John "Jack" Coffee Hays, the rangers became an experienced and feared fighting unit. Their effective use of the Colt revolver helped popularize the weapon. During the Mexican War (1846–48), Hays's rangers served as scouts, spies, and cavalrymen under generals Zachary Taylor and Winfield Scott. Mounted and heavily armed, the Texas Rangers earned a reputation as fiercely independent fighters. Because of their ruthless pursuit of Mexican guerrillas and their rough treatment of citizens, their Mexican counterparts labeled them "los diablos tejanos" (the Texas devils).

From the end of the Mexican War to 1874, the rangers saw little action. The U.S. Army guarded the Texas frontier, leaving the rangers with few responsibilities. They reappeared in 1874, when the state legislature created several ranger companies to deal with Indian attacks in West Texas, Mexican bandits along the Rio Grande, and the growing number of outlaws and desperadoes that infested Texas. In a military role, they assisted the U.S. Army in crushing Comanche and Kiowa resistance during the 1870s. As lawmen, the Texas Rangers traveled thousands of miles while tracking criminals. They gained fame by restoring peace in civil conflicts such as the Sutton-Taylor Feud and by capturing Great Plains outlaws such as gunfighter John Wesley Hardin and train robber Sam Bass.

With the end of the Indian wars and the general establishment of law and order, the duties and responsibilities of the rangers changed. In the 1910s and 1920s rangers guarded the Mexico-Texas border from Mexican revolutionaries, enforced prohibition laws, and policed oil boomtowns. In 1935 the Texas Rangers became a professional law enforcement unit when they were incorporated, along with the state highway patrol, into the newly created Texas Department of Public Safety (DPS). Since then they have been the investigative body of the DPS. Modern-day rangers travel by car, plane, boat, helicopter, and only occasionally by horse. They still do not wear a uniform; the ranger badge is the only common accouterment worn by all rangers. Although their numbers remain small (only 106 rangers were on duty in 1997), the Texas Rangers continue to be the elite of Texas law enforcement.

Mark R. Ellis
University of Nebraska at Kearney

Gillett, James B. *Six Years with the Texas Rangers, 1875–1881.* New Haven CT: Yale University Press, 1925. Samora, Julian, Joe Bernal, and Albert Peña. *Gunpowder Justice: A Reassessment of the Texas Rangers.* Notre Dame IN: University of Notre Dame Press, 1979. Webb, Walter Prescott. *The Texas Rangers: A Century of Frontier Defense.* Austin: University of Texas Press, 1965.

TREATIES

See NATIVE AMERICANS: Treaties

TRIAL OF STANDING BEAR

See PROTEST AND DISSENT: Trial of Standing Bear

UNITED STATES V. SIOUX NATION OF INDIANS

In *United States v. Sioux Nation of Indians* (1980), the U.S. Supreme Court held that an 1877 act of Congress, by which the United States wrested control of the Black Hills of South Dakota from the Sioux Indian Nation, constituted a "taking" of property under the Fifth Amendment, giving rise to an obligation to fairly compensate the Sioux. The Court affirmed a prior decision of the court of claims, which had awarded the Sioux $17.1 million for the taking of the Black Hills, and further held that the tribe was entitled to interest on that amount from 1877. By the late 1990s, the amount due the Sioux had risen to more than $600 million—a payment that the tribe still refuses to accept, choosing instead to continue to seek the return of the land itself.

The 1980 decision represented the judicial culmination of more than sixty years of litigation and lobbying in the Court of Claims, the Indian Claims Commission, the U.S. Congress, and the Supreme Court, in which the Sioux sought retribution for more than a century's worth of bad faith and fraudulent dealings relating to the Black Hills. The fundamental basis for the continuing claim is the 1868 Fort Laramie Treaty, in which the government pledged that the Great Sioux Reservation, including the Black Hills, would be permanently preserved for the "absolute and undisturbed use and occupation" of the tribe. The treaty further provided that no change to the reservation boundaries would be effective unless approved by at least three-fourths of the adult male population of the Sioux Nation. In 1877 Congress enacted a statute that, in effect, unilaterally abrogated the provisions of the 1868 treaty. The act codified the terms of a new treaty, signed under military duress by only about 10 percent of the adult male Sioux population, under which the Sioux purportedly ceded another 7 million acres, including the Black Hills, to the United States.

Some forty years after losing the Black Hills under those dubious circumstances, the Sioux embarked upon a long judicial and legislative quest for their return. In 1920 they brought suit in the Court of Claims, alleging that the government had taken the Black Hills without just compensation in violation of the Fifth Amendment. The Court of Claims ultimately dismissed that claim in 1942, and the Sioux then reasserted their arguments before the Indian Claims Commission, beginning in 1946. The commission held that the 1877 act was in fact a compensable taking for which the Sioux were entitled to $17.5 million, without interest. On appeal, however, the Court of Claims again dismissed the Sioux claim, holding that the tribe's arguments were barred by the Court's 1942 decision. There the matter stood until 1978, when the Sioux obtained a special act of Congress authorizing a new review of the tribe's Black Hills claim without regard to the earlier decisions of the Court of Claims. This time the Court of Claims held that the government had indeed acted in bad faith in taking the Black Hills and that the Sioux were entitled to $17.1 million in damages, plus interest from 1877. When the Supreme Court affirmed the Court of Claims ruling in 1980, the Sioux's long decades of legal tenacity were seemingly vindicated.

Yet even before the Sioux achieved this

monumental Supreme Court victory, controversy arose within the tribe and between some members of the tribe and their attorneys over whether or not a monetary judgment should even be sought, much less accepted. For growing numbers of Sioux, monetary compensation was not acceptable as a resolution of their claims—only the return of the sacred Black Hills themselves would suffice. Those sentiments have controlled subsequent events in this prolonged drama, and the Sioux continue to refuse to accept the payment dictated by the Court's decision.

See also NATIVE AMERICANS: Sioux.

Mark R. Scherer
University of Nebraska at Omaha

Lazarus, Edward. *Black Hills, White Justice: The Sioux Nation versus the United States, 1775 to the Present*. New York: HarperCollins, 1991. Pemberton, Richard, Jr. "'I Saw That It Was Holy': The Black Hills and the Concept of Sacred Land." *Law and Inequality: A Journal of Theory and Practice* 3 (1985): 287–311.

VIGILANTES

Vigilantes are individuals who take the law into their own hands. Vigilante movements have often been viewed in a positive light, and apologists suggest that vigilance committees were necessary because duly constituted legal authorities failed to maintain order and punish alleged criminals. This assumption has never been proven or adequately explored.

Vigilantes, often called stranglers, slickers, white caps, night riders, lynch mobs, and a variety of other names, usually worked as a group at night (sometimes hooded) to assure anonymity, to bolster their courage, to reduce their personal accountability, and to avoid prosecution. They formed committees, and in order to solicit legitimacy for their actions they issued proclamations that suggested that they had to act to "preserve" law and order. Usually vigilantism occurred when a group of citizens believed that the law either was not working or was too slow in prosecuting alleged criminals. Under such conditions local members of the community took action to remedy the situation.

San Francisco vigilante movements in 1851 and 1856 were probably the best-known examples of such extralegal activity. Their methods included organization of community leaders, focus on a particular "problem" in society, the quick apprehension of alleged criminals, and a "speedy trial" followed by punishment such as flogging or, more commonly, death by hanging. Vigilantism spread quickly across the West. Vigilantes who were little better than lynch mobs took retribution against anyone considered to be a threat to Great Plains society. Although the Canadian Plains seldom experienced such violent activities, several examples of vigilante activity took place from 1867 to 1897 in the Kootenay River region in British Columbia that borders western Montana.

Walter van Tilburg Clark in *The Ox-Bow Incident* (1940) correctly perceived that this distinctly American form of violence appealed

University of Colorado football star "The Whizzer" Byron White (right), between 1930 and 1940

to the local community and that the people involved in the activity assumed that their actions were necessary for their community's welfare. Clark also provided the components for the lynch mob action: an alleged crime and criminal, a mob leader, an inflammatory speech, liberal use of alcohol, a rope, and, finally, a tree in town or in a nearby cottonwood grove.

Whether the victim was Sheriff Henry Plummer in Bannack, Montana, Cattle Kate in Wyoming, Frank Blackhawk (Standing Rock Sioux) in Williamsport, North Dakota, William Brown in Omaha, Nebraska, or some nameless Indian, Chinese, or Hispanic victim on a lonely country road, Great Plains vigilantism or lynch mob action was swift and usually fatal. Richard Maxwell Brown provides the following nineteenth-century statistics for vigilante killings in Great Plains states: Texas, 140; Montana, 101; Wyoming, 31; Colorado, 23; Nebraska, 21; Kansas, 18; South Dakota, 10; Oklahoma, 2; and North Dakota, 0. For comparative purposes, California, the birthplace of western vigilantism, had 109 victims. However, these statistics are misleading, since they do not include lynch mob killings.

Some historians claim that vigilantism is not the same as lynching, but David A. Johnson suggests that the distinction between organized vigilance committees and ephemeral lynch parties is a blurred one. Johnson also notes that in the 1850s the term *mob* was seldom used to describe vigilantism, but a decade later *mob* or *lynch mob* had become the predominant terms to describe this type of violence. If one adds lynch mob victims to vigilante killings, the resulting Great Plains totals would be Texas, 475; Montana, 122; Oklahoma, 98; Wyoming, 65; Colorado, 41; Nebraska, 38; Kansas, 40; South Dakota, 23; and North Dakota, 10. Again by comparison, in California vigilantes and mobs lynched at least 380 victims.

Regardless of how one chooses to define "vigilante," it remains a word that stigmatizes those who took the law into their own hands. Historically, it has been convenient to modify what has been called the "shared memory" of a local community in order to "fit the facts," such as in the mysterious hanging of Barrett Scott, a convicted embezzler, on January 19, 1895, at an abandoned farmhouse in northern Nebraska and the attempt to avoid detection by dropping the body in the Niobrara River. Unfortunately for local taxpayers, Scott was not given time to return the money. A jury failed to convict any of the identified vigilantes, who presumably returned to their community "vindicated" by their deadly actions.

See also IMAGES AND ICONS: Frontier Violence.

Clare V. McKanna Jr.
San Diego State University

Brown, Richard Maxwell. *Strain of Violence: Historical Studies of American Violence and Vigilantism*. New York: Oxford University Press, 1975. Hewitt, James W. "The Fatal Fall of Barrett Scott: Vigilantes on the Niobrara." *Great Plains Quarterly* 12 (1992): 107–20. Johnson, David A. "Vigilance and the Law: The Moral Authority of Popular Justice in the Far West." *American Quarterly* 33 (1981): 558–86.

WATER LAW, PRAIRIE PROVINCES

See WATER: Water Law, Prairie Provinces

WHITE, BYRON (1917–2002)

Byron Raymond White was born on June 17, 1917, in Fort Collins, Colorado, but grew up in the nearby sugar beet hamlet of Wellington. His father ran a lumberyard, and his mother was a homemaker. Both Byron and his older brother, Clayton S. (Sam), raised beets and did odd jobs from an early age to help support the family. A full-tuition scholarship took Byron White from this impoverished Plains background to the University of Colorado, where he became class president, all-American in football (second in the 1937 Heisman Trophy vote), and a Rhodes Scholar. (His brother had become a Rhodes Scholar four years earlier.) After a season as the highest-paid player in the National Football League, he went to Oxford, but war forced him to return stateside, where he attended Yale Law School. Following naval service in the South Pacific, he returned to Yale, led his class academically, and then clerked for the chief justice of the United States.

In 1959 John F. Kennedy, whom White had met in England and in the navy, enticed him to help run his impending presidential campaign. After the election, Kennedy appointed White deputy attorney general, and White spent more than a year as the principal administrator of the Department of Justice, with special responsibility for staffing and judicial nominations. He personally went to Alabama in 1961 to oversee treatment of the Freedom Riders. When Justice Charles E. Whittaker of Kansas retired on disability in March 1962, Kennedy named White to the Court, the only Colorado native so honored. White spent three decades on the Court, where he earned a reputation for brilliance if not eloquence and for skepticism toward judicial intervention in social problems unless clearly guided by appropriate legislation. His best-known opinions were dissents involving criminal justice (*Miranda v. Arizona*), abortion (*Roe v. Wade*), and separation of powers (*INS v. Chadha*).

White retired form the Court in 1993 but continued to sit on lower federal courts and to serve the nation in a variety of capacities. He died in Denver, Colorado, of complications from pneumonia, on April 15, 2002.

Dennis J. Hutchinson
University of Chicago

Hutchinson, Dennis J. *The Man Who Once Was Whizzer White*. New York: Free Press, 1998.

WHITE PRIMARY

After Reconstruction, southern states began a campaign to disfranchise African American voters in order to eliminate the Republican Party from Southern politics and safeguard white supremacy. Various methods were used, including poll taxes, literacy tests, and violence, but by the 1920s a widely used method of disfranchisement was the white primary. As a political device, legitimized by state statutes, the white primary effectively eliminated African American voters from the electoral process by barring them from primary elections.

In 1923 the intensity of opposition to the white primary increased when Texas abandoned the white primary by party rule and enacted a law that prohibited the participation of African Americans in a Democratic primary election. From the 1920s through the 1950s the NAACP waged a systematic legal campaign against the white primary, arguing that it violated the Fourteenth and Fifteenth Amendments. When the NAACP prevailed in the U.S. Supreme Court, supporters of white primary statutes returned to state legislatures and enacted laws that they thought would pass constitutional muster. The Supreme Court upheld Texas's white primary statute in *Grovey v. Townsend* (1935), holding that the Democratic Party was a voluntary, private organization that could determine its own membership qualifications.

During the 1940s and 1950s the Supreme Court began to chip away at the legality of the white primary more decisively. In *United States v. Classic* (1941), for example, the Supreme Court reversed the *Townsend* precedent, arguing that the Constitution secured the right to vote. In 1944 the Supreme Court further eroded the power of the Texas white primary in *Smith v. Allwright*, ruling that the state had violated the Constitution by providing ballots at primary elections. This decision largely ended the white primary in Texas. Between 1940 and 1947 the number of registered African American voters in Texas jumped from 30,000 to 100,000. Finally, in *Terry v. Adams* (1953), the Supreme Court prohibited the legacies of the white primary, insisting that the scope of the Fifteenth Amendment included any election in which public issues are decided or public officials are elected. In the end, the persistence of the NAACP and the willingness of the Supreme Court to create a more democratic society eradicated the white primary as a disfranchisement device.

See also AFRICAN AMERICANS: Civil Rights.

Michael W. Combs
University of Nebraska–Lincoln

Combs, Michael W. "The Supreme Court and African Americans: Personnel and Policy Transformations." *Howard Law Journal* 36 (1993): 139–84. Key, V. O., Jr. *Southern Politics*. New York: Vintage Books, 1949. Woodward, C. Vann. *The Strange Career of Jim Crow*. New York: Oxford University Press, 1966.

WINTERS DOCTRINE

See WATER: Winters Doctrine

Literary Traditions

O. D. Wheeler interviewing Cheyennes, including White Bull, about the Battle of the Little Bighorn, June 1901

LITERARY TRADITIONS

Whatever stories the wolves tell, they do not tell to human ears, and the songs of the earliest hunter-gatherers in the Great Plains are now lost to memory. Nonetheless, the extant literatures of the Great Plains are plentiful, rich, and diverse.

The tradition began with the oral literatures of the many Native nations who have lived in the area and with the folktales and dramas of the early European and mixed-blood peoples. The first written literature to come from the Plains was the utilitarian recording of tribal histories as winter counts and the diaries and letters from early European American explorers. In most people's minds, Plains literature is probably associated with the Wild West and with tales that pit humans against a vast and harsh environment or "cowboys" against "Indians," and certainly literature of this sort has been both extremely popular and influential in forming the American self-identity. Popular Prairie fiction in Canada, by contrast, featured order and community. Plains writers in both the United States and Canada also produced a body of realistic fiction dealing with European American settlement and ways of living on the land. Poetry flourishes, though drama has not really become naturalized on the Plains except in the Prairie Provinces of Canada. Meanwhile, the last twenty years have seen a renaissance of writing by Native peoples and other longtime cultures of the Plains, as Métis, Blackfeet, and Chicano peoples, among others, have found a voice in fiction and poetry.

Native Oral Literatures

Living oral tradition as well as transcriptions by literate observers have preserved much oral literature. Narratives of a sacred or semisacred nature explain the origins of the universe, of the particular nation, of the hero figures of the nation, and of the holy ceremonies of the people. Thus the Blackfeet tell how Napi (Old Man) created the universe, and the Kiowa tell of how that nation came into this world through a hollow log. White Buffalo Woman brought the sacred pipe to the Lakotas, and the animals in the medicine lodges gave curing ceremonies to the Pawnee doctors. Orphan Boy among the Omahas, the Tai-Me twins among the Kiowas, and Scarface among the Blackfeet are heroes with long story cycles. Trickster, called Nanabush or Nanapush among the Ojibwas and Crees, Iktome among the Lakotas, and many other names in other languages, is a ubiquitous figure in these narratives. The Winnebagos have a particularly well-developed Trickster cycle, documented by Paul Radin in the early part of the twentieth century and more recently by Winnebago storyteller Felix White. Trickster is neither good nor evil but rather a representation of the human spirit at its most basic level, creation and destruction inextricably mixed.

Songs, chants, and prayers are also characteristic of traditional oral Plains literatures. Much oral literature consists of events in the lives of the people, gossip, campfire stories, and examples of both proper and improper behavior to be told to young people. Winter counts are such ordinary happenings compiled by year, and they serve as both a calendar and a mnemonic device for remembering and recounting the history of the people. Petroglyphs (writing on stone), hide paintings, and, from the nineteenth and twentieth centuries, ledger book drawings are other pictorial narratives of events.

Mexican Folk Literatures

Much of what is now the Southern Plains of the United States was first colonized by Spain and later controlled by Mexico, so it is not surprising that the population of the area, a racial and cultural mixture of Spanish and Indian, should support a folk literature similar to that of Mexico. Semisacred legends regarding the Virgin of Guadalupe have always been important to the Spanish speakers of the Southern Plains, as to other Mexicans. Folk pageants such as dramas based on the Spanish tradition or spectacles showing the Spanish conquest of the Moors or other heroic and romantic action were part of village life.

After the Mexican War and the partition of the territory that had been part of Mexico, the border began to play a part in folk narrative, particularly in the *corridos*, long ballads often printed on cheap broadsheets and sung in the streets. Typically, a *corrido* describes a Mexican outlaw and folk hero who outwits the Texas Rangers and other gringos sent to capture him.

Explorers and Other Travelers

The first non-Native literature of the Great Plains consists of the journals of predominantly European and European American explorers. These men ventured out into the Plains for various pragmatic reasons. They were careful to describe the terrain, its flora and fauna, its human inhabitants, and the patterns of social and economic trade and travel. Missionaries and Indian agents also traveled about the Plains in the eighteenth and nineteenth centuries, recording in journals and letters home what they saw and what they thought. By the mid–nineteenth century, professional travelers like Washington Irving and Francis Parkman were following in the literal steps of the explorers and writing about *A Tour on the Prairies* (1835) and *The Oregon Trail* (1849). Increasing numbers of men and women, professional and amateur writers, traveled west and recorded their experiences.

Plains Fiction

Not until James Fenimore Cooper's *The Prairie* (1827), written in Paris by a man who had never been west of the Alleghenies, did European-style fiction and poetry deal with the Great Plains. Cooper was extremely influential for American literature in general but particularly so for Plains literature. His legacy was twofold, leading to the popular Western, beginning with the dime novel, and also to the nonformula Western, the realistic agrarian or small-town novel. The development of a written European American literature on the Ca-nadian Prairies followed a different pattern and came later.

In both popular and nonformula Plains literature, in both Canada and the United States, the land has been a major force. The vast expanse of earth and sky, at once uplifting and humbling, shapes the lives of all who dwell upon the grasslands of North America. Even in urban literature, where a distinctive Plains environment is marked more by cultural and ethnic enclaves and mixes than by the land itself, the very air proclaims a place that is unlike either East or West. In the mid–nineteenth century, when the United States was first creating for itself a national identity that went beyond the ideals of the American Revolution, poets, philosophers, and painters all postulated that while Europe might have history, America had Nature and therefore a close and transcendental relationship with a deity or first force. This sense of renewal in nature affected Plains writers most strongly. In the vastness of the Plains there was renewal and communion with nature.

Within that nature there was also the Indian, split into the "noble savage" and the "bloodthirsty redskin." In such formulations, the Indian was always an "other" against whom the white characters defined themselves rather than a character deserving development in his or her own right. Again, Cooper set the pattern, with the "good" Mohicans and "bad" Mingos of New York State transformed into the "good" Pawnees and "bad" Sioux of the Plains who help or hinder Leatherstocking and his various white friends and antagonists.

In the United States the genre Western, from the dime novel to John Wayne and from Zane Grey to Louis L'Amour, has become a formative, though excluding, national myth, the embodiment of the "rugged individual" who takes the law into his (rarely her) own hands and plows ahead, overcoming obstacles. The conventions of the Western, of the man living without and above the law, also shaped the cop movie, the hard-boiled detective, and the space fantasy. Cooper's hero, Natty Bumppo, the eponymous Leatherstocking, a white man living outside both white and Indian society and claiming a higher moral law than the conventions of either, is the first fully developed representative of a European American type.

Leatherstocking's popularity fitted in with other frontier culture of the time, particularly that of the Great Plains frontier. Thus the fictional "autobiographies" of Daniel Boone and Davy Crockett as well as of a host of lesser-known or truly fictional frontiersmen showed a hero who was close to nature. Wild and rowdy he might be, but he was also eventually a force for what an emerging society saw as an ideal of order. He venerated "good" women but saw them as representatives of an unduly moralistic and legalistic order that he repudiated. Except in the "autobiographies," he rarely married. The frontier narrative became truly formulaic with the dime novels. As the Deadeye Dick series shows, the hero could be a lawman or an outlaw or swap back and forth. Calamity Jane was a female version of this hero, but sagas featuring such heroines were more likely than those of the male heroes to be marked by unhappy love affairs.

Although the North American settlement frontier did not close in 1890, as the Bureau of the Census claimed, the massive population movement in twentieth- and twenty-first-century North America has been from the farms and small towns to the cities. The mythologized West became the setting for what was frankly escape literature only a generation after the Plains had offered a real escape. Owen Wister's *The Virginian* (1902) is the book that marks this apotheosis of the West as a paradise lost. Wister, a Philadelphia lawyer, found his own restorative in the clean air and vast spaces of Wyoming, and his fable of the romance between a Virginia cowboy and a Vermont schoolmarm in Wyoming proved enormously successful and durable. *The Virginian*, like most Westerns, reflects a great admiration for violence. In Wister's terms, his heroine, Molly, represents the overly moralistic code of "snivilization," as he called it, but she is able to come through in a crisis and rally to her man after he kills the villain, Trampas, in a shoot-out. The book reflects Wister's elitist biases as well as the Anglo-Saxon nationalism that flourished in the decade of the Spanish-American War and was built on the casual denigration of Indians that was implicit in Cooper's "noble savage" formulations. For Wister, the true noble savage was the Anglo-Saxon, whose "nobility" led to lynch laws and commercial success, while the "Indians" were only a plot convention, "bloodthirsty savages" whose attack on the hero allowed the heroine to nurse him back to health and to fall in love.

The Virginian's immediate successors were genial heroes whose appeal has been mostly to a juvenile audience. *Chip of the Flying U* (1906) by B. M. Bowers, one of the few women to write Westerns, and Clarence Mulford's Hopalong Cassidy, introduced in *Bar 20* (1907), are charming but lack the mythic strength of the Virginian. The most successful writer to follow Wister was the enormously prolific Zane Grey. His gutsy heroines, torrid love plots, and action-packed dramas have proved endlessly popular. *Riders of the Purple Sage* (1912) was considered risqué in its portrayal of the two pairs of lovers and was, in a sense, innovative in its use of Mormons, rather than Indians, as the "savage" antagonists. During World War I Grey capitalized on anti-German sentiment to use Germans and Industrial Workers of the World organizers as the bad guys in *Desert of Wheat* (1919). And in *The Vanishing American* he tried in the 1922 serial version to have an Indian war hero vanish by marrying a white girl and assimilating, but a negative response to the marriage led him to return to Cooper's solution in *The Last of the Mohicans*, killing off his hero in the 1925 book version of the story.

Max Brand (Frederick Faust), Luke Short (Frederick D. Glidden), and Ernest Haycox were among the many prolific writers of pulp Westerns who followed Grey. Eugene Manlove Rhodes, a more sophisticated writer who, like Wister, combined his romances with keenly observed realistic details, published a number of innovative Westerns, including *Paso por Aqui* (1926) and the novel *Beyond the Desert* (1934). By the late 1930s the genre was so well developed that it could be used allegorically by Walter Van Tilburg Clark in his novel *The Ox-Bow Incident* (1940), in which the conventions of the lynching in *The Virginian* are turned upside down and the action becomes a parable of fascism and mob rule, not an example, as it had been to Wister, of the workings of a higher moral order. Jack Schaeffer's *Shane* (1949) also works by changing the convention. Schaeffer loosely bases his story on the same Johnson County (Wyoming) range war that Wister had used but makes Wister's rustlers his good guys, a switch that Frederick Manfred also makes in his *Riders of Judgment* (1949). Manfred draws heavily, though without explicit acknowledgment, on historical documents of the range war. While many of Zane Grey's books, set in the Southwest or Far West, like Clark's *Ox-Bow Incident*, set in Nevada, cannot, strictly speaking, be called Plains literature, the conventions of the genre do not allow for meaningful distinctions based on geography. The world of the Western is a region of the mind. The sexual revolution of the 1960s affected the Western as well, to the success of Louis L'Amour's dynastic Westerns and to such role reversals as John Seelye's *The Kid* (1972), in which the "kid" turns out to be a girl and the man who plays the Leatherstocking role is a mute African American man.

Whether in fiction, film, radio, or television, the popular Western hero is a loner who explicitly rejects society as it is represented by law, organized religion, and most women. For Leatherstocking and the dime novel heroes, this divorce from society is final and absolute. For the characters descended from Daniel Boone and the Virginian, it seems possible to have it all, as the hero marries, sires children, and settles down with both wealth and prominence in the community. Schaeffer's Shane, by splitting the hero into the hard-working farmer and the drifter-gunslinger who comes to his aid but then leaves, shows again that the dream of unfettered freedom and thus of violence is inimical to the dream of the garden fruitful in both crops and children.

The second strain in Plains fiction is that dream of the garden. Although it clearly has roots in the classic tradition of the pastoral, it is descended primarily from the literary realism and naturalism that flourished in the United States in the late nineteenth and early twentieth centuries. It deals not with the larger-than-life figure of the cowboy or gunslinger but with the ordinary dirt farmer and not with the individual but with the family. Hamlin Garland's *Main-Travelled Roads* stories, published in the 1890s, are the first full-blown members of this genre. They deal with the details and hardships of farm life on the "middle border," the area running from Wisconsin and Iowa through the Dakotas, and contrast the beauty of the natural landscape with the squalor of the built landscape and the demeaning and destructive demands of organized society. Instead of praising one individual working to bring about an abstract justice outside of the settlement, Garland's work celebrates the efforts of the community to bring about social justice within its borders. His essentially populist view of Plains life has remained pervasive. It appears in Sinclair Lewis's *Main Street* (1920), in which the prairie town is a parasite on the industrious farmers, and in Mari Sandoz's books, particularly *Old Jules* (1935), the fictionalized story of Sandoz's father, and *Capital City* (1939), an allegorical novel deploring the betrayal of the community by the few who have become rich.

The difficulties of Plains settlement were magnified when the settlers were outside the dominant culture. O. E. Rölvaag's *Giants in the Earth* (1927), originally published in two volumes in Norway in 1924 and 1925, remains the classic immigrant novel. It pits Per Hansa, at once the larger-than-life heroic pioneer and the character who does not realize the cultural loss involved in pioneering, against his wife, Beret, a Cassandra-like figure whose warnings that by losing their Norwegian culture they will lose their souls and themselves are not heeded by her fellow settlers. In two sequels, *Peder Victorious* (1929) and *Their Father's God* (1931), Rölvaag explores the emotional consequences of assimilation into an American culture characterized by materialism. While Rölvaag's work is often joyous and shows the miraculous nature of the first plantings of wheat on the Dakota Plains, nature is more agnostic and culture more vital than in either the popular Western or works following Garland's essentially meliorist vision of the Plains.

Rölvaag's work not only presents the Scandinavian experience on the Plains but also serves as a model for the fiction of other ethnic groups. Texas writer Tomás Rivera explicitly patterned his classic of Tejano migrant life, . . . *Y No Se Lo Tragó la Tierra* (. . . *And the Earth Did Not Part*, 1971) on Rölvaag's trilogy. Chicano culture is more problematic for Rivera's characters than Norwegian is for Rölvaag's, however, and Rivera's revolt against the social system that virtually enslaves the migrants is closer to Garland's than to Rölvaag's. Other portraits of ethnic settlers such as Sophus Keith Winthur's Danes in *Take All to Nebraska* (1936) and Hope Williams Sykes's Germans from Russia in *Second Hoeing* (1935) detail the same conflicts between the ethnic culture, the pressures of assimilation, and the oppressive social and economic system in which Plains agriculturalists live and work. Oscar Micheaux's two Plains novels, *The Conquest* (1913) and *The Homesteader* (1917), show the particular pressures on African American settlers.

The two most popular authors in the agrarian tradition are undoubtedly Willa Cather and Laura Ingalls Wilder. Both explicitly reject Garland's populism in favor of stories of the trials and ultimate triumphs of the great individual. Their heroes parallel the traditions of the popular Westerns except for two crucial differences. Their conquests are nonviolent, and their transcendent individuals are women.

Willa Cather's first two Nebraska novels, *O Pioneers!* (1913) and the perennial favorite *My Ántonia* (1918), feature strong heroines possessed of an almost mythical sense of oneness with the land. They create true homes in a demanding environment that stymies most of the men who surround them. Cather is a superb stylist, justly noted for her ability to describe the prairie and to capture its beauty, actually creating a new aesthetic for a landscape that had none of the features of the sublime and picturesque conventions of beauty. Long read as a sunny and feminist hymn of praise to the land and to the pioneer tradition, Cather's work is now being reinterpreted, not least importantly as lesbian literature.

Laura Ingalls Wilder's Little House books, children's classics and the basis for an extremely popular television series, are also more than simple autobiographical narratives of one family's experiences pioneering in the upper Midwest and South Dakota. Reflecting the influence of Wilder's daughter, Rose Wilder Lane, they are libertarian parables about individual liberty within the roles of masculine and feminine provided by the culture. In a somewhat similar vein, L. Frank Baum's Wizard of Oz books are a popular children's series with an explicitly feminist point of view. Like Cather and Wilder, Baum relies on the great individual, his plucky Kansas heroine, Dorothy, to right the wrongs that self-proclaimed reformers have been unable to conquer. *The Wizard of Oz* (1900) is thus both a great American fairy tale and a political parable. Not surprisingly, the works of all three writers include a subtle strain of erasing or undercutting Native claims on the land.

Radicalism made its way into Plains fiction, as into so much else in American culture, in the 1930s. John Steinbeck's *The Grapes of Wrath* (1939), though it actually takes place in Oklahoma east of the Plains and in California, is deservedly the classic Plains novel of the period, expressing both the determination and despair of the farmers who were forced to leave the Plains by the twin disasters of Dust Bowl and Depression. For all their heroism, Steinbeck's characters cannot win until they manage to lick the system and change it to work for them, not to oppress them. Meridel LeSueur and Tillie Olsen expressed the radicalism of the 1930s from the Plains fringe, LeSueur primarily from Minnesota but with some descriptions of Kansas among the stories in *Salute to Spring* (1940) and Olsen from Omaha, although the city is not explicitly named in *Yonnondio* (a novel actually written in 1934 but not published until 1974). Frederick Manfred's *Chokecherry Tree* (1948) and *The Golden Bowl* (1944) also present the plight of the inarticulate, ordinary man during the Depression on the Plains. Manfred is realistic and sympathetic to his male characters—his female characters are another matter—and presents a radical point of view, though he is not as explicitly ideological as the other writers mentioned in this paragraph.

Since World War II, Plains fiction has occupied a rather peculiar position in American

letters. The enormously prolific and talented Wright Morris published a host of favorably reviewed novels, appeared frequently in the *New Yorker*, and yet regularly shows up on lists of the most underrated authors. Morris is little known and little read even in his home state of Nebraska, where almost every schoolchild has read something by Willa Cather. His photo text *The Home Place* (1948) provides in pictures and a spare narrative a powerful look at what has become of the pioneer generation, while *Ceremony at Lone Tree* (1960) examines the legacy of the Western in sanctioned and unsanctioned violence in a West that has both come of age and degenerated. North Dakota novelist Larry Woiwode has suffered something of the same fate of critical acceptance unaccompanied by commensurate fame or readership. Larry McMurtry, on the other hand, has been successful not only with novels much like the formula Western, including *Horseman, Pass By* (1961) and *Lonesome Dove* (1985), but also with the merciless yet tender portrayal of the contemporary Great Plains (his hometown, Archer City, Texas) in *The Last Picture Show* (1966) and its sequel, *Texasville* (1987). Meanwhile, hundreds of extremely talented writers produce and publish short stories and novels that depict the Great Plains with clarity and insight but receive little attention or readership.

Canadian Prairie Fiction

Prairie fiction in Canada developed quite differently from Plains fiction in the United States. While some dime novels were set or written in Canada, mostly by British or American authors quite ignorant of the terrain, the beginning of popular Prairie fiction came from the writers who were explicitly excluded from the popular Western, women and preachers. Ralph Connor's (Rev. Charles Gordon) books of Christian uplift, particularly *The Sky Pilot* (1899) and *Corporal Cameron of the Mounted* (1912), were bestsellers, along with Nellie McClung's *Sowing Seeds in Danny* (1908). Although some later American versions of the Mountie story are nothing but variations on the Virginian, clothed in a scarlet tunic, the homegrown Mountie story, as it starts with Connor's Corporal Cameron, tells a very different story from that of the Western. Here the hero is not the man who stands outside the law but rather the man who represents the law of his country and imperial order. McClung's best-sellers were rooted very firmly in the realities of the Prairie communities in which she lived. Her *Purple Springs* (1921) is a triumphant account of the woman suffrage movement in Prairie Canada, a cause that she also championed in essays and political activism. Other primarily realistic novels include Arthur Stringer's Prairie Trilogy, *The Prairie Wife* (1915), *The Prairie Mother* (1920), and *The Prairie Child* (1922), a curious amalgam of the purest romantic invention and a shrewd and barely sympathetic look at the self-delusions of the Prairie settlers. Robert Stead's several novels move toward a realistic portrayal of homesteading and Prairie farming, culminating in *Grain* (1926). Martha Ostenso's *Wild Geese* (1925) is,

like Stringer's works, a combination of brooding realism and equally brooding romanticism of a gothic sort. Frederick Philip Grove (nee Felix Paul Greve, a truly self-made man) put the seal on the Prairie novel as dour, brooding, and doomed with *Settlers of the Marsh* (1925) and *Fruits of the Earth* (1933). At the same time, his autobiographical sketches, *Over Prairie Trails* (1922), like Cather's work, found a new voice and vocabulary for describing and hence creating for the reader the beauty of the Prairies.

Sinclair Ross's *As for Me and My House* (1941) is a turning point for both Canadian literature and Prairie/Plains literature. Its deceptively simple form—ostensibly, it is the diary of a clergyman's wife during a year in a small Saskatchewan town during the mid-1930s—masks an extremely complex book that asks whether art, as defined by European conventions, is possible in the Prairie Provinces of Canada. The book is open-ended, and the answer is provided at least in part by the subsequent success of Canadian Prairie literature. Like Cather, Ross also provides a homosexual voice in Plains literature.

While American Plains literature has remained either popular culture or a high culture removed from the literary centers of the United States, Prairie literature is at the very center of the Canadian literary canon that has been emerging since *As for Me and My House*. Although Ross's novel vanished almost without a trace until it was republished in 1957, Prairie writers such as Grove, Margaret Laurence, Adele Wiseman, Robert Kroetsch, Rudy Wiebe, and others have consistently won Canada's most prestigious literary awards and are central figures in Canadian literature. Laurence's *The Stone Angel* (1964), like *As for Me and My House*, is one of the acknowledged classics of the canon. Paradoxically, while the Western is perhaps the most enduring form of the American national myth of identity, serious writing by Plains authors is at the fringes of the contemporary American tradition, while Canadian Prairie literature, which from its inception rejected the popular American form, is central to Canadian literature. Not surprisingly, *The Stone Diaries* (1993), written in and about Manitoba by a former American (Carol Shields), is the only recent Plains novel to win a Pulitzer Prize. (It had already won the Governor General's Award for fiction.) Canadian Prairie fiction continues to flourish. Among the many contemporary writers are Sharon Butala and Guy Vanderhaege.

Implicitly or explicitly, Canadian Prairie literature rejects the themes of the Western—the noble savage, the rugged individual, the two-gun man—in favor of community and to some extent of women and family. Women as both writers and characters are central to this fiction, and Ross's choice of a woman's diary for his form draws attention to the diaries and letters by women that have always been part of the literature of European American settlement in the Great Plains. The themes of Prairie fiction are heritage and community. Rather than an American Adam, concerned with starting anew in a new world, the Canadian

Hagar (the name of the heroine of *The Stone Angel*) is a wanderer in a desert that she makes a home partly by connecting it with her ancestors. This is also a theme in the American agrarian novel, both the ethnic novel, in which a European culture fails in transplantation to the New World, and works by old stock Americans such as Garland and Cather. But Canadian literature emphasizes creating a past through stories or art. This is most clear in Margaret Laurence's *The Diviners* (1974), a novel that deals with both the Native and European histories of the land and recognizes both the complicity in oppression and the cultural significance of European settlement in the Great Plains.

Like Laurence, many European Canadian writers have used Native or mixed-blood characters in their fiction. In part this reflects a larger percentage of Native peoples on the Canadian Prairies than on the Plains of the United States, and in part it represents the Canadian search for themes that differentiate Canadians from Americans. It also represents the Canadian commitment, at least in theory, to multiculturalism and the tendency of Prairie writers, unlike American Plains writers, to be toward the left of the political spectrum. In *The Scorched Wood People* (1977) and *The Temptations of Big Bear* (1973), Rudy Wiebe has attempted to show the Red River and North-West Rebellions from the viewpoints of the Métis and the Crees, endeavors that have drawn mixed reactions from critics and Native readers. W. O. Mitchell has used many versions of the noble savage, particularly in *Vanishing Point* (1973), while in *Dance Me Outside* (1977) and subsequent Silas Ermineskin stories W. P. Kinsella has updated the noble savage to a streetwise and astute kid of nineteen. Laurence was most cognizant among these writers of the Native point of view in her decision never to speak for Native people in her characters, while Kinsella is the most controversial of the writers among both Native and European American critics.

Fiction by Native Peoples

Native peoples have shown themselves more than capable of speaking for themselves, not only in oral traditions but in writing. While short writings by Indians and as-told-to autobiographies have existed ever since European contact with the peoples of North America, the first flowering of Native writing in English occurred in the 1920s and 1930s, a period when legal restrictions on cultural, religious, and political freedoms of Native peoples began to be lifted. *Cogewea, the Half Blood* (1927) seems to be the first Plains novel published by an Indian or mixed-blood author, although the author, Mourning Dove (or Hum Ishu Ma or Christine Quintasket), had to work through a fairly intrusive European American editor. In the next decade D'Arcy McNickle published his classic novel of western Montana, *The Surrounded* (1936), and Black Elk (via white poet John Neihardt) and Luther Standing Bear published autobiographical accounts that described and praised traditional Lakota ways.

While Native authors continued to write and sometimes found publishers for their accounts throughout the 1940s and 1950s, it was not until the 1960s that a true cultural renaissance began among the Native peoples of North America. While N. Scott Momaday's Pulitzer Prize–winning novel *House Made of Dawn* (1968) is set primarily in the Southwest, his formally innovative *The Way to Rainy Mountain* (1969) deals specifically with the Kiowas' relationship to the Plains. James Welch's *Winter in the Blood* (1974), *The Death of Jim Loney* (1979), and *Fools Crow* (1986) form a trilogy of great power that traces the survival of the Blackfeet from the late 1870s to the present. In the Southern Plains a similar cultural renaissance has produced a flowering of Chicano fiction, which draws upon oral traditions of both Spanish and Native origins. Rudolfo Anaya's limpid *Bless Me, Ultima* (1972), set in the llano of eastern New Mexico and self-consciously combining Native and Hispanic traditions, is perhaps the best known of these works. More recently, Louise Erdrich's novels of the North Dakota Chippewa, including *Love Medicine* (1984), *The Beet Queen* (1986), *Tracks* (1988), *The Bingo Palace* (1995), and *Antelope Wife* (1998), have been popular best-sellers as well as highly acclaimed. Her use of Nanabush, the trickster, is an example of how the oral tradition is being subsumed into the new written literature.

The Native Canadian renaissance in Plains literature lagged nearly two decades behind that of the United States. It began with nonfiction by two Métis writers, Maria Campbell's *Halfbreed* (1973) and Howard Adams's *Prison of Grass* (1975). Beatrice Culleton's *In Search of April Raintree* (1983) became the first prairie novel by an author of Native descent, followed by Thomas King's *Medicine River* (1989) and *Green Grass, Running Water* (1993). King's infectious humor and ability to blend Native oral tradition and everyday life with history as well as the European–North American literary tradition have enabled him to create a new Great Plains aesthetic. Buoyed by the political resurgence of First Nations peoples in Canada and the creation of Native newspapers such as *Windspeaker* (Edmonton) and First Nations publishing houses such as Theytus and Pemmican, Native Canadian Prairie writing continues to grow in both quality and quantity.

Plains Poetry

Poetry, chant, and song have always been part of the oral literary tradition on the Plains. The contemporary powwow circuit and access to inexpensive, high-quality recording equipment have produced an outpouring of both traditional and newly created songs and chants. A contemporary sacred tradition including both Native American church and Gospel songs has spurred the writing of lyrics in both English and Indigenous languages. Individual performers such as John Trudell and Keith Secola have now written and recorded significant bodies of work.

Written European-style poetry on the North-ern Plains undoubtedly begins with Henry Kelsey's doggerel narrative of his fur-trading expedition in 1690, though similar narratives probably exist in Spanish for the Southern Plains. The monument of the long poem tradition on the Plains is John Neihardt's five-part *Cycle of the West*: *The Song of Hugh Glass* (1915), *The Song of the Three Friends* (1919), *The Song of the Indian Wars* (1925), *The Song of the Messiah* (1935), and *The Song of Jedediah Smith* (1941). These poems, all in heroic couplets and ranging from 110 to 179 pages, are Neihardt's attempt to provide America with its own *Iliad* and *Odyssey*, looking at the struggle for the West from the point of view of the mountain men and the Indians, particularly the Lakotas. Although the work is an impressive achievement, the unidiomatic quality of the heroic couplets has discouraged both readers and successors, while the explicitly Christian imagery works against the Indian content. Tom McGrath, Ed Dorn, Robert Kroetsch, and others, using contemporary speech patterns and such nonliterary genres as seed catalogs (in Kroetsch's 1977 poem of that title), have written long poems both more experimental and more accessible than Neihardt's.

Lyric poetry rather than narrative has been characteristic of the Plains as it has of the rest of the English-speaking world for the last two centuries. For the most part it began with popular newspaper verse. Like butter-and-egg money, pay or prizes for newspaper poetry often helped the farm or small-town wife round out the household budget. This tradition of vernacular poetry is now represented by the "cowboy poets," who work in ballad styles and present their frequently humorous verses to aficionados at "cowboy poetry" gatherings all over the West. By the 1920s the literary magazine, or little magazine, was starting to supplant the small-town newspaper as the major venue for the publication of lyric poetry. Frequently connected to a college or university and more recently to a creative writing program, little magazines such as *Prairie Schooner*, *Midlands*, *Frontier*, and *Dandelion* and small local presses have both provided an outlet for local poets and connected Plains writing to the rest of the continent. Like most writers in English in the twentieth century, Plains poets have frequently chosen variable feet and sound patterns other than end rhymes, although poets like William Stafford manipulate blank verse, slant rhymes, and other traditional forms with marked success.

The differences in theme, outlook, and national audience that distinguish Canadian and American Plains fiction are much less evident in poetry. Neihardt's cycle is similar to Canadian documentary poems such as E. J. Pratt's *Towards the Last Spike* (1952), which sounds the same blend of pride and chagrin at "progress" onto the center of the continent. McGrath's social justice themes are not dissimilar from those of Manitoban Dorothy Livesay. Like William Stafford, Robert Kroetsch is concerned with the past and its traditions, with the domestication and violation of the land and its inhabitants. Contemporary Plains women poets such as Hilda Raz and Lorna Crozier are particularly strong voices whose concerns with naming, with birthing, and with identifying the land as female and as mother are similar on both sides of the border.

The renaissance in Native writing beginning in the 1960s is evident in poetry as well as fiction and frequently involves the same writers. N. Scott Momaday's *Angle of Geese* (1974), James Welch's *Riding the Earthboy 40* (1971), and Louise Erdrich's *Jacklight* (1984) are all highly sophisticated in image, allusion, and technique and unquestionably represent some of the best contemporary Plains poetry. Emma LaRoche is probably the best known of the contemporary Native Canadian poets, while Paula Gunn Allen, Linda Hogan, and Elizabeth Cook-Lynn are among the best known on the U.S. side.

Writers of Asian and African descent in any genre are still extremely rare in the Great Plains. Novelist and filmmaker Oscar Micheaux was a rare African American voice at the beginning of the twentieth century, and Ralph Ellison and Langston Hughes both grew up on the Plains. Fred Wah has become an important contemporary Chinese Canadian writer. Increased immigration, especially to the Prairie Provinces, continues to add new voices to the Prairie mosaic.

Plains Drama

Drama has to a large extent been an import to the Plains. In the nineteenth century touring companies from New York and Chicago followed the railroad lines to present versions of the latest plays and operas from the East and of the classics to city and small-town audiences. No Plains drama comparable to Plains fiction or poetry has developed in the United States, though there are notable local exceptions. Folk drama has remained important on the Southern Plains. Often, as in the Christmas *posadas*, these dramas are religious, but secular patriotic fiestas also include drama. Town pageants, somewhere between mass and folk art, have also attained popularity in some locales throughout the Plains. They may be produced somewhat formulaically by outsiders for a specific occasion such as a town's centennial or written and regularly produced by townspeople.

Community-based drama has been far more successful in the Prairie Provinces, particularly Alberta and Saskatchewan, than in the Plains states. The Banff School of Fine Arts in Alberta began in the 1930s to promote and produce community theater, written and often acted by members of the community. Gwen Pharis Ringwood emerged as the premier playwright of the movement. While the Banff School has moved away from community-based theater to a more traditional and less regional focus since the 1950s, Saskatchewan has more recently become the venue of a vibrant and popular community-based theater that often includes dramas about carefully researched incidents in the province, often improvised or workshopped instead of written by a solitary playwright. These include Theatre

Passe Muraille's *The West Show* (1975) and its successor, the Saskatoon 25th Street Theatre's collective creation of *Paper Wheat* (1982), about the formation of the Saskatchewan Wheat Pool, and, perhaps most remarkable, Linda Griffiths and Maria Campbell's *Jessica* (1982/1986), about a mixed-blood woman's successful attempt to come to terms with her heritage and ancestral spirits in a racist and sexist society. The communal/cooperative nature of this sort of theater, though directly descended from Paul Thompson and the Theatre Passe Muraille of Toronto, seems especially well suited both to Saskatchewan's political history of cooperatives and democratic socialism and to the ethos of Native peoples. An alternative form of documentary by a single playwright is exemplified in the works of Rex Deverell of Regina's Globe Theatre, including *No. 1 Hard* (1978) and *Medicare* (1980). Despite perennial financial problems, theater continues to flourish in the Prairie Provinces. Sharon Pollock and Brad Fraser are among the most successful contemporary playwrights, but many theater groups and the almost endless creativity of the summer fringe festivals guarantee that Prairie theater remains an extremely accessible literary art.

Conclusion

As the world has moved, rockily enough, on into the twenty-first century, it seems likely that the Great Plains will cease to be regarded as the cultural hinterland it has seemed to be in the United States and will become, as it is in Canada, a region generating a particularly innovative and high-quality literature. The popular Western, if it is to become anything other than an endlessly repeating formula, will become more ambiguous and less purely heroic. As an environmentalist consciousness becomes more necessary and accepted for survival, the progress that Owen Wister and his heirs had presented as positive—even as it destroyed the wilderness Eden—will seem more purely destructive. The communitarian ethic and the multicultural point of view characteristic, at least in theory, of Canadian and Native peoples will become the norm, and the search for ancestors in the land will continue and be amplified. The myth of the vanishing American that has haunted portrayals of Native peoples for the past 500 years will pale and recede as it becomes more clear that demographically, politically, economically, and culturally Native peoples are very decidedly not vanishing, despite the often genocidal invasion that was Native peoples' experience of the "pioneering" of the Great Plains. But the land will remain, and the harshness of a continental climate will remain. And the starkness of land and sky will encourage dreamers to write more of what we call Plains literature.

See also AFRICAN AMERICANS: Micheaux, Oscar / EUROPEAN AMERICANS: *Giants in the Earth*; Kelsey, Henry / FILM: *The Last Picture Show* / GENDER: McClung, Nellie / MUSIC: Trudell, John / PROTEST AND DISSENT: McGrath, Tom.

Frances W. Kaye
University of Nebraska–Lincoln

Bredahl, Carl A., Jr. *New Ground: Western American Narrative and the Literary Canon*. Chapel Hill: University of North Carolina Press, 1989. Etulain, Richard. *Re-Imagining the Modern American West: A Century of Fiction, History, and Art*. Tucson: University of Arizona Press, 1996. Fiddler, Don., ed. *Looking at the Words of Our People: An Anthology of First Nations Literary Criticism*. Penticton, British Columbia: Theytus, 1993. Filwod, Alan. *Collective Encounters: Documentary Theatre in English Canada*. Toronto: University of Toronto Press, 1987. Harrison, Dick. *Unnamed Country: The Struggle for a Canadian Prairie Fiction*. Edmonton: University of Alberta Press, 1977. Larson, Charles R. *American Indian Fiction*. Albuquerque: University of New Mexico Press, 1978. Meyer, Roy W. *The Middle Western Farm Novel in the Twentieth Century*. Lincoln: University of Nebraska Press, 1965. Milton, John R. *The Novel of the American West*. Lincoln: University of Nebraska Press, 1980. New, W. H., ed. *Native Writers and Canadian Writing*. Vancouver: University of British Columbia Press, 1990. Olson, Paul, ed. *Broken Hoops and Plains People: A Sourcebook*. Lincoln: Nebraska Curriculum Development Project, 1976. Probert, Kenneth G., ed. *Writing Saskatchewan: 20 Critical Essays*. Regina Saskatchewan. Canadian Plains Research Center, 1989. Quantic, Diane. *The Nature of Place: A Study of Great Plains Fiction*. Lincoln: University of Nebraska Press, 1995. Smith, Henry Nash. *Virgin Land: The American West as Symbol and Myth*. Cambridge: Harvard University Press, 1950. Thacker, Robert. *The Great Prairie Fact and Literary Imagination*. Albuquerque: University of New Mexico Press, 1989. Tuska, Jon, ed. *The American West in Fiction*. Lincoln: University of Nebraska Press, 1982. Western Literature Association. *A Literary History of the American West*. Fort Worth: Texas Christian University Press, 1987.

ALDRICH, BESS STREETER (1881–1954)

Bessie Genevra Streeter Aldrich (Margaret Dean Stevens, her pseudonym until 1918) was born on February 17, 1881, in Cedar Falls, Iowa. She lived there until 1901, when she graduated from Iowa State Normal School with a degree in education. In 1907 she married Captain Charles S. Aldrich; in 1909 they moved with their baby daughter to Elmwood, Nebraska, where they had become co-owners of the American Exchange Bank and where their three sons were born. Aldrich was widowed in 1925 yet put all of her children through college with her writing. She remained in Elmwood until 1945, when she moved to Lincoln, Nebraska, where she lived until her death on August 3, 1954.

Aldrich wrote nine novels, all of which, after her *A Lantern in Her Hand* (1928), were on the best-seller list. In addition, Aldrich wrote more than 100 short stories, which were first published in magazines; many were later republished in two volumes. One story won an O. Henry Award. Aldrich also was the author of one novella and two omnibus editions and served as a scriptwriter for Paramount. Much of her work has been anthologized and produced for radio and television. Her novel *Miss Bishop* (1933) became the movie *Cheers for Miss Bishop* (1941). All of Aldrich's novels remain in print, in standard editions as well as Braille and large print, and in a number of European and Asian languages. Her short stories from 1920 to 1954 also remain in print.

Bess Streeter Aldrich used the rural Midwest and Great Plains for both her long and short works. She is best described as a romantic realist who wrote of rural life in a positive sense, valuing its warmth and generosity of spirit, yet who was honest enough to show that it was not perfect.

Aldrich received an honorary doctorate from the University of Nebraska in 1934 and the Iowa Johnson Brigham Literature Award in 1949, and she was posthumously elected to the Nebraska Hall of Fame in 1973.

Carol Miles Petersen
Omaha, Nebraska

Petersen, Carol Miles. *Bess Streeter Aldrich: The Dreams Are All Real*. Lincoln: University of Nebraska Press, 1995.

BAUM, L. FRANK (1856–1919)

Nine years before he wrote his first children's book, Lyman Frank Baum followed the frontier promise of prosperity to Dakota Territory, embarking on an experience that would contribute greatly to the themes and scenes of his great American fairy tales about the Land of Oz. Critics have long noted that *The Wizard of Oz* (1900) celebrates the values of the agrarian heartland and provided the nation with its first recognizably American (as opposed to European) fairyland. The book and its author have also had lasting impacts on the culture and image of the Great Plains region, from Kansas to North and South Dakota.

Born into a wealthy family in Chittenango, New York, on May 15, 1856, Baum sampled a variety of careers, most involving writing and publishing. When he married Maud Gage, the youngest daughter of national suffrage activist Matilda Joslyn Gage, the couple settled in Syracuse, New York, before the birth of the first of their four sons in December 1883. For the next five years Baum worked in a family business that made axle grease. When the business, like many of his earlier enterprises, failed, Baum looked around for new opportunities. In the early 1880s many of Baum's neighbors, among them members of his wife's family, had headed west to participate in Dakota Territory's boom (1879–87). After a whirlwind trip to the area in September 1888 Baum packed up his family and moved to Aberdeen, a county-seat town in the northeastern corner of what is now South Dakota, where he established Baum's Bazaar to sell a wide variety of luxury goods just as the Dakota boom ended.

By the winter of 1889 drought conditions had brought actual starvation to parts of Dakota, and during the next five years almost 3,000 people abandoned the Aberdeen service area. Baum's Bazaar failed, and in January 1890 Baum took over the weekly newspaper of a fellow Syracuse transplant and began a fifteen-month career as western editor and job printer. His *Aberdeen Saturday Pioneer* reveals in depth his attitudes about politics, suffrage, tolerance, and religion, offering an important key to the themes that later surface in Baum's fiction, especially his fourteen Oz books.

L. Frank Baum, ca. 1900

The year 1890 provided an incredible range of events for an observant editor to comment upon. South Dakota had become a state on November 2, 1889, and the political events of its first year included the formation of an independent party that would evolve into the Populist Party. A campaign to give women the vote brought national personalities such as Carrie Chapman Catt and Susan B. Anthony to stump the state for suffrage, while the Ghost Dance movement among the Lakotas attracted Gen. Nelson Miles and Buffalo Bill Cody. Temperance advocates and liquor dealers exchanged heated rhetoric on the issue of prohibition. To contribute barbed comments to the political brew, Baum created a weekly satirical column entitled "Our Landlady." In April 1891, however, economic conditions forced the editor and his family to join the exodus from Dakota.

From Aberdeen Baum went to Chicago, where he worked as a newspaper editor, crockery salesman, and editor of a trade journal before beginning to write children's books at the age of forty-one. From 1897 until his death in Hollywood, California, on May 5, 1919, Baum wrote more than seventy books, many under pseudonyms, but it is *The Wizard of Oz* (1900) that is most important. In it Baum created a fairy tale that has become a cultural symbol, largely through adaptation to stage and screen (beginning with a musical comedy in 1902). Its characters, attitudes, and values are all distinctly American. Unfortunately, its depiction of Kansas as a drab, drought-stricken hinterland has affected the region for years. On the positive side, the book also created Dorothy Gale, a strong heroine who embodies the assertiveness and ability of those who settled the Plains.

The Wizard of Oz also contains an allegorical commentary on American politics and the Populist movement of the Great Plains region.

The other Oz books, the next of which is *The Marvelous Land of Oz* (1904), continue the tradition of strong female characters and add allegorical commentary on women's rights and utopian concepts. The Dakota prairie and its wildlife—prairie dogs, bison, gophers, crows, and grasshoppers—also provided the setting and characters for some of Baum's shorter fiction, his "Animal Fairy Tales," which appeared in the *Delineator* in 1905, and the "Tinkle Tales," a series of small books for younger children that appeared in 1906 and 1907.

See also FILM: *The Wizard of Oz* / IMAGES AND ICONS: Gale, Dorothy / POLITICS AND GOVERNMENT: Populists (People's Party).

Nancy Tystad Koupal
South Dakota State Historical Society

Baum, Frank Joslyn, and Russell P. MacFall. *To Please a Child: A Biography of L. Frank Baum, Royal Historian of Oz*. Chicago: Reilly and Lee, 1961. Baum, L. Frank. *Our Landlady*, edited and annotated by Nancy Tystad Koupal. Lincoln: University of Nebraska Press, 1996. Koupal, Nancy Tystad. "The Wonderful Wizard of the West: L. Frank Baum in South Dakota, 1888–91." *Great Plains Quarterly* 9 (1989): 203–15.

BIRDSELL, SANDRA (b. 1942)

Sandra Birdsell, who was born in the small town of Hamiota, Manitoba, on April 22, 1942, is the author of two novels, three volumes of short fiction, one collection of short stories, and a children's book. She has also written scripts for television. Her *Agassiz Stories* was chosen by *Macleans* as one of the ten best books of 1987, and her short story "Falling in Love" received the National Magazine Award in 1984.

Most of her adult fiction, essentially realist in style, is set in the fictional southern Manitoba town of Agassiz. Her stories typically concern the encounter of young women either with men who don't deserve them or with unimaginative old people (grandparents, neighbors, accidental acquaintances) who have grown weary of life. Birdsell writes a marvelous short story: "Night Travelers," "Ladies of the House," and "The Two-Headed Calf" all share that irresistibility common to excellent writing. "Night Travelers," for instance, tells of a mixed Mennonite-Métis marriage that has gone wrong. Various members of the family gradually come to know of the wife's infidelity. Birdsell's novels excel at introducing conflicts that the reader longs to see resolved. Middle-aged, eccentric Minnie Pullman starts off *The Missing Child* (1989) with a vision she has while floating naked down the Red River at night that the world is about to experience a second Noah's flood. Young Amy, early in *The Chrome Suite* (1995), is marked for life by a ruffian's kick in the stomach. She manages to blame all the subsequent sufferings and disappointments in her life on this youthful tragedy and the chronic pain beneath her ribs. Birdsell's *The Town that Floated Away* (1997) charms us with the adventures of an irrepressible orphan, Virginia Potts, who faces an ethical dilemma she almost does not solve. Like much of her adult fiction, this story makes use of the theme or symbol of a catastrophic, world-changing flood.

Douglas Reimer
University of Manitoba

BROOKS, GWENDOLYN

See AFRICAN AMERICANS: Brooks, Gwendolyn

BUTALA, SHARON (b. 1940)

Sharon Butala is best known for her descriptions of the physical and spiritual geography of her corner of southwestern Saskatchewan, near the Montana border, where she lives with her husband, Peter Butala, a cattle rancher. In 1996 the Butalas dedicated a portion of their ranch land to Nature Conservancy Canada so that the beauty of the native shortgrass prairie could be preserved. Butala's literary work has similarly been dedicated to preserving and communicating the aesthetic and cultural meanings of the prairie, especially the complex relationships between farming people and the land they work.

Born Sharon LeBlanc on August 24, 1940, in northern Saskatchewan near Nipawin, Butala moved to Saskatoon at age thirteen. After graduating from St. Mary's Roman Catholic School, she attended the University of Saskatchewan, where she earned a bachelor's degree in English and art. A decade later she returned to the university for a bachelor's degree in education, specializing in learning disabilities. She married Peter Butala after her first marriage ended, leaving her urban life behind and embarking on a difficult but fruitful period of reflection, observation, and self-discovery through writing.

Butala's first published work was *Country of the Heart* (1984), which was nominated for the W. H. Smith/*Books in Canada* First Novel Award. Subsequent to this successful debut, she has written extensively, publishing two collections of acclaimed short stories (*Queen of the Headaches*, 1985; *Fever*, 1990), five more novels, two nonfiction accounts, and a collection of essays (*Coyote's Morning Cry*, 1995). She has also written six unpublished plays. Of special interest is her loosely connected novel trilogy about life in rural Saskatchewan, comprised of *The Gates of the Sun* (1986), *Luna* (1988), and *The Fourth Archangel* (1992). *Luna* portrays the special challenges and rewards of rural women's lives, while *The Fourth Archangel* presents a visionary and compassionate account of the provincial farm crisis. These novels belong to the tradition of regional realism, with elements of the mythic and the magical.

Butala's first foray into nonfiction, *The Perfection of the Morning* (1994), tells of the slow process by which she learned to see nature truly. The book remained on best-seller lists for more than a year and brought Butala considerable recognition within Canada. In her sixth novel, *The Garden of Eden* (1998), Butala expanded her geographical parameters to Ethiopia, but her focus remained the capacity of the land to heal and human responsibility for its restoration and protection. *Wild Stone Heart* (2000), a companion volume to *The Perfection of the Morning*, chronicles Butala's respectful exploration of a 100-acre field of unplowed land; seeking to connect with the wild and with an Indigenous worldview in order to heal her spiritual malaise, she investigates the Aboriginal and settler pasts to uncover layers of unknowable presence. While maintaining her interest in emotional journeys and the beauty of the land, Butala's later work has increasingly turned to considerations of the mystical.

Janice Fiamengo
University of Saskatchewan–Saskatoon

CAMPBELL, MARIA (b. 1940)

Métis author and activist Maria Campbell is best known for her remarkable autobiography, *Halfbreed* (1973), the first document of its kind in Canada. In it Campbell describes her early life in a northern Saskatchewan Métis trapping community in the 1940s (she was born at Park Valley in April 1940), the support of her beloved grandmother Cheechum, and the gradual destruction of her family and community by racism, poverty, and alcohol. Left to care for her seven younger siblings after her mother's death, Campbell quit school and married at fifteen. *Halfbreed* tracks the young Maria's struggle through alcohol, drug addiction, and prostitution and, finally, her healing return to the traditions of her Cree heritage.

Campbell's collaborative theatrical work, *Jessica*, based on *Halfbreed*, was first performed in Toronto by Theatre Passe Muraille in 1981. A description of the troubled process of the play's creation was later published with Linda Griffiths under the title *The Book of Jessica: A Theatrical Transformation* (1989).

Campbell's recent writing has been for children and includes informational illustrated works on Plains Indians and Métis heritage. An illustrated collection of narratives, or "told to" stories, from old men of northern Saskatchewan Métis communities, *Stories of the Road Allowance People*, appeared in 1995. Campbell has helped establish emergency shelters for women and community theater groups, and she has encouraged First Nations writers. She has been writer in residence at several universities and in 1999 was teaching creative writing at the University of Saskatchewan. Campbell lives on the land homesteaded by Gabriel Dumont, commander of the Métis forces in the North-West Rebellion of 1885.

Jeanne Perreault
University of Calgary

Bataille, Gretchen M., and Kathleen Mullen Sands. *American Indian Women: Telling Their Lives*. Lincoln: University of Nebraska Press, 1984: 113–26.

CAPTIVITY NARRATIVES

See GENDER: Captivity Narratives

CATHER, WILLA (1873–1947)

In her essay "My First Novels [There Were Two]," Willa Cather recalls a New York critic who responded to *O Pioneers!* by claiming, "I simply don't care a damn what happens in Nebraska, no matter who writes about it." One of Cather's foremost achievements has been to make readers care about the "distinctly déclassé" Nebraska and the Great Plains. Indeed, Cather's own complex ties to the Great Plains underlie much of her best writing.

A quintessential Great Plains writer, Cather lived in Nebraska only thirteen years but was later to claim that her deepest feelings were rooted in her childhood ties to this place. Born in the Back Creek Valley of Virginia on December 7, 1873, Cather migrated with her relatives to Red Cloud, Nebraska, in 1883. Her first experience of "a country bare as a piece of sheet iron" was a traumatic one, memorably retold through the eyes of Jim Burden in *My Ántonia*. After a brief but fierce struggle, Cather grew to love the land and the people she came to know. As an adult she recalled her early years on "the Divide" as among the most important and fulfilling periods of her life. It is also true that a young woman as intelligent, ambitious, and unconventional as Cather felt compelled to explore the world outside Red Cloud, and as soon as she graduated from high school she left her hometown to attend the University of Nebraska. After six years in Lincoln, during which she received her undergraduate degree and established a national reputation as a theater and music critic for the local papers, Cather headed east.

She moved to Pittsburgh in 1896 and worked as a journalist, editor, and teacher while also actively publishing short stories. In 1906 she joined the staff of *McClure's Magazine* and began a residence in New York City. She stayed with *McClure's* for six years, writing her first novel, *Alexander's Bridge* (1912), while also serving as managing editor. Convinced by Sarah Orne Jewett that she could not serve two masters, Cather quit her job at *McClure's* and embarked on a career as a professional novelist. Over the next eleven years she wrote five novels set, completely or in part, in the Great Plains—*O Pioneers!* (1913), *The Song of the Lark* (1915), *My Ántonia* (1918), *One of Ours* (1922), and *A Lost Lady* (1923). After the publication of *A Lost Lady*, Cather turned to other settings in her next four novels. However, late in her career, with the publication of *Lucy Gayheart* (1935) and her best collection of short stories, *Obscure Destinies* (1932), she returned to Nebraska for her artistic material.

Since her death in New York on April 24, 1947, Cather's reputation has grown with an increased recognition of the complexity and allusive depth of her work. No longer classified as a "mere" regional writer, she is now viewed as a regionalist in the tradition of Jewett, Twain, and Faulkner. Her writing provides fertile ground for feminist, lesbian, and gender critics, while the deceptive simplicity of her prose conceals a host of biographical, historical, political, biblical, and literary references. With the recent inclusion of *A Lost Lady* in *Encyclopedia Britannica*'s list of great books and the adaptation of *The Song of the Lark* for Masterpiece Theater's American Collection series, Cather is now considered not only a Great Plains but a great American writer.

Matthew Hokom
University of Nebraska–Lincoln

Rosowski, Susan J. *The Voyage Perilous: Willa Cather's Romanticism.* Lincoln: University of Nebraska Press, 1986. Urgo, Joseph R. *Willa Cather and the Myth of American Migration.* Champaign: University of Illinois Press, 1995. Woodress, James. *Willa Cather: A Literary Life.* Lincoln: University of Nebraska Press, 1987.

CHILDREN'S LITERATURE

The most realistic children's literature about the Plains during the settlement period and into the 1920s can be found in family periodicals. Popular magazines such as *St. Nicholas* and weekly newspapers like the *Youth's Companion* highlighted the sense of adventure to be discovered on the Plains frontier as well as the uniqueness of the various Native American cultures.

Although these periodicals published works by well-known writers of the era, a large percentage of the stories were by lesser-known writers such as Kate M. Cleary, Elia Peattie, and William R. Lighton, who wrote fiction about Nebraska; Charles Askins, John R. Spears, Elizabeth Grinnell, and G. W. Ogden, who set their stories in Kansas and Oklahoma; L. Frank Baum and Franklin Welles Calkins, whose stories depict Wyoming and the Dakotas; and Canadian writers Nellie McClung and Edward McTavish, whose tales center on Manitoba, and Rev. Charles W. Gordon (aka Ralph Connor), whose best-selling fiction represents life in Saskatchewan. Many authors contributed only one story, usually based on personal accounts of Plains life. Serials were especially popular, like *The Little Squatters* by Hamlin Garland, *The Boy Settlers* by Noah Brooks, and *A Banker's Judgment* by Marianne Gauss.

The typical pattern in the stories of Plains settlement is of an initiation, beginning with a physical and emotional separation as the children withdraw into an unknown and often hostile environment. The innocent pioneer versus the complex frontier forms the conflict. Although the stories about boys reaching manhood have various plots and settings, the boys' tasks are mainly physical tests. Stereotypically, the girls achieve a moral rather than physical triumph.

Though strongly informed by this earlier tradition, children's literature of the Plains published since the 1930s has all but eclipsed these periodical writers. In 1932 Laura Ingalls Wilder, with the help of her daughter, Rose Wilder Lane, published *Little House in the Big Woods*, commencing a family saga now known collectively as the Little House books. The genius of Wilder's vision is its blending of adventure and domestic realism, its positing of a feisty, tomboy heroine, Laura, against the ameliorating influence of her gentle sister, Mary, and her firm-handed mother, Caroline. Along the way, readers receive moral lessons, learn songs, poems, and recipes, and gain an understanding of schooling, farming, and town building on the Plains during the late nineteenth century. Wilder's series provided a narrative pattern for many other children's writers of the Plains, including Carol Ryrie Brink (*Caddie Woodlawn* and *Magical Melons*), Lois Lenski (*Prairie School*), Barbara Smucker (*Days of Terror*), Patricia MacLachlan (*Sarah Plain and Tall*), Pam Conrad (*Prairie Songs, Prairie Visions,* and *My Daniel*), Laurie Lawlor (the Addie series), Celia Barker Lottridge (*Ticket to Curlew*), Kathryn Lasky (*The Bone Wars*), Cecil Freeman Beeler (*The Girl in the Well*), and Charlene Joy Talbot (*An Orphan for Nebraska*). Adventure writers like Texan Fred Gipson (*Old Yeller*) continue the tradition of the male initiation story, yet even Gipson's classic novel centers its dramatic plot around the stability of home and a strong mother figure.

Though the history of settlement preoccupies children's writers of the Plains, a number of other significant genres emerged in the twentieth century. In particular, this literature has attempted to provide a more accurate and humane depiction of Plains tribes than found in many settlement novels. Native and non-Native writers alike have worked to replace stereotypes and misrepresentations of Native American life with truthful, unedited retellings of oral tales and balanced portraits of life in biographies and fiction. Mari Sandoz (*The Horsecatcher, The Story Catcher*), Virginia Driving Hawk Sneve (*Betrayed, When Thunders Speak*), Maria Campbell (*People of the Buffalo*), and Paul Goble (*The Girl Who Loved Wild Horses*) have added immeasurably to children's appreciation of Native American/First Nations history, oral storytelling, and art.

Some Plains children's writers focus on contemporary life with all its attendant problems and challenges. In 1967 Oklahoma writer S. E. Hinton changed the course of contemporary young adult literature with her gritty first novel, *The Outsiders*. Ivy Ruckman's bestselling *Night of the Twisters* re-creates modern Grand Island, Nebraska, during the hours of a natural disaster. To this day, literary realism defines children's literature of the Plains. Even the Oz stories of the great fantasist L. Frank Baum bear the imprint of realism. However, Native American writers for children are now adding the fabric of vision, myth, and legend to this tradition of realism, countering European American myths of settlement and creating new narrative patterns inspired by oral storytelling.

Susanne George
University of Nebraska at Kearney
Susan Naramore Maher
University of Nebraska at Omaha

CLEARY, KATE M.

See GENDER: Cleary, Kate M.

COWBOY POETRY

Ever since cattle first trod the Chisholm Trail to Abilene in 1867, cowboys have been composing verse, some of it sung as song lyrics, some of it published in livestock journals, and some of it recited as poetry around campfires or in bunkhouses. In fact, according to cowboy folk song authority Guy Logsdon, no other occupational folk group in this country has produced as much verse, partly because of subject matter (the cowboy's exciting and sometimes dangerous work occurs amidst beautiful natural surroundings) and partly because of opportunity (the cowboy has sufficient leisure, whether on the back of a horse or behind the steering wheel of a pickup, in which to reflect and compose). The cowboy, in essence, puts into practice Wordsworth's theoretical definition of poetry as emotion recollected in tranquility.

In form, traditional cowboy poetry is rhymed and metrically regular, usually cast in ballad stanzas or tetrameter stanzas with second and fourth lines rhyming and with narrative a predominant element. While in earlier years cowboy poetry tended to reflect the episodes and duties of actual ranch work, recently innovative cowboy poets have written in free verse and have expanded their subject matter to include themes such as the environment and economic or governmental threats to the cowboy way of life. In contrast to much mainstream academic poetry, cowboy poetry is marked by accessibility to a general audience and emphasizes public oral performance.

Unlike the more visible aspects of cowboy culture that were earlier adapted into our popular culture, however, authentic cowboy verse remained essentially unknown beyond range country until the first Cowboy Poetry Gathering, held at Elko, Nevada, in 1985. Since then cowboy poetry has enjoyed a renaissance, with scores of gatherings being held throughout the West and performers such as Baxter Black and Waddie Mitchell gaining national prominence. Although this recent surge of popularity has attracted a host of less-than-skilled practitioners, the work of cowboy poets such as J. B. Allen, Wallace McRae, Vess Quinlan, Buck Ramsey, Andy Wilkinson, and Paul Zarzyski, among many others, has the technical skill, intellectual rigor, and universality of emotion that are the hallmarks of lasting poetry.

See also IMAGES AND ICONS: Cowboy Culture / MUSIC: Cowboy Music.

James Hoy
Emporia State University

Cannon, Hal, ed. *Cowboy Poetry: A Gathering.* Salt Lake City: Gibbs Smith, 1985. Lomax, John. *Cowboy Songs and Other Frontier Ballads.* New York: Macmillan Company, 1910. Thorp, N. Howard (Jack). *Songs of the Cowboys.* Boston: Houghton Mifflin, 1921.

CROZIER, LORNA (b. 1948)

Born on May 24, 1948, and raised in Swift Current, Saskatchewan, poet, anthologist, and professor Lorna Crozier writes predominantly of life on the Canadian Great Plains. Frequent reprintings of her new and selected poems, *The Garden Going on without Us* (1985), and her characteristically packed public readings attest to her work's broad appeal. Its humor, rich imagery, and unpretentious language prompt many people to recognize aspects of their own lives. Crozier's sometimes spicy stew of frank sexuality and trenchant but witty feminist critique has, however, overpowered some palettes.

The strength of Crozier's identification with the land is evident in the title of her first collection, *Inside Is the Sky* (1976), while her kinship with its creatures, which in "Inventing the Hawk" makes her feel the bird's scream rising from her belly to echo in her skull, is sometimes stronger than the connection she feels to humans. Her affection for Prairie people is, nevertheless, palpable in everything from the tall tales of "Spring Storm, 1916" to her description in "Home Town" of a freshman history student who identifies the Holy Land as something like Christ's hometown. The warmth of such feelings does not, however, blind her to the racism, misogyny, and pettiness of some hometown people.

Crozier often reworks Christian and patriarchal accounts of origin and existence. Her rewriting of Genesis in "On the Seventh Day" explains the thin strip of earth beneath the massive skies of the Great Plains: a forgetful God was without His wife to remind Him that He had already created light, so He kept repeating this step, leaving scant space for land. *A Saving Grace* (1996) gives new voice and a richer female consciousness to Sinclair Ross's Mrs. Bentley, narrator of *As for Me and My House*, imagining, for example, the kind of domestic violence that might go on in the house of a woman who jumps into a dry well with her baby and lies there silently for three days ("The Kind of Woman").

Susan Gingell
University of Saskatchewan

Gingell, Susan. "Let Us Revise Mythologies: The Poetry of Lorna Crozier." *Essays on Canadian Writing* 43 (1991): 67–82. Hillis, Doris. "The Real Truth, the *Poetic Truth*: An Interview with Lorna Crozier." *Prairie Fire* 6 (1985): 4–15.

DEBO, ANGIE (1890–1988)

Angie Debo was an historian and advocate for human rights who spent all of her life in the Great Plains. She wrote nine books about Native Americans and the development of Oklahoma, edited four other volumes, and was the author of numerous scholarly articles. Several of her books have been used as textbooks in college courses. In addition to writing, she lobbied for civil liberties and for the rights of Native Americans.

Angie Debo was born January 30, 1890, on a farm near Beattie, Kansas. Nine years later her father used a covered wagon to move his family to a new farm near Marshall, Oklahoma. Debo attended rural one-room schools and at age twelve completed the instruction they offered. When she was sixteen and could obtain a teacher's certificate, Debo began teaching in rural schools near Marshall. Finally, the town acquired a four-year high school. Debo graduated from it in 1913 and from the University of Oklahoma in 1918. She then taught in Enid, Oklahoma, until 1923, when she attended the University of Chicago and received a master's degree in 1924. For nine years, from 1924 to 1933, she taught preparatory classes in the history department of West Texas State Teachers College while completing her doctorate at the University of Oklahoma. Debo's doctoral dissertation received wide acclaim upon its publication in 1934 under the title *The Rise and Fall of the Choctaw Republic*. When she was unable to find a college teaching position, she decided to move back to her parents' home in Marshall and devote all her time to researching and writing.

Debo's next book, *And Still the Waters Run: The Betrayal of the Five Civilized Tribes*, became available in 1940. This pioneering work describes the tribes and their relations with the federal government and the courts of Oklahoma. It took almost four years for her to find a willing publisher, largely because she was exposing graft and corruption, topics that heretofore had not been addressed in scholarly works. This and another of her books, *The Road to Disappearance: A History of the Creek Indians* (1941), were used by the U.S. Supreme Court in deciding a 1976 case, *Harjo v. Kleppe*. Other books by Debo include *The Five Civilized Tribes of Oklahoma: Report on Social and Economic Conditions* (1951); *Geronimo: The Man, His Time, His Place* (1976); *Oklahoma: Foot loose and Fancy-free* (1949); *Tulsa: From Creek Town to Oil Capital* (1943); *Prairie City: The Making of an American Community* (1944); and the seminal *A History of the Indians of the United States* (1970).

Debo's study of Native Americans and their relationships with the federal government took her into new areas of research in the 1930s. She said that her only goal was to conduct the research to reveal the truth and to publish it. To achieve this goal she pioneered in writing from the Indian point of view. Her books have been widely recognized as resources for determining Native American property rights. Through her lobbying efforts she contributed to the passage of the Alaska Native Claims Settlement Act and helped Arizona Indians establish land and water rights. Over the years Debo received numerous awards for her research, her writing, and her involvement in efforts on behalf of civil liberties. Shortly before her death in Marshall, Oklahoma, on February 21, 1988, she became the fourth person, and the first woman, to receive the prestigious Award for Scholarly Distinction from the American Historical Association.

Heather M. Lloyd
Oklahoma State University

Angie Debo Papers, Collection 88-013, Oklahoma State University Library, Stillwater. Leckie, Shirley A. *Angie Debo: Pioneering Historian*. Norman: University of Oklahoma Press, 2000. Sandlin, Martha, producer. *Indians, Outlaws and Angie Debo*. Alexandria VA: PBS Video, 1988.

DEVERELL, REX (b. 1941)

Rex Deverell is a Canadian dramatist noted for his children's plays, his full-length plays, and his time as a writer in residence at the Globe Theatre, Regina, from 1975 to 1990. He was born July 17, 1941, in Toronto, raised in Orillia, Ontario, and received a bachelor's from McMaster University, Hamilton, Ontario, in 1963, a bachelor of divinity from McMaster in 1966, and a master of sacred theology from Union Theological Seminary in New York in 1967. He began writing plays in 1966 and has been a prolific writer ever since, with more than twenty children's plays, fifteen full-length plays, and half a dozen plays commissioned by various groups. He has participated in five collective productions and has been an active playwright for CBC radio.

At the Globe Theatre he began as a children's playwright and wrote roughly one children's play a year. His first full-length play, *Boiler Room Suite* (1977), became his best known and most produced. He wrote a number of Saskatchewan-specific documentaries like *Medicare!* (1980), on the introduction of socialized medicine to Canada and the subsequent doctors strike, as well as *Number 1 Hard* (1978) and *Black Powder: Estevan 1931* (1981). He has also written musicals, including *Mandarin Oranges* (1985/1990), and plays that explore religion, including *Righteousness* (1983), about Saint Augustine.

Plays produced in a single year, 1985, give a good cross section of Deverell's work. That year was the centenary of the North-West Rebellion, and Deverell composed both a five hour radio drama for the CBC, *The Riel Commission*, and a play for the Globe, *Beyond Batoche*. He also wrote a musical, a children's play, and another radio drama and worked on a collective show in 1985.

Donald C. Kerr
University of Saskatchewan

Wallace, Robert, and Cynthia Zimmerman, eds. *The Works: Conversations with English Canadian Playwrights*. Toronto: Coach House Press, 1982: 127–41.

DUST BOWL LITERATURE

During the 1930s a number of literary texts illustrated drought, dusters, and economic depression through powerful stories and contributed to aesthetic movements for social realism and cultural regionalism.

John Steinbeck's 1939 novel, *The Grapes of Wrath*, inspired the nation with its tale of a tenant-farm family, the Joads, who lost their home in eastern Oklahoma and searched for a more promising land in California. The novel accentuated human dignity and courage against a mechanistic, exploitative social system. In 1937 Frederick Manfred wrote the first draft of his novel *The Golden Bowl*, which was published in 1944. He portrayed a spirited resistance to fate in the Northern Plains by focusing on Maury Grant, a wandering protagonist who returned to the Dust Bowl and started the cycle of conquest again. After embracing his fate, he and the Thors, a mythic family holding onto a dying land, refused to abandon their homestead.

Set within Kansas during the late nineteenth century, John Ise's *Sod and Stubble: The Story of a Kansas Homestead* (1936) recounts a familial story of remarkable heroism against drought, grasshoppers, fires, dust storms, and economic depression. Women homesteaders in the Dakotas are featured in Edith Kohl's mixed autobiography and novel, *The Land of the Burnt Thigh* (1938).

Lawrence Svobida, a western Kansas farmer turned author, recounted a cautionary tale in his 1940 autobiography, *An Empire of Dust*. Though his wheat farm failed to survive the dust storms and adverse climate, Svobida worked incessantly to win a harvest and to keep the land from blowing away. The story underscores frustration and pride, but it ends in failure.

Paul Sears, a botanist at the University of Oklahoma, authored the most significant ecological text of the decade. Alarmed by the violent dust storms raging across the continent, in *Deserts on the March* (1935) he explained how the rapid conquest of North America had upset the balance of nature. If the nation was headed down such a slippery slope, Sears argued, then the assumptions of frontier progress required reexamination.

Kenneth Porter's prose and poetry, which lament the failures embodied in a dust cloud over Kansas, appeared in a number of magazines in the 1930s. After the Dust Bowl conditions faded from the landscape, Lois Phillips Hudson's *The Bones of Plenty* (1962) and *Reapers of the Dust* (1964) reinvented empty land, solid inhabitants, and frontier myths for subsequent generations. Ann Marie Low's *Dust Bowl Diary* (1984) recalls the difficulties of farm life in North Dakota.

Dust bowl literature thus illuminates the human fight against extreme temperatures, soil erosion, agricultural maladjustment, and swirling winds. While the crisis exposed the nation to a range of anxieties, literature was a vehicle that could bring the Dust Bowl into the experiences of readers outside the region. Limning a powerful landscape in national memory, Dust Bowl literature invented an enduring iconography for the Great Plains.

See also FILM: *The Grapes of Wrath* / MUSIC: Guthrie, Woody / PHYSICAL ENVIRONMENT: Dust Bowl.

Brad Lookingbill
Columbia College

Lookingbill, Brad. "The Living and the Dead Land: The Great Plains Environment and the Literature of Depression America." *Heritage of the Great Plains* 29 (1996): 38–48. Quantic, Diane Dufva. *The Nature of the Place: A Study of Great Plains Fiction*. Lincoln: University of Nebraska Press, 1995.

ELLISON, RALPH (1911–1994)

Ralph Waldo Ellison, best known as the author of the award-winning novel *Invisible Man* (1952), was a "Renaissance man": sculptor, editor, short-story writer, novelist, jazz trumpeter, and photographer. He was born March 1, 1914, in Oklahoma City, Oklahoma, to Lewis Alfred Ellison and Ida Millsap Ellison. The Ellisons had moved to Oklahoma in

1911 in hopes of finding more opportunities in an area free of the severe racism of the Deep South. When Ellison was born, Oklahoma had only been a state for seven years, and it retained its frontier spirit.

Oklahoma had a long history of racism, as evidenced by its maintenance of segregated schools. Ellison graduated in 1931 from the all-black Douglas High School, where he received a rigorous training in music. From 1933 to 1936 Ellison studied music at Tuskegee Institute in Alabama. He played first trumpet in the school orchestra as well as serving as the orchestra's student director.

Ellison decided to spend the summer of 1936 in New York City in order to earn money for the next academic year. He never returned to school. While in New York, Ellison met Langston Hughes and Richard Wright, who encouraged him to write his first story, "Hymie's Bull." He then began to write book reviews, essays, and short stories, and he served as editor of the *Negro Quarterly* for a short time. Ellison's masterwork, *Invisible Man*, received many awards, including the National Book Award in 1953.

Besides his novel, Ellison also published two essay collections, *Shadow and Act* (1964) and *Going to the Territory* (1987). He began a second novel from which he released several sections, but he died April 16, 1994, in New York City before it was published. Six unpublished short stories that predate *Invisible Man* were published posthumously.

Venetria K. Patton
University of Nebraska–Lincoln

O'Meally, Robert G. *The Craft of Ralph Ellison*. Cambridge: Harvard University Press, 1980. Reckley, Ralph. "Ellison, Ralph." In *The Oxford Companion to African American Literature*, edited by William L. Andrews, Frances Smith Foster, and Trudier Harris. New York: Oxford University Press, 1997: 129–31.

ERDRICH, LOUISE (b. 1954)

Since 1984, when she published the collection of poems *Jacklight*, Louise Erdrich has stood out as one of the more captivating and original voices not only in Native American literary circles but also in contemporary American literature generally. Erdrich's popular and critical success stems from her ability to craft evocative narratives that draw heavily on oral storytelling traditions and other aspects of Native American culture.

Born in Little Falls, Minnesota, in 1954, and raised in Wahpeton, North Dakota, Erdrich is a member of the Turtle Mountain Band of the Anishinabe (Chippewas), but she also has German-immigrant roots. She has drawn on these two traditions in her fiction while examining the challenges of coming to terms with mixed ancestry and celebrating the vitality of Chippewa history, culture, tradition, and community in the face of European American intrusion. Drawing on storytelling traditions of the Chippewas, Erdrich repeatedly constructs fictions that employ multiple narrators, including a dog in *The Antelope Wife* (1998), and span several generations, producing what one writer has called a "layered"

point of view. But if her narrative style appears nonlinear and disjointed to the reader, what readily emerges is Erdrich's strong sense of place. These stylistic and thematic features have prompted critics and reviewers to compare Erdrich's North Dakota landscape to Nobel Prize–winning author William Faulkner's Yoknapatawpha County, especially as they emerge in her well-known tetralogy (*Love Medicine*, 1984; *The Beet Queen*, 1986; *Tracks*, 1988; *The Bingo Palace*, 1995; and *The Antelope Wife*, 1998), which focuses on three Chippewa families and others on and around the reservation. Erdrich does not shy away from difficult issues such as alcoholism and broken families that confront Native communities; however, by infusing her tales with humor, folklore, and spirituality, Erdrich treats her subjects with both compassion and sensitivity.

Philip R. Coleman-Hull
Bethany College

Bruchac, Joseph. *Survival This Way: Interviews with American Indian Poets*. Tucson: University of Arizona Press, 1987. Smith, Jeanne Rosier. *Writing Tricksters: Mythic Gambols in American Ethnic Literature*. Berkeley: University of California Press, 1997.

GIANTS IN THE EARTH

See EUROPEAN AMERICANS: *Giants in the Earth*

GORDON, CHARLES W. (1860–1937)

Charles William Gordon was Canada's first best-selling novelist. Born on September 13, 1860, in Glengarry County, Ontario, to Mary Robertson Gordon and Scots missionary Daniel Gordon, Charles was educated at universities in Toronto and Edinburgh, earning a doctor of divinity. He served as a Methodist missionary in pioneer settlements west of Calgary from 1890 to 1893, then as pastor of St. Stephen's Church in Winnipeg until his death on October 31, 1937.

Gordon began writing moral tales under the pseudonym "Ralph Connor" to promote missionary work, but because he happened to be a gifted storyteller, his first three books, *Black Rock* (1898), *The Sky Pilot* (1899), and *The Man from Glengarry* (1901), sold over five million copies—an unheard-of number for a Canadian author. He wrote twenty more, and for a time his popularity could be compared to Zane Grey's. Gordon counted national leaders such as Wilfrid Laurier, Theodore Roosevelt, and Woodrow Wilson among his readers and friends and was himself one of Canada's most prominent citizens, providing leadership in national and international organizations.

Not surprisingly, the Reverend Gordon's romances were didactic, promoting the values of muscular Christianity, the Social Gospel, and the Empire. Their patriarchal, imperialist, and ethnocentric assumptions render them worse than irrelevant today, but Gordon did embrace the more liberal social and political ideas of his time, including public ownership of certain industries.

Only a few of Gordon's romances are set on the Plains or in the foothills, including *The*

Foreigner (1909) and *Corporal Cameron of the North West Mounted Police* (1912). *The Sky Pilot* epitomizes these Western stories, depicting a young tenderfoot missionary winning over the blasphemous ranch hands by proving he is straight and manly. In Gordon's marriage of East and West, counter to the American frontier formula, western vitality is tamed by eastern refinement.

Dick Harrison
Sechelt, British Columbia

Lennox, John. "Charles W. Gordon ["Ralph Connor"] (1860–1937)." In *Canadian Writers and Their Works*, Fiction series, vol. 3, edited by Robert Lecker, Jack David, and Ellen Quigley. Toronto: ECW, 1988: 102–59. Thompson, J. Lee, and John H. Thompson. "Ralph Connor and the Canadian Identity." *Queens Quarterly* 79 (1972): 159–70.

THE GRAPES OF WRATH

See FILM: *The Grapes of Wrath*

GREY, ZANE (1872–1939)

Immensely popular in the 1910s and 1920s as a writer of Western romances such as *Heritage of the Desert* (1910) and *Riders of the Purple Sage* (1912), Zane Grey also wrote sporting and adventure novels and short stories. He was born Pearl Zane Grey on January 31, 1872, in Zanesville, Ohio. He practiced dentistry in New York City from 1896 to 1904 before traveling extensively in the West. He died on October 23, 1939, in Altadena, California.

Vintage Grey features a romantic adventure during which a couple, often two couples, find true love, marriage, and wealth after overcoming obstacles in an environment made ambiguous by conflicting laws. The majestic western land confronts them: beauty, vastness, physical challenge, and a renewing spirit. So does outlaw violence: rustling, gunplay, and threats of seduction, the latter enhancing the erotic appeal. They respond with fists and guns. Splendid horses frequently aid the protagonists. Native Americans, either as enemies or victims, often constitute a disturbing presence.

Sometimes locale specific, sometimes not, Grey's narratives often travel the Great Plains. In *The Trail Driver* (1936), Texas Joe Shipman wins the love of orphan Reddy Bayne on an 1871 cattle drive from Texas to Dodge City. Tough young Andrew Bonning prevails with equally tough runaway Martha Ann Dixon in *Wyoming* (1953). The earlier *U.P. Trail* (1918) celebrates the building of the Union Pacific Railroad. Several Grey novels involve Texas Rangers. Wade Holden in *Shadow on the Trail* (1946) has to escape them to prove himself. In *Lone Star Ranger* (1915) Buck Duane flees from and then secretly joins the Rangers to clear his name. The close reader will find intriguing ironies in Grey; in both *Heritage of the Desert* and *Lone Star Ranger* conflicting and ambiguous laws call into question their very meaning.

Arthur G. Kimball
Huron International University Tokyo

Kimball, Arthur G. *Ace of Hearts: The Westerns of Zane Grey*. Fort Worth: Texas Christian University Press, 1993. Scott, Kenneth W. *Zane Grey: Born to the West: A Reference Guide*. Boston: G. K. Hall, 1979.

GROVE, FREDERICK PHILIP (1879–1948)

Frederick Philip Grove was born Felix Paul Greve in Radomno, East Prussia, on February 14, 1879. As a young adult he earned a meager living translating novels and publishing poetry under various names. He incurred large debts and was jailed in 1903 for defrauding a fellow student. Greve left Germany in 1909, covering his tracks with a fake suicide, and spent three poorly documented years in the United States. He surfaced in Manitoba in September 1912 as Frederick Philip Grove and started teaching first in the predominantly German-speaking Mennonite regions south of Winnipeg and then later in even more remote rural districts. In August 1914 he married Catherine Wiens (1892–1972), and a year later, while in Virden, Manitoba, the couple had a daughter, Phyllis May (1915–27). He graduated with a bachelor of arts degree in French and German from the University of Manitoba in 1922, and he and his wife accepted teaching assignments in Rapid City, Manitoba, where they remained until 1929.

After Phyllis May Grove's tragic death during an appendicitis operation in Minnedosa in 1927, the Groves longed for different surroundings and moved to Ontario. In October 1931 Grove settled on an estate in Simcoe, Ontario, where he hoped to fulfill his dream of living like a gentleman farmer. Despite unfavorable conditions during the Depression and World War II and increasingly poor health, Grove managed to publish almost to the end of his life.

His first novel, *Settlers of the Marsh* (1925), a story of love, murder, and redemption on the Manitoba Prairie (a thinly veiled account of Grove's own affair in Kentucky in 1911 with Else Ploetz, later Baroness von Freytag-Loringhoven), was critically praised but commercially unsuccessful. It was followed in 1927 by the partly autobiographical and partly allegorical novel *A Search for America*, the story of a young European immigrant's settlement in Canada, which earned him both critical acclaim and some prosperity. His later novels, essays, and partly fictional autobiography, *In Search of Myself* (1946), failed to achieve the popular success of *A Search for America*.

Grove always felt underappreciated, although he was the recipient of many honors and his work was taught in schools and universities. The Royal Society of Canada awarded him the Lorne Pierce Medal for literary achievement in 1934 and elected him a fellow in 1941, and Grove obtained honorary doctorates from the University of Manitoba and Mount Allison University, New Brunswick, in 1944.

In May 1946 Grove suffered a debilitating stroke that left him crippled. He died on August 19, 1948. Grove's complicated biography, with its blending of fact and fiction in both his life and his works, was not worked out until 1971, when Douglas O. Spettigue traced the Canadian author back to the minor German literary figure, Felix Paul Greve.

Gaby Divay
University of Manitoba

Frederick Philip Grove Papers, Archives and Special Collections, University of Manitoba Libraries, Winnipeg. Spettigue, Douglas O. *FPG: The European Years*. Ottawa: Oberon Press, 1973.

GUTHRIE, A. B., JR. (1901–1991)

Alfred Bertram Guthrie Jr. is best known for his cycle of six novels spanning the exploration and settlement of the West from the days of the fur trade through the mid–twentieth century (*The Big Sky*, 1947; *The Way West*, 1949; *These Thousand Hills*, 1956; *Arfive*, 1971; *Last Valley*, 1975; *Fair Land, Fair Land*, 1982). He also produced six relatively slight mystery novels, the screenplays for *Shane* and *The Kentuckian*, a children's book, a volume of poetry, and short stories. All the fiction, except the last mystery, are set in the Plains of eastern Montana and at the edge of the Rocky Mountains. His autobiography, *The Blue Hen's Chick* (1965), reveals the influence of the "Big Sky Country" on his vision of the westward movement and the consequences of the closing of the frontier.

Guthrie was born January 13, 1901, in Bedford, Indiana, but moved with his family to Choteau, Montana, six months later. Like his father, he felt a sense of freedom on the Plains and in the mountains, and he made the Choteau area the hub of his fiction. The landscape is significant in all his fiction, and space is a persistent theme.

After graduation from the University of Montana, Guthrie worked at a variety of jobs, including as a newspaper reporter in Lexington, Kentucky. In 1944 a Nieman Fellowship to Harvard gave him the opportunity to work on *The Big Sky*. After publication of his second novel, *The Way West*, he left newspaper work and returned to Montana to write fiction. He died in Choteau on April 26, 1991.

Paul T. Bryant
Radford, Virginia

Bryant, Paul T. "External Characterization in *The Big Sky*." *Western American Literature* 31 (1996): 195–210. Ford, Thomas W. *A. B. Guthrie, Jr.* Boston: Twayne, 1981.

HAYES, KATE SIMPSON

See GENDER: Hayes, Kate Simpson

HOGAN, LINDA (b. 1947)

Contemporary Native American poet, novelist, and essayist Linda Hogan explores the relationship of humans to the natural world, both past and present. She was born in Denver, Colorado, on July 16, 1947, to a Chickasaw father and a mother of German descent. Her father's family in Oklahoma were gifted storytellers, and this heritage and love for the landscape inform her belief in the sacredness of the earth and its inhabitants. A teacher and political activist, Hogan has taught literature and creative writing at the Universities of Minnesota and Colorado. In 1986 she received an American Book Award for her book of poems, *Seeing through the Sun*.

An impassioned political and spiritual leader, Hogan catalogs the voices of the disenfranchised, particularly those who have suffered during the settling of the Great Plains. Her historical novel, *Mean Spirit* (1990), a finalist for a Pulitzer Prize in 1991, depicts the devastating impact of the 1920s Oklahoma oil boom on an Osage Indian community, especially its women.

Throughout her work, Hogan argues for a balancing of spiritual, intellectual, and physical realms based upon traditional Native beliefs that link past and present into one coherent vision. Contrasting the loud and often violent dominant culture with the voices of her ancestors, Hogan argues that chaos, violence, and greed have silenced the wisdom of the land, yet she seeks to lessen this alienation. The long "distances" she often evokes are the space of the Plains as well as the landscape of lost time and space.

In Hogan's work, women learn from experience that destruction of parts leads to destruction of the whole. She documents a history of extinction and the imposition of a philosophy without reverence or a sense of the future. Harshly rewriting the myths of Plains settlement, she nonetheless holds out hope for healing and rebirth, seeking new stories and habits that nurture the creative power of this region. There is hope, she says, in the land, the water, and those that listen.

Mark Vogel
Appalachian State University

Hogan, Linda. *Dwellings: Reflections on the Natural World.* New York: W. W. Norton, 1995. Scholer, Bo. "A Heart Made out of Crickets: An Interview with Linda Hogan." *Journal of Ethnic Studies* 16 (1988): 107–17.

HUGHES, LANGSTON

See AFRICAN AMERICANS: Hughes, Langston

IMMIGRANT LITERATURE

Immigrant literature takes various forms and is usually written by immigrants and second- and/or third-generation Americans. Often autobiographical in nature, these narratives reflect the experience of immigration and acculturation and the associated uneasiness of these processes. The anxiety that immigrant literature exposes is a combination of determination, success, loneliness, and abandonment. Repressed desires of attachment to the homeland juxtaposed with the uncertainties surrounding assimilation assert themselves as underlying conflicts. Added to these struggles are issues of self-identity that stem from the intricacies of cultural adaptation.

Tension in immigrant literature centers on association with the new land, identification of the self and other, and language acquisition. First, the land itself offers a powerful blend of freedom and fear. Whether the landscape is the wilderness that Cotton Mather writes about in *Magnalia Christi Americana* (1702) or the flat expanse of the Great Plains that Per Hansa finds exhilarating and Beret, his wife, renders intolerable in O. E. Rölvaag's *Giants in the Earth* (1927), the New World offers an abundance of possibilities even as it diminishes emotional security. Immigrant writings illustrate ambivalence surrounding the land: the untouched wilderness offers both freedom from past constraints and fear of independence associated with pleasures derived from the land.

Immigrant literature also explores the idea of self and other. The writings seek to affirm the new immigrant self while simultaneously using the other to restructure the immigrant's new identity. Fundamentally, the notion of self and other becomes manifest as the narrators and characters reflect the ambiguities of the immigrant experience. When people emigrate, they strive to give up that which they were in order to become the other, that which they desire to be. The former self remains part of the immigrant's psychological structure. In *Giants in the Earth*, Per Hansa and Beret represent self and other. While Per Hansa sublimates his Old World self by conquering physical obstacles, Beret's transformation to her New World self emerges only after a descent into extreme loneliness. The juxtaposition of these characters reflects the heroic illusion and difficult reality of immigrant life.

A third characteristic of immigrant literature, intertwined with aspects of self and other, is the acquisition of a new language. In many immigrant narratives, acquiring English becomes a traumatic experience. The writings often point out the fact that children become more fluent in English than their parents. The first language of the immigrant is that of the home, containing implications and idioms that make the native language familiar and comfortable. English initially resides outside of the immigrant and belongs to the other. Eventually, the immigrant adopts English to conduct the business of social interactions, education, and commerce. English, however, intrudes on the comfort of the home, creating an abyss that widens with time as the immigrant embraces the new cultural modes of behavior.

As immigrants and settlers moved to the interior regions of America, they brought with them their native languages, cultures, dreams of success, and fears of the unknown. In their writings, relationships of characters and narrators to the physical land, the development of self and other, and the acquisition of language appear as central themes not only in literature written by immigrants and their children who made the trek but also in works by authors who may be generations removed from the actual experience but whose collective past embodies acculturation. The symphony of voices echoing the immigrant experience form a multiethnic framework for the literature of the Great Plains.

See also EUROPEAN AMERICANS: *Giants in the Earth.*

Linda Norberg Blair
Springfield, Virginia

Gunn, Giles. *The Interpretation of Otherness: Literature, Religion, and the American Imagination.* New York: Oxford University Press, 1979. Kolodny, Annette. *The Lay of the Land: Metaphor as Experience and History in American Life and Letters.* Chapel Hill: University of North Carolina Press, 1975.

IN COLD BLOOD

See LAW: *In Cold Blood*

INGE, WILLIAM (1913–1973)

Born on May 3, 1913, in Independence, Kansas, William Inge is best remembered for four theatrical successes: *Come Back, Little Sheba* (1950), the Pulitzer Prize winner *Picnic* (1953), *Bus Stop* (1955), and *The Dark at the Top of the Stairs* (1957). Inge's portraits made him the first successful playwright to re-create small-town Plains life, including its hypocrisy and oppressive judgments. His characters frequently find that they must settle for life as it is and not as they wish it to be.

Before his success with *Come Back, Little Sheba*, which was produced on Broadway in 1950, Inge had worked in a number of occupations, none of which satisfied him. He labored on a highway crew, as an English teacher in the Columbus (Kansas) High School in 1937–38, as an instructor at Stephens College in Columbia, Missouri, from 1938 to 1943, and as a drama critic for the *St. Louis Star-Times* from 1943 to 1946. He once told an interviewer that he felt out of place in Kansas and did not claim it as his past until he moved to New York.

Even after his success with *Come Back, Little Sheba* and the three plays that followed, Inge was plagued by self-doubts. In 1959 *A Loss of Roses* failed critically and financially, and Inge retreated to Florida and began work on his script *Splendor in the Grass*, for which he won an Academy Award in 1961. Inge returned to drama with *Natural Affection* (1963) and *Where's Daddy?* (1966), but both were unsuccessful, confirming his fears that he could not live up to his four Broadway plays of the 1950s. Inge then turned to fiction, hoping to avoid the negative criticism that devastated him. He published two novels, *Good Luck, Miss Wyckoff* (1970) and *My Son Is a Splendid Driver* (1971), but again his work was largely rejected. His earlier anxieties and depression, compounded by chronic alcoholism, left him with an overwhelming pessimism, and on June 10, 1973, in Los Angeles, he killed himself. Inge felt that he could no longer write, and without writing he did not want to live. Although some of his characters manage to settle for a qualified happiness, Inge was unable to make a similar compromise. He was buried in his hometown.

See also FILM: *Splendor in the Grass.*

Elizabeth A. Turner
William Rainey Harper College

Shuman, R. Baird. *William Inge.* Boston: Twayne, 1989.

KREISEL, HENRY (1922–1991)

Born in Vienna on June 5, 1922, Jewish novelist, literary critic, and academic Henry Kreisel escaped to England after the German annexation of Austria in 1938. Along with other German-speaking Jews and political refugees, he was apprehended as an "enemy alien" in May 1940 and sent to an internment camp in New Brunswick, Canada. He described his camp experience as fortunate in that it liberated him from his factory job and, in the debates among the many intellectuals interned with him, proved to be an excellent "university." While interned, he decided to become a writer in English, taking as his inspiration Joseph Conrad. Released in November 1941, he studied at Harbord Collegiate and the University of Toronto and went on to a career at the University of Alberta as professor of English and vice-president. He died on April 22, 1991.

Kreisel conceived of his fiction as seeing Europe (particularly, the Holocaust) through Canadian eyes and Canada (particularly, its political security and naïveté) through immigrant eyes. In his novels *The Rich Man* (1948) and *The Betrayal* (1964) and in the short stories collected in *The Almost Meeting* (1981), most of which are set during the months immediately preceding the Holocaust or the months and years immediately following it, he explores themes of emotional loss and survival, human dilemmas and weakness leading to moral paralysis and betrayal, and human forgiveness.

Kreisel became a strong and perceptive voice defining Prairie fiction in "The Broken Globe" (1965), his story of a Ukrainian immigrant farmer's passionate attachment to his land, and in the essay "The Prairie: A State of Mind" (1968). This essay surveys earlier fiction about the Canadian Prairies, beginning by noting its frequent analogies between the Prairie landscape and the sea in terms of the vacancy, stillness, and wind of both. Arguing that the physical fact of the Prairie landscape produces a state of mind in which men feel compelled to conquer the land while also feeling diminished and spiritually imprisoned in its vastness, he suggests that this landscape is productive of a puritanism subject to occasional eruptions of violence. This essay was one of the first to note that European settlers' writings about the Prairies suppressed the history and presence of Native peoples.

Henry Kreisel played an active role in the development of Canadian literature curricula in the university and was a founding member (1977) of NeWest Press, which defined its publishing mandate in terms of Prairie regionalism.

Shirley Neuman
University of British Columbia

Brenner, Rachel Feldhay. "Henry Kreisel—European Experience of Canadian Reality: A State of Mind." *World Literature Written in English* 28 (1988): 269–87. Henry Kreisel Papers, Mss., Collection of the Library of the University of Manitoba, Winnipeg. Neuman, Shirley, ed. *Another Country: Writings by and about Henry Kreisel*. Edmonton: NeWest Press, 1985.

KROETSCH, ROBERT (b. 1927)

Robert Kroetsch, novelist, poet, essayist, and teacher, was born on June 26, 1927, in Heisler, Alberta. He received degrees in English from the University of Alberta, Middlebury College, and the University of Iowa. After teaching at the State University of New York–Binghamton, he returned in 1978 to Canada and the University of Manitoba. He has served as writer in residence at many universities and is a frequent and popular teacher of creative writing at the Banff Centre in Alberta. Kroetsch sets his writing in and comments directly upon the Great Plains, particularly, central and southern Alberta.

Growing up on a farm in central Alberta, Kroetsch gained an ear for storytelling from the political speeches of his uncles, the family histories of his aunts, the pulp fiction favored by the hired men, and the all-encompassing cosmology of the Bible. His university training emphasized the European–North American literary canon, and Kroetsch himself sought out the trickster and shaman stories of the Cree and Blackfoot peoples who had lived in Alberta for millennia. His fiction combines finely observed details of the places and people of the Great Plains with a postmodern sensibility that disrupts chronology and cause and effect. His narratives are filled with a virtuosic bawdiness. For instance, *The Studhorse Man* (1969), for which he won the Governor General's Award, follows the odyssey of trickster and phallic acrobat Hazard Lepage as he leads his great blue stallion around post–World War II Alberta in search of mares in heat. Other novels dealing with the Great Plains include *Words of My Roaring* (1966), a parody of the 1935 Alberta election; *Gone Indian* (1973); *Badlands* (1975), a retelling of the great dinosaur hunts along Alberta's Red Deer River; and *What the Crow Said* (1978). Kroetsch has also produced a relatively small number of short stories and creative nonfiction essays about the Prairies.

Like his fiction, Kroetsch's poetry accommodates and parodies world influences as well as Prairie narratives. In *Seed Catalogue* (1977) he asks,

How do you grow a prairie town?
The gopher was the model.
Stand up straight:
telephone poles
grain elevators
church steeples.
Vanish, suddenly: the
gopher was the model.

Later, in *The Hornbooks of Rita K* (2001), he writes, more cryptically,

Rita was accustomed to the deceptive
    randomness of
wind and rain and sky, to the violence and
    the blinding
inevitability of prairie sun. She had an
    aversion to
intentional space.

Kroetsch's *Alberta* (1968) is a memoir of place that sets up in a nonfictional genre some of the same themes that appear in his fiction. His essay collection *The Lovely Treachery of Words* (1989) both explores the work of other Prairie writers and sets forth some of the theory underlying his own work, while the autobiographical essays in *A Likely Story* (1995) further explicate his life and craft. Perhaps Kroetsch best explained his aims—and his achievements—in a 1981 interview in which he said that his fiction and poetry "work out new relationships" between men and women as they develop in the new urban centers of the West. Because the Prairies were wiped out, "right down to zero," during the Great Depression, "we started to invent a new concept of self and a new concept of society. Now I'm intrigued to watch that developing in the Prairies."

Frances W. Kaye
University of Nebraska–Lincoln

Lecker, Robert. *Robert Kroetsch*. Boston: Twayne, 1986. Neuman, Shirley, and Robert Wilson, eds. *Labyrinths of Voice: Conversations with Robert Kroetsch*. Edmonton: NeWest Press, 1982. Twigg, Alan. "Robert Kroetsch: Male." In *For Openers: Conversations with 24 Canadian Writers*. Madeira Park, British Columbia: Harbour Publishing, 1981, 107–16.

L'AMOUR, LOUIS (1908–1988)

Louis L'Amour was an extraordinarily successful writer of Western fiction. He wrote more than 100 novels, of which there are more than 225 million copies in print. Dozens of his books were made into movies.

He was born Louis Dearborn LaMoore in Jamestown, North Dakota, on March 22, 1908. His father was a veterinarian who loved horses and athletics; his mother loved to read, write poetry, and tell stories. Louis grew up tough and with a voracious appetite for reading. When the family moved to the Southwest in 1923, Louis quit school. He spent the next two decades going through a string of knockabout jobs, from Texas cattle skinner to deckhand on ocean freighters and finally to World War II tank officer.

His adventures around the world gave L'Amour an appreciation for the sweep of human history that influenced all his writings. Starting in 1946 he concentrated on writing and published his first Western novel in 1950. Eventually, his output rose to three books a year. L'Amour was a dedicated researcher. His novels were known for their authenticity and accuracy, frequent tidbits of advice, and embedded historical lectures on the American West. However, he was foremost a master storyteller and had a superb gift for describing settings, locales, and the past. His action-packed plots and heroic characters provided exciting entertainment for millions of deeply satisfied readers, who lovingly ignored the literary flaws of a writer who claimed never to have revised any of his work. L'Amour died on June 10, 1988, in Los Angeles, leaving outlines of more than fifty novels he had not gotten around to writing.

James A. Janke
Dakota State University

Gale, Robert L. *Louis L'Amour*. Boston: Twayne, 1985.

LAROCQUE, EMMA (b. 1949)

Emma LaRocque is a Plains Cree Métis who was born in a log cabin on January 2, 1949, in Big Boy, northeastern Alberta. Her family made a living from trapping. In *Defeathering the Indian* (1975), she points out that she did not know that she was poor or culturally deprived until she started school. Her book describes a happy childhood, and though she insisted on being sent to school at an early age, in retrospect she is saddened by the fact that this education stole her away from her parents and her culture. LaRocque worked as a teacher on the Janvier Reservation until 1971, then as a reporter and editor for the Alberta Native Communications Society's newspaper, *Native People*. She has earned two master's degrees and is now a professor of Native studies at the University of Manitoba.

LaRocque is both a literary critic and a poet. Her early writing began with cogent discussions of colonization and oppression and how these have affected Métis society. She has since become a powerful political writer in the broader fields of social criticism, human rights issues, women's rights, and family violence. She feels that much of her writing has been constrained by her academic training and deplores the fact that if she draws on information from experts within her culture, it is not accepted by the academy. She also resists what she calls the "ghettoization" of Native literature, whereby it is defined as "Native" when indeed it may address universal issues. LaRocque's poetry does indeed address universal issues, as in "Coffins Fell from the Sky," a lament upon the news that her mother had terminal cancer, but the "angry prairie wind of coldstone Canada" (from the poem "1990") also blows through her poems, lodging them in her Métis Alberta background.

See also NATIVE AMERICANS: Métis.

Agnes Grant
Winnipeg, Manitoba

Lutz, Harmut. *Contemporary Challenges: Conversations with Canadian Native Authors.* Saskatoon, Saskatchewan: Fifth House, 1991. Perreault, Jeanne, and Sylvia Vance, eds. *Writing the Circle.* Norman: University of Oklahoma Press, 1993.

LAURENCE, MARGARET (1926–1987)

Margaret Laurence was born Jean Margaret Wemyss on July 18, 1926, in Neepawa, Manitoba, a small Prairie town 130 miles northwest of Winnipeg. Although both her parents died before she was nine, she remained in Neepawa, where she was raised during the Depression years by her aunt Margaret Simpson Wemyss, who had become her stepmother.

Laurence attended United College, Winnipeg, where she was profoundly influenced by the tenets of the Social Gospel. In 1947 she married John Fergus "Jack" Laurence, an Albertan and veteran of World War II. While he completed his engineering studies, Laurence worked as a journalist in Winnipeg, first for the *Westerner* and then for the *Winnipeg Citizen*, a cooperatively owned Socialist daily. Those newspaper pieces contain her reflections on life and culture in the bustling city of Winnipeg. While living there, Laurence became friends with Adele Wiseman, who would later receive a Governor General's Award for her novel *The Sacrifice*. The friendship between Wiseman and Laurence endured and produced a remarkable correspondence, now published.

Beginning in 1950 Laurence and her husband spent seven years in Africa, where Jack worked on engineering projects in the British Somaliland Protectorate (Somalia) and in the Gold Coast (Ghana). While in Africa, Laurence completed her first book, *A Tree for Poverty* (1954), a collaborative effort that involved a Polish linguist and Somali interpreters. This remarkable achievement was the first English translation of Somali oral literature.

Returning to Canada in 1957 with her husband and their two young children, Laurence embarked on what was to become her best-known fiction: a series of related novels and a collection of short stories, *A Bird in the House* (1970), which deal with a small fictional Prairie town named Manawaka. It was not so much one particular Prairie town, Laurence remarked, but rather an amalgam of many Prairie towns. In 1962 the Laurences separated. Margaret and the children moved to England. The couple divorced in 1969.

Margaret Laurence wrote fifteen books, including several works for children, and a travel memoir, *The Prophet's Camel Bell* (1963). In her Manawaka fiction, with its forthright portrayal of memorable women, characters struggle against stultifying and hypocritical elements in a small Prairie town. Their lives are a paradigm of any individual's struggle with inner forces that must be confronted if one is to live a full life.

In *The Stone Angel* (1964), Hagar Shipley, a ninety-year-old proud Prairie woman of Scots-Irish descent and Presbyterian background, recalls her life and contemplates the approach of death without self-pity or sentimentality. Laurence's last and most structurally complex novel, *The Diviners* (1974), encompasses not only the contemporary story of Morag Gunn as wife, mother, and writer but also stories of Scots ancestors, Canadian pioneers, and Métis. *The Diviners* also examines the nature of memory and explores the ways in which the present and past shape each other.

After Laurence returned permanently to Canada in 1974, she became active in establishing the Writers' Union of Canada and continued to offer encouragement to fellow writers while working for nuclear disarmament and world peace. Although Margaret Laurence settled in Lakefield, Ontario, she remained a Prairie person who believed that her girlhood in Neepawa continued to shape her vision of life. Margaret Laurence's collection *Heart of a Stranger* (1976) contains several essays describing the lasting impact of the Prairie years on her personal growth and on her view of the world. She died in Lakefield, Ontario, on January 5, 1987.

Donez Xiques
Brooklyn College, City University of New York

King, James. *The Life of Margaret Laurence.* Toronto: Alfred A. Knopf Canada, 1997. Morley, Patricia. *Margaret Laurence: The Long Journey Home.* Montreal: McGill-Queen's University Press, 1991. Thomas, Clara. *The Manawaka World of Margaret Laurence.* Toronto: McClelland and Stewart, 1975.

LITERARY ARCHITECTURE

See ARCHITECTURE: Literary Architecture

LITERARY CRITICISM

The predominant critical response to Great Plains writing has been, to paraphrase Henry Kreisel, the effect of the landscape upon the European American imagination. In the United States, the 1920s saw the publication of two studies—Dorothy Dondore's *The Prairie and the Making of Middle America* (1926) and Lucy Lockwood Hazard's *The Frontier in American Literature* (1927)—that identified texts and used them to trace a regional imaginative history derived from Frederick Jackson Turner's frontier thesis. Similar work was done (though with little reference to the frontier theory) in Canada by Edward McCourt, whose *The Canadian West in Fiction* (1949; revised, 1970) laid the basis for the two major Canadian studies, Laurence Ricou's *Vertical Man/Horizontal World* (1973) and Dick Harrison's *Unnamed Country* (1977). Both are nationalist studies that largely ignore material from south of the forty-ninth parallel, and both argue the primacy of the Prairie landscape in informing and shaping a distinctly Canadian point of view, one derived from imaginative interaction with the land itself over time.

Written partially as a response to them, Robert Thacker's *The Great Prairie Fact and Literary Imagination* (1989) is an analysis of the European and European American aesthetic and literary response to the Great Plains landscape from Cabeza de Vaca during the 1530s to Sharon Butala during the 1980s. His conclusion, following Cather in *O Pioneers!* is that "the great fact" is "the land itself." Central to all three post-1970 studies is Wallace Stegner's *Wolf Willow* (1962), a volume that has achieved classic status in Canada owing to its Saskatchewan setting. Beyond these central studies, other recent critical works either adopt individual themes or assert a new critical perspective. Carol Fairbanks's *Prairie Women* (1986) is an instance of the former, as is Steven Olson's *The Prairie in Nineteenth-Century American Poetry* (1994). Arnold E. Davidson's *Coyote Country* (1994) advances a Canadian exceptionalist argument informed by postmodern theory in a treatment of a group of writers succeeding those offered by Ricou, Harrison, and Thacker. Similarly, and despite an attempt to treat Canadian writers along with American ones, Diane Dufva Quantic offers an American exceptionalist argument in *The Nature of the Place* (1995). So too does Joni L. Kinsey in *Plain Pictures* (1996). Kinsey analyzes painted and photographed images in a way that attests to the ongoing pull of the Great Plains landscape upon the imagination.

Robert Thacker
St. Lawrence University

Harrison, Dick. *Unnamed Country: The Struggle for a Canadian Prairie Fiction.* Edmonton: University of Alberta Press, 1977. Ricou, Laurence. *Vertical Man/Horizontal World: Man and Landscape in Canadian Prairie Fiction.*

Vancouver: University of British Columbia Press, 1973. Thacker, Robert. *The Great Prairie Fact and Literary Imagination*. Albuquerque: University of New Mexico Press, 1989.

LITTLE MAGAZINES

If the job of little magazines is to shape literary taste, the Great Plains states have helped shape such taste for the better part of a century. Some of the oldest and most venerable of the country's literary magazines are published in the Great Plains: *Prairie Schooner* has been published continuously at the University of Nebraska since 1926, and *North Dakota Quarterly*, which started in 1910 at Grand Forks as *Quarterly Review*, ceased publication from 1933 to 1955 and then began publication again under its new name. More recent nationally recognized university-based journals include *South Dakota Review* (Vermillion, 1963), *Nebraska Review* (Omaha, 1972), *Cimarron Review* (Stillwater, Oklahoma, 1967), *Denver Quarterly* (1966), *Colorado Review* (Fort Collins, 1956), *Writers' Forum* (Colorado Springs, 1974), *The Texas Review* (Huntsville, 1980) and *Puerto del Sol* (Las Cruces, New Mexico, 1960).

Historically, critics have charged that university-sponsored magazines do not find truly new literary work because their institutions are interested primarily in establishing orthodox reputations, while the little magazine ought to be interested in the unorthodox. In any case, the Great Plains also hosts a number of literary journals independent of academia. The *Bloomsbury Review* has been a highly successful Denver independent since 1980. The magazine's large subscriber base (65,000) and loyal advertisers keep it solvent. Robert Greer, founder and editor of Denver's *High Plains Literary Review* since 1986, is a medical doctor who teaches in the University of Colorado's medical school and writes medical thrillers. He started the magazine to showcase work he felt was not being published in other journals. Volunteers, including editor Polly Swafford, are the reason *Potpourri* (Prairie Village, Kansas, 1989) claims it has been able to continue to publish. However, independent publishers also have problems with censorship, as Michael Hathaway, editor of the *Chiron Review* (St. John, Kansas, 1982), discovered when he had to search for a new printer after the newspaper that printed the quarterly took offense at accepted material.

The Canadian independents, most notably *Prairie Fire* (Winnipeg, 1978) and *Grain* (Regina, 1973), are primarily funded by three sources: provincial writers guilds, the Canada Council for the Arts, and local arts councils, while *Prairie Journal* (Calgary, 1983) is supported by a trust.

Both university-sponsored and independent literary magazines located in the Great Plains have played a significant role in the formation of contemporary literary taste. The tradition promises to remain strong in the twenty-first century.

Ladette Randolph
University of Nebraska Press

Anderson, Elliott, and Mary Kinzie, eds. *The Little Magazine in America: A Modern Documentary History*. Yonkers NY: Pushcart Press, 1978. Council of Literary Magazines and Presses. *Directory of Literary Magazines 1997–98*. Wakefield RI: Asphodel Press, 1997.

LIVESAY, DOROTHY (1909–1996)

Born in Winnipeg on October 12, 1909, to journalist parents, Dorothy Livesay over some sixty-five active writing years published twenty-one volumes of poetry, four of fiction and nonfiction prose, and a myriad of articles, reviews, forewords, agitprop and docudramas, edited volumes of the creative writing of others, journalistic pieces, and uncollected individual short stories and poems. She spent only two phases of her life—her first and sixth decades—in the Prairies and would engage intensely with most of the other places she lived—British Columbia, Ontario, New Brunswick, Africa, England, and France. But Livesay's writing throughout bore the indelible psychic imprint of that first landscape, the Canadian Great Plains: its openness and multiethnicity were powerful influences on her work.

Livesay's family moved to Ontario in 1920, but when she was in her twenties, a moderately Marxist Livesay passed back through the Prairies on a promotional tour for a new leftist periodical. Prairie laborers were mobilizing to break out of the long-standing grip of the Great Depression, which in Canada had hit their region the hardest, and Livesay's contact with Prairie workers from coal miners to sugar beet harvesters encouraged her creative combining of art with her agenda for social change. That aspect of Prairie inspiration continued to inform her thought and technique in her subsequent years in British Columbia and abroad.

Later in life, a seasoned writer and academic, she took two positions as writer in residence in the Great Plains: 1968–71 at the University of Alberta (Edmonton) and 1974–76 at the University of Manitoba. She helped found a new literary journal, *CV/II*, that was a supportive venue for emerging Prairie writers. In the 1980s she spent summers near the Icelandic community at Gimli, Manitoba. These years saw a literary revisiting of her Prairie origins in some poems of *Plainsongs* (1969, expanded 1971) and particularly in the linked stories entitled *A Winnipeg Childhood* (1973), expanded and renamed *Beginnings* (1988). Those stories follow a lightly disguised Dorothy ("Elizabeth") through a vivid rendering of her childhood in a Prairie city, charming readers with its descriptive simplicity, its magic-realist treatment of the commonplace, and its fluid, rhythmic prose.

Livesay absorbed and developed the Canadian Prairie's early-twentieth-century optimistic vision of infinite possibilities, of a new and egalitarian society, passionate and fresh. One must note, however, that she also shared the no less historical Prairie sense of isolation, alienation, exclusion, and marginalization. Yet that personal perspective dovetailed productively with another Great Plains element, the multicultural patchwork of Winnipeg, which

shaped her lifelong interest in social justice and equality and the rights of minorities, a conviction embodied in verse dramas such as her liberatory treatment of the hitherto reviled Métis leader Louis Riel, "Prophet of the New World." The inherent drama of the Prairies, its strong horizontals and majestic skyscapes, the enormity of spaces and intense contrasts of light: all seem connected with both Livesay's preoccupation with nature as well as her gravitation to polarities and complementarities in human relations and the universe. Dorothy Livesay died in Victoria, British Columbia, on December 29, 1996.

See also PROTEST AND DISSENT: Riel, Louis.

Lee Briscoe Thompson
University of Vermont

Thompson, Lee Briscoe. *Dorothy Livesay*. Boston: Twayne, 1987. University of Manitoba Department of Archives. *The Papers of Dorothy Livesay: A Research Tool*. Winnipeg: University of Manitoba, 1986.

MALIN, JAMES C. (1893–1979)

A distinguished historian of the Great Plains, James Malin was born on the homestead of his father, Jared Nelson Malin, near Edgeley, North Dakota, on February 8, 1893, and lived there and at nearby Kulm while his father was by turns farmer, store clerk, real estate and agricultural implement salesman, sheep man, and lay preacher. The family moved to Edwards County, Kansas, in 1903. Young Malin experienced Plains country farming and sheepherding at first hand as well as life in Lewis, Kansas, before entering Baker University at Baldwin City, Kansas, in 1910. Initially enrolled as a mathematics major, he switched to history and also completed the equivalent of majors in philosophy and biology before his graduation in 1914. After periods of high school teaching, graduate study at the University of Kansas, and military service, he completed a doctorate and joined the history department at the University of Kansas in 1921. He retired in 1963. He long served as associate editor of the *Kansas Historical Quarterly* and was president of the Agricultural History Society, the Kansas Historical Society, and the Kansas History Teachers Association. A fellow of the American Association for the Advancement of Science, he served on committees of major associations in American history, geography, and American studies.

Malin wrote fifteen books, more than 100 articles, and many book reviews. He prepared two survey texts during his early career and later published in the philosophy of history, but most of his publications deal with the history of his native state and the adjacent grasslands of the Plains. Several of Malin's books focus on the regional and national politics involved in establishing Kansas Territory and the subsequent state: *Indian Policy and Westward Expansion* (1921), *John Brown and the Legend of Fifty-Six* (1942), and *The Nebraska Question, 1852–1854* (1953). In the early 1930s he began to investigate the accommodation of European Americans to the subhumid environment of the grasslands, innovating methods for studying population turnover and community development and investigating relevant research in other disciplines. He described his results as "history from the bottom up" in articles and books such as "The Turnover of Farm Population in Kansas" (*Kansas Historical Quarterly*, 1935), *Winter Wheat in the Golden Belt of Kansas: A Study in Adaptation to Subhumid Geographical Environment* (1940; reprint, 1944), "Dust Storms, 1850–1900" (*Kansas Historical Quarterly*, 1946), and *The Grassland of North America: Prolegomena to Its History* (1947).

Malin significantly advanced understanding of the history of the North American grassland regions. He particularly illuminated the factors underlying mid-nineteenth-century Indian policy, the activity of political factions in territorial Kansas, the Kansas-Nebraska Act, settler and agricultural adaptation, the incidence of dust storms, and the influence of science and technology in shaping regional development. He was the first American historian to make extensive use of federal and state census returns at the farm level. Alone among western historians of his generation, he drew heavily on ecological research, and he believed that ecology paralleled history in its objectives. However, he disputed some of the generalizations of ecologist Frederic Clements and his followers concerning the American grasslands.

Sensitive to editorial oversight, Malin published most of his own books during the last third of his career, a practice that impeded the circulation of his ideas. Malin died on January 16, 1979, at Lawrence, Kansas.

See also PHYSICAL ENVIRONMENT: Grasses / POLITICS AND GOVERNMENT: Kansas-Nebraska Act.

Allan G. Bogue
University of Wisconsin–Madison

Bogue, Allan G. "James C. Malin: A Voice from the Grassland." In *Writing Western History: Essays on Major Western Historians*, edited by Richard W. Etulain. Albuquerque: University of New Mexico Press, 1991: 215–46. Malin, James C. *History and Ecology: Studies of the Grassland*, edited by Robert P. Swierenga. Lincoln: University of Nebraska Press, 1984.

MANDEL, ELI (1922–1992)

Elias Wolf Mandel, the Canadian poet and critic, was born to a Jewish family in Estevan, Saskatchewan, on December 3, 1922. He grew up there and in Regina, and he was always influenced by his western origins. He first left the Prairies in 1943, when he served in Europe with the Canadian Army Medical Corps. Returning in 1945, he completed his bachelor's (1949) and master's (1950) at the University of Saskatchewan in Saskatoon, then left again to complete a doctorate (on the writings of Christopher Smart) at the University of Toronto (1957). Mandel's academic appointments took him to St. Jean (Quebec), Edmonton (Alberta), and (after his separation from his first wife, the poet Miriam Mandel) to York University in Toronto, where he remained as professor of English and humanities from 1967 until he suffered a major stroke in 1989. He died on September 3, 1992.

Author and editor of twenty books, Mandel

acquired a substantial reputation as a theorist of Canadian poetry (as in *Another Time*, 1977, and the anthology *Contexts of Canadian Criticism*, 1971) and as a poet. Early commentaries on his work (e.g., on *Black and Secret Man*, 1964) described it as mythic, seeing in it the influence of Northrop Frye. Later commentary, responding to *Stony Plain* (1973), *Out of Place* (1977, with photographs by his second wife, the critic Ann Mandel), *Life Sentence* (1981), and *Dreaming Backwards* (selected poems, 1981), recognized that the influences on his work are more wide-ranging. Mandel's interest in mysticism, his wit, and his fascination with doubles, ambiguity, chaos, and the paradox of being an individual in a socially interdependent world, for example, derive from his personal travels (in India, Spain, Peru), his readings in George Steiner and others, and his Jewish Prairie heritage. Increasingly, he meditated on what this heritage meant to him, not so much as a set of received religious traditions but as an accumulation of memories that he associates with place.

William H. New
University of British Columbia

Cooley, Dennis. *Eli Mandel and His Works*. Toronto: ECW Press, 1992. New, W. H. "Interim Conclusion: Reading Eli Mandel's 'The Madwomen of the Plaza de Mayo.'" In *Inside the Poem*, edited by W. H. New. Toronto: Oxford University Press, 1992: 160–64.

MAY, KARL (1842–1912)

Among the most popular German writers of all times, Karl Friedrich May was born February 25, 1842, in Ernstthal, Saxony, the fifth child of fourteen to impoverished weavers. After a difficult youth, May lost the opportunity to become a teacher when he was accused of the theft of a watch and had to serve a jail term. More serious charges of impersonation and fraud later sent him back to prison for a total of eight years.

When May was released at age thirty-two, he was determined to become a writer. By the time of his death on March 30, 1912, in Radebeul outside Dresden, May was wealthy and famous, and his place was firmly established in German history. His enormous success (he wrote some eighty books) rests on the gripping first-person narration of travel stories (translated into more than thirty languages), many set in the American West and six specifically on the Llano Estacado. In May's "Western" stories, the narrator, Old Shatterhand, a German frontiersman, forms a blood-brother bond with a noble, handsome, and intelligent Mescalero Apache chief, Winnetou, a character who may well be the most beloved figure in all of German literature. As described in *The Spirit of the Llano Estacado* (1887–88), these friends ride through dangerous, arid terrain and violently shifting weather patterns portrayed in vivid detail. In response to his fans' clamor, May had cards produced showing him dressed in trapper's clothing and signed "Dr. Karl May, known as 'Old Shatterhand.'"

Revelations in the press concerning May's prison record and the fact that he had never

Karl May dressed as "Old Shatterhand"

been to the United States when he wrote his famous stories assaulted him mercilessly in the last years of his life. The question of May's sources—writers who had actually been in America, such as the Germans Charles Sealsfield, Friedrich Gerstäcker, Balduin Möllhausen, and the Irishman Mayne Reid, who spent time on the Llano Estacado—remains a major issue.

See also PHYSICAL ENVIRONMENT: Llano Estacado.

Meredith McClain
Texas Tech University

Frayling, Christopher. *Spaghetti Westerns: Cowboys and Europeans from Karl May to Sergio Leone*. London: Routledge and Kegan Paul, 1981. Sammons, Jeffrey L. *Ideology, Mimesis, Fantasy: Charles Sealsfield, Friedrich Gerstäcker, Karl May, and Other German Novelists of America*. Chapel Hill: University of North Carolina Press, 1998.

MCGRATH, TOM

See PROTEST AND DISSENT: McGrath, Tom

MCMURTRY, LARRY (b. 1936)

Born June 3, 1936, in Wichita Falls, Texas, to Hazel Rugh McIver and Jefferson McMurtry, Lawrence Jefferson McMurtry grew up with ranch hands and cowboys. He received a bachelor of arts degree from the University of North Texas and a master of arts degree from Rice University and studied creative writing at Stanford. He married Josephine Ballard on July 15, 1959; they divorced in 1966. He has one son, James Lawrence. McMurtry taught creative writing at Rice from 1963 to 1969 and now lives in Archer City, Texas, where he runs a bookstore called Booked Up.

McMurtry has published twenty-one novels and much nonfiction, and he has received numerous literary awards. His trail-driving novel, *Lonesome Dove* (1985), received the Spur Award of the Western Writers of America, the Texas Institute of Letters Prize, and a Pulitzer Prize (1986). McMurtry has written sequels to all of his most popular books. He followed the characters of *Lonesome Dove* in sequels, prequels, and the television miniseries films *The Streets of Laredo* (1995), *Return to Lonesome Dove* (1993), and *Dead Man's Walk* (1996), but he has never managed to improve on the originals. *The Last Picture Show* (1966) was reprised in *Texasville* (1987), and *Duane's Depressed* (1999) and other works are linked by their characters.

What makes McMurtry's *Lonesome Dove* one of the best Westerns ever written is his ability to combine a rip-snorting story full of wonderful characters with a history of and elegy for America's westward migration. *Lonesome Dove* joins *Horseman, Pass By* (1961) and *Leaving Cheyenne* (1963) as McMurtry's Texas trilogy. McMurtry's *In a Narrow Grave* (1968) collects many of his published essays.

Most of McMurtry's novels have a certain wistfulness. Sadness and laconic humor, occasioned by loneliness and an awareness of the uncertainties of life, run through his work in an insistent refrain.

See also FILM: *Hud*; *The Last Picture Show*.

Dorys Crow Grover
Texas A&M University–Commerce

Lich, Lera Patrick Tyler. *Larry McMurtry's Texas: Evolution of the Myth*. Austin: Eakin, 1987. Reynolds, Clay, ed. *Taking Stock: A Larry McMurtry Casebook*. Dallas: Southern Methodist University Press, 1989.

MEMOIRS

From the very first incursion of European Americans into the Great Plains (the Spaniard Cabeza de Vaca, about 1534), the memoir has been a preeminent form for the region's writers. Confronted with an unfamiliar and treeless landscape peopled by culturally alien Natives and roamed over by buffalo (an animal he was the first recorded European to have seen), Cabeza de Vaca recalled his experiences and then wrote and published his *Relación* (1542). It began an autobiographical memoir tradition that continues today through volumes such as Ian Frazier's *Great Plains* (1989), William Least Heat-Moon's *PrairyErth* (1991), and Sharon Butala's *The Perfection of the Morning* (1994). So pervasive is the form that two of the region's best-known novels—Willa Cather's *My Ántonia* (1918) and Sinclair Ross's *As for Me and My House* (1941)—adopt the illusion of memoir for fictional purposes. This was nothing new: when James Fenimore Cooper first used the Great Plains as the fictional setting in his *The Prairie* (1823), his primary source for landscape description was Edwin James's memoir of Major Stephen Long's 1819–20 expedition to the Rocky Mountains.

Cabeza de Vaca's account was followed by Pedro de Castañeda's *Narrative* (1896) of the Coronado expedition of 1540–42, and, as the Great Plains was visited by other explorers through the early nineteenth century, numerous other accounts were written and published. On the Canadian Plains the British fur-trading companies sponsored the explorations

—and ultimately the writing—of early figures such as Henry Kelsey (c. 1667–1724), Anthony Henday (who journeyed through the Plains in the mid-1700s), and David Thompson (1770–1857); of these, Thompson's *Narrative* is the best known and most detailed.

As the United States expanded onto the Great Plains before the Civil War, several aesthetically shaped memoirs appeared: Washington Irving's account of his trip to the Indian Territory, *A Tour on the Prairies* (1835), was but one of three western books published by America's then most acknowledged man of letters. This period also saw Josiah Gregg's *Commerce of the Prairies* (1844) and painter George Catlin's *Letters and Notes* (1841). (Catlin's Canadian counterpart, Paul Kane, published *Wanderings of an Artist* in 1859.) The single most significant memoir of the prewar period, however, is Francis Parkman's *The Oregon Trail* (1849). The young historian was determined, during his overland trip to the Rockies in the summer of 1846, to see and describe Native Americans, their landscapes, and their ways of life.

After the war, as exploration gave way to settlement, pioneering memoirs—both unpublished and published—supplanted travelers' accounts. Of these, Hamlin Garland's various autobiographical memoirs—especially *A Son of the Middle Border* (1917) and *A Daughter of the Middle Border* (1921)—are representative and may be read within the contexts of Garland's fiction. Like such fiction—and that by Cather, Wallace Stegner, Wright Morris, Robert Kroetsch, and others—the Great Plains memoir since settlement has focused on understanding the region—in Morris's phrase—as "home place." Of these, three autobiographical memoirs stand out particularly. Frederick Philip Grove's *Over Prairie Trails* (1922) recounts the author's weekly struggle traveling through the Manitoba bush to reach his family, who lived some distance away. The other two, Mari Sandoz's *Love Song to the Plains* (1961) and Wallace Stegner's *Wolf Willow* (1962), marry each author's personal feelings for the Plains with a recounted history of the region. *Wolf Willow*, the most sustained and complex Great Plains autobiographical memoir, is a profound articulation of the recalled meanings made and found in a single landscape, felt by a single person: "If I am native to anything," Stegner sees at one point, "I am native to this." And, because the Iowa-born Stegner wrote about the Plains borderland region of south Saskatchewan where he grew up, *Wolf Willow* remains better regarded in Canada than in the United States. It need not be, for the book is a paradigm of the Great Plains autobiographical memoir, capturing its most frequently seen characteristics.

Robert Thacker
St. Lawrence University

Grove, Frederick Philip. *Over Prairie Trails*. Toronto: McClelland and Stewart, 1991. Parkman, Francis. *The Oregon Trail*. 1849. Edited by E. N. Feltskog. Lincoln: University of Nebraska Press, 1994. Stegner, Wallace. *Wolf Willow: A History, a Story, and a Memory of the Last Plains Frontier*. New York: Viking Press, 1962.

MITCHELL, W. O. (1914–1998)

William Ormond Mitchell was the most loved of Canadian authors, his fiction and drama spanning the worlds of popular entertainment and literary art. Born on March 13, 1914, in Weyburn, Saskatchewan, to Ormond and Margaret McMurray Mitchell, he grew up on the Prairies and attended the Universities of Manitoba and Alberta. His first and most celebrated novel, *Who Has Seen the Wind* (1947), launched a distinguished literary career, during which he wrote drama for radio, screen, stage, and television as well as short stories and nine more novels, including the critically acclaimed *The Vanishing Point* (1973) and *How I Spent My Summer Holidays* (1981). Mitchell also became a mentor to younger authors as writer in residence at several universities and was awarded the Order of Canada and other honors before his death in Calgary on February 25, 1998.

Mitchell's broadest popularity grew from his *Jake and the Kid* radio series, a humorous look at Prairie life that ran for more than 300 episodes, and from his public performances in the tradition of Charles Dickens, Mark Twain, and Stephen Leacock. As a humorist, Mitchell claimed literary descent particularly from Twain. Mitchell's greatest critical success is *Who Has Seen the Wind*, the story of a Prairie boy's search for meaning that has become a Canadian classic.

Mitchell was, in one respect, a victim of his own success. His lyric evocation of a child's world of innocence is so compelling that readers can be distracted from his enduring themes of the fall from innocence and the problems of human mortality. On the other hand, Mitchell's popularity enabled him to create for all Canadians an ancestral home on the Prairies.

Dick Harrison
Sechelt, British Columbia

Harrison, Dick. "W. O. Mitchell (1914–)." In *Canadian Writers and Their Works*, Fiction series, edited by Robert Lecker, Jack David, and Ellen Quigley. Toronto: ECW Press, 1991: 4: 141–208. Latham, Sheila, and David Latham, eds. *The Art of W. O. Mitchell*. Toronto: University of Toronto Press, 1997.

MOMADAY, N. SCOTT (b. 1934)

House Made of Dawn (1968), N. Scott Momaday's Pulitzer Prize–winning novel about a World War II veteran's experiences at Jemez Pueblo and in Los Angeles, was a groundbreaking literary event that attracted widespread attention to contemporary Native American writing as well as to much older written and oral Native American literature. Since the publication of that novel, Momaday has written another, *The Ancient Child* (1989), and has also gained international recognition as a poet (*The Gourd Dancer*, 1976; *In the Presence of the Sun: A Gathering of Shields, 1961–1991*, 1992; *In the Bear's House*, 1999), an autobiographer and engaging interviewee (*The Way to Rainy Mountain*, 1969; *The Names: A Memoir*, 1976; *Ancestral Voice*, 1989; *Conversations with N. Scott Momaday*, 1997), an essayist

(*The Man Made of Words: Essays, Stories, and Passages*, 1997), and a respected artist.

Navarre Scott Momaday was born in Lawton, Oklahoma, on February 27, 1934. Although he has lived most of his life away from his birthplace, southwestern Oklahoma and other Great Plains landscapes have dominated much of his best fiction and poetry. In *The Ancient Child*, some of his most lyric prose poems capture the majesty and seasonal beauties of Devil's Tower (Bear Lodge) in Wyoming and the Wichita Mountains' high meadows in spring. Several fine poems celebrate striking aspects of the Plains landscape (the "prairie fire" of sunrise in "Plainview 3") and Plains culture (*The Gourd Dancer*, "Rings of Bone," and the "Gathering of Shields" prose poems).

It is in *The Way to Rainy Mountain*, however, that Momaday offers his most sustained and moving testimony to the Great Plains. His father's people, the Kiowa, undertook a migration 300 years ago that traversed the Great Plains from the headwaters of the Yellowstone River to Rainy Mountain in southwestern Oklahoma and continued in later years with horseback travels through Texas to Mexico. For Momaday, the Plains area of southwestern Oklahoma is "a landscape that is incomparable," in part because it grounds and witnesses a grand paradox for his father's people, "a time that is gone forever, and the human spirit, which endures." To capture this landscape in twenty-four two-page sections, Momaday created three "angles of vision": storytelling (tribal narratives and family lore), history-fact, and personal experience. Together these viewpoints acknowledge the harshness of the Plains —blizzards, a summer heat as fierce as "an anvil's edge," tornadoes powered by a wild mythical horse—and document the tragedies of his people: 800 Kiowa horse carcasses rotting near Fort Sill, thousands of buffalo slaughtered, many Kiowas killed and taken into captivity. But in memory, in the present, and in the sense of sacred play of the three perspectives, the vitality of the Kiowa Plains endures in a mountain that "burns and shines" in the "early sun," in a reverence for the grand wanderings of great horsemen, and in the joy of seeing a newborn buffalo that adds life to the returning buffalo herds. Small wonder that Momaday can look at the remote knoll that is Rainy Mountain and see a place "where Creation was begun."

See also NATIVE AMERICANS: Kiowas.

Kenneth M. Roemer
University of Texas–Arlington

Roemer, Kenneth M., ed. *Approaches to Teaching Momaday's "The Way to Rainy Mountain."* New York: Modern Language Association, 1988. Scarberry-Garcia, Susan. *Landmarks of Healing: A Study of "House Made of Dawn."* Albuquerque: University of New Mexico Press, 1990. Schubnell, Matthias. *N. Scott Momaday: The Cultural and Literary Background.* Norman: University of Oklahoma Press, 1985.

MORRIS, WRIGHT (1910–1998)

Wright Morris, novelist and photographer, was born in Central City, Nebraska, on January 6, 1910. His mother died when he was six days old. Morris lived with his father in towns along the Platte and in Omaha before moving to Chicago in 1924. In subsequent years, Morris traveled widely in Mexico and Europe before settling in Mill Valley, California, where he died on April 25, 1998.

Of his more than thirty books, Morris is best known for his photo-texts and the novels that probe origins, identity, and the significance of the Plains in shaping human character and experience. Morris's tone of inquiry is cogently expressed in the photo-text novel *The Home Place* (1948) by protagonist Clyde Muncy: "There's too much sky out here . . . too much horizontal, . . . so that the exclamation, the perpendicular, had to come. Anyone who was born and raised on the plains knows that the high false front on the Feed Store, and the white water tower, are not a question of vanity. It's a problem of being. Of knowing you are there." Muncy's nostalgia is tempered in *The World in the Attic* (1949) by nausea, an emotional reaction that warns him against excessive indulgence in the past. In later novels Morris examines, with comic compassion, the consciousness of those who live where "there is no place to hide"—even, in *Ceremony in Lone Tree* (1960), from the likes of mass murderer Charles Starkweather.

In his final novel, *Plains Song for Female Voices* (1980), Sharon Atkins comes to understand that complete "escape" from the Plains is impossible. Morris explores his own umbilical connections to Nebraska in the photo-text *God's Country and My People* (1968) and his memoir, *Will's Boy* (1981). At its best, his words and photographs salvage the post-Depression era from dissolution by time and human fallibility.

Joseph J. Wydeven
Bellevue University

Knoll, Robert, ed. *Conversations with Wright Morris: Critical Views and Responses.* Lincoln: University of Nebraska Press, 1977. Wydeven, Joseph J. *Wright Morris Revisited.* Boston: Twayne, 1998.

MOUNTIE STORIES

Mountie stories were once the most popular adventure fiction of the Canadian Prairies, but by the 1950s they were overtaken by history and changing fashion. Soon after they came west, the North-West Mounted Police were discovered by the international entertainment industry, with nineteenth-century adventure writers creating various romantic images of the force. British writers such as John Mackie and Harold Bindloss depicted Mounties as well-bred Englishmen defending the ideals of empire. The Mounties of American writers such as James Oliver Curwood were U.S. marshals in red tunics, given to shootouts and extralegal justice. By contrast, the Canadian Mountie hero popularized by Charles Gordon and Gilbert Parker could ride into a hostile Indian camp and arrest the chief's son without unholstering his weapon because he eschewed violence: his uncanny power resided not in himself but in the empire he symbolized.

Mountie stories appeared regularly through the 1940s, but by 1950 virtually none were being published in Canada. Canadian publishers were losing interest probably because, with Canada's growing independence, a hero embodying a discarded myth of empire was an embarrassment. The fictional Mountie was left largely to Hollywood, which had already produced more than 200 movies projecting the American image of the force. Aside from historical studies, Mounties in Canada usually feature in ironic or satiric sketches on radio or television. The crowning irony may be the sale of the rights to the Mountie image to the Disney Corporation in 1995, completing the circle of an old British colonial symbol absorbed in the new American colonization of Canadian culture.

See also LAW: North-West Mounted Police.

Dick Harrison
Sechelt, British Columbia

Dawson, Michael. *The Mountie: From Dime Novel to Disney.* Toronto: Between the Lines, 1998. Harrison, Dick, ed. *Best Mounted Police Stories.* Edmonton: University of Alberta Press, 1978. Walden, Keith. *Visions of Order: The Canadian Mounties in Symbol and Myth.* Toronto: Butterworths, 1982.

NATIVE AMERICAN LITERATURE

Native American literature begins with the oral traditions in the hundreds of Indigenous cultures of North America and finds its fullness in all aspects of written literature as well. Until the last several decades, however, Native American literature has primarily been studied for its ethnographic interest. A fruitful intellectual discussion of the place of Native American literature within global literary study—a discussion that includes Native American intellectuals, artists, and writers themselves—only began during the activist period of the 1960s and 1970s.

The written Native American literary tradition commenced as early as the eighteenth century, when a Mohegan Methodist missionary, Samson Occum, published his *Sermon Preached at the Execution of Moses Paul, an Indian* in 1772. William Apess (Pequot), also a Christian minister, wrote an autobiography that protested non-Indians' treatment of Indians, and he also collected the autobiographies of other Christian Indians in *Experiences of Five Christian Indians of the Pequot Tribe* (1833). Other Native Americans published historical and cultural accounts of their peoples during the nineteenth century: David Cusick (Tuscarora); George Copway, Peter Jones, and William Whipple Warren (Ojibwa); Peter Dooyentate Clarke (Wyandot); Chief Elias Johnson (Tuscarora); and Chief Andrew J. Blackbird (Ottawa). These valuable writings represent a range of genres and reflect cultural issues of the times in which they were written.

Plains Indian oral literature includes literary expressions from cultures as different as Blackfeet (northwestern Montana) are from Kiowa (Southern Plains). By far, autobiographies comprise the bulk of written literary materials. During the late nineteenth and early twentieth centuries, academics—mostly anthropologists and historians—took up the idea that Native testimony or life stories needed to be preserved. Many believed that Native Americans were disappearing and with them their languages and histories; great efforts needed to be made to preserve cultural histories and literatures in writing. While many Native Americans wrote their own autobiographies during this period, many more had their life stories recorded as "as-told-to" autobiographies by anthropologists, ethnographers, and "Indian buffs." Plains Indian life stories, particularly those of warriors and chiefs, were so plentiful that they became a genre unto themselves.

Black Elk Speaks (Lakota) is probably the most famous as-told-to narrative, a text "told through" John G. Neihardt. Because the poet Neihardt was most interested in obtaining Black Elk's story for his poetic work on the American West, he omitted aspects of Black Elk's life that did not fit his own poetic purposes. In his study of *Black Elk Speaks*, entitled *The Sixth Grandfather*, Raymond DeMallie presents the transcripts of the initial interviews with Black Elk, enabling us to study the life of Black Elk and the textual creation of that famous work. Other well-known as-told-to Plains autobiographies include *Pretty Shield: Medicine Woman of the Crows* and *Plenty-Coups: Chief of the Crows* (both as told to Frank B. Linderman in 1932 and 1930, respectively) and *Cheyenne Memories* (by John Stands in Timber and Margot Liberty, 1967). Most notable among the self-generated autobiographies of the early twentieth century are Charles Eastman's (Dakota) *Indian Boyhood* (1902) and *From the Deep Woods to Civilization* (1916) and Gertrude Bonnin's (Lakota) *American Indian Stories* (1921), a mixture of short fiction, autobiography, and nonfiction. Contemporary Lakota as-told-to autobiographies continue, for example, *Lame Deer, Seeker of Visions* (1972) and *Lakota Woman* (1990), both written with Richard Erdoes.

European literary genres such as poetry and fiction, for the most part, began being employed by Native American people in the nineteenth century. John Rollin Ridge (Cherokee) wrote the first Native American novel in English, *The Life and Adventures of Joaquin Murieta* (1854). The most famous Plains Indian writer is N. Scott Momaday (Kiowa), whose first novel, *House Made of Dawn* (1968), won the Pulitzer Prize for literature in 1969. *The Way to Rainy Mountain*, the autobiography he published a year later, traces his journey from the mountains of Montana to Rainy Mountain in Oklahoma, the path Kiowa people followed as their culture was transformed through acquisition of the Tai-Me, the Sun Dance medicine bundle. Momaday's influence since the 1960s cannot be underestimated; through his writing, he created a new voice and a new place for Native American writers in the American imagination.

The era of awakening, dubbed the Native American Renaissance by literary critic Kenneth Lincoln, witnessed the production of many new Indian texts after Momaday's influential novel and autobiographical memoir, including works by Leslie Marmon Silko (Laguna), Simon Or-

tiz (Acoma Pueblo), and Ray Young Bear (Mesquaki) as well as poetry by Roberta Hill (Oneida), Duane Niatum (Klallam), Joy Harjo (Creek), and Wendy Rose (Hopi-Miwok), and others. James Welch, a Plains writer of Blackfeet and Gros Ventre heritage, has been and remains prominent among Native American writers, with five novels, one book of poetry, and a nonfictional book on the Indian point of view of the Battle of the Little Bighorn.

The substantial amount of writing by Native Americans now enables the identification of clusters of work based on genre, tribal affiliation, geography, theme, style, gender, and sexual preference. The blossoming of nonfictional essay writing and literary criticism by Natives themselves bodes well for the future study of Native American literature. Most notable among contemporary essayists is Elizabeth Cook-Lynn (Crow-Creek-Dakota); her collection *Why I Can't Read Wallace Stegner* (1996) hits at crucial contemporary Native American struggles, challenges, and grievances in tough-minded and bold terms. Although primarily a poet and fiction writer, Cook-Lynn presents "a tribal voice" (the subtitle of the text) that cannot be ignored. Most importantly, Native American literature owes its existence to continuing and vibrant oral traditions.

See also RELIGION: Black Elk, Nicholas.

Kathryn W. Shanley
University of Montana

Allen, Paula Gunn, ed. *Studies in American Indian Literature: Critical Essays and Course Designs.* New York: Modern Language Association, 1983. Ruoff, A. LaVonne Brown. *American Indian Literatures: An Introduction, Bibliographic Review, and Selected Bibliography.* New York: Modern Language Association, 1999. Weaver, Jace. *That the People Might Live: Native American Literatures and Native American Community.* New York: Oxford University Press, 1997.

NATURE WRITING

Nature writing has been a component of American Great Plains literature ever since Lewis and Clark captured their impressions of the Plains in their journals. Long before, Native peoples had described their existence in stories about nature, passed on from generation to generation. The land's presence indelibly marks itself in language, making nature a part of Plains fiction, poetry, nonfiction, and drama. Frederick Philip Grove's *Over Prairie Trails* (1922) marks the beginning of a vital body of twentieth-century Great Plains nature writing that has emerged in both the United States and Canada. This literary tradition gazes back upon the irrevocable environmental changes on the Plains, noting the loss of species, the depletion of resources, the economic boom-and-bust cycles that have populated and depopulated areas, and the traumatic displacement of Native peoples. Grove's narrative positions a lone traveler on the Plains both fascinated with and distrustful of the natural forces confronting him. This ambivalence toward such a vast landscape is a signature mood in much Plains nature writing.

The natural landscape today reveals an environment vastly different from that encoun-

tered by Lewis and Clark in 1804. The aftermath of settlement haunts contemporary Plains nature writers such as Gretel Ehrlich, Ian Frazier, Don Gayton, Linda Hasselstrom, Wes Jackson, William Least Heat-Moon, John McPhee, and Wallace Stegner. Least Heat-Moon's metaphor of deep mapping that conflates natural and human history through time and space provides an understanding of contemporary nature writing of the Plains. Like geologists, these writers create cross-sectional narratives of natural history, illuminating the strata in which natural history makes contact with human cultures, in which deep time and human time collide. John Janovy's textual journeys to Keith County, Nebraska, illustrate the complex histories that Plains nature writers create. Evolutionary history is rich in Keith County (and in Don Gayton's Saskatchewan), yet European Americans have rapidly altered what has taken millions of years to create. Plains human history unravels at an even faster pace. Around the abandoned homesteads, ghost towns, and empty schoolyards, nature reasserts its claim. Species become extinct, but the niches will be filled with new plants and animals. In a "tallgrass dream," Gayton ponders the complexity of reestablishing grasslands that are all but gone.

Nature writing of the Plains is as much about the human response to change as it is about the natural world's adjustment to change. It examines the human need for spiritual connection to the land. Kathleen Norris coined the phrase "spiritual geography" to define her search for meaning in western South Dakota, and other nature writers of the Plains, including Loren Eiseley, Sharon Butala, Don Gayton, Linda Hogan, Least Heat-Moon, Norris, and Dan O'Brien have also expressed with memorable poignancy their spiritual hungers. To counter the sense of fragmentation that often accompanies life in embattled communities, these writers seek wisdom in the land. Some, like Linda Hasselstrom, are acutely aware of how tenuous humans' hold on the land is. An entire way of life is threatened when ranchers and farmers face economic hardships. Native writers in particular turn back to the land to re-create their tribal legacies and to recover suppressed spiritual traditions.

Nature writing of the Plains, therefore, expresses multiple themes: to account for loss, to acknowledge mistakes, to preserve and celebrate what remains, and to retrace centuries of change. To accomplish such layered narratives, nature writers of the Plains cross boundaries of genre and discipline, region and country, gender and culture. In voicings rich and variant, they examine complex issues of science, history, and human desire.

Susan Naramore Maher
University of Nebraska at Omaha

Lyon, Thomas J. "The Nature Essay in the West." In *A Literary History of the American West*, edited by J. Golden Taylor. Fort Worth: Texas Christian University Press, 1987: 221–65. Quantic, Diane Dufva. *The Nature of the Place: A Study of Great Plains Fiction.* Lincoln: University of Nebraska Press, 1995. Thacker, Robert. *The Great Prairie Fact and Literary Imagination.* Albuquerque: University of New Mexico Press, 1989.

NEIHARDT, JOHN G. (1881–1973)

Black Elk and John G. Neihardt at the Sioux Victory celebration at Pine Ridge, South Dakota, September 1945

John G. Neihardt was born near Sharpsburg, Illinois, on January 8, 1881. After living for a time in a sod house in western Kansas and then in Kansas City, he moved to Wayne, Nebraska, where he graduated from Nebraska Normal College at age sixteen and wrote and published his first book, *The Divine Enchantment* (1900), which was based on Vedanta philosophy.

In 1900 Neihardt moved to Bancroft, Nebraska. He edited the local newspaper, worked as a clerk on the Omaha Reservation, and wrote lyric poetry, short stories, and novels. *Outing Magazine* commissioned Neihardt to record his experiences on a 2,000-mile trip down the Missouri River in 1908, later published as *The River and I* (1910). That same year, Neihardt married Mona Martinsen, a sculptor and former student of Rodin. They had four children: Enid, Sigurd, Hilda, and Alice.

Neihardt wrote literary columns for a number of newspapers, including the *Minneapolis Journal* (1911–21) and the *St. Louis Post-Dispatch* (1926–38), producing nearly 3,000 essays and reviews. In 1912 Neihardt began work on his five-volume epic *Cycle of the West*. The *Cycle*, completed in 1941, recounts tales of American explorers and fur traders of the trans-Missouri country (*The Song of Hugh Glass*, 1915; *The Song of the Three Friends*, 1919; and *The Song of Jedediah Smith*, 1941) and of the Native peoples dispossessed by those explorers and, later, settlers (*The Song of the Indian Wars*, 1925; *The Song of the Messiah*, 1935). While researching *The Song of the Messiah*, Neihardt met an Oglala Lakota holy man, Black Elk, whose vision he recorded in *Black Elk Speaks* (1932).

In 1921 Neihardt was named poet laureate of Nebraska. From 1949 until 1966 he was poet in residence and lecturer at the University of Missouri. He was working on a second vol-

ume of his autobiography when he died on November 3, 1973, in Lincoln, Nebraska.

See also RELIGION: Black Elk, Nicholas.

Lori Utecht
John G. Neihardt Center

Aly, Lucile T. *John G. Neihardt: A Critical Biography*. Amsterdam: Rodopi, 1977. Whitney, Blair. *John G. Neihardt*. Boston: G. K. Hall, 1976.

OLSEN, TILLIE (b. 1913)

Tillie Olsen, author of *Tell Me a Riddle*, was born Tillie Lerner on a farm near Mead, Nebraska, on January 14, 1913. Like many other Jewish immigrants in Nebraska, the Lerners had left Russia after the failure of the 1905 revolution. The family moved to Omaha in 1917. Olsen's parents were active Socialists, and her father, Samuel, ran for lieutenant governor on the Socialist Party ticket in 1928. Her early life was centered in the family's struggle to make a living and its radical politics. At Central High, Olsen read widely and wrote for the school paper but was not a model student. She dropped out of high school after joining the Young Communist League in 1931. By 1934 she had moved to San Francisco, where she married Jack Olsen and reared four daughters.

Olsen's first story, "The Iron Throat," appeared in 1934 in the *Partisan Review*. The story attracted attention, and Olsen participated in the 1935 Writers Congress. In the 1940s Olsen was active in union and other left-wing activities. In 1961, after her mother's death, Olsen published *Tell Me a Riddle*, a collection of short fiction. The title story, based on her parents' lives, focuses on a mother's memories and the family's responses to her impending death from cancer. Another story is "I Stand Here Ironing." Both stories portray creative women whose lives were subdued by the exigencies of motherhood. These stories received wide critical acclaim and resonated with the emerging feminist ideas of the 1970s. In 1974 Olsen published *Yonnondio*, a novel of the Great Depression she began in the early 1930s. *Yonnondio* also draws on her family history and midwestern roots. The novel focuses on Mazie, a starry-eyed young girl, who moves with her family from the farm to a large meat-packing city like Omaha. In 1978 Olsen published *Silences*, a book of nonfiction essays about pressures that silence women as writers.

Olsen's fiction won national and international notice in the 1970s. She is generally considered a major figure among contemporary women writers.

Linda Ray Pratt
University of Nebraska–Lincoln

ORAL TRADITIONS

Oral traditions are a body of unwritten information and messages preserved in memory and repeated through succeeding generations. In the Great Plains, this information was originally held by Native Americans. Oral traditions have preserved much of the early history of the Plains. Statements repeated from generation to generation, often combining lore and fact,

retained information about human migrations, conflicts among peoples, and changes in societal patterns during the period that preceded European contact. Information and lore, sometimes contained in stories with moral messages, were preserved about specific places and geographical landmarks. The repeated telling of this material, both for entertainment and the maintenance of community identity, preserved the knowledge.

European American migration to the Plains brought people who, though they carried with them their own set of oral traditions, often did not understand the importance of Native American oral traditions. Although much traditional knowledge was lost, some survived in oral form or became part of the written history of the area. For example, in 1930 Nebraska poet John G. Neihardt traveled to the Pine Ridge Agency in South Dakota to interview Oglala Lakota holy man Black Elk. The resulting book, *Black Elk Speaks*, though shaped and written by Neihardt, is an important and revered repository of Lakota belief and history from about 1850 to 1890.

Mari Sandoz drew on stories she had heard as a child from Native American visitors to her family's remote ranch in the Sand Hills of Nebraska when she wrote *Crazy Horse* and other books about Native Americans. Authors such as Gerald Vizenor and N. Scott Momaday rely on the oral tradition while working to identify its role in modern literature. Most recent poetry, fiction, and history of Native Americans on the Plains contains information drawn from oral traditions.

Oral history—as opposed to oral traditions—began in the late 1930s with the advent of modern technology and the availability of recording equipment. Although oral history is the collection of first-hand information from a person, its collection techniques, including the use of a tape recorder and a trained interviewer, have been adapted for use in documenting oral traditions. Interviews with Native Americans in collections held at institutions such as the University of Oklahoma and the University of South Dakota are examples.

Information based on or drawn from oral sources has grown with each succeeding movement of people into the Plains. Stories about the Oregon Trail, the Pony Express, contact between Native Americans and European Americans, pioneer settlement, cattle drives, and professions such as store keeping, soldiering, and teaching, among many others, have become part of the Plains oral tradition and are preserved in universities, historical societies, and local archives. Oral traditions continue to provide insight into the history of the Great Plains and the changes that have occurred throughout the years. Documented and defined by modern research methods, as in Ian Frazier's *Great Plains*, they help provide a unique source of information that extends beyond the written record, retaining the words and stories of and about people and places that might otherwise have been lost.

See also FOLKWAYS: Plains Indian Narratives.

Barbara W. Sommer
BWS Associates

Blaeser, Kimberly M. *Gerald Vizenor: Writing in the Oral Tradition*. Norman: University of Oklahoma Press, 1996. Vansina, Jan. *Oral Tradition as History*. Madison: University of Wisconsin Press, 1985.

OSTENSO, MARTHA (1900–1963)

Martha Ostenso was a Minnesota novelist often claimed by Canadians because she lived in Canada for six years and set four of her novels there. She was born in Norway on September 17, 1900, to Sigurd and Olina Tungeland Ostenso, who migrated to the Midwest in 1902. After the family moved to Manitoba in 1915, Ostenso taught briefly in the interlake area north of Winnipeg. She attended the University of Manitoba for two years before following her creative writing teacher, Douglas Durkin, to New York in 1921. Himself a novelist, Durkin is said to have collaborated with Ostenso in all her novels, including *Wild Geese*, which won the Dodd Mead First Novel Award in 1925. Together they produced a dozen popular novels under her name over the next thirty years, including *The Young May Moon* (1929), *The Mandrake Root* (1938), and *O River, Remember* (1943). They reportedly earned up to $40,000 annually and kept a house in Beverly Hills where they socialized with stars such as Douglas Fairbanks Jr., Mary Pickford, and Henry Fonda, who starred in a 1941 Hollywood remake of *Wild Geese*.

Ostenso's best novel, *Wild Geese*, depicts a tyrannical Prairie patriarch overthrown by the suppressed vitality and moral courage of the women in his family. Hailed as an early contribution to Prairie realism, the novel draws much of its power from its romantic characterization. Ostenso's other novels, set mainly in the rural Midwest, portray family conflicts and the darker reaches of romantic love and often exhibit the author's gift for creating powerful female characters. Ostenso died in Seattle on November 24, 1963.

Dick Harrison
Sechelt, British Columbia

Atherton, Stanley S. "Martha Ostenso (1900–63)." In *Canadian Writers and Their Works*, 4: 210–53, Fiction series, edited by Robert Lecker, Jack David, and Ellen Quigley. Toronto: ECW Press, 1991. Baldwin, Charles C. *Martha Ostenso: Daughter of the Vikings*. New York: Dodd, Mead, 1930.

PERSONAL EXPERIENCE NARRATIVES

See FOLKWAYS: Personal Experience Narratives

PLAINS INDIAN NARRATIVES

See FOLKWAYS: Plains Indian Narratives

POETRY

Nearly all the poetry written in the Great Plains during the last 150 years can be placed in two general categories. In the nineteenth and early twentieth centuries, poetry written in the literary forms of, for example, Keats or Byron was considered respectable, while poetry whose form and rhetoric were an extension of its subject matter was only beginning to seek legitimacy. Imitative poems occasionally made use of the locale or the culture in which the poet lived and wrote, such as the epic and iambic heroic pioneer and Native American poems of John G. Neihardt, but, generally, the main aspiration of the imitative poet was to create what was considered to be respectable "classical" literature, as if to establish the fact that civilization was indeed possible far from the traditional seats of refinement. The worldwide emergence of literary realism established the legitimacy of poems whose forms were "organic"—poems whose free forms seemed a natural extension of content. In the early twentieth century the balance began to tip toward a poem that disdained classical influences while attempting to respond to the life and culture of the poet's immediate locality. Today, poets writing work of this latter kind far outnumber those writing in classical forms, though Plains poetry of all forms does have at least one distinguishing tradition, that of reporting news from the frontier.

Much of Plains literature written during the period of settlement—stories, poems, essays, and newspaper columns—described the joys and sorrows of life on the edge of American or Canadian civilization. Authors customarily addressed their work to a remote, comfortably situated audience, an audience ignorant of what a sod house in Nebraska or a homestead shack in Saskatchewan might offer. It made perfect sense for writers to make such reports because, after all, they had no other audience. Most of the readers in both countries were still "back east." Those frontier writers' principal tools were scenic description and action-filled anecdote, and the emotional stance was one of hard-bitten acceptance of circumstances.

The tradition of reporting from the frontier continues today. During the past 150 years, easterners have come to expect Plains writers to continue writing steady-eyed reports from the "edge of civilization," even though the frontier has long since passed on west and sunk out of sight in the Pacific. For example, Thomas McGrath's epic poem *Letter to an Imaginary Friend*, one of the twentieth century's genuine masterpieces, is in part a report from the frontier of North Dakota.

The contemporary poetry most readily identified as Great Plains writing still follows these general parameters: it is descriptive, anecdotal, noncelebratory, and generally accepting of circumstances. It continues to be the expectation of eastern readers that poets "out there" will continue to provide reports on living conditions in rural America. Sometimes, in an attempt to sell itself to the established eastern literary community, which still maintains authority in matters literary, Plains poetry has suffered by trying to be too entertaining, too clever, too anecdotal, and obsequious toward an eastern audience. A poet who lives in Kansas and who writes in the manner of, say, the New York school—in which setting and environment are suppressed in favor of a more cerebral, talky, unanchored or nonlocal poetry—may find it difficult to find acceptance either in the East or in Kansas.

Probably the most important, most highly acclaimed Plains poet was the late William Stafford (1914–93), who spent his boyhood in Kansas and who continued to write tellingly and movingly about life on the Plains even after he moved to Oregon. Stafford's most notable poems adhere to the traits mentioned above: they are descriptive and anecdotal, and though loss and misery may be described, Stafford never pities himself or the people whose lives he portrays. Generous with his praise for the Kansas landscape and its people, he is never inappropriately boosterish. The people in his poems, such as a small-town spinster schoolmistress dying of cancer in old age, are ennobled by Stafford's dispassionate account of their uncomplaining struggles. Much of Stafford's best work fits into the category of reports from the frontier.

There are hundreds if not thousands of poets living on the Plains in the twenty-first century, many having considerable talent and national recognition. Some of these authors, like the Cherokee writer Diane Glancy, are talented poets and fiction writers as well. Linda Hasselstrom, a ranch woman from South Dakota, is an accomplished poet, diarist, and essayist.

Poetry on the Canadian Prairies is perhaps even more ubiquitous than on the U.S. side. Canada Council and provincial writers guilds not only provide subsidies for publication but also support reading tours by poets and other writers and poet-in-residence grants for libraries in major cities and many small towns. Louis Riel, Canada's most celebrated western rebel, was also an accomplished poet, and his heirs are legion. Just a few are Di Brandt and Bonnie Burnard, Louise Halfe and Beth Cuthand, Dennis Cooley and Anne Szumigalski, Fred Wah and Robert Kroetsch.

Like all authors, Plains poets are at their best when they focus their talents on trying to write well rather than trying to write what is expected of them. Paying too much attention to the expectation and entertainment of outside readers and publishers can lead to the weaknesses of glibness and redundancy. But, on the other hand, bowing to their own traditions, Plains poets continue to have an irrepressible urge to tell the people what life is really like out in this land of wide horizons.

Ted Kooser
Garland, Nebraska

POLLOCK, SHARON (b. 1936)

Playwright, actor, and director Sharon Pollock was born Mary Sharon Chalmers in Fredericton, New Brunswick, on April 19, 1936, the eldest daughter of Dr. Everette Chalmers, physician, a version of whom is the central character in Pollock's most personal play, *Doc*. She was involved in theater in school and in amateur companies, ran a box office, and did considerable acting, winning best actress in the Dominion Drama Festival in 1966. She began writing children's plays and plays for radio and television and in 1971 wrote her first stage play, *Compulsory Option*. She moved in

1976 to Calgary, which has been her home since, though among other positions she was for two years artistic director of Theatre New Brunswick.

Pollock made her name with two historical dramas: *Walsh* (1973), about the relationship between a Mountie and Chief Sitting Bull and the betrayal of the Sioux by the Canadian government (the 1983 version is the anthologized version); and *The Komagata Maru Incident* (1976), about the rejection by Canada in 1914 of Sikh refugees aboard a Japanese ship in Vancouver harbor.

Pollock's best year was 1980, when she produced three plays. *One Tiger to a Hill* is again based on an historical event, a 1975 hostage-taking incident at a maximum-security prison. Both *Blood Relations* and *Generations* are more personal stories. *Blood Relations* is based on Lizzie Borden, acquitted in 1882 in Massachusetts of the axe murders of her father and stepmother. *Generations* is the story of a southern Alberta farm family and the first of Pollock's plays not based on external sources.

Of these plays *Blood Relations* has become the most famous, with productions across Canada and in other countries. It won Pollock her first Governor General's Literary Award for drama, repeated in 1986 with *Doc. Whiskey Six Cadenza*, an extravaganza about the 1920s Crow's Nest Pass, was produced in 1983 and *Doc*, a version of Pollock's family life, in 1984, both in Calgary. *Doc* became a nationally produced play. Since then a one-woman show, *Getting It Straight* (1990), has had a Toronto premiere, and until recently Pollock has been running the Garry Theatre in Calgary.

Donald C. Kerr
University of Saskatchewan

Rudakoff, Judith, and Reta Much, eds. *Fair Play, 12 Women Speak, Conversations with Canadian Playwrights*. Toronto: Simon and Pierre, 1980: 208–20. Zimmerman, Cynthia. *Playwriting Women: Female Voices in English Canada*. Toronto: Simon and Pierre, 1994: 61–97.

PORTER, KATHERINE ANNE

(1890–1980)

Katherine Anne Porter's varied fictional treatments of the Great Plains areas of Texas and the Southwest are important documents in the historical and cultural study of these regions. It must be kept in mind, however, that Porter—like most writers of fiction—freely adapted descriptions of this area for her own aesthetic purposes; hence, absolute realism cannot be expected in her fictional accounts of the Texas Hill Country, where she was born —at Indian Creek on May 15, 1890—and grew to maturity and which provided an important impetus for her creative work.

Among the finely crafted works of short fiction that describe and analyze the Great Plains areas of Texas and the Southwest are *He* (1927), *The Jilting of Granny Weatherall* (1929), *The Grave* (1935), *Noon Wine* (1937), *Old Mortality* (1938), and *Holiday* (1960). Inseparable from the hardscrabble rural landscapes are the memorable characters who are extensions and personifications of the land itself. The domi-

neering grandmother in numerous stories has, in fact, been described as a "metaphor for Texas" because of her determination to survive and prosper despite the hardships and calamities inherent in the prevailing conditions.

Katherine Anne Porter, after a life of accomplishment (including a National Book Award and Pulitzer Prize, both in 1966) and enthusiastic living (she married and divorced three times), died on September 18, 1980, in Silver Spring, Maryland.

James T. F. Tanner
University of North Texas

Givner, Joan. *Katherine Anne Porter: A Life*. New York: Simon and Schuster, 1982. Tanner, James T. F. *The Texas Legacy of Katherine Anne Porter*. Denton: University of North Texas Press, 1991.

POSEY, ALEXANDER (1873–1908)

Alexander Posey, 1908

Alexander Lawrence Posey, a well-known Muskogee Creek poet and journalist, lived in Indian Territory during the turbulent years prior to and one year beyond Oklahoma statehood. He is best remembered for a series of humorous and politically insightful articles printed while he was the owner and editor of the *Eufaula Journal*. "Fus Fixico Letters," some seventy-two in all, became a weekly feature of Posey's newspaper and made use of voices and personae of traditional Creek Indian figures to comment on territorial politicians, elections, members of the Dawes Commission, the issues of coming statehood and an Indian state to be called Sequoyah, as well as the general resistance to "progress" and land allotments led by the Creek historian Chitto Harjo.

Posey was born near present-day Eufaula, Oklahoma, on August 3, 1873, the first child of Nancy and Lewis Henderson Posey. He received his postsecondary education at Bacone Indian University, Muskogee, Oklahoma, where he gained some recognition as a budding poet and as a writer of commencement

orations. He was elected as a clerk in the Creek House of Warriors and appointed as superintendent of the Creek Orphan Asylum near Okmulgee. He married Minnie Harris, a schoolteacher from Farmington, Arkansas. In his writings, Posey emphasized the importance of conforming to the new American society and to what he felt were progressive viewpoints.

Although he had achieved a national journalistic reputation, his interests had expanded to include tribal folkways, land development, and even oil and gas speculation. But his life was cut short by a tragic drowning accident on the morning of May 27, 1908. He was survived by his young wife and two children.

Charles Ballard
University of Nebraska–Lincoln

Littlefield, Daniel F., Jr. *Alex Posey: Creek Poet, Journalist, and Humorist*. Lincoln: University of Nebraska Press, 1992. Posey, Alexander. *The Fus Fixico Letters*, edited by Daniel F. Littlefield Jr. and Carol A. Pretty Hunter. Lincoln: University of Nebraska Press, 1993.

PRAIRIE SCHOONER

The *Prairie Schooner*, founded in 1926 at the University of Nebraska by Lowry C. Wimberly, is widely recognized as one of the premier literary magazines in the world. It has been cited by the *Washington Post* for its "fabulous fiction" and by the *Dictionary of Literary Biography* and *Writer's Digest* as one of the top ten magazines publishing poetry.

The *Prairie Schooner*'s prose and poetry are regularly reprinted in collections such as *Best American Poetry*, *Best American Short Stories*, *Best American Essays*, the *O. Henry* anthology of short stories, and the *Pushcart Prize* anthology. The *Schooner* has also won recognition for special issues devoted to specific national and ethnic literatures.

A consistent goal of the *Prairie Schooner* editorial staff has been to publish works of excellent young writers. That group has included, among many others, Joyce Carol Oates, Eudora Welty, Octavio Paz, Truman Capote, Cynthia Ozick, Tennessee Williams, Raymond Carver, and Richard Russo. Willa Cather, Mari Sandoz, Loren Eiseley, Wright Morris, Ron Hansen, Ted Kooser, and Kathleen West are among the prestigious Nebraska contributors.

The *Prairie Schooner* is supported by the University of Nebraska through the Department of English and the University of Nebraska Press. Its distinguished editors have been Wimberly (1926–56), Karl Shapiro (1956–63), Bernice Slote (1963–80), Hugh Luke (1980–87), and Hilda Raz (1987–present).

Perhaps the best summation of the *Schooner*'s history appeared in the *Literary Magazine Review* several years ago: "[The] Prairie Schooner rolls along, avoiding the quagmires of fads and schisms, steadfastly defining the American idiom."

Lee T. Lemon
University of Nebraska–Lincoln

PROMOTIONAL LITERATURE

See IMAGES AND ICONS: Promotional Literature

PUBLISHING HOUSES

Lacking the population to sustain commercial publishing, the Great Plains has been, in book publishing, largely the domain of university presses, notably those at Oklahoma, Nebraska, and Kansas.

The first influential book publisher in the Great Plains was Haldeman-Julius of Girard, Kansas, publishers of the Little Blue Books. Between 1918 and 1928 Haldeman-Julius published some 2,000 titles, each priced at five cents a copy and sixty-four pages in length, on every imaginable topic, from abridgments of classics of philosophy to religion to politics to sex, and sold 100 million books worldwide. With a distinct skeptical and socialist bent, Haldeman-Julius fed an enormous hunger—and market—for intellectual stimulation among newly literate classes of Americans.

The Little Blue Books were not primarily literary, and a relative dearth of literary publishing has characterized the Great Plains ever since. But a mission to cultivate a literate and informed citizenry was evident in the program of the next significant publisher to arise on the Plains, the University of Oklahoma Press, founded in 1928.

At first the Oklahoma list showed a fondness for the common person and the common voice—the journal *Folk Say* (1929) and the longtime bestseller, E. H. Faulkner's *Plowman's Folly* (1943), come to mind—and at the same time a commitment to making Greek and Latin classics readily available. The list reflected the tastes of the press's second director (from the mid-1930s until the late 1960s), Savoie Lottinville, a Rhodes scholar, classicist, and committed Oklahoman with a vision of greatness, and the hard work of his editor, Mary Stith. Oklahoma made its most lasting contribution by publishing books of scholarly rigor about the people of the Western Hemisphere, notably in the Civilization of the American Indian series, which between 1932 and 1997 had extended to 225 titles. Like Haldeman-Julius, the early University of Oklahoma Press had its own printing plant. Under the motto "Books Worth Keeping," however, Oklahoma went Haldeman-Julius one better, using its plant to produce prize-winning design and high-quality letterpress printing in hard bindings.

It was by capitalizing on new trends in printing and binding that the University of Nebraska Press challenged Oklahoma. In many ways, Nebraska followed Oklahoma's road to success. Oklahoma published histories of the surrounding states. So did Nebraska. Oklahoma reprinted classics of the western frontier and of Native American cultures. So did Nebraska, sometimes reprinting the same public domain books. However, while Oklahoma reprinted regional books by typing fresh manuscripts and reediting, redesigning, and retypesetting them in hot lead, printing them letterpress, and publishing them in cloth bindings, Nebraska took advantage of the rising quality of photo-offset printing technology to publish paperbacks.

The University of Nebraska Press had been founded in 1941, but it was only in 1959, when its editor, Virginia Faulkner, and its hard-working director, Bruce Nicoll, established Bison Books (the first university press quality paperback imprint in the United States), that Nebraska rose to prominence. Today it offers a dynamic list in several areas of scholarship. Nebraska has built a substantial list in Native studies and western history, translations of European literature, creative nonfiction, and sports history.

The third university press to rise to prominence on the U.S. Great Plains, the University Press of Kansas, was founded in 1946 and came into its own in the late 1980s. The press's director, Fred Woodward, its longtime editor, Kate Torrey, and its marketing head, Susan Schott, learned from their predecessors and achieved success by following a specialized editorial program in a very business-like manner. Alone among the three, Kansas publishes books strictly about the United States, including series on the American presidency and natural resource policy. As its name suggests, the University Press of Kansas is supported by a consortium of state campuses.

These three presses, hosted by universities, have focused on scholarship, not on contemporary literature. Literary publishing in the Great Plains has been the domain of several small university presses in Texas; trade houses such as the Swallow Press, originally in Denver; small presses like Frank Parman's Point Riders Press in Norman, Oklahoma, and Ted Kooser's Windflower Press in Lincoln, Nebraska; and a few fine printers like the Abattoir Press at the University of Nebraska at Omaha. Among textbook publishers on the Plains are branches of Harcourt Brace and Holt, Rinehart, and Winston in Texas and, until 1998, when it relocated to Indianapolis, Cliff's Notes.

Canadian Plains publishers include presses at the Universities of Alberta, Calgary, and Manitoba and the Canadian Plains Research Center at the University of Regina. Fifth House in Saskatoon, Coteau in Regina, and NeWest and Hurtig in Edmonton are influential regional presses, while Winnipeg's Pemmican is one of the oldest and best established Native presses in North America, producing books by Native authors and reaching a wide Native audience in Canada.

See also EDUCATION: Cliff's Notes.

Stephen F. Cox
University of Arizona Press

RIGGS, ROLLIE LYNN (1899–1954)

One of Oklahoma's finest playwrights and poets, confidant to Joan Crawford and Bette Davis, and critically acclaimed contemporary of Eugene O'Neill and Tennessee Williams, Rollie Lynn Riggs was an enigma to most who knew him during his short life. He spent his professional career exploring the unique character and spirit of Oklahoma and its precursor, Indian Territory, while shrouding his personal life from public scrutiny. As an acculturated allotment-era Cherokee and a closeted gay man in the first part of the twentieth century, Riggs traveled across the country and the world in search of both artistic acclaim and security. The latter eluded him to the end of his life.

Born in Indian Territory on August 31, 1899, near present-day Claremore, Oklahoma, Riggs was educated briefly at the University of Oklahoma in Norman and lived at various times in Santa Fe, Paris, Chicago, New York, and Hollywood. His poetry and plays focus almost exclusively on the land and people of rural Oklahoma, and he wrote with a dedication to respectfully and accurately representing the speech, philosophies, and cultures of his youth. His poetry follows in much the same fashion but also includes deeply reflective and melancholy elegies and poems of alienation and solitude. His most famous play, *Green Grow the Lilacs* (1929), became the model in 1943 for the Rodgers and Hammerstein musical *Oklahoma!* His only play to focus on Indian issues was also his favorite: *The Cherokee Night* (1930). Lynn Riggs died in New York City on June 29, 1954, of cancer.

See also FILM: *Oklahoma!*

Daniel Heath Justice
University of Toronto

Braunlich, Phyllis Cole. *Haunted by Home: The Life and Letters of Lynn Riggs*. Norman: University of Oklahoma Press, 1988.

RIVERA, TOMÁS

See HISPANIC AMERICANS: Rivera, Tomás

RÖLVAAG, O. E. (1876–1931)

Born April 22, 1876, to Peder Jakobsen Rölvaag and Ellerine Pedersdatter Vaag, Ole Edvart Rölvaag grew up in the Norwegian hamlet of Rölvaag, a small fishing community on Dønna Island just below the Arctic Circle. Rölvaag immigrated to Elk Point, South Dakota, at the age of twenty and represented this immigrant experience throughout his fictional work. Nevertheless, impressions from his early years remained in his use of Norwegian ballads, hymns, folklore, and classic literature; his utilization of sea-going themes and images; and his blend of the romantic and realistic inspired by the stunning beauty of Dønna.

In his first published novel, the autobiographical *The Third Life of Per Smevik* (1912), Rölvaag detailed his hardships as a new immigrant in the West, explored the costs of immigration to America, and began to reveal his ideas on cultural integrity, that is, ensuring cultural identity is not sacrificed in the wake of the American Dream. He continued these themes in subsequent works—*On Forgotten Paths* (1914), *Pure Gold* (1920), and *The Boat of Longing* (1921)—before beginning his tour de force, *Giants in the Earth*, in 1923 while on sabbatical from St. Olaf College. First published in Norway in two parts, the novel revolves around Per Hansa and his wife, Beret. Deftly employing Norwegian folklore and myth, Rölvaag uses *Giants* to artistically examine the physical, cultural, and psychological realities of Plains immigrant life while offering characters who encapsulate more universal themes. Rölvaag wrote two more novels that charted the Hansa saga, *Peder Victorious* (1929) and *Their Father's God* (1931). Lacking the epic grandeur and stylistic brilliance of *Giants*, these two novels are more political in nature as they continue to promote Rölvaag's ideals of cultural integrity. Having already sketched out notes for a sequel to these novels, Rölvaag died of a heart attack on November 5, 1931, in Northfield, Minnesota.

See also EUROPEAN AMERICANS: *Giants in the Earth.*

*Philip R. Coleman-Hull
Bethany College*

Haugen, Einar. *Ole Edvart Rölvaag*. Boston: Twayne, 1983. Jorgenson, Theodore, and Nora Solum. *Ole Edvart Röl-vaag: A Biography*. New York: Harper and Brothers, 1939. Simonson, Harold P. *Prairies Within: The Tragic Trilogy of Ole Rölvaag*. Seattle: University of Washington Press, 1987.

ROSS, SINCLAIR (1908–1996)

James Sinclair Ross was born on a homestead near Prince Albert, Saskatchewan, on January 22, 1908. His parents separated when he was seven, and he was raised by his mother on a series of Saskatchewan farms where she made her living as a housekeeper. After grade eleven schooling, he joined the Royal Bank of Canada in 1924 and, with the exception of service in the Canadian Army in England from 1942 to 1946, continued with the bank in several Saskatchewan towns, Winnipeg, and Montreal until his retirement in 1968. He died in Vancouver on February 29, 1996.

Ross is best known for three titles. *The Lamp at Noon and Other Stories* (1968) collects the works of short fiction he wrote in the 1930s and 1940s. These stories chronicle the physical and psychological hardships of living and working on isolated Prairie farms during the drought and depression of the 1930s. They dramatize the heroic determination that kept the settlers from defeat as well as the pride that cut them off from nearly all contact with others. Ross's major novel, *As for Me and My House* (1941), is the story of the Reverend Philip Bentley and his unnamed wife, their loveless marriage, and their efforts to escape from the small Prairie town in which they are living. Like Ross's short fiction, *As for Me and My House* is set against a 1930s background of dust storms and economic hardship that gives the novel dramatic and historical authenticity. But its lasting interest derives from the way the story is told: in a series of diary entries from Mrs. Bentley's point of view and in a taut, lyrical prose style that renders for the imagining eye both the beauty and the harshness of the Prairie setting. Ross's last novel, *Sawbones Memorial* (1974), is the story of a small Saskatchewan community that looks back over its past on the evening of the local doctor's retirement party. Critics have praised the comic exposure of small-town meanness and prejudice and the skill with which Ross handled an experimental dramatic form. Ross's other two

novels, *The Well* (1951) and *Whir of Gold* (1970), have earned less critical and popular interest.

*David Stouck
Simon Fraser University*

McMullen, Lorraine. *Sinclair Ross*. Boston: Twayne, 1979. Stouck, David, ed. *Sinclair Ross's "As for Me and My House": Five Decades of Criticism*. Toronto: University of Toronto Press, 1991.

ROY, GABRIELLE (1909–1983)

Gabrielle Roy

Born in St. Boniface, Manitoba, on March 22, 1909, Gabrielle Roy entered the world on the threshold of the Great Plains, whose skies, towns, fields, and people she eventually painted with loving strokes in articles, stories, and novels.

Roy graduated with honors from high school and received her teaching certificate in 1929. In 1937, unfulfilled by her teaching career in Manitoba, she traveled to Europe, ostensibly to study acting. Returning to Canada on the eve of World War II, Roy settled in Montreal, where from 1939 to 1945 she enjoyed considerable success as a journalist, publishing more than 100 articles and short stories. This apprenticeship honed her craft and allowed her to travel throughout Canada, meeting the people who would eventually populate her fiction.

In 1945 the publication of her first novel, *Bonheur d'occasion*, brought her immediate renown. Easily Roy's best-known work, this award-winning exposé of the poor, French-speaking population of Montreal gave new direction to the French Canadian novel.

The majority of Roy's writing individualizes the ethnic groups who settled in Canada's Great Plains, documenting the land and the human struggles there through the screen of personal experience and recollection. Whether a Franco-Manitoban family, a dying and careworn Ukrainian woman, or immigrant children, Roy's characters give voice to heretofore silent populations in works such as *La Route d'Altamont* (1966) and *Ces enfants de ma vie* (1977).

The recipient of three Governor General's Literary Awards for fiction and numerous other honors, Roy died in Quebec City on July 13, 1983. Gabrielle Roy's writings depict the lives of the poor, the dispossessed, and the lonely and transform them into sublime truths about the human condition.

*Bill Clemente
Peru State College
Linda Clemente
Ripon College*

Clemente, Linda, and William Clemente. *Gabrielle Roy: Creation and Memory*. Toronto: ECW Press, 1997. Ricard, François. *Gabrielle Roy: Une vie*. Montreal: Boreal, 1996.

SANDOZ, MARI (1896–1966)

Mari Sandoz was born into the hardships of immigrant life in western Nebraska. In her short stories, novels, and histories of the Great Plains, Sandoz dramatized both the human conflicts and the beauty and danger of the arid environment. While Sandoz never directly confronted the replacement of Native Americans with families like her own, she was one of the first to chronicle vividly and sympathetically the cruel removal of Indians from their homelands.

Sandoz was born on May 11, 1896, in the Sandoz homestead on the Niobrara River, south of Hay Springs, Nebraska. The first of six children of Swiss immigrants, Jules and Mary Fehr Sandoz, her childhood and young adult years were difficult. A slight child, she was burdened from the age of six with childcare, kitchen, and garden chores. She faced discrimination as an immigrant in a ranching community and as the offspring of a quarrelsome father who fought with neighbors and abused his wife and children. Mari was nine before she was allowed to attend school and to learn to read and write English. These negative experiences and a brief story of hers published in an Omaha newspaper when she was almost twelve strengthened her determination to succeed as a writer.

Escaping from home into a marriage that eventually failed, Sandoz fled to Lincoln, Nebraska, to find work, enter the state university, and concentrate on writing. In 1935, after a long writing apprenticeship, Sandoz won the *Atlantic Press* nonfiction contest with *Old Jules*, a biography of her father and the communities he helped establish in the Niobrara country. This remarkable characterization of her father and his life, perhaps her best-known work, combines both an objective view of the opinionated, unkempt, brilliant, and well-educated man and an unobtrusive autobiographical view of his eldest daughter, the young Mari. *Old Jules* illuminates basic themes that appear in her later works: the struggle between ranchers and grangers; the need for strong governmental policies to protect freedom and prevent discrimination; respect for Native Americans; and the power and vulnerability of women on the frontier. *Old Jules* also introduces Sandoz's basic style, which is judgmental in its ironic view of human affairs and lyrical when it draws from her intimate experience with the beauty and danger of the Plains environment. Determined to protect the distinctive voice of the West, she fought her editors to protect her idiom and her bold language.

Sandoz's taste for history as story and story as history was whetted by evenings she spent crouched in the wood box behind the kitchen stove, listening to Jules swap stories with visitors: other settlers, old trappers and traders, and Indians. These stories reverberate in Sandoz's Great Plains series, the core of her work. The series includes three biographies—*Old Jules, Crazy Horse: The Strange Man of the Oglalas* (1942), and *Cheyenne Autumn* (1953) —and three histories—*The Buffalo Hunters: The Story of the Hide Men* (1954), *The Cattlemen: From the Rio Grande across the Far Marias* (1958), and *The Beaver Men: Spearheads of Empire* (1964). A seventh book, a partly researched history of oil exploration and exploitation, was unfinished when, on March 10, 1966, she died of cancer in New York City, her last "outpost."

Sandoz's histories have received more positive attention than her novels, which tend to be didactic. However, in her first novel, *Slogum House* (1937), the character of Gulla Slogum, who attempts to capture a frontier county by intimidation, theft, and murder, is strongly enough drawn to have elicited both outrage for its frankness and commendation for its characterization. All her novels are storehouses of the experiences and history of Plains settlement.

In 1950 Sandoz was awarded an honorary doctorate of literature by the University of Nebraska. The citation included recognition of Sandoz as an authority on Plains Indians. Her last history, *The Battle of the Little Bighorn* (1966), was told primarily from Native American perspectives. She insisted on going through the proofs before leaving for the hospital, where she spent her final days, an indication of Mari Sandoz's indomitable will and spirit.

Barbara Wright Rippey
College of Saint Mary

Mari Sandoz Papers, Love Library, University of Nebraska–Lincoln. Stauffer, Helen Winter. *Mari Sandoz, Story Catcher of the Plains*. Lincoln: University of Nebraska Press, 1982.

SMALL PRESSES

Small, independent publishers have been an important presence in the Great Plains since the mid–nineteenth century. During the early days of settlement, nearly every small town had its independent publisher, putting out community newspapers, political pamphlets, collections of sermons, church circle cookbooks, and, occasionally, for a price, a slim volume of poetry.

The principal difference today is that printing—or, better, reproduced writing—has become much less costly and more accessible to people who want to publish their own writing or the work of authors they admire. Until the early to middle years of the twentieth century, aspiring independent publishers had nothing to work with but time-devouring, hand-set lead type and manually operated, sheet-fed printing presses. Offset lithography eventually became the preferable option, but it was cost-efficient only when large numbers of printed materials were ordered, and most small press entrepreneurs did not have the wherewithal to distribute large press runs.

In recent years, inexpensive typesetting programs for home computers and a proliferation of neighborhood copy centers have made an enormous difference to aspiring publishers. Len Fulton, longtime publisher of the annual directory of small presses published by Dustbooks, reports that at the end of 1997 his database showed 195 independent publishers and 73 self-publishers located in the American Plains states. A few of these publishers adhere for aesthetic reasons to original printing technology, creating beautiful limited editions using hand-set type and even handmade paper. These presses, which might publish editions of, for example, 200 stapled chapbooks or 2,000 perfect-bound books, have traditionally specialized in the noncommercial market, offering writing of high literary quality that may be too esoteric for established publishers.

The quality of writing published by small, independent publishers varies greatly, but many noted writers got their start in Great Plains literary magazines such as *Cutbank* (Montana) and the *Cottonwood Review* (Kansas). Native American writers such as James Welch, Diane Glancy, Elizabeth Cook-Lynn, and others appeared in Great Plains small presses long before it became fashionable for eastern literary houses to publish them. As a young, aspiring writer, the important Native American writer Louise Erdrich worked for a time for Plains Distribution Service, a group of small press people dedicated to getting the publications of small, independent presses and authors into bookstores and the hands of readers.

In Canada, small independent presses have also allowed writers to have their say. Perhaps more important are the independent presses, small by U.S. standards but midsize for Canada, that, with the support of Canada Council and provincial writers guilds, publish much of the innovative writing of the Prairies. These include Edmonton's NeWest, Saskatoon's Fifth House, Winnipeg's Peguis and Turnstone, and Regina's Coteau.

Ted Kooser
Garland, Nebraska

STAFFORD, WILLIAM (1914–1993)

Although William Stafford lived most of his adult life in Oregon, he drew heavily on memories of his early days in Kansas for his poetry. Born in Hutchinson, Kansas, on January 17, 1914, Stafford received both his bachelor's and master's degrees from the University of Kansas and later earned his doctorate at the University of Iowa. Following World War II, during which he was a conscientious objector, Stafford began his teaching career at Lewis and Clark College, from which he retired in 1979. He died in Lake Oswego, Oregon, on August 28, 1993.

Though he was widely published in magazines, his first collection, *West of Your City*, did not appear until 1960. It was followed two years later by *Traveling through the Dark*, which received the National Book Award. Other awards include the Shelley Memorial Prize, a Guggenheim Fellowship, a senior fellowship from the National Endowment for the Arts, and an appointment as poetry consultant to the Library of Congress.

A master of the short lyric, Stafford wrote poetry that was deceptively quiet and often focused on natural settings but that frequently contained an implicit criticism of the artifices of urban life. There is a liveliness of imagery and rhythm throughout his work that shows his keen-eyed pleasure in invention. Very active as a public reader of his poetry, he also took part in many writers conferences and workshops throughout his career. His prose—essays, reviews, and interviews—was collected in three volumes. Always responsive to small magazines and presses, he published some sixty collections and chapbooks over the years.

Vern Rutsala
Lewis and Clark College

Holden, Jonathan. *The Mark to Turn: A Reading of William Stafford's Poetry*. Lawrence: University Press of Kansas, 1976. Stitt, Peter. *The World's Hieroglyphic Beauty: Five American Poets*. Athens: University of Georgia Press, 1985.

STEAD, ROBERT (1880–1959)

Robert James Campbell Stead was a pioneer of realist fiction on the Canadian Prairies. Born on September 4, 1880, in Middleville, Ontario, to Richard and May Campbell Stead, he grew up on a farm near Cartwright, Manitoba. Stead quit school at fourteen to work at various jobs, including journalism, and before he was twenty he had founded a rural weekly. By 1913 he was publicity director for the Canadian Pacific Railway's colonization department in Calgary, and in 1919 he moved to Ottawa to direct publicity for federal departments, including immigration and colonization, until his retirement in 1946.

Stead's literary career began with *The Empire Builders* (1908) and other volumes of Kiplingesque patriotic verse. He then wrote a series of popular romances of pioneering, including *The Cow Puncher* (1918), which sold more than 70,000 copies, and *The Homesteader* (1916), which went through multiple editions and was reprinted in 1973 as a classic of its genre, representing the garden view of the Prairies.

What is remarkable about Stead's career is that in the 1920s he abandoned popular (and lucrative) romances for realist fiction. *Grain* (1926), in particular, with its ironic narrative voice and its stumbling hero, Gander Stake, marked an antiromantic shift in his fiction. Stunted by the numbing labor and cultural deprivation of the farm, Gander is unable to relate even to the soil he tills.

With Frederick Philip Grove and Martha Ostenso, Stead is credited with initiating the sober view of European settlers' spiritual alienation from the land that distinguishes Prairie realism. Stead died in Ottawa on June 25, 1959.

Dick Harrison
Sechelt, British Columbia

Fee, Margery. "Robert J. C. Stead." In *Dictionary of Literary Biography*, edited by W. H. New, 92: 370–73. Detroit: Gale Research, 1990. Thompson, Eric. "Robert Stead (1880–1959)." In *Canadian Writers and Their Works*, Fiction series, edited by Robert Lecker, Jack David, and Ellen Quigley, 3: 214–76. Toronto: ECW Press, 1988.

STEGNER, WALLACE (1909–1993)

Wallace Stegner, one of the West's most important authors not only as novelist and short story writer but as historian and environmentalist, made major contributions to both American and Canadian western literatures. Born in Lake Mills, Iowa, on February 18, 1909, to George and Hilda Paulson Stegner, he grew up in towns across the West, wherever his father's restless frontier spirit led the family. Most influential in Stegner's development were the childhood years in Eastend, Saskatchewan, from 1917 to 1920 and his youth in Salt Lake City. He earned a bachelor of arts degree from the University of Utah and a master's and doctorate from the University of Iowa.

Stegner combined his writing with a distinguished teaching career that extended from Harvard to Stanford, where he founded the creative writing program and directed it from 1945 to 1971. His first book of fiction, *Remembering Laughter*, won the Little Brown Novelette Prize in 1937, and he went on to write or edit thirty-two books of history, biography, and fiction, including a dozen novels, as well as scores of articles on the land and literature of the West.

One of Stegner's greatest achievements was his contribution to a sense of place for traditionally uprooted westerners. He gave the western landscape a concrete, vivid, sensory presence on the page, and among the most intensely realized of his western places are the Saskatchewan Plains in his major autobiographical novel, *The Big Rock Candy Mountain* (1943), and in *Wolf Willow* (1962), the book of history, reminiscence, and fiction that became an inspiration to Canadian Prairie regionalists. "Place" also encompasses the people and culture of the West, which became Stegner's explicit subject in nonfiction writings, including the essays in *The Sound of Mountain Water* (1969) and histories such as *Mormon Country* (1942).

While Stegner loved the land, he expressed a lifelong ambivalence toward western American culture. His major writings are charged with a fundamental opposition between frontier individualism and civilizing community. In fiction it takes the dramatic form of tension between characters such as the restless frontiersman Bo Mason and his humane and cultivated wife, Elsa, in *The Big Rock Candy Mountain*. In Stegner's most celebrated novel, *The Angle of Repose* (1971), the polarities are more balanced. Frontier engineer Oliver Ward's succession of idealistic failures are as admirable, in their way, as Susan Ward's devotion to culture and human relations. As historian and environmentalist, Stegner was less ambivalent. He saw westerners as cut off from their past by a frontier myth that obscures and distorts it, and he warned of the folly of unbridled individualism in an environment where survival depends on cooperation. Central to his environmentalism is his biography of conservationist John Wesley Powell, *Beyond the Hundredth Meridian* (1954), and articles in national magazines kept him at the forefront of the movement.

Recognition of Stegner's achievements gathered momentum in his mature years, including a Pulitzer Prize for *The Angle of Repose* at age sixty-two and a National Book Award for *The Spectator Bird* at sixty-eight. Stegner remained an active, major writer, publishing the novel *Crossing to Safety* (1987), his *Collected Stories* (1990), and two collections of essays in the last six years before his death on April 13, 1993.

Dick Harrison
Sechelt, British Columbia

Arthur, Anthony. *Critical Essays on Wallace Stegner*. Boston: G. K. Hall, 1982. Rankin, Charles E. *Wallace Stegner: Man and Writer*. Albuquerque: University of New Mexico Press, 1996. Robinson, Forrest G., and Margaret G. Robinson. *Wallace Stegner*. Boston: Twayne, 1977.

THOMPSON, ERA BELL

See AFRICAN AMERICANS: Thompson, Era Bell

TRAVEL LITERATURE

Whether traveling as part of an exploratory expedition, for trade purposes, as emigrants, or as tourists, since the sixteenth century writers have tried to represent the vast, often disorienting spaces of the Great Plains. Beginning with Francisco Vásquez de Coronado, travelers have created metaphorical links with the familiar in order to convey the unfamiliar to their readers. Coronado compared the Plains to the sea, a trope that remains common in the twenty-first century. Drawing on a European tradition that offered no models of description for such land forms, writers have struggled to describe both the vastness and the sense of disorientation they felt in a Plains landscape.

During the period of exploration, travelers' views depended upon their course and mode of transportation. Whereas French explorers and Lewis and Clark, traveling by river, found beauty and abundant wildlife and vegetation, overland travelers such as Zebulon Pike found a Great American Desert. Others such as Englishman Henry Kelsey, traveling in 1690 across what are now the Prairie Provinces, noted with some exasperation that during the long trek he saw only "Beast and grass." Repeatedly, these travelers registered their own sense of insignificance when confronted with the great openness of the Plains. Most of these accounts take the journal form, which allows readers to better gauge the effect of the Plains on travelers. Through the usually daily journal entries, readers gain a sense of the distances traversed, the harshness of travel conditions, and the unrelenting boredom for travelers with inadequate skills for making distinctions in a land new to them.

Travelers, whether explorers, scientists, traders, immigrants, or tourists, write of the difficulty adjusting to the Plains. They feel disoriented, their accustomed sense of perspective fails them, and they notice odd optical effects. Distances deceive, objects appear much larger, and travelers are tricked by mirages. While these effects tend to make travelers uncomfortable, the Plains offer compensation in the clear and healthy air, the sense of boundless freedom, and the restorative powers of Plains life for the ill and the invalid. Josiah Gregg, Santa Fe trader and author of *Commerce of the Prairies* (1844), felt that his Plains travels healed him, and he only reluctantly returned to the settlements. Many women travelers found the open spaces exhilarating, viewing the Plains in spring as a vast garden. In her 1846 diary, published as *Down the Santa Fe Trail and into Mexico: The Diary of Susan Shelby Magoffin* (1926), Susan Magoffin describes the freedom she felt on the Plains in spite of traveling with Gen. Stephen Kearny's Army of the West.

Yet the great expanses continued to resist attempts at description. Frequently, travelers write of their own inadequacy at representing what they experience. The phrase "words cannot convey" appear repeatedly in many accounts. Many critics claim that words failed so many travel writers because they were too dependent upon European literary models. The well-educated tourist in particular was too attached to aesthetic conventions to see the Plains in any other way than from a "civilized" point of view. And the Plains rarely corresponded with the attributes accorded aesthetic models such as the beautiful, the picturesque, and the sublime. Nevertheless, references to the sublimity or lack thereof dot many accounts. In spite of the writer's scientific or documentary goals, the language of European romanticism prevailed among many educated travelers, with Native Americans compared to Moors in many accounts from the nineteenth century.

Related to this tradition, both nineteenth- and twentieth-century travelers to the Great Plains often lamented what they saw to be the imminent extinction of the bison and the Indians and the very vastness of the Plains. Consequently, accounts from George Catlin's *Illustrations of the Manners, Customs, and Conditions of the North American Indians with Letters and Notes* (1841) to Francis Parkman's *The Oregon Trail* (1849) to Ian Frazier's *Great Plains* (1988) offer a sense of both consequence and urgency for getting the details right.

Many travelers had their sense of the Plains formed by reading earlier accounts before they arrived. Parkman read Prince Maximilian of Wied-Neuwied, Gregg, and John Charles Frémont before his journey, and Susan Shelby Magoffin read Gregg before her trip over the Santa Fe Trail. Classic American writers as diverse as James Fenimore Cooper and Edgar Allan Poe read published accounts and then created characters experienced in Plains life; neither actually traveled to the Plains. Not surprisingly, with published accounts in mind if not in hand, such writers projected their own and others' expectations onto Plains landscapes. While travel writing about the Great Plains offers a fascinating look at the way writers of European descent have struggled with a powerful and unfamiliar landscape, it remained for inhabitants to find a language adequate to convey a sense of place.

See also GENDER: Victorian Women Travelers.

Nancy Cook
University of Rhode Island

Dondore, Dorothy. *The Prairie and the Making of Middle America: Four Centuries of Description*. New York: Antiquarian Press, 1961. Francis, R. Douglas. *Images of the West: Responses to the Canadian Prairies, 1690–1960*. Saskatoon: Western Producer Prairie Books, 1989. Thacker, Robert. *The Great Prairie Fact and Literary Imagination*. Albuquerque: University of New Mexico Press, 1989.

VANDERHAEGHE, GUY (b. 1951)

The publication and reception of Guy Vanderhaeghe's *Man Descending* in 1982 indicated the arrival of a powerful new voice in both western Canadian literature and Canadian fiction in general. Over time, the strength of his narratives and his vision of lives enduring and surviving have been recognized with two Governor General's Literary Awards, the City of Toronto Award, and, in England, the Geoffrey Faber Memorial Prize for fiction as well as other honors. Vanderhaeghe was born in Esterhazy, Saskatchewan, on April 5, 1951. He was educated at the Universities of Saskatchewan and Regina and lives in Saskatoon.

Vanderhaeghe's voice comes out of the traditions and influences of previous writers from the West—Wallace Stegner, Sinclair Ross, Martha Ostenso, W. O. Mitchell, and Margaret Laurence. Like those writers, Vanderhaeghe's "naming" of the Prairies is a significant contribution and, at the least, one of his starting points. In an early interview with David Carpenter in 1982, Vanderhaeghe said that his response to reading Robert Kroetsch's *The Studhorse Man* was precisely in this act of naming: "Even though it was such a mythic book it had a tremendous amount of authenticity for me. . . . I said to myself, even before I had decided to write, this part of the world can be written about." His vision of the Prairie landscape is painted deeply as a strong wash beneath the struggles and images of his characters, especially in *Homesick* (1990) and *The Englishman's Boy* (1996). Though he has hauled the urban landscapes of the Canadian Prairie into the foreground of his work more than some previous writers, particularly in *My Present Age* (1984), it is still true that, as an artist, he has helped celebrate the lyrical beauty and mythical harshness of the Prairie landscape and universalized it in his imagery.

Vanderhaeghe's voice also surfaces within a renaissance of new voices in western fiction: Robert Kroetsch, Rudy Wiebe, David Aranason, Carol Shields, Kristjana Gunnars, Aritha Van Herk, Edna Alford, Sandra Birdsell, and Jack Hodgins. From the early short stories through to the large designs of the novels, the tension between modernist and postmodernist—the positioning between past and present influences—is always present. Like Alice Munro, Vanderhaeghe has pushed realist narrative in a postmodern direction, out into looser, more chaotic forms, while, unlike Munro, he has insisted upon an almost modernist leanness in the images he sets up to control his vision of contemporary life. The latest evidence of this tension is the pull, in *The Englishman's Boy*, between the postmodern, spatial effects of its narrative as it weaves itself back and forth between historical foregrounds and backgrounds and the tight, modernist design of its vision as it echoes Pound, Fitzgerald, and Faulkner in its attempt to superimpose images upon history, force the contradictions and paradoxes of history into stylized resolutions or representations of those things.

This struggle in Vanderhaeghe's narratives is between where he wants to take the traditions of social and psychological realism in his forms and how he tries to organize the play between existence and history in his content. It accounts for a dichotomy in his texts between an ever-loosening abandonment of linearity and closure in form, reminiscent of Kroetsch and Shields, and an almost mannered, throwback design in content, reminiscent of Fitzgerald, Stegner, and Hemingway and fueled, one suspects, by his own background in history and philosophy. That is why the admittedly dark and even limited comedy of *My Present Age* can appeal to some readers who might be suspicious of the lean designs of *The Englishman's Boy*, even though the latter is the stronger work in many ways. It is the looseness, more Kroetsch-influenced hilarity of the former that appeals, with its mirrors of form and content, and it is likely that in further work this tension between the modern and postmodern in Vanderhaeghe's writing will break down, and he will fulfill the brilliance of his voice and vision even more than he already has.

John Hugh Lent
Okanagan University College

Carpenter, David. "Inside Guy Vanderhaeghe." *NeWest Review* 8 (1982): 8–15.

WEBB, WALTER PRESCOTT (1888–1963)

A child of the Great Plains, Walter Prescott Webb was one of the preeminent historians of the region and of the American western frontier. He was born on April 3, 1888, in Panola County, East Texas, on the southern fringe of the Great Plains and grew to manhood in the farmland of the Stephens-Eastland Counties area of West Texas. After graduating from high school and before going on to the University of Texas at Austin for his higher education in 1909, Webb taught in several of the local country schools. At the University of Texas he completed his bachelor's degree in history in 1915 and became a member of the history faculty in 1918. He became a particularly close friend of the western writer J. Frank Dobie and the Texas naturalist Roy Bedichek while at the University of Texas.

Webb earned his master's degree from the University of Texas in 1920, writing his thesis on the Texas Rangers. In 1922, at the age of thirty-four, Webb took a leave of absence from his faculty duties to pursue a doctorate in history at the University of Chicago, but he failed to complete the degree and returned to Austin a year later. Webb finally received his doctorate from Texas in 1932, having submitted the previously published *The Great Plains* (1931) as his dissertation. For his many scholarly achievements (he wrote or edited more than twenty books), the University of Chicago presented him with an honorary doctorate of laws in 1958. Among his accomplishments were the books *The Texas Rangers* (1935), *Divided We Stand* (1937), and *The Great Frontier* (1952). Webb was a Harkness Lecturer at London University in 1938, the Harmsworth Professor of American History at Oxford University in 1942–43, president of the Mississippi Valley Historical Association (Organization of American Historians) in 1954–55, and president of the American Historical Association in 1958.

Webb married Jane Oliphant on September 16, 1916; they had one daughter, Mildred Alice, born on July 30, 1918. Almost two years after Jane's death, Webb married Terrell Maverick, the widow of San Antonio mayor and New Deal congressman Maury Maverick, on December 14, 1961. Webb died in an automobile accident near Austin on March 8, 1963.

Webb drew much of his love and understanding of the Great Plains from his own life and the writings of historians of the American frontier, especially Frederick Jackson Turner. In *The Great Frontier*, Webb even went so far as to expand Turner's ideas on the lure of the frontier into a global arena. But clearly Webb's major work was *The Great Plains*. It is a pioneering work not only in regional and frontier history but also in environmental history and historical geography. Webb argued that the frontier of settlement halted at the eastern edge of the Great Plains (he called it a "cultural fault line") because European American institutions and settlers were not prepared for a semiarid environment with few trees and less water. In Webb's view, settlement proceeded only after technological advancements such as the six-gun, windmill, and barbed wire allowed farmers and ranchers to master the environment. But Webb realized that aridity would continue to be a major regional problem, and because of this he questioned whether large populations could be sustained indefinitely in the Great Plains. Webb also noted the powerful impact of the Plains environment on those who came to settle there and the effect of the region on the rest of the country. Historically and methodologically, Walter Prescott Webb showed how to understand the Great Plains, and more than any other scholar he defined the Plains as a North American region.

See also FOLKWAYS: Dobie, J. Frank.

Dennis Reinhartz
University of Texas at Arlington

Furman, Necah S. *Walter Prescott Webb: His Life and His Impact*. Albuquerque: University of New Mexico Press, 1976. Owens, William A. *Three Friends: Roy Bedichek, J. Frank Dobie, Walter Prescott Webb*. Austin: University of Texas Press, 1967.

WELCH, JAMES (1940–2003)

Born in Browning, Montana, where the mountains break into foothills and then prairie, James Welch, a writer of Blackfeet and Gros Ventre heritage, remained rooted in Montana. His writings reflected a lifetime spent primarily in the magnificent and variable geographic terrain of the West. Welch attended schools in Montana, Oregon, and Alaska before graduating in Minneapolis, Minnesota, in 1958. He received a bachelor of arts degree in liberal arts from the University of Montana in 1965, where he also enrolled in the master of fine arts in creative writing program from 1966 to 1968 but did not earn a degree.

Since the publication of his first novel, *Winter in the Blood* (1974), Welch has been widely recognized as a leading figure in Native American literature. His novels have been translated and published in France, Italy, Germany, Holland, Japan, Sweden, and England. Subsequent to the rave reception his first novel received (it was reviewed on the front page of the *New York Times Book Review*), Welch republished his first and only collection of poetry, *Riding the Earthboy 40* (1971; reprint, 1976). In 1979 *The Death of Jim Loney* appeared, a second novel set around the Fort Belknap Reservation in Montana. Both novels' protagonists grapple with their familial histories, the deaths of loved ones, and excessive alcohol use.

With his third novel, *Fools Crow* (1986), Welch moved to depictions of historical events. Set in the Rocky Mountains, home of the Piegan (Pikuni) band of the Blackfeet Confederacy in the 1870s, *Fools Crow* offers a fictional view of Pikuni life around the time of the virtual extinction of the bison and just before Blackfeet people signed a treaty that forever changed their way of life. Based on historical figures such as Pikuni leader Heavy Runner and U.S. Army officer Gen. William Tecumseh Sherman, the novel takes as its central subject the growth into manhood of White Man's Dog into Fools Crow, a chief. Fools Crow must grapple with what living with honor versus shame is and might be in the face of cultural upheaval. That same year Welch coedited *The Real West Marginal Way* (1986), a volume based on Richard Hugo's life and work, together with his wife, Lois Monk Welch, and Ripley Hugo, widow of Richard Hugo.

In his fourth novel, *The Indian Lawyer* (1990), Welch drew on his ten years of experience as vice chairman of the Montana State Board of Pardons (1979–88) to depict another sort of Indian protagonist. Sylvester Yellow Calf, a descendant of Fools Crow, becomes a lawyer and a Senate hopeful. In *The Indian Lawyer* Welch moves beyond depictions of familial and personal identity struggles to present a man who learns he can make or break himself.

The traumatic events in U.S.-Native relations gripped Welch's imagination more fully after he wrote *Fools Crow* and *The Indian Lawyer*. Along with Paul Stekler, he created a video, *Killing Custer: The Battle of the Little Bighorn and the Fate of the Plains Indians* (1994), that reflects Native American points of view regarding the Battle of the Little Bighorn. In his last novel, *The Heartsong of Charging Elk* (2000), Welch told the poignant story of a Lakota who is left stranded and sick in Marsailles when the Wild West show that had employed him moved on.

Welch occasionally taught at the University of Washington and Cornell University as a visiting professor, and lived in Missoula, where he wrote full-time. Welch died of a heart attack August 4, 2003, in Missoula.

See also WAR: Little Bighorn, Battle of the.

Kathryn W. Shanley
University of Montana

Beidler, Peter G., ed. "James Welch's *Winter in the Blood*." *American Indian Quarterly* 4 (1978): 93–172. McFarland, Ron. *James Welch*. Lewiston ID: Confluence Press, 1986. Velie, Alan R. "James Welch's Poetry." *American Indian Culture and Research Journal* 3 (1979): 22–23.

THE WESTERN

The Western, contrary to the mainstream novel of the American West by authors like A. B. Guthrie Jr., Ole Rölvaag, Willa Cather, and Edna Ferber, is a mass-produced subgenre of popular literature rigidly defined by a formulaic plot, conventional characters, and its setting in the Old West, a semimythical place and time in American history. Rather than describing the settlers' psychological and spiritual relationship to the land or giving a realistic picture of a particular region of western America, the Western is a nostalgic adventure novel, drawing on the dialectic struggle between savagery and civilization, law and lawlessness, and East and West at an imaginary, epic moment when the two opposing poles were believed to be in a precarious balance. Thus the Western is set predominantly in the Great Plains and in the mountains and deserts of the Southwest during the second half of the nineteenth century. According to John Cawelti, the Great Plains is a particularly appropriate setting for the Western because of the region's openness, its inhospitableness to human settlement, its extremes of light and climate, as well as its grandeur and beauty.

The Western traces its roots to the romantic novels of James Fenimore Cooper, notably, his Leatherstocking series, which deplores the relentless eradication of the "savage but noble" Native Americans through the onslaught of European American civilization. This romantic sympathy for the Native Americans soon gave way to the crude juxtaposition of settler and savage in the dime novels of the 1860s and 1870s such as Edward Ellis's *Seth Jones; or, The Captives of the Frontier* (1860). In Edward L. Wheeler's *Deadwood Dick on Deck* (1878), set in the Black Hills, Indians no longer exist even as an opposing force.

The basic formula for the contemporary Western derives from two sources: semifactual accounts of the life of cowboys such as Andy Adams's *The Log of a Cowboy* (1903), a fictional diary of a cattle drive from Texas through the Great Plains to Montana, and Owen Wister's *The Virginian: A Horseman of the Plains* (1902). Set in Wyoming in the 1870s, *The Virginian* introduced to the genre the cowboy hero, the tenderfoot narrator, the Code of the West, the climactic shootout, and the young schoolteacher from the East who tries to civilize the hero but ends up being converted to his Western values in the end. *The Virginian* was written at a time when the frontier was declared closed, when it became clear that American society in the twentieth century would be inescapably secular, urban, and industrial, when gender roles were becoming increasingly blurred, and when waves of immigration from Europe began to change the ethnic composition of the country. Wister's nostalgic glance back at a time and place when these trends might still have been reversed as well as his admonition that the basic values of the Old West must be preserved to guide the country in the right direction struck a responsive chord in a large segment of the population.

The result was countless formulaic imitations of the basic ingredients of *The Virginian*, notably by Zane Grey, Max Brand (pen name of Frederick Faust), Ernest Haycox, and Louis L'Amour. Directing their novels initially at the readers of pulp magazines, these writers reduced the plot of *The Virginian* to a heroic adventure formula with a limited number of variations: the conflict between ranchers and settlers or between cattlemen and sheep men, the story of the cowboy turned gunfighter, the conflict between cavalry and Indians, adventures accompanying the construction of the transcontinental railroad, and the former outlaw-turned-marshal haunted by his past, all revolving around a love story. These "romantic" Westerns reaffirm the dominance of male-dominated western values such as monogamous love, instinctive rather than institutional Christianity, a patriarchal family structure, and the justified use of violence in defense of these values. Females are civilizers and therefore initially hostile to this code of behavior, but they are always converted to accepting the male view in the end. Thus Wister's attempt to represent the allegorical forces vying for dominance in a future American society was reduced to a formulaic erotic struggle between a western male and an eastern female.

This nostalgic fantasy of the victory of male western values became more and more unsustainable as the vision of the Old West was blurred by the counterimage of contemporary urban, industrial society. In the 1950s the tone of the Western became darker and more cynical, the young cowboy heroes giving way to jaded older men, mainly sheriffs and marshals, confronted with an apathetic population, increasingly organized villains, and more ambiguously virtuous women. The optimistic "myth of foundation" of the romantic Western gave way to the "myth of transition," the need to save what could be saved of traditional western values in a modern world that has lost its way. This view is mainly expressed in the classic Western films of the period, notably *High Noon* (1952), *Shane* (1953, based on the novel by Jack Schaefer), John Ford's *The Man Who Shot Liberty Valance* (1962), and *Cheyenne Autumn* (1964, based on the novel by Mari Sandoz).

In the second half of the twentieth century the classic formula of the Western came under pressure from the counterculture of the 1960s and the revisionist New Western historians. Minority groups and women began to claim their rightful place in western popular fiction, and former heroes of the West were now cast in the role of villains, as can be seen in Thomas Berger's *Little Big Man* (1964) and the 1990 film *Dances with Wolves*.

Although the traditional popular Western has been in decline in print, in film, and on television after its heyday in the 1950s, it is too early to pronounce it moribund, as some commentators have done recently. If anything, the Western is moving away from its formulaic, ultraconservative past to become a part of the more sensitive, diverse mainstream of literature about the American West, as evidenced by the novels of Larry McMurtry (*Leaving Cheyenne*, 1962; *Lonesome Dove*, 1985) and Elmer Kelton (*The Day the Cowboys Quit*, 1971; *The Man Who Rode Midnight*, 1987). But for aficionados of the more formulaic Westerns, there are the excellent, historically well-researched Plains Western series of Terry C. Johnston (some thirty novels in his Plainsman series), Richard S. Wheeler (his Barnaby Sky series, which focuses on Plains Indian cultures), Tabor Evans (the prolific author of the Longarm series), and Harry Combs to ensure the continued viability of the most American of literary genres.

See also FILM: *Dances with Wolves*; Westerns.

Franz G. Blaha
University of Nebraska–Lincoln

Cawelti, John G. *The Six-Gun Mystique*. Bowling Green OH: Popular Press, 1971. Durham, Philip, and Everett L. Jones. *The Western Story: Fact, Fiction, and Myth*. New York: Harcourt Brace, 1975.

WIEBE, RUDY (b. 1934)

Canadian author Rudy Wiebe was born on October 4, 1934, near Fairholme, Saskatchewan, four years after his parents emigrated from Russia. Growing up in a German-speaking community, Wiebe did not learn English until he attended school.

Wiebe's best-known novels are set in the Canadian Prairies and explore the lives of Mennonites, his own people, as well as those of historic First Nations and Métis leaders and contemporary Canadians who struggle to understand their regional, cultural, and personal history. *Peace Shall Destroy Many* (1962) describes a community in Saskatchewan during World War II. *The Blue Mountains of China* (1970) traces the migrations of Mennonite refugees from Russia to China, South America, and Canada, where a contemporary Mennonite demonstrates his faith by carrying a cross beside the Prairie highway. In his next two novels, *The Temptations of Big Bear* (1973) and *The Scorched-Wood People* (1977), Wiebe focuses on events culminating in the 1885 rebellion that led to the arrests of Native leaders Big Bear and Poundmaker and to the execution of Louis Riel. *The Temptations of Big Bear*, which won the 1973 Governor General's Literary Award for fiction, is often considered Wiebe's masterpiece. Among his other works are *A Discovery of Strangers* (1994), an epic novel about the first Franklin expedition into the Canadian Northwest, which also won a Governor General's Literary Award for fiction; collections of short stories, including *River of Stone: Fiction and Memories* (1995); a novella about Albert Johnson called *The Mad Trapper* (1980); a play about the Prairies called *Far as the Eye Can See* (1977); essays; and the autobiographical work, *Playing Dead: A Contemplation Concerning the Arctic* (1989), in which Wiebe meditates upon the power of stories to create identity and a sense of place.

Wiebe has taught English and creative writing at the University of Alberta since 1967. In 1987 he was awarded the Royal Society of Canada's Lorne Pierce Medal.

See also NATIVE AMERICANS: Big Bear / RELIGION: Mennonites.

Sherrill Grace
University of British Columbia

Grace, Sherrill. "Western Myth and Northern History: The Plains Indians of Berger and Wiebe." *Great Plains Quarterly* 3 (1983): 146–56. Van Toorn, Penny. *Rudy Wiebe and the Historicity of the World*. Edmonton: University of Alberta Press, 1995.

WILDER, LAURA INGALLS (1867–1957)

Laura Ingalls Wilder was born in a log cabin near Pepin, Wisconsin, on February 7, 1867. She subsequently lived in Kansas, Minnesota, Iowa, and South Dakota before settling in her final home in Mansfield, Missouri, in 1894. She died there on February 10, 1957.

The Little House series, Laura Ingalls Wilder's eight-volume set of autobiographical novels for children (1932–43), is arguably the most influential twentieth-century narrative of female childhood and adolescence on the western frontier. On their publication during the Great Depression, these books were almost immediately canonized as children's "classics," and they have shaped generations of children's and adults' beliefs about European

Laura Ingalls Wilder, 1918

American settlers' lives on the nineteenth-century Great Plains.

Wilder was a sixty-five-year-old Missouri farm woman with a long working life as housekeeper, poultry woman, teacher, and journalist behind her when the first Little House book was published in 1932. Her (unacknowledged) collaborator and adviser was her daughter, nationally known writer Rose Wilder Lane. Much of the power of the Little House series comes from the immediacy of its autobiographical protagonist: it places a spirited girl at the center of the cultural controversies of the 1870s and 1880s Great Plains. In the first book, *Little House in the Big Woods* (1932), Laura Ingalls is four, experiencing the satisfying rhythms of settled farm life with her young parents and sisters. In *Little House on the Prairie* (1935), Pa tires of the Wisconsin farm's predictabilities and persuades his dubious wife to move to Kansas "Indian country," where they settle illegally on Indian lands. Laura is intensely curious about their Native American neighbors, whom Ma fears and hates and Pa (sometimes) admires and emulates. She discovers a passion for the Great Plains country of waving grasses and no visible boundaries. When, after laboriously constructing a little log house, the Ingallses are ordered off their claim by the U.S. government, they backtrack to Minnesota and, in *On the Banks of Plum Creek* (1937), settle on a farm near an established town. Church and school offer cultural advantages, and Laura's domestic education intensifies. But the Ingallses are beset by drought, grasshoppers, and illness, and by the next book (*By the Shores of Silver Lake*, 1939) are glad to leave for a new western homestead in Dakota Territory. In this and the three following books, adolescent Laura learns the boundaries of women's and men's work in a frontier town, surviving blizzards in *The Long Winter* (1940) and, in *Little Town on the Prairie* (1941), seeking adult occupations that engage her energy and agency. The series ends, in *These Happy Golden*

Years (1943), with the interwoven stories of Laura's first adult professional success as a schoolteacher and her courtship and marriage to a young homesteader, Almanzo Wilder.

The Little House series engages important issues of European American settler culture in the Great Plains: the competition of Ma's settled domesticity and Pa's westering wanderlust; the broached and botched possibilities of intercultural contacts between frontier Americans of different races and ethnicities; the gendered alternatives of work, consumption, and courtship offered to female children and adolescents in Plains towns. Recently, critics, historians, and biographers have debated whether Wilder's series confirms or questions the Turnerian account of the settling of the American West, have scrutinized constructions of gender and domestic culture in the series, and have argued about the extent and importance of Rose Wilder Lane's collaboration. Meanwhile, the Little House series has continued to spawn cultural spin-offs that attest to the persistent freshness and importance of this canonical Great Plains narrative.

Ann Romines
George Washington University

Romines, Ann. *Constructing the Little House: Gender, Culture, and Laura Ingalls Wilder.* Amherst: University of Massachusetts Press, 1997. Wilder, Laura Ingalls, and Rose Wilder Lane. *A Little House Sampler*, edited by William T. Anderson. Lincoln: University of Nebraska Press, 1988.

WISEMAN, ADELE (1928–1992)

Canadian writer Adele Wiseman was born on May 21, 1928, and raised in Winnipeg, Manitoba. Her parents had emigrated from the Ukraine in 1923 and spent two years in Montreal before settling in Winnipeg's North End, a vibrant enclave of Jewish, German, Ukrainian, and Slavic immigrants. Wiseman earned a bachelor of arts degree in English and psychology from the University of Manitoba in 1949. Following graduation, she lived in London, Rome, and New York, where she wrote and worked at a number of jobs. From 1964 to 1969 Wiseman lived in Montreal, where she taught English at Sir George Williams (now Concordia) University and Macdonald College of McGill University. She was later writer in residence at several Canadian universities and head of the May Studios (Writing Program) at Banff Centre for the Arts.

Wiseman wrote two novels, *The Sacrifice*, which received the Governor General's Literary Award for fiction in 1956, and *Crackpot* (1974). Both novels employ biblical metaphors, are set in (the unnamed city of) Winnipeg, and explore the lives of Jewish immigrants who settle on the Canadian Prairies. *The Sacrifice* is the tragic story of a butcher who murders a local temptress. The biblical story of Abraham and Isaac resonates throughout Wiseman's narrative. Her own Abraham—once proud and certain—is transplanted from the Old to the New World, where he loses his third son and his precarious hold on life in a novel that charts the demise of a patriarch. *Crackpot* shifts from tragic to comic mode and experiments with narrative form and perspective. The work celebrates the resilience of Hoda, an obese Jewish prostitute whose life, like Abraham's, is shattered by moral and spiritual challenges.

Wiseman also wrote two plays (*The Lovebound*, ca. 1960; *Testimonial Dinner*, 1978); two books for children (*Kenji and the Cricket*, 1988; *Puccini and the Prowlers*, 1992); and three works of nonfiction (*Old Markets, New World*, 1964; *Old Woman at Play*, 1978; *Memoirs of a Book Molesting Childhood and Other Essays*, 1987). Her correspondence with fellow writer and friend is available in *Selected Letters of Margaret Laurence and Adele Wiseman* (1997).

See also CITIES AND TOWNS: Winnipeg, Manitoba.

Ruth Panofsky
Ryerson Polytechnic University

Greene, Elizabeth, ed. *We Who Can Fly: Poems, Essays and Memories in Honour of Adele Wiseman.* Dunvegan, Ontario: Cormorant Books, 1997. Panofsky, Ruth, ed. *Room of One's Own* 16 (1993). Adele Wiseman issue. Adele Wiseman Papers, York University, Toronto.

WOIWODE, LARRY (b. 1941)

Even though Larry Woiwode moved out of North Dakota when he was eight and did not return to live there until 1978, he is imbued with the "Dakota mystique"—a sense of awe at the vast land, a need for family and community, and an awareness of and a faith in God that helps people there survive. Two of his novels (*Beyond the Bedroom Wall: A Family Album*, 1975; *Born Brothers*, 1988), a number of his short stories, and some of his poems focus on North Dakota people and on the Northern Plains experience. Whether a specific work is set in North Dakota or not, a sense of place, of family, and of God permeates Woiwode's writing, especially in his semiautobiographical *Beyond the Bedroom Wall*. One reads this novel as if paging through a family picture album full of places, biographical vignettes, fragments of memories, and longer reminiscences that leave the reader curious about the characters and incidents recorded in the "snapshots." Parts 1 and 2, set in rural North Dakota, trace the history of the family through four generations, until they move to Illinois.

As of 1998, Woiwode had written three other novels (*What I'm Going to Do, I Think*, 1969; *Poppa John*, 1981; *Indian Affairs*, 1992), two volumes of short stories (*The Neumiller Stories*, 1989; *Silent Passengers*, 1993), and two of poetry (*Poetry North: Five Poets of North Dakota*, 1970; *Even Tide*, 1977). In addition to published interviews, Woiwode has short stories, poems, and nonfiction pieces that have not yet been collected. Woiwode is a careful craftsman, a compelling storyteller, and a stylist with a gift for both lyrical and precise expression.

Denis R. Fournier
University of Mary

Gardner, John. "The Family of a Man and the Family of Man." Review of *Beyond the Bedroom Wall: A Family Album*, by Larry Woiwode. *New York Times Book Review*, September 28, 1975, 1–2. Quantic, Diane Dufva. *The Nature of the Place: A Study of Great Plains Fiction*. Lincoln: University of Nebraska Press, 1995.

ZAMORA, BERNICE

See HISPANIC AMERICANS: Zamora, Bernice

ZITKALA ŠA (1876–1938)

Zitkala Ša, a Yankton Sioux, was among the first Native American authors to tell her own story without the aid of an editor or translator, and she was a significant figure in pan-Indian politics during the first part of the twentieth century. She was born Gertrude Simmons on February 22, 1876, on the Yankton Reservation in South Dakota. As a little girl, at the enticement of missionaries, she left her mother and homeland to attend boarding school. In compelling narratives published in the *Atlantic Monthly* and *Harper's Magazine* in the early 1900s, Gertrude described her life on the reservation and her experiences in White's Manual Labor Institute boarding school in Indiana and as a teacher at Carlisle Indian School in Pennsylvania. She also published short stories and a collection of traditional Sioux tales, *Old Indian Legends* (1901). Gertrude renamed her literary and public persona Zitkala Ša, or Red Bird.

In 1901 Gertrude returned to the Yankton Reservation, where she met and married Raymond Bonnin. They worked for the Indian Bureau on the Uintah and Ouray Reservation in Utah, where Gertrude collaborated with William Hanson on the *Sun Dance Opera* (1913) and became involved with the Pan-Indian Society of American Indians. After she was elected secretary in 1916, she and Raymond moved to Washington DC, where they worked for the society and edited and wrote for *American Indian Magazine*.

In 1921 she published her earlier writings along with several new, more political pieces in *American Indian Stories*. With Raymond, she continued her activism, lobbying for the American Indian Citizenship Act of 1924, against violence and injustice on reservations, and for land claims and tribal rights. Zitkala Ša died on January 26, 1938, in Washington DC. She was buried in Arlington National Cemetery.

P. Jane Hafen
University of Nevada–Las Vegas

Rappaport, Doreen. *The Flight of Red Bird: The Life of Zitkala-Ša*. New York: Dial Books, 1997.

Media

Western Union Telegraph Office, Wichita, Kansas, ca. 1912

Media 501

MEDIA

To receive a television signal at our southeastern Montana ranch in the early 1960s our family had to work as a team. My father climbed the old wind-charger tower on which our antenna was mounted. I stayed inside to adjust the set, while my younger sister and brother stood outside the window to relay messages to Dad on the tower behind the house. "Hold it," I'd yell. "There. No. Back just a little the other way. No. Back again slooooowly." I'd shout my instructions out the window to my sister, who shouted to my brother at the corner of the house, and he'd shout up to Dad. The tower was barely within shouting distance on a windy day. With the antenna pointed northeast, we could get stations from Dickinson and Williston in North Dakota. A slight turn west of north picked up the signal from Glendive, Montana. The reward for this effort could be a Saturday evening watching Richard Boone as Paladin in *Have Gun Will Travel*, followed by James Arness as Marshal Matt Dillon in *Gunsmoke*. These network programs were exceptional because local stations had to earn their network programs one at a time in those days. Most of the programs were nonnetwork fare such as old movies and professional wrestling, which Dad enjoyed far more than anyone else in the family. Reception depended upon the weather.

To get a newspaper, we could drive five miles to Ismay to pick up the mail, which carried the previous day's edition of the *Miles City Star*, published sixty-five miles away. Otherwise, we could wait for mail delivery on Tuesdays, Thursdays, and Saturdays. When we'd pick up the mail at the Ismay Post Office, Postmaster Esther Heigh could give an abstract of the day's news as she handed the paper through the old-fashioned counter window. Besides the *Star*, our subscriptions included the weekly *Life* magazine and several farm magazines. The weekly *Fallon County Times* was published in Baker thirty miles away.

We could see a movie at a drive-in twenty miles away. Radio and phonographs provided music. In the time we lived there, KFLN began broadcasting from Baker, carrying agricultural market reports and country music, as did KATAL (the "Cattle Call") from Miles City, but a hill west of our house made reception difficult. Occasionally, we received stations like KFAB in Omaha, WHO in Des Moines, and CKCK in Regina, but none came in well enough for us to become devoted listeners. At night, however, we received several clear-channel stations. As teenagers we listened to rock station KOMA in Oklahoma City. Advertisements on that station promoted events from Oklahoma to Kansas. In the late 1990s KOMA played the same music, but the format then was called "golden oldies." I grew up believing that scratchy radio reception, snowy television, and late newspapers were a way of life in the country.

Early Mass Communication

Linking isolated towns and ranches in the Great Plains with the larger society has always been a challenge. Early settlers, longing for news from major population centers they had left behind, gathered at stage and railroad stations likely to carry mail and newspapers. Taverns and cafes increased their appeal by subscribing to major newspapers. When local newspapers were established, editors often supported their publications with commercial printing. Editors lifted much of their news from the "exchanges," distant newspapers that editors traded so they could borrow news from one another. Editors sought to attract new settlers and subscribers. Because they had a stake in the town's success, editors often boosted the virtues of their towns. Sometimes town developers even gave them lots to sell as an additional incentive.

The earliest mass media in the Great Plains, of course, relied on simple technology. The Washington handpress, for example, printed hundreds of small-town newspapers across the Plains throughout the nineteenth century. This press differed little from the press Benjamin Franklin operated in colonial America, and it allowed one printer to produce the newspaper alone or with a single assistant, apprentice, or slave. A variation patented by Samuel Rust in 1821 moved west in wagons because innovations, like hollow legs, made it lighter to move than its cast-iron competitors. The Ramage press with some wooden components was introduced to compete with Rust. Besides the heavy iron press, printers needed paper, ink, and cases filled with type.

When William N. Byers left Omaha for the mining country with his Washington handpress and related equipment in 1859, the press was so heavy and the streets of Omaha so muddy that the wagon carrying the press got bogged down before it got out of town. The train of wagons sported banners promising a new newspaper without naming a location, but the group set out for Fort Laramie. The wagons covered a mere eight miles on their first day. Byers had already set the forms for half of his first run of the *Rocky Mountain News*, even though he did not know where the newspaper would be published. Spacers were inserted to hold room for the place and date of the first pressrun. When the entourage stopped, the forms were opened and new type was inserted to give the date and place of publication. The outside two pages of the first issue of the *Rocky Mountain News* of April 22, 1859, contained some news that was more than a year old and other items that were not news at all. Throughout the nineteenth century, newspapers carried nonnews items such as fiction, poetry, essays, and morality tales.

Byers started the *News* in Auraria across Cherry Creek from Denver City, Colorado, and it began by appealing to residents of both towns. Timely news was hard to get because the nearest post office was more than 100 miles away at Fort Laramie. Without mail or telegraph service, residents settled for older news. At least it was newer than word of mouth around town. Even after newspapers became established, they often printed the old news on the outside—the front and back pages—of a four-page newspaper. These outside pages could be printed a day or two early and the inside pages printed later with recent news and editorial comment.

In promoting their idea of "progress," editors often attacked the original inhabitants of the land as "savages" who did not deserve to own the land. Some western editors, with the help of eastern "exchanges," exaggerated Indian atrocities and even faked at least one massacre. In 1867 the normally respectable *New York Tribune*, published by Horace Greeley, reported on a massacre of eighty people at the mouth of the Yellowstone River near Fort Buford. The story even gave details of a small number of soldiers holding off thousands of Indians before being overwhelmed. The newspaper said a colonel shot his wife to save her from a fate worse than death. When the *Tribune* discovered that the story was a fake, it admitted that it had been duped. Other major newspapers, however, let the error stand. *Frank Leslie's Illustrated Newspaper* once published a faked story under a picture of "General" George Armstrong Custer talking to the surviving members of a homestead family attacked by Indians. At the end of the story, the newspaper said the event never happened but contended that stories like this often did happen in the West. Especially after each discovery of gold, newspapers in both the East and West said Native Americans stood in the way of national prosperity.

Native American Media

Native American publications in the Great Plains shared many challenges of small-town publications. They faced shortages of supplies and money, carried small subscription lists, confronted dilemmas related to political sponsorship, and found national advertising illusive. Native papers and many Native-owned broadcast stations continue to receive support from their tribal councils, and, as a result, they often face complex political pressures, including the pressure to satisfy patrons while covering the news.

Their traditional dilemmas began with the earliest Native American newspaper, the *Cherokee Phoenix*, published in both English and Cherokee in the late 1820s in the original Cherokee capital at New Echota, Georgia. Editor Elias Boudinot stood up to the power of both the tribal council and their white, racist neighbors. Boudinot waged a courageous fight against white abuse of Cherokees and reported on dissension within the tribal council over Cherokee removal from Georgia to Indian Territory. The editor got caught in tribal factionalism, however, and was killed in Indian Territory in 1839 for signing the treaty that ceded the Cherokees' original land.

The Reverend Samuel Worcester and printer John F. Wheeler, both of whom served Georgia prison time for their work on the *Phoenix*, helped the Cherokees start the *Cherokee Advocate* in 1844 in the new Cherokee capital of Tahlequah in Indian Territory, with William P. Ross, the chief's nephew, as editor. The *Advocate* continued the *Phoenix*'s policies of free distribution and publication in both Cherokee and English. The newspaper's objectives were to spread important news among the Cherokee people, to advance their general interests, and to defend Indian rights. Clearly, the goals reflected a partisan commitment to the cause of Native peoples, but the newspaper also reflected factionalism among the Cherokees and continued, with missionary sponsorship, to advocate assimilation and defend human rights within that context. Although Cherokee law prevented editors from printing personal and partisan items, political debate occasionally became intensely personal and sometimes violent. After the Civil War, the *Cherokee Advocate* was published under the same format until it ceased publication in 1906. The federal government ordered the Cherokee type preserved in the Smithsonian Institution and the rest of the equipment sold in 1911.

The second Native American newspaper, the *Shawnee Sun (Siwinowe Kesibi)*, began in 1835 under the editorship of Johnston Lykins and with the assistance of the Reverend Jotham Meeker, a missionary who took a printing press with him to his duties at the large Baptist mission at Shawnee Mission, Kansas. The press at Shawnee Mission published part of the newspaper in the Shawnee language using the English alphabet. Meeker translated religious messages and songs and published Indian material in the Native language. His press was the first in the area that is now Kansas. The newspaper was published monthly or semimonthly until its suspension in 1839. It resumed publication in 1841 and apparently lasted until 1844.

By the end of the twentieth century, one of the three national Native American newspapers was published in the Great Plains. The editorial headquarters for *Indian Country Today*, formerly the *Lakota Times*, are located in Rapid City, South Dakota. Other examples of Native voices from the Great Plains included the 2000-watt tribally owned KILI, voice of the Lakota Nation, in Porcupine Butte, South Dakota, and its sister station, KINI, in Rosebud.

Newspaper War in the West
When white settlers arrived in Kansas, they immediately engaged in a war of words. The first English-only newspaper in Kansas was the *Kansas Weekly Herald*, published in Leavenworth from 1854 to 1861. The Kansas-Nebraska Act had created such a rush by competing groups to settle Kansas that the first issue of the proslavery *Herald* was published under a tree, even before the rest of the town appeared. Three free-state papers began in Lawrence in January 1855: the *Kansas Herald of Freedom*, the *Kansas Free State*, and the *Kansas Tribune*. More than 100 newspapers were published during Kansas's territorial period between 1854 and 1861. Like many newspapers, the *Tribune* had trouble getting started on a regular footing. Two-dollar annual subscriptions were payable in advance, and early issues appeared sporadically.

After passage of the Kansas-Nebraska Act of 1854 let voters decide whether new states would be slave or free, war broke out over which faction would rule Kansas. Every faction had its newspaper. Local editors risked their lives in this fight. Missouri bushwhackers attacked newspaper offices, destroying presses so they could not be repaired and scattering type into the street. When slave-state raiders from Missouri attacked Lawrence in 1856, they systematically destroyed two newspaper offices and wrecked the presses. Contemporary observers said only someone who understood printing could have done such an effective job of destroying the presses.

Newspaper Rivalries
Elsewhere in the Great Plains, newspaper rivalries were also intense. Like the Lawrence contest over who would be first, two Denver newspapers raced for the same honor in that city. William N. Byers and the *Rocky Mountain News* faced stiff competition in the drive to control the Denver market. In April 1859 John L. Merrick, who had published the *St. Joseph Gazette* in Missouri (probably printed on a press fished out of the Missouri River at Independence after anti-Mormon rioters had sunk it there), moved his newspaper equipment to Denver City to begin the *Cherry Creek Pioneer*. Once the editors became aware of each other, they raced to be first. Byers won by twenty minutes, and Merrick's *Pioneer* folded after the first issue. His primitive press was capable of printing only seven-by-ten-inch sheets one side at a time, putting him at a severe disadvantage. The victorious *News* enjoyed no luxuries. It was published in an attic room above a saloon whose ceiling had to be reinforced to prevent bullets fired into the air from hitting printers at work. Above the press, a leaky roof allowed rain to drip on the equipment.

Like that of its short-term competitor, the *Rocky Mountain News*'s press could also boast a colorful history. Byers's press may have printed Nebraska Territory's first newspaper. The *Nebraska Palladium and Platte Valley Advocate* had appeared on November 15, 1854, in Bellevue and reached a peak of 500 subscribers before its death the following April. The press later issued the *Bellevue Gazette* on October 23, 1856, and ran for about two years, ending when Byers bought it. From the upstairs office in Auraria, Byers moved his office into a new building along Cherry Creek. The press reached a dramatic end when a fast-moving Cherry Creek swept away the *Rocky Mountain News* building, its press, and all its equipment in the flood of May 19, 1864.

Many western newspapers had short lives. One of Byers's most persistent early competitors, Thomas Gibson, tried several times to start newspapers. He started the *Rocky Mountain Gold Reporter and Mountain City Herald* on August 6, 1859, in Mountain City, Colorado, but soon gave up and returned to Omaha. Later he managed the *Western Mountaineer*, owned by the founders of Golden, Colorado. The *Western Mountaineer* began publication on December 4, 1859, and folded in early 1860. Gibson returned to Denver to compete with Byers and started Colorado's first daily newspaper, the *Daily Herald and Rocky Mountain Advertiser*, on May 1, 1860. Gibson started a weekly edition, the *Rocky Mountain Herald*, on May 5, 1860.

The *Denver Evening Post* appeared for the first time in August 1892, but its editors misjudged their audience. They supported the gold standard at a time when their readers supported William Jennings Bryan and free silver, and the paper died after its first year. Determined not to make the same mistake, two new owners, Frederick G. Bonfils and Harry Heye Tammen, revived the *Evening Post* as a daily in 1894. They reached new heights in sensationalism and antiauthoritarianism. The *Post*'s publishers called their red-painted office the "red room," but local residents took to calling it the "bucket of blood." Like William Randolph Hearst in New York, Tammen and Bonfils exploited sensationalism and identified with the common folks by attacking politicians. In one early issue, the *Post* editors attacked child labor in department stores: "As you enter one of them, a little, pale-faced girl opens the door, standing in the dangerous drafts, for people are coming and going. This method of employing child labor at starvation wages which are all the way from $1 to $1.50 a week, for which they work from sixty-five to seventy hours a week, may be fashionable in Baxter Street, New York, but we desire to serve notice on these establishments that it will not go in the great West." A story on the Denver water company said city residents were drinking sewage, among other things: "The site of an old slaughterhouse in Mount Vernon gulch was visited. Water was running through it washing the old bones and eventually finding its way into the city water mains." Editors assumed that journalism was political, and their readers believed in the innocent West, in contrast to a corrupt East, as the reference to New York indicates.

Like other western newspapers both big and small, the *Post* saw itself as an engine of progress. From its first day, the *Post* promised to "devote special and ceaseless attention to the material interests of the state and to the development of her vast and varied resources." It campaigned to "direct its efforts that more acres of land shall be brought under cultivation" and to promote trade, mining, and industrial development. In 2001 the *Denver Post* and the *Rocky Mountain News* entered into a joint operating agreement. The two papers remain competitors in one of the few U.S. metropolitan areas to have competing major newspapers.

Media Standardization Moves West
Despite their local flavor, small-town western newspapers often reflected evidence of mass production. Beginning in the 1870s, syndication services supplied "patent pages" or "ready prints"—pages already printed on one side—to local printers, who then printed on the backs of the pages. Local newspapers could order preprinted pages and simply use the other side of the sheet (two of the newspaper's four pages) for local news and advertising. Some of

the national syndicates also supplied boiler-plate, preset pages of lead type ready to be printed. All these services saved time and money for printers who still set type one letter at a time while standing at a type case. In the 1880s the Linotype machine allowed a typesetter to sit at a keyboard and call up letters as brass forms into which lead was poured one line at a time, making local news easier to print. However, the boilerplate and ready-print services supplied enough material to fill entire pages or parts of pages, leaving little space to be filled locally.

The preset syndication services helped some publishers create "satellite papers" in which several towns could have virtually the same newspaper with some minor changes in the local news columns. Newspapers could then be printed in nearby towns with the printer inserting a minimum of local news. Local governments helped by requiring legal notices, such as claims for cattle brands and homesteads, to be published for several consecutive weeks. With these notices already set for several weeks, the printer did not have to revise entire columns from week to week.

Editors and Their Agendas

Newspapers across the Plains worked to overcome the label of the Great American Desert applied by early explorers. Town boosters reported fantasies as well as facts, hoping their eastern colleagues would reprint articles extolling the virtues of frontier life. Editors in homesteader towns dreamed in print of the day when miraculous farming techniques would transform gumbo flats into blooming gardens. Even winter looked good in booster columns, improving the health and hardiness of residents. Similarly, boomtown newspapers predicted a peaceful future for their towns, while drunken cowboys loped their horses through the streets, yelling and shooting their guns into the air. In Denver, for example, Byers's *Rocky Mountain News* encouraged farming as a source of long-term stability, even while miners celebrated short-term successes. Newspapers in small homestead towns promoted dryland farming on the theory that once the land was plowed the increased moisture in the air would stimulate rain, hence the slogan, "rainfall follows the plow."

On the other hand, some editors in towns dependent upon cattle and mining turned their backs on reformers. Saloons, gambling, prostitution, and tolerance of violence often helped local business for the short term. Editors often became a saloon's best customers. The editor wanted to put a good face on town news, but the saloon, so often a source of conflict, attracted business. Saloons were dependable advertisers; in fact, critics said frontier newspapers contained too many liquor advertisements. Temperance advocates frequently wrote letters and, occasionally, became editors, but they left little evidence that miners showed any interest in receiving temperance lectures through the press.

Reports of minor crimes revealed the usual mix of editorial comment and news. Some newspapers threatened to help enforce the law by printing the names of people who persisted in wild riding through the streets. Editors often balanced calls for law and order with comments about the increasing number of families making their homes within the town. Frontier editors faced a basic dilemma in deciding whether to report the seamy side of town life or to put forth a wholesome image to attract families. Many editors advocated community reform without calling attention to town problems. Editorial campaigns for law and order frequently supported anonymous vigilance committees, ironically operating outside the law to rid the community of undesirables.

Editors in railhead towns at the end of the Texas to Kansas cattle drives in the 1870s boosted their towns in the competition to attract cattle drives. They ignored the indiscretions of visiting trail hands, who deposited their wages at saloons. Town delegations occasionally met the drives on the trail to persuade drovers to come to their towns. The towns also fought over railroads; railroads held out for concessions that could include free land for rights of way, depots, stockyards, and cash payments. Editors participated in this process, defending the promotional expenses to local readers and extolling the town's virtues to readers beyond the local trade area. Cow town editors depended upon the cattle trade because their towns did, and editors received reliable revenue from legal notices necessary for ranchers to establish their ownership of livestock brands. Editors who at first sided with cattle drovers on such issues as street violence and herd laws to protect fenced farms came to see the future differently as railheads moved west and waves of immigrants settled in the country.

Early historians and dime novelists created stereotypes of frontier editors, especially itinerant ones. Two such editors, Legh Freeman and Frederic E. Lockley, have received scholarly attention. Lockley, who had been a journalist in Cleveland and New York City, moved west to cover Indian Territory, Salt Lake City, and several Kansas towns. During one of his two stints as a newspaper owner, Lockley owned the *Arkansas City Traveler* in the Kansas border town founded during the Oklahoma land rush. "I felt myself in a humble way to be a public teacher; a sound and moral newspaper press I thought had much to do with our national life," he wrote at the turn of the century. But he found that his hours reading exchanges, condensing news, and writing editorials were wasted on people who wanted "little local squibs telling who comes and goes and booming the town on all occasions."

While involved in land-speculation and town-promotion schemes, Legh Freeman tried to live the stereotypical life of a frontier scout. His *Frontier Index*, called the "press on wheels" because of his frequent moves, traveled from town to town ahead of the Union Pacific Railroad in Nebraska, Colorado, Wyoming, Montana, and Utah. Like the mythic mountain man Jim Bridger, whom Freeman may have interviewed early in life, the editor tried to stay ahead of advancing civilization. Toward the end of Freeman's life, his wife and family ran the paper while he traveled and sent home columns.

Humorist Edgar Wilson "Bill" Nye followed Mark Twain in writing widely reprinted newspaper columns and popular books and in touring the lecture circuit. Nye, who edited the *Laramie Boomerang* in Wyoming, proposed a school to train frontier journalists, with the training including self-defense, first aid, theology, medicine, and politics (just to keep up on frontier issues). By the age of ninety-five, Nye concluded, "The student will have lost that wild, reckless and impulsive style so common among younger and less experienced journalists." At that point the most pressing question would be whether to invest in government bonds or real estate in a growing town. Like many small-town editors, Nye also worked as postmaster. William Allen White, editor of the *Emporia Gazette* in Kansas, gained national attention in the early twentieth century for his politics and his articulate advocacy of the West.

Great Plains newspapers provided other celebrities as well as national leaders. Canada's fifth prime minister, Mackenzie Bowell, was once a compositor on the *Calgary Herald*. Sir Clifford Sifton, owner of the *Manitoba Free Press*, and his editor, John Wesley Dafoe, became national figures from 1901 through the late 1920s, while Sifton played a major role as a national party and provincial leader in defining Canada's independence from Great Britain. Dafoe's sixty-year journalism career made the *Free Press* a major liberal and progressive voice in the West. George Creel, who headed the U.S. propaganda effort during World War I, had been a *Post* reporter and police commissioner in Denver. Willa Cather worked as a theater and music critic for two newspapers in Lincoln before moving to Pittsburgh and New York City journalism. L. Frank Baum wrote and edited an Aberdeen, South Dakota, newspaper before he wrote *The Wizard of Oz*.

Plains Radio

Like newspapers, radio linked the Plains with the rest of the world. As early as 1917, Plains residents as far away as Texas occasionally heard the daily University of Wisconsin weather and agricultural bulletins broadcast in Morse code for Wisconsin farmers. Texans got their own weather and crop reports from the University of Texas at Austin, where physics professor S. Leroy Brown built a radio station before World War I. During the war, however, the federal government imposed an embargo on radio development except for military purposes.

Unlicensed pirates continued to broadcast through the war and after. In 1920 Ashley Clayton Dixon began broadcasting music by a pickup orchestra among neighbors from his new home near Three Mile Trading Post north of Stevensville, Montana. Dixon and other amateurs around the nation created an interest in radio that was exploited by Westinghouse employees, who began the first commercial radio station, KDKA in Pittsburgh, in 1920. (The world's oldest commercial radio station, CFCF in Montreal, had already gone on the air as experimental station XWA.) Westinghouse immediately saw the value of broadcasting to sell wireless receiving sets while major corporations fought over patent rights.

University of Nebraska faculty, who had experimented with voice transmission in 1921, began offering courses by radio at $12.50 per student. The cost included textbook, exams, and two credits for those who passed. By the spring of 1922 at least nineteen other U.S. academic institutions had radio stations. The University of Texas at Austin had two stations, but they had merged by 1922 into the 500-watt KUT station, which broadcast from 8 to 10 P.M. three nights a week. One of the best-equipped stations in the nation at the time, KUT carried agricultural and marketing reports, music, and lectures. It aired a church service on Sundays and football games in season. In the mid-1920s the station became KNOW in Austin and carried no news, sponsored programs, or commercials. Commercial radio began in Texas in 1922, and by the end of the year the state hosted twenty-five stations, including WBAP and KFLZ in Fort Worth and KGNC in Amarillo. In 1923 WBAP began a country music variety show featuring local talent similar to the style later developed in Nashville as the *Grand Ole Opry*.

Before the government allotted frequencies in 1927 and 1928, many stations tried operating on the same frequencies. The *Kansas City Star* operated WDAF and regularly went off the air at 7 P.M. to allow WHB, also in Kansas City, to have the frequency—until one evening when a local politician was scheduled to appear on WHB to attack the *Star*. WDAF retained control over the frequency that evening to create a weird effect while the man spoke. Consumers buying radios sometimes hoped to receive distant stations, so a Chicago newspaper promoted weekly silent nights—in Kansas City it was Saturday night—during which time the local stations would be silent so residents could listen for distant stations. The silent nights ended by 1927 with recriminations and complaints of revenue losses. The idea of long-distance broadcasting, except for a few clear-channel frequencies, ended with it.

Many early radio stations were formed to promote specific businesses that used radio to sell products. For example, KHD was run by a marble company in Colorado Springs. In 1923 Dr. John Richard Brinkley began one of the most unusual radio stations, KFKB ("Kansas First, Kansas Best" or "Kansas Folks Know Best") in Milford, to promote his combination of fundamentalist religion and miracle cures using goat glands. He also broadcast other church services, Kansas State College courses, Masonic lectures, and orchestra concerts. His broadcasts were so lucrative that he was able to build a large portion of Milford. However, the Federal Radio Commission revoked his license for operating contrary to the public interest, broadcasting indecent material, and using point-to-point communication

for commercial purposes, an illegal activity at the time. The Kansas State Medical Board later revoked his medical license, challenging his goat-gland cures.

After being discredited in the United States, Brinkley persuaded the Mexican government to license him to broadcast from a powerful station, in part as revenge to the United States and Canada for dividing up all the radio frequencies among themselves. In 1931 his XER broadcast from 300-foot towers across the Rio Grande from Del Rio, Texas, and became one of the first superpower "border radio" stations. When the Mexican government sought to prohibit Brinkley's medical broadcasts by keeping him out of the country, he began a remote broadcast from a hotel in downtown Del Rio, with his voice going to the transmitter in Mexico and back into the U.S. airwaves.

Radio grew rapidly across the continent. The American public's investment in equipment grew from $60 million in 1922 to $358 million in 1924. Commercial radio stations in Canada faced stiff competition for both frequencies and listeners from the United States and even from the powerful Mexican border stations. Like U.S. stations, Canadian stations argued over frequencies. In Saskatoon three stations shared the same wavelength in 1925. Canadian National Railways pioneered radio for train passengers and, because of the railway's public ownership, provided a model for the later British and Canadian Broadcasting Corporations. The remoteness of Canadian settlements in the West led to rapid public and private investment in broadcasting, while newspapers retained a primarily local focus through most of the twentieth century. Many Canadian stations forged agreements with U.S. stations to carry American programs, while the Canadian National Railways built what became the CBC with its strategically located stations and telephone links. The Canadian government took control over broadcast regulation and operation of the public network only after 1932.

In Regina the *Leader* newspaper started CKCK, Saskatchewan's first commercial radio station, in 1922. Both the newspaper and the station advised people on how to build their own receiving sets and warned against unscrupulous dealers who exaggerated the reception capabilities of their receivers. Like their American counterparts, Canadian listeners received a heavy dose of weather and agricultural and marketing information. In the days of distance broadcasting, CKCK's toughest competitors for listeners included WLS in Chicago, KOA in Denver, and KFNF in Hastings, Nebraska.

Although Plains stations began by broadcasting with local talent, they eventually adopted standard formats, especially after television usurped the demand for dramatic and musical programming. Many national media personalities such as Johnny Carson and Lawrence Welk starred on the Plains. Carson, an Iowa native who was host of NBC television's *The Tonight Show* for thirty years, started on Nebraska radio stations, including KFAB and

WOW radio and television in Omaha, before moving to Los Angeles and New York. Welk, who grew up in Strasburg, North Dakota, began his broadcasting career on WNAX radio in Yankton, South Dakota. Chet Huntley, who played with his first crystal radio set as a child in Montana, became coanchor with David Brinkley of NBC's *The Huntley-Brinkley Report*, the leading network evening newscast for much of its fifteen years on the air, beginning in 1956. Their chief competitor, Walter Cronkite, who anchored *The CBS Evening News* from 1962 through 1981, spent his early years in Kansas City, Missouri, and worked as a newspaper and wire-service reporter in Houston, Kansas City, Dallas, Austin, and El Paso. His CBS colleague Eric Sevareid developed an interest in journalism as a child in Velva, North Dakota.

The Mass Media Become Concentrated

Despite the myth of individualistic western editors, the mass media became concentrated in regional and national chains almost from the beginning. Montana's notorious copper kings created a major chain when they bought up most of the state's daily newspapers in 1900 during their war over the location of the state's capital. The Anaconda Company controlled those newspapers until it sold them to the Iowa-based Lee Enterprises in the 1950s. Although its major holdings were in the Midwest, Lee owned newspapers and television stations across the Plains by the end of the twentieth century. In Montana Lee continued to own the daily *Billings Gazette*, the *Montana Standard* of Butte, the *Independent Record* of Helena, the *Missoulian* of Missoula, and twelve weekly shoppers and other specialized publications in Montana alone. In Nebraska Lee owned the daily *Lincoln Journal-Star*, the weekly *Plattsmouth Journal*, and KMTV, CBS-affiliated Channel 3 in Omaha. The *Lincoln Journal-Star* was formed in 1995 when Lee Enterprises purchased the *Lincoln Journal*, which had been owned by the Seacrest family for generations. The *Journal* had begun as the *Nebraska Commonwealth* in Nebraska City in 1867 and moved to Lincoln within a year. The first Sunday edition appeared in 1871 and became the *State Journal* in 1882. A year before their merger, the Lincoln newspapers claimed independence from each other through a joint operating agreement.

Newspapers had spread across the Northern Plains of both the United States and Canada in the wake of settlement by the end of the nineteenth century, well after newspapers had been established in the Central Plains. While Kansas newspapers fought the Civil War, European Americans were yet to settle the Northern Plains. North Dakota's oldest daily newspaper, the *Bismarck Tribune*, was founded in Dakota Territory by Clement Lounsberry only in 1873.

Some editors made the purpose of their newspapers clear in their names, like the *Calgary Herald, Mining and Ranch Advocate and General Advertiser*. Despite the pretentious name, this paper had humble origins in a tent beside the Elbow River in 1883. In 1908 William

Southam purchased the Calgary newspaper as his newspaper empire moved westward from its base in London, Ontario. Southam purchased the *Edmonton Journal* in 1912 and engaged in a journalism war of sensationalism with the *Bulletin*, which had a simple slogan: "Read the Bible and the *Bulletin*." The Southam Corporation grew over the century both in the number of newspapers and in other industrial interests, including steel mills, crushed stone, and carriage manufacturing.

In the mid-1990s, the financially troubled Southam Corporation merged with Hollinger International Inc., a newspaper chain controlled by media mogul Conrad Black, who had a reputation for operating newspapers as businesses, holding journalists in contempt, and advocating tougher libel laws. Hollinger's far-ranging interests included the *Jerusalem Post* in Israel, the *Chicago Sun-Times* in the United States, the *London Daily Telegraph* in England, and the *Sydney Morning Herald* in Australia. The merged corporation published hundreds of nondaily newspapers and specialized magazines covering diverse topics such as fishing and trucking. Hollinger has taken a leading role in online publications in each nation.

In response to the growing threat from chains, some smaller newspapers created organizations such as the Southern Saskatchewan Press Association. One of its active members was a newspaper that, like many other Plains publications, followed the railroads west. The *Courier* appeared in Moosomin, Saskatchewan, soon after the settlers disembarked from the Canadian Pacific Railway. The newspaper, now called the *World-Spectator*, celebrated its first century in October 1984. As early as 1918 several Saskatoon residents founded *Turner's Weekly* to be an independent weekly newspaper with literary aspirations for the general public. It died in 1920, but one of its founders, legislator Harris Turner, started the *Progressive* in 1923 with the slogan "Reliable News—Unfettered Opinions—Western Rights." The publication soon became the *Western Producer* weekly newspaper and continued into the twenty-first century.

The *Toronto Sun* founded several newspapers toward the end of the century to compete with Hollinger and Southam. The *Edmonton Sun* opened in 1978 and the *Calgary Sun* in 1980. In October 1996 the employees purchased the *Edmonton Sun* and the *Calgary Sun* from Rogers Communications Inc., a newspaper chain that had been founded twenty-five years earlier and sold to Maclean Hunter and then to Rogers.

The Canadian Broadcasting Corporation was created, in part, to reach isolated residents in the West in the 1930s. Like the CBC, U.S. public broadcasting networks reached into the Plains with an alternative to American commercial broadcasting. Because of government underfunding, the CBC came to rely on commercial stations to buy its services. Some U.S. radio stations on the Northern Plains carried CBC services.

At least one of the world's largest media companies emerged from the Great Plains.

At the end of the twentieth century, Tele-Communication, Inc., of Englewood, Colorado, supplied television to more than 300 markets in North America. Its TCI Cablevision supplied many Plains cities, including the Colorado cities of Denver, Grand Junction, Greeley, Pueblo, and Thornton; the Texas cities of Abilene, Beaumont, Corpus Christi, Dallas, Garland, Harlingen, Port Arthur, and Tyler; and the Wyoming cities of Casper and Cheyenne. TCI also covered Bellevue, Nebraska; Billings, Montana; Topeka, Kansas; and Tulsa, Oklahoma. It owned smaller cable systems throughout the United States.

The Plains Remain Isolated for Some

Although they were a dying breed, many small-town newspapers remained local with local owners. Others joined smaller newspaper groups, like the Yellowstone Newspapers of Montana that controlled the daily *Miles City Star* and *Livingston Enterprise*, the weekly *Glendive Ranger-Review*, and KATL radio in Miles City. From 1969 to 1984 David and Ella Rivenes operated KYUS television in Miles City, one of the smallest stations in the nation. Miles City had competing KATL ("Cattle") radio and KYUS ("Cayuse") television, both occasionally using horses with their logos.

At the beginning of the twenty-first century, then, no one in Ismay, Montana, climbed a tower to turn an antenna by hand the way we did forty years earlier. Like television viewers around the world, residents of Ismay get as much television as they can afford. They can purchase several kinds of disks and then subscribe to satellite services that provide hundreds of channels carrying public affairs, old movies, premium services like HBO and Showtime, regional network affiliates carrying entertainment programs and advertising, and pay-per-view sporting events and movies. Ranchers and small-town residents no longer depend upon local stations to acquire network programming one show at a time. Westerns like *Gunsmoke* and *Have Gun Will Travel* are still available, but only in reruns on cable channels or on video. Small-town values prevail, however, with some folks noticing when a bachelor neighbor has his disk turned in the direction of the Playboy channel. Despite a variety of choices, local news and weather are hard to find on satellite television, especially in remote areas. Some ranchers and their families, however, have chosen not to invest in the disks and transponders necessary to receive the new bounty. Some ranchers say their work takes too much time to warrant investing in recreational television.

See also CITIES AND TOWNS: Denver, Colorado / IMAGES AND ICONS: Rainfall Follows the Plow / LITERARY TRADITIONS: Baum, L. Frank; Cather, Willa / MUSIC: Welk, Lawrence / POLITICS AND GOVERNMENT: Sifton, Clifford / WAR: Bleeding Kansas.

William E. Huntzicker
Bemidji State University

Bennion, Sherilyn Cox. *Equal to the Occasion: Women Editors of the Nineteenth-Century West*. Reno: University of Nevada Press, 1990. Carter, L. Edward. *The Story of Oklahoma Newspapers*. Muskogee: Oklahoma Heritage Association by Western Heritage Books, 1984. Cloud, Barbara. *The Business of Newspapers on the Western Frontier*. Reno: University of Nevada Press, 1992. Dary, David. *Red Blood and Black Ink: Journalism in the Old West*. New York: Alfred A. Knopf, 1998. Huntzicker, William E. "The Frontier Press 1800–1900." In *The Media in America: A History*, edited by William D. Sloan. Northport AL: Vision Press, 2002: 175–98. Karolevitz, Robert F. *Newspapering in the Old West*. Seattle: Superior Publishing Company, 1965. Karolevitz, Robert F. *With a Shirt Tail Full of Type: The Story of Newspapering in South Dakota*. Brookings: South Dakota Press Association, 1982. Kesterson, W. H. *A History of Journalism in Canada*. Toronto: McClelland and Stewart Limited, 1967. Littlefield, Daniel F., Jr., and James W. Parins. *American Indian and Alaska Native Newspapers and Periodicals, 1826–1924*. Westport CT: Greenwood Press, 1984. Lyon, William H., ed. *Journalism in the West*. Manhattan KS: Sunflower University Press, 1980. Rankin, Charles E. "Type and Stereotype: Frederic E. Lockley, Pioneer Journalist." *American Journalist* 14 (1997): 182–204. Schmalz, Wayne. *On Air: Radio in Saskatchewan*. Regina, Saskatchewan: Coteau Books, 1990. Schmitt, Jo Ann. *Fighting Editors*. San Antonio: Naylor Company, 1958. Vipond, Mary. *Listening In: The First Decade of Canadian Broadcasting, 1922–1923*. Montreal: McGill-Queen's University Press, 1992.

AFRICAN AMERICAN NEWSPAPERS

See AFRICAN AMERICANS: African American Newspapers

ARGUS LEADER (SIOUX FALLS)

The *Argus Leader*, published in Sioux Falls, South Dakota, is the survivor of a number of newspapers that have existed in that community since its first founding in 1857. It is the product of a merger of two early papers: the *Sioux Falls Argus*, a weekly paper begun in 1881, and the *Sioux Falls Leader*, which was founded in 1883. The consolidation occurred in 1887, and the name was hyphenated until December 3, 1979. The *Argus-Leader* was originally a Democratic paper, but it switched to the Republican Party during the 1896 McKinley election. (The paper long ago dropped any political party connection.) Begun as a morning paper, it changed to evening publication in 1885 and continued on that schedule for the next ninety-four years.

The *Argus-Leader* nearly joined the town's other failed newspapers in 1889 when it ceased publication for more than a week due to financial problems. At that time, when Sioux Falls had a population of about 10,000, the paper had a total circulation of only 1,000 daily and 900 weekly. New owners moved the paper to 109 N. Main, where it thrived: by 1892 total circulation had risen to 7,500, and the paper had become a statewide publication. This success became clearly visible in 1917 with the addition of a second floor and a new pressroom to the building and the erection of an electric bulletin board and a large electric World Series board on its facade. On January 1, 1928, the *Argus-Leader*'s main competitor, the *Sioux Falls Daily Press*, a morning paper, ceased operations, and its publisher, Fred C. Christopherson, became assistant editor of the *Argus-Leader*. Christopherson continued at the *Argus-Leader* for the next thirty-three years, retiring in 1961 as executive editor.

The *Argus-Leader* experienced major changes after World War II. In 1951 a massive fire destroyed the business office and newsroom. After operating in various temporary quarters, the paper moved to its present site at Tenth and Minnesota in 1954. A year later local owners sold the paper to John A. Kennedy of San Diego, California, who in turn sold it to the Speidel newspaper chain of Reno, Nevada, in 1963. In May 1977 the Gannet Company, Inc., a newspaper chain of fifty-four papers, merged with the thirteen-paper Speidel Company. Through this merger, Allen Neuharth, a native of Eureka, South Dakota, and head of the Gannet Company, became owner of the *Argus-Leader*. It was at this time that the paper switched to being a morning paper and dropped Sioux Falls from its nameplate.

The *Argus Leader*, with a daily circulation of about 52,000 in August 2000, remains the only locally published daily newspaper in Sioux Falls. While its primary focus is Minnehaha and adjacent counties, the *Argus Leader* is also the regional newspaper of "east river" South Dakota, southwestern Minnesota, and northwestern Iowa.

See also CITIES AND TOWNS: Sioux Falls, South Dakota.

Gary D. Olson
Augustana College

Bailey, Dana. *History of Minnehaha County*. Sioux Falls SD: Brown and Saenger, 1899. Hollingsworth, Dave. "Argus Leader Chronology." *Argus Leader*, May 1, 1988. Olson, Gary D., and Erik L. Olson. *Pictorial History of Sioux Falls*. Norfolk VA: Donning Press, 1985.

BILLINGS GAZETTE

The *Billings (Montana) Gazette* can truly claim to have risen from the ashes—the ashes of a fire that consumed its printing plant the night before its maiden edition on May 3, 1885. Displaying frontier grit and resourcefulness, the newspaper's first editor, J. D. Matheson, rescued enough type from the ruins to compose a single sheet, nine by twelve inches, printed on both sides. By the following week the fledgling journal was up to four pages.

The *Gazette* itself was created from a melding of three earlier newspapers, the *Herald*, the *Rustler*, and the *Post*. The latter had been started three years earlier, in 1882, in the neighboring town of Coulson by Abel Kelsey Yerkes, the "Poet of Sourdough Creek." When Yerkes moved his publication to Billings in July 1882, only a handful of buildings dotted the alkali flats by the Yellowstone River, and there were only 500 residents in the town (named after Frederick Billings, former president of the Northern Pacific Railroad). By the following January there were 1,200. The overnight boom led to the enduring nickname the "Magic City."

The *Gazette* rode the growth curve, purchasing the town's first linotype machine in 1901. It editorialized for a better water supply and stronger fire protection. It chronicled the raw energy of the emerging agricultural and railroad center and its denizens, among them Calamity Jane and Liver-Eating Johnson.

After consolidation with the *Billings Evening Journal* in 1908, the newspaper was published under both names until 1916, when the *Journal* name was dropped. Both morning and evening editions were published. The same year the Anaconda Copper Mining Company purchased a controlling interest, as it did with papers in Anaconda, Butte, Helena, Livingston, and Missoula, thereby launching nearly a half century of company-controlled journalism in Montana. The paternalistic ACM treated its employees well and chose to ignore its foes, clamping a lid on news critical of the company or inimical to its interests.

The newspaper grew, expanding its distribution boundaries, first along railroad lines, then more broadly across eastern Montana and northern Wyoming as road networks built up. By 1927 the *Gazette* was the city's largest year-round industry, employing 112 persons and with an annual payroll of $200,000. In 1934 it reported the highest circulation of any daily newspaper in the state, a distinction it still holds. By 1941 there were 20,374 subscribers, and the paper was rolling out as many as five different morning editions.

Finally realizing the incongruity of a mining and processing company owning a string of newspapers, ACM sold them all to Lee Newspapers of Davenport, Iowa, on June 1, 1959. Lee president Don Anderson promoted the *Gazette*'s Duane "Doc" Bowler to managing editor in 1960 with orders to "make a newspaper of it." Under Lee ownership, which continues to this day, the *Gazette* grew even faster. The newspaper moved out of its old offices (jocularly referred to by local newspapermen as the "Fourth House," in reference to three houses of prostitution that had once shared the same corner) to its present headquarters in 1968.

Today, the *Gazette*'s circulation is about 60,000, covering one of the largest regional newspaper distribution areas in the United States, and the newspaper has an editorial staff of eighty. The "phoenix of the Plains," 115 years old at the turn of the twenty-first century, has proven its staying power.

See also CITIES AND TOWNS: Billings, Montana.

Clemens P. Work
University of Montana

Cooper, Myrtle E. *From Tent Town to City: A Chronological History of Billings, Montana 1882–1935*. Billings MT: Friends of the Library, 1981. Gransbery, Jim. "Gazette Rises from Ashes." *Billings Gazette*, May 5, 1985: H4. Wright, Kathryn H. *Billings, the Magic City and How It Grew*. Billings MT: Reporter Printing and Supply Company, 1978.

BISMARCK TRIBUNE

The *Bismarck Tribune* was established in 1873, the first newspaper in Dakota Territory. The remote northern half of Dakota Territory saw few permanent European American settlers until the Northern Pacific Railroad reached the Plains in the early 1870s. In the spring of 1873 a young Civil War veteran sensed an opportunity behind the railroad construction crews. Clement A. Lounsberry had worked for several Minnesota newspapers. In May 1873,

after his coverage of Minnesota's state legislature ended, he moved printing equipment by the first railcar into Bismarck. Issue number one of the *Bismarck Tribune* was published in July.

Most new western towns built around the advancing railroad attracted bawdy houses and lawless drifters, and early Bismarck was no exception. "Colonel" Lounsberry, who kept his old Civil War rank, as was the fashion at the time, hoped to establish order through editorial. Lounsberry asked for a "vigilance committee" to respond to town troublemakers. Dance-hall proprietors Dave Mullen and Jack O'Neil perceived this as a threat. Heavily armed, they confronted Lounsberry at the *Tribune* office. In characteristic words of the "fighting editor" common to the western frontier, Lounsberry claimed he challenged them to go ahead and shoot, boasting that he had "heard bullets fly before." The saloon owners demurred, however, and merely asked him to refrain from issuing attacks in their direction.

The *Tribune* began publishing daily in 1881. Always a relatively small daily (1996 circulation was 31,161), it nevertheless became nationally known for its coverage of two events. In 1937 it received a Pulitzer Prize for its series "Self-Help in the Dust Bowl," aimed at farmers battling the droughts of the 1930s. Better known, however, is its renown as the first newspaper to break the story of "Custer's Last Stand." Gen. George Armstrong Custer left for his last battle from Fort Abraham Lincoln, near Bismarck. Lounsberry sent along reporter Mark Kellogg. Kellogg became one of the casualties of the famous June 25, 1876, battle. His bloodstained notes found their way back to Bismarck, where Lounsberry hogged the town's single telegraph line for twenty-two hours to transmit the story as sometime correspondent for the *New York Tribune*. The eastern editors at first did not believe him, however, and held the story long enough for Lounsberry's own paper to get the scoop.

Lounsberry remained publisher until 1884, when he sold the paper to Marshall Jewell, who had been job shop manager. While still a relatively small daily by national standards, the *Tribune* has traditionally distributed over a vast geographical area in a sparsely populated state. By a 1960s comparison, the *Tribune* still counted a geographic circulation twice that of newspapers in similarly sized eastern cities. Because the Bismarck paper reached so far, however, distribution costs were also three times higher.

In the first quarter of the twentieth century the *Tribune* faced competition from five other newspapers publishing from the state capital. Even in 1930 its circulation was only 6,000, compared to 11,000 claimed by the German-language weekly *Der Staats-Anzeiger*. By 1970, however, the *Tribune* claimed 17,086 subscribers and the German-language paper only 989. Today the *Tribune* is the third largest daily in the state after the *Grand Forks Herald* and *Fargo-Moorhead Forum*. It is owned by Lee Enterprises.

See also CITIES AND TOWNS: Bismarck, North Dakota / WAR: Little Bighorn, Battle of the.

Ross F. Collins
North Dakota State University

Lounsberry, Clement A. *North Dakota: History and People.* Chicago: S. J. Clarke Publishing Company, 1917. Robinson, Elwyn. *History of North Dakota.* Fargo: Institute for Regional Studies, North Dakota State University, 1995. Schmidt, Paul C. "The Press in North Dakota." *North Dakota History* 31 (1964): 216–22.

BRINKLEY, JOHN RICHARD (1885–1942)

John R. Brinkley pioneered radio broadcasting with numerous innovations that influenced the industry for decades. Brinkley was born in Beta, North Carolina, on July 8, 1885. His father was a mountain doctor who apprenticed to learn medicine, much like lawyers learned their craft in the nineteenth century. The son decided on a career in medicine, receiving a degree from the Eclectic Medical University of Kansas City, an institution of questionable standards and ethics. He began practicing in 1918 in the small Kansas town of Milford and pioneered in glandular surgery, developing a lucrative operation that brought him worldwide attention for rejuvenating elderly men with goat glands. He advertised his unique operation over the new medium of radio.

Brinkley presciently envisioned the potential of radio and received a license from the Federal Radio Commission to operate station KFKB in 1923, becoming one of the first commercial broadcasters in the nation. He pioneered radio programming with a twelve-hour daily combination of country music, news, markets, orchestras, local talent, medical advice, and travelogues describing his world journeys, all directed toward a rural audience. He also experimented with bringing college extension courses into the home, utilizing professors from nearby Kansas State College, and allowing politicians free airtime and a citizens forum during which the civic questions of listeners could be answered. His station, broadcasting at 5,000 watts, became popular over a wide area and in 1929 was voted best in the nation in a poll conducted by *Radio Digest*. That same year he conceived the idea for a show called *Medical Question Box*, during which his rustic listeners described their ailments. He read their symptoms over the air, then prescribed remedies available at his pharmacy. After regional pharmacists became upset over this intrusion, Brinkley changed to recommending the prescriptions be filled at his listeners' local drugstore, and pharmacists gave him a cut on each sale.

This competition aroused the ire of the *Kansas City Star*, which owned radio station WDAF, both because of lost revenues from prescription drug advertisements and loss of the popularity contest to Brinkley's station. The American Medical Association was also disturbed over his lack of ethics in advertising, and the two combined to have both his medical and radio licenses revoked in 1930. Brinkley unsuccessfully ran for governor that year, hoping to name a new medical board for Kansas.

Brinkley then moved south of the border, where Mexico licensed him to operate a powerful "borderblaster" station in Villa Acuña. Living and practicing medicine in Del Rio, where he was licensed in Texas, he continued to experiment, developing the techniques of electrical transcriptions and longwire directional antennas, which are still in use. When Mexico increased his power to 500,000 watts, he could reach listeners across North America. Others imitated his borderblaster techniques, and the resulting jumble in the airwaves led to the Treaty of Havana of 1937, a North American agreement to control international radio broadcasting. For the first time Mexico received some fair share, legally, of the airwave allotments and agreed to bring its rogue broadcasters under control.

Once a millionaire through his unusual medical and radio practices, Brinkley began a rapid descent in 1939 when the American Medical Association successfully won a suit against him and disgruntled patients began lawsuits. He died bankrupt in San Antonio, Texas, on May 26, 1942, but his radio techniques endured.

R. Alton Lee
University of South Dakota

Fowler, Gene, and Bill Crawford. *Border Radio: Quacks, Yodelers, Pitchmen, Psychics, and Other Amazing Broadcasters of the American Airwaves.* Austin: Texas Monthly Press, 1987. Lee, R. Alton. *The Bizarre Careers of John R. Brinkley.* Lexington: University Press of Kentucky, 2002.

BROKAW, TOM (b. 1940)

Tom Brokaw, editor, author, and TV anchor, was born in Webster, South Dakota, on February 6, 1940. Brokaw's parents belonged to the generation that would later be featured in his 1998 best-seller, *The Greatest Generation*. During World War II his father, Red Brokaw, was an operator of construction machinery and snowplows on a small air force base at Igloo in western South Dakota. His mother, Jean, was a typical 1940s housewife. Later the family moved to Yankton, South Dakota, where Brokaw worked at a local radio station, KYNT. He graduated from Yankton High School, where he met his wife, Meredith Auld, a former Miss South Dakota.

Brokaw attended the University of Iowa in Iowa City but later finished his college degree at the University of South Dakota at Vermillion. His first professional job on television was in Sioux City, Iowa, with KTIV-TV. From 1962 to 1965 he worked in Omaha for KMTV. Then in 1965 he joined WSB-TV in Atlanta, Georgia. NBC News scouts liked the young investigative reporter's coverage of the civil rights movement, and in 1973 he was hired as NBC White House correspondent. He became cohost of the *Today* show in 1976, a position he held until 1981. He was then appointed anchor of the NBC *Nightly News*.

Brokaw's coverage of world and national news has included the signing on the White House lawn of the historic Middle East peace agreement, the fall of the Berlin Wall, and human-rights abuses in Tibet as well as the first exclusive U.S. one-on-one interview with

Tom Brokaw

Mikhail Gorbachev and an interview with the Dalai Lama. He was the first anchor to report from the site of the Oklahoma City bombing and from the scene of the 1996 TWA Flight 800 tragedy. In 1999 he did the first North American television interview with Russian prime minister Yevgeny Primakov and was the first of the network evening news anchors to travel to Tirana, Albania, during the NATO air strikes in the former Yugoslavia.

Awards for his investigative reporting are numerous. They include a Peabody Award for his report "To Be an American" and Emmy Awards for his "China in Crisis" special reports and for his reports on the 1992 floods in the Midwest. He received the Dennis Kauff Memorial Award for Lifetime Achievement in Journalism from Boston University and the Lowell Thomas Award from Marist College. He was inducted into Broadcasting and Cable TV's Hall of Fame in 1977. He is also a recipient of the Neuharth Award, presented by the Freedom Forum every fall at the University of South Dakota. The Tom Brokaw Award is presented yearly to an outstanding South Dakota media person.

M. L. Cornette
University of South Dakota

Brokaw, Tom. *The Greatest Generation.* New York: Random House, 1998.

CALGARY HERALD

The *Calgary (Alberta) Herald* was first printed in 1883 in a tent at the junction of the Elbow and Bow Rivers. A teacher named Thomas Braden and his friend, printer Andrew Armour, produced the first issue. At that time it was known as the *Calgary Herald, Mining and Ranch Advocate and General Advertiser*. The first edition was four pages long and had a circulation of 150 copies.

The *Calgary Herald*, financed by a five-hundred-dollar interest-free loan from a Toronto milliner, Miss Frances Ann Chandler, was a questionable enterprise during its first few years. The cost for a year's subscription was $3. By 1884 the founders had replaced their tent with a shack and had hired their first editor, Hugh St. Quentin Cayley. At that time, Braden and Armour found that westerners wanted more updated information about the growing Riel Rebellion in the Northwest Territories. One year later, the *Calgary Herald* went daily. To meet demand, a new press was purchased that could print up to 400 papers an hour, if a strong man was turning the crank. The paper was still experiencing growing pains and financial uncertainty in 1894, when J. J. Young took over the paper, saving it from near bankruptcy.

During those early years, the *Calgary Herald* was not so much published as improvised, with updated news provided by bulletins from passengers on the Canadian Pacific Railway. By 1902 business had improved so much that the newspaper bought the city's first two Linotypes, which allowed fresh type to be cast, a line at a time, from molten metal. This revolutionary invention was used to publish the daily paper for the next seventy years.

In 1906 James Hossack Woods was traveling on holiday when he stopped in Calgary. The journalist and advertising man met Young, who offered Woods an option on half the *Calgary Herald*. A year later Woods approached William Southam, who already owned the *Hamilton Spectator* and the *Ottawa Citizen*, to buy a share of the *Herald*. In 1908 Southam bought 301 shares of the newspaper. *Herald* circulation reached 20,000 in 1914, when the advent of World War I placed extraordinary demands on newspapers to provide fast-breaking news. The *Calgary Herald* was becoming an important source of news for Alberta. In 1923 the paper was also influential in founding the Alberta Wheat Pool, which gave farmers more leverage for better grain prices in the marketplace. The newspaper grew and expanded over the course of the twentieth century, covering news about the Great Depression, both world wars, the economic recession during the mid-1980s, and the 1988 Calgary Winter Olympics.

In the early 1990s competing media, new technology, and changing lifestyles began to restrict further growth of the *Calgary Herald*. The eight-month strike of 230 *Calgary Herald* newsroom and distribution-center employees against owner Conrad Black in 1999–2000 also forced the newspaper to retool various departments. New technological innovations were implemented to increase the quality, accuracy, and efficiency of the growing daily.

In November 2000, in Canada's largest media deal to date, CanWest founder and chairman Israel Asper bought the *Calgary Herald* from Hollinger International Inc. chairman Conrad Black. This latest transaction will likely lead to the convergence of the printed word of the *Calgary Herald* with the Internet and broadcasting capabilities owned by CanWest. As of September 2000 the *Calgary Herald*'s circulation was at 114,533 daily Monday through Thursday, 151,374 on Friday, 130,387 on Saturday, and 113,532 on Sunday.

See also CITIES AND TOWNS: Calgary, Alberta.

Diane Howard
University of Calgary

Sumner, Jeff. *Gale Directory of Publications and Broadcast Media*. 134th ed., vol. 2. Detroit: Gale Group, 2000. Vickers, Reg. *The Calgary Herald*. Calgary, Alberta. 1982.

CAPPER, ARTHUR (1865–1951)

Publisher of agricultural journals, governor of Kansas, longtime U.S. senator from Kansas, and philanthropist Arthur Capper was born in Garnett, Kansas, on July 14, 1865. In 1884, after high school graduation, Capper moved to Topeka, where he found employment with the *Topeka Capital* and became a leading reporter. He married Florence Crawford, only daughter of the third Kansas governor. They had no children. Acquiring his first weekly newspaper in 1893, Capper consolidated it with others, forming the *Mail and Breeze*. In 1900 he acquired a monthly agricultural journal. In 1901 he added the *Topeka Capital* and its *Weekly Capital*. Vigorous in increasing the circulation and advertising revenues of all his journals, Capper gained wealth rapidly. He built a five-story plant across the street from the capitol in Topeka and an elaborate mansion nearby.

While some of his publications had a general audience, Capper was best known for his agricultural journals, such as the monthly *Missouri Valley Farmer* (known later as *Capper's Farmer*) and the *Farmer's Mail and Breeze*, which acquired the *Kansas Farmer* and assumed that name. In 1910 he purchased the *Missouri Ruralist*, and for a time he owned Nebraska and Oklahoma farm papers as well as one covering the Rockies. He became partial owner of leading farm papers published in Cleveland, Ohio. All his other journals were published in Topeka, with editorial offices in the states of circulation: *Kansas Farmer*, *Missouri Ruralist*, *Ohio Farmer*, *Michigan Farmer*, *Pennsylvania Farmer*, and *Capper's Farmer* were all well known as the Capper Farm Press.

In 1912, as a Republican, Capper lost a close race for Kansas governor, but he won in 1914 and 1916. In 1918 he was elected to the first of five terms in the U.S. Senate. He was a conservative and the leader of the Farm Bloc but not an initiator of legislation. When he died on December 19, 1951, his beneficiaries were a surviving sister, leading employees, and the Capper Foundation for Crippled Children.

Homer E. Socolofsky
Manhattan, Kansas

Socolofsky, Homer E. *Arthur Capper: Publisher, Politician, Philanthropist*. Lawrence: University Press of Kansas, 1962.

CARSON, JOHNNY (b. 1925)

John William "Johnny" Carson, born in Corning, Iowa, on October 23, 1925, became one of the Great Plains' most significant contributions to American popular culture. His humorously skeptical view of American politics, razor-sharp wit, and self-deprecation made him the television equivalent of Mark Twain and Will Rogers.

Carson grew up in Norfolk, Nebraska, where his outlook was shaped by listening to the family radio. He immersed himself in popular culture, memorizing jokes he heard and writing down routines for subsequent analysis. By age twelve he was performing magic tricks interspersed with a memorized, ostensibly impromptu patter. His first "professional" engagement was for the Norfolk Rotary Club in 1939 as the "Great Carsoni."

Upon graduation from high school in 1943, Carson entered the U.S. Navy and distinguished himself in several combat situations, especially after his ship was hit by torpedoes in 1945. He enrolled at the University of Nebraska in 1946, and in 1949 he wrote a senior thesis entitled "How to Write Comedy Jokes," analyzing dozens of radio performers and their delivery. The main thrust of his thesis was, "A good comedian can get you to buy his sponsor's products."

After college Carson went to work for wow radio in Omaha. *The Johnny Carson Show* aired weekdays, while he was assigned airtime on wow's television affiliate with no particular format. He told jokes, did humorous interviews, and staged turtle races. Television liked him; he was a "cool" performer, casual and relaxed. Radio announcers with stentorian tones did not normally do well in the new medium.

In Los Angeles by 1954, with KNXT-TV, he created *Carson's Cellar*, resembling its counterpart in Omaha. In 1955 Red Skelton hired him for his CBS network show, and for one broadcast Carson successfully substituted as host for Skelton. CBS executives gave Carson his own show in July 1955, but it was canceled in March 1956.

Carson then moved to New York City, working as substitute host for afternoon quiz shows. In 1957 he became full-time host of ABC's *Do You Trust Your Wife?* It was a primordial talk show that soon became the grammatically incorrect *Who Do You Trust?* With it, Carson's stock reached unprecedented heights. By 1962 he had embarked on a rendezvous with television destiny, becoming the host of NBC's *The Tonight Show*.

Jack Paar brought an anxiety-ridden persona to *The Tonight Show*, discussing his personal problems, his family, and his assorted neuroses. Carson was at first reluctant to succeed him, since *The Tonight Show* had become so closely identified with its host. Carson was far more tranquil than Paar, and the first critical evaluations were not in his favor. He realized, however, that a decade in fear of thermonuclear annihilation had left American television audiences ready for an escape from neurosis. NBC executives feared that Carson's appointment had been a sizable blunder; they thought the show bland when compared to Paar's—and in a way they were right. But audiences found comfort in Carson's blandness. Three months after taking over for Paar, Carson was reaching 500,000 more homes than

Paar had. *The Tonight Show* starring Johnny Carson increased its market share year after year, even though television writers continued to pan its host: one said, "He exhibits all the charm of a snickering schoolboy scribbling graffiti on a public wall." Competitors came and went, but Carson remained "King of the Night" for the next three decades, achieving a dominance unprecedented in broadcast history.

Carson had always been a student of entertainment media; he knew the techniques of other performers, the history of broadcasting successes or failures, and the capacity of television to deplete its assets quickly. He also recognized that late-night television was not an intellectual exercise. It was something to which viewers in most cases paid only intermittent attention: people "had the TV on" while they usually did something else. It was the casualness, the seemingly unrehearsed nonintrusiveness of the show, that made Carson so popular.

Carson became the highest-salaried performer in television history, though his salary amounted to a tiny fraction of the revenues his show garnered for the network. When he mentioned that he might retire from *The Tonight Show* in the summer of 1979, stock prices of NBC parent company RCA dropped precipitously—an indication of the fact that *The Tonight Show* alone earned 17 percent of the company's revenue. Carson had become so dominant a figure in popular culture that he had an optical disorder named after him in the *New England Journal of Medicine* called *Carsongenous monocular nyctalopia*, or "Carson night blindness." It occurs when a person watches television late at night with only one eye open, a result of lying in bed on one's side, one eye buried in the pillow, the other fixed on the screen.

Since retiring from *The Tonight Show* in 1992, Carson has returned frequently to his roots in Iowa and Nebraska, contributing large sums for the construction of arts centers in small towns near his boyhood home. In 1992 Carson was awarded the Presidential Medal of Freedom, and in 1993 he was awarded the Kennedy Center Honors Lifetime Achievement Award.

William Grange
University of Nebraska–Lincoln

Corkery, Paul. *Carson*. Ketchum ID: Randt, 1987. Leamer, Laurence. *King of the Night*. New York: William Morrow, 1989. Smith, Ronald L. *Johnny Carson*. New York: St. Martin's Press, 1987.

CAVETT, DICK (b. 1936)

Richard A. "Dick" Cavett, comedian, writer, actor, and, most famously, talk-show host, was born in the small Nebraska town of Gibbon on November 19, 1936. Both his parents were teachers. When Cavett was five his family moved to Grand Island; his high school years were spent in Lincoln. Cavett remembers his Nebraska upbringing fondly: a landscape of idyllic images, darkened only by his mother's death when he was ten, a tragedy from which, he admits, he has never fully recovered.

Cavett started into acting early and performed his magic act at various Lincoln venues. (He first met another rising star, Johnny Carson, at a magic show in a Lincoln church basement.) Cavett was driven by a sense of destiny, a knowledge that he would be famous, and he acted in stage productions at Yale (from which he graduated in 1958) and then, without much success, in New York City. He maneuvered his big break in 1960 when he cornered Jack Paar in a corridor off the set of NBC's *The Jack Paar Tonight Show* and handed him an envelope of jokes. Paar used the jokes and hired Cavett a week later.

During the next few years, Cavett wrote jokes for Paar, Carson, Merv Griffin, and Jerry Lewis and performed in stand-up comedy and on television. His first stint as a television host was on ABC's *The Morning* in 1968. The show lasted only a season, but Cavett was soon in the limelight as host of *The Dick Cavett Show*, which ran on ABC from 1969 to 1974. While Cavett rejects being labeled as intellectual, the urbane tenor of the show and the high caliber of his guests (who included Laurence Olivier and Ingmar Bergman) set it apart from other talk shows.

But the show's ratings were never high enough to suit executives, and, despite receiving three Emmy Awards, it was canceled in 1974. *The Dick Cavett Show* was revived on PBS from 1977 to 1982 and briefly again on ABC in 1986–87. After 1989 Cavett hosted a regular show on the cable network CNBC. Cavett also made numerous other television appearances and acted in many movies (often as himself) during these years. As he makes clear in his autobiographical conversation with Christopher Porterfield, however, despite his successes elsewhere, he remains firmly rooted in his Great Plains background.

David J. Wishart
University of Nebraska–Lincoln

Cavett, Richard A., and Christopher Porterfield. *Cavett*. New York: Harcourt Brace Jovanovich, 1974. Rooney, Terrie M., ed. *Contemporary Theater, Film, and Television*. Detroit: Gale, 1996: 15: 83–85.

CRONKITE, WALTER LELAND (b. 1916)

Walter Leland Cronkite Jr., the American journalist whose objectivity and credibility prompted *Time* magazine to name him the most trusted man in America, greatly influenced the development of national television news reporting while serving as anchor and managing editor at CBS News from 1962 to 1981.

Cronkite was born November 4, 1916, in St. Joseph, Missouri. When his dentist father received a World War I army commission in 1917, the family moved to Kansas City, Missouri. In 1928 the family relocated to Houston, Texas. Cronkite graduated from high school in 1933 and enrolled as a political science major at the University of Texas at Austin. Uncertain about his future vocation, he dropped out of college in 1935 and worked at a wide variety of jobs over much of the Midwest. After his 1940 marriage to Betsy Maxwell, Cronkite and his wife moved to New York City, where he had been assigned to the United Press foreign office.

In 1942 Cronkite accepted a position as a war correspondent based in London, where he distinguished himself for bravery and professionalism. Following the surrender of Nazi Germany in 1945, he was named chief United Press correspondent at the Nuremberg war trials. In 1946 he was sent to Moscow for two years, accompanied by his wife. At Edward R. Murrow's invitation, Cronkite left United Press in 1948 to work at radio station KMBD in Washington DC. In 1951 after joining CBS-owned television station WTOP, his *Man of the Week* program attracted the attention of CBS executives. He was chosen to cover the first televised national political convention in 1952 in Chicago as well as every ensuing convention while he was with CBS News. Cronkite was transferred by CBS to New York City in 1955 to host *The Twentieth Century*, *Eyewitness to History*, and *You Are There*.

In 1961 America was introduced to the space age with Cronkite's televised live launch of Alan B. Shepard, the first American in space. Cronkite covered every manned NASA flight until his retirement. After a 1968 fact-finding trip to Southeast Asia, Cronkite declared his opposition to the increasingly unpopular Vietnam War on a special news program and challenged the misleading optimism expressed by governmental officials. His pronouncement had a powerful impact on American politics, influencing Lyndon Johnson's decision not to run for reelection as president.

Cronkite, an outspoken defender of First Amendment rights, received most of the credit—or blame—for exposing the multifarious criminal activities of members of Richard Nixon's White House staff as they attempted to cover up the Watergate break-in. Intense pressure from the public and news media eventually brought down the entire Nixon administration.

Cronkite was also responsible for opening the dialogue between Israeli prime minister Menachem Begin and Egyptian president Anwar Sadat, giving President Jimmy Carter the opportunity to secure an agreement of cooperation between the two nations in a historic 1979 White House ceremony.

By the time Cronkite retired from CBS in 1981, he had received every major broadcasting honor as well as the Presidential Medal of Freedom awarded to him by President Jimmy Carter.

Doug James
Spring Hill College

James, Doug. *Walter Cronkite: His Life and Times*. Nashville: JMP Press, 1991.

DAILY OKLAHOMAN

When E. K. Gaylord arrived in Oklahoma City in 1902 he found a young town of 7,000 residents with two newspapers, including the one he would work at and own for more than seventy years—the *Daily Oklahoman*. After Gaylord met with Roy E. Stafford, the publisher of the eight-year-old *Oklahoman*, the men reached an agreement for Gaylord to become Stafford's business manager and financial partner.

The newspaper had passed through several hands since its founding in 1894. Gaylord began his duties on January 27, 1903, and two days later the Oklahoma Publishing Company (OPUBCO) was incorporated. In less than a century, Gaylord's original five-thousand-dollar investment in a fledgling newspaper would become a billion-dollar media empire.

Oklahoma became a state on November 16, 1907, and soon the state capital was moved from Guthrie to Oklahoma City. Gaylord chaired the Oklahoma City campaign for the capital site. With the move came higher statewide status for the *Daily Oklahoman*. However, the *Oklahoman*'s early growth was impeded by circulation wars with both paid and free newspapers and a fire that destroyed its building and melted its printing equipment in 1909.

In 1916 OPUBCO purchased the *Oklahoma Times*, which it operated until 1984. That purchase left only one rival, the *Oklahoma City News*, an afternoon daily owned by the Scripps-Howard chain. The *News* folded in the 1970s when afternoon newspapers across America faced circulation declines with the advent of evening television news, making Oklahoma City one of the many cities in American with a single newspaper.

Gaylord's efforts to buy and beat the competition and his courage in facing down political opposition and an advertising boycott impressed the directors of OPUBCO, and in 1916 they named him president of the company, despite the fact that Stafford owned the majority of the stock. Stafford, who perceived the directors' action as a vote of no confidence, quickly sold his interest in the newspaper for $300,000.

Stafford's departure set the stage for a remarkable career for Gaylord as president of a growing newspaper in a growing state, a career that lasted until his death in 1974 at the age of 101. In those years Oklahoma saw both bad times—the Great Depression and the Dust Bowl—and good—the discovery of huge oil fields throughout the state. Through them all the *Daily Oklahoman* steadily maintained its mission to be the newspaper of record for the state. National attention focused on the city and the newspaper in 1995, when the federal building in Oklahoma City was bombed in the largest act of domestic terrorism in the nation's history. Reporters and editors worked nonstop for more than a month, covering the story in a manner praised by consumers and industry insiders alike.

Over the years the *Daily Oklahoman* gained a reputation for embracing new technology, shunning special interests, and encouraging economic growth in the city and state. From their earliest days, radio and television fascinated Gaylord with their possibilities. OPUBCO brought radio to Oklahoma City in 1928 and television in 1949, often pioneering technologies and fostering talent later enjoyed na-

tionwide. Edward L. Gaylord, who followed his father into the OPUBCO presidency in 1974, expanded the OPUBCO media holdings, purchasing television stations in Seattle, New Orleans, Cleveland, and Fort Worth. In 1983 OPUBCO bought the Opryland hotel and entertainment complex in Nashville, Tennessee, and media properties, including the Nashville Network, Country Music Television, WSM Radio, and the Grand Ole Opry, forming the publicly held Gaylord Entertainment in the process.

The *Daily Oklahoman* stands today as the centerpiece of the Oklahoma Publishing Company and is one of the largest family-owned newspapers in the United States, with circulation in excess of 225,000 daily and 330,000 on Sunday.

See also CITIES AND TOWNS: Oklahoma City, Oklahoma.

Philip D. Patterson
Oklahoma Christian University

Daily Oklahoman Archives, Tom and Ada Beam Library, Oklahoma Christian University, Oklahoma City. Dary, David. "A Work In Progress: The Oklahoma Publishing Company Celebrates 95 Years." *Daily Oklahoman*, supplement, November 8, 1998: 1–17.

DALLAS MORNING NEWS

The *Dallas Morning News* traces its roots to the thriving port city of Galveston, where in 1842 Samuel Bangs, a publisher from Boston, founded the *Galveston News*. After the Civil War, a Confederate colonel from North Carolina named A. H. Belo joined the *Galveston News* as bookkeeper. Belo quickly became a full partner, and the newspaper became the foundation of the A. H. Belo Corporation, now one of the largest diversified media companies in the United States.

In 1885 Belo told his mailroom manager, George Bannerman Dealey, to find a place in North Texas to start a sister publication. Dealey chose the small town of Dallas and named the newspaper the *Dallas Morning News*. When the *Dallas Morning News* was launched in 1885, its most serious challenge came from the far-off *St. Louis Post-Dispatch*, which had a greater circulation in Texas than any Texas newspaper. To meet this threat, the *Dallas Morning News* used a special train to deliver copies to McKinney, Sherman, Denison, and other towns in North and East Texas. It also used trains to deliver copies to Fort Worth to the west.

By 1906, the year the predecessor of the *Fort Worth Star-Telegram* began publication, the *Dallas Morning News* had reached a circulation of 38,000, and Dallas was soon to be the major city in North Texas. An often-bitter rivalry developed between Dallas and Fort Worth. Dallas was becoming a sophisticated metropolitan center, while Fort Worth remained a cow town and proudly identified itself as "Where the West Begins." While it had some circulation in the Fort Worth area, the *Dallas Morning News* concentrated most of its circulation efforts in the city of Dallas and cities in the northern and eastern regions of Texas. The *Fort Worth Star-Telegram*, looking

westward, became the newspaper for all of West Texas and into New Mexico.

An almost impenetrable wall grew up along the boundary line that separates Dallas County and Tarrant County, where Fort Worth is located. For most of the twentieth century, the *Dallas Morning News* and the *Fort Worth Star-Telegram* respected that boundary, and other than single-copy newsstand sales, each stayed on its own side of the county line. However, by the 1960s the thirty-mile-wide rural area between Dallas and Fort Worth began to explode in industry and population. Arlington grew almost overnight from 7,500 to more than 300,000. Several other cities in the former no-man's-land had exceeded 100,000 by the end of the twentieth century. This led to a major circulation war between the *Dallas Morning News* and the *Fort Worth Star-Telegram*. Both coveted the rapidly expanding population as possible subscribers and readers. In the 1990s both newspapers established Arlington editions that grew into the *Arlington Morning News* and the *Arlington Star-Telegram*. The circulation battle also includes the area to the north of Arlington known as the Mid-Cities. Most of this disputed territory is in Tarrant County.

Although the *Dallas Morning News* has become one of the largest newspapers in the country and now competes for the Plains border country to the west, it has never approached the influence of the *Fort Worth Star-Telegram* in the West Texas and eastern New Mexico portions of the Great Plains.

Gerald L. Grotta
Texas Christian University

A. H. Belo Corporation: Commemorating 150 Years, 1842–1992. Dallas: A. H. Belo, 1992.

DENVER POST

An integral ingredient in Colorado lore and pride, the *Denver Post* entered unfamiliar peaceful territory in 2001, when the 108-year-old daily newspaper ended a bitter feud with the *Rocky Mountain News* and began working with its former crosstown rival and new business partner. A joint operating agreement effectively ended one of the longest, most ruthless newspaper wars in the country. In its early years, the battle between the *Post* and the *News* included name calling, sensationalism, editorial crusades, and promotional stunts. In the spirit of a Wild West duel, the fight even spilled out into the streets near the state capitol in 1907, when *Post* owner Frederick Bonfils attacked and beat *News* owner Thomas Patterson, who had called Bonfils a "blackmailer" in a cartoon.

The *Denver Post* was founded in August 1892 as a weekly. Three years later, Harry Tammen and Frederick Bonfils purchased the then-daily *Evening Post* for $12,500 and began an all-out war against its four rival dailies, turning Denver's journalism scene into what one historian called "a three-ring circus." (The *Post*, in fact, even owned a circus in the early 1900s.) With its use of red headlines and lurid stories, the *Post* was proud of its yellow journalism. The other newspapers soon died or were merged. In 1926 Scripps-Howard Newspapers bought the *News* and merged it with the *Express*, leaving only the morning *News* and afternoon *Post*. Each newspaper tried furiously to put the other out of business and in the process lost millions of dollars. The *News*, which had been founded in 1859 by William Byers, almost perished around the time of World War II. It then switched to a tabloid format. But for forty years the *Post*, declaring itself "The Voice of the Rocky Mountain Empire," held the dominant position in the market.

The *Post* was sold in 1980 to the Times Mirror Company for $95 million and became a morning newspaper the following year. But its circulation declined until William Dean Singleton's MediaNews Group bought it in 1987, also for $95 million. The circulation war heated up, and both newspapers remained neck and neck in their race to gain the most subscribers. Nevertheless, when the joint operating agreement was announced in May 2000, the E. W. Scripps Company admitted the *Rocky Mountain News* had lost $123 million in the past decade. The *Post* meanwhile reported profits of $192 million in the same period. Both papers had ridiculously low penny-a-day subscription rates to attract readers, and both claimed the largest circulation gains in the country in 2000. The *Post* reported a daily circulation of 420,033 and Sunday circulation of 586,485, while the *News* had a daily circulation of 426,465 and Sunday circulation of 529,681.

The joint operating agreement, which merged business operations such as advertising and circulation under the Denver Newspaper Agency, was approved by U.S. Attorney General Janet Reno in January 2001 in record time. Both companies agreed to split the profits fifty-fifty, but the E. W. Scripps Company and the *News* had to pay $60 million to MediaNews and the *Post* to enter the arrangement. The editorial departments of the two newspapers remained independent, keeping Denver one of the dwindling number of two-newspaper towns (in 2001, fewer than twenty remained in the United States). In 2001 the two newspapers continued to publish competing newspapers Monday through Friday, but the *News* oversaw publication of a single newspaper on Saturdays, and the *Post* oversaw a single Sunday edition. The staffs of both newspapers vowed to continue the journalistic rivalry that has provided more than a century of interesting and colorful reporting to the people of Colorado. In 2000 both newspapers won Pulitzer Prizes for their coverage of the shootings at Columbine High School, the *Post* for reporting and the *News* for photography.

See also ASIAN AMERICANS: Hosokawa, William / CITIES AND TOWNS: Denver, Colorado.

Kris Kodrich
Colorado State University

Anton, Mike. "Battle of Wits, Words Made History." *Rocky Mountain News*, May 12, 2000: A5. Hosokawa, Bill. *Thunder in the Rockies: The Incredible Denver Post*. New York: William Morrow, 1976. Kreck, Dick. "A 108-Year-Old Street Fight: Newspapers Share a Long, Colorful History." *Denver Post*, May 12, 2000: A16.

EDMONTON JOURNAL

The first 1,000 copies of the *Edmonton Journal* rolled off the presses at the back of the Shamrock Fruit Store on November 11, 1903. The paper's founders were John Macpherson, Arthur Moore, and J. W. Cunningham, and the *Journal* faced tough competition from the well-established *Edmonton Bulletin*. In fact, the *Journal* failed to show a profit for five years. By 2002 the *Journal* employed 894 staff and had an average daily circulation of 145,000 copies.

The *Journal* grew with Edmonton, which was incorporated as a city in 1904. From its inception the *Journal* sided with the Conservative Party and therefore against the *Bulletin*, whose co-owner, Frank Oliver, was a Liberal cabinet minister. The *Journal* also was a champion of the development of the "new Northwest," a booster for the city and region, especially when economic times were hard in the 1920s and 1930s.

Under the control of John Imrie, who was publisher from 1921 to 1941, the *Journal* moved into a handsome new building on Bellamy Hill in 1921; branched out into radio, launching CJCA, Alberta's first radio station, in 1922; and won a Pulitzer Prize in 1938, the first time such an award had been made outside the United States. The honor was given for the paper's defense of freedom of the press in resisting William Aberhart's Social Credit government's bill to bring newspapers under government control. The *Journal* battled the bill in front-page editorials and all the way to the Supreme Court, which ruled against the government on March 4, 1938.

On January 20, 1951, the *Bulletin* stopped its presses for good, leaving the *Journal* as Edmonton's only daily newspaper until April 2, 1978, when the *Edmonton Sun*, a morning tabloid, printed its first edition. The *Journal*'s facilities were improved to keep pace with its expanded circulation, which had reached 95,881 in 1956. An addition doubled the size of the paper's building in 1952, a press building was added in 1955, and in 1980 the opening of the Eastgate production plant, complete with offset presses, inaugurated the modern era of the *Edmonton Journal*. For five years, from September 2, 1980, to April 8, 1985, the *Journal* put out both evening and morning editions, but thereafter, in keeping with nationwide trends, the paper published only a morning edition.

Recent years have seen the construction of a new fifteen-million-dollar office complex, which involved the demolition of the old 1921 structure, a landmark that city planners did not want to see erased. (Parts of the old facade were incorporated into the new structure.) The *Journal* also put $1 million into becoming part owner of the Edmonton Oilers, demonstrating again that Edmonton's leading paper not only reports the news of the city and region but also is part of that news.

David J. Wishart
University of Nebraska–Lincoln

EDWARDS, BOB (1864–1922)

One of Canada's leading journalists, Bob Edwards was a critic of government officials and the excessive moralism of the churches as well as a supporter of the emancipation of women and the temperance crusade. He was best known as the one-man staff, editor, and publisher of the *Calgary Eye Opener* and remembered for his off-color tales and jokes. Edwards built the paper's circulation and his own reputation for social criticism combined with humor.

Robert Chambers Edwards was born on September 12, 1864, in Edinburgh, Scotland. He was orphaned at an early age and, with his brother Jack, raised by an aunt. He was educated at Glasgow University, where he studied philosophy and literature. For a brief period, Edwards traveled throughout Europe, settling in the south of France, where he continued the family tradition of newspaper writing and publishing. His first enterprise was an English newspaper named the *Traveler*, which he published on the Riviera and which catered to English gentry traveling abroad.

In 1884 Bob traveled with his brother to the United States and for the next ten years found assorted jobs working on farms and cattle operations in Wyoming, Iowa, and Alberta, Canada. In 1897 he finally settled down in the small town of Wetaskiwin, fifty miles south of Edmonton. There he established the *Wetaskiwin Free Lance*, the first newspaper to be published between Edmonton and Calgary. Edwards wrote less about "real news" and more on the social issues of the day. The editor of the *Calgary Herald* was impressed by Edwards's humor and witty journalistic prose and offered to reprint some of his articles in the Calgary paper.

In 1898 Bob Edwards moved to Calgary, where he continued to publish and write for the *Wetaskiwin Free Lance*. He soon moved on to Winnipeg, where he struggled as a news reporter for the *Winnipeg Free Press*. Disillusioned as a writer for a large daily, Edwards returned to the small-town life he so enjoyed and set up shop in High River, where he published the first edition of the *Eye Opener* in March 1902. The hard-drinking, carefree Edwards created fictional characters and tales considered shocking by small-town standards, and eventually he moved his operation to Calgary. As soon as he was settled, Edwards continued to build his reputation by reporting on various local scandals with satire and wit.

Over the next twenty years Bob Edwards became known for standing up for the common person, highlighting the plight of prostitutes, and revealing the scams of fraudulent real estate developers. Personally, he battled severe alcoholism, so much so that in 1916 he was one of the supporters of prohibition in Alberta. A year later he married a Scottish woman who was less than half his age.

In the summer of 1920 Edwards published a soft-cover book of some of his best stories, editorials, and jokes. It was an enormous success and appeared regularly as an annual edition for the remainder of his life. Edwards died on November 14, 1922, leaving a long legacy of witty writings depicting the political, social, and economic times of the early Canadian western frontier. To honor Bob Edwards, Alberta Theater Projects initiated an award in his name recognizing Canadian writers who exemplify the spirit of freedom of expression.

Diane Howard
University of Calgary

Dempsey, Hugh. *The Best of Bob Edwards*. Edmonton, Alberta: Hurtig Publishers, 1975. Longpré, Kerry, and Margaret Dickson. *Provocative Canadians: In the Spirit of Bob Edwards*. Calgary, Alberta: Bayeux Arts, 1999. MacEwan, Grant. *Eye Opener Bob: The Story of Bob Edwards*. Saskatoon, Saskatchewan: Western Producer Prairie Books, 1974.

EMPORIA GAZETTE

For more than 100 years, the *Emporia Gazette* has covered the city of Emporia, Kansas, its joys, heartaches, and scandals, and surrounding Lyon County, providing Kansas with news and opinion that includes the state, nation, and world. It has endured as one of the state's strongest small dailies and has been a training ground for some of the state's best journalists.

Emporia, from its very beginning, had a strong tradition of newspapers, as did many pioneer communities. Its first newspaper, the *Kanzas News*, began just a few months after the town was founded in 1857, when Senator Preston Plumb started the newspaper to promote development and the Republican Party. A former owner of the *News*, J. R. Graham, founded the *Emporia Gazette* in 1890 but sold it to W. Y. Morgan during the 1893 depression.

Five years after its founding, when newspapers and the country were struggling financially, the *Gazette* was purchased for $3,000 by William Allen White, a twenty-seven-year-old Republican newspaperman ready to hone his reporting and editing talents. After writing for several Kansas publications, White considered purchasing newspapers in several northeast Kansas cities, including Lawrence, but decided on Emporia, the town where he was born and where he had attended college. White borrowed the money to purchase the paper from Governor E. N. Morrill, from the estate of Senator Plumb, from Plumb's brother George, and from Major Calvin Hood. All were paid back quickly, mostly from money made from the sale of White's books and stories, which were gaining popularity.

White played the role of small-town country editor, conscious of his role in bolstering the community. His editorials, often in support of small-town values, were frequently printed in national newspapers and magazines, bringing recognition to the *Gazette*. With new and faster presses and more efficient distribution, larger editions and wider circulation became possible, and the increased subscription rates and advertising revenue put the paper on a sound financial footing.

In many respects, the *Gazette* is similar to most local hometown newspapers. It covers the local area; it reflects its community's tastes; it records the town's history. Unlike most dailies, however, the *Gazette* also gained national prominence, as William Allen White became well known through his political associations, national writings, and Pulitzer Prize. As its reputation grew, the newspaper began to attract starstruck young journalists, who were trained by various *Gazette* managing and city editors. Many went on to become some of the state's best journalists.

To this day, the *Gazette*, appearing six days a week, maintains its roots in community coverage. It has stayed in the White family, first with his son and daughter-in-law, William Lindsay and Kathrine White, then with his granddaughter and her husband, Barbara and David Walker, and now his grandson and his wife, Chris and Ashley Walker. While the newspaper remains a training ground for many novice reporters, its editors help maintain continuity with long careers in the newsroom.

Sally E. Turner
Emporia State University

The Emporia Gazette's Album of Memories. Emporia KS: Emporia Gazette, 1976. Griffith, Sally Foreman. *Hometown News: William Allen White and the "Emporia Gazette."* New York: Oxford University Press, 1998. White, William Allen. *The Autobiography of William Allen White*. New York: Macmillan Publishing Company, 1946.

FORT WORTH STAR-TELEGRAM

In 1936 the *Amarillo Globe* said of the legendary publisher of the *Fort Worth Star-Telegram*: "West Texas is bound on the north by Colorado and Oklahoma, on the west by New Mexico, on the south by Mexico, and on the east by Amon Carter." Thirty years earlier there had been only two newspapers in Fort Worth—the morning *Telegram* and the morning *Record*. Then in 1906 young Amon Carter agreed to become advertising manager of a new evening newspaper, the *Star*.

Initially, the *Star* floundered, and it never managed to break even. Then in 1909, in an audacious move, the near-bankrupt *Star* bought the larger and much more successful *Telegram*, and the *Fort Worth Star-Telegram* was born, with Amon Carter as primary owner and publisher. Together, the new publisher and his newspaper were to become a major force in shaping not only Fort Worth but all of West Texas and eastern New Mexico—a sizable chunk of the Great Plains.

Until then, West Texas had been largely ignored by everybody. However, Amon Carter had a much different vision of the future of this vast expanse of hot, dry, windy plains. That future was to include a great oil boom and irrigated croplands to supplement the historic cattle industry. As Amon Carter would tell audiences, West Texas is larger than New York, Massachusetts, Pennsylvania, and Maryland combined. The *Fort Worth Star-Telegram* embraced the residents of West Texas, and the citizens of West Texas embraced the *Fort Worth Star-Telegram*. The newspaper would eventually serve an area of 350,000 square miles and deliver copies every day to homes up to 700 miles west of Fort Worth, well into New Mexico. It dominated the market in such West Texas population centers as Amarillo, Abilene, Lubbock, Midland-Odessa, and El Paso. By 1913 it had become the fourth-largest newspaper in Texas, with a circulation of 40,000. By 1918 its 66,000 subscribers made it the largest newspaper in all of Texas. Then in 1923 circulation reached 115,000, and it was the largest newspaper in the southern United States—larger than the *Dallas Morning News* or the *Houston Chronicle* or the *Atlanta Journal*. Much of this growth came from subscribers in West Texas and eastern New Mexico. It wasn't until midcentury that newspapers in much larger cities finally passed the *Fort Worth Star-Telegram* in circulation.

The decline of home-delivery circulation throughout West Texas and eastern New Mexico began in the second half of the century. Passenger trains that had delivered the newspaper to those far-flung towns stopped running, and there was no other economical way to spread the newspaper throughout this vast region. People in isolated West Texas communities had used the *Fort Worth Star-Telegram*'s ads from large Fort Worth department stores to order merchandise for mail delivery. When department stores—both independent and chain—began to open in West Texas they reduced the need for mail-order shopping, which in turn reduced the value of West Texas subscribers for the Fort Worth stores. Finally, as cities grew, the newspapers in West Texas began to improve and expand. In a way, the successful development of West Texas that had been fostered by the *Fort Worth Star-Telegram* helped reduce the need for that newspaper in much of the region.

On June 23, 1955, Amon Carter died, and his son, Amon Carter Jr., became publisher. Then in 1974 the *Fort Worth Star-Telegram* was purchased by Capital Cities of New York, and in 1996 Capital Cities/ABC merged with the Walt Disney Company. Within a year, Disney/ABC's publications, including the *Fort Worth Star-Telegram* and the *Kansas City Star*, were purchased by Knight-Ridder, the second largest newspaper group in the country.

By the end of the twentieth century, the *Fort Worth Star-Telegram* had changed its focus from West Texas to the Fort Worth metropolitan area and eastward into the rapidly growing Arlington and Mid-Cities area between Fort Worth and Dallas. But no story of the West Texas region of the Great Plains would be complete without the newspaper that "discovered" West Texas, nurtured it, promoted it, and served it so well for most of the first half of the century.

See also CITIES AND TOWNS: Fort Worth, Texas.

Gerald L. Grotta
Texas Christian University

Flemmons, Jerry. *Amon: The Texan Who Played Cowboy for America*. Lubbock: Texas Tech University Press, 1998. Meek, Phillip J. *Fort Worth Star-Telegram: "Where the West Begins."* New York: Newcomen Society in North America, 1981.

FREEMAN, LEGH (1842–1915)

Legh Freeman was born on December 4, 1842, in Culpeper, Virginia. During the Civil War he served as a telegraph operator in the Confederate army. He was captured in 1864 but later released after swearing allegiance to the Union and agreeing to serve in the American West. In April 1865 Freeman arrived at Fort Kearny, Nebraska, where troops were needed to guard the Oregon Trail. After being mustered out of the service late in 1865, Freeman acquired some old printing equipment and began editing and publishing the *Kearney Herald*. He was joined in 1866 by his brother Frederick, and when the Union Pacific moved past Kearney that fall, the brothers packed up their equipment, renamed their paper the *Frontier Index*, and moved to North Platte. Sometimes called the "press on wheels," the *Frontier Index* then moved from one railroad construction camp to the next, including the future towns of North Platte, Nebraska; Julesburg, Colorado; Laramie, Wyoming; and Ogden, Utah.

One study of Freeman's extant editorials found that 25 percent promoted town sites, 16 percent discussed local nonpolitical affairs, 13 percent local politics, 7 percent Indian issues, and 5 percent the newspaper itself. In his editorials he vociferously attacked Mormons, Chinese, Indians, politicians, opposition editors, construction-camp lawlessness, and President Ulysses S. Grant. On at least one occasion Freeman's biting editorials cost him his press and nearly his life. On November 20, 1868, in Bear River City, Dakota Territory (soon to be Wyoming Territory), a mob of infuriated railroad workers destroyed Freeman's printing equipment and drove him out of town.

Freeman never stayed in one place too long. Like the mountain men he emulated, the editor tried to stay ahead of advancing settlement. Freeman's brother Fred and later his wife, Ada, sometimes ran the paper while he traveled and sent home columns. Freeman stayed in the newspaper business long after the completion of the transcontinental railroad: he published newspapers in Utah, Montana, and Washington. He married three times and had four children. His later years were spent in Washington, where he published the *Washington Farmer* and became involved in the populist movement. Representing himself as the "Red Horse Candidate," Freeman failed twice to obtain a senatorial seat and finished last in the 1914 North Yakima mayoral election. He died February 7, 1915, in North Yakima, Washington.

See also CITIES AND TOWNS: "Hell on Wheels" Towns.

William E. Huntzicker
Bemidji State University

Heuterman, Thomas H. *Movable Type: Biography of Legh R. Freeman*. Ames: Iowa State University Press, 1979. Lent, John A. "The Press on Wheels: A History of the Frontier Index." *Journal of the West* 10 (1971): 662–99. Wright, Elizabeth. *Independence in All Things, Neutrality in Nothing: The Story of a Pioneer Journalist of the American West*. San Francisco: Miller Freeman Publications, 1973.

GARNER, ELMER

See PROTEST AND DISSENT: Garner, Elmer

HALL, MONTE (b. 1923)

Monte Hall, television celebrity and noted philanthropist, was born in Winnipeg on August 25, 1923, and brought up in the close-knit Jewish community there. His maternal grandfather migrated from the village of Poveltch in the Ukraine, stepping off the train in Winnipeg in 1901. Within a few years he had built a successful fruit and vegetable business. Hall traces his strong Jewish roots to lessons learned in his grandfather's home and to the example of his mother, a leading figure among Canadian Jewry. He believes that his Jewish upbringing in his grandfather's home—a home filled with four generations of relatives—gave him the sense of humor that prepared him for his show-business career.

While a student at the University of Manitoba in the early 1940s, Hall acted in musical and dramatic productions and served as a host of Canadian army shows. After graduation with a bachelor of science degree in 1945, he moved to Toronto and continued his career as an actor, emcee, and sportscaster. In New York from 1955 to 1960 he was emcee of NBC's radio show *Monitor*. Hall's big break came in Hollywood in 1963, when he and coproducer Stefan Hatos put together *Let's Make a Deal*, the game show where contestants from the audience dressed in outrageous costumes to get Hall's attention and offered items they had brought with them in exchange for valuable or nonsense prizes hidden in boxes behind a curtain. With Hall as the amiable host, *Let's Make a Deal* ran from 1963 to 1968 on NBC, from 1968 to 1976 on ABC, and briefly again on NBC in 1990–91.

Hall has also devoted his time to myriad charitable and philanthropic endeavors. He was recognized for this work in 1988, when he was made an Officer of the Order of Canada, the country's most prestigious award. Honorary degrees at the Universities of Manitoba (1987) and Haifa (1989) and at the Hahneman College of Medicine (1988) as well as induction into the National Broadcasters Hall of Fame (1995) also attest to Monte Hall's lifetime achievements.

David J. Wishart
University of Nebraska–Lincoln

Hall, Monte. "My Canadian Jewish Childhood." *Western States Jewish History* 26 (1994): 101–11.

HUNTLEY, CHET (1911–1974)

Chester Robert Huntley, the national news broadcaster and commentator, was born on December 10, 1911, in Cardwell, Montana. His father, Percy Adams "Pat" Huntley, was a railroad telegrapher; his mother, Blanche Wadine Tatham, was a former schoolteacher whose relatives had crossed the Plains in a covered wagon. His early life on a northern Montana ranch near the small town of Saco and in a succession of railroad towns in southern Montana greatly influenced his outlook on life and his reporting style, instilling in him a work ethic and an independent stance.

Huntley's broadcasting career began early.

His father copied down play-by-play reports of World Series baseball games as they came over the wire. Huntley announced the action out the depot window to the assembled fans. He graduated from Whitehall High School in 1929 and studied at Montana State College at Bozeman and the Cornish School of Arts in Seattle, Washington, before transferring to the University of Washington at Seattle, where he received his bachelor's degree in 1934.

While still a student, Chet Huntley worked at radio stations in Seattle and Spokane before transferring to KGW in Portland, Oregon. He then worked in Los Angeles for NBC (1937–39), CBS (1939–51), and ABC (1951–55). In 1956 he moved to New York City, where he did a ten-minute radio commentary (*Chet Huntley Reporting*), a Sunday afternoon television program, and a Saturday evening news program. Huntley's reporting style included commentary, although he was quick to note he was not interested in advocacy journalism.

Also in 1956 Huntley was teamed with David Brinkley, NBC's Washington correspondent, to broadcast the national political conventions. They worked so well together that NBC placed them on a fifteen-minute evening newscast, with Huntley in New York City and Brinkley in Washington DC. They did their first program on October 20, 1956. The newscast expanded to half an hour in 1963. NBC executives hoped that Huntley's solemn demeanor, serious tone, and rich voice would help compete with CBS's Edward R. Murrow.

The Huntley-Brinkley Report was an instant success. The show's closing signature ("Good night, Chet. Good night, David. And good night for NBC News") became familiar to the 20 million viewers they reached at the peak of their popularity. Their ratings remained high up to Huntley's departure July 31, 1970. The partnership helped mold the nightly national newscast into the principal daily news source now enjoyed by many Americans. *The Huntley-Brinkley Report* won every major news award, including seven Emmy Awards, four Peabody Awards, and two Overseas Press Club Awards.

Huntley had left CBS in 1951 because his bosses were unhappy with his liberal commentary and because he refused to sign a loyalty oath. One of his most controversial moves came on March 29, 1967, when he crossed picket lines set up by striking members of the American Federation of Television and Radio Artists (AFTRA). His coanchor, David Brinkley, honored the strike. Huntley said at the time he did not think newsmen belonged in a union with singers and dancers.

Huntley stayed active in retirement. He broadcast commentaries, advertised for American Airlines, and got the company to sponsor a television series, *The American Experience*. He also joined an advertising firm, Levine, Huntley, Schmidt, Inc. Chet Huntley died March 20, 1974, three days before the opening ceremonies for his twenty-five-million-dollar recreational complex called Big Sky near Bozeman.

Peter E. Mayeux
University of Nebraska–Lincoln

Chet Huntley Papers (1911–74), Montana State University Library, Bozeman. Huntley, Chet. *The Generous Years: Remembrances of a Frontier Boyhood.* New York: Random House, 1968.

IMMIGRANT NEWSPAPERS

Because the settlement of the Great Plains coincided with a period of heavy immigration to the United States, the immigrant press held a prominent position in the region. One of the primary roles played by immigrant newspapers was to educate the newly arrived. To accomplish this, the immigrant papers were initially printed in the native language of the target audience. Later, as immigrants learned to speak English, some papers abandoned the native language and converted to English. Others printed in both languages, and one, *Die Staatspresse*, was trilingual, printing in English, German, and Norwegian. The papers provided information about the local community, including the culture, economy, and government. News was reported on the national and international levels, especially targeting the immigrants' homeland. Some papers even sent reporters to Europe to gather information firsthand. It was also common for fiction and poetry to be included in the papers. Examples of these broad-based papers are *Den Danske Pionner*, a Danish paper published in Omaha, and the *Dakota Freie Presse*, a German paper published in a variety of locations in the Dakotas and Minnesota.

Other papers served the interests of particular groups. Papers for fraternal organizations, church groups, labor unions, and political parties were published to provide specific information for a relatively narrow audience. The Slovonic Benevolent Society of Texas, for example, published the *Vestnik* every week in West, Texas. The *Mennonite* was published for the Mennonites who lived near Newton, Kansas. The monthly *Katolicky Delnick* was published in Dodge, Nebraska, and, as its title suggests, it served the Czech Catholic workman. Also providing religious information was the *Ukrainski Visti*, serving Ukrainian immigrants in and around Edmonton, Alberta.

The impact immigrant newspapers had on the lives of their readers was twofold. First, the papers aided assimilation into the society and culture of the United States. They provided information that helped immigrants adjust to their new life and to fit in. However, the papers also slowed assimilation. By supplying information in the native language, the papers provided a means for the immigrant to live successfully in the United States with little or no English. In the early twentieth century, for example, the small Kaposvar Colony in Saskatchewan supported a Hungarian-language paper. Not only did the paper provide information in Hungarian, but it was also an advocate for cultural preservation issues such as Hungarian schools with Hungarian teachers to instruct in their native tongue. Some papers helped the ethnic community to grow. In his paper, *Pokrok Zapadu*, Omaha resident John Rosicky encouraged Czechs in Europe to immigrate to Omaha and join the thriving Czech community there. Dr. Friedrich Renner, editor of the *Nebraska Deutsche Zeitung*, declared that the goal of his paper was to spread the news of a territory where there was good land and other employment opportunities. He mailed copies of each issue to Germany, Austria, Alsace, and Lorraine.

Immigrant papers varied greatly in size, frequency of publication, location of publication, circulation, and longevity. They ranged from single page to multipage, from daily to monthly, and from a few hundred subscribers to several thousand. *Den Danske Pionner*, for example, was the largest of all Danish American weeklies, with a mailing list of 40,000 and an estimated readership of 100,000. Some newspapers were published outside the Plains but had wide circulation within the region. Others originated in communities on the Plains. Many of these were published in the larger communities on the periphery of the region, such as Omaha and Denver. Smaller towns, however, also played a part in the immigrant press. Some supported small papers, often with short life spans. The *Kansas Stats Tiding*, for example, survived for only one year in the Swedish settlement of Lindsborg, Kansas. Other small towns such as West, Texas, supported more than one paper, some of which were published well into the twentieth century.

Immigrant newspapers in the twenty-first century serve two audiences. Papers established in the nineteenth and early twentieth centuries are read primarily by the descendants of the original subscribers and those who are interested in maintaining their cultural heritage. Many of these papers have converted to English. The *Western News*, for example, began publishing in Swedish in 1888. In 1941 the newspaper converted to a dual-language format (English and Swedish), a practice it continues today. A few papers still publish in the native language. *Der Staats-Anzeiger*, begun in 1906, continues to publish weekly in German from its Bismarck, North Dakota, office. In Omaha, the *American Citizen* still publishes in Italian. New papers have emerged, serving a second audience of more recent immigrants to the Plains. *Viltis*, for example, has been published in Denver since 1942 for the Lithuanian population. The weekly *Rocky Mountain Jiho* has published in both English and Japanese since 1962. There are also numerous papers serving the Latino populations of the Central and Southern Plains, although many are published in towns lying just outside the boundaries of the region.

Kathleen L. Fimple
Wayne, Nebraska

Park, Robert E. *The Immigrant Press and Its Control.* New York: Harper and Brothers Publishers, 1922. Wynar, Lubomys R., and Anna T. Wynar. *Encyclopedic Directory of Ethnic Newspapers and Periodicals in the United States.* Littleton CO: Libraries Unlimited, 1976.

INDIAN COUNTRY TODAY

Indian Country Today is the most widely circulated and arguably the most influential Native newspaper in the world. Tim Giago (*Nanwica Kciji*, or Defender), Oglala Lakota, established the weekly paper in 1981 as the *Lakota Times*. Giago, born in 1934 on the Pine Ridge Reservation and educated at the Holy Rosary Mission School there, served in the U.S. Navy after high school. He attended San Jose State College in California and earned his bachelor's degree from the University of Nevada–Reno. Giago worked a variety of jobs before becoming an Indian affairs columnist for the *Rapid City Journal* in Rapid City, South Dakota, in 1979; he later became a full-time reporter. In 1981 he established the *Lakota Times* to provide news coverage for Pine Ridge. The paper expanded to cover other reservations in the upper Midwest and by 1986 was distributed to all reservations in South Dakota, North Dakota, Nebraska, and Montana. Unlike most Native American papers, which tend to focus on one tribe or reservation, the *Lakota Times* focused on all tribes and reservations. The paper's offices moved to Rapid City in 1989, and in 1991 the *Lakota Times* claimed a readership of 50,000. By 1999 circulation had reached 77,000, with pass-along readership estimated to be as high as 100,000.

With support from the Gannett Corporation, publisher of *USA Today*, Giago expanded to national coverage in 1992 and changed the name of the paper to *Indian Country Today*. The paper operated bureaus in Albuquerque, New Mexico, and Spokane, Washington, and used freelance reporters to cover other regions. Giago has used the paper and pieces written for national publications such as *USA Today*, the *New York Times*, and *Newsweek* to defend Lakota and other Native American interests. He may be most widely known for criticizing the use of Native Americans as sports team mascots.

Standing Stone Media, Inc., an operation of the Oneida Indian Nation of New York State, bought *Indian Country Today* in December 1998. Corporate headquarters moved to New York, but editorial headquarters remain in Rapid City. The independent paper's sale to a tribal entity raised concern among some members of the Native American Journalists Association, who feared the Oneidas might restrict the paper's editorial voice. Early indications, however, show that the tribe is not changing the paper's editorial process. The paper maintains a bureau in Washington DC and has reporters in the Southwest, California, Oklahoma, and the Northeast. An expanding pool of correspondents provides national coverage. The paper now claims distribution in all fifty states and seventeen foreign countries, and it operates an on-line version.

Todd M. Kerstetter
Texas Christian University

Andreassi, Diane. "Tim Giago." In *Notable Native Americans*, edited by Sharon Malinowski. Detroit: Gale Research, 1995: 164–65. Fitzgerald, Mark. "A 'New Model' for Tribal Ownership?" *Editor & Publisher*, October 23, 1999: 22–26. Riley, Sam G. *Biographical Dictionary of American Newspaper Columnists*. Westport CT: Greenwood Press, 1995.

INTERNET

The information age has early roots on the edge of the Great Plains with the work of John V. Atanasoff, a professor at Iowa State College (now Iowa State University), who led the development of the first all-electronic computer in 1940. The growth of the information age in the Great Plains is especially evident in the spread of the global computer network known as the Internet.

The National Science Foundation's NSFNET, established in 1986, was instrumental in the rise of the Internet from its beginnings in the Department of Defense to its place as a worldwide communications system. The NSFNET was envisioned as a national computer network to connect researchers at universities to the newly established supercomputer centers and to each other. The network design consisted of regional networks connected to a national backbone. The NSFNET was remarkably successful and became the basis of the modern Internet. In the summer of 1986 the NSF funded the creation of MIDnet, a regional network in the heart of the Great Plains. The original NSF grant recipients were eleven universities (predominantly land-grant institutions) in Arkansas, Iowa, Kansas, Missouri, Nebraska, Oklahoma, and South Dakota. In September 1987 MIDnet became the first regional network to be fully operational.

The first MIDnet network consisted of leased lines operating at 56 kilobits per second (Kb/s) connecting routers using the TCP/IP protocol at each campus to the NSFNET backbone through the National Center for Supercomputing Applications (NCSA) at the University of Illinois. Because of the land-grant character of the MIDnet consortium, all but one of the member institutions were located in relatively small cities lacking 56 Kb/s service. "Special assembly" by AT&T, the contractor for the communications lines, caused considerable expense and some delay, but final installation and testing of the lines were completed in September 1987, and MIDnet became operational.

The NSFNET and MIDnet grew quickly. By 1989 the NSFNET backbone had been upgraded to 1.544 Kb/s (T1) with the MIDnet hub at the University of Nebraska–Lincoln. Although MIDnet began as a university research network with a grant spearheaded by Doug Gale at the University of Nebraska–Lincoln, it was soon evident that success would take the Internet far beyond its initial purpose.

MIDnet shifted from being a university-based organization to nonprofit status in 1992. Two years later, MIDnet was acquired by Global Internet, a Palo Alto start-up company whose Network Services Division later was acquired by Verio in 1997. Similarly, the NSFNET was commercialized with the formation of the Internic in 1993 and its transfer to the private sector in 1995. Many businesses in the Great Plains contributed to the commercial development of the Internet. For example, MFS Communications of Omaha, Nebraska, pioneered fiber-optic networks in metropolitan areas around the world and established early commercial network access points (NAPS); and Ameritrade, also based in Omaha, began popularizing stock trading on the Internet in 1995.

The Great Plains Network (GPN) is the next-generation, regional, "Internet 2" network for research and instruction. GPN was founded in 1997, with many of the original MIDNET institutions. The increase in speed from the 56 Kb/s rate of the original MIDNET to the 155 megabits/second (Mb/s) OC3 and 622 Mb/s OC12 rates of the GPN illustrates the great and rapid progress of the Internet in the Great Plains.

The information age will influence greatly the future of the Great Plains. The Internet allows instant, broad communication of work, commerce, education, medical care, and entertainment, thus bridging in new ways the distances that both isolate and insulate residents of the Great Plains. This brings opportunities for benefits and risks of loss. The opportunities are in decentralization, allowing Great Plains residents to engage from distant locales in many more new and diverse activities. Given this new access, for example, the feasibility of economic enterprises locating in formerly stagnant small Plains towns is significantly enhanced. The risks are that communication technologies also create dynamics for efficiency that foster centralization of smaller enterprises from remote areas and for a general homogenization of regional distinctions.

Stephen E. Reichenbach
University of Nebraska–Lincoln
Carol Farnham
Lincoln, Nebraska
Dale Finkelson
University of Nebraska–Lincoln

KANSAS CITY STAR

The *Kansas City Star* was born September 18, 1880, founded by William Rockhill Nelson, who owned a construction business and the *Fort Wayne (Indiana) Sentinel*, and newspaperman Samuel Morss. The two left Fort Wayne's economic problems and moved to Kansas City, then a frontier boomtown with three newspapers that each sold for a nickel. Under "Colonel" Nelson's brash leadership and selling for two cents, the evening *Star* became a national newspaper and dominating political force that championed honest government and civic improvement. One of Nelson's many crusades led to a city park system that became a national model.

On October 19, 1901, Nelson bought a morning competitor, the *Kansas City Times*, and formed the "24-hour *Star*." Nelson died April 13, 1915, leaving one of the nation's best newspapers to heirs who ran it until it was sold in 1926 to thirty employees for $11 million. Roy A. Roberts, a Nelson disciple, became managing editor in 1928. Once a *Star* carrier and reporter, Roberts ultimately was president, editor, and general manager. His powerful influence on regional and national politics and his political acumen helped the *Star* retain its ranking among the nation's best through the 1950s.

The 1940s saw record expansion, but newsprint shortages that began during World War II hampered the *Star*'s growth. In 1945 the company purchased a Park Falls, Wisconsin, paper mill to supply newsprint, but the cost of mitigating the mill's pollution ultimately contributed to the *Star*'s sale. In 1955 the *Star* was found guilty of monopolistic advertising practices. It agreed to change practices and sell WDAF-TV, started in 1949, and WDAF radio, started in 1922. The controversy contributed to a sluggishness that infiltrated some areas, but the news-reporting operation thrived. In 1963 Roberts was succeeded by Richard B. Fowler, whose goal was diversification. But questionable purchases, other financial burdens, and changing national readership habits loomed. On February 15, 1977, Capital Cities Communications Inc. bought the *Star* for $125 million.

James H. Hale, named publisher the day sale papers were signed, made changes newspaper-wide, cutting costs while leading expansions and improvements that yielded record profits. Ultimately, however, declining circulation threatened afternoon newspapers nationwide. The *Times* and *Star* were combined, and the morning *Star* began on March 1, 1990.

On January 4, 1996, Capital Cities/ABC and Walt Disney Company agreed to merge. Ironically, Walt Disney had delivered the *Star* as a boy, but his applications as artist, office boy, and truck driver were rejected. Other celebrities also had ties to the *Star*. Ernest Hemingway worked there in 1917–18, and editor C. G. "Pete" Wellington helped develop Hemingway's writing style. On April 5, 1997, Knight-Ridder, the nation's second-largest newspaper company, bought the *Star* and three other newspapers for $1.65 billion.

The *Kansas City Star*, legendary for local coverage and attention to writing, has won seven Pulitzer Prizes and four George Polk Awards. Its daily circulation was at 275,535 in 2001, and the company's mission statement reflects Nelson's legacy: "Since 1880, The *Star* has been our area's preeminent communications company because of a commitment to one ideal: Building our community through knowledge."

See also CITIES AND TOWNS: Kansas City, Kansas and Missouri / FILM: Disney, Walt.

Bonnie Bressers
Kansas State University

Kansas City Star, Commemorative Centennial Issue, September 14, 1980. Stafford, D. "Sale Is Latest Chapter in *Star* History." *Kansas City Star*, April 15, 1997: A15.

LEADER-POST (REGINA)

The *Leader-Post* is the only newspaper published in Regina, Saskatchewan. It is typical of the monopoly papers operated across Canada by the nation's biggest chain, the Hollinger organization, which owns not only the *Leader-Post* but also the *Star-Phoenix* in Saskatoon and the province's two other dailies in Moose Jaw and Prince Albert.

The *L-P*, as it is popularly known, was

started by Nicholas Flood Davin, a flamboyant Irish lawyer, shortly after Regina was founded in 1882. Davin's small weekly paper, which he modestly called the *Leader*, reflected its owner's feisty personality. Davin, a Conservative, used the paper to propel himself into Parliament, then sold out to Walter Scott, a Liberal. Scott also used the *Leader* as a political stepping stone and eventually became Saskatchewan's first premier.

The *Leader* prospered and became a daily when Regina's economy boomed at the beginning of the twentieth century. After that, the paper went through several owners. Meanwhile, a competing paper, the *Regina Daily Post*, had started up. The Sifton family bought them both in 1928 and amalgamated them, enjoying a monopoly for the next seven decades before selling out to the profit-hungry Hollinger, which promptly fired a quarter of the staff to cut costs.

During its peak under the Siftons, the *Leader-Post* provided solid coverage of the city and southern Saskatchewan. It maintained bureaus in Moose Jaw, Swift Current, Yorkton, Weyburn, and Estevan as well as Ottawa. During those good years, from the 1950s to the 1970s, the *L-P* was the best source of news between Winnipeg and Calgary.

But over the past quarter-century, competition from television, declining reader interest, and a gradual shift in policy toward putting profit ahead of public service have combined to reduce the *L-P* to a shadow of its former self. It no longer holds a preeminent place in the journalistic community, and the remaining newsroom staffers have become so disgruntled that they recently voted to form a labor union.

Today's editions of the paper are filled with wire copy, human-interest features, and other easy-to-get material. The scaled-down newsroom staff attends car accidents and news conferences, but the paper offers little when it comes to enterprise or investigative reporting. An independent rival weekly recently failed, so the *L-P* has no competition and no incentive to improve.

News coverage is not the only thing that has declined. The once-spirited paper has become timid and bland. Today's editorial page comes out in favor of responsible citizenship, good government, and other banalities. The only thing the *Leader-Post* regularly gets upset about is the fate of the Saskatchewan Roughriders football team, which the sports department covers in the minutest detail.

The *L-P* is a big booster of the community, taking part in promotional events and beating the drum for good causes. The paper's appearance is better than its content. Its pages are well laid out, while reproduction of color ads and photos is good, thanks to a high-quality press and a modern plant.

See also CITIES AND TOWNS: Regina, Saskatchewan.

Jim McKenzie
University of Regina

MILITARY POST PUBLICATIONS

U.S. troop newspapers in both Spanish and English appeared in the Great Plains soon after the Mexican War (1846–48). These soldier newspapers included the *Anglo-Saxon*, the *Santa Fe Republican*, the *Flag of Freedom*, and the *Picket Guard*—one of the first substantial troop papers of the U.S. Army. The papers included items on American troop victories, the preparedness of Mexican troops, the need for accurate reporting, the rivalry between regular and volunteer troops, and the need to keep enlisted men's morale high. Although they generally lasted a short time, these small, letter-size sheets accustomed troops to having their own papers, even in combat zones.

In 1864, during the American Civil War, the *Frontier Scout*, a four-page, three-column weekly, appeared at Fort Union, Dakota Territory. The same name was used for a paper started in 1865 farther down the Missouri River at Fort Rice, Dakota Territory. It is likely that the same printing office produced both papers. Prisoner-of-war publications were not uncommon. On a sheet of unruled letter paper, a captain in the Connecticut Volunteers produced a handwritten publication, the *Old Flag*, at Camp Ford, Texas. Each single copy was read aloud to prisoners.

Post publications reflected the military's growing professionalism between the Civil War and the beginning of World War I. Weekly newspapers were established at several Plains military installations to help relieve boredom, inform troops, and recount life on the frontier. In articles, poems, drawings, cartoons, and editorials, readers learned about military policies and were informed about life at the post. Great Plains newspapers included the *Chugg Water Journal*, Fort Laramie; the *Phil Kearny Scout*, Fort Philip Kearny, Dakota Territory; the *Daily Telegraph*, Fort Bridger, Wyoming; and the *Plains*, Fort Larned, Kansas. The frontier soldier papers resembled their civilian counterparts with their mixture of wit and satire and their boosterism.

Publications were also established by veterans and other military groups. In 1888, for example, the United States Cavalry Association issued the *U.S. Cavalry Journal* from Leavenworth, Kansas, and after 1910 the Artillery Association published the *Field Artillery Journal* from Washington DC and Fort Sill, Oklahoma.

During World War I, camp newspapers typically were seven-column, four-page papers costing two cents a copy. Weekly issues aimed to boost troop morale and promote high moral standards. Many soldier papers were launched following the Armistice, including the *Jayhawker* in France, the "Unofficial Organ of the 137th Infantry," a unit with Kansas connections. A hospital paper, the *Fort Bayard News*, was published near Silver City, New Mexico, by the U.S. Army General Hospital. And in 1922 the first monthly issue of the *Military Review* was published at the Command and General Staff College at Fort Leavenworth, Kansas. The *Review* has been labeled the "Professional Journal of the U.S. Army" because of its articles on military philosophy and tactics and its influence on army doctrine.

Long before Pearl Harbor, GI papers were started to help train draftees. Two of these papers were the *Camp Wolters Longhorn*, published near Mineral Wells, Texas, and the *Rainbow Reveille* at Camp Gruber, Oklahoma. During the war, other troop newspapers emerged, including BAM, published in 1943 at the Naval Air Gunner's School, Purcell, Oklahoma. World War II military publications observed tight editorial controls that produced items that were bland, traditional, and predictable. Most were weeklies printed by letterpress or offset, although several were mimeographed issues. Writers with little or no actual journalism experience produced many of the camp papers.

Several Great Plains military post publications continue journalistic traditions that began in the nineteenth century. Some of these are the *Field Artillery Journal* (a magazine) and *Military Review*.

See also WAR: Military Bases.

Peter E. Mayeux
University of Nebraska–Lincoln

Cornebise, Alfred Emile. *Ranks and Columns: Armed Forces Newspapers in American Wars*. Westport CT: Greenwood Press, 1993.

MOYERS, BILL (b. 1934)

Bill Moyers was born Billy Don in Hugo, Oklahoma, on June 5, 1934. He grew up in Marshall, Texas. Marshall was a small town, and books were Moyers's entry into the larger world outside his home. He attributes his love of the spoken and written word to growing up among storytellers in East Texas, including his father, who had only a fourth-grade education but was a well-known spinner of yarns.

Moyers's own first stories were as a print journalist, beginning with a part-time job at the age of fifteen on the local *Marshall Messenger*. He later attended the Southwestern Baptist Theological Seminary and became a fully ordained Baptist minister. Journalistic and ministerial careers were followed by a third one in politics. At twenty-seven he joined the staff of Texas senator Lyndon Johnson, and he served Johnson in one capacity or another from 1959 to 1966. He was on Johnson's staff through the Texas politician's first year as vice president and his first three years as president after John F. Kennedy's assassination. As Johnson's press secretary during the early part of the Vietnam War, Moyers later joked that the administration faced a credibility gap "so bad we didn't believe our own press releases." It was an ironic position for him to be in, considering his later image as journalistic truth seeker, and it occasioned some bitter controversies with critics in later years.

After leaving the Johnson administration Moyers reentered the newspaper business for three years as publisher of Long Island's *Newsday*. In 1970 the paper was bought by the *Los Angeles Times*, and Moyers was replaced. Moyers then began his distinguished career as a journalist and reporter on public television.

More familiar with the worlds of politics and publishing than television when he first appeared on WNET-TV, New York's PBS station, in 1970, Bill Moyers worked alternately out of the Public Broadcasting Service and CBS in a variety of settings and with a wide range of producers. He extended the "think-piece" tradition of Edward R. Murrow in filmed and taped interviews. His dedication to the written word, his ability to provide historical context for central themes in American life, and his moral passion recalled Murrow at his best. In interviews with artists, scientists, politicians, and provocative thinkers of all kinds, Moyers brought to television what he called the "conversation of democracy." The foundation support and funding Moyers elicited in the 1970s and early 1980s gave him degrees of freedom few broadcasters possessed, and he was constantly working to consolidate his position of independence from both network and governmental control. Never a talk-show host in conventional terms, he produced 600 hours of programming (filmed and videotaped conversations and documentary interviews) between 1971 and 1989 alone, or the equivalent of more than half an hour of programming a week for eighteen years.

Many of Moyers's programs have also had significant afterlives. Filmed conversations with mythology scholar Joseph Campbell and poet Robert Bly sold tens of thousands of copies in videocassette after they were aired. One of Moyers's programs, "Marshall, Texas," in the *Creativity* series, celebrated his own hometown. Produced by David Grubin, many consider it one of his finest pieces of work. Moyers also produced books to accompany many of his most successful television series, for example, *The Secret Government* (1988), *A World of Ideas* (1989), *A World of Ideas II* (1990), and *Healing the Mind* (1992). These books consistently placed Moyers on the *New York Times* best-seller list.

What Bill Moyers proved, beginning in the 1970s and then into the 1980s and 1990s, was that television talk could be both subtle and profound—and much more versatile than most people thought. He showed that despite limitations imposed on televised talk by the "commodification" of most talk-show formats, the range of what could be said on television need not be limited to superficialities. From early Great Plains roots, Moyers rose to be considered one of the people who most faithfully followed Edward R. Murrow in raising the standards of journalism, public debate, and inquiry on the most powerful medium of public presentation in the United States: television.

See also POLITICS AND GOVERNMENT: Johnson, Lyndon Baines.

Bernard M. Timberg
Johnson C. Smith University

NATIVE AMERICAN RADIO

Radio stations owned and operated by Native Americans and Native Canadians serve much of the Great Plains. The delivery systems are different in the two countries, but the goals are similar: to help preserve and promote Indigenous languages and cultures.

Broadcast media were once negative forces in Indigenous communities because they bombarded the communities with Western languages, cultures, and values. The media of the dominant culture overwhelmed and imperiled fragile traditional cultures. In recent years, however, electronic media owned and operated by Indigenous people have helped to restore the balance.

The first Native American radio station went on the air in 1973. A scattered few additional stations followed during the rest of the decade, but their development was hampered by a lack of funds. A change in federal government policy in the 1980s provided more resources to equip and operate Native stations, and their numbers grew steadily. As of 1999, some forty stations were broadcasting across the United States, and others were being planned.

Fourteen of the Native stations serve the American Great Plains. Each of the stations operates independently. They are licensed variously to tribal councils, community colleges, church groups, and nonprofit corporations. Half of the stations are located in the Dakotas, with three in North Dakota and four in South Dakota. Montana, Wyoming, and Colorado are each home to one station, and there are four in New Mexico. One is being planned for western Minnesota. There are no Native stations in Nebraska, Oklahoma, Texas, or Kansas.

Some stations receive programming from the National Public Radio network, but most do not because of the expense involved in being a member of the network. Most do receive satellite-delivered programming such as *National Native News* (a newscast) and *Native America Calling* (a call-in program) and other services of the American Indian Radio on Satellite Network (AIROS). Many non-Native stations in the region also broadcast some of these programs. Popular music and public service programs, including coverage of powwows and other cultural events, are also featured on Native stations. Traditional languages are used extensively on some stations, while others do little or no Native-language programming because the languages are seldom used anymore or there are multiple Indigenous languages in a listening area, which limits the use of any single language.

Indigenous stations also serve the Canadian provinces in the Great Plains. Similar to the situation in the United States, Indigenous communities had little control of the media that reached them until the 1980s, when the Canadian government began to fund and support Native-controlled electronic media that would protect and preserve Indigenous languages and cultures. Alberta, Saskatchewan, and Manitoba are each home to sophisticated radio networks that deliver signals to dozens of communities in each province. Corporations in each province provide this service. In Alberta, CFWE-FM radio, owned and operated by the Aboriginal Multi-Media Society, reaches forty-six communities in the province by satellite. In Saskatchewan, the Missinipi Broadcasting Corporation provides the service to more than thirty communities via FM transmitters or cable. In Manitoba, the Aboriginal FM Network of Native Communications Inc. reaches seventy sites. This centralized network system is different from the American model but is an efficient means of reaching the large and sparsely populated regions that are served.

Bruce L. Smith
Southwest Texas State University

Browne, Donald R. *Electronic Media and Indigenous Peoples: A Voice of Our Own?* Ames: Iowa State University Press, 1996. Keith, Michael C. *Signals in the Air: Native Broadcasting in America.* Westport CT: Praeger, 1995. Smith, Bruce L., and M. L. Cornette. "Electronic Smoke Signals: Native American Radio in the United States." *Cultural Survival Quarterly* (spring 1998): 28–31.

NEBRASKA PRESS ASSOCIATION V. STUART

See LAW: *Nebraska Press Association v. Stuart*

NEUHARTH, ALLEN (b. 1924)

Allen H. Neuharth, the founder of USA *Today*, is a self-made multimillionaire who has never forgotten his South Dakota roots. Neuharth's pioneering use of a lighter, brighter style, coupled with a heavy reliance on color and graphics, changed the face of the American newspaper. He also is the founder of the Freedom Forum, a nonprofit, nonpartisan media foundation dedicated to free speech and free press for people around the world.

Born on March 22, 1924, in Eureka, South Dakota, Neuharth watched his mother, Christina, struggle to make ends meet and raise two young children after his father, Daniel, died when Neuharth was a toddler. Neuharth later would describe his mother as the first victim of discrimination he knew; her plight, and that of the state's Native American population, had a profound impact on him.

After Daniel Neuharth's death, the family moved to Alpena so Christina could be near her family. It was there that young Al got his first taste of newspapering, as a delivery boy and later in the composing room of the weekly *Alpena Journal*. He graduated from Alpena High School and enlisted in the army, serving with General George Patton as a combat infantryman in World War II. He received the Bronze Star.

Following the war, Neuharth took advantage of the GI Bill to attend the University of South Dakota in Vermillion, where he majored in journalism and served as the editor of the college paper, the *Volante*. After graduating, Neuharth and a friend founded a statewide tabloid called *SoDak Sports* that lasted only two years before folding. Neuharth attributes that early failure with giving him the courage to take chances and achieve success later in life.

After a series of reporting, editing, and management jobs at newspapers around the country, Neuharth joined Gannett in 1963 and ultimately became president, chairman, and chief executive officer of the company. It was at Gannett that Neuharth founded *USA Today* and became a vocal advocate for the hiring, training, and promotion of women and minorities.

Neuharth makes frequent trips back to his native state, including an annual visit to the University of South Dakota campus for the presentation of the Allen H. Neuharth Award for Excellence in Journalism to a prominent print or broadcast journalist. A two-million-dollar gift from the Freedom Forum in 2000 enabled renovation of a building that was named for Neuharth and houses the Department of Contemporary Media and Journalism, the student newspaper, TV and radio facilities, the Freedom Forum Neuharth Center, and all other media operations on the campus. Through the Freedom Forum, Neuharth also has been instrumental in establishing professional development and recruitment programs for Native American journalists and in providing support for the Crazy Horse Monument in the Black Hills.

Neuharth has two grown children from his first marriage. He and his current wife, Dr. Rachel Fornes, reside in Cocoa Beach, Florida, with their six adopted children.

Cheryl Arvidson
Freedom Forum Newseum

Boye, Will. "The Most Notable Ambassadors of Diversity 2001." *Proud* (winter 2001): 13–23. Neuharth, Allen H. *Confessions of an S.O.B.* New York: Doubleday, 1989.

NYE, BILL (1850–1896)

Edgar Wilson "Bill" Nye was born on August 25, 1850, in Shirley, Maine. His family moved to Wisconsin when he was two years old. Nye attempted farming and teaching but was unsuccessful. He also studied law but did not pass the bar in Wisconsin. Leaving Wisconsin in 1876, he made his way to Laramie City, Wyoming Territory, where he worked as a reporter for the *Laramie Sentinel*. Nye next began a two-year stint as editor of the *Laramie Boomerang*, a newspaper named after his unpredictable mule. His satirical editorials and feature stories soon spread his fame far beyond Wyoming.

In addition to his work as an editor, Nye passed the Wyoming bar and practiced law. He also served as justice of the peace, U.S. commissioner, and U.S. postmaster. In 1877 he married Clara Francis Smith, and together they had seven children. He published two works while living in Wyoming, *Bill Nye and Boomerang* (1881) and *Forty Liars and Other Lies* (1882). In 1883 spinal meningitis forced him to seek healthier surroundings. Following a short recuperative period in Greeley, Colorado, Nye returned to his childhood home of Hudson, Wisconsin.

In 1885 Nye began a second career as a platform lecturer. He was wildly successful, rivaling Mark Twain in popularity. He delivered his humorous lectures, sometimes alone and sometimes with other humorists such as James Whitcomb Riley, until his death in 1896. He was soon a household name, and his gangly, bald figure, familiar through both the lecture circuit and the humorous illustrations included throughout his books, made him a particularly well-known celebrity.

Nye continued to write throughout his career as a lecturer, his style becoming progressively more refined and containing less of the jocular humor that had been in vogue during the previous decades and that reads poorly today. In 1887 he published *Bill Nye's Remarks*, and in 1888 he and his longtime partner, Riley, published *Nye and Riley's Railway Guide*, their take on the popular railroad guides of the era. In 1887 Nye returned to regular newspaper work when he became a writer for the Sunday edition of the *New York World*. He moved to New York City in that year, remaining there until 1891, when his newspaper columns became syndicated in seventy newspapers.

With his health still frail from spinal meningitis, Nye left New York City for Asheville, North Carolina. He continued writing and lecturing, producing his two best-known works, *Bill Nye's History of the United States* (1894) and *Bill Nye's History of England from the Druids to the Reign of Henry VIII* (1896).

A gentle wit, Nye himself was often the focus of his jokes. Regretfully, he also adopted the prejudices of his day. He specialized in lampooning the self-important, including politicians and recent arrivals to the Plains from back east. Although he spent less than ten years in the Plains, the experience proved to be central to his writings. Nye adopted the western love of play on words, exaggeration, and a sense of pragmatism. In early 1896 Nye suffered a series of strokes that finally took his life on February 22 at his home near Asheville, North Carolina.

Charles Vollan
University of Nebraska–Lincoln

Keterson, David B. *Bill Nye: The Western Writings.* Boise ID: Boise State University Press, 1976. Nye, Frank Wilson, ed. *Bill Nye: His Own Life Story.* New York: Century Company, 1926.

OMAHA WORLD-HERALD

In 1885 a young, wealthy lawyer named Gilbert M. Hitchcock and four business partners decided that the booming city of Omaha, Nebraska, needed an independent newspaper. Hitchcock founded the *Omaha Daily World* on August 24, 1885, promising a newsy newspaper for business people. The paper struggled financially in the early years, but Hitchcock, who provided most of the capital and owned almost all the paper's stock, paid $30,000 for the competing morning *Herald*, and on July 15, 1889, the combined *Omaha World-Herald* hit the streets.

Hitchcock's independent stance didn't last, and his interest in Democratic politics helped turn the paper Democratic by 1888. The turn came just in time to boost the political career of young politician William Jennings Bryan. In 1894 Hitchcock and Bryan worked out an arrangement that put Bryan on the *World-Herald* masthead as editor in chief. Bryan wanted a platform for his beliefs, and Hitchcock thought Bryan's editorials would help boost the paper's circulation. Bryan, who received a salary and free rail passes as editor, was mostly absent. Political reporter and editor Richard Metcalfe rewrote Bryan's notes into editorials. The arrangement failed to build circulation, and Bryan left the paper two years later when he first won the Democratic nomination for president.

Hitchcock, who continued as head of the newspaper during his own political career of three terms in the House of Representatives and two terms as a senator, died in 1934. His son-in-law Henry Doorly became president of the World Publishing Company, the publisher of the *World-Herald*. More familiar with the business side of running a newspaper, Doorly worked to standardize ad policies and practices. He became disenchanted with the New Deal and Democrats, switching the paper's political allegiance to the Republican Party.

In 1937 the *World-Herald* became the only paper in the city after the demise of the Hearst-owned *Omaha Bee-News*. After Doorly's retirement in 1955, Walter E. Christenson took over. Harold W. Andersen succeeded Christenson, followed by John A. Gottschalk in 1989.

The *World-Herald*, owned by Hitchcock and family members since 1885, attracted the interest of Samuel Newhouse of the Newhouse newspaper chain in 1962. This interest prompted Omaha construction executive Peter Kiewit to make a successful bid for the paper to keep the ownership local. After Kiewit's death in 1979, ownership was divided, with about 80 percent going to nonunion employee-stockholders and the remaining 20 percent to the Peter Kiewit Foundation.

A regional newspaper with morning and evening editions, the *World-Herald* is distributed across Nebraska and into surrounding states. The paper now takes a moderate conservative stance. In 2001 production switched to a new 100-million-dollar press and plant in downtown Omaha.

The *World-Herald* has won three Pulitzer Prizes. The first went to longtime editor Harvey Newbranch for a 1919 editorial written after a mob lynched a black prisoner. Newbranch's editorial called for sanity. In 1943 the paper won the Public Service Pulitzer for collecting about six million tons in a scrap metal drive. Photographer Earle Bunker won the third Pulitzer in 1944 for a photo of a soldier returning to his family.

See also AFRICAN AMERICANS: Omaha Race Riot / CITIES AND TOWNS: Omaha, Nebraska.

Carol Zuegner
Creighton University

Limprecht, Hollis J. *A Century of Service, 1885–1985.* Omaha: Omaha World-Herald Company, 1985. Roesgen, Bill. "Staying the Course." *American Journalism Review* 21 (1999): 40–46.

PEFFER, WILLIAM ALFRED (1831–1912)

William Alfred Peffer was a prominent newspaper editor who helped organize the People's

Party and became the first Populist U.S. senator. Born in Cumberland County, Pennsylvania, on September 10, 1831, Peffer farmed and taught school in several states before settling in Fredonia, Kansas, in 1870. There he purchased a small newspaper that he renamed the *Fredonia Journal*.

A Republican, Peffer was elected a state senator in 1874 and a presidential elector in 1880, but he was more involved in journalism than politics. In 1875 he moved to Coffeyville, renamed his newspaper the *Coffeyville Journal*, and became active in the Kansas Editors Association. In 1881, leaving a son to run the *Coffeyville Journal*, Peffer moved to Topeka as editor of the *Kansas Farmer*, the state's foremost farm journal and most widely circulated newspaper. He also became an associate editor for the *Topeka Capital*, the state's leading Republican daily. But he followed a nonpartisan course in making the *Kansas Farmer* an influential reform newspaper, advocating railroad regulation, financial reform, antimonopolism, and political democratization. He urged farmers to organize, and the Farmers Alliance made the *Farmer* its official state paper.

In 1890 Peffer's editorials and speeches helped the alliance launch the People's Party of Kansas, which defeated the Republicans and in 1891 elected him senator. Resigning from the *Farmer*, he became the major shareholder of the *Topeka Advocate*, the leading Populist newspaper, and organized and became the first president of the Kansas Reform Press Association. His books, *The Way Out* (1890) and *The Farmer's Side: His Troubles and Their Remedy* (1891), were fundamental Populist literature.

Peffer chaired the 1891 Cincinnati conference that organized the national People's Party, and he became the principal advocate of Populist measures in Congress. He used his official salary to help start the *National Watchman* as a Populist newspaper in Washington DC, and in 1895 he took control of the *Advocate*. He consistently promoted a radical and independent course for the Populist Party but gradually lost influence as it turned to a policy of fusion on the basis of free silver. He was not reelected in 1897 and shortly thereafter sold the *Advocate*. He continued to write for newspapers and magazines on agricultural and economic topics until his death in Grenola, Kansas, on October 6, 1912.

See also POLITICS AND GOVERNMENT: Populists (People's Party).

Peter H. Argersinger
Southern Illinois University

Argersinger, Peter H. *Populism and Politics: William Alfred Peffer and the People's Party*. Lexington: University Press of Kentucky, 1974. Peffer, William A. *Populism, Its Rise and Fall*, edited by Peter H. Argersinger. Lawrence: University Press of Kansas, 1992.

RADIO

Radio was most significant in the social life and economic development of the Great Plains from the early 1920s through the 1960s. An article in *Radio World* in September 1922

Listening to the radio, Aberdeen, South Dakota, November 1940

identified thirty-two radio stations operating in Kansas and Nebraska. The rest of the Great Plains shared another twenty radio stations, the majority located on the perimeter of the region.

There was a great deal of enthusiasm about the arrival of radio. When KDYS in Great Falls, Montana, went on the air in 1922 nearly 800 people crowded around a single radio at a local store to hear the first broadcast. The broadcast was cut short by a mechanical failure, and the radio station went off the air the following year, but the event signified the popularity of radio.

The region's residents eagerly welcomed radio because it reduced boredom and isolation and helped them feel connected with the rest of the country. Rural communities listened to the same news and entertainment programs heard by the rest of the nation. Rural families in the Great Plains, like other families in America, would gather around the radio to listen to their favorite evening programs. NBC was heard over KFYR in Bismarck and KOA in Denver. In Omaha, KOIL aired the NBC Basic Blue Network, while WOW aired NBC Basic Red. CBS was heard over KLZ in Denver, WNAX in Yankton, and WIBW in Topeka. WBAP in Fort Worth aired NBC programming but also carried the Texas Network.

Regional and local radio stations offered a variety of programs that targeted local audiences. Religious services were broadcast for people who could not leave the farm for Sunday services. Educational programs were broadcast from stations such as KOOW of the Oklahoma College for Women in Chickasha, Oklahoma, and KFJM from the University of North Dakota in Grand Forks. The U.S. Department of Agriculture (USDA) recognized the important benefits of radio and sponsored a number of programs that provided radio stations in rural areas with up-to-date agricultural and household information. The USDA programming provided a cost-effective way for small local stations to fill their schedule.

Women were a particularly important market because radio provided companionship during routine daily chores. Home economists working for the USDA, the Rural Electrification Administration (REA), and other groups provided a variety of radio programs that targeted women in rural locations.

A radio was generally inexpensive to own and operate, and in most cases the purchase of a single radio provided years of service. Battery-powered radios were a common appliance in rural homes, and the battery from the family automobile was a useful way to power the radio. The automobile was parked on an incline before the battery was removed so the car could be rolled to a start if the power of the battery had been drained by an evening of listening to the radio. Most rural listeners developed recharging systems to maintain the battery's power. The arrival of REA power during the late 1930s through the early 1950s allowed rural residents to switch to AC-powered radios. REA reports indicate that the AC radio was the most frequently purchased household electrical appliance of new REA electrical users.

In addition to its popularity as a form of entertainment, radio brought significant economic benefits to the Great Plains. Two informational benefits of radio were critical to the economic lives of Great Plains residents. First, the accuracy and availability of weather reports improved. Residents were alerted about approaching violent weather in their immediate area. Weather changes were more accurately tracked as local forecasting improved. This was especially important when deciding a planting or harvesting schedule or when to gather or release livestock. The second major informational benefit of radio was the availability of up-to-date market reports. As early as 1922, KFKA in Greeley, Colorado, regularly provided information about livestock prices in Denver. Radio provided rural communities and residents access to accurate and timely trade information. Decisions about when to buy and sell products and commodities were based on the latest market information from Chicago, Denver, Fort Worth, Kansas City, and other regional trade centers. Radio gave Great Plains residents a greater sense of freedom and control over their economic lives.

Radio also provided local businesses with an advertising medium that could reach into remote areas of their communities and expand their markets. Seed, tires, batteries, and other important farm goods were advertised over the radio, as were household items and clothing. For example, the Gurney Seed and Nursery Company of Yankton, South Dakota, purchased WNAX radio for $2,000 in 1927 and developed a strong local clientele and mail-order business by advertising a wide variety of goods over the radio. The company developed and sponsored some of the most popular music programs in the state and was one of the first stations to feature Great Plains musicians such as the Lawrence Welk Band.

Radio delivered entertainment, companionship, education, religion, weather reports, market reports, and a wide variety of informational programs that made life in the Great Plains easier and more enjoyable. Radio allowed the residents of the Great Plains their first opportunity to feel as though they were in tune with the rest of the nation. The arrival of television in the 1950s and 1960s and the continued development of advanced media delivery systems eventually diminished radio's importance in the region.

Michael Brown
University of Wyoming

Barnouw, Erik. *A History of Broadcasting in the United States*. New York: Oxford University Press, 1966. Smulyan, Susan. *Selling Radio*. Washington DC: Smithsonian Institution Press, 1994. Wik, Reynold. "The Radio in Rural America in the 1920s." *Agricultural History* 55 (1981): 339–50.

RHODES, RICHARD (b. 1937)

Author and journalist Richard L. Rhodes is not to be envied for his childhood. Born in Kansas City, Kansas, on July 4, 1937, Rhodes lost his mother to suicide thirteen months later. His father, a mechanic with the Missouri Pacific Railroad, moved Richard and his older brother, Stanley, from one boardinghouse to another throughout the city. In 1947 Richard's father married a sadistic woman whom, even when he was an adult, Richard still feared. Beaten and starved by their stepmother and ignored by their father, the boys eventually found sanctuary in the Andrew Drumm Institute, a boys home located on a farm near Independence, Missouri. Books were Richard's window to the wider world, and, against all odds, he gained access to that world when he was admitted to Yale.

He graduated in 1959, and, after working as a trainee writer for *Newsweek* and then as an editor at Hallmark Cards, he began writing seriously when he was in his thirties, and he has never stopped. His first book, *The Inland Ground: An Evocation of the American Middle West* (1970), was praised for its portraits of midwestern people and places. His most acclaimed work, *The Making of the Atomic Bomb* (1987), brought Rhodes a National Book Award, the National Book Critics Circle Award, and a Pulitzer Prize. Candid analyses of his own sexuality (*Making Love: An Erotic Odyssey*, 1992) and his harrowing childhood (*A Hole in the World: An American Boyhood*, 1990) are among the twelve nonfiction and four fiction books he has written. Rhodes has also made numerous contributions to newspapers and magazines both as author and editor.

Despite his successes, Rhodes has never forgotten his abusive childhood, and years of heavy drinking took their toll until he quit drinking when he was nearing fifty. He maintains that all his work, whatever the specific subject matter, is a repetition of one theme: men faced with violence who struggle against it and find, perhaps, a ray of hope.

David J. Wishart
University of Nebraska–Lincoln

Jones, Daniel, and Jorgenson, John D., eds. *Contemporary Authors*. New Revisions series. Detroit: Gale Research, 1997: 58: 354–58. Rhodes, Richard. *A Hole in the World: An American Boyhood*. New York: Simon and Schuster, 1990.

SEVAREID, ERIC (1912–1992)

Like many writers who grew up in frontier towns and achieved national reputations, Eric Sevareid, CBS World War II correspondent and TV commentator of the 1960s and 1970s, viewed his youth in Velva, North Dakota (population 800), with ambivalence. As a small boy he climbed the surrounding hills and gazed over the wheat fields, gaining an early sense of the infiniteness of his human possibilities. In his memoir, *Not So Wild a Dream* (1946), he idealizes Velva as a symbol of the spirit of democracy that won World War II. But after moving to Minneapolis at the age of twelve in 1926, following his father's bank failure, he returned only three times, twice as a magazine or TV journalist to write about himself.

Born Arnold Eric Sevareid on November 26, 1912, son of Alfred Eric Sevareid, a local banker, and Clara Hougen, daughter of a Norwegian Lutheran minister and a regal woman who encouraged him to read widely, Sevareid inherited Norwegian reticence and Lutheran moral integrity.

Young Sevareid crammed more adventure into his youth than most men experience in a lifetime. At seventeen, with an older boy, Walter Port, he paddled a canoe 2,000 miles from Minneapolis to the Hudson Bay. He rode the rails to California during the Great Depression to work for the summer in a gold mine. At the University of Minnesota his greatest love was the student paper, the *Minnesota Daily*, and his greatest disappointment was not being named editor because, he was convinced, the university president resented his opposition to ROTC. As a cub reporter for the *Minneapolis Star* he saw the local establishment's use of police power to brutally suppress the truckers strike as one face of domestic fascism; the other face was the Silver Shirts movement, which Sevareid exposed in a series for the *Minneapolis Journal*.

In 1935 he married Lois Finger, the law student daughter of the university's track coach, and they moved to Paris, where Sevareid became a reporter for the Paris edition of the *New York Herald*. Impressed by his coverage of a murder trial, CBS's London-based Edward R. Murrow invited him to join the news team —eventually including William L. Shirer, Charles Collingwood, Winston Burdett, and Howard K. Smith and known as "Murrow's Boys"—that he was putting together to cover the outbreak of World War II. Lois, who had just given birth to twins, Peter and Michael, returned home as Sevareid covered the fall of Paris, which he described as "a beautiful woman in a coma, not knowing or asking why."

Sevareid joined Murrow in London and endured the blitz, then rejoined his family in Washington, amazed to discover that his broadcasts from France and England had made him a celebrity. When his plane crashed in the jungles of Burma on his way to China, he and his party survived two weeks among the Naga tribesmen, and he emerged more famous than ever. He returned to the European front and covered North Africa, the Italian campaign, the invasion of southern France, and the final thrust across the Rhine into Germany.

In the 1950s, in his CBS evening radio news commentaries, Sevareid developed a unique journalistic form, the carefully wrought brief commentary that was erudite without being pedantic, eloquent but clear. He moved reluctantly into television, because the lights made him nervous and because he resented the image being more powerful than the words. But his final two-minute commentaries on Walter Cronkite's CBS *Evening News*, rendered more effective by his dignified appearance, made him one of the most respected American journalists. His high points were in his condemnations of the Vietnam War, his defense of freedom of the press in response to an attack from Vice President Spiro Agnew, and his Watergate commentaries.

In 1959, unable to cope with Lois's manic depression, he fled to Europe with Belen Marshall, a Cuban songwriter whom he married in 1963. They had a daughter, Cristina, and were divorced in 1973. Later, following retirement in 1977, he married Suzanne St. Pierre, a producer for *60 Minutes*. He died in his Georgetown home of stomach cancer on July 9, 1992. Visitors to his rustic country cabin outside Warrenton, Virginia, saw how much it recalled the North Dakota frontier.

Raymond A. Schroth
Fordham College

Schroth, Raymond A. *The American Journey of Eric Sevareid*. South Royalton VT: Steerforth Press, 1995.

SLAUGHTER, LINDA

See GENDER: Slaughter, Linda

SMALL-TOWN NEWSPAPERS

There are hundreds if not thousands of small-town newspapers scattered throughout the Great Plains, and they play an important role in the health and vitality of their communities. In the Canadian Plains, for example, the Saskatchewan Weekly Newspapers Association is composed of eighty weekly newspapers reaching more than 500,000 readers. The Alberta Weekly Newspapers Association is about eighty years old and has 102 member newspapers scattered throughout Alberta and into the Northwest Territories. Some papers have a history that goes back to the 1800s; others are brand new.

Traditionally, the community newspaper was defined as a nondaily publication serving a small community. However, as markets, business models, and technologies have changed over the years, it is no longer feasible to distinguish community newspapers based upon frequency or circulation size. A community newspaper may be published once a week, several times a week, or daily. With the emergence of the Internet, some community newspapers exist only in cyberspace. Regardless of frequency or method of distribution, most community newspapers are committed to providing local information and related services that serve and strengthen their communities.

In frontier days, as people moved west, so too did newspapers, largely because of the portability and durability of the flatbed press. A newspaper became one of the earliest marks of a new Plains community. When a newspaper arrived in Leavenworth, Kansas Territory, in 1854, for example, the town consisted of four tents. Denver's *Rocky Mountain News* was first published in 1859 in a saloon attic. Legh and Frederick Freeman, two former Confederate telegraph operators, started the *Kearney Herald* at Fort Kearny in Nebraska in 1865, then traveled west with the construction of the Union Pacific, setting up their press at every new railhead. They first published their *Frontier Index* in North Platte and then continued into Dakota Territory (later Wyoming Territory).

Evangelists and social activists also pioneered publishing in the Great Plains. Outspoken former lawyers, preachers, teachers, politicians, farmers, miners, and others tried their hand at journalism. A local editor could inspire voters and make himself an important figure in the community. Most editors were men, but women also participated in the region's journalism, first as editors' wives and then leading the papers after their husbands died. Carry Nation, with her *Smasher's Mail*, published in Medicine Lodge, Kansas, in the first years of the twentieth century, promoted temperance and prohibition. Woman suffrage and feminism found early champions in western newspapers.

Editors were expected to serve the local interests of their communities by campaigning for territorial status or statehood, for railroads, and for or against the abolition of slavery. Marriages, deaths, births, social events, prairie fires, lodge meetings, and rumors of gold and silver strikes were included, along with stories of local gunfights. One famous story was the *Bismarck Tribune*'s account of George Armstrong Custer's defeat at the Battle of the Little Bighorn in 1876, an account based on notes retrieved from the body of accompanying reporter Mark Kellogg.

Papers in the West were known for their quirky independence. One radical publication that broke through to a mass audience was *Appeal to Reason*, published in Girard, Kansas. In 1912 it had a circulation of 750,000. Another small-town newspaper that transcended local importance was the *Emporia Gazette*, published by William Allen White from 1895 to 1944.

Until the late 1800s, little thought was given to training editors and reporters. For more than a century, the emphasis was on printing, and future editors learned to set type under the apprentice system. But there were some modest efforts at training. In the 1840s young Native American students in Indian Territory were being trained in printing, and as early as 1848 girls at the Park Hill Seminary were producing a school paper, the *Cherokee Rosebud*. Printing in Indian Territory started with the *Cherokee Almanac*, which began publishing in 1835 at Tahlequah. Another Native American

newspaper, the *Shawnee Sun*, began in 1835 at Shawnee Mission in what would become Kansas. Basic training manuals for journalists existed in the 1860s, and as early as 1873 Kansas State College offered printing classes for rural publishers.

Rural free delivery in 1896 made it possible for large dailies to reach into rural areas, and people predicted the end of rural weeklies. Instead, a special emphasis on local coverage actually strengthened the small-town papers because they no longer had to devote space to world or national events. During World War I local newspapers promoted war bonds, Red Cross campaigns, salvage efforts, and recruitment programs. Personnel problems developed as printers and editors went off to war, and many times wives had to fill in. In the 1920s, despite competition for advertising from radio, many small newspapers, with better equipment and better business methods, attained solid footing in their communities. This did not prevent a large number of failures during the Great Depression. Newspaper editors went back to the old system of bartering because their readers could not afford to buy the paper and businesses could not afford to advertise. Still, the Depression was a time of leadership for many small-town papers. Editorials called for community efforts to overcome local problems and promoted optimism. Papers closed again when World War II broke out, while others carried on with wives, sisters, and mothers assuming the responsibilities of publishing. Newspapers were considered vital to the war effort because of their ability to maintain morale on the home front. When veterans returned home, they flocked to universities, and interest in journalism careers rose, in large part because of the experiences of wartime correspondents.

The years after World War II saw a revolution in production methods and a change in the organization of the publishing business that greatly affected community newspapers. In the 1950s the change from metal to film production accelerated, especially at nondaily newspapers, which could more easily make the switch since they had fewer machines—and people—to deal with. Since new production processes made it easier to start a paper and suburban expansion increased the need for more papers, another development, the newspaper chain, brought change to community newspaper management. Computers in the newsroom, the development of digital cameras, and the convergence of print, audio, and video on the Internet combined to make the last few years of the twentieth century an exciting time for those involved in small-town newspapers. As with any changes, some newspapers embraced the new technologies, while others tried to avoid them.

But the one constant in small-town newspapers is that they strive to provide people with local news about their schools, government, clubs, and activities. They continue to announce births, deaths, weddings, and anniversaries. Editors of small-town newspapers

know that if they chronicle people's lives and the events around them, people will read their papers.

See also CITIES AND TOWNS: Small Towns / PROTEST AND DISSENT: *Appeal to Reason*; Nation, Carry.

Gloria B. Freeland
Kansas State University

America's Premier Community Newspapers. Arlington VA: National Newspaper Association, 1998. Karolevitz, Robert E. *From Quill to Computer: The Story of America's Community Newspapers*. Freeman SD: Pine Hill Press, 1985. Sloan, William David, James G. Stovall, and James D. Startt. *The Media in America: A History*. Scottsdale AZ: Publishing Horizons, 1993.

SPANISH-LANGUAGE PRESS

See HISPANIC AMERICANS: Spanish-Language Press

STAR-PHOENIX (SASKATOON)

The *Star-Phoenix* is the only daily newspaper published in Saskatoon, Saskatchewan. With a circulation of about 65,000, it is the largest and best newspaper in the province. But in recent years, *Star-Phoenix* news executives have struggled to maintain the high quality of coverage the paper has traditionally offered its readers.

This fight to uphold newsroom standards has been particularly difficult since 1996, when the *Star-Phoenix* was purchased by the Hollinger organization. Hollinger, controlled by press baron Conrad Black, is Canada's largest newspaper chain. The Siftons, who operated the paper for seventy years through four generations, always looked after their employees. It was a tradition stretching back to the Great Depression, when the *Star-Phoenix* kept everyone on the job despite tough economic times.

Hollinger promised that nothing would change and that it would maintain the paper's editorial quality. But once the sale was finalized, the profit-hungry Hollinger's first move was to fire one-quarter of the newspaper's staff, including twenty-four people in the editorial department. This mass firing, coupled with a similar move at the *Leader-Post* in Regina, sent shock waves through newsrooms across the nation. That day, March 2, 1996, which has become known as "Black Saturday," has gone down as one of the cruelest and darkest days in Canadian journalistic history.

The *S-P*, as it is popularly called, also came to national attention in 1978, when the Supreme Court of Canada upheld a lower-court judgment against the paper in a libel case. The *S-P* had published a letter to the editor from two law students who accused a Saskatoon alderman named Morris Chernesky of displaying "racist resistance" for opposing the location of an alcoholic rehabilitation center for Indians in a white area. The Supreme Court awarded Chernesky $25,000 and ruled that the newspaper could not use the defense of "fair comment" because the opinions expressed in the letter were not those of the newspaper itself. This ruling prompted several provincial governments to change their libel laws to ensure that newspapers could publish letters from readers who held opinions not necessarily agreeing with those of the paper.

The *Star-Phoenix* has grown up with the city it serves. It began life as the *Phenix* in 1902. The paper, initially printed on a Washington handpress by Westley and Edward Norman, was renamed the *Phoenix* in 1905. It became a daily a year later. A second paper, the *Capital*, was started in 1906 and renamed the *Star* six years later. The *Star* and the *Phenix* were merged in 1928, when both papers were purchased by the Sifton family.

Editorially, the *Star-Phoenix* has frequently shown itself to be sharper and quicker off the mark than the *Leader-Post*, its sister paper in Regina. The *S-P* puts more emphasis on original reporting, and its columnists are more inclined to take controversial stands. This difference is due in part to the fact that while Regina, the provincial capital, is dominated by a civil-service mentality, Saskatoon has a more business-oriented and progressive outlook.

See also CITIES AND TOWNS: Saskatoon, Saskatchewan.

Jim McKenzie
University of Regina

STORZ, TODD (1924–1964)

Omaha, Nebraska, radio broadcasting entrepreneur Robert Todd Storz was described in 1956 by *Time* magazine as the "fastest rising figure in U.S. radio." His Mid-Continent Broadcasting Company and its daytime-only KOWH ruled Omaha's airwaves from 1950 through 1957 with controversial outside stunts and station promotions, listen-to-win contests and games, popular music, razzle-dazzle announcers, and sensational sounding news broadcasts that offered listeners a weekly cash award for the best news tip. Under Storz's direct supervision the company spawned similar independent programming success stories at six other radio stations acquired by the company from 1953 through 1960, creating one of the most innovative and profitable privately held nonnetwork radio groups in the history of post–World War II broadcasting.

Born in Omaha to Robert Herman Storz and Mildred Todd Storz on May 8, 1924, Storz developed an early interest in radio and built a cigar-box crystal set at the age of eight. During his early teens he was a five-meter "bootlegger," transmitting without a license, and by his sixteenth year he was a licensed amateur radio operator. He attended Omaha public schools, leaving that city's Central High School in 1940 to complete his secondary education at the prestigious Choate School in Wallingford, Connecticut. After graduating in 1942 he attended the University of Nebraska for one year. He enlisted in the United States Army and passed specialized Signal Corps cryptography exams with the highest score, becoming the youngest warrant officer in the service.

Following World War II Storz took a twelve-week NBC-sponsored course in radio at Northwestern University at Evanston, Illinois, and worked at several radio stations as an announcer, salesman, and copywriter. In 1947 he was employed at KBON in Omaha, hosting its *1490 Swing Club* program. In 1949 Todd and his father purchased KOWH from the *Omaha World Herald* for $75,000. Todd, age twenty-five, became KOWH general manager and vice president of the new Mid-Continent Broadcasting Company. His father, fifty, was the company's president. By 1951 KOWH had become the nation's top-rated independent radio station.

In 1957 the company changed its name to the Storz Broadcasting Company and sold KOWH to William F. Buckley Jr.'s National Weekly, Inc., for $822,500, an astonishing price for a 500-watt daytime-only radio station. Meanwhile, Storz had acquired AM radio stations in New Orleans, Kansas City, Minneapolis–St. Paul, Miami, Oklahoma City, and St. Louis. Storz was president of the highly profitable company; his father was its chairman of the board. Storz originated the idea of Top 40 music programming with the purchase in 1953 of WTIX in New Orleans.

In 1957 declining network radio revenues prompted ABC to recruit several Storz top management figures. As consultants, they recommended new programming at ABC Radio, including network news and the Top 40 music format at several of its owned and operated radio stations and many of its affiliates.

On April 13, 1964, Todd Storz died from an apparent stroke at his home in Miami Beach, Florida. In 1966 Robert H. Storz returned the company's home office operations to Omaha from Miami Beach. Beginning in 1978 the Storz stations were sold separately, the last in 1985, bringing to a close an important chapter in American radio history.

Richard W. Fatherley
Kansas City, Kansas

TELEGRAPH

The electric telegraph played an important role in the lives of the inhabitants of the Great Plains from its first appearance in the region in the 1860s until well into the twentieth century. Work on a coast-to-coast telegraph line in the United States began when Congress passed the Pacific Telegraph Act in 1860. The Western Union Telegraph Company supervised the construction of the line, which ran from Omaha, Nebraska, through Laramie, Wyoming, to San Francisco, California. Upon its completion in October 1861, the transcontinental telegraph spelled an end to the Pony Express, which had operated during its construction.

Some of the construction crews used electric batteries to give shocks to the Arapaho and Cheyenne inhabitants of the region and frighten them away, creating an atmosphere of hostility between the Native Americans and the telegraph companies. After the Sand Creek Massacre in 1864, the Native Americans realized that the telegraph could be used to summon troops, and they began a campaign to tear down the wires in what is now western Nebraska, eastern Colorado, and southern Wyoming. This continued until 1869, when the lines were moved to the trackside of the newly completed Union Pacific Railroad. As in the United States, the completion of a cross-country telegraph system in western Canada preceded the building of the transcontinental railway. The Canadian Pacific Railway Telegraph was operational clear to the Pacific Coast ten years before the completion of the transcontinental Canadian Pacific Railway in 1885.

Tributary lines soon connected major towns and cities to the main line. A mutually beneficial relationship grew up between the telegraph companies and the railroads. Western Union telegraph operators were stationed in each railroad depot and used the telegraph to signal train movements from one station to the next. When operators were not busy with train orders, they sent personal messages, received commodity reports, and arranged shipments for local farmers and merchants. Although the stereotypical telegraph operator in western lore is a male, women also worked as telegraphers. The percentage of women telegraphers in the Plains states grew from approximately 5 percent in 1870 to 10 percent in 1900.

During the 1870s and 1880s populists and members of the Grange movement accused the railroad and telegraph companies of manipulating commodity prices and shipping rates. The Interstate Commerce Commission, established in 1887 to regulate railroad shipping rates, was chartered to regulate the telegraph industry as well in 1910. The use of the telegraph began to decline after 1900 as it was replaced by the telephone for personal messages and by centralized traffic-control systems for railroad use. The depot telegrapher lived on in movies like *Western Union* (1939) and *Kansas Pacific* (1953) as a nostalgic symbol of a bygone era.

The problems of settling and governing the Great Plains were those of time and space; the telegraph solved these problems elegantly by compressing the time required to communicate between widely separated cities, towns, and forts from days to mere seconds. For newspaper editors the telegraph meant the swift arrival of news from the East. For farmers the telegraph provided a means to arrange the shipment of crops and cattle. And for all ordinary men and women the telegraph enabled personal communications with distant friends and family.

See also TRANSPORTATION: Railroads, United States; Railways, Canada.

Thomas C. Jepsen
National Coalition of Independent Scholars

Burnet, Robert. *Canadian Railway Telegraph History*. Etobicoke, Ontario: Telegraph Key and Sounder, 1997. Gabler, Edwin. *The American Telegrapher: A Social History, 1860–1900*. New Brunswick NJ: Rutgers University Press, 1988.

Jepsen, Thomas. "The Telegraph Comes to Colorado: A New Technology and Its Consequences." *Essays and Monographs in Colorado History* 7 (1987): 1–25.

TELEVISION SHOWS

The Great Plains became an important component of television programming soon after the medium became successful on a national level. Programs included documentaries as well as traditional entertainment.

Noncommercial educational (later called public) broadcasting led the way with a series entitled *Great Plains Trilogy*. The thirty-nine half-hour programs were produced in the 1950s by Jack McBride of KUON-TV at the University of Nebraska. The first thirteen programs dealt with the paleontology of the region. The second set of thirteen programs considered archaeology. The third group emphasized Great Plains history. The Ford Foundation provided the funding, and the series was broadcast on educational/public television stations.

In commercial broadcasting many popular programs about life on the American frontier did not indicate specific locations. Others that might be related to the Great Plains such as *Little House on the Prairie* were actually filmed in other areas. *Dallas*, the highest-rated commercial network program of the early 1980s, included episodes about the Texas Plains even though the city is peripheral to the region.

One of the best known of the series clearly identified with the Great Plains was *Gunsmoke* (CBS, 1955–75), which starred James Arness as U.S. marshal Matt Dillon. *Gunsmoke*, which continued to enjoy success as a syndicated off-network rerun, was set in Dodge City, Kansas, in the 1870s and 1880s. The show's twenty years on the network included thirty-minute as well as sixty-minute versions. Amanda Blake (Kitty), Milburn Stone (Doc), Dennis Weaver (Chester), and Burt Reynolds (Quint) were key characters in this depiction of life in a western Kansas cattle town.

Several other westerns were specifically set in the Plains. *The Dakotas* (ABC, 1963) included Larry Ward, Chad Everett, and Jack Elam as U.S. marshals. *The Cowboys* (ABC, 1974) featured a cattle drive from a New Mexico ranch to Dodge City, Kansas, with a trail crew consisting of eleven nine- to fifteen-year-old children. *The Cisco Kid* (syndicated, 1951), based on the O. Henry character and probably the first television series to be filmed in color, involved a Robin Hood hero (played by Duncan Renaldo) and his partner, Pancho (Leo Carillo), in New Mexico during the 1890s. *Buckskin* (NBC, 1958 and 1965) cast Sallie Brophie as a widow hotel owner in 1880s Montana. Tommy Nolan played her son Jody who, seated on corral fence, plays his harmonica and narrates each story. *Branded* (NBC, 1965) placed Chuck Conners in southeastern Wyoming in the 1870s as a former soldier trying to clear his name. *Alias Smith and Jones* (ABC, 1971–73) followed two bank robbers who, after ending criminal careers, are promised pardons if they prove themselves worthy for twelve months in Kansas during the 1890s. A comedy Western, *F Troop* (ABC, 1965–67), featured Forrest Tucker, Larry Storch, and Ken Berry in the Union army in 1866 in Kansas.

Some programs were not located in identifiable states or towns but depicted the region more generally. One example, *How the West Was Won* (ABC, 1977), a three-part miniseries about a Virginia family homesteading in the Great Plains, brought former *Gunsmoke* star James Arness back to the region with costars Eva Marie Saint and Bruce Boxleitner. Another example, *Wagon Train* (NBC, ABC, 1957–65), followed a wagon master (Ward Bond until his death in 1960, when he was replaced by John McIntire) who led pioneers from a starting point at St. Joseph, Missouri, across the Plains to final destinations in the Far West. The eight-hour miniseries *Lonesome Dove* (CBS, 1989) offered solid performances by Robert Duvall, Tommy Lee Jones, and Anjelica Huston during a cattle drive from Lonesome Dove, Texas, to Montana. *Return to Lonesome Dove* (CBS, 1993) continued the story with Barbara Hershey and William Peterson as the stars.

A different type of series, *Route 66* (CBS, 1960–64), followed the adventures of two young men, played by Martin Milner and George Maharis, as they drove a white Chevrolet Corvette through the Great Plains and points west on that famous highway. The series benefited from successful recordings of the theme song, which was written by Nelson Riddle.

Television programming tends to follow audience trends. Much of the emphasis in the Great Plains followed the interest in Westerns during the early years of the medium. When the Western declined in popularity, the Great Plains tended to fade from the screen. But as specialized locations returned to popularity, programming such as the *Lonesome Dove* miniseries and documentaries on the Oregon Trail, Lewis and Clark, and Native Americans have brought the focus back to the region.

See also IMAGES AND ICONS: Dodge City, Kansas / LITERARY TRADITIONS: The Western / TRANSPORTATION: Route 66.

Larry Walklin
University of Nebraska–Lincoln

Phillips, Louis, and Burham Holmes. *TV Almanac.* New York: Macmillan Publishing Company, 1994. Terrace, Vincent. *Complete Encyclopedia of Television Programs.* New York: Barnes, 1979.

TRILLIN, CALVIN (b. 1935)

Journalist, critic, and novelist Calvin Trillin was born on December 5, 1935, and raised in a middle-class neighborhood in Kansas City, Missouri. Even now, after decades of living in Greenwich Village in New York City, he still regards Kansas City as his primary point of reference.

Trillin's mother and father (so tenderly recollected in his 1996 book, *Messages from My Father*) were second-generation grocers whose own parents had immigrated from Lithuania and the Ukraine, respectively. Trillin's father brought him up to aspire to greater things than being a grocer, yet it was his father's quiet messages and example that had the greatest effect on Trillin.

In 1953 Trillin did what his father had always planned for him and left for Yale, where he edited the *Yale Daily News*. He graduated in 1957. Trillin's first job was as a "floating" journalist with *Time*, writing on subjects as diverse as medicine and religion. In 1963 he moved to the *New Yorker* as a staff writer, and there he quickly established his reputation as a first-rate essayist and journalist. In 1978 he joined the *Nation* as a columnist; since 1990 he has also contributed light but scathing political verse to that magazine.

Trillin has written on a wide range of subjects in his columns, novels, plays, and poems: politics, murder, growing up, food, and American places. Some of his pieces in the Great Plains, for example, his essay on the small town of Protection, Kansas, which for a brief time flourished on the manufacture of concertina barbed wire for use in Vietnam and then reverted to its normal state of barely "holding its own" (*U.S. Journal*, 1971), are filled with Trillin's empathy for ordinary people. Others, like his explication of the sordid relationships behind brutal murders in Emporia, Kansas, in 1983, undermining its "front-porch" image (*American Stories*, 1991), are prime examples of tough investigative reporting. But Trillin is perhaps best known for his political commentary, which generally employs understated humor to lay bare hypocrisies and injustices and to bring inflated egos down to size. Like his father before him, Calvin Trillin has always "given good weight."

David J. Wishart
University of Nebraska–Lincoln

"Trillin, Calvin (Marshall)." In *Contemporary Authors*, New Revision series, 67: 349–53. Detroit: Gale Research. 1981. Trillin, Calvin. *Messages from My Father.* New York: Farrar, Straus, and Giroux, 1996.

WESTERN PRODUCER

A Saskatoon-based weekly newspaper founded in 1924, the *Western Producer* began publishing in 1923 as the *Progressive*. Founders Harris Turner and Pat Waldren proposed establishing a newspaper to the Saskatchewan Grain Growers Association (SGGA), which eventually endorsed the venture, providing $7,000 in loans and 5,000 subscribers. In return, the SGGA was granted three places on the five-member editorial board. To encourage members of the recently created Saskatchewan Wheat Pool (SWP) to subscribe and to avoid association with the federal Progressive Party, the paper's name was changed, printing its first edition under the *Western Producer* banner in September 1924.

Despite the influence of the SGGA, the *Western Producer* became known for its objective, nonpartisan, high-quality reporting. Among its many influential journalists was Violet McNaughton, a prominent SGGA member and woman's rights advocate.

The Great Depression created hardships for the *Western Producer*. Subscriptions began falling, and, in order to avoid ruin, the SWP purchased the paper in 1931, operating it as a subsidiary. Despite the *Western Producer*'s problems, it retained more than 100,000 subscribers during the Depression years. In the 1950s the *Western Producer* ventured into book publishing. Its first monograph appeared in 1958 and led to the creation of Western Producer Prairie Books. By 1983 more than 100 books on several Prairie topics had been printed. Budgetary constraints, however, led to the dissolution of the press in the 1990s.

The *Western Producer* continues to perform vital economic, political, and social functions. In addition to providing agricultural news, the paper includes sections for youth, women, and rural society in general. The *Western Producer* has had a considerable influence on Prairie society and simultaneously embodies Prairie farmers' independence and cooperative spirit.

See also AGRICULTURE: Saskatchewan Wheat Pool.

Kerry Badgley
National Archives of Canada

Fairbairn, Garry Lawrence. *From Prairie Roots: The Remarkable Story of the Saskatchewan Wheat Pool.* Saskatoon, Saskatchewan: Western Producer Prairie Books, 1984.

WHITE, WILLIAM ALLEN (1868–1944)

William Allen White, a dean of American journalism and social commentary through the first half of the twentieth century, was born in Emporia, Kansas, on February 10, 1868. Few at the start of the twenty-first century recall White beyond textbook references to his scathing editorial rebuke of Populism in 1896 entitled "What's the Matter with Kansas?" White was then a conservative Republi-

can and the upstart publisher of the *Emporia Gazette*, which he had purchased in 1895. His editorial was picked up by the national party, which spread the word widely. White soon shifted from conservative to progressive politics. He became an intimate ally of Theodore Roosevelt and a national progressive spokesperson, and he remained in the liberal limelight for half a century.

White was a masterful wordsmith: his *Gazette* editorials were regularly picked up by newspapers, and his commentary and syndicated reporting were published in leading newspapers and magazines such as *McClure's* and the *Saturday Evening Post*. White wrote biographies of Calvin Coolidge (1925 and 1938) and Woodrow Wilson (1924) as well as fiction —his short stories and novels, published into the early 1920s, packed hefty social and political charges. *A Certain Rich Man* (1909) was the most successful, eventually selling close to 300,000 copies. White gained more fame and respect for two editorials written in the early twenties: "Mary White," which eulogized the tragic death of his spirited daughter in 1921, and "To an Anxious Friend," which won a Pulitzer Prize for its defense of free speech in 1922. Collections of his editorials in the *Emporia Gazette* were widely read and greatly influenced the next generation of journalists.

White always retained an active interest in politics. He joined Roosevelt in the 1912 Bull Moose revolt; he defended liberal Republican policies through the 1920s; he generally supported New Deal initiatives in the 1930s; and, while a staunch Republican, he prominently allied himself with Franklin Roosevelt to overcome isolationist sentiment in 1940–41 and chaired the Committee to Defend America by Aiding the Allies.

White died in Emporia on January 29, 1944. He had remained a citizen of that town, but he traveled widely, and he was acknowledged as a national folk hero. White was a strong proponent of small-town values; he advocated the impression of those values upon an urban-industrial America he enthusiastically embraced. His Emporia home is now a historic landmark.

Edward Gale Agran
Wilmington College

Johnson, Walter. *William Allen White's America.* New York: Henry Holt and Company, 1947. Johnson, Walter, and Alberta Pantle. "A Bibliography of the Published Works of William Allen White." *Kansas Historical Quarterly* 15 (1947): 22–41. White, William Allen. *The Autobiography of William Allen White.* New York: Macmillan Publishing Company, 1946.

WINNIPEG FREE PRESS

The *Manitoba Free Press*, precursor of the *Winnipeg Free Press* (the name change took place in 1931), printed its first edition in November 1872, only two years after Manitoba joined the Confederation and two years before its host city, Winnipeg, was incorporated. The founders, John A. Kenny (publisher) and W. F. Luxton (editor), lived above the paper's offices in a tar-paper shack on the corner of Main and James Streets. The early papers were cranked out on a handpress that was surrounded by coal-tar lamps to keep the ink from freezing. From this rudimentary beginning the *Free Press* grew with Winnipeg to become not only Manitoba's leading newspaper but also one of the most respected papers in the country.

Much of the success of the *Winnipeg Free Press* can be attributed to two men, politician Sir Clifford Sifton (1861–1929) and journalist John W. Dafoe (1866–1944). Sifton took over ownership of a rather floundering enterprise in 1898, determined to make the paper the voice of the Liberal Party in the Prairie Provinces. To that end he appointed Dafoe, a young Montreal journalist, as editor in 1901. Dafoe edited the paper until his death. In his editorials Dafoe championed the interests of western Canada, strenuously argued for greater Canadian autonomy from Britain, and promoted the Liberal Party (though not all individuals affiliated with it). In the 1930s his pessimistic editorials candidly chronicled the devastation of drought and unemployment on the Prairies, and in 1938, alone among leading Canadian editorialists, he refused to support the Munich Pact.

Dafoe carefully amassed a superb cast of journalists. For example, he appointed the talented Cora Hind (1861–1942) as agricultural editor in 1901, twenty years after she had been refused a job at the paper because she was a woman. Dafoe also nurtured the career of A. Grant Dexter (1896–1961), who joined the *Free Press* in 1912 and became one of Canada's preeminent political journalists. Dexter went on to edit the *Free Press* from 1948 to 1954.

In 1980 the *Winnipeg Free Press* absorbed its main rival, the *Winnipeg Tribune*. By the year

William Allen White at his Gazette *desk, ca. 1909*

2000 the paper was being read by more than 50 percent of the adults in Winnipeg, its main market. Weekday circulation was 128,988, Saturday circulation was 191,076, and Sunday circulation stood at 144,588. In all, its circulation is more than three times that of its main competitor, the *Winnipeg Sun*. In 1991 the *Free Press* abandoned its cramped downtown offices for a new 150-million-dollar production plant in northwestern Winnipeg. There, three computerized presses can each print papers at the rate of 75,000 an hour. The *Winnipeg Free Press* has come a long way since Kenny and Luxton turned out the first edition.

See also CITIES AND TOWNS: Winnipeg, Manitoba / GENDER: Hind, Cora / POLITICS AND GOVERNMENT: Sifton, Clifford.

David J. Wishart
University of Nebraska–Lincoln

Donnelly, Murray S. *Dafoe of the Free Press*. Toronto: Macmillan Publishing Company, 1968.

Music

The original Light Crust Dough Boys, from left: Herman Arnspiger, Bob Wills, Milton Brown, Truett Kemsey, Borris Mills (official), W. Lee O'Daniel, 1931

Music 529

MUSIC

The people of the Great Plains have created a diverse spectrum of musical practices whose initially autonomous forms have combined to generate a wellspring of acculturative popular music that is now heard throughout the world. Native peoples have maintained a musical life of great spirituality in spite of repression and isolation. White settlers entering the area evolved sturdy uses of European folk music into a sophisticated tradition of American art music, reflected in regional symphony and opera companies as well as university music programs. Evolving through gospel, blues, and ragtime, African American musicians created a distinct jazz style centered on the territory bands. Many facets of African American music were incorporated into rhythm and blues and combined with western swing and rockabilly to help define rock and roll. From Woody Guthrie and Buddy Holly to Lawrence Welk and Garth Brooks, from Jay McShann and Ornette Coleman to Howard Hanson and k. d. lang, musicians from the Great Plains illustrate a diversity that is central to American and Canadian life.

The First Musicians

The earliest music in the great swath of open space dissecting the middle of North America collectively known as the Great Plains has, like the constant winds that scour the open land, been lost to time. The Native peoples of the Great Plains traditionally practiced a musical culture that was rich in diversity yet unified by important issues. Like many tribal societies, especially those seminomadic ones with a minimum of material possessions, the Plains Indians developed much of their cultural expression through music. Music and religion were inseparable, and symbolic ritual maintenance of natural law through ceremonial affirmation played a central role in coordinating tribal life. Prayers for divine intervention in hunting and war, healing songs, and clerical divinatory songs all connected the individual with the supernatural.

Music was also used to regulate the more mundane social needs of the community. The rhythms of narrated songs that perpetuated the history of the people, social singing and dancing at feasts, love songs, boasting songs, work songs, and lullabies, performed by all members of the community, not just a professional elite, filled the daily life of the group. Another commonality the Native Plains peoples shared with other Indigenous groups in North America was the interconnection between music and dance. Musicians moved while singing, and dancers sang and played (with anklets) while dancing. Though many forms of musical expression were lost in the turmoil of the European American incursion, others have persisted and remain a vital part of Native American life and of Great Plains music.

Even more than other regions, the Native American music from the Great Plains was predominantly vocal. Men singing with an ecstatic high register (falsetto) or the unison singing of men and women was the most common (singing in harmony was not practiced). Loud, robust melodies appropriate to the open spaces of the Plains tended to begin in the upper register (in contrast with the European folk song curve, which begins low before reaching a high point near the end). Another important characteristic of Plains singing was, and is, the use of vocables, or "nonsense" syllables. While considered a coded hermetic language by some, most scholars believe nonlexical sounds are used for their euphonious sensuality. Often a song will begin with vocables, giving way in the middle to a text section, often sung by an individual. These lyrics may be altered to fit changing conditions.

As to the question of authorship, the concept of the "composer" is a much different one from that found in European music. In Native cosmologies, all songs are in existence; the individual singer receives the song as a supernatural gift. For example, through the vision quest, the arduous process involving fasting and other self-sacrifices, a song is granted as a gift from the supernatural. Perhaps the most famous result of such divine intervention is the complex series of visions and songs bestowed upon the Lakota chief Black Elk as a boy:

> Then I looked up at the clouds and two men were coming there, headfirst like arrows slanting down; and as they came, they sang a sacred song and the thunder was like drumming. I will sing it for you. The song and drumming were like this:

> Behold, a sacred voice is calling you;
> All over the sky a sacred voice is calling

Another, less cosmic approach to composing consisted of assembling a new song out of sections of other tunes. Contrary to popular opinion, improvisation holds a smaller role in tribal music than is generally believed. While individual songs may change when passed on in the oral tradition from generation to generation, the creative function of the individual is secondary to the continuity of the community; therefore, the songs are conducted within careful structures. The misconception of "primitive" music being primarily improvised was perpetuated by the racist belief in the superiority of notated (nonimprovised) European art music.

Purely instrumental music not connected with singing was uncommon in Native American music. The most important instruments are percussive. Drums, especially the collectively played large tom-tom, are central to Plains Indian music, and their cosmic significance to the community can be compared to the role of the gamelan in Javanese society or the organ in European church music. Smaller drums, rattles, and whistles are also common. String instruments are virtually nonexistent. Flutes were much less common on the Plains than in the Pacific Northwest and the Southwest.

The arrival of Spanish, French, and English explorers, trappers, and settlers, beginning with the Spanish in the 1500s, while influencing Indian music, never led to the kind of acculturated music found in Mexico or parts of South America, where Indigenous elements were more fully integrated into the new society. Rather than blending in with the new cultures, Native Americans remained separate, and music in general tended to unify around a kind of "Pan-Indian" style, much of which was derived from the Plains style. Two important instances of this during the nineteenth century were the Ghost Dance and peyote songs. Begun after 1880 in the Great Basin area of Nevada, the Ghost Dance was an attempt to reverse the recent tragic tide of history. In 1890 the U.S. Congress cited the dance's popularity with Plains warrior groups as an excuse to outlaw it. Similarly, peyote songs, revolving around the sacramental ingestion of peyote buds, which contain the hallucinogen mescaline, originated in Mexico and were introduced to the Plains area by the Apaches. They remain an important element in many Native societies today.

Traditional Native American music today has become dominated by the Plains style and has witnessed a surge in popularity since the 1950s through powwows and the growth of Indian-oriented recording companies such as Canyon Records. While the purity and motives of some of this music, with its obvious appeal to a white, tourist, New Age audience, may be deplored by some, authentic music and ritual true to its ancient and sacred heritage continues to be practiced, representing a vital living tradition as well as an invaluable link to the past.

Contemporary Indian blues, country, and rock can also serve as a powerful vehicle for social statement. The mixing of politics, music, and poetry is particularly evident in the work of John Trudell. Trudell was born in Omaha, Nebraska, and grew up on the Santee Sioux Reservation. He first came to prominence as a national spokesman during the Indians of All Tribes' occupation of Alcatraz in 1969. He was national chairman of the American Indian Movement (AIM) from 1973 to 1979, a period of intense Indian activism. His first album on a major label, AKA Graffiti Man, released in 1992, was highly acclaimed and featured the work of the late Kiowa guitarist Jesse Ed Davis.

O Pioneers

While often lacking the mystical element so important for Native peoples, music for the first European American settlers in the Great Plains played an important functional role in their daily lives. Music was used to cope with an alien environment, alleviate a drab, lonely existence, and perpetuate traditional cultures. In its path from the rural to the urban tradition, pioneer music was defined first and foremost as entertainment, with the emphasis on family singing and community dances. Folk songs inherited from various ethnic backgrounds, popular songs, and hymns (aided by hymnals that contained only the words) constituted the early repertoire. They were sung and passed on by oral transmissions and provided the principal form of home entertainment. Instruments, whether homemade jugs and spoons or fiddles, guitars, banjos, and Jew's harps, were present from the beginning. Later, piano became the most important parlor instrument, a symbol of "civilization" in the Great American Desert. As villages began to grow, organized dances evolved from family jam sessions and became a focal point of community life. Spurred on by the hornpipes and reels of the fiddler, the vigorous dancing provided an important emotional and physical outlet. Similar to these dances were the "play party games," featuring circle and line dancing. In time, these amateur affairs turned into barn dances, hops, and stepping bees featuring more trained musicians.

The legacy of this emphasis on dance survived in polka bands and popular dance bands, including those of Lawrence Welk. Welk, born in Strasburg, North Dakota, in 1903, became a popular television icon in that particular mid-American mold that also produced comedian Johnny Carson and newscaster Walter Cronkite. Welk's long-running program defined an unabashedly sweet, sentimental, "corny" musical idiom drawn from Slavic folk dances and semiclassical and country selections and featured accordion solos that have been copied by legions of lesser-known players. The central European polka heritage has remained particularly vital in the Northern Plains, highlighted by the annual Czech Festival, during which Wilbur, Nebraska, showcases homegrown artists such as Math Sladky and Ernie Kucera.

Classical Music

With the influx of American settlers and the establishment of towns, the musical life of the Great Plains entered a new, more refined existence. The first true professional musicians were probably itinerant singing teachers who taught both round and shape notes and teachers of piano and violin. Communities rushed to acquire fife and drum corps, bands, orchestras, vocal ensembles, and opera companies as status symbols indicating their civilizing position in the "wilderness." For example, as early as 1880 the town of Lincoln, Nebraska, had a philharmonic society, three orchestras, a military band, two string bands, an opera house (opened in 1873), an oratorio society, and two male chorales. European artists, including Ignace Paderewski, Leopold Goldowsky, Josef Hofmann, Pablo Casals, and Jan Kubelik, as well as European opera companies began concertizing the Great Plains. In addition to these public arenas, private musical clubs offering recitals and lectures on the arts proliferated. Eventually, symphony orchestras and opera companies would be established in Fort Worth, Tulsa, Wichita, Omaha, and Colorado Springs. Beginning in 1897, Canadian orchestras were founded in Calgary, Winnipeg, Regina, and Saskatoon. The Royal Winnipeg Ballet, Canada's oldest, was established in 1938.

Concurrent with these developments was the rise of music education. Among the earliest schools of music and conservatories in

the area were those at the Universities of Kansas, Oklahoma, and Colorado. A seminal figure in this movement was Willard Kimball, who, after studying in Leipzig, graduated from Oberlin and lived in Iowa for nineteen years before moving to Nebraska to establish what eventually became the University of Nebraska School of Music in 1894. Kimball also organized the Trans-Mississippi and International Exposition, held in Omaha in 1898. This lavish *fin-de-siècle* World's Fair, which was seen as an important "coming of age" of Plains culture, featured members of the Chicago Symphony and the U.S. Marine Band as well as the famous black cornetist Percy Lowery. The Canadian Prairie Provinces also began developing music programs at universities, beginning with the University of Winnipeg in 1880 and followed by the Universities of Saskatoon (1907), Edmonton (1908), Regina (1911), and Calgary (1945).

The legacy of this rich musical tradition can be appreciated in the number of classical musicians born or educated in the Great Plains who became prominent during the twentieth century. Three important composers from the region helped create an American music that was more homegrown and less dependent on European classical models. Pulitzer Prize winner Howard Hanson (1896–1981) was born in Wahoo, Nebraska, and graduated from the University of Nebraska. He went on to direct the Eastman School of Music in Rochester, New York, which became one of the most prominent in the world. Hanson forged an accessible American romantic style that incorporated material reflecting his Scandinavian ancestry. Roy Harris (1898–1979), born in Lincoln County, Oklahoma, studied in Paris before composing his Third Symphony in 1939, a classic of musical populism. Another Pulitzer Prize winner, Virgil Thomson, born in Kansas City, Missouri, in 1896, expressed regionalism in his operas and film scores and, as music critic for the *New York Herald Tribune*, promoted the cause of American music.

Later composers born or active on the American Great Plains included Anthony Donato, Cecil Effinger, and Robert Beadell. All enjoyed long careers as teachers and composers. Prominent composers from the Canadian Prairie Provinces include Barbara Pentland, who studied at Juilliard before teaching at Toronto and Vancouver; Harry Freedman, who was raised in Medicine Hat, Alberta, and later became composer in residence with the Toronto Symphony; and Sydney Hodkinson, who was born in Winnipeg, later taught at Eastman and Southern Methodist University, and also directed the St. Paul Chamber Orchestra.

From Cowboy to Country: The Importance of the Lone Star State

In spite of the European-derived Plains music described above, for most classically trained musicians, like Willa Cather's heroine in *The Song of the Lark*, Thea Kronenborg, the ultimate success of "making it" necessitated relocation to the East, especially New York. The

unique and significant contribution of music from the Great Plains lies not in replication of an outside aesthetic but in the creation of a vital new form of American popular music that drew its strength from a mixture of European American, African American, and Latino sources. Some of the first stirrings of this truly authentic music originated on the Southern Great Plains, especially in the state of Texas. From a potent mix of Appalachian folk songs, Cajun music from nearby Louisiana, Mexican *norteña*, mariachi, and corridos, along with the influence of a distinctive regional African American blues, Texas musicians created or popularized a host of forms such as the cowboy song, honky-tonk, western swing, and various Tex-Mex hybrids that eventually merged into the country and western music of the late 1940s.

The cowboy, one of the most enduring of American myths, emerged from the brief period of the open-range cattle drives from 1865 to 1885 and endured because of romantic dime-novel portrayals of heroes such as Buffalo Bill Cody (1846–1917). Cowboy song lyrics began to appear in the early twentieth century. Some of the most important were collected by N. Howard "Jack" Thorpe. Thorpe, an authentic cowboy who worked in eastern New Mexico and West Texas, published an important collection of 101 cowboy songs (lyrics only) in 1921. The first recordings of cowboy songs followed in 1925. Among the initial stars of this new genre was Woodward "Tex" Ritter, who became interested in singing while a drama student at the University of Texas at Austin. His first recordings in 1933 are considered among the most authentic. Paradoxically, his famous nickname was acquired in New York while appearing on a popular radio program.

Of all the singing cowboys from Texas, the most famous was undoubtedly Gene Autry. Born on a ranch near Tioga, Texas, in 1907, Autry grew up in neighboring Oklahoma until he ran away from home to join the Fields Brothers Marvelous Medicine Show as an Al Jolson impersonator. Following some advice from Jimmie Rodgers, he adopted the cowboy persona, billing himself as Oklahoma's Yodeling Cowboy. Autry later starred in many movies that elevated him, along with his chief rival, Roy Rogers, to superstar status.

Among the other important musicians from the Lone Star State were the Traveling Troubadour, Ernest Tubb (1914–84), and fiddler Bob Wills (1905–75). Born near Kosse, Texas, Wills formed his first band, the Light Crust Doughboys, in 1931 before moving to Tulsa with his most famous group, the Texas Playboys. Wills and his band were broadcast regularly on radio station KVOO from 1934 through 1942 before moving to Hollywood to pursue a film career. Wills's music helped define an approach that became known as western swing, a hybrid style incorporating instrumental elements of jazz and blues within the country string-band tradition. Another Texan, Roy Orbison, born in the town of Vernon in 1936, became a top rockabilly star after he signed with Sun Records in 1956 before moving to

Nashville. Orbison's ballad style exerted a tremendous influence on both American and British singers, including the Beatles, who opened for Orbison on his 1963 tour of England. The preeminent position of Texas country music has continued unabated with the success of the outlaws who spurned Nashville conventions, including Willie Nelson, Waylon Jennings, and David Allen Coe as well as newer country groups like Asleep at the Wheel.

While only peripherally part of the cowboy tradition, mention must be made of the contributions of folksinger Woody Guthrie, the person who, perhaps more than any other, shaped American folk music. Woodrow Wilson Guthrie was born in Okemah, Oklahoma, in 1912, and as a young man he experienced the deprivations of the Great Depression. Taking to the road as a wandering minstrel, Guthrie created a repertoire of protest songs championing the rights of the poor and oppressed. His songs speak to the plight of migrant workers and coal miners, and he strongly supported the cause of the unions. His song "Pretty Boy Floyd" interprets the outlaw of the 1930s as a Robin Hood character, stealing from the banks and giving to the poor disenfranchised farmers. He published a collection of folk songs and an autobiography and became a major influence on later singers such as Bob Dylan and Bruce Springsteen. In 1961 Dylan made a pilgrimage to Guthrie's bedside in New Jersey as he lay dying from Huntington's disease, and his early composition, "Song to Woody," was his commemoration to this American original.

Black Music on the Plains

Originating at first in segregated isolation, then finally merging with white styles in the period after World War II, black music of the Great Plains developed unique and influential forms of blues, ragtime, swing, and jazz. The first major entry of African Americans onto the Plains began after the Civil War. Between 1868 and 1895 more than 5,000 black cowboys worked the ranges from Texas to Kansas. Like their white counterparts, they passed the lonely time with singing and fiddle music. These cowboy minstrels included "Big" Jim Simpson, who worked the Chisholm Trail before settling in Wyoming, and fiddlers George Washington and Sabrien Bates, who rode with Billy the Kid.

Another access for African American music onto the Great Plains occurred through regimental bands. The black Ninth and Tenth Cavalry and Twenty-fourth and Twenty-fifth Infantry bands served from Texas to the Dakotas.

Emerging out of the African American band tradition was Perry George Lowery (1870–1942). Born in the Flint Hills country of eastern Kansas, Lowery was the product of a small but successful group of self-sufficient African American farmers. He began by playing drums, then switched to cornet. After studying in Boston, Lowery became known as the World's Greatest Colored Cornet Soloist and was featured at the 1898 Trans-Mississippi and International Exposition.

Most distinctive forms of African American music that emerged in the twentieth century were based on the blues. Blues-derived music evolved from slave field hollers and gospel music and had a major impact on jazz, country, and rock. Rooted in the South, the blues developed into several distinctive regional styles. One of these early country blues styles arose in Texas and was characterized by single-string guitar playing and a more relaxed vocal sound than found in the nearby Mississippi Delta. Male blues singers from the Plains region include Roy Brown and Amos Milburn from Texas, Robert Jeffrey and Lemuel Johnson from Oklahoma, and "Gatemouth" Moore from Topeka, Kansas. Two important female blues artists, both from Kansas City, Kansas, were Hattie "Hi Hat" McDaniel and Ada Brown (a cousin of ragtime composer James Scott). McDaniel later moved to Hollywood and became a film star in 1939, when she was awarded the first Academy Award ever given to an African American for her role in Gone with the Wind.

Note should also be made here of another great musician from the Southern Plains who began as a blues guitarist before moving east and almost single-handedly defining the electric guitar as a jazz solo instrument. Charlie Christian, from Bonham, Texas, recorded with Benny Goodman from 1939 to 1941 and also played in with Charlie Parker, Dizzy Gillespie, and Thelonious Monk. Christian created a clean, linear style that became the model for most later jazz guitar players. He died from tuberculosis in 1942 at the age of twenty-five.

The blues also was the basis of a new type of piano music that developed in the Great Plains region. Dubbed boogie-woogie, Texas barrelhouse, or honky-tonk, this exciting style featured a steadfast, rocking bass line synchronized under tremolos and triplets in the right hand. These traits, especially the active bass line, became prominent in later Kansas City jazz, urban blues, rhythm and blues, and rock and roll. Complete with melody, harmony, and bass, blues piano was a self-sufficient music machine, able to provide solo entertainment for dances at roadhouses and private parties. One variation was the house rent party, when guests, for a small fee to help pay a month's rent, would be treated to good food and piano music. Plains pianists included Sammy Price, Pete Johnson, and Jay McShann. At the time of writing, McShann, in his eighties, is still active and a consummate master of virtually every classic jazz piano idiom.

Beginning after World War I and continuing throughout the 1920s until their decline during the Depression, territory bands flourished in the Great Plains. Stated simply, a territory band is an ensemble based in an outlying area, where sparse population necessitated traveling great distances for social activities. Territory bands tended to monopolize the music of these regions, and, like big fish in small ponds, they enjoyed a local but not a regional reputation. Because the early recording industry was centered in the East, many of

these barnstorming groups have not been preserved on vinyl; however, several future jazz and blues stars cut their teeth in territory bands. The goal of most groups was eventually to relocate to the big cities, especially Kansas City, which by the mid-1930s had become a mecca for jazz.

The musical styles of these groups, though varying considerably, involved an approach, distinct from the recorded groups in the East, that eventually became defined in the Kansas City style of the late 1930s and was also an integral component of bebop jazz, which emerged after World War II. A brash exuberance, heavily based on the blues, marked the sound of the territory bands. Using the familiar blues as a framework encouraged improvisation, and some of the arrangements were assembled on the spot without written charts. These "head arrangements" used short, repeated motifs called "riffs" that could be easily picked up by ear and that served as melodies and backgrounds behind soloists. Another ingredient of the sound of these groups was the use of syncopated ragtime rhythms. Much of ragtime was developed in nearby Missouri, especially in Sedalia, with the work of Scott Joplin. The typical instrumentation of these bands consisted of about three saxophones, three or four brass instruments, and a rhythm section of piano, guitar or banjo, bass (tuba later replacing string bass), piano, and drums. Over time, the size of the orchestra was increased with the addition of more reed and brass instruments.

One of the most important Plains territory bands was Andy Kirk and the Clouds of Joy, which originated in Oklahoma City and included future piano sensation Mary Lou Williams. Buster Smith's troop began in Dallas before relocating and gaining fame as the Oklahoma City Blue Devils. This legendary group included Walter Page on bass, the influential Lester Young on tenor saxophone, blues shouter Jimmy Rushing, and the great Bill "Count" Basie on piano. George Morrison's band, which dominated the Denver scene well into the 1940s, served as an apprenticeship for John Lewis (later of the Modern Jazz Quartet) and Jimmy Lunceford.

The most classic synthesis of African American musical evolution on the Plains was Kansas City jazz. In the competitive struggle of the territory bands for preeminence, the band of Bennie Moten and Count Basie won the day. Moten began leading bands in the early 1920s, making his first recording in 1923. Eventually, he lured an impressive lineup away from rival bands, including Walter Page, Jimmy Rushing, trumpeter "Hot Lips" Page, and, most importantly, Count Basie, who joined Moten in 1929. During an East Coast tour, Bennie Moten's Kansas City Orchestra recorded what many scholars feel are the first definitive swing classics. Moten died unexpectedly during minor surgery in 1935, and, after a brief hiatus, the band was reassembled with Basie as the leader. This ensemble featured Lester Young, Walter Page, Freddie Green on guitar, and Jo Jones on drums. Basie's orchestra went on to rival Duke

Ellington's as the most important black ensemble of the period. Its no-nonsense, "straight-ahead" style is still emulated by many traditional big bands of today.

It remained for a native of Kansas City, Kansas, to complete the transformation of the territory band tradition to modern jazz. Charlie "Yardbird" Parker, born in 1920, came of age during the decade of the 1940s, the golden age of Kansas City jazz. Wide-open jam sessions featuring traveling musicians provided a democratic forum for young players to learn and to prove themselves. Playing professionally by age fifteen, Parker made his first important recordings in Wichita, Kansas, in 1940 with Jay McShann's blues-based band. There he also acquired his nickname, "Yardbird" or "Bird." Parker, along with Dizzy Gillespie, Thelonious Monk, and others, went on to create bebop, the first modern jazz style, combining the energy of the blues and territory bands of the Plains with the harmonic sophistication of the East Coast. Parker died in New York City in 1955, a victim of hard living.

The Plains region has proven especially fertile soil for saxophonists. These include tenor saxophonist Ben Webster, born in Kansas City, Missouri, and Herschel Evans, from Denton, Texas. Webster's deep tone was a feature of the great Ellington bands of the 1930s. Evans played with Count Basie alongside Lester Young. Later players included the iconoclastic Ornette Coleman, born in 1930 in Fort Worth, Texas. Playing in a highly original style that combined elements of blues and bebop, Coleman helped create a new, avant-garde language for jazz in the 1960s. More recently, Dewey Redman and Julius Hemphill, both also from Fort Worth, have continued the rich tradition of Plains saxophonists.

Previously separated for the most part by segregation, the streams of black and white music began swimming together after World War II, leading directly to the rock and roll of the 1950s. The most important immediate precursor to rock was rhythm and blues. R&B (the term was first coined by *Billboard Magazine* in 1949) combined elements of earlier blues and gospel, big band swing and boogie-woogie, and resulted in an infectious dance music that appealed to both white and black listeners. Initially shunned by major labels, R&B was recorded by small, independent recording companies and disseminated over radio.

Important R&B artists from the Plains included Wynonie Harris and King Curtis (born Curtis Outen). Harris, born in Omaha in 1915 (or possibly 1913), began as a big band singer before making his most influential R&B recordings with King Records. King Curtis became one of R&B's most sought after saxophonists. Born in Fort Worth in 1934, he went on to record with the Coasters, Wilson Pickett, Sam and Dave, and Aretha Franklin before launching a successful solo career. He was stabbed to death in New York City in 1971.

Rockabilly and Rock and Roll

During the 1950s white musicians began combining elements of rhythm and blues with country music in a classic phase of early rock and roll known as rockabilly. The most important early rock and roll musician from the Great Plains was Buddy Holly. Charles Hardin Holley, born in 1936 in Lubbock, Texas, was one of rock's first great composers, guitarists (he helped popularize the Fender Stratocaster), vocalists, and bandleaders. He had a direct influence on many later artists, including Bob Dylan and the Beatles, whose very name is a tribute to Holly's band, the Crickets. Yet his career, cut short by a plane crash that also claimed the lives of the Big Bopper and Richie Valens, only lasted two years. Holly started out playing western swing, but after his band opened for Elvis Presley in 1957 he turned to rock and roll. Spurred on by the success of his number one hit, "That'll Be the Day," Holly and the Crickets became one of the few white bands to play the Apollo Theater in Harlem. Unlike his chief competitors, Elvis and Jerry Lee Lewis, Holly's success was based more on his musicianship than on a frantic stage demeanor. Another early rock star from the Plains was Eddie Cochran, who like Holly had a spectacular brief career cut short by an accident. He was born in Oklahoma City and enjoyed his greatest success as a singer-guitarist with "Summertime Blues" in 1957. He died in an auto crash in London in 1960.

Perceived as a menace to society and incurring the envy of the major recording companies, rock and roll came under attack at the end of the 1950s, and a clean-cut, toned-down, more acceptable form of rock was created that centered on so-called teen idols. While many of them came from Philadelphia (home of the influential Dick Clark TV program *American Bandstand*), one of these popular singers hailed from Fargo, North Dakota. Bobby Vee got his start when his band filled in for the late Buddy Holly in Moorhead, Minnesota. His innocent songs of teenage love made him a star by the early 1960s. While hardly a teen idol, mention should be made of another popular success from North Dakota, Peggy Lee. Born in 1920 in Jamestown, Lee's long and varied career began as a vocalist with the Benny Goodman Orchestra.

Popular Music of the Sixties

The decade of the 1960s saw an explosion of popular music, the most important of which adopted a political and social agenda not found in the music of the previous decade. Furthermore, the music deepened in technological, compositional, and textual complexity, creating a myriad of styles that combined and reconfigured older forms. While the principal creative arenas for this activity were on the coasts and in England, some prominent rock stars of the 1960s originated in the Great Plains.

The most influential rock styles emanating from the Great Plains quite naturally reflected the region's long background in blues and country music. Buddy Miles was born in Omaha, Nebraska, in 1946. His early solo efforts combined R&B with psychedelic rock. He has also enjoyed a diverse career, playing with Wilson Pickett, Electric Flag, Jimi Hendrix, and Santana. Elvin Bishop, born in Tulsa, Oklahoma, absorbed the Chicago blues style and played with Bob Dylan and the Paul Butterfield Blues Band before leading his own rock band in the 1970s. Other rock musicians from the Plains include Randy Bachman, J. J. Cale, and the band REO Speedwagon. Bachman was born in Winnipeg and was a founding member of the Guess Who. After leaving the band, he went on to form Bachman-Turner Overdrive, which reaped immense success and helped to define a middle ground between the emerging heavy rock of the mid-1970s and more conventional rock idioms. J. J. Cale, born in Oklahoma City, Oklahoma, is a prolific country-blues-rock singer-songwriter whose songs have been recorded by Eric Clapton and Lynyrd Skynyrd.

Just as rock dipped into country music for new fusion possibilities, progressive country purposefully incorporated rock elements to broaden its fan base. Delbert McClinton, born in Lubbock in 1940, has recorded in blues and country styles. Closer to the country style are such well-known performers as John Denver (born in Roswell, New Mexico, in 1943) and Tanya Tucker (born in Seminole, Texas, in 1958). Garth Brooks, born in Tulsa, Oklahoma, in 1962, became country's biggest star of the 1990s. Influenced by diverse bands such as Kiss, Lynyrd Skynyrd, and Styx, combined with traditional models such as Hank Williams Sr. and Lefty Frizzell, Brooks's music appealed to crossover fans of both country and rock. Listed by *Billboard Magazine* as the top grossing country artist from 1991 to 1993, Brooks led the way in creating a new eclectic style and confirmed country's position as the most popular musical genre in America.

Another fusion music developing in the Southern Plains reflects a Latino, Tex-Mex heritage. Joe "King" Carrasco was born in Dumas, Texas, and began working in the Austin area in 1973 performing what he calls "nuevo wavo," a combination of rock, Chicano polkas, and new wave. Brave Combo, also from Texas, blends polka, rock, salsa, and other Latin styles to create a quirky, iconoclastic mix. Both Carrasco and Brave Combo, while enjoying regional fame, have yet to achieve national attention.

Combining the improvisation of bebop with the rhythms and amplified instruments of blues and rock, jazz rock (or fusion) became an important direction in the 1970s. Two Plains bands reflecting two different approaches to fusion are Kansas and Mannheim Steamroller. Kansas, formed in Topeka in 1970, began as a high school garage band before evolving into an ornate art rock ensemble, utilizing classical and jazz elements. Chip Davis and his synthesized Mannheim Steamroller came out of Omaha and have maintained a large following through a commercial, formulaic mix of New Age and fusion patterns.

Although relatively few in number, singer-songwriters from the Canadian Plains exerted their special influence on mainstream popular music. Buffy Sainte-Marie, a Cree Indian, was born in Saskatchewan in 1941. She became the first popular Native American musician, recording extensively from 1964 to 1981. An activist for Native peoples' rights, she also appeared on the children's TV program *Sesame Street* from 1976 to 1981. Joni Mitchell, born Roberta Joan Anderson in Fort Macleod, Alberta, in 1943, began performing while a student at Alberta College of Art in Calgary. Mitchell emerged as a distinctive voice in mid-sixties folk rock with her sophisticated confessional lyrics sung in a unique recitative style. Continuing to evolve, she has incorporated jazz elements and world music into her repertoire. The controversial k. d. lang (Katheryn Dawn Lang) was raised on a farm in Consort, Alberta, in 1962. lang (she prefers the lower case) studied classical piano and guitar before turning to country music with a style partly modeled on that of Patsy Cline. She was voted vocalist of the year by *Rolling Stone Magazine* in 1983 and achieved international recognition with her performance at the 1988 Calgary Winter Olympics. Her open lesbianism and activity as a spokesperson for the "antimeat" movement have imbued recordings such as *All You Can Eat* (1995) with the kind of controversy associated more with rock than country music.

Another seminal figure from the Canadian Plains, one who has defied categorization by covering a variety of rock idioms during his career, is Neil Young. Born in Toronto in 1945, Young moved to Winnipeg when he was fifteen before moving to California in 1966, where he helped form the rock band Buffalo Springfield. An ensuing solo career that has lasted to the present day was punctuated by a stint with Crosby, Stills, Nash and Young, including an appearance at Woodstock. One of the most enduring and consistently creative of the 1960s generation of rock stars, Young has turned out more than fifty albums, ranging in style from acoustic ballads to country rock and especially hard rock.

The Present

The Great Plains region continues to provide a nurturing environment for young musicians: Melissa Etheridge from Leavenworth, Kansas, Matthew Sweet from Lincoln, Nebraska, and Reba McIntire out of McAlester, Oklahoma, are among the most recent in this distinguished parade of artists. The winds that have eavesdropped on so much diverse music still blow unimpeded through the Great Plains, but today this music is no longer lost to the open spaces. Classical music, no longer an imported product from Europe or the East Coast, flourishes in universities and in symphony and opera companies. Community bands with summer concerts in the park as well as the polka bands of the Sokol Halls and roadhouses are still found in numerous Czech, Swedish, and German communities and help maintain a sense of cultural continuity. New country music, especially on the Southern Plains, continues to combine and reinvent itself, while blues and jazz are studied and preserved in schools and community ensembles and played

in venues throughout the region. The underground rock scene prospers in college communities, and, perhaps most significantly, given its longevity, Native American music is alive and evolving while still maintaining its ties to tradition.

See also AFRICAN AMERICANS: Christian, Charlie; Coleman, Ornette; Harris, Wynonie; McDaniel, Hattie; McShann, Jay / FILM: Autry, Gene / NATIVE AMERICANS: Powwows / RELIGION: Black Elk, Nicholas; Ghost Dance; Native American Church; Vision Quest.

Randall L. Snyder
University of Nebraska–Lincoln

Carr, Patrick, ed. *The Illustrated History of Country Music*. New York: Doubleday, 1979. Dyer, Karen. "Music on the Nebraska Plains." Master's thesis, University of Nebraska–Lincoln, 1979. Garofalo, Reebee. *Rockin' Out: Popular Music in the USA*. Boston: Allyn and Bacon, 1997. Hitchcock, H. Wiley. *Music in the United States*. Englewood Cliffs NJ: Prentice-Hall, 1988. Keil, Charles. *Urban Blues*. Chicago: University of Chicago Press, 1966. Neihardt, John G. *Black Elk Speaks*. Lincoln: University of Nebraska Press, 1961. Nettle, Bruno. *Folk Music in the United States*. Detroit: Wayne State University Press, 1976. Romanowski, Patricia, and Holly George-Warren, eds. *The New Rolling Stone Encyclopedia of Rock and Roll*. New York: Fireside, 1995. Russell, Ross. *Jazz Style in Kansas City and the Southwest*. London: University of California Press, 1971. Schuller, Gunther. *Early Jazz*. New York: Oxford University Press, 1968. Southern, Eileen. *The Music of Black Americans*. New York: W. W. Norton, 1983. Thorp, N. Howard. *Songs of the Cowboy*. New York: Clarkson N. Potter, 1966.

AUTRY, GENE

See FILM: Autry, Gene

AXTON, HOYT (1938–1999)

Singer, songwriter, guitarist, and actor Hoyt Axton was born on March 25, 1938, in the small town of Duncan in southwestern Oklahoma. He was the son of Mae Boren Axton (1915–97), who cowrote the 1956 Elvis Presley hit song "Heartbreak Hotel." A football scholarship led to Oklahoma University, though he left in the late 1950s to join the navy.

Axton began writing and performing on his own in West Coast music clubs during the burgeoning folk music revival of the late 1950s and early 1960s. While he built up a loyal following on the folk club circuit, he remained relatively unknown until his song "Greenback Dollar" was recorded by the Kingston Trio in 1962; it led to a recording contract with Horizon Records and albums such as *Balladeer* (1962), *Thunder 'n' Lightning* (1963), and *Saturday's Child* (1963).

The popular rock band Steppenwolf recorded Axton's song "The Pusher" in 1964; it rose to the top levels of the pop charts and was eventually included in the sound track of the 1969 film *Easy Rider*. In the mid-1960s Axton became interested in acting and performed in the television series *Bonanza*, *Bionic Woman*, and *McCloud*. His later motion picture roles included parts in *Black Stallion* (1979), *E.T.* (1983), and *Gremlins* (1984). He was also a guest on many television talk and variety shows.

The rock band Three Dog Night recorded

Axton's "Joy to the World" and "Never Been to Spain" in 1971 and took him on tour as an opening act. Concert tours of the United States, Europe, and Asia followed, along with the recording of many more albums. His songs have also been recorded by Waylon Jennings, Glen Campbell, John Denver, and Ringo Starr. Hoyt Axton died on October 26, 1999, at his home in Victor, Montana.

Bill Markwick
Toronto, Ontario

Clarke, Donald. *The Penguin Encyclopedia of Popular Music*. London: Viking Books, 1989. Stambler, Irwin, and Landon Grelun. *The Encyclopedia of Folk, Country & Western Music*. New York: St. Martin's Press, 1984.

BAKER, CHET (1929–1988)

Chet Baker was a jazz trumpeter and extraordinary musical stylist who helped define the "cool jazz" era of the 1950s. He was born in Yale, Oklahoma, on December 23, 1929. When he was about eleven years old his family moved to California, where the cool jazz movement would later thrive. Baker developed his trumpet-playing ability in the Glendale High School band and in the army. His philosophy of jazz was formed in the jazz clubs along Central Avenue in Los Angeles. In 1951, after his second discharge from the army, he began playing with Charlie Parker after winning an audition that Parker had staged at the Tiffany Club.

But it was Gerry Mulligan, a popular arranger and composer during the 1940s, who launched Baker's career with the Mulligan quartet in 1952. Theoretically, this unique quartet, which consisted only of bass, drums, baritone saxophone, and trumpet but excluded piano and guitar, should have had a thin, dead sound, with limited possibility for creativity. However, due to the players' talent and vision, the Mulligan quartet was very well received, and Chet Baker became famous. He was even named the best trumpeter of 1954 by *Down Beat* magazine. Baker was a member of the Mulligan quartet for only one year. Despite a drug dependency, he maintained a steady international solo career from the time he left the quartet until his mysterious death on May 13, 1988, when his body was found on the sidewalk in front of his hotel in Amsterdam.

Chet Baker is remembered for his velvety tone, his uncanny ability to create beautiful musical lines during improvisation solos, and his masterful phrasing. He was also well known for his smooth, laid-back singing voice. With his handsome face, rebellious gaze, and interpretation of songs like "You've Changed" and "My Funny Valentine," he personified cool and radiated romance.

Jay Wilkinson
University of Oklahoma

Carr, Roy. *A Century of Jazz*. New York: Da Capo Press, 1997. Gioia, Ted. *West Coast Jazz: Modern Jazz in California, 1945–1960*. Berkeley: University of California Press, 1998. Morgenstern, Dan. *Jazz People*. New York: Da Capo Press, 1976.

BORDER RADIO

In 1931 Kansas-native "Doctor" J. R. Brinkley founded radio station XERA (later XERF) in Villa Acuna, Coahuila, Mexico, due south of San Angelo, Texas. It was the first border radio station, positioned just over the Rio Grande and aimed northward at the American audience.

In Mexico, where wildcat station owners were unfettered by the Federal Communication Commission's regulations on wattage output, stations like XERA could transmit in excess of 500,000 watts. In the Great Plains, where the level topography of the land means that radio waves are usually obstructed only by the curvature of the earth, signals (particularly AM frequencies) can travel hundreds, sometimes thousands of miles before fading out. The result was a string of stations just across the Mexican border that garnered massive audiences.

Border radio stations were huge money-makers for station owners who sold programming time, fundamental evangelists, and a stunning array of entrepreneurs who used the airwaves to run mail-order businesses. On the artistic side, music ranged from country and gospel to *conjunto* and rhythm and blues, and musicians like Bob Wills used border radio to widen their audiences. From 1938 to 1939 the Carter family actually lived in Mexico and broadcast live on border radio stations. The stations' massive radius of air coverage also allowed them to serve as a platform for numerous self-made celebrities. Flour salesman Wilbert Lee "Pappy" O'Daniel used border radio to become a western swing music impresario and later governor of Texas. A young disc jockey named Bobby Smith created the persona of Wolfman Jack in the mid-1960s on XERF, where he also served as station manager. He soon parlayed this into national success.

A 1968 Mexico-U.S. treaty finally put a cap on border station wattage. However, nostalgia over these stations has been celebrated in song by the likes of zz Top ("Heard It on the x"), John Hiatt ("Pirate Radio"), and Dave Alvin ("Border Radio").

See also MEDIA: Brinkley, John Richard.

Akim D. Reinhardt
Towson University

Fowler, Gene, and Bill Crawford. *Border Radio: Quacks, Yodelers, Pitchmen, and Other Amazing Broadcasters of the American Airwaves*. Austin: Texas Monthly Press, 1987. Jack, Wolfman, with Byron Laursen. *Have Mercy! Confessions of the Original Rock 'n' Roll Animal*. New York: Warner Books, 1995.

BROOKS, GARTH (b. 1962)

Country music superstar Troyal Garth Brooks was born on February 7, 1962, in Tulsa, Oklahoma. He is the youngest child of Troyal Raymond and Colleen Carroll Brooks. He has one older brother, Kelly, and four older half-siblings. Soon after Brooks's birth, the Brooks family moved to Yukon, Oklahoma, a small town outside of Oklahoma City. Country music was relatively important in Brooks's family (his mother had a short stint as a singer for

Garth Brooks, 1987

Capitol Records in Nashville in the 1950s), but his formative years did not indicate that he was country music royalty in the making.

Growing up, he was more interested in athletics than music. In grade school and high school he played baseball, basketball, and football and ran track. He was influenced by the popular music of the 1970s: American singer-songwriter types such as Jim Croce, James Taylor, Don McLean, and Dan Fogelberg and "arena-rock" bands such as Bob Seger and the Silver Bullet Band, Kansas, KISS, Journey, and Foreigner.

After graduating from Yukon High School in 1980, Brooks went to Oklahoma State University (OSU) in Stillwater, Oklahoma, on a partial track scholarship (javelin throw). Like most OSU freshmen, Brooks quickly discovered that music and nightlife were a significant part of Stillwater culture. Near campus, on Washington Street, was a three-block row of restaurants and bars known as the Strip where local musicians performed nightly for beer-guzzling students.

Inspired by the variety of music and the skill of many of the musicians he met, Brooks began to spend every moment of his free time practicing the guitar—an instrument he'd taken up, along with the banjo, in high school —and singing and writing songs. He eventually made his musical headquarters at Willie's, a bar on the Strip that was saloonlike in style but always hosted an eclectic audience. Over time, Brooks developed a substantial repertoire of different styles of music. Between performing onstage and for the track team, Brooks managed to earn a degree in advertising, graduating in 1984.

In June 1987 Brooks and his band, Santa Fe, moved to Nashville. The band broke up shortly after the move, due to artistic differences. But Brooks confidently presented himself to the Nashville public, eventually catching the eye of former ASCAP executive Bob Doyle. Doyle became Brooks's manager and, less than a year after Brooks had moved to Nashville, landed his charismatic young charge a contract with Capitol Records. In 1988 he released his first album, simply entitled *Garth Brooks*. Less than eight years later, he had become the biggest-

selling solo artist of all time, in the process earning numerous music industry awards and worldwide popularity.

Matt O'Meilia
Tulsa, Oklahoma

O'Meilia, Matt. *Garth Brooks: The Road out of Santa Fe*. Oklahoma: University of Oklahoma Press, 1997.

CHRISTIAN, CHARLIE

See AFRICAN AMERICANS: Christian, Charlie

CLASSICAL MUSIC

On the Great Plains frontier, classical music may seem to have disappeared from the milieu of settlers, and of course its presence was very much diminished. However, traces of its existence could be found in the instruction books and other material to be played on parlor organs (some of which were to be found in the sod structures of the Plains) or to be used in piano instruction for children, an early feature of the settlement era. Private classical instruction in other instruments and voice followed in many communities. A basis for the classical tradition also existed almost immediately in the music of many religious services. Often shortly after the arrival of the railroad, in some localities church choirs were formed that undertook the performance of anthems reflecting the classical tradition if not actually being composed by Handel or Haydn. Eventually, in larger communities, building on the church choir tradition (which still continues), choral societies were formed that presented oratorios. Denver's Musical Union (1867) is among the earliest of these societies. About the same time, the development of independent concert orchestras began. Often consisting of about twenty members, many of these efforts had an ephemeral existence, lasting sometimes for only one or two concerts or perhaps a season before the development of more durable organizations that in turn may have been dissolved themselves during times of depression or war.

The approach of the twentieth century saw the appearance of classical selections on the programs of the many wind bands of the era. Verdi and Wagner were particularly popular, and of one ensemble, that of Frederick Innes, it was said in Omaha in 1898 that "there is but one Wagner, and Innes is his prophet."

With the establishment of railroads came the appearance of touring artists at communities along the line. Before the turn of the twentieth century and after, artists such as Madam Albani, Madam Melba, the Mendelssohn Quintette Club, the Metropolitan Opera, the Theodore Thomas Orchestra, and many others made their way to larger centers in the Great Plains. In some cases these appearances were sponsored by local musical societies, many of which are still important in the musical life of communities. In addition, there are over seventy concert agencies that offer classical artists to the public.

Before the middle of the twentieth century,

universities began to play an important part, which still continues, in the public presentation of classical music, either through their own series of guest or faculty artists or the performance of their campus ensembles such as choirs, orchestras, and wind groups. Most composers of the region have, during this time, become situated at universities. Almost universally, school systems offer experience and instruction in classical music, both vocal and instrumental, to students, as do many hundreds of private instructors.

Prominent artists who have their origins in the region include clarinetist James Campbell (Leduc, Alberta), tenor Jon Vickers (Prince Albert, Saskatchewan), bass Samuel Ramey (Colby, Kansas), composers Roy Harris (Lincoln County, Oklahoma) and Howard Hanson (Wahoo, Nebraska), and composer-critic Virgil Thomson (Kansas City, Missouri). Thomson said of his compositions written during his years abroad: "I wanted Paris . . . to understand the ways we like to think and feel on the banks of the Kaw and the Missouri." Orchestral works reflecting the attributes of the region include Sowerby's *Prairie* (1929) and Thomson's soundtrack to the film *The Plow That Broke the Plains* (1936).

Well over fifty independent symphony orchestras are to be found in the region as well as thirty orchestras maintained by colleges or universities that in some cases include community members. Ten of the orchestras—the Calgary Philharmonic and the Edmonton Symphony in Alberta; the Winnipeg Symphony in Manitoba; the Colorado Symphony (Denver) and Colorado Springs Symphony in Colorado; the Omaha Symphony in Nebraska; the Kansas City Symphony in Missouri; the Wichita Symphony in Kansas; and the Oklahoma Philharmonic and Tulsa Philharmonic in Oklahoma—have budgets in excess of $1 million. Many communities also support wind ensembles over and above those sponsored by educational institutions. In more recent times, youth orchestras independent of educational institutions have been formed in several larger centers.

Choral ensembles presently flourish in considerable number either independently, associated with a symphony orchestra, as a community function of universities or colleges, or as an ensemble exclusively for students. A number of independent children's choruses are also active. Fifteen professional ballet or dance companies presently operate in the region. Larger centers often possess concert facilities specifically designed for classical music such as the Jack Singer Concert Hall in Calgary, the Boettcher Concert Hall in Denver, and the Century II Concert Hall in Wichita.

Bruce Lobaugh
Omaha, Nebraska

American Symphony Orchestra League, Washington DC. *1998–99 North and Central American Directory*. New York: Amateur Chamber Music Players, 1998. *Musical America International Directory of the Performing Arts*. Hightstown NJ: Primedia Information, 1998.

COCHRAN, EDDIE (1938–1960)

Eddie Cochran, the pioneering rock and roll songwriter, singer, and guitarist with the James Dean good looks, was a product of a Plains background, even though his place of birth remains disputed. Some rock references maintain that he was born in Oklahoma City; others have him coming into the world in Albert Lea, Minnesota. The date, October 3, 1938, is not in dispute, nor is the fact that his parents moved from Oklahoma City to Albert Lea at some point during the 1930s. Cochran himself claimed Oklahoma City as his hometown, and the country and western music that his parents absorbed in Oklahoma was a formative influence on the young musician.

By the time the family moved on to California in 1953, Eddie Cochran had become an accomplished guitarist. He started his career as backup guitarist to hillbilly singer Hank Cochran (not related), but his big break came when he teamed up with songwriter Jerry Capehart and obtained a recording contract with Liberty. The hits started coming in 1957, and he soared into prominence in 1958 with "Summertime Blues," that raucous outburst of teenage frustration and rebelliousness. More hits followed, including "C'mon Everybody" and "Somethin' Else," and Cochran seemed positioned to move up alongside Elvis Presley as a superstar when, in 1960, he embarked on a tour of Britain with his friend Gene Vincent. The tour was a great success; both artists were already superstars in Britain. Cochran played his last concert at the Bristol Hippodrome on April 16. The following day, Easter Sunday, on the way to Heathrow Airport, their car crashed into a lamppost, killing Cochran and badly injuring Vincent.

Eddie Cochran, despite his early death, had a lasting impact on rock music. Many artists, including the Sex Pistols and, most famously, the Who, have recorded his songs. He was inducted into the Rock and Roll Hall of Fame in 1987.

David J. Wishart
University of Nebraska–Lincoln

COLEMAN, ORNETTE

See AFRICAN AMERICANS: Coleman, Ornette

COUNTRY MUSIC

Southern white rural music, subsequently called "hillbilly" in the 1920s and "country" in the late 1940s, evolved from the reservoir of folk music brought to North America by Anglo-Celtic immigrants and West African slaves. In its embryonic stages the music was marked by several vocal and instrumental characteristics that had been transplanted to colonial America. A large part of the early country music repertoire was derived from the vast body of Anglo-Scottish-Irish ballads that existed during the colonial period. Compilations of ballads that indicate many of them diffused westward to the Great Plains include John A. Lomax's *Cowboy Songs and Other Frontier Ballads* (1910) and William A. Owens's *Texas Folk Songs* (1950).

Historically associated with the Great Plains are two major country music instruments: fiddle and guitar. The fiddle probably entered the Great Plains with the Lewis and Clark expedition. It was an ideal frontier instrument and, in fact, was often referred to in the nineteenth century as the "royal instrument of the frontier." People moving westward into the Great Plains states carried the small, compact fiddle in their wagons or in their saddlebags. The fiddler could generally be heard anywhere a crowd gathered, including political rallies, militia musters, housewarmings, barn raisings, and fiddle contests.

Fiddlin' Eck Robertson from Amarillo, Texas, who recorded in the 1920s, was one of the first country musicians. Robertson, long known for his fiddling prowess at Texas fiddle contests, recorded "Sally Goodin" for the Victor Company of New York in 1923. Robertson played the song on the WBAP radio barn dance program in Fort Worth about a year later. The WBAP *Barn Dance* lays claim to having produced one of the first radio barn dance programs in the United States, about a year before the WLS (Chicago) *National Barn Dance* and almost three years before the WSM (Nashville) *Grand Ole Opry*.

Most musicologists agree that the guitar filtered northward from Mexico into Texas, where rural blacks mastered the instrument. Long associated with country blues, the guitar spread from the Texas cotton fields eastward to other sections of the Lowland South, especially with the increased migrations of freed blacks following the Emancipation Proclamation of 1863.

Seven substyles of country music emerged during the twentieth century. Four of these originated in the Great Plains states of Texas and Oklahoma: singing cowboy, western swing, honky-tonk, and country rock. The first singing cowboy song to draw national attention was "Home on the Range," created in Kansas in 1873 by Dr. Brewster Higley, a homesteader in Smith County who wrote the words, and Dan Kelly, who lived near Harlan in the same county and composed the music. The first of the singing cowboy stylists were Carl T. Sprague, Goebel Reeves, and Jules Verne Allen, all from Texas. The songs they performed were based on numerous ballads written in the nineteenth century by authentic cowboys while they sat around the campfire or rested in the bunkhouse. Examples include "When the Work's All Done This Fall," "The Cowboy's Prayer," and "Following the Cow Trail." Texas also produced the singing cowboy performers who made the substyle nationally popular— Gene Autry and Woodward Maurice Ritter, better known as "Tex."

Western swing began to evolve in the late 1920s, when Bob Wills (from Kosse, Texas) organized the Wills Fiddle Band and Milton Brown (from Stephenville, Texas) developed the Musical Brownies, both in Fort Worth. The city soon gained a reputation as the "cradle of western swing" because the musicians were from the vicinity and local radio stations were promoting the new sound. After moving to Tulsa in the mid-1930s, Wills made country music history by adding reeds and brass to his band, which then numbered from fifteen to eighteen pieces. Other distinctive instrumental ingredients included multiple fiddles playing harmony; a strong rhythm section composed of drums, bass, and tenor banjo; and the jazzlike improvisation of the steel guitar. Wills created western swing for dancing, and it became the big band sound of the 1930s applied to country music.

After the repeal of Prohibition, hundreds of rural musicians found employment in the bars, roadhouses, and taverns of Texas and Oklahoma. These social institutions, collectively referred to as honky-tonks, were frequented by farmers, truck drivers, and oil field roustabouts who gathered to relax, drink beer, and release their frustration with a round of "hell raising." These activities were coupled with listening and dancing to music. To prevail over the rowdy clientele, the music became louder, and a steady, heavy beat was necessary for dancing. Although many honky-tonkers danced, the substyle was essentially lyric oriented and aimed at working-class listeners. Lyrical content typically dealt with the listener's problems, including drink, illicit love, and divorce. Frequently termed "cryin' in your beer" or "tear in your beer" music, honky-tonk titles included "Divorce Me C.O.D.," "Honky Tonk Blues," and "It Makes No Difference Now." Texans, including Al Dexter, Ted Daffan, Moon Mullican, and preeminently Ernest Tubb, were in the forefront in legitimizing honky-tonk in the 1930s. Later, honky-tonk was further popularized by Texans such as Ray Price, George Jones, and Lefty Frizzell.

Country rock, also known as "redneck rock," "country counterculture," and "progressive country," was first centered in Austin, Texas, especially at the Armadillo World Headquarters, founded in 1970 in an old National Guard armory. It increasingly featured country entertainers, especially Texas musicians, who appealed to both country and rock audiences, including Kinky Friedman and the Texas Jewboys, Frieda and the Firedogs, and Asleep at the Wheel. Two native-born Texans, Willie Nelson and Waylon Jennings, returned to Austin in the 1970s to lead the "Austin Sound" movement. Because of their laid-back lifestyle and exposure to a number of musical cultures, both Waylon and Willie were receptive to the rock forms and musicians already on the Austin scene.

Oklahoma and Texas have been the most prolific Great Plains states in the production of country music performers and composers. According to recent biographical data, Texas ranks first in total production, with more than 100 artists, while Oklahoma has spawned more than 60, ranking it fourth after Texas, Kentucky, and Tennessee in terms of per capita output.

One of the major pioneers in country music vocals was Vernon Dalhart (Marion Slaughter) from Jefferson, Texas. Slaughter, in searching for a stage name, took the names of two Texas towns. Dalhart is noted for recording the first

country music megahit in 1924, "The Prisoner's Song" and "Wreck of the Old 97," which became the biggest selling record (estimated at six million) for the Victor Company during the preelectric recording period. In addition to the Texans who contributed to the singing cowboy, western swing, honky-tonk, and country rock genres of country music, the list of Texas country artists is impressive, including Mickey Gilley, Kris Kristofferson, Kenny Rogers, Barbara and Louise Mandrell, Jim Reeves, Buck Owens, Hank Thompson, Tanya Tucker, Don Williams, Johnny Rodriguez, Larry Gatlin, and Janie Fricke. Moreover, the state continues to produce new talent such as Ronnie Dunn of Brooks and Dunn, Collin Raye, Lee Roy Parnell, Ty Herndon, Tracy Byrd, Junior Brown, Clay Walker, LeAnn Rimes, Lyle Lovett, Neal McCoy, Tracy Lawrence, Mark Chestnutt, George Strait, and Clint Black.

Overlooked country music artists born in Oklahoma include Spade Cooley, known as the King of Western Swing, who reportedly fronted the largest band ever assembled in country music; Otto Gray and his Oklahoma Cowboys, one of the most important groups in the commercialization of country music; and two African American performers and songwriters, Big Al Downing and Stoney Edwards. Several Oklahoma-born women vied for the title of Queen of Country Music during the 1960s, when women were finally beginning to achieve equal status with males: Molly Bee, Wanda Jackson, Norma Jean, Bonnie Owens, and Jeanie Shepherd. In addition to the recent megastars Garth Brooks, Vince Gill, and Reba McEntire, Oklahoma has produced a cadre of new artists such as Joe Diffie, Wade Hayes, Toby Keith, and Bryan White.

Kansas-born country artists include Carson J. Robison (Oswego), one of the pioneer songwriters of the 1920s. His compositions include "My Blue Ridge Mountain Home," "The Wreck of the Number Nine," and "Naomi Wise." Robison's lifelong career in the songwriting business culminated in the 1948 hit, "Life Gets Teejus Don't It." Border radio station entrepreneur and bogus physician Dr. John Richard Brinkley started his first radio station in Milford, Kansas, in 1923. Brinkley's major contribution to country music was his employment of several hillbilly music performers on his station such as Uncle Bob Larkin as well as the use of a hillbilly band in his races for governor of Kansas in 1930 and 1932. Wendell Hall of St. George was one of the first hillbilly singers to sell a million records with his 1923 recording of "It Ain't Gonna Rain No More." Coffeyville's Rodney Lay is best known for his songwriting talents with compositions such as "He's Got a Way with Women," "Seven Days Come Sunday," and "You Could've Heard a Heartbreak." Harry "Hap" Peebles was born in Anthony and promoted artists such as Roy Acuff, Ernest Tubb, and Dolly Parton, served on the Country Music Association (CMA) board of directors for sixteen years, and received the first Promoter of the Year Award from the CMA. The newest country artist from Kansas is Martina McBride from Sharon. Her 1990s hits include "My Baby Loves Me" and "Independence Day."

Tompall and the Glaser Brothers, a family group from Spalding that operated off and on from the 1950s to the 1980s, is the best-known country act from Nebraska. Beginning their career on local radio and television stations in Hastings and Holdredge, the group first appeared on the *Grand Ole Opry* in 1960. In 1968 the brothers opened their own recording studio in Nashville, which became the unofficial headquarters for the flourishing outlaw music movement. Named vocal group of the year in 1971 by the CMA and vocal group of the decade in 1974 by *Record World*, they scored their biggest success in 1981 with "Lovin' Her Was Easier (Than Anything I'll Ever Do Again)."

Grand Forks, North Dakota, boasts one of the most celebrated female country artists of the 1970s. Lynn Anderson's "I Never Promised You a Rose Garden" (1970) topped both country and pop charts and won her the title of best female vocalist in 1971 by the CMA. This Grammy Award winner was voted country artist of the decade by *Record World* magazine for her string of number one hits in the 1970s, including the aforementioned "Rose Garden," "You're My Man" (1971), "How Can I Unlove You" (1972), "Keep Me in Mind" (1974), and "What a Man, My Man Is" (1975).

Montana is the birthplace of two well-known female country performers: Jana Jae of Great Falls and Nicolette Larson of Helena. Jae, often described as the First Lady of Country Fiddle, joined Buck Owens and the Buckaroos in the early 1970s and starred with her blue fiddle on the television show *Hee Haw* during the mid-1970s. Larson is best known for her duet with Steve Wariner on "That's How You Know When Love's Right," which won them vocal duet of the year in 1986 from both the Country Music Association and the Academy of Country Music, and for her work with Neil Young.

Of the Canadian Great Plains provinces, Alberta has produced the only notable country music artists: k. d. lang and George Fox. Kathryn Dawn Lang, born in Consort, Alberta, was named the Canadian Country Music Association entertainer of the year in 1987, 1988, and 1989. Moreover, in 1987, 1988, and 1990 she was honored as the country female vocalist of the year with Juno Awards. Her album *Shadowland* (produced by the legendary Owen Bradley) went gold in 1988 and platinum in 1989 in Canada and gold in the United States in 1992. She has captured Grammy Awards in 1988 ("Crying") and 1990 (*Absolute Torch and Twang*). A talented songwriter and vocalist, k. d. lang has played a major role in linking rock and country in a manner that has made country music more accessible to wider audiences. Fox, a native of Cochrane, Alberta, launched his career in country music in the late 1980s and early 1990s with hits such as "Long Distance," "Angelina," and "I Fell in Love & I Can't Get Out." During this time, he was the recipient of the Vista Rising Star Award, composer of the year, male vocalist of the year, and country artist of the year, all given by the Canadian Country Music Association. His albums include *George Fox* (1988), *With All My Might*

(1989), *Spice of Life* (1991), and *Mustang Heart* (1993). As this full accounting shows, the Great Plains has long been a heartland of country music.

George O. Carney
Oklahoma State University

Carney, George O. "Country Music and the South: A Cultural Geography Perspective." *Journal of Cultural Geography* 1 (1980): 16–33. Koster, Rick. *Texas Music.* New York: St. Martin's Press, 1998. Malone, Bill C. *Country Music, U.S.A.* Austin: University of Texas Press, 1985.

COWBOY MUSIC

Cowboy music is a folk idiom whose musical progenitors include British ballads, familiar European melodies, Mexican and Spanish influences, and the tunes and traditions of America's mountains, rural areas, and southern states. It emerged just after the Civil War with the establishment of the "open range cattle kingdom" in the Great Plains.

Longhorn cattle were plentiful in Texas, and in the summer of 1867 entrepreneurs began driving herds north along the Chisholm Trail to the railhead in Abilene, Kansas, for shipment to eastern markets. Many more cattle drives followed during the ensuing two decades, and by the 1880s the drives extended as far north as Wyoming and Montana, where rich grazing lands on the open range were plentiful. Though the tradition of cowboy music established during those years continues to the present, a majority of the older songs date from approximately 1870 to 1920. Thereafter, the media (via sheet music, recordings, radio, movies, and television) became a potent force in shaping the idiom and people's ideas about it.

Authentic cowboy songs tell the story of the cattlemen, their often solitary way of life, the animals they rode, herded, and guarded against, and the wide expanse of the Great Plains and American West where they worked. Some of the tunes were functional, like the night-herding songs of cowboys who circled the herd as it lay on the bedding ground. These melodies reassured the restive cattle and helped prevent night noises and events from causing a stampede. Other tunes extolled the lives and abilities of cowboys, real and mythical, eulogized those killed in their labors, or celebrated animals that got the better of their human companions. These include "The Old Chisholm Trail," perhaps the most popular song of the Old West, "The Educated Feller" ("Zebra Dun"), which was sung to the tune of "Son of a Gambolier," "Sam Bass," "The Grand Round Up" ("The Cowboy's Sweet By and By"), whose melody was "My Bonnie Lies over the Ocean," "Little Joe the Wrangler," which used the tune of "The Little Old Log Cabin in the Lane," "Whoopie Ti Yi Yo," "Goodbye Old Paint," "Windy Bill," and "The Cowboy's Lament." The songs were usually sung by individuals, not groups, and were constantly reshaped and added to according to the particular tastes of the performers. Poems with Western or cowboy themes appeared regularly in journals, newspapers, and magazines, and many of these were set to music. Often, the words of a given song, poem, or narrative were sung to more than one tune. Cowboy song melodies were often rather simple, using few pitches. Some were pentatonic (using but five different note names), while others had strong triadic (a chord of three tones a third apart) underpinnings. Most importantly, the tunes cowboys favored were easily singable and suitable for the lyrics, which in their original form were sometimes colorful and earthy.

Cowboy music represents a rich and unique part of American cultural life. It is the music that we associate with the American West and represents the musings of countless individuals who worked, slept, ate, and sometimes died on the open prairie.

See also IMAGES AND ICONS: Cowboy Culture / LITERARY TRADITIONS: Cowboy Poetry.

Alfred W. Cochran
Kansas State University

Lomax, John A., and Alan Lomax. *Cowboy Songs and Other Frontier Ballads.* New York: Macmillan Publishing Company, 1938. Orlin, Glenn. *The Hell-Bound Train: A Cowboy Songbook.* Urbana: University of Illinois Press, 1973. White, John I. *Git Along, Little Dogies: Songs and Songmakers of the American West.* Urbana: University of Illinois Press, 1975.

DENVER, JOHN (1943–1997)

John Denver was a popular entertainer and songwriter whose music exalted simple living and the natural beauty of the American West. He was born Henry John Deutschendorf Jr. in Roswell, New Mexico, on December 31, 1943. His parents, Henry John "Dutch" Deutschendorf and Erma Swope, were native Oklahomans who moved frequently due to Dutch Deutschendorf's career as an Air Force flight instructor and test pilot.

The Deutschendorfs were descendants of German Russian colonists who settled on the Ukrainian steppes during the reign of Czar Alexander I. By the 1920s an American branch of the Deutschendorf family had put down roots near Cordell, Oklahoma, along the Washita River. For years afterward, their prairie farmstead in Oklahoma would serve as the home place of the Deutschendorf family. John Denver composed some of his earliest songs while he labored in the dusty wheat fields of western Oklahoma during the summer months. He was only a teenager at the time, but the experience of working so close to the land exerted a profound and lasting influence on his life philosophy and his music.

Henry John Deutschendorf Jr. rose to fame after a song he had written, "Leaving on a Jet Plane," was recorded by the musical trio Peter, Paul, and Mary in 1968. His career as a songwriter soon blossomed into that of a popular performer and also a movie and television actor. By the mid-1970s his new name, John Denver, had become a household word, and both his music and his shy yet upbeat personality endeared him to millions of fans all around the world.

John Denver wrote and recorded many musical hits, including "Rocky Mountain High," "Sunshine on My Shoulders," "Take Me Home, Country Roads," and "Annie's Song." Despite Denver's frequent reference to the Rocky Mountains of Colorado, he also wrote songs about memorable experiences and characters drawn from the Plains of western Oklahoma and Kansas. The song "Matthew," for example, was inspired by real-life wheat farmer and close relative Dean Deutschendorf.

One of the many causes that Denver championed was that of the environment, and it was a theme that dominated the musical compositions of his later years. On October 12, 1997, he was killed in a single-engine plane crash near Pacific Grove, California. A few days later, a memorial service was held for John Denver in Aurora, Colorado, at the edge of both the Rocky Mountains and the Great Plains, the two regions he so proudly celebrated in his distinctive and uplifting music.

See also EUROPEAN AMERICANS: German Russians.

Timothy J. Kloberdanz
North Dakota State University

Denver, John. *Take Me Home: An Autobiography*, with Arthur Tobier. New York: Harmony Books, 1994. Deutschendorf, Abe. "Memories of My Nephew John Denver." *Journal of the American Historical Society of Germans from Russia* 21 (1998): 6–7. Kloberdanz, Timothy J. "Henry John Deutschendorf, Jr.: The World Knew Him as John Denver." *Journal of the American Historical Society of Germans from Russia* 21 (1998): 1–5.

DIXIE CHICKS

The Dixie Chicks erupted onto the national music scene in 1998 with their major label debut album, *Wide Open Spaces.* Sisters Emily Erwin Robison and Martie Erwin Seidel founded the group in 1989 with Laura Lynch and Robin Macy, gaining regional acclaim as a close-harmony bluegrass band that always delivered with a honeysuckle sound and virtuoso instrumentation. Macy left in 1992 and Lynch in 1995. Late in 1995 the Erwin sisters joined their solid musicianship with the craggy, soulful vocal talents of Lubbock native Natalie Maines to develop a musical sound with a decidedly West Texas edge that has proved to be just the right blend for winning millions of new converts as well as die-hard country fans to their distinctive interpretation of rocking Texas roots music.

Wide Open Spaces won a plethora of awards, including a Grammy for best country album, the National Association of Record Merchandisers Award for best-selling recording by a new group, and the Country Music Association Award for album of the year, among many other accolades. In 2002 *Wide Open Spaces* won the group a place in the *Guinness Book of World Records* for the best-selling country debut album of all time.

Fly, the band's second album, followed close behind their first and won them Grammys, *Billboard* awards, and Country Music Association awards in both 1999 and 2000 for their talents and the album. Their 1999 tour promoting *Fly* gained a life of its own, making the Dixie Chicks a pop-culture phenomenon, with young and enthusiastic audiences flocking to their innovative performance spectaculars to hear old-fashioned banjo and fiddle music and contemporary lyrics tuned to a new age.

The Dixie Chicks are consummate musicians. They play their own lead instruments, do their own sessions work, and write their own songs. With the success of *Wide Open Spaces* they gained the commercial opportunity to write many of the songs they recorded on *Fly*, including "Ready to Run" and "Cowboy Take Me Away" by Martie Seidel and Marcus Hammon, "Don't Waste Your Heart" by Emily Robison and Natalie Maines, "Sin Wagon" by Natalie Maines, Emily Robison, and Stephany Smith, and "Without You" by Natalie Maines and Eric Silver.

Pamela H. Brink
Associated Authors and Editors, Inc.

ETHERIDGE, MELISSA (b. 1961)

Melissa Etheridge, gravelly voice rocker and gay rights activist, was born in historic Leavenworth, Kansas, on May 29, 1961. She grew up listening to a variety of types of music, from rock to country and blues, on the local AM stations, and by the age of twelve she was playing guitar in a band. She lists Keith Richards of the Rolling Stones as the main influence on her guitar playing. When she graduated from high school, she struck out for Boston and a year at the Berklee College of Music before landing in Los Angeles in 1982. By that time she had developed her own style as a writer and performer of rock songs tinged with blues.

Etheridge signed with Island Records in 1986 and issued her first album two years later. It went platinum. In 1992 she won her first Grammy for "Ain't It Heavy" from the *Never Enough* album. By 1999 she had put out a total of seven albums, including 1993's *Yes I Am*, which sold more than four million copies and yielded three Top 10 hits, among them the Grammy-winning "Come to My Window." Etheridge has since become a rock celebrity, performing with her friend and hero, Bruce Springsteen, on her MTV *Unplugged* special, singing "Piece of My Heart" at Janis Joplin's induction into the Rock and Roll Hall of Fame, and appearing at Woodstock in 1999. More than this, however, she has devoted herself to social activism, especially as a gay rights advocate. She publicly announced her own lesbianism in 1993. Etheridge does not shy away from controversy in her songs or in her life, but she says (as if with disappointment) that the only place where her concerts have drawn right-wing protests is her hometown of Leavenworth.

David J. Wishart
University of Nebraska–Lincoln

Nickson, Chris. *The Only One*. New York: St. Martin's Press, 1997.

THE FLATLANDERS

In the arts, events need not last long to have long-lasting impact. Such is the case with the Flatlanders, a Lubbock, Texas, band from the early 1970s. Though they were together scarcely over a year and produced only one recording, which wasn't released until almost a decade after they'd gone their separate ways, the influence of their music has spanned generations, genres, and geography.

Joe Ely, Jimmie Dale Gilmore, and Butch Hancock had become acquainted during their high school years in Lubbock. Reconnecting there in the summer of 1971, they discovered their mutual interests in blues, old-time country music (especially the works of Jimmie Rodgers), and songwriting. The three began performing together, with Jimmie Dale handling the lead vocals, Joe adding harmonica and Dobro, and all playing acoustic guitar and singing harmonies. From time to time, they were joined by several other musicians native to the Llano Estacado: John Reed on guitar, Sylvester Rice on acoustic bass, Tony Pearson on mandolin, and Steve Wesson on saw (a carpenter's ripsaw, bent and played with a violin bow).

The band, called the Flatlanders in celebration of the region's topography, cut several demo tracks at a small studio in Big Springs, Texas. Those led to a recording session in Nashville in February 1972, when Ely, Gilmore, and Hancock recorded seventeen songs, joined by Tommy Hancock on fiddle, Rice on acoustic bass, and Wesson on saw. Gilmore and Butch Hancock each wrote four of the tunes, Lubbock native Al Strehli wrote two, and Al's sister Angela wrote another. The selections were augmented with classic songs by Jimmie Rodgers, Willie Nelson, A. P. Carter, and Harry Choates. The company for whom the session was done, Plantation Records, only released two 45s for airplay: "Dallas" and "Jole Blon." It wasn't until 1980 that an English label, Charly Music, released an LP (*The Flatlanders: One Road More*) with all seventeen cuts.

The Flatlanders scattered soon after the release of the two singles, but their music has continued to influence new generations of audiences and musicians. In particular, Joe Ely and Jimmie Dale Gilmore are now internationally known for their songwriting, performing, and recording careers, and Butch Hancock has developed a cultlike reputation for his writing. In 1990 Rounder Records released a CD reissue of fourteen songs from the Nashville session. Aptly, it was entitled *More a Legend than a Band*.

Andy Wilkinson
Lubbock, Texas

FOLK SONGS

See FOLKWAYS: Folk Songs

FRONTIER OPERA HOUSES

Frontier communities regarded opera houses as visual symbols of prosperity—beacons to settlers that a town had permanence, promise, and culture. Though more properly "opera hall," the name "opera house" suggested refinement and elegance to local residents, so it prevailed. The opera house heyday lasted from about ten years after a town's founding until approximately 1917. Often on the second floor of the town's first brick building, opera houses contained an open space large enough for a significant portion of the community to congregate. All contained stages, some had permanent seating, but most consisted of a large room that could be arranged in a variety of configurations depending on need—dances, political meetings, banquets, basketball games, concerts, home talent shows, or professional entertainment.

Opera houses represented all types of vernacular Main Street architecture from the early two-part commercial block second-floor theaters to the one-part community audito-

Lodgepole (Nebraska) Opera House, built in 1911, closed in the late 1940s

rium models favored in the early twentieth century. These theaters functioned as the heart of frontier society, gathering places where folks could celebrate life and escape its daily rigors. Originally owned and managed by a civic-spirited merchant, they eventually passed into public ownership.

The opera house "season" lasted from late fall to early spring, beginning after the crops were in and lasting as long as the rutted roads remained frozen to accommodate evening travel. Frequent dances provided income for fire departments, dancing schools, lodges, bands, commercial clubs, and ball teams. Home talent performances by cornet bands, community instrumentalists, choral unions, local music students, and college or church choirs always earned high praise from local newspaper editors.

Several times each season, an opera house manager contracted for professional entertainment, often through a lyceum bureau booking agency. Unable to accommodate the more pricey offerings of combination companies booked out of New York, most Plains communities settled for concerts or other entertainments by smaller groups such as the Hallowell Concert Company, complete with baritone and lady trap-drummer; Round's Ladies Orchestra; the Schubert Symphony and Ladies Quartette; the Sue Burgess Concert Company, featuring contralto, reader, violinist, and pianist; Blind Boone, a pianist who drew rowdy crowds; and Mrs. Winters, a melodious whistler. More exotic musicians included the Royal Hawaiian Concert Company, Kulolo's Hawaiians, Vierra's Royal Hawaiians, Ramos' Spanish Orchestra, Losseff's Russian Quartet, the Swiss Bell Ringers, and the Chicago Boys' Choir, which traveled with marambophone, bagpipes, tambourine, castanets, and a harp.

Opera houses declined as a performance venue after 1917 for a variety of reasons related to twentieth-century technology. Many had reached the end of their architectural usefulness and could no longer safely support large crowds of people; the devastation of the 1903 Iroquois Theatre fire in Chicago, which killed 600 people, made the nation aware of the dangers of second-floor theaters. Automobiles, shifts in population, and postwar affluence meant smaller audiences in small towns. Most important, motion pictures proved more attractive to audiences and more cost-effective to managers than traveling troupes. Plains towns built no true frontier opera houses after World War I. Today, small Great Plains towns use community auditoriums to fill the non-entertainment functions of the opera house, while larger cities and television provide the performance venues.

D. Layne Ehlers
Bacone College

Ehlers, D. Layne. "This Week at the Opera House: Popular Music Entertainment at Great Plains Opera Houses, 1887–1917." *Great Plains Quarterly* 20 (2000): 183–95. Zivanovic, Judith K., ed. *Opera Houses of the Midwest.* Manhattan KS: Mid-America Theatre Conference, 1988.

GUTHRIE, WOODY (1912–1967)

Woodrow Wilson, or Woody, Guthrie was born in Okemah, Oklahoma, on July 14, 1912. His formative years exposed him to middle-class circumstances in a wild and restless boomtown, although his family life unraveled by 1927. His father, Charlie, became an alcoholic, while his mother, Nora, suffered from Huntington's chorea and was committed to a mental institution.

Relocating to Pampa, Texas, in 1929, Guthrie met and married his first wife, Mary Jennings. While listening to the voices emanating from the region, he developed his musical talents and appropriated cowboy songs, gospel hymns, and hard-luck blues for his repertoire. Soon he discovered a new life as a rambling minstrel, playing folksy songs on his guitar at country dances, rodeos, and carnivals.

In 1937, after experiencing firsthand the blistering heat and sandstorms of the Dust Bowl, Guthrie left his family and took to the road. He arrived in California, where a relative helped him find work. The boom in country music on the radio brought ballads to KFVD in Los Angeles, California, and listeners enjoyed folk songs that described a distant homeland and "cornpone" philosophy. While referencing experiences seemingly long ago and far away, Guthrie's lyrics summoned an audience's recollections of hard times in the heartland. From the beginning of his musical career, he was dubbed the Dust Bowl Troubadour and the Okie Balladeer. After a divorce from his first wife, he married Marjorie Mazia in 1945.

While playing the restless saloon singer, Guthrie matured into a visionary artist. He wrote a column for the *People's Daily World* and crafted poetry, a novel, and an autobiography. Composing more than 1,000 songs, he sang of the Dust Bowl, President Roosevelt's New Deal, antifascist patriotism, union organization, and child's play. His titles ranged from "Jesus Christ" to "Union Maid." His working-class heroes traveled with him in the classic anthem "This Land Is Your Land." Over the course of his journey, he collaborated with Maxine "Lefty Lou" Crissman, Pete Seeger, Leadbelly, Burl Ives, Cisco Houston, and Alan Lomax. By the 1960s, Guthrie had become a legendary icon for a younger generation of protest musicians, including Bob Dylan and Joan Baez. His influence is still seen in the more contemplative songs of Bruce Springsteen.

Guthrie identified with the "Dust Bowl refugees" of the Great Plains and, in effect, reinvented himself. Through the chords of memory he articulated a collective search among plain-folk Americans for a better life. While musing that socialism offered a new hope for this kind of proletariat, he sang about a primitive rebel in a nascent state. The wiry balladeer came to embody the rambling Okie of his songs. After suffering for fifteen years from Huntington's chorea, he died in New York on October 3, 1967.

See also PHYSICAL ENVIRONMENT: Dust Bowl / POLITICS AND GOVERNMENT: New Deal.

Brad Lookingbill
Columbia College

Guthrie, Woody. *Bound for Glory.* New York: E. P. Dutton, 1943. Klein, Joe. *Woody Guthrie: A Life.* New York: Alfred A. Knopf, Inc., 1980. Lookingbill, Brad. "Dusty Apocalypse and Socialist Salvation: A Study of Woody Guthrie's Dust Bowl Imagery." *Chronicles of Oklahoma* 72 (1994–95): 396–413.

HANSON, HOWARD (1896–1981)

Born in Wahoo, Nebraska, on October 28, 1896, to Swedish immigrants, Howard Hanson was a child prodigy, learning piano and cello by the age of fourteen. As a high school junior and senior, he conducted the Wahoo High School Orchestra. Educated at Northwestern University, Hanson was appointed dean of music at the University of the Pacific in 1919 and then studied at the American Academy in Rome, Italy, for three years. In 1924 he was chosen by George Eastman to head the Eastman School of Music at the University of Rochester, a post he held until 1964.

Hanson composed seven symphonies, the opera *Merrymount*, and several other orchestral works. His fourth symphony, *Requiem*, won a Pulitzer Prize in 1944. Several of Hanson's chorales incorporated the poetry of Walt Whitman. Hanson also promoted the works of American composers in concert, on phonograph records, and on the radio. Under Hanson the Eastman School of Music became one of the foremost music schools in America, and he made music education a respected vocation.

Hanson's compositional style has been called American romantic, influenced by music's romantic period of the late 1800s. Hanson described his music as springing from the soil of his native Nebraska and reflecting the broad prairies rather than the city. He died in Rochester, New York, on February 26, 1981. Hanson's birthplace in Wahoo is owned by the Saunders County Historical Society and is open to the public.

Eric J. Bachenberg
Lincoln, Nebraska

Williams, David Russell. *Conversations with Howard Hanson.* Arkadelphia AR: Delta Publications, 1988.

WYNONIE, HARRIS

See AFRICAN AMERICANS: Wynonie, Harris

HISPANIC MUSIC

Most Hispanic communities in the Great Plains maintain Mexican and Mexican American musical and cultural traditions, including musical repertoires, tastes, and practices. The maintenance and persistence of musical traditions and preferences depends in large part on the date of arrival in the area. More recently arrived Mexican immigrants bring musical styles from their home regions: mariachi music from the state of Jalisco, harp music from the state of Michoacán, and border music (*música norteña*, featuring the accordion) from the northern state of Nuevo León, for example. Mexican Americans born in the Great Plains perform, listen, and dance to mainstream North American popular music (rock, rap, pop, blues) and jazz, Tex-Mex musical styles, especially the accordion-led *conjunto* ensemble, and current Latin American and Mexican popular and folk music genres: Colombian *cumbia*, Caribbean salsa, Mexican lyric *canciones románticas* (love songs), and *corridos* (contemporary narrative ballads, often with a strong social or political orientation).

Mexican, Chicano, and Latino popular musicians whose work is well known and appreciated in the Great Plains include a wide range of artists active in a variety of musical styles: the Latin rock group Santana (led by Mexican-born guitarist Carlos Santana); Los Tigres del Norte, the *música norteña* band from the state of Sinaloa noted for the performance of songs with strong social commentary; Panamanian salsa musician Ruben Blades; Selena Quintanilla, the much-lamented *tejana* singer; *tejano conjunto* accordionist Flaco Jiménez; and *tejana* singer Lydia Mendoza, among others.

Hispanic Catholic and Protestant sacred musical styles in the Great Plains have also been influenced by developments in Mexico and the Hispanic Southwest. In Spanish-speaking congregations, Catholic and Protestant sacred musical performance styles and repertoires are related to secular styles, though with a religious context and message. The influence of mainstream North American popular secular music styles can certainly be heard in Hispanic congregations in Great Plains states as elsewhere in the country.

Most of these musical styles and traditions remain generally invisible to the mainstream majority European American population in the Great Plains region. Just as earlier Czech and Swedish musical traditions were often mysterious to outsiders during the peak years of central European and Scandinavian immigration to the Great Plains (though everyone knew, and knows, the polka), so too are many Hispanic musical traditions generally unfamiliar to non-Spanish speakers today. Some possible exceptions include Mexican mariachi music and Tex-Mex *conjunto* music, with its polka roots.

In addition to the Hispanic community's acceptance and use of a heterogeneous mix of Mexican, Mexican American, North American, and Latin American popular and folk music styles, the generally well developed public school music education establishment in the region embraces and involves students of all races and ethnicities, including those with Spanish surnames. As the number of Hispanic students in schools in Nebraska, Kansas, and other Great Plains states grows, so too will their representation in marching bands, wind ensembles, orchestras, jazz bands, and choruses in elementary and secondary schools in the region. Much of the repertoire, with its emphasis on European and European American art and popular music traditions and jazz, performed by these musical ensembles is situated at a distance from the popular and folk music repertoires and styles common in Spanish-speaking communities. However, musical groups featuring Mexican and Latino

repertoire (especially mariachi music) have been established in some public schools in the region (in Fort Worth, for example) in order to foster positive self-identification among Hispanic students. Nevertheless, one should not assume that Hispanic musical life and involvement in the Great Plains is limited to only one tradition or style. Rather, it should be considered as a mosaic made up of many constituent and finely nuanced parts.

John Koegel
California State University, Fullerton

Burr, Ramiro. *The Billboard Guide to Tejano and Regional Mexican Music*. New York: Billboard Books, 1999. Garcia, Juan R. *Mexicans in the Midwest, 1900–1932*. Tucson: University of Arizona Press, 1996. Peña, Manuel. *Música Tejana: The Cultural Economy of Artistic Transformation*. College Station: Texas A&M University Press, 1999.

HOLLY, BUDDY (1936–1959)

Buddy Holly was born Charles Hardin Holley on September 7, 1936, in Lubbock, Texas. He removed the *e* from his last name in 1956. The famously bespectacled Holly, along with his band, the Crickets, was among the most innovative and influential pioneers of rock and roll music, an amalgam of white country and western and black rhythm and blues styles.

The youngest of four children, Holly followed his mother and siblings in learning to play a variety of instruments (guitar, violin, and piano) to accompany country and western and gospel singing. That early influence was later modified by exposure to the black rhythm and blues music he enthusiastically listened to on late-night radio. Further reinforcement came from rock and roll trailblazers Bill Haley and Elvis Presley, for whom Holly opened concerts in Lubbock in 1955.

Holly was brought to the attention of Decca Records through the efforts of an agent, Eddie Crandall, leading in 1956 to commercial recording sessions in Nashville with country and western producer Owen Bradley. Bradley's attempt to force Holly's unique style into a Nashville mold in releases such as "Blue Days, Black Nights" met with little success. Discouraged by the experience, Holly and the Crickets (drummer Jerry Allison, bassist Larry Welborn, and guitarist Niki Sullivan) collaborated in February 1957 with Clovis, New Mexico, performer, producer, and recording engineer Norman Petty to record their first hit record, "That'll Be the Day," in Petty's studio. The recording, released on Brunswick Records, reached number one on the American charts by September; it also topped the British charts. Other hits followed quickly in 1957: "Oh Boy!" and "Peggy Sue," released on the Coral label, rose to the Top 10. The hit records led to additional recording sessions and national tours, including the first performance by a white band at the Apollo Theater in Harlem and television appearances on *American Bandstand* and *The Ed Sullivan Show*.

The year 1958 brought a flurry of recording sessions with Petty and tours to Hawaii, Australia, and England. Holly's influence on the following generations of English rock stars was massive: Paul McCartney and Keith Rich-

ards later testified to his profound impact on the nascent Beatles and Rolling Stones in the BBC documentary *The Real Buddy Holly Story*. On August 4, 1958, Holly and Maria Elena Santiago married. They had no children. In late 1958 Buddy and Maria moved to Greenwich Village, following the dissolution of his managerial arrangement with Petty and the decision by the Crickets to pursue an independent future. In New York Holly resumed writing songs, emphasizing his role as a soloist, and undertook the promotion of other promising young artists, including Waylon Jennings.

A midwestern tour led to the fatal crash on February 3, 1959, of the small plane in which Holly and two other young performers (the Big Bopper and Richie Valens) were attempting to fly from their engagement in Clear Lake, Iowa, to Fargo, North Dakota. More than 1,100 people gathered for Holly's funeral in Lubbock. The hits continued after his death, with the lonesome and defiant "It Doesn't Matter Anymore" climbing to number one in the United Kingdom. Holly was a member of the first group of inductees into the Rock and Roll Hall of Fame in 1986.

Holly's legacy includes the band format of two amplified guitars, bass, and drums, the practice of the artist performing mostly his original compositions, and even the wearing of glasses onstage. Techniques developed in collaboration with Norman Petty—overdubbing, artificial reverberation, and the use of piano, celesta, drumming on a cardboard box, and knee slapping—were later mimicked by others. Also characteristic of his musical style are the rhythmic subdivision of a single syllable (*we-e-e-ell, he-he-he-hey*), extreme shifts of vocal register, intense guitar strumming with consecutive downstrokes, and the pervasive driving percussion of Jerry Allison.

Wayne Hobbs
Texas Tech University

Amburn, Ellis. *Buddy Holly: A Biography*. New York: St. Martin's Press, 1995. Goldrosen, John. *Remembering Buddy: The Definitive Biography*. New York: Da Capo Press, 2000. Griggs, Bill. *Buddy Holly: Day-by-Day*. Lubbock: Rockin' 50's, 1997–98.

JENNINGS, WAYLON (1937–2002)

Among the leaders of the outlaw movement that revitalized country music in the 1970s, Waylon Jennings was born on June 15, 1937, in Littlefield, Texas. He formed his own band at the age of twelve and worked as a radio DJ two years later. He dropped out of high school in the tenth grade to pursue his career. In 1954 Jennings moved to Lubbock, Texas, where he met Buddy Holly the following year. His influences included Hank Williams, Ernest Tubb, Webb Price, B. B. King, and Bobbie "Blue" Bland as well as his early mentor, Buddy Holly.

From 1958 to 1959 Jennings played bass for Buddy Holly, who produced Jennings's first album and taught him that there should be no barriers between the audience and the performer. Jennings gave his seat to the Big Bopper on the fatal flight that also took the lives of

Holly and Richie Valens in February 1959. Following this close call, Jennings returned to Lubbock to regroup before moving to Phoenix, where he started his band, the Waylors, and began to build a diverse audience.

Jennings moved to Nashville in 1965, signing with RCA. Like Willie Nelson before him, Jennings found himself an outcast in Nashville and perhaps a little more "country" than the industry itself. Although he scored several Top 5 hits, including "Only Daddy That'll Walk the Line" and "Walk on out of My Mind," he found success elusive until he began to produce his own records and use his own musicians. In 1969 he married fellow singer Jessi Colter.

By the 1970s Jennings had a series of hit albums, including the first platinum-selling solo country album, Ol' Waylon, in 1977. He was long associated with fellow outlaws Willie Nelson, Johnny Cash, and Kris Kristofferson, with whom he recorded as the Highwaymen in the late 1980s. His teaming with Willie Nelson produced two notable albums, Waylon and Willie (1978), which produced the crossover hit "Mammas, Don't Let Your Babies Grow up to Be Cowboys," and WWII (1982), which went gold.

In addition to his musical work, Jennings acted in films such as Outlaw Justice (with Kris Kristofferson, Willie Nelson, and Travis Tritt, 1999) and the made-for-television Stagecoach (1986) as well as providing the narration for the television show The Dukes of Hazzard. He wrote his autobiography, Waylon (1996), and even produced a children's album, Cowboys, Sisters, Rascals & Dirt (1993). His work was well received, with Jennings winning numerous awards from the Country Music Association: male vocalist of the year (1975), vocal duo of the year with Willie Nelson (1976), album of the year (Wanted: The Outlaws, 1976), and single of the year ("Good Hearted Woman," 1976). He was inducted into the Country Music Hall of Fame in 2001.

Jennings spoke and wrote openly about his troubles with alcohol and drugs. After earning his GED in 1989, he also promoted the equivalency program and worked to encourage children to stay in school.

Despite less than enthusiastic acceptance from the country music industry, Jennings nonetheless attained legendary status due to his outlaw reputation and ability to appeal to rock audiences. Indeed, his popularity is broader and deeper than that of most modern country music stars, despite the lack of airplay that his songs now receive.

Jennings died on February 13, 2002, in Chandler, Arizona, of complications from diabetes.

Charles Vollan
University of Nebraska–Lincoln

KANSAS CITY JAZZ

Like its counterparts in other urban cultural hotbeds, Kansas City jazz emerged in the early decades of the twentieth century with a distinctive sense of place. The unique Kansas City brand of jazz drew on the orchestral ragtime, boogie-woogie, and rural blues of the region; was based largely on repetitive phrases, or riffs; and was performed by big bands. In that respect, it owes little to the more familiar jazz style of New Orleans, which was distinguished by its small group interplay, or polyphony. By contrast, Kansas City jazz is known for its powerful rhythmic drive and the dominance of reed instruments, especially the saxophone.

Kansas City's prominence as a jazz center in the 1920s and 1930s can be attributed in part to geography. A hub for itinerant territory bands that performed throughout the Great Plains and Southwest, Kansas City attracted a talented cross section of musicians. They came from Oklahoma City and Tulsa, from Dallas and San Antonio, from Omaha and Wichita, often stopping in Kansas City for a respite from the road, to hire new band members from the growing stable of players, or to sample the burgeoning nightlife. From disparate musical backgrounds they conceived and gave birth to a new, exhilarating style of jazz.

The long reign of mayor and political boss Tom Pendergast also made it possible for jazz to flourish in Prohibition Era Kansas City. From about 1925 until his indictment in 1938 for income tax fraud, Pendergast virtually controlled the city, awarding construction contracts to friends and relatives and subtly encouraging vice as bootleggers, gangsters, and corrupt politicians exploited the lucrative network of speakeasies and all-night cabarets. Pendergast's permissive political policies unwittingly nurtured Kansas City jazz. During the peak years, the city boasted several hundred nightclubs, ballrooms, and other venues offering live music—a profitable training ground for musicians to learn their trade and develop the individual sound that is the hallmark of jazz.

Dozens of the most popular clubs—including the Sunset Club, the Subway Club, the Boulevard Lounge, the Cherry Blossom, the Lone Star, the Panama, Lucille's Paradise Band Box, Elks' Rest, and the Old Kentucky Bar-B-Que—were clustered in a district bordered by Twelfth Street on the north and Eighteenth Street on the south. Outside the district but still within easy walking distance were the Amos and Andy, Greenleaf Gardens, and the Hey Hay Club. Most famous of all was the Reno Club, where the Count Basie Orchestra got its start.

Kansas City jazz evolved as performance opportunities proliferated in theaters, dance halls, and, most importantly, intimate after-hours clubs. Because many of the early practitioners of Kansas City jazz were traveling musicians staying in town only briefly, the musical arrangements remained simple enough for all to learn quickly, often during informal jam sessions. These so-called head arrangements, many of which incorporated standard three-chord blues patterns, were rehearsed and committed to memory, allowing more freedom for instrumental soloists.

Kansas City's all-night jam sessions are legendary. In some clubs a rhythm section was installed, and guest musicians were encouraged to sit in. In other venues the sessions would begin after the regular evening's entertainment had ended and continue until the last players were ready for bed or breakfast, which was served at many local diners catering to the city's nocturnal revelers. Competitive jam sessions, or cutting contests, among musicians were so prolific that a hierarchy evolved. Only the most skilled musicians were allowed to take the stage at the Sunset, the Subway, and the Reno, while other clubs were reserved for beginners.

The earliest and most important exemplar of the Kansas City jazz style was Bennie Moten's Kansas City Orchestra, which employed many of the best musicians and made some of the music's most memorable recordings such as the standards "Moten Swing" and "Prince of Wails." Other significant bands in the early history of Kansas City jazz were Walter Page's Blue Devils, George E. Lee's Novelty Singing Orchestra, the Alphonso Trent Orchestra, and Troy Floyd's Shadowland Orchestra.

After Moten's sudden death in 1935, several members of the band formed the nucleus of a smaller ensemble led by pianist Bill Basie. It was later expanded to become the Count Basie Orchestra. Until his death in 1984, Basie was the most prominent and most publicized ambassador of the Kansas City jazz style, repeatedly touring the world to popular acclaim.

Other Kansas City bands of note were led by Andy Kirk, Harlan Leonard, and Jay McShann, best known for giving a young alto saxophonist named Charlie Parker his first big break. During a stint with McShann from 1940 to 1942, Parker toured and made his first recordings, although he is better known for later pioneering the bebop style after his move to New York City.

In the competitive, superheated climate of the Kansas City jam sessions, the powerful sound of the tenor saxophone emerged as the dominant instrument. Among the great tenor players who participated in these storied sessions were Lester Young, Coleman Hawkins, Ben Webster, Herschel Evans, Chu Berry, Budd Johnson, and Buddy Tate. Also contributing to the driving swing sound associated with Kansas City jazz were the walking bass technique, the time-keeping function of the rhythm guitar, and the use of the hi-hat for greater rhythmic emphasis. All of these were exemplified by early members of the Basie rhythm section—bassist Walter Page, guitarist Freddie Green, and drummer Jo Jones.

The Kansas City sound was largely instrumental, but it also drew on the blues vocal tradition of the Deep South and Southwest. The blues shouter added variety to the concert repertoire and became a fixture of Kansas City jazz bands. Among the best were Joe Turner, Jimmy Rushing, and Walter Brown. Similarly, boogie-woogie piano players like McShann and Pete Johnson had a role in developing the Kansas City jazz style but with a sound closely related to the blues. Pianist Mary Lou Williams had a more sophisticated jazz keyboard style and also distinguished herself as a composer.

As the era of "Pendergast prosperity" ended

in the early 1940s, so did many employment opportunities for musicians. The popular, dance-friendly Kansas City swing style would eventually be incorporated into mainstream jazz, where its irresistible rhythms can still be heard.

See also CITIES AND TOWNS: Kansas City, Kansas and Missouri.

Tom Ineck
Nebraska Humanities Council

Driggs, Frank. "The Real Kansas City Jazz." Liner notes for the CD *The Real Kansas City Jazz of the '20s, '30s, '40s*, Columbia Records 64855 (March 1996). Robinson, J. Bradford. *The New Grove Dictionary of Jazz*, s.v. "Kansas City jazz." New York: St. Martin's Press, 1988. Russell, Ross. *Jazz Style in Kansas City and the Southwest*. Berkeley: University of California Press, 1971.

KING CURTIS

See AFRICAN AMERICANS: King Curtis

LANG, K. D. (b. 1962)

Singer and songwriter k. d. lang was born Kathryn Dawn Lang on November 2, 1962, in Edmonton, Alberta. Raised in the small town of Consort, she studied music for a year after high school and began performing professionally in Edmonton in 1981. Her recording career began with *A Truly Western Experience* in 1984 with her band, the Reclines. Claiming Patsy Cline as an alter ego, she cultivated an unconventional, occasionally frenetic, and irreverent stage presence during this period in her career. In 1984 she made her U.S. debut and began to tour internationally. Signed to Sire Records, she released *Angel with a Lariat* and *Shadowland* in 1987. "Crying," her duet with Roy Orbison, won her a Grammy in 1988 for best country music collaboration. *Absolute Torch and Twang*, released in 1989, sold 100,000 copies in Canada and 500,000 in the United States and earned her a Grammy in 1990 for best female country vocalist. In Canada she won three Juno Awards from 1987 to 1990.

Although clearly in the mainstream of country music, as demonstrated by the Grammys, Grammy nominations, and awards from the Canadian Country Music Association, lang has suggested that her music, along with that of many other Canadian country musicians, differs in subtle ways from the homogeneous Nashville product because of the ethnic influences—Irish, Scottish, Ukrainian—found on the Canadian Prairies. Three albums appeared in the 1990s: *Ingenue* (1992), *All You Can Eat* (1995), and *Drag* (1997). They represent a significant change in lang's musical style, described by one writer as country-punk turned pop-torch chanteuse. Unifying and to some extent determining the nature of the change has been her instrument, her voice: rich, flexible, and superbly controlled.

Wesley Berg
University of Alberta

Miller, Mark. "k. d. lang." In *Encyclopedia of Music in Canada*, 2nd ed., edited by Helmut Kallman et al. Toronto: University of Toronto Press, 1992.

LEE, PEGGY (1920–2002)

Peggy Lee

Peggy Lee was born Norma Deloris Egstrom on May 26, 1920, in Jamestown, North Dakota. Her love of singing pulled her out of an abusive home and onto local radio by the age of fourteen. After high school she performed throughout the Midwest. She was discovered by Benny Goodman in Chicago in 1941 and recorded her first hits with the Benny Goodman Orchestra. Lee and her husband, guitarist Dave Barbour, left Goodman in 1943 to write and record their own hits, including "It's a Good Day" and "Mañana." The latter marked the start of Lee's lifelong fascination with Latin rhythms. The collaboration and marriage ended in 1951.

Lee's solo career featured recording successes, live concerts, and television appearances. She also appeared in *The Jazz Singer* (1953) and *Pete Kelly's Blues*, which garnered her an Oscar nomination for best supporting actress in 1955. In the same year, she wrote songs for Disney's *Lady and the Tramp* and provided voices for the film. Recording highlights of Lee's career include the 1958 release of "Fever," a million-seller that earned two Grammy nominations and "Is That All There Is," which earned her the 1969 Grammy award for best contemporary vocal performance by a female artist.

During a career that spanned six decades and defies categorization by genre, Peggy Lee recorded more than 60 albums and more than 700 individual songs. She wrote more than 75 songs and published poetry and an autobiography. She was honored by fans and peers for her uniquely sensuous vocal quality, her flawless musicality, and her riveting stage presence. Peggy Lee died of a heart attack at her home in Bel Air, California, on January 21, 2002.

Kate Stevenson
Jamestown College

Lee, Peggy. *Miss Peggy Lee: An Autobiography*. New York: Donald I. Fine, Inc., 1989. Lees, Gene. *Singers and the Song II*. New York: Oxford University Press, 1998. Reich, Howard. "Peggy Lee: A Sensual American Classic, through Illness and Injury, the Amazing Performer Has Managed to Survive." *San Francisco Examiner*, September 5, 1993: D2.

MCSHANN, JAY

See AFRICAN AMERICANS: McShann, Jay

MILLER, GLENN (1904–1944)

The man who would become one of America's best-loved bandleaders was born in Clarinda, Iowa, on March 1, 1904. Alton Glenn Miller's homesteading parents then decided to try their luck in Nebraska; in 1907 they packed up their family and moved into a sod house in the very small town of Tryon. After another move to Missouri the family wound up in Fort Morgan, Colorado, where Miller developed an interest in dance band music. He was talented enough on the trombone to support himself in orchestras through two years at the University of Colorado and in 1924 moved to Los Angeles to play full time in the Ben Pollack Orchestra.

Miller considered himself a mediocre trombone player at best. His real ambition was to make new arrangements of tunes others had written and to use his arrangements to develop a recognizable style for a band of his own. After stints with other big names in the 1930s, including Ray Noble and the Dorsey brothers, he set out to form the first Glenn Miller Band. This one failed, but on his next attempt in 1939 he landed a summer slot at the Glen Island Casino, a big band hot spot with a nationwide radio hookup. Within months, Miller had a national following. Hit after hit followed, beginning with "In the Mood" and including the first gold record ever awarded, for "Chattanooga Choo Choo." The band also made two movies by 1942, giving fans in the hinterlands a chance to see them in action.

World War II intervened, and as Miller saw his young bandsmen joining up or being drafted out of their chairs he wanted to do more for his country. He pestered the army until they gave him a captain's commission and a fifty-member band, complete with a string section, something his civilian band did not include. His morale-building duties included modernizing military music, notably with the "Saint Louis Blues March," and making numerous radio broadcasts and war bond drives.

Miller lobbied hard to take his band overseas to play for the Allied troops in Europe. The army relented in the summer of 1944; for the next six months the Glenn Miller Army Air Force Band kept a relentless schedule of base concerts and radio broadcasts in England. Wanting to get closer to the troops who would most enjoy the little bit of home his music brought them, by-now-promoted Major Miller was making plans to bring his band to Paris when his light plane disappeared over the English Channel on December 15, 1944. Rumors persist that the plane was brought down by friendly fire, most likely by bombs jettisoned by a Royal Air Force squadron flying above it.

The band continued without him and, after several changes in personnel and name, still tours today. Miller's songs are swing band classics, and fan clubs in America and England continue to attract new members. His signature tune, "Moonlight Serenade," the only one of the band's hits written by Miller, evokes the romantic, patriotic, and musical war years yet remains instantly recognizable today.

Scarlett Presley
University of Wisconsin–Madison

Butcher, Geoffrey. *Next to a Letter from Home: Major Glenn Miller's Wartime Band.* Edinburgh: Mainstream Publishing Company, Ltd., 1986. Simon, George T. *Glenn Miller and His Orchestra.* New York: Thomas Y. Cromwell Company, 1974.

MILLER, ROGER (1936–1992)

Roger Dean Miller was an immensely popular country music artist and songwriter whose witty and catchy songs dominated country music from 1964 to 1966. Miller was born in Fort Worth, Texas, on January 2, 1936. When he was thirteen months old his father died, so Miller was raised by his Uncle Elmer on a farm in Erick, Oklahoma. There he learned to play fiddle, banjo, and guitar. After high school, Miller joined the army and served in Korea, then in a country band in Special Services at Fort McPherson in Atlanta. After the army, Miller moved to Nashville in 1957 and pursued a songwriting career. He also performed as a musician, playing for Minnie Pearl, Faron Young, and Ray Price.

His first songwriting hit was "Invitation to the Blues," recorded by Ray Price in 1958. Other early songwriting hits include "Half a Mind," recorded by Ernest Tubb, "Billy Bayou" and "Home," recorded by Jim Reeves, and "You Don't Want My Love," recorded by Andy Williams. Miller recorded for Starday and then RCA Victor before signing with Mercury's Smash label, where in 1964 he began a string of hits with "Dang Me," followed by "Chug-a-Lug," "England Swings," "Engine Engine Number 9," and his biggest song, "King of the Road." Miller won five Grammys for his 1964 work and another six for his 1965 recordings.

In 1966 he hosted *The Roger Miller Show* on NBC, and in 1973 he narrated the voice of the rooster in Disney's *Robin Hood*. In the mid-1980s he wrote the score for the Broadway musical *Big River*, based on the novel *Huckleberry Finn*, for which he won a Tony Award. Miller was diagnosed with throat cancer in 1991 and died in Santa Fe, New Mexico, on October 25, 1992. He was inducted into the Country Music Hall of Fame in 1995.

Don Cusic
Belmont University

MITCHELL, JONI (b. 1943)

Singer, songwriter, guitarist, and pianist Joni Mitchell was born Roberta Joan Anderson on November 7, 1943, in Fort Macleod, Alberta. She grew up in Saskatoon, Saskatchewan. Mitchell studied art for a year in Calgary and then moved to Toronto, where, with her husband, Chad Mitchell, she began to write songs and sing in coffeehouses. She moved to Detroit in 1965 and to New York in 1966 and then settled in Los Angeles in 1968 with a second home near Vancouver.

Mitchell made her reputation initially as a songwriter. Judy Collins recorded Mitchell's song "Both Sides Now" (1967), and other Mitchell songs have been recorded by Gordon Lightfoot, Bob Dylan, and Frank Sinatra. Seventeen albums over thirty years, with a Grammy for *Clouds* (1969), have moved from the folk styles of her coffeehouse origins through the jazz influences of the 1970s and the rock styles of the 1980s to a return to a simpler folk-based style in the 1990s. Mitchell has maintained a long, independent career, and the style of her lyrics and melodies has been influential. In 1979 she said of her music that it had a striding quality that was like long steps across the flat prairies, but she also acknowledged the increasingly urban influences of jazz and rock. Her lyrics since the early 1970s have been autobiographical, dealing with the pain of love, loneliness, and modern life. Although she has made her career in the United States, many of her songs reflect the point of view of the outsider, a Canadian who can never fully be a part of life in Los Angeles and yet can also never return to her small town Plains roots.

Wesley Berg
University of Alberta

Fetherling, Douglas. *Some Day Soon: Essays on Canadian Songwriters.* Kingston, Ontario: Quarry Press, 1991. Miller, Mark. "Joni Mitchell." In *Encyclopedia of Music in Canada*, 2nd ed., edited by Helmut Kallmann et al. Toronto: University of Toronto Press, 1992. Mitchell, Joni. *The Complete Poems and Lyrics.* Toronto: Random House, 1997.

NATIONAL MUSIC MUSEUM

The National Music Museum is one of the great museums of its kind in the world. Housed in a carefully restored Carnegie library building on the campus of the University of South Dakota in Vermillion, the museum's ever-growing collections of more than 7,000 American, European, and non-Western instruments are the most inclusive in the world, rivaled only by similar museums in Berlin, Paris, Oxford, Rome, and Vienna. Included are many of the earliest, best-preserved, and historically most important musical instruments known to survive, along with an extensive library of rare books and archival materials.

The museum serves the people of the Great Plains and the nation as an international center for collecting and conserving musical instruments of all cultures and bringing people together to study, enjoy, and understand our diverse musical heritage.

It has a special responsibility to preserve musical instruments that were either imported to or built in the United States, with emphasis on the musical traditions of the Northern Great Plains. The museum's American musical instrument manufacturers archives has no rival. Complete band libraries from small towns in the region are preserved, along with many unique resources such as the handwritten manuscripts of the music composed by General Custer's bandmaster, Felix Vinatieri (1834–91); the compositions of one of the region's first serious female composers, Marjorie Eastwood Dudley (1891–1961); and the musical arrangements of Stan Fritts (1910–69) and the Korn Kobblers.

Museum facilities also include a specialized library, state-of-the-art conservation laboratory, and extensive study and storage areas.

See also EDUCATION: Museums.

André P. Larson
University of South Dakota

NATIVE AMERICAN MUSIC

Music lies at the heart of Indian culture. From birth to death, all occasions, sacred and secular, personal and tribal, in the life of the Plains Indian are inextricably intertwined with musical performances.

Music serves numerous functions in traditional Indian culture, including religious ceremonies, healing ceremonies, work songs, game songs, courtship, storytelling, songs to bring success in hunting, agriculture, and war, and social songs and dances. As traditional culture has been influenced through contact with non-Indian cultures, the purposes and functions of music have been adapted so that music retains its meaningful role in cultural identity.

The music of the Plains is the most familiar Native American music to non-Indian peoples, due in large part to its use in television and motion pictures (including the Academy Award–winning *Dances with Wolves*, which featured performances by the Porcupine Singers, a well-known Lakota musical group). The high, tense vocal style, the descending melodic pattern, the vocables (meaningful syllables without a direct English translation), and the rhythmic drumming of the Plains are immediately identifiable as "Indian music" throughout the world. Because of its familiarity, it is often erroneously used in entertainment venues to represent the musical practices of all Indians, regardless of tribal or cultural identity. A recent renaissance of interest in Native cultures has, in large part, corrected this misconception.

The defining characteristics of Plains style music include a tense, tight, and rather strained vocal style; among Northern Plains tribes a high vocal range, among the tribes of the Southern Plains a medium range; "collapsible" melodic contour-melodies that begin high, drop drastically lower over the course of a song, and frequently end with repetitions of the tonic pitch; ululations produced by rapidly fluttering the tongue against the roof of the mouth; singing mostly in unison; and, normally, one large drum played by several musicians to accompany songs. Lyrics may be sung entirely in a tribal language, entirely in vocables, in English, or in any combination.

Drums, the best-known type of Indian instrument, are made in many sizes and shapes and from diverse materials. Both small hand drums—twelve to eighteen inches in circumference and covered on one or both sides with a rawhide head and played by one person—and larger "powwow" drums—sometimes the size of a marching band bass drum and played simultaneously by several musicians—are commonly used among Plains tribes. In contemporary practice, the word "drum" refers not only as a noun to the instrument itself but also as a verb to the performers who play it and sing. Many tribes consider the drum to represent the heartbeat of Mother Earth and to offer a means of communication with the supernatural. Because of this significance, tribes often establish strict protocols for playing the drum.

Rattles are the most ubiquitous type of instrument and display great inventiveness with natural materials. Modern Plains Indians have incorporated virtually every type of material imaginable into the construction of rattles: gourds, turtle shells, carved wood, deer hooves, animal horns, animal hide, and tree bark. Other percussive instruments include large dance bells attached to the arms or legs of dancers to provide an ambient accompaniment to dancing, rasps, and wooden sticks.

Flutes and whistles are the primary melodic instruments among Plains Indians. Members of Coronado's sixteenth-century expedition into the Southern Plains provided the first documentation of flute music by non-Indian sources, while Lewis and Clark noted the use of flutes among Northern Plains peoples in the early nineteenth century. In pre-twentieth-century traditional practices, the flute was used primarily to perform courting songs, though some tribes used flutes and whistles in healing ceremonies. Flute performance among Plains tribes, however, had virtually disappeared by the early twentieth century. Kiowa musician Doc Tate Nevaquaya is credited with reviving the tradition of flute making and playing in the late 1940s and 1950s. Contemporary musicians, including Kevin Locke (Lakota), Joseph Fire Crow (Cheyenne), Tom Mauchahty Ware (Comanche-Kiowa), and Robert Tree Cody (Dakota-Maricopa), have expanded the role of the Indian flute far beyond its traditional role in courtship and healing to embrace social songs, dances, and popular songs. The sound of the Indian flute is now heard in motion picture scores and jazz and rock bands in addition to more traditional venues.

Native American music continues to thrive and evolve. Contemporary musicians are exploring combinations of traditional and non-Indian musics to create new styles and genres that retain a distinctively Native American identity. Non-Indian popular music genres such as rock, country, and jazz have been suc-cessfully adapted into the modern Indian repertoire by artists such as Tom Bee (Lakota) performing with XIT, the first commercially successful all-Indian rock band, and Keith Secola (Anishinaabe) and the Wild Band of Indians. Indian musicians such as Buffy Sainte-Marie (Cree) and R. Carlos Nakai (Ute-Navajo) contribute to motion picture and television scores, and the orchestral and choral compositions of Oklahoma-born composer-conductor Louis Ballard (Quapaw-Cherokee) mark the beginnings of Indian symphonic and chamber music. Pianist Paul La Roche (Lakota) combines traditional and New Age elements in his unique works for keyboard.

Powwows and tribal fairs held throughout the Great Plains provide opportunities to experience all musical styles and genres of today's Plains Indians, including generations-old traditional songs and dances as well as contemporary popular music. Modern powwows and tribal fairs are celebrations of Native American culture and include displays of tribal arts and crafts, meals of traditional Native foods, and discussions of social and political issues in addition to the music and dance. They are as much community social events as dance performances. Music and dance include ceremonial performances restricted to initiated members of the tribe; competitive dancing featuring world-class performers of grass dances, fancy dances, jingle dress, and specialty dances; and the after-hours social dances referred to as "forty-nine" dances, the popular music and dance of younger tribal members. Among the larger Plains powwows and tribal fairs held annually are Red Earth Powwow, Oklahoma City, Oklahoma; Gathering of Nations, Albuquerque, New Mexico; Crow Fair, Crow Agency, Montana; and United Tribes Powwow, Bismarck, North Dakota. However, smaller local gatherings offer insights into Indian song and dance in a more intimate setting that allows more interaction among performers and audience members.

See also NATIVE AMERICANS: Powwows / SPORTS AND RECREATION: Crow Fair.

J. Bryan Burton
West Chester University of Pennsylvania

Burton, J. Bryan. *Moving within the Circle: Contemporary Native American Music and Dance*. Danbury CT: World Music Press, 1993. Heth, Charlotte, ed. *Native American Dance: Ceremonies and Social Traditions*. Washington DC: Smithsonian Institution Press, 1992. Laubin, Reginald, and Gladys Laubin. *Indian Dances of North America—Their Importance to Indian Life*. Norman: University of Oklahoma Press, 1989.

NELSON, WILLIE (b. 1933)

Willie Nelson is among America's best-known country music stars. He was born in Abbot, Texas, on April 30, 1933, to Ira and Myrtle Nelson. Nelson's mother abandoned the family when he was five years old, and he and his sister, Bobbie Lee, were raised by their paternal grandparents. The family was musical, and both children studied music through mail-order courses bought by their grandparents. At age six Willie received his first guitar from his grandfather.

Nelson's first musical performance came at age ten, accompanied by Bobbie Lee on piano. By the time he left high school he had his own radio show. After a brief career in the air force, he worked as a DJ and began writing songs, including "Family Bible" and "Night Life." His marriage, the first of several, fell apart, but his career began to climb as his writing ability was quickly recognized. He moved to Nashville in 1959, selling songs to Faron Young ("Hello Walls") and Patsy Cline ("Crazy"). Although his songs were popular when others performed them, Willie himself never found fame as a performer in Nashville. He took the burning of his home there in 1970 as a sign and returned to Texas.

In Texas he began working on his own music, gradually creating a distinctive style that mixed the sound of classic country with a hippie sensibility and earning a reputation as a musical outlaw. His two best-selling albums—*Shotgun Willie* (1973) and *Phases and Stages* (1974)—came out during this era. In 1975 he switched to Columbia, which remained his label until the 1990s. His first album for the new label, *Red-Headed Stranger* (1975), proved to be a breakthrough, confirming his image as an outlaw and romantic hero.

In addition to musical performances, Nelson also acted in several films, including *The Electric Horseman* (1979), *Honeysuckle Rose* (1980), for which he also contributed the soundtrack, *Barbarossa* (1982), and *Wag the Dog* (1997), among others. Nelson founded and has served as the president of Farm Aid, the nearly yearly musical benefit for American farmers. Farm Aid concerts have raised millions for struggling farmers and have taken place in cities from Austin, Texas, and Lincoln, Nebraska, to Columbia, South Carolina.

From 1984 to 1993 Nelson unsuccessfully battled the IRS over $16.7 million in taxes and fines dating back to 1972. Nelson blamed the accounting firm of Price Waterhouse for the mistakes. He eventually settled with the agency. In 1994 he was arrested after police found marijuana in the ashtray of his pickup truck. The search was illegal, and the charges were dropped.

Nelson's career has been propelled by his own intense energy. He has recorded more than 100 albums, written his autobiography, and maintains a grueling concert schedule. His status in American culture is that of pop icon; he has even been the subject of a novel (Richard "Kinky" Friedman's *Road Kill* [1997]). Nelson actively campaigns for farm relief, even testifying before Congress, as well as for the legalization of marijuana. He has cited Mexican American music, blues, western swing, and Frank Sinatra as part of a large list of musical influences; his own work has ranged from country and pop to blues and gospel.

Charles Vollan
University of Nebraska–Lincoln

Nelson, Willie, and Bud Shrake. *Willie: An Autobiography*. New York: Simon and Schuster, 1988; reprint, New York: Cooper Square Press, 2000.

OPERA

Professional opera in the Great Plains began in Denver in 1864 and then was established in Lawrence, Kansas (1869), Kansas City, Missouri (1870), Lincoln, Nebraska (1874), Fort Worth, Texas (1878), Winnipeg, Manitoba (1883), Huron, South Dakota (1885), and various other locations. Its appearance depended on the size and wealth of the community and/or the arrival of the railroad. It was presented largely by touring companies such as those of the soprano Emma Abbott and the British impresario James Mapleson. Amateur local companies specialized in lighter opera. The abbreviated productions of the day often had extraneous selections introduced into them. In the United States, each Plains state boasted as many as several hundred "opera houses," but operas were performed only in a small percentage of them.

Interest in opera had waned by the turn of the century, but the Metropolitan Opera of New York appeared at Omaha in 1890 and intermittently elsewhere in the region through the 1950s. After the turn of the century, touring companies declined when economic conditions worked against their success. Local societies continued, one even presenting Verdi's *Aïda* in Regina in 1932.

Through the 1940s, 1950s, and 1960s, permanent professional opera companies with seasons of varying lengths were formed. They now number nearly ten, the more impressive ones being those in Edmonton, Tulsa, and Kansas City, Missouri. More than twenty universities and colleges of the region maintain opera activities of varying degrees of intensity and scope. Outstanding singers from the region include John Vickers, tenor, and Samuel Ramey, bass. The career of White Eagle, tenor, a Native American from South Dakota who trained in opera in San Francisco, never fully developed before his illness and death in 1995. Opera plots set in the region include Charles Wakefield Cadman's *Shanewis* (1918) as well as Libby Larsen's *Eric Hermannson's Soul* (1998), based on a story by Willa Cather.

H. Bruce Lobaugh
Omaha, Nebraska

Jennings, Harlan F. "Grand Opera in Kansas in the 1880's." Ph.D. diss., University of Cincinnati, 1978. *Musical America International Directory of the Performing Arts.* Hightstown NJ: Primedia Information, 1999. Sadie, Stanley, ed. *The New Grove Dictionary of Opera.* London: Macmillan Publishing Company, 1992.

ORBISON, ROY (1936–1988)

Roy Kelton Orbison was born in Vernon, Texas, on April 23, 1936, and grew up in nearby Wink (population 1,000), where his father worked in the oil fields. Surrounded by the sounds of western swing and honky-tonk, he began singing for audiences at the age of ten. His first band, the Wink Westerners, played pop songs and western standards around West Texas before adapting to the times and, as the Teen Kings, moving into rockabilly. This was a short-lived phase for Orbison, who turned to ballads after 1958 and, recording for Monu-

ment, moved into the ranks of leading stars alongside Elvis Presley and Buddy Holly.

Between 1958 and 1964 a Roy Orbison big-beat ballad was rarely absent from the record charts. His often melancholy songs, including "Only the Lonely," "Running Scared," "Crying," "It's Over," and "Oh, Pretty Woman," sung in an operatic style that often crescendoed to a high note, were standard accompaniments to teenage angst. Working with producer Fred Foster, Orbison pioneered the use of violin backing and abandoned the standard "verse-chorus" song structure in favor of a more complex symphonic style. He was equally popular in the United Kingdom as in the United States, and when he toured the UK in 1963 with the Beatles, who idolized him, Orbison was the main act.

Orbison's career plummeted after 1964, as hard rock displaced the softer, more sentimental songs of the early 1960s. A move to MGM did nothing to rescue declining sales, and, more drastically, Roy's life was struck by tragedy: in 1966 his first wife, Claudette, was killed in a motorcycle accident, and, just over two years later, his two oldest sons, Tony and Roy, died in a house fire while Roy was on tour in Europe.

By 1970 Orbison was virtually forgotten in the United States, though he continued to turn out albums for MGM and later Mercury. Married again in 1969 to a German, Barbara Welhoner, he spent more and more of his time in Europe, where he was still a popular figure. But his mystique was enduring: his black clothes, black shades, and motionless presence on stage still captivated audiences. He continued to tour, playing small towns like the ones he had known in his youth on the Plains.

Moreover, a newer generation of rock artists had not forgotten Roy Orbison. Bruce Springsteen introduced him at his induction into the Rock and Roll Hall of Fame in 1987, and sales of his record "In Dreams" revived after it was featured in David Lynch's bizarre movie *Blue Velvet* (1986). Further new exposure came in the HBO special *Roy Orbison and Friends: A Black and White Night*, in which he was joined and honored by Springsteen, Elvis Costello, Bonnie Raitt, and other rock luminaries whose careers had been so influenced by him. Orbison's career rose to a new zenith in 1988, when he recorded with Bob Dylan, George Harrison, Tom Petty, and Jeff Lynne as a member of The Traveling Wilburys. His new solo album, *Mystery Girl*, shot up the charts in early 1989, but by that time the gentle Texan with the ethereal voice had died on December 6, 1988, in Hendersonville, Tennessee.

Burt Kaufman
Oakland, California

Clayson, Alan. *Only the Lonely: Roy Orbison's Life and Legacy.* New York: St. Martin's Press, 1990. Kaufman, Burt. "Spotlight on Roy Orbison." *Rockin' 50's* 31 (1991): 8–16.

PARKER, CHARLIE (1920–1955)

Charles Parker Jr. was born in Kansas City, Kansas, on August 29, 1920. When he was seven, Charlie moved with his mother, Addie,

to Kansas City, Missouri, which was growing at a boomtown rate. From 1925 to 1938 Kansas City was run by notorious Democratic machine boss Tom Pendergast. Pendergast's machine chose to ignore the prohibition on alcohol imposed by the Volsted Act. Kansas City's bars, nightclubs, and cabarets flourished twenty-four hours a day, providing fertile ground for the emergence of a distinctive blues-based jazz style. Thus, while Parker was receiving his formal education at Crispus Attucks Public School and Old Lincoln High School, he was also receiving his early musical education and inspiration outside famous clubs near 18th and Vine, like the Reno Club and Lucille's Paradise Band Box, listening to the legendary orchestras of Count Basie, Bennie Moten, and Walter Page's Blue Devils. Some say it was this early proclivity for "hanging out" that gave Parker the nickname "Yardbird" (a slang term for chicken), later shortened to "Bird," a more fitting description for the soaring, high-flying artist he was to become.

Bird's chosen instrument was the alto saxophone, but he showed little obvious musical promise with it in his early years. In fact, a famous jazz anecdote has Basie's drummer hurling a cymbal at the young Parker after a particularly ragged solo. At the age of sixteen, after an intensive period of musical study while performing at a resort in the Ozarks, Parker returned home to take the Kansas City music scene by storm. In the late thirties and early forties Parker played with a number of prominent Kansas City ensembles, most notably the Jay McShann Orchestra; but by 1942 Bird had moved his base of operations to New York City. There he emerged as perhaps the single most important creative figure in the birth of what came to be called modern jazz or bebop.

Collaborating with similar-minded musicians, most notably Dizzy Gillespie, Thelonious Monk, Bud Powell, Charles Mingus, and Max Roach, Parker revolutionized the art of jazz composition and soloing. As Louis Armstrong had done before him, Bird influenced all of the serious younger jazz musicians of his day, regardless of their chosen instrument. Parker's rhythmic, harmonic, and melodic innovations proved pivotal in changing the primarily dance-oriented swing jazz of the thirties and forties in the direction of full-blown art music. While many of his compositions are thought to have been created in the most casual of circumstances, such as during taxi rides or recording sessions, compositions such as "Confirmation," "Donna Lee," and "Now's the Time" remain central to the repertoire of jazz standards.

Charlie Parker was perhaps the greatest genius jazz has known. He successfully toured Europe and the United States, his recordings eventually sold millions of copies, and he was so revered in jazz circles during his lifetime that a major jazz club—Birdland—was named in his honor. He became a patron saint of the Beat generation immortalized in Jack Kerouac's *On the Road* (1957), and he was the subject of a major Hollywood film tribute, *Bird* (1988), directed by devoted fan Clint Eastwood. Charlie Parker's genius was tragically short-lived. He died in New York City on March 12, 1955, from complications resulting from long-term substance abuse. Charlie Parker and his mother lie side by side in Lincoln Cemetery, Kansas City, Missouri.

William P. Nye
Hollins University

Giddens, Gary. *Celebrity Bird: The Triumph of Charlie Parker*. New York: Beech Tree/Morrow, 1987. Nye, William. "The Heroic Boon of Charlie Parker." *Popular Music and Society* 15 (1991): 21–31. Riesner, Robert, ed. *Bird: The Legend of Charlie Parker*. New York: Da Capo Press, 1977.

POLKA MUSIC

The polka, a couples dance in duple time, was popular in much of Europe during the second half of the nineteenth century. Since many immigrants from Europe settled in the Great Plains during that period, they brought an affinity for the polka dance and the associated music with them as part of their cultural legacy. Germans and Czechs, in particular, have tended to be the most active in perpetuating the polka tradition in the Great Plains, but Poles, Swedes, Danes, Norwegians, Finns, Italians, Slovenians, Croatians, and other European Americans also identify the polka as part of their ethnic heritage.

The nineteenth-century polka craze also entered Mexico from Europe, and Mexican musicians in Texas interacted with musical German, Polish, and Czech immigrants there to shape the polka style of the Tex-Mex *conjuntos* (bands). During the twentieth century Mexican Americans migrated to many areas of the Great Plains, bringing the conjunto style of polka music and dancing with them.

Polka musicians in the Great Plains play in several distinctive styles. The names of the most influential styles refer to ethnic groups—Czech or "Bohemian," German or "Dutchman," Polish, Mexican, and Slovenian. There is a core constituency of dancers and players from the particular ethnic group in each of the polka "scenes"; however, people from a variety of other ethnic backgrounds participate as well. Mutual influences are common in the music and dancing.

In rural areas, Czechs and Germans have been the most active. There are important concentrations of Czech bands in eastern Nebraska and central Texas. Both the Czech and German polka styles tend to emphasize brass and reed instruments in interaction with an accordion or concertina. The Dutchman style of German American music, originally from southern Minnesota, has also been influential in the Great Plains. Broadcasts of the Whoopee John Orchestra over Minneapolis's clear channel station WCCO were avidly followed on the Plains, and the well-known Dutchman bands toured westward from Minnesota. Thus German bands from the Dakotas to Kansas often use the Chemnitzer type of concertina played by Whoopee John. The Czech bands, on the other hand, tend to utilize the diatonic button box accordion or modern piano keyboard accordion. The German bands strive for a smoother blended brass and reed sound, while the Czech bands opt for an incisive brassy or reedy tone from the wind instruments.

Germans from Russia have developed Dutch Hop, a polka style unique to the Great Plains and played mainly in western Nebraska and eastern Colorado. The hammer dulcimer is an important instrument in Dutch Hop, and the trombone provides the bass line rather than the tuba of the Dutchman and Czech bands.

Polish- and Slovenian-style polka bands are strongest in urban centers like Omaha and Kansas City, although on the western Plains there are also Slovenian bands in mining and mill towns. Polish bands are influenced by Chicago Polish musicians like Lil' Wally and Eddie Blazonczyk. They use the Chemnitzer concertina interacting with brass and reeds played in a raucous and polyphonic style. Slovenian bands foreground the accordion accompanied by tenor or plectrum banjo. Slovenian and Polish bands avoid the tuba, using a string bass, bass guitar, or recently a Midi bass synthesizer played by the accordion player with his or her left hand.

Richard March
Wisconsin Arts Board

Greene, Victor. *A Passion for Polka*. Berkeley: University of California Press, 1992. Keil, Charles, Angeliki V. Keil, and Dick Blau. *Polka Happiness*. Philadelphia: Temple University Press, 1992. Leary, James P., and Richard March. *Down Home Dairyland: A Listener's Guide*. Madison: University of Wisconsin–Extension, 1996.

ROCK AND ROLL MUSIC

The rock music that developed in the Great Plains is derived from many sources, notably the blues, country, and various ethnic folk styles. Many of the artists who were born and raised in the Great Plains have exerted a great influence on the direction that rock music has taken since the late 1950s. Many others have had a more local influence, for every Plains town of any size has its own pulsating rock scene.

The earliest and most influential of the Great Plains musicians are from Texas. Lubbock's Buddy Holly (1936–59), with his band, the Crickets, had several major hits in the late 1950s, beginning with "That'll Be the Day" (1957). Though strongly influenced by rock styles from Memphis and Chicago, the Crickets developed their own rock sound, which incorporated a West Texas feel, that affected the next generation of rockers, including the Beatles, the Rolling Stones, and the Grateful Dead. Other Texas artists associated with Holly include the Big Bopper, J. P. Richardson (1931–59) from Sabine Pass, who was killed in the same plane crash as Holly, and Waylon Jennings (1937–2002) of Littlefield, the bassist for the Crickets who relinquished his airplane seat to Richardson. Jennings emerged in the 1970s as an important figure in outlaw music (country music with a strong rock foundation), in which he was joined by fellow Texan Willie Nelson, who was born in Abbot in 1933.

Jennings and Nelson are crossover artists, equally popular with rock and country fans. Also fatefully associated with Holly is Bobby Vee, who was born in Fargo, North Dakota, in 1943. Vee's band was brought in as a replacement act for the February 3, 1959, concert in Moorhead, Minnesota, that Holly had been scheduled to play. Vee later had several Top 10 hits in the 1960s, including "Take Good Care of My Baby" (1961) and "The Night Has a Thousand Eyes" (1962).

Roy Orbison (1936–1988), from Vernon and Wink, began his career in Texas but eventually moved to Memphis, Tennessee, where he recorded several songs at Sun Studio, the birthplace of rockabilly. Orbison had two number one hit singles, "Running Scared" (1961) and "Oh, Pretty Woman" (1964). Despite several personal tragedies in the late 1960s, Orbison continued to perform in the 1970s and 1980s. In 1988 he joined George Harrison, Bob Dylan, Jeff Lynne, and Tom Petty for a triumphant return to the spotlight in The Traveling Wilburys, but he died of a heart attack shortly after the release of their first album.

Texas remains the most fertile ground for rock music on the Plains. Lubbock produced Jimmie Dale Gilmore and Butch Hancock, Amarillo Joe Ely, and Fort Worth Townes Van Zandt. Gilmore, Hancock, and Ely played together in the acoustic band the Flatlanders in the early 1970s, a suitable name for musicians from the Staked Plains of Texas.

Several artists from Oklahoma significantly contributed to the development of rock as songwriters and performers. Among these are Hoyt Axton, who was born in 1938 in Duncan. Among his many songs are "The Pusher" (recorded by Steppenwolf in 1964) and "Joy to the World" (a hit for Three Dog Night in 1971). Jimmy Webb, born in Elk City in 1946 (and a millionaire by age twenty-one) is another prolific Oklahoma songwriter whose hits include "By the Time I Get to Phoenix" (Glen Campbell, 1967), "Up, Up, and Away" (the Fifth Dimension, 1967), and "MacArthur Park" (Richard Harris, 1968). J. J. Cale (born in Oklahoma City in 1938) was yet another talented Oklahoma musician, composing "After Midnight" (1970) and "Cocaine" (1977) for Eric Clapton and "Call Me the Breeze" for Lynyrd Skynyrd (1974) among many others. Cale became a popular recording artist in the 1970s, offering his own slower, emotional renditions of these songs.

Leon Russell (born in 1941), from Lawton, became a session instrumentalist in Los Angeles in 1958, playing guitar, bass, keyboards, and trumpet. By the 1960s he had established himself as an important writer and producer, working with artists like Glen Campbell, the Byrds, and Gary Lewis and the Playboys. In 1970 Russell was the charismatic musical director for Joe Cocker's Mad Dogs and Englishmen tour, and he later helped organize the band for George Harrison's benefit concert for Bangladesh. Russell composed many memorable songs that were featured on his own down-home albums and recorded by others; for example, "Delta Lady" was a hit for

Joe Cocker in 1969, and "Superstar" was a major success for the Carpenters in 1971. Russell is a consummate session man who has recorded with artists as different as Frank Sinatra, Herb Albert, and Bob Dylan.

Judy Collins, born in Seattle in 1939 but raised in Denver, and John Denver (1943–97), born in Roswell, New Mexico, came out of the western Plains. Collins, who developed her art in Denver's coffeehouses, had hits with pop ballads like "Both Sides Now" (1967) and "Send in the Clowns" (1975). Denver's music is more folk-oriented country rock, praising the virtues of country living, particularly in the Rocky Mountains. Denver's most memorable hits include "Rocky Mountain High" (1972) and "Annie's Song" (1975). After enjoying a great deal of success in the 1970s, Denver's career stalled in the 1980s. He was beginning a comeback in the late 1990s when he was killed in an airplane accident.

Several musicians who were born or raised in the Prairie Provinces have also been influential in the development of rock. Joni Mitchell was born in 1943 in Fort Macleod, Alberta, and studied art in Calgary. She worked the folk scene in Toronto and had her first hit with "Big Yellow Taxi" (1970). A durable and talented artist, Mitchell has incorporated jazz elements in her music, particularly, her album *Mingus* (1979). Neil Young, one of the major figures in American rock music, spent his formative years in Winnipeg before moving back to Toronto (his birthplace, in 1945) and then on to Los Angeles. Influenced by 1950s rock and roll styles, Young came into prominence in the late 1960s as the lead guitarist for Buffalo Springfield. After the demise of the band, Young recorded two albums before joining the supergroup Crosby, Stills and Nash. They recorded the album *Déjà vu* in 1970, but personality conflicts led to Young leaving the group. He recorded several albums in the 1970s, notably, the critically acclaimed *Harvest* (1971), and has continued to record prolifically. Because of his minimalist approach to guitar soloing, Young is also considered to be the "godfather" of alternative rock, as his eulogy to Kurt Cobain (*Sleeps with Angels*, 1994) and his collaborations with Pearl Jam (*Mirror Ball*, 1995) prove.

All members of the Guess Who also came out of Winnipeg. Their numerous hits include "These Eyes" (1969) and "American Woman" (1970). At the height of their popularity, lead guitarist Randy Bachman left the band for personal reasons, and the group disbanded in 1975. Bachman joined his brothers Robbie and Tim and friend Fred Turner to create Bachman-Turner Overdrive. BTO had several hit songs in the 1970s, including "You Ain't Seen Nothing Yet" and "Taking Care of Business" (both 1974), before disbanding in 1977.

Many more Great Plains musicians have contributed to the development of rock music. With few exceptions, these artists are rooted in varying combinations of folk, country, and blues styles. Again, with few exceptions, they were obliged to leave the region, generally for the coasts, to make their names in the business. But Plains Texans often went only as far as Austin, and others like Neil Young and Joni Mitchell still refer to the Plains as home.

Stephen Valdez
University of Georgia

Clifford, Mike. *The Harmony Illustrated Encyclopedia of Rock.* New York: Harmony Books, 1992. DeCurtis, Anthony, James Henke, and Holly George-Warren, eds. *The Rolling Stone Illustrated History of Rock and Roll.* New York: Random House, 1992. Valdez, Stephen. *A History of Rock Music.* Dubuque IA: Kendall-Hunt Publishers, 1999.

SAINTE-MARIE, BUFFY (b. 1941)

Buffy Sainte-Marie is a Cree singer-songwriter, guitarist, mouth-bow player, artist, and educator who was born February 20, 1941, at the Piapot Reserve in Saskatchewan, Canada. Orphaned when a few months old, she was raised by a part Micmac family in Massachusetts and later adopted by a Cree family related to her biological parents. As a college student in the early 1960s, Sainte-Marie became known as a social commentator, initially in New York's Greenwich Village, then internationally in Europe, Canada, Australia, Hong Kong, and Japan. Her songs addressing the plight of Native American people such as "My Country 'Tis of Thy People You're Dying" (1964) generated the most controversy. Several of her songs became widely known in versions by other artists, including "Until It's Time for You to Go" (recorded by Elvis Presley and many others), "Up Where We Belong" (the theme for the film *An Officer and a Gentleman*, which won an Academy Award in 1983 for best song), and the antiwar song "The Universal Soldier" (used as an anthem for the 1960s peace movement).

Sainte-Marie is also noted for her work as a digital artist and as an educator. Her regular performances on the TV show *Sesame Street* (1975–81) taught countless children that Indians still exist. The Cradleboard Teaching Project, founded by Sainte-Marie in 1996, enables mainstream school systems to communicate with Native American communities via computer. Currently residing in Hawaii, Sainte-Marie frequently travels to make recordings, perform concerts, and lecture on a variety of topics, including electronic music, digital art, and Native American women's issues.

Paula Conlon
University of Oklahoma

Miller, Mark. "Buffy Sainte-Marie." In *Encyclopedia of Music in Canada*, 2nd ed., edited by Helmut Kallman et al. Toronto: University of Toronto Press, 1992. Stawarz, Jean. "Songs of Conscience: A Dialogue with Buffy Sainte-Marie." *Runner* (1994): 26–39.

SCHOOLS OF MUSIC

The Great Plains has witnessed the development of many music programs in higher education that are, to a large extent, responsible for the rich musical heritage and culture of its people. These schools and departments of music in the region's colleges and universities have contributed greatly to the quality of life in the Great Plains in addition to training future teachers and professional and amateur musicians. Six music programs in higher education have a tradition of musical excellence and represent the impact that all of the schools and departments of music have had on the people of the Great Plains.

Two of these music programs, the University of Kansas and the University of Nebraska–Lincoln, are among the oldest in the Great Plains. They are geographically close to each other, and their music programs developed at approximately the same time. Both music programs were granted membership in the National Association of Schools of Music (NASM) in 1928, the first year NASM began awarding national accreditation. The first evidence of a music department at the University of Kansas appears in the university catalog of 1877–78, which lists music by special instructors. In 1884 a committee introduced music study to the curriculum to furnish instruction in all branches of music to both amateur and professional students, to combine music with regular collegiate work, and to train teachers. The idea that all three could be offered in a single department was unheard-of before 1884 and was not generally accepted until well after World War I.

The University of Nebraska catalog of 1877 describes the availability of vocal and instrumental study. The names of several different music instructors appear in the records between 1877 and 1887. In 1892 a plan was presented to enhance the music program by establishing a conservatory that would operate as a separate entity by generating its own funds. The conservatory would serve the university by offering instruction for which credit would be granted. The current School of Music at the University of Nebraska–Lincoln evolved from this plan and was officially founded in 1894. The following description of the School of Music appeared in a 1910 issue of the *Musical Courier*: "It stands here in a city of 40,000 inhabitants, situated in the center of a great prairie, isolated from all the great art centers of the United States." The board of regents purchased the School of Music in 1930, and it became an official academic unit of the University of Nebraska–Lincoln.

Two additional institutions developed comprehensive music programs in the Great Plains. The School of Music at the University of Oklahoma became one of the first music programs in the country to be granted membership in NASM in 1931, and the music program at the University of Colorado grew to become a College of Music and was awarded accreditation in NASM in 1941.

Alberta College in Edmonton is one of Canada's oldest arts institutions. The music department, now the Conservatory of Music, was established in 1903 and has become one of the largest music programs in Canada. The School of Music at the University of Manitoba can be traced to 1944, when students in arts and sciences could minor in music with courses in music theory and music history. A degree program in music was instituted in 1963.

Lawrence R. Mallett
University of Nebraska–Lincoln

TEAGARDEN, JACK (1905–1964)

Weldon Leo "Jack" Teagarden was one of the most influential jazz trombonists of the early twentieth century. His playing was among the first examples of individual style in the genre of jazz trombone. He was also a fine vocalist. He has inspired many performers, from jazz trombonists to the concert trombone soloist Christian Lindberg.

Teagarden was born in the Texas Panhandle town of Vernon on August 29, 1905. After his father died in the 1918 flu epidemic, the family briefly moved to Chappell, Nebraska, then headed back south to Oklahoma City. His family was poor, but there was always music: Teagarden was playing the piano at the age of five and the baritone horn by the time he was seven; by age ten he had taken up the trombone. He started playing professionally (in San Antonio) when he was fourteen. His musical influences were varied, but it is obvious from his playing that he took a great deal from black music, especially the blues. Teagarden's recording career began when he was twenty-two years old with a session for Johnny Johnson and his Statler Pennsylvanians. He took part in the first mixed-race recording session when he recorded "Knockin' a Jug" with Louis Armstrong in 1929. Teagarden performed with many of the other jazz greats of his era, including Benny Goodman, Red Nichols, Paul Whiteman, and Eddie Condon. From 1928 to 1933 a great deal of Teagarden's work was as a musical sideman, including with Ben Pollack's band, but he also had his own band for a time. This period produced some of Teagarden's most distinctive and best-known recordings, including "Someone Stole Gabriel's Horn" (1933).

Teagarden led his own band full time from 1939 to 1947, recording (on Decca after 1941) good music but making no money. After his band broke up, Teagarden played with the Louis Armstrong All Stars until 1951, when he formed his own All Star orchestra and achieved considerable success playing Dixieland jazz. Teagarden continued to perform until his death in New Orleans in 1964. He was inducted into the Jazz Hall of Fame in 1996.

Scott L. Anderson
University of Nebraska–Lincoln

Schuller, Gunther. *The Swing Era: The Development of Jazz 1930–1945.* New York: Oxford University Press, 1989. Smith, Jay D., and Len Guttridge. *Jack Teagarden: The Story of a Jazz Maverick.* New York: Da Capo Press, 1976.

TERRITORY BANDS

The term *territory band* refers to those Plains and midwestern dance bands of the 1920s and 1930s that played throughout an expansive geographic area extending from Texas in the south to Nebraska in the north and from St. Louis in the east to Denver in the west. Typically, territory bands were headquartered in the region's major cities, principally, Kansas City, Oklahoma City, Dallas, Houston, Omaha, St. Louis, and Denver. These urban centers, responding to demands for Jazz Age and Swing Era dance music as well as accompaniments for "silent" films, supported large, diversified musical communities. Traveling bands, drawn from such big city talent pools, were assembled by bookers for strings of one-nighters at rural dance halls in the small towns of the surrounding "territory." Unfortunately, the history of territory bands, especially during the 1920s, is sketchy because these ensembles seldom, if ever, had opportunities to record. Among the more than 100 traveling dance bands active in the 1920s were those of Alphonso Trent (Dallas), Doc Ross (Oklahoma City), Troy Floyd (San Antonio), Walter Page (Oklahoma City and Kansas City), and Jesse Stone (Kansas City).

In the 1930s, with the Plains hit hard by the Great Depression, economic necessity brought many of the region's best musicians to Kansas City, a wide-open town where whiskey and jazz flowed twenty-four hours a day, thanks to political boss Tom Pendergast. Aside from supporting its own vibrant nightlife, Kansas City became the center for the area's territory bands. This concentration of so much jazz talent was significant in consolidating a distinctive Kansas City style. Erasing the last influences of the contrapuntal New Orleans tradition by replacing tuba with string bass and banjo with guitar and by expanding the size of groups from combos to big bands, the easygoing and swinging Kansas City style also capitalized on blues and riff-based ensembles, which, while pleasing dancers, also encouraged virtuoso soloing. During the 1930s, the Kansas City–based bands of Bennie Moten, Walter Page, Count Basie, and Jay McShann all took their turns touring the Plains as territory bands.

Chuck Berg
University of Kansas

Kansas City Jazz Museum. *Kansas City . . . and All That's Jazz.* Kansas City MO: Andrew McMeel Publishing, 1999. Pearson, Nathan W., Jr. *Goin' to Kansas City.* Urbana: University of Illinois Press, 1988. Russell, Ross. *Jazz Style in Kansas City and the Southwest.* Berkeley: University of California Press, 1971.

THOMSON, VIRGIL (1896–1989)

Virgil Thomson, classical composer and music critic, was born on November 25, 1896, in Kansas City, Missouri, where he learned piano and played organ at his family's Calvary Baptist Church. After serving in the army during World War I, Thomson studied composition and conducting in New York, Paris, and Boston. He graduated from Harvard in 1923. Returning to Paris in 1925, his home until 1940, Thomson came under the influence of composition pedagogue Nadia Boulanger and French composer Erik Satie, whose clarity, simplicity, and humor he admired.

Thomson's large body of work, which includes operas, symphonies, chamber pieces, songs, and film scores, while reflecting the classicism of his formal studies, is largely rooted in his early musical experiences in Kansas City. Indeed, in his well-known scores for the celebrated documentary films *The River* (1937), *The Plow That Broke the Plains* (1936), and *Louisiana Story* (1948), the last of which earned a Pulitzer Prize, Thomson incorporated familiar American religious and secular melodies. Even in his operas, most famously, *Four Saints in Three Acts* (1934), Thomson employed the musical vernacular of his midwestern background, an example of the "new simplicity" and growing nationalism of American serious music of the 1930s.

In addition to composing, Thomson enjoyed a successful career as a music journalist. Having established himself in the pages of *Modern Music* during the 1930s, he was commissioned to write *The State of Music* (1939), which argued that musicians should produce their own music. On the strength of that work, the *New York Herald Tribune* hired Thomson as its chief music critic. During his reign at the *Tribune* from 1940 to 1954, Thomson's provocative commentaries were anthologized in *The Right of Judging* (1948), *Music Right and Left* (1951), and *Music Reviewed, 1940–54* (1967). In the 1970s and 1980s Thomson devoted himself largely to teaching and lecturing. He died in New York City on September 30, 1989.

See also FILM: *The Plow That Broke the Plains.*

Chuck Berg
University of Kansas

Rockwell, John. *A Virgil Thomson Reader.* Boston: Houghton Mifflin, 1981. Thomson, Virgil. *Virgil Thomson.* New York: Alfred A. Knopf, Inc., 1966. Tommasini, Anthony. *Virgil Thomson: Composer on the Aisle.* New York: W. W. Norton, 1997.

TRUDELL, JOHN (b. 1946)

A Santee Dakota, John Trudell was born in Omaha, Nebraska, on February 15, 1946, and raised on the Santee Sioux Reservation. Initially, he achieved national notoriety for his political activism on behalf of Native Americans. He was a leader of the Indians of All Tribes' occupation of Alcatraz in 1969, and in that capacity he hosted a radio program in 1970, *Radio Free Alcatraz*, that was broadcast in Berkeley, Los Angeles, and New York City. From 1973 to 1979 he served as the national chairman of the American Indian Movement (AIM). After the fire-bombing death of his wife, mother-in-law, and three daughters at their home on the Duck Valley Reservation in Nevada on February 11, 1979, Trudell began moving away from direct political action and devoted more of his time to artistic and intellectual endeavors.

In 1981 he wrote his first book, *Living in Reality.* In 1985 he formed the Graffiti Band with Jesse Ed Davis, a prolific studio guitarist from Oklahoma City who was of Seminole and Kiowa descent. Together they wedded Trudell's poetry, which ranged from political and social commentary to love poems, with Davis's unique musical style. They released AKA *Graffiti Man* and *Heart Jump Bouquet* before Davis's death in 1988. AKA was subsequently rereleased on a major label (Rykodisk) in 1992 and was executively produced by Jackson Browne. It featured the original tapes of Davis and Trudell, which were remastered and fleshed out with additional musicians. Guest appearances were made by Browne and Kris Kristofferson. AKA received high critical acclaim (Bob Dylan called it the best album of the year) and was followed by *Johnny Damas and Me* (1995).

Trudell has also acted in several feature films, including *Thunderheart* (1992), *On Deadly Ground* (1994), and *Smoke Signals* (1998). In 1994 he published his second book, *Stickman*.

See also PROTEST AND DISSENT: American Indian Movement.

Akim D. Reinhardt
Towson University

TUBB, ERNEST (1914–1984)

Ernest Dale Tubb, popular and influential country music singer, was born in Crisp in rural Ellis County, Texas (near Dallas), the youngest of five children in a sharecropping family. His family picked cotton there during the prosperous World War I years and then in about 1920 moved west to the High Plains, pulling cotton in and around Benjamin, Texas. Cowboy music performed by Jules Verne Allen and others was one early influence on Tubb, but his main formative influence was the music of recording star Jimmie Rodgers. Later, while working a succession of radio jobs in San Antonio, San Angelo, Corpus Christi, and Fort Worth, Tubb was influenced by contemporaries such as Rex Griffin, Tommy Duncan, Al Dexter, Floyd Tillman, Ted Daffan, and Moon Mullican. He failed as a Jimmie Rodgers clone on Bluebird Records (1936–37) but developed his own warm, drawling, honky-tonk singing style and a growing following through self-written song hits on Decca Records after 1940, especially 1941's "Walking the Floor over You."

Tubb worked in four Hollywood films of the 1940s—two Charles Starrett Westerns for Columbia Pictures and two musical variety films—and moved his base of operations from Texas to Nashville's *Grand Ole Opry* in 1943. He remained one of the show's biggest stars for the rest of his career and is legendary for the professional helping hand he extended to others, including Hank Williams, Hank Snow, Charlie Walker, Johnny Cash, Stonewall Jackson, the Wilburn Brothers, George Hamilton IV, duet partner Loretta Lynn, and his own one-time Texas Troubadours bandsmen Jack Greene and Cal Smith. Emphysema ended his long career in 1982, and two years later, on September 6, 1984, in Nashville, it took his life. During his seventy years he won all the honors the country music world can bestow, including election in 1965 as the sixth member of the Country Music Hall of Fame.

Ronnie Pugh
Nashville, Tennessee

Pugh, Ronnie. *Ernest Tubb: The Texas Troubadour.* Durham NC: Duke University Press, 1996.

VEE, BOBBY (b. 1943)

Born Robert Thomas Velline on April 30, 1943, in Fargo, North Dakota, Bobby Vee became one of the more enduring popular musicians of the mid– to late twentieth century. After gaining entrance into his older brother's combo because he knew the lyrics to the popular songs of the day, Vee got his first major exposure on the night of February 3, 1959, in Moorhead, Minnesota, as one of the acts filling in for Buddy Holly, Richie Valens, and the Big Bopper, J. P. Richardson, who had died that morning in a plane crash near Clear Lake, Iowa. The success throughout the Northern Plains and upper Midwest of his self-penned and Holly-inspired "Susie Baby" led to his signing with Los Angeles–based Liberty Records in the fall of 1959. He achieved international fame singing about the joys and angst of teenage life and young adulthood on "Devil or Angel," "Rubber Ball," "Take Good Care of My Baby" (which stayed at number one on the *Billboard* charts for three weeks in September 1961), "Run to Him," "The Night Has a Thousand Eyes," "Come Back When You Grow Up," and dozens of other songs released on singles and albums throughout the 1960s. In 1967 Vee starred in the movie *C'mon, Let's Live a Little,* in which he portrayed a rural folksinger adjusting to college life.

Vee still plays to sold-out audiences throughout Europe and North America. His high-energy, positively oriented stage show includes his three sons, who also perform independently as a rockabilly act called the Vees. At his studio located near St. Cloud, Minnesota, Vee continues to record and release songs, old and new, on his Rockhouse label, including novel arrangements and compositions that reveal a diverse and occasionally avant-garde musical intellect.

John Arthur Lindquist
University of Wisconsin–Madison

Nite, Norm N. *Rock On: The Illustrated Encyclopedia of Rock N' Roll.* New York: Thomas Y. Crowell Company, 1974. Rees, Dafydd, and Luke Crampton. DK *Encyclopedia of Rock Stars.* New York: DK Publishing, 1996.

WELK, LAWRENCE (1903–1992)

The sixth of eight children, Lawrence Welk was born on a farm near Strasburg in south-central North Dakota on March 11, 1903, to Ludwig and Christina Schwann Welk, German Russian immigrants from the Odessa region of the Ukraine. Throughout his career, Welk claimed that his lifelong frugality, work ethic, and strong Catholic Church ties were products of his impoverished and strictly disciplined upbringing. A largely self-taught musician, Welk quit school during the fourth grade, purchased his first piano accordion at age seventeen, and left the farm on his twenty-first birthday to begin a career as a regional musician and dance band leader.

In 1926 he began his first significant full-time job in South Dakota as an accordionist and actor with the Peerless Entertainers, a small traveling show led by George T. Kelly, the individual Welk credited with teaching him the basics of advertising, showmanship, and audience sensitivity. From 1927 to 1937 Welk traveled the Plains states with his own six- to ten-piece territory band under various

Lawrence Welk

names (Welk's Novelty Orchestra, the Hotsy-Totsy Boys, and the Honolulu Fruit Gum Orchestra), and from 1927 to 1934 they played live radio shows over WNAX in Yankton, South Dakota. During this period his most notable and regular bookings were in the seven Tom Archer Ballrooms located in Iowa, Nebraska, South Dakota, and Missouri. In 1931 he married Fern Renner in Yankton. They had three children: Shirley (b. 1932), Donna (b. 1937), and Lawrence Jr. (b. 1940).

In late 1937 Welk got his first national exposure under management of the Fredericks Brothers with broadcast performances at the William Penn Hotel in Pittsburgh. It was during this booking in early 1938 that he began distinguishing his musical style as "champagne music," and soon thereafter he had his own waltz-ballad, "You're My Home Sweet Home," rearranged as "Bubbles in the Wine," his signature theme for the remainder of his career. While at the William Penn he also hired the first of seven "champagne ladies" (Lois Best, 1938–40; Jayne Walton, 1940–45; Joan Mowery, 1945–47; Helen Ramsey, 1947–49; Roberta Linn, 1949–53; Alice Lon, 1953–59; and Norma Zimmer, 1960–82). From 1940 to 1950 Welk's band was based in Chicago, where he most often played the Trianon Ballroom.

Welk moved his band in 1951 to the Aragon Ballroom in Santa Monica, California, and was featured from 1952 to 1955 on weekly broadcasts from the ballroom over KTLA television. In 1955 Welk began weekly national broadcasts over ABC. After ABC dropped the show in 1971, it continued in syndication until Welk's retirement in 1982. During the early years of this period Welk hired his most famous band member, accordionist Myron Floren (1950); his personal manager, Sam Lutz (1952); and his musical director, George Cates (1956). All three remained with him until his retirement. In 1956 he hired the four Lennon Sisters as featured singers, the first of a long line of young singers and dancers who would become part of his "musical family" over the next twenty-one years. In order to keep his now famous musical family intact (he paid only union scale salaries, a policy that never changed throughout his career), he initiated a unique profit-sharing plan in 1956 based in part on how long a member of the show remained with the organization.

After building his audience through years of live appearances, he maintained their loyalty as television viewers with the stylistic consistency of his programming, the personalized presentation of his musical family, his famous accent and misstatements, and his simple, North Dakota farm boy demeanor. Welk retired at the end of the 1982 season, and the decision was made not to continue the show without him. Even though his show never received a broadcast award, it remains the most watched and longest running program of its kind in television history. Reruns continue over public television stations. In 1994 Lawrence Jr. opened the Welk Theater and Resort in Branson, Missouri, where the shows are headlined by members of the original television cast. The Lawrence Welk Archive, which contains his scrapbooks, band arrangements, and memorabilia, is located at North Dakota State University in Fargo. Welk died on May 12, 1992, in Santa Monica, California.

Robert W. Groves
North Dakota State University

Schwienher, William. *Lawrence Welk: An American Institution.* Chicago: Nelson-Hall, 1980. Welk, Lawrence. *Wunnerful, Wunnerful: The Autobiography of Lawrence Welk,* edited by Bernice McGeehan. Englewood Cliffs NJ: Prentice-Hall, 1971.

WESTERN SWING

Western swing is ballroom music, a style with a constant beat built around a lead fiddle using a long, smooth bow stroke suitable for two-step dancing. More than the song or the singer, western swing is built on instrumental improvisation, and its strong dance rhythms constitute a significant departure from the listening conventions of traditional country music.

The style had its beginnings in 1931 with a fiddle band that played first over radio station KFJZ, then over WBAP in Fort Worth, Texas, promoting Light Crust flour for the Burrus Mill and Elevator Company. Bob Wills played fiddle, Herman Arnspiger played guitar, and Milton Brown sang, and they called themselves the Light Crust Doughboys. The special talents and distinctive style of this small country band established Fort Worth as the "cradle of western swing" and Bob Wills as a significant musical innovator whose experimentations changed the course, sound, and audience of fiddle music forever.

Initially, band members performed for no fee and worked eight hours a day at the mill, playing just for the chance to be heard and maybe hired for dances in and around Fort Worth. By 1932 they were salaried, and Burrus Mill's general manager, Wilbert Lee "Pappy" O'Daniel, was broadcasting the show in San Antonio, Houston, and Oklahoma, as well as Forth Worth. For the next twenty years, even with a rather constant turnover in musicians, the Light Crust Doughboys remained one of the most popular radio shows in the Southwest and helped launch Pappy O'Daniel as a colorful force in Texas politics.

In late 1932 Milton Brown and his brother Durwood left the Doughboys to form Milton Brown and the Musical Brownies, a very successful band playing in the new western swing style. Until his death in a 1936 automobile accident, Milton Brown helped popularize this new dance music with over 100 recording selections for Victor and Decca.

Bob Wills only stayed with O'Daniel and the Doughboys until 1933. By 1934 he and his band were solidly established in Tulsa, Oklahoma, as Bob Wills and His Texas Playboys. For the next twenty-five years they broadcast over radio station KVOO, made numerous regional and national tours, appeared in almost twenty Hollywood movies, and recorded their music in abundance with major record labels. Through all these venues, Bob Wills and His Texas Playboys established their diverse and continually changing repertoire and folksy yet sophisticated style as elemental influences on American popular music.

Western swing, like traditional country music, posits "humble folk" as its audience but radically expands the definition by adding dance rhythms and mellow vocalists to express both urban and country musical themes. Milton Brown's best-selling recording was "St. Louis Blues." Bob Wills and His Texas Playboys gave their audiences everything from Bob and John Wills's poignant country creation "Faded Love" to Tommy Duncan's crooning rendition of "Right or Wrong" and "I'll String Along with You."

In the beginning both Wills's and Brown's bands were innovative country string bands relying on the fiddle, guitar, banjo, and bass for their distinctive style. Wills, however, soon defied country music conventions and the fiddle band tradition. By adding saxophones, clarinets, trombones, drums, and even mariachi horns to his orchestra, he created a big band sound that embraced both the brassy jazz of the era and the lively two-step rhythms for dancing on the Southern High Plains. Bob Wills consistently responded to the diverse musical traditions of his native region, radically reshaping them to fit his own special brand of swing orchestra.

As a child, Wills had listened to and admired the blues sung by African Americans who worked the cotton harvest with his family in West Texas. "I slurred my fiddle," he explained, "in order to play the blues." This slurring of the strings is a basic characteristic of western swing string instrumentation. Wills's many experimentations with the amplified steel guitar helped intensify these blues rhythms, and, through his influence, the plaintive whine of amplified steel soon became a standard in the expression of country and western music.

Wills also incorporated regional Hispanic influences into his music. While barbering and playing fiddle in Roy, New Mexico, in the late 1920s, Wills composed a piece he called "Spanish Two-Step." A decade later he rearranged it into what became his most famous song, "San Antonio Rose." The Playboys recorded it as a country instrumental in 1938 and in 1940 as the "New San Antonio Rose," with lyrics performed by Tommy Duncan and mariachi horns added to reinforce the Hispanic spirit of the tune. In 1941 Bing Crosby recorded the song, giving Bob Wills's western swing its first national recognition.

In many ways, western swing music is a manifestation of the cultural forces that came together where the geographical isolation and harsh living conditions of the frontier met the electronic age. People still living in dugouts and sod houses on the Southern High Plains became a part of popular culture through the radio and the jukebox, mingling their musical talents and tastes with new sounds introduced to them through the accessibility of phonographs and the airwaves.

By applying new, innovative techniques to playing the fiddle and all the other basic country string instruments, western swing serves as a significant crucible in the development of popular American music, expanding a regional, rural sound into a dynamic, rhythmic style that forms a continuum through rockabilly, rock and roll, crossover country, and what is now called, specifically because of western swing, country and western music.

Pamela H. Brink
Associated Authors and Editors, Inc.

Malone, Bill C. *Country Music USA: A Fifty-Year History.* Austin: University of Texas Press, 1985. Mason, Michael, ed. *The Country Music Book.* New York: Charles Scribner's Sons, 1985. Townsend, Charles. *San Antonio Rose: The Life and Music of Bob Wills.* Urbana: University of Illinois Press, 1976.

WEST TEXAS FAMILY MUSIC MAKING

Defined by the dramatic landscape of the Llano Estacado, a vast mesa 3,000 feet high and 300 miles across with accompanying canyonlands, the high plains of Texas are bordered by Oklahoma on the north, the Edwards Plateau on the south, New Mexico on the west, and I-35 on the east. This land, commonly known as West Texas, possesses a distinctive regional culture shaped by the cattle, cotton, and oil industries, a perennial wind, and a seemingly endless sky. One of the most meaningful manifestations of this regional culture is a tradition of music making that has influenced the shape and style of popular music since Amarillo's Eck Robertson made the nation's first country music recording in 1922.

For the farm families who settled here in the early 1900s, music making was not only a prominent form of family entertainment but also one of the few opportunities available to escape a hardscrabble existence. Those with a talent on the fiddle could earn more money playing for a Saturday night dance than they could chopping cotton for a week.

Bob Wills came from a musical family who moved to Memphis near Amarillo in 1913. His father, John T. Wills, was a famous contest fiddler, often competing against Eck Robertson for championship status. To the Wills family, string band music was a serious study, and by the time Bob Wills was ten years old, he was playing mandolin to his father's fiddle at local dances. As bandleader for Bob Wills and His Texas Playboys, Wills gained international fame by developing and popularizing western swing music through tours, recordings, and Hollywood movies.

The pattern of Wills's career is emblematic of a family music-making tradition that permeates West Texas, a tradition rooted in rigorous fiddle or guitar training learned primarily at home, polished with family members and friends for public performance, and inspired in rhythm and technique by a regional predilection for ballroom dancing based on a strong backbeat. Since Bob Wills, West Texas music has achieved that backbeat with drums.

Hoyle Nix also came from a cotton-farming, musical family and learned the fiddle from his father, Jonah. In 1946 he formed the West Texas Cowboys, based out of Big Spring. Brother Ben played guitar in the band, and Hoyle's son Jody joined the group at age eight as the drummer. The West Texas Cowboys is a classic western swing band featuring lead fiddle, so when Jody took over the band in 1985, he gave up his drums for the fiddle he had been playing in the background since age eleven.

Tommy Hancock, as fiddler and bandleader, and Charlene Condray, as lead singer, met and married in Lubbock while performing with the Roadside Cowboys in the 1950s. They reopened the Cotton Club in Lubbock in the 1960s and welcomed a new generation of musicians to their performance arena. Influenced by the counterculture movement, in the 1970s the Hancocks moved to New Mexico, where their children grew up singing and playing music for entertainment. The family ultimately formed a musical touring group, the Supernatural Family Band, and today Charlene and daughters Traci and Conni still perform together as the Texana Dames.

In instrumental virtuosity, performance style, range of selection, and family ties, the Maines Brothers Band stands as the quintessential West Texas music group. Four of the seven-member band are brothers whose father, Wayne Maines, and uncles, James and Sonny, were the feature artists for the original Lubbock-based Maines Brothers Band popular in the 1950s and 1960s. Brothers Lloyd and Steve took up guitar as teenagers, and Kenny started playing electric bass at age eleven. Soon they were performing with their father's band and playing gigs with their own group. When he was old enough, brother Donnie joined them on drums. Today, besides performing with his brothers, Lloyd Maines coproduces and plays pedal steel and guitars for the Dixie Chicks, which features his daughter Natalie Maines as lead singer.

When the Maines Brothers Band takes the stage, audiences are treated to a primarily guitar-led rhythm celebration of the complete spectrum of West Texas music. A concert might easily include songs made famous by television personalities Mac Davis from Lubbock and Jimmy Dean from Plainview, a rendition of the Rhythm Orchids' "Party Doll," a medley of greats from Wink's Roy Orbison or Lubbock's Buddy Holly, plus favorites by Odessa's Gatlin Brothers and Lubbock's Jimmie Dale Gilmore and Joe Ely. With an instrumental combination that includes a myriad of guitars, harmonica, drums and other percussion, pedal steel, Hawaiian slide, fiddle, mandolin, keyboard, and occasional jazz accordion and horns, the band has the musicianship to entertain with everything from Bob Wills's "San Antonio Rose" to favorites by Terry Allen and Butch Hancock. While Kenny Maines is the primary lead vocalist, band members Steve Maines and Jerry Brownlow also take their turns, and everybody else joins in on harmony, including sister LaTronda Maines.

Versatile instrumentation is the foundation of West Texas music, with vocals serving as just a basic part of the mix. Except for Roy Orbison and Don Williams of Floydada, West Texas music tends to feature craggy-edged lead vocalists who sell a song with spirit rather than tone and tenor. Nowhere is this more apparent than in the list of female stars who hail from West Texas. From Natalie Maines to Seminole's Tanya Tucker, Fort Worth's Lee Ann Barton, Lubbock's Angela Strehli, Anton's Jeannie C. Reilly, and Kermit's Charline Arthur, West Texas female singers tend to project a raw, unschooled bluesy edge and a worldly wise demeanor to match.

Lubbock's Kimmie Rhodes is another example of the raspy-voiced West Texas lead vocalist, but her career points more significantly to the prolific songwriting tradition that emanates from the region. From Amarillo's Susan Gibson and "Wide Open Spaces" to Kimmie Rhodes and Natalie Maines, to Jimmie Dale Gilmore's long list of lyrics and Butch Hancock's even longer list, to Joe Ely, Terry Allen, Angela Strehli, and her brother Al Strehli, current performing artists from West Texas continue to generate volumes of poignant and witty lyrics, many with a decidedly self-conscious regional perspective.

Their talents are equally matched by their predecessors. Buddy Holly is credited with popularizing original songwriting in rock and roll recordings, and his songs have withstood the test of time, including his first hit, "That'll Be the Day," and his "Not Fade Away," which became the unofficial theme song for the Grateful Dead. Waylon Jennings, electric bass player on the final, fatal Buddy Holly tour who gave up his seat to the Big Bopper, penned a number of memorable songs alone and in collaboration with fellow "outlaw" Willie Nelson. Holly's lifelong friend and member of the Crickets, Sonny Curtis, also has many songs to his credit, including *The Mary Tyler Moore Show* theme song and "Walk Right Back."

Woody Guthrie represents yet another generation of West Texas songwriters. Although born in Oklahoma, Guthrie didn't play music until he moved to Texas as a teenager in 1929. He learned guitar from his uncle Jeff and put together the Corncob Trio, which represented Pampa at the 1936 Texas centennial celebration. Guthrie soon left West Texas, as did his contemporaries Hugh and Karl Farr, who joined Roy Rogers in Hollywood to become members of the Sons of the Pioneers. Guthrie remained a lone and significant voice of the people, writing volumes of folk songs, including what has been termed our unofficial national anthem, "This Land Is Your Land."

While the core of West Texas music is the family, a musical kinship runs even deeper, crossing stylistic lines to make manifest an innovative instrumental virtuosity celebrated by every age and social grouping. Tommy Allsup serves as a significant case in point. Allsup began his career playing electric guitar for Bob Wills and the Texas Playboys, organized his own band in Odessa with Moon Mullican as his boogie-woogie pianist, served as a sessions player at the Norman Petty Studio in Clovis, New Mexico, and played lead guitar on the final Buddy Holly tour, giving up his seat on the plane to Richie Valens. Through his Odessa recording studio in 1965, he produced the Zager and Evans hit "In the Year 2525" and in Nashville the two-album set *Bob Wills, For the Last Time*, featuring many of the original Playboys and Hoyle and Jody Nix. His career runs the gamut of popular musical styles, usually defined in ethnic and generational lines, to confirm Waylon Jennings's observation: "I have always felt that blues, rock and roll, and country are just about a beat apart."

Pamela H. Brink
Associated Authors and Editors, Inc.

WILLS, BOB (1905–1975)

James Robert Wills was born in the "black belt" of East Texas near the town of Kosse on March 6, 1905. He grew up in a musical family of fiddle players and in an area famous for African American music that produced Scott Joplin, Victoria Spivey, and Blind Lemon Jefferson. From his family he learned to play frontier fiddle music, which had been part of frontier cultural life from the East Coast to West Texas. From the African Americans he learned blues and jazz. By the time Wills played his first dance as a fiddler at a ranch in West Texas at the age of ten, he had already begun to add blues and jazz idioms to traditional fiddle music. This combination was eventually called western swing and became one of the most distinctive sounds in all of American music. There was hardly an American musical expression that could not be heard at one time or another in Wills' music: ragtime, New Orleans jazz, blues, rhythm and blues, rock, country, and big band swing. Wills blended it all into a swinging dance music that remained popular for seventy-five years.

Wills performed his music for years at country and ranch dances in West Texas before introducing it to the general public on radio stations in Fort Worth. He organized the Light Crust Doughboys, broadcast over the Texas Quality Network in 1933, and soon revolutionized music in Texas. His greatest success was with his band the Texas Playboys in Tulsa, Oklahoma, between 1934 and 1942. During those years he added brass, woodwinds, and drums and developed a band that by 1940 numbered eighteen members. The band could play anything from a fiddle breakdown to a George Gershwin composition and give it a swinging rhythm and solid beat. His recordings sold in the hundreds of thousands and his "San Antonio Rose" in the millions. Wills began making movies in Hollywood in 1940, and when he was discharged from the army in 1943 he moved the Texas Playboys to California. There he was more successful, at least financially, than at any time in his career. Huge crowds at his dances and big-selling records made him one of the highest paid bandleaders in America.

After the war, Wills gave up most of the brass and reeds in his band and used more fiddles, guitars, steel guitars, and mandolins. This emphasis on strings helped him maintain his popularity even after the age of the big bands was over, and he influenced the two musical forces that were destined to dominate American music down to the present, rock and roll and country and western. Western swing had a marked impression on early rockabillies such as Bill Haley and the Comets, Buddy Holly and the Crickets, and Elvis Presley. Wills's greatest influence, however, was on country and western. The Country Music Association gave him its highest honor in 1968, naming Wills to the Country Music Hall of Fame. In 1999 Bob Wills was inducted into the Rock and Roll Hall of Fame in the category of "early influences."

What was it that gave Wills's music such lasting appeal? His music and style had many good qualities, but mainly, his music made people happy. Bob Wills practiced what President Franklin D. Roosevelt had advocated early in the Great Depression—that the right kind of music could help us sing and whistle our way out of hard times or at least live better with them. In this sense, Bob Wills and His Texas Playboys were more than entertainers, they were therapists. They played a practical role in American life during the Great Depression and later during World War II.

When Bob Wills died in Dallas on May 13, 1975, he left the world a much richer place. His compositions like "Faded Love," "Maiden's Prayer," and "San Antonio Rose" are part of the repertoire of country and pop artists and Americana itself. He helped bridge the gap between black and white musical cultures when he began combining them as a boy. Out of that came Bob Wills's richest legacy, his own musical style, the happy lilting rhythms and moving beat of western swing.

Charles R. Townsend
West Texas A&M University

Sheldon, Ruth. *Hubbin' It: The Life of Bob Wills*. Tulsa: Privately published, 1938. Townsend, Charles R. *San Antonio Rose: The Life and Music of Bob Wills*. Urbana: University of Illinois Press, 1976.

YOUNG, NEIL (b. 1945)

Neil Young's forty-year career has established him as one of the most productive and influential folk and rock musicians in North America. Young was born in Toronto, Ontario, on November 12, 1945, the son of Scott Young, an acclaimed Canadian sportswriter. When his parents' marriage dissolved in 1960, Young moved west to Winnipeg, Manitoba, with his mother, Rassy. It was in Winnipeg that the adolescent Young became a musician, first nurtured at the piano of his talented and progressive mother and later plugging in an electric guitar when rock and roll emerged as a major musical genre.

Growing up in Winnipeg, Young felt not only the pop influence of the British Invasion and the lyrical focus of folk music but also the strains of rockabilly and country twang that blew in from the Prairies. Young spoke of his modest Winnipeg upbringing during a 1999 concert in Minneapolis, noting, "I grew up a bit north of here. This was the Emerald City to me." After playing in several high school bands in Winnipeg, Young sought to advance his career first in Fort William and Toronto before heading west to California in 1966. There he joined the folk rock band Buffalo Springfield, and he has been one of rock's stars ever since.

With more than fifty albums to his credit, Young has embraced many musical styles and performed with a diverse assortment of collaborators, yet two particular sounds stand out: his acoustic compositions, which date back to his folk music days in Canada, and the bold electrical offerings created with his longtime backup band, Crazy Horse. Young's acoustic songs blend his distinctive highly pitched vocals with multilayered guitar chords punctuated with bass runs. Young adds a plaintive harmonica to many of his acoustic songs and provides competent backup on the piano and an antique pump organ. When backed by Crazy Horse, Young's music takes on a different personality, with a powerful guitar sound that is part Americana, part blues, and part grunge. Young's electrical guitar roams freely over the music with full, rich chords and piercing solos. Young is a superbly accomplished guitarist whose mastery is best appreciated in live performances.

Young's songs are often composed of fragmented phrases and juxtaposed verses that seldom stand alone as poetry yet when combined with his music take on an evocative meaning that transcends words. An example of this is Young's "Ohio." Written in 1970, the day after National Guard troops killed four protestors at Kent State University and recorded with Crosby, Stills and Nash, the song hit the airwaves within a week of the shootings and became an instant anthem for the antiwar movement. Young had been reluctant to embrace the antiwar cause to the extent of many of his folk music contemporaries, and his later political sentiments were as scattered as his musical styles. Still, his songwriting expertise is evident in this minimalist song that so well captures the heart and soul of the matter.

Young's rural roots and populist tendencies are evident in his passionate involvement in Farm Aid, an annual concert event initiated in 1985 with fellow musicians Willie Nelson and John Mellencamp. Young's commitment to this cause is evident in his extensive onstage discourses on the plight of family farms. This is a marked departure from his usual stage demeanor, which is intensely focused on his music and seldom includes more than a few obligatory greetings thrown in between songs. With two sons suffering from birth defects, Young and his wife, Peggi, have also organized the annual Bridge concert since 1986, supporting a San Francisco–area school for severely handicapped children.

Young has twice been inducted into the Rock and Roll Hall of Fame, first in 1995 as a solo artist and in 1997 as a member of Buffalo Springfield.

Sean Hartnett
University of Wisconsin–Eau Claire

McDonough, James. *Shakey: Neil Young's Biography*. London: Random House UK, Limited, 2002.

Native Americans

Rally marchers leave Pine Ridge, South Dakota, on their way to Whiteclay, Nebraska, on June 26, 1999. The demonstration by Native Americans protested the sale of alcohol and unsolved murders in Whiteclay.

The Plains Indian has been one of the most important and pervasive icons in American culture. Imagine him, for example, as a young man on horseback. Almost without effort, the image conjures up full-blown narratives of buffalo hunts and mounted warfare. Make the "he" into a young woman and imagine romantic tragedies of forced marriage and unrequited love. Make the Indian a wizened elder and see if you don't think of spiritual wonder and almost superhuman ecological communion.

But don't forget that real people peer up from the depths of such timeless images. And while the images can be easily moved to the Hollywood backlot, those real people are not so easily detached from the Great Plains themselves, for this difficult environment framed ongoing historical transformations in Native political organization, social relations, economy, and culture. Along with the nomadic bison hunting popularized in the movies, Native Americans engaged in raiding, trading, pastoralism, agriculture, diplomacy, politics, religious innovation and syncretism, warfare, migration, wage labor, lawsuits, lobbying, and gaming. Through these adaptive strategies, the Plains peoples worked to protect and enhance their political power and their ability to sustain themselves economically, and to maintain their cultural distinctiveness.

Longevity in the Plains

Although some peoples came to the Plains earlier than others, Native Americans have lived there for a long time. Evidence from the Agate Basin site in eastern Wyoming, for example, indicates that humans lived in the Plains at least as early as 8500 B.C. Radiocarbon dating of material from the Lewisville site near Dallas, Texas, suggests Indians and their precursors may have been in the Plains for at least 38,000 years. The oral histories of some tribes refer to long-extinct mammoths and other megafauna. "Star charts" suggest that the Lakota Sioux have associated parts of the Black Hills in South Dakota with astrometrical phenomena since ancient times. Some scholars assert that the Sioux peoples originated in the Great Lakes region and only began moving onto the Plains in the late seventeenth and early eighteenth centuries. Many Lakotas, however, trace the origins of their people to Wind Cave in the Black Hills and suggest that they were simply in the middle of a long, slow migration home after living elsewhere for a time. Clarity on this issue will probably not be forthcoming.

Environmental Adaptations

Their extended tenure in the Plains allowed Native peoples to experience significant alterations in the environment. Between 11,500 and 11,000 before present, precipitation declined, the range of temperatures increased, and free-flowing streams began to turn into small lakes and marshes, eventually becoming part of the expanding grassland. Species adapted to the wetter world—such as mammoths, camels,

and horses—died out, opening ecological niches in the Plains grassland. Most of these niches were filled by bison, which were becoming smaller and more mobile in order to be more effective in the drier climate.

Plains peoples adjusted to these changes as well. Around the time that the larger game disappeared, nomadic hunters shifted from Clovis-style spear points and arrowheads to the smaller Folsom points and heads, which were used until about 8000 B.C. Like more recent Native peoples, Folsom hunters and their successors depended heavily upon the bison and relied upon the more sophisticated social organization necessary for group hunting. Such organization allowed for the creation and use of "buffalo jumps," a large funnel of trees, rocks, poles, and people designed to channel stampeding bison over a cliff. Plains hunters used buffalo jumps like the Head-Smashed-In site in southwestern Alberta as early as 5,500 years ago. Along with the bison, Indian hunters' prey included deer, elk, and other smaller game.

Plains residents began experimenting with pottery and more sedentary villages at least as early as 2,000 years ago. Ancestors of the Mandans and Hidatsas eventually settled in fortified villages along the Missouri River, where they raised corn, beans, and squash. These villages generally ranged in size from ten to ninety lodges and were built from bracing poles and packed earthen cover. Between spring planting and fall harvest, the villagers probably left the river's bottomland to hunt bison.

Some of the crops these villagers grew became part of the extensive trade networks that linked the horticulturalists with Plains hunters and with peoples outside the Plains. The Caddo and Wichita trade networks included some of the Pueblos in present-day New Mexico, Cahokia (a city built by the Illinois people near the confluence of the Mississippi and Missouri Rivers), Hiwasee Island on the Tennessee River, Etowah near the Chattahoochee River, and the Platte River Pawnee communities. The Mandans, Hidatsas, and Arikaras traded with peoples from what is today the American Southwest and with more nomadic Plains hunters like the Crows, Assiniboines, Plains Crees, Cheyennes, Arapahos, Kiowas, and Comanches. Both material goods (agricultural products, dried meat, flint, and animal hides) and cultural products (songs and dances) traded hands.

Migrations

While the rise of sedentary villages and agriculture stood out as a key way that Plains peoples adapted to and shaped their environment, migration played an equally important role in the lives of many Indians. It seems that Plains societies were both amalgamating and splitting apart, and that mobility constituted a common response to both social and environmental factors. The groups that came to be known as Apaches, for example, separated from people in the Northern Plains as early as 600 A.D. They moved south, sojourning in

Nebraska before moving into the Southern Plains between 1450 and 1525. By the late 1600s they and their Kiowa allies had staked out a territory ranging from northwestern Texas to Wyoming and the Black Hills. At the same time, Shoshones moved east from the Great Basin to eastern Montana. Separating from the Hidatsas and Missouri River horticulture, the Crows migrated west to the Montana-Dakota area.

Such migrations accelerated after 1700, as some groups left the Plains and others entered the region. Moving from what is now eastern Montana, a branch of Shoshones that would come to be known as Comanches swept the Apaches south and by 1775 forced them from the Plains entirely. Cheyennes and Arapahos migrated west from the Great Lakes region. Crees and Assiniboines gradually moved into the Canadian Prairies. Iowas, Missourias, Omahas, Osages, Otoes, Poncas, and Quapaws all came to the Plains after living for some time in what is today Arkansas, Missouri, and Iowa.

Horses, Guns, and Diseases

Migrations also brought Europeans to the Plains, beginning in the sixteenth century. The newcomers brought both opportunities and perils for the Plains peoples in the forms of trade and disease. Horses and firearms were the most important European trade items. The Spanish reintroduced horses into the Plains, in part through trading networks that connected Plains peoples with the Pueblos and Apaches. (Horses had existed in the Americas at one time, but they had become extinct.) Indians acted as middlemen and traded horses to more distant Plains peoples. By the late 1600s, for example, Kiowas and Kiowa Apaches traded horses to the Caddos. Comanches often acquired horses by raiding Spanish and Apache settlements and then traded the animals to other tribes. Utes, Cheyennes, and Arapahos moved horses to the north. Because Spanish law forbade the selling or trading of firearms to Natives, the Plains peoples turned to the English and French for guns, and middleman relationships developed with both mobile traders and trade centers in the Arkansas, Missouri, and Red River valleys.

Access to horses and weaponry came at a high cost. European traders brought European epidemic diseases to which Plains Indians had not been exposed and to which they had limited immunity. Even Natives who had never met a European became ill as a result of contact with Native middlemen in the trade who inadvertently exposed them to smallpox, measles, whooping cough, and many other diseases. Regardless of the source, European diseases spread through the Plains and decimated Native populations, especially those concentrated in villages. Epidemics during the late eighteenth and early nineteenth centuries reduced the Arikaras' population by an estimated 80 percent. The Hidatsas, Mandans, Omahas, Poncas, and other relatively sedentary tribes also suffered great losses.

The combination of European diseases and

trade items had a complex impact upon the Plains. Access to horses allowed for the more effective killing and transportation of bison. Consequently, many tribes—such as the Lakota Sioux—rejected a sedentary and horticultural lifestyle and devoted less time to trapping beaver and more time to the hunting of bison. Tribes with the greatest access to horses and firearms could expand their territory and power at the expense of those tribes with fewer guns and horses. The Osages' access to both guns and horses, for example, helped to make them the main power in the region between the lower Missouri and lower Red Rivers by the mid-1700s. The Comanches' control of the horse trade and their alliance with the Kiowas gave them command over the area between the Arkansas and Red Rivers by the end of the eighteenth century. By the mid–nineteenth century, the Sioux, aided by the Arapahos and Cheyennes, dominated the region bounded by the Minnesota and Yellowstone Rivers in the north and the Republican River in the south. The relative power of the nomads was actually increased by disease: they suffered losses, of course, but their dispersed lifestyles made them less vulnerable to epidemics than the concentrated village populations.

Europeans

Unlike their horses, guns, and pathogens, Europeans themselves initially had a relatively limited presence in the Plains. The Spanish first penetrated the region between 1540 and 1542 looking for "cities of gold." When they failed to find the riches they expected, they withdrew and only slowly established missions and colonies in New Mexico and Texas during the seventeenth century. Spain did sponsor an expedition to the Plains under Pedro de Villasur in 1720, but it suffered a military defeat at the hands of the Pawnees and Otoes.

The French expanded into the Southern and Central Plains by the early eighteenth century from bases in the Mississippi Valley. They negotiated commercial and military agreements with Plains tribes. Through these agreements, the French traded with Indians for furs, while using Plains peoples as a defense against rival Europeans and Indians. Few in number and often nomadic themselves, the French posed no threat to Indian autonomy.

In the late eighteenth century, British fur traders from Canada pushed into the Prairie Provinces. Unlike the individualistic French traders, the large British companies built numerous trading posts among the Assiniboines, Plains Crees, Blackfoot, and Gros Ventres, drawing them into market relations. Alcohol, the credit system, and intermarriage created strong linkages and dependencies, but the number of the British and the volume of their trade were too small to dramatically alter the Native cultures. Like the other Plains groups, the Indians of the Canadian Prairies managed to keep their subsistence, political, and cultural systems largely intact until the second half of the nineteenth century.

Americans

When the British, French, and Spanish entered the Plains, they tended to seek peaceful relations with Indian people. In truth, Europeans lacked the power to do otherwise. The same cannot be said, however, of the United States. American expansion into the Plains in the nineteenth century involved the purposeful or incidental destruction and control of those Plains resources upon which Native Americans depended. To be sure, Plains people adopted various responses to the Americans' actions. Nevertheless, by the end of the century, Native peoples had seen their populations decline precipitously, had lost control over much of their land and other economic resources, and faced the prospect of seeing their societies and cultures forcibly annihilated by outsiders.

Fur traders were the first Americans to enter the Northern and Central Plains in significant numbers in the first four decades of the nineteenth century. In the 1840s large numbers of emigrants passed through the Great Plains on their way to Oregon, Utah, and the California goldfields. The construction of railroads across the Plains after the Civil War made accessible a region with limited navigable rivers, and the Homestead Act of 1862 and other laws drew settlers to the Plains by providing land at a relatively small cost.

The influx presented significant problems for the Plains peoples. Many migrants took old Indian routes across the Plains and codified them for other Americans as "trails"—the Overland or Oregon Trail, which traced the Platte River, and the Santa Fe Trail, which ran along part of the Arkansas River. Migration along these trails destroyed the ecosystems of the Platte and Arkansas Valleys. The emigrants drove the bison away, churned the grasslands into mile-wide dust swathes, stripped wood from river bottoms, and polluted water sources—often with diseases such as cholera. Native peoples who depended upon the resources of these areas, such as the Sioux and Pawnees in the north and the Comanches and Kiowas in the south, demanded compensation for this damage and sought substitutes for the lost game. The Comanches and Kiowas, for example, took to raiding for cattle and other items. This led to an escalating series of threats, a cycle of raids, and occasional reprisals by whites.

Treaties, Diplomacy, and Dispossession in the United States

Throughout much of the nineteenth century the U.S. government sought to deal with the conflicts between Indians and non-Indian migrants and settlers through treaties that restricted Native peoples to certain areas. In 1825 the federal government created a Permanent Indian Frontier. Encompassing much of modern-day Nebraska, Kansas, and Oklahoma, it was to serve as a home for displaced eastern tribes. Tribes already in the area, such as the Kansas, Wichitas, Osages, and Pawnees, ceded lands to make room for tribes removed from the east, such as the Delawares and Kick-

apoos. But this was not a Permanent Indian Frontier. In 1854 the Kansas-Nebraska Act opened up vast areas for American settlement. In a flurry of treaty signing in the second half of the 1850s many Indigenous groups ceded their ancestral lands, retaining only small reservations.

On their reservations Plains Indians were placed under great pressure to change. They experimented with new strategies of resistance but enjoyed limited success. Pawnees in Nebraska and Osages in Kansas, for example, found their livelihoods threatened by Sioux raids and by non-Indian migrants who drove off game. The Indians responded by trying to levy tolls of sugar and coffee on emigrants and by occasionally resorting to harassment and cattle raids. American settlers, crowding in around the reservations, called for the Indians' removal. By the mid-1880s the Pawnees and many of the other Native peoples in Kansas and Nebraska had been relocated to Indian Territory (now Oklahoma), the remnant of the Permanent Indian Frontier.

Many Plains peoples engaged in diplomacy with the United States and other tribes as a strategy to deal with the American newcomers. In 1851, at Fort Laramie, federal agents negotiated a treaty with the Arapahos, Arikaras, Assiniboines, Cheyennes, Crows, Hidatsas, Mandans, Lakota Sioux, and others. Two years later the government entered into a treaty with the Comanches, Kiowas, and Kiowa Apaches at Fort Atkinson. In 1855, along the Judith River, representatives of the Bloods, Piegans, Siksikas, and Gros Ventres made their agreements with the United States. These treaties called for peaceful relations, delineated which tribes got which lands, and stipulated that tribes would be given supplies and services to make up for the destruction of game by non-Indians.

Wars

The treaties did not end threats to Indian lifeways and thus failed to forestall violence for long. The Americans' destruction of game intensified competition among the tribes for the remaining bison and other animals. The U.S. military fought several engagements with the Lakota Sioux, Cheyennes, and Arapahos in the mid-1850s. In the two years after the 1858 discovery of gold in Colorado, thousands of gold seekers flocked into Arapaho territory, violating the 1851 treaty. Some Arapahos responded by moving north of the Platte. For the southern bands who remained, relations with the trespassers deteriorated, and on November 29, 1864, white militiamen massacred Black Kettle's and White Antelope's Cheyennes and Arapahos at Sand Creek, Colorado. In response, members of these tribes, along with some Sioux, Comanches, and Kiowas, resorted to war. They launched a series of attacks against posts along the immigrant trails. Relative peace was restored when the Southern Arapahos, some Cheyenne bands, Comanches, and Kiowas agreed in 1865 and 1867 to treaties that would confine them to reservations. In exchange, federal officials guaranteed that the Indians would be protected from attacks by settlers and soldiers and that they would receive goods to offset the destruction of the bison and other game. When the Comanches and Kiowas resumed raiding because the government failed to provide adequate rations, the army destroyed the Indians' winter camps and forced them back to their reservation along the Red River.

In the Central and Northern Plains, bands of Cheyennes, Arapahos, and Lakota Sioux also waged war to protect themselves. The discovery of gold in Montana in 1862 brought large numbers of non-Indians into and through the area. When the federal government built forts to protect the settlers and the route to the goldfields, the Bozeman Trail, Native Americans laid siege to the forts and forced the United States to negotiate a settlement. In the 1868 Treaty of Fort Laramie, federal negotiators agreed to evacuate the forts, to provide a large reservation (the "Great Sioux Reservation") in South and North Dakota, and to guarantee Indian hunting rights.

Sitting Bull (Tantanka Iyotanka), 1885

Nevertheless, the Sioux and their allies ultimately suffered the same fate as the Comanches and Kiowas. When Americans discovered gold in the Black Hills area of the Great Sioux Reservation in 1874, the federal government unsuccessfully attempted to get the Sioux to sell or lease the land. War broke out between the army and the Sioux and Northern Cheyennes in 1876. The Indians, led by Gall and Sitting Bull (both Hunkpapa Sioux), defeated forces under Gen. George Armstrong Custer at the Battle of the Little Bighorn, but the military's winter campaign of 1876–77 forced most of the Sioux and Cheyennes to return to their reservations or to flee to Canada. Among the latter, those led by Sitting Bull returned to the reservation in 1881, while some others settled in Canada permanently. By the time of Sitting Bull's return, all of the Plains peoples had been settled on reservations.

The army's successes over some Plains tribes stemmed in large measure from the assistance of other Plains Indians as scouts and auxiliaries. Pawnees, Arikaras, and Crows helped the American military fight against the Lakotas, while Pawnees, Caddos, and Wichitas allied with the United States against the Comanches. Military service represented a means for some Indians to adapt to changing conditions. By serving as a scout or auxiliary, an Indian could provide himself and his family with material benefits, including extra rations, food, money, and horses captured in battle. Some Plains Natives saw the United States as a lesser threat than tribes like the Sioux. Service in the army also provided an avenue of escape, albeit temporary, from reservation life and an opportunity to gain honor and status through combat. Similar motivations would later prompt Plains Indians to serve in the U.S. Armed Forces in subsequent conflicts, such as World Wars I and II, Korea, and Vietnam.

Treaties, Dispossession, and War in Canada

On the Canadian Prairies, the fur trade remained the principal medium of interaction between the Indians and whites until the late 1860s. A "middle ground" emerged there between the Blackfoot, Gros Ventres, Assiniboines, and Plains Crees on the one side, and fur traders on the other. Interchange of ideas reduced racial prejudices, gifts created fictive kinship ties, intermarriage bonded companies and bands together, and sexual interaction produced a large Métis (persons of mixed Native, French, and British heritage) population. This cultural accommodation came to an end with the decline of the fur trade in the 1860s. In 1870, after years of deteriorating resources and decreasing profits, the Hudson's Bay Company sold Rupert's Land to the Dominion of Canada.

Like their counterparts in the United States, Canadian officials wanted to move Plains Indians and Métis out of the way of non-Indians who settled the Prairie Provinces in greater numbers following the construction of the Canadian Pacific Railway. Hoping to learn from the United States and avoid a series of financially costly wars, Ottawa officials negotiated a series of seven numbered treaties with the Plains peoples between 1871 and 1877. The Natives agreed to the treaties after a movement led by Métis Louis Riel to establish an independent Métis government in 1869 was crushed and because they wanted government aid to offset the loss of the bison. Plains groups with which the government signed treaties included the Red River Anishinaabes (Chippewas), Plains Crees, Plains Anishinaabes, Siksikas (Northern Blackfoot), Bloods, Northern Piegans, Sarcees, and selected Assiniboines. Generally, the treaties stipulated that the Natives would agree to accept reserves and individual allotments of land in exchange for government aid and assistance in agriculture.

Like their counterparts farther south, Canadian Plains peoples found diplomacy did not produce desired results. Construction of the Canadian Pacific Railway destroyed most of the Blackfoot's hunting territory. Canadian officials often failed to provide adequate aid and sometimes withheld promised aid as punishment for those who called for alterations to treaty provisions. Efforts by leaders such as Crowfoot (Siksika Blackfoot) and Big Bear (Cree) to keep the peace between Natives and whites ultimately proved unsuccessful. In 1884 starving Indians robbed government storehouses and killed several local officials. Crees, Assiniboines, and Métis fended off an attack by troops at Cut Knife Hill, but several key Indian leaders were later arrested.

Chief Poundmaker (Pītikwahanapiwīyin)

Troops also crushed the North-West Rebellion of Métis. In March 1885 in Saskatchewan a group of Métis, led once again by Louis Riel, took control of the village of Batoche, arrested the Indian agent, and declared the existence of a new government for the area. Hundreds of Crees and Assiniboines under Big Bear and Poundmaker joined Riel. Government troops recaptured Batoche and eventually forced many of the Métis and Indians, including Riel, Poundmaker, and Big Bear, to surrender (although some escaped to Montana). After a series of trials, the Canadian government hanged Riel and eight others.

Reservations, Allotments, and Assimilation

As a result of the loss of economic resources and military defeats, Plains peoples found themselves confined to reservations in the United States and reserves in Canada. Reservation life represented a radical departure from the Indians' prior existence. Some groups, such as those Cheyennes and Arapahos who had been resettled in Oklahoma, found themselves far from their homelands, where the environment was unfamiliar and adjustment was difficult. Even for those who remained in relatively familiar territory, the mobility integral to their bison-hunting way of life had been lost. Even if Indians were allowed to leave the reservation or reserve to hunt, their main prey, the bison, was virtually extinct by the early 1880s. For the Caddos, Wichitas, and other Plains peoples who depended on agriculture, the reservation lands often proved inadequate for cultivation. Plains peoples, who had once drawn their existence from the soil and the bison, had in many ways become economically dependent upon United States.

For all of the problems with the reservations and reserves, however, they represented homes for peoples and contexts for their cultures. In the United States especially, humanitarian "reformers" worked to take away even this single saving grace. These reformers and their advocates in the government argued that Americans had an obligation to "civilize"— assimilate—Indians by breaking down tribal bonds and absorbing them into white society as individuals.

Several factors helped reformers win support for their ideas. In the context of the Plains Wars and expanding white settlement, absorbing Indians into white society seemed to be the only way to prevent their extinction. Evangelical Christians' desire to create a "righteous empire" in the United States made conversion of the "red heathens" an important goal. Industrialization and increasing immigration of eastern European Catholics and Jews seemed to threaten traditional rural Anglo-Saxon values and fueled a desire to "Americanize" the first Americans. Reformers also felt that assimilation would end the dependence of many Native Americans upon government rations and annuities.

The 1887 General Allotment Act (along with subsequent acts and amendments) ultimately became the vehicle through which reformers sought to eradicate Indian cultures and societies. Sponsored by Massachusetts senator Henry Dawes, the act provided for ending the tribes' communal landownership and allotting reservation land into individually owned plots. Dawes and the reformers argued that the legislation would sever the peoples' bonds with their "backwards" tribal cultures and societies while forcing them to become hardworking farmers. Unallotted reservation land would then be sold as "surplus lands" to non-Indians. This would further facilitate assimilation by reducing the land available for Indians to use for hunting and would allow Indians to learn from their white neighbors.

Allotment did not become such a significant (and damaging) aspect of Indian policy in Canada. The 1869 Indian Act granted band councils the right to assign full title of specific reserve lands to individuals, who subsequently were allowed to sell, rent, or lease their land only to other band members. Hence, non-Indians simply did not have the same opportunities to buy nonallotted "surplus" lands or to eventually gain access to allotted lands.

Canadians did follow the Americans' lead in using education as a means of assimilation. By the mid-1890s both the U.S. and Canadian governments funded a network of Indian day and boarding schools to foster assimilation. These schools provided academic and vocational education while forbidding students from engaging in such Indian cultural activities as speaking Native languages and practicing Native religions.

Officials in Washington and Ottawa suppressed Plains Indian cultural practices in other ways as well. In Canada, the 1876 Indian Act (with subsequent amendments) outlawed traditional tribal and band governments and banned various religious and cultural practices such as the Sun Dance and Thirst Dance. In the United States, federal agents forced Native Americans to attend Christian services, to adopt "citizens'" clothing and hairstyles, to follow only federally approved Indian leaders, and to abstain from such cultural practices as the Sun Dance and polygamy.

Cultural and Economic Adaptations

Native Americans did not passively accept such strictures, and they found many ways to resist. Sometimes such resistance led to violence, as when conflict with some Lakota Sioux over the Ghost Dance religion ended in the Wounded Knee Massacre in December 1890. Emerging in the late 1880s, the Ghost Dance religion anticipated the destruction of the Earth and the creation of a new world occupied by abundant game and deceased relatives. Many Lakotas, including Sitting Bull, embraced the Ghost Dance and began performing the requisite songs and dances. Some believed that certain "Ghost Shirts" would protect them from harm. Fearing that the dances portended an uprising, the Indian agent at Standing Rock Reservation ordered the arrest of Sitting Bull, who had remained a powerful advocate of Lakota resistance. During the arrest an intense fight ensued, and Indian policemen killed the respected leader. Fearing more violence, Miniconjou leader Big Foot and his band fled south to the Pine Ridge Reservation. There, on December 28, 1890, at Wounded Knee Creek, soldiers attempted to disarm the Indians, and gunfire was exchanged. Who pulled the trigger first remains unclear, but the army's superior firepower turned the encounter into a massacre: from 150 to 250 Sioux men, women, and children died, as did twenty-five soldiers. Still, the Ghost Dance continued to attract adherents from the Plains, including Oklahoma Kiowas and Comanches, Saskatchewan Sioux, and Wyoming Shoshones.

Some Plains Indians accepted at least some white ways and policies. Big Tree, a Kiowa war leader imprisoned for a time for his raiding activities, converted to Christianity and became a farmer on his Oklahoma allotment. Others resisted assimilation while adapting to the new world that was being thrust upon them. Omaha half-siblings Susette and Francis La Flesche attended white educational institutions and used their education to conduct a campaign to win public support for allowing the Poncas to return to their home in Nebraska. Susan La Flesche graduated from medical school (making her one of the few American women and the only Native American woman in the nineteenth century to do so) and used her training to treat her people.

Religion was a primary means of preserving cultural distinctiveness. Many Indians became involved with peyotism in the late nineteenth and early twentieth centuries. Involving the ingestion of the peyote plant, peyotism is a syncretistic belief system that combines aspects of Christian and traditional Indian spirituality. A Caddo expression of peyotism, the Big Moon ceremony (later known as Cross Fire ritual) incorporated Jesus Christ, the Bible, and other Christian elements.

Multitribal gatherings pointed toward new "pan-Indian" identities that coexisted with more discrete tribal identifications. Native peoples in the Plains came to share certain kinds of cultural display. The Grass Dance, originating with the Pawnees, became a regular part of the growing number of intertribal gatherings across the Plains. Native peoples in the United States and Canada got permission to perform the dance on their home reservations by billing it as a "tribute" to the nation on American Independence Day (July 4) or Canadian Dominion Day (July 1).

Economically, Plains Indians' adaptations varied. The Osages and a few other tribes generated income from oil or other mineral resources. A growing number depended upon seasonal and wage labor. Some Indians reconciled wage labor with more traditional economic enterprises. Cheyenne women, for example, continued to produce moccasins for other Indians and non-Indians, just as they had since before Lewis and Clark. By the end of World War I Cheyennes and Arapahos served as seasonal agricultural laborers harvesting Oklahoma wheat. Many Sioux helped harvest potatoes in Nebraska. Plains peoples experimented with cattle ranching, which looked to be on the path to success until agents and other non-Indians pressured Indians to sell off their herds during World War I. The Gros Ventres, Pine Ridge Sioux, Comanches, and other Indian ranchers sold or leased much of their land to whites.

The Indian cattle industry temporarily fared better on the Canadian Prairies. In an effort to diversify Native economies, Ottawa officials encouraged the Prairie groups to become stock raisers by issuing large numbers of cattle to them. The cattle industry was well established on the Prairie reserves by 1900, but a long dry spell in the 1920s, together with extensive leasing of grazing lands to non-Indians, subsequently decreased the importance of ranching.

The Indian New Deal in the Plains

By the end of the 1920s many Americans had concluded that allotment and assimilation had not been successful. Nationally, the sale of surplus lands and allotments from 1887 to 1934 reduced the Indian's land base by two-thirds, from 138 million to 52 million acres. Ironically, a policy designed to foster self-support produced dispossession and dependency instead. Such economic devastation undoubtedly helped account for Indians' low incomes and high rates of infant mortality and disease.

The growing recognition of these failures led to a shift in U.S. Indian policy that once again changed the environment in which Indians operated. The new changes, like the old ones, created both opportunities and problems for Indians. In 1933 John Collier, a New York social worker and longtime critic of federal Indian policy, became the commissioner of Indian affairs. Collier believed that white society had become too individualistic and had much to learn from Native Americans' community-oriented cultures. He came to office determined to reverse the assimilation policy and to restore an Indian economic base. Collier's reforms, contained in the 1934 Indian Reorganization Act (IRA), ended allotment, increased tribally owned land, and authorized tribes to organize constitutional governments empowered to negotiate with their federal, state, and local counterparts. The act also allowed greater access to economic resources through the establishment of a revolving credit fund from which tribes could finance economic development projects and by making Indians eligible for social welfare programs available to other citizens.

Many Plains peoples availed themselves of the IRA's political and economic provisions. The Cheyenne-Arapahos of Oklahoma, Caddos, Pawnees, Poncas, Iowas, Blackfeet, Pine Ridge Sioux, and other Plains groups adopted written constitutions under the Indian New Deal. The Blackfeet developed a new law code that provided for wildlife conservation. With a two-million-dollar loan, the Northern Cheyennes developed a livestock enterprise. Thousands of Indians found temporary employment through New Deal work programs like the Indian Civilian Conservation Corps and the Works Project Administration. Funds from the latter agency paid for Shoshones to tan elk hides, while the Civilian Conservation Corps and other relief programs provided work for 85 percent of Rosebud Reservation males. The Indian New Deal facilitated the return of millions of acres of land to Native American control as well.

Nevertheless, the Indian New Deal had its share of problems. The IRA's provisions for organizing tribal governments were based on Collier's understanding of the Pueblos and on European American models and thus were often different from tribes' conceptions of government. The secretary of the interior had the power to "review" many decisions made by the new tribal governments. The money in the credit fund usually proved inadequate and only went to the best credit risks and not to those who most needed money. The question of whether tribes should organize under the act often proved divisive. On the Rosebud and Pine Ridge Reservations, for example, more acculturated residents tended to favor the act for its economic provisions, whereas traditional residents advocated basing relations with the United States on past treaties and thus tended to oppose it.

World War II and Termination

Like the New Deal, World War II had an enormous impact upon Plains Indians. Thousands served in the armed forces of the United States and Canada, and wartime activities promoted economic opportunities. The Sioux, for example, helped build military facilities in the Northern Plains. In other cases, Indians migrated to urban areas to work in war industries, an out-migration from reservations that has continued to some degree ever since. In Canada, many Indians who served in World War II gained citizenship and political rights, giving them more leverage to fight for religious rights and better education, housing, and health programs. Many of these efforts came to fruition with the 1951 Indian Act, which granted the Natives greater freedom to practice religious and cultural ceremonies and the right to raise political funds and consume alcohol outside reserves.

In 1946 Congress passed the Indian Claims Commission Act, which created the Indian Claims Commission. Through the commission Native Americans could win compensation from the federal government for past mistreatment, such as violations of treaties and land seizures. Numerous Plains Indian groups filed claims with the commission. The Pawnee, for example, were awarded $7.3 million by the Indian Claims Commission in 1962 in recognition of past "unconscionably low" payments for their lands.

The Indian Claims Commission, however, was also a mechanism for clearing the backlog of Indian claims as a prelude to severing federal obligation to the tribes. The success that Indians had had serving in World War II, as well as desires to cut federal spending and to promote national unity during the cold war, convinced many that Indians no longer needed special protection and that they should be "rewarded" through integration into the "mainstream." These views produced the "termination" policy between 1953 and the early 1960s. Termination sought to end Indians' eligibility for certain federal services and to abolish the federal trust status of Indian lands. The latter move would subject reservations to state laws and state taxes and other forces that would presumably erode and destroy Native Americans' distinct cultural status. One Plains tribe, the Northern Poncas, was declared terminated. The federal government also funded a voluntary relocation program to encourage Indians to move to urban areas, such as Denver, where they would supposedly have more employment opportunities and would more readily assimilate.

In some ways, relocation to urban areas could be seen as a revival of the old Plains Indian strategy of physical mobility. The results of relocation often proved mixed, however. As much as 40 percent of relocatees eventually returned to their home communities. City life caused or exacerbated such ills as alcoholism, spouse abuse, and poverty. Nevertheless, some relocatees did find employment, and the interaction of people from different tribes helped foster a "pan-Plains" and "pan-Indian" consciousness.

Native Political Adaptations

Whether they migrated to cities or stayed in their home communities, Plains Indians increasingly utilized intertribal organizing and political tactics—direct lobbying and public protests, for example—to protect and advance their interests. Even before World War II ended, Native peoples met in Denver to form the National Congress of American Indians (NCAI). Osages, Gros Ventres, Blackfeet, Oglala Sioux, Cheyenne-Arapahos, and other representatives of the Plains tribes secured important positions in the organization. Helen Peterson (Oglala Sioux) was executive director from 1953 to 1961. Plains Indians also often proved successful in using their positions to lobby Congress to reject or alter several termination bills during the 1950s. Ironically, termination—designed to break down tribal structures—probably strengthened Plains tribes and organizations by providing a coherent threat that united many Indians in opposition.

Native American lobbying and organization ultimately forced a change in federal policy. Instead of termination, federal policy by the early 1960s came to emphasize "self-determination," which involved allowing tribes greater control over their own affairs. Self-determination was facilitated by the 1960s War on Poverty, which gave local organizations access to federal funds and opportunities to administer antipoverty projects. Indians' inclusion in War on Poverty legislation stemmed largely from the 1964 Indian Capital Conference on Poverty held in Washington DC. Plains Indians played prominent roles in the conference, including NCAI executive director Robert Burnette (Rosebud Sioux), congressional representative Benjamin Reifel (Brulé Sioux), honorary conference chairman Walter Wetzel (Blackfoot), and archdeacon Vine V. Deloria Sr. (Standing Rock Sioux).

Many Plains peoples utilized the federal resources that the War on Poverty made available. The Anishinaabe and Cree residents of the Rocky Boy's Reservation in Montana started a crafts cooperative that produced and sold leather goods to customers throughout the country. The Rosebud Sioux used federal assistance to provide prefabricated housing to reservation residents. Indians not only improved their economic situations, but the experience of managing programs and funds strengthened tribal governments and provided a training ground for Indian leaders.

Sometimes, Plains Indians worked for self-determination through more assertive protest. The organization most commonly associated with this approach in the late twentieth century was the American Indian Movement (AIM). Although originally founded in Minneapolis in 1968 as an outgrowth of the pan-tribal Indian communities that developed in urban areas, the group established chapters throughout the Plains states. In South Dakota in 1970, AIM members occupied the Sheep Mountain area—taken from the Pine Ridge Sioux during World War II—and staged another protest at Mount Rushmore. In 1973, the year after the Trail of Broken Treaties caravan to Washington DC and the seizure of the Bureau of Indian Affairs building, Dennis Banks (Anishinaabe), Russell Means (Oglala Sioux, or Lakota), and other AIM members occupied the Pine Ridge Reservation town of Wounded Knee for more than two months. The occupation grew out of a conflict with tribal chairman Richard Wilson, who was seen by AIM as a corrupt puppet of the United States. The occupation was, in some ways, a rejection of both America's Indian policy and of the tribal council form of government itself.

Since the late 1960s, Canadian Indian strategies of protest, lobbying, and lawsuits have forced Ottawa policymakers to acknowledge increased self-government for the Native peoples of the Plains and elsewhere. By the end of the 1960s a growing number of functions once handled for bands by the Canadian government—such as housing and education—had been taken over by Indian councils. Native protests forced the government to reject a termination-style policy recommended by a 1969 White Paper. Indian lobbying and protest also convinced Ottawa policymakers to set up an Office of Native Claims to investigate and negotiate settlements with individual Indians and Native groups who claimed to have lost land because of the government's failure to honor its treaty obligations to the tribes. The government, as part of the 1982 Constitution Act, recognized for the first time Native peoples' title to the land based on Aboriginal status and treaties. However, the measure failed to spell out what such rights entailed, and it did not settle the issue of Natives' relationship with the rest of the country. This became clear in 1990 when Elijah Harper, a Cree and the only Native member of the Manitoba Legislative Assembly, helped block the Meech Lake Accord, which classified French-speaking Quebec as a "distinct" society but failed to recognize the distinct status of Natives. What the future holds for the Plains peoples of Canada and their relationship with other Canadians remains unclear, although legal decisions of the late 1990s point to positive changes in views toward Indian land management and the validity of oral history.

The same uncertainty holds true for the United States as well. In many respects, Plains peoples' adaptive strategies have succeeded in enhancing their opportunities for political power and economic self-sufficiency. Federal legislation such as the Indian Self-Determination and Education Act (1975) and the Self-Governance Project Demonstration Act (1991) have allowed many tribes greater control over their own political affairs. Several Plains Indians—like Northern Cheyenne Ben Nighthorse Campbell, the first Native American to serve in the U.S. Senate—have filled important government positions. Economic development projects, especially the creation of Indian gaming establishments, have increased the incomes of some groups. On the Pine Ridge Reservation, for example, the Prairie Wind Casino was generating several thousand dollars a month in the mid-1990s.

Such political and economic progress has

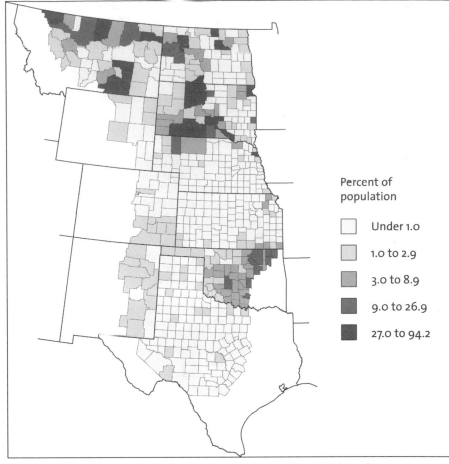

Native American population in the U.S. Great Plains as a percentage of total population, by county, in 2000

Percent of population

- Under 1.0
- 1.0 to 2.9
- 3.0 to 8.9
- 9.0 to 26.9
- 27.0 to 94.2

been accompanied by an even greater success among North American Plains peoples in maintaining distinct identities. Spiritual practices like the Sun Dance are experiencing a revival in both the United States and Canada. By the mid-1990s Buffy Sainte-Marie—a Cree from the Piapot Reserve in Saskatchewan—had recorded several albums of Indian and popular music, written several pieces for Indian publications, and authored a children's book incorporating Indian themes. AIM co-founder and musician John Trudell, a Santee Sioux, mixed Northern Plains Indian musical forms with blues and rock and roll. Trudell, Floyd Westerman, Russell Means, and other Plains Indian actors have appeared in several films. The American Indian Religious Freedom Act (1978) and the Native American Graves Protection and Repatriation Act (1990) —enacted as a result of Indian demands—have provided a legal basis for the protection of Native American religious practices and for the repatriation of Indian remains and cultural items held by museums.

Furthermore, the 2000 census shows that Native Americans in the U.S. Great Plains are increasing significantly in numbers, while most Plains counties are losing population. The overall Native American population in North Dakota grew 20 percent from 1990 to 2000, in South Dakota 23 percent, and in Montana 18 percent. During the same years forty-seven of North Dakota's fifty-three

counties lost population. The resurgence of Native American population is a result of high birth rates but also of a significant return to the reservations, partly because of job opportunities at casinos. The reservations and surrounding counties stand out on the 2000 census map as places having more than 25 percent, and often more than 50 percent, of their population Native American.

In many ways, however, the Plains peoples of the twenty-first century face significant challenges. Large numbers of Natives in Canada and the United States continue to experience poverty, ill health, substandard housing, and poor health care at rates well above the national average. In the mid-1990s unemployment on the Pine Ridge Reservation ranged from 65 to 85 percent, 1,800 families lacked adequate housing, and many people suffered from alcoholism. Cuts in funding for U.S. Indian programs during the 1980s and 1990s have exacerbated such problems and threaten to cancel out recent gains in self-determination and quality of life. States and private concerns have launched concerted attacks on Indian gaming.

Conclusion

Assertions of a "Native renaissance" may be premature. Nevertheless, Plains Native peoples have proven skilled at adapting to hardship and change while making the most of available opportunities. They have traded and raided, farmed and hunted, ranched and worked for wages, negotiated and made war, danced and prayed, lobbied and protested. Such adaptive strategies have allowed Plains Indians to maintain themselves as distinct peoples despite significant obstacles. One could argue that Plains Indian history has been a succession of "Native renaissances," always coming in response to hard times and always changing the nature of Plains cultures. Native peoples are and will continue to be an integral part of life in the Plains for a long time to come.

See also FILM: Hollywood Indians / LAW: Dawes Act / LITERARY TRADITIONS: Hogan, Linda; Momaday, N. Scott; Welch, James / MUSIC: Sainte-Marie, Buffy; Trudell, John / PHYSICAL ENVIRONMENT: Bison / PROTEST AND DISSENT: American Indian Movement / RELIGION: Ghost Dance / WAR: Indian Scouts; North-West Rebellion; Sioux Wars.

Philip J. Deloria
University of Michigan
Christopher K. Riggs
University of Colorado at Boulder

Comeau, Pauline, and Aldo Santin. *The First Canadians: A Profile of Canada's Native People Today.* Toronto: University of Toronto Press, 1990. Deloria, Vine, Jr., and Clifford M. Lytle. *The Nations Within: The Past and Future of American Indian Sovereignty.* Lincoln: University of Nebraska Press, 1984. Fixico, Donald L. *Termination and Relocation: Federal Indian Policy, 1945–1960.* Albuquerque: University of New Mexico Press, 1986. Holm, Tom. *Strong Hearts, Wounded Souls: Native American Veterans of Vietnam.* Austin: University of Texas Press, 1996. Hoxie, Frederick E. *Parading through History: The Making of the Crow Nation in America, 1805–1935.* Cambridge: Cambridge University Press, 1995. Josephy, Alvin M., Jr., ed. *America in 1492: The World of the Indian People before the Arrival of Columbus.* New York: Alfred A. Knopf, Inc. 1992. McNickle, D'Arcy. *Native American Tribalism: Indian Survivals and Renewals.* London: Oxford University Press, 1973. Philp, Kenneth R. *John Collier's Crusade for Indian Reform, 1920–1954.* Tucson: University of Arizona Press, 1977. Smith, Paul Chaat, and Robert Allen Warrior. *Like a Hurricane: The Indian Movement from Alcatraz to Wounded Knee.* New York: New Press, 1996. Trigger, Bruce, and Wilcomb E. Washburn, eds. *The Cambridge History of the Native Peoples of the Americas.* Cambridge: Cambridge University Press, 1996. Van Kirk, Sylvia. *Many Tender Ties: Women in Fur-Trade Society, 1670–1870.* Norman: University of Oklahoma Press, 1983. Wood, W. Raymond, and Thomas D. Thiessen, eds. *Early Fur Trade on the Northern Plains: Canadian Traders among the Mandan and Hidatsa Indians, 1738–1818.* Norman: University of Oklahoma Press, 1985.

ALLOTMENT

Allotment in severalty is the process of dividing collectively occupied lands into individually owned parcels. European Americans applied the concept to Native Americans many times, beginning in the colonial era and culminating in the passage of the 1887 General Allotment (Dawes) Act. It began as a strategy for rewarding cooperative Native leaders with large parcels of land. Later, the government used allotments to appease Indian peoples who opposed being removed from their homelands. When Native Americans were removed from the southeastern United States in the 1830s, treaties granted allotments of land to families who wished to stay, while dictating the terms of

removal to the Southern Plains for all others. Many people who took allotments under these treaties lost them to fraud perpetrated by land speculators.

As the reservation policy emerged in the 1850s, the United States began inserting allotment provisions into land cession treaties. The treaties divided reservation lands into individual parcels at the president's discretion, but this use of allotment served no clear policy objective. In the late 1860s the government reinvented allotment in severalty as an assimilation strategy. Reformers believed that individualized landownership (private property) would help transform Native Americans into farmers, thereby integrating them into the American economy. Development-oriented westerners supported the idea, hoping that allotment would free up "surplus" lands for settlement, mining, ranching, and forestry. The uneasy alliance of these two powerful interest groups helped win passage of the General Allotment (Dawes) Act in 1887, after eight years of congressional debate. Similarly, in the Prairie Provinces in the 1870s and 1880s, newly created reserves for First Nations were allotted into individual and family parcels as part of the assimilation program.

During the debate over severalty legislation in the United States, Native Americans voiced their opinions on the topic. Some, like the Omahas, lobbied for their own allotment acts to secure title to their homelands. Others, like the Five Tribes of Indian Territory, petitioned to be excluded from the Dawes Act, arguing that they were already sufficiently "Americanized."

The Dawes Act mandated the division of reservations into individually owned allotments of land, using a base size of 160 acres for adult males and smaller amounts for other tribal members. Typically, though, allotment sizes were determined on a reservation-by-reservation basis, and often all members of the tribe received the same acreage. Unallotted "surplus" land could be purchased by the federal government and sold to non-Indians. The allotments themselves were to remain in trust (protected against sale and untaxed) for twenty-five years, but Congress eroded this protection in the 1890s and early 1900s.

The president determined which reservations would be allotted, and pressure from development interests usually drove his selections. Tribes in the Plains were singled out more frequently than those in other regions because ranchers and farmers wanted access to their lands. Plains tribes were also disproportionately targeted by competency commissions that decided which allottees were "competent" to handle their own business affairs. "Competent" individuals were compelled to take outright title to their allotments, dissolving the trust status and leaving the land vulnerable to sale.

The Indian Reorganization Act of 1934 officially ended the allotment policy. But many tribes continue to deal with the complex geographic, legal, and economic legacy of the leg-

islation, which turned their reservations into patchworks of tribal lands, allotments, and non-Indian lands.

See also LAW: Dawes Act.

Emily Greenwald
University of Nebraska–Lincoln

Carlson, Leonard A. *Indians, Bureaucrats, and Land: The Dawes Act and the Decline of Indian Farming.* Westport CT: Greenwood Press, 1981. McDonnell, Janet A. *The Dispossession of the American Indian, 1887–1934.* Bloomington: Indiana University Press, 1991. Otis, D. S. *The Dawes Act and the Allotment of Indian Lands.* Norman: University of Oklahoma Press, 1973.

AMERICAN INDIAN MOVEMENT

See PROTEST AND DISSENT: American Indian Movement

APACHES

Apaches, along with Navajos, are the southernmost extension of Athapaskan-language speakers. Scholars disagree on which Apaches first lived in the Great Plains. Specialists traditionally argued for a sixteenth-century Apache entry into the region, in part because early Spanish accounts described them in the Plains of Texas and eastern New Mexico. Scholars assumed they were recent arrivals. Archeological work in the 1970s, however, affirmed an Apachean presence in the Central Plains in the fifteenth and sixteenth centuries. Moreover, the Apaches' own stories place them in the Plains as early as the ninth century.

On the basis of archeological evidence, Karl Schlesier postulated four waves of Apachean migration into the Plains between 50 and 1550 A.D. The first of these is associated with a proto-Athapaskan movement into Saskatchewan and the Northern Great Plains by 50 A.D. Their descendants are the Sarcees (Sarsis). A second movement of people, destined to be known as southern Athapaskans, arrived in Montana around 200 A.D. Schlesier believes that this wave split into three parts, one of which remained in place, while the other two parts continued south into Wyoming and the Black Hills, respectively. From there they moved to the Southern Plains, where Spanish explorers encountered their descendants. A third wave entered the Plains between 950 and 1225 A.D. These people became the Navajos (Déné) and Chiricahua Apaches (N'de). This migration is described in traditional stories of Chiricahua and Mescalero Apache peoples. Navajo accounts place their arrival in Colorado and northern New Mexico at about 1100.

A fourth and final wave of Apachean migration, from 1450 to 1650, brought the ancestors of the Jicarillas, Lipans, and lastly, the distantly related Kiowa Apaches (also called Plains Apaches). These Apaches subsisted by food gathering, hunting, and horticulture, augmented by trade with settled farming communities. Autonomous Apache bands collected near the Pueblos, where they traded or raided as conditions warranted.

Spanish entrance into the Southern Plains in the sixteenth century brought profound changes to Apache ways of life. Colonization and forced conversion of Pueblo trading partners created increased hostility between the mobile and settled peoples. Acquisition of European horses and metal weapons presented new opportunities to raid for additional goods.

Spanish officials in New Mexico and Texas had difficulty identifying Apache tribes by name and location. Frequent changes in designation were required to correct mistakes. By 1700 Apaches in the Plains were identified as follows: Lipans, occupying central Texas; Faroans, in the Texas Panhandle; Mescaleros, in eastern New Mexico; Jicarillas, north and east of the Mescaleros; Carlanas, located along the present Colorado–New Mexico border; and Cuartelejos, in eastern Colorado and adjacent western Kansas. Palomas occupied central Nebraska along the Platte River. Plains (later also known as Kiowa Apaches) Apaches were in and around the Black Hills of South Dakota.

By the mid–seventeenth century Apaches had acquired enough horses that their raids became a major concern for Spanish authorities in New Mexico. Colonial governors tried various policies to subjugate them. Military expeditions against scattered autonomous bands produced limited results. Spanish alliances with Pueblos and Comanches were more productive. After 1700 the Comanches swept the Apaches off the plains of Texas and eastern New Mexico. Spanish territorial governors at times attempted to concentrate Apaches near Pueblo communities through dispersal of trade goods, including guns and alcohol. Some bands accepted Spanish annuities and settled under Spanish rule. Most did not. Spain failed to bring Apache bands in the Plains under control. Mexico fared no better. Apache raids, along with Comanche inroads, became the bane of existence in newly independent Mexico between 1821 and 1846.

In independent Texas (1836–45), policy was hostile to Indian populations, Apaches included. Texas, however, focused on war against Comanches, being less interested in Lipans and Mescaleros, who were generally far enough west to be beyond reach. The United States' annexation of Texas in 1845, and occupation and acquisition of much of northern Mexico in 1848, brought immense changes to the Apaches. Gen. Stephen Watts Kearny pronounced the United States' policy at Las Vegas, New Mexico, in 1846, which called for disarming and forcible settlement of all nomadic raiders. That policy was pursued for more than thirty years to an eventual successful conclusion.

From 1849 to 1851 a severe cholera epidemic along overland trails struck the Apaches. Most Lipans perished. Survivors, harried by Comanches and Kiowas, eventually took refuge with the Mescaleros, who absorbed them.

The United States negotiated treaties with the Apaches in the 1850s, but most were not ratified. The U.S. Army carried on a series of campaigns against specific Apache bands in the 1850s. By 1861 war with Apaches had become general. The Jicarillas were fortunate to find refuge on the immense Maxwell Land Grant in northern New Mexico. In 1863 the army was authorized to carry out a war of extermination against the Apaches. Kit Carson directed a campaign against the Mescaleros that resulted in their surrender. They and other Apache bands were gradually placed, by force or agreement, on reservations in New Mexico and Arizona. Apache resistance ended by 1887.

Mescaleros, with surviving Lipans, were established on a reservation in south-central New Mexico, where they still remain, numbering 3,511 in 1992. Jicarillas finally were granted a reservation of their own in northern New Mexico in 1887, to the west of the Great Plains. The reservation was increased in size in 1907 and again in 1908. Their population in 1992 was 3,100. Chiricahua Apaches were held as prisoners of war in Florida and Alabama until 1893. They were then moved to Fort Sill, Oklahoma, and placed as prisoners on land donated by Comanches and Kiowas. In 1913 most of their lands were annexed to Fort Sill. About two-thirds moved to Mescalero; the rest stayed at Fort Sill. They are the Fort Sill Apaches, numbering just over 100. The Plains Apaches were placed at Fort Sill with Kiowas and Comanches at the conclusion of hostilities with those peoples in the 1870s. Most descendants of the Plains Apaches remain in that area, where they are officially recognized as the Apache Tribe of Oklahoma. They have about 1,600 enrolled tribal members.

Donald C. Cole
Bethany College

Basso, Keith H., and Morris E. Opler, eds. *Apachean Culture History and Ethnology.* Tucson: University of Arizona Press, 1971. Hyde, George E. *Indians of the High Plains: From the Prehistoric Period to the Coming of Europeans.* Norman: University of Oklahoma Press, 1959. Schlesier, Karl H., ed. *Plains Indians,* A.D. 500–1500: The Archaeological Past of Historic Groups.* Norman: University of Oklahoma Press, 1994.

ARAPAHOS

Arapahos referred to themselves as *Hinanaeina* (*hinono'eino*), or "The People." Trappers and traders in the early nineteenth century used the Crow name for Arapahos, *Alappaho* (Many Tattoos), and Arapahos began referring to themselves by that term in their dealings with Americans. Five dialects of Arapaho (an Algonquian language) existed in historical times and correlated with tribal divisions: Hinanaeina (Arapaho); Hitounena (Gros Ventre); and three others, the speakers of which presumably became absorbed by the other divisions.

Arapahos entered the Northern Plains at least by the early eighteenth century, probably from the northeast. The Gros Ventre division remained in the far Northern Plains, while Arapahos moved in a southerly direction. Wealthy in horses, probably since the 1740s, Arapahos ranged from the headwaters of the Missouri to the Platte River, and west as far as the foothills of the Rocky Mountains. By 1806 they allied with Cheyennes, largely to counter the westward movement of the Sioux (Lakota). With the Cheyennes, they drove the Kiowas and Comanches south of the Arkansas River by 1826 and controlled the region between the Platte and Arkansas Rivers. In 1835, diminished by smallpox, they numbered an estimated 3,600.

Arapahos relied on bison for food, clothing, and many other necessities. In the 1830s and 1840s they hunted in the Estes Park area of Colorado (especially the region of the Cache la Poudre River) and the adjacent Plains to the east, which they recognized as their exclusive territory. Men hunted and women dried the meat, collected and dried roots and berries, dressed hides, and made tipi covers, clothing, and containers. The quilled, painted, and, by the nineteenth century, beaded designs applied on hide by women represented prayers for the well being of a relative. After 1857 settlers and miners moved into the Parks area of present-day Colorado, driving off the bison, so that the Arapahos had to hunt more regularly on the open plains east of the Rockies.

Most of the year, Arapahos lived in bands that moved together when large camps were formed or disbanded and affiliated with one of the several named subdivisions of the Hinanaeina, but individuals and households could move from one band to another. Kinship was reckoned on the basis of bilateral descent, although other individuals could be absorbed into kindred by means of "adoption." Arapahos married outside their group of kindred and legalized marriage by gift exchange between the bride's and groom's families.

The Arapaho origin story focuses on Pipe Person's creation of the earth from mud below the surface of an expanse of water. Pipe Person, through prayer-thought, created all life, including the first Arapahos. Arapahos henceforth kept a replica of the Flat Pipe as a symbol of their covenant with the life force or power on which Pipe Person drew. Rites centered on the pipe bundle helped ensure the success of Arapahos generally and of individuals specifically. Seven men's and seven women's medicine bags contained objects and implements that symbolized forms of power, and these passed from one custodian to another. Prayer-thoughts could affect events and lives, and the sincerity of a petitioner's prayer-thought was validated by sacrifices of property or of the body by flesh offerings and fasting. In the major tribal ritual, the Offerings Lodge (also known as the Sun Dance), a petitioner vowed to participate (that is, make a sacrifice) in the ceremony in return for supernatural aid. Individuals also acquired supernatural aid by dreaming or fasting for a vision encounter with a supernatural being. During the early nineteenth century, many of the men's vision fasts were on various peaks in Estes Park, Colorado. Women usually received power in a dream or from a husband or parent.

A governing council and an age-graded series of societies, supervised by the elderly custodians of the medicine bundle, comprised the tribal government. Initiation into each society was precipitated by a religious vow; the age mates of the votary went through the ceremony as a group. Wives were considered to progress through the men's societies with their husbands. These men's groups performed political duties, including keeping order in the camp and supervising the communal hunts. The governing council in the nineteenth century consisted of four leaders representing four tribal subdivisions, the medicine bundle custodians, and the leaders of the men's societies. Beginning in the 1840s "chiefs" served as intermediaries between the governing council and federal officials.

The Arapahos prospered from trading bison robes to Americans in the 1830s, but beginning in the 1840s, American expansion westward disturbed the bison herds. The United States initiated treaty councils, first to prevent troubles along the immigrant routes and later to remove Plains peoples from areas where Americans wanted to settle. In 1851 the Arapahos signed a peace treaty that guaranteed that settlers would not trespass on the tribe's lands in Wyoming and Colorado. Settlers and miners violated the treaty, with little opposition from the federal government, which led to trouble with the Arapahos and Cheyennes. In 1864 Colorado militia massacred a Cheyenne and Arapaho camp at Sand Creek, provoking a two-year war and resulting in the separation of Arapaho bands into politically independent northern and southern divisions. In 1867 the Southern Arapahos, led by Little Raven, signed the Treaty of Medicine Lodge Creek, ending hostilities. In 1868 the Northern Arapahos, having fought for several years to hold onto the bison range in Wyoming and Montana, signed a treaty under Medicine Man's leadership and agreed to settle on a reservation. Intermediary chiefs negotiated with officials during subsequent months, and in 1869 President Ulysses S. Grant created by executive order a reservation for Southern Arapahos and Cheyennes in Indian Territory (later Oklahoma). In 1878 Northern Arapahos obtained permission to settle on the Shoshone reservation in Wyoming.

When they moved to their reservations, the Southern Arapahos numbered about 1,200 and the Northern Arapahos, 1,000. The Southern branch continued to hunt bison until 1878, when game became scarce. During the 1880s Arapahos on both reservations depended for subsistence on the supplies issued by the federal government and disbursed by band leaders, the most important of whom were Black Coal and Sharp Nose in Wyoming and Powderface, Left Hand, and Yellow Bear in Oklahoma. Leaders also organized communal agricultural labor on both reservations and freighting and livestock raising in Oklahoma. The reservation in Oklahoma was divided into individually owned allotments of land in 1892, and unallotted lands were sold to non-Indians. In Wyoming, allotment occurred in 1901, but the unallotted lands were in an area undesirable for farming, and consequently these lands were never sold. In Oklahoma, the federal government facilitated the sale of most of the allotments over the years, while in Wyoming oil was discovered on the tribally owned unallotted lands. Since 1940 all Northern Arapahos have received monthly per capita payments from mineral royalties and bonuses, which have helped to alleviate poverty and have kept land sales to a minimum.

Both the Oklahoma and Wyoming Arapahos had intermediary chiefs until the third decade of the twentieth century. These chiefs worked to defend the treaty rights of their respective tribes. When the federal government encouraged the formation of elective, representative, and constitutional government, Oklahoma Arapahos instituted a "business committee." Wyoming Arapahos rejected the idea of constitutional government, but adopted an elective, representational "business council." In both cases, traditional ideals of leadership became incorporated into the new form of tribal government. Federal programs that created jobs, scholarships, housing, and other kinds of development were introduced, beginning in the 1960s, and these strengthened the role of tribal government. In the late 1990s the population of Arapahos in Oklahoma was about 4,000, in Wyoming at that time there were about 4,400 Arapahos—half of whom live within the boundaries or former boundaries of the reservation. Enrollment in the Northern or Southern Arapaho tribes is contingent on having at least 25 percent Arapaho ancestry; most have more than 25 percent.

The Offerings Lodge continued in Oklahoma until 1939, and thereafter Arapahos took it to Wyoming, where the ceremony continues today, as does the Sacred Pipe ritual. The Ghost Dance movement was important in the 1890s and, in revised form, in the early twentieth century in both the Oklahoma and Wyoming communities. Peyote ritual was introduced to the Southern Arapahos by Plains Apaches in the 1890s and then transferred to the Wyoming Arapahos; the Native American Church continues to be important in both communities. Mennonite and Baptist missionaries introduced Christianity in Oklahoma, and Catholic and Episcopal missionaries in Wyoming. Generally, the practice of Native religion and Christianity are not mutually exclusive. Since the 1970s there has been an elaboration of "traditional" religious and social ritual in both the Oklahoma and Wyoming communities.

See also WAR: Sand Creek Massacre.

Loretta Fowler
University of Oklahoma

Fowler, Loretta. *The Arapaho*. New York: Chelsea House Publishers, 1989. Fowler, Loretta. *Arapahoe Politics, 1851–1978: Symbols in Crises of Authority*. Lincoln: University of Nebraska Press, 1982. Kroeber, Alfred L. *The Arapaho*. Bulletin of the American Museum of Natural History, vol. 18 (New York, 1902–7).

ARCHAIC PERIOD SITES

For approximately 6,000 years, between about 8,000 and 2,000 years ago, the Archaic period in the Great Plains was a time of human adjustment to changing ecological conditions. Paleo-Indian bison hunting decreased markedly after about 9,000 years ago, due to a steady deterioration of ecological conditions. Subsequently there were several late Paleo-Indian groups, such as Lusk, Angostura, Frederick, and James Allen, which were beginning to shift toward the use of small animal and plant resources. By about 8,000 years ago, both bison and human populations in the Great Plains had decreased significantly. Some groups may have moved into the foothills and mountains to the west and others into the prairies on the east. The Plains was not abandoned during the Archaic period, but ecological conditions made it a much less desirable place.

Much of what is known about the Plains Archaic period comes from archeological sites on the edges of, and just outside, the Plains. A widespread change in projectile point styles from lanceolate to notched forms is arbitrarily used to mark the beginning of the Plains Archaic period. Some argue that the change was the result of new groups moving into the area, while others believe it was simply a technological modification accepted by the existing residents. The best evidence for these changes is found in areas adjacent to the Plains and in areas of topographic relief within the Plains, such as the Black Hills of western South Dakota and northeast Wyoming and the Pryor Mountains in southern Montana.

In the Northern Plains, the Early Plains Archaic, also known as the Altithermal, is dated from about 8,000 to 5,500 years ago; the Middle Plains Archaic lasted from about 5,500 to 3,000 years ago; and the Late Plains Archaic lasted from about 3,000 years ago until between 2,000 and 1,500 years ago. A slightly different chronology is used in the Central and Southern Plains. The Early Archaic period there is 8,500 to 6,500 years ago; the Middle Archaic is 6,500 to 4,500 years ago; and the Late Archaic is 4,500 to 2,500 years ago.

Evidence from the Early Plains Archaic suggests that the Black Hills may have been a kind of oasis where bison were able to maintain their numbers. The Hawken site in northeast Wyoming, a 6,500-year-old bison kill site, contained animals that were intermediate in size (probably *Bison occidentalis*), smaller than the ones found in earlier Paleo-Indian kills but larger than the modern bison found in kill sites after about 5,500 years ago. The Itasca site, close to the Plains in Minnesota and dating from between 7,000 and 8,000 years ago, contained similar bison. The Cherokee site in Iowa has Late Paleo-Indian and Early Archaic bison evidence. The Rustad and Smilden-Rostburg sites in western North Dakota are Early Archaic sites with bison remains. The lowest level at the Oxbow Dam site in southern Saskatchewan is Early Archaic. The Logan Creek complex in eastern Nebraska and Iowa and the Sutter site in eastern Kansas are also Early Archaic. Early Archaic sites in the Southern Plains include the Gore Pit site in south-central Oklahoma and the Wilson Leonard site on the Edwards Plateau, which has a stratified sequence of Early through Late Archaic levels.

Pronghorn remains are found in Great Plains sites of all ages. The Trappers Point site at a seasonal migration route along the Green River, just beyond the Plains in western Wyoming, contains communal pronghorn kills dating from about 8,000 to 5,000 years ago and is a strong indicator of similar pronghorn procurement throughout much of the Plains.

The Medicine House and Split Rock pit house sites along the North Platte River in southern Wyoming contain evidence of the use of grinding stones, plants, and small animals. Rock shelters and open sites in the Big Horn Mountains of northern Wyoming and in the Pryor Mountains of southern Montana also hold Early Archaic evidence.

Improved climatic conditions and a resurgence of bison hunting appeared during the Middle Plains Archaic, around 5,500 years ago on the Northern Plains. The Head-Smashed-In buffalo jump near Lethbridge, Alberta, is one of the more spectacular of these bison procurement features, showing continuous use from the end of the Early Plains Archaic into historic times. Oxbow Dam, Mortlach, and Long Creek are deep, stratified sites in southern Saskatchewan with both Middle and Late Archaic levels.

McKean sites, named after the McKean site in the Wyoming Black Hills, are widespread over the Northern Plains. The Scoggin site, for example, a bone bed inside an artificial bison corral, is located in western Wyoming close to the North Platte River. The Laidlaw site in southern Alberta is Middle Archaic, with drive lines and a pit used to trap pronghorns. Flat stone grinding slabs, manos (handheld grinding stones), and stone-filled fire pits are numerous in the southern part of the McKean occupation area, indicating a trend toward broad-spectrum hunting and gathering.

The Middle Archaic of the Edwards Plateau of Texas is well represented at the Wilson Leonard site by a wide variety of diagnostic traits. Middle Archaic levels are also present at the Magic Mountain site on the Front Range west of Denver, Colorado.

Late Plains Archaic sites are widely distributed throughout the Great Plains. First thought to be late Paleo-Indian because of large lanceolate projectile points, the Late Archaic Nebo Hill complex, widespread along the Kansas-Missouri border, contains a wide variety of artifact material, features, and faunal and plant food resources. The Late Archaic Pelican Lake complex, named from sites in southern Saskatchewan, is found over most of the Northern Plains. Pelican Lake levels are found at Head-Smashed-In buffalo jump in Alberta and in jump and arroyo bison kills in Montana. South of the Montana border, Pelican Lake demonstrates less dietary emphasis on bison and more on smaller animals, including pronghorn and deer. Grinding stones and stone-filled food-preparation pits are also common. Along the Powder River in northern Wyoming and Montana are arroyo bison kill sites known as Yonkee from a site in southern Montana, with dates of about 2,500 years ago. Stone circles (tipi rings) are widespread features from this period, most of which are believed to have held down the edges of hide coverings of conical lodges.

Besant cultural groups, another Late Archaic group named from sites in southern Saskatchewan, may have been the most sophisticated pedestrian bison hunters to appear in the Plains. The Ruby site in eastern Wyoming is a large bison corral alongside a religious structure. Farther west is the Muddy Creek site, a large Besant bison corral located in a depression, with a wooden ramp built to stampede the animals into the enclosure. Large stone circle concentrations represent associated living areas, and a large boulder pile on a high point overlooking the site is a religious structure.

In the Central and Southern Plains, the Late Archaic subsistence strategy was broad-spectrum hunting and gathering. There is a 2,600-year-old bison jump at Bonfire Shelter at the mouth of the Pecos River in Texas. Late Archaic groups on the eastern margins of the Great Plains may have been encouraging the propagation of native plants, but there is no evidence of corn, beans, or squash.

Following the Archaic in the Northern Plains was the Late Prehistoric period, between about 2,000 and 1,500 years ago, which witnessed the appearance of the bow and arrow and intensified bison hunting. Avonlea, one of the earliest hunting groups to use the bow and arrow, was contemporaneous with some late Besant groups. On the eastern edge of the Plains, agricultural villagers with ceramics and Central American cultigens appeared and persisted into historic times.

See also PHYSICAL ENVIRONMENT: Bison.

George C. Frison
University of Wyoming–Laramie

Johnson, Alfred E., ed. *Archaic Prehistory on the Prairie Plains Border*. Lawrence: University of Kansas Publications in Anthropology, no. 12 (1980). Larson, Mary Lou, and Julie Francis, eds. *Changing Perspectives on the Archaic on the Northwestern Plains and Rocky Mountains*. Vermillion: University of South Dakota Press, 1997. Wood, W. Raymond, ed. *Archaeology on the Great Plains*. Lawrence: University Press of Kansas, 1998.

ARIKARAS

Long before European Americans entered the Great Plains, the Arikaras, who called themselves *Sahnish*, meaning "People," separated from the Skiri Pawnees and moved northward to the Missouri River valley in present-day South Dakota. From that time on, they were associated more with the nearby Siouan-speaking Mandans and Hidatsas than with their fellow Caddoan-speaking Pawnees to the south.

Like the Mandans and Hidatsas, the Arikaras centered their lives on the river, using its high bluffs for their earth lodge villages and the rich soil of the bottomlands for gardens of corn, beans, squash, sunflowers, and tobacco. In early spring, Arikara women planted and tended the gardens. Then the people left on summer bison hunts. They returned to the village in the fall to harvest the crops. In late fall they undertook another bison hunt before moving to the winter villages in the bottomlands, where there was convenient wood and water. The earth lodges, like those built by other horticultural tribes of the Plains, were dome-shaped structures large enough to house several generations of a family and all their belongings. Arikara women made clay cooking vessels, decorated with stamped or etched designs, and distinctive willow harvest baskets. These square baskets, marked by brown and white geometric patterns woven around bent wood frames, are unique to the Arikaras, Hidatsas, and Mandans. Most other tools and utensils were common to other Plains tribes. The earth lodges, built and owned by the women, were usually occupied by sisters and their families. This kind of system is often associated with matrilineal clans, but there is no evidence for such a system among the Arikaras. It may be that their village organization and voluntary societies or associations replaced the functions of the clans. Some of these societies were military, encouraging their members to participate in raids and warfare, while others acted as police or cared for the poor. Belonging to a society helped a man attain the military successes and religious devotions that were required for village leadership.

Each Arikara village was autonomous, and leadership was diffuse, organized by rank rather than hierarchically. When the fur trader Pierre Antoine Tabeau called a council meeting in 1804, forty-two of the best-known military and religious leaders—called "men of first rank"—attended. The second level consisted of men and women who had been initiated into the honorary society called Piraskani based on their excellence of character. The third group was composed of men who had significant war honors, probably members of important societies. The lowest level included all remaining warriors.

Men who desired leadership positions also had religious duties. Arikara religious beliefs and practices centered around a belief in a principal creator, Nesharu, and a principal helper, Mother Corn. Mother Corn led the Arikaras out of the underworld and taught them what they needed to know to live in this world. Mother Corn instructed them to build the Medicine Lodge where the sacred ceremonies were held and gave each village a sacred bundle to ensure its well-being and continuance. In addition, each man had to seek a spirit guardian, who gave him prayers and objects to put in a personal sacred bundle. Throughout the year, the owners of sacred bundles sponsored ceremonies associated with corn growing and bison hunting. The Medicine Lodge ceremony took from fifteen to twenty days and marked the end of the year with demonstrations of sacred power, feasting, curing, and other sacred events.

Arikara culture changed dramatically in the eighteenth century, as the Lakotas challenged them for bison-hunting territory, and smallpox epidemics decimated the tribe. By 1804, when Tabeau lived with the Arikaras, their eighteen villages had been reduced to three fortified settlements. That same year, Lewis and Clark described the Arikaras as "tenants at will" to the Lakotas. The Arikaras occupied these villages off and on until 1823, when they were attacked by Col. Henry Leavenworth as punishment for Arikara attacks on traders. In 1837, reeling from the effects of another devastating smallpox epidemic, most of the tribe moved north to join the Mandans and Hidatsas at Fort Clark. Ever since, Arikara history has been bound with that of the Mandans and Hidatsas, and in 1862 they settled with them at Like-a-Fishhook Village.

In 1871 the Arikaras, Mandans, and Hidatsas ceded their homeland of about 12 million acres, retaining the eight-million-acre Fort Berthold Reservation (in present-day North Dakota). Allotments subsequently reduced the reservation to about one million acres. At the end of the 1880s Like-a-Fishhook Village was abandoned and the Arikaras settled around the community of Nishu, where they became ranchers and farmers. Spread across the reservation, on both sides of the river, the three tribes led relatively separate lives until 1934, when they accepted the Indian Reorganization Act and adopted the name Three Affiliated Tribes of Fort Berthold Reservation. The damming of the Missouri River in 1954 caused most tribal members to be relocated. The Arikaras centered around the town of White Shield, near some of their most important cultural sites. In the 1970s about 700 Arikaras lived on the reservation, and in 1990 the U.S. census reported a total Arikara population of 1,583.

See also WATER: Pick-Sloan Plan.

Mary Jane Schneider
University of North Dakota

Meyer, Roy W. *The Village Indians of the Upper Missouri: The Mandans, Hidatsas, and Arikaras*. Lincoln: University of Nebraska Press, 1977. Parks, Douglas R. *Traditional Narratives of the Arikara Indians*. Lincoln: University of Nebraska Press, 1991.

ASSIMILATION POLICY

Both the United States and Canada developed assimilation policies for their Native peoples. Americans and Canadians both believed that the only way to save the Indians from extinction, and to make room for settlers, was to locate Indians on reservations and convert them into Christian, self-sufficient farmers, complete with a European American sense of individualism and private property ownership. The paradox should be evident: spatial segregation was supposed to lead to cultural integration.

Although assimilation policies were evident in early federal Indian policy and in treaties with Plains Indians in the 1830s, the intensity of the program deepened in the reservation era after the Civil War. The United States applied the policy to the Southern Plains tribes at the 1867 Treaty of Medicine Lodge Creek and to the northern tribes at the 1868 Treaty of Fort Laramie. Tribal leaders were coerced into agreeing to cede to the United States all but a fraction of their land and to locate on reservations. The treaties also committed the Indians to send their children to government schools and provided for the possibility of private property in land. As compensation for the land ceded, Indians were to receive annual payments in cash and goods, as well as the services of physicians, instructors in agriculture, and other government aid. Similar terms, with only details varying, were negotiated with Plains Indians throughout the region from the 1850s through the 1870s.

It was assumed that within decades the Indians would become assimilated. The outcome was far different. There was almost a decade of bloody fighting before all of the western Plains Indians were even located on reservations, and they remained there only because the bison had been nearly exterminated by the late 1870s and early 1880s. Confined to reservations, frequently hungry, and oppressed by officials pressuring them to send their children to school and abandon cherished religious and social customs, Native Americans led a miserable existence. Indian men showed little interest in farming land that would daunt a seasoned white farmer.

Real assimilation had not taken place by the end of the reservation period. The Indian Office then tried to legislate assimilation when it introduced the allotment policy through the General Allotment Act of 1887. Each Indian was to be given a plot of land, generally 160 acres, on which to begin farming. Any remaining reservation land was sold off as "surplus lands." Congress was increasingly reluctant to fund Indian programs, having been told for decades that assimilation was imminent. In an effort to make Indians more employable, the government restructured education programs to prepare the youth for entry-level jobs—the girls as domestic servants and the boys as farm- and ranch hands and common laborers. The contexts for this assimilative education were day and boarding schools on reservations as well as off-reservation boarding schools, such as those at Genoa, Nebraska, and Haskell, Kansas.

By the 1920s the failure of assimilation policies was apparent. The United States had destroyed one way of life, and the Indians were struggling to salvage some of their cultures and to survive. The abrogation of the allotment policy in 1934 was recognition that it, and assimilation, had failed.

In Canada developments were similar in many respects. From 1871 to 1885, in a series of seven treaties, the Canadian government acquired Indian lands in the Prairie Provinces and settled the Indians on reserves, where they were put under pressure to assimilate. As was the case in the United States, the Bible and the plow were the principal instruments for assimilation. Reserves were often smaller than their equivalents in the United States, and religious groups were more prominent in Indian education. But again, as in the United States, the rhetoric of the government's assimilation policy was not matched by a genuine commitment in investment: farming instructors were often inept, promised agricultural equipment did not arrive, and Indian self-sufficiency remained a pipe dream.

Consequently, by the 1920s assimilation also seemed to have failed in Canada. Nevertheless, in both countries education and intermarriage were having an effect. Some Indians were merging with the general population, and increasingly, the products of the much-maligned schools were playing more important roles on reservations and reserves. However, the Indians' tenacity in preserving their cultures would be rewarded in the 1970s and 1980s when, in both countries, assimilation gave way to the new policy of self-determination.

See also EDUCATION: Indian Boarding Schools, United States; Indian Residential Schools, Canada / LAW: Dawes Act.

William T. Hagan
Norman, Oklahoma

Dickason, Olive Patricia. *Canada's First Nations*. Norman: University of Oklahoma Press, 1992. Hoxie, Frederick E. *A Final Promise*. Lincoln: University of Nebraska Press, 1984. Prucha, Francis Paul. *The Great Father*. Lincoln: University of Nebraska Press, 1984.

ASSINIBOINES

The Assiniboines (the western portion in Alberta are called Stoneys) refer to themselves as *Nakota*. They are Siouan speakers, linguistically situated in the Dakota-Lakota-Stoney language continuum. They have been distinct dialectically since before the sixteenth century, and 250 years of enmity between Assiniboines and Sioux peoples resulted in many Assiniboines denying that they were ever Sioux. Their closest allies were the Crees and, later, the Ojibwas. The name Assiniboine comes from the Ojibwa *assini-pwa-n*, or "stone enemy."

First noted by Europeans in the *Jesuit Relations* of 1640, Assiniboines were reported in 1658 to be living 100 miles west of Lake Nipigon and trading in the western Lake Superior regions. Other Assiniboines were encountered on the northern Prairies by Hudson's Bay Company trader and explorer Henry Kelsey in 1690–91 as far west as the Red Deer River in the Rocky Mountain foothills. During the winter of 1754–55, Anthony Henday of Hudson's Bay Company in central Alberta was assisted by "Assiniboine" families who were certainly those farthest west, antecedents of the contemporary Stoneys.

Their geographic concentrations in the seventeenth century included the areas continuously westward from Lake Winnipeg into central Saskatchewan. The Mortlach Aggregate archeological tradition has been identified in this region as representing the prehistoric and protohistoric Assiniboine. The first accounts of Assiniboines from the mid–eighteenth century report portions of groups active as middlemen and transporters in the initial postcontact trade networks. La Vérendrye joined an Assiniboine trade expedition to the Mandan villages on the Missouri River in 1738. A portion of the population participated in tribal and intertribal transport expeditions from the interior to Hudson Bay. Other portions of the population were hunters and gatherers, living on processing bison into provisions or, in the case of the Stoney populations, utilizing the variety of resources of the Rocky Mountain foothills. The Stoney territories were reached by competing traders in the 1770s. By 1780 Assiniboines were no longer ranging east of the Forks of the Red River of the North and the Assiniboine River; instead their eastern territories became the confluence of the Souris and Assiniboine Rivers and the White Earth River valley to the Missouri.

The Assiniboine subsistence round primarily exploited the parklands between forest and prairie and a series of microclimates found throughout the forests and prairies. The drainages of the Saskatchewan and Assiniboine Rivers to the North, the Milk River in the west, and the Missouri to the south framed their homelands. Bison and other large game were primarily hunted, with smaller animals and a wide range of flora rounding out the food resources before annuities and commercial provisions. Bison skin was the major substance for clothing and for making tipi covers for shelter.

Assiniboine social organization involved autonomous bands, each comprising a group of families who camped together. Many were related by blood and marriage. Consequently, the band was both the basic political and economic social unit and completely sovereign. Individual affiliation was theoretically flexible, and although kinship bound members to one another, new bands and new headmen could emerge. This caused bands to fragment, as individuals and families realigned themselves to the new social formation. The political order was headed by a group of senior males who comprised the *hungabi*, or "little chiefs," and from among them a *hunga* was chosen to be the executor of this council's will. Senior warriors led the *agi'cita*, or "soldiers' society," and they were empowered by the hungabi to fulfill specific tasks that were within their authority.

Assiniboine religion utilizes the long-stemmed pipe, which is the fundamental element in all ceremonies: vision quests, sweat lodges, the Sun Dance (which they call the "Tibi Tanga," or "Big Lodge," also translated as "Medicine Lodge"), hand games (a divinational form of the Pawnee Ghost Dance complex), and feasts, including the Ghost Feast, held within four days of a person's death and during subsequent memorials. Participants in all of these contexts make themselves humble, asking others to pray for them. Individuals pray for their kinsmen and friends and ask that their collective and personal wishes, desires, or vows be fulfilled. A spirit world of helpers is called upon in prayer to prescribe action. Shamans with special powers mediate interpretations and lead ceremonies.

Contemporary Assiniboine life signals an interest in the revival of religious ceremonies and preservation of their language. This has occurred in part because increased numbers of individuals seek advanced education and follow careers that remove them from their reserve communities. Consequently, these communities have become self-reflective about how effectively to reproduce the language and culture in future generations and how best to coordinate or balance individual development and community development, which is mostly economic and cultural.

Estimates of the historic Assiniboine population give a total of 10,000, prior to their decline by as much as half due to the 1780–81 smallpox pandemic. Subsequent recoveries were offset by other disease episodes that left the Assiniboines with fewer than 5,000 individuals on the eve of reserves and reservations in the 1870s. Numbers continued to dwindle as adjustment was made to a sedentary way of life on reservations in the United States after 1873 and on reserves in Canada after 1874. Shortly after 1900, the population began a steady increase to the present. Contemporary populations of Assiniboine communities in Montana, based on the 1990 census are: Fort Belknap, 2,180 (with Atsinas, Gros Ventres, and others resident and enrolled) and Fort Peck, 5,782 (with Sioux and others resident and enrolled). The resident and enrolled populations on Saskatchewan reserves, based on the 1998 census, are: Carry the Kettle, 1,924; Lean Man/Grizzly Bear's Head/Mosquito, 1,042 (with Crees); White Bear, 1,782, (with Crees); Ocean Man, 321; and Pheasant's Rump, 302. The 1998 populations (on and off reserve) for the Alberta reserves are: Southern Stoney communities at Morley, 3,598 (from among the Bearspaw, Chiniki, and Wesley Bands); the same bands at Eden Valley, 479, and at Big Horn, 133; and Northern Stoney communities at Alexis, 1,274, and Paul, 1,438.

Important historic leaders include Crazy Bear, who headed the delegation to the 1851 Fort Laramie Treaty Council; Red Stone among the lower Assiniboines in the same period, who led in the transition to reservations in the mid- to late nineteenth century; and Chiefs Jacob Bearspaw, John Chiniki, and Jacob Goodstoney who were the Stoney signers of Treaty Number 7 in Canada in September of 1877. The earliest documentation of oral history and folklore was by Edwin Thompson Denig in the early 1850s, and the earliest ethnographies were by Robert H. Lowie (1909) and David Rodnick (1938).

David Reed Miller
Saskatchewan Indian Federated College–
University of Regina

Denig, Edwin Thompson. "Indian Tribes of the Upper Missouri." In *Forty-sixth Annual Report of the Bureau of American Ethnology to the Secretary of the Smithsonian Institution, 1928–1929*. Washington DC: Government Printing Office, 1930: 375–628. Lowie, Robert H. "The Assiniboine." *Anthropological Papers of the American Museum of Natural History* 4 (1909). Rodnick, David. *The Fort Belknap Assiniboine of Montana: A Study in Culture Change*. New Haven CT: Yale University Press, 1938.

ASTRONOMY

Like all humans, the Native peoples of the Plains observed the sky, particularly the night sky, and created astronomies. Scholars have used three general methods to describe and understand pre-European astronomies in North America: an examination of myth; archeological data, including astronomical artifacts; and detailed ethnographic and historic studies of specific peoples.

In Blackfoot myth, for example, the Pleiades were small boys who became stars when their parents would not give them yellow buffalo calf robes. Very young calves have yellow hides in May or June, when the Pleiades are not visible, but become dark around September when the Pleiades reappear.

Archeology was used by Waldo Wedel to identify astronomies, which he proposed that "council circles" in central Kansas might be solstice registers. These types of data include the well-known medicine wheels, including Wyoming's Big Horn Medicine Wheel. Such sites are also common in the Northern Great Plains and the Prairie Provinces. The most important is the Moose Mountain Medicine Wheel in Saskatchewan, which is aligned to the summer solstice sunrise. Nearby, others mark the rising of the major summer stars: Aldebaran, Rigel, and Sirius.

One of the most important astronomical artifacts is the Skiri Pawnee star chart, drawn on a buffalo scalp and associated with the Big Black Meteoric Star bundle and ceremony. This star is associated with the northeast star pillar position and the color black. It has been proposed that its position is a point north of the celestial pole, a definite black spot in the heavens. The chart seems to be a pictograph of the night sky with key stars and constellations recorded.

Von Del Chamberlain's elegant analysis of the cosmology of the Pawnees is one of the most brilliant ethnographic studies of Native American astronomy. Chamberlain identifies major constellations in Pawnee astronomy, pointing out that they structured the world around the four cardinal, and especially semicardinal, positions. Morning and Evening Stars are associated with the east and west, and there are North and South Stars and four star pillar positions: the Northeast, Northwest, Southwest, and Southeast. Identifying the particular stars in the heavens with these positions is difficult, but one association is clear: Polaris is the North Star. Chamberlain outlines the problems of identifying the Morning and Evening Stars with the planets, but he settles on Mars and Venus, respectively. The sun and moon are also linked: the Sun is Morning Star's younger brother and the Moon is Evening Star's little sister. The semicardinal positions—the star pillars holding up the earth lodge roof and cosmologically the universe—have several interpretations, including that they refer to no celestial bodies. One view sees them linked to planets: Mercury (red) to the Southeast, Saturn (yellow) to the Northwest, and Jupiter (white) to the Southwest. Northeast is a problem, because its color is black and there is no black star. Another view sees them as the stars along the ecliptic, representing Spica (Southwest), Antares (Southeast), Aldebaran (Northwest), and Regulus (Northeast). A final interpretation has them as the brightest stars: Capella (Northwest), Sirius (Southwest), Vega (Northeast), and Antares (Southeast).

Patricia J. O'Brien
Kansas State University

Chamberlain, Von Del. *When Stars Came Down to Earth*. Los Altos CA: Ballena Press, 1982. Wedel, Waldo R. "The

Council Circles of Central Kansas: Were They Solstice Registers?" *American Antiquity* 32 (1967): 54–63. Wilson, M. N. "Blackfoot Star Myths—The Pleiades." *The American Antiquarian* 15 (1893): 149–50.

BERDACHE

See GENDER: *Berdache*

BIG BEAR (ca. 1825–1888)

Big Bear (Mistahimaskwa) was a leader of the Plains Crees who carried on a nine-year struggle to gain better treaty terms for his people from the Canadian government. Born about 1825 to Ojibwa parents near Fort Carlton, Saskatchewan, Big Bear was part of a transitional camp that spent its summers on the open Plains but in winter hunted and trapped in the woodlands near Jackfish Lake, Saskatchewan. After the death of his father, about 1865, Big Bear became chief of a band of sixty-five lodges. In addition, he received a number of visions and was a religious leader who opposed the work of Christian missionaries.

In 1876 Big Bear refused to sign Treaty Number 6 with the Canadian government. Instead, he said he would wait five years to see if its promises were honored. As starvation began to beset the Crees, many young dissidents flocked to Big Bear's camp, and he became one of the most important chiefs on the Canadian Plains. During this time, he demanded better terms from the government but was unsuccessful. Finally, he was forced to sign the treaty in 1882 when his own sons rebelled against him.

In the spring of 1885, the Métis launched the North-West Rebellion and, at the same time, Big Bear's son, Little Bear (Ayimisis), joined with war chief Wandering Spirit (Kapapamahchakwew) to kill nine white residents of Frog Lake. Several others were taken prisoner. Big Bear tried to stop the killing and later protected the prisoners. However, as chief, he was convicted of treason and was sentenced to three years in prison. He became ill while imprisoned and was released after two years. He died within a year of his release.

See also WAR: North-West Rebellion.

Hugh A. Dempsey
Glenbow Museum

Dempsey, Hugh A. *Big Bear: The End of Freedom.* Vancouver: Douglas and McIntyre, 1984.

BLACK ELK, NICHOLAS

See RELIGION: Black Elk, Nicholas

BLACKFOOT

One of the largest Native American groups of the Northern Plains, the Blackfoot Confederacy, consists of the Siksikas (Blackfoot proper), Kainahs (Bloods), Northern (Canadian) Piegans, and Southern Piegans (or Blackfeet, as they came to be known). The Algonquian-speaking Blackfoot may have migrated from the north and northwestern woodlands into the Plains of southern Alberta and northern Montana sometime in the fifteenth century. If so, they adapted to become one of the defining Plains Indian nations, so much so that their own history places their homeland in the Northern Plains.

Early estimates of Blackfoot population varied from 15,000 to 40,000. Blackfoot territory included the area from the North Saskatchewan River south to the Yellowstone River, and from central Saskatchewan west to the continental divide. By the middle of the eighteenth century, the Blackfoot had acquired horses from other tribes and guns from British traders. Raiding, gathering, hunting, and trading became the mainstays of their economy, and their power and influence grew. Wider contacts, however, made the Blackfoot vulnerable to smallpox, such as during the 1837 epidemic, and to other diseases which periodically decimated them.

The Blackfoot saw themselves as a part of a vibrant, sacred world, regarding the Sun as one of the most powerful beings. Like other Plains tribes, Blackfoot men and women secured their place in this world through vision quests, through ceremonies of sacred bundles to secure the blessing and protection of powerful bird and animal spirits (the "beaver medicine" being considered among the oldest and most powerful ceremonies), and through reliance on the spiritual guidance of medicine men and women. Although no central authority governed the Blackfoot, the Sun Dance eventually emerged as the principal summer ceremony that brought together dozens of independent, dispersed bands.

In 1806 the Lewis and Clark expedition incurred the enmity of the Blackfoot, resulting in periodic attacks on Americans. The Blackfoot gained a reputation for fierceness due to their opposition to the incursion of American fur trappers into their territory. They remained on friendlier terms with the Hudson's Bay Company, which encouraged the Blackfoot to trade at its posts. After the establishment of Fort McKenzie on the Marias River in 1833, contacts with Americans grew. The Blackfoot exchanged buffalo robes, pemmican, elk and deer hides, and furs for manufactured goods. These contacts occasionally led to trader- or trapper-Native marriages and the appearance of a mixed-blood population.

The transition from independence to reservation life was harrowing for the Blackfoot. In 1855 the Blackfoot, with several other tribes, took part in their first American treaty. The so-called Lame Bull's Treaty set aside for the Blackfoot a portion of a reservation in what became Montana in exchange for annuities and other pledges by the U.S. government. Few promises were fulfilled, and in subsequent years, as whiskey peddlers, miners, cattlemen, and settlers moved into the area, conflicts increased and clamor for the reduction of this reservation grew. Congress failed to ratify two such treaties, and in the 1860s the situation led to a series of raids and clashes called the "Blackfoot War." On January 23, 1870, Blackfoot resistance to encroachment on their lands ended with the massacre on the Marias River of 173 men, women, and children by the U.S. Army under Maj. Eugene V. Baker.

In July 1873 an executive order set aside a new reservation for the Blackfeet, Gros Ventres, and River Crows. The 2,750-square-mile reservation was bounded on the west by the continental divide, on the north by the U.S.-Canadian border, on the south by the Missouri River, and on the east by Dakota Territory. In 1874, upon the urging of settlers, Congress restored the land between the Sun and the Missouri Rivers to public domain.

The remaining bands of the Confederacy signed Treaty Number 7 with the British government in 1877. The Blackfoot and the Kainahs, along with the Sarcee (Sarsi), received as their reserve a four-mile by 200-mile strip of land along the Bow River in southern Alberta. The Kainahs subsequently moved to a new reserve between the St. Mary and Belly Rivers, and the Piegans went to a reserve west of Fort Macleod. The land was more suited to hunting than to farming, and the disappearance of the bison from the Northern Plains between 1879 and 1883 brought famine and starvation to the Confederacy. In Canada, an estimated 1,000 Blackfoot died, and almost 600 died of starvation and associated diseases in Montana. As a result, the American Blackfeet were pressured in 1888 and 1896 to trade their only remaining resource, their land, for the prospect of government annuities.

In both countries, efforts to teach self-support through farming and irrigated agriculture initially failed, but by the turn of the century cattle raising began to emerge as a successful enterprise, especially among the growing population of the mixed bloods. In the United States, however, the acts of 1907 and 1919 allotted the reservation, resulting in an erosion of the Blackfeet land base and the crippling of their nascent economy. The Canadian Blackfoot lands were also reduced by the early twentieth century.

The American practice of allotment and assimilation formally ended with the passage of the Indian Reorganization Act in 1934. The Blackfeet chose to organize under this act with a tribal council elected by residents of the various districts of the reservation. Health, education, and economic conditions on the reservation slowly began to improve. During World War II many Blackfeet served in the armed forces and found employment off the reservation. Many consequently chose to relocate to urban centers while maintaining their tribal affiliation. Some entered skilled and professional occupations and pursued higher education.

Since the 1930s the Blackfeet economy has followed the pattern of other tribes with various tribal enterprises—ranching, timber and gas, and light manufacturing industries—which experienced mixed success. The 1.3-million-acre Blackfeet Reservation, adjacent to Glacier National Park (which was once part of it), attracts tourists and visitors. The tribally owned and operated Museum of the Plains Indians houses exhibits and publishes monographs on tribal history and culture. The fully accredited Blackfeet Community College in Browning, Montana, offers standard curriculum as well courses in the language and traditions of the tribe. Tribal enrollment is about 15,000, with about 7,000 residing on the Montana reservation. The registered population of Canadian Blackfoot is about 16,000, with almost 12,000 living on the three reserves.

See also LITERARY TRADITIONS: Welch, James.

Hana Samek Norton
Albuquerque, New Mexico

Ewers, John C. *The Blackfeet: Raiders on the Northwestern Plains*. Norman: University of Oklahoma Press, 1958. Ground, Mary. *Grass Woman Stories*. Browning MT: Blackfeet Heritage Program, 1978. Samek, Hana. *The Blackfoot Confederacy 1880–1920*. Albuquerque: University of New Mexico Press, 1987.

BLACK KETTLE (ca. 1800–1868)

Black Kettle (Moketavato) was a leading chief of the Southern Cheyennes through the difficult years of the 1850s and 1860s. Born in the Black Hills before that area was part of the United States, Black Kettle married a woman of the Wotapio band and lived with his wife's people, as was customary. When the chief of that band, Bear with Feathers, died in 1850, Black Kettle was elected chief. In time, Black Kettle married another three women, all sisters to his first wife, and with them Black Kettle had seventeen children.

Black Kettle was a "Peace Chief," dedicated to strong leadership through nonaggression. After the discovery of gold in Colorado in 1858, the hunting lands of the Southern Cheyennes became increasingly encroached upon by Americans, and resentment developed on both sides. In 1864 Black Kettle and his band, which had avoided hostilities and tried to forge a peace, were camped on Sand Creek, an intermittent tributary of the Arkansas in present-day Kiowa County, Colorado (now called the Big Sandy). On November 28, Col. (and Reverend) John M. Chivington, with 600 to 1,000 men of the Colorado Volunteers, mounted a surprise attack on the village. As Black Kettle hoisted a white flag and an American flag in an attempt to stop the violence, Chivington's men massacred between 100 and 200 Indians, mainly women and children.

The Cheyennes retaliated by killing several hundred settlers during the following four years. Black Kettle worked to reestablish peace. His mark, for example, appears second on the Treaty of Medicine Lodge Creek of October 28, 1867, an attempt to establish peace on the Central and Southern Plains. But Black Kettle's efforts all came to nothing on November 27, 1868, when his sleeping village on the Washita River, in present-day Roger Mills County, Oklahoma, was attacked by troops led by George Armstrong Custer. Black Kettle and more than 100 of his people were killed.

See also WAR: Sand Creek Massacre; Washita, Battle of the.

Bruce E. Johansen
University of Nebraska at Omaha

Hoig, Stan. *The Sand Creek Massacre*. Norman: University of Oklahoma Press, 1961. Moore, John H. *The Cheyenne Nation: A Social and Demographic History*. Lincoln: University of Nebraska Press, 1987.

CADDOS

The Caddo Indians are a tribe whose traditional historic homeland was located along the borders of present Louisiana, Texas, Arkansas, and Oklahoma. In the seventeenth and eighteenth centuries the Caddos occupied a strategic position between Spanish Texas and French Louisiana. In the early nineteenth century, however, Texans forced the tribe out into the Great Plains. After wandering for three decades, they finally settled in western Oklahoma, where most of the Caddos still live today.

The Caddos were the southernmost tribe of the Caddoan language group, whose membership stretched northward to include the Wichitas, Pawnees, and Arikaras. About 2,000 years ago the Caddo peoples settled down in small horticultural villages between the Neches and Arkansas Rivers. By about 1000 A.D., the Caddos had developed complex and socially ranked societies with well-planned civic and ceremonial centers. They conducted elaborate ceremonial practices and mortuary rituals led by a religious and political elite, and engaged in extensive interregional trade.

In 1542 the Caddos were visited by the remnants of Hernando de Soto's Spanish *entrada*, at this point led by Luis de Moscoso. Although the Spaniards spent only a few weeks among the Caddos, they, and later members of other Spanish expeditions, left behind epidemic diseases, which caused the Caddo population to decline catastrophically. By the time Europeans returned to Caddo country in the late seventeenth century, the tribe had abandoned their village sites in the Arkansas Valley. The 10,000 remaining Caddos established permanent farming villages along the Red and the Neches Rivers. The Red River Caddos consisted of the four tribes of the Kadohadacho Confederacy, as well as the Yatasis and Natchitoches. To the west, along the upper reaches of the Neches River in East Texas, were the nine tribes that made up the Hasinai Confederacy. Each individual Caddo tribe was led by a hereditary chief, or *caddi*, who presided over a well-defined chain of command that provided the tribe with strong, efficient government.

By 1730 both the French and the Spanish had established themselves in the Caddos' territory. The French maintained trading posts at the Natchitoches, Yatasi, and Kadohadacho villages, while the Spanish set up three Franciscan missions in Hasinai country, as well as establishing the capital of Texas at Los Adaes, only a few miles west of the French post at Natchitoches. Despite the Spanish presence, all of the Caddo tribes obtained French weapons and metal goods, which, together with the adoption of the horse in the seventeenth century, allowed them to better defend themselves against enemies such as the Lipan Apaches to the west and the Osages to the east. By the mid-eighteenth century, however, the Caddos had abandoned most of their traditional crafts and were increasingly dependent upon European metal goods. When Spain obtained Louisiana from France in 1763, it continued to allow French trade goods to flow to the Caddos and their Wichita and Comanche allies in Texas. When the United States acquired the territory in 1803, the Caddos found themselves occupying an undefined border between American Louisiana and Spanish Texas. Seizing the moment, the Kadohadacho caddi, Dehahuit, expertly played the two rivals against one another to gain even further munificence for all of the Caddo tribes for whom he had become spokesman. After 1821, however, the border between Louisiana and Texas was settled, and both the United States and the newly independent Mexico neglected the Caddos. By the 1830s alcohol, disease, and Osage pressure had caused the Caddo numbers to dwindle to about 1,000, and the original fifteen tribes had coalesced into only three: the Hainais, Nadacos, and Kadohadachos. In 1835 U.S. Indian agent Jehiel Brooks forced the Kadohadachos to sign a treaty by which the tribe agreed to move to East Texas to live with the Hainais and Nadacos.

Unfortunately for the Caddos, Texas gained its independence from Mexico the following year and the Anglo-Americans who ruled the republic after 1836 and the state after 1845 were extremely hostile to the Indians of the region. In 1838 Texan settlers drove all three Caddo tribes from their homes in the forests of East Texas out onto the plains of central Texas, where they lived in various settlements for the next sixteen years. In 1854 the Caddos—along with Wichitas, Tonkawas, and Penateka Comanches—settled on two Indian reservations established by the U.S. government on the Brazos River. On the Brazos Reservation, the three Caddo tribes were led by Nadaco caddi Iesh (or José María), an impressive leader who convinced his fellow tribesmen to accept the federal government's "civilization" program and to assist the United States and the Texas Rangers in their struggle with hostile Comanches. Despite this accommodationist stance, in 1859 Texas vigilantes forced the Brazos Reservation tribes to move north of the Red River into Indian Territory. The Caddos splintered during the chaos of the Civil War, moving into Kansas and Colorado. The federal government finally brought them together on a reservation in 1872. On the Wichita Reservation, between the Washita and Canadian Rivers, the three remaining Caddo groups united into one tribe. Although the Caddos did everything the federal government asked of them in their new homes—farming, stock raising, and submitting to education and Christianity—the Wichita Reservation was dissolved in 1901 and the 534 remaining Caddos went through the allotment process as outlined by the Dawes Act of 1887.

Despite the attempts of the federal government to destroy it, the Caddo tribe remained intact, and a measure of home rule was provided through the terms of the Oklahoma Indian Welfare Act of 1936, which was accepted by the enrolled Caddo voters. The tribe ratified a constitution that remained in effect until 1976, when it was replaced by a completely new document. A measure of compensation for their historical losses came in the 1970s when the U.S. Court of Claims awarded the Caddo tribe $383,475 for abuses in the 1835 treaty and $1,222,800 for inadequate payments for allotments and surplus lands on the Wichita Reservation. Today, the approximately 3,200 Caddos maintain a tribal complex on thirty-seven acres of tribal-controlled land located at Binger, in Caddo County, Oklahoma.

F. Todd Smith
University of North Texas

Carter, Cecile. *Caddo Indians: Where We Come From*. Norman: University of Oklahoma Press, 1995. Smith, F. Todd. *The Caddo Indians: Tribes at the Convergence of Empires, 1542–1854*. College Station: Texas A&M University Press, 1995. Smith, F. Todd. *The Caddos, the Wichitas, and the United States, 1846–1901*. College Station: Texas A&M University Press, 1996.

CALUMET CEREMONY

Native Americans used the calumet ceremony throughout the Plains to trade between different tribes, or between different bands of the same tribe, for food and other needed items. The ceremony evolved in the thirteenth century, possibly among the Wichitas. During the early thirteenth century the climate of the Plains was wetter, supporting more bison and encouraging more tribes to move into the region. Subsequently, as the weather turned drier, many tribes, caught without adequate food supplies following a poor hunt or a local drought, needed to trade with neighbors to survive. In time, the calumet ceremony not only provided food but also often became a primary bond between bands and tribes.

In its fullest form, the calumet was a long and complex ceremony, but even the more common shorter version involved several days of ritual feasting, gift giving, singing, and dancing. The ceremony climaxed with the presentation of the calumet pipe, which made unrelated peoples one "family" through the working of a fictional kinship. Leaders of different bands adopted each other as father or son. Exchanges of gifts then went on for several days, in the later stages accompanied by exchanges between the men and women of each band, who acquired the same fictive father-son relationship to the other band as that established by their leaders. A leader's calumet relationships were considered permanent, and leaders were expected to maintain a number of calumet relationships with other tribes, bands, and villages. The calumet ceremonies also allowed men and women from different bands to meet and court each other, and often trade bonds between bands were supplemented by matrimonial bonds.

Mark A. Eifler
University of Portland

Blakeslee, Donald J. "The Plains Interband Trade System: An Ethnohistoric and Archeological Investigation." Ph.D. diss., University of Wisconsin, Milwaukee, 1975. Fletcher, Alice C. *The Hako: Song, Pipe, and Unity in a Pawnee Calumet Ceremony*. Lincoln: University of Nebraska Press, 1996.

CAMPBELL, MARIA

See LITERARY TRADITIONS: Campbell, Maria

CHEYENNES

Between 1820 and 1869 the Cheyenne nation was the most powerful Indian military force in the Central Great Plains, despite comprising only about 3,500 people. They achieved a dominant military position by allying with the Arapahos and Lakotas, then driving the Shoshones toward the northwest and the Kiowas and Comanches to the south, while keeping the Crows and Pawnees at bay by continual attacks against their villages. Thus, they gained control of the prime bison-hunting areas between the forks of the Platte and on the upper reaches of the Republican and Smoky Hills Rivers, and achieved preferred access to trading posts on the Arkansas and South Platte Rivers.

The Cheyennes were also successful during this period in their warfare against the U.S. Army, which could not catch them on the open Plains, or was often sorry when it did, as at the Fetterman Fight in Wyoming in 1866 and the Battle of Beecher's Island in Colorado in 1868. The military success of the Cheyennes can be attributed mainly to four factors: they could mobilize up to 1,500 warriors, all the active men in the tribe, for a single engagement; their bands were dispersed most of the year so that they could observe anyone entering their territory; their warriors traveled light and took along spare horses for attack, pursuit, and escape; and they maintained ferocious war traditions, which included suicide warfare, dog ropes, medicine lances, and a complex system of war honors that encouraged quick and decisive combat.

The Cheyennes, who speak a language of the Algonquian family and call themselves *Tsistsistas*, did not see themselves as primarily a militaristic people, however, but as a religious people. Even today their traditional culture is organized around the annual Sun Dances, performed on their Oklahoma and Montana reservations, and the Arrow Renewal Ceremony, performed in Oklahoma. In addition, most Cheyennes are involved in the Native American Church, or peyote religion, as well as Christian denominations, especially the Catholic Church in Montana and the Mennonite Church on both reservations.

The Cheyennes entered written history during the seventeenth century in Minnesota around the shores of Mille Lacs, where they collected wild rice and made occasional trips to the Plains to hunt bison on foot. By 1766, however, some Cheyenne bands had acquired horses and moved their base to the Minnesota River to become mounted bison hunters, while at least one other band occupied an agricultural village on the Sheyenne River in North Dakota, a river that bears the name applied to them by their Dakota neighbors, meaning "red talkers," or people of foreign language. Several decades later the various Cheyenne bands were reunited along the middle Missouri River, where they pursued an economy of mixed agriculture and hunting, based in fortified villages on the riverbanks.

Later still, probably about 1790, the Cheyenne bands moved to the vicinity of the Black Hills, where they acquired more horses, which ultimately enabled them to give up agriculture for a nomadic life of full-time bison hunting. They were urged to do this by their prophet Sweet Medicine, who was given four medicine arrows by sacred persons whom he met in a cave at Bear Butte in South Dakota, known to the Cheyennes as *Nowahwas*, or Sacred Mountain. Two of the arrows were for killing bison by magical means, and two for killing their enemies.

The Cheyenne political system had two aspects, war and peace, and two kinds of chiefs, war chiefs, or *notxevoe*, and peace chiefs, or *vehoe*. The peace chiefs led the nation's ten or so bands, supervised their trade, and adjudicated disputes. When war threatened, they gave control of the nation to the war chiefs, who planned strategy and tactics and led the attacks. Ideally, there were forty-four peace chiefs in the Chiefs' Council, four of whom were senior, or "Old Man Chiefs," and each of the seven to ten military societies was led by one to four "Big War Chiefs" and four to sixteen "Little War Chiefs."

Most of the daily work in Cheyenne society was done by women, organized along matrilineal lines. A woman usually worked alongside her mother and mother's sisters, her own sisters, her daughters, and her sisters' daughters for her entire life. Women "ruled the camp" and owned the tipis and furnishings, as well as a number of horses. As workers, they organized guilds that honored women who had made tipi covers and liners, clothing, quillwork, and beadwork. Honorable women received the privilege of smoking a pipe after menopause.

Young women were married by ages sixteen to eighteen, the oldest daughter first. Because of warfare, there were more women than men in Cheyenne society, so if possible a second sister was married to her older sister's husband (sororal polygyny). If a man died, his brother was required to marry his widow to maintain ties between the two extended families. If a woman died, an unmarried sister was required to marry the widower, to take care of the children and maintain ties between the families. If there were no unmarried sisters, then a married sister or other woman related in the female line adopted the children. Modern Cheyenne women often "co-mother" their children, playfully calling the practice "Cheyenne health insurance."

The military societies founded in Aboriginal times are still active. They sponsor dinners and powwows to honor their members and families and raise money for the annual ceremonies. Also in existence are local groups of "War Mothers," which were first organized during World War I to honor servicemen and -women and veterans.

Concerning treaties, the U.S. government now admits its failure to live up to the treaties of Fort Laramie (1851) and Fort Wise (1861), and in 1968 paid compensation of approximately $2,000 to each Cheyenne, far less than the actual value of the land taken and annuities not received. In addition, the government has admitted to defrauding Cheyennes of their reservation land through the Jerome Commission, which was certified by the infamous Lone Wolf decision in 1903. The Cheyennes were never compensated for that fraud or for the 200 noncombatants killed and horses and belongings stolen in 1864 during the Sand Creek Massacre. The descendants of those attacked were promised indemnities under the Treaty of the Little Arkansas in 1865, which have not yet been paid as of 2001, although the Cheyenne Sand Creek Descendants Association continues to make legal efforts to collect the funds.

On their reservations, beginning in the 1870s, the Cheyennes were subjected to an unending series of programs, ostensibly intended to better their condition. Missionary and government schools were set up, and some have continued to modern times. After the passage of the Indian Reorganization Act in 1934 and the Oklahoma Indian Welfare Act in 1936, Cheyennes were able to organize an official government on each reservation and to practice their religion and speak their language freely.

In recent years, the Cheyennes have taken steps to achieve economic self-sufficiency. They have inaugurated bingo halls in Oklahoma and tourist facilities in Oklahoma and Montana. They are presently negotiating with private corporations to bring manufacturing jobs to the reservation areas. Their present population consists of approximately 7,000 Northern Cheyennes enrolled on their reservation in southeastern Montana and another 7,000 Southern Cheyennes enrolled on their reservation in west-central Oklahoma.

See also GENDER: Native American Gender Roles / LAW: *Lone Wolf v. Hitchcock* / WAR: Sand Creek Massacre.

John H. Moore
University of Florida

Berthrong, Donald J. *The Southern Cheyennes*. Norman: University of Oklahoma Press, 1963. Grinnell, George B. *The Cheyenne Indians*. New York: Cooper Square, 1962. Moore, John H. *The Cheyenne Nation*. Lincoln: University of Nebraska Press, 1987.

COMANCHES

The Comanches were the first Native people to adopt the classic horse-mounted lifestyle of the Plains. The ethnonym Comanche probably derives from the Ute word *komantsia*—"anyone who wants to fight me all the time." Their name for themselves is *Nemene*, or "Our People."

Shoshone speakers, including proto-Comanches, probably moved to the Northern Plains in the sixteenth century. In the late seventeenth century the proto-Comanches began a southward movement, and by the early eighteenth century, if not before, they were in contact with the Spaniards of New Mexico. The earliest mention of Comanches in Texas came

in the 1740s. By the 1840s Comanches were regularly crossing the Rio Grande into Mexico on horse raids.

The Comanche economy can be characterized in three modes: a domestic economy of hunting and gathering, a commercial economy of trade and raid, and a political-diplomatic economy. In the domestic economy, Comanches used both individual stalking of bison and group methods. Group hunts usually occurred in late summer and fall when the animals were fat, robes were good, and there were few flies. Group hunts began with scouts locating a herd. After the scouts reported the herd's location to the chiefs, the hunters were admonished to stay together. The actual hunt was under the direction of the chief or a noted warrior. However, once the chase began, each hunter acted separately. Hunters identified their kills by arrow marks. Other men could claim a portion of the meat by counting coup on it, but the hide remained the property of the killer.

There were three general trade contexts: formal and informal trade fairs and bartering in European settlements; trading posts; and exchange with *viageros* or "travelers," later called *comancheros*. Comanches traded horses and the products of the hunt with neighboring peoples for agricultural products and, in postcontact times, European industrial products.

Political relations with other peoples probably always included gift exchanges. Political relations with European Americans developed into an economy with significant ramifications. Items in this economy included elite goods such as silver-headed canes, flags, and uniforms. They also included items that could be redistributed downward through the social structure such as foodstuffs, cloth, and metal goods.

Details of Aboriginal clothing are scanty, but it seems that summer dress was minimal. Men wore perhaps only a shirt, a breechcloth, possibly leggings, and moccasins. By the reservation period, photographs and museum collections show mid-thigh-length shirts decorated with twist fringe at the shoulder and elbow. Some side-seam leggings are represented in museum collections, although late-nineteenth-century photographs also show front-seam style, attached by thongs to the belt at the waist and tied with garters below the knee. From knee to ankle, leggings were decorated with long twist fringe. Moccasins were of the two-piece, hard-sole variety. A long triangular vamp was decorated with fringes and tin cone tinklers. The earliest examples of women's apparel are two-part dresses, consisting of a skirt suspended by straps from the shoulders and a separate poncholike blouse; some mid-nineteenth-century photographs show a separate wrap fastened with broaches. In hot weather, or when nursing or in mourning, the blouse could be removed. The later style was a single-piece dress. By the mid– to late nineteenth century, both men and women wore a cloth about the waist outside both leggings and skirt.

Comanche tipis were distinct, with a four-pole base, but with the rest of the poles set in as in a three-pole tipi. The cut of the skins forming the cover was also apparently unique.

Comanche relations with the supernatural were considered to be an individual's concern, and despite a range of variation in belief and practice, there were broad features common to Comanche religion. Religious practice centered on *puha*, personal power obtained from the supernatural. Power was available to both men and women, both of whom could become *puhacut*, or a "possessor of power."

In prereservation times, there were four levels of sociopolitical organization: simple family, extended family, local band, and division. The simple family consisted of a man, his wife or wives, and various dependents—children, parents, or parents-in-law. The basic social unit was the bilaterally extended family, or *nemenakane*, "people who live together in a house(hold)." Local bands were composed of one or more extended families, as well as attached simple families and individuals, and were called *rancherías* by the Spaniards. The highest level of Comanche political organization was the division, the tribally organized group of local bands linked by ties of kinship and men's societies. The names and numbers of these groups have changed greatly over the course of Comanche history.

The Comanches were assigned a reservation in southwestern Oklahoma following the Treaty of Medicine Lodge Creek in 1867, but not all the bands were on the reservation until 1876. The reservation was allotted after the General Allotment Act of 1887. Most Comanches now live in the vicinity of Lawton, Oklahoma. They are active, although often partial, participants in the mainstream economy. Fort Sill in Lawton, Tinker Air Force Base in Oklahoma City, and Altus Air Force Base in Altus, as well as several other federal installations, provide employment. As a tribe the Comanches have few independent resources. In 1984 a bingo operation was opened, although it has been the focus of much controversy, and its contribution to the Comanche economy is uncertain.

Although more than half of the 1901–6 Comanche allotments are still in Indian hands, few Comanches actively work them. Rather, allotments are held as undivided joint property by multiple heirs of the original allottee and are leased to non-Indian farmers or stockmen. A number of oil wells have been drilled on allotments, and several Comanches have become quite wealthy through such revenues.

There are no reliable Aboriginal population estimates; similarly, details of epidemic diseases are scanty and contradictory. In 1870 it was estimated that there were 3,742 Comanches, including possibly 1,000 off-reservation. In 1875, 1,556 Comanches were reported on the reservation south of the Washita River. In 1900 there were 1,499 Comanches, but a year later measles took ninety-eight lives. The low point of 1,399 was reached in 1904, and it was not until the 1930s that the population again surpassed 2,000. In 1990 the tribal population was approximately 9,000.

See also HISPANIC AMERICANS: *Comancheros*.

Thomas W. Kavanagh
Indiana University

Kavanagh, Thomas W. *Comanche Political History: An Ethnohistorical Perspective, 1706–1875.* Lincoln: University of Nebraska Press, 1996.

CRAZY HORSE

See WAR: Crazy Horse

CROW FAIR

See SPORTS AND RECREATION: Crow Fair

CROWFOOT (ca. 1830–1890)

Crowfoot (Isapo-muksika, or "Crow Indian's Big Foot") was head chief of the Blackfoot (Siksika) tribe. A great orator and warrior, Crowfoot contributed in a significant way to the peaceful settlement of the Canadian West.

Crowfoot was born around 1830 on the Belly River, near present-day Lethbridge, Alberta. He first went to war at about the age of thirteen and showed great bravery in striking an enemy tipi with his whip and rescuing his wounded brother. He was in nineteen engagements with enemy tribes and was wounded six times. His greatest feat of bravery occurred in 1866 when, in full view of his camp, he killed a grizzly bear with a spear. Shortly thereafter he became leader of the Big Pipes Band, and by 1870 he was one of three head chiefs of the tribe.

Crowfoot maintained good relations with the Hudson's Bay Company, appreciating that, unlike American traders, they did not flood the land with alcohol. Crowfoot also befriended the Catholic missionary Albert Lacombe in 1865 and later rescued him when he was in a camp that was attacked by a Cree war party. Crowfoot allowed Lacombe to preach to his people, though Crowfoot himself paid little attention to Christianity.

In 1874, when the North-West Mounted Police extended their control over western Canada, Crowfoot established friendly relations with its commander, James F. Macleod. In 1877 he willingly signed the Blackfoot treaty (Treaty Number 7) with the Canadian government, ceding much of southern Alberta. However, after the Blackfoot were obliged to live, mired in famine, on their reserve east of Calgary, Crowfoot became disillusioned with the government. Nevertheless, he continued to mediate between his people and government officials. By the last decade of his life, most of his children had died of tuberculosis and he was almost constantly in mourning. Crowfoot died on April 25, 1890, in a tipi in the Bow Valley. He is now considered to be one of Canada's national heroes.

See also LAW: Macleod, James.

Hugh A. Dempsey
Glenbow Museum

Dempsey, Hugh A. *Crowfoot, Chief of the Blackfeet.* Norman: University of Oklahoma Press, 1972.

CROWS

The Crow people traditionally call themselves *Apsaalooke* or *Absaroka*, commonly translated as "Children of the Large-Beaked Bird." While likely referring to the raven, this term was misinterpreted by early trappers who began to address the Apsaalooke as the Crows. The Crows attribute their origins, as well as the creation of the world, to the trickster Old Man Coyote. The narrative begins with Old Man Coyote traveling alone in a cold and wet world. As four ducks flew over, Old Man Coyote asked his younger brothers to dive beneath the waters and bring up some earth so he could make the land. The first duck dove but was unsuccessful, as were the second and third ducks. Finally, Old Man Coyote asked the fourth duck, Hell Diver, to bring up some earth. The duck dove deep and, after being down a long time, surfaced with a small piece of mud. With this earth Old Man Coyote traveled from east to west and made the land, mountains, and rivers, animals and plants, and gave them life. But the world was still a lonely place. So Old Man Coyote molded from the earth an image he liked and blew a small breath into it. The first man was made. Old Man Coyote was not satisfied. He tried again and the first woman was created. Old Man Coyote was no longer alone. He taught the people how to live and pray, giving them their language, clan system, and ceremonies.

The historic migration of the Crows from the Lake Winnipeg region of Canada into the Bighorn and Yellowstone River basins of Montana and Wyoming (probably before 1600) predated the arrival of the horse. Horses were acquired by 1750, and the Crows' economic life was transformed from one of sedentary farming to one of bison hunting. The horse became an integral symbol of Crow identity and status. Male leadership roles became predicated on achieving a series of war deeds, such as touching an enemy in combat or leading a successful horse raid against an enemy. Among their enemies were the Blackfeet, Cheyennes, and Lakotas. The Sun Dance became a prominent ceremonial expression, helping unite the tribe and providing a means to obtain spiritual power to avenge the death of a relative.

Despite the changes initiated by the adoption of the horse, the Crows retained elements of their former society. The Tobacco Ceremony, the yearly planting and harvesting of the sacred tobacco seeds, reflected their once-agrarian orientation. The Crows also maintained their matrilineal clan structure, and even today's clan system is based on the thirteen original clans. The Crow language is part of the Siouan family, thus giving them a linguistic affiliation with many other tribes of the region. Today, up to one-third of the population continues to speak their native language.

The central organizing principle around which much of Aboriginal and contemporary Crow society revolves is best understood in the Crow term for clan, *ashammaleaxia*, literally meaning "driftwood lodges." As an individual piece of driftwood has difficulty surviving the powerful eddies and boulders of the Yellowstone or Bighorn Rivers, so too does an individual Crow have difficulty surviving the river of life, full of potential adversaries—formerly Lakotas and Blackfeet but now unemployment, substance abuse, and discrimination. But in tightly lodging itself with other pieces of driftwood along the riverbank, the driftwood is protected. So, too, is an individual Crow protected and nurtured when lodged securely in an extensive web of kinship ties. These are ties made up of both social and spiritual kinsmen and maintained through an extensive pattern of gift exchanges.

The values of ashammaleaxia are clearly evident in oral traditions, kinship relationships, and religious ceremonialism. The story of Burnt Face is an example. A young boy is badly scarred and subsequently ostracized. Burnt Face fasts for several days in the Big Horn Mountains. While on the mountain, he assembles the "Big Horn Medicine Wheel" as a gift to the Sun. Having given of himself, Burnt Face is adopted by the Little People, who remove his scar. He returns to his people and subsequently becomes a great healer, having extended his kinship ties to the Little People.

Of all kinship relations, that of *aassahke*, or "clan uncle and aunt," is pivotal. A clan uncle or aunt is any male and female member of one's father's mother's clan. Such individuals are to be respected, and gifts of food and blankets are provided to them during giveaways. In return, aassahke bestow on a child an "Indian name," sing "praise songs" for accomplishments, and offer protective prayer.

The principles of ashammaleaxia are expressed in a sweat bath, a Catholic Mass, a medicine bundle opening, a vision quest, a peyote meeting, and a Sun Dance. In each instance, individual prayer, the "gift" of sacrificing food and water, or the medicine power of a guardian spirit may be directed at a kinsmen in need. The last "buffalo days" Sun Dance was held in 1875, but with the assistance of the Shoshones, the Crows were again performing the Sun Dance by the 1940s. Today the Shoshone-Crow Sun Dance has become fully integrated into Crow family and religious life. As many as 120 men and women participate in a Sun Dance, several of which are held on the reservation during June and July. Along with the sponsor, each dancer has made a vow to the Creator or his or her own spirit guardian to go without food and water and "dry up" to help another. Typically, dances last three days. During the Sun Dance, individual participants offer prayer for family members, collective morning prayers are given for the welfare of all peoples, the sick are "doctored" by medicine men, and individual dancers may be given a vision.

The ravages of smallpox in the 1830s, the destruction of the bison, the confinement to a reservation in 1868, and its subsequent reduction by treaties and allotment in the late nineteenth and early twentieth centuries all contributed to a decrease in the population to a low of 1,625 by the early 1930s. With improved health care and economic opportunities, the enrolled Crow population had risen to 10,000 by 1998. The Crow Indian Reservation of some two million acres, of which nearly one-third is owned by non-Indians, is located in south-central Montana.

Electing not to adopt most of the specific provisions of the Indian Reorganization Act of 1934, the Crows wrote their own constitution in 1948. It established a general council government made up of every adult member of the tribe. The council elects four officers: a chairman, vice chairman, secretary, and vice secretary. It also establishes various governing committees that oversee such activities as land purchases, industrial development, housing, education, and tribal enrollment.

The resilience of the Crow people is partly the result of persistent great leadership, including Plenty Coups, Pretty Eagle, Medicine Crow, Robert Yellowtail, Angela Russell (a state senator), Bill Yellowtail (a state senator and regional director of the Environmental Protection Agency), and Janine Pease Pretty On Top (president of Little Big Horn College and a 1994 MacArthur Fellow).

See also LAW: *Montana v. United States* / SPORTS AND RECREATION: Crow Fair.

Rodney Frey
University of Idaho

Frey, Rodney. *The World of the Crow Indians: As Driftwood Lodges.* Norman: University of Oklahoma Press, 1987. Hoxie, Frederick. *Parading through History: The Making of the Crow Nation in America, 1805–1933.* New York: Cambridge University Press, 1995. Lowie, Robert. *The Crow Indians.* New York: Holt, Rinehart and Winston, 1935, rev. ed. 1956.

DULL KNIFE (ca. 1810–1883)

He was born in the rugged mountain country of Montana's Rosebud Valley at the beginning of the nineteenth century and died there near century's end. In between, the trajectory of his life encompassed the full sweep of Indian experience on the nineteenth century Northern Great Plains: warrior, chief, signatory to the Fort Laramie Treaty, statesman, reservation citizen, Cheyenne Outbreak leader, hunted quarry, starving survivor, tribal elder.

To his people, the Northern Cheyennes, he was called *Wo'he Hiv'*, or Morning Star. As a boy, it is said that he showed uncommon bravery and leadership. As a young man, he joined in raids against the Crows, Arikaras, Snakes, and Shoshones, earning a reputation for fierceness and courage. On December 21, 1866, he and Lakota war chief Crazy Horse led a decoy party that helped wipe out Capt. William J. Fetterman and all eighty-one of his men. But not long afterward he began to believe war against the whites was hopeless. A gifted orator and skilled negotiator, he visited the forts, talked to the soldiers, and attended peace parleys, looking for a way out for his people.

In 1868 he was among the chiefs who signed the Treaty of Fort Laramie, agreeing he would never again "sharpen his knife" against the

Dull Knife (Wo'he Hiv')

whites. Dull Knife, as he was now known, kept his word. Col. George A. Woodward, commander of Fort Fetterman, recalled an 1871 visit to the fort: "Of the three head-men of the Cheyennes, Dull Knife was, I think, greatly the superior. . . . His manner of speech was earnest and dignified, and his whole bearing was that of a leader with the cares of state."

In June 1876, while others left for the Little Bighorn, Dull Knife stayed in his camp a few miles southwest of the battle. Exactly five months after the Custer fight, a surprise predawn army attack wiped out much of his village. On April 21, 1877, after a winter sharing meager supplies in Crazy Horse's camp, Dull Knife and 553 of his people surrendered at Fort Robinson, Nebraska.

Five weeks later, Dull Knife and his Northern Cheyenne were forcibly marched to a reservation in Indian Territory. After a year enduring starvation, disease, death, and acute homesickness, Dull Knife and Little Wolf, another chief and the tribe's most capable warrior, decided to lead about 300 of their people north on a 1,000-mile freedom flight back to their Montana homeland. They left on September 9, 1878. Six weeks and more than 500 miles later—exhausted, hungry, cold, an estimated 2,000 troops in pursuit—they had made it deep into the Sandhills of northwest Nebraska, where the chiefs made a decision: Little Wolf and the stronger ones would continue to Montana; Dull Knife and the weaker ones would look for Red Cloud's nearby camp.

On October 23, the cavalry caught up with the weaker group, marching Dull Knife and 148 prisoners on a twenty-eight-mile trek to Fort Robinson. The post commander, Capt. Henry Wessells, told Dull Knife and four sub-

chiefs on January 3, 1879, that a decision had been made: the Northern Cheyenne must return immediately to their Indian Territory reservation. "I am here on my own ground," Dull Knife replied, "and I will never go back. You may kill me here, but you cannot make me go back." On January 5, Wessells ordered all food and heating fuel withheld from the defiant Northern Cheyennes. Two days later, he cut off the water supply. Still, Dull Knife and his people refused to leave their barracks.

Shortly before 10 P.M. on the evening of January 9, with the temperature below zero and half a foot of snow on the ground, the Northern Cheyennes broke out of the barracks, fleeing for the protective bluffs across the White River. Skirmishes between the Northern Cheyennes and cavalry troops continued for two weeks. When the shooting ended on January 23, thirty-nine Northern Cheyenne men and twenty-five women and children had been killed. Dull Knife was not among them. He and several family members eventually made it to the safety of Pine Ridge Agency about sixty miles away, surviving the last few nights by eating the soles of their moccasins.

Later that year Dull Knife, then about seventy, was allowed to return to Montana. In November he rejoined Little Wolf, who—after a journey of seven months and more than 1,000 miles—had made it safely back. Dull Knife died of natural causes in his Rosebud Valley homeland in 1883. About a year later, on March 26, 1884, the U.S. government officially set aside a tract of Montana land as the permanent home of the Northern Cheyennes.

See also WAR: Crazy Horse.

Joe Starita
University of Nebraska–Lincoln

Starita, Joe. *The Dull Knifes of Pine Ridge: A Lakota Odyssey.* New York: Putnam, 1995.

EARTH LODGES

See ARCHITECTURE: Earth Lodges.

ECUERACAPA (d. 1793)

Ecueracapa (Leather Cape) was the name the Spaniards of late-eighteenth-century New Mexico gave to the principal chief of the Kotsoteka Comanches. His Comanche name was apparently *Koontyta'nikypa'a,* or "Crane on a Stake," but he was also called Cota de Malla (or Maya), "Coat of Mail." This latter citation has led to continuing confusion between the New Mexican Ecueracapa and at least two Texas Comanches also called Cota de Malla.

Ecueracapa first came to the attention of the New Mexican Spaniards in late 1785 when, after peace had been concluded with the Texas Comanches, Governor Juan Bautista de Anza managed to open communication with the western Comanches. They sent word that Ecueracapa, the "captain most distinguished as much by his skill and valor in war as by his adroitness and intelligence in political matters," was empowered to enter into negotiations, which were conducted in early 1786. In June 1786 a formal agreement was signed at

Pecos Pueblo marking the beginning of a Comanche–New Mexican peace that endured until 1821.

In the following years, Ecueracapa appears a number of times in the historical record. In May 1787 he forestalled retaliation against some Jupe Comanche youths who had stolen Spanish horses, and in early 1790 he was involved in an ill-planned joint Spanish-Comanche expedition against the Pawnees. In 1793 Ecueracapa was "grievously wounded" on a campaign against the Pawnees. He probably died sometime that fall.

Thomas W. Kavanagh
Indiana University

Kavanagh, Tomas W. *Comanche Political History: An Ethnohistorical Perspective, 1706–1875.* Lincoln: University of Nebraska Press, 1996.

ERDRICH, LOUISE

See LITERARY TRADITIONS: Erdrich, Louise

GENÍZAROS

See HISPANIC AMERICANS: *Genízaros*

GHOST DANCE

See RELIGION: Ghost Dance

GROS VENTRES

The Gros Ventres are an Algonquian-speaking people from the area of the Great Plains between the Missouri River, Montana, and the Saskatchewan River in the Canadian Prairies. Their own name is *A'aninin* or *A'ani*, meaning "White Clay People," derived from their belief that they were made from white clay found on the river bottoms.

The Gros Ventres are among the least known tribes of the Northern Plains, partly the consequence of mistaken identity. The name Gros Ventre ("Big Belly" in French) is a misnomer that originated from a mistranslation of the gesture for the A'aninin in the Plains sign language. The Crees referred to the Gros Ventres as the Water Falls People, Falls Indians, or Rapid Indians because the tribe occupied territory inclusive of the southern branch of the Saskatchewan River, where rapids are frequent. The sign for them was the passing of the hands over the body like water falling. This was mistranslated as a sign representing a large stomach, and hence they became known as the Big Bellies, or Gros Ventres. Adding to the confusion, the Gros Ventres are also known as the "Atsinas" in some ethnological sources, a Blackfoot word meaning "Belly People." To distinguish them from the Hidatsas, also known as the Gros Ventres, sometimes they were called the "Gros Ventre of the Prairies."

Earliest mention of the Gros Ventres places them in the region of the Saskatchewan River in the eighteenth century, far removed from their kindred, the Arapahos. When and where these two tribes split is not known. Trappers and traders of the Hudson's Bay Company and the North West Company located the Gros Ventres on the South Saskatchewan River between 1775 and 1790. As the Gros Ventres ventured farther west and south, they quickly adopted the lifestyle of the Northern Plains. They became mobile and followed the buffalo herds for their primary source of food and clothing. They lived in easily moved tipis and excelled at the elaborate and beautiful beadwork and quillwork of that region.

Like other Plains tribes, the Gros Ventres' spiritual practices were rich and complex. Their principal tribal ceremony was the Sun Dance, or "Sacrifice Dance." Their major religious possessions were sacred pipes. The Gros Ventres once possessed ten such pipes, but now have only two; the Flat Pipe and the Chief Medicine Pipe, or Feathered Pipe, are revered as a direct link to the supernatural. Each spring, the two medicine pipes are used to secure blessings from the One Above.

During the early part of the nineteenth century, the Gros Ventres were driven farther south to the Missouri River country by the Crees and Assiniboines. In the 1820s one band of the Gros Ventres joined the Arapahos in the Cimarron Valley, in the present-day Oklahoma Panhandle. The Gros Ventres band remained there for five years before traveling back north in 1833.

The reunited Gros Ventres took up a precarious position on the Northern Plains, settling in an area between the Blackfoot to the west, the Assiniboines to the east, and the Crows toward the south. Smallpox epidemics had struck the tribe in 1781, 1801, and 1829, significantly reducing their numbers. The great smallpox epidemic of 1837–38 devastated the Blackfoot and the Assiniboines but left the Gros Ventres and the Crows comparatively undisturbed. The Crows proved an enduring enemy, and warfare continued between the two tribes even into the reservation period.

Unlike many other Northern Plains tribes, the Gros Ventres generally remained on good terms with non-Indians. They patronized the American traders at Fort McKenzie and were considered among the more receptive tribes in the region. Jesuit missionaries, including Father Pierre-Jean De Smet and Father Nicolas Point, made sporadic visits to the Gros Ventres and found them generally amicable but resistant to Christianization. Isaac Stephens, governor of Washington Territory, held council with the Gros Ventres, as part of the Blackfoot nation, in 1855, out of which came a treaty formalizing relations between the tribe and the United States and pressing for intertribal peace on the Northern Plains.

Gold was discovered in what is now Montana in 1862, bringing more and more non-Indians through the hunting territories that supported the Blackfeet, Assiniboines, Crows, and Gros Ventres. The completion of the Union Pacific Railroad in 1869, and the Northern Pacific Railroad in 1883, brought increasing numbers of settlers and made the region less remote. The impact of such rapid settlement greatly reduced the game herds, particularly the bison, already dwindling in numbers. The last of the buffalo herds had disappeared from the Northern Plains by the time the Gros Ventres were confined to the Fort Belknap Reservation in north-central Montana in 1888. At that time, their population stood at 964, and their tribal numbers fell to a low of 576 in 1900.

In 1935 the tribe reorganized its government, the Fort Belknap Indian Community Council, under the terms of the Wheeler-Howard Act (Indian Reorganization Act). In the twentieth century the tribe petitioned the U.S. government for compensation for questionable land transfers in the nineteenth century and battled with mining corporations in an effort to maintain its land base and protect the environment. Despite sharing the Fort Belknap Reservation with the Assiniboines, the Gros Ventres have worked to maintain a distinct culture. There are now few fluent Gros Ventre speakers; however a vigorous program to teach the language begins in primary school and culminates in classes at a local community college. Their economy is agriculturally based, but the federal and tribal governments remain the primary employers, and unemployment remains high. In 2000 the Gros Ventres numbered some 3,000 members, the majority living on the 652,593-acre Fort Belknap Reservation.

Walter C. Fleming
Montana State University–Bozeman

Bryan, William L., Jr. *Montana's Indians: Yesterday and Today.* Helena MT: American and World Geographic Publishing, 1996. Flannery, Regina. *The Gros Ventre of Montana: Part I, Social Life.* Washington DC: Catholic University of America Press, 1953. Horse Capture, George, ed. *The Seven Visions of Bull Lodge.* Lincoln: University of Nebraska Press, 1992.

HALF-BREED TRACT

The Half-Breed Tract, also known as the Nemaha Half-Breed Reservation or Reserve, was established on July 15, 1830, with the signing of the Treaty of Prairie du Chien in Michigan Territory. The Half-Breed Tract was established to provide a homeland for tribal members of mixed ancestry, at the request of the signatory Native American nations, the Otoe-Missourias, Omahas, and Iowas, and on behalf of the Santees and Yanktons. Article 10 of the treaty ceded approximately 138,000 acres of Otoe-Missouria land that extended from the Missouri River westward between the Great (Big) Nemaha and Little Nemaha Rivers to form a triangular tract located in what is now southeastern Nebraska. This was the first treaty in which Congress authorized the allotment of land in severalty to Native Americans.

On September 10, 1860, following thirty years of controversy regarding the western boundary of the tract, Lewis Neal became the first of 389 individuals to receive a patent of land allotted in severalty. Because there were too many eligible mixed-blood claimants, each allottee received only 320 acres instead of 640 acres originally suggested in the Treaty of Prairie du Chien. By the 1870s most of the land allotted in the Half-Breed Tract had been taken over by white settlers, who sometimes used alcohol to entice mixed-bloods to sell, or who married mixed-bloods and so gained entitlement to allotments. The first test of Native American land severalty in the United States ended in complete failure in terms of the original intention of the Treaty of Prairie du Chien signatories.

William T. Waters
University of Nebraska at Kearney

Chapman, Berlin B. *The Otoes and Missourias: A Study of Indian Removal and the Legal Aftermath.* Oklahoma City: Time Journal Publishing Co., 1965. Johansen, Gregory J. "To Make Some Provision for Their Half-Breeds, The Nemaha Half-Breed Reserve, 1830–66." *Nebraska History* 67 (1986): 8–29.

HARRIS, LADONNA (b. 1930)

LaDonna Harris, a Comanche woman born in 1930 in Walters, Oklahoma, is a well-known political activist. Once shy and retiring, but nonetheless aware of the inequities of being an Indian in America, LaDonna blossomed during her marriage to Fred R. Harris, who was later a U.S. senator from Oklahoma and candidate for president. She put her personality and many talents to work as the founder of Oklahomans for Indian Opportunity (OIO), a Native American charitable and educational nonprofit organization. OIO expanded into civil rights activities in the 1960s and was the forerunner of Americans for Indian Opportunity, with its flagship Ambassadors program, a nationwide project headed by Harris. The Ambassadors project takes some of the nation's brightest and most promising young Indian professionals through an intensive one-year program aimed at rekindling and reinforcing the use of the tribal values in a modern context.

Harris's work takes her all over the country, including Washington DC, where she is well known in Congress as a fighter for, and defender of, Indian rights and programs. She is in demand as a speaker, both locally and nationally, and frequently leaves her home in Bernalillo, New Mexico, to travel in support of Indian issues. Publicly acknowledged by various Indian and non-Indian organizations as a successful activist, LaDonna remains at heart a Comanche woman and returns frequently to her Oklahoma roots, often accompanied by one or more of her three adult children and one grandchild, to draw strength and vitality from her heritage.

H. Henrietta Stockel
Cochise College

Harris, LaDonna. *LaDonna Harris: A Comanche Life*, edited by H. Henrietta Stockel. Lincoln: University of Nebraska Press, 2000.

HEALTH

The history of the health of Great Plains tribes can be characterized as a series of epidemiological transitions highlighted by several distinct eras. Before European American colonization, Plains peoples suffered from low-virulence infections and socially induced mortalities. Paleopathological evidence reveals numerous afflictions: malnutrition, anemia, tuberculosis, treponematosis, and other degenerative, chronic, and congenital conditions. Together with periodic trauma, such as accidents and warfare, these afflictions determined morbidity and mortality patterns.

European American contact brought elevated levels of morbidity and mortality. Most tribes experienced deteriorating health conditions and sustained population declines. The crucial factor was the introduction of Eastern Hemisphere infectious diseases such as cholera, influenza, measles, and smallpox. Even before 1730 Plains populations were exposed to epidemics. Then, between 1730 and 1877, approximately fifty epidemics swept across the Northern Plains; Southern Plains societies suffered similar catastrophes. Smallpox was particularly devastating: the 1837–38 epidemic, for example, killed an estimated 17,200 Indians in the Northern Great Plains, including 8,160 Blackfoot.

Epidemics were accompanied by increased warfare, impairment of subsistence activities and consequent famine, breakdown of social systems, which crippled a tribe's capacity to care for its sick, and deep cultural stress. In response, Great Plains societies employed a number of adaptive strategies, altering their kinship, marital, and adoption practices, and modifying their ideological systems to explain the introduced pathogens. Some tribes accepted select western medical techniques, such as vaccination, adding them to their traditional repertoire of healing practices.

Rudimentary governmental health services were introduced after 1819 under the auspices of the War Department. Army physicians, missionaries, and even traders administered sporadic medical care. Some U.S. government treaties promised medical care, but of the numbered treaties in Canada, only Treaty Number 6 (1876), with the Crees, referred specifically to medical services. Concerted efforts to provide health care for Plains Indians did not occur until long after their confinement to reservations and reserves.

Although epidemics, including influenza, still sporadically occurred, after about 1880 the main causes of morbidity and mortality were afflictions brought about by the impoverished conditions of life on the reservations and reserves, especially tuberculosis, trachoma, and dysentery. For example, in 1898 the high (54 per 1,000) death rate among the Canadian Sarcee (Sarsi) was largely the result of tuberculosis.

In response, in both the Canadian and U.S. Great Plains a rudimentary system of health care delivery was developed that included hospital-based care, civilian physicians, and field matrons. In particular, tuberculosis, trachoma, and high infant mortality rates were targeted. Prior to 1940, however, health care delivery to Plains reservations and reserves was plagued by inadequate facilities, a lack of medical supplies, personnel problems, as well as by a general resistance to western medicine. Western medical practices were rejected both because they were culturally alien and also because they undermined Indigenous healing and associated religious beliefs.

In Canada after World War II the responsibility for Native health services was transferred to Health and Welfare Canada, and then, in the 1970s, to the Department of Indian Affairs and Northern Development. In the United States, since the mid-1960s the goal of the Indian Health Service has been to bring Native American health up to the level of the rest of the nation. Still, the health of Native Americans and First Nations remains well below the national averages.

Indeed, the Native peoples of the Plains have similar epidemiological and demographic profiles to those found in the developing world. They are young, poorly educated, and have low income, and their societies are characterized by high fertility and mortality rates, with prevalent occurrences of chronic diseases and social pathologies. Plains Indians have a life expectancy that is seven years lower than the U.S. and Canadian averages. Infant mortality, though falling, was still 3.5 times higher among First Nations of the Prairies than in Canada as a whole in 1996, and in 2000 the infant mortality rate in the Aberdeen, South Dakota, service area exceeded the national average by more than 50 percent.

With the notable exception of another introduced disease, the human immunodeficiency virus that leads to AIDS, infectious diseases on the reservations and reserves have waned because of improvements in sanitation and, to a degree, rising standards of living. The three leading causes of death are now heart disease, malignant neoplasms (tumors), and accidents. Type 2 diabetes, hypertension, and arthritis are also prevalent, and alcoholism, substance abuse, homicide, and family violence also occur at rates substantially higher than the national averages. To one degree or another, these are all afflictions of poverty and associated dysfunctional lifestyles and behavior.

Although such statistics reveal how large the gap is in health equity between Plains Indigenous and non-Indigenous peoples, improvements are being made on a number of health fronts. Great Plains tribes are assuming greater responsibility in defining their health needs and controlling health resources. They are integrating traditional medical practices with western medical techniques to address their health concerns in a culturally appropriate manner. It is hoped that the result will be sustained improvements in health.

Gregory R. Campbell
University of Montana

Campbell, Gregory R. "Indian Health Service." In *Native America in the Twentieth Century: An Encyclopedia*, edited by Mary B. Davis. New York: Garland Publishing, Inc., 1994: 256–61. Waldram, James B., D. Ann Herring, and T. Kue Young. *Aboriginal Health in Canada: Historical, Cultural, and Epidemiological Perspectives.* Toronto: University of Toronto Press, 1995. Young, T. Kue. *The Health of Native Americans: Towards a Biocultural Epidemiology.* New York: Oxford University Press, 1994.

HIDATSAS

The Hidatsas, an Indian people of the Northern Plains, have lived in what is now west-central North Dakota for nearly a millennium. The name "Hidatsa," which refers to the willows growing on Missouri River sandbars, was once applied to a single band but later encompassed the entire people. Along with the Mandans and the Arikaras, the Hidatsas were the northernmost Plains people to construct large, permanent earth lodge villages and to practice agriculture intensively. Composed in the early historic era of three closely related bands—the Hidatsa-proper, Awatixa, and Awaxawi—each spoke a distinct dialect of Siouan language and maintained unique identities and traditions of separate origin. Awaxawi and Hidatsa-proper traditions describe the people emerging from an underground world near a large body of water, often identified with Devils Lake in eastern North Dakota, and a migration and later meeting with the Mandans, a people with whom the Hidatsa have been intimately associated to the present day. The Awatixa, in contrast, maintain they have always resided on the Missouri River.

During the late eighteenth and early nineteenth centuries, when European and European American observers began to record their encounters with Northern Plains Indians, the Hidatsas lived in three villages perched on bluffs near the junction of the Knife and Missouri Rivers. Archeologists now believe the Hidatsas, specifically the Awatixa, had established themselves in the area as early as 1100 A.D. Although Hidatsas traveled widely and maintained extensive ties, especially trade ties, to other peoples throughout the Northern Plains and beyond, their villages and river valley environs remained at the heart of their collective life. Villages, with their large numbers of domed, multifamily earth lodges, were principally the domain of Hidatsa women, as well as the children and elderly in their care. For men, villages were a place of return and departure, as their lives frequently led them abroad for hunting and raiding. Rivers provided water, clay for pottery, places for recreation and play, and avenues for travel. Spring floods nourished the river-bottom gardens cultivated by Hidatsa women that yielded an abundance of corn, squash, beans, and sunflowers for their own consumption and for an extensive trade. Men found ample game, including white-tailed deer, along wooded bottoms, but they also turned to the High Plains beyond to hunt bison and pronghorn antelope with friends and family in semiannual hunts.

Clans and societies incorporated each Hidatsa person and bound them together in mutual obligation while also providing care, identity, and community. Membership in the seven or eight clans active in the historic era was matrilineal and cut across the three Hidatsa groups, integrating these distinct communities. Men's and women's societies provided various social services, and membership changed over the course of an individual's life. Likewise, religious observation and devotion were woven throughout daily life. The Hidatsas recognized their world as variously endowed with spirits to be acknowledged and respected, and prayer was offered frequently in a recognition of, and request for, assistance from the power inherent in all things. Individuals, often male, pursued visions and sought guidance even in childhood, presenting acts of self-sacrifice as evidence of their reverence and purpose. Rewarded with a successful vision, an individual would make a small personal bundle as a representation of powers to be called upon for assistance. Larger bundles, associated with clans or societies, afforded power and protection but required observation of unique ritual care by a trained owner.

The encounter with European and, later, European American newcomers placed unprecedented challenges before the Hidatsas. Some aspects of change were welcome, including the adoption of horses and the expansion of the long-established Aboriginal trade network to incorporate newcomers. But disease, decline in population, and the necessity of defense from the more numerous Sioux (Lakotas) proved especially daunting. Before the cycle of epidemics, the Hidatsas may have numbered 5,000 to 6,000 people, but at least as early as the 1780s their population began to decline. In 1837 a smallpox epidemic killed half of the Hidatsa people in a matter of months, leaving only 1,200 to 1,400 survivors. These losses, combined with even more devastating losses suffered by the Mandans, led to the establishment of a single, shared village, Like-a-Fishhook, in 1845. There the Mandans and Hidatsas were joined by the Arikaras in 1862. In 1870 the three peoples were placed on the eight-million-acre Fort Berthold Reservation in present-day central North Dakota. By the end of the nineteenth century, the Hidatsa population had declined to some 400 people.

Early in the 1880s, in keeping with the government's assimilation policy, the Hidatsas, Mandans, and Arikaras were encouraged to abandon Like-a-Fishhook Village and to establish family farms on individual allotments. While some Hidatsa families chose to do so, many continued to reside in small towns and communities—Lucky Mound, Shell Creek, and Independence—established close to the Missouri River, where they pursued ranching and other enterprises. The size of the reservation was reduced to less than one million acres by allotments.

The 1930s saw a respite from overt demands for assimilation and a revision of Fort Berthold's tribal government as the Three Affiliated Tribes under the Indian Reorganization Act (IRA) of 1934. But challenges continued. With the construction of Garrison Dam during the 1950s, some 156,000 acres of Fort Berthold Reservation, home to 90 percent of the tribal community, were flooded. Tribal leaders had resisted the project but finally yielded to congressional pressure and accepted a twelve-million-dollar compensation package. Relocation continued even as the water rose, and many Hidatsas moved to the town of Mandaree. An additional $143 million was appropriated by Congress in 1992, but the dislocation and disruption caused by the Garrison Dam are felt to this day.

See also WATER: Pick-Sloan Plan.

J. Wendel Cox
Arizona State University

Ahler, Stanley A., Thomas D. Thiessen, and Michael K. Trimble. *People of the Willows: The Prehistory and Early History of the Hidatsa Indians.* Grand Forks: University of North Dakota Press, 1991. Gilman, Carolyn, and Mary Jane Schneider. *The Way to Independence: Memories of a Hidatsa Indian Family, 1840–1920.* St. Paul: Minnesota Historical Society Press, 1987. Meyer, Roy W. *The Village Indians of the Upper Missouri: The Mandans, Hidatsas, and Arikaras.* Lincoln: University of Nebraska Press, 1977.

HOGAN, LINDA

See LITERARY TRADITIONS: Hogan, Linda

HOLLYWOOD INDIANS

See FILM: Hollywood Indians

HORSE

So much has been written about the coming of the horse to the Western Hemisphere with the Spanish invasion that it is often forgotten that the Americas are the home of the modern, single-hoofed horse, *Equus.* Having evolved from the tiny, one-foot-tall and three-toed *Hyracotherium* some two million years ago, the modern horse migrated from North America to Asia over the Bering Strait land bridge. When the first humans crossed the strait in the opposite direction after about 20,000 B.C., they found the Great Plains teeming with horses, which for several millennia were among the many species of megafauna hunted by the first Plains peoples. Then, some 8,000 to 10,000 years ago, the horse followed the mammoth, camel, and other large American mammals into extinction, apparently as the victim of overhunting and a changing climate.

The ensuing intermission in the history of Plains Indian horse use lasted until the early seventeenth century, when the Spanish reintroduced the animal. Although horses began to infiltrate the Plains soon after the Spanish settled New Mexico in 1598, widespread diffusion began only after the Pueblo Revolt of 1680. The subsequent Spanish abandonment of New Mexico put large numbers of livestock into the hands of Pueblo Indians, who embarked on an active horse trade with Plains nomads. Carried forward by Plains Indian raiders and traders, the horse frontier advanced rapidly, reaching the Missouri River in the 1730s and the Canadian Prairies in the 1770s.

The horse that the Spanish brought to the Americas was the famed barb horse, a mix of Arab and Spanish stock. Bred to survive in the North African deserts, these small but sturdy animals found a fitting ecological niche in the dry, grass-covered Southern Plains. By 1800 Comanches, Kiowas, and other Native groups of the area possessed enormous herds. The region between the Rio Grande and the Arkansas River also supported about two million wild horses, which had propagated from strays left by raiders. However, as the horse frontier expanded northward through the Plains, it lost its momentum. The harsh northern winters reduced horses' reproductive success, and the heavy snowfall made feeding difficult, causing severe winter losses. Combined, these factors prevented most Northern Plains groups from becoming fully mounted. While the Southern Plains Indians had as many as four to six horses per person, only the Piegans in the Northern Plains had enough animals to put all their people on horseback.

Horses revolutionized the Plains Indian way of life by allowing their owners to hunt, trade, and wage war more effectively, to have bigger tipis and move more possessions, and to transport their old and sick, who might previously have been abandoned. The impact of the horse was most dramatic on the Southern Plains, where a true equestrian culture emerged. Comanches, Kiowas, Arapahos, and Cheyennes, who became specialized horse raiders and herders, maintained large herds of surplus animals for trade with other Native groups and European Americans. Horses also became the foundation of status systems by changing relatively egalitarian societies into nascent class societies based on horse ownership. In fact, so attractive was this new horse culture that many groups—most notably Comanches, Lakotas, and Cheyennes—abandoned their traditional homelands for an equestrian existence in the Plains. In doing so, they became some of the most refined and celebrated equestrian societies in history, matched only by the great horse cultures of Asia. However, the large horse herds also disturbed the region's delicate ecological balance, as they competed for water and grass with native species. By the early 1840s the crucial river valleys had already become overexploited, pushing the massive bison herds into an early decline. It is also possible that horses triggered a decline in women's status because the bison hunt became more the domain of the mounted male hunter rather than of the society at large.

The horse culture established weaker roots in the Northern Plains, where the lack of animals prevented the Indians from making a full equestrian transition. Plains Crees, Assiniboines, and other northern groups relied extensively on inferior dog transportation and pedestrian hunting methods. The shortage of animals also encouraged warfare, as tribes tried to stock their herds by raiding their neighbors. Yet another variation of the full-fledged horse culture emerged among the Pawnees, Wichitas, and other horticulturists of the eastern Plains, for whom the horse was a mixed blessing. Horses encouraged these farmers to diversify their economies by allowing them to increase the role of bison hunting in their subsistence cycles. Mandans, Hidatsas, and Arikaras on the upper Missouri River enhanced their role as the paramount traders in the Plains when they started to channel horses from the Southern to the Northern Plains. But horses also overtaxed local ecosystems, obliging the Pawnees, for example, to stay away

from their villages for extended periods of time. Horses also attracted raiders. After 1830 Lakota war parties swept down on Pawnee villages almost every year, seeking horses, corn, and honor, and precipitating the decline of this once-powerful people.

The beginning of the reservation period after 1850 marked the end of the Plains horse cultures, but it did not end the association between Indians and horses. During the difficult early years of reservation life, many previously nomadic groups turned to cattle and horse ranching as an alternative to the forced, alien agrarian lifestyle. Rodeo has offered another important way to maintain the connection with horses. On a more abstract level, most people still link Plains Indians and horses almost automatically, and the Hollywood film industry has sold the visual image of the mounted Plains warrior as the stereotype for all North American Indians. To many Indians the horse continues to symbolize their traditional cultures and lifeways as they existed before the European American takeover. From celebration parades and art to actual herds on reservation fields, horses are still integral to Plains Indian life.

Pekka Hämäläinen
Texas A&M University

Ewers, John C. *The Horse in the Blackfoot Indian Culture.* Washington DC: Bureau of American Ethnology, 1955. Holder, Preston. *The Hoe and Horse on the Plains: A Study of Cultural Development among North American Indians.* Lincoln: University of Nebraska Press, 1970.

HOWLING WOLF

See ART: Howling Wolf

HUNTING

The celebrated horse-mounted bison hunters of the eighteenth and nineteenth centuries in the Great Plains have captured the popular imagination, but their reign represents only a relatively short phase in the long and complex history of Plains Indian hunting. Twelve thousand years ago, the Plains was home to eight-ton mastodons, twelve-feet-tall mammoths, giant bison, and wild horses. A growing number of Clovis people hunted these massive animals by driving them into swamps or box canyons and piercing their hides with sharp, fluted darts and spears using atlatls, or leverlike spear throwers. Such ventures were dangerous, but the rewards were worth the risk: a single kill could keep a hunting group of thirty to fifty people furnished with meat and fat for weeks. By around 9000 B.C., however, warming climate, changing vegetation cover, and, apparently, overhunting pushed the Pleistocene megafauna into extinction, marking the end of the first great hunting culture of the Plains.

The Plains people adjusted to the disappearance of large mammals by concentrating their efforts on smaller animals such as deer, elk, pronghorn antelopes, grizzlies, and modern species of bison. They perfected a wide range of killing techniques: they camouflaged themselves in animal skins and patiently

stalked their prey; ambushed individual animals at water holes; drove entire herds into manmade corrals; or stampeded bison over high bluffs and then slaughtered the crippled animals with spears, darts, and stones. About 2,000 years ago Plains Indians also learned the use of the bow and arrow, which allowed them to kill effectively from a safe distance.

By about 1000 A.D., however, encouraged by a wetter climate, the Plains people began to focus increasingly on farming, and hunting gradually became a secondary economic activity. By the thirteenth century there were still large numbers of nomadic hunters on the western shortgrass Plains (where Spanish explorers would encounter their descendants in the sixteenth century), but most Plains Indians lived along the eastern river valleys, where they based their economies on farming and sporadic hunting excursions.

This trend was suddenly reversed in the seventeenth and eighteenth centuries when horses became available to the Plains Indians. The horse was the missing tool that made it possible for Indians to begin a systematic exploitation of the enormous resource of protein, fat, and hides that was stored in the bodies of an estimated 30 million bison in the Plains. On horseback, hunters could follow the migrating herds more closely and over a wider range, kill the animals more efficiently, and carry back more meat and hides. Attracted by previously unimagined hunting possibilities, Indians poured into the Plains from all directions, creating one of most renowned hunting cultures in history.

By the early nineteenth century the Plains Indians had mastered an array of equestrian bison-hunting techniques that were carefully adapted to the seasonal and geographical variations of the region. In the winter, hunters drove bison into snow-filled gulches or snowdrifts, and in the summer, into swamps, rivers, or corrals. In the Northern Plains, where horses were in short supply, many groups continued to rely on pedestrian hunting techniques, such as the foot surround. Many Plains groups also burned sections of grasslands to make bison migrations and aggregations more predictable. The most popular method was the mounted chase, in which hunters galloped after bison on carefully trained running horses, thrusting lances or shooting volleys of arrows at the sides of the animals. A short bow remained the bison hunters' preferred weapon, because muskets were difficult to load and handle on horseback, and because powder and ball were scarce and expensive, and thus better reserved for warfare.

In the winter and spring Plains Indians usually hunted in small groups of few individuals, but in the summer and fall, when bison congregated into massive herds, hunting became a collective effort of hundreds of people. A typical mass hunt involved several stages, each consecrated by rituals. The preparation began with a bison-calling ceremony, usually a dance, song, or prayer performed by a medicine man. When the herd was located, a camp police of distinguished warriors took over, making sure nobody would try to start the hunt prematurely and stampede the herd. On the chief's order, the entire camp moved out as an orderly column—first the scouts, then medicine men, priests, and leaders, and finally old men, women, and children. Young men rode on both sides of the column, providing protection and ready to charge when the prey came in sight. The actual hunt might take only about thirty minutes, for bison had more endurance than horses and could pull away in few minutes, but that was enough time for most hunters to bring down several animals. After the chase was over, the families moved in to butcher their animals (each hunter used arrows and lances of his own design for recognition), turning the carcasses swiftly into piles of sliced meat, tallow, and hides. A successful hunt ended with ritual smoking, dancing, and feasting, which helped Indians maintain a proper relationship with animal spirits.

Although all Plains groups continued to hunt deer, elk, bears, porcupines, and other animals for clothing, food, tools, and jewelry, by the late eighteenth century most Plains Indians had developed a singular dependency on the buffalo. The western Plains became the domain of highly specialized hunter-nomads who fed, clothed, sheltered, and decorated themselves from the skin, flesh, fat, and bones of the bison. What they could not get by hunting, they acquired by trading surplus hides, dried meat, pemmican, and other products of the hunt. The eastern horticulturists, too, intensified their hunting practices and began to make extended semiannual hunting expeditions to the western Plains.

This emphasis on bison hunting persisted even after the advent of the commercial fur trade in the late eighteenth century. Some northern groups began producing deerskins and beaver pelts for trading posts, but most Plains Indians refused to take up trapping and instead provisioned European American trappers with bison meat and pemmican. From the 1830s on, following the collapse of beaver trade, bison robes became the primary focus of the fur trade, and during the following four decades Plains Indians produced more than 200,000 hides and skins and 40 to 100 tons of pemmican a year for European American markets.

Such reliance on a narrow ecological base ultimately proved unsustainable, pushing the bison populations into a steep decline by the mid–nineteenth century. The traditional Plains Indian hunting culture came to an end in the 1870s and 1880s with the near extermination of the bison by commercial white hunters and the often violent removal of Indians into reservations, where Indian agents endeavored to transform them from hunters into farmers. Some Indians refused to give up their chosen lifestyle and continued to leave reservations in a desperate search for the few surviving bison. By the 1890s, however, all Plains Indians had been forced to abandon their dream of living as hunters. Today, a few Plains Indians make a living by hunting, or by mixing hunting with other economic activities, but even these efforts are threatened by the ongoing legal struggles among tribal, state, and federal governments over hunting rights.

Pekka Hämäläinen
Texas A&M University

Frison, George C. *Prehistoric Hunters of the High Plains*. San Diego: Academic Press, 1991. Isenberg, Andrew C. *The Destruction of the Bison: An Environmental History, 1750–1920*. Cambridge: Cambridge University Press, 2000. Lowie, Robert H. *Indians of the Plains*. New York: McGraw-Hill Book Company, Inc., 1954.

INDIAN AGENTS

See POLITICS AND GOVERNMENT: Indian Agents

INDIAN BOARDING SCHOOLS, UNITED STATES

See EDUCATION: Indian Boarding Schools, United States

INDIAN CLAIMS COMMISSION

See LAW: Indian Claims Commission

INDIAN COUNTRY TODAY

See MEDIA: *Indian Country Today*

INDIAN COWBOYS

Plains Indians have been cowboys for a long time. Their involvement in the cattle industry of the region began in the late nineteenth century and continues to the present. Indian men and women have also been involved for an extended period of time in the world of rodeo. Their participation in ranching and rodeo is significant both in economic and cultural terms.

After the American Civil War, cattle ranching played an important role in the economic development of the Plains. This development came at considerable cost. Native communities lost millions of acres through treaties, agreements, land allotment, land cessions, and long-term leases. With bison hunting no longer possible, Plains Indian peoples had to find alternative means to sustain themselves. Cattle ranching offered Indian men a chance to ride, an alternative to farming, and an opportunity to demonstrate both competence and generosity. Cattle could be given as presents, used to feed people at a gathering, and employed to teach young people about responsibility and reciprocity. Given their needs and given the success their new neighbors were enjoying, it is not surprising that so many Indian individuals and communities turned to cattle ranching. Some, like Quanah Parker, knew spectacular, if too brief, success. Others started ranches that continue to our own day. Many Native cowboys also found work as cowboys on ranches owned by non-Indians.

Progress in the Indian cattle industry during the twentieth century was limited by fluctuating federal policies and market conditions, as well as the problems of fractionated land-ownership because of the division of allotted land through inheritance and sale. Nonetheless, many Indian ranchers continue in the business, either through tribal or community enterprises or as individuals. They know the same satisfactions and experience the same problems as their non-Indian counterparts. Access to better legal counsel has permitted tribes in many instances to obtain more equitable leases or to promote ranching by tribal members.

Plains Indian rodeo dates back to the turn of the century. At agricultural fairs at the Crow Indian Reservation and elsewhere, rodeos began to be featured as prominent components of annual gatherings. The Crows took great pride in their abilities and accomplishments as bronc riders. At Rosebud and other reservations in the Dakotas, Lakota cowboys also demonstrated their talents in various rodeos. The best Indian cowboys, like Sam Bird in Ground (Crow) and George Defender (Standing Rock Sioux), captured world championship titles early in the twentieth century. Tom Three Persons (Blood) won instant immortality by riding Midnight in the first Calgary Stampede rodeo in 1912.

The Plains Indian rodeo tradition continues. Plains Indian cowgirls and cowboys participate in regional competitions, often instructed and judged by relatives eager to pass along their love for the sport, and they have also enjoyed considerable success in the Indian National Finals Rodeo. Names like Gladstone and Guardipee, Bird and Bruised Head are immediately recognizable to all those who cherish the history and heritage of Indian rodeo.

See also AGRICULTURE: Cattle Ranching / SPORTS AND RECREATION: Crow Fair; Rodeo.

Peter Iverson
Arizona State University

Dempsey, Hugh A. *Tom Three Persons: Legend of an Indian Cowboy*. Saskatoon: Purich Publishing, 1997. Iverson, Peter. *When Indians Became Cowboys: Native Peoples and Cattle Ranching in the American West*. Norman: University of Oklahoma Press, 1994. Iverson, Peter, and Linda MacCannell. *Riders from the West: Portraits of Indian Rodeo*. Seattle: University of Washington Press, 1999.

INDIAN POLICE

See LAW: Indian Police

INDIAN REMOVAL

The policy of the U.S. government to move Native Americans from their homelands to other locations was part of the clash of cultures brought about by the colonization of North America. There was no such policy of forcible removals from east to west in Canada; even within the Prairie Provinces, First Nations were given considerable choice in the selection of their reserves. U.S. policy was formalized in the Indian Removal Act of 1830, which gave President Andrew Jackson the authority to make treaties with tribes by which they would exchange land east of the Mississippi River for lands to the west. By that time, however, removals had been taking place for more than two decades.

President Thomas Jefferson initiated the idea of removal with the Louisiana Purchase in 1803. He saw a new western territory where Native Americans could live their traditional lifestyles far removed from often deleterious contact with Americans. The rationale was that moving Native Americans to this Permanent Indian Frontier would open up land in the eastern United States for European American settlers, while protecting them until such time as they were willing and able to assimilate into American society. Jefferson also believed that consolidating Native Americans in the Great Plains would create a barrier that would prevent American settlers from dispersing too widely. In the 1820s and 1830s, Baptist missionary Isaac McCoy even campaigned to create a separate Indian state in the Great Plains, where Native Americans could be taught the precepts of American civilization, but the idea did not receive serious attention in Congress.

As early as 1808 the Sauks and Foxes moved voluntarily from Illinois to Missouri to escape the disruption of their lives by white settlers. From 1817 to 1820 federal agents signed treaties with the Delawares in Ohio and the Kickapoos and Weas in Illinois by which the tribes agreed to exchange their lands for others in Illinois and Missouri. By 1817 leaders of the Cherokees in Georgia had agreed to a treaty that provided individual allotments for those who agreed to be citizens of the state and remain on their land, or a tract of land west of the Mississippi for those who chose to move. The Choctaws signed a similar treaty in 1820. Removal policy led to divisions within tribes between those who agreed to stay in their homelands and adapt to new ways and those who decided to move west and try to retain their cultural identities. Even before formal legislation for Indian removal, some Choctaw and Cherokee families were moving west of the Mississippi to settle on lands guaranteed to them by treaty.

By the time of Andrew Jackson's election to the presidency in 1828, the prospect of ridding the east of Native Americans appealed greatly to land speculators, and Jackson's strong sense of nationalism led him to reject the idea that tribes could exist as sovereign nations within the confines of American territory. Within ten years of the passage of the Indian Removal Act, vast areas of the Midwest and the southeastern United States had been "cleared" and the Native American residents removed to tracts of land in the present-day states of Kansas and Oklahoma.

North of the Ohio River a great variety of Native American communities were shifted west. These included Peorias, Kaskaskias, Sauks and Foxes, Piankashaws, Weas, Shawnees, Ottawas, Wyandottes, Potawatomis, Delawares, and Kickapoos. Many of these groups suffered multiple removals. The Delawares, for example, were originally from eastern Pennsylvania. They subsequently moved to Ohio, Illinois, Missouri, and, in 1829, to Kansas. The Kickapoos also ended up in eastern Kansas in 1832, after first being moved from southern Ohio and then from southwestern Missouri.

By 1841 emigrant Native Americans occupied squared-off tracts along the eastern portions of the Great Plains from present-day Nebraska to Texas. They were settled on land that was purchased from Indigenous Plains tribes, such as the Pawnees and Kaws, and frequently conflicts ensued between the emigrants and the local Native Americans.

Major removal treaties were also negotiated with the southeastern tribes. The Choctaws signed the Treaty of Dancing Rabbit Creek in 1830, in large part because the state of Mississippi extended its laws over the tribe and made illegal the operations of the tribal government. The state of Georgia also sought to regulate the Cherokees. The Creeks, Seminoles, and Chickasaws signed treaties in 1832, and the Cherokees signed the Treaty of New Echota in 1835. As a result of these treaties, approximately 60,000 members of these tribes made the trek west to the land designated as Indian Territory in the eastern half of what is now Oklahoma. For the Creeks, Seminoles, and Cherokees, these were forced marches under the U.S. Army. It is estimated that approximately one-quarter of the refugees died along the trail from illness, exposure, or starvation.

After 1854 the tide of European American settlement reached the Great Plains, and the Permanent Indian Frontier fragmented into reservations, where Indigenous Plains peoples and emigrant tribes were segregated and placed under great pressure to acculturate. In the following three decades, as their reservations were surrounded by settlers, many of these Indians, including the Pawnees, Poncas, Cheyennes, Arapahos, Comanches, Potawatomis, and Kickapoos, made their final migration to Indian Territory, where many of their descendants remain today.

Clara Sue Kidwell
University of Oklahoma

Abel, Annie H. "The History of Events Resulting in Indian Consolidation West of the Mississippi." In *Annual Report of the American Historical Association for the Year 1906*. Washington DC: Government Printing Office, 1908. Foreman, Grant. *Indian Removal: The Emigration of the Five Civilized Tribes of Indians*. Norman: University of Oklahoma Press, 1953.

INDIAN RESIDENTIAL SCHOOLS, CANADA

See EDUCATION: Indian Residential Schools, Canada

INDIAN SCOUTS

See WAR: Indian Scouts

INDIAN TERRITORY

All of Oklahoma was referred to as "Indian Territory" until 1890, when Congress partitioned Oklahoma Territory and made "Indian Territory" the formal name for the Five Civilized Tribes' domain. Indian Territory's relevance to the Great Plains thus spans from the 1820s, when the United States cleared title through treaty cessions by the Quapaws (1818)

and Osages (1825) and designated the area as "Indian Country," to the Oklahoma land runs, beginning in 1889.

The area had long been permanently or seasonally occupied by Great Plains peoples, notably the Wichitas, Kiowas, and Plains Apaches. Comanche, Cheyenne, Arapaho, and Pawnee bison hunters also knew it well in the 1820s, as did hunters from the east, including bands of Cherokees, who came to the Arkansas and Red River areas decades before their nation was forcibly relocated there. The treaties that forced the Five Tribes to remove from their eastern homelands in the 1830s gave them roughly equivalent areas in Indian Territory, overlapping the eastern margin of the Great Plains.

The Five Tribes' three ribbons of Great Plains land included the Cherokee Outlet in the north, a strip between this and the Canadian River shared by the Creek and Seminole Nations, and a wide expanse between the Canadian and North Fork of the Red River owned by the Choctaws and Chickasaws (Texas began west of the North Fork). The Five Tribes' settlements clung to the safe, humid, accessible, alluvial valleys to the east, which left the Kiowas and Comanches to command their western lands.

Beginning in the 1850s western Indian Territory became a dumping ground for dispossessed Plains Indians. When the Chickasaws and Choctaws separated in 1855, they leased the western third of their domain to the United States to resettle Texas Indians. After the Civil War the Five Tribes were forced to cede their western lands to make room for new reservations. The eastern third of the Cherokee, Creek, and Seminole holdings was parceled among a diverse set of Native American refugees, creating a cluster of small, poverty-stricken reservations. The western lands of the Seminoles, Choctaws, and Chickasaws became reservations for the Cheyennes and Arapahos, Comanches, and Kiowas and Apaches, following their brutal suppression by the army in the 1860s and 1870s, which also coincided with the era of the cattle drives through the area.

By the 1880s reservation farming was largely unsuccessful, since the most rational land use for land-rich, capital-poor Indians was to lease land to white cattlemen. For quite different reasons, farmers and humanitarian reformers agreed that the communal land tenure on reservations had to end. In 1887 Congress passed the General Allotment (Dawes) Act, which required tribal members to select 160 acres of land for their own use, although title would be held for a period of years by the government. The acreage that remained was then opened to white settlement. The reservations of western Indian Territory were allotted in the late 1880s and early 1890s. This was immediately followed by land runs and lotteries that brought tens of thousands of white families to the region.

See also POLITICS AND GOVERNMENT: Oklahoma.

Brad A. Bays
Oklahoma State University

Debo, Angie. *And Still the Waters Run: The Betrayal of the Five Civilized Tribes.* Princeton NJ: Princeton University Press, 1940. Gibson, Arrell Morgan. *Oklahoma: A History of Five Centuries.* Norman: University of Oklahoma Press, 1981. Morris, John W., Charles R. Goins, and Edwin C. McReynolds. *Historical Atlas of Oklahoma.* Norman: University of Oklahoma Press, 1986.

INDIAN TRAILS

See TRANSPORTATION: Indian Trails

INTERTRIBAL WARFARE

See WAR: Intertribal Warfare

JUMANOS

Jumano is the standard ethnonym applied by scholars to a Native American people who, between the sixteenth and eighteenth centuries, were variously identified as Jumano, Humana, Xuman, Sumana, and Chouman. Modern interest began in 1890, when Adolph Bandelier observed that the Jumanos, evidently an important Indian nation during the early days of Spanish exploration north of Mexico, had virtually disappeared from the historical record by 1700. Scholars have since ranged far and wide in pursuit of the identity and the fate of the Jumanos: Frederick W. Hodge believed them to be Caddoans, ancestors of the Wichitas; Carl Sauer favored a Uto-Aztecan affiliation, linking them to the Tarahumaras and other Mexican Indians; Jack D. Forbes argued that they were early Apacheans. In 1940 France V. Scholes and H. P. Mera proposed that "Jumano" was simply a generic term that Spanish colonists had used to designate all Indians who painted or tattooed their faces with horizontal lines; in view of the diversity of opinion, it is not surprising that this suggestion found wide acceptance. Recently, Nancy P. Hickerson has reopened the discussion, citing inferential evidence that the Jumanos' language (never recorded) was actually Tanoan, closely related to that of their trading partners in the eastern Pueblos of New Mexico.

Bandelier's data provided no clues to Jumano prehistory, nor did he speculate about their linguistic or cultural links with other tribes. During the intervening century, archival and archeological research has revealed a fuller—if still incomplete—picture of their adaptation and possible origins. The Jumanos ranged from south of the Rio Grande to the Southern Plains. Within this territory they were essentially nomadic, although there were permanent enclaves at La Junta de los Rios (near present-day Ojinaga, Chihuahua), in the Tompiro Pueblos of New Mexico, and perhaps elsewhere. Their eastward movements were timed to coincide with seasonal rains and prime bison hunting in the Plains; the return trip brought the Jumano bands back to spend the winter at or near the communities of their trading partners. There, meat, hides, and other trophies of the hunt were traded for agricultural produce. Such a relationship of reciprocity between related farmers and hunter-gatherers has many parallels and often develops as an adaptation to changing ecological conditions.

The historical importance of the Jumanos rests primarily on their role as intertribal and interregional traders. This role undoubtedly developed as a consequence of their pattern of seasonal migration. The Southern Plains was a hunting area shared by many Native American groups—Caddoan, Tonkawan, Coahuiltecan, and others. The Jumanos established a close relationship with the Caddos and their neighbors (the "Tejas" alliance) and became active agents in trade between these tribes and those along the Rio Grande. Their routes followed and linked several river systems, including the Pecos, Canadian, Brazos, and Colorado of Texas.

The Jumanos' trade sphere expanded when they adopted an equestrian way of life, and it changed in character as they began to deal in horses. Records of French explorer La Salle's visits to the Ceni (Caddos) reveal the impact of the Jumano trade, which provided the Caddo elite with Spanish clothing, swords, religious artifacts, and many horses; on the return trip, hides and peltries were carried for sale in New Spain. At this time the Jumano traders were, in effect, serving as Spanish surrogates in promoting friendly relations between the "Nations of the North" (the Caddoan confederacies) and the Spanish Crown.

Even as their interregional trade reached its height, the Jumanos' territorial base was increasingly under attack. Apaches and Jumanos were in contention, both for hunting grounds and for trade access along the Rio Grande. In 1540 Coronado's expedition witnessed the enmity between Querechos (Apaches) and Teyas (probably Jumanos). By 1600 the Apaches had taken control of the trade at Pecos Pueblo, and they dominated a wide area east of that site. In the Tompiro region, farther south, the Jumano population was augmented by refugees from the war in the Plains. When the Tompiros also came under attack, around 1660, the Jumanos abandoned New Mexico for good; thereafter, La Junta de los Rios was their only foothold on the Rio Grande. The Jumanos' trade continued from La Junta following a route along the lower Pecos and Colorado Rivers. This route was broken around 1690, when Apache bands pushed eastward to the upper Colorado and the Brazos. Thereafter, the Jumanos had no intact territorial base, and their activities as traders came to an end. Remnant groups around La Junta evidently joined forces with their conquerors after 1700, when Apache occupancy extended southward along the Rio Grande below El Paso.

Throughout the seventeenth century there were several occasions in which Jumano leaders acted as spokesmen for their own and allied tribes, seeking Spanish assistance in defending their territories and trade routes. In 1682 the Jumano chief Juan Sabeata addressed such an appeal to New Mexican authorities at El Paso and escorted a party of soldiers and Franciscan friars to meet with representatives of more than thirty Indian nations on the upper Colorado of Texas. When this effort failed, a remarkable transregional economic and political alliance came to an end, and the Jumanos effectively vanished from the history of the Southern Plains.

Nancy Parrott Hickerson
Texas Tech University

Hickerson, Nancy P. *The Jumanos: Hunters and Traders of the South Plains.* Austin: University of Texas Press, 1994. Kelley, J. Charles. "Juan Sabeata and Diffusion in Aboriginal Texas." *American Anthropologist* 57 (1955): 981–95. Scholes, France V., and H. P. Mera. "Some Aspects of the Jumano Problem." *Contributions to American Anthropology and History* 6 (1940): 269–99.

KAWS

The Kaw, or Kanza, Indians refer to themselves collectively as the Kaw Nation. The names Kaw and Kanza appear on the tribe's national seal, but Kaw is the identity used by members. Kaw means "Wind People." The Kaws are part of the Dhegiha branch of the Central Siouan speaking peoples, a group that includes Quapaws, Osages, Omahas, and Poncas. According to their histories, these tribes once lived together along or near the lower Ohio Valley. They began to migrate westward around 1300 A.D., and by the 1700s the Kaws were firmly situated in present northeastern Kansas and northwestern Missouri.

From the late eighteenth century until the late 1820s, the Kaws, numbering about 1,500, lived in a single village near present Manhattan, Kansas. Their territory extended throughout most of the Kansas Valley and the lower reaches of its tributaries from about the Delaware River west to the Solomon and Smoky Hill Rivers. Within this core, the Kaws exercised nearly total territorial control. Their hunting range extended west to the upper Republican River and south to the saline plains of the present Kansas-Oklahoma border.

The Kaws' subsistence operated on an annual cycle of hunting, horticulture, raiding, and trading. Beginning in April, Kaw women planted corn, beans, pumpkins, melons, and squash in small fields around the village. They also gathered nuts, berries, roots, tubers, and wood in the riparian forest adjacent to the Kansas and Blue Rivers. Kaw males pastured their horses on nearby upland prairie and hunted (mostly elk and deer) along the Kansas River. After planting ended in early May, the Kaws left for their annual summer bison hunt. Along the way to the bison grounds, they hunted deer and elk, and small war parties frequently left to raid Pawnee villages. The Kaws primarily hunted along the middle Solomon, Smoky Hill, and Arkansas Rivers, where vast herds of bison sought water in summer. They returned to their village in mid-August to harvest their crops. In winter, the Kaws left their village again and traveled to the woodlands along the Missouri River in present northeastern Kansas and northwestern Missouri. There they scattered into small parties and hunted beaver, deer, elk, turkey, and other smaller game. The furs from these animals were exchanged for goods from French and American traders who regularly traveled the Missouri River. During this season, Kaw war parties raided Otoe, Iowa, Sauk, Fox, and Missouria villages. The Kaws reconvened at their village in mid-March.

This subsistence pattern also provided the Kaws with their material culture (dress, tools, utensils, weapons, and housing). Kaw dress, for instance, consisted of moccasins and leggings (made from deerskins), a breechcloth and girdle (acquired through trade), and a blanket or bison robe. Male warriors often wore necklaces of animal claws or of shells, beads, and metal ornaments (acquired through trade), and they carried a wire apparatus to keep their arms, chins, eyebrows, and scalp plucked (except for a strip of hair on the top of their heads). Both men and women used vermilion to dye their hair.

Circular earth lodges were the most common form of village housing. A lodge measured from thirty to sixty feet in diameter and housed an average of two families (or about ten persons). Each lodge consisted of an outer ring of wooden posts and four taller central posts that were then covered with a frame of stick or twig bundles, over which they laid grass or reed mats, tree bark, and earth. Inside a lodge they maintained a central fire pit (and a hole in the roof's center for smoke to escape) as well as storage pits for dried corn, beans, and other foods. When the Kaws were on the hunt, they lived in portable skin-covered tipis.

Kaw society was patrilineal, and it was divided into two halves, or moieties, each composed of eight clans, or gentes (consisting of several families each), whose members descended from a common ancestor. Politically, the Kaws were organized around a loose confederation headed by several chiefs. There were five civil chiefs, drawn from each of the five leading gentes. There were also several war chiefs, established warriors who ruled in matters of war. Chiefs were elected by a common council of the people because of their demonstrated wisdom, bravery, and generosity. Office was for life and succession was hereditary. Despite the chieftainships, usually no solid ruling authority was recognized. Most matters were still decided through common council, and some degree of factionalism was characteristic of Kaw politics.

In 1825 the U.S. government convinced the Kaws to cede their land and placed them on a reservation in present northern Kansas. For the next two decades, the Kaws were hemmed in by thousands of relocated Indians from the eastern United States. The influx of emigrant Indians and the expansion of the fur trade depleted small game in the region, and missionaries and government employees on the reservation introduced disease. The Kaws intensified their bison hunting, raided enemies with increasing frequency, and stole crops and animals from neighboring reservations and white settlements.

The Kaws maintained their population of 1,500 persons until midcentury, after which their numbers plummeted. The U.S. government restricted the Kaws to progressively smaller reservations (in 1846, 1859, and 1873). When officials opened Kansas Territory in 1854, settlers pushed the bison farther west, depleted grass and wood, peddled whiskey, and brought more disease to the tribe. Starvation was chronic, and frequent outbreaks of smallpox, cholera, and other illnesses continued to plague the tribe. When the Kaws were removed to Indian Territory in 1873, they numbered 500. By 1900 barely 200 full-blooded Kaws remained. Tragedy extended beyond death. Since religious knowledge was preserved within each gente, the demise of entire gente populations meant the loss of beliefs and customs. By the early twentieth century, much understanding of Kaw society, religion, and history was lost forever.

Congress dissolved the last Kaw reservation in 1902, and the lands were divided into individual allotments. Four years later the former reservation became part of Kay County, Oklahoma. Today, many Kaw descendants still reside in Kay County. According to the 1997 tribal enrollment, there are 2,269 Kaw Nation members. The last Kaw full-blood, William A. Mehojah Sr., died in Omaha, Nebraska, on April 23, 2000.

Benjamin Y. Dixon
University of Oklahoma

Unrau, William E. *The Kansa Indians, A History of the Wind People, 1673–1873*. Norman: University of Oklahoma Press, 1971. Wedel, Waldo R. "The Kansa Indians." *Transactions of the Kansas Academy of Science* 49 (1946) 1–35.

KIOWAS

The Kiowas believe that they originated in the Bitterroot Mountains of present-day Montana. They now call themselves *K'oigu*, the "Principal People." Earlier names, *Kwuda*, or *T'epda*, "Coming-Out People," commemorate the Kiowa creation story, when Saynday, the Kiowa trickster, transformed the subterranean-living Kiowas into ants, then commanded them to populate the earth's surface via a hollow cottonwood log. A pregnant woman became lodged in the log, preventing the majority of the ant-people from emerging; hence the small nineteenth century population of approximately 1,000 to 1,100 Kiowas.

Besides Saynday, other mythological culture heroes include the *Zaidethali*, or "Split Boys," who slew numerous monsters before one disappeared forever and the other transformed himself into the eucharistic *Thali-da-i*, or "Boy Medicines," known today as the Ten Medicines. During the height of the horse and buffalo culture (ca. 1750 to 1875), these sacred bundles were possessed by ten keepers whose main duty was to pray for the well-being of the people and to settle civil disputes.

Sometime in the mid–eighteenth century, the Kiowas and culturally affiliated Plains Apaches migrated from the Yellowstone River region southeastward toward the Black Hills and befriended the Crows. Between 1775 and 1805 the Kiowas and Plains Apaches were pushed farther south of the Black Hills by Lakotas and Cheyennes. Migrating south to the horse-rich Southern Plains, they initially came into conflict with the more numerous Comanches. After about 1800, however, the Kiowas, Comanches, and Plains Apaches (later referred to as KCA Indians) made an alliance and followed the migratory bison herds between the Arkansas and Red Rivers.

Mid-nineteenth-century Kiowa society consisted of ten to twenty hunting bands, each composed of several extended family groups, or kindreds. Each kindred was led by the oldest of a group of brothers, and each band was led by the most prominent man among the coalesced kindreds—the *topadok'i*, or "main chief." The Kiowas recognized four classes: *ondedau*, or "rich" people; the *ondegup'a*, "second best"; the *kwwn*, "poor"; and the *dapom*, or "worthless." Relatives were separated by sex and generation; for example, all cousins were classified as "brothers" and "sisters."

Until about 1847 the Kiowas and Plains Apaches occupied present-day western Oklahoma, southwestern Kansas, and the Texas Panhandle. Winter and summer camps were located on branches of the Red, Washita, South Canadian, and North Canadian Rivers. From this core region, intertribal war parties raided south into Texas and Mexico and southwest into present-day New Mexico. Pawnees, Navajos, Utes, Mexicans, and Texans were common enemies. In the Treaty of Fort Gibson of May 26, 1837, for example, signed by ten Kiowa leaders, including the famous Dohausan, principal Kiowa chief between 1833 and 1866, the Kiowas agreed not to raid the Santa Fe Trail and to guarantee safe passage of all Americans crossing the Southern Plains.

Between 1848 and 1868 the Kiowas expanded their territory north and west into central Kansas and southeastern Colorado. During this period, winter and summer camps were located along the Great Bend of the Arkansas River in Kansas and at the confluence of Wolf Creek and the North Canadian River in northwestern Oklahoma. This northward migration resulted from the expansion of Texas settlements and the arrival of immigrant tribes in eastern Kansas and the Indian Territory. Conflicts with the Pawnees and immigrant tribes were inevitable, because population pressures, dwindling bison herds, and shrinking territory in the Central and Southern Plains created competition for scarce resources. As raiding into Texas and Mexico for horses and plunder continued unabated, the Kiowas began kidnapping children to replace their own children, who had fallen victims to infectious disease. Many Kiowas today remark about the large amount of "captive blood" in the tribe and maintain that all Kiowas are part Mexican.

On October 21, 1867, the KCA Indians signed the Treaty of Medicine Lodge Creek and agreed to a reservation in present southwestern Oklahoma, bounded on the north and south by the Washita and Red Rivers. Although the Kiowas abandoned Kansas and Colorado in the fall of 1868, they continued to raid into Texas, which precipitated military action against them. By the end of the 1874–75 Red River War they had capitulated. Renowned Kiowa leaders and warriors were dead or in custody. The remaining topadok'i were demoted to "beef chiefs," in charge of annuity distributions to the former bands, which were now confined in a single village near Fort Sill. The Southern Plains bison herds were extinct by the late 1870s, leaving the Kiowas completely dependent on the government for their subsistence. Most attempts to transform Kiowas into stock herders and farmers failed, so famine persisted during the 1880s and 1890s. Further changes occurred after the Jerome Agreement of 1892, which brought about the allotment of KCA lands. Since the "opening" of the Kiowa Reservation to homesteaders on August 6, 1901, the Kiowas have lived on individual allotments north of the Wichita Mountains, bounded on the west by the town of Lone Wolf and on the east by Anadarko.

Nineteenth-century Kiowa cosmology was based on the concept of *daudau*, or "power," a spirit force that permeated the universe and all natural entities, such as earth, air, mountains, plants, and animals. Power seekers endured vision quests in the Wichita Mountains and other high elevations; the fortunate few who received power visions became great warriors, or curers who painted power symbols on their shields. Before the reservation period several shield societies were in existence, but they died out after 1875. The Sun Dance, the most important Kiowa ceremony, was performed to regenerate the Kiowas and the bison herds. Held in mid-June only if pledged by *ondedau* men, the four dancing days of the ceremony culminated in the final day when the sacred Taime, or Sun Dance bundle, was hung in the forked pole of the Sun Dance altar to bless all tribal members.

Government intervention brought about the demise of the Sun Dance. Although the aborted 1890 Sun Dance "when the forked poles were left standing" marked the death of the Sun Dance religion, the Kiowas turned to the Ghost Dance, which ended in 1891, but was brought back between 1894 and 1916. Missionaries came to Kiowa country in 1887, and by 1918, when the Native American Church of Oklahoma was chartered, most Kiowas were either Christians or peyotists. Today, there are a handful of Kiowa peyote Roadmen, but most Kiowas are Baptist, Methodist, or Pentecostal. Medicine bundle inheritance broke down in the twentieth century, but the eleven tribal bundles—the Thali-da-i and Taime— are still sought out with prayer requests. Despite vast cultural and religious change in the last century, the Kiowas believe that *daudau* still exists in many guises, and that *Dauk'i*, or "God," is in everything.

Approximately 4,000 Kiowas now live in western Oklahoma, and another 6,000 live elsewhere in the United States. Kiowas are very much involved in intertribal powwows and cultural activities that promote their tribal identity. Tribal offices are located in Carnegie, Oklahoma, and at the Bureau of Indian Affairs in Anadarko. Kiowa tribal government, chartered by a constitution, consists of a business committee and a tribal chair. Contemporary Kiowas of note include N. Scott Momaday, 1969 Pulitzer Prize winner for liter-

ature, and Everett Rhoades, former assistant surgeon general of the United States.

See also LITERARY TRADITIONS: Momaday, N. Scott.

Benjamin R. Kracht
Northeastern State University

Mishkin, Bernard. *Rank and Warfare among the Plains Indians.* 1940. Lincoln: University of Nebraska Press, 1992. Mooney, James. *Calendar History of the Kiowa Indians.* 1895–96. Washington DC: Smithsonian Institution Press, 1979. Richardson, Jane. *Law and Status among the Kiowa Indians.* Seattle: University of Washington Press, 1940.

KIOWA SIX

See ART: Kiowa Six

LA FLESCHE, SUSAN (1865–1915)

Physician and Indian reformer Susan La Flesche Picotte was born in June 1865, the youngest daughter of Joseph La Flesche, last traditional chief of the Omaha tribe. Joseph's commitment to education is reflected in her education. She attended the local Presbyterian mission school, the Omaha Agency Indian School, the Elizabeth Institute for Young Ladies in Elizabeth, New Jersey, and Hampton Normal and Agricultural Institute in Virginia, where she graduated in May 1886. Supported by the Connecticut Branch of the Women's National Indian Association, she attended the Woman's Medical College of Pennsylvania, graduating in March 1889 at the head of her class. Following an internship at the Woman's Hospital in Philadelphia, she returned to her reservation to practice medicine.

For the next four years, as government physician at the Omaha Agency Indian School, she dispensed medicine and encouraged tribal members to become Christian. Her religious dedication was rewarded years later, when in 1905 she was appointed medical missionary by the Presbyterian Board of Home Missions. Working out of the Blackbird Hills Presbyterian Church, she read the Bible in the Omaha language and held church services.

Ill health forced her resignation as government physician in 1893. She married Henry Picotte, a Sioux Indian from the Yankton Agency, and upon regaining her strength, resumed her medical practice in Bancroft and later in Walthill, Nebraska, among both Indians and whites. She lobbied for required medical inspection of schools, sanitary ice cream dishes and spoons, and free school drinking fountains; fought against tuberculosis and the common housefly; and campaigned against alcohol following the death of her hard-drinking husband. In addition, she organized the Thurston County Medical Association, served on Walthill's health board, chaired the State Health Committee of the Nebraska Federation of Women's Clubs, and organized a hospital for Walthill in 1913. She also helped organize a new church for Walthill, was active as president of the church missionary society, participated in a new chapter of the Eastern Star, and supported various community projects, lectures, and concerts.

In 1909, when the government arbitrarily ex-

tended the trust period for protecting Omaha land an additional ten years, she was chosen unanimously by the tribe to head a delegation to Washington DC. The Omahas were subsequently declared competent to rent or lease their lands and handle their own monies.

A product of the nineteenth-century reform movement and its assimilationist policy, she in turn helped her people prepare for the twentieth century. She died on September 18, 1915, and was buried in the Bancroft cemetery.

Valerie Sherer Mathes
Sonoma, California

Mathes, Valerie Sherer. "Iron Eyes' Daughters: Susette and Susan La Flesche, Nineteenth-Century Indian Reformers." In *By Grit and Grace: Eleven Women Who Shaped the American West*, edited by Glenda Riley and Richard Etulain. Golden CO: Fulcrum Press, 1997: 135–52. Mathes, Valerie Sherer. "Susan La Flesche Picotte, M.D.: Nineteenth-Century Physician and Reformer." *Great Plains Quarterly* 13 (1993): 172–86. Tong, Benson. *Susan La Flesche Picotte, M.D.: Omaha Indian Leader and Reformer.* Norman: University of Oklahoma Press, 1999.

Classification of Native Languages of the Great Plains

CADDOAN

Arikara
Pawnee
Kitsai
Wichita
Caddo
Jumano (?)

ATHAPASKAN

Sarcee
Kiowa Apache
Jicarilla
Lipan
Jumano (?)

SIOUAN

Mandan
Hidatsa
Crow
Assiniboine
Stoney
Santee-Sisseton
Yankton-Yanktonai
Teton
Iowa
Otoe
Missouria
Winnebago*
Omaha
Ponca
Osage
Kanza (Kaw)
Quapaw*

ALGONQUIAN

Blackfoot
Arapaho
Atsina
Cheyenne
Sutai
Plains Cree

Plains Ojibwa
Kickapoo*
Fox-Sauk*
Peoria*
Miami*
Kaskaskia*
Ottawa*
Potawatomi*
Shawnee*
Delaware*

IROQUOIAN

Cherokee*
Seneca*
Wyandotte*

MUSCOGEAN

Choctaw*
Chickasaw*
Creek*
Seminole*

UTO-AZTECAN

Shoshone
Comanche
Jumano (?)

TANOAN

Kiowa
Jumano (?)

KLAMATH-MODOC

Modoc*

SAHAPTIAN

Nez Perce*

ISOLATES

Tonkawa
*Removed to Great Plains by federal order

LANGUAGES

The Great Plains has long been the home to a multitude of distinct Native voices. The language of each family, band, community, or nation has developed to embrace and describe a dynamic life. Through their oral tradition, communities transmit a rich heritage of spiritual, historical, and practical knowledge to their children. The tools of archeologists, linguists, and historians can be combined with the memories of Native elders to study the rise, decline, and survival of these linguistically diverse communities. One useful linguistic device for organizing the many languages of the Great Plains is the "family." It works by placing languages and dialects into groups that exhibit features suggesting a common linguistic origin at some time in the past. Not all languages can be so easily categorized. For example, the Jumano language family of the Southern Plains has been variously identified as sharing features with the Athapaskan, Caddoan, Uto-Aztecan, and more recently, Tanoan language families.

Prior to the European advent of the Great Plains in the 1500s, two language families, Caddoan and Siouan, were already long represented in the region, and several others could be found along the perimeter. Caddoan speakers are some of the oldest communities of the region to survive into contemporary times. They were distributed from the Southern Plains (Wichitas, Caddos, and Kitsais), through the Central Plains (Pawnees), to the Missouri River in the Dakotas (Arikaras). Siouian speakers were the Mandans and Hidatsas of the middle Missouri River and the Crows of the Montana Plains. Except for the Crows, these Caddoan and Siouan speakers were agriculturalists residing near rivers.

Around the margins of the Great Plains were many communities taking seasonal advantage of bison resources. They represented a variety of language families, including Siouan speakers in the north and eastern periphery, Apachean Athapaskan speakers along the western edge, Uto-Aztecan and Tanoan speakers penetrating from the western mountains and moving southward, Algonquian speakers across the northern regions, and some linguistic isolates such as the Tonkawas in the south. The introduction and spread of the horse after the 1750s, together with increasing pressures from European American interests, encouraged many of these groups to become full-time Plains residents. Some entered into trading arrangements with Plains agriculturalists, Puebloans, or Spanish settlements. Communication between these diverse groups was facilitated by fictive kinship relations established through ceremonial adoptions, intermarriage, sign language, and the multilingual abilities of many Plains residents.

In the 1800s the equestrian nomadic bison hunters came to dominate the Great Plains. Their lifestyle became the stereotyped image of the region, including their use of sign language for intergroup communication. While there is no evidence of a single unified sign system, the dynamics of trade, alliances, and warfare created a need for a rich system of nonverbal communication. The greater mobility and contact with linguistically diverse groups in the Great Plains made sign language a necessity. Short-term alliances, such as the one among the Cheyennes, Sioux, Arapahos, Kiowas, Comanches, Apaches, and others against the Utes, may have served to standardize to some degree the gesture language in use by Plains residents.

After 1830 the federal government sanctioned the forced removal of many eastern, and some western, Native American communities into the Great Plains, which dramatically increased the linguistic diversity of the region, adding new voices from the Siouan, Algonquian, Muscogean, Iroquoian, Klamath-Modoc, and Sahaptian language families. However, catastrophic epidemics and other pressures from both inside and outside of the Native communities worked against the survival of Indigenous languages. Missionary and federal strategies of assimilation operated to vilify and reduce the use of Native languages and the cultural identities and communities they supported. The ongoing effect of such policies has

been the slow strangulation of many Native voices. Languages such as Kitsai, Lipan, Missouri, Quapaw, and Tonkawa have been silenced, while many more have been weakened to a whisper.

Language helps to carry a people's history, culture, worldview, and wisdom. It is our great fortune that a diversity of Native languages has survived in the Great Plains. Geographic isolation and local willpower have assisted some communities in resisting assimilation to an English-only existence. Many more communities are joining a rising tide of Native American language awareness, maintenance, and revival efforts. However, their success is not guaranteed. Revival strategies vary between communities, due to differences in local needs, values, and resources. All are faced with the daunting task of securing a place for their voices when the mainstream language has such an overwhelming presence. Without vibrant Native voices lifting into the air with song, story, and prayer, how can we speak to *our* children about the history of the Great Plains?

Mark J. Awakuni-Swetland
University of Nebraska–Lincoln

Campbell, Lyle, and Marianne Mithun, eds. *The Languages of Native America: Historical and Comparative Assessment.* Austin: University of Texas Press, 1979. Hollow, Robert C., and Douglas R. Parks. "Studies in Plains Linguistics: A Review." In *Anthropology on the Great Plains*, edited by W. Raymond Wood and Margot Liberty. Lincoln: University of Nebraska Press, 1980: 98–109. Schlesier, Karl H., ed. *Plains Indians, A.D. 500–1500: The Archaeological Past of Historic Groups.* Norman: University of Oklahoma Press, 1994.

LAROCQUE, EMMA

See LITERARY TRADITIONS: LaRocque, Emma

LORENTINO, DOROTHY SUNRISE

See EDUCATION: Lorentino, Dorothy Sunrise

MANDANS

The Siouan-speaking people now called Mandans referred to themselves as *Numangkaki,* or "People of the First Man," a name that reflected their creation by First Man. Despite this common name, the people lived in separate, autonomous villages that were identified by their locations on the Missouri River and its tributaries. The two main divisions were the *Nuitadi,* "People of the West Side," and *Nuptadi,* "People of the East Side." Two other divisions, the *Awigaxa* and *Istopa,* mentioned by early European and European American visitors, disappeared under the pressure of epidemics and American settlement.

In 1797 British explorer David Thompson found some Mandans still living in villages on the Missouri while others had settled among the Hidatsa on the Knife River. Mandan villages differed from those of the Hidatsas by the arrangement of the earth lodges around an open space with a shrine in its center. Like the Arikaras and Hidatsas, the Mandans combined bison hunting with corn, beans, squash, and sunflower agriculture, and this combination set the seasonal round of spring planting, summer hunting, fall harvesting, and winter hunting. While hunting, the tribe lived in tipis and carried only the most necessary tools and clothing. At the village, however, the earth lodge provided plenty of room for storing items such as pottery and baskets, which the women made for cooking and harvesting, respectively. Related women, usually sisters, would build and occupy a lodge with their families.

Family relationships were organized on the basis of matrilineal clans. All the women in a family and their children were members of the same clan. A man who married a woman who was not of his clan moved into her earth lodge, but his primary loyalty was to his clan. The clan cared for its members, especially orphans and the elderly, disciplined its children, assisted its members in acquiring membership in military, social, and religious societies, and helped to purchase sacred bundles that allowed a man to perform religious ceremonies. These sacred bundles were earthly manifestations of the Mandans' origins. Each bundle contained objects, songs, and instructions for the sponsor of the ceremony. These ceremonies ensured the continued success of gardening and hunting activities that supported the tribe. The most important ceremony was the Okipa, a dramatization of the creation of the Mandan world by Lone Man and the gift of the animals. Despite their recognition of common identity, the villages were independent in their government. Each village selected two men—one known for his military abilities and the other for diplomacy—from the general council of sacred bundle owners to lead the village. The leaders served only as long as people accepted their ideas.

The first non-Indians to visit the Mandans found them to be hospitable to outsiders, and this established a long tradition of friendship between the Mandans and European Americans. In 1837 a devastating smallpox epidemic killed most of the Mandans and a large number of Hidatsas, leaving the fewer than 200 survivors vulnerable to attacks from hostile tribes. As a defensive measure, the Mandans moved up the Missouri and, with the Hidatsas, established Like-a-Fishhook Village. This became a trade and administrative center for the region, attracting fur traders, government officials, and missionaries. The Arikaras moved to the village in 1862, completing the association that eventually became the Three Affiliated Tribes of the Fort Berthold Indian Reservation.

After forty years, Like-a-Fishhook was overcrowded and the local resources were exhausted. Consequently, in the early 1880s, even before allotment officially began, its inhabitants moved to new, kinship-based communities along the Missouri. The Mandans moved to the west side, where they established the settlements of Charging Eagle, Red Butte, and Beaver Creek. There they lived as farmers and ranchers, sending their children to the community school and attending church events and traditional ceremonies. In 1934 the Mandans, Hidatsas, and Arikaras

voted to accept the Indian Reorganization Act and, under its auspices, established a tribal council, adopted a constitution, and took the name Three Affiliated Tribes of Fort Berthold Reservation.

In 1954 Garrison Dam, part of the Pick-Sloan Plan, turned the Missouri River into Lake Sakakawea, causing major changes in Mandan life. People had to leave the small, kinship-based, bottomland communities and move into new houses in new towns. The new Mandan community of Twin Buttes was built, but not everyone lived there, and tribal activities became more difficult to coordinate. Relatives no longer lived next door to each other, and the removal of the bridge isolated this corner of the reservation from New Town, the new administrative headquarters.

In the years that have passed since the dam was built, the Mandans have strived to maintain their language by teaching it in the elementary school and have revived the Sun Dance and other ceremonies. Nevertheless, marriage with outsiders and work opportunities elsewhere on the reservation continue to draw young people away. A tenacious core of Mandan identity survives, however, and their population, which was only 241 in 1874, has rebounded to more than 1,200.

See also WATER: Pick-Sloan Plan.

Mary Jane Schneider
University of North Dakota

Bowers, Alfred W. *Mandan Social and Ceremonial Organization.* Chicago: University of Chicago Press, 1950. Meyer, Roy W. *The Village Indians of the Upper Missouri: The Mandans, Hidatsas, and Arikaras.* Lincoln: University of Nebraska Press, 1977. Wood, W. Raymond, and Thomas D. Thiessen. *Early Fur Trade on the Northern Plains.* Norman: University of Oklahoma Press, 1985.

MANKILLER, WILMA (b. 1945)

The first woman to lead the Cherokee Nation of Oklahoma, and the tribe's most influential principal chief since John Ross of the nineteenth century, Wilma Mankiller's dedication to her people and their future defines her life of public service and social activism. Among Cherokees and other Native American peoples, Mankiller remains a staunch advocate of Native civil, spiritual, and sovereignty rights, economic independence, women's rights, and education and health reform, all while successfully fighting her own battles with emotional tragedy and personal illness.

Wilma Pearl Mankiller was born at Tahlequah, Oklahoma, on November 18, 1945, to Irene, of Dutch-Irish heritage, and Charlie, a full-blood Cherokee. Material poverty marked her life on the family's allotment tract, known as Mankiller Flats. This poverty would serve as the impetus for her family's move to San Francisco, California, in 1956 as part of the federal government's relocation policies under the auspices of the Bureau of Indian Affairs (BIA). When the BIA's promises of financial security proved false, the family turned to the San Francisco Indian Center for cultural and emotional support. Mankiller and her father developed a particularly strong relationship with the cen-

ter, and she credits her interests in politics to watching Charlie work as an advocate for the Indian community of San Francisco.

In 1963 Mankiller married Hector Hugo Olaya de Bardi, whom she had met while a student at San Francisco State College, and by 1966 she was the mother of two daughters, Felicia and Gina. Her growing activism for Indian rights was heightened by the Indian occupation of Alcatraz Island; while her siblings joined the protesters on the island itself, Mankiller spent much of her time in fundraising activities for the movement. In 1974, due to fundamental differences in political and personal philosophies, Mankiller and her husband divorced, and in 1977 she returned to Mankiller Flats with her daughters.

Mankiller's work with the Cherokee Nation, as an economic stimulus coordinator, began shortly after her arrival but was interrupted by a near-fatal car accident in 1979, in which her best friend, Sherry Morris, was killed when her vehicle struck Mankiller's car head-on while passing on a blind curve. Mankiller's recovery was compounded by the emotional trauma of Morris's death and the onset of myasthenia gravis, a type of muscular dystrophy in which the immune system attacks skeletal muscles. With help from Cherokee medicine people, surgery, and drug therapy, Mankiller fully recovered and in 1980 continued her work with the Cherokee Nation.

By 1983, after directing a highly successful community revitalization program, Mankiller had developed a strong reputation as an efficient organizer and dedicated advocate of Cherokee people, particularly the poor of the nation. Ross Swimmer, then principal chief, asked her to be his running mate as deputy chief. Swimmer and Mankiller narrowly won the election. In 1985 Swimmer resigned to head the BIA in Washington DC, and Mankiller became the first woman principal chief of the Cherokee Nation. She was reelected in a run-off in 1987, and in 1991, a year after repeated hospitalizations and a kidney transplant, she won her second election with 82 percent of the vote.

The move toward tribal revitalization marked Mankiller's tenure as principal chief, during which she focused on Cherokee self-reliance, independence, and pride. She championed a variety of economic, political, educational, and cultural projects, including Cherokee language and literacy classes, rural development and housing construction, health care initiatives, and land claims settlement. Due to continued ill health, including a second kidney operation and treatment for lymphatic cancer, Mankiller declined in 1995 to run for a third term, but she has since remained active in Cherokee affairs and international Indigenous and women's rights. She and her husband, Charlie Soap, a bilingual full-blood Cherokee, are often seen at multitribal cultural and political events; at powwows, Charlie is a noted Plains-style dancer.

Some of the honors Mankiller has received include induction into the International

Women's Forum Hall of Fame, the National Women's Hall of Fame, and the Oklahoma Women's Hall of Fame. She is the recipient of the National Racial Justice award, *Ms.* magazine's Woman of the Year award, and the Oklahoma Federation of Women's American Indian Woman of the Year award, and she was named in the *Marquis Who's Who* as one of the fifty great Americans. In 1998 Mankiller received the Medal of Freedom, the top civilian honor given by the U.S. government, from President Bill Clinton in honor of her work for the rights of women and Native peoples throughout the world.

Daniel Heath Justice
University of Toronto

Mankiller, Wilma, and Michael Wallis. *Mankiller: A Chief and Her People*. New York: St. Martin's Press, 1993.

MÉTIS

The term "Métis," from the French meaning "mixed," is used by scholars to designate individuals and groups who identify their antecedents with historical fur trade communities, and it refers to people who possess a distinctive sociocultural heritage and sense of self-identification. These descendants of Native American women and European men forged a new identity that was distinct from Indigenous bands and from the European American world of the trading posts. The Métis of the Great Plains could be found almost anywhere the fur trade predominated, and by the early nineteenth century distinct communities were emerging in the valleys of the North Saskatchewan, Assiniboine, and Red Rivers in British North America and the Missouri River and its tributaries in U.S. territory.

These communities varied considerably, depending on the locality in which they arose, the Native American bands they were allied to, the ethnicity and nationality of the fur trade fathers, and the particular roles they played within the fur trade economy. What they had in common was that they were bicultural communities that functioned as intermediaries or brokers between European American fur traders on the one hand and trapping bands on the other. It was in these interstitial spaces that unique Métis identities were forged. Being Métis had many advantages in these fur trade worlds. It was an ethnic positioning that allowed individuals to cross boundaries separating Native American and European American societies. It allowed for flexibility in self-definition, whereby an individual could accentuate those personality and kinship aspects to allow entry into both worlds. Some of these communities used "Métis" to identify themselves, though other terms were used, including Michif, Bois Brûlé, Chicot, "Half-Breed," and "Mixed-Blood," among others.

Although these Métis bands were found across the Northern Plains from the Missouri to the Athabasca River, Métis political identity in the early nineteenth century was focused on the Red River Settlement. Their assertion of political rights arose there first in relation to the fur trade wars between the North West

Métis traders, 1872–74

Company and the Hudson's Bay Company following the establishment of the Red River Settlement in 1811. The Plains Métis, closely tied to the various bourgeois of the North West Company by consanguinity and employment, were encouraged to oppose the Hudson's Bay Company's efforts to impose any authority over them. This conflict, which ended in violence and the deaths of twenty-one colonists at the Seven Oaks Massacre in 1816, came to be seen by the Métis as the initiation of a "new nation."

Acting as buffalo-hunting provisioners and trappers in the fur trade of the Great Plains, the Métis considered themselves independent of both fur trade and tribal control. By the 1840s the buffalo-robe trade, complementing the summer provisioning hunt, resulted in the establishment of sizable winter villages wherever buffalo could be found. This move into the territory of the Sioux, Crees, and Blackfoot caused violent confrontations, the most famous of which was the Battle of Grand Coteau, on June 16–19, 1851. Here Métis buffalo hunters from the Red River came under sustained attack from Sioux near the Missouri River. Attacked by a much larger force, the Métis circled their two-wheeled Red River carts to corral their horses and oxen and to shelter their women and children. The men established a perimeter the distance of a gunshot by scraping gun pits in the prairie sod, and from these rifle pits they inflicted enough casualties that the Sioux eventually broke off the attack.

In order to alleviate such hostilities, attempts were made to broker peace treaties between the Métis and the various tribal groups. In 1858 the Métis, Sioux, and Ojibwas met in a Grand Council north of the Sheyenne River, to the west of Devils Lake (present-day North Dakota), to set tribal boundaries and establish peace among the three groups. The Métis, though closely associated with the Ojibwas of the region, were recognized as a separate political and military force and were given the right to hunt in Sioux territory. Still, conflicts would continue to erupt between the Métis and various tribal groups throughout the 1860s and 1870s.

In the treaties negotiated between the United States and Native American groups west of the Great Lakes, various bands insisted that treaties provide some compensation for their "mixed-blood" brothers not living as Indians or as part of the band. When the Red River Métis heard that the American government was planning to negotiate a treaty with the Pembina and Red Lake Chippewas (Ojibwas), many decided to relocate to the American side of the boundary to take advantage of the benefits of this treaty. During the negotiations the Métis claimed that it was their country and that they had long defended and maintained it against the encroachments of enemies. The treaty that was signed between the United States and the Pembina Chippewas on September 20, 1851, however, did not include the Métis as signatories because the government believed it should not treat with people who it regarded "as our *quasi* citizens." The government negotiator did stipulate that he would not object to any just or reasonable treaty stipulation the Indians might choose to make for the Métis' benefit.

With the transfer of Rupert's Land to Canada in 1869–70, the Red River Métis, led by Louis Riel, initiated a political movement to guarantee their rights in the new political order. The Manitoba Act of 1870, which brought the Red River Settlement into the Canadian Confederation, granted the Métis both land rights and some semblance of constitutional recognition. The rush of settlers into Manitoba after 1870, and the continuing profitability of the buffalo-robe trade, however, induced many Métis to sell their landholdings and move farther west. In 1884 Riel, now claiming to be a religious prophet, led another movement, the North-West Rebellion, aimed at recapturing the political power the Métis had lost in the Red River Settlement. Centered in the communities of the South Saskatchewan River, this movement eventually resulted in armed rebellion against the Canadian state in 1885. The uprising was crushed, and Riel was hanged for treason on November 16, 1885.

Following the North-West Rebellion of 1885 and the demise of the fur trade in the Plains, the Métis lost much of their political influence and cohesiveness. They dispersed northward and westward, with many also fleeing to Montana and North Dakota to escape expected reprisals. There they joined preexisting Métis communities that had been established during the heyday of the fur trade. Although Métis communities survived into the twentieth century in both the United States and Canada, poverty, demoralization, and prejudice against them led many individuals to suppress their biracial heritage and identity. Since the 1970s, however, social, cultural, and political developments that have legitimized ethnicity have produced a renaissance of Métis identity and political activity throughout the Northern Plains and Prairie Provinces. In 1982 the Métis were recognized as one of Canada's Aboriginal Peoples under section 35(2) of the Constitution Act.

See also LAW: Pierre-Guillaume Sayer Trial / PROTEST AND DISSENT: Riel, Louis / WAR: North-West Rebellion; Red River Resistance; Seven Oaks Massacre.

Gerhard J. Ens
University of Alberta

Ens, Gerhard. J. *Homeland to Hinterland: The Changing Worlds of the Red River Métis in the Nineteenth Century.* Toronto: University of Toronto Press, 1996. Foster, John E. "Wintering, the Outsider Male and Ethnogenesis of the Western Plains Métis." *Prairie Forum* 19 (1994): 1–13. Peterson, Jacqueline, and Jennifer S. H. Brown, eds. *The New Peoples: Being and Becoming Métis in North America.* Winnipeg: University of Manitoba Press, 1985.

MNI SOSE INTERTRIBAL WATER RIGHTS COALITION

See WATER: Mni Sose Intertribal Water Rights Coalition

MOMADAY, N. SCOTT

See LITERARY TRADITIONS: Momaday, N. Scott

MORNING STAR CEREMONY

See RELIGION: Morning Star Ceremony

NATIONAL CONGRESS OF AMERICAN INDIANS

See PROTEST AND DISSENT: National Congress of American Indians

NATIVE AMERICAN AGRICULTURE

See AGRICULTURE: Native American Agriculture

NATIVE AMERICAN ARCHITECTURE, CONTEMPORARY

See ARCHITECTURE: Native American Architecture, Contemporary

NATIVE AMERICAN ARCHITECTURE, TRADITIONAL

See ARCHITECTURE: Native American Architecture, Traditional

NATIVE AMERICAN ART, TRADITIONAL

See ART: Native American Art, Traditional

NATIVE AMERICAN CHURCH

See RELIGION: Native American Church

NATIVE AMERICAN GENDER ROLES

See GENDER: Native American Gender Roles

NATIVE AMERICAN RADIO

See MEDIA: Native American Radio

NATIVE AMERICAN RIGHTS FUND

See LAW: Native American Rights Fund

OJIBWAS

Within the Great Plains, the Ojibwas reside in Montana, North Dakota, Manitoba, Saskatchewan, and Alberta. The name "Ojibwa" is generally translated as "To Roast Till Puckered Up," an allusion to the puckered moccasins worn in the past. In the Great Plains, however, Ojibwa is more likely to be used as a geographical designation rather than a self-identifying term. In fact, no inclusive terms exist to refer to all the Ojibwa communities in the Great Plains. Generally, the term "Plains Bungi" (or Bungee) refers to the Ojibwas residing in Alberta, Saskatchewan, and western Manitoba. "Saulteaux" is often used to designate Ojibwas living in the area near Lake Winnipeg as well as the region south of the lake and extending to the international border. Within the United States, "Chippewas" is frequently used to identify Ojibwas in North Dakota and Montana. In addition to these terms, "Métis" is employed to refer to descendants of French and Ojibwa, Cree, and/or Chippewa ancestors. The Ojibwas speak dialects of the Algonquian language family.

Ojibwas in the eastern portion of their territory sometimes refer to themselves as Anishinaabes, which means "The People" or "Original Man." According to oral traditions, the Ojibwas once belonged to the three fires of the Anishinaabes. This triad represented a confederacy that included not only the Ojibwas but also the Potawatomis and Ottawas. In

North Dakota, some local Ojibwas also refer to themselves by the Algonquian word *nakkawininiwak*, which means "those who speak differently." This refers to linguistic differences between the Ojibwa spoken by the Plains and Woodland Ojibwas.

The Plains Ojibwas are descended from Algonquian-speaking Woodland groups located in Michigan, Wisconsin, Minnesota, and Ontario. During the late eighteenth century the expansion of the fur trade and the Iroquois resulted in the migration of some Ojibwas into the Great Plains. Many of these migrants settled in forested areas surrounded by lakes. As a result, substantial communities developed near Lake Winnipeg, in the Turtle Mountain region of North Dakota, and the confluence of the Red and Red Lake Rivers in Montana.

In these areas the Plains Ojibwas began hunting bison, elk, deer, and small game. Fur trapping, fishing, and horse raiding also became important activities in the region. Like numerous other Plains populations, the Ojibwas in the area used bison-hide tipis, the horse and travois, and hard-soled footwear. Like their Woodland ancestors, the Plains Ojibwas continued to use floral designs in their beadwork and to make fish-skin containers. Other similarities between the Plains and Woodland Ojibwas continued in the areas of social organization and belief systems.

The Plains Ojibwas retained the concept of nonresidential totemic clans. A number of these patrilineal clans formed bands. Exogamous marriages occurred at both the clan and band level. After marriage, residency was initially matrilocal, due to the two- to three-year bride service (labor due to the bride's family) required of the groom. After that period, the couple practiced patrilocal residency. Husbands practiced mother-in-law avoidance. Joking relationships existed between the wife and her husband's brothers, as well as between the husband and his wife's sisters.

Unlike the Woodland Ojibwas, only a few Plains Ojibwas practiced the Shaking Tent ceremony. Most Plains Ojibwas instead participated in the Sun Dance. Throughout the Ojibwa region, however, belief in Manitou, Windigo, and Nanibush persisted. Manitou refers to a neutral power that permeates all matter. Only through religious training can a person learn to control this essence. Windigo is a giant humanlike monster that resides in the winter forest, and Nanibush refers to a comic hero that continually breaks taboos. During the twentieth century the Native American Church became an important aspect of religious activities among many Ojibwas in the United States.

Currently, the Ojibwas occupy five reserves in Alberta, six in Saskatchewan, two in Manitoba, two reservations in North Dakota, and three in Montana. Generally, members of other Native populations also occupy these reservations and reserves. For example, the Rocky Boy's Reservation in Montana includes Plains Ojibwas, Plains Crees, and Métis, and intermarriage has blurred the lines between the groups.

In Canada, traditional Ojibwa continues to be spoken in many households, while within the United States some adults and fewer children speak the language. Consequently, a number of communities in Montana and North Dakota are establishing bilingual educational programs.

See also LITERARY TRADITIONS: Erdrich, Louise.

Martha L. McCollough
University of Nebraska–Lincoln

Albers, Patricia C. "Plains Ojibwa." In *Handbook of North American Indians*, edited by Raymond J. DeMallie, 13: 652–61. Washington DC: Smithsonian Institution, 2001. LaCounte, Alysia E. "Ojibwa: Chippewa in Montana." In *Native America in the Twentieth Century: An Encyclopedia*, edited by Mary B. Davis. New York and London: Garland Publishing, Inc., 1996: 399–401. Murray, Stanley N. "The Turtle Mountain Chippewa, 1882–1905." *North Dakota History* 51 (1984): 14–37.

OMAHAS

The Omahas have lived near the middle Missouri River since the early 1700s. Their Sacred Legend describes an origin in a wooded, game-filled region near a large body of water, perhaps the Great Lakes. The Sacred Legend tells how the people developed many subsistence skills, implements, and social organizations with focused thought and keen observation. During the course of a slow migration westward, the people adapted to their changing environment. The language they developed is one of five related dialects in the Dhegiha branch of the Siouan language family that also includes the Poncas, Quapaws, Osages, and Kanzas (Kaws). The descriptive name "Omaha" (from umo^nho^n, "against the current" or "upstream") indicates a parting of company from these related peoples during that migration.

After contact with Arikara and Pawnee peoples, the Omahas adopted earth lodge dwellings, bison skin tipis, and local varieties of maize. They settled into the region west of the Missouri between the Platte and Niobrara Rivers. Village sites were situated along running streams where the bottomlands provided tillable soil, fuel, and building materials. $To^n{}'wo^nto^ngatho^n$, or "Big Village on Omaha Creek," was the principal Omaha village from 1775 until 1845, with a population estimated to have been more than 2,000 people in 1795. The Omahas created a complex schedule of seasonal movements that enabled them to produce substantial gardens of maize, beans, and other cultigens, while conducting large-scale communal bison hunts on the western plains of present-day Nebraska and Kansas.

It was during the summer bison hunts that Omaha social organization became graphically visible. When the people paused in their daily travels, all of the tipis were erected in a circle on the prairie. The Omahas are divided into ten patrilineal clans, each of which has one or more subclans. The ten clans camped in designated places around the circle.

The Omahas are further organized in a moiety system, or complementary halves, in which one half of the clans are associated with the earth-female cosmic forces, and the other half with sky-male cosmic forces. Each clan and subclan has a catalog of unique personal names for its members, as well as particular duties, rights, and prohibitions. Marriage is to a person outside the clan and, ideally, outside the moiety. Any tendencies toward factionalism are reduced because all ceremonial and political functions require the presence and assistance of multiple clans.

Seven of the ten clans traditionally provided an individual to sit on the tribal council, which deliberated on community affairs and arbitrated disputes. Their authority was sanctioned by the use of two Sacred Tribal Pipes. The eighth clan, as keepers of the Sacred Tent of War, provided military leadership during times of external assault. The two remaining clans did not have a seat on the council but performed important duties for the maintenance of the community.

The Omahas had several social societies that served to foster martial and civic responsibilities. One of the most important of these was the *Hethúshka*. Membership was restricted to men who had received public war honors. The distinctive dances, songs, and regalia of this society have become the foundation of the "War Dance" of the contemporary Great Plains powwow. Men performing acts of generosity could become members of a chief's society. There were also several doctoring and secret societies.

The Sacred Legend describes the first meeting with Europeans while the Omaha were in the east. This first amicable encounter was followed by the establishment of relations with the French by 1724, the British by 1790, and American traders soon after. The Omahas have maintained a tradition of peaceful relations with European and American visitors ever since. An example of this peace can be seen in the material assistance Omahas rendered to Mormon emigrants residing at their Winter Quarters on the Missouri River in 1846–48.

Until the late nineteenth century amicable relations with nearby Native groups were not always the rule. The need to travel to the western bison-hunting grounds for provisions placed the Omahas in a vulnerable position on two fronts. A successful summer hunt required the presence of religious objects such as the Sacred Pole and the Sacred Buffalo Hide, their aged caretakers, and the entire tribal group. Such a slow-moving company of men, women, children, dogs, and horses burdened with gear made an easy target for enemies. Meanwhile, those people who were too old or infirm to make the journey remained in the earth lodge villages to tend the gardens. The few able-bodied men who stayed to protect them were at a disadvantage if a superior force attacked.

Contact and interaction with European Americans wrought many changes on Omaha society. Subsistence hunting and agriculture shifted to an international fur trade economy. Traditional skills, arts, and crafts declined in favor of the use of trade goods, including firearms. Political and social status shifted as men better able to negotiate trade or hunt successfully for marketable quantities of pelts and bison robes overshadowed customary leaders whose prestige had been gained through oratorical skills, consensus building, and acts of generosity. Women expended more energy in the preparation of furs and hides for market. Recurring epidemic diseases reduced the population several times, causing the Omahas to lose control of the fur trade in their region while becoming increasingly vulnerable to attack by their enemies. They were forced to finally abandon $To^n{'}wo^nto^ngatho^n$ in 1845 and retreat to a village site closer to the mouth of the Platte.

Under such pressures the Omahas signed treaties relinquishing control of land. The 1830 Treaty of Prairie du Chien ceded their claims to land in the present state of Iowa. To protect their own future they signed an 1854 treaty establishing a reservation in exchange for the remainder of their Nebraska land. The Omahas moved to their present reservation in 1855–56.

Many Omahas embraced some of the more visible "Americanizing" efforts of the federal government by adopting frame houses, new farming techniques, Christianity, and English-language education for their children. Important institutions such as the Sacred Pole, Sacred Buffalo Hide, the Sacred Tribal Pipes, and the Sacred Tent of War were put to sleep. Some of the secret and social societies went underground. Other Native organizations, such as the Native American Church, emerged.

In 1882 some Omahas joined with various non-Indian interest groups to push for the allotment of land. Much of the allotted lands was later sold, or it was forfeited because the taxes could not be paid. Allotments that once blanketed the entire reservation at the turn of the century were eroded to a strip of Omaha holdings along the Missouri River bluffs by the 1950s.

The Omahas voted to accept the provisions of the Indian Reorganization Act of 1934, creating a constitutional government with a tribal council elected by popular vote. The Omaha Tribal Council has emerged as the provider of services or space for many of the secular and sacred activities of the community. These efforts were given a boost in 1962 with a $2.9 million award from the Indian Claims Commission for Omaha lands taken in 1854. Reservation lands stranded east of the shifting Missouri River in Iowa were reclaimed and are being developed. Proceeds from these enterprises, including the Casino Omaha, have been applied to social and cultural revival efforts.

In 1994 about 2,000 of the 5,227 tribal members lived on the reservation, most in the Macy, Nebraska, area. A large number of Omahas make their homes in the surrounding urban centers of Omaha and Lincoln, Nebraska, and Sioux City, Iowa. An annual August encampment and powwow is held at Macy that serves as a homecoming opportunity for the off-reservation tribal members.

Many Omahas continue to negotiate their lives between the pressures of mainstream western society and the traditional values of Omaha culture. Leaders continue to emerge out of this struggle, men and women who emulate the values in the Sacred Legend of focused thought and keen observation. It is their strength and dignity that encourage the Omaha people to continue traveling upstream as a proud nation.

Mark J. Awakuni-Swetland
University of Nebraska–Lincoln

Dorsey, James Owen. "Omaha Sociology." In *Third Annual Report of the Bureau of American Ethnology (1881–1882)*. Washington DC: Government Printing Office, 1884. Fletcher, Alice C., and Francis La Flesche. "The Omaha Tribe." *Twenty-seventh Annual Report of the Bureau of American Ethnology (1905–1906)*. Washington DC: Government Printing Office, 1911. Tate, Michael L. *The Upstream People: An Annotated Research Bibliography of the Omaha Tribe*. Metuchen NJ: Scarecrow Press, 1991.

OSAGES

The Osages, Dhegiha Siouan speakers, believed in the beginning that there was chaos in the universe. Amid the chaos, the all-powerful, mysterious, and invisible life force, *Wakonda*, created order by organizing the universe into air, land, and water, creating the Middle Waters. Wakonda brought three groups together, and they became the *Wa-zha-she*, the "Children of the Middle Waters," or the Osage nation.

The location of the Osage creation is cloaked in myth and metaphor, but many believe that they formed as a distinct people in the forests along the Ohio Valley and were pushed onto the prairies by Iroquois attacks. Others argue they were survivors of the Oneota cultural complex of the Plains river valleys. By 1673 the Osages were dwelling along the Osage River (in present-day Missouri), and throughout the eighteenth century they hunted in the Ozark Highlands and out onto the Great Plains. They occupied the region from the Republican River in Kansas south to the Red River of Oklahoma and Texas until the early 1830s. In 1839, to make room for the removed eastern tribes, the Osages were forced onto a reservation in southern Kansas. In 1870, as whites invaded their reservation, they were moved south into Indian Territory.

The Osages were semisedentary people who inhabited wooden longhouses in prairie villages in the spring and fall and spent summers in the Plains and winters in the forest. In the spring, after planting their crops, they left their villages to hunt in the Great Plains. In early July they returned to the villages to harvest their crops and store them for winter. They returned to the Plains in September, where they hunted until winter and then traveled back to the forests. They remained there until spring, when they gathered again to renew their seasonal cycle.

Osage men wore deerskin breechcloths and covered their legs with buckskin leggings. They rarely wore anything on their upper bodies, and only in the winter did they wrap themselves in buffalo robes. Osage women wore red and blue dyed buckskin leggings and buckskin tunics. The Osages became well known for their silk ribbon reverse appliqué,

in which they cut silk in elaborate patterns and sewed them in layers onto their blankets and clothing.

The Osages believed that all things of the universe were manifestations of Wakonda. They sought to live in peace and harmony with the universe. Clan elders possessed sacred songs, rituals, and bundles, and they used them to sanctify important events and solicit the support of Wakonda.

The basic political unit of the Osages was the village, and according to Osage oral traditions, in the beginning all of the Osages lived in a single village along a river. The village contained twenty-four clans and was divided into moieties, the earth people and sky people. Each moiety had a hereditary leader, and these two chiefs shared power with clan elders. Together they made up the village council, which led the people. For a variety of political, economic, and social reasons, as the Osages moved west they separated into three major bands, with the two northern bands, the Big and Little Osages, occupying southern Kansas, and the Arkansas Osages, occupying the Verdigris River valley, just north of the Three Forks of the Arkansas.

The Osages were a numerous people. The earliest account of their population dates to 1719, when Claude-Charles DuTisné estimated there were 200 warriors and 200 lodges in the single village he visited. In 1817 superintendent of Indian Affairs William Clark reported 6,000 Osages. Great epidemics struck the Osages in the 1830s; hundreds died, as they were simultaneously stricken with cholera and smallpox. Later, on their reservation, pneumonia and tuberculosis continued to take a toll, and their population fell to 4,000 by 1870. By 1906 they numbered only 2,000.

In the early twenty-first century, there are now about 10,000 Osages on the tribal roll, but due to the unique nature of the Osage allotment, there are two distinct forms of membership. Osage lands were allotted individually in 1906, but because they had purchased their 1,470,559 acres from the Cherokees and possessed fee simple title to the land, the government had to negotiate with them before they could make more allotments. While allotting the surface rights individually, the Osages successfully preserved communal ownership to the mineral rights to all of their lands. They retain these today. The mineral rights were divided equally into 2,229 shares for the individuals on the roll on July 1, 1907. These shares—headrights—would never be divided, and subsequently, children born to Osage parents were recognized as members of the tribe but were not given additional shares in the tribe's income. After allotment, their reservation became Osage County, where 30 percent of Osages live today. Another 30 percent lives elsewhere in Oklahoma, and the remainder lives in other parts of the United States.

Willard Hughes Rollings
University of Nevada, Las Vegas

Mathews, John J. *The Osages: Children of the Middle Waters*. Norman: University of Oklahoma Press, 1961. Rollings, Willard H. *The Osage: An Ethnohistorical Study of Hegemony on the Prairie-Plains*. Columbia: University of Missouri Press, 1992.

OTOE-MISSOURIAS

The Otoe-Missourias were two separate peoples until they amalgamated in the last years of the eighteenth century. Members of the Chiwere group of Siouan speakers, they were driven westward from the Great Lakes region in the seventeenth century by the Sioux, who were also moving westward under pressure emanating from the expanding orbit of European colonization. By 1714 the Otoes were living in a village on the Salt Creek tributary of the Platte River in what is now eastern Nebraska. They occupied that vicinity for the remainder of the eighteenth century. The Missourias joined them there in 1798 after the Sauks and Foxes had driven them out of their former homeland of present-day northwest Missouri. From that time on the Otoe-Missourias were one nation, though the Missourias remained a distinctive constituent throughout the nineteenth century.

They lived, like the neighboring Pawnees and Omahas, in earth lodge villages and divided their subsistence activities between intensive farming at the villages, biannual bison hunts out on the Plains, and a wide array of food collection. They calibrated their annual cycle closely to the signs and rhythms of the physical environment, and they sanctified their activities with ceremonies that enlisted the support of sacred powers. Their way of life worked because they spread their subsistence base over a broad spectrum of Plains resources, and in 1800 they sustained a population of more than 1,000 people.

But the outside world crowded in, and with the fur traders, missionaries, Indian agents, and settlers came disease and resource depletion. By 1804, when Lewis and Clark passed by, the Otoe-Missouria population had been reduced by smallpox to fewer than 800; subsequent epidemics and depletion of game, bringing famine, continued the downward plunge to 600 by midcentury. Fur traders established a post at Bellevue in the 1820s, just to the east of the Otoe-Missouria village, and alcohol became a disruptive force in their society. Enmities that otherwise might have been settled peacefully erupted into violence. Head chief Big Kaw could not preserve unity, and by the 1840s the Otoe-Missourias had splintered into four separate villages.

Mired in poverty, and with starvation a constant companion, they were forced to sell their only resource, their land, merely to survive. The United States obliged, as it needed land on which to settle refugee Indians from the eastern United States in the 1830s and homes for settlers after 1854. The first sale came in 1830 when, at the Treaty of Prairie du Chien, the Otoe-Missourias surrendered their claims to any lands east of the Missouri and also sold a sliver of land in southeastern Nebraska (the Nemaha Half-Breed Reservation) for the resettlement there of mixed-bloods from various tribes. A cession of about one million acres in southeastern Nebraska followed in 1833. The Otoe-Missourias received 4.1 cents an acre for this prime agricultural land. As with subsequent payments for cessions, the money was used by the United States to provide annuities (blankets, farming equipment, and other items) and to finance its assimilation policy, which aimed to transform communal Indians into self-supporting farmers working on separate 160-acre allotments. Even in 1881, when the Otoe-Missourias abandoned Nebraska for Indian Territory, very few, if any, of their men were farming.

When the Kansas-Nebraska Act of May 30, 1854, opened Nebraska for settlement by European Americans, the Otoe-Missourias sold their remaining homeland for 42.6 cents an acre, retaining only a 162,000-acre reservation straddling the Kansas-Nebraska boundary. This was fertile country, and it soon became clear that, as surrounding population pressure mounted and land values escalated, the Otoe-Missourias would have difficulty retaining it. They lived there, poorly but still defiantly traditional, for twenty-five years. Their agents were generally corrupt until Quakers took over in 1869. Under great pressure to change, and with the old ways increasingly unfeasible, their society cleaved into two opposing segments: one, called the "stable faction" by the Quakers, paid at least lip service to the assimilation policy; the other, the "wild party," led by traditional chiefs Medicine Horse and Ar-ka-ke-ta, remained steadfastly traditional. When the Otoe-Missourias migrated to Oklahoma Territory, following the sale of their reservation in two parts in 1876 and 1881, the division persisted and was not healed until after 1890.

In Indian Territory, the Otoe-Missourias settled on a 129,113-acre reservation in what is now Noble County, Oklahoma. Their population continued to plummet, dropping to 340 in 1894. Thereafter, their numbers gradually rebounded to reach 1,550 by 1990. Their reservation was completely allotted in 1907, but when oil was discovered on their lands in 1912, the trust status of their allotments was abrogated, and fully 90 percent of their land base was lost.

The Otoe-Missourias continued to resist the United States' efforts to reshape them. They refused to set up a constitutional government—which would have abolished their traditional tribal government—until 1984, and they have used their resources to buy back some of their lost lands. In the late 1940s, like most other Plains tribes, they lodged their claims with the Indian Claims Commission, and in 1955 and 1964 received awards of $1,156,035 and $1,750,000 for lands that had been taken in 1830, 1833, and 1854 for payments "so low as to shock the conscience." These awards, large at first sight, diminished to small sums when allocated to individuals. Still, it is remarkable—in fact a triumph—that this small nation, despite the loss of their homeland and the assault on their way of life, has endured into the twenty-first century. Their annual powwow, held in July, and their continued coherence

around kinship groups, ceremonies, and social gatherings, ensure the continuance of their tribal identity.

David J. Wishart
University of Nebraska–Lincoln

Chapman, Berlin Basil. *The Otoes and Missourias: A Study of Indian Removal and the Legal Aftermath.* Oklahoma City: Times Journal Publishing Co., 1965. Edmunds, R. David. *The Otoe-Missouria People.* Phoenix: Indian Tribal Series, 1976. Wishart, David J. *An Unspeakable Sadness: The Dispossession of the Nebraska Indians.* Lincoln: University of Nebraska Press, 1994.

PALEO-INDIANS

Paleo-Indians were the earliest people to inhabit the Americas. Between 30,000 and 11,000 years ago, small, highly mobile groups of hunter-gatherers extended their hunting areas throughout Beringia (the landmass that joined Siberia and Alaska) and into the Western Hemisphere. This "bridging landmass" emerged slowly from beneath the Bering Sea as more than nine million cubic miles of glacial ice accumulated over southern Alaska, Canada, Labrador, and Greenland. About 20,000 to 18,000 years ago an immense "ice dome" (the Laurentide glacier) towered more than one mile over present-day Hudson Bay. Two lobes of ice spread southward over the eastern edge of the Dakotas and deeper into the Midwest. The Central and Southern Great Plains remained unglaciated at this time, yet the mountains of glacial ice to the north exerted pronounced influences upon the everyday lives of the Paleo-Indians throughout the region.

Archeologists believe that Paleo-Indians expanded into certain ice-free areas of North America's interior, or along its coastal margins. The timing of the arrival of Paleo-Indians in the Great Plains and in North America, in general, is under renewed investigation. Recent genetic studies based on mitochondrial DNA suggest that a founding population composed

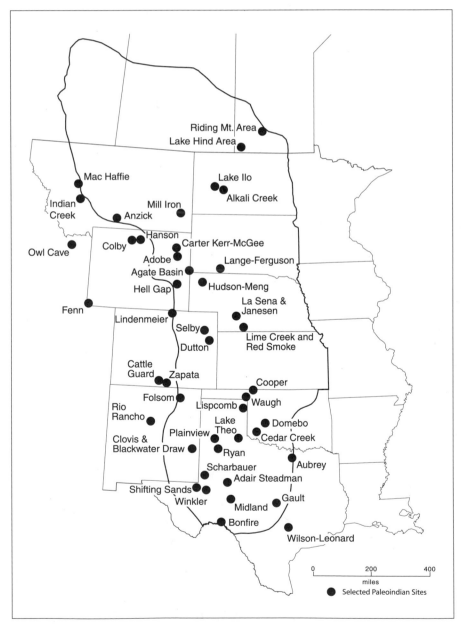

Selected Paleo-Indian sites in the Great Plains

of four distinct genetic lineages appeared in the Western Hemisphere between 37,000 and 23,000 years before present (B.P.). It appears that all contemporary Native Americans are descendants of these Paleo-Indian lineages, including the hunter-gatherers who made their appearance in the Great Plains 18,000 years ago or earlier.

During the last Ice Age, the Great Plains was inhabited by a diverse array of animals, including the Columbian mammoth, musk oxen, caribou, horse, camel, bison, elk, lion, wolf, arctic ground squirrels, arctic shrews, and lemmings. Around 14,500 B.P. the Northern Hemisphere began to warm and the glaciers began to shrink. The ice over North America essentially disappeared by 6,500 B.P. Mosaic communities of plants and animals were reshuffled and sorted into their characteristic zonal patterns of today. Many large herbivorous and carnivorous mammals were unable to make the necessary shifts in diet, reproduction, and morphology and became extinct between 12,000 and 10,000 B.P. Some scientists have attributed the disappearance of many larger mammals to the superior predatory abilities of the Paleo-Indians themselves. There is little reason to believe that Paleo-Indian hunter-gatherers had any significant role in these global animal extinctions; such extinctions had occurred many times before, particularly during abrupt shifts from colder glacial to warmer interglacial periods.

The most abundant physical evidence for Paleo-Indians in the Plains consists of a diverse array of carefully made chipped stone projectile points that were given geographical place-names like Clovis, Goshen, Folsom, Midland, Plainview, Cody, Alberta, Hell Gap, Scottsbluff, and Eden. Hunting weapons were probably constructed from interchangeable parts that were frequently repaired and recycled. Certain chipped stone points (e.g., Clovis, Folsom, and Goshen) were attached to short, fletched "dart" shafts and thrown with the use of a leverlike spear thrower, or atlatl. Paleo-Indian flint knappers developed an extremely efficient eleven-step method for transforming a large flake of high-quality stone into a multipurpose cutting implement and, later, into a Folsom point, two "razor blades," and a "lathe" tool. Larger stone points (e.g., Scottsbluff, Hell Gap, and Alberta) functioned as thrusting spears for dispatching bison that had been driven into natural traps created by parabolic sand dunes, deep gullies, or snowdrifts. Paleo-Indian tool kits also included chipped stone tools required to skin and butcher game, scrape skins and hides, and fashion specialized tools and component parts (e.g., foreshafts, shaft straighteners, and delicate eyed needles) of bone, antler, ivory, and wood.

One of the first documented discoveries of Paleo-Indian stone tools found together with the bones of extinct Ice Age animals in North America was made by H. T. Martin and T. R. Overton in 1895 near Russell Springs, Kansas. A similar find was made by George McJunkin—a cowboy, naturalist, and former black slave—in 1908 near Folsom, New Mexico. But it was not until August 29, 1927, that a fluted spear or "dart" point (Folsom) was found by archeologists among the bones of extinct bison (*Bison antiquus*) at McJunkin's Folsom site. Paleontologists, archeologists, and anthropologists were called to inspect this find in its undisturbed context, and only then did the scientific community agree that humans had lived contemporaneously with these now-extinct animals at the end of the last Ice Age.

These accidental finds sparked the initial systematic studies of the Paleo-Indian presence in the North American Great Plains. In the 1930s Clovis projectile points (dated 11,200–10,900 B.P.) were found with the remains of extinct Ice Age elephants (mammoths) and also bison near Clovis, New Mexico. Later Paleo-Indian occupations (10,000–8,800 B.P.), including the Cody complex on the Northern Plains and the Firstview complex on the Southern Plains, featured a number of chipped stone projectile points. With the development of radiocarbon dating in the 1950s, as well as the excavation of "layer-cake like" sites at Blackwater Draw, New Mexico, and Hell Gap, Wyoming, archeologists outlined the time frame for Paleo-Indian life in the Great Plains that is used today.

Paleo-Indians left a scant "trail" throughout the Great Plains. Geographer Vance Holliday has estimated that archeologists have found roughly two Paleo-Indian campsites for each century of their currently documented 2,400-year-long stay in the Great Plains. In the Southern High Plains, this means that there is one Paleo-Indian campsite per 667 square miles (1,733 square kilometers). Yet Paleo-Indian sites are still being discovered, including campsites (e.g., Mill Iron, Montana; Lake Ilo, North Dakota; and Cattle Guard, Colorado), animal kill sites (e.g., Waugh and Cooper sites in Kansas), tool caches (e.g., Anzick, Montana; Fenn, Wyoming; and Ryan, Texas), and tool stone quarries and/or workshops (e.g., Alkali Creek, North Dakota, and Hanson, Wyoming).

Researchers have also intensified their efforts to revise and to reformulate their reconstructions of past environments and Paleo-Indian life. Archeologists had generally assumed that the Great Plains during the late glacial period supported a widespread boreal forest composed predominantly of spruce trees. This spruce forest reconstruction is not supported by a fossil record that is dominated by grazing and browsing mammals. Also, paleoecologists now suggest that much, if not all, of the spruce and pine pollen was not endemic and had actually been deposited over the Plains by westerly winds.

Recent studies suggest that Paleo-Indian hunter-gatherers, specifically Folsom people, lived in small, multifamily groups. These groups or hunting bands may have established from twelve to thirty-six camps per year throughout an area of more than 52,000 square miles (slightly less than the area of North Dakota). Folsom-age projectile points have been found more than 300 miles (500 km) from their geological source. It appears that Paleo-Indians quickly located sources for the highest-quality tool stone in the Plains, including Knife River flint (western North Dakota), Niobrara jasper (Nebraska), and Edwards chert (Texas).

The Great Plains has played, and continues to play, a central role in the study of Paleo-Indian lifeways in the Western Hemisphere. Recent work by Steve Holen (Nebraska State Museum) at mammoth death sites may push the initial human occupation of the Great Plains back to more than 18,000 years ago. Such recent research also suggests that the earliest Paleo-Indians may have scavenged food from large mammal carcasses. Archeologists are making use of refined radiocarbon dating methods and more dynamic views of prehistoric technology to reassess the static Paleo-Indian "culture histories" that once dominated their thinking. Archeologists working in the Great Plains have now begun to bring the faint outlines of Paleo-Indian existence into better focus.

See also PHYSICAL ENVIRONMENT: Glaciation; Paleoenvironments.

Alan J. Osborn
University of Nebraska–Lincoln

Frison, George C. *Prehistoric Hunters of the High Plains.* New York: Academic Press, 1991. Holliday, Vance T. *Paleoindian Geoarchaeology of the Southern High Plains.* Austin: University of Texas Press, 1997. Stanford, Dennis J., and Jane S. Day, eds. *Ice Age Hunters of the Rockies.* Niwot CO: University Press of Colorado, 1992.

PARKER, QUANAH (ca. 1852–1911)

Born between 1845 and 1852 to the white captive Cynthia Ann Parker and the Quahada Comanche war chief Peta Nocona, Quanah Parker grew up within traditional Comanche society, but his later life was marked by a fusion of white and Indian ways. By the time of the 1874–75 Red River War, Quanah had gained such a sufficient following that he helped lead the momentous attack of as many as 700 Comanches, Kiowas, and Southern Cheyennes against the two dozen buffalo hunters and merchants at the Adobe Walls trading post in the Texas Panhandle. The failure of this attack, and subsequent army victories on the Staked Plains, forced all the Comanches and Kiowas to their reservation at Fort Sill in western Indian Territory.

Because of his white ancestry and his willingness to accept reservation life, Quanah attracted the attention of various civilians and military officers at Fort Sill. Agent P. B. Hunt established him as a band chief, with authority to preside over the issuance of beef rations and other annuities. This provided Quanah with significant leverage among his own people, even to the detriment of some of the traditional elders. By 1886 he had been appointed one of the three judges of the Court of Indian Offenses, and he used this position to champion an assimilationist course.

Despite his cooperation with white authorities and his determination to have his people "walk the white man's road," Quanah steadfastly honored many Comanche traditions. He retained his long hair, participated in ancient ceremonies, spoke mostly in the Comanche language, and preserved the right of polygamous marriage. The fact that he had eight wives, five of them at one time, angered

Quanah Parker

some important whites, and in 1898 this cost him the coveted position of Indian judge. Significantly, however, he won his battle to serve as a leader of the peyote religion that was expanding rapidly among his people.

Even though Quanah drew most of his authority as "principal chief" from whites, his popularity among Comanches also increased, especially because of his diplomatic skills in negotiating leasing agreements with Texas cattlemen. Although many tribal members initially had opposed the leasing of tribal grazing lands, the collective income soon guaranteed majority support. The greatest challenge to the reservation began in 1892 when the Jerome Commission called for the allotment of tribal lands into individual holdings and the sale of all surplus acreage to white settlers. Quanah made repeated trips to Washington DC to fight this assault on the collective land base and Comanche sovereignty, but, yielding to the inevitable realities, he negotiated the best terms possible and accepted the allotment process in 1900.

Throughout the years of reservation life, Quanah Parker closely aligned his personal interests with those of the broader tribe. He received money and other gifts from Texas cattlemen, lived in the spacious "star house" built by their largess, fenced several thousand acres of tribal land for his own cattle herd and to rent to whites, and rewarded supporters and family members with reservation jobs through supportive agents. Yet no one could doubt that Quanah had gained more benefits for the tribe then any other leader of the era. He died on February 11, 1911. His funeral at Lawton, Oklahoma, was the largest ever held in that region,

and was well attended by respectful Indians and whites alike.

See also WAR: Adobe Walls, Battle of.

Michael L. Tate
University of Nebraska at Omaha

Hagan, William T. *Quanah Parker, Comanche Chief*. Norman: University of Oklahoma Press, 1993. Hagan, William T. *United States–Comanche Relations: The Reservation Years*. New Haven CT: Yale University Press, 1976.

PAWNEES

Unlike many Plains Indians, who moved into the area relatively recently, the Pawnees are longtime residents of the Great Plains. Linguistic and archeological evidence indicates that the Pawnees, specifically the Skiri band, have roots in central Nebraska extending back at least as far as the sixteenth century, and perhaps even further to the Upper Republican peoples who occupied villages along the Republican and Loup Rivers from 1100 A.D. to 1400 A.D. This stock was subsequently reinforced by recurrent migrations of other Caddoan-speaking bands from the Southern Great Plains during the seventeenth and eighteenth centuries. The Pawnees' own traditions speak of an origin in the southwestern United States, then a slow migration north, leaving their relatives, the Wichitas, on the Southern Plains. Linguistic analysis suggests that this split occurred in the first few centuries A.D.

By 1800 the Pawnee were a loose confederation of four bands—the Skiris (Loups), Chauis (Grands), Kitkahahkis (Republicans), and Pitahawiratas (Tappages). Their combined population, according to Lewis and Clark, was 6,850. The Skiris lived in a large village (twenty to forty acres in extent) on a terrace of the Loup River near present-day Palmer, Nebraska; the Chauis occupied two villages on the south side of the Platte River near Bellwood and Linwood; and the Kitkahahkis lived to the south on the Republican River between Red Cloud and Guide Rock. By 1811, under pressure from the Kanzas, the Kitkahahkis moved north to the Loup. The location of the Pitahawirata village, if indeed it was separate from the Chaui sites, is unknown.

Each band was largely independent of the others, with its own chiefs, priests, and ceremonies. The Skiris, especially, maintained an independent stance from the other three bands. The identity of each band was encapsulated in their village bundles, the bison hide packs which contained sacred icons and which represented the peoples' original charter with the gods. Every step in the year's cycle of activities was sanctified by the bundles.

The traditional annual cycle of the Pawnees began in April when the first thunder from the south announced that it was time to clear the fields for cultivation. Corn, beans, squash, and sunflowers were planted by the women along the river floodplains. In late June, when the crops were well established, the Pawnees left for their summer bison hunt. They returned to the villages in late August and harvested and stored their crops. In early November they again abandoned their villages for the bison

range, where they remained until March, hunting and camping on the upper reaches of the Republican, Smokey Hill, Solomon, and Platte Rivers. The bison hunts not only provided meat and most of the Indians' raw materials but also allowed the Pawnees and their horses (of which there were 6,000 in 1806) to spread their subsistence base over an extensive area. This annual cycle was a successful adaptation to the transitional environment of the Great Plains, and in most years the Pawnees produced a food surplus and flourished as the dominant power in the Central Plains.

In the nineteenth century the traditional lifestyle of the Pawnees was seriously disrupted by war and disease. Their population in 1800 was already only a fraction of the 15,000 or 20,000 people the villages had sustained in previous years. Smallpox struck in 1798, then again in 1830–31, taking at least half the population in one winter. After each epidemic, the Pawnees partly recovered, but after 1831 diseases struck with increased frequency and the population went on a downward spiral that was reversed only after 1906.

Also, after 1831 the Pawnee found themselves caught in a vise, pressed by the Lakotas from the north and by the expanding American frontier to the east. From that time until their departure from Nebraska in 1876, they lived under the shadow of attack. Hunts and harvests were disrupted, food supplies became more precarious, and death rates soared. In the 1840s, mounting traffic along the Oregon Trail led to the depletion of timber and grass, and the bison were driven west beyond the forks of the Platte. By 1854, when Nebraska Territory was opened to settlers, the Pawnees were a beleaguered people.

Traditionally, the territory occupied and claimed by the Pawnees reached from the Niobrara to the Arkansas and Cimarron Rivers. The southern part of this territory was sold to the United States in 1833, and subsequent cessions left the Pawnees with only a small reservation, later Nance County, Nebraska, on the Loup River. There, between 1857 and 1876, their population dropped to fewer than 2,000 people, and settlers increasingly hemmed in their lives. In the early 1870s a series of disasters, including a massacre by the Lakotas in southwestern Nebraska in 1873 and the destruction of the crops by drought and grasshoppers, persuaded the Pawnees to relinquish their reservation and take up residency near the Wichitas in Indian Territory.

The migration south and subsequent problems of adjusting to the new homeland resulted in further population decline, the nadir being reached in 1906 when only 650 Pawnees remained. In 1892 the Pawnees accepted individual allotments, and the remainder of their reservation was sold to settlers. The Pawnees were given $30,000 a year for this land. Many of their traditions were forgotten, and ceremonies lapsed. Their culture was resilient, however, and their rich traditions were preserved in the early twentieth century by James Murie, a member of the Skiri band. In 1936 the Pawnees gained tribal government recognition under the Oklahoma

Indian Welfare Act. Their identity was further reinforced by lengthy and successful claims-case litigation before the Indian Claims Commission from 1946 to 1962. The Pawnees were eventually awarded $7,316,096 for lands in Nebraska and Oklahoma that had been taken from them for an "unconscionably" low payment in the nineteenth century.

In the late twentieth century the Pawnee population numbered nearly 2,400, most of whom lived around the headquarters of the tribal council in Pawnee, Oklahoma. The tribe owned 726 acres, and another 19,399 acres was allotted to individuals. Unemployment stood at 25 percent. The Pawnees are governed by a council consisting of a president, vice president, and five council members.

David J. Wishart
University of Nebraska–Lincoln

Blaine, Martha Royce. *Pawnee Passage: 1870–1875*. Norman: University of Oklahoma Press, 1990. Weltfish, Gene. *The Lost Universe: Pawnee Life and Culture*. Lincoln: University of Nebraska Press, 1977. Wishart, David J. *An Unspeakable Sadness: The Dispossession of the Nebraska Indians*. Lincoln: University of Nebraska Press, 1994.

PAYIPWAT (ca. 1816–1908)

Payipwat was one of five major chiefs of the Plains Cree (Nehiyawak) after 1860. He was born around 1816, probably in what is now southwestern Manitoba or eastern Saskatchewan, and named Kisikawasan Awasis, or "Flash in the Sky Boy." As a child he and his grandmother were captured and adopted by the Sioux. At age fourteen he was rescued by his own people, and he grew up to be a highly respected spiritual leader among the Young Dogs, a notable Cree-Assiniboine band of the Qu'Appelle Valley region. Because he learned Sioux medicine, his people named him Payipwat (or Piapot), "Hole in the Sioux," sometimes translated as "One Who Knows the Secrets of the Sioux."

An independent and assertive leader, Payipwat agreed to Treaty Number 4 in 1875, after making it clear that it was a "preliminary negotiation." He insisted that the treaty contain a number of additional provisions, and while Treaty 4 was never altered, many of these provisions were written into Treaty Number 6 (1876).

With the disappearance of the bison, Payipwat and other Plains Cree and Assiniboine leaders argued for the establishment of a large Indian territory in the Cypress Hills. However, the plan was thwarted when the federal government coerced their removal to smaller reserves by withholding rations from the starving Indians. The Plains Native coalition for an Indian territory collapsed when the government took advantage of the Métis resistance (1885) to crush it.

Once settled on his reserve near Fort Qu'Appelle, Payipwat continued pressing the federal government to live up to its treaty promises and continued resisting government regulations prohibiting ceremonial practices. Until the end of his life Payipwat resisted Christian conversion and challenged Canadian infringements on Cree sovereignty. A federal order

deposing him as chief of his band was issued the day he died, in late April of 1908, on the Piapot Reserve in Saskatchewan.

Winona Wheeler
Saskatchewan Indian Federated College
Saskatoon, Saskatchewan

Tobias, John L. "Payipwat." In *Dictionary of Canadian Biography*, edited by Ramsay Cook, 13: 815–18. Toronto: University of Toronto Press, 1994. Watetsch, Able. *Payepot and His People, as Told to Bloodwen Davies*. Regina: Saskatchewan History and Folklore Society, 1959.

PITARESARU (ca. 1823–1874)

Pitaresaru (Petalesharo) is a Pawnee name meaning "Chief of Men" or "Man Chief." Two or more outstanding chiefs of this name were members of the Chaui band of the Pawnee (there was also a famous Skiri Pawnee chief named Pitaresaru who died in the devastating smallpox epidemic of 1830–31). The elder Pitaresaru of the Chaui band was born in the late eighteenth or early nineteenth century. His name is on the 1833 treaty whereby the Pawnee ceded what is now southern Nebraska to the United States. His son is believed to have been born around 1823 and died as head chief in 1874 in Nebraska, the Pawnee tribal homeland.

The younger Pitaresaru was described as being over six feet tall and of good appearance. He became a chief when he was twenty-nine. He devoted his life to the good of his people, and, as an excellent orator, he attempted to mollify the U.S. government in its often unreasonable demands and treatment. Pitaresaru's name appears first—indicating his primary importance among all four Pawnee bands—on the 1857 treaty in which the Pawnees ceded the balance of their ancestral lands, retaining only a small reservation on the Loup River. Although honoring his own culture, Pitaresaru accepted U.S. government schools so that Pawnee children could learn to read and write the white man's words. He sought to maintain the sovereignty of tribal leaders and forcefully criticized negligent and dishonest agency employees. When his reservation-bound people endured hunger in the 1860s, he successfully pleaded that the tribe be allowed to go on the bison hunt, an activity that countered government policy of spatial restriction and conversion of the Pawnees into farmers.

When pressure came for the removal of the Pawnees from Nebraska to Indian Territory, at first he was resolutely against it, but later he agreed to the removal with a heavy heart. In 1874, before this sad migration was made, Pitaresaru died under mysterious circumstances; he was shot in the leg by parties unknown and subsequently perished from gangrene.

It was later said by a Skiri Pawnee that Pitaresaru ruled all the bands and was a great man. Today, some of his warrior songs are still sung by the Pawnee people in Oklahoma.

Martha Royce Blaine
Oklahoma City, Oklahoma

Blaine, Martha Royce. *Pawnee Passage: 1870–1875*. Norman: University of Oklahoma Press, 1990. Dunbar, John B. "Pitalesharu." *American History Magazine* 5 (1880): 340–42.

PLAINS APACHES

According to our legends, we, the Plains Apaches or Apache Tribe of Oklahoma, have been here since time began. Our earliest oral histories record our existence with the Sarcees (Sarsis) in Canada. These same histories mention that we split from the Sarcees and established ourselves in the Black Hills of South Dakota. At that time, we were known as Káłt'inde, "Cedar People." This name was given to us by some other tribe. At that time, the Lakotas granted us the territory south of the Black Hills, while they took the territory to the north. We began to make our way to the south, hunting the bison.

Because of the second name our people were given, our elders believe we must have been very proficient hunters. We again came to be known by our former name, Bek'áhe, or "Whetstone," given to us by another tribe. Our elders believe this came about because we were always honing our knives in order to butcher the many bison our hunters killed. The sign for our people, to this very day, is the sign of honing—moving the outside of the right hand back and forth over the thumb side of the left hand. Today we are known in our own language as Ná'isha, "Stealers or Takers." We were given this name by the Kiowas, with whom we have long been closely associated. It seems that we got this name because of our ability to steal horses in the prereservation period.

We also have had multiple English names. We were first known as the Kiowa Apaches. Our elders believe this name was given to us in order to distinguish us from the Fort Sill Apaches. After the 1867 Treaty of Medicine Lodge Creek, we shared the Kiowa Reservation with the Kiowa and Comanche people. In 1894 the U.S. Army brought a number of Chiricahua Apaches to Fort Sill. At that time, it became necessary to distinguish us from the Fort Sill Apaches. Because we had been closely associated with the Kiowas, we became known as the Kiowa Apaches. The name Plains Apache was given to us by anthropologists and government officials. This name stems from our location and our mobile lifestyle.

We came to this area of the country by wandering with the bison, moving south from the Dakotas. We traveled on the eastern side of the Rocky Mountains, into the Southern Plains. We traveled throughout the Plains, from the northern reaches of the Missouri River to Chihuahua, Mexico. We traded extensively, bartering buffalo hides, salt, and meat for produce and other goods. Through trade, we established peaceful relationships with a number of other tribes, including the Pawnees, Arapahos, and Kiowas. Our people preferred trading to raiding for goods, but we were not passive when hostilities occurred.

Warfare and raiding allowed men to gain power and prestige. To become leaders, men were expected to have outstanding character. The leaders were honest, understanding, level-headed men who had shown valor in war or had distinguished themselves as providers.

Our tribe was governed by chiefs, a council of elders, warriors, and medicine people. When a man appeared to hold the qualities that made a good chief, the warriors would suggest that the council consider him for that position. If the council agreed with the warriors, the man was made a chief. Occasionally, sons or grandsons would inherit their father's or grandfather's positions, but only if the young man had the qualifications. If a chief abused his position or acted irresponsibly, he could be run off or killed.

Women also were important in Ná'ishą society. While women did not hold positions of power, they were in charge of maintaining many of the family possessions. Women were responsible for making and repairing the tipis and all items associated with them. Gathering of plant foods and, occasionally, small game, were women's activities as well. Special skill in tipi sewing, clothing decoration, and food location and preparation was recognized by induction into women's societies, which had their own dances and songs.

Today, we are recognized as the Apache Tribe of Oklahoma. This name was established in 1972 when the Kiowa, Comanche, and Apache tribes officially separated. While each tribe had run its own tribal affairs previously, we all had been supervised by the Bureau of Indian Affairs. Upon establishing our independence in 1972, we became an entity separate from the other two tribes, with our own tribal name and government. Government officers are elected in general elections. There are approximately 1,600 enrolled tribal members. The majority of tribal members live in Caddo and Comanche Counties in Oklahoma. Our tribal offices are located in Anadarko, Oklahoma.

Alfred Chalepah Sr.
Irene Poolaw
Houston Klinekole Sr.
Apache Tribe of Oklahoma
Pamela Innes
Deborah Bernsten
University of Oklahoma

Bittle, William. Fieldnotes. Apache Tribe of Oklahoma Culture Office, Anadarko, Oklahoma. Chalepah, Alfred Sr., Irene Poolaw, and Houston Klinekole Sr. Oral histories. Apache Tribe of Oklahoma Culture Office, Anadarko, Oklahoma.

PLAINS CREES

Plains Crees traditionally occupied—and still occupy—a large section of the Canadian Plains, extending through much of central Alberta and central and southeastern Saskatchewan. Most of this territory is within the Parkland Belt, a transitional zone between the open grasslands on the south and the boreal forests to the north. Plains Crees speak a dialect of Algonquian.

Archeological remains (Selkirk composite) attributed to the western boreal forest Crees date from at least A.D. 1350 in northern Saskatchewan. Whether Crees also occupied the Aspen Parklands at this time is not certain, although there are some late archeological materials in this zone that reflect Selkirk influ-

ence. Indeed, when Henry Kelsey, the first European known to have visited the Canadian Plains, traveled through the Aspen Parklands of eastern Saskatchewan in 1690, he met Crees there, along with Nakotas (Assiniboines) Certainly, the detailed observations of Hudson's Bay Company employees in the mid-1700s record the presence of at least four named Cree groups—Susahanna, Sturgeon, Pegogamow, and Kiskatchewan—in the Aspen Parklands of Saskatchewan through to central Alberta. The nature of the social and political organization of these groups remains uncertain. It should be noted that the predominant occupants of the Parklands of Saskatchewan and Manitoba at this time were the Nakotas (Assiniboines), who were friends and allies of the Crees. They often located their camps in close proximity, particularly at bison pounds.

Beginning in the late seventeenth century and continuing through most of the eighteenth century, many of these Crees (and Nakotas) played a prominent role in the developing fur trade. In particular, they acted as middlemen traders, and each summer they took canoe loads of furs to York Factory on Hudson Bay. These they traded for European goods, which, upon returning to the borders of the Plains, they exchanged with other Native peoples for furs. Of particular importance was the Blackfoot-Cree alliance, which formed in the 1730s and continued throughout the eighteenth century. At the heart of this alliance was the provision of guns by the Crees to the Blackfoot in return for furs.

Important changes occurred in the second half of the eighteenth century, including the establishment of a number of fur trade posts on the fringes of the Canadian Prairies, beginning with the French posts in the 1740s and 1750s. By 1780 the Hudson's Bay Company, the North West Company, and some smaller companies operated many posts in the western interior. The Parkland Crees and the Nakotas became much involved in the provisions trade, producing pemmican for the support of the employees of the trading companies. An even more important agent of change was disease, particularly the smallpox epidemics of 1780–81 and 1837–38, which greatly reduced the Cree population. Notably, during 1838 most of the Parkland Crees were vaccinated against smallpox, a reflection of their close relations with the Hudson's Bay Company. Unfortunately, this was not the case with most of the Nakota bands, which were decimated. The Parkland Crees then emerged as the predominant occupants of the Aspen Parklands and adjacent grasslands of central Saskatchewan and Alberta, and very quickly became a new tribal group—the Plains Crees.

Through the mid–nineteenth century, the Plains Crees maintained an economic cycle that positioned them near the grassland/parkland interface during the winter. A common method of taking bison at this season involved building a pound—a circular corral with an opening on one side. Wings extending outward from the opening for a considerable distance were employed to funnel small herds

into the pound where they were dispatched. In the course of the winter, some families traveled into the forest edge to trap fur-bearing animals, an activity that continued through the spring. During the latter season they sometimes built fish weirs on streams in order to intercept spawning runs. Following this they moved out into the Plains for the summer. While the Plains Crees valued horses highly, the number of horses remained low because the northern winters impeded their reproduction and caused a high general mortality. Therefore, dogs remained an important draft animal.

By the second half of the nineteenth century the Plains Crees were divided into eight major bands. Each of these bands had at least one prominent chief who often was the focus of a large camp group; however, all the members of each band gathered together only once a year, during the summer. At this time, in late June or early July, there was a ceremonial gathering at which the Sun (Thirsting) Dance was celebrated. The Plains Crees also observed nine other sacred ceremonies, the most prominent of which was the Smoking Tipi. However, in central Saskatchewan the Goose Dance—a ceremony of certain boreal forest Crees with elements adapted from the Midewiwin (the Grand Medicine Society) of the Ojibwas—was also important.

During the second half of the nineteenth century the bison herds were decimated, their range contracting to the south and southwest. As a result, many Crees were drawn far out onto the grasslands of southwestern Saskatchewan and northern Montana, where they came into conflict with their former allies, the Blackfoot. In the 1870s, with the approaching extirpation of the bison, most of the Plains Cree bands entered into treaty agreements with the Canadian government and took up residence on some twenty-four reserves in Alberta and Saskatchewan, where they survived by farming and ranching.

Over the years, many of the Plains Crees (and Plains Ojibwas) had intermarried with French traders, creating the Métis culture. In 1885, led by chiefs Poundmaker and Big Bear, they joined their relatives in the North-West Rebellion. Defeated after two major battles, Cree leaders were imprisoned, and one group left Canada and eventually settled on the Rocky Boy's Reservation in northern Montana. In the late 1800s the Plains Cree population was about 7,000; by 1998 it had increased remarkably to 62,330 persons, with 37,314 living in Saskatchewan and 25,016 in Alberta. In recent decades there has been considerable out-migration from the reserves to the cities of the Canadian Prairies, and there are now probably more Plains Crees living in urban areas than on the reserves.

See also WAR: North-West Rebellion.

David Meyer
University of Saskatchewan

Ahenakew, Freda, and H. Christoph Wolfart, eds. *Kwayask ê-kî-pê-kiskinowâpahtihicik. Their Example Showed Me the Way.* Told by Emma Minde. Edmonton: University of Alberta Press, 1997. Mandelbaum, David G. *The Plains Cree:*

An Ethnographic, Historical and Comparative Study. Canadian Plains Studies no. 9. Regina: Canadian Plains Research Centre, 1979. Russell, Dale. *Eighteenth-Century Western Cree and Their Neighbours.* Archaeological Survey of Canada Mercury Series Paper no. 143. Hull, Quebec: Canadian Museum of Civilization, 1991.

PLENTY COUPS (1848–1932)

Plenty Coups (*Alaxchiiaahush,* or *Aleck chea ahoos*) was a Crow warrior, diplomat, and mediator. He was born in 1848 at "the cliff that has no pass" in present Billings, Montana. Also known as Bull Who Goes Into (Against) the Wind, he was a Mountain Crow. His parents died when he was about ten years old. Orphaned and in grief, he was encouraged by camp criers to go on vision quests. He was adopted by the Little People and guided by eagles, who became his guardians. In a vision in the Crazy Mountains he saw the buffalo disappear and be replaced by cattle, a windstorm destroy all trees except the one in which the chickadee lived, and himself as an old man sitting by a house.

By his mid-twenties Plenty Coups had accomplished each of four war deeds to achieve the distinction of chieftain, or "good man." He carried a Medicine Pipe and Pipe Holder's bag as a leader of the Fox Warrior Society. One of many Crows who scouted for the U.S. military, he was a leader in the Battle of the Rosebud on June 17, 1876. Years later he stated his reason for aiding the Americans: "[W]e plainly saw that this course was the only one which might save our beautiful country for us." In 1880 he traveled with five other Crow leaders to Washington DC. The main purpose was to negotiate the sale of the western part of the reservation and a Northern Pacific Railroad right-of-way up the Yellowstone Valley. At George Washington's home, he pondered the difficulties of his "small nation." Inspired by the visit, he later willed land in 1928 to be used as a park, recreation ground, and display of his possessions as "a reminder to Indians and white people alike that the two races should live and work together harmoniously." His house, a Montana state park, is a National Historic Landmark.

By 1890 Plenty Coups and Pretty Eagle were recognized as head chiefs of the tribe. Plenty Coups settled in Pryor Valley, on land he had seen in his vision, where he farmed, raised cattle and horses, and established a general merchandise store. He was involved in "pan-Indian" intertribal networks and fought the continual pressure to sell Crow land. In preparation for hearings on yet another bill for opening and settlement of the reservation in 1917, Plenty Coups and other leaders held traditional war ceremonies in a Washington DC hotel room, including burning buffalo chips and offering songs and prayers. He promoted Crow Fair and also led parades at regional fairs. He encouraged Crow support of U.S. efforts during World War I. Chosen to be the representative of all Indians and called "Chief of All Chiefs" for dedication of the Tomb of the Unknown Soldier at Arlington National

Cemetery in 1921, he placed his war bonnet and coup stick before the casket; they are on display there today.

Following the example of the chickadee to be observant and learn from others, Plenty Coups lived according to his own Crow values and also accommodated non-Indian culture. He practiced traditional Crow religion, including the vision quest, sweat lodge, and Sacred Tobacco Society. He was baptized into the Catholic Church at St. Xavier on the Crow Indian Reservation. He was married several times, but his two children died young, so he and his wives adopted and raised other children. He considered all the Crows as his "children." He understood that education is important and donated part of his land for a school. His most famous statement was "Education is your most powerful weapon. With education you are the white man's equal; without education you are his victim." Plenty Coups passed to the "Other Side Camp" on March 4, 1932, at age eighty-four. Funeral services were held according to both Catholic and traditional Crow customs, including proclamation in the Crow language of his deeds. The tribe voted to honor him as their last traditional chief.

See also SPORTS AND RECREATION: Crow Fair.

C. Adrian Heidenreich
Montana State University–Billings

Hoxie, Frederick E. *Parading through History: The Making of the Crow Nation in America, 1805–1935.* New York: Cambridge University Press, 1995. Linderman, Frank B. *Plenty-Coups, Chief of the Crows.* 1930. Lincoln: University of Nebraska Press, 1962.

PONCAS

Since their arrival in the Great Plains, the Ponca Tribe has always been small in numbers. Yet their history and experiences are representative of many of the major themes that have shaped the lives of the Native inhabitants of the region. According to the Poncas' oral history, their original homeland was in the Ohio River valley. For reasons now unknown, the Siouan Degiha speakers (Poncas, Omahas, Kanzas, Osages, and Quapaws) undertook a vast migration: as they followed the Ohio, Mississippi, and eventually the Missouri Rivers, one cognate tribe after another divided off until only the Poncas and Omahas remained together. The Poncas eventually separated from the Omahas and settled in the Niobrara River valley (in present-day northeastern Nebraska) by the early eighteenth century. As a consequence, the Poncas and Omahas speak mutually intelligible dialects and had similar political and social organization, including hereditary chiefs and patrilineal, exogamous clans.

Settling into their new land, the Poncas jettisoned many of their Woodland adaptations in favor of the archetypal Plains Village Tradition of semipermanent earth lodge villages, maize horticulture, and communal bison hunting. In the nineteenth century, however, as a result of epidemic diseases, the Poncas periodically abandoned horticulture in favor of full-time nomadic bison hunting. Still, they never abandoned their homeland near the confluence of the Niobrara and Missouri Rivers, and they continued to return to their sacred sites, villages, and gardens on a regular basis.

The typical seasonal round of the Poncas was organized around the horticultural calendar: planting gardens in the spring and harvesting in the fall, interspersed with communal bison hunts in the summer and winter seasons. Hunting and horticulture were supplemented by gathering wild plants and herbs for food and healing. The Poncas utilized a vast area of the Central Great Plains for trading, hunting, horse raiding, and visiting. In all, they claimed an area extending from the Missouri River on the east to the Black Hills and foothills of the Rocky Mountains to the west, and from the White River in the north to the Platte River in the south.

Given their range, the Poncas had to learn to coexist with their more numerous and powerful neighbors, the Lakotas and the Pawnees. The Poncas forged a tenuous alliance with the Oglala Lakotas, occasionally hunting together and accompanying them on their horse raids against the Pawnees. From the Oglalas the Poncas learned the sacred Sun Dance, but they modified it to fit Ponca horticultural traditions by adding an emphasis on fertility and renewal, consistent with the goals of a horticultural tribe. The Poncas also practiced (and still practice) the sacred pipe religion and expressed a strong belief in their all-powerful creator, *Wakonda.* The Poncas had a more troubled relationship with the Brulé Lakotas, however, which would eventually contribute to their expulsion from their Niobrara homeland.

The Poncas point with pride to the fact that they never engaged in armed conflict with the U.S. government. In all, they signed four treaties, including a treaty that ceded Aboriginal title to the majority of their land and established a reservation near Niobrara, Nebraska, in 1858. The Poncas tried earnestly to succeed in their transition to reservation-based farming. However, those efforts proved futile when the government ceded away title to the entire Ponca Reservation to the Sioux in the Treaty of Fort Laramie in 1868. Overnight, the Poncas found themselves trespassers on their own reservation. The Brulé Lakotas, under Chief Spotted Tail, were relentless in their harassment of the Poncas and eventually weakened them to the point of desperation. Conditions were so grave by the 1870s that the Poncas considered a plan to abandon their homeland in favor of a new reservation in Indian Territory. After traveling to the proposed site in the winter of 1877, a delegation of Ponca chiefs declined the offer. However, the will of the chiefs was disregarded by the government, and the forced removal of the tribe commenced in the spring of 1877.

This event, known as the Ponca Trail of Tears, was a disaster. Plagued by bad weather and inadequate preparations, the Poncas lost more than one-fifth (158 from 730) of their population within the first two years of removal. Dissatisfaction with their circumstances led to a desperate attempt by Chief Standing Bear to return to the Niobrara homeland to honor the dying wish of his son to be buried with his ancestors. On New Year's Day of 1879, Standing Bear led a small party of Poncas—mostly women and children—back to Nebraska. They were arrested, and a trial ensued in federal district court in Omaha, Nebraska. Judge Elmer Dundy declared that "an Indian is a person under the meaning of the law" and that the United States had no authority to return Standing Bear to Indian Territory.

Standing Bear had won his case, but the victory was a hollow one for the Ponca Tribe. The majority of the Poncas, after spending more than two years settling into their new reservation in Indian Territory, opted to remain there. In 1881 the Ponca Tribe was officially dissolved and legally reconstituted as two separate entities: the Northern Ponca Tribe, residing on a portion of the old Ponca Reservation in northeastern Nebraska, and the Southern Ponca Tribe, with a reservation of 101,000 acres in north-central Oklahoma.

The two Ponca tribes, still linked by family, cultural, and linguistic ties, have faced vastly different fates in the twentieth century. The Ponca Tribe of Oklahoma, organized in 1950, is headquartered in White Eagle, named after the Poncas' charismatic paramount chief at the time of removal. In 1996 the Southern Poncas listed 2,581 enrolled members, of whom more than half resided in Kay County, Oklahoma. The Southern Poncas' land base suffered as a consequence of allotment policy, and they eventually lost the vast majority of their land-holdings, including oil-rich lands, to non-Indian interests, particularly the "101 Ranch." The Southern Poncas have been active in the Native American Church, the revitalization of the *Heduska*, or War Dance Society, and the Plains powwow tradition. The economy of the Ponca Tribe of Oklahoma is based on a successful bingo hall, smoke shops, and various tribal economic development initiatives.

The Northern Ponca Tribe also struggled in the twentieth century with land loss and the out-migration of tribal members. The Northern Ponca Tribe was terminated in 1962, joining more than 100 tribes that lost their status as a result of federal termination policy. At the time of termination, only 442 Northern Poncas were listed on the tribal roll, and only 847 of their original 27,000 acres remained. Tribal status was legally restored by Congress in 1990 as a result of a prolonged tribal grassroots effort led by the nonprofit Northern Ponca Restoration Committee. The Ponca Tribe of Nebraska is currently headquartered in Niobrara, Nebraska, near their first reservation. The tribe, denied the opportunity to reestablish their reservation by Congress, delivers services to tribal members residing in fifteen designated counties in Nebraska, South Dakota, and Iowa. Enrollment exceeds 2,000. At the turn of the twenty-first century the tribe was engaged in a number of economic developments and cultural revitalization projects, including the reintroduction of bison on tribal trust lands near Niobrara and the establish-

ment of the Ponca Health and Wellness Center in Omaha, Nebraska.

See also PROTEST AND DISSENT: Trial of Standing Bear.

Beth R. Ritter
University of Nebraska at Omaha

Howard, James H. *The Ponca Tribe*. Washington DC: Government Printing Office, 1995. Ritter, Beth R. "The Politics of Retribalization: The Northern Ponca Case." *Great Plains Research* 4 (1994): 237–55. Wishart, David J. *An Unspeakable Sadness: The Dispossession of the Nebraska Indians*. Lincoln: University of Nebraska Press, 1994.

POSEY, ALEXANDER

See LITERARY TRADITIONS: Posey, Alexander

POUNDMAKER (ca. 1842–1886)

Poundmaker, whose Indian name was *Pītik-wahanapiwīyin*, was born around 1842. The son of an Assiniboine Indian and a mixed-blood mother of French descent, he was a member of a prominent Plains Cree family from the House Band in what today is central Saskatchewan.

Poundmaker was destined to become an influential leader. In 1873 he was adopted by Crowfoot, head chief of the powerful Blackfoot nation of southern Alberta. This happened during a brief truce in the wars between the Crees and the Blackfoot, when Poundmaker visited Crowfoot's camp for the first time. One of Crowfoot's wives, who was grieving the loss of a son in battle, was struck with Poundmaker's resemblance to her dead son and prevailed upon the chief to adopt the Cree as a replacement. For his part, Crowfoot was greatly impressed with Poundmaker's statesmanlike bearing and commitment to peacemaking, and so he readily agreed. The adoption invested Poundmaker with the attributes of a Blackfoot family member; it bestowed new wealth on him in the form of horses gifted by his adoptive family; and it conferred upon him a new Blackfoot name, *Makoyi-koh-kin* (Wolf Thin Legs). When Poundmaker returned home, he was accorded special standing because of his personal connection to a nation that traditionally had been an enemy of the Crees. Within a few years he was elevated to the rank of a councilor, or minor chief, in the River People Band led by Chief Red Pheasant.

Poundmaker proved to be a strong critic of government policy. In 1876, during the negotiation of Treaty Number 6 at Fort Carlton, he took exception to the very notion of confining Indians to reserves. "This is our land!" he protested to the government commissioners. "It isn't a piece of pemmican to be cut off and given in little pieces back to us." He also insisted that the terms offered did not provide adequately for agricultural assistance or for famine relief during hard times. He eventually signed the treaty but remained resistant to taking up reserve life. In 1878, when Red Pheasant agreed to move onto a reserve, Poundmaker formed his own band and made a last-ditch effort to hunt down the few remaining buffalo. A year later he and his starving band accepted a reserve some forty miles west of

Battleford, Saskatchewan. Although he made efforts to master farming, he nevertheless remained a determined critic of the government, which routinely ignored both Indian treaty rights and the starvation that stalked the reserves.

Owing to circumstances beyond his control, Poundmaker was implicated in the North-West Rebellion of 1885. Like most Indian leaders, he did not want to join the disaffected Métis who had clashed with government forces at Batoche and elsewhere. While he was known to criticize government policy and the deplorable conditions on reserves, his main aim was to achieve reform through peaceful means, particularly the renegotiation of Treaty 6. However, soon after the outbreak of hostilities, Poundmaker progressively lost control over his camp, which came to include dissident Métis and a number of Assiniboines who had murdered a farm instructor. At Battleford he was unable to prevent his warriors from looting homes and offices that had been abandoned when the occupants fled for protection to the police barracks nearby. Later, Poundmaker's authority was preempted by his band's warrior society, which, at Cut Knife Hill, Saskatchewan, resisted an assault by government forces led by Lt. Col. William Dillon Otter. Throughout these events Poundmaker cautioned restraint and took steps to protect prisoners. He is also credited with preventing the warriors from inflicting heavy losses on Otter's troops as they retreated in disarray.

Nevertheless, Poundmaker was blamed by a government determined to cripple Indian society by removing its leadership. He was subjected to a humiliating surrender at the hands of Gen. Frederick Dobson Middleton, placed on trial in 1885 for treason, and sentenced to three years in Stony Mountain Penitentiary, Manitoba. He was granted early release in 1886 but died of tuberculosis four months later, on July 4, while visiting Crowfoot. Initially buried at Blackfoot Crossing, Alberta, his remains were reinterred at Cut Knife Hill in 1967.

See also WAR: North-West Rebellion.

F. Laurie Barron
University of Saskatchewan

Jefferson, Robert. *Fifty Years on the Saskatchewan*. Battleford, Saskatchewan: Canadian North-West Historical Society, 1929. Sluman, Norma. *Poundmaker*. Toronto: McGraw-Hill Ryerson Ltd., 1967. Stonechild, Blair, and Bill Waiser. *Loyal till Death: Indians and the North-West Rebellion*. Calgary: Fifth House Ltd., 1997.

POWWOWS

The word powwow is derived from the Narragansett language and refers to a gathering of Native people for the purpose of singing, dancing, celebration, and socialization. It consists of ceremonies, dance competitions, and social dancing. Many are large, annual events and have well-established reputations, such as those held in Calgary, Denver, and Oklahoma City. Powwows are characterized by the use of one or more groups of singers, which are called "drums," and the wearing of elaborate regalia during the dance portions of the event. The style of music and dance that has become stan-

Powwow at Potawatomi Indian Agency, Kansas, ca. 1920

dardized in many Great Plains powwows is termed "intertribal" because it is a hybridization of dance and music from several Native American groups. Powwows vary in size from giant affairs attended by people from a wide variety of locations on the North American continent, to small, local gatherings where the population of one community is the primary audience.

The history of the event demonstrates its dynamic nature. During the first part of the twentieth century, there was a great deal of interaction among Native peoples due to relocation on reservations and through increased availability of transportation technology such as the railroad. Native peoples maintained cultural identity by preserving traditional music and dance styles. Participation in World War I, World War II, and the Korean War gave Native American men who might have been members of warrior societies among their own people the opportunity to become active warriors. Traditional dances were held and songs were composed to honor these men. By 1955 there was a great deal of interest in artistic exchange among tribal groups in the Great Plains, who continued to celebrate their warrior societies through song and dance, especially in Oklahoma. These songs and dances were shared with members of neighboring tribes, and an amalgamation of musical and dance traits resulted that led to the contemporary intertribal powwow.

When these intertribal celebrations began, they did not possess the common elements that can be found today. Although there is still a large amount of variation in format, competition, and participation, many powwows in the Great Plains have an overall form that is predictable and understood by all participants. This form includes a wide variety of events held for specific reasons and, in many cases, in a specific order.

The most impressive event of the contemporary powwow is the Grand Entry, the first part of any dance session. During this time, all dancers who are to compete enter the powwow arena in a specified order. After the Grand Entry, a special ceremony usually takes place that includes the singing of a Flag Song and, sometimes, an Honor Song. After the songs the master of ceremonies may introduce important people at the event, and a prayer is frequently offered. This might be followed by a speech from a dignitary, such as the powwow princess or a visiting politician. During all of this ceremony, the dancers stand quietly in the powwow arena. At its close, the emcee usually calls for an intertribal dance, so that everyone may participate. Several such dances may occur before the competitions begin.

Competition dancing is divided into categories according to the type of songs performed by the drum (the singing group), the type of dance steps and regalia worn by the contestants, and the contestants' ages. Men's categories usually include traditional and fancy dancers. Women are divided into traditional, fancy, and jingle dress dancers. All categories are further classified by age into adult, junior, and tiny tot divisions. Awards for the competitions are presented for dancing technique, such as stopping on the correct foot with the last beat of the drum and appropriate composure during the entire powwow. Prizes may include cash, trophies, and a wide variety of material objects such as blankets, rifles, food, or household items.

A great diversity of music may be heard at any given powwow. Some of the musical styles include the Omaha dance, social dance, and intertribal. Songs are not improvised but are composed by singers who teach them to other members of the drum. These songs are then dispersed among the population through performance at powwows and through recordings. Songs have appropriate drumbeats that accompany them, including the parade beat, the Omaha beat, the social dance beat, accent or

honor beats, and the drum roll. Each of these beats is distinctive, and aficionados will know immediately by the drumbeat which type of song is being performed. The speed of the beat varies according to the type of dance and the style of the drum. Distinctive differences exist between Northern Plains and Southern Plains styles, and these include a faster beat in the north and a slower beat in the south. These differences sometimes make it impossible for a northern-style dancer, for example, to compete while a southern-style drum is playing. For this reason, international drums often perform at powwows in a neutral style so that dancers from both the northern and southern traditions may compete simultaneously.

Competitions are the main focus of the powwow for some participants, but other types of activities occur at various points during the event. Giveaways are common, and intertribal and special dances are interspersed throughout the affair, giving noncompetitive dancers a chance to participate. Raffles are frequently held to raise money in support of the event or to help sponsor the next powwow. After the formal portion of the powwow, young dancers often get together in the late evening for a round of "forty-nine dances." The informal nature of the forty-nines contrasts with the relatively rigid structure of the other powwow dances. This is a time for celebration among young adults who participate often into the early hours of the morning.

Contemporary powwows play an important role in the social and cultural life of Native Americans. They are a celebration of heritage and tradition that has survived in a unique form apart from the daily lives of the participants. Powwows engender a sense of community and belonging among the people who participate, and those who are on the powwow circuit look forward to making new acquaintances and renewing old friendships as much as to the singing, dancing, and competitions. Music and dance are natural media for dissemination of cultural information because they are so visible, and powwows and recordings of powwow songs disperse important features of Native American culture not only among Native American communities but also among members of other communities.

See also SPORTS AND RECREATION: Crow Fair.

Kenton Bales
University of Nebraska at Omaha

Horse Capture, George P. Powwow. Cody WY: Buffalo Bill Historical Center, 1989. Powers, William K. War Dance: Plains Indian Musical Performance. Tucson: University of Arizona Press, 1990.

PUBLIC LAW 280

See LAW: Public Law 280

QUAPAWS

When first encountered by Europeans in the 1670s, some 15,000 to 20,000 Quapaws resided in four permanent villages near the confluence of the Mississippi and Arkansas Rivers. They practiced a mixed economy of agriculture and hunting. Socially they were divided into a myriad of patrilineal clans and subclans. Known to their Dheghia-branch Sioux kinsmen (the Osages, Omahas, Kanzas, and Poncas) as *Ugaxpa*, or "Downstream People," the Quapaws entered into trading and military alliances first with the French and then with the Spanish. The benefits of these relationships hardly compensated for the costs of altered lifeways, weakened social structures, and decimated population (they were reduced to 575 persons by 1800).

In 1803, when the United States acquired Louisiana, American authorities saw the Quapaws as impediments to national expansion. Thirty years later they forced the tribe, led by Chief Heckaton, to remove from its Arkansas homeland to a 150-square-mile reservation in northeastern Oklahoma. The traumatic relocation to Indian Territory divided the tribe into two main groups, one living on the reservation and the other along the Canadian River. Most tribespeople engaged in bison hunting; a few farmed successfully and sent their children to missionary schools.

Tribal fortunes changed markedly with the onset of the American Civil War. Although tribal chiefs War-te-she and Ki-he-cah-te-da signed a treaty with the Confederacy in 1861, within a year the bands had retreated to Kansas with other Indians sympathetic to the Union. There the refugees suffered four years of painful deprivation, resulting in the deaths of one-half of the tribe.

The post–Civil War years brought little relief. In an 1867 treaty with the United States, tribal leaders exchanged reservation land for annuity payments and educational stipends. Led by the last hereditary chief of the Quapaws, Tallchief, a majority of the tribespeople left the reservation to live with their Osage kinsmen. Those who remained leased the domain to non-Indian agriculturists and admitted "homeless" Indians to tribal citizenship. In 1893, fearing forfeiture of the reservation, Quapaw leaders John Medicine and Abner W. Abrams took the unprecedented action of allotting it in 240-acre parcels to 234 enrolled members of the tribe. Federal government approval came after the fact.

In the 1920s and 1930s the discovery of rich lead and zinc deposits on some individual allotments changed the course of Quapaw history. Because wealthy allottees were systematically defrauded, the federal government in 1908 revoked fraudulent leases, obtained higher royalties, and shielded Indian income from local, state, and federal taxes. But this intervention also brought federal control of mining royalties paid to individual allottees. The hated bureaucratic restrictions, however, did not prevent the Quapaws from engaging in uncontrolled spending that left most of them in poverty by 1940. Nor did it prevent a significant number of the wealthy allottees, led by Chief Victor Griffin, from embracing and supporting the Big Moon peyote cult, which had been introduced by John "Moonhead" Wilson in the 1890s.

Because the status quo served the Quapaw leadership well, it rejected the Indian Reorganization Act of 1934 and then refused to organize under the terms of the Oklahoma Indian Welfare Act enacted two years later. The leadership did file a claim under the provisions of the Indian Claims Commission Act of 1946, an action that in 1954 resulted in a favorable judgment of nearly $1 million. In 1961 that money was divided among 1,199 individual Quapaws.

The commission award revitalized the Quapaws both as a people and as a community. Organized in 1956 as the Business Committee, the tribal government adroitly diverted termination pressures in the 1950s. At the beginning of the twenty-first century it manages varying enterprises ranging from a bingo parlor to a quick-stop gasoline station, a nationally acclaimed powwow, and a gleaming new office building southeast of Quapaw, Oklahoma.

W. David Baird
Pepperdine University

Baird, W. David. *The Quapaw Indians: A History of the Downstream People*. Norman: University of Oklahoma Press, 1980. Baird, W. David. *The Quapaws*. New York: Chelsea House, 1989.

RED CLOUD

See WAR: Red Cloud

REPATRIATION

Since the 1970s Native Americans have sought the repatriation of their ancestors' skeletal remains, burial goods, and sacred objects from museums and laboratories. Part of a worldwide Indigenous movement, Native Americans contend that these institutions acquired and retained the remains and objects in violation of the rights of the dead, the tribe, and the sacred. In response, some scholars maintain that the remains provide an important scientific and educational resource and that treatment of the materials has been respectful.

The entire repatriation movement may have started on the fringe of the Great Plains in 1971. An Ihanktonwan (Yankton Sioux) woman, Maria Pearson, protested the differential treatment of Native American remains buried at the edge of a non-Indian, pioneer cemetery near Glenwood, Iowa, that was to be relocated for highway construction. While the non-Indian remains were immediately reburied, the Native remains were taken to the state archeologist's office for study. A court order, Governor Robert Ray's intervention, and substantial media coverage eventually allowed the remains to be reburied.

The case prompted attention by the American Indian Movement (AIM) and the International Indian Treaty Council, which took action against archeologists and their excavations in several locations. Digs in Minnesota and Iowa were disrupted by AIM members. However, other pressing matters, such as the takeover at Alcatraz and Wounded Knee, had turned the attention of AIM elsewhere.

In 1978 the discovery of the massacred remains of nearly 500 individuals from the prehistoric Crow Creek Village along the Missouri River in South Dakota drew international attention when archeologists and the Army Corps of Engineers–Omaha District agreed to rebury the remains after study. After the remains were reburied in 1981, many archeologists and human osteologists were critical of the agreement, contending that new techniques would have allowed substantially more information to be gleaned from the remains if they had been curated for eventual restudy.

In 1982 the International Indian Treaty Council again turned its attention to repatriation. One of its members, Jan Hammil, determined that organizations, with the Smithsonian Institution as the primary example, should be pressured to return remains for reburial. She also pressured the Society for American Archaeology, the primary organization of professional archeologists in the United States, not to pass a resolution against repatriation. This struggle continued until passage of major federal repatriation laws in 1989 and 1990.

During this time, several states debated or enacted laws dealing with repatriation. The most controversial case in the Plains involved the Pawnees' efforts to seek the return of skeletons and grave goods curated in the Nebraska State Historical Society (NSHS). In 1988 Lawrence Goodfox Jr. of the Pawnee Tribe of Oklahoma issued several requests to the NSHS for the repatriation of remains and burial offerings long held by the society. NSHS executive director James Hanson refused to respond to the tribe's request, and a long, nationally visible battle ensued. The Pawnees joined forces with other Nebraska tribes and the Native American Rights Fund to seek legislative relief that would force the NSHS to repatriate the remains. In 1989 the coalition eventually saw passage in the Nebraska legislature of the Unmarked Human Burial Sites and Skeletal Remains Protection Act (LB-340). The law required Nebraska public museums to return all tribally identifiable skeletal remains and burial offerings to tribes that requested them for reburial.

Reburial opponents, led by the NSHS, campaigned to derail the legislation. Even after enactment, the NSHS opposed return of remains from the more distant past, in which determining tribal affiliation is often difficult. Eventually, agreements between tribes and the NSHS allowed the return of many more remains than had been originally sought.

While the Pawnees' campaign was going on, the Omahas were working with Harvard University's Peabody Museum to seek the return of *Umon'hon'ti*, their sacred pole. In 1888, under pressure to abandon their beliefs and accept Christianity, the Omaha tribe had turned Umon'hon'ti and other sacred objects, including the ceremonial war pipes and the sacred shell, over to ethnographer Alice Fletcher for safekeeping. Fletcher transferred them to the Peabody Museum. After an extraordinary effort on the part of the Omahas to reclaim their objects, the Peabody returned the pole in 1989 and has since returned other sacred objects.

In 1989 the World Archaeological Congress met at the University of South Dakota for a forum entitled "Archeological Ethics and the Treatment of the Dead." Archeologists and Indigenous people from twenty countries and twenty-seven Native American nations debated the repatriation issue, eventually passing the Vermillion Accord. This accord influenced the passage of several provincial laws in Canada and ethics codes for both the World Archaeological Congress and the Australian Archaeological Association.

In 1989 and 1990, after lengthy negotiations between the Native American Rights Fund, the National Congress of American Indians, the Society for American Archaeology, and other interested parties, the U.S. Congress passed two important federal laws. Targeting the Smithsonian, the National Museum of the American Indian Act (Public Law 101-185) required that the Smithsonian inventory its collection of skeletal remains so that tribes could claim them for repatriation. The Smithsonian has since returned human remains to Plains tribes, including the Pawnees, Cheyennes, and Wahpeton Sioux. In 1990 the Native American Graves Protection and Repatriation Act (Public Law 101–601) extended the earlier law to all federal agencies or institutions with any level of federal involvement. The act requires return of human remains, grave goods, and items of cultural patrimony. It also demands consultation with tribes and requires that a broader range of information, such as oral tradition, be considered when documenting cultural affiliation of remains. After several years of drafting operative regulations, the law has generally worked, although details remain to be worked out. Demonstrations of cultural affiliation have proved contentious for remains from the distant past, and another key issue is the treatment of remains found on private land.

See also LAW: Native American Rights Fund / PROTEST AND DISSENT: American Indian Movement.

Larry J. Zimmerman
University of Iowa

Echo-Hawk, Walter, ed. Special Edition: Repatriation of American Indian Remains. *American Indian Culture and Research Journal* 16 (1992). Echo-Hawk, Walter, and Roger Echo-Hawk. *Battlefields and Burial Grounds: The Indian Struggle to Protect Ancestral Graves in the United States.* Minneapolis: Lerner Publications Company, 1994. Ridington, Robin, and Dennis Hastings. *Blessing for a Long Time: The Sacred Pole of the Omaha Tribe.* Lincoln: University of Nebraska Press, 1997.

RESERVATIONS

Reservations in the Great Plains are territorial units retained by Native American tribes, either as remnants of their ancestral lands, or as designated areas assigned after removal—from both within and outside the region—following the cession of homelands to the United States. They are places where tribal and federal jurisdictions prevail, to the general exclusion of state jurisdiction, though the legal boundaries here are constantly shifting with new decisions in the courts. Great Plains reservations are generally poor places, mineral resources and revenues from gaming notwithstanding. But they are also treasured homelands where ancestors are buried, sacred sites revered, and cultures preserved; for their Native American residents, they are the surviving geographic connection between past and present.

The first reservations in the Plains, other than the relatively large areas set aside for relocated Indians such as the Delawares in the 1820s and 1830s, were created after the Kansas-Nebraska Act of 1854 opened up the area to European American settlement. Because of this incursion, the idea of a separate, extraterritorial "Indian Country" in the Plains, which had prevailed since 1830, became impractical. Instead, Plains Indians would be restricted to small areas recognized in treaties, laws, or executive orders as belonging to them. The remaining homelands would then be available for resettlement by European Americans. On the reservations, Native Americans would be placed under great pressure to assimilate—to take out individual farms, or allotments, to learn English, and to convert to Christianity. When this occurred, theoretically, the Native Americans would simply merge into the larger society, and any additional reservation lands over and above their allotments would also pass to European Americans. In this sense, then, and despite the recognition in treaties of Indian rights to the lands, reservations were seen by the United States in the mid–nineteenth century as only a temporary expedient until Native Americans assimilated. But Native Americans in the Plains, and elsewhere in the United States, did not disappear through assimilation, or through war and disease. Thus, reservations have remained a significant component of the region's identity.

By 1860 the Indians of eastern Nebraska (e.g., the Pawnees) and eastern Kansas (e.g., the Kaws) had sold their remaining homelands to the United States, retaining only small reservations. In the following decades reservations were created successively west, north, and south (in Indian Territory) from the initial area of European American advance, as tribes, under varying degrees of coercion, were forced to cede their lands. In 1868, for example, at the Treaty of Fort Laramie, the Crows surrendered 38 million acres of their hunting grounds in what is now Montana and Wyoming and agreed to a reservation in south-central Montana. In 1874 and 1888 the Blackfeet relinquished about 27 million acres of land in Montana and took out a reservation where the Plains meets the Rocky Mountains at the forty-ninth parallel. By the latter date, all Plains tribes had been restricted to reservations.

Despite the "recognized" or "reserved" title under which the Plains tribes hold their reservations, their size and the Indians' sovereignty on them have been eroded almost from the beginning. Those early reservations in Kansas and Nebraska were quickly surrounded and coveted by settlers. By 1881 the Kaws, Pawnees, Poncas, and Otoe-Missourias had all been removed to Indian Territory and their reservations thrown open to resettlement. Even when original reservations were retained, as in the cases of the Crows and Blackfeet, the Indians were forced by settlers' demands, and by their own poverty, to sell portions to the United States in return for subsistence. The Crow Indian Reservation, for example, was significantly reduced by cessions in 1882 and 1892, and the size of the Blackfeet Reservation was almost halved in 1895.

Even greater losses from Plains reservations occurred after passage of the General Allotment (Dawes) Act of 1887. At various times thereafter, Indians were allocated individual allotments (generally 160 acres), and the portions of reservations remaining after that allocation were declared "surplus lands" that were opened to European American settlement. In 1904, on the Devils Lake Sioux Reservation in North Dakota, for example, 135,824 acres were allotted to 1,193 Indians, leaving 92,144 acres of surplus lands to be sold to settlers at $1.25 an acre. Subsequently, following a government trust period, many of the allotments were also sold to settlers. As a consequence, non-Indians now own 75 percent of the Devils Lake Sioux Reservation. This is a characteristic pattern on many Plains reservations, which are a "checkerboard" of Indian and non-Indian lands, greatly complicating jurisdiction and compromising tribal sovereignty.

On a map of Indian reservations in the United States, the Northern Great Plains stands out. There are still many Native Americans in Oklahoma, of course, as the successor to Indian Territory, but with the exception of the Osage Reservation, all the reservations were dissolved in the years leading up to statehood. (Many Indian groups in Oklahoma own tribal lands, and some refer to their lands as reservations, but for census purposes they are designated as Tribal Jurisdiction Statistical Areas.) There are no reservations in the Texas Plains, where, after statehood in 1846, the state controlled land disbursement and made no room for the Indigenous inhabitants. There are relatively few (seven) remaining reservations in Kansas and Nebraska, the result of Indian removals in the nineteenth century. But north of the Nebraska–South Dakota border, reservations abound (there are seventeen of them), and most are large. The 1,771,082-acre Pine Ridge Reservation, for example, with its tribally enrolled population of 17,775 in 1995, is one of the largest reservations in the country. It is also one of the poorest places in the country, with 60 percent of families living below the poverty level in 1990. Even on the 2,235,095-acre Crow Indian Reservation in Montana, with its rich resources of coal, oil, and gas, per capita income in 1995 was only $4,243 and unemployment stood at 44 percent.

Despite the promises of the United States, spelled out in treaties and agreements, the status of Plains reservations remains insecure, especially because of state intervention. In an important case in 1981, *Montana v. United States*, the U.S. Supreme Court ruled that the Crow tribe does not have the right to regulate nonmember hunting and fishing on reservation lands that are not owned by, or held in trust for, the tribe. The only exceptions are if the activity threatens tribal integrity or if consensual agreements have been made. Similarly, in federal district court in North Dakota in 1993, the Devils Lake Sioux were held to have the right to contract for electrical services only on lands owned by, or held in trust for, the tribe, which meant only about one-quarter of the area of the reservation. These decisions indicate that the geographic extent of Indian sovereignty is being moved from the exterior boundaries of the reservation to those areas within the reservation held in trust by the tribe or by members of the tribe.

Yet, in other ways, the Indian presence on Plains reservations is resurgent. In a region where rural populations are rapidly thinning, Indian reservations stand out as areas of significant population growth. Birthrates are higher than average, and death rates, though still high, have fallen. Moreover, Indians are returning to reservations to fill jobs created by gaming and other economic development. New revenues mean that reservation lands once alienated can be reclaimed. Far from disappearing, Native Americans and their reservation homelands are reasserting themselves on the landscape of the Great Plains.

See also CITIES AND TOWNS: Reservation Towns / LAW: *Montana v. United States.*

David J. Wishart
University of Nebraska–Lincoln

Marino, Cesare. "Reservations." In *Native America in the Twentieth Century: An Encyclopedia*, edited by Mary B. Davis. New York: Garland Publishing, Inc., 1996. Royce, Charles C. *Indian Land Cessions in the United States.* 18th Annual Report of the Bureau of American Ethnology, 1896–97. Washington DC: Government Printing Office, 1899. Velarde Tiller, Veronica E. *American Indian Reservations and Trust Areas.* Albuquerque: Tiller Research Inc., 1996.

RESERVATION TOWNS

See CITIES AND TOWNS: Reservation Towns

RESERVES

Indian (First Nations) reserves on the Canadian Prairies were the outcome of a series of treaties negotiated between the new Dominion of Canada and Indian leaders whose peoples had occupied the Prairies for generations. Canada's top priority, when it acquired Rupert's Land from the Hudson's Bay Company in 1870, was to extinguish Indian title to the land and to stabilize the Indian population in anticipation of white agricultural settlement. The Indians' priority was to preserve their way of life in the face of inevitable changes on the Canadian Prairies. Consequently, government officials and Indian leaders held very different views on the purpose of the treaties and reserves.

Treaties numbered 1 through 7 were negotiated between 1871 and 1877 and covered the Prairies of the present-day provinces of Manitoba, Saskatchewan, and Alberta. Treaties 1 and 2 were similar in that each Indian band would receive an inalienable reserve of land using a ratio of 160 acres per family of five and an annuity of $15 per family. Liquor sales were prohibited, and schools would be built by the government on the reserves. Gifts of livestock, farming equipment, and clothing, as well as hunting and fishing rights, were mentioned verbally during negotiations but were not written into the treaties. Subsequently, these two treaties were amended in 1875 to bring them into line with Treaty 3, which set precedents for later treaties. Its terms were: 640 acres per family of five, annuities of $5 per person, a gratuity of $12, a suit of clothes every three years, salaries for chiefs and band officers, plus gifts of medals and flags. Hunting and fishing rights in unsettled areas were formally acknowledged, and reserves were to be supplied with livestock, farming equipment, and seed. Agricultural instruction would be provided by the government. The only subsequent change was the provision in Treaty 6 of a "medicine chest"—a provision that was then extended to the other treaty areas. Provision was also made for American Sioux (Lakota) refugees from the Battle of the Little Bighorn: they received reserves based on eighty acres per family of five but no annuities, as they had no lands in Canada to cede. The size of all reserves was based on population levels during the 1870s; no provision was made for subsequent population expansion.

Although the government's declared policy was assimilation, in practice it was segregation. The very concept of a reserve is one of segregation. Indians were supposed to select the location of their reserves, but government agents often intervened and clustered the reserves to facilitate bureaucratic administration. In 1882 all the southern reserves except those in southern Alberta were moved north of the Canadian Pacific Railroad to avoid further cross-border raids with American bands. Agents were to terminate the Indians' roaming over the Prairies, to teach them farming, and to settle them on reserves where they would not interfere with white settlement. After the North-West Rebellion of 1885, agents increasingly took control of affairs on the reserves as the power of Indian chiefs was reduced and Indians became wards of the government. In the area of education the government's practice was indeed assimilationist. Schools on the reserves were run by Christian missionaries who sought to "civilize" and Christianize Indian children by stamping out Aboriginal cultural influences. These practices worked against the Indian ideal of preserving as much of their culture as they could on their reserves.

Refusal of the reserve system was scarcely an option for Prairie Province Indians in the 1870s. A smallpox epidemic in the early 1870s, followed by rapid disappearance of the bison, reduced Indian bands to starvation and dependence on government rations for survival. Their plight was desperate by 1880, and despite the pleas of several chiefs such as Big Bear, who argued for Indian unity and renegotiation with the government, many accepted the government's terms. Big Bear even favored clustering of reserves as a step toward creating Indian solidarity and preservation of Indian culture. But even their hunting and fishing rights along the northern margins of the Prairies were ignored, as agents sought to restrict Indian mobility and to seclude them on their reserves. The Indians' distinctive way of life was subjected to the crushing pressures of starvation: sheer survival was possible only on the government's terms. Nevertheless, Indians retained significant elements of their cultures on these small, inalienable reserves of land that had been set aside for them in the early 1880s.

Major changes to the reserve system came after World War II, in which Indians fought bravely in the Canadian armed forces. Veterans refused to accept second-class citizenship, and a revised Indian Act in 1951 gave Indian bands a measure of control for the first time. Although the policy of assimilation continued, Indians were no longer wards of government but were to advance to full rights as citizens. Indians now determined who belonged to Indian bands and who could live on reserves. The Indian Act of 1876 had declared that only "status" Indians could reside permanently on reserves, and the government reserved the right to determine who was a "status Indian." Men who lived off the reserve could lose their status, and the position of women was even more precarious, especially those who married non-Indians. Resolution of these issues now became a matter for Indian bands, although the troublesome problem of women's status was not finally resolved until 1982, when many women were reinstated as band members.

Other changes came more easily. Schools were secularized during the 1960s, and by 1970 Indian bands began to take direct control of education. Bands also took financial control and increasingly policed their reserves—public consumption of alcohol, for example, was permitted in 1970. By the 1980s a pan-Indian movement had been established, which linked Indian reserves on the Prairies with other reserves across Canada, and, as the drive toward Aboriginal self-government was launched, Big Bear's dream of a century earlier became a possibility.

The Canadian government had been determined to treat Indians better than the United States had. Those lofty goals were never achieved, partly through lack of commitment by the government in Ottawa and partly through internal contradictions in policy, but mostly because Indians' wishes were ignored. The result was a marginalization of Canadian Prairie Indians through segregation similar to that of their American cousins for more than a century.

See also EDUCATION: Indian Residential Schools, Canada / POLITICS AND GOVERNMENT: Indian Agents.

D. Aidan McQuillan
University of Toronto

Canada Royal Commission on Aboriginal Peoples. *For Seven Generations: An Information Legacy of the Royal Commission on Aboriginal Peoples.* Ottawa: Libraxus, 1997. Dickason, Olive P. *Canada's First Nations: A History of*

Founding Peoples from Earliest Times. Toronto: McClelland and Stewart Ltd., 1992. McQuillan, D. Aidan. "Creation of Indian Reserves on the Canadian Prairies, 1870–1885." *Geographical Review* 70 (1980): 379–96.

RIGGS, ROLLIE LYNN

See LITERARY TRADITIONS: Riggs, Rollie Lynn

ROE CLOUD, HENRY

See EDUCATION: Roe Cloud, Henry

SACAGAWEA

See GENDER: Sacagawea

SACRED GEOGRAPHY

While Great Plains Indian religions differ considerably from one another, they all exhibit a sacred geography. All of nature is regarded as being sacred, yet certain geographical features and areas figure more prominently than others on the sacred map.

Sacred places have multiple levels of meaning to Indigenous cultures. First, sacred places are acts of creation, usually designed by a World Maker. The places are revealed through the society's mythology (sacred truth), thereby becoming the physical manifestations of the mythological system. Second, Great Plains Indians hinge both their religious perceptions and their religious ceremonies on sacred places. The locale where a ritual takes place is as significant as the ritual itself. Third, symbolism is an important component of sacred places. Last, the religious perceptions that Plains Indians have of their physical environment lead to a psychological stability evident in a condition referred to as "existential insideness." Existential insideness is knowing that a particular place is where one belongs, completing the self-identity of an individual. Existential insideness is supported through the spiritual system of the culture when there is an acknowledgment of sacred places.

The mythological traditions of many Plains Indians are located in real places. Thus, place is both mythic and geographical. For example, *Pahuk*, meaning "Mound on the Water," located in eastern Nebraska on a high bluff above the Platte River, is one of five known Pawnee sacred sites. The Pawnees believe Pahuk is one of the locales where the Sacred Animals (*Nahu'rac*) held council during mythic times and where a young Pawnee boy learned healing practices from the animal council. The boy took the knowledge to his people, curing his fellow villagers and eventually teaching his skills to other young men of the village. Traditionally, Pawnee doctors would visit Pahuk yearly to renew their healing powers and to give thanks to those mythic beings who bestowed the knowledge on their predecessor.

A place made sacred through mythology is continually consecrated by rituals. The Lakota religion recognizes seven sacred ceremonies. Each of these ceremonies is identified with specific sites where the rituals are performed. The *hanbleceya* (vision quest) ceremony is executed at Bear Butte in western South Dakota near the Black Hills, a place the Lakotas describe as "their most sacred altar." The hanbleceya is a prayer for spiritual guidance. The Lakotas recognize Bear Butte as a particularly worthy site for visions because the seeker is generally successful, and visions experienced there can reveal future events that are necessary for the continuation of humanity.

Symbolism plays a primary role in the recognition of sacredness for Great Plains Indian peoples. Natural landforms or human-manufactured structures often symbolize the cosmos: their shapes possess the power of what they symbolize. The "medicine wheel," to many Plains cultures, represents an organization of the cosmos based on a recognition of the four sacred directions. These circular rock formations are found throughout the Plains region and are regularly visited by Indian people on pilgrimages. The best-known example, the Big Horn Medicine Wheel, is sacred to the Cheyennes, Lakotas, Arapahos, and Shoshones.

Existential insideness, the feeling that one belongs to a particular place, characterizes Plains Indians' relationships with their homeland. According to the Lakotas, their religion cannot be practiced without access to the sacred places. When this bond is severed, severe psychological alienation and cultural disintegration can ensue. Many Native American peoples' sense of identity comes from walking on land also walked on by their ancestors, or by being able to identify places that are not only significant to them as individuals but also significant to their ancestors. To lose this identity, through loss of sacred lands, would have devastating consequences for the generations to come.

Kari Forbes-Boyte
Sacramento City College

Eliade, Mircea. *The Sacred and the Profane: The Nature of Religion*. New York: Harcourt, Brace, and World, Inc., 1957. Vecsey, Christopher. *Handbook of American Indian Religious Freedom*. New York: Crossroad Publishing Company, 1991.

SAINT-MARIE, BUFFY

See MUSIC: Saint-Marie, Buffy

SARCEES

The Sarcees (Sarsis) are an Athapaskan-speaking people living along the eastern foothills of the Rocky Mountains in southwestern Alberta. In 1983 they formally adopted the name *Tsuu T'inas*, which means "Many People" in their own language.

According to Tsuu T'ina legend, all of the Athapaskan-speaking people once lived together in northwestern Canada and Alaska. One winter, when the people were crossing a frozen lake, a young boy asked his grandmother to get him a stick that was protruding from the ice. When she tried to pick it up, she found the stick to be frozen fast in the ice. As the old lady continued to pull and twist the stick, the water was stirred up and the turbulence angered the Underwater Creature. As he rose, a great fissure split the ice. Terrified, the people ran for shore. Those who headed north became the Dénés of Canada and Alaska. Others moved southward, becoming the Tsuu T'inas, Apaches, and Navajos.

Once in the south, the Tsuu T'inas may have first occupied the upper drainages of the Saskatchewan and Athabasca Rivers. By the early nineteenth century they had moved farther south and into a close alliance with the Siksikas (Blackfoot proper). They lived primarily along the central portion of the Bow River and at sites along Wolf Creek (now called Fish Creek), the Weasel Head section of the Elbow River, and at Moose Mountain which assumed sacred significance.

Through their close association, the Tsuu T'inas adopted much of the material and sacred culture of the Blackfoot. Methods and tools for bison hunting and hide preparation, as well as styles of tipis and clothing, all resemble those of the Blackfoot. Because many sacred objects were left with their northern relatives, the Tsuu T'inas incorporated Blackfoot ceremonies into their own belief system. Today, the people are very private about their beliefs and are reluctant to discuss them publicly.

The Tsuu T'inas lived in kin-based groups, which they referred to as clans. The leader of the clan was acknowledged for his good judgment and ability to bring about a consensus. Individuals were free to move from clan to clan, as they saw fit. The Tsuu T'inas presently recognize five clans, although there may have been more before the epidemics and starvation of the late 1800s.

In 1877 Treaty Number 7 was signed between the government of Canada and the Siksikas, Piegans, Kainahs (Bloods), Stoneys, and Tsuu T'inas. At that time, the population of the Tsuu T'inas was estimated to be only 672 persons, and the government suggested that the Tsuu T'inas be included on a large reserve to be set aside for all of the Blackfoot. Bull Head, an influential Tsuu T'ina leader, recognized the importance of having their own place to preserve their language and culture. He argued successfully for a distinct reserve, and a place was eventually set aside along the Elbow River, near the North-West Mounted Police post at Fort Calgary. By 1881, when the Tsuu T'inas were settled on the reserve, the population had dropped to about 450 persons; it continued to decline over the ensuing years.

In 2001 a population of about 1,100 lives on the reserve. The city of Calgary abuts two of its boundaries, while expanding rural subdivisions encroach on the other edges. An elected council of one chief and eleven council members manage the affairs and revenues from resort and golf course developments, oil and gas exploration, and, until recently, rental for land used as a military base. A large office complex houses several federal government offices, whose rent contributes to the tribal revenue.

The Tsuu T'inas have a cultural research program that is actively collecting oral histories. This information is housed at the Tsuu T'ina Peoples Museum.

Jeanette Starlight
Tsuu T'ina Peoples Museum
Gerald T. Conaty
Glenbow Museum

Jenness, Diamond. *The Sarcee Indians of Alberta*. Bulletin no. 90, Anthropological Series no. 23. Ottawa: National Museums of Canada, 1938.

SHOSHONES

"Shoshone" comes from the Shoshone word *sosoni'*, which is a plural form of *sonipe*, a type of high-growing grass. Several tribes on the Plains referred to the Shoshones as the "Grass House People," and this name probably refers to the conically shaped houses made of native grasses (sosoni') used by the Great Basin Indians. The more common term used by Shoshone people is *Newe*, or "People." The name Shoshone was first recorded in 1805 after Meriwether Lewis encountered a group of "Sosonees or snake Indians" among the Crows and noted them in his diary. The Shoshones were also called the "Snake People" by some Plains Indians. The origin of the term Snake People is based on the sign, in Indian sign language, that the Shoshone people used for themselves. The hand motion made during the sign represents a snake to most signers, but among the Shoshones it referred to the salmon, a fish unknown to the Great Plains. Today, many Shoshones have adopted the term Sosoni' to refer to other groups of Shoshones besides themselves. The Shoshone language is spoken by approximately 5,000 people across Nevada, Idaho, and Wyoming. It belongs to the western branch of the Numic group of Uto-Aztecan languages.

Since the Shoshones are widespread across the West, anthropologists have divided them into three groups based on where they live: the Western Shoshones of Nevada, the Northern Shoshones of Idaho, and the Eastern Shoshones of Wyoming. The different bands of Shoshone speakers share many cultural traits. The Eastern Shoshones are the only band that has adopted a Great Plains way of life.

The prehistory of the Shoshone people—how their ancestors (the Numa) were able to occupy a large portion of the Great Basin (Nevada and Utah), in addition to the contiguous areas of Idaho and Wyoming—is a debated topic. The origin of the Numa is believed to be the southwestern corner of the Great Basin. By 1500 Shoshones had crossed the Rocky Mountains and begun their expansion toward the northwestern Plains. By 1700 a group of Shoshones had moved into the Southern Plains and eventually developed their own identity as the Comanches. The current location of the Eastern Shoshones in central Wyoming is the result of a period of intense warfare from 1780 to 1825 against the Blackfeet, Crows, and Assiniboines.

The Eastern Shoshones divided themselves into two groups, based on geographical location and primary food resource. Shoshones living in the Green River and Wind River valleys of Wyoming were known as the Buffalo Eaters (*Guchundeka'*) or the Sage Grass People (*Boho'inee'*). Shoshones living in the Rocky Mountains and Lake Yellowstone areas were known as the Sheep-eaters (*Dukundeka'*) or the Mountain People (*Doyahinee'*).

The subsistence cycle of the Eastern Shoshones in the winter involved the tribe breaking into bands, each loosely associated with a particular mountain or valley. In early spring these bands reunited in the Wind River valley before going to the bison grounds for the spring hunt. After the spring hunt, most Eastern Shoshones spent their early summer in the Wind River valley. Then, in late June and early July, the intertribal rendezvous (or trade fair) was held at Fort Bridger. After the fair the Shoshones broke up into family groups until the fall bison hunt, when the tribe would come together one last time before the winter.

Bison meat played an extremely significant role culturally and economically in the lives of the Eastern Shoshones, accounting for about 50 percent of their diet at the height of the Plains horse culture in the 1700s. Fish caught during the spring and early summer were the second most important resource. Elk, mule deer, beaver, jackrabbit, and mountain sheep were also important sources of protein. Berries were either eaten raw, made into soup, or mixed with dried, powdered meat and fat to produce pemmican. Also, roots were eaten after being baked in earthen ovens.

Shoshone arts and industries exploited wood resources, animal products such as leather, sinew, bone, and minerals such as obsidian, flint, steatite, and slate. Leather working was done mostly by women, except for bowstrings, shields, drums, and rattles, which men produced. Iron, only available through trade, became an important material used in making arrow and spear points as well as knives.

The roles of men and women in Shoshone society were strictly regulated. Women were traditionally in charge of plant gathering, butchering and preparing bison, household chores, crafting items such as tipis and clothing, and child care. Men were in charge of hunting, warfare, and the political and economic decisions for the tribe.

The tribal chief (*daigwahni*) was an older man who had distinguished himself in warfare and possessed supernatural power. The chief controlled collective hunts and the tribe's movements. During times of warfare a special war chief was chosen. There were two Shoshone military societies: the Yellow Brows and the Logs. The Yellow Brows were young warriors who were the advanced forces in battle, whereas the Logs were older men who brought up the rear. These military societies also acted as a police force when the tribe gathered together.

The Shoshone religion is based on belief in supernatural power (*boha*) that is acquired primarily through vision quests and dreams. A shaman (*boha gande*) is a person who uses supernatural power to cure others and also leads special group ceremonies, especially at "Round Dances." The Eastern Shoshones also adopted two pan-Indian religions, the Sun Dance and the Native American Church. The Sun Dance was introduced to the Eastern Shoshones by a Comanche named Yellow Hand around 1800. Originally the Eastern Shoshones had rejected the missionary activities of the peyote religion of the Comanches, but the Native American Church gained influence after it was reintroduced by Arapahos in the early part of the twentieth century.

In 1868 the Shoshones of the Plains ceded their ancestral lands and were placed on a reservation in the lee of the Wind River Range of Wyoming. The Wind River Reservation now extends over 2,268,000 acres and is shared by Eastern Shoshones (who live mainly in the west and northwest) and Arapahos (who live mainly in the east and southeast). The Shoshone population on the reservation was 1,185 in 1988, following years of out-migration in response to dire poverty and high unemployment rates.

Christopher Loether
Idaho State University

Shimkin, Demetri. "Eastern Shoshone." In *Handbook of North American Indians*, edited by William C. Sturtevant, 11:308–35. Washington DC: Smithsonian Institution, 1986. Trenholm, Virginia Cole, and Maurine Carley. *The Shoshones: Sentinels of the Rockies*. Norman: University of Oklahoma Press, 1964.

SIGN LANGUAGE

The Plains Sign Language (PSL) is the most sophisticated Aboriginal sign language known. PSL is a direct signaling system; its symbols are understood without any reference to a spoken language. At its zenith in the mid–nineteenth century, PSL was the principal lingua franca of the trans-Mississippi West. There were three dominant regional dialects: Southern Plains, Northern Plains, and Plateau (the mountainous region north of the Great Basin). The variation between these was mostly in vocabulary, although sign mechanics also varied.

It is not known where or when PSL originated, but it was likely the Texas Gulf Coast, where a large number of mutually unintelligible languages were spoken. Given its complexity and wide use, the PSL must be many centuries old. The earliest probable observations of the PSL by Europeans were by Spaniards in the Southern Plains in the first half of the sixteenth century. During the nineteenth century, the PSL was used throughout the Plains, from the Texas Panhandle to the Missouri River and beyond, eventually reaching the Canadian Prairies. But sign use was also prominent outside this area, wherever tribes were influenced by Plains culture.

During the period when the PSL was an ongoing lingua franca, the Kiowas, Comanches, Cheyennes, and Arapahos were known as especially skilled signers. It may be significant that these tribes, who spoke mutually unintelligible languages, were often allies. Adult men are thought to have been the primary users of PSL, although some women knew and used PSL as well. Apart from conversational uses, PSL was also usual in public storytelling.

This use survives into the present. Signing was also used for oratory, largely before multilingual audiences.

PSL makes heavy use of portrayal of meanings by descriptive gesture, thus PSL is heavily pantomimic, but many signs are also merely conventional. PSL is, then, a mixed system varying from gestures whose reading is obvious, to gestures whose meaning cannot be inferred and which must be learned. All PSL signs are built from around eighty mutually contrasting basic gestures. Each sign usually includes three or four of these, formed with either one or both hands, which may be used in a stationary position or moved about. Signs are normally produced in a continuous flow of motion, but sentences and longer segments of discourse may be set off by brief pauses. When signing is done at a distance, movements are exaggerated in various ways to make the sign more "readable."

Signing was often accompanied by verbal language. Usually the verbal speech had the same meaning as the signed message. But this does not mean that signed messages were a translation of a spoken analog, following the rules of the spoken language. PSL is an independent language with its own rules. The order of words in a signed sentence is fairly free, and the same thing can usually be said with a number of alternate word orders, though a particular word order is usually preferred. In general, subjects precede verbs, and modifiers follow the element modified.

Unfortunately, PSL is now almost completely obsolete, although some signers can still be found here and there on Plains reservations. But time is short. Soon, only memories will remain as testimony to the former existence of the fascinating and colorful system of communication which we know as the Plains Sign Language.

Allan R. Taylor
University of Colorado at Boulder

Clark, William Philo. *The Indian Sign Language.* Lincoln: University of Nebraska Press, 1982. Taylor, Allan R. "Nonverbal Communication in Aboriginal North America: The Plains Sign Language." In *Aboriginal Sign Languages of the Americas and Australia,* edited by Thomas A. Sebeok and Donna Jean Umiker-Sebeok, 2:223–44. New York: Plenum Press, 1978.

SIOUX

The Sioux, and most particularly the Lakota Sioux, are the iconic warrior horsemen of the Northern Plains. They have become perhaps the best known of all Indian nations through paintings and photographs, confrontations with the U.S. military, Wild West shows, and hundreds of Hollywood movies. Sitting Bull, Crazy Horse, Red Cloud, and other Lakota Sioux leaders are among the most famous of all Native Americans, and the Battle of the Little Bighorn in 1876 and the Wounded Knee Massacre in 1890 are among the most widely known events in U.S. history. But the Lakotas are only one division of the Great Sioux Nation.

The Great Sioux Nation, known as *Oceti Sakowin,* or "Seven Council Fires," is a confederation of closely allied cognate bands. They speak three mutually intelligible dialects of the Siouan language family: Dakota, Nakota, and Lakota. They became known as the Sioux, or a word like it, in the seventeenth century, when their enemies, the Ojibwas, told the French that that was what they were called. The word derives from the Ojibwa term *Na dou esse,* which means "Snakeline Ones" or "Enemies." The French spelled the word *Nadousioux,* and the English and Americans shortened it to Sioux. In recent years, the Sioux, like many other Native peoples, have made a concerted effort to replace their imposed, derogatory name by the names they called themselves. Self-identification is commonly based on either band or sub-band names (e.g., Santee, Oglala, or Sicangu), linguistic groups (Lakota, Dakota, or Nakota), or, increasingly, in the twentieth century, by the name of the reservation of origin (e.g., "Rosebud Sioux" or "Cheyenne River Sioux").

The Great Sioux Nation has seven primary divisions, based on their respective places in the Seven Council Fires. The Isantis (Santees), Dakota speakers, occupy the east and are comprised of four council fires: the Mdewakantunwan, the Sisitunwan, the Wahpetunwan, and the Wahpekute. The Wiciyelas, Nakota speakers, occupy the middle division and are composed of two council fires: the Ihanktunwun (Yanktons) and Ihanktunwanna (Yanktonais). The western council fire is occupied by the Titunwans (Tetons), Lakota speakers, composed of seven sub-bands: Oglala (Scatter One's Own), Sicangu or Brulé (Burnt Thigh), Hunkpapa (Those Who Camp At the Entrance), Mnikowoju o Minneconjou (Those Who Plant By the Stream), Itzipco or Sans Arcs (Without Bows), Oohenunpa (Two Kettles), and Sihasapa (Black Feet).

Europeans first encountered the Sioux in the seventeenth century in the mixed hardwood forests of central Minnesota and northwestern Wisconsin. In the mid–seventeenth century, the Sioux began moving westward and southward, pushed by the Ojibwas, who gradually infiltrated into Minnesota from the Lake Superior area, and pulled by the abundant Plains bison herds and the diffusion of horses from the Southern Plains. While some bands had a few horses by 1707, if not earlier, the Lakotas did not fundamentally become Plains horsemen until 1750–75, by which time they had crossed the Missouri River, displacing the previous residents of the region. By the mid–eighteenth century, the Lakotas and Nakotas were closely associated with the Central and Northern Plains. The Dakotas (Santees) remained primarily in Minnesota, where they received reservations in the nineteenth century. The Sioux Uprising of 1862 resulted in the relocation of many Santees to small reservations in South Dakota and Nebraska, although others remained in Minnesota.

As each of the Council Fires adapted to different Plains environments, their lifeways changed and diverged from one another. Yet they maintained their political, economic, and social ties through intermarriage, trade, religious ceremonies, communal hunting, and military alliances.

The Yanktons and Yanktonais, who eventually settled in the eastern Dakotas, became middlemen in a far-flung trade system between the Lakotas, who had pushed westward as far as Wyoming and eastern Montana, and the eastern Santees, who were closely involved in the French fur trade in Minnesota. While the Lakotas became buffalo-hunting, nomadic horsemen, and the principal grain grown by the Santees shifted from wild rice to corn, some Yanktons and Yanktonais adopted many of the traits of the semisedentary Plains villagers, such as the Mandans and Arikaras, including the building of earth lodges. With the horse for transportation and vast herds of bison, the Lakotas prospered and their numbers grew until, by the nineteenth century, they outnumbered all other bands of the Great Sioux Nation combined. By the mid–nineteenth century, the Lakotas and their allies presented a formidable military and political barrier to European American expansion into the Central and Northern Plains.

The Lakotas eventually controlled a vast hunting territory stretching from the Platte River north to the Heart River and from the Missouri River west to the Bighorn Mountains. Their highly flexible social and political organization was well suited to the demands of maintaining such an empire. The basic unit of Lakota society was the *tiyospaye,* a small group of bilaterally related kin, informally led by a headman. Each of the seven Lakota sub-bands had societies, including *akicitas* (police) and *nacas* (civil leaders). Nacas from each of the sub-bands formed a tribal council (*Naca Ominicia*) with executive committees commonly known as *wicasa* (shirt wearers). When the seven sub-bands congregated each summer for the Sun Dance, the nacas of each of the seven sub-bands constituted a national council. Holy men and medicine people were also consulted on important matters, revealing the centrality of Lakota spiritual and ceremonial life.

The belief systems and rituals of the Lakotas and Nakotas reflect many of the values essential for successful nomadic bison hunting in the Northern Great Plains (e.g., individuality, bravery, sacrifice, vision seeking). The Lakotas are further anchored to the Great Plains by their conviction that they were created by *Wakan Tanka* (Grandfather, the Great Spirit) and emerged from a cave (Wind Cave) in *Paha Sapa,* the Black Hills of South Dakota. This place, more than any other, is sacred to the Lakotas. It was in the Great Plains that the Lakotas received their Sacred Pipe and the Seven Sacred Rites, including the Sun Dance, from White Buffalo Calf Woman.

Life within the tiyospaye centered around daily subsistence tasks divided by age and gender. Hunting, raiding, and making tools and weapons were the responsibilities of men, with time leftover for trading, counsels, ceremonies, and leisure activities, such as wagering on foot and horse races. Women's responsibilities included gathering wild resources, such as prairie turnips, processing and tanning hides, cooking, sewing, quillwork, and managing the daily needs of the household. Women were responsible for breaking camp, packing belongings on travois, and setting up camp again at the end of the day. Older children and youth frequently had responsibility for gathering firewood and water and tending to horses and dogs. Grandparents and elders were often entrusted with the primary responsibility for caring for small children and infants and assisting with household tasks. In Lakota society, men were allowed to have more than one wife, and men of high status frequently had several wives, ideally sisters or women from the same tiyospaye.

During the first half of the nineteenth century, at the very time the horse-riding nomadic way of life of the Lakotas was flourishing, the grasslands were being invaded by European Americans. The U.S. government initiated an aggressive military policy in the Plains during the 1860s. This policy included building additional military posts and pursuing Indian groups characterized as "hostile," activities that inflamed already tense relations between the federal government and the Lakotas and their allies. The Great Sioux Nation and its allies proved formidable opponents, militarily and politically, and brought the U.S. government to the negotiating table twice at Fort Laramie (1854 and 1868) to sign treaties. The 1868 Treaty of Fort Laramie established the Great Sioux Reservation, spanning more than half of the modern state of South Dakota (west of the Missouri River), and provided annuities and rations for the Sioux. Economic relief was welcomed by the tribe. Bison were an increasingly scarce resource in the Plains by the mid-1870s, and by the mid-1880s they were virtually extinct. The eradication of the bison, mainstay of their economy, had a devastating impact on the Sioux.

By the 1870s intolerable pressures led to a series of "Indian Wars," the most famous of which was the annihilation of Gen. George Armstrong Custer's Seventh Calvary at the Battle of the Little Bighorn in 1876 by Sitting Bull's Lakotas and their Cheyenne allies. Retribution was swift, and even those Lakotas who held out, including the bands of Crazy Horse and Sitting Bull, were eventually settled on the Great Sioux Reservation. In 1889 Congress broke up the Great Sioux Reservation into several smaller reservations in North and South Dakota. These reservations were loosely based on membership of the sub-bands. Their holdings were further diminished and scattered by allotment in severalty in the 1890s, which forced nuclear families onto small acreages and opened the remaining "surplus" land to non-Indian settlement. Many Lakotas selected their allotments near other members of their tiyospayes, maintaining a semblance of their old organization. The massacre of Big Foot's band at Wounded Knee Creek in 1890 and the killing of Sitting Bull by Indian policemen the same year marked the end of freedom and the preferred nomadic way of life for many Lakotas.

The 1890s were difficult years for the Sioux. Confined to reservations, where indifferent and self-serving Indian agents controlled them, they were expected to farm arid land. Their children were shipped to boarding schools, such as Carlisle Indian School in Pennsylvania, where they were urged to abandon their Indian ways. The Sun Dance, which had always served as an integrating mechanism for the Lakotas, had been banned along with other Lakota rituals in 1882. Although it was banned, the Lakota Sun Dance was never eradicated; it simply went "underground" to await a more tolerant era. In the 1890s other religions, such as the Ghost Dance and peyotism, helped fill the gap.

The first two decades of the twentieth century were periods of adjustment to reservation life on scattered allotments. Some reservations even began to prosper, to a degree, in the 1920s, only to be devastated during the Dust Bowl and Depression of the 1930s. Still, the catastrophe provided an opportunity to introduce radical reforms. These well-intentioned reforms were introduced by John Collier of the new Roosevelt administration and enacted as the Indian Reorganization Act (IRA) of 1934. The IRA was designed to improve subsistence and employment opportunities on the reservations and to ensure that tribal councils were democratically elected (counter to the traditions of the Lakotas and others). Collier and his staff targeted the Sioux reservations in the Dakotas and pressured them to adopt IRA-style governments and constitutions, which they did. The IRA reforms resulted in short-term moderate relief, as the Lakotas took advantage of some of the economic development programs, but they had negligible long-term benefits, with the exception that allotment policy was ended, which allowed the Lakotas to halt the erosion of their land base.

The second half of the twentieth century was a time of far-reaching change and renewal for many Sioux. Reduction in mortality and high birthrates almost doubled their population, which strained employment on reservations. As part of the termination policy, the Eisenhower administration encouraged Indians to leave their reservations with the 1952 Voluntary Relocation Program. In the 1950s and 1960s regional centers such as Denver, Cheyenne, Bismarck, Minneapolis, Sioux Falls, and Sioux City became home to many Sioux. Poorly educated and discriminated against, many young Sioux soon returned to their reservations. The turbulence of this period in federal Indian policy, coupled with the civil rights movement, encouraged the birth of the American Indian Movement (AIM). AIM has maintained a close connection to the Great Sioux Nation, with many leaders—Russell Means, Leonard Peltier, and John Trudell—claiming Sioux ancestry.

By the 1970s the once radical position that Indians should be able to follow their own cultural traditions—rather than be forced to assimilate to European American traditions—became more widely accepted. The publication of Dee Brown's immensely popular *Bury My Heart at Wounded Knee* in 1971 and a new confrontation at Wounded Knee in 1973 led by

AIM, heightened public consciousness of the plight of the Sioux. Moreover, this era confirmed that the sacred Black Hills were not, nor had they ever been, for sale. In 1980 the U.S. Supreme Court reviewed the fifty-seven-year-old Black Hills land claims case of the Great Sioux Nation and concluded that the taking of the Black Hills by the U.S. government was illegal and that the Great Sioux Nation was entitled to compensation for the taking. That award has now grown to more than $600 million and continues to draw interest in the U.S. Treasury because the Great Sioux Nation has refused the settlement, demanding the return of Paha Sapa, the Black Hills, instead.

Despite the gains reaped from the political and economic programs of the self-determination era, the Sioux reservations in North and South Dakota remain some of the poorest places in the United States. Many reservations have chosen to open casinos, and some have enjoyed the benefits of large-scale capital infusions into their local economies; others, because of their remoteness from urban population centers, have seen little improvement in their economies, besides improving joblessness rates, as a result of casinos. Today, although transformed through decades of hardship and deprivation, the Great Sioux Nation is in a vigorous, if difficult, renaissance. Many Lakotas continue to speak their language and practice traditions such as the Sun Dance. Tribal community colleges, frequently named after important Lakota leaders, have sprung up on the reservations and are educating tribal members in the skills required to engage the global economy and simultaneously recapture their tribal heritage and traditions.

See also IMAGES AND ICONS: Wild West Shows / LAW: *United States v. Sioux Nation of Indians* / PROTEST AND DISSENT: American Indian Movement / SPORTS AND RECREATION: Mills, Billy / WAR: Crazy Horse; Little Bighorn, Battle of the; Red Cloud; Sioux Wars; Wounded Knee Massacre.

Guy Gibbon
University of Minnesota

DeMallie, Raymond J., and Douglas R. Parks, eds. *Sioux Indian Religion*. Norman: University of Oklahoma Press, 1987. Howard, James H. *The Canadian Sioux*. Lincoln: University of Nebraska Press, 1984. Price, Catherine. *The Oglala People, 1841–1879: A Political History*. Lincoln: University of Nebraska Press, 1996.

SIOUX WARS

See WAR: Sioux Wars

SITTING BULL (ca. 1831–1890)

Sitting Bull (*Tantanka Iyotanka*) was born in the early 1830s along the Grand River at a place called Many Caches near present-day Bullhead, South Dakota. During the Plains Indian Wars (1865–76) he rose to prominence as a military and political leader among the Lakotas and led resistance against U.S. military and civilian encroachment through their traditional homelands between the mouth of the Grand and the Yellowstone River basin.

Sitting Bull distinguished himself early as a hunter and warrior and rose to prominence among his own people as a generous man and capable war leader; consequently, he was inducted into a number of prestigious warrior societies. In 1866 he gained attention of the American public for his attacks on soldiers and settlers at Fort Buford (located at the confluence of the Yellowstone and Missouri Rivers).

In response to intensifying outside pressures the Hunkpapa and other Lakota bands, principally the Itizipco, Minneconjou, Sihasapa, and a loose alliance of Oglalas under Crazy Horse, attempted to consolidate leadership. In 1866 or 1867 Sitting Bull was recognized as an important political and military leader of these bands. In some accounts he is labeled "supreme chief." Therefore, in 1867 and 1868, when Catholic missionary Pierre-Jean De Smet sought to broker a truce with the Lakotas, he dealt primarily with Sitting Bull. In these negotiations Sitting Bull rejected all overtures and stated his determination to protect his people's homeland and lifeways, a message he repeated often in subsequent years.

For a time tensions abated due to troop withdrawals along the Bozeman Trail as part of the 1868 Treaty of Fort Laramie, which created the Great Sioux Reservation. However, many Lakotas left their agencies to join Sitting Bull when federal officials failed to enforce provisions of the treaty and prospectors poured into the Black Hills after the government-sponsored expedition in 1874, led by George Armstrong Custer, confirmed the existence of gold there. Clashes between the army and "the Sitting Bull people," as they came to be known, were frequent.

In June 1876, during the annual Sun Dance, Sitting Bull had a vision of dead soldiers falling into an Indian camp, and on June 25, 1876, his prophecy came true with the defeat of Custer's command at the Battle of the Little Bighorn. After this fight, the army systematically hunted Native peoples, and by the fall of 1876 Sitting Bull was one of the few leaders still resisting surrender and living outside his agency. In October, Gen. Nelson Miles intercepted Sitting Bull in Montana Territory and demanded his surrender; typically, Sitting Bull stated his determination to continue living in the old way and resist federal demands. By May of 1877 Sitting Bull and about 400 followers had sought refuge in Saskatchewan, settling between Wood Mountain and Fort Qu'Appelle. Starvation was never far away, and the Dominion of Canada would not provide food or other support, so after lengthy discussion with Canadian and American officials, on July 19, 1881, Sitting Bull and 200 followers crossed into the United States and handed over horses and weapons at Fort Buford. Despite the U.S. government's assurances he would be repatriated with the Hunkpapa at Standing Rock Agency, Sitting Bull and about 100 of his people were held in detention at Fort Randall in southeastern Dakota Territory.

In May 1883 Sitting Bull was permitted to join his people at Standing Rock. There he came under the jurisdiction of Indian agent James McLaughlin, and a sustained clash of wills and philosophies ensued. Sitting Bull struggled to maintain a sense of nationhood and to preserve traditional Lakota values, while McLaughlin enforced federal policy. Sitting Bull left the reservation briefly in 1884 and 1885 to tour in two Wild West shows, then returned to Standing Rock to continue his role as outspoken critic of government attempts to divest the Sioux of nine million acres of their land. Nonetheless, the land was lost in 1889, and against this backdrop word of the Ghost Dance spread among the Sioux. Sitting Bull permitted the Ghost Dance in his camp along the Grand River, not far from his birthplace, and Agent McLaughlin quickly seized on this and petitioned the government to order his arrest. On December 12, 1890, arrest orders for Sitting Bull were sent from Washington. By daybreak on December 15, 1890, following an intense fight, Sitting Bull was dead, and eight of his followers and six Indian police lay dead or dying.

See also IMAGES AND ICONS: Wild West Shows / LAW: Indian Police / RELIGION: Ghost Dance / WAR: Little Bighorn, Battle of the.

Carole A. Barrett
University of Mary

Manzione, Joseph. "*I Am Looking North for My Life*": *Sitting Bull, 1876–1881*. Salt Lake: University of Utah Press, 1991. Utley, Robert M. *The Lance and the Shield: The Life and Times of Sitting Bull*. New York: Henry Holt, 1993. Vestal, Stanley. *Sitting Bull: Champion of the Sioux*. Norman: University of Oklahoma Press, 1932.

SOVEREIGNTY

Sovereignty originally referred to the political attributes of a European king. To be sovereign was to be "above everything." Sovereignty was thought to reside in the physical person of the ruler. The formation of the Swiss Confederation in 1291 and the United Provinces (now the Netherlands) in 1581 introduced a new kind of actor on the political stage: democratic republics that did not have individual dynastic rulers. The seventeenth-century Dutch jurist Hugo de Groot (or Grotius) and eighteenth-century Swiss jurist Emmerich Vattel wrote pioneering legal treatises arguing that sovereignty resides collectively in society itself—that is, in the state and its citizens.

European ideas of sovereignty were culturally applicable to some Aboriginal American contexts. The agricultural city-states of the Mississippi Valley were governed by individual chiefs, as attested by early French descriptions of the city of Natchez. On the whole, however, the chiefs and councils of Indian tribes did not assert absolute lawmaking power over their people.

This was especially true in the Great Plains where, as John Moore has demonstrated for the Cheyennes, group boundaries and leadership remained flexible and could change from season to season. Households not only realigned themselves and chose new leaders within the nation, but they often left the nation altogether, for a season or many years, to travel and hunt with relatives in other nations. While the nation collectively defended a distinct territory with which it identified historically and ceremonially, its constituent families and clans, and its leadership, could be extremely fluid. When the camp crier announced that a respected man planned to break camp at dawn, households individually chose whether to follow him.

Great Plains nations were patches in a boundless, endlessly changing web of kinship relationships, landscapes, and languages. Mobility within this web was sufficient to prevent any persistent concentrations of political power. At the same time, solidarity was sufficient to repel intruders who lacked legitimate claims to local hospitality. Although Great Plains nations could mobilize a formidable military power, as the U.S. Army learned, their leaders generally lacked the institutional means or authority to regulate daily life.

To be sure, most Great Plains nations had "police societies," which could promote good behavior and intervene in disturbances within the camp. In extreme cases, camp police could confiscate malefactors' possessions or even banish them from the community altogether, but only to the extent such actions were supported by collective opinion. When internal disputes could not be resolved by means of negotiation and compromise between families, there was always the option of departure from the camp. A leader misguided enough to try to impose his will on the people would find himself without followers. Plains leaders earned their influence through courage, hard work, and generosity, and they retained it by setting a good example and by respecting the autonomy of others. They were "slow thinkers and silent eaters," as Severt Young Bear puts it so well.

It is accordingly difficult to translate "sovereignty" into Plains Indian languages without changing its meaning. In Lakota, Cree, and Blackfeet societies, for example, "sovereignty" is translated into phrases such as "we do things our own way" or "we are ourselves." This equates sovereignty with freedom rather than power. It has no reference to the existence or legitimacy of states, rulers, or human laws.

Early European explorers nevertheless frequently referred to chiefs as "kings" and showered them with presents in the manner of European court ceremony. What is more important historically and legally is the fact that British, French, Spanish, and Dutch colonists routinely made treaties with Indian nations for trade, military alliances, and the right to build settlements in tribal territories. Warfare and diplomacy with Europeans enhanced the status, wealth, and influence of individual Indian leaders within their own societies. The governance of Indian nations gradually became more centralized and coercive, adopting more and more the political culture of Europeans. Meanwhile, ironically, Europeans began to question whether Indian nations were entitled to be respected as sovereign and independent states—especially after signing treaties that placed them under the protection of European kings.

The first generation of American legal scholars turned to the writings of Grotius and Vattel to explain how a republic could claim to enjoy sovereignty in its diplomacy with European kings. John Marshall, who was secretary of state under President John Adams and then chief justice of the Supreme Court, applied Vattel's legal principles to Indian tribes in the case of *Worcester v. Georgia* (1832). Indian tribes continued to be "distinct, independent political communities, retaining their original natural rights," Marshall concluded, even where they had placed themselves under Europeans' protection by treaty. Although the Worcester decision made it clear that tribal sovereignty was limited only by Indians' consent—in a treaty—Marshall's earlier dictum in *Cherokee Nation v. Georgia* (1831) that Indian tribes are "domestic dependent nations" was resuscitated by late-nineteenth-century judges and has introduced a fundamental ambiguity into the issue of tribal sovereignty. More than a century later, Felix Cohen, a lawyer for the Bureau of Indian Affairs from 1933 to 1948, coined the term "residual sovereignty" to describe the political authority of Indian tribes, and it has continued to be used by lawyers and judges in the United States.

The application of the principle of sovereignty to Native American tribes has changed significantly over time. According to *Worcester*, the sovereignty of an Indian tribe is limited only by the express terms of its treaties with the United States. From 1890 to 1903, however, the U.S. Supreme Court upheld a number of federal laws that interfered with Indian property in violation of treaties, reasoning that Congress has superior sovereignty or "plenary power" over Indians. Finally, in *Oliphant v. Suquamish Indian Tribe* (1978), the Supreme Court ruled that accepting the protection of the United States implicitly stripped Indian tribes of political powers that are "inconsistent with their status" as Indians.

As a result of court decisions, the sovereignty of Native American tribes today is limited by what the tribes surrendered by treaty, what Congress has imposed on tribes by legislation, and what the courts consider to be "inconsistent with their status." Depending on the way particular courts interpret treaties and laws, Indian tribes' residual sovereignty can be very great, or nearly nonexistent.

In Canada, a constitutional monarchy in which the queen is the sovereign and head of state, the courts have not applied the term sovereignty to Indian nations. About half of the territory of Canada was acquired through Indian treaties made in the name of the Crown between 1724 and 1929, however, and most of the rest has been acquired through "modern-day treaties" made since 1975. Since the 1970s, moreover, Canada's Indian nations have insisted that, although they respect the Crown, they possess "unsurrendered sovereignty" of their own. The government of Canada continues to resist this argument, although it has acknowledged as a matter of national policy that Indian nations possess an "inherent right to self-government."

Canada amended its national constitution in 1982 to include, among other changes, a declaration that "the existing aboriginal and treaty rights of the aboriginal peoples of Canada are hereby recognized and affirmed." Indian leaders argue that sovereignty and self-government are Aboriginal rights. This argument has not yet been tested in the Supreme Court of Canada, but it was strongly supported by the Royal Commission on Aboriginal Peoples, a seven-member national policy review body that was established in 1992 and published its final report four years later.

Sovereignty has taken on new meanings for Indian nations in the twentieth century as a result of wider economic and cultural changes and conflicts. The process of centralization of power, which began during the treaty-making period, was enhanced by legislation creating elected tribal lawmaking bodies—in the United States by the Indian Reorganization Act in 1934 and in Canada by amendments to the Indian Act in 1951. Federal funding of tribal government operations, mining of tribal lands, and (in the United States) profits from tribally owned gambling casinos have given many Indian tribal governments large infusions of cash and have turned tribal leaders into corporate managers and employers. Jurisdictional disputes with surrounding state and provincial governments have forced the tribes to assert exclusive territorial lawmaking and law-enforcing powers through the courts. More and more, Native American tribes are exercising sovereignty in the European sense of the word.

At the same time, U.S. and Canadian Indian nations no longer insist on complete independence, but rather a limited sovereignty similar to that of individual states within the American federal system, or individual provinces in Canada's confederation. They tend to accept the inevitability of some degree of congressional (or parliamentary) power over their lives and responsibility for their well-being, while demanding the greatest possible authority over their own territories and citizens. In Canada, this kind of arrangement has sometimes been described as "shared sovereignty," a cooperative political partnership under a freely agreed division of labor.

Although similar political changes have been taking place in Indian communities throughout the United States and Canada, some conflicts over power and resources have been specific to the Great Plains. Plains agriculture has long been based on economies of scale—that is, farming and ranching as much acreage as possible as a single unit. There was considerable pressure on federal officials to open large Indian reservations to leasing or permanent settlement, once the surrounding lands had been fenced. The mechanization of agriculture and soaring grain prices during World War I added to the demand for more acreage. The U.S. and Canadian governments both responded by facilitating the leasing of land within Indian reservations and the diminishment of reservation boundaries.

In the United States, Indian tribes have struggled unsuccessfully to maintain jurisdiction over all of the lands within their original reservation boundaries, including non-Indian settlements. The Supreme Court has taken the view that Congress intended to break up the larger Plains Indian reservations rather than place settlers under the authority of Indian governments. Several Sioux reservations have been considerably reduced (or "disestablished") as a result. The most recent Supreme Court decision, *South Dakota v. Yankton Sioux Tribe* (1998), concluded that Congress intended to dissolve the Yankton Sioux Indian Reservation when it purchased land for settlers from the tribe in 1892. An earlier decision, *Brendale v. Confederated Tribes* (1989), ruled that Indian governments lack authority over predominantly non-Indian settlements inside Indian reservations.

In Canada, leasing and cutoffs are the subjects of hundreds of unresolved land claims in the Prairies. Although the Canadian federal government has accepted responsibility for settling these claims on a case-by-case basis through negotiations, Indians have criticized delays and inadequate compensation. In *Guerin v. The Queen* (1985), Canada's Supreme Court ruled that federal officials have a "fiduciary responsibility" to manage Indian land prudently for Indians' benefit, and that they must pay for any losses attributable to mismanagement. The Royal Commission on Aboriginal Peoples called for the establishment of a tribunal, like the former U.S. Indian Claims Commission, to expedite the processing of land claims.

Meanwhile, water has been replacing land as the main source of friction between Indian tribes and their non-Indian neighbors. Irrigation has surpassed mechanization as the competitive edge in farming the Great Plains, and limited supplies of water must be rationed between long-established non-Indian farms and Indian reservations. In a 1908 decision, *Winters v. United States*, the U.S. Supreme Court reasoned that Congress necessarily intended to include sufficient water for Indian farming when it set land aside as reservations. Indian tribes in the Missouri and Colorado River watersheds have used this legal principle to gain ownership of water and to build their own irrigation systems. Their right to sell unneeded water back to non-Indians is now in dispute.

Irrigation promises to be a growing source of conflict over water allocation in the Saskatchewan River basin, comprising much of southern Alberta and central Saskatchewan. Special Indian water rights have not yet been recognized by Canadian courts, however. To establish an "aboriginal right," according to Canada's Supreme Court in *R. v. Van der Peet* (1997), Indian nations would need to prove that water played a significant role in Aboriginal culture, and that it was neither expressly surrendered through treaty nor explicitly expropriated by Parliament. Since most of the Indians of the Saskatchewan River basin were originally hunters who only began farming and ranching after settling on reserves in the 1880s, it may be difficult for them to convince the courts that they enjoy an Aboriginal right to water.

The growing importance of water in the struggle over Indian sovereignty in the Great Plains highlights the issue of change in Indian nations' political organization and social values. In the arid Plains, water was an object of great reverence and careful stewardship. Important ceremonies, sacred bundles, and pipes were dedicated to water and water dwellers, such as the "beaver bundles" among the Blackfoot and Plains Crees. People exercised collective stewardship of water and shared its use; they did not contemplate altering its flow or allowing anyone to enjoy special privileges. Many Indian governments today associate water rights with large-scale reclamation projects, construction jobs, centrally managed agribusiness, cash flow, and political power.

In the Great Plains context, then, sovereignty has come to be associated more strongly with the power of institutions than with the freedom and responsibility of members of society. To a large extent, this shift in perspective is an understandable and justifiable response to continuing encroachments by Europeans and their governments. Indian nations built statelike institutions and greater power because they needed power to defend themselves. But the power to defend is also potentially the power to oppress people and to disrupt ecosystems. Acquiring sovereignty in the European sense brings new kinds of choices and responsibilities. Many contemporary North American Indians would share the critical viewpoint of Meskwaki (Sauk and Fox) poet Ray Young Bear, who wrote, "By replacing the window of the Cosmic Earth Lodge with aluminum panelling, we encouraged a sudden gust of wind to tear it apart, which made us cringe as the other elements gathered around us in force."

See also WATER: Winters Doctrine.

Russel Barsh
University of Lethbridge

Moore, John H. *The Cheyenne Nation: A Social and Demographic History*. Lincoln: University of Nebraska Press, 1987. Young Bear, Ray A. *Remnants of the First Earth*. New York: Grove Press, 1996. Young Bear, Severt, and R. D. Theisz. *Standing in the Light: A Lakota Way of Seeing*. Lincoln: University of Nebraska Press, 1994.

SPOTTED TAIL (1823–1881)

Spotted Tail (*Sinte Galeska*), a major Brulé Sioux leader in the Plains Indian wars, was born to a man named Chunka (Tangled Hair) and a mother named Walks With Pipe, probably along the White River of South Dakota. Known as Jumping Buffalo in his youth, Spotted Tail got his adult name from a striped raccoon pelt that was given to him by a trapper.

In 1855 he was jailed at Fort Leavenworth in retaliation for the defeat of Lt. John Grattan's force the previous year by Brulés, though Spotted Tail had not been involved in the incident. Upon his release in 1856, he balanced Lakota nationalism with conciliation to the United States, as he was convinced of American military superiority. By 1866 he had refrained from hostilities against Americans, unlike his nephew Crazy Horse.

Spotted Tail made several trips to Washington DC on behalf of his people in the 1860s and 1870s. During the most important visit, in 1875, Spotted Tail was among the Sioux chiefs appointed by U.S. officials to negotiate the sale of the Black Hills following George Armstrong Custer's expedition there a year earlier. Spotted Tail, who was one of the few Sioux chiefs who understood the value to Americans of the gold in the hills, demanded that the government's offer of $6 million be declined, but under duress he eventually agreed to its sale.

In the 1870s tension arose between Red Cloud and Spotted Tail after U.S. officials appointed Spotted Tail as chief of the Sioux at the Spotted Tail and Rosebud Agencies, eventually replacing Red Cloud. Throughout the 1870s Spotted Tail was accused by Red Cloud of pocketing the proceeds from a sale of tribal land. Possibly as part of this dissension, Spotted Tail was shot to death on August 5, 1881, by Crow Dog, a Brulé subchief with whom he had several disputes. Crow Dog's murder case provided the gist of the Supreme Court case *Ex Parte Crow Dog* (1883), in which the defendant was eventually freed when the court ruled that the United States had no jurisdiction over the murder, which had occurred on Indian land.

See also LAW: *Ex Parte Crow Dog* (Major Crimes Act) / WAR: Crazy Horse; Red Cloud.

Bruce E. Johansen
University of Nebraska at Omaha

Hyde, George E. *Spotted Tail's Folk*. Norman: University of Oklahoma Press, 1961. Schusky, Ernest Lester. *The Forgotten Sioux*. Chicago: Nelson-Hall, 1975. Utley, Robert M. *The Lance and the Shield: The Life and Times of Sitting Bull*. New York: Henry Holt, 1993.

STANDING BEAR (ca. 1829–1908)

In the Nebraska Hall of Fame in the State Capitol building is a bust of Standing Bear. He is there among other honored Nebraskans because of the pivotal role he played in resisting the United States' efforts to move his people from their homeland and for his victory in a famous trial, which projected American injustices against Native Americans into the public mind.

Standing Bear was born around 1829 in the traditional Ponca homeland near the confluence of the Niobrara and Missouri Rivers. The Poncas sold this homeland to the United States in 1858, retaining a 58,000-acre reservation between Ponca Creek and the Niobrara. In 1865 the reservation boundaries were modified, resulting in a larger reservation that fronted on the Missouri River. On this reservation the Poncas lived a life of deprivation and fear—the United States did little to protect them from attacks from the Brulé Sioux. Furthermore, when the United States created the Great Sioux Reservation in 1868, the Ponca Reservation was included within its boundaries, arguably depriving them of title to their remaining land.

This was the context for the removal of the Poncas to Indian Territory in 1877. Standing Bear was among the chiefs who protested this eviction, and for this he was imprisoned at Yankton in early 1877. But they were forced to move. Standing Bear went with the second, more resistant, group of migrants. On the way, his daughter Prairie Flower died of consumption.

On their new reservation in Indian Territory, the Poncas continued to die in great numbers. Unknown to their agent, Standing Bear and twenty-nine other Poncas had been storing their rations in preparation for the daunting journey back to the Niobrara. They left on January 1, 1879, and trekked through the Plains winter to reach the reservation of their relatives, the Omahas, in mid-March. Standing Bear carried with him the bones of his son to be buried in the familiar earth along the Niobrara.

Again the federal government intervened. Standing Bear and his followers were arrested by order of Gen. George Crook and taken to Fort Omaha, the intention being to return them to Indian Territory. At this point Thomas Henry Tibbles, an Omaha newspaperman, became interested in their plight and secured two Nebraska lawyers to represent them. The lawyers filed a federal court application for habeas corpus to test the legality of the detention. Judge Elmer Dundy, after permitting Standing Bear to make a moving speech, ruled the detention illegal and the prisoners released. Dundy reasoned that Indians were indeed "persons" under the law and entitled to sever tribal connections and to live where they desired.

Standing Bear subsequently toured the eastern United States with Tibbles, arousing support for the reform of federal Indian policy. In the 1880s he lived with his followers in the bend of the Niobrara, farming successfully. They became known as the Northern Poncas, and their lives increasingly separated from the Southern Poncas who had remained in Indian Territory. Standing Bear died in 1908 and was buried alongside his ancestors.

See also PROTEST AND DISSENT: Trial of Standing Bear.

James Lake Sr.
University of Nebraska College of Law

Lake, James A., Sr. "Standing Bear, Who?" *Nebraska Law Review* 60 (1981): 451–503. Tibbles, Thomas Henry. *The Ponca Chiefs: An Account of the Trial of Standing Bear*. Edited by Kay Graber. Lincoln: University of Nebraska Press, 1972. Wishart, David J. *An Unspeakable Sadness: The Dispossession of the Nebraska Indians*. Lincoln: University of Nebraska Press, 1994.

SUN DANCE

See RELIGION: Sun Dance

THORPE, JIM

See SPORTS AND RECREATION: Thorpe, Jim

TIPIS

See ARCHITECTURE: Tipis

TONKAWAS

The Tonkawas were a combination of a number of independent bands. The name "Tonkawa" translates as "they all stay together." From at least the eleventh century until their removal to a reservation in Indian Territory in 1884, the Tonkawas occupied the pin oak prairie and grassland that stretched from the Llano River in central Texas to the Canadian River in Oklahoma.

The Tonkawas, who numbered several thousand before contact with Europeans, were led by a selected tribal chief. Maternal clans were the basic societal unit, with children becoming members of the mother's clan and the husband living with his wife's clan. The Tonkawas subsisted by hunting bison and other game and by gathering a wide variety of wild fruits, roots, and nuts. Unlike most other Plains Indians, they also ate fish and shellfish. They practiced agriculture, unsuccessfully, and only when the elimination of the bison drove them to it. Their traditional homes were short tipis made of bison hides. When this resource was no longer available, in the second half of the nineteenth century, they lived in tipilike structures made of brush and grass, and later in flat huts roofed with brush. The Tonkawa language is thought to be unrelated to any other Native American language.

The Tonkawas initially came in contact with Spanish explorers in the sixteenth century. They came into permanent association with European settlers in 1722, when Juan Rodriguez, the chief of the southern Tonkawas (Ervipiames), demanded and received a mission, San Francisco Xavier de Najera, at San Antonio de Béjar in Texas. Although the Ervipiames and their allies never settled at San Antonio's missions in any numbers, the Tonkawas began to interact with the Spaniards as allies against the Lipan Apaches and Comanches. But Spain saw the advantages of Comanche friendship at the expense of the weaker Tonkawas, and by the 1770s the Tonkawas were left to make a place for themselves on the borderland between the Comanches and the Europeans. Under a chief named El Mocho they aligned themselves with the Lipans and Bidais. While successfully fending off Spanish and Comanche attacks, they moved closer to the forests of East Texas and absorbed the remnants of the Karankawas, a coastal tribe.

By 1821, when Stephen F. Austin's colonists arrived on the Brazos River, the Tonkawas were in need of powerful allies. They offered to serve the American settlers as scouts and fighters. Throughout the years of the Austin Colony, the Texas Revolution, and into the decade of Texas's independence, the Tonkawas served loyally as auxiliaries to the military arm of Anglo Texas in its battles with Iscanis (a subtribe of the Wichitas) and Comanches. Their reward, after the United States had annexed Texas, was to be removed to a reservation on the Clear Fork of the Brazos in 1856, a time when Texans were demanding that all Indians be exiled from the soil of the state. In 1859 the Tonkawas were removed to Fort Cobb on the Washita River in Indian Territory, along with the other tribes of the Texas frontier.

Old enmities died hard, however, as did old friendships. Tonkawas continued to help United States and Texas troops fight the Comanches. With the outbreak of the Civil War, the Tonkawas sided with the Texans, while most Indians at Fort Cobb favored the Union. On October 24, 1862, pro-Union Indians attacked the Tonkawas, killing half the tribe and driving the survivors back into Texas, where Confederate authorities provided them with food and clothing and enlisted them as scouts on the frontier.

When the Civil War ended, the relentless push of Americans westward into Comanche country once again provided the Tonkawas with employment. Enlisted by the U.S. Army as scouts, they were settled at Fort Griffin in north-central Texas and employed continually until the Comanche defeat in 1878. Tonkawa scouts distinguished themselves in every major action of the post–Civil War era in Texas. When the Comanches and their allies had been confined to a reservation, the Tonkawas expected to be rewarded for their long service to the United States. Instead Fort Griffin was abandoned in 1881 and the Tonkawas' funds were cut off. For three years the tribe survived mostly on rations, until they were forcibly removed to lands abandoned by Chief Joseph's Nez Perces near the present-day town of Tonkawa, in Kay County, Oklahoma. In 1896 their reservation was allotted, and their land base was further reduced. They now hold 399 acres of land. Their population plummeted to 34 in 1921, then began a slow revival to 43 in 1936 and 186 in 1993.

In recent years Tonkawas have developed an interest in their past and their role in Texas settlement. A powwow in Austin and local gatherings in Oklahoma have served to create a renewed interest in a people who are among the original settlers of what is now Texas and the most loyal of American allies.

Thomas F. Schilz
San Diego Miramar College

Carlisle, Jeffery D. "Tonkawa Indians." In *The New Handbook of Texas*, edited by Ron Tyler, 6:525–26. Austin: Texas State Historical Association, 1996. Smithwick, Noah. *The Evolution of a State, or Recollections of Old Texas Days*. Austin: Gammel Book Co., 1900.

TRADE

Native peoples of the Great Plains engaged in trade between members of the same tribe, between different tribes, and with the European Americans who increasingly encroached upon their lands and lives. Trade within the tribe involved gift-giving, a means of obtaining needed items and social status. Trade between Plains tribes often took the form of an exchange of products of the hunt (bison robes, dried meat, and tallow) for agricultural products, such as corn and squash. European and American items, such as horses, guns, and other metal products, were incorporated into the existing Plains trade system after the seventeenth century.

Trade among the Plains Indians has a long history. The archeological record shows an active trade in Knife River flint in the Northern Plains beginning before 2000 B.C. Moreover, copper, obsidian, and marine shell artifacts suggest an existence of an early east–west trade route crossing the Northern Plains and connecting to the Great Lakes and the Atlantic Coast in the east and the Rocky Mountains and the Pacific Coast in the west. Farther south, the people living along the lower Missouri, Arkansas, and Red Rivers traded in copper and marine shells with the Mississippi Valley people after 2000 B.C. There is also evidence of local trade for this period. While the Northern Plains trade system remained relatively stable throughout the following centuries, the Southern and Central Plains trade patterns changed dramatically around A.D. 1200, when the ties between the Mississippi valley and the lower Missouri, Arkansas, and Red River societies were cut. Further changes came in the fourteenth and fifteenth centuries, when the Southern Plains societies began to trade in corn, pottery, and bison products with the Pueblos of the Southwest.

At the time of European contact, there were two types of Native American trading sites in the Great Plains. The first was associated with permanent agricultural villages, including those of the Mandans and Hidatsas in present-day North Dakota and the Arikaras in present-day South Dakota. These sites hosted trading parties from the Crows, Shoshones from the west, Assiniboines and Crees from the north, and Plains Apaches, Cheyennes, Arapahos, and Pawnees from the south. Lewis and Clark, who wintered with the Mandans in 1804, noted that traders in the villages obtained items from as far as Mexico and the Pacific Coast. In the Southern Plains, the Wichita villages on the Arkansas and Red Rivers served as trading sites for Jumanos, Apaches, Comanches, and Pawnees.

The second type of trading site was a trade fair, or rendezvous, in which bands met to exchange goods away from a permanent village, generally at a point convenient to nomadic bands. The Dakota rendezvous, held on the James River in present-day South Dakota, and the Shoshone rendezvous, held in southwestern Wyoming, were regular trading fairs at the beginning of the nineteenth century. A major trading site—perhaps as important as those at the Mandan, Hidatsa, and Arikara villages—was operated by the Western Comanches in the valley of the upper Arkansas River from the 1740s to around 1830.

An integral part of the trade system was the middlemen who operated between the various trade centers. The Cheyennes served as intermediaries between the upper Missouri villages and the Southern Plains hunter-pastoralists and carried firearms and other European American goods to the south and horses to the north. The Crows trafficked in horses and firearms between the central upper Missouri and the Shoshone rendezvous. The Assiniboines and Plains Crees carried manufactured goods to the upper Missouri from Canadian fur traders and took back horses and corn. In the Southern Plains, the Jumanos and Apaches and later the Apaches and Comanches competed for the lucrative middleman position between the Wichitas and the Pueblos. By linking the trade centers, these middleman groups integrated the Plains tribes into a compact commercial network that covered the whole region.

The trade systems were maintained through a variety of sustaining mechanisms, including the calumet ceremony, redundancy trading, and sign language. The calumet ceremony made unrelated peoples one family through the working of a fictional kinship. Leaders of different bands or tribes adopted each other as father or son, allowing trade to take place even between traditional enemies. In such exchanges, tribes gained access to foodstuffs that would otherwise have been difficult to acquire. However, Native peoples often exchanged corn for corn, or meat for meat. The Pawnees, for example, traded corn for corn with the Arikaras. This redundancy trading was a security mechanism, setting up avenues for exchange in case of local crop failure. Sign language allowed linguistically diverse tribes to negotiate the terms of the trade.

European traders began to engage in this trade from the edges of the Plains. Spanish settlers in Santa Fe exchanged goods of European manufacture, such as beads, mirrors, and blades, for hides, foodstuffs and services early in the seventeenth century. British traders infiltrated the network from the northeast, and French and Spanish traders pushed up the Missouri River from St. Louis in the late eighteenth century. By the early nineteenth century, American and British fur companies had created networks of fixed trading posts throughout the Missouri and Saskatchewan river drainage basins. At these points European and American manufactured products were exchanged for bison robes, beaver pelts, and other furs and skins. The Plains Indians became the primary producers in an international trade system controlled from New York and London. American and Canadian traders also sought to bypass the traditional middlemen and used alcohol as a means to curry favor. The Indians would not have participated if they had not valued the introduced products (especially guns), but a dependency on outside supplies was created, and when there no longer were furs to trade the Indians could not obtain the goods they had come to rely upon.

The increased market demands resulted in the collapse of the resource base. By 1840 beaver had been eliminated from large parts of the Plains, and the virtual destruction of the bison herds in the 1870s brought an end to the traditional Plains Indian trade. Restricted to reservations in both Canada and the United States, the Indians' trade was often a sale of annuity goods, at inadequate prices, at the local trader's store. Native American conventions of trade continued, and continues, within tribes and in contexts like powwows between tribes, but the traditional Plains trade system that had endured for so long fell victim to imposed European American economies.

Mark A. Eifler
University of Portland

Hämäläinen, Pekka. "The Western Comanche Trade Center: Rethinking the Plains Indian Trade System." *Western Historical Quarterly* 29 (1998): 485–513. Jablow, Joseph. "The Cheyenne in Plains Indian Trade Relations 1795–1840." In *Monographs of the American Ethnological Society*. Vol. 19. New York: J. J. Augustin Publisher, 1950. Swagerty, William R. "Indian Trade in the Trans-Mississippi West to 1870." In *Handbook of North American Indians*, 4:351–74. Washington DC: Smithsonian Institution, 1988.

TREATIES

In both the United States and Canada, negotiated treaties were the instrument for obtaining Indian lands and more generally for extending federal control over Native peoples, while at the same time recognizing the sovereignty they retained. In the United States, the Constitution gave the executive branch the authority to negotiate treaties and the Senate the authority to ratify them. Treaty making was abolished in 1871, but similar bilateral agreements between the federal government and the tribes continued thereafter. In Canada, the provision for a treaty process was established with the Royal Proclamation of 1763, whereby the Crown reserved the sole right to purchase Indian lands. That authority was continued through the British North America Act of 1867, which passed on the Crown's authority over First Peoples to the new Dominion of Canada.

In both Canada and the United States, early treaties proclaimed peace and friendship between the government and the Native peoples. The fact is, neither of the colonizing powers had the military power to defeat the Indians, and treaties were a pragmatic alternative. After 1812, however, the population balance swung in favor of the European Americans, and treaties became the means to acquire Indian lands. Especially in the United States, it was a buyer's market. Pressured by settlers and mired in poverty, Indians rarely had any option but to sell. In many cases, consent to treaties was obtained only through fraud and duress. The surrender of the Black Hills by the Lakotas (Sioux) in 1877 and the sale of the Red River Valley of the North by the Red Lake and Pembina bands of the Chippewas are notable examples of such manipulation.

In the American Great Plains, treaty making for the purpose of obtaining Indian lands began with the cession of what is now southern Oklahoma by the Quapaw in 1818. This land, and vast areas subsequently obtained in the 1820s and 1830s in present-day Oklahoma, Kansas, and southern Nebraska, were bought from Plains Indians to make room for relocated Indians from the eastern United States. The next wave of treaties came in eastern Nebraska and southeastern Dakota Territory in the second half of the 1850s when the Pawnees, Omahas, Poncas, Otoe-Missourias, and Yanktons sold their ancestral lands, retaining only small reservations. European Americans moved in to settle the newly acquired public domain. This process was repeated westward and northward throughout the Great Plains in the following four decades. Indian dispossession, achieved through treaties, was the prerequisite for frontier settlement.

In Canada, the clearing of Indian title to the Prairie Provinces was done more quickly. From 1871 to 1877, in a series of seven numbered treaties, the many bands of Crees, Chippewas, Assiniboines, and Blackfoot relinquished their claims to the land and settled on reserves. The terms of each treaty varied only in detail. Through Treaties 1 and 2, for example, concluded in 1871, the Swampy Crees and Chippewas ceded 52,400 square miles of southern Manitoba and Saskatchewan in return for a

U.S. Army commissioners in council with chiefs, Fort Laramie, Wyoming, 1868

reserve, a school, farm implements, a one-time payment of $3 per person, and an annuity of $3 per person.

Similar types of compensation were given south of the forty-ninth parallel. In both countries, payments for lands—the monies due the Indians—were used to fund the government's "civilization" programs, which aimed to assimilate the Indians as independent, self-sufficient, Christianized farmers. But payments for Indian lands were so low (they averaged ten cents an acre in the Central and Northern Great Plains) and the quality of services and goods so poor, that the end product of treaty making was poverty, not self-sufficiency.

On the one hand, then, treaties can be viewed as a subterfuge, a means of acquiring Indian lands legally and without the more expensive and disruptive warfare. Negotiations took place, the Indians had their say, and the federal governments set the conditions of the divestiture. On the other hand, treaties established reservations and reserves where tribal law and government still prevail despite challenges. Treaties are not merely historical documents; they are contracts between sovereign powers, the foundation of Indian law, and often the legal justification for claims cases.

David J. Wishart
University of Nebraska–Lincoln

Cohen, Felix S. *Handbook of Federal Indian Law*. Buffalo: William S. Hein Co., 1988: 33–67. McQuillan, Aidan D. "Creation of Indian Reserves on the Canadian Prairies, 1870–1885." *Geographical Review* 70 (1980): 219–36. Wilkinson, Charles F. *American Indians, Time, and the Law*. New Haven CT: Yale University Press, 1987.

TRIAL OF STANDING BEAR

See PROTEST AND DISSENT: Trial of Standing Bear

TRIBAL COLLEGES

See EDUCATION: Tribal Colleges

TRUDELL, JOHN

See MUSIC: Trudell, John

URBAN COMMUNITIES

Urban Indian communities are mainly the products of the federal relocation program for Native Americans following World War II, which was associated with the "termination" movement. The relocation impetus derived from the harsh winter of 1947–48 on the Navajo Reservation, where freezing conditions resulted in starvation for both the Navajos and their livestock. The government responded by airdropping hay to sheep and horses and by moving many Navajo families to Denver, Salt Lake City, and Los Angeles. Convinced that this drastic action had been a success, the government sponsored a wider relocation through the Bureau of Indian Affairs. From 1952 to 1973 an estimated 100,000 Native Americans relocated to urban areas such as Chicago, Los Angeles, Seattle, San Francisco, Dallas, and, in the

Great Plains, Wichita, Denver, Oklahoma City, and Tulsa. The relocation program promised Native Americans jobs and housing in the cities, but it actually began a new era of federal efforts to assimilate Native peoples into the mainstream culture of America.

The first Indian relocatees were so-called gatekeepers who helped each other in this urban frontier experience. In the 1950s and 1960s urban Indians lacked sufficient education and needed job skills to compete successfully in the cities. Many did not make this adjustment, and becoming frustrated, they returned to their reservation or resorted to drink. A second generation of Native Americans migrated to the cities in the 1960s and 1970s, often settling near relatives who were already living there. By the 1980s this generation had grown up in the cities and felt closer to Indian friends and relatives there than to those on reservations. They did not know the reservation culture like their parents and grandparents, although they did visit on a regular basis. They developed an urban Indian culture quite unlike the way of life on the reservation. Urban Indian centers, which had been established in the early 1970s with government funding, became stronger, with more independent funding and community support. They provided counseling and sponsored bowling leagues, softball teams, and other outings for their Indian communities. Such centers—in the Great Plains at Fort Worth, Oklahoma City, Tulsa, Wichita, Lincoln, Denver, Rapid City, and Sioux Falls, for example—brought together Native Americans from different tribes, creating a new overall Indian identity.

Los Angeles became the largest urban Indian community, drawing Native Americans from all over the United States but mainly from the Southwest and Oklahoma. About 113,000 Native Americans lived in the greater Los Angeles metropolitan area by 1997. In the Great Plains in the late 1990s, about 25,000 Native Americans, mostly Navajos and Lakotas, called Denver their home; 22,000 to 25,000 Cherokees, Choctaws, Chickasaws, Creeks, and Seminoles, and various Southern and Northern Plains tribes lived in Dallas–Fort Worth; 48,196 Native Americans, drawn mainly from the Five Civilized Tribes and eastern Oklahoma tribes, resided in Tulsa; and 45,720 of the Five Civilized Tribes and western Oklahoma tribes lived in Oklahoma City. Smaller, but significant, Native American populations also lived in Rapid City (10,000 to 12,000, mainly Lakotas) and Sioux Falls (12,000 to 15,000, also mainly Lakotas) in South Dakota and in Omaha and Lincoln, Nebraska (with 10,000 and 1,150 Poncas, Lakotas, and Omahas, respectively).

Donald L. Fixico
University of Kansas

Danziger, Edmund, Jr. *Survival and Regeneration: Detroit's American Indian Community*. Detroit: Wayne State University Press, 1991. Fixico, Donald L. *The Urban Indian Experience in America*. Albuquerque: University of New Mexico Press, 2000. Weibel-Orlando, Joan. *Indian Country, L.A.: Maintaining Ethnic Community in Complex Society*. Urbana: University of Illinois Press, 1991.

URBAN INDIAN RESERVES

See CITIES AND TOWNS: Urban Indian Reserves

VETERANS

Native Americans have served with the U.S. armed forces as auxiliaries, allies, scouts, volunteers, and conscripts since the Revolutionary War, and Canadian First Peoples fought for Great Britain as early as the mid–eighteenth century. During both world wars, Native Americans and First Peoples served (and died) in numbers exceeding their relative populations and distinguished themselves on battlefields from the Argonne Forest to Iwo Jima. For example, more than 4,000 First Peoples enlisted in World War I, including every eligible man in Saskatchewan's File Hill community. Native North Americans' record of service extended to the hills of Korea, the rain forests of Vietnam, and the deserts of Saudi Arabia and Iraq during the Gulf War of 1991 and 2003 invasion of Iraq.

The reasons why Native North Americans enter the armed forces are many and complex. They serve to earn a guaranteed wage or perhaps because they believe that tribal treaty agreements obligate them to volunteer for military duty. For some, military service was a natural step from militarized Indian boarding schools. For Mike Mountain Horse of the Blood Band of Alberta, and no doubt many others, fighting in World War I was proof that the warrior tradition had not been suppressed by reservation life.

Whatever their reasons for entering the military, those who returned had to face challenging problems of readjustment to civilian life. Information from the U.S. Department of Veterans Affairs and statistical data from the Bureau of the Census reveal that by 1980 there were more than 159,000 Native Americans eligible to receive veteran's benefits. The majority of these veterans came from the Great Plains. Many of them rarely used their hard-earned benefits because of the distances involved in traveling from reservations to VA hospitals, benefits offices, and veterans' outreach clinics.

Adjustment to civilian life was much more than taking advantage of veteran's benefits, however. Returning veterans had to readjust emotionally, economically, and culturally. The adjustment was eased for some by strong family relationships and by ceremonies designed to cleanse the veteran of his or her war-related trauma or to honor their sacrifices. Economic adjustment was difficult. Many veterans of the wars of the twentieth century returned to Plains communities, whether urban or reservation, that were among the poorest in the nation, with few opportunities for work. Still, these veterans revived warrior societies, took part in time-honored ceremonies related to warfare, and founded all-Indian VFW and American Legion posts.

Nowhere were these revivals, ceremonies, and organizations as important as in the Great Plains. The Kiowas, for example, rejuvenated the Gourd Dance, a warriors' society ceremony, and the Black Leggings, another warrior sodality, following World War II. Several other societies were revived among the Cheyennes, Lakotas, Arapahos, Pawnees, and Osages. These revivals, initiated and kept alive largely by veterans, have become an important part of the post–World War II movement to preserve tribal cultures.

Militarization quite often has an effect of democratizing societies. It was clear, for example, that after World Wars I and II Native North American veterans were prepared to demand their full rights of citizenship. Their service in the military had, in effect, legitimized their quest for better treatment. A great number of veterans of World War II became tribal officials almost immediately following the conflict. One, a Lakota from the Lower Brulé Agency of South Dakota, was elected tribal chairman at the young age of nineteen. In 1945, all the tribal council members of Crow Creek Reservation (also in South Dakota) were veterans. By 1946 more than one-third of all tribes in the United States had veterans serving as tribal council members. Numerous others went on to lead the fight against the federal policy of termination and later to promote self-determination and tribal self-sufficiency.

Tom Holm
University of Arizona

Bernstein, Alison R. *American Indians and World War II.* Norman: University of Oklahoma Press, 1991. Gaffen, Fred. *Forgotten Soldiers.* Penticton, British Columbia: Theytus Books Ltd., 1985. Holm, Tom. *Strong Hearts, Wounded Souls: Native American Veterans of the Vietnam War.* Austin: University of Texas Press, 1996.

VISION QUEST

See RELIGION: Vision Quest

WELCH, JAMES

See LITERARY TRADITIONS: Welch, James

WICHITAS

When the Spanish explorer Coronado traveled across the Southern Plains in 1541 in search of the fabled riches of Quivira, he encountered large villages of a distinctive tattooed people along the Great Bend of the Arkansas River, near present-day Arkansas City, Kansas. This was the initial European contact with the Native Americans now recognized as the Wichita and Affiliated Tribes.

Early historic accounts from Coronado's *entrada* and the later Oñate expedition found the Wichitas referring to themselves as the *Quicasquiris* or *Quirasquiris* (or *Ki'dikir' eis,* based on interviews conducted with tribal members in 1949). Close study of Spanish and French explorers' visits with the Wichitas reveals a loosely aligned confederacy of a number of bands. These included the Taovayas, Tawakonis, Iscanis-Wacos, and the Wichitas proper. By the eighteenth century the Kitsais, another tribe related to the Wichita subgroups, had been assimilated by the Wichitas.

Linguistically, the Wichita language belongs

Wichita Indian grass house

to the Caddoan language family that also includes the Pawnee, Kitsai, Caddo, and Arikara languages. Historically, Wichita is most closely related to the Northern Caddoan subfamily languages of Kitsai and Pawnee and is more distantly related to Caddo of Proto-Caddoan derivation.

While many Native groups traditionally recognized as Plains societies (for example, the Cheyennes) have a relatively recent history in the Southern Plains, the Wichitas have been there for 2,000 to 2,500 years. They were among a diffuse group of people, possibly from Louisiana or Mississippi, who began a westward movement some 3,000 years ago. This migration gradually extended across the Plains, displacing existing residents. During this expansion, the newcomers began to develop regional distinctions in material culture, means of subsistence, and social, political, and religious organization. Archeologists now link these regional expressions to the historic Caddo, Kitsai, Wichita, Pawnee, and Arikara tribes. Archeological evidence and historic accounts reveal that the Wichitas ranged over much of the Southern Plains, including what is currently north-central Texas, Oklahoma, and south-central Kansas.

Wichita subsistence practices reflected a dual economy based on farming and hunting. During the spring and summer they cultivated sizable plots of corn, beans, and squash and harvested wild plants such as amaranth and sunflower. Bison, deer, and small game were hunted. In the fall and winter the Wichitas conducted large-scale communal bison hunts. Greater reliance on hunting by a traditionally agricultural people was probably connected to the introduction of the horse in the seventeenth century.

The Aboriginal material culture of the Wichitas closely parallels that of other Plains village societies. A variety of natural products, such as animal bones and hides, wood, plant fiber, stone, and clay, were used in the manufacture of domestic goods, clothing, and ornaments. Much of the traditional technology was abandoned by the late nineteenth century in favor of European American goods. The most distinctive aspect of the Wichita material world was their beehive-shaped grass houses. These houses ranged from fifteen to thirty feet in diameter and twelve to twenty feet in height. The dwelling, consisting of fourteen to sixteen cedar posts with a frame of smaller cedar and willow poles, was covered with bundles of coarse grass. Four small poles extended about three feet from the peak of the house, representing the four world quarters or gods. Wichita dwellings were designed to house extended family units of roughly eight to ten people. Villages had from thirty to several hundred such residences. Wichita settlements in the eighteenth century also typically contained a palisade or fortification, although not all the houses of the village would be within this protected area.

Wichita society has been generally viewed as highly egalitarian, with male status acquired through individual achievements in hunting and warfare. However, there are indications that some Wichita subgroups, such as the Tawakonis, had chiefs or rulers with greater authority; inheritance of these positions appears likely to have occurred in some instances. A typical Wichita village would have a principal chief elected by the head warriors, a leader responsible for finding new village locations, shamans or medicine men, warriors, elders, and "no-count men," who were servants to the chief, leader, or priests. Women of the village were responsible for planting and tending the crops as well as most of the labor-intensive tasks, such as building houses, collecting firewood, and hauling water. Men were principally involved in hunting and warfare. As was the case in many Native American farming societies, kinship was matrilinear, or traced through the woman's side, and matrilocal, meaning that the husband moved to the residence of the wife's family after marriage.

The Wichitas recognized a host of sacred figures. These were divided into the gods and goddesses of the earth and sky. Supreme among these was the god known as *Kinnikasus* (Man Never Known On Earth), who was responsible for the creation of the universe and its parts. Other male gods controlled the heavens (with the exception of the moon goddess), whereas goddesses—the goddess of water, for example—reigned on earth. The Wichitas also believed that all animate and inanimate objects possessed a spirit and that everything could assume more than its apparent natural characteristics. These concepts played a significant role in the development of supernatural powers among the medicine men. The Wichitas have also been credited with establishing the calumet ceremony as a means of initiating truce conditions among Plains societies.

The arrival of Europeans on the Southern Plains dramatically transformed Plains tribes. The presence of the horse and European goods, weapons, and diseases brought about drastic changes in demographics, subsistence economies, and political structures of most tribes, including the Wichitas. The French and Spanish also manipulated the tribes, pitting them against each other in an effort to gain control of the Southern Plains. In the seventeenth and eighteenth centuries, the Wichitas had continuous conflicts with the Apaches and Comanches to the west and the Osages to the east. By the mid–eighteenth century, they had established peace with the Comanches. Conflicts continued with the Apaches and Osages. In the 1750s the Osages forced the Wichitas from the Great Bend of the Arkansas River to the middle reaches of the Red River. The Wichitas maintained good relations with the French but never fully embraced Spanish authority. They won a major victory over the Spanish in 1759 when Col. Diego Ortiz Parilla failed in his attack on a Wichita village on the Red River.

The Wichitas may have had a total population of around 10,000 in the 1700s. Subsequently, introduced diseases and continuing conflicts with whites and other Indians led to significant population decline. By the late eighteenth century their population had dropped to about 4,000, and by the 1890s only 153 Wichitas remained.

In 1872 the Wichitas ceded all claims to their ancestral lands in Texas and Indian Territory to the United States and were left with a 743,000-acre reservation in present-day Caddo County, Oklahoma. However, this agreement was never ratified, and their title to the land remained in doubt. In 1901 the reservation was allotted and greatly reduced by the sale of "surplus lands."

The Wichita and Affiliated Tribes currently reside adjacent to the Anadarko Agency just north of Anadarko, Oklahoma. They hold some 1,260 acres of land in common trust with the Caddo and Delaware tribes. In 1995 there were 1,798 Wichitas, most of whom lived in Oklahoma.

Robert L. Brooks
University of Oklahoma

Dorsey, George A. *The Mythology of the Wichita*. Washington DC: Carnegie Institution, 1904. John, Elizabeth A. H. *Storms Brewed in Other Men's Worlds*. College Station: Texas A&M University Press, 1975. Newcomb, W. W. Jr. *The Indians of Texas*. Austin: University of Texas Press, 1961.

WINTERS DOCTRINE

See WATER: Winters Doctrine

WOMEN OF ALL RED NATIONS

See PROTEST AND DISSENT: Women of All Red Nations

WOUNDED KNEE MASSACRE

See WAR: Wounded Knee Massacre

ZITKALA ŠA

See LITERARY TRADITIONS: Zitkala Ša

Physical Environment

Lesser sandhill crane spring flock in Nebraska

PHYSICAL ENVIRONMENT

The Great Plains of Canada and the United States form an enormous piedmont flanking the eastern slope of the Rocky Mountains. Taken as a whole, this piedmont, some 300 to 400 miles wide and 1,800 miles long, is like a stage before the backdrop of the Rockies. Visitors have always been inclined to appreciate that backdrop more than they have the stage, but for the people who live on the Plains it remains a debatable point which of the two is really the more impressive.

Topography

Explorers often used the phrase "great plains" and even put it on maps, but the first person to recognize the Great Plains as a physiographic unit of North America appears to have been John Wesley Powell, writing in 1895. Leading geographers of the early twentieth century, such as William Morris Davis and Isaiah Bowman, picked up the term in this technical sense and soon used it in textbooks. During World War I, Nevin M. Fenneman began work on his still authoritative physiography of the United States, and his map of the physical divisions of the country, published by the U.S. Geological Survey and accompanying his text of 1931, is still in print. It demarcates not only the Great Plains, but also adds subdivisions of the Plains that have now become standard, including such colloquial ones as the High Plains and other, more technical ones such as the Plains Border and the Missouri Plateau. Edwin Hammond in 1964 proposed revisions to Fenneman's map, including dropping the term Great Plains altogether and replacing it with a set of terms including such awkward ones as Upper Missouri River Broken Lands, but Fenneman's terminology has endured.

The Great Plains slopes gently eastward. As defined here, the maximum height of its western edge rises from about 2,000 feet above sea level in Canada to more than 6,000 feet in New Mexico. On its eastern edge, the Plains drop to an elevation of about 1,000 feet along a line from Winnipeg to Kansas City, Oklahoma City, and the toe of the Balcones Escarpment in Texas. The Great Plains, therefore, slopes eastward approximately ten feet per mile, a slant that is wholly imperceptible to the unaided eye.

Most of the Great Plains, it should be stressed, is not especially flat, and this general slope can therefore be misleading. According to Edwin Hammond, the only parts of the Great Plains that are simultaneously both flat and level are the valley of the Platte River in Nebraska, the valley of the Arkansas River in central Kansas, and several former glacial lake beds, especially those now drained by the Red and Souris Rivers in North Dakota and the James River in South Dakota. There are other equally flat but not so level parts of the Great Plains: preeminent among these tilted plains are the High Plains, which extend from the Pine Ridge Escarpment in northern Nebraska south to Midland-Odessa, Texas. (Their most famous subdivision is the Llano Estacado, or

Staked Plains, that extends south from the Canadian River near Amarillo and is spectacularly rimmed on the east by the Caprock Escarpment and on the west, in New Mexico, by the Mescalero Escarpment.) Tilted they may be, but to the eye the High Plains seem as level as they are flat. Indeed, they seem so level and flat that they can strike even the comfortable modern traveler as faintly distressing, for their flatness keeps the horizon always close and can create a sense of confinement. The occasional breaks in the High Plains—and there are several, including the impressive valleys of the Canadian, Cimarron, and Republican Rivers—can therefore be a welcome respite from the sense of being thrust upward and pushed into the lid of the sky. The Great Plains possesses other equally flat but tilted plains as well, but these areas are much smaller than the High Plains; economically, the most important of them is probably the wheat-rich Wichita Prairie of Kansas.

The greater part of the Plains south of the Nebraska Sandhills is composed of irregular or rolling, not flat, ground. Bounding the High Plains, for example, there are tablelands of moderate or considerable relief, both on the west near Raton, New Mexico, and on the east, with the Gypsum Plains of north-central Texas. Farther east, there are low mountains in the Wichitas near Lawton, Oklahoma; there are plains with high hills in the Lampasas Cut Plains of the dissected eastern edge of the Edwards Plateau; there are hills such as the Smoky, Flint, and Osage Hills of Kansas and Oklahoma; and there are huge areas of gently rolling plains, such as the Red River Rolling Plains of Oklahoma and Texas and the Enid Prairie of Oklahoma.

The Nebraska Sandhills, the largest area of sand dunes in the Western Hemisphere, were classified by Hammond as open hills; to their north he delineated a complex topographic mosaic including tablelands along the Missouri, open high hills in the Powder River Basin, low mountains in the Black Hills, and open high mountains in the Bearpaw Mountains south of Havre, Montana.

No classification like Hammond's has been made for the landforms of Canada, but H. S. Bostock of the Geological Survey of Canada has subdivided the Canadian Great Plains into the Alberta, Saskatchewan, and Manitoba Plains. Despite these names, the boundaries of these units follow topographical rather than political features. Thus the Alberta Plain, largest of the three, is bounded on the west by the Rocky Mountain foothills, on the north by the Alberta Plateau, which starts at the Athabaska River, and on the east by the Missouri Coteau, an escarpment that runs from near North Battleford southeasterly into the Dakotas. The Saskatchewan Plain extends eastward below the Coteau to the Manitoba Escarpment, which lies just west of Lakes Winnipegosis and Manitoba. The outstanding topographic feature on the Canadian plains, other than the subdividing escarpments, is the Cypress Hills, which rise southeast of Medicine Hat, Alberta. The Great Plains in Canada, it should again be emphasized, are by no

means either entirely flat or entirely level; extensive areas here, too, are rolling or even hilly.

Strikingly, our knowledge of the topography of the Great Plains remains incomplete. This may be surprising, since the main lines of natural drainage were worked out nearly 150 years ago: those in the United States, for example, were shown in 1857 with startling accuracy on the map prepared by Lt. G. K. Warren of the U.S. Army Corps of Topographical Engineers. In the century that followed, Dominion-land surveyors in Canada and public-domain surveyors in the United States drafted planimetric maps showing almost every creek and hill on the Plains; geodetic and topographic surveyors added elevations. Yet significant details are being discovered even today. Recent digital terrain mapping by Gail Thelin and Richard Pike of the U.S. Geological Survey, for example, has revealed what appears to be an extraordinary set of regional fractures trending from northwest to southeast across the Plains, especially north of the Sandhills. Thelin and Pike suggest that these features were created by the collision and fusion of an ancestral North America with lands farther west.

Geology

As such details suggest, a real understanding of topography requires a knowledge of geology. Much sense can in fact be made of the topography of the Great Plains if we remember that the Great Plains rest upon the North American craton, which is to say the Precambrian continental core. Exposed in the United States primarily in the Superior Upland of northern Minnesota, but exposed far more extensively in the Canadian Shield, these cratonic rocks extend between the Appalachians and the Rockies. At a few places on the Plains they outcrop, most notably in the Black Hills of South Dakota, where they emerge from between encircling sedimentary layers. Less massively, they are revealed in the Little Belt Mountains south of Great Falls, Montana, and in the Wichita Mountains northwest of Lawton, Oklahoma. Elsewhere they are buried, often at tremendous depth. At Amarillo, which is 5,000 feet above sea level, the cratonic rocks lie at a depth of 3,000 feet below sea level; eastward, they plunge to a basin whose surface lies approximately 30,000 feet below sea level.

This great thickness of sedimentary rocks covering the craton accumulated over a period of several hundred million years as sediments from the Appalachians and Rockies were carried across the often submerged but intervening lowland. Periods of uplift and erosion have removed most of the sediments that at one time or another were laid down upon the craton, but, with the few exceptions mentioned above, at least some sedimentary material still remains in place atop the cratonic rocks of the Great Plains.

The surviving sections of the Tertiary, or most recent of these major sedimentary accumulations, form the floor of the High Plains. Most of even these Tertiary rocks—including the greater part of their most famous member, the Ogallala Formation—have been stripped

Badlands, South Dakota, ca. 1930

away by erosion; as a result, the High Plains in Texas and Oklahoma break away on the east to a much older (indeed, Upper Paleozoic) sequence of sedimentary rocks. Even on the west, facing the Rockies from which the Tertiary sediments were derived, erosion has stripped away the Tertiary cover except in southeastern Wyoming, where the so-called Gangplank, near Cheyenne, provides a ramp for both the Union Pacific and Interstate 80 as they climb toward Sherman Summit. South of the Gangplank, the sedimentary rocks exposed in the Colorado Piedmont, which stretches from the Wyoming state line south nearly to Colorado Springs, are older—mostly Cretaceous—and are lower topographically, as well as stratigraphically, than the High Plains materials exposed in easternmost Colorado and in western Kansas. Cretaceous rock is exposed south of the High Plains, too, where an ancient limestone surface forms the Edwards Plateau. Still older rocks are exposed west of the Mescalero Escarpment, the western edge of the High Plains in New Mexico. North of the High Plains, sedimentary rocks of Mesozoic age form most of the surface northward into Canada, where they extend as far as the western margin of Great Bear Lake.

These Mesozoic sedimentary rocks form a surface whose irregularity may probably be ascribed, at least in part, to ancient erosion surfaces exposed when later sediments were removed, but the modern surface of the Plains owes a great deal also to repeated glaciations in the last two million years. The great Laurentide ice sheet, which blanketed all but insignificant bits of central Canada, extended southward at its maximum to about the present-day Missouri River, whose course was profoundly modified by the ice sheet and which, in Montana and the Dakotas, approximately marks the southern limit of the glacial advance.

North of that line, of course, there are many topographic features shaped by ice. Perhaps the most famous is the Missouri Coteau itself, a structural ridge topped with glacial sediments along its entire course from the Saskatchewan River south through the Dakotas. There are countless smaller signs of ancient ice: at Pingree, North Dakota, chains of lakes indicate former meltwater channels; drumlins (depositional hills) may be found near Priddis, Alberta; and the world's largest glacial erratics (boulders), transported 300 miles by ice, sit in huge wheat fields near Okotoks, Alberta.

The effects of the ice and of Ice Age climates are also evident, however, far south of the Missouri River, for north winds blowing over glacial outwash moved fine sand south to form great beds of loess that now cover southern Nebraska with a blanket more than thirty feet thick. (It is no longer clear that the same winds built up the Sandhills, which may have originated at an earlier time.) The loess layer thins drastically to the south, so that the High Plains at Amarillo are topped with a layer about four feet thick; the material, moreover, seems to have come from the Pecos River rather than from the north. Still, the loess of the southern High Plains may well have been transported by unusually strong winds associated with a glacial climate.

Weather and Climate

The climatology of the Great Plains is, of course, a subject in its own right, and one whose foundations go back at least to the seminal work published in 1854 by Lorin Blodget of the Smithsonian Institution. Blodget at that time published maps whose isothermal lines, joining points of equal temperature, were surprisingly accurate. His annual temperature map, for example, showed the 60° isotherm

essentially as modern maps do: coming across central New Mexico, the line was draped over the Llano Estacado and continued eastward to the mouth of Chesapeake Bay. Blodget's precipitation maps accurately indicated relatively wet areas in the Northwest, in the Rockies and Appalachians, and along the Gulf Coast; significantly, they indicated a low in the Great Plains. Blodget in fact drew what we would call a twenty-inch isohyet running very close to the 100th meridian; he even correctly indicated that in the Northern Plains this line, connecting points of equal precipitation, lies slightly east of that meridian but that in the Southern Plains it crosses over to the west of it. (His map, which spoke of the "Great Plains of the Interior," made special mention of the "Desert Plains" where we now recognize the High Plains. Contrary to famous earlier assertions that this part of the country was uninhabitable by Europeans, Blodget wrote that these plains had "much capacity for cultivation.")

With all his pioneering knowledge, Blodget was keenly aware that there was much he did not understand. Things we take for granted, he advanced as tentative truths: that the atmosphere in the midlatitudes has a generally westerly flow; that the Cordilleran chains create rain shadows in their lees; that continentality induces a general decline in winter temperatures at inland locations. (Here, however, Blodget erred by attributing the decline entirely to elevation.) Of other processes much studied today Blodget had little or no conception: air mass analysis was unknown to him; so were such things as winter-storm dynamics, the role of the Rocky Mountains in nurturing the formation of the low pressure systems that contain those storms, and the role of jet streams in guiding storm movement.

The wealth of Great Plains climatological data is now so great that it is difficult to provide a coherent description of the climate of the Plains. An unorthodox but perhaps useful approach is to begin by noticing the dramatic contrast in the frost-free period as one moves northward from Texas. At San Angelo and Abilene, for example, the frost-free period is about 230 days, but as one moves north the period declines to 210 days in Amarillo; 174 days in Garden City, Kansas; 160 days in North Platte, Nebraska; 140 days in Bismarck, North Dakota; and to between 100 and 120 days in southern Alberta and Saskatchewan. The duration of snow cover naturally mirrors this disparity. North of the Black Hills, the ground is white more than three months a year, but the ground is white fewer than ten days annually south of a line drawn from Roswell, New Mexico, eastward through Plainview, Texas, Oklahoma City, and Tulsa. (It is perhaps surprising, given the duration of snow cover in the north and the added fact that snow falls in the Dakotas more than forty days a year, that total snowfall, even in the Northern Plains, is not great by continental standards: in the Dakotas, it averages about thirty-two inches. In the south, of course, accumulations are much less—hardly an inch falls annually on the Edwards Plateau.)

This dramatic contrast in frost-free periods

Blizzard Allen, South Dakota, February 1946

can, however, exaggerate the differences between the Northern and Southern Plains. Granted, in winter the spread between daily average temperatures in Edmonton and Amarillo is fully 30°F, but the temperature spread between Edmonton and Amarillo in summer is only 15°F—and the record highs in those two cities are less than 10°F apart, which, one may be surprised to learn, is about as far apart as the highest temperatures recorded in Amarillo and scorching Midland, only 200 miles to its south. Across the entire sweep of the Plains, moreover, there are common weather elements. Everywhere, days are sunnier more often than they are cloudy: the total sunshine at Regina, for example, exceeds 2,400 hours annually, which is far higher than can be found anywhere else on the continent at that latitude. There is relatively little fog on the Plains, and average relative humidity in the summer is lower than the average relative humidity anywhere to the east. Another point in common across the sweep of the Plains—and a notorious one at that—is windiness: the flow veers seasonally from a generally northerly flow in January, especially in the Northern Plains, to a generally southerly flow in July, especially in the Southern Plains, when in particular the wind flow is exceedingly strong. The Plains are famous, too, for violent storms and sudden weather changes. In May these are classically associated with thunderstorms and—particularly in Oklahoma—with tornadoes, some fifty of which are reported annually in that state alone, where they most commonly form late in the afternoon or early evening, then ominously meander in a generally northeasterly path. In winter, the Plains are associated with cold fronts sweeping south and overnight lowering temperatures by fully 70°F.

To this list of climatic elements that are more uniform than disparate, one finally must add precipitation, which by some measures is the most important of the lot. There can be few more arresting or compelling lines

on the North American map than that of the sixteen-inch isohyet, which, like the neighboring twenty-, twenty-four-, and twenty-eight-inch ones, runs almost straight from Canada to Mexico. Only at the Rockies do the well-behaved lines break up and turn into ovals that encircle highland masses.

The precipitation that falls on the Plains is well distributed for agriculture, with about 40 percent of the annual total occurring during June, July, and August, and with only about 10 percent occurring in December, January, and February. The absolute levels of precipitation on the Plains, however, were something new for settlers from the east, where equally dry climates are unknown, apart from the agriculturally useless lands of northern Canada. The consequences were tragic everywhere on the Plains but perhaps more famously in the south, where higher temperatures raise evaporative potentials to 100 inches a year or more, twice the figure at the Canadian border.

Hydrology

The proportion of Great Plains precipitation that returns directly to the atmosphere through evaporation or transpiration is amazingly great: South Dakota's Standing Rock Indian Reservation, for example, receives very slightly more than three million acre-feet of precipitation annually; of that quantity, 95 percent—2.84 million acre-feet—returns directly to the atmosphere. Runoff from the Great Plains is therefore very limited. Indeed, over most of the Plains hardly more than one inch of precipitation runs off annually, and on the High Plains and substantial parts of the Northern Plains the figure is half that. The rivers of the Plains are often reduced to trickles. Granted, these trickles can turn on a dime to raging torrents that wipe out bridges, farms, and livelihoods, but by continental standards, even the floods of the Great Plains are small things and either very local or exotic, the result of water coming from the Rockies.

Few rivers on the Plains can in fact resist the tendency to flashiness. An exception must be

granted for Nebraska's Sandhills, where the branches of the Loup River are recharged by groundwater and remain remarkably constant. A more typical example, however, would be the Cimarron River near Fairview, Oklahoma. The stream carries a mean annual flow of 330 cubic feet of water per second, but 70 percent of the year its flow is less than 30 cubic feet per second, and for only a quarter of the year does its flow much exceed 200. In short, one rarely sees the stream carrying its average flow. Finding streams like these at moments of average flow can be an exercise in itself, one requiring planning: the North and South Saskatchewan Rivers, for example, peak in June or July, but their tributaries peak in April or May. At first glance this seems anomalous, but the tributaries depend on local snowmelt, while the main streams depend on runoff coming from distant mountains, where high elevations imply a later date for snowmelt.

Most of the year, a visitor to a typical Great Plains stream will be almost lost in a wide floodplain dotted with thickets of cottonwood and filled brim to brim with sand. Highway bridges that come to these valleys are impressively long, but if there are ten cantilever sections to the bridge, chances are that water is flowing under only one of them. The channel below is continually being redefined: even in periods of low flow one will hear splashes almost by the minute. Looking up in expectation of seeing an animal, instead one sees only a lonely caving sandbank and a swirl of turbidity. (Perhaps the rivers of the Plains are siltier today than they were before the arrival of farmers; in any event, the rivers of the Plains rank today as the siltiest on the continent, save only for those of the desert Southwest.)

The rivers of the Plains often mock the long blue lines on maps and disappear altogether, only reemerging miles downstream, as water gently wells up from sandy streambeds. Some portion of that stream flow, of course, percolates underground. Once there, it is by no means forgotten, however, for across the sweep of the Great Plains groundwater is a subject of the keenest interest. It has been so from the earliest period of white settlement, when the windmill became one of the chief icons of the Plains. It remains so today, when people are concerned not only for the quantity of available groundwater but also with its quality.

The most productive wells on the Plains are generally found along watercourses, but the Plains are famous for also having vast aquifers. Individual wells here may not be as productive as those in valleys, but these aquifers in aggregate yield huge quantities of water that can be extracted great distances from any substantial source of surface water. The Dakota sandstone, which takes its name from Dakota County in the northeasternmost corner of Nebraska, is a good example: indeed it is a classic case of an aquifer containing water under sufficient pressure to produce an artesian flow many miles from the point where the water sank underground.

The best known of the Plains aquifers is the

Ogallala, which was named in the 1890s by N. H. Darton of the U.S. Geological Survey. Together with several smaller hydraulically connected formations that with it comprise the Great Plains Aquifer, the Ogallala covers some 177,000 square miles, across which the aquifer is draped like a blanket. Its saturated thickness varies from less than 100 feet in the southern Texas Panhandle to more than 1,000 feet in the Nebraska Sandhills. Some 22 billion acre-feet of sandy material are saturated in the Ogallala with 3 billion acre-feet of water. Two-thirds of the water is in lucky Nebraska. Water enters the aquifer at a rate averaging about six inches annually, but this recharge rate depends on soil porosity and varies from almost nothing in parts of Texas to several feet annually in sandy parts of Nebraska and Kansas. (Another way of looking at this is to note that 80 percent of the total recharge occurs north of a line between Colorado Springs and Hays, Kansas.) The water in the aquifer normally moves eastward and downhill at about one foot per day. Some of it returns to rivers, which generally flow below the local water table; only a few streams—the Cimarron, for example—flow above the water table and contribute to aquifer recharge. More serious groundwater loss, however, has been suffered at the hands of farmers, particularly in the southern half of the aquifer. Willard D. Johnson of the U.S. Geological Survey warned early in the twentieth century that widespread irrigation of the High Plains was not sustainable, but his prescription of stock farming was ignored. Texas has been particularly hard hit, for it has pumped more water from the Ogallala than any other state, even though it began with only about a tenth of the aquifer's stored water. The quality of Ogallala water has changed too; wherever the reservoir underlies farmland rather than rangeland, the water has grown increasingly alkaline.

Biogeography

In the time of Lewis and Clark, such rain and snow as fell on the eastern side of the Plains supported a veritable meadow: grasses six feet high, set among deciduous trees like oak and hickory. To the west, typically at an elevation of 2,000 feet, that virgin prairie gave way to a steppe. Trees were scarce here, except for stream course cottonwoods, and the grass was short—unless one dug up the roots and found that the six inches of buffalo grass that one saw above ground capped a tangle of roots six feet deep.

By 1880, enough was known of America's vegetation for Charles S. Sargent to map America's forested regions with high accuracy. Sargent said little about the sea of grass that is the Great Plains, but he commented on the difference between bottomland forests on the eastern and western sides of the Plains: oaks, walnuts, ash, and box elders disappeared one by one, he wrote, until only cottonwoods survived beyond the 100th meridian. Like many other students, Canadian as well as American, Sargent was well aware, too, of the complex dynamics of this grassland, particularly on the

eastern margin, where trees quickly invaded if fire was suppressed. The importance of fire in grassland modification, relative to soil moisture and other factors, has been the subject of debate ever since.

Twenty years after Sargent's work, which was published as a monograph accompanying the Tenth Census, C. Hart Merriam of the U.S. Biological Survey published the first map of what we today would call ecoregions. The terms he employed, such as the "austral life zone," are little used today, but the concept of an ecoregion is still indispensable. Other key ecological concepts also arose in the Great Plains in the early years of this century. The ideas of plant succession and climax communities, for example, were developed in the Great Plains by Frederick Clements, a Nebraskan by birth and training.

In 1923 Homer Shantz and Raphael Zon published their great map of the natural vegetation of the United States. The map showed a continent forested on the east but coming, as one moved westward, to an oak-hickory forest whose western margin ran from central Texas through the Ozarks to central Michigan. Immediately west of that forest in Texas, and extending to the Pecos River and the High Plains, lay a desert savanna, with mesquite, but from the southwestern corner of Oklahoma due north to Nebraska (where it curved west around the Sandhills and then resumed a northward course) lay a line marking the western edge of a tallgrass prairie, bluestems chiefly, into which the oak-hickory forest penetrated along stream courses. At an elevation of about 2,000 feet the vegetation changed to much shorter grama and buffalo grasses. Shantz, who was responsible for the part of the map showing grasslands, recognized that the line between tall and short grass is not sharp and depends in part upon soil and soil moisture conditions.

Since the 1920s, the study of Great Plains vegetation has focused in large part on getting a better understanding of the distribution of tall and short grasses and their relationship to forests. Much of this work, perhaps inevitably, has led to finer and finer subdivisions of the generalities laid out by Shantz. In 1964, for example, A. W. Kuchler prepared a map of potential natural vegetation that is widely used today and which, following Clements rather than Shantz, recognized transitional categories on either side of the tallgrass prairie. Kuchler saw the eastern part of the tallgrass as a mosaic of bluestem and oak-hickory forest, while the tallgrass prairie proper occupied only a meridional swath reaching from Winnipeg to Topeka, with arms stretching into northwest Iowa and the Nebraska Sandhills. Farther west, Kuchler recognized a bluestem prairie mixed with wheatgrass in the north and grama grass on the south; still farther west lay the shortgrass proper. Kuchler subdivided it latitudinally, with grama and buffalo grasses dominating as far north as Nebraska; to the north lay a domain of wheatgrass in the Dakotas and buffalo grass in still drier Montana. Kuchler did not map Canada, but the same species of western wheatgrass and grama grass

extend north to an encircling arc of aspen savanna, a parkland that itself grades into an aspen-spruce forest or, at the edge of the Rockies, into a spruce-pine forest. As in the United States, forest invasion of the grassland—in this case with aspen advancing by suckering rather than by seed—occurs whenever fire is suppressed, and the small amount of tallgrass prairie that once existed in the Red River Valley of the North has in this way been lost almost entirely. Although shortgrass species such as buffalo grass are now common in the driest parts of the Canadian Great Plains, their dominance appears to be the result of overgrazing in historic times. The potential natural vegetation, in other words, appears to contain taller species like western wheatgrass.

The story of plant geography in the Great Plains can hardly avoid taking notice of the arrival of farming and ranching, which has transformed the vegetation of the Plains, both to our benefit and our loss. Some introduced species are welcomed by farmers and ranchers—brome and wheatgrasses in the Northern Plains are a case in point. Others have become serious problems, among them leafy spurge in the north and prickly pear and eastern red cedar in the south. Today, as a consequence, one must hunt to locate sites where the vegetation may be even approximately virginal. Sites like the Konza Prairie near Manhattan, Kansas, thus acquire special significance.

The impact of European settlement on the animals of the Great Plains was perhaps even more dramatic. Recent research suggests that earlier accounts may have seriously overestimated bison numbers at the start of the nineteenth century and that the real number—perhaps 30 million rather than the 60 million or more often reported—may have been at a momentary and unsustainable peak. Still, the primeval bison herds beg comparison with the herbivore populations of East Africa, and their reduction to fewer than a thousand animals by 1889 is therefore all the more appalling. The pronghorn, once perhaps as numerous as the bison and yet killed off until fewer than 25,000 animals remained, supply almost as gruesome a tale of human destruction. Today, thanks to sustained efforts, the pronghorn population has risen to more than a million animals, perhaps half of them in Wyoming.

It is worth remembering, of course, that the advent of European settlement was not always so devastating. The rattlesnake is not yet endangered, despite a century or more of methodical killing. Some 250 species of grasshoppers still reside on the Plains, to which most of them are naturally restricted, and few night sounds can be as familiar on the Plains as that of the cicada. White settlement even proved a boon for some animal species, at least temporarily. The population of the greater prairie chicken, for example, exploded with the introduction of grain farming. After a peak about 1880, it began to decline with the loss of wetlands and hayfields and with competition from introduced species such as the ring-necked pheasant, a native of China. Chicken populations have recovered enough to sustain legalized hunting today in several states, particularly Kansas and Nebraska, where prairie chicken numbers may exceed those of two centuries ago.

A final point to remember is that a neatly separated discussion of plant and animal geography masks the actual and complex relationships that exist between those organisms. Much effort of late has gone into studying the effect on grassland of intensive but short-duration bison grazing. Smaller animals, too, have influenced the vegetation of the Plains. A good example is the once astronomically numerous prairie dog, which was discovered for science by Meriwether Lewis. We ourselves play not only a major but often an unconscious role in altering these several populations. The shelterbelts that were so widely planted in the 1930s, for example, are now commonly dying of old age. Farmers tend not to replant them but instead to bulldoze and grub them out. One consequence is that local populations of jackrabbits, pheasants, deer, and squirrels are losing habitat. In the absence of data, one can only wonder how many species are declining as unintended consequences of our actions.

Soils

People in an overwhelmingly urban society naturally have a hard time grasping subjects like topography and climatology or geology and biogeography, for all these things are increasingly removed from daily life. They have an almost impossible time, however, trying to muster any interest in soil and soil geography, for these are subjects inescapably linked with pejorative terms like dirt. Like all soils, however, the soils of the Great Plains reflect all the other elements of the physical environment, which can at least in large part be deduced from the crumbly or sandy, moist or dry, warm or cold soil mantle that rests on the earth.

The grass of the Great Plains, after all, is responsible for the dark color that is one of the two diagnostic traits of Great Plains soils. The other diagnostic trait of these soils arises from the climate of the Great Plains and is an alkaline layer, usually calcium carbonate, which occurs at the lowest level in the soil that is seasonally saturated. The two traits overlap. Dark color extends well east of the Great Plains, but the alkaline layer is typical of arid climates and extends well to the west. Hence the logic underlying the statement of Curtis F. Marbut, a pioneer soil scientist, that the Great Plains is simply that part of the country where these two traits overlap.

In a monograph published in 1935 as a part of the USDA's great *Atlas of American Agriculture*, Marbut went on to develop this idea: he pointed out that there is an inverse relationship between light soil color and deep layers of carbonate accumulation. The darkest soils, that is, are found in the wetter east, where the zone of carbonate accumulation lies at a depth of about six feet. Farther west, soil colors are lighter because there is less soil moisture and therefore less organic matter. Here, however,

the zone of alkaline accumulation is much closer to the surface. On the High Plains, it is so well developed that it forms an impervious layer of so-called caliche. Marbut mapped parent material and on this basis distinguished three groups of soils based on where they were formed: glacial deposits, windborne deposits, and from bedrock—the latter lying chiefly in Kansas and the non-panhandle parts of Oklahoma and Texas. Yet when Marbut came to formally classify the soils of the Great Plains, he chose to ignore parent material and instead focus on those two diagnostic criteria we have already noted.

The eastern edge of the Great Plains thus became for Marbut the line beyond which there was enough precipitation that soil moisture percolated through the entire soil profile; there was no permanently dry zone here, and therefore no zone of carbonate accumulation. West of that line, however, one came to what Marbut, using Russian nomenclature, called the chernozems or black soils, though much thinner than the chernozems of Russia. Marbut distinguished a belt of these chernozems centered roughly along the 100th meridian from the eastern Dakotas through central Kansas, western Oklahoma, and Texas as far south as the Rio Grande. East of these chernozems generally lay forested and acidic podsols in the north and "prairie soils" to the south—soils formed under grass but so humid that the soils were degraded. West of the chernozems lay lighter-colored "dark brown" soils that graded on the west into patches of "brown" soils, which occurred in the driest parts of the Plains.

In Canada, soil taxonomists still use this nomenclature, so that most Canadian prairie soils are mapped as chernozems in the wetter and encircling savanna but dark brown and brown in the drier core along the international boundary. In the United States, however, the soil taxonomy used by Marbut was replaced in 1960 by another system, one that introduced an entire lexicon of neologisms and which is therefore exceedingly difficult for all but experts to use comfortably.

This new classification system distinguishes between Great Plains soils neither by parent material nor by color but chiefly by soil temperature and moisture. The Great Plains soils of the United States are thus now classed chiefly as mollisols, or soils formed under a cover of grasses and forbs. Subdivisions are then made on the basis of soil temperature, so that the soils of the Dakotas, where the mean annual soil temperature is below 47°F, are recognized as borolls, while moister soils to the south are recognized generally as udolls or, in Texas, where mean annual soil temperature exceeds 72°F, as thermic udolls. Further subdivision is made on the basis of soil moisture. East of the Missouri Coteau, for example, the soil is recognized as a udic boroll, while to the west the soil is classified as a typic boroll. Similarly, the soils of the Central Plains are divided into udolls when they have sufficient moisture for plant growth much of the year; where moisture is lacking for long periods, the soils are labeled as ustolls; where, as in south-

eastern Colorado, soils are usually dry and therefore low in organic matter, they are called ustic aridosols. Some soils, lacking profile horizons, are mapped instead as entisols: the most extensive areas are the Sandhills and the gray soils developed on the thin glacial debris of southeastern Montana.

It is easy for the layman to despair in the face of such verbal arcana, but there is one final point about soils that is easy to grasp. Like the groundwater and vegetation of the Plains, the soils of the Great Plains have not fared well in the last century. Estimates are that soil losses under range conditions on the Plains today average two tons per acre annually, while losses on cropland are twice that or more. The Southern and Central Plains have been hurt most, both by wind erosion on the High Plains south of the Arkansas River and by severe sheet erosion and gullying in the deep loess south of the Sandhills and in the once extensive cotton lands of Oklahoma. Nearly a century after Willard Johnson's warnings, the question of proper land use remains an open one in the Great Plains, and for all the work of the Soil Conservation Service since its creation in the 1930s, one can still drive for mile after mile across Oklahoma and see the deep and unhealed red scars etched by farmers a lifetime ago.

Significance

How, in sum, are we to comprehend this place? Keep the question simple. Forget about people. Forget about roads and railroads, wires, cables, and pipelines. Forget about towns and cities, wells for water and oil and gas, cultivated fields, and the sorry pastures that have been grazed bare by generations of cattle that have been confined behind endless miles of wretched fence lines. What are we to make of this place as God created it?

A traditional answer would have us see the Plains as a place of economic opportunity, a resource. Such an outlook kept several generations of scientists at work, supported by public funding. Another answer, however, and one more relevant to most people today, can be inferred from the overtones of the question itself. From this perspective, the Great Plains is best comprehended as a place too magnificent for fetters. Unique to the continent in always open and seemingly endless vistas, the Plains is a place to teach us how it feels to be free.

One might think back to Josiah Gregg, who in the 1830s crossed the Plains time and again between the Missouri River and the then Mexican town of Santa Fe. Gregg concluded his famous *Commerce of the Prairies* on an ironic note. Tongue in cheek, he wrote that the reports were accurate: the Great Plains was indeed dangerous. Gregg went on to explain, however, that the danger lay not in Indians but in the freedom of the place: like a magic elixir, the air of the Plains rendered civilized men unfit for the East—its towns full of narrow streets, its houses full of airless rooms, its people confined by girdles and neckties.

We have come a long way in taming the

Plains. Perhaps Josiah Gregg was better off not having seen the fences, better off not having heard the radio stations with their incessant wheedling, better off not having smelled the feedlots that have sprung up so many places. But the Great Plains is by no means defeated. The skies remain as infinite in the day as skies elsewhere can be only at night. Muddy, modest, quietly occupied streams continue to find their lonely ways across the immensity. Grass continues to hiss before the steady wind. Geese still fly over this place; so do white pelicans en route from Great Salt Lake to the Gulf. Scissor-tailed flycatchers and roadrunners still call the Southern Plains home; other birds like meadowlarks and bobolinks, dickcissels and American kestrals are still commonplace. This is still a very physical place, huge enough that the human drama on it can shrink to insignificance. We wish to be important, influential, and so such a thought is not one we welcome. Yet there is comfort in it nonetheless, for no actor on earth could help but be thrilled by the prospect of such a huge stage.

See also WATER: Floods; Ogallala Aquifer; Rivers.

Bret Wallach
University of Oklahoma

Atwood, Wallace W. *The Physiographic Provinces of North America.* New York: Ginn, 1940. Bostock, H. S. "Physiographic Regions of Canada," Map 1254A of the Geological Survey of Canada, 1970. Fenneman, Nevin M. *Physiography of Western United States.* New York: McGraw-Hill, 1931. Flores, Dan. "Bison Ecology and Bison Diplomacy: The Southern Plains from 1800 to 1850." *The Journal of American History* 78 (1991): 465–85. Great Plains Flora Association. *Flora of the Great Plains.* Lawrence: University Press of Kansas, 1986. Hammond, Edwin. "Analysis of Properties in Land Form Geography: Application to Broad-scale Land Form Mapping." *Annals,* Association of American Geographers 54 (1964): 11–19. Kuchler, August Wilhelm. *Potential Natural Vegetation of the Coterminous United States.* New York: American Geographical Society, 1964. U.S. Department of Agriculture. *Atlas of American Agriculture.* Washington DC: Government Printing Office, 1936. U.S. Department of Agriculture. *Climate and Man.* Washington, DC: Government Printing Office, 1941. U.S. Geological Survey. *The National Atlas of the United States of America.* Washington DC: Government Printing Office, 1970. Visher, Stephen Argent. *Climatic Atlas of the United States.* Cambridge: Harvard University Press, 1954. Weaver, J. E. *Prairie Plants and Their Environment.* Lincoln: University of Nebraska Press, 1968.

AGRICULTURAL METEOROLOGY

See AGRICULTURE: Agricultural Meteorology

AMPHIBIANS AND REPTILES

Amphibians and reptiles, collectively called herptiles, are ectothermic or "cold-blooded" vertebrates. Amphibians include frogs and toads, salamanders, and caecilians, the latter not represented in the Great Plains. Reptiles technically do not constitute a distinct biological group, but the term is used here in the vernacular sense to refer to turtles and tortoises, lizards, snakes, and alligators and crocodiles. Amphibians and reptiles, except for rattlesnakes, are not typical icons of the Plains, yet more than 150 different species occur in some part of the region. This number represents about 30 percent of the species occurring in North America. No herp species is limited to the Great Plains, but many species reach one of their distributional limits here. More herps occur in the southern part of the region.

Only eleven species of salamanders extend into the Great Plains, mostly along its eastern periphery. Of these, seven species are restricted to southeastern Kansas, and only *Ambystoma tigrinum*, the tiger salamander, is found throughout the Great Plains. This salamander spends much time underground in burrows and surfaces to feed or reproduce when environmental conditions are favorable.

There are thirty-two species of frogs and toads in the Great Plains, including three that are especially prominent. One species, *Spea bombifrons*, the Plains spadefoot, occurs in all states and provinces of the Great Plains. This species depends on temporary ponds formed after spring and summer thunderstorms. Well known for its rapid tadpole development, it can breed in roadside ditches. *Bufo cognatus*, the Great Plains toad, is abundant and forms large breeding choruses after thunderstorms. The shrill call of thousands of these toads from a "buffalo wallow" can be heard for several miles. A third species, *Rana blairi*, the plains leopard frog, is restricted to the central grasslands, extending from the Great Plains into the tallgrass prairie peninsula as far east as western Indiana. Like other leopard frogs, it is dependent on permanent ponds and lakes because its larvae require several months for metamorphosis.

Of the nineteen species of turtles in the Great Plains, none occurs in all states and provinces. The snapping turtle, *Chelydra serpentina*, occurring in larger ponds, lakes, or rivers, is found throughout the Great Plains except for Alberta. The painted turtle, *Chrysemys picta*, is widely distributed across the Plains except for Texas. This is one of the few herps of the region whose distribution is more northern than southern. It frequents permanent ponds and lakes. *Terrapene ornata*, the ornate box turtle, is a common terrestrial species, especially in sandy soils of the Southern Plains and as far north as South Dakota. This species is often associated with mammal burrows, such as those of prairie dogs, where it will retreat to overwinter.

The thirty-three species of lizards have a distinctly southern distribution: all but one occur in Texas, and none are found entirely throughout the region. *Phrynosoma douglassi*, the short-horned lizard, is the most widespread species, occurring in all states and provinces except Manitoba, Kansas, and Oklahoma. However, this species frequents the plateaus along the Rocky Mountains rather than being a true Plains species. The distribution of *Eumeces septentrionalis*, the prairie skink, is remarkably coincident with the tallgrass prairie from eastern Texas to Manitoba, although its distribution extends eastward into Minnesota and Iowa. The Great Plains skink, *Eumeces obsoletus*, is distributed from the desert Southwest into the Southern Plains and as far north as Nebraska and Wyoming.

Snakes are the most numerous herptiles with fifty-nine species occurring in some part of the Plains. Fifty of these species live on the Plains of Texas. Three species, the plains garter snake (*Thamnophis radix*), common garter snake (*Thamnophis sirtalis*), and western hognose snake (*Heterodon nasicus*), inhabit all states and provinces of the region. Garter snakes are semi-aquatic, occurring along streams and ponds, whereas the hognose is common in open, especially sandy, prairies. The hognose is well known for its feigning-death behavior when disturbed. The racer, *Coluber constrictor*, living throughout the region except for the Canadian provinces, is a common species of the open grasslands. The prairie rattlesnake, *Crotalus viridis*, is found throughout the region except for Manitoba. It is often associated with prairie dog towns and is much maligned because of its poisonous nature. The gopher snake, *Pituophis catenifer*, also occurs throughout except for Manitoba. This harmless snake of the open prairies can be more than six feet long and because of its hissing behavior gives the appearance of being dangerous. In fact, perhaps many of the reports of rattlesnake encounters may actually involve the gopher snake.

Even though amphibians and reptiles are frequently inconspicuous to the casual observer, they are a common and important component of the fauna of the Great Plains.

Royce E. Ballinger
University of Nebraska–Lincoln

Conant, Roger, and Joseph T. Collins. *A Field Guide to Reptiles and Amphibians: Eastern and Central North America.* Boston: Houghton Mifflin Company, 1991. Lynch, John D. "Annotated Checklist of the Amphibians and Reptiles of Nebraska." *Transactions of the Nebraska Academy of Sciences* 13 (1985): 33–57.

ARMADILLOS

The nine-banded armadillo, *Dasypus novemcinctus*, is a member of the order Xenarthra, which includes slow-moving and highly specialized creatures such as sloths and anteaters. Historically a creature of South America, the coastal prairies, and extreme south Texas, the armadillo extended its range during the twentieth century into the Plains region of Texas, Oklahoma, Kansas, and southern Nebraska. Since 1981 the armadillo has been the official state mascot of Texas.

With long claws on all of its toes, the armadillo is a proficient digger. Other physical aspects include a bony carapace protecting the entire dorsal area of the body and nine bands between the rump and shoulders allowing flexibility in body movement. The head, protected by a bony plate, can be withdrawn into the shell when perceived or real danger is near. Overall body coloration is a grayish brown. About 90 percent of the armadillo's diet consists of insects and various species of invertebrates such as crayfish and millipedes.

Population densities within its range vary widely and are dictated by soil types and favorable habitat. Densities tend to be high where loose sandy soil exists along streambeds and in woodlands and lower in areas where

Armadillo

tighter clay-based soils predominate. The denning habit of the armadillo is novel in that a single animal may excavate and occupy several dens within its range. These lairs are located along stream banks, beneath boulders, and around tree trunks. Armadillos do not hibernate, but they do stay underground for extended periods in freezing weather.

The armadillo's reproduction system involves delayed implantation. Breeding occurs in late July, but the fertilized ovum remains in the uterus for about fourteen weeks without development. By November, normal development resumes and the young are born four months later as identical quadruplets of the same sex.

Wyman Meinzer
Benjamin, Texas

Davis, William B., and David J. Schmidly. *The Mammals of Texas*. Austin: Texas Parks and Wildlife Press, 1994. Smith, Larry L., and R. W. Doughty. *The Amazing Armadillo*. Austin: University of Texas Press, 1984.

AUDUBON, JOHN JAMES (1785–1851)

John James Audubon, the artist and naturalist, was born at Les Cayes, Santo Domingue (now Haiti), on April 26, 1785, the illegitimate son of a French sea captain and a French chambermaid. Audubon moved to Philadelphia when he was eighteen to manage his father's property. There he first developed his interest in birds and his career as a naturalist began. To this expertise he added painting after 1810, and by the 1830s he was recognized as the foremost American naturalist.

His encounter with the Great Plains came relatively late in his life, when he was fifty-eight. In fact, it was his last expedition. In 1843, Audubon embarked on what he called his "Great Western Journey," traveling by steamboat up the Missouri River from St. Louis to Fort Union, near what is now the Montana–North Dakota border. He took the trip to fulfill a lifelong dream to see the Great Plains and also to collect specimens and gather information about the mammals of the American West for *The Viviparous Quadrupeds of North America* (1845–54), which he was preparing with John Bachman. Traveling with Audubon were his friend Edward Harris, an ornithologist; John G. Bell, a taxidermist; Isaac Sprague, an artist; and Louis M. Squires, who served as Audubon's secretary.

The party left St. Louis on April 25 aboard the *Omega*, a small steamer belonging to the American Fur Company, on which they were joined by more than a hundred hunters and trappers, also bound for Fort Union, the company's principal trading post. Throughout the trip, Audubon and Harris both kept regular journals and wrote fact-filled letters, which collectively provide a detailed record of their observations and activities. (Audubon's journal, lost for more than fifty years, was discovered in 1896 by two of his granddaughters, one of whom published it the following year.) As the boat made its way upriver, stopping to visit settlements and cut wood for fuel, Audubon drew pictures of the landscape and sketched the rabbits, squirrels, woodchucks, and other small animals and birds his party collected on their occasional hunting trips. Audubon also expressed disappointment at the Native Americans he encountered along the way, believing they fell short of the romantic descriptions and idealized paintings offered by George Catlin. On June 13, after fifty days and 1,400 miles, the *Omega* finally reached Fort Union. It then returned downriver, leaving Audubon and the others to explore the area around the fort, where they remained throughout the summer.

During that time, Audubon observed hunters and trappers at work; he made an overnight trip up the Yellowstone River; he collected specimens of wolves, elk, antelope, deer, and bighorn sheep; and he noted the "immense numbers" of buffalo, which he saw in their natural habitat for the first time. He also mourned the senseless destruction of the buffalo, though that did not prevent his party from hunting these animals at every opportunity. At the end of two months, on August 16, the expedition left Fort Union on a forty-foot mackinaw and returned to St. Louis. "I have no less than 14 New Species of Birds, perhaps a few more," Audubon wrote to Bachman upon his return. "The variety of Quadrupeds is small in the Country we visited, and I fear that I have not more than 3 or 4 New ones." But, he added, "I have brought home good Sketches of Scenery, Drawings of flowers, and also the heads of Antilopes, Big horns, Wolves and Buffaloes."

Audubon's health began to fail in the mid-1840s, but with the help of his sons and Bachman, he completed *Quadrupeds*. Audubon died in New York on January 27, 1851.

Daniel J. Philippon
University of Minnesota, Twin Cities

Audubon, Maria R., ed. *Audubon and His Journals*. New York: Scribner's, 1897. McDermott, John Francis, ed. *Audubon in the West*. Norman: University of Oklahoma Press, 1965. McDermott, John Francis, ed. *Up the Missouri with Audubon: The Journal of Edward Harris*. Norman: University of Oklahoma Press, 1951.

AUGHEY, SAMUEL, JR. (1831–1912)

Samuel Aughey Jr. was a minister and naturalist/geologist in Nebraska and Wyoming from 1864 until 1886. He was born on February 8, 1831, near Mifflin, Pennsylvania, the son of Samuel and Elizabeth Kepner Aughey. He graduated from Pennsylvania College (now Gettysburg College) in 1856 and then attended seminary there. Aughey came to Dakota City, Nebraska, in 1864 as a "home missionary" for the Lutheran Church. After resigning this position in 1867, he worked for the Dakota County government from 1866 until 1869 as superintendent of public instruction and county surveyor. He was named the first professor of natural science at the University of Nebraska in Lincoln in 1871.

Despite heavy teaching responsibilities, Aughey published widely on the geology, botany, and zoology of Nebraska. The work was of uneven quality; when scientific information conflicted with his desire to promote the Plains as an ideal place for settlers, his promotional instincts often won. For example, writing in 1880 during one of Nebraska's wetter periods, Aughey confidently asserted that the act of cultivating the soil was responsible for increased rainfall. This apocryphal theory, "rainfall follows the plow," did not survive the devastating drought of the 1890s. Aughey was also instrumental in the founding of both the Nebraska State Historical Society and the Nebraska Academy of Sciences, serving as the first secretary of the former and the first president of the latter.

Aughey's relationship with the University of Nebraska began to deteriorate in the early 1880s. In 1883, he was involved in a financial scandal that precipitated his resignation from the university. He subsequently became territorial geologist for Wyoming. A smelting accident in 1886 left him with severe heavy metal poisoning and ended his career as a geologist and his time as a resident of the Great Plains.

Aughey had married Elizabeth Catherine Welty on October 14, 1858. They had three children, only one of whom, Helen Barbara, survived childhood. Aughey died on February 3, 1912, in Spokane, Washington.

See also IMAGES AND ICONS: Rain Follows the Plow.

Margaret R. Bolick
University of Nebraska–Lincoln
Hugh H. Genoways
University of Nebraska–Lincoln

Aughey, Samuel. *Sketches of the Physical Geography and Geology of Nebraska*. Omaha: Daily Republican Book, 1880.

BADLANDS

Badlands are a form of intense gullying that results from a combination of four factors: clay-rich material, such as shale, that inhibits water penetration; limited vegetation to impede runoff of precipitation; rainfall concentrated in scattered, intense showers; and downcutting of the drainage system. The four factors cause an intricate, fine-textured drainage network that is characterized by many V-shaped, straight-sided gullies divided by knifelike ridges.

Principal badland areas in the Great Plains are at Badlands National Park in southwestern South Dakota, Theodore Roosevelt National

Park in western North Dakota, and Dinosaur Provincial Park in southern Alberta. Shales of the White River Group (Oligocene), including the Chadron and Brule Formations, form the badlands in South Dakota and northwestern Nebraska. Shales of the Fort Union Formation (Paleocene) form them in North Dakota and eastern Montana, and Cretaceous shales shape the badlands in Alberta. Other, more isolated areas of badlands occur in the Great Plains, typically where impermeable shales outcrop at the land surface and are subject to the conditions named above. Generally, badlands are common along the Little Missouri and Cheyenne Rivers in the Dakotas and along the White River north of Pine Ridge, as at Toadstool State Park in northwestern Nebraska and at Badlands National Park.

See also SPORTS AND RECREATION: National Parks.

Richard G. Reider
University of Wyoming

Bloom, A. L. *Geomorphology, a Systematic Analysis of Late Cenozoic Landforms.* Englewood Cliffs NJ: Prentice-Hall, 1998. Fenneman, Nevin V. *Physiography of Western United States.* New York: McGraw-Hill Book Company, 1931.

BIRD MIGRATIONS

Bird migrations are regular two-way movements of birds that have evolved to assure more space and food for raising offspring as well as increased overwinter survival. Internal rhythms, often related to the reproductive cycle, are triggered by photoperiod (changing amount of daylight), prompting the migration. Weather conditions usually influence date of departure and pace of advancement toward a destination. The result is one of the Great Plains's most spectacular natural events, as millions of birds move northward to breeding grounds and southward to wintering sites over large expanses of grasslands, wetlands, and grain fields.

The endangered whooping crane (*Grus americana*) is probably the most renowned Plains migrant. All of the world's naturally occurring whoopers (about 170 individuals) migrate between Arkansas National Wildlife Refuge, along the Texas coast, and Wood Buffalo National Park, along the borders of Alberta, Saskatchewan, and the Northwest Territories, using a pathway that covers the north to south extent of the Plains region. Most migrant waterfowl common to the Plains, such as the lesser snow goose (*Chen caerulescens*), white-fronted goose (*Anser albifrons*), northern pintail (*Anas acuta*), and mallard (*A. platyrhynchos*), follow the Central Flyway, a locational characterization of seasonal waterfowl movements used for international management of migratory game birds. The flight strategies of other Plains migrants, such as raptors (burrowing owl [*Speotyto cunicularia*] and ferruginous hawk [*Buteo regalis*]), shorebirds (upland sandpiper [*Bartramia longicauda*], long-billed curlew [*Numenius americanus*], and red-necked phalarope [*Libipes lobatus*]), and songbirds (Harris's sparrow [*Zonotricha querula*] and clay-colored sparrow [*Spizella pallida*]), are more temporally and spatially diverse.

Bald eagles (*Haliaeetus leucocephalus*) are the first migrators during early spring. The next arrivals are sandhill cranes (*Grus canadensis*), ducks, and geese. During later spring, shorebirds are followed by songbirds. Some migrant songbirds, such as the dickcissel (*Spiza americana*), arrive on breeding grounds in the Northern Plains while individuals of the same species have already completed their nesting in the Southern Plains and started their migration to wintering grounds. Arctic nesters such as the Harris's sparrow move to the Central Plains for the entire winter, whereas the snow bunting (*Plectrophenax nivalis*) moves in and out of the Central Plains in response to severe weather.

Many Plains migrants use different routes during spring and fall, possibly to optimize feeding opportunities or avoid harsh winds. For example, the American golden plover (*Pluvialis dominica*) breeds from the northern coast of Alaska to the eastern shores of northern Canada, flies southward along the Atlantic coast to its wintering area in southern South America, then forms a migration loop as it returns to its breeding grounds by flying over the Great Plains.

Distances that birds migrate vary within and among species. Individuals that nest in the southernmost part of the lark bunting's (*Calamospiza melanocorys*) breeding range migrate shorter distances to wintering locations (less than fifty miles) than those in the northern part of the breeding grounds (hundreds of miles). Blue-winged teal (*Anas discors*) that nest close to the Arctic Circle and winter in Argentina move a distance of about 7,000 miles. Long-distance fliers rely on a variety of cues for navigation, such as the position of celestial bodies, the magnetic field of the earth, and landscape features. For example, shorebirds and cranes closely follow paths that lie over a series of basin wetlands that extend from the Texas coast to the Northwest Territories.

Long-distance migrants may fly without stopping. Others may spend a few hours, days, or even weeks at a particular location for rest and refueling. Birds that fly long distances before stopping rely on fat reserves for energy or winds associated with weather systems. Shorebirds are especially known for moving great distances in short time periods. The American golden plover for example, can move 4,000 miles in less than three days with the help of winds in the direction of flight. Most Great Plains migrants are not equipped to make such marathon flights. Instead, they make regular refueling and drinking stops.

Locations where migrants land for short duration are referred to as stopover sites. Solitary birds or family groups usually use these sites. Examples are the seasonally flooded fields and shallow wetlands used by whooping cranes for feeding and resting. Habitats used by migrating birds for longer time periods to replenish energy for farther movement or gain weight for reproduction are sometimes referred to as staging areas. Large groups of Plains migrants are often associated with wetland-related staging areas, many of which are protected as state or national conservation areas, such as Bosque del Apache, New Mexico, Cheyenne Bottoms Wildlife Management Area, Kansas, J. Clark Salyer National Wildlife Refuge, North Dakota, and Delta Marsh, Manitoba, Canada. Arguably the best location in the world for viewing bird migrations is the Central Platte River Valley and Rainwater Basin of south-central Nebraska, which attracts up to three million geese, fifty-two species of waterbirds, and the world's largest concentration of cranes (500,000) in spring.

Since 1900, habitat alterations, such as channel flow reduction, wetland drainage, and conversion of grassland to cropland, have rendered migrant species more susceptible to diseases and natural disasters such as drought. Traditionally, conservation efforts for Plains species emphasized breeding and wintering locations. Current studies emphasize understanding habitat requirements during migration and how to most effectively protect migrant species.

See also SPORTS AND RECREATION: National Wildlife Refuges / WATER: Cheyenne Bottoms; Platte River Whooping Crane Maintenance Trust.

Amy L. Richert
University of Nebraska–Lincoln
Kevin E. Church
Nebraska Game and Parks Commission

Alerstam, Thomas. *Bird Migration.* New York: Cambridge University Press, 1990. Farrand, John, Jr., ed. *The Audubon Society Master Guide to Birding.* New York: Alfred A. Knopf, 1983.

BIRDS

It should come as no surprise to learn that the most characteristic birds of the Great Plains are small, mostly dead-grass brownish, and inconspicuous; there are few places to hide or nest in grasslands except among the grasses themselves. Of all of the native terrestrial birds in North America north of Mexico, less than 10 percent, or about thirty species, can be considered as Great Plains endemics. This term describes those species that are not only native to a geographic or ecologic region but are also essentially limited to it.

The 200-plus species of birds that breed within the Great Plains are of special interest for several reasons. First, there are those relatively few grassland endemics that presumably evolved in a semiarid grass-dominated environment and consequently have acquired an array of ecologically adaptive characteristics (ground-nesting, often seed-eating, with well-camouflaged plumages). They also have communication systems (vocalizations and plumage patterns) that are adaptively modified for effectiveness in open-field environments, such as singing in flight rather than from elevated perches. Many have conspicuous wing, tail, or underpart markings that are highly visible while flying but are hidden when on the ground. A dozen species of sparrows, five shorebirds, three grouse species, two meadowlarks, the horned lark (*Eremophila alpestris*), and the Sprague's pipit (*Anthus spraguei*) all closely conform to this combination of traits. A half-dozen predatory birds, which are often open-country species that may also range into deserts, also are grassland adapted. These include the prairie falcon (*Falco mexicanus*), Swainson's and ferruginous hawks (*Buteo swainsoni* and *B. regalis*), northern harrier (*Circus cyaneus*), and the short-eared and burrowing owls (*Asio flammea* and *Athene cunicularia*), although a few of these are tree- or cliff-nesters rather than being strictly ground-nesting. Finally, three aquatic species that are adapted to nesting in prairie marshes, the Wilson's phalarope (*Phalaropus tricolor*), black tern (*Chlidonias niger*), and Franklin's gull (*Larus pipixican*), round out the list of Great Plains endemics.

The second group of birds having particular relevance to the Great Plains are those closely related species occurring in forests both to the east and west of the Plains, but that are largely excluded from the Plains grasslands. These often penetrate and locally cross the Plains only along those predominately east–west river systems supporting sufficient woody growth that provide narrow corridors for the birds to exploit. In many respects these species are of even greater biological interest than are the strictly grassland endemics, because where the western species encounter the eastern near-relatives, interactions can occur between them for the first time since their ancestors were originally separated. This may have happened as long ago as when the Great Plains grasslands originally developed as mountain building to the west produced increasing aridity eastwardly, or at least since the last glaciations had similar isolating effects on the Northern Plains. It is in such ecological and genetic "suture zones," such as those provided by the Platte and Niobrara River valleys in Nebraska, that these populations come into contact and variably interact. Examples of such eastern versus western relatives include the Baltimore and Bullock's orioles (*Icterus galbula* and *I. spurius*), the rose-breasted and black-headed grosbeaks (*Pheuticus ludovicianus* and *P. melanocephalus*), the indigo and lazuli buntings (*Passerina cyanea* and *P. amoena*), and the eastern and spotted towhees (*Pipilo erythrophthalmus* and *P. maculatus*). All of these closely related pairs meet and, to varying degrees, hybridize along river corridors. The extent to which such hybridization results provides a rough index to their genetic disparity and the duration of separation of their populations. The most extensively hybridizing species pairs among the birds mentioned are the towhees and the orioles, which have broad and extensive zones of hybridization and have until recently been considered as subspecies. However, the grosbeaks and buntings show reduced levels of hybridization and their species distinctiveness has rarely been questioned. Yet because of increased degrees of tree planting across the Plains and the progressive growth of riverine forests since the cessation of prairie fires, the frequency of hybridization opportunities for such species pairs may continue to increase.

A third group of birds that nest at least in parts of the Great Plains are other woodland birds that do not necessarily have eastern and western counterparts. Many of these are of nearly universal occurrence throughout the forests of North America and have managed to penetrate the limits of the Great Plains in various regions. Surprisingly, these tree-adapted birds comprise about half of the total Plains avifauna, even though woodlands and forests occupy less than 5 percent of the total area of the region. These birds include groups such as woodpeckers, warblers, vireos, and other mostly insect-eating and tree-foraging or tree-nesting birds.

Although no Great Plains birds have become extinct, many grassland-adapted birds have undergone severe population declines in recent years as native grasslands have disappeared. In an analysis of breeding bird populations based on annual surveys done between 1966 and 1993, only four of twenty-eight monitored grassland species have shown positive, statistically significant population trends. Twenty-one species have exhibited population declines, many of them statistically significant.

Paul A. Johnsgard
University of Nebraska–Lincoln

Johnsgard, Paul A. *Birds of the Great Plains: Breeding Species and Their Distribution*. Lincoln: University of Nebraska Press, 1979. Johnsgard, Paul A. *The Nature of Nebraska: Biodiversity and Ecology*. Lincoln: University of Nebraska Press, 2001. Johnsgard, Paul A. *Prairie Birds: Fragile Splendor on the Great Plains* Lawrence: University Press of Kansas, 2001.

BISON

The North American bison (*Bison bison*) is the dominant symbol of the natural world of the Great Plains. Often referred to as "buffalo," the bison is actually the North American counterpart of a distinct evolutionary lineage stretching back into the Pliocene. While true buffalo are found in Africa and southern Asia, the closest living relative of the North American bison is the European wisent. Bison first appear in the fossil record in China and later spread into North America across the Bering Land Bridge into modern Alaska, reaching the Plains during the Middle Pleistocene (730,000 to 128,000 years ago).

The modern male bison stands roughly six feet tall at the shoulder, is about nine feet long, and weighs 1,800 to 2,000 pounds. Females are smaller, averaging about five feet at the shoulder, seven feet in length, and 700 to 800 pounds. Both sexes have fairly short horns that curve upward and inward, and massive heads and forequarters with a large hump just behind the head, along with relatively slender hips and hindquarters. The bison's thick coat insulates it against Plains winters, and its powerful head and neck allow it to dig through snow for winter forage. As individuals, bison (particularly males) are unpredictable and often aggressive and have been known to attack humans. However, they are extremely social and react more predictably in herds: in particular, bison bunch to-

gether and stampede as a group in response to even slight provocations. Bison are built to run, with males clocked at speeds of thirty miles per hour; a bison can canter far longer than a horse.

Bison herds on the Plains today live in limited areas, including national, state, and local parks and private ranches. Most herds are also managed, to some degree, through selective slaughter and provision of winterfeed. Bison, however, once ranged from northern Mexico to Canada and from Nevada to the Appalachian Mountains, and bison numbers and movements in this vast territory were determined primarily by the natural distributions and amount of forage, water, and winter shelter.

For much of the year, females, calves, and adolescent males tend to form "nursery" herds, separate from "bull" herds comprised primarily of adult males. Both nursery and bull herds form cohesive, hierarchically organized social units, with social positions determined by the outcomes of dominance fights in which pairs of bull bison clash their heads together and attempt to knock each other off balance. Although there are few records of bison herd sizes prior to the nineteenth century, bison probably dispersed into their smallest social groups in winter and early spring when food was least abundant and nutritious. Winter herds may have been larger in the north as animals sought out limited sheltered areas to escape wind and cold. Maximum herd sizes were probably no larger than 10,000 to 20,000.

In unmanaged modern herds too, late winter and early spring are hard times, and "winter-kill" resulting from old age, starvation, predation, and exposure limits population increase. Calves are born in April and May. Throughout the Plains, bison aggregate into larger herds during the summer and early fall, when Plains grasses grow best and provide the highest nutritional yield. Herd sizes particularly increase in late summer, when nursery and bull herds combine for the annual rut. During the rut, fights between males are nearly continuous because victorious (or dominant) males have preferential access to females.

Modern bison and their habits resulted from a long process of evolutionary change. The earliest North American forms (*Bison latifrons*) were much larger than the modern species and had much longer, straighter, and sharper horns. Trends toward smaller bodies with more modern horns were accompanied by skeletal changes in the head and shoulders over time, indicating increasing strength and a greater ability to bear the shock of collisions in dominance battles. Taken together, these changes (particularly the shift to a less lethal horn configuration) imply that dominance clashes became more common, apparently because of increasing herd sizes. These trends reflect changes in the adaptations of the bison, probably caused by alterations in the Plains environment. Bison originated as a forest species and probably lived in small social groups, with dominance fights rare and, given the lethal design of their horns, probably often fatal. The Pleistocene expansion of the Plains grassland and decreasing forage production due to increasing aridity within the last 12,000 years probably favored smaller animals living in larger herds, thereby increasing the frequency of dominance fights and evolution of less dangerous fighting apparatus.

Humans have also profoundly influenced the Plains bison. Native Americans hunted ancient and modern bison for at least 12,000 years, stalking individual animals or slaughtering entire herds by driving animals over cliffs or into corrals or other traps. Within the last 1,000 years, hunter-gatherer groups throughout the Plains hunted both for their own needs and to produce a surplus for trade with their agricultural neighbors.

In the first half of the nineteenth century the fur trade provided a new market for bison robes, and hunting increased significantly. After about 1850, railroad construction, population expansion, and increased commerce in bison hides accelerated the rate at which bison were slaughtered. Bison were also adversely affected by increasing competition with European American and Native American horse and cattle herds for limited winter forage and by cattle-borne diseases. Ultimately, these forces reduced an estimated population in the early nineteenth century of 30 to 50 million animals to fewer than 1,000 by the 1890s.

Bison populations now total some 70,000, thanks to efforts by government agencies and private groups like the National Bison Association and the InterTribal Bison Cooperative. Private groups are particularly motivated by a growing market for bison meat, which is lower in fat and cholesterol than beef.

See also AGRICULTURE: Buffalo Ranching / NATIVE AMERICANS: Hunting.

Douglas B. Bamforth
University of Colorado

Bamforth, D. B. *Ecology and Human Organization on the Great Plains.* New York: Plenum Press, 1988. Flores, Dan. "Bison Ecology and Bison Diplomacy: The Southern Plains from 1800 to 1850." *Journal of American History* 78 (1991): 465–85. Roe, F. G. *The North American Buffalo.* Toronto: University of Toronto Press, 1970.

BLACK HILLS

The Black Hills is an eroded structural dome in northwestern South Dakota and adjacent northeastern Wyoming. Elevations range from about 3,500 feet along its margins to 7,242 feet on Harney Peak near the center. The dome has eroded Precambrian crystalline rocks (granite and schist) exposed near its center, as at Harney Peak and Mount Rushmore National Memorial. Younger rocks lie outward from these. Among them, soft shales form valleys, whereas resistant rocks, such as sandstones and limestones, form plateaus, hogbacks, or homoclines. Paleozoic limestones, principally the Minnekahta limestone (Permian), overlie the crystalline units and form the Limestone Plateau that covers much of the western half of the uplift. Outward from the Paleozoic beds is the Spearfish Formation (Triassic) that forms the Red Valley (or Racetrack) that entirely rims the edges of the Black Hills. Next, the Dakota Sandstone (Cretaceous) forms a prominent

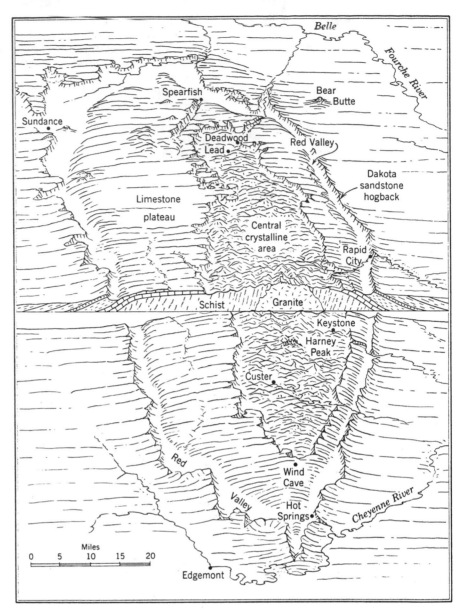

Black Hills diagram

hogback encircling the uplift. Late Mesozoic and Tertiary beds comprise the plains beyond the hogback.

Limestone caverns are common on the Limestone Plateau, as at Jewel Cave National Monument and Wind Cave National Park. Hot springs occasionally occur along the margins of the uplift, as at the town of Hot Springs, South Dakota. Numerous laccolithic peaks (caused by volcanic intrusions) lie north and west of the uplift in South Dakota and Wyoming, including Elkhorn Peak, Crow Peak, Crook Mountain, and Citadel Rock. Devils Tower in Wyoming (a national monument) is a volcanic neck and Bear Butte in South Dakota is an igneous plug. All these volcanic features are Tertiary in age. Gold deposits in the Black Hills are associated with the Tertiary volcanism.

The Black Hills is dominated by ponderosa pine (*Pinus ponderosa*) with open parklands and valleys covered by grasses. Birch (*Betula* sp.) and aspen (*Populus tremuloides*) are also common in higher elevations.

See also LAW: *United States v. Sioux Tribe of Indians* / SPORTS AND RECREATION: National Parks.

Richard G. Reider
University of Wyoming

Fenneman, Nevin M. *Physiography of Western United States.* New York: McGraw-Hill Book Company, 1931. Thornbury, W. D. *Regional Geomorphology of the United States.* New York: John Wiley & Sons, 1965.

BLACK-TAILED PRAIRIE DOG

The black-tailed prairie dog (*Cynomys ludovicianus*) is a medium-sized burrowing rodent that lives in colonies or towns. About five billion prairie dogs inhabited the Great Plains in the early 1900s. The largest prairie dog colony on record, in Texas, measured 100 miles wide by 250 miles long.

Black-tailed prairie dogs are social animals and have twelve distinct calls and various postures that they use to communicate with others. They warn each other of danger with a short series of barks and signal all is clear with a spectacular jump-yip call. Each family group defends an area of about one acre. When two prairie dogs meet, they often touch their teeth together. This "kiss" is used to distinguish a family member from a stranger.

Black-tailed prairie dogs are active year-round. During the day, they feed on grasses, clip tall plants, and maintain their burrows. The vegetation in a colony is shorter and consists of different species than the surrounding grasslands, resulting in unique islands of habitat. More than 200 species of wildlife have been observed in the vicinity of prairie dog towns. Species that are closely associated with prairie dogs include the mountain plover, ferruginous hawk, burrowing owl, and the endangered black-footed ferret. Songbirds and small mammals frequent towns in search of food and shelter. Prairie dog burrows provide homes for deer mice, cottontail rabbits, and prairie rattlesnakes. Prairie dogs also are food for several predators, including the golden eagle, badger, coyote, and swift fox.

Historically, bison grazed on prairie dog towns. Humans replaced the bison with cattle and much of the prairie with crop fields. Since 1900, populations of prairie dogs have been reduced significantly in some areas and eliminated in others, largely due to cultivation of prairie soils, efforts to poison prairie dogs, and residential development. The black-tailed prairie dog was recently proposed for listing as a threatened species under the federal Endangered Species Act. The listing of the black-tailed prairie dog was determined to be "warranted but precluded," and their status is now reviewed annually. Several federal and state agencies, Native American tribes, conservation organizations, and individuals are developing plans and programs to ensure the long-term viability of prairie dog populations and minimize the impacts of prairie dogs on private landowners. Prairie dogs provide recreation for nature observers, photographers, and the sporting public. With proper management, populations can be maintained at levels that ensure the natural heritage and biodiversity of the Great Plains.

Scott E. Hygnstrom
University of Nebraska–Lincoln
Kurt C. VerCauteren
USDA/APHIS/Wildlife Services

Hoogland, John, L. *The Black-tailed Prairie Dog—Social Life of a Burrowing Mammal.* Chicago: University of Chicago Press, 1995. Hygnstrom, Scott E., and Dallas R. Virchow. "Prairie Dogs." In *Prevention and Control of Wildlife Damage,* edited by Scott E. Hygnstrom, Robert M. Timm, and Gary E. Larson. Lincoln: University of Nebraska Cooperative Extension, 1994: 1385–96.

BLIZZARDS

The climate of the Great Plains region is punctuated with extreme variation in both temperature and precipitation, and one of these extreme weather events is the blizzard. A blizzard is a storm with sustained winds in excess of thirty-five miles per hour, temperatures below 20°F, and blowing or falling snow that reduces visibility to less than a quarter mile.

Although most common in winter, Plains blizzards also occur in autumn and spring. The meteorological "stage" is set when a mass of cold polar air moves rapidly southward from higher latitudes and encounters a strong northward flow of moist tropical air from lower latitudes. When a low-pressure cell encounters the energy difference between these two unlike air masses, it rapidly grows in strength, becoming a "deepening low." As the low-pressure cell strengthens, it feeds itself by pulling southward even greater amounts of cold air and northward even larger amounts of warm air and moisture. By the time the blizzard reaches full intensity, it is not unusual to have severe thunderstorms and tornadoes across the southern portion of this major storm. Snowfalls often exceed 1½ feet just north of the path of the low, and wind chill temperatures drop to life-threatening levels across the northern portion of the storm. The winds pack the snow, making it extremely difficult to walk through and to remove from driveways and sidewalks. Although urban highways are usually opened within a day or so of a blizzard, rural roads often remain impassible for many days.

Blizzards have, on rare occasion, occurred as far south as northern Texas, but they increase in frequency northward up the Great Plains. Nebraska, for example, averages one to two blizzards per year while the southern parts of the Prairie Provinces average from three to five blizzards per year. The climate history of the Great Plains is replete with stories of blizzards, but two storms stand out. Most legendary is the "Blizzard of '88," which occurred in January 1888. The region from Texas to Alberta was affected by this paralyzing storm. The suddenness of the blizzard conditions resulted in many people losing their lives as they traveled even short distances to their homes. The blizzard of January 1975, called the "blizzard of the century," struck the Plains from Kansas to Manitoba. This blizzard was so fierce that it set all-time record low-pressure values for the region.

See also FOLKWAYS: Blizzard Stories.

Kenneth F. Dewey
University of Nebraska–Lincoln

BLUEBONNETS

Bluebonnets are lupines that bring to mind visions of beauty and spectacular color. These wildflowers of the Legume family (Fabaceae, alternately Leguminosae), genus *Lupinus*, are breathtaking in full bloom, covering prairies and hills with carpets of solid color ranging from blue-purple to deep blue, pale blue to creamy-white, or pink. There are close to a dozen species that grow within the Great Plains from Texas to Canada.

Bluebonnets are winter annuals, or perennials, that form rosettes in the fall and flowers in the spring. The alternate leaves are palmately compound, bearing four to fifteen leaflets (usually five or seven). Pea-like flowers in terminal clusters have five uniformly colored petals consisting of two wing petals, two keel petals, and an erect banner petal bearing a central white spot, yellow in some species, that turns burgundy-red with age. Interestingly, the main pollinators of bluebonnets, bees and bumblebees, are drawn to the white spot in their nectar search and shun the red spot, which indicates nectar is no longer available.

Emblematic of Texas, bluebonnet is the state flower, but arguments existed for seventy years as to which species should be the "official" one. In 1971, the legislature passed a law naming all the species of *Lupinus* found within the state the official flower. The loveliest and most conspicuous one is *Lupinus texensis* of central Texas.

The genus name derives from the Latin *lupus*, meaning "wolf." The five leaflets were thought to resemble wolflike tracks, and long ago these plants were blamed for robbing the soil of nutrients. Now we know that nodules on the roots contain nitrogen-fixing bacteria, *Rhizobium* spp., that actually enrich the soil.

Zoe Merriman Kirkpatrick
Post, Texas

Kirkpatrick, Zoe Merriman. *Wildflowers of the Western Plains.* Austin: University of Texas Press, 1992. McGregor, R. L., coordinator, and T. M. Barkley, ed. *Atlas of the Flora of the Great Plains.* Ames: Iowa State University Press, 1977. Shinners, L. H. "The Bluebonnets (*Lupinus*) of Texas." *Field & Laboratory* 21(1959): 149–53.

BUFFALO COMMONS

See IMAGES AND ICONS: Buffalo Commons

CAPROCK CANYONLANDS

Encircling the perimeter of the 50,000-square-mile southern High Plains plateau given the name *El Llano Estacado* by Spanish explorers is an area that belies the common perception of the Great Plains as a region of minimal topographic relief. Popularly called the Caprock Canyonlands, this is a brightly colored landscape of red badlands, juniper breaks, and sandstone canyons reaching a depth of 800 feet. This canyon country began to form a million years ago when the westward-eroding Canadian, Red, Brazos, Colorado, and Pecos Rivers sliced into High Plains sediments washed down from the southern Rockies. By 100,000 years ago the Canadian and Pecos had cut to the base of the mountains, creating the Llano Estacado plateau. The central trio of rivers, however, has yet to breach the Llano Estacado. It is their erosion into the plateau, a process that continually exposes the water-bearing gravels of the Ogallala Aquifer, that has formed the present canyon systems of the Red River (Palo Duro, Mulberry, Tule, and the Little Red, Los Lingos, and Quitaque Canyons), the Brazos (Blanco, Yellow House, and Double Mountain Fork Canyons), and the Colorado (Muchaque Canyon).

As sources of water, timber, exposed geology, and often astonishing topography and coloring, the Caprock Canyonlands has played a critical role in human and natural history in the Great Plains. The draws feeding the canyonlands were centers of Clovis and Folsom cultures in the Great Plains, and the canyons themselves were famous rendezvous sites in the trade between Pueblo agriculturalists and Plains buffalo hunters. Coronado was the first European to describe them when he camped in Blanco Canyon in 1540. In the nineteenth century they served as the last sanctuary of the Comanches, Kiowas, and Southern Cheyennes, who were forced to reservations after the Battle of Palo Duro Canyon in 1874. Charles Goodnight proceeded to found his JA Ranch in Palo Duro in 1876. The canyons have largely remained in the hands of ranchers since.

In the twentieth century the Caprock Canyonlands played new roles in human society. The artist Georgia O'Keeffe's initial Western inspiration, for example, came from her encounters with Palo Duro during World War I. Preserving as they do the best remaining wildlands on the Southern Plains, since the 1930s these surprising canyons have increasingly been designated as state parks, wildlife refuges, and nature preserves of various kinds.

See also ART: O'Keefe, Georgia / WAR: Palo Duro Canyon, Battle of.

Dan Flores
University of Montana

Flores, Dan L., and Amy Gormley Winton. *Canyon Visions: Photographs and Pastels of the Texas Plains.* Lubbock: Texas Tech University Press, 1989.

CARLSBAD CAVERNS

Giant Domes, Carlsbad Caverns National Park, New Mexico, 1933–42

Located in southeastern New Mexico where the Great Plains meets the block uplifts of the Basin and Range Province, Carlsbad Caverns is one of the most spectacular and famous caves in the world. Carlsbad Caverns was recognized as a national park in 1930 and as a World Heritage Site in 1995. Twenty miles of rooms and passages have been explored and surveyed, and new discoveries continue to be made. The Big Room is 375 feet from floor to ceiling and is adorned with large, but delicate, stalactites and stalagmites. The cave is home to about a half million Mexican free-tail bats. The bat population was estimated at 8.7 million in the 1930s. DDT use in the United States and Mexico is the apparent cause for the sharp decline in their numbers.

The caverns developed in reef and back-reef limestones that were deposited along the north margin of a rapidly subsiding marine basin during Permian times. The large cave and more than fifty caves nearby lie below a sparsely vegetated, 4,400-foot-high plateau that receives less than fifteen inches of rainfall per year. Most caves form in humid settings through the dissolution of limestone by carbonic acid. (Carbonic acid is produced when carbon dioxide from the root zone mixes with groundwater.) However, clues such as thick gypsum (calcium sulfate) deposits within Carlsbad Caverns indicate that sulfuric, not carbonic, acid generated this cave. Hydrogen sulfide gas is abundant in the deeply buried, petroleum-rich rocks of the basin south of the cave. When this gas migrated upward, it was oxidized by groundwater, thereby generating sulfuric acid. Cavernous pores in the limestone and gypsum deposits are the resulting product.

See also INDUSTRY: Tourism / SPORTS AND RECREATION: National Parks.

David B. Loope
University of Nebraska–Lincoln

Morehouse, D. F. "Cave development via the sulfuric acid reaction." *National Speliological Society Bulletin* 30 (1968): 1–10. Palmer, A. N. "Carlsbad Caverns National Park." In *Geology of the National Parks*, edited by Ann Harris and Ester Tuttle: Dubuque IA: Kendall/Hunt Publishing Company, 1983.

CHINOOKS

Chinooks are warm and dry winds that descend the eastern slopes of the Rocky Mountains and dramatically affect the cold-season weather of the western Great Plains. This term is derived from the Chinook Indians of Oregon, who originally identified a local unseasonably warm wind as a "snow-eater." Air from a mild source region over the Pacific Ocean is further warmed by compression as it descends downslope and replaces a shallow cold air mass. Chinooks are capable of warming regions near the mountains by 50°F to 68°F in time periods as brief as fifteen minutes, leading to a rapid melting of any snow cover that is present. Some of the greatest extremes of temperature change in U.S. history have occurred in the Great Plains due to chinooks, including a warming of 81°F in two minutes in Spearfish, South Dakota, on January 22, 1943.

While chinooks have beneficial temperature effects during the cold season, they may also be accompanied by severe windstorms, especially east of the Front Range of the Colorado Rockies. A stable layer in the atmosphere just above the mountains and a low-pressure trough to the east of the mountains cause westerly winds to accelerate over the Front Range. In this situation, a mountain wave can develop that forces the air above the mountain upward followed by a severe downslope acceleration. In one instance, a chinook windstorm struck Boulder, Colorado, on January 17, 1982, with winds in excess of 200 feet per second, resulting in more than $17 million in damage.

See also FOLKWAYS: Chinook Stories.

Michael A. Palecki
Midwestern Regional Climate Center

Barry, Roger G. *Mountain Weather and Climate.* New York: Methuen & Co., 1981. Geer, I. A., ed. *Glossary of Weather and Climate.* Boston: American Meteorological Society, 1996. Keen, R. A. *Skywatch: The Western Weather Guide.* Golden CO: Fulcrum, Inc., 1987.

CLIMATE

To a large extent, the climate of the Great Plains is determined by its geographic position within North America. The region is affected by several different air mass types that possess very different temperature and moisture properties. Air masses that move south over the region, from the dry, often snow-covered interior sections of central Canada, bring cold, dry air across the Plains. Air masses that form over the Gulf of Mexico and the Caribbean often move northward into the Plains with warm, very moist air. Occasionally, very warm, dry air will enter the Plains with air masses that originate in the desert areas of the southwestern United States and northern Mexico. Finally, air that originates over the Pacific Ocean will often move east, crossing the mountainous region of the western third of the United States into the Great Plains. The transport of this air up the windward side of a mountain barrier and then down the leeward side results in significant warming and drying. Depending on the time of year, one or a combination of these air masses typically dominate much of the Great Plains region.

Another major factor in the climate of the Great Plains is its location near the center of the continent, a great distance from any large body of water. For a given input or output of energy, the temperature of water changes much more slowly than that of soil surfaces. Thus the temperature in an area in close proximity to a large body of water typically experiences a more consistent climate because of the moderating effects of the water (such an area is cooler in the summer and warmer in the winter). As a result of soil surfaces heating and cooling rapidly, regions remote from large water bodies experience large variations in temperature throughout the course of a year and over a twenty-four-hour period.

The Great Plains, therefore, has a large range in both annual and daily temperatures. During the midwinter months (January and February), when cold, dry air from central Canada dominates, temperatures are very cold, with mean temperatures varying from 40°F across the Southern Plains to as low as 10°F across the Canadian Prairies. During midsummer (July and August), when the Plains are dominated by either warm, moist air from the Gulf of

Mexico or warm, dry air from the Southwest, mean temperatures increase to approximately 80°F through the Southern Plains and approximately 66°F across the Canadian Prairies. This gives the region a much larger range in annual temperature than is found elsewhere in North America. For example, the range in mean monthly temperature between January and July in Omaha, Nebraska, is approximately 56°F, while in Philadelphia, Pennsylvania, and San Francisco, California (each at a similar latitude), the ranges are 46°F and 14°F respectively. The daily temperature range across the Plains generally increases to the north and west, away from the moderating influence of the Gulf of Mexico. During July, the mean daily temperature range across the Plains is approximately 30°F, while in the eastern parts of North America the daily range is 20°F and along the Pacific coast only 10°F.

Precipitation across the Great Plains decreases dramatically from southeast to northwest. The main source of atmospheric moisture is the Gulf of Mexico. Areas near the Gulf, in the southeastern portion of the Plains, receive more than forty inches of precipitation annually. This total decreases to less than fourteen inches in eastern Montana and parts of the Canadian Prairies. The annual cycle of precipitation across the Plains is dominated by a summer maximum. During the summer months warm, moist air masses move north from the Gulf of Mexico. These air masses normally produce showers and thunderstorms because of their unstable characteristics. During the spring cold, dry air masses from central Canada often interact with the air from the Gulf to set the stage for the outbreak of severe thunderstorms that can bring heavy rainfall, high winds, hail, and tornadoes to local areas. During the winter snow normally covers a substantial portion of the Plains. Annual snowfall averages from less than one inch across the southern portion of the region to more than forty inches across the north. Because of the cold winter temperatures and the relatively heavy annual snowfall, snow cover blankets the Northern Plains throughout much of the winter season.

The year-to-year variability in temperature and precipitation across the Great Plains is very large. This variability is especially evident in the recurrent problem of drought. The very warm and often dry summer weather that is characteristic of the Plains leads to high evaporation and transpiration (water loss from plants) rates. Soils are often depleted of their moisture, leading to stressed natural and cultivated vegetation. A measure of the lack of available soil moisture for plants, the soil moisture deficit, has been calculated for the entire Great Plains region for the period 1895 through 1994. From this it is clear that the Plains as a whole has undergone recurrent periods of drought over the last century, especially during the 1930s (the Dust Bowl years) and the 1950s. The large annual (within one year) and interannual (year-to-year) variability of Great Plains climate makes the region

a natural laboratory for studying the effects of climate variability on a host of problems associated with the interaction of humans with their environment.

See also AGRICULTURE: Agricultural Meteorology / INDUSTRY: Weather Industry / WATER: Drought.

Daniel J. Leathers
University of Delaware

Borchert, John R. "The Climate of the Central North American Grassland." *Annals of the Association of American Geographers* 40 (1950): 1–39. Lawson, Merlin P., and Charles W. Stockton. "Desert Myth and Climatic Reality." *Annals of the Association of the American Geographers* 71 (1981): 527–35. Rosenberg, Norman J. "Climate of the Great Plains Region of the United States." *Great Plains Quarterly* 6 (1986): 22–32.

COTTONWOODS

Cottonwoods, tall and stately pioneer invaders of the prairies—though few and far between when European Americans first came to the Great Plains—served as prominent landmarks and shady respites for those who traversed the region. They often marked a source of water and provided fuel for campsites. The cottonwood population increased dramatically with the coming of the plow and the demise of prairie wildfires. The seedlings that sprouted on sandbars were collected by early settlers and planted at their homesites for shade and wind shelter.

Today, cottonwoods continue to be an important part of farmstead windbreaks and field shelterbelts. Natural cottonwood stands are one of the main sources of sawtimber harvested in the Great Plains. The lumber, though lightweight and soft, is used for pallets and light construction. These fast growing, easily propagated trees are also used to provide fiber for high-quality paper.

Cottonwoods—members of the genus *Populus* in the willow family (Salicaceae)—are most at home along flowing streams and level, subirrigated uplands where soil moisture is plentiful. They bear wind-pollinated flowers. After pollination capsules release large numbers of tiny, cottony, winged seeds in early summer that must germinate and take root in a matter of hours or perish because they do not contain their own built-in food supply. Most species of *Populus* will also reproduce readily by stump and root sprouts. They can be propagated by hardwood cuttings as well.

Eastern cottonwood (*P. deltoides*) and its western variety plains cottonwood (var. *occidentalis*) grow throughout the Great Plains from the Rio Grande to the Prairie Provinces of Canada. The national cochampion eastern cottonwood stood ninety-six feet tall near Arapahoe, Nebraska, until it was severely damaged by wind. The national champion plains cottonwood stands 105 feet tall near Hygiene, Colorado.

Other cottonwood species native to the Great Plains are the narrowleaf cottonwood (*P. anqustifolia*) and the lancleaf cottonwood (*p. xacuminata*), which is believed to be a natural cross between the eastern and narrowleaf cottonwoods. Closely related family members

—balsam poplar (*P. balsamifera*) and quaking aspen (*P. tremuloides*)—are natives of northern portions of the Great Plains.

Walter T. Bagley
University of Nebraska–Lincoln

American Forestry Association. *National Register of Big Trees*. Washington DC, 1996.

COYOTES

The most opportunistic of all North American predators, the coyote (*Canis laterans*) was familiar to Native Americans, early travelers, and settlers in the Great Plains. Their characteristic yip and resonant howling earned them the title "song dog of the prairie." Figuring prominently in the religious traditions of the Plains Indians, the coyotes of the Great Plains were observed by Lewis and Clark, who termed them the "prairie wolf." Thomas Say of the Stephen Long expedition in 1823 provided more specific information on this ubiquitous western animal and gave it its scientific name.

Smaller in size than its relative the wolf, coyotes usually weigh between eighteen and thirty pounds, are born in litters of five to seven pups, and live up to eighteen years. They are remarkably adaptable animals that can live in almost any environment. As native fauna was reduced through settlement and as domesticated animals were raised in the Great Plains, the omnivorous coyote began to prey upon the chickens, pigs, cattle, and sheep of the emerging farms and ranches. Coyote predation became a problem for European American settlers, and the resources of local, state, and federal government were called upon to address this problem. In the latter half of the nineteenth century, state bounties were placed on coyotes. Trappers hunted, poisoned, and trapped them, but there was only limited success in reducing their numbers. Coyotes remain as one of the most persistent and distinctive members of the fauna of the Great Plains.

Phillip Drennon Thomas
Wichita State University

Leydet, François. *The Coyote: Defiant Songdog of the West*. Norman: University of Oklahoma Press, 1977. Van Wormer, Joe. *The World of the Coyote*. Philadelphia: J. B. Lippincott Company, 1964.

DUST BOWL

The Dust Bowl was an area of drought and severe wind erosion in southwestern Kansas, southeastern Colorado, northeastern New Mexico, and the panhandles of Oklahoma and Texas during the 1930s. This area extended approximately 400 miles from north to south and 300 miles from east to west, although the boundary was never precise because of fluctuations in annual precipitation.

The area was first given the name "Dust Bowl" by Robert E. Geiger, a reporter for the *Washington DC Evening Star*, who used the term in an article following a severe dust storm, known as a black blizzard, on April 14, 1935. Soon, the Soil Conservation Service and the public were using the phrase Dust Bowl to

Dust cloud rolling over western Kansas town, February 21, 1935

identify the area of the Southern Great Plains that experienced the worst drought, wind erosion, and dust storms.

Although drought and dust storms are natural phenomena in the Great Plains, it was the rapid expansion of wheat production following World War I that destroyed soil-holding native grasses and created the Dust Bowl. After drought ruined the wheat crop during the autumn of 1931, the prevailing winds began to lift the soil and plague the region with dust storms by late January 1932.

As the drought and dust storms worsened during the mid-1930s, the federal government responded to the economic and technical needs of the drought-stricken farmers in the Dust Bowl with a host of programs. The Agricultural Adjustment Administration provided funds to farmers who agreed to limit wheat and cotton production, while the Commodity Credit Corporation offered price supporting loans on these crops. The Soil Conservation Service demonstrated terracing, strip cropping, and grass seeding techniques that prevented wind erosion and provided financial assistance that enabled farmers to apply these techniques. The Resettlement Administration and the Farm Security Administration furnished loans to the most destitute farmers who could not receive credit from other lending institutions to sustain their families and agricultural operations. The Farm Security Administration also purchased wind-eroded lands from farmers and returned those areas to grasslands. Originally known as land-utilization projects, they are now identified as national grasslands.

In 1935 the Resettlement Administration filmed the documentary *The Plow That Broke the Plains*, hoping to gain public and congressional support for its program to resettle people from the worst of the eroded lands. In 1937 *Life* magazine published several paintings by Alexandre Hogue that depicted conditions in the Dust Bowl. Residents of the Dust Bowl criticized these works because they seemed to place the blame for the dust storms on the farmers and their new laborsaving technology, such as tractors and combines, rather than on drought. In 1940, Congress ordered the film withdrawn from circulation.

In 1938 wind erosion began to diminish with the return of near-normal precipitation to many areas of the Dust Bowl. By 1940 the drought on the Southern Great Plains had ended. The federal programs that had helped farmers remain on the land, practice soil conservation, and endure the economic crisis of the Great Depression were not without their critics. Given the problems of drought, dust, and economic depression, however, these programs provided essential assistance at a time when abnormal climatic conditions and poor farming practices created unprecedented wind erosion and earned the Southern Great Plains its reputation as the Dust Bowl.

See also AGRICULTURE: Agricultural Adjustment Administration; Farm Security Administration / ART: Dust Bowl Photographers; Hogue, Alexandre / FILM: *The Grapes of Wrath*; *The Plow That Broke the Plains* / MUSIC: Guthrie, Woody.

R. Douglas Hurt
Iowa State University

Hurt, R. Douglas. *The Dust Bowl: An Agricultural and Social History*. Chicago: Nelson-Hall, 1981. Riney-Kehrberg, Pamela. *Rooted in Dust: Surviving Drought and Depression in Southwestern Kansas*. Lawrence: University Press of Kansas, 1994. Worster, Donald. *Dust Bowl: The Southern Plains in the 1930s*. New York: Oxford University Press, 1979.

EISELEY, LOREN (1907–1977)

Loren Corey Eiseley was born September 3, 1907, in Fremont, Nebraska, and was the only child of Daisy Corey and Clyde Edwin Eiseley. After briefly residing in both Fremont and Aurora, the family settled in Lincoln, where in 1925 Loren completed his public schooling, the first member of his family to do so. Having been introduced to the natural history museum on the University of Nebraska campus at age twelve and returning often to be fascinated by its archeological and anthropological exhibits, he entered the university that fall intent on majoring in science. It was at Nebraska that he experienced his first scientific expedition as part of the South Party (Morrill Paleontological Expedition of 1931–33). Professor C. Bertrand Schultz, leader of the expedition,

honored Eiseley some years later by naming a fossil oreodont after him (*hadroleptauchenia eiseleyi*).

Eiseley graduated from the university in 1933 with a Bachelor of Arts in sociology and English and received a doctorate in anthropology at the University of Pennsylvania in 1937. After brief tenure at the University of Kansas and Oberlin College in Ohio, where he served as chair of the Department of Sociology and Anthropology, he returned to Pennsylvania where he remained for thirty years until he ended his teaching career as Benjamin Franklin Professor of Anthropology and the History of Science.

Although his formal education and subsequent livelihood would emphasize scientific application, Eiseley maintained a dedicated and productive interest in literature and composition. In fact, his fiction won him awards from *Atlantic Monthly* as a high-school senior and citation in the Distinctive Index of *Best Short Stories of 1936*, and he wrote three collections of poetry. But it was Eiseley's combination of scientific analysis and poetic sensibility that brought him his greatest acclaim. In books like *The Immense Journey* (1957) and *Darwin's Century: Evolution and the Men who Discovered It* (1958), he interpreted natural history for a wide audience. Eiseley conveyed a sense of awe and wonder when he wrote about nature, a spiritual yearning that reverberated with his readers.

During his lifetime, Eiseley was awarded thirty-six honorary degrees, memberships in distinguished scholarly societies—including the National Institute of Arts and Letters—and was appointed by President Lyndon Johnson to the President's Task Force on the Preservation of Natural Beauty. He was the twelfth recipient of the Distinguished Nebraskan Award. Loren Eiseley died in Philadelphia on July 9, 1977.

Jacquelynn Sorensen
University of Nebraska–Lincoln

Christianson, Gale E. *Fox at the Wood's Edge: a Biography of Loren Eiseley*. New York: Henry Holt and Company, 1990. Heidtmann, Peter. *Loren Eiseley: A Modern Ishmael*. Hamden CT: Archon Books, 1991.

ENDANGERED SPECIES

Endangered species of fauna and flora are those species in imminent danger of becoming extinct unless mitigating actions are taken, particularly in saving critical habitats. The list of endangered species in the Great Plains was developed using the official list of the Division of Endangered Species of the U.S. Fish and Wildlife Service and provincial lists for Alberta, Manitoba, and Saskatchewan prepared by the World Wildlife Fund. The list is dominated by vertebrate species, with six species of mammals, thirteen birds, one amphibian, and six fishes. The only invertebrate is an insect, the American burying beetle, and there are ten species and two varieties of vascular plants.

The most noticeable characteristic of this list is how short it is. There are only thirty-nine endangered species in the entire Great Plains. There are no reptiles on the list, and the only amphibian on the list is the Houston toad, which only marginally enters the Great Plains in central Texas. If all the species that only marginally enter the Great Plains are eliminated, the list would be significantly reduced. Among mammals, the gray bat and the Indiana bat reach the Great Plains only in extreme eastern Kansas, and the ocelot reaches the Great Plains only in south Texas. The grizzly bear and gray wolf may well be extirpated from the Great Plains, although grizzly bears may still be extant along the front of the Rocky Mountains west of Calgary and gray wolves may be found in the Parkland Belt at the northern edge of the region in the Canadian provinces.

Six species of birds on the list—burrowing owl, greater prairie-chicken, loggerhead shrike, mountain plover, piping plover, and sage thrasher—appear in the Great Plains list only because they are on one or more of the Canadian provincial lists of endangered species. The whooping crane and Eskimo curlew only migrate through the Great Plains and do not breed or reside for very long in the region. Five of the six species of fishes (the pallid sturgeon being the exception) are from restricted habitats at the southwestern edge of the Great Plains in Texas. Among the vascular plants, there are four types of cacti that enter the Great Plains in the desert grasslands along the southwestern edge of the region.

The American burying beetle has an extensive geographic range in the eastern United States, but some of the largest and best-studied populations are in Nebraska. The pallid sturgeon is found in the Missouri River and its tributaries. This leaves very few species on the list that have a broad geographic range in the Great Plains, including the black-footed ferret, swift fox, American peregrine falcon, loggerhead shrike, least tern, piping plover, western prairie fringed orchid, small white lady's slipper orchid, and Mead's milkweed.

Endangered status results from complex changes in habitats. The black-footed ferret, for example, has been taken to the brink of extinction because of the decline of its main food source, the black-tailed prairie dog, which now occupies only 2 percent of its former range. The presence of the burrowing owl on the endangered lists of three Canadian Prairie Provinces may be linked to the same cause.

Why does an extensive phytogeographic region such as the Great Plains have so few endangered species? There are at least two answers to this question. First, habitats in the Great Plains cover extensive areas and the phytogeographic regions flow almost imperceptibly from the shortgrass prairie in the west through the midgrasses to the tallgrass prairies of the east. Consequently, there are few habitats in which species can become isolated and vulnerable. Species that do become endangered tend to occupy limited geographic ranges or live in very specialized ecological niches, such as caves, hot springs, or gypsum outcrops. Second, the species that do

occur in the Great Plains have broad geographic distributions and broad ecological resource limits. Species with these characteristics are generally not those that reach endangered status.

Hugh H. Genoways
University of Nebraska–Lincoln
Margaret R. Bolick
University of Nebraska–Lincoln

Benedict, Russell A., Patricia W. Freeman, and Hugh H. Genoways. "Prairie Legacies—Mammals." In *Prairie Conservation*, edited by Fred B. Samson and Fritz L. Knopf. Washington DC: Island Press, 1996: 149–68. Bragg, Thomas B., and Allen A. Steuter. "Prairie Ecology—The Mixed Prairie." In *Prairie Conservation*, edited by Fred B. Samson and Fritz L. Knopf. Washington DC: Island Press, 1996, 53–66. Knopf, Fritz L. "Prairie Legacies—Birds." In *Prairie Conservation*, edited by Fred B. Samson and Fritz L. Knopf. Washington DC: Island Press, 1996: 135–48.

FIRE ECOLOGY

Historically, fire was a ubiquitous component of the Great Plains environment, interacting with other components, such as bison whose grazing patterns resulted in uneven fuel distribution and therefore in diverse fire effects. The frequency of historic fires varied throughout the Great Plains, from every two to three years in the eastern tallgrass prairies, to three to four years in the Nebraska Sandhills, six to twenty-five years in mesic-to-xeric northern mixed-grass prairies, and five to ten years in the western shortgrass prairies and desert grasslands.

Fire effects vary with frequency, season-of-occurrence, and location. Generally repeated fires in any season affect diversity by favoring

Endangered Fauna and Flora of the Great Plains (2001)

FAUNA

Mammals (7)

Canis lupus	gray wolf
Felis pardalis	ocelot
Mustela nigripes	black-footed ferret
Myotis grisescens	gray bat
Myotis sodalis	Indiana bat
Ursus arctos	grizzly bear
Vulpes velox	swift fox

Birds (13)

Charadrius melodus	piping plover
Dedroica chrysoparia	golden-cheeked warbler
Empidonax traillii extimus	southwestern willow flycatcher
Eupoda montana	mountain plover
Falco peregrinus anatum	American peregrine falcon
Grus americana	whooping crane
Lanius ludovicianus	loggerhead shrike
Numenius borealis	Eskimo curlew
Oreoscoptes montanus	sage thrasher
Speotyto cunicularia	burrowing owl
Sterna antillarum	least tern
Tympanuchus cupido	greater prairie-chicken
Vireo atricapellus	black-capped vireo

Amphibian (1)

Bufo houstonensis	Houston toad

Fishes (6)

Cyprinodon bovinus	Leon Springs pupfish
Cyprinodon elegans	Comanche Springs pupfish
Gambusia heterochir	Clear Creek gambusia
Gambusia nobilis	Pecos gambusia
Hybognathus amarus	Rio Grande silvery minnow
Scaphirhychus albus	pallid sturgeon

Insect (1)

Nicrophorus americanus	American burying beetle

FLORA

Vascular Plants (11)

Asclepias meadii	Mead's milkweed
Callirhoe scabriuscula	Texas poppy-mallow
Coryphantha minima	Nellie cory cactus
Coryphantha sneedii var. *leei*	Lee pincushion cactus
Coryphantha sneedii var. *sneedii*	Sneed pincushion cactus
Cypripedium candidum	small white lady's slipper orchid
Echinocereus fendleri var. *kuenzleri*	Kuenzler hedgehog cactus
Erigonum gypsophilum	Gypsum wild-buckwheat
Frankenia johnstonii	Johnston's frankenia
Penstemon haydenii	blowout penstemon
Platanthera praeclara	western prairie fringed orchid

grasses over forbs. Dormant-season fires remove litter and thus may both encourage undesirable plants, such as smooth brome (*Bromus inermis*), sweet clover (*Melilotus* spp.), and Kentucky bluegrass (*Poa pratensis*), and expose soil to surface erosion. However, dormant-season fires have less of an effect on ground-nesting birds and invertebrates. Late-spring fires, the season of most eastern grassland prescribed burning, favor the dominant, warm-season species such as big bluestem (*Andropogon gerardii*) over cool-season species like Kentucky bluegrass, but they often have a major impact on the invertebrate community. Summer (growing-season) fires, which historically occurred most frequently but were smallest in size, reduce plant diversity by favoring grasses over forbs. These fires are less likely to affect invertebrates or ground-nesting birds and are most successful in top-killing woody plants that invade and degrade unburned prairies.

Individual species, however, do not all respond similarly to fire. Thus maintaining a diverse fire regime, interactive with other ecosystem-level components such as grazing, is essential to the long-term, ecological diversity and dynamics of Great Plains grasslands.

Thomas B. Bragg
University of Nebraska at Omaha

Bragg, Thomas B. "Climate, Soils and Fire: The Physical Environment of North American Grasslands." In *The Changing Prairie*, edited by Kathleen H. Keeler and Anthony Joern. Oxford: Oxford University Press, 1995: 49–81. Bragg, Thomas B., and Lloyd C. Hulbert. "Woody Plant Invasion of Unburned Kansas Bluestem Prairie." *Journal of Range Management* 29 (1976): 19–24.

FISH

Aquatic habitats in the Great Plains region were historically dominated by rivers and streams with associated wetlands and few natural lakes. Native fishes are typically riverine species that are in many cases adapted to strong current, turbid water, and a wide range of water temperatures. However, many species that require clear water and cool temperatures are found as relict populations in springs and headwater streams. The native and introduced fish fauna are an important link in food chains for many species and are significant economic resources for many communities.

The native fish fauna of the Great Plains includes representatives of twenty-eight families and more than 100 species. Several other families and many species have been introduced. The minnow family (Cyprinidae) is the most diverse with more than forty species native to the region. Other species-rich families include suckers (Catostomidae), catfish (Ictaluridae), perch (Percidae), and sunfish (Centrarchidae). The fathead minnow (*Pimephales promelas*), sand shiner (*Notropis stramineus*), and red shiner (*Cyprinella lutrensis*) are some of the most widespread species. Other species, like the Topeka shiner (*Notropis topeka*), plains minnow (*Hybognathus placitus*), and plains topminnow (*Fundulus sciadicus*), are nearly confined to the Great Plains.

Before European American settlement, the south-central portion of the region, covering Kansas and part of Colorado, was the most diverse, with 109 native species from twenty families. The north-central region (Nebraska, South Dakota, Wyoming) had ninety-three native species from twenty-two families while the northern Plains states' (North Dakota, Montana) native fishes numbered seventy-six species from nineteen families. The Canadian (Manitoba, Saskatchewan, Alberta) and southern (Oklahoma, Texas, New Mexico) portions of the Great Plains were the least diverse with fifty-eight and sixty-two species respectively. Both regions had seventeen native families, but the southern region included representatives of two families (Characidae, Cyprinodontidae) and eight species found native nowhere else in the Plains. The northern states and Canadian regions contribute two families (Salmonidae, Cottidae) and four species to the native fauna. The Great Plains fish fauna shows a strong influence of its connection to the Mississippi drainage. However, representatives of northern and southwestern faunas are also in evidence.

Since the onset of European American settlement, many of the rivers have been dammed to produce reservoirs ranging in size from small farm ponds to large impoundments. Reservoirs and ponds have provided new habitats where exotic species have flourished after being introduced. Introduced sport fish, especially members of the families Salmonidae, Moronidae, and Centrarchidae, prey upon and compete for food with many native species. Aquatic habitats have also been altered or destroyed by chemical pollution, channelization, erosion, siltation, and water depletion. Habitat alteration, pollution, and introduction of nonnative species have led to the demise of many local populations. Introductions of mosquito fish (*Gambusia affinis*) have competed with a number of native minnows and killifish, such as the plains topminnow. Habitat protection and restoration measures have been initiated by conservation organizations to prevent continued losses from the native fish fauna, but many populations are already in serious jeopardy or have been extirpated.

Edward J. Peters
University of Nebraska–Lincoln

Brown, C. J. D. *Fishes of Montana*. Bozeman: Montana State University, 1971. Cross, Frank B., and Joseph T. Collins. *Fishes in Kansas*. Lawrence: University of Kansas Natural History Museum, 1995. Lee, David S., Carter R. Gilbert, Charles H. Hocutt, Robert E. Jenkins, Don E. McAllister, and Jay R. Stauffer Jr. *Atlas of North American Freshwater Fishes*. Raleigh: North Carolina Biological Survey, Publication No. 1980–12, 1980.

FLORA

More than 2,900 species of vascular plants from some 730 genera in 159 families grow in the Great Plains. The vast majority (all but 81 species in 8 families) are angiosperms (flowering plants). For plants the Great Plains has one of the most stressful climates: hot summers, cold winters, frequent droughts, with dramatic seasonal and annual variation. Consequently, the plants that dominate the region are herbaceous grasses and forbs (wildflowers) derived from the plant families of temperate regions rather than trees or plants from families of tropical regions. The families with the most genera and species are sunflowers (Asteraceae), with more than 100 genera and 430 species, grasses (Poaceae, 76 genera, 260 species), sedges (Cyperaceae, 13 genera, 220 species), and legumes (Fabaceae, 34 genera, 158 species, or 46 genera, and 178 species if Caesalpinaceae and Mimosaceae are included in the Fabaceae). The precise numbers are subject to revision as taxonomists improve their understanding of the flora, but the pattern is unlikely to change. Other groups with numerous species are mustards (Brassicaceae), lilies (Liliaceae), umbels (Apiaceae), mints (Lamiaceae), and the penstemon family (Scrophulariaceae).

Compared to North American deserts and forests, Plains ecosystems formed very recently. Consequently, there are only about 100 endemic species and no endemic genera or families. The most common endemic species are composites (Asteraceae, 27 species), and legumes (Fabaceae, 21 species, especially *Astragalus*). Surprisingly, there are no endemic grasses.

Plants that are naturally rare in this region tend to occur in restricted habitats, especially at the western edge of the region, or in scattered microhabitats, such as salt marshes. However, reduction of formerly widespread ecosystems such as tallgrass and midgrass prairies to tiny fragments is putting many previously common species at risk of extinction. In addition, changes in land use, such as continuous grazing and reduction of fire, pose threats to some species: If a plant decreases under grazing, or requires fire to prosper, it may decline even if the area is otherwise undisturbed and well managed. Historically, both grazing and fire occurred episodically, and some species relied on the changing conditions.

Approximately 12 percent of all Plains species have recently been introduced to the region: plants from the eastern United States (previously excluded by drought, recurrent fire, and absence of tree cover), plants from the western United States (previously unable to cross the mountains), and plants from Europe, Asia, and occasionally Africa and South America brought by humans. Some of these, such as *Salsola* (tumbleweeds), are able to invade natural ecosystems, but most introduced plants remain associated with humans. These can be expected to steadily increase in number and diversity where human impact increases. The introduced plants form the basis for an ongoing evolution of the flora, in some cases changing in response to Plains conditions, and in other cases hybridizing with their native relatives to form new varieties and possibly species.

Great Plains flora is dominated by perennial herbs, plants that die back to the roots each winter then resprout in the spring. Trees are abundant on the edges of the region and in the larger river valleys of the eastern Plains. Beyond these areas, trees and shrubs, because they are more injured by prairie fires than

Generalized Chart of Rocks of the Great Plains

Eon	Era	Period	Epoch	Millions of years ago	Northern (AB, SK, MB, MT, ND)	Central (WY, SD, NE, N. CO)	Southern (KS, OK, NM, TX, S. CO)
Phanerozoic	Cenozoic	Quaternary	Holocene	0.01	alluvium, windblown sand glacial deposits	alluvium, windblown sand glacial deposits, windblown silt	alluvium, lake deposits windblown sand and silt
			Pleistocene	1.6			
		Tertiary	Pliocene	5	alluvium	Broadwater & Long Pine Fms	Blackwater Draw Fm
			Miocene	24	Flaxville Fm / Wood Mountain Fm	Ogallala Group: Ash Hollow Fm, Valentine Fm, Runningwater Fm	Ogallala Fm / Birdwell Fm, Couch Fm
			Oligocene	34	Cypress Hills Fm	White River Group: Brule Fm/Chadron Fm, Chamberlain Pass Fm / Arikaree Group	
			Eocene	58	Golden Valley Fm		
			Paleocene	65	Porcupine Hills Fm / Willow Creek Fm / Fort Union Group	Dawson Arkose / Denver Fm	Poison Cyn Fm / Raton Fm / Vermejo Fm
	Mesozoic	Cretaceous		144	Frenchman Fm / Eastend Sandstone / Hell Creek Fm	Fox Hills Fm / Trinidad Fm / Pierre Shale / Colorado Group	Edwards Limestone
		Jurassic		208	Undivided – mostly mudstones and sandstones		
		Triassic		245	Undivided – mostly limestone, shale, "red beds," and salt		
	Paleozoic			570	Undivided – mostly marine limestone and shale		
	Precambrian				Undivided – mostly metamorphic and igneous rocks		

Note: Unit names are representative and not complete. Time column is not to scale. Shading represents missing intervals of strata.

herbs (especially grasses), were historically found only in areas protected from fire, such as near cliffs or on islands and at bends in rivers. A few shrubs—lead plant (*Amorpha canescens*), for example—survive well within the open grassland. Others, such as sumac (*Rhus*) and dogwoods (*Cornus*), rapidly increase in unburned prairie.

Kathleen H. Keeler
University of Nebraska–Lincoln
James H. Locklear
Nebraska Statewide Arboretum

Great Plains Flora Association. *Flora of the Great Plains.* Lawrence: University Press of Kansas, 1986.

GEOLOGY

Any discussion of the geology of a given physiographic region should distinguish between the history of the present landscape and the older geologic record that, for the most part, lies buried beneath the area. The oldest rocks under the Great Plains belong to the Precambrian era and represent a complex set of primarily igneous and metamorphic rocks. They record the construction of the North American continent as a series of continental plates which collided with an earlier "North America" that was 2.1 billion years old and much farther south than today. These ancient rocks are exposed at the surface within the Great Plains in the Black Hills and the Central Texas and Hartville (eastern Wyoming) Uplifts.

About one billion years ago, the last amalgamation of continental material involving the future Great Plains region was completed, and erosion prevailed over deposition for the next half billion years, leaving little in the way of a rock record in the central part of the continent. Beginning about 540 million years ago, the first of many shallow inland seas ushered in the Paleozoic and later the Mesozoic eras. Shallow ocean waters covered a significant part of the interior of North America, including the region we recognize as the Great Plains, for most of Paleozoic and Mesozoic time. Typically between 5,000 and 10,000 feet of layered sediments, predominantly limestones, shales, and sandstones representing a mixture of seafloor, near-shore, and delta environments, accumulated during the course of almost 480 million years.

This long period of predominantly shallow marine deposition was brought to a close some 70 million years ago when a major period of mountain building (the Laramide Orogeny) created a belt of mountains stretching from Alaska to Mexico. This major shift in geologic processes lasted for more than 20 million years, as the continental seas retreated, to be replaced by the first landscapes of the ancestral Great Plains. Uplift along the eastern margin of the Rocky Mountains was dramatic, and deposits of the Cretaceous seas were raised thousands of feet above sea level. East of the rising Rockies and the flanking basins, gentle warping and uplift raised the former seabeds

from one to a few thousand feet. The Black Hills and the Laramie Range and Hartville Uplift of eastern Wyoming were formed as highlands probably late in the Laramide Orogeny. They reached maximum elevation in the late Paleocene and early Eocene.

The forces of erosion immediately attacked all of these new highlands, and the mud, sand, and gravel produced were transported by eastward-flowing rivers and deposited in low basins on the western margin of the newly created Plains during the Paleocene. The majority of these deposits were preserved in the Northern Great Plains, and no sediment or depositional record has been discovered for the first 25 million years of the Cenozoic era in the Central Great Plains except for the Denver and Raton Basins. Erosion and/or nondeposition was the order of the day for an even longer time, some 50 million years, in the Southern Great Plains. The following discussion will focus on more specific aspects of the geologic history of the Southern, Central, and Northern Great Plains.

The rivers originating in the newly arisen southern Rocky Mountains flowed eastward and carved a series of drainages hundreds of feet deep into the recently uplifted Mesozoic strata. The record in the Southern Great Plains for the first 75 percent of the Cenozoic, however, speaks only of erosion. Only the Raton Basin contains sedimentary rocks of early Cenozoic age. The enormous quantity of debris that was shed off the rising mountains was transported across the region into the Gulf of

Mexico, forming major deltas along the coastline. Enough sediment was delivered in the early Cenozoic to the Gulf that the coastline was pushed more than 100 miles seaward. Finally, about 12 million years ago, braided streams flowing in the valleys began to deposit sand and gravel, and the construction of the Southern High Plains was under way. These valleys did not always completely fill with stream deposits, and in Texas and eastern New Mexico they are often capped by windblown sand and silt, which were also deposited on the adjacent uplands. Near the end of the Miocene and into the early Pliocene, sedimentation rates slowed and extensive calcareous soils (caliches) developed on a relatively stable land surface. These calcareous soils form the hard and durable caprock horizons that cover much of the Southern High Plains. Geologists have included these deposits within the Ogallala Formation or Group. These strata comprise the majority of sediments in the High Plains aquifer, the primary source of groundwater in the Southern and Central Great Plains. The Quaternary deposits of the Southern High Plains are primarily windblown sandy silt and shallow lake sediments.

In the Central Great Plains there is a good record of early Cenozoic (Paleocene) deposition only in the Denver Basin and in the Williston Basin of northwestern South Dakota. The basal Paleocene rocks (Denver Formation) are up to 1,500 feet thick and consist of fine-grained river floodplain, swamp, and lake sediments with scattered coaly beds. These strata are overlain by coarse sandstones and conglomerates (Dawson Formation), representing large alluvial fans deposited by braided rivers that drained the newly arisen Rocky Mountain Front Range. The climate was probably tropical to subtropical throughout most of the Great Plains during the Paleocene epoch. For the succeeding 20 million years, representing most of the Eocene, only a sparse rock record is preserved and erosion or nondeposition was widespread throughout the Great Plains. A major period of sedimentation was then initiated in the late Eocene and continued into the Oligocene. Over the next eight million years, as much as 1,300 feet of predominantly fine-grained sediment, the White River Group, was deposited across much of the Central Great Plains. This deposit is unique because much of it was deposited by the wind, and typically more than 80 percent of the fine-grained mineral grains are shards of volcanic glass or volcanic minerals derived from huge eruptive centers in the Great Basin of Nevada and Utah. There are widespread coarse-grained river deposits in the lower part of the White River Group, but the upper half consists primarily of windblown sandy silt, an ancient dust (loess) deposit that blanketed and built up the landscapes. This interval also marks a change from subtropical to a subhumid (and possibly semiarid) environment in the Central Great Plains.

The next major set of rocks, the Arikaree Group, represents about 10 million years of late Oligocene and early Miocene time and is restricted to western Nebraska and adjoining parts of South Dakota and Wyoming. The basal Arikaree strata were deposited in several valleys as sandy river sediments. However, the remainder of the Arikaree is composed primarily of windblown fine sand and silt. As much as 40 to 70 percent of these grains have a volcanic origin, but they appear to be largely derived from huge volcanic eruptions in Colorado instead of the Great Basin. At the end of Arikaree deposition, about 18 million years ago, the dominant depositional process and accompanying landscape development underwent a major shift. The constructional and widespread windblown deposits of the Arikaree and White River Groups gave way to deposition in restricted river valleys that typifies the Miocene-age Ogallala Group. There was also a cessation of volcanically derived material blown into the Great Plains, and from that time to the present the Rocky Mountains have been the major source (excluding continental glacial deposits) of sediment deposited in the Plains. Ogallala deposition began about six million years earlier here than in the Southern Great Plains, and landscape evolution was more complex, as there are more cycles of valley cutting and filling preserved in the rock record. Sediment transported out of the Central and Northern Great Plains by rivers during the Miocene was probably delivered to the ocean via Hudson Bay rather than the Gulf of Mexico. Observations of ancient soils and mammal fossils of the Arikaree and Ogallala Groups suggest that shortgrass prairies first appeared in the Great Plains in the early Miocene, about 22 million years ago, and that tallgrass prairies did not appear until the late Miocene, about 8 to 10 million years ago.

Ogallala sedimentation ceased across the Central and Southern Great Plains at about the same time, some five million years ago at the end of the Miocene. The region had less local relief than today and would have presented remarkable vistas of vast, nearly unbroken grasslands, sloping gently to the east and ramping westward up onto the Rockies. Most of the present physiographic regions of the Great Plains are a result of erosion in the last five million years. Widespread uplift to the west and in the Black Hills caused rivers draining these highlands to erode the landscape once again and the Great Plains were carved up. One of the few remaining examples of the "climax" Great Plains topography is found in the "Gangplank" area west of Cheyenne, Wyoming. Here the Union Pacific Railroad and Interstate 80 use the gentle slope of the old Ogallala surface to climb to the summit of the Laramie Mountains. Renewed uplift of the Rocky Mountains of northern Colorado and southeastern Wyoming between 3.5 and 2 million years ago (Pliocene epoch), perhaps aided by increased precipitation, delivered coarse sediment out onto the Great Plains via ancestral South and North Platte Rivers. Within Colorado, Wyoming, and western Nebraska, these deposits were confined to valleys no larger than those of the present North and South Platte. In central Nebraska, however, a complex sheet of sand and gravel, as much as 200 feet thick, was deposited over 20,000 square miles. These deposits, referred to as the Broadwater and Long Pine Formations, represent the greatest known volume of coarse material shed into the Great Plains in the last 34 million years.

The Williston Basin, covering 60,000 square miles, contains the most extensive and complete section of Paleocene deposits (Fort Union Group) in the Great Plains. The Fort Union Group consists of as much as 1,800 feet of sandstone, mudstone, and thick coal beds deposited mainly in delta, swamp, and river environments. The last of the great interior seas was slowly retreating toward the northeast and Hudson Bay while the lower part of the Fort Union was being deposited. It left behind a deposit of shale called the Cannonball Formation. The Eocene primarily marks a time of erosion. While late Eocene- to Oligocene-age White River strata were deposited in North Dakota, to the northwest in Saskatchewan the equivalent-age Cypress Hills Formation was deposited. However, it is a coarse-grained river deposit compared to the windblown White River strata. There are a few thin and widely scattered Miocene- and Pliocene-age river deposits found across the Northern Great Plains. It has been estimated that up to two kilometers of sediment were removed by erosion from this region between 34 and 2 million years ago. What is left is only a small fraction of the enormous quantity of material that was moved out of the region, a situation similar to the Southern Great Plains.

During the last two million years, the geologic history of the Central and Northern Great Plains was dominated by the effects of continental glaciation. In the Southern Plains, the record is one of interplay between deposition by running water, winds, and in lake basins.

James B. Swinehart
University of Nebraska–Lincoln

Baars, D. L. "Basins of the Rocky Mountain Region." In *Sedimentary Cover, North American Craton, U.S.*, edited by L. L. Sloss, The Geology of North America, vol. D-2: 109–220. Boulder CO: Geological Society of America, 1988.
Trimble, Donald E. *The Geologic Story of the Great Plains.* Geologic Survey Bulletin 1493. Washington DC: Government Printing Office, 1980.

GLACIATION

During the Pleistocene epoch (from two million to 10,000 years ago), continental glaciers invaded the Great Plains only in the northern portions; nevertheless, their effects on the entire region were profound. Glacial ice repeatedly blocked the rivers that drained eastward, forming ice-marginal lakes and diverting the rivers southward. Wind deflated sand and silt from the floodplains of the rivers that carried sediment-laden meltwater from both the enlarged glaciers in the Rocky Mountains and the continental ice sheet, creating fields of dunes and depositing a loess mantle on the uplands. Permafrost (perennially frozen ground) developed around the ice margin where strong winds swept the blanket of snow from the surface. Lowered temperatures along the glacier margin and southward caused major changes in distribution of the biota of the entire region.

The Laurentide ice sheets that developed in eastern and central Canada expanded to reach the Great Plains at least seven times between about 2.2 million years ago and less than 10,000 years ago, when the margin of the last glacier melted from the area. After each period of glaciation, ice disappeared long enough for soil profiles to form on the sediments left behind.

The early glaciations were the most extensive. They have been dated approximately by the relationships of the tills they deposited in reference to four ashfall deposits, three from the Yellowstone Caldera, and one from Bishop, California. One till lies beneath the oldest of these ash lenses, dating back more than 2 million years, and at least four till units lie between ash lenses deposited from 1.27 million to 610,000 years ago. All of these are now referred to as pre-Illinoian tills. The outer margin of one or more of these early continental glaciers extended into northeastern Kansas and eastern Nebraska, then angled northwestward across the Dakotas and northern Montana, where it approached the piedmont glaciers of the Rocky Mountains.

All the major rivers that drain eastward from the Rocky Mountains built alluvial fans where they left the mountain front and deposited gravel and sand along their routes toward the northeast and east. Uplift in the late Cenozoic period (around two million years ago) resulted in downcutting by those rivers, so that terraces, identified by soil profile, preservation, relative height, and presence of ash lenses, exist along the valleys. Stream diversions and piracy have since changed the courses of many streams in the Central and Northern High Plains. The Missouri River, which formerly drained northeastward into the Hudson Bay Lowland, was ponded several times by ice dams and ultimately diverted into its present course. The ancestral Platte River, its upper course rejuvenated by uplift in the Rocky Mountains and its discharge augmented by increased precipitation and, perhaps, meltwater from late Pliocene mountain glaciers, carried a vast amount of coarse gravel eastward across eastern Wyoming and into west-central and northern Nebraska, where it accumulated as the Broadwater and Long Pine Formations. Across the Central Plains, the ancestral Platte shifted its course repeatedly throughout the Pleistocene in response to local uplift (the Chadron Arch), aggradation, and glacial blocking, finally following its present course after having spread sheets of gravel across wide areas of east-central Nebraska. In the Southern Plains, sand and silt, probably blown from the floodplains of the Pecos and Canadian Rivers, accumulated in a sequence that becomes finer northeastward across western Texas and Oklahoma (Blackwater Draw Formation) and reaches as far as south-central Nebraska. Deposition began more than 1.4 million years ago and continued intermittently until less than 118,000 years ago, with paleosols (ancient soils) recording periods of stability.

Glaciations took place between 610,000 years ago and the first of the Illinoian glaciations, 300,000 years ago, but left no recognizable record in the Great Plains. Nor have tills of Illinoian age been identified with certainty in the Great Plains, although the ice undoubtedly reached the region, and tills of that age should exist buried beneath the deposits of the last, or Wisconsinan, glaciation.

The most complete record of the effects of glaciation in the Great Plains, as elsewhere, is that of the late Wisconsinan ice sheet, which reached its maximum extent about 20,000 years ago and covered the region north of a diagonal line from southeastern South Dakota to southern Alberta. Lobes of Wisconsinan ice expanded into lowlands from the James River basin to the upper Milk River basin in Montana. Meltwater flooded down the Missouri River Valley, as well as down rivers that were fed by alpine glaciers in the Rocky Mountains. Strong northwesterly winds deflated sand and silt from these ribbons of outwash to accumulate as dunes along the rivers and loess over much of the upland.

Strong winds associated with both glaciers and dry interglacial conditions generated dunes from alluvial sediments deposited in central Nebraska along an abandoned mid-Pleistocene route of the Platte River. Late Wisconsinan winds built massive dunes from these sand fields, which were reactivated repeatedly during dry phases over the last 10,000 years. The strong northwesterly winds eroded troughs and ridges in the zone adjacent to the ice margin and swept the zone free of snow so that permafrost developed. Lakes formed where drainage was blocked by the ice. The largest of these, Lake Agassiz, covered more than half of Manitoba and extended into Saskatchewan, Ontario, Minnesota, North Dakota, and the northeast corner of South Dakota. This huge lake drained through the Minnesota River Valley until the retreating ice margin had uncovered outlet routes to the east. By about 11,000 years ago, the ice margin lay along the north side of Lake Winnipeg, although the Laurentide ice sheet did not entirely disappear until about 6,000 years ago.

See also WATER: Kettle Lakes; Lake Agassiz.

William J. Wayne
University of Nebraska–Lincoln

Morrison, Roger B., ed. *Quaternary Nonglacial Geology: Conterminous U.S.*, The Geology of North America, vol. K-2. Boulder CO: Geological Society of America, 1991. Sibrava, Vladimir, D. Q. Bowen, and G. M. Richmond, eds. *Quaternary Glaciations in the Northern Hemisphere*. Oxford: Pergamon Press, 1986.

GRASSES

Grasses are truly the defining feature of the Great Plains landscape. They are key elements in both the aesthetic appeal and the economic value of the Plains. The various shapes, textures, colors, and movements of grasses in a wide sweep of Plains landscape has inspired many artists, naturalists, and casual observers. It is the very existence of grass—providing forage for livestock and fostering nutritious soils for farming—that has made the Great Plains a hospitable place for human settlement and agriculture.

Grasses are the third largest plant family, and grass species are more broadly represented around the world than the species of any other family. Grasses include the plants referred to as "grains," which form the major food group for humans as well as many animals. Many cultivated crops—corn, wheat, sorghum, millet, barley, oats, rice—are grasses that have been domesticated from their wild relatives. Large portions of the Great Plains, particularly the wetter region east of the ninety-eighth meridian, have been converted from natural grasslands to fields that are planted with the cultivated grasses corn, wheat, and sorghum.

Grasses are classified as "monocots," which means that their tissue does not form wood and their stems do not increase in girth as they grow. Monocots have root systems that tend to form a dense, fibrous mat. Such a rooting habit made it possible for early Plains settlers to cut out blocks of soil, held together by the dense mat of roots, to form sod houses. Another diagnostic feature of grasses is the fact that their flowers are quite unlike those of other plant groups. The flowers are so small and inconspicuous that many people have the impression that grasses do not form flowers at all. They do in fact form flowers, but these tend to lack petals and sepals; most grasses are wind-pollinated, so the need to attract pollinators with bright and showy blossoms is minimal. Grass flowers are arranged in tightly packed vertical clusters called spikes, or more branched and spreading clusters called panicles. Although they do not have colorful petals, the most obvious flower part is often the bright yellow, pollen filled anthers protruding from the flower.

In the Great Plains grasses comprise most of the biomass in the plant canopy; they form a matrix in which other herbaceous plants and shrubs are interspersed. While some grasses have an annual growth form, most of the native and abundant species are perennial. The Great Plains region can be subdivided into smaller subregions based on the type of perennial grasses growing in each area. The westernmost portion, adjacent to the Rocky Mountains, consists of shortgrass prairie. This region is one of the driest regions of the Plains because of the rain shadow effect of the Rocky Mountains. Short-statured, drought-tolerant grasses such as *Bouteloua gracilis* (blue grama) and *Buchloë dactyloides* (buffalograss) are the dominant grasses. The easternmost portion is classified as tallgrass prairie. This region receives more moisture than the shortgrass region because of the weakening of the Rocky Mountain rain shadow and the increasing effect of moist air from the Gulf of Mexico. The dominant grasses in the tallgrass prairie are *Andropogon gerardii* (big bluestem), *Panicum virgatum* (switchgrass), and *Sorghastrum nutans* (Indiangrass). Between the short- and tallgrass prairies is a type of grassland referred to as mixed-grass prairie. This is a transitional zone and includes the short- and tallgrass species as well as increased dominance of the species *Schizachyrium scoparius* (little bluestem) and *Agropyron smithii* (western wheatgrass). The mixed-grass prairie can be further subdivided into a northern and southern type. The northern mixed-grass prairie includes greater abundance of the cool season grasses, *A. smithii* and species of *Stipa* (needlegrass) while the southern mixed-grass prairie is dominated by the warm season grasses, *S. scoparius* and *Bouteloua curtipendula* (sideoats grama). Both the northern mixed- and tallgrass prairies extend from the United States northward into Canada and form the majority of what is termed the "Canadian Prairie Province." This area of grassland also includes the fescue prairie, dominated by *Festuca scabrella* (rough fescue). Fescue prairie forms an arc around the northern and northwestern perimeter of the mixed-grass prairie, where grassland gives way to forest.

One often underappreciated ecological role that grasses play is in the formation of the rich soils, called mollisols, that typically underlay grasslands. Why are these soils so rich in nutrients and organic matter? The answer lies in the growth patterns of the grasses themselves. The aboveground portion of grass dies back every year, and the dense, fibrous root system is constantly growing and dying back. All of this results in large inputs of organic matter into the soil. The breakdown of the organic matter supplies nutrients to plants. The presence of the organic matter also increases the nutrient—and water—holding capacity of the soil. The richness of the soil has resulted in the wetter portions of the Great Plains becoming the breadbasket of the world.

A second important ecological role played by grasses is their persistence under drought, grazing, and fire, all forces that can kill other types of plants. Many grasses withstand these forces with little injury. A key reason is that grasses have their perennating organs (from which new growth arises) protected below the surface of the soil. Because of the protection of the perennating organ in the soil, grasses can grow back after their aboveground biomass has been removed by drought, grazing, or fire. In addition to the belowground perennating organs, the large amount of root biomass allows grasses to store resources needed to replace aboveground tissue lost to fire or grazers. The amount of root biomass in grasslands is often greater than the amount of aboveground biomass; in fact, grasslands could be called upside-down forests. Grass roots provide habitat and food for a whole suite of animals, bacteria, and fungi, just as a forest canopy supports an array of life.

The belowground community (as well as the aboveground canopy) is radically altered by plowing and the conversion of natural grasslands to agricultural fields in the Great Plains. This conversion has already claimed more than 90 percent of the tallgrass prairie region, and other grassland types, especially those in areas with reliable sources of water, have also disappeared. Grasses are valuable in both an aesthetic sense and for the critical ecological roles that they play in ecosystems.

More and more conservation efforts are under way to preserve what remains of the natural grasslands in the Great Plains.

See also ARCHITECTURE: Sod Wall Construction.

Mary Ann Vinton
Creighton University

Brown, Lauren. *Grasslands*. New York: Alfred A. Knopf, Inc., 1997. Coupland, R. T., ed. *Ecosystems of the World 8A: Natural Grasslands: Introduction and Western Hemisphere*. Amsterdam: Elsevier Science Publishers, 1992. Estes, J. R., R. J. Tyrl, and J. N. Brunken, eds. *Grasses and Grasslands: Systematics and Ecology*. Norman: University of Oklahoma Press, 1982.

GRASSHOPPERS

Grasshoppers inhabit all grasslands and associated arid regions in the Great Plains, where they eat a varied diet of grasses or herbs. Among native herbivores, grasshoppers rank among the most conspicuous and important consumers of aboveground vegetation in natural grasslands, often rivaling large vertebrate ungulates in impact. The species diversity of grasshoppers is great, with about 750 species found throughout North America and about 400 species inhabiting the seventeen western states. These numbers are similar to bird species diversity. Taxonomically, grasshoppers in the Great Plains are divided into four main groups or subfamilies: Gomphocerines (slant-faced grasshoppers), Oedipodines (band-winged grasshoppers), Melanoplines (spur-throat grasshoppers), and Cyrtacanthacradines. These groupings reflect historical, evolutionary trajectories that loosely predict diet, reproductive characteristics, and habitat use. Migratory locusts, a form of grasshopper, are not found in North America although they do occur in Central America, and the term has been repeatedly misused in popular accounts describing grasshopper outbreaks.

Given the great number of grasshopper species in the Great Plains, it is not surprising that species react to common environmental factors in different ways, with obvious species-specific differences in plant species eaten, courtship behavior, habitat selection, and geographic distribution. Unlike butterflies or leafhoppers, grasshoppers do not specialize on particular host plants, although they are discriminating feeders and will not feed on just anything. Grasshopper assemblies change in species composition along environmental gradients, just as plant communities vary, often in a gradual manner.

Grasshoppers occur year-round at all sites, primarily as eggs or overwintering nymphs during cold months and nymphs or reproductive adults at other times. Seasonal appearances of nymphs and adults of different species result in distinct groups of one-generation-per-year spring and summer species complexes in the Central and Northern Great Plains, and species with extended seasonality or even multiple generations per year populate the Southern Great Plains.

Densities rarely become so great that vegetation of entire regions is denuded with great impact on native plants as well as crops. In most years, however, grasshoppers consume less than 10 percent of the standing vegetation in grasslands. Rocky mountain locusts (*Melanoplus spretus* Walsh) presented a spectacular example of grasshopper outbreaks during the mid– and late nineteenth century, when millions of individuals dispersed from central breeding grounds in the shortgrass prairies of Colorado into neighboring eastern states, causing significant crop damage. A particularly vivid portrayal of such an infestation is given in the novel *Giants in the Earth* (1927), O. E. Rölvaag's vivid saga of pioneer settlement in South Dakota in the 1870s. This species is now presumed extinct for unknown reasons, probably resulting from agricultural development in shortgrass prairie regions.

Grasshopper populations are quite dynamic, with periodic fluctuations in overall numbers for all species about every seven to ten years. Climate and food quality can play important roles in these changes, but many other ecological factors are also involved, including competition for limited food resources. Predators and other natural enemies—primarily birds, spi-

Grasshoppers, Cheyenne River Indian Agency, South Dakota, 1936

ders, other insect predators, and insect parasites—also exert significant limiting effects on population sizes; pathogens, including bacteria, viruses, and fungi, can also kill many grasshoppers in some years.

See also FOLKWAYS: Insect Lore.

Anthony Joern
University of Nebraska–Lincoln

Capinera, J. L., and T. S. Sechrist. *Grasshoppers (Acrididae) of Colorado: Identification, Biology, and Management.* Colorado State University Experiment Station Bulletin No. 548S. Fort Collins: Colorado State University, 1982. Pfadt, Robert E. *Field Guide to Common Western Grasshoppers.* Wyoming Agricultural Experiment Station Bulletin 912. Laramie: University of Wyoming, 1994.

GREAT AMERICAN DESERT

See IMAGES AND ICONS: Great American Desert

HAYDEN, FERDINAND VANDEVEER

(1829–1887)

From 1853 to the late 1870s, Ferdinand Hayden was known to the Sioux as "man-who-picks-up-stones-running." To his contemporaries in the sciences, he was either a fine geologist or an entrepreneur who gave the government and land speculators the information needed to sell large tracts of western land. For the eager U.S. public Hayden was the man who provided a series of government-financed guides to the Great Plains and the Rocky Mountains.

Hayden was born in Westfield, Massachusetts, on September 7, 1829. He graduated from Oberlin College in 1850, and then earned a degree in medicine from Albany Medical School in 1853. His true love, however, was geology.

Hayden's extensive exploration of the American West began immediately upon his graduation with his first visit to the White River Badlands of Nebraska and South Dakota as an employee of James Hall, arguably the most respected paleontologist of the period. This trip was followed the next two seasons by an expedition funded by private interests that surveyed the upper Missouri River basin up to the mouth of the Bighorn River. The summers of 1856 and 1857 found Hayden accompanying his first governmental survey, the Warren expedition of Topographical Engineers, to examine the Yellowstone River and the region to the north. In 1858 Hayden joined his longtime friend, F. B. Meek, on a private survey of northeastern Kansas. In 1859 Hayden again joined the U.S. Topographical Engineers as the surgeon and naturalist of Cap. W. F. Raynolds's expeditions that, in two years, traversed the area of the upper Missouri, the Yellowstone, and the Bighorn Mountains. Hayden's explorations were interrupted in 1861 by the Civil War, which was the only time he truly used his medical degree, but were quickly resumed in 1866 when he returned to the Badlands under the sponsorship of the Academy of Natural Sciences of Philadelphia.

In 1867, Hayden took charge of a geological survey of Nebraska, an enterprise that he expanded into the most comprehensive scientific survey ever made of the American West. Through his reports of his expeditions to Nebraska and adjacent territories in 1867, southern and eastern Utah in 1868, southern and eastern Wyoming in 1870, the upper Yellowstone in 1871, eastern Montana in 1872, Colorado from 1873 to 1876, eastern Idaho and western Wyoming in 1877, and finally, the remaining sections of Wyoming in 1878, Hayden made the Great Plains known to the American public. The Yellowstone report was instrumental in the creation of Yellowstone National Park; the Colorado report was partly responsible for rapid settlement of that state in the late 1870s; and the Nebraska report clarified that the Great Plains was not a Great American Desert, but a richly endowed region, in which even the Sandhills of Nebraska would "yet become a fine pasture ground for herds of sheep, cattle, and horses."

Hayden's surveys, along with those of Clarence King, George Wheeler, and John Wesley Powell, were absorbed into the U.S. Geological Survey in 1879. Hayden was retained by the survey as a staff geologist. After three years in Washington, Hayden's health began to deteriorate, and it was thought that a field assignment might help to rejuvenate him. He was assigned to the USGS office in Montana. Hayden remained there until 1886, when it became obvious that his health was not going to improve, and he was forced to resign his position. He returned to Philadelphia where, after being confined to his home for more than a year, he died on December 22, 1887.

Michael Shambaugh-Miller
University of Nebraska Medical Center

Bartlett, Richard A. *Great Surveys of the American West.* Norman: University of Oklahoma Press, 1962. Foster, Mike. *Life of Ferdinand Vandeveer Hayden: Strange Genius.* Niwot CO: Roberts Rinehart, 1994.

INSECTS

The Great Plains of North America, like every other terrestrial ecosystem, has always depended upon insects for its existence. Insects are essential for maintaining plant life on the Plains through movement of nutrients, improving soil, accelerating organic decay, and pollinating plants. Additionally, insects form the foundation of the animal food web, upon which many species depend. As Plains ecosystems have given way to agroecosystems, the importance of insects has been altered, yet it still remains.

Insects are, by far, the most diverse animals on earth, and this is as true of the Plains as it is of the tropics. More than 100,000 insect species are known to exist in North America, and of these at least tens of thousands occur in the Great Plains. Although most insect groups are represented on the Plains, probably the most common are the insect orders Orthoptera (grasshoppers and crickets), Hemiptera (true bugs, various insects with sucking mouthparts), Diptera (true flies), Coleoptera (beetles), Lepidoptera (butterflies and moths), and Hymenoptera (ants, bees, and wasps).

The intimate association of insects and plants is essential for maintaining prairies. Soil structure and nutrient flow depend largely on the action of ants in moving material from the soil surface to plant root zones. A complex of dung beetle (scarab) species is essential for the rapid decomposition of animal dung, originally from herds of bison and now from herds of cattle. Similarly, other species of beetles and flies are crucial in recycling dead animal tissue. Finally, many prairie plants depend on insect pollinators, especially various species of native bees. Certainly not all associations of insects in the Great Plains have been beneficial or benign. Periodic grasshopper plagues removed so much vegetation that many larger herbivores, like bison, subsequently starved. Also biting flies and various internal and external insect parasites tormented animals, including humans. The plants of the Plains, however, cannot exist without their associated insects.

As some plant species have diminished or disappeared, so too have their associated insects. This is especially true for many prairie butterflies, which have a limited range of host plants. The reduction of the prairie has also led to the decline of other Plains animals and, therefore, of the insects which depend upon them. The American burying beetle (*Nicophorus americus*), an endangered insect species once found in all of eastern North America, now only occurs in scattered populations in the Great Plains (plus one remnant population in Rhode Island). Whether or not the decline of this species is associated with the decline of specific host carrion or other changes in habitat is unclear. Sometimes, as with prairie butterflies and moths, the loss of plant species can be clearly associated with loss of their associated insects. In other instances, the relationships are more problematic. One of the most striking mysteries involves the disappearance of the Rocky Mountain locust (*Melanoplus spretus Walsh*) that swept across the Great Plains in massive swarms of billions through the 1870s but apparently became extinct by the early 1900s. It seems likely that changes in habitat, possibly through agriculture and loss of egg-laying sites, explain the extinction of this grasshopper.

Continuing threats to insect biodiversity of the Plains also are associated with habitat change and loss. The management of existing prairies is of key importance in maintaining biodiversity. In particular fire and its negative impact on invertebrate communities has become a serious issue in managing remnant prairies. Similarly identifying and protecting other unique Plains habitats is another compelling issue for maintaining insect biodiversity. For example, one of the most endangered insects in the United States, the Salt Creek tiger beetle (*Cicindela nevadica lincolniana*), is a member of a complex of tiger beetle species that occur exclusively in salt marshes of the Eastern Great Plains. The decline of these insects directly follows from the destruction of salt marsh habitats through agriculture and urbanization.

Human use of the Great Plains has profoundly influenced the insect fauna, probably in ways we can never completely recognize (given that the Plains was substantially changed before its insect fauna was thoroughly studied). The destruction of the great bison herds and the ecosystems of which they were a part undoubtedly altered insect diversity and abundance. In general, urbanization and agriculture have reduced insect biodiversity. Agroecosystems are simplified as compared to natural ecosystems. This simplification leads to reduced species diversity, but may also result in large population increases of individual species, such as the corn rootworm beetles. Agriculture and urbanization also introduced many nonnative insects to the Great Plains, principally domestic species and pest species associated with crop plants, and this is a continuing process.

The introduction of nonnative plants such as crops not only leads to the introduction of new insects but also to the adaptation of native insects to these new crops. For example, with the introduction of soybean in the 1930s and 1940s, a native beetle, *Cerotoma trifurcata* (bean leaf beetle), rapidly moved from native leguminous hosts to become a soybean pest. A more striking example of this adaptation is the beetle *Leptinotarsa decemlineata* switching hosts from one solanaceous plant, buffalo bur, to another, potato. This insect, now known as the Colorado potato beetle, is one of the most severe potato pests throughout the world (and holds the dubious distinction of being one of the insect species most resistant to insecticides). It diffused from the Central Great Plains in the 1870s to most potato-growing regions of the world in less than a century, highlighting the influence of trade and human commerce on insect distributions.

Human interactions with insects largely have been confrontational rather than appreciative. One exception is that many Native peoples of the Great Plains recognized the importance of insects as an essential feature of nature and speak to the importance of insects in their oral traditions. Some Native people also ate insects, such as grasshoppers and crickets, as an occasional feature of their diet. For European American settlers of the Plains, insects were either ignored or viewed as pests. Black flies and mosquitoes were constant irritants, and insect-borne diseases like malaria and yellow fever were widespread in at least the Eastern Great Plains in the 1800s. Although these diseases no longer occur in the Great Plains, various encephalitis viruses, transmitted by mosquitoes, and Lyme disease, transmitted by ticks, still do present human health risks. Insects, especially through outbreaks of grasshoppers, crickets, and armyworms, also were a serious impediment to crop production as European American agriculture moved onto the Great Plains. Insects are still a significant factor in agriculture on the Plains, not only through exceptional pest outbreaks, but also through the routine occurrence of many pest species.

The future of insect biodiversity on the Plains is inexorably tied to the conservation of their habitats. The legacy of western attitudes toward insects, reinforced by potential health and agricultural risks from insects, is that insects are mostly ignored or despised. However, insects are an essential element of the Great Plains. Their fate, for good or ill, will mirror that of the Great Plains ecosystem itself.

See also FOLKWAYS: Insect Lore.

Leon Higley
University of Nebraska–Lincoln

Costello, D. F. *The Prairie World.* New York: Thomas Y. Crowell Co. 1969. Huggins, D. G. "Insects and Their Relatives." In *Natural Kansas*, edited by J. T. Collins. Lawrence: University Press of Kansas, 1985: 115–29. O'Toole, C. *The Encyclopedia of Insects.* New York: Facts on File Publications, 1987.

LAKE AGASSIZ

See WATER: Lake Agassiz

LLANO ESTACADO

The Llano Estacado is that part of the High Plains south of the Canadian River in northwest Texas and eastern New Mexico. Encompassing more than 30,000 square miles, this vast, semiarid tableland is one of the flattest parts of the United States. Its surface slopes gently toward the southeast at about eight to ten feet per mile, and elevations range from around 2,500 feet on the eastern and southern margins to more than 4,200 feet in the northwest.

The Llano is a coalescent alluvial plain composed of Tertiary and Pleistocene deposits carried east from the Rocky Mountains by east–west trending streams. This alluvium also forms the massive Ogallala Aquifer that underlies the Llano and is the region's major water source. Later the Llano was isolated hydrologically from the rest of the High Plains by the downcutting of the Canadian River and was deprived of runoff from the Rockies by the headward erosion and stream piracy of the Pecos River. Distinct physical boundaries mark three sides: the rugged valley of the Canadian River in the north and the prominent Caprock and Mescalero Escarpments on the east and west respectively. To the south, the Llano merges imperceptibly with the Edwards Plateau. The surface of the Llano is covered with widespread eolian deposits of sands, marls, and loams. Sand sheets and dunes are found in many places, with the largest dune field extending across the New Mexican Llano into Bailey and Lamb Counties, Texas. Among the Llano's topographic features are numerous playa lakes and a few shallow draws that drain southeastward and form the headwaters of the Red, Brazos, and Colorado Rivers. These intermittent streams have cut scenic canyons into the eastern escarpment, most notably Palo Duro Canyon. Nearly all runoff on the Llano, however, accumulates in the thousands of ephemeral, freshwater playa lakes, which capture as much as two to three million acre-feet of water annually, although most of it soon evaporates.

Several theories explain the origin of the name Llano Estacado, though none is universally accepted. At present, a favored theory is that "estacado" refers to the palisaded or stockaded appearance of the caprock in many places, especially the west-facing escarpment in New Mexico.

See also WATER: Playa Lakes.

Otis W. Templer
Texas Tech University

Hunt, Charles B. *Natural Regions of the United States and Canada.* San Francisco: W. H. Freeman and Company, 1974. Leatherwood, Art, and Otis W. Templer. "The Llano Estacado: A Geographic Overview." In *Land of the Underground Rain: Water Usage on the High Plains*, edited by Donald W. Whisenhunt. Portales, NM: Eastern New Mexico State University, 1974: 12–22.

MESQUITE

Mesquite (genus *Prosopis*; family Fabaceae) is a thorny, woody shrub or tree that inhabits many arid and semiarid regions around the world. Honey mesquite (*P. glandulosa*) is native to the Southern Great Plains and is found in central and West Texas, western Oklahoma, and eastern New Mexico. It has increased in density and distribution since the late 1800s. Reasons for the increase are controversial but may include livestock grazing, reduction of fire frequency, climatic change, and increased atmospheric carbon dioxide. Mesquite is widely regarded as a noxious plant because of its interference with livestock production. Control efforts since the 1930s have included herbicide, mechanical, and prescribed fire treatments. Recent research suggests the potential benefits of mesquite if managed as a low-density savanna plant. Such benefits include wildlife habitat, livestock shading, nitrogen fixation, and wood products.

Seedpods of this legume are high in soluble carbohydrates and are consumed by wildlife and domestic livestock. Germination is enhanced by animal ingestion and fecal deposition. Most initial growth is toward taproot development. Potential growth form is few-stemmed and arboreal, but destruction of aboveground tissue stimulates sprouting from meristem at stem bases and causes a multi-stemmed, thorny growth. Leaves are bipinnately compound, winter-deciduous, and unpalatable; flowering is monoecious.

Mesquite is adapted to a variety of soils and environments and can grow a deep taproot as well as extensive shallow lateral roots. Water use can be phreatophytic (drawing from the water table or just above it), but mesquite will also grow on shallow-water sites and tolerate droughts by minimizing transpiration. Capacity to enrich soil fertility through nitrogen fixation and canopy shading may significantly alter flora beneath canopies. Mesquite may serve as a host plant, facilitating establishment of other plant species. Generally, dense stands of mesquite reduce growth of herbaceous plants. Dense stands are thought to reduce off-site water yield, but no studies have yet verified this.

R. James Ansley
Texas Agricultural Experiment Station
Vernon, Texas

Brown, J. R., and S. Archer. "Woody Plant Invasion of Grasslands: Establishment of Honey Mesquite (*Prosopis glandulosa* var. *glandulosa*) on Sites Differing in Herbaceous Biomass and Grazing History." *Oecologia* 80 (1989): 19–26. Simpson, B. B., ed. *Mesquite: Its Biology in Two Desert Ecosystems.* US/IBP Synthesis Series vol. 4. Stroudsberg PA: Dowden, Hutchinson, & Ross, Inc., 1977.

NATIONAL FORESTS

See SPORTS AND RECREATION: National Forests

NATIONAL GRASSLANDS

See SPORTS AND RECREATION: National Grasslands

NATIONAL PARKS

See SPORTS AND RECREATION: National Parks

NATIONAL WILDLIFE REFUGES

See SPORTS AND RECREATION: National Wildlife Refuges

NATURE WRITING

See LITERARY TRADITIONS: Nature Writing

NIOBRARA ECOTONE

The Niobrara ecotone, along the Niobrara River in north-central Nebraska, is an area of transition between habitats, plants, and animals with more eastern, western, southern, and northern distributions. The ecotone is most dramatic from the mouth of Minnechaduza Creek on the Fort Niobrara National Wildlife Refuge to the mouth of Plum Creek north of Ainsworth. In this fifty-mile stretch, the Niobrara flows through a gently rolling grassland in a wooded canyon nearly 400 feet deep. The canyon has developed during the last 20,000 years as local uplifting of the earth's surface has been countered by the actively downcutting Niobrara River. Several geological formations are exposed, leading to an array of soils, slopes, and sun angles. The ecotone is a mosaic of habitats on wet-to-dry and warm-to-cool sites, with shallow-to-deep and fertile-to-sterile soils.

South of the river, paper birch (*Betula papyrifera*) and aspen (*Populus tremuloides-grandidentata*) stands, with northern mannagrass (*Glyceria borealis*) and green orchids (*Habenaria hyperborea*) in the understory, grade into eastern deciduous woodland featuring basswood (*Tilia americana*), hop hornbeam (*Ostrya virginiana*), and hazelnut (*Corylus americana*). These woodlands are replaced by mesic tallgrass prairie stands on subirrigated low terraces, and bur oak (*Quercus macrocarpa*)–ponderosa pine (*Pinus ponderosa*) savanna and then Sandhills prairie on the dry upper slopes. North of the river the ecotone is a transition from western coniferous woodland dominated by ponderosa pine to northern mixed-grass prairie. Riparian woodlands, shrub lands, wetlands, and riverine habitats occur on the valley floor.

The Niobrara ecotone is particularly rich in species because of the many transitions between the distinct woodland, grassland, and wetland habitats in a relatively small area. The ecotone supports nearly two-thirds of the vascular plant species, more than half of the mammal and bird species, more than a third of the butterfly species, and more than a quarter of the fish species found in Nebraska. Fifty-five moss and eighty-six lichen species have been collected within the ecotone.

Whether on the canyon slopes and terraces or in the valley bottom, the forces of moving water, fire, and grazing continue to maintain this dynamic mosaic. Interestingly a northwest to southeast flowing river of the Miocene epoch (5 to 24 million years ago) also supported an impressive ecotone in what is now the middle Niobrara Valley. The fossil remains of a diverse group of browsers, grazers, predators, and aquatic species are represented in numerous quarries excavated in the contemporary Niobrara ecotone.

Allen A. Steuter
The Nature Conservancy

Kaul, Robert B., Gail E. Kantak, and Steven P. Churchill. "The Niobrara River Valley, a Postglacial Migration Corridor and Refugium of Forest Plants and Animals in the Grasslands of Central North America." *The Botanical Review* 54 (1988): 44–81. Steuter, Allen A., Bruce Jasch, Joel Ihnen, and Larry L. Tieszen. "Woodland/Grassland Boundary Changes in the Middle Niobrara Valley of Nebraska Identified by Delta Carbon 13 Values of Soil Organic Matter." *American Midland Naturalist* 124 (1990): 301–8.

OGALLALA AQUIFER

See WATER: Ogallala Aquifer

PALEOENVIRONMENTS

The most recent geologic period in Earth's history has been labeled the Quaternary, extending back approximately two to four million years. This period has been divided into two geologic epochs—the Pleistocene, which ended approximately 12,000 years ago, and the Holocene since that time. Over the course of the Quaternary, dramatic climatic shifts occurred that, to a great extent, shaped the rolling landscape and vegetation of today's Great Plains. Since the Late Pleistocene, three major trends have dominated the environmental history of the region. First, between about 18,000 and 10,000 years ago, glaciers began to waste, and climatic amelioration significantly altered the biota and landscape; second, during the early and middle portions of the Holocene, the climatic trend was toward increased dryness and warmth; and third, there followed a period of greater moisture and cooling in the late Holocene. It should be noted, however, that the climate is "time-transgressive," meaning it does not change simultaneously everywhere, and therefore its effects on Plains biota would have varied over the years and across space.

In recent simulation models large-scale climatic shifts have been shown to be the result of changing atmospheric circulation patterns caused by shifts in the orientation of the earth's axis. At 18,000 years ago, the Laurentide ice sheet, while cooling temperatures across North America, caused a split in the jet stream. A deflection of the southern branch of the jet stream brought moister conditions to what is now the southwestern United States, while anticyclonic winds, generated by the ice sheet, brought prevailing easterlies and dry air to the northwest, instead of the usual moisture-laden westerlies. Shifts in the jet stream also appear to have been a major factor in changing climatic patterns during the Holocene.

Individual faunal species and communities were greatly affected by the Pleistocene climatic and vegetation shifts. Late Pleistocene faunal communities have been referred to as "disharmonious," "intermingled," and "nonanalog assemblages" to describe the heterogeneous nature of the species composition. R. Dale Guthrie, a mammalian biogeographer, described these communities as a "patchy mosaic" that allowed for increased numbers and diversity of herbivores. In the Great Plains a dry and cool wooded parkland existed, with a hardwood forest of oak, aspen, and cottonwood to the east and a coniferous forest to the west. In the open areas, sagebrush was dominant. With glacial retreat, the eastern forest followed the ice northward into southern Manitoba and Saskatchewan, while the western coniferous forest moved upslope into the Rockies.

During the late Pleistocene, faunal communities were compressed, and members of such diverse habitats as alpine tundra and xeric grasslands were living together in the same community. A patchy mosaic of Ice Age plants and animals has also been applied to describe this time period. With glacial retreat came a collapse in the Ice Age communities and a reduction in biotic diversity. More than one-half of North America's large mammals became extinct. Less-nutritious Holocene vegetation communities, which had defensive responses to grazing and browsing, replaced this mosaic of highly nutritious late Pleistocene vegetation. The change was probably too abrupt for the adaptive abilities of many herbivores. Paleoindian hunters may have been an additional cause of the mammals' extinction.

The shift from Pleistocene to Holocene environments was the most dramatic period of climatic change in recent earth history. Profound reorganization of biotic communities resulted, with a pattern of diverse patchy environments being replaced by a pattern of zonal communities—from "plaids" to "stripes," according to Guthrie. The megafaunal species that survived, such as the bison, were significantly smaller in size, but they were able to expand their range to become the predominant species in the Great Plains.

Increased warmth and generally drier conditions characterized the early Holocene. Active stream alluviation occurred throughout the region, with wetlands and marshes common in the Southern Plains. The trend toward increased warmth and decreased precipitation peaked around 8500 B.P. The dominance of the Pacific westerlies and the seasonal peak in solar radiation were important factors during this climatic episode, often referred to as the Hypsithermal or Altithermal. Drought-resistant grasslands expanded, and lake levels dropped in a time-transgressive trend that began first in the Northern Plains and then extended later to the Central and Southern Plains. For example, on the prairies of Manitoba thermal maxima occurred about 7,000 years ago, with summer temperatures as much as 3.5°F warmer and annual precipitation about one inch less than today.

By about 4,500 years ago the onset of modern, or Neoglacial, conditions began, but again this was not uniform across the region. Between 3,000 and 4,000 years ago, the mid-Holocene prairies of northern Alberta and Manitoba were replaced by boreal forests. In the Nebraska Sandhills, increased groundwater, which changed the mid-Holocene marshlands to lakes, signaled the beginning of the Neoglacial in the Central Plains around 3,700 years ago.

While the magnitude of the climatic shift from the mid-Holocene thermal maxima to the Neoglacial was nowhere as severe as the Pleistocene-Holocene shift, significant changes did take place. In the Colorado Front Range, expansion of alpine glaciers occurred, while in the Southern Plains increased moisture permitted soil formation, and an open oak woodland became established in central Texas.

The increased effective moisture of the Late Holocene, particularly between A.D. 1550 and 1880, appears to have had a positive effect on bison populations. It has been proposed that high forage production led to increased population density, larger herds, and decreased migration. Plains groups appear to have taken advantage of this trend, as is evident by large bison kill sites, such as the Glenrock and Vore Sites in Wyoming, and abundant evidence of bison from Central Plains archeological sites.

During the last hundred years the climate has shifted to a warm-dry regime. How long this will last is unknown. It is important to know about Plains paleoenvironments because they provide an understanding of how Holocene biotic communities developed and suggest models for likely future climate change and for the thoughtful management of ecosystems.

See also NATIVE AMERICANS: Archaic Period Sites; Paleo-Indians.

Kenneth P. Cannon
National Park Service
Lincoln, Nebraska

Guthrie, R. Dale. *Frozen Fauna of the Mammoth Steppe: The Story of Blue Babe*. Chicago: University of Chicago Press, 1990. Porter, Stephen C., ed. *The Late Pleistocene*, vol. 1 of *Late-Quaternary Environments of the United States*, ed. H. E. Wright, Jr. Minneapolis: University of Minnesota Press, 1983. Wright, Herbert E., Jr., ed. *The Holocene*, vol. 2 of *Late-Quaternary Environments of the United States*. Minneapolis: University of Minnesota Press, 1983.

PALLISER'S TRIANGLE

James Hector, a member of the British expedition of 1857–60 to the western interior of Canada, led by Capt. James Palliser, described the "arid district" of the Canadian Prairies as "a triangular region," with its apex reaching 52 north latitude and its base extending from 100 west to 114 west along the U.S. border (49 north latitude). This is the genesis of the term "Palliser's Triangle," which is still widely used. The cities of Lethbridge and Medicine Hat, Alberta, and Swift Current, Saskatchewan, are located within Palliser's Triangle, which is better described as experiencing subhumid or semiarid rather than truly arid conditions. Annual precipitation averages ten to fourteen inches, to which winter snowfall contributes two to three inches of water equivalent. This results in a climatic designation of steppe rather than desert or semidesert. Within the triangle, as Hector himself reported, there are localities with more humid environments. These include the Cypress Hills, straddling the Alberta-Saskatchewan border, receiving fifteen to nineteen inches annual precipitation and supporting a forest cover, especially on north-facing slopes. In most of the region, which occupies about 73,000 square miles, shortgrass prairie is the natural vegetation.

The southeast corner of the triangle defined by Hector lies in today's southwestern Manitoba, but the true dry belt of the Canadian Prairies extends only about as far east as 104 west on the forty-ninth parallel. Ranching, dryland wheat cultivation, and oil and gas extraction are the main industries, with some specialized irrigation agriculture around Lethbridge. Near Val Marie in southern Saskatchewan, about 300 square miles have been included in the Grasslands National Park Reserve.

Alexander H. Paul
University of Regina

Hector, James. "On the Capabilities for Settlement of the Central Part of British North America." *Edinburgh New Philosophical Journal*, New Series 14 (1861): 263–68. Spry, Irene M. *The Palliser Expedition: An Account of John Palliser's British North American Expedition, 1857–1860*. Toronto: Macmillan of Canada, 1963. Warkentin, John. *The Western Interior of Canada: A Record of Geographical Discovery*. Toronto: McClelland and Stewart, 1964.

PHYSIOGRAPHY

The Great Plains, as defined in Nevin M. Fenneman's classic work, *Physiography of Western United States* (1931), is a distinct physiographic region that lies between the Rocky Mountains to the west and the Canadian Shield, Central Lowlands, and Gulf Coastal Plain regions to the east, and stretches from the Canadian Prairies in the north to the Edwards Plateau in Texas. Although broadly described as a low relief part of the North American interior, the Plains landscape is complex and diverse and owes its origin to a variety of geologic processes, with specific subregions dominated by fluvial, eolian, volcanic, or glacial landforms. This diversity is best discussed with reference to traditionally recognized subregions.

The High Plains, stretching from Nebraska to Texas, can be thought of as the core of the Great Plains in terms of its geologic history, its current morphological expression, and the perception of a vast featureless landscape. The High Plains's surface is constructional in origin, representing the accumulation of fluvial sediments of Tertiary age that were shed from the Rockies in a series of west-to-east trending river valleys and alluvial plains, with coeval eolian (wind-blown) sediments blanketing the uplands. Following this accumulation phase, major rivers that rise in the Rockies (Platte, Arkansas, Canadian, Pecos), plus rivers that originate on the High Plains surface (Niobrara, Republican, Smoky Hill, Cimarron, Red), cut distinct valleys through this former accumulation surface and formed a series of downward-stepping terraces. Erosionally isolated remnants of the High Plains include Scotts Bluff and Chimney Rock National Monuments, located along the North Platte River in Nebraska, that have long served as landmarks for travelers moving westward. Outside of the major river valleys, eolian and other processes dominate the relatively undissected parts of the High Plains surface. The most notable eolian landscape is the Nebraska Sandhills, the largest sand dune field in the Western Hemisphere. Individual dunes can be more than 300 feet in height and extend for many miles. Although the dunes are now grass-covered, they have been active multiple times during the last few thousand years when regional climates were drier. At the southern end of the High Plains in Texas, on the Llano Estacado, thick accumulations of wind-blown sediments cover Tertiary fluvial deposits and have produced a flat landscape, one that is punctuated by tens of thousands of mostly dry lake basins, or playas, and a series of narrow ephemeral stream channels that are locally referred to as draws.

The northern boundary of the High Plains is defined by the Pine Ridge Escarpment, with three key Great Plains physiographic subregions lying farther to the north. Just north of the High Plains, the Unglaciated Missouri Plateau of eastern Montana, eastern Wyoming, and the western Dakotas consists of broad tablelands where the Tertiary cover has been mostly stripped by the Missouri River and its tributaries. The tablelands are punctuated by a number of isolated mountain ranges and areas of deeply dissected badlands topography where the Tertiary cover is still present. Several mountain ranges in Montana (Highwood, Bearpaw, Little Rocky, Judith, Big Snowy, Big Belt, Little Belt, Castle, and Crazy) originated as masses of intrusive and/or volcanic igneous rock. The best examples of badlands topography are the White River Badlands of Badlands National Park in South Dakota and the Little Missouri Badlands of Theodore Roosevelt National Park in North Dakota. The eastern boundary of the Missouri Plateau is defined by the Missouri Escarpment, where the landscape descends 500 to 650 feet to the glaciated Central Lowlands. The Black Hills of western South Dakota are often treated as a distinct subregion. They originated as a folded and thrusted mass of ancient sedimentary and crystalline rocks similar to, and geologically related to, the Rockies farther west. The presidential faces on Mount Rushmore National Memorial are carved in granites that make up the core of this mountain range, whereas Wind

Cave and Jewel Cave were formed by dissolution of the tilted limestones that encircle the crystalline core. Devils Tower National Monument is a near-vertical erosional remnant of an igneous intrusion on the western periphery of the Black Hills in Wyoming.

Farther north and east are the Glaciated Interior Plains of northeastern Montana, northern and eastern North Dakota, and eastern South Dakota in the United States and Alberta, Saskatchewan, and Manitoba in Canada. For this encyclopedia, the northern limits of the Great Plains in Canada have been defined on the basis of a biogeographic boundary, the Parkland Belt, which roughly corresponds to the Manitoba Escarpment on the east-northeast and the North Saskatchewan River valley on the north. Within this part of the Glaciated Interior Plains, remnants of Tertiary fluvial sediments shed from the Rockies form prominent topographic features, including the Hand Hills and Swan Hills of western Alberta, the Cypress Hills of southern Saskatchewan, Wood Mountain in southern Saskatchewan, northern Montana, and northern North Dakota, and Turtle Mountain in southern Manitoba and northern North Dakota. Elsewhere, the landscape is mostly underlain by sedimentary rocks of Cretaceous age and bears the imprint of the numerous glaciations of the Pleistocene Ice Ages, especially the most recent glaciation that ended 10,000 to 12,000 years ago. Accordingly, Cretaceous rocks are mostly covered by glacial sediments and landforms, and the landscape is flat to gently rolling with numerous shallow internally drained depressions, scattered low-relief hills, and narrow incised river valleys that originated as meltwater channels. The Red Deer River valley, east of Calgary, Alberta, is an example of a former meltwater channel, with postglacial dissection having created the extensive badlands topography that is best known for the fossils discovered at Dinosaur Provincial Park. The numerous glacial advances have also disrupted and diverted the preglacial drainage in the region, so that major rivers that originate in the Canadian Rockies, like the North Saskatchewan and South Saskatchewan, used to flow to Hudson Bay and the Arctic Ocean, but now flow into remnants of large glacial lakes in Manitoba. At an even grander scale, the upper Missouri River used to flow out of Montana and North Dakota to Hudson Bay as well, but it was diverted southeast by the glaciers to join the Mississippi River and flow to the Gulf of Mexico.

The western margins of the High Plains remain connected to the Rockies only along the Gangplank of southeastern Wyoming and along a short reach between Denver and Colorado Springs, which forms the divide between the Platte and Arkansas River drainages. Elsewhere, the Colorado Piedmont lies between the High Plains and the Front Range of the Rockies, at elevations distinctly lower than the High Plains surface, and consists of a series of river terraces on which major urban centers of Colorado (Colorado Springs, Denver, and Fort Collins) have developed. These terraces represent former floodplain levels of the South Platte and Arkansas Rivers and their principal Rocky Mountain tributaries and were formed as they cut down through and removed the old High Plains's surface and its underlying Tertiary fluvial deposits. In many places, terrace surfaces and the surrounding dissected bedrock landscape are covered by small sand dune fields as well. The Raton Section, straddling the border between Colorado and New Mexico, lies between the High Plains and the Rockies and is a landscape dominated by recent volcanic activity, with volcanic rocks covering Tertiary fluvial deposits and older sedimentary rocks. Prominent features include lava-capped tablelands such as Raton Mesa and Mesa de Maya and a variety of volcanic peaks. Capulin Volcano National Monument, for example, rising almost 1,000 feet above the surrounding landscape, is a cinder cone volcano that erupted between 10,000 and 4,000 years ago. Farther south, the broad Pecos Valley lies between the Sangre de Cristo Range of the Rockies and the Mescalero Escarpment, which defines the western boundary to the Llano Estacado. In addition to the Pecos River, which originates in the Sangre de Cristos and flows south through the Edwards Plateau to the Rio Grande, key elements of the landscape here include many sinks, depressions, and caves, referred to collectively as karst topography, that formed as a result of the dissolution of ancient limestone bedrock. The best-known solution features are found at Carlsbad Caverns National Park.

Two subregions can be recognized to the east of the High Plains. The Plains Border of southern Nebraska, Kansas, and northern Oklahoma is a more dissected continuation of the High Plains, as a number of west to east flowing rivers (Republican, Solomon, Saline, Smoky Hill, Arkansas, Cimarron, North Canadian) have cut broad valleys through the Tertiary cover, which is only preserved along relatively narrow stream divides in the western part of this subregion. The Low Rolling Plains subregion farther south in Oklahoma and West Texas is even more dissected, cut by the Canadian, Washita, Red, and Brazos Rivers, and completely separated from the High Plains by the prominent Caprock Escarpment. Both areas have in common westward-dipping pre-Tertiary sedimentary rocks, the dissection of which has produced a series of alternating north–south oriented, relatively featureless plains developed in easily eroded shales and prominent east-facing scarps developed in more resistant sandstones or limestones. In addition to the dissected and scarped terrain, other notable features include the Arbuckle Mountains and Wichita Mountains of south-central Oklahoma, where ancient sedimentary and crystalline rocks were uplifted long ago and still remain at elevations 650 to 1,000 feet higher than the surrounding plains.

The southern limits of the High Plains, or Llano Estacado, merge almost imperceptibly with the Edwards Plateau, the southernmost extension of the Great Plains. The landscape here consists of broad tablelands formed in pre-Tertiary limestones, punctuated by deeply incised bedrock valleys of the major rivers. The Pecos River, for example, flows north to south until it merges with the Rio Grande, whereas the Colorado River and its tributaries drain the northern part of the plateau, and the Nueces, San Antonio, and Guadalupe Rivers drain the southern and southeastern margins. The Central Texas Uplift to the north and east of the Edwards Plateau is actually a topographic basin (often referred to as the Llano Basin) that represents an exhumed landscape of ancient upwarped sedimentary rocks surrounding a crystalline core that was exposed as limestones of the Edwards Plateau were completely removed by the Colorado River and its tributaries. Dissected remnants of limestone tablelands, referred to as the Callahan Divide, occur north of the Central Texas Uplift and Colorado Valley and represent the divide between the Colorado drainage and that of the Brazos River, whereas more continuous dissected limestone topography farther east, wholly within the Brazos drainage, is referred to as the Lampasas Cut Plain. The southeastern margin of the Edwards Plateau is deeply dissected and referred to as the Texas Hill Country, whereas the Balcones Escarpment, at the foot of which the major urban centers of San Antonio and Austin have grown, separates the Hill Country from the Gulf Coastal Plain Physiographic Province.

Michael D. Blum
Louisiana State University

Fenneman, Nevin M. *Physiography of Western United States.* New York: McGraw Hill, 1931. Klassen, R. W. "Quaternary Geology of the Southern Canadian Interior Plains." In *Quaternary Geology of Canada and Greenland*, edited by R. J. Fulton. Ottawa: Geological Society of Canada, 1989: 97–174. Thornbury, William D. *Regional Geomorphology of the United States.* New York: Wiley, 1965.

PLAYA LAKES

See WATER: Playa Lakes

PRAIRIE PRESERVATION

Prairie preservation in both the United States and Canada began under the aegis of the national governments. In Canada efforts began in the second decade of the twentieth century when the parks branch of the Department of Interior sought suitable prairie habitat for restoring pronghorn antelope populations. Three reserves became dominion parks in 1922—Nemiskam, Wawaskesy, and Menissawok—and all subsequently were ceded to the Provinces of Alberta and Saskatchewan during the 1930s and 1940s. Initial U.S. efforts were a reaction to the Dust Bowl. Under the 1934 Bankhead-Jones Farm Tenant Act, the federal government acquired 11.3 million acres of submarginal farmland. Of this, 2.64 million acres in the Great Plains were eventually designated as national grasslands.

Organized efforts to preserve prairies date to the 1930s in the United States, when the Ecological Society of America and the National Research Council began advocating the inclusion of a prairie area in the national park system. During the 1950s, the National Park

Service began to investigate sites in Kansas. The combined efforts of several environmental groups, the National Park Service, and key Kansas legislators finally succeeded in creating a 10,894-acre preserve in the Flint Hills, officially designated as the National Tallgrass Prairie Preserve in 1996. In Canada, the Saskatchewan Natural History Society began lobbying for a prairie national park in the late 1950s. This effort eventually materialized in the Grasslands National Park in Alberta, established 1981.

Among organizations The Nature Conservancy has most aggressively pursued prairie preservation, thanks in large part to the philanthropy of the late Katherine Ordway (1899–1979). As of the mid-1990s The Nature Conservancy had acquired more than 550,000 acres of grasslands in the Great Plains, the largest preserves being Cross Ranch, North Dakota; Samuel H. Ordway Jr. Memorial Prairie, South Dakota; Konza Prairie, Kansas; Tallgrass Prairie Preserve, Oklahoma; and Niobrara Valley Preserve, Nebraska. Although not as visible, the efforts of many smaller organizations are also noteworthy. Such groups target relatively small, diverse, and often isolated prairie remnants. Preserves range from the 26.5-acre St. James Living Prairie Museum in metropolitan Winnipeg, Manitoba, to the 1,114-acre Maddin Ranch near Colorado City, Texas, where the owner, the Native Prairies Association of Texas, is working with the Natural Resources Conservation Service to restore the prairie ecosystem.

Promising, but as yet unproven, efforts are the public-private partnerships that have proliferated since the late 1980s. These partnerships include the North American Waterfowl Management Plan, signed by Canada and the United States in 1986, which gave rise to the Prairie Pothole Joint Venture and the Prairie Habitat Joint Venture. The Great Plains Partnership, initiated by the Western Governors Association, has attempted to coordinate ongoing scientific research and data collection with conservation activities. The Prairie Conservation Act Plan (1989–1995), a product of the World Wildlife Fund and the governments of Manitoba, Saskatchewan, and Alberta, led to a variety of initiatives as well as actual land reserves. More recently, the U.S. Fish and Wildlife Service initiated the Sandhills Management Plan. Although such partnerships may substantially reform land-management practices throughout the Great Plains, the long-term potential for large-scale prairie restoration remains an open question.

See also SPORTS AND RECREATION: National Grasslands.

Rebecca Conard
Wichita State University

Samson, Fred B., and Fritz L. Knopf, eds. *Prairie Conservation: Preserving North America's Most Endangered Ecosystem.* Washington DC: Island Press, 1996.

RATTLESNAKES

Rattlesnakes (*Crotalus* spp. and *Sistrurus* spp.) are found throughout the Great Plains, with ten species (nine *Crotalus*, one *Sistrurus*) ranging from northern Mexico up through the Prairie Provinces of Canada. They live in a number of diverse habitats, including deserts, grasslands, and woodlands. In the Great Plains, rattlesnakes are often associated with prairie dog towns.

During winter, large groups of rattlesnakes can often be found in hibernacula (cavities or burrows where they overwinter), sometimes with other species of snakes. Rattlesnakes give birth to live young, and litter sizes range from one to twenty-five, often depending on the size of the female. Rattlesnakes feed on small mammals, birds, or in some cases, reptiles and amphibians, using infrared sensors located in pits in the front of their heads to locate their prey (hence the name pit vipers). Rattlesnakes have a keen ability to track prey they have envenomated and released. The toxicity of rattlesnake bites varies with the species and size of the snake. Rattlesnake venom causes the necrosis of living tissues and, in some species, includes neurotoxins that affect the nervous system of the prey.

Dangerous and feared, rattlesnakes are widely represented in the folklore, myths, art, and literature of Native American and European American peoples of the Great Plains. Their dangerous reputation (often exaggerated) has led to such traditions as the "rattlesnake roundup" that involves the slaughter of many individuals. Roundups, along with habitat fragmentation, have resulted in drastic consequences for the long-term persistence of rattlesnake populations.

Geoffrey R. Smith
William Jewell College

Klauber, L. M. *Rattlesnakes: Their Habits, Life Histories, and Influence on Mankind.* Berkeley: University of California Press, 1956. Rubio, M. *Rattlesnake: Portrait of a Predator.* Washington DC: Smithsonian Institution Press, 1998.

RIVERS

See WATER: Rivers

ROADRUNNERS

The roadrunner (*Geococcyx californianus*) is primarily a ground-dwelling member of the cuckoo family that inhabits the southern extremes of the Great Plains region. The range of the roadrunner extends across the southwestern United States and into central Mexico. The northern perimeter extends through the Texas Panhandle and Oklahoma into southern Kansas and west into southeastern Colorado. Habitat preference varies widely within this region but includes both desert conditions in the south to grasslands in the north.

The adult roadrunner has a total body length of about twenty-four inches and is designed for speed. With its zygodactyl feet, characterized by two toes forward and two toes back, the roadrunner is an efficient predator on many species of insects and most small reptiles, including the rattlesnake. Both male and female have buff-colored undersides with a mixture of black, bronze, and buff feathers on the breast. Both sexes possess a crest on top of the head.

Nesting habits of the roadrunner are consistent throughout the Plains. Courtship begins in the early spring with nests being constructed in shrubs and small trees at heights of from three to about fifteen feet. Nests are shallow and from eighteen to twenty inches in diameter. The first clutch of eggs (from a total of two or three) is laid in late April to early May. The incubation period lasts about eighteen days, with both parents sharing all nesting chores. Juveniles leave the nest at about fourteen days of age and remain secluded in underbrush for an additional eight to ten days. Parenting chores by adults continue during this period. Upon emergence after the ten-day seclusion period the juveniles are prepared to fend for themselves.

Wyman Meinzer
Benjamin, Texas

Bent, Arthur Cleveland. *Life Histories of North American Cuckoos, Goatsuckers, Hummingbirds, and Their Allies.* New York: Dover Publications, 1948. Meinzer, Wyman. *The Roadrunner.* Lubbock: Texas Tech University Press, 1993.

SANDHILLS

The Central and Southern Great Plains contains the greatest concentration of windblown sand in North America, and the Sandhills, covering 20,000 square miles of central Nebraska, is the largest of these Great Plains sand dune fields. Currently stabilized by prairie vegetation, the Sandhills is one of the world's premier grasslands for cattle grazing. The dune landscape is interspersed with about 2,000 shallow lakes and more than a million acres of wetlands. These diverse wildlife and plant communities present a sharp contrast to the adjacent dryland communities of the dunes.

Three major dune types occur in the Sandhills: barchanoid-ridge and megabarchan dunes, typically 120 to 300 feet high and one to five miles long, formed by unidirectional winds from the northwest; simple linear dunes, forty to sixty feet high and one mile long, formed by winds from two directions; and compound parabolic dunes, fifty to seventy feet high and 1,400 feet long, also formed by unidirectional winds from the northwest. Both linear and parabolic dunes also occur superimposed on the larger megabarchan and barchanoid-ridge dunes. Sand sheets, areas of flat-lying sand with scattered small dunes, are the only portion of the Sandhills that lend themselves to typical Great Plains farming practices.

The most crucial factor in the formation of dune fields, given a supply of sand and sufficient winds, is a sparse vegetative cover. Radiocarbon dating of soils buried by dune sand indicate several periods of widespread blowing sand between 250 and 1,000 years ago that were caused by droughts more severe than any of the past 100 years. These episodes of aridity have made it difficult to document older periods of dune sand activity because they "cannibalized" and buried the earlier history of the dune field.

However, geologists have discovered ancient river valleys within the Sandhills that were blocked and partially filled by dune sand during major droughts. Lakes and marshes that formed behind the sand dams were sites of peat and/or mud deposition, as well as local wind-blown sand layers. Radiocarbon dates from these deposits indicate major periods of dune sand activity during the following times: 13,000 to 12,000 years ago; 8,000 to 5,000 years ago; and 3,500 to 2,800 years ago.

Analysis of the mineral grains that make up the sand in the Sandhills indicates that there is more quartz and less feldspar present than occurs in possible source sediments. These include sandstones of the Ogallala and Arikaree Groups and the North and South Platte Rivers. The most probable explanation for this discrepancy is a reduction of sand-sized feldspar (which is more easily broken than quartz) to dust-sized particles via grain impacts during windstorms. This would require many cycles of aridity and suggests the Sandhills has a history that may extend more than 100,000 years. Only bits and pieces of that record may have been preserved and will require much work to discover and interpret.

See also WATER: Sandhills Lakes.

James B. Swinehart
University of Nebraska–Lincoln

Loope, David B., James B. Swinehart, and Jon P. Mason. "Dune-dammed Paleovalleys of the Nebraska Sand Hills: Intrinsic Versus Climatic-controls on the Accumulation of Lake and Marsh Sediments." *Geological Society of America Bulletin* 107 (1995): 396–406. McIntosh, Charles B. *The Nebraska Sand Hills: The Human Landscape.* Lincoln: University of Nebraska Press, 1996.

SANDHILLS LAKES

See WATER: Sandhills Lakes

SHELTERBELTS

A shelterbelt is an area planted with trees and shrubs arranged in rows to form a barrier to reduce surface winds. Planted throughout the Great Plains, shelterbelts provide wind protection for homes, farms and ranches, highways, livestock, crops, and a diversity of habitats for numerous species of wildlife. This biodiversity helps maintain various predator-prey relationships and contributes to biological control of crop pests.

Shelterbelts were first planted in the region by early settlers. Many brought tree seeds and seedlings from the East or gathered seedlings from local native stands and planted them around their homes for protection, firewood, and beauty. During the agricultural expansion of the early 1900s, much of the native grassland was plowed and planted to wheat. As the drought conditions of the 1920s intensified, many agricultural fields in the region were abandoned, and wind erosion escalated.

In 1935, the U.S. Forest Service undertook the largest tree-planting effort ever conducted, the Prairie States Forestry Project. During the next eight years, with labor provided by the Works Project Administration (WPA), more than 222 million tree seedlings were planted, creating in excess of 18,500 miles of shelterbelts. Most of these shelterbelts were ten to sixteen rows wide and a mile long. Even under the dry conditions of the time, most seedlings survived and for the next thirty to forty years provided protection to the agricultural lands of the region.

While many of these original shelterbelts still exist around farmsteads, most of the wide-row field shelterbelts have been removed to make way for center-pivot irrigation systems or field consolidation. Some have been replaced with single or double-row field windbreaks. Today, the Natural Resource Conservation Service has primary responsibility for shelterbelts and soil conservation efforts. In cooperation with state forestry agencies and local conservation districts, more than 20 million tree and shrub seedlings are planted annually throughout the Great Plains, many in shelterbelts.

Similar efforts occurred in the Prairie Provinces under the direction of the Prairie Farm Rehabilitation Administration. Since the beginning of tree planting efforts in 1892, more than 500 million seedlings have been distributed to landowners, and today four to six million seedlings are distributed to landowners each year.

Shelterbelts work by reducing wind speed on the leeward side of the shelterbelt. The amount of wind speed reduction is determined by the number and arrangement of trees and shrubs in the shelterbelt: the denser the shelterbelt, the greater the reduction. The size of the protected area depends on the length and height of the shelterbelt. For example, a twenty-five-foot tall, moderately dense shelterbelt will reduce wind speed for a distance of 250 to 500 feet leeward. In this sheltered zone, temperature and humidity are increased slightly and evaporation is reduced. The goal of any shelterbelt planting is to use the microclimate created in the sheltered area to the advantage of the landowner. In winter the reduced wind speed means a significant reduction in wind chill temperatures and a 20 to 40 percent reduction in the amount of energy needed to heat a home. Outdoor activities are more pleasant in farmyards or livestock areas when wind protection is available. Livestock that are protected require less feed and suffer fewer heath problems. Field shelterbelts help control wind erosion and increase production of crops on sheltered fields by an average of 12 to 15 percent, providing producers with increased economic returns. Living snow fences of trees and shrubs planted along highways reduce snow removal costs and decrease traffic accidents.

James R. Brandle
University of Nebraska–Lincoln

Brandle, James R., D. L. Hintz, and J. W. Sturrock. *Windbreak Technology.* Amsterdam: Elsevier Science Publishers B.V., 1988. Droze, Wilmon H. *Trees, Prairies, and People: A History of Tree Planting in the Plains States.* Denton: Texas Woman's University Press, 1977. Howe, J. A. G. "One Hundred Years of Prairie Forestry." *Prairie Forum* 11 (1986): 243–51.

SOIL EROSION

Soil erosion is the removal of soil from a position on the landscape. The two main agents of soil erosion are wind and water. The type of erosion that occurs is generally related to climate. Because the climate of the Great Plains is relatively dry, and strong winds are common, wind erosion is widespread throughout the region. On May 12, 1934, for example, winds carried an estimated 200 million tons of soil from the Southern Great Plains over 1,500 miles to the Atlantic Ocean. Ideal conditions for wind erosion are loose, finely divided and dry soil on a bare, smooth surface.

Wind erosion moves soil in three ways: suspension, saltation, and surface creep. Very fine particles (less than 0.05 mm in diameter) can be blown into the air and carried in suspension for long distances. The particles fall out of suspension when the wind velocity is reduced or they are washed out by rain. Soil grains between 0.05 mm and 0.5 mm in diameter are too heavy to be suspended. These grains are lifted briefly in the air, move a short distance, and fall back to the surface. Most soil eroded by wind moves by this type of motion (saltation). Saltating grains generally bounce along the surface of the soil until the wind velocity lessens or they meet some obstruction. These grains may knock other grains into the air. Soil grains between 0.5 mm and 1 mm in diameter are too large to be lifted into the wind stream. They are bumped along the soil surface by saltating grains in a movement called surface creep. Soil grains moving by saltation are the keys to wind erosion. Saltating grains increase the number of smaller and larger particles that move in suspension or by soil creep.

Water erosion is more prominent in humid regions. It does, however, occur in the Great Plains especially on sloping landscapes. In 1992 the average annual water erosion rate on cropland was estimated at 3.1 tons per acre. The movement of soil by water is a complex process that is influenced by the amount, duration, and intensity of rainfall, as well as by the nature of the soil, ground cover, and slope of the land. Raindrops play a substantial part in the movement of soil by water. Soil grains are detached from the soil mass by the force of raindrops striking the soil grains. The soil grains may then be splashed, rolled, slid, or carried in suspension along the land surface.

There are three types of water erosion: sheet, rill, and gully. Sheet erosion is the rather uniform removal of thin layers of soil over the entire soil surface. Sheet erosion is the least recognizable type of erosion. It probably occurs rarely because minute channeling usually takes place soon after erosion begins. Rill erosion occurs in small well-defined channels or streamlets where there is a concentration of flow. These rills are large and stable enough to be seen. However, they can be removed by normal tillage operations. Most rill erosion occurs on recently cultivated soil. Gully erosion produces large channels that cannot be erased by normal tillage operations.

Mark Kuzila
Conservation and Survey Division
University of Nebraska–Lincoln

Schwab, G. O., R. K. Frevert, K. K. Barnes, and T. W. Edminster. *Elementary Soil and Water Engineering.* New York: John Wiley and Sons, Inc. 1957. Stallings, J. H. *Soil Conservation.* Englewood Cliffs NJ: Prentice-Hall, Inc. 1957. Troeh, F. R., J. A. Hobbs, and R. L. Donahue. *Soil and Water Conservation.* Englewood Cliffs NJ: Prentice-Hall, Inc. 1980.

SOILS

Soil is the product of the weathering action of climate and biological organisms on the parent material as modified by the topography of the site and the time the parent material has been in place. Parent materials are those geologic deposits that have remained stable long enough for a soil to form in them. In the Plains, parent materials are for the most part medium textured and calcareous. Plains soils formed under forest and later under grasses. Most upland soils are old enough for weathering to have formed soil horizons in the upper meter of the parent material. Humus content is normally higher in soils of the Northern Plains than in those farther south; this is associated with soil temperature gradients. Lime tends to exist at a more shallow depth in soils of the drier western Plains than in those of the eastern Plains, if all else is equal. In addition High Plains soils tend to contain as much as 60 percent volcanic ash. Topography affects the microclimate of the site and often affects age and ultimately the soil that is forming there. If the condition of all of the interacting factors is known, it is possible to predict soil conditions at any given site.

Classification systems are used to name soils. The United States currently classifies soil with six levels of abstraction: order, suborder, great group, subgroup, family, and series. In Canada the same number of levels are used but with a slightly different approach: order, great group, subgroup, family, series, and type. The U.S. system recognizes "type" but considers it to be a phase of a series rather than a separate taxonomic level. Families in the U.S. system are defined on criteria such as particle size class, mineralogy, temperature groups, and several others. Canadian soils are all "frigid" by the U.S. family designation, because their average temperature at twenty inches is less than 46° F. Mesic and thermic categories (46–59°F and greater than 59°F, respectively) are characteristic of the Southern Plains. Differences in the two classification systems are not great enough to interfere seriously with field operations along the forty-ninth parallel, and both serve their purposes well.

The archetypal Plains soil is classified as an Ustoll in the United States and a Chernozemic soil (Boroll in the United States) in Canada. Chernozemic soils (Borolls) formed in association with tall to short prairie grasses in a semiarid climate and in a temperature zone where the average annual soil temperature is between 32°F and 49°F. For example, a soil in the Elstow series in the Prairie Provinces is in the Chernozemic order, Dark Brown great group, Eluviated subgroup, Elstow series, and Elstow loam type. No family is identified. A similar soil in the United States is the Hol-dredge Series, which falls in the fine silty mixed mesic family, Typic subgroup, Argiustoll great group, Ustoll suborder, and Mollisol order.

Sand fields (dunes and sand sheets), as well as alluvial-colluvial deposits, also exist in many parts of the region. Soils on these deposits are very recent and are classified in the same order (Entisols) to recognize their lack of development. These sandy soils (Psamments) tend to be very low in the organic agents that bind soil particles together into aggregates. This, and the constant bombardment of sand-size particles at the surface, causes sand particles to dislodge and blow in the wind if they are exposed. Southwest Kansas, the Oklahoma and Texas Panhandles, southeastern and northeastern Colorado, and northeastern New Mexico are at risk of this. By far the largest area threatened, however, is the Sandhills region of Nebraska. Roughly one-third of the state consists of aeolian sand that is currently mobile in certain areas and is in delicate balance with its current grass vegetation and the "blow out" areas that continually form. During the 1930s—the longest drought in the Plains in recent time—as much as one-half the topsoil was lost from more than 20 million acres of Plains land. Considering parent material, topography, and soil age, in the windy climate of the Plains, wind erosion is a significant and continuing hazard.

The soils of the Plains can be very productive in most areas if there is water to irrigate them and if accepted erosion-control measures are practiced. Minimum tillage and windbreaks are very useful in this respect. Nitrogen fertilizer is needed for the high crop yields expected, but natural levels are more than adequate for the range grasses that cover large parts of the region. Organic matter has declined, but its condition is such that the amounts remain adequate on the siltier soils, at least. Shortages of elements such as phosphorus, zinc, and sulfur are critical for cropland in some areas because of the low acidity of the soils. If they are carefully managed and treated as part of a fragile ecosystem, the soils of the Great Plains can continue to supply a large part of the earth's food supply for generations.

David Lewis
University of Nebraska–Lincoln

Department of the Interior. Soil Working Group on the Ogallala Aquifer. *Missouri Basin-Great Plains Caucus.* Washington DC: Government Printing Office, 1980: 2–11.

SOIL SURVEYS

A soil survey shows the kinds of soil that exist in a given region and their exact location on a map of the landscape. Names are assigned to soils at these locations in accordance with properties they do or do not possess. Over time all soil surveys monitor changes in the soils as they are altered through agriculture and other types of land use. The surveys also help to predict the success of any use to which the land is put. If used to their potential, soil surveys indicate how long the soil can sustain current practices.

Names are assigned to soils through development and application of a system of classification. Soil surveys in the United States have been developed using several classification schemes, with the first being merely a map of the surficial geologic deposits. C. F. Marbut's classification system was put into use in the early part of the twentieth century. This system was replaced by one devised by C. Kellogg in 1938 that remained in use until 1975, when the current classification system became the standard for soil surveys in the United States. In Canada surveys began later and were initially patterned on the U.S. system. In 1960 a comprehensive soil classification system was developed by Canadian soil scientists to support an expanded soil survey program throughout the agricultural areas of the country. This system was adjusted several times to best fit the soil properties that the ongoing survey discovered. In many ways, it is now like that used in Great Britain.

The earliest soil maps were made using topographic or plane table maps as base maps. Air photos became the base maps on which soil boundaries were placed in the 1930s. They came into use following the placement of the soil survey within the Natural Resources Conservation Service of the U.S. Department of Agriculture. The Canadian Plains began their surveys about the time air photos came into common use. A new generation of soil maps from these photos combined with more recent ones were completed for the Canadian Plains in the early 1990s. Canadian surveys have followed much the same trends, especially since the early 1960s. In both countries, surveys now use new technologies in remote sensing, global positioning, and base maps made from digital images. These maps will become a component of complete geographic information systems being developed in the Great Plains.

David Lewis
University of Nebraska–Lincoln

Ableiter, K. J. "Soil Classification in the United States." *Soil Science* 67 (1949): 183–91. U.S. Department of Agriculture. Soil Survey Staff. *Soil Taxonomy: A Comprehensive System.* Washington DC: Government Printing Office, 1975.

THUNDERSTORMS

Thunderstorms are an integral part of the Great Plains climate and provide a significant proportion of total precipitation. Lightning, moderate to heavy rainfall, strong winds, and frequently hail accompany these events. Thunderstorm season varies greatly from south to north, but it generally coincides with the growing season for crops, contributing to the rains needed for successful dryland agriculture. In the Central and Southern Plains, thunderstorms are most frequent in spring and early summer, with a secondary maximum in the fall. In the Canadian Prairies May through September is thunderstorm season. The number of days per year with thunderstorms ranges from twenty-five to thirty at observation stations in the Prairie Provinces to forty-five to fifty in Plains portions of Kansas, Oklahoma, and Colorado.

Some thunderstorms reach an intensity that causes damage and are referred to as severe thunderstorms. These storms may produce flash flooding and erosion, large hail, intense lightning, damaging winds, and even tornadoes. Rainfalls of several inches in an hour or less occur throughout the Great Plains. Hail is common in severe thunderstorms and may be large and/or abundant, causing heavy losses to both crops and property. Hailstones the size of softballs have fallen on numerous occasions, and the Great Plains holds records for the largest hailstones documented in both the United States (Coffeyville, Kansas, September 1970, 5½ inches diameter) and Canada (Cedoux, Saskatchewan, August 1973, almost 4½ inches diameter).

Alexander Paul
University of Regina

TOPOGRAPHIC MAPS

Topographic maps show the general configuration of the land surface, including its relief and the position of natural and man-made features. The configuration is shown commonly by contour lines, imaginary lines connecting all points of equal elevation on the earth's surface above or below a datum plane such as mean sea level. When the land slope is steeper the contour lines are closer together. Topographic maps at scales of one inch to a mile or greater (shown as 1:63,360 on the map) are used in many ways. They are particularly important in preparation of various types of geologic maps and cross sections that can be used in locating, for example, mineral resources or aquifers.

Explorations of the geology and natural resources of the American West were initiated by the King, Wheeler, Hayden, and Powell Surveys from 1867 to 1879, but major topographic mapping efforts began only after 1881. In December 1885 John Wesley Powell, second director of the U.S. Geological Survey, testified before a joint committee of Congress about the national need for topographic maps of the country. He said that topographic mapping of the country could be completed in twenty-four years. By 1894 about one-fifth of the United States was depicted on topographic maps. Mapping of the U.S. Great Plains at a scale of 1:24,000 was completed in 1994 by the U.S. Geological Survey. Topographic maps of the Canadian Prairie Provinces have been completed at a scale of 1:50,000 by the Canada Map Office.

R. F. Diffendal Jr.
University of Nebraska–Lincoln

Manning, Thomas G. *Government in Science: The U.S. Geological Survey, 1867–1894.* Lexington: University Press of Kentucky, 1967. Stegner, Wallace. *Beyond the Hundredth Meridian.* Boston: Houghton Mifflin, 1953.

TORNADOES

Tornadoes occur more frequently and are more intense in the Great Plains than in any other region on earth. Plains geography, with fringing mountain ranges running predomi-

nantly north to south, allows cold dry air from the north to collide with warm moist tropical air from the south. The jet stream, which seasonally migrates south across the Great Plains, is another essential ingredient in the creation of tornadoes. The highest frequency of tornadoes is in central Oklahoma, but incidence is also high in a zone from northeast Texas through Kansas to eastern Nebraska and Iowa. This region is commonly known as "tornado alley." The tornado season for North America peaks in May; however, there is considerable geographic variation in the timing of peak occurrence. For example, tornadoes in Texas and Oklahoma peak in April, in Nebraska in June, and in the Southern Prairie Provinces in late July and early August.

Tornadoes develop on the backside of particularly strong thunderstorms and hang down from the cloud as if the thunderstorm had a tail. These tornado-producing thunderstorms can occur singly or in a line known as a squall line, which often produces multiple tornadoes. Great Plains tornadoes commonly occur in late afternoon, when surface temperatures are the highest, providing the daily maximum uplift to the moist air near the ground. Most tornadoes move from the southwest toward the northeast; however, they may travel in any direction, and in some rare instances they remain stationary or reverse direction.

Tornado intensity is described by the F-scale. F0 and F1 tornadoes are weak tornadoes, with top wind speeds reaching 112 miles per hour, a typical width of 50 to 100 feet, and a typical life span of only a few minutes. They account for 68 percent of all Great Plains tornadoes. F2 and F3 tornadoes are strong tornadoes, with winds as high as 206 miles per hour, a width of 100 to 400 feet, and a life span of more than twenty minutes. They account for 30 percent of all Great Plains tornadoes. F4 and F5 violent tornadoes are the strongest, with wind speeds that can exceed 300 miles per

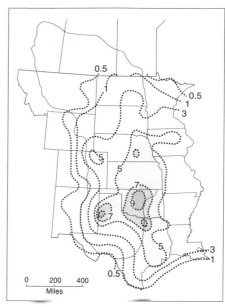

Average annual tornado incidence per 10,000 square miles from 1970 to 1997

hour, a funnel as wide as a mile, and a duration of several hours. Violent tornadoes represent only 2 percent of all tornadoes in the Great Plains, but they account for more than 90 percent of tornado-caused deaths. For the period 1950–97, the annual average number of F2 to F5 tornadoes was twenty-nine for Texas, seventeen for Oklahoma, eleven for Kansas, seven for Nebraska, five for South Dakota, three for North Dakota, and about one per year for each of the Prairie Provinces.

Tornado data have been collected only since the early 1950s. Since that time the data indicate that there has been an increasing trend in tornadoes in the Great Plains. However, this increase has been observed only in the weak F0 and F1 tornadoes; there has been no increase in the number of days with tornadoes. Scientists have concluded that almost all of the apparent increase is due to enhanced public awareness and better reporting methods during the last few decades.

See also FOLKWAYS: Tornado Stories.

Kenneth F. Dewey
University of Nebraska–Lincoln

TREE PLANTING AND CLIMATE CHANGE

See IMAGES AND ICONS: Tree Planting and Climate Change

WEATHER INDUSTRY

See INDUSTRY: Weather Industry

WEEDS

According to the U.S. Department of Agriculture, countless hours and millions of dollars are spent each year to control weeds, and millions more—hours and dollars—are lost in yield reductions. However, what exactly is a weed? And what makes a plant a weed? Many people are surprised to learn that a weed is technically "a plant out of place." So

Tornado at beginning of life, Cordell, Oklahoma, May 22, 1981

one person's weed can be someone else's salad green, pharmaceutical, transgenic crop, or wildflower!

What are the characteristics of plants that often grow out of place? One characteristic is a tendency to reach high numbers rapidly and to replace or slow the growth of more desirable plants. Traits allowing rapid population growth include early development, fast reproduction, and many long-lived seeds. Structures that aid dispersal often help weedy plants colonize far and wide. Finally, many weeds lack effective enemies, such as insects and diseases that reduce plant growth and reproduction.

Most of the economically important weeds in the Plains were introduced, with many coming from Eurasia; most arrived as contaminants of seed brought in to expand agriculture. While each list will be a little different, only a few plants really cause serious problems. Less than 1 percent of the plants listed in the *Flora of the Great Plains* are considered serious weeds, and only 1 percent or so of those are serious enough to be designated as legally noxious. Similar ratios have been found in other regions too, leading to the "tens rule." This rule states that, on average, one out of ten species that are introduced actually establish, and one out of those ten species escape into the wild, and then one out of the ten that escape become pests (0.1 percent).

Given the agricultural economy of the region, weedy plants have a special importance in the Great Plains. Plants that are good at competing with crops or forage plants in pastures and rangeland create problems. Some weeds can reduce crop yields dramatically, such as heavy stands of pennycress (*Thlaspi arvense* L.) in winter wheat or annual grasses like giant foxtail (*Setaria faberi* Herrm.) in row crops. Control of weeds in crops adds to the cost of food production. Plants that invade our gardens, lawns, and golf courses cause consternation, and their control can be expensive, economically and environmentally. Finally plants that invade native plant communities in parks, preserves, and natural roadside stands of prairie jeopardize natural heritage.

Options for reducing weed densities include mechanical, cultural, chemical, and biological methods. Each method has advantages and disadvantages. Mechanical methods include hand cutting and tilling. The advantages, including relatively low input costs, are balanced against disadvantages, such as the time and labor needed to cut weeds. Cultural methods involve reducing the weed's effects on desired plants by altering fertility, managing grass growth, or timing disturbances to suppress weed performance. The advantages are longer-term decreases in weed densities, while the disadvantages include a need for tighter planning and possibly added inputs. Chemical control involves spraying with selective or broad-spectrum herbicides. This has the advantages of speed and coverage but the disadvantages of chemical costs, increasing resistance of weeds, and environmental release of chemicals. Biological control involves the use of natural enemies to lower weed densities, either by intro-

ducing foreign or engineered species or by augmenting native enemies that feed on the weed. Here the advantages are persistence and low maintenance costs, while the disadvantages are more limited control and the risk of side effects to forage and native species. Integrated weed management programs combine methods that reduce weeds and enhance the growth of desired plants. Clearly the strategy that provides for effective limitation of weed density with the smallest economic and environmental cost is preferred.

Weed control does not necessarily mean extermination. Once a species is established it is usually impossible, or at least extremely expensive, to eradicate. Weed control is really a management issue. The issue is a challenging one, involving trade-offs and compromises. One compromise is increasing the tolerance for the presence of some noneconomic, non-environmentally threatening weeds. An indiscriminate "cure" can sometimes be worse than the problem, reducing multiple beneficial species along with the targeted pest plant species. This lesson was learned the hard way, when the side effects of broad-spectrum pesticides and generalist biocontrol agents became evident.

However, weedy species can be valuable as well. For example, some weeds contain chemical compounds of medicinal values (e.g., thistles), and many plant compounds have yet to be researched or used. Others contain genetic material with clues to effective pest control, drought tolerance, or growth acceleration. Still others are important for wildlife, and many contribute to our "feeling of nature" when outdoors. Economically useful weedy plants in the Plains include dandelion for greens, chamomile for tea, thistles for honeybees, and countless species for cover and soil retention. It is likely that researchers will find that wild weedy plants hold secrets to problems that have yet to be identified. So a weed is a potentially useful plant that is sometimes out of place and in the way. Knowing this can increase the ability to appreciate and use plants, while limiting their numbers where it really matters.

Svata M. Louda
University of Nebraska–Lincoln

Great Plains Flora Association. *Flora of the Great Plains*. Lawrence: University Press of Kansas, 1987.

WETLANDS

See WATER: Wetlands

WHITE-TAILED DEER

The white-tailed deer (*Odocoileus virginianus*) is one of two members of the deer family (Cervidae) commonly found in the Great Plains. When alarmed, white-tailed deer hold their tails erect, baring their white underside and white rump. Bucks (males) begin growing bonelike antlers early each summer and by early fall the antlers stop growing and harden. The antlers have a main beam with tines erupting from the top and are used for fighting and establishing rank in the social hierarchy.

White-tailed deer are very adaptable, both

in the habitats they occupy and the foods they eat. The highest densities of whitetails in the Great Plains occur where forests along rivers and streams are flanked by agricultural fields. Wooded areas provide deer with protective cover and natural foods. Agricultural fields provide abundant, high-quality foods. The availability of large tracts of winter cover and travel corridors between seasonal ranges are primary factors limiting populations.

By the early nineteenth century, unregulated harvesting had extirpated white-tailed deer from many areas. However, their ability to adapt to human activities has allowed them to revive throughout the region, and current populations are stable to increasing in rural and urban settings. In fact, their range may be increasing westward. High deer populations can create problems though, for farmers, foresters, rural and urban residents, and motorists. White-tailed deer are the most popular big-game animal in North America. Both deer hunting and habitat manipulation are essential for managing and controlling their populations.

Kurt C. VerCauteren
Scott E. Hygnstrom
University of Nebraska–Lincoln

Halls, Lowell K., ed. *White-Tailed Deer: Ecology and Management*. Harrisburg PA: Stackpole Books, 1984. VerCauteren, Kurt C., and Scott E. Hygnstrom. "A Review of White-Tailed Deer Movements in the Great Plains Relative to Environmental Conditions," *Great Plains Review* 4 (1994): 117–32.

WILDFLOWERS

The term "wildflowers" usually refers to attractive native flowering species. In the Great Plains the category often includes plants that are native elsewhere but have naturalized (reproducing on their own) in the Great Plains region. It rarely includes grasses, because grass flowers are small, but some grass flowers are very colorful and the foliage is often striking. Flowering shrubs and trees are not usually considered wildflowers, but there are a number of handsome natives such as wild plums (*Prunus*) and redbuds (*Cercis*).

The native wildflowers of the grasslands are likely declining in numbers because their natural habitats—native grasslands, forests, and wetlands—have been replaced by fields as well as urban and suburban areas. Some, such as *Liatris* (gay feather) and *Coreopsis*, have been successfully brought into cultivation. Some species, such as purple coneflowers (*Echinacea*), are being collected for their medicinal properties to the point that they are increasingly difficult to find in their natural environment. Other species are decreasing because they depend on parts of the ecosystem that are no longer present, as is in the case of *Ruellia humilis* (Acanthaceae), which was once apparently pollinated by a moth that has become extinct in some areas.

The Great Plains is especially rich in showy flowers of the plant families Asteraceae (sunflowers, asters, coneflowers), Fabaceae (peas, clovers), Onagraceae (evening primroses), and Asclepiadaceae (milkweeds). Native wildflowers are mostly yellow, blue, or purple in color, with true reds being rare. White flowers, especially those with long tubes (corollas), usually open at night and some have wonderful fragrances. Colors reflect the preferences of pollinators: bees, flies, and butterflies prefer bright colors and visit plants by day, while moths and hawkmoths fly by night. Partly white flowers (e.g., *Gaura*) may be visited by both kinds of pollinators.

The flowering of prairie plants can be divided into five seasons: early spring, late spring, early summer, late summer, and fall. Examples of flowers reflecting that seasonal sequence include pasque flower (*Anemone patens*) early in the spring; puccoon (various *Lithospermum* species) in late spring; scurf peas (*Psoralea*) in June; milkweeds (*Asclepias* species) in late summer; and asters and gentians in fall.

A few native wildflowers are found across the entire region, but more often, similar species occur in sequence along east–west and north–south transects. These plants are adapted to the area where they are found, and this local diversity increases the variety of native species. Likewise, in many cases there are distinctive species or varieties confined to special growing conditions, such as sand, rocky outcrops, and wetlands. Milkweeds are a good example. The common milkweed (*Asclepias syriaca*) is found in the Eastern Plains. It is replaced in the Western Plains by the similar showy milkweed (*A. speciosa*). The swamp milkweed (*A. incarnata*), with leaves much narrower and the flowers a more reddish pink than the previous two, is found in marshy areas and wet meadows across the region. And on sand the characteristic milkweed is the green-flowered sand milkweed (*A. arenaria*).

Plants of human-disturbed environments (highway margins, lawns) are usually called weeds. Whether native or introduced, these occur across the entire Great Plains. Many familiar roadside wildflowers, such as goatsbeard (*Tragopogon*), sweet clover (*Melilotus*), and dame's rocket (*Hesperis*), were introduced.

Within our region, forested areas harbor a distinct group of wildflowers. In most cases these are species shared with more extensive forests in the east or southeast, such as spring beauty (*Claytonia virginica*), mayapple (*Podophyllum peltatum*), and touch-me-not (*Impatiens* species).

Since flowers are necessary for plant reproduction, picking bouquets of wildflowers poses a threat to their survival, especially for the nonweedy species. As the human impact in the Great Plains increases and more areas are developed, threats to native wildflowers will only get worse. Digging up native plants as a method of collecting them frequently fails because prairie natives are very deeply rooted and difficult to dig up. This is, therefore, an even greater threat to the survival of prairie species than picking the flowers.

Kathleen H. Keeler
University of Nebraska–Lincoln

Freeman, C. C., and E. K. Schofield. *Roadside Wildflowers of the Southern Great Plains*. Lawrence: University Press of Kansas, 1991. Great Plains Flora Association. *Flora of the Great Plains*. Lawrence: University Press of Kansas, 1987. Weaver, J. E. *Native Vegetation of Nebraska*. Lincoln: University of Nebraska Press, 1965.

WIND

In popular imagination and folklore wind is the weather element that typifies the Great Plains. From the warming chinook winds of the High Plains to howling blizzards and threatening tornadoes, wind shapes how residents and others view the Plains. Wind is an important player in the mythology of Great Plains Native Americans, and the wind is frequently mentioned in other Plains literature, including *The Wonderful Wizard of Oz*. Homesteaders made frequent mention of the wind in their journals. None of this is surprising: apart from some coastal regions, the Great Plains is the windiest portion of North America.

Since the beginning of homesteading on the Plains, wind has been primarily associated with disaster. Blizzards have meant catastrophe for the cattle industry. Grass fires fanned by wind have raced across the landscape, destroying buildings and fences while at the same time renewing the Plains ecosystem. Tornadoes have brought death and destruction to the region, obliging residents to build storm cellars and to reinforce rooms for protection. Farmers and ranchers have planted shelterbelts to shield fields from soil erosion, crops from moisture loss, and cattle from wind-driven snow.

But wind is also a natural resource for the Great Plains. For more than 150 years, ranchers and farmers have used windmills to pump groundwater, without which settlement would have been severely restricted. During the 1930s and 1940s, small electric wind generators were used on remote homesteads to power radios. With the coming of inexpensive and reliable grid-based electricity, the electric wind generator all but disappeared from the Great Plains. By the 1990s, however, large-scale wind projects were being developed in Alberta, North Dakota, Colorado, Kansas, Nebraska, Texas, and Wyoming. It is likely that wind will again become an important energy resource for Plains residents.

The power of the wind also has a major impact on the topography of the Great Plains. Soil erosion and deposition shapes the topography of the region. During the drought years of the 1930s, tons of topsoil were transported east by the wind from the Southern and Central Plains. Despite conservation efforts, blowing dust from plowed fields and tumbleweeds piled against fences are still emblematic scenes on the Great Plains.

See also INDUSTRY: Wind Energy.

David Emory Stooksbury
University of Georgia

WIND ENERGY

See INDUSTRY: Wind Energy

WOODLANDS

Although grassland is the characteristic vegetation of the Great Plains, contact with forests and woodlands occurs at the boundaries of the region, and significant areas of transition between woodland and grassland vegetation exist. Trees are also associated with river systems and various physiographic features within the Plains.

Tallgrass prairie is the dominant vegetation of the eastern Great Plains. In Kansas and Oklahoma a broad transition zone occurs where the tallgrass prairie contacts the deciduous forest of eastern North America, resulting in a mosaic vegetation combining elements of both plant communities. Where prairie dominates and the tree canopy cover is less than 50 percent, the vegetation is called savanna. The trees most commonly associated with savannas are various species of oaks. Bur oak (*Quercus macrocarpa*) dominates the savannas of the northeastern Great Plains. Post oak (*Quercus stellata*) and blackjack oak (*Quercus marilandica*) are the primary tree species in the savanna region, called the Cross Timbers, of Kansas, Oklahoma, and Texas. The balance between tallgrass prairie vegetation and woody plants in savannas was maintained historically by fire. Trees and other woody species increase in number in savannas where fire is suppressed.

In Manitoba, Saskatchewan, and Alberta, where tallgrass and mixed prairie contact the boreal forest of the north, a transition zone, called the Parkland Belt, occurs. This is a region of grasslands interspersed with groves of trees. Bur oak is the most common tree in the eastern portion of this zone and is replaced by aspen (*Populus tremuloides*) to the west. Isolated, islandlike occurrences of aspen/bur oak parklands occur to the south in North Dakota.

In Montana, Douglas fir (*Pseudotsuga menziesii*) forest occurs on the plains east of the Rockies in association with isolated mountains such as the Highwood and Bearpaw. Disjunct occurrences of ponderosa pine (*Pinus ponderosa*) occur as forest and savanna in association with landforms such as the Pine Ridge Escarpment in western Nebraska and the badlands of western North Dakota.

The Black Hills of western South Dakota and adjacent Wyoming are forested with a unique assemblage of trees and other plants dominated by Rocky Mountain species but also including species from the deciduous forest of eastern North America and the boreal forest of Canada. A similar mixing of elements from these three forest types occurs in the Niobrara River valley of north-central Nebraska.

In northeastern New Mexico and adjacent parts of Colorado and Oklahoma, areas of woodland dominated by piñon pine (*Pinus edulis*) and juniper (*Juniperus* spp.) occur in association with escarpments, canyons, and other physiographic features of volcanic origin. Juniper savanna often occurs where the shortgrass prairie comes into contact with these woodlands.

At the southern reaches of the Great Plains in Texas the shortgrass prairie mingles with mesquite trees (*Propsis glandulosa*) to form mesquite savanna. Where the Southern Plains blends into the Texas Hill Country, a mosaic of woodland and grassland occurs with oaks and junipers being the important trees.

In addition to these transition areas at the boundaries of the Great Plains, forest vegetation penetrates the Plains along many river systems. A thin band of eastern deciduous forest dominated by oaks and hickories (*Carya* spp.) borders the Missouri River and its tributaries in eastern Kansas and Nebraska. The diversity of trees and other plant species diminishes upstream. In Oklahoma Cross Timbers savanna extends westward into the Plains along the Cimarron and Canadian Rivers.

Woody vegetation associated specifically with the floodplain zone of streams and rivers is termed riparian forest. Riparian forests occurred historically along much of the major rivers like the Missouri, Platte, and Arkansas. Cottonwood (*Populus deltoides*) was the main tree of these forests and often was the only tree along the western reaches of these rivers. Isolated, western occurrences of cottonwood were sometimes given the name "Big Timbers." Other frequently associated riparian trees include willows (*Salix* spp.), hackberry (*Celtis occidentalis*), boxelder (*Acer negundo*), and elm (*Ulmus* spp.). The Osage orange tree (*Maclura pomifera*), widely planted for hedges and windbreaks by pioneers and farmers, originally occurred in riparian habitat along the Red River in Oklahoma and Texas.

Occurrences of woodlands add significantly to the biodiversity of the Plains, having more associated species of birds, mammals, and other animals than the adjacent grasslands. These areas were also important to the Native peoples of the Plains, providing firewood, lodge poles, bow wood, and other aspects of their material culture, as well as providing sheltered places for camps.

James H. Locklear
Nebraska Statewide Arboretum

Babour, M. G., and W. D. Billings, eds. *North American Terrestrial Vegetation*. New York: Cambridge University Press, 1988. Great Plains Flora Association. *Flora of the Great Plains*. Lawrence: University Press of Kansas, 1986. Küchler, A. W. *Potential Natural Vegetation of the Coterminous United States*. New York: American Geographical Society, 1964. Map.

Politics and Government

John Diefenbaker

POLITICS AND GOVERNMENT

The history of politics in the Great Plains has to do with the formal structures of governmental authority and the process of political decision making, as well as the policies of external political agencies that have affected the region. Before the arrival of Europeans, political authority tended to be local in nature, relating to the authority of Native American leaders over bands or tribes. Since the nineteenth century, however, politics has had not only local but state or provincial and federal dimensions. The most distinctive aspects of Plains politics appeared between 1890 and World War II; since 1945, Plains politics has moved closer to national patterns.

Political Authority before the Arrival of Europeans

Before the arrival of the Europeans and the horse, most of the Indigenous people of the Great Plains lived in permanent villages along streams and rivers. Some—the Blackfoot, for example—lived as nomadic hunters. The basic political unit of the sedentary societies was the village, each with its own structure of authority. The Pawnees, for example, were divided into four bands; the largest of them, the Skiris, had an internal organization based on thirteen villages, a political structure that persisted even after the number of actual villages significantly declined. The chiefs of each village typically joined together as a tribal council that met periodically throughout the year. The Skiris also collaborated with the other three Pawnee bands on significant issues, making this a confederation of independent but mutually supported units.

Patterns of leadership differed among the Plains tribes, but the position of village chief was typically hereditary within certain lineages. A chief's actual authority, however, rested on his ability to provide successful leadership—in dealing with traders, distributing goods, negotiating with outsiders, allocating farmlands, and adjudicating disputes. Those from other families could, through demonstrating their abilities, exercise other forms of leadership. Thus, a village might have one or a few main chiefs, several shamans, and separate leaders for war, buffalo-hunting expeditions, and the various men's societies. Occasionally, a woman might serve as a shaman, but women did not hold any of the other community-wide political roles.

Advent of Europeans and Americans

In 1541 Vásquez de Coronado and the few men under his command became the first Europeans to venture into the Great Plains. Afterward, Spanish authorities did little to establish their political authority there. The Hudson's Bay Company began trading from posts along the eastern shores of Hudson Bay and James Bay in 1670. By 1720 the hinterland of York Factory, the largest of these posts, included the whole of what is now Manitoba and Saskatchewan. Under the terms of its charter the Hudson's Bay Company had governmental and judicial powers, but these were exercised only in a minimal way during the early years of the company's history. French explorers and traders entered the Plains in the early eighteenth century, but French authorities were no more active than the Spanish in establishing their political authority.

Plains Indians experienced the impact of the arrival of Europeans in North America long before significant numbers of Europeans came to the Plains. European settlers along the Atlantic traded with nearby Indigenous peoples, providing guns and manufactured goods, including items of iron and brass. As these trading partners were pushed west by European expansion, they, in turn, equipped with guns and iron weapons, pressured the peoples to their west. This constant pressure from the East, compressing Indian space, bred conflict among the Plains tribes and between Plains tribes and migrating tribes. The Teton and Yankton Sioux, for example, pressured from the East and attracted to the Plains by the horse and bison, crossed the Missouri River by 1800 and began their successful campaign to wrest control of the range from Indigenous groups such as the Pawnees and Kiowas. Farther north the Western Wood Crees entered territory of the Plains Crees, who in turn began to frequent the hunting grounds of the more westerly tribes, resulting in bloody intertribal conflicts.

Among the nomadic Plains tribes, the basic political unit was the band—a relatively small group that traveled together, camped together, hunted together, and made war together. Bands of the same tribe or closely related tribes came together for religious ceremonies, councils, hunting, or war. Political leadership was typically fluid, with different leaders for different purposes, none of whom held supreme authority within the band or tribe. As of about 1800, for example, the Cheyennes had ten bands, each with four chiefs; when the ten bands came together each spring, the four chiefs of each band, plus a few other elders, formed a tribal council. Other men were war leaders or led men's societies.

The Treaty of Paris (1763) gave Spain the entire southern region between the Mississippi River and the crest of the Rocky Mountains, and it gave Britain the vast northern territories formerly held by New France. Spanish authorities exerted little political authority in the Plains, however. In 1800 Spain secretly sold to France the entire Louisiana country north of the Red River. Napoleon, the ruler of France, then sold Louisiana to the United States in 1803.

From the Louisiana Purchase to the Kansas-Nebraska Act

Although claimed by European powers for some 250 years, the Plains had, in fact, experienced very little outside political authority during that time. That changed in 1811 when Thomas Douglas, Lord Selkirk, with the assistance of the Hudson's Bay Company, established an agricultural colony on the Red River of the North at the present site of Winnipeg. Conflict between rival fur traders led Selkirk to secure a small force of mercenary soldiers, recently released from British employ, to reestablish order in the new settlement. Meanwhile, the U.S. government sent explorers into its part of the Plains and then planted small military posts along the Missouri River, but the military exercised little influence. Real political control still rested largely with the villages, bands, and tribes.

In 1830 Congress passed the Indian Removal Act, which uprooted many Native American peoples living east of the Mississippi and removed them to the eastern parts of what are now Kansas and Oklahoma. Many of them had long since adapted to white society, and some—the Cherokees, for example—brought with them political structures modeled as much on the U.S. Constitution as on traditional practices.

Through the annexation of Texas (1845) and war with Mexico and the resulting Treaty of Guadalupe Hidalgo (1848), the United States acquired title to territories that included the Southern Plains. Though Texas claimed most of the Southern Plains, the residents of New Mexico contested that claim. Congress in 1850 attempted to resolve these and other issues arising from the war with Mexico through an elaborate compromise that, among other provisions, set the present western boundary of Texas and established a territorial government for New Mexico.

By 1850 most of the Plains still appeared on maps as "unorganized Indian territory." The major land routes to California, Oregon, and New Mexico crossed this territory. Committed to the idea of a railroad from Chicago to the Pacific Ocean, Stephen Douglas, U.S. senator from Illinois, had long recognized the need to establish territorial organization in the Plains. Early efforts foundered, however, on southern opposition to the creation of territories where the Missouri Compromise (1820) banned slavery. Douglas fashioned a successful compromise in early 1854, creating Nebraska and Kansas Territories, each to decide whether or not to permit slavery within its boundaries. The Kansas-Nebraska Act provoked a great national debate over slavery, precipitated the emergence of the Republican Party, and contributed significantly to a major national political realignment. The organization of Kansas, in turn, initiated a miniature civil war known as "Bleeding Kansas."

From the Kansas-Nebraska Act to the 1890s

The population of Kansas Territory grew rapidly, and Kansas became a state in 1861. Congress also created several more territories in the region: Dakota and Colorado in 1861, Montana in 1864, and Wyoming in 1868. With the end of the Civil War, opportunities in the Plains attracted many new settlers. Nebraska became a state in 1867 and Colorado in 1876.

Even late in the nineteenth century, however, much of the American Plains remained territories. Montana and the Dakotas became states only in 1889 and Wyoming in 1890. Oklahoma and New Mexico remained territories into the twentieth century. Throughout their territorial days, residents could not elect their own governors nor participate in presidential elections, and the election of the territorial legislature had no implications for the election of U.S. senators (who were elected by state legislatures until 1913). What political patronage existed was federal and often allocated in faraway Washington. All this made for low stakes for parties in territorial politics, and some historians have suggested that, in long-time territories, strong party organizations and loyalties were consequently stunted.

In most of the Canadian Plains, provincial status also came relatively late. After the creation of the Dominion of Canada in 1867, the new government entered into negotiations with the Hudson's Bay Company for acquisition of its vast holdings in what is now central and western Canada. After the successful completion of these negotiations, the first significant step toward the organization of territories came in 1870, when the Manitoba Act created a tiny Manitoba province and a huge federally administered unit, the Northwest Territories. The Northwest Territories Act of 1875 provided for local government but left the most important decisions to an appointed lieutenant governor. Both laws made possible the establishment of a dual school system and, after 1877, both recognized French and English as official languages, but these provisions proved to be long-term sources of political conflict. The boundaries of Manitoba were expanded in 1882, and four federal districts were created in the Plains. Thereafter, the Northwest Territories moved toward self-government and integration into federal politics. In the 1890s the school laws of the Northwest Territories made English the language of instruction in all schools, though local school trustees could provide for the study of a language other than English. After a rapid population increase in the 1890s, the districts were consolidated into the Provinces of Alberta and Saskatchewan in 1905. A final boundary adjustment in 1912 gave additional northern territory to Manitoba. As was true in the United States, long-term territorial status seems to have stunted the growth of political parties, though, perhaps, for different reasons.

Unlike the situation in the territories, following the Civil War the political parties in the Plains states had a greater stake in elections, and partisanship developed along regional lines. Kansas, Nebraska, and Colorado emerged as Republican strongholds under the leadership of Union Army veterans who solicited the votes of their numerous fellow veterans. There, Republicans constantly reminded voters of the Homestead Act and Republican largess in promoting western economic development. Party politics in Texas followed as directly from that state's participation in the Confederacy, as westward-moving southern whites assisted the Democrats in "redeeming" the state from Republican rule in 1873 and keeping it securely Democratic thereafter. In Canada, early governments in Manitoba and the territories were nonpartisan. In Manitoba in 1888, a partisan Liberal government replaced the nonpartisan

government of Premier John Norquay, who was of mixed Cree and Scottish ancestry, while territorial administrations remained nonpartisan until the new Provinces of Saskatchewan and Alberta were created in 1905.

Politics of Gender, Ethnicity, and Race

Throughout the late nineteenth and early twentieth centuries, advocates of women's suffrage were active in the Northern and Central Plains. In 1867 Kansas became the first state to vote on the issue, but its voters rejected suffrage. The first session of the Wyoming territorial legislature, in 1869, approved suffrage for women—the first time any state or territory had taken such a step. Some attributed that decision to the belief among Wyoming males that women's suffrage would draw more women to the territory, but others have pointed to diligent lobbying by suffrage advocates. When Wyoming achieved statehood in 1890, it became the first state to fully enfranchise women. Colorado, in 1893, became the first state whose male voters approved women's suffrage. Despite repeated agitation of the issue and several referenda, the other Plains states continued to reject suffrage until 1912 or later, even though women won statewide elective office in North Dakota and Oklahoma.

With or without the suffrage, Plains women took prominent roles in reform movements, especially efforts to banish liquor. In 1878 Kansans amended their state constitution to prohibit the importation, manufacture, and sale of alcohol, but the law was widely violated. Despite referenda in several other Plains states, before 1907 laws banning liquor were passed only in North and South Dakota, and South Dakotans soon reversed that decision.

In the Northern Plains the political battle over prohibition reflected broader ethnic and religious differences. One side, called evangelicals by some historians, consisted of old-stock Americans and immigrants who affiliated with the Methodist, Baptist, Congregational, or Presbyterian denominations, along with Norwegian and Swedish immigrants and their offspring. On the other side were Catholics and many German Protestants, called liturgicals or confessionals by some historians. Whereas evangelicals condemned as sinful any use of alcohol, and often added gambling and dancing, liturgicals found no inherent sin in a stein of beer, a dance, or a lottery. Thus, referenda on prohibition and women's suffrage (closely connected in many voters' minds) often turned on the ethno-cultural values of voters. Identification with the Democratic and Republican Parties in the Northern Plains often had ethnic dimensions, for northern Democrats adamantly opposed prohibition. Republicans usually tried to duck the issue but sometimes issued cautious endorsements. Similar patterns regarding ethnicity, prohibition, and women's suffrage were to be found in the Prairie Provinces, though the time of settlement there meant that the patterns appeared later. There, ethnic conflict often focused as well on denominational schools, especially funding and the extent of civil supervision.

If the struggle over prohibition formed a highly divisive political issue in the Northern Plains, Texas politics sometimes revolved around race. Texas experienced Radical Reconstruction beginning in 1867, and a coalition of black and white Radical Republicans remained in control until 1873, when the Democrats won a gubernatorial election characterized by widespread fraud and intimidation of black voters. With the Democrats' accession to power, a new state constitution was written, severely limiting the legislature but not disfranchising black voters.

In the Central Plains states, the small numbers of African Americans aligned themselves with the dominant Republicans. Some received political patronage in return, and a few were elected to local or state office, including state auditor in Kansas. In Kansas, and later in Oklahoma Territory, black migrants from the South created all-black towns and exercised local political authority.

In the late nineteenth and early twentieth centuries, only in New Mexico did Mexican Americans exercise significant political power. Long-established Hispano communities (most of them not in the Plains), along with the slow pace of in-migration by other groups, meant that Mexican culture dominated many areas. Voters elected Mexican Americans as local officials, territorial legislators, and territorial delegates to Congress. Mexican Americans also secured federal patronage posts, including territorial secretary and governor.

As the American Plains filled up with new residents, Congress moved toward reducing the size of Indian reservations, the largest of which were in Dakota and Montana Territories and in what is now Oklahoma. Outside the jurisdiction of state or territorial officials, these reservations were administered directly by the Bureau of Indian Affairs. In 1871 Congress had specified that the executive branch was no longer to negotiate treaties with Indian tribes. Officials of the Bureau of Indian Affairs, committed to a policy of assimilation, sought to eliminate most traditional practices, including structures of authority and governance. In the Dawes Act of 1887, Congress directed that reservation land be divided among Indian families and owned in severalty (i.e., individually) rather than in common. Remaining land was to be taken out of the reservation system, producing a dramatic reduction in the size of reservations. In 1890 Congress created Oklahoma Territory in the western part of what is now Oklahoma, leaving the eastern region as Indian Territory. In the Northern Plains, the Great Sioux Reservation had been significantly reduced in size in 1877 and was broken up into smaller units in 1889.

In the Prairie Provinces, the 1870s and 1880s also proved crucial to the Native peoples and Métis (those of mixed Indian and European, mostly French, ancestry). The Indian Act of 1876, based on assumptions about assimilation similar to those underlying the Dawes Act, made Canadian Indians wards of the federal government. In the 1870s a series of treaties with the major Plains tribes typically provided for small reserves along with annuities and equipment. The treaties opened large areas for railroad construction, European and Canadian settlement, and agricultural development. An uprising by Métis in 1885, in opposition to Canadian federal authority, was quickly suppressed.

Populism and Silver

By the 1880s political agitators throughout the Plains were calling for new federal policies to counteract steadily declining prices for farm products and to regulate railroad rates, but few established political figures took notice. Texas was an exception, at least with regard to railroad rates. John Reagan, member of Congress from Texas, had advocated regulation through the late 1870s and early 1880s and had contributed to the Interstate Commerce Act in 1886. James Hogg, as attorney general and governor in the late 1880s and early 1890s, made a political reputation in Texas by attacking railroads.

In 1890, in the Central and Northern Plains states, new political parties emerged, claiming to speak for hard-pressed farmers and laborers. Organized at first as state parties under various names, the parties eventually came together as the People's Party, or Populists. The new party called for governmental action to restrict the great corporations that had developed since the Civil War and, the Populists argued, limited the economic opportunities and political rights of ordinary citizens. In the Plains the Populists drew their greatest strength from farmers on marginally productive land, often with large mortgages at high interest rates, for whom the prevailing deflation proved especially ruinous.

The Populists called for sweeping changes in federal monetary and banking policies, especially expansion of the circulating currency to counteract the prevalent deflation; government ownership of the railroads and the telegraph and telephone systems; structural reforms to make government more responsive to voters, including the secret ballot and the initiative and referendum; and other reforms such as the eight-hour workday and a graduated income tax. Populists won office as local and state officials, including governor, and as members of state legislatures and the U.S. Congress.

In most places in the Central and Northern Plains states, the Democrats were reduced to a tiny third party. They often threw their support behind Populist candidates. Such fusions brought gubernatorial victories in 1892 in Colorado, Kansas, and North Dakota, in 1894 in Nebraska, and in 1896 in South Dakota. In Texas, where the Democrats were the dominant party, the growth of Populism brought unsuccessful fusion with the minority Republicans.

In 1896 William Jennings Bryan, a Democrat from Nebraska, won the Democratic presidential nomination on a platform that stressed currency inflation through silver coinage and called for an income tax and other reforms. Most western Populists enthusiastically gave

him their support, and he secured their party's nomination as well. Leading western Republicans broke with their party, formed the Silver Party (or Silver Republicans), and also nominated Bryan. Bryan lost the presidency, though he did well throughout much of the West. The Populist and Silver Republican parties survived for a few years, then faded away. For many voters in some Plains states, party loyalties may have been significantly weakened. In Colorado and Nebraska, the Democrats emerged stronger than they had been before 1890. Republicans and Democrats were closely competitive in those two states and in Montana over the next twenty years. Kansas and the Dakotas, however, could usually be found in the Republican camp.

Racial issues became prominent in Texas politics in the 1890s, when the state's Populists made a strong appeal to black voters and, in coalition with Republicans, registered a strong vote for their gubernatorial candidate in 1896. Texas adopted a poll tax in 1902 but never followed other former Confederate states in creating a more elaborate set of legal or constitutional provisions designed to restrict black participation in politics. Texas Democrats accomplished much the same thing extralegally, though, by barring African Americans from Democratic primaries (and eventually writing that provision into law) and by coercing blacks who insisted on exercising the franchise.

The two-party system remained intact in western Canada until 1917, although there was considerable dissatisfaction with federal policies governing tariffs, railways, grain handling, and grain marketing. That discontent, and the formation of a Union government in 1917 to implement a policy of military conscription, contributed to the breakup of the two-party system and the formation of the National Progressive Party after World War I.

Progressivism

Where the Populists had focused especially on economic problems, other reformers, then and later, raised other issues. By 1910 or so, reformers had adopted the label "progressive" for themselves and their proposals. Every Plains state experienced progressive reform during the two decades before World War I, and those reforms changed both the structure and function of most state governments. In 1898 South Dakota Populists made their state the first to adopt the initiative and referendum. Most other Plains states also adopted the initiative and referendum, though not through Populists' efforts. Other popular structural reforms intended to foster direct democracy included the direct primary, recall, nonpartisan offices, and limits on political parties. Structural reforms to extend the merit system to state employees, to rationalize the structure of state government, and to simplify state budgeting were also adopted in many states.

The initiative, referendum, and recall were also popular in the Canadian Plains. The legislatures of all three Prairie Provinces approved variations on direct-democracy legislation between 1912 and 1916. The Alberta law was

highly limited. That of Saskatchewan was rejected due to low turnout in a referendum (even though those who voted were strongly in favor). Manitoba's law was overturned in the courts. The Progressives, however, and particularly the United Farmers of Alberta, initiated aggressive new direct legislation measures in the 1920s, but these also failed to achieve the desired results. More recently the western-based Reform Party of Canada has again proposed measures such as recall, initiative, and referendum.

Progressives in the Plains states added new functions to state government as they promoted regulation of railroads and public utilities, abolition of child labor, employer liability and workers' compensation, and protection for consumers. Four states set up insurance funds for deposits in state-chartered banks. When Oklahoma became a state in 1907, its constitution included a wide range of progressive innovations, including restrictions on corporations, a graduated income tax, and the initiative and referendum. Oklahoma Democrats showed another side of progressivism, however, when they enacted racial segregation and a literacy test for voting, a device to disfranchise African American voters. Under Gov. Peter Norbeck (1917–21), a progressive Republican, South Dakota launched several state-owned enterprises, including a coal mine, cement plant, hail insurance fund, and hydroelectric plants.

Renewed organizing by women and temperance advocates brought new victories for prohibition and women's suffrage. Oklahomans voted their state dry in 1907, and by 1918 all the Plains states but Texas had done the same. Kansas adopted women's suffrage in 1912 and Montana followed in 1914. In 1916 Montana elected the first woman to serve in the House of Representatives, Jeannette Rankin. South Dakotans and Oklahomans adopted women's suffrage in 1918. In all the other Plains states, women gained the suffrage with the Nineteenth Amendment in 1920. In Canada, in 1916, Manitoba was the first province to extend the franchise to women, followed almost immediately by Saskatchewan and Alberta. The following year the federal government extended the franchise to women in the military and to female relatives of military men, and in 1918 all women in western Canada gained the right to vote in federal elections.

Progressivism in the Plains states differed in important ways from progressivism in eastern states. Like other western progressives, those in the Plains were more likely to favor direct democracy, women's suffrage, and prohibition than their eastern counterparts. Some, like Norbeck, proved more receptive to state-owned enterprise, especially if such enterprises were for the purpose of economic development. And, as events after 1914 were to demonstrate, some were distinctly more isolationist in their views on foreign policy.

In some Plains states, voters endorsed proposals more radical than those proffered by progressives. The Socialist Party, espousing government ownership of key industries, made an especially strong showing in Oklahoma, winning 21 percent of the vote for governor in 1914. Socialists developed strength elsewhere in the Plains states, electing local officials in several places, but failed to win any office higher than member of the state legislature. In North Dakota, by contrast, Arthur C. Townley, a former socialist organizer, was the moving force in the Nonpartisan League (NPL). The NPL won the governorship in 1916 and dominated the state legislature in 1919. They enacted much of their program, including a state-owned bank and terminal grain elevator.

In the Canadian Plains the 1890s and early twentieth century brought increased immigration and development, leading, belatedly, to provincial status for Alberta and Saskatchewan in 1905. In both provinces Liberals established themselves as the majority until after World War I, but Manitoba had a Conservative government from 1900 to 1915. Liberals sustained themselves in the two western provinces by drawing upon federal patronage and by paying close attention to local interests, especially the grain growers who opposed the protective tariff. The Liberals also cultivated a more diverse constituency than did the Conservatives, whose voters and leaders were largely British in ancestry and Anglican in religion. Even so, both parties were predominantly British and Protestant in ethnicity. In Manitoba the Conservatives thrived by painting the Liberals as insufficiently attentive to local concerns. Liberals and Conservatives from the Prairie Provinces sometimes took positions in support of their regional interests that set them apart from their eastern counterparts, just as progressive Republicans and Democrats in Plains states sometimes found themselves in opposition to the national leadership of their parties.

World War I and Depression

Jeannette Rankin of Montana and Sen. George W. Norris of Nebraska were among those members of Congress who voted against the declaration of war in 1917. Throughout the Plains, World War I introduced a period of intense patriotism, encouraged by the administration of President Woodrow Wilson, new state Councils of Defense, and extragovernmental bodies. Suspicion and hostility greeted those of German birth or descent, pacifists (including Mennonites, who were often of German ancestry), and radicals, especially the NPL, Socialists, and the Industrial Workers of the World. Canada had entered the war earlier, at the same time Britain did, and the war there, too, intensified Canadianization drives among both immigrants and French Canadians and brought suppression of radical groups.

The war created a huge demand for wheat and meat. At the end of the war, however, prices for agricultural products fell, initiating an agricultural depression that persisted when the rest of the economy began to roar with the prosperity of the 1920s. By 1922 agricultural distress and reversals for organized labor, especially railroad workers, sparked political protests among farmers and workers in the American Plains. Organized through the Conference on Progressive Political Action, protesting voters put Democrats into the governorship in several Plains states and elected Burton K. Wheeler, a progressive Democrat, to the U.S. Senate from Montana. A similar coalition in Oklahoma elected the governor there. In 1924, the independent presidential candidacy of Robert La Follette drew significant support from farmers and organized labor. He failed to win any Plains state, but he carried many counties across the Northern and Central Plains. Political protest ebbed in the late 1920s, until the onset of the Great Depression in 1929–30.

The economic distress of farmers contributed to the development of a congressional "farm bloc" in 1921. Members of Congress from both parties, including many from the Plains states, joined to support regulation of stockyards and grain exchanges, exempt farm cooperatives from antitrust laws, and make credit more easily available to farmers. Arthur Capper, U.S. senator from Kansas, often took a leading role in the farm bloc. Despite such efforts, however, the farm economy continued to slump.

In the Canadian Plains, the war years and their immediate aftermath produced a new political movement that drew upon traditions from eastern Canada, from Britain (including cooperatives, trade unions, and socialism), and from populism, progressivism, and the NPL in the United States. Launched at a federal level as the National Progressive Party in 1920, it especially drew its voting strength from farmers and scored important victories in the 1921 federal elections, sweeping nearly every seat in the Prairie Provinces. Variations appeared in provincial politics. In Alberta the NPL had scored some early victories in 1917. Pressured by NPL successes, the older and larger United Farmers of Alberta (UFA) moved toward more independent political involvement. In 1919 the UFA and NPL merged, and in 1921 the UFA swept the provincial elections, virtually eliminating all other parties, and remained in power for the next fourteen years. The United Farmers of Manitoba, in 1922, won control of that province and remained a dominant element in various coalition governments until 1958. Both farmer organizations were allied with the Progressives at the federal level. In Saskatchewan the ruling Liberals made substantial concessions to the Saskatchewan Grain Growers Association and forestalled the emergence of a viable farmers' party. Thus, by the mid-1920s party politics in the Prairie Provinces had begun to show distinctive variants from federal patterns.

In 1924 two Plains states elected the nation's first female governors. In Wyoming, the death of the incumbent a month before the election led to the nomination and election of his widow, Nellie Tayloe Ross. Miriam A. "Ma" Ferguson won the governorship in Texas, but she was widely seen as a surrogate for her husband, James E. Ferguson, who was ineligible to run because he had been impeached from the governorship in 1917.

Ma Ferguson's victory in the Texas Democratic primary came despite the opposition of the Ku Klux Klan. Antiblack, anti-Catholic, anti-Semitic, and anti-immigrant, the Klan presented itself as the defender of old-fashioned Protestant morality and became a significant force in Plains politics. Klan-endorsed candidates won local and state office across Texas, Colorado, Oklahoma, and Kansas in the early and mid-1920s. The Klan tried to influence elections elsewhere but declined in most places after the mid-1920s. In 1929, however, in Saskatchewan, the Klan contributed to the defeat of the Liberals.

The nationwide Depression that began in 1929 was a serious economic blow to a region whose farmers had not shared in the more general prosperity of the previous decade. Nature compounded the Depression with drought, beginning in 1933 and lasting until 1938, turning large areas of the Plains into the Dust Bowl. Political repercussions appeared in a few Plains states as early as 1930, when voters elected governors and senators who promised to address their economic problems. The political upheaval intensified in 1932, when Franklin D. Roosevelt became the first Democrat to sweep all of the Plains states' electoral votes. He also carried Democrats into Congress, statehouses, and state legislatures. In North Dakota, a revived Nonpartisan League, led by William Langer, won complete control of state government for the first time since 1919. For most Plains states, elections in the early 1930s marked the biggest protest vote in their history, and Democrats dominated most Plains state governments.

In mid-1932, in some Northern Plains states and nearby areas, the Farmers Holiday Association began efforts to raise farm prices by withholding produce from market and sometimes blocking roads to prevent others from selling. Holiday members joined others in demanding that state governments impose a moratorium on farm mortgage foreclosures, and several Northern Plains states adopted such measures.

Roosevelt's New Deal addressed the farm problem with the Agricultural Adjustment Act, which included provisions for paying farmers and stockgrowers to reduce production. Relief rolls, both state and federal, grew to include a quarter or a third of the population in some Plains states, and sometimes two-thirds or more of those in Dust Bowl counties. Other New Deal programs ranged from construction of schools and bridges to rural electrification, and from tree planting and flood control to social security. One New Deal project, the Fort Peck Dam in Montana, was the largest earthen dam in the world when it was completed in 1939.

By the mid-1930s several Plains states had experienced efforts by Democratic governors and legislatures to create "Little New Deals," but most were modest and unimaginative. Nearly everywhere in the Plains states, governors and legislatures drastically cut state spending to provide property tax relief. Seeking alternatives to property taxes, several states enacted sales taxes or income taxes. Plains states also created the agencies necessary to participate in new federal welfare programs.

In a few instances in the 1930s, states went beyond budget cutting, tax reform, and participation in New Deal programs. In 1936 Colorado voters approved a pension program for those over sixty that proved so costly it absorbed most of the new sales tax. In Nebraska, Senator Norris convinced voters in 1934 to amend the state constitution to create a unicameral, nonpartisan legislature. Norris also provided some of the inspiration for the development of Nebraska's public power districts, most of which used federal funds to construct generating and distribution systems. By 1945 the state's entire electrical power system was publicly owned.

The New Deal also brought important changes to the governance of Indian reservations. Roosevelt appointed John Collier as commissioner of Indian Affairs. A longtime critic of previous federal Indian policies, Collier closed down many boarding schools and ended efforts to suppress traditional religious practices. His "Indian New Deal" included as its centerpiece the Indian Reorganization Act (1934), which promised to end allotments, restore tribal ownership of unallotted lands, and encourage tribal self-government, albeit using European American–styled governments. Tribes could vote on participation, however, and some rejected the reforms.

In 1936 Republicans gave their presidential nomination to Alfred Landon of Kansas, but he was buried in a Roosevelt landslide that continued the Democratic dominance in most of the Plains states. Soon after, however, some leading Democrats, notably Burton Wheeler, became highly critical of Roosevelt. In 1938 and after, Plains voters also expressed their disaffection from the New Deal, as most of the Northern Plains states returned to the Republicans and the Southern Plains states turned to conservative Democrats.

The late 1930s saw isolationism at high tide in the Northern Plains. In the mid- and late 1930s, Sen. Gerald Nye of North Dakota led investigations into the munitions industry and sponsored neutrality legislation. Jeannette Rankin of Montana cast the only vote against American entry into World War II. Isolationism then receded, but Langer voted against joining the United Nations, and both North Dakota senators opposed the North Atlantic Treaty Organization.

The Depression brought permanent changes in the politics of the Prairie Provinces. As the economy worsened, Saskatchewan was especially hard hit. The federal government, in Liberal hands, eventually provided relief grants to the Prairie Provinces and, perhaps most importantly, turned over control of natural resources to the provincial governments, thereby ending a long-standing grievance. When the Conservatives swept into federal office in 1930, they were led by Richard Bennett from Calgary, the first western prime minister.

Bennett's Conservatives failed to carry Alberta and Saskatchewan, both of which were moving toward distinctive provincial party systems. In 1929 Saskatchewan voters finally ended the Liberals' long tenure with a Conservative victory. This was short-lived, and in the mid-1930s control returned to the Liberals. Within Saskatchewan the Conservatives virtually disappeared from provincial politics, and opposition to the majority Liberals came instead from the Cooperative Commonwealth Federation (CCF), a farmer-labor coalition with socialist leanings. Albertans abandoned the UFA in 1935 and turned to a new party, Social Credit. Social Credit owed its appeal, more than anything else, to William Aberhart, a fundamentalist radio preacher who combined old-time religion with a cranky economics that promised to increase consumers' purchasing power. Drawing upon economic distress born of falling prices for farm products and urban unemployment, Social Credit swept Alberta's elections in 1935 and dominated the province's politics until 1971. For much of that time, Alberta practiced virtually one-party politics, with Social Credit sometimes winning 90 percent of the seats. It also attracted a following outside Alberta. From 1922 until 1943 Manitoba had a coalition government led by a veteran of the National Progressive Party, John Bracken. In 1943 Bracken became leader of the federal Conservatives, insisted that the party take the name Progressive Conservatives, and pushed it to adopt at least some of the old Progressive programs, especially opposition to the protective tariff.

Plains Politics since 1945

Prosperity returned to the Plains during World War II. During and after the war, liberals continued on the defensive in most places in the Plains, as conservative Republicans usually held most governorships in the Northern and Central Plains states and equally conservative Democrats held those in Oklahoma and Texas. Except for Montana and sometimes North Dakota, the Northern Plains states usually sent conservative Republicans to represent them in Washington. Between 1956 and the mid-1970s, however, all the Plains states moved toward more competitive two-party systems.

In the late 1950s the national economy entered a recession. When Dwight D. Eisenhower's presidential coattails were removed from state and congressional elections, economically distressed farmers and urban dwellers began to elect liberal Democrats throughout the Northern Plains. By 1959 George McGovern of South Dakota, Quentin Burdick of North Dakota (elected following a fusion of the Democratic Party with remnants of the NPL in 1956), and Gale McGee of Wyoming had joined Mike Mansfield and Lee Metcalf of Montana to make the Northern Plains appear a center of congressional liberalism. Northern and Central Plains states also began electing Democrats as governor, albeit usually moderate or conservative Democrats. Since the late 1950s Nebraska and North Dakota have joined Montana as being more likely to elect Democrats than Republicans as governor or U.S. senator. Underneath those highly visible offices, however, significant majorities of the voters have continued to identify themselves as Republicans.

As Democratic victories made some Northern and Central Plains states more competitive for major offices, a parallel development occurred among Southern Plains Republicans. In 1961 Texans sent a Republican, John Tower, to the U.S. Senate for the first time since Reconstruction. In 1962 Henry Bellmon became the first Republican ever to win the Oklahoma governorship, and Bellmon went on to the U.S. Senate in 1968. By 1973 both Oklahoma senators were Republicans. Like the Northern and Central Plains states, Oklahoma voted consistently Republican for president from 1952 through 1988, excepting only 1964. (Between 1952 and 1996, excepting 1964, all the Northern and Central Plains states voted Republican for president except for Montana and Colorado in 1992.) Though Texas voted Republican for president in 1952, 1956, and 1972, it was not until 1978 that a Republican, Bill Clements, won the governorship, and that office has alternated between the parties since then. Texas has voted Republican in presidential elections consistently since 1980. New Mexico voted Republican in all presidential elections after 1948 except 1960, 1992, 1996, and 2000. However, just as voters in the Northern Plains states have elected Democrats to major offices even though most have remained Republican, so most Oklahomans and Texans seem to have remained Democrats—at least until the late 1980s.

Republican gains in Southern Plains states, like Republican gains in the South more generally, came in part in response to Democratic espousal of civil rights legislation. The civil rights movement had its most direct impact in the Southern Plains, even though the specifics of *Brown v. The Board of Education of Topeka* (1954) concerned Topeka, Kansas. Earlier, the Supreme Court had struck down the Texas white primary law (1944) and had ordered Oklahoma and Texas to integrate their state graduate and professional schools (1950). There were, however, relatively few African Americans in most Plains counties, so the direct political impact of the civil rights movement was more pronounced in the eastern, non-Plains portions of those states. One important exception was Colorado, where Denver residents fought an occasionally violent battle over school integration between 1969 and 1974.

The 1970s also saw increased politicization of other ethnic groups in Plains states. In South Dakota, the American Indian Movement, first organized in Minneapolis in 1968, led demonstrations demanding equal treatment and autonomy and challenging the existing tribal leadership. A confrontation at Wounded Knee in 1973 produced two deaths. A violent, but not deadly, confrontation in 1967 brought an end to the Alianza, a New Mexico group formed to demand the return of land grants. In the early 1970s in Texas, Mexican Americans formed the La Raza Unida Party and won a number of local offices.

During the last quarter of the twentieth century, politics in several Plains states acquired a greater measure of racial and gender diversity. New Mexicans, to be certain, had routinely elected Mexican Americans to state and federal office throughout their state's history. In 1978 Nancy Landon Kassebaum of Kansas won the first of three terms in the U.S. Senate. Coloradoans in 1974 elected George L. Brown, the nation's first black lieutenant governor since Reconstruction, and in 1992 they sent Ben Nighthorse Campbell, a Native American, to the U.S. Senate. Patricia Schroeder, who served in Congress for twenty-four years, left undefeated in 1996 with a national reputation. In Nebraska in 1986, two women, Helen Boosalis and Kay Orr, faced each other as the major party candidates for governor.

In the Prairie Provinces, quite different political patterns evolved after World War II. In Saskatchewan, the CCF, led by Tommy C. Douglas until 1961, defeated the Liberals in 1944. The CCF took office as the first avowedly socialist state or provincial government in Canada or the United States, and it dominated Saskatchewan politics until 1964. A political coalition of farmers, labor, and professionals, the CCF espoused socialism and, in power, enacted a variety of reforms of provincial government as well as creating several government-owned manufacturing ventures, a hospitalization insurance program, and publicly owned transportation facilities. The CCF became part of the New Democratic Party (NDP) in 1961. When the NDP introduced a universal, compulsory, prepaid medical care plan in 1961–62, it precipitated massive resistance by the province's physicians. This, along with some losses among its farm supporters who disliked the NDP's close ties to labor, helped to produce a Liberal victory in 1964. The NDP regained their majority in 1971, lost to the Progressive Conservatives in 1982, but subsequently recovered. The coalition that had governed in Manitoba since the early 1920s came to an end in 1958 with a Progressive Conservative win. Party turnover in Manitoba has been frequent since then, with Progressive Conservatives, Liberals, and the NDP all forming governments at least once. In office, the Manitoba NDP initiated some moderate socialist programs. Alberta, riding a crest of economic prosperity produced by a post–World War II oil boom, continued its maverick political ways, giving usually enormous parliamentary margins to Social Credit through 1971, when it switched to the Progressive Conservatives by similar large margins.

Federal Canadian politics between 1935 and 1957 was dominated by the Liberals. In 1957, however, John Diefenbaker, a charismatic Progressive Conservative from Saskatchewan, narrowly defeated the incumbent Liberals. He achieved a decisive victory in another federal election in 1958. Diefenbaker enjoyed strong support in western Canada, particularly in the rural areas, even after he lost the 1962 federal election. Support in western Canada for the Progressive Conservatives remained strong for decades but was seriously eroded by the massive unpopularity of Brian Mulroney's Progressive Conservative government during its last years in power. Disillusioned conservatives then turned in large numbers to a new political party. Preston Manning, son of a longtime Social Credit premier, founded the Reform Party in 1987 on the principles of conservatism and opposition to special treatment for Quebec and to preferences based on race, language, or culture. In the 1997 federal election, western voters divided their support between Reform, Liberal, and New Democratic Party candidates, with Reform showing particular strength in Alberta and British Columbia, allowing it to become the largest opposition party in the federal parliament.

Throughout most of the Great Plains, net out-migration began after World War II and has persisted in most rural places since. The remaining population became more concentrated in urban areas. Local and state government faced a variety of problems resulting from a diminishing population base, but education often drew the greatest attention. Declining population and increasing accreditation standards caught rural schools in their pincers. Although school consolidation often proved politically divisive, most Plains states witnessed sharp reductions in the number of school districts—by 72 percent in Wyoming between 1952 and 1984, and by 67 percent in Nebraska between 1949 and 1965.

Conclusion

The political history of the Great Plains has much in common with its surrounding regions. Many of its distinctive features are shared with other western or midwestern states. One feature, federal policies aimed at promoting economic development, has been common throughout much of the West. Populism, early approval of women's suffrage, and the western variety of progressivism were perhaps the most distinctive aspects of Plains political development, but they were not unique to Plains states. Populism and progressivism left most Plains states with a legacy of direct democracy and a few Plains states with state-owned enterprises. Populism and western progressivism, born of agricultural adversity and, in the 1920s at least, nurtured by a political alliance of farmers and labor, grew out of a social and economic situation now largely vanished. A similar alliance produced the Cooperative Commonwealth Federation in Saskatchewan, which showed more staying power in the form of the New Democratic Party than did its counterparts south of the border. The substantial decline in the proportion of farmers and stockgrowers in the U.S. Plains population has reduced the potential base for such politics, and the emergence of an agribusiness attitude among many of the survivors seems to have given them a different political outlook.

The emergence of two-party competition throughout most of the Plains states since the late 1950s suggests that the Plains's political subcultures are being homogenized into larger national patterns. Similarly, the half-century pattern of support for most Republican presidential candidates throughout most of the Plains suggests a homogenization into larger patterns of western politics. Finally, the decline in party loyalty in the East and South suggests that even that aspect of western politics is no longer unique. In the Canadian Plains, however, the rise of the Reform Party suggests that western distinctiveness in a Canadian context may be a persistent feature of that nation's politics.

See also AFRICAN AMERICANS: All-Black Towns / EDUCATION: School Consolidation and Reorganization / GENDER: Suffrage Movement / LAW: *Brown v. The Board of Education of Topeka*; White Primary / NATIVE AMERICANS: Indian Removal; Métis; Pawnees; Treaties / PROTEST AND DISSENT: Aberhart, William; American Indian Movement; Ku Klux Klan; Nonpartisan League; Temperance Movement / WAR: Bleeding Kansas.

Robert W. Cherny
San Francisco State University

Abbott, Carl. *Colorado: A History of the Centennial State*. Boulder: Colorado Associated University Press, 1982. Barr, Alwyn. *Reconstruction to Reform: Texas Politics, 1876–1906*. Austin: University of Texas Press, 1971. Brown, Norman D. *Hood, Bonnet, and Little Brown Jug: Texas Politics, 1921–1928*. College Station: Texas A&M University Press, 1984. Cherny, Robert W. *Populism, Progressivism, and the Transformation of Nebraska Politics, 1885–1915*. Lincoln: University of Nebraska Press, 1981. Clanton, Gene. *Kansas Populism: Ideas and Men*. Lawrence: University Press of Kansas, 1969. Friesen, Gerald. *The Canadian Prairies: A History*. Lincoln: University of Nebraska Press, 1984. Gomez-Quinones, Juan. *Roots of Chicano Politics, 1600–1940*. Albuquerque: University of New Mexico Press, 1994. Gould, Lewis L. *Wyoming: A Political History, 1868–1896*. New Haven CT: Yale University Press, 1968. Laycock, David H. *Populism and Democratic Thought in the Canadian Prairies, 1910 to 1945*. Toronto: University of Toronto Press, 1990. Lipset, Seymour Martin. *Agrarian Socialism: The Cooperative Commonwealth Federation in Saskatchewan*. Berkeley: University of California Press, 1971. Lowitt, Richard. *The New Deal and the West*. Bloomington: Indiana University Press, 1984. Macpherson, Crawford Brough. *Democracy in Alberta: Social Credit and the Party System*. Toronto: University of Toronto Press, 1968. Malone, Michael P., and Richard B. Roeder. *Montana: A History of Two Centuries*. Seattle: University of Washington Press, 1976. Morlan, Robert L. *Political Prairie Fire: The Nonpartisan League, 1915–1922*. Minneapolis: University of Minnesota Press, 1955. Saloutos, Theodore, and John D. Hicks. *Agricultural Discontent in the Middle West, 1900–1939*. Madison: University of Wisconsin Press, 1951. Scales, James R., and Danney Goble. *Oklahoma Politics: A History*. Norman: University of Oklahoma Press, 1982.

ABBOTT, GRACE (1878–1939)

Grace Abbott was perhaps the greatest champion of children's rights in American history. She was born (November 17, 1878) and raised in Grand Island, Nebraska. Abbott was part of an accomplished pioneer family. Her father was the first lieutenant governor of Nebraska, her mother was a leader of the early Plains women's suffrage movement, and her sister, Edith, was the first woman in American history to become the dean of a major university graduate school, the University of Chicago. Grace Abbott herself was the first woman nominated for a presidential cabinet post, secretary of labor for Herbert Hoover, and the first person sent to represent the United States at a committee of the League of Nations.

Grace Abbott

As chief of the U.S. Children's Bureau from 1921 to 1934, Abbott was the highest ranking and most powerful woman in the U.S. government when the Depression hit. She was the only trained social worker at the top political levels in Washington DC in those disaster-filled days. Accordingly, she exerted a crucial influence on the momentous relief and welfare efforts that were developed in response to the crisis.

A trusted associate of Nobel Prize–winner Jane Addams, Abbott also made significant contributions to the field of immigration rights during her tenure as director of the Immigrants Protective League of Chicago from 1908 to 1917. She was a vigorous leader in the fight against child labor and a longtime crusader for improved children's health care. She was among the first female broadcasters to a national audience, with "Your Child" on NBC in the 1920s, and her trailblazing social service work has been credited with leading the way to the creation of the Social Security Act and the United Nations' UNICEF program.

Abbott was a woman of intriguing contradictions: a lifelong Republican Party member and a lifelong liberal activist; a native of the Plains frontier who spent much of her adult life in the poorest immigrant quarters of urban Chicago; and an unmarried woman who was nicknamed "the mother of America's 43 million children."

Abbott's courageous struggles—to protect the rights of immigrants, to increase the role of women in government, and to improve the lives of all children—demonstrate a remarkable human ability to seek out suffering and to do something about it. She was a bold and defiant woman who changed our country more profoundly than have many presidents.

Throughout her career, Abbott never lost her profound love for her Great Plains homeland, which she felt had so vitally contributed to her character. As Edith Abbott wrote of her sister, "To the end of her life, Grace was a daughter of the pioneers—with the vigorous 'dash' of the pioneer who is able to accept temporary defeat in the confident belief in ultimate victory . . . even when the odds on the other side are very great."

Edward Keating, congressional representative from Colorado, summed up the feelings of innumerable Americans when, following Abbott's death on June 19, 1939, in Chicago, he stood on the floor of the Congress and said, quite simply: "To me there was something about Grace Abbott which always suggested Joan of Arc."

See also EDUCATION: Abbott, Edith.

John Sorensen
New York City

Abbott, Edith. "A Sister's Memories." *Social Service Review* 13 (1939): 351–408. Costin, Lela B. *Two Sisters for Social Justice: A Biography of Grace and Edith Abbott.* Urbana: University of Illinois Press, 1983. Sorensen, John. "My Sister and Comrade: A Radio Portrait of Grace Abbott." Aired on Nebraska Public Radio, Lincoln, January 20, 21, and 22, 1997.

ALBERTA

Anchoring the northwestern edge of the Great Plains and nestled against the Rocky Mountains, the province of Alberta, Canada, is a unique blend of European and North American influences, a blend that has produced a political system characterized by strong leaders, strong political parties, and strong governments. Interestingly, this uniqueness can be traced to the influence of those who settled the Great Plains on both sides of the forty-ninth parallel. It is a prime example of how geography and human migration have intersected to produce new political behavior.

Canada is a federal state. Like other federations it has a system of government that constitutionally divides power between central and constituent governments. In Canada the latter are called provinces. The institutions of government are modeled largely on the British parliamentary system as it existed in the nineteenth century. There is an elected legislature in each province, with a cabinet consisting of a premier and ministers who are members of the House. Although the Queen is nominally the provincial head of state, in practice this position is occupied by an appointed official called the lieutenant governor. Elections are held on a regular basis, usually every four years, and are contested by several political parties, many of which have unique roots in the province.

Alberta was created in 1905 as one of the new provinces carved out of the old Northwest Territories, which had stretched from Manitoba north to the Arctic Ocean and west and south to the Rocky Mountains. For political reasons the Liberal government of Sir Wilfrid Laurier ignored the advice of those supporting a single province and created several provinces instead. The result was Alberta, Saskatchewan, and an enlarged Manitoba, increasing the number of provinces in Canada by two.

Initially the politics of Alberta followed the traditional British and Canadian model, with elections contested by the Liberal and Conservative Parties. The Liberals, under the leadership of A. C. Rutherford, were in power between 1905 and 1921. However, powerful social

Alberta Legislature building, Edmonton

and economic forces, together with the influx of settlers from the midwestern United States, changed the system dramatically after World War I.

Alberta, like most of the Great Plains jurisdictions, was a society rooted in the agricultural development of the incredibly fertile land of the Prairies. It was a society largely dependent on the production and export of grains. As with any such society, it was subject to the boom and bust cycle of a single industry. Thus, when prices for agricultural products dropped dramatically after 1919, farmers and their supporters looked for solutions to the economic crisis.

They found their solution in radical populist politics. The person most responsible for promoting this approach was Henry Wise Wood, an immigrant from the midwestern United States, who brought with him strong ideas about individualism and group government. These found resonance and took root in the Alberta of the 1920s. Together with other farmers he founded the United Farmers of Alberta (UFA), a movement that contested and won the 1921 election. In defeating the Liberals the UFA began a trend that continues to this day. No political party that has been elected to govern Alberta has ever returned to power after it was defeated.

Populist politics dominated the Alberta scene from 1921 until after World War II. In the mid-1930s the UFA faltered as a result of a series of internal scandals. It was completely wiped out in the 1935 election. Its place in government was taken by a new political party called Social Credit, which ran for the first time in that year under the leadership of William Aberhart, a Protestant minister. Social Credit won a stunning landslide victory in its first electoral contest.

Although Social Credit was a populist party, it differed in many important respects from its predecessor. Its basic ideology was taken from the teachings of Maj. Clifford Douglas, an Englishman who proposed a comprehensive monetary policy for dealing with the role of government in society. While these ideas were soon discarded in practice, the party continued to espouse them in theory until the late 1960s. Finally, while the UFA had been radical democrats, Social Credit was more plebiscitarian and less tolerant of political dissent. After the death of Aberhart in 1943 the party elected E. C. Manning, a protégé of his. (In 2000 his son, E. P. Manning, headed the Reform Party at the national level in Canada.) Social Credit stayed in power until 1971.

The discovery and exploitation of huge oil and gas reserves in Alberta after World War II dramatically changed the economic and social landscape of Alberta. In twenty years the province moved from a largely rural agricultural society to an urban, resource-based community. This brought with it some political changes. In 1971, after thirty-five years in office, the Social Credit Party was defeated. Peter Lougheed, a Calgary lawyer, led the new Progressive Conservative government. It was strongly particularistic and protective of the oil industry and its benefits. It had several confrontations with the federal government over natural resources and the revenue from them.

After 1982, when the New Democratic Party under Grant Notley became the Official Opposition, politics in the province seemed to be adjusting to a left-right division. Notley's death in 1984, and the inability of his successors to hold on to their position, however, resulted in a return to one-party dominance. The Liberal Party, which has not regained power since 1921, is now the Official Opposition, but the Progressive Conservative Party has been firmly in office for twenty-seven years.

The history of politics in Alberta has been dominated by two characteristics. The first is a strong sense of political alienation. Albertans have tended to see their role in Canada as undervalued and ignored. This strong sense of grievance has led them to elect representatives who are prepared to "fight for Alberta and the west." The second is the plebiscitarian nature of politics in the province. Most governments have received strong mandates, with little opposition. However, once rejected, parties have forever remained excluded. In a sense, despite the present strong economic base and the obvious wealth of the province, Albertans continue to exhibit the political behavior of an earlier, more marginal time. Grievance and alienation, once instilled in a political culture, are difficult to remove.

The politics of Alberta today is as fascinating as it was at the turn of the twentieth century. It is a prime example of how the geographical features and settlement patterns of the North American Great Plains have shaped social and political behavior to create unique and interesting societies.

See also INDUSTRY: Petroleum, Canada / PROTEST AND DISSENT: Aberhart, William.

Howard A. Leeson
University of Regina

Calderola, Carle. *Society and Politics in Alberta*. Toronto: Methuen, 1979. Dyck, Rand. *Provincial Politics in Canada*. Scarborough, Ontario: Prentice-Hall Canada, Inc., 1995. MacGregor, James G. *A History of Alberta*. Edmonton: Hurtig Publishers, 1972.

BACA, POLLY

See HISPANIC AMERICANS: Baca, Polly

BELLMON, HENRY (b. 1921)

Henry Bellmon, governor and U.S. senator from Oklahoma, was the pivotal figure in creating Oklahoma's modern two-party politics. Bellmon was born on September 3, 1921, on a farm near Billings, Noble County, Oklahoma. He graduated from Oklahoma A&M University (now Oklahoma State University) in 1942 and served with distinction in the U.S. Marine Corps during World War II. After the war ended, he returned to the family farm and became active in local politics. He was elected to the Oklahoma legislature in 1946 but was defeated for reelection in 1948.

In 1947 Bellmon married Shirley Osborn, and for the next fifteen years he concentrated on farming and raising his three daughters. In 1960 he was elected as chair of the Oklahoma Republican Party and in that capacity worked to make the party competitive at the state and local level. Two years later he announced his candidacy for governor of Oklahoma. He defeated Democrat Bill Atkinson, and in doing so became the first Republican governor of Oklahoma and the first Republican to be governor of any southern state since Reconstruction.

Bellmon was ineligible to succeed himself as governor and left office in 1967. The following year, he ran for the U.S. Senate and defeated incumbent Democrat Mike Monroney. Despite his close association with President Richard Nixon, Bellmon was reelected over Democrat Ed Edmondson in 1974 by a narrow margin. During his two terms in the Senate, Bellmon rose to become ranking minority member of the Senate Budget Committee. He voted a generally conservative line but angered doctrinaire conservatives with his support for the Panama Canal treaty and school integration.

Bellmon declined to run for a third term in 1980 and returned to Oklahoma. He served as a member of the faculty at the University of Oklahoma before running for a second term as governor in 1986. By winning the election, Bellmon became Oklahoma's first Republican to win a second term as governor. During his second term Bellmon presided over the centennial of the Oklahoma Land Run of 1889. He continued to steer a moderate course and implemented important budgetary and educational reforms. Bellmon retired after completing his term in 1991, but he remained active in local and state political activity. Henry Bellmon will be remembered as the architect of modern two-party politics in Oklahoma and as a governor and senator of independence and integrity.

Fred M. Shelley
Southwest Texas State University

Bellmon, Henry. *The Life and Times of Henry Bellmon*. Tulsa OK: Charter Oak Press. 1992.

BENNETT, RICHARD B. (1870–1947)

Businessman, lawyer, politician, and prime minister, Richard Bennett was born in Hopewell, New Brunswick, on July 3, 1870, the eldest son of five children. His father, Henry, was a shipbuilding craftsman who drank heavily and drove his business into bankruptcy. His mother, a schoolmistress of strong religious tenets, poured herself into raising her children, of whom Richard was her favorite. A shy and studious boy gifted with a clear mind, superb memory, compelling voice, and strong tenacity, he spent his childhood and teens in school, church, and household duties. He avoided most other children and their pastimes, including alcohol, tobacco, games, and sports. A devout Methodist, he focused on the goal of living life opposite to that of his father and bringing to his mother the success in life he thought she deserved.

Bennett graduated from eighth grade at age

twelve, joined the militia, and was a teacher from age sixteen. He entered Dalhousie Law School at age twenty, working part-time as a librarian to finance his studies. Called to the bar in the year of his graduation in 1893, he made a striking figure. Tall, lean, and fair-skinned, and with a glib eloquence, he was successful in court. Possessing an insatiable appetite for current affairs and politics in Canada, Britain, and the Empire, he ran for Chatham city council in 1896 and won. His manager was his youthful friend Max Aitken, the future Lord Beaverbrook. He left office after several months of feuding with his fellow councilors. Later that year his law dean at Dalhousie recommended him to Sir James Lougheed of Calgary, who went to Chatham for a personal interview. Bennett was offered a job as Lougheed's law partner, and after several months of hard negotiations, he accepted it. He saw his future on the Prairies.

The young lawyer devoted his career to fame and fortune: fame through the ballot box and fortune through his legal practice. A strict sabbatarian, he never joined in Prairie culture. Uninterested in horses, farming, or ranching, he lived a solitary, bachelor life first in boardinghouses and later in the Palliser Hotel. He worked twelve-hour days, six days a week. Dressed in a stiff hat, topcoat, striped pants, starched wing collar, and cravat, he took his meals at the Alberta Hotel, where he entertained clients at a separate table behind a drawn curtain. By 1913 he was a rotund figure who had his assistants carry his briefcase and law books into court. Bennett became Calgary's premier corporate lawyer. He was legal counsel for the Canadian Pacific Railway (CPR), the Hudson's Bay Company, the Royal Bank, and numerous insurance companies. He also made a fortune buying CPR land and selling it to out-of-town investors. He brought Max Aitken out west and with him created monopolies in grain elevators, electric utilities, and cement. Sitting on corporate directorates and participating in joint ventures, he became president of Calgary Power and a major investor in the Alberta-Pacific Grain Company and Canada Cement. By 1914 he was one of the wealthiest men in the Canadian Prairies.

Bennett had a clear view of his adopted land. He saw its economic potential as unlimited: grains, meats, hydroelectric power, oil and gas, mining, transportation, and settlement. The Canadian Prairies were seen as Britain's hinterland, a place where British culture could flourish in the new industrial world, serving as a counterbalance to the economic power of the American Plains. He saw himself as the conduit between eastern Canadian and British bankers and investors and the development of an industrial, and imperial, Prairie economy. Thus, he was a strong proponent of the British Empire, preferential tariffs, and British foreign policy. He went into politics to develop these ideas. A Conservative, he was elected for Calgary to the territorial assembly in 1898, to the provincial legislature in 1909, and to the Dominion Parliament in 1911. His great lament

was World War I, which split the Empire and brought a depression from which the Prairies would never recover in his lifetime.

The 1920s were a period of transition in Bennett's life. He split in anger with his law partner Lougheed in 1921, lost several elections, and considered moving to Britain. But after he won the seat of Calgary West in 1925, his career turned from law and business to politics and from the Prairies to Ottawa. He became the leader of Canada's Conservative Party in 1927 and prime minister in the election of 1930. He promised aggressive and progressive action, but he could not convert his ideas into legislation. Indecisive, he was unable to gain the confidence of the people or to understand from his hotel suite how they saw the world. Bennett became isolated in his own party by 1934, and his party was defeated in the election of October 1935.

His vision of the Prairies, however, still captured the minds of most of his constituents, who continued to vote for him. In these later years he was one of the major philanthropists of Prairie society. But embittered by the belief that his country did not appreciate him, in 1939 he bought the Mickleham estate in Surrey, England, and moved there. Supported by his friend Max, now Lord Beaverbrook, his wealth and political beliefs brought him the title of viscount in 1941. He died at his estate on June 26, 1947, of heart failure.

See also LAW: Lougheed, James.

Louis A. Knafla
University of Calgary

Bennett Papers. National Archives of Canada, Ottawa, and Glenbow-Alberta Institute, Calgary. Gray, James H. *R. B. Bennett: The Calgary Years.* Toronto: University of Toronto Press, 1991. Knafla, Louis A. "Richard 'Bonfire' Bennett: The Legal Practice of a Prairie Corporate Lawyer, 1898 to 1913." In *Beyond the Law: Lawyers and Business in Canada, 1830 to 1930*, edited by Carol Wilton. Toronto: Osgoode Society, 1990: 320–76.

BRYAN, WILLIAM JENNINGS
(1860–1925)

William Jennings Bryan, known as the "Boy Orator of the Platte" and the "Great Commoner," was a political leader with uncommon oratorical abilities and an affinity for the religious and rural classes. Born on March 19, 1860, in Salem, Illinois, Bryan idolized Abraham Lincoln, who had been born nearby. In Lincoln, Bryan saw a public servant with a strong dedication to the common people and a strong faith in Christian morality. Bryan adopted both.

Bryan attended Illinois College, where he met his wife, Mary Baird, and graduated from Chicago's Union College of Law in 1883. In 1887 he relocated to Lincoln, Nebraska, which would be his home until 1921. He established a law office with his friend Adolphus R. Talbot and practiced until 1895, while establishing himself politically among Nebraska's Democratic leadership. Less business-oriented than other Nebraska Democrats, such as J. Sterling Morton, Bryan was chosen to run in the 1890 congressional elections to appeal to the increasingly political Farmers Alliance, which

would evolve into the Populist, or People's, Party. Although traditionally a Republican state, Nebraska elected Bryan to his first political office. He served in the House of Representatives from 1891 to 1895. From 1894 to 1896 he also edited the Democratic *Omaha World-Herald*.

In 1896 Bryan addressed the Democratic National Convention in Chicago, giving his famous "Cross of Gold" speech, a stirring distillation of the complaints of agrarian and urban people who felt defeated by America's rapid industrialization and entry into world markets. The electrifying speech won Bryan the presidential nomination at age thirty-six. Shortly thereafter, the Populist Party also nominated Bryan but attempted to maintain its independence by nominating a different vice presidential candidate. During his campaign Bryan virtually ignored the Populist Party, although he did champion its ideas, chief among them the remonetization of silver. In part due to fears of political and economic disruption, William McKinley won the election, but Bryan would now be the perennial Democratic presidential candidate.

In 1898 Bryan organized a regiment to fight in the Spanish-American War, but he remained in Florida while the unit went on. Bryan won the Democratic nomination for the presidency again in 1900; his campaign attacked America's imperial role following the Spanish-American and Philippine-American wars. American voters rejected Bryan's anti-imperialism and reelected McKinley by an even larger margin than in 1896. In 1901 Bryan established *The Commoner*, which advanced his liberal political views and conservative religious beliefs.

Bryan received the Democratic presidential nomination a third time in 1908 but lost to Teddy Roosevelt's chosen successor, William Howard Taft. From 1913 to 1915 Bryan served as the secretary of state under President Woodrow Wilson. He resigned in 1915 because he believed that, despite Wilson's professed neutrality toward the belligerent powers in World War I, his pro-British actions would lead America into war. Although Bryan never won the presidency, his influence was immense. He traveled throughout the country and the world speaking to great crowds on various social and political issues, including prohibition and women's suffrage (both of which he supported).

Bryan lived in Lincoln until 1921, when he moved to Florida. In the last decade of his life his religious conservatism overshadowed his liberal political beliefs. His final public appearance was in Dayton, Tennessee, as prosecuting lawyer in the trial of John Scopes, who had been charged with violating a Tennessee law prohibiting the teaching of the theory of evolution in the public schools. The opposing counsel, Clarence Darrow, criticized Bryan's literal interpretation of the Bible, upon which the Tennessee law relied, and placed Bryan on the stand, forcing him to admit to several biblical contradictions. The state won the case, but Bryan's own often self-contradictory testimony highlighted the growing gap between

William Jennings Bryan, between 1900 and 1910

religious fundamentalism and secularism in the United States.

William Jennings Bryan died on July 26, 1925, in Dayton, Tennessee, just days after the Scopes trial. When Bryan championed the cause of the poor rural and urban classes in 1896, he was seen as a radical voice calling for deep societal change, but by 1925 his was a conservative voice. By the close of his life he had come to symbolize American divisions regarding religion. Some found in him a perfect champion of religious conservatism, while others, such as H. L. Mencken, found him to represent intolerant religious extremism. Always controversial, Bryan's career saw his transformation from a crusader for the rights of the common people against organized wealth to an anti-imperialist and, finally, to a proponent of biblical creationism.

Charles Vollan
University of Nebraska–Lincoln

Cherny, Robert W. *A Righteous Cause: The Life of William Jennings Bryan.* Norman: University of Oklahoma Press, 1994. "William Jennings Bryan and His America." Special issue. *Nebraska History* 77 (1996).

BUSH, GEORGE H. W. (b. 1924)

George Herbert Walker Bush served as the forty-first president of the United States. One of three persons elected to the presidency from Texas, Bush shares with John Adams the distinction of having seen his son inaugurated to the presidency.

Bush was born in Milton, Massachusetts, on June 12, 1924, the son of Prescott and Dorothy Walker Bush. His father served as a Republican senator from Connecticut from 1953 to 1965. George Bush grew up in Greenwich, Connecticut, and attended Yale University. In 1942 he enlisted in the U.S. Navy as a pilot and flew fifty-eight combat missions in the Pacific. After the war he returned to Yale and graduated in 1948. He married Barbara Pierce in 1945. They had six children: George W., Robin (who died of leukemia at the age of three), John (Jeb), Neil, Marvin, and Dorothy.

After graduating from college, Bush moved to Odessa, Texas, to begin a career in the oil industry. He cofounded the Zapata Petroleum Corporation in Midland in 1953. In 1958 he moved the company's headquarters to Houston, where he became active in Republican politics. In 1964 he ran as a Republican for a seat in the U.S. Senate but lost to Democrat Ralph Yarborough. Two years later he won a seat in the U.S. House of Representatives and was reelected in 1968. In 1970 Bush decided to run for the Senate again, but he lost to Democrat Lloyd Bentsen, who had defeated the more liberal Yarborough in the Democratic Party primary.

Following Bush's defeat by Bentsen, President Richard Nixon appointed Bush as permanent representative of the United States to the United Nations. In 1973 he became chairman of the Republican National Committee. After Nixon resigned the presidency in the wake of the Watergate scandal in 1974, his successor, Gerald R. Ford, appointed Bush as U.S. ambassador to China and then director of the Central Intelligence Agency. He returned to private life after Ford's defeat in the 1976 presidential election by Democrat Jimmy Carter.

In 1980 Bush ran for the Republican nomination for president of the United States. Although he won several primary elections, he lost the party's nomination to former California governor Ronald Reagan. Reagan asked Bush to serve as the Republican candidate for vice president, and the Reagan-Bush ticket easily defeated Carter and his running mate, Walter Mondale, in the general election.

Bush served as Reagan's vice president from 1981 to 1989. The Reagan-Bush ticket was reelected in a landslide in 1984. Although some conservative Republicans were skeptical of Bush's commitment to conservative policies, Bush was nominated by the Republicans as their presidential candidate in 1988. He and his running mate, Sen. Dan Quayle of Indiana, defeated the Democratic nominees, Gov. Michael Dukakis of Massachusetts and Senator Bentsen.

Bush was inaugurated on January 20, 1989. During his administration, communist governments in eastern Europe and the Soviet Union collapsed. In 1990 Iraqi dictator Saddam Hussein took over Kuwait. After Saddam declined to restore Kuwait's independence, Bush assembled an international coalition to expel Iraq from Kuwait. He received congressional approval to use force, and early in 1991 the U.S.-led coalition used air and ground assaults to oust the Iraqis from Kuwait. Bush also initiated discussions with Mexico and Canada that would lead eventually to the establishment of the North American Free Trade Agreement

Bush's foreign policy successes in the Middle East, eastern Europe, and elsewhere won him widespread popularity. Few anticipated that he would have difficulty being reelected in 1992. However, Bush's opponents accused him of neglecting the economy and other domestic issues. With a recession in 1990 and 1991, and increasing levels of unemployment, he was portrayed as being out of touch with, and unsympathetic to, the difficulties faced by poor and middle-class Americans. He was renominated in 1992 but lost the general election to Democrat Bill Clinton. A third candidate, Ross Perot, won nearly 20 percent of the vote and may have taken enough votes away from Bush to secure Clinton's victory in the general election.

After his defeat by Clinton, Bush retired from public life. However, he had the satisfaction of seeing two of his sons achieve high public office. His oldest son, George W. Bush, was elected governor of Texas in 1994 and 1998 and president in 2000. Son Jeb was elected governor of Florida in 1998.

Fred M. Shelley
Southwest Texas State University

Bush, George H. W., and Brent Scowcroft. *A World Transformed.* New York: Alfred A. Knopf, Inc. 1998. Greene, John R. *The Presidency of George Bush.* Lawrence: University Press of Kansas, 2000. Parmet, Herbert S. *George Bush: The Life of a Lone Star Yankee.* New York: Scribner, 1997.

BUSH, GEORGE W. (b. 1946)

In 2000 George Walker Bush was elected the forty-third president of the United States. He and John Quincy Adams are the only U.S. presidents whose fathers also achieved that high office.

Bush was born on July 6, 1946, in New Haven, Connecticut, the son of George Herbert Walker and Barbara Pierce Bush. At the age of two, he moved with his family to Odessa, Texas, and shortly thereafter to Midland. Following in his father's footsteps, he attended Yale University, graduating in 1968. He later earned a master of business administration degree from Harvard University in 1975. He served as a pilot in the Texas Air National Guard between 1968 and 1973, and married Laura Welch of Midland in 1977.

Bush spent much of his early career in the oil and gas industry in Texas, although he ran unsuccessfully for a seat in the House of Representatives in 1978. In the late 1980s he worked as an adviser and speechwriter in his father's presidential campaign. After his father won the election, the younger Bush purchased the Texas Rangers professional baseball team.

In 1994 Bush ran for governor of Texas. He won the Republican nomination and defeated a popular incumbent, Democrat Ann Richards, in the general election. Bush was a popular governor, emphasizing welfare and education reform along with strong anticrime measures. He was easily reelected in 1998.

In the spring of 2000 Bush began campaigning for the Republican presidential nomination. Turning back a strong challenge by Sen. John McCain of Arizona, Bush won his party's nomination. He selected Richard Cheney, former Wyoming representative and U.S. secretary of defense, as his running mate. In one of the closest and most hotly contested presidential elections in history, Bush and Cheney defeated their Democratic opponents, Vice President Al Gore and Sen. Joseph Lieberman. For five weeks after Election Day, the outcome hung in the balance while allegations of ballot irregularities and flawed voting procedures were investigated in Florida, whose twenty-five electoral votes would determine the outcome. Eventually, the U.S. Supreme Court ruled in Bush's favor, and the Bush-Cheney ticket was elected with a margin of 271 to 266 in the Electoral College, despite the fact that Gore won approximately half a million more popular votes than Bush.

Bush was inaugurated in January 2001. The September 11, 2001, terrorist attacks on the World Trade Center and the Pentagon soon provided a test of Bush's leadership. The administration's response to global terrorism, including military action in 2001 against the al-Qaida network in Afghanistan and the 2003 invasion of Iraq, proved highly popular, and Bush's approval rating remained very high into 2003.

Fred M. Shelley
Southwest Texas State University

Bruni, Frank. *Ambling into History: The Unlikely Odyssey of George W. Bush.* New York: HarperCollins, 2001. Hatfield, James. *Fortunate Son: George W. Bush and the Making of an American President.* New York: Times Books, 1999. Toobin, Jeffrey. *Too Close to Call: The Thirty-six-Day Battle to Decide the 2000 Election.* New York: Random House, 2001.

CHAVEZ, LINDA

See HISPANIC AMERICANS: Chavez, Linda

CIVIL DIVISIONS OF GOVERNMENT

The lands and peoples of the North American Great Plains fall within the territorial jurisdictions of the Dominion of Canada and the United States of America. These countries are federal democracies with three distinct levels of representation and administration: national or federal, state or provincial, and local levels of government. Citizens elect legislators and other officeholders, pay taxes, and are governed by laws enacted at each of the three levels of governance. Canada's more formally centralized parliamentary system is based on the British principle of "responsible government," with members of the national executive cabinet chosen from, and accountable to, the legislature. There is no separately elected executive, as in the U.S. presidential and congressional system.

Lands of the Great Plains north of the forty-ninth parallel fall within Canada's three "Prairie Provinces" of Alberta (provincehood 1905), Manitoba (1870), and Saskatchewan (1905). These provinces were formed from part of the area controlled until 1870 by the Hudson's Bay Company. The unicameral legislatures of each of these provinces have principal authority over such matters as natural resources, education, land tenure, health, property, and civil rights within their territories, and each legislature shares authority with the Canadian national government over inland waterways, railroads, external trade, agriculture, old-age pensions, and foreign immigration to their local regions. Governmental units at the local or third tier of government are formally subdivisions of the provincial governments. Partly because Canadians believed that extreme localism had been one of the precipitating causes of the American Revolution, local governments in Canada generally have been restricted to more limited roles than in the United States. However, distance from the federal capital in Ottawa, combined with the passage of time, encouraged the establishment of stronger local authorities in the Prairie Provinces than in eastern Canada. The three Prairie Provinces are subdivided into about 1,300 urban and rural municipalities. However, some three-quarters of the total population lives in thirty-five of the larger municipalities that are classed as cities. Small populations, weak tax bases, and confusing overlaps between municipal, school district, and hospital district boundaries have forced considerable reorganization and consolidation of local government units in more rural areas of the Prairie Provinces in recent years.

The Great Plains south of the forty-ninth parallel falls within the territories of ten of the fifty states of the United States. These include Colorado (statehood 1876), Kansas (1861), Montana (1889), Nebraska (1867), New Mexico (1912), North Dakota (1889), Oklahoma (1907), South Dakota (1889), Texas (1845), and Wyoming (1890). These states span most of the territories acquired from France via the Louisiana Purchase in 1803 and from Mexico via the annexation of Texas in 1845. Although these states entered the Union relatively late, they all have sovereign status under the U.S. Constitution, which formally reserves all powers not expressly delegated to the federal government to the states and their citizens. While the federal government holds primary jurisdiction over several important matters, such as currency, foreign relations, and national defense, most aspects of governance involve shared or overlapping federal and state responsibilities. Both legally and practically, the powers of state governments are maintained and reinforced by governors and by legislatures whose members are independently elected by the citizens of each state. Except for Nebraska's unicameral, all state legislatures are bicameral.

Partly reflecting the strong localistic aspect of American political culture, the lowest or third tier of American governance tends to be considerably more varied and complex than is the case in Canada. In addition to the federal government and their respective state governments, most Americans also pay taxes to a county government, a city or town government, a school district unit, and several so-called special districts. Although units of local government are formally subdivisions of state governments, they often tend to have considerable legal and practical autonomy over their own local affairs. Thus, levels of local tax effort and pubic service provision can and do vary greatly from place to place within the United States. Moreover, the degree of governmental localism that is encountered in the American Great Plains is often even more intense than elsewhere in the nation. One indicator is the unusually high incidence of patriotic names given to counties, towns, or streets within the region, such as Washington, Lincoln, Franklin, Union, Liberty, Independence, Freedom, or Unity.

Another, more important indicator is the sheer number of local governmental units within the Great Plains. The ten Plains states contain more than 21,000 local governments, including 818 counties, 4,183 municipalities, 4,124 towns or townships, 4,148 school districts, and 8,600 special districts. The citizens of these ten states vote in various constituencies for seventy-eight officials at the federal level (for president, senators, and representatives) and for 2,903 officials at the state level (e.g., governors, attorneys general, judges, legislators). In addition, the citizens of these ten states elect an astonishing 110,328 local officials (e.g., mayors, sheriffs, justices, county commissioners, and members of city or town councils, school boards, and special district bodies). Indeed, in many of the more lightly populated counties of the Central Plains, more than one out of every twenty-five persons is an elected local official of some type. Among the more extreme cases is Arthur County, Nebraska, with a 1990 population of 462 persons and fifty elected local officials in 1992. In comparison, the average for the

United States as a whole is about one elected local official for every 500 people. While the overall average for Great Plains states is about one elected local official for every 285 people, the rate is much higher in many rural areas. Though this indicates a very high rate of direct participation in local government, it must be recognized that efforts to maintain local government services impose substantial burdens on the residents of sparsely populated sections of the Great Plains.

J. Clark Archer
University of Nebraska–Lincoln

U.S. Bureau of the Census. 1992 *Census of Governments.* Washington DC: Government Printing Office, 1994. Zelinsky, Wilbur. *Nation into State: The Shifting Symbolic Foundations of American Nationalism.* Chapel Hill: University of North Carolina Press, 1988.

CLARK, JOE (b. 1939)

Born June 5, 1939, in High River, Alberta, Joe Clark was the first Canadian prime minister to have been born in the Prairies. At age thirty-six he was chosen as the youngest person ever to lead the Progressive Conservative Party. Sworn to office the day before his fortieth birthday, he became his country's youngest prime minister. His government, defeated in the House of Commons on its first budget and by the Liberals in the ensuing general election, remained in office only nine months, from May 1979 to February 1980, one of the briefest governments in Canadian history. From 1984 to 1993 he served first as Canada's minister for external affairs, then as constitutional affairs minister, in the government of Brian Mulroney, the man who had successfully challenged him for the leadership of the Progressive Conservative Party in 1983.

Joe Clark was raised in a Tory (Conservative) and Catholic family, an unusual mix by Canadian standards for much of the twentieth century. His grandfather had published a small-town newspaper in Ontario, and his father moved to Alberta where, just four months after the creation of the province in 1905, he established the weekly paper in High River.

Clark was educated at the University of Alberta, earning bachelor's and master's degrees in political science. Although he spent the greatest part of his adult life in public affairs (either in an elected or behind-the-scenes party position), Clark listed journalism as his chosen profession in his official biographies. Known to cite passages from Wallace Stegner's *Wolf Willow* about the poignant beauty of the Great Plains and about the spirit and virtues imbued by the harsh Prairie environment, Joe Clark was profoundly shaped by the geographic and social diversity of the foothills country south of Calgary in which he spent the first eighteen years of his life. His later championing of the view of Canada as a "community of communities" (dismissed by his political nemesis, Pierre Trudeau, as an affront to the principle of a single Canadian nationhood) was drawn from his early experiences in that part of Alberta.

First elected to parliament in 1972, he was reelected in the five succeeding Canadian general elections. His unexpected victory over ten other candidates for the Tory leadership in 1976 led the press to dub him "Joe Who?" That, together with his badly handled budget vote in 1979 and open dissension within the Tory party over his leadership in the early 1980s, led his opponents to launch an "Anyone But Clark" movement aimed at his removal from the party's top position. When the challenge to his leadership succeeded in 1983, with Brian Mulroney's selection to lead the Progressive Conservative Party, many commentators speculated openly that Joe Clark's political career had come to an end. However, he proved them wrong with his loyalty to his party and its leader in the decade that followed, combined with his handling of the External Affairs ministry and his stewardship of the constitutional affairs portfolio during difficult (and ultimately unsuccessful) consultations and negotiations over Canada's constitutional arrangements. He demonstrated an understanding of foreign policy and Canadian society that helped to remove a measure of the tarnish from his leadership of the Progressive Conservative Party from 1976 to 1983.

Withdrawing from national politics at the time of the 1993 election, Clark established a political consultancy firm in Calgary. With clients in Canada and abroad, the business enabled him to draw on contacts established during his twenty-one years in elected politics. The attractions of public life surfaced once again, however, when in 1998 he successfully sought the national leadership of his party. By then the Conservatives had been reduced, with only twenty members of Parliament, to fifth place in the House of Commons and were heavily in debt. Clark's considerable challenge at that point, made more burdensome because he held no seat in Parliament from which he could attempt to gain daily media exposure, was to rebuild the Tory Party into a national force similar to what it had been during his earlier period in Canadian politics.

See also LITERARY TRADITIONS: Stegner, Wallace.

John C. Courtney
University of Saskatchewan

Courtney, John C. *Do Conventions Matter? Choosing National Party Leaders in Canada.* Montreal: McGill-Queen's University Press, 1995. Graham, Ron. *One-Eyed Kings: Promise and Illusion in Canadian Politics.* Toronto: Collins, 1986. Humphreys, David L. *Joe Clark: A Portrait.* Toronto: Deneau and Greenberg Publishers Ltd., 1978.

COLORADO

Colorado is famous for its high Rocky Mountains, but the eastern one-third of the state consists of High Plains. There is a dynamic relationship between the mountains and the Plains. The rain and snow that falls in the mountains almost every day of the year flows down to the Plains and is used to irrigate highly productive farms and ranches. On the other hand, the mountains create the rainshadow effect that condemns the Colorado Plains to a meager annual average of fifteen inches of precipitation.

Originally, the land area that is now Colorado was part of four other U.S. territories—Nebraska, Kansas, New Mexico, and Utah. The major event in the governmental history of Colorado was the discovery of gold near present-day Denver. The year was 1858, and news of the gold strike attracted large numbers of prospectors and miners to the area. One of the high Rocky Mountains—Pikes Peak—rises above the Plains just seventy miles south of Denver. Gold seekers rushing into the region simply steered their horses and covered wagons toward Pikes Peak, which was readily visible on the western horizon.

As the population around Denver increased, there was a movement to make the gold-mining areas a separate territory and, eventually, a separate state. In 1861 the U.S. Congress went along with this idea, and the same legislation that granted statehood to Kansas created Colorado Territory. The boundary of the new territory was nothing more than a big rectangle drawn around the city of Denver.

The gold mines continued to produce valuable ore, and then silver was discovered. By 1876 there was enough mining activity and population for Congress to grant statehood to Colorado. Because Colorado became a state in the same year as the 100th anniversary of the Declaration of Independence, Colorado adopted the nickname "Centennial State."

The government of Colorado, like that of most states, is based on the national government. The legislative power is vested in a bicameral state legislature, the upper house known as the Colorado Senate and the lower house called the Colorado House of Representatives. Most of the executive power is vested in a governor. Other elected executive officials include the treasurer, the attorney general, and the secretary of state. Starting in 1990 all state elected officials in Colorado, legislative and executive, have been limited to two four-year terms in office.

Because Colorado is a large state with high, isolating mountain ranges, the state government has granted a great deal of power to county and city governments. Cities in particular have strong home-rule powers and are allowed to govern themselves, with reduced interference from state officials or the state legislature. In the Plains counties, which are mainly rural and small town in character, local governments have extensive powers over welfare programs, road paving, and law enforcement.

Colorado mainly votes for Republican Party candidates, but the state has a two-party flavor and qualified Democrats often do win high political office. From 1976 to 2000 the Republican Party enjoyed comfortable majorities in both houses of the Colorado state legislature. In the twenty-four years from 1974 to 1998, however, the Democrats controlled the governorship. Richard Lamm, a Democrat and a nationally known environmentalist, was elected governor in 1974 and served twelve years in office. Roy Romer, a Democrat with many business connections in Colorado, was elected to succeed Lamm in 1986 and also served as governor for twelve years. Romer had to leave the governor's office following the 1998 election when the eight-year term limits took effect. He was succeeded by a Republican, Gov. Bill Owens.

Gold and silver mining are no longer the mainstays of the Colorado economy. During World War II the U.S. government located a large number of military facilities in Colorado, mainly in Denver and Colorado Springs, two cities located in the Plains right at the foot of the Rocky Mountains. As a result, Colorado enjoyed a post–World War II economic and population boom. That boom was sustained in the late twentieth century by a large number of "high-tech" computer and data processing firms locating in Colorado. In 2000 the population of Colorado was 4.3 million persons and continuing to grow.

Most of the economic and population growth in Colorado is concentrated along the Front Range, an urbanized area running from north to south at the eastern foot of the Rocky Mountains. To the east, the High Plains of Colorado did not share in this rapid growth, but the region has remained a productive and successful agricultural area, due in part to irrigation from rivers and from deep wells.

See also AFRICAN AMERICANS: Webb, Wellington and Wilma / HISPANIC AMERICANS: Peña, Federico.

Robert D. Loevy
Colorado College

Cronin, Thomas E., and Robert D. Loevy. *Colorado Politics and Government: Governing the Centennial State.* Lincoln: University of Nebraska Press, 1993. Lorch, Robert S. *Colorado's Government.* Niwot CO: University Press of Colorado, 1991.

COOPERATIVE COMMONWEALTH FEDERATION

The Cooperative Commonwealth Federation (CCF) was established in 1932 in Calgary, Alberta, as a socialist coalition of farmers, laborers, and progressive reformers from western Canada. The institutional impetus for a new political party came from the breakaway "Ginger Group" of Progressive members of Parliament (MPs) in cooperation with two Labor MPs, including James Shaver Woodsworth, who became the party's first federal leader.

The League for Social Reconstruction, a group of urban intellectuals, drafted the Regina Manifesto that the CCF adopted in 1933. The manifesto called for the replacement of capitalism with economic planning, the nationalization of key industries, and the development of cooperatives. Though radical, the socialism of the CCF was nonrevolutionary—most of the party's members were not Marxists but Christian socialists and British Fabians.

Contesting elections federally and provincially, the CCF had its greatest successes in the 1940s: it topped a national public opinion poll in 1943; formed the Official Opposition in Ontario in the same year; formed a government led by Tommy C. Douglas in Saskatchewan in 1944; and elected twenty-eight MPs in 1945. Its

members were adept parliamentarians and innovators of social policy who pushed the federal Liberal government to expand and improve the welfare state in Canada.

With the onset of the cold war, charges of communism dogged the CCF. It tried to moderate its image in 1956 by replacing the Regina Manifesto with the Winnipeg Declaration, but was unsuccessful. In the 1958 federal election, the party's leader, M. J. Coldwell, lost his seat and the CCF was reduced to only eight MPs. The CCF and the Canadian Labour Congress entered a formal alliance to create the New Democratic Party in 1961.

See also PROTEST AND DISSENT: Woodsworth, James Shaver.

Amy Nugent
University of Calgary

Young, Walter D. *The Anatomy of a Party: The National CCF, 1932–61.* Toronto: University of Toronto Press, 1969.

COUNTY SEATS

See CITIES AND TOWNS: County Seats

DEMOCRATIC PARTY

The noted Oklahoma humorist Will Rogers once said, "I belong to no organized party; I'm a Democrat." Rogers's jest conveyed more than a grain of truth. American political parties are nonexclusive in the sense that there are no formal membership requirements other than self-declaration when registering to vote. American political parties are also quite loosely organized, with considerable variation in organizational structure and ideological stance from place to place. The most important roles of American political parties involve the recruitment and selection of candidates for offices at local, state, and national levels. But the importance of local interests and the fragmented nature of political power under the American federal system render unanimity on policy issues quite unlikely.

The antecedents of the modern Democratic Party can be traced to the embryonic Democratic-Republican faction formed under the leadership of James Madison and Thomas Jefferson near the end of the eighteenth century. Democratic-Republican candidates were most successful in frontier settings away from the Tidewater commercial core of the young Republic. In 1800 Jefferson defeated Federalist incumbent John Adams. Shortly after winning the presidency, Jefferson put aside his own concerns about centralized authority to successfully negotiate the Louisiana Purchase of 1803, which brought much of the territory of the Great Plains under American sovereignty.

The Democratic Party is usually deemed to have been formed by supporters of Andrew Jackson who split away from the vanishing Democratic-Republican Party in 1828. The Democratic Party was the first to hold a national convention, to renominate Jackson for president in 1832. The Democratic National Committee was initially formed in 1848 to give the party continuity between quadrennial national nominating conventions. But whichever date of origin is selected—1800, 1828, 1832,

or even 1848—the Democratic Party is generally recognized as the oldest political party still in existence in the entire world.

From 1828 until 1856 the Jacksonian Democratic coalition of Southern white planters, Irish Catholic immigrant laborers, and western frontiersmen was often successful against the opposing Whig coalition of Yankee merchants, "native" English Protestants, and successful midwestern farmers. But Democrats divided sharply over slavery into northern and southern factions, losing the presidency to Republican Abraham Lincoln in 1860. The Republican Party became nationally dominant after the Civil War. The Democratic Party regained strength in the South after Reconstruction, and it also managed to attract considerable support among immigrants in northern cities. However, between 1860 and 1928 Grover Cleveland and Woodrow Wilson were the only Democrats elected to the White House.

The post–Civil War geography of party support in the Great Plains echoed that of the United States as a whole. Republicans dominated from Kansas northward, while Democrats won sweeping electoral victories as soon as federal troops were withdrawn after Reconstruction. For example, in the three U.S. Congresses between 1885 and 1890, every single one of the U.S. senators and all but one of the U.S. representatives from the Central and Northern Plains states of Colorado, Wyoming, Montana, Kansas, Nebraska, and North and South Dakota were Republicans; and every single one of the U.S. senators and representatives from Texas were Democrats. Oklahoma and New Mexico had not yet been admitted to the Union, but they too would become strongly Democratic after their admission in the early twentieth century.

The end of the nineteenth century was an economically and politically tumultuous period in the Great Plains. Drought and low agricultural product prices pressured farmers to demand relief. Reform pledges by Greenback and Populist Party candidates began to draw farmers and townsfolk dependent upon farmers away from their traditional party loyalties. Populist or Populist-Democratic fusion candidates did well in the Central and Northern Plains, winning several U.S. House or U.S. Senate seats in Colorado, Kansas, Nebraska, North and South Dakota, Montana, and Wyoming in elections from 1890 to 1902. In Texas, where "Bourbon" Democrats dominated, white agrarian Populists joined with black Republicans to win fusion Populist-Republican seats in the U.S. House of Representatives in each election between 1896 and 1900.

William Jennings Bryan was the most notable Plains Democrat of the period. Agrarian unrest swept Republicans from Nebraska's U.S. House delegation in the 1890 election, and Bryan was elected to the House of Representatives from Nebraska's First District. The "Boy Orator of the Platte" made his famous "Cross of Gold" speech to the Democratic National Convention in 1896 criticizing tight fiscal policies and calling for several reforms, including greater regulation of railroads and imposition of an income tax in order to expand federal relief efforts. The speech convinced wavering delegates to nominate the "Great Commoner" for president. Bryan was also nominated for the presidency by the Populist Party and by the Silver Party in 1896. After a hard-fought campaign, Bryan lost to Republican William McKinley in the popular and the electoral votes. Bryan carried all the Great Plains states except North Dakota. Bryan was again nominated for president in 1900 and 1908, losing the rematch to McKinley in 1900 and to Republican William Howard Taft in 1908.

The Populist alliance, involving struggling farmers in the South and West, blacks in the South, and recent immigrants in the northern industrial centers, sent shock waves through American politics. Newspapers in eastern financial centers were nearly unanimous in condemning Bryan's proposed Populist reforms, such as relaxing the gold standard, instituting an income tax, and providing for direct election of U.S. senators. Because of their own aversion to mobilizing immigrant workers and low-income farmers, northern Republican elites looked away while southern Democratic elites pushed enactment of "Jim Crow" laws to restrict voting by blacks and disadvantaged whites. Voter participation rates plummeted in several southern states from well over half of the potential electorate in 1896 to less than one-quarter in the early twentieth century. In Texas the total number of presidential votes cast plunged from more than 540,000 in 1896 to 231,000 in 1904.

For much of the next century Republicans continued to dominate the Central and Northern Plains and Democrats the Southern Plains. However, the Populist influence, reflecting voter dissatisfaction with dominant eastern political and economic interests, affected voters in both parties throughout the region over much of the twentieth century. Populist-oriented Democrats have been elected to major offices across the Central and Northern Plains, and populist-oriented Republicans have won elections in the Southern Plains. Many of these persons played major roles in the political history of the twentieth-century United States.

Although Democrats in the South are generally more conservative than those elsewhere, many southern Democrats elected from the Plains states have been noted for their populist and progressive ideas. Their progressive backgrounds and ideas have helped several achieve national prominence. The regularity with which Democratic incumbents were reelected in the Southern Great Plains states tended to bestow advantages under the congressional seniority system. Among those who served as speaker of the U.S. House of Representatives were Texans John Nance Garner (1931–33), Sam Rayburn (1940–47, 1949–53, and 1955–61), and James Wright (1987–89), as well as Oklahoman Carl Albert (1971–77). On the Senate side, Democratic majority leaders have included Lyndon Baines Johnson of Texas (1955–61) and Thomas A. Daschle of South

Dakota (from 2001–3). Johnson was minority leader from 1953 to 1955, as was Daschle from 1995 to 2001 and again in 2003. Two other prominent Plains Democrats in the House of Representatives were George Mahon of Lubbock, Texas, who served fifteen years as chair of the House Appropriations Committee (1964–1979), and Marvin Jones of Amarillo, who was chair of the House Agriculture Committee in the 1930s and early 1940s and played a critical role in the enactment of New Deal farm legislation.

National legislative leadership roles proved to be stepping-stones for two of the Texas Democrats, Garner and Johnson. Garner was elected twice as vice president (1933–41) under Franklin Delano Roosevelt. Johnson was elected vice president on the Democratic ticket with John F. Kennedy of Massachusetts in 1960. Johnson then succeeded to the presidency in 1963 following Kennedy's assassination in Dallas and was elected to the presidency in his own right in 1964. Other nationally prominent Plains state Democrats include U.S. Sen. George McGovern (1963–81) of South Dakota, who ran unsuccessfully as Democratic nominee for president in 1972, and U.S. Sen. Robert Kerrey (1989–2001) of Nebraska, who contested for the Democratic presidential nomination in 1992 and 1996. Hubert Humphrey, who represented Minnesota but was born and raised in South Dakota, served as vice president under Johnson from 1965 to 1969 and ran unsuccessfully as the Democratic nominee for president in 1968.

The long-term pattern of Democratic dominance in the Southern Plains and Republican dominance in the Central and Northern Plains was never complete, and it was less apparent at the end of the twentieth century than it had been at the beginning. When the partisan affiliations of state governors are examined, it is found that eighty Democrats, seventy-three Republicans, and three Independents or Populists served as governor of a Great Plains state between 1900 and 1949. However, there was a fairly sharp geographical division. Among the three Southern Plains states of Texas, Oklahoma, and New Mexico, the gubernatorial split was thirty-eight Democrats and four Republicans. Among seven Plains states to the north, the gubernatorial split from 1900 to 1949 was forty-two Democrats, sixty-nine Republicans, and three Independents or Populists. This pattern changed dramatically in the last half of the twentieth century. Again examining the partisan affiliations of governors, it can be noted that all twenty Texas governors elected between 1898 and 1978 were Democrats. From 1978 to 2001, however, Texas had four Republican and three Democratic governors. For all ten Great Plains states from 1950 to 2000, the gubernatorial partisan division was fifty-one Democrats and fifty-nine Republicans. Among the three Southern Plains states of Texas, Oklahoma, and New Mexico, the numbers were twenty-three Democrats and fourteen Republicans, while among the remaining seven northern Plains states the numbers were twenty-eight Democrats and forty-five Republicans.

Clearly, the partisanship changes were much more significant in the Southern Plains than in the Central and Northern Plains. Among the latter states, Democrats held 37 percent of all governorships from 1900 to 1949, compared with 38 percent of all governorships from 1950 to 2000. Among Southern Plains states, however, the Democratic proportion of all governorships fell from 90 percent during 1900 to 1949, to 62 percent during 1950 to 2000.

Similar patterns can be found while looking at U.S. congressional delegations from the region. In 1900 the Central and Northern Plains states elected three Democrats, thirteen Republicans, and three Populists to the U.S. House of Representatives, compared with thirteen Democrats and no Republicans from Southern Plains states. In 1950 the Central and Northern Plains states elected three Democrats and eighteen Republicans to the U.S. House, while the Southern Plains states elected twenty-nine Democrats and two Republicans. In 2000 the Central and Northern Plains states sent three Democrats and thirteen Republicans to the U.S. House, while Southern Plains states elected nineteen Democratic and twenty Republican U.S. representatives. Between 1950 and 2000 the Democratic share of the Southern Plains delegation in the U.S. House of Representatives fell from more than 90 percent to less than half.

These data illustrate that Democrats have been a minority party for most of the twentieth century in the Central and Northern Plains, although they have won a fair share of elections and produced a number of eminent national leaders. In the Southern Plains the Democrats have lost their once-dominant position, and today the Democrats are less successful in presidential, gubernatorial, and congressional elections in the region than was the case in the past.

J. Clark Archer
University of Nebraska–Lincoln
Fred M. Shelley
Southwest Texas State University

Goldinger, Carolyn, ed. Presidential Elections since 1789. Washington DC: Congressional Quarterly, 1991. Martis, Kenneth C. The Historical Atlas of Political Parties in the United States Congress, 1789–1989. New York: Macmillan Publishing Company, 1989. Wetterau, Bruce. Congressional Quarterly's Desk Reference on the States. Washington DC: Congressional Quarterly, 1999.

DIEFENBAKER, JOHN (1895–1979)

John George Diefenbaker, criminal lawyer, politician, and Progressive Conservative prime minister of Canada from 1957 to 1963, was born at Neustadt, Ontario, on September 19, 1895. Although Diefenbaker was born and died in Ontario, his reputation will be linked forever to the Canadian West and, in particular, to the province of Saskatchewan. He was, as a colleague once described him, "a prairie man to the core." As such, his character was shaped by his early life in Saskatchewan, his priorities influenced by that region's attitudes toward the issues he would face as prime minister, and his policies directed toward making the country's peripheries more important considerations in national decision making.

Diefenbaker moved with his family to the Fort Carlton region of the Northwest Territories in 1903, when it was still a frontier. His early years were spent in small Prairie communities and, after 1910, in Saskatoon. After attending the University of Saskatchewan and serving in World War I, Diefenbaker obtained a law degree and practiced law in Wakaw and Prince Albert, Saskatchewan. In subsequent years his legal career flourished, but he was also drawn to politics.

Diefenbaker was nearly sixty-two when he became prime minister, and the many defeats he endured en route might have deterred a man less convinced of his political destiny. He stood for both Parliament and the Saskatchewan Legislative Assembly twice, and he led the Conservative Party in the provincial election of 1938, in which not one of his candidates was elected, before winning a federal seat in 1940. He also contested the leadership of the national Progressive Conservative Party twice without success before winning it in 1956.

During his years in opposition, however, Diefenbaker developed into a formidable debater and platform performer, skills that served him well in the 1957 and 1958 national election campaigns. He led his party to a minority victory in the first of these, but it was in the second that his "vision" of a new and better Canada captivated the electorate and brought the Conservatives the greatest electoral triumph in Canadian history to that time. His charisma and oratory enthralled his audiences, and he offered hope to a nation thirsting for innovative ideas for strengthening the economy, especially in the outlying regions of the country.

Once in power, Diefenbaker, with the able assistance of a small group of advisers from western Canada, attempted to set the country on a new course after what they believed to have been two decades of drift under the uninspired leadership of the Liberal Party. These men were motivated by Canadian nationalism, a commitment to social justice, and a conviction that government must create the conditions whereby private enterprise could develop all regions of the country. They believed Canada to be a "treasure-house" of wealth waiting to be tapped for the benefit of all Canadians, and they were determined to use these resources for both economic and social goals. Under the auspices of the "New National Policy," they emphasized natural resource development to spur the economy, create employment, and provide additional revenues for much-needed social programs. The Atlantic Provinces Power Development, the South Saskatchewan River Dam, the Roads to Resources that opened the north, and the Resources for Tomorrow conference, which catalogued Canada's potential, rank high on the list of achievements of the Diefenbaker government. So do its actions in aid of Canadian agriculture, including the Agricultural Rehabilitation and Development program and the sale of grain surpluses to communist countries such as China, which not only brought prosperity to Prairie farm communities but also created opportunities for Canadian businesses which remain in place today. Other accomplishments include legislation of Canada's first Bill of Rights, extension of the franchise to Aboriginal Canadians, and the adoption of Diefenbaker's stand against apartheid by the Commonwealth.

Despite these successes, Diefenbaker's staggering victory in 1958 created expectations that probably no leader could have satisfied, and a downturn in the economy of Central Canada and unpopular decisions in the realms of defense and foreign policy led to the defeat of his government in 1963 and the loss of his party's leadership four years later. Diefenbaker remained in his beloved House of Commons until his death in Ottawa on August 16, 1979, but he never regained his former prominence. Nevertheless, during his lengthy career, John Diefenbaker accomplished much of merit. He brought the concerns of western Canada to the forefront of national politics. He rejuvenated the Progressive Conservative Party in all regions of the country. He brought to Canadians a heightened awareness of their potential greatness and the importance of "justice" as a fundamental principle of their polity. Any deficiencies he displayed while prime minister do not outweigh these important contributions to his country.

Patrick Kyba
University of Guelph

Diefenbaker, John G. *One Canada: Memoirs.* 3 vols. Toronto: Macmillan Publishing Company, 1975. Smith, Denis. *Rogue Tory: The Life and Legend of John G. Diefenbaker.* Toronto: MacFarlane Walter and Ross, 1995. Story, D. C., and R. B. Shepard, eds. *The Diefenbaker Legacy: Canadian Politics, Law and Society since 1957.* Regina: Canadian Plains Research Center, 1998.

DIRECT DEMOCRACY

Direct democracy—which includes the plebiscitary devices of initiative, referendum, and recall—is the political process whereby citizens participate directly in the making of public policy by casting their votes on ballot measures. The so-called citizen initiative is the most participatory form of direct democracy. With the initiative, citizens collect a specified number of valid signatures in order to place either a statutory measure or a constitutional amendment on the ballot for fellow voters to adopt or reject. In addition to the initiative, the "popular" referendum allows citizens to petition their legislatures to place a disputed legislative action on the ballot for the voters to reconsider, and the recall enables citizens to collect signatures to force a retention vote of an elected official.

The practice of direct democracy grew out of the doctrines put forth by the Populist (People's) Party, the single-taxers led by Henry George, and the Farmers Alliance during the late nineteenth century. In 1898 the citizens of South Dakota became the first in the Union to adopt the use of the three devices at the state level. The Reverend Robert W. Haire, an activist in the Knights of Labor, is generally credited with devising the original South Dakota scheme. Following the lead of South Dakota, voters in seven other American states in the Great Plains region adopted some form of statewide direct democracy: Montana (1906), Oklahoma (1907), Colorado (1910), New Mexico (1911), Nebraska (1912), North Dakota (1914), and Wyoming (1968). In Canada, more recently, the Prairie province of Saskatchewan adopted a nonbinding initiative in 1991. The citizens of Manitoba embraced the initiative in 1916, but it was subsequently declared unconstitutional.

In the United States during the 1910s, direct democracy was highly prized by progressive reformers as an instrument to return government back to the people. It was viewed as an institutional check on the power of unresponsive state legislatures, which were often seen as being under the thumb of special interests. Today, the initiative process is utilized quite frequently by citizen groups, as well as by special interests, in the Great Plains states where it is permitted, but the popular referendum and the recall election are seldom used.

See also PROTEST AND DISSENT: Haire, Robert.

Daniel A. Smith
University of Denver

Boyer, J. Patrick. *Direct Democracy in Canada: The History and Future of Referendums.* Toronto: Dundurn Press, 1992. Cronin, Thomas E. *Direct Democracy: The Politics of Initiative, Referendum, and Recall.* Cambridge: Harvard University Press, 1989. Munro, William Bennett, ed. *The Initiative, Referendum, and Recall.* New York: D. Appleton and Company, 1912.

DOLE, BOB (b. 1923)

Born on July 22, 1923, in Russell, Kansas, Robert J. "Bob" Dole rose from county attorney to become a five-term U.S. senator, chairman of the Republican Party (1971–72), Republican nominee for vice president (1976), and three-time presidential candidate. In 1996 Dole won the Republican nomination for president but lost in the general election to incumbent President Bill Clinton.

Gravely wounded in the last days of World War II, Dole returned home to Kansas to rehabilitate his shattered body and to complete his education. He was elected to the state legislature in 1951, even before finishing law school at Topeka's Washburn University. Dole impressed state Republicans with his prairie conservatism and capacity for hard work. In 1960, after eight years as Russell County attorney, Dole won the Republican nomination for the U.S. House, where he served for eight years as a solid representative of western Kansas. In 1968 Republican incumbent Sen. Frank Carlson stepped down and encouraged Dole to replace him. After a typically energetic campaign, Dole won the seat and—save for a narrow victory over Rep. Bill Roy in 1974—faced no serious opposition for the remainder of his tenure on Capitol Hill.

A long-time member of the Agriculture and Finance Committees, Bob Dole became a national political figure in the 1970s. He served as chairman of the Republican National Committee (RNC) during the 1972 presidential campaign and was President Gerald Ford's running mate in 1976. Despite his RNC position, Dole played no role in the Watergate affair that brought down Richard Nixon's presidency. As the vice presidential candidate, Dole often took the offensive against the Democrats, thus gaining the reputation as a rough campaigner.

By the late 1970s Dole had risen through the Senate's ranks and had won recognition as an effective legislator whose conservatism was often tempered with pragmatism. After Republicans won control of the Senate in 1980, Dole served first as chairman of the Finance Committee (1981–84) and then as the Republican floor leader (majority leader, 1985–86, 1995–96; minority leader, 1987–94). As a Senate leader Dole demonstrated great talents and even greater patience in forging majorities among his Senate colleagues. Nowhere was this clearer than in his role in "saving" social security in 1983, as he played a central role in putting together a package that was acceptable to Republicans and Democrats in both houses, as well as to the Reagan White House. In 1990, after thirty years of trying, Dole won passage of the Americans with Disabilities Act, which, with the 1972 food-stamps initiative, represent two of his most important substantive legislative legacies.

In 1996 Bob Dole won the Republican presidential nomination, after which he resigned from the Senate to concentrate his attention on the presidential race. He proved incapable of overcoming a healthy economy and President Clinton's strong performance on the campaign trail, and he returned to private life as an attorney for a prestigious Washington law firm. Dole remained active in international affairs—especially on missions to the former Yugoslavia—and in 1997 President Clinton honored him with the Presidential Medal of Freedom. In addition, Elizabeth Dole's continuing prominence as a Republican presidential hopeful kept Bob Dole active in national politics beyond his own period of officeholding and campaigning.

Burdett A. Loomis
University of Kansas

Cramer, Richard Ben. *What It Takes*. New York: Random House, 1992. Dole, Bob and Elizabeth. *Unlimited Partners*. New York: Simon and Schuster, 1998. Thompson, Jake H. *Bob Dole*. New York: Donald Fine, 1994.

DOUGLAS, TOMMY (1904–1986)

Thomas Clement Douglas was born in Falkirk, Scotland, on October 20, 1904. His family moved to Winnipeg, Manitoba, in 1919, where he witnessed the Winnipeg General Strike. After being ordained a Baptist minister in 1930, Douglas moved to Weyburn, Saskatchewan. Motivated by the widespread suffering he saw during the Depression, he decided to pursue a course of political activism.

In 1935 Douglas was elected to the House of Commons as a member of the socialist Cooperative Commonwealth Federation (CCF). In 1944 he resigned from the House of Commons to lead the Saskatchewan CCF, which swept to power to become the first socialist government in North America. Douglas was premier of Saskatchewan for the next seventeen years.

Tommy Douglas

Tommy Douglas was the most beloved premier in Saskatchewan history. He was a spellbinding orator with a ready wit, whose views were informed by the Social Gospel, the notion that people should create heaven on earth by helping others. He was opposed to doctrinaire socialism aimed at overthrowing capitalism; instead, he favored state regulation so that the "little guy" could compete against vested interests. He preached a liberal democratic philosophy based on individual rights, but more than others of his day, he also supported the collective rights of First Nations.

The Douglas government, though not without its failures, introduced reforms of seminal importance. It was the first in Canada to adopt a provincial Bill of Rights. Its social welfare legislation, based on human dignity, was the most enlightened of its day. It was the first provincial government to address the problems of Aboriginal peoples. And, over the objections of doctors, it created a provincial health care system that became a model for the rest of Canada.

In 1962 Douglas returned to the House of Commons in Ottawa to lead the New Democratic Party (NDP), the successor to the federal CCF. He surrendered the leadership of the NDP in 1971 and retired from Parliament eight years later. Tommy Douglas died in Ottawa on February 24, 1986.

F. Laurie Barron
University of Saskatchewan

Barron, F. Laurie. *Walking in Indian Moccasins: The Native Policies of Tommy Douglas and the CCF*. Vancouver: University of British Columbia Press, 1997. McLeod, Thomas H., and Ian McLead. *Tommy Douglas: The Road to Jerusalem*. Edmonton: Hurtig Publishers, 1987. Thomas, Lewis H., ed. *The Making of a Socialist: The Recollections of T. C. Douglas*. Edmonton: University of Alberta Press, 1982.

EISENHOWER, DWIGHT D. (1890–1969)

Dwight D. Eisenhower, the thirty-fourth president of the United States, was born in Denison, Texas, a town near the Texas-Oklahoma border, on October 14, 1890. He was the third of seven sons of David Jacob Eisenhower and Ida Stover Eisenhower. In the spring of 1891 the family returned to the home of their ancestors by moving due north to Abilene, Kansas, where Eisenhower's father worked in a creamery. Eisenhower graduated from Abilene High School in 1909. Lacking financial resources, Eisenhower went on in 1911 to the U.S. Military Academy at West Point, where tuition was free. Upon graduating from West Point in 1915, Eisenhower was assigned to training U.S. Army infantry troops at Fort Sam Houston in San Antonio, Texas. While stationed there, Eisenhower met, and in 1916 married, Mamie Geneva Doud, daughter of a prosperous Denver, Colorado, family. Together they had two children—Doud Dwight Eisenhower, who died of scarlet fever in 1921 at the age of three, and John Sheldon Doud Eisenhower, born in 1922.

Having been turned down for overseas duty several times, Eisenhower spent the World War I years moving from one military post to another. Luckily, while stationed in Camp Meade, Col. George S. Patton moved next door to Eisenhower and introduced him to Brig. Gen. Fox Conner, thus moving Eisenhower into the army's upper echelon. Eisenhower served on Conner's staff in the Panama Canal Zone, and Conner went on to support Eisenhower's admission into the Command and General Staff School at Fort Leavenworth, Kansas. Eisenhower graduated in 1926, first in his class of top army officers. He then served as aide to Gen. Douglas MacArthur, the army chief of staff, following him to the Philippines. When World War II broke out, Eisenhower was asked by Gen. George C. Marshall, who had replaced MacArthur as army chief of staff, to serve in the War Plans Division. Eisenhower went on to become commander of U.S. troops in Europe, head of the Allied invasions of North Africa, Sicily, and Italy, and in February 1943 was promoted to the rank of four-star general. Later that year, President Franklin D. Roosevelt named Eisenhower supreme commander of the Allied Expeditionary Force in Europe, and it was in this capacity that Eisenhower directed the largest seaborne invasion in history—the invasion of Normandy in northern France that came to be known as D day.

After the war Eisenhower returned home a five-star general and war hero. He replaced Marshall as army chief of staff in 1945 and directed demobilization efforts. In 1948 he retired from active military service to become president of Columbia University, and he published his account of the war, *Crusade in Europe* (1948), which became an immediate best-seller and made Eisenhower a wealthy man. Quickly leaving behind his career as an academic administrator, Eisenhower gladly accepted President Harry Truman's invitation to become supreme commander of the North

Dwight D. Eisenhower, June 1952

Atlantic Treaty Organization (NATO) forces in early 1951.

Although both political parties tried to draft him as their candidate, in 1952 Eisenhower retired from the military after thirty-seven years of service and ran as the Republican nominee for president of the United States. In June of that year he defeated, with the help of a Texas delegation, the more conservative Sen. Robert A. Taft of Ohio for his party's nomination, accepted Richard M. Nixon as his vice presidential running mate, and later defeated Gov. Adlai E. Stevenson of Illinois for the presidency.

As president, Eisenhower was known for delegating power and forging a middle ground on policies, thus guaranteeing that he would be criticized by Republicans when he wasn't criticized by Democrats. As the first Republican president since Herbert Hoover, Eisenhower's domestic program, labeled "modern Republicanism," was designed not to dismantle New Deal programs but to hold them in check with Eisenhower's own brand of fiscal probity. He signed into law the Agricultural Act of 1956, which continued the system of flexible price supports, albeit at prices less than farmers wanted, and the Agricultural Act of 1958, which provided for a phased lowering of price supports. He supported expansion of social security coverage to millions of additional workers, including farmers, legislation to raise the minimum wage to $1 per hour while expanding its coverage, and he created the Department of Health, Education, and Welfare. And, although unsuccessful, he attempted to expand medical insurance coverage to the needy. While strongly supporting privatization, Eisenhower also obtained passage of two massive federal public works projects—the St. Lawrence Seaway in 1954 and the Interstate Highway System in 1956.

Although not an outspoken defender of civil rights, Eisenhower did much to advance racial integration. As army chief of staff and later as president he worked to integrate the

army and the navy. He supported the Justice Department in its amicus curiae brief written in support of ending segregation in the *Brown v. The Board of Education of Topeka* case before the Supreme Court and, while refusing to publicly support the Supreme Court in its *Brown* decision, Eisenhower made good his promise to enforce the law by using federal troops to force school desegregation in Little Rock, Arkansas, in 1957. Eisenhower signed into law the Civil Rights Act of 1957—the first major civil rights legislation to be passed since the Civil Rights Act of 1875.

As a former war hero, Eisenhower could speak boldly of "massive retaliation" while working on the side of peace and conciliation. Eisenhower visited Korea and concluded a truce in July 1953, refused to commit U.S. forces in Indochina, worked to relax tensions with the Soviet Union, and did not intervene militarily when uprisings occurred in East Germany and Hungary. A staunch anticommunist, Eisenhower did not support the tactics of Sen. Joseph R. McCarthy but left it to others to publicly rebuke McCarthy. Eisenhower's anticommunist bent could be seen in his support of covert activities by the Central Intelligence Agency aimed at undermining the spread of communism abroad. When the Soviet Union successfully launched Sputnik I, the first man-made satellite to orbit the Earth, Eisenhower responded with another major federal initiative providing funds to increase the study of science in public schools.

Although his critics were numerous, Eisenhower remained popular with the American people and was reelected in 1956, despite his suffering a heart attack in 1955. He was above all a pragmatic president, preaching the gospel of a balanced budget but accepting quite often the reality of budget deficits, especially when the economy was weak. He was the oldest person to hold the office of president up to that time, the first president born in the state of Texas, and the first president to warn against the hazards of the military-industrial complex. Eisenhower left office in January 1961 and retired to a farm near Gettysburg, Pennsylvania, where he completed his memoirs. Eisenhower died on March 28, 1969, in Washington DC.

See also LAW: *Brown v. The Board of Education of Topeka* / WAR: World War II.

Ann Mari May
University of Nebraska–Lincoln

Ambrose, Stephen E. *Eisenhower.* New York: Simon and Schuster, 1983. Perret, Geoffrey. *Eisenhower.* New York: Random House, 1999. Richardson, Elmo. *The Presidency of Dwight D. Eisenhower.* Lawrence: University Press of Kansas, 1979.

FALL, ALBERT (1861–1944)

Albert Bacon Fall served as a U.S. senator from New Mexico and as secretary of the interior under President Warren G. Harding. He was born on November 26, 1861, in Frankfort, Kentucky. The Civil War reduced his family to poverty, and Fall was largely self-educated. As a young adult, he moved to Texas, where he

drove cattle, cooked for cowboys, and sold real estate, insurance, and groceries. In 1883 he moved to Mexico and worked there at a mining job before finally settling, in 1887, on a ranch near Las Cruces, New Mexico. There he practiced law and entered politics as a Democrat. He served as the territory's attorney general, in both houses of its legislature, and on its supreme court. In 1912 he served as a delegate to the New Mexico constitutional convention. Though a resident of New Mexico, Fall established strong connections with industrial concerns in El Paso, Texas, and invested in mines in northern Mexico. He believed strongly in free enterprise, maintaining that natural resources should be exploited by private firms.

Fall admired President Theodore Roosevelt and consequently aligned himself with the Republican Party. In 1912, when New Mexico became a state, he was elected, as a Republican, to serve in the U.S. Senate. There he made close relationships, notably with Warren G. Harding of Ohio, who, like Fall, was an enthusiastic poker player.

After Harding was elected president in 1920, he chose Fall as his secretary of the interior. Under Fall's influence, in 1921 Harding and Secretary of the Navy Edwin Denby transferred authority over naval oil reserves at Teapot Dome, Wyoming, and Elk Hills, California, from the navy to the Interior Department, which then leased them to oilmen Harry F. Sinclair and Edward Doheny (the latter a friend of Fall's from his early mining days).

In 1923 Fall resigned and returned to his ranch in New Mexico. The next year a Senate investigation disclosed that he had received gifts of cash, bonds, and livestock from Sinclair and Doheny. The courts later canceled the leases, and Fall was convicted of accepting a $100,000 bribe from Doheny. He was the first cabinet member convicted of a felony committed while in office, and he served nine and a half months in a Santa Fe prison. Broken financially and physically, he died in poverty, on November 30, 1944, in El Paso, Texas.

Robert D. Parmet
York College of the City University of New York

Bates, J. Leonard. *The Origins of Teapot Dome: Progressives, Parties, and Petroleum, 1909–1921.* Urbana: University of Illinois Press, 1963. Stratton, David H. "New Mexico Machiavellian? The Story of Albert B. Fall." *Montana* 7 (1957): 2–14. Stratton, David H., ed. *The Memoirs of Albert B. Fall.* El Paso: Texas Western Press, 1966.

FEDERAL GOVERNMENT, CANADA

Most of the area covered by Canada's three Prairie Provinces was purchased by the federal government from the Hudson's Bay Company in 1868. The Canadian Plains was a sparsely populated frontier, and the government was anxious to settle the region quickly and uniformly. The North-West Mounted Police force was established, and the government in Ottawa embarked on an aggressive campaign to populate the area. To achieve this goal, control over the land and natural resources of the western interior was retained by the federal

How the Farmer Benefits by
a Protective Tariff

Political cartoon, "Putting on the Screws"

government. In a sense, the three Prairie Provinces are "Children of Confederation" in that they had not existed as self-governing colonies prior to Canadian Confederation in 1867. Manitoba attained provincial status in 1870, but Saskatchewan and Alberta did not become provinces until 1905.

The way in which the Prairie Provinces became part of Canada has given rise to the phenomenon of western alienation. This includes specific complaints about discriminatory treatment, as well as the pervasive feeling among its citizens that Manitoba, Saskatchewan, and Alberta are second-class provinces. They had to wait until 1930 to gain ownership of their land and natural resources. In the American Plains states and in the West more generally, federal ownership and control over large tracts of land created similar resentment.

Settlers to the Prairies came in waves between the turn of the twentieth century and World War II. They came with high expectations fed by extravagant advertising campaigns launched by the federal government and the Canadian Pacific Railway. The Prairies were described as a veritable Garden of Eden. Many newcomers were defeated by the weather, the uncertainty of the grain trade, and difficulty in coaxing a crop out of virgin soil.

Ottawa's policies on tariffs, its decisions on the railway, and its primary role in immigration and homesteading had a crucial impact on the evolution of the Prairie Provinces. Until the onset of World War II, these provinces were isolated from the rest of the country and united in their dependence on the wheat economy. A shared sense of grievance added to their cohesion: national policies favoring Central Canada, particularly in the early years, fueled the perception that the federal government was a remote, insensitive instrument of the manufacturing sector located at the center. There was some justification for these sentiments, since federal domination of the region

in its formative years was unparalleled in the rest of the country.

Common experiences led to a cross-fertilization of ideas on the agrarian frontier on both sides of the international boundary. They were part of the raw material from which populism and nonpartisan ideals were constructed. Ideas popularized by the Nonpartisan League, which originated in North Dakota, were picked up on the Canadian Plains. League candidates were unsuccessful in elections during World War I, but nonpartisan sentiments turned out to be more durable. Canada's political system proved more permeable to new political parties spawned by Prairie discontent; some survive to this day.

More than a century after Canadian Confederation, an identity of interest no longer binds the Prairie Provinces. Their economies have diversified, and powerful provincial governments now articulate the interests and air the grievances of their citizens. However, it is still possible for provincial premiers to mobilize the population by fanning the flames of western alienation. For example, natural resource ownership remains a flashpoint in Alberta, which is home to the bulk of Canada's conventional petroleum resources. Any hint of federal intrusion into this industry is vigorously resisted. There has been minimal change in the division of powers. However, the importance of the powers conferred on the provinces has increased dramatically, while federal responsibilities have declined in importance.

Hinterland status and the problem of being a relatively small population continue to frustrate citizens of the Prairies, to whom the federal government seems as remote as it was before technology compressed time and space.

See also INDUSTRY: Petroleum, Canada.

Doreen Barrie
University of Calgary

Francis, R. Douglas, and Howard Palmer. *The Prairie West: Historical Readings.* Edmonton: Pica Pica Press, 1985. Lower, J. Arthur. *Western Canada: An Outline History.* Vancouver: Douglas and McIntyre, 1983.

FEDERAL GOVERNMENT, UNITED STATES

The role of the U.S. federal government in the development and current status of the Great Plains has been central and often controversial. Most of the Great Plains became part of the United States when the federal government, led by President Thomas Jefferson, bought "Louisiana" from the French in 1803. That same government then commissioned an expeditionary party to explore the massive tract of land. The records of Lewis and Clark constitute the first and, in many ways, the most influential systematic American observations and reflections in the Great Plains.

The land of the Great Plains began its relationship with the federal government as a set of territories, which meant that governmental structures were relatively undeveloped and the federal government, by default, was the crucial player in the few tasks accorded it in those days (law enforcement, mail delivery, develop-

ment of transportation, and the like). As each territory acquired more population and identity, pressure would grow for the territory to be upgraded to statehood. Thus, Texas became a state in 1845, Kansas in 1861, Nebraska in 1867, Colorado in 1876, the Dakotas and Montana in 1889, Wyoming in 1890, Oklahoma in 1907, and New Mexico in 1912.

Statehood brought the Great Plains into a different stage of relationship with the federal government. Theoretically, such designation might have been expected to give the states greater autonomy, but in reality it has not worked out that way. The shifting nature of federalism through the history of the Republic has generally been one of expanding federal authority. The Civil War, various Supreme Court decisions, the New Deal, and the Great Society all shifted power to Washington and away from the state capitals.

Though affecting the entire country, the expanding role of the federal government has probably been resented more in the Great Plains than in any other region except the South. The spirit of individualism may have been romanticized in portrayals of the Old West, but it is not entirely fictitious. Although historically beneficiaries of federal programs beyond their proportion in the U.S. population, citizens of the Great Plains have long been among the loudest complainers about the goings-on in far-off Washington. People residing in the Great Plains still prefer to govern themselves. Current governors of the states of the Great Plains stridently object to the "unfunded mandates" coming from Washington, gun owners decry federal efforts to control guns, farmers drive their tractors to Washington to protest federal policies, antigovernment militias sprout, and distrust of government and bureaucrats is rampant and occasionally transforms into hatred and violence—witness the bombing of a federal building in Oklahoma City and the events following a federal raid on firearms at the Branch Davidian compound near Waco.

The federal government's relationship with Native Americans, many of whom still reside in the Great Plains, has been checkered and inconsistent. At different times it has included breaking legal treaties, forcing people to live in undesirable areas, promoting assimilation with whites, protecting cultural differences, declaring individuals to be wards of the state, and permitting legalized gaming (and therefore substantial profits) on land controlled by Native Americans.

The independent spirit that characterizes people of the Great Plains, regardless of race and ethnicity, makes it unlikely any governmental entity will be embraced warmly. Yet the U.S. federal government, for better or for worse, continues to be intimately involved in the daily lives of people in the Great Plains, whether by providing farm subsidies, assisting the elderly, protecting lightly used air traffic corridors, offering disaster relief, or determining winners and losers in water disputes.

See also IMAGES AND ICONS: Colony of the East / NATIVE AMERICANS: Assimilation Policy; Treaties / PROTEST AND DISSENT: Oklahoma City Bombing / RELIGION: Branch Davidians.

John R. Hibbing
University of Nebraska–Lincoln

Stein, Robert M., and Bickers, Kenneth N. *Perpetuating the Pork Barrel*. New York: Cambridge University Press, 1995. Tolchin, Susan J. *The Angry American*. Boulder CO: Westview, 1999.

FERGUSON, JAMES AND MIRIAM
(1871–1944; 1875–1961)

James and Miriam "Ma" Ferguson were dominant political figures in Texas between World Wars I and II. James Edward Ferguson was born on a farm near Salado, Bell County, Texas, on August 31, 1871, and was educated in local public schools. He studied law at night and was admitted to the bar in 1897. He and Miriam Wallace, a Bell County native born on June 13, 1875, were married in 1899. With strong support from progressive and anti-Prohibition forces, "Farmer Jim" was elected governor of Texas in 1914. He was reelected in 1916 but the following year was impeached on grounds of misusing public funds and removed from office. The conviction forbade Ferguson to hold "any office of honor, trust, or profit" in Texas. In order to keep Ferguson's name in the public spotlight, the Fergusons began to publish a weekly political newspaper, the *Ferguson Forum*.

Ferguson's impeachment decree did not apply to federal offices, and in 1922 Ferguson ran for the U.S. Senate as an opponent of Prohibition and the Ku Klux Klan. He was supported by many rural Populist voters and by enemies of the Klan, but lost to Klan member Earle Mayfield. Arguing that his impeachment was invalid, Ferguson attempted to run for governor in the 1924 Democratic primary. After the party leadership refused to place his name on the ballot, his wife ran in his stead.

Ma Ferguson ran for governor of Texas five times, winning twice. In the 1924 election, Ma opposed the Klan and campaigned on the slogan "two governors for the price of one," making clear that her husband, often called "Pa," would make major decisions. She was elected and so became the first woman to be elected governor of any state. She lost to Dan Moody two years later and lost again in 1930, but was elected for a second two-year term in 1932. She ran one final time in 1940 but lost to W. Lee "Pappy" O'Daniel.

Jim Ferguson died on September 21, 1944, and with his death the era of Ferguson leadership of Texas's rural populists and anti-Klan activists ended. Miriam Ferguson lived quietly in retirement until her death on June 25, 1961. The Fergusons are buried side by side in Austin's State Cemetery.

Fred M. Shelley
Southwest Texas State University

Brown, Norman D. *Hood, Bonnet, and Little Brown Jug: Texas Politics, 1921–1928*. College Station: Texas A&M University Press, 1984. Key, V. O., Jr. *Southern Politics*. New York: Alfred A. Knopf, 1949.

FORD, GERALD (b. 1913)

Gerald Ford, the thirty-seventh president of the United States, was born Leslie Lynch King in Omaha, Nebraska, on July 14, 1913. However, he only lived there for seven weeks. To escape a husband who beat and threatened to kill her, King's mother fled from Omaha to her waiting parents across the state line in Council Bluffs, Iowa. From there, she took her son back to her childhood home in Grand Rapids, Michigan. She eventually married a local paint and varnish dealer, who gave the boy his name—Gerald Rudolph Ford Jr.

Thus, despite the fact that Ford shares with Dwight D. Eisenhower and Lyndon B. Johnson the distinction of being one of only three American presidents born in Great Plains states, Ford's Nebraska roots were not deep. His youth was spent in Grand Rapids and his collegiate years at the University of Michigan, where he excelled in football, and at Yale University, where he took his law degree. After a stint in the U.S. Navy during World War II, Ford was elected to the House of Representatives from Michigan's Fifth District in 1948. He served twenty-five years in the House, nine of them as minority leader, before being tapped by Richard Nixon in 1973 as his choice to succeed Spiro Agnew, who had resigned the vice presidency under a cloud of controversy. Ford acceded to the presidency on August 9, 1974, when Nixon himself resigned amid a spate of Watergate-related charges.

Ford's administration centered around political crises caused largely by his pardon of Nixon, a worsening economy, and a break with the conservative wing of his own Republican Party. It was the latter concern that fed into an issue of great importance to American farmers, particularly wheat farmers in the Great Plains. On September 9, 1975, Ford suspended the sale of American grain to the Soviet Union. Ford argued that his decision was an attempt to force a Soviet commitment to buy more wheat; however, many observers concluded that the decision was an attempt to initiate a "get tough" policy toward the Soviets in an effort to shore up his worsening relations with the Republican Right before the 1976 presidential election. In either event, Plains farmers were outraged. Recognizing the possibility for serious political fallout, by the end of that month Ford had negotiated a deal with the Soviet Union that allowed for the increased purchase of American grain and the lifting of the embargo. Satisfied with Ford's efforts—as well as with his decision to jettison his eastern liberal vice president, Nelson Rockefeller, in favor of Kansas senator Bob Dole—each state of the Great Plains, save Texas, gave a majority of their votes to Ford that fall. It was not enough, however, to save Ford's presidency, as he narrowly lost his bid for reelection to former Georgia governor Jimmy Carter.

Following his defeat, Ford returned to the University of Michigan for a brief tenure as a professor. He then joined several corporate boards and charitable organizations. He briefly entertained a return to politics in 1980 as Ronald Reagan's running mate, but the deal fell through. Out of politics, Ford presently divides his time between homes in California and Colorado.

John Robert Greene
Cazenovia College

Ford, Gerald R. *A Time to Heal*. New York: Harper and Row, 1979. Greene, John Robert. *The Presidency of Gerald R. Ford*. Lawrence: University Press of Kansas, 1995.

FORTY-NINTH PARALLEL

At just under 740 miles, the forty-ninth parallel separating the Prairie Provinces from the Northern Plains states is part of the longest continuous unguarded boundary line in the world. The forty-ninth parallel bisects a borderland region characterized by physical uniformity in its grassland ecosystem and continental climate and by socioeconomic affinity in its predominantly rural and agrarian economy, low population density, and geographical isolation from markets. The kinds of interactions taking place over time, as well as similar geographical conditions, have added to the synthesis within this borderland region. North–south intermingling occurred well before European settlement, as the American and Canadian fur trading systems converged within a frontier context in which the border, first established in an 1818 treaty between the United States and Great Britain, was relatively meaningless. This unsurveyed line, stretching from the Lake of the Woods in southwestern Ontario to the Rocky Mountains and later extended to the Pacific Coast, was ignored by the buffalo and by the whites, Native peoples, and Métis who hunted them. Further integration in the nineteenth century was ensured by the development of north–south trade links between the Hudson's Bay Company and St. Paul and Chicago capitalists who competed for control of the Northern Plains and saw the monopoly of the British firm in Canada as an impediment to their imperialist schemes. Fort Benton, Montana, located at the head of navigation on the Missouri River and functioning as the gateway to the Whoop-Up Trail to Fort Macleod and Calgary, dominated the commerce of the Canadian Plains for twenty-five years (1858–83).

Even after the boundary line was delineated in 1874 by a joint British and American commission, north–south flows continued, primarily in terms of goods and then people. Yet immediately the boundary acquired significance, as it became the focus for changing relations taking place within the borderland region. It cut across the hunting grounds of Native peoples and Métis and erased their former territories. Ironically, these groups viewed it as a "Medicine Line" because it represented refuge from persecution by whites on the other side. During the 1870s the whiskey trade with Natives caused tension along the border and was used by Canadian nationalists to fuel anti-American sentiment. In this context the forty-ninth parallel came to be viewed by Canadians as a "shield" to America's "manifest destiny," while for most Americans, the border shared with Canada was too far removed to acquire much notice at all.

Earthen boundary marker at the forty-ninth parallel

At the beginning of the twentieth century the Prairies held the promise of the "Last Best West" for Canadians, Europeans, and a considerable number of Americans, while the Northern Plains was increasingly viewed as a remote place, a region to be bypassed by those seeking opportunity in the Far West. While integration within the Northern Plains and Prairie borderland region continued to occur because of a common hinterland, migration flows, the diffusion of technology and ideas, and the evolution of capital relations across the border, the east–west flow of trade and migration into the region paralleling the Canadian Pacific Railway and the Great Northern Railroad served to form national ties that counterbalanced the continuing north–south connections. And even though the border was obscured by the migration of settlers from eastern North America and Europe who carried with them an array of social and economic affiliations, their different settlement histories, loyalties, political cultures, urban systems, and core-periphery relations ensured divergence between the Northern Plains and Prairies.

The forty-ninth parallel has served as a major symbol of the predominant east–west development in both countries, and for Canadians it takes on added importance as a territorial axis, defined in terms of their relationship with the United States. In this context, this artificial line has become a matrix for Canadian culture, at least an Anglo-Canadian culture, which is by its nature regional in composition as well as in origin. Today, however, the forty-ninth parallel as a spatial metaphor has become blurred in a world where the forces of new technologies, globalization, and "time-space compression" have challenged the traditional Canadian view of the border as a territorial symbol of sovereignty and separation. In this new global environment, place as defined

by borders is no longer the essential element of identity. Regional differences are diminishing in the face of homogenizing economic forces and a global culture, as is the importance of cartographic lines and compass points that enable inhabitants of this region, regardless of which side of the forty-ninth they inhabit, to orient themselves in time and space.

See also EUROPEAN AMERICANS: Settlement Patterns, Canada / IMAGES AND ICONS: Last Best West / INDUSTRY: NAFTA / TRANSPORTATION: Whoop-Up Trail.

Randy William Widdis
University of Regina

Lecker, Robert, ed. *Borderlands: Essays in Canadian-American Relations.* Toronto: ECW Press, 1991. Sharp, Paul F. "The American Farmer and the 'Last Best West.'" *Agricultural History* 21 (1947): 65–74. Widdis, Randy W. *With Scarcely a Ripple: Anglo-Canadian Migration into the United States and Western Canada, 1880–1920.* Montreal: McGill-Queen's University Press, 1998.

FRAZIER, LYNN (1874–1947)

Lynn J. Frazier, governor and U.S. senator from North Dakota, was born in Steele County, Minnesota, on December 21, 1874, and moved to North Dakota in 1881. He graduated from the University of North Dakota in 1901 and returned to the family farm in Pembina County.

In 1916 the newly organized Nonpartisan League recruited Frazier, who had never run for public office, to run for governor of North Dakota. Frazier was elected in a landslide. He was reelected in 1918 and 1920. During his administration, League reforms that were enacted included a state-owned grain elevator, state-owned bank, and Industrial Commission. In 1921 opponents of Frazier's reform program forced a recall election. Frazier was defeated by Ragnvold Nestos, becoming the first American governor to be recalled from office. In 1922, however, Frazier was re-

cruited to run for the U.S. Senate and was easily elected.

As a senator, Frazier aligned himself with the progressive Republican bloc led by Robert La Follette and George Norris. Frazier and his fellow progressives supported agrarian and other social reforms, organized labor, and public power. He was reelected in 1928 and 1934. By the late 1920s Frazier had turned much of his attention to world affairs. An isolationist and pacifist, Frazier supported efforts by the Women's Peace Union to ban war and introduced a constitutional amendment outlawing warfare. He also supported national referenda to determine whether the United States would become involved in foreign wars. In 1940 Frazier ran for a fourth term but lost the Republican primary to William Langer. He retired to his farm and died on January 11, 1947.

See also PROTEST AND DISSENT: Nonpartisan League.

Fred M. Shelley
Southwest Texas State University

Erickson, Nels. *The Gentleman from North Dakota: Lynn J. Frazier.* Bismarck: North Dakota Heritage Center, 1986.

GARDINER, JIMMY

See AGRICULTURE: Gardiner, Jimmy

HOGG, JAMES (1851–1906)

James Stephen Hogg, born near Rusk, Texas, on March 24, 1851, served Texas as attorney general from 1887 to 1890 and as governor from 1891 to 1895. Walter Prescott Webb described the "People's Governor" as having "the courage of leadership which is part of the Western tradition."

Hogg's influence on the modernization of the Great Plains was a "rough wooing." Hogg, himself a small cattleman, favored the open range over fencing. Perhaps remembering his father's support for homestead exemption during the Texas Republic, Hogg supported protection of homesteads and public school lands. He recovered much acreage from the railroads that had been granted for switches and sidings, but he lost a disputed border area, Greer County, to Oklahoma. In the Scottish tradition of being "agin' the government," he opposed federal crop subsidies. His campaign slogan was "Enforce the law," whether in dealing with two-bit outlawry or corporate robbery. He dissolved the Texas Traffic Association, a combination of railroads that sought to fix rates, and he established the Texas Railroad Commission for railroad regulation. Hogg's regulatory program reflected moderate progressivism. Symbolically, when the railways shunted Coxey's Army of unemployed protesters near Sierra Blanca, Texas, in 1894, Hogg ordered them transported across the state. Although politically based in East Texas, in 1892 Hogg carried a number of Great Plains counties despite opposition from Populists and ranchers. Hogg's administration brought the maverick Plains, fit to be branded, into the twentieth century. Hogg died at Houston on March 3, 1906, and was buried in Austin.

See also AGRICULTURE: XIT Ranch / INDUS-
TRY: Goodnight, Charles.

Gilbert M. Cuthbertson
Rice University

Cotner, Robert C. *James Stephen Hogg: A Biography.* Aus-
tin: University of Texas Press, 1959. Cotner, Robert C., ed.
Addresses and State Papers of James Stephen Hogg. Austin:
University of Texas Press, 1951.

HUMPHREY, HUBERT (1911–1978)

South Dakota native Hubert Horatio Humphrey was vice president of the United States
from 1965 to 1969 under President Lyndon B.
Johnson and served as U.S. senator from Minnesota from 1949 to 1964 and again from 1971
to 1978. Born in Wallace, South Dakota, on
May 27, 1911, Humphrey was the second son
and namesake of a small-town drugstore
owner with roots traceable to New England
and England. His mother, Christine Sannes,
was of Norwegian descent, her father having
migrated from Norway to South Dakota in the
1880s. When Humphrey was six years old, the
family moved from Wallace to neighboring
Doland, where in 1929 he graduated from
Doland High School.

As a child, Humphrey enjoyed the security
and freedom of rural South Dakota. He played
in the open fields, watched for the arrival
of freight trains, sold newspapers after school,
and helped his father in the drugstore. When
African Americans migrated to the area for seasonal road-building work, Humphrey made a
point to welcome them. This idyllic, carefree
childhood was shattered by the arrival of the
Great Depression, which forced his father to
sell their home to keep the drugstore in business. By 1930 his father's business had failed,
and the family moved to the larger town of
Huron to begin again with another store.

Humphrey attended the University of Minnesota in 1929 and 1930, but because of his
family's economic struggle, he left to work in
his father's drugstore. He dedicated the next
six years to his father's business, often working
without a salary. In 1933 he studied for several
intensive months at Denver's Capitol College
of Pharmacy to become a pharmacist. Still,
Humphrey was unhappy with the direction of
his professional life.

In 1936 Humphrey married Muriel Buck.
She supported his desire to go back to college.
With her financial and emotional support,
Humphrey returned to the University of Minnesota in 1937, where he earned a bachelor's
degree in political science. In 1940 he earned a
master's degree from Louisiana State University. He returned to Minnesota to pursue a
doctoral degree but was deflected by opportunities to get involved in politics.

Humphrey had always expressed an interest
in politics. Because he was dynamic, gregari-
ous, and an excellent speaker, he engaged people's attention. When he became director of a
federal workers' education program in Minnesota in the 1940s, he established important
connections with the state's labor leaders and
made his first bid for mayor (which was unsuccessful). In 1944 he facilitated a critical merger
of Minnesota's Farmer-Labor Party with the
Democratic Party, creating the Democratic-
Farmer-Labor Party and making it possible for
Democrats to win political office. In June 1945
Humphrey won the mayoral election in Minneapolis. In 1948 he took his leadership in the
Democratic Party to the national level when he
successfully urged Democrats to adopt a civil
rights plank. In November of that year, Humphrey successfully defeated incumbent Republican Joseph Ball for a seat in the U.S. Senate.

As a senator, Humphrey was a cold war politician who supported stringent anticommunist legislation while also denouncing Sen.
Joseph McCarthy for attacking Communists,
or "red-baiting." Humphrey also paid special
attention to civil rights, labor, taxes, foreign
policy, and agriculture. Initially, Humphrey
faced much opposition from southern Democrats for his outspokenness, especially on civil
rights. However, he became more pragmatic
with experience and especially benefited from
his friendship with Sen. Lyndon B. Johnson of
Texas. Importantly, after winning only incremental gains for civil rights in the 1950s, he
secured Senate support for the landmark Civil
Rights Act of 1964.

Humphrey aspired to the presidency
throughout his political career. He sought the
vice presidency several times, believing this
to be a necessary step to the presidency. When
he succeeded as President Johnson's running
mate in 1964, however, Humphrey found himself marginalized. Although placed in a humiliating, subservient role—exclusion from National Security Council meetings, for example
—Humphrey remained loyal to the president
and supported his Vietnam War policy. When
Johnson withdrew his candidacy for reelection in 1968, Humphrey won the Democratic
Party's nomination. He lost to Republican
Richard Nixon by a substantial margin in the
electoral vote (301 to 191) but by a narrow
margin in the popular vote.

Humphrey returned to the U.S. Senate from
Minnesota in 1971 and won reelection in 1976.
He ran in the Democratic primaries for president in 1972 but lost the nomination to South
Dakota senator George McGovern. A symbol
of postwar liberalism, Humphrey has gained
recognition for his commitment to civil rights.
He died of cancer in 1978 and was survived by
his wife, Muriel (who was appointed to complete her husband's Senate term), four children, and many grandchildren.

Linda Van Ingen
University of Nebraska at Kearney

Humphrey, Hubert H. *The Education of a Public Man: My
Life and Politics.* Garden City NY: Doubleday and Co.,
1976. Solberg, Carl. *Hubert Humphrey: A Biography.* New
York: W. W. Norton Co., 1984. Thurber, Timothy N. *The
Politics of Equality: Hubert H. Humphrey and the African
American Freedom Struggle.* New York: Columbia Univer-
sity Press, 1999.

INDIAN AGENTS

In both Canada and the United States, Indian
agents were responsible for implementing
federal Indian policy. They were the government's representatives on reservations and reserves and, as such, they wielded great power
over Native peoples, even to the extent of
usurping their traditional political authority,
suppressing religious practices, and transforming social roles.

In the United States, Indian policy was
transmitted from a commissioner of Indian
Affairs (operating, after 1849, from the Office
of Indian Affairs in Washington DC) through
regional superintendents, to agents, who were
responsible for a single tribe or a group of
tribes. The agents, in turn, supervised teachers, blacksmiths, farmers, and other agency
employees. In the early nineteenth century in
the U.S. Great Plains, agents like John Dougherty, who was in charge of the Upper Missouri
Agency from 1827 to 1837, were roving ambassadors who strived to maintain peace and to
obtain Indian lands. In the second half of the
nineteenth century agents took up residence
on their designated reservations and promoted the government's assimilation policy.

In Canada, a separate Department of Indian Affairs was not established until 1880, following the Indian Act of 1876. Federal policy
(the federal government was confirmed in its
authority over First Nations in the Constitution Act of 1867) was formulated in Ottawa, in
the "Inside Service" of the Department of Indian Affairs. From there it passed through regional superintendencies (there were three
such districts—headquartered at Battleford,
Qu'Appelle, and Calgary—in the Prairie Provinces in 1897) to agents on the numerous reserves that were established after the treaties of
the 1870s.

In the early nineteenth century, in the
United States, Plains Indian agents were often
traders who moved into the Indian service
when the fur trade collapsed. Later, their
origins were more diverse, but in both Canada
and the United States they tended to come
from eastern states and provinces, and they
were often unsuited for the job. Political patronage played a major role in appointments.
In the late 1860s Quakers and other religious
denominations were put in charge of many of
the agencies in the U.S. Great Plains in an
effort to introduce some honesty into the service; a similar transition occurred in the Prairie Provinces in the 1870s. Military officers
were also appointed as agents on some U.S.
Plains reservations in the late 1860s and 1870s.

Some agents did their jobs honorably amid
the terrible living conditions that prevailed on
the reservations and reserves. They were convinced that the only way the Native peoples
could survive was by becoming individualized
Christian farmers who made a living on their
own pieces of private property. Many others
were corrupt, taking advantage of the remoteness of their situations by skimming their
charges' annuities or by colluding with settlers
to steal Indian lands. Because of dismissals for
corruption or ineptitude and resignations
caused by the hardships of living in such isolated, desperate situations, agent turnover was
high. At the Blackfoot Agency in Montana, for
example, ten agents came and went in the thirteen years from 1863 to 1876; to the south at

the Crow Agency, eight agents served in the nine years from 1869 to 1878. Such frenetic change did not inspire confidence in federal policy.

In the late nineteenth century and early twentieth century, agents imposed the assimilation policy with increasing force. After 1881 on the Canadian reserves, agents were given the powers of justices of the peace and encouraged to use them to control the Indians' behavior, including restricting them to the reserves by enforcing antivagrancy laws. South of the international boundary, agents threatened to withhold the Indians' annuities if they did not put their children in schools or work in the fields. In both countries, agents increasingly took over the political decision making that had previously resided with tribal councils.

In the United States, the post of Indian agent was abolished in 1908 by commissioner of Indian Affairs Francis Leupp. Thereafter, doctors and teachers, officially called superintendents, took over the agents' duties. Leupp believed that they would be more successful in promoting assimilation. On Canadian reserves, agents remained the federal government's representatives, with comprehensive powers to regulate the Indians' lives, until the 1960s. Thereafter, agents were gradually removed from the reserves. The position no longer exists in the Department of Indian Affairs.

See also NATIVE AMERICANS: Reservations; Reserves.

David J. Wishart
University of Nebraska–Lincoln

Abbott, Frederick H. *The Administration of Indian Affairs in Canada.* Washington DC: Board of Indian Commissioners, 1915. Hill, Edward E. *The Office of Indian Affairs, 1824–1880: Historical Sketches.* New York: Clearwater Publishing Co., 1974. *Report of the Royal Commission on Aboriginal Peoples.* Ottawa: RCAP, 1996.

INDIAN COUNTRY

"Indian Country" refers to a variable geographic place where Native Americans reside on trust lands—reserves and reservations. The term is in use in both Canada and the United States, but it bears specific legal meaning only in the latter, where it defines both tribal holdings and individual land allotments, whether still in trust or held in fee (absolute ownership). There is no comparable meaning in Canada, for Native reserves are administered only for Indian communities, not for individual Indians. In both nations the federal government administers most of these lands and thereby generally preempts provincial or state authority over them. Every state and province in the Great Plains includes Indian Country: trust lands abound in the northern tier of states and in the adjacent three provinces—for example, the Rosebud Reservation in South Dakota, the Crow Indian Reservation in Montana, and the Assiniboine Reserve in Saskatchewan. In the Prairie Provinces there are numerous very small reserves, many occupied by brethren of tribes within U.S. borders (e.g., the Blackfeet and Crees); in Alberta there are also a small number of Métis reserves held in

fee simple title. In contrast, reservations on the Americans side of the border are generally much larger, although in the states of Kansas, Nebraska, and Texas, there are only a few small, scattered reservations. Oklahoma—once Indian Territory, to which were relocated tribes from the South, East, and from other parts of the Plains—does not acknowledge Indian Country, despite the existence of the Osage Reservation and so-called former reservations (for the most part, Indian Territory reservations were cancelled through allotment).

Because of conflict and litigation over jurisdiction, other interpretations of Indian Country would apply extralegal meaning in the United States. Such interpretations involve former Aboriginal territory (where, for example, some tribes may continue to hunt and fish but not without controversy); adjudicated claims areas, or lands shown to have historically belonged to tribes, and all former trust lands whether within or outside reservations. State jurisdiction over certain criminal and civil authority may extend to Indians and their lands, but not authority over land use. (Under the Indian Act of 1876 in Canada, provinces do have some jurisdiction over Indians on reserves, but rarely over land in reserves, and provincial zoning authority may apply only if not contrary to that act and constitutional revisions of 1982.)

At one time Indian Country was extraterritorial by treaty and lay beyond local European American jurisdiction. Such was true of the Great Plains until settlers and others, seeking land farther and farther west in both countries, agitated for the cession of tribal reserves or reservations. At first, treaties reserved considerable acreage, as with the Great Sioux Reservation that once dominated Dakota Territory and buffered tribes from adjacent non-Indian communities. Unfortunately, Congress enabled non-Indian homesteading within reservations by declaring remaining acreage "surplus" subsequent to the allotment of tribal lands to individual Indians. Moreover, countless non-Indians also acquired trust lands through sale or inheritance. This aspect of Indian Country is fundamentally inapplicable to Canada.

Where entire counties within Indian Country in some states have become non-Indian in character, litigation has ensued, leading to the diminishment of external boundaries of many allotted reservations. Plains tribes have not escaped this judicial interpretation. In *Rosebud Sioux Tribe v. Kneip* (1977), the Supreme Court determined that four counties in South Dakota were disestablished by earlier allotment laws; consequently, some 2,000 tribal members and seven recognized communities occupying trust acreage on the Rosebud Reservation ended up outside the reservation. South Dakota does not delineate on official state maps those counties once part of reservations that now comprise mostly non-Indian citizenry. Recent court decisions have continued to erode the legal meaning of Indian Country and hence its geographic configuration. Fee lands owned, utilized, and resided on

by non-Indians constitute a strong demographic factor disqualifying tribal jurisdiction over land-use planning and related environmental management. This interpretation has led the courts in *Devils Lake Sioux Tribe v. North Dakota* PSC to exclude non-Indian holdings from tribal jurisdiction on the Fort Totten Reservation (North Dakota); a similar decision has diminished tribal authority on the Crow Indian Reservation (Montana). According to *South Dakota v. Bourland*, the alienation of Cheyenne River (South Dakota) Sioux lands by flood control and other acts eliminated tribal jurisdiction over non-Indians on certain lands adjacent to the Missouri River. In 1998 a similar decision—*South Dakota v. Yankton Sioux Tribe*—excluded from tribal jurisdiction all former trust lands lying outside diminished reservation borders.

See also NATIVE AMERICANS: Reservations; Reserves.

Imre Sutton
California State University, Fullerton

Getches, David H., Charles F. Wilkinson, and Robert A Williams Jr. *Cases and Materials on Federal Indian Law.* St. Paul: West Publishing Co., 1993. Johnson, Ralph W. "Fragile Gains: Two Centuries of Canadian and United States Policy toward Indians." *Washington Law Review* 66 (1991): 643–718. Sutton, Imre. "Preface to Indian Country: Geography and Law." *American Indian Culture and Research Journal* 15 (1991): 3–35.

JOHNSON, LYNDON BAINES
(1908–1973)

Lyndon Baines Johnson, thirty-sixth president of the United States, was one of the most controversial and important chief executives since World War II. Born on a small farm in the scenic Texas Hill Country near the community of Stonewall on August 27, 1908, Johnson grew up in a family where politics and public affairs took center stage. He married Claudia Alta "Lady Bird" Taylor in 1934 while serving as secretary to Texas congressman Richard Kleberg. Johnson served as Texas director of the National Youth Administration in the 1930s and won his first election to Congress in 1937 as a New Deal Democrat and an ardent Franklin Roosevelt supporter. He subsequently won a seat in the U.S. Senate in 1948 by narrowly defeating Gov. Coke Stevenson in one of the most controversial elections in modern political history.

Johnson became Senate majority leader in 1955 and gained recognition for his ability to pass legislation while cooperating with the Republican presidential administration. In 1960 he ran as John Kennedy's vice president to provide experience and balance to the ticket. His presence on the ballot helped deliver key states like Texas, while increasing Democratic votes throughout the Great Plains states. Johnson unexpectedly achieved his goal of the presidency following Kennedy's assassination in Dallas on November 22, 1963. With the sentiment of the nation behind him, Johnson pushed the landmark Civil Rights Act of 1964 through Congress as he planned his election-year strategy.

Lyndon Baines Johnson and Secretary of Agriculture Orville Freeman at LBJ Ranch, November 1964

The Great Plains had provided a bastion of political support for the Republican Party since the demise of the Populist movement. Between 1952 and 1996 the majority of states in the region supported Republican presidential candidates. The only exception was 1964, when Lyndon Johnson steamrolled Republican Barry Goldwater in one of the most lopsided presidential elections in history. In a whirlwind campaign tour through the area, Johnson quoted Texas historian Walter Prescott Webb in saying, "America's frontier is different. It lies inside our country, not at the edge." Johnson rode a wave of sentiment and popularity in sweeping the electoral votes of the Great Plains in 1964, bringing many new Democratic congressmen to Washington on his coattails.

With his popular mandate and an overwhelming congressional Democratic majority, Johnson pushed legislation at a frantic pace. The War on Poverty, the Voting Rights Act, Medicare, Head Start, the National Endowment for the Arts, the National Aeronautics and Space Administration (NASA), and a multitude of other initiatives were launched, greatly expanding the federal presence at every level. His "Great Society" programs exceeded those of the New Deal, as Johnson crafted an agenda that fundamentally reshaped American society and culture. Johnson also wanted an impact on the land itself. As part of his "New Conservation" efforts, Congress passed landmark environmental legislation: the Clean Air Act, the Wilderness Act, the Endangered Species Act, the Water Quality Act, and many more that brought long-term change to America's heartland. Immensely impressed with this record,

Sen. Clinton Anderson (Democrat–New Mexico) called Johnson "the smartest politician I ever knew."

Johnson launched new programs to aid rural America and agriculture. The Food Stamp Act reduced farm surpluses and increased income while setting up a popular program that enabled less-fortunate Americans to purchase basic commodities. More than $2 billion went to the Rural Electrification Administration (REA) to extend electricity and telephones. The largest loan in REA history allowed a North Dakota cooperative to provide electricity to over one million residents in eight states. Personal income levels in the Great Plains during the Johnson years increased in a region still largely dependent on agriculture.

As part of his civil rights program, Johnson sought to bring Native Americans into the national mainstream. In a reversal of federal policies in the 1950s that attempted to relocate Native Americans from their lands to cities, Johnson's administration pushed for aid to expand education and economic opportunities and placed a new emphasis on Indian cultures. More than $10 billion in federal aid went to Indians in an attempt to reduce poverty and unemployment that ran as high as 85 percent on some reservations. He appointed Robert L. Bennett, an Oneida Indian, as the first Native American to head the Bureau of Indian Affairs in the twentieth century. In 1968 Johnson's speech on "The Forgotten American" urged approval of the "Indian Bill of Rights." The legislation extended protection of the U.S. Constitution for Indians in their own tribal constitutions amid a resurgence of Indian sovereignty.

However, foreign affairs diverted Johnson's attention, as he inherited Kennedy's commitment to Vietnam. Johnson expanded the nation's military commitment, and by 1965 the United States assumed primary responsibility for the Vietnam War. Vietnam soon replaced his domestic agenda as the cost of maintaining the war forced the administration to choose guns over butter. Opposition steadily increased at home as casualties mounted with no discernible end to the conflict. Faced with rising opposition within Congress and his own party, coupled with his overall decline in popularity, Johnson surprised the nation on March 31, 1968, when he announced on television that he would not seek reelection, and he called for renewed efforts for peace. Like many others, Sen. Gale McGee (Democrat–Wyoming), a Johnson stalwart, reacted with shock to Johnson's decision: "I had to listen to the replay again to still believe it," McGee said. McGee and others were soon disappointed, as the peace initiatives failed to end the fighting in Vietnam before Johnson left office and Democratic presidential nominee Hubert Humphrey lost a close election to Republican Richard Nixon in November 1968.

Johnson's liberal nationalism left a legacy of achievement but opened the door for conservative reaction and political realignment as a result of his ambitious domestic agenda. His many accomplishments are now part of the

nation's heritage and illustrated his deep conviction to civil rights and economic opportunity to all Americans. His decisions concerning Vietnam demonstrated the limits of American power during the cold war era. In 1969 Johnson and his wife, Lady Bird, retired to their ranch, where he lived until a heart attack ended his life on January 22, 1973.

Patrick L. Cox
University of Texas at Austin

Anderson, Clinton, and Max Magee. Interviews. Oral History Collection. Lyndon Baines Johnson Presidential Library, Austin. Dallek, Robert. *Flawed Giant: Lyndon Johnson and His Times, 1961–1973*. New York: Oxford University Press, 1998. *Public Papers of the Presidents of the United States: Lyndon B. Johnson*. Washington DC: Government Printing Office, 1964–69.

KANSAS

The nation's thirty-fourth state was admitted to the Union on January 29, 1861, after a brief but contentious history. Prior to the Louisiana Purchase in 1803, what is now Kansas was occupied by Native Americans, including the Kaws, Osages, and Wichitas. A number of Europeans, including Spanish explorer Francisco Vásquez de Coronado, had visited the area from 1541 on. Congress initially attached the northern portion of the Louisiana Purchase, to which Kansas was a part, to Indiana Territory. This area became part of Missouri Territory in 1812. After the Missouri Compromise of 1820, which provided for the admission of Missouri to the Union as a slave state, the area of Kansas was considered to be part of "Indian Country" and outside U.S. jurisdiction.

The 1854 Kansas-Nebraska Act was the prelude for the American settlement of Kansas. The act superseded the Missouri Compromise, giving settlers the right to determine whether Kansas should be a free or slave territory. An influx of proslavery advocates from southern states and abolitionists from New England ensued, resulting in bloodshed. The fiery abolitionist John Brown was active in the territory, leading his followers in a massacre of proslavery Missouri settlers at Pottawatomie Creek in Franklin County on May 24, 1856. Later, in 1863, William Quantrill led his proslavery guerrilla forces in raiding and burning a number of Kansas farms and towns (including Lawrence) whose citizens opposed slavery.

Proslavery Democrats controlled the first territorial government and dominated in the early years. But by October 1859, after numerous attempts to draft a constitution, a document reflecting the views of Republican free-state forces was approved by a margin of nearly two to one. Statehood was delayed by national partisan divisions, which led Democratic senators from the South to oppose the addition of a Republican state prior to the 1860 presidential election. It was not until January 21, 1861, after a number of southern senators had left Washington in anticipation of the secession of their states, that Kansas received the necessary votes for admission; the Kansas statehood bill was signed by President James Buchanan eight days later.

Since the granting of statehood, Kansas has

remained one of the most Republican of all states in national politics. The state's political culture has been characterized as "moralistic," and Kansans played prominent leadership roles in a variety of movements such as populism, progressivism, and prohibition. Republican Dwight D. Eisenhower, from Abilene, served as the thirty-fourth president of the United States from 1953 to 1961. Two other Kansans have run (unsuccessfully) for president on the Republican ticket in this century: Gov. Alf Landon in 1936 and former U.S. Senate majority leader Bob Dole in 1996. Kansas's partisan tendencies survived even the powerful political forces that brought about the critical realignments of the 1890s and 1930s. While the agricultural depressions underlying the Populist Revolt and the New Deal enabled third parties and Democrats to gain occasional short-run advantage, there were few permanent voter shifts within the electorate, and the state in each instance quickly returned to its Republican predilections. Kansas rarely deviates from the Republican Party in its presidential voting, and it stands as the only state not to have elected at least one Democratic senator since the 1930s. Republicans hold a 45 to 30 percent registration advantage over Democrats, with 25 percent of registrants choosing to be independents. In 1998 a Republican was governor (elected by a three-to-one margin), Republicans had strong majorities in both houses of the Kansas legislature, and three of the state's four congressmen were Republican.

The Republican dominance has always been a reflection of the state's socioeconomic population mix. Kansas has lacked the economic-cultural-racial diversity that often characterizes two-party competition in other states. Traditionally Democratic minority groups enjoy only a modest presence in the state. Of nearly 2.7 million residents in 2000, only 5.7 percent were African American, 7 percent Hispanic, 1.7 percent Asian, and less than 1 percent Native American. Despite an estimated 80,000 members of organized labor, most affiliated with the AFL-CIO, right-to-work laws have impeded the development of a strong union movement that traditionally offers support to the Democratic Party.

Kansas has an image as a rural, agricultural state, but urbanization has taken place at a rapid pace, particularly in the suburbs adjacent to Kansas City and near Wichita. The number of farms has dwindled while the average size has increased, and the proportion of rural residents in the state is now less than 30 percent. While the rural-based agriculture and oil and gas industries still are important, wholesale and retail trade are now the largest components of the state's economy.

Kansas politics in recent decades has been dominated by divisions within the Republican Party between its rural and suburban wings on such issues as the redistribution of aid from wealthy suburban school districts to the poorer rural school districts. In the late 1980s and the 1990s, abortion policy led to major internal divisions in the Republican Party organization between Christian Right elements and social moderates. Republican factionalism has enabled conservative Democrats to win the governorship on a number of occasions.

See also WAR: Bleeding Kansas

Allan J. Cigler
University of Kansas

Cigler, Allan J., and Burdette A. Loomis. "Kansas: Two-Party Competition in a One-Party State." In *Party Realignment and State Politics*, edited by Maureen Moakley. Columbus: Ohio State University Press, 1992: 163–78. Drury, James W. *The Government of Kansas*. Topeka: University of Kansas, Capitol Complex Center, 1997. Frederickson, H. George, ed. *Public Policy and the Two States of Kansas*. Lawrence: University Press of Kansas, 1994.

KANSAS-NEBRASKA ACT

The Kansas-Nebraska Act of 1854 brought territorial government to that portion of the Louisiana Purchase between the Missouri River and the divide of the Rocky Mountains and from 37° north latitude to the boundary of British America at 49° north latitude. The act created, within this huge area, the territories of Kansas and Nebraska, dividing them at 40° north latitude. In addition to what became the states of Kansas (1861) and Nebraska (1867), portions of what became Colorado were included in the Kansas and Nebraska Territories and parts of what became Wyoming, South Dakota, North Dakota, and Montana were within Nebraska Territory.

The Kansas-Nebraska Act would be crucial in the coming of the Civil War. The Missouri Compromise (1820) had banned slavery in the Louisiana Purchase north of 36°30′ north latitude, except within the borders of the slave state of Missouri that was created by the Compromise. By midcentury there was growing pressure to open the trans-Missouri Indian country to settlement. The Platte Purchase, a 3,139-square-mile area adjoining the Missouri River north and northwest of modern Kansas City, had been carved, with no sectional commotion, from the nonslave area of the Louisiana Purchase and added to Missouri in 1837. In 1846 Iowa entered the Union, extending that state to the Missouri River. Two years earlier Rep. Stephen Douglas of Illinois had offered the first bill to provide territorial government for the trans-Missouri area, called "Nebraska." A Nebraska bill passed the House in 1853 but failed in the Senate, largely because of southern opposition.

In December 1853 Sen. Augustus Dodge of Iowa offered a Nebraska bill that, like the recent House measure, did not address the slavery issue. Stephen Douglas, who chaired the Senate Committee on Territories, recognized that southern opposition to the Missouri Compromise ban upon slavery threatened such legislation. In January 1854 he reported a rewritten bill that embodied the "popular sovereignty" principle, by which the people of the territory ultimately would decide if their prospective state would or would not have slavery. This concept had been basic to his legislation to organize New Mexico and Utah Territories, key parts of the Compromise of 1850. However, southern pressure for explicit repeal of the 36°30′ line was soon evident, and Douglas brought in a bill by adding such a repeal. This revision also called for the establishment of two territories. The latter provision implicitly recognized that frontier Iowa and Missouri boosters had produced separate nuclei of potential settlement in the trans-Missouri country and that diverse transcontinental railroad interests would be served by the creation of two territories, Kansas and Nebraska. Despite northern outrage over the proposed repeal of the Missouri Compromise slavery ban, the Kansas-Nebraska bill passed Congress, and on May 30, 1854, received President Franklin Pierce's signature.

As historian James Malin explained, Douglas saw the Great Lakes–Mississippi Valley region as the "geographical pivot" for continental development. To Douglas, popular sovereignty was a rational policy that would facilitate the nation's spatial and economic development. But this was not a calm, deliberative time, and the Kansas-Nebraska Act brought two tremendous forces—the slavery controversy and national expansion augmented by technology—into collision. The ensuing agitation, including the conflict called "Bleeding Kansas," brought a recasting of political parties that destabilized the Republic and propelled the nation toward war.

See also WAR: Bleeding Kansas

Harl A. Dalstrom
University of Nebraska at Omaha

Malin, James C. "The Motives of Stephen A. Douglas in the Organization of Nebraska Territory: A Letter Dated December 17, 1853." *Kansas Historical Quarterly* 19 (1951): 321–53. Nichols, Roy F. "The Kansas-Nebraska Act: A Century of Historiography." *Mississippi Valley Historical Review* 43 (1956): 167–212. Rawley, James A. *Race and Politics: "Bleeding Kansas" and the Coming of the Civil War*. Philadelphia: Lippincott, Williams and Wilkins, 1969.

KASSEBAUM, NANCY (b. 1932)

Nancy Landon Kassebaum, daughter of the 1936 Republican presidential nominee Alf Landon, was born in Topeka, Kansas, on July 29, 1932. She was first elected to the U.S. Senate from Kansas in 1978 and served two additional terms before retiring in 1996. She had little experience in public office prior to her election, mainly having served only on the school board in the small town of Maize, Kansas, between 1973 and 1975. She capitalized on her prominent family name to win the 1978 Republican primary and then won a relatively close race against a better-known Democratic opponent in the general election. She quickly became a popular figure in the state and won reelection in both 1984 and 1990 by a three-to-one margin.

Senator Kassebaum developed a reputation in the Senate as a conservative on domestic economic issues and a moderate on social issues. She was an aggressive advocate for devolution, the transferring of power from the government in Washington to the states. She deviated from many Senate Republicans by supporting international family planning abroad and pro-choice policies domestically, angering a number of Christian Right Republicans in her home state.

With a master's degree in international relations from the University of Michigan (1956), Senator Kassebaum was an active member of the Senate Foreign Relations Committee. She was a staunch supporter of economic sanctions against South Africa during the Reagan years. She unsuccessfully challenged the Bush administration to cut off food credit guarantees to Iraq prior to the Gulf War, money that was later revealed to be used for that nation's military buildup.

After her retirement from the U.S. Senate, Kassebaum married former Republican Senate minority leader Howard Baker. She currently resides in Tennessee and has been disengaged from Kansas politics since her retirement.

Allan J. Cigler
University of Kansas

LANDON, ALFRED (1887–1987)

Best remembered for his landslide defeat by Franklin D. Roosevelt in the 1936 presidential election, Alf Landon played a major role in Kansas Republican politics from the early 1900s through his death in Topeka—at age 100—on October 12, 1987.

Born in West Middlesex in the western Pennsylvania oil country on September 9, 1887, Landon moved with his family to Kansas when the oil industry sought to exploit the huge Mid-Continent deposits of the Southern Plains. An astute businessman, Landon accumulated an oil-based fortune by the 1920s, and he increasingly turned his attention to Republican politics, first behind the scenes, then as state party chairman, and finally as governor during the mid-Depression years (1933 through 1937).

Landon generally supported the Progressive side of Republican politics, which he practiced in a low-key and congenial style that emphasized bridging differences without compromising principles. As governor, he worked well with the Roosevelt administration on agricultural, petroleum, and welfare issues, among others. Moreover, he lowered taxes and reformed local government finances.

In 1935 Landon easily won reelection, the only Republican governor in the nation to do so. This success, in conjunction with his capacity to bring together various party factions, made him an attractive candidate for the 1936 Republican presidential nomination. Landon represented new leadership for the "Grand Old Party," and he won the nomination with an almost unanimous vote of the convention delegates. Landon waged an energetic and responsible campaign, but Roosevelt overwhelmed him in a defeat of historic proportions. Landon received 38 percent of the major party vote and won only eight electoral votes (Maine and Vermont). For Landon, the results would serve as his political epitaph for the public at large, but he would remain active in national, international, and Republican Party affairs for most of the next fifty years.

Landon's internationalism came to the fore as he articulated measured support for much of Roosevelt's foreign policy in the late 1930s

and through the war years. He continued to speak on international issues in the postwar era, adopting positions that emphasized the value of the United Nations and the need to think seriously about world peace. At the same time, he remained active in the Republican Party, often seeking to influence the outcomes of state and national decisions. However, by the 1950s, with his failure to back fellow Kansan Dwight Eisenhower for the Republican presidential nomination, Landon had become an outsider at both the state and national levels.

For the last thirty years of his life Landon played the role of a Republican elder statesman and was an advocate for strengthening international trade. A lifelong partisan, Landon won bipartisan admiration for his independence, experience, and civility. And he would spend his last years observing the successes of his daughter, Nancy Landon Kassebaum, as she served with distinction in the US Senate and practiced the kind of moderate Republicanism that he had long championed.

Burdett A. Loomis
University of Kansas

Landon, Alfred M. *America at the Crossroads*. Port Washington NY: Kennikat Press, 1971. McCoy, Donald R. *Landon of Kansas*. Lincoln: University of Nebraska Press, 1996. Palmer, Frederick. *This Man Landon*. New York: Dodd, Mead and Company, 1936.

LANGER, WILLIAM (1886–1959)

William Langer, governor and senator from North Dakota, was one of the most colorful political personalities to come out of the Great Plains. Langer was born in Everest, Dakota Territory, on September 30, 1886. He studied law at the University of North Dakota and established a practice in Mandan, North Dakota, in 1916. In 1918 Langer was tapped to be the Nonpartisan League (NPL) candidate for attorney general. He broke with the NPL and ran for governor in 1920 as a Republican coalition candidate but was defeated. In 1932 he was championed as an NPL candidate for governor. Elected, he ordered moratoriums on home and farm foreclosures and a grain embargo on export of the state's wheat (the latter was ruled unconstitutional). In 1934 he was convicted of conspiracy to defraud the United States by arranging for kickbacks to the NPL from state employees on federally funded projects and removed from office. His conviction was overturned on appeal, and in 1936 he again ran successfully for governor. He was elected U.S. senator in 1940 and served until 1959. During his tenure as senator he was a champion of farm programs, rural electrification, health research, and improvements in social security. He was a humanitarian liberal ahead of his time, supporting an equal rights amendment, maternity leave legislation, and the vote for eighteen-year-olds. He was a champion of Native Americans, World War II refugees, and a strong advocate of civil rights legislation. To much of the Senate he was an eccentric who tilted at windmills, as exemplified by his filibuster to deny Earl Warren ap-

pointment to the Supreme Court and his vicious attacks on Winston Churchill.

In his runs for office, Langer often changed factional allegiance or ran as an independent. Langer had no equal in the art of personal politics: he knew tens of thousands of constituents, dealt with their problems, and made them part of his machine. In particular, he was a master in mobilizing the German and German Russian voters of the state, who were critical to his victories, especially in three-way races. Langer died from heart disease in Washington DC on November 8, 1959.

See also PROTEST AND DISSENT: Nonpartisan League.

Theodore B. Pedeliski
University of North Dakota

Geelan, Agnes. *The Dakota Maverick: The Political Life of William Langer*. Bismarck: Prairie House, 1983. Pedeliski, Theodore B. "The German-Russian Ethnic Factor in William Langer's Campaigns, 1914–1940." *North Dakota History* 64 (1997): 2–20.

LEMKE, WILLIAM (1878–1950)

William Lemke, North Dakota politician and unsuccessful third-party presidential candidate, was born in Stearns County, Minnesota, on August 13, 1878. His family moved to Towner County, North Dakota, in 1883. He graduated from the University of North Dakota in 1902, earned a law degree at Yale University in 1905, and returned to Fargo to practice law. In 1915 Lemke became legal adviser to the Nonpartisan League and played an instrumental role in the League's dominance of North Dakota politics. He was elected attorney general of North Dakota in 1920 but was recalled a year later.

In 1932 Lemke was elected to the House of Representatives as a Republican, although he supported Democrat Franklin D. Roosevelt. After Roosevelt refused to support Lemke's proposals for farm mortgage refinancing and bankruptcy, Lemke broke with the president. Backed by a coalition of Roosevelt's opponents, including Father Charles Coughlin, Dr. Francis Townsend, and supporters of the recently assassinated Huey Long, Lemke ran for president in 1936 as the candidate of the Union Party. Lemke hoped to win enough votes to force the election into the House of Representatives, but he won fewer than a million votes.

After his defeat, Lemke resumed his House career. He ran unsuccessfully for the Senate in 1940 but returned to the House in 1942, where he remained until his death in Fargo on May 30, 1950. During his later years in Congress he emphasized natural resources, and he played an instrumental role in establishing the Theodore Roosevelt National Park in North Dakota's badlands.

See also PROTEST AND DISSENT: Nonpartisan League.

Fred M. Shelley
Southwest Texas State University

Blackorby, Edward C. *Prairie Rebel: The Public Life of William Lemke*. Lincoln: University of Nebraska Press, 1963.

LIBERAL PARTY

The Liberal Party is a usually left-of-center Canadian political party that has formed the government at various times at the provincial level in Alberta, Saskatchewan, and Manitoba, and it was the governing party of the whole country for the majority of the twentieth century.

Manitoba was the first new province to join the original four in Confederation in 1867, and it did so in part because of pressure from a Métis provisional government headed by Louis Riel and in part to fulfill Ontario's dreams of western expansion. Its early years are therefore characterized by a latent sense of resentment against the central government and attempts to fashion the province in the image of Ontario. Manitoba's first Liberal premier, Thomas Greenway, for example, was an ardent promoter of Ontario emigration, and during his administration from 1887 to 1899 he reshaped the frontier landscape into a mini-Ontario. This included, most importantly, putting an end to the system of provincially run Catholic schools that had served the early francophone and Métis population of Manitoba and replacing it with a virtual monopoly for the Protestant school system. The Liberal Party in Manitoba failed to have much success after Greenway's government. Liberals fused with the more left-wing Progressives in 1932 and formed a coalition government first under John Bracken and then under Stuart Garson in 1943. With the end of the coalition, Douglas Campbell, an erstwhile Liberal, held the premier's office from 1948 until 1958, but he was criticized for his conservative policies that were not in line with traditional Liberal ideals. Politics in Manitoba tend to be dominated by either the far left or the right, so the Liberal party of the center has generally failed to attract much support.

Political parties were relatively slow to come to the Great Plains of Canada. Before being divided into provinces in 1905, the area known as the Northwest Territories had a territorial government at Regina that was strictly nonpartisan. Influenced by such organizations as the Nonpartisan League in the United States, territorial officials had refused to divide themselves into the Liberals and Conservatives that were the accepted political parties in the rest of the country. The transition to provincial status, however, forced political parties upon the new governments in Alberta and Saskatchewan and ensured the early preeminence of the Liberal Party.

In carving provinces out of territories, a number of structural changes had to be made that affected the political development of the two provinces. Two of the key appointments, made by prime minister of Canada Wilfrid Laurier, were the positions of lieutenant governor for the two provinces. These men would then be responsible for appointing the first premiers of the provinces prior to the establishment of the appropriate electoral machinery. In appointing as lieutenant governors people with known Liberal Party sympathies, Laurier effectively ensured that the new governments of the provinces would also be Liberal. Thus began the early period of Liberal dominance in provinces previously committed to the principles of nonpartisanship.

In Alberta, the Liberal Party remained in power from 1905 until 1921, when it was replaced by a group of loosely organized farmers who were upset with the growing corruption within the Liberal Party and the government's inability to deal with the agricultural recession in the wake of World War I. With a strong sense of nonpartisanship and close ties to agricultural associations in the United States, the United Farmers of Alberta established a government that was in many ways reminiscent of the territorial period. Other similar organizations called United Farmers appeared elsewhere in the country in the 1920s and formed the government in a number of provinces. In Saskatchewan, however, the Liberal Party continued to hold power through the 1920s, in part by appointing the chief proponent of the United Farmer movement, William Motherwell, as minister of agriculture in the Liberal government, effectively silencing the opposition of farmers. The era of Liberal dominance in Saskatchewan ended briefly in 1929 with the election of a Conservative government, but the party returned to power for another decade in 1934. By 1944, however, the Liberal Party in Saskatchewan was increasingly regarded as too conservative, and it was replaced with North America's first socialist government under the Cooperative Commonwealth Federation.

The Liberal Party in Alberta and Saskatchewan has never matched the success of its period in office immediately following the provinces' entry into Confederation. Alberta has not elected a Liberal government since World War I, although the party continues to attract some support and has formed the Official Opposition. In Saskatchewan, Liberals were again elected to form the government in 1964, although the party under Ross Thatcher was regarded as more conservative in its position on government intervention in the economy than is normal for the Liberals.

In addition to being a provincial political party, the Liberal Party is also a national party, although there is often no organizational relationship between Liberals at these two levels of government. Voters in Alberta and Saskatchewan were originally strong supporters of the Liberal Party at the national level, even after the party was no longer in power at the provincial level. The west gave solid support to Laurier at the beginning of the century, continued to vote for the national Liberals under Mackenzie King in the 1920s and between 1935 and 1948, and supported the party through the Louis St. Laurent administration of the 1950s. This support was rewarded: a number of Liberal politicians from the region, such as James Gardiner and Charles Dunning, subsequently found key positions within the national Liberal governments of the 1930s, 1940s, and 1950s. By 1957, however, westerners were disillusioned with the national Liberal party, finding it dominated by the people and the needs of Central Canada and neglecting issues that would have particular resonance in the Great Plains. The Liberal agricultural policy was regarded as especially weak, a problem the party seems curiously unable to rectify. Thus, the Liberals have found little support in the Prairie Provinces since the 1960s, rarely electing more than one or two politicians from all of Saskatchewan and Alberta.

P. E. Bryden
Mount Allison University

Smith, David E. *Prairie Liberalism: The Liberal Party in Saskatchewan, 1905–1971.* Toronto: University of Toronto Press, 1975. Smith, David E. *The Regional Decline of a National Party: Liberals on the Prairies.* Toronto: University of Toronto Press, 1981. Thomas, Lewis G. *The Liberal Party in Alberta: A History of Politics in the Province of Alberta, 1905–1921.* Toronto: University of Toronto Press, 1959.

LOUGHEED, EDGAR PETER (b. 1928)

Edgar Peter Lougheed was born in Calgary on July 26, 1928, he was the grandson of Sir James Lougheed, one of the dominant legal, political, and business figures in early Alberta history. Lougheed earned a bachelor of arts and bachelor of laws from the University of Alberta and master of business administration from Harvard University. Returning to Calgary in 1954, he spent the next eleven years in a successful combination of corporate and private legal practice. In 1965 he turned to politics, assuming the leadership of the moribund Progressive Conservative Party. Lougheed served as premier of Alberta from 1971 until his retirement in 1985.

By the late 1960s postwar oil and gas wealth had created a "new" Alberta. Appealing to this Alberta with the simple slogan "Now," Lougheed and the Progressive Conservatives swept into power in 1971, ending Social Credit's dynasty. While expenditures on traditional responsibilities soared, his government focused much of its attention on joint public–private sector "megaprojects" such as the Athabaska tar sands development. Another landmark initiative, the Alberta Heritage Trust Fund, targeted its oil-derived revenues for both the enrichment of the province's social and cultural fabric and the diversification of its boom-and-bust resource economy.

Disagreements with the federal government over energy resource pricing and taxation simmered throughout the 1970s as Alberta boomed, finally boiling over in 1980 with the National Energy Program (NEP). Lougheed denounced the NEP as an economic and constitutional declaration of war on Alberta. Two years later Alberta's economy and provincial revenues had crashed, but Lougheed won a third landslide reelection by blaming Ottawa while deftly downplaying the role of sliding world oil prices and his own administration's excessively ambitious spending. Although initially dismissed by most non-Albertans as a "blue-eyed sheik" selfishly hoarding the province's windfall resource wealth, his steadfast opposition to both Quebec separatism and Prime Minister Pierre Trudeau's centralizing constitutional vision gradually won him respect.

Lougheed's legacy was a period of remarkable social and economic development that gave Albertans an unprecedented sense of self-confidence and in the process compelled other Canadians to acknowledge Alberta's growing importance in national affairs.

See also INDUSTRY: Petroleum, Canada / LAW: Lougheed, James.

Patrick H. Brennan
University of Calgary

Hustak, Alan. *Peter Lougheed: A Biography.* Toronto: McClelland and Stewart Ltd., 1979. Wood, David. *The Lougheed Legacy.* Toronto: Key Porter Books, 1985.

LOUISIANA PURCHASE

Purchased in 1803 from France for $15 million —about four cents per acre—the Louisiana Purchase added much of the Great Plains to the United States, set the stage for expansion to the Pacific Ocean, and set in motion sectional conflicts over slavery that led to the Civil War.

The territory of Louisiana comprised a significant region of the interior of North America. Its borders were the Mississippi River on the east, the Rocky Mountains on the west, and the Spanish territories of Texas and New Mexico on the south, but the northern border was never clearly defined (although it roughly followed the forty-ninth parallel). Louisiana Territory—under French, Spanish, and American possession—was mainly occupied by Native American peoples until the 1850s. European settlement was limited to river towns (for example, New Orleans and St. Louis) and trading posts along the Mississippi and Missouri Rivers. Until 1763 France controlled most of Louisiana Territory, although Spain intruded on several occasions, including the 1720 Pedro de Villazur expedition into present-day Nebraska. France transferred Louisiana to Spain in 1763 after being defeated in the French and Indian War (Seven Years War in Europe). By the early 1790s the fledgling United States, which was expanding westward toward the Mississippi, relied on the river and the port of New Orleans as an outlet for trans-Appalachian produce. A 1795 treaty with Spain guaranteed Americans access to New Orleans, but by 1801 that privilege was threatened when Spain gave Louisiana back to France. Napoleon hoped to use Louisiana as a base to reestablish its colonial empire in the Caribbean and possibly in North America.

Fearing that access to New Orleans might be blocked by the French presence, President Thomas Jefferson sought to buy or negotiate access to a Mississippi port. In January of 1803 James Monroe traveled to Paris with instructions to offer $2 million for New Orleans and West Florida. Fortunately for the United States, their offer came on the heels of French setbacks in the Caribbean (malaria and yellow fever had ravaged the French military) and the threat of war with England. Fearing that Louisiana would be lost to a British-American alliance, and in need of money to launch further military campaigns, Napoleon ordered his minister to sell all of Louisiana to the American nego-

tiators. The agreed-upon price, $15 million ($11,250,000 for Louisiana and $3,750,000 for American civilian claims against France), gave the United States approximately 828,000 square miles of territory, nearly doubling the land base of the nation. The Senate approved the deal on October 20, 1803.

Exactly what the United States had purchased remained unclear. When asked by Monroe about the boundaries, the French foreign minister responded: "You have made a noble bargain for yourselves, and I suppose you will make the most of it." The Lewis and Clark expedition (1804–6) did just that. The expedition, which wintered near the mouth of the Columbia River in 1805–6, pushed the boundaries of Louisiana beyond the Rocky Mountains to the Pacific Ocean, giving the United States a claim to Oregon. The southern boundary was more difficult to discern, because Spain occupied neighboring Texas and New Mexico. The Adams-Onís Treaty of 1819 finally set the southern boundary at the western bank of the Sabine, Red, and Arkansas Rivers.

The Louisiana Purchase eventually added thirteen states to the nation and brought the Great Plains—America's future breadbasket— into the nation. The purchase also had unforeseen consequences as it sowed the seeds of sectionalism over the expansion of slavery.

Mark R. Ellis
University of Nebraska at Kearney

DeConde, Alexander. *This Affair of Louisiana.* New York: Scribner, 1976. Hermann, Binger. *The Louisiana Purchase.* Washington DC: Government Printing Office, 1898.

MANITOBA

Manitoba became a Canadian province in 1870. Its origins were intimately connected to the fate of First Peoples. Aboriginal title to the lands now constituting much of Manitoba were extinguished by treaties in the 1870s. First Peoples, primarily Crees and Ojibwas, were removed to distant reserves, where they continued to be ruled in colonial fashion by Indian agents until well into the twentieth century. The Red River Métis, people of mixed Aboriginal and European heritage who had founded a distinctive culture at the forks of the Red and Assisiboine Rivers, were similarly dispossessed. The Métis had fought in the Red River Resistance of 1869–70 to protect their rights to the land from a threatened Canadian takeover. Under the leadership of Louis Riel they formed a provisional government whose agents entered into negotiations with Canada, which led to the establishment of the province of Manitoba through the Manitoba Act of July 15, 1870. But the rights that the largely French-speaking Métis believed they had secured in the Manitoba Act were extinguished throughout the 1870s and 1880s, leading to their dispossession and dispersal.

In their wake, settlers of British origin, many migrating westward from Ontario, arrived in the 1870s and 1880s to occupy the rich agricultural land of southern Manitoba. Mennonites and Icelanders also settled in Manitoba in the 1870s, but essentially Manitoba

became culturally and economically an extension of English-speaking Ontario.

In 1896 the great wheat and railway boom took off, creating the economic foundations of twentieth-century Manitoba. The boom was fueled by the massive inflow of eastern European immigrants, who farmed the less-fertile and more northerly lands not occupied by immigrants of British descent, and who formed the core of the labor force that turned Winnipeg into a major manufacturing and distribution center with a hinterland that stretched to the Pacific Ocean. For a short but dramatic period, Winnipeg became the "Chicago of the North."

By 1914 the boom was over. The best prairie land was occupied, most of the railways were built, and the insatiable demand for new supplies and infrastructure was largely filled. The dynamic for growth was exhausted. The shape of Manitoba's economy—a wheat and railway center with significant manufacturing, wholesaling, and financial strength at the hub of an east–west economy—was largely determined for the next fifty years.

A seminal event in shaping Manitoba's politics soon followed in the form of the 1919 Winnipeg General Strike. Winnipeg was a city divided: an aggressive and successful business class of British origins lived in the comfortable south end of the city, and a working class disproportionately comprised of eastern European immigrants was jammed into the teeming, poverty-stricken, multilingual North End. The result was the dramatic, six-week-long General Strike in 1919. Winnipeg's powerful business class responded with a nonpartisan coalition-building strategy intended to ameliorate the class conflict that, as the General Strike made clear, was at the heart of Manitoba's politics. The resulting rurally based coalition governments were successful in governing post–General Strike Manitoba from 1922 to 1958.

In 1958 a Conservative government was elected that finally broke with the fiscally conservative pattern of the previous forty years. Premier Duff Roblin adopted a strategy of public spending to modernize what had become an economically stagnant province. The moderately social democratic New Democratic Party (NDP), elected in 1969, continued Roblin's "Keynesian welfare state" strategy and, with the exception of a hiatus from 1977 to 1981, stayed in office from 1969 to 1988.

The Conservatives under Gary Filmon were reelected in 1988 and served until 1999. Breaking with the economic pattern of the preceding thirty years, they have adopted an economic strategy substantially different from their NDP and Conservative predecessors— one consistent with the neoliberal temper of the times. Their strategy is based on reductions in taxes and public spending to improve the business climate and to attract capital from outside the province, and on increased exports to the United States consistent with the Canada–U.S. and the North American Free Trade Agreements.

As a consequence, Manitoba's economy has

POLITICS AND GOVERNMENT : 673

been rotated on its axis from an east–west to a north–south orientation. The province's historic role as the hub of a pan-Canadian, east–west economy—the "gateway to the west"—has disappeared, replaced by the attempt to create a new role as an export platform at the north end of a midcontinental trade corridor. Manitoba now seeks to become the "gateway to the south."

See also INDUSTRY: NAFTA / NATIVE AMERICANS: Métis / PROTEST AND DISSENT: Winnipeg General Strike / WAR: Red River Resistance.

Jim Silver
University of Winnipeg

Friesen, Gerald. *The Canadian Prairies: A History*. Toronto: University of Toronto Press, 1984. Morton, William Lewis. *Manitoba: A History*. Toronto: University of Toronto Press, 1957. Silver, Jim, and Jeremy Hull, eds. *The Political Economy of Manitoba*. Regina: Canadian Plains Research Center, 1990.

MANSFIELD, MIKE (1903–2001)

Michael Joseph Mansfield was born in New York City on March 16, 1903. He was five years old when his mother died, and shortly thereafter he moved to Great Falls, Montana, to live with his father's aunt and uncle. His father remained in New York, where he was a hotel porter. Although his career took him to many other places, Mansfield once said that he always felt a homesickness when absent from Montana.

After serving in the navy (he enlisted at the age of fourteen), the army, and the marines, he returned to Montana in 1922 and worked in the Butte mines for the next eight years, first as a miner, then as a mucker and mining engineer. Although he had not even completed grade school, Mansfield gained admittance to the Montana School of Mines in Butte in 1927. After his first year, he transferred to Montana State University (later the University of Montana) in Missoula, where he received bachelor's and master's degrees in 1933 and 1934, respectively. His thesis, on Korean-American relations, anticipated a lifelong interest in Asia. He stayed at the university as an administrator and teacher of Latin American and Far Eastern history until 1942. After entering politics, he retained his position as professor of history at the university on permanent tenure.

Mansfield was elected to the U.S. Congress on the Democratic ticket in 1942, carrying eleven of seventeen counties in Montana's First District. He served five terms in Congress. Surviving attacks at the height of McCarthyism for his views on China, he was elected senator from Montana in 1952. Although he won fewer counties than his opponent, Republican Zales Ecton, he was elected with a plurality of 6,600. Mansfield's support came mainly from a belt of counties in the northern half of the state, extending, with few interruptions, from its western to its eastern boundaries. He served in the Senate until 1977. In the early 1960s he was the leading advocate in Washington for stopping the war in Vietnam. As Senate majority leader from 1961 to 1977 (the longest any member ever held that position), Mansfield played a major role in the passage of landmark domestic legislation, including the Civil Rights Act of 1964, the Voting Rights Act of 1965, reduction in the voting age from twenty-one to eighteen, and Medicare, as well as sundry foreign policy landmarks, including the rapprochement between the United States and China. He held the post of American ambassador to Japan from 1976 to 1988 under Presidents Jimmy Carter and Ronald Reagan.

Mike Mansfield died in Washington DC on October 5, 2001, one year after the death of his wife, Maureen, to whom he was married for sixty-eight years.

Angela Unruh
The Maureen and Mike Mansfield Foundation

Mansfield, Mike, and Michael S. Sample. *Mike Mansfield's Montana*. Billings: Goatrock Productions, 1972. Waldron, Ellis. *An Atlas of Montana Politics since 1864*. Missoula: Montana State Press, 1958.

MCGOVERN, GEORGE (b. 1922)

South Dakota senator and 1972 Democratic presidential nominee George McGovern was born on July 19, 1922, in the small town of Avon in southeastern South Dakota. He later moved with his family to Mitchell, where his father served as minister for the town's Methodist Church. McGovern's interest in politics first became apparent in high school, where he was an active member of the debate team, through which he met his future wife, Eleanor Sternberg. He entered Dakota Wesleyan University in Mitchell on an academic scholarship in 1940. Three years later he enlisted in the U.S. Army Air Corps, becoming a highly decorated B-24 bomber pilot in Europe. He completed his bachelor of arts degree at Dakota Wesleyan in 1946.

Following his graduation, McGovern, who had a deep interest in the Social Gospel, enrolled at Garrett Theological Seminary on the campus of Northwestern University in Evanston, Illinois. But after hearing a lecture by the western historian Ray Allen Billington, he opted for graduate work in history. He received his doctorate from Northwestern in 1953. McGovern then began a short career as a professor at Dakota Wesleyan University before being elected to the U.S. House of Representatives in 1956. In 1961 President John F. Kennedy named him director of the Food for Peace program. He left the Kennedy administration the following year to run for Senate and was elected for the first of three terms. Though best known in his Senate career for his outspoken opposition to the Vietnam War, South Dakotans appreciated him most for his efforts on behalf of Plains farmers and his expertise on food and agricultural policy.

McGovern briefly entered the race for the 1968 presidential nomination following the assassination of Robert Kennedy. The widespread outcry over the perceived unfairness of the presidential nomination process led to the creation of a reform commission in 1969, which McGovern chaired. In 1972 he ran again for the presidency, this time winning the Democratic nomination with the help of an army of young volunteers. Pundits were stunned that the junior senator from a small Plains state, widely known as "the prairie populist," could defeat the better-financed favorites of the party leadership.

Although McGovern was a deeply religious family man rooted in the populist traditions of the Great Plains, Republicans and some elements of the Washington media tried to link him with the excesses of the radical counterculture of the day. Abandoned by much of the Democratic Party establishment, badly outspent, and subjected to a series of "dirty tricks" that were later revealed in the Watergate investigation, McGovern lost the election to incumbent President Richard Nixon in one of the biggest landslides in U.S. history. Less than a year later, however, as Nixon's scandals unfolded, public opinion polls showed that were the election held over, McGovern would have won.

McGovern was reelected to the Senate in 1974 but was defeated in 1980 in a stunning upset, along with several other prominent Democrats, in the Republican landslide. He became a part-time lecturer at Northwestern and other universities and continued to speak out on political affairs. He launched an unsuccessful bid for the Democratic presidential nomination in 1984. He became president of the Middle East Policy Council in 1991, calling for a more balanced U.S. policy toward the region. The alcohol-related death of his daughter Terry in 1994 led McGovern to write a widely acclaimed personalized biography of her struggle with alcoholism, and he soon became a prominent spokesperson for the recognition and treatment of the disease. In 1997 President Bill Clinton named him the U.S. permanent representative to the United Nations Food and Agricultural Organization based in Rome.

Stephen Zunes
University of San Francisco

McGovern, George. *Grassroots*. New York: Random House, 1977. Weil, Gordon L. *The Long Shot: George McGovern Runs for President*. New York: W. W. Norton Co., 1973.

MEIGHEN, ARTHUR (1874–1960)

Arthur Meighen has been described as the greatest Canadian parliamentarian ever. Born on June 16, 1874, in the small community of St. Mary's, Ontario, Meighen spent most of his life in politics, becoming prime minister of Canada in 1920 and again briefly in 1926.

Raised in a staunch Protestant environment, Meighen was a quiet and studious youth. His most outstanding characteristics were his abilities as an orator and debater, which he displayed even in his earliest schooling. After studying mathematics at the University of Toronto and trying his luck as a shopkeeper and teacher, Arthur Meighen headed west to seek adventure in the Prairies. After a failed attempt in the dried-fruit industry, Meighen proceeded to article as a lawyer and soon found himself established in the small town of Portage La Prairie, Manitoba. It was here that Arthur Meighen discovered two great loves,

Isabel Cox, whom he married in 1904, and the Conservative Party of Canada.

Arthur Meighen proved to be a most loyal party member. First elected to Parliament in 1908, Meighen became an eloquent defender of a variety of government initiatives, including tariffs, naval policies, and railway nationalization. Meighen was also the author and instigator of several of the most controversial pieces of legislation in Canadian history. During World War I he prepared the Wartime Elections Bill, the War Measures Act, and the Military Service Act, which opponents allege corrupted the electoral process and infringed traditional civil rights.

The aftermath of World War I was an unsettling time in Canada. The Union government that had steered the country through the turbulent wartime years came to an end. When Arthur Meighen became leader of the ruling Conservative Party in 1920, following prime minister Sir Robert Borden's resignation, he faced the difficult task of keeping not only the party but the entire country united. Meighen's uneasy relationship with particular parts of the country limited his effectiveness in this capacity. In 1919 Meighen had acted as mediator in the Winnipeg General Strike. When violence erupted, many criticized him for being unsympathetic to labor concerns. Furthermore, western farmers were angry with Meighen for having sent their sons to war after promising that they would be protected from conscription. This sentiment was echoed in Quebec, where many were also angry with Meighen for introducing wartime conscription.

While Meighen enjoyed international success at the Imperial Conference of 1921, his inability to band the country together resulted in his electoral defeat that year at the hands of his long-time rival, Mackenzie King. Although he formed a minority government in 1926 after a constitutional crisis resulted in King's resignation, Meighen's government was short-lived, lasting only three days. Meighen retreated from the fray to pursue business interests in Toronto, but the lure of politics proved irresistible. On February 3, 1932, he was appointed to the Senate of Canada. Determined to play a leading role, Meighen was one of the first to caution about events developing in Europe, but his warnings went unheeded. Meighen left politics forever in 1942, after suffering a crushing electoral defeat as he sought the Conservative Party leadership a final time. He died on August 4, 1960, in Toronto.

See also PROTEST AND DISSENT: Winnipeg General Strike.

Laura Madokoro
University of Waterloo

English, John. *Arthur Meighen*. Don Mills, Ontario: Fitzhenry and Whiteside Publishers, 1977. Graham, Roger. *Arthur Meighen: A Biography*. Toronto: Clarke, Irwin and Company, 1960–65.

MONRONEY, MIKE (1902–1980)

Almer Stillwell "Mike" Monroney was born in Oklahoma City on March 2, 1902. He graduated from the University of Oklahoma in 1924 with a degree in journalism and a Phi Beta Kappa key. He worked first as a journalist for the *Oklahoma News*, then in 1929 took over management of his father's business, the oldest furniture company in Oklahoma. In 1932 Monroney married Mary Ellen Mellon.

Monroney's first venture into politics as a candidate came in 1937 when he ran unsuccessfully in a special election for congressman from Oklahoma's Fifth District. Running again in 1938, Democrat Monroney won the seat. Monroney's twelve years of service in the U.S. House of Representatives spanned the end of the New Deal and World War II, and the beginning of the cold war and the Korean War. Monroney was a strong supporter of wartime wage and price controls and public housing. His most lasting contribution, however, was the Legislative Reorganization Act of 1946, the first and only major overhaul of congressional machinery in the twentieth century.

In 1950 Monroney was elected to the U.S. Senate, where he authored the legislation establishing the Federal Aviation Administration. He also authored the bill establishing the International Development Association to make low-interest loans to underdeveloped nations. He was reelected in 1956 and 1962.

Monroney came to the Senate during the height of Sen. Joseph McCarthy's controversial hearings on subversive activities, and he played a major role in the censuring of the Wisconsin senator. On more than one occasion, Monroney and McCarthy clashed on the Senate floor. A strong supporter of Adlai Stevenson's presidential bids, Monroney came close to being named to the ticket with Stevenson in 1952. In 1960 he headed the effort to draft Stevenson for a third presidential nomination. Monroney was defeated in 1968 in his bid for a fourth term. He died on February 13, 1980.

Von Russell Creel
Oklahoma City University

Creel, Von Russell, and Bob Burke. *Mike Monroney: Oklahoma Liberal*. Oklahoma City: University of Central Oklahoma and Oklahoma Heritage Association, 1997. Fried, Richard. *Men against McCarthy*. New York: Columbia University Press, 1976.

MONTANA

Long inhabited by various Native American groups, Montana was first systematically explored by Americans in the Lewis and Clark expedition (1804–6). Subsequently, fur traders and trappers entered the area, but the real burst in American migration into Montana started with the discovery of gold in 1858. Prospectors swarmed into the area, and on March 26, 1864, President Abraham Lincoln signed a bill creating the Montana Territory.

Ranchers and homesteaders soon followed, and with the end of the Indian wars the territory's European American population exploded from 38,159 in 1880 to 132,159 ten years later. Settlers vigorously pressed for statehood, and on November 8, 1889, President Benjamin Harrison signed a bill recognizing Montana as the forty-first state.

The basis of representation in the legislature was particularly important in drafting the state constitution. The Great Plains region of Montana, devoted to ranching and with a homestead rush then under way, was relatively unpopulated compared to the mining and timbering counties in the western third of the state. To ensure that their interests were protected, Plains delegates sought and won language for equal representation of each county in the new state senate (one senator per county), while the state house of representatives would be based upon population, but with the proviso that each county was entitled to a minimum of one representative. The battle over apportionment of the state legislature in 1889 in turn reflected the underlying regional divisions in the state that have continued to the present day.

In the wake of statehood, homesteading was actively promoted by the Great Northern Railroad and the Milwaukee Road, and tens of thousands of settlers flooded into the semiarid Plains between 1890 and World War I. This influx of newcomers in turn engendered the creation of dozens of new counties, with the result that the state went from sixteen counties at the time of statehood to fifty-six by the early 1920s. This development further institutionalized rural dominance of the state legislature, and this would remain unchanged until the federal courts mandated change in the 1960s.

From its beginning Montana has been a state whose economy is heavily dependent upon the boom-and-bust cycles of resource extraction (minerals, oil, gas, and timber) and the insecurities of uncertain rainfall and commodity prices in its agricultural sector. In the western counties, where mining and associated activities dominated, progressive politics and labor unionism were relatively strong. In the Plains, after brief flirtations with a variety of third-party experiments, rural and Republican conservatism became firmly entrenched.

These two traditions were manifest in a variety of contradictory expressions. Montana became one of the first states to adopt the initiative and referendum and in 1916 became the first state to elect a woman, Jeannette Rankin, to the U.S. House of Representatives. On the other hand, even in the progressive west, the range of political choice was narrow due to the heavy influence of corporate giants like the Anaconda Copper Mining Company in state and local politics. These clashing traditions came to a head in the gubernatorial election of 1920, in which Democrat Burton K. Wheeler, representing a progressive coalition of workers and farmers ranging from conservative trade unionists to Nonpartisan League dryland homesteaders and socialists and revolutionary communists, was defeated by Republican Joseph Dixon who, though no friend of corporate power, was nonetheless tolerated by it as the lesser of two evils.

After 1920 the Anaconda Company, in alliance with other business giants like the Montana Power Company, wielded pervasive control over the internal politics and policy of the state. The mining company owned most of the state's larger newspapers and wined and dined the legislators when they met for brief sixty-day sessions once every two years. Ironically, the state at the same time would send to Washington liberal and progressive-leaning politicians like Wheeler (elected to the Senate in 1922), Thomas J. Walsh, and later Mike Mansfield and Lee Metcalf. Observers have long tried to account for what some have called the schizophrenia of Montana politics, but certainly one reason is that these individuals were far less threatening to the big business community in faraway Washington DC than they were in the governor's mansion in Helena.

The conservative environment of state politics was also reinforced in part by the malapportionment of the state legislature. Since Montana's fifty-six counties had equality of representation in the state senate and a minimum of one per county in the statehouse, the rural Plains counties were grossly overrepresented in relation to their population: as few as 16 percent of the state's voters could elect a majority of the state senate. But in 1964, in the case of *Reynolds v. Sims*, the U.S. Supreme Court ruled that inequality of population in state legislative districting violated the equal protection clause of the Fourteenth Amendment, which in its judgment required that political subdivisions within a state be as nearly equal in population as practicable. When the Montana State Legislature failed to reapportion in accordance with the standard set, a federal district court did the job for it in 1965.

Reapportionment seemed in turn to trigger a more general drive to reform the constitutional system. In 1970 a call for a convention to write a new state constitution won substantial approval statewide, with support generally highest in the western counties and lowest in the Plains counties. The legislature responded by enacting legislation for the election of delegates and the convening of the assembly, and in the November 1971 special election 100 delegates were duly elected (58 Democrats, 36 Republicans, and 6 independents). The convention then proceeded to write a new constitution that included several innovations. Among these were annual legislative sessions, election of legislators from single-member districts, statewide property tax assessment, apportionment by a nonpartisan and independent districting commission, and fully open and public legislative sessions.

In addition, the new constitution explicitly recognized the individual right of privacy and included articles guaranteeing a "clean and healthful environment" and "equality of educational opportunity." It also mandated voter review of local government every ten years, which allows citizens, if they choose, to review and select new forms of local government, an innovation unprecedented in the United States.

Recognizing the growing importance of the strip-mining of Montana coal, the proposed constitution also established a coal-severance-tax trust fund in which not less than 25 percent of severance tax revenues was to be earmarked for the trust, and it also stipulated that "all

lands disturbed by the taking of natural resources shall be reclaimed." The draft constitution also asserted a public interest in water and its uses and opened up the door for subsequent actions by the legislature and the courts to spell out what public activities constituted a "beneficial use" of the state's water. The document's provisions for the protection of natural resources, including water, and for moving assessment of property values to the state were controversial and appeared to threaten the economic position and assumed property rights of both the mining and agricultural communities, who lobbied vigorously against ratification.

The subsequent referendum vote on the constitution was extraordinarily close, with a winning margin of only 2,532 out of 230,298 votes cast. Further, the vote showed a sharp division of opinion between urban and rural voters. The constitution was approved in only twelve counties, all in the mountain west of the state. In contrast, the constitution lost badly in the Plains counties.

By the 1990s a new political geography appeared to be emerging. Rather than an urban-rural or mountain-plains line of division, the new pattern has isolated Democrats to places where the labor union presence and tradition remain strong, counties with a substantial proportion of Native Americans, and counties with sizable numbers of public employees, such as Lewis and Clark County (Helena) and Missoula County, site of the University of Montana, the state's liberal bastion. Montana appears to be undergoing a critical political realignment, moving from a state in which the two major parties were evenly matched, with strong and consistent regional bases of support, to one dominated by the Republican Party. One expression is Republican control of both houses of the state legislature and the governorship. Another is the growing strength of a radical antitax, antigovernment ideology in which voters now routinely face constitutional initiatives to repeal or abolish taxes, require a public vote on any new taxes, or require a supermajority vote in the legislature to increase taxes. Finally, the state has become identified as an incubator of ultra-right-wing causes like the Militia of Montana and the Montana Freemen, even though such fringe groups have enjoyed little real support.

On at least two issues, however, contemporary Montanans are all agreed. First, they do not want a retail sales tax. In 1971 the people soundly rejected a sales tax referendum. In 1993 they reaffirmed that opinion in a second referendum vote. Montana remains one of a handful of states that does not have a sales tax, and consequently it relies much too heavily on property and personal income taxes to support state and local government. Secondly, there is a strong willingness to use the tools of direct democracy—the initiative and the popular referendum. From 1972, when the new constitution was adopted, to 1999, ninety-four initiative petitions to create new statutes or amend the constitution were circulated for signatures. Of these, thirty-one qualified for

November ballots and eighteen were approved by the voters.

But the most important story about Montana politics today is perhaps the dominance of conservatism. The causes of this are hard to discern, but there are some indicators. First, the state's economy remains heavily dependent on "boom and bust" market forces in the resource and agricultural markets, and throughout the 1990s Montana's income growth was anemic, with significant job growth apparent only in the low-wage service sector, a sector noted for the absence of labor unions. Second, the state's population, which declined by 7 percent in the 1980s, turned around and exploded, with a 10-percentage-point increase between 1990 and 1998. The bulk of the growth in population has occurred in the mountain region. The western counties, with their rugged mountains, evergreen forests, clear lakes, and blue-ribbon trout streams, are being transformed into a "lifestyle frontier." Into these attractive environs come many with comfortable incomes (often in retirement accounts or earned elsewhere). Their needs provide employment in the construction and service economies, the former to build trophy homes and summer cabins, the latter to work at a growing number of pricey restaurants, boutiques, and resorts.

From 1990 to 2000 the population of the state grew by 103,000, but during the same period twenty-two counties experienced population declines, most of them in the Plains. The declines have been the greatest where farming and ranching have remained the predominant economic activity, and it is this uneven economic growth and the increasing disparities in wealth and income that suggest a new Montana configuration is emerging.

In the Plains of Montana the state's eastern boundary is an artificial line on the map—the cultural and economic distances between Jordan, in central Montana, and Belle Fourche, in western South Dakota, are minimal. In contrast, light years of material and psychic distance separate both of these communities and the hundreds like them in the Great Plains from the soft ambience and comfortable affluence of places in Montana like Bozeman, north of Yellowstone National Park, and Big Fork on the shore of Flathead Lake. But both Montanas seem to be merging into one conservative hegemony dedicated to keeping taxes low and government services minimal.

See also PROTEST AND DISSENT: Freemen
Jerry W. Calvert
Montana State University

Lopach, James J., et al. *We the People of Montana: The Workings of a Popular Government*. Missoula: Mountain Press Publishing, 1983. Malone, Michael, Richard B. Roeder, and William L. Lang. *Montana: A History of Two Centuries*. Seattle: University of Washington Press, 1991. Toole, K. Ross. *Twentieth-Century Montana: A State of Extremes*. Norman: University of Oklahoma Press, 1972.

MORTON, J. STERLING (1832–1902)

Born in Adams, New York, on April 22, 1832, Morton grew up in Monroe, Michigan, and was educated at the University of Michigan. He migrated to Bellevue, Nebraska Territory, in 1854 and served as clerk of the Nebraska Supreme Court. In 1855 he became editor of the *Nebraska City News* and was twice elected to the legislature. Morton, a Democrat, was secretary of the territory from 1858 to 1861, and was briefly acting governor.

The Civil War brought an era of Republican domination and political defeats for Morton, who came to concentrate upon his newspaper work. He championed rural development, emphasizing tree planting on the prairies, and made his Nebraska City farm a place for forestation and agricultural innovations. Upon his initiative, the state board of agriculture in 1872 established Arbor Day as an occasion for planting trees. In time, Arbor Day would be widely observed. In 1886 Morton, mindful of environmental change, urged the Nebraska State Historical Society to create an "arboreal bureau" which would compile information on orchard and forestation projects. A "biography of all the planted trees in the state," he said, would "lift into view valuable facts and render humanity a vast service."

A libertarian, Morton opposed railroad regulation, protective tariffs, and prohibition. As secretary of agriculture in Grover Cleveland's second administration, he stressed frugality and civil service while the scientific and marketing functions of the U.S. Department of Agriculture grew. In the monetary struggle of the 1890s, he backed the gold standard but failed to prevent William Jennings Bryan from committing the Democratic Party to free silver.

Morton later established *The Conservative*, a newspaper that heralded his political perspective. Although Nebraska would gain renown for conservative Republicanism, no one better exemplified this conservative heritage than Democrat J. Sterling Morton. However, his environmentalism was his more prominent legacy. He died at the home of his son in Lake Forest, Illinois, on April 27, 1902.

See also IMAGES AND ICONS: Tree Planting and Climate Change.

Harl A. Dalstrom
University of Nebraska at Omaha

Olson, James C. *J. Sterling Morton.* Lincoln: University of Nebraska Press, 1942. Winslow Davis, Kate. "Neighbors to the Mortons." *Nebraska History* 53 (1972): 15–34.

MUNDT, KARL (1900–1974)

Karl E. Mundt was a prominent farm-state Republican who served in Congress for thirty-four years (five terms in the House and four in the Senate). Born on June 3, 1900, in Humboldt, South Dakota, Mundt became a high school teacher and school superintendent in Bryant, South Dakota, after graduating from Carleton College (1923) and obtaining a master's degree from Columbia University (1927). In 1924 he moved to Madison, South Dakota, where he taught and coached the debate team at the Eastern State Normal School while also engaging in an investment business with his father. Although referring to himself as a liberal Republican in getting elected to Congress as representative of South Dakota's First Dis-

trict in 1938, he quickly identified with the conservatives in the party. His first major action as a congressman was a successful effort to remove from circulation the government documentary film *The Plow That Broke the Plains*, which depicted the devastating relationship between mechanized farming and the Dust Bowl.

World War II transformed Mundt from a staunch isolationist into a committed internationalist. Throughout his career he was known primarily to those outside his home state as an outspoken anticommunist. He teamed up with fellow congressman Richard Nixon on the House Un-American Activities Committee during the 1940s and later stood loyally behind Sen. Joseph R. McCarthy in his crusade against alleged internal subversion. Mundt maintained a strong electoral base in his home state by backing price supports for agriculture while maintaining a solid conservative record on other issues. He was a joiner who stayed in close contact with the electorate, affiliating with many organizations, including the Masons, the Elks, the Kiwanis, the El Riad Shrine, and the Methodist Church. He was also an enthusiastic conservationist and active in the Izaak Walton League. A crippling stroke in 1969 incapacitated him and forced his retirement three years later. Mundt died in Washington DC on August 16, 1974.

See also FILM: *The Plow That Broke the Plains.*

John E. Miller
South Dakota State University

Heidepriem, Scott N. *A Fair Chance for a Free People: A Biography of Karl E. Mundt, U.S. Senator.* Madison SD: Karl E. Mundt Foundation, 1988. Mundt, Karl E. Papers. Karl E. Mundt Library, Dakota State University, Madison, South Dakota.

NATIONAL PROGRESSIVE PARTY

The National Progressive Party of Canada was born of frustration and expired in futility. At bottom it was an attempt to achieve regional economic goals at the national level through third-party political action in a traditionally two-party context. The grain growers of the Canadian Plains and their rural allies in Ontario participated in provincial politics as well and with much greater success.

The first small shipment of wheat for export left the Prairies in 1876. But it was not until the completion of the Canadian Pacific Railway in the mid-1880s that the agricultural potential of the area began to be realized. It was capable of producing, in extraordinary quantities, the best hard wheat in the world. For the individual producer, however, it was a costly progress from farm gate to final sale. Along the way lurked predators of many kinds taking their profits from the value of the farmer's wheat. First were the bankers who provided his credit. Then came the local elevator or storage companies, the grain dealers on the Winnipeg Exchange, the railways, the terminal elevators, the shipping lines, the insurance brokers, the importers, and the millers. The international price of the farmer's bushel of

wheat had to satisfy them all. To the individual grain grower, the most vulnerable link in this chain, the game seemed loaded against him.

It was the impotence of the individual farmer that drove them together. In 1902 they formed the Territorial Grain Growers Association, and, after Alberta and Saskatchewan became provinces in 1905, they as well as Manitoba created provincial organizations. For most farmers the critical question was control of production costs. They had to sell their wheat in an uncontrollable world market and buy all their necessities from protected industries in Central Canada. Effective cost control would depend, ultimately, on political action on the tariff.

With the protectionist Conservatives in power in Ottawa after 1911, the western farmers could expect little relief from that direction. When the Nonpartisan League won North Dakota in 1916, Canadian farmers began to dream of a third-party assault on Ottawa. That same year, the Canadian Council of Agriculture, a lobby group, issued the Farmers' Platform demanding lower tariffs, tax reform, and public ownership of transportation and communication facilities.

The move toward independent political action was stalled by the exigencies of the World War I and the disruption of the world wheat market. With Argentina and Australia out of the game because of shipping shortages and submarine threats, Canada and the United States had little choice but to negotiate with Britain a fixed price for wheat and compel all their producers to participate in a regulated market. As it turned out, the price was well above prewar prices. A coalition government was formed by the ruling Conservatives and most Liberals in Canada to prosecute the war vigorously on a nonpartisan basis. The western grain growers gave their support, and their most prominent leader, T. A. Crerar, president of United Grain Growers, a successful farmer-owned cooperative, entered the cabinet as minister of agriculture.

Crerar had not abandoned his low-tariff principles. He made it clear to the prime minister, Sir Robert Borden, that if the government maintained high-tariff policies after the war, he could no longer remain in the cabinet. When the Union government introduced its budget in the late spring of 1919, it contained no provisions for lower tariffs. Crerar promptly resigned and was immediately joined by ten others. They began calling themselves Progressives and were in the unusual position of having a parliamentary delegation before any such party was organized in the country.

The following year the National Progressive Party was formally organized, Crerar was confirmed as leader, and a refurbished Farmers' Platform was their banner. Across the Prairies and in rural Ontario they seemed to carry all before them. When the Union government called a federal election in late 1921, the Progressives permanently disrupted Canadian politics. For the first time since Confederation in 1867 there was a credible third party on the national scene. The Liberals, with a plurality of seats in the House of Commons, formed the country's first minority government. The Progressives had won sixty-five seats and thus became the second-largest group in the House. They declined the role of Official Opposition, to which they were entitled, because they were hamstrung by their own rather confused ideology. Crerar could never enforce party discipline on this "restless and unreliable band."

Largely because they were unwilling and unable to exploit their balance of power position, the Progressives were not successful in national affairs. Prime Minister Mackenzie King quickly realized that the Progressives would never support the high-tariff Conservatives and thus he had little to fear from them. His position, though tenuous, was nevertheless secure. There were inconclusive negotiations about an arrangement between Liberals and Progressives, but King would not commit himself to lower tariffs and risk his Montreal support for undependable assurances from Crerar. The latter, for his part, could not organize his followers into a disciplined political force. So on their major issue of tariff reform, the Progressives gained little. They were able to secure the restoration of favorable freight rates on grain shipments, known as the Crow's Nest Pass rates. It was their only significant achievement.

A year after the election, Crerar resigned the leadership of the Progressive Party. There were personal reasons for his decision, but it was also evident that he had grown discouraged by the internal divisions of the party. As the Progressives disintegrated, the grain growers of the Prairies were turning once again to economic action to serve their needs. The new pooling movement swept them in a new direction. In the election of 1925 they were reduced to twenty-four seats. Most of them drifted into the Liberal Party until only a small group of less than a dozen, known as the "Ginger Group," remained in the House.

What had these angry farmers accomplished? They formed a minority government briefly in Ontario and they came to dominate the politics of the Prairie Provinces, ensuring attention to their demands. On the national level, they ended the two-party system in Canada and forced the restoration of favorable freight rates. Western dissent became an enduring factor in Canadian politics.

J. E. Rea
University of Manitoba

Laycock, David. *Populism and Democratic Thought in the Canadian Prairies, 1910 to 1945.* Toronto: University of Toronto Press, 1990. Morton, William Lewis. *The Progressive Party in Canada.* Toronto: University of Toronto Press, 1950. Rea, J. E. *T. A. Crerar, A Political Life.* Montreal: McGill-Queen's University Press, 1997.

NEBRASKA

The politics and government of Nebraska have been inextricably linked to national events and developments. Statehood was achieved on March 1, 1867, after a decade of political tumult. The major factor influencing the extended debate over statehood was the heightening slavery issue. Once the Civil War settled the slavery argument, Nebraska moved from territorial status, which it had gained with the Louisiana Purchase in 1803, to full statehood, and its governance became primarily a state matter.

The original constitution, which had been hastily drafted and adopted in 1866, proved inadequate for the state, and it was replaced in 1875 with a more relevant document. This revision proved satisfactory until events late in the century, such as rapid population growth fueled by immigration and widespread economic deprivation in the agrarian sector, strained the political system, and another major constitutional update was approved in 1920. Finally, numerous piecemeal amendments proposed by the legislature and the populace, as well as two constitutional revision commissions in the 1970s and 1990s, have kept the structure and powers of state government in step with changing political conditions.

The most distinguishing aspect of Nebraska's governmental structure is the nonpartisan, single-chamber legislature, adopted in 1934 via a popularly initiated constitutional amendment. Its legacy stems from the progressive and populist movements, which succeeded in adopting numerous major policy innovations around the turn of the twentieth century. The unicameral campaign lagged until it was taken up by U.S. senator George W. Norris. Norris also logged an unmatched Nebraska record of political achievement in the national capitol, which included the legal recognition of labor unions, rural electrification, and regional riverbed development. The unicameral legislature system, although widely accepted in Nebraska and generally lauded by political reformers, has not been adoptable in the many states that have reviewed it recently. The nonpartisan feature is less popular, but numerous constitutional amendment attempts to abolish it and revert to a partisan arrangement have fallen short.

Nebraska's executive and judicial branches currently reflect political reform trends evident throughout state government. The governor's office was very restricted prior to the 1920 constitutional changes that lifted the ban on the creation of additional executive agencies, and since the 1950s additional budgetary, appointive, and veto powers have been implemented. The effect of these changes has allowed the governor to contend for leadership in setting state policy. The major areas of judicial improvement involve the selection of judges through a three-stage state system of peer nomination, governor appointment, and voter retention, plus a centralization for administrative purposes of all state and local courts under the chief justice of the state supreme court. Both of these changes came in the 1970s. A major structural change to the Nebraska courts occurred in 1991 after a constitutional amendment was adopted that authorized creation of an appeals court.

Nebraska's political culture instills in its citizenry a mixed set of goals and expectations. Normally the populace abides by a conservatism that sustains long periods of public support for existing political institutions, procedures, and officialdoms. The calm is altered, however, by occasional interruptions fueled by deteriorating economic conditions, especially in the farm sector. This accounts for the long electoral sway the Republican Party has enjoyed in the state's history, but there have been intervals of Democratic preponderance, most notably in the 1910s, 1930s, and again in the 1970s and 1980s. Nebraskans espouse their party membership (or lack thereof) at voter registration time, and in 1998 the tally found the Republicans well ahead with 49 percent, Democrats with 37 percent, and Independents with 14 percent of the registered voters.

The state's population base has been nearly flat for the past half-century and it currently numbers about 1,711,000; this ranks it thirty-seventh most populous among the states. Nebraska was rapidly populated by immigrants after the Civil War and was sustained by economic largess until the Great Depression. Since then, the combined effect of plentiful underground water resources for the agricultural sector and beneficial tax incentives proffered by state and city governments for businesses making capital investments has resulted in a slightly upward movement in both population and economic growth.

See also ARCHITECTURE: Nebraska State Capitol.

Robert Sittig
University of Nebraska–Lincoln

Breckenridge, Adam C. *One House for Two: Nebraska's Unicameral Legislature.* Washington DC: Public Affairs Press, 1957. Miewald, Robert D., ed. *Nebraska Government and Politics.* Lincoln: University of Nebraska Press, 1984. Pedersen, James F., and Kenneth D. Wald. *Shall the People Rule? A History of the Democratic Party in Nebraska Politics, 1854–1972.* Lincoln NE: J. North, 1973.

NEW DEAL

The New Deal's policies affecting the Great Plains may be subdivided into national programs and those aimed explicitly at the region. But the line is at times blurred. National programs had a differential impact depending upon local circumstances.

The absence of large urban centers or industrial concentrations meant that such New Deal initiatives as the National Industrial Recovery Act and the Wagner Labor Relations Act did not have the same importance in the Plains as in the Northeast or Great Lakes states. On the other hand, John Collier's Indian New Deal had an impact in the Plains matched only in the Southwest.

Depressed agriculture—intensified in the Plains by drought from 1930 on—made relief the region's most pressing want. Whether local and state governments in the Plains could have done more to relieve the distress of their citizens is an open question, given the rise in tax delinquencies. But the evidence indicates that lack of will was as much to blame as lack of resources. Responsibility for taking care of those requiring public assistance thus fell upon the Federal Emergency Relief Administration (FERA), headed by Harry Hopkins. Hopkins had to wage a continuing battle with local politicians to impose professionalized administration and gain the demanded matching spending. The major exception to the laggardness of the Plains states in social provision was old-age pensions, because of their relatively high proportion of elderly.

Of primary long-term importance for the Plains was the domestic allotment plan incorporated in the Agricultural Adjustment Act (AAA) of 1933. The goal was to raise farm prices to the level of "parity" by inducing farmers through benefit payments to reduce acreage. After the Supreme Court held unconstitutional the processing tax that funded benefit payments, Congress in 1936 readopted the plan with a conservationist veneer. Farmers would be paid out of general revenues to grow soil-conserving crops instead of soil-exhausting (and surplus) crops, such as wheat and cotton.

By the end of 1935 the AAA paid out slightly over $1.1 billion in benefit and rental payments, with approximately half going to the ten Plains states. North Dakota, South Dakota, Nebraska, Texas, and Oklahoma were the top five states in the percentage of farmer participation in the program. Prices simultaneously rose, though still remaining below the "parity" level. But higher prices were of limited benefit to those whose crops were ruined by the drought. Agricultural prosperity did not return to the Plains until after the return of higher rainfall levels in the summer of 1938 and the subsequent war in Europe.

Because of the drought, the FERA inaugurated in 1934 a special program through its new Division of Rural Rehabilitation to tide farmers over by loans for the purchase of seed, fertilizer, livestock, and equipment. The AAA's emergency cattle purchase program saved from total ruin the livestock raisers of the western Plains, whose herds faced decimation from blowing dust and lack of forage. And the ranching interests were largely successful in controlling Department of Interior policies under the Taylor Grazing Act of 1934. Farm Credit Administration refinancing of mortgages was a boon to a section where debt per farm was among the nation's highest. So was the rural electrification program pushed by the Rural Electrification Administration, given the region's poverty, sparse population, and distances.

The benefits to the Plains from the New Deal work relief programs were mixed. The region lacked the skilled labor and financial resources for matching funds required for the capital-intensive projects of the Public Works Administration. But the large tracts of federally owned land made the area a favored location for Civilian Conservation Corps camps, and the financial boost such camps provided caused communities to vie for their placement. As throughout the country, the Works Progress Administration (WPA)—though giving many communities otherwise unattainable new facilities—failed to provide jobs for all those needing work. And those not taken on by the WPA, or falling into the special categories covered by the Social Security Act, fared

poorly when Washington turned back responsibility for general assistance to the states.

The dust storms that swept over the Plains from 1934 on were the catalyst for the formulation of a program to deal with what were regarded as its long-range problems. There was a consensus among New Deal planners that the crux of the difficulty was an exploitative agriculture ill adapted to the region's climate and soil. Their 1936 report, *The Future of the Great Plains*, called for a multipronged attack to prevent soil erosion and make the fullest possible use of available water. But its capstone was a proposal for a radical restructuring of land use—a shift from the commercial production of row crops to livestock pasturage. Undergirding this proposal was a call for a revolution in "Attitudes of Mind."

The response of Plains dwellers ranged from enthusiastic acceptance to hostility. Despite rhetorical bows to the noble yeoman myth, most Plains farmers were profit-maximizing capitalists. Accordingly, fullest exploitation of available water took highest priority—the more so because the public at large rather than the beneficiaries would bear the bulk of the cost of federal irrigation projects. Despite suspicion about the ambitions of Hugh Hammond Bennett's Soil Conservation Service under the Soil Conservation Act of 1935, the lure of higher outputs through government-subsidized innovations such as contour plowing and listing brought at least partial acceptance. There was, however, strong resistance to including provision for mandatory land-use regulations in the states that were authorizing acts to create soil conservation districts. Even in the states that did so, those provisions remained a dead letter.

More ambitious and/or radical proposals did not find much favor with Congress or—so far as can be ascertained—with Plains dwellers. President Franklin D. Roosevelt's pet erosion solution—building a hundred-mile-wide shelterbelt of trees from the Texas Panhandle to Canada—failed to win legislative backing. Although Roosevelt kept the project going until 1942 with relief funds, the results were a shadow of his vision. The Resettlement Administration and Farm Security Administration continued the FERA rehabilitation loan program, but budget restraints limited what could be accomplished. The few experiments at a more collectivist-style agriculture sparked cries of a communist plot. Even the suggestion of any large-scale resettlement of population from the Plains raised angry protests from local spokesmen. Paradoxically, the New Deal's success in providing immediate relief undercut the likelihood of major behavioral and value changes.

Eight of the top fourteen states in per capita expenditures by major New Deal agencies from 1933 to 1939 were Plains states, but this largess brought no long-term political advantage. Roosevelt carried all the Plains states in 1932 and again in 1936, while Democrats were swept into office throughout the region. But many of those Democrats were Jeffersonian states' righters (such as Edwin C. Johnson in Colorado), demagogues (such as "Alfalfa Bill" Murray in Okla-

homa), or political mountebanks (such as Charles W. Bryan in Nebraska). In Congress, Roosevelt's leading regional supporters were progressive Republicans such as George W. Norris of Nebraska and Bronson Cutting of New Mexico. No Plains state instituted a "little New Deal." Even in North Dakota—the most radically inclined state of the region—Nonpartisan League–backed Gov. William Langer offered more bombast than substance.

Plains lawmakers began swinging away from support for the Roosevelt administration with the 1937 Supreme Court–packing fight. The 1938 election showed a similar movement under way among the public. And in 1940 Roosevelt himself lost Colorado, Kansas, Nebraska, and the Dakotas. Crucial in explaining this rightward shift appears to be the conflict between New Deal policies and Plains dwellers' rugged individualist self-image. Financial desperation led a majority to compromise temporarily what they saw as their principles—a compromise that was rationalized by the justification that people such as themselves were the backbone of the country and thus uniquely deserving of governmental solicitude. But extending that solicitude to the alien and suspect masses of the cities was another matter; nor was it required once the agricultural subsidy programs had become safely institutionalized.

Long-standing rural fears about the threat of centralized power were raised by Roosevelt's Court-packing and executive branch reorganization plans and were reinforced by the intrusion of federal bureaucrats into the daily lives of Plains men and women. The New Deal's growing exploitation of class warfare rhetoric threatened the myth of classlessness with which local elites had long buttressed their own positions. The final blow was Roosevelt's interventionist foreign policies. Plains isolationism had diverse roots—the feeling that American problems should be dealt with first, suspicions of an international bankers' conspiracy, ethnic loyalties and resentments—but the result was to solidify the reaction against the New Deal and its works.

See also AGRICULTURE: Agricultural Adjustment Administration; Farm Security Administration; Taylor Grazing Act.

John Braeman
University of Nebraska–Lincoln

Lowitt, Richard. *The New Deal and the West.* 1984. Norman: University of Oklahoma Press, 1993. Saloutos, Theodore. *The American Farmer and the New Deal.* Ames: Iowa State University Press, 1982. Schuyler, Michael W. *The Dread of Plenty: Agricultural Relief Activities in the Middle West, 1933–1939.* Manhattan KS: Sunflower University Press, 1989.

NEW DEMOCRATIC PARTY

The New Democratic Party of Canada (NDP) was founded in 1961 from an earlier party, the Cooperative Commonwealth Federation (CCF), and the largest trade union federation, the Canadian Labour Congress. The first leader of the NDP, from 1961 to 1971, was T. C. "Tommy" Douglas, who had led the CCF in Saskatchewan to its first victories. The current (2001) national leader is Alexa McDonough, a member of Parliament from Halifax, Nova Scotia, and a former leader of the party in that province.

The NDP has yet to form a federal government, but it has run governments in Saskatchewan, Manitoba, British Columbia, Yukon, and (only once to date) Ontario. Nationally, it has been enormously influential as the "conscience of the country" and by forcing reforms in minority-government situations. Thus, it was instrumental in obtaining the first old-age pension legislation, unemployment insurance, family allowances, and electoral reform (disclosure on funding sources and limits on spending). Its pioneering of public health care—"medicare"—in Saskatchewan in 1944 led to the establishment of a national scheme in the 1960s under a Liberal government. T. C. Douglas is now recognized as the "father of medicare" in Canada.

The NDP caucus, reduced to thirteen members in the federal election of 2000, barely retained official party status in the House of Commons (twelve members is the minimum). This loss of support is likely the result of the growth of the far-right Canadian Alliance Party, fear of which moved NDP voters to the center-left Liberal Party as the party most able to keep the far right out of office. The drop in support has prompted a call for review of the NDP's policies, name, structure, and relations with activist citizens' organizations.

Lynn McDonald
University of Guelph

McDonald, Lynn. *The Party That Changed Canada: The New Democratic Party Then and Now.* Toronto: Macmillan Publishing Company, 1986. Morton, Desmond. *Social Democracy in Canada:* NDP. Toronto: Samuel Stevens, Hakkert, 1977.

NEW MEXICO

In 2000 New Mexico had a population of 1.8 million, a per capita income of $19,936, one of the lowest in the nation (which in 1999 averaged $26,412), and a state government that spent around $6.5 billion, including transfers from the federal government of around $1.6 billion. The state has one large city, Albuquerque, and a varied economy, including high technology, military complexes, agriculture, mining, and tourism. The population is varied and includes twenty-three Indian tribes, Hispanics with multigenerational roots, pioneer ranchers, migrant professionals, new retirees, artists, scientists, and tourism specialists. Geographically, analysts distinguish the Indian Northwest, Hispanic North, Little Texas (the Plains of New Mexico), Albuquerque, and the Southwest Borderlands, each with distinct political behaviors.

At the time of the Spanish conquest, New Mexico was populated by small groups of Navajos and Apaches, and some 30,000 Pueblo Indians scattered in villages along the Rio Grande and west as far as Zuni and Acoma. In 1598 Don Juan de Oñate led a group of settlers from Central Mexico to what is now Espanola, New Mexico, extending the Spanish Empire northward by several hundred miles. His successor, Pedro de Peralta, founded Santa Fe as a capital in 1610, and Franciscan missionaries began a lengthy period of conversion of Natives to Catholicism. In 1680 a revolt by Pueblo Indians forced colonists to retreat until control was regained in 1692. The area remained remote from Spanish rule, however, and under continuous threats from Apache, Navajo, Ute, and Comanche raiders during the eighteenth century.

Isolated even more by the instability that followed Mexican independence from Spain in 1821, New Mexicans began trading with Anglo-Americans through the Santa Fe Trail. After annexation of Texas in 1845, expansionists pressured President James K. Polk to harden his position in a dispute with Mexico over the western boundary. Negotiations failed and the United States declared war in May 1846. Gen. Stephen Kearny marched into New Mexico, ending Mexican control. U.S. troops invaded Mexico at Veracruz, and Mexico ceded California, Arizona, Nevada, Utah, Colorado, and New Mexico in 1848. In 1850 the Territory of New Mexico, including modern New Mexico, Arizona, and parts of Nevada and Colorado, was established, and the boundary with Texas set. The Gadsden Purchase of 1853 fixed the southern boundary, and in 1861 the creation of the Territory of Colorado established New Mexico's northern boundary. When Arizona was separated from New Mexico in 1863, New Mexico's present boundaries were stabilized.

During the territorial period, Spanish-speaking New Mexicans lost much property in predatory land grabs led by unscrupulous agents with political connections. Indians resisting U.S. authority fared even worse. The Apaches' Mescalero lands were invaded by the U.S. Army in 1863, and the tribe was relocated. Col. Kit Carson attacked the Navajos' farmlands at Canyon de Chelly in 1864, forcing 6,000 to surrender in the face of starvation. The Navajos were relocated 300 miles away for four years. When a constitution was written in 1911, a year before statehood, Hispanics, who outnumbered Anglos, secured guarantees protecting language and citizenship. Although granted U.S. citizenship in 1924, Indians did not vote in state and national elections in New Mexico until the late 1940s, and even later in local elections. Hispanic and Indian incomes in New Mexico are still significantly lower than those of Anglos.

In spite of these difficulties, following political reforms in the 1960s Indians and Hispanics in New Mexico integrated more easily into the state's political system. Comprising about 40 percent of the state's population, Hispanics are greatly overrepresented in the Democratic Party, which is dominant in most counties at the local level. In the legislature Hispanics have held most leadership positions since the early 1970s. Two recent governors were Hispanic. With only 11 percent of the state's population, Indians commonly elect legislators in districts with large Indian populations. Navajos also vote in elections for the Navajo Nation, headquartered in Arizona.

Culturally, the Plains area of New Mexico (roughly the eastern third of the state) is the legacy of Anglo ranching and farming pioneers who settled about a hundred years ago. Some of the land was in the Permian Basin and was exploited for oil during the 1920s and 1930s. This area is known as "Little Texas," a designation that summarizes a conservative political culture, a dwindling oil economy, and proximity to Texas. In-migration of Hispanics has recently begun to change the demographic composition and political culture of the region.

New Mexico has a bicameral legislature, unsalaried, which alternates each year between thirty- and sixty-day sessions. The governor, whose powers are relatively weak, shares the executive branch with an elected treasurer, attorney general, auditor, secretary of state, commissioner of public lands, and public regulatory commission. In spite of its diverse population, New Mexico has voted for the winning presidential candidate in all elections since statehood except for 1976, when New Mexico voted slightly in favor of Gerald Ford's losing campaign, and 2000, when the state supported Vice President Al Gore. For national offices, including the U.S. Senate and House, the state is competitive between the two major parties, but for local offices most counties vote strongly Democrat.

Twentieth-century notable political figures include Dennis Chavez, who led a mass migration of Hispanics from the Republican to the Democratic Party during the 1930s and went on to a distinguished senatorial career; Gov. Bruce King, who created a thirty-year Democratic governing coalition of ranchers, liberal urbanites, and Hispanics; Sen. Pete Domenici, a Republican who attracted broad-based support from Democrats after 1972; Jerry Apodaca, who reorganized state government efficiently in 1974 after becoming the first Hispanic governor elected in half a century; and Republican governor Gary Johnson, whose use of the veto became legendary in the late 1990s.

See also HISPANIC AMERICANS: Maxwell Land Grant.

Jose Z. Garcia
New Mexico State University

Vigil, Maurilio E., Michael Olsen, and Roy Lujan. *New Mexico Government and Politics.* Lanham MD: University Press of America, 1990.

NORBECK, PETER (1870–1936)

Peter Norbeck was governor and U.S. senator from South Dakota and a pivotal figure in South Dakota politics in the early twentieth century. Norbeck was born in Clay County, South Dakota, on August 27, 1870. He was the son of the Reverend George Norbeck and Karen Larsen Norbeck, immigrants from Norway. The Norbecks soon moved to Charles Mix County, where Peter grew up. After attending the University of South Dakota, Norbeck invented an improved method of drilling wells to extract water from aquifers. He and his partner, Oscar Nicholson, established a well-drilling business in Redfield, South Dakota. The business prospered in the drought-stricken Great Plains, and Norbeck became wealthy. He married Lydia Anderson in 1900, and they raised four children.

Inspired by the progressive Republicanism of Theodore Roosevelt, Norbeck entered politics. He was elected to the South Dakota Senate in 1908 and served three two-year terms. He was elected lieutenant governor in 1914 and governor in 1916 and 1918. During Norbeck's governorship, statewide populist parties were established in several neighboring states, including the Nonpartisan League of North Dakota and the Farmer-Labor Party of Minnesota. Nonpartisan League organizers tried to establish a similar party in South Dakota, but Norbeck incorporated many of the League's policies into his own platform. Norbeck's popularity among farmers and his progressive views were instrumental in preventing the establishment of a third party in South Dakota, whose Republican Party remained allied with progressives throughout Norbeck's lifetime.

In 1920 Norbeck was elected to the U.S. Senate. He was reelected in 1926 and 1932. As a senator, Norbeck was especially active in agriculture and conservation issues. He played an instrumental role in the establishment of Mount Rushmore as a national memorial. In the 1930s Norbeck generally supported New Deal legislation, but he was distrusted by Republicans who regarded him as too progressive and by Democrats who shunned his loyalty to the Republican Party.

His last years were also overshadowed by the onset of cancer, which led to his death in Redfield, South Dakota, on December 20, 1936. Norbeck is recognized as a leader of the progressive forces of the Northern Plains and as an instrumental figure in preventing a split between progressive and conservative Republicans during the interwar years.

See also IMAGES AND ICONS: Mount Rushmore National Memorial.

Fred M. Shelley
Southwest Texas State University

Fite, Gilbert C., and Peter Norbeck. *Prairie Statesman.* Columbia: University of Missouri Press, 1948.

NORRIS, GEORGE W. (1861–1944)

George William Norris represented Nebraska for forty years in the House of Representatives and U.S. Senate, passing significant liberal legislation as a maverick Republican and Independent. Norris was born on July 11, 1861, near Clyde, Ohio. He grew up on his family farm, where he learned temperance, fear of debt, and Lincoln Republicanism from his widowed mother. After graduating from Northern Indiana Normal School (later Valparaiso University), George failed as a lawyer in Walla Walla, Washington, and Beatrice, Nebraska, before moving to Beaver City and then McCook, Nebraska, where he married the daughter of a prominent family and became county attorney and then district judge.

In 1902 he was elected as a Republican to Congress; he spent the next ten years in growing disenchantment with Republican leaders and extreme partisanship. He led a revolt of insurgents and Democrats to limit the powers of the Speaker of the House, Republican Joe Cannon, in 1910, which earned Norris a chapter in John Kennedy's *Profiles in Courage.* Election to the Senate in 1912, again as a Republican, gave Norris a national platform as a political and economic democrat often at odds with Republican leadership. He supported unreservedly the initiative, referendum, recall, a strong civil service, and abolishing the Electoral College and the poll tax. He opposed the excesses of partisanship.

Endorsing Franklin Roosevelt's successful candidacy in 1932 changed Norris's role from gadfly critic to architect of major legislation. Economic democracy was the recurring theme of Norris's legislation. The Norris-LaGuardia Act of 1932 curtailed federal court injunctions against labor unions. Norris introduced and enabled passage that same year of the Twentieth Amendment to the U.S. Constitution, which ended lame duck sessions of Congress, notorious for special interest influence.

Norris took his greatest satisfaction from passage of the Tennessee Valley Authority Act in 1933, which harnessed hydroelectric power under public ownership. Rural electric cooperatives brought light and power to American farms under the Norris-Rayburn Act of 1936. In Nebraska, Norris successfully led the 1934 petition drive for a nonpartisan unicameral to limit special interest and party boss influence. His final Senate term was as an Independent, and he lost his 1942 reelection bid. An autobiography, *The Fighting Liberal*, was finished eight weeks before his death at McCook on September 2, 1944.

David Landis
Nebraska Legislature

Lowitt, Richard. *George W. Norris: The Making of a Progressive, 1861–1912.* Westport CT: Greenwood Press, 1963. Lowitt, Richard. *George W. Norris: The Persistence of a Progressive, 1913–1933.* Chicago: University of Illinois Press, 1971. Lowitt, Richard. *George W. Norris: The Triumph of a Progressive.* Chicago: University of Illinois Press, 1978.

NORTH DAKOTA

In 1889, Dakota Territory, which had been created in 1861, was divided into the states of North and South Dakota. From earliest statehood, North Dakota was strongly Republican. The delegates to the Constitutional Convention in 1889 were overwhelmingly so. The Republican machine run by railroad lobbyist Alexander McKenzie was challenged by the Farmers Alliance and by reform Republicans and Democrats who were able to elect Gov. Eli Shortridge, a Populist, in 1892, and Gov. John Burke, a Democrat, in 1906, 1908, and 1910. North Dakota became the spawning ground for the Nonpartisan League (NPL), a populist-reform organization that was able to capture the legislature and statewide offices in 1918 and pass a platform including state-owned enterprises such as a state bank, flour mill, and hail insurance program. The NPL was nonpartisan in name only: it filed its candidates on the Republican primary ballot, and the primaries became key to control of state government. The two Republican factions, the NPL and the Independent Voters Association, while bitter foes, would meet to select national party committeemen and divide the delegates selected for the National Republican Convention.

The NPL's dominance lasted only until 1921, when the Independent Voters Association was able to bring about a voter recall of the NPL governor, attorney general, and commissioner of agriculture. The decade of the 1920s was a period of political chameleons who changed political affiliation to run as Democrats if they lost in the Republican primaries. The NPL was not able to regain control of state government until 1932. It refurbished its populist image, adopting diversity rules guaranteeing delegates for women, labor, Native Americans, and veterans. It elected Bill Langer as governor and won complete control of the legislature. After Langer's conspiracy conviction and removal from office in 1934, the state had four governors in seven months. The year 1938 saw a Democrat governor, John Moses, elected with Republican crossover votes. Moses and a conservative Republican-Democrat coalition controlled state politics until 1944.

In 1946 the lines were drawn between the NPL and the Republican Organizing Committee (ROC). The ROC swept state elections, and the NPL faded in influence.

From 1947 until 1956 a movement of "NPL insurgents," along with the Farmers Union and Democrats, worked to move the NPL into filing in the Democratic column. In 1956 the NPL voted to merge with the Democrats, but it took until 1962 before they held a unified convention. They slowly emerged as a competitive party whose candidates won a U.S. Senate seat and the governorship in 1960. The 1980s represented the high-water mark of Democratic Party influence, with election of Govs. Art Link and George Sinner, election of the congressional delegation, a majority of statewide offices, and control of at least one house of the legislature in 1983, 1987, and 1989.

After 1992 the Republicans regained the governorship under Ed Schafer and elected large majorities in the legislature. Majority party leaders in the legislature asserted their dominance over policy vis-à-vis their own governor and moved to establish more legislative checks on executive branch action. Democrats have held onto the state's congressional delegation, but that represents a tendency of state voters to focus on personalities over parties and to favor incumbents efficacious in defending the state's interests in Washington. The swings of power between the NPL and ROC and Republicans and Democrats did not affect some trusted and popular officeholders who were able to serve for decades.

North Dakota politics is an expression of a participatory political culture with high levels of voter turnout. Voters also actively employ the initiative and referendum in their politics. From 1918 to 1998 the state put some 222 constitutional amendments (41 by petition), 65 referrals, and 141 initiatives on the ballot. Signature requirements to put measures on the ballot are quite low (2 percent of population for initiative or referendum, 4 percent for constitutional amendment). Ballot measures have become a vehicle to overturn tax laws and to legislate morality issues (liquor, gambling, Sunday opening) that the legislature seeks to avoid. These mechanisms have also been the sounding board for political mavericks who express their distrust of elected officials and seek to legislate around the legislature. One of the preeminent "referral kings" was Robert P. McCarney, who spent over a decade challenging the legislature in this manner. Until 1998, at least, ultraconservative groups that have had success in putting their agenda on popular initiatives in other states had been unsuccessful in co-opting the North Dakota electorate.

See also PROTEST AND DISSENT: Nonpartisan League.

Theodore B. Pedeliski
University of North Dakota

Howard, Thomas, ed. *The North Dakota Political Tradition.* Ames: Iowa State University Press, 1981. Omdahl, Lloyd B. *Insurgents.* Dakota Territory centennial ed. Brainerd MN: n.p., 1961. Robinson, Elwyn B. *History of North Dakota.* Lincoln: University of Nebraska Press, 1966.

NYE, GERALD (1892–1971)

Sen. Gerald P. Nye of North Dakota gained prominence as one of the most outspoken of Great Plains isolationists in the pre–World War II period. Born in Wisconsin on December 19, 1892, Nye moved to North Dakota in 1916 and became a small-town newspaper publisher. In 1924 he was an unsuccessful independent candidate for Congress. When Sen. Edwin F. Ladd of North Dakota died in 1926, Nye emerged as the dark horse interim appointment of Gov. Arthur G. Sorlie. He won his first election on a platform of "North Dakota for North Dakotans." In his first term he voiced typical populist conspiracy themes of the exploitation of farmers and little people by big business and banks. In the early 1930s he supported Father Charles Coughlin and his goal to control the evils of capitalism and Dr. Francis Townsend's plan to give every person over sixty a pension of $200 a month. He initially supported the National Recovery Administration but then felt it had been completely co-opted by industry.

In 1933 Nye gained national prominence by heading an investigation of the munitions industry in which he cast the industry as profiteers and warmongers. The late 1930s saw Nye's isolationist views come to fruition in the Neutrality Acts of 1936 and 1937. After war broke out in Europe in 1939, Nye worked with the America First Committee and protested any efforts to aid Britain or defend our freedoms on the high seas. He even sought to investigate the movie industry, especially Jewish film producers, alleging bias in demonizing Germany. Pearl Harbor undercut Nye's support. He mellowed his views to offer support for the war, but in 1944 he was defeated. His defeat was less over the war issue than such local issues as his divorce and hasty re-marriage, his Chevy Chase lifestyle, and his failure to bring home the bacon to the home folks. He died in Washington DC on July 18, 1971.

Theodore B. Pedeliski
University of North Dakota

Cole, Wayne. *Senator Gerald P. Nye and American Foreign Relations.* Minneapolis: University of Minnesota Press, 1962.

OKLAHOMA

When Oklahoma became the forty-sixth state in 1907, it brought together two disparate territories. The eastern half of the state was Indian Territory, a place where the federal government had been sending Native Americans since 1817. The western region, officially unassigned land, eventually became Oklahoma Territory. These two regions, reflecting significant topographical differences, were even more distinctive in history, culture, and political orientation.

In the Land Run of 1889, white settlers poured into the "unassigned lands" of what would become Oklahoma Territory. These homesteaders came largely from the Midwest, bringing their Republican politics and the values of frontier individualism. The northern and western Oklahoma Plains was ideal wheat-growing country. Today, it remains sparsely settled, primarily agriculture land. Beginning in the mid-1800s, other settlers, mostly whites from Texas and the South, had begun a relentless invasion of Indian Territory. The land in the southeastern region, with rolling hills and scrub forest, was far less suitable for large farms. Many of the new occupants became subsistence farmers. They brought along their Democratic heritage and a southern cultural and political outlook.

The enduring question remains: is Oklahoma primarily a Plains or southern state? It is both, and distinctive regional differences are still visible today. The northwestern wheat-growing region is still far more Republican than the rural southeast. The political fault line bisects the state from northeast to southwest, largely reflecting the Indian Territory–Oklahoma Territory division at statehood. Old-timers still refer to the southeast as "Little Dixie." It is the poorest part of the state and remains the most Democratic. Since World War II the state's two large metropolitan areas, Oklahoma City and Tulsa, have joined the rural northwest as Republican strongholds.

Statewide, more and more Oklahoma voters have turned to Republican candidates. The last Democratic presidential nominee to carry the state was Lyndon Johnson in 1964. Unlike the states of the Deep South, race has not been a major cause of this shift. With an African American population of about 8 percent, race has never been the defining issue in Oklahoma politics. A key influence in the state's shifting political allegiance has been religion. With an abundance of Protestant fundamentalists and evangelicals, the state has become a bastion of social conservatism. In 2000 the Christian Right dominated the state's Republican Party. Oklahoma's six House members, and senators Don Nickles and Jim Inhofe, were all Republicans, a first in state history. All had 100 percent Christian Coalition voting records.

For statewide offices, the Republicans have fared less well. In the year 2000 Gov. Frank Keating, a Tulsa Republican, was serving his second term. Of the additional ten statewide offices, the Republicans held five. Democrats controlled the state legislature, holding about three-fifths of the seats in the House (60 of 101) and the Senate (33 of 48). Although party registration favors the Democrats (about 57 percent to 35 percent Republican, with 8 percent Independent), more Sooners self-identify as Republicans than Democrats. At the end of the twentieth century a statewide survey of party identification shows 39 percent Republican, 31 percent Democrat, and the balance Independent or other. These figures represent a precise reversal of party identification from the 1980s.

The state's populist-influenced constitution scatters power widely. Boards and commissions abound, mostly controlled indirectly, if at all, by the state's chief executive. In formal power, Oklahoma's governor ranks below average. The office is especially weak on appointment power and the authority to reorganize the executive branch.

Following a 1960s bribery scandal in the state supreme court, the voters approved a constitutional amendment removing the courts from partisan politics. The governor now appoints members of the two highest courts to a six-year term (the supreme court has nine members and the court of criminal appeals five members). The nominees must come from a list of three names provided by a judicial nominating commission. Each six years, the incumbents may seek a new term by appearing on a retention ballot. The voters elect lower-level judges on nonpartisan ballots.

Oklahoma's political culture has been called "frontier individualism" or "agrarian populist." With a pro-gun, antiregulation electorate, the state enjoys a low tax burden. Still, it has a higher than average number of state and local government employees. Such an anomaly results in part from the continued political strength of rural Oklahoma. The state contains seventy-seven counties, each electing eight separate officials, and there are more than 500 independent school districts.

The state's population (about 3.4 million in 2000) grew less rapidly than the nation's as a whole, causing the loss of a congressional seat following the 2000 census. The economy has diversified and is far less dependent today on extractive industry and agriculture. Still, the state's per capita income is below average and is only partly offset by a lower cost of living. As the state's quest for a more diversified economy continues, Oklahoma struggles to find its place in a global technology economy.

See also IMAGES AND ICONS: Boomers / NATIVE AMERICANS: Indian Territory.

David R. Morgan
University of Oklahoma

Markwood, Christopher L., ed. *Oklahoma Government and Politics: An Introduction.* Dubuque IA: Kendall/Hunt Pub. Co., 2000. Morgan, David R., Robert E. England, and George G. Humphreys. *Oklahoma Politics and Policies.* Lincoln: University of Nebraska Press, 1991. Scales, James R., and Danney Goble. *Oklahoma Politics: A History.* Norman: University of Oklahoma Press, 1982.

PETTIGREW, RICHARD (1848–1926)

One of the first two U.S. senators from South Dakota and a successful businessman, Richard Franklin Pettigrew was born July 23, 1848, in Ludlow, Vermont, to abolitionist parents who maintained a station on the Underground Railroad. When he was young his family moved to Wisconsin, where he graduated from Evansville Academy in 1864, attended Beloit College for two years, and studied law at the University of Wisconsin.

In 1870 Pettigrew settled in Sioux Falls, Dakota Territory, where he earned his living as a surveyor and lawyer before establishing himself as a prominent real estate broker. During the next twenty years his business interests expanded to include railroads, mining, and agriculture. Politically astute, he was first elected to the territory's legislature in 1872 as a Republican and later served on the territorial council before winning the position of delegate to the U.S. Congress in 1880.

After South Dakota achieved statehood in 1889, Pettigrew served twelve years in the U.S. Senate. During his first term in office, the Panic of 1893 ruined his business investments, which caused him to abandon his Republican principles for the lure of populism. He advocated the issues of free silver and government regulation of large businesses while personally attacking Republicans and their positions on the gold standard and the annexation of Hawaii and the Philippines. These views eventually doomed his reelection efforts for a third term in the Senate. Disgruntled, he moved to New York City, where he lived for ten years and amassed another personal fortune before returning to Sioux Falls. He died on October 5, 1926, leaving to the community his home to be used as a museum that would preserve the Pettigrew legacy.

Kermit L. Staggers
University of Sioux Falls

Hendrickson, Kenneth E., Jr. "The Public Career of Richard F. Pettigrew of South Dakota, 1848–1926." *South Dakota Department of History Report and Historical Collections* 34 (1968): 143–311. Pettigrew, Richard Franklin. Papers. Siouxland Heritage Museums, Sioux Falls SD.

POPULISTS (PEOPLE'S PARTY)

A dynamic third party of the 1890s, the People's Party sharply challenged the period's economic inequities and the unresponsiveness of the two major political parties. Though Populists, as adherents of the new party were called, were also important in the South and in the Rocky Mountain states, they were especially numerous and influential in the Great Plains.

Populist protest emerged amid an agricultural depression that engulfed the Plains beginning in the late 1880s. A boom spurred by railroad development, town building, ready credit, and good weather collapsed because of drought, low crop prices, falling land values, and onerous debt. To protect their fading interests, distressed farmers demanded reforms, ranging from state laws reducing interest rates and regulating railroads to national laws providing agricultural credits and promoting monetary inflation. Increasing the money supply through an expanded greenback currency and unlimited silver coinage ("free silver") was widely favored to reduce the burden of debt and to increase farm prices.

To the farmers' dismay, the Republican Party, which dominated state legislatures in the region, rejected their reform proposals in favor of untrammeled business development. Nor could the Democratic Party—weak, conservative, and focused on cultural issues—serve as a vehicle for agrarian economic reform.

Mobilized by the Farmers Alliance and other reform organizations, angry farmers therefore created third parties throughout the Plains states in 1890. South Dakota dissidents moved first, forming the Independent Party on June 7, 1890, but it was the formation of the Kansas People's Party on June 12, 1890, that provided the name eventually adopted everywhere.

These initial campaigns achieved considerable success. Led by crusading editors like William Peffer of the *Kansas Farmer* and Henry Loucks of the *Dakota Ruralist* and spellbinding orators like Mary Elizabeth Lease and "Sockless Jerry" Simpson of Kansas and Omer Kem of Nebraska, Populists elected several congressmen and senators and captured control of the legislatures in Nebraska and Kansas while gaining the balance of power in others.

Kansas Populists then led in organizing a national People's Party in 1891. The new party's first national nominating convention met in Omaha, Nebraska, on July 4, 1892. It adopted the famous Omaha Platform, eloquently summarizing the Populists' economic and political reform goals, and nominated James Weaver of Iowa for president. The Populists carried Kansas, Idaho, and Nevada and garnered more than a million popular votes, but the party met little success in the South, where fraud, intimidation, and racism disrupted their potential constituency, or in the industrial East.

But Populists again achieved important victories at the state level in the West, often by cooperating or "fusing" with Democrats on a common ticket. More Populists were elected to Congress, and Kansas, Colorado, and Nebraska elected Populist governors. Despite consistent Republican opposition, Populists eventually enacted important reforms in several states. They passed laws regulating railroads, banks, stockyards, and insurance companies, protecting labor unions, and improving working conditions. They were also largely responsible for democratic political reforms such as women's suffrage in Colorado and the initiative and referendum in South Dakota.

But most Populist objectives required national, not state, action. To achieve national success, Weaver and other Populist leaders, who had already fused with Democrats in state elections, began pursuing a policy to arrange in 1896 a national fusion based on the issue of free silver.

Their strategy went awry, however, when the Democratic Party nominated William Jennings Bryan of Nebraska on a free silver platform. Bryan had worked with Populists in Nebraska, and the fusionists' political logic dictated that the People's Party also nominate him, creating a solid coalition for the silver issue they had labored to promote. Other Populists argued futilely that the party should preserve its independence by adopting a comprehensive reform platform and nominating a Populist rather than being submerged in a Democratic silver campaign.

Not only did Bryan's nomination produce discord, but the fusion campaign tactics further splintered the party and obscured its identity. Subordinating the party and its principles to the Democrats, moreover, brought no reward, for Bryan was soundly defeated by Republican William McKinley. Fusion state tickets did triumph in Kansas, Nebraska, and South Dakota, but these victories were dying gasps, and the disappointing performances of fusionist governors and legislatures further disillusioned the rank and file. Populist candidates lost almost everywhere in the 1898 elections, and wrangling between party officials and antifusion Populists split the national party. The gradual return of prosperity further undermined the Populists' appeal, and Republican legislatures in the Plains states provided the final blow by enacting antifusion laws. Disintegrating, the People's Party soon disappeared completely.

See also PROTEST AND DISSENT: Farmers Alliance; Lease, Mary Elizabeth.

Peter H. Argersinger
Southern Illinois University

Argersinger, Peter H. *The Limits of Agrarian Radicalism: Western Populism and American Politics.* Lawrence: University Press of Kansas, 1995. Cherny, Robert W. *Populism, Progressivism, and the Transformation of Nebraska Politics.* Lincoln: University of Nebraska Press, 1981. McMath, Robert C. *American Populism: A Social History, 1877–1898.* New York: Hill and Wang, 1993.

PRAIRIE FARM REHABILITATION ADMINISTRATION

See AGRICULTURE: Prairie Farm Rehabilitation Administration

PROGRESSIVE CONSERVATIVE PARTY

The name of this party will strike many as an oxymoron. Yet it unintentionally catches something of the party's essence. It has been a coalition of ardent supporters of the free market system and minimal government, and of those (the so-called Red Tories) who have an organic view of society and believe that the state has an obligation to preserve social harmony and to take care of those who cannot easily fend for themselves.

The party came into being in 1854 and was known subsequently as the Conservative Party, until it added the "Progressive" in 1943. Their new federal leader, John Bracken, who for twenty years was premier of Manitoba, insisted on the change. He had been a Progressive, but never a Conservative, until he assumed the party's leadership. Also commonly known as the Tories or the PCs, the party is closest in ideology to the Republican Party in the United States and the British Conservatives (the terms PC, Conservative, and Tory are used interchangeably here). The party was the dominant player in national politics from 1867 to 1896 and spent thirty years in power in the twentieth century. The Progressive Conservatives have been, until recently, the chief rival to the Liberals.

In the Prairie Provinces the party has generally been laissez-faire in economics, socially conservative, skeptical of the ability of government to bring about positive change, and strongly supportive of free trade. (It was a Progressive Conservative national government that negotiated the North American Free Trade Agreement with the United States which came into effect in 1989.) However, the Red Tory element has not been absent, and the party has often been infused with a streak of populism. One example of the former would be Duff Roblin, premier of Manitoba from 1958 to 1967, and of the latter, John Diefenbaker from Saskatchewan, prime minister of Canada from 1957 to 1963.

The Conservative Party in Manitoba was in existence from 1883, being favored by many settlers from Ontario. The party was in power from 1900 to 1915 under the leadership of Sir Rodmond Roblin, a relatively progressive Conservative for his day. However, his government fell in 1915, the result of a financial scandal involving the construction of the legislative building in Winnipeg. Although the party survived, and served in a coalition government during World War II and its aftermath, not until 1958 did it again form a government on its own. Ironically, it was Sir Rodmond Roblin's grandson, Duff Roblin, who came to power in that year. He is widely regarded as perhaps the greatest of all Manitoba premiers. He is credited with breaking the province's Depression mentality and in expanding access to education and other services. Perhaps his most enduring monument is the Floodway, a huge dike around Winnipeg, which has several times saved the city from flooding. The PCs have held office on a number of occasions since Roblin left office. Their premiers have been Walter Weir (1967–69), Sterling Lyon (1977–81), and Gary Filmon (1988–99). Filmon was regarded as a more moderate figure than his two predecessors.

The party has been much less successful in Saskatchewan at the provincial level, though the unique personality and appeal of John Diefenbaker at the federal level made the province for a while the most loyal source of Tory support. In fact, only three times since the province entered Canadian Confederation in 1905 has the party formed the provincial government. J. T. Anderson had the misfortune to win power in 1929. Saskatchewan was hit as badly as any jurisdiction in North America by the Depression, a situation compounded by several years of drought. So, after Anderson's defeat in 1934, the Conservative Party was virtually moribund for years while the Liberals and the Cooperative Commonwealth Federation (later, the New Democratic Party) took turns in office.

In 1982, however, the general Prairie dislike of the federal Liberals undermined support for that party at both levels of government and, after eleven years of New Democratic Party rule, Saskatchewan voters concluded that it was time for a change. So, Grant Devine became the first Tory premier in forty-eight years. Devine's was a generally centrist government. It combined laissez-faire policies (such as the privatization of some public enterprises) with activism (an expansion of the rural hospital system). Devine was defeated by the New Democratic Party in 1991. Since then, the party's reputation has suffered from revelations that several of its cabinet and caucus members, while in office, enriched themselves by illegal means. Thus, there is a rather grim joke in the province that the headquarters of the Saskatchewan PC Party are to be found in the local penitentiary.

Alberta is a profoundly conservative province, where dedication to free enterprise and limited government is stronger than elsewhere. Indeed, Alberta is regarded as the most "American" of provinces. Though the Conservatives did not form a government there until 1971, sixty-six years after the province's entry into Confederation, ideologically conservative parties have been triumphant. The United Farmers of Alberta formed the government from 1921 to 1935, and Social Credit from 1935 to 1971. In the latter year, the old-fashioned image of the government and the widespread desire for change resulted in the election of the Progressive Conservatives under the leadership of Peter Lougheed (1971–85), one of the most charismatic figures in Prairie politics in the last half-century.

Under Lougheed, Alberta's vast economic resources were fully tapped, an equitable pricing agreement for oil and natural gas reached with the federal government, the province's standing in the country enhanced, a Heritage Fund (money set aside for future contingencies) established, and Alberta transformed into a modern economy and society. Frequently at odds with the federal government, Lougheed won repeated reelection with huge majorities. The PCs were still in office in 2001. Lougheed's successors were Don Getty (to 1992) and Ralph Klein since Getty's departure.

Alberta and Manitoba provide a good comparison of the varieties of Canadian and Prairie conservatism. In Alberta, the politics of the Progressive Conservative Party have often been reminiscent of the more radical elements of the Republican Party in the United States.

Manitoba's Progressive Conservatives have tended to be more moderate and centrist.

See also INDUSTRY: NAFTA.

Geoffrey Lambert
University of Manitoba

Campbell, Colin, and William Christian. *Parties, Leaders and Ideologies in Canada.* Toronto: McGraw-Hill Ryerson Ltd., 1995: 25–65. Friesen, Gerald. *The Canadian Prairies: A History.* Toronto: University of Toronto Press, 1987.

RAILROAD POLITICS

"Railroad politics" is the term used to summarize the bargaining among railroads and their investors, employees, customers, and public officials. This bargaining has at different times centered on the location of railroad lines and supporting facilities, the quality of service provided by railroad companies, the wages paid to employees, the profits returned to investors, and, especially, the charges imposed on passengers and freight shippers.

Although the first railroads penetrated the Great Plains of the United States in the 1860s, it was the 1880s that saw enormous expansion. In that decade railroad firms laid more miles of track in the United States than in any comparable time period anywhere in the world. Similarly, north of the forty-ninth parallel the decade of the 1880s saw the completion of the Canadian Pacific, Canada's first transcontinental railway. The result in the Great Plains was a land boom and rapid population growth. The particular location of the rail lines was often a matter of political bargaining. Land speculators, town builders, and municipal officials vied to have railroads come to their favored location because of the economic vitality that rail service promised. Fully three-quarters of the towns incorporated in Alberta were established by railway companies. Towns that did not enjoy direct access to the railroad network either stagnated or died. Locations favored with railroad junctions, railroad yards (sidetracks for the storage and sorting of equipment), terminal facilities, and maintenance shops were especially likely to boom economically in the late nineteenth century in the Plains. Calgary actually bribed the Canadian Pacific to obtain its maintenance shops and freight yards.

Railroad companies built too many lines in the Great Plains for all to be profitable, and by the depression years of the 1890s several major carriers were bankrupt but still operating. Competition for the most profitable long-haul freight and passenger traffic was intense. Although improvements in operating efficiencies had led to lower rates, farmers and merchants dependent on railroad service often complained that charges were too high. Some in the Plains argued for public ownership of the railroads to ensure their operation in "the public interest," a policy advocated by the populist movement. Shippers who complained about unjust freight rates also turned to state and federal regulation.

With a return to prosperity in the first years of the twentieth century, railroads and shippers continued to bargain for advantage, especially through a system of federal regulation strengthened by the Hepburn Act of 1906 and the Mann-Elkins Act of 1910. Railroads sought permission from regulators to increase rates so as to improve facilities and operating efficiencies. Employees seeking higher wages and investors seeking better returns supported the carriers, while shippers viewed rate increase requests suspiciously. The political bargaining among those groups was typically intense, with elected officials in the Great Plains voicing support for local merchants and farmers and expressing hostility toward the carriers.

The intensity of railroad politics gradually eased as improved highways and long-distance motor trucks lessened the dependence of shippers on the railroad serving their local area. Nevertheless, grain farmers depended on railroads for taking their products to market cheaply, and railroads continued to haul large volumes of other agricultural products and manufactured goods as well. After the Staggers Rail Act of 1980 deregulated the carriers, there were widespread mergers of competing railroads, as well as the integration of rail and motor truck freight services. This situation sometimes led to problems, especially in the 1990s when the Union Pacific Railroad was unable to manage operations efficiently after taking over the Southern Pacific lines, and bitter complaints again emerged in Texas and other places in the Great Plains.

See also TRANSPORTATION: Railroads, United States; Railways, Canada.

K. Austin Kerr
Ohio State University

Berk, Gerald. *Alternative Tracks: The Constitution of American Industrial Order, 1865–1917.* Baltimore MD: Johns Hopkins University Press, 1994. Hoogenboom, Ari and Olive. *A History of the ICC: From Panacea to Palliative.* New York: W. W. Norton Co., 1976. Kerr, K. Austin. *American Railroad Politics, 1914–1920: Rates, Wages, and Efficiency.* Pittsburgh: University of Pittsburgh Press, 1968.

RANKIN, JEANNETTE (1880–1973)

Jeannette Rankin, the first woman elected to the U.S. Congress (1916), was born on a ranch near Missoula, Montana Territory, on June 11, 1880. She was the eldest of seven children of Olive Pickering Rankin and John Rankin, who was successful in the ranching and lumbering business. Her early development and subsequent career were no doubt influenced by the relative remoteness of Montana, the freedom and challenges of frontier life, and the harsh environmental demands, all of which required a strong and independent character.

Following graduation from the University of Montana with a bachelor of science degree in biology in 1902, she worked for a time as a country schoolteacher and as a part-time seamstress. In 1908 she left Montana to study at the New York School of Philanthropy (now the Columbia University School of Social Work), and after a brief stint as a social worker in Montana and Washington, she entered the University of Washington in 1909. She became active in the successful state campaign for

Jeannette Rankin

women's suffrage in 1910, which energized her and helped define her subsequent career, focusing on suffrage and then incorporating pacifist issues.

The approval by Montana of female suffrage in 1914 set the stage for her own campaign for one of Montana's at-large seats in the U.S. House of Representatives as a progressive Republican. Her previous work for suffrage in Montana gave her contacts, organizational skills, public speaking ability, and a knowledge of Montana voters that served her well. In her campaign she traveled the vastness of the state by train and automobile (which she drove herself) to speak to groups as disparate as mountain miners, Plains farmers, and women's groups. She spoke on street corners, in lumber camps, union halls, and kitchens. Her brother, Wellington, who became a highly successful lawyer and prominent Republican in Montana, managed her successful campaign.

Jeannette Rankin served two terms in Congress—separated by twenty years—where she worked hard for reform legislation ranging from women's issues to various problems of specific concern to western states. She was defined as a pacifist when her congressional terms (1917–19 and 1941–43) coincided with the outbreak of the two World Wars, and she was the only member of Congress to vote against U.S. entry into both of them. Whereas she received considerable support for her stance in 1917, she was accorded very little support in the different atmosphere of 1941. Failing to win reelection each time, she devoted her efforts to active involvement in various pacifist organizations and to world travels.

She returned briefly to public life in 1968, as part of a women's coalition called the Jeannette Rankin Brigade, to march on Washington in protest of the Vietnam War. Even as she passed the age of ninety, she continued to give interviews and speeches opposing the Vietnam War and supporting women's rights. In 1971 the National Organization of Women named her as the first member of the Susan B. Anthony Hall of Fame, acclaiming her contri-

bution to the cause of women's rights. But her health was deteriorating, and she died in Carmel, California, on May 18, 1973.

See also GENDER: Suffrage Movement.

Forest L. Grieves
University of Montana

Giles, Kevin S. *Flight of the Dove: The Story of Jeannette Rankin.* Beaverton OR: Touchstone Press, 1980. Josephson, Hannah. *Jeannette Rankin: First Lady in Congress—A Biography.* Indianapolis: Bobbs-Merrill Company, Inc., 1974. Richey, Elinor. *Eminent Women of the West: Jeannette Rankin, Woman of Commitment.* Berkeley: Howell-North Books, 1975.

REFORM PARTY

The Reform Party of Canada was founded in 1987 by Preston Manning, son of a former Alberta premier, as a right-wing populist party with strong regional support in western Canada, especially Alberta and British Columbia. Over the next few years the party steadily grew, reaching its zenith in the Canadian election of June 1997, when it won sixty seats (out of a total of 301), thus making it Her Majesty's Official Opposition to the victorious Liberal Party.

The Reform Party's immediate rise stemmed from disgruntlement on the part of a number of prominent western conservatives with the policies of the governing federal Progressive Conservative Party. Reform's cultural and ideological roots, however, were much older. Reform espoused populist notions of direct democracy (referendums, initiatives, and recall), brought to the Canadian West in the early part of the twentieth century by farmers' parties from the American Midwest. Like these parties, much of Reform's appeal arose out of a sense of regional economic and political alienation. Reform's populism, however, was also textured by other, later contacts with the American Great Plains. Particularly influential were American oil companies and their personnel from the states of Texas, Oklahoma, California, and Louisiana who developed Alberta's oil industry after 1947 and who infused that province's local political culture with beliefs supportive of free enterprise, low taxes, and minimal government. Reform was the vehicle for this right-populist and moral conservative tradition in Canada, much as the Republican Party is in the United States.

At the same time, Reform's appeal can only be understood in the specific context of social and political changes that occurred in Canada after the 1960s, including a series of wrenching federal-provincial constitutional conflicts. The Reform Party was particularly opposed to Canada's official policies of bilingualism and multiculturalism, continued high levels of immigration, and "special interest" groups. It was Reform's staunch opposition to the granting of special constitutional status to Quebec, however, that garnered the party its greatest political support.

Reform failed to win a seat in the 1988 Canadian election. Between 1990 and 1992, however, a series of failures to ratify changes to Canada's constitution threatened a political crisis. Quebec separatism was on the rise;

public anger and anxiety outside of Quebec escalated. In this highly charged emotional context, Reform support rose dramatically.

In the 1993 Canadian election, Reform won fifty-two seats. All but one of Reform's victories were in the West: twenty-two seats of twenty-six in Alberta, twenty-four of thirty in British Columbia, four in Saskatchewan, and one in Manitoba. Reform's lone "nonwestern" seat was in Ontario. The results left Reform as Canada's third party, behind the governing Liberals and the separatist Bloc Quebecois, who formed Canada's Official Opposition party.

After 1993 Reform attempted to broaden its national appeal. While the party remained fiscally conservative, it toned down its regionalist rhetoric and attempted to soften its image as intolerant of minorities. These efforts brought mixed results in the election of 1997. Though the party garnered Official Opposition status, it seemed more than ever trapped in its western base. In this context, Manning and others renewed efforts to unite Canada's right wing and create a national alternative to the governing Liberals. In the spring of 2000 Reform Party members voted to transform the party into the Canadian Alliance Party. Subsequently, a new leader was chosen, Stockwell Day, a former Conservative politician in Alberta. Later that same year, Day's Alliance Party won sixty-six seats, repeating Reform's success in becoming the Official Opposition to the victorious Liberals. Again, however, the party's support was largely confined to its western bastion. Moreover, its success was short-lived, as Day and the party quickly fell in the polls amid infighting and widespread perceptions of ineptitude. Alliance's public humiliation made many yearn for a resurrection of its Reform predecessor.

Trevor Harrison
University of Alberta

Flanagan, Tom. *Waiting for the Wave: The Reform Party and Preston Manning.* Toronto: Stoddart Publishing Company Ltd., 1995. Harrison, Trevor. *Of Passionate Intensity: Right-Wing Populism and the Reform Party of Canada.* Toronto: University of Toronto Press, 1995.

REPUBLICAN PARTY

The Republican Party has long been a major political force within the Great Plains, just as major issues involving the Great Plains have long posed significant policy concerns for Republican leaders at various governmental levels, from local to national. Indeed, the very origins of the Republican Party can be traced to mid-nineteenth-century controversies prompted by settlement and statehood questions involving the Great Plains.

One of the most troublesome issues accompanying the westward expansion of the American frontier was the question of whether slavery would be permitted or excluded in newly settled areas. The Missouri Compromise of 1820 admitted Missouri as a slave state and Maine as a free state, while also prohibiting slavery from any future states to be formed from remaining lands of the Louisiana Territory north of 36°30′ north latitude. The un-

easy balance was shattered by the Kansas-Nebraska Act of 1854, which partitioned off these eventual states from the larger Louisiana Territory and authorized residents of each of the two newly organized territories to decide for themselves whether to allow or disallow slavery. "Bloody Kansas" conflicts soon broke out between slaveholders and abolitionists.

Both the Democratic Party and the opposing Whig Party comprised coalitions that included advocates of both proslavery and antislavery positions. In March 1854 antislavery dissidents from these major parties met in Ripon, Wisconsin, along with other abolitionists who were just as outraged by congressional debate leading to the Kansas-Nebraska Act, and formed the Republican Party.

The newly formed party became a formidable political force in the North and West almost immediately. In the election of 1856 the young Republican Party captured ninety seats in the U.S. House of Representatives and made a very credible run for the White House by nominating Gen. John C. Frémont, a hero of the Mexican War, as the party's presidential candidate. Frémont's total of 1.3 million popular votes easily bested the 870,000 votes received by Whig candidate Millard Fillmore, but it trailed Democratic candidate James Buchanan's 1.8 million popular votes. Texas, the only Great Plains state as yet formed, cast its electoral votes for Buchanan, who won the Electoral College ballot with 174 votes, compared with 114 for Fremont, and just 8 for Fillmore.

The Republican juggernaut emerged from the 1858 off-year elections with 116 out of 238 seats in the U.S. House of Representatives. Republicans were just shy of an absolute majority and could easily outvote the eighty-three Democrats who comprised the next-largest voting bloc in the lower house of the U.S. Congress. But while all seats in the U.S. House are decided at each two-year election cycle, only one-third of Senate seats are decided at one time. So Democrats still held a thirty-eight- to twenty-six-seat lead in the U.S. Senate and could continue to block abolitionist proposals, at least temporarily.

The impasse led to an electoral showdown in 1860. As the outcomes of popular contests for seats in the U.S. House and for seats in state legislatures, which would in turn choose new members of the U.S. Senate, began to become known, it looked likely that Republicans might gain effective majorities in both houses of Congress. The presidential contest became crucial, since a moderate or proslavery president might be able to effectively veto abolitionist measures. The Democratic coalition had fractured into northern and southern wings, each of which nominated candidates for the presidency. The rival Constitutional Union Party, which carried the banner for former moderate or proslavery Whigs, also nominated its own presidential candidate. The Republican presidential nominee was Abraham Lincoln of Illinois. More than 1.8 million popular votes were cast for Lincoln, compared with 1.4 million for Northern Democrat Ste-

phen A. Douglas, 850,000 for Southern Democrat John C. Breckinridge, and 591,000 for Constitutional Union candidate John Bell. This gave Lincoln a nearly 40 percent plurality of the popular vote. More importantly, Lincoln's 180 out of 303 electoral votes were more than the absolute majority needed to settle the presidential contest.

Bullets soon followed ballots. Secessionist Southern states broke with the federal Union to form their own rival Confederate States of America. The Civil War began on April 12, 1861, when Confederate forces fired on the Union's Fort Sumter. The stronger Union eventually prevailed in four years of savage warfare, but at the cost of nearly 650,000 Union casualties, compared to about 134,000 Confederate casualties. Most of the major battles were fought on Southern soil, so wartime destruction and financial losses from the emancipation of slaves devastated the plantation economy of the South, including that of the Plains state of Texas.

Southern secession and the outcome of the Civil War were of major importance to the Great Plains. Beforehand, the rivalry over slavery had compounded many of the practical difficulties of settling the region. For example, congressional efforts to authorize the building of a transcontinental railroad were stymied on several occasions by Southerners, who were adamantly opposed to northern routes, or by Northerners, who were equally adamantly opposed to southern routes. The act that finally authorized construction of the Union Pacific Railroad, from Omaha, Nebraska, to Sacramento, California, was passed in 1862, when there were no Southern voices in the halls of the U.S. Congress. Subsequently, railroads served as crucial transport links between Great Plains farms and ranches and the distant markets for their products.

Another important measure passed by mainly Republican proponents in the absence of Southern opposition was the Homestead Act of 1862, which laid the foundation for successive post–Civil War waves of settlement expansion across the Great Plains. The Homestead Act encouraged immigration by providing free government land to settlers who were willing to live upon and improve their properties. After the war, thousands of Union veterans joined many other settlers from the eastern United States and many other countries in obtaining free homestead land throughout the Central and Northern Plains. The Homestead Act specifically forbade Confederate veterans who had taken up arms against the United States from settling homestead lands. Because Union veterans tended to be Republicans and Confederate supporters tended to be Democrats, this ban reinforced the strongly Republican character of the Central and Northern Plains.

The Union Pacific Railroad Act, the Homestead Act, and other related measures endeared many of those who settled in the Great Plains in the late nineteenth century to the candidates of the "Grand Old Party" whose predecessors had pushed those measures through Congress at a time of great turmoil and opportunity. All of the Northern Plains states grew rapidly in population between 1865 and 1890, and by 1890 all had been admitted to the Union.

With increased population and settlement, however, came increasing discontent. In the East and the Great Lakes states, the Republican movement of the 1850s had been based on two key principles—abolition of slavery and support for industrialization. The Civil War settled the first question, and many Republican leaders in the 1870s and 1880s were linked increasingly with large industrial concerns. However, Great Plains farmers found themselves more and more at the mercy of eastern-dominated railroads, banks, and corporations. Many became disenchanted with the conservatism of the Republican Party in the East. By the 1890s the Populist movement, which was oriented to the interests of the small farmer against large corporate interests, had taken hold and was especially strong in the Plains. In 1896 William Jennings Bryan of Nebraska won the presidential nomination of both the Democrats and the Populists. Although he carried all of the Plains states except North Dakota, Bryan was defeated nationally by Republican William McKinley, and he lost again in 1900 and 1908.

Despite the fact that Bryan's three defeats signaled the end of the Populist movement nationally, populism continued to have considerable impact on the politics of the Plains states. Populist-oriented political factions contested statewide and local elections throughout the Central and Northern Plains. For example, the Nonpartisan League emerged as a major force in North Dakota politics before World War I, and it remained important until the 1950s. Throughout the twentieth century, politics in the Central and Northern Plains has generally been dominated by the Republicans, with Democrats making occasional inroads. In the Southern Plains the Democrats were the dominant party until the 1960s, when Republican influence began to increase.

This trend is illustrated in the distribution of governorships across the two parties in the two regions of the Plains. Republicans held 60 percent of the governorships of the Central and Northern Plains states (North Dakota, South Dakota, Nebraska, Kansas, Montana, Wyoming, and Colorado) between 1900 and 1950, and 55 percent between 1950 and 2000. In the Southern Plains states of Texas, Oklahoma, and New Mexico, Republicans held only 9 percent of the governorships between 1900 and 1950 but 35 percent between 1950 and 2000. Similarly, Republicans held 67 percent of Central and Northern Plains House seats in 1900, 81 percent in 1950, and 81 percent again in 2000, while they held no seats in the Southern Plains in 1900, 6 percent in 1950, and 52 percent in 2000.

The Plains has produced many Republican leaders who have held national prominence throughout the past century. Some were strongly influenced by the progressive sentiments of the populist movement, while others have been more conservative. Several Plains politicians have been nominated by the Republican Party for national office. Interestingly, most have had connections to Kansas. In 1928 Republican Charles Curtis of Kansas was elected vice president, but he and his running mate, Herbert Hoover, were defeated in their reelection bid four years later by Franklin D. Roosevelt and his running mate, Texan John Nance Garner. In 1936 the Republicans nominated Gov. Alfred Landon of Kansas, who ran unsuccessfully against Roosevelt. Dwight D. Eisenhower, born in Denison, Texas, and raised in Abilene, Kansas, was elected president in 1952 and 1956. Sen. Robert Dole, who represented Kansas in the Senate for nearly twenty-eight years, was the unsuccessful Republican nominee for vice president in 1976 and for president in 1996. In 2000 two candidates with Great Plains connections—though not to Kansas—were nominated and elected under the Republican Party label. Thus, the first presidential contest of the twenty-first century was won by Gov. George W. Bush of Texas and his vice presidential running mate, former Wyoming U.S. representative Richard Cheney, whose birthplace was Lincoln, Nebraska.

No Plains Republican served as Speaker of the House of Representatives in the twentieth century. Two Republicans have served as their party's leader in the Senate: Kenneth Wherry of Nebraska was minority leader from 1949 to 1951, while Dole was majority leader from 1985 to 1987 and again from 1995 to 1996 and minority leader from 1987 to 1995. Many other Plains Republicans, however, have achieved notable records in Congress. George Norris of Nebraska served thirty-six years in the Senate and was recognized as one of the Senate's leading progressive Republicans throughout his career. Among his many legislative achievements was sponsorship of the bill creating the Tennessee Valley Authority during the New Deal era. Peter Norbeck of South Dakota was a strong supporter of progressive legislation as governor and senator, and his progressive attitudes forestalled the creation of an independent progressive movement in that state. Alan Simpson of Wyoming was prominent in his party's leadership in the 1980s and 1990s, and Henry Bellmon of Oklahoma served two terms in the Senate and two as governor. Among the more conservative long-time Republican members of the Senate were South Dakota's Karl Mundt and Nebraska's Roman Hruska and Carl Curtis.

Fred M. Shelley
Southwest Texas State University
J. Clark Archer
University of Nebraska–Lincoln

Martis, Kenneth C. *The Historical Atlas of Political Parties in the United States Congress, 1789–1989.* New York: Macmillan Publishing Company, 1989. Shelley, Fred M., J. Clark Archer, Fiona M. Davidson, and Stanley D. Brunn. *Political Geography of the United States.* New York: Guilford Press, 1996. Witkoski, Michael. "The Republican Party." In *International Encyclopedia of Government and Politics,* edited by Frank N. Magill. Chicago: Salem Press, 1996: 1167–71.

RICHARDSON, BILL

See HISPANIC AMERICANS: Richardson, Bill

ROSS, NELLIE TAYLOE (1876–1977)

Nellie Tayloe Ross is notable as the nation's first woman governor. She was born in St. Joseph, Missouri, on November 29, 1876, educated in private schools, and taught kindergarten briefly in Omaha, Nebraska. She married a young lawyer from Tennessee named William Bradford Ross in 1902, and the couple moved to Cheyenne, Wyoming. William's law practice in Cheyenne was very successful, and he became one of the leaders of the Democratic Party in Wyoming and was elected governor in 1922. Nellie spent those years as a wife and a mother.

Nellie Ross entered into politics with the death of her husband in 1924. Because William had completed only the first two years of his term as governor, a special election was called to elect a replacement. The Democratic Party chose Nellie as their candidate and she won easily. She was known as a good administrator and a fine public speaker, but she had to work with a Republican-controlled legislature, which limited her achievements. She failed to win reelection by a very narrow margin in 1926.

After her defeat Ross focused on national politics. She campaigned for presidential candidate Al Smith in 1928 and became vice chairman of the Democratic Party. In 1932 she directed the campaign for the women's vote for Franklin D. Roosevelt, and because of her work, President Roosevelt appointed her director of the U.S. Mint in 1933. She was the first woman to hold that position, and she served four five-year terms before retiring from the U.S. Mint and politics in 1952.

Ross spent the remainder of her life traveling, lecturing, writing, and with family. She died in Washington DC on December 19, 1977, at the age of 101.

Monte G. Kniffen
University of Wyoming

Ross, Nellie Tayloe. Papers. American Heritage Center, University of Wyoming, Laramie. Scharff, V. "Feminism, Femininity, and Power: Nellie Tayloe Ross and the Woman Politician's Dilemma." *Frontiers* 15 (1995): 87–106.

SALTER, SUSANNA

See GENDER: Salter, Susanna

SASKATCHEWAN

Saskatchewan, lying between the forty-ninth and sixtieth parallels, is located on the northern edge of the Great Plains. While Saskatchewan extends over 251,700 square miles, only part of this region falls within the Great Plains. Geographically, the province is divided into two equal parts: the southern part belongs to the Great Plains, while the northern part lies in the Canadian Shield. Saskatchewan's southern neighbors are the states of Montana and North Dakota. To its west lies the province of Alberta and to the east, the province of Manitoba. At the sixtieth parallel, Saskatchewan ends and the Northwest Territories begins.

The province of Saskatchewan came into being on September 1, 1905. The province's name, which was originally used as a district of the Northwest Territories, is based on the Cree word for swift-flowing water, or *Kis-is-ska-tche-wan*. Saskatchewan's agriculture has dominated its economy and defined its political culture. The dry climate provides a challenge to farmers, who mostly grow wheat. Perhaps because of the dry climate and resulting crop failures, creating periodic economic crises, the people of Saskatchewan have sometimes rejected the two leading parties, the Liberals and Progressive Conservatives, and sought to create their own parties. The Liberal Party dominated Saskatchewan's politics until 1944, with only a short interlude (1929–34) of Conservative rule. In 1944, under the leadership of T. C. Douglas, the Cooperative Commonwealth Federation (CCF) won the provincial election, forming the first social democratic government in Canada. The CCF governed until 1964. In 1961 the CCF became the New Democratic Party, which subsequently formed the governments in Saskatchewan from 1971 to 1982 and from 1991 to 1999. Intervening governments were formed by the Liberal Party from 1964 to 1971 and by the Progressive Conservative Party (after a long period of quiescence) from 1982 to 1991. In 1995 the Saskatchewan Party replaced the Progressive Conservative Party.

In the early part of the twentieth century, most of the population was rural. Today, most of the population is urban. While the shift of population from rural areas to urban ones has eroded the political power of rural Saskatchewan, agricultural concerns, ranging from inadequate rainfall to low prices, can still dominate the political agenda. However, rural Saskatchewan no longer holds the political reins in Saskatchewan.

Like other Canadian provinces, the government of Saskatchewan is modeled after the British parliamentary system. It has an elected legislative assembly, a party system, and a premier and cabinet. The premier is the head of the executive council or cabinet. Each member of the cabinet is a minister with assigned specific powers and responsibilities. For the government to pass a bill, the Saskatchewan Legislative Assembly must approve the bill by a simple majority vote. The largest opposition party forms the Official Opposition. In 1997 there were fifty-eight elected members of the legislative assembly. The largest party, the New Democratic Party, had forty seats; the Saskatchewan Party had nine seats; the Liberal Party had five seats; one member sat as independent; and three seats were vacant. Premier Roy Romanow was the leader of the New Democratic government. Because of Canada's past colonial status, each province has a lieutenant governor who originally represented the British Crown but who now performs ceremonial functions. In 1999 Jack Wiebe was the lieutenant governor of Saskatchewan.

Canada is a federal state with political powers divided between the federal and provincial governments. The powers held by the provincial government are named in the Canadian Constitution of 1982, which superseded the British North America Act of 1867. Saskatchewan is responsible for its cultural and educational institutions, highways, medical services, natural resources, and social services. To meet these obligations, the Saskatchewan government has the power to tax its citizens and businesses and to receive fees (royalties) from firms exploiting its natural resources. Saskatchewan has never been represented in large numbers in Ottawa, but the province has produced important national political leaders, such as John Diefenbaker, who was prime minister from 1957 to 1963, and "Jimmy" Gardiner, who was minister of agriculture from 1935 to 1957.

While the duration of a government is five years, most call for a new election in the fourth year, especially if conditions for winning the next election appear favorable. But elections in Saskatchewan are never a sure thing. Past experience shows that few governments have held office for more than ten years, and rarely has the winning party garnered more than 50 percent of the votes. The volatility of the Saskatchewan voter is less a swing from the left to the right than a reaction to "good" government. No matter what the ideology of the party in power, eventually the government loses favor with the electorate.

Robert M. Bone
University of Saskatchewan

Bone, Robert M. *The Regional Geography of Canada: A Country of Regions.* Toronto: Oxford University Press, 1999. Dyck, Rand. *Provincial Politics in Canada.* Scarborough, Ontario: Prentice-Hall, 1991.

SIFTON, CLIFFORD (1861–1929)

Sir Clifford Sifton was a successful Manitoba lawyer, entrepreneur, member of the provincial and federal governments, and newspaper publisher. Of Protestant Irish descent, Sifton was born near Arva, Ontario, on March 10, 1861, educated there and in Manitoba, and trained as a lawyer in Winnipeg. He settled in Brandon in 1882, where he established a law practice and speculated in land during the early settlement years of the region. Elected to the provincial legislature in 1888, he became attorney general in the Liberal government of Thomas Greenway in 1891. He led a successful defense of the government's controversial 1890 legislation to create a system of national schools, and his efforts stimulated expansion of the province's railway network.

In November of 1896 he became minister of the interior and superintendent-general of Indian Affairs in the federal Liberal government of Sir Wilfrid Laurier. There he devoted his great energies and organizational abilities to attracting settlers to the Prairie West. Through aggressive advertising in the United States, Great Britain, and Europe, he brought the potential of the Canadian Prairies to the attention of vast numbers of potential immigrants.

He overhauled the system for getting immigrants to the West and actually settled on the land, and he pressured railway and other interests to make available vast tracts of land previously withheld from settlement. His policy of attracting large numbers of settlers from central and eastern Europe, particularly Slavs such as Poles, Ukrainians, and Doukhobors, was intensely controversial; nativist critics believed that the newcomers, who often settled in blocs, would fail to assimilate and would undermine the essential British character of Canadian society. Though unmoved by this argument, Sifton had his own prejudices, believing that these people were peasant races who would succeed in coping with the hardships of Prairie farming where thousands of Britishers had failed. As he later famously remarked, "I think a stalwart peasant in a sheepskin coat, born on the soil, whose forefathers have been farmers for ten generations, with a stout wife and a half-dozen children, is good quality."

Sifton also was responsible for government policy in the Yukon during the gold rush beginning in 1897, and he was Canada's agent-general during the Alaska Boundary Tribunal of 1903. He was chiefly responsible for negotiating lowered freight rates into and out of the West in connection with the building of the Crowsnest Pass Railway in 1897 and was influential in shaping the government's railway legislation in 1903. In 1905, when the government was about to create the new Provinces of Alberta and Saskatchewan, Sifton disagreed with Laurier over the educational provisions of the proposed provincial acts and resigned from the cabinet. He remained in Parliament as a private member until 1911, when he opposed the government's policy with respect to reciprocity with the United States. He played a significant role in helping the Conservative opposition defeat Laurier's government. His last major involvement in politics came in 1917, when during World War I he actively aided in the organization and successful election campaign of a win-the-war Union government, dedicated to implementing a policy of conscription. Sifton was knighted in 1915.

In 1909 Laurier appointed Sifton to head the Canadian Commission of Conservation, a position he held until November 1918. The commission was influential in promoting the efficient management of resources. In 1897–98 he had purchased the *Manitoba Free Press* of Winnipeg to be the major organ of the Liberal Party in western Canada; it was an enormously profitable investment, both politically and financially, owing much to Sifton's selection of the brilliant John W. Dafoe as editor. At his death, in New York City on April 17, 1929, the paper was the most valuable item in the family's considerable portfolio. Sifton had become a figure of national importance, but his reputation rests most securely in his role in developing the Prairie West.

See also MEDIA: Winnipeg Free Press.

David J. Hall
University of Alberta

Dafoe, John W. *Clifford Sifton in Relation to His Times*. Toronto: Macmillan Publishing Company, 1931. Hall, David J. *Clifford Sifton*. Vancouver: University of British Columbia Press, 1985. Sifton, Sir Clifford. Papers. National Archives of Canada, Ottawa.

SILVER REPUBLICANS

Committed to unlimited silver coinage ("free silver"), Silver Republicans opposed the restrictive financial policies of the national Republican Party in the late nineteenth century. They predominated in the West, especially in the Rocky Mountain states, whose silver production would benefit from a larger federal market, and in the Plains states, where troubled farmers favored inflation to reduce their debt burden and to increase farm prices.

From the 1870s on, silverites succeeded in including free silver in Republican state platforms, and they steadily supported silver proposals in Congress. In 1889–90 the "omnibus" admission of six new western states, including North and South Dakota, increased their congressional influence, and they secured passage of the Sherman Silver Purchase Act.

After eastern Republicans joined conservative Democrats under President Grover Cleveland to repeal the Sherman Act in 1893, the silver issue quickly rose to dominate politics and contribute to the realignment of the 1890s. Led by Sen. Henry Teller of Colorado and Sen. Richard Pettigrew of South Dakota, Silver Republicans joined Democrats and Populists in agitating the issue.

When the 1896 Republican platform adopted the gold standard, many Silver Republicans reluctantly acquiesced, but others bolted to organize the Silver Republican Party. It proposed Teller as a candidate acceptable to all silverites but endorsed the subsequent Democratic nomination of William Jennings Bryan on a silver platform. Although the Bryan campaign failed, Silver Republicans had success in state elections in Kansas, Nebraska, and South Dakota, where they fused with Democrats and Populists.

Thereafter, some Silver Republicans rejoined the main party; others continued to fuse with Populists and Democrats but with diminishing success. After Bryan's second defeat in 1900, they dissolved their organization and followed Pettigrew into the Democratic Party.

Peter H. Argersinger
Southern Illinois University

Ellis, Elmer. *Henry Moore Teller: Defender of the West*. Caldwell ID: Caxton Printers Ltd., 1941. Hendrickson, Kenneth E. "The Public Career of Richard F. Pettigrew of South Dakota." *South Dakota Department of History, Report and Historical Collections* 34 (1968): 143–311. Wellborn, Fred. "The Influence of the Silver Republican Senators, 1889–1891." *Mississippi Valley Historical Review* 14 (1928): 462–80.

SORENSEN, TED (b. 1928)

Theodore Sorensen was born on May 8, 1928, in a sod house in Lincoln, Nebraska. He was one of five children born to Christian Abraham Sorensen and Annis Chaikin Sorensen. His father was active in Republican Party politics, rising to become the state attorney general of Nebraska. His mother, an outspoken feminist and pacifist of Russian Jewish heritage, gave her family name to each of her five children as their middle name. The Sorensen household was a regular meeting place for progressive Republicans, and Ted absorbed most of his early ideas from the lively debates that were a regular part of his family life. He attended the public schools in Lincoln, graduating from Lincoln High School in 1945. Sorenson graduated from the University of Nebraska in 1949, entered the University of Nebraska College of Law, where he eventually became editor in chief of the *Nebraska Law Review*. He graduated first in his class in 1951.

Seeking a larger venue for his talents, Sorensen moved to Washington DC, where he took a position as a staff attorney for the Federal Security Agency (1951–52), worked as a staff member for the Joint Committee on Railroad Retirement (1952), and ultimately joined the staff of newly elected Sen. John F. Kennedy (1953–61). Sorensen quickly became Senator Kennedy's chief policy adviser and speechwriter. He did the background research for Kennedy's Pulitzer Prize–winning book, *Profiles in Courage*, and wrote Kennedy's speech that electrified the 1956 Democratic National Convention. Sorensen worked tirelessly to help John Kennedy secure the 1960 democratic presidential nomination, serving as both the campaign's chief policy adviser and speechwriter. Upon his assumption of the presidential office in 1961, John F. Kennedy appointed Sorensen as special counsel to the president, a title created specifically for him. He remained the chief policy adviser and speechwriter for President Kennedy. Sorensen retained this title throughout the Kennedy administration and into the early months of the Lyndon Johnson administration. In 1965 Sorensen published his book *Kennedy*, which became a national bestseller. Two years later, with Robert Kennedy then a U.S. senator from New York, Sorensen became chairman of the New York State Democratic Committee's advisory council, and he served as a delegate to the 1968 Democratic National Convention, a convention at which he had hoped to help Robert F. Kennedy wrest the nomination away from Hubert H. Humphrey and Eugene McCarthy. But an assassin's bullet ended the Kennedy quest in June 1968, just weeks before the convention. Sorensen tried to pick up the pieces of the Kennedy organization and offered himself as the Democratic candidate for the U.S. Senate from New York in 1970. Following his defeat, he returned to the New York law firm of Paul, Weiss, Rifkind, Wharton and Garrison, where he remained in 2000.

Throughout the 1980s and 1990s Sorensen devoted himself to numerous causes, serving as a director of the Twentieth-Century Fund, as a member of the Council on Foreign Relations and the National Democratic Institute for International Affairs, and as a trustee of the New York Academy of Medicine, among many other positions. Over the years he has been awarded honorary degrees from the University of Canterbury, Alfred University, Temple University, Fairfield University, and the University of Nebraska. He is the author or editor of seven books, most recently *Why I Am a Democrat* (1996). He is a member of the bar of the U.S. Supreme Court, the District of Columbia, and the states of New York and Nebraska.

Martin J. Medhurst
Texas A&M University

Sorensen, Theodore. Papers. John F. Kennedy Presidential Library, Boston. Sorensen, Theodore C. *Why I Am a Democrat*. New York: Henry Holt and Company, 1996.

SOUTH DAKOTA

Government and politics of South Dakota are in large measure a reflection of the state's past. Home of the Arikaras, and later the Lakota-, Nakota-, and Dakota-speaking Indians (Sioux), the area that became South Dakota was penetrated by French and Spanish explorers, traders, and trappers before and after the Louisiana Purchase of 1803. However, permanent European American settlers did not begin to arrive in any significant numbers until the establishment of the Dakota Territory in 1861 and approval of the Homestead Act in 1862. The two acts together offered some promise of law and order and economic livelihood through ownership and productive use of the land for American-born, German, Scandinavian, and Irish pioneers. Still, the disruption of the Civil War, isolated Indian outbreaks, and drought and other environmental disasters kept the non-Indian population below 12,000 persons until the start of a population spurt in 1878, following the discovery of gold in the Black Hills and the completion of the railroad to Sioux City, Iowa.

On November 2, 1889, the separate states of North and South Dakota were proclaimed, and the era of the Dakota Territory ended. Rival factions fighting over whether the capital city of the Dakota Territory should be located in the southern territorial city of Yankton or the northern territorial city of Bismarck had much to do with the division of the Dakota Territory into North and South Dakota. Pierre was selected as the capital of South Dakota upon statehood.

The Great Depression destroyed South Dakota's agricultural economy and drove the population down from a high of 697,000 in 1930 to 642,000 by 1940. South Dakota has not experienced another economic or population boom since the Depression, as evidenced by the fact that the 1990 population of 724,000 was not far from the 1930 total. The population according to the 2000 census only increased to 755,000. Economically, the state ranks near the bottom in nonfarm industrial wages and continues to have one of our nation's most rural economies. South Dakota's per capita income ranks thirty-eighth among the fifty states.

The beliefs of pioneer German, Scandinavian, and Irish pioneers permeated the state and continue to contribute to a strong moral overtone in politics and governance that has low tolerance for graft and corruption in public affairs. The values and homeland experiences of German and Scandinavian pioneers favored experimentation with public ownership of economic enterprises and substantial public sponsorship of education from the elementary through postsecondary levels in all corners of the state. The success of the Populist Party in South Dakota in the 1890s and the progressive movement that impacted both the South Dakota Democratic and Republican Parties in the early 1900s can be explained by these immigrant values, as well as by farm problems. Peter Norbeck championed the Republican progressive era as governor from 1917 to 1921, and Tom Berry best represented the Democratic progressive era as governor from 1933 to 1937. Municipal-owned enterprises, the South Dakota Cement Plant, more than 170 public school districts, and six public regional universities are contemporary examples of the manifestation of those beliefs.

There is also a strong strain of fiscal conservatism in South Dakota that emphasizes efficiency in government and limited public revenue to support government. However, the desire for many units of local government to serve a sparse population spread out over a large area contributes to many inefficiencies. Still, the emphasis on efficiency is evident in South Dakota's streamlined State Unified Judiciary, the modern cabinet model of its executive branch, and the part-time, nonprofessional 105-member legislature that meets only seventy-five days during its two-year term.

Native Americans constitute approximately 8 percent of the state's population, including those who reside on the nine reservations that lie wholly or in part within South Dakota and those who live in urban areas. Relations between Indians and non-Indians continue to be a source of conflict, most recently in the state's attempt to disestablish the Yankton Reservation, but otherwise, and despite the much-publicized East River (Missouri) and West River differences and urban-rural disputes, the relatively homogeneous character of the population reduces political dispute in the state. Recent exit polling conducted by Voter News Service following the 1998 election revealed that 40 percent of the South Dakota voters identify themselves as conservatives, 50 percent as moderates, and only 10 percent as liberals. Moderate conservatism is a suitable ideological label for South Dakota.

The moderate conservatism of South Dakota politics also leads to Republican Party domination of state gubernatorial and legislative elections. William Janklow's domination of state politics as governor from 1979 to 1987 and congressman from 1995 to 2004 is an example of Republican success in state elections. Democrats have controlled the state senate for only six years, the state house of representatives for only two years, and the governorship for only ten years since 1938. In fact, from 1889 to the present, Democrats have won only four governorships (1926, 1932, 1958, and 1970). Richard F. Kneip's three gubernatorial election victories in 1970, 1972, and 1974 are the most remembered by Democrats. Democrats do fare much better in congressional races and state constitutional office races when a vacancy exists and an energetic, articulate Democrat runs for election. Once elected, these Democrats have been able to use the advantages of the incumbency to be reelected. Former U.S. senator and Democratic presidential nominee George McGovern and U.S. Senate minority (1995–2001 and again beginning in 2003) and majority (2001–3) leader Tom Daschle are obvious examples of Democratic success stories. Former Republican U.S. representatives and senators Karl Mundt, Francis Case, and Larry Pressler and former Democratic U.S. representative and current U.S. senator Tim Johnson are other major political figures in twentieth-century South Dakota politics.

See also IMAGES AND ICONS: West River Country.

Robert V. Burns
South Dakota State University

Burns, Robert V., and Herbert E. Cheever. "South Dakota: Conflict and Cooperation among Conservatives." In *Interest Group Politics in the Midwestern States*, edited by Ronald J. Hrebenar and Clive S. Thomas. Ames: Iowa State University Press, 1993: 285–304. Farber, William O., Thomas C. Geary, and Loren M. Carlson. *Government of South Dakota*. Vermillion: Dakota Press, 1979. Schell, H. S. *History of South Dakota*. Lincoln: University of Nebraska Press, 1975.

SOVEREIGNTY

See NATIVE AMERICANS: Sovereignty

SWAN, ALEXANDER

See AGRICULTURE: Swan, Alexander

TELLER, HENRY (1830–1914)

Henry Moore Teller represented Colorado in the U.S. Senate from 1876, when Colorado joined the Union, to 1909, with a three-year interlude as interior secretary. Colorado's first nationally prominent political figure, Teller was influential in state and national affairs. The senator was widely respected and known as the "defender of the West" and, affectionately, as "Colorado's Grand Old Man."

Born on May 23, 1830, as one of eight children in a strict Methodist farm family in upper New York, Teller educated himself in the law. He practiced briefly in Morrison, Illinois, then moved to the booming mining territory west of Denver in 1861. There he practiced mining law and participated in mining and railroad businesses. Teller was active in Colorado's Republican politics as leader of the Golden area faction in the protracted intraparty rivalry between the "Denver ring" and the "Golden gang." Throughout his political career he was a spokesperson for the commoner, including miners and homesteaders. He spoke forcefully for western territories and interests and was tenacious in his battles for silver coinage and against the eastern establishment, its banks, and the gold standard. In the U.S. Senate he sponsored the "Teller amendment" pledging U.S. support for Cuban independence.

Senator Teller was a staunch Republican most of his political life, but his relentless crusade for silver interests, along with his populist sentiments, devotion to states' rights, and opposition to imperialism, eventually and inevitably led him to bolt the party. Upon leaving the Republicans in 1896, he organized the Silver Republican Party, worked cooperatively with Populists and Democrats, and received support for the presidential nomination of all three parties. Teller declined and instead supported Democratic presidential nominee William Jennings Bryan. Henry Moore Teller died in Denver on February 23, 1914.

John A. Straayer
Colorado State University

Ellis, Elmer. *Henry Moore Teller: Defender of the West*. Caldwell ID: Caxton Printers Ltd., 1941. Teller, Henry. Papers. Colorado Historical Society, Denver.

TEXAS

Although Texas includes a significant portion of the Great Plains, its politics and government have been far more heavily influenced by two other geographic factors: its proximity to Mexico and its situation in the southern United States.

Texas was originally a northern province of Spanish Mexico. After winning their independence in 1821, Mexicans encouraged immigration from the adjacent United States. This policy backfired in 1836, however, when an army of "Texian" Americans under the command of Sam Houston vanquished a Mexican army under General Santa Anna and achieved independence. From that year to the modern era, persons of Mexican descent have been at an economic and political disadvantage in Texas. Their increasing numbers, plus other historical changes, however, have guaranteed their continuing, and growing, importance in the state.

From the revolution of 1836, when Texas declared itself a republic, through 1845 when it entered the United States, to the end of the Civil War in 1865, the state experienced immigration largely from other Southern states. Southern white farmers, moving west, brought their slaves and the economic, political, and social institutions of slavery with them. Texas, like the other Confederate states, was defeated in the war and occupied in a humiliating fashion by victorious Union troops during Reconstruction, which in Texas lasted until 1874. As with the other Southern states, this searing historical experience exercised a dominating influence over Texas society and institutions for well over a century after the end of the war.

The Southern political culture that dominates Texas even today can best be summarized as "conservatism." With some noteworthy exceptions, such as Lyndon Johnson, Anglo-Texans have opposed an active government, especially on behalf of the disadvantaged. They have defined good government largely in terms of low taxes; when taxes are necessary they prefer the regressive variety, such as sales taxes. Anglo-Texans have also been extremely conservative on social issues. Contemporary public opinion surveys reveal that they oppose affirmative action and gay rights, and support prayer in schools and the death penalty, by wide margins.

As in the other Southern states, after the Civil War Anglo-Texans prevented African Americans from voting by statutes, customs, and violence. The schemes created to prevent black political participation also worked to keep ballots out of the hands of Mexican Americans and poor Anglos. The federal government forced Texas to admit all of its adult citizens to the franchise in the 1960s and 1970s, but the legacy of the suppression of voting rights lives on in the extremely low turnout of the state's minority citizens.

The great Spindletop oil strike near Galveston in 1901 inaugurated a period in which Texas became one of the world's important petroleum-producing provinces and the nation's dominant producer. Production taxes on oil and gas, in many years supplying a third of state government revenue, reinforced the resistance of the population to more direct taxes.

The general conservatism of the dominant Anglo population found further expression in two institutional arrangements. First, Texas was a one-party Democratic state until well into the 1970s. Since the Texas Democratic Party was usually dominated by reactionaries, the one-party system served to reinforce the control of dominant ethnic and economic interests. Second, the state constitution of 1876, written by white farmers nursing grievances against the perceived tyranny of the just-departed Reconstruction regime, "disintegrates" the executive, parceling out legislative and administrative power among several independently elected officials. The governor is weak. Moreover, in seeking to foresee and prohibit every possible misbehavior by state government, the authors wrote in specifically circumscribed grants of power and forbade almost everything not mentioned in the document. The result of this specificity has been both a state government that does comparatively little, and one that must amend the constitution to meet every new contingency. As a consequence, by the late 1990s the constitution, at over 80,000 words, was the second longest among the states and had been amended more than 360 times.

At the turn of the twenty-first century, Texas had a population of about twenty million, making it the second most populous state in the country. Its economy was robust and diverse. The modernity and prosperity of the state, however, existed alongside political institutions and behaviors that exhibited more apparent than real change.

Texas's petroleum production, the foundation of its economy for most of the twentieth century, declined steadily after the 1960s. By the mid-1980s production taxes were supplying less than 5 percent of state government revenue. The legislature responded by raising the sales tax, whose regressive impact fell most heavily on the poor. Texas remained the only large industrial state without an income tax.

When the national Democratic Party became dominated by liberals in the 1960s, it set in motion a slow party realignment among the state's conservative Anglo population. Minority citizens, now fully enfranchised, tended to vote overwhelmingly Democratic, but they still went to the polls in very low percentages. This voluntary abstention meant that the generally greater liberalism of African Americans and Mexican Americans had little impact on elections, and state government remained conservative. By the mid-1990s Republicans filled most state offices.

Nevertheless, the Mexican American portion of Texas's population continues to grow rapidly. If Mexican Americans and African Americans ever began to go to the polls in significant numbers, they could join with the few liberal Anglos in a "rainbow coalition" that might transform the state's politics. At this writing, however, there is no sign that such a transformation is imminent.

See also INDUSTRY: Petroleum, United States.

David F. Prindle
University of Texas at Austin

Barr, Alwyn. *Black Texans: A History of African Americans in Texas, 1528–1995*. Norman: University of Oklahoma Press, 1996. Kraemer, Richard H., Charldean Newell, and David F. Prindle. *Texas Politics*. 8th ed. Belmont CA: West/Wadsworth, 1999. Montejano, David. *Anglos and Mexicans in the Making of Texas, 1836–1986*. Austin: University of Texas Press, 1987.

TEXAS REPUBLIC

The Great Plains was in politics before politics was in the Great Plains. The Llano Estacado and the *tierras lejas* (distant lands) of early maps caused controversy during the Texas Republic, the period of Texas's independent government that lasted from its revolution against Mexico in 1836 to its annexation by the United States in 1845. Even later, some areas in the Texas Plains prided themselves on only having been crossed by Coronado, Comanches, or Lipan Apaches before 1870. The power to ward "hostiles" off the frontier still survives in Texas's constitution.

Comanche raids, including the kidnapping of Cynthia Ann Parker in 1836 and Matilda Lockhart in 1838, necessitated the protection of the western frontier during the Texas Republic and the establishment of "ranging companies" under Capt. John C. Hays. This organization began the development of the law enforcement officers known as the Texas Rangers. One of the most significant episodes of frontier violence was the Council House Fight at San Antonio of March 19, 1840. Representatives of the Comanche delegation were arrested for failing to return all of their captives.

President of the Texas Republic Mirabeau Lamar viewed the Great Plains as part of Texas's "manifest destiny." Imperial Texas extended at least to Santa Fe. Lamar's Santa Fe expedition in 1841 was arrested by Mexican governor Manuel Armijo near Tucumcari on October 5. A retaliatory expedition, led by Jacob Snively in 1843, was halted by Capt. Philip St. George Cooke of the U.S. Army. Part of the Texas annexation settlement required reparations of $10 million for the seizure of the Snively expedition. The expedition's arrest was made on the Arkansas River in an area Texas claimed as its territory.

During the Texas Republic only a few small forts were established west of San Antonio and the Balcones Escarpment. Defense of the trade routes against marauders and protection of settlements west of Lamar's new capital at Austin became major priorities after annexation.

See also LAW: Texas Rangers.

Gilbert M. Cuthbertson
Rice University

Fehrenbach, T. R. *Lone Star*. New York: Macmillan Publishing Company, 1968. Webb, Walter Prescott. *The Texas Rangers*. Austin: University of Texas Press, 1970.

TRIBAL GOVERNMENTS, CONTEMPORARY

One of the most interesting questions that can be asked about contemporary tribal government is, what is its source of authority and power? Unlike the federal government or any state governments, tribal governments in the United States do not have their foundations in the U.S. Constitution. Indigenous North American peoples had sociopolitical organizations that preceded the federal constitutions of both Canada and the United States and were not part of the people or political units that created these federal systems. Treaties in both nation-states provide one source for the ongoing relationships between these nation-states and the Indigenous governments, but these are not the only sources. Executive orders, national legislation, and court cases set further parameters on the interactions of Indigenous peoples with dominant states in North America; however, these are not the sources of tribal authority.

Current research from several directions in the United States and Canada concludes that the most successful tribal development occurs where traditional structures match the contemporary ones. This notion is intuitively satisfying, but it contradicts the historical policy behind the major pieces of legislation affecting the structure of tribal government in the twentieth century. The Indian Reorganization Act of 1934 (IRA) created a centralized corporate model for tribal governments, assuming that traditional systems were inadequate to the demands of modern society. Similarly, the Indian Act in Canada (1876) created band councils. Decision making and development under these model governments has been uneven at best.

One successful fusion of traditional and contemporary governments is the Cheyennes'. Their prophet, Sweet Medicine, gave the Cheyennes their code of sacred laws, including organization of the council of forty-four chiefs for the ten bands of Cheyennes. The council consulted with warrior societies before making its political decisions. While contemporary Northern Cheyenne government is organized under the IRA, traditional values maintain a strong influence. Tribal government is represented at the annual ceremonies, and ceremonial leaders receive tribal grants and, in some cases, a salary. This has the added benefit of continuity in the formal network between the Northern Cheyennes of Montana and the Southern Cheyennes of Oklahoma. Additionally, while the IRA model centralizes decision making, the Northern Cheyennes use a referendum to allow the community a voice on major decisions.

In a different configuration, the basic political unit for the nomadic Lakota (Sioux) was groups of families, or *tiyospayes*, each governed by a *wicasitancan*, or chief. Through the leaders of fraternal societies the local unit became part of the band, then part of the larger Lakota Nation. A signal value for the Lakota was autonomy, and the critical level of allegiance was local, to the *tiyospaye*. Their political structure was designed to maximize and encourage this autonomy. In 1889 the United States forced the Sioux Nation to accept six separate reservations: Cheyenne River, Crow Creek, Lower Brulé, Pine Ridge, Rosebud, and Standing Rock. Those contemporary Lakota governments, later organized under the IRA, emphasize tribal councils, centralized authorities with few mechanisms to include the community or traditional leadership in the decision-making process. Government decisions at the Rosebud and Pine Ridge Reservations have been undermined by local and kinship-based allegiances, as would be expected when the formal governing systems are seen as illegitimate by many in the community.

The influence of tribal values in tribal political approaches at the end of the twentieth century is illustrated in a contemporary interpretation of Treaty Number 7 as considered from the position of the Blackfoot Confederacy of southern Alberta. In the treaty the Blackfeet, Bloods, and other signatories promise to "maintain peace and good order." The clause broadly requires order between and among Indigenous people and with other Crown subjects at the time of the treaty (1877) and in the future. Such an agreement, it is argued, requires or implies the authority and power to implement the treaty terms by the Native nations. One avenue is to participate with the federal and provincial governments through guaranteed representation or comanagement.

Despite the amount of influence or interference from the United States and Canada and their efforts to transform, and even terminate, tribal polities, tribal governments persist. Even Indigenous nations that were forced to relocate several times, or those whose governments were repeatedly dissolved by external forces and whose populations were scattered, seem to find the most success when they draw their source of legitimate authority and power today from historic or traditional structures.

See also NATIVE AMERICANS: Blackfoot; Cheyennes; Sioux.

Roberta Haines
University of California, Los Angeles

Champagne, Duane. *American Indian Societies: Strategies and Condition of Political and Cultural Survival*. Cultural Survival Report 32. Cambridge MA: Cultural Survival, Inc., 1989. Cornell, Stephen, and Joseph P. Kalt. *What Can Tribes Do? Strategies and Institutions in American Indian Economic Development*. Los Angeles: American Indian Studies Center, 1992. Ladner, Kiera L. "Treaty Seven and Guaranteed Representation: How Treaty Rights Can Evolve into Parliamentary Seats." *Great Plains Quarterly* 17 (1997): 85–101.

VOTING PATTERNS, CANADA

The three Prairie Provinces are often regarded as a single entity. In fact, their political histories and voting patterns are quite different.

When Manitoba entered the Canadian Confederation in 1870, its population was mainly Métis. By the turn of the century the dominant group was of Ontario British stock. Later waves of immigration from eastern Europe (especially the Ukraine) and, more recently, from South and Southeast Asia and parts of Latin America added diversity to the social fabric and political culture of the province. It was, however, the Ontario immigration that had the most profound effect on Manitoba politics.

Manitoba is the most politically competitive of the three provinces and arguably the least likely to support radical new parties. In common with other provinces, Farmer and progressive parties did well in the period between the two world wars. However, since the late 1950s the major trends have been the habitual weakness of the Liberals (who last won a Manitoba provincial election in 1953) and the regular alternation in office of the New Democrats and the Progressive Conservatives. In the eight elections between 1969 and 1995, only twice was a government granted a majority of more than five seats in the fifty-seven-member legislature. The New Democrats and Progressive Conservatives have each formed the government after four of those elections. On only one occasion have the Liberals done well enough even to form the Official Opposition.

It has been argued that a diagonal line can be drawn across Manitoba, cutting right through the capital city and dividing the province into two political regions. The Progressive Conservatives' loyal base has been among the largely Anglo-Saxon and Mennonite farmers of the province's southwest and the business and professional communities of the south end of Winnipeg. North of the line are the descendants of the later-arriving ethnic communities who settled on the less-productive land and who tend to vote center-left. Parties win or lose elections depending on their ability to win seats straddling the line.

Saskatchewan has been described as "social democratic." It felt the Ontario influence less than did Manitoba and has had a larger measure of British, eastern European, and American immigration. Its "left-wing" tendencies are demonstrated by the fact that the New Democratic Party and its predecessor, the Cooperative Commonwealth Federation, have held power most of the time since 1944. In a province of small cities and towns, the New Democratic Party, as in Manitoba, does best in the larger communities, but here it also does well in rural areas. Saskatchewan was probably the province worst hit by the Depression, and it has a long history of cooperatives and other collective action in the farming community. The major challenger has been the Liberals. The Progressive Conservatives have formed only two governments since the Depression.

Alberta is commonly regarded as the most "American" of Canadian provinces. Its early settlers (many of them indeed midwestern Americans) brought with them more individualism (and evangelicalism) than was to be found in the other two provinces. The prosperity brought by the oil, gas, and agricultural sectors (Alberta is the wealthiest and lowest-taxed Canadian province) has bred an American-style distaste for government, and as a result basic conservatism is more acceptable there. By contrast, the other Prairie Provinces are less vibrant economically and more dependent on federal government largess.

Alberta has a history of electing parties to power for long periods and with huge majorities. The Liberals held office from the province's entry into Confederation in 1905 until 1921. The United Farmers of Alberta then held office until 1935. Social Credit (a mix of social conservatism, populism, free enterprise, and unorthodox monetary doctrine) then held office for thirty-six years, sustained in power by the booming oil industry. The old-fashioned image of the party and a desire for change led to their replacement by the Progressive Conservatives in 1971. They still held office in 1998. Social Credit has disappeared, the New Democratic Party is weak outside Edmonton and the north, and the Liberals have only recently revived as a viable alternative.

What the three provinces have in common is the greater strength of the right-of-center in the rural areas, the left-of-center in urban core areas, and a relatively high level of competition in the suburbs. Ethnicity is also a factor. Further, the substantial First Nations vote, if mobilized, has tended to go center-left in all three provinces. Where the provinces differ most is in the relative strength of the left–right forces and in the particular parties that have served as a mouthpiece for different interests.

There is perhaps greater affinity among them when one examines voting for the federal House of Commons. All three provinces, to a greater or lesser extent, share the belief that the West has been badly treated by governments dominated by Central Canada (Ontario and Quebec). There have been disputes over resource policy, government discretionary spending, tariff policy, boundaries, and the status of Quebec and the French language, among others. For the last forty years the Liberals (who have been in power nationally most of the time) have enjoyed only occasional support on the Prairies, Alberta being especially resistant to Liberal allures. Even at the height of Liberal popularity elsewhere, the Prairies have remained unimpressed. Both the Progressive Conservatives and the New Democratic Party have had strong representation (though the latter has been weak in Alberta). The long-simmering aftermath of the ill-fated

CF-18 decision in 1986 (a highly controversial aircraft maintenance decision) manifested itself in the dramatic rise of the Reform Party in the elections of 1993 and 1997. Reform, founded in 1987, favors neoconservative economics and social conservatism. The long-dominant Progressive Conservatives won no seats in the region in 1993, and only one in 1997. The New Democratic Party won a small number of seats, while the Liberals did best in Manitoba.

Geoffrey Lambert
University of Manitoba

Dyck, Rand. *Provincial Politics in Canada: Towards the Turn of the Century.* 3rd ed. Scarborough, Ontario: Prentice-Hall, 1995. Wiseman, Nelson. "The Pattern of Prairie Politics." In *Party Politics in Canada,* 5th ed., edited by Hugh G. Thorburn. Scarborough, Ontario: Prentice-Hall, 1985: 242–59.

VOTING PATTERNS, UNITED STATES

The voting patterns of the residents of the American Great Plains demonstrate both the distinctiveness of the political culture of the Great Plains in relation to the political cultures of other major regions of the United States and the existence of discernible local differences of political attitudes and habits within the region itself. Such place-to-place variations in political culture and behavior are facilitated, and even in some respects encouraged, by the federal democratic structure of American governance in which national, state, and local governments each have distinct though overlapping roles and responsibilities. The need for coordination across the three major levels of the American federal system has contributed to the predominance of a two-party system of electoral competition at federal, state, and local levels, although by no means are all electoral contests fought under party labels. The use of single-member-district plurality-system elections to choose members of the U.S. Congress, state legislatures, and many local councils or commissions also encourages two-party competition, as does the complex indirect Electoral College mechanism for electing the U.S. president. But even so, the pressures toward political diversity from one region or locality to the next can and often do outweigh those pressures that tend toward political uniformity within the American federal republic.

Thus, coins engraved with the slogan "e pluribus unum" are legal tender in the American Great Plains, just as elsewhere within the United States, but there is not one mind among Great Plains residents nor among residents of other regions over issues such as the proportion of these coins that ought to be collected in taxes, or the ends toward which the tax monies ought to be expended. Of course, elections are meant to provide citizens their most important means of expressing their views regarding just these sorts of issues.

When it comes to actually exercising their rights and obligations of citizenship at the polls, residents of the American Great Plains are among the most energetic in the United

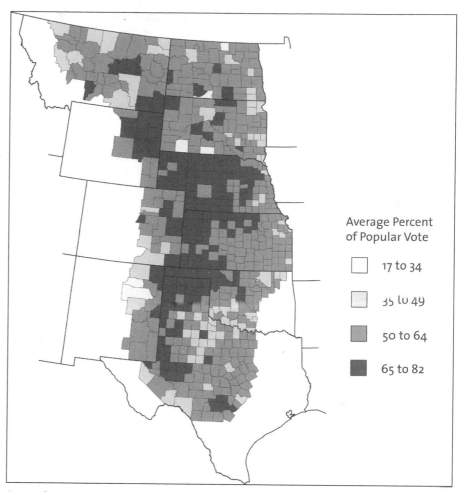

Average Percent of Popular Vote

☐ 17 to 34

☐ 35 to 49

▨ 50 to 64

■ 65 to 82

Support for Republicans, as a percentage of total votes, in presidential elections from 1980 to 2000, by county, in the U.S. Great Plains

States. If national voter turnout in presidential elections is expressed as a proportion of voting-age population, which facilitates comparisons, it can be noted that an average of 52.1 percent of potential voters in the nation as a whole participated in the six presidential elections from 1980 to 2000. In comparison, the state-level average for the ten states of the Great Plains was a presidential voter turnout rate of 56.2 percent. Thus, when the ten Great Plains states are considered together, it is found that the region's potential voters have been notably more likely to exercise their electoral franchise in recent presidential elections than voters in the nation as a whole.

But it is also important to observe that conspicuous geographical differences exist within the region itself. In particular, Central and Northern Plains states tend to have much higher turnout rates than do Southern Plains states. On average for the 1980 to 2000 presidential elections, more than 60 percent of potential voters in the northernmost Plains states of Montana (64.5 percent), North Dakota (62.2 percent), and South Dakota (62.8 percent) cast ballots, compared with fewer than 50 percent of potential voters in the southernmost states of New Mexico (49.3 percent) and Texas (45.2 percent). And the north-to-south latitudes of the remaining states almost perfectly correlate with their average

turnout levels as well, including those of Colorado (56.6 percent), Kansas (56.7 percent), Nebraska (56.7 percent), Oklahoma (52.0 percent), and Wyoming (56.8 percent). This pattern of lower voter participation in the Southern Plains has appeared for most presidential elections of the twentieth century, though differences have diminished since the Voting Rights Act of 1965 outlawed overt efforts to disenfranchise potential minority voters.

The effects and aftereffects of the Civil War and Reconstruction continued to be manifested in the geographical patterns of party preferences within the Great Plains well into the twentieth century. Voters in former Confederate or Confederate-leaning states south of the thirty-seventh parallel, which separates Colorado and Kansas from New Mexico and Oklahoma, usually supported Democratic candidates much more heavily than Republican candidates. In contrast, voters in former Union or Union-leaning Great Plains states north of the thirty-seventh parallel were usually much more inclined to support Republican candidates, although there were notable exceptions during the Greenback and Populist revolts of the 1880s and 1890s. Roughly twenty percentage points usually separated voters to the north and south of this line right through the New Deal era, when about three-quarters of Southern Plains voters supported Franklin

D. Roosevelt's Democratic candidacy. In contrast, Central and Northern Plains voters, who had given Roosevelt a comfortable majority of their votes in 1932 and 1936, gave greater preferences to Republicans Wendell L. Willkie in 1940 and Thomas E. Dewey in 1944.

The second half of the twentieth century saw significant changes in the geography of voting within the region. The nomination of World War II hero Gen. Dwight D. Eisenhower of Kansas as the Republican presidential candidate in 1952 served as a catalyst for change in the Southern Plains. Despite their traditional Democratic loyalties, small majorities of voters in New Mexico, Oklahoma, and Texas joined greater majorities north of the thirty-seventh parallel to give Eisenhower a sweeping victory throughout the Great Plains over his Democratic rival, Adlai E. Stevenson, in 1952. In 1956 Eisenhower's continued popularity shrunk the difference in aggregate Republican voter support north and south of the thirty-seventh parallel from thirteen to seven percentage points.

For the remainder of most of the twentieth century, the aggregate differences in proportions of popular support for Democratic or Republican presidential candidates within the Great Plains remained below seven percentage points to the north and south of the thirty-seventh parallel. The exceptions were in 1968, when George C. Wallace's American Independent candidacy made a differentially greater impact among voters in the Southern Plains, and in 1980, when John B. Anderson's Independent candidacy made a differentially greater impact among voters in the Central and Northern Plains. In striking contrast to earlier periods, voters in the Southern Plains gave greater aggregate support to Republican presidential candidates than to Democratic ones in every election from 1980 to the close of the twentieth century. Indeed, only once during the second half of the twentieth century did Great Plains voters in the region as a whole give more of their ballots to a Democratic than to a Republican presidential candidate. That was in 1964, when Lyndon B. Johnson of Texas led the Democratic ticket. In essence, many voters living in the Southern Plains lost their traditional aversion to the Grand Old Party of the Republic during the second half of the twentieth century. But in the process there were also parallel changes in the policy priorities of the national Democratic and Republican Parties, to the extent that such issues as civil rights or agrarian support, which had been mainly Republican priorities at the start of the twentieth century, were at least as likely to be Democratic priorities by the close of the century.

Although a majority of voters in the Great Plains have supported Republican candidates in presidential elections in recent years, there nevertheless exist notable locational variations in patterns of voter preferences at smaller geographical scales within the region. As shown on the map of average Republican support by county for the six presidential elections from 1980 to 2000 (see p. 693), there is a large and conspicuous subregion of very high Republican support that extends northward from the Texas Panhandle across western Kansas, throughout central and western Nebraska, and into eastern Wyoming. Within this zone, which is economically dominated by ranching and irrigated agriculture, county-level averages of 65 to 82 percent of voters supported Republican candidates in the 1980 to 2000 elections. Other smaller concentrations of very high average Republican support also can be found in each of the Great Plains states. Even in New Mexico, which has been the most Democratic state in the region, about half of all counties show average levels of Republican support of 50 percent or more for the 1980 to 2000 elections. Indeed, of the total of 824 counties in the Great Plains states, 626, or about three out of four, exhibit Republican majorities on average for the 1980 to 2000 elections. The remaining one out of four counties that average less than majority levels of support for Republican presidential candidates tend to be found along the margins of the Great Plains proper. The shadings associated with counties in hillier subsections of southeastern Oklahoma and eastern Texas, together with those along the eastern flank of the Rocky Mountains near the western margin of the Plains, suggest a tendency toward greater Democratic support with greater local topographic relief. Traditional patterns of party sentiment associated with marginal agricultural or nonagricultural economic activities that characterize these areas have perhaps been reinforced by the in-migration of persons of retirement age in recent years. In several states, including the Central Great Plains states of Kansas, Nebraska, and Colorado, isolated counties with larger cities or higher proportions of college or university populations tend to show lower levels of average Republican support than do surrounding agrarian counties. But the counties exhibiting the very lowest levels of Republican support, involving averages of 17 to 34 percent Republican voting in the 1980 to 2000 presidential elections, usually are those with very high proportions of Native American or Latino populations. Indeed, the two Plains counties with the very lowest levels of Republican support in 1980 to 2000 are Shannon County, South Dakota, which contains the Pine Ridge Indian Reservation, and Starr County, Texas, a generally rural county in the lower Rio Grande Valley. In these economically depressed counties, an average of four of five voters cast their ballots in support of Democratic candidates in the presidential elections from 1980 to 2000.

J. Clark Archer
University of Nebraska–Lincoln

Archer, J. Clark, Stephen J. Lavin, Kenneth C. Martis, and Fred M. Shelley. *Atlas of American Politics, 1960–2000.* Washington DC: Congressional Quarterly Press, 2002. Elazar, Daniel J. "Political Culture on the Plains," *Western Historical Quarterly* 11 (1980): 261–83. Shelley, Fred M., J. Clark Archer, Fiona M. Davidson, and Stanley D. Brunn. *Political Geography of the United States.* New York: Guilford Press, 1996.

WARREN, FRANCIS (1844–1929)

Francis Warren

U.S. senator Francis Emory Warren used his seniority and committee assignments to encourage economic development in the West and to build an effective Republican political machine in Wyoming. Born on June 20, 1844, in Hinsdale, Massachusetts, Warren attended local schools and won the Congressional Medal of Honor for his service with a Union Army regiment during the Civil War. Moving westward, he arrived in Cheyenne in 1868, where he clerked in a furniture store. Soon, he purchased and expanded the enterprise (renaming it the Warren Mercantile Company) and established the Warren Land and Livestock Company and a far-flung set of investments in banks, railroads, and public utilities. Possibly the wealthiest individual in Wyoming, Warren maintained close ties to the powerful Wyoming Stock Growers Association and served as president of the National Wool Growers Association.

Business interests quite naturally attracted Warren to politics. Appointed territorial governor in 1885, he sided with business interests and Chinese workers during the Rock Springs massacre of 1885. In 1890 Warren was elected the state's first governor, but he resigned days later after being chosen U.S. senator. He would serve more than thirty-seven years in the Senate, a record unsurpassed until 1964. Warren's seniority, his energy, his unusual knack for political organization and patronage, and his close attention to the state's business interests brought him extensive influence both in Washington and in Wyoming.

Warren chose to use that influence primarily to benefit his state and region. Rejecting charges of conflict of interest, he worked assiduously for high tariffs on raw wool, hides, and beef—positions that clearly favored the sheep and cattle industry. Warren supported federal leasing policies designed to accommodate both interests, he opposed policies that would block fencing on the federal domain, and he promoted the Carey Act of 1894 and a host of irrigation and reclamation projects to advance western interests. He lobbied shamelessly for the construction of federal buildings in Wyoming and used his position on the Senate Military Affairs Committee to enhance Fort Mackenzie in Sheridan, Wyoming, and Fort D. A. Russell (later F. E. Warren Air Force Base) in Cheyenne. As chair of the Senate Appropriations Committee in the 1920s, Warren worked for government economy and high tariffs.

Warren died in Washington DC on November 24, 1929. He was married twice, and a daughter by his first marriage became the wife of Gen. John J. Pershing.

See also WAR: Pershing, John J.

William Howard Moore
University of Wyoming

Gould, Lewis L. *Wyoming: From Territory to Statehood.* Worland WY: High Plains Publishing Company, 1989. Larson, Taft Alfred. *History of Wyoming.* Lincoln: University of Nebraska Press, 1978. Warren, Francis E. Papers. Ms. 00013. American Heritage Center, University of Wyoming, Laramie.

WATTS, J. C.

See AFRICAN AMERICANS: Watts, J. C.

WEBB, WELLINGTON AND WILMA

See AFRICAN AMERICANS: Webb, Wellington and Wilma

WYOMING

With an unforgiving climate, arid plains, rugged mountains, and scarce deposits of precious metals, Wyoming was one of the final western states organized for statehood. The 98,000 square miles that would become the forty-fourth state came to the United States as a result of the Louisiana Purchase of 1803, the settlement of the disputed Oregon boundary line with Great Britain in 1846, and the Mexican cession of 1848 under terms of the Treaty of Guadalupe Hidalgo.

John Colter, a member of the Lewis and Clark expedition (1804–6) who set off on his own to explore the Rocky Mountains, was probably the first white American to visit what is now the state of Wyoming (although the Vérendrye brothers, Louis-Joseph and François, may have pushed that far west in 1742–43). When he returned in 1807, Colter told fantastic stories of the wonders he had seen in the Yellowstone region. Colter was followed by numerous trappers and adventurers who trapped and traded in the Rocky Mountains. By the late 1840s thousands of settlers were annually crossing what some considered the "Great American Desert" on their way to California's gold fields, the Mormon Zion at the Great Salt Lake, or the greener pastures of

Oregon territory. However, few stayed to endure Wyoming's harsh winters. In 1851 a council at Fort Laramie, conducted by Thomas Fitzpatrick and assisted by Jesuit missionary priest Father Pierre De Smet, secured permission from several Native American leaders for the safe passage of pioneers across Indian lands in return for a promise of annuities from the U.S. government. Following an outbreak of warfare in 1865 along the Bozeman Trail, intermittent conflicts persisted until the tribal alliance under Sitting Bull was defeated in 1876. Meanwhile, to protect and govern the remote white settlements along the Union Pacific route, the Wyoming Territory had been created in 1868 by carving off the western section of the Dakota Territory and including parts of what is now Utah and Idaho.

Territorial government for Wyoming was organized on May 19, 1869, in Cheyenne. On December 10, 1869, in an unsuccessful effort to encourage female settlers, the first territorial legislature adopted an act granting women the right to vote. The following year, census figures showed 9,000 inhabitants (not including Native Americans), mostly located in small communities or cattle ranches along the newly completed Union Pacific Railroad line that traversed the southernmost part of the territory. Recognizing the uniqueness of the Yellowstone region, the northwest corner of Wyoming was designated by the federal government as the nation's first national park in 1872. Cattle ranching, and later sheep ranching, soon followed the rail lines and spread northward as the Native American resistance faded. In 1886 the territorial legislature established the University of Wyoming, which remains the state's only baccalaureate and graduate school (seven regional "community colleges" were created after World War II). In 1890 Wyoming's representative to Congress, Joseph M. Carey, claiming the territory had more than 100,000 residents, introduced enabling legislation in the U.S. House of Representatives seeking statehood, and on July 10 the Wyoming Statehood Act was signed by President Benjamin Harrison. An official census conducted that year would show Wyoming's actual population to be only 62,555.

Wyoming's politics are generally conservative and independent-minded, with Republicans usually controlling the legislative and statewide elected offices. Until court-ordered reapportionment of the Senate in 1965, rural interests, headed by the Wyoming Stock Growers Association, dominated statehouse politics. Although Wyoming's constitution has been amended or altered more than sixty times, it remains essentially the same as drafted in 1889,

providing for a bicameral legislature (sixty representatives and thirty senators), which meets for a forty-day session beginning in January in odd-numbered years, and for a twenty-day session in even-numbered years to consider and adopt a budget. The state constitution also granted full voting rights to women, the only state to do so at that time, earning for Wyoming the name "Equality State." The constitution provides for an elected governor, who serves a four-year term, but no lieutenant governor (the secretary of state is next in line of succession). Other elected executive officers include a superintendent of public instruction, auditor, and treasurer. The state supreme court consists of five justices elected to terms of eight years.

Petroleum production, mining (especially coal in the Powder River Basin), and natural gas provide the basis of Wyoming's economy. Although Wyoming still proudly calls itself the "Cowboy State," the agricultural sector produces less revenue and offers fewer jobs than the state's mineral industry or its tourism industry, which attracts several million visitors each summer to Yellowstone Park, Devils Tower, and other scenic vistas, and winter sports enthusiasts to Wyoming's mountains during the long snowy months. Because of a reliance on extractive industries, particularly oil drilling, for its tax base, Wyoming has always been vulnerable to booms and busts. With the decline of oil prices in the 1980s, Wyoming's population, already the smallest of any state in the nation, declined to 456,000 in 1990, but rose to 494,000 in 2000.

Wyoming's most notable political leaders include Chief Washakie (c. 1801–1900) of the Shoshones, who maintained peaceful relations with whites and settled his people on the Wind River Reservation in central Wyoming; Nellie Tayloe Ross (1876–1977), who in 1924 was the first woman elected as governor of a state; and Richard "Dick" Cheney (b. 1941), who served as chief of staff to President Gerald R. Ford (1974–76), Wyoming's lone representative to the U.S. House (1979–89), secretary of defense (1989–1993) in the George Bush administration, and the vice president of the United States in the George W. Bush administration in 2000.

See also EUROPEAN AMERICANS: Vérendrye Family.

Michael J. Devine
University of Wyoming

Gould, Lewis L. *Wyoming: From Territory to Statehood.* Worland WY: High Plains Publishing Company, 1989. Larson, Taft Alfred. *History of Wyoming.* Lincoln: University of Nebraska Press, 1978.

Protest and Dissent

Meeting at Victoria Park, Winnipeg, Manitoba, June 13, 1919

PROTEST AND DISSENT

Protest and dissent have helped shape the history of the Great Plains in the modern era. Dramatic episodes like the 1919 Winnipeg (Manitoba) General Strike and the 1973 occupation of Wounded Knee, South Dakota, are just a few of the many efforts that have made their impact felt in the region and beyond. On numerous occasions, individuals and groups have taken a public stand to denounce a perceived evil or promote a desired good. Sometimes protest was tied to a more permanent effort, such as the labor movement, a farmers' organization, or an ideological cause; other times, it was a single outburst of anger or complaint. Dissenting views also were advanced by the formation of local civil rights groups like Omaha's De Porres Club or radical newspapers like Kansas's *Appeal to Reason*, or even in letters written to the local press. Protest and dissent have not been isolated topics in the Great Plains; rather, they have been major elements in the region's history.

Farm Protest

Much of the protest has an economic origin. Hard-pressed farmers from Texas to Alberta have organized repeatedly in an effort to obtain better prices for their crops and livestock, fairer treatment from railroads and other corporations, and better community and public services. On a number of occasions, farm groups that first organized in the United States spread to Canada's Prairie Provinces. For example, in the late nineteenth century, the Patrons of Husbandry, or the Grange (formed in 1867), preached a gospel of education, economic cooperation, and social activity for the farm family. It met with great success initially when it launched a cooperative crusade in the 1870s. Although its strongest outposts were in the Midwest, the Grange also enjoyed a strong following in some Plains states and in the Prairie Provinces. Its experience was shared by numerous other farm organizations that emerged in the region in subsequent decades. In the early twentieth century, the American Society of Equity (organized in 1902) emerged as an influential transborder movement as well. It focused most of its energies on marketing and cooperatives, although it also lobbied politicians and sponsored social and educational programs. Ultimately, the Society of Equity on both sides of the forty-ninth parallel played a role in the emergence of the Nonpartisan League (NPL), an agrarian political movement that had its origins in North Dakota in 1915.

Time and time again, Great Plains farmers have organized to avoid the middleman, advance the interests of rural people, and preserve the family farm. They met with their greatest successes between 1910 and 1960. In the Prairie Provinces, the Grain Growers Associations, the United Farmers of Alberta (UFA), the United Farmers of Canada, Saskatchewan Section, and the United Farmers of Manitoba were the important farm groups that emerged prior to 1930. They promoted a gospel of farm

Deputies with nightsticks line the highway coming into Omaha, Nebraska, to protect trucks against Farmers Holiday Association demonstrators, September 1, 1932.

cooperatives and agrarian politics. Among their greatest assets was *The Western Producer*, a newspaper that served a major educational and propaganda role for decades. South of the forty-ninth parallel, the comparable movement for American farmers, particularly from the World War I era into the 1950s, was the National Farmers Union (NFU). Cooperatives, education, and political activity were all part of the agenda of this effort, which had its greatest presence in the Plains states, particularly in North Dakota and Oklahoma. There were numerous parallels between the Canadian and American farm movements, one of which was the important role that women often played in sustaining these efforts, but the response to particular problems often differed from province to province and from state to state. For example, the once-nonpartisan UFA entered politics in 1922 and dominated the Alberta provincial government until 1935. In the United States, however, the NFU was never tempted to transform itself into a political organization.

The Great Depression of the 1930s presented an enormous challenge to existing farm groups in the Great Plains. Cooperative marketing was not a remedy for low farm prices, and farmers across the region were threatened with foreclosure and other economic disasters. Government at all levels in the United States and Canada was slow to respond to the unprecedented crisis. What emerged was a grassroots protest movement, or what some have coined the farm revolt of the 1930s. The major American organization was the Farmers Holiday Association, which sponsored farm strikes or withholding actions and interfered with forced farm sales through "penny auctions." The Farmers Holiday Association began in 1932 and spread across the Upper Midwest and Northern Plains. Hun-

dreds and even thousands of farmers took part in demonstrations, penny auctions, and marches on state capitols. In February 1933 an estimated 4,000 farmers gathered on the steps of the new state capitol building in Lincoln, Nebraska, demanding a moratorium law.

But the first skirmishes of the farm revolt of the 1930s were fought by smaller groups. Communist-led organizations, the United Farmers League (UFL) and the Farmers Unity League (FUL), conducted penny auctions before the better-known Farmers Holiday Association came into existence. A Manitoba farm sale was halted by an FUL group in early 1931, and similar episodes soon took place on both sides of the border. For a short time it looked as if the countryside in the Great Plains was in revolt. Ultimately, federal farm programs helped undercut the appeal of agrarian insurgency in the United States. Yet the farm revolt of the 1930s dramatized the plight of American and Canadian farmers, pressured government to provide assistance, and played a role in reconfiguring the political culture of the region.

Farm protest in the more recent era has had less impact. During the 1950s and 1960s a new American farm group emerged, the National Farmers Organization (NFO). It focused its attention on marketing, ultimately opting for collective bargaining. Like the farmers' groups of the 1930s, NFO initially attracted widespread publicity. It, too, sponsored withholding actions or strikes but soon settled down, establishing a niche particularly among dairy and hog farmers. The National Farmers Union of Canada, largely a Saskatchewan group, developed a parallel course of action in more recent years as well. In the late 1970s and early 1980s, farmers again were faced with low prices and high debt and interest rates. A new farm revolt ensued on both sides of the border, and the older farm groups were often bypassed by the insurgency. The main vehicle of this protest in the United States was the American Agriculture Movement, which was formed in 1978. It was accompanied by many smaller groups in the next several years, most of which were organized in the early 1980s. A Canadian Agriculture Movement was formed, and an umbrella group, the North American Farm Alliance, emerged in 1982, open to both American and Canadian membership. The 1980s probably witnessed more farm protest than any time since the early 1930s. These efforts sometimes borrowed tactics and rhetoric from earlier eras; for example, Mary Elizabeth Lease's alleged comment from the late nineteenth century, "Farmers need to raise less corn and more hell," was often quoted with approval. Such efforts again drew attention to the plight of farmers, but there were significantly fewer of them than previously, so their political influence was correspondingly reduced as well. By the end of the twentieth century, the ranks of family farm organizations throughout the Plains fell far short of earlier days, when farm protest and farm votes determined elections on both sides of the border.

Yet the legacies of those earlier efforts are manifest in the region. Farm cooperatives to buy wheat and sell oil and gasoline dot the Plains from Texas to Alberta; North Dakota continues to operate a state-owned bank; Nebraska forbids nonfamily farm corporations from owning and operating farms; and the Canadian medicare system, first promoted by the farmer-dominated Cooperative Commonwealth Federation in Saskatchewan, remains in place.

Labor Protest

Workers in the Great Plains often have protested because of their wages and working conditions. While the region generally has not had the reputation as a center of labor protest, organized labor has had an extended history in Winnipeg, Brandon (Manitoba), Edmonton, Calgary, Regina, Saskatoon, Omaha, and Kansas City, as well as in other railroad and mining centers. Craft unions organized skilled workers such as printers, carpenters, and bricklayers in the late nineteenth century in many communities in the Plains, and they, along with railroad unions, ranked among the most successful unionization efforts in that era. An important effort outside the craft unions was that of the Knights of Labor (organized in 1867), an attempt to organize workers regardless of skill, gender, or race. Although the Knights had their greatest success in the northeastern and midwestern United States, they also had a significant presence in the Plains states and parts of the Prairie Provinces. Winnipeg, Omaha, and Kansas City, Kansas, were among the strongest Knights of Labor communities in the region, and the Kansas City Knights emerged as a strong political force in the 1880s. Then, the Knights seemed a real alternative to the craft union approach. Ultimately, however, the "bread and butter"

Socialist group at Minot, North Dakota, convention, 1910

unionism of Samuel Gompers and the American Federation of Labor prevailed in the United States and in Canada as well.

However, in the early twentieth century a more militant form of unionism—often called industrial unionism because it sought to organize workers in particular industries regardless of job skill—had a strong presence in some cities and in the countryside. The Industrial Workers of the World (IWW) was formed in 1905 and sought to organize all workers into one big union. More radical than craft unions, Wobblies (as IWW members were called) sought to replace the existing economic and political order with workers' rule. Although the IWW tried to recruit members from all occupations, in the Great Plains this union met with its greatest success in the wheat fields, where it organized harvest hands. From 1915 to 1917 thousands of migratory workers from Oklahoma to North Dakota had red cards signifying IWW membership. At one point, a tentative closed shop arrangement between the NPL in North Dakota and the IWW was negotiated, only to be repudiated by the farm group's members soon after. Local authorities often suppressed the Wobblies, two noteworthy crackdowns occurring in Minot, North Dakota, and Mitchell, South Dakota. After the United States entered World War I in 1917, repression of radical groups became the norm, and the Wobblies were harassed repeatedly. During the war years and the anticommunist "Red Scare" that followed World War I, the IWW was decimated in the Plains states.

The "one big union" idea also had appeal north of the forty-ninth parallel, as the IWW established a foothold in western Canada prior to World War I. The war experience itself had a radicalizing effect on many Canadian workers, and western Canada experienced its greatest labor strife in history in 1919. Pent-up resentment, increased militancy, and the example of the Bolshevik revolution in Russia all served to

encourage Canadian unionists to take the offensive after World War I. When the Western Labor Conference met in Calgary in March of 1919, militant labor sentiments were at fever pitch. The gathering denounced the capitalist economic order, extended greetings to the government of the Soviet Union, and opted to form a new union open to all workers, called the One Big Union (OBU). Like the IWW before it, the OBU was a rejection not only of the existing economic order but also of the traditional labor movement led by conservative labor leaders like Samuel Gompers.

Growing labor strife across Canada coincided with the formation of the OBU. A showdown between employers and the new labor militancy occurred in Winnipeg in the summer of 1919. The famous Winnipeg General Strike has been portrayed as both a revolutionary upheaval and a repressive counterrevolution against legitimate trade union aspirations. As a practical matter, the labor troubles in Winnipeg did not grow out of a confrontation between the OBU and local employers. Rather, they were related to more conventional disputes over wages and the right of collective bargaining. When workers went out on strike, many other local unions walked out in sympathy with the strikers. Employers and politicians, however, portrayed the Winnipeg General Strike as the beginning of a revolution and seized every opportunity to suppress the strikers. General strikes in other western Canadian cities followed, as unionists sought to show their support for the Winnipeg strikers. Police, soldiers, employers, and returning veterans all joined in the fray in Winnipeg, and the strikers were routed after three weeks of struggle. This defeat marked the end of an era and a turning point in labor history in the Great Plains. Never again, north or south of the forty-ninth parallel, would there be such a confrontation between employers and workers.

The 1920s were labor's lean years in both the United States and Canada. Kansas miners, Nebraska and Kansas packinghouse workers, and railroad workers across the U.S. Plains all suffered defeat in the early 1920s, as did miners and others in the Prairie Provinces. One noteworthy episode in southeast Kansas involved female relatives of male coal miners. During the coal strike of 1921, these women organized the "Amazon Army," which toured mine sites, picketing and attacking strikebreakers. This strike ended in failure, as did miners' strikes in western Canada in this era.

Organized workers had little to celebrate anywhere in the Great Plains until the mid- to late 1930s, when the labor movement regrouped and launched new organizational drives during the Great Depression. This time, benefiting from new labor legislation and the example of union success elsewhere in the United States, workers organized new unions and flocked to old ones. One of the most important developments was the formation of the Congress of Industrial Organizations (CIO), which was a federation of industrial unions. Workers flocked to the new industrial unions on both sides of the border. (In both Canada and the United States, unions often are referred to as internationals, as they have affiliates in both countries.) Yet union growth was not limited to the new unions. Old craft unions, including the Teamsters, which emerged as a major union for the first time, also enjoyed important organizational successes. With the outbreak of World War II, union militancy was replaced by no-strike pledges, but union membership and political influence continued to grow. In Saskatchewan, a farmer-labor political coalition, the Cooperative Commonwealth Confederation (CCF), first came to power in 1944, and prolabor candidates were elected to ridings in numerous assembly districts there and in Manitoba. South of the border, however, a conservative reaction to labor gains ensued in the war years and the immediate postwar period.

On earlier occasions, anti-union sentiment had resulted in employer counteroffensives known as the open shop movement. The movement had been particularly strong in Omaha and Fargo; the Omaha Business Men's Association asserted that "Omaha is the best open shop city of its size in the United States." Such efforts had been swept away by the late 1930s in the wake of union successes, but employers regrouped following World War II and launched a major effort to revive the open shop. In the Dakotas and Nebraska, they successfully promoted "right-to-work" laws. Both South Dakota and Nebraska amended their constitutions to prohibit the union shop in 1946, and more than a decade later Kansas passed a right-to-work measure as well. These anti-union efforts amounted to a businessmen's protest movement.

Labor membership in Plains states lagged behind that in more industrialized states, but the labor movement continued to represent tens of thousands of workers. Later, in the 1960s and 1970s, as teachers and other public employees opted for unionization across the country, Plains states passed measures providing for collective bargaining, particularly for teachers. One noteworthy episode occurred in South Dakota, when Rapid City teachers went out on strike in 1970. Today, university and college professors in the Prairie Provinces, South Dakota, Nebraska, and Kansas are among public employees exercising their right to bargain for wages and working conditions.

Political Protest and Dissent

Political protest and dissent has been an integral feature of the political culture of the Plains states and Prairie Provinces. Aside from the Populist movement of the 1890s, third parties in the Plains states have been more a vehicle for protest and advocacy than a means of assuming political power. In the Prairie Provinces, on the other hand, third parties such as Social Credit and the CCF (and its successor, the New Democratic Party) have met with much greater electoral success in the twentieth century. There, too, however, minor third parties, including the Communist Party, have played a similar protest role. Socialists often ran for office in the early twentieth century, but their campaigns proved to be more protest than a means of gaining public office. The exception was Oklahoma, where members of the Socialist Party were elected to five state legislatures seats and to more than 100 local offices in 1914.

A key element in the pre–World War I Socialist effort was a highly successful weekly newspaper, *Appeal to Reason*, published in Girard, Kansas, by Julius Wayland. Folksy, well-written, and controversial, *Appeal to Reason* may have had the largest circulation of any political paper in the United States (more than 760,000 of some issues), and subscribers across the country read this paper for years. (Upton Sinclair's novel *The Jungle* first appeared in serial form in the *Appeal to Reason*.)

Itinerant speakers also played a major role in promoting the Socialist cause in the U.S. Plains, and Kate Richards O'Hare was among the best known. She spoke at Socialist encampments in Oklahoma and at other party gatherings across the region. During World War I she was convicted of violating the Espionage Act for antiwar comments she allegedly made in a speech in Bowman, North Dakota.

In the U.S. Great Plains, farmers and small-town folk were more likely than city folk to be Socialists. Beatrice, Nebraska, Sisseton, South Dakota, and Minot, North Dakota, were among the communities that elected Socialist mayors. The emergence of third parties as a kind of protest was behind the more successful NPL that dominated North Dakota politics and took over courthouses in portions of eastern South Dakota and northeastern Montana from 1916 to 1922.

Other third-party political protest involved Communists in the early 1920s and after. Though there never were many Communists in the U.S. Plains, small pockets existed in Finnish settlements in the Dakotas and Montana and in a number of other communities across the Northern Plains at different times. Key Communist leaders Earl Browder and James Cannon both came from Kansas and under-

went their baptism of fire in radical causes there. (Cannon subsequently broke with the Communists and served as the chief leader of the American Trotskyist movement until his death.) Ella Reeve "Mother" Bloor was the most prominent Communist figure in the region during the Great Depression. An energetic agitator despite her age, the sixty-seven-year-old Bloor played a key role in the farm revolt of that era, traveling across the Dakotas, Montana, and Nebraska from 1930 to 1934, speaking and organizing wherever she went. While most of her efforts involved farmers, she was arrested in Nebraska for her role in the 1934 Loup City Riot in which Communists and their allies tried to organize women in a local chicken-processing plant. She ultimately served thirty days in jail.

Communists also played a role in the labor and unemployment struggles of the 1930s. They likely had a stronger presence in the Prairie Provinces than in the U.S. Plains states. Communists had a following in some mining districts, Ukrainian settlements, and Winnipeg's North End. In 1935 they played a key part in the unemployment march across western Canada that was halted dramatically with the Regina Riot. Marchers had trekked to Regina en route to their ultimate destination, Ottawa, where they planned to petition the federal government for relief. At Regina, however, local authorities and the Royal Canadian Mounted Police intercepted the trekkers, attacking a mass meeting and brutally dispersing them.

Communists participated in the larger farm and labor organizations in the region. Their strongest base after the 1930s probably was in Winnipeg and smaller Ukrainian communities. As late as the 1960s, a Communist represented the North End in the Winnipeg City Council. Some Communists had participated in the CCF in Saskatchewan and the NFU in the Northern Plains states at times. Yet their role should not be exaggerated. Opponents often used the "red" issue as a way of discrediting liberal causes, and the NPL, CCF, and NFU all were subjected to such attacks. Many liberal groups in this region often found themselves the target of right-wing protest groups.

Political protest and dissent have not been a left-of-center monopoly. An important early right-wing protest group in the Plains states and Prairie Provinces was the Ku Klux Klan. It quickly attracted a strong following, particularly in Oklahoma, but had a presence throughout the entire region in the 1920s. Governors in both Oklahoma and Kansas went to war with the Klan, though Oklahoma governor John C. "Our Jack" Walton's primary motivation in doing so was to avoid impeachment and removal from office. (This effort failed, as his bizarre and arbitrary behavior alienated many of his former supporters.) The Klan spread to Canada in the mid-1920s and attracted a strong following in both Alberta and Saskatchewan. There, its drawing power came from its anti-Catholic and anti-immigrant stance. Recent historians of the Klan increasingly stress the complexity of this topic, observing that its adherents often were motivated more by a desire to preserve existing moral codes than by racism and anti-Catholicism. While scholars disagree on the significance of the Klan in this era, there seems little question that Protestant clergymen often promoted its cause on both sides of the border.

Right-wing protest probably has come in as many varieties as its counterparts on the left. In the 1930s, coinciding with President Franklin Roosevelt's New Deal (and sometimes in response to it), an articulate right-wing protest element emerged in the Plains. Key figures in this grouping included Gerald B. Winrod and Elmer J. Garner, both then from Wichita. Winrod published the *Defender* magazine, and Garner edited *Publicity*, a newspaper. By the late 1930s both of them identified the New Deal with Jews and communists. Anti-Semitic and isolationist, they saw the Roosevelt administration dominated by Jews and vehemently denounced U.S. foreign policy. Following Pearl Harbor, however, both tempered their remarks. Still, in 1942 they were indicted for sedition, along with twenty-nine other right-wing figures. Garner died two weeks after the trial began, and the case against Winrod and other defendants ended in a mistrial in 1946. Some historians maintain that this prosecution was an overreaction to the right wing, a kind of "brown scare," analogous to the overreaction to the left, or "red scare," of the post–World War II era.

Support for Sen. Joseph McCarthy emerged in the Plains states during the cold war years. While there was no McCarthyite movement per se, McCarthyite attacks were made against many groups and people. For example, in northeast Montana, a Farmers Anti-Communist Club appeared and ran advertisements in two local weekly newspapers in the mid-1950s. The chief target of this group apparently was the NFU, and the advertisements often portrayed the liberal farm group as a Communist front or an organization in which Communists played a major role. Later, in the 1960s, the John Birch Society appeared in the region. Its national leader denounced Dwight Eisenhower's presidency as too liberal, sometimes suggesting that the popular president had been a tool of the Communists. Birch Society members probably had their greatest influence at the local level, particularly on school boards.

An even more extreme right-wing protest movement emerged in the 1980s and 1990s. At the depths of the farm crisis of the 1980s, the Posse Comitatus and other extremist groups recruited among hard-pressed farmers. Built on a racist and anti-Semitic ideology, this movement preached a harsh, antigovernment gospel that justified violence and fraudulent financial practices. Numerous publications, speakers, and workshops promoted this message. While observers differed in their assessment of the recruitment success of these groups, all agreed that the groups built a following in the countryside. Gordon Kahl of North Dakota and Arthur Kirk of Nebraska

were two of their recruits. Both men resisted arrest and died in shootouts with authorities, becoming martyrs to their extremist causes.

The Posse Comitatus has faded from view while continuing as an intermittently active arm of antigovernment protest. Its torch has been picked up by newer organizations, including some militia groups. In Garfield County in northeastern Montana, a group calling themselves the Freemen claimed they had established sovereignty in Justus Township and constructed a stockade around their farm in 1996. They financed their actions by passing millions of dollars' worth of bad checks. A long siege of more than two months ensued before the group surrendered to the authorities, who included a large number of FBI agents. A similar episode occurred in West Texas in 1997. In Jeff Davis County, a right-wing group claimed they had reestablished the Republic of Texas, arguing that the United States' annexation of Texas in 1846 had been invalid. Also heavily armed, this faction subscribed to many of the political ideas of the Posse Comitatus and threatened to shoot anyone who interfered with their activities. After the kidnapping of a local couple, authorities acted and suppressed the would-be secessionist group. Its leaders were sentenced to long prison sentences for kidnapping and passing millions of dollars' worth of bad checks.

Unlike earlier protesters, these contemporary right-wing extremist groups do not seek to change government policy; instead, they want to form their own kind of government outside existing political institutions. In the wake of the 1995 Oklahoma City bombing, the media and others have focused much more attention on right-wing protest groups who preach violence and vigilante-type justice. Once simply characterized as tax protestors, they now are subject to greater scrutiny and concern.

Civil Rights and Ethnic Protest

An early protest involving Native Americans was that of Thomas H. Tibbles and Standing Bear. In 1879 the U.S. government ordered Gen. George Crook to return Standing Bear and his Ponca band from their traditional homeland in northeastern Nebraska to Indian Territory, where they had been removed two years previously. Crook, appalled by the assignment, notified Tibbles, a reporter for the *Omaha Daily Herald*, who used the story to focus attention on citizenship rights for Native Americans. Tibbles also arranged for two local attorneys to file a writ of habeas corpus on behalf of the Ponca leader in federal court. The judge ruled that Standing Bear and his followers were U.S. citizens who had withdrawn from the Ponca tribe, and that the federal government had no basis to order their return to Indian Territory. Following the trial, Crook and Tibbles continued to aid the Ponca cause to regain their land in northeast Nebraska. Susette La Flesche, the daughter of an Omaha chief, joined the effort, later marrying Tibbles. She devoted much of her life to working for Indian rights, including the recognition of their U.S. citizenship.

African Americans often were treated as second-class citizens in the Plains. After World War I there were several violent outbreaks against African Americans, including a 1919 lynching in Omaha and the 1921 Tulsa Race Riot that resulted in the deaths of at least thirty-nine African Americans, and probably many more. Some African Americans organized chapters of the National Association of Colored People (NAACP), while others formed units of Marcus Garvey's back-to-Africa group, the Universal Negro Improvement Association (UNIA). By the mid-1920s Oklahoma City and Omaha had both NAACP and UNIA affiliates, Topeka and Lincoln had NAACP chapters, and Kansas City and Tulsa had UNIA divisions.

Civil rights activism had a long history in the region. Plains blacks protested the film *Birth of a Nation* as racist and sought to eliminate discrimination in employment and education. The U.S. Supreme Court's 1954 landmark decision in *Brown v. The Board of Education*, which paved the way for desegregation of the public schools, was the result of several NAACP lawsuits, including one on behalf of Linda Brown and other black students in Topeka, Kansas. Some African Americans in the Great Plains opted for direct action even before the outbreak of activism in the South in the 1960s. Omaha's De Porres Club, organized in 1947, integrated a Catholic parish and pressured the local Coca Cola bottling works (located in the city's largest black neighborhood) and the transit company to hire blacks. For a time, this group was affiliated with the Congress of Racial Equality (CORE). In 1958 NAACP youth groups in Wichita and Oklahoma City conducted successful lunch-counter sit-ins in order to obtain service for blacks.

One of the region's most dramatic protests was the 1973 takeover of Wounded Knee. The American Indian Movement (AIM) launched a frontal assault on both discrimination against Native Americans and the existing power structure on reservations. In early 1973 AIM took control of the community of Wounded Knee, South Dakota, which was the site of the 1890 massacre of more than 200 Sioux men, women, and children by the U.S. Seventh Cavalry. While AIM sought to dramatize the plight of contemporary Indians, the takeover also was aimed at overthrowing the current tribal leadership on the Pine Ridge Reservation. The occupation lasted seventy-one days. Although AIM was not successful in achieving its stated objectives, this episode heightened media attention on the problems faced by Indians in the region. Canadian Indians supported the South Dakota occupation, and the Ojibwa Warrior Society briefly took over a site across the Manitoba line in western Ontario later the same year. Native American protest on both sides of the forty-ninth parallel became commonplace in the late twentieth century.

Ubiquity of Protest

Not all dissent involves political causes. One noteworthy example of quiet dissent that still resulted in serious controversy was an effort to provide cooperative medical care in the small

Protesting against animal activists in South Dakota

southwestern Oklahoma town of Elk City. A Lebanese immigrant, Michael Shadid, settled in this community in 1911 after graduating from medical school. Determined to provide access to adequate health care, he and the local Farmers Union raised funds to establish a cooperative hospital. Although boycotted and opposed by the local medical establishment, the Elk City facility persisted and provided excellent and inexpensive health care to the community for a generation. Ultimately, in 1964, it became a local community hospital, no longer based on cooperative principles.

A different kind of dissent regarding medical services emerged in Saskatchewan, when the CCF government established medicare in 1962. There, doctors went out on strike, opposing what they saw as socialized medicine. A "Keep Our Doctors Committee" appeared even before the walkout, and most of the hospitals in the province were closed. The strike itself lasted less than a month, but ultimately the medical establishment across Canada became reconciled to publicly funded, universal medical care.

The themes of protest and dissent are also present in the cultural history of the region. One of the most significant examples is the 1978 film *Northern Lights*, which tells the story of an NPL organizer in northwestern North Dakota in 1915–16. Directed by John Hanson and Rob Nilsson, this black-and-white film featured mostly local people in its cast and premiered in the small town of Crosby, North Dakota. It won an award at the 1979 Cannes Film Festival. The film was narrated by Henry Martinson, then in his nineties and poet laureate of North Dakota, who was a veteran of numerous social and political causes dating back to his involvement with the Socialist Party and the NPL of the World War I era.

Perhaps the best-known artist of the Great Plains to emerge out of a protest tradition was songwriter-folksinger Woody Guthrie of Oklahoma. Among his numerous songs and ballads were "Talkin' Dust Bowl Blues" and "This Land Is Your Land." Guthrie met with his greatest success on the East Coast, where he performed and recorded songs. His work was an influence on a number of other singers, including his friend Pete Seeger, Bob Dylan, and Bruce Springsteen. Agnes "Sis" Cunningham was another Oklahoma protest singer who emerged in the 1930s. She participated in a left-wing theater troupe known as the Red Dust Players and helped organize CIO unions in her home state. Later, in the 1940s, she joined Guthrie in New York City as a member of the well-known Almanac Singers.

The literature of the Great Plains also contains dissenting themes. Marie Sandoz's *Capitol City*, while not one of her strongest works, reveals the author's estrangement from the dominant culture and her sympathies with the underdog, including embattled farmers, worried by foreclosures, and striking Teamsters in the 1930s. Another regional protest novel is William Cunningham's *Green Corn Rebellion*. (Cunningham was the older brother of Sis Cunningham). This work, published in 1935, is an example of the proletariat novel that appeared in the 1930s. It treats a rural Oklahoma uprising that was quickly suppressed by local authorities in the wake of the U.S. entry into World War I.

Nonfiction works treating Great Plains topics reflect regional dissenting themes as well. Bruce Nelson's *Land of the Dacotahs*, first published in 1946, offers an episodic history of the Dakotas and Montana. It sides with Indians, homesteaders, and North Dakota's NPL. Unlike Nelson, who was from Minnesota, Angie Debo lived almost all of her ninety-eight years in the Great Plains. Trained at the Universities of Oklahoma and Chicago, she is recognized as one of the leading authorities on the history of Southern Plains Indians. Her most important work may have been *And Still the Waters*

Run, a historical treatment of how white Oklahomans stole large amounts of Indian land. A number of the culprits were still alive and were prominent citizens at the time Debo wrote the manuscript, and the University of Oklahoma administration refused to allow its press to publish the book. Finally, *And Still the Waters Run* was published in 1940 by Princeton University Press. Debo's work was characterized by a strong sympathy toward Indians at a time when that stance was unpopular in Oklahoma.

Critical treatments of the Great Plains sometimes themselves provoked protest. Local responses to Pere Lorentz's 1936 film documentary, *The Plow That Broke the Plains*, and John Steinbeck's novel *The Grapes of Wrath* constituted yet another variety of regional protest. Lorentz's classic twenty-eight-minute film provoked a firestorm of journalistic and political criticism for defaming South Dakota, even though none of its footage was shot in that state. Likewise, *The Grapes of Wrath* was perceived as a libel on Oklahoma by some local editorial writers, especially in Oklahoma City.

Conclusion

Protest and dissent permeate the recent history of the Great Plains. In some cases, especially in regard to farm and labor protest, they constitute an important part of the background of new organizations and institutions. On other occasions, protestors and dissenters have had little lasting effect; their voices were raised or their remarks recorded, and then they faded into obscurity, only to be rediscovered later (if at all) by enterprising journalists or historians. New causes have appeared in recent decades, but they often utilize tactics introduced long ago. In the 1980s and 1990s, for example, protestors on both sides of the abortion issue picketed and sometimes resorted to civil disobedience, following courses of action earlier laid out by the labor and civil rights movements. Historically, many people on numerous occasions have demonstrated their approval or opposition to current practices or proposed changes. The frequency and the geographic extent of their efforts demonstrate that protest and dissent have not been an aberration in the Great Plains; rather, they constitute an irreducible element of the region.

See also AFRICAN AMERICANS: Civil Rights; Omaha Race Riot; Tulsa Race Riot / AGRICULTURE: Corporate Farming / FILM: *The Grapes of Wrath*; *Northern Lights*; *The Plow That Broke the Plains* / LAW: Anti–Corporate Farming Laws; *Brown v. The Board of Education of Topeka* / LITERARY TRADITIONS: Debo, Angie; Sandoz, Mari / MEDIA: *Western Producer* / MUSIC: Guthrie, Woody / POLITICS AND GOVERNMENT: Cooperative Commonwealth Federation; New Democratic Party; Populists (People's Party).

William C. Pratt
University of Nebraska at Omaha

Barthelme, Marion K. *Women in the Texas Populist Movement: Letters to the Southern Mercury.* College Station:

Texas A&M University Press, 1997. Bumsted, J. M. "1919: The Winnipeg Strike Reconsidered." *The Beaver* (June–July 1994): 27–44. Corcoran, James. *Bitter Harvest: Gordon Kahl and the Posse Comitatus: Murder in the Heartland.* New York: Penguin Books, 1990. Dyson, Lowell K. *Red Harvest: The Communist Party and American Farmers.* Lincoln: University of Nebraska Press, 1982. Green, James R. *Grass-Roots Socialism: Radical Movements in the Southwest, 1895–1943.* Baton Rouge: Louisiana State University Press, 1978. Haug, Charles James. "The Industrial Workers of the World in North Dakota, 1913–1917." *North Dakota Quarterly* 39 (1971): 85–102. Henson, Tom M. "Ku Klux Klan in Western Canada." *Alberta History* 25 (1977): 1–8. Joyce, David D. *An Oklahoma I Had Never Seen Before: Alternative Views of Oklahoma History.* Norman: University of Oklahoma Press, 1994. MacPherson, Ian. "Selective Borrowings: The American Impact upon the Prairie Co-operative Movement, 1920–39." *Canadian Review of American Studies* 10 (1979): 137–51. McCormack, A. Ross. *Reformers, Rebels, and Revolutionaries: The Western Canadian Radical Movement 1899–1919.* Toronto: University of Toronto Press, 1991. Monod, David. "The Agrarian Struggle: Rural Communism in Alberta and Saskatchewan, 1926–1935." *Historie sociale/Social History* 35 (1985): 98–118. Pratt, William C. "Workers, Bosses, and Historians on the Northern Plains." *Great Plains Quarterly* 16 (1996): 229–50. Saloutos, Theodore, and John D. Hicks. *Twentieth-Century Populism: Agricultural Discontent in the Middle West, 1900–1939.* Lincoln: University of Nebraska Press, 1964. Sharp, Paul F. *The Agrarian Revolt in Western Canada: A Survey Showing American Parallels.* Minneapolis: University of Minnesota Press, 1948. Shover, L. John. *Cornbelt Rebellion: The Farmers' Holiday Association.* Urbana: University of Illinois Press, 1965. Wilson, L. J. "Educational Role of the United Farm Women of Alberta." *Alberta History* 25 (1977): 28–36.

ABERHART, WILLIAM (1878–1943)

William "Bible Bill" Aberhart was a dominating figure in Alberta political, religious, and educational life during the first half of the twentieth century. Born in Perth County, Ontario, on December 30, 1878, Aberhart moved to Calgary in 1910. While serving as a respected high school principal for the next twenty-five years, he became increasingly involved in Baptist lay preaching, founded the fundamentalist Calgary Prophetic Bible Institute in 1927, and successfully established himself as a pioneer radio evangelist.

By the early 1930s the plight of many Albertans, ravaged by drought and economic depression, was desperate. Aberhart's preaching began to incorporate a personalized version of the "social credit" doctrines of the British economic thinker Maj. C. H. Douglas, and Prophetic Bible Institute study groups became the nucleus of a provincewide Social Credit crusade. After attempting unsuccessfully to convince the United Farmers of Alberta government to adopt social credit policies, he moved in 1934 to transform Social Credit into a full-blown political party.

Aberhart's brand of "social credit" resonated with the traditional Alberta mix of "radical" economic panaceas, grassroots democracy, and Christianity. Political opponents dismissed his program of twenty-five-dollar monthly dividends and attacks on the financial establishment's "Fifty Bigshots" as "funny money" nonsense, and they branded Aberhart himself as a dangerous charlatan. Yet attempts to discredit Aberhart and his message mattered little to growing numbers of small businessmen, urban workers, and farmers; it was enough that he promised action and offered hope.

Aberhart's Social Credit swept into power in 1935 with 54 percent of the popular vote and fifty-six of sixty-three legislative seats. By merely advocating the control, not the elimination, of capitalism, Aberhart's version of "social credit" had appealed to those who rejected the capitalist status quo but feared embracing the socialist Cooperative Commonwealth Federation.

When "dividends" to increase the purchasing power of the poor failed to materialize, Premier Aberhart claimed Albertans had only voted for "good government." Nevertheless, a caucus insurgency fueled by grassroots discontent finally compelled passage of "social credit" financial and economic legislation in 1937–38, only to have it promptly ruled unconstitutional. Thereafter, disillusioned with Aberhart's authoritarian leadership style and his government's failure to act aggressively enough on social and economic reforms, many radical Social Creditors abandoned the party. Press-gag legislation designed to muzzle political criticism further alienated the establishment and frightened intellectuals across the country. Fortunately for Aberhart, a less dramatic agenda of health and education reforms, as well as legislative measures favorable to small business and consumers, enabled Social Credit to stave off stiff challenges from the right and the left in 1940.

World War II revived Alberta's economy and made governing easier, and major oil discoveries immediately following the war altered the province's economy and society almost beyond recognition. The political legacy of William Aberhart, who died suddenly in Vancouver on May 23, 1943, remains controversial. Few disagree, however, that the right-wing path along which he intended to lead the party, and which his protégé and successor, Ernest Manning, would take it during his long tenure as Social Credit premier, was clear after 1940.

Patrick H. Brennan
University of Calgary

Elliott, David, and Iris Miller. *Bible Bill: A Biography of William Aberhart.* Edmonton: Reidmore Books, 1987. Finkel, Alvin. *The Social Credit Phenomenon in Alberta.* Toronto: University of Toronto Press, 1989. Irving, John. *The Social Credit Movement in Alberta.* Toronto: University of Toronto Press, 1959.

AMAZON ARMY

One repercussion of the "Red Scare" following World War I was the attempt by business to reverse the gains made by labor during the war. There followed a series of strikes throughout the nation. In southeast Kansas the coal miners of the United Mine Workers (UMW), led by Alexander Howat, defied both President Woodrow Wilson and the president of the UMW, John L. Lewis, in a series of strikes. When Kansas passed the Court of Industrial Relations law to do away with strikes, Howat called a strike to test the law. His imprisonment resulted in the "Amazon Army."

On December 11, 1921, a mass meeting of women in Franklin, Kansas, prompted 2,000 to 6,000 wives, daughters, mothers, sisters, and sweethearts of striking miners to march in the Kansas coalfields over the next several days. The marchers included Annie Stovich, Mary Skubitz, and her mother Julia Youvain. Mrs. Ted Farrell, Mrs. Felix Azamber, Mrs. William Howe, Mrs. J. R. Supple, Mrs. James Marioth, Mrs. Paul Johnson, and Mrs. Julia Chiararini signed the resolutions at Franklin. The women's march sparked interest across the state and nation. Although controversy exists over whether any violence occurred during the march (red pepper being the "weapon" of choice), the state sent in the militia, including cavalry and some machine-gun units, and some arrests were made. The women's march caused a stir but did not stop coal production, and the strike ended on January 13, 1922.

Thomas R. Walther
Pittsburg State University

Schofield, Ann. "The Women's March: Miners, Family and Community in Pittsburg, Kansas, 1921–1922." *Kansas History: A Journal of the Central Plains* 7 (1984): 159–68.

AMERICAN AGRICULTURE MOVEMENT

The American Agriculture Movement (AAM) originated among Great Plains farm men and women who, in 1977, protested government farm policy, specifically the 1973 and 1977 farm bills, that encouraged increased, large-scale production without corresponding high supports. An unstructured farmers' organization, AAM boldly dramatized the grievances of family farmers: a depressed farm economy, low prices, high operating costs, a disinterested government, and ineffective farm groups. Central to its goals then and now was the call for 100 percent of parity for all domestic and foreign consumer agriculture products. Achieving higher commodity prices has eluded AAM, as has the ability to sustain momentum, which diminished with the loss of media publicity in the early 1980s. Redirecting its strategy away from the early, naively conceived demonstrations toward more effective political lobbying, however, has enabled AAM to maintain a voice in agricultural policymaking.

At the outset of AAM activism, farm men and women were caught in an ever-tightening economic vise of surging fixed costs and rising interest rates. Farming had become increasingly complex, industrialized, efficient, international, and productive throughout the century. The resulting chronic overproduction, low prices, and greater need for capital had altered the nature of farm economics as well, making family farming a vanishing prospect. AAM's demand for parity referred to an economic relationship in which strong agricultural prices boosted farmers' purchasing power to at least equal that of other sectors of the economy. Parity has been the baseline for formulating federal agricultural policy since the 1920s, when agricultural prosperity was measured against the prosperous years of 1909 to 1914, otherwise known as the "golden age of agriculture." After both world wars and until the early 1970s, the agricultural economy was relatively stable, with steady interest rates and prices near 100 percent of parity, aided by government price supports and production controls (incidentally designed to eliminate smaller farms).

Domestic and international developments beginning in the 1960s, however, presaged the agricultural downturn of the 1970s against which AAM would protest. The Agricultural Act of 1965 reduced the strength of American commodity prices on international markets. International crop failures, especially in the Soviet Union, initially enhanced demand for American grain; exports more than doubled between 1968 and 1973, prices jumped, and the government urged farmers to plant and fertilize more. Yet conflicts in the Middle East led to escalating petroleum prices and sharp increases in gasoline, farm machinery, and petroleum-based fertilizers. What looked to be an improving agricultural economy in 1973 was in dissipation in 1976, when international grain production levels recovered and American farm prices tumbled. Additionally, the Agricultural Act of 1977 established a floor on commodity prices that was well under the average for 1973 to 1975. Farmers who signed government contracts would receive a combination of loans and direct payments toward a government-determined "target price" that was notably less than the government's cost of production figures.

Drastically deteriorating agricultural conditions provoked voices of dissent, and strike talk among a small group of Springfield, Colorado, large-scale wheat farmers and farm-related businessmen in September 1977 resonated widely. Within weeks, 600 farm men and women gathered in Springfield supporting the call for a national farm strike by all food and fiber producers. Organizers set the strike date as December 14, at which time producers would cut production levels by 50 percent if legislators failed to address the deficiencies of the two recent farm bills and guarantee 100 percent of parity. The group, initially calling itself the American Agricultural Strike, overestimated both the importance of the family farm to the national economy and the farmers' commitment to the strike. Nevertheless, the movement effectively used the media, rallies, "tractorcades," and pamphlets to attract attention and expand. In October 5,000 farm men and women demonstrated in Amarillo, Texas, and by year's end, the group, now calling itself the American Agriculture Movement, claimed 1,100 local offices in forty states.

Ultimately, AAM's farm strike and political activism floundered. When asked later, the vast majority of AAM leaders conceded they had not adhered to the strike's call to reduce production. While publicity generated interest in AAM's cause, such as coverage of the January 18, 1978, assemblage of some 3,000 farm men and women in Washington DC, it was also used against them by opponents. A second gathering of farmers in Washington on February 5, 1979, damaged credibility when

AAM tractors ensnarled traffic and, according to an unsympathetic Senate, caused $3.6 million in damages to federal property. Despite AAM's assistance to the local community during a blizzard, the negative publicity resulted in a significant loss of support.

Politically, AAM's loose structure and alienation from major farm groups confused legislators. Similar to the American Farm Bureau Federation, AAM relied upon local groups of farmers for its organization, instead of on structured leadership. While in Washington, AAM developed state delegations whereby representatives from each met nightly as the "delegate body" and by day badgered congressional staff with demands for 100 percent of parity, import tariffs, and minimum prices for exports. AAM proposals were opposed by the Carter administration, the Farm Bureau, and other lobbying groups who predicted runaway inflation and higher consumer food costs. Despite winning a moratorium on foreclosures by the Farmers Home Administration and an 11 percent increase in price supports, AAM believed it had been sold out. Consequently, it pursued a more disruptive strategy when it returned to Washington in February 1979.

By June, between 60 and 90 percent of AAM offices had closed, but, unwilling to give up, the group incorporated in August as AAM Inc. with Texas cotton farmer Marvin Meek as chair. Under Meek, AAM Inc. lobbied for higher commodity prices and the manufacture of gasohol, but the government remained unresponsive to the fact that farm prices fell each month during 1981. In 1982 AAM Inc. supporters began pressuring state legislatures for assistance. At this point several factions splintered off and became Grassroots AAM, but AAM Inc. remained the larger and more visible group. AAM Inc. formed a political action committee and pooled the largest resources of any farm group in the 1982 elections. It is currently part of the National Farm Coalition, an organization dedicated to promoting a unified farm program. Today, AAM Inc. also lobbies for rural issues.

See also AGRICULTURE: Agricultural Price Supports.

Ginette Aley
Iowa State University

Browne, William P., and John Dinse. "The Emergence of the American Agriculture Movement, 1977–1979." *Great Plains Quarterly* 5 (1985): 221–35. Dyson, Lowell K. "American Agricultural Movement." In *Farmers' Organizations.* New York: Greenwood Press, 1986: 8–14. Hurt, R. Douglas. *American Agriculture: A Brief History.* Ames: Iowa State University Press, 1994.

AMERICAN INDIAN MOVEMENT

Eddie Benton Banai and Clyde Bellecourt, two Ojibwa prisoners at Minnesota's Stillwater Prison, began organizing fellow Native American inmates in 1963, preaching a doctrine of Indian pride and self-reliance. After receiving parole the following year, Bellecourt took his message to Minneapolis. By 1968 he and Banai had teamed up with two more Ojibwas, George Mitchell and Dennis Banks. They named their

American Indian Movement, Wounded Knee, South Dakota, March 2, 1973

group Concerned Indian Americans. Unhappy with that acronym, they settled upon the American Indian Movement (AIM).

AIM monitored police actions to prevent and report brutality, fought discrimination in jobs and housing, and set up survival schools to equip Indian children with life skills for the urban environment and provide them alternative views of Native history unavailable in public schools. Its approach was also pan-Indian; since the Indian ghettos of American cities contained people from different reservations and tribes, AIM did not represent any single one of them. Instead, they focused on local issues that affected all Indians.

At first, the organization solicited government funds and donations from religious groups. But by 1968 frustration from dealing with these organizations led AIM to adopt a stance that was antagonistic toward mainstream America. They also began to extend their efforts beyond Minnesota. In 1970 an AIM chapter was founded in Cleveland by Russell Means, a Lakota who was born on the Pine Ridge Reservation in South Dakota. Major chapters were subsequently added in Milwaukee, Denver, Chicago, and San Francisco. Throughout its existence, AIM's power structure was largely decentralized, with individual chapters retaining substantial authority and frequently concentrating on local issues. In addition, its national leaders, including Banks, Means, Bellecourt, and Santee Dakota John

Trudell, generally led by force of personality and with support from their followers and colleagues.

AIM went beyond urban concerns and made inroads on the Pine Ridge Reservation when it organized protests in nearby Gordon, Nebraska, in early 1972. A Lakota from the reservation, Raymond Yellow Thunder, had been abducted, publicly humiliated, and beaten to death in the town by white racists. When they were charged with involuntary manslaughter instead of murder, many Pine Ridge Lakotas were outraged. AIM marched on the town and forced concessions from local authorities and the governor, thus cementing its presence and reputation on the reservation.

Later that year, AIM moved onto the national stage through its involvement in the Trail of Broken Treaties, a large-scale civil rights march in Washington DC the week before the presidential election of 1972. When the marchers arrived, inadequate sleeping accommodations and federal red tape led to an altercation with police at the Bureau of Indian Affairs (BIA) building, which quickly turned into a riot. The marchers occupied the building. During the standoff, AIM took control of the occupation and dealt with the media and federal negotiators. The occupation ended after less than a week when the government paid AIM more than $66,000 to transport people back home.

After the BIA building incident, AIM was condemned by Pine Ridge tribal chairman Dick Wilson, who himself was embroiled in a major political dispute; many people on the reservation accused him of corruption and intimidation. As conditions became increasingly violent, AIM came to the support of Wilson's opponents. After Means announced he would run against Wilson in the next election, Wilson had him temporarily jailed.

Tensions increased when the federal government stationed FBI agents and U.S. marshals on the reservation in the midst of Wilson's impeachment trial. After Wilson was acquitted amid confusing circumstances, his opponents decided to make a stand by seizing Wounded Knee, the site of the 1890 massacre of as many as 300 Lakotas by the U.S. Seventh Cavalry. AIM readily supported them. They jointly occupied the hamlet of Wounded Knee on February 27, 1973, and were immediately surrounded by marshals, FBI agents, BIA police, and Wilson's private army, known as the "goon squad."

During the ensuing siege, AIM again took control of the situation, dealing with the national media and negotiating with the federal representatives. After seventy-one days, endless negotiations, the shooting death of two AIM supporters, and the paralysis of one marshal, the siege ended on May 8. It signaled the beginning of the end of AIM.

From then on, AIM endured a two-pronged attack from the federal government. First, a long series of trials against AIM's leaders was designed to bankrupt the organization through costly legal fees and keeping its leaders tied up in court. Meanwhile, the FBI used counter-intelligence programs, later deemed illegal, to infiltrate and disrupt the organization. Government repression reached its zenith with the conviction of prominent AIM member Leonard Peltier in the 1975 shooting deaths of two FBI agents on the Pine Ridge Reservation. During the trial, the government intimidated witnesses, manufactured evidence, and committed numerous other infractions. Nonetheless, Peltier was sentenced to two consecutive life terms in 1977. Efforts to win his freedom have since gained international attention, and Amnesty International currently recognizes him as one of the most important political prisoners in the world.

Meanwhile, a virtual civil war between AIM and the "goons" plagued Pine Ridge during Wilson's post–Wounded Knee tenure (1973–76), resulting in more than fifty unsolved murders of AIM members and supporters. In 1979 the mother-in-law, wife, and three children of AIM's national chairman, John Trudell, were killed in an arsonist's fire. The cause of the fire, which was started while Trudell was protesting the Peltier verdict, remains unsolved.

Bankruptcy, paranoia, and repression, combined with AIM's decentralized structure and leadership patterns, led to a spiraling decline within the organization. Individual leaders increasingly worked on their own projects, political and otherwise, and by the 1980s AIM was defunct as a national entity. The FBI closed its active files on AIM in July 1979. Today, a scattering of local chapters continues to work on local issues, and individual members of national prominence continue to invoke the movement's name on behalf of their own programs.

See also MUSIC: Trudell, John / WAR: Wounded Knee Massacre.

Akim D. Reinhardt
Towson University

Churchill, Ward, and Jim Vander Wall. *Agents of Repression: The FBI's Secret War against the Black Panther Party and the American Indian Movement.* Boston: South End Press, 1988. Smith, Paul Chaat, and Robert Allen Warrior. *Like a Hurricane.* New York: New Press, 1996.

AMERINGER, OSCAR (1870–1943)

Oscar Ameringer, a principal leader of the socialist movement on the Southern Plains, was born in Achstetten, Germany, on August 4, 1870, the son of a cabinetmaker. Evading military service, he emigrated to the United States in 1886 and earned his living as a furniture worker, salesman, painter, and musician. He joined the Socialist Party shortly after it was formed in 1901 and became editor of the *Labor World*, financed by the Brewery Workers Union. He reported on the general strike that tied up the port of New Orleans in 1907. The dockworkers' success there in forging a long-term biracial alliance reinforced Ameringer's commitment to both racial equality and industrial unionism.

After the strike's collapse, Ameringer moved to Oklahoma, where he quickly assumed a leading role in the Socialist Party. Although lacking a sizable industrial working class, Oklahoma boasted the nation's largest Socialist Party, polling close to a third of the statewide vote. On his first speaking tour in 1907, traveling by covered wagon and on horseback, Ameringer realized that Oklahoma's farmers, primarily impoverished tenants, constituted the party's major potential base of support. Ameringer stayed in dirt-floored tenant shacks and homes dug out of hillsides and saw human suffering at its most intense. The Oklahoma farmers' socialist commitment deeply impressed him. He praised their determination by recalling that the man who presided at his first speech had arrived soaked to the skin, having swum across a river in his only suit because the bridge had been washed out.

Ameringer was one of the most popular speakers at the weeklong socialist encampments, frequently held in Oklahoma from 1908 until the U.S. entry into World War I. Farm people numbering in the thousands traveled vast distances, often in covered wagons bearing red flags, to hear Ameringer and other socialist orators. In 1911 Ameringer polled 23 percent of the vote in a three-way race for mayor of Oklahoma City.

In 1910 Ameringer led the fight against Oklahoma's adoption of the so-called grandfather clause, which was introduced by the Democrats to eliminate black suffrage. His effort was opposed by a faction in the Oklahoma Socialist Party based in the Little Dixie section of the state, which resented Ameringer as an outsider and feared losing white supporters. In 1913 this faction assumed control of the Socialist Party in Oklahoma, and Ameringer moved to Milwaukee.

Although opposed to U.S. intervention in World War I, Ameringer advised Oklahoma farmers against launching the Green Corn Rebellion, an abortive uprising to force the government to end the war. The repression it precipitated, along with a decline in farm tenancy, caused the swift collapse of the Oklahoma Socialist Party.

Returning to Oklahoma City after the war, Ameringer published a radical newspaper, the *Oklahoma Leader*, which, as the *American Guardian* from 1931 to 1941, developed a national circulation. Ameringer waged a high-profile campaign in the *Leader* against the Ku Klux Klan, which was highly influential in Oklahoma during the early 1920s. From 1922 to 1931 Ameringer also published the *Illinois Miner* in Oklahoma City, an insurgent newspaper that challenged John L. Lewis's control of the United Mine Workers. He contributed a column under the pseudonym Adam Coaldigger. In his preface to Ameringer's 1940 autobiography, *If You Don't Weaken*, Carl Sandburg, an old socialist comrade and friend, compared him as a humorist to Mark Twain and Will Rogers. Oscar Ameringer died in Oklahoma City on November 5, 1943.

Stephen H. Norwood
University of Oklahoma

Ameringer, Oscar. *If You Don't Weaken.* Norman: University of Oklahoma Press, 1983. Green, James R. *Grass-Roots Socialism: Radical Movements in the Southwest, 1895–1943.* Baton Rouge: Louisiana State University Press, 1978. Meredith, Howard L. "A History of the Socialist Party in Oklahoma." Ph.D. diss., University of Oklahoma, 1969.

APPEAL TO REASON

First published by Julius A. Wayland at Kansas City on August 31, 1895, *Appeal to Reason* was a four-page socialist weekly. In February 1897 Wayland moved the paper to the southeast Kansas coal-mining town of Girard. There, drawing on the talents of some fine editors and numerous nationally known socialist thinkers and writers, the *Appeal* became the leading socialist publication in the United States, with a circulation of 760,000 at its peak in 1913.

Throughout its history, the *Appeal* highlighted the evils of capitalism and the promise of a socialist society. It fashioned itself the champion of a uniquely American brand of socialism and was tremendously successful because it combined this epigrammatic socialism with the right amount of muckraking, scandal, and circulation hustle. During the first decade of the twentieth century, American socialist leader Eugene Debs worked as a staff writer for *Appeal to Reason*, and the paper introduced its readers to Upton Sinclair's attack on poor and unsanitary working conditions in the meatpacking industry. A serialized version of Sinclair's *The Jungle* first appeared in Wayland's weekly, beginning on February 25, 1905.

Upon the death of J. A. Wayland by suicide in November 1912, Fred D. Warren, who had been working as editor for some years, continued publishing the *Appeal*. He was succeeded by Walter H. Wayland, son of the founder, Louis Kopelin, and then Emmanuel Haldeman-Julius. *Appeal to Reason* and its editors came under frequent attack by federal authorities during the years leading up to World War I. Some detractors labeled it the "Squeal for Treason," while Theodore Roosevelt branded it a "vituperative organ of propaganda, anarchy and bloodshed." Nevertheless, to the chagrin of many socialists, *Appeal to Reason* supported President Woodrow Wilson and the crusade to "make the world safe for democracy." It continued its advocacy of socialism and the international movement but changed its name to the *New Appeal*.

Soon after the war ended, the paper reverted back to its old title. It had, however, lost much of its zeal and readership and wilted under the anti-Red reaction of the early twenties. *Appeal to Reason* was discontinued in 1922, but its last editor, Haldeman-Julius, continued the paper's long-standing effort to educate the masses through his immensely popular Little Blue Book series, which brought quality literature to the public in inexpensive pocket books.

Virgil W. Dean
Kansas State Historical Society

Appeal to Reason, Kansas City MO, Kansas City KS, and Girard KS, 1895–1922, Library and Archives Division, Kansas State Historical Society, Topeka KS. Shore, Elliott. *Talkin' Socialism: J. A. Wayland and the Role of the Press in American Radicalism, 1890–1912*. Lawrence: University Press of Kansas, 1988. Wayland, Julius Augustus. Collection. Pittsburg State University Library, Pittsburg KS.

BARNARD, KATE

See GENDER: Barnard, Kate

BLOOR, ELLA R. (1862–1951)

Ella Reeve "Mother" Bloor was a feminist and labor organizer who dedicated her life to the cause of America's industrial workers and farmers. She was born on Staten Island, New York, on July 8, 1862, and brought up in comfortable upper-middle-class circumstances. As a young woman she was drawn to the suffrage and prohibition movements, and after 1902 she devoted herself to labor issues, investigating, for example, the Chicago meatpacking industry and demonstrating for the rights of working women and their children. In 1919 she broke with the Socialist Party because many in its ranks supported World War I, and she joined the newly formed American Communist Party.

In 1929 the Communist Party sent Bloor, then sixty-seven years old, to work with farmers in North and South Dakota. For the next five years much of her focus was in the Great Plains. In 1930 Bloor married North Dakota farmer and fellow Communist Andrew Omholt, and a year later she joined the United Farmers League as an organizer in the Dakotas and Montana. The United Farmers League fought bank foreclosures and organized mass demonstrations, often with Bloor literally leading the parade. When the unrest spread into Iowa and Nebraska as the "Farmers Holiday" movement grew, Bloor continued her role as featured speaker, especially during the dramatic Milk Strike of 1932 in Sioux City, Iowa. She frequently worked alongside her oldest son and party comrade, Hal Ware. In 1934, while protesting on behalf of striking women chicken pluckers in Loup City, Nebraska, Bloor was arrested for the thirty-sixth and final time in her long career. In 1935, after multiple appeals failed, the then seventy-three-year-old woman served thirty days in an Omaha jail—an event that received much sympathetic press even in mainstream publications.

Hailed in a 1937 *Life* magazine piece as the "grand old woman of the U.S. Communist party," Bloor spent her final active years fighting fascism at home and abroad. She died in Richlandtown, Pennsylvania, on August 10, 1951.

Kathleen Banks Nutter
Smith College

Bloor, Ella Reeve. Papers. Sophia Smith Collection, Smith College, Northampton MA. Bloor, Ella Reeve. *We Are Many*. New York: International Publishers, 1940. Dyson, Lowell K. *Red Harvest: The Communist Party and American Farmers*. Lincoln: University of Nebraska Press, 1982.

BRANCH DAVIDIANS

See RELIGION: Branch Davidians

BROWDER, EARL (1891–1973)

Leader of the American Communist Party (CPUSA) during the movement's heyday, Earl Russell Browder was born into an impoverished, radicalized Wichita, Kansas, family on May 20, 1891. Forced to leave school before completing third grade, he rose eventually to become an accountant, while wandering around Kansas City leftist movements. World War I draft resistance sent him to Leavenworth Penitentiary in 1919. Upon release, he located New York Leninists and soon led a delegation to Moscow. There, he befriended Soviet labor expert Solomon Lozovsky. Between 1922 and 1926 Browder assisted domestic working-class hero William Z. Foster and supported Joseph Stalin, who was bureaucratizing the Soviet Union's revolutionary state. In 1926 Browder married Raissa Luganovskaya, a former Russian commissar of justice, who pestered Lozovsky to give Browder a career break. Covert work for the Communist International (Comintern) in China quickly followed. By 1932 Browder led the CPUSA, and soon he was championing Comintern head Georgi Dimitrov's antifascist Popular Front policy, which sought to replace revolution with reformism and advocated collective security with the Soviet Union against Germany. Rapidly the Communists became the largest political party left of the Democrats, bringing unprecedented influence.

In 1939 the Soviet Union signed a non-aggression treaty with Nazi Germany, abandoning the tactic of collective security. Browder vacillated, caught between the Soviet Union's demands and domestic radical needs. In 1941 the U.S. government sent him to Atlanta Penitentiary on an ancient passport technicality. Amid a national "Red Scare," the CPUSA hastily broke official Comintern ties. In June 1941 Germany invaded Russia, and that December the United States entered the war, making possible the Grand Alliance between the Soviet Union and the Western powers. Communists gave the conflict their total support, and President Franklin D. Roosevelt freed Browder on May 16, 1942.

Unlike his experience in Leavenworth twenty years earlier, imprisonment in Atlanta left Browder with permanent psychological damage. Wisely, in 1938 he had secured his sister's release from Soviet secret police work, citing his own high profile. Yet recklessly he maintained espionage contacts because of curiosity, a need to outpace former mentor Foster (now a rival), and to impress the Russians. In 1943 Stalin disbanded the Comintern. Browder, ever vain, assumed he now led an independent Communist movement. By 1944 he considered himself a world Marxist thinker, akin to Chou En-lai. Browder converted the CPUSA into a leftist pressure group, the Communist Political Association. He thereby abandoned the movement's Leninist vanguard role. Once Allied victory became inevitable, a message from Moscow brought the CPUSA's reconstitution and Browder's expulsion. He spent his remaining years a pariah and died on June 27, 1973, unmourned by any Communist publications.

James G. Ryan
Texas A&M University at Galveston

Browder, Earl. Papers. Syracuse University Library, Syracuse University, Syracuse NY. Ryan, James G. *Earl Browder: The Failure of American Communism*. Tuscaloosa: University of Alabama Press, 1997. Ryan, James G. "Earl

Browder and American Communism." In *American Reform and Reformers*, edited by Randall M. Miller and Paul A. Cimbala. Westport CT: Greenwood Press, 1996: 71–82.

BROWN, JOHN (1800–1859)

John Brown, an abolitionist extremist, heightened sectional tensions and fomented violence before the Civil War by leading the "Pottawatomie Massacre" in Kansas in 1856 and the raid against the federal arsenal at Harpers Ferry, Virginia, in 1859. Brown was born in West Torrington, Connecticut, on May 9, 1800, and moved with his family to Hudson, Ohio, at age five. A tanner by trade, Brown married twice and reared twenty children.

Brown inherited from his father a religious antipathy toward slavery that was reinforced by the religious ferment of the Second Great Awakening. He adopted a strict Calvinist belief in predestination, divine election, and human depravity that prompted him to consider slavery a sin, which he was chosen by God to help eradicate. During the 1830s, when abolitionists such as William Lloyd Garrison increasingly appealed to religious conscience, Brown developed an uncompromising hostility toward slavery and joined the radical abolitionist movement that demanded immediate emancipation. While living in Springfield, Ohio, Brown attacked slavery with heightening militancy, aiding runaway slaves, associating with the African American abolitionist Frederick Douglass, writing antislavery essays, and citing the Bible in defense of violent resistance. During the 1840s he developed a reputation for proposing impractical schemes for fomenting rebellion in the South, including guerrilla warfare.

When passage of the Kansas-Nebraska Act in 1854 led to armed resistance in Kansas, Brown settled near Osawatomie with five of his sons and their families. He joined the Free State guerrilla movement and commanded a company of twenty men known as the Liberty Guards. Enraged by the sack of Lawrence, a Free State stronghold, Brown led a raid on May 24, 1856, against a settlement at Pottawatomie Creek, killing five southern settlers. For the next four months, a veritable civil war raged in the territory, claiming 200 lives and earning the label "Bleeding Kansas." After a proslavery counterattack against Osawatomie in August, Brown fled Kansas.

Hailed as a hero among northern abolitionists and excoriated as a lunatic among southern defenders of slavery, Brown accepted support from a group of abolitionists dubbed the "Secret Six." He spent the next three years lecturing, raising funds, aiding runaway slaves, writing, and organizing his raid against Harpers Ferry. On October 16, 1859, Brown seized the federal arsenal at Harpers Ferry with a force of eighteen men, including five free African Americans, in hopes of igniting a widespread slave revolt. By the time federal troops recaptured the arsenal two days later, Brown's followers had killed four men and suffered ten casualties, including two of Brown's sons. Brown's impassioned self-defense as he and six followers underwent trial, conviction, and ex-

ecution made him a martyr among abolitionists and a popular antislavery crusader throughout the North. His execution, on December 2, 1859, became a political issue, inflamed sectional tensions, and inspired the Civil War hymn that began with the line "John Brown's body lies a mould'ring in the grave."

Kenneth J. Winkle
University of Nebraska–Lincoln

Oates, Stephen B. *To Purge This Land with Blood: A Biography of John Brown*. New York: Harper and Row, 1970. Rawley, James A. *Race and Politics: "Bleeding Kansas" and the Coming of the Civil War*. Philadelphia: Lippincott, 1969.

CANNON, JAMES PATRICK (1890–1974)

Ranking Communist Party (CPUSA) figure, American Trotskyist movement founder, and longtime Socialist Workers Party leader, James Cannon was born in Rosedale, Kansas, on February 11, 1890. Poverty radicalized his immigrant father, John, a laborer in a foundry. John introduced the young James to Irish nationalism, the Knights of Labor, populism, and finally the Socialist Party. James displayed a deep and lifelong anger at capitalism and the injustices it spawned. He left high school to organize for the Industrial Workers of the World. Soon he joined the Socialist Party and rose rapidly among its left wing. Cannon had taken a path that would make him an acquaintance of nearly all the era's celebrated radicals.

After Earl Browder's imprisonment during World War I, Cannon edited *Workers World*, the organ of the Socialist Party in Kansas. In 1919 the party expelled its left wing, and Cannon became prominent in the nascent Communist underground. He held important St. Louis and Cleveland posts, then transferred to New York City in 1921. There he helped head the Workers Party, a legal organization, after the "Red Scare" subsided and V. I. Lenin shifted toward nonrevolutionary tactics. Between 1922 and 1928 Cannon served on the Communist International's presidium and headed International Labor Defense, a leftist legal support group. He also backed William Z. Foster's faction of what had become the CPUSA.

Cannon's life took a dramatic turn in 1928 while he was in the Soviet Union. In Moscow, Leon Trotsky offered compelling criticism of Joseph Stalin and the Soviet Union's direction. Cannon returned to the United States carrying Trotsky's writings. That October, Cannon and 100 followers were driven from the CPUSA. They called themselves the Communist League of America (Left Opposition), began publishing a newspaper, *The Militant*, and later a magazine, *New International*. From that time on, Cannon would consider Trotsky the custodian of authentic Bolshevik values. The League helped lead a sensational Minneapolis Teamster strike, fused with A. J. Muste's followers, and in 1936 entered the Socialist Party. The Trotskyists were expelled the following year, and Cannon founded the Socialist Workers Party in 1938. By 1939 the movement had 1,000 American members and a following in labor and intellectual circles.

Success brought schism during the early months of World War II. Socialist Workers Party figures Max Shachtman and James Burnham argued that the Stalinists constituted a new bureaucratic class in the Soviet Union. Cannon, like Trotsky, considered the Soviet Union's nationalized economy worth defending, despite Stalin's dictatorship. In early 1940 Shachtman's faction became the Workers Party. In 1941 federal authorities used the Smith Act to imprison Cannon and seventeen other Socialist Workers Party figures and Minneapolis Teamsters. Supposedly their organizations had advocated the violent overthrow of the U.S. government; actually they opposed American foreign policy. Cannon served thirteen months at Sandstone Penitentiary. During the McCarthy era, a public that drew few distinctions among radicals persecuted the Socialist Workers Party and Communist Party alike.

Cannon retired in 1953 but lived to see the "New Left" of the 1960s and 1970s. He died on August 21, 1974, believing that Vietnam War resisters, African Americans, Hispanics, women, youth, and gays were taking a permanent step toward socialism in the United States.

James G. Ryan
Texas A&M University at Galveston

Cannon, James Patrick. Papers. Wisconsin State Historical Society, Madison WI. Wald, Alan. "James P. Cannon." In *Biographical Dictionary of the American Left*, edited by Bernard K. Johnpoll and Harvey Klehr. Westport CT: Greenwood Press, 1986: 62–65.

COLBY, CLARA

See GENDER: Colby, Clara

COWBOY STRIKE OF 1883

From 1880 to 1883 a new corporate ownership spread throughout the Texas Panhandle. Ranch cowboys no longer knew the owners by name, had any particular trust in the new company, or saw any signs of loyalty or tradition. The cowboy lost his place as a valued member of the ranch family and became only an employee.

The country was in transition. Large urban populations needed to be fed. Cattle were cheap, grass free, and the railroads made transportation possible. But the corporations and cattle syndicates who bought their way into the Plains didn't figure on the cost of freezing winters and stifling drought. General ignorance of livestock became their biggest liability, and the only controllable cost they could find was the cowboy.

Even before the new owners came, a cowboy's job was never easy. Aside from working roundups twice a year, they rode the fence line, branded cattle, and doctored sick animals. They slept in a dank dugout, or perhaps a tent, if anything. Everything they ate came out of one pot. But a ranch hand could take part of his pay in calves, or if he was lucky, he could round up enough maverick cows to begin his own small herd. He was furnished several horses to do his work, and the longer he worked for the ranch, the better the horses he was given.

The new owners decided to claim the orphaned, unbranded cattle as their own, and they put strict limits on the use of ranch horses. No one got more than two horses, and they were to be left in the corral when the day was done. Perhaps even worse, the corporate ranches decided that their men could not carry any weapons, play cards or gamble in any other way, nor could they take a drink of alcohol while in the employment of the ranch.

In the spring of 1883 the cowboys went on strike. Wagons and men from three of the biggest ranches in the Canadian River valley came together for a meeting. The three wagon bosses were not malcontents. They were all respected top hands who had earned their positions only to see their influence diminished. They took a bold step, writing the following proclamation:

We, the undersigned cowboys of Canadian river, do by these presents agree to bind ourselves into the following obligations: First, that we will not work for less than $50 per month, and we furthermore agree no one shall work for less than $50 per month, after 31st of March.

Second, good cooks shall also receive $50 per month.

Third, anyone running an outfit shall not work for less than $75 per month. Anyone violating the above obligations shall suffer the consequences. Those not having funds to pay board after March 31st will be provided for 30 days at Tascosa.

Twenty-four men signed the proclamations. Five copies were made, and each one was delivered to a large ranch.

It was a foolish move. Many of the better cowboys already made more money than the petition called for, and the cowboys reluctantly admitted that some among their ranks were not worth the prescribed $50 a month. Also, there was no shortage of labor in the Panhandle. The cattle business in the lower part of the state was in disarray, and South Texas cowboys were willing to make the long ride for a solid job. As the "scab" crews were put together, the strikers were ordered off the ranches and told that they would never work again on the Texas Plains. In thirty days, the strike was over and the cowboys had lost. Many of them left the Panhandle; those who stayed took jobs in town.

Art Chapman
Fort Worth, Texas

DENVER'S ANTI-CHINESE RIOT

See ASIAN AMERICANS: Denver's Anti-Chinese Riot

DOCTORS' STRIKE

In 1944 the first social democratic government in North America was elected in the province of Saskatchewan. The new government of Premier Tommy Douglas intended to introduce plans to insure both medical and hospital services immediately following the election; however, because of financial limitations, it decided instead to establish a provincewide system of hospital insurance. The Saskatchewan Hospital Insurance Plan, established in 1947 and funded mainly from provincial tax revenue, provided free inpatient hospital care for all residents of the province.

In 1957 the federal government introduced its Canada-wide universal hospital insurance plan, based on the Saskatchewan model. The financial restrictions on the Saskatchewan government, which had delayed the implementation of Medical Care Insurance, were then significantly reduced as money was injected by the federal government into the Saskatchewan government's hospital insurance plan. The Saskatchewan government was, by the end of the 1950s, in a good financial position and, with this federal support, able to turn its attention to developing a Medical Care Insurance plan.

While most doctors in Saskatchewan were in favor of the Hospital Insurance Plan, they were strongly opposed to a Medical Care Insurance plan because they felt it was an infringement on the financial and professional relationship between themselves and their patients. The plan did not place doctors on salary but did control the fees they could charge for consultations and surgeries, which doctors felt would limit their ability to earn income in the future. The Saskatchewan doctors' resistance to the plan, although couched in the language of concern for the plan's impact on patients' well-being, was largely predicated on its impact on physicians' incomes.

Accordingly, on July 1, 1962, the date the Medical Care Insurance Plan was to go into effect, more than 90 percent of the province's doctors withdrew their services. This strike, although relatively short—it only lasted twenty-three days—was very bitter. The government used the threat of bringing doctors in from the British National Health Service as strikebreakers. At the same time, they asked a physician-mediator and peer of the British realm, Lord Taylor, to help settle the dispute. After tireless negotiations, begun on July 16, Taylor brought the two sides together, and the strike was settled on July 23.

Like the pioneering Saskatchewan Hospital Insurance Plan, the Saskatchewan government's Medical Service Plan of 1962 was the first universal, publicly funded insurance scheme to pay for doctors' services in North America. And again, as in the case of the Hospital Insurance Plan, this plan for insuring physicians' services was the model the federal government turned to when it introduced nationwide medical care insurance in 1967.

The 1962 Doctors' Strike was an important point in Canadian medical history. If the doctors had won the strike, it is not clear whether the universal, nationwide, publicly funded system of medicare, as it exists in Canada today, would have been established.

See also POLITICS AND GOVERNMENT: Douglas, Tommy.

Aleck Ostry
University of British Columbia

Badgley, Robin F., and Samuel Wolfe. *Doctors' Strike: Medical Care and Conflict in Saskatchewan.* Toronto: Macmillan Publishing Company, 1967. Ostry, Aleck. "Prelude to Medicare: Institutional Change and Continuity in Saskatchewan, 1944–1962." *Prairie Forum* 20 (1995) 87–105. Tollefson, Edwin A. *Bitter Medicine: The Saskatchewan Medicare Feud.* Saskatoon: Modern Press, 1964.

ESTEVAN STRIKE

On September 29, 1931, almost 400 striking coal miners clashed with local police and the Royal Canadian Mounted Police (RCMP) in the streets of Estevan, Saskatchewan. The battle lasted less than an hour but left three men dead and twenty-three seriously injured. It was Canada's worst day of labor-related violence since "Bloody Saturday" in Winnipeg (June 21, 1919), and before long Estevan's day of infamy became known simply as "Black Tuesday."

Miners in the Estevan-Bienfait region had long complained about their seasonal employment, low wages, and atrocious working and living conditions. However, they lacked a vehicle to voice such grievances until the summer of 1931, when they formed a branch of the Mine Workers Union of Canada (MUWC). By September they had managed to organize virtually the entire workforce.

Coal operators refused to deal with the new union, complaining that it was connected to the procommunist Workers Unity League. In response, the MUWC held a strike vote and on September 8 brought the coalfields to a standstill. Over the next two weeks, the RCMP and private police were brought into the area to maintain order and protect property while employers unsuccessfully attempted to reopen the mines using nonunion men.

Hoping to mobilize public support, striking miners proposed to parade through the streets of Estevan. Although advised by town officials that this would not be permitted, the strikers proceeded as planned, and on September 29, accompanied by their wives and children, they descended upon the town in a convoy of cars and trucks. An early scuffle with the police resulted in the fatal shooting of one miner, which in turn sparked the riot. Subsequent criminal trials and a Royal Commission attempted to allocate responsibility for the breakdown in civil order, but given conditions within the industry, "Black Tuesday" is probably best understood as a tragic accident that had long been waiting to happen.

David Bright
University of Calgary

FARMERS ALLIANCE

Widespread economic distress among farmers in the South and Great Plains in the 1870s and 1880s, resulting from such problems as overproduction, declining commodity prices, inadequate credit, and transportation costs, launched the Farmers Alliance, one of the most influential agrarian protest movements in the United States. At one point three distinct organizations carried the name. The appeal of one National Farmers Alliance, the "northern" sibling organized in Chicago in 1880 and led by farm journalist Milton George, was largely limited to the Midwest. It was soon overshadowed by the far larger and more important National Farmers Alliance that originated in 1877 on the Texas frontier in Lampasas County. Despite its much greater size and geographical reach into the Great Plains, especially Kansas, Colorado, and the Dakotas, as well as to California and the South, it is commonly labeled the "southern" Alliance. The third division, which complemented the latter's evangelical drive to enlist all southern farmers, was the Colored Farmers National Alliance, also founded in Texas, in 1886.

When Charles William Macune, a country doctor, assumed the leadership of the Texas Farmers Alliance in 1886, he offered an ambitious program of economic cooperation and expansion into a new, nonpartisan national organization. Within five years, the "southern" National Farmers Alliance became the largest citizen organization of nineteenth-century America. When neither the Democratic nor Republican Party proved responsive to its demands for agrarian reform, the Alliance became the leading institutional vehicle for the organization of the Populist Party in 1891–92, effectively ending the Alliance's growth and influence by the late 1890s.

Charles W. Macune Jr.
California State University, Northridge

Macune, Charles W., Jr. "The Wellsprings of a Populist: Dr. C. W. Macune before 1886." *Southwestern Historical Quarterly* 90 (1986): 139–58. McMath, Robert C., Jr. *Populist Vanguard: A History of the Southern Farmers' Alliance.* New York: W. W. Norton, 1977.

FARMERS HOLIDAY ASSOCIATION

The Farmers Holiday Association, active from 1932 to 1937, served as the nominal organization behind a protest movement by mostly midwestern and Great Plains farmers in reaction to more than ten years of depressed farm income. During World War I farmers met increased worldwide demand for food by increasing their farm sizes and mechanizing their operations. Both strategies proved to be problematic following the post–World War I crash of the farm economy that occurred when foreign markets contracted and wartime price controls ended. After a decade of neglect by the major political parties, many farmers looked to protest movements and third parties as the Great Depression compounded their economic difficulties.

The Farmers Holiday Association grew out of the National Farmers Union, an organization that lobbied for farm aid and tariff reform, as well as operating purchasing and sales cooperatives. The name referred to the famous "Bank Holiday," farmers noting that if bankers could take a holiday to reorder their business, they should be allowed to do the same. The National Farmers Union and the Farmers Holiday Association remained closely linked, in part because the primary leader of the Farmers Holiday Association, Milo Reno, had also been the head of the Iowa Farmers Union. Milo

Reno remained central to the organization well past its peak in 1933, and the Iowa chapter was the strongest and most active branch of the organization. Although the organization was national, it received greatest support in the Upper Midwest and Northern Great Plains: Iowa, Nebraska, Minnesota, Wisconsin, South Dakota, and North Dakota drew the largest number of followers. Each state chapter acted independently. In Nebraska, the Communist Party attempted to gain some degree of control, but despite considerable activity and media exposure, it had only limited influence.

Most members owned property or had recently become tenants. Association members never constituted a majority of farmers in any region, which weakened their position and virtually guaranteed conflict with their neighbors. The core concept of the movement, cost of production, centered on the belief that farmers must make a profit on their commodities. In an era when many commodities sold for less than they cost to produce, this idea had obvious appeal. Under the system proposed by the Farmers Holiday Association, farmers would be allowed to grow all they wanted, and the federal government would mandate a price high enough to cover the costs of mortgage, seed, equipment, and labor plus guarantee a profit on commodities intended for the domestic market. The government would then sell the surplus on world markets at true market value. Similar ideas, embodied in the McNary-Haugen Bill, failed to win enough support to override President Calvin Coolidge's vetoes in the 1920s. Other positions advocated by the organization included tariff reform and currency inflation.

The mechanism for change would be the farm strike, or "holiday." The original plan, as conceived by Reno and advocated by him as early as 1921, would call for farmers to cease selling their products or buying anything from anyone. What gave the movement power and importance was the unplanned radical behavior of its members, who, acting without instructions from official leadership, barricaded roads and forced nonstriking farmers to turn away from their markets. Strikers, barricade runners, and law enforcement officers all committed acts of violence. There were a few deaths.

Of almost equal importance to the barricades were efforts to stop farm foreclosure sales by transforming them into "penny" or "Sears and Roebuck" sales. Farmers refused to bid more than pennies on the dollar for foreclosed property, even threatening those who attempted to enter higher bids. Following the sale the property would be returned to the original owner. In many cases striking farmers found active sympathy from state and local politicians and from local law enforcement agencies.

The largest strike lasted from early August to early September 1932 but was successful only in Sioux City and Omaha. Nationally, the planned uprising of farmers failed to materialize. Other strikes failed to achieve their stated goals, but they did pressure the authorities to

take action to relieve the crisis. Among the most important results were agreements by major lenders to temporarily halt farm foreclosures and legislation enacting statewide moratoriums on foreclosures in Nebraska, South Dakota, and Minnesota.

The power of the Farmers Holiday Association declined with the election of Franklin D. Roosevelt to the presidency in 1932. Milo Reno urged a temporary halt to action in the belief that Roosevelt supported cost of production. But Roosevelt's secretary of agriculture, Henry Wallace, was opposed, favoring instead control of production coupled with payments for acres taken out of service, and these measures were embodied in the Agricultural Adjustment Act. Although Farmers Holiday Association leaders threatened continued strikes, the organization lost its ability to influence farmers, now mollified by the receipt of government checks. In its latter years, the organization and its leader, Milo Reno, flirted with supporters of radical action, including Huey Long, Father Charles Coughlin, and Francis Townsend, but the movement never again achieved its earlier levels of success. While the strikes were failures, the organization and its members did bring the desperate plight of the Midwest and Plains farm community to the attention of the nation, which resulted in New Deal farm relief legislation.

See also POLITICS AND GOVERNMENT: New Deal.

Charles Vollan
University of Nebraska–Lincoln

Dyson, Lowell K. *Red Harvest: The Communist Party and American Farmers.* Lincoln: University of Nebraska Press, 1982. Shover, John. *Cornbelt Rebellion: The Farmers' Holiday Association.* Urbana: University of Illinois Press, 1965. White, Roland, ed. *Milo Reno: Farmers' Union Pioneer.* Iowa City IA: Athens Press, 1941.

FINLEY, IRA (1886–1981)

Oklahoma socialist and labor leader Ira Monroe Finley twice served in the state legislature and began one of the first organizations for the rights of the unemployed, the Veterans of Industry of America, during the Great Depression.

Born in Missouri on December 7, 1886, to Irish immigrant parents, Finley grew up in rural Arkansas and Texas. His father had been a successful farmer in Missouri, but the farm in Texas failed. After his father's death, Finley restored the family's fortunes, only to be ruined by the Panic of 1907.

The twenty-year-old Finley then moved to Oklahoma, where he engaged in sharecropping and construction work on the Missouri, Kansas, and Texas Railroad. After being laid off the railroad job, Finley became a socialist and soon involved himself in both the Oklahoma Socialist Party and the Oklahoma State Federation of Labor (OSFL). By 1917 he began organizing Oklahoma locals of the United Brotherhood of Railroad Maintenance of the Way Employees. Finley proved so effective that he received an offer from the union's national headquarters to serve as a full-time organizer.

Elected to the state legislature in 1922 as a Democrat and part of the Farmer-Labor Reconstruction League (FLRL) campaign, Finley grew disenchanted with the FLRL's newly elected governor, John C. Walton, and voted to impeach him in November 1923. This was an act of courage on Finley's part, as the OSFL, which elected Finley president in June 1923, had originally organized the FLRL and was dominated by ardent Walton supporters. His actions cost Finley the OSFL's top post in 1925.

He moved to Oklahoma City in the late 1920s and became prosperous in the road machinery sales and real estate businesses. But Finley's interest in politics and public service never died, and in 1930 he won the state House seat for Oklahoma City's Capital Hill district. William H. "Alfalfa Bill" Murray, elected governor in 1930, soon asked Finley to serve as director of Oklahoma's relief efforts. Finley modestly declined, suggesting instead that Murray select Dr. Charles Evans, former president of Oklahoma Normal School (now the University of Central Oklahoma). Murray agreed, on condition Evans seek Finley's advice and Finley direct relief efforts in Oklahoma County. Finley accepted.

During his tenure, Finley came to believe that a "Share the Work" program to redistribute wealth, enforced by state or federal law, was the only effective means to deal with the Depression. Finley shared this idea with other county relief directors, and the men established the Veterans of Industry of America (VIA) on September 28, 1932.

Finley personally rented the new organization's offices and paid for them out of his own pocket. VIA's first efforts involved lobbying for a state law that would tax businesses that made their employees work more than thirty hours a week. Finley also worked to set up local chapters throughout Oklahoma. By October 1933 VIA claimed 40,000 members, mostly unemployed workers and displaced farmers, but also casual workers and even some small businessmen. Separate locals for blacks existed in eastern Oklahoma. All the members carried blue membership cards inscribed with the VIA slogan written by Finley: "Poverty must be wiped out. No nation can call itself Christian or civilized that permits babes, little children and the aged to suffer for food, clothes and shelter."

VIA became an effective pressure group for the unemployed in Oklahoma. It proved especially effective along the Arkansas border, where small farmers and tenants joined VIA boycotts of "slave wage" agricultural employers. VIA members also joined picket lines to help striking union members and worked to discourage the unemployed from becoming strikebreakers.

The Veterans of Industry of America declined during World War II as defense industries created new jobs and reduced the number of unemployed. Finley, however, continued his involvement with Oklahoma labor and Democratic Party affairs until his death on May 4, 1981.

Nigel Anthony Sellars
Christopher Newport University

Green, James R. *Grass-Roots Socialism: Radical Movements in the Southwest, 1895–1943*. Baton Rouge: Louisiana State University Press, 1978. McGinnis, Patrick E. *Oklahoma's Depression Radicals: Ira M. Finley and the Veterans of Industry of America*. New York: Peter Lang Publishing, 1991.

FREEMEN

The Freemen, a lineal descendent of the Posse Comitatus, is part of the antigovernment "Patriot" movement that sprang to life after the passage of federal gun-control legislation (the Brady Bill) and the violent confrontations between the FBI and the Randy Weaver family at Ruby Ridge, Idaho, in 1992 and the Branch Davidian religious sect at Waco, Texas, in 1994. In general, "Patriots" believe that the federal government is tyrannical in character and under the control of a malevolent "New World Order" directed by the United Nations or a worldwide Jewish conspiracy. This justifies, in their minds, the formation of armed, private militias aimed at defending citizens against the threat from Washington DC.

A Freeman is, in theory, anyone who claims to be a sovereign citizen. According to the doctrine, the United States consists of two types of citizens. First are the descendants of individuals who were American citizens before the Civil War and whose status was determined by the Bill of Rights. Second are the descendants of individuals whose rights were assigned to them by the Fourteenth Amendment and subsequent legislation. Citizens of the first kind are potentially "sovereign." These Freemen may dissolve the bonds that exist between themselves and the United States by refusing to obtain driver's licenses or automobile registrations, recognize the jurisdiction of state and federal courts, or pay income taxes. In practice, Freemen have grouped together in townships located on property belonging to one or more of the individuals involved. Members of this community then claim sovereignty for the township, a status that places it beyond the law, or so they believe.

The most widely known of these Freemen townships was the Justus Township located on the Clark ranch near Jordan, Montana. In 1996 its members engaged in an eighty-eight-day standoff with authorities who were seeking to evict some members from the premises and arrest others on a variety of federal and state criminal charges. In contrast to the Ruby Ridge and Waco incidents, this event ended peacefully on June 13, 1996, with the surrender of the Freemen. On July 8 a federal jury in Billings convicted the leader of the group of bank fraud and other charges.

Freemen are vulnerable to criminal charges because of their propensity for issuing bogus checks and money orders and threatening to "arrest" judges and other public officials with whose decisions they disagree. In dealing with such officials, it has become common for Freemen to organize their own "common law" courts, which then may issue fake "liens" against the property of the offending public officeholder. On some occasions these spurious "courts" have found individuals guilty of various offenses and threatened to carry out "sentences" against them. Many Freemen are drawn to Christian Identity theology, which mixes unorthodox biblical understandings with straightforward racism. They believe that God has chosen white, Nordic yeomen, much like the Freemen themselves, to rule America.

Prior to the 1996 Justus Township episode, Leroy Schweitzer, Roy Schwasinger, and other Freemen leaders were able to earn a living by conducting seminars in which farmers, ranchers, and other beleaguered rural folk were trained in the techniques of tax avoidance through the invocation of what observers referred to as "legal magic." After the conclusion of the Justus Township standoff and the subsequent criminal prosecutions, the Freemen movement fell on hard times.

Leonard Weinberg
University of Nevada, Reno

Dyer, Joel. *Harvest of Rage: Why Oklahoma City Is Only the Beginning*. Boulder CO; Westview Press, 1997. Stern, Kenneth S. *A Force upon the Plain: The American Militia Movement and the Politics of Hate*. New York: Simon and Schuster, 1996. Wessinger, Catherine. *How the Millennium Comes Violently*. New York: Seven Bridges Press, 2000.

GARNER, ELMER (1864–1944)

Born in Tama County, Iowa, on January 1, 1864, but raised near Downs in Osborne County, Kansas, Elmer J. Garner was an editor and publisher of the late nineteenth and early twentieth century who moved from Farmers Alliance advocacy in 1890 to the radical "old Christian right" of fellow Kansans Dr. John R. Brinkley and Rev. Gerald B. Winrod. Garner edited papers identified with the People's, Republican, and Democratic Parties, even though he claimed political independence. By some accounts his *Farmers' Advance* (Almena, Norton County) was the first Populist newspaper in Kansas, but during the 1890s Garner's *Logan Republican* also supported prohibitionists and free-silver Democrats such as William Jennings Bryan, as well as many Republican candidates. Despite his chameleonic politics, Garner consistently espoused prohibitionism, nativism, and isolationism; he also frequently employed anti-British, anti-Catholic, and anti-Semitic rhetoric in his advocacy of free silver and farm cooperatives and in his diatribes against the world financial conspiracy.

After a stint in Oklahoma editing the *Oklahoma State Register* (Guthrie) and the *Cimarron Valley Clipper* (Coyle), Garner moved back to Kansas, eventually settling in Emporia, where he ran a print shop and in the mid-1920s a newspaper, the *Kansas State Bugle*, that stood "one hundred percent for Protestant Americanism" and supported the activities of the Ku Klux Klan. Garner then moved to Wichita, where in 1930 he helped organize that city's "Brinkley for Governor Club" and launched *Publicity*, a four-page weekly tabloid devoted to Dr. Brinkley and "Brinkleyism." In this, his final publishing venture, Garner championed the goat gland doctor's political career and "populist" platform: free textbooks for Kansas children; public ownership of natural resources and utilities, including transportation;

support for strong farmers' cooperative and trade union movements; prevention of centralized control of banking, finance, and farming interests; elimination of war profits; and a mandatory referendum to precede any declaration of war. But he also supported much of the New Deal during the mid-1930s until President Franklin D. Roosevelt's emphasis shifted overseas. Editor Garner was virulent in his opposition to a third term and subsequently called for the impeachment of "Roosevelt and his Jewish Camarilla."

Publicity softened its anti-Roosevelt message after Pearl Harbor, but it was too late. The justice department, through a federal grand jury, indicted Elmer J. Garner on sedition charges and eventually put him on trial in Washington DC with twenty-nine other defendants. They were said to have been a part of a nationwide conspiracy to subvert the country's armed forces. The "Great Sedition Trial," or *United States v. McWilliams*, ended for the eighty-year-old Wichita editor on May 4, 1944, about two weeks after it began, when Garner died in a Washington boardinghouse.

See also MEDIA: Brinkley, John Richard.

Virgil W. Dean
Kansas State Historical Society

Dean, Virgil W. "Another Wichita Seditionist? Elmer J. Garner and the Radical Right's Opposition to World War II." *Kansas History* 17 (1994): 50–64. Ribuffo, Leo P. *The Old Christian Right: The Protestant Far Right from the Great Depression to the Cold War*. Philadelphia: Temple University Press, 1983.

GRAIN GROWERS ASSOCIATIONS

Western Canada became a cereal grain and mixed agriculture region as the result of deliberate public and private initiatives that were geared to facilitating the creation of a domestic industrial economy in Canada. The famous "national policy" implemented by successive Canadian governments after 1878 was actually a series of policies. The three foundational policies were the establishment of protective tariffs, the promotion of western settlement, and the construction of a transcontinental railroad. An expanding agricultural population in the West was to provide export cash crops and serve as a captive market for Canadian industry, with the Canadian Pacific Railway providing transportation. Although it took longer to come to fruition than the business and political leaders had envisioned, after 1900 Canada did in fact experience an economic boom. There were, however, underlying structural problems, especially in the West.

The market relations that Prairie farmers engaged in with the grain trade were inherently incompatible because farmers' incomes were dependent on maximizing the price they received for their products, while the profits of grain dealers were maximized by minimizing what they paid the farmer. As a result, farmers began to complain about the trading, marketing, and pricing actions of the grain trade. Given the importance of Prairie settlement in the overall national policy, the Canadian government was quick to intervene. Before 1900

the first of several Royal Commissions investigated the grain trade. The end result of the First Commission was a major regulatory initiative, the Manitoba Grain Act, passed in 1901. The act was designed to regulate and supervise the grain trade so as to provide fair practices and prices. Problems persisted, however.

As a result of a bumper crop in western Canada in 1901, many farmers found themselves unable to market their crops because the grain companies and the Canadian Pacific Railroad were not adhering to the provisions of the Manitoba Grain Act. In order to redress the situation, farmers in what was then the Northwest Territories organized a meeting to discuss their options. Organizers were optimistic that they could get twelve people to attend their meeting in Indian Head (in present-day Saskatchewan), but when the doors opened, about seventy farmers were waiting. The farmers decided to form a nonpartisan organization to represent their interests, and the Territorial Grain Growers Association (TGGA) was born. A year later, when the TGGA held its first general meeting, its membership was 500.

The TGGA deliberately and explicitly did not affiliate with any political party; rather, it was to be the voice of all farmers. As settlement proceeded and new communities developed, locals of the TGGA were established. By 1902 the member of Parliament from the region was bringing resolutions and motions dealing with grain-handling problems, passed at the annual TGGA meetings and by TGGA locals, to the House of Commons, where they were typically enacted as amendments to the Manitoba Grain Act. The farmers had discovered that collectively they could wield considerable political power.

Perhaps the greatest boost to the stature of the TGGA came in 1902 when the organization addressed the continuing problems associated with grain boxcar allocations. It appeared that the Canadian Pacific was ignoring the provisions of the Manitoba Grain Act in its allocation of grain cars. After an unsuccessful visit to the company's offices in Winnipeg, the TGGA convinced the federal government to lay a court charge against the railroad. The company was convicted and forced to comply with the provisions of the legislation. The court victory demonstrated the effectiveness of collective action, and the membership of the TGGA grew even faster. In Manitoba a branch was formed under the name the Manitoba Grain Growers Association. In the years that followed, the TGGA worked closely with its Manitoba counterpart, regularly visiting Ottawa to lobby the government for action on various matters.

When the provinces of Saskatchewan and Alberta were established in 1905, the former Territorial Grain Growers Association disappeared. However, the change was in name only. The name of the Saskatchewan section was changed to the Saskatchewan Grain Growers Association (SGGA), and it went on to play an important role in regional and national economic and political developments. The SGGA

was instrumental in the establishment of subsequent Royal Commissions to investigate the grain trade, as well as in dispatching Prairie firebrand E. A. Partridge to investigate the Winnipeg Grain Exchange, a development that ultimately produced one of the region's first major farmers' cooperative grain companies. While the SGGA experienced internal conflict and eventually fragmented over the question of direct political participation, it and its predecessor laid the foundation for much of the collective activity that shaped the region.

Murray Knuttila
University of Regina

GRANGE

The Order of Patrons of Husbandry, or the Grange, was the first important large organization of farmers in the United States. Founded in 1867, principally by Oliver H. Kelley, a Minnesota farmer and clerk in the U.S. Department of Agriculture, the Grange opened its membership to men and women as a fraternal organization of rural people and worked to facilitate better social life for farm families, to share useful information, and to reduce the hostility of sectionalism after the Civil War.

The first growth of the organization occurred in Minnesota, with chapters outside Minnesota emerging in the early 1870s when farmers suffered economically. The Depression of 1873 especially increased membership. Grangers, as members were called, believed themselves the victims of railroads, which charged oppressive transportation rates and purchased their produce at low prices because of their monopoly powers, and also of various middlemen with whom farmers had to do business. Moreover, farmers in the Great Plains faced additional problems of bad weather and insects, especially grasshoppers. In fact, in 1874 Grangers throughout the nation sent money and supplies to fellow members in the Great Plains suffering grasshopper infestation.

By 1876, while Ohio, Indiana, and Iowa led the way with total number of local chapters, or granges, Nebraska, Kansas, and Montana had the largest number of members per 1,000 population. Most Grangers eventually became interested in Grange-owned marketing cooperatives and farm equipment factories. Additionally, in an effort to accommodate the needs of Grangers, the private mail-order firm of Montgomery Ward and Company was established. And in the Middle West particularly, promoting state regulation of railroad shipping rates became a major concern of Grangers. However, in Kansas and Nebraska, railroad regulation generated little interest, for farmers in still-developing parts of the Great Plains desired increased trackage, not expansion-hindering public oversight.

Grangers throughout the nation did agree on other reform topics, in particular financial and monetary policy, as well as political reforms. While the official position of the National Grange was nonpartisan, advocating issues but not parties, many Grangers joined and even assumed leadership roles in emerging political third parties, such as the state-level Antimonopoly, Reform, and Greenback Parties, and also exerted influence in the major parties. The greatest success of their political activism was the enactment of state railroad regulation, commonly known as the Granger Laws.

By 1880 the Granger movement began to lose its impetus. Even though the U.S. Supreme Court in *Munn v. Illinois* (1877)—and in subsequent Granger cases—upheld the constitutionality of state railroad laws, many states repealed their railroad laws in the face of diminished rail service. The Grangers' marketing and manufacturing efforts failed, as they were undersold by competitors. In all, the number of members of the Grange nationally had shrunk to about 124,000 from a high of 860,000.

But the Grange did not pass away. During the decade of the 1870s, farmers in the West and South had dominated the organization. Thereafter, northeasterners played a leading role in reviving the Grange, which nationally had more than 300,000 members in the 1990s.

Many issues and government programs promoted by the Grange have been successful. Over the years Grangers called for women's suffrage, direct election of U.S. senators, direct primaries, graduated income tax, rural free delivery, parcel post system, better country roads, rural electrification, improved education for farm children and college students (especially at land grant institutions), extension service, federal farm credit programs, and parity price supports. Today, the National Grange continues to lobby for farm policies from its headquarters in Washington DC.

Thomas Burnell Colbert
Marshalltown Community College

Buck, Solon J. *The Granger Movement.* Cambridge: Harvard University Press, 1913. Nordin, D. Sven. *Rich Harvest: A History of the Grange, 1867–1900.* Jackson: University of Mississippi Press, 1974. Woods, Thomas A. *Knights of the Plow: Oliver H. Kelley and the Origins of the Grange in Republican Ideology.* Ames: Iowa State University Press, 1991.

GREEN CORN REBELLION

This short-lived tenant farmers' revolt broke out in three counties along Oklahoma's South Canadian River in August 1917. Ostensibly an uprising against World War I and the Conscription Act, the Green Corn Rebellion actually emerged from a series of long-standing grievances tenant farmers held against local landowners, businessmen, and state and local authorities, especially over the increasing consolidation of agricultural land by a few wealthy landholders. At the time of the rebellion, more than half of Oklahoma's farmers were tenants, many of whom had been forced into that condition by rampant land speculation and outright fraud.

In the early years of the twentieth century, large numbers of tenants and small farmers sought help from the state's Socialist Party and its affiliated organizations, such as the Renters Union. While the Socialists called for expanding the public domain, enacting a graduated

land tax, and creating a cooperative marketing system, some tenants grew frustrated with the political process and turned to night riding or to direct action techniques borrowed from the Industrial Workers of the World (IWW). But the IWW itself rejected the tenant farmers because the union recruited only wageworkers.

The tenants instead joined another organization, the Working Class Union (WCU), based in Van Buren, Arkansas. The WCU locals in Oklahoma soon claimed 35,000 members, a questionable number. WCU membership rose with the collapse of cotton prices at the start of World War I, then grew again with opposition to a 1915 cattle-dipping campaign intended to check the spread of Texas fever. Charging that the chemicals used in the treatment harmed livestock, WCU members dynamited dipping vats and destroyed the property of local officials. But the organization became inactive after cotton prices rose in 1916.

The WCU revived in 1917 after American entry into World War I. Both opposition to the war and the old grievances simmered throughout the summer of 1917. In early August hundreds of men gathered at the Sasakwa, Oklahoma, farm of John Spears, an aging Socialist, to plan a march on Washington to end the war. They intended to live on barbecued beef and roasted green corn, the latter giving the rebellion its name. On August 3 rebels started burning bridges and cutting telegraph lines, but hastily organized posses soon halted the rebellion. Three men were killed and more than 400 others were arrested. Of those, 150 were convicted and received federal prison terms of up to ten years.

In the wake of the rebellion, the state Socialist Party disbanded. State and federal authorities used the uprising as a means to suppress the IWW, which had taken no part in the rebellion.

Nigel Anthony Sellars
Christopher Newport University

Burbank, Garin. *When Farmers Voted Red: The Gospel of Socialism in the Oklahoma Countryside, 1910–1924.* Westport CT: Greenwood Press, 1976. Green, James R. *Grass-Roots Socialism: Radical Movements in the Southwest, 1895–1943.* Baton Rouge: Louisiana State University Press, 1978. Sellars, Nigel Anthony. *Oil, Wheat, and Wobblies: The Industrial Workers of the World in Oklahoma, 1905–1930.* Norman: University of Oklahoma Press, 1998.

HAIRE, ROBERT (1845–1916)

Political and social activist Robert Emmett Haire was born on August 29, 1845, in Freedom, Michigan. He graduated from normal school in Ypsilanti, Michigan, served as a sailor on the Great Lakes, studied law at the University of Michigan, and then joined the clergy of the Roman Catholic Church. Haire formally studied theology at the University of Louvain in Belgium and Saint Mary's of the West in Cincinnati, and remained an independent scholar of literature, economics, and linguistics throughout his life. He took the middle name William prior to his ordination in Detroit, Michigan, on March 1, 1874.

Haire relocated to Dakota Territory in 1879 after serving as a priest in Detroit and Flint,

Michigan. He built a sod church and braved the extremes of the Great Plains climate to tend forty-two mission stations between southwestern Minnesota and present-day southeastern North Dakota. With his outgoing personality, he cultivated friendships with both Protestants and Catholics. Attracted by Haire's activism, the Presentation Sisters established Saint Luke's Hospital and a parochial school in Haire's newly created parish in Aberdeen, South Dakota. Haire also published the *Dakota Catholic American* newspaper to promote social reform in the Northern Plains. His advocacy brought support to the issues of prohibition, women's suffrage, workers' rights, and increased voter participation in the political process. His reformist agenda and presidency of the newly established Dakota Knights of Labor, however, prompted Bishop Martin Marty to suspend him from parish work in May of 1890.

Haire remained a practicing Catholic priest throughout his life, but in his later years he became increasingly involved in politics. He gave strong speeches at Populist Party conventions and specifically promoted the statewide initiative and popular referendum that South Dakota adopted in 1897. Haire's leadership skills led state Republicans to name him commissioner of charities and corrections and Populist governor Andrew E. Lee to nominate him to the state board of regents. By 1900 Haire also claimed founding membership in the Socialist Party, and he remained active in the local branch until his death on March 4, 1916. Catholics and Protestants from diverse backgrounds filled Sacred Heart Church to attend Haire's funeral, testimony to the influential life of this Great Plains activist.

See also POLITICS AND GOVERNMENT: Populists (People's Party).

Robert W. Galler Jr.
Western Michigan University

Atwood, E. Francis. *A Memoir of the Life of Father Robert W. Haire: Pioneer, Priest, and Scholar, Founder of Socialism in the Dakotahs.* Sisseton SD: Socialist Party, 1916. Sannes, Erling N. "Knowledge Is Power: The Knights of Labor in South Dakota." *South Dakota History* 22 (1992): 400–430. Webb, Daryl. " 'Just Principles Never Die': Brown County Populists, 1890–1900." *South Dakota History* 22 (1992): 366–99.

HARPER, ELIJAH (b. 1949)

As the Manitoba legislature's only Aboriginal member, Elijah Harper played a major role in defeating the Meech Lake Accord. A Cree Indian, Elijah was born in his parents' log cabin on March 3, 1949, at Red Sucker Lake near the Manitoba and Ontario border. One of thirteen children, he spent much time with his paternal grandparents, living in their home but seeing his parents everyday. When he was five years old, he became ill and spent six months under the auspices of the Indian Affairs medical staff without any contact with his parents. He left home to pursue an education, marrying during his second year as a university student in Winnipeg. After being active in Native organizations and issues, he and his family returned home, where he was elected chief of Red Sucker Lake in 1978. Three years later he was elected as a New Democrat member for the vast Rupert's Land riding, with about 70 percent of the vote. From his remote reservation he forced Aboriginal issues into the constitutional debate.

Attempting to accommodate Quebec and preserve Canada, the Meech Lake Accord proclaimed that Canada had two distinct founding nations. Harper agreed that Quebec's society was distinct but regarded the exclusion of Native peoples from Canada's founding nations as offensive, as did most Native organizations. Prime Minister Brian Mulroney and the provincial premiers signed the Meech Lake Accord on June 9, 1990. After the signing ceremony the legislatures of Manitoba, Newfoundland, and New Brunswick faced a two-week deadline to approve. Harper delayed the vote on the accord forty-eight hours, and a procedural mistake also delayed the accord's introduction to the Manitoba legislature. When debate extension required unanimous consent, Harper again objected, preventing a vote before the deadline expired. His quiet refusal, with an eagle feather in hand, embodied Native resentment over recent and historic mistreatment. Harper became a national symbol for Native issues. He is also a controversial figure, however, and at times he has appeared to be prone to political self-destruction, such as when he refused to take a Breathalyzer test following a minor traffic accident.

John M. Pederson
Mayville State University

Cohen, Andrew. *A Deal Undone: The Making and Breaking of the Meech Lake Accord*. Vancouver: Douglas and McIntyre, 1990. Comeau, Pauline. *Elijah: No Ordinary Hero*. Vancouver: Douglas and McIntyre, 1993. Hager, Barbara. *Honour Songs*. Vancouver: Raincoast Books, 1996.

INDUSTRIAL WORKERS OF THE WORLD

The Industrial Workers of the World (IWW), or Wobblies, originated in Chicago in 1905 as a loose amalgam of labor and political entities, principally the Western Federation of Miners (WFM) and various socialist political parties. The union aspired to organize all workers by industry (hence the name "Industrial") instead of by skill categories, as did trade unions like the American Federation of Labor. Led by "Big Bill" Haywood from the WFM, the Wobblies moved from organizing eastern factories full of unskilled immigrants and women in the early years to organizing the huge migrant labor force in the western United States that worked in the extractive industries of lumbering, mining and petroleum, and agriculture. Immigrant, homeless, relying on the railroads for transportation, and camping on the edges of towns in so-called jungles, the migrant worker was the ultimate invisible person. The Wobblies created an organization that enlisted migrant workers as the foot soldiers in their "army of the revolution."

The IWW did not see itself as a political party and eschewed involvement with any political system. Rather, it favored "direct action"—the use of labor action to solve labor problems. Rich in symbolism, and using a variety of visual images to present its story to a largely immigrant and often illiterate audience, the Wobblies became identified by the black cat and the French wooden shoe (*sabot*), the symbol for sabotage. Although the Wobbly newspaper *Solidarity* hinted broadly at the advantages of sabotage for realizing goals, it is not clear to what extent sabotage was actually practiced.

In the Great Plains, the Wobblies reached their greatest extent and impact just prior to the World War I with a concerted effort to organize migrant wheat harvesters, the so-called bindlestiffs. They used a "contagion" method of organizing, where any new member could sign up additional new members. Capitalizing on the fact that railroads were really the only means of long-distance transportation, Wobblies took control of boxcars, organizing everyone in the car as the freight trains moved from town to town. Small-town sheriffs had no idea what to do when boxcar after boxcar loaded with singing, shouting Wobblies landed in their town. If they arrested one or two for disturbing the peace, the rest of the union would surround the jail and demand release. Employers were unaccustomed to having migrant workers band together to demand higher pay.

Between 1915 and 1917 the IWW swept across the Plains like a prairie fire. By the summer of 1916 the IWW was collecting dues from more than 18,000 migrant harvesters, and its organizers boasted of an "800-mile picket line" from Oklahoma to South Dakota. The Wobblies' mobility, developed from many years of practice as migrants, allowed them to appear to be everywhere at once.

After the onset of World War I, the image of the saboteur was used effectively against the union by state and federal agencies. When the Wobblies attempted to capture, in the form of increased wages, some of the money being fed into wartime industry, they were accused of sympathizing with Germany. Following the success of the Russian Revolution in 1917, the "army of the revolution" was dealt a serious blow by a series of coordinated government raids on IWW headquarters across the United States in September of that year. Hundreds of IWW leaders were arrested and tried for treason and other charges, draining the union's coffers. Wichita, Kansas, became infamous for its rotating jail cells, in which at least one Wobbly died and many more wasted away waiting for trial. Big Bill Haywood emigrated to communist Russia following the war.

Ultimately, the advent of combine wheat harvesters obviated the need for huge numbers of migrant laborers, and the adoption of the automobile split migrants into small groups that could not be organized as effectively as entire boxcar loads. By the late 1920s the *I Won't Works*, as the Wobblies were nicknamed, were little more than an exciting memory in the Great Plains.

Ted Grossardt
University of Kentucky

Brissenden, Paul F. *The I.W.W.: A Study of American Syndicalism*. New York: Columbia University, 1919. Kornbluh, Joyce L. *Rebel Voices: An I.W.W. Anthology*. Ann Arbor: University of Michigan Press, 1965. Sellars, Nigel Anthony. *Oil, Wheat, and Wobblies: The Industrial Workers of the World in Oklahoma, 1905–1930*. Norman: University of Oklahoma Press, 1998.

JUNTA DE INDIGNACIÓN

While the native Hispanos formed the majority of the population throughout New Mexico's territorial period and into the early statehood years after 1912, they were nevertheless subject to the powerful forces of Americanization. As Anglo-American and foreign settlers prepared New Mexico for full incorporation into the United States, considerable ethnic conflict arose. Seeing many threats to their social and cultural interests, Hispanos responded with ethnic protest. By the turn of the twentieth century, a distinct tradition of Hispano collective resistance emerged. Some of the most significant Hispano protest took place within the vast region that the Spanish *pobladores* (yeoman settlers) first called *las vegas grandes* (the great meadows) and *el llano estacado* (the Staked Plains), which extended from the Rockies onto the western fringe of the Great Plains. Anglo newcomers came upon Hispanos who were already settled in the Plains counties of San Miguel, Mora, Colfax, Union, and Guadalupe.

A major form of protest innovated by Hispanos living in the Plains was *la junta de indignación* (mass meeting of indignation). In the typical junta de indignación, a spontaneous demonstration was organized to deal with an issue suddenly affecting the Hispanos as an ethnic group. One of the biggest and most significant of such juntas took place in Las Vegas in 1901 in response to a Methodist missionary who disparaged in a local newspaper column the "pagan" religious customs of the Hispano folk. A crowd of 600 Hispanos rallied to refute the missionary's alleged "lies" and "calumnies." Typical of the Hispano junta de indignación, a round of speakers denounced the offender in harsh and sarcastic terms. Also typical of this protest genre, the leaders appointed a committee and charged it with crafting resolutions to be published in the press calling for Anglos to cease their racial prejudices.

Hispano ranchers in the Plains also applied la junta de indignación in efforts to keep legal possession of communal lands. On the important Las Vegas Land Grant, for example, a "people's" movement, consisting of hastily convened meetings, formed in response to the actions of a group of elite townsmen who attempted to gain control of the grant. In this case, juntas de indignación intertwined with dramatic court cases and local elections.

Statewide juntas also erupted in 1933 when a psychology professor at the University of New Mexico disseminated negative stereotypes of Hispanos in his racial attitude scale. Protests erupted in the two Plains communities of Springer and Taylor Springs in Colfax County. Both involved the rituals of indignant speakers and a petition calling on the governor to fire the professor whose "slanders" insulted the Hispano people.

As a collective repertoire, la junta de indignación enabled Hispanos to forge a homeland ethnic identity. It served as a means for giving notice that they would not tolerate the denial of rights in the land that their ancestors had settled. The classic turn-of-the-century junta de indignación went out of style in the mid-1930s as the Great Depression and the New Deal caused significant changes in New Mexico's structure of political and civic engagement.

See also HISPANIC AMERICANS: Hispano Homeland.

Phillip B. Gonzales
University of New Mexico

Arellano, Anselmo F. "People Versus Trustees: Protest Activity on the Las Vegas Land Grant." In *Las Vegas Grandes on the Gallinas, 1835–1985*, edited by Anselmo F. Arellano and Julián Josué Vigil. Las Vegas NM: Editorial Teleraña, 1985: 66–74. Gonzales, Phillip B. *Forced Sacrifice as Ethnic Protest: The Hispano Cause in New Mexico and the Racial Attitude Confrontation of 1933*. New York: Peter Lang Publishing, 2001. Gonzales, Phillip B. "La Junta de Indignación: Hispano Repertoire of Collective Protest in New Mexico, 1884–1933." *Western Historical Quarterly* 31 (2000): 161–86.

KU KLUX KLAN

There are three separate and distinct periods of the Ku Klux Klan's history in the United States. The first Klan, founded at Pulaski, Tennessee, in 1865, did not have much of a presence in the Great Plains. Although it began as a local social club with secret rituals and costumes that usually featured flowing robes, pointed hats, and masks, the Klan spread quickly throughout the South with the promise that it would defend the Constitution and help the weak and oppressed. However, the Klan resorted to terror and extreme violence when blacks were given civil and voting rights. In 1877, when Reconstruction came to an end, the Klan officially disbanded.

The second Klan, founded in 1915 by William Joseph Simmons at Stone Mountain, Georgia, had a greater impact in the Plains. Simmons emphasized that the Klan was a fraternal charitable organization that supported white supremacy. The Klan grew rapidly after 1919, when it launched a national campaign to attract members. It was especially strong in urban areas, and by the mid-1920s it was organized in every state. Nationally the Klan claimed 10 million members by 1924, but recent scholars estimate that the membership was closer to two million. It is estimated that between 1915 and 1944, Klan membership in the Plains states made up 20 percent of the Klan's total membership. During this period, Klan membership was strongest in Texas (190,000) and Oklahoma (95,000), and declined northward through Colorado (45,000), Kansas (40,000), Nebraska (25,000), South Dakota (5,000), and North Dakota (3,000). The Klan was also strong in Alberta and Saskatchewan during the 1920s, drawing support for its anti-Catholic and anti-immigrant positions.

The Klan grew rapidly between 1921 and

Ku Klux Klan, probably in Denver, Colorado, between 1921 and 1930

1925 because it was able to exploit the fears and anxieties of post–World War I America. The Klan's promise to preserve traditional values and morals gave people a sense of power, fraternity, and security. Although the Klan still used antiblack rhetoric, especially in the Southern Plains, the Klan's primary message in the 1920s was that it stood for law and order, traditional morality, and most important, "100 percent Americanism." It was successful because it tailored its appeal in every community to respond to local issues and concerns. The Klan's appeal to "100 percent Americanism" allowed local Klans to target any group—blacks, Jews, radicals, immigrants, Mexicans, and especially Catholics.

The Klan used moral suasion, political influence, social pressure, and violence to accomplish its objectives. In the Northern Plains the Klan was rarely involved in acts of violence, and, while it influenced some local elections, it had a negligible impact on the political process. In Texas and Oklahoma, however, the Klan was involved in widespread public whippings, tar and featherings, lynchings, and brutal homicides. In Texas and Oklahoma alone there were as many as 1,000 victims of Klan violence. In Dallas the Klan was credited with sixty-eight floggings in 1922; in Oklahoma there was near civil war in 1923 when Gov. John C. Walton declared marshal law in an effort to control Klan violence. In Texas, Oklahoma, and Kansas the Klan was a major political force, and many Klansmen were elected to local, state, and national offices.

In Texas in the early 1920s the Klan controlled the lower house of the Texas legislature and elected Klansman Earl B. Mayfield to serve in the U.S. Senate. In 1924 in Kansas,

William Allen White, the editor of the *Emporia Gazette*, gained national attention when he ran for governor in an attempt to resist the Klan's efforts to control the Republican Party.

Klan membership declined rapidly after 1925. Escalating violence, organized opposition, and corruption within the Klan organization, as well as the conviction of one the Klan's most important leaders for rape and murder, robbed the Klan of its claim to moral leadership. By the end of the 1930s the Klan was increasingly viewed as un-American. In 1944, when the government sued the Klan for back taxes, it disbanded.

The Klan revived after World War II to resist the civil rights movement. Lacking a national organizational structure, the Klan quickly split into a number of small, violent factions. It was involved in numerous bombings and murders in the South, particularly during the 1960s, but the Klan's nationwide membership numbered only in the tens of thousands. The Klan's violent, un-American reputation limited its appeal in the Plains. Still, by the early 1990s Klanwatch, a project of the Southern Poverty Law Center, reported that although Klan membership nationally had fallen to only 5,000, violent hate crimes were rapidly increasing and that small Klan units were again active in Colorado, Nebraska, Kansas, Oklahoma, and Texas.

Michael W. Schuyler
University of Nebraska at Kearney

Chalmers, David. *Hooded Americanism: The History of the Ku Klux Klan*. New York: New Viewpoints, 1981. Jackson, Kenneth T. *The Ku Klux Klan in the City, 1915–1930*. New York: Oxford University Press, 1967. Lay, Shawn. *The Invisible Empire in the West: Toward a New Appraisal of the Ku Klux Klan of the 1920s*. Chicago: University of Illinois Press, 1992.

LEASE, MARY ELIZABETH (1853–1933)

In the heyday of the Populist Party, 1890–96, Mary Lease was one of the most prominent women in America, celebrated as the "Kansas Joan of Arc." She was born on September 11, 1853, in Ridgway, Pennsylvania, the daughter of Irish immigrants. Her father died as a Union prisoner of war, a calamity that plunged the family into poverty. In 1870 his widow sent twenty-year-old Mary to teach at Osage Mission, Kansas, where she married local pharmacist Charles Lease in 1873. The couple lost everything in the Panic of 1873 and moved to Denison, Texas. While her husband shifted from job to job, Lease took in washing and bore six children, two of whom died in infancy. She also joined the temperance movement and discovered her talent as an orator.

In the 1880s the family moved to Wichita, where Lease became a Knights of Labor organizer and women's suffrage advocate, as well as one of the first women to pass the Kansas bar. When the Populist Party formed in 1890, it seemed poised to address a broad range of Lease's concerns, and she plunged into the campaign. Her speeches were famously fiery, though she did not—as myth has it—urge farmers to "raise less corn and more hell."

Lease's agenda did not match those of many other Populist leaders. Denouncing those who cooperated with Democrats, she also offended anti-imperialists with her 1895 book, *The Problem of Civilization Solved*, advocating U.S. colonization of Latin America. In 1896 Lease declared herself a socialist but stumped reluctantly for William Jennings Bryan. After Bryan's defeat, Lease divorced her husband and moved with her children to New York, where she worked as a lawyer and lecturer until her death on October 30, 1933.

Though Lease repudiated the Populists, she left an enduring legacy from her years in the Plains. According to reports from an 1890 convention, it was she who gave the People's Party its name. She inspired novelist Hamlin Garland to fictionalize her in *A Spoil of Office* (1893). The first woman to be appointed a state superintendent of charities (by a Populist governor in Kansas), she blended with passion the advocacy of women's rights, overseas expansion, and domestic economic reform.

See also POLITICS AND GOVERNMENT: Populists (People's Party).

Rebecca Edwards
Vassar College

Blumberg, Dorothy Rose. "Mary Elizabeth Lease, Populist Orator: A Profile." *Kansas History* 1 (1978): 3–15. Clanton, O. Gene. "Intolerant Populist? The Disaffection of Mary Elizabeth Lease." *Kansas Historical Quarterly* 34 (1968): 189–200.

MALCOLM X (1925–1965)

Malcolm X was born Malcolm Little at University Hospital in Omaha, Nebraska, on May 19, 1925. He was also known later in life by his religious name, El-Hajj Malik El-Shabbazz. His parents, Earl Little and Louise Norton Little, were both active members of Marcus Gar-

Malcolm X

vey's Universal Negro Improvement Association and they wrote for the UNIA paper, the *Negro World*.

The Littles' home was reportedly attacked by Ku Klux Klansmen in December 1926, and they left immediately for Milwaukee, Wisconsin. In January 1928 they moved to Lansing, Michigan. There, Earl Little, as an organizer for the Garvey movement, continued his community activism. In September 1931 his body was found by the railroad tracks, cut in half by a locomotive car. Historical accounts differ: some believe that local white supremacist organizations committed this murder; others have speculated that his death was a suicide. Whatever the case, from 1931 to 1939 the Little family disintegrated. In 1939 Malcolm's mother, Louise, was diagnosed as legally insane and committed to the state mental hospital in Kalamazoo, Michigan, where she remained for more than twenty years. Malcolm began having problems with the social welfare system and was placed in foster care. He also spent time in juvenile detention homes.

By 1941 Malcolm had moved to the Roxbury section of Boston to live with his sister Ella. He held various jobs, such as laborer and porter on the New Haven Railroad line, and he slipped into a life of petty crime. He moved back to Michigan in December 1942 but quickly returned to New York, where he continued working for the New Haven Railroad. From 1944 to 1946 Malcolm was continually involved in illegal activity, ranging from drugs and burglary to gambling and prostitution. In February 1946 he began serving an eight- to ten-year prison sentence at the Charlestown (Massachusetts) Prison for burglary. There, he began a self-taught study in reading and writing. After being relocated to the Concord Reformatory in 1947, Malcolm was exposed to the teachings of Elijah Muhammad by a fellow inmate. His life was transformed. Malcolm's siblings were also converted and accepted membership into the Nation of Islam.

After fifteen months at the Concord Reformatory, Malcolm was transferred to Norfolk Prison Colony, then sent back to Charlestown to serve the remainder of his sentence. Paroled in 1952, he went to live with his brother Wilfred in Inkster, Michigan, where he worked as a furniture salesman. That same year he was assigned his "X" to replace the name that had been taken from his slave ancestors and became an active member in the Nation of Islam.

From this point on, Malcolm X's activity and membership in the Nation of Islam intensified: in the fall of 1953 he became first minister of Boston Temple No. 11; in March 1954 he was assigned acting minister of Philadelphia Temple No. 12; and in June of that year, he was appointed minister of New York Temple No. 7. His message in the temple and on the streets of Harlem stressed black nationalism and lambasted integration as a hoax.

At the same time, Malcolm X also made an important transition in his family life. In 1958 he married Betty X (Sanders). In November his first daughter, Attallah, was born. She was followed in later years by daughters Quibilah (1960), Ilyasah (1962), and Gamilah (1964). When he died, his wife was pregnant with twins and gave birth to daughters, Malaak and Malikah, in November 1965.

Taking on the responsibilities and duties as a national spokesperson for the Nation of Islam, Malcolm traveled widely, expressing his views in television interviews, court cases involving civil rights, and forums on black equality and leadership. By 1963, however, his status was beginning to deteriorate within the leadership circle of the Nation of Islam. That year in Detroit, he gave one of his most influential lectures, "Message to the Grass Roots," arguing for black nationalism and thereby challenging Elijah Mohammad's conception of the Nation of Islam as a purely religious movement. Days later he referred to the death of President John F. Kennedy as "chickens coming home to roost." Immediately after making this comment, he was suspended from his position as national spokesperson for the Nation of Islam and banned from public speaking for ninety days. In March 1964, after his period of suspension, he announced that he was leaving the Nation of Islam to establish Muslim Mosque Incorporated and the Organization of Afro-American Unity. He moderated his views, moving toward accommodation with Martin Luther King's crusade for civil rights.

In April 1964 Malcolm journeyed to Mecca to make hajj, fulfilling his religious requirements and duties. This period also served as time for self-reflection and meditation. When he returned to the United States and founded the Organization of Afro-American Unity, he hoped to link the freedom struggles of blacks in Africa with those in the United States. The end came on February 21, 1965, when he was assassinated by four gunmen while giving a speech at the Audubon Ballroom in Harlem.

Malcolm X was only thirty-nine years old when he died, but in that brief lifespan he became one of the most important African American leaders of the twentieth century. Although often out of step with civil rights leaders because of his separatist views and his refusal to eschew violent means of change, he nurtured pride and self-respect in African Americans, and more than anyone else he re-established their connection to Africa.

See also AFRICAN AMERICANS: Civil Rights / RELIGION: Islam.

James L. Conyers Jr.
University of Nebraska at Omaha

Gallen, David, ed. *A Malcolm X Reader*. New York: Carroll and Graf Publishers, Inc., 1994. Malcolm X, with Alex Haley. *The Autobiography of Malcolm X*. New York: Grove Press, 1965. Perry, Theresa, ed. *Teaching Malcolm X*. New York: Routledge, 1996.

MARTINSON, HENRY (1883–1981)

Born in Minneapolis, Minnesota, on March 6, 1883, Henry Martinson became one of the most prominent figures in the North Dakota labor movement. After trying to farm a homestead in Minnesota, Martinson moved to Minot, North Dakota, in 1907 and became a painter. After reading several labor tracts, he became a socialist and began to write for the labor newspaper *Iconoclast*. He rose to become its editor. He served as secretary of the state Socialist Party until its collapse in 1918, then recruited members for the Nonpartisan League. He remained active in the labor movement and in 1937 was appointed the deputy commissioner of labor for North Dakota. He held the position for twenty-eight years, fighting to improve labor conditions.

After losing his state position in 1965, Martinson remained active as secretary of the Trades and Labor Assembly in Fargo, and he began preserving the early history of labor in the state. He wrote a brief *History of North Dakota Labor* in 1970, expanding on this in articles in *North Dakota History* and in contributions to the film documentaries *Prairie Fire* (1977) and *Northern Lights* (1978). He also wrote and published poetry with regional themes. In 1975 he was named poet laureate of North Dakota. Martinson sought public office many times, always on a socialist platform. He commented wryly late in life that while he should have won these contests, he lacked the votes. Active in the cause of labor to the last, he died in Fargo on November 20, 1981.

See also FILM: *Northern Lights*.

Terry L. Shoptaugh
Moorhead State University

Martinson, Henry. *Comes the Revolution: A Personal Memoir of the Socialist Movement in North Dakota*. Fargo: n.p., 1969. Martinson, Henry. Papers. University of North Dakota Library, Grand Forks ND. Martinson, Henry. *Village Commune Barefoot Boy*. Fargo ND: n.p., 1976.

MCGRATH, TOM (1916–1990)

Perhaps America's most talented political poet, Thomas Matthew McGrath was a man dedicated to protest. Born (on November 20, 1916) and raised on a farm near the tiny Plains town of Sheldon, North Dakota, he returned there through his poetry to relate the simple struggles of his boyhood in the 1920s. The family farm fell into the hands of bankers in the Great Depression. It is such hardships, as well as joys, that he captures in his poems, especially his best and longest, the semi-auto-biographical *Letter to an Imaginary Friend* (published in four parts from 1962 to 1985 and as a combined definitive edition in 1997).

McGrath's father was influenced by the Wobblies and was a storyteller who read poems and sang to his son on the farm. Tom grew up respecting the workingman, and the rhythms and images of the threshing machine influenced his poetry. As a young adult he rode the rails, and in the early 1940s he worked as a welder and union organizer in the New York shipyards. He still found time to earn his bachelor of arts degree from the University of North Dakota in 1939 and his master of arts from Louisiana State University a year later. He received a Rhodes scholarship to study at Oxford, but delayed it until after World War II, during which he served reluctantly in the Aleutian Islands. In 1954 McGrath was ousted from a teaching job at Los Angeles State College of Applied Arts and Sciences for his radical views and his refusal to testify before the House Committee on Un-American Activities.

Following a year in New York, where he wrote what he called "junk fiction," McGrath returned to teach writing at North Dakota State University in Fargo in 1962, and after that, at Moorhead State University in Moorhead, Minnesota, from 1968 to 1982. However, he often took leaves to travel in Europe and Mexico, and he published prolifically. His poetry has been described as a Whitmanesque song about America, though unlike Whitman, he candidly attacks the country's racism, classism, and sectionalism. McGrath was a Marxist, but his communism functioned as a vehicle for his art, a framework within which he could build and render his vision of life. Like Crazy Horse, whom he championed, he was an outsider, rooted in the Plains and a defender of the people.

McGrath received many honors for his poetry, including an American Book Award for *Echoes inside the Labyrinth* in 1983, but his frank, outspoken political views probably prevented him from receiving the recognition he deserved as a great American poet. Tom McGrath died in Minneapolis on September 19, 1990.

Tom Matchie
North Dakota State University

McGrath, Tom. *Letter to an Imaginary Friend*. Port Townsend WA: Copper Canyon Press, 1997. Stern, Frederick C. *The Revolutionary Poet in the United States: The Poetry of Thomas McGrath*. Columbia: University of Missouri Press, 1988.

NATION, CARRY (1846–1911)

Carry Amelia Nation became famous for her exploits as a direct-action prohibitionist in Kansas. Her career began in 1900, when she single-handedly demolished a number of saloons in Kiowa and Wichita, and the notoriety she cultivated during the next ten years made her a catalyst for antiliquor sentiment throughout the country. Always controversial, she was vilified by some as a crank and lauded by others as a saintly friend and benefactor; yet her image as the woman with a hatchet in one hand (commemorating one of the weapons she wielded against saloons) and a Bible in the other achieved iconographic status. At the beginning of the twentieth century, she was arguably the most notorious woman in America.

She was born Carry Moore in Garrard County, Kentucky, on November 25, 1846. Her father, a planter and stock trader, was frequently away on business; her mother was periodically delusional. Most of the nurture she received as a child came from the family's slaves. Her parents' entrepreneurial ambitions made life peripatetic throughout Carry's youth. After several relocations in Kentucky, they moved to western Missouri in 1857. There, sectional tensions along the Kansas-Missouri border were on the rise. In 1860 they finally put down roots in Cass County, just south of Kansas City, but wartime hostilities forced them to relocate several more times before it was safe to stay there permanently. In 1864–65 Carry lived and studied at the Clay Seminary in Liberty, Missouri. Then her mother's condition worsened, and her father, without slaves, needed her at home to care for her five younger siblings.

Carry was desperately unhappy as the family drudge, and when a young physician named Charles Gloyd proposed marriage, she was eager to accept. She married him on November 21, 1867, too headstrong to heed warnings about his alcoholism. She soon acknowledged the extent of his problem and left him after ten months. She returned to her parents' home and gave birth to her daughter, Charlien, on September 27, 1868.

In 1871–72 Carry Gloyd attended the Missouri State Normal School in Warrensburg and earned a teaching certificate, then taught school in Holden until she lost her position to the niece of a school board member. Unemployed and desperate, she fixed her sights on David Nation, a widower with four children. He was nineteen years her senior and generally unpopular, but she married him anyway on December 30, 1874. Carry later declared that the chief benefit of their long, unhappy marriage was that it had given her a new name, one that prophetically declared her mission to "Carry A. Nation" for the prohibitionist cause.

The Nations lived in Warrensburg for two years, then acquired a cotton plantation in Brazoria County, Texas, where they moved in January 1877. The cotton venture failed, but the prospect of starvation prompted Carry to rent a boardinghouse in nearby Columbia. The business grew, and when they moved to Richmond, Texas, in 1881, she was able to buy a large hotel adjacent to the county courthouse. They lived in Richmond for eight years, with Carry as the family's breadwinner, but they were run out of town for supporting freedmen's voting rights.

Carry's life in the Great Plains began in Medicine Lodge, Kansas, where David found work as pastor of the Christian Church in 1889. With no hotel to keep her busy, and with all five children grown and living elsewhere, Carry channeled her energies into prohibitionism. Kansas was a "dry" state, but liquor flowed freely and public officials refused to enforce the law. Carry founded a local chapter of the Woman's Christian Temperance Union (WCTU) in 1892 and spearheaded its successful campaign to close the saloons of Medicine Lodge. Her activism waned between 1894 and 1899, when she and David homesteaded in Oklahoma Territory, but it returned with a vengeance after they moved back to Medicine Lodge. In June 1900 she dreamed that God was commanding her to take violent action, so she abandoned the WCTU's ladylike tactics and launched the "hatchetation" crusade that made her famous.

Carry moved to Topeka in January 1901 and made it her base of operations until 1905, when she shifted her headquarters to Guthrie, Oklahoma Territory, to fight for a "dry" Oklahoma statehood. In 1907 she moved to Washington DC, and in 1908 and 1909 took her crusade to Great Britain. She declared herself semiretired in 1909 and settled in Eureka Springs, Arkansas, but she continued her efforts until paralyzed by a stroke in January 1911. She was hospitalized in Leavenworth, Kansas, where she died on June 9, 1911.

Carry Nation was on the move throughout her career and supported herself by lecturing on the Lyceum, Chautauqua, and Vaudeville circuits, speaking wherever she could find an audience. She also sold souvenir hatchets and copies of her autobiography. With her earnings, she built a home for drunkards' wives in Kansas City, launched a purity farm for boys in Oklahoma, and gave to many causes. She created disturbances wherever she went, was jailed more than thirty times, and endured several beatings at the hands of her opponents. Noteworthy for her support of African Americans, Catholics, and Jews, and for her promotion of women's suffrage, sex education, and public health, she is nevertheless mainly remembered for the things that she opposed—alcohol, tobacco, political corruption, and fraternal organizations.

Karen Kidd
California State University, Fullerton

Nation, Carry A. *Scrapbook and Diary*. Topeka: Kansas State Historical Society. Nation, Carry A. *The Use and Need of the Life of Carry A. Nation*. Topeka: F. M. Steves and Sons, 1909.

NATIONAL CONGRESS OF AMERICAN INDIANS

The National Congress of American Indians (NCAI) is the oldest pan-Indian organization in the United States. Its mission is to "inform the public and the federal government on tribal self-government, treaty rights, and a broad range of federal policy issues affecting tribal governments." The NCAI provides legal aid to protect Indian civil rights and serves as a watchdog in protection of treaty rights.

Organized in Denver, Colorado, in 1944 by well-educated Native American leaders such as D'Arcy McNickle (Flathead), Archie Phinney (Nez Perce), and Charles E. Heacock (Sioux), the NCAI battled against the federal government's policies of termination of tribal status and relocation. The NCAI also scored an important victory in helping create the Indian Claims Commission. By the 1960s, with the threat of termination fading, the NCAI focused on issues such as poverty and public health. However, during the 1960s the NCAI lost its position as the sole voice for Native Americans. More radical groups, such as the American Indian Movement and the National Indian Youth Council, diverged from the moderate policies of the NCAI by taking a more militant stand. During the 1980s and 1990s the NCAI continued to work to protect Native American cultural rights and the repatriation of Indian artifacts and remains.

The NCAI has grown from an original membership of fifty tribes in 1944 to more than 250 member tribes in 2001. The NCAI functions as a legislative body, with tribes electing delegates to represent them at a national convention. With its headquarters in Washington DC, the NCAI continues to operate as a lobbying agent on behalf of all Native American peoples. Issues concerning the NCAI in 2001 included environmental protection and natural resources management, enhancement of Indian health, and the protection of Indian cultural resources and religious freedom.

Mark R. Ellis
University of Nebraska at Kearney

Cowger, Thomas W. *The National Congress of American Indians: The Founding Years*. Lincoln: University of Nebraska Press, 1999.

NATIONAL FARMERS UNION

The National Farmers Union (officially the Farmers Educational and Cooperative Union of America) originated in Point, Texas, in 1902. Farmers Union members saw themselves as continuing earlier efforts by the Farmers Alliance, the Populist Party, and the greenback and free silver movements to minimize the power of monopolies and enhance opportunities for small family farmers to achieve social and economic equality in the United States. The organization spread throughout various regions of the nation, but by the end of World War II was most firmly established in the Great Plains, with its most active affiliates in Nebraska, Kansas, Oklahoma, Montana, and the Dakotas.

The Farmers Union has consistently argued that U.S. government policies often contribute to an unholy alliance between big business and government, which leads to corporate domination of U.S. society. It has opposed protective tariffs as favoring large business enterprises and, in the field of agriculture, has criticized the American Farm Bureau Federation as an arm of the National Association of Manufacturers. The Farmers Union's rejection of a survival of the fittest approach to economic life led it to support the 1949 Brannan Plan calling for agricultural prices to seek their own levels in the marketplace while allowing government supports for smaller producers when prices fell below what was considered a fair return. The Farmers Union's concern for equity also led the organization to cooperate closely with organized labor, particularly in its opposition to the 1947 Taft-Hartley Act and its support for the 1946 Full Employment Act.

More than any other general farm organization, the Farmers Union paid particularly close attention to links between domestic and foreign policy, and it especially criticized U.S. policies abroad in the early years of the cold war. The Union claimed that the actions of the Truman administration, particularly the Marshall Plan to revitalize postwar Europe, contributed to the decline of the small family farmer by helping generate what it termed artificial scarcity at home. The Farmers Union hoped that the United States would move toward a foreign policy stressing, as it believed President Roosevelt had, international cooperation over military and economic competition. The Union's position on U.S. foreign policy generated accusations that the organization sympathized with communists, and the State Department and the House Un-American Activities Committee both kept a close watch on the activities of various Farmers Union spokesmen. Such scrutiny during the height of McCarthyism led to occasional rifts between the national organization and its various state and regional affiliates, a few of which, because of their exceptionally vocal criticism of U.S. policy, were eventually expelled from the Farmers Union.

Despite its outspoken views and its occasionally raucous history, the National Farmers Union still exists. With headquarters in both Washington DC and Denver, Colorado, an announced membership of 300,000 farm and ranch families, and a Web site, the Farmers Union still promotes the contributions rural America can make to a healthy U.S. society.

Bruce E. Field
Northern Illinois University

Field, Bruce E. *Harvest of Dissent: The National Farmers Union and the Early Cold War*. Lawrence: University Press of Kansas, 1998. Flamm, Michael W. "The National Farmers Union and the Evolution of Agrarian Liberalism, 1937–1946." *Agricultural History* 68 (1994): 54–80. Pratt, William C. "The Farmers Union, McCarthyism, and the Demise of the Agrarian Left." *Historian* 58 (1996): 329–42.

NONPARTISAN LEAGUE

United by low commodity prices, high interest rates, shady practices in the grain trade, and thwarted political goals, farmers of North Dakota gathered in the spring of 1915 to form the Nonpartisan League (NPL). Coalescing behind the impressive oratorical and organizational skills of Arthur C. Townley, the NPL served the state, and the nation, as a grand experiment in socialist agrarian reform.

After failing as a farmer and as an organizer

for North Dakota's Socialist Party, Townley drifted to Bismarck to observe the 1915 session of the state legislature, where representatives prepared to debate the creation of a state-owned terminal elevator. The elevator was intended to give North Dakota farmers a degree of control over the marketing of their wheat. In the heated debate, Fargo representative Treadwell Twitchell allegedly told farmers crowding the balcony that "running the state was none of their business" and that they should "go home and slop the hogs."

Rather than returning home, however, Townley met with a number of McHenry County farmers to discuss their growing resentment and frustration with politics as dominated by the grain trade and the railroads. Declaring that the end had come for machine politics, which left no role for farmers or laborers, the assembled men declared the formation of the Farmers Nonpartisan Political League, later renamed the Nonpartisan League.

Familiar with the failure of third-party political movements, Townley determined that the NPL should use existing parties to implement the organization's agenda. Accordingly, the NPL sought to endorse candidates from either of the major political parties in the state's open primaries in order to form a "nonpartisan" ticket that farmers could support in the November election. To gain farmers' support, candidates needed only to promise to uphold the NPL's ever-growing list of demands. By the primary of 1916, the League's platform included state ownership of terminal elevators, flour mills, cold storage plants, and packing plants; formation of a state hail insurance program; and establishment of state-owned banks that would offer farmers low-interest loans. Additionally, the state would inspect grain, exempt farm improvements from taxation, and create a program of public works for the unemployed.

Despite flooding on primary day that kept significant numbers of farmers from the polls, NPL-designated candidates carried all but one state office in June 1916. In the November general election, the NPL claimed control of the governorship, cabinet, and state house of representatives. Its failure to carry the state senate stalled the effort to achieve state socialism, but the organization's 40,000 members still held the day. During the 1917 session, the legislature passed into law much of the progressive agenda called for by NPL members. It created a much-improved grain grading system, established a state highway commission, prohibited rate discrimination by railroads, increased aid to education, and proposed constitutional amendments for female suffrage and the exemption of farm improvements from taxation.

In 1918, claiming near total victory, the Nonpartisan League began implementing what Townley referred to as the "New Day for North Dakota." Aided by constitutional amendments sponsored by the League and interpreted by an NPL-dominated state supreme court, the organization set about its agenda. The NPL utilized the 1919 legislative session to implement much of its platform, creating the North Dakota Mill and Elevator Association, the Home Building Association, the Bank of North Dakota, a state-sponsored hail insurance program, and an industrial commission to oversee the development of further state businesses. The 1919 legislative session also sponsored progressive legislation to provide workman's compensation, reduced hours of labor for working women, the inspection of coal mines, and limited the use of injunctions in labor disputes.

The party's appeal was not limited to North Dakota, and over the course of 1918–19 the movement expanded into the majority of Great Plains and midwestern states. At the height of its popularity, the NPL claimed more than 200,000 members in twenty states. Although the NPL never took control of the reins of state power elsewhere as it did in North Dakota, the political debate in many states clearly felt the influence of the organization.

The work of the NPL did not go unchallenged. Increasingly, the league's leadership came under attack for malfeasance, socialist inclination, and fraud. The primary opposition came from a coalition of disaffected businessmen and Republicans locked out of their own party. Charges from the Independent Voters Association, as well as the defection of major NPL officeholders—Attorney General William Langer, Secretary of State Thomas Hall, and state auditor Carl Kozitsky—and the publication of the salacious *Red Flame*, ultimately brought the NPL era in North Dakota to a close. Equally detrimental to the cause of continued NPL control was the almost universally poor management of the state's new businesses.

On October 28, 1921, NPL governor Lynn J. Frazier suffered the ignominy of being the first state official removed from office under the terms of an NPL-sponsored state constitutional amendment. The same recall election witnessed the removal of Attorney General William Lemke and Commissioner of Agriculture John Hagen. North Dakotans, however, voted to uphold the principles of state-sponsored business. Indeed, much of the program instigated by the NPL remains in place in modern-day North Dakota.

See also POLITICS AND GOVERNMENT: Frazier, Lynn; Langer, William; Lemke, William; North Dakota.

Kimberly K. Porter
University of North Dakota

Coleman, Patrick K., and Charles R. Lamb, compilers. *The Nonpartisan League, 1915–1922: An Annotated Bibliography*. St. Paul: Minnesota Historical Society Press, 1985. Morlan, Robert L. *Political Prairie Fire: The Nonpartisan League, 1915–1922*. St. Paul: Minnesota Historical Society Press, 1985. Robinson, Elwyn B. *History of North Dakota*. Lincoln: University of Nebraska Press, 1966.

O'HARE, KATE RICHARDS (1876–1948)

Born on March 26, 1876, in Ottawa County, Kansas, Kate Richards O'Hare was one of the most popular lecturers, journalists, and socialist reformers of the first decades of the twentieth century, with her strongest support coming in the Great Plains and the Southwest. She was the daughter of Kansas homesteaders who lost their land in the late 1880s and relocated to Kansas City, Missouri. Educated in Kansas, Missouri, and Nebraska, Kate taught school briefly, then turned to temperance and missionary work. Disillusioned, she became a machinist in her father's shop, which introduced her to the labor movement. In 1901 Kate enrolled in a socialist program in Girard, Kan

Kate Richards O'Hare and family

sas, a hub of socialist activism and the home of the newspaper *Appeal to Reason*. She became an organizer for the newly founded Socialist Party of America and, with her new husband, Frank Patrick O'Hare, went on the road to spread the word of socialism.

For five years the O'Hares and their four children homesteaded in Oklahoma Territory, which was then beginning to develop one of the fastest-growing socialist movements in the United States. Kate wrote for the regional socialist press and became the most popular local speaker at the socialist summer encampments in the Southwest, which featured nationally known lecturers and drew thousands of farmers. In 1909 the O'Hares relocated to Kansas City, Kansas, where Kate was a candidate for the U.S. House of Representatives in 1910. Thereafter, they settled in St. Louis, Missouri, where she became a staff writer for the *National Rip-Saw*, an agrarian socialist monthly, alongside her close colleague Eugene Debs.

As a socialist, O'Hare advocated peaceful means to achieve a collectivist system, promoting electoral activity, mass education, and reform measures. In the Socialist Party, she was the voice of the farmers of the Great Plains, one of the few party leaders who understood intimately the farmers' struggle with increasingly overwhelming economic forces. She introduced an agrarian plank to the party's platform and tried to expand its definition of the proletariat to include farmers. Meanwhile, O'Hare toured constantly on the socialist lecture circuit, with her spring and summer itineraries spanning the Dakotas through Texas and Oklahoma.

During World War I O'Hare upheld the Socialist Party's opposition to the war. She was found guilty of violating the Espionage Act for an antiwar speech she delivered in Bowman, North Dakota, in 1917 and served fourteen months of a five-year prison term. Thereafter, her activities focused on penal reform and labor education. In 1928 she divorced O'Hare, and that year married Charles C. Cunningham, a businessman, and gradually abandoned her activism, although she continued to lecture on civic issues until the end of her life. She died in Benicia, California, on January 10, 1948.

Sally M. Miller
University of the Pacific

Basen, Neil K. "Kate Richards O'Hare: The 'First Lady' of American Socialism, 1901–1917." *Labor History* 21 (1980): 165–99. Foner, Philip S., and Sally M. Miller, eds. *Kate Richards O'Hare: Selected Writings and Speeches*. Baton Rouge: Louisiana State University Press, 1982. Miller, Sally M. *From Prairie to Prison: The Life of Social Activist Kate Richards O'Hare*. Columbia: University of Missouri Press, 1993.

OKLAHOMA CITY BOMBING

The bombing of the Murrah Federal Building in downtown Oklahoma City at 9:02 on the morning of April 19, 1995, created emotional, social, and political shock waves that reverberated throughout the Great Plains and beyond. The deaths of 168 people and the wounding of more than 674 tragically confronted heartland

Oklahoma City National Memorial, Field of Empty Chairs

residents with the reality that they were not immune from the violent forces they had mainly perceived as an abstraction.

Previous outbreaks of violence associated with controversial social and political issues had been minor in the Great Plains. The bombings of abortion clinics were a continuing threat in the region, but loss of life and property were limited. In fact, under the criteria of the Department of Justice, such acts were not regarded as terrorism. However, the seeds for discontent continued to be sown as a result of the crisis in family farming and the closing of smokestack industries. That discontent was channeled and manipulated by the militia movement into a distrust and hatred of government, especially federal government. The discontent was greatly magnified by the deadly operations led by the Federal Bureau of Investigation against Randy Weaver and his family at Ruby Ridge in August 1992 and against the Branch Davidian compound near Waco, Texas, on April 19, 1993. The Waco siege had a very personal meaning for Timothy McVeigh, whose visit to the site contributed to his rage against the government, a rage that would be directed at the Murrah Building.

On the morning of April 19, 1995, an air of normalcy marked the beginning of another workday in Oklahoma City and the surrounding communities. The weather, while a little chilly, served as a reminder that spring had finally come to the Plains. Watercooler discussion focused on the continued revitalization of the downtown former factory area known as Bricktown and the prospects of the local triple-A baseball team. But all this would change at 9:02, when a massive explosion rocked the downtown and sent destructive shockwaves over a two-mile area. The explosion could be heard twenty miles away. Initially, those who were not on the immediate scene attributed the explosion to a sonic

boom from a military aircraft at Tinker Air Force Base in Midwest City or a gas explosion in one of the abandoned buildings in a decayed area near downtown. Even when the first pictures were transmitted by the local news helicopter a few minutes after the bombing, the source of the explosion was uncertain. The on-air pictures of the smoke and chaos at the Murrah Building obscured what had happened, even as survivors, bystanders, and first-aid workers sought to initiate rescue operations. It soon became clear from the destruction of the building that Oklahoma City had been subject to a terrorist attack.

Initially, the bombing was attributed to a Middle Eastern terrorist organization. First, a former Oklahoma congressman, with ties to the intelligence community and law enforcement in Washington DC, maintained that officials had indicated to him that a foreign group probably initiated the attack. Terrorist experts who appeared on network television largely shared this "conventional wisdom." Second, there was a state of denial that Americans could have engaged in such carnage against their fellow citizens. This changed with the capture of Timothy McVeigh, but a knee-jerk prejudice was one of the community's first responses to the bombing.

More impressive was the way the community assisted the survivors, their families, and the victims' families. The first responders, including the fire department, the police, and health-care professionals, helped to establish what is now called "the Oklahoma Standard" in dealing with mass destruction. Soon, support became national in scope, as rescue units from around the country converged on Oklahoma City.

The Oklahoma bombing entered a new and still ongoing legal phase with the capture, trial, and execution of Timothy McVeigh and the continuing disposition of the Terry Nichols case. Now almost ten years after the bombing, the inhabitants of Oklahoma City face the challenge of remembering and memorializing the victims and survivors without continuing a cycle of victimization. The Oklahoma City National Memorial is not only a powerful symbol of remembrances but has also become a leading tourist destination in the region. In addition, the Oklahoma City National Memorial Institute for the Prevention of Terrorism was established to study terrorism as well as train first responders to deal more effectively with future incidents.

See also RELIGION: Branch Davidians
Stephen Sloan
University of Oklahoma

OMAHA RACE RIOT

See AFRICAN AMERICANS: Omaha Race Riot

ON-TO-OTTAWA TREK

In early April 1935 hundreds of dissatisfied, disillusioned men walked out of federally run relief camps throughout British Columbia and descended on Vancouver in a bold attempt to reverse their dead-end lives and bring about some kind of "work for wages" program. No one wanted to deal with the men, least of all Conservative prime minister R. B. Bennett, who believed that the Communist Party of Canada had orchestrated the protest. As the stalemate dragged on week after numbing week, the men decided to go to Ottawa and lay their grievances directly before the government.

An estimated 1,000 On-to-Ottawa trekkers left Vancouver by freight train in early June 1935. No attempt was made to stop them. Police and government authorities confidently assumed that the resolve of the workers on relief would melt away like the snow in the interior mountains. But as the freight train the men were riding gained momentum as it rumbled down the Albertan foothills into the Prairies, so too did the trek. The audacity of the men stirred the imagination of those who had suffered through five terrible years of drought and depressed prices. Here were hundreds of young men headed to Ottawa to tell the country's political leaders that they were not doing enough to help ease the hardship and deprivation of western Canada. The Bennett government, on the other hand, saw only an army of single, homeless, unemployed men who had nothing to lose and might to do anything.

As the trek continued east from Calgary, the Canadian government hurriedly made plans to bring it to an end. Not only had the ranks of the trekkers swollen to 1,500 because of a number of new recruits from Alberta, but hundreds more were expected to join in Winnipeg. The federal government consequently announced that the trek would be stopped at Regina, on the grounds that it was an unlawful movement.

The On-to-Ottawa Trek, numbering an estimated 2,000 men, reached Regina on June 14. Over the next two weeks, the two sides tried unsuccessfully to reach some kind of agreement; a special meeting between the trek leaders and the prime minister, for example, quickly degenerated into a shouting match. With no way out of Regina, the trekkers decided at the end of June to return to the west coast. But Ottawa insisted that the group had to disband on federal terms—namely, go to a nearby hurriedly erected holding facility where the men would be processed. The trek leadership balked at this proposal—they wanted nothing to do with a "concentration camp"—and turned to Jimmy Gardiner's provincial government for assistance on the afternoon of July 1.

Later that evening, while the provincial cabinet met to discuss the trek request, the North-West Mounted Police, with the support of the Regina city police, decided to execute warrants for the trek leaders at a public rally at Market Square. The mounted police could easily have made the arrests at any time during the day, but instead, with clubs and tear gas at the ready, chose to pluck the men from a peaceful fund-raising meeting. The raid quickly degenerated into a pitched battle between the police and trekkers and citizens, which spilled over into the streets of downtown Regina. Order was not restored until the early hours of the next day, and only after the police had fired directly into crowds of rioters. The toll was one dead, a good number injured, more than 100 arrested, and thousands of dollars in damage.

In the immediate aftermath of the riot, the Saskatchewan government launched a public inquiry. Three hundred and fifty-nine witnesses provided fifty-three volumes of testimony and one inescapable conclusion—the police had provoked the violence by trying to arrest the trek leaders at a public rally. But in their two-volume report, the commissioners assigned the blame for the riot to the trekkers, while the police were completely exonerated.

The On-to-Ottawa Trek was a testament to how the Canadian government had so miserably failed the country's single, homeless, unemployed population during the Great Depression. It also underscored how the Canadian government was prepared to use force in the interests of "peace, order, and good government."

See also CITIES AND TOWNS: Regina, Saskatchewan / POLITICS AND GOVERNMENT: Bennett, Richard B.

Bill Waiser
University of Saskatchewan

Brown, Lorne. *When Freedom Was Lost: The Unemployed, the Agitator, and the State.* Montreal: Black Rose Books, 1987. Howard, Victor. *"We Were the Salt of the Earth!": A Narrative of the On-to-Ottawa Trek and the Regina Riot.* Regina: Canadian Plains Research Center, 1985. Saskatchewan Archives Board.

PARTRIDGE, EDWARD A. (1861–1931)

Edward Alexander Partridge was born on November 5, 1861, in Dalston, Ontario. After completing school, Partridge earned a teacher's certificate. He taught in Ontario, but he was a restless man, content only when building something. The opening of the Canadian Prairies beckoned, and in 1883 Partridge and his brother headed west to homestead near Sintaluta (now in Saskatchewan), where he resided until 1927. On arrival at Sintaluta, Partridge worked as a schoolteacher. He also fulfilled some of his required homestead residency by serving in the Yorkton Company Militia of Canada for three months during the 1885 Riel Rebellion. He fell in love with Mary Stephens, a young woman from a nearby town. They married in 1886 and devoted their lives to building their farm and raising a family of five.

Partridge quickly developed an analysis of the Canadian social and economic system that was premised on the understanding that capitalism is a class-based system, with inherent patterns of exploitation, domination, and inequities. As a result of his and others' difficulties in marketing grain at competitive prices, he entered into a lifelong mission to change the world through collective struggle. Partridge was present in 1901 when a group of disgruntled farmers organized one of the first western Canadian agrarian political action organizations, the Territorial Grain Growers Association. Partridge quickly concluded that political lobbying was limited in its potential to effect real social change, so in 1908 he campaigned to form a farmers' grain company, the Grain Growers Grain Company (GGGC). Although the GGGC eventually evolved into a successful cooperative, for Partridge it did not represent a real solution. As Partridge and others undertook various campaigns to establish cooperatives, secure political concessions, and generally improve the lot of farmers, they encountered what they considered unfair coverage in the press. In order to present their side of the story, they created an agrarian news journal in 1908. Partridge was the first editor of the *Grain Growers Guide*, but as was typical of his restless spirit, he only lasted one issue before moving on. His next undertaking was a campaign to secure public ownership of the elevator system through the involvement of provincial governments. Although it never came to fruition, the "Partridge Plan" did result in government support for a cooperative elevator company.

In addition to organizing cooperatives and grain companies, Prairie farmers attempted to shape government policies, especially those relating to tariffs. In 1910 hundreds of farmers converged on Ottawa in what became known as the "Siege of Ottawa." Partridge was there. World War I brought a temporary lull to the agrarian agitation; however, it also brought personal tragedy to Partridge and his wife. In 1914 one of their daughters drowned while swimming near the farm. Then, although Partridge was a pacifist, their two sons served and were killed during World War I. Partridge's health remained a problem, in part because he had lost a leg in a farm accident in 1908.

Partridge, undoubtedly supported by Mary, joined the fight for a western political party after the war. He also became involved in organizing a new group, the Farmers Union of Canada, in 1921, and in organizing the Wheat Pool in Saskatchewan. In 1926 he explicated his vision of a better world in a book, *A War on Poverty*. The vision and spiritual message of the book reflect the remarkable resilience of the human spirit; however, he was not able to recover from one last loss, Mary's death while she was gardening on the farm. Partridge left Saskatchewan and ended his own life in Victoria on August 3, 1931.

Murray Knuttila
University of Regina

POSSE COMITATUS

This extreme right-wing group takes its name from the Latin for "power of the county." Its founders, Henry Beach and William Potter Gale, were radical localists who claimed that the county is the highest and only legitimate level of government to which citizens owe allegiance—it is only the county, they argue, headed by a sheriff chosen by the community's white male residents, that possesses the right to enforce the law. According to Posse doctrine, the law itself is derived from the Bible, English common law, the Articles of Confederation, and, more vaguely, the U.S. Constitution. In their minds, no "Jew-dominated" legislature or Congress has the ability to make laws that "real, white Americans" are obliged to follow.

Beach, a member of the pro-Nazi Silver Shirt movement during the 1930s, and Gale, a former World War II army officer and a key figure in the development of the racist and anti-Semitic Christian Identity ideology, organized the Posse Comitatus in Portland, Oregon, in 1969 in the midst of the Vietnam War and the country's racial tensions. But it was during the mid-1970s and 1980s, and in the Great Plains, that this loosely connected organization, whose members sought to retain their anonymity, achieved prominence. The farm crisis of these years created the conditions necessary for their doctrine to attract significant support. Such Posse figures as Gordon Kahl, a North Dakota farmer, James Wickstrom, the Posse's self-proclaimed "counterinsurgency director," and Rick Elliot, a Colorado dairy farmer who became the publisher of the anti-Semitic *Primrose and Cattlemen's Gazette* (its message being that Jews were leading cattlemen down the primrose path), crisscrossed the region explaining to farmers and ranchers why they were under no obligation to repay overdue loans or peacefully accept the foreclosure of their property. This appealed to some indebted and hard-pressed farmers whose entire way of life was in jeopardy. At "seminars" and on country music radio stations such as KTTL-FM in Dodge City, Kansas, Posse spokesmen explained to their listeners that they were under no obligation to pay income taxes to a fraudulent Internal Revenue Service or abide by the judgments of federal or state courts. According to a 1976 FBI report, the Posse had seventy-eight chapters located in twenty-three states, concentrated, for the most part, in the Great Plains and the Midwest.

Some Posse figures attempted to transform their rhetoric—about resisting the government and cleansing the land—into reality. Violent encounters between law enforcement officers and Posse members attracted widespread attention. The most notorious of these incidents—it was later made into a television film—involved Kahl, who in 1983 shot and killed two deputies in a dispute over his failure to pay taxes. He fled to Arkansas, where he murdered a local sheriff and was then himself killed in the ensuing conflict. This was the most dramatic, but hardly the only, episode in which Posse members threatened or carried out violent attacks on individuals they defined as their enemies. Although the Posse Comitatus is not as visible today as in the past, it continues to be an intermittently active faction of antigovernment protest.

Leonard Weinberg
University of Nevada, Reno

Corcoran, James. *Bitter Harvest: Gordon Kahl and the Posse Comitatus: Murder in the Heartland.* New York: Penguin Books, 1990. George, John, and Laird Wilcox, *American Extremists.* Amherst NY: Prometheus Books, 1996. Sargent, Lyman Towered, ed. *Extremism in America.* New York: New York University Press, 1995.

REED, MYRON (1836–1899)

Myron Reed, between 1886 and 1901

Myron Winslow Reed, Civil War veteran, celebrated preacher, and the West's foremost Christian Socialist, demanded justice for Native Americans, women's suffrage, and assistance for the poor without mandating any moral criteria. Reed was born in Windsor County, Vermont, on July 24, 1836, and graduated from Chicago Theological Seminary in 1868. He conducted ministries in New Orleans, Milwaukee, and Indianapolis before moving to Denver to pastor the First Congregational Church (1884–94). A Democratic candidate for Congress in 1886 and a cofounder of Denver's Associated Charities Organization in 1887, Reed felt he would be more effective as a voice for the Populists, laborers, and ordinary folk: he declared that he would speak his mind to all who would listen, and no rich man would own him.

In response to the problems imposed on the West by industrialism, Reed offered Christian Socialism. After the 1886 Haymarket Affair in Chicago, which resulted in deaths of protesting workers and police, the *Rocky Mountain News* published Reed's observations that the nation's newspapers had condemned a version of socialism, but not true socialism. He emphasized a Christian Socialism based on cooperation, not cutthroat competition, and which advocated a new society fashioned by persuasion, not violence. In "The Evolution of the Tramp," four sermons published by the *News* (1886), Reed declared that jobless tramps were victims of industrialism. The tramp, he argued, acted as a warning to society that the social system had failed. Known for his epigrams, Reed said, "It is not a comfortable world while a single soul goes without."

Reed supported the Knights of Labor and the worker's right to organize and bargain collectively. During the 1894 Cripple Creek miners' strike, he publicly backed the strikers. This action resulted in his resignation from his pas-

torate and the subsequent organization of the independent Broadway Temple, which charged no pew rent. Here Reed preached to a full auditorium, emphasizing workers' rights and Christian Socialism. As president of the Brotherhood of the Cooperative Commonwealth, he planned to organize a socialist colony in Colorado, but illness stopped him.

"The people's voice" died on January 30, 1899. More than 6,000 people from all walks of life tried to crowd into the Broadway Temple for his funeral. These mourners confirmed his influence and popularity for all social classes.

James A. Denton
University of Colorado at Boulder

Denton, James A. *Rocky Mountain Radical: Myron W. Reed, Christian Socialist.* Albuquerque: University of New Mexico Press, 1997. Reed, Myron W. *Temple Talks.* Indianapolis: Bowen-Merrill Company, 1898. Szasz, Ferenc Morton. *The Protestant Clergy in the Great Plains and Mountain West, 1865–1915.* Albuquerque: University of New Mexico Press, 1988.

RIEL, LOUIS (1844–1885)

Born on October 22 or 23, 1844, in Red River Colony (Manitoba), Riel was educated in St. Boniface before being sent by Bishop Alexandre Taché to attend the Sulpician College in Montreal in the hope that he would become a priest. Riel was expelled from the college in 1865, after which he wrote poetry, read law, and spent time in the United States.

Returning to Red River in July 1868, Riel quickly became a leader in the agitation that was developing over the annexation of the Northwest. At his urging, the Métis established a provisional government on December 8, 1869, to force Canada to negotiate the entry of the Northwest into Confederation, and he was elected president. In the events that followed, a young Ontario Orangeman, Thomas Scott, was executed by a Métis firing squad, an act that enraged the people of Ontario. To avoid reprisals, Riel fled Red River prior to the arrival of a military expedition, and when the Ontario provincial government posted a five-thousand-dollar reward for the capture of those involved in Scott's death, he sought refuge in the United States.

Riel was elected three times as a member of Parliament for the constituency of Provencher, but he never took his seat and was subsequently expelled from the House of Commons. In December 1875 he underwent a deep religious experience that convinced him he had a special mission to fulfill. Riel's outward manifestations of religiosity resulted in his confinement in asylums in Quebec. Upon his release in January 1878, Riel went to the United States, where he lived with friends. He arrived in Montana in 1880, married a Métis woman, Marguerite Monet *dit* Bellehumeur, acquired U.S. citizenship in 1883, and taught school at Saint Peter's Mission on the Sun River.

On June 4, 1884, a delegation of Métis from the territorial district of Saskatchewan arrived at the mission to ask Riel to return with them and champion the cause of the people of the Northwest. Riel accepted the invitation and

Hanging of Louis Riel in effigy, July 1885

returned to Saskatchewan, where he organized a movement to pressure the Canadian government to redress the grievances of the Northwest.

In the meantime, Riel had religious revelations and claimed to be a prophet with a mission to create a new social order in the Canadian Northwest. On March 19, 1885, Riel formed a provisional government known as the Exovedate, and hostilities broke out a few days later. The Métis eventually were defeated at the village of Batoche, and Riel surrendered on May 15. He was taken to Regina, where he was charged with high treason. He was tried, found guilty, and sentenced to death, despite the jury's recommendation for clemency. Riel was hanged in Regina on November 16, 1885.

His execution contributed to a political revolution in Quebec, strained dominion-provincial relationships, and furthered the division between French and English in Canada. The condemnation of Riel's actions by the Catholic clergy disappointed the Métis and contributed to the emergence of a distinct Métis national consciousness.

See also NATIVE AMERICANS: Métis / WAR: North-West Rebellion; Red River Resistance.

Raymond J. A. Huel
University of Lethbridge

Flanagan, Thomas. *Louis "David" Riel: "Prophet of the New World."* Toronto: University of Toronto Press, 1996. Stanley, G. F. G., ed. *The Collected Writings of Louis Riel/ Les écrits complets de Louis Riel.* Edmonton: University of Alberta Press, 1985.

SILKWOOD V. KERR-MCGEE CORPORATION

Silkwood v. Kerr-McGee Corporation is a dense court decision concerning statutory interpretation and punitive damages. But it is better known for the mystery at its heart: the unexplained 1974 death of Karen Silkwood, a twenty-eight-year-old divorced mother of three small children. In the quarter century since her death, Silkwood has become a symbol of the antinuclear movement in the United States.

The complicated legal action was occasioned by the radioactive contamination of Silkwood, a laboratory analyst at Kerr-McGee's Cimarron nuclear fuel-rod fabrication plant near Crescent, Oklahoma. Silkwood, who had lived most of her life in small Texas and Oklahoma towns, had been working for Kerr-McGee for a little more than two years before a routine radiation check in early November 1974 revealed that she had been contaminated by plutonium, one of the most radioactive substances in existence. Subsequent tests disclosed that the radioactive poison persisted not only in Silkwood's person but in her apartment.

Before these unsettling incidents, Silkwood had complained about what she saw as Kerr-McGee's cavalier disregard for worker safety. Furthermore, as an elected union representative, she had been responsible for bringing the company's safety violations to the attention of the Atomic Energy Commission. So, when she discovered she had been exposed to extraordinarily high levels of radiation, she suspected that she might have been intentionally contaminated for her whistle-blowing. She also believed that the company had doctored photomicrographs of fuel rods in order to meet regulatory standards. On the night of November 13, 1974, she had made arrangements to show a reporter for the *New York Times* evidence of alleged Kerr-McGee illegalities. On her way to the meeting, she was killed in an automobile accident that has never been adequately explained.

After her death, Bill Silkwood, Karen's father and executor, sued Kerr-McGee in federal court for civil damages accruing from Karen's contamination. Because of the suspicious circumstances surrounding the death of a nuclear-industry critic, the Silkwood civil trial became a cause célèbre for the antinuclear movement. The Silkwood family was represented in court by the flamboyant attorney Gerry Spence from Wyoming. At the conclusion of the longest civil litigation in Oklahoma history, the jury found in favor of the Silkwood estate to the tune of $505,000 in compensatory damages and a staggering $10 million in punitive damages.

A myriad of legal motions and appeals stretched the case into the 1980s. The circuit court of appeals eventually overturned the punitive damages portion of the district court verdict. But on further appeal on January 11, 1984, the U.S. Supreme Court, in a five to four decision, reversed the circuit court and reinstated the jury's finding of punitive damages. Although Congress in the Price-Anderson Act of 1957 and the Atomic Energy Act of 1954 had certainly intended to institute a comprehensive regulation of nuclear power, the Supreme Court concluded that the legislators had not meant to preempt the assignment of punitive damages against a nuclear licensee in a civil lawsuit. The holding remains controversial among some legal scholars who question the Supreme Court's reading of relevant nuclear regulatory statutes. Perhaps more importantly, the name Karen Silkwood continues to resonate in the memories of nuclear critics, abetted by books such as *Who Killed Karen Silkwood?* (1981) and popular films such as *The China Syndrome* (1979) and *Silkwood* (1983).

John W. Johnson
University of Northern Iowa

Johnson, John W. *Insuring against Disaster: The Nuclear Industry on Trial.* Macon GA: Mercer University Press, 1986. Kohn, Howard. *Who Killed Karen Silkwood?* New York: Summit Books, 1981. *Silkwood v. Kerr-McGee Corporation,* 464 U.S. 238, 104 Sup. Ct. 615, 78 L. Ed. 2d 443 (1984).

STRONG, ANNA LOUISE (1885–1970)

Anna Louise Strong was a foreign correspondent and social activist whose midwestern idealism and pioneering spirit led her to extended stays in Russia and China. Although never a member of the Communist Party, she sympathized with the Communist cause and wrote of its struggles with a vibrant naivete, believing that a new era of human progress had arrived.

Anna Louise Strong was born on November 25, 1885, in a two-room parsonage in Friend, Nebraska, where her father, Sydney Strong, was a Congregational minister who was deeply involved in progressive movements. When she was not yet two, family lore relates, a late summer cyclone lifted her from the front yard and deposited her, relatively unscathed, in the cow pasture some distance away—an archetypal Plains experience.

Sydney Strong's ministry took the family to various midwestern locations such as Cincinnati, Ohio, and Oak Park, Illinois. A diligent and precocious student, Anna finished high school at fifteen, graduated from Oberlin College summa cum laude, and became, at age twenty-three, the youngest woman to receive a doctorate from the University of Chicago.

In Kansas City in 1911, Strong was director of the Child Welfare Exhibit Program, an organization dedicated to improving the well-being of urban children. It was there that she embraced socialism and decided to devote her life to progressive social causes. In 1919, as editor of the *Seattle Union Record,* she played an important role in the Seattle General Strike. In

1921 she traveled to the new Soviet Union, which became her principal home until 1949, when she was expelled by Stalin as a suspected spy. During this time she made yearly trips and lecture tours back to the United States, while also covering revolutionary developments in China, Mexico, and Spain. Shunned by both the American right and left and labeled a Soviet spy during the McCarthy era, she lived and wrote in California until she decided to take up residence in China in 1958.

Strong was warmly received by the Chinese Communist leaders, who saw her as a valuable propaganda mouthpiece they could use in their dealings with the West. She had interviewed Mao Tse-tung in 1946 at the Communist headquarters in Yenan, where he first used the term "paper tiger" to refer to Western imperialists. Her death in Beijing in March 1970 was an occasion for public mourning and a state funeral. She is buried in the Revolutionary Martyrs' Cemetery in Beijing.

Molly Spitzer Frost
George Washington University

Strong, Anna Louise. *China's Millions*. New York: Coward-McCann, 1928. Strong, Anna Louise. *I Change Worlds*. New York: Holt, Rinehart and Winston, 1935. Strong, Tracy, and Helene Keyssar. *Right in Her Soul: The Life of Anna Louise Strong*. New York: Random House, 1983.

SUFFRAGE MOVEMENT

See GENDER: Suffrage Movement

TEMPERANCE MOVEMENT

The temperance movement arose in the nineteenth century as a result of high rates of liquor consumption, consumption that many observers thought damaging to the individual drinker, to families, to communities, and to society as a whole. This movement operated in both the United States and Canada, as reformers sought to reduce the volume of alcohol consumption. The temperance crusade had roots in the evangelical Protestant churches that sought to remove barriers to the "right behaviors" leading to salvation, in this case overconsumption. There were both separate and common organizations in the two nations. Especially important in common was the Woman's Christian Temperance Union (WCTU), founded in the United States in 1874 and organized in Canada that same year. Each state and province, however, had other temperance organizations; in the United States, for example, the Anti-Saloon League was especially powerful in the first decades of the twentieth century.

Concerned about the human and social wastage brought about by high rates of alcohol consumption, temperance advocates worked to reform the individual drinker. Most typical in this regard were religious revivals and other activities of moral persuasion aimed at obtaining pledges from individuals to reform themselves by abstaining from alcoholic drink. The temperance movement soon moved from persuasion and pledge-taking to legal controls. Reformers worked for measures to prohibit businesses from manufacturing, distributing,

and selling alcoholic beverages. Across the Great Plains, communities turned to "local option" laws. Later they worked to achieve state- or provincewide prohibition laws and, eventually, national laws.

Prohibition was a lively political issue in all of the Great Plains states and provinces for many years. In the United States, federal law applied prohibition to Indian lands from 1834 to 1953. In the 1850s Americans witnessed a wave of state prohibition measures, most of which were repealed within a few years. Prohibition came more permanently to the Great Plains in 1880, when Kansas adopted state prohibition in a popular referendum. The experience in Kansas with prohibition was especially noteworthy. Although prohibition enjoyed strong majority support, a minority of citizens opposed the measure, and illegal distribution and sale continued, with saloons brazenly operating in some communities. With prohibition sentiment building across the nation by the turn of the twentieth century, some Kansas citizens sought better enforcement of their anti-drink statute. The state WCTU successfully used nonviolent demonstrations to close some establishments. Frustrated by continuing illegal operations, however, Carry Nation achieved national notoriety in 1900 and 1901 when she traveled to Kansas communities and physically smashed saloons and their liquor stocks. Her controversial actions stirred the prohibition movement but did little to bring about better enforcement of the law.

The success of the Kansas prohibition referendum in 1880 spurred protestors in other states to enact similar legislation, often with the active campaigning of the WCTU. In Texas, the temperance movement gained strength with the formation of the United Friends of Temperance around 1870 and the state WCTU in 1883. Local option spread in Texas, although the state did not enact prohibition laws prior to the success of the national movement. In 1889 North Dakota became the first state to enter the union under prohibition legislation. Oklahoma also entered as a dry state in 1907, so powerful were its temperance reformers. By 1917 all of the Great Plains states except Texas and Wyoming had enacted prohibition laws. The United States enacted national prohibition under the Eighteenth Amendment to the Constitution, in effect from January 16, 1920, until December 6, 1933, when it was repealed by the Twenty-first Amendment. In the United States, with the end of national prohibition, the repeal movement swept the Great Plains states. Kansas held onto prohibition until 1948 and Oklahoma until 1959.

In Canada, although the Prairie Provinces by 1900 provided for restrictions on alcohol sales, the situation was complicated because the federal government retained the right to regulate the manufacture of alcoholic beverages. Eventually, by popular referendum, prohibition was adopted in Alberta (1915), Manitoba (1916), and Saskatchewan (1917). Prohibition, however, proved short-lived in the Canadian provinces. By 1925 the three Prairie provinces had abandoned prohibition in favor of sales under strict government control.

K. Austin Kerr
Ohio State University

Bader, Robert Smith. *Prohibition in Kansas: A History*. Lawrence: University Press of Kansas, 1986. Franklin, Jimmie Lewis. *Born Sober: Prohibition in Oklahoma, 1907–1959*. Norman: University of Oklahoma Press, 1971. Gould, Lewis L. *Progressives and Prohibitionists: Texas Democrats in the Wilson Era*. Austin: University of Texas Press, 1973.

TOWNLEY, ARTHUR C. (1880–1959)

Arthur C. Townley, founder of the Nonpartisan League, was born near Browns Valley, Minnesota, on December 30, 1880. After failing three times to make a living by farming (in Cheyenne Wells, Colorado, and Beach and Golden Valley, North Dakota) and alienated by an economy that did not reward his efforts, Townley turned to the Socialist Party. His impressive organizational and oratorical skills quickly propelled him into the party's leadership. Unorthodox methods of recruiting, however, frustrated party leaders and led to his expulsion.

Townley then directed his energies to the farmers' cause, and in February 1915, along with A. E. Brown, he founded the Farmers Nonpartisan Political League of North Dakota, otherwise known as the Nonpartisan League (NPL). The NPL platform grew to include state ownership of terminal elevators, flour mills, cold storage plants, and packing plants, as well as a state-sponsored hail insurance program and state-owned banks. By 1918 the organization claimed 200,000 members and controlled the state of North Dakota. Accordingly, the NPL began to implement its platform. The party, however, came under attack for malfeasance, socialist inclinations, and fraud. The NPL fell from power in the autumn of 1921 when a recall election removed one of its leading representatives, Gov. Lynn Frazier, from office. Townley did not hold elected public office himself, preferring to remain behind the scenes as president of the NPL and its master organizer.

Following a ninety-day federal prison sentence in 1922 for discouraging enlistment during World War I, Townley resigned his position as head of the NPL in North Dakota, and the movement soon collapsed. Townley never again captured the limelight. He tried and failed to win political office in North Dakota and Minnesota on several occasions between 1930 and 1958, dabbled in oil promotion and itinerant medicine sales, and supported his stepdaughter's motion picture career. He also took a virulent anticommunist stance during the 1950s, targeting leaders of the Farmers Union. Townley died in a car accident near Makoti, North Dakota, on November 7, 1959.

Kimberly K. Porter
University of North Dakota

Morlan, Robert L. *Political Prairie Fire: The Nonpartisan League, 1915–1922*. St. Paul: Minnesota Historical Society Press, 1985. Remele, Larry R. *The Lost Years of A. C. Townley (After the Nonpartisan League)*. Bismarck: North Dakota Humanities Council, 1988.

TRIAL OF STANDING BEAR

On May 12, 1879, in Omaha, Nebraska, in the U.S. Circuit Court for the District of Nebraska, Judge Elmer Dundy ruled that noncitizen Indians—in this case, a group of Poncas led by Chief Standing Bear—were defined as persons in terms of federal law and entitled to review under habeas corpus protections (a constitutionally based appeal used to determine whether a person is restrained or imprisoned without due process). The writ of habeas corpus specifically stated that Standing Bear and his followers had withdrawn from the Ponca tribe. Standing Bear's case not only played a central role in four crucial decades of Ponca-federal relations, but it also directly influenced landmark Indian policy changes of the 1880s.

In an 1858 treaty, the Poncas ceded all their lands except for a small reservation (in present-day northeastern Nebraska) on the lower Niobrara River. Dutifully taking up farming the white man's way, the Poncas endured terrible hardships when their crops regularly failed and Indian agency supplies remained woefully inadequate. Yet their long-standing friendship with the United States failed to prevent their forced removal to Indian Territory in the spring of 1877. The Poncas' conditions worsened due to the Office of Indian Affairs' complete lack of preparation for their arrival—no lands had been reserved and no appropriation secured to provide food, clothing, and housing. As many as 200 Poncas died from related hardships. In January 1879 Standing Bear and twenty-nine others fled back to their Nebraska homeland. When they reached the Omaha reservation in March, the U.S. Army arrested them and escorted them to Fort Omaha (located four miles north of Omaha, Nebraska).

On March 30 *Omaha Daily Herald* assistant editor Thomas Henry Tibbles interviewed Standing Bear and dispatched a stream of features to newspapers in Chicago, New York, and other eastern cities. Tibbles also inaugurated a legal challenge against Standing Bear's arrest, obtaining the services of two prominent Omaha attorneys, John Lee Webster and A. J. Poppleton. In May, Judge Dundy delivered his extraordinary ruling that habeas corpus safeguards applied to Standing Bear, even though as a Native American he was a noncitizen and in spite of the fact that for all practical purposes he had renounced his Ponca tribal affiliation. Moreover, because federal statutes authorized the army to deliver prisoners only to civil authorities, making the Ponca detainment at Fort Omaha illegal, Dundy ordered Standing Bear and the Poncas released and directed that there would be no appeals to a higher court.

Judge Dundy's bold decision protected Standing Bear's Poncas from being returned to Indian Territory, but it provided no lands for them. In 1890 they finally secured allotments on their former reservation. Equally important, Standing Bear's struggle for justice significantly influenced the national movement to reform Indian policy. In the fall of 1879 Tibbles featured Standing Bear on a highly successful Indian reform tour that included Chicago, Boston, New York, Philadelphia, and Washington. In Boston, Standing Bear's eloquence so impressed Massachusetts senator Henry L. Dawes that he plunged into the Indian reform movement. He joined the Senate Indian Affairs Committee, and his leadership on Indian issues and prominence on the popular issue of Indian assimilation led directly to passage of the 1887 General Allotment (or Dawes) Act. Standing Bear lived on his family allotment on the Niobrara until his death in 1908.

See also NATIVE AMERICANS: Poncas; Standing Bear.

Dennis J. Smith
Morningside College

Hoxie, Frederick E. *A Final Promise: The Campaign to Assimilate the Indians, 1880–1920.* Lincoln: University of Nebraska Press, 1984. Lake, James A., Sr. "Standing Bear, Who?" *Nebraska Law Review* 60 (1981): 451–503. Tibbles, Thomas Henry. *The Ponca Chiefs: An Account of the Trial of Standing Bear*, edited by Kay Graber. Lincoln: University of Nebraska Press, 1972.

TULSA RACE RIOT

See AFRICAN AMERICANS: Tulsa Race Riot

UNITED FARMERS OF ALBERTA

The United Farmers of Alberta (UFA) was established in 1909 as an amalgamation of the Alberta Farmers Association and the Alberta Society of Equity, the latter an offshoot of the American Society of Equity. The UFA's primary aim was to ameliorate the vulnerable economic position of Alberta farmers. It protested the protective Canadian tariff on farm equipment, lobbied for the regulation of marketing practices at grain elevators, and called for an end to government-endorsed railway monopolies.

In 1912 the UFA endorsed women's suffrage and encouraged farm women to become involved in the organization. In 1915 the United Farm Women of Alberta (UFWA) was formed, campaigning for women's suffrage (gained in 1916), temperance, and rural health and education standards. Unlike women's auxiliaries in traditional Canadian political organizations, the UFWA did not mainly bake cookies and stuff envelopes. These women stood with their UFA men as economically disadvantaged farm workers, but they also used annual conventions and agrarian newsletters to raise their gender-specific concerns.

Physically removed from the national center of power in Ottawa and disillusioned by the corrupt and seemingly undifferentiated national political parties, many in the UFA began to advocate direct political action. Henry Wise Wood, president of the organization from 1916 to 1931, was a native Missourian who had witnessed the failures of the Farmers Alliance and the Populist Party. He was therefore skeptical of direct political action by farmers. Nevertheless, he became convinced that direct involvement was needed, and he advocated a theory of group government or political representation based on occupation.

In 1916 the Nonpartisan League, fresh from its political victories in North Dakota, entered Alberta to mobilize farmers into political action. Also in 1916 the UFA endorsed the Canadian Council of Agriculture's "Farmers' Platform," which provided a clear statement of agrarian political goals. Resolved to political action, the UFA merged with the Nonpartisan League in 1919 and contested the 1921 Alberta election. The UFA ran only rural candidates, cooperating in some instances with urban labor candidates. It won the election and remained in office until 1935. Wood refused the premiership, which went instead to Herbert Greenfield (1921–25), then to John Brownlee (1925–34), and R. G. Reid (1934–35). Of particular interest, in 1921 Irene Parlby, former president of the UFWA, became the first woman cabinet minister in Alberta.

Despite Wood's radical theories of group government, the UFA governed in a conventional, efficient manner, establishing wheat, dairy, poultry, and livestock pools and improving provincial health and education services. With the onset of the Great Depression, the UFA attempted to provide debt relief for farmers, but its solutions were ineffective and too orthodox for the Alberta electorate. In 1935 Social Credit swept the UFA out of office, and the UFA then retreated from political activity. Today the UFA operates farm supply stores and petroleum outlets throughout Alberta, sponsors rural youth groups, and remains one of Canada's largest farmer-owned agricultural organizations.

See also POLITICS AND GOVERNMENT: Alberta.

Amy Nugent
University of Calgary

Betke, Carl. "The United Farmers of Alberta, 1921–1935." In *Riel to Reform: A History of Protest in Western Canada*, edited by George Melnyk. Saskatoon: Fifth House Publishers, 1992. Morton, W. L. *The Progressive Party in Canada*. Toronto: University of Toronto Press, 1950.

UNITED FARMERS OF CANADA, SASKATCHEWAN SECTION

An agrarian protest organization that enjoyed considerable popularity from the late 1920s to the 1940s, the United Farmers of Canada, Saskatchewan Section (UFCSS), was founded in 1926 as a result of a merger between the Farmers Union of Canada and the Saskatchewan Grain Growers Association (SGGA). The two groups had formerly been rivals; in fact, the Farmers Union of Canada was established in response to what its members saw as a conservative SGGA leadership that was too closely tied to the provincial government and that had lost touch with rank and file farmers. The amalgamation was ratified at the UFCSS's inaugural meeting in 1927, and long-serving agrarian activist E. A. Partridge was chosen honorary president.

The UFCSS was part of a tradition of dissent on the Canadian Prairies that began to take root in the early 1900s and took shape during a period in which other agrarian organizations (such as the Progressive Party and United

Farmers of Alberta) exerted considerable influence in federal and provincial politics. At the time of the UFCSS's establishment, the United Farm Women of Saskatchewan (UFWS) was also formed. The UFWS worked with the men on several initiatives and also independently on women's issues. Although it experienced problems common to women's organizations that work within male-dominated groups, UFWS members enjoyed more influence than women in most other agrarian associations.

In 1928 the UFCSS passed a resolution that called upon the government to compel all farmers to market their wheat through the Saskatchewan Wheat Pool. To convince farmers of the benefits of the "100 percent pool" plan, American cooperator Aaron Sapiro was recruited to speak on the need for all farmers to participate in the venture. The issue split the UFCSS and the Saskatchewan Wheat Pool, as the latter body maintained that compulsory legislation would destroy the movement. In addition to cooperative marketing, the UFCSS steadfastly supported other forms of cooperation.

Initially, the UFCSS opposed direct political action. Members disliked partisan politics and believed that contesting elections detracted farmers from more important goals, such as controlling the marketing of their produce. Thus, it chose instead to focus on lobbying and education. In the latter field, it embarked upon a program that occasionally competed with that of the Saskatchewan Wheat Pool.

The onset of the Great Depression drove the UFCSS toward direct political action, which it officially endorsed in 1931. Stressing "industrial action" (rather than concentrating on farm issues, as some organizations did), in 1932 the UFCSS merged with the small but influential provincial Independent Labour Party and became known as the Saskatchewan Farmer-Labour Group. Soon after, this body became the Saskatchewan Section of the Cooperative Commonwealth Federation.

In 1946 the UFCSS supported the Alberta Farmers Union's strike, which generated conflict within the movement and with the Saskatchewan Wheat Pool. In 1948 the UFCSS reorganized and was renamed the Saskatchewan Farmers Union. By 1954, it had more than 72,000 members. In the ensuing years, however, with a few exceptions, membership declined. In 1969 the Saskatchewan Farmers Union and other organizations merged to form the National Farmers Union.

See also AGRICULTURE: Saskatchewan Wheat Pool.

Kerry Badgley
National Archives of Canada

Fairbairn, Garry Lawrence. *From Prairie Roots: The Remarkable Story of the Saskatchewan Wheat Pool.* Saskatoon: Western Producer Prairie Books, 1984. McCrorie, James Napier. *In Union Is Strength.* Saskatoon: Centre for Community Studies, 1964.

WINNIPEG GENERAL STRIKE

For six weeks in the early summer of 1919, Winnipeg, then the largest city in the Cana-

Winnipeg General Strike, June 21, 1919

dian Prairies, was shut down by a general strike. More than 30,000 of the city's workers walked off their jobs in a test of strength that was to prove the focal point of a labor explosion that was national and international in scope. The strike was provoked by the refusal of employers to recognize and bargain with the metal and building trades federations of unions. The Winnipeg Trades and Labor Council organized a poll of its affiliates' members, and a general strike was approved by a vote of 11,112 to 524. The response to the strike call on May 15 was overwhelming. Not only did organized workers respond solidly, shutting down factories, newspapers, telephones, and streetcars, but thousands of unorganized workers joined them. The city fell silent.

Longer and more disciplined than the Seattle General Strike the previous February, the Winnipeg confrontation remains without precedent in the history of class confrontation in North America. In the discourse of its opponents, the strike was a drive for revolutionary power by working-class militants. Workers, perhaps too defensively, saw the strike as a struggle for collective bargaining. Traditional accounts of the strike have been shaped by these conflicting narratives, with historians siding with the strikers' portrayal of the strike.

Recent assessments of the strike have rejected this dichotomy and now view the strike as a complex social event with various meanings rooted in the growing social crisis that marked Canadian society in the last years of World War I. Wartime inflation, the dramatic growth in union membership, the movement for industrial unionism, and the determination of workers to press for a new postwar order shaped an unprecedented threat to the state and to business capital interests in 1919. A Royal Commission on Industrial Relations, appointed by the Canadian government to investigate the labor revolt, encountered wide-

spread anger at "profiteering" and heard repeated calls for "production for use and not for profit." Across the country, workers debated various tactics and increasingly adopted the general strike as the best means of fostering solidarity and furthering working-class interests during postwar reconstruction. In 1918 the Winnipeg Trades and Labor Council had debated calling a general strike on four different occasions. When it finally occurred, old animosities among workers, between central and eastern European immigrants and Canadian or British-born workers, and between men and women workers, dissolved before the logic of class unity. Even the swelling ranks of returned war veterans rallied, for the most part, to labor's cause, adding even greater volatility to the developing crisis.

Revolutions in Russia and Germany no longer seemed very remote in Winnipeg in 1919. While trade unions tried to focus negotiations on issues of collective bargaining, employers and those in charge of the federal government were deeply uneasy about the trajectory of this unprecedented working-class mobilization. Determined that the strike had to be crushed, employers formed a "Citizens Committee of One Thousand" to fight the strike and support "established government." Despite the overwhelming British-Canadian character of the strike leadership, they denounced the general strike as an attempt at revolution inspired by "enemy aliens" and called for its immediate suppression by the state. At the behest of the Committee, Winnipeg's entire city police force was dismissed when they refused, en masse, to sign a loyalty oath; the force was replaced with untrained, antistriker "specials."

While the federal government was committed from the outset to the unconditional defeat of the strike, it was determined to avoid provoking a threatened walkout of the railway-running trades across western Canada.

Such a development could easily have unified the wave of local strikes in sympathy with Winnipeg workers into a massive strike from Lake Superior to the Pacific. By separate negotiations, the Canadian minister of labor managed to appease the leadership of the railroad-running trade unions. Early in June, the federal government prepared the legislative groundwork for an assault on strike leadership by amending the Immigration Act to allow for the deportation from Canada of British subjects and broadened the Criminal Code definition of sedition. In late-night raids on June 16–17, the strike leaders were arrested, along with a group of eastern European immigrants, who could serve as evidence of the "alien" character of the struggle. On June 21—Bloody Saturday—a demonstration of pro-strike returned-soldiers was brutally attacked by the specials and the Royal North-West Mounted Police, killing two men and injuring at least two dozen. Following further repression of the strikers' newspaper and the promise of a provincial government inquiry, the General Strike was ended on June 25.

The tide of postwar radicalism did not subside with the state suppression of the strike. Led by A. J. Andrews, members of the Citizens Committee of One Thousand mobilized the authority and resources of the federal Department of Justice in legal and ideological assaults designed to discredit and disperse proponents of labor radicalism in Winnipeg and elsewhere to restore the legitimacy of the existing order. Postwar radicalism was condemned as a form of Bolshevism. The workers' revolt of 1919 was portrayed as a criminal enterprise and its radicals were jailed. Yet the legal and ideological ascendancy of the Citizens Committee and its allies in the government was far from absolute. Rather than produce mass adhesion to the established order, the assault on radicalism generated working-class dissent and antagonism.

See also CITIES AND TOWNS: Winnipeg, Manitoba.

Tom Mitchell and James Naylor
Brandon University

Bercuson, David J. *Confrontation at Winnipeg: Labour, Industrial Relations, and the General Strike.* Montreal: McGill-Queen's University Press, 1990. Heron, Craig. *The Workers' Revolt in Canada, 1917–1925.* Toronto: University of Toronto Press, 1998. Penner, Norman, ed. *Winnipeg 1919: The Strikers' Own History of the Winnipeg General Strike.* Toronto: James Lorimer, 1972.

WINROD, GERALD (1900–1957)

Gerald Burton Winrod was a second-rank leader in the Protestant fundamentalist movement during the 1920s and the foremost far-right activist in the Great Plains during the 1930s. Winrod was born on March 7, 1900, in Wichita, Kansas, where he grew up. In 1925 he founded the Defenders of the Christian Faith, and operating from in his hometown of Wichita, Kansas, he campaigned on the stump, over the radio, and in his *Defender* magazine against Darwinism, liberal theology, and what he called a national "moral sag." A believer in Bible prophecy, he found in world events signs of the rise of the Antichrist and Jesus' imminent return, but except for a fervent defense of Prohibition, he initially paid slight attention to conventional politics.

In 1933 Winrod quickly concluded that the cosmopolitan New Deal represented both the "moral sag" in politics and an alien tyranny. Combining his own premillennial theology with an anti-Semitic conspiracy theory found in *The Protocols of the Learned Elders of Zion*, the notorious forgery concocted by Russian royalists at the turn of the twentieth century, he viewed the Roosevelt administration as part of a venerable Jewish plot extending back to the crucifixion of Jesus. By the mid-1930s, while still trying to convert Jews, he was applauding Adolf Hitler's suppression of alleged Jewish subversives. In 1938, temporarily playing down his anti-Semitism, Winrod ran for the U.S. Senate from Kansas and finished third in the Republican primary with 53,149 votes (21.4 percent).

Winrod's sympathy for Hitler and opposition to American entry into World War II led to his indictment for sedition in 1942. The case ended in a mistrial in 1946, and Winrod resumed his polemical activities, discerning further Jewish conspiracies and continued "moral sag" in the postwar era. A lifelong believer in faith healing, Winrod distrusted orthodox medicine and championed spurious cancer treatments. His refusal to consult a physician contributed in part to his own death from pneumonia in Wichita on November 11, 1957.

Leo P. Ribuffo
George Washington University

Ribuffo, Leo P. *The Old Christian Right: The Protestant Far Right from the Great Depression to the Cold War.* Philadelphia: Temple University Press, 1983.

WOMEN OF ALL RED NATIONS

Women of All Red Nations (WARN) was founded in 1978 in San Francisco, California, and to date remains the most prominent activist Native American women's organization. WARN advocates for Native American treaty rights and for social, economic, and environmental justice for Native American peoples. WARN was created at the height of Indian activism in the 1970s, when the virtually all-male national leadership of Indian activist groups became targeted by federal and state law enforcement agencies and courts. After the national American Indian Movement leaders were prosecuted and imprisoned by the federal legal system, women were called to the fore of Native American issues and WARN was born.

From its beginning, WARN has sent spokespersons to international forums concerning colonialism, land struggles, energy resource protection, and Indigenous rights recognition. WARN was instrumental in stopping the uranium mining that was planned for the sacred Black Hills of South Dakota. The organization built coalitions with non-Indians so that uranium mining would never be conducted in lands sacred to the Lakota, Dakota, and Nakota people.

WARN also conducted a health study of the water on the Pine Ridge Reservation in South Dakota, which found that the groundwater system was highly radioactive. Since then, federal funds have been allocated for the construction of a safe drinking-water system, called *Mni Wiconi*, or the Water of Life, for the greater reservation area. WARN has worked on numerous issues relating to human health, specifically the epidemic proportions of Type II diabetes in Indian Country, as well as the terrible problems associated with fetal alcohol syndrome and fetal alcohol effect.

Today, WARN continues its advocacy, predominantly through the efforts of women's circles in local communities both on and off reservations. WARN's ongoing community organization and advocacy on issues affecting Native Americans at the grassroots level remain highly focused and effective.

Madonna Thunder Hawk
Eagle Butte, South Dakota

WOOD, HENRY WISE (1860–1941)

Henry Wise Wood was a farmer, first in Missouri and then in Alberta. In Canada he became a leader in agrarian organizations, had a weighty influence on agrarian involvement in politics, and was a prominent figure in establishing the Alberta Wheat Pool. Born in Ralls County, Missouri, on May 31, 1860, Wood was educated in a rural school, at a private school in Monroe City, and at Christian University (later Culver-Stockton College) in Canton, Missouri. In 1883 he married Etta Leora Cook, and they had four sons. Following three years in Texas (1878–81) he returned to Ralls County, where he farmed, bred cattle, and joined the Farmers and Laborers Union.

By the time he moved to a farm near Carstairs, Alberta, in 1905, he was widely read in political philosophers such as Karl Marx and John Stuart Mill. The failure of American farmers to enter politics directly, and the corruption of their farm organizations through political engagement, convinced him that Canadian agrarian movements would share the same fate if they embarked on a similar path. Wood was elected president of the United Farmers of Alberta (UFA) in 1916 and became president of the Canadian Council of Agriculture in 1917. His rapid rise in these bodies reflected his energy and skill at organization, as well as his conviction that the future for farmers lay in their willingness to view themselves as an economic class, committed to principles of cooperation more than of competition, and acting effectively to push the goals of farmers upon both government and business while avoiding the siren call of entering politics directly.

By the end of World War I, however, grassroots determination to enter politics left Wood no choice but to try to shape the political activity in accordance with his ideas: the farmers should enter politics as an economic group, which would maintain its integrity as a purely agrarian entity, but be prepared at the same time to cooperate with other economic groups such as labor. At all costs they should avoid participating in the existing corrupt political system. While the

UFA officially supported the Progressive Party, formed after World War I to represent the interests of farmers at Ottawa, Wood's ideas were fundamentally opposed to those of the other major farm representative in politics, T. A. Crerar of Manitoba. Crerar accepted the basic principles of political organization as they existed, but he believed that the Progressive Party's duty was to pressure the traditional major parties, Liberal and Conservative, to adopt policies that were in the interest of farmers. Thus, despite electing sixty-four members to Parliament in 1921 and becoming the second-largest group after the governing Liberals, the Progressives were divided at their core, and the national movement largely disintegrated by the mid-1920s. A major factor was Wood's ideological intransigence. Nevertheless, within Alberta the political wing of the UFA became the government in 1921, holding power as essentially a farmer government until 1935.

Wood also believed in the ideas of the American apostle of cooperation, Aaron Sapiro, who spoke often in western Canada in the 1920s. Indeed, Wood was able to generate the cooperation of businessmen, farmers, and the Alberta government, all under his leadership and that of the UFA, to form the Alberta Wheat Pool, of which Wood became president in 1923. From there he was instrumental in the creation of pools in Saskatchewan and Manitoba and became vice president (1924) of the Central Selling Agency, which marketed the wheat of the three pools.

Wood retired as president of the UFA in 1931, and as president of the Wheat Pool in 1937. In 1935 he received the Grand Cross of Saint Michael and Saint George from King George V, recognizing "his services to the cause of agrarian unity and cooperation." He died in Calgary on June 10, 1941.

David J. Hall
University of Alberta

Morton, W. L. "The Social Philosophy of Henry Wise Wood, the Canadian Agrarian Leader." *Agricultural History* 22 (1948): 114–22. Rolph, William Kirby. *Henry Wise Wood of Alberta*. Toronto: University of Toronto Press, 1950. Wood, Henry Wise. Papers. Glenbow Archives. Calgary, Alberta.

WOODSWORTH, JAMES SHAVER
(1874–1942)

Methodist minister, politician, and social reformer, James Shaver Woodsworth was born on July 29, 1874, near Toronto, Ontario. He moved with his family to the Great Plains in 1882 when his Methodist minister father took a new position in Winnipeg. Woodsworth followed his father into the ministry; he was ordained in 1896 and worked for several years as a circuit rider in the Manitoba Plains. In 1899 he traveled to Oxford, England, where he studied for two years and worked in settlement houses in the slums of East London. The extreme poverty and dire living conditions he witnessed had a profound impact on the minister; thereafter he became a proponent of the "Social Gospel" and strived to improve the living conditions of the poor. By 1904 he was back in the Great Plains, working with immigrants in the slums of Winnipeg's North End. For almost ten years he operated a settlement house called the All Peoples Mission. He also wrote extensively on the plight of poor immigrants and the working class, producing two books, *Strangers within Our Gates* (1909) and *My Neighbor* (1911).

World War I marked a turning point in Woodsworth's career. As a staunch pacifist, he opposed Canadian involvement in the war and spoke openly about his views. He particularly despised the draft and the participation of Methodist ministers as recruiters. Because of his vocal opposition, Woodsworth lost his government job and, unable to find work as a minister in Winnipeg, was forced to move his family to Vancouver. There he became increasingly more politicized, as he worked on the docks, joined the longshoremen's union, and wrote for labor newspapers. In June 1919, while visiting Winnipeg, he was arrested for writing "seditious" editorials during the Winnipeg General Strike. Woodsworth's arrest and his widely read coverage and criticism of the government's handling of the strike boosted his popularity among Canada's working class. In 1921 he was elected to Canada's House of Commons as a member of Manitoba's Independent Labour Party. As a legislator, Woodsworth became one of Canada's leading social reformers; among other reforms, he helped create Canada's Old-Age Pension Plan. In 1932 he helped form the Cooperative Commonwealth Federation (forerunner to the New Democratic Party), a political party comprised largely of labor, farmer, and socialist groups from western Canada. He served as the party's chair and its parliamentary leader until his death.

World War II was Woodsworth's final political battle. Once again, he opposed Canadian involvement, and in 1939 he was the only member of the House of Commons to vote against a declaration of war. Despite Woodsworth's opposition to the war, he remained party chairman and was elected in 1940 to another term in the House of Commons. Weakened by ill health, however, Woodsworth returned with his wife to the family home in Vancouver, where he died on March 21, 1942.

See also POLITICS AND GOVERNMENT: Co-operative Commonwealth Federation.

Mark R. Ellis
University of Nebraska at Kearney

Mills, Allen George. *Fool for Christ: The Political Thought of J. S. Woodsworth*. Toronto: University of Toronto Press, 1991. Woodsworth, James Shaver. *My Neighbor: A Study of City Conditions, a Plea for Social Service*. Toronto: Missionary Society of the Methodist Church, 1911.

Religion

Church in Hettinger, North Dakota, 1942

RELIGION

A rich religious life marks the Great Plains throughout its history. Long before many Native Americans—the Sioux, Blackfoot, Comanches, Apaches, Cheyennes, and Arapahos—moved into the Plains, other Indigenous societies flourished along the rivers and streams of the region. For all of them, religion was not a distinct arena of existence but was interwoven with every other aspect of common life. Identifying particular beliefs and specific activities as religious reflects an understanding of religion more characteristic of the Europeans, whose presence in the Plains began with the Spanish explorers of the early 1500s. In time, efforts first of the Spanish and then in the early 1700s of the French to Christianize tribal peoples planted Roman Catholicism in the Plains. Some of these missions left an influence that endures to the present.

Perhaps the most significant era that shaped the present religious configuration of the Plains was the nineteenth century. By the mid–nineteenth century, thousands of persons of European background began making their way across the Plains. Some remained there while others pushed on to California, Utah, and Oregon. The primary infusion of European Americans came in the latter decades of the nineteenth century and early twentieth century when railroads made access much easier.

The religious styles of these migrants reflected the tremendous diversity that had come to characterize organized religion in Canada and the United States. Most of the Protestant denominations were represented among those settlers who made the Plains their home. But there is an additional ingredient in the story, not only for Protestantism but also for Catholicism: ethnicity. New communities frequently were comprised of persons who shared a common ethnic heritage. To understand the religious life of the Plains, then, we must be sensitive to the particular style, for example, of Norwegian Lutheranism and Czech Catholicism. And we must also be alert to groups such as the Mennonites who fused a shared ethnic identity with a distinctive religious orientation.

In time, other communities, other religious groups, and other social forces were to leave their imprint on Plains religious culture. Japanese immigrants, for example, have made Buddhism a vital part of the religious story of Alberta. Experimental Jewish agricultural communities in the Prairie Provinces and in North Dakota have also given a special dimension to the religious heritage of the Plains. As urbanization came to the Plains, so, too, came a concern for relating religion to public life not only in movements like the Social Gospel but in the establishment of hospitals, educational institutions, and a host of other social service agencies.

Other movements that defy denominational boundaries, such as fundamentalism, Pentecostalism, and revivalism, have likewise left an abiding influence. With the coming of the electronic age, religious broadcasting on radio and television linked the religious life of the Plains to that of the entire North American continent in new ways. But to understand the contours of the religious landscape of the Plains today, we must begin with an appreciation for the religious world of the Native American cultures of the region.

Native American Traditions and Christian Missions

To generalize about the religious dimension of Plains Indigenous cultures is to ignore the distinctive elements of the numerous individual societies that once flourished in the region. Yet there are sufficient common elements to warrant some summary statements. Location was the paramount factor in determining both cultural and religious style. Those who clustered in villages along the Missouri River and its tributaries in the eastern Plains were oriented more toward agriculture, especially cultivation of corn. What later interpreters would identify as religious rites thus tended to focus on fertility, cementing the close relationship between people and the land. Those to the west, approaching the Rocky Mountains, where a semiarid climate precluded agriculture, were more dispersed and migratory, and bison hunting was central to their way of life. Among these peoples, vision quests, which brought individuals into contact with supernatural power, thereby increasing their prowess as hunters while connecting them to powerful mythic figures, were basic to the religious beliefs and practices. Sacred sites, such as Bear Butte in present-day South Dakota were, and are, particularly important for such quests.

The case of the Sioux is instructive, although by no means representative of all the peoples of the Plains. Traditionally from what is today part of Wisconsin and Minnesota, the western Sioux by the mid–seventeenth century were pushed by the Ojibwas and drawn by the bison toward the Great Plains. As the Sioux adapted to Plains life, they moved toward dominance because they quickly incorporated the horse (brought first to the Southern Plains by the Spanish) into their culture, and agricultural pursuits gave way to bison hunting. Adaptation in the religious sphere followed, as the concern for fertility was superseded by concern for success in hunting, and vision quests assumed greater importance. One well-known consequence was the emergence of the Sun Dance, an annual rite symbolically re-creating and renewing the cosmos in order to assure the well-being of the people. The role of shamans, with their ability to call on supernatural power to effect both healing and success in hunting and other tribal endeavors, grew in importance.

External forces, such as increased migration of non-Native Americans into the Plains, government policies that were frequently inimical to tribal life, and Christian proselytizing, spurred other changes. We should here note three currents that had significant long-term consequences: increased efforts among Christian groups to establish missions among the tribes; the rise to prominence of the Ghost Dance; and the development of peyotism.

Three examples of mission work may be taken as examples. Earliest are the missions among Native Americans started by the Spanish. By the mid–eighteenth century the Spanish had sent around 100 expeditions into what is now Texas; many included the establishment of missions designed both to convert and, ostensibly, to civilize Natives by organizing them into something akin to agricultural colonies. The earliest, founded by Franciscans in 1682, lay just outside the Plains near El Paso. Although these missions often served to protect their Native inhabitants from even worse exploitation by the Spanish conquerors, they still disrupted tribal life and represented the imposition of an alien religious style. These missions demonstrate a characteristic that was to mark similar enterprises throughout the Plains, namely the missionary as both friend, who offered security and protection from outside invaders, and foe, whose very presence undermined traditional tribal ways.

To the north, Belgian priest Pierre-Jean De Smet was one of the most influential of the early Catholic missionaries. De Smet's efforts to raise money and call attention to mission needs, beginning in 1838, took him from the Potawatomis in Iowa to the Columbia and Willamette Valleys of the Pacific Northwest. De Smet stands out as well for his genuine appreciation of Native ways, making him repeatedly a valued mediator between tribal peoples and white settlers who encroached on their lands. Twenty years before De Smet began his labors, Joseph-Norbert Provencher assumed leadership of mission work on the Red River of the North, intent on providing spiritual leadership for the French Canadians already there, as well as establishing agricultural colonies and schools for the Indigenous peoples. By the 1830s numerous mission stations were operating, many later sustained through assistance from the French Order of Oblates of Mary Immaculate. Provencher was instrumental in persuading both the Oblates and the Grey Nuns to undertake mission work in western Canada. Also by the 1830s, the Anglican Church Missionary Society, hoping to minister to British Canadians and Native Americans alike, was extending its work from its base along the Red River Valley of the North. Most of these endeavors share another feature that was to mark much mission work, namely the establishment of schools that would provide Native Americans with something like a western-style education. Even here, however, there was a paternalistic assumption of great import, for many harbored the conviction that education would "civilize" or impress western ways on the Indigenous inhabitants, rendering them easier to control and more amenable to conversion to Christianity.

This conviction comes into sharp relief in the third example, the work of Stephen Return Riggs, an agent of the American Board of Foreign Missions from 1837 until his death in 1883, who translated both the Bible and secular works into the Dakota language of the Santee Sioux. Riggs was convinced that education would bring a "higher" standard of living to the tribes by preparing them for participation in "Christian civilization." His work, however, also illustrates another long-term impact of the missionary enterprise. In 1862, when armed conflict erupted between the Sioux and American forces, many of Riggs's converts were loath to participate in the fighting. When they, too, suffered reprisals, many of the Sioux believed that white culture had so destroyed the supernatural powers that once shaped tribal life that conversions to Christianity, the religion of the apparently more powerful white culture, increased.

The Ghost Dance, a fusion of millenarian hopes and rituals uniting the living and the dead, began as a revival of Wodziwob's Round Dance of 1870. A Paiute shaman named Wovoka, who lived on the Walker River Reservation in Nevada, had participated in the 1870 movement and had a vision that gave birth to a new revitalization movement that spread quickly to the Plains tribes during the winter of 1888–89. Wovoka's vision endowed him with a message promising the ultimate restoration of tribal integrity at a time when the cohesion of tribal cultures was increasingly challenged by external forces. Wovoka called for the renewal of traditional tribal mores through the practice of trance dances in which supernatural empowerment would come to the faithful. Short Bull and Kicking Bear, Lakota representatives of the Sioux, visited Wovoka and carried the message back to their people. The Ghost Dance also took firm root among the Canadian Sioux, where the movement was known as New Tidings.

In an effort to exert control over the Plains peoples, the American government had banned ritual enactment of the Sun Dance in 1883. The Ghost Dance appeared to be even more of a threat, as it brought renewed solidarity and hope to the tribal cultures. It also increased militant resistance to further external domination, especially among the Sioux who believed that their "ghost shirts" were bulletproof. The massacre at Wounded Knee Creek in 1890 brought these millennial expectations and the hope for revitalized tribal life to a sudden halt for many Sioux, but Wovoka's religion persisted among the Oklahoma tribes, Canadian Native peoples, and the Great Basin peoples well into the twentieth century.

Among the Canadian Crees, the Ghost Dance had a rather different character, reflecting perhaps the generally less violent nature of tribal relations with the Canadian government. In this context, the Ghost Dance served more as a means for the Prairie tribes to form a united front in their dealings with the government. However, the Riel Rebellion of 1885, which was spurred primarily by the Métis but also counted several Cree bands among its participants, essentially thwarted efforts to maintain this united front.

By the dawn of the twentieth century the disintegration of traditional ways among the Plains tribes was evident. Confined to reservations and increasingly dependent on government annuity payments and assistance from Christian missionaries, who rarely appreciated the richness of Native American religiosity, the tribal peoples of the Plains faced what seemed a bleak future. Some sought to return to traditional practices such as the Sun Dance. Others moved toward assimilation into white culture, manifested in part through the adoption or adaptation of practices associated with Christianity. Yet others hoped to revitalize Native American life through promoting a shared "Indian" consciousness. Peyotism, regarded by many as the most important twentieth-century religious development among Native American peoples, fused aspects of all three adjustments.

Long part of tribal religiosity in Mexico where the peyote cactus grows, peyote rites became part of Kiowa and Comanche life around 1870. Peyotism spread rather slowly, usually making its way into tribal life when its advocates, such as Quanah Parker, traveled from tribe to tribe promoting it. Administered under strict ceremonial guidelines, peyote generates visions that often combine Christian symbols with traditional ones, for example, by linking Christ with the Great Spirit. Peyotism also encouraged a return to traditional ethics that would simultaneously renew tribal integrity and allow more peaceful accommodation with white society.

In the United States, the Native American Church, in which peyote rituals are central, was first legally chartered in Oklahoma in 1918. However, as the larger culture developed increasing concern about use of controlled hallucinogenic substances, sporadic efforts were made to quash the practice, culminating first in a U.S. Supreme Court case in 1990 that upheld the right of states to prohibit the practice, and then in federal legislation enacted in the wake of that court decision that protected the practice. Despite the apprehension of the larger culture, peyotism remains one of the most vital means for sustaining a Native American cultural and religious identity. It is estimated that the Native American Church has 200,000 members.

Christianity in the Plains

For the most part, the planting of Christianity in the Great Plains mirrors patterns of migration of persons of European stock into the region. Today, most of the old-line Protestant groups have pockets of strength in the Plains, as do Roman Catholicism and the Orthodox. This great religious diversity prevents generalization except at the broadest scale. The United Church of Canada is the dominant religion in many parts of the Prairie Provinces, a Lutheran belt (the product of Scandinavian immigration) stretches across much of North and South Dakota, Methodism is the leading religion in much of the Central Great Plains, although this is also the area with the greatest religious diversity in the region, and the Southern Plains, particularly in Texas, is dominated by the Southern Baptist religion. The highest percentage of church membership in the region is in the Lutheran and Southern Baptist belts.

But the story is not simply one of transplanting religious institutions from Europe or the eastern United States and eastern Canada. In many cases there is a vital ethnic component that has given religious communities a distinctive flavor, for in some situations immigrants moved to the Plains as entire communities, where a particular religious style, a cultural tradition, and an ethnic heritage were inextricably intertwined.

Roman Catholic Christianity in the Southern Plains has its roots in Spanish exploration and conquest; the missions to the Native Americans frequently sought to serve the religious needs of soldiers and traders whose presence cemented Spanish control. Even today, given the increase in migration from Mexico into the Southern and Central Plains over the last several decades, Catholicism there retains a vital Hispanic cast.

In the Canadian portion of the Great Plains, institutional Catholicism owes much to those who sought to plant the seeds of Presbyterianism there. In 1812, Thomas Douglas, the Fifth Earl of Selkirk, established his Kildonan colony, populated by Scottish immigrants, along the Red River of the North near today's Winnipeg. As a Scottish community, Lord Selkirk's settlement was overwhelmingly Reformed (Presbyterian) in religious sentiment. But there were already some French Canadian traders in the area who were Roman Catholic by heritage, and in time Selkirk hired German soldiers, largely Roman Catholic as well, to provide protection for his people. What brought Joseph-Norbert Provencher to launch his mission to the Indigenous people in the area was Selkirk's request for a priest to provide spiritual guidance for those who were Catholic. Provencher's work is central to Roman Catholic growth in western Canada, which benefited from the gradual movement of Catholics to the area. In 1847 Provencher became the first bishop of St. Boniface (Manitoba).

As Roman Catholics moved into areas of the Plains, they brought with them their commitment to work in education through parochial schools and to promote health care through the establishment of hospitals—all in some ways also an extension of earlier missions to Native Americans. Other groups were to follow suit, and the story of higher education especially, and the developing networks of health-care institutions, is inextricably tied to the religious history of the Great Plains. For Roman Catholics, much of the labor that sustained such enterprises came from the numerous orders of nuns that sent workers wherever there were Catholic people to be served. For example, the Presentation Sisters have long been recognized as leaders in health care in Montana and the Dakotas.

The Scottish community at Kildonan was also indirectly the key to bringing the Anglican Church to the Prairie Provinces. When these settlers could not procure the services of a Presbyterian clergyman, they turned to the Anglican John West for spiritual leadership. For twenty years West served in Kildonan as the community awaited the arrival of a Presbyterian minister. But West used his post to promote Anglican work, overseeing for a time the labors among Native peoples sponsored by the Anglican Church Missionary Society.

The major influx of Protestants who remained permanently in the region came as a result of two factors: the expansion of railroads that linked the more heavily settled East with the Pacific in both the United States and Canada and the surge in immigration that marked the period after 1880 until restrictions were imposed in 1919 by a Canadian Order in Council and in 1924 by the United States. In Canada, for example, after the Canadian Pacific Railway extended service to Winnipeg in 1881 and to British Columbia in 1885, settlers flocked to Alberta and Saskatchewan. In both the United States and Canada, for several decades the bulk of the organized churches were to be found along the railroad lines. The landscape of towns and rural areas throughout the region was imprinted with churches and graveyards that told the story of the origins of the settlers.

The Scandinavian and German immigrants who came to the Dakotas were largely Lutheran and tended to organize churches based on country of origin. Even when English became the language of education and business, Swedish, Norwegian, and Finnish remained the languages for worship, helping sustain a cultural and ethnic heritage. Not until generations had passed and languages of origin had faded did these groups enter into mergers with other Lutheran bodies, gradually diminishing their ethnic aura. A similar pattern occurred in Canada, where Swedish immigrants organized the Evangelical Covenant Church in Winnipeg in 1904; Norwegian and Danish Lutherans soon replicated the pattern in establishing their Evangelical Free Church.

Three examples bring into bold relief the fusion of religion, culture, and ethnicity among groups intent on preserving a distinctive identity: the Doukhobors, the Mennonites, and the Ukrainians who ultimately separated from the Russian Orthodox Church. The Doukhobors, the largest group of whom is known formally today as the Union of Spiritual Communities in Christ, trace their origins to a schism in the Russian Orthodox Church in the seventeenth century. Many of the more mystical among them began to regroup. Those who were followers of Peter Verigin migrated en masse to Saskatchewan in 1899. At times experimenting with communal living—the last of these attempts was largely done in by the economic turmoil of the Great Depression—the Doukhobors have sustained a Russian mystical pietism that stresses the inward apprehension of the law of God and a divinity that even in seventeenth- and eighteenth-century Russia the more orthodox regarded as heretical. This inner-directed mysticism has also brought conflict with the Canadian government since Doukhobors refused to subscribe to any oaths of allegiance to the government.

Many of the Mennonites who found their way to the Plains also had Russian backgrounds. By 1812 Mennonites from Poland and Prussia had established several colonies in southern Russia, where one group that later called itself the Kleine Gemeinde (today's Evangelical Mennonite Conference) broke away from the larger body. That year they began to migrate in large numbers to Manitoba and Nebraska, although the smaller Nebraska cluster eventually dissipated. Blending their own pietism with the agrarian ways of southern Russia, the Kleine Gemeinde flourished in western Canada, where, by the late twentieth century, adherents spread across five provinces. Yet other Mennonites, forerunners of today's Church of God in Christ, Mennonite, experienced rapid growth in the Great Plains because they were able to gain converts among the increasing numbers of immigrants who came from Russia and Germany to parts of Kansas and Manitoba in the late nineteenth century.

A second wave of Mennonites came particularly to Alberta, Saskatchewan, and Manitoba following World War I. There the availability of land offered promise for sustaining a simple agrarian existence that had been disrupted by the violence and land dispossessions of the Russian Revolution. Mennonite migration had received earlier encouragement when the Canadian government created preserves for the group in Manitoba in the 1870s and in Saskatchewan in the 1890s. Adhering to a quasi-communal way of life and encouraging the young to marry fellow believers, the various clusters of Mennonites represent both a religious community and an ethnic group.

A similar story is that of the Hutterites who came to the Northern Great Plains. With roots in the sixteenth-century Moravian Anabaptist movement that saw adherents persecuted and pushed into the Ukraine and elsewhere, Hutterites came to the United States in the 1870s. They established colonies (Bruderhofs) in South Dakota and Montana, where they hoped to maintain a simple agrarian life in which they shared common ownership of goods and property. But fearing persecution because of their pacifist principles (and because of their largely German heritage), hundreds crossed the border into western Canada during World War I, although some later returned to the United States.

A significant Ukrainian migration into the Canadian Plains also provides an illustration of the fusion of religious, cultural, and ethnic dimensions into a single whole. In the Ukraine, the Russian Orthodox Church had established itself as dominant, but because it was seen as an agency of the state many Ukrainians regarded the church as ethnically Russian, an arm of a regime that imposed its will on the Ukrainian people. Hence, when the Ukrainian National Republic asserted its independence following German occupation during World War I and the disarray that came with the Russian Revolution, some Ukrainians in Canada moved to establish a separate church that would merge a distinctive ethnic heritage with Orthodox Christianity. Thus in July 1918 the Ukrainian Greek-Orthodox Church of Canada was organized in Saskatoon, Saskatchewan. Less tied to Ukrainian nationalism is the Russian/Ukrainian Baptist Union of the United States, formed in 1901. Although now reduced to a handful of churches, this body had its genesis in an immigrant community in Kiev, North Dakota, made up of persons who had come from southern Russia and the Ukraine in the late nineteenth century.

Many other Protestant denominations took root in the Great Plains. Congregationalists, for example, owed their growth largely to those who migrated to the Northern Plains from New England, although when the United Church of Christ was formed through mergers in the twentieth century, many whose origins were in German Congregationalism, as manifested in the Evangelical and Reformed Church, became part of the new venture. Methodism, the largest Protestant body in the United States in the mid–nineteenth century, also traces its strength in the Plains to conventional patterns of migration. But Methodism, which by 1950 boasted having at least one church in every county in the Great Plains south of the Canadian boundary, can also look to its pattern of itinerant ministry, the practice of sending clergy from place to place to minister to a scattered flock, as another reason for its growth. In the Canadian Prairie Provinces, most of the Methodist, Congregationalist, and Presbyterian churches joined their parent denominations in forming the United Church of Canada in 1925.

In the twentieth century, congregations' associations with the Southern Baptist Convention have grown rapidly and extended westward from a traditional stronghold in the South into the Great Plains of Texas, Oklahoma, and New Mexico. In a solid block of counties in West Texas, stretching from Amarillo on the north to Odessa on the south, Baptists account for more than 50 percent of church membership. Beyond this block, in adjacent areas of western Oklahoma and eastern New Mexico, Baptists constitute 25 to 50 percent of church membership. The main exception to this dominant Baptist presence in this entire area is a handful of counties where more than 25 percent of church members are Catholics, the result of Hispanic immigration.

The social conservatism of the Southern Baptist Convention has had a great influence on ways of life in the Southern Great Plains. Their abhorrence of alcohol, for example, delayed the emergence of a successful wine industry in West Texas until the 1970s and today makes difficult the passage of any referendum that proposes easing public access to liquor.

The story of individual Christian groups in the Plains would fill many volumes. Virtually every denomination that is not restricted to a single American region has at least a handful of congregations in the U.S. Great Plains. By the late twentieth century, the same held true for the Canadian Prairie Provinces. But throughout the Plains there are countless independent churches as well. Many of the smaller denominations and independent churches trace their beginnings to religious movements such as fundamentalism or pentecostalism that cut across traditional denominational lines.

Crossdenominational Movements and Currents

Fundamentalism is a many-faceted phenomenon. Many forces coalesced to give it birth in the decades surrounding the start of the twentieth century: a rejection of modern critical methods of biblical interpretation, perceived intellectual threats to orthodox Protestant theological formulation, a surge of interest in biblical prophecy informed by dispensationalism, reactions to immigration, urbanization, industrialization, and a host of others. In the United States, fundamentalism had its greatest early impact in the Northeast, particularly among Baptists and Presbyterians; in Canada, Toronto and the ministry of the controversial and colorful Thomas Todhunter Shields were at the core of early fundamentalism. Fundamentalism's base of support expanded across both nations, in part because of the popularity of the study Bible produced by C. I. Scofield (the Scofield Reference Bible), first published in 1909. Scofield's own career in law and ministry took him to Kansas, Missouri, Colorado, Texas, and Massachusetts. His personal influence in the Southern Plains was enhanced especially by his pastorates in Dallas.

Indeed, it was use of the Scofield Reference Bible that first drew Canadian Presbyterian and then Baptist layman William "Bible Bill" Aberhart into the dispensationalist-fundamentalist orbit. At the heart of dispensationalism lies an understanding that history from Creation to its final consummation is divided into different epochs or dispensations and that humanity now is approaching the final dispensation. Hence there is a passionate concern for unraveling biblical prophecy to identify links with contemporary events. This concern, fostered by a host of prophetic Bible conferences in the United States and Canada that started in the 1880s, means that the Bible itself is of tremendous significance to dispensationalism. The conviction that the Bible is an inerrant guide to history cements the connection between dispensationalism and fundamentalism.

Aberhart was a dynamic Bible teacher based for many years at the Westbourne Baptist Church in Calgary, Alberta, who derived much of his early thinking from a correspondence course written by Scofield. Aberhart was quick to take advantage of advancing media technology to promote his teaching, issuing a monthly fundamentalist magazine (*Prophetic Times*) and in 1929 beginning a regular radio broadcast from Calgary that soon gained a large audience. Indeed, radio was to prove a major medium for the transmission of evangelical and fundamentalist thinking throughout the Plains. Aberhart also founded the Prophetic Bible Institute that served as an educational agency and at times as a church.

Unlike many fundamentalists of the 1920s and 1930s, Aberhart took a keen interest in economics and politics, adapting the economic ideas of C. H. Douglas on "Social Credit" as the foundation for a political party that for a time dominated the Alberta legislature and allowed Aberhart to serve as premier of the province. Many of his social ideas distressed other fundamentalist leaders, who believed that Aberhart had abandoned a religious vocation for political expediency.

A more moderate evangelicalism, albeit laced with some fundamentalist ideas in popular understanding, has remained more deeply entrenched in Protestant religiosity in the Plains. Mass revivalism and deft use of the media are largely responsible for its enduring impact. Evangelist Charles E. Fuller was among the first to make extensive use of radio in addition to organizing revival meetings that drew thousands in attendance. Launching his radio ministry from California in 1930, Fuller found that his program, ultimately named the *Old-Fashioned Revival Hour*, became one of the most popular radio shows of the late 1940s and early 1950s. It reached millions of homes in the Great Plains of the United States and Canada.

Further cementing the presence of evangelicalism in the Plains has been the multifaceted ministry of Billy Graham. Although not a native of the region, Graham has held crusades in many of the major cities of the Great Plains, proclaiming to millions his gospel of simple trust in God as the answer to personal and social problems. Like Aberhart, Graham has deftly used broadcast media, especially radio, and publications ranging from his own *Decision* magazine to *Christianity Today* to make a conservative religious message plausible and respectable. Today, television brings virtually every media preacher into the homes of the Plains.

Modern pentecostalism has also secured a place in the religious life of the Plains. Revivals conducted in 1901 by Charles Fox Parham in Topeka, Kansas, where he had already founded a Bible college, are one of the formative events of neo-pentecostalism, with its emphasis on speaking in tongues and divine healing. A generation later, in 1948, a revival emanating from an independent Bible school at North Battleford, Saskatchewan, was critical in the spread of the Latter Rain Pentecostal movement across North America, giving fresh power to belief in healing through the laying on of hands. Oral Roberts, perhaps the best-known healing evangelist of mid-twentieth-century North America, conducted his own brand of tent revivals in many Great Plains locales. Based in Tulsa, Oklahoma, since 1947, Roberts has been a major force in making a pentecostal style acceptable in many Protestant circles. All of these streams of pentecostalism have helped fuel the growth of both independent churches and denominations, such as the Assemblies of God, that emphasize the reality of charismatic gifts of the Spirit.

More liberal religious currents have also influenced religious developments in the Plains. In the later nineteenth and early twentieth centuries, Social Christianity, or the Social Gospel, emerged as another response to the way industrialization and urbanization were reshaping life in North America. Informed by modernist theological ideas that applied critical analysis to Scripture, the Social Gospel sought to apply the ethical principles derived from the teachings of Jesus to contemporary social issues, particularly those having to do with labor, working conditions in factories, and living conditions in urban slums. In the United States, the more industrialized areas of the Northeast were the major centers of the Social Gospel impulse, but in Canada its core was in Winnipeg. This was the result of the work of the Methodist Salem G. Bland, professor at Wesley College there, and particularly of the efforts of another Methodist, James Shaver Woodsworth, who as head of All Peoples Mission in Winnipeg had a powerful ministry among the unemployed and ill-housed of the city. Woodsworth's *Strangers within Our Gates* (1909) and *My Neighbor* (1911), written for a popular audience, served to instill Social Gospel ideas in the religiosity of ordinary men and women.

Another piece of popular literature helped make Social Gospel principles bywords for the faithful in the United States. In 1896 Topeka, Kansas, pastor Charles M. Sheldon published a series of sermons he had preached to his Sunday evening congregation. Appearing as a novel the following year, *In His Steps* remains in print today. It represents a critical effort to personalize and individualize the corporate ethic of the Social Gospel through its depiction of a band of women and men who covenant for one year to ask the question "What would Jesus do?" before making any business decision. All are driven to abandon the traditional trappings of success for work with the poor and outcast. And although the result is not the social change sought by the larger movement, the individuals involved undergo significant personal transformation. By reaching a mass audience, Sheldon ensured that the Social Gospel's impact would not be restricted to a single denomination in its impact. However, in both the United States and Canada the coming of World War I and then the Great Depression shattered the optimism that undergirded the Social Gospel's hopes for far-reaching, immediate social change. Nevertheless, its heritage lived on in the United States in the enduring strains of progressive politics and in much of the New Deal promoted by Franklin Roosevelt, and in Canada in the policies of the Cooperative Commonwealth Federation government that came to power in Saskatchewan in 1944.

Other Religious Movements and Communities

Countless other religious movements and communities have found the Plains fertile soil for propagating their own visions of life here and hereafter. Some groups have come into the Plains because they believed that conditions there favored their growth. For example, in 1887 Charles Ora Card led a small group of Latter-day Saints, better known as Mormons, from Utah to Alberta, where they founded what is today Cardston. At the time they left Salt Lake City, the U.S. government was placing increasing pressure on the Mormons to renounce the practice of polygamy as a condition for admitting Utah as a state. What drew Card's group to Canada was both the limited toleration of already existing polygamous marriages (although not recognition of future ones) and the availability of land suitable for the irrigation methods developed by the Mormons. From Alberta, Mormon missionaries fanned out across Canada.

The famous mid-nineteenth-century gold rush and then the need for workers to build rail lines brought an upsurge in immigration to Canada and the United States from Asia. Chinese and Japanese settlers helped establish a Buddhist presence in western Canada; Lethbridge, Alberta, has remained the center of a vibrant Japanese Buddhist community. More recently, new immigrants from South Asia have broadened the ethnic and religious pluralism of the Great Plains, though their total numbers remain small. Nonetheless, the presence of a wider range of Asian religions promises to bring new challenges. In Canada, for example, there has been conflict centering on the growing Sikh community, some of whose members have fought government regulations that sought to require them to wear the traditional headgear rather than turbans while serving in the Royal Canadian Mounted Police.

Throughout the Plains, the Jewish population remains small, concentrated more in the larger towns and cities. Yet the Plains plays a significant role in Jewish history in North America. The large emigration from Russia around the turn of the century included thousands of Jews. Although many remained in the major ports of entry for immigrants, several thousand ultimately made their way to the Plains, some as a result of the conscious efforts of Jewish groups to establish agricultural colonies and farm communities. In such settings, it was thought, Jewish identity would be less threatened by the religious pluralism of the larger culture, and immigrants would be able to replicate their traditional agrarian life without the danger of the Russian pogroms that had forced many to leave their homeland. A Jewish farming community was organized in Oxbow, Saskatchewan, in 1892; other Canadian ventures followed in Alberta and Manitoba. Winnipeg remains an important Jewish center. Farther south, the Am Olam, a group of Jewish farmers in eastern South Dakota, owe their genesis as a community to similar impulses. Early in the twentieth century, some Jewish leaders in the United States mustered support for the "Galveston plan," an organized movement to bring immigrant Jews directly to Galveston, Texas, and from there to relocate them in towns and farming communities scattered throughout the interior of North America. As with similar programs, the stated rationale for the Galveston plan was to protect Jewish immigrants from the religious and social corruption of the cities in the East.

Although Islam in North America has witnessed steady expansion since the close of World War II, so that it is now among the fastest-growing religions in the United States and Canada, Muslims have been in the Plains at least since the start of the century. Evidence reveals, for example, that in 1900 a Muslim family in Ross, North Dakota, was using their home as a mosque for communal prayer on a regular basis. Around the same time, Muslim immigrants came to Edmonton, Alberta, working as peddlers. The community there, although small, was sufficiently stable and prosperous that it erected a mosque in 1938. It has continued to grow to the point that in Edmonton, Muslims are now able to take advantage of government provisions that allow for religious instruction in public schools after regular school hours.

An Increasing Diversity

Over the years, the religious life of the Great Plains has become increasingly diverse. Despite years of suppression, the religions of the Indigenous peoples of the Great Plains have endured and adapted to changing circumstances. The westward migration of Americans on both sides of the border and the heavy influx of European immigrants coming in the later nineteenth and early twentieth centuries added greatly to the diversity. In countless towns and communities from Alberta to Texas, the heritage of the immigrant past endures in religious beliefs and landscapes. More recent immigration from Mexico (the latter augmenting a Hispanic and Roman Catholic presence that has existed on the fringes of the Southern Great Plains for centuries) and from Asia has contributed even more detail to this rich tapestry of regional religious life.

See also ARCHITECTURE: Religious Architecture / EDUCATION: Indian Boarding Schools, United States; Indian Residential Schools, Canada / EUROPEAN AMERICANS: Douglas, Thomas (Earl of Selkirk); Jews; Ukrainians / LAW: North Dakota Anti-Garb Law / NATIVE AMERICANS: Sacred Geography / PROTEST AND DISSENT: Aberhart, William; Woodsworth, James Shaver / WAR: Wounded Knee Massacre.

Charles H. Lippy
University of Tennessee at Chattanooga

Ahlstrom, Sydney E. *A Religious History of the American People.* New Haven CT: Yale University Press, 1972. Blau, Joseph L. *Judaism in America: From Curiosity to Third Faith.* Chicago: University of Chicago Press, 1976. Bowden, Henry Warner. *American Indians and Christian Missions.* Chicago: University of Chicago Press, 1981. Epp, Frank H. *Mennonites in Canada, 1786–1920: The History of a Separate People.* Toronto: Macmillan Publishing Company, 1974. Epp, Frank H. *Mennonites in Canada, 1920–1940.* Toronto: Macmillan Publishing Company, 1982. Gaustad, Edwin Scott. *A Religious History of America.* San Francisco: Harper and Row, 1990. Hennesey, James, S.J. *America's Catholics: A History of the Roman Catholic Community in the United States.* New York: Oxford University Press, 1981. Kilbourn, William, A. C. Forrest, and Patrick Watson. *Religion in Canada: The Spiritual Development of a Nation.* Toronto: McClelland and Stewart, Ltd. 1968. Lippy, Charles H., and Peter W. Williams, eds. *Encyclopedia of the American Religious Experience.* New York: Charles Scribners Sons, 1988. Noll, Mark A. *A History of Christianity in the United States and Canada.* Grand Rapids MI: William B. Eerdmans Publishing Co., 1992. Woodcock, George, and Ivan Avakumovic. *The Doukhobors.* Toronto: Oxford University Press, 1968. *Yearbook of American and Canadian Churches.* Nashville: Abingdon Press, published annually.

ADVENTISM

Seventh-day Adventism, which arose in the northeastern United States in the 1840s, holds several doctrinal beliefs. Distinctive of their doctrinal system, and reflected in the denomination's name, is a belief in the perpetuity of the seventh-day Sabbath as the day of rest for Christians and a belief in the visible and literal return of Jesus Christ in the not too distant future. The denomination is evangelical in the sense that it holds for salvation by grace through faith. The church worldwide now has a presence in 205 of the 230 nations recognized by the United Nations.

Members of the Seventh-day Adventist Church first settled in the Great Plains at Omaha, Nebraska, in 1858. As of 1999 the region hosted approximately 50,000 of the 10 million Adventists worldwide. That membership is distributed rather evenly across the Great Plains. The Mid-America Union Conference (headquartered in Lincoln, Nebraska) is the administrative unit that is responsible for most of the region. The southern part of the Great Plains falls within the jurisdiction of the Southwestern Union Conference (Burleson, Texas), while the Canadian Union Conference (or Seventh-day Adventist Church in Canada, with headquarters in Oshawa, Ontario) includes the northern part. Those administrative units supervise the work of eleven local conferences that are included in or intersect the Great Plains. The membership in the Great Plains is, in general, proportionate among the various racial groups of the region. The major exception to that generalization is Native Americans. Although Adventists have missions to the Native American population, those missions have not prospered in relative proportion to other Adventist work in the region.

Adventists in the Great Plains sponsor a large number of elementary schools, several secondary schools ("academies"), and three tertiary institutions: Union College in Lincoln, Nebraska; Southwestern Adventist University in Keene, Texas, near the southern edge of the Plains; and Canadian University College near its northern boundary in College Heights, Alberta. The church also operates several medical facilities in the Great Plains. The most significant are the PorterCare hospitals in Denver, Louisville, and Littleton, Colorado; the Central Texas Medical Center in San Marcos, Texas; and the Huguley Memorial Medical Centers west of Fort Worth, Texas.

George R. Knight
Andrews University

Dick, Everett. *Union College of the Golden Cords.* Lincoln NE: Union College Press, 1967. Knight, George R. *A Brief History of Seventh-day Adventists.* Hagerstown MD: Review and Herald, 1999. Neufeld, Don F., ed. *Seventh-day Adventist Encyclopedia.* Hagerstown MD: Review and Herald, 1996.

ASSEMBLIES OF GOD

The Assemblies of God, headquartered in Springfield, Missouri, was founded in April 1914, when 300 ministers and delegates assembled in Hot Springs, Arkansas, and sought a way to accredit ministers, commission and support missionaries, select a common biblical name, and establish a Bible training school. The convention lasted ten days and was characterized by passionate preaching, heated debate, fervent prayer, and an unusual unity that produced an agreement to form a "cooperative" fellowship of churches that would not be an organization but an "organism" empowered and directed by the Holy Spirit. The result of this meeting was called the General Council of the Assemblies of God.

After Hot Springs, successful evangelistic campaigns were conducted in brush arbors, tents, town halls, and any other place where people could gather and seek God. Meetings were characterized by shouting, unusual physical manifestations, and testimonies of divine healing. Preaching was centered on four cardinal doctrines that included salvation by grace through faith, divine healing as part of Christ's atonement, the baptism in the Holy Spirit initially evidenced by speaking in tongues, and the imminent return of Jesus Christ to earth. Early Assemblies of God ministers called it the full gospel, and it swept through the High Plains like a prairie fire.

By 1922 the Assemblies of God had established regional district councils in North Texas, West Texas, Oklahoma, Kansas, Nebraska, South Dakota, and North Dakota, all part of annual district councils that supervised a growing number of churches. By 1925 the Pentecostal Assemblies of Canada had formed its own organization and begun a prolonged period of growth that is still expanding under the leadership of its present general superintendent, James McKnight.

The Assemblies of God has flourished among the independent and highly individualistic communities of the Great Plains. Two of the largest districts of the Assemblies of God are in the Great Plains. In all, more than 1,700 churches and 190,000 members throughout the Plains make up 10 percent of its total church membership. Outstanding leaders in the Assemblies of God, such as Bert Webb, Bartlett Petersen, Stanley Berg, G. Raymond Carlson, A. G. Ward, A. H. Argue, E. R. Foster, Hugh Cadwalder, A. A. Wilson, and the present general treasurer of the Assemblies of God, James K. Bridges, have all labored in Great Plains districts.

Gene Brown
Waxahachie, Texas

Burgess, Stanley M., and Gary B. McGee, eds. "Pentecostal Assemblies of Canada." In *Dictionary of Pentecostal and Charismatic Movements*. Grand Rapids MI: Zondervan Publishing House, 1988: 695–99. Carlson, G. Raymond. "When Pentecost Came to the Upper Midwest." *Assemblies of God Heritage* 4 (1984): 3–7. Menzies, William W. *Anointed to Serve*. Springfield MO: Gospel Publishing House, 1971.

BAPTISTS

The people called Baptists represent the largest Protestant religious tradition in the United States, claiming more than 30 million members. The Southern Baptist Convention, with its 16 million members, is the largest Baptist denomination, yet there are more than eighty other groups in the United States that claim the appellation "Baptist." Baptists span the theological spectrum from Calvinist to Arminian, from liberal to conservative to fundamentalist, and are deeply divided into three major parties—mainline ecumenical, conservative evangelical, and separatist fundamental—a division found within the Baptist family around the world. There are approximately two million Baptists in the Great Plains, mostly located in Texas, Oklahoma, and Kansas. There are relatively few Baptists in North and South Dakota, Nebraska, Wyoming, Montana, and in the Prairie Provinces. In these areas combined, there are only about 140,000 total adherents. Southern Baptists are by far the strongest Baptist body in the Great Plains.

Despite the differences and disputes that have created numerous variations, the Baptist faith remains an experiential religion, embracing differing ethical, cultural, and doctrinal tenets. Nevertheless, throughout their history Baptists have held to a number of basic principles that set them apart from other Christian bodies. Commonly held Baptist beliefs and doctrines include the following: scripture alone as the authoritative guide for life; church membership that is predicated upon personal faith in Jesus Christ as Savior and Lord; baptism by immersion and the Lord's Supper as the ordinances of the church; the autonomy of each local congregation in its decision making; congregational church government; the priesthood of the believer, or soul competency; and religious liberty and the separation of church and state.

Baptists have long been concerned with bringing persons to faith in Jesus Christ. Thus, Baptists have tended to view the Central and Northern Plains region as a mission field. Originally, Baptists targeted Native Americans and new settlers. In 1842 the Baptist missionary Isaac McCoy founded the American Indian Mission Association in Kansas. Through this organization, which later came under the direction of the Southern Baptist Convention, McCoy worked to see that Native Americans were fairly treated by the government. He also defined areas for relocation of tribes, laid out plans for cities, and initiated Baptist missions at Topeka and Paaoli. The first Baptist work in Nebraska was begun in 1833 by Moses Merrill and his wife when the two started a mission with the Otoe-Missouria Indians. Merrill published a book of hymns in the Otoe language.

The first known Baptists in Dakota Territory, Elijah Terry and James Tanner, arrived in 1852 at Walhalla, in present-day North Dakota, and started a church there. By 1881 the American Baptist Home Mission Society had appointed forty-eight missionaries in the territory who helped establish various foreign-language churches among Swedes, Germans, Norwegians, and Danes. In Canada, Alexander McDonald was sent by Ontario Baptists to Manitoba in 1873; in 1875 he formed a church of seven members. By 1900 there were ninety-nine churches and 170 preaching stations in the Prairie Provinces. As Native Americans and ethnic populations became Americanized and adopted English for their worship services, the bilingual witness of Baptists in the Plains diminished. Church planting continues as the most significant feature of Baptist mission activity in the Great Plains.

Theological education has also been an important facet of Baptist endeavors in the Great Plains. The Central Baptist Theological Seminary in Kansas City, founded in 1901, was jointly sponsored by Southern and Northern (American) Baptist Conventions until Southern Baptists started their own school across the river in Missouri in 1957. The library at Central contains materials related to Native American missions, including a collection related to Charles Journeycake, a Baptist minister who was the last chief of the Delawares. The North American Baptist Conference, the only surviving transborder union of Baptists and the leading Baptist group in the Prairie Provinces, supports the North American Baptist Seminary in Sioux Falls, South Dakota, and Edmonton Baptist Seminary in Edmonton, Alberta. The Canadian Convention of Southern Baptists, which was organized in 1985, supports the Canadian Southern Baptist Theological Seminary at Cochrane, Alberta. While neither a college nor seminary, the Baptist Leadership Training School, located in Calgary, has provided basic training in biblical and pastoral studies since 1949. The institute operates under the auspices of the Baptist Union of Western Canada.

Jerry L. Faught II
Oklahoma Baptist University

McBeth, H. Leon. *The Baptist Heritage*. Nashville: Broadman Press, 1987. Thompson, Margaret E. *The Baptist Story in Western Canada*. Calgary: Baptist Union of Western Canada, 1974. Wardin, Albert W., ed. *Baptists around the World*. Nashville: Broadman and Holman, 1995.

BLACK ELK, NICHOLAS (1866–1950)

Black Elk was probably the most influential Native American leader of the twentieth century. His influence flows from the enduring beauty and power of his religious teachings, his lifetime of engagement with the problems of his people, and the galvanizing effect of the book *Black Elk Speaks* on the revival of traditional religion and culture.

Black Elk was probably born in 1866, the first year after the Civil War. The end of the war brought western expansion, which led to aggressive efforts to confine and assimilate the Plains tribes. Black Elk's early years were spent living the old nomadic life, and he was present at the Custer fight on the Little Big Horn in 1876. He announced his vocation as a holy man by performing the Horse Dance in 1881, but after the government outlawed the Sun Dance and Native healing practices in 1883, his profession could only be practiced underground. Almost all Black Elk's working life as a holy man was spent in this repressive context, and his religious thought is in part a response to the dominant culture's oppression, missioniza-

Nicholas Black Elk and family, between 1890 and 1910

tion, and social engineering. In 1887 Black Elk enlisted with Buffalo Bill Cody and traveled to Europe with his Wild West Show. On his return to the Pine Ridge Reservation in 1889, he became a leader of the Ghost Dance. When the government responded with troops, Black Elk called for armed resistance, and he was present at the Wounded Knee Massacre in 1890.

After Wounded Knee, Black Elk seems to have continued with his medicine practice. In 1904 he accepted Catholicism and became active as a catechist, a position that allowed him to regain a public leadership role. He mastered reservation Catholicism through conversations with the Jesuits, including Eugene Buechel, who cites Black Elk in his Lakota dictionary. In 1931 Black Elk was interviewed by poet John G. Neihardt, which resulted in *Black Elk Speaks* (1932). The book strained Black Elk's relationship with the Jesuits, and he subsequently worked at the Duhamel Sioux Pageant, demonstrating traditional rituals. In 1944 Neihardt interviewed Black Elk for *When the Tree Flowered* (1951). In 1947–48 Black Elk gave an account of Lakota ritual to Joseph Epes Brown that became *The Sacred Pipe* (1953), which provides a Lakota parallel to the seven sacraments and asserts the equal validity of Christianity and traditional religion. Black Elk died at Manderson, South Dakota, on August 17, 1950.

Scholarly work on Black Elk has tended to focus on the authenticity and adequacy of Neihardt's portrait of Black Elk as a traditionalist in *Black Elk Speaks* and on the related issue of the extent of Black Elk's commitment to Catholicism. (The authenticity of *The Sacred Pipe* is a growing topic of discussion.) At one pole of the debate, Michael F. Steltenkamp's *Black Elk: Holy Man of the Oglala* (1993) portrays Black Elk as a progressive Catholic who retains little meaningful commitment to traditional religion. At the other

pole, Julian Rice's *Black Elk's Story: Distinguishing Its Lakota Purpose* (1991) portrays Black Elk's involvement in Catholicism as strategic, a response to oppression. Although this debate is illuminating, it is also misleading, because Black Elk retained a lifelong commitment to the central intention of the Ghost Dance, the revitalization of traditional culture through religious ritual. In terms of culture, Black Elk was undoubtedly a nativist, and the symbolism and hope of the Ghost Dance is seldom far from his teaching. On the other hand, his engagement with Catholicism shows that he could assimilate a very different set of religious symbols, something that seems to have been far easier for him than for academic observers obsessed with the colonialist search for authenticity.

Black Elk was not the broken old man who mourns the death of the dream at the end of *Black Elk Speaks*. Nor was he anybody's anthropological informant, a passive source of information on the past. For Black Elk, the dream never died, and he always spoke to the Lakota present. In the simplest terms, he was a leader of his people during a time of troubles, and those troubles should certainly not be forgotten in evaluating his life and work. Black Elk was one of the most gifted spokesmen for the Lakota wisdom tradition, and his farseeing literary collaborations have disseminated his teachings far beyond their original cultural horizon. Lakota holy men still teach the great lessons of this tradition—respect for sacred power, the relatedness of all beings, and care for the earth—and they still draw on Black Elk's legacy, which continues to confront and challenge European ways of viewing humanity, society, and the cosmos.

See also LITERARY TRADITIONS: Neihardt, John G. / WAR: Wounded Knee Massacre.

> *Clyde Holler*
> *Morganton, Georgia*

DeMallie, Raymond J., ed. *The Sixth Grandfather: Black Elk's Teachings Given to John G. Neihardt*. Lincoln: University of Nebraska Press, 1984. Holler, Clyde. *Black Elk's Religion: The Sun Dance and Lakota Catholicism*. Syracuse NY: Syracuse University Press, 1995. Holler, Clyde, ed. *The Black Elk Reader*. Syracuse NY: Syracuse University Press, 2000.

BLAND, SALEM (1859–1950)

Born August 26, 1859, in Lachute, Quebec, and educated in that province, Salem Goldworth Bland moved to Winnipeg, Manitoba, in 1903 to teach New Testament and church history at Wesley College after twenty years as a popular Methodist minister in eastern Ontario and Quebec. Over the next sixteen years he had a remarkable impact across the Prairie Provinces, where he was in great demand as a preacher of uncommon eloquence and as a popularizer of liberal theology and the Social Gospel. Well-read in secular as in theological matters, he was at once a proponent of German historical critics of the Bible like Adolf Harnack and of reform Darwinists like Henry Drummond and Benjamin Kidd. He became increasingly radical as a result of his association with agrarian, labor, and social reform

activists. His outspokenness about the exploitation of Prairie farmers by the grain trade and of Winnipeg newcomers by employers and landlords who were often active churchmen led to a falling out with wealthy laymen who had at first welcomed him.

Invited to address the convention of the Saskatchewan Grain Growers Association in 1913, he sparked an abortive move toward third-party politics. His dismissal from Wesley College in 1917 on grounds of financial restraint was an academic freedom cause célèbre across the West. For a time he was a columnist for the *Grain Growers Guide* and a lecturer on the Chautauqua circuit. He was courted to run in the wartime election of 1917 but deferred to a returned soldier, Major G. W. Andrews, thus signaling the high hopes he held for a major social and political reconstruction after the war under the inspiration of returning soldiers. He would express this view in a small but wide-ranging and controversial book, *The New Christianity* (1920). Thought by some to be one of the instigators of the Winnipeg General Strike of mid-1919, he had by that time moved to a Toronto pastorate and would soon begin a twenty-year career as a regular columnist for the *Toronto Daily Star* under the byline of "The Observer." He died in Toronto on February 6, 1950.

See also PROTEST AND DISSENT: Grain Growers Associations.

> *Richard Allen*
> *Hamilton, Ontario*

Allen, Richard. "Salem Bland and the Spirituality of the Social Gospel: Winnipeg and the West, 1903–1913." In *Prairie Spirit: Perspectives on the Heritage of the United Church of Canada in the West*, edited by Dennis L. Butcher, Catherine Macdonald, Margaret McPherson, Raymond Smith, and A. McKibbon Watts. Winnipeg: University of Manitoba Press, 1985: 217–32. Allen, Richard. *The Social Passion: Religion and Social Reform in Canada*. Toronto: University of Toronto Press, 1971.

BRANCH DAVIDIANS

The Branch Davidian sect emerged in 1955 from a Seventh-day Adventist reform movement in Central Texas and became widely known in 1993 when federal agents surrounded the group's property outside Waco, beginning a fifty-one-day siege that ended in the fiery deaths of most members.

The Branch Davidians trace their roots to a Seventh-day Adventist reform movement founded by Bulgarian immigrant Victor Houteff in Los Angeles. After a 1929 visionary experience, Houteff began teaching what he claimed was his divinely inspired true interpretation of scripture, thus implying inaccuracies in Seventh-day Adventist practices. Local church leaders charged Houteff with heresy, prompting him to move with his followers to Central Texas. The Davidians agreed with most Seventh-day Adventist doctrine, but Houteff taught his followers that his scriptural interpretations constituted part of an emerging truth, in which Seventh-day Adventist apostasy prevented Christ's return and the apocalyptic events that would usher in the Kingdom of God on earth.

Houteff's wife, Florence, assumed the group's leadership after Victor's death in 1955. Florence Houteff almost immediately published her revelation that the apocalypse would occur on April 22, 1959. When the apocalypse failed to materialize, the Davidians fell into chaos, and Ben Roden, leader of a splinter group dating to 1955 known as the Branch Davidians (this group referred to Jesus Christ as the Branch), emerged as the new leader. When Roden died, his wife, Lois, a prophetess in her own right, took charge. George Roden, Lois's son, fought successfully to gain control in 1985, temporarily defeating his main rival, Vernon Howell, whom Lois Roden apparently intended as her successor. In 1988 Howell, who two years later legally changed his name to David Koresh, wrested control of the group's Mount Carmel community from Roden, marking the beginning of the group's most tragic era.

Koresh assumed leadership when the Branch Davidian community faced economic and political crises, and he used the situation to consolidate power and turn the group in new theological directions. Koresh averted a financial crisis by successfully soliciting monetary contributions to pay back taxes for the Mount Carmel commune. He developed automobile restoration and weapons businesses to provide the group with continued income. Koresh secured his leadership by converting new members and convincing them that he was descended spiritually from King David and was a "sinful messiah" on a mission from God to initiate Armageddon. Koresh prophesied an apocalyptic battle pitting Branch Davidians against the American army, ushering in the Kingdom of God on earth, in which the Branch Davidians would play an important role. He also convinced many followers that his mission included fathering a new line of God's children. Koresh created the "House of David"—the women who became his spiritual wives—and produced a number of offspring. These innovations created jealousies within the group and objections, from within and without, to the induction of underage girls into the House of Koresh.

Combined with alleged violations of weapons laws, the group's social innovations brought increasing attention from outsiders, including the media, anticult activists, and state and federal agencies. Agents from the U.S. Bureau of Alcohol, Tobacco, and Firearms raided Mount Carmel on February 28, 1993, but withering fire from the main residence killed four agents and injured twenty more, thus creating a standoff. The Federal Bureau of Investigation assumed control of the situation that same day and led a fifty-one-day siege. On April 19, 1993, the FBI used two M-60 tanks and four Bradley vehicles to inject tear gas into the Mount Carmel dwelling intermittently for six hours in hopes of flushing the Branch Davidians out of their stronghold. At about noon, a fire swept through Mount Carmel, killing many of the seventy-four of the Branch Davidians inside; others died of gunshot wounds, apparently inflicted by themselves or others inside Mount Carmel.

The April 1993 tragedy bears similarities to the Wounded Knee Massacre of 1890. Both involved religious groups dominated by prophecy and antagonistic to the United States and its dominant cultural and social values, and both groups suffered massive loss of life in conflicts with federal agencies. The events raised questions about the extent of religious freedom in the Plains and the federal government's role in enforcing cultural values and law and order in the region.

Todd M. Kerstetter
Texas Christian University

Tabor, James D., and Eugene V. Gallagher. *Why Waco? Cults and the Battle for Religious Freedom in America.* Berkeley: University of California Press, 1995. Wright, Stuart A. *Armageddon in Waco: Critical Perspectives on the Branch Davidian Conflict.* Chicago: University of Illinois Press, 1995.

BUDDHISM

Buddhism traces its origins to a sixth century B.C. Indian prince who practiced meditation until he became realized as the Buddha, or "enlightened one." During the next two and a half millennia, Buddhism became a major religious tradition, thriving in Southeast Asia as Theravada ("the tradition of the elders"), East Asia as Mahayana ("the great vehicle"), and Central Asia as Vajrayana ("the diamond vehicle"). Common practices in these three "vehicles" are meditation, cultivation of wisdom and compassion, and the development of Buddhist communities.

Buddhist adherents now live mainly in larger towns and cities of the Great Plains in two general populations (although actual census figures are not available). First, there are the Asian American communities of larger cities such as Omaha, Billings, and Calgary. In these cities, recently established immigrants from Asia seek to knit together their ancestral traditions with Buddhist observance. The Vietnamese of Oklahoma City have expressed economic and social confidence with a beautiful new temple; Thai and Laotian communities have established impressive Theravada centers just beyond the Plains borders in Houston, Dallas, and elsewhere in Texas. Other Asian communities have multigenerational history in the Great Plains, and Buddhist temples serve to join religion, spirituality, and culture in a single environment. The Buddhist Churches of America (BCA) was first established around 1900 as the American mission of the Jodo Shinshu, a popular Pure Land sect from Japan. The Denver Buddhist Temple has long owned prime downtown real estate to house not only its temple, but a community center, subsidized housing for seniors, and shopping center.

The second category of adherents, widely distributed throughout the Plains, are "convert" communities, for whom Buddhism is not their ancestral tradition. These groups fall into the three major "vehicles" described above. The Theravada groups practice *vipassana* (insight) meditation with little ritual or cultural accouterments. Vipassana groups gather weekly or biweekly for sitting meditation (*zazen*) and "dharma talks" given on tape or by members or visiting teachers. Small centers based in private homes can be found from Edmonton and Calgary south to Boulder, Santa Fe, and Dallas. They communicate through networking, newsletters, and public posting.

The primary Mahayana meditation practiced is Zen, which originated in Japan and China. Tiny Zen centers dot the Great Plains from Rapid City to Missoula and from Omaha to Amarillo, sporting catchy names like "Laughing Teabowl," "Empty Sky," and "Great Mountain." Many of these centers are associated with the Vietnamese Zen master Thich Nhat Hanh, the monk who played an important role in ending the U.S.-Vietnam War in his homeland. Others trace their lineages to the Japanese traditions of Katagiri Roshi, who established a center in Minneapolis in the 1960s, or of Maezumi Roshi from Los Angeles. The Zen centers also stress *zazen*, scheduled multiple times each week, as well as dharma talks and readings from Zen classics.

Vajrayana Buddhism, associated with Tibet, has centers in Edmonton, Kansas City, and Dallas, but the greatest concentration of Vajrayana practice is in Boulder, Colorado, the home of Naropa University, which in 2000 had an enrollment of 900. The Buddhist-inspired accredited university was founded by Chögyam, Trungpa, a teacher (*lama*) who escaped from the Chinese invasion of Tibet in 1959. Vajrayana communities, centered on authorized teachers, are characterized by sitting meditation, ritual practice, tightly knit communities, rigorous study programs, and dharma talks.

See also ASIAN AMERICANS: Denver Buddhist Temple.

Judith Simmer-Brown
Naropa University

Morreale, Don, ed. *The Complete Guide to Buddhist America.* Boston: Shambhala Publications, 1998. Prebish, Charles S. *Luminous Passage: The Practice and Study of Buddhism in America.* Berkeley: University of California Press, 1999. Seager, Richard Hughes. *Buddhism in America.* New York: Columbia University Press, 1999.

CANADIAN WESLEYAN METHODISM

Whereas Methodism in Upper and Lower Canada had been subjected to the strong imprint of American Methodism and subsequently drew many of its leading lights from Loyalist stock, the missions to the western Canadian Plains were initially dominated by strong English connections. Missionaries, headed by James Evans (1801–1846), came to the Plains under the initiative of the Wesleyan Missionary Society and the jurisdiction of the Hudson's Bay Company in London. Evans established his base at Norway House, on the northern tip of Lake Winnipeg, and from there he and his coworkers branched out westward across the vast territories toward the Rocky Mountains. Robert Terrill Rundle (1811–1896) made his headquarters at Fort Edmonton in 1840 and traveled widely among the Crees and the Blackfoot. Both Rundle and Evans were particularly skilled in the Cree language, the latter fashioning a syllabics system that became the basis of the first published hymnary in western Canada. While Rundle was an effective itinerant preacher, his only permanent legacy was a community at Pigeon Lake, Alberta. Greater success was accorded Henry Bird Steinhauer (c. 1820–1884), an Ojibwa from Ontario, who joined another Methodist missionary, William Mason (c. 1813–1893), in Manitoba. After ordination, Steinhauer went to Alberta and founded the mission at Whitefish Lake, where he stayed for the remainder of his life.

The last decades of the century, however, were marked by the pressures of mass immigration of Europeans to the Prairies, a process accelerated by the Hudson's Bay Company's ceding of the West to the British government in 1869. Thereafter, Methodist influence expanded in the new towns and cities. For example, George Young (1821–1890) of the Canadian Conference established Grace Church in Winnipeg in 1871. Mission programs from churches in eastern Canada swung into play to care for the influx. With this movement, the Methodist tradition shifted away from proselytizing to transforming the vast immigrant crowd into "good" Canadians, and away from condemnation of sin to criticism of the social order. Educational institutions sprouted up, such as Wesley College (1877) in Winnipeg and Alberta College (1903) in Edmonton. By the time Methodists joined with Presbyterians in 1925 to form the United Church of Canada, Methodist agitation for social order, public morality, community focus, and sensitivity to lay concerns had already forged a solid position in Prairie consciousness, an influence that continues to this day.

Earle H. Waugh
University of Alberta

Emery, George. *The Methodist Church on the Prairies, 1896–1914.* Montreal: McGill-Queen's University Press, 2001. French, G. S., and J. W. Grant. "Canada." In *Encyclopedia of World Methodism,* edited by N. B. Harmon. Nashville: United Methodist Publishing House, 1974: 385–401.

CATHOLIC SISTERHOODS

Catholic sisterhoods are groups of Roman Catholic women who are bound by the vows of poverty, chastity, and obedience to live in a community and to serve the church in a wide range of ministries, especially education, health care, and social services. These women arrived in the Great Plains in the 1860s to establish schools, hospitals, and churches for Native Americans from Dakota Territory to Texas. They were among the first representatives of the Catholic Church to reach the frontier for purposes of evangelization. As the sisterhoods attracted more members in later years, they founded a large number of institutions to serve the Catholic population in the Great Plains, including elementary and high schools, colleges, orphanages, homes for women, hospitals, and nursing homes. Much of the Catholic infrastructure in the Great Plains was established by religious sisters.

Between fifty and sixty Catholic sisterhoods serve in the Great Plains today. These groups vary widely in terms of membership, lifestyle, and apostolic activity. The largest groups include the Sisters of Saint Joseph of Carondelet (St. Louis, Missouri), Order of Saint Benedict of Pontifical Jurisdiction (Yankton, South Dakota), Religious Sisters of Mercy (Omaha, Ne-

braska), and the Sisters of the Presentation of the Blessed Virgin Mary (Aberdeen, South Dakota). The smallest community is the Oblate Sisters of the Blessed Sacrament, who minister to Native Americans in Rapid City and Marty, South Dakota. In the Prairie Provinces the most prominent Catholic sisterhoods are the Grey Nuns and the Sisters of Saint Anne.

Since the Second Vatican Council (1965) the sisterhoods have liberalized their rules on dress, cloister, and the types of work they perform. The new areas of ministry include reaching out to the poor and marginalized as directors of soup kitchens, social workers, hospice caretakers, and coordinators of low-income housing and improving the condition of Native Americans.

See also LAW: North Dakota Anti-Garb Law.

James T. Carroll
Iona College

Coburn, Carol, and Martha Smith. *Spirited Lives: How Nuns Shaped Catholic Culture and American Life, 1836–1920.* Chapel Hill: University of North Carolina Press, 1999. Peterson, Susan. "Religious Communities of Women in the West: The Presentation Sisters' Adaptation to the Northern Plains Frontier." *Journal of the West* 21 (1982): 65–70. Peterson, Susan. "Widening Horizons: Catholic Sisterhoods on the Northern Plains, 1874–1910." *Great Plains Quarterly* 5 (1985): 125–32.

CHURCH OF JESUS CHRIST OF LATTER-DAY SAINTS

The Church of Jesus Christ of Latter-day Saints, commonly referred to as the Mormons or Latter-day Saints, had a significant influence on the settling of the trans-Mississippi West. In the spring of 1820 the church's founder, Joseph Smith Jr., claimed to have received a visitation by God and Jesus Christ in upstate New York. In 1823, Smith asserted, the angel Moroni revealed to him the location of golden plates recounting the resurrected Christ's appearance to peoples in the Western Hemisphere. In 1827 Smith acquired these plates and began translating them into the Book of Mormon, a companion scripture to the Bible.

On April 6, 1830, Smith and several followers founded the Church of Latter-day Saints in Fayette, Seneca County, New York. Missionary labors commenced, meeting with significant success at home and abroad. Others, however, greeted the Latter-day Saints and their prophet with skepticism at best and persecution at worst. The Saints sought a more tolerant place to practice their religion and migrated, first to Kirtland, Ohio, and then to various settlements in Missouri. Persecution mounted and mobs forcibly drove the Saints to Nauvoo, Illinois. On June 27, 1844, violence erupted, and a local militia murdered Joseph Smith and his brother Hyrum in Carthage, Illinois.

Persecution intensified, and in 1846 the Saints were driven from Nauvoo. Smith's successor, Brigham Young, and the majority of the Latter-day Saints began the exodus west to Kanesville (Council Bluffs, Iowa) and Winter Quarters (Florence, Nebraska). The following year, a portion of those who had temporarily settled on the Missouri River continued west along the north side of the Platte to Salt Lake City, Utah. From 1847 to 1869 more than

70,000 Mormons migrated across the Plains to the Great Basin. During 1846–47 a Mormon battalion of 549 men, sixty women, and several children volunteers served under Gen. Stephen W. Kearny during the Mexican War. They marched 1,850 miles from Council Bluffs, Iowa, in a southwesterly direction across the Great Plains through Santa Fe to San Diego, California, in perhaps the longest infantry march in American history.

Initially, the Mormons viewed the Great Plains as a barrier to cross in order to reach their "Zion" in the Great Basin. They established temporary settlements, freight stations, ferry crossings, and a Perpetual Emigrating Fund to assist overland emigrants. Although they made their headquarters in Salt Lake City, they also founded more than 400 settlements from Canada to Mexico and from the Pacific to the Great Plains. Initial settlement in the Great Plains took place in the western portions of Colorado, New Mexico, Texas, and Wyoming. By 1895 Mormon settlement of southern Alberta made it the first stake (a group of five to eight wards and branches) organized outside the United States. Today, every major city in the Great Plains has at least one congregation.

Although the Latter-day Saints are America's fifth-largest church, the majority of adherents now live outside North America. In 2000 membership exceeded 11 million and was growing by approximately 400,000 annually. In the Great Plains states and Prairie Provinces, membership exceeded 600,000, with more than 50,000 members each in Alberta, New Mexico, and Wyoming, 100,000 in Colorado, and 200,000 in Texas. Of the church's 100 or more temples, twelve lie within or near the Great Plains: in Albuquerque, New Mexico; Billings, Montana; Bismarck, North Dakota; Cardston, Alberta; Dallas, Texas; Denver, Colorado; Edmonton, Alberta; Houston, Texas; Lubbock, Texas; Oklahoma City, Oklahoma; Regina, Saskatchewan; and Omaha (Winter Quarters), Nebraska.

See also TRANSPORTATION: Mormon Trail.

Jay H. Buckley
Brigham Young University

Allen, James B., and Glen M. Leonard. *The Story of the Latter-day Saints.* Salt Lake City: Deseret Book Company, 1992. Ludlow, Daniel H., ed. *Encyclopedia of Mormonism.* New York: Macmillan Publishing Company, 1992.

COMFORT, E. NICHOLAS (1884–1956)

The Reverend E. Nicholas Comfort, founder of the Oklahoma School of Religion, was a leading southwestern proponent of the Social Gospel. He was born in Brookston, Texas, on May 1, 1884. Overcoming an impoverished youth in eastern Texas and western Oklahoma, Comfort was educated at McCormick Theological Seminary, the University of Chicago, Columbia University, and Union Theological Seminary. In 1924 he returned to Oklahoma to become pastor for Presbyterian students at the state's flagship university in Norman.

Determined to overcome sectarianism and fundamentalism, Comfort established the Oklahoma School of Religion in 1927. During the two decades of its existence, the School of Religion (1927–48) strove to provide interdenominational instruction. In the process, the school, along with Dean Comfort as its director, proved enormously controversial. Comfort propounded the message of the fatherhood of God and the brotherhood of man, while condemning militarism, racism, and economic inequities. As a consequence, both he and the School of Religion experienced ridicule from less ecumenically inclined ministers, self-proclaimed patriots, and right-wing politicians. Investigative committees examined the operations of Comfort and his school, initially resulting in a firestorm of protest from supporters across the state. The emergence of the cold war resulted in an even less hospitable climate, and the School of Religion was forced to close its doors in 1948. By that point, Comfort was preaching as an itinerant minister and building a new, small house on the outskirts of Norman. After suffering two strokes, Comfort and his wife, Esther, moved to Rochester, Minnesota, to be close to one of their three children and the Mayo Clinic. He died there on February 27, 1956.

Robert C. Cottrell
California State University, Chico

Cottrell, Robert C. *The Social Gospel of E. Nicholas Comfort.* Norman: University of Oklahoma Press, 1997. Cottrell, Robert C. "The Social Gospel of Nicholas Comfort." *Chronicles of Oklahoma* 61 (1983–84): 386–409.

DENVER BUDDHIST TEMPLE

See ASIAN AMERICANS: Denver Buddhist Temple

DE SMET, PIERRE-JEAN (1801–1873)

As a missionary to the West, Pierre-Jean De Smet, S.J., had no equal among nineteenth-century Catholics. Born on January 30, 1801, to a wealthy family in East Flanders (Belgium), De Smet journeyed to America in 1821 to join the Society of Jesus, or Jesuits, an order of Catholic men with a special interest in missions and education. Following more than a decade of religious formation, De Smet began his missionary career in 1838 when he established Saint Joseph's Mission for members of the Potawatomi tribe at Council Bluffs. From that date until his death, De Smet baptized many thousands of Native Americans in more than thirty tribes. He traveled some 180,000 miles, including seventeen trips across the Atlantic Ocean, in his efforts to educate others about the spiritual condition of Native Americans, and he ultimately raised more than a half million dollars on their behalf.

For thirty years, in nineteen journeys taken between 1838 and 1868, De Smet traversed the Great Plains from all points of the compass and during all seasons of the year. Intimately familiar with the drainage basins of both the Missouri and Columbia Rivers, De Smet favored the Great Plains because he believed that the natural environment offered exceptional advantages to potential settlers. He used terms like "superb" and "smiling and beauti-

Pierre-Jean De Smet, ca. 1864

ful" to describe the richness of the environment in letters to his family and others in Europe. De Smet encountered the Niobrara, White Earth, and Little Medicine Rivers in his travels in the Great Plains, but it was the attributes of the Missouri and the Platte that received most of the attention in his extensive journals. An avid amateur scientist, De Smet was also a close observer of the region's flora, fauna, and geology.

After 1851 the question of how to reconcile the needs of white pioneers with the rights of Native Americans vexed De Smet. The key to his solution, which he offered several times to high government officials, including President Abraham Lincoln, centered on isolating tribes for a minimum of twenty years while missionaries added elements of "practical civilization" to their already crowded workload of spiritual salvation.

De Smet passed away at his room in the Jesuit community at St. Louis University on May 23, 1873. His ideas, observations, and predictions about the trans-Mississippi western frontier survive in four published books and hundreds of personal letters preserved in archives in Belgium, St. Louis, Missouri, and Pullman, Washington.

Robert C. Carriker
Gonzaga University

Carriker, Robert. "Admiring Advocate of the Great Plains: Father Pierre-Jean De Smet, S.J., on the Middle Missouri." *Great Plains Quarterly* 14 (1994): 243–56. Carriker, Robert C. *Father Peter John De Smet, S.J.: Jesuit in the West.* Norman: University of Oklahoma Press, 1995. Chittenden, Hiram Martin, and Alfred Talbot Richardson, eds. *Life, Letters and Travels of Father Pierre-Jean De Smet, S.J., 1801–1873.* New York: Francis P. Harper, 1905.

DISCIPLES OF CHRIST

The Christian Church (Disciples of Christ) was born in the first third of the nineteenth century on American soil of Presbyterian parentage. Under the guidance of its forebears, Scots Irish immigrants Thomas Campbell (1763–1854), his son, Alexander (1788–1866), Walter Scott (1796–1861), and the Maryland-born Barton Warren Stone (1772–1844), it focused on the restoration of biblical principles that stressed the unity of the church, reliance on New Testament authority, and self-governance of local congregations.

In the formative years no specific orders of clergy or church organization existed, and still today there is no official book of discipline that manages church life. Each congregation was to call and consecrate its own leaders. Those leaders earned their livings as farmers, merchants, bankers, teachers, and doctors in their communities and served as elders, deacons, and preachers in the church. The selection of local leaders, including clergy, remains a tenet of Disciples' practice today.

Adhering to no established creed as a test of fellowship, the movement advocated the blending of reason, a capacity of the human intellect, with revelation through the inspiration of the Bible. Two ordinances (sacraments) continue to be observed: the weekly celebration of the Lord's Supper, commonly called the breaking of bread, and baptism by immersion for the remission of sins offered to those able to confess Jesus as Lord and Savior, commonly referred to as believer's baptism.

There were four guiding principles defined as ideals of this movement: unity, restoration, liberty, and mission. Mission essentially was confined to the United States. Foreign mission fields were of interest but early on were not considered a priority. It was not until the last two decades of the nineteenth century and into the beginning of the twentieth that Disciples engaged in overseas ministries intentionally and with purpose. The home missionary enterprise was active and devoted to building new congregations and chartering educational institutions. Predominantly located in county seats along the American frontier, Disciple evangelists and church planters followed the westward migration of the expanding nation. These new congregations appropriated the rugged individualism and institutional independence that characterized the national mood.

States and territories west of the Mississippi River destined for development were Missouri, Kansas, Oklahoma, and Texas, particularly as the evangelists and planters followed the cattle trails and the railroads in these latter three states. To a lesser extent, church settlements were established in Iowa, Nebraska, and Colorado, with virtually none in Montana and Wyoming. The appeal of the Disciples movement was to western Europeans, especially those from the British Isles. With the exception of Oklahoma, with its unique political configuration of the Indian and Oklahoma territories, there was little expansion into Native lands or mission to Native peoples.

The current membership and number of congregations, according to a 1997 denominational census, reflects little change from earlier days. Twenty-three percent of the total membership and 25 percent of the Disciples of Christ churches in the United States and Canada are located in the Great Plains. Of those figures, 84 percent of the membership and 85 percent of the churches still are concentrated in Kansas, Oklahoma, and Texas, even though the dust of the cattle trails has settled and the boom of the railroads has faded.

John M. Imbler
Phillips Theological Seminary

Garrison, Winfred Ernest, and Alfred T. De Groot. *The Disciples of Christ: A History*. St. Louis: Christian Board of Education, 1948.

DISPENSATIONALISM

Among evangelical Christian churches in the Great Plains, dispensationalism is an influential hermeneutical system or framework intended to make sense of the vast and varied literature of the Bible. The system assumes the existence of a personal God who created the world and humankind; a historical, grammatical interpretation of the Bible (which describes both God's work and providential plan for human history); and a premillennial understanding of eschatology. Although the number of "dispensations," or historical periods, is sometimes thought to be the distinctive feature of dispensationalism, other hermeneutical systems (such as covenant theology) also describe biblical history in terms of such phases. The major periods include the patriarchal, Mosaic, church, millennial kingdom, and eternal kingdom. Dispensationalism relates these to one another as distinct outworkings of God's purposes. For example, God's purposes during the Mosaic dispensation are different from his purposes during the dispensation of the church. Likewise, the relevant entities are distinct: during the Mosaic dispensation people related to God through the nation of Israel and the covenants that God made with that nation. Following the death of Jesus Christ, however, God instituted a new entity, the church, as the vehicle through which he would accomplish his purposes for the present dispensation.

Churches in the Plains that are best known for their dispensational approach to the Bible include the Berean Fellowship of Churches (centered in Nebraska), Independent Fundamental Churches of America (Kansas and Colorado), General Association of Regular Baptist Churches (Kansas, Nebraska, Colorado, Montana), Baptist Bible Fellowship (centered in Missouri), and World Baptist Fellowship (strongest in Texas). There has also been some dispensational influence in the mainline denominations, though it is not extensive. W. A. Criswell has been the best-known dispensationalist in Southern Baptist circles; Lewis Sperry Chafer and John F. Walvoord (both associated with Dallas Theological Seminary) were Presbyterian. The American Sunday School Union has also been influential in beginning Sunday schools in the Dakotas, Ne-

braska, and Colorado. The Rural Home Missionary Association, headquartered in Illinois, is active in ministry in the Plains states.

Dispensational Bible colleges and institutes that are located in the Great Plains include the Rocky Mountain Bible Institute in Denver (now part of Colorado Christian University), Midwest Bible and Missionary Institute (Salina, Kansas, now part of Calvary Bible College and Seminary in Kansas City), Prairie Bible Institute (Three Hills, Alberta), Montana Bible Institute (Lewiston, Montana), and Frontier School of the Bible (LaGrange, Wyoming). The most significant dispensational influences on churches of the Great Plains have been Dallas Theological Seminary and Moody Bible Institute (Chicago), which have trained many of the pastors and teachers for ministry in these institutions.

The two best-known popularizers of dispensationalism in the Plains have been C. I. Scofield and William Aberhart. Scofield was an attorney and politician from Kansas who, after ordination to the Congregational ministry in 1882, edited the dispensational Scofield Reference Bible. Aberhart was a Baptist radio preacher in Calgary who founded the Calgary Prophetic Bible Institute and headed Alberta's Social Credit government from 1935 until his death in 1943.

See also PROTEST AND DISSENT: Aberhart, William.

Rodney J. Decker
Baptist Bible Seminary

Marsden, George M. *Fundamentalism and American Culture: The Shaping of Twentieth-Century Evangelicalism, 1870–1925*. New York: Oxford University Press, 1980. Ryrie, Charles. *Dispensationalism*. Chicago: Moody Press, 1995. Sandeen, Earnest. *The Roots of Fundamentalism: British and American Millenarianism, 1800–1930*. Chicago: University of Chicago Press, 1970.

DISTRIBUTION OF RELIGIONS

The pattern of allegiance to religious groups in the Great Plains is largely a function of immigration history. Although denominational mergers and missionary activities over the years have made linkages to specific ethnic groups difficult to discern in places, they nevertheless remain largely intact. Four broad bands of dominance trend east and west across the region: the United Church of Canada in the Prairie Provinces; a Lutheran-Catholic mix in the Dakotas, Montana, Wyoming, and northern Nebraska; a diverse amalgam headed by Catholicism and Methodism in Kansas, Colorado, and southern Nebraska; and a Southern Baptist hegemony throughout most of Oklahoma and Texas.

The United Church of Canada, a body created in 1925 by a merger of most of the nation's Congregational, Methodist, and Presbyterian congregations, dominates religious life in the Prairie Provinces. This authority is partly by default. Canadian Catholics did not move west from Quebec in large numbers, and most early Prairie settlers avoided the Anglican Church because they associated it with the upper social classes of Southern Ontario. Catholicism (counting both Latin and Byzantine

rites) is the second most important grouping in the region, some of it connected with the early Métis population and some with the Ukrainian colonists who came to the northern fringe of settlement in Manitoba and Saskatchewan. French Canadian settlers established St. Boniface, now a part of metropolitan Winnipeg. Other important religious regions in the Prairies have evolved from two German Russian Mennonite colonies south of Winnipeg and an American Mormon settlement at Cardston in southwestern Alberta.

When Dakota Territory was first settled by Europeans and Americans in the 1870s, it and other parts of the Northern Plains attracted primarily Yankee settlers drawn from the northern tier of American states. They brought with them Congregational, American Baptist, and Unitarian churches. Most of these people decided to move elsewhere after a long drought in the 1890s, however, and left this land to be occupied by a variety of more permanent immigrants and faiths from Bohemia, Germany, Holland, Russia, and Scandinavia. Norwegians and other Scandinavians came first and concentrated their Lutheranism in northeastern Nebraska and in the Red River Valley of eastern North Dakota. Two counties there (Steele and Traill) still report that more than 70 percent of their church membership is Lutheran. Norwegian Lutheranism also dominates across extreme northern North Dakota and into extreme northeastern Montana.

Germans and German Russians settled widely across the Northern Plains and brought along with them Catholic, Hutterite, Lutheran, Mennonite, and Reformed churches. Catholicism is the leading religion in most of the Plains counties of Montana and Wyoming, plus those in the western half of South Dakota. Most of these churches are German and Bohemian-based, but some are the product of successful missionary work among Native Americans. Episcopalians were active on the mission front as well, and this church can claim more than 20 percent of the religious adherents reported in five counties populated by Lakotas. Several of the smaller denominations in the Plains have exceptional strength in certain places, including the United Church of Christ in the Nebraska Sandhills; the (Dutch) Reformed Church in Douglas County, South Dakota; and the Hutterian Brethren (or Hutterites) southwest of Lewistown, Montana. The Native American Church and other Indigenous religions are important in parts of the Northern Plains as well, but reliable statistics for them are unavailable.

In most of the counties of the Central Plains in Kansas and Nebraska, the United Methodist Church claims more members than any other religious body. This preeminence is similar to that found in rural sections of Ohio, Indiana, Illinois, and southern Iowa and reflects the origins in these states of most early immigrants to the midsection of the Plains. Kansans, in turn, extended Methodism southward several counties when they participated in the late-nineteenth-century land rushes into northwestern Oklahoma. In many communities across these states, Methodists account for about a third of the church membership. Catholicism is the other major church in this section. With a strong presence in Kansas City, Omaha, Wichita, and other large cities, this faith actually has the largest number of adherents in the Plains. Catholicism also is important in several rural areas, including the Volga German communities of Ellis County, Kansas.

Neither Catholicism nor Methodism is really dominant over the Central Plains as a whole, because settlers came from a comparatively wide variety of places in the United States and abroad. Northerners scattered American Baptist and Presbyterian churches across the region, for example, and people from the Ohio Valley brought their Disciples of Christ faith. Similarly, various Europeans established Catholic, Lutheran, Mennonite, and other congregations. The biggest of the Protestant immigrant churches is the Lutheran Church, Missouri Synod, with 11 percent of the religious membership in Nebraska and 5 percent in Kansas. This organization was created by German settlers in Illinois and Missouri and it came west with them. Another Germanic faith, Mennonitism, is a major presence in Harvey, Marion, and McPherson Counties in Kansas. The ancestors of local people there bought land from the Santa Fe Railroad.

With the exception of some Germans in the Hill Country of Texas, European settlers generally avoided the Southern Plains. So did emigrants from the northern states. The religious scene in Oklahoma and Texas is thus dominated by the traditional southern denominations, the Southern Baptist Convention and the United Methodist Church. Both faiths grew because they encouraged local leadership and worked hard on the mission front. In the past their strength was nearly equal to one another, but in the 1990s Baptists could claim about 50 percent of the church membership in a typical Southern Plains county and the Methodists only about 15 percent. Fundamentalist Protestantism is a significant and growing presence in the region. The Church of Christ claims 4 percent of the religious adherents in Oklahoma, for example, as does the Assemblies of God, the largest of the nation's pentecostal groups.

The western and southern fringes of the Southern Plains are a transition zone between Latino and Southern culture, and thus between the Catholic and Baptist religious traditions. Expansion of settlers into eastern New Mexico took place nearly simultaneously from east and west, with Latinos seeking irrigation sites and Anglos grass for their cattle. Since 1900 the Latino migration has continued eastward and northward. Some of this is to rural counties, but most has been to urban, industrial areas. Lubbock, Texas, now has a major Catholic presence. So do Pueblo, Colorado, Garden City, Kansas, and Lexington, Nebraska.

See also ARCHITECTURE: Religious Architecture / EUROPEAN AMERICANS: Settlement Patterns, Canada; Settlement Patterns, United States.

James R. Shortridge
University of Kansas

Bradley, Martin B., Norman M. Green Jr., Dale E. Jones, Mac Lynn, and Lou McNeil. *Churches and Church Membership in the United States 1990.* Atlanta: Glenmary Research Center, 1992. Gaustad, Edwin S. *Historical Atlas of Religion in America.* New York: Harper and Row, 1976. *The National Atlas of Canada.* Ottawa: Department of Energy, Mines, and Resources, 1985.

DOUKHOBORS

Originating in seventeenth-century southern Russia, the Doukhobors (Spirit Wrestlers) were one of nearly 200 sects to break away from the Russian Orthodox Church. The Doukhobors renounced all human institutions, including church and government, and became pacifists.

Persecution in Russia and generous immigration policies framed by Clifford Sifton, Canada's minister of the interior, lured a constituent of 7,500 Doukhobors to Canada in 1899. The Canadian government agreed to

their two stated requirements: that they be exempt from military service and that they be permitted to settle in solid blocks. They soon established fifty-seven successful farming communes in east-central Saskatchewan. Sifton wanted experienced farmers to settle the Great Plains, and the Doukhobors certainly qualified. For generations they had tilled the soil, and Leo Tolstoy called them "the best farmers in Russia."

In 1902, without warning, the Canadian government insisted that the Doukhobors individually register their settlement lands by swearing allegiance to the Crown, something the Doukhobor conscience would not allow. Reaction to the demand caused a three-way split among the Doukhobors. One group, composed of 236 families, complied and became known as Independent Doukhobors. They continue to farm in east-central Saskatchewan around the towns of Blaine Lake,

Ruins of a Doukhobor prayer home near Kamsack, Saskatchewan (above), Doukhobor prayer home in Saskatoon, Saskatchewan (below)

Canora, and Kamsack. Another more zealous faction, known as the Sons of Freedom, determined to embarrass the government with a protest march, but the cold October weather drove them back home. The main group (the Community Doukhobors) sent for their leader from Russia, Peter the Lordly Verigin, and he led them to British Columbia, where previously owned lands were purchased that did not require the dreaded oath of allegiance.

The Doukhobor contribution to Plains agriculture cannot easily be exaggerated. By 1903 the community owned sixteen steam engines, eleven threshing machines, six flour mills, and five sawmills. They had amassed 600 horses, 400 oxen, and 865 cows. Just prior to their migration to British Columbia, they managed 258,880 acres of farmland, of which 49,429 acres had been seeded. The land was cultivated the hard way, with oxen, and sometimes even by hand. Although challenged by harsh winds, unpredictable water supplies, and the occasional prairie fire, the Doukhobors prevailed.

The fate of the British Columbia Doukhobors (the Christian Community of Universal Brotherhood, or CCUB) bordered on the tragic. Peter Verigin was killed on October 24, 1924, when the train he was riding from Castlegar to Grand Forks, British Columbia, was hit by an explosion. In 1938, partially in fear of such a large utopian experiment, involving some 10,000 people with property worth $6 million, the Canadian government initiated a surprise foreclosure on the community. Doukhobor lands and properties were seized and sold at prices well below cost, and the CCUB was liquidated.

Eager to keep their vision alive, the Doukhobors formed the Union of Spiritual Communities in Christ (USCC), which continues to sponsor a number of local and national events related to Doukhobor history, spirituality, and culture.

See also POLITICS AND GOVERNMENT: Sifton, Clifford.

John W. Friesen
University of Calgary

Friesen, John W., and Michael M. Verigin. *The Community Doukhobors: A People in Transition*. Ottawa: Borealis Press, 1996. Tarasoff, Koozma J. *Plakun Trava: The Doukhobors*. Grand Forks, British Columbia: Mir Publication Society, 1982. Woodcock, George, and Ivan Avakumovic. *The Doukhobors*. Toronto: McClelland and Stewart Ltd., 1977.

EASTERN ORTHODOX

Divided administratively into fifteen autocephalous (independent) territorial churches, Orthodox Christians claim to be the one holy Catholic and Apostolic Church founded by Christ. They hold to the "orthodox" (right-believing) canons, faith, and doctrines as defined by the seven ecumenical councils convoked in the Byzantine Empire from 325 to 787 A.D. Characterized by their sacramental theology, hierarchical ecclesiology, iconodulism, and rich liturgical tradition, Orthodox Christians number approximately 250 million peo-

Saint Michael's Ukrainian Orthodox Church, Gardenton, Manitoba built in 1935

ple and live primarily in Russia, eastern Europe, the Balkans, and the Middle East. There are about four million Orthodox Christians in North America.

The Russian Orthodox Church established the first Orthodox mission in North American in 1794 and opened a missionary diocese in San Francisco in 1872. Over the next thirty years this diocese welcomed hundreds of thousands of Orthodox immigrants from the Balkans, and more widely from the Ottoman, Russian, and Austro-Hungarian Empires. Greeks, Slavs (Ukrainians, Russians, Belarusans, Macedonians, Montenegrins, Bulgarians), Romanians, and Arabs comprised the bulk of these Orthodox immigrants.

In Canada most Orthodox immigrants became homesteaders in the Great Plains. Between 1890 and 1914, thanks in part to a government policy that encouraged settlement in the western provinces, a quarter of a million Romanians and Ukrainians from Bukovina, Moldova, Galicia, and Banat moved to the Canadian Prairies. Ukrainians formed the first Orthodox parish in the Canadian Plains in 1898; four years later the first Romanian parish opened in Regina. From these small beginnings, the number of Canadian Orthodox Christians has grown to 750,000.

In the United States, by contrast, most Orthodox immigrants stayed in large cities in New York, Pennsylvania, and Illinois, where they worked in mines, factories, and shops. But by the 1890s increasing numbers of Orthodox workers were moving to the Great Plains and taking jobs in rail transport, meatpacking plants, steel mills, and mines. Slavic workers at the Globe smelting plant north of Denver founded the Holy Transfiguration Church in 1898; in 1903 and 1905, respectively, Slavic steelworkers in the Plains towns of

Pueblo and Calhan, Colorado, opened their own parishes.

After 1905 Greeks replaced Slavs as the largest Orthodox ethnic group. Between 1890 and 1920 some 600,000 Greeks arrived in the United States and founded more than 140 parishes. Job opportunities attracted some of these Greeks to the Great Plains. In 1904, for example, a meatpacking strike in Omaha, Nebraska, led manufacturers there to seek out cheaper Greek workers. In 1908 they founded an Orthodox parish, Saint John the Baptist, that survived a vicious anti-Greek pogrom a year later. Between 1906 and 1909 Greeks also founded churches in Denver, Pueblo, and Kansas City.

Smaller ethnic groups also formed Orthodox parishes in the U.S. Plains. In 1902 Lebanese Arabs founded the parish of Saint George in the cattle town of Kearney, Nebraska; sixteen years later Christian Arabs opened a church in Wichita, Kansas. Between 1904 and 1920 Romanians created thirteen parishes in the Midwest.

After the Russian Revolution, the Orthodox community split along ethnic and political lines. By 1930 Greeks, Ukrainians, Romanians, Arabs, Serbs, Bulgarians, and Albanians had established jurisdictions that were wholly independent of the original Russian Orthodox missionary diocese. Disputes over liturgical questions and the church's proper relationship to the Communist government exacerbated these ethnic splits; today there are more than thirty Orthodox jurisdictions in North America.

A minority of the four million American and Canadian Orthodox Christians lives in the Great Plains today, but various Orthodox jurisdictions are working to increase that number. The Ukrainian Orthodox Church of Canada

(UOCC) has 128,000 adherents in 290 parishes, most of which are located in the Prairie Provinces. The UOCC also operates Saint Andrew's College in Winnipeg, Manitoba. Sixty of the 600 parishes of the Orthodox Church of America (the name that the original Russian missionary diocese adopted in 1970) are in the Great Plains. The Greek Orthodox Archdiocese of America opened its Denver bishopric for the Great Plains in 1979 and is currently completing construction of a new diocesan center there. The Antiochian Orthodox Christian Archdiocese of North America, which is subordinate to the patriarch of Antioch in Syria, has moved beyond its Arab ethnic base by encouraging a "Western rite" similar to the Anglican prayer book of 1928. Several old, conservative Episcopalian churches have converted to Antiochian Orthodoxy; for example, in 1991 the archdiocese received Saint Marks of Denver, originally founded as an Anglican church in 1895. Although only 20 of its 159 parishes are located in the Great Plains, the Antiochian Archdiocese in 1995 consecrated a chancery, overseen by auxiliary Bishop Basil (Essey), in Wichita, Kansas.

See also ARCHITECTURE: Ukrainian Architecture / EUROPEAN AMERICANS: Ukrainians.

Eugene Clay
Arizona State University

Martynowych, Orest. *Ukrainians in Canada: The Formative Period, 1891–1924.* Edmonton: Canadian Institute of Ukrainian Studies Press, 1991. Moskos, Charles C. *Greek Americans: Struggle and Success.* New Brunswick NJ: Transaction Publishers, 1989. Stokoe, Mark. *Orthodox Christians in North America, 1794–1994.* Syosset NY: Orthodox Christian Publications Center, 1995.

EPISCOPALIANISM

Episcopalians constitute the American branch or province of the worldwide Anglican Communion. They adopted this name both because of the political sensitivities generated by the American Revolution and because they wished to signal their continuity with that Communion and especially its episcopal tradition. The Episcopal Church of the USA has approximately 2.5 million members, eleven seminaries, and 103 dioceses, of which nineteen are in the Great Plains. The Anglican Church of Canada started in the mid–eighteenth century and has nearly 750,000 members and thirty dioceses, of which nine are in the Great Plains. In the United States, the largest concentrations of communicants are found on the coasts, especially the eastern.

In addition to the episcopal structure that apostolically links the modern church to the first century, the denomination's other distinctive features are its liturgical style and its commitment to social justice. Liturgically, the Episcopal Church maintains both unity and diversity through its Book of Common Prayer. Each Anglican province in the world is responsible for its own prayer book, which thus symbolizes its continuity with the tradition as well as local originality. The earliest prayer books (1549 and 1552) were produced in England largely by Thomas Cranmer, and they reflected both Catholic and Reformation theologies, as does the Episcopal Church's current Book of Common Prayer, last revised in 1979. Unity and diversity are also embodied by the honorific (but not juridical) primacy accorded the archbishop of Canterbury.

The church's commitment to social justice may be seen in traditional arenas such as civil and women's rights. It was the second branch within the Anglican Communion to ordain women as priests and the first to consecrate women as bishops. It can also be discerned in what is often called "Anglican methodology" or the *via media*, which is shorthand for the church's commitment to inclusivism wherever possible and appropriate. This feature is evident in the church's bicameral governing structure, a somewhat cumbersome but deliberately republican form of governance in which laity, priests, and bishops have a significant voice. It is also evident in the fact that the church did not split over the Civil War. Its refusal to take an official stance toward slavery has been interpreted by some as weakness, but by others as a deliberate avoidance of taking any steps that would lead to schism. Regardless, the church resumed its prewar pace both quickly and peacefully after hostilities ceased.

While Episcopalians moved west along with other Christians in the first half of the nineteenth century, their dedication to evangelization lagged behind that of other denominations. This resulted from the denomination's authority structure on the one hand and the general suspicion of any kind of central authority among westerners on the other. In part, it also reflected the fact that many of the early bishops in the Great Plains were "high church" Anglo-Catholics, whereas most priests and laypersons were "low church" evangelicals. The resulting spirituality, occasionally referred to as "evangelical Catholicism," has characterized much Episcopal life and character in the Great Plains ever since.

The General Convention of 1835 designated the church itself as a missionary institution, and all of its members as official missionaries with regard to westward expansion. Ten years later Bishop Jackson Kemper began what one biographer called "the most fruitful single ministry in the annals of the [Episcopal] church." He organized the first dioceses in Indiana, Illinois, Missouri, Iowa, Wisconsin, Kansas, Nebraska, and Dakota. In the Canadian Prairies, the Colonial and Continental Church Society ministered to settlers and maintained Emmanuel College in Saskatoon from 1914 to 1954 for the training of clergy.

Sharing the constants of sparse population, inclement weather, and widespread poverty, parishes and dioceses grew slowly in the Great Plains in the nineteenth century, although rather more quickly in the more urban areas. However, because of increased immigration during the early decades of the twentieth century and the economic surge caused by World War I, the Plains grew in both industrial and agricultural wealth and significance. The Episcopal Church's fortunes rose accordingly, even though the war itself resulted in the closing of various schools and temporarily depressed parochial budgets because of the absence of soldiers and their contributions.

The Great Depression was disproportionately harsh on both church and civil society in the Plains, and many dioceses found themselves at the bottom of national lists with regard to parish offerings, baptisms, ordinations, and the like. As with the previous war, though, World War II generated an increase in the fortunes of the Episcopal Church, though there was a general falloff in membership after 1960 in the Plains and elsewhere. Episcopalians remain a relatively small denomination in the Great Plains—ranked sixth or seventh by number of churches per state—and are most strongly represented in cities of the eastern part of the region. Many counties in the western reaches of the Great Plains, especially in the panhandles of Texas and Oklahoma and in eastern Colorado and western Kansas, have no Episcopal churches at all.

Kern R. Trembath
University of Notre Dame

Albright, Raymond W. *A History of the Protestant Episcopal Church.* New York: Macmillan Publishing Company, 1964. Pritchard, Robert W. *A History of the Episcopal Church.* Harrisburg PA: Morehouse Publishing, 1991. Taylor, Blanche Mercer. *Plenteous Harvest: The Episcopal Church in Kansas, 1837–1972.* Topeka KS: Prepared by the author for the Diocese of Kansas, 1973.

EPP, THEODORE (1907–1985)

Theodore Epp was the founder of the international radio broadcast *Back to the Bible.* Born in Oraibi, Arizona, on January 27, 1907, the son of missionaries to the Hopi Indians, after seminary he pastored several churches in Oklahoma. In November 1934, however, Epp was invited to preach a message on a local radio station and this event changed his life.

On May 1, 1939, Theodore Epp drove to Lincoln, Nebraska, to begin his radio ministry. He had $95 in his pocket, enough to pay for three weeks of airtime on KFOR, at that time a 250-watt station. Less than a year later, the popularity of Epp's Bible teaching created an opportunity to release the program on a much larger station in Grand Island, Nebraska, where he moved. But Theodore Epp soon knew that Lincoln was to be the home of his ministry, and in 1942 his family and he returned to the capital city and began airing *Back to the Bible* on KFAB, a 10,000-watt station.

From these humble beginnings, the influence of Epp's radio broadcast rapidly grew. Today, *Back to the Bible* is heard on more than 900 radio stations, translators, and cable outlets every day. The ministry broadcasts in Chinese, Russian, Spanish, Italian, and twenty-five other languages from ten international offices. Theodore Epp's dream of teaching the Bible on radio has been expanded to include four different daily radio broadcasts, television, video, print, and the Internet. Theodore Epp died on October 13, 1985.

Woodrow Kroll
Lincoln, Nebraska

Berry, Harold J. *I Love to Tell the Story: Back to the Bible's Adventure of Faith.* Lincoln NE: Back to the Bible, 1989. Epp, Theodore. *A Man after the Heart of God.* Lincoln NE: Good News Broadcasting Association, Inc., 1965. Ward, Mark. *Air of Salvation: The Story of Christian Broadcasting.* Grand Rapids MI: Baker Books, 1994.

EVANGELICALISM

Evangelicalism is a Protestant ethos that has fostered denominational, interdenominational, and nondenominational traditions and institutions since its emergence in the late seventeenth and the eighteenth centuries. As an ethos, evangelicalism has been a phenomenon of religious contention as well as revitalization. It encompasses denominations as diverse as the Assemblies of God, the Churches of Christ, the Conservative Baptist Association, and the Evangelical Free Church, yet evangelicalism has had, and continues to have, an influence on many members and groups within other denominations, from the Evangelical Lutheran Church in America to the Reformed Church in America, and on unnumbered independent congregations and other religious organizations.

Confusion about the nature and development of evangelicalism is in part due to popular conflation of the historical ethos with evangel and evangelism. "Evangel" is a rough transliteration of the New Testament Greek word for good news or gospel. While evangelicalism has certainly been concerned with the evangel of Jesus Christ, it has never had exclusive possession of it. Similarly, while evangelism—the intentional propagation of the Christian good news—has also been a central concern in evangelicalism, evangelicals have not been the only Christians to encourage and engage in evangelism.

To the conceptual ambiguity in evangelicalism's name, the historical development of the ethos adds further complexity. As a term, "evangelical" arose in connection with the Protestant Reformation of the sixteenth century. In distinction from Roman Catholicism, Protestants at the time saw themselves as stressing the gospel of justification by faith in the atoning work of God in Jesus Christ. The formative century for evangelicalism, though, was the eighteenth. The convergence of elements of English Puritanism with the newer movement of continental pietism fed a burgeoning network of personal contacts and institutional ties epitomized by the evangelical Anglicans George Whitefield and John Wesley and the Moravian Count Zinzendorf. Itinerant preaching for conversion, publishing religious literature for evangelism and growth in holiness, and founding societies and institutions that downplayed denominational distinctions in the interests of promoting the gospel marked a broad European–North American "evangelical awakening" that encompassed varied local episodes of revivalism and evangelical institution-building.

By the time of European American settlement in the Great Plains in the mid– to late nineteenth century, "evangelical" was a term the majority of North American Protestants would have accepted as an apt one for themselves and their coreligionists. Particularly among Anglo-American Protestants, whether Baptists, Congregationalists, Methodists, or Presbyterians, evangelicalism had become an ethos that stressed transdenominational emphases on personalizing belief in the atoning work of Christ, on the centrality of using the Bible for faith and practice, and on the importance of faith-based activism. In other words, by 1900 the evangelical ethos was conversionist, crucicentric, biblicist, activist, and populist. Late-nineteenth- and early-twentieth-century Protestant evangelists who worked in the Great Plains, whether lesser-known local or denominational figures, or more famous national, interdenominational figures such as Dwight L. Moody, John Wilbur Chapman, and William A. "Billy" Sunday, were evangelicals. So, too, were most nineteenth-century English-speaking Protestant home missionaries, circuit riders, and missionaries to Native Americans. Also, many Protestants who sought to act on the social implications of the gospel in the late nineteenth and early twentieth century were evangelicals.

However, by 1900 the evangelical dominance of North American Protestantism was also showing signs of fraying. Larger social and intellectual trends were leading some elements among otherwise evangelical Protestant groups and institutions to respond by downplaying supernaturalism in favor of divine immanence and by challenging conventional understandings of the Bible's composition, meaning, and authority. Other Protestants accentuated or developed various aspects of the evangelical ethos to counter perceived "modernizing" trends within and outside of the religious community. Dispensationalism, the holiness movement, and pentecostalism arose as distinct movements within evangelicalism that were well represented in the U.S. Great Plains. These movements not only led in many cases to new institutions (e.g., Bible institutes and colleges, the Church of the Nazarene, and the Assemblies of God) but also fed a more militant antimodernist and separatist stream within evangelicalism.

During the same turn-of-the-century era, a Christian restorationist tradition that had always been a minority element within evangelicalism became more institutionally distinct when the Churches of Christ distinguished themselves from the Disciples of Christ in 1906. Symbolic of the strength of the Churches of Christ in Oklahoma and Texas is Abilene Christian University, an important Great Plains religious and educational institution within an anti-institutional evangelical tradition.

After 1920 the more militant antimodernists within evangelicalism were calling themselves fundamentalists. As fundamentalism became the then-newest movement to take shape under the umbrella of the evangelical ethos, evangelicalism in all its burgeoning complexity not only persisted in the U.S. Great Plains through churches, revivalism, periodicals, camps, educational institutions, radio, and later television and film, but it also took root and flourished in the Prairies of Canada. In 1922 Kansan Leslie E. Maxwell arrived in Three Hills, Alberta, and founded the nondenominational Prairie Bible Institute. It is perhaps the most famous of several Canadian Plains evangelical institutions of higher education founded or reorganized since 1920, including the Canadian Bible Institute and Canadian Theological Seminary in Regina, Saskatchewan (Christian and Missionary Alliance), the Canadian Mennonite Bible College, the Canadian Nazarene College, and Catherine Booth College (Salvation Army), all in Winnipeg, Manitoba, and the King's University College in Edmonton, Alberta (Christian Reformed).

In the Great Plains since World War II, evangelicalism has grown in numbers and in its public presence even as the intermingling of its various elements has made for some new forms of old elements. The rise of Oral Roberts illustrates some of the contemporary flexibility of evangelicalism in the Great Plains. Roberts began his adult career before and during the war as a pastor and evangelist for the Pentecostal Holiness Church. Not long after the war, though, the native Oklahoman launched an independent evangelistic and healing ministry that came to be institutionalized in television broadcasts and Oral Roberts University and its associated organizations in Tulsa. Further, in 1968 Roberts reflected a resurgence of a more open rather than separatist evangelicalism when he publicly left the Pentecostal Holiness Church and took ministerial ordination in the United Methodist Church. He also embodies both the strength and weaknesses of another aspect of contemporary evangelicalism: religious fiefdoms built around the charisma of an individual.

While the future vitality of Roberts's religious empire seems in question, another new center of evangelicalism in the Great Plains—Colorado Springs, Colorado—continues to thrive in the twenty-first century. Colorado Springs's electronics firms and military have been joined by a plethora of evangelical institutions, which were either founded or relocated there since 1945. Evangelical groups such as the Navigators, the Christian Booksellers Association, Young Life, and Focus on the Family employed in 1991 some 2,000 people and pumped some $40 million in payroll into the local economy. Moreover, by 1995 local estimates put the self-designated proportion of evangelicals in the city of 300,000 at 40 percent. Particular leaders and institutions and movements embodying the evangelical ethos will continue to come and go, but evangelicalism at large has become a permanent part of Great Plains life.

Douglas Firth Anderson
Northwestern College, Orange City, Iowa

Dayton, Donald W., and Robert K. Johnston, eds. *The Variety of American Evangelicalism.* Downers Grove IL: InterVarsity Press, 1991. Rabey, Steve. "Colorado Springs: Head for the Mountains." *Christianity Today* 35 (Nov. 25, 1991): 47. Rawlyk, George A., ed. *Aspects of the Canadian Evangelical Experience.* Montreal: McGill-Queen's University Press, 1997.

GHOST DANCE

The Ghost Dance, a messianic Native American religious movement, originated in Nevada around 1870, faded, reemerged in its best-known form in the winter of 1888–89, then spread rapidly through much of the Great Plains, where hundreds of adherents died in the 1890 Wounded Knee Massacre.

In 1869 or 1870, Tävibo, a Northern Paiute and first Ghost Dance prophet, preached that white people would disappear from the earth and dead Indians would return to enjoy a utopian life. He also claimed to communicate with the dead and taught followers to perform a ceremonial circular dance that contributed to the movement earning the Ghost Dance label. The movement spread through Nevada and to parts of California and Oregon but subsided after the prophecies failed to materialize. Another Paiute prophet, Wovoka, revived the movement in 1889. Rumored to be Tävibo's son, and certainly influenced by his teachings, Wovoka experienced a vision of the Supreme Being in 1889, after which he preached peaceful coexistence and a strong work ethic and taught ceremonial songs and dances to resurrect dead Indians. According to the vision, if Indians followed these practices, they would be reunited with the dead and whites would disappear. Indians who had already subscribed to the first Ghost Dance tended to reject Wovoka's version, but the second Ghost Dance found acceptance among Plains tribes as far east as the Dakotas, Nebraska, Kansas, Oklahoma, and Texas.

The Ghost Dance affected no group more than the Lakota Sioux bands who adopted it. Several Lakota bands sent emissaries to interview Wovoka about his teachings. They reported in early 1890 Wovoka's message that performing Ghost Dance ceremonies and songs would bring back dead Indians, return plentiful buffalo herds, and induce a natural disaster that would sweep away whites, thus restoring the Indian way of life that had existed prior to European contact. The Ghost Dance provided a hopeful message to all Indians, but it proved particularly enticing to Lakotas suffering poor conditions on reservations and to Lakota leaders such as Sitting Bull (Tantanka Iyotanka), who had resisted U.S. Indian policy. Lakota participants added vestments known as ghost shirts to the ceremonies and songs brought by the emissaries. They believed these white muslin shirts, decorated with a variety of symbols, protected them from danger, including bullets. The Lakotas' white neighbors and reservation officials viewed the movement as a threat to U.S. Indian policy and believed the Ghost Dance ceremonies and ghost shirts indicated that the Lakotas intended to start a war. Reservation officials called on the U.S. government to stop the dancing. The government dispatched the U.S. Army and called for the arrest of key leaders such as Sitting Bull and Big Foot (Si Tanka). Indian police killed Sitting Bull while arresting him. Two weeks later, on December 29, 1890, members of the Seventh Cavalry killed Big Foot and at least 145 of his followers (casualty estimates range to higher than 300) in the Wounded Knee Massacre, thus eliminating key leaders most opposed to the United States and its Indian policy. Many historians have pointed to Wounded Knee as the closing episode in the West's Indian wars.

The Ghost Dance died out among the Lakotas after Wounded Knee, but it survived elsewhere in the Plains. A Dakota Sioux community in Canada, for instance, practiced the Ghost Dance into the 1960s. During the 1970s, Leonard Crow Dog, an Oglala Lakota holy man affiliated with the American Indian Movement, revived the Ghost Dance as part of the Red Power movement. To many, the Ghost Dance represented resistance to U.S. Indian policy and American culture and was a rallying point for preserving traditional Indian culture.

See also NATIVE AMERICANS: Sitting Bull / PROTEST AND DISSENT: American Indian Movement / WAR: Wounded Knee Massacre.

Todd M. Kerstetter
Texas Christian University

Hittman, Michael. *Wovoka and the Ghost Dance*. Lincoln: University of Nebraska Press, 1997. Kehoe, Alice Beck. *The Ghost Dance: Ethnohistory and Revitalization*. New York: Holt, Rinehart and Winston, 1989. Mooney, James. *The Ghost-Dance Religion and the Sioux Outbreak of 1890*, Fourteenth Annual Report of the Bureau of American Ethnology, 1892–93, pt. 2. Washington DC: Government Printing Office, 1896.

HINDUISM

Hinduism is the Western name given to a religious tradition developed over thousands of years in India. Because it has no creed or major institutional structure, it is intricately intertwined with societal systems, and some scholars declare that it is impossible to separate Hinduism as a religion from other aspects of Indian society. This means it is virtually impossible to define precisely what constitutes the Hindu religion, especially when transferred into a different cultural setting such as the Great Plains.

Lacking a set of rigid doctrines, Hinduism encompasses a large diversity of religious beliefs and practices. Nevertheless, devotion to a particular deity expressed through worship (*puja*) is important to most Hindus. The ritual of worship usually occurs individually or with other family members in the home and at local shrines and temples. Traditionally, large congregational meetings were rare, but in recent years within North America, group meetings for worship, spiritual messages, and the celebration of religious festivals have become common.

Both the diversity of beliefs and religious practices by Hindus and the inevitable changes that occur whenever a religion is transported to another cultural setting contribute to a wide diversity in the expression of Hinduism in the Great Plains, especially because Asian Indians who have migrated to North America, primarily during the last half century, have not formed large ethnic enclaves, which might have encouraged centers of orthodoxy. Likewise, the non-Asian citizens of Canada and the United States who have adopted various beliefs and rituals associated with Hinduism have followed a variety of gurus, each emphasizing different aspects of this equivocal religion.

The many societies, ashrams, and study groups (more than 100 are identified in the 1996 edition of *Encyclopedia of American Religions for the United States*) tend to be localized and unrelated to one another. Followers may meet informally in homes, community buildings, and interfaith centers. Also, Hindus in the Great Plains may seek individual spiritual guidance from printed materials and from Web sites on the Internet and by making a special journey to an ashram in India or elsewhere in North America.

Hinduism has not had a major impact on the dominant society in the Great Plains: its arrival in this region occurred generally during only the last three decades of the twentieth century; it tends to be nonproselytizing, with private worship; and its adherents are few in number and scattered. Nevertheless, more than thirty temples and numerous other religious structures contribute to the urban landscapes of Calgary and Edmonton, Alberta; Saskatoon and Regina, Saskatchewan; Winnipeg, Manitoba; Denver, Boulder, Aurora, Fort Collins, and Littleton, Colorado; Shawnee, Kansas; Kansas City, Missouri; Omaha, Nebraska; Oklahoma City and Tulsa, Oklahoma; and Irving, Austin, and Dallas, Texas. Less evident visually but functioning as a part of community life in more than three dozen cities are centers of Hindu-related societies such as Ammachi, Art of Living, Chinmaya Mission West, Integral Yoga, Sathya Sai Baba, Science of Spirituality, and the Theosophical Society, as well as the transcendental meditation programs maintained by the Maharishi Vedic Universities. In addition to participating in special events occurring within the Great Plains, many Hindus travel to neighboring places to attend religious festivals (such as Diwali and Holi), special *pujas*, pilgrimages, and summer camps.

Robert H. Stoddard
University of Nebraska–Lincoln

Gaustad, Edwin Scott, and Philip L. Barlow. *The Historical Atlas of Religion in America*. New York: Oxford University Press, 2000. Melton, J. Gordon. *Encyclopedia of American Religions*. Detroit: Gale Research, 1996. Tweed, Thomas A. "Asian Religions in America: Reflections on an Emerging Subfield." In *Religious Diversity and American Religious History: Studies in Traditions and Cultures*, edited by Walter H. Conser Jr. and Sumner B. Twiss. Athens: University of Georgia Press, 1997: 189–217.

HUBBARD, L. RON (1911–1986)

L. Ron Hubbard developed the spiritual healing technology known as dianetics and the applied religious philosophy of scientology. While some details of Hubbard's life are disputed in scholarly studies of scientology, Hubbard's public achievements are remarkable by any standard of measurement.

Hubbard was born on March 13, 1911, in Tilden, Nebraska, the son of Harry Ross Hubbard, an officer in the U.S. Navy, and Ledora May Waterbury de Wolfe. He traveled the world during his teen years and published a number of adventure stories. By the 1940s he had established himself as one of the most prolific science fiction writers in the world.

Hubbard's career took a dramatic turn during a tour of duty in the U.S. Navy during World War II, when he became interested in discovering the cause of physical and emotional problems. His studies led him to conclude that ideally the mind has control over the body. He developed a new form of psychotherapy, which was spelled out in *Dianetics: The Modern Science of Mental Health*, a perennial best-seller since its publication in 1950. The goal of dianetic therapy was to clear the mind of painful memory blocks called "engrams," which limited the mind's control of the body. Unlike similar-sounding therapies, dianetics claims that these engramatic memories extend to the prenatal period and must be cleared in chronological sequence, beginning with the earliest painful experiences. When the mind is cleared, the person becomes totally self-determined.

Hubbard's experience with dianetic therapy led to the astonishing discovery that his clients were troubled by engrams from previous lives. Hubbard believed that this finding proved conclusively that humans are spiritual beings who inhabit a body and use a mind but are identical with neither. On the basis of this discovery, Hubbard developed the religious philosophy that he called "scientology," a system of spiritual counseling and training to liberate the immortal and omniscient self from all dependence on matter, energy, space, and time.

The first Church of Scientology was established in 1954 to deliver these spiritual services in the precise ways prescribed by Hubbard. Under his personal supervision, a worldwide network of scientology churches was established. During this time, he wrote numerous books and hundreds of papers standardizing the teachings and practices of scientology. Hubbard resigned his position as executive director of the Church of Scientology in 1967 to research higher levels of spiritual attainment and to develop community development programs in literacy, drug rehabilitation, and administrative techniques.

Hubbard died in Creston, California, on January 24, 1986. He left a legacy of fiction and nonfiction works that have been translated into thirty-three languages, with more than 120 million copies in circulation. His nonfiction works serve as the sacred scripture for a worldwide religious movement, whose more than 3,000 churches and missions minister to some eight million people in more than 100 countries and thirty languages. Hubbard is neither idolized nor worshiped by his followers. Rather, he is honored as the founder of a contemporary religion that combines the spirituality of Eastern religions and the rationality of Western science.

Lonnie D. Kliever
Southern Methodist University

Anonymous. *Scientology: Theology and Practice of a Contemporary Religion*. Los Angeles: Bridge Publications, 1998. Wallis, Roy. *This Road to Total Freedom*. New York: Columbia University Press, 1977.

HUTTERITES

The Hutterian Brethren (commonly known as the Hutterites) are a traditional Christian sect who settled in many agricultural colonies across the Great Plains of the United States and Canada. Approximately 36,000 members live and work communally in about 428 collective farms, or *Bruderhofs* (*Bruderhöfe*).

The Hutterian movement began in 1528, when an Anabaptist sect in Austerlitz, Moravia (now the Czech Republic), adopted communal living, rejected the sanctioned practice of infant baptism, and renounced the Catholic doctrine of transubstantiation. Severely persecuted for these heresies, the sect found its current name in 1536 when an early leader, Jakob Hutter, was burned at the stake.

After more than 300 years of persecution and forced migration within eastern Europe and Russia, the Hutterites fled to Dakota Territory between 1874 and 1877. However, they were again persecuted in the United States during World War I due to their strict pacifism and Germanic ethnicity, and all but one colony migrated to Canada in 1918. While many colonies remain in Alberta, Saskatchewan, Manitoba, and British Columbia today, others have returned to, or have been founded in, the United States. These are primarily located in South Dakota and Montana but are also found in North Dakota, Minnesota, and Washington.

Daily life in Hutterian colonies revolves around religion, as Hutterites attend services every evening and twice on Sunday. Their spiritual beliefs discourage selfish interests and emphasize serving the communal good. The tenet of *Gelassenheit*—or "self-surrender"— entails a rejection of material luxury and personal wealth. Modeling themselves after the early Christians (see Acts 2:44–47), the Hutterites practice communal ownership of land and other goods. While individual families live in private apartments, each colony holds all possessions and money in a common trust. Hutterites eat and work collectively, receiving no individual salary but sharing equally in the proceeds of their labor. The colony provides for all basic necessities, such as medical costs, child care, clothing, and furniture.

Hutterian colonies are located in sparsely populated areas to minimize interaction with the outside world and thus focus attention on spiritual goals. Like the well-known Amish and Mennonites (who are not communal), the Hutterites adhere to traditional dress, customs, and language. Unlike these other Germanic Anabaptist sects, the Hutterites employ modern technology and methods of agriculture and manufacturing.

Hutterites learn English but use High German in religious services and informally speak a Tyrolean dialect, which they call Hutterisch. Children learn Hutterite traditions and history in a German-speaking classroom while also studying standard academic topics in a government-mandated school, which they call the "English" school. They are growing more open to conventional education, and some Hutterite teenagers now earn high school diplomas.

Adolescents become adult members at age fifteen and are eligible for baptism at age twenty. At this age, a Hutterite woman generally leaves her colony to marry a man in another colony, which receives a dowry in exchange. The Hutterites practice traditional gender roles, and women cannot vote or hold colony office. Large families are encouraged, and Hutterites have some of the highest birthrates of any ethnic or religious group in the United States, with an average of nine children per family. For this reason, the total number of Hutterites and Hutterian colonies rises steadily. When a colony grows too large (130–150 members), it splits and forms a "daughter" colony.

Some related traditional sects, such as the Bruderhof of New York, Pennsylvania, and Connecticut, or nonagricultural colonies in Japan, England, and Paraguay, have grown out of the Hutterian movement. The Prarieleut are people of Hutterian descent who also settled in the Great Plains but do not live communally, and they often attend Mennonite churches.

Courtney Muir Wallner
Columbia University
James A. Kitts
Cornell University

Hostetler, John A. *Hutterite Society*. Baltimore MD: Johns Hopkins University Press, 1974. Hostetler, John A., and Gertrude Enders Huntington. *The Hutterites in North America*. New York: Holt, Rinehart and Winston, 1967. Miller, Timothy. "A Guide to the Literature on the Hutterites." *Communal Societies* 10 (1990): 68–86.

INDIAN MISSIONARIES

Christian missionaries promoted strategies to transform Native American communities in the Great Plains. By the end of the nineteenth century few reservations and reserves claimed no Protestant or Catholic presence. Over time, tribal members selectively accepted certain cultural components while actively preserving Native traditions. Intercultural relations involved individuals acting within dozens of tribal and denominational traditions, not conflicts between monolithic "Indian" or "missionary" perspectives.

Missionary contact with Great Plains tribes increased during the nineteenth century. Organized in 1810, the interdenominational American Board of Commissioners of Foreign Missions (ABCFM) led the way among Protestant missionary organizations. In 1819 Congress established a "civilization fund," appropriating $10,000 annually to support assimilation programs for Native Americans. Missionaries, spiritually motivated by the Second Great Awakening of the 1820s and 1830s and partially supported by federal funds, flocked into Indian Country. When Congress passed the Indian Removal Act (1830) and forcibly relocated many eastern tribes to the Plains, Christian representatives followed close behind to minister to relocated tribes as well as to Indians. In 1838 Baptist missionary Evan Jones and Cherokee minister Jesse Bushyhead led two of the Cherokee removal parties to Indian Territory. Missionaries exerted little influence over tribal members during early interactions. In fact, Christian ministers often lived on the hospitality of tribal leaders. In 1834 ABCFM-sponsored ministers Samuel Allis and John Dunbar joined the Pawnees during their winter buffalo hunt in the Central Plains. During this five-month journey the missionaries lived beholden to tribal members for linguistic and cultural education, as well as for food and shelter. They developed a better understanding of Pawnee ways during the next few years, but claimed no conversions. Pawnee leaders showed interest in the missionaries but ignored their appeals to abandon their seminomadic lifestyle.

Nineteenth-century missionaries arrived in the Great Plains with little experience in intercultural relations. Religious emissaries were drawn from Roman Catholic, Methodist, Baptist, Presbyterian, Lutheran, Mormon, Episcopal, Quaker, and other denominations. Many had extensive educational backgrounds by nineteenth-century standards. In the Plains they endured harsh weather, epidemics, limited support, and cultural isolation. They proved incapable, however, of recognizing the vitality of Native American societies. Instead, their culturally tainted vision saw tribal members as "lazy," "childlike," and "corrupt" members of "offensive" cultural traditions. Some missionaries disagreed on whether they should first promote Christianity or "civilization" within tribal communities. None questioned the premise of advocating both. Many, including Rev. John West, an Anglican stationed in southern Manitoba during the 1820s, considered principles of Christian mission work as indistinguishable from civilization programs.

Despite ethnocentric biases, religious leaders advocated the potential equality of all Christians. Missionaries provided tribes with support for their bodies and minds while hoping to cultivate Christian souls. Jotham Meeker served the Ottawas in Franklin County, Kansas, for more than twenty years as a physician and Baptist minister. Isabel Crawford taught domestic skills at a remote Kiowa camp in western Oklahoma during the late nineteenth and early twentieth centuries. Catholic sisterhoods, including the Grey Nuns, Sisters of the Presentation, Benedictines, and Franciscans, taught in mission schools and developed health-care facilities.

Missionaries found no single assimilation formula that would work for all Native Americans. The effectiveness of programs varied even within divisions of the same tribe. Distinctive tribal histories and missionaries' personalities produced different outcomes at each mission station. Historic contacts with European Americans, community locations, tribal leadership structures, and other variables influenced tribal acceptance, or rejection, of the Christian agenda. Missionary flexibility, communication skills, and attitudes affected tribal responses. In the 1830s, Jesuits recognized a failed mission to the Potawatomis in Council Bluffs, Iowa, at the same time that they recorded success with Potawatomis at Sugar Creek, Kansas. Similarly, during the 1870s, Quaker representatives had varying success with their efforts among the Pawnees, Otoe-Missourias, and Omahas of Nebraska.

Missionaries did not always practice truly Christian behavior. President Ulysses Grant's "Peace Policy" (1869) restricted reservations to a single Christian denomination, reinforcing denominational competition for tribal support. Self-serving actions often came at the expense of tribal interests. During the 1860s, Baptist leaders colluded with federal agents to defraud Ottawas of thousands of acres of their east-central Kansas land under the guise of creating an Indian university. Despite varied commentary from former students about their boarding-school experiences, countless stories reveal physical and emotional abuse at these institutions.

Why did tribal members seek relationships with missionaries? Some recognized the spiritual power of Christian emissaries. The Blackfoot, for instance, described eminent Jesuit missionary Pierre-Jean De Smet as "the man who talks to the Great Spirit." Others saw missionaries of different denominations as potential allies, capable of supporting them against unpopular federal agents and assimilation programs. After their removal to Kansas in the 1820s, Ohio Shawnees sided with Baptist missionaries while relatives from Missouri cultivated the support of Methodists. On the Lakotas' Pine Ridge Reservation in the 1880s, American Horse's people generally turned to Episcopalians while Red Cloud's folk allied with Jesuit Catholics. In this way, missionary support reinforced preexistent tribal divisions.

Religious leaders often promoted tribal traditions at the expense of the federal assimilation agenda in order to gain converts. Some missions promoted "English only" rules for students in boarding schools while perpetuating adult use of tribal languages. Many missionaries learned tribal languages to cultivate support for their Christian message. ABCFM missionary Stephen Riggs, impatient for the Santee Sioux to understand English, learned the Dakota language to preach Christianity. He also published a Dakota grammar and dictionary in 1851 and *Dakota Odowan*, a hymnbook in 1853. By the end of his life in 1883, he had published a translation of the Bible in Dakota. Presbyterian missionaries Samuel Irvin and William Hamilton unintentionally supported Iowa and Sac traditions. Their recorded observations of these tribal cultures from 1837 to 1853 stand today as significant ethnographic sources despite their obvious ethnocentric biases. Methodist Rev. John McDougall in southern Alberta went so far as to argue against the Canadian policy of suppressing the Sun Dance and Thirst Dance on the grounds of religious liberty.

Tribal members also crossed cultural barriers. Over time, many joined Christian denominations, even serving within organizational structures as true "Indian" missionaries. Still, they retained their tribal identities. Kickapoo leader Kennekuk cloaked himself in Methodist garb while promoting a nativist agenda. The Kickapoo prophet used his prominence to delay for fourteen years his people's removal from their Illinois homelands to Kansas. In addition, he promoted religious traditions that incorporated rituals and beliefs that drew his people, as well as his Potawatomi converts, beyond Methodist norms. Despite his persistent Lakota identity, Black Elk served as a Catholic catechist on the Pine Ridge Reservation.

Canadian religious leaders, perhaps even more than their American counterparts, promoted the cultivation of Native missionaries. Dakota tribal members John Thunder and Peter Hunter, of the Birdtail Creek Reserve in southern Manitoba, gained employment from the Foreign Mission Committee of the Presbyterian Church. From 1887 to 1912 they served as ministers to their Dakota people in the Northern Great Plains. Both men used their missionary offices to improve their people's status within Canadian and American societies. In these capacities, Thunder and Hunter preached Christianity in the Dakota language and promoted an agenda aimed at improved conditions for Native peoples. Some Indian missionaries crossed tribal lines to spread the Christian message. Ojibwa-born Shahwanegezhick of Ontario, who took the name Henry Bird Steinhauer, introduced Methodist tradition to the Crees of Alberta.

Over time, Native Americans across the Great Plains incorporated Christian traditions into their tribal identities. Missionaries erred, however, in their estimation that they could replace tribal traditions with Christianity. On the Omaha Reservation in Nebraska, prominent La Flesche family members claimed elements of Presbyterian tradition that did not clash with their tribal identities. Some contemporary Native Americans choose to blend tribal traditions with Christianity by praying to Jesus in a sweat lodge and the Great Spirit in churches. Other Native Americans see no need for religious exclusivity. They distinctly practice tribal, Christian, and Native American Church traditions throughout their lives. Many contemporary tribal members still essentially ignore Christian traditions.

Missionary practices changed in tone during the twentieth century. By the 1920s some Christian denominations grew more tolerant of certain tribal traditions. Following World War II, urban ministries arose to work with tribal members drawn to cities for economic and educational opportunities. The later decades of the century witnessed declining ministerial staff and revived interest in Native American communities, leading to increased missionary alliances. Pine Ridge, South Dakota, and Bismarck, North Dakota, now host ecumenical ministries serving tribal members from different denominational backgrounds. Ironically, many contemporary clergy grow increasingly involved in tribal rituals, to the point of suggesting potential Christian "conversion" to Native American traditions.

See also NATIVE AMERICANS: Assimilation Policy.

Robert W. Galler Jr.
Western Michigan University

Beaver, R. Pierce. "Protestant Churches and the Indians." In *Handbook of North American Indians*, edited by William C. Sturtevant. Vol. 4: *History of Indian-White Relations*, edited by Wilcomb Washburn. Washington DC: Smithsonian Institution, 1988: 430–58. Bowden, Henry Warner. *American Indians and Christian Missions: Studies in Cultural Conflict*. Chicago: University of Chicago Press, 1981. Burns, Robert I., S.J. "Roman Catholic Missions in the Northwest." In *Handbook of North American Indians*, edited by William C. Sturtevant. Vol. 4: *History of Indian-White Relations*, edited by Wilcomb Washburn. Washington DC: Smithsonian Institution, 1988: 494–500.

ISLAM

Islam has more than one billion adherents who are found in every region of the world, including the Great Plains. There, as everywhere else throughout North America, an extraordinarily diverse Muslim community is growing dramatically, building places of worship, schools, and community centers, and contributing to the broader community.

Islam is a monotheistic faith, recognizing the oneness of Allah, the same God who is known, according to Islam, to Abraham, Moses, Jesus, and others and is worshiped also by Christians and Jews. According to Islam, God's word, the *Qur'an*, was revealed through Muhammad (ca. 570–632) over a twenty-year period. Unlike the Bible, which is mostly in third-person narrative form, the *Qur'an* is considered God's direct speech. Recitation of the *Qur'an* is a major component of Islamic ritual and piety.

The mass immigration to North America in the late nineteenth and early twentieth centuries brought many from traditionally Islamic countries of the Middle East and North Africa. Although these were largely Christians and Jews, some Islamic communities were established, including one in Cedar Rapids, Iowa, just outside the Great Plains. Especially toward the end of this period, there was rising interest in Islam among African Americans, including the foundation of various movements that would coalesce into the Nation of Islam.

After World War II, and especially after 1980, Islam became established as a major religious grouping in the Great Plains, at least in the cities, although the ten largest Muslim population centers in North America were all outside the region.

Demographically, many locales have two main communities—African Americans and "immigrants"—although the latter now includes many individuals who were born in North America, as well as numerous converts. Both communities may be subdivided. Islam has grown tremendously among African Americans. Many youths became Muslims in prison and retained their new religion after their release. The Nation of Islam has always had some authentic Islamic elements, including the *Qur'an*, but its racial teachings and its views about Wallace Fard and Elijah Mohammed (Fard was deified as Allah) are antithetical to normative Islam. Since 1975, when Elijah Mohammed's son W. D. Mohammed broke with this theology, a sizable portion of African Americans practice normative Islam and generally have good ties with the immigrant community. Within the immigrant community, at least in the Great Plains, Sunnis and Shiites form one community, unlike the exclusive situation found in many traditionally Islamic countries. Nevertheless, some demographic scholarship has noted a tendency for mosques to align along ethnolinguistic lines, the major groupings being Arab, Persian, South Asian, and Southeast Asian.

A survey completed in the early 1990s found mosques, student organizations, or Muslim organizations in the Denver metropolitan area, Fort Collins and Greeley, Pueblo and Colorado Springs, Colorado; Lawrence, Wichita, Manhattan, and suburban Kansas City, Kansas; Bozeman and Billings, Montana; Omaha and Lincoln, Nebraska; Portales, New Mexico; Fargo, Minot, and Grand Forks, North Dakota; Stillwater, Tulsa, Oklahoma City, Edmond, Norman, and Ponca City, Oklahoma; Brookings, South Dakota; and Fort Worth and Arlington, Denton, Blanco, Lubbock, Amarillo, Midland, Odessa, Waco, and Austin, Texas. In the Canadian Prairie Provinces, there are Muslim communities in Regina, Saskatoon, Edmonton, and Winnipeg. Many of the major mosques or Islamic Centers serve large university populations. Some of these communities have established Islamic day schools that offer a full general curriculum that meets all state requirements but also provides intensive education in Arabic language, *Qur'an*, and Islamic religion and history.

See also PROTEST AND DISSENT: Malcolm X.

Seth Ward
University of Denver

Bagby, Ihsan, ed. *Muslim Resource Guide: An Essential Guide for Media and Government*. Fountain Valley CA: Islamic Resource Institute, 1994. *Directory of Masjids and Muslim Organizations in North America*. Fountain Valley CA: Islamic Resource Institute, 1994. Smith, Jane I. *Islam in America*. New York: Columbia University Press, 1999.

JONES, HAROLD (1909–2002)

Harold Stephen Jones, a Santee Sioux, was the first Native American to be elected bishop of any major denomination. Born in Mitchell, South Dakota, on December 14, 1909, Jones was raised by his grandparents, the Reverend William Holmes, an early Indian Episcopal priest, and his wife, Rebecca, a Caucasian. This dual heritage fostered his eventual ability to serve successfully in a racially conflicted church and society.

Jones's childhood was spent in Niobrara, Nebraska, and Wakpala, South Dakota, where his grandfather served mission churches. His grandfather died while Jones was in his teens. Then came a struggle with discrimination and poverty as he helped support his grandmother and continued his education. He graduated from Northern State College in 1935 and received a licentiate in theology from Seabury-Western Theological Seminary, Evanston, Illinois, in 1938. He married Blossom Steele, a Lakota, in December of 1938, a week after his ordination as deacon.

Beginning with Messiah Chapel in Wounded Knee, Jones was assigned in rapid succession to four small chapels on the Pine Ridge Reservation. There was never adequate compensation, which led to mounting debts on top of unpaid college loans. Three children were born into the Jones family, with only the daughter, Norma, surviving. Moves to the Cheyenne River Reservation in 1947 and back to Pine Ridge in 1952 brought added responsibilities but no financial relief. That finally came when he was called in 1956 to serve a white congregation in Wahpeton, North Dakota.

In 1968 the national Episcopal Church called him to take over the Navajo mission field in Arizona, where he had to adapt to a different language and culture. While there he was elected suffragan (assistant) bishop of South Dakota and was consecrated in a great multiracial service in Sioux Falls on January 11, 1972. His ministry as bishop was severely limited by a stroke after less than a year of service to both white and Indian congregations, and he had to take an early retirement in 1976. Subsequently, the Rt. Rev. Harold Jones lived with his daughter in Chandler, Arizona, and died there on November 12, 2002.

Mary E. Cochran
Tacoma, Washington

Anderson, Owannah. *Four Hundred Years: Anglican/Episcopal Mission among American Indians*. Cincinnati: Forward Movement Publications, 1997. Cochran, Mary E. *Dakota Cross-Bearer: The Life and World of a Native American Bishop*. Lincoln: University of Nebraska Press, 2000. Sneve, Virginia Driving Hawk. *That They May Have Life: The Episcopal Church in South Dakota*. New York: Seabury Press, 1977.

JUDAISM

In terms of numbers of adherents, Judaism has never had a large presence in the Great Plains. In 1990 only two counties—El Paso County, Colorado, home to Colorado Springs, and Tarrant County, Texas, with Fort Worth—had as many as two Reform Judaism congregations, and only twenty-one other counties in the region had even a single congregation. Most were urban counties, such as Cass County (with Fargo) and Burleigh County (with Bismarck), North Dakota. There were even fewer Conservative and Orthodox Judaism congregations in the region. Yet Judaism has been part of the religious landscape of the Plains since the beginnings of European American settlement. Eventually, Jews would come from all over Europe and from other parts of North America. Many came first as peddlers and became merchants, newsmen, and politicians; relatively few came as homesteaders and not many of those stayed on the land.

Denver, for example, was founded in 1858 by merchants and prospectors drawn to the gold rush. Among these were at least ten Jews, who gathered on Rosh Hashanah for what is believed to be the first religious services held in the city. While firmly attached to their Jewish heritage, these pioneers were apparently not observant Jews; most felt the need for a service only on Rosh Hashanah, with prayer being conducted by the most knowledgeable man. An early need was a Jewish cemetery, and usually the first organization was the Jewish Burial Society. This would frequently evolve into the Hebrew Benevolent Society, the core organization for the development of synagogues, welfare services, and schools.

Jews came to the Great Plains in significant numbers in the late nineteenth century from eastern Europe and Russia, where anti-Semitism was on the rise. By 1890, for example, there were 1,000 Jews in Omaha, Nebraska. Others, sponsored by such agencies as the Industrial Removal Office (founded in New York in 1901), sought to make a living on the land. By 1910 there were at least 1,200 Jewish farmers in central North Dakota. Jewish farm families also settled in southern Alberta.

Maintaining culture and religion was difficult in these thinly settled areas. There were usually not enough people in a given area to establish a synagogue, hire a rabbi, support a kosher butcher, or maintain a *cheder* (Jewish elementary school). In Burleigh County, North Dakota, Jewish women arranged for a Bismarck rabbi to rotate from one locale to another, teaching Hebrew to children, performing ritual slaughtering of animals, and conducting services. But generally, rural Jewish settlers stayed on the land only long enough to prove up their homesteads. Then they sold the property and moved to towns within, and beyond, the Great Plains.

Because the Jews of the Great Plains came from every quarter of Europe and from every economic class, there were sometimes ethnic, political, and theological tensions. For example, in 1884 the Reform rabbi of Denver's Temple Emmanuel was told to stop ridiculing Orthodox Jews, and in the 1930s Zionist versus anti-Zionist arguments swept through Jewish communities. In the Wichita German Jewish community in the late nineteenth century, Reform Judaism was embraced by those who sought a degree of cultural assimilation. Dietary laws were relaxed, and prayer was given in English rather than Hebrew. Weekly services took place in homes and were often conducted by a layman. Later Jewish arrivals in Wichita from eastern Europe practiced a more traditional faith, forming a Hebrew congregation in 1906. But the tensions between the two groups were minor: there were so few Jews that religious compromise was imperative if the community was to survive.

Today the Jews of the Great Plains are largely urban. Communities are under the aegis of the Jewish Federation of each city. However, folk wisdom has it that, in any small town in which a Jew would wish to settle there would be a Jew there to meet him, or her, at the station.

See also EUROPEAN AMERICANS: Jews.

Gladys Sturman
Western States Jewish History

Gaustad, Edwin Scott, and Philip L. Barlow. *New Historical Atlas of Religions in America.* Oxford: Oxford University Press, 2001. Rothman, Hal. "'Same Horse, New Wagon': Tradition and Assimilation among the Jews of Wichita, 1835–1930." *Great Plains Quarterly* 15 (1995): 83–104. Schulte, Janet E. "'Proving Up and Moving Up': Jewish Homesteading Activity in North Dakota, 1900–1920." *Great Plains Quarterly* 10 (1990): 228–44.

LAC STE. ANNE PILGRIMAGE

This pilgrimage is the most famous and the most popular of the Roman Catholic pilgrimages in western Canada. It is held annually at Lac Ste. Anne, about forty miles west of Edmonton, Alberta, in the third week of July, to coincide with the feast day of Saint Anne (July 26). Saint Anne, mother of the Virgin Mary, is also the patron saint of childless women and miners, as well as the miracle worker of Canada. The pilgrimage was inaugurated in 1889 by Joseph Lestanc, a Missionary Oblate of Mary Immaculate, who, while visiting the shrine of Saint Anne of Auray in his native Brittany, felt the need to work ardently to revive the cult of Saint Anne and to institute pilgrimages in her honor. Upon Lestanc's return to Canada, a new chapel was built at the Lac Ste. Anne Mission, and he obtained a statue of the saint that had touched the famous relics at Sainte Anne de Beaupré in Quebec.

Religious services associated with the pilgrimage include penitential rites, mass and Holy Communion, recitation of the rosary, the blessing of the sick, the stations of the cross, benediction of the Blessed Sacrament, and the blessing of the lake. First Nations languages such as Cree and Blackfoot are used extensively in these services. Today the annual pilgrimage attracts thousands of Indians and Métis from the western provinces and the Northwest Territories, and it reflects a blend of traditional Catholic practices implanted long ago by French-speaking Oblate missionaries and traditional Native ceremonies and rituals.

Raymond J. A. Huel
University of Lethbridge

Provincial Archives of Alberta, *Fonds Oblat de la province Alberta-Saskatchewan, Lac Ste Anne, 6, Codex historicus,* Edmonton, Alberta: Provincial Archives of Alberta, 1889–1964.

LUTHERANISM

Lutherans are members of a Protestant tradition flowing from the life and thought of Martin Luther, the sixteenth-century German monk turned theologian, pastor, and family patriarch. Lutherans became a major religious group in the Great Plains of North America in the latter half of the nineteenth century, and as the twenty-first century began, they continued to color the society and culture of various locales in the Plains and their borderlands.

Theologically, Lutherans have identified themselves as evangelical in that Luther in his break with Roman Catholicism stressed the Gospels and the evangel of justification by faith in the gracious work of God in Jesus Christ. An individual's ultimate standing before God, in other words, is not gained by moral works or by keeping God's law; rather, it is by *sola gratia* (grace alone) and *sola fides* (faith alone). *Sola scriptura* (Scripture alone) has also been a key affirmation of Lutherans, indicating that the canonical books of the Bible, not any church office, institution, or theological tradition, are the ultimate norm

for Christian life and thought. Nevertheless, confessionalism has always been a strong component in Lutheran identity. Next to the ecumenical creeds of the early church, the two most important confessional documents for Lutherans have been the Augsburg Confession (1530) and Luther's Small Catechism (1529). These and other documents were gathered in 1580 into the Book of Concord, a collection that remains formally important for Lutheran theology.

Lutheran immigrants to the Great Plains brought with them not only a strong theological tradition but also conceptions of church order and elements of an ethos that shaped the social and cultural institutions they constructed. In the German and Scandinavian states from which the vast majority of Great Plains Lutherans came in the nineteenth century, Lutheranism was formally established. In the Plains of North America, however, legal nonestablishment, together with the vastness of the region, reinforced the primacy of the local congregation in Lutheran life. At the local level, Lutheran leadership is still formally embodied in the pastorate and also in elected lay officials. The office of bishop has become widespread among Lutheran groups, but as a useful administrative office rather than one representing apostolic succession. Above this local level, Lutherans organized regional synods based largely on differences in ethnicity. Only in the latter half of the twentieth century, as ethnicity has softened, has the plethora of Lutheran synodical bodies represented in the Great Plains begun to significantly diminish through mergers. Since 1988 the vast majority of Plains Lutherans are affiliated with either the Evangelical Lutheran Church of America (ELCA) or the Lutheran Church, Missouri Synod (LCMS), the former theologically and socially more pluralist than the latter.

An important aspect of a Lutheran ethos in the North American Plains has been pietism, a diffuse revitalization movement of the seventeenth and eighteenth centuries that was later reinforced by similar revitalization movements in the nineteenth century. This pietist stream reinforced among many Lutherans a stress on personalizing belief. It also stressed the embodiment of such commitment through "godly" practices and the avoidance of "worldly" practices. Also worth noting in a Lutheran ethos are the patriarchal family, enacted by Luther himself and carried on symbolically through the present by the local pastor and his family, and Lutheran corporate worship, which has consistently stressed the proclamation of the Word, the importance of the sacraments of baptism and the Lord's Supper, and the role of music, particularly chorales, in engaging the participation of the entire community.

The arrival of Lutherans in the Plains began with major migrations of Germans and, to a lesser extent, Scandinavians to the central and upper portions of the Mississippi River basin in the 1840s and 1850s. The political and economic upheavals of an industrializing and liberalizing Europe were factors that prompted emigration, but economic opportunity, particularly land, was the most pervasive pull. By the time the American Civil War began in 1861, Wisconsin, Minnesota, Missouri, and a section of Texas had received thousands of these Lutheran emigrants. The English-speaking descendants of colonial-era Lutherans, primarily concentrated in Pennsylvania, and the more recent German-speaking Lutherans centered in Ohio held relatively little appeal for these newly arriving Lutherans. Instead, the emigrants formed new synods, most notably the Missouri Synod (1847), but also Hauge's Synod (Norwegian, 1846), the Texas Synod (German, 1851), the Norwegian Synod (1853), and the Augustana Synod (Swedish, 1860). The founding of Augustana College in Sioux Falls (now South Dakota) in 1860 foreshadowed what this planting of Lutheranism in the eastern borderlands of the U.S. Great Plains would bring once the Civil War ended.

Lutherans secured their initial planting in the Plains proper with two phases of settlement after 1865. The earlier phase was in the Northern Plains between roughly 1865 and 1900. The regional shape and depth of this migration is suggested by the establishment of Lutheran institutions of higher education. By 1900, in addition to Augustana College, the following had been founded: Bethany College (Augustana Synod) and Saint John's College (Missouri Synod) in Kansas; Dana College (United Danish), Midland College (General Synod), and Concordia Teachers College (Missouri Synod) in Nebraska; and Texas Lutheran College (Texas Synod).

The second phase was the spilling over of this migration into the Canadian Prairie Provinces between 1890 and 1914. The Lutheran population swelled enough so that in 1915 the General Council of Lutherans organized the Saskatoon Theological Seminary, Saskatchewan.

Lutheran communities in the Great Plains have received their finest literary depiction to date in the novels of Ole Rölvaag, who lived and worked on a farm in South Dakota for three years in the late 1890s before attending Augustana College. Prior to World War I, Lutherans in the Great Plains were comparatively isolated geographically and insulated culturally. Whether in Block Corners, Kansas, Dalesburg, South Dakota, or some other German or Scandinavian enclave in the Plains, community life for observant Lutherans was centered around church and school. The pastor and, in the most conservative communities, the Lutheran schoolteacher provided the theological, social, and cultural leadership locally that was integral to sustaining ethnic as well as religious identity until well into the twentieth century. The church building, and sometimes a separate school building, provided a material center for community life, which was expressed formally in corporate worship, in congregational and school events such as picnics and mission festivals, and, by the turn of the nineteenth and into the twentieth century, women's groups and youth groups as well. Home missions by various Lutheran synods, while similar in most respects to those undertaken by various anglo-phone Protestant denominations, were limited to organizing congregations among the sending group's ethnic compatriots rather than seeking to evangelize outside the ethnic group.

The twentieth century's world wars and economic depression were major catalysts for undermining isolation and insulation. Lutheran ethnicity has not disappeared, however; it has merely softened its tone and expanded and blurred its borders. Radio storyteller Garrison Keillor's Norwegian Lutherans, while fictional and nostalgic, are evocative of a persistent ethos as much Lutheran as it is ethnic, and Lake Wobegon is a place almost as much Plains as it is Prairie. As of 1990 the political units of the Great Plains with the largest percentages of the population expressing a Lutheran affiliation are North Dakota (36 percent), South Dakota (30 percent), and Nebraska (16 percent). Such proportions suggest that, whatever changes may come to Plains Lutherans as a collective religious tradition and community, they will remain a significant element in the region.

See also LITERARY TRADITIONS: Rölvaag, O. E.

Douglas Firth Anderson
Northwestern College, Orange City, Iowa

Coburn, Carol K. *Life at Four Corners: Religion, Gender, and Education in a German-Lutheran Community, 1868–1945.* Lawrence: University Press of Kansas, 1992. Gjerde, Jon. *The Minds of the West: Ethnocultural Evolution in the Rural Middle West, 1830–1917.* Chapel Hill: University of North Carolina Press, 1997. Nelson, E. Clifford, ed. *The Lutherans in North America.* Philadelphia: Fortress Press, 1975.

MENNONITES

Mennonites are a Christian sect that originated in southern Germany, Switzerland, and the Netherlands in the sixteenth century. They have lived in the Great Plains since the 1870s, when thousands emigrated there at the encouragement of state officials and railroad companies who desired to settle the region. Entire Mennonite villages often migrated en masse from Europe to the Great Plains to flee religious persecution. These mass migrations helped Mennonites create several distinctive population hearths in this region. Today, from a worldwide membership of slightly over one million, approximately 10 percent reside in the Great Plains.

Manitoba became a principal Canadian settlement site because of the East and West Reserve lands, established south of Winnipeg by Canadian officials in 1873 and 1876, respectively, which offered settlers the autonomy they sought. There, Mennonites built their own schools and replicated the economic and social patterns practiced in Europe. In the mid–twentieth century a majority of Mennonites in the Prairie Provinces lived on farms, but this percentage has declined dramatically in recent decades. Today, Winnipeg has the largest concentration of Mennonites of any urban center in the region.

In the United States, Mennonite immigrants found land and a climate that encouraged settlement around Henderson, Nebraska, in 1874, and near Freeman, South Dakota, in 1873. In Kansas, the area near Newton became a major cultural hearth starting around 1874, largely through the construction of liberal arts colleges, hospitals, and relief agencies. In south-central Kansas, land shortages following World War II and economic pressures forced Mennonites off farms and into communities, where they quickly built institutions and businesses that reflected their Mennonite ideology. For example, Mennonite entrepreneur Lyle Yost founded Hesston Corporation (today known as Hay and Forage, Incorporated), a leading agricultural machinery manufacturer.

The multiplicity of Mennonite origins in Europe means that the Mennonites of the Great Plains are by no means a homogeneous group, having brought with them differing traditions and emphases in their faith. The various Mennonite strains do, however, have many practices in common, including adult baptism, separation from the larger culture, simple living, and pacifism. Traditionally, pacifism has meant not complying with conscription (conscientious objection) and not supporting militarism. This pacifistic stance has often put them at odds with the state and non-Mennonites in general, both in Europe and in North America. Today, support for community-based nonviolent campaigns and conflict mediation agencies have become the primary outlet for these pacifist beliefs. Battles with the state over conscription are increasingly rare. In fact, because of the publicized efforts of the Mennonite relief agencies, such as Mennonite Central Committee, service, rather than strident pacifism, became the group's defining trait in the latter half of the twentieth century.

Initially, the Great Plains appealed to Mennonites because of the group's traditional rural bias, derived from centuries of persecution in Europe. Certainly Mennonitism in the Great Plains once was very parochial, as they were a reserved people, speaking Germanic dialects, wearing distinctive, simple garb, and living in isolated rural enclaves. Most Mennonites believed that their faith was incompatible with urban life. Although Mennonites are still widely perceived as a rural people, more frequently Mennonites are making their homes in Plains towns, living and working alongside non-Mennonites. Distinctive dress, language, and physical isolation have given way to service work and conflict resolution as the defining elements of Mennonitism today.

See also INDUSTRY: Swather.

Steven V. Foulke
Emporia State University

Foulke, Steven V. "Shaping of Place: Mennonitism in South-Central Kansas." Ph.D. diss., University of Kansas, 1998. Redekop, Calvin. *Mennonite Society.* Baltimore MD: Johns Hopkins University Press, 1989. Smith, C. Henry. *The Coming of the Russian Mennonites: An Episode in the Settling of the Last Frontier, 1874–1884.* Berne IN: Mennonite Book Concern, 1927.

METHODISM, UNITED STATES

Methodism emerged as a lay organization within the Church of England in the mid–

eighteenth century and separated from that parent body in 1784. By that time, Methodist evangelists had been active in North America for more than twenty years, spreading a religion that emphasized the primacy of the Bible, but also the importance of reason, experience, and social action. The sermons of John Wesley, the founder of Methodism, and the inspirational hymns of his younger brother Charles were, and are, the heart of the theology.

In the United States, Methodism quickly became the most successful frontier religion, spreading westward in step with the expansion of the nation. (See the entry on Canadian Wesleyan Methodism for the Canadian story.) The emphasis on personal salvation, the galvanizing effect of Charles's hymns, and especially the groundswell of conversion through circuit rider preaching and camp meetings accounted for this rapid growth. By 1830 Methodism dominated more American counties than any other denomination. Also by 1830 Methodism had reached the Great Plains, with the establishment of the Shawnee Mission in what is now Kansas. Over the next thirty years, Methodist missions were established in Kansas and Indian Territory for the Delawares (1832), Choctaws (1832), Kickapoos (1833), Peorias (1833), Potawatomis (1837), Senecas (1839), Quapaws (1843), and Sauk and Fox (1860).

The Methodist Church established conferences—its system of regional organization—in Nebraska and Kansas soon after the Civil War and continued its extraordinary rate of expansion into the Great Plains. Only a series of schisms, mainly over the issues of centralized control and slavery, slowed the advance. By 1890 most counties in the eastern half of Kansas and across the entire breadth of southern Nebraska had more than eleven Methodist churches; many had more than twenty.

Methodism continued to gain members in the Great Plains and in the country as a whole to about 1970, when national membership reached about 11 million. Most of the branches of the denomination were reunited in 1939 and in 1968 as the United Methodist Church. By 1950, while the number of Methodist churches per county in the core area of Kansas and Nebraska had fallen, as other denominations became established, most counties in the Great Plains had at least three Methodist churches. But thereafter, and in common with many other mainline Protestant denominations, church membership declined nationally and regionally. In 1990 Methodists accounted for 17.8 percent of denominational membership in Kansas (compared to 28.5 percent in 1890), second only to Roman Catholics. In Texas, Methodists ranked third behind Roman Catholics and Baptists, with 9.3 percent of denominational membership (compared to 32.3 percent in 1890), and in Nebraska Methodists accounted for 14.5 percent of denominational membership (compared to 22.1 percent in 1890), behind Catholics and Lutherans. In other Great Plains states in 1990, Methodism ranked third in New Mexico in denominational membership (6.2 percent), second in

Oklahoma (15.6 percent), fifth in Colorado (7.2 percent), sixth in Wyoming (4.9 percent), third in South Dakota (9.2 percent), third in North Dakota (4.9 percent), and fifth in Montana (5.7 percent).

Despite the recent decline, however, Methodism continues to exert a major influence on Great Plains land and life. Methodism has always emphasized education, and fifteen theological seminars, universities, and colleges in the Great Plains are associated with the Methodist Church. Among them are Iliff School of Theology (Denver, Colorado), Dakota Wesleyan University (Mitchell, South Dakota), Rocky Mountain College (Billings, Montana), Nebraska Wesleyan University (Lincoln, Nebraska), Baker University (Baldwin City, Kansas), Oklahoma City University (Oklahoma), and Texas Wesleyan University (Fort Worth, Texas). While many rural Methodist churches are humble frame buildings, some church structures are prominent landscape features. Trinity Methodist, completed in Denver in 1887, has a 182-foot spire and once dominated the city's skyline; and the Art Deco–style Boston Avenue Methodist Church of Tulsa, Oklahoma, designed in 1926 by Bruce Goff, has a 280-foot tower and an auditorium that can hold 1,800 worshipers. In Kansas, Methodism is the leading denomination in most counties, and Methodism is still regarded as one of the two foundations of Kansas culture, the other being the Republican Party.

See also ARCHITECTURE: Goff, Bruce.

David J. Wishart
University of Nebraska–Lincoln

Gaustad, Edwin Scott, and Philip L. Barlow. *New Historical Atlas of Religion in America.* Oxford: Oxford University Press, 2001. Szasz, Ferenc M. *The Protestant Clergy in the Great Plains and Mountain West, 1865–1915.* Albuquerque: University of New Mexico Press, 1988.

MORNING STAR CEREMONY

The Morning Star bundle ceremony among the Skiri Pawnees (who lived in what is now central Nebraska) reasserted devotion to the power of the rising Eastern Star (Mars). It was their only ritual involving human sacrifice and was one of only a few not tied to seasonal cycles. For the ceremony to occur, a male member of the tribe had to announce that he had seen Morning Star in a dream and, upon awakening, perceived it rising in the east. Ritual tradition then called for dispatch of the dreamer (now deemed the "warrior leader") to secure a girl captive by raiding neighboring villages. The power of the ceremony was to provide for success in war and for fertility.

Preparation for the ceremony, which ended in a ritual feast and dance by the entire village, involved several stages and sacred songs. After being dressed by the Morning Star priest in sacred raiments from the Morning Star bundle and anointed with red ointment, the captive stayed with the Wolf man, who brought her daily to the warrior leader for meals eaten with utensils from the Morning Star bundle.

On the appropriate predawn morning, the Wolf man led the captive to the scaffold, con-

structed of different symbolic species of wood. The killing was carried out with a ceremonial bow and arrow. Immediately a stone knife incision was made near the heart, and specially prepared buffalo meat held to receive drops of the victim's blood before being prepared for feasting. Before the body was removed and placed in the prairie facing east, the entire village, including children, lodged dozens of arrows in the victim's back. The Skiris believed that this ceremony allowed the victim's spirit to ascend to the sky to become a star, while her body returned to the earth.

The last known Morning Star Ceremony sacrifice took place on April 22, 1838, with the killing of Haxti, a fifteen-year-old Lakota girl. The United States subsequently suppressed the ceremony, but it also seems that some Skiris themselves wished to stop the human sacrifice.

See also NATIVE AMERICANS: Pawnees.

Byron Cannon
University of Utah

Dorsey, George A., and James Murie. *Notes on Skidi Pawnee Society.* Chicago: Field Museum of Natural History, 1940. Murie, James. *Ceremonies of the Pawnee.* Lincoln: University of Nebraska Press, 1989.

NATIVE AMERICAN CHURCH

Native Americans have long been subjected to various policies of the United States in an attempt to "civilize" them. Conversion to Christianity was among such policies. As with most issues dealing with Native Americans, the picture is not complete without providing some insight into both the traditional and legal backgrounds.

Many denominations of mainstream Christianity made initial forays into Indian Country in the attempt to convert Native Americans to Christianity and as part of federal policy. The success of these efforts is reflected by the single Christian creed professed by various tribes. For example, many Omahas originally adhered to Mormonism. Some Sioux tribes are substantially Catholic or Episcopalian. It depended upon who arrived first to begin the conversion process.

In the early part of the twentieth century, a unique Native Christian religion founded upon the basic tenets of Christianity began to sweep throughout Indian Country. While conversion to Christianity was a slow and painful process, the tenets of the Native American Church were most readily accepted. While the exact origins of the Native American Church and its incorporation of peyote as a sacrament of communion are shrouded in oral history, Native believers generally agree that it began in the Southwest and worked its way up from Mexico. Among the Plains Indians, the Omahas, Poncas, Winnebagos, and Sioux readily accepted the belief system of the Native American Church.

The tenets of the Native American Church are similar to mainstream Christianity. The leap from traditional belief in a universal creative, mysterious, and holy power (God) who now has a son, Jesus Christ, was initially surprising. However, ready acceptance of God having a son was not that difficult, as all things were believed to be possible through the Creator. Peyote is also considered sacred and holy as a sacrament and the means in which to commune with God and Jesus Christ.

The use of peyote, a cactus plant of the mescal family, within the Native American Church has spawned both case law and federal legislation. The legal controversy over peyote resulted in its legal classification as a controlled drug. Therefore, only card-carrying members of the church are allowed to possess, transport, and use peyote for religious purposes.

The Indian Religious Freedom Act of 1978 was passed to provide legal protection for the Native American Church in its use of peyote. All peyote has to be transported from Texas, where it grows. Of the fifty states, only twenty-eight states have enacted laws similar to, or in conformance with, federal regulation intended to protect its use. However, in the U.S. Supreme Court case of *Employment Division v. Smith* (1990), the Court held that the First Amendment does not provide protection for practitioners of the Native American Church. Two subsequent amendments, in 1994 and 1996, intended to clarify and provide the much-needed protections.

As for the actual religious ceremony itself, it is an act that requires deep commitment and faith. It is generally held in a tipi or, in inclement weather, a large area indoors. The Native American Church also requires that a pastor, priest, or elder conduct the services. This person is referred to as the Roadman, who from time to time must travel from tribal community to community, similar to early Christian missionaries who covered wide geographical areas.

The Roadman is assisted by a Fireman, whose task is to care for the holy fireplace by making sure that it burns continuously throughout the night. His own instruments for conducting the church services are the prayer staff, his eagle feather, a beaded and feathered gourd, a small drum, cedar, and the peyote chief, which is always present at the altar. Other peyote is ground finely or made into a mush and passed around in a circle to all participants as a sacrament to commune with God and his Son. The Roadman's wife or other female relative prepares seven sacramental foods and the "second breakfast" that are part of the church services. Her part takes place very early, between 4:30 and 5:00 in the morning. The seven sacramental foods are water, shredded beef, corn mush, rice, strawberries, cookies, and soft, individually wrapped candies. To counterbalance the bitterness of the peyote consumed during the services, the sweet foods were added later. The second breakfast is like any other breakfast. It generally includes boiled eggs, toast, hash brown potatoes, coffee, and juice. This meal is served well after sunrise and just prior to the closing of the church services.

Church services are not regular Sunday occurrences but are held in accordance with special requests by a family for celebrating a birthday, or for a memorial or funeral service. Services begin at sundown on either a Friday or Saturday evening and end at sunrise. Thus, a participant "sits up" all night, giving up a full night's rest as part of a small sacrifice to the Great and Holy Spirit and his Son.

The church services culminate in a feast for the whole community the following day. Because peyote is a stimulant, all of the participating members are wide awake, so they, too, attend the feast. The need for sleep is generally felt in the late afternoon, particularly after the feast. Gifts are given to the Roadman and all his helpers by the sponsoring family at the feast to show deep appreciation for all his hard work.

Wynema Morris
Walthill, Nebraska

OKIPA

The *Okipa* was the most powerful religious ceremony of the Mandan people of North Dakota. The four-day ceremony was performed every year during the summer. It retold the history of the creation of the Earth and all living things. The main characters are the Okipa Maker, or Lone Man, who created the Mandan and gave them their rituals; *Hoita*, or Speckled Eagle, who created the animals; and *Oxinhede*, the Foolish One, who did not believe in the power of Okipa and was cast out of the village at the end. These three dancers are joined by others impersonating buffalo, bald eagles, holy women, swans, snakes, grizzly bears, night, day, wolves, coyotes, meadowlarks, and antelopes. They are supported by drummers playing sacred turtle drums.

The dancers performed inside the Okipa lodge, which was filled by men fasting, praying, and seeking visions. Sacred bundles, containing objects such as buffalo hair, a stuffed raven, a porcupine headdress, buffalo teeth, and a warbonnet of raven and swan feathers, were also presented. These objects represented key elements in the history of the people. The younger men generally underwent torture to demonstrate their bravery. Long wooden skewers were pushed through cuts in the skin on their backs or chests, and they were hung by ropes from beams. Their bodies were weighted down with buffalo skulls hung from other skewers thrust into their thighs and calves. The torment was extreme, but crying out was a sign of cowardice, and those best able to stand the pain became Mandan leaders. Women were not allowed inside the lodge, although some would sit on the roof, where they would fast.

The purpose of the ceremony was to reaffirm the bond between the people and the natural world and to unify the Mandans through a ritual of suffering and bloodshed. The Okipa had been performed for hundreds of years when the artist George Catlin witnessed the ceremony in 1832. The Okipa was probably last held on Fort Berthold Reservation in 1889 or 1890, after which it was suppressed by the United States.

See also NATIVE AMERICANS: Mandans.

Leslie V. Tischauser
Prairie State College

Bowers, Alfred. *Mandan Social and Ceremonial Organization.* Chicago: University of Chicago Press, 1950. McHugh, Tom. *The Time of the Buffalo.* Lincoln: University of Nebraska Press, 1972. Meyer, Roy W. *The Village Indians of the Upper Missouri: The Mandan, Hidatsas, and Arikaras.* Lincoln: University of Nebraska Press, 1977.

PARHAM, CHARLES FOX (1873–1929)

Charles Fox Parham, who was born in Muscatine, Iowa, on June 4, 1873, is regarded as the founder and doctrinal father of the worldwide pentecostal movement. A sickly youth, Parham nevertheless enrolled in Southwest Kansas College in 1890, where he became interested in the Christian ministry. After receiving a call to preach, he left college before graduating, and in 1893 accepted the pastorate of a Methodist church in Linwood, Kansas.

In Linwood, Parham soon became involved in the holiness movement, which was spreading in Methodist circles at the time. This movement stressed instant second-blessing sanctification as taught by John Wesley. It was in the Plains that the most radical elements of the holiness movement took root. By 1895, as controversy over the second blessing divided the church, Parham became so enmeshed in holiness theology that he left the Methodist Church to follow a career as an independent holiness evangelist and teacher. He soon began to emphasize newer doctrines, such as divine healing and the instant premillennial second coming of Christ. For the rest of his life, he also rejected any type of church organization.

In 1898 Parham opened his own "Bethel Bible School" and healing home in Topeka, Kansas, where in 1899 he began publication of a magazine called the *Apostolic Faith.* It was in this school that Parham and his students studied the differing teachings of the holiness movement relating to the "baptism in the Holy Spirit" described in Acts 2:4. Through a student consensus, with some help from Parham, the student body concluded that speaking in tongues (glossolalia) was the "Bible evidence" of such an experience.

On January 1, 1901, a student in the school, Agnes Ozman, spoke in tongues, electrifying the school and the Topeka area through sensational stories in local newspapers. Parham's teaching that speaking in tongues was the necessary "Bible evidence" of baptism in the Holy Spirit became known as the "touch felt round the world" that, according to J. Roswell Flower of the Assemblies of God, "made the Twentieth Century Pentecostal Movement." Parham also began to teach that glossolalia also constituted zenolalia (i.e., "missionary tongues"), whereby missionaries could go to the corners of the earth and preach miraculously in known human languages that they had not learned. In a short time, all Pentecostals except Parham dropped this belief due to unsuccessful efforts at preaching in unknown tongues in India and other places.

By 1906 the pentecostal movement had spread to Los Angeles through a black preacher, William Joseph Seymour, who learned pentecostal theology as Parham's student in another Bible school in Houston, Texas. From the Azusa

Street Mission led by Seymour, the pentecostal movement spread rapidly throughout the world.

In October 1906 Parham visited Azusa Street and denounced the Los Angeles meetings as being dominated by "holy rollers and hypnotists" that featured "darkey camp meeting stunts." He was thereupon expelled from Azusa Street by Seymour and his elders. For the rest of his life, Parham denounced his former student and the Azusa Street revival as "spiritual power prostituted." In 1907 Parham was accused of sodomy in San Antonio during a local healing crusade. Although he was acquitted of the charge, his influence as a major leader in the pentecostal movement was over. In the last two decades of his life, Parham retired to his home in Baxter Springs, Kansas, where several thousand of his followers attended his annual camp meetings until his death on January 29, 1929. He is buried in Baxter Springs.

A century after Parham's movement began in Topeka, the Pentecostals had grown to be the second largest family of Christians, with more than 500 million members in the pentecostal and charismatic churches and movements that had spread from Topeka to practically every nation of the world. Major American denominations produced by the pentecostal movement include the Assemblies of God, the Church of God in Christ, the Pentecostal Holiness Church, the Church of God (Cleveland, Tennessee), the United Pentecostal Church, and the Pentecostal Church of God.

Vinson Synan
Regent University

Burgess, Stanley, Gary McGee, and Patrick Alexander. *Dictionary of Pentecostal and Charismatic Movements.* Grand Rapids MI: Zondervan Publishing House, 1988. Goff, James R. *Fields White unto Harvest: Charles Fox Parham and the Missionary Origins of Pentecostalism.* Fayetteville: University of Arkansas Press, 1988. Synan, Vinson. *Holiness-Pentecostal Tradition.* Grand Rapids MI: William B. Eerdmans Publishing Co., 1997.

PRESBYTERIANISM

Presbyterians trace their theology to the Reformed tradition of John Calvin and their church structure to the Scottish reformer John Knox. The title Presbyterian describes the leadership in each church of "presbyters," otherwise known as elders or bishops. The Presbyterian system of government involves a series of three courts: the session, comprised of the pastor and elders of a local congregation; the presbytery or synod, comprised of the pastors and elders from a region; and the general assembly, a denominationwide meeting held annually. The growth of Presbyterianism in the Great Plains was driven by a missionary zeal to win Christian converts among Native peoples, a need to organize churches for the spreading American and Canadian populations, and a desire to promote a Protestant Christian civility.

Even preceding the arrival of missionaries in the Great Plains, Presbyterianism took root in the Red River Settlement in 1812, with its predominantly Scottish population. Missionary activity began in earnest in the 1830s with sponsorship from the Board of Foreign Missions. Rev. John Dunbar and Samuel Allis were sent to live—in difficult and often dangerous circumstances—with the Pawnees from 1834 to 1845. The father and son team, Reverends T. S. Williamson and John P. Williamson, ministered to the Lakotas from 1835 to 1898. Both Dunbar and the Williamsons learned the Native languages and translated parts of the Bible into them. Their program was to change the entire cultures—religion, education, and ways of life—in order to prepare the Native peoples for responsible American citizenship. To this end, John Williamson also established a school and a Dakota-language newspaper, *Word Carrier,* in 1871. Presbyterian missionaries to the Plains were also sponsored by the Board of Home Missions after 1870.

Presbyterianism spread into the Plains in the second half of the nineteenth century with European American settlement. In the Canadian Prairie Provinces, Presbyterians played an important role in the Social Gospel movement, which sought to apply the principles of Christianity to social reform. In the United States the establishment of numerous Presbyterian churches was accomplished by Sheldon Jackson, who was sent west by three presbyteries in the synod of Iowa in 1869. In the first year alone, he traveled 29,000 miles and organized twenty-two churches. Still, despite the western expansion, the core areas of Presbyterianism in both Canada and the United States remained in the East. Although there are now more than 1,500 Presbyterian churches in the U.S. Great Plains, Presbyterianism tends to rank third or fourth in numbers among Protestant denominations, behind Methodists (in the Central Plains), Baptists (in the Southern Plains), and Lutherans (in the Northern Plains).

Stu Kerns
Lincoln, Nebraska

Coleman, Michael C. *Presbyterian Missionary Attitudes toward American Indians, 1837–1893.* Jackson: University Press of Mississippi, 1985. Drury, Clifford M. *Presbyterian Panorama: One Hundred and Fifty Years of National Missions History.* Philadelphia: Presbyterian Church in the United States of America Board of Christian Education, 1952. Szasz, Ferenc Morton. *The Protestant Clergy in the Great Plains and Mountain West, 1865–1915.* Albuquerque: University of New Mexico Press, 1988.

PROVENCHER, JOSEPH-NORBERT
(1787–1853)

Born on February 12, 1787, at Nicolet, Quebec, Joseph-Norbert Provencher (baptized Joseph) was ordained in 1811 and served as a curate until he was sent to the Red River Settlement (Manitoba) in 1818 to establish the Catholic Church in the Canadian West. Described as moral, humble, tenacious, and devout, Provencher was consecrated titular bishop in 1822 and first bishop of the diocese of the Northwest, founded in 1847 at St. Boniface (Manitoba). He died there on June 7, 1853.

Bishop Provencher worked tirelessly as an ecclesiastic administrator. He built churches and schools to serve the newly arriving Irish, Scottish, and French Canadian Catholic settlers. He sent priests out to the Métis hunters and traders to solemnize their mixed-race marriages. He created "itinerant missions" with priests who traveled with various Plains Native peoples, attempting to convert them to Christianity—an endeavor that was largely unsuccessful during this period. Provencher even sent missionaries as far afield as Lake Athabasca and the Pacific Northwest to establish the Catholic presence. He skillfully avoided conflict with rival Protestant groups and received, like them, an annual grant from the Hudson's Bay Company to assist in his activities. During his career, Provencher made numerous trips to Quebec, and two to the United States and Europe, to garner Catholic support for mission development. In total, Bishop Joseph-Norbert Provencher brought thirteen secular priests from Quebec and during the 1840s persuaded both the Oblates of Mary Immaculate and the Sisters of Charity of the Hôpital Général at Montreal (commonly known as the "Grey Nuns") to establish themselves in the Canadian West.

James G. Mullens
University of Saskatchewan

Frémont, Donatien. *Mgr. Provencher et son temps.* Winnipeg: Editions de Liberté, 1935. King, Dennis. *Joseph Norbert Provencher.* Winnipeg: Peguis Publishers, 1982. Provencher, Joseph-Norbert. "Lettres de monseigneur Joseph-Norbert Provencher, premier évêque de Saint-Boniface," Soc. Hist. de Saint-Boniface, *Bulletin* 3 (1913). St. Boniface, Manitoba.

QUAKERS

Quaker settlements began to appear in the Great Plains in Kansas in the 1850s when families moved together from Quaker communities in Indiana and Iowa. Lured by the prospect of choice land, they were also motivated by benevolent concern for Native Americans and the opportunity of voting against slavery in this newly opened territory. Homes and churches were constructed of logs and prairie sod.

Historically, Quaker worship consisted of a simple gathering in silence, without clergy, planned program, or sacrament. Worshipers prayed or spoke as they felt moved by God. Influenced by frontier revivalism, many Quakers in the latter third of the 1800s embraced the evangelistic methods and pastoral leadership characteristic of others. Thereafter, much of the spread of Quakerism in rural Oklahoma and Nebraska reflected this new development.

Maintaining the dignity and equality of all persons and leadership by women as well as men have been encouraged. Numerous Quaker schools across Kansas, Oklahoma, and Nebraska made education available before the advent of public schools. Not limited to Quakers, Barclay College (Haviland, Kansas) and Friends University (Wichita, Kansas) continue to provide education at the adult level. Work with Native Americans, initiated in Kansas at Shawnee Mission (1836), continued in Nebraska in the late 1860s, when Quakers were appointed as agents to the Pawnees, Omahas, and Otoe-Missourias, and subsequently in Oklahoma and New Mexico.

Approximately a dozen isolated Quaker Meetings (worship groups) can be found in Nebraska, and there is a small, unprogrammed group in each of the five major cities of the Prairie Provinces of Canada. The highest concentration of Quakers in the Great Plains, however, is found in southern Kansas, northern Oklahoma, and southeastern Colorado, where the pastoral leadership style of worship tends to prevail. Membership among Quakers within the Great Plains is approximately 6,000, with about 75 percent located in Kansas and Oklahoma.

Leroy Brightup
Friends University

Barbour, Hugh, and J. William Frost. *The Quakers*. Richmond IN: Friends United Press, 1994. Dorland, Arthur Garratt. *The Quakers in Canada: A History*. Toronto: Ryerson Press, 1968. Elliott, Errol T. *Quakers on the American Frontier*. Richmond IN: Friends United Press, 1969.

ROBERTS, ORAL (b, 1918)

Born on January 24, 1918, in Pontotoc Country, Oklahoma, Oral Granville Roberts was one of the chief architects of a pentecostal/charismatic revival that flourished in the twentieth century, significantly altering the religious demography of the world. The son of Ellis Roberts, an itinerant evangelist in the Pentecostal Holiness Church, Roberts believed that he was divinely healed of tuberculosis while a teenager, and shortly afterward he was ordained by the Pentecostal Holiness Church. In 1947 he made a bold decision to give up his position as pastor of a church in Enid, Oklahoma, to launch an independent healing ministry. In the second half of the twentieth century, Roberts was the most famous pentecostal evangelist in the world; he developed fresh methods of fund-raising and collected hundreds of millions of dollars to support a diverse assortment of ministries. In addition to conducting revivals in many nations, in the 1950s he launched innovative radio and television ministries. In 1965 Roberts opened Oral Roberts University in Tulsa. In 1980 Roberts set out to add a hospital and medical school to the university. While the university was a successful educational enterprise, the medical school survived for only seven years. By the end of the 1980s Roberts had turned over most of the responsibility for his ministry and the university to his son, Richard Roberts.

Roberts's choice of Tulsa as his home base was a calculated decision. His roots went deep into the soil of Oklahoma; he was proud that his maternal great-grandmother had been a full-blood Cherokee Indian. He imbibed the Wild West enthusiasm of post–World War II Tulsa; it was a place, he believed, where "great ideas can be had and great movements can be launched." Roberts's presence in Tulsa attracted other evangelists to the city, making it a hub of conservative religious activities in the last half of the twentieth century.

Often ridiculed during his early years as a "fake healer" and charlatan, Roberts usually had an uneasy relationship with the press and

Prayer Tower at Oral Roberts University

with mainstream American religious leaders. However, in the late 1960s Roberts made a series of decisions that for a time improved his public image. In 1968 he stopped holding tent revivals and discontinued the television programs that had featured people lining up to be healed. A few months later, in a risky and expensive venture, Roberts released a series of professionally produced television specials that were aired in prime time. At the same time, Roberts left the Pentecostal Holiness Church to become a member of the prestigious Boston Avenue Methodist Church in Tulsa. In the 1980s Roberts's public image once again plummeted. He was criticized by many Tulsa leaders who opposed the building of the huge City of Faith Hospital and by the media because of the extravagant fund-raising tactics he used to fund his excursion into medical education. In addition, while no hint of scandal ever touched Roberts and his wife, Evelyn, his ministry suffered because of widespread criticism of televangelists following the exposés of Jim Bakker and Jimmy Swaggart in the late 1980s.

Oral Roberts was a pivotal figure in twentieth-century Protestantism. He pioneered many of the television techniques that made possible the rapid expansion of religious television in the 1970s and 1980s, and he also devised many of the fund-raising strategies used by later television ministers. Probably more important in the long run, in the 1960s Roberts anticipated the spread of the pentecostal emphasis on the gifts of the Holy Spirit and divine healing into mainstream Protestant churches and the Roman Catholic Church. As early as the 1950s, Roberts's tent campaigns included people from many different churches, and in the 1960s Roberts consciously turned his attention to ministering to nonpentecostal Christians. Through his writings and in scores of conferences at Oral Roberts University, Roberts encouraged a revising of pentecostal theology that made it more palatable to mainstream Christians. By the end of the twentieth century, Oral Roberts had become a guiding figure to millions of charismatic Christians around the world.

David Edwin Harrell Jr.
Auburn University

Harrell, David Edwin Jr. *Oral Roberts: An American Life*. Bloomington: Indiana University Press, 1985. Robinson, Wayne A. *Oral: The Warm, Intimate Unauthorized Portrait of a Man of God*. Los Angeles: Acton House, 1976.

ROMAN CATHOLICISM

Roman Catholicism was the first European church to be introduced into the Great Plains, and it remains the single largest denomination in the region. This reflects the diversity of Protestant denominations, of course, as well as the continued importance of Catholicism. But Catholicism in the Plains, as elsewhere in North America, is by no means homogeneous. At least through the middle of the twentieth century, it was an ethnically diverse church, and the various cultures of Catholicism in the region have much to do with the history of immigration.

As early as 1680, Spanish Franciscan missions lined the valley of the upper Rio Grande and spilled out onto the Great Plains to the east of Santa Fe. The number of these missions was reduced over the course of the following century, but Spaniards intermarried with Native Americans, and the religious legacy, reinforced by subsequent waves of Latino migrations in the 1920s, 1950s, and in recent decades, has persisted. In 1990, in almost all of the Plains counties of New Mexico and Colorado, Roman Catholicism is the largest denomination.

Spaniards, and Catholicism, did not extend significantly into the Southern Great Plains from the Franciscan missions that were established on the Gulf Coast Plain of Texas in the eighteenth century—the Comanches and Apaches formed a formidable barrier. Witness the destruction of Mission Santa Cruz de San Sabá (built in 1757 at a site near present-day Menard, Texas) by a force of 2,000 Comanches and other Indians on March 16, 1758, which left two of the three Franciscan missionaries dead.

The next nucleus of Catholicism in the Great Plains emerged in the Red River Valley of the North in the early nineteenth century. In 1818 Lord Selkirk (Thomas Douglas) requested Catholic missionaries to serve his nascent colony of Scots, Irish, and Métis settlers. One of their number, Joseph-Norbert Provencher, was appointed bishop and apostolic vicar of the Northwest in 1820, and he later became the first bishop of St. Boniface. Alexandre-Antonin Taché, of the Oblates of Mary Immaculate, followed Provencher to the Red River Settlement in 1845. Working as an assistant to

Mexican Catholic Church, Deming, New Mexico, 1910–1919

Provencher, Taché was a tireless missionary to the Indians, Métis, and new settlers in the interior. He was appointed bishop of St. Boniface in 1853 and archbishop in 1871. Catholicism in the Prairie Provinces grew through conversion and in-migration of French Canadians and, later, eastern and southern Europeans. Roman Catholics remain the most numerous religious group in the Prairie Provinces, except for a belt of counties in southern Alberta, Saskatchewan, and Manitoba, where the United Church of Canada predominates. Lac St. Anne, situated forty miles to the west of Edmonton, is the most important Catholic pilgrimage site in western Canada.

Roman Catholic missionaries were also active to the south of the forty-ninth parallel. The peripatetic Jesuit missionary Pierre-Jean De Smet began his work at the Saint Joseph's Mission to the Potawatomis at Council Bluffs in 1838, and he baptized thousands of Indians and Métis in the Northern Plains over the course of the next thirty years. In the Southern Plains, in present-day Kansas, Catholic missions were established for the Potawatomis (1838), Miamis (1847), and Osages (1847).

The ranks of Catholics in the Plains were greatly increased by immigrants after 1854—first Irish and Germans, then Germans from Russia, Poles, Czechs, Slovaks, Hungarians and others from eastern Europe, Italians, and most recently, Latinos. In North Dakota, Germans from Russia, clustering in the south-central counties, were the most numerous Catholics. Germans from Russia also settled in Ellis County, in west-central Kansas, while Catholics from the Rhineland, Alsace, and Westphalia settled to the northwest of Wichita. Such clustering was encouraged by Louis Fink, bishop of Kansas, because it facilitated preaching and encouraged cohesion.

By the late nineteenth century, the Catholic Church in the Great Plains was divided into national parishes, which were distinct from official territorial parishes, though often under the same bishop. Italians, German Catholics, Irish,

and others listened to services in their own languages and worshiped their own saints, continuing the traditions of their homelands. Even in the mid–twentieth century, such diverse expression prevailed. Integration has since occurred, with Hispanic Catholics remaining most distinct.

By 1890 Catholics ranked first in terms of religious adherents in the states of North Dakota (44.4 percent), Montana (77.5 percent), South Dakota (30.1 percent), Wyoming (61.4 percent), Colorado (54.3 percent), New Mexico (95.1 percent), and Nebraska (26.5 percent); second in Kansas (20.1 percent, behind Methodists) and Oklahoma (25.9 percent, behind Methodists); and third in Texas (14.7 percent, behind Baptists and Methodists).

A century later, Catholicism had lost ground to other denominations in much of the Plains, especially to Baptists in the Southern Plains, Lutherans in the Northern Plains, and Mormons in Wyoming, while still remaining generally the largest denomination in the region. In the 1990s Catholicism ranked first in number of adherents in the states of Montana (36.9 percent), Wyoming (27.5 percent), Colorado (37.3 percent), Nebraska (33.3 percent), and Kansas (27.3 percent); second in North Dakota (35.8 percent, behind Lutheranism), South Dakota (30.0 percent, behind Lutheranism), and Texas (32.8 percent, behind Baptists); and fifth in Oklahoma (6.8 percent, behind Baptists, Methodists, and various Pentecostal and Holiness groups). The religious landscape of the Plains is still filled with Catholic churches, schools, seminaries, hospitals, orphanages, and monasteries (of which there are four in both North and South Dakota).

In some parts of the Plains, especially areas of Latino in-migration, the number of Catholics is increasing. The diocese of Lubbock, Texas, for example, was established in 1983 in response to the growing population of adherents. But more generally in the region, the future for Catholicism is clouded. Since the 1960s the numbers of priests and nuns have

declined significantly, and many now are aged. Few young men and women are replacing them. There are relatively few counties in the Plains where every congregation has a resident priest. In each of Pembina and Stutsman Counties, North Dakota, and Custer County, Nebraska, in 1990, for example, there were more than six congregations without resident priests. The trend suggests that, barring radical changes, such as allowing priests to marry or women to be ordained, the number of parishioners served by each priest is only going to increase as Roman Catholicism is stretched thin over much of the Plains.

See also EUROPEAN AMERICANS: Douglas, Thomas (Earl of Selkirk) / HISPANIC AMERICANS: San Sabá Mission and Presidio / LAW: North Dakota Anti-Garb Law / WAR: San Sabá Mission, Destruction of.

David J. Wishart
University of Nebraska–Lincoln

Abramson, Harold J. *Ethnic Diversity in Catholic America.* New York: John Wiley and Sons, 1973. Gaustad, Edwin Scott, and Philip L. Barlow. *New Historical Atlas of Religion in America.* Oxford: Oxford University Press, 2001.

SANAPIA (1895–1984)

Sanapia (Memory Woman), the last known Comanche Eagle Doctor, was born at Fort Sill, Oklahoma, in the spring of 1895. She was one of the most powerful Native women in the Plains during the middle decades of the twentieth century. Her father was a converted Christian and her mother was a traditional Comanche-Arapaho. Sanapia's mother, maternal uncle, and maternal grandmother were Eagle Doctors, and her grandmother reared the girl in traditional Comanche ways.

From ages seven to thirteen Sanapia was educated at the Cache Creek Mission School in southern Oklahoma. Thereafter, she began training with her mother. She was reluctant at first, but her uncle had cured her of influenza as a child and had made her promise to pursue training as an Eagle Doctor when she was older. He named her Memory Woman to remind her of her pledge. Training included learning herbal medicine, healing skills (including sucking), and eagle power. Tradition, however, stipulated that she could not begin practicing until after menopause.

Sanapia was married three times, the first time, briefly, at the age of seventeen. When her second husband (with whom she had two children) died in the 1930s, Sanapia's grief led her to a period of drinking, gambling, and depression. In 1945 she healed a child at her sister's behest, and subsequently she assumed her role as an Eagle Doctor. She eventually incorporated elements of the Native American Church and Christianity into her traditional teachings.

By the 1960s she was the last surviving Comanche Eagle Doctor with maximum powers. Concerned that she would not be able to pass on her powers before dying, she allowed anthropologist David E. Jones to write an account of her life and her healing powers. They produced a book in 1972, which she hoped would serve as a training manual for the future generations.

See also NATIVE AMERICANS: Comanches.

Akim D. Reinhardt
Towson University

Jones, David E. *Sanapia, Comanche Medicine Woman*. New York: Holt, Rinehart and Winston, 1972.

SHELDON, CHARLES (1857–1946)

Born February 26, 1857, at Wellsville, New York, son of a poor congregational preacher, Charles Monroe Sheldon was the author of some thirty Christian social novels, including *In His Steps* (1897), a phenomenally successful instructional novel. His latter youth was spent in the Dakotas. Subsequently educated at Brown University and Andover Theological Seminary, he ministered at Waterbury, Vermont, for two years before accepting a call to Central Congregational Church in Topeka, Kansas (1889), where he remained for the rest of his life.

Sheldon began writing in his teens and seems never to have stopped. At Central Church he delivered Sunday evening serial sermons dealing in a fictional manner with the challenge to church and society of a host of contemporary ills: unemployment, poverty, the alienation of upper and lower classes, exploitation by landlords, racial discrimination, the menace of the liquor trade, sensationalism in the media, corruption at city hall, labor extremists and radical nostrums, hypocrisy in the churches, and the failure of philanthropy and the gospel of wealth to cure an ailing world. First published by installment in religious magazines and then as full novels, Sheldon's works reflected his own unceasing activism as a social reformist minister. He made an indelible impact, bringing the larger world of Christian social reform to Topeka and the Great Plains and making the region's single most important contribution to the popular Christian social movement that was at the core of early-twentieth-century progressivism.

In His Steps was the best-seller among a growing genre of Christian social novels welling up out of the 1870s and 1880s, whose success owed much to the widespread Protestant proscription of reading secular fiction but probably owed more to the anxiety among middle- and upper-class Protestants in the face of dramatic social changes undermining both their sense of community and their sense of social control. Entirely unsophisticated in plot, characterization, theology, or social analysis, the novels prescribed a simple, enduring formula: "What would Jesus do?" Sheldon presented the resulting encounter of upper- and middle-class Protestants with working-class America in unabashedly sentimental and melodramatic terms that touched the consciences of millions.

Sheldon gave no sign of the radical Christian socialism of George Herron in Iowa or W. D. P. Bliss in Boston, with whom he, however, had considerable contact, and he seems not to have recognized the strain of labor Christianity among labor leaders like Eugene Debs, although he saw more potential in the working class than was normally allowed in midcentury Christian novels. Like his counterpart best-selling western Canadian Christian social novelist Ralph Connor (Rev. C. W. Gordon), Sheldon's locus of social progress lay in changing the hearts of persons of standing, which linked him in certain ways with the contemporary revivalism of Dwight Moody. Sheldon died in Topeka on February 24, 1946, after a long, active retirement increasingly focused on the cause of world peace.

See also LITERARY TRADITIONS: Gordon, Charles W.

Richard Allen
Hamilton, Ontario

Boyer, Paul S. "*In His Steps*: A Reappraisal." *American Quarterly* 23 (Apr. 1971): 60–78. Ferré, John P. *A Social Gospel for Millions: The Religious Bestsellers of Charles Sheldon, Charles Gordon, and Harold Bell Wright*. Bowling Green OH: Bowling Green State University Press, 1988. Miller, Timothy. *Following in His Steps. A Biography of Charles M. Sheldon*. Knoxville: University of Tennessee Press, 1987.

SUN DANCE

The Sun Dance is a distinctive ceremony that is central to the religious identity of the Indigenous peoples of the Great Plains. It developed among the horse-mounted, bison-hunting nations who populated the Great Plains in the eighteenth and nineteenth centuries. Those nations at the core of its practice in the bison-hunting era that have continued its practice into the contemporary period include the Arapahos, the Cheyennes (Southern and Northern), the Blackfoot (who include the Siksikas or Blackfoot proper, the Bloods or Kainahs, and the Northern and Southern Piegans or Pikunis), and the Sioux (including in particular the westernmost Sioux, who are the seven tribes of the Lakota nation, but also including the Yanktons and Santees, who comprise the six tribes of the Dakota nation). From these four nations, the Sun Dance ceremony spread to the Kiowas and Comanches, who ranged the Southern Plains, and to Northern Plains nations such as the Plains Crees of Saskatchewan and the Sarcees of Alberta, as well as to virtually every other Plains nation in the land between these two extremes, including the Arikaras, Assiniboines, Crows, Gros Ventres, Hidatsas, Mandans, Pawnees, Plains Ojibwas, Poncas, Shoshones, and Utes.

The Canadian and U.S. governments perceived this ceremony as superstitious rather than religious and suppressed it, and full liberty to practice the Sun Dance was regained only after the mid–twentieth century. Some Sun Dances, including the Kiowa, Comanche, and Crow ceremonies, ended in the nineteenth century. Others persisted clandestinely through the time of suppression. The Crows in 1941 formally renewed practice of the ceremony by receiving the Shoshone form as their own.

The name Sun Dance derives from the Sioux identification of it as *Wi wanyang wacipi*, translated as "sun gazing dance." Other Plains peoples have names for the ceremony that do not refer to the sun. The Arapaho, Cheyenne, and Blackfoot names for the ceremony all refer to the medicine lodge within which the ritual dancing occurs. The medicine lodge is constructed of pole rafters radiating from a sacred central pole. However, the best-known and most widely practiced contemporary form of the ceremony is that of the Sioux, who do not construct a medicine lodge. Instead, the Sioux make a *hocoka*, or ritual circle, with a sacred cottonwood tree erected in the center and a circular arbor built around the entire perimeter, except for an open entrance to the east, so that the dancing takes place within a central arena that is completely open to the sky and to "sun gazing." However, both traditions, whether that of the medicine lodge or of the hocoka, involve ritual ways of making local space sacred as a setting for renewal of the people's relationship with the land itself and with all the beings of their life-world, both human and other-than-human.

The ceremony is highly variable because its performance is intimately connected to the authoritative guidance of visions or dreams that establish an individual relationship between one or more of the central participants and one or more spirit persons. In all cases, however, the primary meaning is understood to be the performance of acts of sacrifice in ritual reciprocity with spiritual powers so that the welfare of friends, family, and the whole people is enhanced. The Arapaho, Cheyenne, Blackfoot, and Sioux nations all practice sacrificial acts of piercing the flesh, often described pejoratively as "torture" by outsiders. Others, such as the Ute, Shoshone, and Crow nations, perform sacrificial acts of embodying their spiritual intentions through fasting and intense dancing, but not through piercing.

Some Indigenous interpreters have suggested an analogy between the piercing of sun dancers and the piercing of Jesus on the cross, seeing both as acts of voluntary sacrifice on behalf of other beings and the cosmic welfare. While this interpretation may facilitate understanding for some, interpreters must be wary of imposing any religious category that clashes with the central concern of the Sun Dance: to establish and maintain kinship with all the people's relatives, including other humans, the animal and plant relatives of this earth, and the cosmic relatives of the spirit realm.

See also ARCHITECTURE: Native American Traditional Architecture.

Dale Stover
University of Nebraska at Omaha

Densmore, Frances. *Teton Sioux Music and Culture*. Lincoln: University of Nebraska Press, 1992. Dorsey, George Amos. *The Arapaho Sun Dance: The Ceremony of the Offerings Lodge*. Field Columbian Museum Publication, no. 75. Chicago: Field Museum of Natural History, 1903. Farr, William E. *The Reservation Blackfeet, 1882–1945: A Photographic History of Cultural Survival*. Seattle: University of Washington Press, 1986.

SWEAT LODGE

The sweat lodge is a contemporary religious ritual of ancient origin used by Native Americans throughout the Great Plains. Eastern Indian groups removed to the Plains by the U.S. government also engage in ceremonial sweating. Groups like the Cherokees and Chickasaws originally utilized permanent, dome-shaped log houses with subterranean floors that were also used for sleeping in winter. This entry will focus on the original Plains groups, among whom the ceremony takes place in a small, circular domed structure constructed of pliable saplings (often willow) with a single entrance facing a specific cardinal direction. The frame of this impermanent structure is tightly covered, formerly with skins but today with blankets, tarps, and sometimes sheet plastic. A pit is dug in the lodge to receive stones that are heated in a fire outside the lodge. This fireplace and frequently a mounded altar constructed of earth excavated from the interior pit are aligned with the entrance of the lodge.

The ceremony consists in entering the lodge, filling the pit with hot stones that are reverenced as ancient and spiritual in nature, pouring water on the hot rocks, praying, singing, speaking from one's heart, closing and opening the door a set number of times, and emerging from the lodge. Important elements in the ceremony that vary in emphasis from group to group are communication with the spiritual realm, moral and/or physical purification, the humbling of oneself, healing of self and/or others through the physical and/or spiritual agency of the sweat, and voluntary suffering to achieve a specific need or to fulfill a pledge for requests already granted.

Variations in the ceremony and structure of the lodge are accounted for by three factors: historic era, cultural group, and specific ritual leader. Nevertheless, there is remarkable consistency in the core ritual and structure across time and among different Plains groups. Variations include the incorporation of a prayer pipe and a variety of symbolic objects such as a buffalo skull placed on the altar outside of the sweat lodge; the erection of a pole on which to tie offerings; the use of switches made of sage, willow, cherry, buffalo tail, or horse hair; song accompaniment with a drum and/or rattle; the sacred use of plants such as sage, cedar, or pine needles; the pouring of herbal infusions on the rocks; drinking water between rounds and sometimes pouring it on oneself; spiritual supplication through crying; spiritual talks, particularly by the leader and sometimes other participants; joking when the door is open; and bathing in a cold stream at the conclusion of the ceremony.

The sweat lodge can be a ceremony in itself but is also used in preparation for other ceremonies such as the Sun Dance, sacred bundle ceremonies, vision quests, and sometimes Native American Church meetings. Among some tribes, men and women sweat together, while in others they are segregated. There are ritual restrictions for women in menses.

The ritual is widely used for marking significant life events, consoling and encouraging, protecting the group from misfortune such as disease, succeeding in battle and hunting, predicting future events, and averting future disaster. Many traditional stories of the revival of the dead through the agency of the sweat lodge attest to the great power of this ceremony.

The ceremony has markedly increased in practice since the beginning of the twentieth century, not only by Indian people on the reservations but more recently in urban areas, correctional facilities, veterans groups, and substance abuse treatment facilities. The spiritual strengthening and social conviviality inherent in the sweat serve to unite family members, Indians from different tribes, and non-Indians, although the proper place and role of outsiders in the sweat lodge and in Indian ritual in general are controversial.

See also ARCHITECTURE: Native American Traditional Architecture.

Raymond A. Bucko
Le Moyne College

Bruchac, Joseph. *The Native American Sweat Lodge: History and Legends.* Freedom CA: Crossing Press, 1993. Bucko, Raymond A., S.J. *The Lakota Ritual of the Sweat Lodge: History and Contemporary Practice.* Lincoln: University of Nebraska Press, 1998. Vecsey, Christopher. "The Genesis of Phillip Deere's Sweat Lodge." In *Imagine Ourselves Richly: Mythic Narratives of North American Indians,* edited by Christopher Vecsey. New York: Crossroad, 1988: 206–32.

TACHÉ, ALEXANDRE-ANTONIN (1823–1894)

Born on July 23, 1823, in Rivière-du-Loup, Quebec, Alexandre-Antonin Taché completed his classical studies at the Saint Hyacinthe College and studied theology at the Seminary of Montreal prior to entering the noviciate of the Oblates of Mary Immaculate in Longueuil. In 1845 he was sent as a subdeacon to serve in the Red River missions, thereby becoming the first French Canadian Oblate to serve in the Canadian Northwest. He was named coadjutor bishop of St. Boniface in 1850, bishop in 1853, and archbishop in 1871.

As a pioneer missionary and bishop, Taché contributed significantly to the establishment of the Catholic Church in western Canada. In 1870 he was asked by the Canadian government to be its mediator during the events known as the Red River Resistance. He was instrumental in negotiating a settlement but later criticized the government for having broken its promise to grant a complete amnesty to all participants, including Louis Riel. Taché regarded Manitoba as a sister province of Quebec, and hence, he and his clergy strove incessantly to promote French Canadian immigration to the Northwest. He was also a vigilant defender of the linguistic and educational rights of French-speaking Catholics in the Northwest. The last years of Taché's life were involved in the controversy surrounding the abolition of confessional schools in Manitoba and the suppression of French as an official language. He wrote numerous pamphlets and letters denouncing this legislation. He died in St. Boniface on June 22, 1894.

See also EUROPEAN AMERICANS: French Canadians / PROTEST AND DISSENT: Riel, Louis / WAR: Red River Resistance.

Raymond J. A. Huel
University of Lethbridge

Archives de l'Archidiocèse de Saint-Boniface, Fonds Taché. Dom Paul Benoît. *Vie de Mgr Taché, Archêveque de Saint-Boniface.* Montréal: Librairie Beauchemin, 1904.

UNITARIANISM

The Unitarian movement originated in sixteenth-century Europe among radical Christians who affirmed the undivided unity of God and promoted a form of religion in which human unity would be based upon individual freedom and reliance upon reason and conscience. In New England the movement emerged early in the nineteenth century, but it was slow in spreading westward, being predominant among the middle class and well educated, and therefore ill adapted to frontier conditions. The same was not true of a parallel movement, the Universalists, but by the time they reached the Great Plains in the 1860s, they had already lost much of their momentum. In 1961 the Unitarians and Universalists merged to form the Unitarian Universalist Association, though most individual congregations retained their single name.

Early Unitarian attempts at extension into the Great Plains bore fruit only in the major cities, all of which had congregations by the end of the nineteenth century. The first was at Omaha in 1869; the largest, that in Tulsa, was exceptional in not having been founded until 1921. Fellowships that now exist in smaller communities have all been established or re-established since 1950. The congregation in Sioux Falls may serve as an example. It mushroomed in 1887, erecting a fine stone church, but was forced by the economic depression to disband ten years later, bequeathing its building to the city as a public library. The present congregation dates from 1961. The inclusion of both Unitarians and Universalists in the original Sioux Falls congregation was typical for the Great Plains but unusual elsewhere. So also was the fact that it was founded and led by women ministers at a time when these constituted no more than a tiny fraction of the active ministry in either denomination as a whole.

A third characteristic shared by all congregations in the Plains was that they were from the outset much more theologically radical than their coreligionists on the East Coast, who continued to maintain a more or less exclusively Christian emphasis. Thus, the new "Bond of Union" adopted by the Omaha congregation in 1890 simply affirmed moral and religious purpose rather than making any specific statement of belief. Such openness paved the way for the strong emergence of nontheistic humanism in the congregations of the Great Plains during the twentieth century.

Unitarians have typically worked in projects for the betterment of the entire community. An outstanding leader in this field was Arthur L. Westerly, a minister in Lincoln, Nebraska (1908–19 and 1929–42), who was active in a wide variety of civic projects and social reforms. The Joslyn family in Omaha likewise contributed heavily to the artistic and musical life of the community.

The congregations have been composed chiefly of persons coming from other parts of North America rather than from overseas. The only exceptions were small-scale movements among Scandinavian immigrants and a much more substantial one among the Icelanders who settled in North Dakota and the Prairie Provinces of Canada. The Icelandic Unitarian Church in Winnipeg was founded in 1891, and until the 1920s most Unitarians in Manitoba and Saskatchewan attended services conducted in Icelandic.

Unitarians have been large in influence but not in numbers, and this has been markedly true in the Great Plains. Figures from 1998 show between 8,000 and 9,000 congregational members, of whom about 750 are in Canada.

Phillip Hewett
Unitarian Church of Vancouver,
British Columbia

Gudmundson, V. Emil. *The Icelandic Unitarian Connection*. Winnipeg: Wheatfield Press, 1984. Lyttle, Charles H. *Freedom Moves West*. Boston: Beacon Press, 1952. Tucker, Cynthia Grant. *Prophetic Sisterhood*. Boston: Beacon Press, 1990.

UNITED CHURCH OF CANADA

The action that brought into being the United Church of Canada was the culmination of successive initiatives beginning with the merger of the four sections of Presbyterianism in 1875 to form the "Presbyterian Church in Canada." The Methodists followed suit in 1884 and the Congregationalists in 1906. The actual negotiations leading up to the formation of the United Church of Canada began when the Board of Home Missions of both the Presbyterian and Methodist Churches, concerned over the duplication of services, especially in the West, adopted a plan of amalgamation. The initial step was to develop a "Basis of Union," founded on goodwill, concession, and compromise and which included a strategy for informing and educating members and adherents. The first meeting of the Joint Union Committee was held in Toronto, on April 21, 1904. It reached the unanimous conclusion "that organic union is both desirable and practicable." Invitations were extended to the Church of England and the Baptist churches in Canada. Although cordially received, the judicatories of these bodies respectfully declined to participate in a wider dialogue of church union. By 1908 a basis of union was agreed upon and was subsequently ratified by plebiscites.

In the meantime, there came into existence in western Canada, mainly in Saskatchewan, a large number of local union churches, which formed the "General Council of Local Union Churches." Beginning in 1921, representatives of the council were welcomed to the early meetings of the Joint Union Committee. Draft bills for the Parliament of Canada and provincial legislatures were prepared and carefully considered during the years 1921–24. These were approved by the supreme courts of the churches. The necessary legislation was enacted in 1924 by Parliament, and from 1924 to 1926 by the legislatures of the various provinces. On June 10, 1925, the union of the three churches was solemnly consummated in the Mutual Street Arena, Toronto, in the presence of more than 8,000 members.

The United Church of Canada is the largest Protestant denomination in Canada. In 1990 it was the leading denomination in much of southern Alberta, southern Saskatchewan, and southwestern Manitoba, and the second largest denomination, after Catholicism, elsewhere in virtually all of rural Alberta and in those parts of southern Saskatchewan and southern Manitoba where it was not first in church membership.

The United Church is dedicated to being a uniting church, reaching out to diverse sectors of Canadian society. It covers a wide spectrum of beliefs and is committed to ecumenism. The church has a strong tradition of voluntary services and a larger share of rural congregations than most other denominations. Women have been able to become ordained ministers since 1936. The liberal thinking of the church is perhaps best exemplified by the statement of the General Council on August 15, 1986, which strongly repudiated the policies of its Methodist and Presbyterian forebears in promoting assimilation programs among Native Canadians, policies that continued into the twentieth century in the context of residential boarding schools. The council asked Native peoples to forgive the church for the irreparable damage it had done and looked toward a future of reconciliation and healing.

See also EDUCATION: Indian Residential Schools, Canada.

Bill Cantelon
Edmonton, Alberta

Gaustad, Edwin Scott, and Philip L. Barlow. *New Historical Atlas of Religion in America*. Oxford: Oxford University Press, 2001. Noll, Mark A. *A History of Christianity in the United States and Canada*. Grand Rapids MI: William B. Eerdmans Publishing Co., 1992.

VISION QUEST

For thousands of years, the nations of the Great Plains celebrated their interdependency with nature in ceremonies such as the vision quest. They accounted the environment that sustained them to be sacred. They saw how the buffalo gave itself to the people, how the grass gave itself to buffalo, how the rain gave itself to grass—how the people, like all their earthly relations, gave themselves back to the vast Plains that sustained them. They called the dark earth "Mother" and the great sun "Father," and they revered the Great Creator, not as some abstract principle but as the palpable design, function, and constant presence of their environment.

Hence, the great sun, the dark earth, and the endless horizon, particularly as viewed from the traditional precincts of Mateo Tepee (Devils Tower), the Black Hills, and the Northern Rockies, became the Great Creator's initiation ground, the passageway for individuals in life transition. Their rites involved spiritual education that was fundamental to their existence. If, indeed, they lived in the home of the Great Creator, then clearly they would consider the significant growth events of their lives to be occasions for ceremony and spiritual edification.

Largely "confirmatory" in function (marking the attainment of changed social status), these rites followed the classic anthropological definition of rites of passage: severance—preparation to leave the former life and go into a sacred time and space, including rites of purification in a sweat lodge; threshold—existence (often three or four days and nights) alone in a sacred world of taboo and self-abnegation, where the individual sacrificed the self to a greater whole and attained "medicine" or visionary power; and incorporation—return to a council of elders and subsequent reintegration within the community as individuals with changed social status.

The objective of the threshold, or mountaintop, experience, was a medicine vision of benefit to the people as a whole. Without food, water, companionship, shelter, or defenses against predators, sometimes in great pain from self-inflicted wounds, the body longed for spiritual answers. The sacred ancestors sent dreams to console and inspire, and the Great Spirit provided "allies" or "helpers." When the initiates returned from this time with the Great Creator and the sacred ancestors, they were considered to have confirmed visionary intent. If the intent were not confirmed, the candidates would often return again—and again until signs from nature indicated that the quest had been consummated. Thus, the community was blessed by the spiritual growth of its members, and every vision took its place in the legendary annals of the people.

Many forms of what, in the English language, has become known as the vision quest were practiced among the people of the Great Plains. Traditions were passed down from medicine men to their apprentices for many generations. The most widely published traditions were recorded by observant Europeans when medicine chiefs were willing to teach them the old ways. Black Elk's *Sacred Pipe* (as told to Joseph Epes Brown) contains a classic depiction of the seven rites of the Oglala Sioux, including a thorough description of the *hanblecheyapi*, or "crying for a vision." Similar noble rites existed among the Crows, Blackfoot, Cheyennes, Arapahos, Pawnees, Kiowas, Crees, and many other peoples, including the Native nations of the Northwest Coast, Great Basin, Eastern Woodlands, and Southwest.

This same ritual vision-quest archetype is known by many other names in cultures throughout the world. Although this tradition has declined in the face of modern life, the rite is still practiced among the Indigenous people of the Great Plains.

See also NATIVE AMERICANS: Sacred Geography.

Steven Foster
School of Lost Borders
Big Pine, California

Brown, Joseph Epes. *The Sacred Pipe: Black Elk's Account of the Seven Rites of the Oglala Sioux*. Norman: University of Oklahoma Press, 1953. Mails, Thomas E. *The Mystic Warriors of the Plains: The Culture, Arts, Crafts, and Religion of the Plains Indians*. New York: Mallard Press, 1972. Van Gennep, Arnold. *The Rites of Passage*. Chicago: University of Chicago Press, 1972.

WOODSWORTH, JAMES SHAVER

See PROTEST AND DISSENT: Woodsworth, James Shaver

Sports and Recreation

Six-man football, McCool Junction, Nebraska, 1998

SPORTS AND RECREATION

In many respects, sports and recreation in the Great Plains are no different from those activities in other North American regions. Every weekend, parents take their boys and girls to play in local soccer leagues, college football teams compete for honors on the gridiron, and golfers stride the fairways. But in important ways, there are attributes of sports and recreation that are particular to the Great Plains or are particularly emphasized in the Great Plains and that are, therefore, distinguishing characteristics of the region's personality. Six-man football, for example, is a Plains innovation, a response to a sparse population in rural areas and the inadequate supply of players for the conventional game. There are annual events such as the Calgary Stampede, the Crow Fair, and the Sturgis Motorcycle Rally that are purely Plains affairs, and there are the great sportsmen and sportswomen such as Jim Thorpe, Gordie Howe, and Nancy Lopez whose achievements have brought distinction to the region. More mundanely, there is the small-town ritual of "cruising around" from the Dairy Queen to the cornfields and back; the tractor pull, a featured event at county and state fairs; and the softball game, a true community event and intergenerational activity. Any discussion of sports and recreation in the Great Plains, however, must start with Native American games, which were played throughout the region for centuries.

Native American Traditions

Traditionally, Native American games were inseparable from their religions. Native American creation stories often involved contests between two opposing Twin Gods armed with clubs or bows and arrows. Games were replays of those creation stories while at the same time providing forums for achievement, recreation, and gambling.

Native American games fall into two broad categories: games of chance and games of dexterity. The former includes dice games and hidden ball games; the latter includes archery, the snow snake, the hoop and pole game, and various ball and running games. Many of these games were played throughout Native North America, but all had their local expressions in the Great Plains.

Dice games, involving dice made from many different materials, were played by every Plains tribe. They were generally played at night after the day's labor was done, and they sometimes went on all night, with considerable stakes involved. More often than not, they were played by women. Blackfeet women in Montana, for example, used four elaborately etched bison rib bones as dice. Sitting opposite each other, the women threw the dice on the ground, adding scores according to which side was up, until a winning score of twelve was attained. Omaha and Cheyenne women used plum stones with patterns burned into one side, and the dice were thrown into a wooden bowl or basket.

The hand game was one of the most widely played games of chance. Because it was done entirely by gesture, it could be played between members of different tribes who did not speak each other's language. In this game, an object made of bone, wood, shell, or hide was moved rapidly from hand to hand by one of the players. The opposing player, carefully tracking the sleight of hand, had to judge which hand held the object. The performance was accompanied by singing, which started out low and built to a crescendo as the swaying player switched the object back and forth until a hand was chosen. This was a man's game and often an occasion of competition between members of different tribes. There is an account of such a game on a Kiowa calendar from 1881–82. A Kiowa leader, Buffalo Bull Coming Out, was challenged by an Apache chief and medicine man. Both claimed the supernatural powers necessary to win. A large crowd waged prized possessions on the outcome, and the victory went to the Kiowa chief.

Games with bows and arrows were ubiquitous in the Great Plains and took many forms. For example, Pawnee boys or men would try to shoot arrows across another arrow that had been placed on the ground. The winner took all the arrows. In one Mandan version, young men, having paid an entry fee of a bison robe or other valued item, would shoot arrows in the air, one after the other. The winner who kept the most arrows in the air at one time took the prizes home.

The snow snake was another game of dexterity that was played wherever frozen conditions prevailed. Played by men and women, young and old, it involved sliding polished rocks, shaped bones, or spears along a track in the ice or snow. The player who slid the implement the farthest or the most accurately to a designated point was the winner.

The hoop and pole game, in a great variety of versions, was played throughout the region. A hoop made of wood, often covered with rawhide and netted in various designs, was rolled down a flattened track. The contestants (two men) tried to throw rods through the hoop or across the hoop as it started to fall. Again, there was gambling on the outcome of the game, but this did not obscure its religious implications. The Skidi Pawnee, for example, played the game to attract the bison, the rods representing bison bulls and the hoop a bison cow.

Lacrosse was played on the Northern Great Plains and in Indian Territory in the second half of the nineteenth century, although it was more common in eastern North America. Shinny, played with a curved wooden bat and a wooden or buckskin ball, was more prevalent on the Plains. Shinny was particularly a woman's game, although it was also played by men and sometimes by men against women. The objective was to knock the ball through the opponent's often-distant goal. Footraces were also common, and, for a man, being a celebrated runner, especially over long distances, was valued only behind being a successful warrior and hunter.

Many of these games died out as European American games and sports were adopted. Of the introduced sports, none was more suited to Native American skills and tradition than rodeo, which continues the horsemanship skills of the Plains Indians. Continuity is also apparent in other developments. The contemporary powwow combines ceremony, gift giving, and the athleticism and grace of dance competition. Gaming, which so rapidly developed on reservations in the 1990s, clearly continues the deeply rooted Native American tradition of gambling. Long-distance running remains a Native American specialty, epitomized by Billy Mills, a Lakota from Pine Ridge Reservation who shot from the pack during the final 200 meters of the 10,000-meter final race at the 1964 Tokyo Olympics, breaking the Olympic record in the process. And in any list of the twentieth century's top athletes, Jim Thorpe of the Sauk and Fox Tribe of Oklahoma must surely rank near the top.

Sports and Recreation on the Great Plains Frontier

On the overland trails in the 1840s and 1850s and on the farms and ranches that were the foundation of nineteenth-century Plains society, there was little time for sports and recreation. On the trails, in the evening, when the horses were tethered and the dinner dishes cleared away, the sounds of a fiddle and laughing dancers might attest to a brief period of recreation before the serious business of a good night's sleep intervened. On the farm, the end of the harvest became an occasion for celebration and perhaps a community picnic, and work tasks like quilting and raising barns were facilitated by bringing neighbors together in a social event.

The Great Plains frontier was not only rural, however. In fact, towns were often created first: there had to be central places to provide land offices, goods and services, and market outlets for prospective farmers. These towns were points of connection, via railroad, telegraph, and newspaper, to the larger and more sophisticated cities to the east. Fads and fashions diffused westward, including new varieties of recreation and sports.

At the booming Kansas cattle towns of Wichita, Caldwell, and Dodge City in the 1880s there were two distinct seasons of recreational activities and two distinct social groups to pursue them. During late spring and summer, the cattle drives reached the towns, and the streets and saloons became a constant carnival. During the fall and winter season, the towns were left to their sedate, permanent populations and their respectable church socials and dances. These two groups represent, perhaps in exaggerated form, the larger American society of the time: the growing middle class, with its Victorian mores, emphasizing hard work and self-control, values that were antithetical to exciting sports and idle recreation; and the underclass (along with debauched aristocrats), which placed a much higher premium on play.

When the cattlemen reached the railhead towns, the respectable population withdrew. The towns filled up with actors, musicians, and other showmen. Bustling street scenes featured cockfights, bear baiting, pugilists, organ grinders with their monkeys, and tightrope walkers. The saloons and dance halls throbbed. The only time the two social strata mixed were when the circus (a European import) came to town or at an occasional polo game, which seemingly was genteel enough for the upper crust yet a natural for the cowboys.

When the cowboys left, resident social life took over. Culture was emphasized, with traveling acting troupes staging Shakespeare as well as popular melodramas. An opera house was essential. Light opera, particularly Gilbert and Sullivan, dominated the stage. Drama and literary societies flourished: the dawn of the "machine age" had ushered in an era of leisure for the middle classes, and in the Victorian era, leisure was to be used in edifying ways.

Individual, though again genteel, sports became popular in the 1880s. Croquet, suitable for women constrained by corsets, was the rage in the Kansas cattle towns in the 1880s. It provided a suitable context for courting. The contemporaneous American bicycle craze, however, did not take hold in Plains towns where the streets were often mud and everyone rode horses or, another innovation, drove a horse and buggy. Roller-skating was also very popular and the only one of the individualized sports to be commercialized. In 1884, for example, the citizens of Caldwell converted the lower floor of the Grand Opera House into a 65-by-15-foot rink. Not to be outdone, the following year Dodge City opened a skating rink and opera house with a 100-by-300-foot floor and a gallery for spectators, a relatively new development in sports and recreation.

Organized spectator sports were in their infancy in the 1880s throughout North America. Horse racing was an attraction for the citizens of the cattle towns, but baseball was the main spectator sport. Settlers coming into Kansas brought the sport with them. By 1867 Leavenworth was home to the Frontier Baseball Club, and by the 1880s there were competitive teams in Dodge City, Wichita, and Caldwell. The rules favored the batter (more effective overhand pitching was not permitted until 1884), which explains how Wichita could defeat Emporia by a score of 58 to 27.

Plains towns were not only importers of eastern fads; they also produced their own entertainers. On July 4, 1882, William F. Cody first featured his combined rodeo-circus-drama at North Platte, Nebraska. By 1887 Buffalo Bill's Wild West show was touring Europe. At the same time, the Dodge City Cowboy Band, regaled in exaggerated Western outfits, was playing to enthusiastic reviews throughout the Midwest. Significantly, these shows were not as popular in their home states, where they seemed phony, as they were in distant places, where they confirmed stereotypes.

The late nineteenth century also saw the beginning of organized sports in the Prairie Province region of Canada. This was allowed by the same developments that were taking place in the United States, not least of which were improved transportation systems that enabled teams and spectators to move between venues. But the situation in the Prairie Provinces was different from that in the American Great Plains in significant ways. A stronger British heritage was expressed in the greater popularity of sports such as cricket, rugby, soccer, and especially curling. The long and frigid winters reinforced the popularity of curling and stimulated the growth of ice hockey as well as indoor sports such as basketball. However, the isolation of the Prairie Provinces from the coasts, even after the completion of the Canadian Pacific Railway in 1885, resulted in north–south connections across the international boundary, which eventually introduced a strong American influence into the regional sporting scene, displacing traditional British sports.

The initial British influence on Prairie Provinces sports and society is shown, for example, in the founding of the Qu'Appelle, Saskatchewan, hunt club in 1889. The club purchased its hounds from the Toronto Hunt Club. The earliest introduced competitive team sports in the region were cricket and soccer. There was a Northwest Cricket Club in Manitoba, for example, in 1864. Soccer was often played by North-West Mounted Police teams against teams from local communities. Curling, introduced from Scotland (and still governed by the parent body based in Scotland as late as 1900), was both a major competitive sport and the main winter pastime of urban and rural dwellers throughout the region. Manitoba was generally the national curling champion in the 1920s and 1930s.

By 1905 ice hockey was the main competitive sport in the Prairie Provinces; every town, no matter how small, had a rink and a team. From its origins in Montreal in the 1880s, the game expanded to Manitoba by 1890. In its early years, ice hockey was a middle-class sport and strictly amateur. The first city leagues in Winnipeg, Regina, and Edmonton were sponsored by colleges, banks, newspapers, and churches. The institutionalization of ice hockey in the schools ensured a steady supply of players, and gradually Prairie Provinces teams were able to compete with the established eastern teams. In 1920, at the Antwerp Olympics, the Winnipeg Falcons proved that the Canadians were the best in the world by winning all their games and the gold medal. The tradition has continued: the Edmonton Oilers of the 1980s were one of the finest teams of all time.

The Prairie Provinces, however, were also receptive to the developing American national sports, basketball, baseball, and football. This was largely the result of the northward migration of Americans across the forty-ninth parallel in the late nineteenth and early twentieth centuries. The Mormon community in Raymond, in southern Alberta, was particularly influential in the establishment of basketball. In this area, basketball was also aided and abetted by the warm chinook winds, which frequently melt the ice, thus impeding outdoor curling and ice hockey. Basketball caught on widely: from 1915 to 1940 the Edmonton Grads were the best women's team in the world.

Baseball and American football (with Canadian variations) developed at the expense of cricket and rugby, demonstrating the growth of the American influence on Canadian society in general. Baseball became the main summer sport and recreational activity in the Prairie Provinces soon after 1900. No sports day or Dominion Day in a small town was complete without an intercommunity game. At the professional level (money was involved in Canadian baseball from the start), teams from Edmonton and Winnipeg were playing American rivals from Grand Forks, Fargo, and Jamestown by 1905. Similarly, Canadian football teams, often associated with universities, were competing against teams from North Dakota by 1920. Clearly, in the arena of competitive sports in the early twentieth century, the Northern Great Plains and the Prairie Provinces were part of the same region.

Twentieth-Century Scenes

In the twentieth century, Plains sports, like sports elsewhere in North America, became institutionalized and commercialized to an extent that could not have been imagined when organized sports were in their infancy in 1900. Baseball led the way, complete with its hierarchy of leagues, its famous stadiums, and its World Series. Top players, both heroes and villains, were as famous as Hollywood stars. Far from this glamour, in small towns throughout the Plains young men played in the summer minor leagues, dreaming of emulating their heroes or at least of making enough money to attend college. For two generations before 1950, baseball held the promise, an illusion for most, of a life beyond the local.

After 1950 television changed the nature of sports (for example, adding at least thirty minutes of commercials to each professional football game) and moved the spectator into the living room. This, in turn, changed recreational patterns, resulting in some people spending a substantial amount of time in the armchair in front of television sports. Countering this, and partly in reaction to it, was the rise of mass participation in sports and leisure activities as the foundation for a healthy lifestyle. Indeed, in the second half of the twentieth century, as the following examples demonstrate, some people's identities were linked as much to what they did in their leisure time as to what they did for a job.

Football, particularly college and high school football, is the preeminent competitive sport and a powerful shaper of community identity over much of the Great Plains. The professional game is also important but less pervasive on the American Plains, because the region's teams are few (the Denver Broncos and the Kansas City Chiefs) and in peripheral locations. In the Prairie Provinces, the Canadian version of football (with its larger field, twelve-man teams, and three downs to advance the ball ten yards) is well represented in successful professional teams in Calgary, Edmonton, and Winnipeg. But there, ice hockey has pride of place in both allegiance and participation.

College football on the American Great Plains is more than a sport. For better or worse, the prestige and self-respect of states are intimately connected to the fortunes of their university football teams. There has, indeed, been great success: the University of Oklahoma was national champion in 1950, 1955, 1956, 1974, 1975, and 2000, the University of Nebraska–Lincoln won the honor in 1970, 1971, 1994, 1995, and 1997 (shared), and the University of Colorado was the nation's best college team in 1991 (shared). Eleven Heisman Trophy winners have rushed and passed their ways out of Plains universities. Stadiums are consistently filled on game days. Memorial Stadium in Lincoln, Nebraska, temporarily becomes the state's third largest population concentration when the Cornhuskers are playing at home. Iconography abounds as supporters don their team's colors, and team flags proclaim allegiance up and down the block. Stores, restaurants, and bars do more business than the rest of the week combined. Universities do well too: the football coach is often the highest paid employee, and successful teams like Nebraska have athletic department budgets (garnered from merchandise sales, concessions, television contracts, and game receipts) that small countries might well envy.

The heart of Plains football, however, beats fastest in the innumerable small towns that punctuate the region's sparsely populated spaces. Local high school teams are emblems of community pride. Their successes are proclaimed on the sign that greets the visitor to the town (Class C State Champions, 1954), and their failures are lamented in taverns and coffee shops. Within the Great Plains, there is no more important high school football tradition than in Texas and Oklahoma.

Sports geographer John Rooney has proven, quantitatively, that the Southern Great Plains is one of the two most important areas of high school football in the United States, producing more players for the college game than any others. (The other region is the northern Appalachians of Pennsylvania, Ohio, and West Virginia, significantly, an early source for many migrants to the Texas and Oklahoma oil fields.) The counties centered on the Texas oil towns of Midland and Odessa, the Texas Panhandle, and a broad zone reaching from about Abilene, Texas, into western Oklahoma turn out approximately four times as many college football players per capita than the national average. Rugged individualism, the lack of alternative outlets for achievement, deep-rooted traditions, and strong community support are some of the reasons for this preeminence. In some small towns in Texas, more than 50 percent of the males try out for the football team, and stadium capacities often exceed the communities' populations. There is a dark side to this, however. Enthusiasm crosses over into fanaticism, performance in the classroom becomes less important than performance on the field, and people's lives are collapsed into football, which is, after all, only a game.

Rodeo is also more prominent in the Great Plains than in other Canadian and American regions. The sport emerged from the Plains open range cattle era and remains closely connected to ranching. The first "cowboy tournaments" ("rodeo," from the Spanish *rodear*, which means "to encircle," was not used until the early twentieth century) took place on the range in the 1870s, as practical skills of roping and riding were displayed in competitions between different outfits. The contests evolved, attracted spectators, and moved from the range to towns. Early competitions were often associated with Wild West shows, which featured bucking, roping, and steer-wrestling competitions. Cheyenne Frontier Days, first held in 1897 (and held annually since that time), initially combined these rodeo contests with Wild West activities such as sham battles and stagecoach holdups.

As rodeo evolved, its procedures were formalized, and professional governing bodies were organized. The Rodeo Association of America was formed in 1928, later to mature into the Professional Rodeo Cowboys Association. The Canadian Rodeo Association was organized in 1944. In 1929 the Rodeo Association of America began naming an all-around champion based on performances in bareback riding, bull riding, calf roping, saddle bronc riding, and steer wrestling. These events remain standard in any rodeo, regardless of location. Barrel racing is included in some rodeos but often as a side event: in the predominantly male world of competitive rodeo, this is the only event that women and girls are allowed to enter. Women as rodeo queens, do, however, play important roles in rodeos, especially in promoting the event. There are separate women's rodeos, sponsored by the Women's Professional Rodeo Association of Blanchard, Oklahoma, and the greatest of all women rodeo stars, Barbara Tad Lucas, is from the Plains. There is also a junior circuit, with another Plains organization, the Little Britches Rodeo Association of Colorado Springs, a major sponsor. The primacy of the Great Plains region in this sport is further confirmed by the location of the headquarters of the Professional Rodeo Cowboys Association in Colorado Springs and the Canadian Rodeo Association in Calgary.

The prestigious rodeos such as Cheyenne Frontier Days and the Calgary Stampede are major economic and cultural events. In the 1980s, by one estimate, more than $3 million flowed into Cheyenne businesses during rodeo days. So ingrained is cowboy culture in the thoroughly modern city of Calgary that when a new indoor sports arena was constructed for the 1988 Winter Olympics it was named the Saddledome, and the roof was shaped accordingly. But, like high school football, the foundations of rodeo are local. In hundreds of communities from spring to fall, at fairs and carnivals, at colleges and impromptu affairs, the cowboy heritage of the Great Plains is celebrated in human-animal competitions, reinforcing the regional sense of rugged individualism.

Hunting, of course, also harks back to the region's recent frontier past, to a time when relations with nature were adversarial. Hunting for food may not be the necessity that it once was, but there is no denying that hunting retains its elemental role in Plains life. In every one of the Plains states, adults hunt, fish, and participate in other wildlife-associated recreation to a degree well above the national average. In North Dakota, for example, in 1985 45 percent of the adult population hunted, fished, or engaged in such "nonconsumptive" activities as wildlife observation and activity. These sporting and recreational activities earned $108 million for North Dakota that year from trip-related expenses, equipment, and permits. Some of this income is applied to wildlife preservation.

However, only 18 percent of North Dakotans hunt exclusively. In fact, there is concern in Plains states that hunting is a dying tradition. Although more women are hunting, the total number of hunters has been falling in recent years. Young people are not joining the ranks of hunters as much as in the past, despite efforts by states, through hunter education courses, to encourage them to do so. Opposition groups such as the Fund for Animals may be partly responsible for the decline of hunting. In the late 1990s the Fund for Animals offered a mountain bike valued at $1,000 to the first Wyoming youngster to turn in his or her permit for a special elk hunt and give up hunting for a season. No one took up the offer, but it does underscore the serious nature of activism against hunting. Other societal trends such as urbanization and multiple jobs, which reduce leisure time, may also be causes of the decline of participation in hunting.

Hunting and fishing are also controversial in other ways in the Great Plains. The landmark case *Montana v. United States*, which was decided by the Supreme Court in 1981, concerned the right of the Crow tribe to regulate hunting and fishing on lands within its reservation owned by non-Indians. The Court agreed that the Crows have the right to regulate non-Indian hunting on Indian lands on the reservation but denied that they have the right to regulate non-Indian hunting on non-Indian lands unless hunting threatened the tribe's political or economic security. Reservations up and down the Plains are patchworks of Indian and non-Indian lands, so hunting and fishing on reservations becomes a complicated matter, both practically and legally, involving contentious issues of sovereignty between tribes and states.

There is ample opportunity for Great Plains residents and visitors to enjoy the physical environment and cultural heritage of the region in lands set aside expressly for that purpose. Innumerable state parks, many of them the product of the Civilian Conservation Corps in the 1930s, are scattered throughout the Great Plains. North of the international boundary provincial parks provide similar hunting, fishing, and scenic amenities.

National parks are relatively few (Theodore Roosevelt National Park in North Dakota, Badlands and Wind Cave National Parks in South Dakota, Carlsbad Caverns National

Park in New Mexico, Riding Mountain National Park in Manitoba, and Elk Island National Park in Alberta), but there are many national monuments, national historic sites, and national recreation areas throughout the region.

As might be expected, national forests are also few. Indeed, the presence of any—for example, the McKelvie National Forest in the Nebraska Sandhills, which, after frequent fires, looks more like a savanna than a forest—may well seem like an ecological anomaly. The Great Plains, however, stand out on the map of national grasslands: seventeen of the twenty largest sites in the United States are in the region, including the largest, the Little Missouri National Grassland of North Dakota. That state also has the nation's major concentration of national wildlife areas, places put aside for the protection of endangered species or for the conservation of animals for hunting. Fully 108 of the total 844 national wildlife areas in the United States are in the prairie pothole lands of North Dakota.

Finally, it should be noted that from Denver and Calgary as well as from smaller urban concentrations in the lee of the Rocky Mountains, ski slopes and other sporting and recreational riches of the High Country are right at hand. Plains residents may be proud of their wide horizons and flowing grasslands, but that's no reason to eschew convenient mountains.

Future Scenarios

Given the accelerating pace of change in Great Plains sports and recreation over the last century, from the croquet craze in the Kansas cattle towns to the proliferation of spectator sports options in the age of television, it is difficult to anticipate future scenarios. New legislation can radically alter the sporting scene in a relatively brief period of time. Title IX of the Education Amendments Act of 1972, for example, ushered in a new era of competitive women's sports at American universities. There is now no fiercer rivalry in Plains sports than the Texas Tech–University of Texas women's basketball game. Changes in society can mean the demise of traditional sports. With continuing rural depopulation and associated school consolidation, six-man football will probably fade from the scene. Changes in technology can produce unforeseen opportunities for recreation. The abandonment of railroad tracks and their conversion into biking, hiking, and bridle trails (Rails to Trails) have greatly enhanced recreation in the Great Plains in recent years, allowing access into the countryside instead of around the perimeters of gridded farmland. Through satellite dishes, cable, and the Internet, Great Plains residents, no matter how isolated, now have easy access to international sports such as soccer or rugby that may well compete with national sports like football and rodeo for allegiance in the future. Still, the hold of those homegrown sports is tenacious. They are rooted in the region's past, and they continue to define its identity.

See also CITIES AND TOWNS: Cattle Towns / GENDER: Rodeo Queens / IMAGES AND ICONS: Cowboy Culture; Friday Night Football; Wild West Shows / LAW: *Montana v. United States* / MUSIC: Frontier Opera Houses.

Jeff Stuyt
Lubbock, Texas
David J. Wishart
University of Nebraska–Lincoln

Bissinger, H. G. *Friday Night Lights: A Town, a Team, and a Dream.* New York: HarperCollins, 1990. Culin, Stewart. *Games of the North American Indians.* Bureau of American Ethnology, 1902–3. Washington DC: Government Printing Office, 1907. Fredriksson, Kristine. *American Rodeo: From Buffalo Bill to Big Business.* College Station: Texas A&M University Press, 1985. Haywood, C. Robert. *Victorian West: Class and Culture in Kansas Cattle Towns.* Lawrence: University Press of Kansas, 1991. Howell, Maxwell L., and Reet A. Howell. *History of Sport in Canada.* Champaign IL: Stipes Publishing Company, 1985. Lawrence, Elizabeth Atwood. *Rodeo: An Anthropologist Looks at the Wild and Tame.* Chicago: University of Chicago Press, 1982. Metcalfe, Alan. *Canada Learns to Play: The Emergence of Organized Sport, 1807–1914.* Toronto: McClelland and Stewart Ltd., 1989. *National Survey of Fishing, Hunting, and Wildlife-Associated Recreation: North Dakota.* Washington DC: Department of the Interior, 1989. Rader, Benjamin G. *American Sports: From the Age of Folk Games to the Age of Televised Sports.* Englewood Cliffs NJ: Prentice-Hall, 1996. Rooney, John F., Jr. *A Geography of American Sport: From Cabin Creek to Anaheim.* Reading MA: Addison-Wesley Publishing Company, 1974. Zinser, Charles I. *Outdoor Recreation: United States National Parks, Forests and Public Lands.* New York: John Wiley and Sons, 1995.

ALEXANDER, GROVER CLEVELAND

(1887–1950)

Grover Cleveland Alexander

One of baseball's greatest pitchers, Grover Cleveland Alexander was inducted into the National Baseball Hall of Fame in 1938. His twenty-year career produced 373 victories, tying him with Christy Mathewson for most victories by a National League pitcher and placing him behind only Cy Young and Walter Johnson for major-league wins.

The son of an Elba, Nebraska, farmer, Alexander was born on February 26, 1887. His major-league career began in 1911 with the Philadelphia Phillies. At the end of his rookie season, he led the league in victories, shutouts, complete games, and innings pitched. From 1913 to 1917 Alexander's record was a stunning 143 wins and 50 losses. In the 1915 World Series he pitched the Phillies' only victory.

From 1919 to 1925 Alexander was the mainstay of the Chicago Cubs pitching staff. Placed on waivers in 1926, he was picked up by the St. Louis Cardinals and helped them clinch a pennant. The 1926 World Series against the New York Yankees produced Alexander's most remembered achievement, as he won two games and, in game seven, struck out Tony Lazzeri with the bases loaded.

After his 373rd victory in 1929, Alexander went on a drinking binge that ended his season. With the Phillies in 1930, he lost three starts, and his major-league career was over. Drinking problems marred his remaining years. He died in St. Paul, Nebraska, on November 4, 1950. A 1952 film biography starring Ronald Reagan, *The Winning Team*, highlighted Alexander's 1926 World Series heroics while downplaying his alcoholism.

Andrea I. Faling
Nebraska State Historical Society

Faling, Andrea I. "His Own Worst Enemy: The Rise and Fall of Grover Cleveland Alexander." *Nebraska History* 71 (1990): 3–12. Kavanagh, Jack. *Ol' Pete: The Grover Cleveland Alexander Story.* South Bend IN: Diamond Communications, 1996.

BASEBALL

The Plains states made important contributions to professional baseball throughout the course of the twentieth century. Among the hundreds of Plains natives who have played in baseball's major leagues are several players who have been recognized for their achievements as World Series champions, most valuable players, and members of baseball's Hall of Fame.

During the first half of the twentieth century, several Plains natives had careers that immortalized them in the history of America's national pastime. Tris Speaker, the "Grey Eagle" of Hubbard City, Texas, was regarded as one of baseball's great outfielders while playing for the Boston Red Sox and Cleveland Indians in the 1910s and 1920s. Speaker's 3,514 lifetime hits rank fifth in major-league history, and his 792 doubles and 309 triples rank him first all-time in both categories. Joe Tinker—one-third of the Chicago Cubs' famous "Tinker to Evers to Chance" infield—hailed from Muscotah, Kansas. Another Hall of Famer from baseball's early years is Sam Crawford of Wahoo, Nebraska.

Rogers Hornsby of Winters, Texas, starred for several teams. With the St. Louis Cardinals, Hornsby batted .424—the highest single-season batting average in major-league history—in 1924. "Rajah" won six consecutive batting titles between 1920 and 1925, and his career average of .358 is second in baseball history only to Ty Cobb. The Waner brothers, Paul and Lloyd, grew up in Harrah, Oklahoma, and starred in the outfield of the Pittsburgh Pirates in the 1920s and 1930s. Another Oklahoman, "Pepper" Martin of Temple, turned in what is still regarded as the best individual performance in a World Series in 1931, leading the St. Louis Cardinals to the championship with a .500 batting average.

Two of the era's outstanding pitchers were Grover Cleveland Alexander, a native of Elba, Nebraska, and Walter Johnson, who was born in Humboldt, Kansas. Alexander (who was played by Ronald Reagan in the movie, *The Winning Team*) starred for several teams and may be best remembered for his heroics in the 1926 World Series for the Cardinals. Johnson, who spent his career with the Washington Senators, held the career strikeout record for many years. Johnson's 417 lifetime victories rank him second to Cy Young in major-league baseball history, and Alexander ranks third with 373. Fifth on the all-time victory list is Warren Spahn, who has lived much of his adult life on a ranch near Hartshorne, Oklahoma.

The Plains continued to contribute players to the major leagues after World War II. Mickey Mantle of Commerce, Oklahoma, starred for the New York Yankees in the 1950s and 1960s. Mantle ranks fifth on the all-time home run list and is still regarded as one of baseball's greatest sluggers and most popular players. Among Mantle's Yankee teammates was fellow Oklahoman Allie Reynolds. Reynolds was born in Oklahoma City and starred at Oklahoma State University, whose baseball stadium is now named for him. In 1951 he became the first pitcher to throw two no-hitters in a single season. Bob Gibson of Omaha, Nebraska, was one of baseball's dominant pitchers in the 1960s. Gibson won seven World Series games with the St. Louis Cardinals in 1964, 1967, and 1968 and still holds the all-time record for most strikeouts in a World Series game. Richie Ashburn of Tilden, Nebraska, starred for the Philadelphia Phillies in the 1950s and later spent many years as the team's broadcaster before his death in 1997.

Johnny Bench of Binger, Oklahoma, is often regarded as the best catcher to play the game. Bench was selected most valuable player in the National League in 1970 and 1972 with the Cincinnati Reds. Bench teamed with Joe Morgan, who was born in Bonham, Texas, and was most valuable player in 1975 and 1976, to lead the "Big Red Machine" to consecutive championships. Willie Stargell, most valuable player with the Pittsburgh Pirates in 1979, was born in Earlsboro, Oklahoma. Stargell's American League counterpart as most valuable player, Don Baylor, was from Blanco, Texas. Baylor went on to additional success as manager of the Colorado Rockies in the 1990s. One of the top stars of the 1990s was Joe Carter of Oklahoma City. In 1993 Carter's ninth-inning home run won the final game of the World Series for the Toronto Blue Jays.

Although the Canadian portion of the Plains has not produced many major-league baseball players, pitcher Reggie Cleveland of Moose Jaw, Saskatchewan, and outfielder Terry Puhl of Melbourne, Saskatchewan, had notable careers in the 1970s and 1980s.

See also AFRICAN AMERICANS: Baseball, Interracial.

Fred M. Shelley
Southwest Texas State University

Porter, David L., ed. *Biographical Dictionary of American Sports: Baseball*. Westport CT: Greenwood Press, 2000.

BASEBALL, INTERRACIAL

See AFRICAN AMERICANS: Baseball, Interracial

BASKETBALL

The sport of basketball has a long and productive history in the Great Plains. Plains states and their universities have contributed many important players and coaches to this popular American sport.

Basketball was invented by Dr. James Naismith in Springfield, Massachusetts, in 1891. Naismith later moved to Lawrence, Kansas, as an instructor of physical education at the University of Kansas and the university's head basketball coach. Under Naismith and his successors, Kansas ranks third on the all-time National Collegiate Athletic Association (NCAA) victory list. The two universities with more victories were coached for many years by Plains natives Adolph Rupp of Halstead, Kansas (at Kentucky), and Dean Smith of Emporia, Kansas (at North Carolina).

Several college basketball teams from the Plains states have won national championships. Wyoming won in 1943, and Oklahoma State (then known as Oklahoma A&M) won titles in 1944 and 1945. The Cowboys were led by Bob Kurland, who became college basketball's first dominant big man. The University of Texas at El Paso (then Texas Western) won in 1966. The University of Kansas won the title in 1988.

Several Plains natives have been recognized as all-Americans for their achievements on the basketball court. Bob Boozer of Omaha twice won all-American honors at Kansas State University in the 1950s. Wichita, Kansas, produced all-Americans Darnell Valentine of the University of Kansas (1980) and Antoine Carr of Wichita State University (1981). Wayman Tisdale, born in Fort Worth, Texas, and raised in Tulsa, Oklahoma, became the first freshman to achieve all-American status at Oklahoma in 1983. He repeated as all-American in 1984 and 1985. Another Sooner, Stacey King of Lawton, Oklahoma, was an all-American in 1989. Mark Price of Enid, Oklahoma, became an all-American for Georgia Tech in the late 1980s. Bryant "Big Country" Reeves of Gans, Oklahoma, was an all-American center at Oklahoma State University in 1995.

Many of these college stars went on to fame as professional basketball players. In addition, Bill Sharman from Abilene, Texas, was a member of the Boston Celtics dynasty, which won eleven National Basketball Association (NBA) championships between 1957 and 1969. Sharman also coached the Los Angeles Lakers to the NBA title in 1971. The NBA's all-time leader in win percentage for coaches is coach Phil Jackson (Chicago Bulls/Los Angeles Lakers) of Williston, North Dakota. Two of the old American Basketball Association's stars were Zelmo Beaty of Hillister, Texas, and Ron Boone of Oklahoma City, Oklahoma.

In addition to organized professional and college basketball, the Plains states have been home to several important amateur basketball teams. Premier among these were the 66ers of Bartlesville, Oklahoma. Sponsored by the Phillips Petroleum Company, the 66ers attracted Kurland and other college stars of the 1940s and 1950s. They won several Amateur Athletic Union championships, and 66er players formed the core of U.S. basketball teams that won gold medals at the Olympic Games in 1948 and 1952. The 66er players also held professional positions with Phillips. Kurland eventually became mayor of Bartlesville, and several other 66ers rose to high executive positions with the company.

The Plains states have been a particularly productive source of women's basketball players and coaches. The Edmonton Grads were the best women's basketball team in the world in the 1920s and 1930s. Jody Conradt of Goldthwaite, Texas, the longtime coach of the University of Texas women's basketball team, is the all-time victories leader among women's coaches. Conradt was elected to the Basketball Hall of Fame in 1998. Two Plains natives have won the Wade Trophy, which is awarded annually to the outstanding player in women's college basketball. Kamie Ethcridge of Lubbock, Texas, who won in 1986, played for Conradt at the University of Texas. Lynette Woodard of Wichita, Kansas, who won the Wade Trophy in 1981 while playing for the University of Kansas, is women's college basketball's all-time leading scorer. Sheryl Swoopes of Brownfield, Texas, was the outstanding player in the women's Final Four in 1993 while leading Texas Tech to the national championship.

Fred M. Shelley
Southwest Texas State University

Douchant, Mike, ed. *The Encyclopedia of College Basketball*. Detroit: Gaines, 1995. Porter, David L., ed. *Biographical Dictionary of American Sports: Basketball and Other Indoor Sports*. Westport CT: Greenwood Press, 1989.

BROWNING, KURT (b. 1966)

Kurt Browning, sometimes called "Gene Kelly on Ice," set a new standard in the world of figure skating. The Canadian earned worldwide popularity due to his remarkable talent, showmanship, and sense of humor.

Born on June 18, 1966, in Rocky Mountain House, Alberta, Browning grew up playing hockey in Caroline, Alberta. He showed a natural talent for figure skating and at the age of sixteen moved to Edmonton to train. On March 25, 1988, he added his name to the *Guinness Book of World Records* by becoming the first person to successfully land a quadruple jump in competition. This athletic ability, in addition to his artistry, led to four Canadian championships and four world championship gold medals. The only amateur achievement that eluded him was an Olympic medal. The 1994 Olympic Games were not unrewarding, however, as he was given the honor of carrying the Canadian flag at the opening ceremonies.

Browning retired from amateur competition in 1994 and continued improving his skills at the professional level. He captured the titles of world professional champion three times, Canadian professional champion four times, and U.S. professional champion twice. He was inducted into the Canadian Figure Skating Hall of Fame on January 30, 2000.

The town of Caroline is proud of its hometown hero, and Browning still maintains his connections to the Plains. He serves as the honorary spokesperson for KidSport Society of Alberta, dedicated to "overcoming the obstacles that prevent some young people from playing sport." He was also proud to be named honorary captain for the Edmonton Oilers hockey team. In 1996 Kurt married Sonia Rodriguez, a principal dancer with the National Ballet of Canada, and they now live in Toronto, Ontario, when he is not on the road entertaining.

Sonja Rossum
University of Nebraska–Lincoln

Browning, Kurt. *Kurt: Forcing the Edge.* New York: HarperCollins Publishers, 1991.

CALGARY WINTER OLYMPICS

In 1988 Calgary, Alberta, welcomed the winter sport athletes of the world by hosting the XV Winter Olympic Games. For sixteen days in February, 2,300 athletes and team officials from fifty-seven countries participated in ten medal sports, one demonstration sport (curling), two demonstration events (freestyle skiing and short track speed skating), and one exhibition event (disabled skiing). Approximately 4,900 members of the media covered the events. Great Olympic champions like Katarina Witt and Raisa Smetanina shared the limelight with more eccentric competitors such as British ski jumper Michael Edwards ("Eddie the Eagle") and the Jamaican bobsled team.

The games cost $700 million (Canadian), about half of which funded the building of new sports facilities. Revenues totaled about $850 million, about 50 percent from the federal, provincial, and municipal governments, 35 percent from the ABC television contract, and the remaining 15 percent from marketing, licensing, and ticket sales. The financial legacies from the games have never been equaled by any other winter or summer games. The approximately $150 million left in the bank in 1988 had grown to about $280 million by 1998 and along the way had also provided about $30 million from earned interest to finance the operation of the various sport facilities and to support athletes.

The first indoor 400-meter speed-skating oval, a new physical education complex, and new residences (the Athletes' Village) were built at the university. Bobsled, luge, ski-jumping facilities, and a museum were built at Canada Olympic Park on the western edge of the city. A new alpine ski area was developed in the Kananaskis Valley, and a new Nordic Center was built at Canmore. A 19,000-seat arena, the Saddledome, was built for hockey and figure skating. Ten thousand volunteers were utilized at the time of the games, and 20,000 had been involved since the games were awarded in 1981 at the International Olympic Committee (IOC) Congress in Baden Baden, Germany.

To this day, these games are still considered by the IOC as truly exceptional, perhaps the finest games ever held, winter or summer. For a Prairie cow town of 640,000 residents, nestled close to the Rocky Mountains, such accolades may at first be surprising. The reasons for this success were the superb organization, the extensive continuing benefits, and, most significantly, the attitude of the people of Alberta. It was their warm welcome, their enthusiasm to host the visitors, their willingness to make the extra effort to ensure that strangers were well taken care of that made a positive impression. Local residents explain that this is the natural way Prairie communities have collaborated for the past 150 years. There seems to be an innate need to welcome strangers, particularly those from the big cities. Alberta is comprised of people from all parts of the world who still maintain cultural traditions from their countries of origin. Therefore, the Belgian-born chocolate maker in Calgary became the assistant to the Belgian team, and the Austrian Club of Calgary hosted the Austrian team and families every evening at its club.

Calgary always has been a sports-minded community, active for more than a century with curling, hockey, skating, baseball, and many other sports and having competitions from the earliest days with its Prairie neighbors. It is known internationally as the home of the Calgary Stampede rodeo. Today, the city is also known throughout the world as the host of the superb Calgary Winter Olympic Games.

See also CITIES AND TOWNS: Calgary, Alberta.

Roger Jackson
University of Calgary

Findling, John E., and Kimberly D. Pelle. *Historical Dictionary of the Modern Olympic Movement.* Westport CT: Greenwood Press, 1996.

CLEMENT, AMANDA (1888–1971)

Amanda Clement was born on March 20, 1888, in Hudson, South Dakota. She became the first paid female umpire in men's baseball. Her career occurred quite by accident. Two lodge teams were scheduled to play a game before her brother's semipro game when the umpire did not show up. Her brother suggested that they ask Amanda. Clement's umpiring was so fair that her brother's team and other semipro teams enlisted her services.

Subsequently, from about 1904 to 1911, she umpired about fifty semipro games each summer in the Dakotas, Nebraska, Minnesota, and Iowa, earning between $15 and $25 per game.

Being a professional umpire in the early twentieth century was not only a man's occupation but was also dangerous. Several minor-league umpires lost their lives, and many minor and major leaguers were assaulted by angry fans. Yet Clement never experienced any abuse. Fans and players respected her expertise. Gamblers liked her because her calls could not be bought. Baseball promoters delighted in her drawing power as the "Only Lady Umpire in the World." And sportswriters enjoyed bragging that "South Dakota has a woman umpire who is said to be about the best preserver of the peace in the whole northwest."

Amanda Clement in many ways epitomized the modern woman. An all-around athlete, she made her mark in history by being the first woman baseball umpire, but she also worked as a newspaper reporter, city assessor, justice of the peace, and social worker. She died on July 20, 1971, in Sioux Falls, South Dakota.

Gai Ingham Berlage
Iona College

Berlage, Gai Ingham. *Women in Baseball: The Forgotten History.* Westport CT: Praeger, 1994.

COACHES

The Great Plains states have produced many successful professional and college sports coaches. Plains natives have coached their teams to numerous national and international championships.

Several prominent professional baseball managers were born in the Plains. Although they were better known as players than as managers, Hall of Famers Tris Speaker of Hubbard City, Texas, and Rogers Hornsby of Winters, Texas, managed world championship teams. Speaker's Cleveland Indians won the World Series in 1920, and Hornsby's St. Louis Cardinals won in 1926. Billy Southworth, who was born in Harvard, Nebraska, managed the Cardinals to World Series titles in 1942 and 1944. Ralph Houk of Larned, Kansas, managed the New York Yankees to world championships in 1961 and 1962.

George "Sparky" Anderson, born in Rapid City, South Dakota, is the only manager to win the World Series in both major leagues. Anderson won with the Cincinnati Reds in 1975 and 1976 and with the Detroit Tigers in 1984. The most successful baseball manager of the 1990s was Bobby Cox, a native of Tulsa, Oklahoma. Cox managed the Atlanta Braves in four World Series, winning in 1995. Mike Hargrove of Perryton, Texas, managed the Cleveland Indians in the World Series in 1995 and 1997.

In college football, Tom Osborne, a native of Hastings, Nebraska, and coach at the University of Nebraska, retired after the 1997 season with 254 victories, ranking him sixth among all National Collegiate Athletic Association (NCAA) Division I coaches in history. Osborne's Cornhuskers won national championships in 1994 and 1995 and shared the title in 1997. Frank Leahy, born in O'Neill, Nebraska, and raised in Winner, South Dakota, coached Notre Dame between 1941 and 1953. Leahy's Fighting Irish won national titles in 1943, 1946, 1947, and 1949. Darrell Royal of Hollis, Oklahoma, coached national champions at the University of Texas in 1963, 1969, and 1970.

Professional basketball's most successful coach of recent years, Phil Jackson, was born in Deer Lodge, Montana. Under Jackson, the Chicago Bulls won National Basketball Association (NBA) titles in 1991, 1992, 1993, 1996, 1997, and 1998. His regular-season winning percentage of .738 (as of 2002) is unmatched in NBA history. Jackson subsequently coached the Los Angeles Lakers to the title in 2000, 2001, and 2002. Another Plains native to earn an NBA title as head coach is Bill Sharman of Abilene, Texas, who won with Los Angeles in 1971.

The Plains has been an especially fertile source of successful college basketball coaches. The two winningest men's coaches and the winningest women's coach are all from the Plains states. Adolph Rupp of Halstead, Kansas, coached the University of Kentucky Wildcats to NCAA basketball titles in 1948, 1949, 1951, and 1958. Dean Smith, born in Emporia and raised in Topeka, Kansas, coached at the University of North Carolina from 1962 to 1997. Smith's Tar Heels won national championships in 1982 and 1993, and Smith holds records for most career and most NCAA tournament victories.

Several other NCAA tournament–winning coaches come from the Plains. Everett Shelton of Cunningham, Kansas, led Wyoming to the NCAA title in 1943. In 1966 the University of Texas at El Paso (then Texas Western), coached by Don Haskins of Enid, Oklahoma, became the first team with an all–African American starting lineup to win the NCAA title, beating Rupp's Kentucky team in the championship game. In 1994 El Paso, Texas, native Nolan Richardson coached the University of Arkansas to the title. Lute Olson of Mayville, North Dakota, won the championship with the University of Arizona in 1997. Other highly successful college basketball coaches from the Plains include Eddie Sutton of Bucklin, Kansas, Billy Tubbs of Tulsa, Oklahoma, Dale Brown of Minot, North Dakota, Gene Keady of Larned, Kansas, Ralph Miller of Chanute, Kansas, Lou Henson of Okay, Oklahoma, Ted Owens of Hollis, Oklahoma, and "Tex" Winter of Wellington, Texas. The winningest coach in NCAA women's basketball, Jody Conradt of the University of Texas, was born in Goldthwaite, Texas. In 1998 Conradt was elected to the Basketball Hall of Fame.

Fred Shelley
Southwest Texas State University

Porter, David L., ed. *Biographical Dictionary of American Sports: Basketball and Other Indoor Sports*. Westport CT: Greenwood Press, 1989. Porter, David L., ed. *Biographical Dictionary of American Sports: Football*. Westport CT: Greenwood Press, 1988.

COLLEGE WORLD SERIES

College baseball players don't necessarily talk about reaching the College World Series; that's a mouthful. Instead, most of them say they dream of going to Omaha.

Because of the National Collegiate Athletic Association (NCAA) Division I College World Series (CWS), which has been played in Omaha at Johnny Rosenblatt Stadium since 1950, Omaha has become synonymous with the sport, and no one wants to see the association end. "When you look at it, how many events are held in the same city for that long a time?" said Dennis Poppe, the NCAA's director of baseball and football operations. "The Masters, the Kentucky Derby, the Indy 500. Sporting events are moved around a lot nowadays. For a city to have an association with the same event for fifty years is a tremendous accomplishment."

The eight-team CWS was a struggling three-year-old event when it first came to Omaha in 1950 after two years in Kalamazoo, Michigan, and one in Wichita, Kansas. (Future president George Bush played for Yale in the first two series in 1947 and 1948, losing to California and Southern California in the three-game series.) Rosenblatt Stadium was two years old at the time but has since gone through numerous renovations to stay modern, fan-friendly, and profitable, keeping the series in Omaha. It now seats 24,000 fans, and attendance for the entire tournament regularly exceeds 200,000. Many of the fans are regulars, season-ticket holders who come back to Rosenblatt every year for the CWS.

Another steady visitor is Louisiana State University, which under coach Skip Bertman has made eleven trips since 1986. The Tigers and their many fans—easily identified by their purple and gold Mardi Gras beads—have become such Omaha regulars that visitors are as likely to find red beans and rice at Rosenblatt as they are red meat. LSU annually leads Division I teams in attendance at more than 7,000 fans per game, and its fans have seen the Tigers win five CWS titles from 1991 to 2000. Texas, with such famed coaches as Bibb Falk, Cliff Gustafson, and Augie Garrido, has earned a record twenty-eight CWS berths, but not even the Longhorns can match Southern California for series tradition. The Trojans rank second, with twenty-one appearances, despite a sixteen-season absence from 1979 to 1994. Southern California has won the event twelve times, more than twice as many as any other program. Coach Rod Dedeaux is credited with ten of those titles, though he was co-coach of an eleventh crown, the 1948 team. Dedeaux's teams won championships in 1951, 1955, 1958, 1960, 1961, 1963, 1964, 1966, and 1968, then won five straight from 1970 to 1974 before one last title in 1978. Coach Mike Gillespie, who replaced Dedeaux after the 1984 season, took USC back to Omaha in 1995 and won the CWS in 1998.

John Manuel
Baseball America

CROSBY, BOB (1897–1947)

Among the best and most colorful steer ropers and all-around hands in early rodeo, Bob Crosby was born on February 27, 1897, in Midland, Texas. Raised around Kenna, New Mexico, he developed into a seasoned cowhand prior to becoming a rodeo contestant in 1923 at New York's Yankee Stadium.

Known as "Wild Horse Bob" on the circuit, Crosby always competed aggressively. In 1925, 1927, and again in 1928 he captured the combined all-around titles at both Pendleton and Cheyenne, thus retiring the coveted Roosevelt Trophy. This remarkable feat—amassing the most cumulative points among the bronc-riding, steer-roping, bulldogging, and wild horse–racing events—amounted to three world championships in the era before official titles were declared.

Bob Crosby specialized in the roping events. He won the calf-roping title at Madison Square Garden three times and the steer-roping title twice at Cheyenne and four times at Pendleton. In the late 1930s and 1940s, while operating his Cross B Ranch near Roswell, New Mexico, Cosby took part in a series of celebrated, matched steer ropings against Carl Arnold and the Weir brothers. He is remembered for his lucky black hat, his string of great roping horses, and his tenacity in competing and winning even with serious injuries.

Once declared the "King of the Cowboys" by *Life* magazine, Wild Horse Bob Crosby died in a Jeep accident near his New Mexico ranch on October 20, 1947. He was inducted into the National Cowboy and Western Heritage Museum's Rodeo Hall of Fame in 1966.

Richard C. Rattenbury
National Cowboy and
Western Heritage Museum

Bob Crosby, Biographical File, National Cowboy and Western Heritage Museum Archives, Oklahoma City. Porter, Willard H. *Who's Who in Rodeo*. Oklahoma City: Powder River Book Company, 1982. Westermeier, Clifford P. *Man, Beast, Dust: The Story of Rodeo*. Lincoln: University of Nebraska Press, 1987.

CROW FAIR

Crow Fair, called the "Tipi Capital of the World," is an annual event held the third weekend in August on the Crow Reservation in Montana. It is one of the largest Native American events in North America and is run by a committee of the Crow tribe. Crow Fair combines a celebration of Crow culture, reunion of family groups, powwow, rodeo, horse racing, and commercial vendors. Native Americans of various tribes and many non-Indian people, including visitors from around the world, gather to celebrate and enjoy themselves. There may be 1,000 tipis, along with wall tents, pickup campers, trailers, and mobile homes. Each family has its own camp area, and people visit and eat under arbor shades and awnings.

These camps surround an open circular dance arbor with bleachers. Immediately around the dance arbor are commercial booths that serve food as well as sell Native crafts, arts, supplies, and children's carnival toys. Social and popular dances are held for young people in the Round Hall. An all-Indian rodeo and horse races are held at the racetrack arena adjacent to the fairgrounds. Crow Fair runs four days for the tribe and general public. A fifth day is devoted to Crow tribal members and their immediate friends and includes dances, giveaways, feasting, and the Parade Dance around camp with a salute to the mountains.

Each morning there is a parade, and spectators line the edges of the road, sitting on folding chairs, in cars, or in the beds of pickup trucks, many holding umbrellas for shade. The procession is led by a color guard of Native American veterans. The main parade includes people on horseback, on foot, and riding on cars and floats. Most are dressed in powwow finery, wearing traditional Plains regalia, including fancy beaded vests, eagle-feather bonnets, shawls, and elk tooth dresses, mixed with cowboy dress. Many horses are outfitted with traditional Crow saddles, beaded or painted saddlebags, Pendleton blankets, beaded rifle bags, and cradleboards. Vehicles and floats also are covered with traditional finery; along the sides, draped banners declare titles of tribal or family affiliation. The floats have displays such as a small tipi and arbor with elders and children or a drum group with dancers. The paraders smile, wave to the people lining the roadside, and throw candy to the children. The current Crow Fair princess leads "visiting royalty" who have won princess titles at other reservations and powwows. Awards are given for the best dress outfits, decorated horses, and floats.

Drum groups, dancers, and spectators assemble at the central dance arbor for the afternoon and evening powwow. The grand entry is led by an Indian veteran color guard, followed by distinguished individuals, honored guests and elders, and then male traditional dancers, male fancy dancers, women traditional dancers, girl's shawl or fancy dancers, jingle dress, grass dancers, and tiny tots. The powwow includes announcements, jokes, dance competitions in various categories and age groups, and intertribal and social dances. Honor songs and dances, giveaways, and adoption and naming ceremonies occur. After the powwow, there are sometimes forty-nine dances and tipi doorway singing. The all-Indian rodeo and horse races are held at the nearby racetrack arena. The rodeo includes saddle bronc and bareback riding, bull riding, bulldogging, calf roping, team roping, and barrel racing. Quarter horse and Thoroughbred racing are featured. There is much betting on the outcomes of the races.

Crow Fair started in 1904, when the Bureau of Indian Affairs agent and Crow leaders agreed that a country fair format would help induce the Crows to become self-supporting farmers while at the same time allow the people to showcase aspects of Crow culture. Crow women exhibited traditional Native foods, clothing, and handicrafts. People brought ponies, calves, pigs, turkeys, and chickens for exhibit as well as potatoes, pumpkins, squash,

grain, jellies, pies, bread, butter, and cakes. Schoolchildren exhibited basketry, embroidery, and various crafts and played band music. A committee of chiefs and elders scheduled entertainment events and arranged a parade, foot and horse racing, relay races, rodeo (including bucking broncos), and dancing to the beat of singers around drums. Storytelling of war deeds by veterans, victory dances, sham battles and reenactments, and the distribution of gifts to tribal members and visitors became popular. Prizes were given for the best-pitched and decorated tipis, tipi-pitching races, farm exhibits, horse work teams and wagons, buggies, and races.

Federal Indian policy at that time generally forbade traditional singing, dancing, and ceremonies, but the combination of agricultural assimilation and traditional culture coincided with public interest in tourism. Visitors included non-Indians as well as members of many other tribes. The fair became a successful national model for Indian events. After World War II the agricultural aspects of Crow Fair were dropped, and the combined Crow and modern pan-Indian event has grown to become one of the most popular cultural celebrations in the world.

See also NATIVE AMERICANS: Crows; Powwows.

C. Adrian Heidenreich
Montana State University, Billings

Baasaxpilua: Northern Plains Celebration. Video. Denver Museum of Natural History, 1982. Loeb, Barbara. "Crow Fair." *Native Peoples* 3 (1990): 16–24. Wisherd, Edwin L. "The Friendly Crows in Festive Panoply." *National Geographic* 52 (1927): 315–22.

CUNNINGHAM, GLENN (1909–1988)

Glenn Cunningham was born on August 4, 1909, in Atlanta, Kansas. He overcame a near-crippling childhood accident to become one of the world's leading track and field athletes during the 1930s. An Elkhart, Kansas, schoolhouse fire left him at age seven unable to walk for nearly six weeks. After regaining his ambulatory ability, Cunningham began running to strengthen his badly scarred legs. In 1930 he was the nation's premier high school mile runner, winning state and national titles, establishing a national high school mile record of 4:24.7, and earning a scholarship to the University of Kansas.

In 1932 Cunningham won the first of three consecutive indoor and outdoor Big 6 (now Big 12) Conference mile championships and the National Collegiate Athletic Association (NCAA) 1500-meter title. He finished fourth in the 1500 meters in the Olympic Games in Los Angeles, California. As the 1933 champion in the NCAA mile and the Amateur Athletic Union (AAU) 800 and 1500 meters, he received the Sullivan Award as the nation's top amateur athlete. In 1934 Cunningham established an outdoor world record of 4:06.7 for the mile and won the AAU indoor 1500-meter title. He won the AAU indoor 1500-meter title again in 1935, 1938, and 1939. In 1935 Cunningham established an indoor world record of 3:50.5 for

1500 meters and secured the first of four consecutive AAU titles in the 1500 meters outdoors. In addition to winning the silver medal in the 1936 Olympic Games in Berlin, he established an outdoor world record of 1:49.7 for the 800 meters.

Educated at the University of Kansas (bachelor of arts, 1934), the University of Iowa (master of arts, 1936), and New York University (doctorate, 1938), Cunningham later served as the director of physical education at Cornell College in Mount Vernon, Iowa. After a stint in the navy during World War II, he married Ruth Sheffield in 1947 and established the Glenn Cunningham Youth Ranch for orphans, juvenile delinquents, and underprivileged youths near Burns, Kansas, and later Augusta, Kansas. Cunningham financed the ranch entirely through his income as an inspirational speaker. He died on March 10, 1988, of a heart attack less than two weeks after participating in a relay race of former champions at the 100th anniversary of the AAU indoor track and field championships.

Adam R. Hornbuckle
Alexandria, Virginia

Cunningham, Glenn, with George X. Sand. *But Never Quit.* Lincoln VA: Chosen Books, 1981.

CURLING

The winter ice sport of curling was introduced to the Great Plains by Scottish immigrants. The minimal equipment needed—ice, brooms, and stones—made it easy for these sportsmen to continue the tradition, especially in the early days when the playing stones weren't always uniform. Curling involves two teams of four players each alternately sliding stones (today, each stone weighs forty-two pounds) along an ice lane toward a target of concentric circles. Points are scored for having more stones closer to the "tee" (the center of the circles).

With long, cold winters and many ponds, lakes, and rivers, the northern parts of the Great Plains are especially suited for curling. In the Canadian provinces of Manitoba, Saskatchewan, and Alberta, the length of the playing season quickly helped curling surpass other sports such as baseball and cricket in popularity. Curling developed as more than a competitive game. During the winter the social fabric of the Prairie communities centered around each town's curling rink.

Just as the railroad's expansion helped establish new settlements in western Canada and the United States, so, too, did it help to spread curling, especially when Scotsmen were part of the railway gangs. Manitoba first recorded curling in 1876, and by 1888 pioneers there had formed the province of Manitoba and Adjoining Territories branch of the Royal Caledonian Curling Club of Scotland. A year later the branch hosted the world's largest bonspiel, or tournament, of the times, with sixty-two rinks (teams) competing in Winnipeg. In 1888 the 100th annual Manitoba Curling Association bonspiel drew a world-record 1,280 rinks.

Curling was played in the territory of Sas-

Curlers from the Dakotah Curling Club, Drayton, North Dakota, 1900–5

katchewan as early as 1880, when tamarack blocks shaped to resemble curling stones were fitted with iron handles and slid across the frozen Saskatchewan River. The dedication of Saskatchewan's curlers is best illustrated by the journey undertaken by a Prince Albert team intent on playing in the 1890 Winnipeg bonspiel. The foursome walked 200 miles, their stones carted by ponies, just to catch a train that required another three days to reach Winnipeg. The roots of curling are still strong in the province today: the Saskatchewan Curling Association is the largest of its kind in the world. At its peak in 1960–61, the association had 578 member clubs. Among the province's best-known curlers was Regina's Richardson family rink, which in 1959 won the first of four national and world championships in five years.

Curling stones were also regularly thrown in Alberta by the 1880s, shortly after the arrival of the railroad. In 1959 Calgary's Big Four Curling Club became the world's largest, boasting forty-eight sheets divided between two levels. Calgary was also the site of the first world championship held outside of Scotland, in 1964, and of the Olympic curling demonstration in 1988.

Curling filtered across the U.S. Great Plains much as it did across Canada but with additional influence from the north. Initial members of the Manitoba Curling Association included clubs in Butte, Montana, and St. Paul, Minnesota. However, the sport has never become as established in the United States as it has in Canada, the "Curling Capital of the World." The three Canadian Prairie Provinces are each home to about 14 percent of that country's estimated 1.5 million curlers. Altogether, the twenty existing clubs in the seven Great Plains states with curling (including western Minnesota) have approximately 1,500 curlers out of 15,000 nationwide. North Dakota's twelve clubs are the largest concentration in the region. The Drayton Curling Club, whose first "home" was a stretch of ice on the Red River, celebrated its centennial in 2001. The Great Plains states have been home to twenty-four national curling champions in the history of U.S. men's, women's, and mixed events, including nine junior men's teams, two of which won world titles.

Manitoba has produced twenty-five national men's champions alone since the Canadians first contested for a title in 1927. Saskatchewan boasts eleven women's champions and is also home to the team that won the women's gold medal in the 1998 Winter Olympic Games in Nagano, Japan, where curling first became a full-medal sport. Alberta also has many national champions, including eighteen men's and thirteen junior men's teams. Altogether, the three provinces have also welcomed home thirty-one world curling champions.

Rick Patzke
U.S. Curling Association

Argan, Wm. P. *Saskatchewan Curling: Heartland Tradition*. Regina: Saskatchewan Curling Association, 1991. Haig, Senator John T. *1948 Manitoba Curling Association Yearbook*. Winnipeg: Manitoba Curling Association, 1948. Smith, David B. *Curling: An Illustrated History*. Edinburgh: John Donald Publishers Ltd., 1981.

DUDE RANCHING

Dude ranching has long been an important part of recreation in the Great Plains. The first dude ranches were generally family-operated cattle ranches that diversified during hard economic times by offering services to travelers. Known as dudes, these people visited ranches to ride horses, fish, and take part in cattle ranch activities. Dude ranches first appeared in the late nineteenth century, and they continue to operate at the beginning of the twenty-first century.

One of the early dude ranches was the Custer Trail Ranch, founded in 1879 by Howard, Willis, and Alden Eaton at Medora, Dakota Territory. The brothers were hosts to visitors in 1882, and in the following year Howard Eaton led guests on the first of his many pack trips to Yellowstone Park. The primary interest for most dudes was horseback riding, but eventually they wanted to experience other outdoor adventures such as cattle drives, fishing trips, and visiting mountainous country and national parks. In order to satisfy their guests better, the Eaton brothers moved their operation in 1904 to the Bighorn Mountain area in Wyoming. Eatons' Ranch has operated there since that move. By the 1890s dude ranches had also developed in Colorado, Wyoming, and Montana.

In 1926 railroad officials helped dude ranchers form the Dude Ranchers Association (DRA), an organization that continues to operate. The number of dude ranches reached its peak in the 1930s, when it was estimated that there were more than 350 in the United States and 1 in Canada. Then the numbers declined, partly due to the Great Depression but also to changing habits of travelers and more varied tourist destinations. The DRA directory for 2000 lists 105 member ranches in the United States and 3 in Canada. Most are located in Colorado, Wyoming, and Montana.

Lawrence R. Borne
Northern Kentucky University

Borne, Lawrence R. *Dude Ranching: A Complete History*. Albuquerque: University of New Mexico Press, 1983. Rodnitzky, Jerome L. "Recapturing the West: The Dude Ranch in American Life." *Arizona and the West* 10 (1968): 111–26. Roundy, Charles G. "The Origins and Early Development of Dude Ranching in Wyoming." *Annals of Wyoming* 45 (1973): 5–25.

EDMONTON GRADS

The Edmonton Commercial Graduates (Grads) dominated women's basketball in North America during the interwar years. Percy Page started the team in 1915 with students and graduates from Edmonton's McDougall Commercial High School, where he was a teacher, and only twice during the Grads' twenty-five years did girls who had not been at McDougall High play for the team.

From 1915 until the team disbanded in 1940, when their practice area was taken over for military purposes, the Grads won 502 of 522 games. At one point in their history they had a winning streak of 147 games, followed by a 78-game winning streak. They won their first Canadian title in 1922 and never surrendered it. In 1923, against Cleveland, they won the first international series for the Underwood Trophy. They defended it successfully for seventeen years. The Grads competed in Fédération Sportive Féminine Internationale (FSFI) championships held in the same cities as the men's Olympics on four occasions (1924, 1928, 1932, and 1936) and won the unofficial world championship each time, with twenty-seven consecutive victories.

Everywhere the Grads played they drew large crowds, including the record attendance of 6,792 for an Underwood Trophy match against the Chicago Taylor-Trunks in Edmonton in 1930. However, the Grads did not forget their Prairie roots, and they staged basketball exhibitions in several small Alberta communities. Coach Page expected his Grads to behave "like ladies" both on and off the court, and his teams established a reputation for sportsmanship, dedication, and determination. Significantly, they demonstrated that they could play the more vigorous men's rules and yet retain their femininity. When asked about the Grads' secret of success, Page replied, "They were champions because they were whole-hearted, sport-loving girls in whom the spirit of the Prairie was born and bred."

Ronald S. Lappage
Lakehead University

Fitness and Amateur Sport Canada. *For the Record: Canada's Greatest Women Athletes.* Toronto: John Wiley and Sons Canada Ltd., 1981. Kidd, Bruce. *The Struggle for Canadian Sport.* Toronto: University of Toronto Press, 1996.

FISHING

Recreational fishing in the Great Plains is about as diverse as any angler wants to make it. Cold-water species such as trout and salmon can be found in the foothills of the Rocky Mountains and even out onto the Plains in cold-water streams and in stocked winter fisheries. Cool-water species—northern pike, walleye, smallmouth bass, and yellow perch, to name a few—abound in the northern part of the Plains and in some of the deeper artificial reservoirs. And, of course, warm-water species abound in the multitude of farm ponds, small lakes, reservoirs, and stream and river systems that drain this rich agricultural region. These species include the catfish, largemouth bass, crappie, other sunfish species, white bass, the landlocked striped bass, the relatively new hybrid wiper and saugeye, and a myriad of other game and non game fishes.

When it comes to fishing opportunities, anglers in the Great Plains probably have more different opportunities than anywhere else in the United States and Canada. In the northern part of this region, walleye rank high on the popularity list, while the southern angler would likely put the black bass at or near the top. In the Central Plains, catfish are an important item on the anglers' list. But specialized anglers who belong to a striper tournament circuit, a fly-fishing organization, or a local bass club, who fish in the yearly carp derby, or who simply dunk a worm for anything they can catch are everywhere.

Nationwide in the United States, fishing remains the number two water-related outdoor sport, with nearly 45 million participants, according to a 1997 survey from the National Sporting Goods Association. Among all indoor and outdoor sports, fishing is seventh. Statistics from the 1996 National Survey of Fishing, Hunting, and Wildlife-Associated Recreation conducted by the U.S. Fish and Wildlife Service indicate that recreational fishing produced $108 billion and created more than 1.2 million full-time jobs in 1996. In Kansas in 1996, for example, fishing was worth $357 million to the state's economy and created the equivalent of 4,922 full-time jobs. In Nebraska, the economic benefit of fishing to the state was even greater, at $427 million and 6,448 jobs. Texas ranks second in the nation, behind only California, with $6.4 billion in revenues from fishing and 80,282 associated jobs (these figures include parts of Texas that are not part of the Great Plains). Clearly, throughout the Great Plains fishing is a significant economic enterprise as well as an integral part of regional culture.

See also PHYSICAL ENVIRONMENT: Fish.

Tommie Berger
Kansas Department of Wildlife and Parks

American Sportsfishing Association. *Economic Impact of Sportsfishing in the United States.* Alexandria VA: American Sportsfishing Association, 1996.

FOOTBALL, AMERICAN

Football has been a mainstay of sports and team-oriented recreation in the Great Plains region for more than a century. Since early settlers opened schools and towns began to organize community sporting activities, football has played a prominent role in the culture and identity of the region. High school, college, and professional football teams in the Great Plains have enjoyed great success throughout the twentieth century and now into the twenty-first century.

High school football in the Great Plains is played by eight-player teams in the smallest communities and on the simplest of playing fields as well as by students in some of the largest and best-equipped school districts in the United States. The latter is especially true in the region's largest state, Texas, where some high schools have facilities and budgets that would be the envy of many smaller college programs. The role of high school football in serving as a community identifier is visible every day on the local landscapes, where many small towns and larger cities have signs and water towers proclaiming the successes of the local team. The level of community identification with the high school football team has also been well established in the popular media, as is evident in several major motion pictures such as *Varsity Blues* (1999). The impact of high school football on the West Texas communities of Midland and Odessa was also critically chronicled by Pulitzer Prize–winning journalist H. G. Bissinger in his book *Friday Night Lights*.

While high school and Little League football continue to play a major role in the everyday life of people throughout the Great Plains region, no form of sport has brought more recognition to the region than college football. Legendary college basketball coaches have parlayed their talents in the region, and college baseball and other sports have also achieved much, but it is the college football teams from the Great Plains that have had unparalleled success over the past fifty years. During that time, Plains schools have won outright or shared sixteen national titles, as determined by the year-end polls of sportswriters and coaches, with the University of Oklahoma winning seven, Nebraska five, Texas three, and Colorado one.

These four teams represent the most successful of the region's college football programs, but they are not the only ones that have triumphed on the gridiron. In 1958 the Big 8 Conference, one of college football's most important leagues, was created. This conference was comprised of Iowa State University, Kansas State University, Oklahoma State University, and the Universities of Colorado, Kansas, Missouri, Nebraska, and Oklahoma. Two of these universities are outside the formally defined Great Plains region (Iowa State University and the University of Missouri); the remaining six are located along the peripheries of the region. While not all of these programs have not had the accomplishments of the dominant programs in the league, all have had their moments in the college football spotlight. Oklahoma State thrived in the 1980s, not least because of Heisman Trophy winner Barry Sanders, who set numerous conference and national rushing records during his time with the Cowboys. The University of Kansas launched the Hall of Fame running back Gale Sayers, and in the 1990s the Kansas State Wildcats became one of college football's most successful teams after decades of suffering as one of the nation's poorest programs.

The Big 8 Conference became synonymous with the Great Plains region, but prior to the 1990s, college sports in Texas were dominated by the Southwest Conference (SWC). This conference was comprised of eight universities from Texas (the University of Texas, University of Houston, Texas Tech, Baylor University, Southern Methodist University, Texas Christian University, and Texas A&M University), together with the University of Arkansas. Unfortunately, this group of programs came to symbolize the problems afflicting college football in the late 1980s and 1990s. At one point seven of the eight Texas programs were on probation with the National Collegiate Athletic Association (NCAA) for various rules violations, and Southern Methodist University is the only program in college football history to suffer the "death penalty": the suspension of the program for one or more years. While rules violations were rampant in the SWC, the Big 8 was not without its own problems. Oklahoma and Oklahoma State were found to have committed major rules violations as well. By 1995 major college football in the region was in disarray, so a plan was put in place to restore respect in the sport. The Big 12 Conference was formed in 1996, comprising the Big 8 programs plus four of the schools from the SWC: the University of Texas, Texas A&M University, Texas Tech, and Baylor University. In the first five years of the conference's existence, two schools from the league won or shared the national title—Nebraska in 1997 and Oklahoma in 2000.

Colorful coaches and players are often part of college football, and the Great Plains region is no exception. Oklahoma has benefited from the coaching careers of Bud Wilkinson, Barry Switzer, Chuck Fairbanks, and now Bob Stoops; Nebraska has contributed coach Bob Devaney and the twenty-five-year head coaching career of Tom Osborne; and Texas was led by legendary coaches Dana X. Bible and Darrell Royal. U.S. Supreme Court Justice Byron "Whizzer" White was an all-American at Colorado.

Professional football in the region has had a shorter but also a successful past. Both the Denver Broncos and Kansas City Chiefs were charter members of the original American Football League in 1960. Each of these teams has won the ultimate pro football prize, the Super Bowl, with Kansas City winning in 1970 and Denver winning twice, in 1997 and 1998, the latter game closing out the storied career of quarterback John Elway. Like the major college programs of the region, these teams are located along the periphery of the Great Plains. The most successful of the professional football teams located on the edge of the region is the Dallas Cowboys. Founded in 1960 as an expansion team in the National Football League, the Cowboys were led for twenty-nine years by coach Tom Landry. After an uneventful first five seasons, the Cowboys played in more Super Bowls than any professional football team, winning the title five times.

The rough-and-tumble sport of football in the Great Plains can be seen as a parallel to life in this often difficult region—hard but leading to triumph and attainment. The Great Plains has seen success in football at all levels, from the small high schools around which family life and Friday nights are often centered in small prairie towns to the national championships of wealthy college and professional teams.

See also AFRICAN AMERICANS: Sanders, Barry; Sayers, Gale / IMAGES AND ICONS: Friday Night Football / LAW: White, Byron.

G. Allen Finchum
Oklahoma State University

Bissinger, H. G. *Friday Night Lights: A Town, a Team, and a Dream.* New York: HarperCollins, 1990. Dortch, Chris, ed. *Blue Ribbon College Football Yearbook: 2001 Edition.* Dulles VA: Brasseys, Inc., 2001. Watterson, John Sayle. *College Football: History, Spectacle, and Controversy.* Baltimore MD: Johns Hopkins University Press, 2000.

FOOTBALL, CANADIAN

Because Canada was a British colony, Canada's football had its roots in the United Kingdom. It was the version in vogue at the British public school of Rugby that arrived in Canada through immigration, the civil service, and military garrisons.

By the 1860s the game was being played in Montreal, where a city group, the Garrison, and McGill University formed teams. In 1874 McGill took its hybrid form of the Rugby game to Harvard University and introduced it to the United States. Harvard in turn promoted it to neighboring academic institutions. Changes in the traditional British game were much slower in Canada than in the United States. In 1882 the scrum method of putting the ball in play was modified slightly in Canada by "heeling" it back to the quarterback; in the United States it was snapped back, a regulation that was not accepted universally in Canada until 1921.

Even though it was understood that the Canadian game was different from English rugby, that term continued to be used in Canada until the 1950s. Growth of the game was assisted by the formation of governing bodies, regional and national. The Quebec Rugby Football Union (QRFU) was formed in 1882; the Ontario Rugby Football Union (ORFU) in 1883; the Canadian Rugby Union (CRU) in 1892; the Canadian Intercollegiate Rugby Football Union (CIRFU) in 1898; the Interprovincial Rugby Football Union (IRFU) in 1907; and the Western Interprovincial Rugby Football Union (WIRFU) in 1911. The latter was the governing body for unions in Manitoba, Saskatchewan, and Alberta. Dominion championships have been held since 1892. A new trophy, the Grey Cup, named after Governor-General Lord Grey, was introduced in 1909 and symbolized Canadian football supremacy. In 1966 the CRU turned over the trusteeship of the cup to the Canadian Football League (CFL) and changed its name to the Canadian Amateur Football Association (CAFA).

Teams representing cities in the Great Plains have played a major role in the development of Canadian football. In 1921 the Edmonton Eskimos were the first western team to challenge for the Grey Cup; the Winnipeg Blue Bombers won that trophy in 1935, the first western team to do so. They were greatly aided by the nine American players the team had recruited from the so-called Swede belt of the Dakotas and Minnesota. That action caused the CRU to impose a restriction on the number of Americans who could play in the national championship. In 1998 team rosters were thirty-seven players: sixteen imports (typically Americans), eighteen nonimports (typically Canadians), and three quarterbacks (no restrictions).

In 1948 the Calgary Stampeders turned the national championship into a celebration when supporters arrived in Toronto, the site of the game, with western regalia, horses, chuck wagons, "cowboys and Indians," and flapjack breakfasts. The Edmonton Eskimos won consecutive Grey Cups in 1954, 1955, and 1956. In a 1998 poll, Jackie Parker of that era was selected as the top player ever to play in the CFL. The Eskimos later won five consecutive cups from 1978 to 1982. Regina was the host of the Grey Cup game of 1995. It was also the first time that an American team, the Baltimore Stallions, won the Grey Cup when they defeated the Calgary Stampeders 37 to 20. It will probably be the last for some time, since all the American teams disbanded after the season, cutting short the American expansion experiment by the CFL.

Professional football in Canada is under the direction of the CFL and had eight teams in 1998: Montreal Alouettes, Toronto Argonauts, Hamilton Tiger-Cats, and Winnipeg Blue Bombers in the Eastern Division; Saskatchewan Roughriders, Calgary Stampeders, Edmonton Eskimos, and British Columbia Lions in the Western Division. The field is 110 yards long and 65 yards wide. End zones are 20 yards long. There are twelve players on each team. The rules allow unlimited motion by the backs and three downs to make ten yards. Opposing teams are separated by a one-yard scrimmage line. Scoring is six points for a touchdown, one for the extra point after, three for a field goal, two for a safety touch, and one for a single point from a punt or missed field goal where the ball is not returned from the end zone.

Canadian university football is under the aegis of the Canadian Intercollegiate Athletic Union (CIAU). It has a national championship and trophy, the Vanier Cup, also named for a Canadian governor-general, Georges Vanier. Playoffs are held among the champions of the four regions: Atlantic University Athletic Association (AUAA), Ontario Universities Athletics (OUA), Ontario-Quebec Intercollegiate Football Conference (OQIFC), and Canada West Universities Athletic Association (CWUAA). Junior football as well as recreational flag and touch football are promoted by the CAFA and its provincial affiliates.

Recreationally, as flag football grows in popularity with girls as well as boys, impromptu games of throwing, catching, running, and kicking are as common as traditional Prairie games of baseball, soccer, road hockey, and curling.

Frank Cosentino
York University

Cosentino, Frank. *Canadian Football: The Grey Cup Years.* Toronto: Musson Book Company, Ltd., 1969. Cosentino, Frank. *A Passing Game.* Winnipeg: Bain and Cox, 1995.

FOOTBALL, SIX-MAN

Invented in 1934 by Stephen Epler, a Chester, Nebraska, teacher who wanted students at small high schools to experience playing football, six-man football is a special Plains phenomenon. After envisioning a modified version of traditional football, Epler spent the summer of 1934 at the University of Nebraska developing his ideas in a project for a summer graduate education course. The first game was played in Hebron, Nebraska, on September 26, 1934, before more than 1,000 fans. In the only six-man game that year, players from Chester and nearby Hardy lined up against boys from Alexandria and Belvidere high schools, resulting in a 19 to 19 tie. The next year uniforms and equipment were purchased for several six-man teams, and enough schools decided to take on this new Plains sport to form a league.

At its height in 1951, six-man football was played in 2,463 schools in forty-eight states. Plains states claimed five of the top ten, with Nebraska second at 167, Texas third at 163, North Dakota sixth at 120, Montana eighth at 85, and South Dakota ninth at 83 schools. In 1997 only 158 schools in seven states (six of them Plains states) fielded six-man football teams: Texas (90), Nebraska (21), Colorado (17), Montana (14), New Mexico (12), Kansas (2), and California (2). With increasing pressure on smaller schools to consolidate, fewer and fewer six-man football teams will be organized. For example, after the 1997 season Nebraska lost seven teams, leaving only fourteen; 1998 marked the last year for the sport in a high school tournament, because future school consolidations will reduce the number below a critical mass necessary for a legitimate play-off system.

Six-man football is different in several ways from eleven- and eight-man football. Perhaps the most colorful rule—one that has resulted in at least two distinctive Plains phrases—is that if an opponent achieves a lead of forty-five points or more in the second half, the game is called. In Texas, this is the slaughter rule, and so "to be slaughtered" takes on a new meaning. In Nebraska small towns, local expressions include "to be forty-fived," which is a phrase residents hope will never be said about their team. Other noteworthy differences in this high-scoring game include a first down requiring advancing the ball fifteen rather than ten yards; the six-man field being 80 (not 100) yards long; all players being eligible for a pass, which can make even the center a "skill" position; and the quarterback having to lateral the ball in order for the offense to advance the ball (since 1998 the quarterback is also able to make a handoff). Scoring is also distinctive. Because preventing a kick from being blocked is very difficult, a successful field goal counts four points in six-man football, and a kick after a touchdown counts two points, while an extra point scored by a pass or run is only one point. Since size, speed, agility, and finesse are as important for successful six-man football players as they are for eleven- and eight-man team members, these teams have produced players who have gone on to star in college football programs and even professional leagues.

In 1993 a *Wall Street Journal* reporter visited several small towns in West Texas and described a Friday night six-man football game in Amherst, a *Last Picture Show* kind of town. At the time the reporter thought that the game's popularity was making a comeback, but that observation seemed premature in the late 1990s. Much more accurate was his notion that six-man football boosts the spirit of small Plains communities.

See also EDUCATION: School Consolidation and Reorganization.

Peter Maslowski
University of Nebraska–Lincoln
John R. Wunder
University of Nebraska–Lincoln

Ingersoll, Bruce. "You Might Call This Football Lite, but It Keeps a Ritual Alive." *Wall Street Journal*, December 3, 1993. Secter, Bob. "A Revival of Six-Man Football." *Los Angeles Times*, October 23, 1991.

FRIDAY NIGHT FOOTBALL

See IMAGES AND ICONS: Friday Night Football

GAMING

Gambling was common in mining towns in South Dakota and Colorado during the late nineteenth century. Gambling, or gaming, reappeared in the Great Plains in response to antitaxation sentiments in the 1980s, when state, provincial, and local governments sought an alternative source of revenue. Many states and provinces began with lotteries to supplement their general revenue funds. Today, six Plains states (Colorado, Kansas, Montana, Nebraska, South Dakota, and Texas) and all three of the Prairie Provinces operate lotteries.

Following the adoption of state lotteries in the United States, local, tribal, and private interests turned toward gambling as well. In the late 1980s the city of Deadwood, South Dakota, looked to its colorful gambling history to revitalize its economy. The Deadwood You Bet Committee used the state's initiative process to introduce a constitutional amendment to allow gambling in Deadwood. To sell gambling as a revenue source, the Deadwood progambling movement focused on gambling's entertainment value and pledged any revenues to historic preservation. In 1988 64.3 percent of voters in South Dakota approved limited stakes gambling, and in November 1989 gaming began in Deadwood. Deadwood expected 100 new jobs and $2 million in bets in the first year. However, even with betting limits of $5, there were an estimated 1,183 new jobs and $93 million in bets generated during the first six months.

On the heels of Deadwood's revenue success, three historical mining communities in Colorado pushed for gaming. The Central City Preservation, Inc. Committee used Colorado's initiative process and won a constitutional amendment to allow limited stakes gaming in the cities of Black Hawk, Central City, and Cripple Creek. By 1995 Deadwood, Black Hawk, Central City, and Cripple Creek had forty-seven, nineteen, thirteen, and twenty-three casinos, respectively. All four cities noted increased congestion and higher property values; the Colorado cities reported losing local services and local establishments to tourism development. One year into gaming in Colorado and three years into gaming in Deadwood, respondents to a survey in all four cities perceived the gaming industries as having an influence over local government greater than that of citizens. Only Deadwood respondents reported a significant increase in historic preservation efforts.

The gaming landscape of the Great Plains also includes at least twenty-two casinos (Class III gaming) on Indian reservations. Most of the tribal casinos are in South Dakota and North Dakota, with eight and six each, respectively. Tribal casinos closer to urban centers and those casinos that can draw visitors from nearby states where gaming is not legal have been particularly successful. For example, tribal gaming endeavors in western Iowa have benefited from tighter laws in Nebraska. Riverboat casinos in Sioux City and Council Bluffs, Iowa, as well as the pari-mutuel gaming and slots available in Council Bluffs have also gained. Riverboat casinos in St. Joseph and Kansas City, Missouri, also lure visitors from the population centers of Kansas City, Kansas, and Omaha, Nebraska.

Unlike the privately run casinos in the United States, gaming and casino operations in Canada fall to the provincial governments. Charitable gaming began in Canada in 1969, and in 1985 the provinces gained exclusive control over gaming. All three Prairie Provinces have lotto, video lottery, and Indian casinos. Manitoba and Saskatchewan also have government-operated casinos, and both Saskatchewan and Alberta have casinos run for charity. The widespread availability of gaming in Manitoba, Saskatchewan, Alberta, Montana, and North Dakota has discouraged the growth of gaming towns along the Canadian-U.S. international border.

The spatial distribution of gaming in the Great Plains ranges from an absence of casino and Class III tribal gaming in the Southern Plains to widespread gaming in the Northern Plains and Prairie Provinces. The difference in gaming availability between states as well as the location of population centers at the eastern periphery of the Plains have encouraged the growth of several gaming towns and attractions along state borders. Whether presented as a way to revive the past and preserve history, as a harmless form of entertainment, or as a way to generate revenue without additional taxation, gaming is changing the economic, political, social, and cultural landscapes of the Great Plains.

See also IMAGES AND ICONS: Deadwood, South Dakota.

Erin Hogan Fouberg
Mary Washington College

Campbell, Colin S., and Garry J. Smith. "Canadian Gambling: Trends and Public Policy Issues." *Annals of the American Academy of Political and Social Science* 556 (1998): 22–35. Fouberg, Erin Hogan. "South Dakota Gaming: A Regional Analysis." *Great Plains Research* 5 (1996): 179–212. Long, Patrick T. "Early Impacts of Limited Stakes Casino Gambling on Rural Community Life." *Tourism Management* 17 (1996): 341–53.

GOWDY, CURT (b. 1919)

Curtis Gowdy was a major figure in televised sport during the 1960s and 1970s, coinciding with that medium's increasing impact on American society. Gowdy was born in Green River, Wyoming, on July 31, 1919, and raised in Cheyenne. He grew up loving team and outdoor sports. He excelled in basketball and softball during his high school years and at the University of Wyoming from 1938 to 1942. After a back injury ended his service in the Army Air Corps in 1943, he began a career as a broadcaster in Cheyenne and later Oklahoma City, Oklahoma.

Gowdy reached broadcasting's big markets in 1949, starting a two-year tour as Mel Allen's partner with the New York Yankees. This exposure led to a job as the announcer for the Boston Red Sox from 1951 to 1966. Gowdy quickly became a popular figure with the large New England audience. Like most broadcasters he covered all major sports and hosted various programs. He impressed network officials and peers with his versatility, preparation, and good humor.

Gowdy reached national prominence during the 1960s as the play-by-play broadcaster of the young American Football League. Teamed with former Missouri quarterback Paul Christman and backed by the managerial and technological innovations of Roone Arledge, Gowdy attracted listeners to the rival league with his enthusiasm, knowledge, and fairness. When the National Broadcasting Company took over the AFL rights in 1966, the network hired Gowdy as its main football and baseball announcer. He announced every World Series and major AFL telecast from 1966 through 1975. In addition, he broadcast college football bowl games and basketball championships. He described his life and announcing philosophy in *Cowboy at the Mike* in 1966.

Gowdy's stature enabled him to launch the *American Sportsman* series in 1967. The program took celebrities on hunting, fishing, and camera trips around the globe and introduced millions of urbanites to the beauties of wilderness, augmenting the fledgling environmental movement. Gowdy received numerous accolades: four Emmys; sportscaster of the year recognitions in 1965 and 1967; a George Foster Peabody Award in 1970; and membership in the Sports Broadcasters, National Baseball, and American Sportscasters Halls of Fame. He served as president of the National Basketball Hall of Fame, and that organization's media award was named in his honor. The creation of Curt Gowdy State Park in Cheyenne in 1971 was yet another recognition.

Gowdy's work on so many sportscasts led to his overexposure in an industry that constantly demanded new faces, and his network appearances declined after 1975. He branched into production and ownership and hosted a critically acclaimed nostalgia series, *The Way It Was*, on PBS during the 1980s. He wrote *Seasons to Remember: The Way It Was in American Sports, 1945–1960* in 1993. Gowdy retired to Palm Beach, Florida, in the 1990s. His son, Curt Gowdy Jr., is an Emmy Award–winning producer of sports programs.

Jim W. Harper
Texas Tech University

Smith, Curt. *Of Mikes and Men: From Ray Scott to Curt Gowdy: Broadcast Tales from the Pro Football Booth.* South Bend IN: Diamond Communications, 1998. Smith, Curt. *Voices of the Game.* South Bend IN: Diamond Communications, 1987.

GRETZKY, WAYNE (b. 1961)

Wayne Gretzky was not born in the Great Plains, but his name will always be associated with Great Plains ice hockey. Gretzky, born on January 26, 1961, in Brantford, Ontario, is one of the greatest ice hockey players of all time. He started his professional career in the World Hockey Association (WHA) by playing for the Indianapolis Racers and Edmonton Oilers before moving in 1979 into the National Hockey League (NHL) with the Oilers, wearing number 99. His nine seasons with the Oilers established him as arguably the greatest ever to play

the game. While in Edmonton, Gretzky was awarded the Hart Trophy, given to the NHL's most valuable player, every year from 1980 to 1987 and again in 1989 as well as the Art Ross Trophy for the league's scoring leader eight times (1981–87, 1990–91, and 1994). During the 1981–82 season he scored the fastest fifty goals and 100 points in one season (thirty-eight games). He holds fourteen NHL career records and led the Oilers to five Stanley Cups.

Gretzky became a hockey icon in Edmonton and developed similar followings playing for the Los Angeles Kings (1988–95), St. Louis Blues (1995–96), and New York Rangers (1996 to his retirement in 1999). With his popularity among the fans and his numerous trophies, awards, and honors, it is easy to understand why Wayne Gretzky was named the top player of all time in 1998 by the *Hockey News* and was inducted into the Hockey Hall of Fame in 1999.

Lisa M. DeChano
Western Michigan University

National Hockey League. *The Official Guide and Record Book, 1996–1997.* Chicago: Triumph Books, 1997.

GYMNASTICS

Although gymnastics has had its greatest development in the Midwest, Northeast, and Pacific region of the United States, universities, high schools, and clubs in the Great Plains, especially in Nebraska and Oklahoma, are known for their gymnastics traditions and successes. Men's teams at the Universities of Nebraska and Oklahoma have been among the finest in the nation. Under coach Francis Allen, Nebraska won eight men's National Collegiate Athletic Association (NCAA) championships between 1979 and 1994. After 1964 Nebraska won thirteen Big 8 Conference titles. Nebraska gymnasts such as James Hartung have stood out at the highest levels of competition. The University of Oklahoma has won three men's NCAA championships and seven Big 8 titles. Oklahoma's best-known gymnast is Bart Conner, a 1984 Olympic gold medal winner. Oklahoma women won the Big 8 title five times and placed second in the 1997 Big 12 championships; Nebraska women won the 1997 Big 12 event.

Other colleges such as the University of Denver, the United States Air Force Academy, the University of North Dakota, Texas Tech, Hardin-Simmons, and Odessa College have sponsored varsity or club gymnastics. The U.S. Olympic Committee maintains a training center in Colorado Springs, Colorado. The Maverick Boys Club and Nard's Trampoline Club in Amarillo, Texas, were among the earliest gymnastics clubs in the region, and the Sokol (ethnic Czechoslovakian) Clubs of Omaha, Nebraska, and Fort Worth, Texas, have long gymnastics traditions. The most accomplished gymnastics Olympian of the region is Shannon Miller of the Dynamo Gymnastics Club in Edmond, Oklahoma, who won seven medals in the 1992 and 1996 games.

Richard V. McGehee
University of Texas at Austin

HALL OF FAME MUSEUMS

There are almost forty major Halls of Fame in the Great Plains region, with the greatest number in Texas (nine), Oklahoma and Kansas (six each), and Colorado (five). There are three in the Plains region of Canada.

Many of these Halls of Fame are museums, such as the National Softball Hall of Fame and Museum in Oklahoma City; the Pro Rodeo Hall of Fame and the Museum of the American Cowboy in Colorado Springs; the National Motorcycle Museum and Hall of Fame in Sturgis, South Dakota; and the Olympic Hall of Fame and Museum in Calgary, Alberta. Some of the Halls of Fame are museums by other names, such as the National Cowboy Hall of Fame and Western Heritage Museum in Oklahoma City; the National Agricultural Center and Hall of Fame in Bonner Springs, Kansas; and the wonderfully titled Gallery of Also Rans in Norton, Kansas.

A number of Halls of Fame are only part of larger museums, including the Roller Skating Hall of Fame in the National Museum of Roller Skating in Lincoln, Nebraska; the International Space Hall of Fame in the Space Center in Alamogordo, New Mexico; the Petroleum Hall of Fame in the Permian Basin Petroleum Museum, Library, and Hall of Fame in Midland, Texas; and Canada's Aviation Hall of Fame in the Reynolds-Alberta Museum in Wetaskiwin, Alberta.

Sometimes Halls of Fame are housed in other types of facilities. For example, the North Dakota Sports Hall of Fame is in the Jamestown Civic Center; the United States Racquetball Hall of Fame is in the United States Racquetball Association headquarters in Colorado Springs; the National Baseball Congress Hall of Fame is in Lawrence-Dumont Stadium in Wichita, Kansas; and the National Fish Culture Hall of Fame is in the D. C. Booth Historic Fish Hatchery in Spearfish, South Dakota.

Halls of Fame take many forms. The National Hall of Fame for Famous American Indians in Anadarko, Oklahoma, is primarily an outdoor sculpture garden; the West Texas Walk of Fame is on a sidewalk outside the Lubbock Memorial Civic Center in Texas; and the Denver Broncos' Ring of Fame is displayed along the facade of Mile High Stadium. Hall of Fame facilities range from a few hundred feet, such as the 325-square-foot National Fish Culture Hall of Fame, to several hundred thousand feet, such as the 220,000-square-foot National Cowboy Hall of Fame and Western Heritage Museum in Oklahoma City.

Most often, Halls of Fame are started by individuals or groups of people interested in the subject matter. They want to honor outstanding achievement, encourage the activity, and promote the area. Others are initiated by sports clubs, professional associations, or governmental bodies. Hall of fame inductees—which run from a handful to thousands—usually are honored with plaques, biographical information, photographs, and displays of memorabilia and artifacts. Some exhibits also make use of interactive displays and slide, film, and video presentations.

Many Halls of Fame are visited by only a few thousand people a year, but some are extremely popular, attracting large crowds. These include the National Cowboy Hall of Fame and Western Heritage Museum, which has an annual attendance of 300,000, and the International Space Hall of Fame at the Space Center, which attracts about 200,000 visitors each year.

See also EDUCATION: Museums.

Victor J. Danilov
University of Colorado–Boulder

Danilov, Victor J. *Hall of Fame Museums: A Reference Guide*. Westport CT: Greenwood Press, 1997.

HEISMAN TROPHY WINNERS

The first Great Plains Heisman Trophy winner was Texas Christian University's Davey O'Brien, who claimed the honor in 1938, the third year it was awarded to the nation's outstanding college football player. It would be fourteen years before another Plains star, Billy Vessels of Oklahoma, won the award in 1952, unless Nile Kinnick, who had attended high school in Omaha but won the trophy while at Iowa in 1939, is counted. A second Heisman drought hit the Plains after Vessels's victory, this time lasting until 1969, when Oklahoma's Steve Owens ended the dry spell and began a steady stream of Plains Heisman champions. In 1972 Nebraska's Johnny Rodgers was honored, followed in 1977 by Earl Campbell of Texas, Oklahoma's Billy Sims in 1978, Nebraska's Mike Rozier in 1983, Barry Sanders of Oklahoma State in 1988, Colorado's Rashaan Salaam in 1994, Ricky Williams of Texas in 1998, and Eric Crouch of Nebraska in 2001.

Of these eleven Heisman heroes, however, only four—Billy Vessels, Johnny Rodgers, Barry Sanders, and Eric Crouch—were home-grown products of the Plains.

Billy Vessels, of tiny Cleveland, Oklahoma, has been called the first Heisman winner of the modern era because it was his outstanding play in a nationally televised game, against Notre Dame in 1952, that moved him to the front of that year's Heisman class. When informed that he had won the Heisman, Vessels replied, "What's the Heisman?" The growing presence and influence of television and its fondness for spectacles like the awarding of the Heisman make it likely that Vessels was the last winner who had no knowledge of the award.

In contrast to Vessels and his small-town background, 1972 winner Johnny Rodgers grew up on the streets of Omaha's north side. At Nebraska he was known for his incredible runs as a wide receiver and punt returner, most notably, a 72-yard return against Oklahoma in the 1971 "Game of the Century." But he was also known for his run-ins with the law. Heisman voters struggled with the issue of awarding the trophy to a convicted felon, but in the end Rodgers's failings seemed to pale when compared to his successes in overcoming great adversity in his life. He was only the third wide receiver to win the award.

Barry Sanders attended high school at Wichita North. He dreamed of attending the University of Oklahoma but was turned down by coach Barry Switzer because he was only five feet seven inches tall and weighed only 175 pounds. Instead, he was welcomed at Oklahoma State, where he shattered National Collegiate Athletic Association (NCAA) rushing records. "We just blew it," Switzer later said about passing over Sanders. "I admire talent, and Barry Sanders is a phenomenal talent." After winning the Heisman during his junior year in 1988, Sanders moved to the National Football League, where he became the acclaimed running back of the Detroit Lions.

Eric Crouch graduated from Millard North High School in Omaha and from the University of Nebraska–Lincoln. With his forty-yard dash time of 4:47, Crouch holds the NCAA Division I-A quarterback record with fifty-nine career rushing touchdowns, but he also completed 51.5 percent of his passes during his college career, and, when called upon, as in the 2001 victory over Oklahoma, he dazzled as a receiver.

Thomas P. Jundt
Brown University

Bell, Jack, et al., eds. *The Heisman: Sixty Years of Tradition and Excellence*. Bronxville NY: Adventure Quest, 1995. Brady, John T. *The Heisman: A Symbol of Excellence*. New York: Athenaeum, 1984. Rader, Benjamin G. *American Sports: From the Age of Folk Games to the Age of Televised Sports*. Englewood Cliffs NJ: Prentice-Hall, 1999.

HOGAN, BEN (1912–1997)

William Benjamin "Bantam Ben" Hogan, America's premier golfer during the 1940s and 1950s, was born on August 13, 1912, in Dublin, Texas. At the age of nine his father committed suicide, forcing the family to move to Fort Worth. As a youngster Ben helped supplement the meager family income by selling newspapers and working as a caddie at Glen Garden Country Club. Hogan began playing on his days off and quickly became a proficient golfer after switching from a left- to a right-handed swing.

He turned professional at the age of seventeen but struggled for the first decade of his golfing career due to a propensity for slicing the ball. Throughout his early golfing career he was forced to take odd jobs to support his wife, Valerie, whom he had married in 1937. By 1940, however, after countless hours at the driving range perfecting his swing, Hogan finished the year with five tournament wins and was the country's leading money winner. His professional career was put on hold between 1942 and 1945 due to military service in the Army Air Corps, but he returned to the professional tour in 1946 and won the Professional Golfers' Association (PGA) Championship.

Hogan's career and life nearly ended in 1949 when a bus hit his car head-on and it seemed that he would never walk again. Determined to prove his doctors wrong, Hogan recovered and returned to the tour in 1951, winning the U.S. Open and the Masters tournaments that year. Lingering injuries, however, limited Hogan to only seven tournaments a year. In 1953, arguably his finest year, Hogan won five of six tournaments, including his fourth U.S. Open title, his second Masters, and the British Open. Hogan continued to win tournaments until his retirement in 1960.

Hogan was known as a fierce competitor. With his signature white visor pulled low over his eyes, he intimidated opponents by blocking out everything around him as he drove toward the green. Hogan ended his career with sixty-three tournament wins (third all-time), including four U.S. Opens and two Masters titles. He was a four-time PGA player of the year and is a member of every golf Hall of Fame, including the PGA Hall of Fame.

After retiring Hogan focused on the golf equipment business that he had established in Fort Worth during the 1950s. Although he sold the company in 1960, he remained as the chairman and played an important role in golf club design for the next twenty years. Hogan died on July 25, 1997, in Fort Worth, Texas.

Mark R. Ellis
University of Nebraska at Kearney

Sampson, Curt. *Hogan*. Nashville: Rutledge Hill Press, 2001.

HORNSBY, ROGERS (1896–1963)

Many baseball experts consider Rogers Hornsby to be the greatest right-handed hitter in the game's history. He was born on April 27, 1896, in Winters, Texas, and later moved to Fort Worth, where he developed his baseball skills on city league and high school teams. In 1914 Hornsby joined a Class D minor-league team in Hugo, Oklahoma. After that franchise folded, he returned to Texas when a team in Denison purchased his contract. While playing for Denison, the infielder impressed a scout for the St. Louis Cardinals, who then bought his contract in September 1915.

Over the next decade Hornsby established himself as one of the most feared hitters in the major leagues. From 1920 to 1925 he won a phenomenal six straight batting titles and two Triple Crowns. Hornsby's .424 batting average in 1924 is still a modern record. Hornsby was an aggressive player with a controversial gambling addiction, and his abrasiveness led to frequent difficulties with his team's front office. As a result, St. Louis traded Hornsby following the 1926 season. He played for five different teams until his retirement in 1937.

During and following his playing days, Hornsby managed several teams, including minor-league franchises in Fort Worth and Beaumont, Texas. Despite his gruff personality, Hornsby's baseball accomplishments made him a hero to thousands of Texans. He finished his Hall of Fame career with 301 home runs and a .358 lifetime batting average, the highest ever for a right-handed hitter. Hornsby died on January 5, 1963, in Chicago.

Kent M. Krause
University of Nebraska–Lincoln

Alexander, Charles C. *Rogers Hornsby: A Biography*. New York: Henry Holt and Company, 1995. Dewey, Donald, and Nicholas Acocella. *The Biographical History of Baseball*. New York: Carroll and Graf Publishers, Inc., 1995.

HOWE, GORDIE (b. 1928)

Like many boys growing up in the Prairie Provinces (he was born at Floral, Saskatchewan, on March 31, 1928), Gordie Howe dreamed of someday playing in the National Hockey League (NHL). At the age of eighteen, Howe's dreams were fulfilled when he took to the ice with the Detroit Red Wings. Over the next thirty-four years, including six in the World Hockey Association (WHA), Howe would enjoy a spectacular, durable career, wreaking havoc on the opposition with his tenacious style of play.

Considered one of the greatest players of all time, Howe was a six-time scoring champion and six-time Hart Memorial Trophy winner, awarded to the league's most valuable player, during his twenty-five-year stint as a Red Wing. Only Wayne Gretzky has won more scoring titles (seven) and has accumulated more MVP awards (nine) than Howe.

As a right-wing forward, Howe amassed 801 goals and 1,850 points in his NHL career, both of which are second to Gretzky's record totals. He helped guide Detroit to four Stanley Cups in six years, from 1950 to 1955, and seven consecutive regular-season titles (1948–54). He dominated the league in the 1951–52 and 1952–53 seasons, racking up eighty-six and ninety-five points, respectively. His forty-seven goals in the 1951–52 season were sixteen more than the second-leading scorer (Chicago's William Mosienko), and he tallied thirty-nine assists, which tied for third best in the league. The next year he recorded a career-high forty-nine goals. But Howe's best year, statistically, occurred in 1968–69 at the age of forty, when he established a career high in points (103), eight more than his previous high. He recorded forty-four goals and fifty-nine assists, his all-time best, and finished third in the scoring race.

Howe's vigor and resiliency were keys to his longevity on the ice. He holds the NHL record for most seasons played (26) and most games played (1,767). However, in his third year, Howe's career was nearly cut short when he collided with Toronto's Ted Kennedy during a play-off game and crashed head-on into the sideboards, suffering a severe brain injury. The injury left him with a slight facial tic, which occasionally caused his eyes to blink uncontrollably. Thus, his teammates nicknamed him Blinky.

At six feet and 205 pounds, Howe was powerful and fearless. He racked up 2,418 career penalty minutes. In 1959 he broke Lou Fontinato's nose in a game against the New York Rangers and caused other extensive damage to Fontinato's face, which required reconstructive surgery.

Howe retired with the Red Wings in 1971, having been named to the NHL all-star team twenty-one times in twenty-five years, and was inducted into Toronto's Hockey Hall of Fame in 1972. He returned to the game in 1973 to join sons Marty and Mark with the WHA Houston Aeros. He closed out his career in 1979 at the age of fifty-two, playing one last year in the NHL with the Hartford Whalers.

Nathan E. Odgaard
Kansas City Kansan

Gale Research, Inc. *The Complete Encyclopedia of Hockey*. Detroit: Associated Features, Inc., 1993.

ICE HOCKEY

Ice hockey has its roots in Europe. Several versions of the sport were played for more than 100 years before they were introduced in North America. British soldiers garrisoned at Kingston, Ontario, were the first to play a form of hockey, called shinny, in the mid-1800s. Ice shinny, in conjunction with the various other European forms of the game, evolved into modern ice hockey. Prior to 1917 there was one exclusively professional league, the Ontario Professional League, and many amateur leagues. The creation of the National Hockey League (NHL) brought the sharpest shooters, quickest goalies, and hardest hitters into one league.

The Great Plains is the hotbed for ice hockey. Two-thirds of all Canadian NHL players come from the Prairie Provinces. Saskatchewan is the province with the highest percentage of players in the NHL, with Alberta and Manitoba also having major representation. In the United States, most of the American-born NHL players hail from a core region extending from North Dakota to New England. Many Plains cities host or have hosted several NHL teams: Kansas City, Missouri; Winnipeg, Manitoba; Calgary and Edmonton, Alberta; and Denver, Colorado. The World Hockey Association (WHA), which lasted from 1972 to 1979, also included teams in the Plains cities of Calgary, Edmonton, and Winnipeg.

The Hockey Hall of Fame has inducted many players from the Plains. Manitoba, with eighteen, has the most inductees of the Prairie Provinces. Hockey greats such as Mervyn "Red" Dutton (1958 inductee), player and NHL president (1943–46), and Terrance "Terry" Sawchuck (1971 inductee), one of the greatest goalkeepers in hockey history, top the list of Manitobans in the Hall of Fame. Saskatchewan boasts fifteen inductees, including one of the most prominent players, "Mr. Hockey" Gordie Howe (1972 inductee); longtime Detroit Red Wings star Eddie Shore (1947 inductee), the only defenseman to win the Hart Trophy for most valuable player four times; and, most recently, Bryan Trottier (1997 inductee), who in the early 1980s led the New York Islanders to four consecutive Stanley Cup victories. Alberta has seven inductees in the Hall of Fame, including John Bucyk (1981 inductee), longtime star of the Boston Bruins, and Bill Gadsby (1970 inductee), three-time first team and three-time second team all-star. Kansas is the only Plains state to have a hometown player inducted into the Hall. Silas "Si" Griffis, known during his hockey tenure as the fastest man in hockey, was inducted in 1950 for his play with the Kenora Thistles (1902–6) and the Vancouver Millionaires (1911–18).

Amateur hockey has long been an impor-

tant part of Great Plains culture. Many high school players from the core regions go on to play collegiate hockey. The Western Collegiate Hockey League (WCHA) is one of the foremost college hockey leagues in the United States, winning thirty national titles since 1951. The University of North Dakota currently owns the record for all-time winning percentage in National Collegiate Athletic Association (NCAA) tournament play. The NHL drafts a large proportion of players while they are still in high school, or the players are drafted before they graduate from college. The WCHA has produced more than 275 NHL players and 140 Olympic hockey players. In 1997 the WCHA placed more than 350 players in the NHL, more than any other collegiate league. Many well-known NHL players, including Jack McCarten, the first U.S. NHL player, Tony Esposito, Ed Belfour, and Brett Hull played in the WCHA. In Canada the Prairie Provinces host eleven of the eighteen teams in the World Hockey League (WHL). Manitoba supports the volunteer actions of Hockey Manitoba, which promotes ice hockey in the province at every age. Recently, the organization began clinics for female hockey players.

Local Plains culture has also been greatly influenced by the sport. By 1905 ice hockey had filtered into every corner of Canada, making it a major component of winter activity. Many leagues were set up, often with support from local schools and churches because of hockey's importance in the education of boys. Everywhere in the Prairie Provinces boys are found practicing their skills year-round and watching NHL games, aspiring to be the next Gordie Howe or Wayne Gretzky.

Lisa M. DeChano
Western Michigan University

MacFarlane, Brian. *60 Years of Hockey: The Intimate Story behind North America's Fastest, Most Exciting Sport. Complete Statistics and Records*. Toronto: McGraw Hill Ryerson, 1976. Metcalfe, Alan. *Canada Learns to Play: The Emergence of Organized Sport, 1807–1914*. Toronto: McClelland and Stewart, 1987. The National Hockey League. *The Official Guide and Record Book, 1995–1996*. Chicago: Triumph Books, 1995.

JACKSON, PHIL (b. 1945)

Born on September 17, 1945, in Deer Lodge, Montana, and brought up in Williston, North Dakota, Phil Jackson is one of the most successful coaches in the history of the National Basketball Association. Between 1990 and 2002 Jackson's Chicago Bulls and Los Angeles Lakers teams won nine NBA championships. Through the 2001–2002 season, Jackson had the highest career-winning percentage in NBA history in regular season games (.738) and play-off games (.742).

Jackson's success is a study in contrasts. At a time when the NBA vigorously promotes its individual stars, he wins by preaching selfless team play. In a game requiring the highest levels of physical skill, he emphasizes the mental and spiritual condition of his players. The coaching philosophy underpinning this approach is an amalgam of influences ranging from Jackson's native Great Plains to the Far

East. "The day I took over the Chicago Bulls," he writes in his book *Sacred Hoops*, "I vowed to create an environment based on the principles of selflessness and compassion I'd learned as a Christian in my parents' home; sitting on a cushion practicing Zen; and studying the teachings of the Lakota Sioux." The son of two Pentecostal ministers, Jackson was a devoted student of the Bible, and his parents had hopes of him entering the ministry. He was also a gifted athlete, a pro prospect in baseball and a standout basketball player on the 1963 Williston High School state championship team. He accepted a basketball scholarship to the University of North Dakota, where he played under future NBA coach Bill Fitch. While twice earning all-American honors on the court, Jackson studied psychology, philosophy, and religion in the classroom and became involved in the charged politics of the Vietnam War era. He graduated in 1967.

A second-round draft choice of the New York Knicks in 1967, Jackson spent ten of his thirteen seasons with that team. He was never a star, but the gangly six-foot-eight-inch Jackson was a valuable role player on a team that featured several future NBA Hall of Fame players, including Bill Bradley, the future senator and presidential candidate. During this time Jackson broadened his personal horizons, exploring various religious and meditative traditions and conducting summer basketball clinics on the Pine Ridge Reservation in South Dakota.

In 1978 Jackson was traded to the New Jersey Nets and got his first taste of coaching as a player/assistant coach. After retiring as a player, he spent the 1980s learning the coaching craft and paying his dues in the Continental Basketball Association and the Puerto Rican summer leagues. In 1987 Jackson accepted an assistant coaching job with the Chicago Bulls, a team with a prodigiously gifted young player named Michael Jordan and a losing record. In 1989, frustrated by more mediocre seasons, Bulls' management offered the head coaching job to Jackson. Within two years, the Bulls were NBA champions. By the end of the 1990s Jackson was recognized as one of the game's all-time great coaches, a reputation solidified by his continued success as head coach of the Los Angeles Lakers.

Roger Holmes
Lincoln, Nebraska

Jackson, Phil, and Hugh Delahanty. *Sacred Hoops.* New York: Hyperion, 1995.

LOPEZ, NANCY

See HISPANIC AMERICANS: Lopez, Nancy

LUCAS, BARBARA (1902–1990)

"Rodeo's First Lady" was born Barbara Inez Barnes on September 1, 1902, on a ranch near Cody, Nebraska. As the youngest of twenty-four children (hence the nickname "Tadpole," shortened to Tad), she was familiar with competition from the start. Riding from a very young age, she was winning steer-riding con-

tests by the time she was fourteen, and by twenty she was a full-time professional cowgirl. She met and married cowboy James Edward "Buck" Lucas shortly before heading to London, where she competed in trick riding for the first time.

The 1920s and early 1930s were a Golden Age for women in rodeo, giving them the opportunity to compete as rough stock riders, trick riders, and relay racers. Fascinated by trick riding, Lucas mastered stunts such as a back drag (arching back so her head was just shy of the galloping hooves) and changing sides of a running horse by crawling under its belly. A fearless performer, she was the only woman ever to ride a Brahma bull in Madison Square Garden. Her trick-riding skills won her an assortment of titles across the country, and starting in 1928 Lucas proved the diversity of her abilities by winning the all-around champion at Madison Square Garden three years in a row, retiring the prestigious ten-thousand-dollar MGM Trophy.

During World War II many women's rodeo competitions were dropped, so in 1948 the Girls Rodeo Association (now the Women's Professional Rodeo Association) set out to revive women's role in the sport. As a charter member, Lucas added credibility to this new organization, and her undisputed success and popularity eventually earned her a place in all three rodeo Halls of Fame: the National Rodeo Hall of Fame (1967, first woman elected), the National Cowgirl Hall of Fame and Western Heritage Museum's Rodeo Hall of Fame (1978), and the Pro Rodeo Hall of Fame (1979).

Lucas retired from her long career at the age of fifty-six. Her daughter Dorothy hated rodeo, but second daughter Mitzi loved it enough to become a respected trick rider herself. Tad Lucas died on February 23, 1990, in Fort Worth, Texas. The Tad Lucas Memorial Award honors women who excel in any field related to western heritage.

Sonja Rossum
University of Nebraska–Lincoln

Lecompte, Mary Lou. *Cowgirls of the Rodeo: Pioneer Professional Athletes (Sport and Society).* Urbana: University of Illinois Press, 2000.

MANTLE, MICKEY (1931–1995)

One of the most recognized names in baseball history, Mickey Mantle starred for the New York Yankees in the 1950s and 1960s. Born in Spavinaw, Oklahoma, on October 20, 1931, he later moved with his family to nearby Commerce. Mantle's father, a lead and zinc miner, spent countless hours developing his son's baseball talent. While growing up, Mantle played on numerous local sandlot and youth teams. He graduated from Commerce High School in 1949 and was signed by the Yankees to play for their Class D minor-league team in Independence, Kansas. In 1950 he played in Joplin, Missouri, for a Class C team, and in the off-season he returned to Oklahoma to work with his father in the mines.

After an impressive spring training in 1951,

Mantle was promoted by New York to the major leagues. Over the next eighteen seasons the "Commerce Comet" established himself as the greatest switch-hitter in the game's history. Among his numerous achievements, Mantle led the league in home runs four times and won three most valuable player awards and one Triple Crown. Elected to the National Baseball Hall of Fame in his first year of eligibility, he finished his career with a .298 batting average and 536 home runs. Mantle's impressive statistics could have been even better had he not been plagued by numerous injuries. Following his retirement, Mantle's legend grew, and he was still a hero to millions in the 1990s. After decades of heavy drinking, he required a liver transplant in June 1995 and died on August 13 of the same year.

Kent M. Krause
University of Nebraska–Lincoln

Borst, William A. "Mantle, Mickey Charles." In *A Biographical Dictionary of American Sports: Baseball*, edited by David L. Porter. Westport CT: Greenwood Press, 1987. Falkner, David. *The Last Hero: The Life of Mickey Mantle.* New York: Simon and Schuster, 1995. Mantle, Mickey, with Herb Glick. *The Mick.* Garden City NY: Doubleday, 1985.

MARIS, ROGER (1934–1985)

In 1961 Roger Maris hit sixty-one home runs and broke baseball's most-hallowed single-season record. He was born in Hibbing, Minnesota, on September 10, 1934, but spent his formative years in North Dakota. As a teenager in Fargo, Maris excelled in football at Shanley High School and also starred with the town's American Legion baseball team. Although the University of Oklahoma recruited Maris to play football, he instead signed a contract to play baseball for the Cleveland Indians in 1953. Maris played for several Cleveland farm teams, including their Class C club in Fargo, before making his major-league debut in 1957.

In 1958 Cleveland traded Maris to the Kansas City Athletics, who then dealt the outfielder to the New York Yankees in December 1959. In 1961, despite facing intense media pressure as well as opposition from fans who did not want him to pass Babe Ruth's single-season mark of sixty home runs, Maris broke the record on the last day of the season. While this achievement made him famous, it proved to be a mixed blessing for Maris, because many never forgave him for surpassing the legendary Ruth. Nevertheless, over the next thirty-seven years Maris's mark was annually the subject of intense media speculation and fan excitement. This culminated in 1998, when his record was finally surpassed by Mark McGuire.

Maris's 1961 season overshadowed a very respectable career in which he hit 275 home runs, won two most valuable player awards as well as a Gold Glove Award, and played in seven World Series. Maris died on December 14, 1985, after a yearlong battle with cancer.

Kent M. Krause
University of Nebraska–Lincoln

Allen, Maury. *Roger Maris: A Man for All Seasons.* New York: Donald I. Fine, Inc., 1986. Maris, Roger, and Jim Ogle. *Roger Maris at Bat.* New York: Duell, Sloan and Pearce, 1962.

MILLS, BILLY (b. 1938)

Billy Mills, an Oglala Sioux, achieved one of the Olympic Games' most astonishing upsets by winning the gold medal in the 10,000 meters in Tokyo, Japan, in 1964. William Mervin Mills was born on June 30, 1938, on the Pine Ridge Reservation in South Dakota. He entered Haskell Institute, an Indian school in Lawrence, Kansas, after being orphaned at age twelve. Active in various sports, he discovered a penchant for distance running and, in 1957, obtained an athletic scholarship to the University of Kansas.

Mills won several Big 8 Conference cross-country and indoor and outdoor track titles before graduating from the University of Kansas in 1962. He joined the U.S. Marine Corps and, after a two-year break from competitive running, qualified for the 1964 U.S. Olympic team in the 10,000 meters and the marathon. A relative unknown in the 10,000 meters, Mills outran favorites Ron Clarke of Australia and Mohamed Gammoudi of Tunisia in the final few meters, establishing an Olympic record of 28:24.4. He joined Louis Tewanima, another Native American who had won the silver medal in the 10,000 meters in 1912, as the only Americans to garner medals in the event. Mills also won national Amateur Athletic Union (AAU) titles at three miles indoors and six miles outdoors in 1965.

After retiring from running, Mills established insurance and public relations firms in California. From 1971 to 1974 he served as an assistant commissioner of Indian affairs in the Office of Recreation and Physical Fitness. In that role, Mills revived the National Track and Field Hall of Fame and the American Indian Athletic Hall of Fame. In 1980 he founded the Billy Mills Leadership Institute to improve social and economic conditions of Native Americans. The 1984 film, *Running Brave,* depicted his rise to Olympic success.

Adam R. Hornbuckle
Alexandria, Virginia

Mills, Billy. *Wokini: A Lakota Journey to Happiness and Self Understanding.* New York: Crown, 1994.

NATIONAL FORESTS

The geographical extent of the National Forest System in the Great Plains is approximately equally divided between land designated as national forest and as national grassland. The national grasslands occur in semiarid environments that are characteristic of the greater portion of the Great Plains. With the exception of the two national forests in Nebraska, the national forests occur in areas of higher elevation, including many uplifted mountain ranges, where a cooler and more humid climate prevails.

Only three national forests are totally within the Great Plains: the Black Hills National Forest (South Dakota, Wyoming); the Nebraska National Forest (Nebraska); and the Samuel R. McKelvie National Forest (Nebraska). All of the Custer National Forest (South Dakota, Montana) is in the Great Plains except for the portion in the Middle Rockies west of Red Lodge, Montana, and another portion west of the Bighorn National Recreation Area, Montana. Approximately half of the Lewis and Clark National Forest (Montana) is found in mountainous uplifts that are surrounded by the Great Plains: the Big Snowy Mountains, the Highwood Mountains, and the Little Belt Mountains. The other part of the Lewis and Clark National Forest is located where the Great Plains end and the Northern Rocky Mountains rise to the Continental Divide. Almost half of the Helena National Forest (Montana), in the Big Belt Mountains east of Helena, and a portion of the Gallatin National Forest (Montana), in the Bridger Range and Crazy Mountains northeast of Bozeman, are also within the Great Plains. The three national forests wholly within the Great Plains and the parts of the other four that are within the Great Plains total about 4 million acres, a very small percentage of the 187 million acres in the 155 national forests found across the entire nation.

Many people are surprised to learn that the seventeen national grasslands that cover 3.8 million acres in the Great Plains are part of the National Forest System. This represents 95 percent of the total acreage classified in this category in the twenty national grasslands of the National Forest System. Originally, many of these grassland areas were plowed for farming, but because of poor soil, recurrent drought, and other factors, they were eroded and were purchased by the federal government during the 1930s and early 1940s and taken out of cultivation. They were managed by the Soil Conservation Service from 1938 through 1953. Through proper management, the grasslands were largely revegetated. A large portion of this land was transferred to the states and nonfederal and other federal agencies. The remaining land was designated by the secretary of agriculture as national grasslands, and in 1953 the Forest Service was charged with administering them. In 1960 an administrative order designated 3,804,000 acres as nineteen national grasslands.

Black Hills National Forest covers 1.25 million acres in western South Dakota and adjacent eastern Wyoming. It extends across much of the Black Hills uplift dome. The plains surrounding the Black Hills have altitudes of 3,000 to 3,500 feet, compared with an altitude of 7,242 feet for Harney Peak, the highest point in the United States east of the Rocky Mountains. From a historic lookout tower on the summit of Harney Peak, one has a panoramic view of parts of South Dakota, Nebraska, Wyoming, and Montana as well as the granite formations and cliffs of the 10,000-acre Black Elk Wilderness, a unit of the National Wilderness Preservation System. Numerous caves, including Wind Cave National Park, are located on the limestone plateau that immediately surrounds the central crystalline core of the Black Hills. Two scenic byways providing access to the forest are the Peter Norbeck (70 miles) and Spearfish Canyon (twenty miles). The Forest Service provides more than 100 developed recreation sites. There are more than 600 miles of trails open to hikers, mountain bikers, cross-country skiers, snowmobilers, and horse and motorbike riders. Mount Rushmore National Memorial is surrounded by the national forest.

The Nebraska National Forest (142,000 acres) and Samuel R. McKelvie National Forest (116,000 acres) include the only human-planted forests in the National Forest System. The Nebraska National Forest consists of two different sections separated by 150 air miles. In central Nebraska in the Sandhills is the human-planted Bessey District. In northwest Nebraska naturally occurring ponderosa pine is found in the Pine Ridge District, which occupies the north facing Pine Ridge Escarpment. Seventy miles north of the Bessey District in the Sandhills of north-central Nebraska is the Samuel R. McKelvie National Forest. Developed recreation facilities in the two national forests are primarily in the Bessey District. Visitors seeking a developed campground or lodging in the Pine Ridge District are well served by adjacent Chadron State Park, Nebraska's first state park. There is a small campground in the Samuel R. McKelvie National Forest at Steer Creek. The 9,600-acre Soldier Creek Wilderness Area in the Pine Ridge District is one of only two units of the National Wilderness Preservation System in Nebraska (the other is at Fort Niobrara National Wildlife Refuge). Also in the Pine Ridge District, south of the Soldier Creek Wilderness Area, is the Pine Ridge National Recreation Area. Horseback riding is a popular activity in both the wilderness and national recreation areas. The same forest supervisor in Chadron, Nebraska, who is responsible for the administration of the Nebraska and Samuel R. McKelvie National Forests is also responsible for administering three national grasslands: the Oglala National Grassland (94,480 acres) located west of Chadron in northwestern Nebraska; the Buffalo Gap National Grassland (595,538 acres) in southwestern South Dakota; and the Fort Pierre National Grassland (115,997 acres) located south of Pierre in central South Dakota.

The 1.3 million–acre Custer National Forest extends in a scattered pattern of over 300 miles from northwestern South Dakota to south-central Montana. Much of the forest is surrounded by rolling prairie and farmland. In the Sioux Ranger District in southeastern Montana and the northwestern corner of South Dakota, the eight separate units of federal land are often described as islands of green in a sea of rolling prairie. These national forestlands are hills or mesas covered with ponderosa pine. Two significant National Natural Landmarks are located in this district: the Castles, a massive limestone uplift that resembles a medieval castle; and Capitol Rock, a white limestone uplift that resembles the nation's capitol. To the west, still in southeastern Montana, is the Ashland Ranger District, which has the largest grazing program of any national forest ranger district. The area is rich in coal and wildlife.

Four national grasslands are administered by the Custer National Forest. The 1,028,051-acre Little Missouri National Grassland in western North Dakota is the largest and most diverse national grassland in the United States. The grassland surrounds the Theodore Roosevelt National Park and consists of rolling prairie and spectacular badlands scenery. The Little Missouri National Grassland also contains the largest free-roaming herd of elk in North Dakota as well as the only herd of bighorn sheep, excellent populations of sharp-tailed grouse, numerous archaeological sites, and rich dinosaur fossil beds. This is cattle and oil and gas country. Trail riding, hiking, and big game and bird hunting are popular recreation activities. The Sheyenne National Grassland (70,268 acres), in the extreme southeastern corner of North Dakota, is composed of rolling sand dunes vegetated by tall prairie grass and contains the largest population of prairie chickens in the state. The Cedar River National Grassland (6,717 acres) is located in southern North Dakota along the South Dakota border west of the Standing Rock Indian Reservation, and the Grand River National Grassland (155,075 acres) is located in northwestern South Dakota along the North Dakota border. They are composed of rolling mixed-grass prairie, some badlands, and river bottoms. The Canadian goose is common to this area, and pheasant, sharp-tailed grouse, other waterfowl, antelope, and mule and white-tailed deer are also hunted. The grasslands provide important seasonal forage for livestock.

The 1.8 million–acre Lewis and Clark National Forest is scattered over seven separate mountain ranges in west-central Montana. Almost half of this national forest is in the Rocky Mountain Division, which is located outside of the Great Plains. The six remaining mountain ranges, in the Jefferson Division of the forest, spring from the surrounding prairie lands, creating a majestic rise in the flattened agricultural landscape. The Highwood, Little Belt, Castle, Big Snowy, Little Snowy, and northern portions of the Crazy Mountains are included in this division.

The Thunder Basin National Grassland (571,971 acres) is located in the Powder River Basin of northeastern Wyoming and administered by the Douglas Ranger District of the Medicine Bow–Routt National Forests. Almost all of the grassland provides forage for livestock. The ancient sediments below the surface contain enormous coal, oil, and gas reserves; other resources include uranium and bentonite, a type of clay mineral with many uses. Six surface coal mines operate on the Thunder Basin National Grassland; the Black Thunder is the largest surface coal mine in North America. There are diverse recreational activities but no developed campgrounds and no potable water.

There are two national grasslands in Colorado—the 435,319-acre Comanche National Grassland in the southeast and the 193,060-acre Pawnee National Grassland in the northeast— and one in Kansas—the 108,175-acre Cimarron National Grassland. These national grasslands are administered as ranger districts of the Pike–San Isabel National Forests. The Comanche National Grassland is located in two separate units—the Timpas Unit near La Junta and the Carrizo Unit near Springfield. The Comanche is characterized by diverse and often spectacular landscapes, ranging from short and midgrass prairies to deep canyons and arroyos branching off the Cimarron and Purgatoire River valleys. The land is managed for many natural and cultural resources, including wildlife, recreation, water, livestock, and minerals as well as for the protection of archaeological, historic, and paleontological resources. Wagon ruts of the Mountain Route of the Santa Fe Trail may be observed in many locations. A wealth of paleontological, prehistoric, and historic sites can be experienced at the Picket Wire Canyonlands, which were added to the Comanche in 1991. There, along the banks of the Purgatoire River, is found one of the largest known trackways of dinosaur footprints in the world.

The Pawnee National Grassland is located in two units, one thirty miles east of Fort Collins and the other on the Wyoming border twenty miles northeast of Greeley. Photographers, bird-watchers, and hikers will find the Pawnee Buttes, in the East Unit of the grassland, an interesting landmark. The buttes are sedimentary rock formations, half a mile apart, rising 350 feet above the Plains. The cliffs in this area are a preferred nesting area for many birds of prey. The Crow Valley Recreation Area, in the West Unit, is the only camping facility in the Pawnee.

The Cimarron National Grassland, the largest parcel of public land in Kansas, is a midgrass prairie and is located in the extreme southwestern corner of the state. Rock cliffs, cottonwood groves, grassy fields, yucca, and sagebrush are scattered throughout the rolling to hilly land. There are ten fishing ponds, hiking trails, three picnic areas, and one campground. Also located on the Cimarron National Grassland are twenty-three miles of the historic Santa Fe Trail, the longest portion of the trail with public access. Oil and gas is being produced from twenty-three fields within the grassland. The White Arrow Travel Management System restricts motor vehicle travel in and along the Cimarron River corridor. It is designed to decrease the amount of resource damage caused by motorized vehicles, to preserve wildlife habitat along the river, and to protect the soil.

The Kiowa (New Mexico), Rita Blanca (Texas, Oklahoma), McClelland Creek (Texas), and Black Kettle (Oklahoma, Texas) National Grasslands are administered by the Cibola National Forest, with forest headquarters in Albuquerque, New Mexico. The first two are operated out of the Clayton Ranger District in Clayton, New Mexico, and the latter two are operated out of the Black Kettle Ranger District

in Cheyenne, Oklahoma. The Kiowa National Grassland (136,417 acres) consists of two discontinuous areas in northeastern New Mexico. The westernmost of these two sections includes fifteen miles of the Canadian River Canyon, an 800-foot-deep canyon that forms a wildlife island for mountain lions, wild turkey, bald and golden eagles, mule deer, antelope, bear, Barbary sheep, and waterfowl. The one developed recreation site in the Kiowa National Grassland is the Mills Canyon Campground. There are still two miles of wagon ruts visible along a portion of the Cimarron Cutoff of the Santa Fe Trail. The Rita Blanca National Grassland (92,989 acres) straddles the border in the extreme southwestern corner of the Oklahoma Panhandle and the extreme northwestern corner of the Texas Panhandle. The two developed recreation areas in the Rita Blanca are the Thompson Grove Picnic Area in Texas and the Felt Picnic Area in Oklahoma. The McClelland Creek National Grassland (1,449 acres) is located midway between Amarillo and the Oklahoma border in the Texas Panhandle and has the distinction of being the smallest national grassland in the country. Its central feature is 350-acre Lake McClelland, with facilities for water sports, fishing, and camping. The Black Kettle National Grassland (31,286 acres) is almost entirely in western Oklahoma, except for a 575-acre tract that surrounds 63-acre Lake Marvin in the Texas Panhandle. There are two camping areas at Lake Marvin. Most of the other recreational use in the grassland takes place at Dead Indian, Skipout, and Spring Creek Lakes in Oklahoma.

The Caddo National Grassland (17,784 acres) and Lyndon B. Johnson National Grassland (20,309 acres) are located in north-central Texas, north and northeast of the Dallas–Fort Worth metropolitan area. They are sparsely forested and provide grazing lands for privately owned livestock. They also provide recreation areas and lakes, hunting and fishing, and habitat for wildlife. Oil and gas wells are a common sight on the grasslands. The Caddo National Grassland contains three lakes, two of which have developed recreation sites. The one developed recreation area in the Lyndon B. Johnson National Grassland is at Black Creek Lake. The National Forests in Texas administer these national grasslands from the supervisor's office in Lufkin, Texas. The National Grassland Ranger District is located in Decatur, Texas.

See also PHYSICAL ENVIRONMENT: Badlands; Black Hills.

Charles I. Zinser
Plattsburgh State University

Zinser, Charles I. *Outdoor Recreation: United States National Parks, Forests and Public Lands.* New York: John Wiley and Sons, 1995.

NATIONAL GRASSLANDS

The national grasslands were created in the 1930s, when the Great Plains was withered by a long drought and the Great Depression had left farm families destitute. President Franklin Roosevelt approved a radical social program to purchase submarginal Great Plains grasslands and resettle farm families into planned cities and subsistence homestead villages. A portion (3.8 million acres) of the 11.3 million acres purchased became nineteen national grasslands on June 20, 1960. Butte Valley National Grassland in northern California was added in 1991. All but three of the national grasslands are located in the Great Plains, from Texas and New Mexico to North Dakota.

In the 1920s scientists led by L. C. Gray examined the use and abuse of private and public lands in the West and studied land utilization practices for production and soil conservation. A 1929 federal act began the process of removing marginal lands from cultivation, leading to a national land utilization conference in 1931. In 1933 President Herbert Hoover proposed a government leasing program of submarginal land, removing it from production, and this was expanded by Roosevelt.

In December 1933 Roosevelt authorized $25 million in emergency relief funds to start the process to buy 75 million acres. Three different agencies began buying land and planning facilities for resettling farm families, but they were soon replaced by the Resettlement Administration, headed by Rexford G. Tugwell. The Resettlement Administration bought the land through foreclosures, condemnations, and voluntary purchases and constructed hundreds of small homes in scattered subsistence farmstead projects to resettle farm families. This social experiment lasted until political pressures forced Tugwell out after the 1936 election. The Farm Security Administration then took over and, with authorization from the Bankhead-Jones Farm Tenant Act, began approving loans to tenants to buy farms and continued federal land purchases. In all, 11.3 million acres were bought for an average of $4.40 per acre in scattered land utilization projects in eleven states.

From 1938 to 1953 the Soil Conservation Service administered the lands, and large portions were distributed to states, Indian reservations, and other federal agencies. The Forest Service took over in 1953 and had control of 5.5 million acres by 1961, with 3.8 million designated as national grasslands. The Plains grasslands and their acreages are Comanche (435,319) and Pawnee (193,060), Colorado; Cimarron (108,175), Kansas; Oglala (94,480), Nebraska; Kiowa (136,417), New Mexico; Cedar River (6,717), Little Missouri (1,028,051), and Sheyenne (70,268), North Dakota; Black Kettle (31,286) and Rita Blanca (92,989), Oklahoma and Texas; Buffalo Gap (595,538), Fort Pierre (115,997), and Grand River (155,075), South Dakota; Caddo (17,784), Lyndon B. Johnson (20,309), and McClelland Creek (1,449), Texas; and Thunder Basin (571,971), Wyoming.

Today, while livestock grazing permits to private ranchers represent the largest use of national grasslands, each also has a multiple use management plan that includes public recreation, wildlife habitat, soil conservation and watershed protection, improved range utilization techniques, and resource protection during mineral operations. Oil and gas leases bring in more than $30 million annually, and grazing permits yield about $2.5 million. The combined annual budgets of the grasslands is about $8.2 million. More than a million people visit the grasslands annually, using twenty-five campgrounds and ten picnic areas.

See also AGRICULTURE: Farm Security Administration.

Francis Moul
Chadron State College

Hurt, R. D. "The National Grasslands: Origin and Development in the Dust Bowl." In *The History of Soil and Water Conservation*, edited by Douglas Helms and Susan L. Flader. Washington DC: Agricultural History Society, 1985. West, Terry. "USDA Forest Service Management of the National Grasslands." *Agricultural History* 64 (spring 1990): 86–98.

NATIONAL PARKS

The Great Plains has thirty units of the U.S. National Park System, three Canadian national parks, and fifteen national historic sites. The thirty U.S. units total slightly over 500,000 acres, which is only 0.6 percent of the 376-unit, 83,431,000-acre U.S. National Park System. In Canada the Great Plains is much better represented in the 38-unit, 55 million–acre Canadian National Park System.

To most people it is the unit classified as "national park" that comes to mind when thinking of the U.S. National Park System. There are fifty-four national parks across the country that cover 47 million acres. Badlands National Park (242,756 acres) in South Dakota occupies almost 50 percent of the total National Park System acreage in the Great Plains. The three other national parks in the U.S. Great Plains are relatively small: Theodore Roosevelt National Park (70,477 acres), North Dakota; Carlsbad Caverns National Park (46,766 acres), New Mexico; and Wind Cave (28,295 acres), South Dakota.

Badlands National Park, located in southwestern South Dakota, consists of sharply eroded buttes, pinnacles, and spires that blend with the largest protected mixed-grass prairie in the United States. The prairie grasslands support bison, bighorn sheep, deer, and pronghorn antelope. Much of the 100-mile-long Badlands Wall, a prominent physiographic feature, is located within the park. Carved by the erosive force of water, this scenic landscape contains the world's richest Oligocene epoch fossil beds, 23 to 35 million years old. Established as Badlands National Monument in 1939, the area was redesignated a national park in 1978. The park is surrounded by the Buffalo Gap National Grassland on the north and the Pine Ridge Reservation on the south. One-quarter (64,000 acres) of the park has been designated as a unit (Sage Creek Wilderness) of the National Wilderness Preservation System and is the site of the reintroduction of the black-footed ferret, the most endangered land mammal in North America. Most visitors experience the North Unit of the park, which is conveniently located near Interstate 90, and drive the Badlands Loop; the Ben Reifel Visitor Center is located along this route. The South Unit is more remote and is almost entirely undeveloped. Despite temperatures that can reach above 100°F, summer is the most popular season to visit Badlands National Park. Lodging is available within the park at the Cedar Pass Lodge and at the one developed campground, the Cedar Pass Campground. The park receives approximately a million visitors per year, but most visitors stay only about four hours.

Theodore Roosevelt National Park is located in the extreme west-central portion of North Dakota in the colorful North Dakota Badlands along the Little Missouri River and is unique among the national parks in that it not only preserves an extraordinary landscape but also serves as a living memorial to a president of the United States and his enduring contribution to the conservation movement. The park was originally established in 1947 as Theodore Roosevelt National Memorial Park but was redesignated a national park in 1978. Roosevelt first came to the area in 1883. The following year he established the Elkhorn Ranch, where many of his attitudes about nature and conservation were shaped and refined. Almost half (29,920 acres) of this park has been designated by Congress as the Theodore Roosevelt Wilderness Area. The park consists of two main units (the North and South Units) and the Elkhorn Ranch Site and is almost completely surrounded by the largest national grassland in the United States, the Little Missouri National Grassland. Nearly fifty miles separate the North and South Units. Interstate 94 borders and passes through the South Unit; the Painted Canyon Visitor Center and the Medora Visitor Center are located there. A major feature of the South Unit is a paved, thirty-six-mile scenic loop with interpretive signs that explain some of the park's historical and natural phenomena. The North Unit is more scenic but due to its isolation is more lightly visited. It also has a scenic drive (twenty-eight miles). The Elkhorn Ranch Site is located thirty-five miles north of the Medora Visitor Center. The ranch buildings no longer exist. Although the park is open all year, some of the park roads may close in the winter. There are developed campgrounds in each unit of the park. The park attracts about 500,000 visitors every year.

Carlsbad Caverns National Park is located at the southern end of the Guadalupe Mountains in the Chihuahuan desert in southeastern New Mexico. The park contains seventy-six separate caves, including the nation's deepest (1,567 feet) and third longest. Originally proclaimed as Carlsbad Caverns National Monument in 1923, it was established as Carlsbad Caverns National Park in 1930. Seventy percent of this park has been designated as part of the National Wilderness Preservation System. Visitors have a choice of two different tours in these spectacular caverns. The Blue Tour begins at the surface and goes belowground at the cave's natural entrance. It is three miles and about three hours long and ends at the Big Room. The Red Tour is one and a quarter miles long and takes about an hour and a half. During this tour an elevator ride descends 755 feet to the edge of the Big Room. The Big Room, 1,800 feet at its longest, 1,100 feet at its widest, and 255 feet at its highest, is one of the largest underground chambers in the world. The chamber is resplendent with cave formations, including the sixty-two-foot-high Giant Dome, Carlsbad's biggest stalagmite. One of the park's most spectacular sights is the mass exodus at dusk of thousands of Mexican free-tailed bats, which fly from the Big Room for a night of feasting on insects. On the surface the 9.25-mile Walnut Canyon Desert Drive is a gravel, one-way loop through dramatic desert mountain scenery. There is no lodging or developed campground within the park. The park receives about 500,000 visitors a year.

Only four national parks are smaller than the Wind Cave National Park, established in 1903. It is located at the edge of the Black Hills of southwestern South Dakota and is bordered on the west by the Black Hills National Forest and on the north by Custer State Park. Wind Cave contains fifty-five miles of passages, making it one of the longest caves in the world. It received its name from the strong air currents that flow in and out of its mouth. The cave contains many unusual mineral formations called boxwork, which are thin calcite fins resembling honeycomb. Aboveground, the park serves as a wildlife sanctuary for the restoration of bison, elk, and pronghorn antelope to the Black Hills. Starting with fourteen bison donated by the Bronx Zoo in 1913, the herd now numbers about 350. Seventy-five percent of the surface of the park is open grassland, and the rest is forested with ponderosa pine. The Elk Mountain Campground is the only option for those who want to stay overnight. Although the park receives 700,000 visitors a year, most of these visits are very short. Among the fifty-four national parks, only urbanized Hot Springs National Park (Arkansas) has shorter average visits.

The establishment of Tallgrass Prairie National Preserve in 1996 in the Flint Hills region of east-central Kansas filled a major void in the National Park System by including the first unit whose major ecosystem is tallgrass prairie. Tallgrass Prairie National Preserve is a new kind of park with a unique public/private managing concept. It is approximately 11,000 acres in size, but most of that land will remain under the ownership of the National Park Trust, which purchased the Z Bar/Spring Hill Ranch in 1994. The National Park Service will own 180 acres, yet the legislation calls for the entire acreage to be managed cooperatively by the National Park Service and the National Park Trust.

Of the ten units of the National Park System in the Great Plains classified as national monuments, four are geological and six are historical in nature. Devils Tower National Monument (1,350 acres) in the northeastern corner of Wyoming is an 865-foot tower of columnar rock, the remains of a volcanic intrusion. It was proclaimed by President Theodore Roosevelt as the first national monument in 1906. Capulin Volcano National Monument (800 acres) is a nearly perfectly shaped cinder cone that stands 1,200 feet above the surrounding High Plains of northeastern New Mexico. A two-mile paved road spiraling to the volcano rim makes this one of the most accessible volcanoes in the world. Jewell Cave National Monument (1,300 acres) is located in the Black Hills of southwestern South Dakota and is the third longest cave in the world. It is known for spectacular formations of various types. Agate Fossil Beds National Monument (2,700 acres) in northwestern Nebraska contains numerous well-preserved Miocene mammal fossils. Alibates Flint Quarries National Monument (1,100 acres) is located in the Texas Panhandle adjacent to Lake Meredith National Recreation Area. For more than 10,000 years, Native Americans dug agatized dolomite from quarries here to make projectile points, knives, scrapers, and other tools.

Salinas Pueblo Missions National Monument (1,071 acres) is located at the western edge of the Great Plains in central New Mexico. This park preserves and interprets the best remaining examples of seventeenth-century Spanish Franciscan mission churches and *conventos*. At Fort Union National Monument (720 acres) in northeastern New Mexico, three U.S. Army forts were built during the second half of the nineteenth century; they were key supply points along the Santa Fe Trail. The largest visible network of wagon ruts on this trail can be seen here. Little Bighorn Battlefield National Monument (765 acres) in southeastern Montana is the site of the Battle of the Little Bighorn between the Seventh Cavalry and the Sioux and Northern Cheyenne Indians in 1876. Homestead National Monument of America (195 acres) in southeastern Nebraska was established to commemorate the Homestead Act of 1862. The massive promontory of Scotts Bluff that rises 800 feet above the valley floor in Scotts Bluff National Monument (3,000 acres) in the western Nebraska Panhandle was a prominent natural landmark for emigrants on the Oregon Trail. This site preserves the memory of the Oregon, California, and Mormon Trails. The Summit Road allows visitors to drive to the top of Scotts Bluff for a spectacular view of the North Platte River valley.

Three national recreation areas in the National Park System are located within the Great Plains. Chickasaw National Recreation Area (9,900 acres), named to honor the Chickasaw Indian Nation, is located in south-central Oklahoma at the eastern edge of the Great Plains. This area was originally designated as Sulphur Springs Reservation in 1902, then redesignated as Platt National Park in 1906. In 1976 Platt National Park and Arbuckle National Recreation Area were combined, and the area was renamed Chickasaw National Recreation Area. The partially forested rolling hills and the springs, streams, and lakes are the setting for a diverse number of outdoor recreation activities that attract 1.5 million visitors per year. Two reservoirs in Texas serve as important centers for water-based recreation, with each recording 1.5 million visits annually: Amistad National Recreation Area (58,500 acres), in the U.S. section of the Amistad Reservoir along the Rio Grande near Del Rio, and Lake Meredith National Recreation Area (46,000 acres), which surrounds Lake Meredith on the Canadian River in the Texas Panhandle.

There is one unit in each of the classifications of national historical park and national memorial in the Great Plains. Lyndon B. Johnson National Historical Park (1,570 acres) is located in the Texas Hill Country of southern Texas north of San Antonio and consists of the birthplace, boyhood home, and ranch of the thirty-sixth president, his grandparents' log cabin, and the Johnson family cemetery. The humble nature of Lyndon Johnson is reflected in this simple cemetery under the live oaks on the banks of the Pedernales River, with his pet beagles buried nearby. At Mount Rushmore National Memorial (1,250 acres) in the Black Hills of southwestern South Dakota colossal heads of Presidents George Washington, Thomas Jefferson, Abraham Lincoln, and Theodore Roosevelt were sculpted by Gutzon Borglum on the face of a granite mountain. The memorial has a new visitor center and the Presidential Trail, which runs along the base of the mountain.

The ten units of the National Park System in the Great Plains that are classified as national historic sites vary in size from the 1.85-acre Brown v. Board of Education National Historic Site (Kansas) to the 1,750-acre Knife River Indian Villages National Historic Site (North Dakota). Six of these national historic sites are forts that relate to key events in westward expansion: Bent's Old Fort (Colorado), Fort Larned (Kansas), Fort Scott (Kansas), Fort Union Trading Post (North Dakota, Montana), Fort Davis (Texas), and Fort Laramie (Wyoming). Two of these parks are dedicated to Native American themes: Knife River Indian Villages (North Dakota) and Washita Battlefield (Oklahoma). Two parks are dedicated to African American themes: Brown v. Board of Education (Kansas) and Nicodemus (Kansas).

Linear units of the National Park System in the Great Plains that are located in the region for at least part of their extent include seven trails in the National Trail System and one national river. The trails are North Country National Scenic Trail (North Dakota), Lewis and Clark National Historic Trail (Nebraska, South Dakota, North Dakota, Montana), Mormon Pioneer National Historic Trail (Nebraska, Colorado), Santa Fe National Historic Trail (Kansas, Colorado, Oklahoma, New Mexico), Oregon National Historic Trail (Kansas, Nebraska, Wyoming), Pony Express National Historic Trail (Kansas, Nebraska, Wyoming), and California National Historic Trail (Kansas, Nebraska, Wyoming). The Missouri National Recreation River (Nebraska, South Dakota) is one of the last free-flowing stretches of the river, extending from Gavin's Point Dam near Yankton, South Dakota, to Ponca, Nebraska.

In Canada, Parks Canada manages the three national parks in the Great Plains. Riding Mountain National Park (741,312 acres) is located on the eastern edge of the interior Plains, west of the Canadian Shield in southwestern Manitoba. The park occupies part of the rugged landscape of the 500-mile-long Manitoba Escarpment west of Lake Manitoba, standing 1,500 feet above the surrounding plains. In 1895 the federal government designated the Riding Mountain area as a timber reserve. It was redesignated as a national park in 1930, taking its name from the park's dominant landform feature—Riding Mountain. The park has three distinctive vegetation zones, creating some of the greatest natural diversity in Canada. The park is essentially an area of boreal forests surrounded by aspen parkland. A third major forest type, eastern deciduous forest, occupies the lowest and warmest areas in the park on the rich soils that have built up along the base of the escarpment. The park is known for the number of its wildlife species. Large mammals include black bears, moose, elk, wolves, and coyotes. Waterfowl and beavers are plentiful along the waterways, and a herd of bison is kept in a large enclosure near Lake Audy. The seventy-eight-mile road system allows access throughout the park for sightseeing, wildlife viewing, and canoeing. There are 250 miles of hiking, biking, and horse trails in the park. The main area of recreational development is at Wasagaming on Clear Lake, a Victorian-style resort that features one of the finest collections of log buildings in Canada. Five campgrounds with a total of 600 sites are located in the park. There are also two group campsites that can accommodate a maximum of 100 people. Although the park is open all year, complete facilities are available only from mid-May to mid-October. On the escarpment in the east is located Agassiz Ski Hill for downhill skiing in the winter.

Grasslands National Park is located in southwestern Saskatchewan near the Saskatchewan-Montana border. This is one of the largest pieces of virtually undisturbed mixedgrass prairie in North America. It may be several years before the park is fully established, so interim management guidelines have been established to direct the management of park lands, visitor activities, and sensitive resources. The park, when fully established, will encompass 350 square miles in two distinct blocks. The West Block includes the Frenchman River valley. This glacial meltwater channel features deeply dissected plateaus, coulees, and the conspicuous Seventy Mile Butte. The park's East Block features the Killdeer Badlands of the Rock Creek area and is representative of the Wood Mountain Upland. The Killdeer Badlands, untouched by glaciation, reveal the multicolored hues of 60,000 years of eroded strata and are the location of the first recorded discovery of dinosaur remains in Canada (1874). Among the wildlife species found in the park are prairie dogs, golden eagles, prairie rattlesnakes, badgers, mule deer, and pronghorn antelope. Ranching operations are still ongoing in much of the area that is in private ownership. There are no designated campgrounds within the park boundaries. Only primitive, random tent camping is available. Limited essential services and a fully developed campground are located in Val Marie, just outside the boundary of the West Block. Near the East Block of the park, the town of Wood Mountain provides very limited services.

The 48,000-acre Elk Island National Park, located in the Beaver Hills region twenty-eight miles east of Edmonton, Alberta, is an oasis for rare and endangered species attracted by its lakes, ponds, forests, and meadows. Originally established in 1906 to protect a herd of twenty elk, the park is home to moose, bear, beaver, and coyote. The park is also a special venue in which to enjoy spectacular prairie sunsets. It is open all year, and most recreation facilities center on Astotin Lake. Sixty miles of trails are popular with hikers and cross-country skiers.

Parks Canada administers the following national historic sites in the Great Plains: in Manitoba, Linear Mounds, Riding Mountain Park East Gate Registration Complex, Riel House, The Forks, St. Andrews Rectory, and Lower Fort Garry; and in Saskatchewan, Frenchman Butte, Fort Battleford, Batoche, Battle of Fish Creek, Fort Livingstone, Fort Pelly, Motherwell Homestead, and Fort Esperance.

See also IMAGES AND ICONS: Homestead National Monument of America; Mount Rushmore National Memorial / PHYSICAL ENVIRONMENT: Badlands; Carlsbad Caverns; Prairie Preservation.

Charles I. Zinser
Plattsburgh State University

Zinser, Charles I. *Outdoor Recreation: United States National Parks, Forests and Public Lands.* New York: John Wiley and Sons, 1995.

NATIONAL WILDLIFE REFUGES

The National Wildlife Refuge System is a network of U.S. lands and waters that are managed specifically for wildlife, especially migratory birds and endangered species. This 92,873,832-acre system is comprised of 512 national wildlife refuges, 198 waterfowl production areas, and 50 coordination areas as well as 3 wildlife research centers, 41 administrative sites, 64 national fish hatcheries, and 6 fishery research stations. The Fish and Wildlife Service in the Department of the Interior administers the system. In the Great Plains there are 110 national wildlife refuges on 1.8 million acres (22 percent of the number of refuges but only 2 percent of the acreage nationwide). The greatest concentration of the refuges in the Great Plains is in North Dakota and Montana. These refuges range in size from 27-acre Stump Lake (North Dakota) to 903,300-acre Charles M. Russell (Montana). Additionally, the "prairie pothole" land (often referred to as "duck factories") of North and South Dakota contains 84 percent of the waterfowl production areas in the country (1,107,300 acres in North Dakota and 966,000 acres in South Dakota). These waterfowl production areas are wetland areas acquired pursuant to the Migratory Bird Hunting and Conservation Act and administered as part of the National Wildlife Refuge System.

The National Wildlife Refuge System represents the most comprehensive wildlife resource management program in the world.

The refuges are managed to maintain habitat, food supplies, and water for animals. In the Great Plains water is the prime factor determining their location. The conservation aspect of resource management governs the National Wildlife Refuge System. Hunting, growing agricultural crops, cutting hay, logging, and trapping are allowed, yet the preservation aspect dominates in seven refuges where eight units of the National Wilderness Preservation System have been designated on 64,743 acres: Medicine Lake National Wildlife Refuge (11,366 acres), Montana; Bend National Wildlife Refuge (20,819 acres), Montana; Fort Niobrara National Wildlife Refuge (4,635 acres), Nebraska; Bitter Lake National Wildlife Refuge (Salt Creek Wilderness, 9,621 acres), New Mexico; Chase Lake National Wildlife Refuge (4,155 acres), North Dakota; Lostwood National Wildlife Refuge (5,577 acres), North Dakota; and Wichita Mountains National Wildlife Refuge (Charons Garden Wilderness, 5,723 acres, and North Mountain Wilderness, 2,847 acres), Oklahoma.

Although refuges are not managed specifically for recreation, a broad range of recreational opportunities is possible on many of them; virtually all of these recreational opportunities revolve around wildlife. Activities vary with each refuge and may depend on the season. Some refuges have elaborate visitor centers and are equipped to handle a large number of visitors, but others are not. Some of the national wildlife refuges in the Great Plains are major tourist attractions and receive very heavy visitation; others are so lightly used that visitation data are not even collected.

Kansas has four national wildlife refuges. Although the Quivira (21,800 acres) is the largest, most visitation occurs at the Kirwin (10,800 acres) and the Flint Hills (40,650 acres). Kirwin is a valuable recreational resource on the North Fork of the Solomon River in north-central Kansas where a Bureau of Reclamation Dam (Kirwin Dam) impounds the river.

In Montana fourteen national wildlife refuges extend over 1,055,00 acres, but most of this acreage is in the huge Charles M. Russell Refuge, the second largest refuge in the lower forty-eight states. This refuge, named after this country's most venerable cowboy artist, extends for almost 150 miles upstream on the Missouri River above the Fort Peck Dam. Motor vehicles are permitted on over 700 miles of designated refuge road, and boating, fishing, exploring, camping (backcountry), and seasonal hunting are all popular. There are developed state park and Army Corps of Engineers recreational facilities adjacent to the refuge. A twenty-mile, thirteen-stop interpretive tour that takes about two hours provides a good overview of the refuge. The UL Bend National Wildlife Refuge borders Charles M. Russell. Medicine Lake National Wildlife Refuge (31,500 acres) is located in the glaciated rolling plains of northeast Montana and contains 11,366 acres of the National Wilderness Preservation System.

Nebraska has eight national wildlife refuges on 148,633 acres. Most of the recreational use occurs at just one refuge, the DeSoto, which lies in both Iowa (3,500 acres) and Nebraska (4,300 acres) and includes an old oxbow lake that was once the course of the Missouri River. The section open for public use is on the Iowa side of the refuge. Sitting on the shore of De-Soto Lake is one of the finest visitor centers and museums to be found on U.S. public lands. Artifacts from the 1860s stern-wheeler *Bertrand* (recovered in 1968 from the sunken ship) are on display here. Other large refuges in Nebraska include the Valentine (71,500 acres) in north-central Nebraska and the Crescent Lake (45,800 acres) in western Nebraska. Nebraska's newest refuge (September 30, 1997), the Boyer Chute, began with the donation of 1,953 acres from the Papio Missouri River Natural Resource District.

In the Great Plains of New Mexico there are four national wildlife refuges on 40,100 acres. The greater portion of this acreage is in one refuge, the Bitter Lake (25,000 acres). This refuge and the Las Vegas (8,700 acres) are by far the leaders in visitation.

North Dakota has sixty-two national wildlife refuges that cover 289,300 acres. The largest of these is J. Clark Salyer (59,400 acres), named after the individual credited with being "the father of the National Wildlife Refuge System." A twenty-two-mile-long interpretive auto tour route threads its way through marshlands, grasslands, sandy hills, and forested areas. Designated as a unit of the National Canoe Trail System, a thirteen-mile stretch of the Souris River offers opportunities for exploration and wildlife observation by canoe. The refuge attracting the most visitors is the Upper Souris (32,300 acres), which is located west and upstream on the Souris River from J. Clark Salyer. Most of Chase Lake (4,155 from 4,400 acres) and 5,577 acres of Lostwood (26,900 acres) are two of the eight units of the National Wilderness Preservation System on national wildlife refuges in the Great Plains. A small refuge on the south shore of Devils Lake, Sullys Hill (1,675 acres), has a unique historical background. President Theodore Roosevelt proclaimed it a national park in 1904, but in 1931 Congress transferred it to the National Wildlife Refuge System. The refuge is one of four managed by the Fish and Wildlife Service for American bison and elk.

Of the six national wildlife refuges in Oklahoma, encompassing 116,100 acres, the Wichita Mountains (59,000 acres) in southwest Oklahoma is the largest and receives the most visitors (1.5 million annually). This refuge was first set aside as the Wichita Forest Reserve in 1901. It became the Wichita Forest and Game Preserve in 1905 and received its present designation in 1934. In 1907 a fence was built and the New York Zoological Society donated fifteen bison, and in 1927 thirty head of Texas longhorns were introduced. These herds have increased to about 525 bison and 300 longhorns today. This refuge offers as wide a range of recreational opportunities as can be found at any refuge in the country. Another very popular refuge in Oklahoma is the Salt Plains (150,000 annual visitors and 32,100 acres) in

the north-central part of the state. The refuge is divided into almost equal parts of salt flats, open water, and vegetated land (marsh, woods, grassland, and cropland).

There are 48,000 acres in six national wildlife refuges in South Dakota. The largest (22,000 acres) and most visited (almost 100,000 visitors annually) is Sand Lake, twenty-five miles north of Aberdeen. The James River supplies water to the Mud and Sand Lakes, which cover over half the refuge. The Lacreek National Wildlife Refuge, with 35,000 annual visitors and covering 17,000 acres, ranks second in the state in both categories.

Very few national wildlife refuges are located in the Great Plains of Colorado, Texas, and Wyoming. Colorado has only one refuge in the Great Plains: Rocky Mountain Arsenal (17,000 acres). The Fish and Wildlife Service has only secondary jurisdiction over this refuge and will not receive primary jurisdiction until a contamination cleanup is completed. There are only four refuges totaling 17,000 acres in the Texas Plains. Muleshoe (5,800 acres) hosts one of the largest concentrations of sandhill cranes in North America from October through March. Balcones Canyonlands (3,500 acres) offers a valuable public hunting area in the Texas Hill Country. Only 5 acres of Grulla National Wildlife Refuge are in Texas; 3,230 acres are in New Mexico. In the Great Plains of Wyoming there are three refuges on 19,900 acres, most of which are accounted for by Pathfinder Refuge (16,800 acres).

See also WATER: Wetlands.

Charles I. Zinser
Plattsburgh State University

Zinser, Charles I. *Outdoor Recreation: United States National Parks, Forests and Public Lands.* New York: John Wiley and Sons, 1995.

PICKETT, BILL

See AFRICAN AMERICANS: Pickett, Bill

POWWOWS

See NATIVE AMERICANS: Powwows

RIDING AROUND

Riding around is a time-honored rural recreation in the Great Plains. When evening comes, families like to pile in the car and take a leisurely drive down familiar country roads to shake off the cares of the day. A multigenerational activity lasting about an hour at a time, riding around, in its purest form, has no particular destination or set purpose. It is primarily a way for families and sometimes close friends to enjoy each other's company and the countryside they know and love. It is also a tried-and-true technique for putting babies to sleep and a traditional time for humming or singing favorite old songs.

Riding around is a simple celebration of loved ones, the landscape, and the seasons. In the summer, when a high evening wind comes up to blow away the heat of the day, riding around might easily include appreciative ob-

servations of a corn, grain sorghum, or sunflower crop nearing harvest, the aroma of alfalfa in bloom, or the slow meander of a hawk also making evening rounds. Autumn weather is a natural enticement for outings that can't help but include cottonwood groves and a maple tree or two decked out for the season. Winter and spring are traditional wheat times, when every inch of growth in the crop draws attention, admiration, and sometimes great worry.

Riding around is not always an evening activity. Some families and friends like to take a drive in the very early morning or after church on Sunday. However, evening is the preferred time. It seems that nothing else inspires Plains people quite so consistently as a sunset sweeping the sky, and taking to the country roads is one of the most satisfying ways to experience the drama of a Great Plains sunset. Taking to the country roads is also one of the most satisfying ways to participate in the unencumbered landscape of the region and enjoy the spirit of freedom it engenders. Since the introduction of the automobile, riding around has been a distinctive Plains tradition. It remains today the same undemanding, meditative recreation rooted in a rural lifestyle that keeps people close to each other and close to the land.

Pamela H. Brink
Associated Authors and Editors, Inc.

RODEO

Rodeo is distinctive, if not unique, among major American spectator and participant sports because it is based on the working skills of a real occupation, even though the roping and riding that take place in a rodeo arena are far more refined than those that occur during the daily work of a ranch. The origins of rodeo lie in the impromptu competitions that naturally arise among men working cattle from the backs of horses—dares to ride an especially cantankerous bucking horse, bets at a calf branding on who can heel more calves without missing, challenges to be first to rope a herd-quitting steer.

The precursors of modern rodeo can be found in the horse sports and races and the riding and roping exhibitions that occurred at the fiestas of Spanish missions in Mexico and California in the late eighteenth and early nineteenth centuries. In the United States rodeo-like activities coincided with the big cattle drives that followed the Civil War—a bronc-riding contest between trail-driving crews near Deer Trail, Colorado; steer-roping contests at Pecos, Texas, and Dodge City, Kansas; tryouts for Buffalo Bill Cody's Wild West show at North Platte, Nebraska. The first complete rodeo, in a modern sense, took place at Prescott, Arizona, in 1888, and contestants paid to enter roping and riding contests in which they competed for trophies and cash prizes before an audience of paying spectators. The best-known American rodeo, Cheyenne Frontier Days, began in 1897. The equally famous Calgary Stampede began in 1912. Many early rodeos were held in pastures, a circle of buggies

Homer Holcomb waves a cape at a Brahma bull, while another clown is thrown at the Colorado State Fair Rodeo in Pueblo, Colorado, between 1920 and 1930.

and automobiles serving as an arena. Bucking horses were held by mounted snubbers while riders saddled them in the open.

Unscrupulous promoters often took advantage of cowboys in the early days of rodeo, but in 1936 a strike by contestants at the big eastern rodeos resulted in the formation of the Cowboys' Turtle Association, the forerunner of today's Professional Rodeo Cowboys Association (based in Colorado Springs). In addition to the hundreds of rodeos sanctioned each year by the association, there are also thousands of so-called amateur rodeos, many of them sanctioned by smaller regional associations. The National Intercollegiate Rodeo Association (which sponsors the national finals at Montana State University in Bozeman), the National High School Rodeo Association (headquartered in Denver), and youth rodeos of various types also sponsor many hundreds of rodeos each year. Rodeo as organized sport also is found in Australia and New Zealand.

Although early-day rodeos often had a dozen or more contest events for both men and women contestants, a contemporary rodeo has seven standard events for men and a cloverleaf barrel race for women. Rodeos generally begin with quasi-patriotic ceremonies that include a grand entry of riders led by the American flag. The first contest event is bareback bronc riding, in which the contestant holds onto the handle of a leather rigging cinched around a horse confined in a narrow bucking chute. To qualify, the rider must spur the horse above the point of the shoulders on the first jump out of the chute, ride for eight seconds, and not touch either himself or the horse with his free hand. Two judges score both the rider and the animal a maximum of 25 points each for a possible total of 100 points. The same rules also apply to saddle bronc riding, during which the contestant

rides in a standard saddle whose design has been approved by the Professional Rodeo Cowboys Association holding onto a buck rein attached to a halter. Bull riding, the last of the rough stock events, has similar rules, except that the rider holds onto a flat-plaited loose rope and is not required to spur the animal out of the chute.

Timed contests include calf roping, steer roping, team roping, and steer wrestling, the latter two the only events requiring two competitors. In each of these events the animal, held in a chute, is given a head start, ensured by a barrier rope that, if broken, results in a ten-second penalty. A roper must catch the calf, throw it to the ground, and tie three legs with a shorter rope called a pigging string. The calf must stay tied for six seconds for a qualified time, with the quickest time winning. Single steer roping follows the same rules except that the roper downs the steer by flipping the rope over the steer's hip and tripping him. In team roping the header catches the steer by the horns, the heeler by the two back legs; catching only one leg results in a five-second fine. In steer wrestling, sometimes called bulldogging, the wrestler comes out of the chute on the left side of the steer, while his helper, called a hazer, comes out on the right to help keep the steer running straight. The dogger must jump off his running horse onto the back of the steer, pull him to a stop, and twist his horns to bring him to the ground with all four legs pointing in the same direction.

Previous to World War II, cowgirls competed among themselves in both roping and riding events and sometimes competed against men in trick-riding and trick-roping events. Today, although women compete in riding and roping events in rodeos sanctioned by the Women's Professional Rodeo Association, most female rodeo competitors are essentially

limited to the barrel race, a timed event in which three barrels must be circled in a cloverleaf pattern.

As professional rodeo has become more popular in recent decades, attracting many participants from urban backgrounds, it has also become more removed from its ranching roots. As a result, a backlash in the form of ranch rodeo has arisen, beginning in Texas in the 1980s and spreading from there throughout most of the western states. In contrast to the individual competition of regular rodeo, ranch rodeo features cooperation among a four-member team competing in events such as calf branding, sorting, and wild cow milking that are more closely attuned to actual ranch work. Although not as accessible to the general population, ranch rodeo has nevertheless proven quite successful in bringing rodeo back to its ranch-country roots.

See also GENDER: Rodeo Queens.

James Hoy
Emporia State University

Fredriksson, Kristine. *American Rodeo: From Buffalo Bill to Big Business.* College Station: Texas A&M University Press, 1985. Westermeier, Clifford. *Man, Beast, Dust: The Story of Rodeo.* Lincoln: University of Nebraska Press, 1987. Wooden, Wayne S., and Gavin Ehringer. *Rodeo in America.* Lawrence: University Press of Kansas, 1996.

RYUN, JIM (b. 1947)

James Ronald Ryun was the world's fastest miler in the mid-1960s. Born on April 29, 1947, Ryun grew up in Wichita, Kansas, and began running as a gangly freshman at East High School. Ryun became the first high school runner to break four minutes in the mile, running 3:59.0 in 1964 as a seventeen-year-old. Later that year, Ryun finished third in the U.S. Olympic 1500-meter trials and competed in the Tokyo Olympics, advancing to the semifinals.

In 1965 Ryun ran 3:58.3 to win the Kansas state meet, then lowered his high school record to 3:56.8 when he finished second to New Zealand's Olympic champion and world record holder Peter Snell in Bakersfield, California. Two weeks later, at the Amateur Athletic Union (AAU) championship in San Diego, Ryun unleashed a powerful sprint during the last lap that carried him past Snell to finish in 3:55.3 and win his first of three straight national titles. Not only did the eighteen-year-old Ryun improve on his high school record, but he also shaved a tenth of a second off Jim Greelle's American record.

Following in the footsteps of world-class milers Glenn Cunningham and Wes Santee, Ryun matriculated to the University of Kansas for his collegiate career. His high school coach, Bob Timmons, joined Ryun in Lawrence and directed a challenging interval-training program based on running numerous repeat quarter miles. This intense training produced spectacular results: Ryun broke the world record for the half mile on June 10, 1966, running a time of 1:44.9 in Terre Haute, Indiana. Five weeks later, on July 17, Ryun claimed the world mile record in Berkeley, California, with a stunning 3:51.3 that trimmed 2.3 seconds off

Michael Jazy's mark. *Sports Illustrated* honored Ryun as the sportsman of the year in 1966, and he was also recognized by the Sullivan Award as the top U.S. amateur athlete.

On June 23, 1967, Ryun lowered his mile world record to 3:51.1 in Bakersfield, California, with superb demonstration of his sit and kick strategy, as he patiently ran in the pack before sprinting his final quarter-mile lap in 52.5 seconds. Two weeks later, he broke the world record for 1500 meters, clocking 3:33.1 in Los Angeles.

Despite being the world's fastest middle-distance runner, Ryun was bettered by the masterful Kenyan Kip Keino in the 1968 Olympic 1500-meter race in Mexico City. An Olympic silver medal was little consolation. After a disappointing start to the 1969 season, the twenty-two-year-old Ryun succumbed to the stresses of adolescent stardom and intensive training and racing and announced his retirement. Three years later, Ryun came out of retirement for another run at an Olympic gold medal. He was quick to regain form, qualifying for the U.S. 1500-meter team. Ryun's Olympic misfortunes continued, however, when a mid-race collision sent him sprawling to the Munich track in the semifinals. The ill-fated record holder pounding the track in frustration proved to be the final scene of his amateur career.

A measure of Ryun's achievements can be found in the longevity of some of his records. His world record in the mile lasted almost eight years, until Tanzanian Filbert Bayi ran 3:51.0 in 1975, shaving a mere tenth of a second off Ryun's mark. At the end of the twentieth century, Ryun still held all four middle-distance American junior records for athletes under twenty years of age, and his 3:55.8 high school record was still three seconds faster than any other American prep had run. It was finally bettered in 2001.

Two decades later, Jim was back running, this time for political office. Running as a conservative Republican in Kansas's Second District, Ryun was elected to Congress in 1996 and reelected in 1998 and 2000.

Sean Hartnett
University of Wisconsin–Eau Claire

SANDERS, BARRY

See AFRICAN AMERICANS: Sanders, Barry

SAYERS, GALE

See AFRICAN AMERICANS: Sayers, Gale

SHOULDERS, JIM (b. 1928)

Perhaps the finest rough stock contestant ever to compete in professional rodeo, Jim Shoulders was born on May 13, 1928, in Tulsa, Oklahoma. Familiar with ranch stock from childhood, he entered his first rodeo competition in 1943 at Oiltown, Oklahoma, winning the evidently inspiring sum of $1,800.

Shoulders dominated rodeo throughout the 1950s, capturing an unequaled sixteen cham-

Jim Shoulders rides an unknown bareback bronc at the Capitol Hill Night Rodeo in Oklahoma City, Oklahoma, 1950.

pionship titles against other greats like Casey Tibbs and Harry Tompkins. His strength, coolness, and flamboyant spurring style won him five all-around champion cowboy titles (1949, 1956–59), an unprecedented seven bull-riding titles (1951, 1954–59), and four bareback bronc–riding titles (1950, 1956–58). This cumulative record has been challenged but never duplicated.

A professional in business as well as sport, Jim Shoulders has done much to promote the future of rodeo. In addition to media promotion as a member of the Miller Lite All-Stars, he has worked in the rodeo production business and maintained fine contract bucking stock, including the famed "weather" bulls Cyclone, Hurricane, Twister, and Tornado, who was ridden only once in six seasons. Shoulders also opened the first rough stock training school (1961–89) for aspiring rodeo contestants at his ranch in Henryetta, Oklahoma.

Renowned in his chosen field, Jim Shoulders was among the first to be inducted into the National Cowboy and Western Heritage Museum's Rodeo Hall of Fame in 1955. Other honors include induction into the Pro Rodeo Hall of Fame in 1979 and the Oklahoma Sports Hall of Fame in 1989.

Richard C. Rattenbury
National Cowboy and
Western Heritage Museum

Fredriksson, Kristine. *American Rodeo: From Buffalo Bill to Big Business.* College Station: Texas A&M University Press, 1985. Porter, Willard H. *Who's Who in Rodeo.* Oklahoma City: Powder River Book Company, 1982.

SPORT HUNTING

Although the cultural influence of hunting today bears little resemblance to that experienced by Native Americans prior to European American settlement, the human desire to hunt still dictates the seasonal activities of millions of Great Plains inhabitants. These outings not only affect hunters personally but also generate revenue for rural economies and political momentum for wildlife conservation.

As elsewhere, hunting in the Great Plains is shaped by the diversity of game species present. Owing to the region's paucity of exclusive endemic bird and mammal species (i.e., those found in the region and nowhere else), only greater and lesser prairie chickens are hunted exclusively in the Great Plains. However, because the Plains encompass a zone where both eastern and western species intermingle, the region boasts perhaps the richest array of game animals and hunting opportunities in North America. Primary large game mammals include white-tailed deer, mule deer, and pronghorn antelope, with elk, moose, and bighorn sheep occurring mainly in the montane western or wooded northern peripheries of the region. Furbearers such as coyote and raccoon and small mammals such as cottontails and fox squirrel are also widely hunted. Primary game birds include ring-necked pheasant, northern bobwhite, prairie grouse (sharp-tailed grouse, sage grouse, and greater and lesser prairie chickens), gray partridge, scaled quail, wild turkey, mourning dove, sandhill crane, and several species of ducks and geese.

Opportunities to pursue these species are enjoyed by more than two million hunters living in states and provinces lying entirely or partly within the Great Plains and by hundreds of thousands more traveling from outside the region. In the Plains states and provinces, about 10 percent of the resident population hunts (more than 90 percent of them males), spending a total of 45 million days afield per year. About 74 percent of Plains states hunters pursue big game, 42 percent pursue resident small game birds and mammals, and 28 percent hunt migratory birds. In all, hunters spend more than $3.7 billion per year during the course of their activities in the Great Plains.

The considerable economic and social impacts of hunting have affected regional biodiversity and governmental responsibilities for wildlife conservation. License fees and excise taxes paid on hunting equipment are spent by state and provincial wildlife agencies to buy land for habitat protection and public access, improve habitat on private land, and enforce wildlife-related laws. These funds have also been used to restore species such as elk and wild turkey in areas of the Great Plains where they had been absent for decades. Furthermore, the ring-necked pheasant and gray partridge, native to Asia and Europe, respectively, were introduced in the Great Plains by wildlife agencies and private individuals in the early 1900s to provide additional hunting opportunities. Both species thrived in agricultural areas not generally habitable by native game birds and have become firmly established. In particular, the ring-necked pheasant is now perhaps the most ubiquitous and well recognized of the region's small game species and is responsible for much of the revenue and days afield associated with Great Plains upland bird hunting. As a rather ironic testament to its cultural importance, the Asian native is the state bird of South Dakota.

Hunting-related customs and laws vary

markedly within the Great Plains. For example, Kansas hunters traditionally shoot prairie chickens in late fall as they fly into crop fields to feed, whereas Nebraskans traditionally walk through rangeland and shoot them as they flush. However, perhaps most important are regional differences in methods used to gain access to hunt on private land, because this is where most hunting occurs in the Great Plains. In Texas, hunters (particularly those pursuing deer, quail, and turkey) are generally expected not only to gain trespass permission but also to pay the landowner a daily or seasonal access fee. Conversely, in North Dakota, hunters may hunt private land without the permission of the landowner unless the land has been clearly posted otherwise. Obviously, these variations in private land access can have significant effects on hunter participation and expenditures.

As might be expected from the diversity in species and customs, there is also variation in the reasons people hunt in the Plains. Residents hunt as part of family or community traditions, for food, to experience a tangible connection with nature, or as a combination of these and other motivations unique to each individual. Hunters from outside the Plains come for all the above reasons as well as to take advantage of a quality or diversity of hunting opportunities unavailable where they live. Regardless of the reasons, people will likely always hunt and in turn value places that best provide the necessary ingredients for that experience. Judged by this standard, the Great Plains is one of the most highly regarded hunting regions in North America.

See also NATIVE AMERICANS: Hunting.

J. Scott Taylor
Nebraska Game and Parks Commission

Federal Provincial Task Force for the 1987 National Survey on the Importance of Wildlife to Canadians. *The Importance of Wildlife to Canadians in 1987: Highlights of a National Survey.* Publ. CW66-103/1989E, 1989. Kellert, Stephen R. "Attitudes and Characteristics of Hunters and Antihunters." *Transactions of the Forty-Third North American Wildlife and Natural Resources Conference* 43 (1978): 412–23. U.S. Department of the Interior, Fish and Wildlife Service, and U.S. Department of Commerce, Bureau of the Census. *1996 National Survey of Fishing, Hunting, and Wildlife-Associated Recreation.* Publ. FHW/96 NAT, 1998.

STECHER, JOE (1893–1974)

Long before Hulk Hogan, "The Rock," or "Stone Cold" Steve Austin wrestled before national television audiences, Joe "The Scissors King" Stecher grappled for world titles with wrestling stalwarts such as Ed "Strangler" Lewis, "Masked Marvel" Mort Henderson, and "Tiger Man" John Pesak. Born to Bohemian immigrants near Dodge, Nebraska, on April 4, 1893, Stecher was a three-time world champion and, at the age of twenty-two, was the youngest man to ever hold the title.

Stecher was a superb athlete. In high school he played nearly every sport, excelling at baseball, swimming, and wrestling. Stecher developed a powerful physique while working on the family's 400-acre farm (at the peak of his career he stood over six feet and weighed 220 pounds). He reportedly perfected his signature move, the scissor hold, by wrapping his powerful legs around 100-pound sacks of grain and squeezing until they burst open.

By his senior year in high school Stecher was focusing solely on wrestling. In 1912, at the age of nineteen, Stecher turned professional and quickly became a sensation after a string of victories against some of the best wrestlers in the nation. By 1915 promoters recognized Stecher's potential to become the next great champion and organized a championship bout in Omaha, Nebraska. On July 5, 1915, before a crowd of 15,000 spectators, he defeated Charlie Cutler for the world championship. Over the next few years Stecher traveled the nation in defense of his title, using his feared scissors hold on one opponent after another. In January 1916, for example, he defeated the "Masked Marvel" Mort Henderson in New York City. Stecher's first defeat (and the loss of his title) came on April 4, 1917, at Omaha to Earl Caddock. Stecher regained his title from Caddock in 1920 at Madison Square Garden in what many experts have called one of the greatest matches ever. His second title run was short-lived, however, as Ed "Strangler" Lewis defeated him ten months later. Stecher continued to battle opponents during the next five years, and on May 5, 1925, he defeated Stanislaus Zbyszko to become the first three-time world champion. "The Scissors King" defended his final title for another three years before losing it on February 20, 1928, to "Strangler." Although Stecher continued to grapple for titles for another six years, shoulder injuries and age caught up with him, and he never regained his championship form.

Stecher retired from wrestling in 1934 at the age of forty-one. Shortly thereafter, Stecher's wife left with their children, and the ex-champion suffered a mental breakdown. Mental problems plagued Stecher for the remainder of his life; his last thirty years were spent in an institution in St. Paul, Minnesota. He died there on March 29, 1974. In 2000 Joe Stecher was inducted into the International Wrestling Institute and Museum's Hall of Fame.

Mark R. Ellis
University of Nebraska at Kearney

STORM CHASING

The attempt to intercept supercell thunderstorms and tornadoes from as close a distance as possible is known as storm chasing. The prevalence of flat terrain and a scarcity of trees combine with a climatology rich in spectacular and violent weather to make the Great Plains the optimal arena for storm chasing. Each spring, people from all corners of the country and beyond visit "Tornado Alley," an area of the Great Plains stretching from North Texas to Nebraska that is the breeding ground of more tornadoes per area than anywhere in the world, to storm chase. In addition to meteorological researchers, amateur weather enthusiasts, photographers, and videographers chase storms as a hobby, and emergency management "storm spotters" and television news crews chase to provide early warnings to the public.

Storm chasing was formally begun by a handful of scientists at the National Severe Storms Laboratory (NSSL) in Norman, Oklahoma, in the mid-1970s to obtain ground truth information in support of the development of weather radar. Storm chasing is extremely hazardous, especially when attempted by those without adequate meteorological training and experience, but the recent swell of attention given the endeavor by the media and the popularity of the Hollywood movie *Twister* (1996) have led to its dramatic increase as a recreational pursuit. Nationally televised programs regularly take viewers on virtual chases by following research teams and other chasers around the Plains each storm season. Storm-chasing tour companies now take vanloads of paying storm tourists on weeklong voyages in search of storms. Customers come from all backgrounds, and "chase vacations" in the Great Plains have become popular with weather enthusiasts from as far away as Europe and Japan.

Large-scale, research-oriented storm intercept projects also became more numerous in the late 1990s as meteorologists sought to improve warning technologies and understand tornado genesis. Field intercept projects of note include the Verification of the Origins of Rotation in Tornadoes Experiment (VORTEX), an ongoing multimillion-dollar research project begun in 1994 and headquartered at NSSL. VORTEX utilizes four to ten vehicles equipped with Mobile Mesonets, an array of sensors mounted on car tops that measure and record weather data very near and around tornadoes. Mobile weather balloon units, video and photogrammetry crews, and radar-equipped "hurricane hunter" aircraft are sometimes used.

Despite their relative frequency on the Plains, tornadoes are still rare events. Even the most experienced and schooled chasers face poor odds of success. Forecasts must be made hours before a tornado touches down, and it is common for chases to cover more than 1,000 miles in a day to and from a "target area." An intercept rate of one tornado witnessed per ten chases is considered a respectable average. In spite of these odds, scientific storm chasing has resulted in the collection of valuable weather data. The success of such field research operations coupled with the high profile storm chasing has gained from media coverage of recent tornado events such as the 1999 Oklahoma City outbreak has stirred widespread fascination with violent weather and made storm chasing an activity likely to remain part of Great Plains science and recreation.

See also FOLKWAYS: Tornado Stories / PHYSICAL ENVIRONMENT: Tornadoes.

Matthew D. Biddle
University of Oklahoma

Bedard, Richard. *In the Shadow of the Tornado.* Norman OK: Gilco Publishing, 1996. Bluestein, Howard. *Tornado Alley: Monster Storms of the Plains.* New York: Oxford University Press, 1999.

STURGIS MOTORCYCLE RALLY

The Sturgis Motorcycle Rally, popularly known as Sturgis, is one of the largest motorcycle rallies in the world. The event draws its name from the town in southwestern South Dakota that hosts the event each year. This Great Plains gathering evokes memories of the fur trade rendezvous or the end-of-the-summer country fair and carnival, drawing people together for one more celebration before the autumn.

The first full week of August turns the sleepy ranching community of Sturgis into a motorcycle Mecca. Enthusiasts come from all fifty states and from around the world to attend the rally. For one week Sturgis is transformed into a large city in which all the inhabitants have one thing in common: motorcycles. Most people camp out in tents, and the traffic in Sturgis resembles Park Avenue in Manhattan. The motorcyclists come to Sturgis with their families and friends for many reasons. They are eager to find old friends, meet new ones, and share stories of the past year. They also enjoy examining each other's motorcycles. Motorcycling organizations sponsor races and tours through the nearby Black Hills, and motorcycle manufacturers host trade shows that provide a glimpse at the new model-year motorcycles and accessories. Sturgis attracts people from all walks of life to spend a week talking about their motorcycles and their motorcycling experiences and creates a strong sense of camaraderie and an amiable atmosphere.

The rally has reached epic proportions; during the fiftieth anniversary in 1990 an estimated 400,000 bikers attended. However, the beginnings of the Sturgis Motorcycle Rally are much more humble. In 1938 J. C. "Pappy" Hoel, a local motorcycle shop owner, encouraged his friends to come to town for two days of racing and fun. The first rally, sponsored by the local motorcycle club, the Jackpine Gypsies, attracted around eighty people to watch nineteen racers on a quarter-mile dirt track at

the Sturgis Fairgrounds. The rally grew, based on word of mouth, encouraging its founders to extend the event and add additional attractions. During the 1980s an increase in motorcycle popularity produced a new generation of enthusiasts eager to experience the Sturgis Motorcycle Rally and races.

Motorcycle racing continues to be a focus at the rally, but Main Street is now the center of attention. The main thoroughfare through town is blocked to automobile traffic, and motorcycles are parked along each curb and two deep along the center line. Guiding their motorcycles through this narrow corridor, riders blast their throttles, releasing a deafening, ever-present thunder. While the street is the domain of the motorcycle, the sidewalks host thousands of vendors selling T-shirts and clothing, patches and stickers, motorcycle accessories, tattoos, food, beverages, and more.

Carlton L. Bonilla
Marymount University

Bonilla, Carlton L. "A South Dakota Rendezvous: The Sturgis Motorcycle Rally and Races." *South Dakota History* 28 (1998): 123–43.

THORPE, JIM (1887–1953)

James Francis Thorpe, widely acknowledged as the greatest American athlete of the twentieth century, was born on May 28, 1887, near Prague, Indian Territory, in what is now the state of Oklahoma. His impoverished parents, Hiram and Charlotte Thorpe, were members of the Sauk and Fox Indian Nation. They gave their son the Native American name Wa-Tho-Huk, or Bright Path. To this day, Thorpe remains the only American athlete to perform at the world-class level in three major sports: track and field, baseball, and football.

Thorpe grew up hunting, fishing, and breaking horses with his twin brother, Charlie. Charlie died of pneumonia at age nine, and Thorpe came to believe he inherited a measure of his brother's physical energy and

Jim Thorpe

strength. Thorpe's mother died when he was a teenager, and his father subsequently sent him to the Carlisle Indian Industrial School in Pennsylvania, one of several schools founded by Richard Henry Pratt with the intent to assimilate Native American youths into European American society. After he enrolled at Carlisle, Thorpe returned to the Great Plains only intermittently throughout the remainder of his life.

While playing halfback for Carlisle, Thorpe earned football all-American honors in 1911 and 1912, leading Carlisle to the collegiate national championship in 1912. Although he did not become an official citizen of the United States until 1917, Thorpe was a member of the U.S. track and field team at the Olympic Games of 1912 held in Stockholm, Sweden. His gold medal performances in both the pentathlon and decathlon inspired King Gustav V of Sweden to remark, "You, Sir, are the greatest athlete in the world." Thorpe's gold medals were stripped from him by the Amateur Athletic Association when it was revealed that he had previously played semiprofessional baseball, but these medals were posthumously restored to him in 1982. It has been argued that the worldwide publicity inspired by Thorpe's accomplishments in Stockholm helped to ensure the future viability of the Olympic Games.

After his triumph in Stockholm, Thorpe signed a five-thousand-dollar contract to play baseball with the New York Giants. He played major-league baseball for seven seasons, with New York, the Boston Braves, and the Cincinnati Reds. In 1915 Thorpe agreed to play football for the Canton Bulldogs. He led Canton to unofficial world championships in 1916, 1917, and 1919. Thorpe went on to play football for an assortment of teams, including the New York Giants and the Chicago Cardinals. In 1920 he become the first president of the American Football Association, which later became the National Football League. After retiring from sports, Thorpe worked as an actor and casting director in Hollywood, lectured around the country on Native American

Sturgis (South Dakota) Motorcycle Rally and Races

culture, and during World War II served in the U.S. Merchant Marine. He died in his trailer in Lomita, California, on March 28, 1953. He is buried in the eastern Pennsylvania town that bears his name.

Thorpe was elected to the Pro Football Hall of Fame in 1963. In 1999 the Associated Press ranked Thorpe third on its list of the 100 top athletes of the century, behind only Babe Ruth and Michael Jordan. In the same year, both the U.S. Senate and the U.S. House of Representatives passed resolutions that designated Thorpe "American Athlete of the Century." Prior to the 2000 Super Bowl, ABC Sports honored Thorpe as "Athlete of the Century," and the National Football League renamed its most valuable player award in his honor.

Russ Cunningham
Poway High School

Schoor, Gene. *The Jim Thorpe Story: America's Greatest Athlete*. New York: Messner, 1951. Wheeler, Robert W. *Jim Thorpe: World's Greatest Athlete*. Norman: University of Oklahoma Press, 1981.

TIBBS, CASEY (1929–1990)

The Great Plains is the home of the open range cattle kingdom, Wild West shows, and an enduring ranching industry, so it is not surprising that the region has produced some of the greatest rodeo champions ever. One of these was Casey Tibbs. Tibbs was born at Mission Ridge, South Dakota, on March 5, 1929, and grew up as a traditional ranch hand, working horses out of his family's log house at the mouth of the Cheyenne River. When he began hitching-to contests in the 1940s, the slightly built Tibbs's uncanny "rhythm riding" drew the derision of older, more powerful riders. They could not argue with his success, however, and by decade's end Tibbs was the youngest world champion in history. As his collection of tack and buckles grew in the 1950s, Tibbs became a darling of the postwar decade alongside major-league baseball stars. His striking good looks, purple luxury sedans, and silk shirts became legendary both in and out of rodeo circles.

By the time of his retirement in 1959, Tibbs had won eighteen world championships (nine Professional Rodeo Cowboys Association and nine International Rodeo Association). His list of championships was matched only by his flamboyant personality. Tibbs had a knack for capturing and in some cases creating the limelight. In 1951 *Life* magazine featured the photogenic South Dakota cowboy on its cover, the only cowboy ever to earn that distinction, and set the stage for Tibbs's post-rodeo careers in acting and overseas Wild West shows. Tibbs died on January 28, 1990, in Ramona, California.

John Michael Duffy
Mission, South Dakota

Fredriksson, Kristine. *American Rodeo*. College Station: Texas A&M University, 1985. Porter, Willard H. *Who's Who in Rodeo*. Oklahoma City: Powder River Book Company, 1982.

Transportation

Burlington Route depot, Beldon, Nebraska

TRANSPORTATION

Although transportation has played a vital role in the history of every American region, it has been especially important in the Great Plains. Having few navigable bodies of water and limited overland roads, the region desperately needed a replacement technology for the river steamboat and the covered wagon and benefited enormously from the appearance of the "iron horse." The Railroad Age solved most of the Great Plains's chronic transport problems and gave the region some of its distinctive characteristics. The thousands of communities spawned and nurtured by the rails often sported a flavor of standardization that the later network of all-weather roads with its automobiles, buses, and trucks helped to sustain.

Native American Transportation

For the Native peoples, the Great Plains was a world of enormous distances. All Indigenous groups of the Plains, whether nomads or seminomads, spent much of their time following the wide-ranging bison herds. In addition, the scarcity of streams and scattered distribution of springs, the primary sources of water, forced these peoples to cover enormous distances on a daily basis. Finally, most Plains tribes were engaged in long-distance commerce at trade centers such as the Arikara and Mandan-Hidatsa villages on the upper Missouri River, which, for some tribes, meant covering hundreds of miles.

The primary reason that made the distances so demanding was the lack of efficient transportation facilities in the period before contact with Europeans. Native Americans lacked large beasts of burden such as camels and horses. Their only domesticated animal was the dog, which was used to carry loads and to draw the travois. Native peoples employed the travois to transport household utensils, weapons, tools, tipi covers, firewood, and meat, but a dog could haul only about sixty pounds, which meant that human beings, particularly women, did most of the carrying themselves.

Most Plains rivers were dry for too long each year to be useful channels for water transportation. As a result, only a few Plains tribes, including the Assiniboines, Blackfoot, and Crees, used canoes, while others relied only on land transportation. The Assiniboines, Blackfoot, and Crees were particularly skillful in using the canoe. In the early eighteenth century, for example, the Blackfoot canoed to the Hudson Bay to trade with the British. More locally, the tribes along the Missouri River developed bullboats—small, light, bowl-shaped vessels made of bison hides—for transportation of goods.

The event that changed the traditional transportation system was, of course, the introduction of the horse to the Plains by the Spanish. (Actually, the proper term would be *reintroduction*, for horses had lived on the Plains until they became extinct around 8000–6000 B.C.) Coronado and other early Spanish conquistadors explored the Southern Plains on horseback in the sixteenth century, but

horses did not begin to spread among the Indians until the Spanish established a permanent colony, New Mexico, at the southwestern edge of the Plains at the end of the sixteenth century. Gradually, through trade and theft, horses spread from the New Mexican ranches in all directions, so that by the end of the eighteenth century all Plains tribes were mounted.

In time, the introduction of the horse was to have far-reaching cultural, economic, and political effects among the Plains Indians, but the most immediate consequence was a transportation revolution. The horse was about eight times as efficient as the dog: it could carry on its back or haul on a travois a load four times heavier than the load a dog could manage, and it could travel twice as far in a day. Thus, horse transport allowed Indians to carry more tools and utensils, extra foodstuffs, and larger tipis, and suddenly nomadism did not require giving up all but the bare minimum of possessions. It also made it possible for Indians to hunt bison more effectively, and this enticed horticulturists—the Omahas, for example—to increase the role of hunting in their economies. Interaction between tribes increased as sheer distance became less of an obstacle. In short, like railroads in the late nineteenth century, horses reduced the friction of distance, opened new economic possibilities, and raised the standards of living on the Plains.

The adoption of horses also resulted in the abandonment of canoes, usually within a generation after the Indians received their first horses. Dogs, on the other hand, continued to be used for transportation throughout the prereservation period. This was particularly the case on the Northern Great Plains, where distance from the source of horses and cold winters, which made herding more difficult and labor intensive, reduced the availability and numbers. The Southern Plains Indians, who had the largest herds, continued to use dogs to carry small items such as moccasins and household utensils.

Waterways

When European Americans entered the Great Plains, they often paddled or floated along thousands of miles of meandering waterways. In the late eighteenth century, when the rival Hudson's Bay and North West Companies extended their fur-trading hinterlands to the Prairies and Parkland Belt, they introduced to the region the water transportation systems they had developed in the Petit Nord (the area bounded by Hudson Bay, Lake Superior, and Lake Winnipeg) during the preceding century. The trading posts were linked to the Hudson Bay and the St. Lawrence River by annual brigades traveling primarily by birch-bark canoes. Paddling along the Saskatchewan River to Lake Winnipeg, then either to the Hudson Bay along the Nelson or Hayes Rivers or to the St. Lawrence along the Winnipeg River and the Great Lakes, the brigades moved furs and other cargoes effectively. The light, maneuverable birch-bark canoe had a cargo capacity of almost 3,000 pounds and allowed a crew of

five or six men to achieve a speed of five or six miles per hour. Such swiftness was crucial, because the northern rivers were navigable for only a few months between the spring thaw and fall freeze.

In contrast to their canoe-using counterparts, the American fur companies along the Missouri River system were able to use larger vessels such as keelboats and mackinaws. Powered by oars, sail, or cordelle (that is, pulled by a rope by men who laboriously walked the bank), keelboats could cover a distance of fifteen to twenty miles a day upstream, carrying a load of twenty to thirty tons of cargo. The broad, flat-bottomed mackinaws, which were used only for downstream shipments, were up to twenty feet long and carried a crew of five or six men and as many as 2,500 bison robes. Driven by the current, they could achieve up to 100 miles a day. For low-bulk and short-distance carriage, the American traders used pirogues (a construction of two canoes fastened together with planks), dugout canoes, and bullboats.

Although mackinaws, canoes, and bullboats continued to be used by fur traders and others at least until the 1870s, the advent of the steamboat on the Missouri River in 1831 revolutionized navigation. By the 1860s, paddle wheelers served as great beasts of burden along the principal streams, particularly the churning 2,285 miles of the Missouri River from its mouth near St. Louis to Fort Benton, a military post in present-day Montana. Supplies for farmers, miners, ranchers, soldiers, and trappers moved by water, as did cargoes of cattle, grain, furs, and mining machinery.

Steamboating posed challenges. Rivers on the Plains were generally unreliable, as they were often braided and shallow, and most flowed through areas of comparatively light annual precipitation. Melting winter snows, spring freshets, and sometimes-heavy autumn rains swelled portions of these streams, but during much of the year they contained inadequate water levels. The Missouri, for example, could be continuously navigated only from mid-March to late June. Even if ample depths existed, snags and sawyers often cluttered the waterways. Rocky shoals, rushing rapids, and shifting channels commonly hindered passage. High prairie winds, too, buffeted vessels, blowing them onto sandbars or into the banks or even causing them to capsize.

A special type of steamboat facilitated navigational ventures. Boats on Plains rivers were ideally suited for the difficult conditions. The use of compact, high-pressure, yet powerful steam engines, which permitted construction of inexpensive and easily maintained crafts with shallow drafts, allowed these vessels to ply relatively shallow streams. Some boats allegedly required only a "heavy morning dew" to navigate.

During the heyday of steamboating on Plains rivers, traffic could be brisk. An individual vessel might handle scores of passengers and considerable quantities of freight. In the late 1870s boats traveling the waters of the

Red River of the North between Fargo and Fort Garry carried settlers with their possessions and supplies northbound and pushed barges loaded with buffalo hides and wheat southbound.

Yet commercial steamboating on Plains rivers was largely ephemeral. Service on some streams ended as soon as a railroad penetrated the territory. Residents along the Brazos River, for example, benefited from limited navigation from the Gulf of Mexico northwestward to Washington, Texas, a distance of approximately 250 miles. By the Civil War, the Houston and Texas Central Railroad had siphoned away nearly all of the river traffic, mostly bales of cotton. Even along the Missouri River stagecoaches and later passenger trains quickly attracted travelers, but steamboat freight movements continued, albeit in diminishing amounts. By the 1920s service was nearly gone, lost to railroads and emerging motor carriers. In subsequent years federal dams made long-distance commerce impossible on the upper Missouri, although towboats and barges continued to serve customers between Sioux City, Iowa, and other downriver points. More recently, commercial inland water operators could call at the Port of East Tulsa, Oklahoma, the western terminus of the "canalized" Arkansas River.

Early Roadways

The trails and traces used by roaming herds of bison and traveling Native Americans provided the earliest practical avenues for European Americans who traversed the supposedly "trackless wilderness" of the Great Plains. Yet these original land routes, particularly in Canada, were immeasurably inferior to water routes. They were superceded by an array of "quasi" roads on which ox, mule, and horse power provided practical transport. By the close of the Civil War, immigrants, prospectors, soldiers, traders, and others could move along principal arteries such as the Central Overland Road (or Oregon-California Trail), parts of which were used by the Pony Express; the Smoky Hill Road, which traversed Kansas and Colorado between communities along the Missouri River and Denver; and the old Santa Fe Trail, the direct link between Missouri and New Mexico, first established in the 1820s. Farther north, an extensive oxcart trail system that crisscrossed the Prairie Provinces in the late nineteenth century was the closest Canadian equivalent of the famous American overland routes.

Other roads also became important arteries for commerce. Some were maintained by the military; others were largely private affairs. Several routes in the Dodge City, Kansas, region illustrate the less-remembered byways. The Dodge City–Fort Supply Trail (also called the Military Road), the Tascosa–Dodge City Trail, and the Jones and Plummer Trail connected the famous Kansas cow town and trading center with areas to the south. While coach and horse travel flourished for about a score of years after the Civil War, construction of railroads like the Rock Island and the Santa Fe brought changes. The "iron horse" killed

off stagecoach service, which federal mail contracts had heavily subsidized, and took over freighting activities, which also had depended upon federal payments for drayage to military posts.

The history of the first major phase of roads on the Plains roughly paralleled the saga of steamboating. Both forms were largely transitory. The stagecoach era lasted but a generation or two for the transport of passengers, mail, and express. However, in the West River Country of South Dakota, stagecoaches rumbled over the mostly unimproved roads until the early part of the twentieth century. As with freight moving on water, overland freight transport by wagon usually enjoyed a longer existence. Significantly, intermodal dimensions developed for both transportation forms. Stagecoach drivers met steamboats at their wharfs and, later, passenger trains at local depots; likewise, wagon teamsters traveled to dock facilities and then to railway freight stations.

Surely the most romantic form of land commerce on the Plains was the cattle trail of the post–Civil War era. For a brief period, a network of these unimproved paths across the grasslands linked the Southern Plains with railheads on the Central Plains, army posts in the Rocky Mountain West, Indian reservations, and other commercial destinations. Altogether, more than six million head of cattle were driven north from Texas from 1866 to 1885. This was one of the few times during the European American period of settlement when the region was integrated lengthwise instead of being laterally connected from east to west. By the 1880s this latter orientation had been reestablished when the barbed-wire fences of settlers closed off the open range. As this grid was laid across the Plains, the cattle trails were dislodged westward: the Chisholm Trail to Abilene, Kansas, gave way to the Western Trail to Dodge City, Kansas, and points north and finally to the Goodnight-Loving Trail, which traced the eastern flank of the Rockies from Texas to Cheyenne, Wyoming. Facing the inevitable closure of the open range, Texas cattle interests made a last, unsuccessful attempt to preserve their industry in 1885 when they proposed a National Cattle Trail linking Texas and Canada, a six-mile-wide cattle highway that would be kept out of private ownership. The day of the cattleman was over, though it still has a powerful place in the American historical imagination.

Railroads

The railroad metamorphosed life in the Great Plains, penetrating the isolation of the region and making possible modern life. Railroad companies did more than penetrate the Plains with a plethora of main, secondary, and branch lines; they peddled land, some from public land grants; they established towns, usually through town-site subsidiaries; and they vigorously (and at times misleadingly) promoted their service territories as ideal places for settlement.

The Railway Age began much later in the Great Plains than in most parts of the United States and Canada, but it lasted longer. While the 1850s witnessed extensive railroad building

in New England, the South, the Old Northwest, and Atlantic Canada, little happened in the West. The 1860s saw some construction on the Plains, most notably the strategic Union Pacific–Central Pacific transcontinental system that sliced through the heart of the region. The first great wave of railroad construction did not begin in the United States in earnest until after depressed conditions, triggered by the Panic of 1873, lifted. During the 1880s railroad expansion boomed. The Chicago and North Western and the Chicago, St. Paul and Milwaukee, for example, covered eastern South Dakota like a web; the two roads spiked down nearly 2,000 miles of track, and this building spree brought the "steam car civilization" to the emerging state.

In the Prairie Provinces, additional incentives for rail building included the desire to consolidate the newly born Dominion of Canada (1867) and the need to confront the rapid —and threatening—westward expansion of the United States. Transcontinental railroads became a national imperative. The Canadian Pacific Railway was chartered in 1881 and completed four years later with the aid of generous government cash and land grants, tax concessions, and rights-of-way. The building of the Canadian Pacific across the Prairies involved a fierce dispute between Edmonton and Calgary. The initial route was planned to follow the northern fringes of the Prairies, but eventually, to Edmonton's bitter disappointment, a more southerly route was chosen. A larger debate focused on whether the Canadian Pacific should be built along a circuitous and expensive route across the inhospitable and sparsely populated terrain north of Lake Superior or a more direct and profitable course through American territory. The company opted for the all-Canadian route, reflecting the nationalistic policies of the period, but it also created an expensive freight rate structure that was disadvantageous for the Prairie farmers.

The hard times of the late 1880s and much of the 1890s halted rail construction, but a second great building boom marked the period from the turn of the century to World War I. This was particularly the case in the Prairie Provinces. Between 1905 and 1914, two competing and partly parallel transcontinental systems— the privately owned Canadian Northern Railway and the Grand Trunk Pacific Railway, a joint attempt by the federal government and the Grand Trunk Railway to break the Canadian Pacific's unpopular monopoly in the West —were constructed to the region's northern sector, which had been left vacant by the Canadian Pacific's decision to take the southerly route across the grasslands. Moreover, the competing transcontinentals launched extensive branch line programs in the Prairie Provinces, covering the region with a thick local track network by 1915.

Even though the railroad map of the Great Plains had largely crystallized by 1920, additional trackage still appeared, especially in the Prairie Provinces of Canada. A third wave of rail building took place in the 1920s and continued in some places into the early 1930s, a century after the railroad's debut in North America. "From all corners of the state come the predictions that South Dakota, within the next few years will see another era of rail building," editorialized a Huron, South Dakota, newspaper in May 1929. "That era, from indications, is now upon us." Indeed, it was.

Rail building in the Great Plains went quickly because it was usually affordable. The generally flat or rolling terrain made construction costs much less per mile than they were in most other sections of the continent. Some Plains pikes were merely rails and untreated ties laid on a gently graded dirt roadbed. When crews of the Union Pacific pushed across Nebraska in the 1860s, they wisely followed the nearly level valley of the Platte River. Shaping the roadbed required little more than the use of inexpensive farm equipment, which semiskilled laborers could easily handle. Only the occasional bridge work posed many financial and engineering challenges. Developmental carriers like the Canadian Northern and the Kansas Pacific built inexpensive lines and made improvements later after revenues increased. Unlike construction in Europe or in eastern North America, most original Plains lines were hardly built for unborn generations. Some exceptions existed, notably the Canadian Pacific, which by 1885 possessed a quality "Dominion from Sea to Sea" route.

Few residents of the Plains ever challenged the notion that the magic touch of a railway, well built or not, promised a bright future for everyone in the surrounding areas. The arrival in 1887 of the Fort Worth and Denver City Railway in the Texas Panhandle village of Quanah prompted a local journalist to predict that the community and its trade area were headed "toward the *Ultima Thule* of commercial and financial success." Such sentiments were ubiquitous.

Yet a love-hate relationship developed between residents of the Great Plains and railroads. The largest companies, usually the transcontinentals, often held local or even regional monopolies. In Nebraska, for example, distinct Burlington and Union Pacific territories had evolved by the latter part of the nineteenth century. Both roads tried to prevent other firms like the Missouri Pacific, North Western, and Rock Island from entering their "spheres of influence." Although railroad freight rates generally dropped during this period, public perceptions were frequently negative about most carriers.

Antirailroad sentiment on the Plains was expressed in various ways. These feelings frequently led to popular support for construction of additional routes; local governments especially subscribed to issues of stocks and bonds. Individuals similarly responded. They also might make gifts of real estate to the future projects. South of the forty-ninth parallel but most of all in the Dakotas, much talk and some action occurred in the 1890s and later for the creation of "farmers' railroads." Disgruntled shippers (or those who lacked adequate rail facilities) would incorporate the company, publicize organizational meetings,

survey the route, and direct construction. Since capital would be limited, farmers and townspeople—anyone who lived along the projected line—would be asked to donate rights-of-way and to contribute their labor. Animal teams would shape the roadbed, and crossties would be harvested from nearby stands of trees. When grading was completed and ties had been furnished, the infant road would be bonded to raise funds to purchase the cheapest suitable rail and rolling stock. The ultimate fate of the finished project usually remained flexible. The road might be sold or leased to a major trunk carrier with the understanding that customers would receive the lowest possible rates and best service. Or, more likely, the line would be operated indefinitely as a cooperative enterprise. Except for several pikes, most notably the Farmers' Grain and Shipping Company and the Fairmount and Veblen, the movement at best produced only "paper" or "hot air" schemes in the United States. In the Prairie Provinces, the "farmers' railways" played an even more limited role. Prairie farmers suffered from high freight rates, but they were partly mitigated by the dense branch line system, which left few areas in need of rail facilities.

The failure of self-help in the railroad sector, reminiscent of the earlier collapse of state exchanges of the Farmers Alliance (which sought to put control of selling farm produce and buying supplies in the hands of farmers), prompted the disaffected residents of the Great Plains to flock to the standard of the People's Party (Populists) and to make loud demands for public ownership of the railroad enterprise. Not all residents of the Plains, however, considered the railroad industry to be a public enemy. In Nebraska, for instance, townspeople frequently refrained from confrontation with the carriers, realizing that an all-out assault on them might damage their abilities to attract outside capital and therefore hinder development.

While differences emerged between residents of the Great Plains about how they should respond to railroad policies and practices, nearly everyone endorsed industry efforts to develop what once had been considered the "Great American Desert." Railroad companies, which usually worked through their affiliated town-site firms, helped to create communities that benefited the general populace, whether urban or rural. Although railroads sought to profit from lot sales, they primarily wanted to settle the territory along their routes. "There is no attempt to make large sums from the sale of these town sites," explained an official of the Atchison, Topeka and Santa Fe Railway, "but rather to build up the country and serve the general interests of the railway company." Settlers on the land meant boxcars filled with grain. A similar sentiment prevailed in the Prairie Provinces, where, in the early nineteenth century, the Canadian Pacific launched elaborate irrigation projects to promote the region's agricultural capacity and settlement.

Railroads left an indelible mark on the Great Plains from Canada to the Rio Grande.

Since rails usually preceded settlement, carriers and their town-site satellites selected the station locations, usually every five to fifteen miles along their lines; acquired the necessary real estate; and surveyed lots and streets. A public auction might take place for the sale of the commercial and residential parcels, and newspaper, pamphlet, and broadside advertising would follow to "boom" the infant community, surely a "New Chicago" or a "New Toronto." Sometimes, as in the case of Winnipeg, the reality was more astounding than even the boosters had dared to dream. Situated on the eastern edge of the Prairies, midway between the Atlantic and Pacific Oceans, Winnipeg was the natural focus of trunk lines. The transcontinentals made Winnipeg the most important interior transportation point and launched the city into an economic and political boom that is unequaled in Canadian urban history: between about the mid-1880s and the end of the century, Winnipeg matured from an unimpressive cluster of wooden sheds and shacks into the leading industrial, financial, and administrative center of the Prairie Provinces.

Railroad-created communities in the Great Plains often had a look-alike appearance. Author Hamlin Garland called them "flimsy little wooden towns." On the Plains, especially the northern sections, it became common to have Main Street run at a right angle to the depot and tracks. The resulting "T-town" was immensely practical. The retailing core stood directly adjacent to the depot, and beyond were the seat of government (if the community won the bid to become the county seat), churches, and houses. The other side of the tracks likely became the locus of major commerce: grain elevators, coal and lumberyards, and the like. This configuration meant that patrons of these businesses, with their carts and wagons, would not clog the commercial thoroughfare and principal residential streets. Thus the railroad corridor, which sliced through the town, sported a practical symmetry: side tracks beyond the main line for local industries and retail and residential sections segregated for their own functions. Hundreds of these T-towns appeared at trackside, including future state and provincial capitals such as Bismarck, North Dakota, Cheyenne, Wyoming, Lincoln, Nebraska, and Regina, Saskatchewan.

Once the railroad network in the Great Plains was set by the early 1930s, it remained stable until the 1960s, particularly to the south of the forty-ninth parallel. Although several carriers, including the Katy, North Western, and Rock Island, fell into bankruptcy during the Great Depression, court-supervised reorganizations revamped these victims of hard times. The enormous traffic generated by World War II energized virtually every road. After the war years companies mostly enjoyed a sizable financial reserve to carry them through forthcoming downswings in the economy. Moreover, a replacement technology, the diesel-electric locomotive, which had been widely adopted by the early 1950s, further aided the balance sheet.

Yet all was not well with the railroads that

served the Great Plains. Tough and at times unreasonable regulation, products of aggressive and well-meaning progressive reforms early in the twentieth century, forced companies to maintain hundreds of unnecessary small-town depots with agents who might work only a few minutes a day. Companies also had to operate money-losing local and branch line passenger trains. With farm-to-market roads and other highway construction and improved waterways, numerous rail appendages, especially ones that handled mostly seasonal grain traffic, became financial liabilities. And "full crew" laws, actually "excess crew" statutes, escalated labor costs. A Nebraska measure, for example, required an extra flagman on every intrastate passenger train.

Change, however, was forthcoming. The Transportation Act of 1958 and other reforms permitted carriers to reduce their fixed costs, including closing scores of rural depots (eventually nearly all of them), eliminating most passenger service with the creation of Amtrak in 1971, and abandoning thousands of miles of lightly used trackage. Then, in the 1960s, railroad mergers greatly affected the region. Some roads, for example, the North Western and Soo Line, expanded by acquiring smaller properties, and efforts began for megamergers. That phenomenon struck the region in 1970 with the formation of Burlington Northern, an amalgamation of the Burlington, Great Northern, and Northern Pacific Railroads. Enactment of the Staggers Act in 1980 further relaxed regulation and gave railroad managers more flexibility, especially in matters of rate setting. New labor accords were also reached with the unions. By the 1990s the roads that served the Plains were in good financial health, with supercarriers Burlington Northern–Santa Fe and Union Pacific dominating the region. In 1995 the latter announced that it would acquire the Southern Pacific, a major carrier in Texas and owner of the former Rock Island's Tucumcari line between New Mexico and Kansas City. Trackage unwanted by the rail giants yet still economically viable commonly emerged as a short line or larger "regional" operation. After the early 1980s companies like the Dakota, Minnesota and Eastern; Farmrail; Kiamichi; Kyle; and Red River Valley and Western appeared on the rail map of the Plains. Throughout the Great Plains, abandoned rail routes were transformed into a new, more recreational transportation system: bike paths.

Although drastic changes occurred in the railway systems in the United States in the twentieth century, they pale in significance compared to the developments in the Prairie Provinces. Intense competition, overexpansion of lines, and financial exigencies during World War I wrecked the two transcontinental companies, the Canadian Northern and Grand Trunk Pacific. These companies, together with three other financially troubled railroads, were amalgamated between 1918 and 1923 into the government-owned Canadian National Railway. Further changes occurred in the 1930s, when the Canadian Pacific and Canadian

National, distressed by the economic depression, began to cut back their dense branch line network in the Prairies, a process that has continued. The railroads also responded to the economic stress by systematically diversifying their activities. The Canadian National expanded its holdings into marine operations, resource industries, hotels, and radio (early on, the company had launched Canada's first radio network), while the Canadian Pacific extended its operations to fields such as mining, real estate, and telecommunications, some of which have been much more profitable than the rail operations. Moreover, the two railway companies established the two largest airlines operating in Canada today. The Trans-Canada Airline (since 1964 Air Canada) began in 1937 as a wholly owned subsidiary of the Canadian National, while Canadian Pacific Airlines was founded in 1942 by the Canadian Pacific.

The growing public ownership of railways and increasing government regulation of transportation companies have given rise to intense ideological debates. One of the most controversial issues has been the regulation of freight rates, which in 1903 became the responsibility of the Board of Railway Commissioners, an independent, quasi-judiciary regulation agency. Reorganized in 1938 as the Canadian Transport Commission, the board has faced the difficult task of finding a balance between the railway companies, which have demanded higher rates as a compensation for their loss of patronage and rising costs, and the Prairie farmers, who have pressed for lower rates. More recently, the debate has shifted to the privatization of the Canadian National, which was accomplished in 1995.

Electric Interurban Railways

While the Great Plains could never claim to be the heartland of the electric interurban railway, promoters from Manitoba to Texas made numerous efforts from the late 1890s until the early 1920s to realize their traction dreams. Distinct from the electric street railway, commonly found in the major towns and cities on the Plains after 1890, which provided local service and possibly a short extension into the nearby countryside to serve an amusement park, cemetery, or special facility, the interurban was designed to connect two or more communities with services similar to those provided by steam railroads, hauling passengers, express, and often carload freight.

Interurban enthusiasts believed that their alternative transport form held advantages, at least for modest distances, over their steam railroad competitors. Unlike the railroad, the electric car promised "no cinders, no dirt, no dust, no smoke." Electric roads could be operated with greater frequency than steam lines, since interurbans had generally lower operating costs. Most passenger interurbans ran on hourly or semihourly schedules and stopped virtually anywhere, while steam trains usually made only several daily trips, pausing at a limited number of points. There was also the attraction of transportation at cheaper rates. Typical charges for interurban travel were less

than those of steam carriers. This made intercity traction particularly attractive in a period of intense consumer unrest throughout the Plains in the late nineteenth and early twentieth centuries.

In the Great Plains, electric interurbans appeared mostly in the central and southern sections. Only one interurban served the Prairie Provinces. The Winnipeg, Selkirk and Lake Winnipeg Railway, partially built in 1904 as a steam road, became electrically powered four years later and developed into a nearly forty-mile traction system. No "true" interurban ever operated in North Dakota, although in 1912 the state claimed twenty-six miles of urban trolley lines. South Dakota received only a small interurban in the Black Hills and about twenty miles of electric street railways. Nebraska fared better. Although residents never rode a bona fide interurban, three electric railways with interurban names actually appeared: Omaha, Lincoln and Beatrice Railway; Omaha and Southern Interurban; and the Omaha and Lincoln Railway and Light Company. These firms in reality were urban trolleys with rural extensions, part of nearly 250 miles of streetcar operations in the state. Kansas, Oklahoma, and Texas, however, built a host of interurbans. Kansas carriers, with about 250 miles of intercity line under wire, chiefly served metropolitan Kansas City, or the Tri-State Mineral Belt of the southeast. A smaller mileage, about 150 miles, laced sections of Oklahoma, but Sooner state companies were more scattered. The principal system, the seventy miles owned by the Oklahoma Railway, radiated out of Oklahoma City in three directions: north to Guthrie, west to El Reno, and south to Norman. Texas had the most interurbans and the greatest mileage. Eleven companies built approximately 500 miles, about 350 miles of which were in the greater Dallas area. Complementing the interurban mileage in these three states were nearly 900 miles of electric street railways.

Scores of interurbans were projected throughout the Great Plains. These "paper" projects proliferated during the two boom periods immediately preceding and following the Panic of 1907. Some schemes were monumental. Early in the century a group of promoters suggested a high-speed electric railway from Winnipeg to the Gulf of Mexico. The mileage of unbuilt interurbans in Texas alone exceeded 20,000 route miles, the most projected in any American state.

An important characteristic of interurbans on the Plains was their relative durability. They often developed carload freight capabilities and could interchange rolling stock with connecting steam roads. Interurbans like the Arkansas Valley Interurban, Kansas City–Kaw Valley, Northeast Oklahoma, and Texas Electric, generally built to steam road standards, became viable freight short lines or switching operations and lasted long after the general demise of the interurban industry during the late 1920s and early 1930s. Several segments of track continue to serve freight consumers. But in general, electric roads failed to develop a competitive freight business and died because of the onslaught of motor, especially automobile, competition.

Autos, Buses, and Trucks

Even though the Great Plains possessed an ample network of rail lines, the appearance of internal combustion vehicles in the early part of the twentieth century prompted residents to demand better public roads. By World War I, good roads associations were pushing hard to lift the region out of the mud and dust. During the 1920s, extensive programs of road improvements, especially paving projects, had been implemented. By the midtwenties the federal government had embarked upon road improvements, and pioneer endeavors such as the 3,331-mile coast-to-coast Lincoln Highway, the "Main Street across America," became part of the national system of highways. Whether for short trips or to take an "auto vacation," a rapidly growing number of citizens made car travel part of their daily routine.

More than motorists drove the roadways of the Great Plains. Motor truck operators, largely unregulated by the states until the 1920s and not by the federal government until 1935, siphoned off lucrative shipments that previously had moved by rail. Yet some executives of mid-American railroads applauded the coming of the truck. After all, these versatile vehicles could feed traffic to important rail arteries, allowing carriers to abandon money-losing appendages and eliminating the need for further branch line construction. This position was, for example, advocated by Ralph Budd, president of the Great Northern Railway.

Bus operators made their debut about the same time in the Great Plains. Resembling early providers of trucking services, these firms were usually small affairs, often mom-and-pop enterprises. But that changed quickly. While trucking remained highly atomized until after World War II, buses in the region tended to be operated by large concerns. The Greyhound Corporation emerged during the formative years of the bus and by 1930 provided coast-to-coast and interregional service.

Railroads, too, played a major role in the bus business. The Union Pacific Railroad is a good example. In 1929 the company purchased Interstate Transit Lines, which mostly served communities in Nebraska, and used the firm to launch a series of interstate passenger routes in the Great Plains and to destinations such as Chicago (with a Chicago and North Western bus affiliate), California, and the Pacific Northwest. Entry by the Union Pacific into bus transportation generated profits and gave residents of the Central Plains even better public transportation. As other carriers did, the Union Pacific used some of its bus routes to make its case to regulators that unprofitable passenger trains could be removed, since patrons had an alternative public transit choice.

After World War II the level of bus service started to decline in the Great Plains and elsewhere. Railroads sold off their bus routes and equipment to other bus carriers, usually to the

Trailways System, or else liquidated their assets. Yet, unlike in some parts of the country, some national, regional, and local bus companies remained on the Plains. This usually happened because alternative forms of public transportation were frequently lacking and also because the percentage of elderly customers who could not or would not drive was high.

All forms of motor transport, private and public, benefited from updated highways. By the early 1950s inadequate roadways troubled and even angered residents of the Great Plains. Bridges and roads did not meet travel requirements; often they were too narrow, at times they were clogged with vehicles, and they regularly suffered from physical deterioration caused in part by the same freezing and thawing that produced annual spring breakups. Construction of the Trans-Canada Highway in the 1950s and 1960s (the longest national highway in the world) and, in the United States, an extensive system of interstate highways made possible by the National Defense Highway Act of 1956 best typified this massive modernization. These improvements instantly gave motorists and truckers the power to drive at much higher speeds for longer unbroken stretches. Traffic boomed accordingly. Better roads did not create a transportation utopia, but they were extremely popular.

Aviation

Because of long distances between major regional centers, residents of the Great Plains early on enthusiastically embraced commercial aviation and quickly developed airmindedness. While barnstormers had been visiting fairs and other outdoor events to perform their daring acts of aerial wizardry since before World War I, commercial aviation emerged only during the mid-1920s. In 1925 Congress passed the Kelly Act, under which the federal government turned over operation of airmail routes from the army to private parties. With mail contracts in hand, commercial passenger operators had the opportunity to make their services financially viable. Since pioneer aircraft could carry few people, subsidies were essential.

Within a decade the Great Plains arguably was enjoying better air service than any other region in the United States. The Plains benefited from stops by the newly established transcontinental carriers, American Airways, Transcontinental and Western Air, and United Airlines. After all, the range of the era's propeller craft was limited, and nonstop flights for major distances were impossible. By the early 1930s nearly a dozen distinctly Plains airlines complemented the ever-expanding network of commercial routes. For example, Braniff Airways linked Bartlesville, Oklahoma, Kansas City, Oklahoma City, and Tulsa; Reed Airline tied Oklahoma City with Wichita Falls; and US Airways connected Denver with Kansas City and provided intermediate stops at the Kansas communities of Goodland and Salina. Canadian carriers, too, bound the country from coast to coast, and firms like Air Canada tied

together interior places such as Winnipeg and Brandon, Manitoba.

As with other commercial transportation forms, the aviation industry hardly remained static. Companies emerged, expanded, merged, and failed. Establishment in 1938 of the Civil Aeronautical Authority (later the Civil Aeronautics Board or CAB), which controlled airline routes and fares, brought general stability to the industry. Service in the Great Plains continued to be good after federal intervention, but other regions, especially the Far West, offered better financial opportunities and therefore received greater attention.

When partial federal deregulation occurred in 1978, inhabitants of the American Plains quickly felt this opening shot in the regulatory revolution. The phenomenon took several forms. Trunk carriers like Northwest and United often reduced the number of flights or ended service outright, particularly to less-populated destinations like Jamestown, North Dakota, and North Platte, Nebraska. These large carriers concentrated on maximizing the profit potentials that were inherent in jet aircraft, introduced in the late 1950s. To fill the void, residents of the Plains frequently saw formation or expansion of a host of commuter airlines. Air Midwest, launched in 1965 and based in Wichita, Kansas, for example, moved from being a largely Kansas operation into serving other parts of the Central and Southern Plains. Air Midwest was more successful than most firms; some airline companies have histories that can be measured in months rather than years. With the dissolution of the CAB, entry into commercial aviation became relatively easy, but financial risks were frequently high and failures common.

By contrast, in the Prairie Provinces, particularly in Alberta, commercial aviation has grown much more steadily. For example, Calgary and Edmonton experienced the largest increases in passenger traffic among all major Canadian cities in the 1970s, and Pacific Western Airlines, with headquarters in Calgary, emerged as the largest regional airline in Canada. This growth can largely be attributed to the favorable overall economic development of the region, although the aviation industry in the Prairie Provinces has also benefited from increasing air traffic to northern centers such as Yellowknife since World War II.

The early development of aviation in the Great Plains led to another facet of this transportation form: extensive aircraft manufacturing. Wichita emerged early as an important center for airplane building. By 1928 the city could proudly proclaim itself as the "Air Capital." Companies such as Beech Aircraft Corporation (1932–present), Boeing Wichita (1934–present), Cessna Aircraft Company (1927–present), and Learjet (1962–present) became nationally, even internationally, famous. Beech Aircraft, for one, supplied airplanes to individuals, companies, and commuter airlines like Air Midwest. Kansas aircraft manufacturers between 1908 and 1993 produced approximately 266,500 aircraft, including kits, for the commercial market.

Conclusion

Transportation has been and will continue to be a vital part of life in the Great Plains. A palimpsest of sorts can readily be detected. The region is dotted with remnants of its water, road, rail, and aviation past: the ruts of the Oregon Trail, for example, are still etched into the landscape in places a century and a half after the last wagons headed west. These physical remains underscore the evolving nature of transport. With great distances to conquer, Plains residents repeatedly have demonstrated their willingness to embrace the best and most practical technologies. It is hardly surprising that dependability and speed have been the factors in regional transportation that have enjoyed widespread public support.

See also CITIES AND TOWNS: T-Towns; Wichita, Kansas; Winnipeg, Manitoba / INDUSTRY: Aerospace; Automotive; Canadian Pacific Railway; Fur Trade / NATIVE AMERICANS: Horse / WATER: Rivers.

H. Roger Grant
Clemson University

Athearn, Robert G. *Union Pacific Country*. Chicago: Rand McNally, 1971. Gard, Wayne. *The Chisholm Trail*. Norman: University of Oklahoma Press, 1954. Grant, H. Roger. *The North Western: A History of the Chicago and North Western Railway System*. De Kalb: Northern Illinois University Press, 1996. Hidy, Ralph, et al. *The Great Northern Railway: A History*. Boston: Harvard Business School Press, 1988. Hofsommer, Don L. *Katy Northwest: The Story of a Branch Line Railroad*. Boulder CO: Pruett Publishing Company, 1976. Hunter, Louis. *Steamboats of the Western Rivers: An Economic and Technological History*. Cambridge: Harvard University Press, 1949. Lamb, W. Kaye. *History of the Canadian Pacific Railway*. New York: Macmillan Publishing Company, 1977. Martin, Albro. *James J. Hill and the Opening of the Northwest*. New York: Oxford University Press, 1976. Quastler, I. E. *Air Midwest: The First Twenty Years*. San Diego: Airline Press of California, 1985. Regehr, T. D. *The Canadian Northern Railway: Pioneer Road of the Northern Prairies, 1895–1918*. Toronto: Macmillan Publishing Company, 1976. Rhodes, Jack. *Intercity Bus Lines of the Southwest*. College Station: Texas A&M University Press, 1988. Stevens, G. R. *History of the Canadian National Railways*. New York: Macmillan Publishing Company, 1973. Winther, Oscar Osburn. *The Transportation Frontier: Trans-Mississippi West, 1965–1890*. New York: Holt, Rinehart and Winston, 1964.

AUTOMOBILES

Automobility revolutionized life in the Great Plains. Marked by vast distances and low population widely scattered on farms and ranches, the region was characterized by isolation, loneliness, and provincialism. Before 1900, railroads controlled transportation on the Plains. To be viable, farms had to be close to rail lines. Crops and cattle went to market on the rails; goods and equipment arrived the same way. Residents of the Plains, on horseback or in carriages and wagons, rarely traveled outside a ten- or twelve-mile radius. Automobility meant personally controlled freedom to travel, and for Plains families, cars and trucks opened new economic and social worlds.

Rural Americans were initially suspicious of automobiles. Expensive, fast, noisy, unreliable, dangerous, the playthings of the urban rich, it was hard to imagine that they could ever have value in the lives of country folk. The town

Fritchie Electric on cross-country trip, Denver, Colorado, 1908

council of Mitchell, South Dakota, expressed the thoughts of many when it banned automobiles from within town limits. But by 1905 cars had become more reliable and less expensive. Henry Ford, who had founded his car company two years before, concluded that the secret to success in the automobile business lay in the production of a light, rugged, powerful, inexpensive car that virtually anyone could afford. In 1908 he introduced the Model T.

The touring car, a five-passenger vehicle with a canvas top and side curtains, was the staple of Model T production. With 22 horsepower to pull 1,200 pounds, the car could go virtually anywhere and do practically anything. Cowboys ran cattle in Model Ts, and farmers carried grain and calves to market in them. Model Ts put Plains farmers and ranchers on wheels and introduced them to a whole new world.

Throughout its production, from 1908 to 1927, virtually the only thing that changed about a Model T was its price, which declined from $850 to $290. Other models were available, including the popular two-seat runabout, which was even less expensive, and a much more costly sedan, but the touring car outsold them all and became by far the most common car on the roads.

Great Plains farmers and ranchers, enjoying remarkable prosperity prior to the 1920s, snapped cars up in numbers that astonished everybody. In 1910 the ratio of adult population to cars was 65 to 1 in Nebraska and 72 to 1 in North Dakota, ranking them fourth and fifth in the nation. Kansas and South Dakota were fourteenth and nineteenth. In the early 1920s, after millions of cars had been sold, the rankings told a similar story—Nebraska and Kansas were third and fourth, South Dakota was seventh. By 1936 five Great Plains states

were in the top ten in car ownership as a proportion of population, with Wyoming in third place with a population to motor vehicle ratio of 3 to 1. The national average in 1936 was nearly 5 to 1. Such figures document the extraordinary popularity—and necessity—of motor vehicles among the residents of the Great Plains. Purchasing cars and trucks in much larger numbers than buyers elsewhere, they were targeted by the automakers as the best market in the country.

Prior to 1930, over half of these vehicles were Fords. Chevrolet rapidly gained preeminence, however, thanks to the introduction in 1929 of a six-cylinder engine that came in four-door sedan trim for only $675. Ford never regained its earlier dominance of the market, even with its introduction in 1932 of an efficient and powerful V8. Between the two there was little room left for other makes, although hopeful Great Plains entrepreneurs entered the automobile business. At least 142 firms organized to manufacture cars and trucks for sale in the exploding local market. Some, such as the Great Smith of Topeka and the Patriot of Lincoln, enjoyed brief success, but none could effectively compete.

Car ownership liberated Plains residents from the isolation and loneliness of life and expanded their world beyond the limitations imposed by horse-drawn travel and stationary rails. At the same time, the freedom of movement drastically changed Great Plains society. One-room schools gave way to consolidated county schools; country doctors moved to towns, opened offices, and associated themselves with local hospitals; and crossroads general stores closed while farm families whizzed by on their way to department stores in town. Town churches absorbed rural members while country churches withered. Indeed, towns became the focus of rural life.

At the same time, fertile land too distant from rail lines to be profitable could now be farmed, and with acreage once devoted to keeping horses put into market production, yields soared. The overproduction and collapsing prices of the 1920s were, in part, also the result of automobility. The transformation of the Plains was the result of the desires of thousands of individuals to free themselves from the dreary loneliness of life in isolation. Automobiles made that transformation possible.

See also INDUSTRY: Automotive / SPORTS AND RECREATION: Riding Around.

Michael D. Green
University of North Carolina

Berger, Michael L. *The Devil Wagon in God's Country: The Automobile and Social Change in Rural America, 1893–1929.* Hamden CT: Archon Books, 1979. Flink, James J. *The Automobile Age.* Cambridge MA: MIT Press, 1988. Wik, Reynold M. *Henry Ford and Grass-Roots America.* Ann Arbor: University of Michigan Press, 1972.

AVIATION

The history of air transport in the Great Plains has been shaped by several factors. The diffuse population and moderate size of urban centers in the Great Plains, along with the greater volume of travel between the larger urban centers, limited the development of regional air travel and freight. Nevertheless, the technological evolution of aircraft, especially the increasing reliability of engines, range, and load capacity, gradually made air a viable alternative to other forms of transport. The evolution of the necessary supporting infrastructure of airports, navigation aids, and weather forecasting also allowed broader public access to and confidence in the new airlines. Finally, the interplay of private business interests and government regulation in both Canada and the United States played a central part in the character of the new industry and its role in the Great Plains.

The high profile of aviation during World War I and its legacy of trained pilots and cheap surplus aircraft prompted an immediate postwar interest in the possibilities of civil aviation. This was especially so in the Great Plains because of the great distances and limited rail connections between urban centers. However, the restricted utility of ex–war machines and the lack of even the most basic support facilities failed to attract capital investment.

Nevertheless, the barnstorming of the early 1920s did play an important role in capturing the public's imagination. By the end of the decade many Plains municipalities were building airports, anxious to connect with the new mode of transportation. Federal contributions in both Canada and the United States were initially limited to the development of aeronautical aids in the form of charts and navigation beacons and airmail subsidies for the air transport industry. In the American Great Plains, small interurban airlines were established on largely north–south routes to act as feeders to the transcontinental railways. Farther north, Canadian companies similarly developed a north–south network, but there the

Fuel truck and biplane at Denver (Colorado) Municipal Airport, between 1929 and 1935

airlines were more involved in air freight, supporting the development of a mining industry beyond the reach of roads and rail.

Regional aviation was largely left to the private sector. However, national interests in a stable air transport industry led to a highly regulated environment. While this included the creation of a Canadian government national airline, in both countries it reinforced and institutionalized a split between large national carriers that crossed the country and regional airlines that fed into this larger network.

Civil aviation boomed after World War II, fostered by the expanded wartime aviation infrastructure, the availability of trained pilots and mechanics, and the establishment of a successful aircraft manufacturing industry within the region. Public confidence in air travel also grew, and by the late 1960s air had surpassed rail in passenger travel. Government regulation remained a prominent feature of the industry but was soon to decline in importance with consequent changes in air transport structure and character.

The expansion of the highway system through the 1950s and 1960s, heavily subsidized by the national government, began to undermine the utility of the short-haul airlines that served Great Plains cities. The deregulation of the airline industry in the late 1970s and 1980s also removed government support for regional service, and less-profitable service to many communities was abandoned. The previous separation between national and regional carriers dissolved, and smaller companies operated in a hub-and-spoke system largely centered on cities outside of the Great Plains, further eroding levels of service to many Plains communities.

See also GENDER: Earhart, Amelia.

David Neufeld
Parks Canada

Bilstein, Roger E. *Flight in America 1900–1983: From the Wrights to the Astronauts.* Baltimore MD: Johns Hopkins University Press, 1984. Davies, R. E. G. *Airlines of the United States since 1914.* New York: Putnam, 1972. Main, J. R. K. *Voyageurs of the Air: A History of Civil Aviation in Canada, 1858–1967.* Ottawa: Canada Department of Transport, 1967.

BOARD OF RAILWAY COMMISSIONERS

The Board of Railway Commissioners of Canada regulated all the major railways in Canada under the authority of the Railway Act of 1903. A broad coalition of interests, including Prairie farmers and merchants, supported the creation of this independent regulatory commission, similar to the American Interstate Commerce Commission. The Canadian government appointed three commissioners to supervise a wide range of activities, including the establishment of rules and regulations for employees, the inspection of new lines, the installation of safety devices, and the investigation of accidents. In 1908 an additional three commissioners were appointed and were expected to regulate the railway, express, telegraph, telephone, and hydroelectric business. The commissioners' most publicly visible activity involved the regulation of freight and passenger rates, and their actions influenced the rate structure in Canada, nowhere more dramatically than in the Prairie Provinces.

Between 1907 and 1914, the commissioners gradually eliminated a number of rate advantages enjoyed by merchants in Winnipeg, Manitoba, since the nineteenth century. These changes allowed rapidly growing business communities in Regina, Calgary, and other towns to compete with Winnipeg as distributing and service centers. Western business leaders continued to complain that the railways granted lower rates to their competitors outside the region, in central Canada. To address these concerns, the commissioners consistently recommended higher rate increases in central than in western Canada during and immediately following World War I. As a result, between 1914 and 1921, a 34 percent difference between central Canadian and Prairie western rates on fifth-class freight (the most common classification of merchandise distributed in carloads) had been narrowed to 14 percent. Thereafter, the railway commissioners addressed more specific Prairie grievances, particularly related to commodities such as grain and livestock. Against the advice of the railway commissioners, the Canadian government reintroduced the 1897 Crow's Nest Pass rates on grain in 1922, rates that remained in effect and controversial until the 1980s.

Ken Cruikshank
McMaster University

Cruikshank, Ken. *Close Ties: Railways, Government and the Board of Railway Commissioners, 1851–1933.* Montreal: McGill-Queen's University Press, 1991. Darling, Howard. *The Politics of Freight Rates.* Toronto: McClelland and Stewart, 1980. MacGibbon, D. A. *Railway Rates and the Canadian Railway Commission.* New York: Houghton Mifflin, 1917.

BOZEMAN TRAIL

The Bozeman Trail served as the most direct route from Julesburg, Colorado, through the Powder River Country to the gold fields of Montana in the mid-1860s. Mapped and marked by John M. Bozeman and John M. Jacobs, the road veered northwest from the Oregon-California Trail at Bridger's Ferry (Fort Fetterman after 1867) on the North Platte River in eastern Wyoming, skirted the Big Horn Mountains to the Yellowstone River valley, and crossed Bozeman Pass to Virginia City, Montana.

Lakotas, enraged by this invasion of their hunting grounds, attacked travelers along the route. The U.S. army provided protection with military escorts and by establishing Forts Reno, Phil Kearny, and C. F. Smith in 1866. Nevertheless, Lakota, Cheyenne, and Arapaho warriors continued warring against construction parties and wagon trains. The Native Americans experienced both dramatic victories and demoralizing defeats. Following their Sun Dance in the summer of 1867, the Lakotas planned to destroy all the forts. Their advantage disappeared when the army replaced their muzzle-loaders with the more accurate, faster-shooting Springfield breech-loading rifles. During two decisive conflicts in August 1867, the Hayfield fight near Fort C. F. Smith and the Wagon Box fight near Fort Phil Kearny, small military detachments repelled overwhelming numbers of Indian attackers. In 1868 Red Cloud signed the Fort Laramie Treaty, agreeing to settle his Lakotas on the Great Sioux Reservation. In return, the United States abandoned the Bozeman Trail.

See also WAR: Sioux Wars.

Jay H. Buckley
Brigham Young University

Hebard, Grace R., and Earl A. Brininstool. *The Bozeman Trail: Historical Accounts of the Blazing of the Overland Routes into the Northwest, and the Fights with Red Cloud's Warriors.* Lincoln: University of Nebraska Press, 1990. Murray, Robert A. *The Bozeman Trail: Highway of History.* Boulder CO: Pruett Publishing Company, 1988.

CANADIAN PACIFIC RAILWAY

See INDUSTRY: Canadian Pacific Railway

CATTLE TRAILS

Ranchers used specific routes, known as cattle trails, to move their animals from grazing lands to market. The most famous trails of the Great Plains ran from Texas northward to Kansas cow towns or railheads. Trail drives defined the classic golden age of the cowboy, as herders drove millions of cattle north from the mid-1860s through the mid-1880s.

Cattlemen in the Great Plains had an interest in moving their animals to more profitable markets to the north and east as early as the 1840s. Edward Piper blazed the first documented cattle trail in 1846, when he drove a thousand head from Texas and sold them in Ohio. Another early route, known initially as the Kansas Trail and later as the Shawnee Trail, opened in the 1840s. The full route ran from Brownsville in southern Texas north through Dallas. After crossing Indian Territory into southeastern Kansas, the trail branched to Missouri railheads at Kansas City, Sedalia, and St. Louis. Quarantines against Texas cattle carrying ticks and the interruptions of the Civil War closed the Shawnee Trail and ended the first phase of Great Plains trail drives.

During the Civil War untended herds in Texas multiplied quickly as Union blockades cut the state off from market outlets. The Texans knew that their four-dollar-per-head cattle in Texas could bring $40 to $50 apiece in eastern markets. Thus, after the war ranchers looked for ways to move their large herds to market. In 1866 Charles Goodnight and Oliver Loving blazed the famous cattle trail that bears their names. It ran northwest from Palo Pinto County, Texas, to Pope's Crossing in southeastern New Mexico, and on north to Fort Sumner and Fort Bascom. From Fort Sumner, Loving continued the route northwest through Raton Pass and on to markets in Colorado. In 1867 the 600-mile Chisholm Trail became the main trail, and it was used extensively until 1871. Illinois cattle buyer Joseph G. McCoy laid out the trail along an old trade path initially developed by merchant Jesse Chisholm. It ran north from San Antonio to Fort Worth, Texas, through Oklahoma and ended at Abilene, Kansas. McCoy built stock pens in Abilene to hold cattle awaiting shipment on the Kansas Pacific Railroad. In 1874 he published the first major account of life on the cattle trail, *Historic Sketches of the Cattle Trade.*

Additional cattle trails developed for a number of reasons. Conflicts with Native Americans, rustlers, or local farmers and ranchers fearful of tick-born "Texas fever" convinced some Texans to seek more peaceful routes. As railroads proliferated in Kansas and Nebraska, new cow towns and markets required new trails to reach them. Ranchers also tried to find better routes with reliable supplies of grass and water and with the fewest major hazards such as major river crossings.

In 1867 ranchers in southern Texas began moving animals along a route that ran parallel to but east of the Chisholm Trail. This Eastern Trail ran through the Cherokee Strip, passed through Wichita and Newton, Kansas, and then went on to Abilene. A decade later, Lucien Maxwell struck out to the northwest from Belton, Texas. This route, known as the Western Trail, ran through Fort Griffin northward to Doan's Store on the Red River and across the Oklahoma Panhandle. Herds could be marketed at Dodge City, Kansas, or Ogallala, Nebraska, or driven to the Northern Great Plains on the Jones and Plummer Trail. Drovers continued to utilize the Western Trail until 1892, when homesteaders settled and fenced off the route in Oklahoma Territory.

On the Northern Plains, drovers moved cattle along several routes, including the Bozeman, Northern, Oregon Cattle, and Jones and Plummer Trails. John Bozeman, born in Georgia, aspired to find a shortcut to the Montana gold deposits. In 1863 he trekked along the Yellowstone River, turned south toward the Big Horn Mountains, and arrived at Deer Creek Settlement. The trail continued in use until it was abandoned in the summer of 1868. From 1869 until about 1875, cattlemen in the Pacific Northwest pushed herds eastward into Wyoming over the Oregon Cattle Trail. Another route, the Northern Trail, paralleled the Oregon Cattle Trail from eastern Oregon through Idaho before joining the latter at South Pass, Wyoming.

Historian Philip Ashton Rollins estimated that cattle drives required about one man for each 250–350 head of cattle. In addition to the drovers, crews included a trail boss, a cook, perhaps an assistant foreman, and a horse wrangler to care for the six to eight mounts needed by each man. Cattle and horses acted up more often early on the trail. After a few weeks the animals became "trail broke" or "road broke" and easier to handle.

Cattle trails became some of the most storied places of the Great Plains. Some cowboys, beginning with Charles A. Siringo in 1885, penned memoirs of life on the trail. Siringo's book, *A Texas Cow Boy*, set off a flood of similar cattle drive books of variable quality and veracity. Countless novels and movies such as *Red River* (1948), starring John Wayne, would popularize the lightning storms, stampedes, rustler attacks, and dangerous river crossings that cowhands actually endured on the trail.

Cowboys drove some 600,000–700,000 animals north from Texas during 1871 alone. In 1884, however, Kansas enacted a quarantine against Texas cattle that effectively killed the large northern drives. The final blow to the drives came when railroads pushed trunk lines southward so that cattle could be shipped directly from Texas. Sporadic drives continued on a reduced basis for another decade, but the great era of the cattle trails had ended.

See also CITIES AND TOWNS: Cattle Towns / FILM: *Red River* / FOLKWAYS: Siringo, Charles / IMAGES AND ICONS: Dodge City, Kansas.

Richard W. Slatta
North Carolina State University

Gard, Wayne. *The Chisholm Trail.* Norman: University of Oklahoma Press, 1988. McCoy, Joseph G. *Historic Sketches* of the Cattle Trade of the West and Southwest, edited by Ralph P. Bieber. Lincoln: University of Nebraska Press, 1985. Skaggs, Jimmy M. The Cattle-Trailing Industry. Norman: University of Oklahoma Press, 1991.

COVERED WAGONS

Covered wagons were the most common means of transportation for pioneers traveling across the Great Plains in the mid–nineteenth century. Fashioned after the larger and heavier Conestoga wagons, developed by the Pennsylvania Dutch a century earlier, the design produced a vehicle strong enough to carry loads of 2,000–3,000 pounds yet light enough to avoid excessive strain to the teams of oxen and mules that pulled it. Wagon beds were constructed of hardwoods such as maple, hickory, and oak and averaged four feet in width and ten to twelve feet in length. The undercarriage housed the wheels, axle assemblies, and support systems, with iron utilized in the construction only to reinforce those wagon parts under the greatest amount of stress such as the wooden wheels. A wagon's rear wheels might reach six feet in height to allow for clearance on the Plains, while its shorter front wheels provided for some maneuverability.

The most familiar feature of the covered wagon of the Great Plains, its billowing cover, was usually a heavy-duty canvas that served as the pioneers' only protection against the elements and other hazards. A frame of hardwood bows supported this cover, and strong ties secured it to the sides of the wagon bed. Many pioneers designed the canvas cover to be rolled and tied back during the summer months to allow for better circulation. The full outfitting of the covered wagon of the Great Plains was not an inexpensive endeavor and could cost as much as $1,500.

Brenda K. Jackson
Washington State University

Mattes, Merrill J. The Great Platte River Road: The Covered Wagon Mainline via Fort Kearny to Fort Laramie. Lincoln: Nebraska State Historical Society, 1969.

DODGE, GRENVILLE (1831–1916)

Born in Danvers, Massachusetts, on April 12, 1831, Grenville Mellen Dodge graduated from Norwich University and Partridge's Military School, both in Norwich, Vermont, as a military and industrial engineer. During the 1850s he surveyed and constructed railroads in Iowa and engaged in business and banking in Council Bluffs in addition to trading with Plains Indians.

Dodge used both his engineering and his military skills during the Civil War, rising from captain to major general. During the conflict's final months, as commander of the Department of the Missouri, his command was expanded to reopen Plains mail routes and protect telegraph lines. Dodge was appointed chief engineer of the Union Pacific Railroad in January 1866 and occupied that position until 1870. His work for the Union Pacific was his greatest accomplishment and won him renown as a railroad builder.

Dodge resigned from the road in January 1870 (although he continued to be associated with the line for many years) and devoted the next three decades to building railroads and organizing railroad companies. These lines lay in the southern United States, Mexico, and Cuba. He also served as consultant to German and Italian engineers as they constructed a tunnel through the Alps.

Dodge devoted his final years to promoting railroad legislation, working in patriotic organizations, and writing on engineering and military subjects. He died at his home in Council Bluffs, Iowa, on January 3, 1916, survived by his wife, Anne, whom he had married on May 29, 1854, and three daughters.

Liston E. Leyendecker
Fort Collins, Colorado

Dodge, Grenville M. How We Built the Union Pacific Railway. Washington DC: Government Printing Office, 1910. Hirshon, Stanley P. Grenville M. Dodge: Soldier, Politician, Railroad Pioneer. Bloomington: Indiana University Press, 1967.

DURANT, THOMAS (1820–1885)

Thomas Clark Durant was born in Lee, Massachusetts, on February 6, 1820. He graduated from Albany Medical College in 1840 and married Heloise Hannah Timbrel in 1847. They had two children. Durant briefly served as a professor of medicine at Albany Medical College but subsequently channeled his energy into business. A railroad promoter and contractor, Thomas Durant's importance to the Great Plains lies in his controlling of route choice and construction as vice president of the Union Pacific Railroad.

To encourage what Robert W. Fogel has called a "premature enterprise," in 1862, 1864, and 1866 Congress provided incentives and set standards for a transcontinental railroad. The Union Pacific was organized to gain the promised loans and land. Besides his vice presidency in the Union Pacific, Durant had major financial interests in the companies he used to grade and lay the track, companies that were paid in money and Union Pacific stock.

With ongoing control of the company assured, the contractors, through Durant, chose a line that maximized construction profits with little concern for potential traffic or later operating costs and profits. In the race with the Central Pacific for subsidized mileage, the Union Pacific did not go through the existing Plains settlement at Denver. The expected expenses and slow progress of a line pushed through the rugged mountains to the west were too great. On the Plains Durant's chosen route followed the Platte River to Lodgepole Creek and the relatively easy Gangplank over the Laramie Range. As Congress intended, the railroad strengthened Council Bluffs and Omaha, but it was Durant's direction that founded new towns westward to Cheyenne and beyond.

Following charges of defrauding the Union Pacific Durant was dropped from the company's directorate in May 1869. In 1870 he sold almost all of his Union Pacific stock. Much of his fortune was lost in the panic of 1873. With his health deteriorating, Durant retired to the Adirondacks. He died at North Creek, New York, on October 15, 1885.

Alan H. Grey
Provo, Utah

Fogel, Robert W. The Union Pacific Railroad: A Case in Premature Enterprise. Baltimore MD: Johns Hopkins University Press, 1960.

EARHART, AMELIA

See GENDER: Earhart, Amelia

ELECTRIC INTERURBAN RAILWAYS

Twenty electric interurban railways operated during the early twentieth century in the Great Plains. Most were built in the early 1900s, with commuters generating most of the revenue. The light-rail interurbans used self-propelled trolley cars resembling standard streetcars. Unfortunately for the largely local owners, almost all interurbans fell victim to a combination of the Great Depression and the rise of the automobile.

Half of the Great Plains interurban companies and almost half of the 1,000 miles of track were on the eastern edge of the Great Plains in the Dallas and Kansas City, Missouri, areas. Dallas had 350 miles of tracks, most of them belonging to the Texas Electric Railroad, which stretched north to Denison and south to Waco. Kansas City had four short interurban railways extending to Lawrence, Leavenworth, and suburban Olathe and Zarah.

The interurbans were a series of unconnected parts. Only four were built in the vast area of Nebraska, South Dakota, North Dakota, and the Prairie Provinces. In Manitoba, a road connected Winnipeg to beach resorts on Lake Winnipeg. South Dakota had the four-mile-long Deadwood Central, and Omaha had two glorified streetcar lines. Half a dozen other interurbans ran in Kansas and Oklahoma: small systems connected Pittsburg, Kansas, with Joplin, Missouri, and the seventy-seven-mile-long Union Electric Railway thrust south from Parsons, Kansas, to Nowata, Oklahoma. At the advent of interurbans, steam railroads already ran through just about all of the important urban centers, so no pressing need existed for an interurban network. Few of the region's interurbans came close to achieving the inexpensive, frequent, and fast service promised by their promoters.

Lawrence H. Larsen
University of Missouri–Kansas City

Hilton, George W., and John F. Due. The Electric Interurban Railways in America. Stanford CA: Stanford University Press, 1960.

GOOD ROADS MOVEMENT

There have been three major road-building movements in the United States. The first good roads movement was for water-bound macadam roads funded by state and local government bonds. This extended from roughly 1880 to 1921 and was confined to the northeastern states and California. The second movement, from 1921 to 1956, saw massive federal funding using taxes raised from gasoline sales to build a nationwide network of bituminous macadam and concrete two-lane roads. This movement had a tremendous effect in the Great Plains. The third movement, which extended nationwide federal funding to high-speed interstate highways, began in 1956 and is essentially now completed.

The first good roads movement had two periods. From 1880 to 1900, farmers granges, the U.S. Post Office, and the organization of bicyclists known by the charming name of the League of American Wheelmen agitated for farm-to-market roads. These were constructed of graded rock bound together with water on the principles laid down in the late eighteenth century by Scottish engineer John Loudon McAdam. Macadam roads lowered the costs of getting farm produce to local railheads, allowed rural free delivery, and made bicycle tourism possible. After 1900 automobilists proved an even more powerful lobby than bicyclists. The first automobiles, imported and expensive, were purchased by wealthy easterners who soon influenced road development, diverting it from farm-to-market roads. As early as 1910, the suburban, intercity, and touring networks of highways funded in states such as Massachusetts and New York were clearly being shaped by elite automobile owners.

During the mid-1910s, automobiles severely damaged the water-bound macadam roads. Trucks, also coming into wide use by the mid-teens, added to the problem because of their much greater weight and power. A surface was needed that could resist the torque of wheels turned by internal combustion engines. California, which came late to the first good roads movement, proved that concrete and bituminous macadam highways held up far better than the early water-bound macadam, although they were considerably more expensive.

With federal funding the second good roads movement extended to the entire country between 1921 and 1956 the lessons learned during the first. A 1914 map showed that none of the Plains states had any improved highways. In 1921 federal funding of the good roads program provided jobs for World War I veterans returning to rural areas. This movement had a huge and enduring impact on mobility in the Great Plains, especially when combined with the rapid appearance of ever-cheaper automobiles and professional engineering of the road network. Henry Ford was mass-producing his Model T by 1913, prices had fallen below $300 by the early 1920s, and there was a dealer in most county seats in the country by the late 1920s. In 1919 Thomas H. Macdonald, a Colorado native, left his position as chief engineer of the Iowa Highway Commission to become chief of the U.S. Bureau of Public Roads. The bureau embodied the best Progressive Era politics: centralized standards set by professional engineers and experts but localized decision making with regard to the resulting network.

Macdonald's management of public spending during the 1920s and the Great Depression

heavily favored rural, less-populated states and renewed the first movement's emphasis on farm-to-market roads. In 1924 Colorado, Kansas, Nebraska, North Dakota, South Dakota, Montana, and Wyoming only had 12 percent of the country's improved roads by mileage, but by 1939 they had 21 percent. Yet in 1938 these states had only 6.5 percent of the country's registered motor vehicles and generated only 5.5 percent of the fuel tax receipts, which were the major source of funding for good roads. By 1939 these seven states had decent statewide networks of two-lane hard-surfaced roads, thanks to the good roads movement.

Peter J. Hugill
Texas A&M University

Hugill, Peter J. "Good Roads and the Automobile in the United States 1880–1929." *Geographical Review* 72 (1982): 327–49. Seely, Bruce. *Building the American Highway System: Engineers as Policy Makers.* Philadelphia: Temple University Press, 1987. Wixom, Charles W. ARBA *Pictorial History of Roadbuilding.* Washington DC: American Road Builders Association, 1975.

HARRIMAN, EDWARD HENRY (1848–1909)

Edward Henry Harriman was born February 28, 1848, in Hempstead, Long Island. A product of Jersey City schools and two years at Trinity School in New York City, he turned to a career on Wall Street but became increasingly interested in railroading. By 1893, after helping reorganize the Erie Railroad, he began rehabilitating other railways.

In December 1897 Harriman joined the board of the bankrupt Union Pacific. A year later he became chairman of the board of directors of the Union Pacific and in ten years put the road in first-class shape. In 1900 Harriman acquired the Southern Pacific but was prevented from entering the northwestern railroad complex by James J. Hill and by his own participation in the Northern Securities Company, which was found guilty of monopoly by the Supreme Court in 1904. Harriman sold his northwestern railroad interests at a substantial profit, which he invested in various railroad companies throughout the country.

This action led the Interstate Commerce Commission to investigate Harriman during 1906 and 1907. The inquiry uncovered the vastness of his ventures and his use of the Union Pacific as a holding company for other railroad corporate funds. The findings of the Interstate Commerce Commission, together with Harriman's interests in both railroads and insurance, not to mention his seeming disdain of public opinion, led Americans to label him a robber baron. Few knew the magnitude of his charitable activities.

Harriman married Mary W. Averell on September 10, 1879, and they had six children. He died on September 9, 1909, at his home in New York.

Liston E. Leyendecker
Fort Collins, Colorado

Kennan, George H. *Edward Henry Harriman: A Biography.* Boston: Houghton Mifflin Company, 1922.

HILL, JAMES (1838–1916)

James J. Hill, known as the Empire Builder, was one of the most important railroad leaders of the nineteenth century. He was born September 16, 1838, in Eramosa Township, Ontario, and died in St. Paul, Minnesota, on May 29, 1916. Hill built the Great Northern Railway and merged it with the Northern Pacific and Burlington Railroads to form a transcontinental railroad that connected Puget Sound with the Great Lakes and the Gulf of Mexico. This railroad system later became the Burlington Northern Railroad.

Hill began his business career in St. Paul, Minnesota, in 1856 as a bookkeeper for a steamboat company. By the 1860s he was a transportation agent handling freight transfers to and from wagons, railroads, and steamboats. This experience enabled him to enter the coal business in the late 1860s, the steamboat business on the Red River of the North in 1870, and the railroad business in 1878. During 1877 Hill formed a group—later dubbed "The Associates"—consisting of himself, Norman Kittson, Donald Smith, George Stephen, and John S. Kennedy to gain control of the bankrupt St. Paul and Pacific Railroad. The Associates renamed the railroad the St. Paul, Minneapolis and Manitoba (SPM&M), and with Hill as president the railroad became a great success. Hill was a sophisticated manager who built his railroads to the highest standards.

Hill built the SPM&M north along the Red River to the Canadian border and received a Minnesota land grant for completing it on time. He transported immigrants (many from Norway and Sweden) north before the winter was over at low rates and sold them homesteads from the Minnesota land grant at $2.50 to $5.00 an acre. This allowed settlers to be on the land in time to plant a crop that spring, and it built up the population around the railroad.

Hill used this same technique when he expanded the SPM&M (later renamed the Great Northern) into Montana in the late 1880s and to Puget Sound in 1893. He charged a nominal fee to transport immigrants in return for their settling along the route. The Great Northern was the only transcontinental built without public subsidies and the only one that did not go bankrupt in the 1890s.

Hill was a strong supporter of soil conservation and scientific farming. He traveled extensively throughout the upper Midwest and Northwest making public speeches at county fairs, encouraging farmers to adopt more advanced methods of farming. He published numerous articles on his views of farming and the value of education. However, Hill's efforts were not always successful. Many of the farmers who were induced by Hill to settle the high plains of Montana failed.

In 1896 Hill established steamship service between Seattle and ports in Asia, making Seattle a world port. In 1901 Hill and Edward H. Harriman engaged in a titanic battle for control of the Burlington and Quincy Railroad. With the aid of J. P. Morgan, Hill eventually won control of the Burlington, enabling him to complete his vision of a transportation empire that linked Asia with the Great Lakes and the Gulf Coast. Hill was known as the Empire Builder largely because he built up population around his railroads rather than building his railroads around a population.

Keith T. Poole
Carnegie Mellon University

Martin, Albro. *James J. Hill and the Opening of the Northwest*. St. Paul: Minnesota Historical Society Press, 1976. Stover, John F. *American Railroads*. Chicago: University of Chicago Press, 1997.

HOLLADAY, BEN (1820–1887)

A giant in the history of transportation in the United States, Ben Holladay was born into a poor Kentucky family in 1820. In 1836 he moved to St. Louis, Missouri, where he gained practical business experience working as a store clerk, liquor salesman, and tavern keeper. Holladay became seriously involved in the transportation business during the Mexican War in 1846, when he contracted with Gen. Stephen W. Kearny to supply wagons and provisions to the U.S. Army. After the war, he formed a partnership with Theodore W. Warner for transporting supplies to Salt Lake City, where they were sold to westbound emigrants. Holladay prospered greatly through his trade with Brigham Young and the Mormons.

Following the 1857 Mormon War, Holladay capitalized on the Pikes Peak gold rush by associating with the staging firm of Russell, Majors and Waddell. The disruption of the Butterfield Overland Mail during the Civil War provided another business opportunity. In March 1862 he gained control of the Central Overland California and Pikes Peak Express Company and its 1,200 miles of stage lines. Holladay improved and expanded the company, increasing the number of stations, obtaining a fleet of new Concord stages, and updating the numerous routes. He also secured government mail contracts amounting to $650,000 annually. By 1866 the Holladay Overland Mail and Express Company extended from Atchison to Denver and Salt Lake City. Nonetheless, Holladay, tired of increasing conflicts with Native Americans and aware that rail transport would soon supplant his stage lines, sold out to Wells, Fargo and Company on November 1, 1866, for $1.5 million cash, $300,000 worth of Wells, Fargo and Company stock, and numerous other perks.

Ben Holladay played a major role in opening up the Great Plains and the West to trade and settlement. While remembered primarily for his success in staging, Holladay held interests in steamships bound for Asia, river-bound stern-wheelers, and numerous western railroads. He also helped establish the Pony Express. Ben Holladay, the flamboyant Stagecoach King, died in Portland, Oregon, on July 8, 1887.

Derrick S. Ward
Ventura, California

Frederick, James V. *Ben Holladay, the Stagecoach King: A Chapter in the Development of Transcontinental Transportation*. Glendale CA: Arthur H. Clark, 1940.

HOLLIDAY, CYRUS K. (1826–1900)

Cyrus Kurtz Holliday, founder of the Atchison, Topeka and Santa Fe Railroad, was born April 3, 1826, in Carlisle, Pennsylvania. He became a leading abolitionist in Kansas, established a settlement at Topeka, and battled Missouri border ruffians before achieving lasting fame and fortune as a railroad builder.

As a young man, Holliday dreamed of building a railroad that would follow the old Santa Fe Trail to the Southwest. His involvement in the struggle over slavery in "Bleeding Kansas," however, put his railroading career on hold. In 1854, when Congress passed the Kansas-Nebraska Act, Holliday moved to Kansas, joined the Free Soil Party, and resided briefly in the small settlement of Lawrence. That fall, he helped found the settlement of Topeka and became that future state capital's first mayor. Throughout the fall of 1855, Holliday, an outspoken antislavery activist, wrote extensively for the *Kansas Freeman*, an abolitionist newspaper. As guerrilla warfare erupted around him, he was named colonel and commanded the Second Kansas Regiment at the December siege of Lawrence. When proslavery guerrillas renewed their incursions into Kansas six weeks later, Colonel Holliday was promoted to brigadier general, and he repulsed the Missourians.

During the late 1850s, Holliday served in the legislature and once again pursued his dream of a career in railroad building. In 1859 the Kansas Territorial Legislature granted him a state charter for the Atchison and Topeka Railroad, and in 1863 President Lincoln signed an act granting Holliday's railroad 2,928,928 acres of land in Kansas and millions more over time in states farther west. On November 24, 1863, the line was renamed the Atchison, Topeka and Santa Fe Railway. Holliday spent half a decade raising the funds needed to get this railroad started. Finally, in 1868, ground was broken at Topeka. The line was a success, soon reaching Colorado and New Mexico and eventually stretching on to Los Angeles.

In 1874, after saving the Atchison, Topeka and Santa Fe from bankruptcy, Thomas Nickerson, a Boston financier, replaced Holliday as the company's president. Holliday returned to serve as president of the reorganized Santa Fe rail system from July 1, 1896, until his death on March 29, 1900.

See also WAR: Bleeding Kansas.

Derrick S. Ward
Ventura, California

Marshall, James. *Santa Fe: The Railroad That Built an Empire*. New York: Random House, 1945.

INDIAN TRAILS

Plains Indians traveled long distances to hunt, trade, make war, and visit sacred places. To do so, they used trails such as the Great North Trail that ran south from Canada along the eastern front of the Rocky Mountains into New Mexico. A trail that crossed it on the north bank of the Arkansas River ran east to the vicinity of Kinsley, Kansas, then overland to cross the southern part of Missouri to the mouth of the Ohio River. These and many other trails created a web across the face of the Great Plains.

The trails were designed to meet the needs of pedestrian travelers. The most important of these needs was water. People using pack dogs can only travel about ten miles per day, and the most heavily used trails had water holes spaced no farther apart than ten miles. Stream crossings and steep hills were avoided whenever possible; as a result, many trails ran along the divides between stream valleys. Although they were sinuous, these routes had the additional advantage of allowing the traveler to see long distances while passing by the headwater springs of numerous creeks.

Trails converged at good fords across streams and at the rare groves of trees in the High Plains. In some instances, such as the ford across the Kansas River in the Flint Hills, the geologic stratum underlying the divide along which a trail ran created a rocky ford where the ridge was cut by a river. Groves provided shade, vegetable foods, fuel for shelter, and a variety of game animals to hunt. The "Big Timbers" of the Arkansas in Colorado, of the Smoky Hill River in western Kansas, and of the Republican River in southwestern Nebraska were some of the favored campgrounds.

Operating in cultures that lacked systems of writing and mapmaking, Plains Indians took advantage of natural landmarks whenever possible. This was especially necessary because massive bison herds could erase in a single day pathways worn by decades of human travel. When natural landmarks were absent, stone or sod cairns were sometimes built. Cairns had varied functions. In some spots they marked the main course of a trail, in others they marked a good spring not visible from the trail itself, while in still other places they indicated the route to be used to regain the trail after a river crossing. Some cairns acted as shrines at which travelers added a stone as a prayer.

Well-designed Indian trails had a pronounced effect on the early European American history of the Great Plains. Native guides led explorers along them, traders built their posts beside them, and battles were fought near them. Emigrant trails such as the Oregon and Santa Fe Trails developed from Indian trails, although wagon traffic sometimes necessitated modifications to the routes. The well-spaced water holes and gentle grades of many trails led to the use of some as cattle trails and railroad routes. Thus their effects continue to be felt today.

Donald J. Blakeslee
Wichita State University

Blakeslee, Donald J., and Robert Blasing. "Indian Trails in the Central Plains." *Plains Anthropologist* 33–119 (1988): 17–26. Mead, J. R. "Trails in Southern Kansas." *Transactions of the Kansas State Historical Society* 5 (1896): 88–93.

LINCOLN HIGHWAY

The Lincoln Highway, one of the United States' major historic east–west routes, crosses the Great Plains states of Nebraska and Wyoming. Referred to as the nation's first transcontinental highway, it originated in 1912 when automobile manufacturers and businessmen formed the Lincoln Highway Association in Detroit. The highway was intended to be a paved, toll-free memorial to Abraham Lincoln that would offer the most direct route from New York to San Francisco. In 1913 the route was designated along existing roads through twelve states: New York, New Jersey, Pennsylvania, Ohio, Indiana, Illinois, Iowa, Nebraska, Wyoming, Utah, Nevada, and California.

The Lincoln Highway entered Nebraska at Omaha and followed section line roads through small towns in the historic transportation corridor of the Platte River valley. The highway closely paralleled the Union Pacific main line, nineteenth-century immigrant trails, and a portion of the Pony Express route. The route of the Lincoln Highway evolved as segments were straightened and improved. In some places it is still possible to find one or more versions of the highway as gravel section line roads, brick streets, and abandoned roadbed along the Union Pacific tracks.

From 1913 until it disbanded in 1928, the Lincoln Highway Association mounted a national publicity campaign to raise funds to mark and improve the route. A network of state and local boosters, or "counsels," was established to aid in these efforts. In addition to publishing a series of guidebooks that provided maps and described road conditions, the association encouraged towns and cities along the route to rename appropriate streets as "Lincoln Way." Kearney, Nebraska, for example, renamed the route through the city on Central Avenue as Lincoln Way. Although the name has since reverted in Kearney, the route through downtown Cheyenne, Wyoming, is still known as Lincoln Way.

Another promotional effort of the Lincoln Highway Association was the sponsorship of "seedling miles." These demonstration road segments varied in length from one to several miles and were constructed with portland cement using funds supplied by the Lincoln Highway Association and local organizations. Seedling miles were constructed in Ohio, Illinois, Indiana, Iowa, and Nebraska. The program was implemented between 1915 and 1917. When seedling miles were constructed at Fremont, Grand Island, and Kearney, the concrete road segments represented some of the only pavement along hundreds of miles of the Lincoln Highway from Nebraska west.

By the late 1920s, when the federal highway numbering system went into effect, the work of the Lincoln Highway Association was largely finished. Through the years, federal and state funds had aided in the improvement of the route. Before it disbanded, the Lincoln Highway Association lobbied to have the Lincoln Highway's new designation as U.S. Route 30 apply to the entire transcontinental route. Instead, U.S. Route 30 diverged from the Lincoln Highway in western Wyoming to continue north and east to Portland, Oregon. Meanwhile, the Lincoln Highway became a series of federal and regional routes through western Wyoming, Nevada, and Utah, terminating at Lincoln Park in San Francisco.

Carol Ahlgren
National Park Service

Ahlgren, Carol, and David Anthone. "The Lincoln Highway in Nebraska: The Pioneer Trail of the Automotive Age." *Nebraska History* 73 (1992): 173–79. Hokanson, Drake. *The Lincoln Highway: Main Street across America.* Iowa City: University of Iowa Press, 1988. Lincoln Highway Association. *The Complete Official Road Guide of the Lincoln Highway.* Tucson AZ: Patrice Press, 1993.

MERIDIAN HIGHWAY

The Meridian Highway, now U.S. Route 81, is a major north–south route that transects the Great Plains from Canada to Mexico. The highway follows the land division grid of the Great Plains from Winnipeg, Manitoba, through North Dakota, South Dakota, Nebraska, Kansas, Oklahoma, and Texas to Mexico, parallel to the sixth principal meridian. Established in 1911–12, it was originally known as the Meridian Road. Later renamed the Meridian Highway, it has been called North America's first international automotive highway.

The Meridian Highway evolved primarily as a farm-to-market road, important to the rural areas, small towns, and cities through which it passed. The original route followed section line roads, running perpendicular to historic east–west transportation corridors. Reflecting its creation from existing farm-to-market rural roads, the original highway passed through each county seat along its route. In 1911 the Meridian Road Association was formed to mark, map, and promote the highway; in 1919 it became the Meridian Highway Association. Similar to contemporaneous good roads organizations, the Meridian Highway Association consisted of representatives from the states, counties, and cities along the route. The Meridian Highway promoters, however, perhaps in recognition of its divergence from more established routes, emphasized the absence of mountain passes and proclaimed that motorists could travel from Canada to Mexico without shifting gears. The association sold memberships and instituted widely publicized tours. When the association was a year old, in 1912, an automobile caravan was organized to travel the route south to Mexico, an event that was irregularly repeated in subsequent years.

As a north–south route that cut through the heart of the Great Plains, the Meridian Highway was relatively unrestricted by geographic barriers. The highway's few major river crossings, therefore, were of tremendous importance. A significant evolution of the route into a modern highway was the completion of the Meridian Highway Bridge in 1924 at the Missouri River between Yankton, South Dakota, and Nebraska.

Like other early named highways, the Meridian changed from its inception with road improvements that included abandonment of the route through urban areas and the establishment of improved two- or four-lane sections. In recent years, the Meridian Highway Association was reestablished as the U.S. 81 Association. Its goals include promotional activities to provide economic benefit for states and communities along the route. The association, however, is less concerned with preservation of the original route and instead hopes to transform U.S. 81 into a major four-lane north–south highway.

Carol Ahlgren
National Park Service

Francis L. Long Papers, Record Group 2171, Nebraska State Historical Society, Lincoln NE. *Yankton Daily Press and Dakotan*, Meridian Highway Bridge Souvenir Edition, Oct. 10–11, 1924.

MORMON TRAIL

The Mormon Pioneer National Historic Trail stretches 1,297 miles from Nauvoo, Illinois, to Salt Lake City, Utah. Although the Mormons, members of the Church of Jesus Christ of Latter-day Saints, did not actually blaze the trail and did not travel it exclusively, their improvements and extensive use permanently affixed their name to it.

The first part of the Mormon exodus commenced on February 4, 1846, when 1,600 Mormons crossed the Mississippi and began the journey to Kanesville (Council Bluffs, Iowa) and Winter Quarters (Florence, Nebraska). In 1847 a group led by Brigham Young began the second portion of the trail, tracing the Platte River's north bank and joining the Oregon-California Trail at Fort Laramie. Four hundred miles later, at Fort Bridger, they diverged from the Oregon-California Trail and continued west to the Great Salt Lake. From 1846 until the completion of the transcontinental railroad in Promontory, Utah, in 1869, 70,000–80,000 Mormons emigrated west over the Oregon-California and Mormon Trails. Approximately 6,000 died along the route.

In 1849 a Perpetual Emigrating Fund was established to enable converts to borrow funds for their trip and repay them after settling in Utah. During the late 1850s Mormon leaders also cut travel time and expenses by implementing two-wheeled handcart travel. Between 1856 and 1860, ten companies comprising 2,962 Mormons used this successful mode of transportation. In 1856, however, the Martin and Willie Companies left too late in the year and were trapped by the Wyoming winter. More than 200 perished before a rescue party arrived.

The Mormon Trail experience was highly organized and less marked by disease or Indian attack than other overland journeys. It served as an initiation, a rite of passage, and was a unifying element for early Mormons. Dramatic reenactments and celebrations of the Mormon Trail occurred in 1897, 1947, and 1997. In 1947 a "Centennial Caravan" consisting of seventy-two automobiles with simulated covered wagon tops and plywood oxen made the journey from Nauvoo to Salt Lake. In 1996 and 1997 an estimated 10,000 joined the sesquicentennial wagon train for a day, a week, or more. The Pioneer Cemetery and Mormon Trail Center at Historic Winter Quarters, Rebecca Winter's grave near Scottsbluff, Nebraska, Fort

Caspar in Casper, Wyoming, the Mormon Handcart Visitors Center on the west side of Devil's Gate, Wyoming, and "This Is the Place" State Park in Salt Lake City memorialize the trail, portions of which are still visible in western Nebraska near North Platte and Sutherland and in various places in Wyoming.

See also RELIGION: Church of Jesus Christ of Latter-day Saints.

Jay H. Buckley
Brigham Young University

Hafen, LeRoy R., and Ann W. Hafen. *Handcarts to Zion: The Story of a Unique Western Migration, 1856–1860.* Lincoln: University of Nebraska Press, 1992. Kimball, Stanley B. *Historic Sites and Markers along the Mormon and Other Great Western Trails.* Urbana: University of Illinois Press, 1988. Stegner, Wallace. *The Gathering of Zion: The Story of the Mormon Trail.* Lincoln: University of Nebraska Press, 1981.

OREGON TRAIL

The Oregon Trail began as a fur traders' route across the Great Plains in 1824 with the discovery of South Pass through the Rocky Mountains. The pack trains and, later, the wagon caravans that supplied the mountain rendezvous started up the trail from Independence and Westport Landing in the present-day Kansas City area. They moved northwestward, tracing the Kansas and Little Blue Rivers to the Platte, then followed its southern bank westward across the Plains. Other traffic left Bellevue, south of present-day Omaha, to follow the north side of the Platte to the rendezvous.

The fur trade era had shaded into that of the Pacific Coast migrations by the early 1840s. The first missionaries and emigrants bound for California and Oregon accompanied fur trade caravans, and former mountain men guided the first emigrant trains. These early migrants generally came from the Mississippi River valley, and farm families predominated. Some 875 settlers traveled the Oregon Trail in 1843, and by 1847 the migration across the Central Plains had swelled to 4,000–5,000 people.

Emigrants used all manner of conveyances, though mostly the familiar canvas-topped wagons. These wagons generally had light bodies and flat beds caulked for stream crossings. Oxen pulled the majority of the wagons; mules and horses hauled the rest. Settlers formed themselves into trains and, within trains, into "messes," or a team of travelers sharing a wagon. Various guides for emigrants, available at the points of departure, described in detail what was needed for the trip.

In the mid-1840s American leaders decided that this growing migration merited protection. In 1848 Fort Kearny was founded in the central Platte River valley, and a year later, Fort Laramie was remodeled from the fur trading post, Fort John, near the mouth of the Laramie River. These two major forts offered provisions, postal and blacksmith services, and medical care.

California gold inspired migrations in 1849 and 1850 that dwarfed the earlier migrations. About 50,000 emigrants went overland to Oregon and, mainly, California in the latter

A man shows the width of the Oregon Trail, between 1920 and 1930

year. This new wave featured a greater proportion of single men and husbands traveling without families, seeking quick wealth rather than new homes. These gold seekers generally came from the upper Mississippi River valley and were more urban in origin than earlier travelers. The upriver towns of Weston and St. Joseph, Missouri, joined the Kansas City area as major departure points, as did the site of the first abortive Fort Kearny at present-day Nebraska City, Nebraska. Farthest north, Kanesville (Council Bluffs), Iowa, served an important stream of travel up the north side of the Platte. After a drop in 1851, heavy traffic to California resumed in 1852, this time with more families. Thereafter, migration continued at a more moderate pace, with something like 250,000–300,000 people traveling the trail across the Plains through 1866.

These later migrants followed well-established routes. Several streams of traffic converged east of Fort Kearny in the central Platte River valley. The south-side throng moved west and crossed the South Platte at three main crossings to Ash Hollow and the North Platte valley. The Upper or Old California Crossing involved a descent into Ash Hollow down Windlass Hill. Otherwise, travelers entered Ash Hollow from the east. The road then lay along the south side of the North Platte through Robidoux and Mitchell Passes, which featured trading posts and blacksmith facilities. From the late 1850s the Later California Crossing near Julesburg, Colorado, led to a new route that reached the North Platte at Courthouse Rock. The south-siders made a dangerous crossing of the Laramie River at the fort. Meanwhile, north-siders from Council Bluffs gathered at the site of present-day Fremont, Nebraska, then negotiated the dangerous Loup River crossing. From there they moved up the north side of the Platte and North Platte to join the south-siders at Fort

Laramie. By the early 1850s precarious toll bridges and ferries existed at the Fort Laramie crossings. From Fort Laramie, travelers hoped to reach South Pass by around July 4, having ideally left the Missouri River around April 15.

Naturally, months on the road through a sometimes harsh land took a toll on travelers, though emigrant mortality probably did not much exceed that among the general American population. Despite apprehensions, few died at the hands of Plains Indians. Many more died from accidents: mishaps with firearms, drownings, and injuries suffered while driving wagons or handling livestock. Disease, especially Asiatic cholera, by far killed the most.

The trail developed new features as emigration continued. Government mail contracts stimulated increasingly reliable stagecoach service from 1850 on. Military contracts launched large-scale freighting on the trail in 1855. The Pikes Peak gold rush of 1859 created a thriving commerce between Colorado and the Nebraska river towns, which replaced the northwestern Missouri towns as the dominant outfitting and departure points. This new traffic brought about a string of stage stations and road ranches, which, along with proliferating bridges and ferries, eliminated much of the hazard of overland travel.

Abandonment of the Oregon Trail began in 1862. In that year stagecoaches began to follow the new Overland Trail, moving southwest from Julesburg, avoiding Indian depredations beyond Fort Laramie. Emigrant travel followed. The North Platte valley thus became largely a military road, except for new civilian travel bound for the Montana gold fields. In 1866 Union Pacific rails were laid down opposite Fort Kearny, and the great era of the Oregon Trail ended.

See also LAW: Overland Trail Constitutions.

Paul Collister
Lincoln, Nebraska

Federal Writers' Project. *The Oregon Trail: The Missouri River to the Pacific Ocean.* New York: Hastings House, 1939; reprint, Somerset Publishers, 1972. Mattes, Merrill J. *The Great Platte River Road: The Covered Wagon Mainline via Fort Kearny to Fort Laramie.* Lincoln: Nebraska State Historical Society, 1969. Unruh, John D., Jr. *The Plains Across: The Overlanders and the Trans-Mississippi West, 1840–60.* Urbana: University of Illinois Press, 1979.

PARKING METER

World's first installed parking meter, Oklahoma City, Oklahoma, 1935

On December 21, 1932, Carl C. Magee of Oklahoma City filed for a patent on the first "coin-controlled parking meter," an invention designed to eliminate a major nuisance of the automobile age, urban parking congestion. Magee, as chair of the Oklahoma City Chamber of Commerce's traffic committee, had been asked to devise an effective method of controlling Oklahoma City's growing parking problem. The capital city was Oklahoma's largest urban area. The city's thoroughfares were used by 10 percent of the state's 550,000 registered automobiles, and all-day workers in the downtown area preempted parking spaces needed by customers of retail establishments. Up to this time, Oklahoma City officials, like those in other large cities, had attached fixed time periods to downtown parking spaces, with traffic officers enforcing the limits by chalking the tires of parked cars and issuing tickets to drivers who parked too long in the same spot. This method proved to be only 5–10 percent effective.

Magee, a New Mexico newspaper reporter who had arrived in Oklahoma City in 1927 to buy and edit a weekly paper, the *Oklahoma News*, quickly became involved in civic work and volunteered to "solve" the city's problem. He conceptualized a spring-operated timing device, articulated precise specifications, and

in late 1932 filed for a patent. Then, in cooperation with Dean Phillip S. Donnell, engineering professor H. G. Thuesen, and other faculty at the Oklahoma State University College of Engineering, Magee sponsored a design competition. Criteria for the device were simple: it had to be small, attractive, windable, and cheap to manufacture.

Unfortunately, none of the submissions proved entirely usable, and in 1933 Thuesen, in concert with Gerald A. Hale, his former student and an OSU engineering instructor, developed the "Black Maria," a spring-wound timing device that followed Magee's concept and met his design criteria. Additional technical work was accomplished by Adolph Schillinger, a machinist from Sand Springs, Oklahoma, and a working model of a manually wound, coin-operated parking timer resulted. In November 1933 Magee filed the patent for this device as well, and in 1935 he incorporated the Dual Parking Meter Company, with himself as president. Refinements were added by the chosen manufacturer, the MacNick Company of Tulsa, makers of timing devices for "shooting" oil wells with nitroglycerin. Magee's third patent, filed on May 13, 1935, was approved on May 24, 1938.

First trademarked as the "Dual" and later as the "Park-O-Meter," Magee's brainchild was adopted by the Oklahoma City council, and in July 1935 175 units were installed in a fourteen-block area of central downtown. Five cents bought an hour's rent on a parking space, and a twenty-dollar fine resulted if the car remained after time expired. Many similar inventions and "improved" models quickly came on the market, creating a thriving industry in Oklahoma and elsewhere. Although its legality was challenged in court, the oft-maligned parking meter was soon adopted by cities across the United States for parking regulation and revenue production.

Dianna Everett
Oklahoma State Historical Society

Fischer, Leroy, and Robert E. Smith. "Oklahoma and the Parking Meter." *Chronicles of Oklahoma* 47 (1969): 169–208. Hale, Gerald A. "Gerald A. Hale: Parking Meter Reminiscences." *Chronicles of Oklahoma* 48 (1970): 341–52. Thuesen, H. G. "Development of the Parking Meter." *Chronicles of Oklahoma* 45 (1967): 112–42.

PONY EXPRESS

The Pony Express was a short-lived fast mail service between St. Joseph, Missouri, and Sacramento, California. In 1855, responding to the desires of his California constituents, Senator William M. Gwin proposed a government-supported express mail service to Congress. Failing to secure congressional aid, Gwin turned to William H. Russell, the lead partner in the overland freighting firm of Russell, Majors and Waddell. After persuading his reluctant partners, Alexander Majors and William B. Waddell, to undertake the risky venture, the enterprising Russell rushed to open Pony Express service.

Preparations were costly. Russell, Majors and Waddell agents bought about 500 of the finest horses and hired approximately 200 riders. Furthermore, they built, outfitted, and staffed 182 stations along the 1,966-mile route that ran by way of Fort Kearny, the Platte River valley, South Pass, and Salt Lake City. The mail run was ceremoniously opened on April 3, 1860, when riders were dispatched from both ends of the trail.

During its eighteen months of operation the Pony Express carried 34,753 pieces of mail and traveled 650,000 miles. To minimize weight and thus increase speed, letters were written on tissue-thin paper, and the riders were small men whose average age was nineteen. Riders on the weekly service ran twenty-four hours a day year-round. Their fastest time was seven days, seventeen hours, and in the spring, summer, and fall they averaged twelve days, two less than winter. Mail costs were extraordinarily high—$10 an ounce in the early days of the service.

Ruins of Three Crossings stage station along the route of the Pony Express, Wyoming, 1870

With the completion of the transcontinental telegraph on October 26, 1861, the Pony Express ended. Economically, it was a disaster. The loss of some $200,000 soon propelled Russell, Majors and Waddell into bankruptcy. Despite its financial failure, the Pony Express remains as a major symbol of an often romanticized American West.

William E. Lass
Mankato State University

Godfrey, Anthony. *Historic Resource Study: Pony Express National Historic Trail.* Washington DC: National Park Service, 1994. Smith, Waddell F., ed. *The Story of the Pony Express.* San Rafael CA: Pony Express History and Art Gallery, 1960.

PORTAGES

A portage is the carrying of goods or boats across land between navigable waters and around obstructions in streams. Portages were paths originated by game; Native Americans and subsequently European Americans modified them when directness, gradient, or footing dictated. Portages along the extensive inland waterways of the Prairies and Northern Plains played a major role in the fur trade, especially after the Hudson's Bay Company moved into the western interior of Canada in 1774 in response to competition and American fur-trading companies began in earnest to exploit furs in the trans-Missouri West after 1806.

All cargo had to be unloaded from a canoe or boat to be carried over the portage. To expedite this process, furs or trade goods were parceled into ninety-pound packs. A man could carry two packs for about half a mile, drop them, then return for two more. With loading and unloading, a mile-long portage could take one hour. Most portages around rapids were a few hundred yards in length, while height-of-land portages (for example, the nine-mile Grand portage between the Hudson Bay and St. Lawrence drainages) could entail several miles. The cumulative effect of all portages on a route included substantial human and economic costs: drowning; injuries and deaths from lifting, straining, and exhaustion; snake bites; Indian attacks; and increased risk of infectious diseases at congestion points were reported by the traders and voyageurs. Increased economic costs included labor and capital equipment costs, opportunity costs (when men took up space for trade goods and supplies) or when low water levels limited supplies and types of vessels used, and damage to goods from increased handling. Portages constituted transportation bottlenecks in a finely tuned economic system that operated only within the short season of open water.

See also INDUSTRY: Fur Trade.

Jody F. Decker
Wilfrid Laurier University

Decker, Jody F., and Donald B. Freeman. "The Role of Portages in Shaping the Economic Geography of the Western Canadian Fur Trade, 1774–1820." In *Canada: Geographical Interpretations. Essays in Honour of John Warkentin,* edited by James R. Gibson. *York University–Atkinson*

College Geographical Monograph 22 (1993): 31–67. Morse, Eric W. *Fur Trade Canoe Routes of Canada/Then and Now.* Toronto: University of Toronto Press, 1971.

RAILROAD DEPOTS

See ARCHITECTURE: Railroad Depots

RAILROAD LAND GRANTS

Rail lines have played a crucial role in the development of the Plains. After the Civil War, rail lines such as the Canadian Pacific Railway, Union Pacific Railroad, and Northern Pacific Railway accepted huge gifts of land to subsidize railroad construction and operations across the American Plains and Canadian Prairies. Leaders in both countries contended that whoever controlled access across this region would control the Pacific Coast.

The construction of railroads in the Plains and Prairies differed from that in eastern North America in that it preceded the settlement of the land. These lines, rather than the communities themselves, shaped the architecture, layout, and placement of towns. In the United States, federal, state, and local governments as well as individuals gave railroad companies gifts of land to build their lines through the Plains. Railroads received an estimated 185 million acres of land from these sources. The largest contributor by far was the federal government, which made the grants directly to the companies or through state government intermediaries. Under grants to the Union Pacific and Central Pacific lines, the federal government offered twenty square miles of land for each mile of track laid in territories and ten square miles of land for each mile of track laid in states. The land grants were in alternate sections, next to government reserved lands, and laid out in a checkerboard pattern. The government reserved lands were in escrow and could not be claimed by homesteaders until the railroads received their full shares. In Canada, railways received more than 38 million acres of land. Most went to the Canadian Pacific line.

During construction and afterward, critics debated whether the land grant was a reasonable subsidy or an opportunity to plunder the landed wealth of the Prairies and Plains. Apologists for the railroad grants admit that the legislation appropriating the lands was often poorly drawn and contradicted land settlement plans. However, they note that building and running a railroad was an expensive and unstable business. Land grants, they write, offered companies immediate revenues and the means to meet future capital costs. The rail lines that bound the Atlantic and Pacific together certainly would not have been constructed so early without the subsidies. Especially in the United States, no other method to promote railroads in the Plains was politically possible.

Critics of the railroad land grants in the U.S. Plains point out that the gifts made railroads the "proprietors of the West." While they were in escrow, railroads did not pay taxes. Worse, they effectively blocked settlement within

the checkerboard patterns. For example, the Northern Pacific reserved a 120-mile swath of land between Minnesota and Puget Sound that was withheld from settlement.

See also EUROPEAN AMERICANS: Land Laws and Settlement.

Michael J. Grant
Lincoln, Nebraska

Gates, Paul W. *Fifty Million Acres: Conflicts over Kansas Land Policy, 1854–1890.* Ithaca NY: Cornell University Press, 1954. Hedges, James B. *The Federal Railway Land Subsidy Policy of Canada.* Cambridge: Harvard University Press, 1934. Mercer, Lloyd J. *Railroads and Land Grant Policy: A Study in Government Intervention.* New York: Academic Press, 1982.

RAILROADS, UNITED STATES

In the last third of the nineteenth century railroads transformed the Great Plains of North America from a sparsely populated, primarily Native American territory to the agricultural heartland of both the United States and Canada.

The post–Civil War period saw the first extension of standard gage tracks across the American Great Plains with the construction of the Union Pacific Railroad, a vital component of the first transcontinental line, completed in May 1869. At that time the Plains were perceived as space to cross as expeditiously as possible, linking the East Coast with the Pacific Coast. The Plains terrain, gradually sloping west to east, and the broad, flat river valleys permitted relatively easy construction and rapid expansion of the rail network. Although extractive and exploitative economic activities had been previously conducted in the Great Plains (for example, fur trading, bison hunting, cattle ranching, and mining), the region was not extensively settled and developed by European Americans until the latter third of the nineteenth century, when railroads made possible the farmers' advance into the area. While railroads made farming expansion onto the Plains possible, high freight rates, caused in part by lack of concern for farmers' well-being but also by the high cost of shipping often empty cars to a sparsely populated region to be filled with agricultural products, led to protest movements, most notably the Grange and the Farmers Alliance, both of which were successful, to a degree, in achieving government regulation of railroads by the 1870s and 1880s.

As an instrument of development, railroads transformed the Great Plains into an integrated part of both the United States and Canada by carrying passengers, including inbound immigrants, and by hauling agricultural products out and building materials in. After the Union Pacific, more than a dozen other railroads laid tracks across the Plains, including the Southern Pacific and the Northern Pacific. They began aggressively to articulate their networks in an effort to capture service territory. Although their progress was interrupted by financial panics and other temporary setbacks, the Great Plains had been laced together with ribbons of steel by the late nineteenth century. Later, similar development occurred in Canada. The first line to cross the Canadian Great Plains was the Canadian Pacific Railway, completed in 1885. Other railroad companies followed. Eventually the northern section of the Plains would have a rail pattern similar to that of its southern neighbor.

Thus, a railroad landscape, as a feature of a larger cultural landscape, came into existence. As the agricultural settlement pattern became fixed upon the Great Plains railroad companies continued to build thousands of miles of secondary and branch lines on both sides of the international border. The zenith of Plains railroad development occurred in the early 1920s, when approximately 42,000 miles of track crisscrossed the region.

Railroads greatly influenced Great Plains urban patterns. Railroad officials located and founded the majority of the region's towns and cities. The distance between the towns was generally about eight to ten miles, which was considered a reasonable hauling distance for farm products, especially small grains. Elevator capacity of about 30,000 bushels necessitated a town for every one or two townships. Consequently, the semihumid eastern Great Plains developed a fairly dense urban settlement pattern (too dense, in fact, and many of the towns eventually failed). The railroads also platted out the towns, generally in a T form, with the Main Street perpendicular to the tracks and the elevator, lumberyard, and other shipping facilities on the other side. Areas west of the 100th meridian generally exhibited a more dispersed pattern, due to their unsuitability for traditional farming techniques. Other railroad sites were set up as locomotive watering and repair points, division offices, and bridging locations on major rivers. The only European American sites that preceded railroad towns in the Great Plains were riverboat ports, fur-trading posts, forts, mining camps, and prerailroad settlements within reach of the Missouri River in territorial Kansas, Nebraska, and Dakota.

After World War II and especially since the 1960s, three themes have characterized railroading in the Great Plains. The first is abandonment of unprofitable branch and secondary lines. Since the 1950s in excess of 8,000 miles of track have been torn up, leaving many Plains towns without rail service (and bikers and hikers richly endowed with trails that cut diagonally across the otherwise right-angled grid of the Plains landscape). South Dakota, Kansas, Texas, Nebraska, and Oklahoma have each lost more than 1,000 miles of track; only Wyoming has gained, the result of expansion in the coal-rich Powder River Basin. Second, the number of rail carriers has declined through numerous consolidations and mergers. The Great Plains is crossed by only a handful of Class A (major carriers) railroads today. A number of regional and subregional freight lines (short lines) have emerged from the infrastructures of the defunct carriers, some of which are successful financially. State railroad authorities have purchased trackage in an effort to maintain vital services such as the delivery of coal to large-scale electric power generating stations. Third, some

railroads operating in the region have transformed themselves into long-haul bulk carriers, with unit coal and grain trains that often consist of more than 100 railcars. Tonnage has been increasing as the Class A railroads continue to haul greater and greater amounts of raw materials that are either produced in the Great Plains (in the Wyoming coal fields, for example) or transported across them. Double tracks support several high-volume routes that cross the Central Great Plains, and single track in both the Northern and Southern Plains is used to capacity. Also, several Plains rail corridors function as "dry canals" for the transcontinental movement of trains hauling only ship container cargoes.

The belief that the Great Plains was a barrier to be crossed in an east–west direction, coupled with separate national strategies to connect East with West, resulted in very little articulation of the U.S. and Canadian railroad networks across the international border. North–south connections were not well developed, especially on the U.S. side, although a plan was promoted before World War I to connect Winnipeg, Manitoba, to Galveston, Texas, via the eastern Plains. The only major connection, a Canadian Pacific Railway route, traces a diagonal line across the Northern Great Plains from Saskatchewan through Minnesota. Six passenger corridors traverse the Plains, operated today by the Amtrak (U.S.) and Via Rail (Canadian) systems. The passage is essentially east–west across the region with only one north–south line on the southeastern Plains periphery. Relatively little passenger traffic is generated at Plains station stops, because few large cities are located along the respective routes.

The efficiency and economics of bulk cargo movement as well as the lesser environmental impacts of railroads compared to trucks on roads and highways continue to promote the use of railroads. A distinctive Great Plains railroad geography manifests itself across the region in the general settlement fabric and in the spectacular coalescence of lines at major towns. Sounds of diesel locomotive horns and rushing freight trains moving from horizon to horizon will continue to reverberate across the Plains into the foreseeable future.

See also ARCHITECTURE: Railroad Depots / CITIES AND TOWNS: T-Towns / PROTEST AND DISSENT: Farmers Alliance; Grange.

Donald J. Berg
South Dakota State University

Hudson, John C. *Plains Country Towns*. Minneapolis: University of Minnesota Press, 1985. Kirby, Russell S. "Nineteenth-Century Patterns of Railroad Development on the Great Plains." *Great Plains Quarterly* 3 (1983): 156–70. Vance, James E., Jr. *The North American Railroad: Its Origin, Evolution, and Geography*. Baltimore MD: Johns Hopkins University Press, 1995.

RAILWAYS, CANADA

Railways provided absolutely essential economic and commercial transportation and auxiliary services for all Prairie people during the pioneer settlement period, and they re-

main one of the most important components of the region's economic infrastructure. They not only provided basic transportation services but also influenced and shaped many other aspects of Prairie life.

The first railway in western Canada was opened for traffic in 1878. It was a short government-built line from Winnipeg to the U.S. border, where it connected with American railroads to Duluth, Minnesota. From Duluth, Canadian traffic was carried by lake steamers to Ontario ports. That first railway was part of a cautious scheme that used water transport on rivers and lakes, wherever possible, with rail links where needed. A much more ambitious all-rail transcontinental scheme had been proposed. It went down in scandal in 1873 but was revived in 1880. The Conservative government elected in 1878 provided substantial cash and land subsidies and turned over all of its surveys and the rail links already built, including the little Manitoba line, to a syndicate of railway promoters who organized the Canadian Pacific Railway Company. The Prairie portion of the new railway was built between 1881 and 1883.

The railway determined the course and patterns of settlement on the Canadian Prairies. When the promoters, in an effort to fend off competition from American railroads, chose a route across the relatively arid southern Prairies rather than a more northerly route through the fertile and already partially settled parklands, new settlers took up homesteads or bought railway land close to the tracks. Those living farther north were served by north–south branch lines from Regina to Prince Albert and from Calgary to Edmonton, which were built in the late 1880s and early 1890s. Thousands of new towns and villages were created. Older ones served by the railway prospered; those bypassed by the railway languished, or, in a few cases, the buildings of bypassed towns were moved to new locations adjacent to the railway. Town sites were laid out approximately eight or ten miles apart, that being the distance it was thought farmers could haul a load of grain and return home the same day if the primitive dirt roads and trails were in good condition. Farmers farther away from the railway and those traveling in inclement weather faced sharply increased costs and frustrations.

Two political and economic issues—freight rates and branch lines—dominated early railway history on the Canadian Prairies. Freight rates in western Canada were higher than in eastern Canada or in the United States. Canadian Pacific officials insisted this was necessary because they had built and were operating an expensive 1,000-mile line north of Lake Superior and another 600-mile line across the Rockies. Neither generated appreciable local traffic. In eastern Canada freight rates had to be set to meet competition by water carriers and rival American railroads. On the Prairies effective measures were taken to keep out rival American railroads, and rates were then set to pay for the costs of carrying traffic to and from western Canada, including the operating costs of the unproductive Lake Superior and mountain sections. Vehement protests resulted in modest rate reductions in the late 1880s, followed by an agreement in 1897, under the terms of which the Canadian Pacific agreed to more substantial rate cuts in return for federal financial assistance to build a major branch line through the Crow's Nest Pass in southern British Columbia.

There were also persistent complaints about lack of adequate service for farmers far removed from the railway's main line. They demanded construction of branch lines. Railway officials argued that remote and sparsely settled areas did not generate sufficient traffic to justify construction of a branch line railway. Settlers responded with claims that growth was impossible until a region had rail service.

The resulting frustrations led to demands for railway competition. In 1895 two former Canadian Pacific contractors built a small, competitive branch line in Manitoba with government financial assistance. They gradually expanded their railway until, in 1901, the Manitoba government agreed to provide financial help if the contractors would build a railway from Winnipeg to Lake Superior that would compete directly with the Canadian Pacific. The ambitious contractors, who had in the meantime reorganized their railway as the Canadian Northern Railway, built and operated the new line as cheaply as possible but drastically reduced freight rates and continued to expand their lines with further government assistance. The federal government tried, with limited success, to regulate freight rates and other railway operations when it established the Board of Railway Commissioners in 1903.

The rapid settlement of the Canadian Prairies after 1900 prompted Canada's oldest and largest railway, the Grand Trunk Railway, to expand westward. The railway tried first to acquire the economically weak but politically popular Canadian Northern Railway. Failure to provide assurances that it would carry freight at Canadian Northern rates scuttled Grand Trunk efforts to take over the Canadian Northern. Instead, the Grand Trunk sought and obtained federal and provincial assistance to build its own railway across the Prairies. A frenzy of railway construction by the Canadian Pacific, Canadian Northern, and Grand Trunk Railways followed. Thousands of miles of new rail lines were built on the Prairies. Many, however, were located in ways designed to injure competitors rather than to provide the broadest possible coverage. The result was wasteful crowding of new lines in some areas and neglect of other more remote regions. Even more disastrous was the decision of the managers of both the Canadian Northern and Grand Trunk Railways to build or make arrangements to expand their systems from coast to coast, including new lines north of Lake Superior and across the Rockies.

Rumors and threats of war after 1911 and then the actual outbreak of war in 1914 resulted in financial crises and inflated costs that pushed the new and as yet incomplete transcontinental railways to the edge of bankruptcy. They were only rescued when the federal government nationalized the Grand Trunk and Canadian Northern systems and amalgamated them with other government-owned railways to form Canadian National Railways. There was new construction in the 1920s, particularly on the Prairies, to integrate previously competitive Canadian Northern and Grand Trunk lines into a single system capable of competing with the privately owned Canadian Pacific. Neither system prospered in the dismal conditions of the 1930s. The Canadian Pacific, with its very low debt charges, survived, and the federal government paid most of Canadian National's much heavier debt charges inherited from its predecessor companies.

The railways were always much more than merely a transportation system. They were the harbingers of a new way of life and as such seriously disrupted the lives of the Native and mixed-blood peoples living on the Canadian Prairies. They made possible extensive settlement and the development of commercial agriculture. As holders of large tracts of land they influenced and on occasion dictated the nature and progress of settlement in particular districts. Their preference for experienced farmers, including many from central and eastern Europe, changed the ethnic composition of many Prairie communities. Canadian Pacific interest in arid land in southern Alberta resulted in the development of massive irrigation projects organized or assisted by the railway. Ownership of thousands of lots in hundreds of prospective towns along the right-of-way of the new railways made the railways key players in the development of towns and villages throughout western Canada, and their large holdings in urban real estate properties made them a dominant force in the shaping of all urban centers in western Canada.

The railways also acquired or participated in numerous ancillary enterprises, ranging from telegraph services to mining and lumbering and later oil and gas ventures. Huge land grants made them partners with the federal government in promoting aggressive federal immigration, homestead, and settlement policies.

During the Great Depression of the 1930s the railways in western Canada became unique symbols of the nation's failing economic system as hundreds of unemployed and angry young men moved about the country, riding illegally on railway freight cars. About 1,800 unemployed men, riding the rails with plans to stage a massive protest demonstration in Ottawa, were forcibly disbanded, with considerable violence, by the police in Regina in 1935. But the railways also performed valuable Depression Era services in moving animals and settlers from the drought-stricken southern to more northerly communities and animal fodder and other supplies from the northern communities southward.

Essential wartime services partially reestablished the reputation of the railways. They were, and still are, the most efficient carriers of bulky western Canadian export products. They carried all manner of military supplies and made possible massive troop movements and the shipment of food products from western Canada to eastern ports and to Great Britain.

After the war Canadian railways faced serious competition in their freight business as a result of the conversion of wartime industrial production plants to the production of, among other items, automobiles and trucks as well as major government initiatives in the construction of better highways. They never recovered from a damaging strike in 1957 during which they lost much of their time-sensitive, high-cost, small-volume freight to the trucking industry. Airline competition gradually inflicted even greater damage on the passenger service offered by the railways in spite of a very costly effort, particularly by the Canadian Pacific in the late 1950s and early 1960s, to offer the best possible passenger service on the most modern passenger, observation, and dining cars. Canadian, like American, railways have abandoned or surrendered the passenger service to independent operators—Via Rail in Canada, Amtrak in the United States, both of which are heavily subsidized.

A contentious postwar issue, particularly in western Canada, has been the abandonment of tens of thousands of miles of branch lines and the decline or death of thousands of small Prairie towns served by those branch lines. With better road transport facilities, railway shipping points at six- to eight-mile intervals are no longer needed, but longer hauling distances increase costs to farmers and divert business from the small towns to larger centers. Nevertheless, the railways continue to provide an essential service in the transportation of bulky western Canadian agricultural and natural resource commodities to market. The increasing importance of that business is, perhaps, most clearly demonstrated by the move in the 1990s of Canadian Pacific headquarters from Montreal to Calgary.

The Canadian railway system was an essential building block in the development of Prairie society and in the integration of the trade of the Canadian Prairies with other parts of Canada. Passage of the North American Free Trade Agreement has resulted in the flow of more western Canadian traffic southward, and the major Canadian railways have acquired or strengthened their links with vital American railroads, but on the Canadian Prairies they continue to provide essential economic services.

See also EUROPEAN AMERICANS: Settlement Patterns, Canada / INDUSTRY: Canadian Pacific Railway / PROTEST AND DISSENT: On-to-Ottawa Trek.

Ted D. Regehr
University of Saskatchewan and University of Calgary

Eagle, John A. *The Canadian Pacific Railway and the Development of Western Canada.* Montreal: McGill-Queen's University Press, 1989. Lamb, W. Kaye. *History of the Canadian Pacific Railway.* New York: Macmillan Publishing Company, 1977. Regehr, T. D. *The Canadian Northern Railway: Pioneer Road of the Northern Prairies, 1895–1918.* Toronto: Macmillan Publishing Company, 1976.

RED RIVER CARTS

Developed in the Prairie Provinces in the nineteenth century by the Métis, the Red River cart was a small, two-wheeled wooden rig drawn by oxen or horses. It had two long shafts attached to an axle and could be strapped to a single draft animal. The shafts supported a platform with wooden rails on two sides. The cart was well designed for Plains travel. Constructed entirely of wood and tied together with leather, it could be easily manufactured in the Red River country, where oaks and poplars thrived in river valleys, bison were abundant, but metal goods were scarce. Large, spoked wheels made the carts easy to draw through the tall grasses, rugged terrain, and shallow streams of the Prairie Provinces. Thanks to their simple design, the carts could be easily repaired when long journeys across the Plains took their toll.

The Métis initially designed the Red River cart for carrying hides, dried meat, and tallow from their semiannual bison hunts on the Plains. Each cart could carry as much as 1,000 pounds—the hides, meat, and grease of five or six buffalo. By the late nineteenth century, the Prairie Provinces were crisscrossed by Métis cart roads, the most important of which was the Carlton Trail from Fort Garry, the supply depot of the Red River settlement, to Fort Carlton on the Saskatchewan River. Each year, several hundred carts trundled back and forth along the road, filling the air with their distinctive ear-piercing screech, caused by the rubbing of wooden wheels against wooden axles. At first, the Métis sold most of their bison products to the fur trade posts in the Red River country, but in the 1850s they began to organize cart brigades to present-day St. Paul, Minnesota. Primarily a long-distance transport device, the Red River cart was replaced in the late nineteenth century by the steamboat and railway.

See also NATIVE AMERICANS: Métis
Pekka Hämäläinen
Texas A&M University

RIDING AROUND

See SPORTS AND RECREATION: Riding Around

ROUTE 66

Route 66 is one of the most famous highways in the world. It runs some 2,200 miles from Chicago to Los Angeles through eight states, cutting across the Great Plains through fourteen miles of southeastern Kansas, then on to Tulsa, Oklahoma City, Amarillo, Albuquerque, and points west. It was originally part of the U.S. highway system established in 1926. It was fully paved by 1938 but was later replaced by the present interstate system. Recently, some remaining segments have been designated as Historic Route 66, and in 1999 Congress passed and President Bill Clinton signed into law the National Route 66 Preservation Bill that will preserve and restore historic properties along the route. Throughout most of its existence as a highway, Route 66 was not very important at either terminus, but it was crucial for communication and transportation in the Southern Plains and the Southwest. The route linked hundreds of rural communities, locally carried farmers' products, and, as one of the few diagonal long-distance highways, was a major trucking artery.

The route earned real fame with John Steinbeck's novel *The Grapes of Wrath* (1939), in which the Joad family and other Okies fled the Great Depression from Oklahoma to California on Route 66. Steinbeck called 66 the "mother road," and some 400,000 people traveled west on it during the 1930s. The 1940 film by John Ford based on Steinbeck's novel further embedded the shield-shaped road sign of Route 66 into the American imagination. Later Route 66 movies include *Easy Rider* (1969) and *Bagdad Cafe* (1987). The highway was also featured in the 1960s television series *Route 66*, starring Martin Milner and George Maharis.

Folksinger Woody Guthrie wrote several songs in which Route 66 was mentioned as the "Main Street" of the Dust Bowl refugees. The most famous of the many Route 66 songs is "(Get Your Kicks on) Route 66," written by Bobby Troup and recorded by Nat King Cole in 1946. Perhaps more than anything else, this song has made Route 66 an American icon. Several museums and Web sites and a Route 66 magazine commemorate the highway's glory days, and the National Historic Route 66 Federation works to preserve both the route and its memory.

See also FILM: *The Grapes of Wrath* / MUSIC: Guthrie, Woody.

Markku Henriksson
University of Helsinki

Snyder, Tom. *Route 66 Traveler's Guide and Roadside Companion*. New York: St. Martin's Griffin, 1995. Wallis, Michael. *Route 66: The Mother Road*. New York: St. Martin's Press, 1990. Witzel, Michael Karl. *Route 66 Remembered*. Osceola WI: Motorbooks International, 1966.

RUSSELL, MAJORS AND WADDELL

The freighting and staging firm of Russell, Majors and Waddell, formed in 1854 to supply military posts in the American West and Southwest, played a significant role in the history of transportation in the Great Plains. Among the firm's achievements was the creation of the legendary Pony Express.

The founding of Russell, Majors and Waddell was rooted in the U.S. Army's need for an efficient means of transporting military supplies between a new depot in Santa Fe and six new army posts in New Mexico Territory, all established at the end of the Mexican War in 1848. In 1854 the War Department decided the best way to efficiently supply these and other posts would be to award two-year contracts to private freighting companies. The quartermaster awarded the first of these contracts to the firm of Russell, Majors and Waddell, a partnership of William H. Russell, Alexander Majors, and William B. Waddell, headquartered in Leavenworth, Kansas. They also transported civilian freight on a large scale.

The company's dealings with the government, rewarding at the start, eventually cost them financially. This downward financial spiral began in 1857, a busy year during which the firm moved nearly five million pounds of supplies to army depots and military posts across Kansas, New Mexico, and Utah. At the outbreak of the 1857 Mormon War, the quartermaster at Fort Leavenworth requested that Russell, Majors and Waddell move some 2.5 million pounds of freight to Salt Lake City, a load far exceeding the firm's contractual obligations for the year. Rather than jeopardize its position as chief army contractor in the West by refusing the excess freight, Russell, Majors and Waddell borrowed to fulfill the request and incurred heavy losses waiting for future reimbursement from the government. A series of transactions in 1858 put the company in debt, and the decision to launch the Central Overland California and Pikes Peak Express, a staging and express concern, further eroded the firm's finances.

In 1860, despite growing financial trouble, Russell created the firm's most enduring legacy by convincing his two reluctant partners to support the establishment of the Pony Express as a means of publicizing the superiority of the central route over the lengthier southern route then employed in the trans-Mississippi West by the Overland Mail Company. That same year, Russell found that he could no longer honor his financial obligations. He became entangled in the most serious financial scandal of the period, a scheme involving high-level Interior and War Department officials. Indicted in the scandal, Russell's involvement effectively destroyed the financial standing of all three partners, and Russell, Majors and Waddell went out of business in 1862.

Derrick S. Ward
Ventura, California

Settle, Raymond W., and Mary Lund Settle. *War Drums and Wagon Wheels: The Story of Russell, Majors, and Waddell*. Lincoln: University of Nebraska Press, 1966.

SANTA FE TRAIL

For most nineteenth-century European Americans the Great Plains represented primarily a transportation challenge, a vast expanse that had to be crossed to gain access to greater riches beyond its boundaries. The Santa Fe Trail, the principal trade route connecting the eastern United States and the Southwest, was one of the most successful solutions to that challenge. The trail opened in 1821, when newly independent Mexico abolished restrictive Spanish laws and allowed foreign traders to enter its New Mexican outposts. The first to capitalize on the new markets was William Becknell, a struggling Missouri merchant who arrived in Santa Fe in the fall of 1821 and sold his goods at a huge profit. The following year, Becknell ventured again from Franklin, Missouri, to Santa Fe, pioneering the Cimarron Cutoff across the Oklahoma Panhandle.

Becknell had tapped a vast commercial potential. The isolated New Mexicans had surpluses of mules, silver, and furs, but they lacked manufactured goods and therefore were eager to have access to U.S. markets. Stimulated by mutual benefits, the trade flourished. During the following six decades, first dozens, then hundreds, and finally thousands of wagons moved each year along the Santa Fe Trail, carrying calico, leather goods, hardware, clothing, beaver pelts, and silver coins across the Plains. By the 1850s the annual value of merchandise shipped over the trail exceeded $5 million. The trail served as a commercial artery until 1880, when the completion of the Atchison, Topeka and Santa Fe Railroad made it obsolete.

By the 1830s a generally accepted routine had developed along the trail. The traders usually left Independence, Missouri (Franklin, the first terminus, was destroyed by a flood in 1828), in mid-May, when Plains grasses were tall enough to provide sufficient forage for draft animals. Most traders used Murphy wagons, three-foot-wide and sixteen-foot-long canvas-topped vehicles with four-inch-thick iron tires to protect the wooden wheels during the arduous, 775-mile trek. After ten days of travel, the traders paused at Council Grove, Kansas, where they gathered into larger caravans led by an elected captain and division lieutenants and typically consisting of 25 freight wagons and 300 oxen and mules. After the break, the caravans headed toward the Big Bend of the Arkansas, traveling ten to fifteen miles a day. The wagon trains followed the northern flank of the Arkansas River valley to the Middle Crossing, where the trail divided into two branches. The longer Mountain Branch followed the Arkansas River to Bent's Fort and then proceeded southwest through Raton Pass to Santa Fe. The more heavily trafficked Cimarron Cutoff first crossed the Cimarron Desert and then followed a direct route to Santa Fe.

Whichever route they chose, the caravans could not escape the harsh Plains elements—dry spells, torrential rains, wolves, fires, and stampeding bison herds. River crossings were particularly troublesome. Although shallow, Plains rivers were filled with sinkholes, quicksand, and other hazards that required careful maneuvering. Traders also needed flexible Indian policies. Caravans moved in parallel columns that could be quickly formed into a protective corral to repel raiders, but they had to be equally ready to welcome trading parties with gifts of coffee, bacon, and tobacco. As the Native economies began to crumble the raids intensified, making the Santa Fe trade a dangerous business. Besides physical landmarks such as the double-peaked Rabbit Ears on the Cimarron Cutoff, the trail was in later years marked by an unbroken string of destroyed wagons and animal remains.

The Santa Fe Trail played a crucial role in shaping North American history. It was critical in absorbing New Mexico into the American commercial orbit and, after the Mexican War, in incorporating the province into the national economy. During the California gold rush, the trail also took thousands of emigrants across the Plains. The trail increased geographic knowledge of Plains rivers, springs, and topography and made Bent's Fort one of the most lucrative commercial centers in the West. But the Santa Fe Trail also launched the European American assault on Plains ecosystems. The iron-rimmed wheels and the hundreds of thousands of animals and people destroyed native vegetation, accelerated erosion, polluted springs, brought new diseases, and disturbed bison herds. By the 1850s the Arkansas River valley, once a haven for Indians and bison, had become a mile-wide dust highway.

Pekka Hämäläinen
Texas A&M University

Brown, William E. *The Santa Fe Trail: The National Park Service 1963 Historic Sites Survey*. St. Louis MO: Patrice Press, 1988. Walker, Henry Pickering. *The Wagonmasters: High Plains Freighting from the Earliest Days of the Santa Fe Trail to 1880*. Norman: University of Oklahoma Press, 1966. West, Elliott. *The Way to the West: Essays on the Central Plains*. Albuquerque: University of New Mexico Press, 1995.

STAGECOACHES

Stagecoaches were vehicles that transported passengers, mail, and light freight over designated routes. Patterned after the English coach and four, which was introduced into the American colonies, the name of the vehicles described both the enclosed carriage and traveling in stages between stations.

Stagecoaching in the Great Plains was stimulated by the California gold rush and the need for faster service than could be supplied by wagons. In 1857 James E. Birch of the California Stage Company contracted with the federal government to run a biweekly mail service over the 1,500-mile route from San Antonio, Texas, to San Diego, California. But the next year the contract was awarded to the Butterfield Overland Mail. After the outbreak of the Civil War the Overland Mail was transferred to the central or California route that ran through the Platte River valley and South Pass. Butterfield subcontracted with Russell, Majors and Waddell, the leading overland freighters, to run stages from the Missouri River to the recently opened Colorado gold fields. After the bankruptcy of Russell, Majors and Waddell, Ben Holladay, who came to be known as the Stagecoach King, dominated the business for several years before selling out to Wells, Fargo and Company in 1866. Wells Fargo and many local companies adjusted to the construction of transcontinental railroads by providing feeder service to those lines. Stagecoaching was finally discontinued after the establishment of railroad networks.

The Concord, manufactured in Concord, New Hampshire, was the most famous stagecoach. Because of its large size, rugged construction, and attractiveness, it was preferred by large companies. As a symbol of frontier life the stagecoach has captured the popular imagination, which continues to be fed by movies and television.

William E. Lass
Mankato State University

Greeley, Horace. *An Overland Journey from New York to San Francisco in the Summer of 1859*. New York: C. M. Saxton, Barker and Company, 1860. Winther, Oscar Osburn. *The Transportation Frontier: Trans-Mississippi West, 1865–1890*. New York: Holt, Rinehart and Winston, 1964.

TRANS-CANADA HIGHWAY

In 1949 the government of Canada passed an Act to Encourage and to Assist in the Construction of a Trans-Canada Highway. The act specified a set of construction criteria for a two-lane highway to connect Canada's east and west coasts by the most direct route. The federal government would pay 50 percent of the construction costs. The highway was officially opened in 1962, and the federal government continued to make payments under the act until 1971. The federal share was over $900 million, and the total cost was estimated at $1.4 billion. At 4,860 miles, it is the longest national highway in the world.

The highway crosses the Prairie Provinces following the route of the transcontinental railway built between 1881 and 1883, linking together five of the eleven largest cities in the region. Leaving the Canadian Shield country of Ontario, it becomes the main street of Winnipeg, Manitoba, then pushes west to the province's second largest city, Brandon. Regina, Saskatchewan, is the next city on the highway, followed by Moose Jaw, Saskatchewan, and Medicine Hat, Alberta. The highway is a major expressway through Calgary, then, heading west, it enters the Rockies via Banff National Park. This route makes the highway an important truck route for provincial and interprovincial trade. Most of the highway across the Prairie Provinces has now been widened to four lanes, and the twinning process continues.

Since the construction of the Trans-Canada Highway, the social custom of gathering for coffee has shifted from the centers of the small towns near the highway to the restaurants and service stations at highway intersections. Further, improved transportation has led to the loss of services and the economic decline of some towns, while those towns near cities have taken on a dormitory function.

Like the railway, the highway was also built for symbolic reasons: to demonstrate Canadian unity. The highway is designated Highway 1 and has the Canadian maple leaf signage. During the summer months it is heavily used by hitchhikers, cyclists, mobile homes, and automobile tourists. Banff National Park receives over five million visitors annually.

Many diaries and coffee-table books have been published reflecting personal experiences along the highway. It has been described as "the artery through which the soul of the nation pulses . . . dedicated to the freedom to travel without restriction." Across the vastness of the Prairie Provinces this is particularly noticeable. In some ways it is the Canadian equivalent of U.S. Route 66.

During the 1970s, a northern route through the Parkland Belt was designated the Yellowhead Highway. Following the Trans-Canada Highway west from Winnipeg for fifty miles, it turns northwest to Saskatoon, Saskatchewan, and Edmonton, Alberta, and enters the Rockies through Jasper National Park and the Yellowhead Pass. It has also been designated as a trans-Canada highway route, although the Yellowhead name is still in more general use.

William R. Horne
University of Northern British Columbia

Howarth, William. *Traveling the Trans-Canada*. Washington DC: National Geographic Society, 1987. Ratausky, Wes. *Silver Highway: A Celebration of the Trans-Canada Highway*. Markham, Ontario: Fitzhenry and Whiteside, 1988.

TRANSCONTINENTAL MOTOR CONVOY

In August 1919 thousands of people in Nebraska and Wyoming greeted U.S. army soldiers with curiosity, patriotic cheer, and generous amounts of food and drink as they drove a convoy of early heavy trucks across the Great Plains.

Among the caravan's nearly 300 soldiers was twenty-eight-year-old Lt. Col. Dwight D. Eisenhower, who became the supreme allied commander during World War II and, in 1952, the thirty-fourth president. President Eisenhower initiated the Federal Highway Trust Fund, which built the nation's 46,000-mile interstate highway system, and he would later credit the convoy experience for teaching him that a quality paved-road system is essential to a nation's economic and military security.

Officially named the Transcontinental Motor Convoy of 1919, the caravan was composed of eighty-one army vehicles and numerous nonmilitary autos and trucks. Its main objective was to determine the military value of assorted vehicles the army had acquired but not put into service during World War I. The convoy also served as a war game, a recruiting drive, a campaign for long-haul trucking, and, not incidentally, a parade observed by millions along its route.

For more than sixty-two bone-jarring days the truck train traveled 3,251 miles from Washington DC to San Francisco on the Lincoln Highway, which later became U.S. Route 30. In 1919 the Lincoln Highway through Nebraska and Wyoming was mostly a rough dirt road, often little more than a deeply rutted trail with weak or nonexistent bridges. The convoy needed twenty days to forge its way through the two Plains states. West of North Platte, Nebraska, the soldiers and machines became mired in a 200-foot stretch of quicksand for more than seven hours.

Overcoming the obstacles of rudimentary vehicles and rugged road conditions with hard work and persistence, the convoy reached San Francisco on September 6 with 90 percent of the vehicles that started still running. Beyond its military value, the convoy helped make the case to the nation that improving cross-country roads was a federal, not just a local, priority—a point Eisenhower would make as president.

See also POLITICS AND GOVERNMENT: Eisenhower, Dwight D.

Tom White
Lincoln, Nebraska

Caught in time between prairie schooners and eighteen-wheelers, the 1919 khaki-covered truck train exits Nebraska.

TRAVOIS

Unique to the Plains, the travois is a wooden load-bearing frame fastened by a leather harness to a dog or horse. The basic dog travois consists of two aspen or cottonwood poles lashed together at one end with buffalo sinew. The other ends rest splayed apart. Crossbars are lashed between the poles near the splayed ends. The finished frame looks like a large letter A with extra crossbars. The apex of the A, wrapped in buffalo skin to prevent friction burns, rests on a dog's shoulders, while the splayed ends drag over the ground.

Used by Plains Indian nations, travois were perfectly suited to their environment. Over native grasslands the dragging travois ends sweep silently and nearly without friction; they appear almost to float through the same prairie that cracks and breaks wheel axles. Outside of grasslands the travois is not much use, for bush and gullies are impassable.

Native women both built the travois and managed the dogs, sometimes using toy travois to train puppies. Bison meat and firewood were typical travois loads. Dogs could tack up and down grassy hill slopes and ford shallow rivers with a travois. But temperature was a serious constraint on travois work, for on warm days dogs overheated easily.

In historic times Plains Indians constructed much larger versions of the dog travois and hitched them to horses. Horse travois allowed the transport of the increased material wealth accumulated by some Native nations skilled in the mounted bison hunt. Children or ill adults could ride on the horse travois load rack as well. Their rack ride was smooth, but the legs of the saddle-rider, typically female, hung uncomfortably over the travois poles.

Norman Henderson
University of East Anglia, England

Ewers, John. *The Horse in Blackfoot Indian Culture*. Bureau of American Ethnology Bulletin 159. Washington DC: Smithsonian Institution, 1955. Henderson, Norman.

Husky and travois

"Replicating Dog Travois Travel on the Northern Plains." *Plains Anthropologist* 39 (1994): 145–59.

WATER TRANSPORTATION

People have always used Plains rivers for transport, but it has never been easy. The nature of the Plains and its rivers conspires against water transport, and many are the explorers and entrepreneurs who set out in boats and ended up on foot or horseback. In the eyes of many, horses and trains came to be seen as the "natural" ways to travel the Plains. In 1931 the historian Walter Prescott Webb went so far as to suggest that since the Lewis and Clark Expedition traveled so much by water, resorting to land travel only when forced to, the expedition experienced little of the "Plains proper" and was therefore not really a Plains venture. Yet a river view of the Plains, although to the modern mind somewhat unusual, is as legitimate as an overlander's perspective.

Native Americans were the first to travel Plains rivers. They used the bullboat, a roughly circular, framed, tublike craft. Made from bent willow branches and buffalo skins sewn with sinews, the bullboat is light enough for one person to carry slung over the shoulders. Although ingeniously simple technology, the bullboat has serious limitations. When wet, the skins rot quickly, so a boat might last only a few days. Bullboats are also difficult to steer and impossible to paddle upstream. Bullboats were primarily useful to cross rivers like the Missouri or for extended one-way trips downstream.

European explorers and traders introduced the birch-bark canoe to the Plains, a craft indigenous to the northeastern North American woodlands. The newcomers experienced roughly a century and a half of frustration trying to push out onto the Plains with this "foreign" technology. Birchbark canoes require almost daily repair, but on the Plains there were no birch trees for bark, nor pine trees for pitch, nor spruce trees for gum.

The rivers themselves work against canoe travel too. Plains rivers tend to meander, slowing progress. They are typically shallow and full of shifting sand and mud bars that ground the traveler's craft, and they conceal snags that pierce the hull. Northern Plains rivers in particular have highly seasonal flows and are shut down by ice in winter. Unlike those in boreal North America, water linkages between Plains watersheds are usually nonexistent, which means that the traveler in any case must develop some overland transport alternative for travel between river systems. The experiences of explorers like Pierre Gaultier de Varennes, sieur de La Vérendrye, who abandoned his canoes on the Assiniboine River in 1738, Zebulon Pike, who exchanged his boat for horses along the Osage River in 1806, Stephen Long, who ascended the Platte River in 1820 by land, and Henry Hind, who abandoned his canoes on the Qu'Appelle River in 1858, are illustrative of the limitations of canoes in the Plains.

Alongside continuing canoe traffic, timber small craft, both flat-bottomed and keeled, were employed on Plains rivers by fur traders, travelers, and explorers. These were sturdier than canoes, but the flat-bottomed boats were only effective going downstream, while keelboats were often grounded. Both types were variously rowed, poled, or even sailed, depending on conditions. It was common, too, for keelboats to be hauled upstream by men or pack animals.

In the nineteenth century steamboats inherited all the Plains river navigation problems of small boats and were also vulnerable to high winds. Steamboats were active in both the Canadian and American Plains but were most important on the Missouri River. In 1832 a steam-driven side-wheeler reached Fort Union at the junction of the Yellowstone and the Missouri. From then on steamers regularly rode the high spring waters at least as far as Fort Union and, when conditions allowed it, continued on farther, with shallow-draft steamers reaching as far as Fort Benton in 1859.

These steamers gave the American Fur Trading Company an advantage over its rivals, particularly the Hudson's Bay Company to the north, in the contested Plains borderlands between the Missouri and South Saskatchewan Rivers. In fact, steam and small boat transport, difficult as they were, are at the root of the division of the Plains between America and Canada. Although the international boundary appears quite unrelated to natural features, the forty-ninth parallel roughly divides the Plains into Hudson Bay and Gulf of Mexico watersheds and reflects the division of fur trader influence between the British operating out of Hudson Bay and the American traders operating from the Mississippi watershed.

From the 1860s onward railroads began to cut into Plains steamer cargoes, putting an end to most commercial traffic by 1890. After World War I the U.S. federal government took a renewed interest in inland waterways, and there was a slow increase in traffic. There are now two significant routes, both completed in the 1970s, maintained for river freight between the Mississippi River and the eastern Plains. The Missouri is kept navigable as far upstream as Sioux City, while the Arkansas-Verdigris project maintains a nine-foot channel as far as Catoosa, near Tulsa. Modern commercial traffic primarily consists of boat-barges. Typically, several flat-bottomed barges carrying bulk goods are tied together in a "tow" and pushed by a diesel-driven towboat.

Lacking the axis of the Mississippi to work from, there has been no rebirth of commercial water traffic on the Canadian Plains. Given the high cost of waterway construction and maintenance and modern environmental concerns, it seems unlikely there will be expansion of the limited U.S. Plains routes either.

The most important modern cargoes of the typical Plains river flow by below the surface—agricultural runoff and urban effluent. Ecologist James Malin was correct to emphasize that the natural state of Plains rivers was muddy and brown, but modern farming, especially cultivation, increases soil runoff, while Plains cities contribute effluent to natural flows. The resulting sediment load is carried by Plains currents until it is dropped in dam reservoirs or in slow-moving rivers like the Mississippi. This transport is not costless, for infilling reservoirs lose their efficiency, dredging to maintain navigability is expensive, and sediment-laden water is difficult or impossible to use for many domestic and industrial purposes. Many of these costs fall on people downstream of the Plains.

See also WATER: Rivers.

Norman Henderson
University of East Anglia, England

Henderson, Norman S. "The Canoe as Failure on the Canadian Plains." *Great Plains Research* 6 (1996): 3–23. Hunter, Louis C. *Steamboats on the Western Rivers: An Economic and Technological History.* New York: Dover, 1993.

WELLS, FARGO AND COMPANY

Wells, Fargo and Company, which developed express, stagecoaching, overland freighting, and banking divisions, was formed in New York in 1852. Its principal founders, Henry Wells and William G. Fargo, both experienced expressmen, had earlier started the American Express Company in association with John Butterfield. Butterfield's unwillingness to extend expressing to California caused Wells and Fargo with other associates to create a separate company.

Based in San Francisco, Wells Fargo soon became California's leading express and banking firm. Aggressively branching out, in 1848 the firm acquired a financial interest in the Butterfield Overland Mail. After purchasing Ben Holladay's Overland Mail and Express Company in 1866, Wells Fargo became dominant in Great Plains and western stagecoaching. Simultaneously, the company opened a freighting division, which, among other things, transported government and private freight by wagon westward from the railhead of the advancing Union Pacific Railroad.

The completion of the Union Pacific in 1869 caused Wells Fargo to deemphasize stagecoaching and freighting in favor of its transcontinental express service. Nonetheless, the firm extended stagecoach and wagon express into new frontiers such as the gold-producing Black Hills. By the 1890s, when railroad networks had finally replaced stagecoaching, Wells Fargo was almost completely devoted to railroad expressing and banking.

In the twentieth century, Wells Fargo's banking interests expanded rapidly. First it became one of the major financial institutions in California and other western states, and then in 1998 it merged with Norwest Corporation of Minneapolis under the Wells Fargo name. The merger made it the principal banking firm on the Northern Great Plains.

William E. Lass
Mankato State University

Beebe, Lucius, and Charles Clegg. *U.S. West: The Saga of Wells Fargo.* New York: E. P. Dutton and Company, 1949. Hungerford, Edward. *Wells Fargo: Advancing the American Frontier.* New York: Random House, 1949.

WESTERN TRAIL

The Western Trail was the long cattle trail that succeeded the Chisholm Trail. The boom in driving Texas longhorns to Kansas railheads started soon after the Civil War. By 1867 Abilene, at the end of the Chisholm Trail (sometimes called the Eastern Trail), was the main cattle market. Abilene boomed for five years, but farmer hostility to cattle drives and westward-advancing railroads led Chisholm Trail herders to shift to Newton, Wichita, and Ellsworth, which soon succumbed to further railroad advances. These circumstances coincided with the Atchison, Topeka and Santa Fe Railroad's 1872 arrival in Dodge City.

As the new cattle market, Dodge City initially received its longhorns over a branch of the Chisholm Trail. But Texas drivers soon laid out the Western Trail, thereby saving themselves 150 miles. The new route, which experienced its first boom year in 1875, ran from near San Antonio northward by Fort Griffin and then by way of a Red River crossing on the northern edge of present-day Wilbarger County and through the western part of Indian Territory. North of Dodge City the trail was extended to Ogallala, Nebraska, on the Union Pacific Railroad. The heyday of the Western Trail was 1875 to 1884. The trail north from Ogallala was first run to the Black Hills. By the early 1880s, when the Northern Pacific Railroad was being extended into the Yellowstone River valley, the Black Hills portion of the Western Trail was continued to the Fort Buford area in present-day western North Dakota, and another branch was opened from Ogallala to Miles City, Montana Territory, by way of Cheyenne.

After the mid-1880s the Western Trail was not important. Its cattle business had been ruined by a combination of an outbreak of Texas fever, rapid advances of the farming frontier into grazing land during a wet cycle, and railroad land sales to incoming farmers.

William E. Lass
Mankato State University

Hunter, J. Marvin, comp. and ed. *The Trail Drivers of Texas.* New York: Argosy-Antiquarian, 1963.

WHOOP-UP TRAIL

Although the origins of the name Whoop-Up Trail are unclear, the fabled history and significance of this trail, which ran from Fort Benton in Montana to the notorious whiskey fort, Fort Whoop-Up (Fort Hamilton), and later Fort Macleod on the Oldman River in Canada, are not debated. Playing an important role in the history of the U.S.-Canadian frontier from the 1850s until the late 1880s, this trail of approximately 240 miles roughly paralleled or followed the Great North Trail along which Native Americans had traveled for millennia on the eastern side of the Rocky Mountains. Founded in 1850, Fort Benton, on the west side of the Missouri some 3,575 miles from its mouth, became a center for trade for northern Montana and southern Alberta for more than four decades.

From 1860 to 1890 more than 600 steamboat landings allowed goods and commerce to reach both U.S. and Canadian frontier communities. Passing through grasslands with few physical barriers, the trail was traversed on foot, on horseback, by mule train, and by trade wagons by Native Americans, fur trappers, whiskey traders, the U.S. Army, the North-West Mounted Police (NWMP), cowboys, miners, ranchers, and settlers. Through Fort Benton passed many of the bison robes that made their way to eastern markets from 1865 to 1882. Furs, whiskey, and trade goods were a staple of the commerce on this trail, although with the coming of the NWMP to western Canada in 1874, the whiskey forts and the whiskey trade began to decline. Supplies for the NWMP and Indian reservations became part of the goods carried by bull trains (consisting of six to twelve yoke, or pair, of oxen) across the border. The coming of the railroad lessened the need for the trail, and by 1890 it no longer played a significant role in the economic life of this region.

Phillip Drennon Thomas
Wichita State University

Berry, Gerald L. *The Whoop-Up Trail.* Edmonton, Alberta: Applied Art Products, 1953. Cushman, Dan. *The Great North Trail.* New York: McGraw-Hill Book Company, 1966. Sharp, Paul E. *Whoop-Up Country: The Canadian-American West, 1865–1885.* Norman: University of Oklahoma Press, 1973.

YELLOWSTONE TRAIL

The Yellowstone Trail was one of the first transcontinental highways. In April 1912 a group of local businessmen began to create an improved highway from Ipswich, South Dakota, to nearby Aberdeen. This effort was led by local booster, state senator, and "good roads" advocate Joseph W. Parmley. Parmley saw that the automobile would come to dominate commerce in the years ahead and was determined that his town not be left behind.

From this humble beginning the Yellowstone Trail Association was organized in October 1912 to promote a marked highway from the Twin Cities to Yellowstone National Park via Aberdeen. Boosters along the route began painting the association logo—a yellow circle with a black arrow pointing in the direction of Yellowstone—on roadside poles, trees, and even rocks. The association achieved a major victory in 1914 by successfully lobbying the National Park Service to allow private autos into Yellowstone Park.

The Yellowstone Trail quickly emerged as the most important northern highway and the primary auto tourist route to and from Yellowstone. During its heyday in the early 1920s the Yellowstone Trail Association maintained a permanent office in Minneapolis along with numerous tourist bureaus in prominent cities along the route. Information tents were placed at strategic highway junctions to entice travelers to take the Yellowstone Trail instead of some other route. The Yellowstone Trail Association was supported by private memberships held by businesses along the route.

Private highway associations began to decline in 1926 after the passage of federal highway legislation, which established the U.S. Route numbering system and placed the federal government in the forefront of highway construction. With the federal government now marking and funding highways, the primary functions of the private highway association disappeared. In the late 1920s, like so many other highway groups, the Yellowstone Trail Association fell on hard economic times. It was permanently disbanded in 1930.

Mike Bedeau
Virginia City, Nevada

War

Cheyenne Indian scouts at Fort Reno, Indian Territory

WAR

The Great Plains has been home to a great diversity of peoples for thousands of years. Although coexistence and commerce have dominated most of the relationships among these divergent populations, intermittent conflict has also defined these contacts. Intertribal warfare among Native Americans involved a fluctuating pattern of alliances and attacks, as tribes attempted to protect their resources, attain powerful positions within trading networks, and expand their domination over larger areas. Raids directed against neighboring peoples also secured wealth, gained captives for trade and adoption, and allowed warriors a mechanism for proving their courage and enhancing their personal honor. Despite the relative frequency of these raids, casualties were minimized, except when groups were fighting for survival, or where vengeance demanded bloody retribution.

By the early eighteenth century the European colonial powers of Spain, France, and Great Britain had established relationships with Plains tribes through an extended network of trade. A variety of trade goods was introduced into Indian communities, but the horse and gun had the greatest impact. Horses increased mobility, bringing more tribes into conflict over resources and producing a new style of mounted raid and counter-raid. Firearms, although initially scarce and inferior to bows and arrows in durability, soon became highly prized objects for warriors and as barter items within intertribal trade.

Spanish and Mexican Periods

Because the colonial powers did not attempt to occupy the Great Plains during the eighteenth century, their impact there was largely measured by the strength of their Indian alliances. In the summer of 1720, when Spanish authorities learned of an alleged French penetration of trading zones in the Central Plains, they dispatched Don Pedro de Villasur with forty-two soldiers and sixty Pueblo auxiliaries from Santa Fe to present-day Nebraska. On August 14, Pawnees and Otoes launched a surprise attack by firing a volley from muskets. Only thirteen of Villasur's men escaped. As a result the Spaniards withdrew their trading interests to the Southern Plains.

Thirty-seven years later, Spanish authorities in Texas attempted to spread their influence beyond the narrow coastal belt that linked settlements in the Rio Grande Valley with those in East Texas. Col. Diego Ortiz Parrilla led approximately 400 soldiers, settlers, and missionaries to found the Mission Santa Cruz de San Sabá and a nearby presidio on the San Saba River near present-day Menard, Texas. They hoped to win converts and allies among the Lipan Apaches and other nomadic Indians of West Texas, but the mission was too far southeast to attract many neophytes. Most importantly, the overt diplomacy between Spaniards and Lipan Apaches antagonized Comanche bands, who had a long-standing feud with the latter and opposed any disruption in their growing dominance of western

Texas. Two Comanche attacks against the settlement in 1758 and 1759 left several dozen defenders dead, crops destroyed, and the mission burned.

Drawing a force of more than 600 Spanish soldiers and Indian auxiliaries from as far away as San Antonio, Ortiz Parrilla attacked the Comanches and allied Wichitas at their fortified village of Tawehash on the Red River. The large numbers of Indians repulsed the attack of October 7, 1759, sent Ortiz Parrilla into a full retreat, and compelled Spanish authorities to give up their hopes of a mission settlement on the periphery of the Texas Plains. Periodic punitive expeditions dispatched from southern Texas and the Rio Grande settlements of New Mexico occasionally inflicted significant casualties among the Comanches, Kiowas, and Apaches, but Spain failed to dominate the Southern Plains at the time of Mexican Independence in 1821. Mexican leaders inherited this volatile situation and continued Spanish strategies of diplomacy, trade, and occasional military forays with about the same degree of effectiveness.

American Military Exploration and Manifest Destiny

As the nineteenth century dawned, Americans received their first impressions of the Great Plains through the reports of military explorers and civilian artists. The 1804–6 reconnaissance of Capt. Meriwether Lewis and Lt. William Clark up the Missouri River and to the Oregon coast whetted America's collective appetite to learn more about the exotic lands. Although private traders and trappers made the first regular transits of the Plains in the 1820s, it was army officers who provided the best written records of the vast area. Zebulon Pike's 1806 journey across the Central Plains and Stephen Long's 1819–20 westward march along the Platte River and return along the Canadian River provided important scientific information. Unfortunately, their complex conclusions were oversimplified by a popular literature that emphasized Long's restricted phrase "Great American Desert" as if it implied that the entire Great Plains was a vast wasteland.

Although large numbers of settlers did not move into the region until after the Civil War, the Army Topographical Engineers opened new trails, discovered marketable resources, and sought to impress resident Native Americans with American power. Capt. John C. Frémont's major explorations of the Plains and Far West during the 1840s paved the way for overlanders to the Pacific Coast and heightened tensions between the United States and Mexico. Espousing a philosophy of manifest destiny, which proclaimed American superior virtues and moral authority over Hispanic institutions, proponents of expansionism viewed the Mexican American War of 1846–48 as a golden opportunity to annex Mexican territory. Although no battles occurred in the Plains during this relatively brief war, the region served as a conduit for moving soldiers and supplies to arenas of combat in New Mexico and California.

Plains Indian Campaigns in the 1850s

After the Treaty of Guadalupe Hidalgo, which ended the Mexican American War in 1848, the government turned its attention to Indian affairs within the Great Plains and the Far West. The 1850s witnessed a flurry of treaty signings that placed many Plains Indians on reservations and limited others to ill-defined hunting ranges. New military posts were rapidly added to the Plains, especially in Texas, where an expanding white population demanded protection, and in Indian Territory, where the removed tribes demanded that the nomadic Comanches and Kiowas be corralled.

Military budgets and troop authorizations remained too small to meet the growing task. In 1853 there were only 10,495 men in the army. Fully four-fifths of them were stationed west of the Mississippi River, with the majority seeing service in the Plains. Some posts, such as Fort Kearny and Fort Laramie, guarded the well-traveled trail along the Platte River. Others, such as Fort Leavenworth, Kansas, were rear-guard posts that coordinated the rotation of men and supplies to more remote places. And still others, particularly in Texas, were established in interlocking arrangements of interior and exterior forts that could protect exposed frontier settlements against Indian raids. Many of these stations never achieved more than temporary status.

Although no sustained Indian wars occurred in the Plains during the 1850s, significant military campaigns were launched. Most of the problems were initiated by white treaty violations and government misunderstandings about Indian intentions. In August 1854 an overzealous and inexperienced Lt. John L. Grattan tried to arrest a Lakota warrior for killing a Mormon emigrant's cow near Fort Laramie. When negotiations with Brulé Lakota leader Conquering Bear failed, Grattan began firing into the Indian encampment, killing Conquering Bear. Grattan's entire command of thirty men was wiped out. In response, on September 3, 1855, a 600-man force commanded by Col. William S. Harney attacked the village of Little Thunder at Ash Hollow, killing approximately eighty-five inhabitants and capturing another seventy women and children. This overreactive strike only bred more resentment and retaliatory raids against innocent Americans passing through the area to California and Oregon.

Bleeding Kansas and Civil War

In addition to campaigns against Plains Indians, the army saw service in the slavery conflict that spilled over into the Great Plains. In Kansas during the 1850s, proslavery and antislavery factions vied with each other for control of county governments and the territorial legislature. Tirades gave way to civil insurrection during the era known as "Bleeding Kansas" between 1856 and 1861. Because federal officials could not count on an impartial territorial militia to stand above the contentious slavery debate, they had to rely on army officers to separate the feuding factions. This thankless task garnered enemies on both sides for the army while simultaneously overtaxing military strength that was needed in other frontier areas. For instance, several companies of the Second U.S. Cavalry had to be rotated out of northwestern Texas during 1857 for civil duty in eastern Kansas. This occurred just at the crucial time when additional soldiers were needed to protect two newly created Indian agencies on and near the Clear Fork of the Brazos. The agencies lay exposed to attacks by angry frontiersmen who ultimately drove the peaceful Caddo and southern Comanche bands into present-day western Oklahoma.

The most significant Civil War battle between Plains troops occurred in late March 1862 approximately twenty-five miles east of Santa Fe, New Mexico. Confederate troops commanded by Gen. Henry Sibley had fought a series of successful battles and skirmishes up the Rio Grande Valley as they attempted to wrest New Mexico from Union hands. This operation represented the first leg of a Confederate plan to push their control into Colorado and as far west as the California coast. At the Battle of Glorieta Pass, Union regular and militia forces under Col. John P. Slough and Maj. John M. Chivington destroyed Sibley's supply train and inflicted a major defeat on rebel forces. This "Gettysburg of the West" proved decisive not in terms of casualties (fewer than seventy men were killed in the battle), but in terms of forcing the supply-starved Confederates out of New Mexico and ending their dream of a southwestern empire.

Plains Indian Wars, 1865–1890

Meanwhile, as Americans fought each other, on November 29, 1864, Col. John M. Chivington and his Colorado Volunteers massacred at least 150 Southern Cheyennes and Arapahos (most of them women, children, and elderly) belonging to Black Kettle's band at Sand Creek, Colorado. This massacre propelled the Central and Northern Great Plains toward a heightened Indian-American confrontation after the Civil War.

At the end of the Civil War, the U.S. Army mustered almost a million men out of service. By 1874, at the height of the Great Plains Indian Wars, the entire army consisted of only 25,000 enlisted men and approximately 2,000 officers. Inadequate budgets frequently led to deterioration of quarters and equipment, slow promotions, poor pay, and a general decline in morale.

Government policy in the late nineteenth century aimed at removing Plains Indians from the path of white settlement, placing them on isolated reservations, and promoting an assimilation program designed to wean them away from traditional ways. Native Americans resisted this concentrated assault on their land base and cultures, and the Great Plains provided the setting for some of the most determined resistance anywhere in the nation's history.

Hatreds left from the 1862 Sioux Uprising in Minnesota and the Sand Creek Massacre still seethed in the Northern Plains in 1866 when the government dispatched Col. Henry Car-

rington to build three posts in the prime bison range of the Powder River country. Forts Reno, Phil Kearny, and C. F. Smith soon guarded the Bozeman Trail, which led to the mining camps of western Montana. Lakota Sioux leaders such as Red Cloud opposed this incursion. On December 21, 1866, Sioux, Cheyenne, and Arapaho warriors killed eighty soldiers under Capt. William J. Fetterman near Fort Phil Kearny. Subsequent attacks against troops from Fort C. F. Smith (Hayfield Fight, August 1, 1867) and Fort Phil Kearny (Wagon Box Fight, August 2, 1867) failed only because outnumbered soldiers were able to maximize their firepower with rapid fire, breech-loading Springfield rifles. Unable to adequately protect the bloody Bozeman Trail, the government signed the Fort Laramie Treaty in 1868. Among the guarantees to the Indians was the army's abandonment of its three new posts.

In the Southern Great Plains, the Medicine Lodge Treaty of October 1867 unrealistically assigned specific ranges of land to the Comanches, Kiowas, Southern Cheyennes, and Arapahos, but not until after several military campaigns had forced the issue. Maj. Gen. Winfield Scott Hancock led the way with a spring 1867 operation across western Kansas involving approximately 1,400 soldiers and militiamen. This huge force did little to stop the increasing Indian depredations or to convince the Southern Cheyennes that the government's word could be trusted.

Following this failure, Gen. Philip Sheridan organized a winter 1868 campaign across the western areas of Indian Territory against the same Southern Cheyenne and Arapaho bands. This operation culminated in Lt. Col. George Armstrong Custer's November 27, 1868, attack on Black Kettle's village on the Washita River. Black Kettle, who still represented a mostly peaceful group of people, was killed.

The final chapter in the Southern Plains confrontations emerged in the Red River War of 1874–75, which pitted 1,400 soldiers of five converging columns against the most defiant bands of Comanches, Kiowas, and Southern Cheyennes. The purpose of converging columns was to squeeze the elusive Indians into a confined area, burn their villages and equipment, capture part of their large horse herds, and inflict a major battlefield defeat on them. Although several dozen engagements occurred during these operations, the decisive battle came at Palo Duro Canyon in the Texas Panhandle. Col. Ranald S. Mackenzie achieved the element of surprise by moving 450 cavalrymen from the canyon's dry rim into the verdant valley where Comanches and Kiowas possessed adequate food, water, and forage to wait out their enemy. Mackenzie's bold strike of September 28, 1874, resulted in few casualties on either side, but he burned the camp and slaughtered more than 1,000 Indian horses and mules. Without the ability to operate in their former Panhandle strongholds during the winter, the various bands gradually headed for the reservation at Fort Sill in western Indian Territory. The war in the Southern Plains was virtually over.

With men and resources now available for a similar sweep of the Northern Plains, Sheridan ordered a general campaign against the Teton Sioux, Northern Cheyennes, and Arapahos during the summer of 1876. Three converging cavalry and infantry columns under Gen. Alfred Terry, Gen. George Crook, and Col. John Gibbon moved to the Yellowstone River in eastern Montana. Crook made the first contact on June 17 in the Battle of the Rosebud, and although he claimed victory, he and his 1,200-man command were compelled to retreat southward into Wyoming to await reinforcements.

Meanwhile, General Terry ordered his second-in-command, Lieutenant Colonel Custer and the Seventh Cavalry, to conduct a reconnaissance up Rosebud Creek and locate any signs of an expected Indian encampment. Scouts reported the village directly west on Little Bighorn, and the Seventh attacked it on June 25, 1876. Unlike previous attacks against lightly defended Plains Indian camps, the soldiers here faced perhaps 1,500 warriors. Custer and approximately 250 of his cavalrymen were killed that day in what Indians referred to as the Battle of the Greasy Grass, and eastern newspapers called Custer's Last Stand.

This greatest single victory by Plains Indians proved to be the beginning of the end for their freedom. A determined Congress and Sheridan ordered the army to continue a relentless winter campaign. One by one, the various bands found their camps destroyed at places such as Slim Buttes, South Dakota (September 9, 1876), and Red Fork of the Powder River, Wyoming (November 25, 1876). By May 1877 Crazy Horse had brought some of the last roaming groups of Oglala Lakotas into the Pine Ridge Agency, and Sitting Bull found temporary protection in Saskatchewan, Canada, for his followers. Dull Knife's Northern Cheyennes surrendered and were sent for the time being to an unhealthy reservation in western Indian Territory. Most of the Arapahos were transferred to the Wind River Reservation in western Wyoming.

During the following thirteen years, Indians on Plains reservations found themselves subject to a fast-changing world that was antithetical to their cultural values and threatened their very survival. In this environment of poverty and death the Ghost Dance found a deeply devoted following among the Northern Plains tribes. Many Sioux converted to the new teaching, which promised a return to the old days that existed before the white man had spread over the land. As the number of faithful increased, paranoia grew among agents and settlers bordering the Sioux reservations. Soldiers began to concentrate in western areas of Nebraska and the Dakotas during the fall of 1890, just as frontier newspapers stirred up anti-Indian hysteria.

The December 15, 1890, killing of Hunkpapa Lakota leader Sitting Bull by tribal police precipitated the panicked flight of Ghost Dancers under Miniconjou Lakota leader Big Foot toward the assumed safety of Pine Ridge Reservation. They were intercepted by troops from the Seventh Cavalry, who escorted them to the hamlet at Wounded Knee to await further orders. On December 29, 1890, amid a search of Indian men and women for concealed weapons, a fight began which led to desperate hand-to-hand combat. Simultaneously, rapid-fire Hotchkiss guns rained down small exploding projectiles. Before the day was done, more than 250—and possibly as many as 300—Lakotas were dead, including 44 women and 18 children. Others fled into the cold expanses of the countryside, where they were killed by pursuing soldiers. The army lost twenty-five men and thirty-nine were wounded. The Wounded Knee Massacre and its followup military operations were not "the last Indian War" that some books claimed. Rather, they were a needless anticlimax to decades of cultural misunderstanding, land pressure, government deceit, and countless calls for revenge.

Canadian-Indian Relations in the Plains

Many Canadians have traditionally viewed their "winning of the West" as a process built upon consensus rather than conflict. They point out that in the lands that became the provinces of Manitoba, Saskatchewan, and Alberta, Indian-white conflict was infrequent when compared with the horrific record below the forty-ninth parallel. They argue that Canadian policies were relatively fair to Indians, giving little cause for resistance. More recent scholarship, however, has challenged this older view and has identified a long history of Canadian injustices toward Native Americans.

Historians such as George Stanley have argued that in the western United States, pioneers enveloped the frontier areas before government authority could be established. In this unregulated environment, frontiersmen stirred up numerous controversies with the tribes as they coveted the land and its resources. By contrast, the argument goes, Canadians established governing and enforcement authorities such as the North-West Mounted Police well in advance of the influx of white population. Thus, conflicts could be minimized by law enforcement officers, and pioneers could feel relatively safe in their new environment.

While Stanley's contention holds merit, it omits the Indian view of this relationship. Canadian Plains tribes such as the Bloods, Piegans, Blackfoot, Assiniboines, Plains Crees, and Ojibwas repeatedly complained about treaty violations and delays in shipments of supplies. Many of these tribes also lived and hunted on the U.S. side of the border, and they were concerned that the Americans might extend their authority to the north. The Boundary Commission Survey of 1872–74 especially disturbed tribal leaders who felt that this might be the opening salvo in a complete transfer of the Plains. They were likewise concerned about the frequent movements of the U.S. Army along the border and its forays into Canada to capture specific Indians.

The most serious threat to the relatively peaceful situation in the Prairie Provinces came from Louis David Riel Jr. and his Métis, mixed-blood people of Indian and French Canadian descent who lived in the Red River Settlement of Manitoba. On the eve of the Hudson's Bay Company sale of the Métis' territory of Rupert's Land to Canada in 1869, a "Red River resistance" developed. Riel helped organize the Comites National des Métis to defend farm ownership, protect hunting rights, and ensure the barter economy of the region. They blocked the new governor, William McDougall, from entering the territory and briefly occupied Fort Garry. Col. Garnet Wolseley marched 1,200 volunteers to the relief of the post, but because of delays in crossing hostile terrain, they did not arrive until August 1870. By then, Riel had withdrawn his followers and a compromise agreement was being hammered out.

Riel remained a hunted man even though he was elected three times to the Canadian House of Commons by the people of Manitoba. In 1884 he heeded the call again to help the Métis people of Saskatchewan who were resisting the inroads of farmers and the Canadian Pacific Railway. The initially peaceful protest turned into the North-West Rebellion, with Riel proclaiming himself president of the separatist state. Skirmishes broke out with North-West Mounted Police near Fort Carlton, and other Indians joined the conflict near Frog Lake. Riel gave up on May 15, 1885 and was hanged for treason on November 16, amid a national uproar over the injustice.

From Frontier Setting to Internationalism

The 1890s brought a change in military activity in the Great Plains, as policymakers shifted their attention from western expansion to matters of international scope. With the Indians now on reservations, many military posts—Forts Buford and Assiniboine, for example—were closed. The shift to international issues began in 1898 with the Spanish American War and continued from 1899 through 1902 in the Philippine-American War. Plains states were affected in two ways by these conflicts. First, regular army troops were redeployed from the frontier posts to overseas duty. At installations across the Plains only handfuls of civilian employees remained to guard against pilfering. In some cases, troops never returned to their previously assigned posts, which were soon closed.

The second impact in the Plains states came in the mobilization of state National Guard units. Many of these units got no further than training camps, but the First Nebraska Infantry, for example, made it to the Philippines and saw active fighting against Spaniards and subsequently during the Philippine-American War.

New concerns for the American military began in 1911 with the outbreak of the Mexican Revolution. Rebel raids that spilled over into American territory throughout 1914 and 1915 forced the United States to augment its protection of the extensive boundary from Texas to California. On May 9, 1916, President Woodrow Wilson mobilized the National Guards of New Mexico, Texas, and Arizona to help defend the border. Little more than a month later, the National Guards of all states were called into action, and by late July, 111,000 guardsmen had moved to the international boundary, including units from all Plains states. Sporadic rebel raids obliged the United States to maintain troops in the region until 1921.

World War I

American response to the war in Europe sent repercussions through Plains agriculture virtually as soon as the struggle began. Immediately after the German invasion of Belgium in 1914, Kansans began donating wheat to area millers who voluntarily ground it into flour for shipment to Europe. With German supplies of potash cut off, American farmers had to look elsewhere for this key fertilizer ingredient. Ten new potash plants were developed in west-central Nebraska. This industrial boom led to the creation of several new communities, most of which failed when the importation of cheaper German potash resumed after the war. The war also stimulated the production of Great Plains oil. The oil fields of Wyoming doubled their output after 1916.

After America's entry into the war in April 1917, President Wilson appointed Herbert Hoover to the newly created U.S. Food Administration. Needing to stimulate food production, Hoover initiated programs for federal subsidies to producers of wheat, corn, cotton, hogs, and sugar. The prices of corn, oats, and hay doubled, while the price of wheat nearly tripled. In Montana, the number of new homesteads peaked as farmers went into debt to plow grasslands for crop production. All across the Plains, patriotic citizens planted vegetable gardens and observed the federally encouraged "wheatless" and "meatless" days.

Military preparations significantly changed home-front Plains communities. In June 1917 construction began on an enormous training facility at the Fort Riley, Kansas, military reserve. Construction of the camp for 50,000 soldiers, and the requisite support services for men in training, created a nearby "Army City," which had four blocks of stores, theaters, barbershops, and pool halls. A similar site, Camp Doniphan, grew on the grounds of Fort Sill, Oklahoma, after 1917.

The new science of "aero-technology" saw its first use in World War I, and the Plains produced two balloon-training facilities. As early as 1900 the U.S. Army Signal Corps had organized a Balloon Detachment, eventually locating all its dirigible activities at Fort Omaha, Nebraska. The program was abandoned in 1909, but when the United States entered the war, the military began using piloted balloons to make more accurate battlefield observations. Fort Omaha was the logical place to expand training operations since the hangar and its companion hydrogen plant were still operational. In July 1917 the Fort Omaha Balloon School received the first of the 16,000 men it would eventually train in balloon skills. A second Plains balloon school opened at Fort Sill, Oklahoma, in September 1917. The Fort Sill balloon operation remained functional into the 1930s, but all the equipment and staff of the Fort Omaha school were moved to Belleville, Illinois, in 1921.

There was little tolerance for anyone appearing un-American during World War I. Montanans' harassment of German Americans and Scandinavians, who preferred that the United States remain neutral, led to considerable unrest. "Liberty Committees" were created in some towns to police suspected antiwar activities. In Glendive a mob nearly lynched a German Mennonite minister who favored peace. In February 1918 the Montana Defense Council, which had already banned any use of the German language, convinced the governor to call a special legislative session, which passed the Montana Sedition Law, making it illegal to criticize the federal government, the armed services, or state government in wartime. This became the model for the federal Sedition Law of 1918.

In the Canadian Prairie Provinces, the outbreak of war in 1914 also improved the farm economy, which had plummeted into debt and depression after 1912. Farmers quickly responded to war needs with sizable quantities of horses, oats, and flour. Acres were rushed into production and nearly 40,000 new farms were created by 1921. The price of land rebounded, wages for farm laborers rose, and unemployment dropped.

World War I also produced economic changes in the postwar Plains. Because many cavalry animals remained to be cared for after the war, the U.S. War Department created the Remount Board in 1919 to establish remount depots, which would condition horses and mules for military use as well as train necessary personnel in animal care and management. With funding in 1921, two permanent remount depots were established in the Great Plains—one at Fort Robinson, Nebraska, and another at Fort Reno, Oklahoma. Fort Robinson quickly became the world's largest remount station, housing 17,000 horses and mules by the late 1930s.

World War II

The outbreak of war in Europe in September 1939 marked the beginning of the end of the Great Depression. Although the United States continued to maintain its isolationist stance against military participation during the first two years of the conflict, the government's "cash and carry" policy of allowing Great Britain and France to purchase necessary supplies meant increased production and employment in most sections of the country, including the Great Plains. The upsurge of production, coupled with the need for soldiers in the armed forces, gradually reduced the surplus of labor. By 1942 the labor pool was drained, and an exhaustive search for manpower was under way in the military, agricultural, industrial, and service sectors of the American economy. Women entered the workforce in record numbers. Forty percent of the employees at Oma-

ha's Martin Bomber Plant and one-half of Remington Arms Company personnel in Denver were women. Prisoners of war were used to bolster the labor force in nonthreatened regions of the country such as the Plains.

After Pearl Harbor the Great Plains benefited greatly from war production and from numerous sectors of the economy that were tied to military expansion. Most of the expansion monies were funneled through the Defense Plant Corporation, a subsidiary of the New Deal's Reconstruction Finance Corporation, created in August 1940. Plains states created their own booster groups to lobby for federal contracts. For example, North Dakota's businessmen organized two groups—the North Dakota War Resource Committee and the Greater North Dakota Association—to procure some of the lucrative government contracts.

During the war, the remoteness of parts of the Great Plains became a virtue that attracted new industries. Most Plains states benefited from the tremendous growth of the wartime aviation industry. Plains spaces were defensibly secure and wide open for the creation of landing strips and for the testing of armaments. Texas established forty air bases, including Avenger Field at Sweetwater, which trained women for the Women Air Force Service Pilots. The clear skies over Midland Army Air Field proved to be an excellent location for the training of aerial bombardiers. The national headquarters of the Air Force Training Command was housed at Fort Worth's Carswell Field, and aircraft factories were also built in the Dallas–Fort Worth area.

In 1942 Montana became the site of Malmstrom Air Force Base, constructed by the Army Air Corps near Great Falls. The Air Corps also established Lowry Field near Denver after the city donated the land from an old sanatorium site. Buckley Field, east of Denver, and Peterson Field, near Colorado Springs, were added to the growing list of Plains airfields. In Wyoming, the Casper Army Air Base was built in the summer of 1942, and Cheyenne became the new home of United Air Lines pilot training. The city was also the site of a modification center that installed new armaments and instruments on thousands of B-17s and smaller bombers. The economic impact of these installations on the local economies was tremendous.

The Prairie Provinces were just as appealing. The British Commonwealth Air Training Plan (BCATP) was formulated in the months before Canada declared war on Germany in September 1939 and was intended to train aircrews for the British armed forces. The BCATP served as Canada's primary contribution to the war effort and drew trainees from Britain, Canada, Australia, New Zealand, and India, as well as recruits from nations that fell to German forces. Administered by the Royal Canadian Air Force, the plan established training schools and runways at more than thirty sites in the Prairies, from Edmonton and Penhold, Alberta, to Winnipeg and Portage la Prairie, Manitoba. By August 1945, 131,553 pilots and

aircrew members had been trained in the Prairie Provinces.

To the south, Wichita, Kansas, became a center in the aviation industry during the war and continues as such to the present day. In 1940 Boeing Aircraft Corporation received a government contract to expand the Beech Aircraft Company in Wichita. By early 1942 Boeing was turning out parts for their B-17 Flying Fortress, and the government had established the National Defense Training School to train aircraft workers. The aircraft industry and its associated schools brought thousands of job seekers to Wichita. Pratt Airfield was completed with government funds in 1943 and became home to heavy bomber groups. All totaled, aircraft plants in Wichita and Kansas City, Kansas, turned out 24,000 planes during the war.

In September 1940 Offutt Field at Bellevue, Nebraska (near Omaha), was selected as a site for the production of B-26 bombers. Construction of the plant immediately brought 3,000 new residents to the sleepy village. The plant opened in early 1942 and employed 14,572 people at its peak. Traffic in and out of the plant led to construction of the first divided highway in Nebraska. During the course of the war, the Bellevue plant produced 1,500 B-26s and more than 500 B-29s, including two modified B-29s—the *Enola Gay* and *Bock's Car*—which dropped the atomic bombs on Hiroshima and Nagasaki to end the war in the Pacific.

The mobilization of thousands of guardsmen during the last quarter of 1940 had a major impact in the Great Plains. Facilities could not be constructed rapidly enough. Near Cheyenne, Fort Warren was expanded to 284 buildings at a cost of more than $5 million. The Wyoming post housed 19,000 men and women at its peak. Soldiers' dependents lived in the city itself and spent millions of dollars annually. The monthly payroll for Fort Warren alone was greater than that of any of the state's industries. In Kansas, Fort Leavenworth expanded its facilities by becoming a training site that pumped $50 million into the Kansas economy in 1940 alone. Other army training sites at Salina's Camp Phillips and nearby Fort Riley as well as naval air corps training facilities at Hutchinson and Olathe forced the prices of consumer goods in those areas to increase by 25 percent between 1939 and 1944.

Defense industries boomed. Again, the relative security of Plains isolation proved to be the drawing card that brought rocket, mine, and bomb production facilities to Sidney, Grand Island, Hastings, and Mead, Nebraska. In Denver, Remington Arms manufactured small-caliber ammunition, the Kaiser Company finished artillery shells, and Rocky Mountain Arsenal produced poisonous gases. Most of these expansive facilities closed within weeks of the war's end in 1945, but some found new uses after the war. The Remington Arms Company buildings ultimately became Denver's Federal Center. The Grand Island Cornhusker Ordnance Plant was reopened for service during the Korean and Vietnam conflicts, finally closing permanently in 1973. However, lack of waste disposal standards throughout their years of operation has endowed a legacy of soil and water pollution for residents presently living near many wartime Plains ordnance plants.

War needs extended into other areas of the home front as well in the early 1940s. In Denver, foundries that once manufactured mining equipment and sugar refining gear began to make oil production machinery. In general, the Plains oil industry expanded. But the Plains industries most positively affected by the war were agriculture and livestock production. The pressure to mechanize increased as much of the traditional farm labor force was pressed into military service. Improved financing for farm machinery allowed many farmers to acquire tractors, which subsequently displaced some two million horses and mules between 1941 and 1945, while increasing the amount of arable land in the Plains by 5 percent. Farmers' cash receipts rose throughout the Plains during the war years, doubling, for example, in Wyoming.

The war touched the Plains in yet another way. As Allied forces made gains against the Axis powers in southern Europe and northern Africa through 1941, guarding and housing the enemy prisoners became a tremendous burden for Allied troop commanders. Beginning early in 1942, the War Department ordered the transfer of all captured enemy personnel to detention camps in the United States. By late 1944 forty-six prisoner-of-war (POW) camp networks were in place in the Great Plains. As replacement labor in United States industries, prisoners were not permitted to undertake any degrading work, nor were they permitted within ten miles of sensitive military installations. Prisoners in a network of nineteen camps in Nebraska and northern Kansas picked beets and corn. POWs in Wyoming's system of eleven camps also undertook agricultural jobs, as they did in Texas.

Another kind of detention camp in the Great Plains revealed America's insensitive treatment of her own citizens—Japanese American internment camps. In February 1942 President Franklin Roosevelt directed that all Japanese Americans were to be evacuated from sensitive areas in the West. Construction of the Amache internment camp near Granada, Colorado, was a boost to the local economy, employing 1,000 men at a cost of $4.2 million. But a total of 7,567 Japanese, over two-thirds of whom were American citizens, were housed in deplorable conditions—cardboard houses, few lights, and no running water. The site was not completely evacuated until October 1945.

In February 1942 the Canadian government undertook similar measures against all people of Japanese extraction living in the "defense zone," a 100-mile-wide strip along the coast of British Columbia. By June 1942 nearly 2,250 Japanese Canadians had been deported to southern Alberta, where they took up residence in the inadequate housing formerly used by seasonal beet workers. Canada faced the same labor shortages found in the United States, and displaced Japanese Canadians harvested Alberta's sugar beets and worked in the Broder Canning Factory at Lethbridge.

Despite the Great Plains's remoteness from both coasts, the Japanese managed to "bomb" several Plains locations with balloon bombs—incendiary devices intended to terrorize Americans and set forests and cities ablaze. Between November 1944 and August 1945, 6,000 armed balloons were launched from Honshu by the Japanese military. Only 300 of them ever reached the United States, most of them exploding on the Pacific Coast. But a sizable number of the balloons drifted inland and exploded over the Plains. South Dakota, for example, reported at least nine balloon explosions.

Cold War

The cold war was born in the sniping between the new superpowers of the United States and the Soviet Union at the Potsdam Conference in July 1945. One month later, the United States unleashed the force that remained for nearly fifty years the primary ingredient of the cold war—the atomic bomb. The ever-present threat of a nuclear holocaust compelled the U.S. Army Air Force to create the Strategic Air Command (SAC). In 1948 SAC's central operations were placed at Offutt Air Force Base, near Omaha, Nebraska, making the Central Plains "ground zero" in any nuclear confrontation and ushering in a new age of defense spending throughout the Great Plains.

The federal government felt obliged to challenge the American public into steadfastly supporting its tough national security measures. The defense plan adopted in 1950 by the Truman administration contained two components: national prevention of nuclear war and public management of atomic war should it ever occur. Government leaders in the Plains responded to the challenge, and in early 1951 Nebraska and South Dakota met with four other midwestern states to outline plans for civilian defense and mutual aid. Practice drills were encouraged on a community level, and on December 5, 1954, Denver residents evacuated the city in a mass preparedness drill designed to make sure that citizens could quickly take shelter in surrounding rural counties.

Over the next two decades, concern for protection from nuclear fallout led some Americans to build their own fallout shelters. In June 1962 Artesia, New Mexico, dedicated the first school building built entirely underground to protect inhabitants from fallout. Eventually, the belowground levels of many public buildings were designated as fallout shelters. Similarly, in 1961 an eastern Nebraska dairy built a thirty-five-thousand-dollar shelter designed to protect 200 head of dairy cattle from fallout. But despite strong federal encouragement and the dissemination of copious amounts of construction "how-to" data, only 1,500 private bomb shelters had been built by 1960.

The threat of Soviet attack drew the American and Canadian portions of the Great Plains closer together. Alberta was located on the flight path of any Soviet bomb squadron headed for either eastern Canada or the United States. Thus, in 1947 Canada appointed a national civil defense coordinator to encourage provincial civil defense. Alberta's civil defense plans were well ahead of those of other Prairie Provinces, and by 1952 the province was using forest fire spotters to watch for enemy aircraft. By 1955 Alberta had trained 25,000 civil defense volunteers to assist in the event of a Soviet attack.

The United States and Canada joined parts of their ground defense forces early in the postwar era, and in 1948–49 Canada created the Mobile Striking Force and placed its joint army–air force headquarters in Winnipeg. In 1958 the two countries formally created a continental network of anti-aircraft defenses. The North American Aerospace Defense Command (NORAD) set up radar defenses as far north as the Arctic Circle and coordinated the system from headquarters at Colorado Springs, Colorado. The headquarters facility, which was built deep inside Cheyenne Mountain, was completed in 1966 at a cost of $142.4 million.

Colorado Springs was the recipient of more Department of Defense dollars after the air force was created as a separate branch of the armed forces. Established in 1948, the air force originally drew from a variety of sources for its officers, but in 1954 Congress granted approval for the creation of an Air Force Academy at Colorado Springs. The government authorized $126 million to purchase the 15,100 acres of ranch land and to construct the buildings. Until the academy was completed, Lowry Air Force Base in Denver was the temporary facility, and the government spent $1 million to ready the base for its role.

Linking the continent together in a web of communications became vital in the postwar era, and in view of those needs, pressure to construct an interstate highway system increased. Although such a network had been envisioned as early as 1944, federal funds had not materialized, and the Korean War only increased the strain on existing highways. Despite the tremendous costs involved, President Dwight Eisenhower signed legislation in 1956 authorizing a twenty-five-billion-dollar interstate highway system. Between 1956 and 1974 construction of the interstate system connected the Great Plains, greatly boosting local economies.

Cold war industrial output in the Plains centered on the manufacture of military aircraft, and Wichita, Kansas, became a major Great Plains component in the military-industrial complex. The end of World War II had meant closure of one of the city's Boeing Aircraft plants, reducing Boeing's Wichita workforce of more than 29,000 by 50 percent. But as cold war tensions increased in the late 1940s, Boeing reopened its Wichita plants to build 1,371 B-47s—the revolutionary Stratojet. Another Wichita aerospace manufacturer, Loadcraft, built carriers for the Honest John missile throughout the 1950s. Nearby McConnell Air Force Base was activated in 1951 to train the B-47 pilots. The base continued its service into the late twentieth century as part of the Strategic Air Command.

The greatest contribution of the Great Plains to America's cold war defenses was its service as a permanent home for the Strategic Air Command's air defense missile system. The construction of intercontinental ballistic missile (ICBM) sites in Wyoming, as well as in adjacent areas of Nebraska and Colorado, pumped $100 million into the regional economy. Similar economic benefits were reaped from the installation of Atlas missile sites in eastern Nebraska and Kansas, and at Altus AFB, Oklahoma, Dyess AFB in Texas, and Walker AFB in eastern New Mexico.

Missile technology continued to evolve through the Titan series of missiles, and by 1960 the advanced Minuteman series was ready for deployment. Upon testing, the missile's range was shy of its intended 5,500-mile reach, so selection of missile sites was confined to the Northern Plains because of the region's closer proximity to the Soviet Union. The first location chosen for installation of the Minuteman missiles was Malmstrom Air Force Base near Great Falls, Montana. The Cuban missile crisis of October 1962 forced the rapid completion of the first ten missile sites and their manned launch-control facility.

The second site chosen for deployment of 150 Minuteman missiles was Ellsworth Air Force Base east of Rapid City, South Dakota. Construction required approximately 3,000 workers who needed housing and other facilities. By the end of 1967, 600 Minuteman missiles had been installed. During the 1970s newer Minuteman II and Minuteman III missiles augmented or replaced Minuteman I ICBMs at 1,000 sites in the Northern Plains.

In 1983 the Reagan administration announced its intention to replace fifty Minuteman III missiles assigned to Warren Air Force Base in Wyoming with the advanced MX Peacekeeper missiles, which could carry more warheads and had greater range and targeting flexibility. The project was completed in 1989 at a cost of $16.6 billion nationally for installation, evaluation, and research. The economic impact on the region was phenomenal: $232 million alone for hardened-silo upgrades.

The cold war faded with the fall of the Berlin Wall in November 1989. In July 1991 President George H. W. Bush and Soviet leader Mikhail Gorbachev signed the Strategic Arms Reduction Treaty, placing limits on the worldwide number of intercontinental ballistic missiles. In September of that year President Bush announced that all 450 operational Minutemen II missiles would be withdrawn, including all those at South Dakota's Ellsworth Air Force Base. The bomb wing there also closed in late 1995, but the base remained open. Because of the ICBM's importance to America's cold war defenses, two missile sites at Ellsworth AFB are being considered for possible historic preservation.

Reduced federal spending due to the end of the cold war had a negative economic impact on many parts of the Great Plains. Near Lubbock, Texas, Reese Air Force Base was closed, with the loss of an estimated $82 million to the local economy. Also closed was Lowry Air Force Base in Denver, which had served as a Titan missile site and as a training center for aircraft maintenance and weapons loading. More than 10,000 military and civilian employees had worked at the base, creating a positive economic impact greater than $600 million annually. Closing the base in 1992 cost 6,000 jobs in the metropolitan area.

At the beginning of the twenty-first century, the Great Plains continues to play an important role in North America's military activities. The wide-open vistas still evoke images of a not-so-distant frontier past in which the Plains served as a military corridor to the Far West and as a place of conflict between immigrant peoples and Native Americans. Cities spread rapidly into those vistas in the twentieth century, and many served as production sites for the new technology that put military strategy into the air. Men and women from the very ethnic groups whose confrontations are part of Plains history now work together in military activities at home during times of natural disaster, or as far away as Haiti and Bosnia in their attempts to restore peace instead of waging war.

See also ARCHITECTURE: Cold War Architecture / ASIAN AMERICANS: Amache Internment Camp / EDUCATION: United States Air Force Academy / EUROPEAN AMERICANS: Villasur, Pedro de / HISPANIC AMERICANS: Guadalupe Hidalgo, Treaty of; San Sabá Mission and Presidio / IMAGES AND ICONS: Custer, George Armstrong; Missile Silos / INDUSTRY: Aerospace; Potash / LAW: North-West Mounted Police / NATIVE AMERICANS: Assimilation Policy; Métis / PROTEST AND DISSENT: Riel, Louis / RELIGION: Ghost Dance.

Michael L. Tate
Jo Lea Wetherilt Behrens
University of Nebraska at Omaha

Clendenen, Clarence C. *Blood on the Border: The United States Army and the Mexican Irregulars.* Toronto: Macmillan Publishing Company, 1969. Conrad, Peter C. *Training for Victory: The British Commonwealth Air Training Plan in the West.* Saskatoon, Saskatchewan: Western Producer Prairie Books, 1989. Goetzmann, William H. *Army Exploration in the American West, 1803–1863.* New Haven CT: Yale University Press, 1959. Haley, James L. *The Buffalo War: The History of the Red River Indian Uprising of 1874.* New York: Doubleday and Co., 1976. Hoig, Stan. *The Sand Creek Massacre.* Norman: University of Oklahoma Press, 1961. Holsinger, M. Paul. "Amache." *Colorado Magazine* 41 (1964): 50–60. Hutton, Paul Andrew, ed. *Soldiers West: Biographies from the Military Frontier.* Lincoln: University of Nebraska Press, 1987. Larson, T. A. *Wyoming's War Years, 1941–1945.* Stanford CA: Stanford University Press, 1954. Reprint, Cheyenne: Wyoming Historical Foundation, 1993. Leckie, William H. *The Buffalo Soldiers: A Narrative of the Negro Cavalry in the West.* Norman: University of Oklahoma Press, 1967. McGinnis, Anthony. *Counting Coups and Cutting Horses: Intertribal Warfare on the Northern Plains, 1738–1889.* Evergreen CO: Cordillera Press, Inc., 1990. Nash, Gerald A. *The American West Transformed: The Impact of the Second World War.* Bloomington: Indiana University Press, 1985. Rickey, Don, Jr. *Forty Miles a Day on Beans and Hay: The Enlisted Soldier Fighting the Indian Wars.* Norman: University of Oklahoma Press, 1963. Smith, Sherry L. *The View from Officers' Row: Army Perception of Western Indians.* Tucson: University of Arizona Press, 1990. Stanley, George F. G. *The Birth of Western Canada: A History of the Riel Rebellions.* Toronto: University of Toronto Press, 1960. Thompson, John
Herd. *The Harvests of War: The Prairie West, 1914–1918.* Toronto: McClelland and Stewart Ltd., 1978. Utley, Robert M. *Frontier Regulars: The United States Army and the Indian, 1866–1891.* New York: Macmillan Publishing Company, 1973. Utley, Robert M. *Frontiersmen in Blue: The United States Army and the Indian, 1848–1865.* New York: Macmillan Publishing Company, 1967. Wooster, Robert. *The Military and United States Indian Policy, 1865–1903.* New Haven CT: Yale University Press, 1988.

ADOBE WALLS, BATTLE OF

This battle between buffalo hunters and approximately 700 Comanche, Kiowa, and Southern Cheyenne warriors resulted in an Indian defeat, one among several during the course of the large-scale military operation known as the Red River War of 1874–75. Inspired by a recent Sun Dance and Comanche medicine man Isatai's promise of easy victory, the warriors sought to inflict a mortal blow against the hated buffalo hunters who were destroying the vast southern herds in the Texas Panhandle. The young Comanche Quanah Parker joined Isatai as nominal leaders of the raid against the twenty-eight men and one woman residing in Adobe Walls, a small complex of trading stores and a saloon in present-day Hutchinson County, Texas.

During the early dawn hours of June 27, 1874, the Indians attacked the residents, quickly killing two hunters who were sleeping in a wagon. The others were alerted immediately because they had remained awake during the night while repairing a broken beam in the saloon. They held off several assaults, losing only two other defenders—one to Indian gunfire and one to the accidental discharge of a rifle. The siege continued for five days. Indian casualties mounted to several dozen, and faith in Isatai's power faded. On the second day of the siege, Billy Dixon fired his fabled shot, hitting a mounted warrior fully eight-tenths of a mile away. Following abandonment of the Adobe Walls settlement six weeks later, the Indians burned it to the ground. Yet the battle had been a bitter setback for them, and it presaged the larger defeat that would soon follow at the hands of the army.

See also NATIVE AMERICANS: Parker, Quanah.

Michael L. Tate
University of Nebraska at Omaha

Dixon, Olive K. *Life of "Billy" Dixon.* Dallas: P. L. Turner Co., 1927. Gard, Wayne. *The Great Buffalo Hunt.* New York: Alfred A. Knopf, Inc., 1959. Haley, James L. *The Buffalo War.* New York: Doubleday and Co., 1976.

AMACHE INTERNMENT CAMP

See ASIAN AMERICANS: Amache Internment Camp

ARIKARA EXPEDITION

Early 1823 proved deadly along the upper Missouri River after a series of Indian attacks on fur trappers and trading posts caused staggering economic losses, especially to the Missouri Fur Company. In particular, the Arikaras opposed American attempts to move upriver, which would eliminate their middleman role in the fur trade. On June 2 they attacked William Ashley's trapping party, which was camped near their villages, close to the confluence of the Grand and Missouri Rivers, killing fourteen men. When the survivors limped into Fort Atkinson (in present-day Nebraska) on June 18, Col. Henry Leavenworth and Indian agent Benjamin O'Fallon decided that American military strength had to be demonstrated. This would be the first major U.S. expedition against the Plains Indians.

Leavenworth left Fort Atkinson on June 22 with 230 men of the Sixth U.S. Infantry and two cannons to punish the Arikaras. Joining him five days later was trader Joshua Pilcher, head of the Missouri Fur Company, with sixty men and a howitzer. Ashley's men added eighty to the force, and about 700 Lakotas joined in to fight their enemies, the Arikaras. As the force neared the villages on August 9, the Lakotas rode ahead and engaged the Arikaras, killing ten to fifteen of them. At dawn on August 10, Leavenworth trained his artillery on the stockaded Arikara villages, but they mainly overshot the target. When the Lakotas deserted the fight to raid the Arikaras' cornfields, the troops were forced to face an expected battle alone. Seizing an opportunity to negotiate with Arikara leaders, Leavenworth asked them to return Ashley's property and to promise future good behavior. The Arikaras were allowed to leave their besieged villages on the night of August 14. Ashley seemingly accepted this outcome, but Pilcher was infuriated.

On August 15 Leavenworth and his troops headed downriver, followed by Pilcher with his contingent of trappers. Angry at the dismal show of force against the Arikaras, Pilcher set fire to both of their villages. This action naturally further alienated the Arikaras, who continued to resist American inroads on the upper Missouri. Forced to seek a new route to the trapping grounds, Ashley and his men forged the overland route into the Central Rockies through South Pass. The new trail set the stage for the enormous future pioneer migration along the Platte Valley and into the West in the 1840s.

See also INDUSTRY: Fur Trade / NATIVE AMERICANS: Arikaras.

Jo Lea Wetherilt Behrens
University of Nebraska at Omaha

Meyer, Roy Willard. *The Village Indians of the Upper Missouri: The Mandans, Hidatsas, and Arikaras.* Lincoln: University of Nebraska Press, 1977. Morgan, Dale L. *Jedediah Smith and the Opening of the West.* Lincoln: University of Nebraska Press, 1964.

ARMY TOPOGRAPHICAL ENGINEERS

From 1777 until 1863 the U.S. Army included topographical engineers among its professional officers. The Topographical Bureau was created as a branch of the U.S. Army Corps of Engineers on March 3, 1813, and remained only a small, elite corps until John James Abert, a graduate of the U.S. Military Academy at West Point, became its head in 1829. A good politician as well as a capable engineer,

Abert succeeded in getting the Corps of Topographical Engineers created in 1838 as an independent army unit separate from the U.S. Army Corps of Engineers. Sixty-four of its seventy-two officers were West Point men, testifying to the unit's superior composition. The Corps was in tune with the romantic interests of a nation curious about the West and anxious to unlock its secrets. On March 3, 1863, Congress eliminated the independent unit, merging it with the Army Engineers.

One of the first six officers in the Corps, Stephen H. Long explored along the Platte, Arkansas, and Red Rivers in 1820. His report included a map of the Great Plains across which was printed "Great American Desert." Although the description is today considered incorrect, Long (and Zebulon Pike before him), in their pessimistic forecasts denying the possibility of white settlement, were accurate within the context of the technology of the times.

The Topographical Engineers were most active in the 1840s and 1850s. John C. Frémont's western explorations began in 1841 with an exploration of the North Platte River. Frémont's next exploration took him west to present Pueblo, Colorado, then north to the Laramie Plains. Returning east a year later, Frémont took a southerly route via Bent's Fort on the Arkansas River. His report of this two-year reconnaissance (1843–44) greatly expanded the geographical knowledge of the Great Plains.

The Southern Plains gained official attention with the advent of the Mexican War. Topographical engineers accompanied military forays searching out the best routes, and sites for artesian wells, into New Mexico and California. They were involved in the running of the Mexican American boundary. Colonel Abert's son, Lt. James W. Abert, Bvt. Maj. William Hemsley Emory, Lt. Amiel Weeks Whipple, and Lt. James H. Simpson are but four of the many topographical engineers whose activities added further to the knowledge of the Southern Plains.

The Topographical Engineers were deeply involved in the Pacific Railroad surveys. These explorations resulted in the delineation of several viable railroad routes ranging, in the north, from St. Paul, Minnesota, to Oregon and, in the south, from Vicksburg to southern California. Lt. Gov. K. Warren, Capt. John W. Gunnison, Isaac I. Stevens, and Capt. William F. Raynolds were among the engineers who traversed the Great Plains in the course of their assignments. In addition, scientists accompanied the surveys, and their Pacific Railroad reports—magnificent volumes gathering dust in research libraries—offer a proud beginning to the scientific investigation of the entire West, including the Great Plains.

Richard A. Bartlett
Florida State University

Goetzmann, William H. *Army Exploration of the American West, 1803–1863.* New Haven CT: Yale University Press, 1959. Goetzmann, William H. *Exploration and Empire.* New York: Alfred A. Knopf, Inc. 1966. Wallace, Edward S. *The Great Reconnaissance.* Boston: Little, Brown and Co., 1955.

BEECHER ISLAND, BATTLE OF

The Battle of Beecher Island was one of the most publicized engagements fought between Plains Indians and the U.S. Army. On September 17, 1868, on a sandbar in the middle of the Arickaree River in eastern Colorado, a large group of Cheyenne Dog Soldiers, Arapahos, and Lakotas attacked fifty citizen scouts under the command of Maj. George A. Forsyth. The scouts held off repeated charges before the Indians departed.

The scouts survived by eating the meat of their horses for nine days before reinforcements arrived from Fort Wallace, Kansas. Forsyth's command sustained losses of five scouts killed and eighteen wounded. Included among the dead was Lt. Frederick H. Beecher, the nephew of the outspoken New York abolitionist Henry Ward Beecher. Forsyth named the battle in memory of Lieutenant Beecher.

The Indian records obtained years later by George Bent and George B. Grinnell accounted for nine warriors killed and an unknown number wounded. One casualty was the esteemed warrior Roman Nose, a Northern Cheyenne member of the Crooked Lance Society. The Cheyennes referred to the battle as "the fight where Roman Nose was killed." Although the battle held little significance for the Indians, the scouts' successful defensive stand against extreme odds was inevitably compared to the Battle of the Little Bighorn, and consequently came to hold epic and symbolic importance for Americans. The sensationalism it generated indirectly led to an infusion of new troops into the Plains, culminating in the Washita campaign.

John H. Monnett
Metropolitan State College of Denver

Monnett, John H. *The Battle of Beecher Island and the Indian War of 1867–1869.* Niwot: University Press of Colorado, 1992.

BLACK REGIMENTS

See AFRICAN AMERICANS: Black Regiments

BLEEDING KANSAS

Bleeding Kansas is the term used to describe the violence that flared in Kansas Territory from 1855 to 1856 (and continued on a smaller scale until 1861). Behind this lay the nation's territorial expansion, beginning with the Louisiana Purchase in 1803, of which Kansas formed a part. Westward migration into the Mississippi Valley, steam-powered transportation, the prospect of a transcontinental railroad through the central United States, an unending land hunger, and acquisition of further western territory from 1845 to 1848 all spurred settlement of the midwestern prairies and sharpened the sectional rivalry between slave and free states.

In 1854, by the Kansas-Nebraska Act, Congress repealed a prohibition on extending slavery in the Louisiana Territory north of 36°30′. The outcome was tumultuous, inaugurated by angry debates in Congress and the press. There followed the birth of the Republican Party, dedicated to the nonextension of slavery, the demise of the nationalist Whig Party, and sectional division of the Democratic Party, sponsor of the law.

The Kansas-Nebraska Act authorized formation of a territorial government in Kansas, lying directly west of slaveholding Missouri. Missourians, concentrated in the slave-owning, hemp-growing northwestern corner, feared that formation of a free territory would jeopardize their interests. Violence, fraud, murder, rivalry for land, and a supine federal response created the "Kansas Question," which dominated national politics from 1854 to 1858. In 1855 some 5,000 Missourians helped elect a proslavery legislature. Gov. Andrew Reeder declined to repudiate the fraud and allowed the legislature to establish a proslavery government. Antislavery groups drafted a "free-state" constitution, held elections, and established an antislavery government. Two territorial governments now existed, one fraudulent but recognized by President Franklin Pierce, the other extralegal and rejected by him. Tension erupted into violence in November and December 1855 in the "Wakarusa War," participated in by 1,500 "border ruffians." Temporarily quelled by the territorial governor, violence little short of civil war again broke out in 1856 when border ruffians sacked the free-state town of Lawrence. In response, a small band led by the fanatical abolitionist John Brown murdered five proslavery settlers, and guerrilla warfare raged. "Bleeding Kansas" brought death to about 200 persons and destroyed about $2 million in property.

Congress bitterly debated a proslavery constitution, refusing to accept it, though it enjoyed President James Buchanan's support. The national crisis was marked by the near-victory of the newborn Republican Party in the presidential election of 1856, the Dred Scott decision of the U.S. Supreme Court in 1857, which mandated that Congress could not constitutionally prohibit slavery in the territories, and the Lincoln-Douglas debates in 1858 that dramatically argued the territorial question.

Congress referred the proslavery constitution to Kansans, resulting in a resounding rejection tied to a stipulation that rejection entailed postponement of statehood. By the time of the vote—August 2, 1858—migration of free-state settlers had decided the issue. Contrary to myth, neither antislavery New Englanders nor Deep South settlers affected the result. The peopling of Kansas followed a more normal migrational pattern. The census of 1860 showed that all slave states had contributed 27,440 persons; three free Ohio Valley states—Ohio, Indiana, Illinois—alone sent 30,929 settlers of a total population of 107,204. The census ironically disclosed that only two blacks lived in Kansas Territory; the next year Kansas entered the Union a free state. But the issue of federal authority over slavery in the territories endured, splitting the nation in 1861.

See also POLITICS AND GOVERNMENT: Kansas-Nebraska Act of 1854.

James A. Rawley
University of Nebraska–Lincoln

Rawley, James A. *Race and Politics: "Bleeding Kansas" and the Coming of the Civil War*. Philadelphia: Lippincott, 1969.

BRITISH COMMONWEALTH AIR TRAINING PLAN

The British Commonwealth Air Training Plan (BCATP) was an agreement signed in Ottawa on December 17, 1939, soon after World War II began, by the governments of Britain, Canada, Australia, and New Zealand. The instruction scheme was centered in Canada, which provided infrastructure and a pool of potential trainees, as well as paying the lion's share of the costs. The plan's schools in Canada graduated 131,553 personnel (72,835 of them homegrown), almost half the total pilots and aircrew employed on British and Commonwealth flying operations during the war. President Franklin D. Roosevelt called Canada the "aerodrome of democracy."

Relative to population, the Prairie Provinces made an enormous overall contribution to the BCATP. Two of the four training command headquarters were situated there: No. 2 in Winnipeg and No. 4 in Regina. The region was well suited to flight training because of climate and terrain. "Pilot factories" were heavily concentrated in the southern parts of Alberta, Manitoba, and Saskatchewan, where there were thirteen Elementary Flying Training Schools and twenty Service Flying Training Schools. Saskatchewan had some fifty schools, bases, and training facilities of various kinds; that province alone trained one-fifth of all BCATP pilots and as much as 30 percent of some categories of aircrew. The influx of people and resources had a positive effect on local economies emerging from the Depression—by encouraging housing starts and small business, for example. Social interactions between localities and the BCATP bases in their midst were characterized by complex levels of integration and friction.

Norman Hillmer
Carleton University

Douglas, W. A. B. *The Official History of the Royal Canadian Air Force*. Vol. 2: *The Creation of a National Air Force*. Toronto: University of Toronto Press, 1986. Hillmer, Norman, and Brereton Greenhous. "The Impact of the British Commonwealth Air Training Plan on Western Canada: Some Saskatchewan Case Studies." *Journal of Canadian Studies* 26 (1981): 133–44.

CHEYENNE MOUNTAIN

In a hollowed-out mountain in the Colorado Rockies, overlooking the Great Plains, is the command center that would sound the first alarm of ballistic missile or air attacks against North America. The North American Aerospace Defense Command (NORAD), hidden in Cheyenne Mountain Air Force Station, near Colorado Springs, Colorado, keeps watch on aircraft, missiles, and space systems posing a threat to the United States and Canada. Cheyenne Mountain is the hub of a communications system that uses satellites, microwave, and fiber-optic links, carrying information from computers around the world to the NORAD commander in chief and his advisers in the command center. There, they constantly assess the aerospace situation on computer screens that display missile warning and aerospace surveillance information.

Built between 1961 and 1966, at a total cost of $142.4 million, the construction required more than one million pounds of explosives and removed more than 693,000 tons of granite. The main excavation consists of three chambers, each 45 feet wide, 60 feet high, and 588 feet long. Seven thousand tons of steel were used for the fifteen two- and three-story buildings inside the mountain. The facility has built-in utilities and services to make it fully self-sufficient for up to thirty days in case of national emergency. The massive blast doors, each more than three feet thick and with a swing weight of thirty tons, can be closed in forty-five seconds. Approximately 200 men and women from the army, navy, marines, air force, and Canadian forces staff the operations centers at Cheyenne Mountain. About 20,000 tourists visit each year.

David C. Arnold
United States Air Force Academy

Air Force Space Command Public Affairs. *Cheyenne Mountain Air Force Base*. August 1993.

CIVIL WAR

The Civil War, from 1861 to 1865, focused on Northern efforts to prohibit slavery in western territories, including the Great Plains. Most battles occurred east of the Mississippi River. Federal officials considered the western theater secondary. They withdrew regular troops from the Great Plains and recruited volunteers, most of whom served in militias, to stay in the West and fight Native Americans. Partisans waged a guerrilla war, especially in eastern Kansas and western Missouri. In the long run, the war intensified federal authority in the Plains, speeding the dispossession of Native Americans, consolidating the reservation system, and escalating the Plains Indian Wars.

In the Southern Plains, the war divided the Five "Civilized" Tribes, who had been removed from the Southeast to Indian Territory during the 1830s. All five signed treaties with the Confederacy but provided troops to both armies and fought an internal civil war. In reprisal, the Union recruited Native "home guards," invaded Indian Territory, and seized one-half of tribal lands to create reservations for Native Americans removed from Kansas. On the western Plains, Colorado militias warred against Cheyennes and Arapahos, massacring 150 at Sand Creek. In the Northern Plains, the United States forced the Sioux out of eastern Dakota Territory after the Santee Sioux Uprising of 1862 in Minnesota. Congressional initiatives, including the Homestead Act, transcontinental railroad land grants, the Land Grant College Act (Morrill Act), and the Department of Agriculture, encouraged rapid agricultural settlement of the Plains. The Civil War intensified westward expansion, dispossession, the reservation system, and the military subjugation of the Plains Indians.

Kenneth J. Winkle
University of Nebraska–Lincoln

Josephy, Alvin M. *The Civil War in the American West*. New York: Random House, 1991.

COLD WAR

The cold war was primarily a struggle between the United States and the Soviet Union to decide which of their respective economic and ideological systems—free-market capitalism or centrally controlled socialism—would dominate world affairs. Beginning during the closing years of the 1940s, the conflict deepened during the 1950s as the two powers sought to influence events around the globe. As the ideological battles played out, technological advances in weaponry increased the threat of thermonuclear holocaust. This threat nearly became reality in 1962, when the world went to the brink of war during the Cuban missile crisis. The cold war ended in 1991 when the Soviet Union collapsed and reformed into the Federation of Independent States.

Profoundly altering American culture and life, the protracted conflict affected every region of the United States, including the Great Plains. The influence of the cold war in the Great Plains began shortly after World War II. In 1948 the Strategic Air Command (SAC) established its headquarters at Offutt Air Force Base outside Omaha, Nebraska. SAC served as the air arm of the nation's offensive strategy for waging nuclear war, and it existed as an icon of American military power for the duration of the cold war. Throughout the 1950s this power was projected by the presence of long-range bombers, such as the B-36 and B-52, planes that were capable of deployment into Soviet airspace. With the introduction of intercontinental ballistic missiles (ICBMs), the primary importance of bombers waned, and various generations of missiles, including the Atlas, the Titan, the Minuteman, and the Cruise, gained strategic prominence. Deployed across the Great Plains, the weapons systems were housed at air force bases located at Schilling, Kansas; Altus, Oklahoma; Lincoln, Nebraska; Ellsworth, South Dakota; and other sites. Supporting the missiles and bombers were early-warning radar installations existing in three lines across the Northern Plains and the Prairie Provinces. The various installations served as economic engines, providing well-paid and secure civilian support employment to local inhabitants in host communities.

While the cold war brought economic benefits to many of the inhabitants of the Great Plains, it extracted a price as well. Most significantly, the presence of bombers and missiles across the region meant that inhabitants faced a high probability of being targeted during a nuclear attack. In recognition of this, the federal government initiated a widespread civil defense effort. In 1948 federal officials appointed Russell J. Hopley, president of Northwestern Bell Telephone of Omaha, Nebraska, as the first director of the Office of Civil Defense Planning. By October of that year, Hopley had published *Civil Defense for National Security*, a manual that detailed protection techniques that Americans could use in the advent of war. The manual advocated a philosophy of crisis relocation—the swift evacuation of urban populations. The manual also stressed the importance of combating panic through a public information campaign. This philosophy eventually gave way to another approach that promoted personal responsibility for civil defense: the home-based fallout shelter.

During the early 1950s, in one installment of the CBS television network show *Retrospect*, national news host Douglas Edwards interviewed the Brown family of Topeka, Kansas, about their "experiment in survival." The exercise involved both parents and their eight children spending a week in a fallout shelter. It so happened that the father was a commercial builder who had built the featured structure. In retrospect, the show was more a marketing ploy for a business than a depiction of how a middle-class American family might survive a nuclear attack.

In reality, the civil defense effort proved little more than a psychological salve for the American populace. By the mid-1950s the Eisenhower administration recognized that nuclear war meant national suicide. Nevertheless, the administration continued to promote the myth of personal responsibility for civil defense in order to avoid demoralizing the American public. Ironically, the civil defense shelters provided little, if any, protection against the fallout threat people faced from the nearest actual threat, government-conducted atmospheric testing of nuclear weapons at the Nevada Test Site.

The cold war never flared into open hostility between the United States and the Soviet Union. The weapons of mass destruction that dotted the Great Plains served to threaten and deter aggression from a society the U.S. government viewed as a danger to the American way of life and American global economic aims. Such protection proved expensive, however. By 1995 the costs associated with the cold war had exceeded $5 trillion. The Great Plains emerged from its cold war experience with deep ties to the federal defense budget, and with fallout shelters now used for storing canned goods and for refuge from tornadoes.

See also ARCHITECTURE: Cold War Architecture / IMAGES AND ICONS: Missile Silos.

Scott D. Hughes
Albuquerque, New Mexico

May, Elaine Tyler. *Homeward Bound: American Families in the Cold War*. New York: Basic Books, 1988. Oakes, Guy. *The Imaginary War: Civil Defense and American Cold War Culture*. New York: Oxford University Press, 1994. Pessen, Edward. *Losing Our Souls: The American Experience in the Cold War*. Chicago: Ivan R. Dee, 1993.

COUNTING COUP

Counting coup, or striking an enemy, was the highest honor earned by warriors participating in the intertribal wars of the Great Plains. Native peoples recognized precise systems of graduated war honors, and usually the greatest exploit was counting coup. Key to a man's success in Plains combat was demonstrating his own courage by proving superiority over his opponent and, in a competitive sense, over his own comrades. Killing was part of war, but showing courage in the process was more important for individual status. This was best accomplished by risking one's life in charging the enemy on foot or horseback to get close enough to touch or strike him with the hand, a weapon, or a "coupstick."

Humiliating the enemy also played a part in this fighting, as illustrated by an account from the Jesuit missionary Father Pierre-Jean De Smet. In De Smet's 1848 visit to the Oglala Lakotas, the Oglala leader Red Fish related to the priest how his men had just suffered a disgraceful defeat at the hands of the Crows. The Crows killed ten Oglalas, then chased the others for a distance. The Crows then were content merely to repeatedly count coup on their enemies with clubs and sticks, thus demonstrating to the Oglalas that they were not worth the ammunition needed to kill them.

Counting coup carried over into the battles against American troops. For example, the Northern Cheyenne warrior Wooden Leg related how, as a young man at the Battle of the Little Bighorn, he and his friend Little Bird chased a soldier across the river, counting coup on him with their whips and grabbing his carbine. They did not kill him, said Wooden Leg, because after counting coup it did not seem particularly brave, and besides, it would waste bullets. Counting coup, then, was the epitome of a type of warfare that pitted the skill and daring of one man against another.

See also: RELIGION: De Smet, Pierre-Jean.

Anthony R. McGinnis
Lyons, Colorado

McGinnis, Anthony R. *Counting Coup and Cutting Horses: Intertribal Warfare on the Northern Plains, 1738–1889*. Evergreen CO: Cordillera Press, Inc., 1990.

CRAZY HORSE (ca. 1840–1877)

Crazy Horse was born near Bear Butte, South Dakota, around 1840. He was the son of Crazy Horse, a distinguished Oglala Lakota warrior and medicine man, and Rattle Blanket Woman, a Miniconjou Lakota.

The life of Crazy Horse nearly bracketed the years of violent contact between the Lakotas and the United States. A war chief of the Oglala, Crazy Horse contested American expansion into Lakota lands in the Northern Great Plains. During Red Cloud's War, Crazy Horse demonstrated his military prowess in the Fetterman Fight at Fort Phil Kearny (1866), the Hayfield Fight (1867), and the Wagon Box Fight (1867). The Lakotas' military success persuaded the government to negotiate, and after prolonged discussions Red Cloud and some Lakota chiefs signed the Fort Laramie Treaty of 1868. Crazy Horse and other Lakota leaders, however, refused to acknowledge the treaty.

Crazy Horse's reputation as a war leader earned the admiration of the Lakotas and Northern Cheyennes and of tribal enemies of the Lakotas such as the Crows. His unyielding opposition toward the demands of the U.S. government and toward the reservation regime made him a central figure among the nontreaty Oglala and Miniconjou Lakotas and the Northern Cheyennes, who increasingly looked to him for leadership after 1868. Crazy Horse earned his highest formal honor in 1868 when he was selected as one of the head war riors, or shirt-wearers, of the Oglalas.

Crazy Horse was a shirt-wearer until 1871, when an affair with a married woman (Black Buffalo Woman, Red Cloud's niece) cost him this prestigious position. Crazy Horse kept a sizable following, however, because of his determined opposition to the United States. By the mid-1870s government officials and army officers recognized him as one of the most prominent leaders of the Lakota resistance.

The 1874 discovery of gold in the Black Hills strengthened the determination of the government to purchase the Black Hills, which angered nearly all Lakota leaders, whether they were signatories of the 1868 Fort Laramie Treaty or not. Negotiations between the government and the Lakotas broke down, and in December of 1875 the government ordered Lakota bands living in the unceded areas along the Yellowstone and Powder Rivers to report within six weeks to the reservations or face military action.

Not wishing to move their villages during the winter and unsure of the government's intention, Crazy Horse and other Lakota and Northern Cheyenne leaders refused. The government insisted on the move, and in March 1876 army units attacked a Northern Cheyenne village mistakenly identified as that of Crazy Horse. The army's destruction of the Northern Cheyenne village convinced Crazy Horse to prepare for an all-out defensive war against the army.

On June 17, 1876, Crazy Horse and approximately 1,500 warriors defeated a military column led by Brig. Gen. George Crook on Rosebud Creek in southern Montana. On June 25, 1876, Crazy Horse was involved in the destruction of Custer's Seventh Cavalry at the Little Bighorn. Despite these defeats, the army persevered against the Indians in the Powder River–Yellowstone River region through the winter of 1876–77. On May 7, 1877, Crazy Horse and his band surrendered at Fort Robinson, Nebraska.

His contempt for reservation life notwithstanding, Crazy Horse realized there was no viable alternative for the beleaguered Lakotas. Initially government officials and army officers sought him out, and their attention caused jealousy among Oglala and Sicanju (Brulé) Lakota chiefs, who spread false rumors about Crazy Horse. Junior army officers were persuaded that Crazy Horse was plotting rebellion and they decided to arrest him. On September 5, 1877, during an attempt to imprison Crazy Horse at Fort Robinson, an army sentry bayoneted him. He died a few hours later. He was survived by two wives and no children.

See also IMAGES AND ICONS: Crazy Horse Monument.

Joseph C. Porter
University of North Carolina at Chapel Hill

Ricker, Eli S. Collection. Nebraska State Historical Society, Lincoln, Nebraska. Sandoz, Mari. *Crazy Horse: The Strange Man of the Oglalas*. New York: Alfred A. Knopf, Inc., 1942.

CROOK, GEORGE (1828–1890)

Gen. George Crook

George Crook was born on September 8, 1828, near Taylorsville, Ohio, to Elizabeth Matthews and Thomas Crook, farmers. He graduated from the U.S. Military Academy at West Point in 1852 and served in California and Oregon fighting Indians until 1861. After serving in the Civil War as colonel of the Thirty-sixth Ohio Volunteer Infantry, Crook returned to the Pacific Northwest.

In 1871 the army ordered Lieutenant Colonel Crook to Arizona to quell the Apaches. After a successful campaign, Crook was promoted to brigadier general in 1873. In 1875 he assumed command of the Military Department of the Platte in Omaha, Nebraska.

In December 1875 the government ordered the army to force Lakotas and Northern Cheyennes from the Powder River country to Indian reservations in Nebraska. On June 17, 1876, Crook's Wyoming Column with 1,300 fighting men (including 175 Crow and 86 Shoshone warriors) fought approximately 1,500 Lakotas and Cheyennes led by Crazy Horse in the fierce six-hour Battle of the Rosebud, Montana, where Crazy Horse stopped Crook's advance. Crook and other officers campaigned throughout 1876 and early 1877, destroying Indian villages and disrupting their hunting. Crazy Horse and other nontreaty Lakotas and Cheyennes were compelled to surrender during the spring of 1877.

Crook, who believed that Americans were to blame for the Indian wars, consistently advocated Indian rights. In 1878 the government ordered Crook to arrest members of the Ponca Tribe who had returned to their Nebraska homeland from Indian Territory. Crook, seeing the injustice in this, convinced others to initiate a lawsuit to stay his orders. In the resulting case, *Standing Bear v. Crook*, Judge Elmer Dundy ruled for the first time in American history that "an Indian is a person within the laws of the United States."

In 1882 Crook returned to Arizona, where he achieved his finest military accomplishment. In 1883 he led nearly 200 Western Apache scouts and about fifty soldiers into the Chiricahuas' sanctuaries in the Sierra Madre of Mexico. After one skirmish, Crook negotiated the Chiricahuas' peaceful return to their Arizona reservation. Crook's superior officer, Gen. Philip Sheridan, publicly criticized Crook's Apache policy, and relations between the two deteriorated to the point that in 1886 Crook asked to be relieved of his command in Arizona. Crook returned to the Department of the Platte until 1888, when he became a major general and was assigned to command the Division of the Missouri, headquartered in Chicago. Crook died there on March 21, 1890. He was survived by his wife, Mary.

See also NATIVE AMERICANS: Standing Bear / PROTEST AND DISSENT: Trial of Standing Bear.

Joseph C. Porter
University of North Carolina at Chapel Hill

Greene, Jerome A. "George Crook." In *Soldiers West: Biographies from the Military Frontier*, edited by Paul Hutton. Lincoln: University of Nebraska Press, 1987: 115–36.
Schmitt, Martin F., ed. *General George Crook: His Autobiography*. Norman: University of Oklahoma Press, 1960.

FRÉMONT, JOHN C. (1813–1890)

John Charles Frémont explored large sections of the Central Great Plains in the 1840s and subsequently was military commander of much of the region for the Union during the Civil War. As the first presidential candidate of the Republican Party, he also sought to prevent slavery's spread to Kansas and Nebraska territories in 1856.

Frémont grew up in Charleston, South Carolina, where he attended the College of Charleston. He gained western experience by assisting Joseph Nicollet in mapping the region between the Mississippi and Missouri Rivers in the late 1830s. Appointment as a second lieutenant in the U.S. Army Corps of Topographical Engineers in 1838, and a famous elopement in 1841 with Jessie Benton, the daughter of Missouri's powerful Sen. Thomas Hart Benton, set the stage for Frémont's emergence as a celebrated western explorer.

In 1842 Frémont inherited Nicollet's command of an army expedition to report on the emigrant trail to Oregon as far as Wyoming's South Pass. Frémont's expedition traveled along the Kansas and Platte Rivers, then followed the Sweetwater River to the famous pass in the Rocky Mountains. On a second expedition in 1843–44, Frémont crossed the Kansas plains to Colorado, then traced the Oregon Trail to its conclusion at Fort Vancouver. Frémont then embarked on an exploration of the Great Basin and a risky winter crossing of the Sierra Nevada into Mexican California.

With the help of his wife, Jessie, Frémont prepared engaging official reports of his expeditions. Along with Frémont's maps of the emigrant trail (completed with the assistance of Charles Preuss), his popular reports provided overland travelers practical information as well as a new vision of the western Plains. Unlike earlier dire images promoted by explorers Zebulon Pike and Stephen Long, Frémont stressed the attractive features and potential of the Plains environment. His travels along the region's rivers led him to remark on the relatively well-timbered valleys; his wife's romantic inclinations probably account for the vivid descriptions of the oceans of green grass speckled with beautiful prairie flowers. Landmarks of the region, including Chimney Rock and Courthouse Rock, entered the national imagination through the Frémonts' captivating account.

Frémont's third expedition, in 1845–46, culminated in his leadership of the Bear Flag Revolt, which helped secure California from Mexico. After a brief term as California's first U.S. senator, two unsuccessful private expeditions to map a central railroad route across the Plains and Rockies, and a fortunate gold claim in California, Frémont accepted the Republican Party's first nomination to the presidency in 1856. His pledge to resist slavery's expansion to the territories of Kansas and Nebraska earned him majority support in the free states, but he failed to overcome Democrat James Buchanan. Nonetheless, Frémont's impressive showing guaranteed him a prominent appointment in the pending national crisis.

In July 1861 Major General Frémont assumed command of the Union's newly created Western Department, headquartered at St. Louis and with responsibility over the vast expanse from the Mississippi to the Rockies. Complications in war-torn Missouri, as well as crippling shortages of men, money, and material, kept Frémont from giving much attention to the Plains. Political intrigues and Frémont's ill timed effort to dismantle slavery in Missouri precipitated his removal from command in November 1861.

Thereafter, Frémont retired to private (and largely unsuccessful) business pursuits, although he did serve as governor of Arizona Territory from 1878 to 1883. Frémont died in New York in July 1890 from an attack of peritonitis. His exploits were not forgotten, however. Cities, counties, lakes, and streams from Nebraska to California still bear his name.

Vernon L. Volpe
University of Nebraska at Kearney

Jackson, Donald, and Mary Lee Spence, eds. *The Expeditions of John Charles Frémont*. 4 vols. Urbana: University of Illinois Press, 1970–1984. Nevins, Allan. *Frémont: Pathmarker of the West*. Lincoln: University of Nebraska Press, 1992. Volpe, Vernon L. "The Frémonts and Emancipation in Missouri." *The Historian* 56 (1994): 339–54.

FRONTIER FORTS

British, Canadian, French, Spanish, and American forts were distributed from the Prairie Provinces to West Texas and from the Missouri River to the Rocky Mountains, although not evenly and not all having a strictly military purpose. In the early nineteenth century, American forts helped to secure and maintain sovereignty in the face of Native American opposition and European schemes to limit the new nation's expansion. Outposts proved a critical line of defense in the south, especially after the Mexican War, 1846–48, but not in the Northern Plains, where the long international border lay virtually undefended.

Fort Laramie, Wyoming

Broadly defined, Great Plains forts fell into two groups. Forts of the first group were places from which to carry on commerce, a staging area for traders of furs and robes. Forts of the second group, detailed here, were places from which to execute war, a staging area for soldiers. Fort Leavenworth (1827), Kansas, for example, the oldest active army post west of the Mississippi, was the starting point for several western explorations. Camp Supply (1868) in present-day Oklahoma served as George A. Custer's departure point for a punitive expedition against the Southern Cheyennes. Fort Abraham Lincoln (1872), North Dakota, played a similar—and less successful—role in 1876 in Custer's foray against the northern tribes. Fort Laramie, which passed from private to public ownership in 1849, became an administrative center at which to negotiate peace, the Fort Laramie Treaty of 1868 its most notable legacy.

Great Plains forts invariably stood at strategic points on the landscape, based on four relationships: to Native American groups; to predominantly east–west transportation lines and communication networks; to burgeoning settlements and urban centers; and to the military chain of command. Since the Plains Indians posed the greatest barrier to westward expansion in the United States, most American forts were located in this region and became, as Gen. William T. Sherman proclaimed, "a picket line of civilization."

Forts were concentrated along historic transportation and communication routes, including the Arkansas, Missouri, Platte, Rio Grande, and Yellowstone Rivers, the Bozeman, Oregon-California, Santa Fe, Smoky Hill, and Southern Overland Trails, the Butterfield Overland Mail and Pacific Telegraph lines, and the Kansas Pacific, Northern Pacific, Southern Pacific, Union Pacific, and Santa Fe Railroads. Fort Dodge (1865), Kansas, first guarded the Santa Fe Trail, then the Santa Fe rail line. Fort Wallace (1865), Kansas, experienced the same transformation when the nearby Kansas Pacific Railroad replaced the Smoky Hill Trail.

As the country looked to the Pacific Coast, the command structure of the U.S. Army and its system of posts, subposts, and cantonments reflected this east–west shift. Omaha, Nebraska, the terminus of the Union Pacific and site of Fort Omaha (1868), also headquartered the Department of the Platte. St. Paul, Minnesota, shared the same relationship with the Department of Dakota and the Northern Pacific and Great Northern Railroads. Both military departments, in turn, reported up the chain to Division of the Missouri headquarters in Chicago, the preeminent rail, commercial, and industrial center in the Midwest.

The history of American forts in the Great Plains falls into three time periods, each roughly bracketed by wars (War of 1812, Mexican War, Civil War, and Spanish-American War). These events focused the attention of the U.S. Army on new enemies and new missions.

The first period is defined by the early posts, which extended north–south from Fort Snelling (1819), Minnesota, to Fort Jesup (1822), Louisiana. Others in this chain included Fort Atkinson (founded in 1819 as Cantonment Missouri) and the first Fort Kearny (1846) on the Missouri River in Nebraska; Fort Leavenworth and Fort Scott (1842), Kansas; Fort Gibson (1824), Fort Towson (1824), and Fort Washita, Oklahoma; and Fort Smith (1817), Arkansas. The early forts were successful in their limited purposes—to protect settlers, to control Native Americans, and to foster the growth of the fur trade. The period concluded with hostilities with Mexico, the annexation of Texas, and the discovery of California gold. With the passage of the Kansas-Nebraska Act in 1854 and the opening of Indian Country to settlers, the emphasis changed from an impenetrable north–south barricade between Native Americans and frontier whites to safe east–west travel corridors for emigrants and entrepreneurs.

Two Platte River forts, the second Fort Kearny and Fort Laramie, define the early years of the second period. To the annoyance of their commanders, emigrants came to depend upon these outposts for essential services such as resupply, medical attention, and blacksmithing. Increased traffic also resulted in more armed conflicts with Native Americans, which in turn increased the military resources poured into the Plains. Such forts symbolized a continual compromise by the army—building large, fixed posts to fight a mobile people, or at least to encourage them with treaty-secured inducements to live away from the trails. Ultimately, the forts that guarded the trails, and their countless feeder lines and alternates, proved more valuable as bases of operations against the Native Americans than as purely defensive systems.

Threats of trail closure in the 1850s came from the Lakotas on the Oregon-California Trail, the Cheyennes on the Smoky Hill Trail, and the Comanches and Kiowas on the Santa Fe Trail. Indian threats, combined with international disputes, provoked the greatest military response, in terms of sheer numbers of new forts, on the expanding Texas frontier. There, an elaborate defense system protected Texans from raiders and defined the southwestern military frontier. The initial chain of forts in central Texas ran northeast–southwest, from the Red River to the Rio Grande, from Fort Washita to Fort Worth, Fort Graham, Fort Gates, Fort Croghan, Fort Inge, and Fort Duncan (all six founded in 1849). The next set shifted west, still running northeast–southwest, consisting of Forts Belknap on the Brazos River (1851), Phantom Hill (1851), Chadbourne (1852), McKavett (1852), Mason (1851), and Clark (1852) near the Rio Grande. Another line ran from the Rio Grande west, from Fort Davis (1854) to Fort Bliss (1848) to Santa Fe's Fort Marcy (1846), each designed first to counter the Mexican Army, then to control area tribes. New Mexico boasted its own string of forts along the Rio Grande and the El Paso–Santa Fe Road, including Forts Craig (1854), McRae (1863), and Selden (1865). This massive infrastructure also ensured a continuous line of communication across the southern part of the transMississippi West.

In the 1850s the Santa Fe Trail became truly a military road, besides a route for emigration and commerce, beginning with Kansas's Fort Riley (1853) and Fort Larned (1859) and ending with Colorado's Fort Lyon (1860) and New Mexico's Fort Union (1851). A bustling center of frontier defense in the Southwest for four decades, Fort Union was the largest U.S. military post and supply depot in the region. To the north, the navigable reaches of the Missouri River had a string of forts: Fort Pierre (1855), replaced by Fort Randall (1856), and Forts Sully (1863), Rice (1864), Stevenson (1867), Buford (1866), Bennett (1870), Abraham Lincoln (1872), and Yates (1874). At the fringe of the Great Plains, Fort Abercrombie (1858) guarded the head of navigation on the Red River of the North.

The Civil War drew off regular army garrisons from the Plains, and Confederate and volunteer surrogates proved to be poor replacements. Native Americans were successful in closing some routes, most notably the Platte Valley route in 1864–65 and later the Bozeman Trail. Fort Fetterman (1867), Wyoming Territory, assumed even greater importance when the army bowed to Indian demands and abandoned the three Bozeman forts farther north—Reno (1865), Phil Kearny (1866), and C. F. Smith (1866); all were burned to the ground in 1868.

The post–Civil War period, when railroads supplanted the trails, was a time of clear military objectives. The army regarrisoned its forts to protect railroad construction crews and later the masses of settlers the new lines brought west. Forts lined the Union Pacific Railroad from Omaha to the Rockies: Forts Omaha, Kearny, McPherson (1863), and Sidney (1867) in Nebraska; Fort Sedgwick (1864) in Colorado; and Forts Bridger (1858), Sanders (1866), D. A. Russell (1867), and Fred Steele (1868) in Wyoming. Ironically a fort's success in protecting railroad construction crews and promoting settlement usually led to its obsolescence.

In post–Civil War Texas, new forts were established—Forts Concho, Griffin, and Richardson in 1867—and old ones reactivated—Forts Stockton (1858), Davis, Quitman (1858), and Bliss. They joined Forts Clark and McKavett in an irregular line running from El Paso to the state's northeast border. Just to the north, Fort Sill (1869) guarded the nearby Kiowa-Comanche Agency. Fort Reno and the Darlington Agency for the Cheyennes and Arapahos were no longer at the frontier's edge, but now in the center of Indian Territory. Fort Sill became a major base from which the Red River War (1874–75) could be waged, ending armed resistance from the Southern Plains tribes. With Fort Laramie as its major base, the Sioux War of 1876–77 accomplished the same in the Northern Plains, after which few new significant posts were established. Fort Assiniboine (1879), Montana, was founded to keep the Lakota leader Sitting Bull, not Canadians, in Canada. Across the border the North-West Mounted Police formed in 1873 and established several outposts in the Prairie region, most notably Fort Macleod (1874), Alberta, and Fort Walsh (1875), Saskatchewan. Together with the occasional subpost on the international border, their slim garrisons sought to prevent smuggling, intertribal clashes, and the introduction of diseased American cattle. It was more police than military work.

The 1880s brought consolidation of the American forts, regiment-sized garrisons, and the replacement of many small posts. The ring of "guardian forts" around the Indian reservations tightened. In the Northern Plains these were Fort Niobrara (1880) and Fort Robinson (1874), Nebraska; Fort Meade (1878), South Dakota; Fort Custer (1877) and Fort Keogh (1876), Montana; and Fort Washakie (1869), Wyoming. With large forts now placed in urban centers, such as Denver's Fort Logan (1887) and Omaha's Fort Crook (1891), authorities had a handy police force to quell civil disturbances.

By the time of the Spanish-American War in 1898 there were barely a dozen posts in the Northern Plains, as compared to three dozen in 1880. Troops—and forts—were spread more or less equally over the entire nation. The military frontier in the Great Plains was closed.

See also ARCHITECTURE: Fort Architecture.

R. Eli Paul
Nebraska State Historical Society

Prucha, Francis Paul. *A Guide to the Military Posts of the United States, 1789–1895.* Madison: State Historical Society of Wisconsin, 1964. Utley, Robert M. *Frontier Regulars: The United States Army and the Indian, 1866–1891.* New York: Macmillan Publishing Company, 1973. Utley, Robert M. *Frontiersmen in Blue: The United States Army and the Indian, 1848–1865.* New York: Macmillan Publishing Company, 1967.

GALVANIZED YANKEES

Galvanized Yankees were Confederate prisoners of war who took an oath of allegiance and enlisted in the U.S. Army, garrisoning western forts and protecting overland trails from 1864 to 1866. During the Civil War, Native American grievances erupted in increased attacks upon emigrants traveling up the Missouri River and along the overland trails. Unable to fill depleting Union lines in the East and the West, President Abraham Lincoln quietly authorized enlistment of repentant Confederate prisoners of war into service in December 1863. The First U.S. Volunteers enlisted from January through June 1864 at Point Lookout, Maryland, where their peers dubbed them "galvanized Yankees." Gen. Ulysses Grant ordered the regiment to garrison forts along the Minnesota-Dakota frontier. Enduring bitter cold and debilitating diseases, the First U.S. Volunteers built Fort Rice on the upper Missouri. They fought the Sioux, thwarted illegal Indian trade, aided overland emigrants, and gathered intelligence.

Five other regiments entered federal service in 1865 from prison pens in Illinois, Indiana, Ohio, and Maryland. The Fourth U.S. Volunteers replaced the First Regiment on the upper Missouri, while the other 4,000 "galvanized Yankees" marched west from Fort Leavenworth to occupy forts and stations and protect travelers along the Oregon, Santa Fe, and stage trails. Overcoming great physical hardship, these U.S. Volunteers fought Indian raiders, repaired telegraph lines, and convoyed supply trains and stagecoaches that crossed the Plains between Montana and New Mexico through November 1866.

Michèle T. Butts
Austin Peay State University

Brown, Dee. *The Galvanized Yankees.* Lincoln: University of Nebraska Press, 1986. Butts, Michèle T. "Galvanized Yankees on the Upper Missouri." Ph.D. diss., University of New Mexico, 1992.

GRANT, CUTHBERT

See IMAGES AND ICONS: Grant, Cuthbert

HARNEY, WILLIAM (1800–1889)

Gen. William S. Harney was born in Haysboro, Tennessee, on August 22, 1800. He first visited the Great Plains in 1825, when he accompanied the Col. Henry Atkinson and Benjamin O'Fallon expedition to sign treaties with the upper Missouri tribes. Harney fought in the Sauk and Fox wars in 1832, serving as Gen. Zachary Taylor's assistant inspector. In 1837 he participated in the Second Seminole War. Harney left Florida with a reputation as an Indian fighter, having performed several daring, and sometimes ruthless, actions against the Seminoles.

Between 1846 and 1848 Harney fought in the U.S.-Mexican War. After the war, Harney was assigned to inspect military posts and control Indian raids in Texas. In 1855 he assumed command of a campaign against the Brulés, who were involved in conflicts with immigrant travelers on the overland trails. On September 3, Harney's troops routed Little Thunder's village at Blue Water Creek (Ash Hollow) in western Nebraska, killing about a half of the 250 band members. The Lakotas named Harney "Mad Bear" because, following the attack on their village, he marched across the Badlands to Fort Pierre, Dakota Territory, challenging the Lakotas to a winter fight. The success of his campaign encouraged Harney to suggest that mobile units might replace permanent posts.

Harney was promoted to brigadier general in 1858, and in 1863 he retired to St. Louis. He returned to the Great Plains as a member of the 1865 and 1867 peace commissions to negotiate treaties with tribal leaders. In 1868 he also received a temporary assignment to establish three Sioux agencies on the Missouri River—at Whetstone Creek, Cheyenne River, and Grand River. Harney died in Orlando, Florida, on May 9, 1889.

Richmond L. Clow
University of Montana

Clow, Richmond L. "General William Harney on the Northern Plains." *South Dakota History* 16 (1986): 229–48.

HAZEN, WILLIAM (1830–1887)

William B. Hazen was a frontier army officer with eighteen years of service in the Great Plains. Born September 27, 1830, in Hartfort, Vermont, he grew up in Ohio, graduated from the U.S. Military Academy at West Point, fought Indians in Oregon, and was seriously wounded in a skirmish with Comanches in Texas in 1859. He served with distinction in the Civil War.

As commander of the Southern Military District at Fort Cobb, Indian Territory, in 1868–69, Hazen helped implement the reservation system in the Southern Plains. During the Washita campaign in 1868, he prevented Gen. Philip Sheridan and Lt. Col. George Custer from attacking his Kiowa charges, which created an animosity that lasted throughout their careers. In 1869 he helped select the site for Fort Sill in Indian Territory. That same year, he was named commander of the Sixth Infantry, a commission he held until 1880.

Hazen's assignments took him into every Great Plains state and territory. Always controversial, he opposed the railroads and land speculators by publishing articles warning prospective settlers that the arid lands of the High Plains were not worth "one penny an acre" for agricultural purposes. He also opposed Sheridan's plan to wipe out the buffalo herds as a means of subjugating the Indians, and in 1872 he exposed corruption of post traders at Fort Sill, which resulted in the impeachment and resignation of Secretary of War William Belknap. In retaliation, Belknap and Sheridan collaborated to exile Hazen to Fort Buford, Dakota Territory, the army's Siberia.

After his friend James Garfield was elected president in 1880, Hazen gained appointment as brigadier general and chief signal officer. In 1871 he married Mildred McLean, a member of a prominent newspaper family. He died in Washington DC on January 16, 1887.

Marvin E. Kroeker
Ada, Oklahoma

Kroeker, Marvin E. *Great Plains Command: William B. Hazen in the Frontier West*. Norman: University of Oklahoma Press, 1976.

INDIAN SCOUTS

From the time of the conquest of Mexico onward, Native American–European American conflicts in North America were seldom clear-cut; some Native Americans almost always participated on the side of the European Americans, and in conflicts between colonizers, they were likely to be present on both sides. This pattern held true in the campaigns fought in the Great Plains. Pueblo auxiliaries helped Spanish forces in New Mexico defeat the Comanches in the 1780s. Lakota Sioux auxiliaries cooperated with Col. Henry Leavenworth's expedition against the Arikaras in 1823, and Cheyenne and Crow scouts rode with the regular army in the Ghost Dance troubles of 1890–91, the last "Indian war" in the West, though they were not present at the Wounded Knee Massacre.

The very idea of Native Americans assisting European Americans in their conquest has always seemed incongruous to some, leading to distrust by whites at the time, and later to charges by Native Americans that Indian scouts and auxiliaries were mercenaries consciously betraying their own people. In most cases the scouts themselves would have found such accusations meaningless and irrelevant. They often saw themselves as fighting, beside the best available allies, against bitter—and frequently stronger—enemies who constituted the greater immediate menace. This was the situation with the Pawnees, Arikaras, Crows, and Shoshones who joined the U.S. Army against their enemy, the Sioux, in the 1860s and 1870s. When some Sioux joined up to fight other Sioux who were resisting the United States, they did so hoping for favorable terms for their own bands and for an eventual reduction of further suffering by the "hostile" bands.

The earliest sustained conflicts between European Americans and Plains Indians began in Texas in the 1830s. There, frontiersmen and Texas Rangers, however bitterly they might fight the Kiowas and Comanches, still enlisted the aid of Tonkawas, Lipans, and Delawares, following a pattern set by frontier rangers and Indian fighters in colonial times. As the U.S. Army became increasingly involved in conflict with the Plains tribes after 1848, they followed the frontiersmen's example. The rising tide of conflict during and after the Civil War led in 1866 to a congressional act authorizing the enlistment of Indians as scouts, on the same terms as regular army soldiers, but for shorter terms. As soldiers they could receive pay, rations, weapons, and noncommissioned rank, and a few received the Medal of Honor for bravery. They served not only as individual trackers and intelligence gatherers but often in large contingents of company or even battalion strength. A few units served for extended periods of time, notably the Pawnee scouts under Maj. Frank North, who took the field in 1864 and 1865, served through the Sioux and Cheyenne campaigns of the late 1860s, and campaigned for the last time in the Sioux War of 1876–77. They were admired and praised by the army commanders they served.

Scouts were valued because of their specialized skills and knowledge acquired over a lifetime: knowledge of how to follow a trail and observe the enemy without being seen, knowledge of the country, and ability to identify vital information from tracks. These skills made it possible for soldiers operating in an alien environment to locate and surprise elusive enemies in their own country and greatly enhanced the ability of the military to carry out their mission.

Thomas W. Dunlay
Lincoln, Nebraska

Dunlay, Thomas W. *Wolves for the Blue Soldiers: Indian Scouts and Auxiliaries with the United States Army, 1860–98*. Lincoln: University of Nebraska Press, 1982.

INTERTRIBAL WARFARE

Intertribal warfare was intense throughout the Great Plains during the 1700s and 1800s, and archeological data indicate that warfare was present prior to this time. Human skeletons from as early as the Woodland Period (250 B.C. to A.D. 900) show occasional marks of violence, but conflict intensified during and after the thirteenth century, by which time farmers were well established in the Plains. After 1250, villages were often destroyed by fire, and human skeletons regularly show marks of violence, scalping, and other mutilations. Warfare was most intense along the Missouri River in the present-day Dakotas, where ancestors of the Mandans, Hidatsas, and Arikaras were at war with each other, and towns inhabited by as many as 1,000 people were often fortified with ditch and palisade defenses. Excavations at the Crow Creek site, an ancestral Arikara town dated to 1325, revealed the bodies of 486 people—men, women, and children, essentially the town's entire population—in a mass grave. These individuals had been scalped and dismembered, and their bones showed clear evidence of severe malnutrition, suggesting that violence resulted from competition for food, probably due to local overpopulation and climatic deterioration. Violence among farmers continued from the 1500s through the late 1800s.

Archeological data on war among the nomadic Plains hunters are few, but some nomads were attacking farmers on the edges of the Plains by at least the 1500s. By the eighteenth century, war was common among the nomads, apparently largely because of conflicts over hunting territories.

Prior to the introduction of European horses and guns, Plains warfare took two forms. When equally matched forces confronted each other, warriors sheltered behind large shields, firing arrows; individual warriors came out from behind these lines to dance and taunt their opponents. This mode of combat was largely for show and casualties were light. However, sometimes, large war parties surprised and utterly destroyed small camps or hamlets. Increasing interaction with Europeans from the eighteenth century on changed these patterns dramatically. Massed shield lines could neither stand against mounted warriors nor protect against firearms; this mode of battle largely disappeared with the introduction of horses and guns, although equally matched mounted war parties sometimes used the old tactics. Early access to horses also allowed some groups, notably the Comanches, to overwhelm and displace neighboring tribes who lacked such access. Documentary and archeological evidence indicate that horses and guns contributed mightily to this more destructive mode of Plains warfare, most intensively along the Missouri River.

Raids for horses by small groups of warriors became a primary form of conflict after about 1750, particularly among the nomadic groups. Horse raiders usually entered enemy camps at night to take horses picketed close to their owners. Such raids were dangerous—raiders were killed when caught in the act—and successful raiders often achieved high status. The relation between war and status in the Plains is similarly evident in the practice of counting coup, in which a living enemy (or sometimes a dead enemy) was touched with the hand or a special stick. This act signified ultimate bravery in most Plains tribes and gave a warrior great prestige.

The prestige attached to stealing horses and to counting coup rather than killing has contributed to the view that Plains warfare was a moderately dangerous kind of game driven by individual quests for status rather than "real" war driven by competition for resources. This is misleading. Individual warriors sought status and sometimes avoided killing enemies in battle, but destructive high-casualty warfare was widespread, with documented battles involving thousands of warriors and hundreds of fatalities. Other massacres like that at Crow Creek are known from the eighteenth and nineteenth centuries, and archeological and documentary evidence show great changes in tribal territories resulting from war before and after white contact.

Destructive war in the Plains intensified after contact because of migrations of eastern tribes (the Cheyennes and Lakotas, for example) into the Plains as settlement moved west,

because Europeans and Americans manipulated traditional hostilities, and because tribes competed for access to European and American trade, especially in fur-rich areas of the Northern Plains and Prairie Provinces. Contact-period war ended some long-standing hostilities: for example, the Mandans, Hidatsas, and Arikaras, decimated by disease and raiding, banded together for mutual protection during the 1860s. Other hostilities continued, and expanding European Americans exploited them: for example, Crows and Pawnees scouted in military campaigns against the Cheyennes and Lakotas. Intertribal violence in the Plains subsided with the confinement of the tribes to reservations in the late nineteenth century.

Douglas B. Bamforth
University of Colorado at Boulder

Bamforth, Douglas B. "Indigenous People, Indigenous Violence: Pre-Contact Warfare on the North American Great Plains." *Man* 29 (1994): 95–115. Galloway, Colin G. *Our Hearts Fell to the Ground: Plains Indian Views of How the West Was Lost.* New York: Bedford Books of St. Martin's Press, 1996.

LINCOLN COUNTY WAR

William H. Bonney (Billy the Kid), ca. 1879

When lawyer Alexander McSween and a young Englishman, John H. Tunstall, began competing with local merchants Lawrence G. Murphy and James Dolan in the tiny community of Lincoln, New Mexico, in the late 1870s, the result was the Lincoln County War. From February 18, 1878, to February 18, 1879, the rivals fought for economic supremacy, first through the legal system and then with bullets, until law and order finally collapsed.

Tunstall's murder by a sheriff's posse in February 1878 prompted his supporters, now styled "the Regulators," to regroup around

McSween. On April 1, Regulators shot Sheriff William Brady and his deputy on Lincoln's main, and only, street. George W. Peppin replaced Brady as sheriff. In the following weeks, McSween and his partisans skirmished with Peppin's posses. McSween led his Regulators back into Lincoln on July 14, and for five days the town was rocked with gunfire. Pleas for help from a frightened resident brought Lt. Col. N. A. M. Dudley and his men from nearby Fort Stanton, but Dudley only stood by as Sheriff Peppin and his men besieged McSween's house. McSween died in a hail of gunfire, as a young outlaw going under the name of William Bonney, or simply "the Kid," led a desperate escape from the burning building.

As a result of the violence, President Rutherford Hayes dismissed territorial governor Samuel Axell and appointed Lew Wallace, a former general (and later, author of *Ben Hur*), in his place. The U.S. Army was brought in to help civilian law officers, and the violence died away gradually. Governor Wallace's amnesty permitted most of the outlaws to go free; only William Bonney was convicted for the murder of Sheriff Brady. Bonney, by then known as "Billy the Kid," rode away from Lincoln branded forever with a reputation as an outlaw.

See also IMAGES AND ICONS: Frontier Violence / LAW: Billy the Kid.

John P. Wilson
Las Cruces, New Mexico

Nolan, Frederick. *The Lincoln County War: A Documentary History.* Norman: University of Oklahoma Press, 1992. Utley, Robert. *High Noon in Lincoln: Violence on the Western Frontier.* Albuquerque: University of New Mexico Press, 1987.

LITTLE BIGHORN, BATTLE OF THE

On Sunday, June 25, 1876, Lt. Col. George Armstrong Custer led 210 men of the U.S. Seventh Cavalry to their deaths at the Battle of the Little Bighorn. It was the army's worst defeat of the Plains Indian Wars.

The prelude to "Custer's Last Stand" began at the 1868 Treaty of Fort Laramie, which created the Great Sioux Reservation, including the Black Hills, as a homeland for the bands of the Lakotas and Cheyennes. The government's objective was to settle the Indians down on the reservation, where they could be more easily controlled. In 1874 rumors of gold in the Black Hills were confirmed by a geological team accompanying Custer's expedition, and white miners invaded the sacred land. This abrogation of the treaty rights by Americans encouraged the Lakotas and Cheyennes to resist restriction to the reservation and to continue bison hunting on the ranges of Nebraska, Wyoming, and Montana. In December 1875 the United States gave the tribes a thirty-day deadline to return to their reservations or be subject to military reprisals.

In the spring of 1876 the United States launched a three-pronged campaign against the Cheyennes and Lakotas. The first prong, under Col. John Gibbon, marched east from Fort Ellis (near present-day Bozeman, Montana). The second prong, led by Gen. Alfred Terry (and including Custer) headed west from Fort Abraham Lincoln near present-day Bismarck, North Dakota. The third prong consisted of Gen. George Crook's men moving north from Wyoming into Montana. These three units planned to meet near the end of June in the vicinity of the Little Bighorn. Unknown to Terry and Gibbon, Crook encountered the Indians near Rosebud Creek in southern Montana and was defeated by them about a week before Custer's battle. After this, his force withdrew to Wyoming, breaking one side of the triangle. Meanwhile, Terry was moving west up the Yellowstone River to the Little Bighorn. The Seventh Cavalry, under Custer, scouted ahead on June 22. On the morning of the 25th, they reached the divide between Rosebud and the Little Bighorn Rivers. From a spot known as the Crow's Nest, they observed a large Indian camp. Worried the Indians might escape, Custer decided to attack down the valley of the Little Bighorn. Custer assumed his approximately 600-member command would face at the most 800 warriors. Instead he found a camp of 5,000 to 8,000 Indians, with about 2,000 of them warriors.

Custer divided the Seventh Cavalry into three elements during the early phases of the battle and then subdivided his immediate command into wings. The Lakota and Cheyenne warriors, although surprised by the army's attack, quickly rallied and put all elements of the Seventh Cavalry's attack on the defensive. The Indians fought in small, loosely affiliated groups. They used their superior numbers, took advantage of available cover, and sniped at the soldiers from long distances. The soldiers deployed in open skirmish order, as they were trained, with the result that they were widely dispersed and became easy targets for the warriors' guns. Encircled by mounted forces led by Crazy Horse and Gall, Custer's entire command perished.

The news of Custer's defeat reached the American public during the celebration of the nation's centennial. The reaction was outrage and military reprisals that confined most of the Lakotas and Cheyennes to the reservation by the spring of 1877. Following the Battle of the Little Bighorn, the Black Hills were confiscated by the United States in direct contradiction of the terms of the 1868 treaty. The site of the battle is now the Little Bighorn Battlefield National Monument (previously, before December 10, 1991, the Custer Battlefield National Monument).

See also FILM: Custer Films / IMAGES AND ICONS: Custer, George Armstrong.

Douglas Scott
National Park Service

Scott, Douglas D., Richard A. Fox, Melissa A. Conner, and Dick Harmon. *Archaeological Perspectives on the Battle of the Little Bighorn*. Norman: University of Oklahoma Press, 1989. Utley, Robert. *Cavalier in Buckskin: George Armstrong Custer and the Western Military Frontier*. Norman: University of Oklahoma Press, 1988.

LONG, STEPHEN H. (1784–1864)

Stephen Harriman Long, army engineer and explorer, helped foster the idea that the Great Plains was the Great American Desert. Son of Moses and Lucy Long, he was born on December 10, 1784, at Hopkinton, New Hampshire. In 1809 he graduated from Dartmouth College, and for the next five years he taught school and worked as a surveyor. Near the end of the War of 1812, Long became a second lieutenant in the Army Corps of Engineers. He remained an army officer for nearly fifty years.

Long hoped to become the next important western explorer after Lewis and Clark, and in 1818 he received orders to organize and lead a scientific expedition west. That year he designed a steamboat, the *Western Engineer*, to carry the scientists up the Missouri River, but it proved unable to navigate that river successfully. In 1820 Long led a small party of scientists and soldiers west to the Rocky Mountains. They examined the land, streams, animals, plants, and minerals along the way. At the Rockies they turned south, searching for the headwaters of the Red River without success. After nearly starving in the Plains, they returned to Fort Smith, Arkansas, late in the summer.

The explorers brought back specimens of plants and animals, as well as new geographic information about the Central Plains. Their report and maps clearly labeled the region as desert. When taken with similar comments from Zebulon Pike, Long's descriptions persuaded many that the Plains was unfit for agriculture. After this, his duties shifted to planning railroads and clearing obstructions out of some of America's larger rivers. His army career ended in 1863, and he died the next year at Alton, Illinois, on September 4.

See also IMAGES AND ICONS: Great American Desert.

Roger L. Nichols
University of Arizona

Nichols, Roger L., and Patrick L. Haley. *Stephen Long and American Frontier Exploration*. Newark: University of Delaware Press, 1980.

MACKENZIE, RANALD (1840–1889)

Ranald Slidell Mackenzie was one of the most capable officers in the frontier army and would probably be one of the most famous were it not for the circumstances of his retirement and death. Mackenzie was born on July 27, 1840, near Tarrytown, New York. He entered the U.S. Military Academy at West Point in 1858 and graduated first in his class in 1862. During the Civil War, Mackenzie gained a reputation for bravery and distinguished leadership and finished the war with the rank of major general.

After the war, Mackenzie served briefly with the Army Corps of Engineers before being assigned to a field command. In 1871 he was given command of the Fourth Cavalry Regiment with the rank of colonel. In the next few years Mackenzie pioneered the use of large bodies of troops on the Llano Estacado in Texas, fought several engagements with Co-

manches and Kiowas, and led a controversial raid on a Kickapoo village in northern Mexico. Mackenzie's most famous fight was his victory at the Battle of Palo Duro Canyon, which was instrumental in putting an end to the Red River War. In 1876 Mackenzie participated in Gen. George Crook's campaign against the Northern Plains Indians. He spent the rest of his active career as a roving troubleshooter on the Texas border and in New Mexico, Arizona, and Colorado.

In November 1883 Mackenzie, now a brigadier general, established his headquarters in San Antonio as the new commander of the Department of Texas. By this time he was behaving in an erratic manner, and his condition quickly deteriorated. After an incident that left him beaten and tied to a wagon wheel, Mackenzie's aides put him on a train to New York, where he was briefly committed to the Bloomingdale Asylum. He was released after a few weeks but never regained mental stability. He died on January 19, 1889, almost forgotten by the general public, and was buried at West Point, New York.

Michael D. Pierce
Tarleton State University

Pierce, Michael D. *The Most Promising Young Officer: A Life of Ranald Slidell Mackenzie*. Norman: University of Oklahoma Press, 1993. Wallace, Ernest, ed. *Ranald S. Mackenzie's Official Correspondence Relating to Texas, 1871–1879*. Lubbock: West Texas Museum Association, 1967–68.

MILES, NELSON (1839–1925)

Nelson Appleton Miles ranks among the army's most effective leaders in the Indian wars of the late nineteenth century. Born at Westminster, Massachusetts, on August 6, 1839, he joined the Union army following the First Battle of Bull Run. Though lacking in formal military training, he proved an excellent combat leader. He participated in all of the Army of the Potomac's major campaigns except Gettysburg, suffered three wounds, and emerged from the war a brevet-major general. He supervised the imprisonment of former Confederate president Jefferson Davis at Fortress Monroe, Virginia, from May 1864 to August 1865.

In September 1866 Miles became a full colonel in the reorganized post–Civil War regular army. In April 1869, following Reconstruction-related duty in North Carolina, he was transferred with the Fifth Infantry Regiment to Kansas. During the next decade Miles commanded troops in a succession of campaigns against Native Americans in the Great Plains—the Red River War (1874–75), the Sioux War (1876–77), and the Nez Perce campaign (1877). He was promoted to brigadier general in 1881 and later helped to organize the capture of Geronimo. After securing a second general's star, he oversaw the Ghost Dance campaign of 1890–91.

In 1895 Miles was appointed commanding general of the army. He led the invasion of Spanish-occupied Puerto Rico during the Spanish-American War but later lost credibility by making sensational, though unsubstantiated, charges that the War Department had distributed "embalmed beef" to American soldiers. He also opposed much-needed structural reform within the army. Upon reaching the mandatory retirement age of sixty-four, Miles retired from active military duty and later unsuccessfully campaigned for the 1904 Democratic presidential nomination. He died in Washington DC of a heart attack while attending the circus with his grandchildren on May 16, 1925, and was buried at Arlington National Cemetery. Egotistical and a shameless self-promoter, Miles had nonetheless established a superb combat record against the Confederates, several groups of Native Americans, and the Spanish.

Robert Wooster
Texas A&M University at Corpus Christi

Wooster, Robert. *Nelson A. Miles and the Twilight of the Frontier Army*. Lincoln: University of Nebraska Press, 1993.

MILITARY BASES

The Great Plains, with wide-open spaces permitting weapons testing and troop maneuvers in empty areas and flight practice under clear skies, as well as interior-of-the-continent security, is a major military region. From Offutt Air Force Base just south of Omaha, Nebraska, the United States Strategic Command (USSTRATCOM) wields its awesome power over a vast arsenal of bombers, missiles, submarines, subsidiary bases, and about 119,000 military and civilian personnel worldwide. The Canadian Land Command is also Plains-based, with its headquarters at Winnipeg, Manitoba. Altogether, in 1995 there were fifty-seven military bases in the Great Plains, their distribution reaching from Canadian Forces Air Base at Cold Lake, Alberta, to Laughlin Air Force Base at Del Rio, Texas. These bases include air force, army, or land command, national guard and reserves, as well as military medical centers, training sites, arsenals, and combat ranges. (Recruiting stations, though they are strictly speaking also bases, are excluded from this count.)

Some of the bases are massive, both in terms of personnel and extent. In 1995 Fort Carson Army Base, for example, on the south side of Colorado Springs, Colorado, had 16,200 active duty personnel and stretched over 373,000 acres, and Fort Sill Army Base at Lawton, Oklahoma, had 17,795 men and women on active duty. Eight other bases had more than 5,000 active personnel. Some bases, however, have only small maintenance staffs. Pueblo Army Depot, fourteen miles to the east of Pueblo, Colorado, has two people on active duty, and the Cornhusker Army Ordnance Plant at Grand Island, Nebraska, has a lonely staff of one.

Military bases, as frontier forts, had proliferated in the Great Plains in the 1860s and 1870s at the height of the Indian wars. Most of these posts were closed by the 1890s as the Indians, defeated more by famine and disease than in battle, were restricted to reservations. Some of the contemporary bases, however, link back to nineteenth-century military posts.

Fort Leavenworth Army Base, at Leavenworth, Kansas, was founded in 1827, and Fort Riley, just west of Manhattan, Kansas, has been an army base since 1853. Military installations again proliferated during World Wars I and II, but most were disassembled when the wars ended. Others were continued: seventeen of the contemporary American bases were established from 1941 to 1943. These include Goodfellow Air Force Base near San Angelo, Texas; Cannon Air Force Base near Clovis, New Mexico; and Ellsworth Air Force Base near Rapid City, South Dakota.

The larger military bases are substantial settlements in their own right. Fort Carson, in addition to its active personnel, employed more than 4,000 civilians in 1989 and was home to 39,000 family members. There were four schools on the base, a day-care center for 287 children, a 195-bed hospital, and various stores. Relatively few Plains towns can boast a population and array of services like this.

Because military bases are such an integral part of the settlement fabric in many parts of the Great Plains, a base closing can be calamitous to the functioning of nearby communities. Recent closures include Canadian Forces bases in Penhold and Calgary, Alberta, Lowry Air Force Base in Denver, and Carswell Air Force Base in Fort Worth, Texas. Some proposed closures were resisted. Goodfellow Air Force Base was scheduled to be closed in 1978. It was saved by the energetic campaigning of a "Blitz Committee," formed by the San Angelo City Council, aided by the behind-the-scenes lobbying of Sen. John Tower. Nevertheless, a military base is a precarious foundation for the local economy, particularly in phases of reduced government expenditures.

David J. Wishart
University of Nebraska–Lincoln

Cragg, Dan. *Guide to Military Installations.* Harrisburg PA: Stackpole Books, 1988. Evinger, William. *Directory of United States Military Bases Worldwide.* Phoenix: Oryx Press, 1995. Hoover, Karl D. *Base Closure: Politics or National Defense Issue? Goodfellow Air Force Base, Texas, 1978–1981.* San Angelo TX: Headquarters Air Training Command History and Research Office, 1989.

NATIONAL GUARDS

National Guards in the Great Plains developed later than in states to the east or west. Territorial status and sparse population hindered guard development, as did limited financial support. South Dakota, for example, appropriated only $500 for its guard in 1895, and Texas, despite its large population, could support only 3,000 guardsmen until 1910. In part, Great Plains states appropriated limited funds for the guard because few of them faced labor disorders or urban upheavals. Colorado was the great exception, with labor turbulence in its mining region from the 1880s through the "Ludlow Massacre" of 1914. But even with an extensive record of policing mining regions, the Colorado guard garnered only limited state support.

The Great Plains National Guard became efficient only after 1900, when federal subsidies

began to underwrite state military budgets. Guardsmen continued to assist state officials during natural disasters and civil disorders, but increased federal support inevitably led to greater federal control. By the 1980s federal support accounted for more than 90 percent of the guard's support. Federal aid also imposed mandatory service on guardsmen. Great Plains guardsmen have served in World War I, World War II, Korea, the Persian Gulf War in 1991, and Iraq in 2003 under this obligation. The National Guard remains a locally oriented institution, proudly aware of its state and regional identification, but is nonetheless more a product of the federal government than of the states.

Jerry Cooper
University of Missouri, St. Louis

Cooper, Jerry. *The Rise of the National Guard: The Evolution The American Militia, 1865–1920.* Lincoln: University of Nebraska Press, 1997.

NIMITZ, CHESTER (1885–1966)

Chester William Nimitz was born in Fredericksburg, Texas, on February 24, 1885, to Chester Bernard, a cattle driver, and Anna (Henke) Nimitz. Chester's father died before he was born. He was raised by his mother and his paternal grandfather, Charles H. Nimitz. The grandfather, a German immigrant and lover of the sea, built a steamboat-shaped hotel in Fredericksburg, the Nimitz Hotel, that still existed at the beginning of the twenty-first century. Young Chester listened with wide eyes to stories of his grandfather's youth in the German merchant marines.

Nimitz graduated from the U.S. Naval Academy in Annapolis, Maryland, on January 30, 1905, seventh in a class of 114. For thirty-five years Nimitz performed his duties in the U.S. Navy, rising to the rank of admiral. On December 17, 1941, ten days after the bombing of Pearl Harbor, Nimitz was appointed commander in chief of the Pacific Fleet. Admiral Nimitz quickly rebuilt the fleet into the largest military armada ever assembled and launched an offensive, with raids on Wake Island, the Gilbert Islands, the Marshall Islands, and New Guinea. He handed the Japanese their first major setback at Midway Island in June 1942 and continued the offensive in the Pacific until the Japanese defeat. Along with Gen. Douglas MacArthur, Nimitz signed the Japanese surrender agreements.

Chester Nimitz was the first naval officer to acquire five stars. In response to Nimitz's generosity in returning to the Japanese their samurai swords, the Japanese government built a Garden of Peace behind the Nimitz Hotel in Fredericksburg as a tribute to his goodwill. Nimitz died on February 20, 1966, near San Francisco and was buried in Golden Gate National Cemetery.

Dede Weldon Casad
Dallas, Texas

Driskill, Frank A., and Dede Weldon Casad. *Chester W. Nimitz: Admiral of the Hills.* Austin TX: Eakin Press, 1983.

NORTH-WEST REBELLION

The North-West Rebellion, also known as the second Riel Rebellion or the Saskatchewan Rebellion, took place in Saskatchewan's Qu'Appelle River valley in 1885 and was closely related to the earlier Métis resistance at Red River, Manitoba, in 1869–70.

After the Red River Resistance, Louis Riel fled to the United States to escape arrest. With their leader labeled a traitor, the Métis of Manitoba were now seen by the Canadian government as squatters on potential homestead lands. Stripped of their lands, and seeing few alternatives, the majority of the Métis people moved farther west along the Saskatchewan River system into what is now Saskatchewan and Alberta (then the Northwest Territories).

By 1884 the Northwest was home to several thousand Native and Métis peoples. Joining them were a large number of non-Native settlers, recent arrivals from the Canadian provinces, giving a total population of about 10,000 people. In this period the Northwest Territories were administered by a lieutenant governor appointed in Ottawa and a small council made up of appointed and elected representatives. By 1884 the number of elected representatives on the council numbered only five, and the residents of the region did not have territorial representation in the federal House of Commons or Senate.

In the Prince Albert–Batoche area, the Métis and non-Native settlers alike were discontented. Many of them had moved from the Red River region more than a decade earlier to establish prosperous farms along the South Saskatchewan River. Conflict over land tenure, hunting reserves, government surveys, tariff structures, and frustration from the absence of government representation led the Métis and whites to organize in 1884. As no clear leader emerged, the Métis sent a delegation to Montana to ask Louis Riel to return to unite the English- and French-speaking Native, white, and Métis residents of the region. Riel, now an American citizen, agreed, and he arrived in Batoche amid much fanfare in May 1884. At the same time, the Plains Crees, under the leadership of chiefs Big Bear and Poundmaker, also began to demand the renegotiation of their treaties.

In a move reminiscent of his Red River days, Riel took up the reins to lead the white and Métis settlers, challenging the legitimacy of the Canadian government in the Northwest and proclaiming the formation of a provisional Métis government at Batoche in March 1885.

On March 26 a detachment of the North-West Mounted Police at Fort Carlton (twenty miles from Batoche) sent 100 men to Duck Lake to head off a possible attack and to prevent the Métis from seizing arms and ammunition stored there. Gabriel Dumont and a large group of Métis met the Mounted Police at Duck Lake, and in the resulting skirmish the Métis killed twelve Mounties and wounded another eleven.

The Duck Lake victory (often called the Duck Lake Massacre by non-Natives) rallied the Native troops and convinced the Crees to join forces with Riel. Cree chiefs Big Bear and Poundmaker tried to maintain calm within the tribes, but the Duck Lake victory had emboldened many of the young Cree warriors who laid siege to Fort Battleford on the North Saskatchewan River. On April 2, 1885, a group of warriors from Big Bear's band attacked the Hudson's Bay Company post at Frog Lake, killing nine non-Native men. Within a few days, the Canadian government sent forces to Batoche, Battleford, and Frog Lake. The main force under Maj. Gen. Frederick Middleton took Batoche on May 12, where Riel surrendered on May 15. Poundmaker surrendered on May 12 and Big Bear on July 2.

Immediately upon his capture, the Canadians brought Riel to Regina for trial. On July 31, 1885, the all-white jury convicted Riel of treason, ignoring both his American citizenship and questions regarding his sanity. Despite a huge public uproar in the province of Quebec, Louis Riel was hanged on November 16, 1885. He was followed to the gallows eleven days later by eight of the Cree warriors who had been involved in the North-West Rebellion.

The Métis gained little from the rebellion. Many of their leaders fled to Montana or were jailed. Citizens of the Northwest received representation in Parliament, but the Métis were forced to either assimilate or move still farther to the margins. The Crees, forced to settle their treaty claims as best they could, suffered under the tightened control of western Indian agents and were relegated to reserve lands, where their death rates climbed rapidly and their population fell dramatically over the next five decades.

See also LAW: North-West Mounted Police / NATIVE AMERICANS: Big Bear; Métis; Poundmaker / PROTEST AND DISSENT: Riel, Louis.

Charlene Porsild
Montana Historical Society

Beal, Bob, and Rod Macleod. *Prairie Fire: The 1885 North-West Rebellion*. Edmonton: Hurtig Publishers, 1984. Flanagan, Thomas. *Louis "David" Riel: "Prophet of the New World."* Toronto: University of Toronto Press, 1996.

PALO DURO CANYON, BATTLE OF

A battle between Kiowas, Comanches, Cheyennes, and 400 troopers of Col. Ranald S. Mackenzie's Fourth U.S. Cavalry took place early on the morning of Monday, September 28, 1874, deep in this great canyon of the Red River, 1,000 feet below the level plains of the Texas Panhandle. Some Tenth and Eleventh U.S. Infantry assisted Mackenzie's command at a base camp. His command comprised part of a five-pronged campaign against several bands of Native Americans who either had left their reservations in Indian Territory for hideouts in the Staked Plains or who had not yet submitted to reservation life. The Palo Duro Canyon fight was the largest engagement in the Red River War and marked the end of the Southern Plains Indians' military resistance.

Led by Tonkawa scouts, Colonel Mackenzie marched his men most of the night, arriving at the rim of the canyon at daybreak. They made their way to the floor of the canyon and attacked. Indian women and children retreated up the canyon, while the men engaged the soldiers in combat to allow their families to escape. The Kiowa band was led by Mamanti, the Comanches by O-ha-ma-tai, and the small band of Cheyennes by Iron Shirt. By noon the Indians had escaped, leaving their lodges and horses behind. Mackenzie ordered the lodges searched, then burned. The next day he had his men shoot 1,048 horses to prevent the Indians from recovering them. The Indians straggled into the reservations, having been left with no supplies for the approaching winter. Mackenzie reported that three Indians and one cavalry trooper died.

See also PHYSICAL ENVIRONMENT: Caprock Canyonlands.

J'Nell L. Pate
Tarrant County Junior College, Fort Worth

Carter, Robert G. *On the Border with Mackenzie*. Washington DC: Eynon Printing Co., Inc., 1935. Pate, J'Nell L. "Colonel Ranald Slidell Mackenzie's First Four Years with the Fourth Cavalry in Texas, 1871–1874." Master's thesis, Texas Christian University, 1964.

PERSHING, JOHN J. (1860–1948)

Spanning America's emergence as a world power, John Joseph Pershing's military career began in the Great Plains as a junior cavalry officer in 1886 and concluded as army chief of staff in 1924. Born September 13, 1860, in Laclede, Missouri, Pershing graduated from the U.S. Military Academy at West Point in 1886. Following duty in South Dakota and in the Southwest, he served as military science professor at the University of Nebraska from 1891 to 1895, founding the drill team now famed as the Pershing Rifles. He taught Willa Cather and included Roscoe Pound and William Jennings Bryan among his friends. He married Frances Warren, daughter of Wyoming senator Francis Warren, in 1905.

The Spanish-American and Philippine-American Wars proved Pershing's first career break, when he came to future president Theodore Roosevelt's attention in Cuba and then performed well in the Philippine Islands. Promoted over 862 senior officers to brigadier general in 1906, Pershing gained national prominence in 1916 with command of the punitive expedition against Mexican revolutionary Pancho Villa. Meanwhile, on August 27, 1915, Pershing lost his wife and three of his four children in a fire at their house at San Francisco's Presidio.

Pershing moved onto the international stage after President Woodrow Wilson selected him to command the American Expeditionary Force when the United States entered World War I in April 1917. Despite its late entrance into the war, the army played a vital role, assisting in blunting Germany's offensives in March and July of 1918, then successfully attacking the Saint Mihiel salient and in the Meuse-Argonne sector as the war ended.

Promoted to general of the armies on Sep-

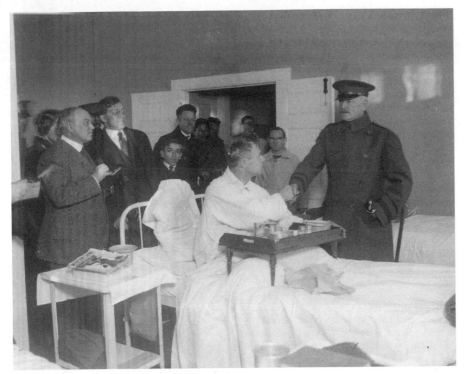

Gen. John J. Pershing shakes hands with army soldier at U.S. Army General Hospital No. 21 (now called Fitzsimons), January 13, 1920.

tember 3, 1919, Pershing ended his career in 1924 as chief of staff. He retired to chair the American Battle Monuments Commission and perform ceremonial duties. On September 2, 1946, he secretly married Michiline Resco. Pershing died in Washington DC on July 15, 1948.

Mark Van Rhyn
University of Nebraska–Lincoln

Smythe, Donald. *Pershing, General of the Armies.* Bloomington: Indiana University Press, 1986.

PIKE, ZEBULON (1779–1813)

Zebulon Montgomery Pike, army officer and explorer, substantially added to early-nineteenth-century knowledge of the Central and Southern Plains. He is remembered mainly for his description of the region as a "Great Sandy Desert" and for Pikes Peak, the Colorado mountain that bears his name.

Son of an army officer, he was born at Lamberton (today Lamington), New Jersey, on January 5, 1779. In 1794 young Pike became a cadet, and five years later he was commissioned as a second lieutenant of the infantry. In 1805, while serving in Illinois, he led a small party up the Mississippi River to locate its source and to select sites for future army posts. The next spring he received orders to lead a party across the Central Plains to find the headwaters of the Arkansas and Red Rivers. The expedition, including twenty-one soldiers, an interpreter, and a civilian doctor, rode west out of St. Louis on July 15, 1806. They crossed Kansas to the Rocky Mountains and into Spanish territory. There, severe winter threatened their survival, forcing them to surrender to the Span-

ish. They were taken south to Chihuahua, Mexico, but in 1807 President Thomas Jefferson secured their release. Early in the War of 1812, Pike was promoted to brigadier general. He died on April 27, 1813, in an explosion of a British powder magazine during the capture of York (Toronto), Ontario.

See also IMAGES AND ICONS: Great American Desert.

Roger L. Nichols
University of Arizona

Hollon, W. Eugene. *The Lost Pathfinder: Zebulon Montgomery Pike.* Norman: University of Oklahoma Press, 1949. Jackson, Donald, ed. *Journals of Zebulon Montgomery Pike.* Norman: University of Oklahoma Press, 1966.

RED CLOUD (1821–1909)

Lakota Sioux chief Red Cloud, regarded by many historians as the most influential of the Native American leaders living in the Great Plains during the late nineteenth century, was born on Blue Water Creek in May 1821 in what is now Garden County, Nebraska. The creek, a tributary of the North Platte River, was located in a neutral hunting ground disputed by the Lakotas and their hated rivals, the Pawnees. Red Cloud's father, Lone Man, was a Brulé, one of the seven Lakota, or western Sioux, tribes that migrated from the woodlands of Minnesota to the Northern Plains during the sixteenth and seventeenth centuries. His mother, Walks-as-She-Thinks, was an Oglala, another of the seven Lakota tribes. When Lone Man died of alcoholism, a sad result of the early commerce with white traders and trappers, Red Cloud, along with his brother and sister, went to live with his mother's people, who were then under the leadership of an Oglala chief named Smoke.

In 1834, when the Oglalas, led by the domineering Sioux leader Bull Bear, were drawn southward to the North Platte River valley by the commercial possibilities of a trading post, which later became Fort Laramie, Red Cloud, a thirteen-year-old member of Smoke's band, joined this important migration. For more than two decades, Smoke's people frequently encamped near Fort Laramie, allowing Red Cloud to learn more about the ways of the whites than most tribal leaders in the Great Plains. Red Cloud also became a great warrior during these years, killing his first enemy in combat at the age of sixteen. As a result of his participation in battles with enemy tribes, such as the Crows, Pawnees, Utes, and Shoshones, Red Cloud allegedly earned eighty coups, a record never matched by any of his tribal rivals.

Red Cloud became prominent in political affairs when he got involved in a bitter brawl in 1841 that resulted in Bull Bear's death; in his autobiography he took personal credit for firing the fatal shot. He later gained the respect and fear of whites, with whom he had been on good terms, when he closed the Bozeman Trail through Wyoming to prospectors heading north to the Montana gold fields by engineering the decisive Fetterman Fight on December 21, 1866. The aftermath of this battle and two others from the so-called Red Cloud's War was the Treaty of Fort Laramie in 1868. In this treaty the Lakotas were assigned an enormous reservation in Dakota Territory, and their hunting territory in Wyoming's buffalo-rich Powder River country was recognized as unceded. The Lakotas subsequently lost the Black Hills in 1877, partly in retaliation for their victory in the Battle of the Little Bighorn, and had their reservation divided and drastically reduced in size in 1889.

Red Cloud's influence in Lakota affairs, which was dominant for a quarter of a century, was diminished as a result of the Ghost Dance, the chief ceremony of an Indian religious movement Red Cloud eventually opposed, and one that ultimately led to the Wounded Knee Massacre on December 29, 1890. The venerable leader died on the Pine Ridge Reservation in South Dakota in 1909 at the age of eighty-eight.

Although Red Cloud has been accused of cruelty in tribal warfare during his younger years and of stubbornness in his negotiations with federal authorities during his older years, his unwavering political and diplomatic leadership on behalf of his people cannot be ignored. Indeed, he demonstrated unusual dedication in his efforts to maintain those provisions in the Treaty of Fort Laramie that he insisted should be honored.

See also NATIVE AMERICANS: Sioux; Treaties / RELIGION: Ghost Dance.

Robert W. Larson
Denver, Colorado

Larson, Robert W. *Red Cloud: Warrior-Statesman of the Lakota Sioux.* Norman: University of Oklahoma Press, 1997. Paul, R. Eli, ed. *Autobiography of Red Cloud: War Leader of the Oglalas.* Helena: Montana Historical Society Press, 1997.

RED RIVER RESISTANCE

In 1869 the Métis of Red River, led by Louis Riel, formed a provisional government to stop the Canadian annexation of Rupert's Land. This territory, encompassing most of today's Prairie Provinces, was under Hudson's Bay Company rule and was scheduled to be transferred to Canada in 1869. During the negotiations between the company, the British government, and the Canadian government for the transfer of sovereignty, no one consulted the Métis, who were the vast majority of the 12,000 residents in the Red River Settlement in the present-day province of Manitoba. Worried about their status in the new Dominion, the Métis took matters into their own hands.

During the summer of 1869, the Métis, comprised of English-speaking Protestant "mixed-bloods" and French-speaking Catholic Métis, held several public meetings to determine how to respond to the proposed transfer. Two competing factions emerged. One, led by William Dease, argued that the Métis should form a provisional government and negotiate with Canada on the basis of their Aboriginal rights. Louis Riel and the Catholic clergy led a second faction, who argued that the transfer represented the annexation of Red River Settlement by Protestant Ontario and threatened the religious rights of the Catholic Métis. Controlling the largest army, and having the Catholic Church on his side, Riel triumphed in this power struggle. In early November 1869 he seized Upper Fort Garry and effective control of the settlement.

Riel and his Métis supporters suppressed internal dissension in the settlement by imprisoning dozens of Métis opponents and Canadians, and then forged a consensus by calling a number of representative conventions. In January 1870 Red River residents elected a representative provisional government to negotiate the terms of their entry into the Dominion. The resulting Manitoba Act of 1870 created the province of Manitoba, guaranteed the property rights of the Métis, provided for bilingual institutions and denominational schools to protect the interests of the Catholic Church, and granted 1.4 million acres of land to Métis children.

The Manitoba Act and Manitoba's entry into the Dominion was a victory for the Red River Métis that Riel was unable to enjoy. During the Resistance, which lasted from October 1869 until August of 1870, Riel's provisional government had executed an Ontario Orangeman by the name of Thomas Scott. This act made it politically impossible for the Canadian government to grant Riel's government an unconditional amnesty for actions taken during the Resistance. Riel fled to the United States in August 1870 when Canadian troops arrived in Manitoba.

See also POLITICS AND GOVERNMENT: Manitoba / PROTEST AND DISSENT: Riel, Louis.

Gerhard J. Ens
University of Alberta

Ens, Gerhard J. "Prologue to the Red River Resistance: Pre-liminal Politics and the Triumph of Riel." *Journal of the Canadian Historical Association* 5 (1994): 111–23. Stanley, George F. G. *Louis Riel*. Toronto: Ryerson Press, 1963.

RIEL, LOUIS

See PROTEST AND DISSENT: Riel, Louis

SAND CREEK MASSACRE

Southern Cheyennes and Arapahos will forever remember the Sand Creek Massacre, which occurred on November 29, 1864, when Col. John M. Chivington and his men of the Colorado Third Volunteer Regiment attacked their camp. Cheyennes called this ordained Methodist minister a "holy-speaking white man," yet his statement "Damn any man who is in sympathy with an Indian" expressed his antipathy toward them.

Two opposing forces caused the massacre. On one hand were the men of the volunteer Third Colorado Cavalry, known as the "Bloodless Third" because their 100-day enlistment had nearly expired without action against Native Americans and led by Colonel Chivington. On the other were the Cheyenne Dog Soldiers, who were opposed to the peaceful goals of Black Kettle and who had been making raids on white settlements—raids that were traced to some warriors of Black Kettle's band. These raids, and blatant land greed thwarted by the failure to acquire mineral-rich Cheyenne and Arapaho lands in treaty conferences in 1851 and 1861, led Gov. John Evans to order Chivington's command to attack.

Black Kettle's mostly peaceful band reported to Fort Lyon as "friendlies" and were told by the sympathetic commanding officer, Maj. Edward Wynkoop, that they should camp near Fort Lyon under military protection. Vister, a Cheyenne woman, described their sense of safety as they settled in along Sand Creek on the night before the attack. At dawn they were surprised by the attack, in which Chivington ordered his men to take no prisoners. Vister recalled that a male relative brought her a pony, striking it on its flanks to flee. Instead, she turned to find her younger brother, whom she pulled up behind her as bullets whizzed around them. One bullet struck her in the leg as they raced away from the besieged camp that flew a U.S. flag and a white flag on a lodgepole.

Vister's wound healed, but the trauma ran deep in her spirit. Cheyennes and Arapahos carry the memory of this massacre. In his testimony before a congressional committee, interpreter John Smith described the atrocities: "All manner of depredations were inflicted on their persons; they were scalped, their brains knocked out; the men used their knives, ripped open women, clubbed little children, knocked them in the head with their guns, beat their brains out, mutilated their bodies in every sense of the word."

Upon their return to Denver, Chivington and his men displayed scalps and other body parts from their victims to a cheering crowd in the Denver opera house. Reaction in the East could not have been more opposite—shock and outrage greeted the news, especially when details of the large number of women and children killed, as well as the way in which they died, became public knowledge. The military held an investigation and Congress held two, which transcended their original purpose and became investigations of all U.S. Indian policy. Congress condemned Chivington and his men, but as their enlistments had run out, they were no longer under military jurisdiction.

In response to the massacre, some Cheyennes and their allies the Arapahos and Lakota Sioux initiated raids all over the Northern Plains, particularly along the Platte River. It was the start of roughly ten years of war in the Northern Plains.

On October 14, 1865, U.S. government commissioners negotiated the Treaty of the Little Arkansas River, which read in part, "The United States being desirous to express its condemnation of, and, as far as may be, repudiate the gross and wanton outrages perpetrated against certain bands of Cheyenne and Arrapahoe Indians, on the twenty-ninth day of November, A.D. 1864, at Sand Creek, in Colorado Territory, while the said Indians were at peace with the United States, and under its flag, whose protection they had by lawful authority been promised and induced to seek, and the Government being desirous to make some suitable reparation for the injuries then done, will grant 320 acres of land by patent," as well as individual payments for property lost to survivors. This promise has not yet been kept.

In 1996 the General Conference of the United Methodist Church adopted a resolution apologizing "for the atrocities committed at Sand Creek, Colorado, by one of their own clergy members." They also offered to "extend to all Cheyennes and Arapahos a hand of reconciliation, and ask forgiveness for the death of over 200 mostly women and children."

See also NATIVE AMERICANS: Black Kettle.

Henrietta Mann
Montana State University–Bozeman

Hoig, Stan. *The Sand Creek Massacre*. Norman: University of Oklahoma Press, 1961.

SAN SABÁ MISSION, DESTRUCTION OF

Mission Santa Cruz de San Sabá, founded for the eastern Apaches in April 1757, near present-day Menard, Texas, was sacked and burned on March 16, 1758, by an allied Native American force of about 2,000 Comanches, Tejas, Tonkawas, and others. At least eight persons, including two of the three Franciscan missionaries present, were slain during the attack. The nearby presidio, San Luis de las Amarillas, four miles farther up the San Saba River, was powerless to intervene. Although the Spanish Franciscan friars, headed by Fray Alonso Giraldo de Terreros, had failed to congregate the Apaches for religious instruction, the allied northern tribes had been alarmed at the prospect of a Spanish-Apache alliance.

The attack represented the first major conflict between Comanches and European American settlers in Texas. Combined with the failed Spanish punitive military expedition to a Wichita (Taovaya) village on the Red River a year later, it demonstrated that the Spanish faced a new type of enemy with greatly expanded capabilities. French firearms had replaced bows and arrows, and the allied Indians had vastly superior numbers. No longer was a ragged Spanish militia, drawn randomly from untrained civilian settlers, capable of holding the frontier. The Spanish advance from Texas toward the Great Plains was halted.

Robert S. Weddle
Bonham, Texas

Weddle, Robert S. *The San Sabá Mission: Spanish Pivot in Texas*. Austin: University of Texas Press, 1964.

SEVEN OAKS MASSACRE

The chain of events leading to the Seven Oaks Massacre began in the spring of 1816, when the Hudson's Bay Company destroyed the North West Company's Fort Gibraltar at the junction of the Red and Assiniboine Rivers. The attack was a part of the companies' intense struggle for the control of the Northern Plains fur and meat trade; its immediate goal was to expel the Nor'westers from the Red River Settlement by cutting off their supply lines from the Plains. As a counterstrike, the North West Company sent Cuthbert Grant and about sixty Métis provisioners to open and secure the road to the Red River.

On June 19, 1816, Grant's force encountered a Hudson's Bay Company party at an oak hill near the destroyed Fort Gibraltar. The group, about twenty-five strong, was led by Robert Semple, the governor of the Red River Settlement, who was determined to get rid of the Nor'westers. The Semple party opened fire, and a fierce fight broke out. The more-numerous Métis caught their opponents in a deadly crossfire and killed Sample and twenty of his followers while suffering only one casualty themselves.

The Seven Oaks Massacre was the bloodiest incident in the forty-year struggle between the Hudson's Bay and North West Companies. It initiated a period of extremely tense relations and provoked the Hudson's Bay Company to attack Fort William in August 1816. The violent cycle continued until 1821, when the companies merged under the name of the Hudson's Bay Company.

See also IMAGES AND ICONS: Cuthbert, Grant / NATIVE AMERICANS: Métis

Pekka Hämäläinen
Texas A&M University

SHERIDAN, PHILIP (1831–1888)

Philip Henry Sheridan, five feet five inches tall and unimpressive looking, was commander of the Military Division of the Missouri during controversial stages of Native American conflict with post–Civil War westward expansion. Sheridan was born on March 6, 1831, in (probably) Albany, New York, and grew up in Ohio. A rather undistinguished student, Sheridan graduated from the U.S. Military Academy at West Point in 1853 and served in Texas and the Pacific Northwest. He rose to the rank of major general by serving with distinction during the Civil War as commander of the Army of the Potomac's cavalry division. After the Civil War, Sheridan performed short stints in Reconstruction-era Texas and Louisiana before going to Fort Leavenworth, Kansas, in the spring of 1868. He was given command of the Military Division of the Missouri in 1869 and promoted to lieutenant general. In 1875 he would marry Irene Rucker, his quartermaster's daughter, and together they had four children.

Too few soldiers, many with less than desirable attitudes and character, too many forts to garrison, and too large an area to defend were just some of the problems confronted by the careful and deliberative commander. Directed by the "peace policy" of the politicians, eastern philanthropists, and social reformers, Sheridan soon developed his strategy. He had two main principles for dealing with Native Americans, for whom he showed little sympathy. The first was to place all Indians on well-guarded reservations and have the U.S. government feed and clothe them. The second was to capture and punish any Indians found off their reservation. To institute this policy, Sheridan ordered a new type of warfare against Native Americans—winter campaigning. His offensive efforts, typified by Lt. Col. George Armstrong Custer's winter battle at the Washita River against the Cheyennes (November 17, 1868), proved successful. Columns of lightly supplied cavalry troops converged on the Indians in winter quarters, where they were immobile because of women, children, and weakened ponies.

Sheridan campaigned widely in the Plains in the 1870s, against the Lakotas in the Sioux War and against the Comanches, Kiowas, Southern Cheyennes, and Southern Arapahos in the Red River War. He was promoted to general in chief of the army in 1883 and general of the army in 1888. That same year, on August 5, he fell victim to a fatal heart attack at Nonquitt, Massachusetts.

Gary Trogdon
Lincoln, Nebraska

Hutton, Paul. *Phil Sheridan and His Army*. Lincoln: University of Nebraska Press, 1985. Morris, Roy, Jr. *Sheridan: The Life and Wars of General Phil Sheridan*. New York: Crown Publishers, Inc., 1992.

SHERMAN, WILLIAM TECUMSEH (1820–1891)

A leading Union general in the Civil War, William Tecumseh Sherman was also a driving force in the postwar settlement of the Great Plains. Sherman was born in Lancaster, Ohio, on February 8, 1820, and brought up in the family of Thomas Ewing, a leading politician. After graduation from the U.S. Military Academy at West Point, he served in the Second Seminole War and in the Mexican War. His success was assured by his leadership and victories in the Civil War, where he put into practice his strategy of property destruction as a means of war, a strategy he would continue against Plains Indians. From 1866 to 1869 he commanded the Military Division of the Missouri, covering the area from the Mississippi River to the Rocky Mountains (with Texas ex-cluded). In 1869 he became commanding general of the entire U.S. Army, a position he held until his retirement in 1884.

Throughout these years, though his responsibilities were wide-ranging, Sherman focused much of his attention in the Great Plains. There, the great transcontinental railroads were built and the Native Americans struggled against the ever-increasing encroachment of the United States. As white settlers poured into the region, Native Americans tried to stem the tide, but the U.S. Army, under Sherman's leadership, thwarted the effort. With the completion of the first transcontinental railroad in 1869 and the subsequent building of other rail lines, Indians could not compete against increasingly mobile soldiers and the mass of settlers. Sherman advocated all-out war aimed at destroying the Indians' subsistence base. Sherman's view of the struggle was a complex one. On one hand, he opposed civilian reformers who proposed a more humanitarian policy toward the Indians, though he did serve on the peace commission at the Medicine Lodge Creek (1867) and Fort Laramie Treaties (1868), respectively. On the other hand, he believed that the main cause of war was American expansion onto tribal lands, and that it was best, for all concerned, to force an end to the painful struggle by militarily controlling the tribes. Through it all, Sherman insisted that progress and order demanded that the Indians move aside for the white settlers, even as he recognized the unjust aspects of the fight. His love for the region never wavered, and he regularly left the frustrations of Washington to tour the Great Plains and the entire American West, where he found a peace of mind not available to him elsewhere. Sherman died in New York City on February 14, 1891.

John F. Marszalek
Mississippi State University

Athearn, Robert G. *William Tecumseh Sherman and the Settlement of the West*. 1956. Reprint, Lincoln: University of Nebraska Press, 1995. Marszalek, John F. *Sherman, A Soldier's Passion for Order*. New York: Free Press, 1993; Vintage, 1994. Sherman Family Papers. Archives of the University of Notre Dame, South Bend IN.

SIOUX WARS

During the last half of the nineteenth century, Lakota Sioux and their Cheyenne and Arapaho allies defended their homelands and natural resources against incursions by the federal government and European American settlers. Collectively known as the Sioux Wars, major engagements included the Grattan Massacre (1854), Fetterman Fight (1866), Battle of the Rosebud (1876), Battle of the Little Bighorn (1876), and the Wounded Knee Massacre (1890).

The first violent conflict in the Plains involving the Lakota Sioux and the federal government grew out of increased travel along the Oregon Trail. To protect overland travelers, the federal government built Fort Kearny in present-day Nebraska and purchased Fort Laramie in present-day Wyoming. Government agents also negotiated the Fort Laramie

Treaty of 1851, which guaranteed the safe passage of emigrants in exchange for annuities and the recognition of tribal territories. Peace held until 1854 when a trivial event—the theft of an emigrant's cow by young Lakotas—led to the Grattan Massacre and subsequent army retaliations. On August 19, 1854, Lt. John Grattan led a detachment of twenty-nine men to recover the stolen cow from the village of Conquering Bear along the North Platte River. Misunderstandings and a belligerent Grattan sparked violence. When the shooting stopped, Grattan and all of his men lay dead; Conquering Bear was the lone Lakota casualty. Army retaliation was certain. The following summer, Col. William S. Harney destroyed a Sioux village at Ash Hollow (present-day Nebraska), killing more than 100 men, women, and children. Harney then pushed into Lakota territory, briefly occupying Fort Pierre (South Dakota) and finally establishing Fort Randall on the Missouri River. Harney's invasion of the Sioux homeland caused the Sioux to move away from the roads, soldiers, and forts and, in combination with the federal government's preoccupation with the Civil War (1861–65), led to almost ten years of relative peace.

Trouble flared again in 1865–67 when emigrants, in violation of the 1851 Treaty of Fort Laramie, moved along the Bozeman Trail to the Montana goldfields. This pathway cut through the heart of Plains Indian hunting grounds in the Powder River area. Persistent Lakota raids against settlers and soldiers along this route prompted the federal government to build Forts Reno, C. F. Smith, and Phil Kearny to protect emigrant travel. Despite the heavy military presence, Indian attacks continued, and in the second half of 1866 Lakotas led by Red Cloud and Crazy Horse battled federal troops. The most notorious engagement was the Fetterman Fight (December 21, 1866) near Fort Phil Kearny, Wyoming Territory, where eighty men under Capt. William Fetterman were killed. Public cries for decisive action against the Sioux reached a fever pitch, but Congress voted to broker peace with the warring tribes. Red Cloud signed the Fort Laramie Treaty (1868), which guaranteed, among other things, abandonment of the Bozeman Trail forts and creation of a large reservation that included the Black Hills. After agreeing to this treaty, Red Cloud and many Lakota bands moved onto this Great Sioux Reservation, while Sitting Bull, Crazy Horse, and Gall continued to resist encroachment on their lands. They openly rejected the treaty and continued to pursue their traditional life.

Hostilities erupted once again after an 1874 military expedition into the Black Hills confirmed rumors of gold. Gold seekers flooded into Paha Sapa (the Black Hills)—a clear violation of the 1868 Fort Laramie Treaty—forcing leaders such as Crazy Horse and Sitting Bull to defend Sioux territory. To avoid conflict, the federal government in 1875 offered to purchase the land from the Sioux. Overwhelmingly, the Sioux rejected this, and the government provoked a military showdown by issuing an ultimatum requiring all Sioux to

report to an agency by January 31, 1876, or be considered hostile. The off-reservation people, now loosely allied under Sitting Bull, were scattered in the Powder River area (southeastern Montana and northwestern Wyoming) in small winter camps, and they largely ignored this arbitrary, impossible demand.

In May 1876 the army launched a three-pronged campaign to force the Lakotas back onto the Great Sioux Reservation: Col. John Gibbon advanced eastward from Fort Ellis (Montana), Gen. George Crook moved north from Fort Laramie, and Gen. Alfred Terry (with George Custer) moved westward from Fort Abraham Lincoln (North Dakota). The military's campaign began to crumble when on June 17, 1876, the Sioux, led by Crazy Horse, routed and turned back Crook's command at the Battle of the Rosebud. On June 25–26, 1876, in the most famous fight of the offensive, Lt. Col. George Custer's Seventh Cavalry attacked an enormous Indian encampment on the Little Bighorn (Greasy Grass) River. Custer divided his command and attempted to strike the village from both ends but was quickly overwhelmed by superior numbers. Custer and 210 men in his immediate command (263 total) were killed.

After this victory, the Sioux and their allies fragmented into small bands and dispersed. The army initiated a winter campaign and relentlessly hunted down those bands that had not returned to their agencies. In May 1877, Crazy Horse surrendered at Fort Robinson, Nebraska; he was killed four months later, reportedly while trying to escape. Sitting Bull fled to Canada with as many as 2,000 followers. In retaliation for defeat at the Little Bighorn, Congress annexed the Black Hills from the Great Sioux Reservation on February 28, 1877.

Essentially, these events marked the end of the Sioux Wars and the start of the reservation era. After Sitting Bull returned to the United States in 1881, all Lakota Sioux bands lived on reservations and any hope of effective resistance was gone. The final conflict between the Sioux and the federal government—the Wounded Knee Massacre—was hardly a military confrontation. Militarily defeated, the Sioux readily adopted the Ghost Dance religion but with a more militaristic twist—some believed they would be impervious to bullets and most believed that if they danced and prayed with enough fervor the European Americans would be driven from the country. Their newfound focus caused great fear in the Plains, leading to a confrontation with federal troops. On December 29, 1890, while attempting to disarm a fleeing band of Lakotas, the Seventh Cavalry killed more than 250 Lakotas (mostly women and children) on the Pine Ridge Reservation in South Dakota. This massacre marked the end of Sioux resistance and the last chapter in the Plains Indian Wars.

See also: IMAGES AND ICONS: Custer, George Armstrong / LAW: United States v. Sioux Tribe of Indians / RELIGION: Ghost Dance.

Carole A. Barrett
University of Mary

Olson, James C. *Red Cloud and the Sioux Problem*. Lin-

coln: University of Nebraska Press, 1965. Utley, Robert M. *The Indian Frontier of the American West, 1846–1890*. Albuquerque: University of New Mexico Press, 1984.

STEPHENSON, WILLIAM SAMUEL
(1896–1989)

Sir William Stephenson, a fourth-generation Manitoban who played a major role in intelligence in World War II, was born in Winnipeg on January 11, 1896, the son of a pioneer family. As a teenager, he was fascinated with radio and enjoyed making and using radio transmitters and receivers. In 1914 Stephenson volunteered for the Royal Canadian Engineers. He was sent to France as a private and earned a commission in the field at the age of nineteen. He was gassed and returned to England as an invalid "disabled for life." He recovered but was still considered unfit to return to the trenches. He turned down an administrative desk job, joined the Royal Flying Corps, and returned to France. He shot down twenty-six planes, for which he was decorated with the Distinguished Flying Cross, the Military Cross, and from the French, the Legion of Honor and the Croix de Guerre with Palms.

In London following World War I, Stephenson started his radio empire with the purchase of a controlling interest in the General Radio Company. He patented a process that enabled photographs to be transmitted electronically, now known as a facsimile, or "fax." He was involved in the aircraft industry, and a plane developed and built in one of Stephenson's factories won the King's Cup air race and ultimately evolved into the Spitfire.

In 1940 Churchill appointed Stephenson to the position of director of British Security Coordination in the Western Hemisphere. In all his wartime work he sought anonymity, operating under the code name of "Intrepid." In this capacity, directing espionage and counterintelligence, he was pivotal to the Allied campaign.

In 1945, at the conclusion of hostilities, Stephenson was knighted by King George VI, and President Harry Truman awarded him the Presidential Medal of Merit, the highest honor available to a civilian. In Manitoba he was appointed chairman of the Manitoba Economic Advisory Board, awarded a doctor of laws degree from the University of Winnipeg, and presented with the province's top honor, the Order of the Buffalo Hunt, Chief Hunter. Sir William Stephenson died January 31, 1989.

Terry Smythe
Winnipeg, Manitoba

STRATEGIC AIR COMMAND

The Strategic Air Command (SAC) was established on March 21, 1946, to deter threats from communist nations, prevent nuclear warfare, and wage the cold war. SAC served to project a global military presence as the bomber leg of the United States nuclear triad that included submarine-launched missiles and land-based intercontinental ballistic missiles. Not solely devoted to deploying nuclear weapons, SAC made significant contributions to conventional warfare in Vietnam and Iraq during the Gulf War.

SAC languished from inadequate funding and unclear direction during its first years under commander Gen. George C. Kenney. As a result of the Berlin blockade and airlift of 1948, however, the mission of SAC crystallized. The Berlin crisis had exposed serious structural and logistical problems that threatened the ability of the United States to enforce its policy of containment against the Soviet Union. In response, Gen. Curtis E. LeMay assumed command of SAC and set about building a credible airborne fighting force. After moving its headquarters from Andrews Field, Maryland, to Offutt Air Force Base near Omaha, Nebraska, LeMay instituted fundamental changes in training, housing, food services, and recreation. A pragmatic leader, LeMay prepared SAC for a war that could begin at any time and for air combat and bombing missions that would have to be deployed immediately. By 1949, when the Soviets exploded their first atomic bomb, SAC had mobilized its resources and crew competence to levels sufficient to meet this new challenge.

In the wake of the Soviet nuclear detonation, the beginning of the Korean War, and new initiatives detailed under NSC-68, the National Security Council's blueprint for waging the cold war, the role of SAC in the worldwide defense of American interests grew. By 1950 SAC had 225 atomic bomb–carrying aircraft (including B-29s, B-50s, and thirty-four B-36s). As cold war relations deteriorated and both the United States and the Soviet Union developed thermonuclear weapons, SAC expanded its role in providing strategic defensive and offensive capabilities. In June 1955 SAC accepted delivery of the first B-52, the jet bomber that became its trademark symbol. In January 1957 SAC headquarters moved to a new control center. From a two-tiered building, comprised of a three-story aboveground administrative structure and a three-story belowground war command center, SAC coordinated its global presence, controlling both bomber and missile systems.

In late 1957, under its new commander, Gen. Thomas S. Powers, SAC assumed its well-known motto, "Peace Is Our Profession." Also during 1957, with cold war tensions increasing, the American military establishment put its nuclear forces on alert status. This condition continued until September 28, 1991, when President George H. W. Bush issued a stand-down order, ending a thirty-five-year period when American nuclear weapons were on launch-ready status and a certain percentage of the American nuclear bomber force continuously remained airborne. SAC ceased to exist on June 1, 1992, when the U.S. Strategic Command (USSTRATCOM), also headquartered at Offutt Air Force Base, took over control of the nation's strategic forces for the post–cold war era.

Scott D. Hughes
Albuquerque, New Mexico

Hopkins, J. C., and Sheldon A. Goldberg. *The Development of SAC, 1946–1986: The Fortieth Anniversary History.* Offutt Air Force Base, Nebraska: Office of the Historian, 1988.

SUMMIT SPRINGS, BATTLE OF

The Battle of Summit Springs, on July 11, 1869, was one of the most decisive engagements fought between the U.S. military and the Southern Plains Indians. In retribution for raids on Kansas settlements in 1868 and 1869, Brig. Gen. C. C. Augur, commander of the Department of the Platte, organized the "Republican River Expedition." His orders to expedition leader Maj. Eugene A. Carr were to clear Indians from the Republican River country with eight companies of the Fifth Cavalry and 150 Pawnee scouts under Maj. Frank North. The command was also to rescue two white prisoners, Maria Weichell and Susanna Alderice.

The campaign, which began from Fort McPherson, Nebraska, was directed against the famed Dog Soldier warrior society of the Southern Cheyennes led by Tall Bull. After eluding the soldiers, Tall Bull stopped on the south side of the swollen South Platte River in Logan County, Colorado. On July 11, under the cover of fog, the command advanced on the village of eighty-five lodges. Carr divided his troops into two attack wings and launched the assault about 3:00 P.M. The Pawnee scouts reached the village first, taking the Dog Soldiers by surprise. Guided by Two Crows, women and children took refuge in a nearby ravine. Tall Bull died defending his people, as did the highly regarded Wolf With Plenty of Hair, allegedly the last Dog Soldier to "stake himself out" with a symbolic "dog rope" in warfare. Carr officially reported one trooper wounded, fifty-two Indians killed, and seventeen women and children captured. Susanna Alderice was killed in the attack, and Maria Weichell was severely wounded.

Summit Springs ended conflict with Native Americans in the Colorado Plains. According to George Bent, who later related the history of the Cheyenne people, the Dog Soldiers were never again an important factor.

John H. Monnett
Metropolitan State College of Denver

Grinnell, George B. *Two Great Scouts and Their Pawnee Battalion: The Experiences of Frank J. North and Luther H. North.* Lincoln: University of Nebraska Press, 1973. Monnett, John H. *The Battle of Beecher Island and the Indian War of 1867–1869.* Niwot: University Press of Colorado, 1992.

TEXAS REVOLUTION

The events known as the Texas Revolution separated Texas from Mexico in 1836. It resulted from efforts of Texas residents, mostly Anglo Americans who had emigrated from the United States, to retain their virtual political autonomy. Disputes over immigration policy and slavery had led to growing tensions and protests between them and the government of Mexico. These became irreconcilable in 1835, when Mexico abandoned its federalist constitution in favor of a centralized order. Texas resistance brought a military response from Mexico, which in turn resulted in war, beginning in October 1835. To promote internal unity and elicit support from Mexican federalists, provisional authorities refrained from declaring independence until March 2, 1836.

The war involved about an equal total number of soldiers on each side (approximately 4,000), but the Texas armies consisted of undisciplined volunteers, including many from the United States. They served in units headed by elected officers and often without an overall commander. The war consisted of two offensive campaigns. The first, by the Texas army under Stephen F. Austin and others, resulted in the capitulation of Bexar (San Antonio) and surrender of Mexican forces on December 10, 1835. The second, under President Antonio López de Santa Anna, focused on redeeming that loss by attacking the Alamo, while other Texas armies succumbed to indecision and a swift movement of Mexican forces under José Urrea. Texas volunteers then rallied under Gen. Sam Houston and retreated deep into East Texas until they halted and assaulted the Mexicans at San Jacinto on April 21. A captive himself, Santa Anna ordered the remainder of Mexican forces to withdraw from Texas and gave his own recognition to the Texas Republic, though this act, conducted under compulsion, did not bring a true accord. In 1837 Sam Houston was elected the first president of the Republic of Texas.

Paul D. Lack
McMurry University

Barr, Alwyn. *Texans in Revolt: The Battle for San Antonio, 1835.* Austin: University of Texas Press, 1990. Lack, Paul D. *The Texas Revolutionary Experience: A Political and Social History, 1835–1886.* College Station: Texas A&M University Press, 1992.

TROPA DE GENÍZARO

During the eighteenth century, Indian slavery and the slave trade were important components in relations between the New Mexican Spanish and Native Americans of the Great Plains. Captives who had been acculturated and paid their ransom debt were discharged by their Spanish masters and entered Spanish society as *genízaros*. The term is from "janissary," which referred to Christian captives who entered Turkish service.

The genízaros, many of whom came from the ranks of such Plains tribes as Plains Apaches, Jumanos, Comanches, Kiowas, Pawnees, Wichitas, and possibly Crows, lacked legal and social status and land; consequently, they settled at frontier outposts from El Paso to north of Santa Fe, where they received land and protected the colony from surrounding Indian raiders—Apaches, Comanches, Navajos, and Utes. In time they developed civilian (trader, weaver, rancher, farmer) and military occupations. Many traded with Plains Indians during peaceful times. They continued as an unorganized military force known for their bravery and fighting ability, both as militia troops and scouts. Their economic status improved with the horses, livestock, and other goods that they were allowed to keep from successful campaigns.

The genízaro militia was officially recognized and formally organized in 1808 as the Tropa de Genízaro. It was commanded by a corporal from their own ranks and based in Santa Fe. They had an organized supply system, which provided the militia with equipment and expendable supplies. With the end of Spanish rule in 1821, the segregated genízaro troops disappeared as they merged with the regular Mexican militia.

See also HISPANIC AMERICANS: Genízaros.

Russell M. Magnaghi
Northern Michigan University

Magnaghi, Russell M. "Plains Indians in New Mexico: The Genízaro Experience." *Great Plains Quarterly* 10 (1990): 86–95.

UNITED STATES AIR FORCE ACADEMY

See EDUCATION: United States Air Force Academy

VILLASUR EXPEDITION

In 1720 the Spanish governor of New Mexico, Antonio Valverde y Cosío, under orders from the viceroy in Mexico City, sent out an expedition to investigate rumors of a French thrust toward New Mexico. The force of forty-two soldiers, sixty Pueblo Indian auxiliaries, and three settlers was led by Lt. Gov. Don Pedro de Villasur. Fray Juan Mínguez went as chaplain. There was also a French interpreter, "Juan de Archebeque" (Jean L'Archevêque), a survivor of the La Salle expedition that had landed on the Texas coast in 1685.

Having left Santa Fe in mid-June 1720, the Villasur expedition encamped in early August on a large river that most authorities identify as the Platte, not far from a sizable Pawnee village. An exchange of messages with the Pawnees proved unsatisfactory, and Villasur, suspecting treachery, prepared to withdraw. On the morning of August 14, while the Spaniards were gathering their horses, they were attacked with musket fire by the Pawnees and Otoes. Taken by surprise, the Spanish camp was thrown into confusion. Only thirteen of the soldiers escaped. Villasur himself perished along with forty-five others, including Mínguez and L'Archevêque. The Villasur catastrophe severely weakened New Mexico's defenses, for the province had lost a third of its fighting force.

See also EUROPEAN AMERICANS: Villasur, Pedro de.

Robert S. Weddle
Bonham, Texas

Jones, Oakah L., Jr. *Pueblo Warriors and Spanish Conquest.* Norman: University of Oklahoma Press, 1966. Thomas, Alfred Barnaby, trans. and ed. *After Coronado: Spanish Exploration Northeast of New Mexico, 1696–1727.* Norman: University of Oklahoma Press, 1935.

WAR CHIEFS

Since superior performance in warfare constituted a principal measure of leadership potential, many Native American societies of the Great Plains during the preconquest era embraced the concept of a war chief (e.g., *toyopki* to the Kiowas; *blotahunka* among the Oglala Sioux) and constructed a cultural order that reinforced a military tradition. For instance, male warriors belonging to Plains tribes such as the Arapahos, Blackfoot, Cheyennes, Comanches, Crows, Kiowas, and Lakotas elevated their status by winning battle distinctions. As honors accrued, men embellished brave deeds through public recitations and symbolic ornamentation. Assiniboine males acquired eagle feathers for each martial exploit; Blackfoot warriors accumulated white weasel skins; and successful Crow soldiers attached wolf tails to the heels of their moccasins. Such recognition did not require the killing of an enemy or the taking of a scalp. In fact, in many Plains societies the practice of counting coup, or touching an enemy with one's hand or a special stick, outranked killing as a heroic deed. A Blackfoot warrior, for example, always dwelt on the number of horses and guns he captured, not on the quantity of enemies extinguished. One of the principal avenues for achieving exalted warrior status was affiliation with a military society. Sporting names such as the Dog Soldiers, Fox Soldiers, and Kit Foxes, war societies extended membership only to the most promising young men of the band.

Most Indigenous societies of the Great Plains practiced some form of hereditary chieftainship and recognized a head chief. In theory, the head chief presided over a council composed of war chiefs, headmen, warriors, and holy men. In practice, however, charismatic, self-made war-party leaders often exercised the most significant authority, especially in times of crisis. The career of the Oglala Lakota leader Red Cloud is illustrative. Red Cloud became a war chief of an Oglala band in the early 1840s. His power and prestige increased over the next two decades as a result of military successes against the Crows, Pawnees, and Shoshones, as well as his strategic intervention against whites along the Bozeman Trail. By the late 1860s the American government regarded Red Cloud, who still retained only war chief status among the Oglalas, as the principal Lakota chief. American officials sought Red Cloud's influence in negotiating a peaceful resolution to the warfare raging in the Northern Plains at the time.

Conflict among the Plains tribes, regardless of warfare's exalted status, was not a "natural" condition or simply the result of the "aggressive instincts" of male warriors. Instead, wars took place primarily in light of pragmatic considerations—acquiring horses, expanding trade, capturing hunting grounds, or defending compatriots from the incursions of the U.S. military. In addition, the dynamics of Plains Indian warfare changed over time in relation to the shifting cultural landscape. For example, the acquisition of horses from the Spanish Southwest during the seventeenth and eighteenth centuries accelerated the nomadic lifestyle of bison hunters like the Kiowas, Cheyennes, and Lakotas, thereby intensifying the competition for buffalo hunting grounds. In conjunction with the horse, the procurement of guns from French, British, and American traders between the seventeenth and nineteenth centuries contributed to various military imbalances in the Great Plains, to the benefit of groups such as the Blackfoot, Comanches, and Lakotas. During the late eighteenth and early nineteenth centuries, the spread of disease pathogens exacerbated these imbalances. Horticultural peoples like the Arikaras, Mandans, and Hidatsas suffered grievously from smallpox epidemics. On the other hand, migratory hunters like the Lakotas escaped the wholesale ravages of disease, enjoyed unprecedented population growth in the early 1800s, and used their demographic advantage to dominate much of the Central and Northern Plains by the mid–nineteenth century.

By the 1850s, however, the onrush of white competitors into the trans-Missouri West posed new military challenges for Native Americans and forced innovative responses. The mounting threat gave rise to alliances among various Plains groups, formed to protect resources as well as one another from the white invasion. In the Northern Plains, the Lakotas, Arapahos, and Cheyennes joined forces; to the south, the Comanches and Kiowas built alliances with the Cheyennes and Arapahos. Emphasis on military accomplishment within tribes assumed even greater significance in the nineteenth century, when white intrusion made martial readiness a prerequisite to a group's survival. Consequently, the closing frontier era produced some of the most notable war chiefs, including Quanah Parker (Comanche), Satank (Kiowa), and Crazy Horse (Oglala Lakota).

James O. Gump
University of San Diego

Mishkin, Bernard. *Rank and Warfare among the Plains Indians.* Lincoln: University of Nebraska Press, 1992. Secoy, Frank Raymond. *Changing Military Patterns of the Great Plains Indians.* Lincoln: University of Nebraska Press, 1992. Utley, Robert M. *The Indian Frontier of the American West, 1846–1890.* Albuquerque: University of New Mexico Press, 1984.

WARTIME PRICES AND TRADE BOARD

The Canadian government formed the Wartime Prices and Trade Board (WPTB) on September 3, 1939. The board was given a critical and massive mandate: to control all supply, manufacture, distribution, and pricing of consumer goods and services. Donald Gordon, appointed in 1941 as WPTB director, reported directly to finance minister J. L. Ilsey, who was a member of Prime Minister Mackenzie King's cabinet. Gordon was responsible for the work of five coordinations and fifty-seven separate commodity administrations. The scope of concerns that fell under the purview of the operations of the WPTB were as varied as sugar rationing, complaints of shortages of baby diapers, price ceiling of consumer goods, garment design restrictions, limitations on distances traveled by commercial vehicles, black market operations, distribution of import quotas to manufacturers, and control of the cost of living. To deal with these issues, the WPTB had the power to promulgate its own orders to ensure equitable and economically sound distribution and sale of the necessaries of life.

Eventually, the WPBT employed nearly 6,000 Canadians; many of the public service administrators worked for the board for $1 per year. Each province had a regional office and several local offices in smaller centers. In the Canadian Prairies, the capitals of Winnipeg, Regina, and Edmonton were supported by a total of twenty additional offices in such locations as Flin Flon, Manitoba; Prince Albert, Saskatchewan; and Medicine Hat, Alberta.

There was an additional volunteer corps of more than 16,000 women across the nation. They played a crucial role in the work of the board's consumer branch under the direction of fourteen Women's Regional Advisory Committees. In the Winnipeg region alone, which covered the area from the Saskatchewan border through Manitoba to western Ontario, more than 900 volunteers worked for thirty-two English- and French-speaking subcommittees to monitor and collect information on such activities as rationing, labeling, clothing conservation, housing shortages, and price checking. In their work we find the origins of the Consumers Association of Canada.

Susan G. Turnbull Caton
University of Manitoba

Taylor, K. S. "Canadian Wartime Price Controls 1941–1946." *Canadian Journal of Economics and Political Science* 13 (1947): 81–98.

WASHITA, BATTLE OF THE

The Battle of the Washita occurred on November 17, 1868, in western Indian Territory, about one mile west of present-day Cheyenne, Oklahoma. Before dawn, Lt. Col. George Armstrong Custer peered over a snow-encrusted ridge into the valley of the Washita River. There he saw a large Cheyenne village in a wooded bottom on the south side of the stream. At daybreak, 700 men of the Seventh U.S. Cavalry struck the village of Black Kettle, a Cheyenne peace chief. Completely surprised, the warriors offered only token resistance as women and children fled to the surrounding woodlot and hills. Troopers occupying the village began burning its fifty lodges, killing approximately 800 horses and destroying supplies. Throughout the day, soldiers skirmished with a growing number of warriors from camps downstream who converged on the smoldering village. In late afternoon, Custer assembled his troops and withdrew, with fifty-three captives. Cavalry casualties included twenty-two men killed and thirteen wounded. Also, Indians murdered Clara Blinn, a white captive, and her young son during the attack. Precise Native losses are unknown. Some estimates placed the dead at nine to twenty men, including Black Kettle, and eighteen to forty women and children, while others suggest that as many as 103 were killed in total.

"Gathering up the dead," Wounded Knee, South Dakota

The Battle of the Washita emerged as the only significant engagement of the winter campaign of 1868–69. Frustrated by elusive Cheyenne and Arapaho warriors who raided the Central Plains frontier the previous summer, Gen. Philip H. Sheridan had organized the expedition to chastise the Indians. He also hoped a show of force would coerce the Cheyennes and Arapahos onto a reservation created for them by the 1867 Treaty of Medicine Lodge Creek. Custer's attack on Black Kettle's village, some of whose warriors participated in the summer raids, accomplished both of Sheridan's objectives. In 1997 the battlefield was designated a National Historic Site by the National Park Service.

See also NATIVE AMERICANS: Black Kettle.

William Corbett
Northeastern State University

Hoig, Stan. *The Battle of the Washita: The Sheridan-Custer Indian Campaign of 1867–1869.* Garden City NY: Doubleday and Co., 1976. Utley, Robert M. *Cavalier in Buckskin: George Armstrong Custer and the Western Military Frontier.* Norman: University of Oklahoma Press, 1988.

WORLD WAR II

At the beginning of World War II, American political leaders in the Great Plains went to Washington to lobby for location of war industries in the region. As early as December 1940, Gov. John Moses of North Dakota and the Greater North Dakota Association, a group of businessmen, presented plans for the establishment of industrial plants in their home state. Again, in March 1942, a North Dakota War Resources Committee went to the nation's capitol in search of war contracts. They met with little success. By 1945 North Dakota had received only $9 million of such contracts, out of a national total of $225 billion. This was less than any other state.

Still, Plains states did make significant contributions to the national war effort, especially in the production of crops, cattle, and oil. Plains states also profited from the expansion of federal military installations, training centers, and new airfields. Some urban areas fared particularly well. For example, Wichita, Kansas, became an important aircraft manufacturing city. There, the Stearman Aircraft Company received military orders for more than 7,000 trainers, and when the Boeing Aircraft Corporation of Seattle expanded its production of B-29s, it made Wichita, with its secure interior location, a primary facility. Employment at the Boeing plant rose from 2,500 in 1941 to 27,000 in 1945, and 1,644 B-29s were produced, more than at any other plant. The plant closed at the end of the war but was later reopened.

Kansas also secured aircraft modification centers. By the time a plane was off the production lines, the demands of combat often required substantial changes. In March 1942 the War Department pressured Boeing to modify 200 B-24 trainer planes for immediate combat duty in the Pacific. Time was of the essence in providing the craft with heavier armaments. Company officials lined up the planes on four Kansas airstrips freshly made from farmland. Six thousand Boeing workers labored night and day, braving blizzards, to modify these planes to military specifications.

The war affected the Great Plains in Canada more than in the United States. At the beginning of the conflict, political leaders in Manitoba, Alberta, and Saskatchewan complained that they were being left out of the mobilization program. The government in Ottawa addressed these concerns after 1941. Winnipeg, Manitoba, received orders for aircraft parts, and the General Motors plant in Regina, Saskatchewan, converted to manufacturing explosives. Regina, along with Winnipeg and Calgary, Alberta, was also a major site for the British Commonwealth Air Training Plan, which trained aviators and repaired and overhauled aircraft engines. Calgary became an important refining center, especially for high-octane aviation gasoline. The Prairie Provinces also became sites for German and Italian prisoner-of-war camps. As in the U.S. Plains states, the Prairie Provinces' population as a whole did not increase, but urban populations did. Winnipeg, Edmonton, and Calgary boomed, as Canadians from rural areas and smaller cities moved to centers of war production. Canadian farmers prospered as they had not done for more than a decade, and mechanization increased the efficiency of agriculture.

In both countries, therefore, the war accelerated existing trends, such as the decline of rural population and of the number of farms. It encouraged the movement of younger men and women into industrial or service occupations in towns and cities within the Great Plains and elsewhere. In both Canada and the United States, the government programs paid veterans to enroll in vocational programs and universities. In sharp contrast to the Great Depression, World War II invigorated the economy of the Great Plains and provided considerable opportunities for its residents.

See also CITIES AND TOWNS: Wichita, Kansas.

Gerald D. Nash
University of New Mexico

Bothwell, Robert, Ian Drummond, and John English. *Canada, 1900–1945.* Toronto: University of Toronto Press, 1987. Nash, Gerald D. *World War II and the West: Reshaping the Economy.* Lincoln: University of Nebraska Press, 1990.

WOUNDED KNEE MASSACRE

On December 29, 1890, on Wounded Knee Creek in southwestern South Dakota, a tangle of events resulted in the deaths of more than 250, and possibly as many as 300, Native Americans. These people were guilty of no crime and were not engaged in combat. A substantial number were women and children. Most of the victims were members of the Miniconjou band of the Lakota Sioux who had been intercepted by military forces after they fled their reservation in South Dakota for refuge in the Badlands.

The story begins in October 1890, when Daniel F. Royer arrived at Pine Ridge Agency, home of the Oglala Lakotas, to assume responsibility as agent. His selection as agent could not have been worse: he knew nothing about Native Americans and was irrationally fearful of them, and from the time of his arrival the dispatches he sent back to Washington were peppered with warnings of an outbreak similar to the one in Minnesota in 1862 in which hundreds of settlers were killed by Santee Sioux. Royer's appointment was also ill timed. In 1890 drought replaced the bountiful rainfall of the 1880s, resulting in crop failures and economic depression. On their reservations, Native Americans were forced into dependence on the federal government for food and clothing. When Royer took over as agent, there was widespread anxiety among the Oglalas regarding the adequacy of government provisions.

A year earlier, the Ghost Dance had appeared on the Pine Ridge Reservation. Born from the vision of a Paiute named Wovoka (aka Jack Wilson), the Ghost Dance blended the messianic account of Christianity with traditional Native beliefs. This new religion told of the return of the Messiah to relieve the suffering of Native Americans and promised that if they would live righteous lives and perform the Ghost Dance in the prescribed manner, the European American invaders would vanish,

the bison would return, and the living and the dead would be reunited in an Edenic world. But in Royer's paranoid mind the Ghost Dance was a war dance that threatened imminent bloodshed. His dispatches to Washington urged that troops be sent to protect citizens from war.

In mid-November 1890 President Benjamin Harrison responded to the fears of an Indian outbreak by ordering troops into the area. Regular troops were sent from Fort Robinson, Nebraska, and on November 18, 1890, the Second Nebraska Infantry left Fort Omaha in two special trains. On the train was also a cadre of newspaper reporters. From that point on, the crisis at Pine Ridge was a significant news item in newspapers across the country and around the world.

The trains unloaded their travelers at Rushville, Nebraska, on November 20, 1890, and from there the troops and reporters made their way to Pine Ridge Agency, where they all soon discovered that there was no crisis to be found. Soon a regular fare of rumors and lies began to appear in the national press, fed by merchants who wanted to keep the reporters, and their expense accounts, engaged in the economically strained communities south of the Pine Ridge Reservation. These fantastic stories fed a growing national anxiety about impending war. They also appeared on the reservations, where Lakotas who had been educated in the nation's Indian schools read the reports of troop activities and the rumors of outbreak to other members of their community. In this manner, the press became an important factor in stoking the anxiety both on and off the reservation.

By mid-December 1890 the combination of news reports, governmental reports (particularly those of the panic-stricken Royer), and Ghost Dancing had every nerve in the region on edge. The Lakotas polarized into political camps commonly referred to in the press as "hostiles" and "friendlies," a distinction between those who were opposed and those who were reconciled to reservation life. The Ghost Dancers were generally assigned to the "hostiles" camp. On December 15, 1890, the Hunkpapa holy man and Ghost Dance leader, Sitting Bull, was killed at Standing Rock Agency. Sitting Bull's death was seen by many as the fate that awaited all who failed to accept reservation life. To the south, at Cheyenne River Agency, the Miniconjou Lakotas grew nervous. Their leader, Big Foot, was also engaged in the Ghost Dance, and though not considered a major threat, he was under close observation by the military. In an attempt to quiet the Miniconjous, the military asked a local squatter named John Dunn to persuade them to acquiesce to the military's wishes that they stay in their own village on the reservation. Dunn's tactics are inexplicable: he is reported to have told the Miniconjous that the military planned to take their men prisoner and deport them to an island in the Atlantic Ocean. He apparently advised them to take sanctuary on Pine Ridge Reservation.

On December 23, the Miniconjous left their

village in the dead of night and fled south toward the Badlands. Big Foot soon contracted pneumonia, which slowed the escape. Nonetheless, the tribe managed to avoid the military pursuit for five days. But on December 28, the Seventh Cavalry intercepted the ailing Big Foot and his people and ordered them into confinement on Wounded Knee Creek. On the morning of December 29, Col. James W. Forsyth convened a council with the Miniconjous. He demanded that they surrender all their firearms and told them that they would be relocated to a new camp. The order to a new camp was interpreted by the Miniconjous as exile, probably to Indian Territory, a prospect that they found intolerable.

While these discussions proceeded in the Lakota camp, a number of Indians began singing Ghost Dance songs, with some rising to throw handfuls of dirt in the air. The troops who surrounded them perceived the singing and dirt throwing as signals to attack, and at this tense moment the fuse was lit. A man named Black Coyote (sometimes called Black Fox) refused to surrender his rifle to a soldier. The two began wrestling over the gun, and in the struggle it discharged. Immediately the nervous troops began firing, while the Miniconjous retrieved their weapons and returned fire. The military's rifle fire was complemented with cannon rounds from Hotchkiss guns, whose accuracy and exploding shells were formidable. The outnumbered and outgunned Lakotas fled, and for several hours intermittent gunfire continued, with the military in pursuit. Bodies were found as far away as three miles from the camp. Firing ceased, and by midafternoon the troops had gathered up their dead and wounded, as well as Lakota wounded, and returned to Pine Ridge Agency. The fear of a reprisal attack kept troops and civilians entrenched at the agency until January 3, 1891, when a military-escorted civilian burial party proceeded to the site of the massacre. There they buried 146 Lakotas in a single mass grave. Other dead were accounted for later, bringing the total to more than 250 Lakotas; the Seventh Cavalry lost twenty-five men.

Photographers accompanied the burial detail and made a total of sixteen photographs. A snowstorm that occurred shortly after the massacre added a cold and grim edge to the scene of carnage. The photographs sold well and, together with news stories, carried the story of the massacre at Wounded Knee worldwide. Soon the event developed a meaning that transcended the reality of the tragic loss of life, and Wounded Knee became, and remains, the symbol of the inhumanity of U.S. government policy toward Native Americans.

See also NATIVE AMERICANS: Sitting Bull / RELIGION: Ghost Dance.

John E. Carter
Nebraska State Historical Society

Jensen, Richard E., R. Eli Paul, and John E. Carter. *Eyewitness at Wounded Knee.* Lincoln: University of Nebraska Press, 1991. Mooney, James. *The Ghost-Dance Religion and the Sioux Outbreak of 1890.* Fourteenth Annual Report of the Bureau of Ethnology, Smithsonian Institution. Washington DC: Government Printing Office, 1896. Utley, Robert. *The Last Days of the Sioux Nation.* New Haven CT: Yale University Press, 1963.

Water

Flooding in Grand Forks, North Dakota, and East Grand Forks, Minnesota, 1997

People have always struggled to adapt their water uses to the windswept, periodically dry Great Plains. This simple fact has remained true for Native Americans, Europeans, and Americans. Cultural values determine how people view water, and consequently how they use and develop it. Native Americans on the Plains stressed the spiritual and communal aspects of water. European Americans, on the other hand, conceived of water mainly in terms of economic development, with the result being an escalating manipulation of the water resources of the Great Plains. First surface irrigation, then dam building, and, most recently, extensive groundwater pumping have furnished the key resource for agriculture and towns, but these processes have also altered the ecosystems of the region to such an extent that environmentalists have sounded alarms. Ultimately, the success or failure of human societies on the Plains has always depended upon how well each developed a sustainable form of water use.

Great Plains Hydraulics

The sources of most major rivers in the Great Plains are in the Rocky Mountains. In the Prairie Provinces, the South and North Saskatchewan, Red Deer, Bow, and Frenchman Rivers flow generally northeastward from the mountains. On the Northern Great Plains the Missouri and its major tributaries, the Milk and Yellowstone Rivers, flow, respectively, on easterly, southeasterly, and northeasterly courses from the Rockies. The Assiniboine, Qu'Appelle, and Souris Rivers are the main exceptions to the hydrogeography in that they rise within the Prairie Provinces.

Farther south, the North and South Platte and Arkansas Rivers rise toward the Rocky Mountains of Colorado before taking their gentle descent eastward. These rivers, and irrigation dependent upon them, benefit from the melt of snowpack in the mountains that sends water to the Central Plains when it is needed most, during the growing season. Farther south again, the Canadian River has its source in the Sangre de Cristo Range, then flows south along its eastern slope before crossing the High Plains of Texas into Oklahoma. The Pecos River folds around the southern edge of the same range, then cuts a trench southward to join the Rio Grande. In Texas the Brazos and Colorado Rivers gather force on the Llano Estacado before following courses to the Gulf of Mexico.

Underlying approximately 174,000 square miles of the Central and Southern Great Plains is a precious resource, the Ogallala (or High Plains) Aquifer. Today this underwater reservoir, "fossil" water that is the remnant of ancient glacial melts, contains more than 3.25 billion acre-feet of drainable water that is tapped by about 200,000 irrigation wells. The aquifer is thickest and most extensive in Nebraska. In its southern reaches, in southwest Kansas and the Texas Panhandle, excessive pumping has exceeded rates of recharge and lowered levels by more than 200 feet.

Precipitation accounts for surface flows and a significant amount of groundwater recharge. Rainfall and snowfall generally increase from west to east from around fourteen inches annually near the Front Range to more than twenty inches by the 100th meridian, and more than forty inches in southeastern Kansas as the rain shadow of the Rocky Mountains is left behind. Variability of rainfall is great everywhere, with extended periods without rain each year and a longer, more widespread drought occurring every twenty years or so. The drought hazard is greatest in winter. Moisture availability for plants is also hampered by the torrential nature of rainfall and its rapid runoff. It is not uncommon for as much as one-quarter of the annual precipitation to be delivered locally in a single storm.

Evaporation and temperature also influence people's adaptations to their hydraulic environments. Evaporation rates, which during the growing season vary from thirty-six inches in the northern reaches of the Plains to more than fifty inches in the Southern Plains, help produce a relatively similar vegetation in both areas despite variance in precipitation. But temperature differences mean shorter growing seasons from south to north. The Southern Plains have an average of more than 200 frost-free days, whereas the Northern Plains often have fewer than 100.

These climatic differences from north to south and west to east have many repercussions for water development. The paucity of reliable streams in the south hindered irrigation until the invention of center pivots that tap the Ogallala Aquifer. The Central Plains proved most conducive to water development because of the favorable combination of water availability (from both surface and groundwater sources) and relatively lengthy growing season.

Native American Use and Spanish Influences

Long before European Americans built their hydraulic society in the Great Plains, Native Americans understood the crucial importance of the limited and variable water resources in the region. The water uses of Plains Indians were founded upon deep spiritual beliefs, but they were also adaptations to variations in precipitation. The ancestors of the historic Pawnees, for example, moved their villages westward along the stream courses of the Solomon and Republican Rivers during times of increased rainfall, and when precipitation levels fell they removed eastward toward the Missouri River. According to Pawnee Indian cosmology, water formed the fourth creation, preceded by the earth, life, and timbers, and followed by cultivated seeds and people. To the Pawnees, failure of rains and stream flows implied broken bonds in the reciprocal relationship between people and water. The Pawnees gave respect to water to maintain the agriculture that was so important in the annual cycle of their lives.

Water was equally important in terms of the bison hunt. Twice a year the Pawnees conducted the Great Cleansing Ceremony before leaving on their hunts. Sacred objects of Pawnee Indian cosmology were taken to the river near their villages and symbolically washed. Afterward the villagers cleaned their dwellings and the streets, then themselves. The priests had a sweat lodge constructed for them, then called all the people to race to the river. The priests followed, entered the stream, and then returned to their sweat lodge for a steam bath. Then the remaining villagers leaped into the stream, bathing and playing in the water, so all were cleansed for the hunt.

Horse-mounted bison hunters like the Arapahos, Blackfeet, Cheyennes, Comanches, Kiowas, and Sioux also gave great consideration to the water resources of the Great Plains. They often made their winter camps and sheltered their vast horse herds in riparian ecosystems where timber and grass, as well as water, were available. The small ponds and springs scattered throughout the Plains were also essential resources, places to camp or to water horses on long journeys. Historically, on the High Plains there were few areas more than fifteen miles from a spring. During dry spells many of these ponds evaporated. Rivers and streams became sandy beds or flowed intermittently. Such times exacted terrible tolls on both people and their animal herds.

When the Spanish colonized the Southwest, beginning in 1598, they practiced a communal form of irrigation by combining their own with Pueblo Indian practices. All people shared in the governance and maintenance of the *acequia madre*, the mother canal, which the community owned in common. Hispanics were still practicing this form of irrigation at the site of present-day Pueblo, Colorado, during the 1840s and early 1850s.

As a result of the Spanish and Pueblo influences, Plains Indians attempted irrigation practices in the region before 1700. In 1637, Taos Indians rose up against the Spanish, then fled eastward into the Great Plains. There they found support among the Plains Apaches, and together they built a small pueblo with irrigation works at a spring in western Kansas, near the present-day town of Scott City. The Spanish called the place *El Curatelejo*, or distant quarter. After the Pueblo Revolt of 1680, more refugees joined the people at El Curatelejo, but an expedition by Juan de Ulibarri forced them back to New Mexico in 1706. The Plains Apaches tried to retain the village and the practice of irrigated agriculture, but eventually Comanches forced them to abandon it sometime after 1750.

Irrigated agriculture was connected to the Spanish attempt to control the Comanches, and later to the U.S. attempt to change the Southern Cheyennes and Arapahos into sedentary farmers. In the summer of 1787, the Spanish tried to convince Comanches under the leadership of Paruanarimuco to relinquish bison hunting and embrace irrigated agriculture. The Spanish located a village site where the San Carlos (Saint Charles) River emptied into the *Rio de Napestle* (today called the Arkansas River) and began constructing housing and irrigation works, tilling land, and planting crops while simultaneously instructing the Comanches in agricultural practices. By January 1788, under the supervision of master craftsman Manuel Segura, the *Jupe* band of Comanches occupied their new homes. But Parunarimuco's wife died that same month, and in accordance to Jupe custom, the Comanches abandoned the site. Governor Fernando de la Concha briefly considered having the pueblo colonized by New Mexicans but decided that the expense of protecting the village would be too costly. So ended the first, and only, attempt of the Spanish to convert Plains Indian peoples to irrigation.

Hispanic water practices contributed to the development of Mormon communal irrigation systems. Beginning in 1846, a group of Mormon emigrants observed Hispanic agriculture around present-day Pueblo, Colorado, where they learned to integrate their utopian values with communal irrigation practices. The Mormons moved to Salt Lake City two years later and most likely introduced cooperative irrigation in the "Wasatch Oasis."

Hispanic community irrigation also influenced Native Americans in the Plains in the two decades before the American Civil War. Traders and Native Americans in the Central and Southern Great Plains recognized the depletion of game animals. Yellow Wolf, a Southern Cheyenne, sought an economic alternative to the fur trade and, with the aid of the Indian agents in the Upper Arkansas Agency, petitioned the U.S. government to build an irrigation colony for the Southern Cheyennes and Arapahos who wanted to farm. Provisions for building an irrigation system and support facilities were part of the Fort Wise Treaty of 1861. Little came of this project, however, as the Civil War diverted federal resources away from the initial work near Fort Lyon in southeastern Colorado. By 1864, the Bureau of Indian Affairs had enough of the project operational to grow a small corn crop. But in the early fall of that year, Southern Arapahos, outraged by ill treatment by the United States, raided the works, stole the stock, and killed some of the bureau's employees. The experiment came apart in the aftermath of the Sand Creek Massacre in November 1864. Later the abandoned system became the foundation of an irrigation system for European American settlers.

Conceptions of Water
Soon after the creation of Colorado Territory in 1859, Coloradans began establishing an elaborate system of water law and regulation. Although some did attempt to create communal irrigation works, they treated water differently than the Spanish, Mormons, and Plains Indians. The United States used law to transform water into a marketable commodity to serve the needs of an economic system based on individual opportunity and gain. The aggressive attitude toward water, and toward environment in general, made possible the resettlement of the Great Plains by Europeans and Americans, but it also resulted in escalating pressures on ecosystems.

When prospectors flocked to the goldfields of Colorado in the early 1860s, they created a demand for agricultural products. Some miners left the hard rock of the mountains for the soft soils of the river valleys in the Colorado Piedmont, where they flourished by supplying food to the miners and ranchers. David Hall and William Brantner developed small, but highly successful, irrigation systems on the South Platte River. Others, like George Washington Swink, constructed lucrative irrigation systems along the Arkansas River, supplying ranchers in the Central Great Plains. Horace Greeley, the famous editor of the *New York Tribune*, eschewed market-oriented irrigation and tried to perfect utopian, communal irrigation at Union Colony in the city that bore his name, Greeley, Colorado. But even the utopians of Greeley soon set aside their agenda of social reform for an emphasis on market agriculture.

As irrigation systems multiplied, draining watercourses on the western edge of the Plains, the need arose for water diversion regulatory laws. It also became apparent that the traditional, common-law-based doctrine of riparian rights, which formed the foundation of water laws in the eastern United States, was an inadequate method for allocating water resources in the semiarid Great Plains. According to this doctrine, water rights were restricted to people who owned land along watercourses. In addition, all riparian owners were entitled to receive an equal amount of water flow. These principles caused numerous problems when applied in the Great Plains. The restriction of the use of water to riparian lands hampered the development of agriculture in areas that were not adjacent to rivers or streams. Even riparian owners themselves could not use the water for intensive irrigation because they were not allowed to diminish the downstream flow of water. Finally, by giving all riparian owners equal claims to the water resources, the doctrine made it impossible to allocate water on the basis of priority needs during droughts, which frequently plagued the Plains.

A solution to these problems was provided by the prior appropriation system of water rights, which many historians argue originated in the California goldfields. The miners created codes to protect the rights of any person who first developed a "beneficial" water use, known otherwise as "first in time, first in right." A miner had a right only to the water that he could use in his operations and, as the first to develop his right, could divert this amount of water before anyone else along the watercourse.

Coloradans developed the first system of prior appropriation in the Great Plains. Colorado lawmakers may have incorporated some elements of Hispanic traditions in defining water as a public, rather than a private, resource. However, they relied to a great extent upon a commodity notion of water rights in defining "beneficial use" solely in terms of domestic, agricultural, and industrial applications. Moreover, prior appropriation encour-

aged the rapid economic development of stream flows by giving people priority to divert water in the chronological order in which each perfected his or her right. Anyone who waited too long to acquire a water right may have received little, if any, actual water because of the priority given to people with earlier dated rights.

The Colorado Doctrine of water rights relied upon the courts to determine individual rights. A person petitioned the state courts for a right, and the judge granted and recorded the right once he or she had presented the appropriate documentation. In 1881 the state legislature created a state engineer's office to regulate water rights. The office was also responsible for dam and irrigation system safety. Locating the origin of rights within the courts, and the regulatory duties in the state engineer's office, made water conflicts in Colorado a highly litigated realm and underwrote a flourishing cadre of water lawyers.

A more centralized system of water doctrine and management developed in Wyoming. Elwood Mead, a civil engineer who was guided by an ethic of conservation stressing the scientific management of natural resources, formulated a more centralized notion of water regulation than that of Colorado. The Wyoming legislature implemented his plans, which called for a state engineer's office that not only regulated the operation of a prior appropriation system of water rights, but also granted all water rights applications in the state. In Wyoming the whole focus of water regulation fell upon the state engineer's office, whereas in Colorado the state engineer's office and the state courts shared the responsibility. In time, the other Great Plains states adopted some form of the prior appropriation system and the creation of an engineer's office along either the Wyoming or Colorado lines, both of which established the legal basis for putting water to economic use.

In the Canadian Prairie Provinces ownership and regulation of water resources (and other resources, such as land) was, and is, derived from British Common Law. In practice this meant that the federal government had authority to use or alienate water resources in the three Prairie Provinces until 1930 when such rights passed to the provincial governments.

The Irrigation Crusade
As irrigation promoters planned their works, they had to move quickly to perfect their water rights. Many promoters envisioned grand irrigation systems crisscrossing the Great Plains. In 1872 William Jackson Palmer dreamed of an irrigation system beginning near Pueblo, Colorado, and terminating somewhere well within western Kansas. In 1873 President Ulysses S. Grant delivered a speech in Denver outlining an extraordinary plan for building a canal from where the South Platte River exits the Rocky Mountains eastward hundreds of miles to a juncture with the Missouri River. In 1889 Willis R. Bierly, a North Dakota newspaper editor, advocated constructing a 230-mile canal from Fort Stevenson on the upper Mis-

souri River to Grand Forks, and from there to Upper Red Lake in Minnesota, then south to Grand Rapids, and eventually emptying into Lake Superior near Duluth. None of these plans materialized.

Others with similar grandiose schemes launched projects designed to transform the shortgrass prairie into a garden. Promoters felt a sense of urgency because they needed to perfect viable water rights for their systems, and this meant laying claim to a flow of water for beneficial uses before anyone else. Failing in this meant the ruin of many projects, as western water courses became "over-appropriated," meaning that people had attached more rights to a stream than its flow could accommodate. Among the notable promoters between 1870 and 1900 were Theodore C. Henry in Colorado, Joseph M. Carey in Wyoming, Asa Soule in Kansas, W. R. Akers in Nebraska, the lawman Pat Garrett in New Mexico, and S. B. Robbins in Montana.

One plainsman in particular achieved notoriety for promoting irrigation as a solution for social and economic problems. William Ellsworth Smythe, from Worcester, Massachusetts, heeded Horace Greeley's call for young people to head west. Trained as a newspaperman, Smythe became the editor of *The Enterprise* in Kearney, Nebraska. He noted how farm families were broken during the droughts that prevailed on the Plains in the early 1890s. He toured New Mexico and observed how Hispanic community-based irrigation systems provided successful crops regardless of the dry climate. When he returned to Nebraska he organized a convention to advertise the virtues of irrigation, and later he took his mission throughout the West. He convened a national forum on irrigation in Salt Lake City in 1891, bringing delegates from all the western states and territories. The attendees returned to their homes full of enthusiasm for irrigation. Also in 1891, Smythe began publishing *Irrigation Age*, a journal dedicated to trumpeting the benefits of irrigation throughout the West. The "republic of irrigation," Smythe pronounced, was at hand.

Infected with irrigation fever, several irrigation promoters rushed into poorly conceived ventures, overestimated water users' needs, and recklessly invested their own and others' funds. T. C. Henry's massive irrigation system in southeast Colorado failed to provide water for the 100,000 acres it was supposed to serve. By the early 1890s the farmers of the La Junta and Lamar Irrigation Company, Henry's enterprise, were in desperate straits. In populistic zeal they turned to the courts of Colorado, where they found a sympathetic forum. By 1896 they had wrestled control of the system away from Henry and collectively acquired possession of the system and the right to govern it according to their mutual self-interest.

Asa Soule, a New York–born traveling salesman, failed even faster than Henry. He underwrote the building of the 100-mile-long Eureka Ditch, constructed in 1884 near Dodge City, Kansas. Soule invested more than $750,000 of his own money, but the system never succeeded in delivering enough water to the farmers tapping the main canal. In just a couple of years Soule, his investors, and irrigators had lost their fortunes on the shortgrass prairies of southwest Kansas. No one ever attempted to revitalize Soule's dream, and only the grass-covered canal banks mark his failed dream of transforming the semiarid grasslands into lush, water-intensive croplands.

Enter the Government

Spectacular failures like those of T. C. Henry and Asa Soule along with the high costs involved in launching irrigation systems ushered the federal government into the irrigation business. The Carey Act of 1894 was the first of a series of federal laws that regulated Plains irrigation practices. Joseph M. Carey, a senator from Wyoming, together with notable investors like Francis E. Warren, a powerful state politician, organized the Wyoming Development Company. In 1883 the company began constructing a system that eventually irrigated about 60,000 acres near Wheatland in southeastern Wyoming. The company completed more than 100 miles of the main canal by 1885, but farmers, recognizing the company's lack of title to the public land, refused to invest. The Carey Act, unsurprisingly, addressed the needs of the Wyoming Development Company very well by allowing the state to select one million acres for reclamation and to receive patents to the land once irrigators were making use of it. The sale of the land to the irrigators either repaid the state or a private company for building the irrigation works, and any remainder returned to the state treasury for the purchase of other reclamation lands. In the case of Wyoming, the state held the land patents in trust for the Wyoming Development Company, and the company received compensation for its construction costs through the land sales and for maintenance through water delivery charges. The act, however, had little effect beyond the borders of Wyoming.

John Wesley Powell, director of the U.S. Geological Survey (USGS), was determined to bring greater federal control and planning to the development of irrigation in the West, including the Great Plains. In 1878, Powell published his famous *Report on the Lands of the Arid Region of the United States* in which he proposed a radically changed federal land policy that called for regional planning around river basins. Under Powell's plan, farmers would acquire 80 acres designated for irrigation, ranchers 2,560 would get acres for their stock, and regulated timber companies could harvest the watershed forests. In 1888 Congress provided Powell with funding to survey public lands and assess their suitability for irrigation. State engineers, state politicians, and business people feared that this centralized mapping and planning would eliminate any lucrative possibilities for local developers. Senator Carey from Wyoming and E. S. Nettleton, a former state engineer of Colorado and an employee in the USGS, worked with Elwood Mead to undermine Powell's political support in Congress. Their unwillingness to embrace Powell's notions of ecological planning, which included criticism of the prior appropriation system, led to Powell's downfall. The end of Powell's survey, however, did not mark the end of government aid to irrigation on the Plains; rather it presaged further governmental support after the creation of the Reclamation Service.

In 1902 Congress passed the Reclamation Act to subsidize irrigation in the West and to build new projects. Renamed the Bureau of Reclamation in 1927, the service bolstered and expanded water developments such as the Elephant Butte project on the Rio Grande south of Albuquerque, New Mexico. The bureau, however, had little effect on High Plains irrigation before 1940. The region lacked the grand dam sites like those in the steep-walled canyons of the West, and by the twentieth century little suitable public land remained in the Plains for the federal government to develop.

The bureau did attempt one innovative irrigation project: a pump irrigation system near Garden City, Kansas. J. W. Gregory, an influential participant in Smythe's irrigation crusade and the editor of a Garden City newspaper, spearheaded a campaign to secure governmental support for a pumping project. Charles S. Slichter's survey of the groundwater resources in the vicinity of Garden City enabled the realization of Gregory's aspirations. Irrigators formed the Finney County Water User's Association in order to contract for water from the service. By 1905 all of the paperwork, studies, and organization had been completed, and the bureau was ready to build.

The bureau anticipated having the pumps ready for the 1908 growing season, but the only result was conflict with local irrigators over the operation of the system. The farmers of the association received little benefit from the project because the pump machinery broke down and the government's ditches leaked. Moreover, in 1909 the Arkansas River was so full that farmers refused to contract for any pump water from the bureau. This resulted in a protest from Frederick Newell, director of the project, who accused farmers of reneging on their repayment pledges to the bureau. In 1910 an angry Newell wrote off the whole pumping experiment as a failure, and the federal government never again ventured into pump irrigation projects.

In the early twentieth century, the federal courts and the growth of the sugar beet industry did more to regulate irrigation on the Plains than the Bureau of Reclamation. The U.S. Supreme Court established the most important national precedents regulating interstate water rights and federal rights to water. Two cases stand out: *Kansas v. Colorado* (1907), which established the doctrine of equity; and *Winters v. United States* (1908), which defined reserved rights.

Kansas v. Colorado stemmed from the artificial division of the Arkansas River by the Kansas-Colorado state line. This boundary inhibited the development of a cooperative approach in using the resources of the river basin as advocated by John Wesley Powell in his *Report on the Lands of the Arid Region of the United States* of 1879. Instead, Kansans and Coloradans on each side of the state line worked hard to put the flow of the river to economic use without regard for the needs and plans of the other. Coloradans, of course, had the advantage because of their upstream position. As early as the 1890s, Kansans, including the irrepressible irrigation promoter Charles "Buffalo" Jones, noted dwindling flows as diversions proliferated in Colorado. Jones was unable to finance interstate litigation before the Supreme Court to remedy the situation. Marshall Murdock, a powerful newspaper editor from Wichita, Kansas, possessed the political clout that Jones lacked, and he persuaded the Kansas legislature to support a case of original jurisdiction in the Supreme Court against Colorado. Kansas attorneys filed their opening briefs in May 1901, initiating the largest interstate suit to have ever reached the Court. In May 1907 Justice David Brewer, a native Kansan, wrote the Court's opinion, later known as the "doctrine of equity." Brewer had tallied economic gains made throughout the Arkansas River valley and noted how the economies in both states had steadily grown regardless of the decreasing river flows into Kansas. Consequently, he ruled that Kansans had not made a case for restraining Colorado's water uses. Kansans, Justice Brewer noted, would have a case only when they could connect economic distress with decreasing river flows. From this time on, the doctrine of equity, the weighing of relative economic gains made through the use of water, governed nearly all interstate water suits.

The court took a completely different tack in deciding how to protect Native American water rights. In the case *Winters v. United States*, known also as the Winters Doctrine, Justice McKenna defined "reserved rights." The case was a result of the Bureau of Indian Affairs's effort to develop farming on the Fort Belknap Reservation in northern Montana. Non-Native farmers built irrigation works along the Milk River, and by 1905 Native American farmers on the Fort Belknap Reservation had little flow to divert for their own lands. The U.S. Attorney General's office came to their aid and won the suit in both district and appeals courts. The Supreme Court upheld the Native Americans's "reserved" rights, those rights inherent in the creation of a reservation. Secondly, the Court's decision preserved Native American water rights even if unused, and it allowed for an unquantified amount of Indian water so long as the flows were used to pursue economic goals on the reservation. Ever since, the Winters Doctrine has guided Supreme Court decisions relating to Native American water rights.

Even more than Supreme Court decisions, sugar beets gave stability to the irrigation economy in the Great Plains. In 1890 Henry Oxnard, a Bostonian who had learned sugar cane refining in the South, but later turned to beet refining, built a large refining factory at Grand Island, Nebraska. Soon after, he built another at Norfolk, Nebraska. His American Crystal Sugar Company became a dominant economic enterprise on the Central Great Plains. In 1900 he built the Rocky Ford factory, and in 1907 the Las Animas factory, in the Arkansas River valley of Colorado. Other sugar beet companies, like the Holly Sugar Company of eastern Colorado and the United States Sugar and Land Company near Garden City, Kansas, offered Oxnard all the competition he could handle. By the 1950s, however, the beet economy had fallen on hard times, and most of the factories stood idle. Nonetheless, sugar beet growing, which requires irrigation, anchored a regional farm economy before advances in pump irrigation made other crops economically feasible.

Irrigation in the Great Plains received an additional boost during the 1930s. When the Great Depression struck, the federal government responded with water projects for the farm economy. The states needed bureaus that could coordinate state water planning with these federal relief projects. In 1936 Montanans were the first to create such a board, the Montana Water Conservation Board, with wide powers to coordinate state planning with the largess of the federal government. Soon after, other Great Plains states followed suit with the creation of their own water boards. A professional class of water lawyers serving private irrigation companies, and hydraulic engineers serving both as consultants and bureaucrats, grew alongside these state agencies, and together they guided a complex and highly fractionalized hydraulic society. Water lawyers such as Judge Watson McHendrie and engineers such as Steven Reynolds, Michael Creed Hinderlider, and George Knapp became regional household names. Even though water development in the Great Plains has been a male-dominated enterprise, women have also made their marks. During the 1930s and 1940s, Vena Pointer worked as an effective water lawyer in the Arkansas River valley of Colorado, and at the time of this writing Anne Bleed serves as the chief hydrologist for the state of Nebraska.

A new development involved the allocation of water resources through the writing of interstate compacts and international treaties. Frederick Newell first proposed compacts while giving testimony during *Kansas v. Colorado*, and Delph Carpenter, a capable and shrewd water lawyer from Colorado, developed the idea. Through these means the hydrologists, engineers, irrigators, and lawyers from the states involved devised the system to regulate interstate water flows to their mutual benefit. During the 1930s and 1940s negotiators concluded compacts on several Great Plains rivers including the Arkansas, Republican, and Canadian. The International Joint Commission, representing the United States, the western states, the Prairie Provinces, and the national government of Canada, negotiated treaties to develop the Milk River, which flows in and out of Montana and Alberta. Compacts and treaties worked simultaneously to promote economic individualism, to stabilize and augment the water supply to existing systems, and to develop new water projects. The Bureau of Reclamation contributed by building massive transmountain water diversion projects for the plains of eastern Colorado. Powerful irrigation interests around Greeley promoted the construction of the Big Thompson Transmountain Water Project. Coloradans in the Arkansas River valley massed enough political clout to have Congress underwrite the Frying Pan Transmountain Water Project. Both of these projects tap the alpine tributaries of the Colorado River and divert flows to the semiarid plains of Colorado rather than heading toward the Pacific.

The Pick-Sloan Plan

No one federal project, however, transformed the Great Plains hydraulics as much as the Pick-Sloan Plan. In 1927 the Mississippi River overflowed its banks and destroyed property from Minnesota to Louisiana. As a result, Congress authorized the Army Corps of Engineers to study flood control for its entire drainage basin. The corps's studies stretched to the upper reaches of the Missouri River, and, empowered by the Omnibus Flood Control Act of 1936, the corps began constructing a series of "flood control" projects throughout the Great Plains in the watersheds of the Missouri, Arkansas, Canadian, and Pecos Rivers among others. The corps initiated its building spree on the Missouri River with the Fort Peck Dam on the northern reaches of the plains of Montana. This project was completed in 1940. In 1943 the Missouri River flooded, and this gave additional impetus to the corps to "control the Missouri River." The corps leader, Col. Lewis Pick, emphasized flood control and paid little heed to irrigation.

The Bureau of Reclamation, fearful of being outdone by the corps, devised its own plans for the Missouri River. In his design, William G. Sloan, a bureau planner, paid particular attention to hydroelectric power production and irrigation. Congress had two contending plans from which to choose, but President Franklin Roosevelt settled the score by endorsing basinwide planning for the Missouri River premised on the Tennessee Valley Authority. Troubled that a regional agency could put them out of business, the bureau and the corps merged their designs and won over Congress by appealing to representatives and senators who disliked centralized planning on the lines of the TVA. Congress backed the Pick-Sloan Plan and began funding in earnest in the late 1940s.

Great Plains residents have expressed great ambivalence about the merits of the Pick-Sloan Plan. The Mandans, Arikaras, and Hidatsas who live on the Fort Berthold Reservation in North Dakota came to rue the day they ever heard of the Garrison Dam, one of the major dams on the mainstem of the Missouri River. The Pick-Sloan project flooded and destroyed their best grassland pastures and ruined their lucrative ranches. The final terms by which these tribes relinquished their lands denied them the right to fish in the reservoir, to water their cattle from it, or to graze their animals near it. "The members of the tribal council sign this contract with heavy hearts," said George Gillette, the tribal business council president, when he put his name on the bill in 1948. Canadians also vigorously protested the Garrison Dam. They claimed that the dam would introduce parasites and fish species from the Missouri into the streams feeding Lakes Winnipeg and Manitoba and consequently destroy the trout and pike fishing in those lakes.

In another case, environmentalists and farmers gathered to protest the bureau's plans for an irrigation project to tap the Oahe Reservoir on the Missouri in South Dakota. One reason that Senator George McGovern lost his bid for reelection in 1980 was because of his rigorous support of the project. The bureau has not attempted to build this system. In general, the bureau has trimmed its ambitious planning as cost overruns became all too common. For example, the bureau promised Montanans that 368,000 acres of irrigation would come their way, when, in actuality, Montana irrigators had only benefited from an additional 48,000 acres by 1987. Critics have even questioned the value of the Pick-Sloan Plan for flood protection. For example, hydrologists remain divided as to whether or not this mass of dams and reservoirs aggravated or ameliorated the effects of the floods of 1993. Whatever the case, the Missouri River has been so drastically altered by dams and the creation of large "prairie lakes" that it would be unrecognizable to Lewis and Clark.

Groundwater
Even more than the federal government's direct subsidy of surface irrigation, it was center pivots that made irrigated agriculture a paying proposition throughout the Great Plains. From the 1880s and 1890s, when hydrologists first began exploring the various levels of groundwater beneath the Plains, irrigators understood that with the right technology they could bring these waters to the surface. Windmills provided a start, but the feeble lift of the machines limited the ways in which farmers could use them. Irrigators could draw only from alluviums and shallow groundwater depths and supply only five acres with a single windmill. After World War II, efficient natural gas and gasoline-powered engines drove powerful pumps that could lift deep groundwater. Still, farmers found even this technology limiting in that they had to level their fields carefully for drainage, monitor siphons, and watch the progress of water flowing down furrows. In 1949 a Colorado tenant farmer, Frank Zybach, patented his center-pivot irrigation system in hopes of alleviating much of the handwork and costly field preparation associated with pump irrigation. These aluminum pipe megamachines mounted to A-frame towers riding on tandem wheels circle a center-post swivel where ground pipes tap the water that is drawn to the surface by pumps. A contemporary system can irrigate about 133 acres out of a 160-acre quarter section.

Center pivots made possible the extensive use of the Ogallala Aquifer. Essentially, the aquifer is the collection of Ice Age runoffs entombed by the accumulations of soil and sand. The total "drainable" aquifer holds enough water to fill Lake Huron, third largest of the Great Lakes. The saturated thickness of the aquifer varies, so that some irrigators have very deep sources beneath their land. Saturated thickness is an important indicator given the slow recharge of the aquifer. For example, some farmers around Lubbock, Texas, have completely pumped all of the water below their feet and have been obliged to return to dryland farming. By contrast, in the mid-1980s in Nebraska, where the saturated thickness of the aquifer is at its greatest, irrigators had used less than 1 percent of the water that was available in the aquifer prior to pumping. By one estimate at least, with 1980 pumping rates, center-pivot systems will be unable to supply 80 percent of the area presently irrigated through this system by the year 2020.

Great Plains irrigators and state legislatures have taken steps to regulate their use of the aquifer through laws and institutions. In 1927, for example, New Mexico became the first of the Great Plains states to bring groundwater (defined as a public rather than private resource) under state control; the state engineer regulates the depletion rates within declared groundwater basins. Elsewhere, management systems vary from state to state, but all the states from Nebraska to Texas that are fortunate enough to have this underground water endowment have institutions and regulations to manage its exploitation.

Irrigation in the Prairie Provinces
As in the American Great Plains, the first irrigation systems in the Prairie Provinces were developed by private individuals and local communities. The beginning of irrigation in the Prairie Provinces is often attributed to John Gleen, who, in 1879, began to irrigate his claim near Calgary. The first major irrigation systems were introduced to the region, in southwestern Alberta, by Mormon emigrants from Utah in the late nineteenth century. After the passage of the Northwest Irrigation Act in 1894, the federal government assumed a more active role in promoting irrigation projects. The central role of the federal government was made possible by the fact that it held jurisdiction over natural resources in the three Prairie Provinces until 1930; other Canadian provinces had received rights to their resources through the British North American Act of 1867 and several subsequent court decisions.

Lacking financial assets, the federal government at first used its extensive rights in the Prairie Provinces by giving huge land grants to the railway companies. The Canadian Pacific Railway, for example, was granted 25 million acres under its own charter in 1881 and acquired about 7 million additional acres from charters of other companies it took over. The rationale behind the policy was that the companies would promote settlement on their lands, and this in turn would result in increased use of their transportation facilities. Under their charters, in 1894 the Pacific Railway Company selected a huge area of land in southwestern Alberta with the intention of introducing irrigation. The plan involved a diversion of the Bow River near Calgary in order to irrigate an enormous, three-million-acre "irrigation block." Although the Bow River Irrigation Project never materialized in its entirety, in 1914 it resulted in the construction of the huge Bassano Dam, which made available a supply of water for the irrigation of nearly 247,000 acres and helped to create a new agricultural hinterland for Calgary.

Such subsidies exemplify the federal government's early, primarily indirect, attempts to promote irrigation in the Prairie Provinces. A period of more direct involvement began in the 1930s when the double disaster of economic recession and prolonged drought hit the Prairie Provinces. In 1935 as large numbers of people migrated from Alberta, Saskatchewan, and Manitoba to other parts of Canada, the federal government established the Prairie Farm Rehabilitation Administration (PFRA) to improve the farm economy and to arrange more efficient use of the limited water resources. At first, PFRA launched several small-scale emergency projects, including building of on-farm "dugouts" (shallow, rectangular excavations designed to hold water), small dams to conserve local runoff, and irrigation works for gardens and small fields. Later, PFRA also assisted in more extensive water projects such as construction of large reservoirs for water storage in the Milk, Red Deer, Bow, and South Saskatchewan River basins.

By far the most ambitious water projects in the Prairie Provinces have focused on river diversions and dam constructions. These large-scale, long-term projects have had at least a triple purpose: to create hydroelectrical power, to limit flood damages, and to increase irrigation acreage. Due to heavy capital costs, a policy was adopted in 1942 that encouraged cooperation between the federal and provincial governments in planning and construction. In general, the federal government has been responsible for the building of the main dams and reservoirs, while the provincial governments have undertaken the construction of distributive networks. Of the three Prairie Provinces, the most extensive cost-shared water projects have taken place in Alberta, which has, for example, Canada's largest irrigation project, the St. Mary River Irrigation District. Saskatchewan and Manitoba, which lack Alberta's advantageous location along the eastern slope of the Rocky Mountains, where snowmelt feeds numerous streams, have been involved with fewer and less ambitious water projects. Nevertheless, both provinces, together with the federal government, have launched several significant developments, the most notable of which are the Red River Floodway in Manitoba, which is aimed to prevent flooding in the Winnipeg area, and the multipurpose Gardiner Dam in Saskatchewan.

Thanks to the federal and provincial governments' extensive river diversion and dam construction projects, surface water has supplied most of the irrigation water in the Prairie Provinces. However, recent years have also witnessed a notable increase in the use of groundwater. Between 1973 and 1986, irrigation acreage in the Prairie Provinces increased from more than 620,000 acres to nearly 1.4 million acres. Center-pivot irrigation is now extensively developed, drawing from groundwater as well as canals, ditches, and reservoirs.

Environmentalism and Water

Conservation of groundwater does not address the serious and mounting problem of water pollution in the Great Plains. People throughout the region face growing levels of nitrates in their groundwater. This poses a special health threat to infants and children. Surface irrigation has also contributed to high levels of salinity in stream flows in the Southern Plains. Riparian soils, abundantly impregnated with salts, produce poor crops when converted to dryland farming. In fact, these soils will not even support the growth of former indigenous grasses like buffalo grass, blue grama, or short bluestem. Along the streams in the Southern Plains, salt cedar, a tree imported to the United States as an ornamental in the mid-1800s, flourishes in the salt-rich soils and has significantly altered former plant and animal communities. Almost 2,000 miles to the north, the St. Mary Dam in Alberta has destroyed the cottonwood riparian ecosystem below the dam. In other places, oil well drilling has created saltwater incursions into fresh groundwater supplies. Minimum or zero tillage, introduced to conserve moisture, has also increased pollution because chemicals are now used to control weeds that had previously been eliminated through the cultivation process. This situation poses a future threat to many urban water supplies. Pesticides such as atrazine are present at high levels in many stream courses as a result of modern farming practices.

Beginning in the 1970s, wetland and wildlife preservation added another aspect to debates swirling around the environmental effects of water use and development in the Great Plains. For example, according to a Kansas Geological Survey report in 1986, more than 600 miles of streams in the state rarely flowed. As streams dry up, wetlands rapidly disappear throughout the Great Plains. In 1980 Canadian environmentalists estimated that the Prairie Provinces had lost 40 to 70 percent of its wetlands. Consequently, farmers and environmentalists often find themselves embroiled in controversies over the preservation of these ecosystems. In one case the U.S. Fish and Wildlife Service has taken an active stance in working to preserve the Prairie Potholes, millions of depressions in glacial drift formed more than 12,000 years ago by retreating glaciers. These hollows, which cover large areas of Alberta, Saskatchewan, North Dakota, and South Dakota, hold precipitation and are important to migrating fowl. The formation of the Platte River Whooping Crane Maintenance Trust in 1979 represented concerns for the protection of wildlife

by maintaining the flow of the Platte River. In 1992, the Kansas chief engineer, David Pope, restricted pump irrigation in favor of the prior "recreational" water rights of Cheyenne Bottoms, a crucially important wetland along the Central Flyway. Environmentalists in Texas have become alarmed at the depletion of the Playa Lakes in the Panhandle. Questions of wildlife preservation are difficult to resolve as they call into question the historical practices and ideology of water development in the Great Plains.

The struggles over water uses have surely reflected the social and economic realities of the Great Plains. Undoubtedly, some Plains people have wrung fabulous riches from water development. Many others have persisted on the land because of advances in water use. However, water development has also created degraded river basins, giving rise to growing environmental demands for the preservation of free-flowing streams. Environmentalists, irrigation companies, urban planners, and Native Americans face great difficulties as they grapple with the consequences of a century of escalating water uses in the Great Plains. Critics doubt the viability of a legal system that accords water mainly as a commodity value subject to technological manipulation while aquifers and rivers disappear. They point to the erosion of not only an environment, but also of a quality of life as water continues to flow uphill to money in the Great Plains. Advocates, on the other hand, note the critical role irrigation has played in the economy of the region. While they may recognize some of the shortcomings of irrigation, they place great faith in water conservation through technological advances in sprinkler systems and in the development of new, less water-intensive crops. The future of water development in the Great Plains is unclear, but change is in the air.

See also AGRICULTURE: Sugar Beets; Prairie Farm Rehabilitation Administration / LAW: Brewer, David / NATIVE AMERICANS: Pawnees / PHYSICAL ENVIRONMENT: Climate.

James E. Sherow
Kansas State University

Clark, Ira G. *Water in New Mexico: A History of Its Management and Use.* Albuquerque: University of New Mexico Press, 1987. Dunbar, Robert G. *Forging New Rights in Western Waters.* Lincoln: University of Nebraska Press, 1983. Green, Donald. *Land of the Underground Rain: Irrigation on the Texas High Plains, 1910–1970.* Austin: University of Texas Press, 1973. Howard, Stanley W. *Green Fields of Montana: A Brief History of Irrigation.* Manhattan KS: Sunflower University Press, 1992. Kromm, David, and Stephen E. White, eds. *Groundwater Exploitation in the High Plains.* Lawrence: University Press of Kansas, 1992. Kuzelka, Robert, et al., eds. *Flat Water: A History of Nebraska and Its Water.* Lincoln NE: Conservation and Survey Division and Institute of Agriculture and Natural Resources, 1993. "North Dakota Water History: Politics and Dreams." *North Dakota History: Journal of the Northern Plains* 59 (1992). Opie, John. *Ogallala: Water for a Dry Land: A Historical Study in the Possibilities for American Sustainable Agriculture.* Lincoln: University of Nebraska Press, 1993. Reisner, Marc. *Cadillac Desert: The American West and Its Disappearing Water.* New York: Viking Penguin, 1986. Sherow, James E. *Watering the Valley: Development along the High Plains Arkansas River, 1870–1950.* Lawrence: University Press of Kansas, 1990. *The State of Canada's Environment.* Ottawa: Minister of the Environment, 1991. Tyler, Daniel. *The Last Water Hole in the West: The Colorado-Big Thompson and the Northern Colorado Water Conservancy District.* Niwot: University Press of Colorado, 1992.

APPROPRIATION DOCTRINE

The appropriation doctrine is a system of water rights that gives an individual the right to use a quantifiable amount of water. The appropriation doctrine is also referred to as prior appropriation because the right to use water is prioritized on the basis of the date the use was established. This characteristic is often summed up in the phrase "first in time, first in right." Under appropriation law, the first person to obtain an appropriation right receives the right to use a fixed amount of water without regard for other water users. In the case of a water shortage, the holder of the first prioritized right receives his or her entire amount to the possible exclusion of all others. Subsequent appropriative rights are filled based on the order of the dates of acquisition, until there is no more water available.

Traditionally there are three elements necessary to acquire an appropriative right: intent to use the water, a physical diversion of the water from the natural stream course, and an application of the water diverted to a beneficial use. Once acquired the right can be bought and sold. Water obtained under the appropriation doctrine can be used in a manner not consistent with the use existing at the time the right was acquired, so long as it is considered a "beneficial" use. An appropriative right is a usufructuary right, or right to use the water, as opposed to owning the water itself. There is no requirement that the water be applied to riparian land or even to land within the same watershed. Thus the appropriation doctrine promotes the consumptive use of water as a commodity, without regard to the location of the use or location of the source.

The rationale of the doctrine comes from personal property law theory. Traditionally, society is deemed enriched as individuals transform nature into usable economic commodities. For example, the law gave individuals incentives to capture wild animals or to mine gold by giving the person title to that which he or she had brought into possession. In like manner, water meandering through the Great Plains was captured by individuals and transformed into an economic commodity usable to settlers.

The appropriation doctrine originated in California as nineteenth-century miners looked for ways to augment the supply of water needed for mining operations. The doctrine first became law in the Great Plains in 1882 as a remedy for conflicts arising from agricultural water use in northeastern Colorado. Promoted by agricultural interests in the Great Plains, the appropriation doctrine was widely adopted as an alternative to riparian rights because of a common vision of future growth and a perception of water scarcity in the region. The doctrine promoted settlement because it allowed water to be detached and used in areas remote from the stream. Appropriation law rewarded those who had diverted water for use in a dry environment by giving them a secure right to a quantifiable amount of water upon which to base their operations. In North Dakota, South Dakota, Nebraska, and Kansas, appropriation is now the exclusive means of acquiring water rights, and in Oklahoma the conflicting doctrine of riparian rights is restricted to household and livestock uses.

Theron Josephson
Ferris State University

Dunbar, Robert G. *Forging New Rights in Western Water.* Lincoln: University of Nebraska Press, 1983. Hutchins, W. A. *Water Rights in the Nineteen Western States.* Washington DC: Government Printing Office, 1974. Trelease, Frank J., and George A. Gould. *Cases and Materials on Water Law,* 4th ed. St. Paul MN: West Publishing Company, 1986.

BOW RIVER IRRIGATION PROJECT

The Bow River Irrigation Project developed the waters of the Bow River for irrigation purposes in the semiarid districts of south-central Alberta. It was not the first irrigation project in western Canada, but eventually it became one of the largest. The project serves an area of 530,000 acres of land lying between the cities of Medicine Hat, Calgary, and Lethbridge in southern Alberta and has brought approximately 210,000 acres under irrigation.

The Bow River Irrigation Project traces its origins to the Grand Forks Cattle Company, which was incorporated in 1903. That company was a successful ranching operation, but in 1906 its operations were taken over by the Robins Irrigation Company, which applied to the federal government of Canada for authority to purchase 151,180 acres of land as well as for water rights to develop irrigation works for 95,143 acres of that land. Difficulties in raising the required capital resulted in a reorganization under which the Southern Alberta Land Company acquired the assets of the former Grand Forks Cattle Company and of the Robins Irrigation Company.

The Southern Alberta Land Company began construction of water diversion works in 1909, but failure or legal inability to sell irrigation lands before it had completed construction of all the irrigation works, coupled with a major accident at one of its headgates and a severe tightening of the financial markets in London just before the outbreak of World War I, forced the Southern Alberta Land Company into receivership in June 1914. Difficult and legally contentious negotiations resulted in acquisition of the assets and obligations of the Southern Alberta Land Company by the Canada Land and Irrigation Company in 1917.

Water for irrigation purposes was first delivered by the Canada Land and Irrigation Company in 1920, but severely depressed prices for wheat in 1922–23, and even more disastrous drought and commodity price declines after 1929, made it impossible for the company to meet its financial obligations. Its operations were taken over in 1935 by the Prairie Farm Rehabilitation Administration (PFRA), which continues to operate the huge irrigation works today.

The Bow River Irrigation Project brought the benefits of irrigation to more than 200,000 acres of arid and semiarid prairie. Irrigation has dramatically increased the productive capacity of vast tracts of prairie lands, but, at least in dry years, those irrigation projects have exhausted the available water supplies. They now threaten the ecology of the entire Bow River drainage basin.

See also AGRICULTURE: Prairie Farm Rehabilitation Administration.

Ted D. Regehr
University of Saskatchewan and
University of Calgary

Gilpin, John. *Prairie Promises: History of the Bow River Irrigation District.* Vauxhall, Alberta: Bow River Irrigation District, 1976. Kirk, D. W. *The Bow River Irrigation Project: The History and Development of the Bow River Irrigation Project up to and Including Its Purchase by the Government of Canada in 1950.* Regina, Saskatchewan: Prairie Farm Rehabilitation Administration, 1955.

CENTER PIVOTS

See INDUSTRY: Center Pivots

CHEYENNE BOTTOMS

Cheyenne Bottoms is a 41,000-acre elliptical basin, formed during the late Pleistocene, north of the great bend on the Arkansas River in Barton County, Kansas. This depression, surrounded by agricultural land and mixed-grass prairie, contains the largest remnant wetland in Kansas and is an important stopover site for tens of thousands of migratory waterfowl and shorebirds, as well as a nesting haven for herons, ducks, rails, gulls, and terns. It has been estimated that more than 90 percent of the continental populations of several shorebird species east of the Rocky Mountains stop at the bottoms during their spring migration from the Southern Hemisphere to the Arctic. No other location in the Great Plains attracts even 10 percent of the number of shorebirds during migration.

The site has been designated as a Wetland of International Importance by the Ramsar Convention and is listed as a Hemispheric Reserve by the Western Hemisphere Shorebird Preserve Network. Since 1949, half of the area has been managed by the Kansas Department of Wildlife and Parks, which uses diverted surface water to provide habitat for migrant and breeding waterbirds. However, increasing competition for limited surface flows and continued withdrawal of groundwater for irrigation has threatened the state's ability to maintain this wetland. The conflict went to court and was resolved, ensuring that the bottoms will receive at least some of its allotted water. During the past decade, an additional 6,500 acres of prime wetland within the basin have been preserved by The Nature Conservancy.

See also PHYSICAL ENVIRONMENT: Bird Migrations.

John L. Zimmerman
Kansas State University

COLORADO DOCTRINE

The Colorado Doctrine set the standards under which a jurisdiction accepts appropriation water law as the fundamental and exclusive water law. The Colorado Doctrine is also known as the doctrine of pure appropriation. It contrasts with systems under which appropriative law coexists with other types of water law.

The doctrine was developed in the late nineteenth century and is named for the state in which it originated. Colorado had adopted appropriation law in its constitution upon statehood (1876), declaring that rivers in the state belonged not to the federal government but to Coloradans, who could appropriate them. Still, questions remained as to the application of common law riparian rights in conjunction with appropriation rights. Up until that time most decisions regarding appropriation law mirrored those in California, where appropriation originated. However, at the time of Colorado statehood California's water law system had evolved to also recognize common law riparian rights, appropriative water rights, and Spanish pueblo rights.

In 1882 the Colorado Supreme Court settled Colorado's water law issue in the case of *Coffin v. Left Hand Ditch Company*, a water dispute between agricultural interests in northeastern Colorado. The court found that the water user who had established the first use of the water had the superior right to continue his or her use despite a riparian claim by an opposing party. The court concluded that riparian law did not exist in Colorado and established the appropriation doctrine as the exclusive water law of the state. Later, among Plains states, Wyoming (1896), New Mexico (1900), and Montana (1921) adopted the Colorado model.

Theron Josephson
Ferris State University

Dunbar, Robert G. *Forging New Rights in Western Water.* Lincoln: University of Nebraska Press, 1983. Hutchins, W. A. *Water Rights in the Nineteen Western States.* Washington DC: Government Printing Office, 1974. Trelease, Frank J., and George A. Gould. *Cases and Materials on Water Law,* 4th ed. St. Paul MN: West Publishing Company, 1986.

DOCTRINE OF EQUITY

The doctrine of equity is a principle of interjurisdictional water allocation developed by the U.S. Supreme Court in response to interstate water conflicts. It is a doctrine of necessity because of the juxtaposition of the legal theory allowing each state to develop its own form of water law against the physical reality that streams flow from one state to another. The doctrine states that when there is a disagreement over the water use of an interstate stream, the court must fashion an equitable apportionment of the water that serves the needs of water users in both states. Equitable apportionment of the water is not based on any mathematical formula but on a fair consideration of all the interests involved.

The doctrine originated in the Great Plains, where water flows not only from west to east but also from appropriation water law jurisdictions to riparian water law jurisdictions. Water allocation and consumptive uses of water by an upstream state have significant consequences when downstream states seek to use water of the same stream. Such was the case with the states of Colorado and Kansas. In 1901 Kansas sued Colorado on behalf of water users of the Arkansas River in western Kansas, alleging that Colorado, through its appropriation law, had encouraged its citizens to consume the water of the Arkansas to the detriment of the people in Kansas. Colorado countered, maintaining that as an independent state it had the right to use all the water it needed, even to the detriment of Kansas residents. By 1904, the case, *Kansas v. Colorado*, had reached the U.S. Supreme Court. In 1907 the Supreme Court rejected both positions. Justice David Brewer, a native of Kansas, wrote the court's opinion. While the Court did not find that Colorado had injured residents of southwestern Kansas to any great degree, it did establish the principle of the "equality of right," which fashioned a remedy requiring courts to ensure each state an equitable opportunity to use interstate stream water. This balancing of relative economic advantages continues to determine decisions on interstate water disputes.

See also LAW: Brewer, David.

Theron Josephson
Ferris State University

Dunbar, Robert G. *Forging New Rights in Western Water*. Lincoln: University of Nebraska Press, 1983. Hutchins, W. A. *Water Rights in the Nineteen Western States*. Washington DC: Government Printing Office, 1974. Trelease, Frank J., and George A. Gould. *Cases and Materials on Water Law*, 4th ed. St. Paul MN: West Publishing Company, 1986.

DROUGHT

Drought is a normal feature of the climate for virtually all portions of the United States and some portions of Canada, but it is one of the defining characteristics of the North American Great Plains. Early maps referred to this region as the Great American Desert, a belief attributed to the explorations of Zebulon Pike across the Southern Plains in 1806 and of Stephen Long across the Central Plains in 1819–20. The drought of the 1890s and, in particular, the Dust Bowl years of the 1930s define the region's climatic past. More recently, droughts have occurred at regular intervals, affecting, at one time or another, all portions of the region.

Drought is the consequence of a natural reduction in the amount of precipitation received over an extended period of time, usually a season or more in length. Drought is never the result of a single cause but, rather, the result of many causes that are synergistic in nature. Prolonged droughts in the Great Plains occur when large-scale anomalies in atmospheric circulation patterns become established and persist for periods of months, seasons, or longer. Impacts are complex, vary on spatial and temporal scales, and depend on the societal context of the drought. The impacts of drought in the Great Plains consequently differ from those experienced in other portions of the United States and Canada.

Historical climate records for the Great Plains only reach back to about 1900, and at only a few locations. Tree-ring data have been used to reconstruct the earlier drought history of the region, and these data illustrate a pattern of periodic and extended droughts, sometimes continuing for several decades. For example, H. E. Weakly identified a drought period of thirty-six years from 1631 to 1667 from an analysis of tree rings in western Nebraska.

A number of conclusions can be drawn from the occurrence of severe to extreme drought in the Great Plains over the last 100 years. First, the percentage of the area in drought is highly variable from year to year. The peak drought year was 1934, when 95 percent of the region experienced severe to extreme drought. Second, it is rare for severe drought not to occur somewhere in the region every year. Third, clusters of drought years, although rare, appear in the 1890s, 1930s, mid-1950s, late 1970s, late 1980s to early 1990s, and, to date, the first three years of the twenty-first century.

Drought produces a complex web of impacts that not only reverberate throughout the region's economy but may also affect other regions, extending even to the global scale (if, for example, harvests fail and crop exports are reduced). These impacts are commonly classified as economic, environmental, and social. Many economic impacts occur in broad agricultural and agriculturally related sectors, because these sectors are dependent on surface and subsurface water supplies. In addition to crop and livestock production losses, drought is associated with increases in insect infestations, plant disease, and wind erosion. The incidence of wildfires increases substantially during extended droughts, which in turn places human and wildlife populations at greater risk. Income loss is another indicator used to assess drought, because so many sectors are affected. Reduced income for farmers has a ripple-down effect as their purchasing power is reduced, leaving small-town businesses without customers.

Environmental losses are the result of damages to plant and animal species, wildlife habitat, and air and water quality; forest and range fires; degradation of landscape quality; loss of biodiversity; and soil erosion. Some of the effects are short-term, and conditions quickly return to normal after the drought. Other environmental effects linger for some time or may even become permanent. For example, short-term effects might entail a reduction of fish or wildlife species or impacts on air quality. Permanent or long-term effects could be reduced soil productivity from soil erosion or an extinction of fish or wildlife species.

Social impacts mainly involve public safety, health, conflicts between water users, reduced quality of life, and inequity in the distribution of impacts and disaster relief. Many of the impacts that are considered economic and environmental have social components as well. The economic hardships of the 1930s drought, for example, caused significant population out-migration from and massive flows of aid into the Great Plains.

Although drought is a natural hazard, vulnerability to its impacts can be reduced. Improving management of drought effects requires identifying both the natural and social repercussions. The Great Plains has historically had a very high incidence of drought, and there is no reason to believe that this incidence will diminish in the future. Vulnerability, on the other hand, is determined by factors such as population numbers, demographic characteristics, technology, government policy, and social behavior. These factors change over time, and vulnerability may increase or decrease in response to these changes. There was relatively little dust blowing in the 1890s drought, for example, for much of the grass cover had not yet been removed by farming.

Much has been done to lessen societal vulnerability to drought in the Great Plains. Irrigation, conservation tillage practices, soil evaporation reduction measures, snow management, and irrigation scheduling have all proved effective in stabilizing agricultural production in a region exposed to the vagaries of weather.

The impacts of recent droughts, however, illustrate the continuing vulnerability. In 1988, drought affected nearly 40 percent of the nation and resulted in nearly $16 billion in agricultural losses. In the Great Plains, this drought reduced spring wheat yields by 54 percent. In 1996, drought in the Southwest and the Southern Great Plains resulted in substantial agricultural losses, increased incidence of forest and range fires, municipal water supply problems, and losses in recreation and tourism. In Texas alone, drought losses were estimated to be $6.5 billion. In 1998, drought in Texas and Oklahoma was estimated to have resulted in $5.8 billion and $2 billion in losses, respectively.

Drought planning is one mechanism that states and provinces have employed to reduce the economic losses and personal hardships. The goal of such plans is to improve the effectiveness of response and preparedness efforts through improved monitoring and early warning; impact and vulnerability assessment; and mitigation programs. These plans are also directed at improving coordination and building partnerships within state government agencies and between state and provincial, local, and federal governments. Most Great Plains states currently have drought plans in place. Plans recently developed by New Mexico and Nebraska are the most progressive because they incorporate mitigation actions as a key component of the planning process. Formal drought plans do not exist in the Prairie Provinces.

Drought is a complex, recurrent, and insidious natural hazard that inflicts considerable pain and hardship on Plains residents. The economic, social, and environmental repercussions of drought result from complex interactions between physical and social systems, and they are difficult to quantify. Scientists and policymakers must understand the characteristics of drought and appreciate the magnitude and complexity of impacts in order for viable assessment, response, and mitigation strategies to be established.

See also ART: Dust Bowl Photographers / PHYSICAL ENVIRONMENT: Climate; Dust Bowl.

Donald A. Wilhite
National Drought Mitigation Center

Hurt, R. Douglas. *The Dust Bowl: An Agricultural and Social History*. Chicago: Nelson-Hall Publishers, 1981. Wilhite, Donald A., ed. *Drought Assessment, Management, and Planning: Theory and Case Studies*. Boston: Kluwer Academic Publishers, 1993.

FLOODS

The history of flooding in the Great Plains displays a marked diversity of types. Most common are short-lived flash floods on small watersheds following intense cloudburst storms. Less common, but usually more destructive, are longer-lived main-stem river floods. These result from heavy rains dispersed over a wide area, fast ice and snowmelt, or a combination of both. On Northern Great Plains streams, ice dams during the spring runoff also lead to flooding. No stream escapes flooding. It is part of a river's natural processes. The primary response of humans to these floods has been through engineering: dams, levees, drainage channels, and land-use modification. Yet the underlying reason humans in the Great Plains have repeatedly suffered from floods is their tendency to occupy floodplains.

Three of the most dramatic and devastating flash floods in the Plains were those of June 1921 on the upper Arkansas; May 1951 on the Little Nemaha at Syracuse, Nebraska; and June 1972 at Rapid City, South Dakota. In the first case, moisture-laden winds blowing westward created a swirling vortex against the Front Range above Pueblo, Colorado, on June 3, 1921. Torrential rains fell from orographic cooling, producing flash floods on the upper Arkansas during the next two days. Pueblo residents stood on the town's levees to watch the flood along the straightened and channeled river that ran through the business district. An unknown number of people lost their lives when flood crests topped the levees; seventy-eight bodies were eventually recovered.

Another example of a cloudburst flood was the record-breaking (in terms of discharge per drainage area) flood on Nebraska's Little Nemaha River at Syracuse on May 8–9, 1951. It was caused by runoff arriving together from two intense thunderstorms over separate watersheds. The flood flow from this event was 225,000 cubic feet per second from a watershed of 218 square miles. Twenty-three people died, and among other damages, sloping fields on uplands lost topsoil in depths "up to the plow sole," while fields at places down on the floodplain were covered by five feet of that topsoil.

A historical benchmark of flood devastation in the Plains was the flood of June 9, 1972, at Rapid City, South Dakota. An intense stationary supercell thunderstorm in the Black Hills dropped up to 15.5 inches of rain—close to the average annual amount—in six hours in the hills to the west of Rapid City. Failure of a dam brought a flood crest on Rapid Creek through town near midnight. Its flood flow was ten times the previous flood record. Homes, businesses, and 5,000 automobiles were destroyed, more than 3,000 people were injured, and 237 died.

Wider areal precipitation produced two of the most devastating floods in the Central Plains. Following a month of above-average rainfall in the watershed, extremely heavy rains fell—up to twenty inches in places—on the south fork of the Republican River in eastern Colorado and western Kansas during the night of May 30–31, 1935. More than 100 people lost their lives, 20,000 head of livestock drowned, and massive destruction of railroad tracks, bridges, and levees occurred. The high loss of life in the upper valley resulted from the arrival of the flood in the middle of the night, with little or no warning. After daylight, many others died when they refused to heed warnings and tried to save livestock and personal belongings.

The 1951 flood of the Kansas and Missouri Rivers at Kansas City followed intense widespread rainfall in the Kansas River basin. The watercourse through Kansas City was notoriously constricted, with much of the industrial district protected behind twenty-foot levees. At the time much of the flood protection work authorized under the Pick-Sloan Plan remained incomplete. After floodwaters topped the levees, nearly $1 billion in damages was sustained. The Missouri at Kansas City also flooded in 1993 when heavy summer rains over much of the Midwest caused the most devastating flood in U.S. history to the Mississippi River basin. Part of this extraordinary event was the particularly severe flooding on the lower Missouri, which brought a river crest at Kansas City on July 27 at nearly three feet above the devastating 1951 flood level.

The Red River of the North holds a special place in the history of Great Plains flooding. As the major northward-flowing river in the United States, it is subject to a distinctive flood potential. Spring floods occur as snow at the headwaters to the south begins to melt. These waters pool behind ice dams to the north. Because the river flows in a relatively flat valley (the bed of ancient glacial Lake Agassiz), the waters rise gradually. A great flood in 1897 followed this pattern, and repeatedly damaging floods have occurred in the cities of Grand Forks, Fargo-Moorhead, and Winnipeg. Movie newsreels in 1950 followed the slowly rising waters, sandbagging efforts, and flooding that went on for weeks across Manitoba in the Red and Assiniboine River valleys. Provincial and dominion governments wrestled with responsibility and assistance in the face of the unprecedented disaster. Southern Manitoba had 530 square miles inundated. Television news in 1997 showed the dramatic burning of Grand Forks's flooded downtown when the Red River flooded on both sides of the border. This flood produced a "Red Sea" in Canada nearly as large as Lake Manitoba. Canadians responded with the enormous engineering project of the Greater Winnipeg Floodway, a twenty-six-mile diversion ditch. Its construction required moving an amount of dirt equal to that of the Panama Canal.

See also CITIES AND TOWN: Fargo, North Dakota; Grand Forks, North Dakota; Winnipeg, Manitoba / PHYSICAL ENVIRONMENT: Climate.

Will Guthrie
University of Kansas

Bumsted, J. M. *Floods of the Centuries: A History of Flood Disasters in the Red River Valley, 1776–1997*. Winnipeg: Great Plains Publications, 1997. Hoyt, William G., and Walter B. Langbein. *Floods*. Princeton: Princeton University Press, 1954. Smith, Keith, and Roy Ward. *Floods: Physical Processes and Human Impacts*. Chichester, England: John Wiley & Sons, 1998.

GARDINER DAM

Located sixty miles south of Saskatoon on the South Saskatchewan River, the Gardiner Dam was named in honor of federal Minister of Agriculture James G. Gardiner, who fought for its creation for many years. Construction began in 1958 and the dam was completed in 1967. It is 210 feet in height and 16,700 feet in length. Diefenbaker Lake, the reservoir the dam created, is 140 miles long with a shoreline of about 475 miles; it covers an area of 109,600 acres and has a total storage capacity of 8 million acre feet. At the time of its construction the Gardiner Dam, which cost $121 million, was second only to the St. Lawrence Seaway in terms of Canadian publicly funded projects. A Saskatchewan study in 1996 placed the cost in today's money at $1 billion. It is the largest earth-filled dam in Canada and one of the largest in the world.

The political will that fueled the undertaking flowed directly from the experience of the "dirty thirties." The dam is located in a region described by the explorer James Palliser in 1859 as being unfit for human habitation, an area known for extreme droughts, with crop failures expected three years out of ten. During the 1930s it was the home of Canada's Dust Bowl, when topsoil was torn from its base and carried by prevailing westerlies in huge black masses, leaving the farmlands barren and houses and hedges all but buried. Crops were ruined and farm life was left in disarray. Some farmers were driven from the land and some to madness and suicide. The purpose of the Gardiner Dam was to mitigate the effects of such drought by supplying irrigation as well as providing electrical power, urban water supply, flood control, and recreational opportunities.

Power generation was the first benefit to make an impact. From the moment it went online, electricity generation began to produce $10 million a year in savings. Urban water supply was soon benefiting as well. A secondary dam was built upstream from the main structure to provide a controlled flow by canal running south to serve the needs of Moose Jaw and the capital city of Regina. Other towns and hamlets and several industrial sites are also being serviced, and access to water is placed within reach of 40 percent of Saskatchewan's population.

The main reservoir and a half dozen satellite lakes fed by canals add substantially to recreational opportunities: six vacation villages, twelve fully developed parks, and three major marinas have been established. Flood control is generally a minor consideration, but in years of high river runoff it is crucially important, and in an average year it is responsible for a savings of $44,000 in flood damage by controlling the flow through the dam's spillways.

Irrigation is the most significant aspect of the project. There are now almost 100,000 acres under irrigation, which has resulted in a shift to new crop mixtures, notably peas, fava beans, pinto beans, lentils, grasses, potatoes, rapeseed, mustard, and, in some isolated instances, small orchards. Oddly enough, for this part of the country, there has been a recent move into mint production—a processing plant has been established in the region, with all of its production being exported to the United States, United Kingdom, as well as Japan and other Asian markets. Most of all, the project has in large part eliminated the fear of drought. As one farmer observed, "In the past ten years I have never had a crop failure on irrigated land."

See also AGRICULTURE: Gardiner, Jimmy.

Max Macdonald
University of Regina

Fairley, Brad. *South Saskatchewan River Basin Study*. Regina: Canada Department of the Environment, 1997.
Kulshreshtha, Suran, et al. *Social Evaluation of the South Saskatchewan River Project*. Ottawa: Queen's Printer, 1988.
Macdonald, Max. *Oasis for a Desert*. Regina: Canadian Plains Research Center, 1999.

IRRIGATION

In response to moisture deficiency, farmers irrigate more than 20 million acres in the Great Plains. Plains irrigation gives water stability to agriculture, permits a wider diversity of crops than possible with rain-fed cultivation, and promotes economic growth through increased productivity and associated processing and livestock feeding activities. Irrigation is most commonly used in the western reaches of the region, where it is drier and there is available groundwater and rivers sustained by Rocky Mountain meltwaters.

Small-scale irrigation in the nineteenth century involved diverting water onto fields or using windmills to pump water from shallow aquifers. By 1900 community and corporate ditch irrigation enterprises were expanding on the Platte and Arkansas Rivers, and, through the efforts of Mormon settlers and railroads, along various rivers in southern Alberta. Windmills were commonly used to pump water for people, stock, and gardens from Texas north to the Dakotas and Manitoba. A huge windmill near Garden City, Kansas, provided enough water to irrigate fifteen acres.

In the American Great Plains large-scale irrigation began with the Reclamation Act of 1902 that authorized the secretary of the interior to construct reservoirs, diversion dams, and distribution canals in the West, including the Plains states. Subsequently, pump tech-

Center-pivot sprinkler irrigation system, Alberta

nologies of the 1930s made it possible to lift water from the Ogallala and other formations of the High Plains Aquifer. In the Prairie Provinces, the federal government of Canada and provincial government of Alberta passed legislation supporting irrigation. The Alberta Irrigation District Act of 1915 enabled farmers to organize into districts that could raise capital to finance construction of dams, canals, and other irrigation works.

The Canadian irrigation districts and American reclamation projects provide water to farmers through a system of dams on rivers, on- and off-stream storage reservoirs, diversion canals, and smaller ditches that lead directly to fields. Gravity flow is most common, but in some newer districts in Saskatchewan and rehabilitated facilities elsewhere, water is provided under pressure. Farmers receive a specified amount of water at a set price, with the district or project maintaining the diversion, storage, and distribution system. Farmers from Nebraska south to Texas pump groundwater directly from the Ogallala Aquifer. Each farmer holds the right to use a given amount of water, measured in acre-feet (the volume of water needed to cover one acre to a depth of one foot). Allocations usually range between two and three acre-feet a year. The depth to the aquifer varies greatly, but a majority of irrigators pump their water from between 100 and 200 feet. Electricity, diesel fuel, or natural gas power most of the pump engines. Alternative sources of water for irrigation, such as effluent from livestock operations or urban areas, provide water in limited areas.

Most Plains farmers apply water to their fields using either surface or sprinkler methods. The main form of surface irrigation is furrow, whereby furrows are plowed between crop rows along which water flows from a pipe with holes called gates. Furrow irrigation is employed when the land is relatively flat and the soils absorb water slowly. The leading form of sprinkler irrigation is the center pivot.

It is a lateral pipe—with spray nozzles, often suspended on drop tubes and mounted on wheeled structures called towers—that is anchored at the center of the field and automatically rotates in a circle. A typical center pivot has a one-quarter-mile radius and waters approximately 130 acres. More or less ground can be irrigated by adding or subtracting pipeline and towers. Center-pivot systems require more capital investment than furrows, but they take less labor to operate and can water uneven terrain and fast absorbing soils.

Irrigation is most developed in areas of good soils where the saturated thickness is greatest or where irrigation districts and reclamation projects have diverted river flow. In 1998 Nebraska led the Plains states with more than 6.3 million irrigated acres, followed by Texas with more than 4.4 million irrigated acres in the Plains part of the state. Next in importance were Kansas (2.7 million acres), Colorado (1.7 million acres in the Plains), and Alberta (1.5 million acres). Montana, Oklahoma, New Mexico, South Dakota, Saskatchewan, Wyoming, and North Dakota each had between 180,000 and 800,000 irrigated acres; Manitoba irrigated some 32,000 acres. Most of the irrigated land in Nebraska, Texas, and Kansas relies on water from the High Plains Aquifer system. At the beginning of the twenty-first century irrigated acreage continued to increase in nearly all areas.

A wide array of crops is irrigated in the Great Plains. Corn occupies about two-fifths of the irrigated land. Nebraska irrigates more than 4.7 million acres of corn and Kansas nearly 1.2 million acres. Hay, grown throughout the region, accounts for nearly 12 percent of the acres irrigated. It is relatively most important in Wyoming and Montana, where irrigated pasture is also significant. Irrigated wheat is most important in Oklahoma, Kansas, Alberta, and Texas. Grain sorghum is irrigated on about 1.4 million acres, nearly two-thirds of which is in Texas, where feedgrains are replacing once-dominant cotton. The irrigated area for all these crops is expanding, as it is also for soybeans, sugar beets, and potatoes.

The sustainability of irrigation in the Great Plains is threatened by soil salinization and by groundwater depletion. Most irrigation-induced soil salinity results from water losses in transport, where seepage from canals raises the water level and brings natural salinity nearer to the surface and within the root zone of crops. Lining irrigation canals and ditches reduces the problem, but it can be very expensive. In Alberta much of the 4,500 miles of canals in the conveyance system has been rehabilitated in this way. Poor on-farm management of irrigation water also can cause salinity, especially in low-lying areas where water ponds and soil become salinized after evaporation. Soils with saliency programs can be reclaimed if the water table is brought below the root zone and the excess salts are leached out of the soil. The depletion of the High Plains Aquifer concerns farmers, as saturated thickness (the vertical extent of the watered zone in the aquifer) is limited in many areas, especially in Texas and New Mexico, and recharge is minimal. In some areas there is not enough water remaining to support irrigation. The distance to the water increases as irrigation lowers the water table, and lifting water becomes too costly when energy prices are high. There also is concern for groundwater quality when agricultural chemicals reach an aquifer.

In response to groundwater depletion, the desire to increase irrigation, and competing demands for water, irrigation efficiency has become a priority for most Plains irrigators. Water-saving practices have been widely adopted by farmers. Furrow irrigation has become less water-consumptive through the use of surge flow, whereby water is intermittently released from the gated pipes to discharge in surges that achieve relatively even watering along the entire length of a row. Center-pivot sprinklers are being fitted with low-energy precision application (LEPA) systems that use low-pressure emitters on drop tubes to apply the water directly on or near the soil. Drip irrigation, wherein water drips or trickles from perforations in a low-pressure pipe placed alongside the base of a row of plants, and subsurface drip irrigation, with the water carried directly to the root of the plants, have moved from experimentation to actual field use. Most farmers employ some form of irrigation scheduling to apply only the water required by a crop under different evaporative conditions. Water-saving innovations extend the available water supplies to assure the continuance of irrigation in the Great Plains.

See also INDUSTRY: Center Pivots.

David E. Kromm
Kansas State University

Green, Donald E. *Land of the Underground Rain: Irrigation in the Texas High Plains, 1910–1970.* Austin: University of Texas Press, 1973. Kromm, David E., and Stephen E. White, eds. *Groundwater Exploration in the High Plains.* Lawrence: University Press of Kansas, 1992.

KETTLE LAKES

Kettle lakes are a landscape feature characteristic of glacial terrain. When glaciers that covered the Northern Great Plains melted, the rock materials that were incorporated in and on top of the glaciers remained on the land surface. These materials commonly enclosed blocks of glacial ice that took many years to melt because they were insulated from solar radiation by the surrounding rock materials. When the buried ice blocks finally melted, they left a depression in the landscape. If the area was wet enough to have a high water table, the depressions filled with water to form kettle lakes. These lakes commonly are isolated from one another with respect to surface drainage. They accumulate water from precipitation, overland runoff, and groundwater, and they lose water to evaporation and seepage to groundwater.

The region of the Great Plains most recently covered by continental glaciers lies within the southern parts of Alberta, Saskatchewan, and Manitoba in Canada, and north and east of the Missouri River in Montana, North Dakota, and South Dakota in the United States. Kettle lakes, commonly called prairie sloughs in Canada and prairie potholes in the United States, are a defining landscape feature in this region because of their abundance. The great majority of kettle lakes are very shallow (less than ten feet deep), but a few are nearly as deep as the thickness of the glacial deposits that surround them (as much as 100 feet deep).

See also PHYSICAL ENVIRONMENT: Glaciation.

Thomas C. Winter
U.S. Geological Survey, Denver

LAKE AGASSIZ

Ten thousand years ago, glacial Lake Agassiz was the largest body of freshwater in North America. At its maximum extent, the lake covered an area of some 135,000 square miles and had a maximum depth of around 700 feet. Lake Agassiz was a product of widespread deglaciation that marked the closure of the last great Ice Age. By 11,700 years ago, the ice front had retreated far enough north to permit impoundment of glacial meltwater—incipient Lake Agassiz—in the extreme southern end of the Red River Valley of the North near the junction of present-day North Dakota, South Dakota, and Minnesota. As the ice sheet retreated the lake gradually expanded northward across the First Steppe (or Manitoba Plain) and over much of the adjoining Precambrian Shield. Initially, drainage flowed southward via the Minnesota and Mississippi Rivers. The level of the lake rose and fell, and its margins correspondingly expanded and contracted, several times in response to a sequence of ice frontal readvances and retreats that alternately opened and closed its outlets into the Lake Superior basin.

Migration made possible by extensive riverine connections with other drainages to the south, east, west, and northwest culminated in a varied fish population in Lake Agassiz. The lake's huge size, however, precluded human occupation of a sizeable portion of the northeastern Plains periphery, while adjacent areas to the south and west were inhabited by generations of hunters and gatherers.

The lake began its final phase of drainage just over 9,000 years ago. Around 1,000 years later a much-diminished Lake Agassiz discharged into ancestral Hudson Bay as the last vestiges of the once-formidable ice dam finally disintegrated.

See also PHYSICAL ENVIRONMENT: Glaciation.

Leo Pettipas
Manitoba Museum of Man and Nature

Teller, James T., and Lee Clayton, eds. *Glacial Lake Agassiz.* St. John's, Newfoundland: Geological Association of Canada, 1983. Teller, James T., and Alan E. Kehew. "Introduction to the Late Glacial History of Large Proglacial Lakes and Meltwater Runoff along the Laurentide Ice Sheet." *Quaternary Science Reviews* 13 (1994): 795–99.

MEAD, ELWOOD (1858–1936)

Elwood Mead was born on a farm near Patriot, Indiana, on January 16, 1858, and was educated at Purdue University. He would go on to write the laws (though they were seldom adopted in full) that became the late-nineteenth-century model for water management in Great Plains and Rocky Mountain states. Mead ended his career as commissioner of the U.S. Bureau of Reclamation.

Mead first became interested in irrigation in Colorado when he taught math and physics at Fort Collins in 1882. He was appointed assistant state engineer in 1885. Three years later he became the first territorial engineer of Wyoming. In 1889–90, at the age of thirty-one, Mead wrote the water law in the constitution and statutes for the new state of Wyoming, aiming to avoid other western states' mistakes and create a new system of active state ownership and supervision of water. Mead believed water law could foster strong agricultural communities, and he sought to eliminate speculation in water rights. Under Mead's system, putting water to use and filing a claim could not create a legal right to use water, as had been the case in most of the West. He required water users to obtain state permits; the permits could be denied if a project was deemed unwise. A panel of engineers served as the primary tribunal in matters of establishment, loss, and change of water rights. Water rights were tied to actual use on designated land to avoid speculation, a concern that means cautious analysis of transfers of water rights in Wyoming even today.

Mead's system was influential throughout the Great Plains, Rocky Mountains, and Canada. Nebraska adopted the entire system; most states (for example, Oklahoma, North Dakota, and South Dakota) balked at supplanting judges with engineers and adopted only the permit system portion.

Mead left Wyoming in 1898 for a career in what he called social engineering—designing irrigation colonies and promoting rural settlement programs in Australia, California, and Washington State. He became commissioner of the Bureau of Reclamation in 1924. He later mentored New Dealers on rural community building and masterminded the Hoover Dam (creating his giant namesake Lake Mead) on the Colorado River. Mead died in Washington DC on January 16, 1936.

Gordon W. Fassett
Cheyenne, Wyoming
Anne MacKinnon
Casper, Wyoming

Kluger, James R. *Turning on Water with a Shovel: The Career of Elwood Mead*. Albuquerque: University of New Mexico Press, 1992. Mead, Elwood. Papers, 1900–42. Water Resources Center Archives, University of California, Berkeley.

MNI SOSE INTERTRIBAL WATER RIGHTS COALITION

The Mni Sose Intertribal Water Rights Coalition was organized in 1993 to enable the twenty-eight American Indian Nations in the Missouri River basin to seek legal, administrative, economic, and physical control over their water resources. Since its inception, the coalition has been engaged in a constant effort to educate U.S. agencies and congressional committees about the treaty and trust responsibilities of the federal government. For example, under the Flood Control Act of 1944, which authorized the Pick-Sloan Plan, eight reservations relinquished a total of 350,000 acres, or 23 percent of the total land appropriated for the construction of the five earthen dams to control flooding along the Missouri River. Although a $1.3 billion economic benefit is derived from these projects each year, the tribes have shared in little of the revenues. However, based upon the efforts of the coalition, the tribes are now in the process of approving contracts for allocations of hydropower from the Pick-Sloan dams, which will ultimately result in lower electrical rates on the reservations.

The coalition is also working with federal and other agencies to develop partnerships with tribes to support tribal water uses, conduct research, and encourage technology transfer to improve water resource development and cultural protection of the environment. With the assistance of the Mni Sose Intertribal Water Rights Coalition, tribes are moving from a passive to an active role in protecting their tribal homelands. They are now acquiring the legislative, administrative, and operational capabilities to govern, manage, and protect their tribal water resources.

Richard Bad Moccasin
Mni Sose Intertribal Water Rights Coalition

NORTHWEST IRRIGATION ACT

The Northwest Irrigation Act, amending and consolidating the Northwest Irrigation Acts of 1894 and 1895, was passed by the Canadian federal government in 1898. It defined and provided for the regulation and control of water rights in the territories that became the provinces of Saskatchewan and Alberta in 1905. Drought conditions in the 1880s and 1890s, together with the arrival of Mormon settlers familiar with irrigation techniques and increased interest in irrigation by the Canadian Pacific Railway, had made it necessary for the federal government to regulate the orderly use of the water resources of the semi-arid Southern Canadian Prairies.

The Northwest Irrigation Act unequivocally revoked or rescinded common law riparian rights, declaring that the water in all streams, lakes, ponds, springs, or other sources belongs to the Crown. It then defined the conditions under which federal officials could grant water rights or concessions to companies or individuals for a variety of uses. Those applying for water rights for irrigation purposes had to define the quantity of water required, the specific lands to be irrigated, and the irrigation works to be constructed. Successful applicants were given indisputable title to the water granted them under their licenses, provided that they used it only in accordance with the terms and conditions of their application. The licensees also enjoyed rights of expropriation of land needed for the development of approved works. But failure to develop the works, or misuse of the water, could result in the revocation of the rights granted. Decisions of government officials regarding revocations were final and without right of appeal to the courts.

Creation of the new provinces of Alberta and Saskatchewan in 1905 necessitated passage of a new federal irrigation act that granted the new provinces some very limited local powers but left regulation of water resources in the new provinces in federal hands. In 1930 the federal government transferred control of the natural resources in Alberta and Saskatchewan to those provinces but retained significant control over water resources under the terms of a new Water Resources Act.

Supporters of the Northwest Irrigation Act, and of later Canadian legislation regulating the use of water for irrigation purposes, insist that the clear enunciation of basic principles and easily understood and enforceable detailed regulations resulted in an almost complete absence of the kind of litigation pertaining to irrigation laws in other, mainly U.S., jurisdictions.

Ted D. Regehr
University of Saskatchewan and
University of Calgary

Dawson, A. S. *Irrigation Development in Western Canada, Address to the Calgary Board of Trade, April 15, 1921*. Calgary: Calgary Board of Trade, 1921. U.S. Department of Agriculture. *Irrigation Laws of the Northwest Territories of Canada and of Wyoming*. J. S. Dennis. Washington DC: Government Printing Office, 1901.

OAHE UNIT

Originally approved by Congress in 1944 as part of the federal government's Pick-Sloan Plan to harness the Missouri River, the Oahe (pronounced a-WA-he) Unit was designed by the U.S. Bureau of Reclamation to divert water from the Missouri River's Oahe Reservoir to irrigate 750,000 acres of land in northeastern South Dakota. The federal government offered the irrigation project to South Dakota as compensation for the loss of approximately 500,000 acres of land as the result of four federal dams built on the South Dakota portion of the Missouri River. Although the Oahe Unit plan was eventually downsized to include only 190,000 acres of irrigation along the James River, support in South Dakota for the project was enthusiastic and widespread. For three decades, every major politician and the most influential businesses in South Dakota, particularly the media, championed the project, and it appeared that construction of the project was inevitable.

But information in the Oahe Unit's environmental impact statement, released in 1973, energized a small group of farmers and landowners already concerned about the project. Their grassroots group, United Family Farmers, quickly grew into a large, sophisticated organization aimed at stopping the project. United Family Farmers members were mostly farmers and ranchers whose lands would have been severed by project canals and ditches, drowned by regulatory reservoirs, mitigated for wildlife purposes, or taxed to build and maintain the project. They accused the Bureau of Reclamation of bullying and mistreating landowners and misleading the public about the irrigation project. Oahe was rare among federal reclamation projects because many farmers scheduled to receive irrigation water resisted the project. Their primary concern was that their land could not survive continual watering. Soil experts hired by United Family Farmers verified that concern. Environmentalists also opposed the Oahe Unit because the project would have destroyed wetlands, channelized the James River and many small, prairie streams, and worsened water pollution problems in the James River.

By 1976, United Family Farmers boasted nearly 2,000 members, and the organization entered candidates for elections to the Oahe Conservancy Sub-district's board of directors. The conservancy sub-district had been formed by the state of South Dakota in 1960 to provide project supporters and the Bureau of Reclamation with a government agency in the Oahe Unit area that would promote and help develop and maintain the irrigation project. United Family Farmers candidates in the 1976 elections ran against board incumbents who were supported by an organization called Friends of Oahe. This group had been organized by South Dakota's banking and construction industries and Senator George McGovern to compete with United Family Farmers. The rivalry between the two groups was vicious.

Until United Family Farmers contested conservancy sub-district elections, positions on the sub-district's eleven-person board of directors had been held only by individuals who supported Oahe. Surprisingly, United Family Farmers candidates soundly defeated Friends of Oahe candidates in the November 1976 election, and the farm group assumed control of the sub-district. That impressive accomplishment, coupled with President Jimmy Carter's plan to reform federal water project planning and construction, encouraged Congress to discontinue funding for the Oahe Unit in 1977, which led to Oahe's demise.

United Family Farmers, now recognized as one of the most innovative and successful grassroots groups to oppose a Bureau of Reclamation project, conceived and advocated a congressional proposal that in 1982 traded discontinuation of the Oahe Unit for authorization of the WEB (Walworth-Edmunds-Brown) water pipeline. WEB eventually became the largest domestic water pipeline system in the United States, delivering treated Oahe Reservoir water to farms and communities in an area the size of Connecticut in northeastern South Dakota. WEB is headquartered in Aberdeen, South Dakota.

Peter Carrels
Aberdeen, South Dakota

Carrels, Peter. *Uphill against Water: The Great Dakota Water War.* Lincoln: University of Nebraska Press, 1999

OGALLALA AQUIFER

The Ogallala, or High Plains, Aquifer is a porous body of complex sediments and sedimentary rock formations that conducts groundwater and yields significant quantities of water to wells and springs. The principal sediments and rocks of the aquifer range in age from 33 million years old to sediments being deposited today, but the majority is less than 12 million years old. Much of the aquifer is composed of the Ogallala Group or Formation. The dominant sediments in the Ogallala and the other hydrogeologic units in the aquifer are river- and wind-deposited sands.

The aquifer underlies about 174,000 square miles of the High Plains. The water-saturated part of the aquifer varies in thickness and is more than 1,000 feet thick in places. Both the thickest and the most extensive areas are in Nebraska. The water from the aquifer is being pumped by nearly 200,000 irrigation wells, most of them installed since the 1940s. Installation rates have varied, with the highest rates generally occurring during dry years. In places, particularly in the southern region, pumping has lowered water levels as much as 200 feet.

Across the Great Plains, many rivers, smaller streams, and springs periodically go dry; consequently water from wells is a more reliable source. Since the late nineteenth century, the U.S. government has recognized the importance of finding sources of underground water to meet the needs of settlers in the Great Plains. Robert Hay (1895), N. H. Darton (1898, 1899), and Willard Johnson (1901, 1902) of the U.S. Geological Survey (USGS) conducted surveys of the region that helped to locate adequate supplies. Several types of surface sediments that accumulated during the Quaternary period (the last 1.6 million years of geologic history) were recognized in their reports. The Ogallala Formation of late Tertiary age was described first by Darton in some detail from study of the unit in western Nebraska. Darton also identified Tertiary sediment and rock layers older than the Ogallala, called the Arikaree Formation, Gering Formation, and the still older Brule Clay in parts of western Nebraska.

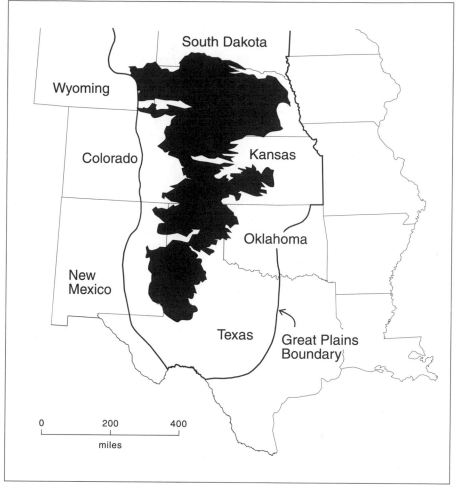

Ogallala Aquifer

Later geologists have recognized that the Ogallala in Nebraska can be subdivided into formations and have raised the Ogallala to a higher level called a group. The Gering Formation has been included in the Arikaree. The name Brule Clay has been changed to Brule Formation, and several widespread subdivisions of the Brule strata have been recognized. The distributions of the Brule, Arikaree, Ogallala, and the Broadwater Formations, all of which were deposited in the middle to late Tertiary period (an interval from 33 million to 1.6 million years ago), have been mapped in Nebraska and adjacent Great Plains states. Only the Ogallala is known from Kansas south. Most of these deposits yield water to wells and springs and are thus parts of an aquifer system, which has been called both the Ogallala Aquifer and the High Plains Aquifer.

Water is present in interconnected openings or pore spaces passing through the formations or between sediment grains of the formations. If the openings are large enough to allow the water to move through them, the formations are said to be permeable. Most of the water in the High Plains Aquifer moves through the narrow, interconnected pore spaces between grains of gravel and/or sand (here gravel is any sediment grain larger than two millimeters in intermediate diameter; sand, 2–0.0625 mm; silt and clay have smaller intermediate diame-

ters). Larger fractures and openings enlarged by water erosion have been observed in the several units of the aquifer but are only locally important. Rocks beneath the High Plains Aquifer are generally impermeable and thus act as a seal that prevents water from moving into them.

The origins and natures of the various units differ. The upper parts of the Brule Formation are primarily composed of volcanic dust and ash, carried by winds from erupting volcanoes in the west to the northern High Plains and deposited as blankets over the region. After the Brule was deposited, rivers draining across the developing High Plains eroded valleys into the formation. The deeper parts of the valleys were filled with river deposits, consisting largely of reworked volcanic debris of the Gering Formation. Most of the remainder of the Arikaree Group is wind-deposited volcanic ash that fills the parts of the ancient valleys above the Gering. The Ogallala Group is a complex and heterogeneous mass of sediment mostly composed of river alluvium derived from erosion of the southern Rocky Mountains. During deposition of the Ogallala and the younger Broadwater Formation, rivers repeatedly eroded valleys and then filled these valleys. Minor finer-grained lake sediments, volcanic ash deposits, and lime-cemented soil horizons occur throughout the Ogallala sequence. Wind deposited sands are common in the Ogallala in the Southern High Plains. Quaternary river alluvium, wind deposits, lake beds, and volcanic ash layers cover much of the High Plains and fill parts of valleys cutting across the High Plains.

The USGS estimates that in 1980 the aquifer contained about 3.25 billion acre-feet of drainable water (an acre-foot is the volume of a one-acre area one foot thick or 43,560 cubic feet). If impounded on the surface, this volume of water would cover the High Plains region to an average depth of about thirty feet. Most of the water in the aquifer comes from precipitation on the High Plains. With the increase of irrigated agriculture, water levels have dropped in places where the groundwater from the aquifer was pumped out faster than water from precipitation moved through the sediments and rocks to replace it. In other areas, water levels have risen where precipitation has allowed water to infiltrate the aquifer at rates greater than those at which water was pumped out, or where reservoirs and canals have lost water to the aquifer at rates greater than the withdrawal.

See also PHYSICAL ENVIRONMENT: Geology.

R. F. Diffendal Jr.
University of Nebraska–Lincoln

Darton, N. H. "Geology and Water Resources of Nebraska West of the One Hundred and Third Meridian." *U.S. Geological Survey 19th Annual Report, Part 4* (1899): 719–85. Dugan, J. T., and Sharpe, J. B. "Water-level Changes in the High Plains Aquifer—Predevelopment to 1994." *U.S. Geological Survey Water-Resources Investigations Report 95–4208* (1996). Johnson, W. D. "The High Plains and Their Utilization." *U.S. Geological Survey 22nd Annual Report, Part 4* (1902): 631–69.

PICK-SLOAN PLAN

Also known as "Big Muddy," the Missouri River meanders 2,341 miles from its origins in the Rocky Mountains of Montana before joining the Mississippi River at St. Louis, Missouri. The river drains roughly one-sixth of the United States, including portions of ten states, the homelands of twenty-eight Native American tribes, and a small portion of Canada. Before 1940 this great river was almost completely uncontrolled.

A series of extreme droughts during the 1930s and severe flooding in 1943 that covered many areas along the Missouri River, including much of Omaha and Kansas City, prompted a surge of interest in water planning for the Missouri River basin. Planners felt that increased management of the river and its tributaries would not only reduce future flooding, but also benefit the region's economy through increased irrigation and hydropower production, enhanced navigation, and job opportunities for veterans returning from World War II. Two federal agencies, the U.S. Bureau of Reclamation and the U.S. Army Corps of Engineers, were the leading water development agencies at the time, and both were called on by Congress to compose plans to harness the unruly river. The Bureau of Reclamation's subsequent plan, sponsored by William G. Sloan, focused on increasing irrigation for agricultural stability and hydropower production for regional economic growth. The Corps of Engineers's plan, sponsored by Col. Lewis A. Pick, concentrated primarily on reducing floods and increasing navigation within the basin. The two plans were eventually merged into the Missouri River Basin Development Project, commonly known as the Pick-Sloan Plan, during a conference in Omaha, Nebraska, on October 17, 1944. The combined plan was submitted to Congress and enacted on December 22 as part of the Flood Control Act of 1944. In appreciation of Colonel Pick and William Sloan's efforts in the development of the plan, the project was officially dedicated as the Pick-Sloan Missouri Basin Program in 1970.

Under the initial $1.9 billion plan, 316 separate projects were authorized, aiming to create 112 dams, 4.3 million acres of irrigation, 2.6 million kilowatts of hydroelectric generating capacity, and hundreds of miles of levees and other flood protection structures. The highlight of the plan was to be the construction of five, large multipurpose dams along the upper main stem of the Missouri River: Garrison, Oahe, Big Bend, Fort Randall, and Gavins Point, along with improvements to the previously constructed Fort Peck Dam in Montana. Under the compromise, the Corps of Engineers would determine reservoir capacities for flood control and navigation and the Bureau of Reclamation would determine capacities for irrigation. The following year, Congress also authorized the Missouri River Bank Stabilization and Navigation Project under the 1945 Rivers and Harbor Act, which allowed for a nine-foot-deep navigation channel to be created on the Missouri River downstream from Sioux City, Iowa. Together, these projects constitute the majority of engineering works on the Missouri River.

To assist in the cooperative management of these projects, Congress authorized the establishment of the Missouri Basin Inter-Agency Committee in 1945, consisting of various federal and state members. The name and structure of this committee has changed several times over the years. In 2001 it was known as the Missouri River Basin Association to reflect the addition of tribal and other interest groups. Through these cooperative efforts, the region was to receive a fair allocation of flood control, enhanced navigation, cheap hydroelectric power, irrigation, and programs to increase public recreation facilities, municipal and industrial water supplies, and fish and wildlife populations. However, since the inception of the Pick-Sloan Plan, many environmental, water rights, and cost-benefit issues have arisen that have forced planners to revise the design and operation of projects. So many concerns surfaced that in 1964 Congress mandated that any Pick-Sloan project not yet initiated would have to be authorized by Congress. Although most of the primary projects have been completed, many other works have been modified, are still under review, or have been eliminated.

The region has received many significant benefits from the Pick-Sloan Plan. Farms, residences, and businesses worth approximately $17.6 billion benefit from flood control measures provided by the mainstem reservoir system. Generated hydropower provides more than 9 percent of the energy use in Iowa, Minnesota, Nebraska, North Dakota, and parts of Illinois, Montana, and Wisconsin. Many irrigation projects were eventually scaled down or eliminated because of inappropriate soil types or lack of interest, but there are approximately 1,600 water intakes on the mainstem reservoir system, supplying much-needed water for municipal, agricultural, industrial, and domestic water uses. In addition, the river and its lakes provide recreational opportunities that contribute $87.1 billion annually to basin states as well as benefiting navigation on the lower river.

Although these and other benefits have been derived from the Pick-Sloan Plan, the project has also caused significant problems for many local people and the natural river ecosystem. Filling the dams involved flooding approximately 1.6 million acres of fertile bottomlands along the river and the voluntary or forced relocation of thousands of people, including more than 900 Native American families. Damming of the upper portions of the river and channelization of the lower reaches have also created new ecosystems to which plants and animals have been forced to adapt. On the upper reaches, lake environments have replaced much of the free-flowing river, and interlake reaches are affected by lower water temperatures and reduced sediment loads. On the lower river, channelization has reduced river depth diversity and eliminated sandbars and river connections with side channels and backwaters. Natural river flows have also been transformed, with high spring flows now captured in reservoirs and low summer and fall flows supplemented with reservoir releases. These modifications have caused significant changes to the habitats and populations of many river fish and bird species, some to the extent that they are now federal- or state-listed as endangered or threatened species or species of special concern.

Overall, the Pick-Sloan Plan has provided local states and tribes with significant benefits. The project has brought much-needed revenue, employment, flood control, cheap hydroelectric power (to some portions of the region), enhanced navigation, recreation, water supply, and a host of other benefits to an economically depressed area. However, this development comes at a great cost. Besides the ever-increasing amounts of money spent on construction and management of the project, other losses have been incurred that cannot be calculated. The cultures and livelihoods of people relocated by the projects were often severely disrupted, and the natural ecosystem of the river has been forever altered. Because of such concerns, attempts are now being made to take a more balanced approach to water management within the Missouri River Basin.

Cody L. Knutson
University of Nebraska–Lincoln

Ferrell, John R. *Big Dam Era: A Legislative and Institutional History of the Pick-Sloan Missouri Basin Program.*

Omaha: U.S. Army Corp of Engineers, 1993. Lawson, Michael L. *Dammed Indians: The Pick-Sloan Plan and the Missouri River Sioux, 1944–1980*. Norman: University of Oklahoma Press, 1982.

PLATTE RIVER WHOOPING CRANE MAINTENANCE TRUST

The Platte River Whooping Crane Maintenance Trust is a nonprofit organization dedicated to conservation of migratory bird habitat along Nebraska's Platte River. The trust's mission is to protect and maintain the physical, hydrological, and biological integrity of the river as a life-support system for whooping cranes, sandhill cranes, waterfowl, and other migratory birds. The trust acquires land and water rights, manages and protects habitat, and conducts research on migratory birds.

In the 1970s, the Missouri Basin Power Project proposed the Grayrocks Dam on the Laramie River (a tributary of the North Platte) in Wyoming. The state of Nebraska and the National Wildlife Federation objected to Grayrocks, claiming it would jeopardize irrigation and wildlife habitat downstream in Nebraska. In 1978 a court-approved settlement provided for certain mitigation and enhancement measures, including the creation of the trust. These measures satisfied the requirements of the Endangered Species Act and allowed construction of Grayrocks to continue.

The trust was initially funded by a $7.5 million payment from the project developers. Income from the fund is used to finance land and water rights acquisition, research, and land management. Three trustees appointed by each of the parties to the settlement agreement administer the trust. Through fee title and conservation easements, the trust protects and manages approximately 10,000 acres. These lands are in active farming and ranching operations, where such activities are compatible with management of migratory bird habitat. The trust also continues to pay property taxes. In addition to land management activities, the trust has participated in legal proceedings, including the Federal Energy Regulatory Commission's relicensing of Nebraska's McConaughy Reservoir and a lawsuit between Nebraska and Wyoming to ensure long-term protection of river flows. A licensing settlement was reached in 1998 with the Nebraska Public Power District and the Central Nebraska Public Power and Irrigation District, in which water stored in an environmental "account" can now be released specifically for wildlife needs. *Nebraska v. Wyoming*, a legal dispute over the allocation of Platte River flow, was settled in 2001, with Wyoming agreeing to further restrictions on its consumptive water use.

See also PHYSICAL ENVIRONMENT: Bird Migrations.

Paul J. Currier
Platte River Whooping Crane
Maintenance Trust

PLAYA LAKES

Playa lakes are integral wetlands of the Southern Great Plains. Playas, meaning "beach" in Spanish, are found in semiarid environments throughout the world but are most numerous in the Playa Lakes Region of southwestern Kansas, southeastern Colorado, the Oklahoma Panhandle, eastern New Mexico, and northwestern Texas. There are approximately 21,000 playa lakes on the Llano Estacado of Texas and New Mexico alone.

Playas are the most apparent topographical aspect of the essentially flat southern High Plains. They are small depressional wetlands, underlain by a clay soil, with a closed watershed. Perhaps the most ephemeral wetlands in North America, playas are dependent on localized, unpredictable, late spring and summer thunderstorms to collect and hold water. Playas can therefore be dry or flooded at any given time, and the plants and animals associated with them have to be able to adapt to such changeable conditions. Playas collect nearly 90 percent of the precipitation runoff on the southern High Plains and are the primary source of flood control. Most overlie the southern portion of the Ogallala Aquifer, and they provide approximately 80 percent of its annual water recharge. This is a critical function of playas, because the southern High Plains are heavily cultivated and grazed, and both endeavors are dependent on the Ogallala Aquifer.

Because of the dominance of agriculture, playas are the primary remaining wildlife habitat in the region. Most wildlife species in the area depend on playa habitats for existence. Thirty-seven mammalian species and almost 200 bird species have been reported in playas. Playas constitute vital nesting, migration, and wintering habitats for wetland birds, including shore and wading species. It has been estimated that nearly two million ducks, 600,000 geese, and 500,000 sandhill cranes winter in playas during wet years. Playas are also the principal breeding sites for amphibians in the region.

A total of 346 plant species are associated with playas. These include not only traditional wetland species but also many prairie plants no longer found in the surrounding uplands. Playas therefore serve as a seed repository for the flora of the region.

Threats to playas include physical alteration, direct application of agricultural chemicals, overgrazing, and sedimentation. Of these, sedimentation is the most serious. Approximately 90 percent of playas surrounded by cropland have lost their original volume due to sedimentation. At the current rate, all playas could fill with sediment within ninety-five years. Fortunately, measures are being taken to prevent or slow future sedimentation effects, restore degraded playas, and conserve these precious wetlands. These include taking land out of production through the Conservation Reserve Program, erosion control through contour farming, and creating buffers of native vegetation around the playas.

See also PHYSICAL ENVIRONMENT: Bird Migrations.

David A. Haukos
Texas Tech University

Haukos, David A., and Loren M. Smith. *Common Flora of the Playa Lakes*. Lubbock: Texas Tech University Press, 1997. Luo, Hong-Ren, Loren M. Smith, B. L. Allen, and David A. Haukos. "Effects of Sedimentation on Playa Wetland Volume." *Ecological Applications* 7 (1997): 247–52.

PORTAGES

See TRANSPORTATION: Portages

RAINMAKING

It is not surprising that European American settlers in the Great Plains, dependent on agriculture and plagued by drought, would develop an interest in rainmaking. The earliest attempts involved the concussion method, which was premised on the theory that gunpowder explosions triggered friction and generated nuclei to produce rain. In 1890 Congress appropriated funds to put this theory into practice. The task was given to Gen. Robert St. George Dyrenforth. Experimentation began on the C Ranch in Andrews County, Texas, in 1891 and continued at San Antonio, Texas, in 1892. No rainfall occurred. General Dyrenforth was dubbed "General Dryhenceforth," and the remaining funds appropriated for rainmaking experiments reverted to the Department of the Treasury.

The public did not give up on rainmaking. Frank Melbourne of Australia, the "rain wizard" who claimed to possess a "secret formulae" to produce rain, launched a successful career in Goodland, Kansas, in 1891. Although Melbourne guarded his techniques, other rainmaking companies soon claimed knowledge of his method. By 1892, the Goodland Artificial Rain Company and the Swisher Rain Company competed for business in South Dakota, Nebraska, Kansas, Oklahoma, Texas, Colorado, Utah, and California. By 1893, five rainmaking companies hailed from Kansas, all claiming use of Melbourne's method. Even then doubters were still in abundance across the Great Plains. Not much had changed since the early days of rainmaking: once while Melbourne was working in the Nebraska Panhandle, Old Jules Sandoz rode down to watch; following the performance that produced thunder, wind, and a few drops of rain complete with double rainbow, Old Jules remarked to his neighbors, "I'll keep catching skunks for a living." Eventually, fraudulent practices disillusioned farmers, and rainmaking companies lost support.

By the end of the nineteenth century, interest in irrigation had supplanted interest in rainmaking in Kansas. Still, Americans' faith in science and progress carried the rainmaker into the twentieth century. The cereal manufacturer, C. W. Post of Texas, maintained belief in the concussion method. From 1911 to 1914, Post executed "rain battles" near Post City, Texas, detonating dynamite along the Caprock Escarpment. Inspired by an occasional rainfall, Post optimistically predicted that rainmaking would one day replace irrigation.

By World War I, as public interest in traditional methods of rainmaking waned, scientists turned to airplanes and cloud seeding with sand, dust, and dry ice. This method used existing clouds, rather than the earlier attempts to create clouds, and met with some local success.

See also INDUSTRY: Post, C. W.

April L. Whitten
Omaha, Nebraska

Mason, Basil John. *Clouds, Rain, and Rainmaking.* Cambridge: University Press, 1962. Spence, Clark C. *The Rainmakers: American "Pluviculture" to World War II.* Lincoln: University of Nebraska Press, 1980. Townsend, Jeff. *Making Rain in America: A History.* Lubbock: Texas Tech University Press, 1975.

REPORT ON THE LANDS OF THE ARID REGION

One of the most famous documents in American environmental history, the *Report on the Lands of the Arid Region of the United States* (1878) was less than 200 pages long. The authors were members of the Geographical and Geological Survey of the Rocky Mountain Region, under the direction of John Wesley Powell, intrepid explorer of the Colorado River and the Grand Canyon. Powell's own contribution to their report to Congress was the first two chapters, which were characteristically bold and visionary.

The nation was moving into a vast region marked by aridity, Powell warned, and the traditional system for disposing of the public domain to private citizens—the 160-acre farming homestead—was badly adapted to that condition. Powell relied on data collected by the Smithsonian showing that beyond the 100th meridian rainfall was less than twenty inches a year, on average, which was insufficient for most crops. Successful settlement would require laws that encouraged smaller-scale farms based on communal irrigation and, more generally, laws that encouraged a pastoral economy of sheep and cattle ranches.

Separating the arid from the humid region was the Great Plains (which Powell called the Sub-humid Region), stretching over nearly one-tenth of the country. He predicted that much agricultural wealth would come out of this "beautiful prairie country," whose rich soils seemed ready for the plow. He foresaw, however, that the Plains would experience many disastrous droughts, leaving people disappointed and bankrupt, and he recommended developing surface irrigation to mitigate some of this uncertainty.

Donald Worster
University of Kansas

Stegner, Wallace. *Beyond the Hundredth Meridian: John Wesley Powell and the Second Opening of the American West.* Boston: Houghton Mifflin, 1954. Worster, Donald. *An Unsettled Country: Changing Landscapes of the American West.* Albuquerque: University of New Mexico, 1994.

RIPARIAN DOCTRINE

The riparian doctrine is a system of water law that gives the owner of land bordering a stream or river, or riparian land, the legal right to use the water of the stream. The right to water use comes from the spatial connection between the stream or river and the riparian land. The riparian right cannot be bought or sold. Nor can a riparian right be extinguished due to nonuse or inefficient use of the water. The riparian right cannot be separated from the land and thus is a permanent benefit of owning riparian land.

Riparian rights are correlative, which means all riparian landowners have an equal right to use the stream or river. Under the riparian doctrine, a riparian landowner has the right to use a reasonable amount of stream water to supply needs naturally arising from living next to a watercourse. However, uses of water must not significantly reduce stream quantity, diminish the quality of the water, or change the spatial pattern of flow, as these alterations may affect the rights of others living along the stream.

Normal riparian uses are not extensive. Traditionally these include domestic water uses, such as supplying household needs and stock watering. Some nonconsumptive commercial uses such as powering a mill are also acceptable. Alternate uses are presumed to be legitimate so long as the use does not negatively affect other riparian rights to the same stream. Riparian rights are based on the theory that most of the water used on riparian land will eventually return to the stream because the water is used in the same drainage basin.

The riparian doctrine was the pioneering water law in the legal landscape of the Great Plains. The first riparian rights were introduced into Texas by the Spanish more than 200 years ago. Subsequently, the riparian doctrine, bundled as part of the common law, came to the Great Plains with the westward expansion of European American settlement in the nineteenth century.

The riparian principles of water law had worked well for settlers in the eastern parts of North America. However, as settlers moved to the drier climates of the western Plains, riparian methods of environmental adaptation did not necessarily yield the same results as those achieved in more humid environments. As population in the marginal environments of the Great Plains increased, and as the settlers tried to duplicate the lifestyles and population densities of the east, demands for water also increased. This led to competition for scarce water and a demand for more efficiency in water usage. Early disputes centered over irrigation diversions, and riparian rights were increasingly circumscribed by allowing only "reasonable" uses of water. Court decisions in Dakota Territory (1866), Nebraska (1903), and Kansas (1905) established this principle. Gradually the competing doctrine of appropriation rights displaced riparian rights in Plains states, with the exception of Texas. But even in Texas,

grants of state lands have not conveyed riparian rights since 1895.

Theron Josephson
Ferris State University

Dunbar, Robert G. *Forging New Rights in Western Water.* Lincoln: University of Nebraska Press, 1983. Hutchins, Wells A. *Water Rights in the Nineteen Western States.* Washington DC: Government Printing Office, 1974. Trelease, Frank J., and George A. Gould. *Cases and Materials on Water Law*, 4th ed. St. Paul MN: West Publishing Company, 1986.

RIVER COMPACTS

Interstate river compacts are used extensively in the Great Plains to voluntarily apportion interstate rivers among two or more states. In addition, although the Canadian Constitution does not provide for interprovincial compacts, a series of four agreements collectively known as the Prairie Provinces Water Apportionment Agreement apportions water among Alberta, Saskatchewan, and Manitoba. Regional rivers subject to compacts, in whole or in part, include the Arkansas, Belle Fourche, Big Blue, Canadian, Niobrara, Pecos, Red, Republican, and Platte in the United States, and the Saskatchewan, Churchill, Assiniboine, and Qu'Appelle in Canada.

With few exceptions, rights to use surface waters, including the waters of interstate streams, are created and administered under state law. If interstate flows are not apportioned among riparian states, interstate conflicts over use are inevitable. The U.S. Supreme Court has held that each riparian state is entitled to an equitable share of a river's flow. Thus an upstream state cannot, by virtue of its geographical position alone, claim all of the water that originates in, or flows through, the state. A state that suffers actual injury as a consequence of another state's water development activities can bring a suit against the offending state under the original jurisdiction of the Supreme Court. Such suits, known as equitable apportionment suits, ask the Court to equitably divide the river among the competing states. However, equitable apportionment suits are costly, time-consuming, and notoriously unpredictable. Moreover, they can be pursued only after serious water conflicts have arisen. In theory, interstate compacts offer riparian states an opportunity to negotiate an equitable distribution of a river's benefits before serious conflicts develop.

An interstate river compact is in the nature of a treaty among riparian states. The compact limits the sovereign powers that each of the compacting parties might otherwise exercise over river flows within their borders. Although some river compacts address issues such as pollution, flood control, and water management, the primary purpose of most river compacts is to allocate flows among competing states. Apportionment can limit consumption in an upper state or mandate delivery to a lower state. Given variations in annual flow, the choice of method can be significant. Moreover, the delivery obligation or the consumption limitation can be stated on a volume basis or as a mandated rate of flow. Compliance can be measured annually or with reference to multiyear averages. An unresolved issue in most river compacts is whether groundwater that is hydrologically linked to surface waters is also subject to allocation or regulation under the compact.

The process of negotiating a river compact is deceptively simple and analogous to negotiating a contract. Typically, the process begins with Congress authorizing riparian states to negotiate a compact, although nothing prevents states from negotiating without a congressional invitation. Participating states appoint representatives to negotiate a draft agreement. If state representatives reach agreement on a draft text, the text is introduced as legislation in each of the participating states. States indicate their willingness to be bound by compact terms by enacting the legislation. The compact does not become a legally binding document, however, until Congress ratifies it. Congressional ratification is required by the Compacts Clause of the U.S. Constitution. Apparently, framers of the Constitution were concerned that without such an approval mechanism, groups of states might amass political power at the expense of the federal government. This concern is readily apparent with respect to river compacts, given the significant federal interest in interstate river systems.

The process of congressional ratification transforms an interstate compact agreement into federal law. As federal law, terms of the compact preempt and supercede any inconsistent provisions of state or local laws. With respect to river compacts, any state water law provisions that are inconsistent with terms of the compact are preempted. Thus, state constitutional provisions purporting to create unlimited rights to divert and appropriate water are, after compacting, limited to the share of a river's flows that have been allocated to the state in question. Apportionment of water by compact also binds individual water users, whether or not they were parties to the compact negotiations, although many river compacts provide that they have no effect on preexisting water rights. On the other hand, congressional ratification permits states to reach agreements that would otherwise comprise an unconstitutional interference with the export of water to other states.

Compact commissions administer most river compacts. Typically, each state will have one or more voting representatives on the commission. The federal government often has a nonvoting representative. The precise structure of the compact commission and the powers that it can exercise are set forth in the compact agreement. Commission powers can be extensive or limited. One theoretical advantage of compacts over litigation in apportioning river benefits is that compacts can provide for continuing administration to respond to changed conditions or new facts developed over time. In practice, however, most river compacts give commissions little power to respond to changed conditions. Typically, commission powers and duties are limited to data collection, compliance monitoring, and report drafting.

In the absence of strong compact commissions, enforcement of river compacts is typically a matter for negotiated settlement or interstate litigation. Suits between states for breach of a compact obligation are within the original and exclusive jurisdiction of the U.S. Supreme Court. The Court may issue authoritative interpretations of compact language, order states to comply with terms of the agreement, or award damages for past failures to comply with terms of the agreement. Historically, the Court has often expressed its preference that states negotiate and compromise their differences rather that resorting to litigation. Many compacts specifically provide that they can be amended, usually through a process that requires formal state ratification and congressional consent. Most also provide that they can be terminated by unanimous consent of the party states.

Recent litigation among Plains states has focused on the extent to which interstate compacts were intended to apply to groundwater pumping. Developments in hydrology have demonstrated that some groundwater sources are linked hydrologically with surface water flows. While a few compacts, such as the Kansas-Nebraska Big Blue River Compact, specifically address the impact of groundwater pumping on surface water flows, most compacts are silent about groundwater. The Arkansas River Compact, for instance, makes no mention of groundwater, but it does provide that future water development may not materially deplete river flows to the detriment of water users in Colorado and Kansas. In *Kansas v. Colorado* (1997), the U.S. Supreme Court upheld the contention of Kansas that postcompact groundwater pumping in Colorado had caused material depletions of the usable state line flows of the Arkansas River in violation of the compact. Similarly, in ongoing litigation between Kansas and Nebraska over use of water in the Republican River basin, Kansas has alleged that the Republican River Compact should be interpreted as apportioning groundwater that is hy-

drologically related to the river flow, despite the absence of specific language in the compact that would mandate that result. Both cases illustrate the difficulty of trying to reconcile principles of modern hydrology with agreements negotiated before groundwater–surface water relationships were clearly perceived.

Norman W. Thorson
University of Nebraska–Lincoln

Grant, Douglas L. "Water Apportionment Compacts Between States." In *Waters and Water Rights*, edited by Robert E. Beck. Charlottesville VA: Michie Law Publishers, 1996: 639–65. Muys, Jerome C. *Interstate Water Compacts: The Interstate Compact and Federal-Interstate Compact.* Arlington VA: National Water Commission, 1971.

RIVERS

Characteristics of rivers in the Great Plains reflect the climatic transition from arid environments in the lee of the Rocky Mountains eastward to subhumid and humid tallgrass prairies. There is much less runoff to the rivers in the western than in the eastern Great Plains; for example, yearly runoff averages 0.2 inch in eastern Colorado compared to eight inches in eastern Kansas.

About one-half of the major Plains rivers begin in the Rocky Mountains at altitudes of 8,000 to 11,000 feet and receive substantial flows from mountain snowmelt. After entering the Great Plains, most of those rivers contribute some of their flows to extensive irrigation projects. Rivers originating in the Plains generally have less flow available in their western reaches, where water for irrigation is most needed. The characteristics of the major rivers are summarized below from north to south in the Great Plains.

Kis-is-ska-tche-wan, which means "swift flowing," was the Cree Indian name for the North and South Saskatchewan Rivers. Rapid flow and flood conditions are most extreme in June or July of years when snowmelt in the mountains coincides with major rainstorms

Platte River State Park, Nebraska, May 1989

Data for Selected Rivers

Gaging station name	Drainage area (square kilometers)	Period of discharge analysis	Average discharge (cubic meters per second)
Missouri River at St. Joseph, Missouri	1,100,000	1958–96	1,300
Missouri River at Bismarck, North Dakota	480,000	1954–96	650
Missouri River near Culbertson, Montana	240,000	1958–95	300
Platte River at Louisville, Nebraska	220,000	1953–96	200
Yellowstone River near Sidney, Montana	180,000	1967–96	360
Kansas River at DeSoto, Kansas	150,000	1918–97	210
South Saskatchewan River at St. Louis, Saskatchewan	150,000	1980–96	190
Arkansas River at Ralston, Oklahoma	140,000	1977–95	170
North Saskatchewan River at Prince Albert, Saskatchewan	130,000	1980–96	230
Red River of the North at Emerson, Manitoba	100,000	1912–95	100
Colorado River at Austin, Texas	100,000	1937–96	55
Red River near Gainesville, Texas	80,000	1937–97	94
Pecos River near Girvin, Texas	77,000	1939–96	2
Brazos River near Glen Rose, Texas	67,000	1970–96	34
Canadian River at Purcell, Oklahoma	67,000	1980–95	22
Cheyenne River at Cherry Creek, South Dakota	62,000	1961–94	23

in the foothills. Dominating water resources development in Saskatchewan is Lake Diefenbaker, which was created by Gardiner Dam on the South Saskatchewan and serves a variety of purposes, including electricity generation, irrigation, and recreation.

The Assiniboine River receives flow from large tributaries, including the Qu'Appelle and Souris Rivers, before joining the Red River of the North. A connection with the South Saskatchewan has existed since the late 1960s when the water level of Lake Diefenbaker has been high enough for water to be released to the Qu'Appelle River.

From its origin in western Montana to its confluence with the Mississippi River, the Missouri is the longest river in the United States and has the second largest drainage area. Early writers described the Missouri as a muddy and a hungry river, constantly eating at its banks. A strong current would tear away an entire strip of forest, blocking the river with tree trunks that hindered navigation. Control works have since reduced these characteristics, but landowners along the banks where the river is not impounded still become apprehensive every time the river rises. The Missouri provides water supplies for Great Falls, Montana, Omaha, Nebraska, and St. Joseph and Kansas City, Missouri. It also provides irrigation water and hydroelectric power from six reservoirs on the main stem upstream from Sioux City, Iowa. The reservoirs in North and South Dakota extend so far along the river that less than a quarter of the river's length in those states has not been inundated.

Snowdrifts on the side of Yount's Peak, near Yellowstone National Park, melt to produce streams that combine into the Yellowstone River, which has the upstream half of its drainage area outside the Great Plains. After making a journey of more than 671 miles and providing water supply for the city of Billings, the Yellowstone joins the Missouri at the Montana–North Dakota boundary.

Although tributaries of the North and South Platte Rivers are less than ten miles apart in northern Colorado, the course of the rivers diverges through Wyoming and Colorado until they finally flow near each other in Nebraska and join at the city of North Platte. The Platte River then flows eastward 310 miles across Nebraska to join the Missouri River at Plattsmouth. The Platte and its largest branches provide irrigation water for vast acreages of crops. The South Platte and tributaries provide part of Denver's water supply. Between Lincoln and Omaha, the Platte provides Lincoln's water supply and part of Omaha's supply by contributing induced recharge to wells in the adjoining alluvium.

The Kansas River has the fifteenth largest drainage area in the United States; however, the river bearing that name has a length of only 185 miles. Topeka, Lawrence, and much of Johnson County, including the densely populated suburbs of Kansas City, obtain water supplies from the Kansas River.

The Arkansas River is the sixth longest in the United States and has the ninth largest drainage area. It supplies water for Pueblo, Aurora, and Colorado Springs, and for extensive irrigation. In western Kansas during much of the year it is nearly dry. In eastern Oklahoma, the Arkansas receives the Canadian River, which, with tributaries, provides about half of the water supply for Oklahoma City.

The headwaters of the Red River are in the New Mexico part of the level, arid Llano Estacado. Eastward, the Red River forms much of the Oklahoma-Texas boundary, and tributaries provide the Wichita Falls water supply. Similarly the Brazos and Colorado Rivers begin on the Llano Estacado, supplying Waco and Austin near the eastern edge of the Great Plains.

Developments on several rivers have resulted in both benefits and unwelcome changes. Well-documented changes include degradation of riverbeds downstream from dams and large reductions in channel width of some rivers.

See also TRANSPORTATION: Water Transportation.

Paul R. Jordan
Lawrence, Kansas

Bartlett, Richard A., ed. *Rolling Rivers*. New York: McGraw-Hill, 1984. Department of the Interior, Geological Survey. *National Water Summary 1985—Hydrologic Events and Surface-Water Resources*. Reston VA: Water-Supply Paper 2300, 1986. Richards, J. Howard, and Ka Iu Fung, eds. *Atlas of Saskatchewan*. Saskatoon: University of Saskatchewan, 1969.

RIVER TOWNS

See CITIES AND TOWNS: River Towns

SANDHILLS LAKES

In the Nebraska Sandhills, there are an estimated 175 square miles of shallow lakes and ponds, about 100 square miles of marsh, and more than 1,500 square miles of subirrigated meadows. These water-dominated landscape features make the Sandhills the second most productive waterfowl region in the United States. Lakes and wetlands occur where low-lying, flat valley floors between grass-stabilized sand dunes intersect the vast groundwater resource of the High Plains, or Ogallala, Aquifer. There is little or no surface water runoff into these lakes. Sandhills lakes range in size from less than 10 acres to more than 800 acres. Lake areas fluctuate seasonally, depending on the dynamic interaction of climatic and hydrologic processes. The deepest Sandhills lake is Blue Lake in Garden County, which is about fifteen feet deep. More characteristic depths are between two and four feet.

Chemical data indicate that the lakes are compositionally diverse, ranging from fresh to brine (total dissolved solids vary from less than 200 milligrams per liter to more than 100,000 milligrams per liter). Alkalinity, as calcium carbonate, ranges from less than 200 to greater than 100,000 milligrams per liter; pH is usually greater than 8.0. Groundwater, primarily derived from local precipitation, is the principal source of water and dissolved solids for the lakes. Differences in the chemistry between lakes are a function of local hydrologic variability, related to the magnitude of inflow and outflow of water from a lake and the age of the lake.

See also PHYSICAL ENVIRONMENT: Sandhills.

David C. Gosselin
University of Nebraska–Lincoln

Gosselin, David C. "Major-ion Chemistry of Compositionally Diverse Lakes, Western Nebraska, U.S.A.: Implications for Paleoclimatic Interpretations." *Journal of Paleolimnology* 17 (1997): 33–49. Rundquist, Donald C. *Wetland Inventories of Nebraska's Sandhills.* Resource Report 9, Conservation and Survey Division, University of Nebraska–Lincoln, 1983.

SPANISH WATER LAW

Spaniards who explored and settled the Great Plains from the sixteenth through the early nineteenth centuries brought with them a set of legal and cultural values about water that had been fostered over the centuries in Spain and later in central Mexico. The arid and semiarid stretches of northern New Mexico, southern Colorado, and western Texas, which constituted the far northern frontier of New Spain, shaped settlement patterns as colonists sought water to sustain rural economic activities. Access to, and control over, this natural resource influenced the rhythms of daily life and not infrequently precipitated conflict between individuals and communities. As a result, knowledge and application of Spanish water rights became the purview of farmers, lawyers, judges, and irrigators.

Spanish water law in America was heir to a long and dynamic legal tradition that began in Spain under the Roman Empire and continued after subsequent invasions by Germanic and Muslim peoples. In 1265, Alfonso X ordered the codification of disparate legal codes and customs and, although elements of Germanic and Islamic law can be found in the compilation, the *Siete Partidas* was the adaptation of Roman Law to a medieval Spanish reality. With a few modifications and additions over the years, the Siete Partidas remained the primary legal code that governed water rights. After the Spanish conquest of Mexico and Peru in the sixteenth century, the general principles of Spanish jurisprudence were given a distinctly American context in a legal code written specifically for Spain's vast empire. In 1681, the Spanish crown promulgated the *Recopilación de las leyes de los reynos de las Indias*, constituting the foundation of Spanish water law in America. It vested original ownership of all land, water, and minerals in the Spanish Crown, which was empowered to alienate from its domain these resources to private individuals, towns, and informal rural communities.

Spanish jurisprudence recognized two kinds of property rights that are fundamental to understanding Spanish water law. Surface water was *propiedad imperfecta*, which meant that it was subject to qualification and measured against the rights of others. The Spanish civil law of property did not recognize riparian rights to running streams or rivers. If a piece of property fronted on a stream, for example, the owner could only use the water for domestic purposes. The Spanish Crown did convey surface water rights, however, for agricultural or industrial purposes through a specific grant (*merced de agua*). On the far northern frontier of New Spain a judicial procedure known as *repartimiento de aguas* often was used to convey such rights. But it was more common for surface water to be granted automatically if the land classification itself reflected a conveyance (e.g., if a plot of land was designated as *tierras de pan llevar*, or irrigable land, then the subsequent grant carried water rights). Groundwater, however, was *propiedad perfecta*. Ownership of spring water and rainwater was nearly absolute, and landowners could not be easily deprived of these waters once conveyance was extended, even if use of it caused damage to neighbors.

Three social entities with juridical personality competed for water on Spain's far northern frontier: Spanish towns, Indian pueblos, and informal rural communities known today as *acequia* (ditch) associations. Judges who presided over water disputes allocated resources according to seven principles: just title, prior use (not the same as prior appropriation in Anglo common law), need, legal right, intent, noninjury to third party, and equity and the common good. The dry expanse of the Great Plains fashioned a legal atmosphere that eschewed water monopolies, and judges applied a combination of these principles to facilitate community harmony and social tranquility. Even after Mexico's independence from Spain in 1821, judges continued to employ these principles as Spanish water law maintained its full vigor.

Moreover, Spanish water law survives today in the Great Plains because the Treaty of Guadalupe Hidalgo, which ended hostilities between the United States and Mexico in 1848, obliged the American government to respect the property of those Mexicans who suddenly found themselves residing north of the newly created boundary. Since water was considered property under Spanish and Mexican law, the U.S. courts act as surrogates for Hispanic water law.

See also HISPANIC AMERICANS: Guadalupe Hidalgo, Treaty of; Hispano Homeland.

Michael M. Brescia
State University of New York, Fredonia

Ebright, Malcolm. *Land Grants and Lawsuits in Northern New Mexico.* Albuquerque: University of New Mexico Press, 1994. Meyer, Michael C. *Water in the Hispanic Southwest: A Social and Legal History, 1550–1850.* Tucson: University of Arizona Press, 1996. Tyler, Daniel. *The Mythical Pueblo Rights Doctrine: Water Administration in Hispanic New Mexico.* El Paso: Texas Western Press, 1990.

STOCK PONDS

Stock ponds, generally small and sometimes transitory, are nevertheless the most ubiquitous source of water in the Great Plains. They occur from Texas to Alberta, wherever there is free-ranging livestock and sufficient surface water or available groundwater. Frequency of occurrence varies also with soil type: there are fewer ponds on permeable soils, such as loess, than on clay soils, which hold the water at the surface. On the Southern Plains they are known as tanks.

There are two types of stock ponds: the embankment pond, which dams a stream or periodic runoff channel, and the excavated pond, where a hole is dug to intersect the water table. The latter—common on floodplains and in other areas, such as the Nebraska Sandhills, where the water table is high—is more dependable because groundwater fluctuates less than surface runoff. Since the nineteenth century, farmers have constructed their own ponds using basic farm equipment; now larger projects may necessitate heavy excavating equipment, and subsidies are available through various conservation programs.

Critics argue that the ponds contribute to the depletion of river flow by impounding runoff. In the balance, however, advantages outweigh any disadvantages. The ponds are a good source of livestock water, allowing well-watered cattle to range widely across pastures. They are often stocked with fish for recreational purposes, and they are points of attraction for wildfowl, which breed there. And aesthetically, the muddy stock pond, ringed by attendant cattle, is a defining Plains scene.

David J. Wishart
University of Nebraska–Lincoln

TRANSMOUNTAIN WATER DIVERSION PROJECTS

When settlers arrived in the Great Plains they noticed that more water was available in the mountains than on the adjacent flatlands, and they developed transmountain water diversion projects, as well as other schemes, to capture mountain runoff in storage reservoirs for use during dry periods. Today, much of the water supply of the Great Plains region near the mountains is based on stored mountain water. Without this imported water, the region could not support as many farms and cities as it does.

A good example of transmountain water diversions is the Colorado–Big Thompson Project. In this project, water flows thirteen miles through a tunnel under Rocky Mountain National Park from the Colorado River headwaters to the East Slope. The project diverts 230,000 acre-feet to serve some 2,428 farms and communities on the East Slope. It involves extensive facilities that include twelve reservoirs, thirty-four miles of tunnel, ninety-five miles of canals or conduits, six hydroelectric plants, and three pumping stations. The project was long in the making and embroiled in political controversy. The preliminary survey was made in 1884; northern Colorado had organized for the "Grand Lake Project" by 1933; and it was completed in 1956. Water management remains a controversial issue in the region, and it is doubtful that more large transmountain water diversion projects will be built.

Neil S. Grigg
Colorado State University

Tyler, Daniel. *The Last Water Hole in the West: The Colorado-Big Thompson Project and the Northern Colorado Water Conservancy District.* Niwot: University Press of Colorado, 1992.

UNION COLONY

The Union Colony of Greeley, Colorado, was one of the most successful irrigation-based settlements in the Great Plains. It was organized by Horace Greeley, who, following his own famous advice, traveled west in 1859 and included a visit to Colorado. Ten years later, he sent a colleague, Nathan Meeker, to search out a suitable site for a colony based on irrigated farming. A site near the junction of the Cache la Poudre and South Platte Rivers was chosen in 1870—a block of land purchased from the Denver Pacific Railroad—and by May colonists were arriving from Chicago, Buffalo, Boston, and New York.

Requirements for membership in the colony included a $155 fee and a good moral character. From the beginning, the success of the colony depended upon control of water. In exchange for their fee, colonists received a farming tract of five, ten, twenty, or forty acres, the size increasing with distance from the central hub of Greeley, as well as guaranteed water rights. Within a month, water was flowing through ditches to cultivated fields of wheat, corn, and vegetables. Within a year, thirty-six miles of main canals had been built, and a grid of lateral ditches brought a potential 60,000 acres within reach of irrigation. The largest canal was twenty-seven miles long, thirty feet wide, and four and one-half feet deep and carried water from the floodplain to the adjacent benchlands. The town of Greeley flourished, reaching a population of 1,500 in May of 1871. The growth was sustained, and by 1873 the colony structure was unable to accommodate the expansion and was disbanded. However, from this successful start, Greeley and the surrounding area have remained one of the most productive portions of the Colorado Piedmont and are still a center of irrigated farming.

David J. Wishart
University of Nebraska–Lincoln

Willard, James F. *The Union Colony at Greeley, Colorado, 1869–1871*. Boulder: University Press of Colorado, 1918.

U.S. ARMY CORPS OF ENGINEERS

The U.S. Army Corps of Engineers (COE) dates back to 1779, when Congress formed the unit for military support purposes. Public works projects, employing citizens outside the military to work for the COE, began in 1824 with work to improve navigation on the Ohio and Mississippi Rivers. The initial and continuing focus of the Army Corps of Engineers in the Great Plains is the Missouri River.

The Corps's presence on the Plains began in 1867 when Capt. Charles W. Howell spent three months on a survey of the Missouri River from Sioux City, Iowa, to Fort Benton, Montana. His purpose was to map major sandbars and snags for those using the Missouri for military purposes or for transportation to the Montana goldfields.

Since that first expedition, the objectives of the COE on the Missouri have been to control bank erosion, improve navigation, and provide flood control. All three goals were placed within reach in the 1950s with the completion of six dams on the river from Montana to South Dakota. Financed mostly by the Pick-Sloan Plan, the dams reduced floods sufficiently to allow the COE to complete their work on bank stabilization and to create a nine-foot-deep navigation channel from the mouth of the Missouri at St. Louis to Sioux City. The COE has also constructed smaller dams on Salt and Papillion Creeks in southeastern Nebraska and constructed levees along hundreds of miles of Missouri River tributaries, including the Big Sioux and Floyd Rivers of Iowa.

The very nature of the Missouri River has been changed by COE intervention. What was once a shallow, swift-flowing river that ranged in width and was capable of moving tremendous loads of silt and sand has been transformed into a relatively narrow, uniform, low-sediment transportation route. Views of the river near Plattsmouth, Nebraska, taken from 1934 to 1983, show the dramatic transformations that have taken place. The strategic placement of wooden and rock dikes has encouraged sediment deposition near the stream banks, leaving flow to be concentrated in the nine-foot-deep navigational channel, which is self-scouring and normally does not require dredging.

The changing nature of society in the Great Plains is reflected in the current debate over the prioritized operation of Missouri River dams. For example, flood protection and navigation have been important priorities when deciding on water releases from the dams. However, because of increased recreational benefits at the reservoirs and the occurrence of several endangered species throughout the river system, there have been calls for expanded priorities. The revision of the COE's Master Manual for the operation of the main stem dams is a subject of ongoing work and controversy.

The COE is organized into eight divisions spanning the United States. The Great Plains is contained within the recently formed Missouri River Region of the Northwest Division, comprising the Missouri and Columbia River basins. The Missouri River Region is composed of the Kansas City and Omaha Districts.

Rollin H. Hotchkiss
University of Nebraska–Lincoln

Brey, Debra, Connie Carman, and Kettie Parks, eds. *The Federal Engineer: Damsites to Missile Sites. A History of the Omaha District of the U.S. Army Corps of Engineers*. Washington DC: Government Printing Office, 1984. *Essayons (Let Us Try): The History of the U.S. Army Corps of Engineers*. Washington DC: Government Printing Office, 1991.

WATER LAW, PRAIRIE PROVINCES

The origin of European-based water law in the Canadian Prairie Provinces lies with the Hudson's Bay Company and the century of company administration that followed establishment of its first inland trading post on the Saskatchewan River in 1774. Along with the company's trade goods came a less tangible but equally powerful force of change: English civil and criminal law. Included within this complex web of principles and procedures was the doctrine of riparian rights. Under this doctrine, water rights are restricted to those who have title to property abutting upon bodies of water, and each shoreline or riparian owner is entitled to receive the flow of water to his or her property undiminished except for that quantity withdrawn by upstream riparians for their domestic purposes. Given the situation where water resources far outstripped the needs of the small population settled along the Red River and at the handful of company fur posts farther west and north along the Prairie fringe, the accepted doctrine of riparian rights remained uncontroversial during the first decades of European settlement.

Canada's purchase of the Hudson's Bay Company's Rupert's Land territory in 1869 brought a new but nonetheless common law–based administration. While the shared common law tradition assured continuity in such matters as riparian rights, federal authority over navigable waterways was anchored in the Canadian Constitution. A more direct and far-reaching manifestation of Canadian authority came in 1870 with the Manitoba Act that created the first Prairie Province and governing institutions for the territory beyond. The act stipulated that control of all public lands within the new province would remain in federal hands, a precedent followed when Alberta and Saskatchewan became provinces in 1905. The manner in which Ottawa intended to administer public or Crown lands in the West was outlined in the 1872 Dominion Lands Act. Based largely upon the U.S. Homestead Act, the Canadian statute implicitly recognized homesteaders' riparian rights. As settlement moved farther west on to the semiarid southwestern Prairie known as Palliser's Triangle, the shortcomings of the riparian rights doctrine in water-scarce regions soon became apparent. Following a comprehensive review of water legislation in the western United States and elsewhere, Parliament, guided by irrigation enthusiast William Pearce, passed the Northwest Irrigation Act (1894). Closely modeled upon the Australian Crown Colony of Victoria's 1886 Irrigation Act, the Canadian legislation marked a radical departure from the Anglo-Saxon riparian rights doctrine in favor of the principle that surface waters should be reserved for the public in the name of the Crown, which would allocate water rights in the common interest. Withdrawal of water for other than domestic purposes was subsequently managed through a licensing system.

As the self-proclaimed arbiter of water access in the dry belt, Ottawa immediately had to confront the delicate issue of proposed water diversion schemes on rivers that traversed the Canadian-American border. The mechanism to resolve differences was found in the International Joint Commission, a Canadian-American intergovernmental body established by the Boundary Waters Treaty (1909).

Power sites and facilities that relied on water embraced another aspect of federal water management. At first regulation was facilitated under the general provision of the Dominion

Land Act requiring the proper management of public lands, but by 1919 the electricity needs of a growing and increasingly urban population required the passage of a specific act. The Dominion Water Power Act provided for the granting of rights to the use of water for power purposes, and where there were applications to use the same supply of water for different purposes, these could be adjusted with reference to the two acts (Power and Irrigation), bearing in mind that the Irrigation Act specified that priority be given to water required for domestic and municipal purposes, followed by irrigation.

In 1930 federal jurisdiction over lands and natural resources in the Prairie West was surrendered to the provinces of Manitoba, Saskatchewan, and Alberta. With regard to water law, the principles established in the federal statutes were incorporated into provincial law with only minor changes, and they remain the foundation of contemporary legislation.

David H. Breen
University of British Columbia

Cochrane, M. F. *Water Powers of Canada: The Prairie Provinces and the Northwest Territories.* RG89, vol. 304, file 4801, National Archives of Canada, Ottawa, 1922. Gisvold, Per. *A Survey of the Law of Water in Alberta, Saskatchewan, and Manitoba.* Pub. 1046. Ottawa: Economics Division, Canada Department of Agriculture, 1959. Percy, David R. "Water Rights in Alberta." *Alberta Law Review* 15 (1977): 142–65.

WATER QUALITY

The Great Plains contains the High Plains (or Ogallala) Aquifer, the largest aquifer system in the United States that stretches from South Dakota to Texas, and has a myriad of rivers, lakes, and prairie wetlands. Vast amounts of groundwater are contained within the sands and gravels with silt lenses of the Miocene age Ogallala Formation, the Brule and Arikaree Formations in western Nebraska, and overlying Quaternary age sands and gravels.

Water quality indexes as measurements of the suitability of water for irrigation, human and animal consumption, and fish and wildlife have been developed by the U.S. Environmental Protection Agency (EPA) and the U.S. Department of Agriculture (USDA). Different limits of exposure are based on human and plant health and environmental considerations. No single compilation of water quality over the vast Plains region exists, though various local assessments have been made. Investigations of groundwater quality in the High Plains Aquifer in the early 1980s were an outgrowth of studies of water depletion from irrigation. The investigations confirmed that mining of groundwater by irrigators since the 1940s had lowered the groundwater table by more than 100 feet in parts of Texas, eastern New Mexico, the Oklahoma Panhandle, and Kansas. Follow-up studies indicated that water table declines greater than forty feet occurred from 1980 to 1995. Total dissolved solids (TDS), a measure of water purity, increased from north to south in the aquifer, suggesting an association between mining and deteriorating quality. Very high TDS levels occurred in the Ogallala Formation groundwater beneath southwestern Kansas and the Texas Panhandle. According to the USDA salinity scale, irrigation with this groundwater will promote development of saline soil conditions that render the soil useless. High TDS levels are generally encountered in deeper, older waters that have become more mineralized with time. Upward movement of naturally occurring chemicals from underlying bedrock is a major source of increased TDS. In Kansas and Texas, underlying Permian age bedrock contains salt beds and saline water, providing high amounts of TDS to the Ogallala Aquifer. Wells in these areas also generally contain elevated sodium concentrations that are known to adversely affect plant growth and soil properties.

Although the Ogallala Aquifer has received intense scrutiny, the focus of Great Plains water quality concern is now on the impact of agrichemicals and the generation of animal wastes by agriculture. Areas that are most sensitive to contamination are alluvial valleys with less than fifty feet to groundwater. These river and stream valleys generally have rich, well-drained bottomland and terrace soils that are heavily irrigated by shallow wells and have been row-cropped for decades. Agriculture, the economic mainstay of the Great Plains, is heavily reliant on agrichemicals. In areas vulnerable to leaching, underlying groundwater commonly contains nitrate and herbicides in levels that may adversely affect human health. Nebraska and Kansas have very high incidences of nitrate in well water. The nitrate is derived from commercial fertilizer and animal waste and exceeds public health limits. The herbicides atrazine and metolachlor are used throughout the region on corn land and are frequently detected in surface water and in many shallow aquifers. In soils and water, pesticide transformation occurs, and the resulting degradates are often detected in concentrations that considerably exceed those of the parent pesticides. These degradate compounds may present a future health hazard and environmental concern. Pesticides are also a problem in surface water. Each spring, pesticides are flushed from farms in the Great Plains in runoff. These pesticides accumulate in lakes and reservoirs and can be introduced into municipal wells situated next to creeks and rivers. In addition to nitrate, ammonia from animal and human waste lagoon overflows has been responsible for several fish kills in the Plains. Other chemicals found in groundwater include carbon tetrachloride and ethylene dibromide, which were used as fumigants and commonly occur beneath and near grain elevators.

Contaminants associated with military bases and industries are also a problem in the Great Plains region. In these locations the groundwater may be contaminated with munitions such as RDX and TNT as well as the commonly used degreaser trichloroethylene. Large trichloroethylene plumes in Hastings, Nebraska, and Wichita, Kansas, are the result of industrial solvent disposal.

Roy F. Spalding
University of Nebraska–Lincoln

Exner, Mary, and Roy F. Spalding. *Occurrence of Pesticides and Nitrate in Nebraska's Ground Water.* Lincoln: University of Nebraska Water Center, 1990. Kolpin D. W., E. M. Thurman, and D. A. Goolsby. "Occurrence of Selected Pesticides and Their Metabolites in Near-Surface Aquifers of the Midwestern United States." *Environmental Science and Technology* 30 (1997): 335–40.

WATER TOWERS

Nebraska Public Power District structure, April 1991

A water tower, or elevated tank, is designed to hold enough water to provide a supply area with sufficient amounts for periods of peak use and, in the case of a system failure, one day's use. A water tower, however, is so much more than a reservoir for water. Along highways, they mark the location and declare the name of countless small and large communities. They also provide an opportunity for ardent fans of high school sports, young lovers, and graduating seniors to declare themselves in height-defying graffiti. The need for water and the need to express pride in hometowns and relationships have made the water tower an enduring feature of the Great Plains landscape.

Water towers are generally constructed from steel. Many were produced by companies known to residents of Plains states from bridge nameplates. A wide variety of shapes are used including those referred to as doorknobs, lattice towers, and fully enclosed domes. Many smaller communities used a shape that one author, Anne Dingus, has likened to the head of the Tinman in the classic movie, *The Wizard of Oz*. After the tank is erected, the steel is given a protective coat of paint. The name of the town and sometimes a logo is then painted on the tank. Repainting is performed to maintain the condition of the tank as well as to cover graffiti. Water towers can seem deceptively small in appearance because of their height. However, they can hold anywhere from 15,000 gallons to as much as 3 million gallons of water.

The operation of a water tower is fairly simple. Because it needs to be elevated above the rest of a water system, it is constructed on a scaffold or, in the case of a tank, positioned on a hill. The height—usually between 100 and 300 feet—of a water tower is necessary in order to provide pressure. Water is pumped from a treatment plant or a well into a city's water system and also into the tower. Because the water tower is providing storage, the system's pump can be sized to supply average rather than peak demand. During any period, if the city's system needs more water, water is allowed to flow from the tank and increase the supply through the pipes. If demand decreases, the water flows into the tank and is then stored until it is needed.

Because of the simplicity of their design, water towers have survived since the first half of the twentieth century. Towers are familiar and well-remembered landmarks to former and current residents of communities. They stand as sentinels over stable and growing communities as well as over towns that have been bypassed by highways and economic development. The real importance of a water supply and the symbolic importance of the water tower ensure that the it will continue to be an elemental part of the Plains landscape.

Dori M. Penny
LTA, Inc., Laramie, Wyoming

Dingus, Anne. "The Water Tower." *Texas Monthly.* 1998.

WATER TRANSPORTATION

See TRANSPORTATION: Water Transportation

WETLANDS

Although they account for only about 6.4 percent of the earth's land surface, wetlands are extremely important ecosystems. Wetlands are ecotones, or transitional environments between deeper water systems and terrestrial uplands. They are characterized by the presence of water at or near the surface, unique soil conditions, and hydrophytes (plants suited to wet conditions). Several formal definitions have been written during the past twenty years for regulatory purposes, including the often-cited U.S. federal definition: "The term wetlands means those areas that are inundated or saturated by surface or ground water at a frequency and duration sufficient to support, and that under normal circumstances do support, a prevalence of vegetation typically adapted for life in saturated soil conditions." Thus, wetlands include marshes, bogs, swamps, fens, wet meadows, peatlands, playas, and a number of other aquatic ecosystems that fall under a variety of names.

Wetlands can be categorized into five main types: marine, estuarine, lacustrine, riverine, and palustrine. The latter three types occur in abundance throughout the Great Plains. Indeed, this region includes two of the most important wetland areas in North America: the

expansive Prairie Potholes region of the Prairie Provinces and north-central United States, and the Nebraska Sandhills. Scientists further group wetlands into subsystems and classes based upon their seasonal hydrology (e.g., intermittent or permanent standing water), bottom substrate material (e.g., rock or soft sediment), and the predominant plants (fifty-six subcategories in all). Lacustrine wetlands are typically associated with ponds and lakes, forming the shallow areas along the margins, while riverine wetlands occur along rivers or streams and are often fed by floodwaters. Palustrine wetlands include the remaining shallow water systems that are typically identified as wetlands, including marshes, swamps, and bogs.

Wetlands are dynamic systems, exhibiting major changes in vegetation during the growing season, as surface and subsurface water levels change, sometimes dramatically. Consequently, they provide habitat for a large number of plants and animals, some adapted strictly to aquatic existence and others capable of living in the water for short periods of time during their life cycle. Many aquatic insects, for example, require water for their preadult stages, then emerge as winged adults: dragonflies, damselflies, midges, and many other insects are common members of the wetland community. Aquatic plants, being less mobile, must have adaptations that allow them to live underwater or in saturated sediments, adaptations such as air chambers in their leaves and stems for gas exchange to roots anchored in oxygen-depleted muds.

On a per acre basis, wetlands produce more plant and animal biomass than any other ecosystem on earth. The vast majority of this production is hidden to the untrained eye: hydrophytes in the wetland bottom in the form of roots, rhizomes, and other storage structures, and microscopic plants called algae, which are attached to hydrophytes or bottom mud or occur free-floating in the water. The propensity of wetlands to produce plant and animal biomass is a reflection of their ability to rapidly take up and cycle basic nutrients such as phosphorus and nitrogen. Consequently, wetlands are also now recognized as ideal systems for treating municipal waste, storm water runoff, agricultural runoff, and animal waste. Many wetlands are being constructed each year for this purpose, and natural and restored wetlands are also used. Thus, wetlands have been termed biological filters or the "kidneys" of the landscape. They serve a variety of other important functions as well, including flood control, sediment trapping, erosion control, and groundwater recharge, in addition to their recreational benefits for camping, hunting, canoeing, fishing, and bird watching.

Perhaps the most significant role of wetlands is in maintaining biodiversity. It has been estimated that one-half of the fish, one-third of the birds, and one-sixth of the mammals on the U.S. threatened and endangered species list occur in wetlands. The Prairie Potholes region, for example, is home to twelve of

the thirty-four species of breeding ducks in North America. Nevertheless, wetlands continue to be lost at an alarming rate. Conversions of wetlands to croplands and urban development have resulted in a cumulative loss of 53 percent of all wetlands in the continental United States. South Dakota and Nebraska have lost approximately 35 percent of their wetlands. Federal efforts to preserve and restore many wetlands have increased in the past ten years in the Great Plains, but the decline continues.

Kyle D. Hoagland
University of Nebraska–Lincoln

Mitsch, William J., and James G. Gosselink. *Wetlands.* New York: Van Nostrand Reinhold Co., 1993. Niering, William A. *Wetlands.* New York: Alfred A. Knopf, 1985. van der Valk, Arnold G., ed. *Northern Prairie Wetlands.* Ames: Iowa State University Press, 1989.

WILD AND SCENIC RIVERS

In 1968 the U.S. Congress created the National Wild and Scenic Rivers System. Intended to protect selected rivers exhibiting "outstandingly remarkable" values, the Wild and Scenic Rivers Act declared, "the established national policy of dam and other construction . . . needs to be complemented by a policy that would preserve other selected rivers . . . in their free-flowing condition to protect the water quality . . . and to fulfill other vital conservation purposes." Federal agencies and others involved in river conservation have long debated whether the intent of Congress was to establish a system that would protect only a few "crown jewel" rivers, or whether rivers representing all physiographic regions of the country and all various river types should be included. Whatever the congressional intent, what cannot be overlooked is that few of the rivers of the Great Plains have received this unique protection since 1968. Through 1998, only parts of three rivers—the Upper Missouri in Montana, the Missouri between South Dakota and Nebraska, and the Niobrara in Nebraska—have been included in the National Wild and Scenic Rivers System.

This lack of wild and scenic river designations is an indicator of socioeconomic values rather than a reflection on the quality of rivers in the Great Plains. Wild and scenic rivers tend to be concentrated in areas where there is a great deal of public land—for example, Alaska and the Pacific Northwest—where concerns over impacts on private lands are less pronounced. This is not to say, however, that rivers of the Great Plains are less deserving of inclusion in the National Wild and Scenic Rivers System. In January 1982, the National Park Service released the Nationwide Rivers Inventory that identified rivers that, at first inspection, were potentially eligible for designation. Through this and subsequent revisions, more than fifty rivers within the Great Plains have been identified as deserving further study or consideration as wild and scenic rivers.

The designated wild and scenic rivers in the Great Plains, and those listed on the Nationwide Rivers Inventory, are generally characterized by abundant plant and animal species diversity due to the presence of water and travel corridors. Humans were also drawn to Great Plains rivers: the designated rivers have important cultural and historical significance, such as the route of Lewis and Clark along the Missouri River and the cultural landscape of ranching along the Niobrara River. It should be noted, however, that human impacts are not readily apparent within the designated boundaries of these rivers; they were designated in large part because they represent presettlement conditions.

Canada also has a national rivers program. Established in 1984, the Canadian Heritage Rivers System is a cooperative program, developed and run by the federal, provincial, and territorial governments. As established, the program has little regulatory authority, instead relying on the foresight and good intentions of the involved governments. The objectives of the program are to give national recognition to Canada's outstanding rivers and to ensure long-term management and conservation of their natural, cultural, historical, and recreational values. None of the Prairie Provinces' rivers has received Heritage River designation to date.

See also PHYSICAL ENVIRONMENT: Niobrara Ecotone.

Dan Haas
National Park Service

Coyle, Kevin J. *The American Rivers Guide to Wild and Scenic River Designation: A Primer on National River Conservation*. Washington DC: American Rivers, 1988. Interagency Wild and Scenic Rivers Coordinating Council. *Wild and Scenic Rivers Reference Guide*. Washington DC: U.S. Departments of the Interior and Agriculture, 1997.

WINTERS DOCTRINE

The judicially crafted Winters Doctrine (1908) provides water for the needs of Native Americans who reside on federally reserved lands. This judicial guarantee, while not absolute, is highly significant given the demands for this critical natural resource in a region where water is often not abundantly available.

Water policy in the Great Plains is shaped by powerful political forces. Economic demands translate into political pressures and ultimately into water law. State water laws are generally designed to allocate water for "beneficial uses," following the doctrine of prior appropriation. Stressing uses, rather than needs, is inconsistent with Native American ideals, whereby water, like other aspects of the environment, is connected to a higher sacred order. Consequently, European American water schemes have often been in conflict with Native American concepts.

In 1908, however, Native Americans prevailed in the landmark case *Winters v. United States*. The case involved the Gros Ventres and Assiniboines of the Fort Belknap Reservation in Montana and their right to use the water of the Milk River. When farmers upstream diverted water from the river the United States brought an injunction against them, reasoning that this left insufficient water for agriculture on the reservation. The farmers appealed. On January 6, 1908, the Supreme Court ruled in favor of the United States and the Native Americans, arguing that the establishment of the Fort Belknap Reservation entitled the Native Americans to perpetual use of the water that it contained. Their rights were "reserved" at the date of establishment (1888), and, contrary to the doctrine of prior appropriation, those rights could not be lost through nonuse.

The Winters Doctrine was a major victory for all Native Americans, serving notice that state laws are secondary to federally reserved water rights and preventing prior appropriation schemes from extinguishing Native American needs. In 1976, in *Cappaert v. United States*, the doctrine was extended to groundwater use on or near federally created reservations. Subsequently, however, an increasingly conservative Supreme Court has ruled against tribes in a number of water rights disputes. While the Winters Doctrine protects Native American water rights, this protection is still vulnerable to changes in the prevailing political climate.

Peter J. Longo
University of Nebraska at Kearney

Burton, Lloyd. *American Indian Water Rights and the Limits of Law*. Lawrence: University Press of Kansas, 1991. Hundley, Norris. "The Winters Decision and Indian Water Rights: A Mystery Reexamined." In *The Plains Indians of the Twentieth Century*, edited by Peter Iverson. Norman: University of Oklahoma Press, 1985: 77–106.

Index of Contributors

General Index

Canada Jurisdiction Act (1803), 443
Canada Land and Irrigation Company, 851
Canada: The Granary of the World (pamphlet), 379
Canada–United States Trade Agreement, 410, 423
Canadian Agriculture Movement, 699
Canadian Alliance Party, 680, 686
Canadian Broadcasting Corporation, 504, 505
Canadian Council on Boys' and Girls' Clubs, 196
Canadian Football League, 773
Canadian Group of Painters, 117
Canadian Heritage River System, 867
Canadian Mosaic, **379**
Canadian National Railway, 202, 244, 796, 809
Canadian Northern Railway, 794, 809
Canadian Pacific Airlines, 796
Canadian Pacific Limited, 413
Canadian Pacific Railway, **413**; artists given free passes by, 109; Brandon, 160; Calgary, 160, 413, 809; in Chinese immigration, 135, 141; Crow's Nest Pass Agreement, 410, 678, 688, 809; cutbacks in the Prairies, 796; depot design, 91; and Fertile Belt, 385; Freer's film sponsored by, 277; and grain growers associations, 712; and Kate Simpson Hayes, 330; headquarters moved to Calgary, 809; and Indian reserves, 187; irrigation promoted by, 29, 795, 849; in Italian immigration, 237; in Japanese immigration, 136, 144; land grants to, 240, 807; Native Americans and, 557; and New Finland, 231; in Norwegian immigration, 242–43; oil discovered by, 429; radio for passengers, 504; railroad politics, 684; Regina, 179; Saskatoon, 183; settlement patterns affected by, 29–30, 244, 733; telegraph system, 522; as transcontinental railroad, 413, 794, 808; and wheat cultivation, 56
Canadian Plains Research Center, **199–200**
Canadian Prairies region, 29–30. *See also* Prairie Provinces
Canadian River, 623, 845, *862*
Canadian Rodeo Association, 765
Canadian Shield, 613
Canadian Transport Commission, 796
Canadian Wesleyan Methodism, **738–39**
Cannon, James Patrick, 701, **708**
Cannon, Joe, 681
canoes, 793, 813
canola, **37**; in Canadian Prairies, 29; oilseeds, 428
Capital City (Sandoz), 470, 703
capitols, state and provincial, **95**
Caponigro, Paul, 118
Capote, Truman, 452–53
Cappaert v. United States (1976), 867
Capper, Arthur, **508**, 650
Caprock Canyonlands, **623–24**, 634
captivity narratives, **326**
Capulin Volcano National Monument, 637, 782
Card, Charles Ora, 734
Cardinal, Douglas, 87
Cardston (Alberta), 734, 741
Carey, Joseph M., 163, 695, 847
Carey Act (1894), 847
Carhenge, 290, **380**

Carlisle Indian Industrial School, 193, 202, 602
Carlsbad Caverns, 436, **624**, 637, 781–82
Carlsbad Caverns National Park, 624, 781–82
Carlsbad NM, 427, 433
Carnegie Foundation libraries, 90
Carney, Frank and Dan, 188, 432
Carpenter, Delph, 848
Carr, Antoine, 767
Carr, Eugene A., 838
Carr, Ralph, 144, 145
Carrasco, Joe "King," 532
Carrington, Henry, 818
Carson, Dolly, 302
Carson, Johnny, 504, **508–9**
Carson, Kit, 164, 244, 562, 680
Carter, Amon G., 168, 512
Carter, Joe, 767
Carver, William F., 399
Case, Francis, 690
casinos, 774
Casper WY, **161–62**
Casselton ND, *290*
Castañeda, Pedro de, 485
Cather, Willa, **475–76**; on expansiveness of Great Plains, xiv; and family farm, 44; heroes of, 470–71; and images of Nebraska and Kansas, 377; on isolation of Plains women, 330; as Lincoln resident, 172; on literary architecture, 87; literary education of, 215; museums and work of, 209, 375; *My Ántonia*, 471, 475, 485; on Nebraska as material for a country, 373; newspaper work of, 475, 503; *O Pioneers!*, 471, 475; and Elia Peattie, 334; and John J. Pershing, 833; and Plains town, 321, 322; *The Song of the Lark*, 475, 530
Catholic Church. *See* Roman Catholicism
Catlin, George, 107, 109, **114**, 485, 494, 619
cattle: barley feed for, 35; branding, 36; buffalo chips, 379; cattle codes, **449–50**; guards, 289, 292, *292*; coyotes preying on, 625; in Eastern Feed Grains and Livestock region, 31; feedlots, 418; grazing on prairie dog towns, 623; in Great Plains agriculture, 27–28, 403, 409; longhorns, 347, 365, 375, 377, **392**; and meatpacking industry, 426; Mexican *comancheros* trading in, 347; Native Americans hunting, 442; Native Americans raising, 558, 577; ranching, **37–38**, 48–49, 403–4; in Sandhills region, 31; Spanish bringing to Western Hemisphere, 365; Alexander Swan, 54; Texas fever, 55, 800, 814. *See also* cattle towns; cattle trails; cowboys; trail drives
cattle towns, **162**; recreation in, 763–64; violence in, 387
cattle trails, **800**; Chisholm Trail, 794, 800, 814; in transportation of Great Plains, 794; Western Trail, 800, 814. *See also* trail drives
caves: in Black Hills, 622; Carlsbad Caverns, 436, 624, 637, 781–82; Jewell Cave National Monument, 782; Native Americans living in, 61
Cavett, Dick, **509**
Cedar River National Grassland, 780
Cedarvale communist community, **227**
celebrations, seasonal, **313**
cemeteries, **70–71**; Boot Hill, 378; Czech, 74; grave markers in, 289, *289*, 296, 302–3

Center for Great Plains Studies at Emporia State University, **200**
Center for Great Plains Studies at the University of Nebraska–Lincoln, 110, **200**
Center for Rural Affairs, **39**
center pivots, **413**, 849, 850, 854, *854*, 855
Central Americans, 349, **353**
Central Flyway, 620
Central Interstate Low-Level Nuclear Waste Compact, 428
Central Overland Road, 794
Central Pacific Railroad, 146, 807
Central Texas Uplift, 637
cereals. *See* grain
Cervantez, Pedro, **353**
Cervin, Olof Z., 65
Cessna Aircraft Company, 797
Chadron NE, 163, 164, 257
Chadron State College, 164
Chafer, Lewis Sperry, 741
Chaikovsky, Nicholas, 227
chain migration, 246, 249
Chalmers, John, 95
Chamberlain SD, 180, 193, 203
Chamberlain, Von Del, 566
Chaney, Lon, 255, **261**
charter culture, 225
Chautauqua, **200–201**
Chavez, César, 349
Chavez, Dennis, 680
Chavez, Linda, 350, **353–54**
cheerleaders, 386
Cheney, Richard, 687, 695
Chernesky, Morris, 521
chernozemic soil, 29, 617, 640
Cherokee Advocate (newspaper), 501–2
Cherokee Bill, 6
Cherokee Nation v. Georgia (1831), 442, 456, 604
Cherokee Phoenix (newspaper), 501–2
Cherokees: Wilma Mankiller, **583–84**; missionaries to, 747–48; removal from Georgia, 578
Cheyenne Bottoms, 850, **851**
Cheyenne Mountain CO, 821, **824**
Cheyenne River, 862
Cheyennes, **569–70**; and Arapahos, 562; in Battle of Beecher Island, 823; in Battle of Summit Springs, 838; in Battle of the Little Bighorn, 830–31; in Battle of the Washita, 568, 818, 840; Black Kettle, 568; contemporary tribal governments, 691–92; counting coup, 825; Dog Soldiers, 823, 838, 839; Dull Knife, 572, 818; Howling Wolf, 121; Indian scouts, 815; law of, 441; in Native American trade, 606; political leadership among, 647; in Red River War, 818, 822; in Sand Creek Massacre, 556, 568, 835; sign language, 600; Sun Dance among, 757; war chiefs, 839
Cheyenne WY, **162–63**; Botanic Gardens, 67; Frontier Days, 163, 335, 765, 784; as gateway city, 152, 154; as "Hell on Wheels" town, 170; libraries in, 206; main street of, 1869, *162*; Alexander Swan, 54; as T-town, 795; Union Pacific Railroad depot, *153*; Warren Air Force Base, 72, 163, 392, 695, 822
Chicago and North Western Railroad, 794
Chicago, St. Paul and Milwaukee Railroad, 794
Chickasaw National Recreation Area, 782

chicken-fried steak, 301
Chief Sam expedition, 10
children's literature, **476**; Rex Deverell's plays, 477
chili, 300
Chilocco OK, 193, 203, 206
Chinatowns: Calgary, **140–41**, 161; Deadwood, **141–42**; Denver, 137, **142**
Chinese, **141**; Asian Canadians, 139, *139*; Asian exclusion legislation, 139–40; Denver's anti-Chinese riot, 135, **142–43**, 146; Female Employment Act of 1912, 143; literature of, 473; pioneer settlers, 135; proverbs and proverbial sayings of, 310; settlement in Great Plains, 136; Chin Lin Sou, 146; *Territory of New Mexico v. Yee Shun*, 146–47; Fee Lee Wong (Wing Tsue), 148. *See also* Chinatowns
Chinese Exclusion Acts, 135, 140, 141
chinooks, **624**; stories, **292–93**, 314
Chip of the Flying U (Bowers), 470
Chisholm Trail, 794, 800, 814
Chittenden, Hiram Martin, 302
Chivington, John M., 279, 568, 818, 835
Choctaws, 578
Chouteau, Auguste, 363
Chouteau, Pierre, Jr., 410, **413–14**
Christian, Charlie, **12**, 531
Christian Identity movement, 711, 721
Christianity, 732–34; Christian Socialism, 722, 734, 757; crossdenominational movements and currents, 734; gender-role rigidity in, 329; Indian missionaries, 747–49; and Native Americans, 558, 597, 731–32, 747–49; Social Gospel, 728, 731, 734, 739–40. *See also* Church of Jesus Christ of Latter-day Saints; Eastern Orthodoxy; Protestantism; Roman Catholicism
Christmas, 313
chuck wagons, 420
churches. *See* religious architecture
Churches of Christ, 745
Churchill, Ward, 269
Church Missionary Society (Anglican), 731, 733
Church of God in Christ, Mennonite, 733
Church of Jesus Christ of Latter-day Saints (Mormons), **739**; crossing Great American Desert, 389; Ben Holladay and, 803; Indian missionaries, 748; irrigation practices of, 846, 856; and Mormon Trail, **804–5**; moving into Canada, 245, 734, 739, 741
ciboleros, 346, 347, **354**
Cimarron (film), 257, **261–62**, 275
Cimarron National Grassland, 780
Cimarron River, 615, 616
The Cisco Kid (television show), 523
cities and towns, **149–89**; building and urban culture, 156–57; college towns, 163–64; in continental context, 151–52; as county seats, 153, 157, 165, 246; European Americans in, 225; frontier law of, 443; gateway, 99, 152, 153–54, 155; of Great Plains, *151*; "Hell on Wheels" towns, 162, 170–71; lumberyards in, 425; Mexican American plazas, 347; origins of individual places, 153; overplatting of, 72; periods of urban life in, 152–53; railroads in development of, xv, 795, 808; reservation towns, 179–80; river towns, 152, 153, 180–81; rural-urban

population change, 181–82; small-town decline, 152–53; sources of early populations of, 154–55; three urban archetypes, 155–56; urban Indian reserves, 187; urban Native American communities, 608; urban roles and town-country relations, 153–54; warehouse districts, 99–100, 155, 225; water towers marking, 865; women and Plains towns, 321–22. *See also* all-black towns; boomtowns; cattle towns; ghost towns; Main Street; small towns
civil defense, 821, 825
civil divisions of government, **657–58**
Civilian Conservation Corps, 679
civil ribaldry, 304
civil rights, **12–13**; and African Americans, 5, 12–13, 702; for gays and lesbians, 329; Lyndon Baines Johnson and, 669; Ku Klux Klan opposing, 715; and *McLaurin v. Oklahoma State Regents*, 197, 207; in Oklahoma City, 176; and politics of Great Plains, 651; protest for, 702. See also *Brown v. The Board of Education of Topeka*
Civil Rights Act (1957), 663
Civil Rights Act (1964), 668
Civil War, **824**; Battle of Glorieta Pass, 818; Galvanized Yankees, 828; Republican Party during, 686; Philip Sheridan, 836; William Tecumseh Sherman, 836; and Texas, 690
Clamorgan, Jacques, 363
Clark, Charles Badger, Jr., 299
Clark, Ed "Dutch," 178
Clark, Jim, **414**
Clark, Joe, **658**
Clark, Walter von Tilburg, 464, 470
Clark, William: graffito at Pompey's Pillar, 436; in Lewis and Clark expedition, 240–41; Manuel Lisa and, 360; and Alfred Jacob Miller, 124; name carved at Pompey's Pillar National Monument, 159; on Sacagawea, *336*; slave York, 3, 7, 24. *See also* Lewis and Clark
Clark SD, 405
class (socioeconomic), 407
classical music, **534–35**; development in Great Plains, 530, 533; Howard Hanson, 530, 539; Virgil Thomson, 530, 548
Clay, Henry, 6
Clay, John, 54
clay construction, **71–72**; in bricks, 70, 289; clay-wall construction, 64; puddled, 69, 74
Cleary, Kate M., **326–27**, 476
Clement, Amanda, **768**
Clements, Bill, 651
Clements, Frederick, 616
Clendenen, Newt, 6
Cleveland, Grover, 689
Cleveland, H. W. S., 86
Cleveland, Reggie, 767
Cliffs Notes, **201**
Clift, Montgomery, 255, **262**, 277
climate, **624–25**; climatology of Great Plains, 614–15; as icon of Great Plains, 373; Native American adaptation to change in, 555; paleoenvironments, 635–36; Palliser's Triangle, 30, *30*, 385, 636, 853, 864; tree planting and change of, **398**; variability in Great Plains, xiii. *See also* drought; weather
Clinton, Bill, 656, 661
clothing: of Comanches, 570; of cowboys, 294, 382; of Kaws, 580

cloud seeding, 860
Clouds of Joy, 531
Clovis points, 576, 589
Clutter family, 452
coaches, **768–69**; in college football, 773; Phil Jackson, 767, 769, 777–78
coal, **414–15**; Estevan strike, 709; Great Plains deposits of, 406; miners strike of 1921, 701, 704; in Montana, 414, 415, *415*, 676; railroad transportation of, 808
Coburn, James, 255
Cochran, Eddie, 532, **535**
Cody, Buffalo Bill (William F.), **380–81**; Buffalo Bill's Wild West show, 291, 380, 399, 400, 737, 764, 784; in Cheyenne, 163; film company of, 257, 269; Wild Bill Hickok performing for, 390; in hunting lore, 305; as icon of Great Plains, *380*
Cody, Iron Eyes, **262**
Coe, David Allen, 531
Coffeyville Raid, **450**
Cohen, Felix, 604
Colby, Clara, **327**
Cold War, **825**; architecture of, **72**; and defense industries, 407; Great Plains and, 821–22; Hubert Humphrey and, 667; North American Air Defense Command, 821, 824; Strategic Air Command, 838
Coldwell, M. J., 659
Cole, Jack, 201
Coleman, Ornette, **13–14**, 532
Coleman, William, 188, **415–16**
collective bargaining, 701
College Park TX, 206
colleges. *See* higher education
College Station TX, 208
college towns, **163–64**
College World Series, **769**
Collier, John, 194, 212, 559, 602, 651, 678
Collins, Judy, 547
Colonial Revival style, 66
Colony of the East, **381**
Colorado: air bases in World War II, 820; Amache internment camp, 138–39; "A&M" program, 196; Anglo-Canadians in, *226*; Arapahos in, 562–63; and Polly Baca, 351; Battle of Summit Springs, 838; biotechnology in, 412; Cheyenne Mountain, 821, 824; civil divisions of government, 657; coal in, 414; Cripple Creek miner's strike, 722; drought, 28; farm consolidation, 44; Farm Security Administration sponsoring irrigation in, 45; gaming and, 774; and Ferdinand Vandeveer Hayden in survey of, 633; Hispanic Americans in, 348, 350, 359; Hungarians in, 235; immigration board of, 236; international trade and, 423, 424, *424*; in Irrigated High Plains region, 31; in Irrigated Valleys region, 31, 32; irrigation, 854; Italians in, 237; Japanese in, 135–36, 140, 142, 144; Jim Crow laws in, 454; Kansas-Nebraska Act and, 670; land-grant university in, 204, 208; land laws and settlement in, 240; libraries in, 206; and Maxwell Land Grant, 361; Methodism in, 752; NAFTA and, 427; national wildlife refuges in, 784; oil in, 430–31; Federico Peña and, 350, 364; Pikes Peak gold rush, 805; Poles in, 243; politics in, 648, 649, 651,

Edmonton, University of, 530
Edmonton Eskimos, 773
Edmonton Grads, 767, **771–72**
Edmonton Journal (newspaper), **511**
Edmonton Oilers, 764, 775
Edmonton Sun (newspaper), 505
education, **191–215**; Edith Abbott and, 198; adult, 198; agricultural, 196; arboretums in, 67; architectural, 65; art, 109; William H. H. Beadle, 198–99; Boys Town, 199; Canadian Plains Research Center, 199–200; Center for Great Plains Studies at Emporia State University, 200; Center for Great Plains Studies at the University of Nebraska–Lincoln, 200; Chautauqua, 200–201; Cliff Notes, 201; collective bargaining for teachers, 701; distance, 201; *Escuela Tlatelolco*, 356; Frontier College, 202; high schools, 195–96; Susan La Flesche and, 581; Orin Libby and, 205; Dorothy Sunrise Lorentino and, 206–7; *McLaurin v. Oklahoma State Regents*, 197, 207; *Meyer v. Nebraska*, 457; National Cowboy Hall of Fame and Western Heritage Center, 110, 209–10, 377; National Ranching Heritage Center, 210; for Native Americans, 193–94, 197, 206–7, 212; North Dakota Institute for Regional Studies, 210; public school development, 194–96; resistance to developments in, 197; Henry Roe Cloud and, 212; Linda Slaughter and, 336–37; state and provincial historical societies, 213. *See also* higher education; libraries; museums; schools
Edwards, Bob, **511–12**
Edwards, Henrietta Muir, 320, 335
Edwards, James, 8
Edwards, Stoney, 536
Edwards Plateau, 30, 32, 634, 636, 637
Eells, Myra Fairbanks, 341
Effinger, Cecil, 530
Egleston, N. H., 398
Eiseley, Loren, **626**
Eisenhower, Dwight D., **662–63**; and Herbert Brownell, 448; Eisenhower Birthplace State Historical Park, 209; Eisenhower Library and Museum, 206, 209, 436; interstate highway system, 663, 812, 821; John Birch Society on, 702; Kansas politics and, 377, 670; politics since 1945, 651; and Republican Party, 687; in transcontinental motor convoy, 812; and voting patterns, 694
Eisenhower, Milton, 388
El Curatelejo, 845
electric interurban railways, 796–97, **801**
electronics industry, 407
Elk City OK, 703
Elkhart KS, 165
Elk Island National Park, 783
Elliot, Rick, 722
Ellison, Ralph, xviii, 473, **478**
Ellsworth KS, 162
Ellwood, Isaac L., 35
El Salvador, 353
Ely, Joe, 538, 546
Emma Lake artists' workshops, **116**
Emporia KS: *Emporia Gazette*, 503, **512**, 521, 524; and meatpacking industry, 362; quiltmaking in, 335; Calvin Trillin on murders in, 523; Welsh in, 251

Emporia Gazette (newspaper), 503, **512**, 521, 524
Emporia State University (Kansas State Normal School): Center for Great Plains Studies at, 200; establishment of, 197; library education at, 206
empresarios, **355–56**
emptiness (as definition of Great Plains), **384–85**
endangered species, **626–27**
Endangered Species Act, 669, 859
energy: National Energy Programme (Canada), 429, 430, 672; Small Farm Energy Project, 39; wind energy, **437**. *See also* fossil fuels
Englewood CO, 505
"English only" ordinances, 362
Enlarged Homestead Act (1909), 240
environment. *See* physical environment
Episcopalianism, **744**; distribution of religions, 741; Indian missionaries, 748; Harold Jones and, 749
epitaphs, 303
Epler, Stephen, 773
Epp, Theodore, **744**
equitable apportionment suits, 860
Erdoes, Richard, 487
Erdrich, Louise, xviii, 322, 473, **478**, 493
erosion. *See* soil erosion
Escobar, José, 368
Escuela Tlatelolco, **356**
Esteban (slave), 3, 7
Estevan strike (1931), **709**
estray statutes, 450
ethanol, **416–17**
Etheridge, Kamie, 767
Etheridge, Melissa, 533, **538**
ethnicity: and architecture, 65–66; and cemeteries, 71; ethnogenesis, 222–23; folk speech influenced by, 299–300; folkways of ethnic groups, 285–86; and foodways, 301; in Great Plains regionalism, xv–xvi; and jokes, 304; museums of, 208; in Plains fiction, 470; politics of, 648; protest regarding, 702; and religion, 223, 731, 732–33; of towns, 156. *See also* African Americans; Asian Americans; European Americans; Hispanic Americans; Native Americans
Etting, Ruth, 255
Eureka Ditch, 847
European Americans, **217–52**; archipelago of communities of, 219–20; art and, 106–8; assimilation of, 221–22; and biogeography of Great Plains, 616–17; cultural transformation of, 221; environmental adaptation of, 220–21; ethnogenesis and, 222–23; Peter Fidler, 229–30; Anthony Henday, 234–35; Maximilian, Prince of Wied-Neuwied, 111, 241–42; Native Americans and, 556; political authority with advent of, 647; political participation by, 223–24; Lord Selkirk, 127, 229, 230, 247, 381; settlement patterns in Canada, 244–46; settlement patterns in United States, 246–47; George Simpson, 247; in urban centers, 225; World War I as watershed for, 224–25. *See also* Anglo-Canadians; Czechs; French Canadians; Germans; Hungarians; Hutterites; Irish; Italians; Jews; Lewis and

Clark; Poles; Russians; Scandinavians; Scots; Spaniards; Ukrainians; Welsh
evangelicalism, 734, **745**
Evans, Herschel, 532, 541
Evans, James, 738
Evans, John, 165, 835
Evans, John Thomas, 251, 363
Evans, Terry, 110, **116**
Evans, Walker, 45, 115, 118
evaporation rates, 845
Exodusters, **14**; as African American pioneers, 7; and ethnic diversity of Great Plains, xvi, 286; in Kansas settlement, 3, 7, 9, 448; in Oklahoma Territory settlement, 4, 7; Pap Singleton, 21
exotic animals, **43**
Ex Parte Crow Dog, 442, **451**, 605
expeditions: art and, 107; Canadian Red River Exploring Expedition, 385; of Coronado, 7, 227, 247, 345, 359; of John Charles Frémont, 164, 178, 231, 495, 686, 817, 823, 826–27; of Henry Kelsey, 239, 301–2; of Manuel Lisa, 247, 301, 360, 414, 419; literature of explorers and other travelers, 469; of Stephen H. Long, 106, 126, 374, 403, 817, 823, 831; of Mallet brothers, 241; of Maximilian, Prince of Wied-Neuwied, 111, 241–42; of Missouri Company, 346, 362–63; of John Palliser, 30, 152, 236, 385; of Zebulon Pike, 164, 178, 257, 817, 823, 834; Spanish, 247–48, 345; of David Thompson, 249; of Pedro Vial, 250–51. *See also* Lewis and Clark

Fahlbusch, Albert, 316
Fairbanks, Chuck, 773
Fairbanks, Douglas, Sr., 255, **266**
fairs, **43**; Native American trade rendezvous, 606; quilting competitions at, 311; tourism, 435; tribal, 544
Fall, Albert, **663**
fallout shelters, 821, 825
family farm, **44**; and anti-corporate farming laws, 445; corporate farming, 40; inheritance practices, 294–95
Fargo ND, **167**; fire of 1893, 167, *167*; as gateway city, 152, 154; Melroe Company, 427; North Dakota Institute for Regional Studies, 210; in Northern Spring Wheat region, 30; open shop movement in, 701; public sculpture in, 157
Fargo, William G., 167
Farmer-Labor Party, 681
Farmers Alliance, 661, 683, **709–10**, 807
Farmers Holiday Association, 650, 699, 699, 707, **710**
Farmers Home Administration, 45
Farmers Nonpartisan Political League of North Dakota. *See* Nonpartisan League
Farmers Unity League, 699
farm implements, **417–18**; agricultural technology, 28; in industry of Great Plains, 405; Melroe Bobcat and, 426–27; small-town industrialization, 433; swather (windrower), 434–35; World War II and, 821
farming. *See* agriculture
farms: consolidation of, **44–45**, 246–47; farmsteads, **78**; inheritance practices for, **294–95**; lore about, **295**; noon meal on, 301. *See also* family farm

Fort Hays KS, 11

Fort Kearny NE: adobe construction at, 71; establishment of, 827; Legh Freeman at, 513; "Hell on Wheels" town near, 170; newspaper at, 521; on Oregon Trail, 805, 836; in Plains Indian campaigns of 1850s, 817; Pony Express passing, 806

Fort Laramie WY: adobe construction at, 71, 80, 98; American Fur Company and, 71, 410, 414; as frontier fort, 827, *827*; and Oregon Trail, 805, 817, 836

Fort Laramie, Treaty of (1851), 556, 570, 695, 836–37

Fort Laramie, Treaty of (1868): army commissioners in council with chiefs, *607*; and assimilation policy, 565; Crazy Horse opposing, 825; Crows surrendering territory in, 597; Dull Knife signing, 572; and *Ex Parte Crow Dog*, 451; Indian uprising leading to, 557, 602, 818; Red Cloud signing, 800, 834, 837; William Tecumseh Sherman, 836; troop withdrawals in, 603

Fort Larned KS, 11, 516

Fort Leavenworth KS: discrimination against black soldiers at, 11; as frontier fort, 827, 832; and Leavenworth Penitentiary, 455; museum at, 436; as rearguard post, 817; *U.S. Cavalry Journal*, 516; in World War II, 820

Fort Mandan ND, 241

Fort McKenzie, 425, 567, 573

Fort Omaha NE, 819–20, 827

Fort Peck Dam, 848, 858

Fort Peck Lake MT, 376

Fort Phil Kearny, 325, 516, 800, 818, 827, 828, 837

Fort Pierre SD, 178, 180, 410, 419

Fort Pueblo CO, 178

Fort Randall Dam, 858

Fort Raymond, 360, 419

Fort Reno, 800, 815, 818, 820, 828, 837

Fort Riley KS, 436, 819, 820, 832

Fort Robinson NE, 820

forts: architecture of, **79–80**, 97–98; closing in 1890s, 819; frontier forts, **827–28**; in Plains Indian campaigns of 1850s, 817; and urbanism, 152. See also *by individual name*

Fort Scott KS, 19–20, 827

Fort Sill OK: Apaches and, 562; architecture of, 80, *80*; William Hazen in site selection of, 829; Lawton and, 171; number of personnel at, 832; in World War I, 819, 820

Fortune, Bob, 8

Fort Union ND: architecture of, 63; in fur trade, 180, 410, 414, 419; as tourist site, 436

Fort Union NM, 828

Fort Union Group, 630

Fort Union National Monument, 782

Fort Wallace KS, 827

Fort Warren NE, 820

Fort William, 836

Fort Worth TX, **167–68**; African Americans in, 4, 5; agricultural services, 405; Asians in, 136; botanical garden in, 68; Ornette Coleman and, 13–14; King Curtis and, 16; first Great Plains television station in, 267; *Fort Worth Star-Telegram*, 510, 512; as gateway city, 152; Hispanic Americans in, 361; Jews in, 238; H. J. Justin and Sons, 424; as livestock marketing center, 410; oil industry in, 168, 175, 176; opera in, 545; C. W. Post and, 432; radio in, 504, 519; Texas Spring Palace, 66; urban Native American community of, 608; weather industry in, 437; western swing, 535–36, 550

Fort Worth and Denver Railway, 158, 188

Fort Worth Star-Telegram (newspaper), 510, **512**

Forty-eighters, 235

forty-ninth parallel, **665–66**

fossil fuels: in Great Plains industry, 406. See *also* coal; natural gas; oil

Foster, Gus, 110

Foster, William Z., 707, 708

Foucart, Joseph, **80–81**

4-H Clubs, 196

Fox, George, 536–37

Fox, Michael J., 255

Fraser, Brad, 473

Fraser, Frances, 292

Frazier, Ian, xiii, xviii, 485, 487, 494

Frazier, Lynn, **666**, 719

Fredericksburg TX, 301, 832

Freedman, Harry, 530

Freedman's Academy, 21

Freeman, Andrew, 421

Freeman, Daniel, 391

Freeman, Frederick, 513, 521

Freeman, Legh, 503, **512–13**, 521

Freemen, xvi, 702, **711**

Freer, James, 255, 267, 277

freight-handling facilities, 155

Fremont NE, 805

Frémont, John Charles, **826–27**; as Army Topographical Engineer, 817, 823, 826; and Colorado Springs, 164; French Canadians in expedition of, 231; Francis Parkman reading, 495; and Pueblo, 178; as Republican presidential candidate, 686, 827

French Canadians, **231–32**; and Canadian Confederation, 222; in Canadian Mosaic, 379; Catholicism of, 732, 741; few migrating west, 244; folk music of, 298; Mallet brothers, 241; missions of, 731; political participation of, 223; Gabrielle Roy, 492; Vérendryes family, 231, 250

French language, 197, 231, 245, 692

Frey, William and Mary, 227

Friere, Paolo, 356

Fritchle, Oliver P., 410

Frizzell, Lodisa, 386

frogs, 618

Frontier College, **202**

frontier forts, **827–28**

Frontier Index (newspaper), 170, 503, 513, 521

frontier opera houses, **538–39**

frontier thesis, 44, 221, 380

frontier violence, **387**; gunslingers, 389–90, 457

Frying Pan Transmountain Water Project, 848

F Troop (television show), 523

Fugate, Caril Ann, 462

Fuller, Charles E., 734

Fulton, Len, 493

fundamentalism, 734, 745

Fund for Animals, 765

fur trade, **419**; Anglo-Canadians in, 226; architecture influenced by, 63; Pierre Chouteau Jr. and, 410, 413–14; in Edmonton, 166; frontier law and, 443; in industry of Great Plains, 403; lore of, **301–2**; Kenneth McKenzie and, 425–26; Métis in, 584; Missouri Fur Company, 247, 360, 419, 823; Native Americans and, 419, 556, 567, 592, 607; Oregon Trail, 804; portages in, 807; river towns, 180; trading posts, 97–98, 403, 419, 607; and urbanism, 152; Vérendryes family, 250; waterways used in, 793; Whoop-Up Trail in, 814; women in, 341. See also American Fur Company; Hudson's Bay Company; North West Company

The Future of the Great Plains (report), xiii, 679

Gadsby, Bill, 777

Gadsden Purchase, 680

Gale, Dorothy, 280–81, **387–88**

Gale, Doug, 515

Gale, William Potter, 721, 722

Gall, 557, 831, 837

Galvanized Yankees, **828**

Galveston plan, 735

gambling. See gaming

games: farm children's, 295; folk, 288; Native American, 763; at seasonal celebrations, 313. See also games of chance

games of chance: Native American, 763. See *also* gaming

gaming, **774**; in Deadwood, 383, 774; Native American, 763, 774

Gangplank, 614, 630, 637

Gantt, John, 71

Garcia, Frances, 350

the garden, **388**; as icon of Great Plains, 374; Nikka Yuko Garden, 145–46; in Plains fiction, 470

Garden City KS: frost-free period, 614; and meatpacking industry, 185, 350, 353, 359, 362, 426; pump irrigation project near, 847; Vietnamese in, 137, 147, *147*; windmill near, 854

Garden of Eden (Lucas KS), 312, 313

Gardenton (Manitoba), *743*

Gardiner, Jimmy, *46*, 672, 688, 721, 853

Gardiner Dam, 849, **853–54**

Garland NE, 59

Garland, Hamlin, 44, 330, 334, 470, 476, 485, 716, 795

Garner, Elmer J., 702, **711–12**

Garner, John Nance, 660

Garreau, Joel, 378

Garrett, Pat, 446

Garrison Dam, 575, 583, 848–49, 858

Garvey, Marcus, 702, 716

gas, natural. See natural gas

Gaspard, Leon, 112

gas stations, 93–94

Gates, John W. "Bet-a-Million," 35

Gateway, Inc., **419–20**

gateway cities, 99, 152, 153–54, 155

Gauss, Marianne, 476

Gavins Point Dam, 858

gay and lesbian life, **329**

Gaylord, E. K., 509–10

Geiger, Robert E., 625

Geins, Vladimir, 227

gender, **317–42**; in *Albert v. Albert*, 323–24; *berdache*, 324–25; and captivity narratives,

gender (*cont.*)
326; gendered space, 330; and interregional differences, 321; and masculinity, 323; Native American roles and, 333–34; politics of, 648; and sense of place, 329–30; from women to, 320–21. *See also* gay and lesbian life; women
General Allotment Act (1887). *See* Dawes (General Allotment) Act
genízeros, **356**; trade by, 354; *Tropa de Genízero*, **838–39**
Genoa NE, 193, 203
geographic center of the United States, **388**
geology, **629–30**; generalized chart of rocks of Great Plains, 629; Ferdinand Vandeveer Hayden, 633; physical environment of Great Plains, 613–14
George, Henry, 661
George, Milton, 710
Gerald, Rossano V., 13
Gerber, Philip L., 320
German-American Alliance, 223, 224
German Russians, **232**; in Canadian West, 245; Dutch Hop, 546; folklife of, 285; folk medicine of, 288; iron grave crosses of, 289, 296, 303; in North Dakota, 232, 376; in Plains fiction, 470; and religion, 741; in sugar beet cultivation, 232, 232, 352; and winter wheat cultivation, 246. *See also* Black Sea Germans; Volga Germans
Germans, **233–34**; in Canadian West, 245; cultural transformation of, 221; in earlier waves of immigration, 219; ethnogenesis in, 222; folklife of, 285–86; folk songs of, 298; and gender relations, 321; German architecture, **81–82**; immigrant newspapers, 514; Lutheranism of, 733, 750; *Meyer v. Nebraska*, 457; political participation by, 223–24; polka music, 546; in Prairie Provinces, 220; and Prohibition, 223; proverbs and proverbial sayings, 310; and religion, 733, 741; Roman Catholicism and, 756; seasonal celebrations of, 313; and women's suffrage, 223; and World War I, 224–25, 650, 819. *See also* German Russians
Getty, Don, 684
Ghost Dance, **746**; of Assiniboines, 566; Black Elk and, 737; Red Cloud and, 834; as response to European settlement, 731, 732, 818; Sitting Bull and, 558, 603, 746; and Wounded Knee Massacre, 558, 732, 558, 603, 746, 837, 841
ghost stories, **302**
ghost towns, xv, **168–69**, *374*
Giago, Tim, 514
Giant (film), 256, **267–68**, 269, 275
Giants in the Earth (Rölvaag), xiv, xv, **234**, 256, 470, 480, 491–92, 632
Gibbon, John, 818, 830, 831, 837
Gibbs, David W., 95
Gibson, Bob, 767
Gibson, Hoot, 255
Gibson, Paul, 169
Gibson, Thomas, 502
Gilbert and Sullivan, 764
Gilcrease, Thomas, 117, 187
Gilder, Robert, 117
Gilmore, Jimmie Dale, 538, 546
Gilpin, Laura, **117–18**
Gilpin, William, 379, 394

Girard KS, 521, 707
Glaciated Interior Plains, 637
glaciation, **630–31**; kettle lakes, 855; Lake Agassiz, 631, 855; paleoenvironments, 635; physiography and, 637
Gladstone NM, *373*
Glancy, Diane, 493
Glass, Hugh, 302
Gleen, John, 849
Glidden, Joseph F., 35, 158
Glorieta Pass, Battle of, 818
Glyde, H. G., 113
Gnadenau KS, 99
goats, **46**
Godwin, Ted, 116, 127
Goff, Bruce, 67, **82**, 83
Gohlke, Frank, 110, **118**
gold: Black Hills gold rush, 178, 180, 404, 837; in Colorado, 658, 805; at Cripple Creek, 164; Homestake Mine, 154, 404, 421–22; in Yukon, 688
The Golden Bowl (Manfred), 471, 477
golden plovers, 620
"Goldilocks on the Oregon Trail" narrative, 308
Goldthorpe, Lucy, 339
Goldwater, Barry, 669
golf: Ben Hogan, 776; Nancy Lopez, 351, 360–61
Gonzalez, Rodolfo "Corky," 349, 356, **356–57**
Goodfox, Lawrence, Jr., 596
Goodhue, Bertram Grosvenor, 66, 89, 95, 157, 172
Goodland KS, 859
Goodnight, Charles, 48, 181, **420**, 800
Goodnight-Loving Trail, 181, 420, 794, 800
good roads movement, **801–2**
Goon, Sin, 141
Gordon, Charles W. (Ralph Connor), 471, 476, **478–79**, 486, 757
Gordon, Donald, 839
Gore OK, 428
Gorecki, Lucy, 340
Gorras Blancas, 347, **357–58**, 358
Goshen points, 589
Gothic Revival style, 66, 80, 90, 92, 94
Gould, Charles N., 431
Gourd Dance, 608–9
government. *See* politics and government
Government Rustic style, 76
Gowdy, Curt, **774–75**
graduated income tax, 649
Graham, Billy, 734
Graham, J. R., 512
grain: barley, 30, 35; barns for storing, 68–69; as breadbasket of North America image, 378–79, 420; custom combining of, 41–42; farm implements for, 417; growers associations for, 712; millet, 47; Post breakfast cereals, 432–33; railroad transport of, 409, 410, 808; rye, 49; Saskatchewan Grain Growers Association, 336, 523, 650; Saskatchewan Women Grain Growers, 336. *See also* corn; grain elevators; grain processing; sorghum; wheat
grain elevators, **82–83**; industrialization of, 409; in gateway cities, 155; in southwestern Alberta, 25; in town development, xv, 186; Wolcott photograph of, *132*
grain growers associations, **712**

Grain Growers Grain Company, 721
grain processing, **420–21**; becoming concentrated, 409–10; flour mills, 409–10, 416, 420–21; in Great Plains, 405; small-town industrialization, 433, 434
Grand Forks Cattle Company, 851
Grand Forks ND, 169; Lynn Anderson, 536; as college town, 163; flood of 1997, 169, 843, 853; headbolt heater development in, 421; in Northern Spring Wheat region, 30
Grand Island NE, 359, 820–21, 832, 848
Grand River National Grassland, 780
Grand Trunk Pacific Railway, 244, 794, 809
Grange, 699, **712–13**, 807
Grant, Cuthbert, **389**, 836
Grant, James B., 12
Grant, Ulysses S., 846
The Grapes of Wrath: film, 255, 256, 257, **268**, 282, 810; novel by Steinbeck, 471, 477, 703, 810
grasses, **631–32**; flora of Great Plains, 628–29. *See also* grasslands
grasshoppers, 305–6, 314, 388, 616, **632–33**, 634, 635
grasslands: biogeography of Great Plains, 616; as icon of Great Plains, 373; national grasslands, 766, 780, **780–81**; openness of, xiv; ranching and, 403; range management, 49; sod-wall construction, 94; wildflowers of, 642. *See also* prairie
Grasslands National Park, 783
Grasslands National Park Reserve, 636
Grattan, John L., 817, 836
Grattan Massacre (1854), 817, 836, 837
Graulich, Melody, 321
grave markers, 289, 289, 296, **302–3**
Gray, Coleen, 255, **268**
Gray, L. C., 781
Gray, Mary, 341
Gray, Otto, 536
Grayrocks Dam, 859
grazing lands: overgrazing, 403; Taylor Grazing Act of 1934, 55, 679
Great American Desert, **389**; Edwin James on, 374, 389; Stephen Long on, xiii, 106, 374, 389, 817, 823, 831; Zebulon Pike on, xiii, 257, 494, 817, 823, 834, 852; and Plains-as-colony thesis, 381; versus Plains as garden, 388; versus Plains as pastoral region, 394; and promotional literature, 394, 395; and "rainfall follows the plow," 395; Walter Prescott Webb on, 389
Great Depression: all-black towns disappearing during, 10; architecture of, 76; banking in, 411; and Canadian settlement patterns, 245–46; farm consolidation during, 44; farm protest, 699; and health-care industry, 406; Joe Jones's paintings of, 122–23; On-to-Ottawa trek, 720–21; and politics of Great Plains, 650–51; Will Rogers and, 278; and small-town newspapers, 521; and socialism in Prairie Provinces, 376
Greater Winnipeg Floodway, 853
Great Falls MT, 30, **169–70**
Great Lakes of the Dakotas, 376
Great March, 460
Great Northern Railway, 144, 675, 797, 802–3
Great Plains, xiii–xviii; birth rates in, 340; as defined in this encyclopedia, *xiv*; as

higher education (*cont.*)
college basketball in, 767; college football in, 765, 772–73; college ice hockey in, 777; college towns, 163–64; College World Series, 769; establishment of colleges and universities, 196; Lutheran, 751; Methodist, 752; National Japanese American Student Relocation Council, 145; Quaker, 754; research libraries at, 206; schools of music, 547; in small-town economy, 185; tribal colleges, 213–14; United States Air Force Academy, 164, 214, 821; women in, **214–15**. *See also* Kansas, University of; Kansas State University; land-grant universities; Nebraska, University of; Oklahoma, University of; Oklahoma State University; Texas, University of; *and other colleges and universities by name*
High Noon (film), 263, 280, 497
High Plains: in physiography of Great Plains, 613, 636; soil, 640. *See also* Llano Estacado
High Plains Aquifer. *See* Ogallala Aquifer
high schools, 195–96
highways. *See* roads and highways
Higley, Brewster, 535
Hill, H. B., 113
Hill, James J., 169, **802–3**
Hill City KS, 156
Hillegass, Cliff, 201
The Hi-Lo Country (film), 256
Hilton, H. R., 395
Hind, Cora, **330–31**, 524
Hind, Henry Youle, 30, 385, 813
Hind, W. G. R., 109
Hinduism, **746**
Hinton, Richard, 386
Hinton, S. E., 476
hired girls, **331**
Hispanic Americans, **343–69**; activists, 349; architecture of, **84–85**; Polly Baca, 350, 351; *betabeleros*, 348, 351–52; Bracero Program, 349, 352–53, 359, 366; Central Americans, 349, 353; Pedro Cervantez, 353; Linda Chavez, 350, 353–54; *ciboleros*, 346, 347, 354; clay construction, 72; *comancheros*, 346, 347, 354–55, 368–69; and cowboy culture, 381; *curanderismo*, 288; Fabiola Cabeza de Baca, 355; *empresarios*, 355–56; *Escuela Tlatelolco*, 356; fiction by, 472; folk dances of, 297; folk literature of, 469; folk music of, 287, 289; folk songs of, 298; folkways of, 285; *genízeros*, 356, 388–89; in *Giant*, 267–68; Rodolfo "Corky" Gonzalez, 349, 356–57; *Gorras Blancas*, 347, 357–58; Guadalupe Hidalgo treaty, 347, 358; José Angel Gutiérrez, 349, 357, 358; Juan José Herrera, 358; Hispanic population geography, **359**; impact of, on Great Plains, 350–51; Luis Jimenez, 360; Latinos and the Plains in twentieth century, 348–50; Manuel Lisa, 247, 301, 341, 360; Nancy Lopez, 351, 360–61; in meatpacking industry, 348, 349–50, 352, 359, **361–62**, 426; Mexican Americans and the Plains, 1846–1900, 347–48; Mexican cuisine, 301, 351, 359, 362; music of, 532, **539–40**; in New Mexico, 350, 359, 680; Miguel Antonio Otero, 350, 363; and party politics, 648; *pastores*, 347, 359, 363–64, 367; Federico Peña, 350, 364; as percentage of Great Plains population, *350*; in Plains

fiction, 470; Plan of San Diego, 364; politicization of, 651–52; proverbs and proverbial sayings of, 310–11; in railroad work, 347, 348, 352, 359, 361; ranching heritage of, 365–66; repatriation to Mexico, 349, 366; Bill Richardson, 350, 366; Tomás Rivera, 366–67, 470; Roman Catholicism of, 756; Casimero Romero, 367; settlement patterns of, 246; South Americans, 367–68; south to north migration of, xvi; in sugar beet cultivation, 348, 350, 351–52, 359, 361; José Piedad Tafoya, 355, 368–69; Tejanos, 351, 359, 369; Bernice Zamora, 351, **369**. *See also* Hispanos
Hispanos: Hispano homeland, 359, **359–60**; *junta de indignación*, 714–15; territorial expansion of, 248, 359
historians: Angie Debo, 477; James C. Malin, 483–84; Walter Prescott Webb, 495–96
historical societies: county, 375; state and provincial, **213**
Hitchcock, Ethan Allen, 456
Hitchcock, Gilbert M., 518
Hobbema (Alberta), 187
hockey. *See* ice hockey
Hodges, Ben, 6
Hodgins, Jack, 495
Hodkinson, Sydney, 530
Hoffman, Frank, 112
Hoffman, Milton, 19
Hogan, Ben, **776**
Hogan, Linda, 473, **479–80**, 487
Hogg, James, **666–67**
Hogue, Alexandre, 112, *119*, **119–20**, 127, 626
Hoistad, Mark, 88
Hokazano, Naokichi, 135, 136
Hokeah, Jack, 124
Holabird, John, 95
Holcomb, Homer, *785*
Holcomb KS, 426, 452
holiness movement, 745, 753
Holladay, Ben, **803**, 811, 813
Holliday, Cyrus K., 186, **803**
Holliday, Doc (John Henry), 307, 384, **390–91**
Hollinger International Inc., 505, 508
Holly, Buddy, xviii, 532, **540**, 546, 549, 551
Hollywood Indians, **269**
Holoun, Hal, 121
home economics, 355
"Home on the Range" (song), 287, 306, 535
Homestake Mine, 154, 404, *404*, **421–22**, *422*
Homestead Act (1862), 239, 320, 339, 340, 374, 686
The Homesteader (film), 18, 256
homesteading: Boomers, 377; breaking the land, 27; Solomon Butcher's photographs of, 112; in Canadian Prairies, 240, 430; films about, 256; health care lacking in, 406; Homestead National Monument of America, **391**, 782; Kinkaid Act, 7, 31, 240; in Montana, 675; in promotional literature, 394; settlement patterns for, 246; sod houses of, 288; in west river country, 399; women and, 319, 320, 337, **339–40**
homicides: by Billy the Kid, 446; in cattle towns, 162; in Dodge City, 383; frontier violence and, 387; gunslingers and, 389–90; by Doc Holliday, 390; *In Cold Blood*, 452–53; by Charles Starkweather, 452, 462
homosexuality: gay and lesbian life, **329**;

Evelyn Hooker's work on, 331–32; Native American *berdache* and, 324–25
Honduras, 353
Hong Kong (China), 137
honky-tonk, 536
Hooker, Evelyn, **331–32**
Hooker, George, 7
hoop and pole game, 763
Hoople ND, *211*
Hoover, Herbert, 652, 687
Hopkins, Harry, 678–79
Hopley, Russell J., 825
Hopper, Dennis, 255, 267, **269–70**
Hopwood v. University of Texas (1996), 13
Horn, Tom, 163
Horne, Elsie Burnett, 308
Hornsby, Rogers, 766–67, 768, **776**
horse, **575–76**; as draft animals, 42; in intertribal warfare, 830; Native Americans and, 555–56, 575–76; as transportation, 793; in World War I, 820
horse racing, 764
Horvath, Steven, 356
Hosokawa, William, 136, **143–44**
hotels: commercial architecture of, 73; in gateway cities, 155; in T-towns, 186
hot-iron branding, 36
hot springs, 622
Houche Ranch, 379
Hough, F. B., 398
Houk, Ralph, 768
house barns, 289, *289*
Houser, Allan, **120**
Houston, Sam, 838
Houston and Texas Central Railroad, 794
Houston TX, 406, 431, 548
Howard, Joseph Kinsey, 381
Howat, Alexander, 704
Howe, Gordie, xviii, 376, **777**
Howe, Oscar, *106*, *120*, **120–21**, 126
Howell, Charles W., 864
Howling Wolf, **121**
How the West Was Won: film, 280; television show, 523
Hoy, Jim, 288, 289
Hruska, Roman, 228, 687
Hubbard, L. Ron, **746–47**
Hud (film), 256, *270*, 274, 275
Hudson, John, xv, 168
Hudson, Lois Phillips, 478
Hudson's Bay Company, **422–23**; and Blackfoot, 567; and conflict with North West Company, 229, 389, 419, 584, 836; Crowfoot and, 571; Peter Fidler and, 229–30; and frontier law, 443; in fur trade, 341, 403, 419, 422–23; Cuthbert Grant and, 389; Anthony Henday and, 234–35; Henry Kelsey and, 239, 301–2; and merger with North West Company, 422, 443; Métis and, 229, 230, 422, 443, 584; north-south trade links of, 665; Pierre-Guillaume Sayer trial, 443, 461; and Plains Crees, 592; political authority under, 647; and Joseph-Norbert Provencher, 754; Rupert's Land relinquished by, 240, 385, 413, 422–23, 460; Scots employed by, 244; Lord Selkirk and, 229; George Simpson and, 247; David Thompson and, 249; trading through hole in wall, 442; and water law, 864; waterways used by, 793

Benjamin "Pap" Singleton, 21–22; sorghum, 51; Southeast Asians in, 137; Spanish exploration of, 247; state historical society of, 213; statehood for, 3, 647, 657, 664, 669; state symbols of, 397; stone houses, 96; Swedes in, 248; swine, 54, 55; tornadoes, 641; tornado stories, 315; tourism and, 435, 436; tribal colleges in, 213; urban population of, 151; Vietnamese in, 147; vigilantes, 464; viticulture, 56; Volga German architecture in, 99; voting patterns in, 693–94; Welsh in, 251; wheat, 27, 56, 221, 420; in Winter Wheat region, 31; *The Wizard of Oz*, 257, 280–81, 387–88; women's suffrage in, 327, 336, 337, 338, 648, 649; woodlands, 643; in World War II, 840. *See also* Abilene; "Bleeding Kansas"; Dodge City; Emporia; Flint Hills; Fort Leavenworth; Garden City; Kansas City; Lawrence; Leavenworth; Topeka; Wichita; *and other towns and cities by name*

Kansas (musical group), 532

Kansas, University of: basketball at, 767; in Big 8 Conference, 772; black student union at, 13; in Lawrence, 163; liberal arts curriculum of, 215; Gale Sayers, 20; school of music at, 547; university press of, 491

Kansas Blackman (newspaper), 7

Kansas City KS, **171**; African Americans in, 6, 171; all-black towns near, 9; interracial baseball in, 10; Knights of Labor in, 700; Mexican Americans in, 361; as river town, 180

Kansas City MO, **171**; African Americans in, 4, 5, 171; Robert Altman and, 255, 258; Aviation Weather Center, 437; Wallace Beery and, 260; civil rights organizations in, 702; Country Club Plaza of, 73, 86; Walt Disney and, 265; and economic services for Great Plains, 407; electric interurban railways, 801; European immigrants drawn to, 225; floods, 853; fringe position of, 153; as gateway city, 152; and Hallmark Cards, Inc., 421; Jean Harlow and, 255, 269; inclusion in Great Plains, xvii; *Kansas City Star*, 515; as livestock marketing center, 410; Jay McShann and, 17–18; and meatpacking industry, 171, 348, 361, 362, 426; opera in, 545; packinghouse strike of 1904, 144; Poles in, 243; radio in, 504; as river town, 180, 181; Spanish-language press in, 368; Calvin Trillin and, 523; warehouse district, 99; Wright buildings in, 101. *See also* Kansas City jazz

Kansas City (film), 255, 258

Kansas City Chiefs, 773

Kansas City jazz, **541–42**; African American music of the Plains, 531–32; Kansas City, 171; Charlie Parker and, 545; and territory bands, 4, 548

Kansas City Monarchs, 10, 171

Kansas City Star (newspaper), **515**

Kansas-Nebraska Act (1854), 3, 177, 647, 669, **670**, 686, 823–24

Kansas Pacific Railroad, 305

Kansas People's Party, 683

Kansas River, 862, *862*

Kansas State Agricultural College. *See* Kansas State University

Kansas State Normal School. *See* Emporia State University

Kansas State University (Kansas State Agricultural College): as land-grant institution, 204, 208, 214; landscape architecture program at, 86; in Manhattan, 163; women students at, 214–15

Kansas v. Colorado (1907), 847–48, 852, 861

Karcher, John, **424–25**

Karlson, Louise, 339

Kassebaum, Nancy, 188, 652, **670–71**

Kaws, **579–80**

Kearney, Denis, 142

Kearney, Stephen Watts, 130, 680, 739

Kearney NE, 170, *201*, 804, 847

Keating, Frank, 682

Keaton, Buster, xviii, 255, *255*, 258, **271**

keelboats, 793, 813

Keillor, Garrison, 323, 751

Keller, Will, 315

Kelley, Oliver H., 712

Kellie, Luna and J. T., 319

Kellogg, Mark, 506, 521

Kelly, Dan, 535

Kelly, Fanny, 326

Kelly, Joan, 320

Kelsey, Henry, **239**, 301–2, 472, 494, 592

Kem, Omer, 683

Kenderdine, Augustus F., 109, 116

Kennedy, John F., 689

Kennedy, Mifflin, 48

Kennedy, Robert F., 689

Kennekuk, 748

Kenny, John A., 524

Kent, J. B., 273

Kent, J. H., 95

Kerrey, Robert, 660

Kerr-McGee Corporation, 723

Kessler, Gerald, 86

Ketcham, Rebecca, 308

kettle lakes (prairie potholes), 850, **855**, 866

Kickapoos, 578

KidSport Society of Alberta, 768

Kiefer OK, 176

Kimball, Thomas Rogers, 65, 66, **85**, 89

Kimball, Willard, 530

King, Bruce, 680

King, Clarence, 633, 641

King, John, 293

King, Mackenzie, 675, 678

King, Richard, 48

King, Stacey, 767

King, Thomas, 472

King Ranch, 48, 278

Kinkaid Act (1904), 7, 31, 240

Kinnick, Nile, 776

Kinsella, W. P., 472

Kinsley KS, 388

Kiowa National Grassland, 780

Kiowas, **580–81**; animal lore of, 291; and Gourd Dance, 608–9; Kiowa Six, 124; law, 441; *Lone Wolf v. Hitchcock*, 456; migrations of, 555; on openness of the plains, xiv; peyotism among, 732; in Red River War, 818, 822; sign language, 600; Sun Dance among, 757; war chiefs, 839

Kiowa Six, **124**

Kirk, Andy, 531, 541

Kirk, Arthur, 702

Kittson, Norman, 226

Klein, Ralph, 684

Knapp, Seaman, 33

Kneip, Richard F., 690

Knights of Kaleva, 232

Knights of Labor, 700, 716, 722

Knode, W. F., 430

Knudsen, Kirsten, 340

Kobata, Toshira, 136

Koch, William E., 287, 288

Kogawa, Joy Nozomi, 139, **145**

Kohl, Edith Eudora, 320, 478

Kolodny, Annette, 321, 323

Kommers, Peter, 88

Konza Prairie, 616

Kool-Aid, **425**

Koreans, 136

Koresh, David (Vernon Howell), 738

Kozitsky, Carl, 719

Krebs OK, 225

Kreisel, Henry, **480–81**

Kroetsch, Robert, 471, 472, **481**, 495

Kuchler, A. W., 616

Ku Klux Klan, **715**; in Canadian West, 245; James E. Ferguson opposing, 665; in politics of Great Plains, 650; as protest group, 701–2; and Tulsa Race Riot of 1921, 22, 187

Kuralt, Charles, 316

Kurland, Bob, 767

Kuroki, Ben, 136

labor: Ella Reeve "Mother" Bloor and, 701, 707; cowboy strike of 1883, 708–9; Cripple Creek miner's strike, 722; Estevan strike, 709; Ira Finley and, 710–11; Industrial Workers of the World, 470, 700, 714; in Kansas, 670; Knights of Labor, 700, 716, 722; labor protest, 700–701; Henry Martinson and, 717; miners' strike of 1921, 701, 704; in Montana, 676; Norris-LaGuardia Act and, 681; *Silkwood v. Kerr-McGee Corporation*, 723; Winnipeg General Strike of 1919, 376, 673, 675, 700, 726–27

Lacombe, Albert, 571

lacrosse, 763

Lac Ste. Anne pilgrimage, **750**, 756

Ladies of Kaleva, 232

La Flesche, Susan, 558, **581**, 702

La Follette, Robert, 650, 666

Lake, John, 183

Lake, Stuart N., 384, 387

Lake Agassiz, 631, **855**

Lake Meredith National Recreation Area, 782

lakes: Great Lakes of the Dakotas, 376; kettle lakes, 850, **855**, 866; lacustrian wetlands, 866; Sandhills lakes, **862–63**

Lakewood CO, 166

Lakota Sioux, **601–2**; in Battle of Beecher Island, 823; in Battle of the Little Bighorn, 601, 602, 830–31; Black Hills sold by, 607; Bozeman Trail attacked by, 800; contemporary tribal governments of, 692; and counting coup, 825; Crazy Horse, 818, 825–26; Ghost Dance among, 558, 732, 746, 818; Indian Claims Commission case by, 453, 463; Indian police, 453, 454; missionaries to, 748; Red Cloud, 834; rodeo and, 577; sacred sites of, 599; and settlement in Great Plains, xv, 555; Sitting Bull, 602–3, 818; Spotted Tail, 451, 605; Sun Dance among, 757; war chiefs, 839; west river country, 399; at Wounded Knee Massacre, 601, 602, 841. *See also* Sioux Wars

Lamar, Mirabeau, 691

Lamb, Agnes, *339*

Lambert, John, 386

Lame Bull's Treaty (1855), 567

Lamm, Richard, 658

L'Amour, Louis, 470, **481**, 496

Lampasas Cut Plain, 637

Landes, Ruth, 325

land grants, railroad, **807**

land-grant system, Mexican, 346–47

land-grant universities, **204–5**; for African Americans, 205, 215; art departments founded at, 108; barn architecture influenced by, 69; establishment of, 196, 208; Morrill Act and, 196, 204, 208, 214; women at, 196, 205, 214

The Land Institute, **47**

land laws and settlement, **239–40**; alien land laws, 140, 144, 444

Land of the Dacohtas (Nelson), 703

Landon, Alfred, 225, 651, 670, **671**, 687

Land Ordinance (1785), 44, 239, 246

Landry, Tom, 773

landscape architecture, **85–86**; Ernst Herminghaus, 84, 86, 172

Lane, George, 49, 404

Lane, Rose Wilder, 471, 476, 497

lang, k. d., 533, 536, **542**

Lange, Dorothea, 45, 109, 115

Langer, William, 650, 651, 666, **671**, 679, 681, 719

Langston OK, 4, 9, 14

Langston University, 4, 207, 215

Langtry TX, 446

language: "English only" ordinances, 362; and ethnogenesis, 222; folk speech, 286–87, **299–300**; French, 197, 231, 245, 692; of immigrant newspapers, 514; and *Meyer v. Nebraska*, 457; Native American, **581–82**; nicknames, 307; Louise Pound's work on, 211–12; sign language, 299, 582, **600–601**, 607. *See also* Spanish language

Laotians: Buddhism of, 738; folk beliefs of, 296; settlement in Great Plains, 137

Laramid Orogeny, 629

Laramie WY, 170, 522

La Raza Unida Party, 349, 357, 358, 651

lariats, 382

Larkin, Uncle Bob, 536

LaRocque, Emma, 473, **481–82**

Larson, Nicolette, 536

Last Best West, 376, **391–92**, 666

The Last Picture Show: film, 256, **271**, 274, 275, 280; novel by McMurtry, 471

Latinos. *See* Hispanic Americans

Latter Rain Pentecostal movement, 734

Laurence, Margaret, 471, 472, **482**

Laurentide ice sheet, 631, 635

Laurier, Sir Wilfrid, 688

law, **439–65**; *Albert v. Albert*, 323–24; American legal frontier, 442–43; anti-corporate farming, 445–46; Asian exclusion legislation, 139–40; Judge Roy Bean, 446; Herbert Brownell Jr., 448; Canadian legal frontier, 443–44; cattle codes, 449–50; contemporary issues, 444–45; Female Employment Act, 143; Emmett Hall, 452; Ella Haskell, 452; Indian Claims Commission, 453, 463; land and settlement, 239–40; James Lougheed, 456; *McLaurin v.*

Oklahoma State Regents, 197, 207, Native American indigenous, 441; Native American Rights Fund, 458–59; Native Americans and European American legal systems, 441–42; for North Dakota anti-garb, 459–60; Overland Trail constitutions, 460–61; "Persons Case," 320, 333, 334–35; Pierre-Guillaume Sayer trial, 443, 461; poison porridge case, 135, 146; Roscoe Pound, 461; Scott family, 21; *Silkwood v. Kerr McGee*, 723; Trial of Standing Bear, 594, 605, 702, 725; twentieth-century developments in, 444; white primary, 465, 649, 651. *See also* civil rights; courts; crime; Dawes (General Allotment) Act; fencing laws; Jim Crow laws; judges; policing; prisons; Supreme Court; treaties; water law

Lawrence, Atwood, 323

Lawrence KS: civil rights, 13; as college town, 163, 164; Langston Hughes, 16; Native American school in, 193, 203, 212, 213; as river town, 153

Lawrie, Lee, 89

Lawton OK, **171–72**

Lay, Rodney, 536

Layton, Solomon, **86–87**, 95

Lead SD: as boomtown, 153; Finns in, 230; Homestake Mine, 154, 404, *404*, 421–22

Leader-Post (newspaper), **515–16**

Leahy, Frank, 769

Learjet, 797

Lease, Mary Elizabeth, 188, 683, 699, **716**

Least Heat-Moon, William, 388, 485, 487

Leavenworth, Henry, 565, 823

Leavenworth KS: first newspaper in, 521; Frontier Baseball Club, 764; as river town, 180; siting of, 153. *See also* Fort Leavenworth

Leavenworth Penitentiary, **455**

Leavitt, Bob, 6

Lebanon KS, 388

Lebret (Saskatchewan), 193

ledger paintings, 125

Lee, Andrew E., 713

Lee, Peggy, xviii, 532, **542**

Lee, Russell, 115

Lee Enterprises, 504, 506

legends, 287

Leighton, A. C., 113

Lelar, Henry, 451

LeMay, Curtis E., 838

Lemke, William, **671**, 719

Lennon Sisters, 550

lesbian and gay life, **329**

Lestanc, Joseph, 750

LeSueur, Meridel, 321, 471

Lethbridge (Alberta): Czechs in, 228; Head-Smashed-In buffalo jump near, 555, 564; Japanese in, 136, 137, 139, 735; Nikka Yuko Garden in, 137, 139, 145–46; oil in, 429; in Palliser's Triangle, 636, 735

Leupp, Francis, 668

Levi Strauss, 382

Levitt, William, 72

Lewis, John, 531

Lewis, John L., 704

Lewis, Meriwether, 240–41, 336, 600, 617. *See also* Lewis and Clark

Lewis, Sinclair, 322, 470

Lewis and Clark, **240–41**; on animal

resources, 403; on Arikaras, 564; and Blackfoot, 567; Clark's slave York accompanying, 3, 7, 24; on coyotes, 625; and federal government, 664; French Canadians and, 231; and fur trade, 419; and fur trade lore, 301; and garden image, 388; Great Falls, 169, 170; as military exploration, 817; in Montana, 675; on Native American trade, 606; and Pierre (SD), 178; and Sacagawea, 336, 341; and Shoshones, 600; water transportation used by, 813

Lewis and Clark National Forest, 779, 780

Lewiston MT, 313

Lexington NE, 185, 350, 353, 359, 362

Libby, Orin, **205**

Liberal KS, 426

Liberal Party, **672**; in Alberta, 653–54, 692; constituency of, 650; Jimmy Gardiner, 46, 672; Great Depression and, 651; immigrants and, 223; in Manitoba, 692; in politics since 1945, 652; in Prairie Provinces, 692–93; in Saskatchewan, 688; Sir Clifford Sifton and, 688

Liberty Committees, 820

libraries, **205–6**; architectural character of, 90

life-cycle customs, 288

Light Crust Dough Boys, 527, 530, 550, 552

Lighton, William R., 476

Like-a-Fishhook Village, 565, 575, 583

Lillie, Gordon W. "Pawnee Bill," 399, 400

limberjack, 300

limestone, 95

Lincoln, Abraham, 659, 686

Lincoln County War, 446, **830**

Lincoln Highway, 97, 163, 797, **803–4**, 812

Lincoln Motion Picture Company, 16, 257

Lincoln NE, **172**; civil rights organizations in, 702; as college town, 172; Davis and Wilson architects, 75–76; Theodore Epp, 744; Farmers Holiday Association demonstration in, 699; Friday night football in, 386; Ernst Herminghaus, 84; Italians in, 237; Jews in, 238; Lincoln Highway, 804; Main Street, 173; Nebraska State Capitol, 89; opera in, 545; John J. Pershing, 172, 833; Charles Starkweather, 462; Swedes in, 248; as T-town, 186, 795; Unitarians in, 759; Urban League, 4; urban Native American community of, 608; Waltz Service Station, 93; warehouse district in, 99

Lincoln NM, 830

Lindgren, Elaine, 320

Lindley, James G., 139

Lindoe, Luke and Vivian, 113

Lindsborg KS, 96, *217*, 220, 248, 288, 297, 301

Link, Art, 681

Linotype, 503, 508

Lipset, Seymour, 407

Lisa, Manuel, 247, 301, 341, **360**, 414, 419

Litchfield NE, 145

literary architecture, **87**

literature, **467–98**; Bess Streeter Aldrich, 473–74; L. Frank Baum, 281, 387–88, 471, 474; Sandra Birdsell, 474–75; Sharon Butala, 471, 475, 485, 487; Maria Campbell, 472, 473, 475; Canadian Prairie fiction, 471–72; captivity narratives, 326; Willa Cather, 470–71, 475–76; children's literature, 476; Kate

Mandans (*cont.*)
  Native American trade, 606; *Okipa* ceremony of, 753; Sun Dance among, 757
Mandel, Eli, **484**
Manfred, Frederick, 470, 471, 477
Manhattan KS, 163, *163*, 164
manifest destiny, 389, 817
Manitoba, **673–74**; Asians in, 136; barley, 35; British Commonwealth Training Plan, 824; Canadian Northern Railway, 794, 809; canola, 37; corn, 39; curling, 770, *771*; eastern as not in Great Plains, xvii; floods, 853; French Canadians in, 231; German Russians in, 232; Germans in, 233–34; Elijah Harper, 560, 713–14; Hispanic Americans in, 351; Hungarians in, 235; and ice hockey, 777; Icelanders in, 235, 673; initiative, referendum, and recall in, 649; International Peace Garden, 391, 398; Irish in, 236; irrigation, 849–50, 854; Japanese in, 144; Jews in, 245; Liberal Party in, 672; libraries in, 206; Mennonites in, 733, 751; Meridian Highway, 804; Native American radio stations in, 517; Norwegians in, 243; out-migration from, 246; Parkland Belt, xvi–xvii; Poles in, 243; politics in, 648, 650, 652, 673–74, 692; Prairie Farm Rehabilitation Administration, 48; Prairie Provinces Water Apportionment Agreement, 860; Progressive Conservative Party in, 684; Prohibition in, 724; provincial capitol, 95; provincial status for, 648, 664; provincial symbols, 397; public school development in, 195; Red River Floodway, 849; Riding Mountain National Park, 782–83; "schools question," 197; Sir Clifford Sifton, 688; sunflowers, 53; Ukrainian architecture, 98; United Church of Canada in, 759; United Farmers of Manitoba, 650, 699; vocational education, 196; voting patterns in, 692; wheat, 420; women's suffrage in, 337, 649; woodlands, 643; in World War II, 840. *See also* Winnipeg; *and other towns and cities by name*
Manitoba, University of, 86, 196, 206, 482, 547
Manitoba Act (1870), 584, 648, 673, 835, 864
Manitoba Agricultural College, 196
Manitoba Curling Association, 770
Manitoba Free Press (*Winnipeg Free Press*) (newspaper), 504, **524–25**, 688
Manitoba Grain Act (1901), 712
Manitoba Grain Growers Association, 712
Manitoba Technical Institute, 196
Mankiller, Wilma, **583–84**
Manly, C. M., 122
Mann, Delbert, 257, **272–73**
Mann-Elkins Act (1910), 685
Mannheim Steamroller, 532
Manning, Ernest C., 225, 654, 704
Manning, Preston, 654, 685, 686
Mansfield, Mike, 651, **674**, 676
Mantle, Mickey, 767, **778**
manufacturing: electronics industry, 407; in Great Plains, xvi, 154. *See also* aerospace industry
maps, topographic, **641**
Marbut, Curtis F., 617
Mariadahl KS, 248
Maris, Roger, **778–79**

Marley, 432
Marling, Karal Ann, 290
Marquette, Pierre, 419
marriage: *Albert v. Albert*, 323–24; between European men and Native American women, 341; mail-order brides, 332. *See also* weddings
Marshall TX, 517
Marshall, John, 442, 604
Marshall, Thurgood, 5
Martin, "Pepper," 767
Martinson, Henry, **717**
Mason, William, 739
masonry construction: brick masonry, **70**; in Czech architecture, 74; stone masonry, **95–96**
Masterson, Bat, **457**; and Wyatt Earp, 383, 384; as gunslinger, 390, 457; and Doc Holliday, 390; killing his brother's murderer, 162, 457; media in stature of, 387; nickname, 307; as walking both sides of the law, 443
mastodons, 576
Matador Land and Cattle Company, 48–49, 244
Mather, Cotton, 480
Matheson, J. D., 506
Maximilian, Prince of Wied-Neuwied, 111, **241–42**, 495
Maxwell, Edward and William S., 95
Maxwell, Leslie E., 745
Maxwell Land Grant, *361*, 562
May, Karl, **484**
Mayfield, Earl B., 715
McBeth, Sally, 308
McBride, Martina, 536
McCabe, Edward P., 4, 9
McCall, Jack, 387, 390
McCarney, Robert P., 682
McCarthy, Joseph R., 663, 667, 675, 677, 702
McCarty, Henry. *See* Billy the Kid
McClelland Creek National Grassland, 780
McClinton, Delbert, 532
McClung, Florence, 127
McClung, Nellie, 320, **333**, 335, 337, 471, 476
McCook NE, 101
McCool Junction NE, *761*
McCoy, Isaac, 736
McCoy, J. C., 171
McCoy, Joseph G., 188, 800
McCurry, W. A., 378
McDaniel, Hattie, **17**
McDonald, Alexander, 736
McDonough, Alexa, 679–80
McDougall, John, 748
McDougall, William, 819
McGee, Gale, 651, 669
McGovern, George, 651, 660, 667, **674**, 690, 849, 856
McGrath, Tom, 472, 489, **717**
McGuire, Dorothy, **273**
McIntire, Reba, 533
McKay, Arthur, 116, 127
McKean sites, 564
McKenzie, Alexander, 681
McKenzie, Kenneth, 244, 422, **425–26**
McKinney, Louise, 320, 335
McLaughlin, James, 603
McLaurin v. Oklahoma State Regents (1950), 197, **207**

McLean, Archie, 404
McMurtry, Larry, xiii, 256, 271, 471, **484–85**, 497
McNickle, D'Arcy, 472, 718
McShann, Jay, **17–18**, 531, 541, 545, 548
McTavish, Edward, 476
McVeigh, Timothy, 720
McVicar, Peter, 448
Mead, Elwood, 846, 847, **855–56**
Means, Russell, 560, 602, 705–6
meat, 300–301; barbecue, 171, 300; beef, 300–301, 394, 410, 418; World War I creating demand for, 650. *See also* meatpacking
"meat and potatoes" diet, 301
meatpacking, **426**; as agribusiness, 409; "Big Five" packers, 404; cattle ranching and, 404; European immigrants in, 225; Hispanic Americans in, 348, 349–50, 353, 359, **361–62**, 426; in Kansas City, 171, 348, 361, 362, 426; new slaughterhouses in Great Plains, 405; in Oklahoma City, 176; in Omaha, 54, 177, 243, 348, 426; Poles in, 243; settlement patterns and, 246; in Sioux Falls, 184; small-town industrialization, 185, 433, 434; Vietnamese in, 147; westward movement of, 29, 410, 426
media, **499–525**; concentration of, 504–5; early mass communication, 501; in frontier violence image, 387; *Nebraska Press Association v. Stuart*, 459; religion in, 734. *See also* broadcasting; film; Internet; journalism; newspapers
medicine: John Richard Brinkley, 504, 507; folk, 288, 297; Menninger Clinic, 186, 207–8. *See also* health-care industry
Medicine, John, 596
Medicine Hat (Alberta), 636
Medicine Lodge KS, 718
Medicine Lodge Creek, Treaty of (1867), 563, 565, 568, 580, 818, 836
medicine wheels, 566, 599
Medora SD, 242
Meech Lake Accord, 560, 713, 714
Meek, F. B., 633
Meek, Joe, 302
Meek, Marvin, 705
Meeker, Jotham, 502, 748
Meeker, Nathan, 864
Meiere, Hildreth, 89
Meighen, Arthur, **674–75**
Melbourne, Frank, 859
Melroe Bobcat, **426–27**
melting pot, 380
memoirs, **485**
men: competitive cooking by, 300; farming associated with, 320–21; masculinity, 323; sense of place of, 329–30
Menninger, C. F., 186, 207
Menninger, Karl, **207–8**
Mennonites, **751**; adobe construction of, 71; Canadian settlement grants for, 219, 222, 232, 240, 244–45, 733, 751; cultural transformation of, 221; distribution of religions, 741, 742; ethnogenesis in, 222; Germans, 233, 234; house barns of, 289, *289*; *Mennonite* newspaper, 514; political participation by, 223; and Prohibition, 223; and wheat cultivation, 31, 56, 221; Rudy Wiebe on, 497; and women's suffrage, 223; and World War I, 224, 650

Nebraska, University of (*cont.*)
200; and Aaron Douglas, 14; and Loren
Eiseley, 626; first African American medical
graduate at, 8; and football, 375, 377, 765,
768, 772, 773; Great Plains Film Festival at,
258; as land-grant institution, 204, 208, 214;
in Lincoln, 172; MIDNET, 515; and John J.
Pershing, 833; and Louise Pound, 211–12;
Prairie Schooner magazine published by,
490; radio research at, 504; Mari Sandoz
papers at, 206; school of music at, 547; and
Ted Sorenson, 689; university press of, 491;
and Roger Welsch, 316; women in art
faculties at, 108
Nebraska Academy of Sciences, 619
Nebraska City NE, 180, 184, 436
Nebraska Consolidated Mills, 416
Nebraska National Forest, 779
Nebraska Press Association v. Stuart, **459**
Nebraska State Capitol, **89**; architecture, 66,
67; as compared to other state capitols, 95,
157; landscape architecture of, 84, 86; in
Lincoln, 172
Nebraska State Historical Society, 596, 619
Nebraska State Normal School, 197, 214
Negro National League, 10, 171
Neihardt, John G., 302, 472, 487, **488**, 489, 737
Nelson, Bruce, 703
Nelson, William Rockhill, 515
Nelson, Willie, 531, 541, **544**, 546
Neodesha KS, 175, 430, 431
Nesharu, 564
Neth, Mary, 321
Nettleton, E. S., 847
Neuharth, Allen, **517–18**
New Deal, **678–79**; Agricultural Adjustment
Administration, 32, 650; architecture
affected by, 76; Dwight D. Eisenhower and,
663; Farm Security Administration, 45;
Lyndon Baines Johnson and, 668, 669;
Native Americans and, 559, 651, 678; and
politics of Great Plains, 650–51; right-wing
protest and, 702; Social Gospel and, 734;
Treasury Section of the Fine Arts of, 122;
William Allen White supporting, 524;
Gerald Winrod on, 727; *The Wizard of Oz*
and, 281
New Democratic Party, **679–80**; in Alberta,
654, 692; creation of, 652, 659; health care
plan of, 652, 680; in Manitoba, 673, 692; in
Saskatchewan, 688, 692; as symbol of
socialistic reform, 375, 376
Newell, Frederick, 847, 848
Newell, Robert, 302
New Finland (Saskatchewan), 231
New Jerusalem (Saskatchewan), 238
New Mexico, **680**; Anglo-Canadians in, *226*;
Apaches in, 561–62; Battle of Glorieta Pass,
818; and Billy the Kid, 446; civil divisions of
government in, 657; coal, 414, 415, *415*;
Colorado Doctrine, 851; and Coronado,
227; cotton, 40, 41, 405, 416; Czechs in, 228;
drought plan, 852; Ecuecapa, 572–73;
European settlement patterns in, 246;
exotic animals, 43; Albert Fall, 663;
genízeros, 356; German Russians in, 232;
groundwater under state control in, 849;
Hispanic Americans in, 350, 359, 680;
Hispanic architecture, 84–85; Hispanos,
359–60; international trade, 424, *424*;

irrigation, 854; Italians in, 237; Japanese in,
144; junta de indignación, 714–15; Kansas-
Nebraska Act and, 670; land-grant
university in, 208; land laws and settlement
in, 240; libraries in, 206; and Lincoln
County War, 446, 830; Llano Estacado, 634;
Mescalero Escarpment, 613, 614;
Methodism in, 752; Mexican rule in, 346–
47; national wildlife refuges in, 784; oil, 431,
680; Georgia O'Keeffe's paintings of, 126;
"Operation Wetback" in, 349; and Miguel
Antonio Otero, 363; *pastores*, 363–64;
politics in, 651, 660, 680, 687, 693–94;
potash, 405, 406; proverbs and proverbial
sayings of, 310; and Bill Richardson, 366;
Roman Catholicism in, 755, 756; and
Casimero Romero, 367; Route 66, 810;
Santa Fe Trail in, 810–11; sheep, 50, 365;
Southern Baptists in, 733; as Spanish
colony, 345, 346; Spanish settlement in, 247,
680; statehood for, 657, 664; state symbols
of, *397*, *398*; as territory, 647–48; *Territory
of New Mexico v. Yee Shun*, 146–47; Reies
López Tijerina's political activism in, 349;
tourism and, 436; tribal colleges in, 213;
Pedro Vial, 250–51; voting patterns in, 693–
94; woodlands, 643. *See also* Roswell; Santa
Fe
New Negro movement, 14
New Salem ND, 312
newspapers: African American, 7, 22; *Appeal
to Reason*, 521, 701, 707; *Argus-Leader*, 505–
6; *Billings Gazette*, 506; *Bismarck Tribune*,
506–7, 521; *Calgary Herald*, 507–8; Arthur
Capper, 508; concentration of, 504–5; *The
Conservative*, 677; *Daily Oklahoman*, 509–
10; *Dallas Morning News*, 510; *Denver Post*,
502, 510–11; as early mass communication,
501; editors and their agendas, 503;
Edmonton Journal, 511; *Emporia Gazette*,
503, 512; and ethnic community, 223; *Fort
Worth Star-Telegram*, 510, 512; Legh
Freeman, 503, 512–13, 521; *Frontier Index*,
170, 503, 513, 521; Elmer J. Garner, 702, 711–
12; immigrant, **514**; *Indian Country Today*,
514; Japanese, 136; *Kansas City Star*, 515;
Leader-Post, 515–16; military post
publications, **516**; Native American, 501–2,
521; *Omaha World-Herald*, 518; quilt
patterns in, 311, 335; rivalries between, 502;
Rocky Mountain News, 501, 502, 503, 510,
511, 521; small-town industrialization of,
433, 434; in small-towns, **520–21**; Spanish-
language press, **368**; standardization of,
502–3; *Star-Phoenix*, 521–22; *Tulsa Star*,
22; USA *Today*, 517–18; *Western Producer*,
523–24; *Winnipeg Free Press*, 504, 524–25,
688
newsreels, 274
New Town ND, 290
Nicaragua, 353
Nichols, J. C., 73, 86, 171
Nickles, Don, 682
nicknames, **307**
Nicodemus KS, 3–4, 9, 14, 156, *156*, 286
Nicoll, Bruce, 491
Nicoll, Marion, 113
Nicollet, Joseph, 826
Nikka Yuko Garden, 137, 139, **145–46**
Nimitz, Chester, **832**

Ninth Cavalry Regiment, 3, 7, 10
Niobrara ecotone, **635**, 643
Niobrara River, 866
nitrification of groundwater, 29, 850, 865
nitrogen fertilizer, 45, 52
Nix, Hoyle, 551
Nixon, Richard, 665, 667, 674, 677
Noble, Charles S., 245
Nolte, Nick, 255, **274–75**
Nonpartisan League, **718–19**; American
Society of Equity and, 699; Communists
and, 701; Lynn Frazier, 666, 719; influence
in Canada, 664, 672, 677; and William
Langer, 671, 679, 719; and William Lemke,
671, 719; and New Deal, 679; and Peter
Norbeck in South Dakota, 681; in North
Dakota politics, 650, 666, 671, 681; in
Northern Lights, 275, 703; and populism,
687; as protest, xvi, 701; as symbol of
socialistic reform, 375, 376; and Arthur C.
Townley, 650, 718–19, 724; and United
Farmers of Alberta, 650, 725
Norbeck, Peter, 393, 649, **680–81**, 687, 690
Norman OK, 163, 164, 437
Norman, Westley and Edward, 522
Norquay, John, 648
Norris, Frank, 379
Norris, George W., 377, 650, 651, 666, 678,
679, **681**, 687
Norris, Kathleen, 487
Norris-LaGuardia Act (1932), 681
Norris-Rayburn Act (1936), 681
North American Air Defense Command
(NORAD), 164, 821, 824
North American craton, 613
North American Farm Alliance, 699
North American Free Trade Agreement. *See*
NAFTA
North American Waterfowl Management
Plan, 638
North Atlantic Treaty Organization, 651
North Battleford (Saskatchewan), 734
North Dakota, **681–82**; African Americans in,
4, 5; Anglo-Canadians in, 226, 226–27;
anti–corporate farming laws in, 445; anti-
garb law of, **459–60**; appropriation
doctrine, 851; Badlands, 620; barley, 35;
cattle, 28; civil divisions of government,
657; coal, 414, 415, *415*; corporate farming
in, 40; curling, 771; Czechs in, 228; Danes
in, 229; on eastern edge of Great Plains,
xvii; ethnic groups in, xvi, 376; European
settlement patterns in, 246; farm
consolidation, 44; farmers' railroads, 795;
fertilizer use, 45; Finns in, 230; flax, 46; folk
monuments, 290; and Lynn Frazier, 666,
719; German Russians in, 232, 376;
Germans in, 233; Hidatsas in, 575; Hispanic
Americans in, 348; hockey, 375; hunting,
765; Icelanders in, 235; images and icons of,
376; initiative and referendum in, 681–82;
and International Peace Garden, 391, 398;
international trade, 424, *424*; in Irrigated
Valleys region, 31; irrigation, 854;
isolationism in, 651; Italians in, 237; Jews in,
238, 750; Kansas-Nebraska Act and, 670;
land-grant university in, 204, 208; land
laws and settlement in, 240; and William
Langer, 671, 681, 719; and William Lemke,
671, 719; Orin Libby as historian of, 205;

libraries in, 206; Little Missouri National Grassland, 766; Lutherans in, 751; and Henry Martinson, 717; and Meridian Highway, 804; Methodism in, 752; NAFTA and, 427; national wildlife refuges in, 766, 783, 784; Native American population growth, 560; Nonpartisan League, xvi; in *Northern Lights*, 275; in Northern Spring Wheat region, 30; Norwegian businessmen in, 155; Norwegians in, 242, 376; Gerald Nye, 651, 682; oil, 431; Poles in, 243; politics in, 649, 651, 660, 681–82, 687, 693–94; population decline in, 169; and Prohibition, 648, 724; and Public Law 280, 461–62; Red Belt in, 225; Roman Catholicism in, 756; rye, 49; school consolidation and reorganization, 212; snowfall, 614; soybeans, 52; State Capitol of, 95, 157; state historical society of, 213, 337; statehood for, 647, 657, 664, 681; state-sponsored enterprise in, 719; state symbols of, 397, 398; sugar beets, 52, 434; Swedes in, 248; Era Bell Thompson, 97, 376; and Arthur C. Townley, 650, 718–19, 724; tribal colleges in, 213; Ukrainian architecture, 98; in Unglaciated Missouri Plateau region, 30; urban population of, 151; urban trolley lines, 796; and vigilantes, 464; voting patterns in, 693–94; and war contracts in World War II, 840; wheat, 56, 420; wind energy, 437; Larry Woiwode writing on, 498; women's suffrage in, 337, 648; woodlands, 643. *See also* Bismarck; Fargo; Fort Union; Grand Forks; Nonpartisan League; *and other towns and cities by name*

North Dakota, University of, 169, 519, 777

North Dakota anti garb law, **159–60**

North Dakota Institute for Regional Studies, 210

North Dakota State University, 86, 167, 204, 208, 210, 214

North Dakota War Resources Committee, 840

The Northern Lights (film), 257, **275**, 703, 717

Northern Pacific Railway Company: in Billings, 159; in Bismarck, 97, 159; and bonanza farming, 35; Calamity Jane and, 325–26; in Grand Forks, 169; merger with Burlington, 796; and Western Trail, 814

Northern Spring Wheat region, 29, 30

North Platte NE, 141, 170, 359, 614

North Platte River, 862; in Casper, 161; and hydraulics of Great Plains, 845; in Irrigated Valleys region, 31

North Saskatchewan River, 615, 861–62, 862

North Sioux City SD, 419

North Texas, University of, 206

North West Company: conflict with Hudson's Bay Company, 229, 389, 419, 584, 836; in fur trade, 419, 592; and Kenneth McKenzie, 426; merger with Hudson's Bay Company, 422, 443; and Red River Settlement, 230, 584; waterways used by, 793

Northwest Cricket Club, 764

Northwest Irrigation Act (1898), **856**, 864

North-West Mounted Police (NWMP), **460**; and alleged Indian crime, 442; creation of, 444, 460; dissolution of, 444; and federal government in Canada, 663; and James

Macleod, 456–57; as minimizing conflict with Native Americans, 819; mounted troop at Fort Walsh, Saskatchewan, *439*; Mountie stories of, 486; in North-West Rebellion, 460, 833; and On-to-Ottawa trek, 721; and Jerry Potts, 394; in Winnipeg General Strike of 1919, 727

North-West Rebellion (1885), **833**; Big Bear in, 567, 833; Crees in, 732, 833; European-Native conflict in, 442, 819; Cuthbert Grant and, 389; as of lasting historical importance, xviii; Métis sense of nationhood and, 389; and North-West Mounted Police, 460, 833; Poundmaker and, 594, 833; and the reserves, 598; Louis Riel in, 442, 460, 557, 585, 723, 819, 833; suppression of, 567, 585

Northwest Territories Act (1875), 648

Norwegians, **242–43**; assimilation of, 222; as businessmen, 155; in Canadian West, 245; cultural transformation of, 221; in Grand Forks, 169; immigrant newspapers, 514; Lutheranism of, a 13, 733, 751; in North Dakota, 242, 376; and Prohibition, 223; Rölvaag's *Giants in the Earth* and, xiv, xv, 234, 491

Notley, Grant, 654

nuclear war, 821, 825, 837–38

nuclear waste sites, **427–28**

Nye, Bill, 503, **518**

Nye, Gerald, 651, **682**

Oahe Dam, 858

Oahe Reservoir, 849, 856, 857

Oahe Unit, **856–57**

Oakley, Annie, 380

Oakley KS, 165

O'Brien, Davey, 776

O'Brien, Patrick, 200

Occum, Samson, 486

Ochsner, Ernest, 121

O'Daniel, Wilbert Lee "Pappy," 534, 550, 665

Odessa TX, **175**; football in, 386, 765, 772; and Midland, 174; oil industry in, 175, 176, 406

O'Fallon, Benjamin, 823, 829

Offutt Air Force Base NE, 820, 821, 825, 832, 838

Ogallala Aquifer, **857–58**; hydrology of Great Plains, 616, 845; irrigation from, 54, 174, 359, 849, 854; and Llano Estacado, 623, 634; meatpacking industry using, 426; playa lakes over, 859; viticulture for conserving, 56; water quality of, 865

Ogallala Formation (Group), 613, 630, 857, 865

Ogallala NE, 162, 378, 387, 814

Ogden, G. W., 476

Oglala Lakota College (Pine Ridge Reservation), 88, *88*

Oglala SD, 270

O'Hare, Kate Richards, 701, **719–20**

oil: Anna Anderson No. 1, *401*, 432; and boomtowns, **175**, 397; in Calgary, 160, 175, 176, 406, 429, 430, 431; in Fort Worth, 168, 175, 176, 406; as icon of southern Great Plains, 377; in industry of Great Plains, 406; and international trade, 423, 424; in Midland-Odessa, 174, 175, 176, 406, 431; museums of, 208; oil field films, **275–76**; oil towns, 153, 154; Petro-Canada, 429;

petroleum in Canada, **429–30**; petroleum in United States, **430–31**; Phillips Petroleum, 432; reflection seismography for locating, 424, 425; Reform Party and, 685; in Regina, 179; roughnecks and roustabouts, 397; tall tales about, 315; in Tulsa, 176, 186, 406; in Wichita Falls, 188, 189; World War I and, 819; World War II and, 821

oilseeds, 41, 405, 412, **428**

Ojibwas, **585–86**

Okajima, Kinji, 144

OK Corral (Tombstone), 384, 390, 391

O'Keeffe, Georgia, **125–26**, 624

Okies, 377, **393**

Okihiro, Gary, 145

Okipa, **753**

Oklahoma, **682–83**; African American newspapers in, 7; African Americans in, 5, 682; all-black towns in, 9; and Oscar Ameringer, 706; "A&M" program in, 196; Anglo-Canadians in, 226; anti–corporate farming laws of, 445; Arapahos in, 563; arboretums, 67; and Gene Autry 259; Baptists in, 733, 736; and Kate Barnard, 324; and Henry Bellmon, 651, 654, 687; Boomers of, 377; Caddos in, 568–69; in Central Interstate Low-Level Nuclear Waste Compact, 428; Cheyennes in, 570; civil divisions of government, 657; and civil rights, 13; Comanches in, 570; and Coronado, 227; corporate farming in, 40; cotton, 31, 40, 41, 416; country music, 536; Czechs in, 228; drought, 28, 852; eastern as not in Great Plains, xvii; electric interurban railways, 796; European settlement patterns in, 246; farm consolidation, 44; fertilizer use, 45; film companies in, 257; in films, 257, 261–62, 276; and Ira Finley, 710–11; football in, 375, 765; and Joseph Foucart, 80–81; German Russians in, 232; Germans in, 233; ghost stories of, 302; Green Corn Rebellion, 713; and Herb Greene, 83–84; gymnastics, 775; Hispanic Americans in, 348, 350–51, 359; Hispanic architecture in, 84–85; images and icons of, 377; and Indian Country, 668; and Indian Territory, 578, 648; Indian Welfare Act of 1936, 568–69, 570; and international trade, 424, *424*; in Irrigated High Plains region, 31; irrigation in, 854; Italians in, 237; Japanese in, 144; Jim Crow laws, 8, 454, 455, 649; Juneteenth, 288; Ku Klux Klan in, 701, 715; land-grant university in, 204, 208; land rushes, 377; libraries in, 206; *McLaurin v. Oklahoma State Regents*, 197, 207; Meridian Highway, 804; Methodism in, 752; and Mike Monroney, 675; NAFTA and, 427; national wildlife refuges in, 784; oil boomtowns in, 176; oil industry in, 406, 431; "Okie" image of, 377, 393; Plains Apaches in, 591–92; Poles in, 243; politics in, 651, 660, 682–83, 687, 693–94; and Prohibition, 649; Quakers in, 754, 755; and racism of first state government, 8, 9; reservations in, 597; and Rollie Lynn Riggs, 491; rock and roll music in, 546; and Will Rogers, 278; Roman Catholicism in, 756; Route 66 through, 810; rye, 49; South Americans in, 367; soybeans, 52; Spanish

Parker, Quanah, 577, **589–90**, 732, 822, 839
parking meters, **806**
Parkland Belt, xiv, xvi–xvii, 29
Parkman, Francis, 469, 494
parks: Government Rustic architecture in, 76; prairie preservation, 637–38; state and provincial, 765. *See also* national parks
Parks, Gordon, 4–5, **19–20**, 255
Parlby, Irene, 320, 335, 725
Parmley, Joseph W., 814
Paroth, Frederick W., 66
Partridge, Edward A., 712, **721**, 725
pasta, 301
pastoral region, **393–94**
pastores, 347, 359, **363–64**, 367
pattern books (architectural), 65
Patterson, Thomas, 510
Pawnee National Grassland, 780
Pawnees, **590–91**; cosmology of, 566; Indian Claims Commission case, 453; lodges of, 62, 88; missionaries to, 748, 754; Pitaresaru, 591; political authority among, 647; relocation of, 556, 590; repatriation, 596; reservations of, 597; sacred sites of, 599; Skiris, 566, 590, 591, 647, 752; Sun Dance among, 757; trade of, 606, 607; Villasur expedition defeated by, 247, 251, 345, 556, 817, 839; water use by, 845
Payipwat, **591**
Payne, David L., 378
Peabody Museum (Harvard University), 596
Peale, Titian Ramsay, **126**
Pearce, William, 864
Pearson, Lester B., 452
Pearson, Maria, 596
Peattie, Elia, **334**, 476
Pecos Bill, **307**, 315
Pecos River: and Caprock Canyonlands, 623; data on, *862*; and hydraulics of Great Plains, 845; physiography of Great Plains, 637; rock art and, 128
Pecos Valley Railway, 181
Peebles, Harry "Hap," 536
Peffer, William Alfred, **518–19**, 683
Pei, I. M., 67
Peltier, Leonard, 270, 602, 706
Pembina District, 226
Peña, Federico, 350, **364**
Peñalosa, Diego de, 395
Pender, Lady Rose, 339
Pendergast, Tom, 541, 545, 548
Penn, Robert Lee, *103*, **126**
Penrose, Spencer, 164
Pentecostal Assemblies of Canada, 736
pentecostalism: Assemblies of God, 735–36, 745; and evangelicalism, 745; in Great Plains, 734; and Charles Fox Parham, 734, 753–54; and Oral Roberts, 734, 745, 755
Pentland, Barbara, 530
People's Party, **683**; and Mary Elizabeth Lease, 683, 716; and William Alfred Peffer, 518–19
Peralta, Pedro de, 680
Perkins, Edwin E., 425
Perkins OK, 174
Permian Basin, 431
Perot, Ross, 656
Pershing, John J., 172, **833–34**
personal experience narratives, **307–8**
"Persons Case," 320, 333, **334–35**
pesticides, 850, 865

Peters, Susie, 124
Peterson, Helen, 559
Petro-Canada, **429**
petroleum. *See* oil
Pettigrew, Richard, **683**, 689
peyotism, 558; among Arapahos, 563; among Cheyennes, 569; among Crows, 571; in Native American Church, 732, 753; and Quanah Parker, 590, 732; among Quapaws, 596; as response to European settlement, 558, 731, 732; among Shoshones, 600
Philip, Scotty, 244
Phillips, Walter, 113
Phillips Petroleum, **432**, 767
philosophy: Cornel West, 23–24
Phinney, Archie, 718
phosphorus fertilizer, 45, 46
photography: of Robert Adams, 110–11; of Solomon Butcher, 107, 112; of Evelyn Cameron, 113; Dust Bowl era, 45, 109–10, **115**; of Terry Evans, 110, 116; of Laura Gilpin, 117–18; of Frank Gohlke, 110, 118; of William Henry Jackson, 121; of Martin and Osa Johnson, 270; of Wright Morris, 486; of Gordon Parks, 19–20; of settlement period, 107; of Marion Post Wolcott, 45, 115, 132
physical environment, **611–44**; John James Audubon and, 619; Samuel Aughey Jr. and, 395, 396, 619; biogeography, 616–17; buffalo commons, xiii, 375, 379; Caprock Canyonlands, 623–24; Loren Eiseley and, 626; hydrology, 615–16; nature writing on, 487; Niobrara ecotone, 635; paleo-environments, 635–36; physiography, 636–37; topography, 613, 641. *See also* Badlands; Black Hills; caves; climate; desert; Dust Bowl; fire; flora; geology; glaciation; grasslands; lakes; Llano Estacado; parks; prairie; rivers; soils; water; weather; wetlands; wildlife; wind; woodlands
physiography, **636–37**
Pick, Lewis A., 848, 858
Pickett, Bill, 7, **20**, 400
Pick-Sloan Plan, 848–49, 853, 856, **858**, 864
pie making, 301
Pierre SD, **178**; Native American school in, 193, 203; as river town, 180; selected as capital, 689; siting of, 153
Pierre-Guillaume Sayer trial, 443, **461**
Pike, Richard, 613
Pike, Zebulon, **834**; and Colorado Springs, 164; on Great American Desert, xiii, 257, 494, 817, 823, 852; and Pueblo, 178
Pikes Peak, 164, 178, 805, 834
Pilcher, Joshua, 823
Pine Ridge Escarpment, 636, 643
Pine Ridge Reservation SD: American Indian Movement at, 706; Black Elk at, 748; casino at, 560; Indian police at, 453, 454; Harold Jones at, 749; Oglala Lakota College, 88, *88*; and Leonard Peltier incident, 270; size and population of, 597; tribal government at, 692; unemployment at, 560; Women of All Red Nations study of, 727; and Wounded Knee Massacre of 1890, 841; and Wounded Knee protest of 1973, 702
Pingree ND, 614
Pinkerton, Allan, 244, 314

pioneers: African American, **7–8**; American legal frontier and, 442–43; Canadian legal frontier, 443–44; mad pioneer women, **392**; museums of, 208; music of, 529–30; public schools built by, 194; settlement process for, 246; sports and recreation among, 763–64; tourism and, 435. *See also* homesteading
Pirsig, Robert, xvii
Pitaresaru, **591**
Pitt, Brad, 255
pizza, 301, 432
Pizza Hut, 188, 301, **432**
Plains Apaches, **591–92**
Plains Border region, 637
Plains country towns, 153, 155–56
Plains Crees, **592–93**; beaver bundles, 605; in North-West Rebellion, 732, 833; Payipwat, 591; Poundmaker, 594; Sun Dance among, 757; trade of, 606–7
Plains Indians. *See* Native Americans
The Plainsman (film), 263, 280
Plains Sign Language, 600–601
Plainview TX, 414, 614
Plan of San Diego, 364
plants. *See* flora
Platte River, 862; data on, *862*; Farm Security Administration sponsoring irrigation, 45; glaciation and, 631; in Irrigated Valleys region, 31; Oregon Trail and, 805
Platte River State Park NE, *861*
Platte River Whooping Crane Maintenance Trust, 850, **859**
Platte Valley, 377
playa lakes, 850, **859**
play party, **309–10**, 530
plazas, 347, 363
Plenty Coups, **593**
Plessy v. Ferguson (1896), 449
The Plow That Broke the Plains (film), 256–57, **276–77**, 626, 677, *703*
Poe, Edgar Allan, 495
poetry, **489**; by Gwendolyn Brooks, 11–12; cowboy poetry, 472, *476*, 537; by Lorna Crozier, 473, 476–77; by Louise Erdrich, 473, 478; by Langston Hughes, 16; by Dorothy Livesay, 472, 483; by Tom McGrath, 472, 489, 717; by Native Americans, 472, 473; by John G. Neihardt, 488; in Plains literature, 472–73; by William Stafford, 472, 489, 493; by Bernice Zamora, 369
Poinsett SD, 231
Point, Nicolas, 573
Pointer, Vena, 848
poison porridge case (1907), 135, **146**
pole buildings, 78
Poles, **243**; in Canadian West, 245; clay construction of, 71; folk arts of, 296; in later waves of immigration, 219; in mining, 225, 243; polka music, 546; Roman Catholicism of, 756
policing: differences between American and Canadian, 444; by Wyatt Earp, 384; Indian police, **453–54**; by Bat Masterson, 457; Native American, 603; by Texas Rangers, 443, **462–63**, 829; and vigilantes, 387, 443, **464–65**. *See also* North-West Mounted Police
politics and government, **645–95**; Grace

symbols of, 397–98; public school development in, 195–96; publishing houses in, 491; Quakers in, 755; radio, 504; railways, 794, 808–9; ranches, 49; rapidity of settlement of, xv; Reform Party in, 685–86; reserves in, 598–99; rivers, 845; Roman Catholicism in, 756; rural-urban population change, 182; school consolidation and reorganization in, 212; settlement patterns in, 244–46; shelterbelts, 639; small presses in, 493; soils, 617, 640; Swedes in, 248–49; teacher training, 197; Telus, 435; topography of, 613; tourism and, 436; trading posts, 98; Trans-Canada Highway, 797, 811–12; Ukrainian architecture, 98; Ukrainians in, 249–50; urban Indian reserves, 187; urbanization of, 152; Victorian women travelers, 339; Vietnamese in, 147; vigilantes, 464; vocational education, 196; voting patterns, 692–93; water compacts, 848; water law, 846, 864–65; Welsh in, 251–52; wheat, 56, 409, 420; women in higher education, 213; women's suffrage in, 322, 337–38; in World War I, 224, 650, 820; in World War II, 820, 840–41. *See also* Alberta; Manitoba; Saskatchewan

Prairie Provinces Water Apportionment Agreement, 860

Prairie Schooner, **490**

Prairie-style architecture, 66, 76, 101

prairie turnip, 309

Pratt, E. J., 472

Precambrian rocks, 629

precious metals: in industry of Great Plains, 404; silver, 404, 649, 683. *See also* gold

precipitation: agricultural meteorology, 33; annual rates of, 615; and climate of Great Plains, 625; as hail, 423, 640, 641; in hydraulics of Great Plains, 845; Palliser's Triangle, 30, *30*, 385, 636, 853, 864. *See also* drought; rainfall; snowfall

predatory birds, 621

Preemption Act (1841), 240

Presbyterianism, **754**; dispensationalism, 741; distribution of religions, 742; fundamentalism in, 734; and Indian missionaries, 748, 754; in Red River Settlement, 732, 754

Presentation Sisters, 732, 739, 748

Presley, Elvis, 15

Pressler, Larry, 690

Preston, Liz, 143

Price, Mark, 767

Price, Sammy, 531

price supports: agricultural, **34**; Agricultural Adjustment Administration, 32–33; and sustainable agriculture, 54

Price Tower (Bartlesville OK), 101

prisoner-of-war (POW) camps, 821

prisons: Leavenworth Penitentiary, 455; in small town economies, 185; twentieth-century legal development of, 444

Professional Rodeo Cowboys Association, 765, 785

Progressive Conservative Party, **683–84**; in Alberta, 653–54, 684, 692; Joe Clark, 658; constituency of, 650; John Diefenbaker, 660–61; Great Depression and, 651; immigrants and, 223; and Edgar Peter Lougheed, 654, 672–73; in Manitoba, 673, 684, 692; and Arthur Meighen, 674–75; in politics since 1945, 652; Reform Party and, 685; in Saskatchewan, 688

Progressive movement: and Lynn Frazier, 666; in Kansas, 377, 670; and Peter Norbeck, 681, 689; in politics of Great Plains, 649–50

Prohibition: William Jennings Bryan supporting, 655; Eighteenth Amendment and, 724; immigrants and, 223; in Indian lands, 724; in Kansas, 377, 648, 724; Kansas City jazz during, 541; Carrie Nation and, 717–18, 724; in Oklahoma, 649; in Prairie Provinces, 724; temperance movement and, 724; women and, 338, 648, 649

promotional literature, **394–95**

pronghorns, 616, 786

protest and dissent, **697–728**; William Aberhart, 704; American Agriculture Movement, 704–5; *Appeal to Reason*, 707; Kate Barnard, 324; Ella Reeve "Mother" Bloor, 701, 707; Earl Browder, 701, 707; John Brown, 3, 377, 669, 708; James Patrick Cannon, 701, 708; civil rights and, 702; Clara Colby, 327; cowboy strike of 1883, 708–9; Denver's anti-Chinese riot, 135, 142–43, 146; Doctors' Strike of 1962, 709; Estevan strike of 1931, 709; ethnic, 702; farm, 699–700; Farmers Alliance, 661, 683, 709–10; Farmers Holiday Association, 710; Ira Finley, 710–11; Freemen, 702, 711; Elmer J. Garner, 702, 711–12; grain growers associations, 712; Grange, 699, 712–13; Great Plains as source of, xvi; Green Corn Rebellion, 713; Elijah Harper, 560, 713–14; Industrial Workers of the World, 470, 700, 714; Junta de Indignación, 714–15; labor, 700–701; Mary Elizabeth Lease, 699, 716; Malcolm X, 716–17; Tom McGrath, 717; National Congress of American Indians, 559, 718; National Farmers Union, 699, 701, 702, 710, 718; Kate Richards O'Hare, 701, 719–20; Omaha Race Riot of 1919, 4, 12, 19; On-to-Ottawa trek, 720–21; Edward A. Partridge, 712, 721; political, 701–2; Posse Comitatus, 375, 702, 711, 721–22; Myron Reed, 722; Louis Riel, 722–23; right-wing, 701–2; *Silkwood v. Kerr-McGee Corporation*, 723; Anna Louise Strong, 723–24; Arthur C. Townley, 650, 718–19, 724; Trial of Standing Bear, 594, 605, 702, 725; Tulsa Race Riot of 1921, 12–13, 22–23, 186–87, 702; ubiquity of, 702–3; United Farmers of Canada, Saskatchewan Section, 699, 725–26; Gerald Winrod, 727; Women of All Red Nations, 727; Henry Wise Wood, 654, 725, 727–28; James Shaver Woodsworth, 659, 728. *See also* American Indian Movement; Ku Klux Klan; Nonpartisan League; radicalism; suffrage movement; temperance movement; United Farmers of Alberta

Protestantism: assimilation of Protestant immigrants, 221; Canadian Indian boarding schools of, 203–4; and church architecture, 92; Disciples of Christ, 740–41, 745; dispensationalism, 741, 745; distribution of religions, 741; and education, 195, 197; and ethnicity, 731, 732–33; evangelicalism, 734, 745; Irish and, 236; and Prohibition, 223; railroads and, 733; of Swedes, 248; Unitarianism, 741, 758–59; United Church of Canada, 732, 733, 741, 759; Gerald B. Winrod, 727. *See also* Adventists; Baptists; Congregationalists; Episcopalianism; Hutterites; Lutheranism; Mennonites; Methodism; pentecostalism; Presbyterianism; Quakers

Provencher, Joseph-Norbert, 731, 732, **754**, 755–56

proverbs and proverbial sayings, **310–11**

public buildings, **89–90**; county courthouses, 76, 90, 157, 186; state and provincial capitols, 95

Public Law 280, **461–62**

public purpose doctrine, 455

Public Works Administration (PWA), 76, 679

publishing houses, **491**; Native American, 472; small presses, **493**

puddled-clay construction, 69, 74

Pueblo CO, 10, **178**, 248, 823, 853

Pueblo Revival style, 85, 97

Puhl, Terry, 767

Purcell OK, 184–85

Purnell, John G., 356

Quakers, **754–55**; as Indian agents, 667, 754; as Indian missionaries, 748

Quanah TX, 795

Quantrill, William, 669

Quapaws, **595–96**; cession of southern Oklahoma by, 607

Qu'Appelle Hunt Club, 764

Qu'Appelle Industrial School (Saskatchewan), *204*

quarrying, 95

Quebec separatism, 685–86

Queen Anne style, 65

quilting, **311–12**; circles, **335**

Quivira, **395**

Raban, Jonathan, xiv

race: politics of, 648, 649. *See also* ethnicity; racial discrimination; racial violence

racial discrimination: anti-Semitism, 238, 702, 711, 721, 727; Asian exclusion legislation, 139–40; against Chinese, 135, 139–40, 141, 142; against Japanese, 136; against Mexicans, 348; white primary, 465, 649, 651. *See also* Jim Crow laws

racial violence: against African Americans, 4, 12; against African American soldiers, 11; against Chinese, 135, 141; Denver's anti-Chinese riot, 142–43, 146; of Ku Klux Klan, 715; in Omaha, 177; Omaha Race Riot of 1919, 4, 12, 19; Tulsa Race Riot of 1921, xviii, 12–13, 22–23, 186–87

radicalism: of Germans, 650; Industrial Workers of the World, 470, 700, 714; in Plains fiction, 471; Red Belt, 225; Red Scare, 700, 704, 708; in small-town newspapers, 521; and World War I, 700. *See also* Communist Party; socialism

Radin, Paul, 469

radio, **519–20**; at border, **534**; and John Richard Brinkley, 504, 507, 534, 536; development in Great Plains, 503–4; *Jake and the Kid*, 485; Native American stations, 502, **517**; religious broadcasting, 734, 744; Spanish language, 351; Todd Storz, 522

651; and populism, 649; and Jeannette Rankin, 685; and Franklin D. Roosevelt, 651; Silver Republicans, **689**, 690; in South Dakota, 690; and Henry Teller, 689, 690; in Texas, 691; voting patterns in Great Plains, 693, 693–94; and Francis E. Warren, 694–95; and women's suffrage, 648; in Wyoming, 695

Republican River Expedition, 838

reservations, **597–98**; allotments, 561; Indian Country, 668; Native Americans confined to, 557–58; reducing size of, 648; reservation towns, **179–80**; termination policy, 602, 604, 718

reserves, **598–99**; Indian Country, 668; urban Indian reserves, **187**

reservoirs: Diefenbaker Lake, 853, 862; federal government constructing, 849; fish in, 628; in Great Plains recreation, 376, 435; Oahe Reservoir, 849, 856, 857; in transmountain water diversion projects, 863

restaurants: Asian, 137, 139, 141; foodways, 300–301; Mexican, 351, 359; tourist architecture, 96. *See also* fast-food restaurants

retailing: Country Club Plaza shopping center, 73, 171; department stores, 73; Jews and, 238; Main Street, 173

revivalism, 734

Reynolds, Allie, 767

Reynolds, F. W., 633

Rhoades, Everett, 581

Rhodes, Dennis Sun, 88

Rhodes, Eugene Manlove, 470

Rhodes, Kimmie, 551

Rhodes, Richard, **520**

rhythm and blues (R&B): African American music, 532; King Curtis, 16, 532; Wynonie Harris, 15, 532

Richardson, Bill, 350, **366**

Richardson, J. P. *See* Big Bopper

Richardson, Nolan, 769

Richthofen, Walter, Baron von, 394

Ricketts, M. O., 8

Riders of the Purple Sage (Grey), 470

Ridge, John Rollin, 487

riding around, 763, **784**

Riding Mountain National Park, 782–83

Riel, Louis, **722–23**; execution of, 557, 585, 723, 819, 833; father of, 461; as icon of the Great Plains, 376; in Plains protest, xvi, 376; as poet, 489; provisional government formed by, 673; Rebellion of 1885, 442, 460, 557, 585, 723, 732, 819, 833; in Red River Resistance, 460, 557, 584, 722, 819, 835

Riggs, Rollie Lynn, **491**

Riggs, Stephen Return, 731–32, 748

right-to-work laws, 701

Riley, Glenda, 321, 322, 323

Rindisbacher, Peter, 109, **127**

ring-necked pheasants, 786

Ringwood, Gwen Pharis, 473

Rio Grande (River), xvii

Rio Grande Valley, 347, 351

riparian doctrine, 443, 846, **860**, 864

Rita Blanca National Grassland, 780

Rittenberry, E. F., 66

Ritter, Woodward "Tex," 530, 535

Rivera, Tomás, **366–67**, 470

river compacts, 848, **860–61**

rivers, **861–62**; floods, 853; forts built near, 827; geology of Great Plains, 629–30; glaciation and, 631; hydrology of Great Plains, 615, 845; riparian doctrine, 443, 846, 860; riparian forest, 644; river compacts, 848, **860–61**; sources of Great Plains', 845, 861; as transportation, 793–94, 813; wetlands, 866; wild and scenic rivers, **866–67**. *See also* dams

river towns, 152, 153, **180–81**

roadrunners, **638**

roads and highways: bridges, 615; early roadways, 794; good roads movement, 801–2; interstate system, 663, 797, 812, 821; Lincoln Highway, 97, 163, 797, 803–4, 812; for motor traffic, 797, 802; NAFTA and construction of, 427; roadside architecture, 93–94; Route 66, 97, 393, 810; tourist architecture, 97; Trans-Canada Highway, 797, 811–12; Yellowstone Trail, 814

roadside architecture, **93–94**

roadside attractions, 290, **312–13**

Roberts, Oral, 734, 745, **755**

Roberts, Roy A., 515

Roberts, Stephen, 89

Robertson, Eck, 535, 550, 551

Robins Irrigation Company, 851

Robinson, Cliff, 113

Robinson, Doane, 393

Robison, Carson J., 536

Robison, Emily Erwin, 537

Roblin, Duff, 673, 684

Roblin, Sir Rodmond, 684

rockabilly, 532

rock and roll music, **546–47**; Hoyt Axton, 533, 546; Eddie Cochran, 532, 535; John Denver, 532, 537, 547; Melissa Etheridge, 533, 538; The Flatlanders, 538, 546; Buddy Holly, 532, 540, 546, 551; of 1950s, 532; of 1960s, 532; Roy Orbison, 530–31, 545, 546; underground style of, 533; Bobby Vee, 532, 546, 549; Neil Young, 533, 547, 552

rock art, **127–28**

rock circles, 61

rock corrals, 363–64

Rock Island Railroad, 186

Rock Springs WY, 135

Rocky Flats Nuclear Weapons Plant, 427

Rocky Ford CO, 144

Rocky Mountain locust, 305–6, 632

Rocky Mountain News (newspaper), 501, 502, 503, 510, 511, 521

Rocky Mountain Oysters, 301

Rocky Mountains: Cheyenne Mountain, 821, 824; geographical knowledge of, 301; geology of Great Plains, 630; ghost towns in, 168; as Great Plains boundary, xvi, 636; Pikes Peak, 164, 178, 805, 834; rivers of Great Plains arising in, 845, 861; skiing in, 766; South Pass, 301

Rocky Mountain Trade Corridor, 427

rodeo, **784–85**; African American cowboys, 6–7; at Cheyenne's Frontier Days, 163, 335; College National Finals Rodeo, 161; Bob Crosby, 769; at fairs, 43; hall of fame, 377; Indian, 577, 763; Barbara Lucas, 765, 778; National Cowboy Hall of Fame and Western Heritage Center, 210; Bill Pickett, 7, 20; in Plains recreation, 765; rodeo queens, **335–36**, 765; Jim Shoulders, 786; as

source of local pride, 375; Casey Tibbs, 789; tourism and, 435, 436; Wild West shows, 400; women in, 765, 778, 785

Rodeo Association of America, 765

Rodgers, Johnny, 776

Rodgers, Patsy, *317*, 335

Rodriguez, Juan, 606

Roe Cloud, Henry, **212**

Rogers, Will, 259, **278**, 377, 436, 659

roller skating, 764

Rollins, Philip Ashton, 381

Rölvaag, O. E., **491–92**; *Giants in the Earth*, xiv, xv, 234, 256, 470, 480, 491–92, 632; on immigrant experience, 470; on Lutheran communities, 751

Roman Catholicism, **755–56**; assimilation of Catholic immigrants, 221; Canadian Indian boarding schools of, 203–4; Catholic sisterhoods, **739**, 748; cemeteries, 70; and church architecture, 92; of Czechs, 228; Pierre-Jean De Smet, 573, 603, 695, 731, 740, 756; distribution of religions, 741–42; and education, 195, 197; and ethnicity, 731, 732–33; and Robert Haire, 713; Indian missionaries, 748; Irish and, 236, 237; Ku Klux Klan and, 715; Lac Ste. Anne pilgrimage, 750, 756; of Mexican Americans, 347; and North Dakota anti-garb law, 459–60; and political participation, 223; and Prohibition, 223, 648; and Joseph-Norbert Provencher, 731, 732, 754, 755–56; and Alexandre-Antonin Taché, 755–56, 758

Romanesque Revival style, 80, 90, 92, 167

Roman Nose, 823

Romanow, Roy, 688

Romer, Roy, 658–59

Romero, Casimero, *367*, 368

Rooney, John, 765

Roosevelt, Franklin D.: Agricultural Adjustment Administration, 32; and basinwide planning for Missouri River, 848; electoral victory of 1932, 650; electoral victory of 1936, 651; electoral victory of 1940, 679; Farm Security Administration, 45; and Elmer J. Garner, 712; and Japanese internment during World War II, 136, 137, 821; and William Lemke, 671; and Nellie Tayloe Ross, 687; voting patterns in Great Plains for, 693–94; *The Wizard of Oz* and, 281. *See also* New Deal

Roosevelt, Theodore, 305

Root, John W., Jr., 95

Roper, Edward, 109

Rorty, Richard, 24

Roschynialski, Mary Zwfka, 71

Rose, Edward, 3

Rosebud, Battle of the (1876), 279, 325, 593, 818, 826, 831, 836, 837

Rosebud Reservation SD, 18, 451, *454*, 692

Rosenberg, Julius and Ethel, 448

Rosicky, John, 514

Ross, Doc, 548

Ross, Nellie Tayloe, 650, **687**, 695

Ross, Sinclair, 471, 477, 485, **492**

Ross, William Bradford, 687

Roswell NM, **181**; Hispanos in, 248; and Nancy Lopez, 351, 360; and aliens, **396–97**; snow cover duration for, 614

Rothstein, Arthur, 109, 115

Smith-Lever Act (1914), 33
Smithsonian Institution, 596, 597
Smoky, Lois, 124
Smoky Hill River, 62
Smoky Hill Road, 794
Smythe, William Ellsworth, 847
snakes: folk beliefs about, 297; rattlesnakes, 616, 638; reptiles of Great Plains, 618; tall tales about, 314
Snow, Frank H., 395
snowfall: annual rates of, 614, 625; in hydraulics of Great Plains, 845
snow snake game, 763
Soap, Charlie, 583
soccer, 764
Social Credit Party, 704; and William Aberhart, 704, 734; in Alberta, 654, 684, 692; electoral success of, 701; and newspapers, 511; in politics since 1945, 652; as symbol of socialist reform, 375, 376; and United Farmers of Alberta, 725
Social Gospel, 728, 731, 734, 739–40
socialism: and Oscar Ameringer, 706; and *Appeal to Reason*, 521, 701, 707; Christian Socialism, 722, 734, 757; and Henry Martinson, 717; and Tillie Olsen, 488; as political protest, 701; in Prairie Provinces, 376. *See also* Socialist Party
Socialist Party: and Oscar Ameringer, 706; and Ella R. Bloor, 707; and James Patrick Cannon, 708; and Ira Finley, 710–11; and Green Corn Rebellion, 713; and Kate Richards O'Hare, 720; in politics of Great Plains, 649–50; and Arthur C. Townley, 724
Socialist Workers Party, 708
sod-wall construction, 63, 64, **94–95**, 96
softball, 763
Soil Bank, 29, 39, **50–51**
Soil Conservation and Domestic Allotment Act, 33
Soil Conservation Service, 679
soil erosion, **639–40**; agricultural technology, 29; Conservation Reserve Program, 29, 39; drought and, 852; wind in, 639, 643
soils, **640**; and architecture, 61; borolls, 30, 617, 640; chernozemic, 29, 617, 640; classification of, 617, 640; defense plants polluting, 821; drought and, 625; fertilizers and, 45–46; of Great Plains, 617; mollisols, 617, 632, 640; riparian, 850; salinization of, 850, 855; soil surveys, **640**; in sustainable agriculture, 53–54; udolls, 617. *See also* soil erosion
Sokol, 228
Solano, Cipriano, 354
Soldier Blue (film), 256, 269, **278–79**
songbirds, 620
The Song of the Lark (Cather), 475, 530
Sons of Norway, 243
sorghum, **51**; drought and, 28; in Great Plains agriculture, 32; irrigation for, 854; in sustainable agriculture, 54
Sou, Chin Lin, **146**
Soule, Asa, 847
Southam, William, 504–5, 508
South Americans, **367–68**
South Dakota, **689–90**; absence of features in, as regional characteristic, xv; Anglo-Canadians in, 226; anti–corporate farming

laws, 445; appropriation doctrine, 851; Arikaras in, 564–65; Badlands, 619, 620; biotechnology in, 412; cattle, 28; civil divisions of government, 657; corn, 39; Czechs in, 228; on eastern edge of Great Plains, xvii; electric railways, 796; ethnic groups in, xvi; European settlement patterns in, 246; farm consolidation, 44; farmers' railroads, 795; Finns in, 230; flax, 46; foreign investment in, 419; gaming in, 774; German Russians in, 232; and Robert Haire, 713; Hispanic Americans in, 348, 361; hockey, 375; Hungarians in, 235; Hutterites in, 733; images and icons of, 376; and Independent Party, 683; initiative and referendum in, 649, 661, 683; and international trade, *424*; irrigation, 854; Italians in, 237; Kansas-Nebraska Act and, 670; land-grant university in, 204, 208; land laws and settlement in, 240; libraries in, 206; Lutherans in, 751; and George McGovern, 651, 660, 667, 674, 690; Mennonites in, 751; Meridian Highway, 804; Methodism in, 752; and Karl Mundt, 677, 687, 690; NAFTA and, 427; national wildlife refuges in, 783, 784; Native Americans in, 560, 690; and Peter Norbeck, 393, 649, 680–81, 687, 690; Oahe Unit, 856–57; oil, 431; and Richard Pettigrew, 683, 689; Poles in, 243; politics in, 649, 651, 660, 687, 689–90, 693–94; and Prohibition, 648; Red Belt in, 225; reservations and, 180, 597; right-to-work law, 701; Roman Catholicism in, 756; rye, 49; school consolidation and reorganization in, 212; sheep, 50; snowfall in, 614; soybeans, 52; State Capitol of, 95; state historical society of, 213; statehood for, 647, 657, 664, 689; state-owned enterprises in, 649; state symbols of, *397*; Swedes in, 248; tornado stories from, 315; tourism and, 376, 435, 436; tribal colleges in, 213; in Unglaciated Missouri Plateau region, 30; urban population of, 151; and vigilantes, 464; voting patterns in, 693–94; and Wall Drug, 312, 398–99; Welsh in, 251; west river country, 399; wetland loss, 866; wheat, 56, 420; women's suffrage in, 337. *See also* Black Hills; Deadwood; Lead; Mitchell; Pierre; Pine Ridge Reservation; Rapid City; Sioux Falls; Vermillion; *and other towns and cities by name*
South Dakota, University of, 120, 163, 215, 543
South Dakota State University, 163, 204, 208, 214
South Dakota v. Yankton Sioux Tribe (1998), 604, 668
Southeast Asians: and settlement in Great Plains, 137. *See also* Cambodians; Laotians; Vietnamese
Southern Alberta Land Company, 851
Southern Baptist Convention, 736; dispensationalism, 741; and settlement in Great Plains, 733; in Southern Plains, 732
Southern Pacific Railroad, 446, 685, 796, 802
Southern Saskatchewan Press Association, 505
South Pass, 301
South Platte River, 862; hydraulics of Great Plains, 845; in Irrigated Valleys region, 31–32; irrigation along, 846

South Saskatchewan River, 615, 861–62, *862*
Southworth, Billy, 768
sovereignty, Native American, **603–5**
soybeans, **51–52**; in Great Plains agriculture, 32; insect pests, 634; in Nebraska, 52, 409
Spade Ranch, 48
Spaniards, **247–48**; Adams-Onís Treaty, 346, **351**, 673; and Apaches, 562; Álvar Cabeza de Vaca, 3, 7, 247, 345, 485; and the Caddos, 568; and conflicts with Native Americans, 817; Coronado, 7, 227, 247, 345, 359, 394–95, 609, 624; and Ecueracapa, 572–73; *genízaros*, 356, 838–39; horses brought by, 575; missions of, 731, 755; in New Mexico, 247, 680; and the Plains, 1540–1821, 345–46; political authority under, 647; Quivira, 395; San Sabá mission and presidio, 345, 367, 755, 817, 835–36; Spanish-Comanche treaties, **368**; and Tonkawas, 606; Pedro Vial, 250–51; Pedro de Villasur, 247, 251, 345, 556, 673, 817, 839; water law, 845–46, **863**. *See also* Spanish language
Spanish Colonial Revival style, 66, 85, 97
Spanish-Comanche treaties, **368**
Spanish language: as first European language spoken in Great Plains, 359; folk speech influenced by, 299; press, **368**; radio stations, 351; widespread use of, 197
Spanish water law, 845–46, **863**
Spaulding, Eliza, 341
Speaker, Tris, 766, 768
Spearfish SD, 624
Spears, John R., 476
Spitzenbogenstil, 66
Splendor in the Grass (film), **279**, 480
sport hunting, 765, **786–87**
sports and recreation, **761–89**; cheerleaders, 386; Crow Fair, 769–70; curling, 764, 770–71; figure skating, 767–68; fishing, 772; on the frontier, 763–64; future scenarios for, 766; Curt Gowdy, 774–75; gymnastics, 775; hall of fame museums, 775–76; national forests, 766, 779–80; national grasslands, 766, 780–81; national wildlife refuges, 766, 783–84; and Native Americans, 763; powwows, 544, 594–95; riding around, 763, 784; as source of local pride, 375; sport hunting, 765, 786–87; storm chasing, 787; Sturgis Motorcycle Rally, 788; on television, 764, 774–75; in twentieth century, 764–66; wrestling, 787. *See also* baseball; basketball; coaches; games; golf; ice hockey; Olympic Games; parks; rodeo; track and field
Spotted Tail, 451, **605**
Spotted Wolf, 278–79
Springfield CO, 705
springtails, xv
Sprint, **434**
Spruce, Everett, 112
spurs, 293–94, 382
square dancing, 297
Stafford, Roy E., 509–10
Stafford, William, 472, 489, **493**
stagecoaches, **811**; Ben Holladay, 803; railroads killing, 794; Wells, Fargo and Company, 813
Stage Coach Mary (Mary Fields), **14–15**
Staggers Rail Act (1980), 685
Standing Bear, 594, **605**, 702, **725**, 826
Standing Bear, Henry, 382

Vietnam War, 669, 674, 685

Vigil, Cleotes, 354

vigilantes, 387, 443, **464–65**

villages, Native American, 61–62

Villasur, Pedro de, **251**; expedition of, 247, 251, 345, 556, 673, 817, **839**

Vincent, Lloyd D., 183

The Virginian: film, 256, 262–63; novel by Wister, 470, 496

Virgin of Guadalupe, 469

vision quest, 599, 731, **759–60**

visual arts: Terry Allen, 111; Stan Herd, 110, 118–19; Bradbury Thompson, 130. *See also* drawing; illustration; painting; photography; sculpture

viticulture, **56**, 733

Vizenor, Gerald, 488

vocational education, 195, 196

Volga Germans: architecture, **99**; Catholicism of, 742; "Dutch hop," 287; folklife of, 285; gender relations of, 321; German Russians, 232; iron grave crosses of, 289; and Prohibition, 223

Voluntary Relocation Program, 602

voting patterns: Canada, **692–93**; United States, **693–94**

Waco TX, 664, 720, 737–38

Waddell, William B., 806, 810

Wagon Box Fight (1867), 800, 818, 825

wagons: chuck wagons, 420; covered wagons, 801; Red River carts, 810

Wagon Train (television show), 523

Wah, Fred, 473

Waitt, Ted, 419–20

Wakarusa War (1855), 824

Waldren, Pat, 523

Walker, Mary Richardson, 341

Wallace, Daniel Webster "80-John," 8

Wallace, George C., 694

Wallace, Henry, 710

Wallace, J. Laurie, 117

Wallace, Lew, 830

Wall Drug, 312, **398–99**

Walsh, James, 460

Walsh, Thomas J., 676

Walton, John C. "Our Jack," 701, 715

Walvoord, John F., 741

Waner, Lloyd, 767

Waner, Paul, 767

war, **815–41**; counting coup, 825, 830; from frontier to internationalism, 819; intertribal warfare, 556–57, 829–30; Lincoln County War, 446, 830; Mexican-American War, 347, 358, 647, 680, 817, 823; Seven Oaks Massacre, 229, 389, 443, 584, 836; in Spanish and Mexican period, 817; Texas Revolution, 838; *Tropa de Genízero,* 838–39; Villasur expedition, 247, 251, 345, 556, 673, 817, 839. *See also* "Bleeding Kansas"; Civil War; Cold War; Indian wars; military; North-West Rebellion; Red River Resistance; World War I; World War II

War Chief (newspaper), 378

war chiefs, **839**

Ware, John, **23**

warehouse districts, **99–100**, 155, 225

War on Poverty, 559

Warren, F. E., Air Force Base, 72, 163, 392, 695, 822

Warren, Francis E., 163, **694–95**, 833, 847

Warren, G. K., 613

Wartime Prices and Trade Board, **839–40**

Washakie, 695

Washburn College Bible, 130, *130*

Washburn University, 21, 449

Washington, George, 531

Washington handpress, 501

Washita, Battle of the (1868), 568, 818, **840**

Waste Isolation Pilot Project, 427–28

water, **843–67**; agricultural technology, 28; conceptions of, 846; environmentalism and, 850; and frontier law, 443; hydrology of Great Plains, 615–16, 845; *Kansas v. Colorado,* 448; Native American use of, 845; *Report on the Lands of the Arid Region,* 240, 847, 848; in soil erosion, 639; Spanish water practices, 845–46; stock ponds, 863; in sustainable agriculture, 53–54; tankhouses for storing, 96; transmountain water diversion projects, 863; U.S. Army Corps of Engineers projects, 864; quality of, 865; towers for, 865–66. *See also* floods; groundwater; irrigation; lakes; precipitation; reservoirs; rivers; water law; water pollution; water transportation; wetlands

waterfowl, 620, 638, 783, 851

water law: appropriation doctrine, 443, 846, 850–51; Colorado Doctrine, 846, 851; doctrine of equity, 848, 851–52; *Kansas v. Colorado,* 847–48, 852, 861; Elwood Mead's system of, 846, 847, 855–56; Mni Sose Intertribal Water Rights Coalition, 856; Native American "reserved" rights, 848, 867; Native American sovereignty and, 604–5; in Prairie Provinces, 846, **864–65**; riparian doctrine, 443, 846, 860, 864; Spanish, 845–46, **863**; in Wyoming, 846

water pollution: by agriculture, 29, 850, 865; from defense plants, 821, 865; water quality, 865

water quality, **865**

water rights. *See* water law

water towers, **865–66**

water transportation, **813**; canoes, 793, 813; keelboats, 793, 813; portages, 807; steamboats, 793–94, 813, 814; in transportation of Great Plains, 793–94

Watson, Ella ("Cattle Kate"), 307

Watts, J. C., **23**

Wayland, Julius A., 701, 707

weather: agricultural meteorology, 33; blizzard stories, 291–92; chinook stories, 292–93; climatology of Great Plains, 614–15; farming lore, 295; folk beliefs about, 297; as icon of Great Plains, 373; radio giving information about, 519; tall tales about, 314; tornado stories, 315; weather industry, **436–37**. *See also* climate; precipitation; storms

Weatherford TX, *154*

Weaver, James, 683

Weaver, Randy, 711, 720

Webb, Jimmy, 546

Webb, Walter Prescott, **495–96**; and Lewis and Clark traveling by water, 813; on Plains as colony, 381; on Plains as desert, 388, 389; on Plains as men's country, 319; on Plains requiring new ways of living, xiii; on sign language, 299

Webb, Wellington and Wilma, 5, **23**

Webster, Ben, 532, 541

Webster, Lee, 725

weddings: mock, **306**; shivarees, 313–14

Wedel, Waldo, 566

weeds, **641–42**

Weidman, Charles, **131**

Weir, Walter, 684

Welch, James, 472, 473, 487, 493, **496**

Welk, Lawrence, 504, 519, 530, **549–50**

wells, 615

Wells, Fargo and Company, 167, 811, **813**

Welsch, Roger, 68, 287, 288, **316**

Welsh, **251–52**; folklife of, 286; David Thompson, 249, 251

Wessells, Henry, 572

West, Cornel, **23–24**

West, John, 732, 748

Westerly, Arthur L., 759

Western Air, 797

Western Canada Sedimentary Basin, 429

The Westerner (film), 263

Western Labor Conference (1919), 700

Western Producer (newspaper), **523–24**, 699

Westerns (film), **279–80**; and changing tone of 1950s, 497; *Cimarron,* 257, 261–62, 275; *The Covered Wagon,* 262, 280; Custer films, 256, 263–64; *Dances with Wolves,* 255, 256, 264, 269, 280, 326, 497, 543; *Days of Heaven,* 256, 264–65, 280; at Great Plains films, 255–56; *High Noon,* 263, 280, 497; *How the West Was Won,* 280; *Hud* and, 270; *The Iron Horse,* 280; *Little Big Man,* 256, 263, 269, 271–72, 280, 497; of Miller Brothers, 273; oil field films, 275–76; *The Outlaw Josie Wales,* 280; *The Plainsman,* 263, 280; *Red River,* 253, 256, 262, 268, 277–78, 280, 800; *Soldier Blue,* 256, 269, 278–79; *The Virginian,* 256, 262–63; *The Westerner,* 263; Wyatt Earp films, **281–82**

Westerns (literature), **496–97**; Zane Grey, 470, 479, 496; Louis L'Amour, 470, 481, 496; Larry McMurtry, 256, 271, 471, 484–85, 497; in Plains fiction, 469–70

western swing, 299, 530, 535–36, **550**, 552

Western Trail, 794, 800, **814**

Western Union Telegraph Company, 499, 522

west river country, **399**

West Texas family music making, **550–51**

West Union NE, 283

Westwood KS, 434

wetlands, **866**; bird migration and, 620; Cheyenne Bottoms, 850, 851; fish, 628; paleoenvironments, 635; playa lakes, 850, 859; preservation, 850

Wharton OK, 411

wheat, **56–57**; Alberta Wheat Pool, 508, 727, 728; breadbasket of North America image, 378–79; in *Days of Heaven,* 264–65; drought, 28; durum, 30, 56, 57, 301, 420; fertilizer use, 45; German Russians bringing red winter, 246; grain processing of, 301, 420–21; in Great Plains agriculture, 27, 405, 409; immigration spurred by, 245; international trade, 423; irrigation and, 854; and limit of midwestern settlement, 377; Mennonites in cultivation of, 31, 56, 221; National Progressive Party and, 677–78; Red Fife, 376; Saskatchewan Wheat Pool, 50, 179, 721, 726, 728; in Winter Wheat region, 31; World War I creating demand for, 650

Wheat Triangle, 30

Wheeler, Burton K., 650, 651, 675–76

Wheeler, Edward, 325

Wheeler, George, 633, 641

Wheeler, John F., 501

Wheeler, O. D., *467*

Wheeler, Richard S., 497

Wherry, Kenneth, 687

White, Byron, *464*, **465**, 773

White, Felix, 469

White, William Allen, 377, 503, 512, 521, **524**, 715

White Bull, *467*

White City KS, 186

Whiteclay NE, *553*

White Eagle, 545

white primary, **465**, 649, 651

White River Group, 630

White-Smith, Sarah Gilbert, 341

white-tailed deer, **642**, 786

Whitman, Narcissa, 341

Whitman ND, 169

Whittredge, Worthington, **131**

whooping cranes, 620, 627, 850, 859

Whoop-Up Trail, **814**

Wichita KS, **188**; aviation industry, 188, 408, 797, 820, 821, 840; as cattle town, 162; Chinese in, 141; in Cold War, 821; and William Coleman, 415–16; Wyatt Earp, 384; founding of, 151; as gateway city, 152; Industrial Workers of the World members jailed in, 713; interracial baseball in, 10; Jews in, 238; and Hattie McDaniel, 17; oil industry, 176; pioneer recreation and, 763–64; Pizza Hut in, 301, 432; and Jim Ryun, 785; and Barry Sanders, 20; sit-in of 1958, 5, 13; Southeast Asians in, 137; tourism and, 435; urban Native American community of, 608; Western Union office, ca. 1912 in, *499*; in World War II, 820, 840; Frank Lloyd Wright buildings in, 101

Wichita Falls TX, **188–89**, 431

Wichitas, **609–10**

Wickstrom, James, 722

Wiebe, Jack, 688

Wiebe, Rudy, 471, 472, 495, **497**

Wilber, Charles Dana, 395

wild and scenic rivers, **866–67**

Wilder, Laura Ingalls, 305, 375, 470, 471, 476, **497–98**

wildflowers, **642–43**

wildlife: and agriculture, **57**; amphibians, 618; armadillos, 618–19; beaver, 403, 419, 607; black-tailed prairie dog, 617, 622–23; coyotes, 625, 786; drought and, 852; grizzly bear, 241; national refuges, 766, 783–84; Titian Ramsay Peale's illustrations of, 126; playa lakes as habitat for, 859; preservation of, 850; pronghorns, 616, 786; sport hunting, 765, 786–87; white-tailed deer, 642, 786. *See also* birds; bison; endangered species; fish; insects; reptiles

wild turkeys, 786

Wild West shows, **399–400**; Buffalo Bill's, 291, 380, 399, 400, 737, 764, 784; of Miller Brothers, 273, 399, 400; rodeo in, 765

Wilkes, Charles, 126

Wilkes, George, 386

Wilkinson, Bud, 773

Williams, Docia Schultz, 302

Williams, Don, 551

Williams, Mary Lou, 531, 541

Williams, Ricky, 776

Williamson, John P., 754

Williamson, T. S., 754

Willis, Dorothy, 113

Williston Basin, 630

Williston ND, 180

Wills, Bob, **551–52**; and Light Crust Dough Boys, 527, 530, 550, 552; and Texas Playboys, 550, 552; and western swing, 299, 530, 535–36, 550, 552; and West Texas family music, 551

Wills, John T., 551

Wilson, John "Moonhead," 596

Wilson, Richard, 560, 706

Wilson, Walter F., 75–76

Wilson, Woodrow, 364, 655, 819

Wimar, Carl, **131–32**

wind, **643**; as energy, **437**; on the Great Plains, 615; in soil erosion, 639, 643. *See also* chinooks

Wind Cave National Park, 782

windmills, **400**; Currie windmill, *400*; and groundwater, 615, 849, 854; and water management, 28; wind for, 643

Wind River Reservation WY, 600

wine: viticulture, 56, 733

Wing Tsue (Fee Lee Wong), **148**

Winkler (Manitoba), 405

Winnipeg (Manitoba), **189**; Asians in, 137, *139*; Salem G. Bland, 734, 737; Canadian Land Command at, 821, 832; Canadian Prairies, 29; as "Chicago of the North," 189, 673; Communists and, 701; European immigrants drawn to, 225; folk traditions in, 286; foreign investment in, 418; freight-handling facilities, 155; fur trade and, 152; futures market, 410; as gateway city, 152; General Strike of 1919, xvi, 376, 673, 675, 700, **726–27**, 728; Germans in, 234; in Great Plains agriculture, 405; and the Guess Who, 547; and Kate Simpson Hayes, 330; Hudson's Bay Company in, 423; Hungarians in, 235; immigrant women and children, ca. 1909 in, *219*; Italians in, 238; Jews in, 238, 239; Knights of Labor in, 700; Manitoba Technical Institute in, 196; and meatpacking industry, 426; Mennonites in, 751; opera, 545; as railroad terminus, xv, xvii, 795, 808; in regional economy, 407; Royal Winnipeg Ballet, 530; siting of, 153; Social Gospel in, 734, 737; Swedes in, 249; Ukrainians in, 250; warehouse district, 99; *Winnipeg Free Press*, 524–25; and James Shaver Woodsworth, 728, 734; in World War II, 840; and Neil Young, 552

Winnipeg, Lake, 631

Winnipeg, University of, 530

Winnipeg Blue Bombers, 773

Winnipeg Free Press (*Manitoba Free Press*) (newspaper), 504, **524–25**, 688

Winnipeg School of Art, 117

Winnipeg, Selkirk and Lake Winnipeg Railway, 796

Winrod, Gerald B., 702, 711, **727**

wintering houses, 98

Winter Olympics: Calgary, 161, 765, **768**; curling, 771

winter: temperatures during, 615, 624. *See also* blizzards; snowfall

Winters Doctrine, **867**

Winters v. United States (1908), 604, 847, 848

Winter Wheat region, 29, 31

Winthui, Sophus Keith, 470

Wisconsinan ice sheet, 631

Wiseman, Adele, 471, **498**

Wishart, David J., 322

Wister, Owen, 470, 496

The Wizard of Oz: book by Baum, 471, 474, 643; film, 257, **280–81**, 377, 387–88

Wohnstallhaus, 81

Woiwode, Larry, 471, **498**

Wolcott, Marion Post, 45, 115, *132*, **132**

The Wolf Hunt (film), 257

Wolfman Jack (Bobby Smith), 534

Wolseley, Garnet, 819

Woman's Bible, 327

women: in agriculture, 330, **340–41**; in Amazon Army, 701, 704; in art culture of Great Plains, 108; in basketball, 767, 771–72; in captivity narratives, 326; in Cather's fiction, 470–71; in country music, 536; farming lore about, 295; as field matrons, **328–29**; first female governors, 650, 687; first, in Congress, 685; in fur trade, **341**; gendered space for, 330; in higher education, **214–15**; as hired girls, **331**; as homesteaders, 319, 320, 337, **339–40**; at land-grant universities, 196, 205, 214; mad pioneer, **392**; as mail-order brides, **332–33**, 337; as newspaper editors, 521; personal experience narratives of, 308; pie making by, 301; and Plains towns, 321–22; promotional literature and, 394–95; putting them into the Plains picture, 319–20; and quilting, 311–12, 335; in rodeo, 765, 778, 785; as rodeo queens, **335–36**, 765; Saskatchewan Women Grain Growers, 336; sense of place of, 329–30; Title IX for, 766; in travel literature, 494; United Farm Women of Alberta, **338**; Victorian women travelers, **338–39**; and Wartime Prices and Trade Board, 840; in water law, 848; West Texas singers, 551; from women to gender, 320–21; in workforce during World War II, 820. *See also* Native American women; suffrage movement

Women Air Force Service Pilots, 820

Women of All Red Nations, **727**

Women's Christian Temperance Union (WCTU), 336, 338, 718

Women's Professional Rodeo Association, 765, 778, 785

Wong, Fee Lee (Wing Tsue), **148**

Wood, Grant, 109

Wood, Henry Wise, 654, 725, **727–28**

Woodard, Lynette, 767

Woodbury, Daniel P., 94

wooden frames, 64, **100–101**

Wooden Leg, 825

woodlands, **643–44**; of Great Plains, xiv; national forests, 766, **779–80**

Woods, James Hossack, 508

Woodsmen of the World, 303

Woodsworth, James Shaver, 659, **728**, 734

Woodward, Fred, 491

Woodward, George A., 572

wool, 50, 347

Worcester, Samuel, 501

Worcester v. Georgia (1032), 442, 604

Working Class Union, 713

Works Progress Administration (WPA), 76, 86, 109, 353, 679

World War I, 819–20; *Appeal to Reason* supporting, 707; Food Production Act of 1917, 33; German Americans and, 224–25, 650, 819; Native Americans in, 608; John J. Pershing and, 833–34; and politics of Great Plains, 650; and radicalism, 700; William Samuel Stephenson and, 837

World War II, **840–41**; British Commonwealth Training Plan, 824; Dwight D. Eisenhower and, 662; Great Plains and, 820–21; and isolationism, 651; Japanese internment during, 136, 138, 143–44, 145, 821; Native Americans in, 559; Native American veterans of, 609; Chester Nimitz and, 832; William Samuel Stephenson and, 837; Wartime Prices and Trade Board, 839–40

Worster, Donald, 381

Wounded Knee confrontation (1973), 560, 602, 651, 702, *705*, 706

Wounded Knee Massacre (1890), **841**; Black Elk at, 737; Branch Davidian tragedy compared with, 738; "Gathering Up the Dead," *840*; Ghost Dance and, 558, 732, 746, 834, 837, 841; Lakota Sioux at, 601, 602, 841; lasting historical significance of, xviii; in Sioux wars, 558, 819, 836, 837; in Wild West Shows, 400

Wounded Knee SD, 376

Wovoka, 732, 746, 841

wrestling: Joe Stecher, 787

Wright, Frank Lloyd, 66, 70, **101**

Wright, James Claude "Jim," 168, 660

Writing-on-Stone Provincial Park (Manitoba), 128

Wyatt Earp (film), 281

Wyoming, **695**; air bases in World War II, 820; Anglo-Canadians in, *226*; Arapahos in, 563; and Bracero Program, 349; cattle, 27, 28; civil divisions of government, 657; coal, 414, 415, *415*; Colorado Doctrine, 851; corn, 39; Czechs in, 228; and William Dubois, 77; farm consolidation, 44; female governor of, 650; folk monuments in, 290; and Gerald Ford, 665, 695; German Russians in, 232; ghost stories, 302; Ferdinand Vandeveer Hayden in survey of, 633; Hispanic Americans in, 351; images and icons of, 376; and international trade, *424*; in Irrigated Valleys region, 31; irrigation, 854; Italians in, 237; and Jim Crow laws, 454, 455; Johnson County War of 1892, 48; Kansas-Nebraska Act and, 670; land-grant university in, 204, 208; land laws and settlement in, 240; Lincoln Highway, 803–4; Methodism in, 752; Esther Morris as first woman magistrate of, 458; NAFTA and, 427; national wildlife refuges in, 784; oil, 431; politics in, 651, 660, 687, 693–94, 695; in Rangelands region, 32; Roman Catholicism in, 756; and Nellie Tayloe Ross, 650, 687, 695; sheep, 50; State Capitol of, 95; statehood for, 647, 657, 664, 695; state symbols of, *397*; sugar beets, 52, 434; tourism and, 436; and vigilantes, 464; voting patterns in, 693–94; and Francis E. Warren, 163, 694–95; water doctrine, 846, 855; Welsh in, 251; wind energy, 437; women's suffrage in, 322, 337, 648; woodlands, 643. *See also* Casper; Cheyenne; Fort Laramie; *and other towns and cities by name*

Wyoming, University of, 204, 208, 214, 695

Wyoming Basin, xvi

Wyoming Development Company, 847

Wyoming Stock Growers Association, 694, 695

XIT Ranch, 38, 48, **57**

Yankton SD, 76–77, 152, 180, 184, 519, 549, 804

Yarborough, Ralph, 656

Yates Center KS, *304*

Yellowstone Expedition, 383

Yellowstone National Park: establishment of, 695; Ferdinand Vandeveer Hayden and, 633; William Henry Jackson's photographs of, 121; Yellowstone Trail, 814

Yellowstone newspapers, 505

Yellowstone River, 862; Billings, 159, 862; Ferdinand Vandeveer Hayden in survey of, 633; in Irrigated Valleys region, 31; river towns, 180

Yellow Thunder, Raymond, 706

Yerkes, Abel Kelsey, 506

York (slave), 3, 7, **24**

York Factory, 647

Yost, Lyle, 435

Young, Lester, 4, 531, 541

Young, Neil, xviii, 533, 547, **552**

Young Bear, Ray, 605

Zamora, Bernice, 351, **369**

Zanuck, Darryl F., 255, 268, **282**

Zen Buddhism, 738

Zimmerman, Anna, 340

Ziolkowski, Korczak, 382

Zitkala Ša, **498**

Zon, Raphael, 616

Zybach, Frank, 413, 849

Illustration Credits

Introduction. *Great Plains Region:* Map by Sonja Rossum. *Population Density:* Map by J. Clark Archer. Source: U.S. Census Bureau, "Census 2000 Redistricting Data (Public Law 94-171 Summary File) Table QT-PL Race, Hispanic or Latino, and Age: 2000." Statistics Canada, 1991 Census of Canada: "Profile of Census Divisions and Subdivisions, Part A" (electronic product). *Great Plains Regional Boundary:* Map by Sonja Rossum.

African Americans. *Frontispiece:* Kansas State Historical Society. E185.1876*1. *African Americans:* Map by J. Clark Archer. U.S. Census Bureau, "Census 2000 Redistricting Data (Public Law 94-171 Summary File) Table QT-PL Race, Hispanic or Latino, and Age: 2000." *African American Cowboys:* Denver Public Library, Western History Collection, Call Number: x-21934. *All-Black Towns:* Photo by Drover, McAlester, Oklahoma. Archives & Manuscripts Division of the Oklahoma Historical Society (Photo No. 3377.D). *Black Regiments:* Library of Congress, African American Odyssey Collection, LC-US2C4-6161 DLC. *Brown, "Aunt" Clara:* Denver Public Library, Western History Collection, Call Number: z-275. *Civil Rights:* Denver Public Library, Western History Collection, Call Number: x-28759. *Harris, Wynonie:* Courtesy of Preston Love. *Hughes, Langston:* Library of Congress LC-USW3-033841-C. *Little, Cleavon:* Courtesy of the American Academy of Dramatic Arts. *Love, Nat:* Denver Public Library, Western History Collection, Call Number: z-147. *McDaniel, Hattie:* Denver Public Library, Western History Collection, Call Number: z-105. *Parks, Gordon:* Kansas State Historical Society. *Sanders, Barry:* Photo courtesy of Oklahoma State University Athletic Department. *Tulsa Race Riot:* Ella Mahler Collection. Courtesy of the Archives & Manuscripts Division of the Oklahoma Historical Society (Photo Number: 20280.4).

Agriculture. *Frontispiece:* Photo courtesy of University of Nebraska–Lincoln Department of Geography. *Agriculture:* Photo by David J. Wishart. / Map by John C. Hudson. *Alfalfa:* NARA-NWDNS, ID 115-JG-521, Gallery of the Open Frontier at *gallery.unl.edu. Branding:* NARA-NRE, ID 75-FB(PHO)-394, Gallery of the Open Frontier at *gallery.unl.edu. Campbell, Hardy Webster:* Image copied from *Bailey's Cyclopedia of American Agriculture,* Vol. 1, 1907. *Cattle Ranching:* Photo courtesy of Southwest Collection/Special Collections Library, Texas Tech University, Lubbock,

Texas. Frank Reeves Photograph Collection, 1925–1975, FR103. *Corn:* U.S. Department of Agriculture, 1997. *Cotton:* Courtesy of Wayne Smith. *Fairs:* Kansas State Historical Society, FK2.55 T.65 F.1918*1. *Sorghum:* Photo courtesy of Gary C. Peterson. *Sugar Beets:* NARA-NWDNS, ID 115-JG-196, Gallery of the Open Frontier at *gallery.unl.edu. Suitcase Farming:* Kansas State Historical Society, FK2.G8 .31P. *4. Wheat:* Photo courtesy of John E. Simmons.

Architecture. *Frontispiece:* D. Murphy photograph, June 1978. *Architecture:* NARA-NWDNS, ID 111 SC 82520, Gallery of the Open Frontier at *gallery.unl.edu.* / Photo courtesy Nebraska Capitol Archives. Sid Spelts Collection. 24-14-4(1). / NARA-NWDNS, ID 106-IN-1248, Gallery of the Open Frontier at *gallery.unl.edu. Barns:* Photo by Ron Van Zee and courtesy of the BARN AGAIN! Program. *Cemeteries:* Photo by Irving Rusinow, NARA-NWDNS, ID 83-G-41952, Gallery of the Open Frontier at *gallery.unl.edu. Fort Architecture:* NARA-NWDNS, ID 111-SC-87874, Gallery of the Open Frontier at *gallery.unl.edu. Grain Elevators:* Photo courtesy of George O. Carney. *Hispanic Architecture:* Photo courtesy of Chris Wilson. *Layton, Solomon:* Courtesy of the Archives & Manuscripts Division of the Oklahoma Historical Society (Photo Number: 19279.1). *Native American Contemporary Architecture:* Photo copyright Carol Herselle Krinsky. *Roadside Architecture:* Nebraska State Historical Society, RG2183. *Warehouse Districts:* Photo by Lynn Meyer.

Art. *Frontispiece:* The John R. Van Derlip Fund. The Minneapolis Institute of Arts. *Art:* Copyright, The University of South Dakota, 1981. From the collection of the University of South Dakota, Vermillion, South Dakota. / Christlieb Collection, Great Plains Art Collection, University of Nebraska–Lincoln, photographed by Roger Bruhn. / The Metropolitan Museum of Art, Arthur H. Hearn Fund, 1932. (32.84). / Gift of Dr. Leon S. McGoogan and the Friends of the Center for Great Plains Studies, Great Plains Art Collection, University of Nebraska–Lincoln. *Herd, Stan:* Jon Blumb Photograph. *Hogue, Alexandre:* Museum purchase. The Philbrook Museum of Art, Tulsa, Oklahoma. 1946.4. *Howe, Oscar:* The University of South Dakota, Vermillion, South Dakota. *Jackson, William Henry:* Denver Public Library, Western History Collection, Photo by Cecil Hayes, Call Number: x-22212. *Jones, Joe:* Collection of

Whitney Museum of American Art, Purchase. 36.144. Photograph © 2000: Whitney Museum of Art. *Kane, Paul:* Photographs courtesy of the Royal Ontario Museum © ROM. *Rock Art:* Photograph courtesy of Ralph Hartley. *Stanley, John Mix:* From Isaac I. Stevens, *Explorations and Surveys for a Railroad from the Mississippi River to the Pacific Ocean.* War Department, House Misc. Doc. 36th Congress, 1st session, 1860. Facing p. 59. Iowa City: University of Iowa Libraries. *Thompson, Bradbury:* Special Collections Mabee Library, Washburn University, Topeka, Kansas. *Wolcott, Marion Post:* Library of Congress LC-USF-34-058135-D.

Asian Americans. *Frontispiece:* Glenbow Archives NA-2798-6. *Asian Americans:* Map by J. Clark Archer. U.S. Census Bureau, "Census 2000 Redistricting Data (Public Law 94-171 Summary File) Table QT-PL Race, Hispanic or Latino, and Age: 2000." *Amache Internment Camp:* B-624, Joe McClelland, 6/20/43. Courtesy Colorado State Archives. *Asian Canadians:* Statistics Canada, 1991, Catalogue 93-315. *Hosokawa, William:* Photo by Tom Parker, NARA-NWDNS, ID 210-G-E664, Gallery of the Open Frontier at *gallery.unl.edu. Vietnamese:* Photo by Janet Benson. *Wong, Fee Lee:* Adams Museum, Deadwood, South Dakota.

Cities and Towns. *Frontispiece:* Kansas State Historical Society FK2.S5 T.5 KanA.7s *5. *Cities and Towns:* Photo courtesy of Michael Conzen. / Photo courtesy of Michael Conzen. / Map by Michael Conzen. / Redrawn by Michael Conzen. / Redrawn by Michael Conzen. *Calgary, Alberta:* Photo courtesy of Calgary Inc. *Cheyenne, Wyoming:* Photo by William Henry Jackson, NARA-NWDNS, ID 57-HS-708, Gallery of the Open Frontier at *gallery.unl.edu. College Towns:* Photograph by Rob Clark, Kansas State Collegian, University Archives, Kansas State University. *Colorado Springs, Colorado:* Courtesy, Colorado Historical Society, Call Number: CHS.J4270, Photo by William Henry Jackson. *Denver, Colorado:* Tom Noel Collection. *Fargo, North Dakota:* Institute for Regional Studies, NDSU, Fargo. *"Hell on Wheels" Towns:* Wyoming State Archives, Department of State Parks and Cultural Resources. *Main Street:* Photo courtesy of Richard Longstreth, 1997. *Oklahoma City, Oklahoma:* NARA-NWDNS, ID 111-SC-87337, Gallery of the Open Frontier at *gallery.unl.edu. Omaha, Nebraska:* Courtesy, Colorado Historical Society, Call Number: CHS.J3318, Photo by

William Henry Jackson. *San Angelo, Texas:* NARA-NWDNS, ID 111-SC-07377, Gallery of the Open Frontier at *gallery.unl.edu*. *Sioux Falls, South Dakota:* Sioux Falls Chamber of Commerce. *Small Towns:* Photograph by Matt Engel.

Education. *Frontispiece:* Fred Hultstrand History in Pictures Collection, NDIRS-NDSU, Fargo. 2028.358. *Education:* Provincial Archives of Manitoba. Negative Number N 10264. *Chautauqua:* Photography by S. D. Butcher. Nebraska State Historical Society. RG2068-2924. *Indian Residential Schools, Canada:* National Archives of Canada/C-037113. *Musuems:* Photo courtesy of John E. Simmons. *One-Room Schoolhouses:* Fred Hultstrand History in Pictures Collection, NDIRS-NDSU, Fargo. 2028.361. *United States Air Force Academy:* Photo courtesy of the United States Air Force Academy.

European Americans. *Frontispiece:* Kansas State Historical Society. FK2M3 L.52. 1961 *10. *European Americans:* The United Church of Canada/Victoria University Archive, Toronto. 93.049P/311 N. / National Library of Canada/Bibliothèque nationale du Canada. C-11553. / Photo by L. B. Foote. National Archives of Canada/PA-122664. / National Archives of Canada/C-000683. *Anglo-Canadians:* U.S. Published Censuses, compiled by Randy Widdis. *German Russians:* W727-7 Hattie Plum Williams Collection No. II. Original property of American Historical Society of Germans from Russia Archives. Photo courtesy of the American Historical Society of Germans from Russia. *Germans:* Nebraska State Historical Society. 917.82 B92g. *Italians:* The UT Institute of Texan Cultures, No. 99-243. Courtesy of Institute of Texas Cultures. *Jews:* Denver Public Library, Western History Collection, Call Number: x-28908. *Kelsey, Henry:* Hudson's Bay Company Archives. Provincial Archives of Manitoba/HBCA Documentary Art, P-392 (N13494). *Scots:* Courtesy, Colorado Historical Society, Call Number: CHS-l1826, Photo by Charles S. Lillybridge.

Film. *Frontispiece:* Copyright 1955, United Artists Corporation. The Museum of Modern Art, New York. *Film:* Photo courtesy of David J. Wishart. *Autry, Gene:* Courtesy of the Autry Museum of Western Heritage. *Brooks, Louise:* Collection Louise Brooks Society. *Chaney, Lon:* Courtesy of Jon Mirsalis. *Days of Heaven:* Copyright 1978 by Paramount Pictures Corporation. Photo by Edie Baskin. The Museum of Modern Art, New York. *Giant:* Copyright Warner Bros. Pictures Distributing Corporation. The Museum of Modern Art, New York. *Movie Houses:* Photo courtesy of Richard Longstreth. *The Plow that Broke the Plains:* The Museum of Modern Art, New York. *Taylor, Robert:* Gage County Historical Society, Beatrice, Nebraska.

Folkways. *Frontispiece:* Photographed by Solomon D. Butcher. Nebraska State Historical Society, RG2608.PH-1048.

Folkways: Photo courtesy of Timothy J. Kloberdanz. / Photo courtesy of Timothy J. Kloberdanz. / Photo courtesy of Timothy J. Kloberdanz. / Photo courtesy of Timothy J. Kloberdanz. *Cattle Guards:* Photograph courtesy of Jim Hoy. *Cowboy Crafts:* Richard Collier, courtesy Wyoming State Museum. *Folk Art:* Photo by Dan Koeck. Courtesy of the North Dakota Council on the Arts. *Grave Markers:* Photo courtesy of John Gary Brown. *Humor:* Photo courtesy of David J. Wishart. *Quilting:* Reprinted from *Nebraska Quilts and Quiltmakers* by P. Crews and R. Naugle by permission of Lincoln Quilters Guild, Lincoln, Nebraska. *Roadside Attractions:* Photo courtesy of John E. Simmons.

Gender. *Frontispiece:* Photo courtesy of Patricia Henderson. *Calamity Jane:* Negative #03, American Heritage Center, University of Wyoming. *Earhart, Amelia:* Denver Public Library, Western History Collection, Photo by Harry M. Rhoads, Call Number: RH-89. *Hind, Cora:* Winnipeg Free Press. *Slaughter, Linda:* State Historical Society of North Dakota. A5418. *United Farm Workers of Alberta:* Glenbow Archives NA-2691-35. *Women Homesteaders:* Photo courtesy of Jerome D. Lamb.

Hispanic Americans. *Frontispiece:* Nebraska State Historical Society. RG1571-36. *Hispanic Americans:* Map by J. Clark Archer. U.S. Census Bureau, "Census 2000 Redistricting Data (Public Law 94-171 Summary File) Table QT-PL Race, Hispanic or Latino, and Age: 2000." *Ciboleros:* Drawing by William J. Baron. *Gonzales, Corky:* Denver Public Library, Western History Collection, Call Number: x-21576. *Gutiérrez, José Angel:* Denver Public Library, Western History Collection, Call Number: x-21628. *Meatpackers:* Kansas State Historical Society. FK2.W7 K.3 F.Arm *1.

Images and Icons. *Frontispiece:* Photo by Charles d'Emery. *Images and Icons:* Photo by Sarah Disbrow. / Reprinted from *Twenty-first Annual Report of the United States Geological Survey to the Secretary of the Interior, 1899–1900* by Charles D. Walcott. Washington DC: Government Printing Office, 1901. / NARA-NWDNS, ID 111-SC-87733, Gallery of the Open Frontier at *gallery.unl.edu*. *Boomers:* NARA-NWDNS, ID 111-SC-87352, Gallery of the Open Frontier at *gallery.unl.edu*. *Deadwood, South Dakota:* NARA-NWDNS, ID 111-SC-87741, Gallery of the Open Frontier at *gallery.unl.edu*. *Earp, Wyatt:* NARA-NWDNS, ID 111-SC-94117, Gallery of the Open Frontier at *gallery.unl.edu*. *Hickok, Wild Bill:* NARA-NWDNS, ID 111-SC-94122, Gallery of the Open Frontier at *gallery.unl.edu*. *Last Best West:* Glenbow Archives Calgary, Alberta, Canada NA-789-104(a). *Roswell Aliens:* Photo courtesy of the International UFO Museum and Research Center. *Roughnecks and Roustabouts:* Oklahoma Heritage Association. *State and Province Symbols:*

Compiled by David J. Wishart. *Wall Drug:* Photo courtesy of Wall Drug. *Windmills:* Courtesy of T. Lindsay Baker.

Industry. *Frontispiece:* Photo courtesy of Phillips Petroleum Company, Corporate Archives. *Industry:* Denver Public Library, Western History Collection, Call Number: x-62647. *Banking:* NARA-NWDNS, ID 233-TW-6, Gallery of the Open Frontier at *gallery.unl.edu*. *Coal:* Coal Industry Annual, 1997. Figures compiled by Daniel Daly. *Farm Implements:* Denver Public Library, Western History Collection, Call Number: x-9090. *Feedlots:* Photograph by Matt Engel. *Headbolt Heater:* Courtesy of Andrew Freeman. *Homestake Mine:* Courtesy of Department of Anthropology and Geography, University of Nebraska–Lincoln. *International Trade:* Table compiled by Craig R. MacPhee. *Justin, H. J., and Sons:* Courtesy of Justin Industries, Inc. *Petroleum, United States:* Photo courtesy of Southwest Collection/Special Collections Library, Texas Tech University, Lubbock, Texas, Rister, Carl Coke Papers 1834–1956, Box 17 of 31, A329.5C.

Law. *Frontispiece:* National Archives of Canada, Stuart Taylor Wood Collection c18046. *Law:* Photo by Marion Post Wolcott. Library of Congress, LC-USF34-058504-D. *Bonnie and Clyde:* Photo courtesy of L. J. Hinton. *Indian Police:* Denver Public Library, Western History Collection, Call Number: x-31567. *Jim Crow Laws:* Photo by Russell Lee. Library of Congress, LC-USF33-012327-M5. *Morris, Esther:* Wyoming State Archives, Department of State Parks and Cultural Resources. *North Dakota Anti-Garb Law:* Photo courtesy of Sacred Heart Monastery. *Texas Rangers:* Denver Public Library, Western History Collection, Photo by M. E. Jacobson, Call Number: z-2572. *White, Byron:* Denver Public Library, Western History Collection, Photo by Harry M. Rhoads, Call Number: RH-1285.

Literary Traditions. *Frontispiece:* Photo by L. A. Huffman. Montana Historical Society, Helena. 981-149. *Baum, L. Frank:* Photo courtesy of Alexander Mitchell Library, Aberdeen SD. *May, Karl:* Courtesy of Meredith McClain. *Neihardt, John G.:* John G. Neihardt, Papers, c. 1858–1974, Western Historical Manuscript Collection-Columbia MO. *Posey, Alexander:* Archives and Manuscripts Division of the Oklahoma Historical Society, Barde Collection, Photo Number 4213. *Roy, Gabrielle:* Photo by permission of Fonds Gabrielle Roy. *Wilder, Laura Ingalls:* Herbert Hoover Presidential Library-Museum, Negative Number: RWC 136.

Media. *Frontispiece:* Archives Center, National Museum of American History, Smithsonian Institution, SI neg. #941820. *Brokaw, Tom:* Photo courtesy of Tom Brokaw. *Radio:* Photo by John Vachon. Library of Congress, LC-USF34-061682-D. *White, William Allen:* Photo courtesy of David Walker and Barbara White Walker,